1982

BRITANNICA
BOOK OF THE YEAR

1982

BRITANNICA
BOOK OF THE YEAR

ENCYCLOPÆDIA BRITANNICA, INC.

CHICAGO, GENEVA, LONDON, MANILA, PARIS, ROME, SEOUL, SYDNEY, TOKYO, TORONTO

THE UNIVERSITY OF CHICAGO

The Britannica Book of the Year is published with the editorial advice
of the faculties of the University of Chicago.

CONTENTS

SPECIAL REPORTS

STRUGGLING FOR NATIONHOOD: THE BIRTH OF ZIMBABWE

by Robert Mugabe, Prime Minister of Zimbabwe

When, in 1652, Jan van Riebeeck, representing the Dutch East India Company, landed at the Cape of Good Hope at the southern tip of Africa and laid the foundations of a future Dutch Cape Colony, no one could have foreseen that the process thus begun would assume such proportions 250 years later. It engulfed, in successive stages, not just the Cape Colony but also the Orange Free State, the Transvaal, Natal, Basutoland, Swaziland, Bechuanaland, Southern Rhodesia, and Northern Rhodesia. The national liberation struggle that transformed Southern Rhodesia into Zimbabwe was an event in this process and was the sum of many linked events.

Colonial Background. In the competitive game of colonial adventures played out in Africa and the Far East during the 15th to the 19th century, the law of the survival of the fittest ruled just as it did in the jungle. The Portuguese eliminated the Arabs, the Dutch the Portuguese, while the French and British, as they struggled for supremacy, together annihilated the Dutch in many areas. Having survived alone in the Cape, the British began pursuing the Dutch settlers moving northward in search of greater freedom. This northward movement by the Afrikaners resulted in the establishment of two republics: the Orange River Republic (now the Orange Free State) and the Transvaal Republic (now Transvaal), whose northern border was the Limpopo River.

Cecil John Rhodes, a British empire builder who had become prime minister in the Cape, saw the growing British Empire threatened by the northward thrust of the Boers. He determined to curb it in the interest not only of the British Empire but also of his own quest for mineral fortune. A zone of British influence had, therefore, to be carved out north of the Transvaal. Rhodes had already foiled the territorial ambitions of the Boers in Bechuanaland (Botswana) through a treaty signed by Chief Khama and the British government. North of the Limpopo, the strategy, apart from treaties signed in 1888 with Chief Lobengula of the Ndebele tribe, was that of occupation. The occupation of the territory, later

Robert Mugabe is Prime Minister and Minister of Defense of Zimbabwe. He was the co-founder and president/general of the Zimbabwe African National Union (ZANU).

called Southern Rhodesia, was the realization of one of Rhodes's grandest dreams.

In 1889 Rhodes secured a royal charter from Queen Victoria for the British South Africa Company, now charged with the task of effecting the occupation. Thus began a colonial history that led to one of the bloodiest conflicts ever fought in Africa: the bitter war between the Ndebele and the settlers in 1893 and, subsequently, the first national liberation war (Chimurenga or Chindunduma) of 1896–97. Having obtained an agreement from the Africans conferring on him the grant of mineral rights, Rhodes turned it into an instrument of political and socioeconomic control. The Africans were both cheated and invaded, and they resorted to war. The 1896–97 war, with its surprise attacks and ambushes, was aimed at exterminating the enemy. In Matabeleland, for example, 130 European settlers were killed within the first week of the war, and the survivors were driven into hiding. In Mashonaland some 450 settlers were annihilated as the uprising, beginning in Chief Mashayamombe's area in the Hartley district, spread to other regions. Peace negotiations with the Ndebele were conducted by Rhodes himself. In Mashonaland British reinforcements defeated the Shonas, and their leaders were executed.

The settlers' victory led to repressive measures against the Africans. All administrative power was vested in the British South Africa Company until 1923, when Britain granted the right of self-government to the settler communities. In 1930 the Land Apportionment Act legalized what already existed in practice: the division of land between the whites and the blacks, with the whites owning 19.9 million ha (49.1 million ac) out of a total of 40.3 million ha (99.6 million ac). From this act, discrimination in the social, economic, and educational spheres also came into being. Since all urban, mining, and industrial areas were designated as white, no African could acquire a permanent home there. Schools, hospitals, and social amenities were all within the white areas. There was racial discrimination in labour conditions and job opportunities as well.

The Failure of Politics. The early nationalist and trade union movements, aware that the institutions of power were fully controlled by the settlers' gov-

Supporters of Robert Mugabe celebrated their election victory in March 1980, after his ZANU (Patriotic Front) party won the right to form a new government.

ernment, confined themselves to correcting the grievances arising from racial discrimination by non-violent means. The Southern Rhodesian African National Congress (1934–57) was the first real national grouping, but for a long time it lacked organization and drive. The National Youth League, formed in 1955 by James Chikerema, George Nyandoro, Edson Sithole, and Dunduzu Chisiza, merged with it in 1957, thus providing a broader basis for the mobilization of popular support.

The establishment of the Central African Federation (Federation of Rhodesia and Nyasaland) in 1953, combining the territories of Southern Rhodesia, Northern Rhodesia, and Nyasaland, was widely regarded by the African nationalist leaders of the three territories as a plot conceived by the white settlers (especially those in Southern Rhodesia) to thwart African aspirations and as a strategy to delay the independence process in Malawi (Nyasaland) and Zambia (Northern Rhodesia). During the federal period (1953–63) the Africans of all three territories were pitted against the whites and the tensions between them were intensified. Feeling their systems threatened, the white governments banned the African National Congress (ANC) of Southern Rhodesia and Nyasaland and later the Zambia Congress, and nationalist leaders, including Kamuzu (Dr. Hastings)

Banda and Kenneth Kaunda, were detained. In Southern Rhodesia the National Democratic Party (NDP) and the Zimbabwe African People's Union (ZAPU), both led by Joshua Nkomo, were successively proscribed in 1961 and 1962.

For a long time, the African Zimbabwean leadership believed that a solution to the political problem of the country lay in using political pressure to compel Britain to call a constitutional conference. However, when a Southern Rhodesian constitutional conference was held in London and Salisbury in 1960 and 1961, respectively, only 15 parliamentary seats out of 65 were given to the Africans. The mood of the whites under Prime Minister Sir Edgar Whitehead was not inclined to compromise. Less compromising still was the mood of the rightist Dominion Party (later the Rhodesia Front), which rejected the 1961 constitution and later proceeded to win the general elections in December 1962. In 1964 it rejected the liberal Winston Field as leader in favour of the more conservative Ian Douglas Smith, thus setting the scene for the defiant and rebellious course that led to Southern Rhodesia's unilateral declaration of independence from Great Britain on Nov. 11, 1965. The principle of majority rule was rejected as anathema by the white minority. Meanwhile, the failure of the Federation spelled the end

of white supremacy in Northern Rhodesia and Nyasaland, both of which moved on to independence in 1964.

Armed Struggle Begins. The realization by a core of the ZAPU leadership that the old political methods had failed and that a new leadership had to be found to confront the enemy by force of arms led to the formation of the Zimbabwe African National Union (ZANU). From its inception, ZANU aimed at armed struggle as the main thrust of national effort. Within a few months of its formation it began recruiting cadres for training in China and Ghana.

It must, however, be stated on behalf of the National Democratic Party that it was the first nationalist organization to distinguish clearly between the remedial approach to grievances and a basic approach that attacked the main cause of grievances against an unjust system. The NDP agitated for political change leading to majority rule based on one man, one vote. ZANU, however, went further by emphasizing that one man, one vote could only be gained by an armed revolutionary struggle.

The unilateral declaration of independence in 1965 rendered the traditional political methods of struggle (strikes, demonstrations, noncollaboration, and appeals to Britain) impotent. In fact, both ZANU and the People's Caretaker Council had been banned in August 1964, leaving them no option but to operate as underground movements.

In those circumstances, external bases became necessary, and these were established in Zambia and Tanzania. As Mozambique became independent, another base area presented itself. In April 1966 ZANU engaged the enemy in what has become known as the Battle of Sinoia. That battle inspired many other encounters with the enemy during 1966–68. ZANU reckons that the second War of Liberation (Chimurenga II) began in April 1966.

It became evident that the strategy of conventional battles was costly in terms of losses—human and material—because the enemy was stronger in manpower and equipment. A revision of strategy and tactics was called for, and a period of tutelage of ZANU cadres occurred in the Tete area of Mozambique between 1970 and 1972. ZANU then relaunched the struggle in December 1972, in the northeastern part of Zimbabwe, after having cultivated popular support over a period of nearly two years. Thenceforth, the struggle was sustained until the cease-fire arranged under the Lancaster House Agreement, save for a brief period in 1974–75 under a détente arrangement.

In the wake of the détente exercise, sharp contradictions developed in ZANLA, the armed wing of ZANU, as some commanders turned renegade after being infiltrated by the enemy. The enemy strategy was clearly to destroy the forces that now covered most of the northeastern zone. Thomas Nhari and Dakarai Badza, who became leaders of the rebellion, kidnapped some members of DARE (the Revolutionary Council) headed by Herbert Chitepo, and at the rear camp base of Chifombo, on the Zambian side near Tete, they assassinated scores of cadres, male and female, for refusing to join them. Nevertheless, the rebellion was crushed.

The enemy was not deterred by this failure. Within four months of the release of the detained nationalist leaders as a result of the détente, Herbert Chitepo was killed on March 18, 1975, when a bomb blew up his car. For most of 1975 the armed struggle made no progress and indeed suffered serious reversals, especially since the newly formed ANC umbrella organization, led by Bishop Abel Muzorewa, had neither direction nor set purpose other than that of stopping the war and negotiating with the Smith regime. The ZANU wing of the new composite body felt offended by the tactics employed against them by the front-line states (Tanzania, Zambia, Mozambique, Botswana, and Angola), which had coerced them into joining the ANC.

Following the shocking death of Herbert Chitepo, the ZANU Central Committee met in March 1975 to review the party's strategy. It was decided at that meeting that the writer, then secretary-general of the party, should leave the country immediately for Mozambique and Tanzania where he would undertake the reorganization of the party's external wing and its fighting wing, ZANLA. The writer requested that a companion, Edgar Tekere, then secretary for youth in ZANU, accompany him. On April 4, 1975, we left for the eastern border where, at Nyafaro, we were joined by Chief Tangwena who led us into Mozambique.

The Conflict Intensifies. The failure of the Victoria Falls talks held between the Smith delegation and that of the ANC led by Bishop Muzorewa convinced the front-line states that Smith was still not amenable to political change. There was no alternative but the continuation of the liberation war, which was rekindled in January 1976 using Mozambique as a rear base. After some dissension the ZANLA commanders finally began to work in unison, expanding their military zones stage by stage and transforming many of them into liberated and semiliberated zones. By 1978 the armed struggle had had such remarkable progress that the collapse of the Smith regime was just a matter of time. But between the Victoria Falls conference in 1975 and the final constitutional conference at Lancaster House in 1979, two other constitutional conferences occurred: the 1976 Geneva Conference based on the Kissinger proposals and the meetings based

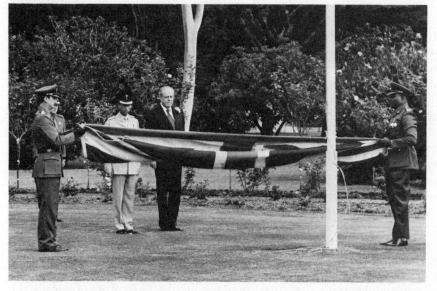

The British Union Jack came down in Salisbury on April 18, 1980; Zimbabwe had become an independent nation at midnight on April 17. Present at the ceremony were Prince Charles of Britain and Lord Soames.

on the Anglo-American proposals, held first in Malta in January 1978 and then in Dar-es-Salaam, Tanzania, in March 1978.

As the idea of a conference to discuss the plan proposed by U.S. Secretary of State Henry Kissinger —which aimed at stopping the war on the basis of ultimate majority rule—took shape, all the leaders of the nationalist groups were invited to a meeting with the front-line states. At this meeting ZANU stood as ZANU for the first time. The meeting had been called to provide a forum for reaching some modicum of unity on nationalist strategy for the prosecution of the struggle. As this could not be done with the ANC, now completely divorced from the war, Pres. Julius Nyerere of Tanzania took various nationalist leaders aside and advised them to form a political front so the political leadership could agree on a common political strategy for the proposed Geneva Conference. It was this idea that led to the formation of the Patriotic Front, which was to adopt a common position for all future constitutional conferences. The Geneva Conference, however, was a fiasco. Smith would not accept the British proposals and the Patriotic Front rejected the Kissinger plan completely.

ZANU strategy following the failure of the Geneva Conference was twofold. First, the ZANU leadership had to be restructured. Second, the liberation war had to be intensified, and more arms had to be procured from allies and friends. The political restructuring of ZANU affected mainly the composition of its Central Committee. At a meeting held at a ZANLA military rear base outside Chimoio which lasted for nearly two weeks, it was decided that the new Central Committee would consist of elected members chosen from various constituencies. It was at this meeting that the writer was elected president of

the party; Simon Muzenda, vice-president; Edgar Tekere, secretary-general; Josiah Tongogara, secretary of defense; Meya Urimbo, national political commissar; Teurai Ropa, secretary of women's affairs; and several others to various positions. For the first time, several members of the ZANLA high command were now also members of the Central Committee so that they too could participate in the policymaking function of the party. The successful restructuring of the party marked a final phase in the protracted effort to save ZANU and establish it as the national vanguard movement.

At the end of 1977, Britain and the United States published their so-called Anglo-American proposals. The result was the Malta meeting between the Patriotic Front and an Anglo-American team at which the Patriotic Front emphasized the need for accepting certain fundamental democratic principles, such as universal adult suffrage, free elections, restructuring of public service, and the disbanding of the Smith regime's illegal army. Negotiations on these principles failed.

Victory in Sight. In the absence of a political solution, armed struggle remained the only option open to ZANU. Formation of the Patriotic Front had resulted in the recruitment of many cadres for the military struggle, but these activities became confined to the northwest and western areas of Zimbabwe and never reached the magnitude of the more comprehensive and more effective ZANLA operations. They complemented the ZANLA operations, however, and by the end of 1979 martial law had been extended to 95% of the country. Between December 1972 and December 1979 (when a ceasefire was agreed to at Lancaster House) the death toll amounted to about 20,000 people.

The "internal settlement" of 1978 that gave rise to

the Muzorewa regime in what was called Zimbabwe-Rhodesia only worsened the situation and invited more daring raids from the guerrilla forces. ZANU, having concentrated on party restructuring in 1977, termed 1978 the Year of the People, when the party and the people would be united so that ZANU and the people would be one. The following year, 1979, was designated Year of the People's Storm (*Gore regukurahundi*), when the struggle would escalate and enemy bases and administrative centres would be stormed and destroyed. The collapse of the Muzorewa-Smith regime was inevitable.

On Aug. 1, 1979, a few days before the Commonwealth heads of government meeting opened in Lusaka, Zambia, Prime Minister Margaret Thatcher told the British Parliament that her government was "wholly committed to genuine majority rule in Rhodesia." The Commonwealth meeting produced an agreement on Rhodesia that recognized the principle of new elections based on one man, one vote under British authority. Britain undertook to convene a constitutional conference to be attended by both the black and white leadership. A cease-fire also had to be established to create an atmosphere of peace for the elections.

The Lancaster House Negotiations. The Lancaster House conference was attended by the Patriotic Front (ZANU and ZAPU) delegation, jointly led by the writer and Joshua Nkomo, and by the Zimbabwe-Rhodesia delegation, with Bishop Muzorewa, Silas Mundawarara, Ian Smith, and Ndabaningi Sithole as the principal members. The British delegation was led by Lord Carrington, who chaired the conference. Lord Carrington's diplomacy was characterized by a bias in favour of the Muzorewa group. Muzorewa's strategy became one of refraining from opposing any of the British constitutional proposals, and the Patriotic Front poked fun at his delegation and referred to its members as "the yes men." On the other hand, the Patriotic Front put up a firm and principled stand and won some useful concessions, although they too conceded ground. They refused to be driven into walking out of the conference, as desired by the Muzorewa group and some members of the British team.

The proposals that caused serious debate were:
> *1. The composition of the House of Assembly and Senate which granted disproportionate racial representation to the white community. In the House of Assembly they have 20 out of 100 seats, and in the Senate 10 out of 40 seats.*
> *2. The need to pay prompt and adequate compensation for the deprivation of property especially as this affected the right to acquire land for the resettlement of the peasants. The issue here was that Britain had to raise large funds for this purpose.*
> *3. A constitutional amendment procedure requiring 100% concurrence of the total membership of the House of Assembly on certain issues.*
> *4. The cease-fire arrangements and positioning of the warring forces during the cease-fire.*
> *5. The status of the guerrilla forces which Lord Carrington finally accepted as "lawful forces," while at the same time refusing to accord them an equal status with the white Rhodesian ones.*

The Zimbabwe constitution agreed at the Lancaster House conference and granted by Britain represents a hard-earned political victory achieved principally through a sustained and bitter armed struggle. It was far from perfect, but it contained more positive than negative aspects and, insofar as it granted independence within a democratic political order, it constituted a viable base on which political power could be built. It was basically this inherent potential that made it acceptable to the Patriotic Front.

The constitution is the supreme law of the country. There is also a formidable Declaration of Rights enshrining the fundamental rights and freedoms of the individual and protecting the rights to life, personal liberty, and freedom from slavery, forced labour, and inhuman treatment. It grants protection against the arbitrary deprivation of property and arbitrary searches of persons or their property. It secures the protection of the law, the protection of the freedoms of conscience, of expression, of assembly, and of association. It also protects freedom of movement and forbids discrimination on the grounds of race, tribe, place of origin, political opinion, colour, or creed.

The constitution creates the usual organs of government—Parliament, which consists of the Senate and a House of Assembly; the Executive, whose authority is vested in the president acting on the advice of the Cabinet; and the Judiciary. Elections to the House of Assembly are every five years and on the basis of adult suffrage (18 years and upward).

A New Nation Is Born. The first elections were held in early March 1980, and of the 80 common roll seats, ZANU (PF) won 57, PF (ZAPU) won 20, and the UANC 3. All the 20 white seats were won by the Rhodesia Front (now the Republican Front). The Senate, 14 of whose seats are filled by an electoral college of the common roll seat holders in House of Assembly, is dominated by representatives of ZANU (PF).

The resounding ZANU (PF) electoral victory was undoubtedly an expression of the unity and solidarity built over many years between the party and the people through the instrumentality of the armed struggle.

The Rhodesia public, for years fed on propaganda that Robert Mugabe was a rabid racist full of animosity and vindictiveness, was shocked to hear the new prime minister call, in his first post-election address to the nation, for national reconciliation so that those who had been enemies might recognize their inevitable oneness as dedicated Zimbabweans with a common destiny. The prime minister proceeded to demonstrate the meaning of national unity and reconciliation by including in his Cabinet four (now five) ZAPU members and two whites (one later resigned for reasons of health). ZAPU also has three deputy ministers.

Another dimension of the prime minister's policy of reconciliation was a request to Lord Soames, who administered the country during the three-month transitional period, to join hands with him in running the country until independence. Under a gentlemen's agreement, Lord Soames remained governor until April 18, 1980, when the Union Jack gave way to the Zimbabwe flag.

Confidence having been established, the most urgent tasks of the new government became the creation of greater peace, the unity of the people, the resettlement of refugees, the rehabilitation of communities affected by the war, and the rebuilding of the economy. Homes were quickly found for the refugees returning from Mozambique, Zambia, and Botswana, numbering a quarter million, and the internally displaced persons, numbering nearly two million, and they were given plots for cultivation. The United Nations High Commissioner for Refugees, other international agencies, and friendly countries assisted generously with resettlement aid. The program went so smoothly that, despite the existing land hunger among the peasants, a bumper maize (corn) harvest has been realized.

The manufacturing, commercial, and mining sectors also performed well during the first year of independence, and a growth rate of 14% was achieved, most of it due to the manufacturing sector. The need for new machinery and spare parts, however, stands in the way of greater expansion.

Zimbabwe's mineral resources include gold, chrome, asbestos, nickel, iron ore, coal, copper, tin, and emeralds. Its major agricultural products are tobacco, maize, cotton, wheat, sugar, groundnuts (peanuts), soybeans, beef, and dairy products. The country's infrastructure—its railway and road systems, hydroelectric and water systems—is very sound, despite a current railway locomotive shortage and a need for better roads in the rural areas.

The Task Ahead. In March 1981 the government convened a Zimbabwe Conference on Reconstruction and Development (Zimcord). During the Lancaster House conference, Britain had proposed that,

Prime Minister Robert Mugabe attended the June 1981 meeting of the Organization of African Unity in Nairobi, Kenya.

since the resources it was able to give Zimbabwe would be inadequate, it could help Zimbabwe sponsor a donors' conference to solicit aid for land development and reconstruction. The Zimbabwe Ministry of Economic Planning and Development took the proposal seriously, assessed the financial requirements needed over a three-year Transitional National Development Plan, and convened the conference in Salisbury. It had been estimated that Z$1.2 billion would be needed, but in reality about Z$1.3 billion was pledged by donor countries, the largest single amounts coming from Britain and the United States. Soon the Transitional National Development Plan will be announced. Its emphasis will be on raising the development in the peasant sector, neglected for decades by successive colonial regimes.

During the war years the Zimbabwe African National Union adopted a socialist philosophy based on Marxist-Leninist principles. Socialism is the guiding philosophy of the present government. Upon the attainment of independence, however, the government made it clear that its programs would occur in a socioeconomic context in which the historical, traditional, and objective circumstances of the country were recognized. Outright nationalization of the various sectors is not a feasible proposition, given the lack of technology, managerial skills, business experience, and even ideological consciousness among the majority of the people. The working class must first develop worker consciousness in

terms of its roles, needs, and duties. Similarly, the workers' technical and managerial skills must be substantially developed before any self-management programs can be undertaken.

Most of these aspects will be taken care of under the development plan, which is the formulation of the policy enunciated as "Growth with Equity" in preparation for Zimcord. To the extent that the promised funds become available, it should be possible to fulfill most of the objectives the government is setting for itself and for the people during the next three years.

Since its assumption of power the present government has taken some revolutionary steps in reforming the socioeconomic system. Primary education has been made free, and health care free for all those earning less than Z$150 dollars a month. Secondary education is now available for every child who completes his or her primary education, although this is not yet free. Racial discrimination has been abolished. The public service is fast being africanized. The monthly minimum wage, starting at Z$75 in July 1980, went up to Z$85 in January 1981 and to Z$105 in January 1982 for industrial, mining, and commercial workers, although the monthly minimum wage for farm and domestic workers has risen only from Z$30 to Z$50 over the period.

Zimbabwe has become a member of the Organization of African Unity, the United Nations and agencies, the Nonaligned Movement, and several other international organizations. It has, by joining the Nonaligned Movement, declared itself committed to the principles of that organization. Within the southern African region, Zimbabwe found itself, upon independence, within the brotherhood of the front-line states. It thus participates in discussions and consultations regularly held by these states on matters of mutual concern, especially on the problems posed by the system of apartheid in South Africa and that country's continued illegal occupation of Namibia in defiance of the United Nations, as well as by its acts of unprovoked aggression and sabotage against neighbouring states. Alongside other front-line states, Zimbabwe insists that Namibia must be granted independence on the basis of UN Security Council Resolution 435, which was passed in 1978.

Zimbabwe has also become a member of the Southern African Development Coordination Conference, whose inaugural meeting was held in Arusha, Tanzania, in 1979, followed by a conference held in Lusaka of heads of government of nine southern African states: Angola, Botswana, Mozambique, Tanzania, Zambia, Swaziland, Zimbabwe, Lesotho, and Malawi. The objectives of SADCC are stated in the Lusaka Declaration of April 1, 1980:

1. The reduction of economic dependence, particularly, but not only, on the Republic of South Africa.
2. The forging of links to create a genuine and equitable regional integration.
3. The mobilization of resources to promote the implementation of national, interstate, and regional policies.
4. Concerted action to secure international cooperation within the framework of our strategy for economic liberation.

In July 1981 a summit meeting was held in Salisbury to appraise the work so far accomplished at the ministerial level of SADCC. Each of the members has been assigned a task. Zimbabwe is to develop a Southern African Food Security Plan. A simple coordinative machinery was also decided upon. The headquarters would be in Gaberones and the president of Botswana, Quett Masire, would remain as chairman of SADCC. Zimbabwe was chosen to provide an executive secretary. These two officials, assisted by a secretariat in Gaberones, will have the responsibility to steer, coordinate, and administer the work of SADCC. Zimbabwe submitted its nominee for the post of executive secretary to SADCC and at the present writing approval is still being awaited.

The Ongoing Struggle. In conclusion, the writer has attempted to retrace the dramatic story of the Zimbabwean national struggle for independence by depicting the causes of the conflict arising from the imposition by Rhodes of a colonial system on a society that had neither invited it nor agreed to it. The writer has also tried to portray the national struggle and to show how a progressive transformation occurred until revolutionary armed struggle, based on the Maoist theory of popular support, brought about the collapse of the colonial system. Throughout the years of the armed struggle ZANU was the undoubted political and revolutionary vanguard of the people's struggle for freedom and independence. Its main arm was always ZANLA, without which independence would not have come as early as it did.

There has also been a focusing on the problems facing the country immediately upon independence and how the present government has attempted to solve them. The reader has been provided with an insight into the policies and plans of the ZANU government for the future of the country. In the view of the ZANU government, the struggle for independence must operate on the basic economic struggle of Marxist-Leninist socialist principles. When our government finds itself in conflict with the established capitalist system it must, in due course, assert its paramountcy and find practical application, again through popular support, in replacing the latter. Independence is thus a starting point of a new type of national struggle.

A luta continua!

Background to a Fateful Year in Poland's History

"NOT A SINGLE POLISH PROBLEM CAN BE SOLVED BY VIOLENCE"

Gen. Wojciech Jaruzelski
December 13, 1981

by K. M. Smogorzewski

The revolution that started in Poland in August 1980 was not the unexpected eruption of a dormant volcano. It was the fourth and the most vigorous protest by the Polish people against the totalitarian system of government imposed on their country after the end of World War II in 1945—a design planned by Joseph Stalin and acquiesced in by Pres. Franklin D. Roosevelt and Prime Minister Winston Churchill.

Poland was the first country to resist Hitler's aggression, fighting alone against an enemy superior in numbers and in modern weapons. Inevitably, Poland lost the September 1939 campaign, but the Polish people continued the armed struggle at home and outside their country. In the final battles of World War II, Polish divisions under Allied command entered Germany from the West and the East. The liberators in the East, however, carried with them an alien Communist regime that the minds and hearts of the Polish people never assimilated, a system allegedly Marxist-Leninist but in reality merely an outward cloak legitimizing the machinery of despotism.

Poles had not forgotten the major part that tsarist Russia played in the partitions of their country at the end of the 18th century. At that time, the Russian rulers were fearful of the Polish national revival signaled by the establishment in 1773 of a Ministry of Education, the first in Europe, and the adoption by the Sejm (parliament) on May 3, 1791, of a democratic constitution, greeted by the British statesman Edmund Burke as "the noblest benefit received by any nation at any time."

The people of Poland also remembered that World War II was preceded by a five-month-long

A London-based writer on contemporary history, Kazimierz Smogorzewski has been a frequent visitor to Poland in recent years and was present at Solidarity's congress at Oliwa in September 1981. He was founder and editor of Free Europe *during World War II, and his publications include* Poland's Access to the Sea *and* The United States and Great Britain.

secret negotiation between Nazi Germany and Soviet Russia which culminated in a pact signed in Moscow on Aug. 23, 1939. Formally it was a nonaggression treaty, but its secret annex mapped a partition of eastern Europe in general and of Poland in particular. Once the two dictators had decided that the Polish state should never rise again, their urgent task was to deprive the Polish nation of its leadership on both sides of the partition line. Hitler gave orders to Heinrich Himmler and Stalin to Lavrenti Beria, his chief of internal security. The latter

Five thousand workers in a flax factory at Zyrardow staged an extended strike in October on behalf of the Solidarity labour movement.

GIANSANTI—SYGMA

One of the leading figures in Poland was Stefan Cardinal Wyszynski (left), shown in 1978 with Karol Cardinal Wojtyla (now Pope John Paul II).

organized the deportation of 1.5 million Poles from eastern Poland to the gulags and the massacre of 15,000 Polish Army officers captured by the Red Army. The officers were executed in April 1940 at Katyn and elsewhere.

Stalin's Polish Policy. The idyll of Nazi-Soviet relations was brutally ended on June 22, 1941, when Hitler launched his Wehrmacht against the U.S.S.R. In the new situation, Stalin had to revise his strategy and to reverse his Polish policy. In 1938 he had signaled to Hitler that he was not interested in Poland's future when he ordered the dissolution of the Communist Party of Poland (KPP) and the execution of hundreds of its members who had taken refuge in the U.S.S.R. The revival of this party, albeit under a new name, became an urgent political necessity. Some members of the old KPP cadre remained in the Soviet Union while others were hiding in German-occupied Poland, among them Wladyslaw Gomulka. In November 1943 Gomulka became secretary-general of the Polish Workers' Party (PPR), which in Stalin's design was to form the nucleus of the future government of the Polish People's Republic, independent on paper but indissolubly linked with the Soviet Union.

In German-occupied Poland a delegation of the legal Polish government-in-exile and a 300,000-strong underground Home Army (AK) continued to be active. When the Red Army forces under Marshal Konstantin Rokossovsky were approaching the Vistula River near Warsaw, both Stanislaw Mikolajczyk, the Polish premier, and Gen. Tadeusz Komorowski, the AK commander, took a militarily risky and politically mistaken decision to start an anti-German uprising in the capital city. As soon as Stalin learned of the uprising, which began on Aug. 1, 1944, he

ordered Rokossovsky to halt his offensive in order to make the Poles aware of their dependence on the Red Army. The 40,000 AK soldiers fought heroically for 63 days, but on October 2 Komorowski was forced to surrender. The loss of human life was enormous: 10,200 men and women of the AK were killed in combat and 13,900 were missing; of the 950,000 civilian population, about 700,000 were forcibly evacuated by the Germans and some 200,000 perished in the fighting. Immediately after the surrender Hitler ordered the total destruction of the city of Warsaw.

The Sovietization of Poland. Shortly after the "liberation" of the ruins of Warsaw on Jan. 17, 1945, Gen. Ivan A. Serov, a high-ranking assistant of Beria, arrested 16 leaders of the Polish underground. They were flown to Moscow, where a show trial was staged at the very time when Vyacheslav Molotov, the Soviet commissar for foreign affairs, together with the U.S. and U.K. ambassadors, was busy with the formation of a "really democratic" Polish government. On June 21, 12 of the 16 leaders, charged with "organizing terrorist acts in the rear of the Red Army," were sentenced to up to ten years' imprisonment. Seven days later the Polish "government of national unity" of 21 ministers, including 15 Communists, was formed, while Boleslaw Bierut, an old Comintern agent, was picked by Stalin to be president of the Polish republic.

The sovietization of Poland began. Dozens of Soviet advisers were apportioned to Polish ministries, and a Soviet-type political police was formed and manned by officers of Soviet and Polish citizenship. Thousands of AK members were arrested and deported to the U.S.S.R. On Sept. 26, 1946, Bierut signed a decree by which 76 generals and colonels in the armed forces who had fought in the West were deprived of Polish nationality. Two years later 19 officers, mainly airmen, who had served in the West and had returned to Poland after 1945, were arrested, falsely accused of spying, and sentenced to death. (They were rehabilitated in October 1956.) The Polish Army formed in the U.S.S.R. after 1943 was officered mainly by Russians. One of the few exceptions was Gen. Michal Zymierski, a prewar Polish officer who became the first minister of defense, but in November 1949 Bierut, on Stalin's orders, appointed Marshal Rokossovsky to this post.

Bierut, who saw in Gomulka a dangerous rival, resolved to remove him from his position as PPR secretary-general. Gomulka, the first Communist leader in the Soviet bloc who dared to defy Stalin, considered that the dictatorship of a single party was neither essential nor expedient. He opposed the collectivization of agriculture; he refused to denounce Tito; and he proclaimed that the Polish So-

cialist Party rendered greater services to the nation than the pro-Soviet Social-Democracy, led by Feliks Dzierzynski. No wonder that in September 1948 Gomulka was dismissed from the post of secretary-general and Bierut was elected in his place. Expelled from the party, Gomulka was arrested in July 1951, and Bierut ordered that he be brought to trial for "rightist-nationalist deviation." Gomulka escaped the fate of the Czechoslovak Rudolf Slansky and the Hungarian Laszlo Raik most probably because Stalin died in March 1953. Bierut finally released his prisoner in April 1955.

Bierut also led an unrelenting struggle against the Roman Catholic Church, whose principal defender in Poland was Stefan Cardinal Wyszynski. By the beginning of 1954 Wyszynski, six other bishops, and more than 900 priests and civilian Catholics were either interned or imprisoned.

Bierut died in March 1956, leaving the leadership of the Polish United Workers' Party (PUWP), as it was now called, deeply divided. No member of the Politburo had any prestige or authority. On March 20 Edward Ochab, a low-key personality, was elected secretary-general.

The 1956 Uprising. On June 28, 1956, an event of historic importance brought to an end the pretence of popular support for the Communist regime. Industrial workers of Poznan staged a general strike, and a large procession carrying the national white and red flags of Poland demanded not only more bread but also freedom and the departure of the Soviets. "We will cut off the hand that dared to threaten our social order," said Premier Jozef Cyrankiewicz in a radio broadcast. The next day Marshal Rokossovsky ordered an armoured unit to use firearms to crush the revolt. At least 53 people were killed and a few hundred wounded.

Following First Secretary Nikita Khrushchev's speech at the 20th congress of the Communist Party of the Soviet Union on Feb. 25, 1956, in which he denounced Stalin's crimes, political turmoil spread across the Soviet bloc, turmoil that was particularly intense in Poland and Hungary. Within the PUWP three trends were apparent: the "dogmatists" opposed all kinds of "democratization"; the "revisionists" requested the uprooting of Stalinist ideas and methods; and the "pragmatists" supported changes which would revive party unity and authority. Ochab and Cyrankiewicz, the leading representatives of the third trend, came to the conclusion that only Gomulka could achieve their aim, and in this they were supported by the second group. They started negotiations with Gomulka, who accepted the mission offered to him on two conditions: that he be solemnly rehabilitated, and that not one of his Stalinist enemies remain in the Politburo. The condi-

tions were met, and Gomulka was restored to party membership.

On October 19, when the PUWP Central Committee had assembled to elect the new Politburo proposed by Gomulka, Khrushchev quite unexpectedly landed in Warsaw; with him were three other members of the Soviet Politburo as well as Marshal Ivan Konev, commander in chief of the Warsaw Pact forces. Knowing that Soviet divisions had gathered on the Polish frontiers with East Germany and the Soviet Union, and that two Soviet divisions stationed inside Poland were moving toward Warsaw, the Central Committee, after coopting Gomulka as its new member, decided that the old Politburo, including Gomulka, would discuss Polish-Soviet relations with the Soviet visitors.

This meeting, which took place on the night of October 19–20 at the Belweder Palace, was stormy. Brave words were pronounced by Ochab and Gomulka. The Polish leaders explained to the Soviets that the people's democracy of Poland wished to be an equal, independent, and sovereign state bringing its own creative contribution to the development of the Soviet bloc. Khrushchev understood that by supporting the "dogmatist" group he was risking bloodshed. Accordingly, the visitors retreated and on October 20 returned to Moscow.

On October 21 the Central Committee elected the new nine-member Politburo. In a secret ballot, Gomulka obtained 74 votes. Immediately afterward he made a lengthy speech, not only to the 75-member Central Committee but, via radio, to the nation. He said that to represent the Poznan tragedy as the work of "imperialist agents" was politically naive. Without the confidence of the working class, Gomulka insisted, no government was possible. Announcing his program, he proclaimed that four-fifths of the country's arable land would remain the property of three million private farmers. That reform, still in force, was the first major anomaly differentiating Poland from other countries of the Soviet bloc.

In November Rokossovsky and 32 other Soviet officers serving in the high command of the Polish armed forces returned to Moscow. At the same time, certain financial problems between Poland and the U.S.S.R. were satisfactorily settled. Gomulka was very popular throughout the country, but three years after his triumphant return to power he purged the party of the young "revisionists," curtailed the press, and dissolved the workers' councils. When the people of Warsaw were asked what had changed most in Poland since the return of Gomulka, the answer was, "The mind of Gomulka." Actually he remained what he had always been: a Communist and a martinet. Although in October 1956 he

released Cardinal Wyszynski and five bishops from confinement, he soon picked fresh disputes with the church. Ignoring the fact that he ruled a Catholic country, in January 1966 he opposed the issuing of a passport to Cardinal Wyszynski, who was due in Rome to attend the celebration of 1,000 years of Christianity in Poland. Consequently, Pope Paul VI canceled his visit to Poland.

In March 1968 Gomulka tolerated the "anti-Zionist" campaign, and in August he allowed Polish troops to take part in the Soviet invasion of Czechoslovakia. Under Soviet pressure, Poland supplied tanks and antiaircraft artillery to North Vietnam.

The 1970 Shipyard Strikes. In December 1970 Gomulka announced considerable price increases on basic foodstuffs, fuel, and clothing. When workers from the Gdansk, Gdynia, and Szczecin shipyards went on strike and riots occurred, he used force against "counterrevolution" and 44 people, according to official sources, were killed by security units. After this bloody tragedy—the second since Poznan—Gomulka was driven out of power.

On Dec. 20, 1970, Edward Gierek, the party first secretary in the highly industrialized province of Katowice, was elected first secretary of the PUWP. Three days later, at the behest of Soviet leader Leonid Brezhnev, he accepted Piotr Jaroszewicz, a former deputy premier, as chairman of the Council of Ministers (premier). Gierek began with a clever tactical move. While Gomulka had opposed the reconstruction of the Warsaw Royal Castle, destroyed in 1944 on Hitler's order, Gierek decided that this historic edifice would be rebuilt, an announcement that roused the patriotic feelings of the nation.

On May 17, 1972, the West German Bundestag (parliament) ratified the Warsaw Treaty of Dec. 7, 1970, which recognized that the Oder-Neisse line "forms the western state frontier of Poland." The German Democratic Republic had recognized this border on July 6, 1950. On June 28, 1972, the Holy See adjusted the external borders of the new western and northern Polish bishoprics to the internationally recognized frontiers. This act opened a new era in Polish-Vatican relations. On Nov. 12, 1973, Stefan Olszowski, the foreign minister, was the first member of the Polish government received in private audience by the pope. From that day a second anomaly distinguished Poland from other members of the Soviet bloc—namely, the free pursuance by the Roman Catholic Church of its spiritual activities.

In mid-1976 the Gierek regime was shaken by large-scale workers' demonstrations resembling those of 1970. When, on June 24, Premier Jaroszewicz, in spite of Gierek's opposition, announced price increases averaging 60% on many staples, industrial workers in Radom and elsewhere went on strike. The following day Jaroszewicz informed the public that his decree was being withdrawn. On this occasion there was no bloodbath, but hundreds of protesters were arrested, beaten, and sentenced to imprisonment. In September a group of Polish intellectuals headed by Edward Lipinski, a well-known economist, Jerzy Andrzejewski, a distinguished writer, and Jacek Kuron (see BIOGRAPHIES) set up the Committee of Workers' Defense (KOR) to protect them from repression and to collect money for their families.

Poland's Economic Crisis. The year 1976 was eventful for Gierek in another way, the significance of which was not immediately apparent to the Polish people. Shortly after his arrival in power, Gierek applied to the Polish economy the so-called "specific maneuver." Assuming that prosperity in the West would continue, he sought considerable foreign credits to buy licenses and plants for the expansion of Polish industry. Because wages in Poland were lower than in the West, he expected to gain a competitive edge for Polish exports in Western markets and to repay the debts from hard-currency profits. But the severe recession that affected the developed market economies in 1974 seriously reduced the plan's chances of success.

Poland's hard-currency debt in 1971 stood at $764 million; in 1975 it jumped to $7.4 billion, and in 1979 it amounted to $21 billion. Polish imports at current prices rose from $3.6 billion to $19.1 billion between 1970 and 1980, while exports grew from $3.5 billion to $17 billion during the same period. Poland's major supplier and customer, covering one-third of the total exchanges each way, was the U.S.S.R. Despite its rich reserves of coal (extraction reached 201 million tons in 1979), Poland imported, mainly from the U.S.S.R., crude petroleum (16.6 million tons in 1979), iron ore (20.1 million tons in 1980), and cotton (172,000 tons in 1980). For these and other imports, Poland paid its eastern neighbour with industrial products. One-fifth of Soviet merchant shipping was built in Polish shipyards; two-thirds of railway freight cars produced in Poland were exported to the Soviet Union; the U.S.S.R. was the chief customer for electrical appliances, aircraft engines, coal-mining machinery, machine tools, telephones, and computers. More than 50 Soviet plants producing sulfuric acid were constructed by Poles.

Until 1975 the price of goods and services exchanged between Poland and the U.S.S.R. was generally based on the world price expressed in U.S. dollars. In 1976 Premier Jaroszewicz agreed that all commercial transactions with the U.S.S.R. would henceforward be settled in "conversion" (*perevod*) rubles, that is, in units of account. Originally, the

exchange rate for the *perevodny* ruble was 90 kopeks to U.S. $1. When the dollar was devalued in 1971 in terms of gold content, the Soviet Gosbank started revising its price within the area of the Council for Mutual Economic Assistance (Comecon). In 1976 the dollar was valued at 77 kopeks and in 1980 at 64 kopeks.

The consequence of using the "conversion" ruble in Polish-Soviet exchanges was bitter. The Polish engineering industry produced machinery that included equipment bought in the West and paid for in hard currency, but Poland sold this to the U.S.S.R. for paper units inconvertible on the world market. Thus an important part of the Polish credits obtained in the West was sucked out by the East.

The Emergence of Solidarity. At the eighth congress of the PUWP, held in Warsaw in February 1980, Gierek warned the workers that, considering the difficult position of Poland's economy, real wages would not rise by more than 9–11% over the next five years, and they must be linked to higher productivity. As the shops were becoming almost empty of foodstuffs and household goods, industrial workers began local strikes. Premier Edward Babiuch, Jaroszewicz's successor, branded them as "political" and recommended the use of force. Gierek went to the Crimea to seek guidance from Brezhnev, who on July 31 advised him to reach a reasonable compromise with the strikers.

Shortly afterward, on August 14, the entire work force of 17,000 stopped production at the Lenin Shipyard in Gdansk. The strike spread throughout the country like a bush fire. An Interfactory Strike Committee (IFSC) was formed with the charismatic Lech Walesa as its leader. On August 24 Gierek sacked Babiuch and appointed as head of government a moderate man, Jozef Pinkowski. To Gdansk he sent Mieczyslaw Jagielski, a senior deputy premier and since 1971 Poland's representative on the Comecon executive committee. Jagielski began negotiating with Walesa and the IFSC on August 23.

The negotiations were difficult but they succeeded. On August 31 Jagielski and Walesa signed the 21 points of a charter providing for "free trade unions, independent from political parties and employers"; guaranteeing "the right to strike"; and ensuring "respect for freedom of expression and of publication." The agreement also stated that the new organization, called Solidarnosc (Solidarity), would "adhere to the principles defined in the Polish constitution" and recognized "the leading role of the PUWP in the state" as well as "Poland's international alliances." The agreement was a truly historic compromise, a triumph of common sense.

On September 1, however, the Kremlin warned for the first time that it would not sanction the agreement. An article signed "Aleksey Petrov" appeared in *Pravda* warning the PUWP that "antisocialist elements" were attempting to overthrow the Polish Communist system. Gierek suffered a heart attack, and on September 6 Stanislaw Kania was elected first secretary. On September 27 *Pravda* renewed its warnings. The mysterious "Petrov" wrote menacingly: "The Polish people remember full well how their country regained its freedom and who really helped the Poles to ensure the very existence of the Polish nation."

Despite the continuous and alarming reports from the Soviet news agency, Tass, that pictured Poland as a country on the brink of chaos, the Gdansk Charter was approved on October 24 by the Warsaw District Court, and Solidarity was registered as a legal organization. On October 30 Kania and Pinkowski paid a visit to Moscow, where they met Brezhnev and Premier Nikolay Tikhonov. The official communiqué said that the meeting was held "in a cordial atmosphere," but the Polish leaders returned to Warsaw with mixed feelings, since their hosts had insisted that they restore the leading role of the PUWP in the state.

On Feb. 11, 1981, a momentous reconstruction of the Polish government took place: Pinkowski was dismissed and Gen. Wojciech Jaruzelski (see BIOGRAPHIES) became premier. Perhaps this exceptional choice signaled an oblique admission that within the PUWP Central Committee there was a penury of men with the necessary prestige and ability to head the government in a critical situation. Those who had suggested Jaruzelski obviously wanted at the helm a military man with authority either to establish working cooperation with Solidarity or to proceed with its dismantlement.

Shortly after this move, two events occurred that exerted a profound influence on Polish patriotic feelings. On May 28 Cardinal Wyszynski died (see OBITUARIES). Primate of Poland and one of the best intellects of his time, he was a man of strong character but also a wise diplomat who considered that his mission was not only to avoid an open struggle between the state and the church but also to seek an honourable modus vivendi between the lords spiritual and temporal. Previously, on May 13, a Turkish assassin attempted to kill Pope John Paul II, formerly Karol Cardinal Wojtyla, archbishop of Krakow, whose views were identical with those of Cardinal Wyszynski. There is no doubt that shortly before Cardinal Wyszynski died he informed Pope John Paul II who should be the next archbishop of Gniezno and Warsaw. On July 7 the pope appointed Bishop Jozef Glemp (see BIOGRAPHIES), who immediately declared himself in favour of continuing the dialogue between the state and Solidarity.

In the meantime, Kania and Jaruzelski discussed their plan of action. On August 14 they flew to the Crimea to be received by Leonid Brezhnev and were told once more that the strengthening of the Polish Marxist-Leninist party was their major task.

Solidarity's First Congress. On September 5 the constituent congress of Solidarity, the largest such organization Poland had ever seen, opened at Oliwa, near Gdansk. Its 9.5 million members, grouped in 43 regional associations, elected 892 delegates who filled the ground floor of the huge sports hall in which the congress was held, while invited guests and press representatives sat in the balconies. The first part of the congress, mainly procedural, lasted six days. The second opened on September 26 and ended on October 7. The congress elected the union's officers and adopted Solidarity's program. Lech Walesa, a moderate, was elected chairman of the 107-member National Commission on the first ballot; he received 426 votes, more than double the 201 votes cast for his radical opponent, Marian Jurczyk.

The program consisted of 38 theses, the most important being the stipulation: "A sense of responsibility compels us to respect the power setup which emerged in Europe after World War II." While Solidarity did not suggest that it was trying to become a political party, it served notice that it must have a share of state power. It called, for instance, for a truly democratic electoral system which would be submitted to the Sejm, after consultation with Solidarity, not later than Dec. 31, 1981.

The debates at the constituent congress were orderly, free, and businesslike, but also at times demagogic and often anti-Soviet. The prevailing tone of the discussions was typically Western European and, considering that all this was happening 500 km east of the iron curtain, Western spectators were exhilarated.

The Kremlin, however, interpreted the debates as an "unbridled campaign of lies and slander against the U.S.S.R." Boris Aristov, the Soviet ambassador in Warsaw, was instructed to call on Kania and Jaruzelski on September 1 and demand "prompt and resolute measures against the counterrevolutionaries." Convinced that Aristov's démarche was an expression of Soviet criticism of his soft approach to Solidarity affairs, Kania resigned as first secretary on October 18 and Jaruzelski, already the fourth premier since February 1980, was elected to the post with overwhelming support. He thus became the third party leader since September 1980.

General Jaruzelski took the helm of a country in political disarray and with a decaying economy. By 1981 Poland's hard currency debt had reached $26 billion and gross national product had fallen by 15%

compared with 1980. Extraction of hard coal shrank in 1980 to 196 million metric tons and in 1981 to 162 million—a 20% fall in two years. Exports of coal—Poland's main source of hard currency—sank between 1979 and 1981 from 41.4 million tons to 16.8 million. Because of shortages of electric power, some raw materials, industrial equipment, and spare parts for machinery purchased abroad—as well as protest strikes—industrial production was at 50 or 60% of capacity. Thanks to favourable weather conditions, arable farming production in 1981 was higher than the average of many years' standing. The grain harvest, at 20 million tons, was 2 million tons above the previous year's. That amount, however, was not sufficient to meet demand, and 7 million tons had to be imported. Livestock production in 1981 was 10% below that of 1980. Shortages of food and of practically all household goods were acute, and the long queues of people in front of shops became an everyday phenomenon in Polish towns and villages.

Martial Law. Premier Jaruzelski knew that the Soviet leaders had reluctantly reconciled themselves to two Polish anomalies within the Soviet bloc: absence of compulsory collectivization of agriculture and spiritual bonds linking the Roman Catholic Church with the Polish people. He did not attempt to discuss with Walesa the third anomaly canvassed by Solidarity. He also knew that Marshal Dmitry Ustinov, the Soviet minister of defense, had signaled by his maneuvers on the Polish borders that he was eager to crush Solidarity. To avoid Soviet military intervention, Jaruzelski chose to act alone.

As first secretary of the PUWP, Jaruzelski on November 4 invited Archbishop Glemp and Lech Walesa (whom he had never met) to discuss his idea of a seven-member Council of National Understanding. Such an advisory institution did not appear attractive to Walesa, and from his skepticism it was construed that no agreement could be reached with Solidarity.

Having completed the plan of his military operation in every detail, Jaruzelski invited Gen. Victor Kulikov to Warsaw. As commander in chief of the Warsaw Pact forces, Kulikov was entitled to know what was going to happen. On the night of December 12–13 the crackdown started. Broadcasting to the nation at 6 AM as chairman of the newly created Military Council of National Salvation (composed of 15 generals, an admiral, and 4 colonels), Jaruzelski explained that the council was not striving for a military dictatorship. Maintaining that "the extremists were planning to destroy Poland's socialist statehood," he proclaimed that he had to act and "tie the hands of the gamblers before they push the homeland into the abyss of fratricidal struggle." Jaruzelski

admitted that "a preventive internment of a group of persons threatening the security of the state" had been carried out. Also interned were a few dozen people who "were personally responsible for bringing the state to profound crisis" and "abusing their office for personal profit."

Jaruzelski added: "We want a strong Poland, strong through its achievements, culture, forms of social life, and place in Europe." In this Poland, he went on, "A special place belongs to the party; notwithstanding its mistakes and bitter defeats, the party remains an active and creative force . . . and we will purify the eternally living sources of our ideas." In this Poland, he continued, there was also room for "the healthy, working-class trend in Solidarity which by its own efforts would remove from its ranks the criers of counterrevolution." In this part of his speech, Jaruzelski also made mention of the Roman Catholic Church: "It is thus that we understand the idea of national accord, that we support it, and respect the diversity of world outlooks in the country and evaluate the patriotic positions of the Church."

Martial law was imposed on Poland, and the country became isolated from the outside world. Brutal by definition, the military confrontation could not avoid being bloody. Warsaw radio admitted that in the first days eight miners had been killed in Katowice. A list of 57 arrested "extremist activists" of Solidarity was published on December 16. It included the three opponents to Walesa's presidency; Tadeusz Mazowiecki, editor in chief of the weekly *Solidarnosc*; Janusz Onyszkiewicz, press spokesman for the Mazowsze regional organization; and Kuron. A list of 32 discredited party members was also published, naming, among others, Gierek, Jaroszewicz, and four former Politburo members.

Lech Walesa was arrested in Gdansk and transported to a villa near Warsaw. It was alleged that he had been asked by a member of the Military Council to broadcast to the nation. It was not known what his captors wanted him to say, but he refused to speak in public before meeting his colleagues from Solidarity's Presidium. He also asked to see Archbishop Glemp, but both requests were declined. When invited to meet Jaruzelski, Archbishop Glemp replied that there would be no point in discussing anything without Walesa's presence.

In spite of the internment of 5,069 (the officially released figure) Solidarity leaders and officials, passive resistance continued throughout the country. Jaruzelski restored order of a sort, but he knew that Polish workers would not dig coal, produce steel, or build machinery under threat of terror; that Polish peasants would not deliver their cattle or pigs to the state slaughterhouses even for fat rewards of zlotys

The first national conference of the Polish Solidarity labour union convened at Oliwa, near Gdansk, in September.

if they were unable to buy the agricultural implements and artificial fertilizers they needed.

In the address quoted above, Jaruzelski said that "not a single Polish problem can be solved by violence." Indeed it seemed ever more likely as 1981 drew to its close that Poland's problems could be solved only by fair negotiations between the state and the true spokesmen for the workers, the peasants, and the professional men and women.

That also was the opinion of the world's most eminent Pole, Pope John Paul II, who in his message on New Year's Day threw the weight of his personal authority, and that of the Roman Catholic Church, behind Solidarity which, he said, expressed the struggle for the dignity of working men and as such belonged "to the actual patrimony of the working men of my country." But the pontiff said nothing tending to equate the present Polish regime with Soviet rule, or to suggest that the church leaders in Poland might not be free to speak in defense of human rights. Addressing a crowd of more than 50,-000 in St. Peter's Square, John Paul proclaimed: "Workers have the right to set up autonomous trade unions whose role is to guard their social, family, and individual rights."

JANUARY

1 *New Year's Day*

6 *Epiphany*

18 *200th anniversary of Daniel Webster's birth*

25 *Chinese New Year; 100th anniversary of Virginia Woolf's birth*

26 *Australia Day; Republic Day in India*

30 *100th anniversary of Franklin D. Roosevelt's birth*

18 **200th anniversary of Daniel Webster's birth.** At age 18, shortly before graduating from Dartmouth College, Daniel Webster was invited by the citizens of Hanover, N.H., to deliver the annual Fourth of July oration. It was the first of many such invitations extended to the famous orator, whose long and distinguished political career began in 1812 when he was elected to the U.S. House of Representatives from New Hampshire. After moving to Boston, he served four more years in the House and 14 years in the Senate. For two years he held the position of secretary of state under Presidents Harrison and Tyler, then returned to the Senate. At the time of his death Webster was again serving the nation as secretary of state. Webster was a staunch defender of the Union. In a speech to U.S. senators he uttered the much-quoted phrase: "Liberty *and* Union, now and forever, one and inseparable!" He manifested his belief in a strong union on another dramatic occasion when, though despising slavery, he supported Henry Clay's Compromise of 1850. One of Webster's best remembered achievements as secretary of state was his role in negotiating the Webster-Ashburton Treaty of 1842, which set the boundary between Maine and Canada. Webster sought the U.S. presidency but never attained it.

25 **100th anniversary of Virginia Woolf's birth.** Born Virginia Stephen on Jan. 25, 1882, in London, Virginia Woolf was the second daughter of Sir Leslie Stephen. She married Leonard Woolf in 1912 and published her first novel, *The Voyage Out*, in 1915. In 1917 the couple founded Hogarth Press, which published all her books, including a reprint of *The Voyage Out*. Critics recognized Woolf's promise in her first two novels (the other was *Night and Day*, 1919), but she was dissatisfied with her work. Underlying her dissatisfaction was the belief that contemporary fiction laid undue emphasis on events, clearly defined characters, and material circumstances. Woolf chose to stress the continuous flow of experience, the indefinableness of character, and external circumstances as they impinge on consciousness. She was also interested in the way time is experienced both as a sequence of disparate moments and as the flow of years and centuries. Her contributions to the develop-ment of the novel can be seen in *Mrs. Dalloway* (1925), *To the Lighthouse* (1927), *Orlando* (1928), *The Waves* (1931), *The Years* (1937), and *Between the Acts* (1941). Though remembered chiefly as a novelist, Woolf published a substantial amount of criticism and two biographies. She drowned herself near her Sussex home on March 28, 1941, during a recurrence of mental illness.

FEBRUARY

2 *Candlemas Day; Groundhog Day; 100th anniversary of James Joyce's birth*

6 *Waitangi Day in New Zealand*

12 *Lincoln's Birthday*

14 *St. Valentine's Day*

21 *Brotherhood Week begins*

22 *250th anniversary of George Washington's birth*

23 *Shrove Tuesday pancake race*

24 *Ash Wednesday; 400th anniversary of Gregorian calendar*

2 **100th anniversary of James Joyce's birth.** Afflicted with vision problems and beset by financial troubles throughout much of his life, James Joyce nevertheless managed to achieve a distinguished place among the literary greats of his time. Though difficult reading for most people, *Ulysses* is considered Joyce's masterpiece and one of the great works of modern literature. In it Joyce explores the stream of consciousness of a group of Dubliners, a technique that deeply influenced other writers. Other well-known works include *A Portrait of the Artist as a Young Man*, *Dubliners*, and *Finnegans Wake*.

22 **250th anniversary of George Washington's birth.** George Washington was born in 1732 to Augustine and Mary Ball Washington at Popes Creek, Va. Augustine had four children by his first wife and six by his second; George, who was the firstborn of the second marriage, began a military career when just out of his teens and quickly rose through the ranks. In 1775 the Continental Congress appointed him commander in chief of the Continental Army. After the War of Independence and the signing of the Treaty of Paris (1783), Washington resigned his commission and returned to his plantation at Mount Vernon with his wife, Martha, whom he had married in 1759. Dissatisfaction with the progress of the nation he had helped forge soon prompted Washington to return to public life, and in 1789 he was unanimously elected first president of the U.S. He won reelection unanimously in 1792. Historians agree that Washington's leadership and good judgment were crucial factors in guiding the young nation though its first shaky years as an independent republic. Washington was the first of eight presidents born in Virginia and the only president who never lived in Washington, D.C.

24 **400th anniversary of Gregorian calendar.** On Feb. 24, 1582, Pope Gregory XIII issued a papal bull bringing the Julian calendar more exactly into line with the solar year and correcting the ten-day error that had accumulated over the centuries. The length of the tropical year, previously reckoned at 365.25 days, was recalculated at 365.2422 days. The ten-day accumulated error was corrected by changing October 5 to October 15. The change went into effect immediately in the Papal States and in Roman Catholic countries but was not adopted in Britain and the American Colonies until 1752. Russia held out until 1918.

MARCH

9 *Jewish feast of Purim*

12 *150th anniversary of Charles Boycott's birth*

15 *Ides of March (Julius Caesar assassinated, 44 BC)*

20 *Vernal equinox in the Northern Hemisphere; autumnal equinox in the Southern Hemisphere*

25 *Independence Day in Greece*

29 *Academy Awards presentations*

12 **150th anniversary of Charles Boycott's birth.** Charles Cunningham Boycott, whose surname is now firmly fixed in the English language, hardly seemed destined for immortality when he was born a century and a half ago. The son of a parson in Norfolk, England, Boycott pursued his career in the Army, retired with the rank of captain, then in 1873 went to work as an agent for the estates of the earl of Erne in County Mayo, Ireland. Shortly after Boycott arrived, Ireland experienced a series of bad harvests, prompting fears of another famine and causing the Irish tenant farmers to form the Land League in 1879. One of the first things the Land League did was to tell Boycott that he must reduce rents by 25%. Boycott refused and instead attempted to serve writs of eviction. The tenants responded by refusing to harvest the crops and by having nothing further to do with Boycott. Thus was born the word boycott. The farmers' nonviolent strategy forced Boycott to import labourers from Ulster, along with 900 armed guards. Boycott left Ireland that year, and conditions eased after Gladstone's Land Act of 1881 set up fair rent tribunals.

29 **Academy Awards presentations.** Hollywood has produced dozens of hits over the years, but the perennial favourite is the annual gathering of the stars themselves at the Academy Awards presentations. The Academy of Motion Picture Arts and Sciences was founded by 36 members in 1927, with Douglas Fairbanks,

Sr., as its first president. The Academy presented its first awards in 1929 for achievements during the year from Aug. 1, 1927, to July 31, 1928. The initial winners included *Wings* for best picture, Emil Jannings for best actor in *The Last Command* and *The Way of All Flesh*, and Janet Gaynor for best actress in *Seventh Heaven*, *Street Angel*, and *Sunrise*. The Academy presented the awards at a banquet on May 16 at the Hollywood Roosevelt Hotel with slightly more than 300 persons attending. By contrast, there are now in the neighbourhood of 4,300 members of the Academy, and the world-wide audience—thanks to television—numbers in the hundreds of millions. Members of the Academy select the winners in each category by secret ballot. In most cases members of the Academy may vote only in the categories to which they belong. Thus, performers vote for performers, directors vote for directors, and so on. The winners in each category receive golden statuettes called Oscars. At the 1981 Academy Awards presentations a film called *Ordinary People* won the Oscar for best picture. For the same film, Robert Redford won best director and Timothy Hutton best supporting actor. Other winners in '81 included Robert De Niro for best actor in *Raging Bull*, Sissy Spacek for best actress in *Coal Miner's Daughter*, and Mary Steenburgen for best supporting actress in *Melvin and Howard*.

APRIL

1 *April Fools' Day*
4 *Palm Sunday*
8 *First Day of Jewish feast of Passover; first day of Masters Golf Tournament*
9 *Bataan Day in the Philippines; Good Friday; La Salle discovered the mouth of the Mississippi (300th anniversary)*
11 *Easter Sunday*
14 *Pan American Day*
18 *Easter in Orthodox churches*
29 *Emperor's birthday in Japan*

8 **Masters Golf Tournament.** Each year many of the best golfers in the world gather at the Augusta National Golf Club in Georgia to see who can play four rounds of golf over these venerable links in the fewest number of strokes. The first winner was Horton Smith, who came in with a 284 in 1934. The course record for a Masters Tournament is 271, set by Jack Nicklaus in 1965 and equaled by Ray Floyd in 1976. Lloyd Mangrum set the competitive course record for one round in 1940 by firing a 64. Five players have since equaled that score: Jack Nicklaus in 1965, Maurice Bembridge in 1974, Hale Irwin in 1975, Gary Player in 1978, and Miller Barber in 1979. Nicklaus, with five victories, has won the Masters more times than anyone else.

9 **La Salle discovered the mouth of the Mississippi.** Robert Cavelier, better known as sieur de La Salle, tried to reach the mouth of the Mississippi River in 1679–

80 but managed only to get close to the site of the present city of Peoria, Ill. This attempt to reach the mouth of the great river began at Ft. Frontenac on the northern shore of Lake Ontario. In early 1682 La Salle and his party once again set out from Ft. Frontenac in canoes, portaging at Chicago and continuing the rest of the way via the Illinois and Mississippi rivers. They reached the mouth of the Mississippi at the Gulf of Mexico on April 9, 1682, 300 years ago. La Salle claimed all the lands drained by the Mississippi and its tributaries in the name of Louis XIV of France and in the king's honour called the vast territory Louisiana. Later, King Louis named La Salle governor of the territory. On a return visit originating in France in 1684, La Salle and his party overshot the river and ended up in Texas. During an attempt to find an overland route to the Mississippi, La Salle's men mutinied and killed him in 1687.

MAY

1 *Kentucky Derby; May Day*
5 *Cinco de Mayo*
8 *VE Day (1945)*
9 *Mother's Day in the U.S.*
21 *Lindbergh landed in Paris (1927)*
30 *Pentecost; Indianapolis 500 auto race*
31 *Memorial Day in the U.S.*

1 **May Day.** Well before the time of Christ it was customary in many parts of Europe and certain other parts of the world to herald the arrival of spring. The Druids in Ireland, Scotland, England, and parts of northern Europe kindled sacred bonfires. The Romans paid homage to Flora, the goddess of flowers, by staging dramatic productions, scattering petals, and adorning small statues of the goddess with blooms. The Celtic custom of lighting bonfires persisted well into the 18th century, and the little Flora dolls the Roman girls decorated were transformed, with the coming of Christianity, to Virgin Mary dolls. By the Middle Ages, maypoles were standard equipment in the villages of England, and it was common to see groups of people "bringing in the May"; that is, gathering blooms and other signs of spring and carrying them home before dawn. May queens were chosen to reign over these and other festivities, and in the 16th and 17th centuries women rose early to bathe their faces in the "May Dew," believed to be a preserver of beauty. The spirit of the first May Days persisted well into our own time with such customs as maypole dances and the exchange of May baskets among children.

5 **Cinco de Mayo.** On the fifth of May 1862 a force of 2,000 Mexicans under Gen. Ignacio Zaragoza soundly defeated French forces that were three times their number. The background, briefly, was this: Mexico had earlier defaulted on bonds to France, Spain, and England. In October 1861 the three powers decided to stage a joint naval demonstration to compel repay-

ment to the bondholders. Leaders of the naval expedition announced that they had no desire for conquest but simply wanted to collect the overdue payments. A conference was arranged and a preliminary agreement was reached. With that, the Spanish and British fleets sailed for home. The French, however, remained behind in the belief that they could easily defeat the Mexicans and establish a centralized monarchy for their emperor, Napoleon III, who was desirous of attaining hegemony in Spanish America. Though the attack failed, the French eventually did conquer Mexico and in 1864 installed Archduke Maximilian of Austria on the throne. He reigned for three years before being deposed and shot on June 19, 1867. Cinco de Mayo is a national holiday in Mexico and is celebrated with much gusto. The day is also celebrated by Mexican-Americans in several cities of the Southwest.

JUNE

6 *Anniversary of D-Day (1944)*
11 *Kamehameha Day in Hawaii*
12 *Queen's "official" birthday in Great Britain; Philippine Independence Day*
15 *Magna Carta Day (1215)*
20 *Father's Day in the U.S.*
21 *Summer solstice in the Northern Hemisphere; winter solstice in the Southern Hemisphere*
23 *First day of Ramadan*

12 **Philippine Independence Day.** The struggle for independence in the Philippines began in 1521 when the Portuguese explorer Ferdinand Magellan landed there and claimed the islands for Spain. The Filipinos won that round; they repelled the invaders and killed Magellan. But Magellan's death did not deter the Spanish. In 1564 they tried again, dispatching a fleet of ships from Mexico. This time the invasion succeeded. With the exception of a period of British control (1762–63) during the Seven Years' War, the Spanish ruled the islands, with varying degrees of success, for well over three centuries. Revolution broke out in 1843, followed by a series of uprisings until 1898. On May 1 of that year Commodore George Dewey and his U.S. fleet defeated the Spanish in the Battle of Manila Bay. On June 12 the revolutionary leader Emilio Aguinaldo, who had returned from exile in Hong Kong, proclaimed the islands independent. With support from Aguinaldo and his followers, U.S. Army Gen. Wesley Merritt attacked the city of Manila, and the Spanish surrendered the following day. The Treaty of Paris, ratified by the U.S. Senate on Feb. 6, 1899, ended the Spanish-American War and resulted in U.S. acquisition of the Philippines in return for the payment of $20 million to Spain. Expecting the islands to be granted immediate self-determination, Aguinaldo once again called for independence, and his followers rose up in revolt against the U.S. even before the treaty was ratified. Though guerrilla war-

fare continued for several years, a commission established by Pres. William McKinley in 1899 concluded that, after a period of training and experience in self-government, the Philippines should be granted independence. U.S. influence was gradually phased out, though the process was delayed by the invasion of the Japanese during World War II. Full independence was granted on July 4, 1946. In 1962 Philippine Pres. Diosdado Macapagal changed the date to June 12, the date in 1898 on which Aguinaldo had proclaimed independence from Spain. The day also honours José Rizal, the revolutionary leader whom the Spanish had executed in 1896.

21 Summer solstice. This is the first day of summer in the Northern Hemisphere, or the exact moment when the Sun appears to reach its northernmost point above the celestial equator, "stop," and begin moving southward again. (The word solstice comes from Latin *solstitium*, *sol* meaning "sun" and *sistere*, "to stand still.") The apparent movement of the Sun from north to south is caused by the changing declination of the Earth's axis as the Earth orbits the Sun. The summer solstice always occurs on or about June 21. In 1982 it will occur at exactly 1:23 PM, Eastern Standard Time, on June 21. In the Southern Hemisphere this marks the beginning of winter.

JULY

15 St. Swithin's Day. According to an old English legend, if it rains on St. Swithin's Day, it will rain for 40 more days. At the time of his death (July 2, 862), Swithin was bishop of Winchester. Before he died he ordered that his remains be buried in a churchyard location that the townspeople had long felt was either cursed or unfit for burial. Why Swithin chose to be buried in this particular spot remains a mystery, but he may have wanted to terminate the superstitions about the plot. In any event, the townspeople followed his instructions. In the decades following his death, Swithin's popularity increased; stories circulated that prayers directed to him resulted in miraculous cures. It was decided, therefore, that Swithin should be reinterred in a more suitable place. More than 100 years after his death, a lavish ceremony was arranged to reinter Swithin's remains in Winchester Cathedral. According to the legend, a great downpour disrupted the ceremony and continued for 40 days. This deluge convinced the do-gooders that

Swithin wanted to remain where he was and also sparked the legend of the 40 days of rain. Nevertheless, the people of Winchester eventually prevailed, and on July 15, 971, Swithin's remains were transferred to Winchester Cathedral, apparently under clear skies.

22 Id al-Fitr. On the Muslim calendar, July 22, 1982, is called Id al-Fitr, the first day of the month of Shawwal, the tenth month of the year. It is one of two great feast days celebrated by Muslims; the other is Id al-Adha, celebrated on the tenth day of the 12th month (Dhu al-Hijjah). Id al-Fitr follows immediately upon Ramadan, a month-long period of fasting and other forms of self-denial for Muslims. During Ramadan, Muslims abstain from food, liquids, and sexual intercourse from sunrise to sunset. They are also expected to say extra prayers and work hard to avoid all forms of sin. Thus, in addition to being one of the two great feast days granted Muslims by Allah, Id al-Fitr also celebrates the end of the penitential season. The day is customarily observed with reunions of friends and relatives and exchanges of gifts.

AUGUST

2 Dublin Horse Show. Everybody from stable boys to members of the international jet set shows up for the Dublin International Horse Show—besides riders, breeders, and others directly involved in equestrian sports, there are thousands of others who just like horses. The event is one of the most important and prestigious horse shows in the world. It was started in the 1860s by the Royal Dublin Society, which dates back even earlier to 1731. Today the program requires five full days and involves something on the order of 2,000 horses. They come from all over the world and represent every imaginable type of horse: jumpers, ponies, Thoroughbreds, hunters, riding cobs, polo ponies, draft horses, and even donkeys. Many of Ireland's fox hunting clubs stage their annual balls during horse show week. Thursday, Ladies Day, brings out elegant hats and fashionable gowns, many designed by the world's leading couturiers. At other times, visitors can enjoy the traditional trade show, arts and crafts exhibits, folk dancing demonstrations, and the annual flower show sponsored by the Royal Horticultural Society. Marching bands provide constant music.

15 Independence Day in India. Thirty-five years ago, in 1947, political power in India passed from the British to the Indians. The new constitution was enacted by the Constituent Assembly in November 1949 and came into force on Jan. 26, 1950. India is a sovereign democratic republic, but by virtue of its voluntary membership in the Commonwealth continues to maintain friendly relations with its former colonial master. It is the second most populous nation in the world.

SEPTEMBER

11 Miss America Pageant. Margaret Gorman, a blue-eyed blonde from Washington, D.C., became the first Miss America in 1921. She was 16 years old, stood 5 ft 1 in, weighed 108 lb, and measured 30–25–32. Since Miss Gorman's time, pageant winners have generally been bigger and older, and emphasis on the bathing suit competition has lessened. The modern-day Miss America must also perform in a talent competition and undergo a personal interview. Contestants share in over $2 million in college scholarships at the local, state, and national levels. Miss America herself receives a $20,000 scholarship, plus a one-year promotional tour that is valued at tens of thousands of dollars. Winners often parlay the Miss America title into lucrative careers in the entertainment industry. Among the Miss Americas who have done so are Bess Myerson, Lee Meriwether, and Phyllis George.

18 Oktoberfest begins in Munich. Oktoberfest, despite the name, usually begins in September. This happens because the festival traditionally begins on a Saturday, runs for slightly more than two weeks, and always ends on the first Sunday of October. It all began in 1810 when Crown Prince Louis married Princess Therese of Saxe-Hildburghausen and decided to stage a celebration outside the gates of Munich. The main event was a horse race, and throngs of Bavarian subjects showed up to watch. So popular was this forerunner of the modern Oktoberfest that the Bavarians decided to perpetuate it. Today, Oktoberfest draws visitors from many lands and claims to be the largest folk festival in the world. Colourful beer tents and all manner of carnival rides flank a mammoth midway dominated by an imposing Ferris wheel. Brass bands fill the air with typical oompah.

Gaily decorated brewers' carts parade down the streets. But the chief activities seem to be eating and drinking. In a typical year, Oktoberfesters put away three dozen or more spit-roasted oxen, 30,000 grilled fish, 400,000 pairs of pork sausages, half a million chickens, and over a million gallons of beer.

OCTOBER

1 *Founding of People's Republic of China (1949)*
4 *25th anniversary of Sputnik*
5 *Day of the Republic in Portugal*
11 *Thanksgiving Day in Canada*
12 *Columbus Day*
18 *Alaska Day*
22 *20th anniversary of Cuban Missile Crisis*
24 *United Nations Day*
31 *Reformation Sunday; Halloween*

4 25th anniversary of Sputnik. The space age, and the space race, began on this date in 1957 when the Soviet Union launched Sputnik 1, the first successful man-made Earth satellite. Sputnik, which was fired into orbit from the U.S.S.R.'s Tyuratam launch site, transmitted radio signals for 21 days. The U.S. successfully launched its first Earth satellite, Explorer 1, on Jan. 31, 1958. The first man in space was Soviet cosmonaut Yuri Gagarin, who began his historic journey on April 12, 1961. The most dramatic of all space achievements occurred on July 20, 1969, when Americans Neil Armstrong and Edwin ("Buzz") Aldrin set foot on the Moon.

31 Halloween. Halloween is actually the short form of All Hallows Eve, the night before All Saints' Day, though the original observances took place centuries before Christ and were anything but saintly. Research into the origins of Halloween have generally concluded that those primarily responsible for the present-day events were pre-Christian Celtic Druids. The Celtic year ended on October 31, and it was Druidic practice at that time to celebrate a joint festival. On this day the Druids honoured both the Sun God and the Lord of the Dead. The Sun God was thanked for the harvest; the Lord of the Dead was appeased with sacrifices of horses and human beings. The sacrifices were also intended to frighten away evil spirits: the Druids believed that departed souls roamed abroad on the night of October 31, often playing tricks and indulging in various supernatural antics in order to frighten the living. These pagan beliefs persisted long after Pope Gregory IV made All Saints' Day and Eve part of the church calendar in the 9th century. In Ireland, Scotland, Wales, and parts of England, country folk were attempting to frighten away evil spirits with bonfires as late as the 19th century. Various kinds of mischief were also commonly practiced in the British Isles. The Irish gave new life to the prankish side of Halloween after immigrating to the U.S. in the 1840s. In the

20th century the mischievous side of Halloween began to include acts of vandalism. Parties and parades also became common. Today children still don costumes and go trick or treating, but instead of candy they often collect money for the United Nations Children's Fund (UNICEF).

NOVEMBER

7 *Anniversary of the Bolshevik Revolution (1917)*
11 *Veterans Day*
20 *Anniversary of Mexican Revolution (1910)*
22 *Pres. John F. Kennedy assassinated (1963)*
25 *Thanksgiving Day in the U.S.*
26 *150th anniversary of Mary Edwards Walker's birth*
28 *First Sunday in Advent*

11 Veterans Day. The U.S. honours its soldiers and its war dead on this day. Originally called Armistice Day, the custom began on Nov. 11, 1919, one year after the Armistice that ended World War I. At the 11th hour of the 11th day of the 11th month in 1918, hostilities between the Allies and Germany formally ended. November 11 became a U.S. federal holiday in 1938. In 1920 Britain and France added ceremonies honouring "the unknown soldier"; the U.S. adopted the same custom the following year. Armistice Day also celebrated the beginning of what many thought would be a lasting era of peace. Ten million soldiers had been killed during the war; few thought such a tragedy could happen again. But it did; in World War II the toll was more than double. Because Armistice Day had lost much of its original significance following World War II and the Korean War, the U.S. Congress passed a bill in 1954 specifying that Armistice Day would henceforth be known and commemorated as Veterans Day. In 1968 Pres. Lyndon B. Johnson signed a bill making Veterans Day a Monday holiday, but veterans groups and others objected and the observance gradually reverted to the traditional date. The federal changeover to the traditional date took effect in 1978.

26 150th anniversary of Mary Edwards Walker's birth. One hears very little about Mary Edwards Walker these days, yet she was one of the best known women of her time. Born on Nov. 26, 1832, she earned a degree in medicine, became the first female surgeon in the U.S. Army, served four months in a Confederate prison during the Civil War, and won the Medal of Honor, the first and only woman ever to do so. She also wrote several books on women's rights and campaigned for women's suffrage. A government review board revoked Walker's Medal of Honor in 1917 on the grounds that she was never an official member of the Army, but Walker continued to wear the medal until her death in 1919. In 1977 the medal was posthumously restored to her by the secretary of the Army.

DECEMBER

5 *200th anniversary of Martin Van Buren's birth*
10 *Human Rights Day*
11 *First day of Jewish feast of Hanukka*
22 *Winter solstice in the Northern Hemisphere; summer solstice in the Southern Hemisphere*
25 *Christmas Day*
29 *Massacre at Wounded Knee (1890)*
30 *Total eclipse of the Moon (North America, Asia, Australasia)*
31 *New Year's Eve*

5 200th anniversary of Martin Van Buren's birth. The eighth president of the U.S., Martin Van Buren, was born on Dec. 5, 1782, and died on July 24, 1862. He was the first U.S. president born after the Declaration of Independence, the first president born in New York State, and the first who was born a U.S. citizen. His seven predecessors, though born in America, began life as British subjects. Van Buren held many political offices during his lifetime, including U.S. senator from New York, governor of New York, and vice-president under Andrew Jackson. He was elected president of the U.S. in 1836 but was defeated by William Henry Harrison in the election of 1840. Van Buren's defeat has been attributed in part to a severe economic depression at that time, to his antislavery sentiments, and to his opposition to the annexation of Texas. He sought the presidency twice more, in 1844 and 1848, but failed miserably in both of these attempts.

11 First day of Hanukka. The Jewish holiday of Hanukka dates back to the 2nd century BC and the victory of the Maccabees over the Syrians. The war started when the Syrians, under the Greek-Syrian King Antiochus IV Epiphanes, attempted to hellenize the Jews. The Syrians suppressed the Jewish religion, desecrated the Temple of Jerusalem, and promoted the worship of pagan gods. When the Maccabees resisted, war broke out. The war lasted three years, and when it was over the Maccabees, under Judas Maccabeus, had won. Without delay they cleansed the Temple, rededicated the altar, and celebrated with sacrifices and songs of praise. The celebration took place on the 25th day of the Jewish month of Kislev in the year 165 BC. Jews celebrate Hanukka for eight days in a number of ways. One is by lighting candles in a multibranched candelabrum called a menorah: one burns on the first day, two on the second, and so on until eight have been lighted. The lighted candles symbolize the faith of the Jewish people and their love of freedom. Other observances include parties, gifts for children, and readings from the First and Second Books of Maccabees and from the Torah. Though not generally considered one of the most important of Jewish holidays, Hanukka has taken on added significance since the creation of the modern state of Israel.

JANUARY

1 *Greece joins European Communities*

Greece was formally admitted into the European Communities (EC) as the tenth member nation. Pres. Konstantinos Karamanlis, who as prime minister of Greece had played an important role in the negotiations, viewed the event as a turning point in modern Greek history. His country's delegation was allotted 5 of the 63 votes that are cast during meetings of the EC's Council of Ministers.

Diouf becomes Senegal president

Abdou Diouf, premier of Senegal since February 1970, was sworn in as president of the West African republic following the resignation of the nation's 74-year-old president, Léopold Sédar Senghor. Senghor, who became head of state in 1960 when Senegal gained independence from France, had groomed 45-year-old Diouf as his successor.

Iceland fights inflation

Gunnar Thoroddsen, prime minister of Iceland, launched a broad and multifaceted austerity program aimed at reducing the annual inflation rate to 40% by the end of the year; during 1980 the rate had been running between 50 and 60%. The government plan included currency reforms and an immediate 10% increase in the cost of bus rides, postage, telephone service, and other government-provided services. Private enterprise, however, was placed under a strict price freeze. The króna was replaced by a new króna, worth 100 of the old units.

5 *"Yorkshire Ripper" believed caught*

British police formally charged Peter W. Sutcliffe, a 35-year-old truck driver, with the November 1980 murder of a 20-year-old female student in Leeds. When Sutcliffe was taken into custody on January 2, police were confident they had finally captured the "Yorkshire Ripper," who was believed responsible for brutally murdering 13 women over five years.

6 *Chad and Libya to merge*

After four days of talks in Tripoli, Libya, between Pres. Goukouni Oueddei of Chad and Libyan leader Col. Muammar al-Qaddafi, Libya announced that the two countries would merge. Though Libya denied it had been involved militarily in the Chadian civil war, its troops had helped Oueddei's supporters take control of the capital city of N'Djamena in December 1980.

7 *U.S. auto sales fall sharply*

Figures published on the U.S. automobile industry showed that domestically manufactured passenger car sales fell 20% below the level of the previous year, making 1980 the industry's worst year since 1961.

AFL-CIO unions help Solidarity

According to reports, some $160,000 contributed by members of AFL-CIO-affiliated labour unions or by their locals had been used to purchase duplicating machines and other office equipment for Solidarity, the independent federation of Polish trade unions. Spokesmen for the U.S. workers said the gifts were a direct response to Solidarity's request for help.

9 *Portuguese premier sworn in*

Francisco Pinto Balsemão, who 18 days earlier had been designated premier by the president of Portugal, was formally sworn in, together with members of his Cabinet. Pinto Balsemão, who headed a three-party coalition government, promised that what remained of the 1974 Marxist revolution would be eradicated during his four years in office. He succeeded Francisco Sá Carniero, who had been killed in a plane crash in December 1980.

10 *Mugabe demotes Joshua Nkomo*

Prime Minister Robert Mugabe of Zimbabwe transferred Joshua Nkomo from the home affairs ministry to the public service ministry because "criticism of the police became [unjustified] criticism of Comrade Nkomo." Nkomo indicated he would not accept the demotion. After Mugabe and his Zimbabwe African National Union (ZANU) party soundly defeated Nkomo and his Zimbabwe African People's Union (ZAPU) party in the March 1980 election, ZAPU had been given four Cabinet posts in the Patriotic Front coalition. But during the months that followed, Nkomo had vigorously objected to many government policies.

13 *Marshal Kulikov visits Poland*

Soviet Marshal Viktor Kulikov, commander in chief of the Warsaw Pact armies, was reported to be in Poland for talks with Communist Party officials and military leaders. Outside observers believed the meetings were calculated to intimidate supporters and members of Solidarity, the independent federation of Polish trade unions, which was formally recognized by the government in October 1980.

15 *Terrorists release D'Urso in Rome*

A member of the Italian terrorist organization Red Brigades notified a news agency in Rome where Giovanni D'Urso could be found unharmed. A director general in the Ministry of Justice, D'Urso had been

A smiling Ronald Reagan and wife Nancy greeted the crowds as they drove to the White House after his inauguration as U.S. president on January 20.

GENE FORTE—CONSOLIDATED NEWS PICTURES/KEYSTONE

kidnapped on Dec. 12, 1980, and forced to reveal government procedures for tracking down terrorists.

17 Marcos lifts martial law

Philippine Pres. Ferdinand E. Marcos declared an end to martial law but stipulated that decrees he had issued during the "emergency," which began in September 1972, would remain in force unless they were specifically changed. Anticipating an end to martial law, a group called the United Democratic Opposition issued a statement on January 15. It questioned the significance of Marcos's impending declaration because such basic democratic freedoms as free speech and a free press would not have been restored. Marcos had informed reporters on January 10 that he intended to remain in office until elections were held in 1984.

18 Trudeau ends trip abroad

Canadian Prime Minister Pierre E. Trudeau returned to Canada after talks with Mexican Pres. José López Portillo. Mexico was the last stop on Trudeau's itinerary, which also included Europe, Africa, and South America. Canada's desire to help bridge the gap between developed and less developed countries was described as support for "a revolution in international morality."

Begin announces new elections

Israeli Prime Minister Menachem Begin announced that new parliamentary elections would be scheduled for July 7, about four months before his term of office was due to expire. The news followed the resignation of Finance Minister Yigael Hurwitz, the sixth Cabinet-level official to desert the Begin government. Moshe Dayan had resigned as foreign minister in October 1979 and Ezer Weizman as defense minister in May 1980.

20 Reagan assumes U.S. presidency

Ronald Wilson Reagan was sworn in as the 40th president of the United States during a noontime ceremony at the nation's Capitol. At 69 years of age, Reagan became the oldest person ever to assume the U.S. presidency. During his inaugural address, Reagan declared that big government was the cause of many of the nation's current economic woes.

Iran frees U.S. hostages

After 444 days of captivity, 52 U.S. citizens were finally permitted to leave Iran aboard an Algerian airliner that carried them to Algiers after a brief refueling stop in Greece. The former hostages were then officially turned over to the custody of U.S. government representatives and flown to the U.S. Air Force base at Wiesbaden, West Germany. Algerians had acted as intermediaries during the final stages of the highly complex negotiations

SVEN SIMON/KATHERINE YOUNG

Fifty-two U.S. citizens, held hostage in Iran, returned to the U.S. on January 25 after 444 days of captivity.

that revolved around frozen Iranian assets, the late shah's wealth, U.S. claims against Iran, and related issues. On January 25 the 52 landed at New York's Stewart Airport, near the U.S. Military Academy, at West Point, where they were expected to remain for a few days in semiprivacy with their families.

21 Mexico and Cuba sign energy pact

Mexico and Cuba signed a comprehensive agreement that would, in various ways, help resolve many of Cuba's most vital energy needs. Mexico would, among other things, train Cuban personnel, supply or help procure needed equipment, and join Cuba in exploring for oil and gas.

23 Kim Dae Jung gets reprieve

South Korean Pres. Chun Doo Hwan commuted the death sentence of Kim Dae Jung, former leader of the opposition New Democratic Party, to life imprisonment. Earlier in the day Kim's conviction on charges of sedition was upheld by the nation's Supreme Court. Chun, who noted that Kim had expressed regrets for past actions and had asked for clemency, said he hoped the reprieve would help end "confrontation politics" in South Korea.

24 President lifts martial law in South Korea

Pres. Chun Doo Hwan decreed an end to martial law in South Korea after deciding

that the country had sufficiently regained the stability it lost after the assassination of Park Chung Hee in October 1979. The midnight to 4 AM curfew, however, would still be observed as it had been since 1945.

25 China sentences "gang of four"

Jiang Qing (Chiang Ch'ing), widow of Chinese Communist Party Chairman Mao Zedong (Mao Tse-tung) and leader of the "gang of four," was sentenced to death for crimes against the state. The sentence, which was handed down by a Beijing (Peking) court, was suspended for two years to give Jiang a chance to save her life by admitting her guilt and expressing remorse. Zhang Chunqiao (Chang Ch'un-ch'iao), formerly mayor of Shanghai and member of the Political Bureau of the Chinese Communist Party Central Committee, received the same sentence. Less severe sentences were handed out to Jiang's two other associates and to an additional six defendants who stood trial at the same time.

28 Iran to get no U.S. arms

U.S. Secretary of State Alexander Haig announced during a news conference that Iran would get no military equipment from the U.S. "either under earlier obligations and contractual agreements or as yet unstated requests." Haig added that the $550 million Iran had already paid for such equipment would be returned.

FEBRUARY

Border fighting flares between Peru and Ecuador

An old border dispute between Peru and Ecuador was rekindled when Ecuadorian troops set up a military camp 13 km (8 mi) inside Peruvian territory. After Ecuadorean Pres. Jaime Roldós Aguilera asked the Organization of American States (OAS) to intervene, representatives of both sides agreed to a cease-fire during a meeting of the OAS in Washington, D.C., on February 2.

Parliamentary elections set in South Africa

P. W. Botha, prime minister of South Africa since September 1978, informed Parliament that new elections would be held on April 29, more than a year and a half earlier than required by law. During the campaign Botha planned to emphasize national security and progress.

29 *Spanish premier resigns*

Adolfo Suárez González unexpectedly resigned as premier of Spain and leader of the Union of the Democratic Centre party, which was in turmoil. Suárez, who had been premier since July 1976, said he hoped his resignation would further the cause of Spain's fledgling democracy.

Islamic nations end summit meeting

The Organization of the Islamic Conference concluded a meeting in Taif, Saudi Arabia, after discussing major issues confronting the Muslim world. The delegates called for greater Arab unity, statehood for the Palestinians, an end to Israeli occupation of East Jerusalem and Arab lands, and the withdrawal of Soviet troops from Afghanistan. Iran's refusal to send a delegation to the conference dashed any hope of directly settling the Iran-Iraq conflict.

30 *Norway's prime minister resigns*

Odvar Nordli resigned as prime minister of Norway "for reasons of health." A firm supporter of NATO and of Norway's participation in the organization, Nordli had been under attack by members of his own Labour Party who opposed the stockpiling of U.S. weapons in their country. Gro Harlem Brundtland succeeded Nordli on February 4.

31 *France and Brazil formalize trade and financial agreement*

At the conclusion of a five-day visit to Paris, Brazilian Pres. João Baptista Figueiredo formalized a complex agreement between his country and France. The pact obligated Brazil to purchase certain French-manufactured items. France would reciprocate by guaranteeing bank loans and helping Brazil advance its development program.

FEBRUARY

2 *Korean president visits U.S.*

South Korean Pres. Chun Doo Hwan and President Reagan, meeting in Washington, D.C., announced that their two countries would "resume immediately the full range of consultations" that Pres. Jimmy Carter had interrupted because he was dissatisfied with certain of Chun's domestic policies. Reagan also assured Chun that U.S. troops would remain in South Korea. Several days later a Reagan administration official confirmed a report that F-16 fighter planes would be sold to South Korea.

Yugoslavia gets IMF loan

The International Monetary Fund was reported to have approved a record three-year loan of $2.1 billion to help Yugoslavia stabilize its economy. By expanding its export markets, Yugoslavia hoped to curb the inflation rate, which reached more than 35% during 1980, and reduce the $2.2 billion trade deficit it had incurred during that same year.

5 *Reagan outlines economic plan*

President Reagan, in his first televised address from the White House, called upon lawmakers and ordinary citizens to support his dramatically new economic program so as to prevent "an economic calamity of tremendous proportions." Basically, Reagan asked for three successive annual 10% reductions in the income tax rates for individuals, accelerated depreciation allowances for plant and equipment, and a drastic reduction in the growth of government spending. The

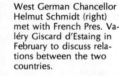
West German Chancellor Helmut Schmidt (right) met with French Pres. Valéry Giscard d'Estaing in February to discuss relations between the two countries.

AGIP

plan, which had never been tried, was designed to slow the rate of inflation, increase productivity, and decrease unemployment. Though Reagan warned that his planned budget cuts would affect "virtually every department of government," he gave assurances that "the truly needy" would be cared for.

Military court convicts Garwood

A jury of five U.S. Marine Corps officers convicted 34-year-old Pfc. Robert R. Garwood of collaborating with the enemy and assaulting a fellow soldier while he was held as a prisoner of war in Vietnam. During the trial former prisoners testified that Garwood had helped the Vietnamese interrogate them, had informed on them, and had lived with his captors. The prosecutor pooh-poohed Garwood's plea of insanity as his only hope of acquittal. On February 13 Garwood received a relatively mild sentence that included reduction to the rank of private and a dishonourable discharge. A U.S. Court of Claims would decide whether or not he would receive $147,000 in back pay that had accumulated while he was a prisoner of war.

6 *Poles end ten-day strike*

Some 100,000 Polish workers in the southern industrial city of Bielsko-Biala ended their ten-day general strike after the government agreed to meet seven demands, the most important of which was the removal of the governor and three of his aides. All were accused of building private villas for themselves, ignoring overdue tax bills involving their friends, and expropriating government cars and buildings for private use.

Schmidt and Giscard hold talks

West German Chancellor Helmut Schmidt and French Pres. Valéry Giscard d'Estaing concluded two days of talks in Paris. One segment of their joint communiqué urged that Poland be allowed to solve its serious domestic problems "without external interference," a clear reference to the persistent threat of a Soviet invasion. Giscard reportedly wanted to set forth in detail the consequences of a Soviet invasion, but Schmidt was said to prefer implied warnings couched in words that were less confrontational.

8 Sihanouk's plan for Kampuchea encounters indifference

Prince Norodom Sihanouk offered to lead a movement to oust the Vietnamese from Kampuchea (Cambodia). The call to arms elicited such weak response that the former head of state canceled the proposed venture on February 27, noting from his exile in North Korea that many Kampuchean exiles living in France were unwilling to associate with guerrillas who had once been loyal to the deposed Pol Pot government.

9 Opposing groups strike in Spain

Two general strikes were called in Spain: the first to protest the murder of a nuclear engineer by radical members of the ETA (Euzkadi ta Azkatasuna, "Homeland and Liberty"), a Basque separatist organization seeking independence for its area of the country; the second, one week later, to protest the death in prison of an ETA supporter.

José María Ryan, an engineer working at a nuclear plant under construction near Bilbao, was murdered on February 6, eight days after he had been kidnapped by the radical wing of the ETA; its members opposed construction of the nuclear installation. A general strike was observed on February 9, the day after Ryan's burial, and huge crowds demonstrated in various cities, apparently to voice outrage against the ETA for using such violence to attain its goals.

The second general strike, on February 16, was organized by the ETA to protest the death in a prison hospital of José Ignacio Arregui Izaguirre, the victim of alleged torture. Arregui, a suspect in the killing of two Civil Guards, had been held incommunicado since his arrest on February 4. When news of Arregui's death was made public, a two-day period of rioting began in San Sebastián, Vitória, and Bilbao.

General becomes Polish premier

Jozef Pinkowski, chairman of the Council of Ministers (premier) since August 1980, was dismissed from office during a plenary session of Poland's Communist Party Central Committee. He was replaced by the 57-year-old defense minister, Gen. Wojciech Jaruzelski, who became a full member of the Politburo in 1978. That same day between 100,000 and 300,000 workers in Jelenia Gora began a general strike that had been brewing for several weeks over the status of a public hospital. Independent farmers also contributed to the general labour unrest and, indirectly at least, to Pinkowski's downfall by demanding that Rural Solidarity be given the status of an officially recognized union.

10 Premier named in Spain

Leopoldo Calvo Sotelo, who had been serving the government in the Department of Economic Affairs, was named premier of Spain by King Juan Carlos. With the approval of the Cortes (parliament), he would succeed Adolfo Suárez González, who recommended the promotion after resigning on January 29.

11 Corsican separatists resort to bombings at home and in Paris

The Corsican National Liberation Front was presumed responsible for 46 bombings that began late at night on the French island of Corsica. Earlier in the day eight Corsican separatists had been sentenced to prison in Paris after being found guilty of the 1980 kidnapping of three persons who opposed autonomy for Corsica. No personal injuries were reported either in Corsica or in three bombing incidents in the Paris area for which the organization claimed credit; extensive damage, however, was inflicted on property, vehicles, public buildings, and stores.

13 Nonaligned nations meet in India

After five days of debate, delegates representing more than 90 nations associated with the nonaligned movement adopted a resolution calling for the withdrawal of foreign troops from Afghanistan and Kampuchea (Cambodia). Though the U.S.S.R. and Vietnam were unmistakably the targets of the resolution, neither country was mentioned by name. Among other matters, the conference went on record as opposing "the military presences of all the great powers" in the Indian Ocean. UN Secretary-General Kurt Waldheim addressed the gathering on February 11, the 20th anniversary of the founding of the nonaligned movement.

16 Prominent Iranians accuse their government of tyranny

A group of 38 Iranian lawyers, writers, and academics began circulating a letter that accused the government of commit-

STEINBERG—GAMMA/LIAISON

Rescue workers removed the wounded after some 200 Civil Guards stormed a session of the Spanish Cortes (parliament) and seized the Cabinet and about 350 legislators as hostages. The coup did not succeed, and the hostages were released the next day.

FEBRUARY

ting "major acts of tyranny." The signatories, some of whom had been imprisoned during the reign of the deposed shah, cited violations of human rights, legal injustices, torture of prisoners, the suppression of ethnic minorities, and maltreatment of political dissidents. They also deplored the open enmity manifested toward higher education, culture, and the arts.

Pope John Paul II visits Asia

Pope John Paul II began his first visit to Asia with a brief stop in Pakistan; he then flew on to the Philippines, the only predominantly Roman Catholic nation in Asia. During a speech delivered in the presence of President and Mrs. Ferdinand E. Marcos on February 17, the pope pointedly noted that even in exceptional situations there is no justification for "any violation of the fundamental dignity of the human person or of the basic rights that safeguard this dignity." During his tour of the country, John Paul singled out two groups for special attention: the poor of Tondo, a notorious Manila slum, and victimized workers labouring in sugar plantations on the island of Negros. The address he delivered to Chinese Catholics in Manila was also beamed to China. After a brief stop in Guam, the pope flew to Japan, where he met with Emperor Hirohito, Prime Minister Zenko Suzuki, and leaders of various religious groups. He told an audience gathered in Hiroshima Peace Memorial Park: "To remember Hiroshima is to abhor nuclear war. To remember Hiroshima is to commit oneself to peace."

Soviets training PLO officers

During a lecture in Beirut, Lebanon, a high-ranking member of the Palestine Liberation Organization (PLO) declared that hundreds of Palestinian military officers, capable of commanding "major sectors, such as brigades," had completed their training at Soviet military academies. The spokesman, who resides in Moscow, also affirmed that 2,000 Palestinians were enrolled in Soviet schools, many in fields relating to science and technology.

17 U.S. aid to El Salvador gets congressional support

After U.S. Secretary of State Alexander Haig briefed a bipartisan group of senators and congressmen on the situation in El Salvador, the Reagan administration received substantial backing for its plan to send military and economic aid to the strife-torn Central American nation. The Reagan administration claimed to have "very solid, increasing evidence" that the leftist guerrillas, with Soviet connivance, were receiving large quantities of military supplies from outside the country. On February 14 Vladillen M. Vasev, a senior Soviet diplomat in Washington, D.C., had denied that his government was sup-

plying arms to the Salvadoran rebels, but he acknowledged that no restrictions were placed on the transshipment of Soviet military equipment after it reached Cuba and Ethiopia.

18 U.S. to observe hostage pact

After a month of careful study, the Reagan administration announced that it would "faithfully implement the agreements" that brought about the release on January 20 of the 52 U.S. citizens held hostage in Iran since November 1979. A State Department spokesman, however, warned that the decision "does not represent a precedent for future actions by the United States government in similar actions. The present administration would not have negotiated with Iran for the release of the hostages. Future acts of state-supported terrorism against the U.S. will meet swift and sure punishment." On February 24 Reagan signed an executive order implementing the agreements.

Kaunda replaces prime minister

Zambian Pres. Kenneth Kaunda named Nalumino Mundia prime minister and Humphrey Mulemba secretary-general of the United National Independence Party, the only legal political entity in the country. Both men were apparently deemed more acceptable to the powerful trade unions than were their respective predecessors, Daniel Lisulo and Mainza Chona.

19 UN mediator fails to terminate Iran-Iraq conflict

Olof Palme, acting as the personal representative of UN Secretary-General Kurt Waldheim, ended his third mission to the Middle East without substantially improving the chances of soon resolving the Iran-Iraq conflict. Palme was convinced, however, that any final settlement would include joint control over the Shatt al-Arab, the vital waterway used to get huge quantities of oil into the Persian Gulf and onto international sea-lanes.

Basques kidnap foreign envoys

Members of the moderate wing of the ETA (Euzkadi ta Azkatasuna, "Homeland and Liberty"), a Basque organization seeking separation of its homelands from Spain, kidnapped the Uruguayan consul from his home in Pamplona and the honorary consuls of Austria and El Salvador from their homes in Bilbao. Similar attempts against the Portuguese and West German consuls in San Sebastián failed. During a radio broadcast the following day, the ETA demanded independence from Spain and the release of 300 Basque prisoners. On February 28 the three diplomats were released unharmed.

20 Dutch to sell subs to Taiwan

Prime Minister Andreas van Agt of The Netherlands gave final approval for the

sale of two Dutch-built submarines to the Chinese Nationalist government in Taiwan. The People's Republic of China quickly denounced the deal as "outrageous interference" in the internal affairs of China and on February 27 formally recalled its ambassador from The Hague. It also requested the Dutch ambassador to leave Beijing (Peking).

22 Iran frees British missionaries

Three British Anglican missionaries, arrested in August 1980 on charges of spying, were released from an Iranian prison after officials acknowledged that documents linking them to the U.S. Central Intelligence Agency were forgeries. A fourth Briton, an employee of a Dutch-Iranian helicopter service company, remained in prison to face charges of espionage and embezzlement.

23 Right-wing coup in Spain fails

During a session of the Spanish Cortes (parliament), which had convened in Madrid to debate approval of Leopoldo Calvo Sotelo as premier, some 200 Civil Guards under the command of Lieut. Col. Antonio Tejero Molina burst into the chamber firing automatic weapons. The Cabinet and about 350 legislators were taken hostage. Tejero, well known as a right-wing extremist, then announced he was taking over the government. In a prepared manifesto, he embraced "true democracy" but denounced regional terrorism. The following morning King Juan Carlos delivered a televised address to the nation. He firmly repudiated the coup and all "actions or personal attitudes that aim at interrupting by force the democratic process." The coup was doomed because the king had overall support from the military. By midday Tejero and the guards were in custody and the hostages released. On February 27 some one million people marched in Madrid to express support for their democratic form of government.

Brezhnev calls for summit talks

During a speech to the 26th congress of the Soviet Communist Party, Pres. Leonid I. Brezhnev proposed a summit meeting between President Reagan and himself to restore "normal relations" between their two countries because it is "universally recognized that in many ways the international situation" depends on their policies. The suggestion was coolly received in Washington. Before adjourning on March 3, the congress reelected all members of the Politburo to new five-year terms, a most unusual action, and approved without change the membership of the party Secretariat.

25 Chun Doo Hwan elected president

South Korea's electoral college, which since the national elections of February 11 had consisted mainly of those bearing the

Democratic Justice Party label, elected Chun Doo Hwan to his first full term as president. The former general, who assumed the presidency in August 1980, received more than 90% of the 5,271 electoral votes cast.

Zia suppresses opposition

Scores of political figures were arrested in various cities of Pakistan after they demanded an end to martial law. Some had signed a petition early in the month urging elections within three months. The government of Pres. Mohammad Zia-ul-Haq had been facing a rising tide of political unrest that was given added impetus on February 7 with the formation of the

Movement for the Restoration of Democracy. The strongest element of the organization, which had the support of left-wing students, was the Pakistan People's Party, headed by the widow and the daughter of Zulfikar Ali Bhutto, a former president who had been hanged in April 1979 for allegedly conspiring to murder a political opponent. In an attempt to avert potential trouble, the government had also closed some universities and jailed or restricted the movements and activities of certain political leaders.

China revamps economic plans

Chinese Vice-Premier Yao Yilin (Yao I-lin), head of the State Planning Ministry,

told the Standing Committee of the National People's Congress that the government would have to reduce spending an additional $9.8 billion to balance its budget. Faced with a huge 1980 deficit of about $12 billion, the government seemed determined to regain control of expenditures even though it meant canceling contracts on such high-priority projects as the Baoshan (Pao-shan) steel complex near Shanghai and vital chemical plants in Nanjing (Nanking), Shandong (Shantung) Province, and elsewhere. Because the Japanese had already invested heavily in carrying out the first phases of the contracts, they were deeply disturbed by the cancellations and appeared determined to seek just compensation.

MARCH

1 Thatcher ends U.S. visit

British Prime Minister Margaret Thatcher left the U.S. after wide-ranging talks with President Reagan and some of his top administrators. On February 27 Thatcher told an audience at Georgetown University that she was "impressed with the striking similarity" between her own policies and those of the Reagan administration. "The president's goal is a stable price level. Ours too. The president's aim is to free the individual from government restraint. Ours too. The president's objective is to reduce public spending and cut direct taxes. Ours too."

2 Pakistanis hijack airliner

Three Pakistani gunmen hijacked a domestic airliner, then diverted the flight to Kabul, Afghanistan. On March 4 the gunmen released 29 of the estimated 148 persons aboard the Boeing 720, but on March 6 they shot and killed one hostage, a member of the Pakistani embassy in Iran. The next day four more hostages were freed. Then on March 9, after reportedly obtaining automatic weapons in Kabul, the gunmen ordered the pilot to head for Damascus, Syria. On March 12, fearful that the terrorists would carry out their threat to blow up the plane and kill all aboard, the Pakistani government finally agreed to release specific prisoners to secure the safe release of the remaining hostages. The crisis ended on March 14 when the three gunmen, all thought to be followers of the late president Zulfikar Ali Bhutto, surrendered to Syrian authorities. Pakistan had already released 54 prisoners and allowed them safe passage out of the country. Syria announced on March 19 that it would not comply with Pakistan's request to extradite the hijackers and the former prisoners.

UN keeps ban on South Africa

The UN General Assembly voted 112–22 against allowing South Africa to reoccupy

the seat it was denied in 1974 because its delegation was not thought to represent South African blacks, who far outnumber the white population. Western nations and Israel opposed the UN action, questioning the right of the General Assembly to determine specific qualifications for membership. On March 6 the General Assembly went one step further when it approved a resolution urging the UN Security Council to impose mandatory sanctions against South Africa for not relinquishing control of South West Africa/Namibia.

3 Thai coalition disintegrates

Thailand's coalition government collapsed when eight members of the Social Action Party (SAP) resigned their Cabinet posts in the government of Prime Minis-

ter Prem Tinsulanond. The trouble began when Chatichai Choonhaven, the minister of industry and a member of the minority Chart Thai party, accused his deputy, a member of SAP, of having tried to subvert an oil deal with Saudi Arabia. When Prem rebuked the deputy for undercutting the minister's negotiations in order to arrange a deal of his own through an agent in Hong Kong, the deputy and other members of SAP resigned their government posts. On March 10 Prem announced the formation of a new five-party coalition that controlled 170 of the 301 seats in the lower house of Parliament.

4 Ivory Coast gets IMF loan

The Ivory Coast was reported to have been granted $626 million in loans by the

The last remaining hijacked passengers on a Pakistani plane were released in Damascus, Syria, after being held for 13 days. The hijackers, who demanded the release of certain prisoners, had killed one of the hostages to demonstrate their determination.

JACQUES PAVLOVSKY—SYGMA

MARCH

International Monetary Fund, which hoped the money would help stabilize that nation's economy. The Ivory Coast had been in financial difficulties for several years, mainly because the market value of coffee and cocoa, its main exports, had declined.

5 Atlanta given federal funds

President Reagan announced that the city of Atlanta, Ga., would receive $979,000 in federal funds to help counter the effects of terror resulting from a series of child murders over the past 19 months. At least 21 black children between the ages of 7 and 15 had disappeared, and 19 of them were subsequently found dead; most were boys. The money would finance social and mental health programs designed to ease the anxiety and fear experienced by young children in the area. An intensive investigation involving local, county, and state police, as well as FBI agents, had produced no solid leads.

6 Peru-Ecuador peace pact set

Peru and Ecuador agreed that Argentina, Brazil, Chile, and the U.S. should mediate the two countries' long-standing border dispute. An earlier cease-fire had been declared on February 2, but it did not hold. In accepting an "immediate peace," Ecuador modified its demands and said it would be satisfied with guaranteed access to the Amazon River, which would provide the country with an outlet to the Atlantic Ocean.

China names new defense minister

At the end of a nine-day meeting, the Standing Committee of China's National People's Congress announced that Geng Biao (Keng Piao), a civilian, would head the Ministry of National Defense. The post had been held by 79-year-old Marshal Xu Xiangqian (Hsü Hsiang-ch'ien), who resigned his vice-premiership in September 1980. Geng was considered a loyal supporter of Vice-Chairman Deng Xiaoping (Teng Hsiao-p'ing) and a defender of Deng's ambitious plans to modernize China.

10 Persian Gulf nations confront regional problems

The foreign ministers of Bahrain, Kuwait, Oman, Qatar, Saudi Arabia, and the United Arab Emirates established a Gulf Cooperation Council during a meeting in Muscat, Oman. The six Persian Gulf nations hoped to improve security and stability in their part of the world by coordinating their economic and political, as well as security, policies.

11 Pinochet begins new term in Chile

Maj. Gen. Augusto Pinochet Ugarte renewed his claim to the presidency of Chile under terms of a new constitution that was approved by plebiscite in Sep-

tember 1980. Pinochet, who simply read a declaration stating that he was beginning an eight-year term, had suspended the 1926 constitution after seizing power in 1973.

Belizeans face uncertain future

Belize, Great Britain, and Guatemala approved the basic principles of an agreement that would grant independence to Belize in the relatively near future. The negotiators, who met in London, also granted Guatemala certain territorial rights. Though some details of the treaty were still to be worked out, news of the general settlement intensified already existing tensions between pro- and anti-independence factions within the British colony. The opposition United Democratic Party, which viewed the pact as near total surrender to Guatemalan demands, called for an immediate referendum on the basic issues. Prime Minister George Price and his pro-independence People's United Party wanted the referendum delayed until all details of the settlement had been worked out and formalized. On April 2 the British governor of Belize felt compelled to declare a state of emergency to bring an end to several days of rioting and violence. Despite such turmoil, British and Belizean officials met in London on April 6 to complete the draft of a constitution under which the people of Belize would presumably live in the future.

Reagan and Trudeau confer in Canada

President Reagan ended a two-day visit to Canada during which he and Canadian Prime Minister Pierre E. Trudeau discussed issues affecting their two countries and other parts of the world. No progress was made on an East Coast fisheries pact, but Reagan promised that the U.S. Coast Guard would not try to keep Canadian fishing vessels outside disputed waters.

15 Dacko wins six-year term

David Dacko was reelected president of the Central African Republic with slightly more than 50% of the vote. He faced four other candidates. Six weeks before the election, the voters gave overwhelming approval to a new democratic constitution. Dacko had promised to restore democracy when he deposed Emperor Bokassa I in a bloodless coup in September 1979. At that time he publicly thanked France and those African nations that had helped him end Bokassa's tyrannical rule.

Growth of world trade down

The international organization known as the General Agreement on Tariffs and Trade reported that world trade had increased only 1% during 1980, the third worst performance (after 1958 and 1975) in 30 years. The decline was largely attributable to weaker demands for oil. During that same period, trade between the

U.S. and the Soviet Union was almost halved, according to the Soviet foreign trade ministry. Combined exports between the two countries fell from $4.1 billion in 1979 to $2,170,000,000 in 1980, an overall decrease of 47%.

16 Coup fails in Mauritania

The government of Mauritania announced that it had foiled an attempted coup led by two military officers who had earlier deserted to Morocco. The two countries had long fought each other and the Popular Front for the Liberation of Saquia el Hamra and Río de Oro (Polisario Front) for control of the Western Sahara after it was abandoned by Spain. Morocco gained control of the upper two-thirds of the region in November 1975. When Mauritania decided to stop fighting in August 1979, it ceded the area it controlled to the Polisario, a native group seeking independence for the territory.

Los Angeles ends school busing

The Los Angeles Board of Education voted to end the mandatory busing of children to achieve racial integration in its schools. On March 11 the California State Supreme Court had refused to rule on whether or not a referendum endorsed by the voters of California in November 1979 was constitutional even though it sought to ban all court-ordered busing not designed to correct deliberate school segregation. The action taken by the Los Angeles school board was unprecedented and would likely inspire officers on other school boards across the nation to seek to dismantle their own school busing programs.

19 Polish police attack workers

Labour unrest in Poland reached a new danger point when local riot police in Bydgoszcz severely injured several workers who had refused to leave the local assembly. Representatives of local farmers had been invited to address the assembly council but then were denied permission to speak. The following day some 500,000 workers affiliated with local chapters of Solidarity staged a two-hour strike to protest the beatings as totally unjustified. When the government seemed, by its inaction, to condone the attacks, Solidarity called for a warning strike on March 27 and for a strike of undetermined duration to begin four days later.

20 Isabel Perón convicted

Isabel Perón, president of Argentina for 21 months after the death of her husband, Juan Perón, was convicted in Buenos Aires on two counts of corruption. A judge declared her guilty of embezzling $700,000 from a charity fund and $1 million from a flood disaster fund while holding public office. Perón would be eligible for parole in July because she had already completed nearly two-thirds of her eight-year sentence.

U.S. Secret Service agents rushed to the assistance of White House Press Secretary James Brady (on the ground at right), who was hit by a bullet during an assassination attempt on Pres. Ronald Reagan. A wounded Washington, D.C., policeman lies on the ground at left. The assailant is being held by police and agents in background.

22 *More U.S. military advisers reach El Salvador*

A group of 12 Green Berets arrived in El Salvador, thereby raising to 54 the number of U.S. military advisers in that country. All were military specialists whose mission was to train Salvadoran troops to fight the leftist guerrillas. The U.S. soldiers would be confined to training areas and would not accompany any government troops during their combat operations. A U.S. State Department official had announced on March 14 that the Reagan administration planned to increase economic aid to El Salvador to a total of $125 million because that kind of assistance was considered more vital to the nation than military aid.

25 *South Korea elects National Assembly*

The Democratic Justice Party (DJP) of South Korea won an absolute majority in the newly constituted National Assembly. Two-thirds of the 276 Assembly seats were decided by the popular vote: the DJP captured 90 seats; the Democratic Korea Party (DKP) finished second with 57; the Korean National Party (KNP) was third with 25. Five other parties won the remaining 19 seats. According to law, four other parties that failed to win 2% of the popular vote and failed to send at least one member to the National Assembly would be disbanded. The remaining 92 seats were allotted proportionally to the three parties that were most successful in the general election, giving a final total of 151

seats to the DJP, 81 to the DKP, and 25 to the KNP.

26 *U.K. gets new political party*

The Social Democratic Party (SDP) gained official recognition in Great Britain and immediately became the third most important political party in Parliament. The organization included 14 members of Parliament, all but one of whom had defected from the Labour Party. In its statement of goals and principles, the SDP sought to position itself between the ruling Conservatives and the Labourites.

29 *Argentine president sworn in*

Gen. Roberto Eduardo Viola, named president-elect of Argentina in October 1980 by the ruling three-man military junta, began his three-year term in office. He succeeded Gen. Jorge Rafael Videla, who took over the government in March 1976 after leading a successful coup against Pres. Isabel Perón. Viola's new 13-member Cabinet included seven civilians, but because the country's two major political parties had decided to reject all offers of positions in the government, neither was represented.

30 *President Reagan shot outside Washington, D.C., hotel*

President Reagan was shot in the chest by a lone gunman who lay in wait outside a Washington, D.C., hotel. The president's press secretary, 40-year-old James Brady, was also severely wounded by a bullet

that pierced his brain. Timothy J. McCarthy, a 31-year-old Secret Service agent, and Thomas Delahanty, a 45-year-old local police officer, were also felled by bullets. All four victims were rushed to hospitals, where they underwent emergency surgery. Doctors issued an optimistic prognosis for the president after removing a bullet from his left lung. Brady's chances of recovery, however, were considered slight by his attending physicians. The two others who were injured were expected to recover. The assailant, who was immediately apprehended, was identified as 25-year-old John W. Hinckley, Jr., of Evergreen, Colo. He had used a .22-calibre "Saturday night special" loaded with devastator bullets that fragment on impact.

Solidarity suspends general strike

Leaders of the Polish labour federation Solidarity agreed to suspend a general strike scheduled to begin the following day. The decision followed tense negotiations with government officials, who finally agreed to most of Solidarity's major demands. Those directly responsible for the beating of workers in Bydgoszcz on March 19 would be put on trial, and the role of local authorities in that incident would be investigated. The government also agreed to give serious consideration to Rural Solidarity's request for legal status. On March 27 millions of Polish workers had participated in an orderly four-hour general strike, an explicit warning that an indefinite general strike would begin in four days unless the government seriously addressed the workers' grievances.

31 *Indonesian hijackers slain*

Four of five Indonesian terrorists were shot and killed in Bangkok, Thailand, after hijacking a domestic DC–9 Garuda airliner on March 28. None of the 55 hostages was injured when Indonesian commandos stormed the plane with the approval of Thai authorities. The hijackers had demanded freedom for 80 persons imprisoned in Indonesia, punishment of Vice-Pres. Adam Malik for allegedly taking kickbacks from a U.S. aircraft company, and expulsion "of all Jewish officials and Israeli militarists" from Indonesia.

U.S. coal miners reject contract

By a margin of more than two to one, union coal miners in the eastern portion of the U.S. refused to approve a new three-year contract that had been negotiated by their leaders on March 23. The rejection raised the spectre of a long strike, which had already begun on March 27 when the old contract expired. Many miners criticized the substitution of widows' pensions for royalties unionized coal companies have had to pay for nonunion coal. The latter provision had increased the cost of nonunion coal and thus protected the jobs of unionized miners.

APRIL

NEVEU-NAYTHONS—GAMMA/LIAISON

Troops loyal to the government took back control of military quarters and communications centres in Bangkok, ending an abortive military coup in Thailand in April.

1 Khomeini wants courts purged

Ayatollah Ruhollah Khomeini suggested that delegations be formed to study Iran's courts and then "dismiss unsuitable judges and prosecutors." Those who deviated from Islamic standards would be viewed as unfit to hold office. Khomeini also urged the prosecution of Revolutionary Guards who violated the principles of Islam by "interfering in matters which are up to the courts and other institutions."

2 Violence in Lebanon escalates

In the worst violence in Lebanon since the 1976 cease-fire, 37 persons were reported killed during intense fighting in Beirut, the capital, and in Zahle, a Christian city some 48 km (30 mi) to the east. During the following days hundreds more were killed or wounded. On April 8, Lebanese Pres. Elias Sarkis ordered a cease-fire, but few believed it would hold. On April 13 Syrian troops took complete control of the hills surrounding Zahle, which relied on Israeli supplies for survival. Because Israel had repeatedly warned that it would never permit the Lebanese Christians to be overwhelmed by Syrian or Palestinian forces, there were widespread fears that the fighting could intensify.

3 Thai coup fails to win support

Troops loyal to Prime Minister Prem Tinsulanond peacefully took back control of military quarters and communications

centres in Bangkok, thereby ending an attempted military coup. After Gen. Sant Chipatima's bloodless revolt on April 1, a Revolutionary Council dissolved Parliament and suspended the constitution; but Prem and King Bhumibol Adulyadej, both of whom had fled to the city of Nakhon Ratchasima, were able to dissuade Thai soldiers from deserting the established government.

4 Red Brigades leader arrested

Italian police in Milan arrested Mario Moretti, generally considered to have been the most important member of the Red Brigades still at large. Moretti was thought to have personal ties with members of terrorist groups outside Italy and to have organized local Red Brigades activities. Three other individuals, all suspected members of the Red Brigades, were arrested with Moretti.

6 Belgian prime minister sworn in

Mark Eyskens was sworn in as prime minister of Belgium. He replaced Wilfried Martens, who resigned March 31 when it became evident that his coalition government was hopelessly split over the issue of continuing automatic wage increases directly linked to increases in the cost of consumer goods.

Ethnic riots rock Yugoslavia

A Yugoslav Communist Party official confirmed that the intensity of recent eth-

nic riots in Kosovo, one of Yugoslavia's two autonomous provinces, had come as a surprise. About three-quarters of Kosovo's 1.5 million inhabitants were ethnic Albanians, whose more extreme leaders wanted the status of Kosovo changed to that of a republic. Some spoke of then seceding from Yugoslavia and perhaps becoming part of neighbouring Albania.

7 Philippines holds plebiscite

In a national plebiscite, Philippine voters overwhelmingly approved modifications in the nation's 1973 constitution. The changes would, for example, permit Pres. Ferdinand E. Marcos to run for another six-year term and would establish a parliamentary form of government with a strong presidency. On April 8 the United Democratic Opposition (UDO) called the plebiscite "a complete farce" but subsequently said it would field a presidential candidate in the June elections if the government agreed to extend the campaign from 45 to 120 days, give the UDO equal access to the news media, sanction UDO representation on poll canvassing boards, and use only verified lists of eligible voters. Marcos was reportedly unwilling to meet all the conditions.

10 Poland's Sejm bans strikes

Poland's Sejm (parliament) approved a resolution banning strikes for a period of two months. Wojciech Jaruzelski, chairman of the Council of Ministers (premier), had threatened to resign if the proposal was voted down. Leaders of Solidarity, the federation of trade unions, warned that no act of the Sejm could prevent a strike if Solidarity's security was seriously threatened.

Uganda upheaval continues

Members of the Uganda Freedom Movement (UFM), an antigovernment organization, took credit for a bombing in Kampala, the nation's capital. Two persons were injured. For more than two months various rebel groups had been seeking to undermine the government of Pres. Milton Obote by ambushing government troops, bombing power stations, destroying businesses, and raiding army barracks to obtain weapons. Government troops, which retaliated with a vengeance, were reportedly also responsible for outrages that served to intensify opposition to the central government.

11 China evaluates Mao Zedong

China's Renmin Ribao (Jen-min Jih-pao, "People's Daily"), the official news organ of the Communist Party, carried a long

discussion on Mao Zedong's (Mao Tse-tung's) place in Chinese history. The article endorsed the opinion of Vice-Chairman Deng Xiaoping (Teng Hsiao-p'ing) that, overall, Mao's merits outweighed his faults. Though Mao was blamed for the havoc wreaked during the Cultural Revolution and for other failings, other high-ranking party members were said to share the blame for the unhappy events that occurred during Mao's final years.

12 U.S. launches first space shuttle

The U.S. launched the world's first space shuttle from Cape Canaveral, Florida. The "Columbia" completed 36 orbits of the Earth during its 54½-hour flight, then glided to a smooth landing at Edwards Air Force Base in southern California. John W. Young, a 50-year-old veteran of four space flights (including two to the Moon), commanded the highly sophisticated space vehicle, and Capt Robert L. Crippen, a 43-year-old astronaut making his first flight into space, served as pilot. At launch time the entire shuttle system weighed about two million kilograms (2,200 tons). Construction of the "Columbia" took three years longer than originally expected and cost about $9.9 billion. The shuttle, which could be used for scientific, commercial, and military purposes, was expected to make scores of flights during the 1980s.

Brixton area of Greater London erupts in violence

More than 150 policemen and some 60 civilians were injured during two days of violence that began on April 11 in the Brixton district of Lambeth, a borough of Greater London. Though the area had a heavy concentration of West Indians, the rioting was not viewed as essentially racial in nature. Rather, it seemed to have been an emotional venting of pent-up frustrations over such social problems as unemployment and an expression of long-smoldering resentment against the large number of police assigned to the Brixton area because of its high crime rate. The officers were accused of frequently harassing members of the community.

16 Trudeau and premiers still at odds

Canadian Prime Minister Pierre E. Trudeau and provincial premiers reached another impasse on the makeup of a new federal constitution. Trudeau refused to accept a compromise proposal endorsed by eight premiers that would permit provinces to reject constitutional amendments by a simple majority vote of their respective legislatures. Trudeau reiterated his belief that Canada's national will would become enfeebled unless it had a strong central government.

17 Rural Solidarity approved

Representatives of the Polish government and of the nation's independent farmers

The U.S. space shuttle "Columbia" made a perfect landing at Edwards Air Force Base in California after completing 36 orbits around the Earth.

signed an agreement that guaranteed official status to Rural Solidarity within a few weeks. In resolving the explosive issue, both sides were convinced that farmers would now work more effectively toward solving the country's food shortages.

19 Terrorists in Davao kill 13

Thirteen persons were killed and scores more were seriously injured in Davao City, Phil., when Filipino terrorists hurled hand grenades into the Roman Catholic cathedral during Easter services. Two arrested suspects reportedly confessed that they belonged to the New People's Army, the military branch of the illegal Philippine Communist Party.

20 U.S. agrees to indemnify Japan for ship sunk by submarine

A spokesman for the U.S. Navy announced that the U.S. was accepting full responsibility for the sinking of the "Nissho Maru" on April 9. The 2,350-ton Japanese merchant vessel went down some 177 km (110 mi) off the southern tip of Japan after being struck by the U.S. submarine "George Washington." Anger in Japan reached a high degree of intensity because there was no indication that officers aboard the submarine made any serious attempt to rescue the Japanese crew. The ship's captain and first mate were both lost at sea, but 13 others were picked up by a Japanese destroyer after spending 18 hours in the water.

24 Reagan lifts grain embargo

President Reagan officially ended an embargo that had severely restricted U.S. grain sales to the Soviet Union during the preceding 15 months. He did not remove the embargo placed on shipments of high-technology goods to the U.S.S.R. The trade sanctions had been imposed by

President Carter shortly after the Soviet Union invaded Afghanistan in December 1979. On April 25 the French government approved the sale of 600,000 tons of grain to the U.S.S.R. but made it clear that France still vigorously opposed the presence of Soviet troops in Afghanistan.

27 Poland's financial problems eased

Fifteen Western nations helped Poland avoid bankruptcy by rescheduling about one quarter of the roughly $10 billion that Poland was obligated to repay various sources before the end of the year. Payment of the remainder was expected to be settled by new credits or by extensions granted by Eastern-bloc nations and international banks.

29 Qaddafi visits Soviet Union

Col. Muammar al-Qaddafi, Libya's chief of state, ended a three-day visit to Moscow that was marked by great cordiality on both sides. Aware that the U.S. and other Western nations had severely castigated Libya for engaging in international terrorism and had criticized the Soviet Union for supporting such activity, the two countries, in a joint communiqué, sought to separate "the liberation struggle of peoples" from the category of "international terrorism."

30 Vetoes doom UN sanctions against South Africa

Great Britain, France, and the U.S. vetoed four UN Security Council resolutions calling for political and economic sanctions against South Africa because it refused to relinquish control over South West Africa/Namibia. The Western nations favoured independence for Namibia but refused to associate themselves with proposals made by certain other UN members regarding that independence.

MAY

1 *Japan to limit auto exports to U.S.*

The Japanese government announced that it would limit its passenger car exports to the U.S. during the next three years. The decision was taken after U.S. legislators informed their Japanese counterparts that the U.S. Congress was prepared to impose import quotas if Japan did not act on its own. During 1980 Japanese car manufacturers captured 21.3% of the U.S. market, while U.S. automakers suffered a combined loss of about $4 billion.

4 *U.S. pledges arms talks*

U.S. Secretary of State Alexander Haig, during a NATO meeting in Rome, informed other members of the alliance that the Reagan administration was now willing to hold discussions with Soviet officials on the reduction of middle-range nuclear missiles in Europe. Haig also disclosed that President Reagan had written to Soviet Pres. Leonid I. Brezhnev informing him of this fact but cautioning that progress in such discussions would depend in part on the Soviet Union's conduct in international affairs.

5 *Bobby Sands dies in Belfast prison*

Robert ("Bobby") Sands, a 27-year-old member of the outlawed Irish Republican Army (IRA), died of starvation in the hospital wing of Maze Prison near Belfast, Northern Ireland. Death came on the 66th day of a hunger strike that Sands and oth-er IRA inmates had undertaken to pressure British authorities into reclassifying them as political prisoners. Sands, who was serving a 14-year sentence for firearms violations, had recently been elected to the British Parliament. News of his death triggered riots in Roman Catholic areas of Belfast.

6 *U.S. expels Libyan diplomats*

The U.S. ordered Libya to close its diplomatic mission in Washington, D.C., and to move its staff outside the country within five days. According to a State Department spokesman, the order reduced U.S.-Libyan ties to the "lowest level consistent with maintenance of diplomatic relations." The Libyans were cited for "a general pattern of unacceptable conduct," which included support for international terrorism and assassinations of dissident Libyans living abroad.

7 *Long strike in Bermuda ends*

Some 1,200 government workers in Bermuda accepted a two-year compromise contract, thus ending a 25-day strike that had brought the country's vital tourist industry to a virtual standstill.

8 *Suzuki confers with Reagan*

Japanese Prime Minister Zenko Suzuki ended two days of talks with President Reagan in Washington, D.C. The joint communiqué included a reference to "the alliance between Japan and the United States," which was based on "their shared values of democracy" and the need for "an appropriate division of roles" for defense. The mention of an alliance between the two countries created such an uproar in Japan, which is constitutionally prohibited from rearming except for purposes of self-defense, that Foreign Minister Masayoshi Ito felt compelled to resign on May 16.

9 *El Salvador announces six arrests in murder of U.S. churchwomen*

The defense minister of El Salvador announced that six members of the country's armed forces had been arrested on April 29 as suspects in the Dec. 2, 1980, murder of three U.S. nuns and one of their female lay co-workers.

10 *Mitterrand elected in France*

François Mitterrand, the 64-year-old leader of France's Socialist Party, defeated incumbent Valéry Giscard d'Estaing in the runoff election for the presidency. His victory meant that France would have its first left-wing president since Charles de Gaulle inaugurated the Fifth Republic in 1958. During the campaign Mitterrand had pledged to nationalize certain industries and give French voters an opportunity to select a new National Assembly. At his installation on May 21, Mitterrand declared that the only victor on May 10 was hope. He then added: "May it become the best-shared asset in France." His choice for premier was Pierre Mauroy, the Socialist mayor of Lille.

12 *Reagan calls for changes in Social Security laws*

President Reagan proposed fundamental changes in Social Security legislation to restore the system to a sound financial basis. Suggestions included a substantial reduction in benefits for those who retire before age 65, full benefits after age 65 for those who continue to work, tightened requirements for disability benefits, a less generous formula in computing basic retirement benefits and pensions for survivors, and a reduction in Social Security taxes within a few years.

13 *John Paul II shot in Vatican City*

Pope John Paul II was shot and seriously injured as he rode in an open car through St. Peter's Square in Vatican City. The pontiff was rushed to a nearby hospital, where surgeons removed parts of his intestines during a five-hour operation. The doctors also treated wounds in the pope's right arm and left hand. Two women tourists from the United States were

Thousands of mourners lined the streets in Belfast, Northern Ireland, to view the funeral procession of Bobby Sands, who died of starvation in Maze Prison. Sands had been on a hunger strike for 66 days.

FRANCOIS LOCHON—GAMMA/LIAISON

French Pres. François Mitterrand left the Elysée Palace for a ceremonial occasion after taking the oath of office.

also injured by bullets during the attempted assassination. The lone gunman, who was immediately apprehended, was identified as Mehmet Ali Agca, a 23-year-old Turkish terrorist who had escaped from prison in November 1979 while on trial for murder.

15 Yugoslavia rotates leadership

Following a predetermined order of succession, Sergej Kraigher began his one-year term as president of Yugoslavia. The present nine-member collective leadership was elected in 1979, before President Tito's death, by parliaments of the nation's six republics and two autonomous provinces.

18 Italy retains right to abortion

Italians voted by a margin of 2–1 to retain a law permitting abortions for a variety of reasons, including those based on socioeconomic conditions. The Roman Catholic Church and the ruling Christian Democratic Party supported repeal. At the same time, the voters rejected a referendum that would have given women under 18 an unrestricted right to abortions and allowed doctors to perform abortions outside of hospitals.

21 WHO votes against baby formulas

The World Health Organization (WHO) voted overwhelmingly that the use of baby formulas be discouraged in third world countries. The vote was 118–1,

with the U.S. casting the only dissenting vote; Argentina, Japan, and South Korea abstained. According to one estimate, the use of baby formulas had contributed to perhaps one million infant deaths a year, often because the formulas were prepared with contaminated water or given to infants in unsterilized bottles. The WHO recommendation, which was presented as an international code of ethics, discouraged the marketing and advertising of baby formulas (except in "legitimate" cases) in favour of breast-feeding. The U.S. defended its vote on various grounds, but two of its senior officials at the Agency for International Development resigned to protest the U.S. stand.

Begin demands removal of Syrian missiles from Lebanon area

Israeli Prime Minister Menachem Begin, who had earlier demanded that Syria remove its surface-to-air missiles from Lebanon, said Israel was now insisting that such missiles also be withdrawn from Syrian territory bordering Lebanon. The prime minister's expanded demands came in the wake of reports that Syria was moving new missiles into the region. Begin had informed the Knesset (Israeli parliament) on May 11 that a planned air strike against the missiles on April 30 had been scrubbed because of bad weather and that a second planned attack had been postponed at the urging of the U.S., which hoped the explosive situation could be defused by special envoy Philip C. Habib's mission to the Mideast.

22 Helmut Schmidt visits U.S.

West German Chancellor Helmut Schmidt and President Reagan concluded two days of talks at the White House. Major topics of discussion included future U.S.-Soviet arms negotiations, Europe's nuclear weaponry vis-à-vis that of the Soviet Union, high U.S. interest rates, and the new Socialist government in France.

"Yorkshire Ripper" sentenced

Peter W. Sutcliffe, the convicted "Yorkshire Ripper," who had been charged with 13 murders and 7 attempted murders, was sentenced in London to life imprisonment. The jury had rejected Sutcliffe's claim of temporary insanity, which was linked to an admission of guilt for the lesser crime of manslaughter.

23 Gunmen seize Barcelona bank

An uncertain number of gunmen seized control of the Central Bank in Barcelona, Spain, and took more than 200 persons hostage. They then demanded the release of one general and three lieutenant colonels, all allegedly involved in the unsuccessful military coup in February. The next day police stormed the bank and captured nine of the terrorists. Others, however, escaped, apparently passing in the confusion as freed hostages. On May 25 a government spokesman said the gunmen seemed to be ordinary criminals and anarchists hired by right-wing extremists.

24 Crash kills Ecuador president

Ecuadorean Pres. Jaime Roldós Aguilera was killed in a plane crash along with his wife, the minister of defense, and two military aides. The 40-year-old chief executive, the youngest president in the Western Hemisphere, had been elected in April 1979 by the largest majority in the nation's history. He was immediately succeeded by Vice-Pres. Osvaldo Hurtado Larrea.

25 Turkish hijackers captured

Four Turkish hijackers, all members of a Marxist guerrilla organization, were overpowered by their hostages at an airport in Burgas, Bulg. The gunmen, who 30 hours earlier had commandeered the plane as it was flying from Istanbul to Ankara, had demanded $500,000 and the release of 47 persons held in Turkish jails.

26 Italian government toppled by Masonic scandal

The coalition government of Italian Premier Arnaldo Forlani collapsed when hundreds of important government officials were named as members of Propaganda Two, a secret Masonic lodge. Magistrates investigating Licio Gelli, the grand master of the lodge, claimed that the secret organization "had combined

JUNE

business and politics with the intention of destroying the constitutional order of the country and of transforming the parliamentary system into a presidential system." Gelli was accused of using highly placed persons to destroy the traditional separation that existed between the "political, administrative, military, and economic spheres" of Italian society.

OPEC cartel freezes oil prices

During their semiannual meeting in Geneva, 12 members of OPEC agreed after much wrangling to freeze their current oil prices and to cut production by at least 10%. Saudi Arabia, which vainly hoped that the current oil glut would force other OPEC nations to reduce their prices to $34 a barrel for 18 months, expressed its dissatisfaction by announcing it would continue its current high level of production and maintain its crude oil prices at $32 a barrel.

27 *Habib reports on Mideast mission*

Philip C. Habib, the U.S. special envoy to the Middle East, returned to Washington, D.C., to report the results of his three-week diplomatic mission to Jerusalem, Damascus, and Beirut. When he departed the U.S. on May 6, Syria and Israel appeared to be heading toward a military showdown. Israel was threatening to destroy Syrian missiles in Lebanon unless they were removed. Though Habib was unable to work out a final agreement acceptable to the Israeli, Syrian, and Lebanese leaders, his first round of talks kept alive hopes that the problem could be resolved without war.

29 *U.S. coal strike settled*

Negotiators for some 160,000 members of the United Mine Workers union in the East and Midwest approved a new 40-month contract worked out with representatives of the soft-coal industry. Nearly 70% of the union workers approved the contract on June 6, thereby ending a strike that began on March 27 and cost the miners about $710 million in wages.

30 *Bangladesh president slain*

Ziaur Rahman, president of Bangladesh, was assassinated during his sleep in the port city of Chittagong. A number of his aides and bodyguards were also slain during the attempted military coup. On June 1 the government announced that the leader of the coup, Maj. Gen. Mohammad Abdul Manzoor, and other top officers had been arrested near Chittagong. The following day Manzoor and two of his aides were reported killed by outraged bystanders. Zia, who became president in April 1977, had reportedly incurred Manzoor's wrath by transferring him to Chittagong in 1979, a move that diminished Manzoor's political importance.

JUNE

3 *Mitterrand implements program*

French Pres. François Mitterrand began to fulfill his campaign pledges by raising the minimum wage by 10% and by increasing some social benefits. The government also warned that, with the approval of Parliament, new taxes would be imposed on wealthy individuals, on luxury goods, and on excessive profits made by financial institutions and oil companies. Parliament would also be asked to abolish the State Security Court, which secretly tried suspected terrorists and spies; the convicted had no right of appeal.

4 *Sadat and Begin meet in Sinai*

Egyptian Pres. Anwar as-Sadat and Israeli Prime Minister Menachem Begin met in the Sinai, mainly to exchange views on the situation in Lebanon. Sadat agreed that Syrian troops should be withdrawn from Lebanon and called upon Pres. Elias Sarkis to express his views on the presence of such forces inside his country. Sadat also criticized Begin for continuing to attack Palestinian bases inside Lebanon. The divisive issue of Jerusalem's future status was reportedly not discussed because neither leader had given any indication he was willing to abandon long-held views.

6 *Pope appoints Canton bishop*

Pope John Paul II announced the appointment of Msgr. Deng Yiming as Roman Catholic archbishop of Canton, China. Despite signs that China might be relaxing its strictures on religious activities, the government refused to recognize Deng's appointment, which was described in the *Beijing Review* as an example

ALAIN KELER—SYGMA

Egyptian Pres. Anwar as-Sadat (centre) and Israeli Prime Minister Menachem Begin (centre right) met in the Sinai in June to discuss the conflict in Lebanon.

of Rome's "utter disregard of the self-governing rights of the Chinese church" and as "interference in the internal affairs of China." Deng had been imprisoned in China for 22 years after the establishment of the People's Republic.

7 *Israel destroys Iraqi reactor*

Israel used eight U.S.-made F-16 bombers and six F-15 fighter planes to destroy completely Iraq's Osirak nuclear reactor near Baghdad. Israel defended its surprise attack by saying that the soon-to-be-completed facility was designed to produce atomic bombs that could be used against Israel. The U.S. was but one of many nations that condemned the attack. France, which had sold the reactor to Iraq, said on June 17 that the continued presence of French personnel at the reactor site guaranteed that Iraq could not have used it to produce atomic weapons secretly.

9 *Spain accepts "social contract"*

In an effort to cut Spain's unemployment rate, which stood at around 12%, the na-

tion's major labour unions and employers entered into a "social contract" that placed limits on wage increases in 1982. The government planned to create some 350,000 jobs to help alleviate unemployment and hoped that restraints on wages would provide more than $1.5 billion for investments that would stimulate employment.

11 *Karmal resigns prime ministership*

Pres. Babrak Karmal of Afghanistan resigned the post of prime minister in favour of Sultan Ali Keshtmand. The top-level government shake-up also affected other high-ranking officials, including Abdur Rashid Arian, who was ousted as first deputy prime minister and minister of justice but was given a seat on the Revolutionary Council's presidium.

12 *U.S. baseball players strike*

The U.S. major league baseball season came to an abrupt halt when the owners of the franchises and the players could not agree on the compensation owners should receive when star players become free agents and sign contracts with other teams. No early settlement of the strike was expected because negotiations that had been going on for more than a year had failed to resolve the differences.

14 *Swiss women win equality*

In a national referendum, Swiss voters approved an amendment to the constitution that would grant women equal rights with men. To pass, the referendum needed not only a majority of the nation's popular vote but popular approval in a majority of the cantons. The referendum was rejected by fewer than 40% of the voters nationwide and in only 9 of the 26 cantons.

15 *Oil consumers meet in Paris*

The International Energy Agency concluded a one-day meeting in Paris after agreeing to hold oil imports to the current level of 19 million to 21 million bbl a day. The ministers, who represented 21 oil-importing nations, also underscored the need to expand the use of other fuels because the energy situation was "still precarious" despite the current surplus of oil on world markets.

16 *China to get U.S. weapons*

Alexander Haig, the U.S. secretary of state, announced that his government was now willing to sell certain weapons to the People's Republic of China. He then noted that a Chinese delegation would visit the U.S. in August to compare China's military needs with equipment the U.S. would be willing to sell.

Marcos reelected in Philippines

Philippine Pres. Ferdinand E. Marcos was reelected to a six-year term. An over-

PHILIPPE LEDRU—SYGMA

Iranians demonstrated in Teheran in June against the policies of former president Abolhassan Bani-Sadr, who was ousted from office by Ayatollah Ruhollah Khomeini.

whelming victory was assured because he was opposed by only minor candidates. After Marcos was nominated by his New Society Movement party on April 25, he upbraided the United Democratic Opposition, which planned to boycott the election on the grounds that it would be neither free nor fair.

Bulgarian leader replaced

Stanko Todorov, chairman of the Bulgarian Council of Ministers (premier) since 1971, was removed from office by the National Assembly and replaced by Grisha Filipov, a member of the Politburo who served the ruling Communist Party as secretary of its Central Committee.

19 *Muslims battle Copts in Cairo*

During three days of fighting between Coptic Christians and Muslims in Cairo, at least 10 persons were killed and 55 injured. The incident was reportedly sparked by a dispute over which group would build a religious edifice on a vacant lot. On June 22 Pres. Anwar as-Sadat asserted that the Communist and Socialist Labour parties had deliberately exploited the dispute to foster violence.

21 *French Assembly takes shape*

The Socialist Party won an impressive absolute majority in France's final round of elections for the National Assembly. The 286 seats it and affiliated parties captured more than doubled its representation during the previous administration of Valéry Giscard d'Estaing. The Rassemblement pour la République lost 67 seats, giving it a new total of 88. The Union pour la Démocratie Française, which lost 57 rep-

resentatives, finished third with 62 seats. The Communist Party won 44 seats, down from 86; independents retained 11 seats. The members of the National Assembly were elected to five-year terms. After the election results were known, Pres. François Mitterrand reappointed Pierre Mauroy premier. He had temporarily assumed that position after Mitterrand's election on May 10.

Atlanta murder suspect held

A 23-year-old man was arrested in Atlanta, Ga., and charged with murdering the last of 28 persons who had disappeared or whose bodies had been found in the Atlanta area during the previous 22 months. The suspect, Wayne B. Williams, was a black free-lance photographer, who had earlier been taken into custody, questioned, and released. Authorities were unwilling to say whether Williams would later be charged with other murders.

22 *Bani-Sadr ousted as president*

Abolhassan Bani-Sadr, who was dismissed as chief of Iran's armed forces on June 10, was ousted from his post as president by Ayatollah Ruhollah Khomeini. The Majlis (parliament), dominated by clerical fundamentalists who opposed Bani-Sadr's relatively moderate positions, had declared the president incompetent the previous day. The dismissal of the president heightened tensions between Bani-Sadr's supporters and extremist elements in Iran.

Spain approves civil divorce

Spain's Parliament passed legislation permitting civil divorce in cases where both

JULY

parties, after a period of separation, wished to dissolve the marriage. Hundreds of thousands of Spaniards were expected to file for divorce under the new law. The ruling Union of the Democratic Centre party had supported the bill despite strong opposition from the Roman Catholic church.

23 *U.K. unemployment rate swells*

The British government announced that the nation's unemployment rate had climbed to 11.1%, the highest it has been in half a century. Prime Minister Margaret Thatcher warned that unemployment would continue to rise during the months ahead because her more immediate goal was to continue the fight against inflation, which had already dropped to 11.7% from 21.9% in 1980.

25 *U.S. high court rules on draft*

The U.S. Supreme Court announced its ruling on the constitutionality of having only males register for a potential military draft. The court did not directly consider the advisability of having women drafted into military service; rather, it focused on the clear constitutional right of Congress "to make rules for the government and regulation of the land and naval forces." That authority, the court decided, includes the right to decide who should be required to register for military service. Justice William Rehnquist, writing for the 6–3 majority, also noted that it was not the court's role to agree or disagree with any such judgment because Congress is a separate branch of government. In effect, the court overruled a three-judge federal district court that had declared that a male-only draft registration was unconstitutional.

27 *Kampuchea names new leaders*

Heng Samrin was elected president of Kampuchea's (Cambodia's) Council of State by members of the National Assembly. Pen Sovan became president of the Council of Ministers after relinquishing his post as minister of defense, which was then given to Chan Si. Chea Sim, who had been minister of the interior, became president of the Assembly.

28 *Iranian leaders killed by bomb*

A powerful explosion, set off by anti-government elements in Iran's capital city of Teheran, killed 72 people, including Chief Justice Ayatollah Mohammad Beheshti, four members of the Cabinet, eight deputy ministers, and at least 20 members of the Majlis (parliament). The bomb detonated near the podium while Beheshti was addressing members of the fundamentalist Islamic Republican Party. Prime Minister Mohammad Ali Raja'i and Speaker of the Majlis Ayatollah Hashemi Rafsanjani had left the area moments before and so escaped death.

Spadolini becomes Italian premier

Giovanni Spadolini, who had been a member of the Italian Senate, was sworn in as premier of a new five-party coalition government. Spadolini, who had also been serving as secretary of the Republican Party, became the first non-Christian Democrat Party politician to head the Italian government since the end of World War II. Besides Republicans and Christian Democrats, who were given a majority of the Cabinet posts, the coalition included Socialists, Social Democrats, and Liberals.

29 *Chairman Hua Guofeng resigns*

The Central Committee of the Chinese Communist Party announced that Hua Guofeng (Hua Kuo-feng) had resigned as party chairman and would be replaced by party Secretary General Hu Yaobang (Hu Yao-pang). Hua, who had been personally chosen party leader by the late Mao Zedong (Mao Tse-tung), had been made to share the blame for many of the problems China had faced in recent years. Foreign observers noted that the promotion of Hu was another victory for Vice-Chairman Deng Xiaoping (Teng Hsiao-p'ing) and his policies, but Hua's ouster reportedly had been delayed by pro-Maoist factions within the party who sought assurances that Hua would be named a vice-chairman and also wished to ensure that public criticism of Mao and his policies would be less severe than Deng would have liked.

30 *Canadian mail halted by strike*

Some 23,000 members of the Canadian Union of Postal Workers began a strike after their representatives failed to settle differences with the Treasury Board. The main issues involved pay and time off from work.

Ireland elects prime minister

Garret FitzGerald was elected prime minister of Ireland by the Dail (lower house of Parliament). In addition to the 65 votes he received from members of his own Fine Gael Party, FitzGerald had the support of 15 members of the Labour Party and of one independent Socialist. This gave him a close 81–78 victory over former prime minister Charles Haughey, whose votes all came from members of the Fianna Fail Party.

Israel's election inconclusive

Israel's ruling Likud coalition, led by Prime Minister Menachem Begin, won a narrow victory in parliamentary elections but faced a difficult task in organizing a viable coalition government. The Likud coalition won 48 seats in the 120-seat Knesset (parliament), and the Labour Alignment won 47. The remaining 25 seats were won by politicians from eight other parties.

JULY

2 *Court backs Iran settlement*

The U.S. Supreme Court, in a unanimous decision, ruled that Presidents Carter and Reagan had had the legal authority to enter into and carry out the agreements with Iran that freed the U.S. hostages after 444 days in captivity. The justices thus upheld the power of the U.S. president to act in such a situation, with at least the implicit approval of Congress, even when it meant nullifying certain court orders and suspending private lawsuits against Iran as a condition for resolving the international crisis. The court's verdict also cleared the way for the eventual release of Iranian assets that had been frozen by Carter in November 1979.

3 *Riots sweep across Britain*

Asian youths in the predominantly Indian neighbourhood of Southall in West London fought with a band of "skinheads," white youths with close-cropped hair. Molotov cocktails were thrown and fires started before the police were able to quell what was termed a race riot. The next day violence erupted in Liverpool as youths from various ethnic backgrounds battled police. During the next week and a half some 30 cities and towns experienced similar violence. On July 27 Prime Minister Margaret Thatcher unveiled a plan that was intended to alleviate unemployment, especially among the young.

6 *Isabel Perón set free*

Isabel Martínez de Perón, former president of Argentina, was freed from house arrest by a federal court. Four days later she departed for Spain. Perón rose to power after the death of her husband in July 1974, but in March 1976 she was ousted by the military who charged her with embezzlement and other crimes.

10 *Fruit fly threatens California produce*

John Block, U.S. secretary of agriculture, warned California farmers that the federal government would quarantine their produce unless state agencies took more

effective measures to control the devastating infestation of the Mediterranean fruit fly. That same day California Gov. Jerry Brown reluctantly ordered extensive aerial spraying with the insecticide malathion. Just two days earlier Brown had rejected such spraying because of the risks entailed in "subjecting 500,000 people, including pregnant women, infants, and children, to six or more aerial applications of a toxic pesticide." California normally shipped about $15 million worth of produce each day to other parts of the country.

11 TV writers in U.S. end strike

Members of the Writers Guild of America announced the end of their 13-week strike against film and television producers after being guaranteed, for the first time, a share in revenues that would otherwise have gone exclusively to the producers. The 8,500-member guild was mainly concerned about revenues coming from rapidly expanding markets involving pay television, videodiscs, and videocassettes. The strike would delay the opening of the fall TV season by several weeks.

13 Mitterrand and Schmidt confer

French Pres. François Mitterrand and West German Chancellor Helmut Schmidt ended a two-day meeting in Bonn, West Germany, during which they discussed national and international issues. Both agreed that high interest rates in the U.S. were adversely affecting the economies of their respective countries and that NATO needed to bolster its military capabilities in Europe to offset the Soviet Union's introduction of SS-20 missiles and Backfire bombers.

14 Poland's Communist Party holds emergency session

Poland's Communist Party met in emergency session to grapple with the urgent economic and political problems confronting the country. In an unprecedented procedure, delegates were chosen by secret ballot and secret balloting was permitted for the first time during the party congress. Before the meeting adjourned on July 20, Stanislaw Kania was narrowly reelected party first secretary, but many members of the Politburo and the Central Committee lost their posts. The delegates also voted to expel Edward Gierek and other well-known former leaders from the Communist Party. Although Gierek had led the party for ten years, he and the others were blamed for having brought Poland to its present state of crisis.

15 France moves to decentralize

The Socialist government of French Pres. François Mitterrand approved a plan that would grant greater powers to regional and departmental councils. Premier Pierre Mauroy called decentralization

UPI

Cars were overturned and stores were looted after rioting broke out in London and several other cities in Britain.

"the most important business of our seven-year term." Total implementation of the three-step plan would take some three years.

16 Malaysia gets new prime minister

Datuk Seri Mahathir bin Mohamad, who had been unanimously elected president of the ruling United Malays National Organization on June 26, became prime minister of Malaysia. He replaced Datuk Hussein bin Onn, who retired. Mahathir, a Malay, had been expelled from his party after publishing The Malay Dilemma (1970) in Singapore. The book was banned in Malaysia because, among other things, it criticized Abdul Rahman, the nation's first prime minister.

House subcommittee rejects UNESCO plan for press controls

The U.S. House of Representatives Foreign Affairs Subcommittee on Human Rights and International Organizations went on record as opposed to UNESCO's plan for a "new world information order." The plan, which includes the licensing of journalists, had earlier been rejected by independent news organizations at the Voices of Freedom Conference held in France on May 17. Critics of the plan viewed it as an assault on free speech and as an attempt to stifle criticism of authoritarian regimes.

Saudis offer Iraq reactor

Muhammad Abdu Yamani, Saudi Arabia's minister of information, announced that his country was willing to pay the entire cost of replacing the nu-

clear reactor that had been destroyed in Iraq on June 7 by Israeli planes. The French government also indicated it was prepared to consider supplying another reactor, provided it was operated under strict conditions.

17 Israeli planes bomb Beirut

Israeli planes, for the first time in seven years, bombed Beirut, the capital of Lebanon. Several hundred persons were reported killed. The main targets were the offices of al-Fatah, the chief guerrilla unit of the Palestine Liberation Organization, and the offices of the Democratic Front for the Liberation of Palestine, another guerrilla organization. Israeli Prime Minister Menachem Begin warned that military targets "purposefully located in the vicinity of or within civilian concentrations" would no longer be spared because modern weapons used by the Palestinian guerrillas posed a growing threat to Israel. During the escalation of violence during the preceding weeks, Palestinians had hit the Israeli towns of Nahariya and Kiryat Shemona with Soviet-made Katyusha rockets.

21 World leaders meet in Ottawa

Seven leaders of the world's major industrialized democracies ended a two-day meeting near Ottawa. Economic questions were given top priority because high U.S. interest rates were creating serious problems for other countries. At the end of the conference President Reagan publicly thanked those in attendance for understanding and supporting current U.S. fiscal policies, but West German Chancellor Helmut Schmidt underscored

AUGUST

DIEGO GOLDBERG—SYGMA

A summit meeting of leaders of seven major industrialized nations took place near Ottawa in July. Leaders came from the U.S., Canada, France, Japan, West Germany, Great Britain, and Italy.

the intractability of the difficulties when he remarked: ". . . when I go back to Bonn, my government will begin to take decisions concerning the fact that unfortunately, for the time being, we still have to deal with high interest rates." Other participants at the conference, which was chaired by Canadian Prime Minister Pierre Trudeau, were French Pres. François Mitterrand, British Prime Minister Margaret Thatcher, Italian Premier Giovanni Spadolini, and Japanese Prime Minister Zenko Suzuki.

22 Pope's assailant convicted

An Italian court found Mehmet Ali Agca guilty of attempting to assassinate Pope John Paul II on May 13. The 23-year-old Turk, who was sentenced to life imprisonment, had contended that the Italian government had no authority to prosecute a crime committed in Vatican City, a sovereign state. The Italian court, however, ruled that provisions of the 1929 Later-

an Treaty permitted such legal actions as long as the Vatican approved.

24 Raja'i replaces Bani-Sadr

Mohammad Ali Raja'i, prime minister of Iran, was elected president by a huge majority of the popular vote. He replaced Abolhassan Bani-Sadr, who had been ousted from office by Ayatollah Ruhollah Khomeini on June 22. The former president, fearing for his life, had gone into hiding on June 12; on July 29 he escaped to Paris where he was granted political asylum.

25 New Zealanders disrupt tour of South African sports team

A group of New Zealanders, who first protested the arrival in New Zealand of South Africa's national rugby team on July 19, intensified their opposition during the matches to such a degree that the police commissioner called the rioting the

"worst civil disturbance in the history of the country." The protest focused on South Africa's racist apartheid policies, which severely restrict the country's non-white population.

28 Poland to receive U.S. corn

The U.S. Department of Agriculture announced its favourable response to Poland's request for emergency shipments of grain to avert a wholesale slaughter of poultry and hogs. With $55 million in new credits coming from the U.S. Food for Peace program, Poland would be able to procure some 350,000 tons of corn. This was somewhat less than Poland had requested, but additional food would be provided through the Catholic Relief Agency which had the Reagan administration's approval to buy surplus U.S. food at low prices for shipment to Poland.

29 Prince Charles and Lady Diana marry in gala ceremony

The prince of Wales, heir to the British throne, married Lady Diana Spencer in an elaborately staged ceremony in St. Paul's Cathedral, London. About one million people lined the route from Buckingham Palace to St. Paul's to catch a glimpse of the 32-year-old prince and his 20-year-old bride. An estimated 700 million people worldwide watched the ceremonies on television.

30 U.S. proposes new refugee and immigration policies

U.S. Attorney General William F. Smith announced proposed changes in U.S. immigration laws that would, among other things, levy fines of $500 to $1,000 against any employer of four or more workers who knowingly hired an illegal alien. After calling attention to the past and future importance of the country's immigration policies, President Reagan pledged to "work toward a new and realistic immigration policy, a policy that will be fair to our own citizens while it opens the door of opportunity for those who seek a new life in America."

AUGUST

1 Torrijos dies in plane crash

Gen. Omar Torrijos Herrera, who for many years had been the de facto ruler of Panama, was found dead along with three other persons who were aboard a plane that crashed in a jungle area of western Panama.

3 PATCO disregards federal law and begins strike

More than 85% of those belonging to the Professional Air Traffic Controllers Or-

ganization (PATCO) went on strike across the U.S. despite repeated government warnings that any controller who refused to work would be fired. Government negotiators had offered a compromise settlement, but it was judged unacceptable by members of the union. PATCO's demands included a four-day, 32-hour workweek, a $10,000 across-the-board raise in salaries, and additional retirement benefits. When the strike began, a federal judge in Washington, D.C., found the union in contempt of court. He ordered the union to pay $250,000 in fines

the first three days and $1 million a day thereafter. On August 5 five union officials were jailed and 55 controllers notified of their dismissal. Meanwhile, some 2,000 nonstriking members of the 15,000-member PATCO union and an equal number of nonunion air traffic controllers manned the towers with the help of supervisory personnel.

5 Begin forms new government

Israeli Prime Minister Menachem Begin won Knesset (parliamentary) approval of

his new four-party coalition government, which held 61 of the 120 seats in the legislature. Begin's Likud Party had won only 48 seats in the June 30 national election, but 13 members of three minor religious parties helped form a new government after gaining certain concessions that mandated, among other things, a stricter observance of the Sabbath throughout the country.

8   *Fidel Castro visits Mexico*

Cuban Pres. Fidel Castro ended a 26-hour visit to Mexico during which he and Pres. José López Portillo discussed, among other things, the North-South economic summit scheduled to be held in Cancún, Mexico, in October. Mexico supported Cuban participation, but President Reagan had made it clear he would boycott the meeting if Castro was invited. Since the success of the summit hinged on U.S. cooperation, it seemed that Cuba could not force the issue without sabotaging the meeting itself.

10   *Canada's mail strike ends*

The Canadian Union of Postal Workers ended its 42-day strike after more than 80% of its 23,000 members approved a new two-year contract. The agreement included a wage increase of 70 Canadian cents per hour and a continuation of cost-of-living adjustments. Other key issues were settled when both sides accepted a period of 17 weeks for maternity leave at 93% of gross salary and four weeks of vacation after eight years of service.

U.S. producing neutron weapons

U.S. Secretary of Defense Caspar Weinberger announced that, with President Reagan's approval, the U.S. had already begun producing neutron warheads. In 1978 President Carter had sanctioned the manufacture of individual components of neutron weapons but had forbidden their integration. Production figures were set at 380 missiles that would be compatible with existing Lance missile launchers and some 800 artillery shells suitable for firing from eight-inch howitzers. None of the neutron weapons would be deployed in a NATO country without the specific approval of that country.

French allowed to leave Iran

After several days of anxious delay, 57 French citizens were allowed to leave Iran after authorities made certain they were leaving no unsatisfied debts behind. Mindful of what had happened earlier to American citizens in Iran, French Pres. François Mitterrand had urged his fellow countrymen to leave the country because anti-French sentiments had been inflamed over Mitterrand's refusal to extradite former Iranian president Abolhassan Bani-Sadr. On August 12 a second group of Frenchmen departed from Iran without incident.

ELIZABETH MARSHALL—LIAISON

Supervisory personnel manned control towers at airports in the U.S. after air traffic controllers went on strike in August.

11   *Balsemão quits as premier*

Portuguese Premier Francisco Pinto Balsemão submitted his resignation to Pres. António Ramalho Eanes because, he said, it was impossible to function under the three-party coalition. The three parties, which comprised a comfortable majority in the Parliament, applauded Balsemão's decision but reaffirmed their intention to remain united and continue running the government.

13   *Reagan's budget and tax plans become law*

President Reagan signed into law the Omnibus Reconciliation Act of 1981 and the Economic Recovery Tax Act of 1981, two pieces of legislation that, he said, "mark an end to the excessive growth in government bureaucracy and government spending and government taxing." The budget bill called for a reduction of $35.2 billion in fiscal year 1982 and almost four times that amount during the following three years. To restrict spending, Congress substantially cut some programs and totally eliminated others. The other bill cut a total of $37.7 billion from taxes that individuals and businesses would otherwise have had to pay in 1982 and mandated an additional reduction of $280.3 billion over the following three years.

14   *Liberia executes rebels*

Five members of Liberia's People's Redemption Council were executed for participating in the attempted assassination of Master Sgt. Samuel K. Doe, the head of state. All five were military men who had backed Doe when he seized power in April 1980.

17   *Israel to receive U.S. jets*

U.S. Secretary of State Alexander Haig announced that the U.S. would no longer

hold up the delivery of promised F-16s and F-15s to Israel. Delivery was suspended on June 10 after Israel used U.S.-made planes to destroy a nuclear reactor in Iraq. The suspension was further extended in July when Israeli planes bombed Beirut. The raid against Iraq sparked a sharp controversy about a possible violation of Israel's 1952 agreement with the U.S. that it would not use U.S.-supplied equipment except for defensive purposes. Israel contended that the attack was "defensive" because Iraq was about to produce nuclear bombs for use against Israel.

19   *U.S. downs two Libyan jet fighters*

Two U.S. Navy F-14 Tomcat fighters shot down two Libyan SU-22s that attacked the U.S. aircraft about 95 km (60 mi) from the coast of Libya. The U.S. insisted that the brief dogfight occurred in international airspace over the Gulf of Sidra even though Libya claimed the area as part of its territory in 1973. The confrontation took place during U.S. military maneuvers that, it was later admitted, were staged in that region of the Mediterranean to underscore U.S. rejection of Libya's claim to sovereignty over what the U.S. insisted were international waters.

24   *South Africa invades Angola*

South Africa ordered two armoured columns and air units to attack Angola from Namibia, which South Africa controls and still calls South West Africa. On August 28 South Africa said it was withdrawing its troops after successfully attacking Angola-based guerrillas fighting for Namibian independence. Angola claimed that hospitals and schools were hit by bombs. Before the attack South Africa reported that Soviet-made radar and surface-to-air missiles had been positioned in southern Angola to impede the pursuit of guerrillas returning to their Angolan sanctuary. Angola earlier admitted it was being supported by Cuban

SEPTEMBER

KALARI—SYGMA

The president of Iran, the prime minister, and three members of the Supreme Defense Council were killed when a bomb went off in a government building in Teheran on August 30.

troops. On September 1 South Africa claimed it had captured a Soviet warrant officer during the raid and had killed other Soviet Army officers.

25 Voyager 2 scans Saturn

Voyager 2, an 820-kg (1,800-lb) unmanned U.S. spacecraft, transmitted spectacular data back to Earth. The vehicle passed within 101,000 km (63,000 mi) of the cloud top that covers the giant planet. Scientists learned for the first time that Saturn's rings number in the thousands, but they found no evidence of moonlets, which would have provided at least one plausible explanation for the existence of the mysterious rings. Despite a wealth of new data supplied by Voyager 2, scientists were still at a loss to explain many of Saturn's other phenomena. Having completed its survey of Saturn, Voyager 2 headed for Uranus, which it was expected to reach in 1986.

26 Church leader pleads for end to Polish strikes

Archbishop Jozef Glemp, Roman Catholic primate of Poland, urged government officials and workers to begin working together for the good of the country. Both groups were described as self-righteous in their determination to control the course of future events. Glemp called for a 30-day moratorium on strikes so that work could be resumed "without tension." It was the first such plea by a church official.

26 North Korea fires missile at U.S. plane

The U.S. claimed that North Korea fired an antiaircraft missile at a high-flying U.S. surveillance plane while it was over South Korea or in international airspace. The U.S. warned it would take "whatever steps are necessary to assure the future safety of our pilots and planes."

28 France and Mexico suggest role for El Salvador guerrillas

In a joint declaration presented to the UN Security Council, France and Mexico described El Salvador's antigovernment guerrillas as a "representative political force" that should be recognized as such and accorded a role in negotiating a cessation of hostilities with the ruling civilian-military junta. The U.S. readily agreed that the people of El Salvador alone should determine their future, but it did not accept the fact that the guerrillas represented a substantial portion of the population.

30 More Iranian leaders slain

Iranian Pres. Mohammad Ali Raja'i, Prime Minister Mohammad Javad Bahonar, and three other members of the Supreme Defense Council were killed when a bomb exploded in Bahonar's office and started a conflagration. Although the attack occurred in a tightly guarded building, a person or persons belonging to an antigovernment group apparently succeeded in passing security checkpoints without arousing suspicion. Raja'i had been president for only 27 days.

SEPTEMBER

1 Alberta and Ottawa sign oil pact

The Canadian government and the province of Alberta, the nation's principal producer of petroleum, ended their bitter controversy over oil when Prime Minister Pierre Elliott Trudeau and provincial premier Peter Lougheed signed a five-year agreement. The pact permits a series of price increases that must, however, keep the price of Alberta oil 25% below world market prices. The accord also established a new ratio for distributing oil revenues shared by oil companies, Alberta, and the federal government.

2 President of Central African Republic replaced

Gen. André Kolingba, the armed forces chief of staff, proclaimed himself head of state of the Central African Republic. He then suspended the constitution, appointed an all-military government, and outlawed activities by political parties. Radio Bangui announced that David Dacko had resigned the presidency for reasons of health at the request of General Kolingba.

5 Sadat ousts Coptic patriarch

In an address before Egypt's Parliament, Pres. Anwar as-Sadat announced that he was deposing Shenuda III, the spiritual leader of some six million Coptic Christians, and giving his authority to a committee of five bishops. Sadat, who accused Shenuda of using his position to build a political power base, also denounced the Muslim Brotherhood as "illegitimate." The fundamentalist group had been active in several Arab countries. Sadat's address followed the arrests on September 3 and 4 of some 1,500 politicians, journalists, and religious activists who were accused of fostering religious tensions between Copts and Muslims.

7 U.S.S.R. warns Spain against joining NATO

The Soviet embassy in Madrid sent a note to the Spanish government warning that world tensions would increase if Spain carried out its plan to join the North Atlantic Treaty Organization (NATO). Spain's foreign minister rejected the note as unacceptable interference in Spain's internal affairs. The Spanish government, according to its foreign minister, preferred membership in NATO to its bilateral defense treaty with the U.S. because

NATO membership would guarantee that present U.S. military bases in Spain would become an integral part of Europe's defense system.

9 France pushes nationalization

The Cabinet of French Pres. François Mitterrand approved legislation that would nationalize 36 large banks and some major industries. The action would not affect 136 foreign-owned banks, but it would mean that about 95% of all bank deposits would reside in state-run institutions. The nationalization program would also extend government control to certain major industries producing such things as textiles, electronic equipment, glass, chemicals, and metals. All investors would receive "full and fair compensation." In many cases this would take the form of 15-year state-backed bonds, but some foreign investors were likely to be offered cash reimbursements.

10 Solidarity wants Parliament freely elected

Solidarity, the Polish federation of independent trade unions, demanded free parliamentary elections during its first national congress. The decision in effect challenged the Communist Party leadership which traditionally arranged elections to ensure that party-approved candidates would maintain near-absolute control at all levels of government. The Soviet Union immediately characterized the congress and Solidarity's demands as "an antisocialist and anti-Soviet orgy." On September 16 Poland's Politburo warned Solidarity that it was engaged in a "program of political opposition that hits at the vital interest" of the nation and threatens bloodshed.

11 Chile extends ban on politics

Chilean Pres. Augusto Pinochet Ugarte, in a nationwide address marking the eighth anniversary of the coup that toppled the regime of Marxist president Salvador Allende Gossens, warned that the ban on political activities would continue in full force for eight more years. Pinochet said Chile had become a bastion of liberty during his administration but authoritarian policies would still be necessary to protect the nation against "the Marxist threat." Under provisions of the six-month-old Chilean constitution, the president had shown no reluctance to invoke his wide powers to control political opposition.

12 Top Italian terrorists seized

A spokesman for Scotland Yard announced in London that nine suspected Italian terrorists, seven men and two women, had been arrested. Though most faced charges of armed robbery and subversion, some were also prime suspects in the 1980 bombing of a Bologna train station that killed more than 80 people.

UPI

Prime Minister George Price of Belize accepted constitutional documents from British officials when the Central American country became independent in September.

15 Pakistan accepts U.S. aid package

Pakistan officially accepted a six-year, $3.2 billion U.S. aid package that included both economic assistance and military credits. Pakistani Pres. Mohammad Zia-ul-Haq concluded the agreement only after the U.S. pledged to deliver within 12 months the first 6 of 40 F-16 fighter planes. In earlier negotiations, the U.S. had said the initial deliveries could not be made for 26 months. Since the U.S. Congress had the right to reject the aid program if it saw fit, Undersecretary of State James L. Buckley sought to reassure members of the House Foreign Affairs Committee who were concerned about reports

that Pakistan was planning to produce nuclear fuels that could be used in nuclear weapons. Buckley said that Pakistan knew "without a doubt" that the detonation of a nuclear device would seriously jeopardize the entire U.S. aid agreement.

Egypt expels 1,500 Soviets

Egypt accused the Soviet ambassador, six members of the Soviet embassy, and two Soviet correspondents of fostering religious unrest in Egypt in order to topple Pres. Anwar as-Sadat's regime. The Soviets were then ordered to leave the country. Egypt also closed the Soviet military liaison office in Cairo and notified 1,500 Soviet technicians to be out of the country within a week. Egypt's actions fell just short of breaking off diplomatic relations with the Soviet Union. Two days later the U.S.S.R. responded by expelling Egyptian military personnel living in Moscow.

17 PLO centre in Lebanon bombed

A bomb planted inside a car that was parked outside the command centre of the Palestine Liberation Organization (PLO) in Sidon, Lebanon, exploded a short time before PLO leaders and Lebanese leftist militia commanders were scheduled to meet. At least 20 persons were reported killed and more than 100 others injured. In addition, six buildings were damaged and a dozen cars destroyed by fire. According to anonymous callers, the Front for the Liberation of Lebanon from Aliens, an underground right-wing organization, was responsible for the bombing.

19 Unions sponsor anti-Reagan rally

An estimated one-quarter million people attended a rally in Washington, D.C., to

Sandra Day O'Connor became the first female justice of the U.S. Supreme Court when she was sworn in on September 25.

OWEN—BLACK STAR

OCTOBER

protest policies of the Reagan administration, especially government cutbacks in social programs. The rally was organized by the American Federation of Labor-Congress of Industrial Organizations (AFL-CIO).

21 Belgian government falls

Prime Minister Mark Eyskens, head of Belgium's Social Christian-Socialist coalition government, resigned when an impasse developed over financing the newly merged steel company of Cockerill and Hainault-Sambre in southern Belgium. French-speaking Socialists from the area demanded long-term government assistance to guarantee survival of the ailing company, but other members of the coalition refused to meet the Socialists' demands.

U.S.-U.S.S.R. trade soars

The U.S. embassy in Moscow revealed that trade between the Soviet Union and the U.S. during the first six months of 1981 had increased nearly 50% over the corresponding period of 1980. U.S. exports to the Soviet Union rose to $1,070,-000,000, an increase of 54%, while Soviet exports to the U.S. increased to $210 million, a gain of 28%. The main items involved were U.S. food and Soviet oil.

Belize gains independence

After more than 300 years under British domination, Belize—long known as British Honduras—gained full independence. In 1964 the Central American colony was granted self-rule, with George Cadle Price as prime minister. With independence, Price continued in office as the first prime minister of the new nation. Many Belizeans were apprehensive of the future because neighbouring Guatemala had long claimed the territory as its own. For this reason some 1,600 British troops were to remain in Belize indefinitely to provide security.

24 U.S.-U.S.S.R. arms talks set

The U.S. and the U.S.S.R. jointly announced that negotiations to limit nuclear weapons in Europe would begin in Geneva on November 30. A spokesman for the U.S. Department of State later affirmed that theatre nuclear forces (medium-range weapons) would be the main subject of the negotiations.

25 Sandra O'Connor becomes justice of U.S. Supreme Court

Sandra Day O'Connor was formally sworn in as an associate justice of the U.S. Supreme Court, the first woman to hold that position. The 51-year-old justice had formerly served as majority leader in the Arizona state senate and as a judge on the Arizona State Court of Appeals. On July 7 President Reagan announced that O'Connor was his choice to replace retiring Justice Potter Stewart. In mid-September, after three days of confirmation hearings that frequently focused on O'Connor's past and present views on legalized abortion, the Senate Judiciary Committee approved the nomination by a vote of 17–0. Republican Sen. Jeremiah Denton of Alabama preferred not to vote, but on September 21 he was among the 99 senators who voted unanimously in favour of the nomination.

Polish workers granted authority in factories

The Polish Sejm (parliament) approved two new laws giving workers a greater say in the management of certain factories. According to an agreement sanctioned by representatives of Solidarity, the Polish federation of independent trade unions, the government would permit workers' councils to share authority in naming certain directors. In cases of dispute, differences of opinion would be settled by a court. Both sides had made significant concessions before agreement could be reached.

28 Canadian high court rules on federal constitution

In a 7–2 decision, the Canadian Supreme Court ruled that Prime Minister Pierre Elliott Trudeau's effort to obtain the patriation of the Canadian constitution was in the strict sense legal. But the same court also ruled in a 6–3 vote that concurrence by Canada's provinces was "a matter of constitutional convention." The court then attempted to clarify its seemingly ambiguous pronouncement by saying: "It is true that Canada would remain a federation if the proposed amendment becomes law. But it would be a different federation, made different at the instance of a majority in the House of the federal Parliament acting alone. It is this process itself which offends the federal principle." Since 1867 Canada had been governed by the British North America Act.

World stocks fluctuate wildly

Stock markets around the world plunged dramatically following a prediction by U.S. analyst Joseph Granville that September 28 would "go down in financial history as a 'Blue Monday.'" However, when the U.S. stock markets rebounded after an initial drop, other markets quickly recovered also. Among the markets most seriously affected were those in Tokyo and Hong Kong, but fear also sparked panic selling in such cities as Brussels, Frankfurt, London, Milan, Paris, and Zürich.

29 U.S. debt reaches $1 trillion

For the first time in history, the ceiling on the U.S. federal debt was raised to more than one trillion dollars. The Senate approved the measure 64–34 after Sen. William Proxmire of Wisconsin pleaded with his colleagues to hold down government spending. He spoke against the bill for more than 16 hours but to no avail. The new limit had been approved earlier by the House of Representatives.

OCTOBER

2 Solidarity reelects Walesa

Solidarity, Poland's federation of trade unions, reelected Lech Walesa as its chairman but gave him only about 55% of the total vote. Those who opposed a new two-year term for Walesa criticized his policies as too moderate and his leadership as too authoritarian. After Walesa's victory the delegates elected numerous radicals to a newly created 107-member policymaking commission.

3 Maze Prison hunger strike ends

A hunger strike by six Irish nationalists being held in Maze Prison near Belfast,

Northern Ireland, was called off when five of the men learned that their families intended to order medical treatment for them as soon as they lost consciousness. Ten prisoners had already voluntarily starved themselves to death during the seven-month protest. The nationalists had demanded status as political prisoners and changes in their treatment, but the British government adamantly refused to discuss any changes so long as the strike persisted.

5 Iran elects new president

Sayyed Ali Khamenei was officially declared winner of Iran's presidential elec-

tion held October 2. Khamenei, a clergyman and since September 1 head of the ruling Islamic Republican Party, was a personal spokesman of Ayatollah Ruhollah Khomeini.

Sudan's Parliaments dissolved

Sudanese Pres. Gaafar Nimeiry dissolved the nation's two parliaments, one in the north, the other in the semiautonomous southern region. The government explained that in the future the National People's Assembly in the north would be nearly 60% smaller and that provinces would be given greater authority over such matters as education and health.

Egyptian Pres. Anwar as-Sadat was photographed just before he was assassinated at a military parade in Cairo.

6 Sadat assassinated in Cairo

Egyptian Pres. Anwar as-Sadat was assassinated during a military parade in Cairo. The attackers, who jumped from a military truck when it reached the reviewing stand, hurled hand grenades and fired automatic weapons as they raced toward the dignitaries. Sadat, who was among those mortally wounded, was rushed by helicopter to a military hospital but died within three hours. Vice-Pres. Hosni Mubarak was standing next to Sadat but was only slightly injured. That evening he officially announced to the nation that the president was dead. On October 9 the Ministry of Defense identified the leader of the plot as the brother of a man who had been arrested during the September crackdown on dissident elements. The commandos were said to be Muslim fundamentalists. Sadat's funeral on October 10 was attended by dignitaries from all over the world, including all three living former U.S. presidents. Most leaders of Muslim countries, however, stayed away because they had opposed Sadat's rapprochement with Israel.

9 U.K. Social Democrats meet

Britain's seven-month-old Social Democratic Party ended its first conference. To give meaning to its commitment to decentralized government, the conference was opened in Perth, Scotland, moved on to Bradford, England, and adjourned in London. During the conference several members of Parliament announced they were leaving the Labour Party to join the ranks of the Social Democrats. The new recruits, who included a former adviser to James Callaghan when he held the post of

Labour prime minister, gave the party 21 representatives in Parliament and marked it as a potentially serious political power.

10 China makes offer to Taiwan

Hu Yaobang, chairman of the Chinese Communist Party, invited Pres. Chiang Ching-kuo and other leaders of the Nationalist government in Taiwan to visit their "native places" in China. On October 7 Chiang Ching-kuo, speaking at a Nationalist Party meeting, pledged never to negotiate with the Chinese Communist government because to do so "is to invite death."

Demonstrators march in Bonn

An estimated 250,000 people marched in Bonn, the capital of West Germany, to protest NATO's announced plans to deploy nuclear weapons in Western Europe. Some called for a total ban on nuclear weapons, including those deployed by the Soviet Union. The demonstrators included private individuals as well as many affiliated with churches, labour unions, environmental groups, and left-wing organizations. Chancellor Helmut Schmidt, a firm backer of NATO's decision, was particularly annoyed that some fellow Social Democrats supported the demonstration. In the following weeks similar marches were organized in other European cities.

13 Mubarak elected in Egypt

Hosni Mubarak was overwhelmingly confirmed as president of Egypt in a national referendum that gave voters the option of approving or disapproving his

nomination. During his inaugural address the following day, Mubarak paid homage to former president Anwar as-Sadat and said he would continue the policies of the slain leader.

14 Norway gets new government

Kåre Willoch became prime minister of Norway and the head of a minority Conservative Party government after efforts to form a coalition with the Christian People's and Centre parties failed. Willoch told Parliament that he accepted membership in NATO as the foundation of Norway's security, but would also seek good relations with the Soviet Union.

15 Reagan extols free market

President Reagan, in an address delivered before the World Affairs Council of Philadelphia, outlined his policy on world economic development. After saying that "development and economic freedom go hand in hand," he noted that a mere handful of industrialized countries that couple "personal freedom with economic reward now produce more than one-half the wealth of the world." Defending the U.S. against charges that its capitalist system was the cause of world hunger and poverty, he asserted that each year the U.S. "provides more food assistance . . . than all other nations combined."

16 Turkey curbs political parties

Turkey's National Security Council, headed by Gen. Kenan Evren, dissolved

India's Prime Minister Indira Gandhi and Mexico's Pres. José López Portillo were among 22 world leaders who attended an economic conference in Cancún, Mexico, in October.

NOVEMBER

all the country's political parties and confiscated their assets. Evren said the move would pave the way for new parties "that would direct their activities toward the future and not to their past struggles."

18 *Socialists win Greek election*

For the first time since the end of World War II, Greek voters chose a Socialist government. The Panhellenic Socialist Movement party (Pasok), under the leadership of Andreas Papandreou, captured 172 seats in the 300-seat Parliament, giving it a comfortable majority. The ruling New Democracy Party wound up with a total of 115. The remaining seats went to Communist Party candidates. On October 21 Papandreou became prime minister and promised to carry out the "mandate for change" he had received.

Kania ousted in Poland

Stanislaw Kania, leader of Poland's Communist Party, was removed from office during a stormy session of the party's Central Committee. The main points of disagreement centred on ways to solve the nation's perilous economic situation and on measures needed to curtail Solidarity, the federation of trade unions, many of whose members had disrupted production by wildcat strikes. Kania was replaced by Wojciech Jaruzelski, an army general who served as Poland's defense minister before being appointed premier in early February.

Reagan and Mitterrand confer

French Pres. François Mitterrand and President Reagan met for the first time, in Williamsburg, Va. During their discussions, the two reportedly agreed on the need to improve Western Europe's military capabilities. They also saw eye to eye on the need for vigorous efforts to bring about a successful conclusion to the Camp David accords. Differences over El Salvador remained; whereas the U.S. supported the existing government, France recognized the guerrillas as a legitimate political faction. Mitterrand was also more committed than Reagan to major programs to aid less developed countries.

21 *NATO confirms intention to deploy nuclear weapons in Europe*

At the end of a two-day conference in Gleneagles, Scotland, representatives of NATO publicly reaffirmed their intention to deploy U.S. nuclear weapons in Western Europe but for the first time indicated a willingness to cancel the plan if the Soviet Union was willing to remove weapons it had targeted at Western Europe.

Yasir Arafat visits Asia

Yasir Arafat, leader of the Palestine Liberation Organization (PLO), ended a two-week visit to Asia and the Soviet Union. After traveling to North Korea, Arafat met in Beijing (Peking) with Chinese Premier Zhao Ziyang, who expressed firm support for the PLO. During Arafat's three-day "unofficial" visit to Japan, he held discussions with Prime Minister Zenko Suzuki and Foreign Minister Sunao Sonoda. Before Arafat's arrival, certain Japanese politicians had tried to force a cancellation of the visit because it was no longer possible "to balance" Arafat's visit with one from the late president of Egypt, Anwar as-Sadat, a moderate Arab. From Japan Arafat flew to Vietnam and then to the Soviet Union where officials granted full diplomatic status to their Arab guest.

22 *PATCO union decertified*

The U.S. Federal Labor Relations Authority voted 2–1 to decertify the Professional Air Traffic Controllers Organization (PATCO) as bargaining representative of air traffic controllers employed by the Federal Aviation Administration. All three members had first reached the conclusion that PATCO called, condoned, and was a party to the illegal strike that began on August 3 and resulted in the firing of all controllers who defied a government order to return to work.

23 *World leaders meet in Cancún to discuss economic aid*

Leaders representing eight industrialized and 14 less developed nations ended a two-day economic conference in Cancún, Mexico. All agreed that greater cooperation was needed between richer and poorer nations, but substantial disagreement surfaced over specific proposals. President Reagan refused to endorse any "gigantic new international bureaucracy" but expressed a willingness to "continue negotiations as to how all of us can help resolve" the discrepancy that exists between the more wealthy "North" and the less developed "South." In his speech, Reagan also expressed his belief that "economic growth and human progress make their greatest strides in countries that encourage economic freedom."

27 *Finnish president resigns*

Urho Kekkonen, the 81-year-old president of Finland, resigned after taking a six-week leave of absence because of poor health. The government announced that in January 1982 voters would select 301 electors whose responsibility it would be to elect a successor to Kekkonen, the nation's president for more than 25 years.

28 *Saudis to get U.S. AWACS planes*

The U.S. Senate gave President Reagan a stunning foreign policy victory when it approved 52–48 the sale of $8.5 billion worth of sophisticated aircraft and other military equipment to Saudi Arabia. The House of Representatives had rejected the sale (301–111) on October 14 and the Senate was expected to do likewise. But, in a dramatic last-minute realignment of votes, several senators who had reserved judgment on the issue, and some who had publicly expressed opposition to the sale, announced they would support the Reagan administration by voting approval. Rejection by both houses of Congress was needed to kill the deal. The controversy centred on five airborne warning and control system (AWACS) surveillance planes, but also extended to electronic ground stations and equipment that would enhance the capability of the 62 F-15 fighter aircraft on order by Saudi Arabia. Israel strenuously opposed the sale on the grounds that turning such equipment over to Saudi Arabia, an Arab state, would imperil Israel's security.

NOVEMBER

1 *Israel rejects Saudi peace plan*

Israeli Prime Minister Menachem Begin attacked Saudi Arabia's peace plan for the Middle East, saying it was a formula for "how to liquidate Israel in stages." The eight-point plan, originally made public in August, gained new importance on October 29 when President Reagan said it was significant because it recognized Israel "as a nation to be negotiated with." The text affirmed "the right of all countries [according to some translators: 'the right of all people'] of the region to live in peace." However, it also contained a number of provisions that Israel found to be unacceptable.

5 *Canadian premiers and Trudeau reach compromise*

The nine premiers of Canada's English-speaking provinces and Prime Minister Pierre Elliott Trudeau reached a compromise on a formula for amending the country's planned first constitution. French-speaking Quebec, however, continued to oppose the majority on the grounds that the proposed constitution would deprive it of basic legislative powers that the province currently enjoyed. Once Canada's Parliament added its approval, the British Parliament would be in a position to take legal steps to make Canada, in a technical and legal sense, a fully independent country.

JAN COLLSIÖÖ—PRESSENS BILD/UPI

A Soviet submarine is escorted into open waters by Swedish ships in November. The Soviet vessel had run aground in restricted Swedish waters.

6 Sweden releases Soviet submarine

The Swedish government released a Soviet submarine that had run aground inside Sweden's territorial waters on October 27. Sweden's foreign minister said his government had "made unprecedented protests in the strongest possible language" over the violation of its territory. The government and the general public were especially incensed that the submarine had ventured into waters near the Karlskrona Naval Base, a restricted area. On November 2 the captain of the vessel finally agreed to be questioned aboard a Swedish naval vessel in the presence of Soviet diplomats, but his explanation was rejected as unacceptable. On November 5 Sweden revealed that radiation had been detected near the front of the submarine, an indication that it was probably armed with nuclear weapons.

8 Mubarak outlines Egypt's future

In a televised address before the Egyptian Parliament, Pres. Hosni Mubarak asserted that Egypt was "an African state" that was "neither East nor West" and would, consequently, "never be within the orbit of this or that country, or this bloc or that bloc." He also pledged that his economic policies would give special attention to helping the nation's underprivileged.

9 Burma chooses new president

U San Yu, a retired army general, was elected president of Burma by the nation's Parliament. He replaced 70-year-old U Ne Win, who retired for personal reasons but was expected to remain an important influence in government.

India gets record IMF loan

The International Monetary Fund (IMF) approved a record $5.8 billion loan to India. The U.S., which opposed the loan on the grounds that it was in fact destined for development and therefore not the IMF's proper concern, abstained in the voting. The loan would be disbursed over a three-year period and, according to the IMF, would not be granted except to cover balance of payments deficits, which conformed to the purposes for which the IMF was established.

10 U.S. claims U.S.S.R. used toxic weapons in Asia

Richard Burt, director of the U.S. Department of State's Bureau of Politico-Military Affairs, informed a Senate foreign relations subcommittee that the government now had clear evidence that the U.S.S.R. had engaged in chemical warfare in Asia. The evidence, reportedly gathered from water and rocks in Laos and Cambodia, consisted of fungal poisons that were not native to that part of the world. The findings were said to confirm earlier U.S. charges that the "yellow rain" reported by inhabitants of the region was in fact toxic chemicals. The Soviet Union vehemently denied the charges, and some scientists who studied the reports hesitated to call the evidence conclusive.

Libyan leader warns of civil war in Chad

Col. Radan Salah, leader of the Libyan troops in Chad, predicted that civil war would once again engulf the country after the soldiers under his command were re-

placed by an African peacekeeping force. Although Chad's president, Goukouni Oueddei, had regained control of his country in December 1980 with the help of Libyan tanks, troops, and aircraft, he informed Libya that he no longer wanted its military forces stationed inside Chad's territory.

11 Greece to ban nuclear weapons

A spokesman for the Greek government told reporters that his country wanted to negotiate the speedy removal of nuclear weapons from its territory and establish a nuclear-free zone in the Balkans. He also noted that Bulgaria, Romania, and Yugoslavia desired the same thing, as did the Soviet Union. According to reports, the only nuclear weapons on Greek soil have been confined to U.S. military bases.

14 Egypt indicts Sadat's killers

The Egyptian government indicted 4 persons for the assassination of Pres. Anwar as-Sadat and 20 others for complicity in the same crime. The accused were also charged with the murder of 7 others who died in the attack and with the attempted murder of 29 who were wounded.

The Gambia and Senegal unite

The Gambia announced that it was forming a new confederation with Senegal. The tiny West African republic on the lower Gambia River is virtually surrounded by much larger Senegal, but its short western border provides access to the Atlantic. The new confederation would be known as Senegambia.

"Columbia" completes second flight

The U.S. space shuttle "Columbia" returned to Earth after completing only one-half of its scheduled five-day mission. The journey was nonetheless historic because it marked the first time any manned vehicle had been reused for a voyage into space. The "Columbia," which was flown by 49-year-old Joe Engle and 44-year-old Richard Truly, was powered by three identical fuel cells. When one malfunctioned not long after blastoff, NASA officials in Houston studied the problem, then took steps to render the fuel cell "inert and safe." After a revised flight plan was drawn up, the astronauts completed their 36th orbit of the Earth and then brought the "Columbia" down at Edwards Air Force Base in California.

15 Bangladesh elects president

Abdus Sattar, a 74-year-old candidate of the Bangladesh Nationalist Party, was elected president of Bangladesh with 66% of the popular vote. He had assumed the duties of president following the assassination of Pres. Ziaur Rahman on May 30. Sattar's strongest rival was Kamal Hossain, candidate of the Awami League. Hossain described the election results as

NOVEMBER

Lord Carrington (centre), Britain's foreign secretary and the president of the European Communities Council of Ministers, attended a meeting of the Arab League in Fez, Morocco, that lasted only a few hours because of a disagreement over Saudi Arabia's proposal for a peace plan for the Middle East. At right is Prince Salman, governor of Riyadh.

"laughable" because of ballot box stuffing and other irregularities.

Khomeini delegates authority

Ayatollah Ruhollah Khomeini, the ultimate political and religious authority in Iran, authorized Ayatollah Hussein Ali Montazeri to select someone to supervise the Revolutionary Guards. It was the second time in two months that the ailing 82-year-old Khomeini had delegated authority to the man who was expected to succeed him.

18 Reagan ready to limit arms

President Reagan, in an address before the National Press Club in Washington, D.C., said he had sent Soviet Pres. Leonid I. Brezhnev "a simple, straightforward, yet historic message" calling for removal of Soviet SS-20 missiles targeted at Europe in exchange for NATO's scrapping the planned deployment in Europe of Pershing II and cruise missiles. Reagan told his audience: "I believe the time is right to move forward on arms control and the resolution of critical regional disputes at the conference table." The president's talk had special significance because the U.S. and the U.S.S.R. were to begin arms control discussions on November 30.

19 AFL-CIO snubs Reagan and attacks Stockman

The American Federation of Labor-Congress of Industrial Organizations ended its annual meeting in New York City after snubbing President Reagan, who was not

invited to address the assembly, and repeatedly ridiculing David Stockman, director of the Office of Management and Budget. Stockman had laid himself open to attack by casting doubt on the Reagan administration's economic plan during a series of interviews with a reporter who published the remarks in a magazine article that became public knowledge on November 10–11. The following day Stockman was summoned to the White House. He offered to resign because of his "poor judgment and loose talk," but the president settled for a severe reprimand. Among other remarks, Stockman was quoted as saying "none of us really under-

U.S. delegate Paul Nitze (left) and U.S.S.R. delegate Juli Kvitsinski (right) began disarmament talks between the two nations in November.

stands what's going on with all these numbers" in the budget. He also expressed doubt that the administration's economic program would work. Stockman had been the chief architect of the program.

20 Turkish junta jails Ecevit

Bulent Ecevit, who served as prime minister of Turkey three different times, faced four months in prison when the martial law commander failed to challenge the sentence handed down by a martial law court on November 3. Ecevit was convicted of deliberately violating a ban on political statements.

Europe to get Siberian gas

A West German consortium and the Soviet Union signed an agreement that would pave the way for the construction of a multibillion-dollar pipeline designed to carry Siberian gas to Western Europe. The U.S. opposed the deal on the grounds that Western Europe would become too dependent on the Soviet Union for a vital commodity.

22 Brezhnev visits Bonn

Soviet Pres. Leonid I. Brezhnev arrived in Bonn, West Germany, for three days of talks with Chancellor Helmut Schmidt. Though several "important international problems" were discussed by the two leaders, arms control outweighed all other issues. Schmidt reportedly sought many times to persuade Brezhnev that President Reagan was sincere when he called for a mutual reduction of arms, but Brezhnev gave no indication that he was any less wary of U.S. intentions than he was before visiting Bonn.

25 Arab League meeting collapses

A meeting of the Arab League in Fez, Morocco, was cut short after just a few

hours when it became apparent that the acrimonious debate over Saudi Arabia's proposed peace plan for the Middle East was destroying whatever hope there was for Arab unity. The meeting began on an inauspicious note when Libyan chief of state Muammar al-Qaddafi, Iraqi Pres. Saddam Hussein, and Syrian Pres. Hafez al-Assad announced they would not attend. The Palestine Liberation Organization also sided with the hard-line group that refused to compromise or negotiate with Israel.

26 Social Democrats in U.K. score first election victory

Shirley Williams, co-founder of Britain's new Social Democratic Party (SDP), was elected to Parliament from the district of Crosby, which had voted Conservative for more than 60 years. Williams, who

became the first SDP candidate to win an election, exulted: "There is not a single safe seat left in the country."

28 New Zealand holds election

New Zealand voters appeared to have denied Prime Minister Robert D. Muldoon's National Party a majority in the Parliament. Preliminary results of the national election indicated that the National Party had won 46 seats in the 92-seat legislature and the Labour Party 44; the remaining two seats were given to the Social Credit Political League. Final results depended on some 250,000 absentee ballots, still uncounted.

29 Bomb kills 90 in Syria

A car loaded with explosives blew up outside side a schoolbuilding in Damascus,

Syria, killing 90 persons and wounding scores of others. Numerous structures in the crowded area were also badly damaged. Pres. Hafez al-Assad's ruling Ba'ath Socialist Party claimed that Muslim Brotherhood terrorists, who had long sought to overthrow Assad, were responsible for the attack.

30 U.S.-U.S.S.R. arms talks begin

Representatives of the United States and the Soviet Union held their first talks in Geneva on the reduction of medium-range nuclear weapons in Europe. Both sides issued positive statements to reporters, indicating that the atmosphere was cordial despite the seriousness of the issues under discussion and the increasing tension between the U.S. and the U.S.S.R. over such matters as the situation in Poland.

DECEMBER

2 Canada's House of Commons backs new constitution

Canada's House of Commons voted 246–24 in favour of Prime Minister Pierre Trudeau's proposal to provide the country with its first true constitution and make it legally independent of Great Britain. After the government-appointed Senate gave its expected consent, the British Parliament would be free to take steps to formalize the new relationship. Canada indicated it would remain a member of the Commonwealth and continue to recognize the British monarch as its official chief of state.

Libyan assassination squads reported to be in the U.S.

The White House confirmed that it had received detailed information about Libyan-trained assassins who had entered the U.S. with the intention of killing President Reagan and other top government officials. Libya's head of state, Col. Muammar al-Qaddafi, ridiculed the report and called Reagan a liar. On December 7 Reagan responded: "We have the evidence, and he knows it." On December 10 the U.S. requested all its citizens to leave Libya immediately and invalidated U.S. passports for travel to that country.

South Africa frees hijackers after Seychelles coup fails

South Africa released 39 of 44 mercenaries who had hijacked an Air India jet after failing to overthrow Pres. France-Albert René of Seychelles. The other five hijackers were charged with crimes that carry relatively light sentences. The plot was uncovered when the mercenaries, purporting to be rugby players, landed in Seychelles on a commercial flight with weapons hidden in their baggage. The

abortive coup was the third against René, who had been accused of trying to turn his archipelago nation into a Soviet base.

3 Israel conditionally accepts European force in Sinai

Israel and the U.S. issued a joint statement accepting Great Britain, France, Italy, and The Netherlands as part of a peacekeeping force in the Sinai after the withdrawal of Israeli troops in April 1982. The statement also insisted on the Camp David accords as "the only viable and ongoing negotiating process" in the search for

a lasting peace in the Middle East. Syria and other Arab nations had warned that endorsement of the Camp David accords would deal "a blow to the Euro-Arab dialogue." The Israeli Cabinet, which had to approve the plan, said it would demand that the Europeans accept the Camp David declarations as the sole framework for future negotiations.

4 Haig explains U.S. position on Central America

U.S. Secretary of State Alexander Haig, during a meeting of the Organization of

Lech Walesa (foreground), leader of Poland's Solidarity union, conferred with other leaders before the Polish government imposed martial law on December 13.

DECEMBER

American States in St. Lucia, warned that the military buildup in Nicaragua was "a prelude to a widening war in Central America." He offered to work toward establishing "proper relations" between the U.S. and Nicaragua provided Nicaragua adopted a new policy regarding "interventionism and militarization."

U.S. unemployment grows

The U.S. Department of Labor announced that the country's unemployment rate had reached 8.4% of the work force in November. The lack of job opportunities was attributed to high interest rates and a slowdown in industrial production and retail sales.

7 *Pol Pot's party organization said to be disbanded*

The Communist Party organization of Pol Pot, whose Khmer Rouge regime in Kampuchea (Cambodia) had been overthrown in January 1979 by the Vietnamese-backed forces of Heng Samrin, was no longer functioning, according to a statement reportedly broadcast from southern China by Pol Pot forces. The surprise announcement was interpreted by some observers as an attempt by Pol Pot to shed his disreputable image.

8 *Danish election inconclusive*

In parliamentary elections, Denmark's ruling Social Democratic Party headed by Prime Minister Anker Jørgensen suffered a net loss of nine seats, leaving it with only 59 of the 179 seats in the legislature. The voters gave the right and left nearly equal representation. Jørgensen said he would resign but was subsequently persuaded by Queen Margrethe to try to form a minority government.

Three hijacked Venezuelan planes land in Cuba

Two Venezuelan DC-9s and one Boeing 727, simultaneously hijacked over Venezuela, landed in Havana after refueling on the island of Aruba and later in Colombia, Honduras, Guatemala, and Panama. None of the several hundred passengers was injured. Cuban police arrested the 11 hijackers, who were reported to include Puerto Rican nationalists, Salvadoran leftists, and Venezuelans seeking a ransom and the release of political prisoners.

9 *Muldoon's party retains majority*

New Zealand Prime Minister Robert Muldoon's National Party won 47 seats in the 92-seat Parliament, according to an announcement following the counting of absentee ballots. The Labour Party captured 43 seats and the Social Credit Party, 2. Preliminary reports after the November 28 election had indicated that the National Party would not attain an absolute majority.

CANADIAN PRESS

Canadian legislators applauded Prime Minister Pierre Elliott Trudeau after the Commons voted on December 2 in favour of Trudeau's constitutional package.

10 *Sakharovs end hunger strike*

The head of the Soviet Academy of Sciences announced that Andrey Sakharov, an eminent physicist and dissident, had ended his hunger strike on December 8. Sakharov and his wife had begun to refuse food on November 22 to protest the Soviet government's refusal to grant their daughter-in-law, Yelizaveta Alekseyeva, permission to join her husband in the U.S. A few days after the Sakharovs' hospitalization was announced December 4, Alekseyeva was notified by Soviet authorities that she would be issued travel documents.

11 *Argentina's president is ousted*

Argentine Pres. Roberto Eduardo Viola was removed from office by a three-man military junta and replaced by Lieut. Gen. Leopoldo Galtieri. The new chief of state was expected to complete Viola's term, which was due to expire in March 1984, while retaining his post as head of the Army. Argentina was burdened by growing unemployment and an annual inflation rate of about 120%.

13 *Martial law imposed on Poland*

The Communist government of Poland, faced with growing social unrest and mounting economic problems, declared a state of emergency and imposed martial law on the entire country. The previous day the leaders of Solidarity, the federation of labour unions, had called for a national referendum on Poland's remaining a Communist state. The government's emergency measures began with a raid on Solidarity's headquarters in Gdansk, a near total shutdown of communications facilities, and a nationwide roundup of numerous former government officials and union activists, including Lech

Walesa, Solidarity's leader. Pope John Paul II immediately pleaded with his countrymen not to spill Polish blood. The severity of the crackdown announced by Gen. Wojciech Jaruzelski, the head of Poland's Communist Party and the nation's premier, prompted President Reagan to declare on December 14 that Poland would not receive any U.S. economic assistance until martial law was lifted. On December 17 he unequivocally blamed the Soviet Union for the imposition of martial law. Unconfirmed reports indicated that thousands had been arrested and that several of the coal miners in Silesia who defied the government by refusing to work had been killed.

Leaders of East and West Germany hold rare meeting

Helmut Schmidt, chancellor of West Germany, and Erich Honecker, chairman of East Germany's Council of State, ended three days of talks outside Berlin. It was the first meeting between the leaders of East and West Germany since Willy Brandt and Willi Stoph held talks in 1970. Although Schmidt agreed to grant East Germany certain credit concessions, there were no indications that any significant diplomatic breakthrough was expected.

14 *Israel annexes Golan Heights*

The Israeli government announced, after an emergency Cabinet meeting, that it was formally extending its "law, jurisdiction, and administration" over the Golan Heights, which it had captured from Syria during the 1967 war. The U.S., which considered the Golan as occupied territory, immediately expressed its "deep concern over, and opposition to, any effort to change the status of the Golan unilaterally." The European Communities and the UN Security Council

were among those who declared the annexation illegal. Israeli Prime Minister Menachem Begin, who had anticipated the negative reaction, asserted that "no one will dictate our lives to us, not even the United States." A spokesman for the Israeli Foreign Ministry explained that Israel had become "saturated" with Syrian war threats.

Belgian government formed

Wilfried Martens, who had already served as prime minister of Belgium four times during the past three years, announced the formation of a new coalition government composed of fellow Social Christians and Liberals. The former government of Mark Eyskens fell on September 21. Martens said the new coalition, which held 113 of the 212 seats in the Chamber of Representatives, would seek emergency powers through 1982 so that it could initiate certain economic reforms without having to wait for Parliament's approval.

15 *UN General Assembly elects Pérez as Waldheim successor*

The UN General Assembly elected 61-year-old Javier Pérez de Cuéllar as successor to Secretary-General Kurt Waldheim. The Peruvian diplomat, whose five-year term would commence on Jan. 1, 1982, was nominated on December 11 after 16 previous ballots had failed to break a deadlock. China had repeatedly vetoed Waldheim's reelection and the U.S. had consistently vetoed China's choice, Salim A. Salim of Tanzania.

Iraqi embassy in Beirut bombed

The Iraqi embassy in Beirut, Lebanon, was totally destroyed by explosives planted, according to various reports, either in an automobile or at the base of structural columns of the building. About 30 persons were killed and some 100 injured. Iraq blamed Iranian and Syrian terrorists for the attack.

17 *U.S. general abducted in Italy*

Brig. Gen. James L. Dozier, a U.S. Army officer, was kidnapped from his apartment in Verona, Italy, by members of the Red Brigades, a leftist terrorist organization that had kidnapped and then murdered former Italian premier Aldo Moro in 1978. Dozier was serving NATO as deputy chief of staff for logistics and administration for land forces in southern Europe. Italian police launched an intensive search for Dozier but without success. On December 31 the kidnappers sent a picture of Dozier to a U.S. news agency in Rome, apparently to indicate that he was still alive.

18 *U.S. suspends pact with Israel*

The U.S. suspended the memorandum of understanding it had signed with Israel on November 30. The pact was meant to strengthen the bonds of unity between the two nations in the face of threats to the Middle East "caused by the Soviet Union or Soviet-controlled forces from outside the region." The Reagan administration reportedly took the unexpected step against Israel to protest its sudden annexation of the Golan Heights and to deter Israel from launching a major military operation in southern Lebanon.

Albanian premier commits suicide

Mehmet Shehu, premier of Albania since 1954, took his own life "at a moment of nervous distress," according to a government announcement. The 68-year-old politician had been expected to succeed Enver Hoxha, the ailing founder and longtime head of Albania's Communist Party.

20 *Polish ambassadors to U.S. and Japan defect to West*

The Polish ambassador to the U.S., Romuald Spasowski, defected to the U.S. to protest the imposition of martial law in Poland. Four days later Zdzislaw Rurarz, the Polish ambassador to Japan, appeared with his family at the U.S. embassy in Tokyo to ask for political asylum. Rurarz said he could no longer represent "a regime which denies the fundamental rights of the Polish people."

China criticizes U.S. policy toward Korea

During a visit to North Korea, Chinese Premier Zhao Ziyang said the United States was responsible for the continued division between North and South Korea. China's official Xinhua news agency quoted Zhao as also saying that the presence of U.S. troops in South Korea was "wanton intervention" in the internal affairs of Korea.

29 *Reagan penalizes U.S.S.R. for role in Polish crackdown*

President Reagan announced a series of sanctions against the Soviet Union, saying that it "bears a heavy and direct responsibility for the repression in Poland." The list of sanctions included a suspension of export licenses for high technology, the closing of U.S. ports and airfields to Soviet ships and planes, an indefinite delay in discussing a new long-term grain sales agreement, and a ban on new licenses to sell U.S. oil and gas equipment, notably, equipment destined for use on the natural gas pipeline from Siberia to Western Europe. On December 23 Reagan had imposed economic restrictions on U.S. dealings with the Polish government to hasten an end to martial law and the "outrages" that accompanied it.

31 *Coup succeeds in Ghana*

Jerry J. Rawlings directed a bloody coup that overthrew Ghanaian Pres. Hilla Limann. In a radio broadcast, Rawlings reminded the nation that after he toppled the military government in June 1979, he voluntarily returned the government to civilian rule three months later. He did not, however, indicate how long the present Provisional Military Council would retain power. In explaining the reasons for the coup, Rawlings described Limann and his associates as "a pack of criminals who bled Ghana to the bone" and brought about the country's "total economic ruin."

Javier Pérez de Cuéllar of Peru (centre) was met by reporters when he arrived in New York City on December 13 after he had been nominated to be secretary-general by the UN General Assembly.

WIDE WORLD

DISASTERS OF 1981

The loss of life and property from disasters in 1981 included the following:

AVIATION

January 14, Ramstein, West Germany. A U.S. Air Force C-130 Hercules transport plane crashed just short of a U.S. ammunition dump in Ramstein; all nine men aboard were killed.

February 7, Leningrad, U.S.S.R. An airplane crash on the outskirts of Leningrad reportedly killed 70 Soviet officers, including as many as 24 admirals and generals. The Soviet armed forces newspaper, *Krasnaya Zvezda*, gave only sketchy details of the disaster.

April 17, Loveland, Colo. A twin-engine commuter airplane carrying 13 passengers and a small private craft carrying 5 sky divers collided in midair about 2.4 km (1.5 mi) from Fort Collins-Loveland Airport; everyone on the commuter plane was killed, but 3 parachutists and the pilot bailed out of the other crippled craft and jumped to safety. Two other chutists also jumped but were killed after they apparently sustained head injuries while parachuting from the plane.

May 6, Walkersville, Md. An EC-135-A airplane, a $50 million missile-and-satellite-tracking aircraft, burst into flames in midair and crashed with 21 persons aboard; there were no survivors.

May 7, Near Buenos Aires, Arg. An Argentine jetliner that had made two unsuccessful attempts to land during a thunderstorm at the Buenos Aires Metropolitan Airport crashed into the Rió de la Plata; all 30 persons aboard were killed.

May 26, Off the coast of Florida. An EA-6B Prowler electronic warfare jet airplane crash-landed on the flight deck of the aircraft carrier "Nimitz," destroying $200 million of aircraft, killing 14 men, and injuring some 48 others. The accident was the worst involving a U.S. aircraft carrier in peacetime.

August 22, Near San-yi, Taiwan. A Boeing 737 en route to Kaohsiung exploded and crashed 150 km (93 mi) southwest of Taipei; all 110 persons aboard were killed.

Late August, Caquetá, Colombia. An airplane crashed into a mountain in Caquetá; 48 persons were killed.

September 2, Paipa, Colombia. A chartered airplane crashed after experiencing mechanical difficulties; 15 of 20 technicians and engineers working for Intercorp, a subsidiary of Exxon, were killed.

September 6, Northern Thailand. A police helicopter carrying a Cabinet minister and five members of Parliament disappeared during a storm over the northern section of the country; all 11 occupants were presumed dead.

September 22, Near Babaeski, Turkey. A Turkish Air Force jet fighter crashed and exploded in a bivouac area used for NATO exercises; the pilot apparently was practicing a diving run and could not maneuver the airplane out of its descent. At least 26 persons were killed and some 75 others were injured.

October 28, Northern Nicaragua. A helicopter crashed into the side of a hill shrouded in fog and killed 15 men; the craft was carrying government airmen who were chasing right-wing gunmen.

November 8, Near Altamirano, Mexico. A Mexican DC-9 jet slammed into the side of a rugged mountain slope some 190 km (120 mi) southwest of Mexico City; 12 passengers and 6 crew members were killed.

December 1, Ajaccio, Corsica. A Yugoslav DC-9 jetliner slammed into Mt. San Pietro minutes before making its approach to land at Ajaccio Airport; all 178 persons aboard were killed.

FIRES AND EXPLOSIONS

January 9, Keansburg, N.J. An early-morning fire at the 54-room Beachview Rest Home claimed the lives of 30 elderly residents, who were either disoriented, under heavy sedation, or too terrified to escape the blaze.

January 11, East St. Louis, Ill. A residential fire killed 11 children who had been left home alone overnight by their mother.

January 17, Near Bogotá, Colombia. An explosion rocked a water dam under construction some 64 km (40 mi) from Bogotá, killed 10 persons, and injured 20 others.

January 18, London, England. A fire broke out shortly after dawn at a three-story house during an all-night teenage birthday party; ten persons who were trapped in the basement were killed.

February 7, Bangalore, India. A fire swept through the main tent of the Venus Circus near the conclusion of a three-hour matinee attended by 4,000 persons; of the 66 persons killed, some were engulfed in flames but others, mostly children, were trampled to death.

February 10, Las Vegas, Nev. A fire that was started by a busboy on the 8th floor of the Hilton Hotel reached the 29th floor in 15 minutes when flames leaped outside through shattered windows; 8 persons were found dead and 198 others were injured, including 3 firemen who were in critical condition.

February 14, São Paulo, Brazil. A Saturday fire in a 20-story office building claimed the lives of at least 17 persons, many of them custodians, and gutted the downtown building.

February 14, Dublin, Ireland. An early-morning fire at the Stardust discotheque claimed the lives of 46 persons and injured 129 others who were attending a dance competition; thick black smoke, burning foam rubber chairs, and the flaming ceiling tiles hampered their escape.

February 19, Southern Philippines. A land mine exploded as a truck ran over it on a U.S.-owned rubber estate; 16 persons were killed.

March 4, Lima, Peru. A riot between two rival gangs at El Sexto prison claimed the lives of 27 prisoners who fled to their cells to avoid the fight; a master bar was pushed across their cells and the prisoners were burned alive when rioters doused their cells and mattresses with kerosene.

March 14, Chicago, Ill. An early-morning blaze at a four-story residential hotel was caused by faulty wiring in the basement laundry room; the fire, which swept up the stairways, trapped and killed 19 persons.

April 19, Davao City, Phil. Two hand grenades exploded in San Pedro Cathedral, which was filled with some 5,000 worshipers; 13 persons were killed by the blast.

April 27, Szczecin, Poland. A fast-burning fire, which started in the restaurant of a three-story building, was fueled by flammable decorations and floor and ceiling covers; noxious fumes from the blaze killed 13 persons.

August 13, Anyang, South Korea. A propane gas explosion in a two-story restaurant reduced the building to rubble; 12 persons were killed when propane gas containers exploded and the structure became a flaming inferno.

September 19, Southern India. An explosion in a fireworks factory claimed the lives of at least 30 persons.

October 24, Hoboken, N.J. A fast-burning fire swept through a five-story apartment building and claimed the lives of 11 persons, 7 of whom were children.

A plane damaged in the crash of another plane on the deck of the U.S. aircraft carrier "Nimitz" is removed from the crash scene. Fourteen men died in the accident.

WIDE WORLD

December 6, Ahmedabad, India. A five-story wood and canvas structure, modeled after the Himalayan mountain range, caught fire and trapped many visitors at the top; at least 49 persons lost their lives in the blaze.

MARINE

January 6, Northern Brazil. A wooden double-decker ferryboat carrying some 500 persons sank while traveling through treacherous currents in a tributary of the Amazon River; 230 persons, including 50 children, were drowned.

January 16, Near Faridpur, Bangladesh. An overcrowded motor launch capsized in the Arial Khan River; 17 persons were killed.

January 16, Off the coast of Crete. A Turkish merchant ship, the "Deniz Sonmez," sank off the coast of the Greek island of Crete; the 34 crew members aboard were feared drowned.

January 25, Java Sea. An Indonesian passenger ship, the "Tampomas II," caught fire and sank in the turbulent Java Sea; rescue efforts were hampered because of driving rain and stormy seas, and at least 431 of the more than 1,100 persons aboard the ferry were drowned.

February 26, Tsugaru Strait, Japan. A 5,923-ton Soviet freighter, the "Komsomolets Nakhodki," sank in stormy seas after issuing a distress signal; patrol boats were unsuccessful in rescuing any of the 38 crewmen.

February 28, Near the Aleutian Islands. The "Dae Rim," a South Korean cargo ship, caught fire and was abandoned by its 22 crewmen; only 2 survived the near-freezing water overnight and were rescued by Soviet ships.

March 8, Off the coast of Bermuda. The 203-m (666-ft) Israeli freighter "Mezada" sank in stormy seas some 160 km (100 mi) southeast of Bermuda; 11 crewmen were rescued by the U.S. Coast Guard, 12 were known dead, and 12 others were missing and presumed drowned.

March 13, Bering Sea. The "Daito Maru 55," a Japanese fishing boat, sank in stormy seas some 610 km (380 mi) northwest of Atka Island in the Aleutians; all 26 crewmen drowned.

May 30, Pacific Ocean. A 6-m (20-ft) cabin cruiser carrying 21 persons on a routine 97-km (60 mi) ferry trip from Abaiang Island to Tarawa, Kiribati, on March 26 was blown 2,090 km (1,300 mi) off course by wind and ocean current; the craft, which drifted for two months, was spotted 1,120 km (700 mi) southeast of Guam by men searching for tuna in a helicopter. Nine persons had died during the course of the ordeal, but rescuers saved 12 others who had survived by living on rainwater, salt water, and a shark, which they caught bare-handed.

September 19, Óbidos, Brazil. An Amazon riverboat, the "Sobral Santos," began taking on water after docking in the northern jungle port of Óbidos; when its 500 passengers panicked and scurried to the other side of the boat, the vessel sank and at least 300 persons drowned.

September 20, Off Calayan Island, Phil. A fierce typhoon packing 185 km/h (115 mph) winds forced a Philippine Navy destroyer to run aground; despite rescue efforts by U.S. helicopters, 52 crewmen drowned and 27 others were missing.

October 26, Off the coast of Miami, Fla. An overloaded homemade 9-m (30-ft) boat capsized less than 1.6 km (1 mi) from shore with 67 Haitian refugees aboard; 33 people drowned and 34 others swam to shore.

November 1, Off the coast of India. A devastating tropical storm that hit the coast of India with tidal waves and winds of up to 145 km/h (90 mph) caused the disappearance of more than 500 fishermen who were sailing in the Arabian Sea during the storm.

November 26, Off the coast of Bermuda. A 7,500-ton West German cargo ship, the "Elma Tres," overturned and sank after being buffeted by high winds in rough seas; of the 24-member crew only one survivor was rescued by a Liberian ship.

Early December, Off the coast of Malaysia. A boat carrying Vietnamese refugees capsized during a monsoon in the South China Sea; 19 persons drowned.

December 2, Off the coast of Japan. The "Crystal Star," a South Korean-registered freighter, apparently sank in rough seas around Japan; there was no trace of the ship or the 38 seamen aboard.

December 20, Off the coast of England. The "Union Star," a 1,400-ton British coaster, slammed onto rocks off the southwest coast of England during high seas; 16 persons were killed.

December 29, Bay of Biscay. The Italian freighter "Marina d' Equa" sank in the Bay of Biscay during a storm; four empty lifeboats were found and the 30 crewmen aboard the freighter were presumed dead.

MINING

February 13, Bhadua, India. An unlicensed mine in the village of Bhadua in Bihar state caved in and heaped tons of mud on 500 workers; 400 labourers escaped unharmed but at least 100 others were missing and feared dead.

March 13, Mawad, Phil. A cave-in at an abandoned gold mine at the foot of Mt. Mainit claimed the lives of 41 amateur prospectors, including 6 women and 4 children; those buried under tons of rock had hoped to profit from soaring gold prices.

April 15, Redstone, Colo. A methane gas explosion at Dutch Creek No. 1 coal mine claimed the lives of 15 miners, who died instantly from the force of the blast.

May 7, South Africa. A methane gas explosion in a coal mine near the Indian Ocean claimed the lives of ten miners.

September 3, Zaluzi, Czech. An explosion ripped through the Pluto coal mine and killed 65 miners; it was the country's worst mining disaster in 20 years.

October 16, Near Sapporo, Japan. A methane gas leak in a coal mine poisoned and killed 83 miners and 10 rescue workers.

December 8, Near Whitwell, Tenn. A coal mine explosion caused by the emission of methane gas killed 13 miners; it was the third mining disaster in six days. On December 3, three miners were crushed to death when a roof caved in at Bergoo, W.Va., and on December 7, eight men lost their lives in Topmost, Ky., in another explosion linked to methane gas.

MISCELLANEOUS

February 8, Piraeus, Greece. A stampede occurred after Greek soccer fans surged to the exit after cheering their club, the Olympiakos, to a 6–0 victory over an Athens team; at least 24 persons at the front of the crowd were trampled to death when the excited throng pushed forward and tried to force their way through the locked exit gate.

March 6–7, Abidjan, Ivory Coast. Suffocation caused the deaths of 46 prisoners who were arrested and confined in rooms that were too small and inadequately ventilated.

March 10, Beni Suef, Egypt. Two neighbouring houses, one of which had been slated for demolition, collapsed and killed 23 occupants and injured 15 others.

March 27, Cocoa Beach, Fla. A five-story building caved in while workers were pouring the concrete on the unfinished roof; 11 men were buried beneath the rubble.

Early July, Bangalore, India. Illicit liquor, believed to contain methyl alcohol, killed at least 308 persons in the southern Indian city of Bangalore. The same liquor also took the lives of 16 persons living in Mysore, some 130 km (80 mi) south of Bangalore.

July 17, Kansas City, Mo. Two crowded 32-ton skywalks collapsed at the Hyatt Regency Hotel, hurled dancers off the ramps, and crashed into the lobby. A third-level walk apparently snapped from the steel rods that suspended it from the ceiling and crashed onto the skywalk directly below it. Of the hundreds of people trapped beneath the tons of steel, glass, and concrete, 113 died.

July 17, South Korea. Thirty-two persons, who had taken to the beaches to escape the heat and celebrate a national holiday, drowned at various beaches.

Early August, Banda, Indon. An outbreak of cholera killed at least 10 persons and hospitalized 40 others in the city of Banda on the island of Sumatra.

Late August, Spain. A poisonous cooking oil, sold illegally door-to-door, killed an estimated 200 persons from early May to late August and affected at least 11,000 others. The olive oil was mixed with rapeseed oil that had been treated for industrial use. Police arrested 25 people under suspicion that they had manufactured and sold the oil.

November 15, Mérida, Mexico. The 1.8-m (6-ft) wall of a bullring collapsed when some youths tried to climb over it in order to attend a political rally where a politician was promising to give away stoves and refrigerators; at least 48 persons were trampled

Workers remove the bodies of people who were killed when a wall collapsed at a bullring in Mérida, Mexico. Many of the victims were trampled to death.

WIDE WORLD

UPI

A great pile of rubble remained after two skywalks collapsed in the lobby of a Kansas City hotel. A total of 113 persons lost their lives in the disaster.

to death and 70 others were injured when the crowd of nearly 10,000 persons panicked.

November 17, Manila, Phil. The collapse of the ceiling at the uncompleted multimillion-dollar Manila Film Festival Center killed at least 30 construction workers.

November 18, Ibagué, Colombia. The collapse of a grandstand in a soccer stadium resulted in the deaths of 17 persons.

November 19, Taif, Saudi Arabia. The roof of a two-story building collapsed on some 800 persons while they were attending two weddings; 50 persons were killed and more than 90 others were seriously injured.

December 4, New Delhi, India. A stampede down the darkened staircase of the Qutb Minar, one of the oldest Islamic monuments in India, resulted in the deaths of 45 persons, most of them school-children; the sightseers reportedly panicked during a power failure when someone shouted that the tower was falling.

NATURAL

January, Northern India. A month-long cold wave and heavy snow that blocked roads to the capital cities of Srinagar in Jammu and Kashmir State and Simla in Himachal Pradesh killed at least 270 persons.

January, Southern Philippines. Heavy rains ravaged the area of Mindanao, severely damaged roads and bridges, killed nearly 200 persons, and left some 300,000 others homeless.

Early January, Japan. Snowstorms and avalanches claimed the lives of at least 61 persons and injured some 350 others in Japan.

January 19, Irian Jaya, Indonesia. A severe earthquake measuring 6.8 on the Richter scale obliterated Stolo Valley of western Irian Jaya; some 1,500 of its 3,000 residents were killed or missing.

January 24–25, Laingsburg, South Africa. Torrential rainfall caused the Buffels River to overflow its banks and send a 2-m (6-ft) wall of water on the farming community of Laingsburg; at least 200 persons were drowned.

February 24, Greece. Two earthquakes and a series of earth tremors rocked Athens, caused chips of marble to fall from the Parthenon, and jolted the city of Corinth, which was declared a disaster area. At least 16 persons were killed and tens of thousands of others camped in the streets in fear of another quake.

March 22, Yugoslavia. Heavy rains triggered a landslide that swept two cars of a train into the Morava River, some 190 km (120 mi) south of Belgrade; 12 persons lost their lives and 35 others were injured.

Late March–April, Northeastern Brazil. Ten days of continuous rain inundated drought-ridden Brazil; 30 persons were drowned and some 50,000 others were left homeless.

Mid-April, Colombia. After a week of flooding in central and northern Colombia, 65 persons were killed and 14,000 others were left homeless.

April 12, Noakhali, Bangladesh. A tornado ripped through the southeastern coastal district of Noakhali and destroyed 15,000 homes and many fields of crops; some 70 persons were killed and 1,500 others were injured.

April 17, Celebes, Indon. A landslide claimed the lives of 23 persons living in northern Celebes (Sulawesi).

April 17, Eastern India. A devastating tornado ripped through the four villages of Kakundi, Erandi, Dhanbendi, and Rengadadpa in Orissa state; more than 120 persons were killed, hundreds were injured, and at least 2,000 homes were destroyed.

Mid–Late April, Venezuela. Two weeks of heavy tropical rainfall caused severe flooding and mud slides that killed at least 27 persons and left some 4,000 others homeless. Hardest hit was Caracas, where many people were buried in their hillside shanties by mud slides.

May 3, Khorasan Province, Iran. Extensive flooding caused by heavy rain killed or injured 100 persons and isolated some 30 villages in the eastern province of Khorasan.

Mid-May, Java, Indon. Heavy rains caused Java's worst flooding in 150 years; a flood of mud and water descended the slopes near Mt. Semeru, and a dam 7 m (23 ft) high burst because of the raging floodwaters. At least 127 persons were known dead, 170 others were missing, and 38 were injured.

May 25, Austin, Texas. Flash floods triggered the overflow of Shoal Creek, which sent torrents of water swirling through the state capital; 10 persons were known dead and eight others were missing.

June 11, Kerman Province, Iran. A powerful earthquake measuring 6.8 on the Richter scale struck southeastern Iran; hardest hit was Golbaf, where two-thirds of the area was destroyed; officials estimated that more than 1,000 persons were killed.

June 21, Mt. Rainier, Washington. Boulder-size blocks of ice, which broke free from a glacier, buried 11 of 29 mountain climbers who were attempting to reach the summit of the 4,392-m (14,410-ft) peak. The accident, the worst ever recorded on Mt. Rainier, occurred 460 m (1,500 ft) above Camp Muir.

June 23, Ayacucho Province, Peru. A series of violent earth tremors measuring 6.0 on the Richter scale killed at least 10 persons and injured 100 others.

July 1, Central Philippines. Tropical storm Kelly pelted the country with heavy rains, which precipitated flooding and landslides in 12 villages; 140 persons were reported killed.

July 12–14, Sichuan (Szechwan) Province, China. Three days of monsoon rains caused the swollen Chang Jiang (Yangtze River) and its tributaries to overflow or burst their banks and send cascading waters through central and southern China; 1.5 million people were left homeless, some 1,300 were killed or missing, and more than 28,000 were injured. The damage to homes and crops was estimated at $1.1 billion.

July 13, Northern Nepal. Flash floods raged through the northern part of the country, damaged the border bridge between China and Nepal, and killed nearly 100 persons.

July 19, Northern Taiwan. Tropical Storm Maury caused massive flooding and landslides; 26 persons lost their lives in the storm.

July 19, Northwestern and northeastern India. Floods in the states of Assam, Uttar Pradesh, and Rajasthan killed some 500 people and left 120,000 others homeless.

July 28, Kerman Province, Iran. A devastating earthquake, measuring 7.3 on the Richter scale, rocked the province and killed some 1,500 persons in a sparsely populated area. It was the second major earthquake in Iran in seven weeks.

August 17, Saravena, Colombia. After the Salamina River burst its banks, the town of Saravena was inundated; some 150 persons were reported dead or missing.

Mid-August, Sichuan Province, China. A new wave of flooding killed 15 persons in southwest China. Chinese officials and scientists criticized China's 30-year deforestation program, which denuded most of the province's watershed areas near the Chang Jiang. Consequently, the river overflows and floods the area.

August 23, Central and Northern Japan. Typhoon Thad, packing winds of up to 130 km/h (80 mph) and accompanied by driving rain, slashed its way across the central and northern prefectures of the country; 40 persons were known dead and 20,000 others were left homeless.

September 1, South Korea. Typhoon Agnes lashed the country with 70 cm (28 in) of rain in two days; 120 persons were reported dead or missing in the worst downpour in South Korea in this century.

September 3, El Eulma, Alg. Flooding inundated the town of El Eulma and killed 43 persons.

September 12–13, Near Gilgit, Pak. A strong earthquake struck two northern Pakistani valleys and killed more than 210 persons.

September 21, U.K. Storms, with winds gusting to 130 km/h (80 mph), led to the deaths of at least 12 persons.

September 21, Fujian (Fukien) Province, China. Typhoon Clara rampaged across the southern section of the province and destroyed some 33,600 ha (83,000 ac) of rice and sugar crops; many people were feared dead.

September 23, Bombay, India. Torrential rains precipitated landslides and caused homes to collapse; at least 15 persons died as a result of the storm.

September 29, Nepal. Heavy rains resulted in flash flooding in many parts of the country; some 500 persons were reportedly killed or missing in the swirling waters.

October, Sichuan Province, China. Continued flooding followed by landslides claimed the lives of 240 persons.

October 7, Northern Mexico. Tropical storm Lydia pelted the northern Pacific coast of Mexico and caused widespread flooding that broke two dams; 65 persons, most of them in coastal and mountain villages, were killed.

October 9, Southern Philippines. A thundering avalanche in a copper mining camp buried sleeping miners and their families; eight buildings serving as bunkhouses were demolished and more than 200 persons were believed killed.

October 17, Border of Venezuela and Colombia. An earthquake sent tremors along Colombia's northern border with Venezuela and killed ten persons.

November 18, Kosovo Province, Yugos. An avalanche swept away two houses and killed 11 persons in the village of Kosutani.

November 19–20, Michigan and Minnesota. A major storm that dumped a foot of snow in the cities of Muskegon and Grand Rapids, Mich., and knocked down power lines contributed to the deaths of at least 17 persons. The weight of the snow also caused the collapse of the fabric roof of the Hubert H. Humphrey Metrodome in Minneapolis, Minn.

November 24, Philippines. Deadly Typhoon Irma roared through the Philippines packing winds of 225 km/h (140 mph) and devastated the coastal towns of Garchitorena and Caramoan; more than 270 persons were killed, some 150 others were injured, and more than 250,000 people were left homeless. The estimated damage to property and crops was put at $10 million.

Early December, Thailand. Week-long monsoon rains and flash flooding battered southern Thailand and left at least 37 persons dead.

December 3, Brazil. Floods and mud slides developed after 20 hours of relentless rain; more than 40 persons were killed, 23 others were injured, and at least 700 persons were left homeless.

December 6, Java, Indon. A landslide, triggered by heavy rains, struck the village of Dasun in eastern Java and killed at least 17 persons.

December 11, Bangladesh and India. A fierce typhoon blasted southwestern Bangladesh and eastern India, knocked down power lines, and destroyed crops; at least 27 persons were believed dead.

RAILROADS

January 1, Pakistan. A passenger train derailment some 275 km (170 mi) north of Karachi resulted in the deaths of 10 persons; more than 150 others were injured.

March 8, Northern Taiwan. A high-speed passenger train struck a truck at a crossing, causing the derailment of five of its ten cars as it proceeded over a bridge; 28 persons were killed and 130 others were injured in Taiwan's worst rail disaster.

March 8, Coronel Brandsen, Arg. A passenger train carrying tourists from the beach resort of Mar del Plata to Buenos Aires slammed into two derailed freight cars; 45 persons were killed and 120 others were injured.

May 14, Near Kyongsan, South Korea. A Seoul-bound passenger train, which struck a motorcycle at an unguarded crossing and then backed up from the wreck, was rammed from behind by a commuter train; 65 persons were killed and at least 240 others were injured in one of South Korea's worst rail disasters.

June 6, Near Mansi, India. A nine-car passenger train carrying more than 500 people plunged off a bridge into the Baghmati River when the driver braked to avoid a cow; the official death toll was put at 268, but over 300 others were still missing.

Late June, Near Gagry, U.S.S.R. A collision involving an express train and a local train near a Black Sea resort claimed the lives of 70 persons and injured 100 others, according to a Moscow report.

July 31, Near Bahawalpur, Pakistan. Six coaches of a passenger train derailed after two retaining plates had been removed from the tracks; 43 persons were killed and 50 others were injured. Authorities did not rule out sabotage as a cause of the accident.

TRAFFIC

February 18, Quantico, Va. A commuter bus carrying as many as 62 passengers crashed through a guardrail on Interstate 95 and fell down a 25-m (80-ft) embankment into about 30 cm (12 in) of water in Chopowamsic Creek; 10 persons were killed and 14 others were injured, two of them critically.

February 19, Morton, Ill. A fiery collision between a semitrailer, a van, and several other vehicles in dense fog resulted in the deaths of nine persons, eight of them occupants of the van.

March 22, Near Zitácuaro, Mexico. A passenger bus plunged off a cliff known as Devil's Curve some 120 km (75 mi) west of Mexico City; 35 persons were killed and 12 others were injured.

April 11, Pakistan. A bus returning from a religious pilgrimage ran off the road and careened into a canal some 320 km (200 mi) north of Karachi; 42 persons were killed.

April 25, Near Culiacán, Mexico. A crowded bus smashed into a truck while traveling from Tijuana to Mexico City; 30 persons were killed and some 15 others were injured.

May 5, Serbia, Yugos. The collision of a truck and a bus in eastern Serbia claimed the lives of 11 persons and injured 10 others.

May 19, Chiapas, Mexico. A truck and a bus collided in the town of Arriaga in the southern state of Chiapas and resulted in 33 deaths and 15 serious injuries; most of those killed were local farmworkers.

June 26, San Bernardino, Calif. A bus carrying 25 people to a family reunion in Alabama burst into flames and then began rolling downhill after the driver had stopped to help rescue those inside; 10 persons were killed and several others were injured when the flaming bus crashed into a truck and slid down a 3-m (10-ft) embankment.

September 12, Near Kampala, Uganda. A bus exploded in a forest after tripping a land mine planted by guerrillas; 20 persons lost their lives in the blast.

September 12, Northern Taiwan. A truck carrying 12 persons sped through a railroad crossing and was hit by a train; nine passengers were killed together with the driver, who apparently disregarded the warning signals at the crossing.

September 15, Punjab State, India. A bus smashed into the iron guard railings of a bridge and then plunged into a river; 27 passengers were killed and 19 others were injured.

September 28, Quintanar de la Orden, Spain. A bus taking members of Spain's Communist Party home after an annual picnic collided head-on with a truck; at least 25 persons were killed and some 25 others were injured.

October 25, Near Dacca, Bangladesh. A crowded bus attempting to board a ferry toppled into the Meghna River when strong currents pulled the ferry away from the dock; at least 80 persons were feared drowned.

November 7, Faisalabad, Pak. Two separate bus accidents, occurring within hours of each other, resulted in the deaths of 14 Muslim pilgrims who were returning from a shrine.

November 16, Near Gaya, India. A bus collided with a truck and then rolled into a nearby creek; at least 13 persons were killed and 20 were injured, 9 of them critically.

November 22, Near Pusan, South Korea. An overloaded speeding bus experienced brake failure and careened off a narrow mountain road when the driver was unable to negotiate a curve; 33 persons were killed and 37 others were injured.

November 27, Chile. A truck collided with a passenger bus some 320 km (200 mi) south of Santiago on the Pan-American Highway; 32 persons were killed and 10 others were injured.

December 15, Near Gokulpur, India. A train crashed into a bus at a railroad crossing; 16 passengers aboard the bus were killed.

MONETARISM— NEITHER KILL NOR CURE

by Samuel Brittan

Two catchphrases dominated the discussion of economics in English-speaking political circles as the 1980s began. They were "monetarism" and "supply-side economics." "Monetarism" was the dominant slogan in Great Britain, while "supply-side economics" was the key term in the United States. Of the two, monetarism was the more fundamental. Even in the U.S., supply-side economics was mainly a shop window item, while monetarism was the weapon behind the counter. Monetarists were more heavily represented in Pres. Ronald Reagan's Treasury Department and Council of Economic Advisers (CEA), appointed in 1981, than under any previous administration. The pursuit of "monetarist" policies was the proximate, although not the fundamental, reason for the escalation of short-term interest rates in that year to above 20%, causing worldwide alarm in financial markets and political conflict between the U.S. and its allies.

The Keynesian Background. Often the best way to understand a doctrine is to ask what it challenges. Most new theories, or revivals of old ones, have arisen when the conventional wisdom of the time failed to account for a growing number of events or to provide help with contemporary problems.

Supply-side economics and monetarism were linked by the fact that they both challenged the previously reigning "Keynesian demand management"—the attempt by governments and central banks to achieve full employment by boosting demand. This involved varying the budget balance or the ease or tightness of money in an endeavour to achieve target levels of output, and thus employment. Whether or not these policies faithfully reflected the teachings of John Maynard Keynes (1883–1946), a great British economist of subtle and frequently changing views, the label has stuck.

Samuel Brittan is an assistant editor and chief economic columnist of the Financial Times, London. His publications include a Hobart Paper for the London Institute of Economic Affairs entitled How to End the "Monetarist" Controversy and Capitalism and the Permissive Society. His Encounter essay Hayek, The New Right and the Crisis of Social Democracy won the 1981 George Orwell Prize for political journalism.

The big blank in post-World War II Keynesian doctrine was that it said very little about the price level. In Britain many Keynesian economists, especially of the older generation, believed that domestic prices were mainly determined by wage costs, which were themselves dependent on largely noneconomic institutional forces such as the attitudes of union leaders. Their main suggested weapon against inflation was thus incomes policy. This could mean either broad-brush wage and price controls or government deals—misleadingly known as "social contracts"—with union chiefs.

North American Keynesians never washed their professional hands of wages and prices to that extent. Although they flirted with wage-price "guideposts," they also believed that there was a trade-off, known as the Phillips curve, between unemployment and inflation, with more of one bringing less of the other.

Breakdown and Crisis. After two decades of apparent success, Keynesian economics increasingly failed to deliver the advertised benefits. Not only did inflation begin to rise to alarming proportions but so did unemployment—a combination of events that completely contradicted the notion of a simple trade-off between them. Trouble was apparent in the late 1960s when the "misery index"—the sum of the unemployment and inflation percentages shown in Chart 1—began rising in country after country. The deterioration was reflected in the increasing difficulty of maintaining the postwar Bretton Woods system of fixed exchange rates against the dollar and a fixed dollar price of gold. The system finally broke down in 1971 when Pres. Richard M. Nixon formally suspended the last remaining vestiges of dollar convertibility. But the crisis did not really become apparent to the man in the street until the fourfold increase in world oil prices in 1973. Although the Arab-Israeli Yom Kippur War of that year triggered the oil price explosion, an important underlying cause was worldwide inflation resulting from the synchronized effects of industrial countries trying to spend their way out of an earlier recession.

While all countries suffered in the post-1973 growth slowdown, shown in the table, countries

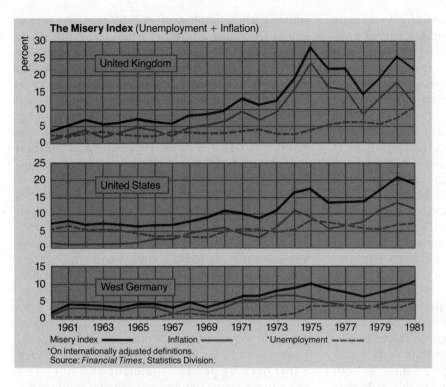

The Misery Index (Unemployment + Inflation)

percent

United Kingdom

United States

West Germany

1961 1963 1965 1967 1969 1971 1973 1975 1977 1979 1981

Misery index ——— Inflation ——— *Unemployment - - - -
*On internationally adjusted definitions.
Source: *Financial Times*, Statistics Division.

The "Misery Index" reflects world-wide rates of unemployment and inflation from the 1960s through 1981.

such as the U.K. and France that tried to spend themselves back into prosperity did worse, even from the point of view of output and jobs, than countries such as West Germany, Japan, and (intermittently) the U.S. that pursued sound money policies. Eventually, even the high-spending countries were forced by currency crises to call a halt.

The Counterrevolution. The crisis in Keynesian economics provided an opportunity for a group of academic economists, among whom Milton Friedman was the most prominent, who had been preparing an intellectual counterrevolution. This had, and has, three main contentions:

1. Governments cannot spend their way to target levels of output and employment. The long-run effects of boosting demand are entirely on the price level. Both the beneficial effects of demand stimulation on output and employment and the adverse effects of demand restriction on these variables are transitional.

To say this implies that there is an underlying rate of unemployment and output growth which is the best that can be sustained in prevailing circumstances. This has been called the "natural" rate, but the name is misleading because there is nothing "natural" about it. It can indeed be changed, but only by structural reforms of markets that are working badly. A better, although less memorable, name that has recently come into use is the "nonaccelerating inflation rate of unemployment" or NAIRU.

2a. The key long-run influence on monetary demand, and thus the main determinant of the nominal national product or national income, is the quantity of money.

2b. There is a clear-cut division between money and other financial assets; the supply of money can be controlled readily by central banks, and the relation between the quantity of money and the national income is predictable and stable. Advocates of this final set of propositions can be called "narrow monetarists" in a descriptive and nonpejorative sense.

The essence of the counterrevolution, and the reason for the political heat of the debate, is contained in the first proposition about the inability of demand management to achieve target levels of employment. This first and key proposition says nothing specifically about money, and one can believe it without believing the other more technical contentions. It can be demonstrated in different ways. Basically, it follows if one accepts two assumptions: first that the prices of all services, including the rewards of labour, are sensitive to market conditions; and second that market participants cannot be fooled by inflation indefinitely.

A stable trade-off between unemployment and inflation, of the kind shown in the traditional Phillips curve, can exist only if wage earners continue to believe that "a dollar is a dollar," irrespective of inflation. The trade-off is thus between unemployment and *unanticipated* inflation. Once, however, "money illusion" vanishes—that is, once inflation is taken into account—wage earners who formerly settled for 3% annual pay increases, for example, insist

on 3% plus an inflation premium. If governments pursue sufficiently accommodating financial policies, they will be able to obtain what they want. But, on the same policy assumptions, these larger wage increases will be passed on in larger price increases, which in turn will stimulate still more rapid inflation, and so on ad infinitum.

The conclusion is that *attempts by governments to spend their way into levels of employment above the sustainable or* NAIRU *rate will lead not merely to inflation but to accelerating inflation and, eventually, to a very nasty stabilization crisis in which unemployment will shoot up for a time to rates far higher than if the expansionary attempt had never been made.* (For a more detailed explanation, *see* the author's *How to End the "Monetarist" Controversy.*)

This proposition is frequently misunderstood. It does not say that stable prices are more important than high employment. The proposition is about cause and effect, which leaves governments free to pursue any price level objective they wish. But it gives notice that tolerating high inflation will not buy more employment. A warning to this effect was given by both Milton Friedman and another economist, Edmund Phelps, writing independently in 1967, several years before the 1970s stagflation.

Further reflection on the consequences of rapid inflation suggests that any long-run relationship is in the opposite direction to that suggested by the Phillips curve. Double-digit inflation, in practice, is never steady or predictable in its speed. The resulting instability distorts the signaling functions of the price system, which makes it more difficult for markets to work effectively. Employment is therefore likely to suffer.

Postwar Success. Why, then, did policies aimed at full employment work so well for two decades? The truth is that as long as the Bretton Woods system prevailed, the overriding aim of economic policy for most countries—despite their Keynesian rhetoric—was to maintain their currency parities against the dollar. Full employment demand-management policies did not come to the U.S. until well into the 1960s. For most of the postwar period, U.S.

administrations followed noninflationary "sound money" policies, and other countries, if they were to avoid devaluing against the dollar, had to imitate them. Thus, until the breakdown of the postwar system, most countries followed sound money policies, although some of them did not know it; and sound money policies proved compatible with full employment. In the late 1960s and early 1970s demand was boosted more vigorously and inflation accelerated, but "unsound" policies failed to prevent unemployment from rising sharply.

Thus the true message of the counterrevolution is that when the underlying forces are making for high rates of employment and growth, Keynesian policies are not needed; and when the underlying forces are making for low growth and employment rates, Keynesian policies do not work. These underlying forces have to be changed, if they can be, by nonmonetary means—which is why the label "monetarism" is so misleading. By its nature, monetary policy can neither kill nor cure real-world ills. *The essence of the counterrevolutionary message is that because demand stimulation cannot give a permanent boost to employment and growth, demand management might as well aim at zero or low inflation and thus gain whatever spillover benefits can be obtained from a more stable price environment.*

Shocks. No sensible exponent of the counterrevolution would deny that shock disruptions to important supplies, such as oil, or major wage breakthroughs by key public-sector unions in countries such as the U.K., can give a once-for-all boost to prices. A counterrevolutionary could accept wage push as a fact of life in the Keynesian era, but he would argue that it was the reflection of a pernicious environment, in which financial policy was adjusted to accommodate whatever level of wages and prices was thrown up by day-to-day events.

The basic strategy suggested by the counterrevolution may be expressed in many different technical ways. But they all amount to an undertaking that governments will refuse to finance a permanently higher rate of inflation brought about as a result of external or internal shocks. The best summary of a so-called monetarist strategy for the medium term is simply "No accommodation of wage or price push." No financial strategy can prevent an increase in unemployment resulting from an increased exercise of union monopoly power, but a preannounced policy can, if believed, minimize increases in unemployment arising from mistaken beliefs about inflation or likely market conditions.

The Quantity Theory. If variations in the quantity of money are the main long-run influences on monetary demand, and if demand movements ulti-

The Growth Slowdown

Average annual compound % rise
in real Gross Domestic Product

Country	1960–73	1973–80
United States	4.0	2.5
United Kingdom	3.0	1.0
France	5.5	3.0
West Germany	4.5	2.5
Japan	10.5	4.0

Source: *Financial Times*, Statistics Division.

mately affect prices rather than output or employment, there is a clear link between changes in the amount of money and changes in the price level. Such a link is the main assertion of the quantity theory of money, which is reached by combining propositions 1 and 2a above. The narrow monetarists, who also embrace 2b, go a step further in their assertions about the measurability and ease of control of the quantity of money and the predictability of its relation to total national expenditure, measured by "money," or "nominal," gross domestic product (GDP).

It was unfortunate for the course of the debate that these more technical propositions about money were formulated by Friedman first, before the wider proposition about the futility of governments trying to spend themselves into full employment. To make matters worse, both the Keynesian and monetarist camps placed excessive emphasis on the performance of their respective short-term forecasts, whereas the real debate related to the longer term. Thus there was hopeless confusion in the public debate between issues on which every citizen has a right to be informed; questions of general economic theory; and highly technical questions best left to a few banking specialists.

Of course these topics needed expert ventilation, but at times it seemed as if a congressman could not decide whether to support the president, or a British citizen how to vote, before deciding whether to follow M1, M1B, M2, or M3 as a definition of money supply or whether to follow a credit measure instead. (In the U.S. M1 [which has been relabeled M1A in some recent statistical publications] consists of currency plus demand or "sight" deposits. M1B includes, in addition, "other checkable deposits" such as negotiable orders of withdrawal [NOW accounts]. There is a broader measure known as M2 which includes most interest-bearing deposit and savings accounts, whether checks can be drawn on them or not. Its coverage is roughly comparable to the British "Sterling M3.") The duke of Wellington's remark about his troops—"I don't know what effect they have on the enemy, but by god they frighten me"—could have been applied to "monetarist" economists by a critical sympathizer.

Unemployment. Neither counterrevolutionaries in general, nor narrow monetarists in particular, need be committed to any particular theory of unemployment. Their message on the subject is negative: demand-boosting policies will not reduce unemployment below the NAIRU or "natural rate." Their positive message is that policy should concentrate on achieving stable growth of monetary demand (i.e., total spending); this will produce rough price stability—or at least a stable and predictable

trend rate of inflation—with deviations in either direction offsetting each other.

Counterrevolutionaries and monetarists, however, tend also to be market economists. Their analysis of the futility of demand-boosting is grounded in a theory of response to changing supply and demand in the labour market. The monetary element in their approach to inflation is based on the view that if the quantity of anything is increased, then, other things being equal, its unit value will drop. And this rule applies to money as it does to bananas, even though money may be more difficult to define and count.

Whatever their detailed views on the nature of money and the forces affecting it, market economists will be impressed by the inescapable evidence connecting major historical inflations with monetary disturbances. One has to be very clever not to link the inflation of imperial Rome with the debasement of the denarius, the 16th-century inflation in Europe with the inflow of precious metals from the New World, or the post-World War I German inflation with the billionfold increase in the quantity of Reichsmarks. Whatever the ultimate initiating force —the burden of defending imperial Rome or of German reparations payments—a necessary condition on all such occasions was an increase in the quantity of currency.

The same market approach extended to jobs suggests that if the price of labour—i.e., wages and any other employment costs incurred by the would-be hirer—is raised by union or government action,

Len Murray, general secretary of the British Trades Union Congress, at a press conference in August, explained the TUC's new plan to review government spending, bring down the unemployment rate, and regenerate the decaying economy.

The British Financial Experiment

The importance of carefully presenting financial strategy is underlined by the British experience under Prime Minister Margaret Thatcher's Conservative government, which came to office in 1979. Contrary to popular belief, the commitment to monetary targets and to limits on public-sector borrowing was actually inaugurated by the previous Labour government. It occurred mainly after the sterling crisis of 1976, when Britain had to make a large drawing from the International Monetary Fund.

The innovation of the Conservative government was not the introduction of financial targets but (1) its willingness to rely on them without the crutch of wage and price controls and (2) its attempt, in its Medium-Term Financial Strategy (MTFS), to shift from the hand-to-mouth, year-to-year setting of financial targets to a framework covering the period 1980–84. As far as the first change was concerned, there really was no alternative. Wage controls had already crumbled in the "winter of discontent" in early 1979, when a wave of strikes in the public services contributed to Labour's election defeat. The important change was the MTFS. It was disliked on the left and by mainstream Keynesian economists because of its financial emphasis and by many Conservatives (including some Thatcherite ministers) because of its element of planning and forward projection, but it was the one economic innovation for which the Thatcher government might be remembered.

It is hardly surprising that initial mistakes were made. The MTFS did not succeed in its key task of discouraging unions and employers from pricing workers out of jobs until it was too late and unemployment was approaching three million. It was not even published until the government's second budget in 1980, and by then a wage round averaging over 20% had already been negotiated. The medium-term strategy only hit the public consciousness in 1981, when it was cited to justify the tax increases imposed that year.

Another mistake was that the strategy was stated in terms of one particular definition of money, Sterling M3 — roughly, notes and coin plus all resident sterling deposits. When Sterling M3 exploded in the summer of 1980 (rising by an annualized rate of 20%), a body blow was dealt to the strategy's credibility — even though many of those who sneered the most, inconsistently blamed excessively "tight" government policy for the rise in unemployment.

Still more important was a mixture of bad luck and bad judgment at a less technical level. The second oil price rise of 1978–80 led to a "shock" increase in prices and a setback to output throughout the world. Instead of reassessing its programs and promises in the light of events, the Conservative government superimposed on the influence coming from oil an increase in value-added and other sales taxes that raised prices a further 4%. Even more important, the new government went ahead with an ill-advised election pledge to honour the pay raises, averaging about 23%, awarded to public-sector workers by the Clegg Commission. Such errors contributed to the credibility gap that led workers to price themselves out of jobs on a massive scale.

Eventually, however, there were notable successes on the inflation front. Despite the failure to stay within monetary targets, the British inflation rate in 1980–81 dropped from over 20% to just over 10%. This resulted from the rise in the sterling exchange rate, caused by international portfolio shifts of a kind unknown to insular monetarism. Sterling's popularity in 1979–80 was due to a mixture of factors: North Sea oil, initial confidence in the Thatcher government, and the increase in footloose OPEC funds. At its peak in January 1981, the trade-weighted sterling exchange rate index was 25% higher than it had been two years earlier. Even after sterling fell later in 1981, it was still at around early 1979 levels. If it had followed the movement of international costs of purchasing power parities, it would have fallen a further 20%.

The steep rise in the real exchange rate — *i.e.*, the exchange rate adjusted for international cost differences — not only brought inflation down more quickly than most observers expected but it put great pressure on the profit margins of all British producers exposed to international competition. It thus contributed to the sharp rise in unemployment.

The profit and employment squeeze had a silver lining in that it brought about improvements in manning levels and a reduction in restrictive practices. The unemployed thus represented a potential for future growth in output and living standards. The government received both blame for the rise in unemployment and, occasionally, praise for its courageous strategy, but neither was merited. No government would have dared to embark on a deliberate policy of squeezing out surplus labour, an outcome that was neither planned nor foreseen. In fact, the role of policy was largely negative. The Thatcher government in the crucial 1979–80 period feared the effects on the money supply of either intervening in the foreign exchange market to hold sterling down or reducing interest rates enough to have the same effect.

Britain's unemployment problem, over and above the general stagflation of the West, was due to a more deep-seated industrial malaise. The exchange rate squeeze merely precipitated a shakeout that would have happened in any case, but over a slightly longer period. Organized British workers — and in many cases managers — too long refused to adapt to a world in which many of their existing products and processes were obsolete or could be undertaken far more cheaply in the newly industrialized countries. Nor were they willing to accept the level of real earnings that would have priced them into work in their existing occupations. More than one wit remarked that Britain had always had millions of unemployed; the difference was that previously they were unemployed "on the job."

On July 29 Pres. Ronald Reagan, after appealing directly to the public on television, won his battle in Congress for the largest tax cut in U.S. history.

less employment will be provided. It also suggests that the supply of workers will be related to the cost of not working. In other words, a tax and social security system that narrows the gap between income from work and income on the dole will discourage job seeking and raise the unemployment figures.

Prime Minister Margaret Thatcher's government in Britain, during its initial period, was very reluctant to make even piecemeal attacks on union legal privileges or to remove other impediments to more competitive labour markets. Its inaction had far more to do with the high levels of unemployment in the early 1980s than the mythical "doctrinaire monetarism" of which it was so often accused.

Supply-siders. U.S. supply-side economists did not lose too much sleep over such issues, because they promised far more dynamic benefits from their policies than just stable prices. One reason for the contrasting emphasis on the two sides of the Atlantic was that, by the 1980 presidential election, monetarism had long been familiar in the U.S. Together with the balanced budget doctrine, it had become the economic "old-time religion." Even in the narrow sense of strict control over monetary growth, it had been on the scene as early as 1966–67, when Pres. Lyndon B. Johnson's tax increases seemed impotent to curb the Vietnam war-induced inflation until they were supported by restrictive Federal Reserve policies. President Nixon announced he was a Keynesian in the 1971 recession, but once reelected he went back to the old-time religion. So, even more energetically, did Pres. Gerald Ford, who succeeded him in 1974.

Even Pres. Jimmy Carter, who began by trying to spend his way to growth and employment targets, had gone back to at least a milk-and-water version of the old-time religion by 1979, when he appointed Paul Volcker chairman of the Federal Reserve

Board. In that year, too, U.S. monetary growth passed its peak. Thus by 1980 the Reagan Republicans were looking for something with more novelty and sex appeal than monetarism, and this was provided by the supply-siders.

The beauty of the term supply side is that people can read almost any meaning into it they like. It can mean that policy should try to improve the supply response of the economy by removing distortions from particular markets. This has been the theme of every major economist from Adam Smith on—and It takes on additional importance if demand stimulation is as impotent as monetarists claim. In the U.S. debate, however, supply-side economics came to mean a specific emphasis on the evils of high taxes. In this sense, Prime Minister Thatcher was as much a supply-sider as President Reagan but was prevented from cutting public spending as she would have liked. The political resistance of her colleagues and the burden of recession were the most publicized obstacles—yet the fact that the easy cuts had already been made by the preceding Labour government was just as important.

But supply-side economics has a narrower meaning still, associated with the Laffer curve, named after the U.S. economist Arthur Laffer. The curve, which looks like an inverted saucer, simply illustrates that as tax rates rise, government revenues first increase, then reach a maximum, and finally fall. The maximum point had almost certainly been passed for marginal rates in the 80 to 90% bracket levied up to 1979 on British citizens at the top end of the income scale. But the extreme supply-siders took it for granted that the majority of U.S. citizens, paying marginal rates of well under 50%, were on the downward sloping section of the curve, and they were therefore in favour of tax cuts even without spending cuts. The recipe of the supply-siders was identical with that of many Keynesians, except that

the former claimed to be stimulating supply and the latter demand—the same free lunch in different wraps.

Supply-siders were not clear whether they expected their measures to cut inflation, as well as stimulate production, or whether they would have to rely on the Fed to hold back prices. Some monetarists were prepared to live with the supply-siders by taking risks with budget deficits, as long as monetary goals were closely observed. Not all supply-siders returned the compliment, and one even told the press that nothing would go right until the monetarist undersecretary of the treasury, Beryl Sprinkel, was whipped in public.

The private riposte of one CEA member—"What is new in supply-side economics is not true, and what is true is not new"—proved prophetic. As time went on, the Reagan team moved further and further from the free-lunch aspects of supply-side theory. The tax "cuts" announced for individuals in 1981 involved no more than catching up with the "fiscal drag" produced by inflation, which pushes people into higher tax brackets and is often handled in Europe by semiautomatic indexation. Even these reliefs were at risk when estimates began to circulate that the U.S. faced possible budget deficits exceeding $100 billion per annum. These deficits could not be written off as an automatic effect of recession but were expected to continue up to the 1984 fiscal year when President Reagan had originally promised to balance the budget. The concern of David Stockman to raise taxes or find more spending cuts, expressed in the celebrated *The Atlantic* article, reflected a wider concern within the administration.

Thus by the end of 1981 the much vaunted differences between the Reagan and Thatcher approaches had worn very thin. Both governments were giving priority to counterinflationary goals, and both had realized that these required a cautious fiscal policy that would support instead of impede the achievement of monetary targets. So, too, did Chancellor Helmut Schmidt's Social Democrat–Free Democrat government in West Germany. By contrast, the newly elected Socialist government in France was committed to one more attempt to make Keynesian demand management work.

Problems of Monetary Policy. The abusive and ill-informed nature of the attacks on monetarism hid from view important unsolved problems facing a sound money approach. The futility of attempts to spend one's way to target levels of output and employment and the fact that inflation is a monetary phenomenon are relatively easy to establish. But this does not mean that it is easy either to measure the effective quantity of money or to control its growth in a noninflationary way. In other words, proposi-

tion 2b is the most dubious of those listed under *The Counterrevolution* above.

During the two and a half centuries of broad price stability that England enjoyed from the reign of Charles II to World War I, there was no conscious attempt to regulate the money supply; it was automatically checked by the link with gold. In none of the periods covered by Friedman and Anna Schwartz in *A Monetary History of the United States, 1867–1960* was there a conscious money supply policy. The Federal Reserve, established in 1913, acted to maintain the gold value of the dollar or—especially in later decades—to influence interest rates. The main finding of narrow monetarism—the stability of the demand for money in relation to total national income—applied to a period when no one was consciously controlling the quantity of money. Thus it did not matter exactly what the definition of money was. Different definitions simply yielded different long-term changes in velocity and hence slightly different numbers for the long-term growth of money supply consistent with stable prices.

All this was bound to change once central banks established monetary targets, as the Fed began to do in the 1970s. Goodhart's Law (named after some obiter dicta by Bank of England economist Charles Goodhart) states that *any* monetary target becomes distorted once it has been selected for policy purposes. In the U.S. the growth of NOW accounts and money market funds on which checks could be

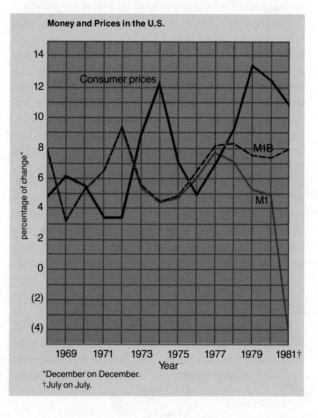

Money and Prices in the U.S.

Consumer prices

M1B

M1

percentage of change*

14
12
10
8
6
4
2
0
(2)
(4)

1969 1971 1973 1975 1977 1979 1981†

Year

*December on December.
†July on July.

drawn were deliberate attempts to utilize deposits outside the Fed's old target definition, known as M1 (see above). Chart 2 shows how the earlier relationship, under which prices followed monetary movements with a lag of around two years, began to weaken in the 1970s. The relatively modest growth rates of M1 in 1971–72 and 1977–78 gave no warning of the inflationary explosions to follow. In 1979–80 M1B was initiated to include the new money substitutes, and it had to be redefined frequently as more substitutes were invented. Market economists had no right to be surprised. Goodhart's Law merely emphasized the well-known propensity of markets to find substitutes for any commodity subject to official control.

The biggest weakness of narrow monetarist theory is that it is formulated in parochial terms. Even so-called international monetarists, who have made the exchange rate the main transmission mechanism between a country's monetary policy and its inflation rate relative to the rest of the world, operate in terms of what Ronald McKinnon has called the "insular economy." This assumes that the demand to hold a country's currency comes mainly from its own citizens and is fairly stable. The removal of exchange controls and the development of world capital markets made nonsense of this assumption, especially after the two oil price explosions. As oil prices skyrocketed, hundreds of billions of dollars of surplus overseas reserves were accumulated by members of the Organization of Petroleum Exporting Countries (OPEC), funds that were often footloose and ready to go wherever the prospects seemed best. It was still true that low-inflation countries (with inflation related to traded goods) were, other things being equal, likely to have exchange rates that were rising relative to countries with high inflation. But a great many other things tend not to be equal. Political hopes and fears—relating, for instance, to the effects of the Polish crisis on West Germany or the vulnerability or safety of energy supplies—are also important. Even the evaluation of economic policies can change overnight.

A Medium-Term Strategy. One response would be for a country like Britain to peg its currency to that of a country such as West Germany, expected to have a low inflation rate, and to direct its own monetary policy toward making the chosen exchange rate stick. This is what was done with parity against the dollar in Bretton Woods days. The problem is that the buck would simply be passed to the countries managing the main currencies, such as the mark, dollar, and yen, who would still have to devise their own counterinflationary policies.

An alternative response, which could apply to one country or to any group of countries acting together,

would be to state medium-term demand-management objectives in terms of money, or nominal, GDP, which is also equal to the quantity of money times its velocity of circulation (MV). This, after all, is what the final objective of policy should be. There would still need to be intermediate objectives for the monetary aggregates, of course, but these could be varied in response to changes in international portfolio demand or internal substitution between financial assets without abandoning basic objectives.

Political Implications. Contrary to what is often supposed, there is nothing inherently right-wing or conservative in "monetarist" doctrines, whether stated in narrow technical terms or in terms of the broader counterrevolution. Even if policies aimed toward stable prices involve a move to balanced budgets (a connection disowned by Friedman), there is nothing in monetarist doctrines to indicate whether public spending should be cut or taxes raised. Indeed, monetarism as such has nothing to say about the level of public spending as distinct from how it is financed.

Monetarist ideas have come to the public wrapped in political packages that contain many other elements. These may be good or bad, but they have nothing to do with either the counterrevolution against Keynesian economics or the monetary approach to inflation. There was, for instance, no logical connection between the desire of the Thatcher and Reagan administrations to rein back government spending and their monetarism. In fact, the pioneering move toward a more monetarist orientation had been taken by Roy Jenkins and Denis Healey, who looked after Britain's finances in the Labour administrations of the 1960s and 1970s, respectively. Farther east, the "hard money" attitudes of Communist governments are proverbial, while true Marxists have always been scornful of the ability of budget deficits and cheap money to overcome unemployment problems.

The so-called monetarists are on trial because of the modesty rather than the extravagance of their claims. If it acquires political credibility (which it has yet to do), the skillfully executed control of monetary demand can provide reasonable price stability over a period of years, reduce fluctuations of the stop-go, boom-slump variety, and ensure against a collapse of demand of the kind that occurred in the 1930s. But it cannot eliminate quarter-to-quarter or year-to-year changes in the inflation rate caused by unpredictable but inevitable shocks and disturbances. Nor can it cure a rising underlying unemployment rate or NAIRU, the fundamental causes of which are not financial. Still less can it provide a cure for low growth or for tensions among rival groups over distribution of the national product.

LETTER FROM WASHINGTON

Henry Adams, a direct descendant of two presidents of the United States, spent much of his life watching the world from the sidelines in Washington, D.C. This led him in his later years to a bleak pessimism about where Man was taking Thought and vice versa. In 1900 he wrote his brother, "All we can say is that at the rate of increase of speed and momentum as calculated over the last 50 years, the present society must break its damned neck in a definite but remote time, not exceeding 50 years more. . . . Either our society must stop or bust . . . that is the affair of those who are to run it."

Adams was clearly wrong on his timing. But he has not been alone in worrying about where Thought is taking Man. A young doctoral candidate, searching the data amassed by the U.S. Department of Commerce on how Americans earn their living, reached a startling conclusion: sometime during the nation's bicentennial span—1976 to 1989—the U.S. would be crossing a continental divide when more than half the national payroll is spent for the manipulation of symbols rather than the making of things. Information processing—to use a term covering everything from auditing to xerography—has become the dominant activity of an economy that once devoted its principal energies to the tilling of soil, and later to the manufacture of goods.

Any report from Washington attempting to delineate significant changes in progress must take such a development into account. What does it mean? For one thing it means that strong centripetal forces are at work in the information industry, even as the nation's current politics pull in the opposite direction toward the devolution of power and the rebirth of federalism among our states and communities. It means that technology versus tradition will be having to make important trade-offs as we move relentlessly into the information society. Lewis Thomas, perhaps the country's most imaginative scientist, likens mankind's evolving community to the ant colony and asks the question: "One thing I'd like to know most of all: when those ants have made the Hill, and are all there, touching and exchanging, and the whole mass begins to behave like a single huge creature, and thinks, what on earth is that thought? And while you're at it, I'd like to know a second thing: when it happens, does any single ant know about it? Does his hair stand on end?"

John McCloy, statesman extraordinaire now approaching his 87th birthday, described our politics best: "America is a continent constantly struggling to become a nation." As we settle into the decade of the 1980s, the struggle in Washington goes on unabated. This year, our new president confidently declared at his inaugural, marks "a New Beginning." Others would assent without necessarily agreeing how different and how durable this new beginning may prove to be. President Reagan's partisans speak of a "sea change" in government that will reverse a half century's drift toward centralized government and welfare statism. Other partisans retort that the conservative swing will last just so long as the Democrats take to get their act together, possibly no longer than the congressional elections of 1982.

In a city where ideology hardly ever plays a dominant role, two economic doctrines now stand in fierce contention. One, tracing its intellectual heritage to the British theoretician John Maynard Keynes, stresses that when the economy is underemployed government must intervene to stimulate consumer demand. Though Franklin D. Roosevelt entered the presidency a half century ago pledged to frugality, his brain trusters soon seized on Keynesian doctrine to justify large-scale government spending as a means of ending the Great Depression. Critics now claim that this emphasis on "demand-side" economics has unleashed inflation while discouraging private entrepreneurs who could save and invest. They argue that "supply-side" economics—stern monetarism, heavy cuts in government spending, a balanced budget, and lowered taxes—will stimulate the private sector to achieve higher productivity and yield higher revenues.

Both demand-side and supply-side theories depend more on faith than on proven works. Throughout the New Deal years government pump-priming failed to lift the economy out of its slough; only the massive expenditures during World War II brought full employment to the nation. More recently, heavy deficit spending by government appears to be producing "stagflation," in which soaring costs are accompanied by a stagnant market.

But supply-side economics demands a similar leap of faith. No one can predict for certain what it takes to rejuvenate the entrepreneur. In Great Britain the best effort of the Tory prime minister, a determined supply-sider, has been met by deeper recession and higher unemployment. Just how long can Reaganomics await a renaissance of the private sector once the pains of budget cutting begin to be felt? It would be ironic, but entirely possible, for neither demand-side nor supply-side economics to receive adequate testing in the political marketplace.

Professional president watchers, who now constitute a sizable chunk of the Washington community, are forever assigning labels to the latest occupant of the White House. "Strong" or "weak"; "great," "mediocre," or "poor." In more recent times concern is regularly voiced about the rise of the "imperial" presidency. This strangely fails to take into account that six of our last seven presidents failed either to win or to serve out a second term. Eisenhower, hero-warrior, was the exception; Kennedy was assassinated. All the others—from Truman on—were, in one way or another, defenestrated.

This succession of one-termers raises the question of how Ronald Reagan will survive the splendid misery of his high office. At 70, oldest of any president at inauguration time, his age alone would seem to be working against him. Yet he has confounded those who were predicting a swift political burial for the ex-movie actor-turned-leader by finishing his first year in office with vigour undiminished. Henry Adams wrote of a long ago president, "He appeared as an intermittent energy, immensely powerful when awake, but passive and plastic in repose." While one doubts that a modern president could afford the public appearance of passivity (not to mention plasticity), Reagan has successfully cut down the working hours in the White House, which during Carter's occupancy had soared all out of bounds. He does not seem to have the obsession with being on camera that afflicted several of his predecessors. He fits quite well into the rhythms of the laid-back era, though his intermittent energies have brought one surprise after another to those who tried to catch him unaware. He has demonstrated so far that a purposeful president can work his will in dismantling government about as effectively as in putting it together. And he measures up fully to Henry Adams' description of bygone leaders: "None doubted. All were great men; some, no doubt, were greater than others; but all were supported, lifted, inspired by the moral certainty of rightness."

Little has changed on that score. No latter-day politician worth his salt, when confronting the cameras and tape recorders of the media, dares admit doubt about even the most vexatious issues. But what has changed is the speed and volume of the words flowing from Washington and instantly reaching the citizen along with far-off friend and foe. What has changed even more radically is the never-ending drama of government provided by the television image, creating the illusion that we have become a Greek marketplace of direct democracy.

Much has been speculated about the coming of a new politician who would suit the demands of the electronic era. He has been slow in arriving, and now, with Reagan, he may turn out to be not so new after all. Indeed, by speech and gesture, the president manages to convey all the old-fashioned virtues, most especially deep sincerity. His opponent's best argument can be demolished during televised debate by the off-handed jest— "There you go again!"—a response familiar to almost every connubial clash from time immemorial.

A good many observers of government believe that this country celebrated the wrong bicentennial year in 1976. The more significant anniversary comes in 1987 when we commemorate the miracle at Philadelphia where our founding fathers laboured throughout a long hot summer to form "a more perfect union." Their document has withstood the testing of time with remarkably few printed alterations, even though the living Constitution has been stretched considerably. The draftsmen's genius was to create a system of government balanced by "a separation of power" —executive, legislative, judicial; and federal, state, local. In fact, as has been pointed out, what we now have are separated institutions sharing powers. Governing in America has been marked by growing complexity of this sharing process.

One cannot read the U.S. Constitution the way a hard-shelled Baptist reads his Bible. Examine how the three co-equal branches really work. The President, of his own volition, now serves as chief legislative draftsman of the government and fairly well determines the basic agenda of Congress. Congress, in turn, has developed its power of legislative "oversight"—a word nowhere mentioned in the Constitution—into a forceful way of intervening at every stage of executive decision-making. And the Judiciary, by its unchallenged role as interpreter of the Constitution, has served as a principal instigator of societal reform. These encroachments into one another's constitutional territory go on daily in Washington without much regard for who is in office. They are likely to continue under a leader who has pledged himself to "take federal government off the backs of the people." Even in the carrying out of his mandate, paradoxically, Ronald Reagan must constantly test the outer limits of presidential authority.

How will America continue, in John McCloy's phrase, its struggle to become a nation? Will centripetal or centrifugal forces prevail? Or will we maintain a happy balance in this young country which is also the world's oldest democracy?

DOUGLASS CATER

PEOPLE OF THE YEAR

Biographies 68

Nobel Prizes 97

Obituaries 100

BIOGRAPHIES

The following is a selected list of men and women who influenced events significantly in 1981.

Alvarez Armelino, Gregorio Conrado

Lieut. Gen. Gregorio Alvarez, who succeeded Aparicio Méndez as president of Uruguay on Sept. 1, 1981, was one of the most important military figures in the regime that had seized power in 1973, overturning the country's long democratic tradition. Alvarez stood out among his fellow officers for his undoubted political abilities, but it was not clear how much freedom of action he would have. Though he inherited a policy of holding general elections and a new constitutional referendum in November 1984, details of the process remained vague— especially concerning the situation of the political parties and the trade unions.

Born into a military family on Nov. 26, 1925, in Montevideo, Alvarez entered the nation's military academy in 1940. His first important military posting was as chief of mounted police in Montevideo in 1962. He rose rapidly, becoming a general in 1971 at the age of 45. He was then designated as chief of the Combined Armed Forces Command (Esmaco), which ran the counterinsurgency operation against the Tupamaros. Alvarez was reportedly one of the officers who used information obtained from captured guerrillas to crack down on corruption in Pres. Juan Bordaberry's administration. In February 1973 the Army issued a 19-point ultimatum under which the National Security Council (Cosena) assumed veto power over Bordaberry's regime. (Alvarez was permanent secretary of Cosena by virtue of his Esmaco position.)

By 1977 Alvarez appeared to be losing influence. As commander of the 4th military region he was due for promotion to head the 1st, but he was passed over. Despite the setback he became commander in chief of the Army in February 1978 and held the post for a year. On retirement and when his position was taken by his rival, Lieut. Gen. Luis Queirolo, Alvarez's star again seemed to be in decline. Nevertheless, in the 1979 round of promotions many of his supporters moved up a rank. In the spring of 1981 a

loan scandal involving gambling led to the dismissal of key opponents. Some claimed that Alvarez engineered the incident to ensure his presidential chances.

(MICHAEL WOOLLER)

Anderson, Ken

The 1981 National Football League season began with Ken Anderson throwing an interception that the other team returned for a touchdown. It ended with Anderson's hometown of Batavia, Ill., throwing a Ken Anderson Day party for the quarterback who led his team into the Super Bowl.

Anderson, named most valuable player in the NFL by virtually everyone who gave an MVP award, hoisted the Cincinnati Bengals up from the cesspool of 4–12, 4–12, and 6–10 seasons the previous three years to a record of 12–4. He had the NFL's best passer rating, 98.5 on a scale in which 100 stands for excellence, and he also led the league with a .626 completion percentage and a .021 interception percentage. With only ten interceptions all season, he improved his NFL career interception percentage to .035. Though Cincinnati lost to San Francisco 26–21 in the Super Bowl, Anderson set Super Bowl records for number of passes completed, 25, and completion percentage, 73.5%.

With Anderson tugging their bootstraps, the Bengals rose from 27th in the league in scoring and 21st in passing in 1980 to third in both categories. His two best games, when he perforated Denver's league-leading pass defense for 396 yd and completed 26 of 32 passes for four touchdowns against Cleveland, climaxed a five-game winning streak that catapulted the Bengals to the top of their division.

Before that, though, Anderson nearly lost his job. The Bengals trailed 21–0 in that first game against Seattle when Anderson was replaced after throwing two interceptions and ten incompletions in the first quarter. The next week Bengal coach Forrest Gregg planned to start quarterback Turk Schonert, who had rallied Cincinnati to a 27–21 victory over Seattle. Having recently achieved a law degree, Anderson thought about retiring. But Gregg changed

his mind, and Anderson guided the Bengals to a come-from-behind victory in the second game. He was starting quarterback thereafter.

Born Feb. 15, 1949, Kenneth Allan Anderson matured late, and no college offered him an athletic scholarship. He played in the lowest division of National Collegiate Athletic Association schools, at Augustana College in Rock Island, Ill., where then Cincinnati assistant coach Bill Walsh left the beaten path of NFL scouts to watch him. On Walsh's recommendation, the Bengals made Anderson a third-round draft choice in 1971. Under Walsh's tutelage Anderson became the first player ever to lead NFL passers in consecutive years, in 1974 and 1975.

(KEVIN M. LAMB)

Baryshnikov, Mikhail

The darling of the U.S. ballet world since defecting from the Soviet Union in 1974, Mikhail Baryshnikov graduated in 1981 from stellar dancer to artistic director of the American Ballet Theatre (ABT). The move, regarded by press and public as one rich in eventual promise if not immediate success, was not inevitable. Baryshnikov had seen, after all, most of the best of all possible worlds in dance. Born in Riga on Jan. 27, 1948, he studied with the legendary Aleksandr Pushkin, joined the Kirov Ballet as a soloist at 18, rose fast to *premier danseur noble*, and won the Nijinsky Prize and the U.S.S.R. State Award of Merit. After defecting he starred at ABT for four years, appeared in the highly acclaimed dance movie *The Turning Point*, and joined George Balanchine's New York City Ballet.

Baryshnikov's two-year tutorial with Balanchine was a mixed success. The celebrated choreographer has a reputation for driving his dancers to extreme physical limits and his rigorous style involves movements for which Baryshnikov was not trained. Moreover, Balanchine emphasizes ensemble dancing that makes his ballerinas the ultimate stars. "The Balanchine experience undoubtedly increased Baryshnikov's physical potential by developing his coordination and, most important, reinforcing his intellectual attitude toward dancing," biog-

rapher Gennady Smakov wrote. "His attempt to extend the boundaries of his Russian experience was most successful. But Mischa was no longer able to carry on, because Balanchine's style began to take its toll on his body." Still, Smakov concluded, "When Baryshnikov begins to compose ballets at ABT, possibly Mischa's 'education sentimentale' with Balanchine and his incredibly imaginative work will be reflected in his own works. His control has grown, and in all his future experiments, the experience with Balanchine will help him."

As for the future fortunes of ABT, one observer remarked halfway through Baryshnikov's first season that while it appeared "tame, half-baked," it was not "wishy-washy. . . . The company shows clear signs of vision at the helm and the ability to implement it." (PHILIP KOPPER)

Begin, Menachem

A reconciliation among previously disunited Arab nations and a serious rift in Israel's relations with the U.S. would seem to be the worst possible developments from the Israeli point of view. Yet by means of a series of initiatives during 1981 that disconcerted friend and foe alike, Prime Minister Menachem Begin of Israel had brought about just that state of affairs by the year's end. As a result the continuance of the Camp David peace process seemed as seriously threatened by Begin's actions as it had at first by the assassination of Egyptian Pres. Anwar as-Sadat.

The culmination of Begin's uncompromisingly hard-line policy, the earlier manifestations of which had been the June air raid that destroyed the Iraqi nuclear reactor at Daura and a series of punitive ground and air attacks into Lebanon, came in mid-December. Begin, perhaps reacting to apparent U.S. ambivalence to the Saudi peace plan that he had declared totally unacceptable, pushed legislation through the Knesset (parliament) that virtually annexed to Israel the Golan Heights area taken from Syria in 1967. The resultant U.S. suspension of the strategic cooperation agreement concluded during Begin's September visit to Washington, D.C., brought a vitriolic response from Begin: "The people of Israel have lived for 3,700 years without a memorandum of understanding with America and will continue to live without it for another 3,700 years."

Begin's domestic policies in the first half of the year were aimed at winning the election called for June 30. The government appeared to be losing support, and opinion polls showed Begin's Likud Party gaining only 20 seats, compared with the 43 it had won in 1977. In the election Likud won a narrow victory over the Labour opposition, and Begin formed a new coalition government on August 4.

Begin was born in Brest-Litovsk, Poland (now Soviet Union), on Aug. 16, 1913. As a law student at the University of Warsaw he was active in the nationalist Betar Youth Movement opposed to the more moderate Zionist establishment. Deported to Siberia in World War II, he was later released to join the Polish Army in exile and was sent to Palestine. In 1943 he took command of the underground Irgun Zvai Leumi extremist organization in the struggle for independence. During 1967–70 he was a member of the National Unity government, and in 1973 he became joint leader of the Likud Party. (JON KIMCHE)

Bird, Vere Cornwall

The attainment of independence on Nov. 1, 1981, for Antigua and Barbuda brought to fruition for Vere Cornwall Bird the dream of a lifetime. At the age of 71 the new prime minister was the last of the old school of Caribbean politicians still in office, having spent his life fighting against inequality and for the independence of Antiguans.

Born on Dec. 7, 1910, in one of Antigua's worst slums, Bird grew up surrounded by poverty and squalor. The victim of a system that limited the educational opportunities available to Antiguans, he received only an elementary education at St. John's Boys' School. As a teenager he joined the Salvation Army and saw, through being posted in other parts of the region, that conditions similar to those in Antigua also existed elsewhere. Though his time in the Salvation Army gave him the leadership and organizational skills that were to prove essential in later life, he broke with the organization when it became apparent that no black person could hope to attain high rank.

In 1939 Bird was one of the few young men to respond to calls for the establishment of trade unions in the Caribbean region to fight for workers' rights and better conditions for the people. He was a founding member of the Antigua Trades and Labour Union and rose rapidly to become its president. In 1945 he ran for the Legislative Council and was easily elected. By 1951 he had successfully fought a number of significant political battles against the plantation aristocracy who then dominated Antiguan life. Through encouraging union members to run for public office, he formed the future basis for the Antigua Labour Party.

In 1960 Bird became the island's first chief minister, retaining office, with the title of premier, when the island achieved associated statehood in 1967. A split within labour lost him his seat in elections in 1971. However, in 1976 and again in 1980 he was returned to power and led the final constitutional negotiations in London in 1980 that brought the two-island state to independence.

A towering 6 ft 9 in tall, Bird was by nature a strong leader with great personal charm. Politically to the left of centre and firmly committed to closer regional links, he perhaps best demonstrated the unique blend of socialism and capitalism characteristic of the mixed economies of the eastern Caribbean. (DAVID A. JESSOP)

Botha, Pieter Willem

South Africa's eighth prime minister since the union was established in 1910, P. W. Botha succeeded B. J. Vorster after the latter's resignation in 1978 and was returned to power, though with a reduced majority, in the 1981 general election. As prime minister Botha held out prospects of an era of evolutionary political reform. His declared policy was one of gradual abolition of hurtful discriminatory measures, marked by self-determination for whites and all other ethnic groups, intergroup cooperation and consultation on matters of common interest, and the concept of a constellation of states of southern Africa. He broke fresh

ground by periodically holding multiracial conferences on national problems with business and other leaders. The main criticisms against him were, from the left, that he did not go far enough and from the right —particularly from the recently formed Herstigte Nasionale Party of Jaap Marais (q.v.)—that he was going too far and "selling out" the white man.

Born into a farming family in the small Orange Free State town of Paul Roux on Jan. 12, 1916, Botha was a law student in Bloemfontein when he attracted the attention of D. F. Malan, a former Nationalist Cabinet minister who was then leader of the breakaway Purified National Party after J. B. M. Hertzog and J. C. Smuts had formed the coalition United Party in the early 1930s. In 1936 Malan appointed Botha organizing secretary of his party in Cape Province. The old National Party (NP) was reunited under Malan on the outbreak of World War II, becoming the official opposition to Smuts's government. By that time Botha had gained a national reputation as an able party organizer and efficient administrator who had done much to strengthen Malan's political base, especially in the Cape. In 1946 he became the first secretary of the NP's youth organization, the Nasionale Jeugbond, and two years later he was made chief secretary of the party in the Cape, a post he held for ten years.

In the crucial 1948 election, which brought the NP into power with Malan as prime minister, Botha entered Parliament as MP for George, a seat he continued to hold. His first Cabinet appointment occurred in 1961, when Prime Minister H. F. Verwoerd named him minister of community development and of Coloured affairs, to which the portfolio of public works was later added. In 1965 Botha was moved to the Department of Defense, into which he threw all his energies with the aim of building up a modern defense force to meet what he visualized as potentially a "total onslaught" from black Africa. (LOUIS HOTZ)

Botham, Ian Terence

The cricketing exploits of England's Ian Botham against Australia in 1981 were saluted by cricketers everywhere as phenomenal. His 149 not out in the third test gave England a narrow win after all seemed lost when he began his innings. His five wickets for one run in 28 balls ensured another surprise win in the fourth test, and in the fifth he gave one of the greatest displays of powerful hitting ever seen in test cricket in making 118 to ensure victory. He ended a memorable season by taking six wickets in an innings in the drawn sixth test match.

Botham was born at Heswall, Cheshire, on Nov. 24, 1955, the son of a chief petty officer in the Royal Navy. At the age of 18 he was picked for his first county match for Somerset, and in the following year, in a one-day match against Hampshire, he showed the fierce determination and courage which, when allied to his natural talents, marked him out for future greatness. Coming in to bat when Somerset had lost eight wickets, he stood up to the speed of the West Indian Andy Roberts and, though hit in the face, refused to leave the crease and went on to make 45 not out and win the match.

Typically, he took five wickets in an innings in each of his first two tests against Australia. In New Zealand he made his first century, took eight wickets, and made three marvelous catches. In 1978 against Pakistan he made a century and took eight wickets in an innings at Lord's and then followed with 20 wickets in two tests against New Zealand. In 1979 in a Golden Jubilee match in Bombay he gave his greatest all-round performance, making a century and taking 13 wickets.

All these thrilling deeds, admittedly against some weak opponents, seemed to mark him out for captaincy, and at the age of 25 he was appointed captain of England. But he had no experience of leadership, his form suffered, and he resigned on the day the selectors had already decided to appoint J. M. Brearley to replace him. Like magic, his old flair returned, and almost single-handedly he won the next three tests against Australia.   (REX ALSTON)

Bryant, Paul ("Bear")

The South's living piece of Americana, Paul ("Bear") Bryant on November 28 broke Amos Alonzo Stagg's coaching record for college football victories with his 315th. It happened in his University of Alabama team's final regular-season game, against state rival Auburn. Then, with a congratulating Pres. Ronald Reagan at his ear, media flashbulbs in his eyes, and the world at his feet, Bryant gave credit to his players and assistant coaches—to everybody but himself.

His legions of fans and worshipers scarcely believed Bryant when he called himself "tired and dotty-headed" any more than they expected him to slow down now that he had achieved the record.

Bryant's 315 victories in 37 years of college football coaching gave him an 8.5-victory-per-year pace that was far ahead of the 7.2 mark of runner-up Woody Hayes. He won six national championships from 1961 through 1977 and was named national coach of the year in 1961, 1971, and 1973. He took Alabama to 28 postseason Bowl games.

Bryant was always more a refiner than an innovator. He adjusted well to changing circumstances. He adjusted to Penn State's weak defensive secondary by having Alabama throw long passes from its run-oriented wishbone formation for his 314th victory. He adjusted to black fullback Sam Cunningham's heroics when Southern California trounced his all-white 1970 team by finally breaking the colour barrier the next year. He adjusted to the more questioning nature of 1960s students by giving more answers. Bryant has said that his greatest strength is as an organizer, that he coaches his assistants and they coach the players, but associates have pointed out his gift for making people believe in themselves, for molding rules to individuals while appearing the ironfisted disciplinarian.

Bryant was born Sept. 11, 1913, in Moro Bottom, Ark., one of 11 children in a farm family. He earned his nickname as a schoolboy in a barehanded wrestling match with a bear. At the University of Alabama he played end on football teams that compiled a record of 23–3–2 in 1933–35.

After six years as an assistant coach and a stint in the U.S. Navy during World War II, Bryant took his first head coaching job at the University of Maryland in 1945. The next year he moved to the University of Kentucky, where he won the school's only Southeastern Conference championship. After several years there and at Texas A & M he returned in 1958 to Alabama as head coach.   (KEVIN M. LAMB)

Burnett, Carol

Celebrities, by virtue (or vice) of seeking the limelight, forsake some of the privacy that other people cherish. Gossipy attention "goes with the territory" of star status. But as actress and comedienne Carol Burnett proved in 1981, there are limits to such treatment. A Los Angeles jury decided she had been libeled by the tabloid *National Enquirer* and awarded her $1.6 million in general and punitive damages, later reduced to $800,000.

The case began five years earlier when

UPI

the *National Enquirer* reported that Burnett became "boisterous" in a Washington, D.C., restaurant. According to the report, she "had a loud argument with another diner, Henry Kissinger," spilled wine on someone else, and tried to share her dessert with everyone in sight. "They portrayed me as drunk," she complained. She agreed that in fact she had dined at the sedately chic Rive Gauche, had "two, maybe three" glasses of wine, and did speak with the former secretary of state. But she maintained that she was not drunk and had not made a scene.

The *Enquirer* had printed a retraction, which might have reduced its culpability if the judge had ruled that the weekly was a newspaper instead of a magazine under California law. The large judgment reflected the jury's belief that the *Enquirer* had flagrantly disregarded the truth.

After the verdict, *Enquirer* editor Iain Calder said, "Our job is to provide our readers with interesting, informative and accurate articles, and this is what we will continue to do." That remained to be seen since nearly a dozen other suits were pending, most of them brought by other celebrities. A consensus among journalists held that the *Enquirer* did not have a legitimate defense under the free speech amendment to the Constitution. Responsible reporting and fair comment were the issues in the Burnett trial, not free speech.

Born in San Antonio, Texas, Burnett has been a stage, television, and film star since 1957. Her material features good-natured humour involving more uplift than put-down. Much more entertaining than the libel suit was her 1981 film, *The Four Seasons*. It presented the bittersweet vicissitudes of three married couples whose vacations are upset by one man's divorce and remarriage.   (PHILIP KOPPER)

Callwood, June

One of Canada's best-known journalists and broadcasters, June Callwood has established herself as a leading political observer in a career spanning almost 40 years. She wrote on political subjects for Canadian periodicals and was host of the Canadian Broadcasting Corporation's "In Touch," a television public affairs program (1975–78). Following a discussion with her of Canadians' reactions to some of the actions of the Canadian government, the publishing firm Doubleday & Co., Inc., commissioned Callwood to write a book explaining the Canadian mentality to the U.S. public. A history of Canada from 1480 to 1980, *Profiles of Canada* (1981) was the result. Among Callwood's conclusions in the book was that no matter how liberal its appearance to the world, Canada has always been a nation of people very much on the side of authority.

Born in Chatham, Ont., on June 2, 1924, Callwood has worked as a writer for most of her life. In 1979 she became head of the Writers' Union of Canada. Her interests include the role emotions play in life, which led to her writing of *Love, Fear, Anger* (1964). In conjunction with other prominent individuals she co-authored several books, notably *A Woman Doctor Looks at Life and Love* (1957) with Marion Hilliard; *Mayo, The Story of My Family and Career* (1968) with Charles Mayo; *How to Talk to Practically Anybody About Practically Anything* (1973)

with Barbara Walters; and *We Mainline Dreams* (1974) with Judianna Denson-Gerber.

When her son joined Toronto's hippie community in the 1960s, Callwood became involved in helping him and his friends. From simple fund raiser she quickly moved to full-time social activist, working on behalf of young people, women, and prisoners. She was a founder and past president of Nellie's, a Toronto hostel for battered wives, and served as president of Justice for Children (1979–80). In 1965 she became vice-president of the Canadian Civil Liberties Union and was co-chairman of the first annual conference of the federal Human Rights Commission (1978). With lawyer Marvin Zuker, Callwood wrote two books on women and the law, *Canadian Women and the Law* (1971) and *The Law Is Not for Women* (1976). In 1978 she was made a member of the Order of Canada, the nation's highest honour. (DIANE LOIS WAY)

Calvo Sotelo y Bustelo, Leopoldo

Following the resignation of Premier Adolfo Suárez González and the abortive coup of Feb. 23–24, 1981, Deputy Premier Leopoldo Calvo Sotelo took over the premiership on February 25 and with it the task of guiding Spain's uneasy transition from the authoritarianism of the Franco regime to Western European-style democracy. His task was rendered more difficult by conflict within the ruling Unión Centro Democrático (UCD) between right-wing Christian Democrats and "Suaristas" (followers of former premier Suárez). Calvo Sotelo's election as UCD president in November, replacing Agustín Rodríguez Sahagún (Suárez's brother-in-law), would, it was hoped, consolidate the party under his leadership.

Born in Madrid on April 14, 1926, Leopoldo Calvo Sotelo came from one of Spain's best-known political families, with links to both the right and the centre of the governing coalition and Socialist parties. He trained as a civil engineer and, after experience in various small-scale firms, began working for the multinational conglomerate Unión Explosivos Río Tinto, at that time a full subsidiary of the metals giant Río Tinto. During 1967–68 he was president of the Spanish national railway network. Although he held ministerial office from the end of the Franco era, he first gained political prominence for his role in helping to organize the Christian Democrats and groups further to the right into the UCD in time to win the June 1977 elections. In the subsequent administration he was rewarded with the post of minister without portfolio, in charge of negotiating Spain's accession to the European Communities (EC).

Calvo Sotelo was regarded as a superb administrator and surrounded himself with able technocrats. If his political talents were less marked than those of his predecessor, his credibility with the private sector and trade unions enabled him to achieve the lowest wage settlement in Spain's recent history. His critics faulted him for his lack of success, initially at least, in demonstrating his independence from the preceding government and for his lack of progress (through little fault of his own) in negotiating an agreement with the EC. (MICHAEL WOOLLER)

Cenac, Winston Francis

One of the least expected developments in the Caribbean in 1981 was the appointment in May of Winston Francis Cenac as prime minister of St. Lucia. Most observers had expected that the 18-month-long power struggle within the ruling St. Lucia Labour Party would have resulted in one of the more established party members emerging as leader.

Following the failure of Alan Louisy, prime minister since the 1979 general election, to pass his budget through Parliament, a constitutional crisis developed. After attempts by the anti-Louisy faction in the Labour Party to form their own government, Cenac emerged as a compromise candidate. By offering the major portfolios —foreign affairs, trade and industry, and tourism—to his remaining principal rival within the Labour Party, Peter Josie, he was able to secure the support of enough members of his party in Parliament to obtain a wafer-thin overall majority of one.

By nature Cenac was not a politician, having spent all his working life in the practice of law. Though he was able to bring to St. Lucia a public aura of calm after the bitter political infighting, it was by no means clear by the end of 1981 whether he had the ability to motivate the party to carry out its program. Those who knew him well indicated that, though personally charming, he lacked the grasp of the complex local and regional issues that others with years of political experience had.

Born on Sept. 14, 1925, Cenac was educated at St. Mary's College, St. Lucia. On leaving he worked at the district court as chief clerk and at the registry of the Supreme Court as deputy registrar. While employed in the service, he obtained a law degree as an external student of the University of London. In 1954 he was admitted to Lincoln's Inn and was called to the bar in February 1957. After a number of legal appointments during 1962–67, he was successively attorney general of St. Lucia, St. Vincent, and Grenada. In 1967 he was appointed to the post of director of public prosecutions in Grenada. In 1969 he returned to St. Lucia and entered private practice, and in 1971 he was appointed to act as puisne judge in St. Vincent. In 1972 he was appointed puisne judge for St. Kitts-Nevis and the British Virgin Islands. (DAVID A. JESSOP)

Chambers, George

The selection of George Chambers as prime minister of Trinidad and Tobago following the death of Eric Williams (*see* OBITUARIES) on March 29, 1981, came as a surprise to many; nevertheless, he was perhaps the most qualified of the four main contenders. Chambers had a reputation for honesty and hard work and, in addition to having served in all the major ministries, he had none of the drawbacks of being associated with the racial politics that had in the past been a divisive influence in Trinidad. Politically, he typified the nationalistic yet broadly socialist approach of the People's National Movement (PNM) by offering every encouragement to private enterprise while maintaining social welfare programs and a substantial state sector. Unlike his predecessor, he was eager to convene

a Caribbean heads-of-government meeting to try to solve major regional differences of opinion.

Chambers used his self-effacing style to brilliant effect from the moment of his appointment and endorsement by the PNM, knowing that he had to campaign in a general election before the end of the year. He announced a minimal Cabinet reshuffle. Unlike his predecessor, he actually spoke to the local media and to the electorate at large, emphasizing the need for political continuity. It was a winning formula, and as a result he won a startling election victory on November 9. Many commentators had forecast a close finish as a new party, the Organization for National Reconstruction, had mounted a major campaign. However, Chambers was able to increase the PNM's parliamentary majority by two and thereby ensure his hold on the party leadership.

Born in Trinidad on Oct. 4, 1928, Chambers left school in his mid-teens with only a rudimentary education and developed his intellect by correspondence courses and by voracious reading of all types of books. He began his working life as an office boy with a local firm of lawyers and later worked with the legal office of an oil company. After entering politics in 1966, he held at different times the portfolios of finance, public utilities and housing, national security, education, industry and commerce, and agriculture, lands, and fisheries. Though his political career was not always smooth —Williams once removed him from office as minister of finance—he never lost support within the party. (DAVID A. JESSOP)

Charles, Prince of Wales

See DIANA, PRINCESS OF WALES.

Cheysson, Claude

Claude Cheysson was appointed France's foreign minister in the Socialist government formed on May 22, 1981, following the election of Pres. François Mitterrand. Cheysson was one of the architects of the Lomé Convention linking the European Economic Community to 60 countries of Africa, the Caribbean, and the Pacific, and a man who believed that third world development was an absolute necessity. He constantly bore in mind the question of human rights and seemed liable to create some divergence between the French and U.S. positions, especially on Central America. But Cheysson was certainly not, on the other hand, one who leaned toward the Soviet Union; he was profoundly "nonaligned."

After Mitterrand's victory in the second round of the presidential election on May 10, the future incumbent of the new post of minister of foreign relations recalled that the new president, like his predecessors since Charles de Gaulle, would surely wish to make this area his particular province. But the natural alignment of Cheysson's views with those of President Mitterrand gave Cheysson a different status from that of his predecessors. Once in office he undertook an intense program of foreign visits (including attendance at the North-South summit at Cancún, Mexico).

Cheysson was born on April 13, 1920, in Paris. He studied at the École Nationale d'Administration, the École Normale Supérieure, and the Polytechnique—a remarkable academic career—before joining the Foreign Ministry in 1948 and becoming head of the liaison service with the West German authorities the following year. Subsequently, he served as counselor to the president of the government of Vietnam in 1952, chef de cabinet to Premier Pierre Mendès-France (1954–55), general secretary of the Commission for Technical Cooperation in Africa (1957–62), director of the Organisme Saharien (1962–65), ambassador to Indonesia (1966–69), and finally from 1973 a member of the European Communities (EC) Commission in Brussels; from 1978 he was EC commissioner in charge of relations with less developed countries.

(JEAN KNECHT)

Christopher, Warren

In November 1979 Iranian militants seized the U.S. embassy in Teheran, captured 53 diplomats and military personnel, and then held them hostage to a series of demands. U.S. Pres. Jimmy Carter froze Iran's assets in the United States and tried vainly to negotiate the hostages' release. Failing, five months later he launched an abortive commando raid to free the captives. For the remainder of his term the problem cast an emotional cloud over his administration.

Carter continued to work for the hostages' freedom, but 12 months after their capture he lost the 1980 election in a landslide to Ronald Reagan. Negotiations were quickly resumed by the lame duck administration's diplomatic agent, Deputy Secretary of State Warren M. Christopher, who had become actively involved in them two months earlier. Four days before Carter left office in January 1981 he gave Christopher the Medal of Freedom in recognition of his work on the hostage problem. Christopher received the honour in absentia, however, because a change of mind by the Iranians had deadlocked the negotiations again. An agreement was finally hammered out, in part because Iran realized it might have to start bargaining from scratch with an un-

tested but apparently less conciliatory president.

Barely hours after Carter left office, Christopher's work bore fruit. The 52 remaining hostages (one ill diplomat had been released earlier) were flown out of Iran. After a hiatus at a U.S. Air Force hospital in West Germany, they reached home.

Born Oct. 27, 1925, in Scranton, N.D., Christopher graduated with honours from the University of Southern California and Stanford University law school. He clerked for U.S. Supreme Court Justice William O. Douglas and then joined a California law firm. He served as deputy attorney general during the presidency of Lyndon B. Johnson. After Reagan's inauguration he returned to private law practice with his old firm. (PHILIP KOPPER)

Cisneros, Henry

San Antonio, best known for the Alamo massacre in the last century, gained national attention again in 1981 when it elected 33-year-old Henry Cisneros as mayor. A hometown boy with a Harvard University degree, a year as a White House fellow, and three terms in the city council to his credit, he was the first Mexican-American to win such an important municipal post.

Cisneros won 62% of the vote over John Steen, a 59-year-old insurance executive and Reagan supporter. His victory followed a heated campaign in which the two men agreed on the need for stimulating the city's economic growth but differed on appropriate methods for doing so. Steen, representing the old guard, favoured conservative programs, while Cisneros advocated aggressive ones. During the campaign Cisneros stated that he hoped to wean the city away from federal grants and concentrate on attracting new industry. If residential water rates must be raised to finance the modern water facilities needed by new industry, so be it.

As a city councilman Cisneros had been an able mediator. When one leading minority organization demanded what he considered unreasonable salary guarantees for unskilled workers in prospective plants, he persuaded them to back off. "Talk to anyone," he declared. "Discuss anything that will bring jobs to San Antonio." Eventually he helped attract a dozen new companies to the town and create 8,400 new jobs.

The son of a retired U.S. Army colonel, Cisneros was raised in a barrio near which he still lives today. Educated at Texas A & M, Harvard, and George Washington University, where he earned a doctorate in public administration, he has taught at the local University of Texas campus. His election culminated a long struggle by San Antonio Hispanics, now 53% of the city's population, to put one of their own in the mayor's office. (PHILIP KOPPER)

Clausen, A. W.

Chief executive of the Bank of America since 1970, A(lden) W(inship) Clausen became head of the World Bank in July 1981. After serving as director of the bank since 1968, Robert McNamara announced that he would retire in 1981. Choosing as his replacement the Republican he had reportedly wanted earlier to be his secretary of the treasury, U.S. Pres. Jimmy Carter obtained Republican presidential candidate Ronald

Reagan's agreement to support Clausen. The agreement between Carter and Reagan forestalled growing sentiment among the bank's 139 member nations that the U.S. should relinquish the executive suite of the $40 billion institution, which finances development in less developed countries. Since the bank—formally the International Bank for Reconstruction and Development—was founded after World War II, its chairman has always been from the U.S.

During McNamara's 13-year tenure, the bank's annual lending rate rose from $1 billion to $12 billion. These loans, to perhaps 100 countries a year, support rural electrification, agriculture, mining development, and road construction. McNamara in 1980 had embarked on a campaign to more than double the institution's capital, but that would require vastly increased support from the U.S., which provides about 20% of the funds. Neither Congress nor the new administration was too willing to go along with so ambitious and expensive a plan during a period of domestic austerity. One of Clausen's major tasks was to persuade the Reagan White House that the bank deserves strong U.S. support. His most persuasive argument was that continued development abroad expands U.S. export markets.

Clausen was born in Hamilton, Ill., on Feb. 17, 1923. He attended Carthage College, then achieved a law degree at the University of Minnesota and attended Harvard University's Advanced Management Program. Joining the Bank of America in 1949, he became its chief executive in 1970.

(PHILIP KOPPER)

Davis, William

The Ontario provincial election of March 19, 1981, was won by the Progressive Conservative Party led by William Davis, thus extending the 38-year reign of the party in Ontario for another four years. Davis, premier of Ontario since 1971, was returned to office with a comfortable majority. During 1980 and 1981 he had been in the forefront of the national debate over the Canadian constitution. Along with Premier Richard Hatfield of New Brunswick, he had supported the stand of Prime Minister Pierre Trudeau against the opposition of the premiers of the other eight provinces. Trudeau wished the Canadian government to gain control over the Canadian constitution, which, as an act of the British Parliament, was still under the control of the U.K. Also along with Trudeau, Davis endorsed a strong role for the federal government to counter Canada's increasingly assertive provinces.

Born in Brampton, Ont., on July 30, 1929, Davis began his political involvement at an early age. At 13 he was a delegate to a national students political convention, and at 20 he was president of the Peel Riding Progressive Conservative Association. After graduation from the University of Toronto in 1951 and Osgoode Hall Law School, Toronto, in 1955, he practiced law with his father's Brampton law firm (1955–59). However, he soon made politics his career. He was first elected to the Ontario legislature to represent Peel Riding in 1959 and was reelected in six subsequent elections between 1963 and 1981. He served as Ontario minister of education (1962–71) and Ontario minister of university affairs

WIDE WORLD

(1964–71). In the latter position he presided over the reshaping and expansion of the province's educational system.

In 1971 Davis replaced John Robarts as leader of the Ontario Progressive Conservative Party, and on March 1, 1971, he was sworn in as premier of Ontario. While a member of the legislature, Davis had served on the select committee studying the executive and administrative problems of the government. As premier, he used his administrative skills and thorough knowledge of government to initiate and carry out a complete reorganization of governmental structures. (DIANE LOIS WAY)

Deng Xiaoping

In 1981 Deng Xiaoping (Teng Hsiao-p'ing), a vice-chairman of the Chinese Communist Party, emerged more clearly than ever as China's most powerful leader. One of his most important political victories was the shunting aside of the late Communist Party chairman Mao Zedong's (Mao Tse-tung's) handpicked successor, Hua Guofeng (q.v.; Hua Kuo-feng), and the installation of 66-year-old Hu Yaobang (Hu Yao-pang) in his place.

Deng also accomplished the delicate task of downgrading Mao's personal legacy to the nation and the importance of ideology when it obstructed "progress." Both steps were deemed necessary if China was to move in a new direction. To stimulate production and thus move China along the road to modernization, Deng sanctioned higher wages and other benefits for workers and gave greater scope to individual initiative. Even though he preferred to leave the party chairmanship in the hands of his close associate Hu, Deng assumed personal direction of the Central Committee's Military Affairs Commission, which runs the Army. Both in the limelight and behind the scenes, Deng was clearly the man drafting the blueprints for China's future.

Deng was born into a family of landlords in southwestern Sichuan (Szechwan) Province in 1904. He left home at 16 to study in Paris, where he became a close friend of Zhou Enlai (Chou En-lai). After returning home in 1926 he became active in the Communist movement. Deng then participated in the historic Long March (1934–35) and played a decisive role in the final elimination of Chiang Kai-shek's Nationalist forces from the mainland.

With the establishment of the People's Republic in 1949, he was made a vice-premier and general secretary of the party. Though purged during the Cultural Revolution, he returned to power in 1973, having apparently been chosen to succeed Premier Zhou Enlai. But three months after Zhou's death in January 1976, the radical "gang of four" engineered Deng's dismissal from all party, government, and army posts. It was only after the gang of four lost power that Deng regained his former status and the power to test his program for transforming China into a modern industrial state. (WINSTON L. Y. YANG)

Diana, Princess of Wales, and Charles, Prince of Wales

It was to be the year of the fairy tale come true: the announcement was made on Feb. 24, 1981, that the prince of Wales, Prince Charles, heir to the British throne, was to

marry a 19-year-old kindergarten teacher, the Lady Diana Spencer. There was, it emerged, one truly fairy-tale aspect to the royal romance. Prince Charles, born Nov. 14, 1948, was to end his media-imposed reign as the world's most eligible bachelor by marrying the girl next door.

Prince Charles in recent years had become an increasingly popular member of the royal family. Well beloved of the press for his mixed fortunes in sporting activities, he also emerged as a serious though unofficial promoter of British business interests abroad. The British public, however, was more concerned to see him take seriously his own statement of some years past that "a chap like me might expect to marry at about the age of 30."

Lady Diana, by the time the engagement was announced, had already passed the media test with flying colours. The press photographers had guessed the secret months earlier, and had followed her on her patriotic way to work in her British-Leyland-built Metro and snapped her among her small charges in Pimlico. She was judged to be discreet—no small point in favour of the future wife of the heir to the throne—almost to the point of shyness, a trait that was later belied by her lively sense of humour.

Diana was born the Honourable Miss Diana Frances Spencer on July 1, 1961, at Park House, the home that her parents rented on Queen Elizabeth's estate at Sandringham, Norfolk, and where her childhood playmates were the queen's younger sons Prince Andrew and Prince Edward. The third child and youngest daughter of Edward John, Viscount Althorp, heir to the 7th Earl Spencer, and his first wife, Frances Roche, she became Lady Diana Spencer when her father succeeded to the earldom in 1975. Riddlesworth prep school, Norfolk, and West Heath near Sevenoaks, Kent, provided the young Diana's schooling, during which time she spent summer holidays with her mother in Scotland (her parents divorced when Diana was six). At finishing school in Switzerland she became a competent skier.

But little of her previous life could have prepared Lady Diana for her new role as the princess of Wales. The wedding itself,

on July 29 in St. Paul's Cathedral, London, was a spectacular royal occasion and one of national festivity for the British public, shared in by many visitors from abroad and by millions around the world who watched the ceremony on television. More royal news was to follow when, in early November, the couple announced that they were expecting a child in June.

(LOUISE WATSON)

Diouf, Abdou

On Jan. 1, 1981, Abdou Diouf was sworn in as president of Senegal, becoming the constitutional successor of Léopold Sédar Senghor, who had voluntarily retired from political life. On January 15 Diouf was nominated general secretary of the ruling Senegalese Socialist Party, also replacing Senghor.

Previously considered to be a technocrat with little capacity for decisive political leadership, Diouf soon altered that impression. One of his first actions was to lift the restrictions imposed by his predecessor on the number of authorized political parties. Then, in August, when rebels in The Gambia (which forms an enclave in Senegal's territory) attempted to overthrow the government of Sir Dawda Jawara (q.v.), absent in Britain at the time, Diouf sent in troops to restore order. Soon afterward Diouf and Jawara agreed that their countries should be joined in a confederation to be known as Senegambia.

Diouf was born on Sept. 7, 1935, at Louga in the centre of the Senegalese peanut basin. The son of a post office employee of the Serer people, as a Muslim he first attended a Koranic school. He then went on to the École Brière de l'Isle in Saint Louis and to the Lycée Faidherbe in the same city. In 1958 he completed his degree in public law in Paris while attending the École Nationale de la France d'Outre-Mer, formerly the École Coloniale.

At the age of 25 Diouf joined the Senegalese public service. When only 26 he was appointed governor of the Region of Sine-Saloum, and in the following year he became director of the departmental staff of the Ministry of Foreign Affairs, serving in the same capacity for the president of the republic from May 1963 to December 1965. General secretary to the presidency until March 1968, he was then appointed to the government as minister of planning and industry. On Feb. 28, 1970, President Senghor made him premier, the first to benefit from a constitutional change that created this post. He was to spend 11 years in the shadow of Senghor and was known as a top civil servant of considerable skill and experience, moderate and able but at the same time uncompromising, before finally emerging at the forefront of the political scene. (PHILIPPE DECRAENE)

Domoto, Hisao

Hisao Domoto stands apart from most Japanese painters creating Western-style works. His art education began in traditional fashion at the Academy of Fine Arts in Kyoto, where he studied classical Japanese painting. He then went on to Nitten (Academy of

Japan), where he won the 1951 and 1953 grand prizes. But Domoto was still searching for something that seemed to elude him, so he boarded a cargo ship in 1955 and headed for France, where he enrolled in l'Ecole des Beaux-Arts in Paris to study engraving. After a time he was drawn to the Art Informel movement, which satisfied his yearning for greater freedom. He also took over the Left Bank atelier of Sam Francis, an American painter.

In 1957 Domoto's works were shown in Italy and Spain and at a world contemporary art exhibition in Tokyo. Some of his paintings also became part of the International Art of a New Era exhibition, which was shown in Japan, Europe, and the U.S. the following year. Still restless, the 30-year-old native of Kyoto was attracted to the avant-garde Gutai group and with it became involved in action painting and creative happenings; their works were frequently irrational in the Zen sense of seeming vagueness and pointlessness.

During the 1970s and '80s Domoto produced his Cosmos series, some of his most interesting and beautiful paintings. They drew from the iconography of Gibbon Sengai, a 19th-century Zen priest. Sengai reduced form to the circle as ultimate simplicity. Domoto chose circles as symbols of infinity and the eternal, drenching them with acrylic colours that move into one another and often unite circles with triangles and squares—an allegorical statement that the world and human destiny take shape as various forces drift and mingle and sustain one another. The motifs of circles, squares, and triangles pervade other Domoto works as well: "Réaction en Chaîne," "Eclipse," and "Solutions de Continuitées," among others.

After ten years in Paris Domoto decided that the cultural heritage of, say, a Jean Dubuffet was not his own. He also concluded that oils were unsuitable for Japanese painters and began to use acrylics exclusively. The successes that attended Domoto's recent exhibitions, notably in Osaka and Paris, seemed to indicate that he had already been accorded international recognition as an artist of unusual merit.

(BARBARA THOREN)

Duarte, José Napoleón

On Dec. 13, 1980, José Napoleón Duarte, a leading Christian Democrat and member of the ruling junta, became president of El Salvador for the second time in his life. In 1972 he had been promptly banished from the country upon election and exiled to Venezuela for the next seven years; this time he was sworn in by the Army, with Col. Jaime Abdul Gutiérrez as his vice-president and commander in chief of the armed forces.

Duarte was born on Nov. 23, 1925, in San Salvador. He was graduated from the University of Notre Dame in the U.S. in 1948 with a degree in civil engineering. A practicing engineer until 1964, mayor of San Salvador, and a founder and first general secretary of the Christian Democrat Party in the 1960s, Duarte as president in 1981 found himself in the midst of a civil war in which

UPI

about 200 people were being killed weekly. The land reforms and nationalization of the banks attempted by the five-man junta, including Duarte, had failed; they succeeded only in polarizing the left, who felt they did not go far enough, and the right, who felt that their power was seriously threatened.

During his ten-day visit to the U.S. in September Duarte admitted: "It is not yet a victorious position. The guerrillas have forces that create problems. The Army has problems of discipline, internally among the low ranks. There are abuses of authority." Simultaneously, the business community, with support from the right, staged a rally in San Salvador in protest against the government that received far greater coverage in the local press than did Duarte's talks with U.S. Pres. Ronald Reagan or his speeches at the UN in New York.

Successive attempts to mediate by the Socialist International, the European Parliament, and France and Mexico all failed. Duarte was not prepared to recognize the leftist Frente Democrático Revolucionario (FDR) as a "representative political force" unless it dissociated itself from its military wing, the Frente Farabundo Martí para la Liberación Nacional. Instead, he put all his hopes in the proposed legislative elections to be held in March 1982 (with presidential elections scheduled for 1983). But with the existing level of violence in the country, the prospect of free voting and, indeed, of Duarte's survival seemed doubtful.

(LUCY BLACKBURN)

Ellis, Perry

In a fashion footnote to the Jan. 20, 1981, inauguration of Ronald Reagan as president of the United States, chroniclers might note that Perry Ellis designed the gray suits that Ronald Reagan, Jr., and his wife, Doria, wore to the swearing-in ceremony. Fashion analysts credited the increasing popularity of U.S. designer Ellis not only to the new aura of opulence associated with the Reagan administration but also to the sophistication and sense of humour expressed by Ellis's clothing.

Ellis is best known for his separates. His trademarks include oversize shirts and sweaters and floppy trousers, which typify his freewheeling style of sportswear. Ease, casual comfort, subtle colour mixtures, and fine natural fabrics used in an informal, often whimsical or romantic manner set Ellis's designs apart. His fall 1981 styles, for example, took elements from a variety of peasant cultures. One result was an Irish-knit fez. Another design incorporated several prints into a single ensemble. His skirts were very long and full, and his pants voluminous. Fur-trimmed boots or high-laced shoes completed many of the outfits.

In 1980 the New York Times identified Ellis as one of 22 designers who have "global influence." His work has been recognized by the Nieman Marcus Award, two Coty Awards (1979 and 1980), and an invitation to represent the U.S. at an international fashion extravaganza entitled "The Best of Five, '81" in Tokyo. The retail volume of his work was expected to reach $20 million in 1981. Yet Ellis insisted that people should keep fashion in perspective. He believes that fashion dies when it is taken too seriously.

Perry Ellis was born on March 3, 1940, grew up in Portsmouth, Va., and earned degrees in business and retailing. After working as a buyer for a Richmond, Va., department store, he became design director of John Meyer of Norwich, a Connecticut clothing manufacturer, in 1967. He later worked for Portfolio, a division of Vera Sportswear, before establishing his own firm under Manhattan Industries, Vera's parent company, in 1979.

(JOAN N. BOTHELL)

Evans, Harold Matthew

After 15 years at The Sunday Times, Harold Evans moved on to what might well be regarded as the crowning achievement of any newspaper editor's career when he took up the post of editor of The Times of London at the beginning of March 1981. From the outgoing editor of The Times, William Rees-Mogg, he won description as "a great journalist," and for readers his appointment allayed some of their fears for the future of the paper under the new chairman of Times Newspapers Ltd., Rupert Murdoch (q.v.).

Evans brought to the position a wealth of journalistic experience and a reputation as a weighty spokesman in the battle for freedom of information, for a press free from the shackles of official secrecy. "Had the Watergate burglars been in Smith Square or Transport House, the half-free press of Britain would have been muzzled," he said in 1974. His years as editor of The Sunday Times (1967–81) were characterized by a succession of investigations, many entailing legal battles in order to ensure publication of their results. Most celebrated, perhaps, was the paper's long quest to publish the facts about the thalidomide case, when tragically deformed children were born to mothers who had been prescribed thalidomide in the early 1960s. The battle to publish was finally won at the European Court of Human Rights.

Born June 28, 1928, Evans joined the Manchester Evening News in 1952 after graduating from the University of Durham. He remained in the north of England, later as editor of the Northern Echo (1961–66), until he was appointed chief assistant to the editor of The Sunday Times in 1966. His work won him many awards: Atlas World Press

Review's International Editor of the Year (1975) and the Institute of Journalists' Gold Medal Award (1979), to name but two. His own massive five-volume work on *Editing and Design* (1972–77) gained him recognition as, above all, a working journalists' editor. His concern with newspaper layout and design became evident in his first months at *The Times*; traditionalists watched in horror as news appeared on the back page and some of the paper's headlines were set in capital letters. Few could deny, however, that the end result was a more readable newspaper.   (LOUISE WATSON)

FitzGerald, Garret

Garret FitzGerald became *taoiseach* (prime minister) of Ireland on June 30, 1981, when his Fine Gael Party joined with the Irish Labour Party to form a coalition government following the June 11 general election. Born in Dublin on Feb. 9, 1926, FitzGerald was the son of a Roman Catholic father from southern Ireland and a Protestant mother from the North, both of whom espoused the cause of Irish freedom. He was educated at Belvedere College and University College, Dublin, where he achieved a degree in history, French, and Spanish. He later studied law, though he was never to practice it.

FitzGerald first entered mainstream politics in 1969, thereby fulfilling his father's wish that any son taking up a political career should do so on the merits of his own performance rather than on the memory of his father's. By 1973 he had become minister for foreign affairs. During his period in office he greatly enhanced Ireland's status in the eyes of his European colleagues and was remembered particularly for his work in completing the complex Lomé Convention negotiations with African, Caribbean, and Pacific countries. A high point in this period was Ireland's presidency of the European Communities' Council of Ministers in the first half of 1975, during which time he introduced many new initiatives in the decision-making mechanism of the Communities. When Liam Cosgrave resigned the leadership of the Fine Gael Party in 1977, FitzGerald was unanimously chosen to succeed him. He immediately set about reorganizing and revitalizing the party. He visited every constituency, set up a youth movement, and employed additional professional staff.

FitzGerald was deeply committed to solving the problems of Northern Ireland and was a frequent visitor there. He initiated discussions on Articles 2 and 3 of the Irish constitution, believing that their assertion of intent to establish a 32-county republic comprising the whole island of Ireland was offensive to Northern Protestants and should be removed. After he took office in June, Anglo-Irish relations were initially strained as a result of the hunger-strike crisis in Northern Ireland. But after a meeting with British Prime Minister Margaret Thatcher in London in November, when it was agreed to set up an Anglo-Irish intergovernmental council, FitzGerald stated, "We are moving step by step toward a new relationship."   (MAVIS ARNOLD)

Francis, Dick

Victory in Britain's Grand National Steeplechase of 1956 was snatched from jockey Dick Francis when his mount, Devon Loch, owned by Queen Elizabeth, the queen mother, inexplicably spread-eagled himself less than 50 yd from the finish line while leading comfortably. Francis put the catastrophe behind him. Encouraged by his wife, Mary, he launched into a new career as a thriller writer. He was spectacularly successful, publishing his 21st book, *Twice Shy*, in 1981 and enjoying total sales of several millions and film and television versions of his work.

Francis first published an autobiography, *The Sport of Queens* (1957; since reprinted). Then, turning to thrillers, he introduced his readers to international horse racing as a world of high potential for violence and crime. His taut style charged his well-plotted stories—their great variety of settings accurately researched—with tension and menace, and he was recognized quickly as a top class professional. His popular bestsellers attracted a cult following.

His first thriller, *Dead Cert* (1962), was succeeded by *Nerve* (1964), *For Kicks* (1965), and *Odds Against* (1965), after which his books appeared annually. *Forfeit* (1968) won the 1970 Edgar Allan Poe Award, and *Whip Hand* (1979) won the 1980 Golden Dagger Award of the Crime Writers' Association. After *Flying Finish* (1966) Francis and his wife started a small plane charter service, which provided the background for *Rat Race* (1970).

Francis was born at the village of Coedcanlas, Pembrokeshire (now Dyfed), Wales, on Oct. 31, 1920, and was a child star at pony shows. After leaving school at Maidenhead, he helped his father in Berkshire in showing horses. He joined the Royal Air Force and served during World War II as a flying officer. After the war he took up horse race riding over hurdles and fences as an amateur jockey, turning professional in 1948. He rode Roimond, Silver Fame, and Finnure for Lord Bicester and in 1953 joined the stable of royal trainer Peter Cazalet as first jockey. In 1953–54 he was National Hunt champion jockey. After a heavy fall in January 1957 he gave up race riding.   (R. M. GOODWIN)

Gandhi, Rajiv

Like his grandfather Jawaharlal Nehru and his mother, Indira Gandhi, before him, Rajiv Gandhi entered politics at the top. But he came into it reluctantly. After the dramatic suddenness of the death of his younger brother, Sanjay Gandhi, in an airplane crash in mid–1980, there were persistent demands in the Youth Congress that he be drafted into a political career. Rajiv Gandhi finally agreed to offer himself as a candidate in a by-election to the House of the People (Lok Sabha) from Amethi, where Sanjay Gandhi had lost in 1977 and won in 1980. He was declared elected on June 15, 1981, polling 258,994 out of the 307,523 votes cast and defeating his nearest rival by a margin of 237,696. In the same month he also became a member of the national executive of the Youth Congress.

The first child of Feroze and Indira Gandhi, Rajiv was born on Aug. 20, 1944. His parents had been arrested and imprisoned in 1942 in what was known as the "Quit India" movement. They were released in 1943 and set up a home in Allahabad. Not long afterward Jawaharlal Nehru assumed office as vice-chairman of the viceroy's Ex-

R. B. BEDI—CAMERA PRESS

ecutive Council (September 1946) and as free India's first prime minister (August 1947). Indira Gandhi moved to New Delhi to look after and help her father. Rajiv and his brother, Sanjay (b. December 1946), grew up in the official residence of the prime minister, where they had the opportunity to meet distinguished people from all parts of the country and the world. Rajiv studied at Welham's School and the Doon School, Dehra Dun, and St. Columba's School, New Delhi, after which he went to the University of Cambridge to study engineering. He did not complete his course, but there he met his future wife, Sonia Maino, an Italian girl. They were married on Feb. 25, 1968.

After obtaining a commercial pilot's license Rajiv joined Indian Airlines, the domestic air service of India. He was a pilot until his resignation in May 1981. He was a person of few words but had the capacity of the Nehrus for unremitting hard work. In the press he was often called the "Mr. Clean" of Indian politics.

(H. Y. SHARADA PRASAD)

Glemp, Msgr. Jozef

On the advice of Stefan Cardinal Wyszynski (*see* OBITUARIES), then primate of Poland, Pope John Paul II had in March 1979 nominated Msgr. Jozef Glemp as ordinary of the Warmia diocese with its see in Olyztyn, where on April 21 he was consecrated bishop. On July 7, 1981, John Paul II appointed Bishop Glemp archbishop of Gniezno and Warsaw and primate of Poland. Glemp thus became the 6th primate to have come from Warmia and the 56th since 1418, when the Council of Constance had bestowed this honorary title on metropolitans of Gniezno, the first capital of the kingdom of Poland. After the restoration of Poland's independence in 1918, Warsaw became again its capital, and the concordat concluded by Poland with the Holy See on Feb. 10, 1925, created a personal union between the archbishoprics of Gniezno and Warsaw.

Glemp was born on Dec. 18, 1929, in Inowroclaw, to a working-class family. Ordained a priest in 1954, he devoted himself

KEYSTONE

to the education of incurably ill children and later was engaged in religious teaching in the Poznan archdiocese. From 1959 to 1964 he studied in Rome, where he obtained the degree of doctor of canon and civil law. From October 1967 he worked in Cardinal Wyszynski's secretariat. He also lectured on Roman law at the Academy of Catholic Theology in Warsaw.

Shortly after his appointment as head of the Polish Catholic hierarchy, he went to the Jasna Gora monastery in Czestochowa, where on August 26 he read his first homily. His investiture took place in Gniezno on September 13 and in Warsaw on September 24. Earlier, on September 5, the new primate read a homily at the cathedral of Oliwa, near Gdansk, the occasion being the opening of the first congress of Poland's free trade union Solidarity. On October 21 Archbishop Glemp met Wojciech Jaruzelski (q.v.), head of the ruling Polish United Workers' (Communist) Party and of the state administration. They expressed the view that Poland's need was for national accord, social calm, dedicated work, and efficient management. A further meeting between the two, on November 4, was also attended by Lech Walesa, the leader of Solidarity. (K. M. SMOGORZEWSKI)

Granville, Joseph

On Tuesday, Jan. 6, 1981, the approximately 3,000 subscribers to stock forecaster Joseph Granville's early warning service received a message: "Sell everything. Market top has been reached. Go short on stocks having sharpest advances since April." And sell they did. The next day Wall Street was deluged with orders. The Dow Jones industrial average fell 31 points before closing down 23.80, and the New York Stock Exchange (NYSE) registered a record volume of 92.9 million shares traded. Only three days earlier Granville's 13,000 regular subscribers had received the *Granville Market Letter* advising them to "buy aggressively." The abrupt change, Granville said, came when the Dow Jones average broke 1,000 on January 5, and an analysis of other indicators failed to confirm the upward trend.

During the rest of the year Granville registered his own highs and lows. In April he prophesied that Los Angeles would be destroyed by a major earthquake. Five months later he predicted that Monday, September 28, would "go down in financial history as 'Blue Monday'" on the NYSE. Investors in Europe, Hong Kong, Tokyo, and Australia, anticipating a replay of the January plunge, panicked. In London the *Financial Times* index declined 17.2 points (the second worst day in history), and in Tokyo the Nikkei Dow Jones indicators experienced their greatest one-day loss ever. But Wall Street stubbornly refused to cooperate and, after an early decline, rallied to close at 842.56, up 18.55.

Rarely has one man had so much influence on world stock prices, but the 57-year-old self-professed guru of Wall Street was no ordinary man. The son of a Yonkers, N.Y., banker who lost everything in the 1929 stock market crash, Granville studied economics at Duke and Columbia universities. He wrote a market letter at the E. F. Hutton brokerage house for several years before starting his own advisory service, where he was consistently wrong during the 1973–74 bear (falling) market. His "technical" theory of investment disregards traditional political and economic indicators in favour of a complex analysis of internal market trends.

Always a maverick, the flamboyant Granville conducted investment seminars that often resembled vaudeville routines. He has been known to appear with chimpanzees, belly dancers, and elaborate costumes and once made his entrance in a coffin. Although his specific stock recommendations were often incorrect, even his severest critics had to admit that Granville's successful long-term track record would be impossible to ignore in the future.

(MELINDA SHEPHERD)

Graves, Michael

U.S. architect Michael Graves has been called a "high priest" of postmodern architecture, a movement that favours the use of decoration, colour, and historical allusion in its buildings as opposed to the austere glass-box constructions that have characterized modernism. His highly controversial design for the Portland (Ore.) Public Office Building, under construction in 1981 and scheduled for completion in 1982, has been variously called an overblown jukebox or a masterpiece. When completed, it will be the first major civic building in the postmodern style in the United States.

Graves's design, which won a heated competition in 1980, calls for a 13-story rectangle decorated with ceramic tiles. A stepped green base supports tall terra-cotta columns topped by a keystone form. A small pavilion surmounts the structure. The architect's plan to decorate the building with a three-story female figure, called "Portlandia," was scrapped after a furor arose over the design.

For Graves all elements of a building or a room are highly symbolic. The base, middle, and top of a building may represent the foot, body, and head of the human form or the features of a natural landscape. His use of soft, muted colours is intended to allude to natural materials and patterns: green represents grass, blue symbolizes water and

sky, yellow is associated with sunshine. Moreover, Graves's work is full of allusions to Greek and Roman motifs, as well as to the Renaissance and Romanticism.

In March 1981 Graves won another design competition, this for the construction of the San Juan Capistrano (Calif.) Public Library. Again his design aroused controversy, critics calling it ugly and awkward. The plan calls for a complex of buildings set around a central courtyard, and, while it alludes to the traditional Spanish colonial architecture of the region, it also represents Graves's unique style.

Graves was born in Indianapolis, Ind., on July 9, 1934. He studied painting as well as architecture, first at the University of Cincinnati and then at Harvard University. He did postgraduate work at the American Academy in Rome. Graves has taught at Princeton University since 1962 and heads his own architectural firm.

(JOAN N. BOTHELL)

Gretzky, Wayne

At an age when most hockey players were graduating from the junior leagues, Wayne Gretzky already had become the standard of excellence with which his 20-year-old contemporaries were compared. He won the National Hockey League's most valuable player trophy twice in his first two NHL seasons, prompting Los Angeles's Marcel Dionne to ponder: "Can you imagine him five or six years from now?"

As the NHL's youngest player in 1980–81, Gretzky set league records for scoring (164 points) and assists (109). The records he broke had not been threatened in the ten years they had stood. He was involved in 50% of his Edmonton team's goals and became the first player in 63 years to average more than two points per game. He also tied a Stanley Cup record with five assists in his first play-off game and almost single-handedly dismantled the last remnants of the Montreal Canadiens' dynasty, earning a standing ovation from demanding Montreal fans. Gretzky's Edmonton Oilers, with the NHL's 14th best record, swept their three-game series with Montreal because when Gretzky was on the ice and the teams were at equal strength, Edmonton outscored Montreal 11–0. Gretzky began the 1981–82 season in similar fashion by scoring 50 goals in the first 39 games, breaking the 50 in 50 record held jointly by Maurice ("Rocket") Richard and Mike Bossy.

There had been doubts about whether Gretzky, at 5 ft 11 in and 165 lb, could withstand the NHL's notorious pounding when the Oilers moved from the folding World Hockey Association to the NHL for the 1979–80 season. But instead of joining in on the muggings, Gretzky avoided them. As Bobby Orr had done for defensemen a hockey generation earlier, Gretzky rewrote the guidelines for playing centre. Playing against bigger people most of his life, Gretzky learned to avoid getting hit by staying away from the side boards and setting up behind the net, which he used to shield himself when passing the puck.

Gretzky's father, Walter, had him on his backyard rink within three years after Wayne was born Jan. 26, 1961, in Brantford, Ont. When he was six, Gretzky played in a league for ten-year-olds. He played against 20-year-olds when he was

16, the year people started calling him "the Great Gretzky," and at 17 he was the WHA rookie of the year, ranking third in scoring with 46 goals and 64 assists. At 18 he tied Dionne for the NHL scoring lead with 137 points. (KEVIN M. LAMB)

Habib, Philip Charles

Troubleshooting in the Middle East, it may be said, is like playing one of the new electronic space games: the more troubles you shoot, the more appear. One man who is intimately familiar with the assignment's frustrations is Philip C. Habib, whom Pres. Ronald Reagan made top U.S. troubleshooter in the Middle East in 1981.

Habib had retired in 1978 after a distinguished foreign service career that brought him to the rank of undersecretary of state for political affairs. His retirement came as a result of a heart attack suffered after a negotiating trip to the Middle East with the then secretary of state, Cyrus Vance. Reagan called Habib out of retirement to deal with the region's latest crisis—the placement of Soviet-made surface-to-air (SAM) missiles in Lebanon by Syria. Syrian forces were supposed to be in Lebanon to keep the country's various warring factions apart. In fact, however, Syria had been fighting a protracted war against Lebanon's Christian Phalangists who, in turn, were supported by Israel. The Israeli government regarded the SAM's as a threat to its aircraft and demanded their removal.

Bouncing back and forth between the key capitals of the area, Habib managed to keep the lid on but could not find a true settlement. Above all, he was able to persuade the Israelis not to attack the SAM sites. But on June 7 Israel bombed an Iraqi nuclear reactor outside Baghdad, and the following month heavy fighting broke out between Israeli forces and troops of the Palestine Liberation Organization in southern Lebanon. Finally, on July 24, thanks largely to Habib's efforts, a cease-fire was arranged, although the SAM's remained in place. By November the situation was again deteriorating, and Habib, who had returned to the U.S., flew back for a two-week round of diplomacy in the world's most persistent trouble spot.

Habib was a specialist in Far Eastern affairs before serving as Vance's principal adviser on the Middle East and Soviet relations during the Carter administration. Born in Brooklyn on Feb. 25, 1920, of Lebanese parents, he was graduated from the University of Idaho and obtained a doctorate from the University of California at Berkeley. (STANLEY W. CLOUD)

Haig, Alexander M., Jr.

When U.S. Pres. Ronald Reagan named Gen. Alexander M. Haig, Jr., to be his secretary of state, he chose a man who seemed admirably qualified by training and temperament. Haig had had a brilliant army career and had previously served as assistant to Henry Kissinger on the National Security Council and as White House chief of staff in the final 20 months of the Nixon administration. But in spite of this previous top-level experience, Haig's first year at the Department of State was marked more by tension than by triumph.

Tension between the White House, Haig, and the Department of State built up

in a series of incidents that began on inauguration day, when Haig submitted a plan to organize decision-making with regard to foreign policy. To longtime Reagan loyalists this looked like a naked power play, and Haig received a setback when the president named Vice-Pres. George Bush to be the foreign policy "crisis manager." Haig reportedly was ready to resign but then proclaimed his willingness to be a team player on the Reagan squad.

A major flap occurred when Haig announced on television that he was "in control" of the government while Bush was flying back to Washington after President Reagan was wounded in an assassination attempt. Within the Cabinet there was occasional disagreement between Haig and Secretary of Defense Caspar Weinberger on a number of issues. And, as always, there was the normal Washington gossip about an ongoing struggle between the National Security Council and the State Department.

Haig appeared to have won that battle as President Reagan reaffirmed his supremacy in the conduct of foreign policy. But when a columnist reported that Haig would soon be replaced, he responded with charges that an unnamed member of the White House staff was waging "guerrilla warfare" against him. It prompted the president to warn that he would tolerate no more squabbling at the top level of his administration.

Haig was born Dec. 2, 1924, in Philadelphia. He received a bachelor's degree from the U.S. Military Academy and a master's degree from Georgetown University. In 1947 he entered the U.S. Army as a second lieutenant, and in 1966–67 he commanded a battalion and brigade in the war in Vietnam. He served as supreme allied commander in Europe from 1974 to 1978. (HAL BRUNO)

Healey, Denis Winston

In the long struggle between left and right for control of the British Labour Party, Denis Healey's hold on the deputy leadership was challenged from the left by Tony Benn. The party was deeply divided by the battle for votes in a new electoral college system of election, and Healey held on to the post by only a small margin in the September 1981 party conference.

One of the best known and most experienced of European politicians, in the 1970s Healey seemed the most likely successor to James Callaghan as leader of the party, but in 1980 he was beaten by Michael Foot in the first of a series of confrontations between left and right. Healey had antagonized the left by rejection of unilateral disarmament and by what were held to be right-wing economic measures when he was chancellor of the Exchequer in the Labour government of 1974–79. His commitment to a defense policy based on nuclear deterrence was rooted in his experience as defense minister for six years (1964–70).

The sharpness of the conflict with the Bennite wing was exacerbated by Healey's blunt assertion of his own pragmatic approach to politics and of his distaste for the theorists of the left. In a statement he issued shortly before the deputy leadership election he said: "Anyone concerned with doing things in the real world and improving the situation of real people knows that to try and develop a detailed blueprint of the sort

of society you want, and then to go for it through thick and thin, is a recipe for either disaster or dictatorship."

Born in Mottingham, Kent, on Aug. 30, 1917, Healey was a brilliant student at Oxford in the 1930s. After World War II he went into the Labour Party secretariat and was head of its international department for seven years before becoming a member of Parliament in 1952. He won a reputation in Parliament as a tough-minded man who was always prepared to say what he thought and give as good as he got. This did not endear him to his critics, but he once said, "I am not in politics to be loved." (HARFORD THOMAS)

Helms, Jesse

During his first term in the U.S. Senate (1974–80), Republican Jesse Helms of North Carolina was known, to the extent he was known at all, as a right-wing curmudgeon, a backer of lost causes, a maker of unheard speeches. But all that changed in 1980 when U.S. voters put fellow conservative Ronald Reagan in the White House and the Republicans in charge of the Senate.

With a conservative president, a much more conservative Congress, and such New Right groups as the Moral Majority making their presence felt, Helms—second only to Reagan in the hearts of many right-wingers—was in his element. From his position as chairman of the Senate Agriculture Committee, he set himself up as a kind of one-man litmus tester of Reagan appointees, managing to delay (if not prevent) several appointments on the grounds that the nominees were too liberal. He also played a major role in backing the administration's budget cuts—even as he fought (successfully) to retain subsidies for his state's tobacco farmers.

Moreover, Helms now had more power to push legislation dealing with the so-called social issues that were at the heart of the New Right's complaints against modern society. Among other things, Helms advocated a "human life bill" that would establish legal rights for human fetuses at conception. He was also backing a proposal to deny the Supreme Court jurisdiction in school-prayer cases. President Reagan paid lip service to many of Helms's favourite causes, but neither the president nor his administration showed much inclination to fight for them in 1981. Even so, Helms's following among New Rightists made him—and his issues—a part of the national agenda.

Helms was born in Monroe, N.C., on Oct. 18, 1921. He attended Wingate (N.C.) Junior College and Wake Forest College in Winston-Salem. In 1948 he became news and program director for a Raleigh radio station and in that position began to be well known for his right-wing views. He was elected to the Raleigh city council in 1957 and never lost an election thereafter. (STANLEY W. CLOUD)

Herriot, James

When The Lord God Made Them All reached the New York Times Book Review best-seller list in May 1981, where it remained a per-

manent feature for eight months and out-sold no less formidable a challenge than *Miss Piggy's Guide to Life*, this latest success for its British author, James Herriot (the pen name of James Alfred Wight), firmly underlined his popularity on the other side of the Atlantic from his home. Based on his own experiences as a veterinary surgeon in Yorkshire, that most fiercely independent-minded of English counties, his books had already traveled around the world, translated into a host of languages.

Herriot's first two novels, *If Only They Could Talk* (1970) and *It Shouldn't Happen to a Vet* (1972), achieved a fair success in Britain in the early 1970s. Then the two were combined to form the first "omnibus" edition of Herriot's work, titled anew as *All Creatures Great and Small*, and launched in the U.S. The book rocketed onto the best-seller lists, was the subject of television adaptations on both sides of the Atlantic and also of a motion picture, and ensured the immediate success of Herriot's subsequent publications. The rich vein of veterinary stories was further tapped in *Let Sleeping Vets Lie* (1973), *Vet in Harness* (1974), *Vets Might Fly* (1976), and *Vet in a Spin* (1977), and the subsequent "omnibus" editions, *All Things Bright and Beautiful* (1973), *All Things Wise and Wonderful* (1977), and *The Lord God Made Them All* (1981).

Herriot's subject matter might at first glance seem unsuited to the wide popularity it has received. But a lifetime's experience of general veterinary practice in the Yorkshire dales brought to his remembrances the quiet humanity with which he demonstrated his regard for his fellow creatures. His anecdotes were laced with a sense of humour, always ready to burst through at the most inopportune moments. Often the stars of his tales emerged as the animals, from stubborn bull to wretchedly spoiled lapdog; the laconic Yorkshire folk; and the moors and dales of Yorkshire itself.

Perhaps the most surprising aspect of his own success story was the fact that Herriot did not begin to write until he was 50 years old. Another surprise was the fact that he grew up not in Yorkshire but in Glasgow, Scotland. Born Oct. 3, 1916, he studied at Glasgow Veterinary College and began general practice at Thirsk, Yorkshire, in 1940.

(LOUISE WATSON)

Heseltine, Michael Ray Dibdin

In a deepening conflict between the U.K. central government and the local authorities, the man at the heart of the controversy was Michael Heseltine, secretary of state for the environment in Margaret Thatcher's Conservative Party Cabinet. His giant department had responsibility not only for protection and conservation of the environment but also for town and country planning, housing, and general oversight of local government.

To curb high-spending local authorities, Heseltine proposed legislation that would require a referendum of local rate (property tax) payers when spending limits imposed by his department were exceeded. (The proposal was later dropped.) In his role as

guardian of the national heritage, he was criticized because his Wildlife and Countryside Bill failed to prevent destruction of the landscape by intensive farming. Heseltine kept his post in the autumn government reshuffle, though he was one of the Cabinet ministers who had made clear his doubts about Thatcher's unyielding commitment to monetarist economic policies.

Born on March 21, 1933, into a well-to-do army family in South Wales, Heseltine took the traditional path via public school, Oxford (where he made a political mark as president of the Union), the Welsh Guards, and on into business. By the mid-1960s he had made his fortune, as a chartered accountant, from property development, and then in setting up the highly successful Haymarket Press specializing in trade and technical publications. He first entered Parliament in 1966 as MP for Tavistock, and from 1974 he represented Henley. He was a junior minister in Edward Heath's government of 1970–74.

Heseltine found himself on the liberal wing of the Thatcher government, and he chose to make that plain in an emotional speech at the 1981 Conservative Party conference in October when he insisted that it was in the Conservative tradition of "one nation" to bring practical help to the deprived communities of the inner cities. In December he followed this up with the announcement that the government was to allocate an additional £95 million for this purpose.

(HARFORD THOMAS)

Horne, Lena

Lena Horne, 48 years an entertainer, enjoyed another success on Broadway in 1981 and won a special Tony award. However, *Lena Horne, the Lady and Her Music*, which won glowing reviews, was for the singer and actress an epiphany. "That's what I always wanted to be, a Broadway star," said Horne, who had achieved fame largely through films, nightclubs, and recordings. She had been an unwilling sex symbol and, less reluctantly, a light-skinned symbol of black talent, a celebrity whose public glitter hid a painful private life.

Born in Brooklyn, N.Y., June 30, 1917, she was the daughter of an actress who abandoned her to tour the country in tent shows and of a numbers runner who simply

UPI

departed. Surviving a series of foster homes in the South, she ended up back in her grandmother's Brooklyn brownstone. Cora Calhoun Horne was a singular lady, an early power in such organizations as the National Urban League, the National Association for the Advancement of Colored People, and the Women's International League for Peace. Emotionally distant but steadfast, she taught Lena to be "bright, well read, independent . . . to survive at any cost."

The girl doted on her absent mother, who took just enough interest in the teenager to hire her out as a dancer in Harlem's Cotton Club. "Nobody really knows what went on in that place," Horne said recently. "I tried to escape once and the gangster boys came in and beat up my stepfather, and then smashed his head in the toilet."

When she did escape, it was as a black Baptist minister's bride, but the marriage, which produced two children, did not last. At Billie Holiday's urging, Horne then spent years singing in Greenwich Village, where Teddy Wilson and Duke Ellington became her musical mentors and actor Paul Robeson her closest friend. Moving to Hollywood, she became the protégé and then the wife of Metro-Goldwyn-Mayer studio musical director Lennie Hayton, and their interracial marriage scandalized the town.

An outspoken civil rights activist, in Hollywood Horne was the first black actress to break casting stereotypes, accepting no maid or mammy parts. During World War II she refused to entertain white troops unless blacks were also admitted, later demanding the same of the nightclubs in which she performed. In those years she became a spellbinding singer, whose distinctive style, phrasing, and delivery influenced a generation of later performers.

(PHILIP KOPPER)

Hu Yaobang

Hu Yaobang (Hu Yao-pang) became one of China's most powerful leaders in June 1981 when he was elected chairman of the Chinese Communist Party. In a behind-the-scenes power struggle, he replaced Mao Zedong's (Mao Tse-tung's) handpicked successor, Hua Guofeng (Hua Kuo-feng). Hu's elevation, engineered by Vice-Chairman Deng Xiaoping (q.v.; Teng Hsiao-p'ing), shifted the balance of power in Chinese leadership to a broader acceptance of programs designed to speed up China's economic growth.

A close associate of Deng since the early 1940s, Hu headed a small group of relatively young but experienced leaders selected to carry out China's program of modernization and ensure a smooth transition of authority. It was his responsibility to direct party affairs and mobilize party workers for the modernization drive that Premier Zhao Ziyang (Chao Tzu-yang) was pushing forward as the nation's chief executive. In his first speech as chairman, Hu said China's climb to modernization would be as long and tortuous as an ascent of famous Mount Tai. He also expressed strong confidence in the future and stressed that down-to-earth policies would characterize economic development.

Born into a poor peasant family in Hunan Province in 1915, Hu was a member of the Communist Party by 1933. A veteran of the

WIDE WORLD

Long March (1934–35), he served as political commissar under Deng in the 2nd Field Army during the war against the Nationalists. In 1949 he and Deng led the Communist Army into Sichuan (Szechwan), where both remained until 1952. Hu headed the Young Communist League until purged at the beginning of the Cultural Revolution in 1966. After being twice purged and twice rehabilitated, he was made propaganda chief, a member of the Politburo, and general secretary of the party.

A self-taught party veteran, Hu was known for his simple way of life, demanding style, moderate views, pragmatic policies, explosive energy, and quick intelligence—all important qualities for a man destined to help shape China's future.

(WINSTON L. Y. YANG)

Jackson, Maynard

In 1981 Maynard Jackson retired to private life. He had served two terms as the mayor of Atlanta, Ga., and was the first black man ever to hold office as chief executive of a major southern U.S. city.

Jackson's successor was Andrew Young, also black, who won a two-man runoff election in late October. The campaign between Young, whom Jackson backed, and Sidney Marcus, a white state representative with strong support from the business community, resulted in a vote that generally followed racial lines. Though both candidates tried to avoid race as an issue, Jackson injected it into the campaign when he referred to Marcus's black backers as "shuffling, grinning . . . Negroes."

The mayoralty campaign was preceded by months of racial tension that resulted from a series of 28 unsolved murders and disappearances of young blacks in Atlanta. The murders, which began in 1979, brought Atlanta worldwide publicity. Since the victims were all black, the murders became a racial issue with some blacks convinced that the killer was white.

Caught in the middle of this uproar, Jackson tried to keep Atlanta calm while the police hunted for the killer. A liberal Democrat who had always received support from white voters, he had sought as mayor to

bridge differences between the races. On June 21, 1981, Wayne Williams, a 23-year-old black free-lance photographer, was arrested in Atlanta and charged with "one count of criminal homicide" in the murder of Nathaniel Carter, 27, one of the 28 victims. (See CRIME AND LAW ENFORCEMENT.)

Maynard Holbrook Jackson was born on March 23, 1938, in Dallas, Texas, into a family with a long history of education, achievement, and leadership. After graduating from Morehouse College in Atlanta at the age of 18, he held several jobs over five years until he entered law school at North Carolina Central University. Upon graduation he found employment with the Emory Legal Services Center in Atlanta, where he represented low-income people with legal problems. In 1968, largely on impulse and admittedly as a kind of protest, Jackson unsuccessfully challenged Herman Talmadge, Georgia's incumbent U.S. senator, in the Democratic primary. A year later he organized a serious and victorious campaign for vice-mayor of Atlanta. In 1973 he ran for the office of mayor and won. He was reelected four years later but could not by law seek a third term.

(VICTOR M. CASSIDY)

Jaruzelski, Wojciech Witold

The election of Gen. Wojciech Jaruzelski on Feb. 11, 1981, as chairman of the Council of Ministers (premier) and his election on October 18 as first secretary of the Polish United Workers' (Communist) Party (PUWP) were anomalous events within the Soviet bloc. As a rule Communist parties in power kept their generals well under control. The PUWP, however, was in disarray under the increasing pressures of the Solidarity campaign; its Central Committee, to save it from disintegration, evidently concluded that Jaruzelski, whose Communist orthodoxy was beyond doubt, was the only Politburo member capable of pulling the party from the quagmire and reinvigorating its role in the state. But the train of events proved impossible to control. Jaruzelski was unable to reach an understanding with Solidarity, and with the prospect of Soviet intervention looming ever closer, on December 13 he declared martial law. (See Feature Article on page 15.)

Jaruzelski was born on July 6, 1923, at Kurow, Lublin Province. His father, a member of the patriotic small gentry of the Bialystok region, was a cavalry officer who became administrator of an estate in the Lublin area. He sent his only son to the Marian Fathers' college at Bielany, a Warsaw suburb. When World War II broke out, the young Jaruzelski and his family were trapped by the invading Red Army. Jaruzelski was deported to the Soviet Union, where he worked at the Karaganda coal mines in Kazakhstan. In 1943 he joined the Polish Army formed in the Soviet Union under Gen. Zygmunt Berling. After graduating from the Soviet cadet school at Ryazan, he participated in the battles on the Vistula and at the Magnuszewo bridgehead and in the liberation of the ruins of Warsaw.

After the war Jaruzelski graduated with honours from the Polish Higher Infantry School and later from the General Staff Academy. He subsequently progressed through various staff appointments—with

promotion to brigadier general at the early age of 33—to become chief of the central political board of the armed forces (1960–65), deputy minister of defense (1962–68), and chief of the general staff (1965–68). In March 1968 he was appointed minister of defense. Jaruzelski, who joined the PUWP in 1947, was elected a member of its Central Committee in 1964 and a member of the Politburo in 1971, being reelected in 1975 and 1981. (K. M. SMOGORZEWSKI)

Jawara, Sir Dawda Kairaba

The Gambia's Pres. Sir Dawda Jawara came perilously close to being overthrown by an armed coup at the end of July 1981. He was in England for the wedding of Prince Charles at the time but successfully appealed to his neighbour, Pres. Abdou Diouf (q.v.) of Senegal, to send in his Army to quell the leftist-led uprising. This violent episode activated a long-standing plan to link The Gambia, with a total population of little more than half a million, in a confederation with Senegal. Although the official language of the former is English while that of Senegal is French, their populations are ethnically closely related. On November 14 Diouf and Jawara signed a formal agreement setting up the confederation of Senegambia, of which they would be, respectively, president and vice-president.

The violent coup attempt came as a surprise because President Jawara had maintained a democratic system of government ever since he led his country into independence in 1965. He won three general elections and placed great value on maintaining a parliamentary opposition. However, economic frustration, especially felt among young people, anger over corruption, and an element of Muslim extremism all contributed to the making of the coup.

Sir Dawda was himself a Muslim, although he was briefly converted to Christianity when he married in 1955. The son of a Mandingo trader, the president was born May 16, 1924, at Barajally. He was educated in Methodist schools in The Gambia before going to Ghana to take a veterinary science degree at Achimota College. He subsequently trained as a veterinary surgeon at the University of Glasgow (Scotland). After his return home he entered politics in 1959 and built up the People's Progressive Party. Minister of education in 1960–61, he became premier in 1962 and prime minister in 1963 when The Gambia achieved full self-government. He continued as prime minister until 1970, when The Gambia became a republic and Jawara its first president.

Knighted by Queen Elizabeth II in 1966, Jawara was renowned for his commitment to human rights. He played a key role in the decision of the Organization of African Unity to establish a human rights charter for Africa. (COLIN LEGUM)

Jenkins, Roy Harris

After four years as president of the European Commission, Roy Jenkins returned to the U.K. not to the well-earned retirement to which he would have been entitled at the age of 60 but to help create a new political party, the Social Democratic Party (SDP).

Despairing of the disarray into which the Labour Party had fallen, Jenkins joined with David Owen, Shirley Williams, and William Rodgers (all of them Cabinet ministers in the last Labour government) to form a Council of Social Democracy, which later became the SDP. Jenkins, the oldest of the four, was the first to contest a by-election, at Warrington in July. With 42% of the votes, he came close to winning a supposedly impregnable Labour stronghold. He thus had put a new centre party on the map of British politics.

Jenkins had become increasingly uneasy with the adversarial politics of the British two-party system. In BBC television's Dimbleby lecture in 1979 he had outlined his thinking and had argued the case for proportional representation to give a more effective voice to alternative parties. The Warrington vote showed that he was not only a deeply concerned political thinker but also a tough, experienced campaigner and vote-getter. He had been a member of Parliament (MP) for working-class constituencies, first in London and then in Birmingham, for 28 years. From 1970 to 1972 he served as deputy leader of the Labour Party, a position he resigned because of disagreements over European policy. In the Harold Wilson government of 1964–70 he had been home secretary and chancellor of the Exchequer. But the 1970s found him increasingly at odds with his own party. He resigned his House of Commons seat in 1976 to take the presidency of the European Commission, saying it was "the most important enterprise in my life." His four-year term in Brussels was in some ways a disappointment, but he was the prime mover in establishing the European Monetary System.

Jenkins's critics complained of his patrician style, all the more so because of his working-class origins. He was born on Nov. 11, 1920, at Abersychan, near Pontypool, South Wales; his father was first a miner, then a miners' union official, and later a Labour MP who became parliamentary private secretary to Deputy Prime Minister Clement Attlee.   (HARFORD THOMAS)

John Paul II

On Pentecost, June 7, 1981, Pope John Paul II appeared in public for the first time since the May 13 attempt on his life. (See RELIGION: Roman Catholic Church.) From the tribune at the back of St. Peter's he spoke of the Council of Constantinople, whose 1,600th anniversary was being celebrated. But the congregation was more concerned with the state of the pope's health than with what he had to say. Though he walked with evident difficulty, his voice, though not at its best, was strong and firm—a great contrast to the quavering, breathless sound that had been heard Sunday by Sunday on Vatican Radio. But by the following Saturday John Paul was back in the Gemelli Hospital with a high temperature. Its cause was later identified as a cytomegalovirus infection. The pope made a slow recovery and did not leave the hospital until August 14.

Before May 13 John Paul's pontificate had been conducted at his usual dizzying pace.

His journey to the Philippines and Japan in February was another marathon. In January he had received Polish union leader Lech Walesa at the Vatican and did not conceal his support for the independent union Solidarity (and his anxieties about its future). Well authenticated was the remark that in the event of a Soviet invasion of Poland, "I would not stay with arms folded." Nor did John Paul stand idly by as the Italian referendum campaign on abortion got under way. He committed himself publicly to the pro-life position, was accused by the "lay" parties of "interfering in the internal affairs of the republic," and was rebuffed by the voters, who were 67.9% in favour of the status quo (i.e., abortion under certain conditions).

Back at work after mid-October, John Paul never quite managed to recapture his previous tempo. There was no travel, not even within Italy. He resumed his Wednesday audience lectures on human sexuality, found time to take control of the Jesuits by appointing an 80-year-old Italian to be his "personal delegate to the Society of Jesus," and completed his third encyclical, Laborem Exercens ("On Human Work"). On more than one occasion following the declaration of martial law in Poland, the pope expressed concern for his native country.

Born at Wadowice in southern Poland on May 18, 1920, Karol Wojtyla was the son of a noncommissioned officer in the Polish Army. He studied literature at the Jagiellonian University of Krakow, wrote poetry, and acted in a group called "Rhapsodic Theatre." Determined to become a priest, during World War II he took refuge in the palace of the archbishop of Krakow. He was ordained in 1946, appointed auxiliary bishop in 1958, archbishop in 1963, and cardinal in 1967, and elected pope on Oct. 16, 1978.   (PETER HEBBLETHWAITE)

Jones, George

His ruggedly handsome face has the look of someone who has plunged into despair and resurfaced only to plunge and resurface again. The scars still show, the despair in his case being over alcohol, finances, and broken marriages; but this time he is in top form with a positive attitude and the solid support of his friends and fans. In 1981 George Jones received the Grammy award for best male country vocal performance and the Country Music Association award for male vocalist of the year.

The "Possum," as he is known to his fans, was born Sept. 12, 1931, in Saratoga, Texas. His exposure to music came early as both his parents were nonprofessional musicians. Shortly after receiving his first guitar when he was nine years old, he began performing at local events. Jones served with the U.S. Marines during the Korean War, returning afterward to Texas and a job as a house painter. He still entertained locally without thinking that it could become his profession. By 1954 his reputation as a performer had spread to other parts of Texas, and he attracted the attention of H. W. ("Pappy") Daily, a veteran music executive at Starday Records in Houston. The next year he recorded a hit on that label entitled "Why, Baby, Why."

The early 1960s were perhaps the classic George Jones period, a time when he recorded songs that not only would become

country standards but standards that would remain associated with his name, such as "Window Up Above" (1961), "She Thinks I Still Care" (1962), "We Must Have Been Out of Our Minds" (1963), and "The Race Is On" (1964). The style that makes a song distinctly his incorporates honky-tonk and Texas country. He uses few backup musicians and sings in an unadorned, straightforward baritone. The songs most often identified with him are about strong men who have been devastated by unfaithful women, the key to their success perhaps being that he sings them as though he means them.

Jones's first marriage ended in divorce, but in 1967 he met Tammy Wynette, already an established country singer, and married her soon thereafter. For several years the two were the king and queen of country music, and while they were married their duet albums, such as We're Gonna Hold On, were immensely popular. After their divorce in 1975 Jones experienced some difficult years, but in 1981 he had regained his place in the front rank of country music singers.   (JULIE KUNKLER)

Juan Carlos I

Spain's popular King Juan Carlos played a major role in the events surrounding the attempted military coup of Feb. 23, 1981, when members of the Civil Guard took over the Spanish Cortes (parliament) and held its members hostage. The king's rapid and effective reaction in rallying wavering military commanders and appearing on television early the following morning helped to defuse and stabilize a potentially explosive situation and no doubt prevented bloodshed.

More usually, the king sought to distance himself from actions that could be construed as involving him in political favouritism. He saw his role as being separate from the nation's day-to-day political and economic problems and consciously avoided identification with specific interest groups, preferring to remain the symbol of a strong democratic Spain. In pursuit of this he traveled extensively overseas. The first king of Spain to visit the Americas, in October he was greeted enthusiastically by U.S. Pres. Ronald Reagan in Washington, D.C. Their talks, three times longer than programmed, touched on subjects of mutual interest: the Middle East situation, NATO and East-West relations, the U.S.-Spanish

defense treaty, and the Cancún, Mexico, meeting of world leaders. Juan Carlos was also the first crowned monarch to pay an official visit to mainland China and at the same time the first Spanish head of state to visit a Communist country. The king and Queen Sophia did not attend the royal wedding in London in July, as the Spanish government considered it inappropriate that Prince Charles and his bride should start their honeymoon cruise from Gibraltar, British sovereignty over which was disputed by Spain.

Juan Carlos Alfonso Victor María de Borbón y Borbón was born in Rome on Jan. 5, 1938, the great-great-grandson of Queen Victoria and the grandson of Alfonso XIII, the last king of Spain before the republic was set up in 1931. In 1947 Gen. Francisco Franco's succession law specified that there would be a return to monarchy in Spain, and Franco picked Juan Carlos as the future king in preference to his father, Don Juan de Borbón y Battenberg, who had opposed Franco. Juan Carlos underwent traditional military training and was commissioned into the three armed services. A jet-fighter and helicopter pilot, Olympic yachtsman, accomplished horseman, and black-belt karate expert, in 1962 he married in Athens Princess Sophia of Greece. He acceded to the throne on Nov. 22, 1975, two days after Franco's death.   (MICHAEL WOOLLER)

Khamenei, Hojatoleslam Sayyed Ali

The official candidate of the Islamic Republican Party (IRP), Hojatoleslam Sayyed Ali Khamenei was elected the third president of the Islamic Republic of Iran on Oct. 2, 1981. He was Iran's third president during 1981: Abolhassan Bani-Sadr had been stripped of his presidential powers by the Majlis (parliament) in June, while his successor, Mohammad Ali Raja'i (see OBITUARIES), was assassinated on August 30, only 37 days after his election. Khamenei was the first religious leader to become president (Ayatollah Ruhollah Khomeini had previously barred the clergy from the office), and his election symbolized the complete domination of the Majlis by the IRP. The first weeks of his presidency were characterized by continuing reprisals against the leftist Mujaheddin-i Khalq, to which the exiled Bani-Sadr had allied himself.

Born in 1940 at Mashhad in northeastern Iran, Khamenei went to Qom in 1958 to study at the Shi'ah theological school of Khomeini. From 1963 he was actively involved in the Islamic antishah movement, for which he was imprisoned several times by Shah Mohammad Reza Pahlavi's security forces. Khamenei became closely associated with Khomeini immediately after the latter's return from exile in France in 1979; he was appointed to the Revolutionary Council and, after its dissolution, became deputy minister of defense and Khomeini's personal representative on the Supreme Defense Council.

A fiery orator in support of the IRP, Khamenei seemed to lose some of his vitality as a result of a serious injury sustained on June 27, 1981; a bomb, concealed in a tape recorder at a press conference, exploded just beside him, wounding his lungs and neck. Because he was in the hospital undergoing a five-hour operation for his own wounds, he escaped the huge explosion of June 28 that killed Ayatollah Mohammad Beheshti (see OBITUARIES), secretary-general of the IRP, along with 71 other leading IRP members. As a result he became a "living martyr" of the revolution, and during the second half of the year he gained greater and greater power. When Hojatoleslam Mohammad Javad Bahonar (see OBITUARIES), Beheshti's successor, was killed along with Raja'i in the August 30 explosion, Khamenei was appointed to the influential position of IRP secretary-general. Just two weeks later he announced his intention to stand in the presidential elections.

(K. M. SMOGORZEWSKI)

Kirkpatrick, Jeane J.

Jeane J. Kirkpatrick's nomination to the post of U.S. ambassador to the United Nations was confirmed by the U.S. Senate on Jan. 29, 1981. A lifetime Democrat appointed by Republican Pres. Ronald Reagan, Kirkpatrick is known as a neoconservative, a term applied to a number of prominent former liberals who have in the past decade moved to the right. In general, they advocate a hard-line anti-Communist, particularly anti-Soviet Union, foreign policy, but remain somewhat more liberal than traditional conservatives on some domestic issues. Kirkpatrick traced her own disenchantment with the Democratic Party to the antiwar, counterculture movement of the 1960s.

Kirkpatrick's most important task in her first year as ambassador was her negotiation of a UN resolution in response to Israel's June 7 attack on an Iraqi nuclear reactor. The U.S. position was that the attack should be condemned but that no sanctions should be imposed on Israel, which maintained that the bombing was intended to prevent Iraq from manufacturing nuclear weapons to be used against Israel. After intense private negotiations with Iraq's foreign minister, Saadun Hamadi, Kirkpatrick achieved a draft resolution that "strongly condemned" the attack but required no arms embargo against Israel and imposed no new restrictions on Israel's military suppliers. The resolution was unanimously approved by the Security Council.

UPI

While many UN observers called this resolution a triumph of diplomacy and President Reagan called Kirkpatrick a "heroine," some analysts believed that Israel deserved no condemnation whatsoever. Moreover, the warm glow of victory was somewhat cooled when aides of U.S. Secretary of State Alexander Haig criticized Kirkpatrick's handling of the matter, claiming that Haig had had to intervene to prevent a resolution too damaging to Israel. Haig himself later disavowed this criticism.

Kirkpatrick was born on Nov. 19, 1926, in Duncan, Okla. A political scientist, she studied at Barnard College and Columbia University, from which she received her Ph.D. in 1967. She later taught at Georgetown University in Washington, D.C. Her books include *Political Woman* (1974) and *The New Presidential Elite* (1976).

(JOAN N. BOTHELL)

Kolingba, André

Gen. André Kolingba was chief of staff of the armed forces of the Central African Republic when, on Sept. 1, 1981, he succeeded David Dacko as president of the republic. A month before, on July 30, his predecessor had promoted him to the highest military rank in the country at a time when continuing internal unrest had forced the authorities in Bangui to proclaim a state of siege and order Kolingba to apply it strictly. He had won Dacko's confidence after playing a signal role in reorganizing the Central African Army, a task that he helped to accomplish after the collapse of the former empire of the exiled Jean-Bédel Bokassa.

It was this element of trust in the relationship between the two men that, among other things, led to the belief that they were in agreement on the transfer of power that was to result in Kolingba's accession to the presidency. After the transfer a Military Committee of National Recovery was formed with Kolingba as chairman; he was also responsible for defense, veterans' affairs, and the armed forces.

In an interview shortly after his accession General Kolingba said that, providing the necessary conditions were fulfilled, there would be a progressive return to democratic government. However, a transitional period of six months to a year would be needed for a fair assessment of the new regime's policies. Stressing the need for foreign aid, he said that France's support would be sought first but that in view of the country's perilous economic and financial state, help would be welcome from any source.

Kolingba was born in Bangui on Aug. 12, 1935. Before his country became independent, he served with the French Army, notably in Indochina and in Cameroon. In terms of ethnic origin he came from the same people as Pres. Mobutu Sese Seko of Zaire.   (PHILIPPE DECRAENE)

Koornhof, Pieter Gerhardus Jacobus

As South Africa's minister of cooperation and development, responsible for the whole complex range of white-black relations, Piet Koornhof stood committed to the view that

essentially "apartheid is dead" and that the nation's policies of racial discrimination had to be ended. But he remained bound by party policy, and in 1981 the realities of apartheid—manifested in the confrontation with black squatters in the Cape Town area—made his task a formidable one.

The product of two historic seats of learning—South Africa's Stellenbosch and Britain's venerable Oxford—Koornhof served a lengthy apprenticeship in a wide range of Afrikaner cultural and unofficial political movements before entering Parliament at the age of 39 and, four years later, obtaining his first junior ministerial post. This was no reflection on his abilities. By that time he had engaged in the youth and other organizational activities of the National Party and in the Federation of Afrikaans Cultural Associations and the secret Afrikaner Broederbond, of which he was appointed general secretary in 1962.

The son of a Dutch Reformed Church minister, Koornhof was born at Leeudoringstad, Transvaal, on Aug. 2, 1925. Graduating from Stellenbosch with all-round distinction, he won a Rhodes scholarship to Oxford. There he gained a doctorate of philosophy with a thesis on "The Drift from the Reserves of the South African Bantu," in which he argued that the efforts to halt the drift and stop black urbanization were futile. This led, on his return to South Africa, to his appointment as a research officer in the Department of Bantu Administration and Development; there, 16 years later, he obtained his first ministerial post.

In 1972 Koornhof was appointed by Prime Minister B. J. Vorster as minister of mines, immigration, and sport and recreation, the last-named being a particularly sensitive portfolio in view of the national and international problems of racially mixed sports. Koornhof, who by then had given evidence of considerable dexterity and flexibility in handling delicate issues, helped to modify national attitudes toward sports by, among other things, giving his patronage to a South African national games tournament open to all races. In 1978 the new prime minister, P. W. Botha (q.v.), moved Koornhof to the Ministry of Cooperation and Development, formerly Bantu Administration and Development.

(LOUIS HOTZ)

Kuron, Jacek

On Nov. 22, 1981, police raided the Warsaw home of Poland's main dissident leader, Jacek Kuron, to break up a meeting that was planning to found a new opposition party. Nobody was arrested, but for Kuron this was not the first brush with the guardians of Communist legality. For his courageous fight for freedom this disillusioned Communist had been twice imprisoned and constantly harassed by the police.

Kuron was born in Lvov on March 3, 1934, into a professional family. In 1949 he joined the Communist-led Union of Polish Youth and in 1953 the Polish United Workers' (Communist) Party (PUWP). A few months later he was thrown out of the party because he refused to confess to some ideological deviations and write his "auto-critical"

cism." In 1956, during the Polish October upheaval, he was reinstated as a party member and started to study history at the University of Warsaw. Together with a group of fellow students he founded in 1957 a political debating club, which a year later was suppressed. In 1964 Kuron and his friend Karol Modzelewski wrote an open letter to party members in which they critically analyzed the PUWP's policy, proposing a revised definition of Marxist socialism. Both authors were dismissed from the party, charged with sedition, and sentenced to three years in prison. They were freed in May 1967 but were arrested again on March 8, 1968, as organizers of a mass meeting of students on the Warsaw university campus protesting against the excesses of censorship and appealing for a genuine democratization of public life. For this they were sentenced to 3½ years in prison.

In 1975 Kuron was one of the authors of a manifesto signed by 59 intellectuals protesting against the proposed amendments to the Polish constitution that would further limit civil liberties. In June 1976, when thousands of Polish workers went on strike in protest against drastic increases in food prices, Kuron stood at their side. He was instrumental in setting up the Workers' Defense Committee (KOR), a dissident group that helped found the Solidarity labour union. When in August 1980 Lech Walesa started to organize free trade unions under the "Solidarity" banner, he invited Kuron to be his political adviser.

(K. M. SMOGORZEWSKI)

Livingstone, Kenneth

The name of Ken Livingstone, left-wing leader of the Labour Party majority on the Greater London Council (GLC), was linked with controversy from the moment he was elected leader; the Labour councillors, after winning the May 1981 elections with Andrew McIntosh as their leader, voted the following day to oust McIntosh and replace him with Livingstone. The right wing of the Labour Party protested, but Livingstone's supporters were in the majority, having gambled and won in their policy of contesting marginal seats.

During the summer Livingstone's views on Northern Ireland (British troops should not be there), private medicine (there should be none), and other matters often made the headlines in Britain's national press and earned him the sobriquet "Red Ken." He declared his support for the hunger-striking members of the Irish Republican Army in prison in Belfast and was strongly criticized for overstepping his responsibilities as GLC leader. Livingstone himself blamed the publicity on lack of news during the traditional "silly season" of the parliamentary recess and maintained his willingness to discuss Labour's plans to implement its manifesto.

Against the threat of increased household rates (property taxes), Londoners in May had approved a proposal that aimed to reduce fares on London Transport, to revive moribund housing schemes, and to create employment. It was the first of those aims, however, that encountered insurmountable trouble. The GLC levied a "supplementary" midyear tax to subsidize substantially reduced fares on the underground (subway) and buses. After a lengthy legal battle the

GLC was ruled to have acted illegally in abandoning business principles and breaking its duty to taxpayers.

Born June 16, 1945, in south London, Livingstone worked as a cancer research technician and trained as a teacher before becoming a full-time politician. He was elected to the GLC in 1974 and ran unsuccessfully as a candidate for Parliament in 1979. A member of the Labour Party since 1968, he maintained "the only way to achieve socialism in this country is by carrying the mass of the people with you." By the end of the year, however, his socialist experiment came under further threat as right-wing Labour councillors considered defecting to the newly formed Social Democratic Party.   (LOUISE WATSON)

Lougheed, (Edgar) Peter

A tough yet skillful and consistent politician, Peter Lougheed by the 1980s had become the embodiment of the new urban Alberta. As premier of that province he strove to make Alberta's voice in the Canadian confederation stronger. Although Alberta had entered the confederation in 1905, ownership of the province's natural resources was not transferred from the federal government until 1930. The oil and gas boom that developed in the 1960s and 1970s gave Alberta the highest economic growth rate in Canada. It also brought the province into conflict with the federal government over the pricing and sharing of the oil and gas reserves. Lougheed, a former football player with the Edmonton Eskimos, became the man to fight for Alberta. The battle began in 1973 when the federal government put an export tax on crude oil. Finally, after years of wrangling, haggling, and political maneuvering, the province and the federal government reached an agreement on oil pricing on Sept. 2, 1981. By the terms of this pact the federal government would receive 25% of the oil revenue and Alberta 75%.

Born in Calgary, Alta., on July 26, 1928, Lougheed was graduated from the University of Alberta with a bachelor's degree in 1950 and a law degree in 1952. He also received a master's degree in business administration from Harvard University in 1954. After a short time practicing law in Calgary, he joined the Mannix Co. Ltd. and rose quickly from secretary in 1956 to director in 1960.

In 1965 Lougheed became leader of the Alberta Progressive Conservative Party. At that time his party did not have a single seat in the Alberta legislature, but he quickly reversed the party's fortunes. He was first elected in 1967 to represent Calgary West in the legislature. In the 1971 provincial election the Progressive Conservative Party gained a majority of seats, and Lougheed became premier of Alberta. His goal as premier was to convert the money earned from oil revenues into permanent capital to yield a self-sustaining economy once the nonrenewable resource base was exhausted. To this purpose his government established with oil revenues the Alberta Heritage Fund, a financial base from which to finance future industrialization and development in the province.

Lougheed disclaimed any ambition in federal politics. In 1975 he was his party's first choice for national leader, but he de-

clined the offer, preferring to stay in Alberta to work for the province.

(DIANE LOIS WAY)

Lustiger, Msgr. Jean-Marie

On Feb. 2, 1981, Pope John Paul II entrusted to Msgr. Jean-Marie Lustiger the most important and distinguished Roman Catholic archdiocese in France, that of Paris. The appointment came only 15 months after Msgr. Lustiger had been made bishop of Orléans, an unusually rapid advancement in the Catholic hierarchy and perhaps especially so for one who was by birth a Jew. Like John Paul, Lustiger was of Polish origin, but what principally united the two men was their affinity on the doctrinal and apostolic plane, their enthusiasm for the ecumenical movement, and their similar independence of mind.

Aaron Lustiger was born in Paris in 1926 of Polish-Jewish immigrant parents. In 1943 his mother died as a deportee in Auschwitz. In 1940, while a schoolboy, Lustiger became a convert to Catholicism and was looked after by Catholic friends in Orléans, thus avoiding deportation. Renamed Jean-Marie, he went into the Carmelite seminary and gained his degree in scholastic philosophy and theology at the Institut Catholique in Paris. After the war he received an arts degree at the Sorbonne.

Ordained priest in 1954, Lustiger was especially interested in young people and became chaplain to the university parish in Paris and to the arts and science students at the Sorbonne and various *grandes écoles*; he was also director of the Richelieu Students' Centre in Paris. He became noted for the sincerity of his spiritual life and his determination not to follow either traditionalist or progressive trends but to seek new apostolic solutions. During 1969–79 he served as parish priest at the Church of Sainte-Jeanne-de-Chantal in the 17th arrondissement in Paris and made considerable efforts to develop means of participation and communication among his parishioners.

A month after his appointment to succeed 76-year-old François Cardinal Marty as archbishop of Paris, Lustiger said on Israeli television that by embracing Christianity he had not renounced his Judaism but, on the contrary, had fulfilled it. "I was born a Jew and a Jew I shall remain, even if many find this unacceptable," he told the Jewish Telegraph Agency. This aroused some hostility from integrationist Catholic circles and from such leading French Jews as Jacob Kaplan, former chief rabbi of France, who declared: "A person cannot be at the same time a Jew and a Christian. He must make a choice." (JEAN KNECHT)

MacCready, Paul

Icarus, purportedly the first man to fly and the first fatality, might have landed safely had not his wax-and-feather wings melted in the Sun. Paul MacCready, a 56-year-old Connecticut Yankee, worked the kinks and feathers out of his design to make a flying machine that harnessed the light that felled the hero of Greek myth. In 1981 his unlikely airplane crossed the English Channel on solar power alone.

"Solar Challenger" was the latest in a series of unusual aircraft that MacCready had designed and built. A physicist, he reworked the accepted aerodynamic formulas and employed space-age materials for all of them. Plastics, carbon fibre, piano wire, and other such materials kept down the weight of the solar vehicle. Then, to power "Solar Challenger," he surfaced its flat wings with 16,128 solar cells borrowed from an abortive U.S. National Aeronautics and Space Administration project. When struck by sunlight, the cells produce weak electrical currents, which, in sufficient numbers, add up to useful power.

MacCready's system generated enough power to drive two motors at 300 rpm and produce 2.7 hp, enough for the plane to fly 69 km/h (43 mph) and carry a light pilot across the Channel. "It's actually the most ridiculous use I can think of for solar cells," MacCready said. "But we wanted to point out just how much solar power can do."

Before "Solar Challenger" MacCready designed and built "Gossamer Condor," the first man-powered plane to negotiate a short figure-eight course. The "Condor" now hangs in the Smithsonian Institution's Air and Space Museum. Then came the "Gossamer Albatross," which also crossed the Channel, powered by bicycle works and the pilot's legs.

MacCready has been doing odd things with air and aircraft since his boyhood in New Haven, Conn. As a teenager he was a champion model maker and novice pilot of bigger craft. Graduating with honours from Yale University in 1947, he then gained a doctorate from California Institute of Technology. During those years he also won three U.S. soaring championships and a world glider title. Head of a California company that makes drag-reduction devices for trucks, efficient windmills, and tidal turbines, he has served on a national panel studying objects from outer space.

(PHILIP KOPPER)

Mahathir bin Mohamad Iskandar

Datuk Seri Dr. Mahathir bin Mohamad Iskandar became prime minister of Malaysia in July 1981, the most controversial figure ever to have assumed that office. As a young man he had challenged the federation's first prime minister, Tunku Abdul Rahman, on behalf of Malay radicalism and was expelled from the United Malays National Organization (UMNO), the dominant party within the ruling coalition. In the political wilderness he wrote an intellectual testament, *The Malay Dilemma*, which was banned. This book, which attempted to identify the problems of and prescribe solutions for the retarded condition of the Malay community, captured the mood of Malay grievance and expectations and in time came to constitute conventional wisdom in Malaysia.

Mahathir was born on Dec. 20, 1925, in Alor Star, the principal town of the state of Kedah. His father was a schoolmaster, and his family was believed to have originated in what is now Bangladesh. He was educated at Sultan Abdul Hamid College and then at the University of Malaya in Singapore, where he studied medicine. Mahathir became involved in politics while still at school after World War II with the onset of the Malay campaign against the Malayan Union. Under a pseudonym he wrote political articles for the local *Sunday Times*.

After graduation in 1953 Mahathir worked as a government medical officer until 1957 and then entered private practice. He was first elected to Parliament in 1964. In 1969, after losing his seat in an election in which UMNO's majority dropped, he made an abortive attempt to oust Tunku Abdul Rahman and was expelled from the party. When Tun Abdul Razak became prime minister, Mahathir resumed membership in UMNO and in 1972 was reelected to its Supreme Council. He was reelected to Parliament in 1974 and then appointed minister of education. When Datuk Hussein bin Onn succeeded Tun Abdul Razak after the latter's death, he appointed Mahathir as his deputy in March 1976. In that office Mahathir consolidated his political position and in June 1981, soon after Datuk Hussein had announced his retirement because of ill health, he was elected unopposed as president of the UMNO, which ensured his succession as prime minister.

Unlike his predecessors, Mahathir had no special ties with Great Britain. Indeed, as a nationalist, he reacted strongly to British initiatives deemed harmful to Malaysian interests. (MICHAEL LEIFER)

Mansouri, Lotfi

Although he did not see an opera performed until he was 21 years old, Lotfi Mansouri later became one of the most highly reputed opera stage directors in the world. In 1976 he was chosen from among 127 qualified persons to replace Herman Geiger-Torel as the general director of the Toronto-based Canadian Opera Company. Soon he had expanded the company's season from 137 to 212 performances. For the company's 30th anniversary season (1980–81) he directed four productions himself and brought Joan Sutherland to Toronto to sing in Vincenzo Bellini's *Norma*.

Born on June 15, 1929, in Teheran, Iran, Mansouri was sent by his family to study medicine in the United States in 1948. He chose to study in southern California because, as an "unabashed movie nut," he wished to be near Hollywood. While studying for his master's degree in psychology at the University of California at Los Angeles, Mansouri, a tenor, took singing lessons and studied voice on a scholarship with Lotte Lehman (1951). He then gave up medicine for opera and studied at the Music Academy of the West in Santa Barbara, Calif. His operatic debut was in Giacomo Puccini's *Tosca* with the Los Angeles Grand Opera (1959). To support himself while studying music, he once did a television beer commercial and a comedy act with a then-unknown comedienne named Carol Burnett.

During rehearsals at the UCLA Opera Workshop, Mansouri broke his arm and was relegated to the position of stage director for Richard Strauss's *Ariadne auf Naxos*. He went on to become stage director of the Zürich (Switz.) Opera House (1960–65) and also director of dramatics at the Zürich International Opera School (1961–65) and at the Centre Lyrique in Geneva (1967–72). At the Grand Theatre of Geneva, where he served as head stage director from 1965 to 1975, he complemented his artistic duties with extensive administrative work.

A much-sought director, Mansouri has been acclaimed for his productions in such

cities as Vienna, Milan, Salzburg, San Francisco, and Chicago. His Canadian debut took place in 1967 when he directed Puccini's *The Girl of the Golden West* in Vancouver. One of his goals when he went to Toronto was to form a resident corps of young Canadian singers. This was realized in 1980 with the formation of the Canadian Opera Company Ensemble, which was to be employed by the Canadian Opera Company on a year-round basis.

(DIANE LOIS WAY)

Maradona, Diego Armando

The brilliant Argentine midfield soccer player Diego Maradona was the subject of a record transfer fee when in 1981 Boca Juniors made his club, Argentinos Juniors, a successful offer of $8 million for his services. The Spanish club Barcelona had already failed in 1980 with a bid of $6 million for him. Maradona joined Boca and lost no time in helping it win the Argentine first division title in 1981; the fee was to have been paid in installments, but Boca defaulted and Maradona returned to Argentinos.

Maradona was born in Lanes, Buenos Aires, on Oct. 30, 1960, one of a family of eight children. He spent his early years in the near-traditional style of kicking a can, or other object, around the back streets of Villa Fiorito, a poor suburb of the capital. Soon showing above-average talent, he was taken under the wing of the Argentinos Juniors club and progressed so well that he was selected as a member of Argentina's winning squad in the World Youth Cup in Tokyo in September 1979. There he attracted attention with his powerful running and skill, and he scored in the 3–1 final victory over the U.S.S.R.

Though a midfield player, Maradona was a prolific scorer and was top marksman in the Argentine first division in 1979 and in 1980. He made his international debut at 16, playing as a substitute in Argentina's 5–1 victory over Hungary in Buenos Aires in February 1977. Cesar Menotti, Argentina's national team manager, decided not to use him in the successful World Cup campaign the following year because of his age, but from 1979 he was a regular on the national team.

Despite the fame and riches thrust upon him, Maradona remained levelheaded. He said his first ambition was to earn enough money so that his father would not have to work so hard to support the family, and his second was to buy a pair of trousers of his own. With a salary of about $1 million per year, he was able to achieve both ambitions well before his 21st birthday.

(TREVOR WILLIAMSON)

Marais, Jacob Albertus

An ultraconservative South African Nationalist politician and leader of the Herstigte Nasionale Party (HNP, or Reformed National Party), Jacob Marais was an almost unknown political figure when he entered public life in 1957 as an ardent supporter of H. F. Verwoerd's ideology of apartheid—separate development on racial lines. Previously employed in a clerical post on the staff of the Council for Scientific and Industrial Research, Marais (born Nov. 2, 1922) resigned to campaign for Parliament as a National Party (NP) candidate in the 1958 general election. He lost but won in a Pretoria constituency later in the year. He soon made his mark as an uncompromising advocate of rigid apartheid and of white supremacy (*wit baasskap*).

In the 1960s, after Verwoerd's assassination and the accession of B. J. Vorster to the leadership of the NP and the premiership, Marais became a more and more outspoken critic of government policies that he regarded as a deviation from orthodox Nationalist principles. He openly disagreed, among other things, with Vorster's efforts to establish détente with black Africa and the exchange of diplomatic relations in some cases, and he was critical of increasing signs of closer interracial consultation and contacts within South Africa. In association with Albert Hertzog, the strongly conservative son of the former Nationalist and later United Party prime minister J. B. M. Hertzog, Marais formed a right-wing group in the NP, which led to his expulsion from the party.

Hertzog, with Marais as his lieutenant, in 1969 established the HNP, pledged to adhere strictly to the basic principles of Afrikaner Nationalism as laid down by Verwoerd. Marais, who took over the leadership after Hertzog's resignation, claimed that the HNP was gaining an increasing measure of grass-roots support and financial backing among the Afrikaans-speaking middle class and in the urban working-class and rural areas.

In its first test, the 1977 general election, the HNP fared badly, with almost all its small number of candidates losing their deposits. In the election of 1981, with more candidates and a better organization, the HNP came close to winning one or two seats in Transvaal and polled 14% of the votes cast. Marais saw in the result clear evidence of a mounting white backlash against what he described as the policies of "surrender" to the black and Coloured population by the "watering down" of apartheid.

(LOUIS HOTZ)

Mauroy, Pierre

Appointed premier by newly elected Pres. François Mitterrand in May 1981, Pierre Mauroy had long been second in command in the French Socialist Party. His massive frame, unhurried manner, and warm and direct oratory were thus already familiar to the French public. He had the calm, the refusal to be swayed by haste or fashion, and the timeless style of *la France profonde*. He spoke in an old-fashioned way, with simple words straight from the heart. No one could be further from a technocrat: cold abstraction set his teeth on edge. A born conciliator and a prudent man, the new premier was a reassuring presence. He was the apostle of "everyday Socialism" and the decentralization of power.

Mauroy was born in Cartignies (Nord) on July 5, 1928, the grandson of a woodcutter and the son of a schoolmaster, the oldest of seven children. At 16 he joined the youth wing of the Section Française de l'Internationale Ouvrière (SFIO), became its national secretary in 1950, and remained in that post until 1958. As a teacher in technical education in the Paris suburbs, he set up in 1951 the Fédération Nationale des Foyers Léo-Lagrange, a popular educational and leisure movement. In 1963 he became a member of the national executive bureau of the SFIO, where he was an active supporter of Socialist unity. At the congress of Épinay-sur-Seine in 1971 he was one of those who helped Mitterrand to gain control of the Socialist Party. With Mitterrand as first secretary, Mauroy joined the national secretariat and became a faithful ally of Mitterrand and his official deputy in the party. Although at the 1979 party congress Mauroy sided with Michel Rocard in the moderate minority faction within the party, he rallied again to Mitterrand when in November 1980 the latter decided to be a presidential candidate; during the campaign he was Mitterrand's spokesman.

Mauroy owed his strength in the Socialist Party to his regionally based support. He gained his parliamentary seat as deputy for the Nord département in 1973 and in the same year was elected mayor of Lille. In 1974, after his election to the regional council for the combined Nord and Pas-de-Calais départements, he became its chairman. He was reelected mayor in 1977 and deputy in 1978.

(JEAN KNECHT)

Maxwell, Cedric

Cedric Maxwell bounded out of the shadows to win the most valuable player award for the National Basketball Association's 1981 championship series when he led the Boston Celtics to a four games to two triumph over the Houston Rockets. Maxwell had long since shown he could maneuver through the forest of bigger men under NBA baskets, and against Houston he shone through the shadow cast by all-star teammate Larry Bird.

When Bird was having trouble scoring and the series was tied 2–2, Maxwell scored 28 points and grabbed 15 rebounds in his eyeball-to-Adam's-apple confrontation with huge Moses Malone. For the six-game series Maxwell led the Celtics with 34 offensive rebounds and led them in scoring three times, averaging 17.6 points. "Being named MVP was a great vindication for me, a great boost to my ego," Maxwell said.

His ego had been pushed aside to make room for Bird's much-heralded arrival in the 1979–80 season, Maxwell's third with Boston. Although he had had his best season the previous year, averaging 19 points and leading the NBA in shooting percentage, the Celtics had their worst season in 30 years. Maxwell's scoring average dropped to 16.9 with Bird alongside, but he led the NBA with a .609 shooting percentage that set a league record for forwards, and the Celtics made the play-offs.

Maxwell always has been a good shooter, as "Good to the last shot" banners attest. He fakes well, draws abundant fouls, has a soft touch, and would set an NBA record for shooting percentage if he could stay close to the .587 pace of his first four seasons.

Not until 1980–81 did Maxwell become a threatening defensive player by using his 39-in reach and the loose-limbed aggressiveness that generally leaves his shirttail untucked. It was hard work for the relatively slight, strong forward at 6 ft 8 in and 227 lb, but basketball never came easily to Maxwell, who did not make his high-school team in Kinston, N.C., until he was a se-

nior. Maxwell, born Nov. 21, 1955, in Kinston, got his best college scholarship offer from the fledgling program at the University of North Carolina at Charlotte.

He put UNCC on the basketball map while earning degrees there in geography and black literature. He was the National Invitation Tournament MVP as a junior and carried his team to within one point of reaching the college basketball championship game as a senior, when he averaged 22.2 points and 12.1 rebounds in 1976–77.

(KEVIN M. LAMB)

Meese, Edwin, III

In a city where status is measured by accessibility to power, Edwin Meese III ranked at the top of the Washington pecking order in 1981. As counselor to U.S. Pres. Ronald Reagan, the California lawyer was the number one man in the White House and, at times, was jokingly referred to as "President Meese." He disclaimed such a role for himself, insisting that Reagan made the decisions. But when reporters asked the president an impromptu question, it sometimes was Meese who answered or advised Reagan that he did not have to answer. When U.S. fighter planes shot down two Libyan jets, Meese waited five and a half hours to wake the president and inform him of the incident.

Meese described his working arrangement with the president as a "lawyer-client" relationship, with himself as the adviser and Reagan as the decision maker. In fact, Meese began his public service career as legal affairs secretary when Reagan was governor of California and later served as his chief of staff in the statehouse. He served as director of the 1980 Reagan presidential campaign and quickly emerged as boss of that operation. There never was any doubt that he would play the same role in the Reagan administration.

It was said that Meese thought like Reagan, and it was he who cut through complex issues, reducing them to a series of options for the president to consider. At times he was criticized for being overly protective in shielding Reagan from differences of opinion within the staff and for being a conservative ideologue. There also was criticism that he failed to see political booby traps looming up, such as the ill-fated and ill-timed plan to cut Social Security benefits while the administration was working to cut the budget. But the consensus in Washington was that Meese had served his president well during their first year in office.

Meese was born in 1931 in Oakland, Calif., son of the treasurer and tax collector of Alameda County. After gaining a bachelor's degree at Yale University, he studied law at the University of California, and was graduated in 1958. From 1958 to 1966 he was a deputy district attorney in Alameda County.

(HAL BRUNO)

Miles, Bernard James Miles, Baron

For actor-manager Bernard Miles, created a knight in 1969 and a life peer in 1979 and now in his 75th year, 1981 was a year of fond memories: the 50th anniversary of his acting debut in *Saint Joan* and of his marriage to actress Josephine Wilson, and the 30th of their joint foundation of the Jacobean-style Mermaid Theatre at Puddle Dock, London, the first professional play-

house in the City of London in over 300 years. On July 7 the theatre reopened, after reconstruction, on its existing Thames-side site as part of an office building.

The Mileses erected the first Mermaid in their London garden in 1951. It moved to the Royal Exchange in 1953 and opened on its present site in a converted warehouse in 1959, only closing for rebuilding in 1979. During those 20 years Miles presented uniquely successful annual seasons of international drama ("from Sophocles to Pinter") that earned the Mermaid the nickname of "London's one-man national theatre." A sometime schoolmaster who had been for five years a provincial designer, stage manager, stage carpenter, property master, character actor, and scenic artist, he settled in London in 1938 and launched into a secondary career as music-hall artist in a one-man sketch featuring an elderly country yokel. The list of his other professional credits—which included authorship and films along with acting and directing—was as long as that of his friend and contemporary, his fellow theatrical peer Lord Olivier.

The reopening of the new Mermaid with a pop-musical version of *Eastward Ho!*, first done by Miles when at the Royal Exchange, was clouded by its box-office failure and by building delays. Despite the success of the prizewinning production of *Children of a Lesser God*, which, like so many Mermaid plays before it, Miles transferred to a West End theatre, financial problems caused the cancellation of two ambitious projects. Too old now to return to his favourite role of Long John Silver, Miles nonetheless saw the year out with the most recent revival, the 14th, of his ever popular stage version of *Treasure Island.* (OSSIA TRILLING)

Miller, Marvin

Major league baseball owners surprisingly celebrated on the night it became apparent that their players would strike. It would be a costly strike, wiping out 713 of the 1981 season's 2,106 games from June 12 through August 9 and depriving the 26 teams of an estimated $72 million in lost revenue. But when a court decision kept the owners' ledgers private, touching off the strike, the owners had accomplished something they had never done before. They had won a battle against Marvin Miller.

While Marvin Julian Miller was the Major League Baseball Players Association's executive director, average players' salaries had increased from $22,000 in 1970 to $46,-000 in 1975 to $143,756 in 1980. Miller had won for them a flourishing pension, a lucrative licensing plan for group promotions, a system of impartial arbitration for salary disputes, and, most significantly, freedom to choose their employers in a business that had left that choice solely to management from 1879 until 1976.

When the bidding owners were unable to contain themselves, occasionally signing below-average players to million-dollar contracts, their brethren provoked the 1981 strike by trying to increase the restrictions on free-agent player movement. Miller proposed an arrangement that would give the owners the compensation they wanted, in the form of a major-league player for a team losing a high-quality free agent, but he would not agree to discourage teams

from signing free agents by making only those teams give up players. The compensation was to come from a pool stocked by all teams eligible to sign free agents, and that pool was the foundation of the eventual agreement.

The Players Association had fought for its survival through brief earlier strikes in 1972 and 1980 and an owners' lockout in 1976. So had Miller, a Brooklyn, N.Y., native born April 14, 1917. He had not been a baseball man when he took over the Players Association July 1, 1966, after 16 years with the United Steelworkers of America, the last 5 as assistant president. Miller was an economist from Miami University and New York University and a career labour negotiator, and the career baseball people resented him for it. They made no secret of their desire to break this interloper.

But with Miller's finger between the ribs of baseball's establishment, the sport did not go broke and the best teams did not become better, as owners predicted. In 1980 major league attendance set a record, and the four division winners were all different from those of the previous season.

(KEVIN M. LAMB)

Mitterrand, François Maurice

It was not enough for François Mitterrand, the leader of France's Socialist Party, to demonstrate a keen political sense—which he undoubtedly possessed. He also learned not to give up and to keep on taking risks rather than bowing to events. Three times during World War II he tried to escape from German prisoner-of-war camps before finally succeeding. Three times too he campaigned for the French presidency: in 1965 he threw down the gauntlet to Charles de Gaulle, who was then at the height of his powers; in 1974 he ran as a symbol of hope to the left; and finally, on May 10, 1981, summarizing his past efforts and harvesting what he had sown, he wrested the long-sought prize from the grasp of Valéry Giscard d'Estaing and became France's 21st president.

KARSH—CAMERA PRESS

It would be hard to explain such obstinacy if it were not based on profound convictions. Evidently, Mitterrand believed that it was his task to lead France along the road of freedom and a socialism that, despite appearances, was very far from Marxism. On December 9, in his first postelection television interview, he defined the objectives of his "French-style" socialism and called on the people of France to mobilize themselves against the international economic crisis.

By background Mitterrand was not a "man of the people." He was born into a bourgeois family on Oct. 26, 1916, at Jarnac (Charente), the son of a stationmaster who had eight children and later went into business. After training as a lawyer in Paris, he was elected deputy for the Nièvre in 1946. Established in the region of the Morvan, for nearly 30 years he kept in touch with local politics and local feelings, especially in Chateau-Chinon, of which he became mayor in 1959.

After serving as minister in 11 short-lived governments under the Fourth Republic, Mitterrand was president of the Fédération de la Gauche Démocrate et Socialiste during 1965–68 and, from 1971, first secretary of the Socialist Party. Although he established a formal alliance with the Communist Party in 1972 to fight the following year's legislative elections, their "common program" evaporated in 1977; Mitterrand's energies had always been devoted to making the Socialists, at the expense of the Communists, the majority party of the left.

Even his opponents always granted to Mitterrand the temperament of a born writer. No one denied that he possessed the gift of a style that recalled that of Pascal, Chateaubriand, and Jules Renard. It was displayed in the dozen or so books that he had published since the early 1960s.

(JEAN KNECHT)

Morita, Akio

Akio Morita would probably never want to be prime minister of Japan because, in a sense, he was already a king. As chairman and chief executive officer of Sony Corp., his empire extended to virtually every corner of the world.

Akio Morita was born on Jan. 26, 1921, in Nagoya, Japan. Had his father prevailed, he would have carried on the 14-generation family business of brewing sake. Instead, he devoted himself to science and engineering, graduating from Osaka Imperial University in 1944 with a major in physics. During World War II he was assigned to the Air Armoury at Yokosuka, where he met Masaru Ibuka, industry's representative on the Wartime Research Committee. The two worked together developing thermal guidance systems and nocturnal vision devices.

After the war, when Morita heard that Ibuka was struggling to establish the Tokyo Communications Laboratory (TCL), he offered to help part-time while supporting himself as a teacher at the Tokyo Institute of Technology. Morita joined TCL full-time when Gen. Douglas MacArthur banned former military officers from serving in teaching posts.

In 1946 Morita and Ibuka co-founded the Tokyo Telecommunications Engineering Corp., which changed its name to Sony Corp. in 1958. The company gave Japan its first magnetic tape recorder in 1950. Within a few years Japan was providing the world with a whole series of new products: the semiconductor Esaki Tunnel Diode, the PV-100 all-transistor portable videotape recorder, the Trinitron colour television picture tube, the U-matic videocassette system, the Betamax videotape recorder, and the PCM (pulse-code modulated) audio unit.

In 1980 Sony produced the first CCD (charge-coupled device) colour video camera, the noiseless Typecorder, a compact single-unit colour videocassette recorder system, and the virtually noiseless CD (compact-disc) digital audio system. In 1981 Sony added a totally new dimension to photography when it marketed the Mavica, a camera that produces still colour pictures without using film. Late in the year Morita agreed to head a special commission to search for new ways to solve the serious trade problems that had developed with other countries. Ironically, the problems were rooted in the remarkable success Sony and other Japanese manufacturers had had in selling their products overseas.

(BARBARA THOREN)

Mubarak, Muhammad Hosni

Following the assassination of Pres. Anwar as-Sadat (see OBITUARIES) on Oct. 6, 1981, Vice-Pres. Muhammad Hosni Mubarak, Sadat's chosen successor, was confirmed as president of Egypt in a referendum held on October 13. Differing markedly in manner and personality from his flamboyant predecessor, Mubarak had little experience of government on becoming vice-president in 1975. However, 6½ years as Sadat's second in command had given him time to absorb statecraft, and in his first appearances as president he gave a strong impression of matter-of-fact efficiency. Indications were that he would devote more time than Sadat to domestic policy, though without abandoning Egypt's commitment to a Middle East settlement based on Camp David. He criticized Israel's December annexation of the Golan Heights as a "direct blow" to the peace process.

Mubarak was born in northern Egypt in 1929 in the same desperately poor Nile Delta province of Menoufia as Sadat. He was graduated in 1949 from Egypt's military academy, joined the Air Force, and first met Sadat at an El Arish military base in the early 1950s. During 1952–61 Mubarak attended pilot training courses in the Soviet Union, where he was trained as a bomber pilot. In 1969 he was appointed general and air force chief of staff. Three years later Sadat appointed him air force commander in chief and deputy war minister. Mubarak's role in planning for the 1973 October war with Israel earned him rapid promotion to Sadat's inner group of advisers. On Oct. 6, 1973, Mubarak launched the surprise air attack against Israel that enabled Egyptian forces to cross the Suez Canal. For Sadat, Mubarak was a model of what he termed the "October generation"—the class of technocrats capable of meeting the Israelis on their own ground and restoring Egypt's pride damaged by the 1967 defeat. In February 1974 Mubarak was appointed air marshal, and in April 1975 he became

sole vice-president, replacing Hussein Shafei. In 1978 he took over a key position as vice-president of the ruling National Democratic Party. After Sadat started his peace initiative in 1977, Mubarak assumed more responsibility for day-to-day affairs. Despite his familiarity with the Soviet Union, Mubarak was outspokenly anti-Communist.

(JOHN WHELAN)

Muldowney, Shirley

"It is strange to see a woman drive one of these cars competitively. . . . I beat the fellows, I don't just sandbag. I'm in there to win, not just because I'm a woman." So says Shirley ("Cha Cha") Muldowney, the only woman in the world who is professionally licensed to drive a Top Fuel dragster. This machine covers a quarter-mile track in less than six seconds, attaining a final speed of about 250 mph (400 km/h). The 2,500-hp engine, which is pushed to its performance limit with extreme speed, may explode or catch fire. If this happens, and it has happened more than once to Muldowney, large quantities of burning nitromethane fuel fly everywhere. The very rapid acceleration of a dragster puts the driver's body under stresses that are two or three times the force of gravity. According to Muldowney, driving under such conditions is like "controlling a runaway roller coaster."

Muldowney, who was about 40 in 1981, began to race cars at the age of 14 in the streets of Schenectady, N.Y. When she was 16 she dropped out of school to marry Jack Muldowney, an auto mechanic. Together they raced stock cars and dragsters. She drove, and he repaired the engines. The marriage ended after 15 years, and Shirley Muldowney continued racing on her own. In 1981 her crew included her grown son John.

Not all male drivers welcomed Muldowney into their ranks, and she has some unpleasant memories of hostile treatment while she was on her way up. Even when she won the national Top Fuel dragster championship in 1977, the previous titleholder declared afterward that he was "not above punching her out." In spite of this Muldowney refuses to be angry.

"They're all my friends now," she says. "Now they don't hate me."

(VICTOR M. CASSIDY)

Murdoch, (Keith) Rupert

The question people asked about Rupert Murdoch was whether he was really a journalist or just a tycoon. He was both. As tycoon he had put together a newspaper empire with its roots in Australia but reaching out to London and New York. As journalist he was the son of one of Australia's most eminent newspapermen, Sir Keith Murdoch (d. 1952). Born in Melbourne, Australia, on March 11, 1931, Rupert Murdoch worked as a journalist briefly on London newspapers in the early 1950s before returning to Australia to take charge of a small afternoon paper in Adelaide. His ambition then was to establish a nationwide quality paper, which he did later with the *Australian.*

It was not until the late 1960s that he extended his interest to London, where he bought the most sensational of the U.K.'s Sunday papers, the *News of the World* (circulation six million), and the failing left-of-centre daily *Sun* (circulation 900,000). He turned the *Sun* into a raucous tabloid and lifted its circulation to almost four million by a policy focusing on sex, scandal, crime, and sports. In the 1970s he moved into the U.S., buying the *New York Post, New York* magazine, and other papers and fighting a running battle with the *New York Daily News.*

Murdoch's chance for a historic coup came when Lord Thomson, chairman of the International Thomson Organization, decided to be rid of his strike-torn and money-losing London papers *The Times* and *The Sunday Times.* For a knockdown price of £12 million, Murdoch acquired these troubled but famous quality newspapers. But to get them he had to disavow his interest as journalist and to commit himself as proprietor not to interfere in their editing. He agreed to make the appointment or dismissal of an editor subject to the consent of a panel of independent directors.

These restraints on his control of *The Times* and *The Sunday Times* followed criticism of the support given to Margaret Thatcher in the 1979 British general election campaign by the *Sun* and the *News of the World.* There had been similar criticism of support given by the *New York Post* to Ronald Reagan in the 1980 U.S. presidential election. Back in Australia, anxiety was expressed about the power of the Murdoch interests in newspapers and broadcasting, and moves were made to block bids that would widen his holdings in television companies. Murdoch's itch to get down to the job of journalist was well known. But his right to do so as a proprietor was being challenged. (HARFORD THOMAS)

Noonan, the Rev. James P.

"You tell the people, 'Don't blame God. He's not responsible for the unequal distribution of wealth in your country. It's your responsibility to do something about these conditions.' " Thus did the Rev. James P. Noonan, the superior general (chief executive) of Maryknoll, known officially as the Catholic Foreign Mission Society of America, defend his order's way of combining social activism with missionary work.

The Maryknoll order was much in the news during 1981. In April one of its missionary priests in El Salvador vanished without warning for ten days and then reappeared to announce that he had been conferring with antigovernment guerrillas. Soon afterward, Honduras accused the order of aiding an insurgent group there and refused admission to any new priests. In June a Maryknoll missionary was expelled from the Philippines. Authorities there alleged that he had preached revolution. In the U.S., government officials, including Secretary of State Alexander Haig, were sharply critical of the order. Conservative spokesmen called the Maryknolls "Marxist-oriented."

Father Noonan denied that his missionary priests were fomenting revolution. "Our concerns are the moral issues in the countries where we work," he declared. "Sometimes the moral issues are not much different from the political issues." Noonan contended that the new missionary is, therefore, both an evangelical and a political person. He said that his detractors simply do not accept his interpretation of the Gospels.

Noonan was born on Aug. 1, 1934, in Burlington, Vt. He completed high school in 1951 and began studies for the priesthood at St. Thomas Seminary in Bloomfield, Conn. After work at seminaries in Arkansas and Massachusetts, he was ordained in 1960. Noonan served as a priest in Burlington, Vt., for one year but concluded that the missions needed him more. In 1961 he joined the Maryknolls and one year later received his first missionary assignment, to the province of Mindanao in the southern Philippines. Noonan remained in the Philippines until 1978, when he was elected to a six-year term as superior general.

(VICTOR M. CASSIDY)

O'Connor, Sandra Day

As both governor of California and president of the United States, Ronald Reagan had never been especially popular with feminists. Among other things, he opposed the Equal Rights Amendment to the Constitution and favoured an amendment that would prohibit abortions. Thus, it was all the more remarkable when he revealed in July 1981 that he was nominating Judge Sandra Day O'Connor of the Arizona State Court of Appeals to be the first woman on the Supreme Court bench.

Almost from the moment that Justice Potter Stewart, 66, announced his retirement, the White House encouraged speculation that Reagan might pick a woman for the court. Many felt there was no better way for the president to score points with the feminists at little or no risk, assuming he could find a female judge with whom he felt ideologically at ease. And the choice of O'Connor, noted for her meticulous, if not very creative, legal mind, was applauded by liberals, moderates, old-guard conservatives like Sen. Barry Goldwater of Arizona—and by feminists. As a judge, O'Connor had a reputation for being tough but fair. While she favoured "judicial restraint" and was a conservative Republican politically, her performance on the bench had not been notably ideological.

Only on the far right did the nomination encounter any significant opposition. "We

feel betrayed," said Paul Brown, head of the Life Amendment Political Action Committee. He and others, including the Rev. Jerry Falwell of Moral Majority, charged that O'Connor favoured abortion and ERA. In the Arizona state senate, where she served prior to her appointment to the court of appeals, O'Connor did advocate that Arizona ratify the ERA, but her votes where abortion was concerned were more equivocal. In any case, the opposition seemed to offend more people than it persuaded, including Goldwater, whose conservative credentials had always been unassailable. The result was that O'Connor's nomination won easy approval in the Senate.

Born March 26, 1930, in El Paso, Texas, to parents who owned a huge ranch on the Arizona-New Mexico border, O'Connor completed both her undergraduate and law studies at Stanford University in only five years. Her husband, John, is also a lawyer.

(STANLEY W. CLOUD)

Page, George

The U.S. National Aeronautics and Space Administration's space shuttle "Columbia," the first reusable extraterrestrial vehicle, finally got off the ground for a low-orbit flight in April 1981, landed again, was refitted, and made a second, longer orbital flight in November. This mission proved in practice what space engineers had been promising for years: they could build a vehicle that would perform a job in orbit, return, and then fly again for different purposes as flexibly as a rental car. The achievement was both a relief and a milestone for George Page, NASA's director of space shuttle operations and winner of the agency's Distinguished Service Medal.

The leader of the long-term project was born in Pittsburgh, Pa., in 1924 and started tinkering with flying machines when he joined the U.S. Army Air Corps at the age of 18. After serving in Africa and the Persian Gulf, he married an Iranian-born U.S. embassy secretary, gained an engineering degree at Pennsylvania State University, and worked on experimental engines for Westinghouse Electric Corp. and on launch operations for General Dynamics Corp. He joined NASA in 1963. Involved in nearly 50

unmanned lift-offs, he supervised most of the two-man Gemini space flights and the Apollo Moon missions.

The space shuttle, said to be the most complex machine ever built, is not the most perfect. Its construction was delayed by a series of problems, many of them centring on the 31,000 tiles that shield the craft from the heat of reentry. Some of the tiles came off during the first flight. The second mission, scheduled to last five days and 83 Earth orbits, was shortened to 54 hours and 36 orbits after a fuel cell failed. Nonetheless, astronauts Joe Engle and Richard Truly completed 90% of the planned scientific work. They mapped geologic faults, measured atmospheric gases, surveyed ocean algae that attract commercially important fish, and took infrared pictures that would be correlated with ground surveys to locate mineral lodes on Earth.   (PHILIP KOPPER)

Papandreou, Andreas

In the Greek general elections of Oct. 18, 1981, Andreas Papandreou led his Panhellenic Socialist Movement (Pasok) to a spectacular victory that gave Greece its first Socialist government in history. Shortly after forming his government (October 21), Papandreou promised to tread softly. "We have no desire to take our country into any adventure," he declared. Nevertheless, there was speculation in the West as to what attitude he might adopt toward Greece's membership in the European Communities and NATO.

Andreas Papandreou was following in the footsteps of his late father, Georgios Papandreou, who, on becoming prime minister in 1963, induced his son to give up a successful academic career teaching economics in U.S. universities, and his U.S. citizenship, to carry on the family name in Greek politics. His rapid rise in government and the party hierarchy sowed the seeds of dissension that eventually led to the fall of his father's government (despite its 53% majority at the polls) following a clash with the king in 1965 over control of the Army.

In 1967, when it became clear that the Papandreous were headed for power in the elections scheduled for May of that year, a military junta seized power one month before the elections and jailed them both.

CAMERA PRESS

Andreas was eventually allowed to leave Greece. He went abroad and organized the Panhellenic Liberation Movement (PAK) to stimulate resistance against the military dictatorship. Later, when democracy was restored in 1974, PAK formed the nucleus for the creation of Pasok. In the 1974 elections Papandreou's party won just over 13% of the vote, but in 1977, thanks to good organization and the deft exploitation of growing anti-Americanism in Greece, his share of votes was doubled to 25%, and in 1981 it almost redoubled to 48%.

Born on Feb. 5, 1919, on the Aegean island of Chios, where his father served as local governor, Papandreou was educated at the U.S.-financed American College and later attended the law school at Athens University. After obtaining his Ph.D. in economics at Harvard University (1943), he became professor of economics, first at the University of Minnesota (1951) and later at the University of California (1955).

(MARIO MODIANO)

Peacock, Andrew Sharp

The supporters of Andrew Peacock were delighted in 1981 when their hero began his long-awaited attempt to unseat Malcolm Fraser from the leadership of Australia's Liberal Party. Peacock created a political crisis in April by resigning his portfolio of industrial relations in the Liberal-National Country Party government and delivering a blistering personal attack on Prime Minister Fraser, whom he described as stubborn, unreasonable, and determined to get his own way. Peacock added point to his attack by couching his resignation speech in the same terms that Fraser had himself used when, in 1971, he had acted as the missile that destroyed his parliamentary leader, John G. Gorton. Peacock clearly hoped that history would repeat itself a decade later and that anti-Fraser factions would support his bid for parliamentary leadership when an opportunity presented itself.

Before his resignation Peacock had been one of the most able of the Liberal Party ministers. He was elected to Parliament in 1966 as the replacement to no less a statesman than Sir Robert Menzies on Menzies's retirement after 17 years as prime minister, and the young man (born Feb. 13, 1939) was clearly seen as a potential prime minister as early as the mid-1960s. He held portfolios of the Army (1969–72), assistant to the treasurer (1971–72), external territories (1972), foreign affairs (1975–80), and industrial relations (1980–81). In the last two of these posts he came into direct opposition to Fraser.

Peacock considered that he had been betrayed by the prime minister's failure to end the recognition of the Pol Pot regime in Kampuchea (Cambodia), and he was outraged at Fraser's lack of finesse in dealing with management and labour unions in industrial relations. When Peacock resigned, many Liberals feared that the chances of a Liberal victory in the next election would be seriously reduced, as he had the style, charisma, confidence, and lack of arrogance that gave him a wider electoral appeal than his master. In the first paragraph of his resignation speech Peacock said, "My resignation is not based on rivalry, nor is it inspired by personal ambition." Few believed him, and both the Liberal and the Australi-

an Labor parties were thrown into uncertainty as to what policies they should pursue and how they should act if Malcolm Fraser were deposed. (A. R. G. GRIFFITHS)

Pinto Balsemão, Francisco José Pereira

A pragmatist and conciliator, Francisco Pinto Balsemão was the opposite of Francisco Sá Carneiro, whom he succeeded as Portugal's premier on Jan. 9, 1981, following Sá Carneiro's death in a plane crash in December 1980. The two had been co-founders of the Social Democratic Party (PSD) in 1974, but the former leader's abrasive personality had caused numerous defections from the party. Those who picked Balsemão to succeed Sá Carneiro saw him as a more flexible manager who could steer Portugal through the difficult task of revising the 1976 Socialist constitution and preparing the country for membership in the European Communities. Balsemão maintained the free market-private enterprise slant of the PSD but with a much more urbane style, knowing that he would need a two-thirds majority in the Assembly to get his party's planned constitutional amendments passed.

Born in 1937, Balsemão trained as a lawyer but turned to journalism, becoming editor in chief (1961–63) of the review Mais Alto and publisher from 1973 of the Expresso, which he quickly made into the best of the country's weekly newspapers. Strongly critical of the Salazar-Caetano regime, it expressed the frustration over the unwinnable African wars and the regime's international isolation that eventually led to the military coup of 1974. In 1975 Balsemão was vice-president of the Constituent Assembly and in 1977, opposition spokesman on foreign affairs.

Balsemão's critics underestimated his role in keeping the PSD together when Sá Carneiro's intolerance of dissidents threatened to fragment the party. However, he had yet to convince the political and business communities of his determination in pursuing the PSD's program. An August crisis in which Balsemão called his critics' bluff and challenged them to find a replacement ended in triumph for him. The incident served to strengthen his hand and forced the dissidents to accept their share of the responsibility of running the country in a difficult period.   (MICHAEL WOOLLER)

Poli, Robert Edmund

It was reminiscent of a scene from one of those B movies in which Ronald Reagan used to star: two antagonists coming down the street toward one another, neither willing to give an inch. Only this time Reagan was president of the United States, his antagonist was the president of a labour union—and the drama was not make-believe.

Facing Reagan was Robert E. Poli, born Feb. 27, 1937, in Pittsburgh, Pa., a career air traffic controller and president of the Professional Air Traffic Controllers Organization. PATCO represented some 85% of the 17,500 federal employees directing U.S. air traffic. For years the controllers had complained to the Federal Aviation Administration about what they saw as unsatisfactory working conditions, but in 1980, when Poli moved up from union vice-president to president, their demands became more militant.

Negotiations for a new contract began in February 1981. Among the union's demands: across-the-board, $10,000 pay increases (from a current average of $33,000 a year); a 32-hour workweek for the high-pressure profession; an earlier retirement age; and higher pension benefits. Faced with a June 22 strike deadline, the two sides stayed far apart until the 11th hour, when the government offered a $40 million package, including a 6.6% salary boost.

Poli called off the strike, but PATCO's rank and file rejected the new package by an overwhelming margin. Further negotiations went nowhere, and Poli led his union onto the picket lines when a new deadline passed. Reagan publicly warned that, since strikes by federal employees were illegal, anyone who walked off the job would be fired. Within a week, controllers who failed to report back to work were sent dismissal notices, as Reagan had promised.

All but a relative handful remained on strike the rest of the year—even after the federal courts stripped the union of its status as a bargaining agent. The FAA replaced the strikers with nonstrikers, supervisory personnel, trainees, military controllers, and—as they became available—new graduates of the air controllers' training program. There were delays and cutbacks in service, but the system seemed to be working relatively well by year's end. On December 31 Poli announced his resignation as PATCO president, saying that he hoped this would smooth the way to rehiring of the striking controllers. President Reagan had said they would be considered for other government jobs but not for their old positions. (STANLEY W. CLOUD)

Price, George Cadle

The style of politics and government of Belize's first prime minister, George Cadle Price, was variously described as philosophical, low key, or low profile. His approach, one that avoided dramatic gestures and instead emphasized quiet negotiation, appeared to owe much to his early training for the priesthood.

Born on Jan. 15, 1919, Price grew up in Belize City and was educated at the Holy Redeemer primary school and St. John's College before he enrolled at St. Augustine's Seminary at Bay St. Louis at the age of 17. Later he attended the National Seminary in Guatemala City, intending to become a priest. When his father fell ill, however, he left the seminary and returned home to Belize. It was an experience that was to affect the rest of his life. Price still lived in great simplicity, dressed accordingly, and for relaxation preferred nothing more than to read and reread the novels of Graham Greene.

Price's political involvement first came to the fore in the late 1940s, when the devaluation of the Belizean dollar caused serious economic hardship for many of the people of what was then called British Honduras. As a result, he was closely involved in the establishment of a People's Provisional Committee, which later became the People's United Party (PUP). From 1954 onward he engaged in national politics and made his way up through the PUP political ranks so that by 1961 he was appointed first minister. Following constitutional changes in 1964, he became premier and then prime

minister when Belize gained independence on Sept. 21, 1981.

The PUP's long stay in power owed much to Price's personal brand of politics. It was hard to classify his political philosophy, which took in many Socialist views yet encouraged the development of private enterprise and investment. Though there were suggestions that certain of the left-leaning younger members of the government might wish to take a stronger line on Central American political issues, Price resolutely steered Belize on a middle course.

(DAVID A. JESSOP)

Qaddafi, Muammar Muhammad al-

Ever since he seized power in Libya in September 1969 and immediately, and skillfully, exploited a strong bargaining position in the world oil market, Col. Muammar al-Qaddafi had been in the news. Throughout 1981 the U.S. administration of Pres. Ronald Reagan seemed intent on keeping Qaddafi's newsworthiness at front-page level. In August two Libyan jets, challenging the presence of U.S. naval and aerial power in or over territorial waters claimed by Libya, were brought down by U.S. Navy planes. The incident led to much posturing by the Libyan and U.S. leaderships but scarcely affected the level of exchange of oil and expertise. The Libyan bureau in Washington, D.C., remained closed, as did the U.S. embassy in Tripoli, but oil continued to flow to the U.S. at the level decreed by the market. Then, in December, the U.S. accusation that Qaddafi had dispatched a hit squad to assassinate President Reagan brought relations between the two countries to their nadir.

Born in a Bedouin tent in the desert south of Tripoli in September 1942, Qaddafi was almost unknown until 1969, when he led a coup that deposed King Idris. Thereafter, as chairman of the Revolutionary Command Council until 1977 and then de facto president, he dominated the regime. From 1976 Qaddafi implemented a progressively socialist policy at home with urban property, banking, and retail distribution all centrally controlled. Industry, as in most Middle Eastern oil states, was also centrally planned and financed, and the future of agricultural resources and their development was by 1981 a central government responsibility.

In 1981 Qaddafi had to accommodate to changed and unpleasant economic circumstances. Saudi Arabia dominated world oil exports and forced the smaller exporters to cut back on shipments. Libya, consequently, was producing less than one-third of the two million barrels per day normal in the late 1970s. The effect on foreign policy was dramatic. Libya mended many broken fences, notably with Morocco, long embarrassed by Libya's financing of Polisario, the Western Saharan independence movement. Qaddafi visited the Gulf states and made conciliatory gestures to the Saudi royal family. He remained firm, however, in his rejectionist-front posture toward Israel and was not alone in the Arab world in rejoicing over the assassination of Egyptian Pres. Anwar as-Sadat; he was also hostile to Egypt's ally Sudan. His late-1980 intervention in Chad came to an end in November 1981.

(J. A. ALLAN)

Questiaux, Nicole Françoise

Delicate features framed by snow-white hair, a measured voice, a clear glance, and gentle persuasion made up Nicole Questiaux. As France's minister of national solidarity she was the highest ranking of the six women members of the Socialist Party government formed in May 1981 after the election of Pres. François Mitterrand. The Ministry of National Solidarity, one of three new ministries set up by President Mitterrand's administration, combined responsibility for social security and welfare, immigrant affairs, and the broad direction of social policy.

Questiaux's first major problem was the growing deficit in the social security budget. Her plan, submitted in November, called for a raising of contributions by employers and employees and pleased no one. The deficit was partly due to the government's measures to aid families, the handicapped, and old people but partly also to the rise in unemployment. Therefore, the solution consisted of controlling health expenditures—a matter that concerned everyone in France—but above all in stimulating economic growth.

Born Nicole Valayer on Dec. 19, 1930, in Nantes, the daughter of an engineer, Questiaux gained her diploma at the Institut d'Études Politiques in Paris and studied at the École Nationale d'Administration (1953–55). In 1955 she joined the Conseil d'État, where in 1963 she was appointed government commissioner to deal with disputes, the first woman to hold such a post. She was already a specialist in social affairs and had contributed to several works on the subject. Georges Dayan, an old friend and mentor of Mitterrand, allegedly introduced Questiaux to the Convention des Institutions Républicaines, which was a meeting place for many supporters of the future president.

In 1970 Questiaux chaired the national delegation for Socialist unity, which brought together Socialists, members of the Convention, and other representative figures with the aim of uniting Socialist forces in France. This undertaking led to the Congress of Socialist Unity in June 1971. A member of the leadership committee of the Socialist Party (PS), she was appointed national delegate to the European Communities in February 1975 but resigned six months later. In 1979 she joined the left-wing group within the PS.

(JEAN KNECHT)

Rattle, Simon

Perhaps the most gifted of Britain's young orchestral conductors, Simon Rattle was born in Liverpool, England, in 1955. As a boy he played percussion with the city's Royal Philharmonic Orchestra and received impromptu lessons from revered French conductor Pierre Boulez, but it was while he was an 18-year-old student at London's Royal Academy of Music that he first gained public attention, organizing and conducting a performance of Gustav Mahler's mighty *Resurrection Symphony* that had even seasoned critics gasping at its compulsive blend of fire and absolute command.

There was little surprise, therefore, when the following year Rattle took first honours at the John Player-sponsored International Conducting Competition and was immediately appointed assistant conductor of Bournemouth's Symphony Orchestra and chamber Sinfonietta. Debuts rapidly followed; Rattle's formal London premiere in 1975 at the capital's Royal Festival Hall, where he appeared for the first time with the Philharmonia Orchestra, was received with rapturous acclaim by critics and public alike. A debut the following year was with Glyndebourne Festival Opera's touring company.

From that time Rattle's career blossomed, guest conducting commitments taking him to Sweden, Denmark, West Germany, and The Netherlands. His U.S. debut, with the Los Angeles Philharmonic, followed in 1979, in which year he also directed the Chicago Symphony and appeared at the Hollywood Bowl. In 1980 he was invited for the first time to direct both the San Francisco and Toronto symphony orchestras and returned (following a popularity poll among the players) for a further concert series with the Los Angeles Philharmonic. The same year he took up appointments as principal and artistic adviser of both the City of Birmingham (England) Symphony Orchestra and the London Choral Society.

In 1981 Rattle signed an exclusive contract with Angel-EMI. First salvos in what promised to be a thoroughly rewarding album career were issues of Deryck Cooke's definitive performing edition of Mahler's unfinished tenth symphony, Holst's *The Planets* suite, and Leos Janacek's *Glagolitic Mass*. Rattle subsequently succeeded Pinchas Zukerman as artistic director, for 1981–83, of London's South Bank Summer Music Festival. (MOZELLE A. MOSHANSKY)

Reagan, Ronald Wilson

Did Ronald Reagan receive a "mandate" from the voters when they elected him president of the United States in 1980? Reagan and his partisans believed he did; others believed that Reagan's large margin of victory was primarily an indication of popular dissatisfaction with the lacklustre leadership provided by Reagan's opponent and predecessor in the White House, Jimmy Carter.

The debate was largely of academic interest, however, because Reagan had no sooner taken office in 1981 than he began to use his considerable political talent to create a mandate for his "supply-side" economic policies. Reagan wanted to cut government spending in order to bring inflation under control and cut taxes to stimulate new growth. He argued that such an unprecedented, combined approach would result in lower federal deficits and a balanced budget by 1984.

Many economists disagreed with Reagan's optimistic forecasts, insisting that they were rooted more in wishful thinking than economic reality. Nevertheless, by lopsided margins and after a flurry of bargaining with various special interests, Congress did the president's bidding, cutting back on projected federal spending for fiscal

UPI

year 1982 by $35.1 billion and approving a three-year, 25% reduction in personal and business income taxes.

Despite these victories, however, trouble lay ahead for Reagan. His budgetary planners discovered that revenue losses caused by the tax cut were unlikely to be offset by spending cuts or new economic growth. Deficits of $60 billion or higher for the next three years were forecast. Largely because of such forecasts, interest rates remained high and the stock market took a nosedive. To make matters worse, the economy sank into a recession during the last quarter of the year, and Reagan conceded that his goal of a balanced budget in 1984 probably would not be met.

Faced with these gloomy prospects, Reagan called for $16 billion in additional budget savings and insisted that, given time, his supply-side theories would work. By now, however, Congress was having second thoughts, and it seemed doubtful that Reagan would again be able to enjoy the full fruits of his "mandate."

The year was also marked for Reagan by an attempt to assassinate him, in Washington on March 30. John W. Hinckley, Jr., a 25-year-old drifter from Colorado, succeeded in seriously wounding the president, but Reagan made a remarkably speedy and complete recovery. (STANLEY W. CLOUD)

Regan, Donald T.

No one ever doubted Donald Regan's qualifications to be secretary of the treasury in the Cabinet of U.S. Pres. Ronald Reagan. As chairman of Merrill Lynch & Co., the nation's largest securities and brokerage firm, Regan was known on Wall Street as a tough, smart financial innovator.

But he also had a reputation for being an intensely private person and an autocratic boss. There were questions as to how he would adapt to political compromise and the open, give-and-take of life in Washington. There also was uncertainty whether the blunt ex-Marine would fit the "team player" mold required of President Reagan's Cabinet members and whether he could accept the administration's economic theories so as to become an effective sales-

man for the president's program. Finally, there was anticipation that Regan might have problems protecting his territory from David Stockman (q.v.), the ambitious and aggressive director of the Office of Management and Budget.

But by the end of the first year it was Regan who had emerged as the loyal team player and effective spokesman. There were some rough exchanges with Congress and the Washington press corps at the start, when it appeared that he was at odds with some of the administration's goals and strategies. He was skeptical that the federal budget could be balanced by 1983 or 1984 as the president had promised.

As it turned out, Regan was right. The president admitted that achieving a balanced budget by the end of his current term in 1984 had "become an unlikelihood because of unforeseen changes," and it was revealed that Stockman had confessed to a newsman that he had little faith in the "supply-side" economic theory. And there were also signs that Regan had taken hold of the massive Treasury Department and was becoming an administration leader.

Born Dec. 21, 1918, in Cambridge, Mass., Regan was graduated from Harvard University. He served during World War II in the Marines, where he rose to the rank of lieutenant colonel. After the war he joined Merrill Lynch as an account executive. Beginning in the mid-1960s he led his firm into banking, real estate, and insurance activities. (HAL BRUNO)

Sattar, Abdus

The acting president of Bangladesh after the assassination of Pres. Ziaur Rahman on May 30, 1981, Justice Abdus Sattar was elected president by a wide margin on November 15. Sattar had been active in public life for more than 40 years in all three countries of the subcontinent, India, Pakistan, and Bangladesh. Despite failing health (he was in the hospital when Zia was killed) and old age, he quickly earned the reputation of being an able administrator as he took full control of the government machinery and kept it running smoothly and effectively during the interim period before the presidential election. His credibility in the public eye rose when he personally intervened in the settlement of a nationwide bank strike and stood up to agitators protesting the execution of the 12 condemned army officers who had led the May 30 rebellion.

Born in Bengal, India, in 1906, Sattar received his early education in Calcutta and began his career as a lawyer in the Calcutta High Court in 1941. He was elected chief executive officer of the Calcutta Corporation in 1945. After the partition of India in 1947, Sattar chose to live in East Pakistan (now Bangladesh) and resumed his legal career in Dacca. He entered politics in 1954, when he campaigned for election to the Constituent Assembly of Pakistan and won. In 1956 he was appointed minister of the interior of Pakistan. He quit his ministerial post the following year and was appointed a judge of the High Court. Subsequently he was chosen as a judge of the Supreme Court of Pakistan. Appointed chief election commissioner of Pakistan in 1969, he conducted the 1970 general election in which the pro-independence Awami League of Sheikh Mujibur

Rahman emerged as the majority party of East Pakistan, ultimately leading to the establishment of Bangladesh as an independent nation in 1971.

After independence Sattar held a number of public posts, including chairman of the wage board for journalists. He was appointed special assistant in 1975 by Pres. Abu Sadat Mohammed Sayem. After General Zia took over as president in 1977, Sattar retained his advisory post and later was appointed vice-president of the republic. Sattar actively helped Zia in drafting the new constitution of Bangladesh and played major roles in organizing the ruling Bangladesh Nationalist Party and in its eventual triumph in the parliamentary election of February 1979.   (GOVINDAN UNNY)

Scorsese, Martin

Martin Scorsese, whose *Raging Bull* brought the life of prizefighter Jake La Motta to the motion-picture screen, won the National Society of Film Critics' best director award in 1981. The film, starring Scorsese's frequent collaborator Robert DeNiro, won box-office popularity and mixed reviews.

It pursued two themes that Scorsese had explored before: raw violence and human isolation within crowded cities. "At once Scorsese's sparest and most mysterious work, it spells out his early obsessions in black and white," wrote Diane Jacobs in *Horizon* magazine. "Who could more perfectly embody violence with a mission than the ambitious boxer? Where is the impulse towards faith and love more dramatically foiled . . . than in the troubled life and career of this man?" Jacobs went on to point out that in *Raging Bull*, as in his earlier films *Mean Streets* and *Taxi Driver*, Scorsese uses his subject to explore the violence underlying the human condition. His manipulation of powerful images and his careful direction of talented performers allow him to accomplish the seemingly impossible: to make the audience feel for his brutal characters. Scorsese communicates the grim view that many of the ugliest inclinations he portrays exist to some extent in everyone.

The director, like many of his characters, was an Italian-American slum kid. Born in New York City on Nov. 17, 1942, he grew up on Manhattan's tough Lower East Side. Asthmatic, frail, and lonely, he escaped neighbourhood realities as a boy by going to the movies with his father, a garment worker. For a while he contemplated entering the priesthood, but he was expelled from a junior seminary for roughhousing and then left the church entirely after hearing a sermon praising U.S. participation in the war in Vietnam as a holy cause. He gained two degrees in filmmaking at New York University, where he also taught, and then turned his hand to documentaries, assisting in the production of *Woodstock*. Scorsese was influenced by producer Roger Corman, director John Cassavetes, and actress Ellen Burstyn, who won an Academy Award for her performance in his atypically soulful *Alice Doesn't Live Here Anymore*.
(PHILIP KOPPER)

Sendak, Maurice

The publication in 1981 of *Outside Over There*, the most recent children's book written and illustrated by Maurice Sendak, was hailed by most critics as an artistic triumph.

At the same time, it reopened the controversy surrounding Sendak's portrayal, in books for children, of possibly frightening monsters that might generate strong emotions. In *Outside Over There*, goblins steal an infant, leaving an ice-baby in her place. Ida, the baby's clever, plucky nine-year-old sister, manages to overcome her own deep fears and rescue the infant.

This latest book is actually the final volume of a trilogy that began with *Where the Wild Things Are* (1963). *Wild Things* vividly represents grotesque monsters and a child's rage at his mother. One critic warned: "It is not a book to be left where a sensitive child may come upon it at twilight." Yet a psychoanalyst argued that the book helps children deal with basic emotions. Sendak himself, in accepting the Caldecott Medal for the book, said, "The fact [is] that from their earliest years children live on familiar terms with disrupting emotions, that fear and anxiety are an intrinsic part of their everyday lives, that they continually cope with frustration as best they can. And it is through fantasy that children achieve catharsis. It is the best means they have for taming Wild Things."

The second volume of Sendak's trilogy, *In the Night Kitchen* (1970), again generated a controversy, for the young hero's nudity disturbed some parents and librarians, as did his obvious sexuality. Admirers claim that Sendak accurately presented a child's dream.

Sendak was born on June 10, 1928, in Brooklyn, N.Y. After graduating from high school, he was employed creating commercial window displays. Ursula Nordstrom, a children's book editor, commissioned his first work, illustrations for Marcel Aymé's *The Wonderful Farm* (1951). The following year his illustrations for Ruth Krauss's *A Hole Is to Dig* made him a major figure in the children's book world. In 1970 he won the prestigious Hans Christian Andersen Award for his contribution to children's literature. By 1981 Sendak had illustrated more than 80 books.

Recently, Sendak moved into new fields. "Really Rosie," an animated special for television, appeared on television in 1975. A musical version of this work, for which Sendak wrote the libretto and designed the sets, opened off Broadway in 1980. He also designed sets and costumes for the Houston (Texas) Opera's 1980 production of Mozart's *The Magic Flute* and for the New York City Opera's 1981 production of Leos Janacek's *The Cunning Little Vixen*.
(JOAN N. BOTHELL)

Sharon, Ariel

It required considerable pressure from his government, from the armed forces, and from events in general before Prime Minister Menachem Begin agreed, in the wake of his election victory of June 30, 1981, to appoint Maj. Gen. Ariel Sharon, Israel's foremost soldier-politician apart from Moshe Dayan, as the nation's new minister of defense. At 53 Sharon was 15 years younger than the prime minister and at the peak of his political activity and ambition. He was considered to be one of the two people most likely to succeed Begin, the other being Foreign Minister Yitzhak Shamir. It was understandable that the prime minister hesitated, and was encouraged to hesitate

by some of his colleagues, before succumbing to Sharon's insistent claim to the Defense Ministry. Unlike almost all other Cabinet ministers, he would be no yes-man in his new office, and he would have a considerable centre of power at his disposal.

Born in 1928, Sharon displayed aggressive abilities that were noticed early by Israel's best talent spotter and the country's first prime minister, David Ben-Gurion. Before the war of independence in 1948, Sharon became a platoon commander in the Alexandroni Brigade, a crack unit, and in his early army career he became involved in intelligence and reconnaissance work in particular. In charge of Unit 101 (1953–57), he carried out many reprisal raids across the Israeli borders and was in command of a controversial attack on Jordan in 1953. He studied law at Tel Aviv University and spent some time at the British Staff College at Camberley. Resigning from the Israeli Army in July 1973, he was recalled for the October 1973 Yom Kippur war. He spearheaded the Israeli counterattack across the Suez Canal that took the Egyptian armed forces and its commander totally by surprise and led to Egyptian Pres. Anwar as-Sadat's acceptance of a cease-fire.

Sharon was instrumental in the formation of the Likud Front in September 1973 and became a member of the Knesset (parliament) that year. He was adviser to Labour Prime Minister Yitzhak Rabin (1975–77) before joining Begin's Likud administration in 1977 as minister of agriculture in charge of settlements. He remained in that post until his appointment to the Defense Ministry.   (JON KIMCHE)

Sliwa, Curtis

Deciding that the New York City police could not always keep the streets and subways safe, a group of young people decided to have a go at it themselves. Led by Curtis Sliwa, the Guardian Angels grew to more than 1,000 who patrolled high-crime areas, especially the most notorious subway lines at night. Attracting the attention of the U.S. and Canadian press, Sliwa, 26, characterized his followers as "deterrents of crime." They were credited with a substantial number of arrests.

The group offered a sense of militant belonging to energetic youths who might otherwise join outlaw gangs. Sliwa offered the chance to perform hazardous duty for a respectable cause. Building his group from within, he insisted that candidates be recommended by members in good standing and then prove themselves as rookies on patrol. After that, a Guardian Angel typically would pull two four-hour shifts a week, riding the trains and patrolling stations. Spotting a crime in progress, they would scare off the thug, give chase, call policemen, and gather information from witnesses and victims.

A number of citizens and columnists applauded their work but predictably, perhaps, city authorities were wary of their youthful exuberance. "There's a potential for real abuse if they're overzealous," the Transit Police chief warned. When one of their number was arrested in a conflict with

BOOK OF THE YEAR

subway police, the movement got a black eye. But the shiner was on the city's face when a woman testified that the Angel was escorting her through the subway when the police officers roughed him up. Afterward, the mayor's office, which had bluntly told the self-appointed troubleshooters to become police recruits or mind their own business, took a more conciliatory view.

Meanwhile, Sliwa began to expand his organization. By the years end several other cities found themselves with their own bands of Guardian Angels. Their reception was mixed. On December 30 an Angel on patrol in Newark, N.J., was killed by a policeman who allegedly mistook him for a burglar, though Sliwa disputed the explanation. It was the first such death since the Angels were founded.   (PHILIP KOPPER)

Smith, Bailey Ezell

Is the Bible free of error? Rev. Bailey Smith thinks so, and his supporters do too. On June 9, 1981, they reelected him president of the Southern Baptist Convention for a second one-year term. Smith's moderate opponents do not subscribe to his strict code of biblical inerrancy.

Alleged anti-Semitism was a second issue that created controversy during Smith's first term as head of the Southern Baptist Convention, an organization representing 13.6 million members of 35,600 churches. While speaking before a political rally during the summer of 1980, Smith had remarked that "God Almighty does not hear the prayer of a Jew." This statement was widely reported; several Jewish leaders and organizations condemned Smith. He subsequently regretted in public that the remark had been made, but he did not retract it.

Regardless of their opinions on other matters, observers agreed that Smith was a remarkable preacher and organizer. After he took over as pastor of the First Southern Baptist Church in Del City, Okla., in 1973, membership more than doubled from 6,600 to 15,500. In 1980 First Southern performed 2,027 baptisms, more than any other Baptist church in the U.S. and the first time one church had baptized more than 2,000 in a single year. Smith's followers searched the neighbourhoods of Del City, a suburb of Oklahoma City, for new converts and never missed an opportunity to spread the Gospel.

Smith was born in Dallas, Texas, on Jan. 30, 1939. Both he and his wife were descended from Baptist ministers. He completed his undergraduate studies at Ouachita Baptist University in Arkadelphia, Ark., in 1962 and received a bachelor of divinity degree from Southwestern Baptist Theological Seminary in Fort Worth, Texas, four years later. He served churches in Warren, Ark., and Hobbs, N.M., before coming to First Southern.

(VICTOR M. CASSIDY)

Sobhuza II

The world's longest reigning monarch, King Sobhuza II of Swaziland celebrated his diamond jubilee on Sept. 4, 1981, in the presence of dignitaries from many countries. Born on July 22, 1899, he was installed as the *ngwenyama* of the Swazi nation in

1921. Although he received a modern education at the Zombodze National School and at South Africa's famous missionary-run Lovedale College, the king jealously cherished and preserved Swazi traditions. Five years after Swaziland became independent in 1968, the king tore up the Westminster-style constitution designed by the British and restored the more ancient system of government in which all effective power remains in the royal capital, while a system of village government, known as the *tinkundlu*, operates at the grass roots. His one concession to modern government was to establish a Cabinet system and a prime minister, but all ministers were chosen by the king himself.

Sobhuza's own life-style reflected a synthesis of the old and the new African; on formal state occasions he appeared in top hat and full dress, but on most other occasions he wore his traditional regalia of scarlet silk loincloth and feathers. While remaining strong in his advocacy of traditional herbal medicines, he at the same time encouraged open-heart surgery and corneal grafts.

With a kingdom wedged between white supremacist South Africa and Marxist Mozambique, Sobhuza trod a careful path to maintain good relations with both his neighbours. He was a strong supporter of the Organization of African Unity but refused to allow Swaziland to be used as a base for guerrilla attacks against South Africa. Vehemently anti-Communist, the king maintained his strong Western ties. His was among the very few African countries that maintained close diplomatic and economic ties with Israel and Taiwan.

Under the king's firm rule, Swaziland enjoyed a remarkable degree of stability and a measure of economic growth. But the question marks for the future were who among the royal princes entitled to succeed Sobhuza would be chosen and whether the successful candidate would be strong enough to continue his traditions.   (COLIN LEGUM)

Spadolini, Giovanni

In June 1981 Giovanni Spadolini became Italy's 41st premier since World War II, pledging to clean up a political scandal that surfaced as a result of revelations concerning membership in a secret Freemasons' lodge called P2. He was the first non-Christian Democrat head of government in the history of the Italian republic. His success in putting together a five-party coalition, announced on June 26, was seen as setting an important precedent in limiting the Christian Democrat Party's long power monopoly in postwar Italy.

Spadolini was a latecomer to national politics, having spent his earlier career primarily in journalism and as an academic. He had served as minister of the environment (1974–76) and of education (March–August 1979) in Christian Democrat-led coalitions before succeeding Ugo La Malfa as leader of the small but influential Republican Party in 1979. As premier, he retained his connections and professional interest as a contemporary historian as he struggled with the aftermath of the P2 affair, severe economic problems, and the continued growth of terrorist violence.

Born in Florence on June 21, 1925, Spadolini read law at the University of Flor-

ence and at the early age of 25 was appointed professor of contemporary history in the faculty of political science there. Simultaneously, he began his journalistic career, writing on politics for several newspapers. In 1955 he was given the job of editor of the Bologna newspaper *Il Resto del Carlino*; during his editorship the paper doubled its circulation. In 1968 he moved to Milan to take over editorship of the *Corriere della Sera*, which has the largest circulation in Italy. He left daily journalism in 1972, was later elected senator, and began his rapid ascent in politics.   (DAVID DOUGLAS WILLEY)

Springsteen, Bruce

By 1981 singer and songwriter Bruce Springsteen had achieved secure status as a rock 'n' roll superstar. His most recent album, *The River* (released in 1980), had been highly praised by critics and avidly purchased by his fans. The rock magazine *Rolling Stone* described the lyrics of *The River* as "filled with uncommon common sense," the singing as "unsparing," the album as "a rock and roll milestone."

During the summer of 1981 Springsteen enjoyed a highly successful concert tour in Europe, beginning with a wildly enthusiastic reception in Hamburg, West Germany, and climaxing with sold-out shows in London. The tour was followed by an appearance in Los Angeles at a rally opposing nuclear power and nuclear weapons, a cause that had engaged Springsteen in recent years.

Springsteen has often been touted as a new Bob Dylan, a reference to his abilities as a lyricist. Themes of alienation, that of individuals from one another and of workers from their jobs, recur in his songs. Cars and the nighttime, street life and death, love and the loss of love, all appear prominently in *The River*.

That album completed a trilogy that Springsteen began with *Born to Run* (1975) and continued in *Darkness on the Edge of Town* (1978). Springsteen's first commercial success, *Born to Run*, traces a day in the life of a New Jersey shore teenager, describing the urban boredom and desperation, the hours of cruising the highways.

Like the people he writes and sings of, Springsteen is a product of an urban environment. He was born on Sept. 23, 1949,

into a working-class family in Freehold, N.J., and became a largely self-taught musician, playing guitar, harmonica, and piano. His career began in New Jersey and New York nightclubs in the 1960s. Signed by Columbia Records in 1972, he had his first album, *Greetings from Asbury Park, N.J.,* released the next year. Though reviewers liked the record, its sales were slow, a pattern repeated with his second album, *The Wild, the Innocent and the E Street Shuffle,* which appeared later in 1973. However, Springsteen's live performances drew increasingly enthusiastic crowds. He achieved national recognition with the release as a single of the song "Born to Run" shortly before the album of that title appeared.   (JOAN N. BOTHELL)

Stockman, David

Even before the administration of U.S. Pres. Ronald Reagan took office, David Stockman was its most visible figure next to the president himself. As director of the Office of Management and Budget (OMB), Stockman became the "point man" in the battle of the economy, leading an uphill charge to reduce federal spending, cut taxes, and, it was hoped, balance the budget by the end of President Reagan's first term.

The ambitious plan featured a mixture of conservative fiscal ideology and "supply-side" theories. The budget and tax cuts were expected to stimulate savings and investment, resulting in economic growth, increased employment, and reduced inflation. For Stockman, implementation of the plan was an awesome challenge. He launched an all-out attack, putting in 16-hour days as the administration pushed its budget and tax cuts through Congress.

But things went wrong almost as soon as the cuts were passed. Wall Street and the financial community failed to respond with a show of confidence, as interest rates remained high and the stock market dropped. The federal deficit continued to grow, and President Reagan was forced to ask an increasingly hostile Congress for a new round of budget cuts.

Then came the revelation that, in a series of tape-recorded interviews with a newsman, Stockman had expressed his own lack of faith in some aspects of the program. He was quoted as saying that the $35 billion budget cut figure came from an "artificial" base, that Kemp-Roth (the original supply-side tax bill) "was always a Trojan horse to bring down the top [income-tax] rate," and that "the supply-side formula was the only way to get a tax policy that was really 'trickle-down.'" Stockman admitted that the administration "didn't add up all the numbers" and that the program had been put together too fast.

It was a devastating blow to the administration, providing fresh ammunition for the Democratic opposition. Stockman offered his resignation to the president. It was refused, but a much-subdued budget director came out of the Oval Office to apologize publicly and reaffirm his belief in "Reaganomics." Born Nov. 10, 1946, at Camp Hood, Texas, Stockman grew up in Michigan, was graduated from Michigan State University, and later attended the Harvard University Divinity School. In 1976 he was elected to the House of Representatives from Michigan.   (HAL BRUNO)

Takemitsu, Toru

Toru Takemitsu is a maverick in a country that often admires its nonconformists without giving them much outright encouragement. The fact that Takemitsu became Japan's leading composer without relying on traditional education was eloquent testimony to his dedication, determination, and musical genius. He trusted his ear to a degree few would dare to imitate because he was less concerned with memorable melodic lines than with timbres, textures, and relationships between sounds and silence. His creations were characteristically atmospheric and austere—sound streams with asymmetrical balance that somehow give coherence to the whole.

In 1948 Takemitsu, who was born in Tokyo on Oct. 8, 1930, began to study intermittently with Yasuji Kiyose, a composer of vocal and chamber music who drew inspiration from German Romanticism and French Impressionism as well as from Japanese folksongs. But Takemitsu was not born to be a follower. Striving to create something new, he turned to such things as improvisation, the sounds of nature, and visual effects, and he used Japanese instruments in ways that were strikingly original.

Takemitsu's first major work, *Requiem* for strings, was first performed in 1957 but was not widely appreciated until Igor Stravinsky heard and praised it several years later. In 1951 Takemitsu collaborated with other composers and artists in organizing Jikken Kobo, an experimental workshop for mixed media in Tokyo. Seven years later he joined the Institute for 20th-Century Music. His works included compositions for the piano in unconventional rhythm and no bar lines and pieces for wind instruments emphasizing their sonorities.

Takemitsu developed an interest in traditional Japanese instruments, particularly the *biwa*, which he used for the first time in 1962, when his score for the film *Seppuku* was awarded first prize at the Mainichi Music Festival. His 73 film credits include the scores for *Woman of the Dunes, Kwaidan,* and *Empire of Passion.* But it was not until his *November Steps,* a sort of double concerto for *biwa* and *shakuhachi* commissioned for the 125th anniversary of the New York Philharmonic in 1968, that Takemitsu attained true international renown. John Rockwell, writing in the *New York Times,* recognized Takemitsu's special genius when he called him "probably the best composer ever to emerge from Japan."   (BARBARA THOREN)

Tebbit, Norman Beresford

With unemployment in the U.K. totaling almost three million, the key post of secretary of state for employment was given to Norman Tebbit in the autumn government reshuffle. Tebbit had held only junior posts at the Departments of Trade and Industry, but he was highly regarded by Prime Minister Margaret Thatcher for his tough, nononsense, and often abrasive approach to industrial relations and the trade unions. He took over from the much more conciliatory James Prior the responsibility for controversial legislation designed to curb the power of the unions.

Tebbit's initial proposals for a bill to be put before Parliament in 1982 were issued as a consultative document on Nov. 23, 1981.

They included limitation of the legal immunities of unions, dismissal of strikers refusing to return to work after a set period, secret ballots on wage offers, and increased compensation for unfairly dismissed nonunion members. In December Tebbit proposed a £1,000 million scheme for the further training of school leavers unable to find work.

In Parliament in the 1970s Tebbit won a reputation as one of the most belligerent MP's in the House of Commons. As a minister he adopted a different style, calm, precise, well-briefed, efficient. Though he said, after his appointment to the Cabinet, "We want to avoid confrontation of any sort," he was as determined as ever to impose legal constraints on what he called politically motivated trade unionism. Decidedly on the right wing of the Conservative Party, he was said to express the conscience of the Tory suburbs.

Born in the North London suburb of Edmonton on March 29, 1931, Tebbit was educated at the local grammar school. He then served in the Royal Air Force, training as a pilot. After brief spells on a London newspaper and in advertising, he returned to flying. As a civil airline pilot during 1953–70, he was actively involved in the British Airline Pilots Association—the pilots' trade union. On entering Parliament in 1970 (first as MP for Epping, then, from 1974, for Chingford), he noted in *Who's Who* that his recreations were "formerly politics, now aviation." There was no doubt about his total commitment to his own hard-line version of Thatcherite conservatism.

                    (HARFORD THOMAS)

Thatcher, Margaret Hilda

Halfway through the five-year term allowed to British parliaments, the Conservative Party government headed by Prime Minister Margaret Thatcher in 1981 was deeply divided about economic policy and hardly bothered to conceal it. Thatcher's response was to dismiss or shunt aside her most outspoken critics in an autumn reshuffle of Cabinet posts and to create around her a ring of dependable Thatcherites. The argument was about the lack of success of monetarist economic policy in bringing down inflation however much it deepened the recession, and this at a time when Britain's North Sea oil production was approaching its peak.

Thatcher remained adamant. Economic policy was brought even more closely under the control of monetarists. Her critics in the Conservative Party and among businessmen who traditionally backed the party feared that the cure was killing the patient, namely, Britain's industrial base. Thatcher insisted that the squeeze was making British industry leaner and more competitive. Her critics, seeing Conservative support slide in the opinion polls, feared that the government was heading for disaster at the next general election. Thatcher, to judge by her program for the 1981–82 session of Parliament announced in November, would not change course.

All this was in keeping with the image she had cultivated as "the iron lady" for

whom there would be no U-turns. The British Cabinet system had been criticized as presidential government in disguise, but few British prime ministers had adopted such an uncompromisingly autocratic style. Yet she began to say in her speeches that she was not so inflexible as she had been made out to be.

Margaret Thatcher was Britain's first woman prime minister. She did not come from the traditional Conservative establishment but was one of a new generation of Conservative politicians who had made their way up in the world by their own efforts. Born on Oct. 13, 1925, she was the daughter of a successful grocer who became the mayor of the market town of Grantham. From the local school she made her way to the University of Oxford, where she took a degree in science. She was elected to Parliament in 1959, became minister of education and science in Edward Heath's government of 1970–74, and succeeded Heath as leader of the Conservative Party in 1975.

(HARFORD THOMAS)

Thomson, Virgil

As a gift in honour of his 85th birthday, U.S. composer Virgil Thomson was presented on Nov. 13, 1981, with a revival of his own now-classic opera entitled *Four Saints in Three Acts*. The first full-length production of this work in more than a decade was staged at Carnegie Hall by the Orchestra of Our Time.

Four Saints in Three Acts, composed to a text by Gertrude Stein, premiered in Hartford, Conn., in 1934 and later moved to Broadway. This work first brought Thomson national attention. With its theme of the religious life, the opera has as its main characters St. Teresa of Avila and St. Ignatius Loyola and the confidant of each. The composer, inspired by the musicality and clear diction he had heard in Harlem, called for an all-black cast. As with other works by Thomson, the music is often described as deceptively simple, entertaining, witty, original, and highly accessible to listeners. Its use of American musical sources—folk ballads, hymns, and other popular 19th-century tunes—is also characteristic of many of Thomson's later compositions.

In the 1930s Thomson, a pioneer in applying serious musical composition to film, composed scores for two government-sponsored documentaries, *The Plow That Broke the Plains* (1936) and *The River* (1937). His score for another motion picture, *Louisiana Story* (1948), won the composer a Pulitzer Prize.

Thomson has written in many musical forms. His first symphonic piece was *Symphony on a Hymn Tune* (1928), and he also wrote one ballet, *Filling Station* (1937).

The composer is perhaps almost as well known as a critic and writer. From 1940 to 1954 he served as the music critic for the *New York Herald Tribune*. His columns, highly acclaimed for their breadth, their insight into new musical directions, and their literary quality, have been collected in several books.

Thomson was born in Kansas City, Mo., on Nov. 25, 1896. He interrupted his studies at Harvard University to spend a year in

Paris and then returned to the U.S. to complete his degree in 1922. Three years later he went back to Paris, where he was strongly influenced by Erik Satie, and remained there until 1940. The recipient of numerous awards, Thomson was honoured in 1966 with the gold medal of the National Institute of Arts and Letters.

(JOAN N. BOTHELL)

Timerman, Jacobo

One morning in April 1977, some 20 armed men dressed as civilians invaded the apartment of Jacobo Timerman in Buenos Aires, Arg. Timerman was handcuffed, covered with a blanket, thrown into the back of his car, and taken away. Timerman, a Jew and the publisher of the newspaper *La Opinión*, was not charged with any crime. Told that he was "a prisoner of the First Army Corps in action," he was held for 30 months in solitary confinement, beaten regularly, humiliated and insulted in every possible way, and tortured with electric shock. His captors presumably wanted him to confess to treason. Timerman never did, and in 1979 international pressure secured his release. He immigrated to Israel and wrote an account of his ordeal that was published in English during the spring of 1981 under the title *Prisoner Without a Name, Cell Without a Number*.

In addition to describing his confinement and torture, the 58-year-old Timerman, who had come to Argentina as a child from his birthplace in the Ukraine, charged that Argentina was a neofascist society with no respect for human rights. He declared that he was tortured because he was Jewish and claimed that Argentina resembled Nazi Germany.

The book became a centre of controversy in the United States after Irving Kristol, a conservative political scientist, charged late in May that Timerman was imprisoned because of his association with David Graiver, a financier who allegedly served as a bagman for Argentina's leftist guerrillas, the Montoneros. Graiver had owned 45% of *La Opinión*, a fact not mentioned in Timerman's book. In response to Timerman's allegations, Jewish leaders in Argentina denied that anti-Semitism was rampant there.

The uproar continued through the summer of 1981 with more charges and countercharges. It eventually affected U.S. foreign policy, contributing to the vote against confirming Ernest W. Lefever as assistant secretary of state for human rights and humanitarian affairs in the Foreign Relations Committee of the U.S. Senate. Lefever would have favoured a low-key approach toward human rights in authoritarian countries such as Argentina.

(VICTOR M. CASSIDY)

Tinker, Grant

The turnover in television's executive suite in 1981 gave critics a field day. "Hi-ho Silverman, away!" wrote the *New Leader*'s correspondent. In a mock TV situation comedy synopsis, *Time* magazine chortled, "The Supertrain is commandeered by Freddie, a brilliant but unstable technician who rearranges the schedule, fires the porters, loses most of his passengers and nearly derails the crack RCA express." Apropos of Grant Tinker's appointment to the network's chairmanship, *Time* added, "At its current

nadir NBC may need more than a Tinker ... a tailor, soldier and spy as well."

The ballyhoo followed a comparatively stately transition. The man who had hired Fred Silverman stepped down as RCA chairman to be succeeded by Arco Oil Co. head Thornton Bradshaw. Silverman, who had run both ABC and CBS during years when they won the ratings game, asked his new boss for a vote of confidence, did not get it, and resigned. Bradshaw, who had done some quiet scouting, then told network affiliates that Tinker would be the new man for the job.

Tinker was regarded as a talented programmer with taste, imagination, and a proven knack of delegating authority to able, creative people. Born in Stamford, Conn., on Jan. 11, 1926, he attended Dartmouth College. After holding several jobs in broadcasting and advertising, he became NBC's West Coast vice-president for programming in the 1960s. He gained his first widespread acclaim as head of MTM Enterprises, which showcased his then wife, Mary Tyler Moore, in her celebrated weekly television comedy series, "The Mary Tyler Moore Show." Spin-off hits for MTM from this show included "Lou Grant" and "Rhoda." Tinker's latest critical success was "Hill Street Blues." (PHILIP KOPPER)

Tojo, Teruo

Teruo Tojo, according to the Japanese press, has the manner of an affable small-town mayor. But appearances can be deceiving. The new president and chief executive officer of Mitsubishi Motors Corp. (MMC), a subsidiary of Mitsubishi Heavy Industries (MHI), is in fact a top-flight engineer and a dynamic executive of unusual ability. His past successes include work on the YS 11, Japan's first passenger plane, and the MU 2, an executive aircraft. In his new position at MMC, Tojo was expected to further enhance his reputation, even though he was sure to face very difficult problems in very difficult times.

During 1980 MMC accounted for only 6.9% of Japan's exports to the U.S. This happened mainly because financially strapped Chrysler Corp. had been granted sole distribution rights for MMC cars marketed in the U.S. Tojo faced the problem squarely, and Chrysler agreed to let MMC operate its own U.S. dealer network until 1990. Tojo's broader goal was to develop his company's engineering capabilities while keeping an eye on future world markets.

Teruo Tojo was born in Tokyo on Sept. 23, 1914, the second son of Hideki Tojo, the man who would be serving as Japan's prime minister when the U.S. entered World War II. After graduating from Tokyo Imperial University in 1937, Tojo joined MHI to study aeronautical engineering. He became closely involved in designing the Zero fighter plane and the Hiryu heavy bomber but never served in the armed forces because of poor eyesight.

Between 1949 and 1959 Tojo designed trucks and buses for Kawasaki Machine Works. He was then picked to head the design division of Japan Aircraft Manufacturing Co. In 1971 he became director and general manager of the Nagoya Aircraft Works, which he had joined in 1963. Tojo returned to Tokyo in 1974 as managing director and general manager of MHI's aircraft

headquarters but in 1980 was named executive vice-president and director of MMC. During fiscal year 1980–81 MMC showed a net profit of $37.7 million on net sales of $5 billion. Tojo expected MMC to do a great deal better than that during his stewardship.

(BARBARA THOREN)

Torrelio Villa, Celso

Selected as the only man in Bolivia's governing military junta who was above U.S. suspicion of involvement in the drug business (ex-president Hugo Banzer Suárez and ex-president Luis García Meza Tejada's supporters had been named as firm suspects), Celso Torrelio Villa took power as Bolivia's president on Sept. 4, 1981. The U.S. reestablished diplomatic relations with Bolivia in early November.

The transfer of power was smoother than predicted, with outgoing president García Meza continuing to live in the presidential palace for some time after the changeover. Relations between the two men did not appear to be strained; indeed, the new president (born in Sucre, June 3, 1933) was widely reported to be García Meza's friend. The acceleration in Torrelio Villa's career could well have been due to García Meza's influence. It took Torrelio Villa 25 years to rise from sublieutenant to brigadier general but only seven months to win his next promotion to general of division on July 23, 1981. He was chosen to join the junta by virtue of his seniority, and his appointment as president followed from his position as senior member of that body.

President Torrelio Villa's actions in promising a return to democracy over the next three years, an increased role for foreign firms in the mining, metallurgical, and petroleum sectors, freedom from fears of nationalization, and acceptance of an International Monetary Fund presence in running the economy marked him as someone who rejected the nationalistic economic model in place in Bolivia since 1952.

(MICHAEL WOOLLER)

Valenzuela, Fernando

He looked out of place ambling to the pitcher's mound. His arms swung mechanically, his cherubic face was expressionless, and his general appearance suggested a chubby schoolboy on his way home for lunch. Not until Fernando Valenzuela began throwing baseballs was it clear that the only people lost were the batters trying to hit them.

As a 20-year-old rookie, Valenzuela kept the Los Angeles Dodgers on course in 1981 for their first World Series championship in 16 years. He was the National League's rookie of the year, and he also won the league's Cy Young award for the best pitcher. He was the *Sporting News* player of the year. He led the league with 180 strikeouts in 192 innings, allowed just 140 hits and 61 walks, won 13 games, lost 7, and had a 2.48 earned run average.

Beyond all his numbers and honours, Valenzuela gave the strike-scarred major leagues a touch of innocence and a healthy dose of good, pure baseball. He won his first eight starts, five of them shutouts, with a 0.50 earned run average. He befuddled hitters and bedazzled experts with his uncanny control of the difficult screwball and with his ability to throw his whole repertoire of pitches from the same motion, in

UPI

which he kicked high and looked straight up just before letting the ball fly.

He was a national sensation and an international treasure. Fellow Mexicans in the Los Angeles area became baseball fans simply because Valenzuela was a baseball star. Posh restaurants had to post guards at his table. Stadiums sold out 12 times for his regular-season starts; he brought the New York Mets alone an extra $310,000.

The public learned that Fernando Valenzuela was born Nov. 1, 1960, the youngest of 12 children. He grew up in a five-room house in Etchohuaquila, Mexico, a tiny farm town of 150 in the Yaqui Valley, 565 km (350 mi) south of the Arizona border. He began playing on men's baseball teams when he was 13, dropped out of high school to play baseball at 15, and signed at 17 to play for the Yucatán Leones, becoming the Mexican League's rookie of the year. Three years later the left-hander became the youngest pitcher ever to win a World Series game, rescuing the Dodgers after they had lost the first two games in the best-of-seven series.

(KEVIN M. LAMB)

Virata, Cesar

"I have to rely on people I have known quite well for a long time so that I don't just get a fair weather report." This was how Cesar Virata, the new prime minister of the Philippines, gauged public reaction to his policies. This serious-minded and conscientious approach was typical of Virata. In a career that had combined business, the academic world, and government service, he had acquired an international reputation as a meticulously honest and hard-working technocrat.

Strictly speaking, Virata was prime minister of the fourth Philippine Republic, which began formally in Manila on July 28, 1981, when the Batasan (legislature) approved the new 18-member Cabinet of Pres. Ferdinand Marcos. The fourth republic, which was modeled after the French parliamentary system, represented a return to political normality after more than eight years of martial law rule. Virata held the posts of prime minister and minister of finance concurrently, also serving as head of the Cabinet's Executive Committee,

which was expected to work closely with Marcos on day-to-day government problems.

After introducing his new Cabinet, President Marcos listed the major problems of the Philippines: overpopulation, unemployment, underemployment, poor productivity in industry and agriculture, unbalanced regional development, and excessive dependence on foreign oil. Cesar Enrique Virata y Aguinaldo had the training and experience to meet these economic challenges. Born on Dec. 12, 1930, in Manila, he earned bachelor's degrees in business administration and mechanical engineering at the University of the Philippines in 1952 and a master's degree in business administration at the University of Pennsylvania one year later. He then taught business administration at the University of the Philippines, eventually becoming a dean there. For a time he was a partner in a major Manila accounting firm. In 1965 the newly elected President Marcos invited Virata to join his transition team and to help solve problems of the rice industry. Virata performed this task and returned to the academic world, only to be summoned by Marcos once more in March 1967. Three years later he became minister of finance, a post he continued to hold in 1981.

(VICTOR M. CASSIDY)

Watt, James Gaius

During his first year as U.S. secretary of the interior, James G. Watt became a symbolic rallying point, both for the conservatives who supported him and for the conservationists who opposed him. But a negative reaction from environmental groups was expected when Pres. Ronald Reagan nominated him. Born Jan. 31, 1938, in Lusk, Wyo., and now a lawyer in Denver, Colo., Watt had been chief counsel for the Mountain States Legal Foundation, a law firm that specialized in fighting environmental restrictions in the West. He had engaged in numerous court battles against the policies of the Interior Department he was about to head. But his pro-development views were said to be in tune with the Reagan administration, and it was hoped that the furor would die down after his Senate confirmation hearing.

Instead, the storm around Watt increased in intensity, partly because of his blunt, sometimes abrasive, style. Environmental organizations that seldom agreed on anything united in opposition to him. On the other side, he became a sought-after speaker for business and industry meetings and fund-raising events for conservative causes.

Under his aggressive leadership, many of Interior's protective programs restricting development of federal lands were relaxed or dismantled. He halted the practice of allowing the federal government to preempt state water rights, planned to lease a billion acres for offshore oil and gas exploration, moved to break a congressional moratorium on development in a Montana wilderness area, eased restrictions on strip mining adjacent to national parks, and advocated a policy of rehabilitating existing national parks instead of acquiring land for new

ones. The result was a flood of lawsuits, angry demonstrations, and editorials. Environmental groups gathered more than a million signatures on petitions calling for his ouster.

His proposal to open four of California's offshore oil tracts to exploratory drilling provoked an outraged reaction from the state's Republican leaders as well as from environmentalists, and he was forced to retreat. The White House cautioned him to check before stepping into any other political minefields. But in most cases, he appeared to have administration backing, despite rumblings that he was turning into a political liability. Certainly he had become an issue in the ongoing debate over the future of the nation's natural resources.

(HAL BRUNO)

Weinberger, Caspar Willard

He is known as "Cap the Knife," and it is a sobriquet Caspar W. Weinberger worked hard to earn. Born Aug. 18, 1917, in San Francisco, he served as California's finance director under then-governor Ronald Reagan, as director of the office of Management and Budget under Pres. Richard M. Nixon, and as secretary of health, education, and welfare under Presidents Nixon and Gerald R. Ford. And in each job his budget-trimming tendencies were the talk of the bureaucracy.

When Reagan was elected president in 1980, he tabbed his old friend Weinberger to be secretary of defense in the new Republican administration. But this time Weinberger was not asked to make budget cuts. Indeed, while the rest of the federal budget was being slashed, defense expenditures in fiscal year 1982 were allowed to grow. All told, Weinberger would be presiding over the biggest spurt in military spending in at least a decade.

Still, Cap the Knife's reputation for efficiency was not entirely unneeded in the Pentagon—even a Pentagon under Reagan. Many experts in and out of government have called the Defense Department the most wasteful of federal agencies. Weinberger, like many a defense secretary before him, set out to streamline its operation. Among other things, the new secretary sought to cut down on internal budgetary paperwork and to delegate more authority to his subordinates, keeping himself free for long-range decision-making.

During his first year in office, Weinberger also found time for some internecine gamesmanship with Reagan's secretary of state (and former army general), Alexander Haig (q.v.). In public and in private the two disagreed on such matters as the U.S. role in El Salvador and the advisability of using a "demonstration" nuclear explosion to scare off an actual Soviet threat to Western Europe. By the end of the year Weinberger was receiving generally favourable comment, despite a growing feeling in Congress that defense expenditures should not be immune to the administration's budget-cutting ax. Some even said Weinberger was doing so well that he might eventually replace the uneven and abrasive Haig at State.

(STANLEY W. CLOUD)

Willoch, Kåre Isaachsen

Kåre Willoch became prime minister of Norway on Oct. 14, 1981, at the head of the country's first purely Conservative government in more than 50 years. In the general election a month earlier he had led his party to its best result since 1924. It won 54 seats in the 155-member Storting (parliament), taking votes not only from its chief opponent, the Labour Party, but also from two small non-Socialist parties with which it was pledged to form a coalition. Together the three—Conservatives, Centre (agrarian) Party, and Christian Democrats—won 80 seats, against the 69 secured by Labour and its parliamentary ally, the small Socialist Left Party. When formation of a coalition proved impossible, because of Christian Democratic demands for reform of the abortion law, Willoch agreed to form an all-Conservative minority Cabinet, relying on the Christian Democratic and Centre parties to provide parliamentary support on most issues.

The Conservatives' victory was very much a personal triumph for Willoch. In the media the election campaign had been dominated by a series of political duels between him and Gro Harlem Brundtland, prime minister of the preceding minority Labour government. Their lively exchanges made good viewing and rallied the faithful in both camps. Ignoring the substantial areas of agreement between the two major parties—on offshore oil development, for instance—the debates stressed traditional differences, such as the Conservative belief in private initiative, lower taxes, and the need to "get Norway moving again," contrasted with Labour's commitment to a regulated, caring society—the familiar concept of the Scandinavian welfare state. In a country riding on an oil prosperity boom, with more people than ever in high tax brackets, Willoch's message won the most converts.

Born in Oslo on Oct. 3, 1928, Kåre Willoch was a veteran of Norwegian politics. He was first elected to the Storting—as a proxy member—in 1953, the year that he graduated in economics from the University of Oslo. He was elected a full member in 1957 and was reelected in every subsequent contest. He served as minister of trade and shipping in Norway's first post-World War II non-Socialist coalition Cabinets (August–September 1963 and 1965–70). In 1970 he became chairman of his party's group in the Storting.

(FAY GJESTER)

Wilson, Lanford

Playwright Lanford Wilson won a Pulitzer Prize in 1980 for *Talley's Folly* and followed the triumph in 1981 with his third play about the Talley family, *A Tale Told*. If that output seemed impressive, it was typical of this new exponent of dramatic realism. By the end of 1981 he had written 34 plays. More important than sheer quantity, according to *Newsweek* magazine's Jack Kroll, "He adores and honors the language and he can shape it to the music of anguish, tenderness or nutball humor."

Born in Lebanon, Mo., April 13, 1937, Wilson grew up there and in two other Missouri towns, Springfield and Ozark. After attending Southwest Missouri State College, he left to live with his father, who had

raised a second family in California. At San Diego State College, Wilson discovered a knack for dialogue while taking a short-story course. Moving on to Chicago and a job in commercial art, he continued writing stories, which were regularly rejected by magazines. There he also discovered the excitement of theatre and tried a few scripts before going to New York City in 1962. He saw every play on Broadway and disliked each one, but he found his element in the experimental off-Broadway stage.

Caffe Cino, an off-off-Broadway establishment, was the first to stage a Wilson play: his one-act *So Long at the Fair* in the summer of 1963. The following May the same stage offered *The Madness of Lady Bright*. Like much of his work, it had autobiographical origins; the title character, Leslie Bright, was based on a desk clerk at the hotel where Wilson took reservations. More one-act plays followed, including *Sand Castle*, which Ellen Stewart presented at the celebrated Cafe La Mama. *Balm in Gilead*, Wilson's first full-length effort, opened at the Cafe La Mama in 1965 and drew such large crowds that fire officials threatened to close the little Greenwich Village house. Perhaps his best-known work, *The Hot L Baltimore*, won the Obie and New York Drama Critics' Circle awards for best play of 1973 and ran for nearly 1,200 performances at the Circle in the Square theatre.

(PHILIP KOPPER)

Zerbo, Saye

On Nov. 25, 1980, Col. Saye Zerbo, commander of the combined forces regiment in Ouagadougou, overthrew his ranking superior, Maj. Gen. Sangoulé Lamizana, president of Upper Volta since 1966, and became the country's new ruler at the head of a Military Committee of Recovery for National Progress. Born in August 1932 in Tougan, the same village as his predecessor, Zerbo was publicly rumoured to be Lamizana's cousin and, despite the latter's confinement to house arrest after the coup—which involved no loss of life—it was said that they had acted in agreement.

At the age of 18 Zerbo joined the French Army and was transferred to the armed forces of Upper Volta in 1961, a year after the country had become independent. A former parachutist, he served in Indochina and Algeria and then received advanced training at a school in Fréjus, France, that was reserved for future cadres in the armed forces of Africa and that trained many political leaders who later came to power in sub-Saharan Africa. In 1971 he entered the École Supérieure de Guerre, leaving in 1972 as the first officer from Upper Volta to gain his diploma from the school. Zerbo was appointed Upper Volta's minister of foreign affairs in 1974, but he left that post in 1976. After holding various commands he became director of the Bureau of Studies of the armed forces staff.

Speaking in December 1981 on the anniversary of the establishment of the republic in 1958, Zerbo referred to the "spectres of thirst, famine, disease, and ignorance" that the nation had to continually struggle to overcome. He said that although progress had been made, minimal needs had not yet been met, and that self-sufficiency in food would be the Military Committee's first priority.

(PHILIPPE DECRAENE)

The 1981 Nobel Prize for Peace went to the Office of the United Nations High Commissioner for Refugees, a humanitarian agency that had also won the award in 1954. Elias Canetti, a Bulgarian-born writer who lives in London, received the Prize for Literature. The economics award was given to James Tobin of Yale University. The Prize for Physiology or Medicine was shared by Roger W. Sperry of the California Institute of Technology and by David H. Hubel and Torsten N. Wiesel, both of Harvard University. All three were honoured for studies of brain organization and function. The Prize for Chemistry was shared by Roald Hoffmann of Cornell University and Kenichi Fukui of Kyoto University, Japan. They were chosen for having worked out rules that predict various chemical reactions on the basis of quantum mechanics, a set of principles that previously had mainly theoretical significance. The Prize for Physics was given to Kai Siegbahn of the University of Uppsala, Sweden, Arthur L. Schawlow of Stanford University, and Nicolaas Bloembergen of Harvard. The latter two were cited for their pioneering work in the field of laser spectroscopy. Siegbahn, the son of a 1924 Nobel laureate, was honoured for work in the related area of electron spectroscopy. The 1981 honorarium for each category amounted to $180,000.

Prize for Peace

In 1948 the UN General Assembly established the International Refugee Organization to provide legal and political protection for refugees. At that time the greatest number of refugees were Europeans displaced by World War II. Three years later the agency was renamed the Office of the United Nations High Commissioner for Refugees (UNHCR), and it won the Nobel Prize for Peace in 1954. Its selection again in 1981, one U.S. news magazine remarked, achieved the Nobel committee's prime goal: "to avoid controversy." One widely read newsweekly registered a protest by failing to mention the peace prize, though it covered all the other Nobel Prizes.

Nonetheless, Poul Hartling, former prime minister of Denmark and the current head of the UN Refugee Commission, said the award "could not have come at a better time." There are more refugees in the world today—mostly in Africa, Asia, and Latin America—than at any time since the end of World War II. During its existence, UNHCR has helped some 25 million people, but there are still about 10 million refugees throughout the world.

Hartling believes the problem is rooted in the emergence of so many new nations. Since the UN was founded, the community of nations had tripled to 154, many with totalitarian regimes. "Democracies usually will not produce refugees because a refugee by definition is a person who is persecuted for his political opinions or his race," Hartling told an interviewer.

With headquarters in Geneva and small offices scattered around the world, the UNHCR serves as an "ambassador" and domestic advocate for refugees, potential and actual. It represents people about to be exiled from their native countries, working to assure their legal rights, especially with regard to passports and exit visas. In situations where an exodus may occur, the agency often provides food, medical care, and emergency shelter. Then it tries to arrange for resettlement of displaced people. The work of the UNHCR has become more difficult in recent years because many traditional havens no longer accept refugees as readily as they once did.

Prize for Economics

James Tobin won the 1981 Nobel Memorial Prize in Economic Science for work that illuminated the practical financial behaviour of investors, consumers, and corporations. The Swedish Academy of Sciences said he has provided the "basis for understanding how subjects actually behave when they acquire different assets and incur debts." This accomplishment hardly seemed to suit a man who called himself "an ivory tower economist" when U.S. Pres. John F. Kennedy asked him to join the Council of Economic Advisers 20 years earlier.

Born in Champaign, Ill., on March 5, 1918, Tobin earned two degrees at Harvard University before World War II, then joined a naval officer training program. He served in the Navy four years, rising to second in command on the destroyer USS "Kearney." After the war he returned to Harvard to teach and take a doctorate. In 1950 he moved to Yale, where he has been a stellar member of the economics faculty, reputedly one of the finest in the nation.

Tobin, who studied with John Maynard Keynes, describes himself as a post-Keynesian in that he takes issue with some of his mentor's unresolved hypotheses and oversimplification of monetary theory. He remains within the Keynesian fold, however, in opposing the view that monetary policy, *i.e.*, control and manipulation of the money supply, is the keystone of effective economic policy. Instead, he holds that such factors as inflation and unemployment rates have a substantial effect on an economy's overall health.

One of Tobin's most significant single achievements was construction of the "portfolio selection theory." In this he demonstrated that investors rarely seek only the highest rates of return. Rather, they tend to balance high risk investments with less speculative ones that pay lower returns, in effect "hedging their bets." Another of his influential ideas involves the "Q-ratio," which measures the relationship of physical assets and their replacement costs. In practice this can be used to predict how industry will handle capital investment programs during times of high and low interest rates.

"Tobin's creative and extensive work on the analysis of financial markets and the transmission mechanisms between financial and real phenomena has unquestionably inspired substantial research during the 1970s on the effects of monetary policy, the implications of government budget deficits and stabilization policy in general," the Academy wrote. "The lively and qualified research in progress in these areas is to a large extent based on Tobin's fundamental contributions.... Few economic researchers of today could be said to have gained so many followers or exerted such influence in contemporary research."

During 1981 Tobin was one of the most outspoken critics of U.S. Pres. Ronald Reagan's economic policies and the tight-money stance adopted by the Federal Reserve Board.

Prize for Literature

"A more ideal recipient of the 1981 Nobel Prize for literature . . . would have to be invented," one magazine critic wrote of Bulgarian-born Elias Canetti. His "sensibilities, like those of last year's winner, Polish poet Czeslaw Milosz, are those of Europe's prewar culture. A polylingual resident of England, who writes in high, lapidary German, he is fashionably obscure . . . widely praised but little known."

The 1981 Nobel Prize winners (left to right): Nicolaas Bloembergen (Physics), Arthur L. Schawlow (Physics), Kai M. Siegbahn (Physics), Kenichi Fukui (Chemistry), Roald Hoffmann (Chemistry), Roger W. Sperry (Physiology or Medicine), David H. Hubel (Physiology or Medicine), Torsten N. Wiesel (Physiology or Medicine), Elias Canetti (Literature), and James Tobin (Economics).

SVENSKT/PICTORIAL PARADE

The Swedish Academy noted: "His oeuvre consists of a novel, three plays, several volumes of notes and aphorisms, a profound examination of the origin, structure and effects of mass movements, a travel book, portraits of authors, character studies and memoirs. But these writings, pursued in such different directions, are held together by a most original and vigorously profiled personality."

Perhaps Canetti's most widely celebrated work is the novel *Die Blendung* ("The Deception"), translated in England as *Auto da Fé* and in the U.S. as *Tower of Babel*. It traces the decline of a scholar haunting his book-filled apartment in Vienna, a man for whom words become the only reality when he puts the torch to his library and immolates himself. Apropos, the Academy wrote that the widely traveled author "has one native land, and that is the German language."

Canetti was born July 25, 1905, in Ruschuk, Bulg. The grandson of a Turkish merchant who knew 17 languages, Canetti first spoke Ladino, the Spanish dialect of exiled Jews. As a small boy he went to England with his parents but was educated in Zürich, Frankfurt, and Vienna, where he took a doctorate in chemistry. For a thumbnail biography he listed his interests as "anthropology, history, psychiatry, history of religions, philosophy, sociology, psychology, and the civilizations of Egypt, Sumer, Greece, Rome, Persia, India, China, Japan, Mexico, Maya, Inca. . . . It is ridiculous to have so many, but they are equally important to me."

His "magisterial work," according to the Academy, is *Crowds and Power*, a multidisciplinary study of mass movement and the search for power by individuals. Joachim Neugroschel, who won the PEN-Goethe House Award for translating Canetti, said: "His early work has a very complex syntax. But his memoirs are lucid, straightforward and animated. Even though he writes in German, it is still an acquired language for him, which possibly gives his writing a greater accuracy, variety and richness."

(PHILIP KOPPER)

Prize for Physiology or Medicine

The Nobel Prize for Physiology or Medicine was divided among three investigators of the details of the workings of the brain. Half of the prize was awarded to Roger W. Sperry of the California Institute of Technology, who was cited for his studies of "the functional specialization of the cerebral hemispheres." The other half of the prize was shared by David H. Hubel and Torsten N. Wiesel, both of the Harvard University Medical School, for their collaborative discoveries concerning "information processing in the visual system."

Neurologists have recognized for a long time that the two halves of the human brain are not interchangeable as are the kidneys or the lungs. That is, a person is not fundamentally affected by the loss of one lung or one kidney because these paired organs are simple duplicates: either can perform the task normally shared by the pair. The cerebral hemispheres, on the other hand, although they are superficially alike, have been shown to differ in their responses to perceptions of the surroundings and in the kinds of mental tasks that they undertake.

Sperry, who is regarded by some experts in his field as the world's leading authority on the brain, has developed many of the surgical and experimental techniques that are necessary in testing theories concerning distinguishable mental activities and in locating the regions where they take place. The studies leading to his Nobel Prize evolved from experiments he conducted—in the late 1940s at the University of Chicago—upon fish, in an investigation of the transfer of learning from one side of the brain to the other. Extension of this work to cats and monkeys entailed disconnecting the halves of the brain by cutting through the nerve bundles, called commissures, that make it possible for the intact animal to choose its actions by integrating the complementary but different mental processes occurring in the separate hemispheres.

In the early 1960s two neurosurgeons, Joseph Bogen and Philip Vogel, applied the nerve-cutting procedure, called commissurotomy, to a group of patients suffering from epilepsy that had been uncontrollable by all other treatments. After recovering from the operation, the patients experienced relief from their seizures and improvement of their general health; they also permitted Sperry and his co-workers to evaluate their psychological condition.

The findings conclusively showed that the left hemisphere is superior to the right in assembling logical sequences that are expressed in speech or writing. The right hemisphere is superior in recognizing faces, copying drawings, or distinguishing objects by feeling them.

Sperry, who was born in Hartford, Conn., in 1913, earned a bachelor's degree in English literature and a master's degree in psychology from Oberlin (Ohio) College and a doctorate in zoology from the University of Chicago in 1941. He then became an associate of the late Karl Lashley, first at Harvard and then at the Yerkes Laboratories of Primate Biology in Orange Park, Fla. In 1946 he joined the faculty of the University of Chicago and in 1954 moved to the California Institute of Technology as Hixon professor of psychobiology.

Hubel and Wiesel, who met when they were both associated with the Johns Hopkins Medical School, have been partners in research on the visual system of mammals since 1959, when they and the late Stephen W. Kuffler joined the faculty of the Harvard Medical School, becoming the nucleus of its department of neurobiology. One of their outstanding achievements has been the analysis of the flow of nerve impulses from the eye to the visual cortex, which is located in the occipital lobes of the cerebrum. They have used tiny electrodes to detect the electrical discharges occurring in individual nerve fibres and brain cells as the retina responds to light and the patterns of information are processed and passed along to the sensory and motor centres of the brain.

Their work has revealed many of the structural and functional details of the visual cortex. They have shown that, although many of these details are determined by genetic mechanisms that operate during prenatal development, visual experience during the first few months after birth can modify them to some extent. Their results support the view that prompt surgery is imperative in correcting certain eye defects that are detectable in newborn children.

Wiesel was born in 1924 in Uppsala, Sweden, and earned a medical degree from the Karolinska Institutet in Stockholm. After remaining there for a year as an instructor in physiology, he accepted a research appointment at the Johns Hopkins University Medical School in 1955. He moved to Harvard in 1959 and was named the Robert Winthrop professor of neurobiology. He remains a Swedish subject.

Hubel was born in 1926 in Windsor, Ont., and attended McGill University in Montreal, receiving a bachelor's degree in 1947 and a doctorate in medicine in 1951. He held positions at the Montreal Neurological Institute, at the Johns Hopkins Medical School, and at the Walter Reed Army Institute of Research in Washington, D.C., before joining the faculty of the Harvard Medical School in 1959. In 1965 he became professor of physiology and, in 1968, the George Packer Berry professor of neurobiology. He became a U.S. citizen in 1953.

Prize for Chemistry

The Nobel Prize for Chemistry was divided equally between Kenichi Fukui of Kyoto University, Japan, and Roald Hoffmann of Cornell University, Ithaca, N.Y., for their independent researches that have led to a remarkably reliable theory regarding the influence of the electronic structures of molecules on the course of reactions that they undergo.

Most of the substances of interest to chemists are composed of particles called molecules, which are stable assemblages of atoms held together by the mutual attraction of adjacent pairs of atoms or pairs of electrons. The linkages between atoms, holding them at particular distances and angles, are called covalent bonds, and chemical reactions are events in which old bonds break and new ones form. Although dozens or hundreds of covalent bonds may be present in a molecule, only a few of them are susceptible to change under ordinary circumstances, and much of the art of the experimental chemist resides in the ability to recognize these and to choose conditions that favour the breaking or formation of a covalent bond between given atoms.

The mechanisms of reactions—that is, the sequences of motions of atomic nuclei and electrons by which molecules of starting materials are converted to molecules of products—have been intensively and fruitfully studied for several decades. The reactions that have become best understood have been those in which one bond breaks or forms at one time, or those in which several such one-bond steps occur in succession.

Many reactions, however, have been observed that involve simultaneous changes in several covalent bonds. These reactions appear to be subject to driving forces different from those previously recognized; their courses and even their possibility could not be accounted for by the older theories.

The achievements of Fukui and Hoffmann are grounded in quantum mechanics, a mathematical analysis of the properties of systems of small particles. The quantum mechanical description of a molecular struc-

ture relies on the solution of a differential equation first formulated by the Austrian theoretician Erwin Schrödinger, whose accomplishment was recognized by the Nobel Prize for Physics in 1933. The Schrödinger equation takes into account the interactions among all the electrons and atomic nuclei in the molecule as well as the wave properties exhibited by these entities. The solutions of the equation, called orbitals, specify a set of energies and spatial distributions of the electrons. Exact solutions of the equation yield results in excellent agreement with experimental observations, but such solutions have been obtained only for systems of a few particles; that is, for molecules too simple to be of much interest to chemists. Approximate solutions have been developed for larger systems, however, and the orbitals of large molecules are now understood well enough to form a useful part of the chemist's methods of evaluating reactions.

In 1954 Fukui published his first exposition of the concept that the crucial process in many chemical reactions consists of an interaction between the highest occupied molecular orbital of one compound and the lowest unoccupied orbital of the other. In effect, one molecule shares its most loosely bound electrons with the other, which accepts them at the site where they can become most tightly bound. The interaction results in the formation of a new, occupied orbital that has properties intermediate between those of the two former ones. Fukui designated these labile orbitals "frontier orbitals" and provided examples of their significance in reactions that produce important classes of organic compounds.

Hoffmann undertook the research leading to his share of the prize when he and Robert B. Woodward sought an explanation of the unexpected course taken by a reaction that Woodward and his colleagues had hoped to use in the synthesis of the complicated molecule of vitamin B_{12}. Hoffmann and Woodward discovered that many reactions involving the formation or breaking of rings of atoms take courses that depend on an identifiable symmetry in the mathematical descriptions of the molecular orbitals that undergo the most change. Their theory, expressed in a set of statements now called the Woodward-Hoffmann rules, accounts for the failure of certain cyclic compounds to form from apparently appropriate starting materials, though others are readily produced; it also clarifies the geometric arrangement of the atoms in the products formed when the rings in cyclic compounds are broken.

Fukui was born in Nara Prefecture, Japan, in 1918. He took little interest in chemistry before enrolling at Kyoto University, where he studied engineering, receiving a Ph.D. in 1948. He has been professor of physical chemistry at Kyoto since 1951.

Hoffmann was born in Zloczow, Poland, in 1937 and immigrated to the U.S. in 1949. He graduated from Columbia University and received his Ph.D. from Harvard in 1962. He collaborated with Woodward at Harvard for the next three years, then joined the Cornell faculty in 1965.

Prize for Physics

The Nobel Prize for Physics was divided among three scientists who have revolutionized spectroscopy, the analytical study of the interaction of electromagnetic radiation with matter. Half of the prize was awarded to Kai M. Siegbahn of the University of Uppsala; the other half was shared by Nicolaas Bloembergen of Harvard University and Arthur L. Schawlow of Stanford University.

Siegbahn formulated the principles underlying the technique called ESCA (electron spectroscopy for chemical analysis) and refined the instruments used in carrying it out. ESCA depends on a fundamental phenomenon, the photoelectric effect, which is the emission of electrons when electromagnetic radiation strikes a material. The effect is displayed by all kinds of materials—solid, liquid, or gaseous—and is brought about by radiation of many wavelengths—visible, ultraviolet, X-rays, and gamma rays.

Einstein in 1905 postulated that the energy of the radiation that causes a material to emit an electron must be exactly equal to the sum of two other quantities of energy: the amount of energy required to detach the electron from its bound state in the material, and the kinetic energy possessed by the electron as it moves away.

The energy of the incoming radiation can be controlled very precisely; Siegbahn's achievement has been the development of ways to measure the kinetic energies of electrons accurately enough to permit the determination of their binding energies. He has shown that each chemical element binds electrons with characteristic energies that are slightly modified by the ionic or molecular environment. The compound sodium thiosulfate, for example, contains atoms of the element sulfur in two different states of combination. Irradiation of this substance with X-rays liberates electrons that had been bound with energies characteristic not only of sulfur but of its two states in the compound.

During the 1970s ESCA was adopted all over the world for analyzing materials, including the particles in polluted air and the surfaces of solid catalysts used in petroleum refining.

Siegbahn—the son of Karl Manne Siegbahn, who received the Nobel Prize for Physics in 1924 for his discoveries relating to X-ray spectroscopy—was born in Lund, Sweden, in 1918. He was awarded his Ph.D. in physics by the University of Stockholm in 1944. In 1951 he was appointed professor at the Royal Institute of Technology in Stockholm, and in 1954 he moved to the University of Uppsala.

Bloembergen and Schawlow earned their share of the Nobel Prize by investigating phenomena that are not detectable without lasers, rather than those that are obvious extensions of established spectroscopic practice.

An inherent difficulty in the measurement of wavelengths of radiation emitted or absorbed by atoms and molecules arises from the motion of these particles in all directions at the same time that they are interacting with the radiation. This motion affects the wavelength of emitted radiation in the same way that the motion of an automobile affects the pitch at which the sound of its horn reaches the ears of a stationary listener. The result of these so-called Doppler shifts is that an absorption or emission spectrum (a graph of intensity against frequency or wavelength) does not consist of a series of sharp peaks, each corresponding to a different interaction; the peaks are broadened and smeared into rounded and overlapping hills and valleys from which it is hard or impossible to pick out the desired information.

Among Schawlow's accomplishments was an ingenious demonstration of a way to circumvent the Doppler broadening and thus to locate precisely the wavelengths of light absorbed by the hydrogen atom. The results of this experiment were a set of highly precise values of the energy levels of the hydrogen atom; these, in turn, led to a new, accurate determination of one of the fundamental physical constants.

Bloembergen became involved with the fundamental principles of masers and lasers while he was engaged in his doctoral research at Harvard in the late 1940s. Within two years after Charles Townes had demonstrated the maser in 1953, Bloembergen provided the specifications for an improved version that has become the most widely used microwave amplifier.

James Clerk Maxwell in the 19th century had presented a satisfactory explanation of the nature and behaviour of electromagnetic radiation that does not appreciably alter the properties of the media through which it propagates. The electric and magnetic fields within a laser beam, however, are so intense that they affect the properties that govern the behaviour of light beams. Bloembergen and his associates have recast Maxwell's formulations to accommodate these effects, thereby establishing the theoretical basis for a new scientific specialty called nonlinear optics. Numerous practical applications of nonlinear optical phenomena have already been developed; these include means of producing laser beams of previously unavailable wavelengths, and a promising method of inducing unusual chemical reactions by focusing energy on any specific covalent bond among many in complex molecules.

Bloembergen was born in Dordrecht, Neth., in 1920 and received bachelor's and master's degrees from the University of Utrecht. In 1946 he accepted a research appointment at Harvard, where he undertook the studies for his doctorate. His Ph.D. was granted by the University of Leiden in 1948. Returning to Harvard, he became an associate professor in 1951 and Gerhard Gade university professor in 1980. He became a U.S. citizen in 1958.

Schawlow was born in Mount Vernon, N.Y., in 1921; shortly thereafter his family moved to Canada, where he attended the University of Toronto, receiving his Ph.D. in 1949. In that year he joined Townes at Columbia University in the maser-laser project that led to Townes's share of the Nobel Prize for Physics in 1964. Townes and Schawlow wrote *Microwave Spectroscopy*, a monograph published in 1955. In 1951 Shawlow went to the Bell Telephone Laboratories; after returning to Columbia as a visiting professor in 1960, he moved to Stanford. In 1978 he was appointed J. G. Jackson and C. J. Wood professor of physics.

(JOHN V. KILLHEFFER)

The following is a selected list of prominent men and women who died during 1981.

Acland, Sir (Hugh) John (Dyke), New Zealand farmer (b. Jan. 18, 1904, Christchurch, N.Z.—d. Jan. 26, 1981, Mount Peel, South Canterbury, N.Z.), was a member (1947–72) of the New Zealand Wool Board and its chairman from 1960 to 1972. He also concurrently served as vice-chairman of the International Wool Secretariat. Acland was active in local government and represented the Temuka district in the New Zealand Parliament (1942–46). He was knighted in 1968.

Albertson, Jack, U.S. actor (b. June 16, 1907, Malden, Mass.—d. Nov. 25, 1981, Hollywood Hills, Calif.), showed his versatility as an actor by garnering awards in three acting media; he won a Tony award for his Broadway performance as the surly Irish father in *The Subject Was Roses*, an Academy Award for best supporting actor in the 1968 motion picture version of the play, an Emmy award (in the 1975–76 season) for his portrayal of the disgruntled garage owner in the television series "Chico and the Man," and another Emmy for a guest appearance on the "Cher" show in 1975. A onetime pool hustler, Albertson launched his career in vaudeville, first as a dancer and then as a straight man; he later formed a partnership with Phil Silvers. Albertson gained acclaim as a comedian when he replaced Eddie Foy in the 1945 Broadway revival of *The Red Mill* and also won praise for the revue *Tickets Please!* In the 1950s and 1960s Albertson appeared in a string of motion pictures, notably *Top Banana* (1954), *Man of a Thousand Faces* (1957), *Lover Come Back* (1962), *How to Murder Your Wife* (1965), *The Flim-Flam Man* (1967), and *The Poseidon Adventure* (1972). Also in 1972 he triumphantly returned to Broadway in *The Sunshine Boys*. His last motion picture, *Dead and Buried*, was released in 1981.

Alexandrovitch, Prince Andrew, grandson of Tsar Alexander III of Russia (b. Jan. 25, 1897, St. Petersburg [now Leningrad], Russia—d. May 8, 1981, Provender, Kent, England), narrowly escaped death after the Russian Revolution and was freed by German troops shortly before the World War I armistice. He fled to Paris with his father, Grand Duke Alexander Mikhailovitch, and later joined the rest of the family in Britain. As the nephew of Nicholas II, Prince Andrew became head of the exiled Russian imperial family; during his exile he devoted himself to painting and stamp collecting.

Alice, Princess (Alice Mary Victoria Augusta Pauline), COUNTESS OF ATHLONE, member of the British royal family (b. Feb. 25, 1883, Windsor, England—d. Jan. 3, 1981, London, England), was the last survivor of Queen Victoria's 37 grandchildren. Married in 1904 to Prince Alexander of Teck, she became countess of Athlone when he abandoned his German title. She accompanied her husband on his many travels, including those undertaken as governor-general of South Africa (1923–31) and of Canada (1940–46). Her adaptability, unaffected manner, and unfailing cheerfulness contributed greatly to her husband's success in these posts. Though she fulfilled fewer public engagements after his death in 1957, she served as chancellor of the University of the West Indies from 1950 to 1971. In 1966 she published her memoirs, *For My Grandchildren*.

Amory, Derick Heathcoat Amory, 1ST VISCOUNT, British politician (b. Dec. 26, 1899, Tiverton, Devon, England—d. Jan. 20, 1981, Tiverton), was chancellor of the Exchequer (1958–60) in the Conservative government of Harold Macmillan. Amory entered national politics after World War II, being elected Conservative member for Tiverton in 1945. In 1951 he was appointed minister for pensions and subsequently served as minister of state at the Board of Trade (1953–54) and as minister of agriculture, fisheries, and food (1955–58). In January 1958, when the three Treasury ministers simultaneously resigned, Macmillan offered Amory the chancellorship. Self-effacing and moderate, he initiated no major changes in economic strategy. Amory was created a viscount when he retired from politics in 1960 and then served (1961–63) as U.K. high commissioner in Canada.

Ansett, Sir Reginald Myles, Australian aviation pioneer (b. Feb. 13, 1909, Inglewood, Victoria, Australia—d. Dec. 23, 1981), founded Ansett Airways Ltd. (later Ansett Transport Industries Ltd.) in 1936 and built it into one of the major airlines in Australia. Ansett was educated at Swinburne Technical College, Victoria, and, starting with one £A50 car, built up a taxi fleet in western Victoria. He also learned to fly, and when local transport regulations prevented him from extending his taxi business to Melbourne, he bought a small monoplane to carry up to six passengers. Ansett's air transport business expanded rapidly, and by 1957 he was able to purchase Australian National Airways for over £A3 million. His other business interests included hotels, television, and road transport. Ansett was knighted in 1969. In 1979 his company was taken over by newspaper proprietor Rupert Murdoch.

Astaire, Adele Marie (ADELE MARIE AUSTERLITZ), U.S. dancer and actress (b. Sept. 10, 1898, Omaha, Neb.—d. Jan. 25, 1981, Phoenix, Ariz.), with her brother, Fred, became theatrical sensations in the U.S. and England in the early part of the century, dancing in a series of 11 musical comedies. When she was only nine, Astaire toured the vaudeville circuit with seven-year-old Fred as her partner. In 1917 they appeared on Broadway in their first hit, *Over the Top,* followed by *The Passing Show of 1918.* A pixieish comedian, Astaire was a natural for such shows as *Funny Face, Lady Be Good, Smiles, For Goodness Sake,* and *The Band Wagon.* In 1931, at the height of her career, Astaire gave up dancing to marry Lord Charles Cavendish the following year. Three years after Lord Charles's death in 1944, she married investment banker Kingman Douglass, whom she also survived.

Asther, Nils, Swedish actor (b. Jan. 17, 1897, Malmö, Sweden—d. Oct. 13, 1981, Stockholm, Sweden), was one of Hollywood's leading actors during the late 1920s and early 1930s, playing opposite Greta Garbo in *Wild Orchids* (1929) and *The Single Standard* (1929). Asther, who made films in Germany before moving to the U.S. (1926) to work with the director Mauritz Stiller, also appeared in *Our Dancing Daughters* (1928) and *The Bitter Tea of General Yen* (1932). In 1934, however, his career was irreparably damaged when he was blacklisted for breach of contract. He moved to London, then returned to Hollywood in 1938 but failed to achieve his former success. Asther lived in poverty and in 1958 went back to Sweden, where he worked for television. He then took up painting and sculpture after his retirement from acting.

Auchinleck, Sir Claude (John Eyre), British field marshal (b. June 21, 1884, Aldershot, England—d. March 23, 1981, Marrakesh, Morocco), defeated Gen. Erwin Rommel's better-armed forces at Cyrenaica, Libya, in 1941 and, though he was subsequently forced to retreat, helped to minimize

British losses and pave the way for victory against the Germans in North Africa. Educated at Sandhurst, Auchinleck served in India and performed with distinction in the Middle East in World War I. He returned to India to command the Peshawar Brigade against the Upper Mohmands in 1933 and by the outbreak of World War II had been appointed deputy chief of the general staff at army headquarters. He commanded British forces in Norway and India until his 1941 appointment to the Middle East, where he replaced Sir Archibald Wavell as commander in chief. After his defeat of Rommel, Auchinleck was replaced because of his questionable defensive strategy. It was not until 1943 that he was given his next major command, again as commander in chief in India. He was promoted to field marshal in 1946 and as supreme commander in India administered the splitting of the Indian Army following the creation of Pakistan. In November 1947 he resigned in open disagreement with the Indian leaders. He frequently returned to the country after his retirement, however, to maintain business connections.

Bagnold, Enid, British writer (b. Oct. 27, 1889, Rochester, England—d. March 31, 1981, London, England), wrote *National Velvet* (1935), the best-selling story of a horse-loving girl who trains and rides a gelding to victory in the Grand National Steeplechase; in 1944 the novel was made into a successful film starring Elizabeth Taylor. This charming fantasy, however, revealed only one facet of a talent that also produced the play *The Chalk Garden* (published 1956), a study of eccentricity, neurosis, and love, praised for its wit and fine language. Bagnold's *Autobiography* (1969) tells of her youthful experiences in bohemian Chelsea and her service as a nurse and ambulance driver in World War I. She also recorded her wartime adventures

in such controversial books as *Diary Without Dates* (1918) and *The Happy Foreigner* (1920). Her novel *Serena Blandish* (1924), subtitled *The Difficulty of Getting Married,* was published anonymously after her marriage in 1920 to Sir Roderick Jones, chairman of Reuters news agency.

Bahonar, Mohammad Javad, Iranian politician (b. 1933, Kerman, Iran—d. Aug. 30, 1981, Teheran, Iran), succeeded Ayatollah Mohammad Hossein Beheshti, who died in an explosion in June 1981, as a leader of the Islamic Republican Party. Bahonar had been imprisoned for his opposition to the shah's regime, but after the overthrow of the shah in 1979, he helped draft the new constitution. In March 1981 he was appointed minister of education and carried on the work started by Mohammad Ali Raja'i in purging the universities of Western cultural influences. After the fall of Pres. Abolhassan Bani-Sadr in June 1981 and Raja'i's election as president in July, Bahonar was appointed prime minister. He was in the midst of trying to restore stability to the country in the face of armed attacks by opponents of the Islamic regime when he and Raja'i were killed in a bomb blast.

Baird, Tadeusz, Polish composer (b. July 26, 1928, Grodzisk Mazowiecki, Poland—d. Aug. 4, 1981, Warsaw, Poland), was a leader of the younger generation of Polish composers. Baird was a pupil of Boleslaw Woytowicz and Kazimierz Sikorski during World War II and later of Piotr Rytek and Piotr Perkowski at the Warsaw Music Conservatory. With Jan Krenz and Kazimierz Serocki, Baird formed "Group 49," whose members adhered to the then ideologically acceptable line of "socialist realism." Baird's later compositions owed more to Western influence. His *Four Essays for Orchestra* won first prize both at the 1958 Grzegorz Fitelberg Competition in Katowice and at the 1959 International UNESCO Composers' Rostrum in Paris. Baird became a professor at the Warsaw State Higher School of Music in 1974 and also was a founder, with Serocki, of the annual Warsaw Autumn Festival.

Baldwin, Roger Nash, U.S. civil rights activist (b. Jan. 21, 1884, Wellesley, Mass.—d. Aug. 26, 1981, Ridgewood, N.J.), was the founder with Norman Thomas, Felix Frankfurter, and others (1920) of the American Civil Liberties Union (ACLU) and a tireless crusader for individual rights guaranteed in the U.S. Constitution and Bill of Rights. Because of this commitment, Baldwin defended a host of extremist groups including Nazis, Communists, and Ku Klux Klansmen and was labeled a leftist himself. During Baldwin's tenure as head of the ACLU, the organization acquired such clients as teacher John T. Scopes in the 1925 Tennessee "Monkey Trial"; the Jehovah's Witnesses, which won free press rights in 1938; James Joyce, who had the ban lifted from his novel *Ulysses;* and Henry Ford, who was granted the right to distribute antiunion pamphlets. The ACLU also took part in the murder trial of Sacco and Vanzetti and successfully challenged (1938 and 1939) Mayor Frank Hague's interference with civil liberties and the CIO in Jersey City. In 1940, though, Baldwin became disenchanted with the Communists and removed them from the ACLU's board of directors; he was also instrumental in ousting his longtime Communist friend Elizabeth Gurley Flynn from the board of directors when she refused to resign. Before his affiliation with the ACLU, Baldwin received a B.A. from Harvard University in 1904 and an M.A. in 1905 and taught sociology at Washington University in St. Louis, Mo. He also served (1907–10) the city as chief probation officer and produced a book with Bernard Flexner, *Juvenile Courts and Probation* (1912), which became a standard work. In 1917 Baldwin became head of the American Union Against Militarism (predecessor of the ACLU), which mostly defended draft resisters and conscientious objectors. The following year Baldwin was sentenced to a year in prison for refusing to go to war. After his release he founded the ACLU and was, for the remainder of his life, in the vanguard of thousands of cases involving the underdog and the oppressed. For many years Baldwin taught at the University of Puerto Rico. In 1981 Pres. Jimmy Carter presented Baldwin with the nation's highest civilian honour, the Medal of Freedom.

Barber, Samuel, U.S. composer (b. March 9, 1910, West Chester, Pa.—d. Jan. 23, 1981, New York, N.Y.), achieved early and lasting fame with his lyric and romantic compositions, including the orchestral piece *Adagio for Strings* (1936) and two Pulitzer Prize-winning works, the opera *Vanessa* (1958) and *Piano Concerto* (1962). At the age of seven Barber composed his first piece, "Sadness," and at ten he attempted his first opera, entitled *The Rose Tree.* In 1924 he entered the Curtis Institute of Music in Philadelphia to study composition with Rosario Scalero, singing with Emilio de Gogorza, and piano with Isabella Vengerova. While still a student he wrote *Serenade for String Quartet* (1929), *Dover Beach* (1931), and his Overture to *The School for Scandal* (1933), which established his reputation after it was given a world premiere by the Philadelphia Orchestra under Alexander Smallens. His virtuosity was given further testimony by the renowned Italian conductor Arturo Toscanini, who in 1938 conducted world premieres of two of Barber's compositions: *Adagio for Strings* and his first *Essay for Orchestra.* Inducted into the U.S. Army in 1943, Barber was soon transferred to the Army Air Forces and commissioned to write the Second Symphony (1944). In this work Barber used a special electronic instrument to imitate radio signals for air navigation; his 1947 revised version substituted an E-flat clarinet. Barber, virtually all of whose works have been recorded, also composed *Violin Concerto* (1941), *Cello Concerto* (1946), and *Piano Sonata* (1949). His admiration for 19th-century poets Percy Bysshe Shelley and Gerard Manley Hopkins and such latter-day authors as James Joyce and James Agee inspired such works as *Music for a Scene from Shelley* (1933), "A Nun Takes the Veil" (1937), *Fadograph of a Yestern Scene* (1971), and *Knoxville: Summer of 1915* (1947).

Barnetson, William Denholm, BARON, British newspaper executive (b. March 21, 1917, Edinburgh, Scotland—d. March 12, 1981, London, England), who, after becoming chairman of United Newspapers Ltd. in 1966, was responsible for the group's rapid expansion and the acquisition of *The Yorkshire Post* and *Punch* in 1969. Barnetson interrupted his studies at the University of Edinburgh to cover the Spanish Civil War as a free-lance writer. After World War II he helped reorganize the West German newspaper industry, launching *Die Welt* in 1946. From 1948 to 1961 he held journalistic and management posts with the *Edinburgh Evening News* and was active in many allied fields, including television. Barnetson was named chairman of Thames Television Ltd. in 1979. Earlier he had chaired Reuters news agency (1968–79), the Press Association (1967–68), the Commonwealth Press Union Council (1972–77), and *The Observer's* governing board (1976–80). Knighted in 1972, Barnetson became a life peer in 1975.

Barnett, Stephen Frank, British veterinarian (b. Aug. 10, 1915—d. Aug. 18, 1981, Cambridge, England), made important contributions to the understanding of tick-borne diseases in livestock and hence to the control of such diseases and the improvement of tropical agriculture. He was particularly noted for his work on East Coast fever, a protozoan disease of cattle, and he acted as adviser to many countries in Africa, South America, and the Middle East. Barnett studied at the Royal Veterinary College in London and in 1939 joined the Kenya Department of Veterinary Services. After obtaining his doctorate at the University of London in 1947 he continued his research in Chicago and East Africa before becoming university lecturer in animal pathology at the University of Cambridge in 1964.

Barr, Alfred Hamilton, Jr., U.S. museum curator (b. Jan. 28, 1902, Detroit, Mich.—d. Aug. 15, 1981, Salisbury, Conn.), as the enterprising director (1929–43) of the Museum of Modern Art (MOMA) in New York City, expanded the realm of the traditional museum to include departments of architecture, education, industrial design, and photography, as well as sculpture and painting. An unqualified showman, Barr freely experimented with a gamut of exhibitions that included such impressive displays as "Picasso, 50 Years of His Art" (1946) and "Matisse: His Art and His Public" (1951). His unconventional and innovative exhibitions, which included a fur-lined teacup, a gasoline pump, an oval wheel, and an elaborate shoeshine stand, created an uproar, and the latter nearly cost him his job. As director, Barr expanded the public awareness of what art is and set forth a model for other museums to emulate. He also established MOMA as one of the most influential museums for modern art information and education in the world. A highly respected tastemaker and connoisseur of modern art, Barr nonetheless had a dictatorial manner that was resented by museum colleagues, who dubbed him "The Pope." In 1943 Barr was replaced as director but in 1947 was named director of collections, a post he held until his retirement in 1967.

Barrington, Kenneth Frank, British cricketer (b. Nov. 24, 1930, Reading, England—d. March 14, 1981, Bridgetown, Barbados), was one of Britain's most reliable post-World War II batsmen and an energetic manager of touring teams. Because Barrington was a serious player and remained aloof from the spectators, he was sometimes criticized for unexciting play. But in his first-class career for Surrey and England he scored a total of 31,714 runs (an average of 45.63), including 6,806 runs in Test cricket (an average of 58.67 in 82 matches). Only two players exceeded his 20 centuries in play for England. His Test career, cut short by a heart attack in 1968, started in 1955 when he toured South Africa, and by 1959 he was recognized as one of the most consistent and reliable batsmen on the English team. He made his highest score, 256 runs, against Australia in 1964. After his retirement he managed tours to India, Pakistan, and New Zealand, and he was assistant manager of the England team on its West Indies tour at the time of his death.

Beheshti, Ayatollah Mohammad Hossein, Iranian politician (b. 1929, Isfahan, Iran—d. June 28, 1981, Teheran, Iran), was leader of the Islamic Republican Party (IRP) and was killed in an explosion at the party headquarters together with 71 other participants during a meeting. Beheshti, who on Feb. 3, 1979, was appointed a member of Iran's Islamic Revolutionary Council by Ayatollah Ruhollah Khomeini, soon became the council's first secretary. In the Majlis (parliament) inaugurated on May 28, 1980, Beheshti led the religiously oriented IRP, the most important parliamentary group. A key figure in Iran's Islamic revolution, Beheshti was reputed to be a cunning manipulator behind the scenes. He played a leading part in the U.S. hostage crisis and was instrumental in the dismissal in June 1981 of Abolhassan Bani-Sadr, first president of the Islamic Republic.

Benchley, Nathaniel Goddard, U.S. novelist (b. Nov. 13, 1915, Newton, Mass.—d. Dec. 14, 1981, Boston, Mass.), was overshadowed by the celebrity status of his father, Robert, a well-known novelist and humorist, and his son Peter, the author of the best-seller *Jaws,* but was himself a highly talented writer and humorist for over 40 years. Benchley, the author of several acclaimed children's books, also wrote novels that combined elements of satire, comedy, farce, and melodrama. His most popular book, *The Off-Islanders,* was later adapted for the screen with the title *The Russians Are Coming, the Russians Are Coming* (1966). Other writings include *Side Street* (1950), *Catch a Falling Spy* (1963), *The Visitors* (1965), *The Hunter's Moon* (1972), and two biographies, *Robert Benchley* (1955) and *Humphrey Bogart* (1975).

Bennett, Robert Russell, U.S. composer and conductor (b. June 15, 1894, Kansas City, Mo.—d.

Aug. 18, 1981, New York, N.Y.), as the fluent orchestrator of some 300 Broadway musicals, repeatedly demonstrated his uncanny ability to assemble a musical number from memory after seeing it rehearsed only a few times. Bennett's impressive list of credits included orchestrations for such Broadway productions as *Annie Get Your Gun; Kiss Me, Kate; Show Boat; South Pacific; Oklahoma!; My Fair Lady; The King and I;* and *The Sound of Music.* He also scored such motion pictures as *The Hunchback of Notre Dame, Show Boat,* and *Oklahoma!,* for which he won an Academy Award in 1955. He also orchestrated Richard Rodgers's music for the 26-episode television series "Victory at Sea." Bennett, who studied under Carl Busch, also composed serious music, conducted symphony orchestras, and served as musical director of the National Broadcasting Co.

Berryman, Sir Frank Horton, Australian Army officer (b. April 11, 1894, Geelong, Victoria, Australia—d. May 28, 1981, Sydney, Australia), was the senior Australian staff officer in the southwest Pacific during World War II and represented Australia at the Japanese surrender on Sept. 2, 1945. He had previously shown considerable ability as a field commander in the Middle East and New Guinea. Berryman studied at Sydney University and at the Royal Military College, Duntroon, before gaining the DSO during World War I. He continued his military training during the interwar period and held various appointments in Australia. During World War II Berryman was promoted to lieutenant general (1944) and served as general officer commanding, I Australian Army Corps. He was awarded the U.S. Medal of Freedom with Silver Palm for his services with the Allied forces under Gen. Douglas MacArthur. After serving as general officer in charge of the Australian Eastern Command during 1946–50 and 1952–53, he directed the Commonwealth jubilee celebrations and the 1954 royal visit to Australia. Berryman, who was knighted the same year he retired (1954), became a director (1954–61) of the Royal Agriculture Society, Sydney, and a colonel commandant of the Royal Australian Artillery (1956–61).

Betancourt, Rómulo, Venezuelan politician (b. Feb. 22, 1908, Guatiré, Miranda, Venezuela—d. Sept. 28, 1981, New York, N.Y.), was a self-proclaimed leftist and anti-Communist who helped restore Venezuela to democracy while twice serving as its president (1945–48 and 1959–64). As a student at the University of Caracas, Betancourt led demonstrations against the dictatorial regime of Juan Vicente Gómez, for which he was jailed and then exiled. He was a member of the Communist Party in Costa Rica for a short time before secretly returning to Venezuela in 1936. He lived in hiding for two years until he was apprehended and again expelled. In 1941 Betancourt was allowed to reenter the country, and in the same year he helped found Acción Democrática, a left-wing anti-Communist party. In 1945 the party came to power after a bloody coup that ousted Gen. Medina Angarita, and Betancourt was installed as president. Although he resigned his presidential office in 1948, another coup ousted his successor and again forced Betancourt into a ten-year exile. He directed the activities of his outlawed party from the U.S., Cuba, Costa Rica, and Puerto Rico, and when Gen. Marcos Pérez Jiménez was overthrown in 1959, Betancourt returned to his homeland. In the same year his party won an absolute majority in Congress, and Betancourt was elected president. During his tenure Betancourt inaugurated agrarian reform, pushed industrial development, and approved the 50–50 formula that gave Venezuela half the profits of the oil companies. In 1964 Betancourt left office as poor as when he was elected and spent the next eight years in Switzerland. In 1972 he returned to Venezuela as an elder statesman and a champion of democracy.

Bliss, Ray Charles, U.S. politician (b. Dec. 16, 1907, Akron, Ohio—d. Aug. 6, 1981, Akron), diligently worked behind the scenes to reinforce the strength of the Republican Party as both Ohio state chairman (1949–65) and national chairman (1952–69) of the party. Bliss effectively demonstrated his organizational skills as state chairman by systematically investigating every complaint; under his leadership the Republicans outscored the Democrats in three of four presidential races and congressional and state elections. In 1965, as head of the Republican National Committee, he helped restructure the fragmented party after the decisive defeat of Barry Goldwater by Lyndon B. Johnson in the 1964 presidential election. Bliss also contributed to the presidential victory of Richard M. Nixon, who later replaced Bliss with Rogers C. B. Morton in 1969. Bliss retired from his seat on the Republican National Committee in 1980.

Böhm, Karl, Austrian conductor (b. Aug. 28, 1894, Graz, Austria—d. Aug. 14, 1981, Salzburg, Austria), established his international reputation after World War II as a conductor of opera and symphonic works with his concert performances and recordings of Richard Strauss, Beethoven, Brahms, Alban Berg, and, above all, Mozart, whose work was the great love of his musical life. He studied law, but in 1920 he was appointed first conductor at the Graz Opera House and in the following year joined the Munich Opera. Encouraged by Karl Muck and Bruno Walter, Böhm became musical director at Darmstadt in 1927, at Hamburg in 1931, and at Dresden in 1934, replacing Fritz Busch, who had been forced to resign by the Nazis. This appointment and his replacement of Bruno Walter at Salzburg in 1938 under similar circumstances damaged his reputation in the postwar years. Böhm directed the State Opera in Vienna from 1943 to 1945 and from 1954 to 1956. In the following year he conducted at the Metropolitan Opera in New York and from 1962 was perhaps the best-known interpreter of Wagner through his work at the Bayreuth Festivals. He was dedicated to the search for precision, and his rigorous interpretations were sometimes criticized for their lack of vision, but his best qualities emerged in his recordings of Strauss and Wagner and at performances of their operas, to which he brought warmth, subtlety, and lyricism.

Boone, Richard Allen, U.S. actor and director (b. June 18, 1917, Los Angeles, Calif.—d. Jan. 10, 1981, St. Augustine, Fla.), portrayed Paladin, a onetime army officer who became a San Francisco-based professional gunslinger during the 1870s in the classic television Western "Have Gun—Will Travel" (1957–63). Garbed in black and armed with a Colt .45, he sold his services to those who were unable to protect themselves. Boone also starred in the television shows "Medic" (1954–56), "The Richard Boone Show" (1963–64), and "Hec Ramsey" (1971–72). After Boone made his motion picture debut in *The Halls of Montezuma* (1951), his craggy face became familiar in such films as *The Desert Fox* (1951), *Ten Wanted Men* (1955), *Big Jake* (1971), and *The Shootist* (1976).

Boyle of Handsworth, Edward Charles Gurney Boyle, BARON, British politician (b. Aug. 31, 1923, Kent, England—d. Sept. 28, 1981, Leeds, England), was minister of education in the Conservative government from 1962 to 1964 and a leading representative of the liberal wing of the Conservative Party. Educated at Eton College and the University of Oxford, Boyle worked in journalism while attempting to enter Parliament. He succeeded in 1950 as member for Handsworth and in 1955 became economic secretary to the Treasury. He was parliamentary secretary (1957–59) to the minister of education, then financial secretary to the Treasury. As minister of education, he steered a middle course between those who favoured retention of the grammar school system with traditional selection and curriculum and supporters of the comprehensive school. Boyle set up the Plowden inquiry into primary education in 1963. In the following year he was made minister of state with special responsibility for higher education and became opposition spokesman on home affairs, then on education after the Conservative defeat in the 1964

election. He fell out with the right wing of the party over his support for an incomes policy and his liberal attitudes to immigration. Boyle, who became director of Penguin Books in 1965, was made a life peer in 1970 and in 1971 was appointed chairman of the Top Salaries Review Board.

Bradford, The Rev. Robert John, Northern Irish Methodist clergyman and politician (b. 1941?—d. Nov. 14, 1981, Belfast, Northern Ireland), had served as Unionist member of the U.K. Parliament for seven years when he was assassinated by militants of the Irish Republican Army (IRA). A known opponent of any conciliatory moves toward the IRA, a supporter of more vigorous security measures in Northern Ireland, and a proponent of the death penalty for terrorist activities, Bradford was engaged at the time of his death in a campaign to discredit the IRA in the eyes of its U.S. supporters. Educated at Queen's University, Belfast, he was ordained a Methodist minister and first stood for the Northern Ireland Assembly in 1973. In the general election of 1974 he was elected to Parliament as United Ulster Unionist Coalition member for Belfast South. Expelled from the party as a supporter of power sharing, he came to revise this view and in 1975 joined the Official Unionist Party, retaining the seat for it in 1979. He was a leading member of the Orange Order and a close friend of the Rev. Ian Paisley, who shared Bradford's opposition to the ecumenical movement. He also advocated extreme conservative policies in social matters, such as opposition to the recent reform of the laws on homosexuality.

Bradley, Omar Nelson, U.S. Army officer (b. Feb. 12, 1893, Clark, Mo.—d. April 8, 1981, New York, N.Y.), graduated from West Point in 1915 but never saw a day of action on the battlefield until 1943, when he was appointed deputy commander of the U.S. II Corps in Tunisia under Gen. George S. Patton and Gen. Dwight D. Eisenhower. His lack of combat experience was countered by methodical textbook planning, and Bradley soon led U.S. armies through some of the bloodiest fighting of World War II. He quickly established a reputation as a brilliant tactician after the defeat of the Germans' Afrika Korps and the invasion of Sicily. He further enhanced his record as commander of the U.S. 1st Army in the D-Day invasion of German-occupied Normandy on June 6, 1944. Bradley's folksy demeanour and dedication to avoiding risky tactics made him a favourite with infantrymen, who dubbed him the "GI's general." He favoured calculated assaults using bombers, tanks, and field guns to protect the infantrymen. Later in 1944 Bradley was named commander of the U.S. 12th Army Group, which included 1.3 million troops—the largest U.S. force ever placed under one man's command. After the Allies' near defeat at the Battle of the Bulge (1945), Bradley led his troops across the Rhine River, through the heart of Ger-

UPI

many (where they captured 325,000 German prisoners), and on to the joining of U.S. and Soviet troops at the port city of Torgau on the Elbe River. In 1945, after the war, Bradley was appointed head of the Veterans Administration, and in 1949 he became first chairman of the Joint Chiefs of Staff. In this post Bradley received a fifth star with his promotion to the rank of general of the army. This distinction had been held by only four other men since the Civil War: George Marshall, Douglas MacArthur, Henry H. Arnold, and Dwight D. Eisenhower. Bradley, who served as chairman of the Bulova Watch Co. from 1958 to 1973, never formally retired from the Army because a congressional act stipulated that all five-star generals are subject to immediate recall. He thus served 69 years on active duty—longer than any other soldier in U.S. history.

Brassens, Georges, French singer and songwriter (b. Oct. 22, 1921, Sète, France—d. Oct. 30, 1981, Sète), held a unique place in the affections of the French public and, during a career of nearly 30 years, had more than 20 million long-playing records sold. His songs, which won the poetry prize of the Académie Française in 1967, belonged to a tradition reaching back to the medieval jongleurs. They combined bawdy humour, tenderness, and contempt for the self-importance of bigots and authority figures. After arriving in Paris in 1940, he worked in the Renault car factory and was conscripted for war work in Germany. Brassens deserted but was given refuge by a couple, to whom he dedicated many of his songs. In 1952 Brassens was discovered by Jacques Grello and made his debut in a nightclub owned by the singer Patachou. His warm voice and emphatic guitar accompaniment were heard at the Olympia, the Alhambra, and the Palais de Chaillot, but he was at his best in his regular appearances in the unpretentious surroundings of the Bobino music hall. Brassens's only motion picture role was in René Clair's *Porte des lilas* (1957). He also published poems and a novel, *La Tour des miracles* (1953).

Breit, Gregory, Russian-born physicist (b. July 14, 1899, Nikolayev, Russia—d. Sept. 13, 1981, Salem, Ore.), was a highly esteemed theoretical physicist who, in 1942, joined the Manhattan Project in Chicago and began making designs for an atomic bomb. Although Breit resigned from the project to embark on ballistics research at the Aberdeen Proving Ground, Md., his expertise was needed again some seven years later when scientists feared that an explosion of a hydrogen bomb might set off a worldwide chain reaction. Breit's calculations discounted this theory, and he backed up his conclusion with tests using a new cyclotron at Oak Ridge (Tenn.) National Laboratories. He was also credited with helping to develop the resonance theory of nuclear reactions and with contributing to the first "atom smashers." For the latter he was awarded a National Medal of Science in 1967. During his long career Breit taught at the University of Minnesota (1923–24), was a physicist in the department of terrestrial magnetism at Carnegie Institution (1924–29), and was professor at New York University (1929–34), the University of Wisconsin (1934–47), Yale University (1937–68), and the State University of New York at Buffalo (1968–73).

Breuer, Marcel (Lajos), Hungarian-born architect and designer (b. May 21, 1902, Pécs, Hung.—d. July 1, 1981, New York, N.Y.), was instrumental in creating modern furniture and building designs that were indicative of a technological age. Breuer was a leading exponent of the International Style, which was characterized by the use of open space and utilized reinforced concrete construction. From 1920 to 1928 he studied and then taught at the famous Bauhaus school of design. Under the tutelage of its master, Walter Gropius, Breuer designed prefabricated housing and modular furniture. In 1925, inspired by the shape of bicycle handlebars, he fashioned his classic Wassily chair, which featured leather straps slung across a tubular steel frame. In 1928 Breuer set up his own architectural firm in Berlin and created the Cesca chair, a tubular

steel dining chair with a cane back and seat. During this time he completed two outstanding projects: the Harnischmacher House (1932) in Weisbaden, Germany, and the Dolderthal Apartments (1934–36) in Zürich, Switz. Breuer then worked for a brief period in London with the architect F. R. S. Yorke. He designed some laminated plywood furniture that became widely imitated. In 1937 Breuer accepted a teaching position at Harvard University's School of Architecture and joined his old associate Walter Gropius. Together with Gropius he designed a series of wood-frame houses that combined elements of the International Style and American materials, resulting in a light, boxlike structure similar to many of his earlier European projects. Examples of this style were Breuer's house at Lincoln, Mass. (1939), and the Chamberlain cottage, Wayland, Mass. (1940). After his move to New York in 1946, Breuer's work became more heavy and sculptural. Some of his major commissions included the Sarah Lawrence College Theatre, Bronxville, N.Y. (1952); UNESCO Headquarters, Paris (1953–58; with Pier Luigi Nervi and Bernard Zehrfuss); St. John's Abbey, Collegeville, Minn. (1953–61); De Bijenkorf department store, Rotterdam, Neth. (1955–57); the IBM research centre, La Gaude, Var, France (1960–62); the Whitney Museum of American Art, New York City (completed 1966); and the headquarters for the Department of Housing and Urban Development (HUD), Washington, D.C. (1963–68). Among his numerous awards and tributes, Breuer received the coveted gold medal of the American Institute of Architects in 1968, and in 1976 he received the gold medal of the French Académie d'Architecture. He retired in the same year.

Brown, Christy, Irish writer (b. June 5, 1932, Dublin, Irish Free State—d. Sept. 7, 1981, Parbrook, Somerset, England), overcame virtually total paralysis to become a successful novelist and poet. Brown was born with cerebral palsy that left him unable to control any of his limbs except his left foot. His mother, who had 12 other children, refused to have him confined to an institution and taught him to read and, using his only viable limb, to write and eventually to type. In 1954 he published his highly successful autobiography, *My Left Foot*, and in 1970 the best-selling *Down All the Days*. Thanks mainly to the devoted care of his mother and his wife, Mary, whom he married in 1972, and to his own determination, his speech and muscular control improved. He published *A Shadow of Summer* in 1974 and *Wild Grow the Lilies* two years later. His last novel, *A Promising Career*, was due to appear in 1982.

Burn, Joshua Harold, British pharmacologist (b. March 6, 1892, Barnard Castle, England—d. July 13, 1981, Oxford, England), was professor of pharmacology at the University of Oxford (1937–59), the author of many standard works on the subject, and a pioneer in research into the measurement of vitamins and hormones. Burn studied at the University of Cambridge and, after service during World War I, finished his studies at Guy's Hospital. He joined the Medical Research Council in 1920. In 1925 he became director of the Pharmacological Laboratories of the Pharmaceutical Society, heading an important research team. He was elected fellow of the Royal Society in 1942 and in 1979 became the first recipient of the British Pharmacological Society's Wellcome Gold Medal.

Butler, Reg (REGINALD COTTERELL BUTLER), British sculptor (b. April 28, 1913, Buntingford, Hertfordshire, England—d. Oct. 23, 1981, Berkhamstead, Hertfordshire, England), gained notoriety in 1953 with his prizewinning entry in an international competition for a monument to "The Unknown Political Prisoner." The work, a semiabstract construction, was greeted with bewilderment by the public, and there was parliamentary opposition to a proposal that it should be sited on the Dover cliffs. The model was defaced in the Tate Gallery by a Hungarian refugee. Butler, who trained as an architect, taught at the Architectural Association School from 1937 to 1939. As a conscientious objector during World War II, Butler worked as a blacksmith, gained considerable experience in

metalworking techniques, and began making forged iron sculptures. After holding his first exhibition in 1949, he produced two metal sculptures for the 1951 Festival of Britain and represented Britain at the 1952 Venice Biennale. In the mid-1950s he returned to modeling and produced a series of studies of figures in space that are among his best work. His later works include painted bronzes.

Cargill, Sir (Ian) Peter Macgillivray, British administrator (b. Sept. 29, 1915, India—d. July 10, 1981, London, England), as senior vice-president (1974–80) of the World Bank was particularly associated with development aid to the Indian subcontinent. Cargill was educated at the University of Oxford and in 1938 entered the Indian Civil Service. He joined the World Bank in 1952, became director of its Asian departments in 1961, and in 1974 became vice-president in charge of finance. As senior vice-president he was responsible for coordinating the work of the bank's vice-presidents and departmental directors. This administrative task grew to immense proportions as the bank continued to increase its aid and commitments to the less developed countries. Cargill was knighted in 1981.

Carmichael, Hoagy (HOAGLAND HOWARD CARMICHAEL), U.S. composer and actor (b. Nov. 22, 1899, Bloomington, Ind.—d. Dec. 27, 1981, Rancho Mirage, Calif.), was a floundering lawyer before he found his niche as the songwriter of the smash hit "Stardust" and such others as "Lazy River," "Georgia on My Mind," "Old Buttermilk Sky," "Skylark," and "Lazybones." While studying for his law degree Carmichael associated with jazz cornetist Bix Beiderbecke, who greatly influenced his style. Carmichael's first composition, "Riverboat Shuffle," was recorded by Beiderbecke and the Wolverines in 1924 and became a jazz classic. In 1927 Carmichael wrote "Washboard Blues," but it was not until "Stardust" was recorded (1930) by Isham Jones's orchestra that his songs were in demand. Other favourites include "Rockin' Chair," "The Nearness of You," "Two Sleepy People," "Memphis in June," "I Get Along Without You Very Well," and "In the Cool, Cool, Cool of the Evening," for which he won an Academy Award in 1951. The self-taught pianist and singer then embarked on a highly successful acting career and was featured in such films as *To Have and Have Not, Johnny Angel, Young Man with a Horn, The Best Years of Our Lives,* and *Canyon Passage.*

Caroe, Sir Olaf Kirkpatrick, British administrator (b. Nov. 15, 1892—d. Nov. 23, 1981, Steyning, Sussex, England), was serving as governor of the North-West Frontier Province in 1946–47 during the difficult period preceding the transfer of British power in India. Educated at the University of Oxford, he served in the Army during World War I before commencing a distinguished career in the Indian Civil Service. Caroe became a recognized expert on the Indian Ocean region and on the Middle East and published such valuable works of political analysis as *Wells of Power* (1951) and *The Soviet Empire* (1952). As governor of the North-West Frontier, he aroused opposition by proposing to hold a referendum to decide the fate of the region; he resigned his post as a guarantee of non-interference while voting took place. The province voted to join Pakistan.

Chagla, Mohomedali Currim, Indian official (b. Sept. 30, 1900, Bombay, India—d. Feb. 9, 1981, Bombay), was dedicated to preserving Indian civil liberties; while serving under Prime Minister Indira Gandhi in 1966–67 he became highly critical of her increasingly authoritarian government. A respected liberal lawyer and jurist, Chagla was chief justice of the Bombay High Court from 1947 to 1958 and a judge to the International Court of Justice at The Hague from 1957 to 1960. He served as ambassador to the U.S., Cuba, and Mexico from 1958

to 1961 and was high commissioner to Britain and ambassador to Ireland from 1962 to 1963. Chagla then became minister of education (1963–66), leader of the Indian delegation to the UN Security Council during the debates on Kashmir (1964–65), and minister for external affairs (1966–67). In 1978 he received a National UNESCO Award for Distinguished Service to Human Rights.

Chambers, Sir (Stanley) Paul, British economist and industrialist (b. April 2, 1904—d. Dec. 23, 1981, London, England), as chairman (1960–68) of Imperial Chemical Industries Ltd. (ICI), Britain's largest industrial group, helped the company to expand into Europe and the U.S. and made an unsuccessful bid to acquire the textile group Courtaulds Ltd. Chambers also became known for his outspoken views on British economic policy. He was educated at the London School of Economics and after graduating in 1928 joined the Inland Revenue and served as secretary and commissioner of its board until he joined ICI in 1947. In the following year he was made finance director and in 1952 deputy chairman. As chairman from 1960 he reorganized the structure of the company but failed in his much-publicized bid for Courtaulds. The latter was a serious blow to his prestige; however, he served on several government committees and in 1967 formed the Industrial Policy Group to study the problems of the British economy. After his retirement from ICI, he became treasurer of the Open University and prochancellor of the University of Kent. Chambers was knighted in 1965.

Chapin, Harry, U.S. singer and songwriter (b. Dec. 7, 1942, New York, N.Y.—d. July 16, 1981, Long Island, N.Y.), by combining elements of folksinging and rock, devised his own "story songs" describing lost opportunities, cruel twists of fate, and disappointments in love. In 1972 his ballad "Taxi" hit the top of the record charts. Other hits included "Cat's in the Cradle," "WOLD," and "Sniper." Chapin, a persistent social activist, gave benefit concerts to raise money for a variety of causes and organizations. He raised thousands of dollars for the Performing Arts Foundation of Long Island, for the Multiple Sclerosis Foundation, for environmental and consumer causes, and for a campaign to combat world hunger. In 1979 Pres. Jimmy Carter named Chapin a commissioner on the Presidential Council on World Hunger. Chapin was killed when his car was hit from behind by a truck.

Chavanon, Christian, French lawyer and administrator (b. March 12, 1913, Pontivy, Morbihan, France—d. June 6, 1981, Neuilly, France), was honorary vice-president of the French Council of State (the administrative supreme court, which advises the government on the drafting of bills and orders) from 1979 to 1981. Trained as a lawyer, he practiced in Bordeaux until 1941. Chavanon then held various administrative posts in government as a legal adviser until becoming director of the Société Nationale des Entreprises de Presse (1953–55). In 1958 Gen. Charles de Gaulle appointed him director general of radio, and in 1961 he became director of the Agence Havas news agency. Chavanon then became (1973) head of the financial section of the Council of State. He was a skillful politician, known for his acid tongue and his ability to survive despite changes of regime.

Chayefsky, Paddy (SIDNEY STYCHEVSKY), U.S. playwright and screenwriter (b. Jan. 29, 1923, New York, N.Y.—d. Aug. 1, 1981, New York), was first heralded for his sensitive television play "Marty," a heartwarming story about a fat lonely butcher and his courtship of a plain schoolteacher; he later adapted "Marty" (1955) for the screen and won his first Academy Award for scriptwriting. Chayefsky received two other Academy Awards for scriptwriting for the frenetic satiric films *Hospital* (1971) and *Network* (1976). The pervasive theme in Chayefsky's plays and scripts is of people "caught in the decline of their society." Besides his plays

UPI

for television, including "The Catered Affair" and "The Bachelor Party," Chayefsky had three Broadway hits: *Middle of the Night, The Tenth Man,* and *Gideon.* After *The Passion of Joseph D.* flopped, Chayefsky rejected Broadway and embarked on a highly successful screenwriting career. His achievements include *The Goddess* (1958), *The Americanization of Emily* (1964), *Ice Station Zebra* (1967), *Paint Your Wagon* (1969), and his last, *Altered States* (1979).

Clair, René (RENÉ CHOMETTE), French film director (b. Nov. 11, 1898, Paris, France—d. March 15, 1981, Neuilly, France), was a noted experimental filmmaker (*Paris qui dort,* 1923; *Un Chapeau de paille d'Italie,* 1927) who made the transition to sound with the delightful musical *Sous les toits de Paris* (1930). Its sentimental charm, its delight in his native city, and its concern for the lives of ordinary people also characterized his best works: *Le Million* (1931), *À nous la liberté* (1932), and *Quatorze Juillet* (1932). There was much of the same verve in *The Ghost Goes West* (1935), made in England, but his exile in Hollywood during the 1940s took him outside his true milieu, and the films he made there, including *I Married a Witch* (1942) and *It Happened Tomorrow* (1943), lacked the unaffected gaiety of his earlier work. *Les Grandes Manoeuvres* (1955), *Porte des lilas* (1957), and *Tout l'Or du monde* (1961), made after his return to France in 1946, struck a more sombre note. By the mid-1960s the France he celebrated had vanished, and the cinema was dominated by a "new wave" of directors. In 1960 Clair became the first filmmaker to be elected to the Académie Française.

Cockburn, Claud, British journalist and humorist (b. April 12, 1904, Peking, China—d. Dec. 15, 1981, Cork, Ireland), founded the newssheet *The Week* in 1933 and established his reputation as the irreverent gadfly of British journalism. *The Week,* which frequently risked prosecution for libel under the Official Secrets Act, circulated among policymakers throughout the world and provided a mixture of rumour and fact not available elsewhere. Cockburn came from a distinguished Scottish family and was the son of a consular official in China. He was educated at Kebel College, Oxford, and joined the staff of *The Times* in 1929 but resigned in 1932 to devote himself to left-wing politics. He joined the Communist Party, fought in the Spanish Civil War, and reported for the *Daily Worker.* In 1946 he ceased to edit *The Week* and became a free-lance writer for such publications as *Punch* and *Private Eye.* He also wrote an autobiography, *I, Claud* (1967), and several other books including *Reporter in Spain* (1936), *Nine Bald Men* (1956), *Bestseller* (1972), *Jericho Road* (1974), and *Union Power* (1976).

Cohen, Albert, Swiss writer (b. Aug. 16, 1895, Corfu, Greece—d. Oct. 17, 1981, Geneva, Switz.), remained relatively unknown until the publication in

1968 of *Belle du seigneur,* which won the Grand Prix of the Académie Française. A massive, Rabelaisian work, it developed the themes of his earlier novels, *Solal* (1930) and *Mangeclous* (1938). Cohen, whose parents emigrated to France while he was still a child, studied law and in 1922 joined the International Labour Office in Geneva, where he spent his working life. His small literary output also included *Le Livre de ma mère* (1954) and *Les Valeureux* (1969), originally intended as part of *Belle du seigneur* but published separately. Although Cohen was an atheist who claimed to venerate God, he was profoundly conscious of his Jewish background and in 1927 founded *La Revue juive,* contributors to which included Einstein and Freud.

Coia, Jack (IACOMO ANTONIO COIA), Scottish architect (b. July 17, 1898, Wolverhampton, England—d. Aug. 14, 1981, Glasgow, Scotland), as senior partner in the firm of Gillespie, Kidd and Coia was noted in particular for his designs of Roman Catholic churches in or near his home town of Glasgow. They included St. Columba's, Mayhill, built in 1937, St. Bride's, East Kilbride (1964), and Our Lady of Good Counsel, Dennistoun (1966). His work was remarkable for its uncompromising application of plain brickwork and modern styles to the design of communal buildings. Coia trained at the Glasgow School of Architecture, and after qualifying in 1924, he went abroad. In 1927 he returned to Glasgow to set up practice. His firm also designed schools, housing projects in Cumbernauld and East Kilbride, St. Peter's College, Cardross, housing for the University of Hull, and Robinson College, Cambridge. Coia was president of the Glasgow Institute of Architects and the Royal Incorporation of Architects in Scotland. A fellow of the Royal Institute of British Architects from 1941, he was awarded the Royal Gold Medal for Architecture in 1969.

Cole, "Cozy" (WILLIAM RANDOLPH COLE), U.S. jazz musician (b. Oct. 17, 1909, East Orange, N.J.—d. Jan. 29, 1981, Columbus, Ohio), was a versatile jazz percussionist whose drumming career was highlighted by the 1958 hit "Topsy," the only drum solo ever to sell more than one million records. After making his recording debut (1930) with Jelly Roll Morton, Cole performed with several major bands, including Stuff Smith's comedy jazz group. In 1938 he joined Cab Calloway's band, and his drumming was featured on "Crescendo in Drums," "Paradiddle," and "Ratamacue." Cole became one of the first black musicians on a network musical staff when he was hired (1942) by CBS radio to play with Raymond Scott's orchestra. In the next year he appeared in the Broadway musical *Carmen Jones* doing "Beat Out Dat Rhythm on a Drum" and later played with Benny Goodman's Quintet in

WIDE WORLD

Seven Lively Arts (1945), another musical. From 1949 to 1953 he toured with Louis Armstrong's All Stars and in the late 1950s was a regular at the Metropole in New York City. In 1962 the U.S. Department of State sent Cole and his band on a tour of Africa. After playing in the quintet of trumpeter Jonah Jones (1969–76), Cole became artist in residence and student lecturer at Capital University in Columbus, Ohio.

Coon, Carleton S(tevens), U.S. anthropologist and archaeologist (b. June 23, 1904, Wakefield, Mass.—d. June 3, 1981, Gloucester, Mass.), often conducted anthropological studies in conjunction with archaeological investigations and was the author of the highly controversial work *Origin of Races* (1962). In 1949 Coon unearthed approximately 31,000 agricultural artifacts, some dated at about 6050 BC, while exploring Belt Cave in northern Iran. Two years later Coon returned to Iran and excavated Hotu Cave, which contained thick rock deposits that revealed an unbroken cultural sequence encompassing the Iron Age, Bronze Age, and New Stone Age. Beneath a layer of rock that had fallen from the ceiling of the cave, Coon found layers of sand and gravel from the last glacial period. Ninety-three metres (39 ft) down he discovered the fossilized bones of human beings. These findings culminated in the publication of *The Story of Man* (1954), which traced the history of man 50,000 years from the Ice Age to modern times. Coon set forth the controversial theory that five distinct major races of man existed before the emergence of *Homo sapiens* as the dominant species. This theory was disputed and then largely ignored by scientists. Coon, who received both undergraduate and graduate degrees from Harvard University, spoke ten languages, including some used by the tribes he studied. He taught anthropology at his alma mater before becoming professor of anthropology at the University of Pennsylvania and curator of ethnology at the University Museum in Philadelphia in 1948. Coon was a prolific writer, and some of his other notable works included: *Tribes of the Rif* (1931), *The Races of Europe* (1939), *A Reader in General Anthropology* (1948), and *The Seven Caves* (1957). His autobiography, *Adventures and Discoveries*, was to be published posthumously.

Coper, Hans, German-born potter (b. April 8, 1920, Germany—d. June 16, 1981, Somerset, England), was a dominant figure in European pottery and perpetuated a purely European tradition free from the influence of Oriental ceramics of the style produced by Bernard Leach and his school. Coper studied engineering in Germany before turning to painting and sculpture. He then went to Britain and, inspired by Lucie Rie, he turned to pottery, producing work that was sculptural and sometimes figurative. Coper taught at the Camberwell School of Art and Crafts and the Royal College of Art, influencing many students of ceramics. In 1969 the Victoria and Albert Museum chose him as the first living potter to become the subject of a major exhibition.

Corbett Ashby, Dame Margery (Irene), British women's rights pioneer (b. April 19, 1882, Sussex, England—d. May 15, 1981, Horsted Keynes, Sussex, England), was a founding member of the International Alliance of Women in 1904 and its honorary president from 1946. She also edited the *International Women's News*. The daughter of C. H. Corbett, a classical scholar and Liberal member of Parliament, Corbett Ashby studied classics at Newnham College, Cambridge, then entered the struggle for women's rights. She traveled extensively, spoke several languages, and was particularly active in the less developed countries. After World War I she helped to form a women's police service in Germany and to found the British Townswomen's Guilds; in 1932 she was an alternate delegate to the Disarmament Conference. She was twice chairman of the National Union of Women's Suffrage Societies. Corbett Ashby had a doctorate of laws degree from the University of St. Andrews and was made Dame Commander of the Order of the British Empire in 1967. Though never elected to Parliament, she stood as a Liberal candidate and was president of the Women's Liberal Federation.

Corcoran, Thomas Gardiner, U.S. lawyer and government official (b. Dec. 29, 1900, Pawtucket, R.I.—d. Dec. 6, 1981, Washington, D.C.), was an influential lawyer who was instrumental in funneling much of Pres. Franklin D. Roosevelt's New Deal legislation through Congress and helped write the Securities Act of 1933, the Securities Exchange Act of 1934, and the Fair Labor Standards Act of 1938. Corcoran, who was dubbed "Tommy the Cork" by Roosevelt, graduated at the head of his class at Harvard University Law School. After practicing law for five years, he was appointed (1932) by Pres. Herbert Hoover as counsel to the newly formed Reconstruction Finance Corporation in Washington. After Hoover's defeat by Roosevelt, Corcoran strengthened his role in the government and the White House and was made assistant to the secretary of the treasury. Corcoran was also a key figure in Roosevelt's failed attempt to add six more justices to the U.S. Supreme Court and to defeat certain members of Congress in the 1938 election. Corcoran's power-broker tactics eventually earned him the enmity of Congress, which thwarted his appointment to a high government post in 1941. Frustrated in his efforts to advance, Corcoran reentered private law practice in 1941 and successfully represented major businesses and defense contractors.

Corner, George Washington, U.S. anatomist and embryologist (b. Dec. 12, 1889, Baltimore, Md.—d. Sept. 28, 1981, Huntsville, Ala.), specialized in analyzing the function of hormones in the female reproductive system and, with Willard M. Allen, identified the hormone progesterone, an ingredient used in oral contraceptives. Their findings led to the development of birth control pills, many of which contain a mixture of a synthetic progestational agent and a small amount of estrogen. Corner received (1913) his M.D. from Johns Hopkins University and taught there and at the University of California until 1923. He then served (1923–40) as professor of anatomy at the University of Rochester School of Medicine, director (1940–55) of the department of embryology at the Carnegie Institution in Washington, historian (1955–60) of the Rockefeller Institute, and executive officer (1960–77) of the American Philosophical Society in Philadelphia.

Cronin, A(rchibald) J(oseph), Scottish physician and novelist (b. July 19, 1896, Cardross, Dumbartonshire, Scotland—d. Jan. 6, 1981, Glion, Switz.), attracted a huge readership during the 1930s and 1940s with a series of novels that combined social realism with a touch of romance, an element of melodrama, and a dash of social criticism. Cronin,

who was forced to abandon his career as a physician in a Welsh mining village because of ill health, published a wealth of novels that were later adapted for the screen. These include: *Hatter's Castle* (1931, filmed 1941); *The Stars Look Down* (1935, filmed 1939); *The Citadel* (1937, filmed 1938); and one of his most popular, *The Keys of the Kingdom* (1942, filmed 1944), the story of a Roman Catholic priest sent to China as a missionary. After publishing his autobiography, *Adventures in Two Worlds*, in 1952, Cronin drew on his experiences as a doctor to create episodes for the television and radio series "Dr. Finley's Casebook."

Crowther, Bosley (FRANCIS BOSLEY CROWTHER, JR.), U.S. journalist and film critic (b. July 13, 1905, Lutherville, Md.—d. March 7, 1981, Mount Kisco, N.Y.), penned some 200 incisive film reviews each year for the *New York Times* as its influential film critic from 1940 to 1967. Crowther served as a general reporter (1928–32), assistant drama editor (1932–37), and assistant screen editor (1937–40) before being named screen editor and film critic in 1940. Aware that his critiques were often decisive in making or breaking the careers of screenwriters, actors, and directors, Crowther always weighed his words carefully to present what he considered an honest and objective evaluation of any performance he reviewed. He personally preferred films with a social message and, though he vigorously opposed film censorship, he strongly criticized motion pictures containing brutal violence. He was also the author of such books as *The Lion's Share: The Story of an Entertainment Empire* (1957), *Hollywood Rajah: The Life and Times of Louis B. Mayer* (1960), *The Great Films: Fifty Golden Years of Motion Pictures* (1967), *Vintage Films* (1977), and *Reruns* (1978).

Curran, Joseph Edward, U.S. labour leader (b. March 1, 1906, New York, N.Y.—d. Aug. 14, 1981, Boca Raton, Fla.), was the feisty founder (1937) and longtime president (1937–73) of the National Maritime Union (NMU). Curran, who had only a seventh-grade education, held a variety of jobs before going to sea at age 16. He worked as an able seaman and boatswain before becoming the ringleader in a 1936 strike by East Coast seamen who were protesting an agreement by the International Seaman's Union (ISU) and the shipowners to give West Coast seamen $5 more per month than their counterparts on the East Coast. The dispute cost Curran his job and precipitated a ten-week strike by East Coast seamen, who wanted the fired seamen reinstated. Curran was then installed as chairman of the Seaman's Defense Committee, a rank-and-file strikers' group. In October a second strike erupted and beached 50,000 seamen and 300 ships. In 1937 the committee declared itself a union and attracted 30,000 members from the ISU. As president of the NMU Curran bolstered the union with 100,000 members and secured hefty pay raises for its members. However, he was often criticized for supporting left-wing causes, for allowing Communist infiltration into the union, and for flaunting his generous union salary. He became a vice-president of the CIO in 1940 and of the AFL-CIO in 1955. Curran retired in 1973 with a pension totaling $1 million after choosing his successor, Shannon J. Wall.

Darlington, Cyril Dean, British biologist (b. Dec. 19, 1903, Chorley, England—d. March 26, 1981, England), was Sherardian professor of botany at the University of Oxford (1953–71) and the author of remarkable and sometimes controversial works on human population and genetics. The first of these, *Recent Advances in Cytology* (1932), virtually established nuclear cytology as a scientific discipline. It appeared while Darlington was a member of the staff at the John Innes Horticultural Institution, which he had joined in 1923. He also served as director there from 1939 to 1953. His second major book, *The Evolution of Genetic Systems* (1939), adopted a still broader perspective in its study of population and evolution and had a far-reaching effect on the

development of biological ideas. In 1969 Darlington published *The Evolution of Man and Society*, a wide-ranging synthesis of human genetics and cultural history in which the author drew controversial political conclusions from his study of the role of genetic variations. A fellow of the Royal Society from 1941 and recipient of its Royal Medal in 1946, he was president of the Genetical Society (1943–46) and a foreign member of the Italian Accademia Nazionale dei Lincei and the Royal Danish Academy of Sciences and Letters.

Davis, Jim, U.S. actor (b. Aug. 26, 1915, Edgerton, Mo.—d. April 26, 1981, Northridge, Calif.), portrayed Jock Ewing, the tough, gravel-voiced patriarch of the oil-rich Ewing family on "Dallas," the top-rated U.S. television series. Davis appeared in more than 150 films, including *Strange Cargo, Little Big Horn,* and *The Parallax View,* and in such television shows as the "Maisie" series with Ann Sothern, "Rescue 8," "The Cowboys," and "Streets of San Francisco." It was his gruff characterization of Jock Ewing, though, that catapulted him to stardom. Because producers felt that Davis had made the role of Ewing uniquely his own, no plans were made to recast his part.

Dayan, Moshe, Israeli soldier and statesman (b. May 20, 1915, Degania Alef, Palestine—d. Oct. 16, 1981, Tel Aviv, Israel), was a charismatic figure in Israel's public life and at the time of the 1967 Six-Day War became a symbol of the nation's victory over its Arab adversaries. He was twice minister of defense (1967; 1969–74) and was foreign minister in Menachem Begin's Cabinet from 1977 until his resignation in 1979. As a youth Dayan trained in the Haganah, a Jewish volunteer defense force, and in 1937 served with British Capt. Orde Wingate's night patrols against Arab raiders. In 1939 he was sentenced to ten years' imprisonment for membership in the Haganah (declared illegal by the British mandatory authorities) but in 1941 was released for service in the British forces. While leading a Jewish company against the Vichy French in Syria, Dayan lost his left eye and thereafter wore the black patch that became a distinguishing mark. He remained an intelligence officer with the Haganah until 1948 and commanded the Jerusalem area during Israel's war of independence. In 1953 Dayan was appointed chief of staff of the Israeli Army. In this capacity he engineered the plan for the invasion of Sinai, which he brilliantly executed in 1956 in collusion with the British and the French during the ill-fated Suez adventure. After retiring from military service in 1958 he joined the Mapai (the labour party), was elected to the Knesset (parliament) in 1959, and became minister of agricul-

ture under Prime Minister David Ben-Gurion. When Levi Eshkol became prime minister, Dayan resigned, and in 1965 he joined Ben-Gurion in leaving Mapai and in forming the Rafi Party. In June 1967, when the threat of Arab aggression was acute, Eshkol appointed Dayan minister of defense. Dayan's collaboration with Maj. Gen. Itzhak Rabin then led to Israel's overwhelming victory in the Six-Day War. Six years later, when Egypt and Syria unexpectedly attacked Israel on Oct. 6, 1973 (Yom Kippur), Dayan was pilloried for the country's lack of preparedness. When Rabin succeeded Golda Meir as prime minister in June 1974, he dropped Dayan from the Cabinet. Four years later, as Begin's foreign minister, Dayan became one of the chief architects of the Camp David accords. Then, angered by Begin's plan to assert Israeli sovereignty over the occupied West Bank area, legally still part of Jordan, he resigned in October 1979. In 1981 he formed a new party, Telem, which advocated unilateral Israeli disengagement from the territories occupied in the 1967 war.

Dean, Paul ("DAFFY"), U.S. baseball player (b. Aug. 14, 1913, Lucas, Ark.—d. March 17, 1981, Springdale, Ark.), together with his brother "Dizzy" Dean pitched for the St. Louis Cardinals when they won the 1934 World Series championship. The legendary Gashouse Gang won the championship in seven games with brothers Paul and Dizzy winning two games each against the Detroit Tigers. During his first two years (1934 and 1935) with the Cardinals, Dean won 19 games each year and pitched a no-hitter against the Brooklyn Dodgers. But his career was cut short when he developed an arm injury in 1936 and was traded to the New York Giants after the 1939 season. His career record included 50 wins, 34 losses, and an earned run average of 3.75.

De Banzie, Brenda, British actress (b. *c.* 1916, Manchester, England—d. March 5, 1981), was ideally cast as Phoebe Rice in the original production of John Osborne's play *The Entertainer* (1957); this role proved to be the climax of her distinguished theatrical career. De Banzie had previously made her name as the star of musical comedies during the 1940s and in Christopher Fry's *Venus Observed* (1950), playing opposite Laurence Olivier. In the same year she appeared in Jean Anouilh's *Point of Departure* and starred in several other successful London and New York productions before joining Olivier in *The Entertainer*. De Banzie also appeared in films for British and Canadian television.

de Graff, Robert F(air), U.S. publisher (b. June 9, 1895, Plainfield, N.J.—d. Nov. 1, 1981, Mill Neck, N.Y.), marketed the first 25-cent paperback books in the U.S. as the enterprising founder of Pocket Books in 1939. De Graff launched his venture with backing from two publishers, Richard L. Simon and M. Lincoln Schuster, and with about 10,000 copies each of ten best-selling books, including *Lost Horizon, Wuthering Heights,* and *The Bridge of San Luis Rey*. The remarkable reception of his paperback books stunned publishers who had insisted that the public would refuse to buy them. When de Graff left Pocket Books in 1957, its annual sales were $15 million.

Delbrück, Max, German-born molecular biologist (b. Sept. 4, 1906, Berlin, Germany—d. March 9, 1981, Pasadena, Calif.), with Alfred D. Hershey and Salvador E. Luria won the 1969 Nobel Prize for Physiology or Medicine for research and discoveries on bacteriophages (viruses that infect bacteria). After Delbrück earned his Ph.D. in physics at the University of Göttingen in 1930, he worked with Otto Hahn and Lise Meitner just prior to their discovery and investigation of uranium fission. While serving as a research assistant at the Kaiser Wilhelm Institute for Chemistry in Berlin (1932–37), Delbrück became interested in molecular genetics and the manner in which complex molecular systems can replicate themselves identically. He began his pioneering work on bacteriophages while on the faculties of the California Institute of Technology (1937–39) and Vanderbilt University

(1940–47). Through a key experiment in 1939, he discovered a one-step process for growing bacteriophages in bacterial cells by which new virus particles would be formed and the cell would die. Delbrück and Hershey also discovered that the genetic material of different kinds of viruses can combine to create new and different types of viruses. In 1947 Delbrück returned to the California Institute of Technology, where he was professor of biology until his retirement in 1977.

De Lullo, Giorgio, Italian theatrical director (b. April 24, 1921—d. July 10, 1981, Rome, Italy), gained an international reputation as founder and director of the Compagnia dei Giovani, which performed in the London World Theatre seasons and at the Paris Théâtre des Nations. A graduate of the Academy of Dramatic Art in Rome, De Lullo made several successful stage appearances before founding the company in 1954 with Romolo Valli, Rossella Falk, and Elsa Albani. They specialized in plays by Shakespeare, Luigi Pirandello, and Carlo Goldoni and won many prizes including the Nettuno d'Oro in 1964. De Lullo won the director's prize at the Théâtre des Nations in 1961. After the Compagnia dei Giovani disbanded in 1971, De Lullo formed the Compagnia di Morelli-Stoppa, which he directed until 1973. De Lullo was best remembered for his company's productions of *Six Characters in Search of an Author, Twelfth Night,* and *The Rules of the Game*.

Denny-Brown, Derek Ernest, New Zealand-born neurologist (b. June 1, 1901, Christchurch, New Zealand—d. April 20, 1981, Cambridge, Mass.), was professor of neurology at Harvard University from 1941 to 1972 (J. J. Putnam professor, 1946–67) and an authority on the neuropathology of the nervous system. Denny-Brown was educated at the Otago University, New Zealand, and at Magdalen College, Oxford, before holding posts at the National Hospital and Guy's Hospital in London. He later worked at St. Bartholomew's Hospital and, again, at the National Hospital. His published works included *The Basal Ganglia* (1962) and *Cerebral Control of Movement* (1966). Denny-Brown was made an Officer of the Order of the British Empire in 1942.

Donskoy, Mark (Semyonovich), Soviet filmmaker (b. March 6, 1901, Odessa, Ukraine—d. March 24, 1981, Moscow, U.S.S.R.), adapted novelist Maksim Gorky's autobiography to make a trilogy of films that are among the finest achievements of Soviet cinema. The first, *The Childhood of Maksim Gorky,* was made in 1938; it was followed over the next two years by *In the World* and *My Universities*. Often deeply moving, universally accessible, and imbued with the artistic qualities of the Soviet silent cinema, the trilogy is an astonishing work to have emerged from the intellectual climate of the Stalinist period. Donskoy studied psychology and law before becoming a pupil of the great silent film director Sergey Eisenstein. Though Donskoy's later films failed to reach the heights of the Gorky trilogy, they included such notable works as *The Village Teacher* (1947), *Mother* (1956), and *Foma Gordeyev* (1959).

Doubrovska, Felia (FELIZATA DLUZHNEVSKA), Russian ballerina (b. 1896, St. Petersburg, Russia—d. Sept. 18, 1981, New York, N.Y.), gave extraordinary performances as the bride in *Les Noces* (1923) and as the Siren in *Prodigal Son* (1929) while dancing with Sergey Diaghilev's Ballet Russes. Doubrovska's tall figure and long legs earned her the admiration of the Russes' leading choreographer, George Balanchine, who cast her in *Pastorale, The Gods Go a-Begging,* and *Apollo*. After graduating from the Imperial Ballet School in St. Petersburg, Russia, Doubrovska joined the Maryinsky Ballet. In 1920 she became part of Diaghilev's company in France and created leading roles until he died in 1929. Doubrovska moved to the U.S. when her husband, the outstanding dancer Pierre Vladimiroff, accepted a teaching position at the School of American Ballet in 1934. From 1949 to 1980 Doubrovska taught advanced girls' classes at the School of American Ballet.

SVEN SIMON/KATHERINE YOUNG

Douglas, Donald Wills, U.S. aircraft designer (b. April 6, 1892, New York, N.Y.—d. Feb. 1, 1981, Palm Springs, Calif.), was the pioneering founder (1920) of the Douglas Aircraft Co. and the manufacturer of the twin-engine DC-3 (military C-47) transport, which ushered in the era of mass airline travel and played a major role in the Allied air victory during World War II. Besides developing such military aircraft as the A-20 attack bomber, the A-3D jet attack bomber, the SBD (Dauntless) dive bomber, and the D-558 and X-3 research planes, Douglas designed the Cloudster, the first airplane to lift more than its own weight in payload, and the World Cruiser biplane, which completed the first around-the-world flight in 1924. After the war his company manufactured the DC-8, DC-9, and DC-10 jet transports and the A-4 (Skyhawk) attack bomber. In the late 1950s the company began producing rockets and guided missiles including the Nike Ajax, Nike Zeus, Honest John, Sparrow, and Genie. His company also designed and developed (1955) the Thor intermediate-range ballistic missile, which later evolved into the highly reliable Delta space launch vehicle used by NASA. In 1957 Douglas retired, and ten years later the Douglas Aircraft Co. merged with the McDonnell Aircraft Corp.

Douglas, Melvyn (MELVYN EDOUARD HESSELBERG), U.S. actor (b. April 5, 1901, Macon, Ga.—d. Aug. 4, 1981, New York, N.Y.), as a debonair leading man pursued such glamorous stars as Greta Garbo, Claudette Colbert, Gloria Swanson, and Joan Crawford in a series of 1930s and 1940s romantic comedies. Douglas made his film debut in *Tonight or Never* (1931). From 1931 to 1942 he starred in over 40 motion pictures including *As You Desire Me* (1932), *She Married Her Boss* (1935), *Ninotchka* (1939), and *Third Finger, Left Hand* (1940). Douglas and his wife, Helen Gahagan Douglas, were both outspoken, prominent liberals. He was briefly the director of the Arts Council of the Office of Civil Defense before serving in the Army during World War II. Douglas then made fewer films and re-

UPI

turned to the stage, appearing in such Broadway productions as *Inherit the Wind, Two Blind Mice, The Bird Cage,* and *Spofford*; in 1960 he received a Tony award for *The Best Man.* He returned to films as a character actor in *Billy Budd* (1962). The following year Douglas won the Academy Award for best supporting actor for his portrayal of an aging cattleman in *Hud.* He received his second Academy Award at the age of 79 for his role as an ailing power broker in *Being There* (1979). Douglas was also awarded a 1968 Emmy for "Do Not Go Gentle into That Good Night." Other memorable films included *The Americanization of Emily* (1964), *I Never Sang for My Father* (1969), *The Seduction of Joe Tynan* (1979), and *Tell Me a Riddle* (1980). Shortly before his death Douglas completed filming the thriller *Ghost Story.*

Downer, Sir Alexander Russell, Australian politician (b. April 7, 1910, Adelaide, Australia—d. March 31, 1981, Williamstown, Australia), was high commissioner in the U.K. from 1964 to 1972. Downer, who was the son of Sir John Downer, twice premier of South Australia, was educated at Geelong Grammar School and Brasenose College, Oxford, where he read law. He was called to the bar by the Inner Temple, London, in 1934 and the South Australian bar in 1935. Captured by the Japanese during World War II, Downer spent three and a half years in Changi prisoner-of-war camp in Singapore. After returning to Australia he was elected to the House of Representatives and was minister for immigration from 1958 to 1963. During his eight-year term as Australia's high commissioner in London he defended the special relationship between the two countries during the British negotiations for entry to the European Economic Community. A man of wide culture and broadly conservative outlook, Downer enjoyed considerable respect in Britain: he was made a freeman of the City of London in 1965, a fellow of the Royal Society of Arts in 1968, and was knighted in 1965.

Drysdale, Sir (George) Russell, Australian painter (b. Feb. 7, 1912, Bognor Regis, Sussex, England—d. June 28, 1981, Sydney, Australia), was among the most representative of modern Australian painters and the first to become widely known outside his own country. Drysdale's vision of the desolate landscape of the outback, expressed in his paintings and drawings of the 1940s, was influenced by English artists of the time but depicted a purely Australian reality. His parents immigrated to Australia when he was 11, and he began painting while recovering from an eye operation. Drysdale's work was first exhibited in London in 1950, establishing his international reputation, and is represented in the Tate Gallery in London and the Metropolitan Museum of Art in New York City, as well as in all Australian state galleries. He was knighted in 1969 and made a Companion of the Order of Australia in 1980.

Durant, Will (WILLIAM JAMES DURANT), U.S. historian and philosopher (b. Nov. 5, 1885, North Adams, Mass.—d. Nov. 7, 1981, Los Angeles, Calif.), and **Ariel** (IDA KAUFMAN), U.S. historian (b. May 10, 1898, Proskupov, Russia—d. Oct. 24, 1981, Hollywood Hills, Calif), who together chronicled the achievements of man over 10,000 years in the monumental work *The Story of Civilization* (11 vol., 1935–75) and won the 1968 Pulitzer Prize for general nonfiction for the tenth volume, *Rousseau and Revolution* (1967). Will Durant, who established a reputation for lucid writing with *Philosophy and the Social Problem* (1917) and *The Story of Philosophy* (1926), which sold some three million copies, was able to finance *The Story of Civilization* with the proceeds from his first two books. The popularity of the latter was attributed to his emphasis on the

AMOS CARR—SIMON AND SCHUSTER

cultural achievements of man in art, literature, philosophy, and science rather than on political, economic, or military events. His work was also appealing to the general public, which enjoyed his anecdotes and picturesque detail. His other books included the autobiographical *Transition* (1927), *Tragedy of Russia* (1933), and *Interpretations of Life: A Survey of Contemporary Literature* (1970), an anecdotal appraisal of modern literature for the general reader. Although his wife helped research the first six volumes of *The Story of Civilization,* her name did not appear as co-author until the publication of the seventh volume, *The Age of Reason Begins.*

Eberly, Bob, U.S. singer (b. 1916, Mechanicsville, N.Y.—d. Nov. 17, 1981, Glen Burnie, Md.), was only 17 when he made his singing debut with the Dorsey Brothers Orchestra, one of the biggest Swing Era big bands. When Jimmy and Tommy Dorsey split up, Eberly remained with the former to popularize such hits as "Tangerine," "Green Eyes," "Blue Champagne," and "The Breeze and I." During his 45-year career Eberly made frequent concert, nightclub, and television appearances; his last performance was in 1980 at the Top of the World in Disney World, Florida.

Elliott, James F. ("JUMBO"), U.S. track and field coach (b. July 8, 1914, Philadelphia, Pa.—d. March 22, 1981, Juno Beach, Fla.), led Villanova University's Wildcats to eight national collegiate team championships and coached 28 Olympic competitors during his 46 years as the university's remarkable track and field coach. After graduating from Villanova in 1935, Elliott assumed the coaching duties at his alma mater while continuing to work as a business equipment contractor. His coaching produced 66 individual NCAA crowns and 377 IC4A individual titles; experts lauded him as the finest coach in the sport. His students included Olympic gold medal winners Ron Delany, Charlie Jenkins, Don Bragg, Paul Otis Drayton, and Larry James and such track stars as Marty Liquori, Dick Buerkle, and Don Paige. His athletes also shine in the prestigious Penn Relays, winning 75 events since 1955.

Euwe, Max, Dutch chess champion (b. May 20, 1901, Watergrafsmeer, Neth.—d. Nov. 26, 1981, Amsterdam, Neth.), was world chess champion (1935–37) and 12 times winner of The Netherlands championship during 1921–56. He combined chess with an active career as a mathematics teacher. Euwe learned to play at the age of four and was established as the leading player in The Netherlands by the time he first met Alexander Alekhine in 1926. In 1935 he defeated Alekhine for the world championship and held it until the rematch in 1937. Euwe gave up match play during the German occupation of the Low Countries, and in the world championship in 1948 Euwe was badly defeated by Alekhine. However, he remained an outstanding player and a brilliant theorist of the game whose *Judgment and Planning in Chess* (1954) and studies of the openings were standard works. During the 1960s he worked in the field of computer sciences. He was president (1970–78) of the International Chess Federation (FIDE).

Exeter, David George Brownlow Cecil, 6TH MARQUESS, British athlete (b. Feb. 9, 1905—d. Oct. 21, 1981, London, England), was an outstanding hurdler and runner whose athletic career, from 1924 to 1933, culminated in his victory in the 400-m hurdles at the Olympic Games in Amsterdam in 1928. Four years later in Los Angeles, he won a silver medal with the British 4 × 400-m relay team. Exeter was later president of the British and the International Amateur Athletic associations, a member of the International Olympic Committee, and the chairman of the committee that organized the 1948 Olympic Games in London. From 1931 to 1943 he was Conservative member of Parliament for Peterborough, and he served as governor and commander in chief of Bermuda from 1943 to 1945.

Fawzi, Mahmoud, Egyptian diplomat (b. Sept. 19, 1900, Cairo, Egypt—d. June 12, 1981, Cairo), was foreign minister under Pres. Gamal Abdel Nasser and prime minister from 1970 to 1972. A lawyer, he obtained his doctorate from the University of Rome after studying in Egypt, Britain, and the U.S. He joined the diplomatic service and served in various posts before his appointment as consul general in Jerusalem (1941–44). He became Egyptian representative at the UN in 1947 and ambassador to Britain in 1952. After the 1952 revolution his linguistic skills and diplomatic experience were invaluable to the new regime; he was foreign minister from 1952, first of Egypt, then, after the union with Syria, of the United Arab Republic. Fawzi remained a diplomat rather than a politician, and his appointment as Pres. Anwar as-Sadat's prime minister was seen as a compromise, stressing the civilian bias of the new leadership. He stayed on as vice-president of Egypt until his retirement in 1974.

Fisk, James Brown, U.S. physicist (b. Aug. 30, 1910, West Warwick, R.I.—d. Aug. 10, 1981, Elizabethtown, N.Y.), helped develop microwave magnetrons for high-frequency radar during World War II as an electronic research engineer at Bell Telephone Laboratories, which he joined in 1939. Fisk served as president of Bell Laboratories from 1959 to 1973, and under his leadership research teams developed the transistor, industrial lasers, and satellite communications systems. Fisk also established a reputation as a tough negotiator and on more than one occasion left Bell to serve the U.S. government. Under Pres. Dwight D. Eisenhower, Fisk headed a U.S. government scientific delegation that negotiated nuclear disarmament with Nikita S. Khrushchev. He also served under Presidents John F. Kennedy and Lyndon B. Johnson. In 1947 Fisk was named first director of the division of research of the Atomic Energy Commission but resigned in 1948 to become Gordon McKay professor at Harvard University. In 1973, a year before his retirement, Fisk became chairman of the board of Bell Laboratories.

Fitzsimmons, Frank Edward, U.S. labour leader (b. April 7, 1908, Jeannette, Pa.—d. May 6, 1981, San Diego, Calif.), was relatively inconspicuous in the International Brotherhood of Teamsters union until Jimmy Hoffa handpicked him in 1966 to serve as stand-in president while Hoffa served a prison sentence for jury tampering, conspiracy, and fraud. Hoffa was released from prison in 1971 after agreeing not to hold any union office, and Fitzsimmons was elected president in his own right. Although Fitzsimmons headed the nation's largest union, he wielded little political influence. He won large contracts in national master freight negotiations and increased the membership of the two million-strong union, but his leadership, unchallenged after the 1975 disappearance and presumed death of Hoffa, was clouded by charges of corruption, mismanagement of union pension funds, and reports of links to organized crime.

Fletcher, Harvey, U.S. physicist (b. Sept. 11, 1884, Provo, Utah—d. July 23, 1981, Provo), headed the scientific research team that developed and demonstrated (Jan. 24, 1934) stereophonic sound, a system of sound recording and reproduction that utilizes two or more independent sound channels of information. This discovery revolutionized the motion-picture and recording industries, which turned out movies, phonograph records, and magnetic tapes featuring stereophonic sound. After earning a Ph.D. from the University of Chicago, Fletcher served for five years as head of the physics department at Brigham Young University in Provo, Utah. He then joined (1916) the staff of Bell Telephone Laboratories. In 1933 he was named head of Bell's physical research lab, overseeing pioneer work in the fields of speech, music, and hearing. In 1949 he moved to Columbia University in New York City and three years later returned to

Brigham Young as director of research. There he also served as chairman of the engineering department, dean of the College of Physical and Engineering Sciences, and professor of physics. Even after his formal retirement, Fletcher continued to write scholarly papers analyzing the sounds of musical instruments and to experiment at his echo-free laboratory at Brigham Young. His work on the fundamentals of psychoacoustics is detailed in *Speech and Hearing* (1929).

Fox, Carol, U.S. opera producer (b. June 15, 1926, Chicago, Ill.—d. July 21, 1981, Chicago), was the resolute co-founder in 1952 of the Lyric Theatre of Chicago (which became the Lyric Opera of Chicago) and its energetic general manager for more than 25 years. Through sheer determination, Fox not only built the company into one of the nation's most distinguished opera houses but shaped its international reputation as well. She was responsible for introducing some of the top Italian singers to the Lyric, including the tempestuous soprano Maria Callas, who made her U.S. debut there in 1954. Fox's predilection for Italian casts and repertory prompted both critics and supporters alike to dub the Lyric "La Scala West." Partly in response to this criticism, an apprentice program was instituted in 1973 for aspiring U.S. singers. Fox retired as general manager in early 1981 because of ill health.

Fox, Terrence ("Terry") Stanley, Canadian student and national hero (b. July 28, 1958, Winnipeg, Man.—d. June 28, 1981, Vancouver, B.C.), was afflicted with cancer while a student at Simon Fraser University in British Columbia and, in spite of the amputation of his right leg, was determined to raise money for cancer research by running a "Marathon of Hope." Fox set out from St. John's, Newfoundland, on April 12, 1980, and logged 5,-375 km (3,339 mi) before lung cancer forced him to abandon his run on Sept. 1, 1980, in Thunder Bay, Ont. His original goal of raising $1 million was far surpassed with contributions exceeding $23 million to the Canadian Cancer Society and other organizations. His sincerity and fortitude served as an inspiration to the citizens of Canada, who enthusiastically cheered him as he made his way across the nation. Fox, who was presented with numerous awards, including the Order of the Dogwood, British Columbia's highest honour, was also twice named Canadian of the Year by the Canadian Press and on September 19 became the youngest Companion of the Order of Canada. His funeral was broadcast nationwide.

Franjieh, Hamid, Lebanese politician (b. 1905?, Zghorta, Lebanon—d. Sept. 5, 1981, Beirut, Lebanon), was foreign minister when his country became independent in 1943 and served in that post several times for different governments until his resignation in 1955. He came from an influential Maronite Christian family and was the brother of former president Suleiman Franjieh. Hamid also aspired to the presidency, which constitutionally must be held by a Maronite, but was defeated in 1952 by Camille Chamoun, who had greater support from central Lebanon. Trained at the French Law School in Beirut, Franjieh practiced as a lawyer before entering politics as a fervent nationalist and representing his country as foreign minister. After his resignation Franjieh, who was then associated with a group supporting the policies of Egyptian Pres. Gamal Abdel Nasser, was forced to withdraw from political activity in 1957 because of illness.

Fraser of North Cape, Bruce Austin Fraser, 1st Baron, British naval officer (b. Feb. 5, 1888, Acton, Middlesex, England—d. Feb. 12, 1981, London, England), as commander in chief (1943–44) of the Home Fleet during World War II directed operations off northern Norway that culminated in the sinking of the German battleship "Scharnhorst" on Dec. 26, 1943. The son of an army general, Fraser joined the Royal Navy at age 14. He became a commander in 1919 after serving as a gunnery officer throughout World War I. After staff appointments and a period on the East Indies station,

he took command of the aircraft carrier "Glorious" in 1936. Two years later he was promoted to rear admiral and became chief of staff of the Mediterranean Fleet. As third sea lord and controller at the Admiralty, he was responsible for building up the Navy's strength immediately prior to and in the first years of World War II. In 1942 he again went to sea as second in command of the Home Fleet, becoming commander in chief the following year. In 1944 Fraser was promoted to admiral, and as commander in chief (1945–46) of the British Pacific Fleet, he was Britain's signatory to the Japanese surrender on board the USS "Missouri" on Sept. 2, 1945. Fraser ended his career in the "senior service's" highest office, as first sea lord and chief of naval staff (1948–51). Fraser became 1st Baron Fraser of North Cape in 1946.

Frederika, former queen of Greece (b. April 18, 1917, Blankenburg, Saxony, Germany—d. Feb. 6, 1981, Madrid, Spain), married Crown Prince Paul of Greece in 1938 and became queen on his accession to the throne in 1947. A direct descendant of both Queen Victoria and Kaiser Wilhelm II, she was accused of pro-Nazi sympathies before World War II but won respect for her courage during the war and for her devoted efforts in welfare work during the years of hardship and instability following the liberation. But Frederika could not escape her enemies, who saw her as an autocratic power behind the throne; they were particularly afraid when her 23-year-old son, Constantine, became king after the death of King Paul in 1964. Her political influence made her the focus of an antimonarchist attack, even though Constantine remained a popular figure. Eight months after the seizure of power in April 1967 by a military junta, the king attempted an unsuccessful countercoup, and the royal family was forced into exile. Frederika went to Rome and then to India to study philosophy, realizing that her intervention could only harm Constantine's chances of regaining the throne. She wrote an autobiography entitled *A Measure of Understanding.* Even her death, which occurred while she was visiting her daughter, Queen Sophia of Spain, threatened to revive controversy when the Greek government gave permission for her to be buried in Greece.

Fuller, Hoyt William, U.S. editor (b. Sept. 10, 1927, Atlanta, Ga.—d. May 11, 1981, Atlanta), was the influential executive editor (1961–76) of *Black World* (formerly *Negro Digest*) who encouraged young black writers to develop a black aesthetic by drawing on black culture and their own experiences in their writings. After *Black World* ceased publication in 1976, Fuller founded and became executive editor of the literary journal *First World.* Fuller, who sometimes wrote under the pseudonym William Barrow, contributed articles to such publications as *The New Yorker, The New Republic,* and the *Christian Science Monitor.* He also published a book, *Journey to Africa* (1971).

Galamian, Ivan Alexander, Persian-born violinist and teacher (b. Jan. 23, 1903, Tabriz, Persia [now Iran]—d. April 14, 1981, New York, N.Y.), stressed attention to technical detail and mental control in his training of such virtuoso violinists as Itzhak Perlman, Pinchas Zuckerman, Michael Rabin, Erick Friedman, and Jamie Laredo. Opposed to strong regimentation, Galamian helped to develop the individual style of each student. While some became concertmasters, others were chamber musicians, conductors, and teachers. Galamian studied under Konstantin Mostras in Moscow and Lucien Carpet in Paris before making his Paris debut in 1924. He taught at the Russian Conservatory in Paris from 1924 to 1937 and performed with European orchestras before moving to the U.S. in 1937. He was appointed to the Curtis Institute in Philadelphia in 1944 and two years later to the strings faculty at the Juilliard School of Music, where he taught until his death.

Gance, Abel, French film director (b. Oct. 25, 1889, Paris, France—d. Nov. 10, 1981, Paris), was a flawed genius whose silent masterpiece *Napoléon* (1927) remains, despite its romantic exaggeration,

a seminal work in cinema history. Designed as the first part of a vast epic, badly remade, disastrously cut, and eventually considered lost, it reemerged triumphantly in 1980 after reconstruction by Kevin Brownlow. Gance's "Polyvision" (the use of three screens) and his later experiments with sound were among his imaginative technical innovations that foreshadowed Cinemascope. But his total lack of business acumen made him unable to reap the financial rewards of his genius. An actor and writer, he set up a film company in 1911 and established himself during World War I when ill health excused him from military service. His *J'Accuse* (1918) was a melodramatic and highly individual protest against the war, and in *La Roue* (1923) he produced a lyrical tribute to the mechanics and the romance of rail, using such daring technical experiments as intercutting, montage, and split screen, all of which were later developed more fully in *Napoléon*. The 1980 revival of *Napoléon*, which was shown in London, Paris, Rome, and the U.S., revealed Gance's prolific talent for invention at a time when advances in cinema technique had permitted the film to be shown, virtually for the first time, as its creator intended.

Garnett, David, British novelist (b. March 9, 1892, Brighton, England—d. Feb. 17, 1981, Montcuq, France), won the Hawthornden Prize and the James Tait Black Memorial Prize in 1923 with his fantasy *Lady into Fox* (1922); this was followed by *A Man in the Zoo* (1924). After studying botany at the Royal College of Science, Garnett disobeyed parental advice to avoid a literary career. Following World War I he set up a bookshop and joined Francis Meynell as a partner in the Nonesuch Press. A friend of D. H. Lawrence and a member of the Bloomsbury circle, he depicted Bloomsbury in *No Love* (1929), sometimes considered his best novel. Garnett, who continued to write well into his 80s, made a notable contribution to scholarship with his edition of Thomas Love Peacock's novels, published in 1948. Garnett also published *Pocahontas: Or the Nonparell of Virginia* (1933) and autobiographical works.

Gérin, Winifred (Mrs. John Lock), British writer (b. 1900, Germany—d. June 28, 1981, London, England), established a reputation late in life as a biographer of the Brontës and maintained her prominence with notable studies of other famous women. Her first marriage was to the Belgian cellist Eugène Gérin, with whom she escaped from occupied Belgium and France at the start of World War II. They then worked in the British Foreign Office together until his death in 1945. Gérin married John Lock in 1954, and their shared interest in the life and works of the Brontë family led to her biography of Anne (1959) and subsequently of Branwell (1961) and the other two Brontë sisters, Charlotte (1967), and Emily (1971). Gérin also published the biographies *Horatio Nelson* (1970), *Elizabeth Gaskell* (1976), and *Anne Thackeray Ritchie* (1981).

Gibbs-Smith, Charles Harvard, British aeronautical historian (b. March 22, 1909, Teddington, England —d. Dec. 3, 1981), began his career in 1932 as assistant keeper at the Victoria and Albert Museum, London, in charge of the photographic collections. During World War II he worked for the photographic division of the Ministry of Information, became its director in 1945, and there developed his interest in aviation. He returned to the museum in 1947 as keeper in the department of public relations and was responsible for organizing many important exhibitions. Gibbs-Smith continued his research into aeronautical history, wrote several books on the subject for the Science Museum, and became a research fellow there after his retirement in 1976.

Gielgud, Val Henry, British radio producer (b. April 28, 1900, London, England—d. Nov. 30, 1981), was production director and later head of sound drama at the British Broadcasting Corporation (BBC) from 1929 to 1963. He was a member of a notable theatrical family (the brother of Sir John Gielgud) and a playwright and theatre producer. Gielgud

also revealed the huge potential of radio as a medium for all kinds of drama, from classical plays to soap opera and educational features. After he created the BBC Drama Repertory Company in 1939, Gielgud gained a massive audience for such regular productions as "Saturday Night Theatre" and acquired actors with remarkable talent. During the post-World War II period radio was steadily eclipsed by the rise of television, and Gielgud's experience in the rival medium from 1950 to 1952 was not a success. His tastes were somewhat conservative, but his achievement in establishing the pattern of BBC radio drama and attracting a large and faithful audience was considerable. Gielgud was made a Commander of the Order of the British Empire in 1958.

Gimbel, Sophie Haas, U.S. fashion designer (b. 1902, Houston, Texas—d. Nov. 28, 1981, New York, N.Y.), as head of the Saks Fifth Avenue Salon Moderne (1931–69) was noted for her chic and elegant fashions, which were worn by such celebrities as Claudette Colbert, Rose Kennedy, and Mrs. Lyndon B. Johnson, for whom she created the American beauty red coat and dress that Johnson wore at the 1965 inauguration of her husband. After designing costumes for a Philadelphia theatrical production in 1921, Gimbel was hired by a lingerie firm to modernize its undergarments. She was credited with transforming the voluminous lady's bloomer into a fashionable panty brief. Gimbel was then enlisted by Saks to revitalize the floundering custom-order Salon Moderne. She designed costumes for more than 50 Broadway shows in two years and presented a less expensive line of ready-to-wear garments called Sophie Originals. Thus when she married Adam Gimbel, president of Saks, her belief in her record of success allowed her to ignore fashion industry rumours about her ability. Believing that U.S. fashions should remain functional and feminine, she later introduced the culotte, or divided skirt. Gimbel, who retired in 1969, was a member of the Fashion Hall of Fame.

Glueckauf, Eugen, German-born scientist (b. April 9, 1906, Eisenach, Germany—d. Sept. 15, 1981, Chilton, England), was head of the radiochemistry branch at the Atomic Energy Research Establishment (AERE), Harwell, and made a notable contribution to the management of nuclear wastes. Glueckauf studied at the Technische Hochschule in Berlin but left Germany in 1933 to escape Nazi persecution. He joined the staff of Imperial College, University of London, then went to Durham Colleges (later University) to conduct research on atmospheric gases. In 1947 he was appointed to the chemistry division at Harwell and continued his earlier work on the separation of gases. He became one of the first to investigate disposal of nuclear wastes in glass. Glueckauf also contributed to the development of seawater desalination and to the study of diffusion of fission products. He published numerous scientific papers on these and other topics. One of his major achievements was his early proposal for a self-contained site for the recycling and disposal of nuclear wastes. Glueckauf was elected a fellow of the Royal Society in 1969. After retirement in 1971 he served as a consultant to the Atomic Energy Research Establishment until 1980.

Golden, Harry (Lewis), U.S. humorist and editor (b. May 6, 1902, New York, N.Y.—d. Oct. 2, 1981, Charlotte, N.C.), pronounced his witticisms in *The Carolina Israelite* as its founder (1941) and only editor. The chief target of Golden's sardonic humour was racism. His tongue-in-cheek proposals included the "Golden Vertical Negro Plan," which called for the removal of seats in public places because whites did not seem to object to standing next to blacks, only to sitting next to them, and the "White Baby Plan," which urged blacks to rent white children so they could escort them to the theatre and thereby be allowed to take a seat. Golden compiled his humorous essays in the best-selling books *Only in America* (1958), *For 2¢ Plain* (1959), and *Enjoy, Enjoy!* (1960). He ceased publication of *The Carolina Israelite* in 1968.

Goolden, Richard Percy Herbert, British actor (b. Feb. 23, 1895, London, England—d. June 18, 1981, London), was best remembered by generations of young audiences as Mole in the children's Christmas play by A. A. Milne, *Toad of Toad Hall,* a part that he played off and on for almost 50 years. Goolden was educated at Charterhouse and the University of Oxford, where his theatrical career began as a member of the dramatic society. After army service in World War I, he joined the Oxford Playhouse company and while still a young man began to take the parts of old men. An eccentric and endearing character, he appeared in *The Cherry Orchard, Hamlet,* and, with Donald Wolfit, in *King Lear* and *Volpone* as well as in modern dramas.

Gopallawa, William, Sri Lankan politician (b. Sept. 17, 1897, Dullewe, Matale, Ceylon—d. Jan. 30, 1981, Colombo, Sri Lanka), was governor-general of Ceylon (1962–72) until the country became the Republic of Sri Lanka in 1972, when he became its first president. A Buddhist, he trained as a teacher and as a barrister before serving on the municipal councils in Kandy and Colombo. In 1958 he was appointed ambassador to China and in 1961 to the U.S., Cuba, and Mexico. An austere figure, respected for his nonpartisan statesmanship, he intervened to ensure the resignation of Sirimavo Bandaranaike's government in 1965 after her party's defeat in the general election. As a result of constitutional changes made by Prime Minister J. R. Jayawardene, the presidency became elective in 1978, and on February 4 of that year Gopallawa retired and was succeeded by Jayawardene.

Grasso, Ella T. (Ella Rosa Giovanna Oliva Tambussi), U.S. politician (b. May 10, 1919, Windsor Locks, Conn.—d. Feb. 5, 1981, Hartford, Conn.), became governor of Connecticut in 1975 and in so

SVEN SIMON/KATHERINE YOUNG

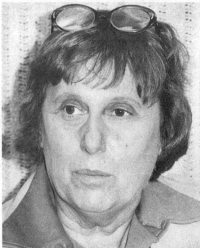

doing became the first woman to be elected governor in her own right. Her credentials included two terms in the state House of Representatives (1953–54 and 1955–57), 12 years as Connecticut's secretary of state (1959–70), and two terms in the U.S. Congress (1971–72 and 1973–74). As governor, Grasso exercised great frugality. She kept state spending low by limiting aid to cities and welfare recipients and by reducing the number of state employees. The state flourished under her direction, but her popularity suffered as a result of these austerity measures. Her success with Connecticut's economy, however, ultimately gained her a second term as governor. Grasso was forced to resign on Dec. 31, 1980, because of fast-spreading cancer.

Green, Paul Eliot, U.S. playwright (b. March 17, 1894, Lillington, N.C.—d. May 4, 1981, Chapel

Hill, N.C.), was one of the first white playwrights to portray sensitively the problems of poor blacks living in the South. Green's most powerful dramatic work, *In Abraham's Bosom,* relates the struggle of a black man attempting to establish a school and improve the lives of his peers. The poignant drama was produced at the Provincetown Theatre in New York City in 1926 and was awarded a Pulitzer Prize the following year. Green's other plays, which explored such themes as chain gangs, lynchings, and prejudice, included *The House of Connelly* (1931), *Roll, Sweet Chariot* (1934), *Hymn to the Rising Sun* (1936), and *Johnny Johnson* (1936). His dramatization of Richard Wright's powerful novel *Native Son* was successfully staged on Broadway (1941). Green also wrote screenplays for leading stars of the era.

Gundelach, Finn Olav, Danish diplomat (b. April 23, 1925, Vejle, Denmark—d. Jan. 13, 1981, Strasbourg, France), played a major role in negotiating Denmark's entry into the European Communities (EC) while serving as ambassador to the EEC from 1967 to 1972. He later became a vice-president of the European Commission, with special responsibility for fisheries and later also for the controversial common agricultural policy (CAP). A member of the Danish resistance during World War II, he studied economics at the University of Århus and after graduation joined the Danish Foreign Ministry. During 1956–59 he was Denmark's permanent representative to the UN at Geneva. There he joined the secretariat of the General Agreement on Tariffs and Trade and was involved in the Kennedy Round negotiations. After becoming Denmark's first EC commissioner in 1973, he conducted difficult fisheries talks with Iceland in 1976 and was considered an outstanding expert in the complex field of agricultural policy.

Guthrie, William Keith Chambers, British classical scholar (b. Aug. 1, 1906, London, England—d. May 17, 1981, Cambridge, England), was Laurence professor of ancient philosophy at the University of Cambridge from 1952 to 1973 and the author of *A History of Greek Philosophy.* Five volumes of the work appeared during 1962–78 and a sixth was published some months after his death. Guthrie was also master (1957–72) of Downing College, Cambridge, a fellow of the British Academy from 1952, and president (1967–68) of the Classical Association. His extensive knowledge of all periods of Greek thought made it possible for him to undertake his comprehensive history of the subject. He was also a specialist on Aristotle and published works on Greek religion. Educated at Cambridge, Guthrie spent his entire career there except for a period of wartime service in the Intelligence Corps. He was active in university life at Cambridge, particularly as orator of the university from 1939 to 1957.

Hailwood, (Stanley) Michael Bailey, British racing motorcyclist (b. April 4, 1940—d. March 23, 1981, Birmingham, England), was ten times world motorcycle champion and won 14 Isle of Man Tourist Trophies (TT's). These feats established Hailwood as a legendary figure in the world of motorcycle racing. Hailwood won his first world championship at the age of 21. From then until 1967 he dominated the sport and delighted his "home" crowd on the Isle of Man. His subsequent career in auto racing was less successful, and his unassuming personality was always uneasy in the more pretentious atmosphere of cars. In 1973 he received the George Medal for saving the Swiss driver Clay Regazzoni from a burning car in the South African Grand Prix. After crashing in 1974, Hailwood retired, but four years later he made a triumphant return to the motorcycle track, broke the Isle of Man lap record, and won the world championship. In the following year he won the Formula One championship again in the TT. Hailwood and his nine-year-old daughter died in a car crash two years after he had retired to manage a motorcycle business.

Haley, Bill (WILLIAM JOHN CLIFTON HALEY, JR.), U.S. rock 'n' roll singer and bandleader (b. July 6, 1925, Highland Park, Mich.—d. Feb. 9, 1981, Harlingen, Texas), together with his band, the Comets, laid the groundwork for the emergence of rock 'n' roll

PHOTO TRENDS

with such hits as "Rock Around the Clock" and "Shake, Rattle and Roll." He and the Comets (originally the Saddlemen) began as a Western swing band, and by blending a touch of black rhythm and blues into their style, they prefigured rock 'n' roll. In 1952 Haley renamed the band and in the following year gained attention with "Crazy Man Crazy." His version of Joe Turner's "Shake, Rattle and Roll" earned Haley a gold record. After being featured in the 1955 motion picture *Blackboard Jungle,* "Rock Around the Clock" became a huge success and had sold some 22.5 million copies by the time of his death. Haley's star waned in the U.S. after the emergence of Elvis Presley and other new performers, but he retained his popularity in Europe, where he played to packed concert halls. Other hits by Bill Haley and the Comets included "See You Later, Alligator," "Razzle Dazzle," and "Rip It Up." In the late 1960s and early 1970s Haley once again excited U.S. audiences with a series of rock 'n' roll revival shows; in 1969 a New York City audience gave his group an 8½-minute ovation after their set.

Handler, Philip, U.S. biochemist (b. Aug. 13, 1901, New York, N.Y.—d. Dec. 29, 1981, Boston, Mass.), was president (1969–81) of the National Academy of Sciences and an internationally acclaimed biochemist who made significant studies on pellagra, a disfiguring disease that disturbs mental and nervous function and causes a red sore tongue and gastrointestinal disturbances. After earning a Ph.D. in biochemistry at the University of Illinois, Handler in 1939 joined Duke University to help conduct research on pellagra. Handler found that the disease, which afflicted people in the Southeast living on corn-based diets, was caused by poor quality corn products that prevented the human body from manufacturing its own nicotinic acid. He was instrumental in the passage of a North Carolina law making it mandatory to fortify cornmeal products with nicotinic acid, iron, and riboflavin. During World War II Handler and a group of scientists developed the pressure bandage used to treat severely burned soldiers; the bandage eliminated inflammation and toxicity and saved hundreds of lives. In other research at Duke University, Handler studied the relationship between diet and high blood pressure in kidney disease. He concluded that a low-protein diet would relieve hypertension but would also reduce the production of a key hormone, ACTH, by the pituitary gland. During his career Handler was credited with discovering at least 15 enzymes. In 1950 he was named chairman of the biochemistry depart-

ment at Duke, where he remained until his 1969 appointment as president of the National Academy of Sciences.

Hanson, Howard, U.S. composer, conductor, and educator (b. Oct. 28, 1896, Wahoo, Neb.—d. Feb. 26, 1981, Rochester, N.Y.), was a prolific composer who won a Pulitzer Prize for his Fourth Symphony (1943) and was one of the nation's most renowned music educators as director of the Eastman School of Music in Rochester, N.Y., from 1924 to 1964. After spending three years (1921–24) in Italy as the winner of the American Academy's Prix de Rome, Hanson returned to the U.S. and began his long association with the Eastman. As director he promoted the works of contemporary American composers through the annual American Music Festival, conducting over 1,000 works by aspiring composers. He also organized the Eastman Philharmonia, a student orchestra. Hanson produced compositions in the conservative post-Romantic tradition and was adamantly opposed to progressive trends in American classical music. Included among his orchestral works are the First Symphony (*Nordic;* 1922), Second Symphony (*Romantic;* 1930), Fifth Symphony (*Sinfonia Sacra;* 1954), and *Lux Aeterna* (for orchestra and chorus; 1923). He also composed the highly popular opera *Merry Mount* (1933), which was commissioned by the Metropolitan Opera, and the choral work *Lament for Beowulf* (1925). In later years he was the distinguished guest conductor of the Boston, NBC, and New York Philharmonic symphonies.

Harburg, E. Y. (EDGAR ["YIP"] HARBURG), U.S. lyricist (b. April 8, 1898, New York, N.Y.—d. March 5, 1981, Los Angeles, Calif.), won an Academy Award by using his lively imagination to write the pensive lyrics of "Over the Rainbow" for the 1939 musical *The Wizard of Oz.* While studying at the City College of New York, Harburg collaborated with classmate Ira Gershwin on a light verse column for the college newspaper. He also contributed verse to Franklin P. Adams's column "The Conning Tower" in the *New York World.* After graduation in 1921, Harburg and a college classmate became proprietors of an electrical appliance company, which by 1929 was worth about a quarter of a million dollars. The Depression left Harburg with only his literary wit, so he turned to writing lyrics for such Broadway productions as *Ballyhoo of 1932* and *Americana,* for which he wrote "Brother, Can You Spare a Dime" (with Jay Gorney). Some of his best remembered songs include "It's Only a Paper Moon," "April in Paris," and "We're Off to See the Wizard." In Hollywood he penned the lyrics for the films *Cabin in the Sky, Can't Help Singing,* and *Centennial Summer,* as well as many others. After being blacklisted in Hollywood after World War II, he returned to Broadway, where he was lyricist and co-author with Fred Saidy and Burton Lane of *Finian's Rainbow.* Harburg remained productive during the 1960s and 1970s and lamented over modern songwriters for their "lack of craftsmanship, their imitative music and poor rhymes."

Harrison, Wallace Kirkman, U.S. architect (b. Sept. 28, 1895, Worcester, Mass.—d. Dec. 2, 1981, New York, N.Y.), played a leading role in designing such magnificent New York City structures as the United Nations headquarters, Rockefeller Center, Lincoln Center for the Performing Arts, and the Metropolitan Opera House, as well as the Empire State Plaza in Albany and the Trylon and Perisphere theme centre for the 1939 New York World's Fair. After World War I, Harrison studied at the École des Beaux-Arts, Paris, returning to New York to work for Bertram Goodhue. Harrison was then invited by Wiley Corbett to become his partner in the firm of Corbett, Harrison & MacMurray, which was asked to join other architects in the design of the Rockefeller Center complex. Later, Harrison was appointed head of an international team of consultants working on the UN headquarters. In 1945 he formed a partnership with Max Abramovitz and established Harrison & Abramovitz, which became one of the largest architectural firms in the U.S. Their design specialty

was office buildings, including the Alcoa Building in Pittsburgh, Pa. (1953), and the Socony Mobil Building in New York City (1956). Harrison's design for the First Presbyterian Church in Stamford, Conn., with its fish-shaped interior and luminous stained glass windows, was also highly regarded. In 1979 Harrison set up his own firm in Rockefeller Center.

Hassel, Odd, Norwegian chemist (b. May 17, 1897, Kristiania [now Oslo], Norway—d. May 11, 1981, Oslo), shared the 1969 Nobel Prize for Chemistry with Sir Derek Barton of Britain for their work in determining the actual three-dimensional shape of certain organic compounds. After studies at Oslo, Munich, and Berlin universities, Hassel returned to Oslo as lecturer in 1925. His early work in crystallography resulted in an important book, *Kristallchemie,* which appeared in English and Russian translations. In 1934 Hassel was appointed professor at the University of Oslo, where he headed the physical chemistry department until his retirement in 1964. After research in crystallography Hassel turned to the study of the structure of gas molecules by means of electron diffraction; this led to the establishment of conformational analysis, the study of the three-dimensional geometric structure of molecules. This Nobel Prize-winning work proved to be vital in the creation of synthetic molecules used in developing new drugs.

Hays, Lee, U.S. folksinger (b. 1914, Little Rock, Ark. —d. Aug. 26, 1981, Tarrytown, N.Y.), was the bass-singing co-founder of the Weavers, a folksinging quartet composed of Hays, Pete Seeger, Ronnie Gilbert, and Fred Hellerman. The group, an outgrowth of the Almanac Singers, which had included Woody Guthrie and Millard Lampard, helped start the folk music boom of the 1950s. The Weavers made their debut in 1949 to rave reviews but were blacklisted and forced to disband in 1952. In 1955 they appeared in Carnegie Hall to a thunderous ovation and continued performing (without Seeger after 1958) until 1963. Hays collaborated on such all-time favourite songs as "If I Had a Hammer," "Kisses Sweeter than Wine," and "Lonesome Traveler."

Head, Alice Maud, British editor (b. May 3, 1886, London, England—d. July 25, 1981, London), was a highly successful magazine editor. Head joined Country Life Ltd. as a secretary at the age of 19 and by the time she was 22 was editor of *Woman at Home.* Later she worked for the National Magazine Co., William Randolph Hearst's London-based enterprise. Besides editing *Good Housekeeping* (1924–39), she was appointed managing director of the company and became Hearst's trusted personal representative in Europe. She later returned to George Newnes Ltd. to edit *Homes and Gardens* and to became a director of Country Life Ltd.

Head, Edith, U.S. fashion designer (b. Oct. 28, 1907, Los Angeles, Calif.—d. Oct. 24, 1981, Hollywood, Calif.), during her 50-year career outfitted such motion picture stars as Mae West, Marlene Dietrich, Bette Davis, Ingrid Bergman, and Elizabeth Taylor and won a record eight Academy Awards for her designs for *The Heiress* (1949), *Samson and Delilah* (1950), *All About Eve* (1950), *A Place in the Sun* (1951), *Roman Holiday* (1953), *Sabrina* (1954), *The Facts of Life* (1960), and *The Sting* (1973). Head, who was noted for the simplicity and elegance of her costumes, joined Paramount Studios in 1923 as a sketch artist and became chief designer there in 1938. Although her designs were stunning, Head herself remained inconspicuous with her subdued two-piece suits and tortoiseshell glasses. She subtly rotated the limelight to the stars for whom she designed and gained a reputation for being able to placate temperamental actresses and directors. Although she did not generally set trends, Head was credited with the popularity of the sarong, which she created for Dorothy Lamour. Head joined Universal Studios in 1967 and at the time of her death had just completed the costumes for *Dead Men Don't Wear Plaid,* starring Steve Martin. She was also the author of two books: *The Dress Doctor* and *How to Dress for Success.*

Heald, Sir Lionel Frederick, British lawyer and politician (b. Aug. 7, 1897, Parrs Wood, Lancashire, England—d. Nov. 7, 1981, Guildford, England), was attorney general (1951–54) in Winston Churchill's government after a successful legal career. He studied at the University of Oxford, served in the Royal Engineers during World War I, and completed his law studies in 1923. After World War II he entered politics and was elected to Parliament in 1950. Heald continued as Conservative member for Chertsey until his retirement in 1970. As attorney general, he defended Britain in the 1952 Persian Oil dispute before the International Court of Justice. After leaving office he remained a noted back-bench member of Parliament, justice of the peace, and chairman of the Air Public Relations Association. He was also a member of the 1960 Monckton Commission, which investigated the future of the Central African Federation, and in 1956 he chaired a Conservative lawyers' committee that produced an influential report on capital punishment.

Hennessy, Sir Patrick, British industrialist (b. April 18, 1898, Middleton, County Cork, Ireland—d. March 13, 1981, Theydon Bois, Essex, England), was managing director (1948–57) and chairman (1956–68) of the Ford Motor Co. in Britain, helped to make it a market leader in the U.K. and a major exporter, particularly in agricultural and commercial vehicles. After serving in World War I, he joined (1920) Ford in Cork and in 1931, when the firm expanded to England, became purchase manager at its factory in Dagenham. He was knighted for his services at the Ministry of Aircraft Production during World War II and in 1948 was appointed managing director of Ford of Britain. As chairman of the company he oversaw the production of its popular postwar models and the development of the diesel engines that established Ford's supremacy in the commercial range.

Henry, Albert Royle, Cook Islands politician (b. June 11, 1907, Aitutaki, Cook Islands—d. Jan. 2, 1981, Rarotonga, Cook Islands), became prime minister of the New Zealand territory of the Cook Islands in 1965 when it was granted internal self-government. Henry was returned to office in four consecutive elections but in 1978 was dismissed and charged with electoral bribery and corruption. He pleaded guilty in 1979 and was barred from politics for three years, but on appeal the order was rescinded. Henry was stripped of the knighthood conferred on him by Queen Elizabeth II in 1974.

Heppenstall, (John) Rayner, British writer (b. July 27, 1911, Huddersfield, England—d. May 23, 1981, Deal, England), was a scholar of French literature and a notable author whose fiction was influenced by contemporary French writing. His novels, including *The Connecting Door* (1962), *The Woodshed* (1962), and *Two Moons* (1977), were experimental works, critically underrated but constituting perhaps the most notable attempt by a British writer to assimilate the technical innovations of French writers. Heppenstall studied in France and at the University of Leeds. He lived as a writer before World War II, served with the Army, and then joined the British Broadcasting Corporation. Heppenstall wrote several radio plays and did translations. His interest in criminal behaviour, revealed in his novel *The Shearers* (1969), produced a series of studies of French crimes, among them *Bluebeard and After* (1972). He also published three volumes of memoirs.

Hirshhorn, Joseph Herman, Latvian-born financier and patron of the arts (b. Aug. 11, 1899, Mitau, Latvia—d. Aug. 31, 1981, Washington, D.C.), a skilled broker and market analyst, he amassed a second fortune as a mining tycoon and assembled one of the largest private art collections in the world, which included thousands of sculptures and paintings. During his childhood in Brooklyn, N.Y., Hirshhorn learned that "poverty has a bitter taste." At the age of 14 he became an office boy on Wall Street; in three years he was working as a broker on the Curb; and a year later he had made $168,000 on his $255 initial investment in the market.

His insight also led him to cash in his stocks some two months before the 1929 stock market crash. In the 1930s Hirshhorn's interest turned to prospecting; he placed a full-page advertisement in the *Toronto Northern Miner* that read: "Canada, your day has come. The world is at your feet, begging you to release your riches cramped in Mother Earth." Three years later he backed the near-defunct Preston East Dome Mines Ltd. with $25,000 for a drilling program and struck gold within a few months. In the 1940s and '50s Hirshhorn turned to uranium mining and formed Pronto Uranium Mines and Algoma Uranium Mines to exploit the uranium-rich Algoma Basin in Ontario. It was reported that Algoma was producing more uranium than all of the more than 600 uranium companies in the U.S. Hirshhorn's financial successes enabled him to realize a boyhood fantasy and acquire art. He became interested in the Abstract Expressionists, and his highly personal purchases included works by Willem de Kooning, Larry Rivers, and Henry Moore. In 1966 Pres. Lyndon B. Johnson persuaded Hirshhorn to donate his massive collection to a museum bearing his name. The Joseph H. Hirshhorn Museum and Sculpture Garden opened in Washington in 1974. Although some critics complained that the collection was uneven, the public response was overwhelmingly positive: more than one million patrons visited the museum in 1980.

Holden, William (WILLIAM FRANKLIN BEEDLE, JR.), U.S. actor (b. April 17, 1918, O'Fallon, Ill.—found dead Nov. 16, 1981, Santa Monica, Calif.), portrayed a tough romantic hero in scores of films and won an Academy Award for best actor as the cynical and opportunistic U.S. prisoner of war in *Stalag 17* (1953). After his first starring role as a violinist-prizefighter in *Golden Boy* (1939) opposite Barbara Stanwyck, Holden was featured in such films as *Our Town* (1940), *I Wanted Wings* (1941), and *Blaze at Noon* (1947). In 1948 he escaped what he termed his "Smiling Jim" roles when he was cast as a psychopathic gangster in *The Dark Past.* One of his

best-known performances was as the ill-fated lover of Gloria Swanson in *Sunset Boulevard* (1950); that portrayal of a young writer won him his first Academy Award nomination. Other films include *The Moon Is Blue, Executive Suite, Sabrina, The Country Girl, The Bridges at Toko-Ri, Love Is a Many-Splendored Thing, Picnic, The Bridge on the River Kwai, The World of Suzie Wong,* and *Network,* for which he gained his third Academy nomination. His last film was *S.O.B.*

Hollowood, (Albert) Bernard, British journalist, economist, and cartoonist (b. June 3, 1910, Burs-

lem, Staffordshire, England—d. March 28, 1981, Shamley Green, Surrey, England), edited the humour magazine *Punch* from 1957 to 1968 and expanded the magazine's format to include serious political and social comment as well as humour. He studied at the University of London School of Economics and taught at Loughborough College before joining the staff of *The Economist* (1944–45). As a cartoonist he began to contribute to *Punch* in 1942. At its best his work was witty and concise, qualities that were particularly evident in the topical "pocket cartoons" that he later contributed to *The Times* of London.

Hörbiger, Paul, Austrian actor (b. April 29, 1894, Budapest, Hun.—d. March 5, 1981, Vienna, Austria), was a leading player with the Vienna Burgtheater and an immensely popular motion picture actor. Hörbiger made his debut in 1919, joined the Prague German Theatre, and in 1926 was invited to Berlin by Max Reinhardt. In 1940 Hörbiger became a member of the Burgtheater and appeared there in many outstanding productions, notably Ferdinand Raimund's *Der Alpenkönig und der Menschenfeind.* Arrested by the Gestapo in 1944, Hörbiger was condemned to death for his resistance activities, but the war ended and he resumed his career. Though he often portrayed a typically Viennese character, he was an actor of great versatility. His range was evident in the variety of parts he played in some 300 films that included *Congress Dances* (1931) and *The Third Man* (1949); he was also frequently seen on television, notably in the series "The Old Judge."

Humes, Helen, U.S. singer (b. June 23, 1913, Louisville, Ky.—d. Sept. 9, 1981, Santa Monica, Calif.), was a sensational jazz and blues singer who performed with Count Basie's orchestra (1938–42) and recorded such songs as "If Papa Has Outside Lovin'," "Do What You Did Last Night," and "Everybody Does It Now." Humes, who was noted for her high-pitched, sweet-toned voice, was especially associated with "Sub-Deb Blues," but she preferred singing such songs as "He May Be Your Man but He Comes to See Me Sometimes" and "The Million Dollar Secret." After leaving Basie's band Humes made the famous hit single "Be-Baba-Leba." She made several comebacks between periods of taking care of her ailing parents. Humes's last appearances included those in the late 1970s at the Cookery in New York City and on tour in Europe.

Ichikawa, Fusae, Japanese feminist and legislator (b. May 15, 1893, Onishi, Aichi Prefecture, Japan—d. Feb. 11, 1981, Tokyo, Japan), campaigned for women's right to vote as the dynamic founder (1924) of the Woman's Suffrage League in Japan. Earlier Ichikawa organized the New Woman's Association (1920), which lobbied for the inclusion of women participants at political gatherings. The law was revised in 1922 to include women. In 1940 the Woman's League was dissolved by the military, but women were granted the right to vote in 1945 under the Allied occupation. Ichikawa was first elected to the Diet in 1953 and was reelected five times. She was defeated in 1971, but in 1974 she made a comeback and was reelected in 1980.

Jackson of Lodsworth, Barbara Mary Jackson, Baroness (Barbara Mary Ward), British economist (b. May 23, 1914, York, England—d. May 31, 1981, Lodsworth, West Sussex, England), was a persuasive spokesman for a closer Western unity and concern for the interests of third world countries. Ward's Roman Catholicism was a major influence on her outlook and convinced her of the need for a juster and less wasteful economic order. She was president of the International Institute for Environment and Development from 1973 and its chairman from 1980. Ward studied at the University of Oxford and wrote a book on colonial problems, *The International Share-Out* (1938), before becoming assistant editor of *The Economist* in 1939.

During World War II she was well known as a panelist on the British radio program "The Brains Trust" and as a lecturer for the Ministry of Information. She was visiting scholar (1957–68) and Carnegie fellow (1959–67) at Harvard University and Schweitzer professor of international economic development (1968–73) at Columbia University. Pres. Lyndon B. Johnson was among those influenced by her advocacy of world economic cooperation. In 1967 she was appointed to the Vatican Pontifical Commission for Justice and Peace and in 1971 became the first woman to address a Vatican Assembly. Her books included *India and the West* (1961), *The Rich Nations and the Poor Nations* (1962), *Spaceship Earth* (1966), and *Only One Earth,* written with René Dubos for the 1972 UN Conference on the Human Environment. She was made a Dame Commander of the Order of the British Empire in 1974 and a life peer in 1976.

Jaffee, Irving, U.S. speed skater (b. 1907?—d. March 20, 1981, San Diego, Calif.), dazzled spectators at the 1932 Winter Olympic Games when he won gold medals in the 5,000- and 10,000-m speedskating events. Four years earlier at St. Moritz, Switz., Jaffee was declared Olympic champion in the 10,000-m race after melting ice prevented some skaters from competing. The International Skating Federation, however, labeled this victory an unofficial one, and he received no gold medal that year. In 1940 Jaffee was inducted into the U.S. Skating Hall of Fame. In later years he made several unsuccessful attempts to recover his Olympic and other medals that had been pawned during the Depression.

Jessel, George, U.S. entertainer (b. April 3, 1898, New York, N.Y.—d. May 24, 1981, Los Angeles, Calif.), earned the title "toastmaster general of the United States" because of his skill in serving as master of ceremonies, after-dinner speaker, and eulogist at hundreds of funerals. During his comedic career, which he began at the age of nine, Jessel entertained his audiences with anecdotes about his poor Jewish upbringing in Harlem in New York City, and during his heyday he performed a vaudeville act that featured a phone conversation with his mother, climaxed by a tender song. His success on Broadway was heightened by his performance in *The Jazz Singer* (1925). His acting career continued in such productions as *The War Song, Joseph,* and *Sweet and Low.* From 1943 to 1953 Jessel pursued a

UPI

career in Hollywood and produced films for 20th Century-Fox, among them *Meet Me After the Show, Golden Girl,* and *Wait till the Sun Shines, Nellie.* Often making guest appearances at fund raisers, rallies, and political meetings, he wore a self-styled uniform adorned with medals, stars, and ribbons. His services were given recognition in 1970 when he received the Jean Hersholt Humanitarian Award of

the Academy of Motion Picture Arts and Sciences. Jessel, who was especially proficient at delivering eulogies, issued his own epitaph: "I tell you here from the shade, it is all worthwhile."

Johnson, Pamela Hansford (Lady Snow), British novelist (b. May 29, 1912, London, England—d. June 19, 1981, London), was for many years a prominent figure in London's literary life. Her novels treated moral concerns with a light touch and covered a wide range of social milieus. They met with critical acclaim but achieved less popularity than those of her husband, C. P. Snow. In her youth Johnson was a close friend of Dylan Thomas, and in 1934 she published a book of verse, *Symphony for Full Orchestra.* Her first novel, *This Bed Thy Centre* (1935), was followed by 18 others, the last being *A Bonfire* (1981). *Too Dear for My Possessing* (1940), *An Avenue of Stone* (1947), and *A Summer to Decide* (1948) formed a trilogy covering a related group of people from the 1920s to the end of the 1940s. Later novels, more satirical in approach, were *The Unspeakable Skipton* (1959), *Night and Silence Who Is Here?* (1963), and *Cork Street, Next to the Hatter's* (1965). Johnson also wrote plays and criticism and a collection of essays, *Important to Me* (1974).

Kardiner, Abram, U.S. psychoanalyst (b. Aug. 17, 1891, New York, N.Y.—d. July 20, 1981, Easton, Conn.), together with Monroe Meyer and Bert Lewin founded (1930) the New York Psychoanalytic Institute, the first psychiatric training school in the U.S. In the 1950s he joined the Columbia University faculty and was director of Columbia's Psychoanalytic Institute. Kardiner, who graduated from Cornell University Medical College, New York City, had just completed his psychiatric residency at Manhattan State Hospital on Ward's Island when Sigmund Freud accepted him as a student-patient for six months in Vienna. When Kardiner returned to the U.S., he discarded Freud's teachings about latent homosexuality but was more accepting of his Oedipal theory, which he considered the crux of Freud's teachings. Kardiner was a leading proponent of a school of psychiatry that combined psychoanalysis and cultural anthropology and that emphasized the interplay of culture with the psyche. He also wrote several clinical books, including *The Individual and His Society* (1939; with Ralph Linton), *The Psychological Frontiers of Society* (1945; with others), *They Studied Man* (1961; with Edward Preble), and *My Analysis with Freud* (1977).

Kelly, Patsy (Bridget Veronica Kelly), U.S. actress (b. Jan. 21, 1910, New York, N.Y.—d. Sept. 24, 1981, Hollywood, Calif.), was a much-loved comedian who was best remembered for her disarming wisecracks, often as an Irish maid. She perfected this role in the Broadway production of *No, No, Nanette,* for which she won a Tony award in 1971. By age 16 Kelly was trouping across the country to appear in a series of revues with such celebrities as Will Rogers and Al Jolson. She then went to Hollywood and made numerous two-reelers with Thelma Todd, Pert Kelton, and Lyda Roberti. Kelly appeared in such films as *The Girl from Missouri, Pigskin Parade,* and *Topper Returns.* After a stint on radio during the mid–1940s, she performed in nightclubs and summer stock before securing a small part in the touring company of *Dear Charles,* which starred her friend Tallulah Bankhead. In the 1960s Kelly made a comeback in films and won wide acclaim for her performances as the maid in *Please Don't Eat the Daisies* (1960) and as a witch in *Rosemary's Baby* (1968).

Kemper, James Scott, U.S. insurance executive (b. Nov. 18, 1886, Van Wert, Ohio—d. Sept. 18, 1981, Chicago, Ill.), was the brash founder of the Kemper Group, the 14th-largest property and casualty insurance company in the U.S. Kemper was a junior insurance clerk before becoming manager of the Lumbermens Mutual Casualty Co., which he founded in 1912. During his tenure (1919–45) as president of the company, Kemper built it into a worldwide conglomerate with assets of $5 billion. Kemper's success was attributed to the quick set-

tlement of claims, the expansion of the mutual casualty carrier into automobile insurance, and public disclosure of the various companies' investments, which increased the confidence of policyholders. A wealthy conservative Republican, Kemper also served as chairman (1944–46) of the Republican National Finance Committee and treasurer (1960–64) of the party's National Committee. In 1953 Kemper was appointed U.S. ambassador to Brazil but relinquished the job 18 months later after being criticized for his blunt diplomacy. He retired as chairman and chief executive officer of the Kemper Group in 1966.

Kennedy, Daisy, Australian-born violinist (b. 1893, Burra, South Australia—d. July 30, 1981, London, England), gave recitals and concerts in major cities of the world and was often asked to give the first performance of new works for the violin. Kennedy grew up in South Australia and was educated at the University Conservatorium in Adelaide. She moved to Prague in 1908, where she studied with Otakar Sevcik, her longtime tutor. After making her Vienna and London debuts in 1911, Kennedy toured New Zealand and Australia (1919–20) and the U.S. (1920, 1925).

Knight, John Shively, U.S. newspaper magnate (b. Oct. 26, 1894, Bluefield, W.Va.—d. June 16, 1981, Akron, Ohio), was the founder of the Knight newspaper empire and the Pulitzer Prize-winning writer of the column entitled "The Editor's Notebook." Knight served as sportswriter and managing editor of the *Akron Beacon Journal* before inheriting the paper when his father died in 1933. His business acumen was evidenced with the acquisition of such newspapers as the *Miami Herald* and the *Times-Press* of Akron. By 1973 Knight owned 15 daily newspapers, and in 1974 Knight merged with Ridder Publications, increasing his

John Shively Knight

UPI

newspaper holdings by 19 dailies. By 1981 the Knight-Ridder chain included 34 daily newspapers in 17 states and boasted the largest weekly circulation of any chain in the country with 25 million copies. Knight was honoured in 1968 with a Pulitzer Prize for his editorial column. He fervently championed freedom of the world press and denounced censorship. In the same year two of Knight's newspapers, the *Detroit Free Press* and the *Charlotte* (N.C.) *Observer,* also won Pulitzers; thus the publisher received three prizes, an unprecedented feat in journalism. In 1976 Knight retired as editorial director of the Knight-Ridder chain.

Kondrashin, Kyril, Russian-born conductor (b. March 6, 1914, Moscow, Russia—d. March 7, 1981, Amsterdam, Neth.), revitalized the Moscow Philharmonic Orchestra as its musical director from 1960 to 1975. As one of the foremost conductors in the Soviet Union, he introduced works of such contemporary composers as Prokofiev and Shostakovich. His direct interpretations of older

composers earned him the nation's highest honour, People's Artist of the U.S.S.R. But Kondrashin, who continued to be drawn to Western music, felt artistically stifled in the Soviet Union and defected to The Netherlands in 1978. The following year he became conductor of the Amsterdam Concertgebouw. Kondrashin studied at the Moscow Conservatory and joined the Nemirovich-Danchenko Music Theatre as assistant conductor in 1934. From 1936 to 1943 he was conductor with the Maly Theatre in Leningrad, and he then spent 13 years with the Bolshoi Theatre in Moscow.

Kotarbinski, Tadeusz Marian, Polish philosopher and educator (b. March 31, 1886, Warsaw, Poland—d. Oct. 3, 1981, Warsaw), was professor of philosophy and logic (1919–61) at the University of Warsaw and rector (1945–49) of the University of Lodz. One of the founders of praxiology, he was the author of many books, including (in English translation) *Praxiology: An Introduction to the Sciences of Efficient Action* (1965) and *Gnosiology: The Scientific Approach to the Theory of Knowledge* (1966). Kotarbinski also served as president of the Polish Academy of Sciences (1957–62).

Krebs, Sir Hans Adolf, German-born biochemist (b. Aug. 25, 1900, Hildesheim, Germany—d. Nov. 22, 1981, Oxford, England), shared the 1953 Nobel Prize for Physiology or Medicine with Fritz A. Lipmann of the U.S. and was professor of biochemistry at the universities of Sheffield (1945–54) and Oxford (1954–67). Krebs began his work in metabolic biochemistry in Berlin and Freiburg before Hitler's rise to power prompted him to leave Germany for England. In 1935 he was appointed lecturer in pharmacology in Sheffield, where he continued his pioneering study of the synthesis of urea and the oxidation of carbon compounds in living creatures to produce carbon dioxide. During World War II he undertook nutritional research. He also directed the Medical Research Council's unit for research in cell metabolism. After retirement in 1967 Krebs continued research at the Radcliffe Infirmary, Oxford. He was made a fellow of the Royal Society in 1947 and knighted in 1958.

Krleza, Miroslav, Yugoslav writer (b. July 7, 1893, Zagreb, Yugos.—d. Dec. 29, 1981, Zagreb), was a prolific and outspoken literary figure who played a major role in Yugoslav letters between the wars and after World War II. Krleza was trained at the Ludoviceum Military Academy and served with the Austro-Hungarian Army during World War I. He then joined the Communist Party and founded a literary journal, *Plamen.* In 1920 Krleza began publishing a series of novels describing the decadence of the Croatian bourgeoisie, and in 1932 he wrote *The Return of Philip Latinovicz* (Eng. trans., 1960), a metaphysical novel. After World War II he was appointed director of the Yugoslav Institute of

Lexicography and president of the Yugoslav Writers' Union. In 1952, at the writers' congress in Ljubljana, he strongly attacked the doctrines of "socialist realism" and called for genuine cultural and creative freedom.

Lacan, Jacques, French psychologist (b. April 13, 1901, Paris, France—d. Sept. 9, 1981, Paris), acquired extraordinary celebrity status in France after the publication of *Écrits* (1966) and gained an international reputation as an original, controversial, and, for some, inspiring interpreter of the work of Sigmund Freud. He claimed to have purged Freudian psychoanalysis of the distortions introduced by post-Freudians and emphasized the primacy of language as the mirror of the unconscious mind. His work was associated with the fashionable theories of structuralism, and its influence extended well beyond the field of psychoanalysis to make him one of the dominant figures in French cultural life during the 1970s. Lacan founded the École Freudienne in Paris but dissolved it in 1980. He intended to replace it with a new school, still more closely aligned to Lacanian orthodoxy. He also wrote poetry and published several volumes of *Séminaires.*

Lancefield, Rebecca Craighill, U.S. bacteriologist (b. Jan. 5, 1895, Fort Wadsworth, N.Y.—d. March 3, 1981, New York, N.Y.), while conducting research at Rockefeller Institute (now Rockefeller University) created a system of classification of more than 60 different types of Group A streptococcal bacteria. Lancefield's studies were vital in proving that one type of streptococcal bacterium could cause a number of diseases, including scarlet fever, erysipelas, or a sore throat; physicians previously had believed that each type of clinical infection was caused by a specific type of streptococcal bacterium. Lancefield's research also led to a more efficacious treatment of streptococcal infections related to such conditions as scarlet fever, rheumatic fever, and glomerulonephritis, an acute inflammation of the kidneys. Lancefield graduated from Wellesley (Mass.) College and in 1918 became a technical assistant at Rockefeller Institute. She later obtained a Ph.D. in immunology and bacteriology at Columbia University. Lancefield spent her entire career (1918–80) at Rockefeller University.

Lasker, Edward, German-born chess master (b. Dec. 3, 1885, Kempen, Germany [now Poland]—d. March 23, 1981, New York, N.Y.), won chess titles in Berlin (1909) and London (1914) before immigrating to the U.S. and capturing five U.S. Open championships between 1916 and 1921. Lasker also gained recognition as the author of the standard work *Chess Strategy* (1915). In 1945 the opus was revised and retitled *Modern Chess Strategy.* His other works included *The Adventure of Chess* (1950), *Chess for Fun and Chess for Blood* (1942), and *Chess Secrets* (1951). As a member of the Marshall Chess Club in New York, Lasker charted yet another victory when he won first prize at the chess masters' tournament in Mexico City in 1954. From 1956 to 1960 he served as president of the club.

Lauwerys, Joseph Albert, Belgian-born educationist (b. Nov. 7, 1902, Belgium—d. June 29, 1981, Blackheath, Surrey, England), was an internationally renowned authority in the field of comparative education and served as director of the Atlantic Institute of Education, Nova Scotia (1970–76), associate professor at the Sorbonne, Paris (1969–74), and professor of comparative education at the University of London Institute of Education (1947–70). After completing his education in England, Lauwerys briefly taught science. In 1932 he joined the London Institute of Education as a lecturer and became reader in 1941. During World War II he cooperated with the education ministers of governments in exile in their plans to rehabilitate the educational systems of occupied countries. Immediately after the war he took part in the estab-

lishment of UNESCO, was a consultant from 1946 to 1948, and was a member of its Good Offices and Conciliation Commission from 1971. He was co-editor (1947–70) of the *World Year Book of Education* and the author of the article on the history of education in *Encyclopædia Britannica.* His many books included *Film in the School* (1936), *The Roots of Science* (1947), *Morals, Democracy and Education* (1958), *Essays in Comparative Education* (3 vol., 1969), and *Science, Morals and Moralogy* (1977).

Leander, Zarah Stina, Swedish singer and actress (b. March 15, 1907, Karlstad, Sweden—d. June 22, 1981, Stockholm, Sweden), began her long career as a star of stage and screen in 1929, when she made her first appearance in revue. Leander was an immediate success: her output of records, films, revues, and plays over the next few years was prolific. From 1936 to 1943 she stayed in Berlin to star in Nazi-made films. After World War II Leander was shunned by the Swedish people, who could not forgive her disloyalty. However, when she returned to the Swedish stage in 1949 in a Karl Gerhard revue, she regained her popularity.

Leavis, Q(ueenie) D(orothy), British literary critic (b. Dec. 7, 1906, London, England—d. March 17, 1981, Cambridge, England), married F. R. Leavis in 1929 and, through their joint editorship (1932–53) of the review *Scrutiny,* exercised a considerable influence on criticism and the academic study and teaching of English literature. Although she collaborated on many of her husband's books, her only major work was *Fiction and the Reading Public* (1932). This work was originally written as a thesis for her Ph.D. under the supervision of I. A. Richards at Cambridge. As co-editor of *Scrutiny,* Leavis showed her uncompromising belief in the need to maintain critical standards. Her work was an essential complement to that of her husband, though she never received the same recognition that he did. They wrote *Lectures in America* (1969) following a stay at Harvard, and the collaboration continued until F. R. Leavis's death in 1978.

Lee, Bernard, British actor (b. Jan. 10, 1908, London, England—d. Jan. 16, 1981, London), played character roles in more than 100 films but was best known as "M," the acerbic spymaster in the James Bond film series. Lee made his stage debut at age six, appearing with his father in a music-hall sketch. After studying at the Royal Academy of Dramatic Art, he maintained a steady career in repertory and on the London West End stage. After his army service in World War II Lee started acting in films. He also appeared in numerous television productions.

Leeder, Sigurd, German-born dancer and choreographer (b. Aug. 14, 1902, Hamburg, Germany—d. June 20, 1981, Herisau, Switz.), was influential in the development of modern dance in Europe. Leeder, who was a pupil of the dance theorist Rudolf Laban, was also a founder (1923) with Kurt Jooss of the Neue Tanzbühne in Münster. In 1927 the group moved to Essen, where they formed the Folkwang Dance Theatre Studio. In 1934, after Hitler came to power, they emigrated to England. As co-director of the Jooss-Leeder School of Dance and of the Ballets Jooss based at Dartington Hall, Devon, Leeder developed the school's teaching methods and created dances, including the popular *Sailor's Fancy.* In 1947, when the company disbanded, Leeder opened a school in London. After a six-year interval in Chile, he moved to Switzerland, where he continued to teach.

Lenya, Lotte (KAROLINE BLAMAUER), German singer and actress (b. Oct. 18, 1898, Penzing, Austria—d. Nov. 27, 1981, New York, N.Y.), was a raspy-voiced singer who became universally identified as a symbol of the glamour and toughness of Germany amid the despair of the 1930s through her portrayal of the prostitute Jenny in the satiric *Die Dreigroschenoper* (*The Threepenny Opera*), written by Bertolt Brecht and her husband, Kurt Weill. Lenya, who studied (1914–20) ballet and drama before marrying Weill in 1926, appeared in the first Brecht-Weill collaboration, *Singspiel* (*Little Mahagonny,*) and in the expanded version, *Aufstieg und Fall der Stadt Mahagonny* (*The Rise and Fall of the City of Mahagonny*). In 1933 Lenya and her husband fled Nazi Germany and emigrated to Paris. There Brecht and Weill composed their only work written specifically for Lenya, the drama-ballet *Die sieben Todsünden* (*The Seven Deadly Sins*). Two years later they moved to the U.S., and Lenya briefly appeared on stage in *The Eternal Road* and *Candle in the Wind.* After Weill's death in 1950, Lenya launched a large-scale revival of his European works and returned to the Broadway footlights in *The Threepenny Opera,* for which she won a Tony award, *The Seven Deadly Sins, Brecht on Brecht,* and *Cabaret.* She also appeared in such films as *The Roman Spring of Mrs. Stone, From Russia with Love,* and *Semi-Tough.*

Le Patourel, John Herbert, British historian (b. July 29, 1909, Guernsey, Channel Islands—d. July 22, 1981, Ilkley, West Yorkshire, England), was professor of medieval history at the University of Leeds from 1945 to 1970 and an expert on Franco-British relations during the Middle Ages. Le Patourel studied at Jesus College, Oxford, and in 1937 published his first book, on the medieval administration of the Channel Islands. At Leeds he founded the Medieval Group and was president of the Thoresby Society and the Yorkshire Archaeological Society. In 1966 he founded the journal *Northern History.* His work on Anglo-Norman studies resulted in *The Norman Empire* (1976). Le Patourel was elected a fellow of the British Academy in 1972.

Lewis, David, Canadian politician (b. June 23, 1909, Swislocz, Poland—d. May 23, 1981, Ottawa, Ont.), was a founder (1961) and leader (1971–75) of Canada's socialist New Democratic Party (NDP). Lewis, who helped lay the foundations for the Co-operative Commonwealth Federation as its secretary from 1937 to 1950, transformed the party into the NDP in 1961. The following year he was elected to the House of Commons but lost his seat in 1963. He regained his seat in 1965 and retained it in the 1968 and 1972 elections. His greatest success came in 1972 when he launched a campaign against "corporate welfare bums" who were receiving government concessions and aid and led the NDP to its strongest position ever, with 31 seats and the balance of power in the Commons. During this period Lewis used his influence and oratorical skill to increase benefits for veterans and the elderly and to establish a national oil company, Petro-Canada. In 1974 the NDP withdrew its support from the Liberal government, and in the subsequent elections Lewis lost his own seat. He retired from politics in 1975.

Lidell, (Tord) Alvar Quan, British radio announcer (b. 1908—d. Jan. 7, 1981, London, England), was recognized by millions of BBC listeners during World War II by his clear, authoritative voice, which reassured audiences that the reports they heard were reliable and objective. His broadcasts began with the phrase, "Here is the news and this is Alvar Lidell reading it." Lidell was later associated with music broadcasting and, after his retirement in 1969, recorded many "talking books" for the blind. After studying at Oxford University he worked as a teacher and an actor before joining the BBC in Birmingham. He moved to London in 1933 and announced such historic news events as the abdication of King Edward VIII (1936) and Prime Minister Neville Chamberlain's declaration of war on Germany in September 1939.

Liebman, Max, U.S. television producer (b. Aug. 5, 1902, Vienna, Austria—d. July 21, 1981, New York, N.Y.), brought a semblance of theatre to television as the producer of the smash hit variety program "Your Show of Shows" (1950–54), which featured such performers as Sid Caesar, Imogene Coca, Carl Reiner, and Marge and Gower Champion. Liebman's talented entertainers imitated the professionalism of a Broadway production by playing to live audiences with cameras and technicians hidden offstage. He introduced such writers as Mel Brooks and Neil Simon and was responsible for the 1950 television debut of Bob Hope. Liebman, who made his debut as a television producer in 1949 with "The Admiral Broadway Revue," was sometimes referred to as the "Ziegfeld of TV" because of the lavishness of his weekly 90-minute "Your Show of Shows."

Lilienthal, David E(li), U.S. government official (b. July 8, 1899, Morton, Ill.—d. Jan. 15, 1981, New York, N.Y.), was chairman of the Tennessee Valley Authority (TVA) and as first chairman of the Atomic Energy Commission was instrumental in the development of nuclear energy. Lilienthal, originally a utilities lawyer by profession, won a telephone-rate controversy that eventually resulted in a $20 million refund to Chicago telephone subscribers. A few years later, as a member of the Wisconsin Public Service Commission, he skillfully reorganized the utilities statutes for that state in such a way that they became a model for six other states. This drew the attention of Pres. Franklin D. Roosevelt, and when the TVA flood-control project was approved by Congress, Roosevelt named Lilienthal director of the TVA's power program in 1933. In 1941 he was appointed chairman of the project, and by 1943 the TVA was the largest producer of power for war in the Western Hemisphere, according to Lilienthal. By becoming the first chairman of the Atomic Energy Commission (AEC) in 1947, Lilienthal assumed power over the U.S. nuclear development program, which had previously been supervised by the Army. As chairman, Lilienthal was committed to improving and expanding plants for fissionable plutonium and uranium, to building up a stockpile of atomic bombs, and to developing nuclear weapons. He resigned from the AEC in 1950 and in 1953 became chairman and chief executive officer of Development and Research Corp., where he continued formulating a coordinated resource development program that included dams, irrigation, electric power, and flood control. His books included *Big Business, a New Era* (1953), *Change, Hope and the Bomb* (1963), and *Atomic Energy, a New Start* (1980).

Lindstrom, Fred Charles ("LINDY"), U.S. baseball player (b. Nov. 21, 1905, Chicago, Ill.—d. Oct. 4, 1981, Chicago), delighted New York Giant baseball fans when he joined the team at age 18 as a third baseman and outfielder and had ten hits against the Washington Senators in the 1924 World Series. Lindstrom, who played for the Giants (1924–32), Pittsburgh Pirates (1933–34), Chicago Cubs (1935), and Brooklyn Dodgers (1936), batted .300 or better from 1926 through 1931. His career batting average was .311, and he was inducted into the Baseball Hall of Fame in 1976. After retiring from baseball in 1936, Lindstrom was baseball coach at Northwestern University for 12 years and the postmaster in Evanston, Ill., for 17 years.

Ling, Hung-hsün, Chinese engineer (b. 1894, Canton, China—d. Aug. 15, 1981, Taipei, Taiwan), was a master railroad builder who constructed major railways including the Canton–Hankow line. Ling was chancellor of Chiao-Tung University in Shanghai, where he had received his education. From 1945 to 1949 he served as deputy minister of communications in Chiang Kai-shek's government, but when the Communists seized power in 1949, he fled to Taiwan with the Nationalists. There he was named chairman of the board of the Chinese Petroleum Corp., a position he held until his retirement in 1971. A noted scholar, Ling was also widely known as the author of *Railway Engineering* and *A Comprehensive Survey of Railway Development in China.*

Link, Edwin Albert, U.S. inventor (b. July 26, 1904, Huntington, Ind.—d. Sept. 7, 1981, Binghamton, N.Y.), was the fascinating inventor (1929) of the Link flight simulator, a mechanical device used to train millions of military and commercial airline pilots to make instrument landings. At first Link's invention was distributed to amusement parks, but in 1934, after dozens of U.S. Army pilots had been

killed making landings, Link's "blue box" was bought to train new pilots. In 1935 he founded Link Aviation Inc. and served as its president until the company became a subsidiary of General Precision Equipment Co. in 1954. He then became president of General Precision until it merged with the Singer Co. in 1968. Link, who was also responsible for introducing trainers for jet fighters, bombers, and transpolar celestial navigation, unveiled (1958) a high-density air navigation system that helped pilots avoid air collisions. During his later years Link turned increasingly to oceanographic exploration because he was convinced that the ocean held the key to food and energy for future generations. In order to facilitate undersea archaeological pursuits, Link co-developed (1960) the "Sea Diver," a bullet-shaped underwater scooter that towed a diver behind it. In the same year he co-invented the "Shark," a mobile, unmanned television camera used to explore the ocean depths and relay photos to a ship via cable. His other contributions include: the "lock-out submarine deep diver," the first submersible with an exit hatch for divers; the "submersible, portable, inflatable dwelling," an air-conditioned underwater home for undersea workers; and the "Sea Link," a rotorless helicopter able to transport four persons down to a depth of 4,575 m (1,500 ft). In 1980 Link was named recipient of the Charles A. Lindbergh Award, given for achievement in science and technology combined with preservation of the natural environment.

Llewelyn-Davies, Richard Llewelyn-Davies, BARON, British architect (b. Dec. 24, 1912—d. Oct. 27, 1981, London, England), was an authority on hospital design and served as professor of urban planning at University College, London, from 1969 until his death. Llewelyn-Davies trained in London and Paris and worked on railway station design before being appointed (1953) by the Nuffield Foundation to head a team investigating the design of hospitals. In 1960 he was appointed professor of architecture at University College, London, and simultaneously built up his architectural practice. His firm's designs for an extension to the Tate Gallery aroused controversy in 1965 and were eventually abandoned. His company designed the new Stock Exchange Tower in London, produced plans for the New Towns at Washington, County Durham, and Milton Keynes, and worked extensively abroad, notably in the U.S., Africa, and the Middle East. In 1963 Llewelyn-Davies became the first architect to be awarded a life peerage. He was president of the Society of Ekistics in 1965 and became an honorary fellow of the American Institute of Architects in 1970.

Lloyd, Sir Hugh Pughe, British air chief marshal (b. Dec. 12, 1894, Leigh, Worcester, England—d. July 13, 1981, Cheltenham, England), was in command of air force operations in Malta for 14 months during World War II and achieved remarkable success in disrupting German supply lines to North Africa. Lloyd was later responsible for British bombing operations in the Far East and after the war was air officer commander in chief of the Bomber Command (1950–53). His first experience of flying was in World War I, when he joined the Royal Flying Corps. He received the Distinguished Flying Cross and remained with the Air Force in India during the 1920s and 1930s. At the outbreak of World War II he was given command of a bomber squadron and by May 1940 had been promoted to senior air staff officer to No. 2 (Bomber) Group. A year later Lloyd was given command of the air forces on Malta and made a major contribution to the allied war effort by harassing enemy supply lines; he described his tactics in *Briefed to Attack* (1949). It was for this achievement that Lloyd was knighted in 1942.

Loeb, William, U.S. newspaper publisher (b. Dec. 26, 1905, Washington, D.C.—d. Sept. 13, 1981, Burlington, Mass.), as the influential right-wing publisher of the *Manchester* (N.H.) *Union Leader* and the *New Hampshire Sunday News,* penned vitriolic editorials printed in boldface, that lambasted presidential candidates and greatly swayed public opin-

ion. His blunt diatribes included attacks against Nelson Rockefeller, whom he termed a "wife swapper," and Pres. Dwight D. Eisenhower, whom he called a "stinking hypocrite." Loeb labeled Sen. Eugene McCarthy a "skunk's skunk," Pres. Richard M. Nixon "a foul ball" for having established diplomatic relations with China, Henry Kissinger "a tool of the Communist conspiracy," and Pres. Gerald R. Ford "a jerk." The target of his most damaging assault was Democratic Sen. Edmund Muskie. During the 1972 presidential campaign a spurious letter was printed in the *Union Leader* that charged Muskie with laughing at ethnic slurs aimed at French Canadians. A front-page editorial further claimed that Muskie's wife was overly fond of liquor. These charges and Muskie's tearful rebuttal to them were believed by many to have ruined his chances for the Democratic presidential nomination. In 1941 Loeb purchased his first newspaper, the *St. Albans* (Vt.) *Daily Messenger,* with money borrowed from his mother. In 1946 he bought a share of the *Union Leader,* which grew to a circulation of 65,000 and became New Hampshire's largest and only statewide daily. Loeb also voiced his views on lower-level politics: he ardently opposed state income and sales taxes and frequently berated state government administrators. In later years Loeb, who found himself in deep financial difficulties, was the subject of criticism when he borrowed $2 million from the Teamsters' Central States Pension Fund and became a champion of the union's jailed president, Jimmy Hoffa. In 1979 Loeb announced that 75% of his newspaper stock was being held in trust for his employees, but his will gave control to his wife and, after her death, to a nine-member board of trustees.

Loos, Anita, U.S. novelist and screenwriter (b. April 26, 1888, Sissons, Calif.—d. Aug. 18, 1981, New York, N.Y.), earned celebrity status with her classic roaring '20s story *Gentlemen Prefer Blondes* (1925), originally serialized in *Harper's Bazaar;* it became a smash hit musical in 1949. The spoof on sex and materialism featured the blonde vamp Lorelei Lee, who insisted that "diamonds are a girl's best friend." Loos contended that she modeled Lorelei after a woman whom her friend H. L. Mencken was dating. The book became an international best-seller with 85 editions and was translated into 14 languages. A child actress who began writing at an early age, Loos's first film scenario, *The New York Hat,* was produced by D. W. Griffith in 1912. With her husband, John Emerson, Loos wrote the subtitles for such silent films as *A Virtuous Vamp, The Perfect Woman,* and *Learning to Love.* She wrote numerous screenplays and such Broadway plays as *The Whole Town's Talking* (1923), *The Fall of Eve* (1925), and *Happy Birthday* (1946). Her books include *But Gentlemen Marry Brunettes* (1928), *A Mouse Is Born* (1951), and her memoirs, *A Girl Like I* (1966).

Lopokova, Lydia Vasilievna (LADY KEYNES), Russian-born ballerina (b. Oct. 21, 1892, St. Petersburg [now Leningrad], Russia—d. June 8, 1981, Sussex, England), excelled in roles that gave rein to her exuberant vitality and humoristic sense, such as Mariuccia in *The Good-Humoured Ladies.* A pupil at the St. Petersburg Imperial Ballet School, she made her first stage appearance in 1901 at the Maryinsky Theatre. After dancing some solo parts with the Imperial Russian Ballet, Lopokova was chosen by Sergey Diaghilev for his 1910 production of *The Firebird,* in Paris. She then spent some years in New York, rejoining Diaghilev's Ballets Russes in 1915. As well as creating the part of Mariuccia in 1917, she won great acclaim as the Lilac Fairy in Diaghilev's 1921 London production of *The Sleeping Beauty.* In 1925 Lopokova married the economist J. M. Keynes and thereafter danced rarely.

Louis, Joe (JOSEPH LOUIS BARROW), U.S. boxer (b. May 13, 1914, Lafayette, Ala.—d. April 12, 1981, Las Vegas, Nev.), was the much admired heavyweight champion of the world for 12 years and perhaps the greatest boxer in the history of the sport. Louis first donned the heavyweight crown when he knocked out James J. Braddock on June 22, 1937; over the next 12 years he defended his title 25 times, scoring 21 knockouts. After begin-

ning his boxing career in Detroit, Louis went on to win the national Amateur Athletic Union light-heavyweight championship in 1934. His first professional bout was against Jack Kracken on July 4, 1934, but his claim to fame came the following year in New York when he knocked out Primo Carnera. Louis's devastating left jabs and hooks earned him the title "Brown Bomber." His repeated victories, coupled with his willingness to risk his championship by taking on all challengers, won him widespread popularity. Louis sustained his first professional loss in 1936 at the hands of Max Schmeling, but in 1938, after having beaten Braddock, Louis fought Schmeling with a vengeance and knocked him out in a record two minutes and four seconds. During the peak of his career (1939–42) Louis displayed remarkable durability, defending his title seven times between December 1940 and June 1941. After joining the U.S. Army in 1942, Louis gave 96 boxing exhibitions before two million soldiers scattered around the world. His record includes knockout victories over such champions as Buddy Baer, Jack Sharkey, and "Jersey" Joe Walcott. After defeating the latter a second time, the undefeated champion retired on March 1, 1949. He made a comeback in 1950 against champion Ezzard Charles but lost in 15 rounds. His last fight of consequence was in 1951 when he lost to Rocky Marciano. In 1954 Louis, who had won 68 professional fights while losing only three, was elected to the Boxing Hall of Fame. Although he had made over $4 million in the ring, he was unable to account for much of it. By 1960 the Internal Revenue Service calculated that Louis owed the government approximately $1,250,000 in taxes. In later years Louis tried to support himself as a professional wrestler. In 1969, after he collapsed on a New York street, he confessed he had been using cocaine. The following year Louis entered a mental hospital to be treated for paranoia. His final years were spent as an official greeter at Caesar's Palace in Las Vegas, Nev. He was buried in Arlington National Cemetery at the request of Pres. Ronald W. Reagan.

Lubalin, Herb(ert) Frederick, U.S. graphic designer (b. March 17, 1918, New York, N.Y.—d. May 24, 1981, New York), was a top-notch graphic designer, best known as the inventor of the avant-garde typeface. An unassuming perfectionist, Lubalin

redesigned such diverse periodicals as *Reader's Digest*, *The Saturday Evening Post*, and *The New Leader*. His flair for design was also showcased in graphics for advertising. He turned out designs for the soft drink Sprite, for Bazooka bubble gum, and for Chicken of the Sea tuna. After serving as art director for various advertising agencies, Lubalin became vice-president, art director, and creative director of Sudler & Hennessey. In the mid-1960s he was president of his own company, Herb Lubalin Inc., but he eventually joined forces with associates and founded Lubalin, Peckolick Associates.

Ludden, Allen (Ellsworth), U.S. game show host (b. Oct. 5, 1918?, Mineral Point, Wis.—d. June 9, 1981, Los Angeles, Calif.), was the quick-witted emcee of such television game shows as "The General Electric College Bowl" (1959–63) and "Password," an immensely popular daytime game show that ran from 1961 to 1967, was revived in 1971, and continued, under varying formats, names, and networks, to the current season. Ludden retired as host in 1979.

Lyons, Dame Enid Muriel, Australian politician (b. July 9, 1897, Leesville, Tasmania—d. Sept. 2, 1981, Canberra, Australia), was the first woman member of the Australian House of Representatives (1943–51) and of the federal Cabinet (1949–51). At the age of 17 she married Joseph Lyons, then minister of education and later prime minister. After his death in 1939, she served (1949–51) as vice-president of the Executive Council, Australia, and then as a member of the board of control of the Australian Broadcasting Commission until 1962. In 1937, visiting Britain for the coronation of King George VI, she was invested with the Grand Cross of the Order of the British Empire; in 1980 she was made Dame of the Order of Australia. Lyons wrote two volumes of autobiography, *So We Take Comfort* (1965) and *Among the Carrion Crows* (1973).

MacDonald, Malcolm John, British politician (b. August 1901, Lossiemouth, Scotland—d. Jan. 11, 1981, near Sevenoaks, Kent, England), was an active diplomat who played a major role in Commonwealth affairs and the son of Britain's first Labour prime minister, James Ramsay MacDonald (1866–1937). MacDonald was elected to Parliament in 1929 as Labour member for Bassetlaw and served as secretary of state for the colonies in 1935 and again from 1938 to 1940. The following year he went to Canada as high commissioner, remaining in that post until his appointment in 1946 as governor-general of the Malayan Union and Singapore. There he presided over the difficult years of Communist terrorist activity and helped make the transition to Malayan independence a smooth one. During 1948–55 he was commissioner-general for the U.K. in Southeast Asia. After five years (1955–60) as high commissioner in India, he headed the British delegation at the Geneva conference on Laos. In 1963 he was sent to Kenya as governor and was responsible for reinstating into Parliament Jomo Kenyatta, who had been imprisoned by previous British administrators. By bringing Kenyatta to leadership, MacDonald helped to ensure the country's progress to a stable independence in 1964. He was Kenya's governor-general (1963–64) and high commissioner (1964–65) until Prime Minister Harold Wilson appointed him Britain's roving envoy in Africa. After MacDonald's retirement in 1970, he continued to travel extensively and wrote several books on ornithology and travel. He was chancellor of the universities of Malaya (1949–61) and Durham (from 1970). A privy councillor from 1935, he was awarded the Order of Merit in 1969.

McKenzie, Robert Trelford, Canadian sociologist (b. Sept. 11, 1917, Vancouver, B.C.—d. Oct. 12, 1981, London, England), became professor of sociology at the London School of Economics and Political Science (LSE) in 1964 and won fame as a television interviewer and political commentator. McKenzie studied, and later lectured, at the University of British Columbia. After World War II McKenzie wrote a doctoral thesis at the LSE that was later published as *British Political Parties* (1955), an original and controversial analysis of the power structure of the Conservative and Labour parties. He became a lecturer at the LSE in 1949. During the early 1950s McKenzie gave occasional talks on radio and television, but in 1955 he appeared on television as an election commentator and launched his most celebrated role. His name became linked (1964) with the "swingometer," on which he demonstrated the emerging trends as the election results came in. But his personal qualities were more evident in his television interviews, notably those with former prime minister Harold Macmillan. McKenzie was twice chairman of the LSE sociology department and was a much admired teacher. He continued to take an interest in Canadian politics and in 1969 was awarded an honorary doctorate at Simon Fraser University, Vancouver.

Maeght, Aimé, French art dealer (b. April 27, 1906, Hazebrouck, France—d. Sept. 6, 1981, Saint-Paul-de-Vence, France), handled the work of leading contemporary artists and became a central figure in French cultural life as a publisher of fine art editions, exhibition organizer, impresario, and creator in 1964 of the Fondation Maeght, a unique art centre in Saint-Paul-de-Vence. Trained as a lithographic printer, Maeght first met leading contemporary artists while working on posters and programs in Cannes. When World War II broke out, the small gallery he had opened acquired a precious collection of paintings from dealers whose Paris galleries had closed because of the German occupation. Maeght himself had to leave Cannes because of his aid to the Resistance and moved to Venice, where he gave shelter to Bonnard and was a neighbour of Matisse. After the liberation Maeght went to Paris and opened a gallery to exhibit works by these painters and other major contemporary artists, including Braque, Chagall, Miró, and Giacometti.

Malina, Frank Joseph, U.S. aeronautical engineer (b. Oct. 2, 1912, Brenham, Texas—d. Nov. 9, 1981, Paris, France), was a pioneering rocketeer who with Theodore von Kármán founded in the late 1930s what became known in 1944 as the Jet Propulsion Laboratory (JPL). Malina, who earned a Ph.D. from the California Institute of Technology in 1940, served as the first director of the JPL from 1944 to 1946. In 1942 he formed Aerojet-General, which became a major aerospace firm. He and Kármán developed solid-fuel rockets that gave propeller-driven aircraft faster takeoffs, and they also helped design (1945) the WAC Corporal, one of the country's first high-altitude sounding rockets. Their original research helped the U.S. put the first man on the Moon. In 1946 Malina moved to France to join UNESCO's scientific research division, which he later headed.

Maltese, Michael, U.S. cartoon animator and writer (b. 1908, New York, N.Y.—d. Feb. 22, 1981, Los Angeles, Calif.), with Charles ("Chuck") Jones created such delightful Warner Bros. cartoon characters as the ever elusive Road Runner, the frustrated Wile E. Coyote, and the debonair skunk Pépé le Pew. Maltese also wrote scripts and devised endless capers for Woody Woodpecker, Daffy Duck, Elmer Fudd, and Yosemite Sam. In 1957 Maltese joined Hanna-Barbera, where he worked on "Yogi Bear," "Huckleberry Hound," and "The Flintstones." After his retirement in 1971, Maltese wrote comic books and helped Jones make "The Return of Duck Dodgers to the 24½ Century."

Mao Dun (MAO TUN), Chinese writer (b. May 27, 1896, Tongxiang [T'ung-hsiang], Zhejiang [Chekiang] Province, China—d. March 27, 1981, Beijing [Peking], China), was born Shen Dehong (Shen Te-hung) but was best known as one of modern China's greatest Realist novelists under the pseudonyms Shen Yanbing (Shen Yen-ping) and Mao Dun, the latter being the Chinese term for contradiction. After leaving Peking University because of lack of funds, Mao Dun became involved in left-wing activities as a proofreader, then editor and translator, at the Commercial Press; as a member of the Literary Research Association; and as editor (1920–23) of the journal *Hsiao-shuo yüeh-pao* ("Short Story Magazine"). In 1926 Mao Dun joined Chiang Kai-shek's Northern Expedition against the warlords as secretary to the propaganda department of the Kuomintang (KMT) Central Executive Committee. But when left-wing KMT members broke with the Chinese Communists, Mao Dun pleaded illness and went to Kuling. In 1930 he helped organize the Left-Wing Writers League and in the same year published his famous trilogy, *Shih* ("Eclipse"), a brilliant account of a group of young intellectuals before and during the Northern Expedition. His objective analysis and psychological realism chronicled modern Chinese society and prompted Western critics to proclaim *Shih* his masterpiece. It was *Tzu-yeh* (1933; *Midnight*, 1957), however, an indicting portrayal of Shanghai's bustling industrialism, that made Mao Dun the foremost novelist of his day. During the Sino-Japanese War Mao Dun continued his leftist literary activities, but after the Communist government took power in 1949, he wrote virtually no more novels, short stories, or plays. Mao Dun was China's minister of culture (1949–65) and was appointed to a number of other positions, which were in most cases more honorary than politically significant. At the time of his death Mao Dun's reminiscences, written some 30 years earlier, were about to be published for the first time.

Marley, Bob (ROBERT NESTA MARLEY), Jamaican reggae singer and composer (b. Feb. 6, 1945, St. Ann, Jamaica—d. May 11, 1981, Miami, Fla.), brought reggae to an international audience and became a noted ambassador for his country and his music. Marley's "dreadlocks," his Rastafarian faith, and his uncompromising lyrics set the tone for the assertion of black consciousness in the 1970s and, despite his fame, he remained close to the disinherited youth of the Jamaican slums. Marley made his first record in 1961 and formed his group The Wailers with Bunny Livingstone and Peter Tosh in 1963. In 1972 he signed a contract with Island Records and became an international star with such albums as *Catch a Fire*, *Natty Dread*, and *Exodus*. Marley, who tried to remain aloof from Jamaican partisan politics, was a victim of an assassination attempt in 1976, apparently for political reasons. In 1978 he brought together the country's two rival party leaders at a "peace concert" and was invited to attend the Zimbabwe independence celebration in 1980. Marley was awarded the Jamaican Order of Merit shortly before his death from cancer.

Marshall, Thomas Humphrey, British sociologist (b. Dec. 19, 1893, London, England—d. Nov. 29, 1981, Cambridge, England), was a pioneer in the academic study of sociology and in the application of sociological concepts to social policy. His major work, *Social Policy in the Twentieth Century* (1965), became a classic in the field, and his approach was informed by his awareness of work in other disciplines, notably in economic history. He read history at Cambridge and, after World War I, became a fellow of Trinity College. After Marshall joined the London School of Economics as lecturer in 1925, he became (1930) reader in sociology, headed the social science department (1944–50), and served as Martin White professor of sociology (1954–56). During 1956–60 he was director of the Social Science Department of UNESCO. Marshall, who helped found the *British Journal of Sociology*, also published *Sociology at the Crossroads, and Other Essays* (1963) and *The Right to Welfare* (1981).

Martin, Sir James, British engineer (b. 1893, County Down, Ireland—d. Jan. 5, 1981, Denham, Buckinghamshire, England), invented the Martin-Baker aircraft ejector seat, a safety device for military aircraft that has protected over 4,700 airmen in their escape from fighter planes. The seat was first tested in 1946, and Martin steadily improved the design to keep pace with the development of supersonic aircraft and to protect pilots ejecting at

high altitudes. He trained as an engineer in Belfast before founding the Martin Aircraft Co. in 1929, which five years later became the Martin-Baker Aircraft Co. Martin was also responsible for improving the armament of World War II fighter aircraft and for inventing a device to cut barrage balloon cables. He was knighted in 1965, was named Officer of the Order of the British Empire and Commander of the Order of the British Empire and received the Royal Aero Club Gold Medal.

Martin, Ross (MARTIN ROSENBLATT), U.S. actor (b. March 22, 1920, Grodek, Poland—d. July 3, 1981, Ramona, Calif.), portrayed Artemus Gordon, an ingenious U.S. government agent who used various disguises, foreign accents, and sophisticated gadgets to thwart or capture an assortment of villains in the fantasy Western television series "The Wild, Wild West" (1965–69). Martin, who launched his acting career on radio with three roles in the "Janice Gray" radio series, was also featured in such television shows as "Mr. Lucky" and the game show "Stump the Stars." His film credits included *Experiment in Terror, The Great Race,* and *The Ceremony.*

Matthews, Jessie, British actress (b. March 11, 1907, London, England—d. Aug. 19, 1981, London), became an international star of stage and screen musicals during the 1930s and was immensely popular after World War II playing the lead role in the radio soap opera "Mrs. Dale's Diary." Matthews studied ballet and by 1923 had her first break in C. B. Cochran's *The Music Box Revue.* She was spotted by André Charlot, who took her with his *Revue of 1924* to New York, where, as Gertrude Lawrence's understudy, she had her first major role. From then on, in *This Year of Grace, Ever Green, Hold My Hand,* and *Wake Up and Dream,* she gained success after success; the film (1933) *The Good Companions* made Matthews an international star. After World War II she appeared in many stage and television plays and in 1963 took over the part of Mrs. Dale. She was made an Officer of the Order of the British Empire in 1970, and her autobiography, *Over My Shoulder,* was published in 1974.

Maudsley, Ronald Harling, British jurist (b. April 8, 1918, Cheshire, England—d. Sept. 29, 1981, San Diego, Calif.), was professor of law at the New York Law School from 1977 to 1981. Maudsley, who studied at the University of Birmingham, later taught for 20 years as a fellow of Brasenose College, Oxford. From 1966 to 1977 he was professor of law at King's College, London, before moving to the U.S. Together with E. H. Burn, Maudsley wrote *Land Law* (1967) and *Trusts and Trustees* (1973), but he was best known for his study of *The Modern Law of Perpetuities* (1979).

Maugham, Robin (ROBERT CECIL ROMER MAUGHAM, 2ND VISCOUNT MAUGHAM), British novelist (b. May 17, 1916, London, England—d. March 13, 1981, Brighton, England), was the author of many novels that were often set against exotic backgrounds and dealt with complicated personal relationships. He also wrote books of reminiscences, including some about his uncle, the writer W. Somerset Maugham (*Conversations with Willie*). Maugham, whose father served as lord chancellor in the late 1930s, was educated at Eton and Cambridge. Seriously wounded in World War II, he worked briefly at the Middle East Intelligence Centre before leaving the Army in 1944. Abandoning a brief legal career, he began to publish novels, among them *The Servant* (1948), later adapted for the stage and the cinema. His other novels included *The Man with Two Shadows* (1958) and *The Second Window* (1968). His autobiography, *Escape from the Shadows* (1972), revealed his homosexuality and was followed by *Search for Nirvana* (1975), also autobiographical.

Mayer, Stefan Antoni, Polish Army officer (b. Sept. 25, 1895, Rawa Ruska, Poland—d. March 24, 1981, London, England), led the intelligence team that cracked the German Army's cipher machine Enigma during the 1930s. The Polish models of Enigma, passed on to the British and French intelligence services shortly before the outbreak of World War

II, were of immense value to the Allied war effort. Mayer studied law and during World War I was a member of Jozef Haller's anti-Communist brigade in the Ukraine. He stayed in the Polish Army after the 1921 peace treaty with the Soviet Union. In 1930 he became head of the intelligence service and supervised the breaking of the Enigma ciphers. When a more complex version of the machine was introduced in 1938, the Polish team was equally successful in mastering it and in the following year offered it to Britain and France. When war broke out, Mayer escaped through France to Britain.

Menuhin, Hephzibah (HEPHZIBAH MENUHIN HAUSER), U.S. pianist (b. May 20, 1920, San Francisco, Calif.—d. Jan. 1, 1981, London, England), was a child prodigy whose exceptional piano playing provided a superb accompaniment for the violin of her brother, Yehudi Menuhin. After winning France's Prix du Disque (1932) for their first recordings, the two made their debut as a duo in Paris in 1934. Their closeness as siblings resulted in a unique and long-lasting musical collaboration that Yehudi described as their "Siamese soul." Besides performing with her brother, Menuhin made solo appearances throughout the world and was active in London social work and in disarmament causes during the 1960s and '70s.

Milward, Sir Anthony Horace, British airline executive (b. March 2, 1905, Redditch, England—d. May 12, 1981, Cheltenham, England), was chairman of British European Airways (BEA) from 1964 to 1970. After starting his career in a textile firm, he learned to fly and during World War II joined the Fleet Air Arm. Milward served as an operational pilot and, while gaining experience in experimental flying, tested new instruments and techniques. He worked briefly for British Overseas Airways Corp., then joined BEA as general manager when it was formed in 1946. Ten years later he became its director. After his retirement he was chairman (1971–76) of the London Tourist Board and then its president. He was made Commander of the Order of the British Empire in 1960 and knighted in 1966.

Montale, Eugenio, Italian poet (b. Oct. 12, 1896, Genoa, Italy—d. Sept. 12, 1981, Milan, Italy), was, with Giuseppe Ungaretti, the leading voice in 20th-century Italian poetry; his achievement was recognized in Italy when he was made a life senator in 1967 and internationally when he was awarded the 1975 Nobel Prize for Literature. His work, notable for its compression and pessimistic intellectuality, was classified with that of Ungaretti under the label Hermeticism. His uncompromising opposition to Fascism earned wide respect during the post-World War II period, when he was regarded as the Grand Old Man of Italian literature. Montale originally intended to become an opera singer, but instead he published his first poems after military service during World War I. His first major work, *Ossi de seppia* (1925), justified its title ("cuttlefish bones") both by the presence of the sea motif in many of the poems and by a style pared to the essentials of language and meaning. He won wide recognition with *Le occasioni* (1939), which appeared shortly after his dismissal from the post of director of the Vieusseux Library in Florence because of his refusal to join the Fascist Party. He spent the war years in Florence but moved to Milan in 1948, joining *Corriere della Sera* as music critic. *La bufera e altro* appeared in 1956, *Xenia* in 1966, and the collected poems in 1977. He was also a noted translator who helped introduce Italian readers to the work of T. S. Eliot, a poet to whom he was often compared.

Montgomery, Robert (HENRY MONTGOMERY, JR.), U.S. actor and director (b. May 21, 1904, Beacon, N.Y.—d. Sept. 27, 1981, New York, N.Y.), was a versatile leading man of the 1930s who turned in superb performances as the spirited, sophisticated gentleman playing opposite Norma Shearer in *The Divorcee* (1930), Helen Hayes in *Vanessa* (1935), and Joan Crawford in *The Last of Mrs. Cheyney* (1937). After Montgomery established his reputation as an actor in *The Big House* (1930), he appeared in a series of comedies opposite the leading ladies of Holly-

wood's "Golden Age." He later gained acclaim for dramatic roles, including that of a pathological murderer in *Night Must Fall* (1937), a gangster in *The Earl of Chicago* (1940), and a saxophone-playing fighter in *Here Comes Mr. Jordan* (1941). In 1949 Montgomery went into radio broadcasting but turned to television the following year with a highly successful dramatic program, "Robert Montgomery Presents" (1950–56). His directing debut came in 1945 when he finished directing *They Were Expendable* for the ailing John Ford. Montgomery then acted in and directed *Lady in the Lake* (1946), *Ride the Pink Horse* (1947), *Once More, My Darling* (1949), and *The Gallant Hours* (1960). In 1952 Montgomery gained national political attention as the television coach for Pres. Dwight D. Eisenhower. Montgomery became the first show business personality to occupy a White House office. In later years he turned to directing Broadway productions, including *The Desperate Hours* (1955) and *Calculated Risk* (1962). Montgomery was also one of the early presidents of the Screen Actors Guild.

Moses, Robert, U.S. builder (b. Dec. 18, 1888, New Haven, Conn.—d. July 29, 1981, West Islip, N.Y.), who more than anyone else transformed the New York landscape with a gigantic network of 35 highways, 12 bridges, 810,000 ha (2 million ac) of parks, 658 playgrounds, numerous housing projects, and two hydroelectric dams, all of which influenced planning in other U.S. cities. Moses studied political science at Yale, Oxford, and Columbia universities before entering New York politics in 1914. From 1924 to 1968 Moses, who never held elective office, maneuvered his power so that he maintained 12 separate city posts simultaneously. He was unwavering in his vision, so much so that he would threaten to resign if his plans were not implemented. He spent huge sums of money because he knew politicians would never leave a half-finished project as a monument to their own incompetence. Some of his most gigantic undertakings included Lincoln Center, the 1964 World's Fair, Shea Stadium, the Triborough Bridge, and Jones Beach State Park. He was also instrumental in bringing the UN building to the East River waterfront. In 1928 Franklin D. Roosevelt was elected governor of New York, and Moses's rise in power abruptly ended. The two spent endless hours in bitter controversy, and Roosevelt forced Moses out of his position as secretary of state of New York. However, Moses did hold onto his parks jobs owing to public support. When Fiorello H. La Guardia became mayor of New York City in 1933, Moses was appointed head of the City Parks Department and head of the Triborough Bridge and Tunnel Authority. In 1934, in his first and only

UPI

117

bid for elective office, Moses ran for governor and lost by a record 800,000 votes. During the 1940s and 1950s Moses built huge public housing towers, which became less and less attractive to the public. In 1959, his popularity waning, Moses relinquished his city posts and became president of the World's Fair. He lost most of his state jobs in 1962 when Nelson Rockefeller unexpectedly accepted his routine resignation. In 1968 Moses was stripped of his last post. Moses's accomplishments were placed under critical scrutiny when the book *The Power Broker*, by Robert Caro, was published in 1974. The 1,246-page work won Caro a Pulitzer Prize. He acknowledged Moses as "the greatest builder in America," while Moses's critics continued to point up the immensity and impersonality of his projects.

Muncey, Bill, U.S. hydroplane driver (b. 1929?—d. Oct. 18, 1981, Acapulco, Mexico), dominated unlimited-class hydroplane racing for more than 25 seasons with over 60 victories, 7 national titles, and 8 Gold Cups, more than any other competitor. He was killed when he lost control of his "Atlas Van Lines" boat during the final heat of the $175,000 World Championship race and the boat flipped over, severing his spinal cord.

Neel, Louis Boyd, British conductor (b. July 19, 1905, London, England—d. Sept. 30, 1981, Toronto, Ont.), was a leading exponent of Baroque music whose own orchestra, founded in 1932, was noted for its performances of new works and revivals of little-known music from the past. In 1952 he moved to Canada to become dean at the Royal Conservatory of Music in Toronto and founded the Hart House Orchestra (1955). His orchestra was particularly associated with the music of Bach and Handel and with modern works such as Britten's *Variations on a Theme of Frank Bridge*, which he took to Salzburg in 1937. He was made Commander of the Order of the British Empire in 1953 and received the Order of Canada (1973).

Newton, Ivor, British pianist (b. Dec. 15, 1892, London, England—d. April 21, 1981, London), was a versatile accompanist who worked with opera singers and variety artists in music halls and on the concert stage. In a career spanning more than 60 years he accompanied Dame Nellie Melba, Kirsten Flagstad, Beniamino Gigli, Maria Callas, Giuseppe Di Stefano, Clara Butt, and Gracie Fields. He also accompanied the instrumentalists Yehudi Menuhin and Pablo Casals. Newton's career began before World War I at seaside concert parties and in the variety theatre. After the war he studied lieder and became not only the most versatile accompanist of his time but also a musician who raised the art of accompaniment to the level of a respectable branch of the profession. He traveled widely and in 1973 accompanied Callas and Di Stefano on highly successful tours. His autobiography, *At the Piano—Ivor Newton* (1966), recalled with humour and admiration the great artists with whom he had worked. He was made Commander of the Order of the British Empire in 1973.

Ney, Marie, British actress (b. July 18, 1895, London, England—d. April 11, 1981, London), made her stage debut in Melbourne in 1916 but established her reputation as a Shakespearean actress in London, where she first appeared in 1923. During the Old Vic season of 1924–25 she played many leading roles, including Viola, Ophelia, and Lady Macbeth. For more than 30 years she was continuously employed, appearing in *The Constant Nymph, Arms and the Man, Dangerous Corner, The Lake,* and many other successful plays. Ney acted abroad for the British Council and ENSA (Entertainments National Service Association—the organization that provided entertainment for the forces) during World War II and returned to the London stage during the postwar years.

Nishio, Suehiro, Japanese politician (b. March 28, 1891, Nagasaki Prefecture, Japan—d. Oct. 3, 1981, Tokyo), helped organize the Marxist-oriented Japan Socialist Party but became impatient with its lack of pragmatism and founded the centre-left Democratic Socialist Party in 1960. Nishio was first elected to the Diet (parliament) in 1929 and in 1932 founded the Social Mass Party. He strongly opposed national mobilization and compared the military proponents to "Hitler and Stalin." This remark led to his ouster from the Diet. After World War II he played a leading role in the Japan Socialist Party and became chairman of the party's Central Committee in 1947. In the same year he was named chief secretary of Japan's first postwar coalition Cabinet headed by Prime Minister Tetsu Katayama. The following year he resigned his post as deputy prime minister in the coalition Cabinet of Hitoshi Ashida because he was implicated in a bribery case. He was later proved innocent. Nishio, who served as chairman of the Democratic Socialist Party from 1960 to 1967, retired from his post to make way for fresh leadership. For the next five years he remained in the Diet and served as the elder statesman of Japan's leftist opposition. He retired from politics in 1972.

Northrop, John Knudsen, U.S. aircraft designer (b. Nov. 10, 1895, Newark, N.J.—d. Feb. 18, 1981, Glendale, Calif.), was one of the most ambitious aircraft designers in the history of aviation and an early proponent of all-metal airplane construction and the flying-wing airplane design. Northrop cofounded Lockheed Aircraft Corp. in 1927 and designed the Lockheed Vega monoplane, which set many speed and endurance records. In 1928 Northrop founded the Avion Corp. (bought by United Aircraft and Transport in 1930), where he developed the Alpha (1930), one of the first modern, low-wing monoplanes. He left United in 1931 to form the Northrop Corp. in El Segundo, Calif. There he constructed the Northrop Gamma, the A-17 and A-17A attack planes, the Navy BT-1 dive-bomber, and various other military craft for foreign countries. In 1937 the company became the El Segundo division of Douglas Aircraft Co. Northrop's pioneering spirit led him to found Northrop Aircraft Inc. in 1939 and to design such planes as the XB-35 flying-wing bomber; the YB-49, a jet-powered version of the XB-35; the N-1M, the world's first successful all-wing plane; the P-61 Black Widow night fighter; the F-89 Scorpion jet fighter; and the B-35 and B-49 bombers for the U.S. Air Force. Northrop retired as director in 1952, and his company was renamed Northrop Corp. in 1959. During World War II Northrop employed wounded hospitalized veterans for small assembly jobs related to his night fighter. After the war he established a prosthetic department, where he developed an improved prosthetic arm and hand.

Nummi, Seppo, Finnish composer (b. May 30, 1932, Oulu, Finland—d. Aug. 1, 1981, Tampere, Finland), was a central figure in contemporary Finnish musical life both as a composer and as founder and director (1969–79) of the Helsinki Festival. Nummi also revived the Savonlinna Opera Festival and was an honorary member of the Finnish Cultural Foundation. After studying at Helsinki University and at the Sibelius Academy, he continued his studies in Germany and Italy. Nummi's works include a string quartet and many songs and madrigals, as well as compositions for the piano. He also served as music critic of the daily newspaper *Uusi Suomi.*

Oakley, Kenneth Page, British anthropologist (b. April 7, 1911—d. Nov. 2, 1981, Amersham, England), used scientific methods of analysis to expose the 1953 Piltdown hoax. The Piltdown skull, allegedly discovered in Sussex in 1912, had been accepted as the remains of *Eoanthropus*, a primitive man who provided the "missing link" between man and ape. Oakley's application of fluorine analysis for dating, using a technique he had developed, proved that the remains were fraudulent. He studied at University College in London and earned a Ph.D. in 1938. He worked with the Geological Survey and the British Museum (Natural History) and investigated sites in Britain and abroad. Oakley also contributed articles and chapters to major publications in the field of paleontology and published his own *Frameworks for Dating Fossil Man* (1964). Besides winning the Prestwich and Henry Stokes Memorial medals, he was a fellow of the British Academy and of University College and served as president of the Anthropological Section of the British Association in 1961.

O'Connor, Sir Richard Nugent, British Army officer (b. Aug. 21, 1889—d. June 17, 1981, London, England), was a much decorated army officer who engineered the brilliant advance (1940–41) against the Italian Army in Libya. O'Connor, who was trained at the Royal Military Academy at Sandhurst, was commissioned in 1909. He fought on the Western Front during World War I, was made a Companion of the Distinguished Service Order with bar, and received the Military Cross and the Italian Silver Medal for valour. His interwar career was equally impressive: during the 1930s he saw active service in the Khyber Pass, and from 1938 to 1939 he was military governor of Jerusalem. After being transferred to Egypt, O'Connor helped draw up the plans for the 1940 offensive against the Italian Army. In early December he launched a surprise attack: 40,000 Italian prisoners were captured, and only 133 British were killed. He went on to take Bardia and Tobruk and, in a final phase of the campaign, virtually destroyed the Italian 10th Army. Taken prisoner in April 1941, he escaped three years later, joined the invasion of Normandy, and once more saw distinguished service in the liberation of France. In 1945 O'Connor was stationed in India as commander in chief of the Eastern Command and promoted to general. O'Connor was knighted in 1941, served (1946–48) as aide-de-camp to King George VI, and was appointed lord lieutenant of Ross and Cromarty after his retirement. He also held the French Croix de Guerre and Legion of Honour.

Oldfield, Sir Maurice, British military intelligence chief (b. Nov. 16, 1915, Derbyshire, England—d. March 11, 1981, London, England), was head of MI-6, Britain's secret intelligence service, from 1973 to 1978. Oldfield was believed to have been the model for "M" in Ian Fleming's James Bond series and for George Smiley in John Le Carré's spy novels. After he was identified in 1968 as a prominent member of MI-6 by the double agent Kim Philby, Oldfield helped restore U.S. confidence in the British intelligence services. Following his graduation from Manchester University in 1938, Oldfield joined the secret service while serving in the Middle East during World War II. He joined the foreign service after leaving the Army and was posted to the Far East; in 1960 he was transferred to Washington, D.C., as MI-6 liaison with the Central Intelligence Agency. Oldfield returned to London in 1965 and was appointed "C" (for "Control," the code designation for the head of MI-6) in 1973. He was knighted in 1978 and acted as security coordinator in Northern Ireland until he was forced to retire in 1980 because of ill health.

Pagnani, Andreina, Italian actress (b. Nov. 24, 1906, Rome, Italy—d. Nov. 22, 1981, Rome), was a remarkable talent who established her reputation in classical drama but achieved equal success in comedy and on film. Born Andreina Gentili, she came from a theatrical family and scored her first triumph in 1922 when she won an amateur dramatic contest. During her nearly 40-year career she played for many leading Italian directors in works by Pirandello, Goldoni, Wilde, Shakespeare, and Shaw. In 1938 she joined the company at the Eliseo in Rome and after World War II was a member of the Venice Biennale company, which traveled to London and Paris. Her voice, her stage presence, and her emotional range were exceptional, and she continued to gain new admirers for her work in films and on television.

Palar, Lambertus Nicodemus, Indonesian diplomat (b. June 5, 1902, Indonesia—d. Feb. 12, 1981, Jakarta, Indonesia), attended the University of Amsterdam, was a member of the Netherlands Labour Movement from 1929 to 1947, and was elected to the Netherlands Parliament in 1939. As a member

of Parliament after World War II Palar lobbied to hold Indonesia and The Netherlands together, but in 1947 he moved to New York City and argued before the UN Security Council for a free Indonesia. Indonesian independence was unilaterally proclaimed on Aug. 17, 1945; however, formal recognition from The Netherlands and the UN was not secured until 1949. In 1950 Indonesia became the 60th member of the UN, and Palar was Indonesia's chief delegate (1950–53 and 1962–65). He also served as ambassador to India (1953–56), West Germany (1956), the U.S.S.R. (1956), Canada (1957–62), and the U.S. (1965–66). After retiring from government service in 1966, Palar was resident scholar at the East-West Center in Hawaii before returning to Indonesia.

Parrington, (Francis) Rex, British paleontologist (b. Feb. 20, 1905—d. April 17, 1981, Surrey, England), was director of the Cambridge University Museum of Zoology and an expert on fossil vertebrates. He was also a noted teacher whose lectures and informal contacts with students communicated his passion for his subject. Parrington studied at Sidney Sussex College, Cambridge, and became Strickland curator at the Museum of Zoology. He spent much of the 1930s on field trips to Africa, North America, and Scotland doing research into fossil fish and reptiles. In 1938 he was appointed lecturer in zoology and director of the Museum of Zoology at Cambridge. He returned to these posts after serving as an artillery officer during World War II. Parrington was elected fellow of the Royal Society in 1962 and appointed reader in vertebrate zoology in the following year. The symposium on vertebrate paleontology and comparative anatomy that he started in 1953 became an annual event and brought together the leading specialists in the field from all parts of the world.

Patrick, Nigel, British actor (b. May 2, 1913, London, England—d. Sept. 21, 1981, London), started his stage and film career before World War II and established himself as a noted comedy actor whose manner and temperament were ideally suited to play the suave English gentleman. Patrick made his stage debut in 1932 and appeared in his first film in 1939. After serving with the Army, he returned to the stage in 1946 and appeared in *The Schoolmistress* (1949), *The Remarkable Mr. Pennypacker* (1955), *The Pleasure of His Company* (1959), and *Present Laughter* (1965). He also enjoyed a highly successful career in films with *The Browning Version, The Sound Barrier,* and *The Pickwick Papers*. In later years he turned increasingly to directing for both stage and screen, his productions during the 1970s including *Blithe Spirit* and *Night Must Fall*. He was widely applauded for one of his last stage appearances, in *Dear Daddy* (1976). Patrick's last performance was in a television play in 1979.

Piccard, the Rev. Jeanette Ridlon, U.S. scientist and Episcopal priest (b. Jan. 5, 1895, Chicago, Ill.—d. May 17, 1981, Minneapolis, Minn.), made a historic ascent into the stratosphere when in 1934 she piloted a spherical balloon of 17,000 cu m (600,000 cu ft) in volume to a height of 17,557 m (57,564 ft) above Lake Erie with her husband, Jean Piccard, as her aide. During her ascent Piccard made studies of the cosmic rays in the stratosphere and became the first balloonist in the U.S. to fly successfully through a layer of clouds. Piccard, who held a B.A. in philosophy and psychology, an M.A. in organic chemistry, and a Ph.D. in education, had a wide range of interests. From 1964 to 1970 she was consultant to the director of NASA's Johnson Space Center, and in her mid-70s she began theological studies. In 1971 she was ordained a deacon of the Episcopal Church and in 1974 was the eldest of 11 women to be ordained priests.

Pilinszky, Janos, Hungarian poet (b. Nov. 25, 1921, Budapest, Hung.—d. May 27, 1981, Budapest), established his reputation with the 18 poems of his first collection, *Trapez es Korlat* ("Trapeze and Parallel Bar"; 1946), a powerful and moving testimonial to the horrors of war. A Catholic by upbringing, he reemerged after the Stalinist era and confirmed his position as one of the most respected Hungarian poets of his time. He was able to travel, notably to England, where his *Selected Poems*, translated by Ted Hughes and Janos Csokits, appeared in 1976.

Plugge, Leonard Frank, British politician and scientist (b. Sept. 21, 1889, London, England—d. Feb. 19, 1981, California), was a research scientist, a pioneer of commercial radio, and a Conservative member of Parliament from 1935 to 1945. He studied at University College, London, and at the University of Brussels and served with the Royal Air Force in World War I before joining the Department of Scientific Research at the Air Ministry. In 1930 he formed the International Broadcasting Co., which ran Radio Normandie, a commercial station broadcasting to Britain from France. From 1939 to 1943 he was chairman of the Parliamentary Scientific Committee. After his defeat in the 1945 election, he returned to scientific research and invention. Plugge was a fellow of the Royal Aeronautical Society, a member of the New York Academy of Sciences, and a recipient of the French Legion of Honour.

Polevoy, Boris (Boris Nikolayevich Kampov), Soviet writer (b. March 17, 1908, Moscow, Russia—d. July 12, 1981, Moscow, U.S.S.R.), was the author of *The Story of a Real Man* (1946), a book inspired by the career of legless Soviet flying ace A. P. Maresiev. Polevoy studied at technical college and started his writing career while working in a textile factory. He was war correspondent for *Pravda* during World War II, reporting from the Western Front and concentrating on the effects of war on the private soldier. After the success of *The Story of a Real Man,* which was translated into several languages, he published novels and fictionalized documentaries. A prominent figure in Soviet literary life, Polevoy twice received the Order of Lenin and was named a Hero of Socialist Labour.

Ponselle, Rosa (Rosa Melba Ponzillo), U.S. opera star (b. Jan. 22, 1897, Meriden, Conn.—d. May 25, 1981, Baltimore, Md.), was a gifted dramatic soprano who reigned for 19 seasons (1918–37) as a principal singer of the Metropolitan Opera. She was noted for her splendid coloratura technique and a voice of great beauty, breadth of tone, and control. Ponselle, who with her sister, Carmela, performed in vaudeville as the Ponzillo Sisters, came to the attention of the tenor Enrico Caruso. Having had virtually no formal training, she made her debut (1918) at the Metropolitan Opera in the role of Leonora in Verdi's *La Forza del Destino* opposite Caruso. She also became famous in the title roles of Bellini's *Norma*, Verdi's *Aïda*, and Ponchielli's *La Gioconda*. After leaving the Met in 1937, she devoted herself to making recordings, teaching, and serving as artistic director of the Baltimore Civic Opera.

Postan, Sir Michael Moissey, Bessarabian-born economic historian (b. September 1899, Tighina, Bessarabia—d. Dec. 12, 1981, Cambridge, England), was professor of economic history at the University of Cambridge from 1938 to 1965 and made an outstanding contribution to the study of medieval economic history. He completed his education in England and in 1927 became lecturer in economic history at University College, London, and then, from 1931, at the London School of Economics. In 1935 he moved to Cambridge, and three years later he succeeded Sir John Clapham as professor of economic history. Postan played an important role in editing the *Cambridge Economic History of Europe* and in stimulating research. His own work on the medieval economy combined a deep understanding of the period with a knowledge of contemporary economic theory and techniques. Postan was named editor of the *Economic History Review* in 1935, and in 1960 he helped to organize the first International Congress on Economic History in Stockholm. After his retirement he edited volumes of the *Cambridge Economic History of Europe* and gave lectures at U.S. universities. His publications included *British War Production* (1952), *Fact and Relevance* (1971), and his general work on the medieval English economy, *The Medieval Economy and Society* (1973). Postan was knighted in 1980.

Potter, Mary, British artist (b. April 9, 1900, London, England—d. Sept. 14, 1981, Aldeburgh, Suffolk, England), painted atmospheric landscapes of the Suffolk countryside. She was married to the writer Stephen Potter and in her later years worked in a studio built for her at Aldeburgh by the composer Benjamin Britten. There, on the Suffolk coast, Potter found a subject ideally suited to her individualistic style of painting. Her work is exhibited in the collections of leading galleries in Britain, the U.S., Canada, and Australia. At the time of her death Potter's work was revived and was shown in the 1981 Arts Council touring exhibition.

Procope, Russell Keith, U.S. jazz musician (b. Aug. 11, 1908, New York, N.Y.—d. Jan. 21, 1981, New York), was showcased as a solo saxophonist and clarinetist with Duke Ellington's orchestra for nearly three decades and performed with such jazz greats as Chick Webb, Fletcher Henderson, Jelly Roll Morton, and the John Kirby Sextet. In 1945 Procope joined the Ellington band, contributing his low, warm chalumeau clarinet sound. His playing was most closely associated with the song "Mood Indigo" and with such pieces as "4:30 Blues," "Blues to Be There," "Second Line," and "Things Ain't What They Used to Be." After Ellington's death in 1974 Procope played in a trio with drummer Sonny Greer and pianist Brooks Kerr. In 1978 he organized a quintet that featured much of Ellington's music.

Rahman, Ziaur, Bangladeshi soldier and statesman (b. Jan. 19, 1936, Shylhet, East Bengal, India—d. May 30, 1981, Chittagong, Bangladesh), served as president of Bangladesh from 1975 to 1981. Zia came to political prominence following the August 1975 military coup in which Sheikh Mujibur Rahman, the new nation's first leader, was killed. Zia was appointed chief of army staff by the new president, Khandakar Mushtaque Ahmed, and attained still greater powers under Ahmed's successor, Abu Sadat Mohammad Sayem. When Sayem resigned the presidency for health reasons in April 1977, General Zia was the heir apparent. He promised reform and a return to democratic elections, but an attempted coup in November 1977 slowed the process. Nevertheless, eight months later Bangladesh's first elections held under universal suffrage took place. The results endorsed Zia's policies. During Zia's presidency, Bangladesh's relations with Pakistan improved, though there were continued border tensions with India. Zia was assassinated during a coup attempt led by Maj. Gen. Mohammad Abdul Manzoor, who in 1971 had fought beside him in the battle to win independence for Bangladesh (formerly East Pakistan).

Raja'i, Mohammad Ali, Iranian politician (b. 1933, Kazvin, Iran—d. Aug. 30, 1981, Teheran, Iran), was killed by a bomb blast at the prime minister's office in Teheran little less than a month after taking office as his country's president. Raja'i had previously served for a year as prime minister, aligning himself with the fundamentalists of the Islamic Republican Party. By using his working-class background and oratorical skills, Raja'i gained popular support. After leaving school he worked as a bricklayer and then joined the Air Force, studying in his spare time to eventually teach. He also became involved in militant opposition to the shah's regime and was arrested and tortured by the security police, Savak; in 1980 he exhibited the scars on his feet to the UN Security Council. He became an active member of the central committee of the Association of Islamic Teachers and after the 1979 revolution was appointed minister of education. In 1980 Pres. Abolhassan Bani-Sadr nominated him prime minister, whereupon he joined in a bitter struggle against the president's authority, attacking all Western influence in Iran and increasingly identifying the Western-educated Bani-Sadr with the forces holding back the Islamic Revolution. When Bani-Sadr fell from power, Raja'i was elected president by an overwhelming majority.

Reeve, the Right Rev. Arthur Stretton, British Anglican clergyman (b. June 11, 1907, Croydon, England—d. Jan. 27, 1981, Ashford Carbonell, Salop, England), was bishop of Lichfield (1953–74) and served as chaplain to King George VI (1945–52) and Queen Elizabeth II (1952–53). The son of a vicar and grandson of a bishop, he read theology at the University of Cambridge and was ordained in 1930. After serving as domestic chaplain to the bishop of Winchester, he became vicar of Christ Church, Highfield, Southampton, and remained there during the early part of World War II. In 1943 he was appointed vicar of Leeds and as a member of the Leeds Hospital Regional Board began to play a major role in relations between the church and the health service. Reeve also became known as an outspoken critic of the decline in sexual morals.

Reiniger, Lotte, German animated-film producer (b. 1899, Berlin, Germany—d. June 19, 1981, Dettenhausen, West Germany), made *The Adventures of Prince Achmed* (1926), usually acknowledged as the first full-length animated cartoon, and remained a creative force in cinema throughout her career. Fascinated by the art of silhouette, Reiniger entered the world of cinema in 1918 doing titles for Paul Wegener. Her first film in 1919 was followed by short animated films based on myths, opera, and fairy tales. After the success of *Prince Achmed,* her genius for silhouette cutting and animation was widely recognized; with her husband, Carl Koch, she worked on Jean Renoir's *La Marseillaise* (1937). They lived in Britain and several other European countries before finally immigrating to Britain in 1949. In the 1950s they made cartoons for television, including *The Gallant Little Tailor,* which won first prize at the 1955 Venice Film Festival. After Koch's death in 1963 Reiniger retired from film work, but she reemerged during the 1970s, making *Aucassin and Nicolette* and *The Rose and the Ring.* Among the many awards and honours she received were the Golden Film Strip prize in 1972, a special jury prize at the Ottawa 1976 International Animated Film Festival, and in 1979 the Cross of the Order of the Federal Republic of Germany.

Rennie, Sir John Ogilvy, British diplomat (b. Jan. 13, 1915—d. Sept. 30, 1981), was head of Britain's Secret Intelligence Service from 1968 to 1974, after a successful career as a diplomat. Rennie studied at Balliol College, Oxford, and worked in advertising in the U.S., where he joined the British information services during World War II. He returned to Britain in 1946 and went into the Foreign Office Information Policy Department, served in Washington, D.C., and Warsaw, and in 1953 became head of the Information Research Department, where he remained until 1958. After further service in North and South America, he was appointed in 1966 deputy undersecretary responsible for defense. Two years later he took over as director-general of MI-6, the secret intelligence service, and proved a successful and respected leader in a highly sensitive post. After his retirement he devoted his time to sailing and painting. Rennie was knighted in 1967.

Rhyl, (Evelyn) Nigel Chetwode Birch, Baron, British politician (b. Nov. 18, 1906, London, England—d. March 8, 1981, Swanmore, Hampshire, England), was economic secretary to the Treasury from 1957 to 1958 before resigning to protest the high level of government expenditure. A consistent critic of inflationary policies, Nigel Birch belonged to the right wing of the Conservative Party and was one of its most admired parliamentarians. Before World War II he made a fortune as a financier and, after army service, was elected to Parliament in 1945. He was secretary of state for air from 1955 to 1957 but always made his greatest impact as a speaker on economic affairs. He advocated policies that were then at odds with those of mainstream Conservatism. His resignation, with those of Enoch Powell and Peter Thorneycroft, was dismissed at the time by Prime Minister Harold Macmillan as "a little local difficulty." But the move profoundly impressed some of his colleagues and seemed vindicated some 20 years later, when the Margaret Thatcher administration adopted a program similar to their own. Nigel Birch never held office again but was an active back-bencher. His speech at the time of the 1963 Profumo affair helped to bring about Macmillan's retirement. He was created a life peer in 1970.

Riad, Mohammed, Egyptian diplomat (b. 1923—d. Sept. 27, 1981, Ljubljana, Yugoslavia), was minister of state for foreign affairs and in 1979 became secretary-general of the Arab League in succession to Mahmoud Riad. He entered the diplomatic service in 1946 and after the revolution of 1952 held leading posts under Presidents Gamal Abdel Nasser and Anwar as-Sadat. He was Egyptian consul in Paris and from 1950 to 1964 a member of the Egyptian delegation to the UN.

Richter, Karl, German conductor (b. Oct. 15, 1926, Plauen, Germany—d. Feb. 15, 1981, Munich, West Germany), established an international reputation as an interpreter of the works of J. S. Bach, particularly the choral works that Richter performed with his Munich Bach choir and orchestra. Together they toured Europe, the U.S., and the U.S.S.R. and recorded all of Bach's major choral and orchestral works, mostly for Deutsche Grammophon. Richter's style, considered revolutionary in the 1950s, was brisk and rigorous, though expressive, and lacked the exaggerated dynamics of 19th-century performance. In later years, however, he was not attracted by the new generation's search for authenticity with original Baroque instruments and orchestra sizes. Richter was trained as an organist and played at Bach's own church, St. Thomas, in Leipzig. In 1951 he went to Munich and taught at the Musikhochschule.

Rocha, Glauber, Brazilian filmmaker (b. March 14, 1938, Vitória da Conquista, Bahia, Brazil—d. Aug. 23, 1981, Rio de Janeiro, Brazil), was a leading representative of the Cinema Nôvo movement, combining political commitment and poetic vision in works that at their best conveyed the contradictions of Brazilian life. Rocha began as a film critic and director of documentaries before making his first feature, *Barravento,* in 1962. With his 1964 film, *Deus e o Diabo na Terra do Sol* (commonly known as *Black God, White Devil*), Rocha found the mixture of violence, myth, and baroque lyricism that was to characterize his work. He also reached an international audience following the film's success at the Cannes Festival. His next features, *Terra em Transe* (1967), a political opera, and *Antonio das Mortes* (1969), were also critically well received abroad, but his popularity in Brazil was declining and the political content of his work brought him into conflict with the authorities. He left for Europe, where he made *Der Leone have Sept Cabecas* (a Franco-Italian production filmed mostly in the Congo), *Cabecas Cortadas,* and *Claro,* in each of which his style became more metaphoric and obscure. Feeling compromised by the commercialism of the international cinema, he sought a new language for political films but failed to convince the critics or the public. At the end of the 1970s he returned to Brazil and wrote a novel and a study of Cinema Nôvo.

Roldós Aguilera, Jaime, Ecuadorian politician (b. Nov. 5, 1940, Guayaquil, Ecuador—d. May 24, 1981, near Guachanama, Ecuador), ended nine years of civilian and military dictatorships when he was elected president of Ecuador on April 29, 1979. Roldós ran as a populist stand-in candidate for his wife's uncle, Assad Bucaram, who had been barred from the race by the military government because his parents were not Ecuadorians. In a surprising and overwhelming victory, Roldós captured 68.4% of the vote and became the youngest president in the Western Hemisphere. Although he was viewed as a left-of-centre candidate, his presidency was more centrist and conservative. During his two years in office, Roldós adopted a middle-of-the-road stance and in so doing renounced many of his campaign promises. His policies increasingly came into conflict with those of Bucaram, who was head of Congress. As a result, Roldós was thwarted in many of his attempts to get legislation passed. In 1980 he left Bucaram's party to form a more moderate party called People, Change, and Democracy. Roldós, together with his wife, Marta, the minister of defense, and other aides, was killed in an airplane crash in the Andes Mountains.

Rosen, Samuel, U.S. ear surgeon (b. 1897, Syracuse, N.Y.—d. Nov. 5, 1981, Beijing [Peking], China), discovered that otosclerosis, a deafening condition in which the bony wall dividing the middle and inner ear thickens, could be alleviated by mobilizing the tiny stapes (or stirrup) bone, one of the chain of minute bones in the middle ear that transmit sound vibrations from the eardrum membrane. During a 1952 diagnostic operation, Rosen made a probe of the stapes bone to ensure that it was rigid before proceeding with fenestration surgery; he found that his patient's hearing was completely restored when he pried loose the fixed stapes. This delicate surgery, on the tiniest bone in the human body, revolutionized ear surgery when its effectiveness was finally recognized in 1955. Rosen, who conducted these operations while on the staff of Mt. Sinai Hospital in New York City, met resistance from colleagues, who, he felt, resented his political stands, his race, and possibly the loss of high fees surgeons had been earning for fenestration surgery. Rosen introduced and demonstrated his technique in at least 40 countries, never accepted a fee for operations outside New York, and donated his instruments so instrument makers could study their unique design. In addition to his affiliation with Mt. Sinai, Rosen was professor emeritus of otolaryngology at the College of Physicians and Surgeons of Columbia University.

Rudenko, Roman, Soviet lawyer (b. 1907—d. Jan. 23, 1981, Moscow, U.S.S.R.), was chief Soviet prosecutor at the Nürnberg trials of leading Nazis after World War II and from 1953 was procurator-general of the U.S.S.R. It was Rudenko who led the 1960 prosecution of Francis Gary Powers, the pilot of a U.S. Lockheed U-2 aircraft shot down on a reconnaissance flight over the Soviet Union. Powers was convicted of espionage and sentenced to ten years' imprisonment but in 1962 was exchanged for the Soviet spy Rudolf Abel.

Russell of Liverpool, Edward Frederick Langley Russell, 2nd Baron, British soldier and lawyer (b. April 10, 1895, Liverpool, England—d. April 8, 1981, Hastings, England), wrote two best-selling books on atrocities committed during World War II: *The Scourge of the Swastika* (1954) and *The Knights of Bushido* (1958). In 1966 he won his case against the magazine *Private Eye,* which alleged that he had written the books solely to make money from the public's prurient interest. Educated at Liverpool College and St. John's College, Oxford, he won the Military Cross for his service in World War I but left the Army in 1930 because of ill health. In the following year he was called to the bar, and in 1934 he joined the judge advocate general's office, where he remained until official displeasure over publication of *The Scourge of the Swastika* led him to resign and devote himself to writing.

Sadat, (Muhammad) Anwar as-, Egyptian soldier and statesman (b. Dec. 25, 1918, Mit Abu al-Kom, Nile Delta, Egypt—d. Oct. 6, 1981, Nasr City, near Cairo, Egypt), as the charismatic president of Egypt from 1970 to 1981 took a historic step toward Middle Eastern peace when he visited Jerusalem and addressed the Knesset (Israel's parliament) at the invitation of Israeli Prime Minister Menachem Begin in November 1977. The trip initiated negotiations that continued at Camp David, Md., and led to the conclusion of an Israeli-Egyptian peace treaty in March 1979. Earlier the 1978 Nobel Prize for Peace had been awarded jointly to Sadat and Begin. In his address to the Knesset, Sadat explicitly accepted the existence of Israel while reiterating his belief that a just and lasting peace depended on an Israeli withdrawal from all occupied Arab territories and recognition of the rights of the Palestinians.

Sadat's peace initiative was at first well received by the Egyptian public but not by most other Arab leaders, especially those who craved Israel's destruction and knew that without Egypt their desire was unattainable. Only Sudan and Morocco fully endorsed it, while Jordan expressed cautious approval. Egypt's principal ally, Saudi Arabia, was dismayed that Sadat had broken the Arab front. Syria, the Palestine Liberation Organization, Iraq, and Libya denounced him as a traitor. In Egypt, too, disillusionment ensued when no improvement was visible in the ailing domestic economy. Earlier in his career Sadat had turned to dramatic action under the pressure of domestic unrest. His crossing of the Suez Canal in October 1973 was in effect an essential prelude to the peace initiative, for it restored the self-respect of the Egyptian Army and raised Sadat, its commander in chief, to the stature of a world statesman.

Sadat began his military career in 1938 after graduating from the Cairo Royal Military Academy. During World War II he plotted to liberate Egypt from British domination and contacted German agents residing in Cairo. He was arrested by the British in 1942 for spying, escaped, but was again arrested in 1945 on a charge of participating in an assassination attempt against the Wafd Party leader Nahas Pasha, then prime minister. In 1950 Sadat was readmitted to the Army, joined Gamal Abdel Nasser's Free Officers, and after their coup that overthrew King Farouk in 1952 held various high offices under the new regime. He was minister of state (1955–56), vice-chairman (1957–60) and chairman (1960–68) of the National Assembly, general secretary of the Egyptian National Union (1957–61), chairman of the Afro-Asian Solidarity Council (1961), speaker of the National Assembly (1961–69), and twice vice-president of the republic (1964–66; 1969–70). When Nasser died in 1970, Sadat became interim president. He was confirmed in office in October of that year, winning more than 90% of the votes in a national referendum. In 1973–74 and again from May 1980 he was also prime minister. In July 1972, dissatisfied with the scale of Soviet military aid after two visits to Moscow earlier in the year, Sadat put an end to the Egyptian-Soviet military collaboration by expelling some 15,000 Soviet military personnel and their dependents. In March 1976 he abrogated Egypt's 1971 treaty of friendship with the U.S.S.R., thus opening the way for even closer collaboration with the U.S.

Like many aspects of his life, the circumstances of Sadat's death were dramatic. While reviewing troops on the eighth anniversary of the crossing of the Suez Canal by Egyptian forces, he was shot dead in a hail of bullets fired by the crew of an army truck, part of the passing parade of vehicles, that came to a halt in front of the reviewing stand. The assassins were thought to be Muslim fundamentalists. (See EGYPT.)

Sands, Bobby (ROBERT GERARD SANDS), Northern Irish member of the Irish Republican Army (b. March 1954, Belfast, Northern Ireland—d. May 5,

1981, Belfast), became an international symbol of Irish Republican resistance to British rule in Northern Ireland before he died in the medical wing of the Maze Prison after refusing food for 66 days. After serving for two and a half years as an apprentice auto worker, Sands joined the IRA. In 1973 he was sentenced to five years' imprisonment for armed robbery and possession of firearms. He was freed in 1976 but was arrested again and sentenced to 14 years for possession of firearms and ammunition with intent and to 10 years for possession of firearms and ammunition in suspicious circumstances. Sands began his hunger strike on March 1, 1981, to gain political prisoner status from the British government. Other IRA prisoners in the Maze's H block later joined the fast. Four days after Sands began to refuse food, Frank Maguire, a member of Parliament for the Northern Ireland constituency of Fermanagh and South Tyrone, died. Standing as an anti-H block candidate, Sands won the subsequent by-election, though he was never installed in his seat in Westminster. As Sands's condition deteriorated, worldwide attention focused on the troubles in Northern Ireland. The British government continued to maintain that the IRA prisoners had committed criminal acts and therefore should be treated as criminals. Meanwhile, neither a group of members of Parliament from the Irish Republic nor an emissary from Pope John Paul II could persuade Sands to abandon his hunger strike.

Saroyan, William (SIRAK GORYAN), U.S. author and playwright (b. Aug. 31, 1908, Fresno, Calif.—d. May 18, 1981, Fresno), lifted the spirits of thousands of Depression-era readers with lively, original short stories and plays that proposed humour and courage as means of conquering adversity. With his first collection of stories, *The Daring Young Man on the Flying Trapeze* (1934), Saroyan immediately received widespread attention. A prolific and spontaneous writer who never revised his work, Saroyan wrote more than 500 stories between 1934 and 1940, including the large collection *Inhale and Exhale* (1936). His first play, *My Heart's in the Highlands* (1939), was performed by the Group Theatre. It was followed by *The Time of Your Life* (1939), written in only six days, for which he won and refused a Pulitzer Prize. His novels, which were generously laced with autobiographical tidbits, included *The Human Comedy* (1943). After World War II Saroyan's optimistic autobiographical hero turned into an older, gloomy man, whose dim views on marriage and divorce were revealed in *Rock Wagram* (1951) and *The Laughing Matter* (1953). He also wrote such melancholy memoirs as *Not*

Dying (1963) and *Don't Go, but If You Must, Say Hello to Everybody* (1969). Saroyan, who supposedly once boasted that he was the world's greatest author, remarked shortly before his death that "Everybody has got to die, but I have always believed an exception would be made in my case."

Sauter, Eddie (EDWARD ERNEST SAUTER), U.S. composer and arranger (b. Dec. 12, 1914, Brooklyn, N.Y.—d. April 21, 1981, Nyack, N.Y.), was an innovative jazz composer and arranger whose influential pieces energized the big bands of Benny Goodman and Ray McKinley. Though he played trumpet and mellophone with Red Norvo's band, Sauter primarily served as an arranger and composer. Beginning in 1939 he provided Goodman's orchestra with prime arrangements featuring the bandleader's clarinet, notably "Clarinet à la King" and "Benny Rides Again." He also arranged "Moonlight on the Ganges," "April in Paris," and "Maid with the Flaccid Air" for Artie Shaw. During the 1950s, with Ray McKinley, Sauter released some of his finest scores, including "Hangover Square," "Sandstorm," and "Borderline." In 1952 he teamed up with Bill Finegan to form the Sauter-Finegan Orchestra. Their studio recordings were eagerly received by radio disc jockeys looking for fresh material. Yet when the orchestra, playing live, tried to modify its style to accommodate a rhythm for dancers, its popularity faded. In later years Sauter turned to writing arrangements for Broadway musicals.

Savage, Sir (Edward) Graham, British educationist (b. Aug. 31, 1886—d. May 18, 1981, London, England), was influential in helping to introduce comprehensive schools into the English educational system. As education officer (1940–51) to the London County Council he expounded his view that secondary schools should cater to a complete cross section of children of eligible age. Savage was educated at Downing College, Cambridge, and taught in England and overseas before joining the Board of Education as a district inspector. He became senior chief inspector in 1933. When he moved to London in 1940, his most pressing task was to ensure the continued education of London's children despite the German bombing raids. The concept of nonselection in school admission, noted by Savage on a trip to New York State in 1925, was preserved in his paper on the future of London schools, which he presented in 1947. His pioneering work resulted in a network of comprehensive schools throughout England.

Scott, Hazel Dorothy, U.S. pianist and singer (b. June 11, 1920, Port of Spain, Trinidad—d. Oct. 2, 1981, New York, N.Y.), was a child prodigy who by the time she was five years old was already improvising songs on the piano. Although she was too young to enter the Juilliard School of Music at age eight, one of its teachers, Paul Wagner, heard her unique playing and agreed to give her private lessons. Scott, who added her own modern-jazz interpretations to the classical works of Rachmaninoff and Liszt, made her piano debut at Carnegie Hall in 1940 playing the latter's Hungarian Rhapsody No. 2 with her own syncopated arrangement. After Scott's father died, her mother organized a band for which Hazel played the piano and trumpet. In 1938 she appeared in the Broadway production *Sing Out the News*, and when Scott belted out "Franklin D. Roosevelt Jones," she stopped the show. After her stunning performance on the keyboards in Broadway's *Priorities of 1942*, she appeared in such motion pictures as *Something to Shout About*, *Broadway Rhythm*, and *The Heat's On*. She was also noted for her 1945 marriage to U.S. Rep. Adam Clayton Powell, Jr.

Ségard, Norbert, French politician (b. Oct. 3, 1922, Aniche, France—d. Feb. 1, 1981, Lille, France), was secretary of state, then minister, for external trade (1974–76) and secretary of state for posts and telecommunications (1976–80). From 1980 until his death, he served as a special minister-delegate attached to the prime minister. Ségard gained respect both for extending the telecommunications network and for his courage in publicly announcing and confronting the cancer that eventually killed him. A latecomer to politics, he was trained as a physicist and teacher and established his political

reputation as an energetic promoter of technical education in northern France. He was also a member of the Higher Council of National Education. Ségard was encouraged by François-Xavier Ortoli, then minister of industrial and scientific development, to enter politics and in 1973 was elected a Gaullist deputy. A devout Catholic and a convinced Gaullist, he failed in his attempt to become mayor of Lille in 1977.

Seper, Franjo Cardinal, Yugoslav prelate of the Roman Catholic Church (b. Oct. 2, 1905, Osijek, Croatia—d. Dec. 30, 1981, Rome, Italy), was prefect of the Sacred Congregation for the Doctrine of the Faith from 1968 to 1980. He succeeded the leading conservative Alfredo Cardinal Ottaviani as head of the Sacred Congregation, formerly known as the Holy Office, and maintained a traditional stance on social and doctrinal matters, thereby attracting criticism for his handling of the controversies surrounding Hans Küng and Edward Schillebeeckx. Seper had been expected to take a more liberal attitude than his predecessor, in part because of his less conservative background. He was ordained in 1930 and became a bishop in 1954, acting as secretary to Aloysius Cardinal Stepinac, archbishop of Zagreb, and succeeding him in 1960. A cardinal from 1965, he made some noted contributions to the debates in the Second Vatican Council (1962–65) and was a well-known participant in the international synods. But as prefect of the Sacred Congregation for the Doctrine of the Faith, he maintained the church's traditional uncompromising condemnation of homosexuality and premarital sexual relations and its opposition to the admission of women to the priesthood; he also asserted the church's right to discipline those like Küng and Schillebeeckx who called for more open attitudes on these and other doctrinal questions.

Serocki, Kazimierz, Polish composer (b. March 3, 1922, Torun, Poland—d. Jan. 31, 1981, Warsaw, Poland), was a founder-member, with Jan Krenz and Tadeusz Baird, of the "Group 49" movement that helped gain international recognition for post–World War II Polish music. Serocki studied with Kazimierz Sikorski in Lodz and with Lazare Lévy and Nadia Boulanger in Paris. In 1952 his piano suite *Suita Preludiow* won him his first national music prize; other prizes followed in 1963 and 1972. His *Freski Symfoniczne* (1964) for full orchestra received a UNESCO award in 1965, and *Pianophonie* (1978) won the 1979 Prix Italia. Serocki was a cofounder, with Tadeusz Baird, of the Warsaw Autumn Festival.

Shankly, Bill, British soccer player (b. 1914, Glenbuck, South Ayrshire, Scotland—d. Sept. 29, 1981, Liverpool, England), had a brilliant career with Preston as a halfback, played for the Scottish national teams, and was a legendary manager (1959–74) of the Liverpool Football Club. Shankly played more than 300 matches for Preston, including cup finals in 1937 and 1938, forging the combination of skill and dogged determination that was to characterize his managerial career. He took Liverpool into the First Division and steered them to victory in three League championships, two FA Cups, and the UEFA Cup. His team, tough and aggressive, idolized its manager, and even after Shankly's retirement he remained a hero to the club's fans.

Sheares, Benjamin Henry, Singaporean politician and physician (b. Aug. 12, 1907, Singapore—d. May 12, 1981, Singapore), was a noted gynecologist and professor of medicine at the University of Malaya in Singapore before being unanimously elected president of Singapore by the Parliament on Dec. 30, 1970. Sheares, who served two and a half terms as president, held a largely ceremonial role insofar as he had no executive powers in Prime Minister Lee Kuan Yew's government. Sheares's approval, however, was imperative if an act of Parliament was to become law.

Shehu, Mehmet, Albanian politician (b. Jan. 10, 1913, Corush, Albania—d. Dec. 18, 1981, Tirana, Albania), was chairman of the Council of Ministers (premier) of Albania from 1954 to 1981 after having served as minister of the interior from 1948 to 1954. He was also minister of defense from 1974 to 1980. Shehu graduated from Tirana Technical College and in 1935 was sent by King Zog I to the Military Academy in Naples, Italy. After he was expelled from the academy for his pro-Communist sympathies, Shehu fought in the Spanish Civil War and was later interned in France. He escaped to Albania in 1942 and joined a partisan unit supported by Tito. After World War II Shehu went to the Voroshilov Military Academy in Moscow and in 1946 was appointed chief of staff of the Albanian Army. A member of the Albanian (Communist) Party of Labour Politburo from 1948, Shehu was party leader Enver Hoxha's trusted aide. Together they opposed Tito's attempt to include Albania in the Yugoslav federation. According to Radio Tirana, Shehu killed himself in a moment of nervous depression. However, since there was no national mourning and no state funeral was held, it appeared that Shehu might have fallen into disgrace.

Shirley-Smith, Sir Hubert, British civil engineer (b. Oct. 13, 1901, London, England—d. Feb. 10, 1981), designed steel bridges in many parts of the world and was a noted writer on engineering topics. His popular contributions to this field included *The World's Great Bridges* (1953) and the article on bridges in *Encyclopædia Britannica*. As a member of the firm of Sir Douglas Fox and Partners (later Freeman, Fox and Partners), he was involved in the design of the Sydney Harbour Bridge. During the 1930s he worked on the design of bridges in the north of England, Rhodesia, and India and during World War II set up the shipyard where tank landing craft were constructed for the Normandy invasion. In 1951 he joined the board of the Cleveland Bridge Co. and traveled to sites in Africa, Asia, and Australasia. Shirley-Smith worked on the Rovaniem Bridge in Finland, did structural designs for the London Shell Centre, and worked on the Forth Road Bridge. Knighted in 1969, he was an active member of many associations of civil engineers; he served as president (1967–68) of the Institution of Civil Engineers and acted as consultant (1969–78) to W. V. Zinn and Associates after his formal retirement.

Shonfield, Sir Andrew (Akiba), British economist and writer (b. Aug. 10, 1917, Tadworth, England—d. Jan. 23, 1981, London, England), was chairman (1969–71) of the Social Science Research Council, director (1972–77) of the Royal Institute of International Affairs (Chatham House), and professor of economics at the European University Institute in Florence, Italy, from 1978 until his death. Shonfield demonstrated his remarkable ability to comprehend economic problems in relation to broader social issues in his two major works, *Attack on World Poverty* (1960) and *Modern Capitalism* (1965). Educated at Oxford University, he served with the Royal Artillery during World War II before his tenure (1947–57) as a staff member of the *Financial Times*. He was then economic editor of *The Observer* from 1958 until he joined Chatham House in 1961 as director of studies. A moderate Socialist, he favoured British entry into the European Economic Community and, as a member of the Royal Commission on Trade Unions (1965–68), argued in favour of greater legal controls on union activities. He was knighted in 1978.

Smith, Joe (JOE SULTZER), U.S. performer (b. Feb. 17, 1884—d. Feb. 22, 1981, Englewood, N.J.), was part of the illustrious vaudeville comedy team of Smith and Dale, who for 73 years performed together in theatres, on television, and in motion pictures. In one of their first engagements, Joe Sultzer and Charles Marks were billed as Smith and Dale because of a printing error. They adopted that name and later, after appearing in the Catskills with Will Lester and Jack Coleman as the Avon Comedy Four, also became known as Smith and Dale of the Avon Comedy Four. The perennial appeal of Smith and Dale, who met when they were teenag-

ers, was their marvelous sense of timing and their mastery of their craft. The team's sketches included "The Card Game," "The New School Teacher," and "Hungarian Rhapsody," but their all-time favourite skit was the classic "Dr. Kronkheit," which never failed to evoke laughter. The lives of the two talented performers formed the basis of the 1972 play and 1975 film *The Sunshine Boys*.

Sondheimer, Franz, German-born scientist (b. May 17, 1926, Stuttgart, Germany—d. Feb. 11, 1981, Stanford, Calif.), with R. B. Woodward was the first to achieve total synthesis of a nonaromatic steroid, a procedure used in the preparation of cholesterol and cortisone. Sondheimer conducted this work at Harvard University in the early 1950s and continued his research after his appointment to the Syntex Pharmaceutical Co. research laboratories in Mexico. In 1956 he became head of the organic chemistry department at the Weizmann Institute of Science in Israel. There his work on compounds of benzene proved what had until then only been predicted by theory and consequently had far-reaching implications for the whole field of organic chemistry. In 1964 he returned to England and worked as research professor at the University of Cambridge (1964–67) and later at University College, London. He made further notable contributions to the synthesis of organic compounds and attracted collaborators from many countries to his laboratories. He was elected a fellow of the Royal Society in 1967.

Speer, Albert, German architect (b. March 19, 1905, Mannheim, Germany—d. Sept. 1, 1981, London, England), was Hitler's chief architect and the minister for armaments and ammunition in the German government from 1942 to 1945. Tried at Nürnberg, he was the only leading Nazi to plead guilty to war crimes, and he served 20 years in Spandau prison, Berlin. Speer studied architecture and taught at the Technical University in Berlin before joining the Nazi Party and being chosen to design the stadium in Nürnberg, the Berlin Chancellery, and other massive monuments of Nazi architecture. He became a personal friend of Hitler, who mesmerized his young protégé and in 1942 appointed him to succeed Fritz Todt as armaments minister, responsible for the slave labour that supported the German wartime economy. Speer proved brilliantly successful and even raised production from 1942 to 1944, despite increased Allied bombing. He also showed remarkable foresight by encouraging the production of synthetic substitutes for oil. But Speer was also one of the first to foresee Germany's eventual defeat and in 1945 was one of a group that attempted to kill Hitler. Later Speer expressed his guilt and remorse for German war crimes and admitted responsibility for

KEYSTONE

what had been done by the Nazi government. After his release from Spandau in 1966 he wrote *Inside the Third Reich* (1970), in which he admitted and attempted to come to terms with his management of the German industrial machine, which, he said, had presented him with a great challenge and given him "incredible satisfaction."

Stanner, William Edward Hanley, Australian anthropologist (b. Nov. 24, 1905, Sydney, Australia —d. Oct. 8, 1981, Canberra, Australia), helped found the Australian Institute of Aboriginal Studies in Canberra and the Gallery of Aboriginal Australia. Stanner was professor of anthropology and sociology at the Australian National University from 1964 to 1970. After studying at the London School of Economics, he conducted research work in Kenya and after World War II became founding director of the East African Institute of Social Research, Makerere, Uganda. As a newspaper reporter during the 1930s he became aware of the plight of the Aborigines and began to campaign on their behalf. Stanner was a member of the Commonwealth Council for Aboriginal Affairs from 1967 to 1977 and in 1979 became a founding member of the Aboriginal Treaty Committee. His broadcast lectures, "After the Dreaming," reached a wide audience, and he published *White Man Got No Dreaming* (1979), a collection of articles. Stanner was appointed Companion of the Order of St. Michael and St. George in 1972.

Stein, Jules Caesar, U.S. show business entrepreneur (b. April 26, 1896, South Bend, Ind.—d. April 29, 1981, Los Angeles, Calif.), abandoned his career as an ophthalmologist in 1924 to found the Music Corporation of America, a small-time band-booking agency that became a colossal entertainment empire. Stein, who paid his way through medical school by playing the saxophone and violin, as well as leading bands, discovered that booking bands was a lucrative and enjoyable sideline to practicing medicine. With MCA he innovatively scheduled one-night stands instead of full-season bookings and fostered the company's growth and power by introducing the exclusive contract; that is, all of his clients' bookings had to be managed solely by him. By the mid-1930s, after signing Guy Lombardo, Stein's agency had gained enough momentum to snare more than half of the nation's major bands. By the end of the 1930s MCA's tentacles reached to Hollywood, where Stein represented such superstars as Bette Davis, Joan Crawford, Greta Garbo, Frank Sinatra, and Jack Benny. Less than a decade later the organization had cornered possibly half of the motion picture industry's top performers. With its acquisition of Universal Studios in the late 1950s, and entry into the production of motion pictures and television programs, MCA was nicknamed "the octopus." In 1962 a federal antitrust suit cited a conflict of interest, and MCA withdrew its talent agency. Stein served as president of MCA until 1946, and as chairman of the board he distributed 53% of the MCA stock to his employees. In later years Stein donated and helped raise millions of dollars for eye research. The entertainment mogul once stated, "If I am remembered for anything, it will not be for anything I did in show business, but for what I did to prevent blindness."

Strelcyn, Stefan, Polish scholar (b. June 28, 1918, Poland—d. May 19, 1981, Manchester, England), was one of the foremost authorities in the field of Ethiopian studies. Strelcyn studied at the University of Warsaw and returned there as associate professor of Semitic studies in 1950. He held the post of professor for 15 years before going to London in 1969 as a visiting lecturer at the School of Oriental and African Studies. Strelcyn was by this time established as a major authority on Ethiopian studies. In the course of his long academic career he cataloged Ethiopic collections in a number of libraries throughout the world; his work gained him the Haile Selassie Award for Ethiopian Studies in 1967. His major publication was *Médicine et plantes d'Ethiopie* (2 vol., 1968 and 1973). The last 11 years of his life were spent at the University of Manchester teaching Semitic languages.

Sudets, Vladimir, Soviet air force officer (b. 1904, Nizhnedneprovsk, Ukraine—d. May 5, 1981, Moscow, U.S.S.R.), became a Soviet war hero following his exploits as a fighter pilot and flight commander during World War II. After the war he was sent to Poland to organize its air force. After returning to Moscow in 1955 he was appointed commander of Soviet strategic air forces, and from 1962 he served as deputy minister of defense and commander of antiaircraft defense forces until 1966.

Sun Yat-sen, Madame (SOONG CH'ING-LING), Chinese political figure (b. Jan. 27, 1893, Shanghai, China—d. May 29, 1981, Beijing [Peking], China), played no significant role in Chinese politics, but she acquired great symbolic importance in Communist China as the widow of the great revolutionary leader Sun Yat-sen and, after his death, as a staunch opponent of Chiang Kai-shek, her

WIDE WORLD

sister's husband. Soong, who married Sun Yat-sen in 1915 after he abandoned his wife and three children, was one of three illustrious sisters who made remarkable marriages. Her elder sister, Soong Ai-ling, wed Kung Hsiang-hsi, a director of the Bank of China, while her younger sister, Soong Mei-ling, married Chiang Kai-shek. During her marriage to Sun Yat-sen, Madame Sun served as his secretary, chief confidant, and inseparable companion until his death in 1925. In 1927 Madame Sun disrupted family unity by accusing Chiang Kai-shek of betraying her husband's "Three People's Principles," the foundation on which the Republic of China was established. The rift widened when Madame Sun decided to remain in China when Chiang Kai-shek's Nationalist forces fled to Taiwan in 1949. In that year she was named vice-chairman of the Central People's Government, and from then on she was engaged in state activities. When Liu Shaoqi (Liu Shao-ch'i) succeeded Mao Zedong (Mao Tse-tung) as head of state in 1959, Madame Sun was named one of two vice-chairmen of the republic, a largely ceremonial post equivalent to that of vice-president. Madame Sun was admitted to membership in the Communist Party only a few weeks before her death and was honoured with a state funeral.

Taurog, Norman, U.S. film director (b. Feb. 23, 1899, Chicago, Ill.—d. April 8, 1981, Rancho Mirage, Calif.), was known for his talent in the direction of children and dogs and won an Academy Award in 1931 for *Skippy* (a comedy about two boys and a dog), starring child actor Jackie Cooper. Taurog's other directing credits include: *Boys Town,* with

Spencer Tracy and Mickey Rooney; *Adventures of Tom Sawyer; Young Tom Edison; Little Nellie Kelly* and *Presenting Lily Mars,* both with Judy Garland; *Blue Hawaii* and *Speedway,* starring Elvis Presley; and *The Caddy* and *You're Never Too Young,* featuring Jerry Lewis and Dean Martin. After becoming blind in his later years, he served as a director at the Braille Institute in Los Angeles for 17 years.

Taylor, Gordon Rattray, British author (b. Jan. 11, 1911, Eastbourne, England—d. Dec. 7, 1981, Bath, England), specialized in writing popular works on broad scientific and social issues. His two books warning of the possible dangers of technological and scientific progress, *The Biological Time Bomb* (1968) and *The Doomsday Book* (1970), were bestsellers and were translated into many languages. After studying at Trinity College, Cambridge, he began a career in journalism in 1933. During World War II he worked with the British Broadcasting Corporation's monitoring service and with the Psychological Warfare Division of Supreme Headquarters, Allied Expeditionary Headquarters. Although he mainly free-lanced after the war, Taylor was chief science adviser to the BBC during the 1960s and also edited the television series "Horizon." His first successful book, *Sex in History* (1953), was followed by *How to Avoid the Future* (1975) and *The Natural History of the Mind* (1979). Taylor's last book, *The Great Evolution Mystery,* was scheduled for publication in 1982.

Tewson, Sir (Harold) Vincent, British trade unionist (b. Feb. 4, 1898, Bradford, England—d. May 1, 1981, Letchworth, England), in 1946 succeeded Sir Walter Citrine as general secretary of the Trades Union Congress (TUC), a post he held for 20 years. Tewson's involvement with the trade union movement began when he left school at age 14 and started working as an office boy at the headquarters of the Amalgamated Society of Dyers. The qualities that guided him in his early union work were recognized by Citrine, who appointed him to the staff of the TUC in 1926. Tewson became general secretary at a time when the movement was under great pressure. The TUC was anxious to support the new Labour government that came to power after World War II, and at the same time union members at the grass-roots level were restless for change. Tewson, patient and deliberate, steered a cautious path through these postwar rapids.

Thomas, Gwyn, Welsh novelist (b. July 6, 1913, Cynner, Porth, Wales—d. April 12, 1981, Cardiff, Wales), drew on his experiences as a young man in the industrial mining communities of South Wales for his novels and short stories. The son of a miner, Thomas won a scholarship to St. Edmund Hall, Oxford, where he studied Spanish. From 1942 to 1962 he taught at Barry Grammar School. He achieved his first major success with the publication of a collection of short stories entitled *Where Did I Put My Pity?* (1946) and the novel *The Dark Philosophers* (1947). In 1949 he published *All Things Betray Thee,* set in 19th-century industrial Wales and sometimes considered his best work. In his novels, as in his frequent contributions to radio and television, he combined imagination and humour with an underlying bitterness at the destructive forces threatening the Welsh community. However, he had no nostalgia for the past or sympathy with Welsh nationalism. Thomas also wrote several plays, including *The Keep* (1961), and in 1968 published his autobiography, *A Few Selected Exits.* The Welsh Arts Council awarded him its Honour (principal prize) in 1976.

Thomas, Lowell, U.S. radio broadcaster (b. April 6, 1892, Woodington, Ohio—d. Aug. 29, 1981, Pawling, N.Y.), was the exuberant pioneering radio broadcaster whose sonorous voice was heard by billions of listeners during his more than 50 years on the airwaves, an unmatched record. Thomas, who began his radio career by replacing Floyd Gibbons on the nation's first network news show in

123

1930, worked for NBC and CBS before also becoming the voice of "Movietone News" in 1935. A renowned globetrotter, he traveled to France, Italy, the Philippines, India, and the Middle East, where in 1917 he photographed and interviewed Col. T. E. Lawrence ("Lawrence of Arabia"). In 1919 Thomas assembled his films of Lawrence and produced *The Last Crusade*, a highly romantic film and lecture presentation about Lawrence of Arabia that played to packed houses in New York and London. Still brimming with tales of adventure, he then published his most famous book, *With Lawrence in Arabia* (1924). A fruitful writing career resulted in a flood of more than 50 books, including *Raiders of the Deep* (1928), *The Hero of Vincennes (1929)*, and *India: Land of the Black Pagoda* (1930). Thomas successfully combined his dual careers as a broadcaster and professional traveler to create exciting programs that featured his exchanges with presidents, astronauts, royalty, and the Dalai Lama of Tibet. He flavoured his shows with his adventures as a tiger hunter in India, his experiences traversing the U.S. in the "See America" campaign, and his stint in Europe as a reporter during World War II. After his nightly news program was taken off the air in 1976, Thomas launched the series "Lowell Thomas Remembers," which included old newsreel footage of historical events. In 1980 he started a syndicated radio program, "The Best Years," which chronicled the achievements of famous personalities in their later years. The first volume of his two-part autobiography, *Good Evening, Everybody*, was published in 1976, and the second, *So Long Until Tomorrow*, appeared in 1977.

Thornton, Charles Bates ("TEX"), U.S. industrialist (b. July 22, 1913, Haskell, Texas—d. Nov. 24, 1981, Holmby Hills, Calif.), was the visionary president (1953–61) and board chairman (1953–81) of Litton Industries, a giant conglomerate with some 5,000 products and sales of over $1 billion a year by 1966. During World War II Thornton rose to the rank of Army Air Forces colonel and devised a statistical control system to monitor the military's global resources. After the war he was dubbed the leader of the "Whiz Kids," a team of nine army colleagues who assisted the ailing Ford Motor Co. in 1946. Two years later Thornton joined the Hughes Aircraft Co. as vice-president and general manager and increased its sales from $150 million to $200 million, but in 1953 he purchased Litton, a tiny electronics company, and immediately began his plan to diversify. By 1981 the company's annual sales had increased to nearly $5 billion.

Thurman, Howard, U.S. clergyman, author, and educator (b. Nov. 18, 1900, Daytona Beach, Fla.—d. April 10, 1981, San Francisco, Calif.), was committed to making Christianity "live for the weak as well as the strong—for all peoples whatever their color, whatever their caste," and founded the Church for Fellowship of All Peoples in San Francisco. Thurman taught religion at Morehouse College in Atlanta, Ga., and at Howard University in Washington, D.C., before making an "evangelical tour" to India in 1935, where he met Mohandas Gandhi. Thurman was deeply moved by Gandhi's contention that Christianity "fostered segregation." The concept of founding an interracial, nondenominational religious fellowship became so attractive to Thurman that he left his theological post at Morehouse in 1944 to start such a church with Alfred Fisk. He served as co-pastor until 1953, when he was appointed dean of the chapel and professor of religion at the Boston University School of Theology. He was the first black to become a full-time faculty member there. Thurman was a poet as well as an author. His books include: *The Greatest of These, Deep River: An Interpretation of Negro Spirituals, The Creative Encounter*, and *Meditations of the Heart*. His autobiography, *With Head and Heart*, appeared in 1980.

Torrijos Herrera, Omar, Panamanian ruler (b. Feb. 13, 1929, Santiago, Panama—d. July 31, 1981,

UPI

western Panama), was brigadier general of Panama's National Guard and the country's de facto strong man for 13 years. Torrijos was probably best known, however, as the formidable negotiator in the 1977 treaties that provided for the transfer by the U.S. of the Panama Canal by the year 2000. In 1968 he led the National Guard in a coup that ousted Pres. Arnulfo Arias Madrid. Torrijos then took complete control of the government and served as chief of government from 1972 to 1978. In the latter year he relinquished that post and set elections for 1984. The cigar-chewing Torrijos, who was backed by the 8,000-man National Guard, was heavily supported in power by the peasants and by left-wing students, although Torrijos represented no clear ideology. This enigmatic leader, who ruled Panama with an iron hand, occasionally consorted with Cuba's Fidel Castro and Libya's Col. Muammar al-Qaddafi. Conversely, he allowed the deposed shah of Iran, Mohammad Reza Pahlavi, to reside on the Panamanian island of Contadora in December 1979; he was also responsible, together with the Vatican, for persuading the Argentine government to release former president Isabel Martínez de Perón from house arrest and permit her exile to Spain. He was killed when his air force plane crashed in the jungle.

Toynbee, (Theodore) Philip, British novelist and journalist (b. June 25, 1916, Oxford, England—d. June 15, 1981, St. Briavels, Lydney, Gloucestershire, England), was a diverse writer who made his mark in the field of journalism and as the author of fiction, criticism, and memoirs. As a novelist he aroused greatest critical interest when he experimented with time and symbolic elements, as in *Tea with Mrs. Goodman* (1947) and *The Garden to the Sea* (1953) and in the verse novels *Pantaloon* (1961), *Two Brothers* (1964), *A Learned City* (1967), and *Views from a Lake* (1968). Toynbee's earlier novels were more conventional in form and reflected the bohemianism prevalent among his contemporaries at Oxford in the 1930s; they included *The Savage Days* (1937), *School in Private* (1941), and *The Barricades* (1943). The intellectual ferment of his youth was also the theme of his memoir *Friends Apart* (1954). Toynbee's father was the eminent historian Arnold Toynbee, and in *Comparing Notes* (1963) they collaborated in bridging the gap between their generations. Toynbee's journalistic career began as editor (1938–39) of a provincial newspaper. After service in World War II, he joined (1950) *The Observer*, first as foreign correspondent and later as its influential book reviewer.

Trifonov, Yury Valentinovich, Soviet writer (b. Aug. 28, 1925, Moscow, U.S.S.R.—d. March 28, 1981, Moscow), managed to retain official acceptance of his work despite its anti-Stalinist overtones. His father, a hero of the Bolshevik Revolution, was executed during the purges in 1938, and his mother was sent to a prison camp.

Trifonov worked in an aircraft factory, then studied at the Gorky Literary Institute. His first novel, *Students* (1950), won the Stalin Prize in 1951. Trifonov also went as a journalist to Central Asia, where he reported on the building of the Kara-Kum canal, the subject of his novel *Thirst Quenching* (1963). Much of his work during the 1960s appeared in *Novy Mir*, the periodical edited by his friend Aleksandr Tvardovsky. His later works, including *The Exchange* (1969), *Preliminary Results* (1970), *The Long Goodbye* (1971), and *The House on the Embankment* (1976), were honest and fearless explorations of contemporary Soviet life. *The Literary Gazette* accused Trifonov of being one-sided and unjust in his portrayal of the cynicism and opportunism fostered by the Stalinist system, but his works were immensely popular, some of them being adapted for stage and screen and several of them translated.

Trippe, Juan Terry, U.S. aviation pioneer (b. June 27, 1899, Sea Bright, N.J.—d. April 3, 1981, New York, N.Y.), significantly influenced the formation and expansion of the international airline industry as the founder of Pan American World Airways. After serving as a naval aviator during World War I, Trippe became president of Long Island Airways, which he founded in 1922 with friends from Yale. From 1924 to 1926 he headed Colonial Air Transport, which secured the first Post Office contract to deliver U.S. airmail on a route between New York City and Boston. In 1927 Trippe felt that the domestic competition was increasing, so, having acquired an airmail route between Miami and Havana, he entered the international field with a single Fokker three-engine monoplane. Successful in establishing himself as a farsighted leader in the aviation business, Trippe was at the forefront of nearly every major development in commercial aviation during the next 40 years. Under his direction Pan Am became the first airline to fly across the Pacific and Atlantic oceans; to order commercial jets (1955), which effectively halved flying time and made air travel a popular form of transportation; and to buy the wide-bodied Boeing 747 jets (1966) for long-distance travel. Trippe also pioneered the use of amphibian "clipper" planes for low-fare service on the North Atlantic (1952) and the concept of selling overseas flight tickets to be paid on an installment basis (1954). After Trippe retired as president and chief executive director of Pan Am in 1968, he served as honorary chairman of the board.

Tyerman, Donald, British journalist (b. March 1, 1908, Middlesbrough, England—d. April 24, 1981, Westleton, Suffolk, England), was editor of *The Economist* from 1956 to 1965. Crippled by polio as a child, Tyerman gained a scholarship to Brasenose College, Oxford, then taught at the University of Southampton until he joined the staff of *The Economist* in 1937. From 1944 to 1955 he was assistant editor of *The Times*, and both there and at *The Economist* he played an important role in post-World War II British journalism by encouraging new talent. Tyerman was a leading member of the International Press Institute and the British and Commonwealth Press councils. As editor of *The Economist*, he not only modernized the paper by changing its layout but established it firmly in a centrist position in politics, opposing Britain's intervention at Suez in 1956 and supporting Labour Party leader Harold Wilson in the 1964 general election.

Urey, Harold Clayton, U.S. chemist (b. April 29, 1893, Walkerton, Ind.—d. Jan. 5, 1981, La Jolla, Calif.), was awarded the 1934 Nobel Prize for Chemistry for his discovery in 1931 of deuterium, a heavy isotope of hydrogen. After earning his Ph.D. from the University of California at Berkeley in 1923, Urey studied the theory of atomic structure with Niels Bohr in Copenhagen. In 1929 he joined the faculty of Columbia University, where he discovered deuterium while working with George M. Murphy and Ferdinand G. Brickwedde. Urey had correctly predicted that the distillation of liquid hydrogen would contain the heavy isotope. The discovery led eventually to the devel-

opment of the hydrogen bomb, which uses deuterium and the heavier hydrogen isotope tritium as its fuel. During World War II Urey worked for the top-secret Manhattan Project, where his research on the separation of uranium isotopes by gaseous diffusion was a major contribution to the development of the atomic bomb. In spite of his pioneering efforts in atomic research, Urey later campaigned for an international ban against nuclear weapons. After the war he moved to the University of Chicago and in 1947 published a paper on the thermodynamic properties of isotopic substances that provided much of the theoretical basis for isotope geochemistry. At Chicago Urey also began his studies of astrophysics and the origins of the solar system. In a celebrated experiment in 1953 he and a graduate student, Stanley Miller, demonstrated that the Earth's primordial ingredients of methane, ammonia, hydrogen, and water could have been forced by lightning discharges to combine into amino acids, the building blocks of protein. His book *The Planets: Their Origin and Development* (1952) was the first systematic and detailed chronology of the origin of the Earth, the Moon, meteorites, and the solar system. Urey left Chicago in 1958 to join the faculty of the University of California at San Diego (La Jolla), where he continued his investigations of geochemistry, the history of the solar system, and the origins of life. During the 1970s he helped analyze the Moon rocks retrieved by the Apollo astronauts and served as a consultant on the Viking missions to Mars.

Urrutia Lleo, Manuel, Cuban judge and politician (b. Dec. 8, 1901, Yaguajay, Las Villas Province, Cuba—d. July 4, 1981, New York, N.Y.), was handpicked by Fidel Castro to serve as the country's first president after the revolution. Urrutia took office on Jan 2, 1959, but was ousted six months later when Castro accused him of being a traitor. Urrutia endured years of house arrest and asylum in the Venezuelan and Mexican embassies in Havana before securing a safe-conduct pass to the U.S. in 1963. There he denounced the Castro government in the book *Fidel Castro & Company, Inc.: Communist Tyranny in Cuba* (1964) and in the same year announced the formation of the Democratic Revolutionary Alliance, comprised of 22 anti-Castro exile groups. Before his presidential appointment, Urrutia had served as a municipal judge. He was forced to resign from the bench in 1957 by the government of Pres. Fulgencio Batista because he acquitted 150 youths charged with rebellion in Santiago de Cuba. Urrutia spent the following years in self-imposed exile before being chosen as a figurehead president by Castro in 1959.

Vanbremeersch, Claude, French Army officer (b. Jan. 3, 1921, Paris, France—d. Feb. 10, 1981, Paris), was head of the French president's military staff from 1975 and chief of staff of the French armed forces from July 1979 to January 1981. Trained at the Saint-Cyr military academy, he was sent to Buchenwald concentration camp in 1943 because of his resistance activities; he rejoined the Army on his liberation in 1945. Vanbremeersch served in the French colonial wars in Indochina and Algeria, joined the general staff, and in 1966 took command of the 35th Infantry Regiment in Belfort. He was head of studies at the military academy from 1968 to 1970 and, after promotion to major general in 1973, took command of the 3rd French Division at Freiburg, West Germany. As chief of staff he stressed the need to modernize France's nuclear forces. He was a grand officer of the Legion of Honour and held three Croix de Guerre.

Vera-Ellen (VERA-ELLEN ROHE), U.S. actress (b. Feb. 16, 1926, Cincinnati, Ohio—d. Aug. 30, 1981, Los Angeles, Calif.), was the lithe blond dancer who starred in a number of 1940s and '50s Hollywood musicals with such masterful dancing partners as Fred Astaire, Gene Kelly, and Danny Kaye. Vera-Ellen, who was discovered by Samuel Goldwyn while appearing on Broadway in *By Jupiter*, made her film debut in *Wonder Man* (1945) opposite Danny Kaye. She also starred with Fred Astaire in *Three Little Words* and *The Belle of New York*, with Gene

Kelly in the famous ballet "Slaughter on Tenth Avenue" in *Words and Music*, and with Bing Crosby in *White Christmas*. Shortly after her last film, *Let's Be Happy* (1956), Vera-Ellen retired.

Vinson, Carl, U.S. politician (b. Nov. 18, 1883, near Milledgeville, Ga.—d. June 1, 1981, Milledgeville), served half a century (1914–64) in the U.S. House of Representatives, longer than anyone else in history, and was the influential chairman of the House Naval Affairs Committee (which in 1947 combined with the House's other military panels to form the House Armed Services Committee). Vinson, who remained obdurate in his fight for military preparedness, was called the Swamp Fox because he shrewdly controlled the Pentagon from his seat in the House. As chairman of the House Naval Affairs Committee he instituted a naval replacement and rebuilding program that later helped the U.S. recover from the 1941 bombing of Pearl Harbor. He worked closely with three U.S. presidents prior to their terms in office: Franklin D. Roosevelt, Dwight D. Eisenhower, and Lyndon B. Johnson. In 1973 a nuclear-powered aircraft carrier was named after Carl Vinson. This honour made Vinson the only living person to ever have a major U.S. Navy ship named for him.

Von Zell, Harry, U.S. radio announcer and actor (b. July 11, 1906, Indianapolis, Ind.—d. Nov. 21, 1981, Calabas, Calif.), was best remembered as the portly announcer on the "Burns and Allen" radio and television show and as the CBS announcer who inadvertently introduced U.S. Pres. Herbert Hoover as "Hoobert Heever." Von Zell, who had an infectious laugh, was also the network announcer on the radio shows of Will Rogers, Jack Benny, Eddie Cantor, and Dinah Shore. After making his motion picture debut in *It's in the Bag*, Von Zell appeared in more than 30 films, including *Uncle Harry*, *I Can Get It for You Wholesale*, and *Son of Paleface*. Von Zell also was a commentator on early "March of Time" programs.

Waldock, Sir (Claud) Humphrey Meredith, British jurist (b. Aug. 13, 1904, Colombo, Ceylon [now Sri Lanka]—d. Aug. 15, 1981, The Hague, Neth.), was president (1971–74) of the European Court of Human Rights and president of the International Court of Justice from 1979 until his death. Educated at Oxford, he returned there to teach law as fellow of Brasenose College in 1930 and was appointed Chichele professor of international law in 1947. During World War II he worked with the Admiralty and in 1946 was a commissioner on the Italo-Yugoslav Boundary Commission. He served subsequently with many such international committees and accompanied the UN mission to Beijing (Peking) in 1951 to negotiate the release of U.S airmen shot down in the Korean War. Waldock also played a major role in drafting the Convention on the Law of Treaties adopted at Vienna in 1969. He joined the European Court of Human Rights in 1966 and became British judge on the International Court of Justice in 1973, gaining admiration for the impartiality of his judgments. He was co-author of *The Law of Mortgages* and editor (1955–74) of *The British Yearbook of International Law*. He was knighted in 1961.

Walker, Mickey (EDWARD PATRICK WALKER), U.S. boxer (b. July 13, 1901, Elizabeth, N.J.—d. April 28, 1981, Freehold, N.J.), was the fearless "Toy Bulldog" who held the world welterweight (1922–26) and middleweight (1926–31) championships before making an unsuccessful bid for the light-heavyweight crown. During his 17-year (1919–35) pugilistic career, Walker, who never weighed more than 77 kg (170 lb) in the ring, consistently displayed his aggressiveness. He won the welterweight championship from Jack Britton in 1922, captured the middleweight crown from Tiger Flowers in 1926, and attempted to beat light-heavyweight champions Tommy Loughran and Maxie Rosenbloom. Undaunted by these defeats, Walker met such heavyweight champions as Jack Sharkey, with whom he boxed a 15-round draw, and Max Schmeling, who knocked Walker out in eight rounds. His professional record included 160

bouts with 60 knockouts. After retiring in 1935, Walker took up painting and in 1955 displayed his work at the Associated American Artists Galleries in New York. He was elected to the Boxing Hall of Fame in 1955.

Wallace, (William Roy) DeWitt, U.S. editor and publisher (b. Nov. 12, 1889, St. Paul, Minn.—d. March 30, 1981, Mount Kisco, N.Y.), used his ingenuity and creativity to found *Reader's Digest* (1921), a pocket-size monthly magazine that attained the largest circulation of any magazine in the world. Wallace conceived the idea of offering condensed magazine articles that had wide appeal, lasting interest, and uplifting themes. In 1919 he began compiling his first condensations while recovering from war wounds. When publishers showed no interest in printing the magazine, Wallace raised $5,000 in provisional subscriptions and, together with his wife, Lila Bell Acheson Wallace, published the first issue in February 1922 from a Greenwich Village basement office in New York City. In a year they had 7,000 subscriptions, and by 1939 they had moved their headquarters to Chappaqua, N.Y., circulation having reached three million copies. In the same year a British edition was started, and in 1940 the first foreign-language edition began. When the circulation rose substantially, Wallace was forced to begin paying for reprinting rights, and by 1955 production costs had become so steep that the *Digest* was forced to run advertisements, though none pertaining to liquor was allowed until 1979 and cigarette ads continued to be prohibited. Although the *Reader's Digest* was sometimes criticized for being socially conservative and culturally middle-brow, it had a circulation of 30.5 million copies in 16 languages by 1981 and had made Wallace a multimillionaire. When asked about an appropriate epitaph, Wallace replied: "The final condensation."

Warburg, Fredric John, British publisher (b. Nov. 27, 1898, London, England—d. May 25, 1981, London), as chairman (1936–71) and later president of Secker and Warburg Ltd. built up a large and varied list of fiction authors, among them George Orwell. Warburg founded the firm after leaving George Routledge & Sons Ltd., where he was junior managing director, and purchasing the ailing Martin Secker Ltd. In the final months of World War II, with the Soviet Union still a fighting ally of Britain, Warburg was the only publisher willing to publish Orwell's masterpiece *Animal Farm* (1945). Orwell's usual publisher, Victor Gollancz, had already turned down this fierce anti-Stalinist allegory. However, Warburg was rewarded with a best-seller and Orwell's next and final novel, *Nineteen Eighty-Four* (1949). Controversy continued to surround Warburg; in 1954 he stood trial at the Old Bailey on a charge of publishing an obscene libel. The novel in question was Stanley Kaufmann's *The Philanderer*. The jury's decision to acquit Warburg led to alterations in the obscenity laws. Warburg gave his account of the case in a long article published in *The New Yorker* magazine (April 20, 1957) entitled *A Slight Case of Obscenity*. He also wrote two volumes of autobiography, *An Occupation for Gentlemen* (1959) and *All Authors Are Equal* (1973).

Ward, Barbara: *see* Jackson of Lodsworth, Baroness.

Ward-Perkins, John Bryan, British archaeologist (b. Feb. 3, 1912—d. May 28, 1981, Stratton, Gloucestershire, England), won international distinction for his archaeological research and was director of the British School at Rome from 1946 to 1974. In 1936, two years after graduating from New College, Oxford, he became an assistant at the London Museum under Mortimer Wheeler. In 1939 Ward-Perkins spent six months as professor of archaeology at the Royal University of Malta, where he surveyed the island's prehistoric monuments. During World War II he served as an artillery officer in North Africa and the Middle East and organized

the military government's antiquities department in Tripoli and Cyrenaica. After the invasion of Italy Ward-Perkins became director of the military government's Monuments and Fine Arts Subcommission there. After the war he returned to Italy to assume his directorship of the British School at Rome, where he helped found the International Association for Classical Archaeology, of which he was president (1974–79). He also directed excavations in Tripolitania (1948–53), Istanbul (1953), Italy (1957–71), and Cyrenaica (1969–71; 1978–79). His numerous publications include *The Shrine of St. Peter* (1955), *The Historical Topography of Veii* (1961), *The Cities of Ancient Greece and Italy* (1974), and, with Amanda Claridge, *Pompeii AD 79*.

Warner, Jack (JOHN WATERS), British actor (b. Oct. 24, 1896, London, England—d. May 24, 1981, London), became almost completely identified with his role as the eponymous policeman hero of BBC television's long-running series "Dixon of Dock Green." Brother of the famous cockney variety comedian Elsie and Doris Waters, Warner too began his career as a cockney entertainer. His first role as a policeman came in the film *The Blue Lamp* (1950). The image of an avuncular London "bobby" stuck, and Warner was chosen to play Constable Dixon (later promoted to sergeant). "Dixon of Dock Green" began in 1955 and continued for an astonishing 21 years.

Warren, Harry (SALVATORE GUARAGNA), U.S. songwriter (b. Dec. 24, 1893, New York, N.Y.—d. Sept. 22, 1981, Los Angeles, Calif.), used his inherent musical talent to become the prolific composer of more than 300 popular songs and the winner of three Academy Awards for "Lullaby of Broadway" (1935), "You'll Never Know" (1943), and "On the Atchison, Topeka and the Santa Fe" (1946). Warren, who never had a music lesson, left school at age 16 and worked as a drummer, a pianist, and an assistant director for motion pictures before joining the Navy. After World War I he published (1922) his first song, "Rose of the Rio Grande." In the 1920s and early '30s Warren wrote songs for such Broadway musicals as *Sweet and Low* and *Crazy Quilt*. He began collaborating with librettist Al Dubin in 1932, and together they turned out songs for a string of smash hit motion pictures including *42nd Street*, the *Gold Diggers* series, and *Wonder Bar*. During the 1940s Warren teamed up with lyricist Mack Gordon; the two wrote songs for such films as *Down Argentine Way*, *Sun Valley Serenade*, *Springtime in the Rockies*, and *Sweet Rosie O'-Grady*. Warren also created the songs for the motion pictures *An Affair to Remember* and *Separate Tables*. Some of his most enduring melodies are: "Shuffle Off to Buffalo," "Chattanooga Choo Choo," "Serenade in Blue," "I Found a Million Dollar Baby," "You're My Everything," "Jeepers Creepers," "That's Amore," "So This Is Venice," and "September in the Rain." In 1973 Warren was inducted into the Songwriters' Hall of Fame.

Waugh, Alec (ALEXANDER RABAN WAUGH), British writer (b. July 8, 1898, Hampstead, London, England—d. Sept. 3, 1981, Tampa, Fla.), caused a sensation in 1917 with the publication of his first novel, *The Loom of Youth*, which dealt with the subject of homosexual behaviour in British public schools, and scored a triumphant success with his best-seller *Island in the Sun* (1956), which sold nearly a million copies and was made into a popular film. His first novel upset the authorities at his school, Sherborne, which he left to attend Sandhurst Military Academy and then join the Army. Toward the end of World War I he was taken prisoner, and he described his experiences in *The Prisoners of Mainz* (1919). Waugh wrote prolifically for many years but enjoyed little success, unlike his younger brother, Evelyn. Waugh wrote many novels and travel books, including *The Hot Countries* (1930), before serving with Army Intelligence in Iraq during World War II. His later works included two autobiographical volumes, *My Brother Evelyn*

and Other Profiles (1967) and *The Best Wine Last* (1978), and an essay, "In Praise of Wine."

Whitaker, Rogers E. M., U.S. writer and editor (b. Jan. 15, 1900, Arlington, Mass.—d. May 11, 1981, New York, N.Y.), helped shape the style of *The New Yorker* as a longtime writer and editor with the magazine. Whitaker, who joined the staff in 1926, only one year after the inception of the publication, was perhaps best known as the widely traveled railroad buff E. M. Frimbo. In his column Whitaker chronicled his adventures over 2,748,636.81 mi of railroad tracks. In 1934 Whitaker inherited the football column, signing it with the initials J. W. L. He also wrote under the pseudonym The Old Curmudgeon in "Talk of the Town" pieces. In the world of New York nightlife, which he reviewed in the magazine's "Goings On About Town" section and his "Tables for Two" column, he was known as Popsie. Although he retired as a *New Yorker* editor in 1975, he continued to contribute to some of its columns.

Widgery, John Passmore Widgery, BARON, British judge (b. July 24, 1911, South Molton, Devon, England—d. July 26, 1981, London, England), was lord chief justice of England from 1971 to 1980. Widgery, who was educated in his native Devon, left school to become an articled clerk. He qualified as a solicitor in 1933, but after World War II he decided to become a barrister. It was not long before he made his mark; only 15 years after he was first called to the bar, Widgery was appointed a high court judge. As lord chief justice during the 1970s he was companion to controversy, but his lucid judgments occasioned great respect. He conducted an exhaustive inquiry into the events of "Bloody Sunday" (Jan. 30, 1972), when 13 civilians were killed by British soldiers in Londonderry, Northern Ireland. Widgery was knighted in 1961 and made a life peer in 1971.

Wilkins, Roy, U.S. civil rights leader (b. Aug. 30, 1901, St. Louis, Mo.—d. Sept. 8, 1981, New York, N.Y.), was the articulate leader (1955–77) of the National Association for the Advancement of Colored People (NAACP) during a period of racial turbulence and mass protest. After graduating from the University of Minnesota in 1923, Wilkins became managing editor of the *Kansas City Call*, a black newspaper. Wilkins's editorials urged blacks to use their vote and were instrumental in the defeat of U.S. Sen. Henry J. Allen, whom Wilkins termed "a militant racist." Wilkins's efforts were noticed by Walter White, executive secretary of the NAACP, who made him his chief assistant in New York in 1931. His investigation of the working conditions of blacks on Mississippi levees resulted in a 1932 report that prompted congressional action. From 1934 to 1949 Wilkins edited *Crisis* magazine, the official NAACP publication. Wilkins, who felt that social justice could best be achieved by constitutional means, won a historic 1954 Supreme Court decision that overturned the doctrine of "separate

KEYSTONE

but equal" educational facilities. An erudite speaker known for his calm, reflective thinking, Wilkins instilled a sense of pride in his fellow blacks and was widely respected. In the early 1960s he worked on Pres. John F. Kennedy's civil rights bill and helped organize the civil rights March on Washington. Because Wilkins remained adamantly opposed to violence and rejected black separatism in any form, he angered many black militants. By the early 1970s some factions within the NAACP felt Wilkins should relinquish his directorship, but he refused to step down. In 1977, after fighting for civil rights for some 50 years, an ailing Wilkins retired.

Williams, Eric Eustace, Trinidadian politician (b. Sept. 25, 1911, Trinidad—d. March 29, 1981, Port-of-Spain, Trinidad), led his People's National Movement (PNM) to victory in the 1956 elections, becoming chief minister of Trinidad and Tobago and, after independence in 1962, prime minister. A writer and academic, he entered politics late in life and enjoyed considerable respect at home and abroad. However, his long period in office failed to live up to the hopes it had inspired: his regime, plagued by corruption, was unable to solve Trinidad's economic and racial problems, while his autocratic style of government was the price paid for stability. Williams studied at St. Catherine's Society (later College), Oxford, and went on to teach political science at Howard University, Washington, D.C. His many books included two authoritative works on colonialism, *The Negro in the Caribbean* (1942) and *Capitalism and Slavery* (1944). His prestige as a scholar led to his membership in the Caribbean Commission, and in 1955, with the creation of the PNM, he entered politics. From the following year his party was consistently in power and faced little serious opposition until the 1970s. He led the country to independence, withdrew it from the West Indian Federation in 1962, and declared it a republic in 1976. Although originally opposed to U.S. influence, Williams was forced by Trinidad's economic circumstances to encourage an increasingly high level of U.S. investment. Black Power militancy, racial tensions, and labour unrest during the 1960s obliged him to take repressive measures that strengthened his regime but represented a failure of his ideals; in 1973 he threatened to resign, and in the elections of the following year he campaigned against the corruption in his own government. He left a legacy of political stability and a measure of prosperity but was unable to solve the underlying problems of his country.

Williams, Mary Lou (MARY ELFRIEDA SCRUGGS), U.S. jazz musician (b. May 8, 1910, Atlanta, Ga.—d. May 28, 1981, Durham, N.C.), earned top honours as the first prominent woman jazz artist with her driving two-fisted piano style, fresh, avant-garde arrangements, and original ragtime, Dixieland, swing, and bebop compositions. Williams's contributions during her almost 60-year reign as the "first lady of jazz" were legion. She brought new spice to the Kansas City jazz world during the late 1920s while performing with Andy Kirk's band. In 1931 she became a permanent pianist and arranger with Andy Kirk's Twelve Clouds of Joy and over the next 11 years contributed such compositions as "Froggy Bottom," "Walkin' & Swingin'," "Cloudy," "Twinklin'," and "Little Joe from Chicago." With the emergence of the swing era, Williams produced some of her finest work, including "Trumpets No End" for Duke Ellington, "Roll 'Em" and "Camel Hop" for Benny Goodman, and "What's Your Story, Morning Glory" for Jimmy Lunceford. Williams was very influential in the 1945 bebop evolution, writing the hit "In the Land of Oo-Bla-Dee" for Dizzy Gillespie and composing "The Zodiac Suite," which she played with the New York Philharmonic. From 1954 to 1957 Williams abandoned her international concert tour to devote her time to prayer and meditation. After converting to Roman Catholicism in 1957 she was persuaded by two priests and Gillespie to return to jazz. Her deep religious convictions inspired her first major religious work, *St. Martin de Porres* (1962). She then wrote three masses, includ-

ing the sedate *A Mass for the Lenten Season* and *Music for Peace* (which later became known as *Mary Lou's Mass* because of its strong, joyful qualities). In 1977 Williams became artist in residence at Duke University in Durham, N.C.

Wood, Natalie (NATASHA GURDIN), U.S. actress (b. July 20, 1938, San Francisco, Calif.—d. Nov. 29, 1981, Santa Catalina Island, Calif.), was an endearing child actress who captivated audiences as the small girl who warily puts her trust in Santa Claus in *Miracle on 34th Street* (1947) and later evolved into one of Hollywood's most beautiful actresses. Al-

KEYSTONE

though Wood never won an Academy Award, she was nominated on three occasions, for *Rebel Without a Cause* (1955), *Splendor in the Grass* (1961), and *Love with the Proper Stranger* (1963). She also won critical acclaim as the lovely Maria in the motion picture version of *West Side Story* (1961) and in the title role of the film *Gypsy* (1963). The glamorous star was twice married (1957–62 and 1972–81) to actor Robert Wagner. At the time of her death she was filming the motion picture *Brainstorm*. It was thought that Wood lost her footing while boarding a small inflatable motorized dinghy and drowned.

Wurf, Jerry (JEROME WURF), U.S. union official (b. May 18, 1919, New York, N.Y.—d. Dec. 10, 1981, Washington, D.C.), served for 17 years as national president of the American Federation of State, County, and Municipal Employees, the largest union of public employees in the U.S. and from 1978 the largest unit of the AFL-CIO. Wurf was largely credited with building the union membership from 200,000 to more than one million by using his powers of persuasion and by actively recruiting women and blacks. Wurf was appointed a vice-president of the AFL-CIO in 1969.

Wyler, William, French-born motion-picture director (b. July 1, 1902, Mulhouse, France—d. July 27, 1981, Beverly Hills, Calif.), was an exceptional film director who, besides winning Academy Awards for *Mrs. Miniver* (1942), *The Best Years of Our Lives* (1946), and the biblical epic *Ben Hur* (1959), directed such classics as *Dead End* (1937), *Jezebel* (1938), and *The Letter* (1940). Wyler, who worked as an office boy, script clerk, and publicity agent before securing a directorship, was equally at home with vastly differing subject matters. He directed some 50 Westerns from 1925 to 1927 before establishing his reputation with *Counsellor-at Law* (1933). His most glittering successes, though, were screen adaptations of fiction and drama, including Sinclair Lewis's *Dodsworth* (1936), Emily Brontë's *Wuthering Heights* (1939), and Lillian Hellman's play *The Little Foxes* (1941). During World War II he directed two outstanding documentary films, *The Memphis Belle*

(1944) and *Thunderbolt* (1945). His list of credits also includes *Roman Holiday* (1953), *The Big Country* (1958), *The Collector* (1965), and *Funny Girl* (1968). Besides his own three Academy Awards, his films earned Oscars for some 40 other artists.

Wyszynski, Stefan Cardinal, Polish prelate of the Roman Catholic Church (born Aug. 3, 1901, Zuzela, Poland—d. May 28, 1981, Warsaw, Poland), was from 1948 archbishop of Gniezno and Warsaw and 55th primate of Poland. The son of a church organist, he studied at the Wloclawek seminary and was ordained on Aug. 3, 1924. After taking a doctorate in law at Lublin Catholic University in 1929, he spent a year in Rome and in 1931 was appointed professor at Wloclawek. Shortly after the outbreak of World War II the Germans annexed western Poland, including the Wloclawek diocese, and his bishop, Msgr. Michal Kozal, ordered Wyszynski to leave Wloclawek. Thus he escaped the fate of 1,811 Polish priests, including Bishop Kozal, who perished in German concentration camps. In March 1945 Wyszynski returned to Wloclawek as rector of the seminary, but a year later he was appointed bishop of Lublin. On Nov. 16, 1948, Pope Pius XII transferred Msgr. Wyszynski to the primatial see of Gniezno and Warsaw. As primate he sought to withdraw the church from political controversy in order to ensure its freedom to teach and counsel its believers unmolested. In 1950, with his approval, a modus vivendi was reached between the episcopate and the government, but in February 1953 the latter violated the agreement and claimed the right to appoint, dismiss, or transfer members of the church's hierarchy. Wyszynski (made cardinal on Jan. 12, 1953) protested in an open letter to Boleslaw Bierut, the Communist premier, and was arrested. In October 1956, on orders from Wladyslaw Gomulka, the new Communist leader, Cardinal Wyszynski was released and resumed his office. A new agreement between the church and the state was reached in December, abolishing the decree of Feb. 9, 1953, and permitting the appointment of five residential bishops in the new western territories. But in 1966 Gomulka refused to issue a passport to Cardinal Wyszynski to attend the Polish millennium cele-

SVEN SIMON/KATHERINE YOUNG

brations in Vatican City. All foreign bishops who planned to visit Czestochowa in August were also denied visas. In view of the controversy, Pope Paul VI had to cancel a planned trip to Poland. In June 1976, when Edward Gierek's regime was shaken by workers' demonstrations, the cardinal combined calls for domestic peace with defense of workers and intellectuals and support of the newly formed Workers' Defense Committee (KOR).

Yates, Dame Frances Amelia, British Renaissance scholar (b. Nov. 28, 1899—d. Sept. 29, 1981, Claygate, Surrey, England), was reader in the history of the Renaissance at the Warburg Institute, London, and made a remarkable contribution to the study of the period. Yates studied French at Univer-

sity College, London, and during the 1930s published *John Florio: The Life of an Italian in Shakespeare's England* (1934) and *A Study of Love's Labour's Lost* (1936). She joined the Warburg Institute in 1941 and was appointed reader in 1956. *The Valois Tapestries* (1959) was followed by a massive study, *Giordano Bruno and the Hermetic Tradition* (1964). Her abiding interest in Shakespeare found expression in *Shakespeare's Last Plays* (1975). Yates's other major works included *The Art of Memory* (1966) and *Astrea* (1975). An honorary fellow of the Warburg Institute from 1967, she was made a Dame Commander of the Order of the British Empire in 1977.

Younghusband, Dame Eileen (Louise), British sociologist (b. Jan. 1, 1902, London, England—d. May 27, 1981, Raleigh, N.C.), brought her organizational and keen analytical powers to bear on the problem of reforming social work in Britain and established improved training facilities for social workers both within and outside the universities. Her achievements in this field won international recognition, and during 1961–68 she was an influential president of the International Association of Schools of Social Work. Though Younghusband had a privileged and sheltered childhood in Kashmir, she nevertheless studied for a diploma in sociology at the London School of Economics. She later returned there as lecturer in social studies (1929–39 and 1944–57). Younghusband then became (1959) chairman of the Ministry of Health Working Party on Social Workers in the Health and Welfare Services. Her most comprehensive book, *Social Work in Britain: 1950–1975*, was published in 1978. Younghusband was made a Dame of the Order of the British Empire in 1964.

Yukawa, Hideki, Japanese physicist (b. Jan. 23, 1907, Tokyo, Japan—d. Sept. 8, 1981, Kyoto, Japan), was awarded the 1949 Nobel Prize for Physics for his theories on subatomic particles. In 1935 Yukawa proposed that mesons (small energized particles) were responsible for binding protons and neutrons in atomic nuclei. During his tenure (1949–53) as visiting professor at Columbia University, New York, Yukawa's theory on the existence of mesons was confirmed in laboratory tests, and he became Japan's first Nobel laureate. After Yukawa graduated from Kyoto Imperial University he lectured there briefly (1932–33) before serving on the faculty at Osaka Imperial University (1933–39). In 1939 he returned to Kyoto, where he continued his theoretical work. Yukawa was invited to the Institute for Advanced Study in Princeton, N.J., in 1948 and in the following year became visiting professor at Columbia University. He returned to his alma mater in 1953 and served as director of Kyoto University's Research Institute for Fundamental Physics until his retirement in 1970.

Zhivkova, Lyudmila, Bulgarian politician (b. July 26, 1942, Sofia, Bulg.—d. July 20, 1981, Sofia), was a daughter of Todor Zhivkov (first secretary of the Bulgarian Communist Party and chairman of the State Council) and from 1979 was on the party's 12-member Politburo. In 1971 she was elected to the Bulgarian Committee of Arts and Culture, of which she became chairman (a ministerial post) in 1975. Zhivkova studied history at the University of Sofia and spent a year at St. Anthony's College, Oxford. After her mother's death in 1971 Zhivkova became Bulgaria's "first lady," accompanying her father on his foreign visits.

Zuckerman, Yitzhak, Polish-born Israeli kibbutznik (b. 1915—d. June 17, 1981, Tel Aviv, Israel), succeeded Mordechai Aniliwitz as commander of the Warsaw Ghetto dwellers who during World War II rebelled against the German occupation authorities. Zuckerman and other survivors, including his future wife, escaped through the city's sewers. Zuckerman settled in Palestine in 1947 and together with others founded the Lohamei Hagetaot kibbutz. There he also set up a documentation centre on the Holocaust and Jewish resistance.

Not all the news events of 1981 made prominent headlines. Among items reported less breathlessly in the worldwide press were the following:

Prodigies, by definition, are relatively rare, but it should come as no surprise that China, with one-quarter of the world's population, claims a share of wonder kids. Shi Fengshou, for instance, takes about eight seconds to multiply two ten-digit numbers in his head. Shen Kegong, an 11-year-old, astonished a panel of expert mathematicians by mentally calculating the value of 625^9 in 20 seconds. He also mentally solved a number of other problems, including: $639 \times 33 + \sqrt[3]{884,736}$. Another prodigy, Li Yuejiang, could reportedly read 2,500 Chinese characters at the age of six—an impressive accomplishment for even the most studious high school graduate. But 12-year-old Wei Ruoyang has been acclaimed by friends to be the Chinese prodigy of prodigies. They say he has X-ray eyes that can detect hidden tumours, material objects placed behind brick walls, and the course of an underground canal or river. When asked how he was able to do such things, Wei said he simply sees these things with his ears. Any other questions?

In mid-June, George Foster found a $100 McDonald County bond on the shelf of his Ginger Blue Lodge and Resort in southwestern Missouri. According to notations on the back of the 1871 certificate, county officials couldn't redeem the bond for $100 in 1874, 1875, or 1876 because there wasn't enough money in the county treasury. Nor does the county have enough money to pay off the bond now. Counting interest, Foster figures he is entitled to about $3.5 million.

Joseph Granville's financial predictions shook up the U.S. stock market in January, but in April his earthquake predictions weren't able to rattle the San Gabriel Mountains in California. Granville made news by saying that the Los Angeles area would be hit by a devastating earthquake at, more or less, 5:31 AM (Pacific time) on April 10. But the Earth didn't tremble as Granville's statistical analysis indicated it would, so the would-be seismologist found himself standing on very shaky ground.

Driving after drinking can be dangerous, but taking a taxi home after a party also has its risks. After attending a gathering at the Hyatt Regency Chicago, Bruce Borys decided to take a cab rather than drive the 65 km (40 mi) to his suburban home in Round Lake Beach. Al Hardy, Jr., the cabbie, simply did what he was told. He headed north on Interstate 94 and waited to be told where to turn off. Some 275 km (170 mi) later Borys woke up in Wisconsin. He finally got home by phoning his boss, who came and picked him up. But there's more to the story than that. Hardy not only wanted the $235 registered on the meter but $114 for a fine he was assessed for making an illegal U-turn to head back to Illinois. Unable to pay the fine, he spent the night in jail, then picked up a $40 ticket for speeding on his way back home. He figured Borys should pay that fine also. Since neither party was willing to yield, the matter was headed for the courts.

Midyear graduations are always something special, but when 35-year-old John Hull Francis III received his diploma from Southern Oregon State College in June, all eyes were upon him. He had graduated with distinction after completing difficult courses in science and math. And during all that time he had not uttered a single word. Eight years earlier he had begun an experiment in nonverbal communication that suited him so well he chose not to speak any more, even though he was quite capable of doing so.

Six families showed up at the same address in a Houston suburb expecting to move into the three-bedroom house they had all separately rented after reading an ad in a Texas newspaper. They came with their children from as far away as Colorado, Ohio, Minnesota, Oklahoma, and Missouri. The sixth family was already living in the Houston area. All had been victimized by a man and woman who rented a house they did not own and then vanished with nearly $5,000.

Work-related death has been given a startling new interpretation by Administrative Law Judge Leo J. LaPorte of Pontiac, Mich. Though the decision was being challenged in an appeals court, 37-year-old Domenico Signorelli's widow and two children were awarded $167 a week for 500 weeks. Signorelli, a project engineer, was sent to England by his employer, GKN Automotive Components Inc. of Birmingham, Mich. While there, he and a woman employee of a GKN subsidiary engaged in sex in the woman's flat after business hours. Signorelli was overcome by carbon monoxide, went into a coma, and died a week later. In a written opinion, Judge LaPorte stated that Signorelli's "work assignment in England exposed him to situations and hazards that were different in nature and degree" from those found in Michigan. If a higher court concurs with the judge's reasoning and final ruling, the engineer's family could receive as much as $250,000 in workman's compensation benefits.

The business card was stuck on a tree in New York City's Central Park. It read: "Quality grass delivered. Money back guarantee." That was all, except for a phone number. A woman jogger who spotted the card had been thinking about a new lawn for quite some time, so she passed the card on to her husband. When he phoned, the conversation didn't quite make sense. He wanted to know the cost per square foot, but the supplier quoted his price in ounces. Both soon realized they were talking about very different varieties of grass.

Nipper will never realize it, but she played a significant role in the July wedding of Britain's Prince Charles and Lady Diana Spencer. The tiny female ferret was commissioned to pull a nylon thread through a small pipe that ran underground from Buckingham Palace to the Victoria Memorial. The thread was attached to the end of a television cable that was drawn through the pipe so that commentators could provide live coverage of the royal procession.

WIDE WORLD

Editors at the *Far Eastern Economic Review* in Hong Kong were happy to receive a complimentary copy of Leonard Silk's *Economics in Plain English* from the U.S. consulate. But they were somewhat surprised to discover that the only thing in plain English was the cover. Everything else was in Chinese.

Chinese herbal medicine has been dispensed by doctors for thousands of years, but some patients in Sichuan (Szechwan) Province are now being sent to a restaurant rather than to a hospital. The menu includes over 100 dishes for various ailments. Diabetics are instructed to order the special dumpling soup; those with fevers, the sliced pork spiced with chrysanthemums; and people with edema, the carp and red beans. The recommended cure for stomach problems, neuroses, and heart trouble is ginseng soup. And if you don't know what ails you, you need only describe your symptoms to the assistant manager, an expert in traditional Chinese medicine, and he'll tell you what to order.

Sundials came first, then clocks and watches in a bewildering array of forms and styles. There were water, sand, and oil lamp clocks, then mechanical devices that used springs, pendulums, and weights. Much later, electrical clocks made an appearance, some relying on batteries for their power. And for scientists, there are now atomic clocks, the ultimate in accuracy. One of the newest watches to go into production is called the OMNI Voice Master. It looks like an ordinary digital watch, but when a button is pushed a voice announces the time of day. The tiny alarm is also new. At the designated moment, the wearer hears the time announced, then about 20 seconds of Boccherini's popular *Minuet*. And the next development? Only time can tell.

When a burglar tried to invade the Phoenix, Ariz., home of Gladys Kastensmith in the wee hours of the morning, he must have thought he'd have an easy time of it. But he was only halfway through the doggie door when he looked up and saw a woman pointing a .38-calibre pistol at his head. The 77-year-old woman must have told her unwanted guest she had learned to shoot in the wide open spaces of Montana, because he was huddled on the floor when the police arrived.

Brian Heise had more than his share of luck in July, and most of it was bad. When his apartment in Provo, Utah, became flooded from a broken pipe in the upstairs apartment, the manager told him to go out and rent a water vacuum. That's when he discovered his car had a flat tire. He changed it, then went inside again to phone a friend for help. The electric shock he got from the phone so startled him that he inadvertently ripped the instrument off the wall. Before he could leave the apartment a second time, a neighbour had to kick down the apartment door because water damage had jammed it tight. While all this was going on, someone stole Heise's car, but it was almost out of gas. He found the car a few blocks away but had to push it to a gas station, where he filled up the tank. That evening Heise attended a military ceremony at Brigham Young University. He injured himself severely when he somehow sat on his bayonet, which had been tossed onto the front seat of his car. Doctors were able to stitch up the wound, but no one was able to resuscitate four of Heise's canaries that were crushed to death by falling plaster. After Heise slipped on the wet carpet and badly injured his tailbone, he said he began to wonder if "God wanted me dead, but just kept missing."

A bank robber in Brisbane, Australia, escaped arrest by stashing his loot under some bushes as police cars came screeching to a halt in front of the bank. He then mingled with the crowd until the commotion subsided. But when he returned to gather up the $35,000, it was gone. Police eventually traced the bank robber to Sydney, but before they could begin their interrogation the suspect insisted on filing a police report against the unknown thief. As police pondered the case, they wondered what charges could be brought against the second man if he were ever caught. He certainly was not guilty of robbing the bank, and he certainly hadn't taken anything that belonged to the man who accused him of stealing.

When does a hole in one go down on your scorecard as an unspectacular par three? Bill Mette can tell you all about it. He, Bill Pratt, and their wives were shooting a round of golf at the Shoreacres course outside Chicago when it happened. Mette teed off at the 127-yd (115-m) 12th hole and watched with amazement as his ball rolled into the cup for a hole-in-one. That unforgettable swing was Mette's second shot. The first ball landed in water for an automatic two-stroke penalty.

The Archives of Surgery reported during the year that when less experienced surgeons are involved, surgical staples are safer than traditional sutures for closing incisions. But some surgeons with long experience also opt for staples because they are faster and thus permit patients to be transferred from operating room to recovery unit sooner.

Taking an aspirin can be hazardous to your health, at least if you use a table knife to dislodge a pill that has stuck in the throat. An unidentified man in Seattle, Wash., did just that. He succeeded in loosening the aspirin but in the process swallowed the knife. Surgeons at Swedish Hospital removed the knife, which had fallen into the esophagus.

Jinichi Sato hopes to make millions marketing powdered alcoholic drinks manufactured in Japan. He's convinced that travelers won't be the only ones snapping up his products because everyone will find it delightfully convenient to conjure up a shot of whiskey, brandy, or Japanese sake with just plain water and a swizzle stick. Sato's brainstorm has already created quite a stir among distillers.

Vocabulary building is so important to teacher Karol Scott that she offered extra credits to her junior high school students in Northglenn, Colo., if they could find 25

Shar-Peis are a rare and still unrecognized breed that masters seem to prize for their loose skin effect. This Shar-Pei is so wrinkled it seems to have been squeezed out of a tube of putty by a fun-loving sculptor. Ernest Albright, owner of Fawn 2nd, thinks his Shar-Pei sets a new norm for loose and wrinkled skin. Others apparently agree because in early August the one-year-old animal won first place in the Ugly Dog Contest held in Petaluma, Calif.

specified words in newspapers. Three did. They got the promised credits when they presented a newspaper ad that read: "Exorbitant, motley, augment, atheist, agnostic, acumen, embryo, hypocrite, fortitude, forlorn, inanimate, impromptu, opaque, mesmerize, vogue, moral, morose, nocturnal, nonchalant, obtuse, prudent, stationery, sagacious, recite, apiary." They simultaneously demonstrated that they had already learned the meaning of ingenuity: they had placed the ad in the newspaper themselves.

At a rate of thousands of characters per second, it doesn't take the computer long to print bills for Blue Cross policyholders in New York. But when it makes mistakes, the computer's highly vaunted speed can be its downfall. In early April, the computer routinely addressed a $183.03 bill to George and Mary Blagmon, then began spewing out a veritable blizzard of duplicates. Within a few days the Blagmons had received 2,500 bills calling for a cumulative payment of $457,575.

Bank employees in Port Huron, Mich., sounded an alarm and locked all the bank's doors after a robber got away with $1,250. While they waited inside for the police to arrive, a patron pounded on the door so insistently that an assistant manager was sent to investigate. The bank robber explained through the closed door that he had had a change of heart and wanted to return the money.

Edward Szuluk's wife was clearly upset when a magistrate in Gloucester, England,

For Hideaki Maruyama, getting from place to place is as simple as putting one foot down after the other. His employer, the Honda Motor Co. of Japan, was so taken with the unique design that it ordered one manufactured just for kicks.

remanded her husband to custody for another week on an assault charge. Determined to stick by her mate, she entered the court's detention room and tightly squeezed her husband's hand. The couple were then taken by ambulance to the Gloucester Royal Hospital's accident unit, where doctors slowly dissolved the superglue that 25-year-old Wendy had smeared on her hand before being searched by security guards outside the detention room.

Raiza Ruiz, a 26-year-old medical student at Venezuela's Central University, was just two months away from graduation when her family was notified she had been killed in a plane crash in the Amazon jungle. In due time the coffin was turned over to the Ruiz family and buried in Caracas. Six days after the crash the girl, still very much alive, found her way out of the jungle and contacted her family. When authorities opened up the coffin it was found to contain animal bones and quicklime. Raiza received her medical diploma in November, but lawyers were still trying to bring her back to life. Government documents certifying to her death and burial meant that Ruiz was still legally dead.

Boiling Springs, Pa., is not known as a convention town, but the conventioneers it welcomed in July were somewhat special. None of the 70 delegates wore a name tag because each belonged to an organization open only to those named Jim Smith.

After visiting a bazaar in Solo, Indonesia, a group of boys headed for Kranggan, their native village. Suddenly they realized one of their number had disappeared. They searched for two hours before hearing his

cries for help. According to *Berita Buana*, a newspaper in Jakarta, the boy was found at the top of a coconut tree. Bandriyo swore he had been transported there by a ghost that had kidnapped him.

When Shirley Rider became an unwed mother in Adelaide, South Australia, she put up her son for adoption. During the ten years that followed she married, had two more children, and then divorced. In time she met a divorced man and they fell in love. Before their planned marriage, the two began discussing their respective backgrounds. It was then that they realized Shirley's first child had been adopted by the man she now planned to marry.

Minnie Hall was fined $250 for selling marijuana after pleading guilty before Judge Ken Porter in Sevierville, Tenn. After expressing regret for what she had done, the 82-year-old criminal told the judge her 98-year-old mother had warned her that she would get into trouble for selling pot.

During September the small African kingdom of Swaziland paid tribute to its ruler, 82-year-old King Sobhuza II. The Lion of Swaziland was obviously happy that so many of his relatives could attend the festivities that marked the 60th year of his reign. Among those present were some hundred wives, five or six hundred children, and an untold number of blood relatives belonging to later generations.

When Harry Chase returned home from his summer vacation, he knew his house in New Orleans, La., had been broken into. That in itself did not surprise or upset him

because the 80-year-old retired seaman was mainly concerned with the kitchen table. The $51 in bills were gone, as was the $30 or so in change that he had placed on the table with a note. Chase smiled contentedly. The unknown intruder had complied perfectly with Chase's written request: he had not ransacked the house.

Five new homes costing about $70,000 each could have been built with the government money that was poured into an experimental project in Michigan alongside Interstate 94. The project earned the state Department of Transportation's first Silver Sow award for profligate spending at a time when social programs were being cut back. In making the award, state Rep. Richard Fitzpatrick felt that $348,000 was a bit much to spend on a solar-powered restroom at a freeway rest stop.

Who discovered America? In 1975 scuba diver Bob Meistrell discovered debris from an old shipwreck in shallow water off the coast of southern California. It was a huge doughnut-shaped stone that weighed some 125 kg (275 lb). After years of research and consultation with experts in Asia, two marine archaeologists from the University of San Diego, Calif., became convinced that the stone relic fits the pattern of anchors used by Chinese seamen more than 2,000 years ago. Other relics that were later found in the same area, they say, reinforce the belief that traditional views of the discovery of America are wrong. The scientists feel certain that Chinese reached America hundreds of years before Columbus or any other European explorer.

Persons arrested for speeding on California highways often insist they could not have been traveling as fast as the arresting officer claimed. Not so with 19-year-old Michael Coyer. When he was nabbed in July on Interstate 15, the officer clocked him at 72 mph (116 km/h) in Cajon Pass. Cooper insisted he was going 75 mph and said he had witnesses who could back up his claim. After all, why be satisfied, he reasoned, with 3 mph less when you've just set a new world record for speed on a skateboard.

In August 1979 Charles Adams stopped at a service station in Georgia and asked for $3 worth of gas. The attendant set the pump for that amount but it reached $4.10 before Adams noticed what had happened. Since he had only $3 in his pocket, he offered to drive home and get the rest of the money, but he refused to leave his driver's license as security. The police were called and Adams was jailed. In early April 1981, after a Muscogee County jury found Adams innocent, the Southland Corp., which owns the gas station, was ordered to pay Adams $100,000 in punitive damages because he had been arrested without cause.

"All the lion wants is for you to have pleasant dreams and sleep in peace and quiet." That was the message to Brazilian taxpayers who had already filed honest reports by early April. But for those who had not met their obligations, authorities sent a dire warning that "you have irritated the lion." To reinforce the message, the tax bureau used advertisements showing a startled

balding man in pajamas awakened by a lion with bared teeth. Taxpayers who filed suspiciously low income figures were notified that the lion would like to see the real numbers. A doctor in Rio de Janeiro who received such a message immediately sat down and wrote a supplementary check for $9,000. After cross-referencing patients' reported payments to their respective doctors, the tax bureau notified one doctor that he still owed the lion $270,000.

During the year, American Tourister aired a televison commercial featuring an ape that tried in vain to damage a piece of luggage. The consumer affairs section of WAGA-TV in Atlanta, Ga., decided to let Willie B., a 200-kg (450-lb) gorilla repeat the experiment in his cage at the local zoo. He not only ripped off the leather cover but tore the suitcase in two so he could use one part for a drinking cup. The TV reporter later learned that the ape in the commercial was a large chimpanzee that weighed some 135 kg (300 lb) less than Willie B.

Waiting in line at a Battle Creek, Mich., post office became so frustrating for a group of patrons in June that they decided to do something about it. After they began chanting "We want service!" a third clerk suddenly appeared and opened up a service window. The patrons were so elated over the success of their clamouring that they decided to give it another try. Amazingly, a fourth clerk opened another window just seconds after the chanting was renewed.

When Janakabai Dhangar began operating her illegal still in Nasik City, India, she trained a band of monkeys to act as lookouts. Whenever the animals spotted the khaki uniforms of policemen, they swung into action and ripped off the officers' clothes. That gave the bootlegger plenty of time to stash the evidence. But the next time the police showed up, they hauled Dhangar off to jail. They had put an end to the monkey business by dressing in ordinary clothes and tossing peanuts to the lookouts.

Respect for life has special meaning for Buddhists, so the news from Osaka, Japan, seemed strange only to those who did not understand. Takeo Kasabo wanted to erect a modest memorial to commemorate living things that had been destroyed during scientific experiments undertaken for the benefit of mankind. So in May a stone inscription was placed in Kyoto's Manju-in temple above a buried Buddhist prayer scroll and the ashes of *Bacillus subtilis*, which represented the many microorganisms that have been destroyed in the course of scientific research.

In June, Lady Luck smiled on a discouraged prospector in South Africa. Boet Sonneburg, who was about to give up his private claim near Windsorton, found an 18-carat diamond that he sold for $25,000. Just three days later he found another gem, a 148-carat diamond worth an estimated $1 million. The 40-year-old prospector decided to keep on digging because "Good things come in threes, don't they?"

Luther ("Smokey") Ward, according to Elka Ward, is a kind and gentle man. Daph-

ney M. Elliott affirmed that Smokey made her feel safe and secure. Both were quick to defend Ward even after they discovered they were apparently married to the same man at the same time. But Marie Marshall Ward was not so tolerant when she learned about the other women in Smokey's life. In mid-September Sheriff Donald Giardino, who charged Ward with bigamy, said he had so far located eight of Smokey's wives —a Connie in Missouri, a Barbara in Montana—and was still counting.

In 1975 a U.S. treasury agent visited Lannie Martorell at her own request. She had an unusual penny and wanted to know more about it. The agent took the penny, then personally returned it some two years later. He also gave Martorell a written statement certifying that she owned "one genuine silver 1975-D one-cent coin inadvertently struck on a Nepalese 25-piasa blank." Martorell says a penny is still a penny, so she has done nothing about it, but a collector of unusual coins would gladly try to convince her it is worth a great deal more if only she would part with it.

Pam Johnson of Mira Loma, Calif., admits Jonathan can be a little silly now and then. And she ought to know. Her Thoroughbred horse sometimes pulls the stable fire alarm, then gives the firemen who arrive to put out the blaze the big hee-haw.

U.S. congressmen are forbidden to hire members of their immediate families. But Rep. Billy Lee Evans of Georgia needed urgent office help, so on St. Valentine's Day he put his wife of several years on the payroll. No one saw any reason to criticize. Billy and April had divorced about three weeks earlier.

Singapore Airlines, which operates flights across the Pacific, added a diversion for travelers in late August. The seven battery-operated slot machines, however, were so overworked that not one slot was operational by the time the plane set down in San Francisco.

Bernadette Scott is not a suspicious person, though the 23-year-old woman has had plenty of reasons to become so. Her husband, Peter, insured her life for more than half a million dollars, then tried to take her life six times—twice by poison, twice by setting fire to the house while she was ill and confined to bed, and twice by trying to entice her to the edge of a cliff. But all the while Bernadette suspected nothing. Then Peter, a computer programmer, persuaded his wife to stand in the middle of a road in order, he told her, to test their car's suspension system. As Peter sped toward his intended victim, he had a sudden change of heart and swerved away at the last moment. Bernadette then learned the awful truth. Peter later pleaded guilty to a variety of charges and was sentenced to life imprisonment by a British court.

Chicago's annual lakefront air and water show is ballyhooed as one of the city's most spectacular summer events. That's one reason, perhaps, why Britain's Royal Air Force accepted an invitation to participate and show off its mammoth Vulcan bomber.

Encyclopaedia Britannica defines a unicorn as "a mythological animal resembling a horse or a kid with a single horn on its forehead." Visitors to Marine World, an amusement complex not far from San Francisco, are sure that Lancelot, a young Angora goat, is real. That being the case, Lancelot must be a real mythological unicorn.

Squadron leader Dave Thomas was given coordinates that, he was told, would give spectators an awesome view of his aircraft: 41°53' N, 87°38' E. Had Thomas followed directions, his Vulcan would have been viewed by startled inhabitants of China's northwest Xinjiang Uygur (Sinkiang Uighur) Autonomous Region. Incidentally, 12-year-old Chicagoan Janice Hay was among the first to point out that 87° E should have been 87° W.

Donald Pallett of Vale, Ore., didn't want to file federal income tax returns for 1977 and 1978, but he was worried about the consequences of simply doing nothing. So instead of reporting incomes of $7,300 and $13,000 for those two years, respectively, he mailed in tax forms that contained only his personal identification and a statement claiming the constitutional right to withhold information that could be incriminating. During Pallett's court trial in May, after all the evidence had been presented, U.S. District Court Judge James Burns instructed the jury that Pallett's defense could be legitimate if he honestly believed that truthful answers could incriminate him. On that basis he was acquitted.

Airline passengers sometimes find out after landing that their baggage was left behind. In October several passengers on a morning flight from Newark, N.J., to Washington, D.C., had no such worry because their luggage had been put aboard. A short time later, however, it was prematurely delivered to the roof of a Sherwin-Williams paint manufacturing complex and a nearby backyard when the plane's cargo door opened in midflight.

OUR CHANGING CITIES

by Richard Whittingham

Modern cities in the United States as well as in Europe are in a constant state of flux. The nature of 20th-century society and the needs, whims, and ambitions of its inhabitants have created an endless procession of people streaming into the metropolises as well as another marching out of them, bound for the suburbs or other locales. The transiency in urban residency over the last 100 years was as real as the kaleidoscopic changes that had been wrought on the cities' concrete faces by men and machines relentlessly building, razing, and renovating the urban landscape.

There was, however, a distinct pattern to this activity, a pair of trends that have been traced and defined by a wide variety of sociologists, urbanologists, and demographers and that now, in the 1980s, appeared to be undergoing a kind of juxtaposition of their historical directions. They were significant because they revealed quite a bit about the lifestyles, priorities, designs, and desires of the people of the U.S. and of modern society in general.

The first trend was the large-scale migration from rural areas to the central cities, a movement that began in the 1800s and accelerated at a breathtaking pace in the 1900s. It was followed by a major if not mass defection of urbanites to the suburbs in the middle of the 20th century, creating substantial entities dubbed metropolitan areas—cities and their surrounding communities.

Now, in the 1980s, there appeared to be a new and not necessarily anticipated turnabout within the pattern that actually involves two movements, one the beginning of an inflow back to the central cities and the other an outflow from the urban-suburban complexes to nonmetropolitan areas, especially in the West, Southwest, and the Mountain States. The latter trend, although still admittedly small in the overall scheme, was simply a reversal of the first trend, one that prompted U.S. Department of Agriculture demographer Calvin Beale to observe, "How do you keep them down in Paree after they've seen the farm?"

Richard Whittingham is a free-lance writer and editor. He is the author of Martial Justice *and many other books on contemporary affairs.*

City dwellers are not nomadic by nature. They do not, generally speaking, move for the sake of moving merely to slake some desire for a new environment, a different vista, a change of neighbours. There are distinct sociological and economic factors at the root of these trends, and it is their effects that impel the throngs to move in specific directions to or from the city. It is the recent turnabout, in its dual nature, that is the most curious. Because it has happened so recently it is less substantiated, but there is clear evidence that noteworthy changes are taking place in the traffic between the cities and suburbs and also between the metropolitan and nonmetropolitan areas.

Rise of the Cities. The city in the U.S. began to assume its modern form in the 19th century at the same time that its counterparts in Europe were growing and changing character, the results of the sweeping effect of the Industrial Revolution. As the cities grew larger, they encouraged a proliferation of individual enterprise but also generated large increases in crime and slums and new and complicated problems for mass transportation and public education.

The U.S. did not become what could be called an urban nation until the early 1900s. Cities, of course, had been established throughout the country, but it really was not until about 1912 that the decline of the rural population would intersect the rise of the urban once and forever on the chart of a changing society. New York City, for example, until 1898 consisted only of the island of Manhattan and parts of the Bronx; with a population of 1.5 million, it was a thriving city but hardly the vast complex it would become with the full annexation that year of what today are the boroughs of the Bronx, Brooklyn, Queens, and Richmond (Staten Island). It was the most dramatic example of the move toward large and politically powerful cities, which were just beginning to take their place on the national scene.

Cities began to blossom everywhere in the U.S., not just on the East Coast but in the Middle West and a few other areas as well. Among those growing the fastest were Chicago, St. Louis, Cleveland, Buffalo, San Francisco, Cincinnati, Pittsburgh, New Orleans, Detroit, and Milwaukee. Outward and upward

"Cities began to blossom everywhere in the U.S., not just on the East Coast but in the Middle West and a few other areas as well."

they began to grow as people came for the jobs, the higher pay, the opportunities that were much more abundant there than back on the farms or in the small rural towns. The skyscrapers soared; the shopping districts grew; the one-story bungalows and the row houses were often overshadowed by multi-flat apartment buildings—all the result of the growth of industry and of the nation's economy.

In 1900, according to the U.S. Bureau of the Census, only 39.6% of the nation's population lived in metropolitan areas (the central cities and their suburbs); in 1910 this figure reached 45.6%, and by 1920 it had grown to a majority of 51.2%. The trend continued until the depression of the 1930s, when the rural exodus stalled notably; only 0.4% abandoned the farms for the city from 1930 to 1940, the lowest percentage since the 1810–20 period. Still, by 1940 approximately 56.5% of the population resided in urban areas.

Move to the Suburbs. World War II then came along and changed everything. Millions of Americans, from their late teens through their 30s, left both the cities and the rural expanses to serve in the armed forces. Industry for the war effort operated at peak capacity, and the cities, with their factories and plants, were the hubs of that activity. But the war would also prove to be the fulcrum on which the trend of U.S. migration turned away from the central city, which for half a century had been the destination of most migrants. When the fighting came to an end, a new and major movement of people would occur from the city to the suburbs, although there

would still be a continued emigration from the farms to the metropolitan areas.

When all of America's Johnnys had marched home again, they were vitally different from the young GI Joes who had left a few tumultuous years earlier, hardly the same young men who had grown up or toiled in the relatively tranquil days before the war. And the country that had industrially mobilized for the war effort was a far cry from the depression-ridden economy that had preceded the years of combat. Never had so many of the nation's key wage earners been so uprooted, sent off to foreign soils, and forced to live in such proximity to and on such terms of interdependency with those whom they might otherwise never have met. This experience contributed substantially to the conformism of the early postwar years and the ease with which these veterans of the military life adapted to the large corporate systems that were then evolving.

An important aspect of the era was the "baby boom," an obvious consequence of the warriors' return. With it in the late 1940s came the desire for safer, roomier, and more pleasant surroundings in which to raise those families, an environment less harsh than that now harboured in the central cities. The logical recourse was to suburbia. With the exception of some old, well-established, wealthy communities close to the large central cities, such as New York's Scarsdale, Chicago's Winnetka, and Cleveland's Shaker Heights, land was cheap and existing housing relatively inexpensive. There were also large tracts of sparsely developed land ready for

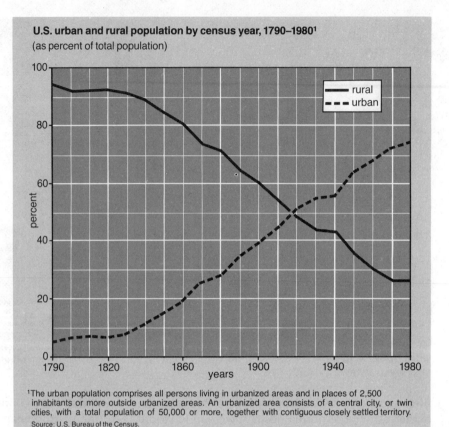

U.S. urban and rural population by census year, 1790–1980[1]
(as percent of total population)

[1]The urban population comprises all persons living in urbanized areas and in places of 2,500 inhabitants or more outside urbanized areas. An urbanized area consists of a central city, or twin cities, with a total population of 50,000 or more, together with contiguous closely settled territory.
Source: U.S. Bureau of the Census.

new construction. The U.S. government helped fuel the movement by making available low-cost mortgage loans, especially through the Veterans Administration, and the entire economic climate was favourable for large-scale construction, creating both homes and jobs in the process.

Suburbia had its fundamental enticements for postwar families. Writers of the time called it the American Dream—a home of one's own with the symbolic white picket fence, backyard barbecues, friendly neighbours who were close enough but not too close, tree-shaded lanes, safe streets, and good schools. It is not hard to imagine the course that upward-bound urbanites of the late 1940s and early 1950s would choose, and soon suburbs were growing at the same phenomenal rate that cities had in the earlier days of the century.

At the same time, the exodus took its toll on the central cities. This happened in several ways. With the departure of a good portion of the middle- and upper-middle-class families, neighbourhoods in the city deteriorated, the percentage of poor and less advantaged increased, and income was lost as the new expatriates spent their paychecks at stores in the suburbs instead of those in the city. Government also played a role that proved harmful to the cities. Federal and state moneys were often earmarked for such projects as the creation of networks of roads

and highways and the expansion of public transportation to enable suburbanites to get to and from their jobs, which at that time were mostly within the central cities. As a result, many of the needs of the city and its inhabitants were unfunded, compounding the urban problems. The metropolitan structure became what George Sternlieb and James W. Hughes referred to in a 1980 article in *Scientific American* as the "doughnut complex." As they explained, "In many places the hole in the doughnut is a decaying central city and the ring is a prosperous and growing suburban . . . region."

The reasons for moving to suburbia became further nourished as the problems of the city grew. And, of course, those problems did grow. Crime rose, racial tensions increased, job opportunities declined, unemployment grew, slums spread, public education foundered for lack of interest and funding, and other human and community services were curtailed. As William Severini Kewinski wrote in the *New York Times Magazine*, "The massive migration changed the cities, robbing them of resources while leaving poorer populations behind."

It was only a matter of time until the inner suburban communities filled to capacity. The migration continued, however, to areas even farther from the central city—to "exurbia," the name coined by writer-editor A. C. Spectorsky in 1955 to describe the

outlying communities that were being developed around the established suburbs. Small businesses flourished in both the suburbs and exurbs, many of them having moved out from the cities along with their owners. And many suburban governing bodies and chambers of commerce began programs to lure large companies away from the city. By the 1960s the suburbs of America were growing at a rate four times that of the central cities.

The term Standard Metropolitan Statistical Area (SMSA) was chosen by the U.S. government as the standard for describing the new urban-suburban complex. Today an SMSA is defined by the Bureau of the Census as a central urban area of at least 50,000 inhabitants and the adjacent communities that have a high degree of economic and social integration with the central area.

The move from city to suburb did not initially affect the flow of people leaving rural America for its urban areas, although now it would be looked at more in terms of relocation to metropolitan areas than to the central cities as it had been in the past. In fact, the biggest single increase in rural migration to urban areas came during the 1940s, when the mass migration to the suburbs was in full swing.

By the 1970s more people were living in the suburbs than in the central cities of America. According to the Bureau of the Census, 85,843,000 lived in metropolitan areas outside central cities, while only 67,850,000 lived in the core cities themselves. From 1960 to 1970 jobs had increased 44% in the suburbs, while in the central cities they had declined by 7%. And the suburban plan to woo large companies into moving not only their corporate offices but their factories and plants as well to the more pristine countryside was becoming a marked success, further isolating the central cities as many workers now commuted from their suburban homes to their suburban jobs. By 1973 the suburbs provided more jobs than the central cities.

In the 1970s many of the exurbs throughout the country grew into "minicities," as they came to be called. Their populations were in the 50,000 to 100,-000 range, and their economic structures made them self-sufficient, much like the small central cities of old. At the same time many metropolitan areas had become so swollen that they now were contiguous with one another, which gave rise to another government definition, the Standard Consolidated Statistical Area (SCSA), a geographic unit made up of adjoining SMSA's that are closely interrelated socially and economically, such as New York-Newark-Jersey City, Los Angeles-Long Beach-Anaheim, and Dallas-Fort Worth. Some demographers went even further, describing large metropolitan agglomerations as "strip cities." The largest of these is "Bos-

"At the same time, there was strong evidence of at least a trickle of people once thought to be rock-ribbed suburbanites back into the central cities."

wash," which stretches from Boston down to Washington, D.C., embracing New York City, Philadelphia, Baltimore, and all of New Jersey and Delaware as well (currently having about 43 million inhabitants).

While the suburbs had gained in population over the last four decades, the nation's central cities had continued to lose population. New York City lost more than 860,000 from 1970 to 1980, and Chicago almost 383,000, according to U.S. Department of Commerce figures. It was an almost universal trend in the nation, with the exception of the so-called Sun Belt, an area of mild climate in the South and Southwest. Those locales experienced increases in both suburban and central-city populations, part of another trend that began to accelerate in the 1970s.

Countertrends. Although the suburbs continued to grow in the 1970s, the utopia was collapsing. The American Dream was wilting. It was perhaps best put in perspective by Charles Haar, the Louis D.

Brandeis professor of law at Harvard University Law School, as he was quoted in the *New York Times*: "People thought of the suburbs as their refuge from the toils of the world, where Norman Rockwell would paint their daily life. But particularly in the last ten years, the suburbs in the East and the Midwest have become the heirs to their cities' problems. They have pollution, high taxes, crime. People thought they would escape all those things in the suburbs. But like the people in Boccaccio's *Decameron*, they ran away from the plague and took it with them."

The things that Haar was talking about have indeed infested much of modern suburbia, in many ways as naturally as they earlier had the central cities. In 1981 there were suburban neighbourhoods that were as crime-ridden as those in the central cities. There were horrendous traffic jams that clogged the outlying expressways and freeways as well as the arterial suburban streets. There were ominous columns of smoke billowing from plants and refineries, poisoned waterways, and sometimes eye-watering smogs.

One of the most critical problems that emerged in suburbia in the 1970s was the cost of housing, which soared with rocketlike propulsion in that decade, accompanied by equally astronomical mortgage interest rates. While the median price of a suburban home in 1970 was in the vicinity of $25,000, by 1980 it was more than $64,000. Interest rates for a conventional home loan that were about 7% in 1970 had risen to 17% and more, and lending institutions were asking "points," 3–4% of the loan to be paid up front, as well as loan service fees of several hundred dollars. In a survey of 15 major metropolitan areas in 1981, *U.S. News & World Report* found that the average mortgage payment for a home purchased in the preceding year was $810 a month, not including real-estate taxes or home insurance.

The result was that fewer and fewer people could afford to live in the suburbs. The typical first-home owner was no longer a young family with one breadwinner and children. Instead, it was a married couple with two incomes and no children, and that kind of family often had more in common with the city life-style than that of the more sedate suburbs.

The energy crisis was another factor affecting the suburbs of the 1970s. With gasoline prices in 1980 quadruple what they had been ten years earlier, the idea of the suburban two-car family dependent on automobiles to get to work, to the store, to wherever the children had to be taken began to seem much less appealing.

Nevertheless, suburban areas continued to grow, registering an 18.2% increase in population during the 1970s. But the rate of growth had decreased drastically. While New York's doughnut ring increased by 23.7% in the 1960s, it grew by only 0.2% in the 1970s; Chicago's suburban growth rate dropped from 34.9% in the 1960s to 13.2% in the 1970s, while that of Los Angeles declined from 34.9 to 18.1% during the same period.

On the other hand, there has been a significant rise in the population of nonmetropolitan areas. Such regions grew at a rate of 15.1% during the '70s, almost 5% higher than the growth rate of SMSA's, the first time in U.S. history such a turnabout had occurred. Also, businesses and manufacturing plants were moving not only to the Sun Belt but also to nonmetropolitan regions throughout the U.S. Thus, the first epic migration within the U.S., that from the country to the city, was being reversed.

At the same time, there was strong evidence of at least a trickle of people once thought to be rock-ribbed suburbanites back into the central cities. There were obvious economic considerations to warrant such a move. For one, there was still a large job market in most of the central cities, and there were strong efforts being made to increase it. In more and more cases, young people who could not afford the high cost of housing in the suburbs were staying in the city.

Many were indulging in what has come to be called "gentrification," the process of moving into rundown neighbourhoods and investing money in rehabilitating what were once fine houses or apartments. The results in many cases were good homes in improving neighbourhoods at a cost much lower than that of a home in the suburbs or exurbs. And this new development, too youthful yet to fully evaluate in terms of overall population movement, may signal a reversal of what had been the wholesale flight from city to suburb.

The cities themselves had certainly made concerted efforts recently to coax not only residents but also industry and business back within their boundaries. Vast capital investments in construction projects had been made in many cities in order to enrich the urban economic situation as well as to create jobs. The $350 million Renaissance Center in Detroit was one example, and the proposed North Loop redevelopment project in Chicago was another. Almost all major cities were planning similar kinds of growth programs, although most were on a more modest level.

It was still too early to predict the eventual overall effect of these new trends back to the hinterlands and into the hearts of the cities or even to forecast whether they would be sustained in the 1980s. But from all outward appearances they seemed to offer the substance both for urban revitalization and for rural growth.

THE CHANGING FACE OF AMERICA

by Manuel D. Plotkin

The 1980 U.S. census, the 20th enumeration of the nation's population, was required by the Constitution to serve as a basis for apportioning membership in the House of Representatives among the states. In addition to collecting the data necessary to fulfill this primary purpose, the decennial census provides a great wealth of information and insights into national demographic, social, and economic trends. Analyses of 1980 census data already published, together with findings of comprehensive demographic surveys conducted in recent years, confirm that the past decade was one of profound changes in the growth, distribution, and composition of the U.S. population and in the life-styles of the American people.

Total Population in the U.S. Final national counts show that there were 226,504,825 persons residing in the United States on April 1, 1980. This represents an increase of 23,202,794 people, or 11.4%, over the 203,302,031 persons counted in 1970. U.S. military and civilian personnel living abroad at the time of the census are not included in these figures.

Although the population increase reported for the decade was somewhat greater than expected by professional demographers, the rate of growth was the smallest in U.S. history, except for the depression years of the 1930s. The 11.4% increase compares with growth rates of 13.4% in the 1960s and 18.5% in the 1950s. This confirms earlier indications that the nation had resumed the long-term downward trend in population growth that began in the 19th century and was interrupted for almost two decades by the post-World War II "baby boom."

The principal reason for the decline in population growth in the 1970s is the surprisingly sharp drop in birthrates to historic lows. The estimated 1980 fertility rate (births per 1,000 women, 15 to 44 years old) implies a lifetime average of 1.9 children per woman, about 25% below the 2.5 rate for 1970 and even substantially lower than the rate of 2.1 children per woman that is necessary for natural replacement of the population.

Manuel D. Plotkin is division vice-president and group practice director, The Austin Company, Management Consulting Division, and a former director of the U.S. Bureau of the Census.

Because of large increases in the number of women of childbearing age, the population of the United States should continue to grow by natural increase well into the 21st century, even if fertility rates remain at present low levels. But the *rate* of growth is expected to decline as these women become older and are replaced by a smaller number of women in the childbearing-age category. Census demographers now anticipate population increases of less than 10% in the 1980s and less than 7% in the 1990s. These estimates are based on predictable changes in the age distribution of the population and the assumption that fertility rates will increase only slightly from present levels.

Population by Regions and States. Wide variations in the patterns of population growth rates by region and by state occurred from 1970 to 1980, with the western and southern regions increasing at about twice the national average and accounting for approximately 90% of the total U.S. population increase. The West had the highest rate of growth, continuing a trend that began in 1850 when it was first included in the census; its population was up 24%. The South was the second fastest growing region, with an increase of 20%, but it reported the largest absolute growth and accounted for more than half of the total U.S. increase. In sharp contrast, the population of the Northeast remained virtually unchanged (0.2% increase), and the North Central (Midwestern) region increased by only 4% during the decade. (*See* Map.)

These diverging trends reflect the substantial migration of population from the northern states to the South and the West, attracted by greater economic opportunities and the warmer climate of the "Sunbelt." Recent studies suggest that these trends will continue well into the 1980s.

During the past decade, every state in the West grew faster than the U.S. average, as did all states in the South except Delaware, Maryland, and the District of Columbia. In the Northeast, population declines in New York and Rhode Island were offset by increases in the other seven states in the region. All of the Midwestern states experienced some growth, but at rates considerably below the national average.

The three states with the largest numerical population gains in the decade were California, which

Table I. Population and Area of the United States, 1790–1980

Census year	Resident population	Increase over preceding census number	Increase over preceding census %	Land area (sq mi)	Persons per sq mi of land area
CONTERMINOUS U.S.*					
1790	3,929,214			864,746	4.5
1800	5,308,483	1,379,269	35.1	864,746	6.1
1810	7,239,881	1,931,398	36.4	1,681,828	4.3
1820	9,638,453	2,398,572	33.1	1,749,462	5.5
1830	12,866,020	3,227,567	33.5	1,749,462	7.4
1840	17,069,453	4,203,433	32.7	1,749,462	9.8
1850	23,191,876	6,122,423	35.9	2,940,042	7.9
1860	31,443,321	8,251,445	35.6	2,969,640	10.6
1870	39,818,449	8,375,128	26.6	2,969,640	13.4
1880	50,155,783	10,337,334	26.0	2,969,640	16.9
1890	62,947,714	12,791,931	25.5	2,969,640	21.2
1900	75,994,575	13,046,861	20.7	2,969,834	25.6
1910	91,972,266	15,977,691	21.0	2,969,565	31.0
1920	105,710,620	13,738,354	14.9	2,969,451	35.6
1930	122,775,046	17,064,426	16.1	2,977,128	41.2
1940	131,669,275	8,894,229	7.2	2,977,128	44.2
1950	150,697,361	19,028,086	14.5	2,974,726	50.7
1960	178,464,236	27,766,875	18.4	2,968,054	60.1
UNITED STATES					
1950	151,325,798	19,161,229	14.5	3,552,206	42.6
1960	179,323,175	27,997,377	18.5	3,540,911	50.6
1970	203,302,031	23,978,856	13.4	3,540,023	57.4
1980	226,504,825	23,202,794	11.4	3,543,883	63.9

*Excludes Alaska and Hawaii.
Source: U.S. Bureau of the Census.

increased 3.7 million (18.5%); Texas with 3 million (27.1%); and Florida with 2.9 million (43.4%). The increase in these three states alone accounted for 42% of the total national population increase. Nevada led the nation in percentage growth (63.5%), followed by Arizona (53.1%) and Florida. Only two states recorded population losses in the decade: New York, which lost 684,103 persons (3.8%), and Rhode Island with a loss of 2,569 persons (0.3%). The District of Columbia also lost population—119,017 persons (15.7%). (See Table II.)

Reapportionment. The population counts for the nation, by state, were reported to the president for transmittal to the Congress in December 1980. One important result of the population changes in the past decade will be the transfer of 17 congressional seats from the North to the South and West. As a consequence, the majority of the House of Representatives will shift out of the North for the first time in this century.

The Northeast will lose nine seats and the North Central region will lose eight seats, while the South will gain eight seats and the West nine seats. The Northeast will have 95 representatives, the North Central region 113, the South 142, and the West 85. The largest losses in congressional representation by state will occur in New York, which will lose five seats, and Illinois, Ohio, and Pennsylvania, two seats

each. The largest gains will be in Florida, with four additional seats, Texas with three seats, and California with two seats. These changes in congressional representation are expected to affect significantly the formation of public policy on a wide range of national issues.

Standard Metropolitan Statistical Areas. During the 1970s there was a surprising reversal of the trend toward concentration of population in metropolitan areas. The 318 Standard Metropolitan Statistical Areas (SMSA's) had an average growth rate of 10.2%, compared with an increase of 15.1% in nonmetropolitan areas. This was the first time in the nation's history that nonmetropolitan population had grown more rapidly than the metropolitan population. In the 1960s metropolitan areas had increased by 17.1%, compared with nonmetropolitan growth of only 3.9%.

Although this reversal of trend is striking, it should not obscure the fact that the U.S. continues to be largely a metropolitan nation. Almost 170 million persons, or 75% of the total population, lived in the 318 SMSA's in 1980. There was a net addition of 75 areas that had qualified as SMSA's since the previous census, when 69% of the population lived in 243 SMSA's. (See Table III.)

The slower rate of growth in the metropolitan areas from 1970 to 1980 was primarily attributable to population declines or modest rates of increase in some of the largest metropolitan areas. Of the seven metropolitan complexes with a 1970 population of more than 3 million, New York experienced a loss of more than 900,000, while Philadelphia, Detroit, and Boston had small losses and Chicago a small gain. Only the Los Angeles and San Francisco metropolitan areas had significant increases: of 15.2% and 11.9%, respectively. Together, these seven very large areas had a net growth of only 2.0% in the 1970s, compared with 16.2% for the same areas in the 1960s.

Metropolitan areas of 500,000 to 3 million population also show a lower rate of growth in the 1970 to 1980 decade than in the 1960s. The smaller metropolitan areas, however—those with populations below 500,000—grew at a somewhat faster rate during the 1970s than they did in the 1960s: 17.4% versus 15.5%, based on preliminary estimates. Thus the smaller metropolitan areas generally grew faster than the larger ones during the 1970s, while metropolitan areas of all three size groups had roughly similar rates of growth during the 1960s.

The causes of the greater population growth in nonmetropolitan areas and in the smaller SMSA's are varied, but most are associated with economic forces. Some nonmetropolitan growth can be attributed to outer suburban development, where less

Table II. Population of the United States by Region, Division, and State, 1980 and 1970 Censuses; with Changes in Congressional Representation

Region, division, or state	1980 in 000	1970 in 000	1970–80 Change in 000	% change	Congressional representation based on 1980 census number	change
Northeastern states	49,137	49,061	76	0.2	95	−9
New England	12,348	11,847	501	4.2	24	−1
Maine	1,125	994	131	13.2	2	−
New Hampshire	921	738	183	24.8	2	−
Vermont	511	445	67	15.0	1	−
Massachusetts	5,737	5,689	48	0.8	11	−1
Rhode Island	947	950	−3	−0.3	2	−
Connecticut	3,108	3,032	75	2.5	6	−
Middle Atlantic	36,788	37,213	−425	−1.1	71	−8
New York	17,557	18,241	−684	−3.8	34	−5
New Jersey	7,364	7,171	193	2.7	14	−1
Pennsylvania	11,867	11,801	66	0.6	23	−2
North Central states	58,854	56,590	2,264	4.0	113	−8
East North Central	41,670	40,263	1,407	3.5	80	−6
Ohio	10,797	10,657	140	1.3	21	−2
Indiana	5,490	5,195	295	5.7	10	−1
Illinois	11,418	11,110	308	2.8	22	−2
Michigan	9,258	8,882	377	4.2	18	−1
Wisconsin	4,705	4,418	288	6.5	9	−
West North Central	17,184	16,328	857	5.2	33	−2
Minnesota	4,077	3,806	271	7.1	8	−
Iowa	2,913	2,825	88	3.1	6	−
Missouri	4,917	4,678	240	5.1	9	−1
North Dakota	653	618	35	5.6	1	−
South Dakota	690	666	24	3.6	1	−1
Nebraska	1,570	1,485	85	5.7	3	−
Kansas	2,363	2,249	114	5.1	5	−
Southern states	75,349	62,813	12,536	20.0	142	+8
South Atlantic	36,943	30,679	6,264	20.4	69	+4
Delaware	595	548	47	8.6	1	−
Maryland	4,216	3,924	293	7.5	8	−
District of Columbia	638	757	−119	−15.7	−	−
Virginia	5,346	4,651	695	14.9	10	−
West Virginia	1,950	1,744	205	11.8	4	−
North Carolina	5,874	5,084	790	15.5	11	−
South Carolina	3,119	2,591	528	20.4	6	−
Georgia	5,464	4,588	876	19.1	10	−
Florida	9,740	6,791	2,949	43.4	19	+4
East South Central	14,663	12,808	1,855	14.5	28	+1
Kentucky	3,661	3,221	441	13.7	7	−
Tennessee	4,591	3,926	665	16.9	9	+1
Alabama	3,890	3,444	446	12.9	7	−
Mississippi	2,521	2,217	304	13.7	5	−
West South Central	23,743	19,326	4,417	22.9	45	+3
Arkansas	2,286	1,923	362	18.8	4	−
Louisiana	4,204	3,645	559	15.3	8	−
Oklahoma	3,025	2,559	466	18.2	6	−
Texas	14,228	11,199	3,030	27.1	27	+3
Western states	43,165	34,838	8,327	23.9	85	+9
Mountain	11,368	8,290	3,078	37.1	24	+5
Montana	787	694	92	13.3	2	−
Idaho	944	713	231	32.4	2	−
Wyoming	471	332	138	41.6	1	−
Colorado	2,889	2,210	679	30.7	6	+1
New Mexico	1,300	1,017	283	27.8	3	+1
Arizona	2,718	1,775	942	53.1	5	+1
Utah	1,461	1,059	402	37.9	3	+1
Nevada	799	489	310	63.5	2	+1
Pacific	31,797	26,548	5,249	19.8	61	+4
Washington	4,130	3,413	717	21.0	8	+1
Oregon	2,633	2,092	541	25.9	5	+1
California	23,669	19,971	3,697	18.5	45	+2
Alaska	400	303	98	32.4	1	−
Hawaii	965	770	195	25.3	2	−
TOTAL UNITED STATES	226,505	203,302	23,203	11.4	435	−

Source: U.S. Bureau of the Census.

Table III. Population of the United States by Metropolitan Status

	Population in 000		Population changes Number	
	1980	1970	in 000	%
United States	226,505	203,302	23,203	11.4
All Standard Metropolitan Statistical Areas (318)	169,405	153,694	15,711	10.2
Central cities (429)	67,930	67,850	80	0.1
Metro areas outside central cities	101,475	85,843	15,631	18.2
Nonmetropolitan areas	57,100	49,608	7,492	15.1

Source: U.S. Bureau of the Census.

Table IV. Age Distribution of U.S. Population— 1970 and 1980

	Population in 000		Change Amount	
Age group	1980	1970*	in 000	%
Under 5	16,344	17,163	−818	−4.8
5–9	16,697	19,969	−3,272	−16.4
10–14	18,241	20,804	−2,563	−12.3
15–19	21,162	19,084	2,078	10.9
20–24	21,313	16,383	4,930	30.1
25–34	37,076	24,923	12,153	48.8
35–44	25,631	23,101	2,530	11.0
45–54	22,797	23,235	−437	−1.9
55–64	21,700	18,602	3,098	16.7
65 and over	25,544	19,972	5,572	27.9
Total	226,505	203,235	23,270	11.4

* 1970 data do not reflect corrections made after the census.
Source: U.S. Bureau of the Census.

expensive housing and uncongested locations provide attractive residential areas for persons employed in cities. A major part of the growth, however, is attributable to employment opportunities in smaller communities, where locations for manufacturing are often cheaper than in the large metropolitan areas. The expansion of the interstate highway network, and the resulting improvement in access to supplies and markets for many nonmetropolitan areas and the smaller SMSA's, served as a stimulus to the movement of manufacturing facilities and employment opportunities to these areas. Relocation of the growing number of retired persons was also a major factor in some areas.

Nearly all of the growth in the total population of metropolitan areas occurred in suburban communities. Central city population during the decade was virtually unchanged, while the suburban population increased by 18.2%, somewhat higher than the 15.1% growth of nonmetropolitan areas. Many individual cities reported substantial gains in population during the decade, especially the smaller cities in the West and the South, but these gains were offset by declines in others, particularly the older and larger cities in the North.

Age, Race, and Ethnicity. Dramatic changes occurred in the age composition of the U.S. population from 1970 to 1980, as the median age rose from 28 to 30 years. Most striking was the increase in the number of persons aged 25 to 34 years, born during the post-World War II baby boom. This age group increased by 12 million persons, or 48.8%. At the same time, the number of children (the population under 15 years of age) decreased by almost 7 million, or 11.5%, because of the "baby bust" that began in the mid-1960s. At the other end of the age spectrum, senior citizens (the population aged 65 years and over) rose 5.5 million, or 27.9%, influenced primarily by increasing longevity trends.

There will continue to be wide swings in the age composition during the 1980s as a result of the declining fertility rates discussed earlier, the aging of the baby boom cohorts, and continuing increases in

longevity of the population. These changes are likely to have substantial impact on the nation's politics and economy. (See Table IV.)

There were also significant changes in the racial and ethnic composition of the population during the 1970s. Improved coverage and differences in census definitions cloud some of the comparisons of 1980 and 1970 data. However, the general patterns reported should prevail.

The black population increased by 17% to 26.5 million in 1980, compared with an 11.4% increase for the total population. Persons of Spanish origin registered a 61% increase to 14.6 million, affected by immigration, improved coverage, increased group awareness, and changes in questionnaire design. The number of Asians and Pacific Islanders increased to 3.5 million from a reported 1.5 million in 1970; immigration was also the principal factor of change for this group. Early tabulations of the 1980 census counts show that, of the total population in 1980, 83.2% reported themselves as white, 11.7% as black, 1.5% as Asian and Pacific Islander, 0.6% as American Indian, Eskimo, and Aleut, and 3% as persons of "other" races.

LOCHER—©1981 CHICAGO TRIBUNE

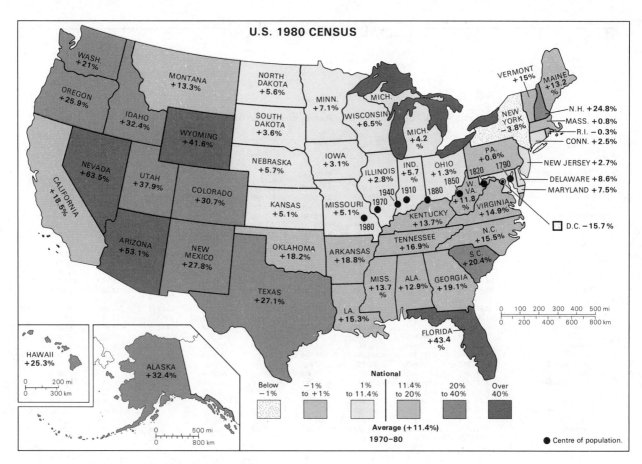

U.S. 1980 CENSUS

WASH. +21%
OREGON +25.9%
MONTANA +13.3%
NORTH DAKOTA +5.6%
MINN. +7.1%
IDAHO +32.4%
SOUTH DAKOTA +3.6%
WISCONSIN +6.5%
MICH.
MICH. +4.2%
VERMONT +15%
MAINE +13.2%
WYOMING +41.6%
NEBRASKA +5.7%
IOWA +3.1%
NEW YORK -3.8%
N.H. +24.8%
MASS. +0.8%
R.I. -0.3%
CONN. +2.5%
NEVADA +63.5%
UTAH +37.9%
COLORADO +30.7%
ILLINOIS +2.8%
IND. +5.7%
OHIO +1.3%
PA. +0.6%
1820
1790
NEW JERSEY +2.7%
CALIFORNIA +18.5%
KANSAS +5.1%
MISSOURI +5.1%
1940
1910
1880
1850
W. VA. +11.8%
DELAWARE +8.6%
MARYLAND +7.5%
1970
KENTUCKY +13.7%
VIRGINIA +14.9%
1980
D.C. -15.7%
ARIZONA +53.1%
NEW MEXICO +27.8%
OKLAHOMA +18.2%
ARKANSAS +18.8%
TENNESSEE +16.9%
N.C. +15.5%
S.C. +20.4%
TEXAS +27.1%
MISS. +13.7%
ALA. +12.9%
GEORGIA +19.1%
LA. +15.3%
FLORIDA +43.4%

HAWAII +25.3%
0   200 mi
0   300 km
ALASKA +32.4%
0   500 mi
0   800 km

0 100 200 300 400 500 mi
0 200 400 600 800 km

National

| Below -1% | -1% to +1% | 1% to 11.4% | 11.4% to 20% | 20% to 40% | Over 40% |

Average (+11.4%)
1970-80

● Centre of population.

Percent gain or loss of population by state (1970–80).

Households and Living Arrangements. The number of households in the United States increased at about two and a half times the rate of increase in the total population between 1970 and 1980. This resulted in a decline of the average household size to a historic low. According to census data, the count of households in 1980 was 80.4 million, a 27% increase over the 63.4 million in 1970. Average household size declined to 2.75 persons from the 1970 average of 3.11 persons.

There were wide variations in the rates of growth of different types of households during the decade. Although 1980 census data by household type were not yet available, the March 1980 Current Population Survey conducted by the Census Bureau provides good estimates. These estimates show that the number of family households increased by approximately 14% in the 1970s and accounted for 74% of all households at the end of the decade. (Family households are maintained by a married couple or by a man or woman who shares the living quarters with relatives but not with a spouse.) However, among family households, the number of married couple families increased by only 8% while households maintained by women with no husband present grew by 55%.

Nonfamily households, most of which consisted of one person living alone, rose by 73% and accounted for more than half of the increase in the total number of households. Primary contributing factors were the growing numbers of young single persons leaving home to live independently and the rising incidence of separation and divorce.

* * *

Analyses of national demographic trends in the past decade confirm several important emerging diversities in the U.S. population. These include changes in migration patterns, age distributions, ethnic affiliations, household arrangements, and life-styles. Many of these changes have vast implications for American political institutions, social values, economic policies, and business directions.

Table V. U.S. Population by Sex, Racial, and Ethnic Group, 1980

Region/Division/State	Total	Male	Female	White	Black	American Indian, Eskimo, and Aleut	Asian and Pacific Islander[1]	Spanish origin[2]	Other
Northeastern states	49,136,667	23,479,591	25,657,076	42,328,154	4,848,786	78,182	559,759	2,604,261	1,321,786
New England	12,348,493	5,923,926	6,424,567	11,585,633	474,549	21,597	81,005	299,145	185,709
Maine	1,124,660	546,235	578,425	1,109,850	3,128	4,087	2,947	5,005	4,648
New Hampshire	920,610	448,462	472,148	910,099	3,990	1,352	2,929	5,587	2,240
Vermont	511,456	249,080	262,376	506,736	1,135	984	1,355	3,304	1,246
Massachusetts	5,737,037	2,730,893	3,006,144	5,362,836	221,279	7,743	49,501	141,043	95,678
Rhode Island	947,154	451,251	495,903	896,692	27,584	2,898	5,303	19,707	14,677
Connecticut	3,107,576	1,498,005	1,609,571	2,799,420	217,433	4,533	18,970	124,499	67,220
Middle Atlantic	36,788,174	17,555,665	19,232,509	30,742,521	4,374,237	56,585	478,754	2,305,116	1,136,077
New York	17,557,288	8,338,961	9,218,327	13,961,106	2,401,842	38,732	310,531	1,659,245	845,077
New Jersey	7,364,158	3,532,719	3,831,439	6,127,090	924,786	8,394	103,842	491,867	200,046
Pennsylvania	11,866,728	5,683,985	6,182,743	10,654,325	1,047,609	9,459	64,381	154,004	90,054
North Central states	58,853,804	28,607,239	30,246,565	52,183,794	5,336,542	248,505	389,747	1,276,405	695,216
East North Central	41,669,738	20,235,410	21,434,328	36,138,962	4,547,998	105,881	302,748	1,067,794	574,149
Ohio	10,797,419	5,217,027	5,580,392	9,597,266	1,076,734	12,240	47,813	119,880	63,366
Indiana	5,490,179	2,665,805	2,824,374	5,004,567	414,732	7,835	20,488	87,020	42,557
Illinois	11,418,461	5,533,525	5,884,936	9,225,575	1,675,229	16,271	159,551	635,525	341,835
Michigan	9,258,344	4,513,951	4,744,393	7,868,956	1,198,710	40,038	56,731	162,388	93,909
Wisconsin	4,705,335	2,305,102	2,400,233	4,442,598	182,593	29,497	18,165	62,981	32,482
West North Central	17,184,066	8,371,829	8,812,237	16,044,832	788,544	142,624	86,999	208,611	121,067
Minnesota	4,077,148	1,998,406	2,078,742	3,936,948	53,342	35,026	26,533	32,124	25,299
Iowa	2,913,387	1,416,195	1,497,192	2,838,805	41,700	5,453	11,577	25,536	15,852
Missouri	4,917,444	2,365,827	2,551,617	4,346,267	514,274	12,319	23,108	51,667	21,476
North Dakota	652,695	328,409	324,286	625,536	2,568	20,157	1,979	3,903	2,455
South Dakota	690,178	340,370	349,808	638,955	2,144	45,101	1,728	4,028	2,250
Nebraska	1,570,006	765,902	804,104	1,490,569	48,389	9,197	6,996	28,020	14,855
Kansas	2,363,208	1,156,720	1,206,488	2,167,752	126,127	15,371	15,078	63,333	38,880
Southern states	75,349,155	36,577,674	38,771,481	58,944,057	14,041,374	372,123	469,762	4,473,172	1,521,839
South Atlantic	36,943,139	17,870,778	19,072,361	28,647,762	7,647,743	118,656	260,638	1,193,823	268,340
Delaware	595,225	286,998	308,227	488,543	95,971	1,330	4,132	9,671	5,249
Maryland	4,216,446	2,042,558	2,173,888	3,158,412	958,050	8,021	64,276	64,740	27,687
District of Columbia	637,651	295,039	342,612	171,796	448,229	1,031	6,635	17,652	9,960
Virginia	5,346,279	2,618,068	2,728,211	4,229,734	1,008,311	9,336	66,209	79,873	32,689
West Virginia	1,949,644	945,408	1,004,236	1,874,751	65,051	1,610	5,194	12,707	3,038
North Carolina	5,874,429	2,852,012	3,022,417	4,453,010	1,316,050	64,635	21,168	56,607	19,566
South Carolina	3,119,208	1,516,905	1,602,303	2,145,122	948,146	5,758	11,807	33,414	8,375
Georgia	5,464,265	2,641,030	2,823,235	3,948,007	1,465,457	7,619	24,461	61,261	18,721
Florida	9,739,992	4,672,760	5,067,232	8,178,387	1,342,478	19,316	56,756	857,898	143,055
East South Central	14,662,882	7,088,606	7,574,276	11,699,604	2,868,268	22,454	41,041	119,315	31,515
Kentucky	3,661,433	1,789,330	1,872,103	3,379,648	259,490	3,610	9,971	27,403	8,714
Tennessee	4,590,750	2,216,395	2,374,355	3,835,078	725,949	5,103	13,963	34,081	10,657
Alabama	3,890,061	1,869,003	2,021,058	2,869,688	995,623	7,561	9,695	33,100	7,494
Mississippi	2,520,638	1,213,878	1,306,760	1,615,190	887,206	6,180	7,412	24,731	4,650
West South Central	23,743,134	11,618,290	12,124,844	18,596,691	3,525,363	231,013	168,083	3,160,034	1,221,984
Arkansas	2,285,513	1,104,258	1,181,255	1,890,002	373,192	9,411	6,732	17,873	6,176
Louisiana	4,203,972	2,039,012	2,164,960	2,911,243	1,237,263	12,064	23,771	99,105	19,631
Oklahoma	3,025,266	1,476,719	1,548,547	2,597,783	204,658	169,464	17,274	57,413	36,087
Texas	14,228,383	6,998,301	7,230,082	11,197,663	1,710,250	40,074	120,306	2,985,643	1,160,090
Western States	43,165,199	21,367,791	21,797,408	34,884,785	2,261,516	719,385	2,081,368	6,252,045	3,218,145
Mountain	11,368,330	5,645,983	5,722,347	9,958,545	268,660	363,169	98,416	1,441,480	679,540
Montana	786,690	392,625	394,065	740,148	1,786	37,270	2,503	9,974	4,983
Idaho	943,935	471,155	472,780	901,641	2,716	10,521	5,948	36,615	23,109
Wyoming	470,816	241,284	229,532	447,716	3,364	7,125	1,969	24,499	10,642
Colorado	2,888,834	1,433,737	1,455,097	2,570,615	101,702	18,059	29,897	339,300	168,561
New Mexico	1,299,968	640,643	659,325	976,465	24,042	104,777	6,816	476,089	187,868
Arizona	2,717,866	1,337,666	1,380,200	2,240,033	75,034	152,857	22,098	440,915	227,844
Utah	1,461,037	724,501	736,536	1,382,550	9,225	19,256	15,076	60,302	34,930
Nevada	799,184	404,372	394,812	699,377	50,791	13,304	14,109	53,786	21,603
Pacific	31,796,869	15,721,808	16,075,061	24,926,240	1,992,856	356,216	1,982,952	4,810,565	2,538,605
Washington	4,130,163	2,051,369	2,078,794	3,777,296	105,544	60,771	102,503	119,986	84,049
Oregon	2,632,663	1,296,355	1,336,308	2,490,192	37,059	27,309	34,767	65,833	43,336
California	23,668,562	11,666,949	12,001,613	18,031,689	1,819,282	201,311	1,253,987	4,543,770	2,362,293
Alaska	400,481	212,321	188,160	308,455	13,619	64,047	8,035	9,497	6,325
Hawaii	965,000	494,814	470,186	318,608	17,352	2,778	583,660	71,479	42,602
TOTAL	226,504,825	110,032,296	116,472,530	188,340,790	26,488,218	1,418,195	3,500,636	14,605,883	6,756,986

[1] Some Asian and Pacific Islander groups such as Cambodian, Laotian, and Thai are included in "other."
[2] Persons of Spanish origin may be of any race.
Source: U.S. Bureau of the Census.

Table VI. Metropolitan Areas of 1,000,000 or more[1]

Rank	Name	Population in 000			Change in 000		% Change	
		1980	1970	1960	1970–80	1960–70	1970–80	1960–70
1	New York-Newark-Jersey City SCSA	16,120	17,035	15,405	−915	1,631	−5.4	10.6
2	Los Angeles-Long Beach-Anaheim SCSA	11,496	9,981	7,752	1,515	2,229	15.2	28.8
3	Chicago-Gary-Kenosha SCSA	7,868	7,726	6,895	142	932	1.8	13.7
4	Philadelphia-Wilmington-Trenton SCSA	5,549	5,628	5,024	−79	604	−1.4	12.0
5	San Francisco-Oakland-San Jose SCSA	5,182	4,631	3,639	551	992	11.9	32.6
6	Detroit-Ann Arbor SCSA	4,618	4,669	4,122	−51	547	−1.1	13.3
7	Boston-Lawrence-Lowell SCSA	3,448	3,526	3,193	−78	333	−2.2	10.4
8	Houston-Galveston SCSA	3,101	2,169	1,571	932	598	43.0	38.1
9	Washington, D.C.	3,060	2,910	2,097	150	813	5.2	38.8
10	Dallas-Fort Worth	2,975	2,378	1,738	597	640	25.1	36.8
11	Cleveland-Akron-Lorain SCSA	2,834	3,000	2,732	−166	267	−5.5	9.8
12	Miami-Fort Lauderdale SCSA	2,640	1,888	1,269	752	619	39.8	48.8
13	St. Louis	2,355	2,411	2,144	−56	267	−2.3	12.4
14	Pittsburgh	2,263	2,401	2,405	−138	−4	−5.7	−0.2
15	Baltimore	2,174	2,071	1,804	103	267	5.0	14.8
16	Minneapolis-St. Paul	2,114	1,965	1,598	149	368	7.6	23.0
17	Seattle-Tacoma SCSA	2,092	1,837	1,429	255	408	13.9	28.6
18	Atlanta	2,030	1,596	1,169	434	426	27.2	36.5
19	San Diego	1,862	1,358	1,033	504	325	37.1	31.4
20	Cincinnati-Hamilton SCSA	1,660	1,613	1,468	47	146	2.9	9.9
21	Denver-Boulder	1,620	1,240	935	380	305	30.6	32.6
22	Milwaukee-Racine SCSA	1,570	1,575	1,421	−5	154	−0.3	10.8
23	Tampa-St. Petersburg	1,569	1,089	809	480	279	44.1	34.5
24	Phoenix	1,508	971	664	537	308	55.3	46.4
25	Kansas City	1,327	1,274	1,109	53	165	4.2	14.9
26	Buffalo	1,242	1,349	1,307	−107	42	−7.9	3.2
27	Portland	1,242	1,007	822	235	185	23.3	22.5
28	New Orleans	1,187	1,046	907	141	139	13.5	15.4
29	Indianapolis	1,167	1,111	944	56	167	5.0	17.7
30	Columbus	1,093	1,018	845	75	173	7.4	20.4
31	San Antonio	1,072	888	736	184	152	20.7	20.7
32	Sacramento	1,014	804	626	210	178	26.1	28.5

[1] Standard Metropolitan Statistical Area, SMSA, unless otherwise indicated; SCSA is a Standard Consolidated Statistical Area and combines two or more contiguous SMSA's.
Source: U.S. Bureau of the Census.

Table VII. Population of States by Amount and Percentage of Change, 1970 to 1980; along with percent urban and rural

Rank by amount of change	Name	Population change 1970–80	% Change 1970–80	Rank of % change	% Urban 1980	% Rural 1980
1	California	3,697,493	18.5	18	91.3	8.7
2	Texas	3,029,728	27.1	10	79.6	20.4
3	Florida	2,948,574	43.4	3	84.3	15.7
4	Arizona	942,467	53.1	2	83.8	16.2
5	Georgia	876,335	19.1	16	62.3	37.7
6	North Carolina	790,018	15.5	21	48.0	52.0
7	Washington	716,919	21.0	14	73.6	26.4
8	Virginia	694,831	14.9	24	66.0	34.0
9	Colorado	679,238	30.7	8	80.6	19.4
10	Tennessee	664,732	16.9	20	60.4	39.6
11	Louisiana	559,335	15.3	22	68.6	31.4
12	Oregon	541,130	25.9	11	67.9	32.1
13	South Carolina	528,495	20.4	15	54.1	45.9
14	Oklahoma	465,803	18.2	19	67.3	32.7
15	Alabama	445,707	12.9	29	60.0	40.0
16	Kentucky	440,722	13.7	26	50.8	49.2
17	Utah	401,764	37.9	5	84.4	15.6
18	Michigan	376,518	4.2	40	70.7	29.3
19	Arkansas	362,191	18.8	17	51.6	48.4
20	Nevada	310,446	63.5	1	85.3	14.7
21	Illinois	308,176	2.8	43	83.0	17.0
22	Mississippi	303,644	13.7	25	47.3	52.7
23	Indiana	294,787	5.7	35	64.2	35.8
24	Maryland	292,549	7.5	32	80.3	19.7
25	Wisconsin	287,514	6.5	34	64.2	35.8
26	New Mexico	282,913	27.8	9	72.2	27.8
27	Minnesota	271,045	7.1	33	66.8	33.2
28	Missouri	239,821	5.1	38	68.1	31.9
29	Idaho	230,920	32.4	6	54.0	46.0
30	West Virginia	205,407	11.8	30	36.2	63.8
31	Hawaii	195,087	25.3	12	86.5	13.5
32	New Jersey	193,046	2.7	44	89.0	11.0
33	New Hampshire	182,929	24.8	13	52.2	47.8
34	Ohio	139,996	1.3	46	73.3	26.7
35	Wyoming	138,400	41.6	4	62.8	37.2
36	Maine	130,938	13.2	28	47.5	52.5
37	Kansas	114,137	5.1	38	66.7	33.3
38	Alaska	97,898	32.4	6	64.5	35.5
39	Montana	92,281	13.3	27	52.9	47.1
40	Iowa	88,019	3.1	42	58.6	41.4
41	Nebraska	84,673	5.7	35	62.7	37.3
42	Connecticut	75,359	2.5	45	78.8	21.2
43	Vermont	66,724	15.0	23	33.8	66.2
44	Pennsylvania	65,962	0.6	48	69.3	30.7
45	Massachusetts	47,867	0.8	47	83.8	16.2
46	Delaware	47,121	8.6	31	70.7	29.3
47	North Dakota	34,903	5.6	37	48.8	51.2
48	South Dakota	23,921	3.6	41	46.4	53.6
49	Rhode Island	−2,569	−0.3	49	87.0	13.0
50	District of Columbia	−119,017	−15.7	51	100.0	0.0
51	New York	−684,103	−3.8	50	84.6	15.4

Source: U.S. Bureau of the Census.

Table VIII. Population of 30 Largest Cities

Rank	Name	1980	1970	1970 rank	% Change 1970–80
1	New York City	7,071,030	7,895,563	1	−10.4
2	Chicago	3,005,072	3,369,357	2	−10.8
3	Los Angeles	2,966,763	2,811,801	3	5.5
4	Philadelphia	1,688,210	1,949,996	4	−13.4
5	Houston	1,594,086	1,233,535	6	29.2
6	Detroit	1,203,339	1,514,063	5	−20.5
7	Dallas	904,078	844,401	8	7.1
8	San Diego	875,504	697,471	14	25.5
9	Phoenix	789,704	584,303	20	35.2
10	Baltimore	786,775	905,787	7	−13.1
11	San Antonio	785,410	654,153	15	20.1
12	Indianapolis	700,807	736,856	11	−4.9
13	San Francisco	678,974	715,674	13	−5.1
14	Memphis	646,356	623,988	17	3.6
15	Washington, D.C.	637,651	756,668	9	−15.7
16	San Jose	636,550	459,913	29	38.4
17	Milwaukee	636,212	717,372	12	−11.3
18	Cleveland	573,822	750,879	10	−23.6
19	Columbus	564,871	540,025	21	4.6
20	Boston	562,994	641,071	16	−12.2
21	New Orleans	557,482	593,471	19	−6.1
22	Jacksonville	540,898	504,265	26	7.3
23	Seattle	493,846	530,831	22	−7.0
24	Denver	491,396	514,678	24	−4.5
25	Nashville-Davidson	455,651	426,029	32	7.0
26	St. Louis	453,085	622,236	18	−27.2
27	Kansas City	448,159	507,330	25	−11.7
28	El Paso	425,259	322,261	45	32.0
29	Atlanta	425,022	495,039	27	−14.1
30	Pittsburgh	423,938	520,089	23	−18.5

Source: U.S. Bureau of the Census.

Table IX. Population by Age, Sex, Racial, and Ethnic Group
In 000

Age	Total	Male	% of total male pop.	Female	% of total female pop.	Racial and ethnic groups					
						White	Black	Amer. Indian, Eskimo, and Aleut	Asian and Pacific Islander[1]	Spanish origin[2]	Other
Under 5	16,344	8,360	7.6	7,984	6.9	12,631	2,436	149	293	1,663	835
5 to 9	16,697	8,538	7.8	8,159	7.0	13,031	2,490	146	302	1,537	728
10 to 14	18,241	9,315	8.5	8,926	7.7	14,460	2,673	156	280	1,475	672
15 to 19	21,162	10,752	9.8	10,410	8.9	16,958	2,983	170	289	1,606	762
20 to 24	21,313	10,660	9.7	10,652	9.1	17,283	2,724	149	320	1,586	836
25 to 29	19,518	9,703	8.8	9,814	8.4	15,983	2,321	125	369	1,376	721
30 to 34	17,558	8,676	7.9	8,882	7.6	14,643	1,888	107	371	1,128	549
35 to 39	13,963	6,860	6.2	7,103	6.1	11,759	1,457	84	277	854	385
40 to 44	11,668	5,708	5.2	5,961	5.1	9,825	1,251	69	221	712	302
45 to 49	11,088	5,388	4.9	5,701	4.9	9,456	1,143	58	181	622	251
50 to 54	11,709	5,620	5.1	6,089	5.2	10,157	1,129	52	158	564	214
55 to 59	11,614	5,481	5.0	6,133	5.3	10,237	1,037	45	130	454	166
60 to 64	10,086	4,669	4.2	5,416	4.7	8,974	871	34	98	321	109
65 to 69	8,781	3,902	3.5	4,879	4.2	7,811	777	28	80	264	85
70 to 74	6,797	2,853	2.6	3,944	3.4	6,094	563	20	58	193	61
75 to 79	4,793	1,847	1.7	2,945	2.5	4,309	387	14	39	136	43
80 to 84	2,934	1,019	0.9	1,915	1.6	2,685	200	7	21	66	22
85 +	2,240	681	0.6	1,558	1.3	2,045	159	6	14	49	16
All ages[3]	226,505	110,032	100.0	116,473	100.0	188,341	26,488	1,418	3,501	14,606	6,757
Median	30.0	28.8		31.3		31.3	24.9	23.0	28.6	23.2	22.3

[1] Some Asian and Pacific Islander groups such as Cambodian, Laotian, and Thai are included in "other."
[2] Persons of Spanish origin may be of any race.
[3] Detail may not add to total due to rounding.
  Source: U.S. Bureau of the Census.

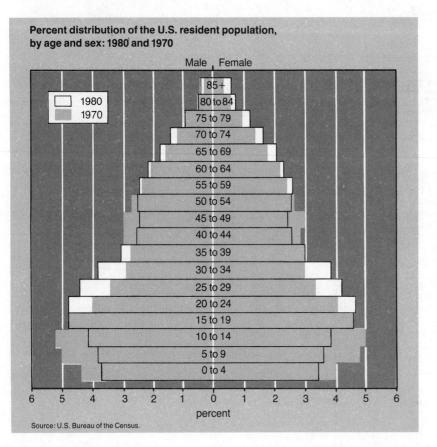

Percent distribution of the U.S. resident population, by age and sex: 1980 and 1970

Male | Female

☐ 1980
▨ 1970

85+
80 to 84
75 to 79
70 to 74
65 to 69
60 to 64
55 to 59
50 to 54
45 to 49
40 to 44
35 to 39
30 to 34
25 to 29
20 to 24
15 to 19
10 to 14
5 to 9
0 to 4

6 5 4 3 2 1 0 1 2 3 4 5 6
percent

Source: U.S. Bureau of the Census.

Population of U.S. Cities over 5,000
1970 and 1980 Censuses

Place	1970	1980
ALABAMA		
Alabaster	2,642	7,079
Albertville	9,963	12,039
Alexander City	12,358	13,807
Andalusia	10,092	10,415
Anniston	31,533	29,523
Arab	4,399	5,967
Athens	14,360	14,558
Atmore	8,293	8,789
Attalla	7,510	7,737
Auburn	22,767	28,471
Bay Minette	6,727	7,455
Bessemer	33,428	31,729
Birmingham	300,910	284,413
Boaz	5,635	7,151
Brewton	6,747	6,680
Brighton	2,277	5,308
Chickasaw	8,447	7,402
Childersburg	4,831	5,084
Clanton	5,868	5,832
Cullman	12,601	13,084
Decatur	38,044	42,002
Demopolis	7,651	7,678
Dothan	36,733	48,750
Enterprise	15,591	18,033
Eufaula	9,102	12,097
Fairfield	14,369	13,040
Fairhope	5,720	7,286
Fayette	4,568	5,287
Florence	34,031	37,029
Fort Payne	8,435	11,485
Fultondale	5,163	6,217
Gadsden	53,928	47,565
Gardendale	6,537	7,928
Greenville	8,033	7,807
Guntersville	6,491	7,041
Haleyville	4,190	5,306
Hartselle	7,355	8,858
Homewood	21,245	21,271
Hoover	688	15,064
Hueytown	7,095	13,309
Huntsville	139,282	142,513
Irondale	3,166	6,521
Jackson	5,957	6,073
Jacksonville	7,715	9,735
Jasper	10,798	11,894
Lanett	6,908	6,897
Leeds	6,991	8,638
Midfield	6,399	6,536
Mobile	190,026	200,452
Monroeville	4,846	5,674
Montgomery (c.)	133,386	178,157
Mountain Brook	19,474	17,400
Muscle Shoals	6,907	8,911
Northport	9,435	14,291
Opelika	19,027	21,896
Opp	6,493	7,204
Oxford	4,361	8,939
Ozark	13,555	13,188
Pelham	931	6,759
Pell City	5,602	6,616
Phenix City	25,281	26,928
Piedmont	5,063	5,544
Pleasant Grove	5,090	7,102
Prattville	13,116	18,647
Prichard	41,578	39,541
Rainbow City	3,107	6,299
Roanoke	5,251	5,896
Russellville	7,814	8,195
Saraland	7,840	9,833
Scottsboro	9,324	14,758
Selma	27,379	26,684
Sheffield	13,115	11,903
Sylacauga	12,255	12,708
Talladega	17,662	19,128
Tarrant City	6,835	8,148
Troy	11,482	12,587
Tuscaloosa	65,773	75,143
Tuscumbia	8,828	9,137
Tuskegee	11,028	12,716
Vestavia Hills	12,250	15,733
ALASKA		
Anchorage	48,081	173,017
Fairbanks	14,771	22,645
Juneau (c.)	6,050	19,528
Ketchikan	6,994	7,198
Sitka	3,370	7,803
ARIZONA		
Apache Junction	...	9,935
Avondale	6,626	8,134
Bisbee	8,328	7,154
Casa Grande	10,536	14,971
Chandler	13,763	29,673
Coolidge	5,314	6,851
Douglas	12,462	13,058
Eloy	5,381	6,240
Flagstaff	26,117	34,641
Gilbert	1,971	5,717
Glendale	36,228	96,988
Globe	7,333	6,708
Holbrook	4,759	5,785
Kingman	7,312	9,257
Lake Havasu City	...	15,737
Mesa	63,049	152,453
Nogales	8,946	15,683
Paradise Valley	6,637	10,832
Payson	...	5,068
Peoria	4,792	12,251
Phoenix (c.)	584,303	789,703
Prescott	13,631	20,055
Safford	5,493	7,010
Scottsdale	67,823	88,364
Sierra Vista	6,689	25,968
Somerton	2,225	5,761
South Tucson	6,220	6,554
Tempe	63,550	106,743
Tucson	262,933	330,537
Winslow	8,066	7,921
Yuma	29,007	42,433
ARKANSAS		
Arkadelphia	9,841	10,005
Batesville	7,209	8,263
Benton	16,499	17,437
Bentonville	5,508	8,756
Blytheville	24,752	24,314
Camden	15,147	15,356
Clarksville	4,616	5,237
Conway	15,510	20,375
Crossett	6,191	6,706
Dumas	4,600	6,091
El Dorado	25,283	26,685
Fayetteville	30,729	36,604
Fordyce	4,837	5,175
Forrest City	12,521	13,803
Fort Smith	62,802	71,384
Harrison	7,239	9,567
Helena	10,415	9,598
Hope	8,830	10,290
Hot Springs	35,631	35,166
Jacksonville	19,832	27,589
Jonesboro	27,050	31,530
Little Rock (c.)	132,483	158,461
McGehee	4,683	5,671
Magnolia	11,303	11,909
Malvern	8,739	10,163
Marianna	6,196	6,220
Mena	4,530	5,154
Monticello	5,085	8,259
Morrilton	6,814	7,355
Mountain Home	3,936	7,447
Newport	7,725	8,339
North Little Rock	60,040	64,419
Osceola	7,204	8,881
Paragould	10,639	15,214
Pine Bluff	57,389	56,576
Pocahontas	4,544	5,995
Rogers	11,050	17,429
Russellville	11,750	14,000
Searcy	9,040	13,612
Sherwood	2,754	10,586
Siloam Springs	6,009	7,940
Springdale	16,783	23,458
Stuttgart	10,477	10,941
Texarkana	21,682	21,459
Trumann	6,023	6,044
Van Buren	8,373	12,020
Warren	6,433	7,646
West Helena	11,007	11,367
West Memphis	26,070	28,138
Wynne	6,696	7,805
CALIFORNIA		
Alameda	70,968	63,852
Albany	15,561	15,130
Alhambra	62,125	64,615
Anaheim	166,408	221,847
Anderson	5,492	7,381
Antioch	28,060	43,559
Arcadia	45,138	45,994
Arcata	8,985	12,338
Arroyo Grande	7,454	11,290
Artesia	14,757	14,301
Arvin	5,199	6,863
Atascadero	...	15,930
Atherton	8,085	7,797
Atwater	11,640	17,530
Auburn	6,570	7,540
Azusa	25,217	29,380
Bakersfield	69,515	105,611
Baldwin Park	47,285	50,554
Banning	12,034	14,020
Barstow	17,442	17,690
Beaumont	5,484	6,818
Bell	21,836	25,450
Bellflower	52,334	53,441
Bell Gardens	29,308	34,117
Belmont	23,538	24,505
Benicia	7,349	15,376
Berkeley	114,091	103,328
Beverly Hills	33,416	32,367
Blythe	7,047	6,805
Brawley	13,746	14,946
Brea	18,447	27,913
Buena Park	63,646	64,165
Burbank	88,871	84,625
Burlingame	27,320	26,173
Calexico	10,625	14,412
Camarillo	19,219	37,732
Campbell	23,797	27,067
Capitola	5,080	9,095
Carlsbad	14,944	35,490
Carpinteria	6,982	10,835
Carson	71,150	81,221
Ceres	6,029	13,281
Cerritos	15,856	52,756
Chico	19,580	26,601
Chino	20,411	40,165
Chowchilla	4,349	5,122
Chula Vista	67,901	83,927
Claremont	24,776	30,950
Clovis	13,856	33,021
Coachella	8,353	9,129
Coalinga	6,161	6,593
Colton	20,016	27,419
Commerce	10,635	10,509
Compton	78,547	81,286
Concord	85,164	103,251
Corcoran	5,249	6,454
Corona	27,519	37,791
Coronado	20,020	16,859
Corte Madera	8,464	8,074
Costa Mesa	72,660	82,291
Covina	30,395	33,751
Cudahy	16,998	17,984
Culver City	34,451	38,139
Cupertino	17,895	25,770
Cypress	31,569	40,391
Daly City	66,922	78,519
Davis	23,488	36,640
Delano	14,559	16,491
CALIF.—Cont.		
Del Mar	3,956	5,017
Desert Hot Springs	2,738	5,941
Dinuba	7,917	9,907
Dixon	4,432	7,541
Downey	88,573	82,602
Duarte	14,981	16,766
El Cajon	52,273	73,892
El Centro	19,272	23,996
El Cerrito	25,190	22,731
El Monte	69,892	79,494
El Paso de Robles	7,168	9,163
El Segundo	15,620	13,752
Escondido	36,792	62,480
Eureka	24,337	24,153
Exeter	4,475	5,619
Fairfax	7,661	7,391
Fairfield	44,146	58,099
Farmersville	3,456	5,544
Fillmore	6,285	9,602
Folsom	5,810	11,003
Fontana	20,673	37,109
Fort Bragg	4,455	5,019
Fortuna	4,203	7,591
Foster City	...	23,287
Fountain Valley	31,886	55,080
Fremont	100,869	131,945
Fresno	165,655	218,202
Fullerton	85,987	102,034
Galt	3,200	5,514
Gardena	41,021	45,165
Garden Grove	121,155	123,351
Gilroy	12,684	21,641
Glendale	132,664	139,060
Glendora	32,143	38,654
Grand Terrace	...	8,498
Grass Valley	5,149	6,697
Grover City	5,939	8,827
Half Moon Bay	4,023	7,282
Hanford	15,179	20,958
Hawaiian Gardens	9,052	10,548
Hawthorne	53,304	56,447
Hayward	93,058	94,167
Healdsburg	5,438	7,217
Hemet	12,252	23,211
Hercules	252	5,963
Hermosa Beach	17,412	18,070
Hillsborough	8,753	10,451
Hollister	7,663	11,488
Huntington Beach	115,960	170,505
Huntington Park	33,744	46,223
Imperial Beach	20,244	22,689
Indio	14,459	21,611
Inglewood	89,985	94,245
Irvine	...	62,134
King City	3,717	5,495
Kingsburg	3,843	5,115
La Canada Flintridge	...	20,153
Lafayette	20,484	20,879
Laguna Beach	14,550	17,860
La Habra	41,350	45,232
Lake Elsinore	3,530	5,982
Lakewood	83,025	74,654
La Mesa	39,178	50,342
La Mirada	30,808	40,986
Lancaster	...	48,027
La Palma	9,687	15,663
La Puente	31,092	30,882
Larkspur	10,487	11,064
La Verne	12,965	23,508
Lawndale	24,825	23,460
Lemon Grove	...	20,780
Lemoore	4,219	8,832
Lindsay	5,206	6,924
Livermore	37,703	48,349
Livingston	2,588	5,326
Lodi	28,691	35,221
Loma Linda	...	10,694
Lomita	19,784	17,191
Lompoc	25,284	26,267
Long Beach	358,879	361,334
Los Alamitos	11,346	11,529
Los Altos	25,062	25,769
Los Altos Hills	6,871	7,421
Los Angeles	2,811,801	2,966,763
Los Banos	9,188	10,341
Los Gatos	22,613	26,593
Lynwood	43,354	48,548
McFarland	4,177	5,151
Madera	16,044	21,732
Manhattan Beach	35,352	31,542
Manteca	13,845	24,925
Martinez	16,506	22,582
Marysville	9,353	9,898
Maywood	16,996	21,810
Mendota	2,705	5,038
Menlo Park	26,826	25,673
Merced	22,670	36,499
Millbrae	20,920	20,058
Mill Valley	12,942	12,967
Milpitas	26,561	37,820
Modesto	61,712	106,105
Monrovia	30,562	30,531
Montclair	22,546	22,628
Montebello	42,807	52,929
Monterey	26,302	27,558
Monterey Park	49,166	54,338
Moraga	...	15,014
Morgan Hill	5,579	17,060
Morro Bay	7,109	9,064
Mountain View	54,132	58,655
Napa	36,103	50,879
National City	43,184	48,772
Newark	27,153	32,126
Newport Beach	49,582	63,475
Norco	14,511	21,126
Norwalk	90,164	85,232
Novato	31,006	43,916
Oakdale	6,594	8,474
Oakland	361,561	339,288
Oceanside	40,494	76,698
CALIF.—Cont.		
Ojai	5,591	6,816
Ontario	64,118	88,820
Orange	77,365	91,788
Oroville	7,536	8,683
Oxnard	71,225	108,195
Pacifica	36,020	36,866
Pacific Grove	13,505	15,755
Palmdale	8,511	12,277
Palm Desert	...	11,801
Palm Springs	20,936	32,271
Palo Alto	56,040	55,225
Palos Verdes Estates	13,631	14,376
Paradise	...	22,571
Paramount	34,734	36,407
Pasadena	112,951	119,374
Perris	4,228	6,740
Petaluma	24,870	33,834
Pico Rivera	54,170	53,459
Piedmont	10,917	10,498
Pinole	13,266	14,253
Pismo Beach	4,043	5,364
Pittsburg	21,423	33,034
Placentia	21,948	35,041
Placerville	5,416	6,739
Pleasant Hill	24,610	25,124
Pleasanton	18,328	35,160
Pomona	87,384	92,742
Porterville	12,602	19,707
Port Hueneme	14,295	17,803
Rancho Cucamonga	...	55,250
Rancho Mirage	...	6,281
Rancho Palos Verdes	...	35,227
Red Bluff	7,676	9,490
Redding	16,659	41,995
Redlands	36,355	43,619
Redondo Beach	57,451	57,102
Redwood City	55,686	54,965
Reedley	8,131	11,071
Rialto	28,370	35,615
Richmond	79,043	74,676
Ridgecrest	7,629	15,929
Riverbank	3,949	5,695
Riverside	140,089	170,876
Rocklin	3,039	7,344
Rohnert Park	6,133	22,965
Rolling Hills Estates	6,735	9,412
Rosemead	40,972	42,604
Roseville	18,221	24,347
Sacramento (c.)	257,105	275,741
Salinas	58,896	80,479
San Anselmo	13,031	11,927
San Bernardino	106,869	118,057
San Bruno	36,254	35,417
San Buenaventura	57,964	74,474
San Carlos	26,053	24,710
San Clemente	17,063	27,325
San Diego	697,471	875,504
San Dimas	15,692	24,014
San Fernando	16,571	17,731
San Francisco	715,674	678,974
San Gabriel	29,336	30,072
Sanger	10,088	12,558
San Jacinto	4,385	7,098
San Jose	459,913	636,550
San Juan Capistrano	3,781	18,959
San Leandro	68,698	63,952
San Luis Obispo	28,036	34,252
San Marcos	3,896	17,479
San Marino	14,177	13,307
San Mateo	78,991	77,561
San Pablo	21,461	19,750
San Rafael	38,977	44,700
Santa Ana	155,710	203,713
Santa Barbara	70,215	74,542
Santa Clara	86,118	87,746
Santa Cruz	32,076	41,483
Santa Fe Springs	14,750	14,559
Santa Maria	32,749	39,685
Santa Monica	88,289	88,314
Santa Paula	18,001	20,552
Santa Rosa	50,006	83,205
Saratoga	26,810	29,261
Sausalito	6,158	7,090
Scotts Valley	3,621	6,891
Seal Beach	24,441	25,975
Seaside	36,883	36,567
Sebastopol	3,993	5,500
Selma	7,459	10,942
Shafter	5,327	7,010
Sierra Madre	12,140	10,837
Signal Hill	5,588	5,734
Simi Valley	59,832	77,500
Soledad	4,222	5,928
Sonoma	4,259	6,054
South El Monte	13,443	16,623
South Gate	56,909	66,784
South Lake Tahoe	12,921	20,681
South Pasadena	22,979	22,681
South San Francisco	46,646	49,393
Stanton	18,186	21,144
Stockton	109,963	149,779
Suisun City	2,917	11,087
Sunnyvale	95,976	106,618
Susanville	6,608	6,520
Taft	4,285	5,316
Temple City	31,034	28,972
Thousand Oaks	35,873	77,797
Tiburon	6,209	6,685
Torrance	134,968	131,497
Tracy	14,724	18,428
Tulare	16,235	22,475
Turlock	13,992	26,291
Tustin	22,313	32,073
Ukiah	10,095	12,035
Union City	14,724	39,406

Place	1970	1980
CALIF.—Cont.		
Upland	32,551	47,647
Vacaville	21,690	43,367
Vallejo	71,710	80,188
Victorville	10,845	14,220
Villa Park	2,723	7,137
Visalia	27,130	49,729
Vista	24,688	35,834
Walnut	5,992	9,978
Walnut Creek	39,844	53,643
Wasco	8,269	9,613
Watsonville	14,719	23,543
West Covina	68,034	80,094
Westminster	60,076	71,133
Whittier	72,863	68,872
Woodlake	3,371	5,375
Woodland	20,677	30,235
Woodside	4,734	5,291
Yorba Linda	11,856	28,254
Yreka City	5,394	5,916
Yuba City	13,986	18,736
COLORADO		
Alamosa	6,985	6,830
Arvada	49,844	84,576
Aurora	74,974	158,588
Boulder	66,870	76,685
Brighton	8,309	12,773
Broomfield	7,261	20,730
Canon City	9,206	13,037
Cherry Hills Village	4,605	5,127
Colorado Springs	135,517	215,150
Commerce City	17,407	16,234
Cortez	6,032	7,095
Craig	4,205	8,133
Denver (c.)	514,678	491,396
Durango	10,333	11,426
Edgewater	4,910	5,714
Englewood	33,695	30,021
Evans	2,570	5,063
Federal Heights	1,502	7,846
Fort Collins	43,337	64,632
Fort Morgan	7,594	8,768
Fountain	3,515	8,324
Golden	9,817	12,237
Grand Junction	20,170	28,144
Greeley	38,902	53,006
Greenwood Village	3,095	5,729
Gunnison	4,613	5,785
Lafayette	3,498	8,985
La Junta	8,205	8,338
Lakewood	92,743	112,848
Lamar	7,797	7,713
Littleton	26,466	28,631
Longmont	23,209	42,942
Louisville	2,409	5,593
Loveland	16,220	30,244
Montrose	6,496	8,722
North Glenn	27,785	29,847
Pueblo	97,774	101,686
Sheridan	4,787	5,377
Steamboat Springs	2,340	5,098
Sterling	10,636	11,385
Thornton	13,326	40,343
Trinidad	9,901	9,663
Westminster	19,512	50,211
Wheat Ridge	29,778	30,293
CONNECTICUT		
Ansonia	21,160	19,039
Avon	8,352	11,201
Berlin	14,149	15,121
Bethel	10,945	16,004
Bloomfield	18,301	18,608
Branford	20,444	23,363
Bridgeport	156,542	142,546
Bristol	55,487	57,370
Brookfield	9,688	12,872
Cheshire	19,051	21,788
Clinton	10,267	11,195
Cromwell	7,400	10,265
Danbury	50,781	60,470
Darien	20,336	18,892
Derby	12,599	12,346
East Hampton	7,078	8,572
East Hartford	57,583	52,563
East Haven	25,120	25,028
Ellington	7,707	9,711
Enfield	46,189	42,695
Essex	4,911	5,078
Fairfield	56,487	54,849
Farmington	14,390	16,407
Glastonbury	20,651	24,327
Granby	6,150	7,956
Greenwich	59,755	59,578
Groton	8,933	10,086
Guilford	12,033	17,375
Hamden	49,357	51,071
Hartford (c.)	158,017	136,392
Ledyard	14,837	13,735
Madison	9,768	14,031
Manchester	47,994	49,761
Meriden	55,959	57,118
Middlebury	5,542	5,995
Middletown	36,924	39,040
Milford	50,858	49,101
Monroe	12,047	14,010
Montville	15,662	16,455
Naugatuck	23,034	26,456
New Britain	83,441	73,840
New Canaan	17,451	17,931
New Fairfield	6,991	11,260
New Haven	137,707	126,109
Newington	26,037	28,841
New London	31,630	28,842
New Milford	14,601	19,420
North Branford	10,778	11,554
North Haven	22,194	22,080
Norwalk	79,288	77,767
Norwich	41,739	38,074
Old Saybrook	8,468	9,287
Orange	13,524	13,237
Plainfield	11,957	12,774
Plainville	16,733	16,401
Plymouth	10,321	10,732
Portland	8,812	8,383
Prospect	6,543	6,807
Putnam	6,918	6,855
Redding	5,590	7,272
Ridgefield	18,188	20,120
Rocky Hill	11,103	14,559
Seymour	12,776	13,434
Shelton	27,165	31,314

Place	1970	1980
CONN.—Cont.		
Simsbury	17,475	21,161
Somers	6,893	8,473
Southbury	7,852	14,156
Southington	30,946	36,879
South Windsor	15,553	17,198
Stamford	108,798	102,453
Stratford	49,775	50,541
Suffield	8,634	9,294
Thomaston	6,233	6,276
Tolland	7,857	9,694
Torrington	31,952	30,987
Trumbull	31,394	32,989
Vernon	27,237	27,974
Wallingford	35,714	37,274
Waterbury	108,033	103,266
Watertown	18,610	19,489
Westbrook	3,820	5,216
West Hartford	68,031	61,301
West Haven	52,851	53,184
Weston	7,417	8,284
Westport	27,414	25,290
Wethersfield	26,662	26,013
Willimantic	14,402	14,652
Wilton	13,572	15,351
Windsor	22,502	25,204
Windsor Locks	15,080	12,190
Wolcott	12,495	13,008
Woodbridge	7,673	7,761
Woodbury	5,869	6,942
DELAWARE		
Dover (c.)	17,488	23,512
Elsmere	8,415	6,493
Milford	5,314	5,356
Newark	21,298	25,247
Seaford	5,537	5,256
Wilmington	80,386	70,195
DISTRICT OF COLUMBIA		
Washington	756,668	637,651
FLORIDA		
Altamonte Springs	4,391	22,028
Apopka	4,045	6,019
Arcadia	5,658	6,002
Atlantic Beach	6,132	7,847
Auburndale	5,386	6,501
Avon Park	6,712	8,026
Bartow	12,891	14,780
Belle Glade	15,949	16,535
Boca Raton	28,506	49,505
Boynton Beach	18,115	35,624
Bradenton	21,040	30,170
Brooksville	4,060	5,582
Callaway	3,240	7,154
Cape Canaveral	4,258	5,733
Cape Coral	...	32,103
Casselberry	9,438	15,247
Chattahoochee	7,944	5,332
Clearwater	52,074	85,450
Clermont	3,661	5,461
Clewiston	3,896	5,219
Cocoa	16,110	16,096
Cocoa Beach	9,952	10,926
Coconut Creek	1,359	6,288
Cooper City	2,535	10,140
Coral Gables	42,494	43,241
Coral Springs	1,489	37,349
Crestview	7,952	7,617
Dania	9,013	11,811
Davie	5,859	20,877
Daytona Beach	45,327	54,176
Deerfield Beach	16,662	39,193
De Funiak Springs	4,966	5,563
De Land	11,641	15,354
Delray Beach	19,915	34,325
Dunedin	17,639	30,203
Edgewater	3,348	6,726
Eustis	6,722	9,453
Fernandina Beach	6,955	7,224
Florida City	5,133	6,174
Fort Lauderdale	139,590	153,256
Fort Meade	4,374	5,546
Fort Myers	27,351	36,638
Fort Pierce	29,721	33,802
Fort Walton Beach	19,994	20,829
Gainesville	64,510	81,371
Greenacres	1,731	8,843
Gulf Breeze	4,190	5,478
Gulfport	9,976	11,180
Haines City	8,956	10,799
Hallandale	23,849	36,517
Hialeah	102,452	145,254
Holly Hill	8,191	9,953
Hollywood	106,873	117,188
Homestead	13,674	20,668
Indian Harbour Beach	5,371	5,967
Jacksonville	504,265	540,898
Jacksonville Beach	12,779	15,462
Jupiter	3,136	9,868
Key West	29,312	24,292
Kissimmee	7,119	15,487
Lake City	10,575	9,257
Lakeland	42,803	47,406
Lake Park	6,993	6,909
Lake Wales	8,240	8,466
Lake Worth	23,714	27,048
Lantana	7,126	8,048
Largo	24,230	58,977
Lauderdale Lakes	10,577	25,426
Lauderhill	8,465	37,271
Leesburg	11,869	13,191
Lighthouse Point	9,071	11,488
Live Oak	6,830	6,732
Longwood	3,203	10,029
Lynn Haven	4,044	6,239
Maitland	7,157	8,763
Margate	8,867	36,044
Marianna	7,282	7,074
Melbourne	40,236	46,536
Miami	334,859	346,931
Miami Beach	87,072	96,298
Miami Shores	9,425	9,244
Miami Springs	13,279	12,350
Milton	5,360	7,206
Miramar	23,997	32,813
Mount Dora	4,646	5,883
Naples	12,042	17,581
New Port Richey	6,098	11,196
New Smyrna Beach	10,580	13,557

Place	1970	1980
FLA.—Cont.		
Niceville	4,155	8,543
North Lauderdale	1,213	18,479
North Miami	34,767	42,566
North Miami Beach	30,544	36,481
North Palm Beach	9,035	11,344
North Port	2,244	6,205
Oakland Park	16,261	21,939
Ocala	22,583	37,170
Ocoee	3,937	7,803
Opa-ocka	11,902	14,460
Orange Park	5,019	8,766
Orlando	99,006	128,394
Ormond Beach	14,063	21,378
Pahokee	5,663	6,346
Palatka	9,444	10,175
Palm Bay	7,176	18,560
Palm Beach	9,086	9,729
Palm Beach Gardens	6,102	14,407
Palmetto	7,422	8,637
Palm Springs	4,340	8,166
Panama City	32,096	33,346
Pembroke Pines	15,496	35,776
Pensacola	59,507	57,619
Perry	7,701	8,251
Pinellas Park	22,287	32,811
Plantation	23,523	48,501
Plant City	15,451	19,270
Pompano Beach	38,587	52,618
Port Orange	3,781	18,756
Port St. Lucie	330	14,690
Punta Gorda	3,879	6,797
Quincy	8,334	8,591
Riviera Beach	21,401	26,596
Rockledge	10,523	11,877
Safety Harbor	3,103	6,461
St. Augustine	12,352	11,985
St. Cloud	5,041	7,840
St. Petersburg	216,159	236,893
St. Petersburg Beach	8,024	9,354
Sanford	17,393	23,176
Sarasota	40,237	48,868
Satellite Beach	6,558	9,163
Sebring	7,223	8,736
South Daytona	4,979	9,608
South Miami	11,780	10,884
Springfield	5,949	7,220
Starke	4,848	5,306
Stuart	4,820	9,467
Sunrise	7,403	39,681
Sweetwater	3,357	8,251
Tallahassee (c.)	72,624	81,548
Tamarac	5,193	29,142
Tampa	277,714	271,523
Tarpon Springs	7,118	13,251
Temple Terrace	7,347	11,097
Titusville	30,515	31,910
Treasure Island	6,120	6,316
Valparaiso	6,504	6,142
Venice	6,648	12,153
Vero Beach	11,908	16,176
West Melbourne	3,050	5,078
West Miami	5,494	6,076
West Palm Beach	57,375	62,530
Wilton Manors	10,948	12,742
Winter Garden	5,153	6,789
Winter Haven	16,136	21,119
Winter Park	21,895	22,314
Winter Springs	...	10,475
Zephyrhills	3,369	5,742
GEORGIA		
Adel	4,972	5,592
Albany	72,623	73,934
Americus	16,091	16,120
Athens	44,342	42,549
Atlanta (c.)	495,039	425,022
Augusta	59,864	47,532
Bainbridge	10,887	10,553
Blakely	5,267	5,880
Brunswick	19,585	17,605
Buford	4,640	6,697
Cairo	8,061	8,777
Calhoun	4,748	5,335
Camilla	4,987	5,414
Carrollton	13,520	14,078
Cartersville	10,138	9,508
Cedartown	9,253	8,619
Chamblee	9,127	7,137
Cochran	5,161	5,121
College Park	18,203	24,632
Columbus	155,028	169,441
Conyers	4,890	6,567
Cordele	10,733	10,914
Covington	10,267	10,586
Dalton	18,872	20,743
Dawson	5,383	5,699
Decatur	21,943	18,404
Doraville	9,157	7,414
Douglas	10,195	10,980
Douglasville	5,472	7,641
Dublin	15,143	16,083
Eastman	5,416	5,330
East Point	39,315	37,486
Elberton	6,438	5,686
Fitzgerald	8,187	10,187
Forest Park	19,994	18,782
Fort Oglethorpe	3,869	5,443
Fort Valley	9,251	9,000
Gainesville	15,459	15,280
Garden City	5,790	6,895
Griffin	22,734	20,728
Hapeville	9,567	6,166
Hinesville	4,115	11,309
Jesup	9,091	9,418
Kennesaw	3,548	5,095
La Fayette	6,044	6,517
La Grange	23,301	24,204
Lawrenceville	5,207	8,928
Macon	122,423	116,860
Marietta	27,216	30,805
Milledgeville	11,601	12,176
Monroe	8,071	8,854
Moultrie	14,400	15,708
Newnan	11,205	11,449
Peachtree City	793	6,429
Perry	7,771	9,453
Quitman	4,818	5,188
Riverdale	2,521	7,121
Rome	30,759	29,654
Roswell	5,430	23,337

Place	1970	1980
GA.—Cont.		
Sandersville	5,546	6,137
Savannah	118,349	141,634
Smyrna	19,157	20,312
Snellville	1,990	8,514
Statesboro	14,616	14,866
Swainsboro	7,325	7,602
Sylvester	4,226	5,860
Thomaston	10,024	9,682
Thomasville	18,155	18,463
Thomson	6,503	7,001
Tifton	12,179	13,749
Toccoa	6,971	9,104
Valdosta	32,303	37,596
Vidalia	9,507	10,393
Warner Robins	33,491	39,893
Waycross	18,996	19,371
Waynesboro	5,530	5,760
Winder	6,605	6,705
HAWAII		
Honolulu (c.)	324,871	364,048
Hawaii has no incorporated places. The city of Honolulu is coextensive with the county of Honolulu.		
IDAHO		
Blackfoot	8,716	10,065
Boise City (c.)	74,990	102,451
Burley	8,279	8,761
Caldwell	14,219	17,699
Chubbuck	2,924	7,052
Coeur d'Alene	16,228	20,054
Idaho Falls	35,776	39,590
Jerome	4,183	6,891
Lewiston	26,068	27,986
Meridian	2,616	6,658
Moscow	14,146	16,513
Mountain Home	6,451	7,540
Nampa	20,768	25,112
Payette	4,521	5,448
Pocatello	40,036	46,340
Post Falls	2,371	5,736
Rexburg	8,272	11,559
Rupert	4,563	5,476
Twin Falls	21,914	26,209
ILLINOIS		
Addison	24,482	28,836
Algonquin	3,515	5,834
Alsip	11,608	17,134
Alton	39,700	34,171
Anna	4,766	5,408
Arlington Heights	65,058	66,116
Aurora	74,389	81,293
Barrington	8,581	9,029
Bartlett	3,501	13,254
Bartonville	7,221	6,110
Batavia	9,060	12,574
Beardstown	6,222	6,338
Belleville	41,223	42,150
Bellwood	22,096	19,811
Belvidere	14,061	15,176
Bensenville	12,956	16,124
Benton	6,833	7,778
Berkeley	6,152	5,467
Berwyn	52,502	46,849
Bethalto	7,074	8,630
Bloomingdale	2,974	12,659
Bloomington	39,992	44,189
Blue Island	22,629	21,855
Bolingbrook	7,651	37,261
Bourbonnais	5,909	13,280
Bradley	9,881	11,008
Bridge View	12,506	14,155
Broadview	9,623	8,618
Brookfield	20,284	19,395
Buffalo Grove	12,333	22,230
Burbank	...	28,462
Cahokia	20,649	18,904
Cairo	6,277	5,931
Calumet City	33,107	39,673
Calumet Park	10,069	8,788
Canton	14,217	14,626
Carbondale	22,816	27,194
Carlinville	5,675	5,439
Carmi	6,033	6,264
Carol Stream	4,434	15,472
Carpentersville	24,059	23,272
Cary	4,358	6,640
Centralia	15,966	15,126
Centreville	11,378	9,747
Champaign	56,837	58,133
Charleston	16,421	19,355
Chatham	2,788	5,597
Chester	5,310	8,027
Chicago	3,369,357	3,005,072
Chicago Heights	40,900	37,026
Chicago Ridge	9,187	13,473
Chillicothe	6,052	6,176
Cicero	67,058	61,232
Clarendon Hills	6,750	6,857
Clinton	7,581	8,014
Collinsville	18,224	19,613
Country Club Hills	6,920	14,676
Countryside	2,864	6,538
Crest Hill	7,460	9,252
Crestwood	5,770	10,712
Crete	4,656	5,417
Creve Coeur	6,440	6,851
Crystal Lake	14,541	18,590
Danville	42,570	38,985
Darien	7,789	14,968
Decatur	90,397	94,081
Deerfield	18,876	17,430
De Kalb	32,949	33,099
Des Plaines	57,239	53,568
Dixon	18,147	15,659
Dolton	25,990	24,766
Downers Grove	32,544	39,274
Du Quoin	6,691	6,594
East Alton	7,309	7,123
East Chicago Heights	5,000	5,347
East Moline	20,956	20,907
East Peoria	18,671	22,385
East St. Louis	70,169	55,200
Edwardsville	11,070	12,460
Effingham	9,458	11,270

Place	1970	1980
ILL.—Cont.		
Eldorado	3,876	5,198
Elgin	55,691	63,798
Elk Grove Village	20,346	28,907
Elmhurst	46,392	44,251
Elmwood Park	26,160	24,016
Evanston	80,113	73,706
Evergreen Park	25,921	22,260
Fairfield	5,897	5,954
Fairview Heights	10,050	12,414
Flora	5,283	5,379
Flossmoor	7,846	8,423
Forest Park	15,472	15,177
Fox Lake	4,511	6,831
Franklin Park	20,348	17,507
Freeport	27,736	26,406
Galesburg	36,290	35,305
Geneseo	5,840	6,373
Geneva	9,049	9,881
Glen Carbon	1,897	5,197
Glencoe	10,542	9,200
Glendale Heights	11,406	23,163
Glen Ellyn	21,909	23,649
Glenview	24,880	30,842
Glenwood	7,416	10,538
Granite City	40,685	36,815
Grays Lake	4,907	5,260
Greenville	4,631	5,271
Gurnee	2,738	7,179
Hanover Park	11,735	28,850
Harrisburg	9,535	9,322
Harvard	5,177	5,126
Harvey	34,636	35,810
Harwood Heights	9,060	8,228
Hazel Crest	10,329	13,973
Herrin	9,623	10,040
Hickory Hills	13,176	13,778
Highland	5,981	7,122
Highland Park	32,263	30,611
Highwood	4,973	5,452
Hillside	8,888	8,279
Hinsdale	15,918	16,726
Hoffman Estates	22,238	38,258
Hometown	6,729	5,324
Homewood	18,871	19,724
Hoopeston	6,461	6,411
Itasca	4,638	7,948
Jacksonville	20,553	20,284
Jerseyville	7,446	7,506
Joliet	78,827	77,956
Justice	9,473	10,552
Kankakee	30,944	30,141
Kewanee	15,762	14,508
La Grange	17,814	15,681
La Grange Park	15,459	13,359
Lake Forest	15,642	15,245
Lake in the Hills	3,240	5,651
Lake Zurich	4,082	8,225
Lansing	25,805	29,039
La Salle	10,736	10,347
Lawrenceville	5,863	5,652
Lemont	5,080	5,640
Libertyville	11,684	16,520
Lincoln	17,582	16,327
Lincolnwood	12,929	11,921
Lindenburst	3,141	6,220
Lisle	5,329	13,625
Litchfield	7,190	7,204
Lockport	9,861	9,017
Lombard	34,043	37,295
Loves Park	12,390	13,192
Lyons	11,124	9,925
McHenry	6,772	10,908
Macomb	19,643	19,632
Madison	7,042	5,915
Marion	11,724	14,031
Markham	15,987	15,172
Matteson	4,741	10,223
Mattoon	19,681	19,787
Maywood	29,019	27,998
Melrose Park	22,716	20,735
Mendota	6,902	7,134
Metropolis	6,940	7,171
Midlothian	14,422	14,274
Milan	4,873	6,264
Moline	46,237	45,709
Monmouth	11,022	10,706
Morris	8,194	8,833
Morton	10,811	14,178
Morton Grove	26,369	23,747
Mount Carmel	8,096	8,908
Mount Prospect	34,995	52,634
Mount Vernon	16,270	16,995
Mundelein	16,128	17,053
Murphysboro	10,013	9,866
Naperville	22,794	42,330
New Lenox	2,855	5,792
Niles	31,432	30,363
Normal	26,396	35,672
Norridge	17,113	16,483
North Aurora	4,833	5,205
Northbrook	25,422	30,735
North Chicago	47,275	38,774
Northfield	5,010	5,807
Northlake	14,191	12,166
North Riverside	8,097	6,764
Oak Brook	4,164	6,641
Oak Forest	19,271	26,096
Oak Lawn	60,305	60,590
Oak Park	62,511	54,887
O'Fallon	7,268	10,217
Olney	8,974	9,026
Orland Park	6,391	23,045
Ottawa	18,716	18,166
Palatine	26,050	32,166
Palos Heights	8,544	11,096
Palos Hills	6,629	16,654
Pana	6,326	6,040
Paris	9,971	9,885
Park Forest	30,638	26,222
Park Forest South	1,748	6,245
Park Ridge	42,614	38,704
Pekin	31,375	33,967
Peoria	126,963	124,160
Peoria Heights	7,943	7,453
Peru	11,772	10,886
Pontiac	10,595	11,227
Princeton	6,959	7,342
Prospect Heights	...	11,808
Quincy	45,288	42,352
Rantoul	25,562	20,161
Richton Park	2,558	9,403
Riverdale	15,806	13,233
River Forest	13,402	12,392

Place	1970	1980
ILL.—Cont.		
River Grove	11,465	10,368
Riverside	10,357	9,236
Robbins	9,641	8,119
Robinson	7,178	7,285
Rochelle	8,594	8,982
Rock Falls	10,287	10,624
Rockford	147,370	139,712
Rock Island	50,166	47,036
Rolling Meadows	19,178	20,167
Romeoville	12,888	15,519
Roselle	6,207	16,948
Round Lake Beach	5,717	12,921
St. Charles	12,945	17,492
Salem	6,187	7,813
Sauk	7,479	10,906
Schaumburg	18,531	52,319
Schiller Park	12,712	11,458
Shelbyville	4,887	5,259
Silvis	5,907	7,130
Skokie	68,322	60,278
South Elgin	4,289	6,218
South Holland	23,931	24,977
Springfield (c.)	91,753	99,637
Spring Valley	5,605	5,822
Steger	8,104	9,269
Sterling	16,113	16,273
Stickney	6,601	5,893
Streamwood	18,176	23,456
Streator	15,600	14,769
Summit	11,569	10,110
Swansea	5,432	5,347
Sycamore	7,843	9,219
Taylorville	10,644	11,386
Tinley Park	12,572	26,171
Urbana	33,976	35,978
Vandalia	5,160	5,338
Vernon Hills	1,056	9,827
Villa Park	25,891	23,185
Warrenville	3,281	7,519
Washington	6,790	10,364
Washington Park	9,524	8,223
Watseka	5,294	5,543
Wauconda	5,460	5,688
Waukegan	65,134	67,653
Westchester	20,033	17,730
West Chicago	9,988	12,550
Western Springs	13,029	12,876
West Frankfort	8,854	9,437
Westmont	8,832	16,718
Wheaton	31,138	43,043
Wheeling	13,243	23,266
Wilmette	32,134	28,229
Winnetka	14,131	12,772
Winthrop Harbor	4,794	5,438
Wood Dale	8,831	11,251
Woodridge	11,028	22,322
Wood River	13,186	12,449
Woodstock	10,226	11,725
Worth	11,999	11,592
Zion	17,268	17,861
INDIANA		
Alexandria	5,600	6,028
Anderson	70,787	64,695
Angola	5,117	5,486
Auburn	7,388	8,122
Bedford	13,087	14,410
Beech Grove	13,559	13,196
Bloomington	43,262	51,646
Bluffton	8,297	8,705
Boonville	5,736	6,300
Brazil	8,163	7,852
Brownsburg	5,751	6,242
Carmel	6,691	18,272
Cedar Lake	7,589	8,754
Charlestown	5,933	5,596
Chesterton	6,177	8,531
Clarksville	13,298	15,164
Clinton	5,340	5,267
Columbia City	4,911	5,091
Columbus	26,457	30,292
Connersville	17,604	17,023
Crawfordsville	13,842	13,325
Crown Point	10,931	16,455
Decatur	8,445	8,649
Dyer	4,906	9,555
East Chicago	46,982	39,786
Elkhart	43,152	41,305
Elwood	11,196	10,867
Evansville	138,764	130,496
Fort Wayne	178,269	172,196
Frankfort	14,956	15,168
Franklin	11,477	11,563
Gary	175,415	151,953
Gas City	5,742	6,370
Goshen	17,871	19,665
Greencastle	8,852	8,403
Greenfield	9,986	11,439
Greensburg	8,620	9,254
Greenwood	11,869	19,327
Griffith	18,168	17,026
Hammond	107,983	93,714
Hartford City	8,207	7,622
Highland	24,947	25,935
Hobart	21,485	22,987
Huntingburg	4,794	5,376
Huntington	16,217	16,202
Indianapolis (c.)	736,856	700,807
Jasper	8,641	9,097
Jeffersonville	20,008	21,220
Kendallville	6,838	7,299
Kokomo	44,042	47,808
Lafayette	44,955	43,011
Lake Station	9,858	14,294
La Porte	22,140	21,796
Lawrence	16,353	25,591
Lebanon	9,766	11,456
Linton	5,450	6,315
Logansport	19,255	17,899
Lowell	3,839	5,827
Madison	13,081	12,472
Marion	39,607	35,874
Martinsville	9,723	11,311
Merrillville	...	27,677
Michigan City	39,369	36,850
Mishawaka	36,060	40,224
Monticello	4,869	5,162
Mooresville	5,800	5,349
Mount Vernon	6,770	7,656
Muncie	69,082	77,216
Munster	16,514	20,671
New Albany	38,402	37,103
New Castle	21,215	20,056

Place	1970	1980
IND.—Cont.		
New Haven	5,346	6,714
Noblesville	7,548	12,056
North Manchester	5,791	5,998
North Vernon	4,582	5,768
Peru	14,139	13,764
Plainfield	8,211	9,191
Plymouth	7,661	7,693
Portage	19,127	27,409
Portland	7,115	7,074
Princeton	7,431	8,976
Richmond	43,999	41,349
Rochester	4,631	5,050
Rushville	6,686	6,113
Salem	5,041	5,290
Schererville	3,663	13,209
Scottsburg	4,791	5,068
Seymour	13,352	15,050
Shelbyville	15,094	14,989
South Bend	125,580	109,727
Speedway	14,523	12,641
Tell City	7,933	8,704
Terre Haute	70,335	61,125
Tipton	5,313	5,004
Valparaiso	20,020	22,247
Vincennes	19,867	20,857
Wabash	13,379	12,985
Warsaw	7,506	10,647
Washington	11,358	11,325
West Lafayette	19,157	21,247
Whiting	7,054	5,630
Winchester	5,493	5,659
IOWA		
Algona	6,032	6,289
Altoona	2,883	5,764
Ames	39,505	45,775
Ankeny	9,151	15,429
Atlantic	7,306	7,789
Bettendorf	22,126	27,381
Boone	12,468	12,602
Burlington	32,366	29,529
Carroll	8,716	9,705
Cedar Falls	29,597	36,322
Cedar Rapids	110,642	110,243
Centerville	6,531	6,558
Charles City	9,268	8,778
Cherokee	7,272	7,004
Clarinda	5,420	5,458
Clear Lake City	6,430	7,458
Clinton	34,719	32,828
Clive	3,005	5,906
Coralville	6,130	7,687
Council Bluffs	60,348	56,449
Creston	8,234	8,429
Davenport	98,469	103,264
Decorah	7,237	7,991
Denison	6,218	6,675
Des Moines (c.)	200,404	191,003
Dubuque	62,309	62,321
Estherville	8,108	7,518
Fairfield	8,715	9,428
Fort Dodge	31,263	29,423
Fort Madison	13,996	13,520
Glenwood	4,421	5,280
Grinnell	8,402	8,868
Harlan	5,049	5,357
Independence	5,910	6,392
Indianola	8,852	10,843
Iowa City	46,850	50,508
Iowa Falls	6,454	6,174
Keokuk	14,631	13,536
Knoxville	7,755	8,143
Le Mars	8,159	8,276
Maquoketa	5,677	6,313
Marion	18,028	19,474
Marshalltown	26,219	26,938
Mason City	30,379	30,144
Mount Pleasant	7,007	7,322
Muscatine	22,405	23,467
Nevada	4,952	5,912
Newton	15,619	15,292
Oelwein	7,735	7,564
Oskaloosa	11,224	10,629
Ottumwa	29,610	27,381
Pella	6,668	8,349
Perry	6,906	7,053
Red Oak	6,210	6,810
Sheldon	4,535	5,003
Shenandoah	5,968	6,274
Sioux City	85,925	82,003
Spencer	10,278	11,726
Storm Lake	8,591	8,814
Urbandale	14,434	17,869
Vinton	4,845	5,040
Washington	6,317	6,584
Waterloo	75,533	75,985
Waverly	7,205	8,444
Webster City	8,488	8,572
West Des Moines	16,441	21,894
Windsor Heights	6,303	5,632
KANSAS		
Abilene	6,661	6,572
Arkansas City	13,216	13,201
Atchinson	12,565	11,407
Augusta	5,977	6,968
Bonner Springs	3,884	6,266
Chanute	10,341	10,506
Coffeyville	15,116	15,185
Colby	4,658	5,544
Concordia	7,221	6,847
Derby	7,947	9,786
Dodge City	14,127	18,001
El Dorado	12,308	10,510
Emporia	23,327	25,287
Fort Scott	8,967	8,893
Garden City	14,790	18,256
Goodland	5,510	5,708
Great Bend	16,133	16,608
Hays	15,396	16,301
Haysville	6,531	8,006
Hutchinson	36,885	40,284
Independence	10,347	10,598
Iola	6,493	6,938
Junction City	19,018	19,305
Kansas City	168,213	161,087
Lansing	3,797	5,307
Lawrence	45,698	52,738
Leavenworth	25,147	33,656
Leawood	10,645	13,360
Lenexa	5,549	18,639
Liberal	13,862	14,911
McPherson	10,851	11,753

Place	1970	1980
KAN.—Cont.		
Manhattan	27,575	32,644
Merriam	10,955	10,794
Mission	8,125	8,643
Newton	15,439	16,332
Olathe	17,917	37,258
Ottawa	11,036	11,016
Overland Park	77,934	81,784
Parsons	13,015	12,898
Pittsburg	20,171	18,770
Prairie Village	28,378	24,657
Pratt	6,736	6,885
Roeland Park	9,760	7,962
Russell	5,371	5,427
Salina	37,714	41,843
Shawnee	20,946	29,653
Topeka (c.)	125,011	115,266
Wellington	8,072	8,212
Wichita	276,554	279,272
Winfield	11,405	10,736
KENTUCKY		
Ashland	29,245	27,064
Bardstown	5,816	6,155
Bellevue	8,847	7,678
Berea	6,956	8,226
Bowling Green	36,705	40,450
Campbellsville	7,598	8,715
Central City	5,450	5,214
Corbin	7,474	8,075
Covington	52,535	49,013
Cynthiana	6,356	5,881
Danville	11,542	12,942
Dayton	8,751	6,979
Edgewood	4,139	7,230
Elizabethtown	11,748	15,380
Elsmere	5,161	7,203
Erlanger	12,676	14,433
Flatwoods	7,380	8,354
Florence	11,661	15,586
Fort Mitchell	6,982	7,297
Fort Thomas	16,338	16,012
Frankfort (c.)	21,902	25,973
Franklin	6,553	7,738
Georgetown	8,629	10,972
Glasgow	11,301	12,958
Harrodsburg	6,741	7,265
Hazard	5,459	5,429
Henderson	22,976	24,834
Hillview	...	5,196
Hopkinsville	21,395	27,318
Independence	1,715	7,998
Jeffersontown	9,701	15,795
Lawrenceburg	3,579	5,167
Lebanon	5,528	6,590
Lexington	108,137	204,165
Louisville	361,706	298,451
Madisonville	15,332	16,979
Mayfield	10,724	10,705
Maysville	7,411	7,983
Middlesborough	11,878	12,251
Monticello	3,618	5,677
Morehead	7,191	7,789
Mount Sterling	5,083	5,820
Murray	13,537	14,248
Newport	25,998	21,587
Nicholasville	5,829	10,400
Owensboro	50,329	54,450
Paducah	31,627	29,315
Paris	7,823	7,935
Princeton	6,292	7,073
Radcliff	8,426	14,519
Richmond	16,861	21,705
Russellville	6,456	7,520
St. Matthews	13,152	13,354
Shelbyville	4,182	5,308
Shively	19,139	16,819
Somerset	10,436	10,649
Versailles	5,679	6,427
Williamsburg	3,687	5,560
Winchester	13,402	15,216
LOUISIANA		
Abbeville	10,996	12,391
Alexandria	41,811	51,565
Baker	8,281	12,865
Bastrop	14,713	15,527
Baton Rouge (c.)	165,921	219,486
Bogalusa	18,412	16,976
Bossier City	43,769	49,969
Breaux Bridge	4,942	5,922
Bunkie	5,395	5,364
Covington	7,170	7,982
Crowley	16,104	16,036
Denham Springs	6,752	8,412
De Ridder	8,030	11,057
Donaldsonville	7,367	7,901
Eunice	11,390	12,479
Franklin	9,325	9,584
Gonzales	4,512	7,287
Gretna	24,875	20,615
Hammond	12,487	15,043
Harahan	13,037	11,384
Houma	30,922	32,602
Jeanerette	6,322	6,511
Jennings	11,783	12,401
Jonesboro	5,072	5,061
Kaplan	5,540	5,016
Kenner	29,858	66,382
Lafayette	68,908	81,961
Lake Charles	77,998	75,051
Lake Providence	6,183	6,361
Leesville	8,928	9,054
Mandeville	2,571	6,076
Mansfield	6,432	6,485
Marksville	4,519	5,113
Minden	13,996	15,074
Monroe	56,374	57,597
Morgan City	16,586	16,114
Natchitoches	15,974	16,664
New Iberia	30,147	32,766
New Orleans	593,471	557,482
Oakdale	7,301	7,155
Opelousas	20,387	18,903
Pineville	8,951	12,034
Plaquemine	7,739	7,521
Ponchatoula	4,545	5,469
Port Allen	5,728	6,114
Rayne	9,510	9,066
Ruston	17,365	20,585
St. Martinville	7,153	7,965
Shreveport	182,064	205,815
Slidell	16,101	26,718
Springhill	6,496	6,516

Place	1970	1980
LA.—Cont.		
Sulphur	14,959	19,709
Tallulah	9,643	10,392
Thibodaux	15,028	15,810
Vidalia	5,538	5,936
Ville Platte	9,692	9,201
Westlake	4,082	5,246
West Monroe	14,868	14,993
Westwego	11,402	12,663
Winnfield	7,142	7,311
Winnsboro	5,349	5,921
Zachary	4,964	7,297
MAINE		
Auburn	24,151	23,128
Augusta (c.)	21,945	21,819
Bangor	33,168	31,643
Bath	9,679	10,246
Belfast	5,957	6,243
Biddeford	19,983	19,638
Brewer	9,300	9,017
Brunswick	16,195	17,366
Cape Elizabeth	7,873	7,838
Caribou	10,419	9,916
Ellsworth	4,603	5,179
Fairfield	5,684	6,113
Farmington	5,657	6,730
Freeport	4,781	5,863
Gardiner	6,685	6,485
Gorham	7,839	10,101
Hampden	4,693	5,250
Houlton	8,111	6,766
Kennebunk	5,646	6,621
Kittery	11,028	9,314
Lewiston	41,779	40,481
Limestone	10,360	8,719
Lincoln	4,759	5,066
Lisbon	6,544	8,769
Madawaska	5,585	5,282
Millinocket	7,742	7,567
Oakland	3,535	5,162
Old Orchard Beach	5,404	6,291
Old Town	8,741	8,422
Orono	9,989	10,578
Portland	65,116	61,572
Presque Isle	11,452	11,172
Rockland	8,505	7,919
Rumford	9,363	8,240
Saco	11,678	12,921
Sanford	15,812	18,020
Scarborough	7,845	11,347
Skowhegan	7,601	8,098
South Portland	23,267	22,712
Topsham	5,022	6,431
Waterville	18,192	17,779
Westbrook	14,444	14,976
Windham	6,593	11,282
Winslow	7,299	8,057
Winthrop	4,335	5,889
Yarmouth	4,854	6,585
York	5,690	8,465
MARYLAND		
Aberdeen	7,403	11,533
Annapolis (c.)	30,095	31,740
Baltimore	905,787	786,775
Bel Air	6,307	7,814
Bladensburg	7,977	7,691
Bowie	35,028	33,695
Cambridge	11,595	11,703
Cheverly	6,808	5,751
College Park	26,156	23,614
Cumberland	29,724	25,933
District Heights	7,846	6,799
Easton	6,809	7,536
Elkton	5,362	6,468
Frederick	23,641	27,557
Frostburg	7,327	7,715
Gaithersburg	8,344	26,424
Greenbelt	18,199	16,000
Hagerstown	35,862	34,132
Havre de Grace	9,791	8,763
Hyattsville	14,998	12,709
Laurel	10,525	12,103
Mount Rainier	8,180	7,361
New Carrollton	14,870	12,632
Rockville	42,739	43,811
Salisbury	15,252	16,429
Seat Pleasant	7,217	5,217
Takoma Park	18,507	16,231
Westminster	7,207	8,808
MASSACHUSETTS		
Abington	12,334	13,517
Acton	14,770	17,544
Acushnet	7,767	8,704
Adams	11,772	10,381
Agawam	21,717	26,271
Amesbury	11,388	13,971
Amherst	26,331	33,229
Andover	23,695	26,370
Arlington	53,524	48,219
Ashland	8,882	9,165
Athol	11,185	10,634
Attleboro	32,907	34,196
Auburn	15,347	14,845
Avon	5,295	5,026
Ayer	8,325	6,993
Bedford	13,513	13,067
Belchertown	5,936	8,339
Bellingham	13,967	14,300
Belmont	28,285	26,100
Beverly	38,348	37,655
Blackstone	6,566	6,570
Boston (c.)	641,071	562,994
Bourne	12,636	13,874
Boxford	4,032	5,374
Braintree	35,050	36,337
Bridgewater	12,911	17,202
Brockton	89,040	95,172
Brookline	58,689	55,062
Burlington	21,980	23,486
Cambridge	100,361	95,322
Canton	17,100	18,182
Chatham	4,554	6,071
Chelmsford	31,432	31,174
Chelsea	30,625	25,431
Chicopee	66,676	55,112
Clinton	13,383	12,771
Cohasset	6,954	7,174
Concord	16,148	16,293
Dalton	7,505	6,797
Danvers	26,151	24,100
Dartmouth	18,800	23,966

Place	1970	1980
MASS.—Cont.		
Dedham	26,938	25,298
Dracut	18,214	21,249
Duxbury	7,636	11,807
East Bridgewater	8,347	9,945
Easthampton	13,012	15,580
East Longmeadow	13,029	12,905
Easton	12,157	16,623
Everett	42,485	37,195
Fairhaven	16,332	15,759
Fall River	96,898	92,574
Falmouth	15,942	23,640
Fitchburg	43,343	39,580
Foxborough	14,218	14,148
Framingham	64,048	65,113
Franklin	17,830	18,217
Gardner	19,748	17,900
Georgetown	5,290	5,687
Gloucester	27,941	27,768
Grafton	11,659	11,238
Granby	5,473	5,380
Great Barrington	7,537	7,405
Greenfield	18,116	18,436
Hamilton	6,373	6,960
Hanover	10,107	11,358
Hanson	7,148	8,617
Harwich	5,892	8,971
Haverhill	46,120	46,865
Hingham	18,845	20,339
Holbrook	11,775	11,140
Holden	12,564	13,336
Holliston	12,069	12,622
Holyoke	50,112	44,678
Hopkinton	5,981	7,114
Hudson	16,084	16,408
Hull	9,961	9,714
Ipswich	10,750	11,158
Kingston	5,999	7,362
Lawrence	66,915	63,175
Lee	6,426	6,247
Leicester	9,140	9,446
Lenox	5,804	6,523
Leominster	32,939	34,508
Lexington	31,886	29,479
Lincoln	7,567	7,098
Longmeadow	15,630	16,301
Lowell	94,239	92,418
Ludlow	17,580	18,150
Lynn	90,294	78,471
Lynnfield	10,826	11,267
Malden	56,127	53,386
Manchester	5,151	5,424
Mansfield	9,939	13,453
Marblehead	21,295	20,126
Marlborough	27,936	30,617
Marshfield	15,223	20,916
Mattapoisett	4,500	5,597
Maynard	9,710	9,590
Medfield	9,821	10,220
Medford	64,397	58,076
Medway	7,938	8,447
Melrose	33,180	30,055
Methuen	35,456	36,701
Middleborough	13,607	16,404
Milford	19,352	23,390
Millbury	11,987	11,808
Milton	27,190	25,860
Monson	7,355	7,315
Nantucket	3,774	5,087
Natick	31,057	29,461
Needham	29,748	27,901
New Bedford	101,777	98,478
Newburyport	15,807	15,900
Newton	91,263	83,622
North Adams	19,195	18,063
Northampton	29,664	29,286
North Andover	16,284	20,129
North Attleborough	18,665	21,095
Northborough	9,218	10,568
Northbridge	11,795	12,246
North Reading	11,264	11,455
Norton	9,487	12,690
Norwell	7,796	9,182
Norwood	30,815	29,711
Orange	6,104	6,884
Oxford	10,345	11,680
Palmer	11,680	11,389
Peabody	48,080	45,976
Pepperell	5,887	8,061
Pittsfield	57,020	51,974
Plymouth	18,606	35,913
Quincy	87,966	84,743
Randolph	27,035	28,218
Raynham	6,705	9,085
Reading	22,539	22,678
Rehoboth	6,512	7,570
Revere	43,159	42,423
Rockland	15,674	15,695
Rockport	5,636	6,345
Salem	40,556	38,220
Salisbury	4,179	5,973
Saugus	25,110	24,746
Scituate	16,973	17,317
Seekonk	11,116	12,269
Sharon	12,367	13,601
Shirley	4,909	5,124
Shrewsbury	19,196	22,674
Somerset	18,088	18,813
Somerville	88,779	77,372
Southborough	5,798	6,193
Southbridge	17,057	16,665
South Hadley	17,033	16,399
Southwick	6,330	7,382
Spencer	8,779	10,774
Springfield	163,905	152,319
Stoneham	20,725	21,424
Stoughton	23,459	26,710
Sudbury	13,506	14,027
Swampscott	13,578	13,837
Swansea	12,640	15,461
Taunton	43,756	45,001
Tewksbury	22,755	24,635
Topsfield	5,225	5,709
Uxbridge	8,253	8,374
Wakefield	25,402	24,895
Walpole	18,149	18,859
Waltham	61,582	58,200
Ware	8,187	8,953
Watertown	39,307	34,384
Wayland	13,461	12,170
Webster	14,917	14,480
Wellesley	28,051	27,209
Westborough	12,594	13,619

Place	1970	1980
MASS.—Cont.		
West Boylston	6,369	6,204
West Bridgewater	6,070	6,359
Westfield	31,433	36,465
Westford	10,368	13,434
Weston	10,870	11,169
Westport	9,791	13,763
West Springfield	28,461	27,042
Westwood	12,750	13,212
Weymouth	54,610	55,601
Whitman	13,059	13,534
Wilbraham	11,984	12,053
Williamstown	8,454	8,741
Wilmington	17,102	17,471
Winchendon	6,635	7,019
Winchester	22,269	20,701
Winthrop	20,335	19,294
Woburn	37,406	36,626
Worcester	176,572	161,799
Wrentham	7,315	7,580
MICHIGAN		
Adrian	20,382	21,186
Albion	12,112	11,059
Allen Park	40,747	34,196
Alma	9,611	9,652
Alpena	13,805	12,214
Ann Arbor	100,035	107,316
Battle Creek	38,931	35,724
Bay City	49,449	41,593
Belding	5,121	5,634
Benton Harbor	16,481	14,707
Berkley	21,879	18,637
Beverly Hills	13,598	11,598
Big Rapids	11,995	14,361
Birmingham	26,170	21,689
Buchanan	4,645	5,142
Burton	...	29,976
Cadillac	9,990	10,199
Center Line	10,379	9,293
Charlotte	8,244	8,251
Cheboygan	5,553	5,106
Clawson	17,617	15,103
Coldwater	9,155	9,461
Davison	5,259	6,087
Dearborn	104,199	90,660
Dearborn Heights	80,069	67,706
Detroit	1,514,063	1,203,339
Dowagiac	6,583	6,307
East Detroit	45,920	38,280
East Grand Rapids	12,565	10,914
East Lansing	47,540	48,309
Ecorse	17,515	14,447
Escanaba	15,368	14,355
Farmington	10,329	11,022
Farmington Hills	...	58,056
Fenton	8,284	8,098
Ferndale	30,850	26,227
Flat Rock	5,643	6,853
Flint	193,317	159,611
Flushing	7,190	8,624
Fraser	11,868	14,560
Garden City	41,864	35,640
Grand Blanc	5,132	6,848
Grand Haven	11,844	11,763
Grand Ledge	6,032	6,920
Grand Rapids	197,649	181,843
Grandville	10,764	12,412
Greenville	7,493	8,019
Grosse Pointe	6,637	5,901
Grosse Pointe Farms	11,701	10,551
Grosse Pointe Park	15,641	13,639
Grosse Pointe Woods	21,878	18,886
Hamtramck	26,783	21,300
Hancock	4,820	5,122
Harper Woods	20,186	16,361
Hastings	6,501	6,418
Hazel Park	23,784	20,914
Highland Park	35,444	27,909
Hillsdale	7,728	7,432
Holland	26,479	26,281
Houghton	6,067	7,512
Howell	5,224	6,976
Huntington Woods	8,536	6,937
Inkster	38,595	35,190
Ionia	6,361	5,920
Iron Mountain	8,702	8,341
Ironwood	8,711	7,741
Ishpeming	8,245	7,538
Jackson	45,484	39,739
Kalamazoo	85,555	79,722
Kentwood	20,310	30,438
Kingsford	5,276	5,290
Lansing (c.)	131,403	130,414
Lapeer	6,314	6,225
Lincoln Park	52,984	45,105
Livonia	110,109	104,814
Ludington	9,021	8,937
Madison Heights	38,599	35,375
Manistee	7,723	7,566
Marquette	21,967	23,288
Marshall	7,253	7,201
Marysville	5,610	7,345
Mason	5,468	6,019
Melvindale	13,862	12,322
Menominee	10,748	10,099
Midland	35,176	37,250
Milford	4,699	5,041
Monroe	23,894	23,531
Mount Clemens	20,476	18,806
Mount Pleasant	20,524	23,746
Muskegon	44,631	40,823
Muskegon Heights	17,304	14,611
Negaunee	5,248	5,189
New Baltimore	4,132	5,439
Niles	12,988	13,115
Northville	5,400	5,698
Norton Shores	22,271	22,025
Novi	9,668	22,525
Oak Park	36,762	31,537
Owosso	17,179	16,455
Petoskey	6,342	6,097
Plymouth	11,758	9,986
Pontiac	85,279	76,715
Portage	33,590	38,157
Port Huron	35,794	33,981
River Rouge	15,947	12,912
Riverview	11,342	14,569
Rochester	7,054	7,203
Romulus	...	24,857
Roseville	60,529	54,311
Royal Oak	86,238	70,893

Place	1970	1980
MICH.—Cont.		
Saginaw	91,849	77,508
St. Clair Shores	88,093	76,210
St. Johns	6,672	7,376
St. Joseph	11,042	9,622
Saline	4,811	6,483
Sault Ste. Marie	15,136	14,448
Southfield	69,285	75,568
Southgate	33,909	32,058
South Haven	6,471	5,943
South Lyon	2,675	5,214
Springfield	3,994	5,917
Sterling Heights	61,365	108,999
Sturgis	9,295	9,468
Swartz Creek	4,928	5,013
Taylor	70,020	77,568
Tecumseh	7,120	7,320
Three Rivers	7,355	7,015
Traverse City	18,048	15,516
Trenton	24,127	22,762
Troy	39,419	67,102
Utica	3,504	5,282
Walker	11,492	15,088
Warren	179,260	161,134
Wayne	21,054	21,159
Westland	86,749	84,603
Wixom	2,010	6,705
Woodhaven	3,566	10,902
Wyandotte	41,061	34,006
Wyoming	56,560	59,616
Ypsilanti	29,538	24,031
MINNESOTA		
Albert Lea	19,418	19,190
Alexandria	6,973	7,608
Andover	...	9,387
Anoka	13,298	15,634
Apple Valley	8,502	21,818
Arden Hills	5,149	8,012
Austin	26,210	23,020
Bemidji	11,490	10,949
Blaine	20,573	28,558
Bloomington	81,970	81,831
Brainerd	11,667	11,489
Brooklyn Center	35,173	31,230
Brooklyn Park	26,230	43,332
Burnsville	19,940	35,674
Champlin	2,275	9,006
Chanhassen	4,879	6,359
Chaska	4,352	8,346
Chisholm	5,913	5,930
Cloquet	8,699	11,142
Columbia Heights	23,997	20,029
Coon Rapids	30,505	35,826
Cottage Grove	13,419	18,994
Crookston	8,312	8,628
Crystal	30,925	25,543
Detroit Lakes	5,797	7,106
Duluth	100,578	92,811
Eagan	...	20,532
East Bethel	2,586	6,626
East Grand Forks	7,607	8,537
Eden Prairie	6,938	16,263
Edina	44,046	46,073
Elk River	2,252	6,785
Eveleth	4,721	5,042
Fairmont	10,751	11,506
Falcon Heights	5,530	5,291
Faribault	16,595	16,241
Fergus Falls	12,443	12,519
Fridley	29,233	30,228
Golden Valley	24,246	22,775
Grand Rapids	7,247	7,934
Ham Lake	...	7,832
Hastings	12,195	12,827
Hermantown	...	6,759
Hibbing	16,104	21,193
Hopkins	13,428	15,336
Hutchinson	8,031	9,244
International Falls	6,439	5,611
Inver Grove Heights	12,148	17,171
Lake Elmo	3,565	5,296
Lakeville	7,556	14,790
Litchfield	5,262	5,904
Little Canada	3,481	7,102
Little Falls	7,467	7,250
Mankato	30,895	28,651
Maple Grove	6,275	20,525
Maplewood	25,186	26,990
Marshall	9,886	11,161
Mendota Heights	6,565	7,288
Minneapolis	434,400	370,951
Minnetonka	35,776	38,683
Montevideo	5,661	5,845
Moorhead	29,687	29,998
Morris	5,366	5,367
Mound	7,572	9,280
Mounds View	10,599	12,593
New Brighton	19,507	23,269
New Hope	23,180	23,087
New Ulm	13,051	13,755
Northfield	10,235	12,562
North Mankato	7,347	9,145
North St. Paul	11,950	11,921
Oakdale	7,795	12,123
Orono	6,787	6,845
Owatonna	15,341	18,632
Plymouth	18,077	31,615
Prior Lake	1,114	7,284
Ramsey	...	10,093
Red Wing	10,441	13,736
Redwood Falls	4,774	5,210
Richfield	47,231	37,851
Robbinsdale	16,845	14,422
Rochester	53,766	57,855
Rosemount	1,337	5,083
Roseville	34,438	35,820
St. Anthony	9,239	7,981
St. Cloud	39,691	42,566
St. Louis Park	48,883	42,931
St. Paul (c.)	309,866	270,230
St. Peter	8,339	9,056
Sauk Rapids	5,051	5,793
Shakopee	6,876	9,941
Shoreview	10,978	17,300
South St. Paul	25,016	21,235
Spring Lake Park	6,417	6,477
Stillwater	10,191	12,290
Thief River Falls	8,618	9,105
Vadnais Heights	3,411	5,111
Virginia	12,450	11,056
Waseca	6,789	8,219
West St. Paul	18,802	18,527

Place	1970	1980
MINN.—Cont.		
White Bear Lake	23,313	22,538
Willmar	12,869	15,895
Winona	26,438	25,075
Woodbury	6,184	10,297
Worthington	9,916	10,243
MISSISSIPPI		
Aberdeen	6,507	7,184
Amory	7,236	7,307
Bay St. Louis	6,752	7,891
Biloxi	48,486	49,311
Booneville	5,895	6,199
Brandon	2,685	9,626
Brookhaven	10,700	10,800
Canton	10,503	11,116
Clarksdale	21,673	21,137
Cleveland	13,327	14,524
Clinton	7,289	14,660
Columbia	7,587	7,733
Columbus	25,795	27,383
Corinth	11,581	13,839
Forest	4,085	5,229
Greenville	39,648	40,613
Greenwood	22,400	20,115
Grenada	9,944	12,641
Gulfport	40,791	39,676
Hattiesburg	38,277	40,829
Holly Springs	5,728	7,285
Indianola	8,947	8,221
Jackson (c.)	153,968	202,895
Kosciusko	7,266	7,415
Laurel	24,145	21,897
Leland	6,000	6,667
Long Beach	6,170	7,967
Louisville	6,626	7,323
McComb	11,851	12,331
Meridian	45,083	46,577
Moss Point	19,321	18,998
Natchez	19,704	22,015
New Albany	6,426	7,072
Ocean Springs	19,160	14,504
Oxford	8,519	9,882
Pascagoula	27,264	29,318
Pass Christian	2,979	5,014
Pearl	...	20,778
Petal	...	8,476
Philadelphia	6,274	6,434
Picayune	9,760	10,361
Ridgeland	1,650	5,461
Senatobia	4,247	5,013
Starkville	11,369	15,169
Tupelo	20,471	23,905
Vicksburg	25,478	25,434
Waynesboro	4,368	5,349
West Point	8,714	8,811
Winona	5,521	6,177
Yazoo City	11,688	12,426
MISSOURI		
Arnold	...	19,141
Aurora	5,359	6,437
Ballwin	10,656	12,750
Bellefontaine Neighbors	14,084	12,082
Belton	12,270	12,708
Berkeley	19,743	16,146
Black Jack	...	5,293
Blue Springs	6,779	25,927
Bolivar	4,769	5,919
Boonville	7,514	6,959
Breckenridge Hills	7,011	5,666
Brentwood	11,248	8,209
Bridgeton	19,992	18,445
Brookfield	5,491	5,555
Cape Girardeau	31,282	34,361
Carthage	11,035	11,104
Caruthersville	7,350	7,958
Charleston	5,131	5,230
Chillicothe	9,519	9,089
Clayton	16,100	14,219
Clinton	7,504	8,366
Columbia	58,812	62,061
Crestwood	15,123	12,815
Creve Coeur	8,967	12,694
Dellwood	7,137	6,200
De Soto	5,984	5,993
Des Peres	5,333	8,254
Dexter	6,024	7,043
Ellisville	4,681	6,233
Excelsior Springs	9,411	10,424
Farmington	6,590	8,270
Ferguson	28,759	24,740
Festus	7,530	7,574
Florissant	65,908	55,372
Fulton	12,248	11,046
Gladstone	23,422	24,990
Glendale	6,981	6,035
Grandview	17,456	24,502
Hannibal	18,609	18,811
Harrisonville	5,052	6,372
Hazelwood	14,082	12,935
Independence	111,630	111,806
Jackson	5,896	7,827
Jefferson City (c.)	32,407	33,619
Jennings	19,379	17,026
Joplin	39,256	38,893
Kansas City	507,330	448,159
Kennett	10,090	10,145
Kirksville	15,560	17,167
Kirkwood	31,679	27,987
Ladue	10,306	9,376
Lebanon	8,616	9,507
Lee's Summit	16,230	28,741
Lexington	5,388	5,063
Liberty	13,704	16,251
Macon	5,301	5,680
Malden	5,374	6,096
Manchester	5,031	6,191
Maplewood	12,785	10,960
Marshall	12,051	12,781
Maryville	9,970	9,558
Mexico	11,807	12,276
Moberly	12,988	13,418
Monett	5,937	6,148
Neosho	7,517	9,493
Nevada	9,736	9,044
Normandy	6,236	5,174
Northwoods	4,607	5,831
O'Fallon	7,018	8,654
Olivette	9,156	8,039
Overland	24,819	19,620
Perryville	5,149	7,343
Pine Lawn	5,745	6,662

Place	1970	1980
MO.—Cont.		
Poplar Bluff	16,653	17,139
Raytown	33,306	31,759
Richmond	4,948	5,499
Richmond Heights	13,802	11,516
Rock Hill	6,815	5,702
Rolla	13,571	13,303
St. Ann	18,215	15,523
St. Charles	31,834	37,379
St. John	8,960	7,854
St. Joseph	72,748	76,691
St. Louis	622,236	453,085
St. Peters	486	15,700
Sedalia	22,847	20,927
Shrewsbury	5,896	5,077
Sikeston	14,699	17,431
Springfield	120,096	133,116
Sullivan	5,111	5,461
Trenton	6,063	6,811
Union	5,183	5,506
University City	47,527	42,738
Warrensburg	13,125	13,807
Washington	8,499	9,251
Webb City	6,923	7,309
Webster Groves	27,457	23,097
West Plains	6,893	7,741
MONTANA		
Anaconda-Deer Lodge County	9,771	12,518
Billings	61,581	66,798
Bozeman	18,670	21,645
Butte-Silver Bow	23,368	37,205
Glendive	6,305	5,978
Great Falls	60,091	56,725
Havre	10,558	10,891
Helena (c.)	22,730	23,938
Kalispell	10,526	10,648
Laurel	4,454	5,481
Lewistown	6,437	7,104
Livingston	6,883	6,994
Miles City	9,023	9,602
Missoula	29,497	33,388
Sidney	4,543	5,726
NEBRASKA		
Alliance	6,862	9,869
Beatrice	12,389	12,891
Bellevue	21,953	21,813
Blair	6,106	6,418
Chadron	5,921	5,933
Columbus	15,471	17,328
Falls City	5,444	5,374
Fremont	22,962	23,979
Gering	5,639	7,760
Grand Island	32,358	33,180
Hastings	23,580	23,045
Holdrege	5,635	5,624
Kearney	19,181	21,158
La Vista	4,858	9,588
Lexington	5,654	6,898
Lincoln (c.)	149,518	171,932
McCook	8,285	8,404
Nebraska City	7,441	7,127
Norfolk	16,607	19,449
North Platte	19,447	24,479
Ogallala	4,976	5,638
Omaha	346,929	311,681
Papillion	5,606	6,399
Plattsmouth	6,371	6,295
Ralston	4,731	5,143
Scottsbluff	14,507	14,156
Seward	5,294	5,713
Sidney	6,403	6,010
South Sioux City	7,920	9,339
Wayne	5,379	5,240
York	6,778	7,723
NEVADA		
Boulder City	5,223	9,590
Carson City (c.)	15,468	32,022
Elko	7,621	8,758
Henderson	16,395	24,363
Las Vegas	125,787	164,674
North Las Vegas	46,067	42,739
Reno	72,863	100,756
Sparks	24,187	40,780
NEW HAMPSHIRE		
Bedford	5,859	9,481
Berlin	15,256	13,084
Claremont	14,221	14,557
Concord (c.)	30,022	30,400
Derry	11,712	18,875
Dover	20,850	22,377
Durham	8,869	10,652
Exeter	8,892	11,024
Franklin	7,292	7,901
Goffstown	9,284	11,315
Hampton	8,011	10,493
Hanover	8,494	9,119
Hooksett	5,564	7,303
Hudson	10,638	14,022
Keene	20,467	21,449
Laconia	14,888	15,575
Lebanon	9,725	11,134
Littleton	5,290	5,558
Londonderry	5,346	13,598
Manchester	87,754	90,936
Merrimack	8,595	15,406
Milford	6,622	8,685
Nashua	55,820	67,865
Newport	5,899	6,229
Pelham	5,408	8,090
Plymouth	4,225	5,094
Portsmouth	25,717	26,254
Rochester	17,938	21,560
Salem	20,142	24,124
Somersworth	9,026	10,350
NEW JERSEY		
Absecon	6,094	6,859
Allendale	6,240	5,901
Asbury Park	16,533	17,015
Atlantic City	47,859	40,199
Audubon	10,802	9,533
Barrington	8,409	7,418
Bayonne	72,743	65,047
Beachwood	4,390	7,687
Belleville	37,629	35,367
Bellmawr	15,618	13,721
Belmar	5,782	6,771
Bergenfield	29,000	25,568

Place	1970	1980
N.J.—Cont.		
Berlin	4,997	5,786
Bernardsville	6,652	6,715
Bloomfield	52,029	47,792
Bloomingdale	7,797	7,867
Bogota	8,960	8,344
Boonton	9,261	8,620
Bound Brook	10,450	9,710
Bridgeton	20,435	18,795
Brigantine	6,741	8,318
Burlington	12,010	10,246
Butler	7,051	7,616
Caldwell	8,677	7,624
Camden	102,551	84,910
Carlstadt	6,724	6,166
Carteret	23,137	20,598
Chatham	9,566	8,537
Clayton	5,193	6,013
Clementon	4,492	5,764
Cliffside Park	18,891	21,464
Clifton	82,437	74,388
Closter	8,604	8,164
Collingswood	17,422	15,838
Cresskill	8,298	7,609
Dover	15,039	14,681
Dumont	20,155	18,334
Dunellen	7,072	6,593
East Orange	75,471	77,025
East Rutherford	8,536	7,849
Eatontown	14,619	12,703
Elizabeth	112,654	106,201
Elmwood Park	20,511	18,377
Emerson	8,428	7,793
Englewood	24,985	23,701
Englewood Cliffs	5,938	5,698
Fair Haven	6,142	5,679
Fair Lawn	38,040	32,229
Fairview	10,698	10,519
Fanwood	8,920	7,767
Florham Park	9,373	9,359
Fort Lee	30,631	32,449
Franklin Lakes	7,550	8,769
Freehold	10,545	10,020
Garfield	30,797	26,803
Glassboro	12,938	14,574
Glen Ridge	8,518	7,855
Glen Rock	13,011	11,497
Gloucester City	14,707	13,121
Guttenberg	5,754	7,340
Hackensack	36,008	36,039
Hackettstown	9,472	8,850
Haddonfield	13,118	12,337
Haddon Heights	9,365	8,361
Haledon	6,767	6,607
Hammonton	11,464	12,298
Harrison	11,811	12,242
Hasbrouck Heights	13,651	12,166
Hawthorne	19,173	18,200
Highland Park	14,385	13,396
Highlands	3,916	5,187
Hillsdale	11,768	10,495
Hoboken	45,380	42,460
Hopatcong	9,052	15,531
Irvington	59,743	61,493
Jersey City	260,350	223,532
Keansburg	9,720	10,613
Kearny	37,585	35,735
Kenilworth	9,165	8,221
Keyport	7,205	7,413
Kinnelon	7,600	7,770
Leonia	8,847	8,027
Lincoln Park	9,034	8,806
Linden	41,409	37,836
Lindenwold	12,199	18,196
Linwood	6,159	6,144
Little Ferry	9,064	9,399
Little Silver	6,010	5,548
Lodi	25,163	23,956
Long Branch	31,774	29,819
Madison	16,710	15,357
Manasquan	4,971	5,354
Manville	13,029	11,278
Margate City	10,576	9,179
Matawan	9,136	8,837
Maywood	11,087	9,895
Metuchen	16,031	13,762
Middlesex	15,038	13,480
Midland Park	8,159	7,381
Milltown	6,470	7,136
Millville	21,366	24,815
Montclair	44,043	38,321
Montvale	7,327	7,318
Morris Plains	5,540	5,305
Morristown	17,662	16,614
Mountainside	7,520	7,118
Neptune City	5,502	5,276
Newark	381,930	329,248
New Brunswick	41,885	41,442
New Milford	19,149	16,876
New Providence	13,796	12,426
Newton	7,297	7,748
North Arlington	18,096	16,587
North Caldwell	6,733	5,832
Northfield	8,646	7,795
North Haledon	7,614	8,177
North Plainfield	21,796	19,108
Northvale	5,177	5,046
Nutley	31,913	28,998
Oakland	14,420	13,443
Ocean City	10,575	13,949
Oceanport	7,503	5,888
Oradell	8,903	8,658
Orange	32,566	31,136
Palisades Park	13,351	13,732
Palmyra	6,969	7,085
Paramus	28,381	26,474
Park Ridge	8,709	8,515
Passaic	55,124	52,463
Paterson	144,824	137,970
Paulsboro	8,084	6,944
Penns Grove	5,727	5,760
Perth Amboy	38,798	38,951
Phillipsburg	17,849	16,647
Pine Hill	5,132	8,684
Pitman	10,257	9,744
Plainfield	46,862	45,555
Pleasantville	14,007	13,435
Point Pleasant	15,968	17,747
Point Pleasant Beach	4,882	5,415
Pompton Lakes	11,397	10,660
Princeton	12,311	12,035
Prospect Park	5,176	5,142
Rahway	29,114	26,723

Place	1970	1980
N.J.—Cont.		
Ramsey	12,571	12,899
Raritan	6,691	6,128
Red Bank	12,847	12,031
Ridgefield	11,308	10,294
Ridgefield Park	13,990	12,738
Ridgewood	27,547	25,208
Ringwood	10,393	12,625
River Edge	12,850	11,111
Rockaway	6,383	6,852
Roseland	4,453	5,330
Roselle	22,585	20,641
Roselle Park	14,277	13,377
Rumson	7,421	7,623
Runnemede	10,475	9,461
Rutherford	20,802	19,068
Salem	7,648	6,959
Sayreville	32,508	29,969
Secaucus	13,228	13,719
Somerdale	6,510	5,900
Somers Point	7,919	10,330
Somerville	13,652	11,973
South Amboy	9,338	8,322
South Orange	16,971	15,864
South Plainfield	21,142	20,521
South River	15,428	14,361
Spotswood	7,891	7,840
Spring Lake Heights	4,602	5,424
Stratford	9,801	8,005
Summit	23,620	21,071
Tenafly	14,827	13,552
Tinton Falls	8,395	7,740
Totowa	11,580	11,448
Trenton (c.)	104,786	92,124
Union Beach	6,472	6,354
Union City	57,305	55,593
Upper Saddle River	7,949	7,958
Ventnor City	10,385	11,704
Verona	15,067	14,166
Vineland	47,399	53,753
Waldwick	12,313	10,802
Wallington	10,284	10,741
Wanaque	8,636	10,025
Washington	5,943	6,429
Watchung	4,750	5,290
West Caldwell	11,913	11,407
Westfield	33,720	30,447
West Long Branch	6,845	7,380
West New York	40,627	39,194
West Orange	43,715	39,510
West Paterson	11,692	11,293
Westwood	11,105	10,714
Wharton	5,535	5,485
Woodbury	12,408	10,353
Woodcliff Lake	5,506	5,644
Wood-Ridge	8,311	7,929
NEW MEXICO		
Alamogordo	23,035	24,024
Albuquerque	244,501	331,767
Artesia	10,315	10,385
Aztec	3,354	5,512
Belen	4,823	5,617
Carlsbad	21,297	25,496
Clovis	28,495	31,194
Deming	8,343	9,964
Espanola	4,528	6,803
Farmington	21,979	30,729
Gallup	14,596	18,161
Grants	8,768	11,451
Hobbs	26,025	28,794
Las Cruces	37,857	45,086
Las Vegas city	7,528	14,322
Lovington	8,915	9,727
Portales	10,554	9,940
Raton	6,962	8,225
Roswell	33,908	39,676
Santa Fe (c.)	41,167	48,899
Silver City	8,557	9,887
Socorro	5,849	7,576
Truth or Consequences	4,656	5,219
Tucumcari	7,189	6,765
NEW YORK		
Albany (c.)	115,781	101,727
Amityville	9,794	9,076
Amsterdam	25,524	21,872
Auburn	34,599	32,548
Babylon	12,897	12,388
Baldwinsville	6,298	6,446
Batavia	17,338	16,703
Bath	6,053	6,042
Bayville	6,147	7,034
Beacon	13,255	12,937
Binghamton	64,123	55,860
Briarcliff Manor	6,521	7,115
Brockport	7,878	9,776
Bronxville	6,674	6,267
Buffalo	462,768	357,870
Canandaigua	10,488	10,419
Canton	6,398	7,055
Cedarhurst	6,941	6,162
Cobleskill	4,368	5,272
Cohoes	18,653	18,114
Colonie	8,701	8,869
Corning	15,792	12,953
Cortland	19,621	20,138
Croton-on-Hudson	7,523	6,889
Depew	22,158	19,819
Dobbs Ferry	10,353	10,053
Dunkirk	16,855	15,310
East Aurora	7,033	6,803
East Hills	8,624	7,160
East Rochester	8,347	7,596
East Rockaway	11,795	10,917
Elmira	39,945	35,327
Endicott	16,556	14,457
Fairport	6,474	5,970
Farmingdale	9,297	7,946
Floral Park	18,466	16,805
Fredonia	10,326	11,126
Freeport	40,374	38,272
Fulton	14,003	13,312
Garden City	25,373	22,927
Geneseo	5,714	6,746
Geneva	16,793	15,133
Glen Cove	25,770	24,618
Glens Falls	17,222	15,897
Gloversville	19,677	17,836
Great Neck	10,798	9,168
Great Neck Plaza	6,043	5,604

Place	1970	1980
N.Y.—Cont.		
Hamburg	10,215	10,582
Harrison	...	23,046
Hastings-on-Hudson	9,479	8,573
Haverstraw	8,198	8,800
Hempstead	39,411	40,404
Herkimer	8,960	8,383
Hornell	12,144	10,234
Horseheads	7,989	7,348
Hudson	8,940	7,986
Hudson Falls	7,917	7,419
Ilion	9,808	9,190
Irvington	5,878	5,774
Ithaca	26,226	28,732
Jamestown	39,795	35,775
Johnson City	18,025	17,126
Johnstown	10,045	9,360
Kenmore	20,980	18,474
Kings Point	5,614	5,234
Kingston	25,544	24,481
Lackawanna	28,657	22,701
Lake Grove	8,133	9,692
Lancaster	13,365	13,056
Larchmont	7,203	6,308
Lawrence	6,566	6,175
Lindenhurst	28,359	26,919
Little Falls	7,629	6,156
Lockport	25,399	24,844
Long Beach	33,127	34,073
Lynbrook	23,151	20,431
Malone	8,048	7,668
Malverne	10,036	9,262
Mamaroneck	18,909	17,616
Manlius	4,295	5,241
Manorhaven	5,488	5,384
Massapequa Park	22,112	19,779
Massena	14,042	12,851
Mechanicville	6,247	5,500
Medina	6,415	6,392
Middletown	22,607	21,454
Mineola	21,845	20,757
Monroe	4,439	5,996
Monticello	5,991	6,306
Mount Kisco	8,172	8,025
Mount Vernon	72,778	66,713
Newark	11,644	10,017
Newburgh	26,219	23,438
New Hyde Park	10,116	9,801
New Rochelle	75,385	70,794
New York City	7,895,563	7,071,030
Niagara Falls	85,615	71,384
Northport	7,494	7,651
North Syracuse	8,687	7,970
North Tarrytown	8,334	7,994
North Tonawanda	36,012	35,760
Norwich	8,843	8,082
Nyack	6,659	6,428
Ogdensburg	14,554	12,375
Olean	19,169	18,207
Oneida	11,658	10,810
Oneonta	16,030	14,933
Ossining	21,659	20,196
Oswego	20,913	19,793
Patchogue	11,582	11,291
Peekskill	19,283	18,236
Pelham	2,076	6,848
Pelham Manor	6,673	6,130
Penn Yan	5,293	5,242
Plattsburgh	18,715	21,057
Pleasantville	7,110	6,749
Port Chester	25,803	23,565
Port Jefferson	5,515	6,731
Port Jervis	8,852	8,699
Potsdam	10,303	10,635
Poughkeepsie	32,029	29,757
Rensselaer	10,136	9,047
Rochester	295,011	241,741
Rockville Centre	27,444	25,405
Rome	50,148	43,826
Rye	15,869	15,083
Salamanca	7,877	6,890
Saranac Lake	6,086	5,578
Saratoga Springs	18,845	23,906
Scarsdale	19,229	17,650
Schenectady	77,958	67,972
Scotia	7,370	7,280
Sea Cliff	5,890	5,364
Seneca Falls	7,794	7,466
Solvay	8,280	7,140
Spring Valley	18,112	20,537
Suffern	8,273	10,794
Syracuse	197,297	170,105
Tarrytown	11,115	10,648
Tonawanda	21,898	18,693
Troy	62,918	56,638
Tuckahoe	6,236	6,076
Utica	91,373	75,632
Valley Stream	40,413	35,769
Walden	5,277	5,659
Wappingers Falls	5,607	5,110
Waterloo	5,418	5,303
Watertown	30,787	27,861
Watervliet	12,404	11,354
Webster	5,037	5,499
Wellsville	5,815	5,769
Westbury	15,362	13,871
West Haverstraw	8,558	9,181
White Plains	50,346	46,999
Williamsville	6,878	6,017
Williston Park	9,154	8,216
Yonkers	204,297	195,351
NORTH CAROLINA		
Albemarle	11,126	15,110
Archdale	4,874	5,305
Asheboro	10,797	15,252
Asheville	57,820	53,281
Boone	8,754	10,191
Burlington	35,930	37,266
Carrboro	5,058	7,517
Cary	7,640	21,612
Chapel Hill	26,199	32,421
Charlotte	241,420	314,447
Clinton	7,157	7,552
Concord	18,464	16,942
Dunn	8,302	8,962
Durham	95,438	100,831
Eden	15,871	15,672
Edenton	4,956	5,264
Elizabeth City	14,381	13,784
Fayetteville	53,510	59,507
Forest City	7,179	7,688

Place	1970	1980
N.C.—Cont.		
Garner	4,923	9,556
Gastonia	47,322	47,333
Goldsboro	26,960	31,871
Graham	8,172	8,415
Greensboro	144,076	155,642
Greenville	29,063	35,740
Havelock	3,012	17,718
Henderson	13,896	13,522
Hendersonville	6,443	6,862
Hickory	20,569	20,757
High Point	63,229	64,107
Hope Mills	1,866	5,412
Jacksonville	16,289	17,056
Kernersville	4,815	6,802
Kings Mountain	8,465	9,080
Kinston	23,020	25,234
Laurinburg	8,859	11,480
Lenoir	14,705	13,748
Lexington	17,205	15,711
Lumberton	16,961	18,340
Mint Hill	...	9,830
Monroe	11,282	12,639
Mooresville	8,808	8,575
Morganton	13,625	13,763
Mount Airy	7,325	6,862
New Bern	14,660	14,557
Newton	7,857	7,624
Oxford	7,178	7,580
Raleigh (c.)	122,830	149,771
Reidsville	13,636	12,492
Roanoke Rapids	13,508	14,702
Rockingham	5,852	8,300
Rocky Mount	34,284	41,283
Roxboro	5,370	7,532
Salisbury	22,515	22,677
Sanford	11,716	14,773
Shelby	16,328	15,310
Smithfield	6,677	7,288
Southern Pines	5,937	8,620
Spring Lake	3,968	6,273
Statesville	20,007	18,622
Tarboro	9,425	8,634
Thomasville	15,230	14,144
Washington	8,961	8,418
Waynesville	6,488	6,765
Whiteville	4,195	5,565
Williamston	6,570	6,159
Wilmington	46,169	44,000
Wilson	29,347	34,424
Winston-Salem	133,683	131,885
NORTH DAKOTA		
Bismarck (c.)	34,703	44,485
Devils Lake	7,078	7,442
Dickinson	12,405	15,924
Fargo	53,365	61,308
Grafton	5,946	5,293
Grand Forks	39,008	43,765
Jamestown	15,385	16,280
Mandan	11,093	15,513
Minot	32,290	32,843
Valley City	7,843	7,774
Wahpeton	7,076	9,064
West Fargo	5,161	10,099
Williston	11,280	13,336
OHIO		
Ada	5,309	5,669
Akron	275,425	237,177
Alliance	26,547	24,315
Amherst	9,902	10,638
Ashland	19,872	20,326
Ashtabula	24,313	23,449
Athens	24,168	19,743
Aurora	6,549	8,177
Avon	7,214	7,241
Avon Lake	12,261	13,222
Barberton	33,052	29,751
Bay Village	18,163	17,846
Beachwood	9,631	9,983
Beavercreek	...	31,589
Bedford	17,552	15,056
Bedford Heights	13,063	13,214
Bellaire	9,655	8,241
Bellbrook	1,268	5,174
Bellefontaine	11,255	11,888
Bellevue	8,604	8,187
Belpre	7,189	7,193
Berea	22,465	19,567
Bexley	14,888	13,405
Blue Ash	8,324	9,506
Bowling Green	14,656	25,728
Brecksville	9,137	10,132
Broadview Heights	11,463	10,920
Brooklyn	13,142	12,342
Brook Park	30,774	26,195
Brunswick	15,852	27,689
Bryan	7,008	7,879
Bucyrus	13,111	13,433
Cambridge	13,656	13,573
Campbell	12,577	11,619
Canfield	4,997	5,535
Canton	110,053	94,730
Celina	8,072	9,137
Centerville	10,333	18,886
Cheviot	11,135	9,888
Chillicothe	24,842	23,420
Cincinnati	453,514	385,457
Circleville	11,687	11,700
Cleveland	750,879	573,822
Cleveland Heights	60,767	56,438
Clyde	5,503	5,489
Columbus (c.)	540,025	564,871
Conneaut	14,552	13,835
Cortland	2,525	5,011
Coshocton	13,747	13,405
Crestline	5,965	5,406
Cuyahoga Falls	49,815	43,710
Dayton	243,023	203,588
Deer Park	7,415	6,745
Defiance	16,281	16,810
Delaware	15,008	18,780
Delphos	7,608	7,314
Dover	11,516	11,526
East Cleveland	39,600	36,957
Eastlake	19,690	22,104
East Liverpool	20,020	16,687
East Palestine	5,604	5,306
Eaton	6,020	6,839
Elyria	53,427	57,504
Englewood	7,885	11,329
Euclid	71,552	59,999
Fairborn	32,267	29,702

Place	1970	1980
OHIO—Cont.		
Fairfield	14,680	30,777
Fairlawn	6,102	6,100
Fairview Park	21,699	19,311
Findlay	35,800	35,594
Forest Park	15,139	18,675
Fostoria	16,037	15,743
Franklin	10,075	10,711
Fremont	18,490	17,834
Gahanna	12,400	18,001
Galion	13,123	12,391
Gallipolis	7,490	5,576
Garfield Heights	41,417	33,380
Geneva	6,449	6,655
Germantown	4,088	5,015
Girard	14,119	12,517
Grandview Heights	8,460	7,420
Greenfield	4,780	5,034
Greenville	12,380	12,999
Grove City	13,911	16,793
Hamilton	67,865	63,189
Harrison	4,408	5,855
Heath	6,768	6,969
Highland Heights	5,926	5,739
Hilliard	8,369	8,008
Hillsboro	5,584	6,356
Hubbard	8,583	9,245
Huron	6,896	7,123
Independence	7,034	8,165
Ironton	15,030	14,290
Jackson	6,843	6,675
Kent	28,183	26,164
Kenton	8,315	8,605
Kettering	71,864	61,186
Kirtland	5,530	5,969
Lakewood	70,173	61,963
Lancaster	32,911	34,953
Lebanon	7,934	9,636
Lima	53,734	47,381
Lincoln Heights	6,099	5,259
Logan	6,269	6,557
London	6,481	6,958
Lorain	78,185	75,416
Louisville	6,298	7,873
Loveland	7,126	9,106
Lyndhurst	19,749	18,092
Macedonia	6,375	6,571
Madeira	6,713	9,341
Mansfield	55,047	53,927
Maple Heights	34,093	29,735
Marietta	16,861	16,467
Marion	38,646	37,040
Martins Ferry	10,757	9,331
Marysville	5,744	7,414
Mason	5,677	8,692
Massillon	32,539	30,557
Maumee	15,937	15,747
Mayfield Heights	22,139	21,550
Medina	10,913	15,268
Mentor	36,912	42,065
Mentor-on-the-Lake	6,517	7,919
Miamisburg	14,797	15,304
Middleburg Heights	12,367	16,218
Middletown	48,767	43,719
Milford	4,828	5,232
Montgomery	5,683	10,088
Moraine	4,898	5,325
Mount Healthy	7,446	7,562
Mount Vernon	13,373	14,380
Napoleon	7,791	8,614
Newark	41,836	41,200
New Carlisle	6,112	6,498
New Lexington	4,921	5,179
New Philadelphia	15,184	16,883
Niles	21,581	23,088
North Canton	15,228	14,228
North College Hill	12,363	10,990
North Olmsted	34,861	36,486
North Ridgeville	13,152	21,522
North Royalton	12,807	17,671
Northwood	4,222	5,495
Norton	12,308	12,242
Norwalk	13,386	14,358
Norwood	30,420	26,342
Oakwood city	10,095	9,372
Oberlin	8,761	8,660
Olmsted Falls	2,504	5,868
Oregon	16,563	18,675
Orrville	7,408	7,511
Oxford	15,868	17,655
Painesville	16,536	16,391
Parma	100,216	92,548
Parma Heights	27,192	23,112
Pepper Pike	5,382	6,177
Perrysburg	7,693	10,215
Piqua	20,741	20,480
Port Clinton	7,202	7,223
Portsmouth	27,633	25,943
Ravenna	11,780	11,987
Reading	14,617	12,879
Reynoldsburg	13,921	20,661
Richmond Heights	9,220	10,095
Rittman	6,308	6,063
Rocky River	22,958	21,084
Rossford	5,302	5,978
St. Bernard	6,131	5,396
St. Clairsville	4,754	5,452
St. Marys	7,699	8,414
Salem	14,186	12,869
Sandusky	32,674	31,360
Sebring	4,954	5,078
Seven Hills	12,700	13,650
Shaker Heights	36,306	32,487
Sharonville	11,393	10,108
Sheffield Lake	8,734	10,484
Shelby	9,847	9,645
Sidney	16,332	17,657
Silverton	6,588	6,172
Solon	11,147	14,341
South Euclid	29,579	25,713
Springdale	8,127	10,111
Springfield	81,941	72,563
Steubenville	30,771	26,400
Stow	20,061	25,303
Streetsboro	7,966	9,055
Strongsville	15,182	28,577
Struthers	15,343	13,624
Sylvania	12,031	15,527
Tallmadge	15,274	15,269
The Village of Indian Hill	5,651	5,521
Tiffin	21,596	19,549

Place	1970	1980
OHIO—Cont.		
Tipp City	5,090	5,595
Toledo	383,062	354,635
Toronto	7,705	6,934
Trenton	5,278	6,401
Trotwood	6,997	7,802
Troy	17,186	19,086
Twinsburg	6,432	7,632
Uhrichsville	5,731	6,130
Union	3,654	5,219
University Heights	17,055	15,401
Upper Arlington	38,727	35,648
Upper Sandusky	5,645	5,967
Urbana	11,237	10,762
Vandalia	10,796	13,161
Van Wert	11,320	11,035
Vermilion	9,872	11,012
Wadsworth	13,142	15,166
Wapakoneta	7,324	8,402
Warren	63,494	56,629
Warrensville Heights	18,925	16,565
Washington	12,495	12,682
Wauseon	4,932	6,173
Wellston	5,410	6,016
Wellsville	5,891	5,095
West Carrollton	10,748	13,148
Westerville	12,530	23,414
Westlake	15,689	19,483
Whitehall	25,263	21,299
Wickliffe	20,632	16,790
Willard	5,510	5,674
Willoughby	18,634	19,329
Willoughby Hills	5,969	8,612
Willowick	21,237	17,834
Wilmington	10,051	10,431
Wooster	18,703	19,289
Worthington	15,326	15,016
Wyoming	9,089	8,282
Xenia	25,373	24,653
Youngstown	140,909	115,436
Zanesville	33,045	28,655
OKLAHOMA		
Ada	14,859	15,902
Altus	23,302	23,101
Alva	7,440	6,416
Anadarko	6,682	6,378
Ardmore	20,881	23,689
Bartlesville	29,683	34,568
Bethany	22,694	22,130
Bixby	3,973	6,969
Blackwell	8,645	8,400
Broken Arrow	11,018	35,761
Chickasha	14,194	15,828
Choctaw	4,750	7,520
Claremore	9,084	12,085
Clinton	8,513	8,796
Cushing	7,529	7,720
Del City	27,133	28,424
Duncan	19,718	22,517
Durant	11,118	11,972
Edmond	16,633	34,637
Elk City	7,323	9,579
El Reno	14,510	15,486
Enid	44,986	50,363
Frederick	6,132	6,153
Guthrie	9,575	10,312
Guymon	7,674	8,492
Henryetta	6,430	6,432
Holdenville	5,181	5,469
Hugo	6,585	7,172
Idabel	5,946	7,622
Jenks	2,685	5,876
Lawton	74,470	80,054
McAlester	18,802	17,255
Marlow	3,995	5,017
Miami	13,880	14,237
Midwest City	48,212	49,559
Moore	18,761	35,063
Muskogee	37,331	40,011
Mustang	2,637	7,496
Norman	52,117	68,020
Oklahoma City (c.)	368,164	403,213
Okmulgee	15,180	16,263
Owasso	3,491	6,149
Pauls Valley	5,769	5,664
Perry	5,341	5,796
Ponca City	25,940	26,238
Poteau	5,500	7,089
Pryor	7,057	8,483
Sallisaw	4,888	6,403
Sand Springs	10,565	13,246
Sapulpa	15,159	15,853
Seminole	7,878	8,590
Shawnee	25,075	26,506
Stillwater	31,126	38,268
Sulphur	5,158	5,516
Tahlequah	9,254	9,708
Tecumseh	4,451	5,123
The Village	13,695	11,049
Tulsa	330,350	360,919
Vinita	5,847	6,740
Wagoner	4,959	6,191
Warr Acres	9,887	9,940
Weatherford	7,959	9,640
Wewoka	5,284	5,480
Woodward	9,563	13,610
Yukon	8,411	17,112
OREGON		
Albany	18,181	26,546
Ashland	12,342	14,943
Astoria	10,244	9,998
Baker	9,354	9,471
Beaverton	18,577	30,582
Bend	13,710	17,263
Canby	3,813	7,659
Central Point	4,004	6,357
City of the Dalles	10,423	10,820
Coos Bay	13,466	14,424
Corvallis	35,056	40,960
Cottage Grove	6,004	7,148
Dallas	6,361	8,530
Eugene	79,028	105,624
Forest Grove	8,275	11,499
Gladstone	6,254	9,500
Grants Pass	12,455	14,997
Gresham	10,030	33,005
Hermiston	4,893	9,408
Hillsboro	14,675	27,664
Klamath Falls	15,775	16,661
La Grande	9,645	11,354
Lake Oswego	14,615	22,868

Place	1970	1980
ORE.—Cont.		
Lebanon	6,636	10,413
Lincoln City	4,198	5,469
McMinnville	10,125	14,080
Medford	28,973	39,603
Milton-Freewater	4,105	5,086
Milwaukie	16,444	17,931
Monmouth	5,237	5,594
Newberg	6,507	10,394
Newport	5,188	7,519
North Bend	8,553	9,779
Ontario	6,523	8,814
Oregon City	9,176	14,673
Pendleton	13,197	14,521
Portland	379,967	366,383
Prineville	4,101	5,276
Redmond	3,721	6,452
Roseburg	14,461	16,644
St. Helens	6,212	7,064
Salem (c.)	68,725	89,233
Seaside	4,402	5,193
Silverton	4,301	5,168
Springfield	26,874	41,621
Sweet Home	3,799	6,921
Tigard	6,499	14,286
Troutdale	1,661	5,908
Tualatin	750	7,348
West Linn	7,091	12,956
Woodburn	7,495	11,196
PENNSYLVANIA		
Aliquippa	22,277	17,094
Allentown	109,871	103,758
Altoona	63,115	57,078
Ambler	7,800	6,628
Ambridge	11,324	9,575
Archbald	6,118	6,295
Arnold	8,174	6,853
Avalon	7,010	6,240
Baden	5,536	5,318
Baldwin	26,729	24,598
Bangor	5,425	5,006
Beaver	6,100	5,441
Beaver Falls	14,635	12,525
Bellefonte	6,828	6,300
Bellevue	11,586	10,128
Berwick	12,274	12,189
Bethel Park	34,758	34,755
Bethlehem	72,686	70,419
Blakely	6,391	7,438
Bloomsburg	11,652	11,717
Braddock	8,795	5,634
Bradford	12,672	11,211
Brentwood	13,732	11,907
Bridgeville	6,717	6,154
Bristol	12,085	10,867
Brookhaven	7,370	7,912
Butler	18,691	17,026
California	6,635	5,703
Camp Hill	9,931	8,422
Canonsburg	11,439	10,459
Carbondale	12,478	11,255
Carlisle	18,079	18,314
Carnegie	10,864	10,099
Castle Shannon	12,036	10,164
Catasauqua	5,702	7,944
Chambersburg	17,315	16,174
Charleroi	6,723	5,717
Chester	56,331	45,794
Clairton	15,051	12,188
Clarion	6,095	6,664
Clarks Summit	5,376	5,272
Clearfield	8,176	7,580
Clifton Heights	8,348	7,320
Coatesville	12,331	10,698
Collingdale	10,605	9,539
Columbia	11,237	10,466
Connellsville	11,643	10,319
Conshohocken	10,195	8,475
Coraopolis	8,435	7,308
Corry	7,435	7,149
Crafton	8,233	7,623
Danville	6,176	5,239
Darby	13,729	11,513
Dickson City	7,698	6,699
Donora	8,825	7,524
Dormont	12,856	11,275
Downingtown	7,437	7,650
Doylestown	8,270	8,717
Du Bois	10,112	9,290
Dunmore	18,168	16,781
Duquesne	11,410	10,094
Duryea	5,264	5,415
Easton	29,450	26,027
East Stroudsburg	7,894	8,039
Economy	7,176	9,538
Edinboro	4,871	6,324
Edwardsville	5,633	5,729
Elizabethtown	8,072	8,233
Ellwood City	10,857	9,998
Emmaus	11,511	11,001
Ephrata	9,662	11,095
Erie	129,265	119,123
Exeter	4,670	5,493
Farrell	11,000	8,645
Folcroft	9,610	8,231
Forest Hills	9,561	8,198
Forty Fort	6,114	5,590
Fox Chapel	4,684	5,049
Frackville	5,445	5,308
Franklin	8,629	8,146
Franklin Park	5,310	6,135
Gettysburg	7,275	7,194
Glassport	7,450	6,242
Glenolden	8,697	7,633
Greensburg	17,077	17,558
Green Tree	6,441	5,722
Greenville	8,704	7,730
Grove City	8,312	8,162
Hanover	15,623	14,890
Harrisburg (c.)	68,061	53,264
Hatboro	8,880	7,579
Hazleton	30,426	27,318
Hellertown	6,615	6,025
Hollidaysburg	6,262	5,892
Homestead	6,309	5,092
Honesdale	5,224	5,128
Huntingdon	6,987	7,042
Indiana	16,100	16,051
Jeannette	15,209	13,106
Jefferson	8,512	8,643
Jim Thorpe	5,456	5,263
Johnstown	42,476	35,496
Kennett Square	4,876	7,415

Place	1970	1980
PA.—Cont.		
Kingston	18,325	15,681
Kittanning	6,231	5,432
Lancaster	57,690	54,725
Lansdale	18,451	16,526
Lansdowne	14,090	11,891
Latrobe	11,749	10,799
Lebanon	28,572	25,711
Lehighton	6,095	5,826
Lewisburg	5,718	5,407
Lewistown	11,098	9,830
Lititz	7,072	7,590
Lock Haven	11,427	9,617
Lower Burrell	13,654	13,200
McKeesport	37,977	31,012
McKees Rocks	11,901	8,742
Mahanoy City	7,257	6,167
Manheim	5,434	5,015
Meadville	16,573	15,544
Mechanicsburg	9,385	9,487
Media	6,444	6,119
Middletown	9,080	10,122
Millersville	6,396	7,668
Milton	7,723	6,730
Minersville	6,012	5,635
Monaca	7,486	7,661
Monessen	15,216	11,928
Monongahela	7,113	5,950
Monroeville	29,011	30,977
Montoursville	5,985	5,403
Moosic	4,646	6,068
Morrisville	11,309	9,845
Mount Carmel	9,317	8,190
Mount Joy	5,041	5,680
Mount Pleasant	5,895	5,354
Munhall	16,574	14,532
Municipality of Murrysville	...	16,036
Nanticoke	14,638	13,044
Nazareth	5,815	5,443
New Brighton	7,637	7,364
New Castle	38,559	33,621
New Cumberland	9,803	8,051
New Kensington	20,312	17,660
Norristown	38,169	34,684
Northampton	8,389	8,240
North Braddock	10,838	8,711
Norwood	7,229	6,647
Oakmont	7,550	7,039
Oil City	15,033	13,881
Old Forge	9,522	9,304
Olyphant	5,422	5,204
Palmerton	5,620	5,455
Palmyra	7,615	7,228
Perkasie	5,451	5,241
Philadelphia	1,949,996	1,688,210
Phoenixville	14,823	14,165
Pittsburgh	520,089	423,938
Pittston	11,113	9,930
Pleasant Hills	10,409	9,676
Plum	21,932	25,932
Plymouth	9,536	7,605
Port Vue	5,862	5,316
Pottstown	25,355	22,729
Pottsville	19,715	18,195
Prospect Park	7,250	6,593
Punxsutawney	7,792	7,479
Quakertown	7,276	8,867
Reading	87,643	78,686
Red Lion	5,645	5,824
Ridgway	6,022	5,604
Ridley Park	9,025	7,889
St. Marys	7,470	6,417
Sayre	7,473	6,951
Schuylkill Haven	6,125	5,977
Scottdale	5,818	5,833
Scranton	102,696	88,117
Selinsgrove	5,116	5,227
Shamokin	11,719	10,357
Sharon	22,653	19,057
Sharon Hill	7,464	6,221
Sharpsville	6,126	5,375
Shenandoah	8,287	7,589
Shillington	6,249	5,601
Shippensburg	6,536	5,261
Somerset	6,269	6,474
Souderton	6,366	6,657
South Williamsport	7,153	6,581
State College	32,833	36,130
Steelton	8,556	6,484
Stroudsburg	5,451	5,148
Sugar Creek	5,944	5,954
Sunbury	13,025	12,292
Swarthmore	6,156	5,950
Swissvale	13,819	11,345
Swoyersville	6,786	5,795
Tamaqua	9,246	8,843
Tarentum	7,379	6,419
Taylor	6,977	7,246
Titusville	7,331	6,884
Turtle Creek	8,308	6,959
Tyrone	7,072	6,346
Uniontown	16,282	14,510
Vandergrift	7,889	6,823
Warren	12,998	12,146
Washington	19,827	18,363
Waynesboro	10,011	9,726
West Chester	19,301	17,435
West Mifflin	28,070	26,279
Westmont	6,673	6,113
West Pittston	7,074	5,980
West View	8,312	7,648
Whitehall	16,450	15,206
White Oak	9,304	9,480
Wilkes-Barre	58,856	51,551
Wilkinsburg	26,780	23,669
Williamsport	37,918	33,401
Wilson	8,406	7,564
Windber	6,332	5,585
Wyomissing	7,136	6,551
Yeadon	12,136	11,727
York	50,335	44,619
RHODE ISLAND		
Barrington	17,554	16,174
Bristol	17,860	20,128
Central Falls	18,716	16,995
Coventry	22,947	27,065
Cranston	74,287	71,992
Cumberland	26,605	27,069
East Greenwich	9,577	10,211
East Providence	48,207	50,980
Glocester	5,160	7,550
Johnston	22,037	24,907

Place	1970	1980
R.I.—Cont.		
Lincoln	16,182	16,949
Narragansett	7,138	12,088
Newport	34,562	29,259
North Kingstown	29,793	21,938
North Providence	24,337	29,188
North Smithfield	9,349	9,972
Pawtucket	76,984	71,204
Portsmouth	12,521	14,257
Providence (c.)	179,116	156,804
Scituate	7,489	8,409
Smithfield	13,468	16,886
Tiverton	12,559	13,526
Warren	10,523	10,640
Warwick	83,694	87,123
Westerly	17,248	18,580
West Warwick	24,323	27,026
Woonsocket	46,820	45,914
SOUTH CAROLINA		
Abbeville	5,515	5,863
Aiken	13,436	14,978
Anderson	27,556	27,313
Barnwell	4,439	5,572
Beaufort	9,434	8,634
Belton	5,257	5,312
Bennettsville	7,468	8,774
Camden	8,532	7,462
Cayce	9,967	11,701
Charleston	66,945	69,510
Cheraw	5,627	5,654
Chester	7,045	6,820
Clemson	6,690	8,118
Clinton	8,138	8,596
Columbia (c.)	113,542	99,296
Conway	8,151	10,240
Darlington	6,990	7,989
Dillon	6,391	7,042
Easley	11,175	14,264
Florence	25,997	30,062
Forest Acres	6,808	6,033
Gaffney	13,131	13,453
Georgetown	10,449	10,144
Goose Creek	3,825	17,811
Greenville	61,436	58,242
Greenwood	21,069	21,613
Greer	10,642	10,525
Hanahan	...	13,224
Hartsville	8,017	7,631
Lake City	6,247	5,636
Lancaster	9,186	9,603
Laurens	10,298	10,587
Marion	7,435	7,700
Mauldin	3,797	8,245
Mount Pleasant	6,879	13,838
Mullins	6,006	6,068
Myrtle Beach	9,035	18,758
Newberry	9,218	9,866
North Augusta	12,883	13,593
North Charleston	...	65,630
Orangeburg	13,252	14,933
Rock Hill	33,846	35,344
Seneca	6,573	7,436
Simpsonville	3,308	9,037
Spartanburg	44,546	43,968
Summerville	3,839	6,368
Sumter	24,555	24,890
Union	10,775	10,523
Walterboro	6,257	6,036
West Columbia	7,838	10,409
Woodruff	4,690	5,171
York	5,081	6,412
SOUTH DAKOTA		
Aberdeen	26,476	25,956
Brookings	13,717	14,951
Huron	14,299	13,000
Madison	6,315	6,210
Mitchell	13,425	13,916
Pierre (c.)	9,699	11,973
Rapid City	43,836	46,492
Sioux Falls	72,488	81,343
Spearfish	4,661	5,251
Sturgis	4,536	5,184
Vermillion	9,128	9,582
Watertown	13,388	15,649
Yankton	11,919	12,011
TENNESSEE		
Alcoa	7,739	6,870
Athens	11,790	12,080
Bartlett	1,150	17,170
Bolivar	6,674	6,597
Brentwood	4,099	9,431
Bristol	20,064	23,986
Brownsville	7,011	9,307
Chattanooga	119,923	169,565
Clarksville	31,719	54,777
Cleveland	21,446	26,415
Clinton	4,794	5,245
Collierville	3,651	7,839
Columbia	21,471	25,767
Cookeville	14,403	20,350
Covington	5,801	6,065
Crossville	5,381	6,394
Dayton	4,361	5,913
Dickson	5,665	7,040
Dyersburg	14,523	15,856
East Ridge	21,799	21,236
Elizabethton	12,269	12,431
Fayetteville	7,691	7,559
Franklin	9,497	12,407
Gallatin	13,253	17,191
Germantown	3,474	20,459
Goodlettsville	6,168	8,327
Greeneville	13,722	14,097
Harriman	8,734	8,303
Hendersonville	412	26,561
Humboldt	10,066	10,209
Jackson	39,996	49,131
Jefferson City	5,124	5,612
Johnson City	33,770	39,753
Kingsport	31,938	32,027
Knoxville	174,587	183,139
LaFollette	6,902	8,176
La Vergne	...	5,495
Lawrenceburg	8,889	10,175
Lebanon	12,492	11,872
Lenoir City	5,324	5,446
Lewisburg	7,207	8,760
Lexington	5,024	5,934
McKenzie	4,873	5,405
McMinnville	10,662	10,683

Place	1970	1980
TENN.—Cont.		
Manchester	6,208	7,250
Martin	7,781	8,898
Maryville	13,808	17,480
Memphis	623,988	646,356
Milan	7,313	8,083
Millington	21,177	20,236
Morristown	20,318	19,683
Murfreesboro	26,360	32,845
Nashville (c.)*	426,029	455,651
Newport	7,328	7,580
Oak Ridge	28,319	27,662
Paris	9,892	10,728
Pulaski	6,989	7,184
Red Bank	12,715	13,297
Ripley	4,794	6,366
Rockwood	5,259	5,767
Savannah	5,576	6,992
Shelbyville	12,262	13,530
Signal Mountain	4,839	5,818
Smyrna	5,698	8,839
Soddy-Daisy	7,569	8,388
Springfield	9,720	10,814
Tullahoma	15,311	15,800
Union City	11,925	10,436
Winchester	5,256	5,821
TEXAS		
Abilene	89,653	98,315
Addison	593	5,553
Alamo	4,291	5,831
Alamo Heights	6,933	6,252
Alice	20,121	20,961
Allen	1,940	8,314
Alpine	5,971	5,465
Alvin	10,671	16,515
Amarillo	127,010	149,230
Andrews	8,625	11,061
Angleton	9,906	13,929
Aransas Pass	5,813	7,173
Arlington	90,229	160,123
Athens	9,582	10,197
Atlanta	5,007	6,272
Austin (c.)	253,539	345,496
Azle	4,493	5,822
Balch Springs	10,464	13,746
Bay City	13,445	17,837
Baytown	43,980	56,923
Beaumont	117,548	118,102
Bedford	10,049	20,821
Beeville	13,506	14,574
Bellaire	19,009	14,950
Bellmead	7,698	7,569
Belton	8,696	10,660
Benbrook	8,169	13,579
Big Spring	28,735	24,804
Bonham	7,698	7,338
Borger	14,195	15,837
Bowie	5,185	5,610
Brady	5,557	5,969
Breckenridge	5,944	6,921
Brenham	8,922	10,966
Brownfield	9,647	10,387
Brownsville	52,522	84,997
Brownwood	17,368	19,203
Bryan	33,719	44,337
Burkburnett	9,230	10,668
Burleson	7,713	11,734
Cameron	5,546	5,721
Canyon	8,333	10,724
Carrizo Springs	5,374	6,886
Carrollton	13,855	40,591
Carthage	5,392	6,447
Cedar Hill	2,610	6,849
Center	4,989	5,827
Childress	5,408	5,817
Cleburne	16,015	19,218
Cleveland	5,627	5,977
Clute City	6,023	9,577
Coleman	5,608	5,960
College Station	17,676	37,272
Colleyville	3,342	6,700
Colorado City	5,227	5,405
Commerce	9,534	8,136
Conroe	11,969	18,034
Copperas Cove	10,818	19,469
Corpus Christi	204,525	231,999
Corsicana	19,972	21,712
Crockett	6,616	7,405
Crowley	2,662	5,852
Crystal City	8,104	8,334
Cuero	6,956	7,124
Dalhart	5,705	6,854
Dallas	844,401	904,078
Deer Park	12,773	22,648
Del Rio	21,330	30,034
Denison	24,923	23,884
Denton	39,874	48,063
De Soto	6,617	15,538
Diboll	3,557	5,227
Dickinson	...	7,505
Dimmitt	4,327	5,019
Donna	7,365	9,952
Dumas	9,771	12,194
Duncanville	14,105	27,781
Eagle Pass	15,364	21,407
Edinburg	17,163	24,075
Edna	5,332	5,650
El Campo	9,332	10,462
El Paso	322,261	425,259
Elsa	4,400	5,061
Ennis	11,046	12,110
Euless	19,316	24,002
Everman	4,570	5,387
Falfurrias	6,355	6,103
Farmers Branch	27,492	24,863
Forest Hill	8,236	11,684
Fort Stockton	8,283	8,688
Fort Worth	393,455	385,141
Fredericksburg	5,326	6,412
Freeport	11,997	13,444
Friendswood	5,675	10,719
Gainesville	13,830	14,081
Galena Park	10,479	9,879
Galveston	61,809	61,902
Garland	81,437	138,857
Gatesville	4,683	6,260
Georgetown	6,395	9,468
Gilmer	4,196	5,167
Gladewater	5,574	6,548
Gonzales	5,854	7,152
Graham	7,477	9,055
Grand Prairie	50,904	71,462
Grapevine	7,049	11,801

*Consolidated government with Davidson County in 1963; formerly called Nashville-Davidson.

Place	1970	1980
TEX.—Cont.		
Greenville	22,043	22,161
Groves	18,067	17,090
Haltom City	28,127	29,014
Harker Heights	4,216	7,345
Harlingen	33,503	43,543
Hearne	4,982	5,418
Henderson	10,187	11,473
Hereford	13,414	15,853
Highland Park	10,133	8,909
Hillsboro	7,224	7,397
Hitchcock	5,565	6,655
Hondo	5,487	6,057
Houston	1,233,535	1,594,086
Humble	3,272	6,729
Huntsville	17,610	23,936
Hurst	27,215	31,420
Ingleside	3,763	5,436
Iowa Park	5,796	6,184
Irving	97,260	109,943
Jacinto City	9,563	8,953
Jacksonville	9,734	12,264
Jasper	6,251	6,959
Katy	2,923	5,660
Kermit	7,884	8,015
Kerrville	12,672	15,276
Kilgore	9,495	10,968
Killeen	35,507	46,296
Kingsville	28,915	28,808
Kirby	3,238	6,385
Lake Jackson	13,376	19,102
La Marque	16,131	15,372
Lamesa	11,559	11,790
Lampasas	5,922	6,165
Lancaster	10,522	14,807
La Porte	7,149	14,062
Laredo	69,024	91,449
League City	10,818	16,578
Leon Valley	2,487	8,951
Levelland	11,445	13,809
Lewisville	9,264	24,273
Liberty	5,591	7,945
Littlefield	6,738	7,409
Live Oak	2,779	8,183
Lockhart	6,489	7,953
Longview	45,547	62,762
Lubbock	149,101	173,979
Lufkin	23,049	28,562
Luling	4,719	5,039
McAllen	37,636	67,042
McKinney	15,193	16,249
Mansfield	3,658	8,092
Marlin	6,351	7,099
Marshall	22,937	24,921
Mathis	5,351	5,667
Mercedes	9,355	11,851
Mesquite	55,131	67,053
Mexia	5,943	7,094
Midland	59,463	70,525
Mineral Wells	18,411	14,468
Mission	13,043	22,589
Missouri City	4,136	24,533
Monahans	8,333	8,397
Mount Pleasant	9,459	11,003
Nacogdoches	22,544	27,149
Navasota	5,111	5,971
Nederland	16,810	16,855
New Braunfels	17,859	22,402
North Richland Hills	16,514	30,592
Odessa	78,380	90,027
Orange	24,457	23,628
Palestine	14,525	15,948
Pampa	21,726	21,396
Paris	23,441	25,498
Pasadena	89,957	112,560
Pearland	6,444	13,248
Pearsall	5,545	7,383
Pecos	12,682	12,855
Perryton	7,810	7,991
Pharr	15,829	21,381
Plainview	19,096	22,187
Plano	17,872	72,331
Pleasanton	5,407	6,346
Port Arthur	57,371	61,195
Portland	7,302	12,023
Port Lavaca	10,491	10,911
Port Neches	10,894	13,944
Raymondville	7,987	9,493
Richardson	48,405	72,496
Richland Hills	8,865	7,977
Richmond	5,777	9,692
River Oaks	8,193	6,890
Robinson	3,807	6,074
Robstown	11,217	12,100
Rockdale	4,655	5,611
Rockwall	3,121	5,939
Rosenberg	12,098	17,995
Round Rock	2,811	11,812
Rowlett	2,243	7,522
Saginaw	2,382	5,736
San Angelo	63,884	73,240
San Antonio	654,153	785,410
San Benito	15,176	17,988
San Diego	4,490	5,225
San Juan	5,070	7,608
San Marcos	18,860	23,420
Santa Fe	. . .	5,413
Schertz	4,061	7,262
Seagoville	4,390	7,304
Seguin	15,934	17,854
Seminole	5,007	6,080
Sherman	29,061	30,413
Silsbee	7,271	7,684
Sinton	5,563	6,044
Slaton	6,583	6,804
Snyder	11,171	12,705
South Houston	11,527	13,293
Stephenville	9,277	11,881
Sugar Land	3,318	8,826
Sulphur Springs	10,642	12,804
Sweetwater	12,020	12,242
Taylor	9,616	10,619
Temple	33,431	42,483
Terrell	14,182	13,225
Texarkana	30,497	31,271
Texas City	38,908	41,403
The Colony	. . .	11,586
Tulia	5,294	5,033
Tyler	57,770	70,508
Universal City	7,613	10,720
University Park	23,498	22,254
Uvalde	10,764	14,178
Vernon	11,454	12,695
TEX.—Cont.		
Victoria	41,349	50,695
Vidor	9,738	12,117
Waco	95,326	101,261
Watauga	3,778	10,284
Waxahachie	13,452	14,624
Weatherford	11,750	12,049
Weslaco	15,313	19,331
West University Place	13,317	12,010
Wharton	7,881	9,033
White Settlement	13,449	13,508
Wichita Falls	96,265	94,201
Windcrest	3,371	5,332
Woodway	4,819	7,091
Yoakum	5,755	6,148
UTAH		
American Fork	7,713	12,417
Bountiful	27,751	32,877
Brigham City	14,007	15,596
Cedar City	8,946	10,972
Centerville	3,268	8,069
Clearfield	13,316	17,982
Clinton	1,768	5,777
Draper	. . .	5,530
Kaysville	6,192	9,811
Layton	13,603	22,862
Lehi	4,659	6,848
Logan	22,333	26,844
Midvale	7,840	10,144
Moab	4,793	5,333
Murray	21,206	25,750
North Ogden	5,257	9,309
North Salt Lake	2,143	5,548
Ogden	69,478	64,407
Orem	25,729	52,399
Payson	4,501	8,246
Pleasant Grove	5,327	10,669
Price	6,218	9,086
Provo	53,131	73,907
Richfield	4,471	5,482
Riverton	2,820	7,293
Roy	14,356	19,694
St. George	7,097	11,350
Salt Lake City (c.)	175,885	163,033
Sandy City	6,438	51,022
South Jordan	2,942	7,492
South Ogden	9,991	11,366
South Salt Lake	7,810	10,561
Spanish Fork	7,284	9,825
Springville	8,790	12,101
Sunset	6,268	5,733
Tooele	12,539	14,335
Vernal	3,908	6,600
Washington Terrace	7,241	8,212
West Jordan	4,221	26,794
VERMONT		
Barre city	10,209	9,824
Barre town	6,509	7,090
Bennington	14,586	15,815
Brattleboro	12,239	11,886
Burlington	38,633	37,712
Colchester	8,776	12,629
Essex Junction	6,511	7,033
Middlebury	6,532	7,574
Montpelier (c.)	8,609	8,241
Rutland	19,293	18,436
St. Albans	8,082	7,308
St. Johnsbury	8,409	7,938
Shelburne	3,728	5,000
South Burlington	. . .	10,679
Springfield	10,063	10,190
Winooski	7,309	6,318
VIRGINIA		
Alexandria	110,927	103,217
Bedford	6,011	5,991
Blacksburg	9,384	30,638
Bluefield	5,286	5,946
Bristol	14,857	19,042
Buena Vista	6,425	6,717
Charlottesville	38,880	45,010
Chesapeake	89,580	114,226
Christiansburg	7,857	10,345
Clifton Forge	5,501	5,046
Colonial Heights	15,097	16,509
Covington	10,060	9,063
Culpeper	6,056	6,621
Danville	46,391	45,642
Fairfax	22,727	19,390
Falls Church	10,772	9,515
Farmville	4,331	6,067
Franklin	6,880	7,308
Fredericksburg	14,450	15,322
Front Royal	8,211	11,126
Galax	6,278	6,524
Hampton	120,779	122,617
Harrisonburg	14,605	19,671
Herndon	4,301	11,449
Hopewell	23,471	23,397
Leesburg	4,821	8,357
Lexington	7,597	7,292
Lynchburg	54,083	66,743
Manassas	9,164	15,438
Manassas Park	6,844	6,524
Marion	8,158	7,029
Martinsville	19,653	18,149
Newport News	138,177	144,903
Norfolk	307,951	266,979
Petersburg	36,103	41,055
Poquoson	5,441	8,726
Portsmouth	110,963	104,577
Pulaski	10,279	10,106
Radford	11,596	13,225
Richlands	4,843	5,796
Richmond (c.)	249,332	219,214
Roanoke	92,115	100,427
Salem	21,982	23,958
South Boston	6,889	7,093
Staunton	24,504	21,857
Suffolk	9,858	47,621
Vienna	17,146	15,469
Vinton	6,347	8,027
Virginia Beach	172,106	262,199
Waynesboro	16,707	15,329
Williamsburg	9,069	9,870
Winchester	14,643	20,217
Wytheville	6,069	7,135
WASHINGTON		
Aberdeen	18,489	18,739
WA.—Cont.		
Anacortes	7,701	9,013
Auburn	21,653	26,417
Bellevue	61,196	73,903
Bellingham	39,375	45,794
Bonney Lake	2,700	5,328
Bothell	5,420	7,943
Bremerton	35,307	36,208
Camas	5,790	5,681
Centralia	10,054	10,809
Chehalis	5,727	6,100
Cheney	6,358	7,630
Clarkston	6,312	6,903
College Place	4,510	5,771
Des Moines	3,951	7,378
Edmonds	23,684	27,526
Ellensburg	13,568	11,752
Enumclaw	4,703	5,427
Ephrata	5,255	5,359
Everett	53,622	54,413
Fircrest	5,651	5,477
Grandview	3,605	5,615
Hoquiam	10,466	9,719
Issaquah	4,313	5,536
Kelso	10,296	11,129
Kennewick	15,212	34,397
Kent	17,711	23,152
Kirkland	14,970	18,779
Lacey	9,696	13,940
Longview	28,373	31,052
Lynnwood	17,381	21,937
Marysville	4,343	5,080
Mercer Island	19,047	21,522
Moses Lake	10,310	10,629
Mountlake Terrace	16,600	16,534
Mount Vernon	8,804	13,009
Oak Harbor	9,167	12,271
Olympia (c.)	23,296	27,447
Pasco	13,920	17,944
Port Angeles	16,367	17,311
Port Townsend	5,241	6,067
Pullman	20,509	23,579
Puyallup	14,742	18,251
Redmond	11,020	23,318
Renton	25,878	30,612
Richland	26,290	33,578
Seattle	530,831	493,846
Sedro-Woolley	4,598	6,110
Shelton	6,515	7,629
Snohomish	5,174	5,294
Spokane	170,516	171,300
Sunnyside	6,751	9,225
Tacoma	154,407	158,501
Toppenish	5,744	6,517
Tumwater	5,373	6,705
Vancouver	41,859	42,834
Walla Walla	23,619	25,618
Wenatchee	16,912	17,257
Yakima	45,588	49,826
WEST VIRGINIA		
Beckley	19,884	20,492
Bluefield	15,921	16,060
Bridgeport	4,777	6,604
Buckhannon	7,261	6,820
Charleston (c.)	71,505	63,968
Clarksburg	24,864	22,371
Dunbar	9,151	9,285
Elkins	8,287	8,536
Fairmont	26,093	23,863
Grafton	6,433	6,845
Huntington	74,315	63,684
Keyser	6,586	6,569
Martinsburg	14,626	13,063
Morgantown	29,431	27,605
Moundsville	13,560	12,419
New Martinsville	6,528	7,109
Nitro	8,019	8,074
Oak Hill	4,738	7,120
Parkersburg	44,208	39,967
Point Pleasant	6,122	5,682
Princeton	7,253	7,493
St. Albans	14,356	12,402
South Charleston	16,333	15,968
Vienna	11,549	11,618
Weirton	27,131	24,736
Weston	7,323	6,250
Wheeling	48,188	43,070
Williamson	5,831	5,219
WISCONSIN		
Antigo	9,005	8,653
Appleton	56,377	59,032
Ashland	9,615	9,115
Ashwaubenon	. . .	14,486
Baraboo	7,931	8,081
Beaver Dam	14,265	14,149
Beloit	35,729	35,207
Berlin	5,338	5,478
Brookfield	31,761	34,035
Brown Deer	12,582	12,921
Burlington	7,479	8,385
Cedarburg	7,697	9,005
Chippewa Falls	12,351	11,845
Cudahy	22,078	19,547
Delavan	5,526	5,684
De Pere	13,309	14,892
Eau Claire	44,619	51,509
Elm Grove	7,201	6,735
Fond du Lac	35,515	35,863
Fort Atkinson	9,164	9,785
Fox Point	7,939	7,649
Franklin	12,247	16,871
Germantown	6,974	10,729
Glendale	13,426	13,882
Grafton	5,998	8,381
Green Bay	87,809	87,889
Greendale	15,089	16,928
Greenfield	24,424	31,467
Hales Corners	7,771	7,110
Hartford	6,499	7,046
Hartland	2,763	5,559
Howard	4,911	8,240
Hudson	5,049	5,434
Janesville	46,426	51,071
Jefferson	5,429	5,647
Kaukauna	11,308	11,310
Kenosha	78,805	77,685
Kimberly	6,131	5,881
La Crosse	50,286	48,347
Lake Geneva	4,890	5,607
Little Chute	5,522	7,907
Madison (c.)	171,809	170,616
Manitowoc	33,430	32,547
WIS.—Cont.		
Marinette	12,696	11,965
Marshfield	15,619	18,290
Menasha	14,836	14,728
Menomonee Falls	31,697	27,845
Menomonie	11,112	12,769
Mequon	12,150	16,193
Merrill	9,502	9,578
Middleton	8,246	11,779
Milwaukee	717,372	636,212
Monona	10,420	8,809
Monroe	8,654	10,027
Muskego	11,573	15,277
Neenah	22,902	23,272
New Berlin	26,910	30,529
New London	5,801	6,210
Oak Creek	13,928	16,932
Oconomowoc	8,741	9,909
Onalaska	4,909	9,249
Oshkosh	53,082	49,678
Platteville	9,599	9,580
Plover	. . .	5,310
Plymouth	5,810	6,027
Portage	7,821	7,896
Port Washington	8,752	8,612
Prairie du Chien	5,540	5,859
Racine	95,162	85,725
Reedsburg	4,585	5,038
Rhinelander	8,218	7,873
Rice Lake	7,278	7,691
Ripon	7,053	7,111
River Falls	7,238	9,036
St. Francis	10,489	10,066
Shawano	6,488	7,013
Sheboygan	48,484	48,085
Sheboygan Falls	4,771	5,253
Shorewood	15,576	14,327
South Milwaukee	23,297	21,069
Sparta	6,258	6,934
Stevens Point	23,479	22,970
Stoughton	6,096	7,589
Sturgeon Bay	6,776	8,847
Sun Prairie	9,935	12,931
Superior	32,237	29,571
Tomah	5,647	7,204
Two Rivers	13,732	13,354
Watertown	15,683	18,113
Waukesha	39,695	50,319
Waupun	7,946	8,132
Wausau	32,806	32,426
Wauwatosa	58,676	51,308
West Allis	71,649	63,982
West Bend	16,555	21,484
Whitefish Bay	17,402	14,930
Whitewater	12,038	11,520
Wisconsin Rapids	18,587	17,995
WYOMING		
Casper	39,361	51,016
Cheyenne (c.)	41,254	47,283
Cody	5,161	6,790
Douglas	2,677	6,030
Evanston	4,462	6,421
Gillette	7,194	12,134
Green River	4,196	12,807
Lander	7,125	9,126
Laramie	23,143	24,410
Powell	4,807	5,310
Rawlins	7,855	11,547
Riverton	7,995	9,588
Rock Springs	11,657	19,458
Sheridan	10,856	15,146
Torrington	4,237	5,441
Wheatland	2,498	5,816
Worland	5,055	6,391

Aerial Sports

Aerial sports history was made twice in 1981, with the first balloon flight across the Pacific Ocean and the first flight of a solar-powered aircraft. The 26-story helium balloon "Double Eagle V," whose crew included Ben Abruzzo and Larry Newman, two of the three men who made the first Atlantic balloon crossing in "Double Eagle II" in 1978, flew 8,500 km (5,300 mi) from Nagashima, Japan, to a point 225 km (140 mi) north of San Francisco in nearly five days, shattering the existing balloon distance record by almost 3,200 km (2,000 mi). Abruzzo, 51, commander of the flight, had hoped to go farther but was happy to settle for the transpacific mark when his craft crash-landed in trees along a ridge in the Mendocino National Forest late on November 12.

The 11,300-cu m (400,000-cu ft) polyethylene balloon was supposed to have maintained a cruising altitude of 5,450 m (18,000 ft), but because of heavy icing and a suspected helium leak it fell as low as 1,500 m (5,000 ft), and at one point the crew prepared to parachute. The other crew members were Ron Clark, 41, like Abruzzo and Newman, 34, a resident of Albuquerque, N.M., and Rocky Aoki, 43, of Miami, a Japanese citizen and owner of the Benihana restaurant chain, who bankrolled the $250,000 enterprise.

The second history-making event was yet another aeronautical breakthrough by Paul MacCready (see BIOGRAPHIES), designer of the "Gossamer Condor," the first man-powered aircraft to fly, and the "Gossamer Albatross," the first man-powered aircraft to cross the English Channel. On July 7 MacCready's "Solar Challenger" became the first solar-powered aircraft to fly and to cross the English Channel, completing a 265-km (165-mi) trip from Cormeilles-en-Vexin, France, near Paris, to the Manston Royal Air Force Base on the southeastern coast of England at an average speed of 48 km/h (30 mph) and a cruising altitude of approximately 3,353 m (11,000 ft).

The U.S. Experimental Aircraft Association had recorded flights in 1979 of an electric battery-powered aircraft that used solar cells to charge the batteries, but the "Solar Challenger," piloted by 28-year-old Stephen Ptacek of Golden, Colo., was the first to be kept aloft solely by solar power transmitted directly to a plane's engine. The 16,128 solar cells were imbedded in the 95-kg (210-lb) aircraft's 14-m (47-ft)-long wings and 4-m (13-ft) horizontal stabilizer. With its two tiny electric motors producing only 2.7 hp, the plane required eight takeoff attempts before it was able to gain sufficient altitude for the flight.

Eighty-one pilots from 25 countries took part in the 17th world gliding championships, held May 24–June 6 at Paderborn, West Germany. George Lee of the U.K. successfully defended his 1979 Open Class championship crown by taking first place in his Nimbus 3 with 6,685 points. First place in the 15-m class was taken by Göran Ax of Sweden with 5,223 points in an AS-W 20. The standard class championship was won by Marc Schroeder of France with 5,769 points in an LS-4.

Among the world's gliding records broken in 1981, Hans Werner Grosse of West Germany set a new mark for distance around a triangular course in a single-place glider, flying 1,306.86 km (812 mi) in an AS-W 17 from Alice Springs, Australia. Susan Martin of Australia set a woman's world record for speed around a 300-km (185-mi) triangular course in a single-place glider, averaging 129.52 km/h (80.48 mph) in a Ventus A from Waikerie, Australia. Adela Dankowska and Slawomira Piatek of Poland broke the women's multiplace 500-km (310-mi) triangular course record, averaging 93.7 km/h (58.2 mph) from Leszno, Poland. In March David Bigelow of the U.S., flying a Phoebus B, became the first glider pilot in history to achieve the prestigious Diamond badge for altitude in the Hawaiian Islands, reaching an absolute altitude of 6,066 m (19,900 ft) over Oahu.

On July 7 the "Solar Challenger" became the first solar-powered aircraft to fly across the English Channel, completing a 265-km (165-mi) trip from France. The unusual craft was designed by Paul MacCready, who also designed the first man-powered aircraft that flew successfully.

The first helium-filled balloon to fly across the U.S. landed in Georgia in October after a 4,050-km (2,515-mi) flight from California. Dubbed the "Super Chicken III," the ten-story-high craft made the journey in a little more than 55 hours.

In October the first balloon flight in history across the U.S. from the Pacific coast to the Atlantic coast was completed by John Shoecroft and Fred Gorrell, both of Phoenix, Ariz., sailing the ten-story-high helium balloon "Super Chicken III" 4,-050 km (2,515 mi) from Costa Mesa, Calif., to Blackbeard Island, Ga., in 55 hours and 25 minutes. The two braved temperatures of −40° C (−40° F) and were on oxygen the entire flight.

A world distance record for AX-9 balloons of 1,139.2 km (707.8 mi) was set in March by Kristian Anderson of the U.S., flying a Raven AX-9 experimental from Lakeland, Minn., to Fish Creek, W.Va. Thomas R. Smith of the U.S. established a new world distance record for AX-5 balloons with a flight of 198.7 km (123.5 mi) from Gowanda, N.Y., to Van Etten, N.Y.

First place in the eight-task World Hot-Air Balloon Championships held at Battle Creek, Mich., June 19–27, was won by Bruce Comstock of the U.S. with 6,840 points. David Bareford of the U.K. was second with 6,631 points, and Janne Balkedahl of Sweden finished third with 6,617.

In the World Relative Work Parachuting Championships, held at Zephyr Hills, Fla., October 9–18, the U.S., Canada, and Australia finished first, second, and third in the eight-member team competition. The U.S., Canada, and Britain placed first, second, and third in the four-way contest.

The Fédération Aéronautique Internationale (FAI) confirmed the world record for the largest free-fall parachute formation, set by a 40-member U.S. team at Davis, Calif., in October 1980, and also the record for biggest night free-fall formation, set by 27 U.S. chutists at Perris Valley, Calif., in September 1980. The 2.7-second ten-man star record made by a Soviet team at Telavi, U.S.S.R., in October 1980 was also confirmed. Records in 1981 included a four-man 18-formation longest day sequence record set by a U.S. team in July at Muskogee, Okla., and a 7-formation longest night sequence record set by a four-man Soviet team at Vesprem, Hung., in April. A U.S. four-way team set a longest sequence combined record of five formations at Coolidge, Ariz., in January.

In May Jim McGowan of King of Prussia, Pa., became the first paraplegic to make a parachute jump, dropping 900 m (3,000 ft) from an airplane to the waters of Pennsylvania's Lake Wallenpaupak with his legs taped together to avoid injury. Divers swam to McGowan's aid after he landed in the water.

The world helicopter championships held in August at Piotrkow Trybunalski, Poland, were won by the U.S. team led by George Chrest. Second was the West German team with G. Pipke as pilot. The Polish team, led by pilot A. Szarawara, was third. The four cumpulsory events included lowering a magnum of champagne through a hole in the roof of a house without breaking the bottle.

The December 1980 speed-around-the-world record for Class C-1-c piston engine aircraft, claimed by Britain's Judith Chisholm, was confirmed by the FAI. She averaged 111.5 km/h (69.3 mph) in a Cessna Centurion. Marie McMillan and Gloria May of the U.S. set 14 light aircraft speed records, in a Beech Bonanza over Arizona, Nevada, and Mexico, in January and February.

The world's largest aviation event, the 29th Annual International Experimental Aircraft Association Convention and Sports Aviation Exhibition held August 1–8 at Oshkosh, Wis., drew 500,000 people and 11,000 aircraft from 59 countries. The Design, Antique, Classic, Rotorcraft, Warbird, and Ultralight Grand Championships were won by U.S. fliers. The Reserve Custom Built Grand Championship was won by an Australian.

(MICHAEL D. KILIAN)

Afghanistan

Afghanistan

A people's republic in central Asia, Afghanistan is bordered by the U.S.S.R., China, Pakistan, and Iran. Area: 652,090 sq km (251,773 sq mi). Pop. (1981 proj.): 16,276,000, including (1978 est.) Pashtoon 50%; Tadzhik 25%; Uzbek 9%; Hazara 9% (UN estimate is 14,176,000, taking into account the exodus to Pakistan and Iran). Cap. and largest city: Kabul (pop., 1979 est., 891,750). Lan-

Afghan rebels continued their attacks against regular Afghan army troops and Soviet forces in the southern part of Afghanistan near Pakistan.

guage: Persian and Pashto. Religion: Muslim 99% (including 80% Sunni; 20% Shi'ah); Hindu, Sikh, and Jewish 1%. President of the Revolutionary Council in 1981 and prime minister to June 11, Babrak Karmal; prime minister from June 11, Sultan Ali Keshtmand.

The stalemate in the Afghan crisis continued throughout 1981. Pres. Babrak Karmal's government rejected negotiations except on its own terms, and the Soviets showed no desire to withdraw or reduce their military presence. In September the scene shifted to the UN in New York City where, during the General Assembly session, UN Secretary-General Kurt Waldheim and Javier Pérez de Cuellar, UN special representative for Afghanistan, had separate discussions with the Afghan foreign minister, Shah Mohammad Dost, and Pakistan's Foreign Minister Agha Shahi. Efforts to bring the two parties together with or without the presence of a UN representative did not succeed, though it was agreed that Pérez de Cuellar would continue his mediation efforts. The New York meetings were a consequence of a November 1980 General Assembly resolution that called for withdrawal of foreign troops from Afghanistan and appealed to all parties to create conditions for a political solution.

On Aug. 25, 1981, President Karmal announced a new set of proposals for negotiations with Pakistan and Iran, either separately or together; this was a slight departure from proposals he had made in May and in December 1980. The democratic revolutionary government of Afghanistan, he said, would be prepared to hold tripartite talks with Pakistan and Iran under the aegis of UN Secretary-General Waldheim or his representative. The government wanted a political settlement that would ensure "a full and reliable end to armed and other interference from outside into Afghanistan's internal affairs, and the creation of conditions un-

der which such interference would be excluded in future." The Soviet troops could withdraw if such international guarantees were given and implemented.

Iran, itself going through a period of internal chaos, reacted negatively to the Kabul proposal, while Pakistan at first considered it "flexible" and later rejected it. Pakistan maintained its earlier stand that any direct negotiation with a representative of the Karmal government would amount to recognition of the regime, contrary to the ruling of the Islamic Conference. Indian Foreign Minister Narasimha Rao and Soviet Deputy Foreign Minister Nikolay Firyubin made separate trips to Islamabad, but they failed to persuade Pakistan to moderate its rigid stance. Meanwhile, India looked on Pakistan's arms buildup as a threat to its own security and even accused Pakistan of prolonging the Afghan crisis in order to obtain sophisticated weapons from the United States. India also tried to persuade Moscow to alter its position, but without results.

Attempts by the European Economic Community and the nonaligned nations to work out a political solution resulted in proposals unacceptable to Moscow and Kabul. At the nonaligned foreign ministers' conference in New Delhi, India, in February, Foreign Minister Dost expressed reservations over the proposals reached through consensus. They called for withdrawal of foreign forces from Afghanistan, noninterference in its internal affairs, and respect for its independence and nonaligned status.

Rebel resistance against the Soviet presence intensified throughout the country, despite all-out efforts by the 85,000-strong Soviet force and the Afghan Army to curb it. The Afghan Army, 80,-000–100,000 strong at the time of the Soviet intervention, continued to suffer depletion as a result of large-scale desertions. Appeals to teachers and stu-

dents from schools and universities to register for military service went unheeded.

There were reports of widespread fighting between the *mujaheddin* (Islamic guerrillas) and the security forces in vast areas stretching from Qandahar in the south to Badakhshan on the Soviet border. Towns in Qandahar Province and the Panjsher valley were said to have changed hands many times. The presence of rebels brought reprisals from the Soviet forces, and helicopter gunship and artillery attacks devastated several villages. Although there were no official estimates, Soviet casualties were also believed to be heavy.

The flight of refugees, doctors, engineers, lawyers, intellectuals, and farmers across the border to Pakistan also continued. By March 1981, according to UN statistics, 1.7 million Afghans had fled to Pakistan and some 400,000 to Iran in order to escape the strife in their country. Although Pakistan denied the allegation, there was said to be evidence of a regular arms flow to the *mujaheddin* inside Afghanistan from across the border. In November 1980 it was disclosed that Egypt was sending arms to the *mujaheddin*, while in March 1981 Saudi Arabia was said to have sent $15 million to the rebels via the Islamic Conference.

In June President Karmal gave up the post of prime minister; he was succeeded in that position by Sultan Ali Keshtmand, another trusted member of the Parcham faction of the People's Democratic Party. Keshtmand was also put in direct charge of the National Patriotic Front, set up in December 1980 with the intention of rallying the people behind Karmal's Marxist revolutionary government. Western reports spoke of continued Soviet attempts to reorganize the country's political structure on the Soviet model. Hundreds of

Soviet citizens were reportedly functioning as advisers, while thousands of Afghan students and young party functionaries were being sent to the Soviet Union for ideological training.

In February Karmal visited Moscow, where he signed a series of agreements, mainly economic, with Soviet leaders. The Afghan economy was moving further and further into the orbit of the Soviet bloc, which took most of its exports in return for food grains and consumer goods. Under a series of trade agreements signed in the first half of the year, large quantities of Soviet bloc consumer goods, including motor vehicles, fertilizers, and foodstuffs, were to be sent to Afghanistan. Afghanistan's electric power distribution grid was to be linked with the Soviet grid under a new agreement announced in September.

(GOVINDAN UNNY)

African Affairs

Africa's continued preoccupation during 1981 was with the rapid decline of the economies of virtually all of its 61 countries. The greatest single problem remained the need for food imports to make up for the progressive failure of most countries to grow enough to feed themselves. (*See* Special Report.) What was remarkable in these circumstances was the relative stability of the continent's political systems.

The Organization of African Unity. The 50-nation Organization of African Unity held its 18th annual summit in June in Nairobi, Kenya, whose president, Daniel arap Moi, became OAU chairman for 1981–82. The main political issues were again the Western Sahara, Chad, South West Africa/Namibia, and South Africa. The Western Sahara issue was defused by an unexpected détente between two of the main adversaries, Morocco and Libya, and by Morocco's acceptance of an earlier OAU proposal for a referendum in the disputed area. The Libyans found themselves under considerable pressure to withdraw their military forces from Chad, as soon as an African peacekeeping force could be assembled to police the country while free elections were arranged. A proposal to hold the next OAU summit in Tripoli, Libya, was accepted after a heated debate. Several countries, including Egypt, Sudan, Uganda, and Senegal, announced their intention to boycott the summit if it were held in Tripoli; others, led by Nigeria, stated as their condition for attending that Libyan troops be withdrawn from Chad six months before the meeting.

The OAU reiterated its demand for total economic sanctions against South Africa unless it agreed to immediate implementation of the UN Security Council resolution 435, which provided a framework for achieving Namibian independence. An attempt by Algeria and Libya to censure Egypt, because of its peace negotiations with Israel, was defeated. The OAU reaffirmed its strong support for the Palestinians' right to an independent state.

Southern Africa. Attention in southern Africa focused on the issue of Namibia's independence. The initial reluctance of U.S. Pres. Ronald Reagan's

AFGHANISTAN

Education. (1978–79) Primary, pupils 942,787, teachers 30,518; secondary, pupils 92,391, teachers 6,530; vocational, pupils 12,735, teachers 889; teacher training, students 6,629, teachers 406; higher, students 11,367, teaching staff 1,012.

Finance. Monetary unit: afghani, with (Sept. 21, 1981) a free rate of 54 afghanis to U.S. $1 (101 afghanis = £1 sterling). Gold and other reserves (June 1981) U.S. $331 million. Budget (1978–79 est.): revenue 16,455,000,000 afghanis; expenditure 12,385,000,000 afghanis. Money supply (March 1981) 40,934,000,000 afghanis.

Foreign Trade. (1980–81) Imports U.S. $438 million; exports U.S. $670 million. Import sources (1977–78): U.S.S.R. 22%; Japan 21%; Iran 13%; West Germany 6%; India 5%. Export destinations (1977–78): U.S.S.R. 37%; Pakistan 12%; U.K. 12%; India 8%; West Germany 6%. Main exports: fruits and nuts 32%; natural gas 32%; carpets 16%; cotton 6%; karakul (persian lamb) skins 5%.

Transport and Communications. Roads (1978) 18,752 km. Motor vehicles in use (1978): passenger 34,506; commercial 22,100. Air traffic (1980): c. 163 million passenger-km; freight c. 21 million net ton-km. Telephones (Jan. 1979) 31,200. Radio receivers (Dec. 1977) c. 823,000. Television receivers (Jan. 1980) c. 120,000.

Agriculture. Production (in 000; metric tons; 1980): wheat c. 2,700; corn 797; rice 421; barley 321; grapes c. 460; cotton, lint c. 25; wool, clean c. 15. Livestock (in 000; 1979): cattle c. 3,980; karakul sheep c. 7,000; other sheep c. 16,000; goats c. 3,000; horses c. 400; asses c. 1,295; camels c. 300.

Industry. Production (in 000; metric tons; 1979–80): coal 132; natural gas (cu m) 2,327,000; cotton fabrics (m) 64,600; rayon fabrics (m) 21,000; nitrogenous fertilizers (nutrient content) 106; cement 98; electricity (kw-hr) c. 908,000.

Sam Nujoma (centre), president of the delegation of the South West Africa People's Organization (SWAPO), and his delegation attended a UN conference in January in Geneva to seek a solution to the question of independence for Namibia.

administration to endorse UN Security Council resolution 435 threatened to undermine the joint initiative begun in 1977 by the contact group of five Western members of the UN Security Council (the U.S., Britain, France, West Germany, and Canada), which sought to find a peaceful settlement to the conflict through negotiations. However, a determined stand by the other four countries — all NATO allies of the U.S. — brought the U.S. back into line in support of the resolution. The U.S. then set out to achieve a new agreement with South Africa by introducing changes in resolution 435. The contact group endorsed a proposed amendment to the resolution which provided constitutional guarantees for minority groups in an independent Namibia along the lines set out in the UN's Universal Declaration of Human Rights.

The U.S. was also persuaded not to link the issue of the withdrawal of Cuban troops from Angola with Namibia's independence. This change of U.S. policy was facilitated by official Angolan declarations that once Namibia was independent and its own borders were no longer threatened by South Africa, Angola would not require the presence of a Cuban military force. In October the contact group resumed attempts to persuade the neighbouring African nations, South Africa, and the South West Africa People's Organization (SWAPO) to agree to implement the first stages of resolution 435 in 1982. However, in the same month the U.S. Senate began moves to repeal a ban on military aid to Jonas Savimbi's guerrilla force, the Union for the Total Independence of Angola (UNITA).

Meanwhile, the level of armed violence in the region continued to rise. The South African Army made several attacks deep into Angola. South African commandos also made a lightning offensive on Mozambique in an attempt to cripple the operations of the African National Congress (ANC). Mozambique accused South Africa of supporting a small dissident armed group that was engaging in successful sabotage against it. Lesotho, too, alleged

that South Africa was involved in supporting the armed attacks of the opposition Basutoland Congress Party, while Zambia claimed that armed units of South Africans were active inside its borders. Prime Minister Robert Mugabe of Zimbabwe accused South Africa of being engaged in attempts to destabilize his country by obstructing the passage of traffic from Zimbabwe to South African ports.

Uneasy relations between South Africa and its neighbours increased the urgent need felt for strengthening the nine-member Southern African Development Coordination Conference (SADCC), the aim of which was to lessen the dependence of its members on South Africa's economy. A pledging conference to provide aid for SADCC projects was well attended by Western nations, a number of Arab countries, and China, though no members of the Soviet bloc were there.

The Horn of Africa. The buildup of naval and other military forces by both the U.S.S.R. and the U.S. in the Indian Ocean and the Red Sea was given a fresh impetus after the assassination of Pres. Anwar as-Sadat (see OBITUARIES) of Egypt in October. Apart from increasing its military visibility in Egypt, the U.S. speeded up the supply of $100 million in arms aid to Sudan. Although it established a formal naval and air presence in Berbera, Somalia, the U.S. preferred to use the better facilities on offer in Kenya and also to complete the infrastructure of its military base on the island of Diego Garcia in the Chagos Archipelago. There were reports of a small but significant number of Soviet warships in the Indian Ocean. African and South Asian coastal nations of the Indian Ocean intensified their pressure to have that sea declared a zone of peace, free from nuclear weapons and foreign military forces.

Despite considerable Soviet military and economic support, efforts to establish a full-fledged Marxist regime in Ethiopia still faltered, partly because of continuing divisions within the ruling

party and partly because of the armed resistance in Eritrea, the Ogaden, Tigre, and Bale. The leaders of Ethiopia, Libya, and South Yemen met in Aden in August to coordinate their opposition to the regimes of Sudan, Somalia, and Egypt, which they identified as U.S. military allies. The U.S.S.R. publicly endorsed their objectives.

Coups and Inter-African Affairs. There was only one successful coup in the continent, the overthrow of Pres. David Dacko in the Central African Republic. A military coup attempt in The Gambia against Pres. Dawda Jawara (*see* BIOGRAPHIES) was defeated only because of military intervention by neighbouring Senegal. Several plots to unseat Pres. Kenneth Kaunda of Zambia were uncovered, and Morocco was accused of being involved in an attempt to overthrow the regime in Mauritania.

Libya's relations with at least a dozen African countries continued to be troubled. The plotters in The Gambia were said to have made contact with Libya's Col. Muammar al-Qaddafi (*see* BIOGRAPHIES); Sudan, Uganda, Senegal, Niger, and Mali accused Libya of plotting against them. Algeria, which had maintained close relations with Libya, was upset by Qaddafi's détente with Morocco, which, in its view, delayed the independence of Western Sahara. Although the Libyans publicly rejoiced in the killing of President Sadat, the Egyptians only accused them of indirect responsibility for the deed. However, the Libyan venture in Chad failed to prosper. Not only was there no progress toward the objective of unifying Libya and Chad, but Pres. Goukouni Oueddei of Chad demanded the withdrawal of all Libyan troops from his country in October.

Political Systems. The trend toward greater liberalization of government continued despite the setback to multiparty politics in The Gambia resulting from the abortive coup. Tunisia fulfilled its promise to hold elections on a multiparty basis; however, the November elections resulted in a sweep for the ruling Parti Socialiste Destourien. In Uganda, notwithstanding armed political violence, Pres. Milton Obote maintained a multiparty parliamentary democratic system. However, in Zimbabwe Prime Minister Mugabe formally announced his aim of establishing a single-party system as the best way of creating a viable nonracial society, but he also promised that no move would be made without the consent of the electorate. Sudan continued its experiment of devolving power from the centre by creating a system of regional assemblies.

External Relations. The election of President Reagan was initially viewed with considerable apprehension by most African leaders. They mistrusted his advocacy of the use of friendship toward South Africa as the best way of changing its system of racial separation; his promised military support to UNITA as a means of ousting the Cubans from Angola and undercutting Soviet influence there; the higher priority he gave to military aid as compared with economic aid; and his generally more interventionist policies in fighting those identified as hostile to U.S. interests. Although some of President Reagan's electoral policies softened during the first year of his administration, he continued to be viewed with suspicion by all but a few countries that stood to gain most by qualifying for large-scale arms supplies—notably Egypt, Sudan, Morocco, and, to a lesser extent, Tunisia.

The election of Pres. François Mitterrand in France was widely welcomed. Most African leaders saw his advent to power as spelling the end of the Gaullist policies of intervention in Africa and as promising more constructive Franco-African cooperation. There was satisfaction with U.K. Prime Minister Margaret Thatcher's strong support for Mugabe's government in Zimbabwe and her government's commitment to securing Namibia's independence and willingness to deal in a friendly fashion with Mozambique and Angola,

UN Secretary General Kurt Waldheim (right) was welcomed for a meeting of the Organization of African Unity in Nairobi, Kenya, by OAU Secretary General Edom Kodjo (left) and Kenyan Foreign Minister Robert Ouko (centre).

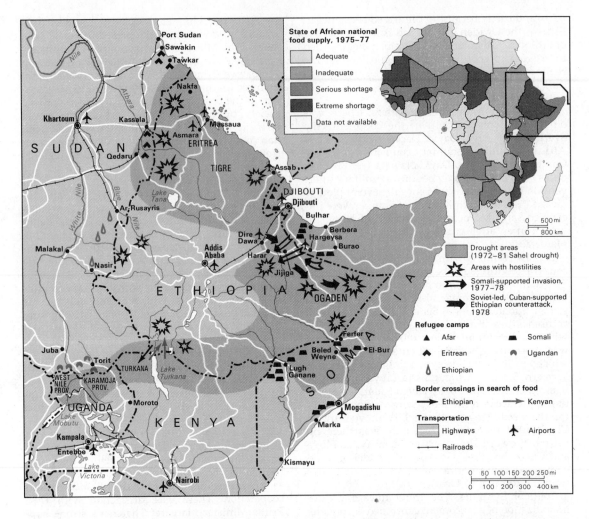

State of African national food supply, 1975–77
- Adequate
- Inadequate
- Serious shortage
- Extreme shortage
- Data not available

Drought areas (1972–81 Sahel drought)
☆ Areas with hostilities
⇨ Somali-supported invasion, 1977–78
➡ Soviet-led, Cuban-supported Ethiopian counterattack, 1978

Refugee camps
▲ Afar ▬ Somali
♠ Eritrean ♦ Ugandan
♦ Ethiopian

Border crossings in search of food
→ Ethiopian → Kenyan

Transportation
▬ Highways ✈ Airports
+—+ Railroads

but there was criticism of British aid cuts and, especially, the decision to increase greatly the fees charged to those from overseas studying in the U.K. The policies of Australia and Canada won general approval, along with those of the Nordic countries.

The Soviet bloc continued to display a keen interest in Africa, concentrating particularly on Ethiopia, Angola, Mozambique, and Libya. Although a number of African countries, including Zambia, were eager to buy arms from the U.S.S.R., the feeling grew that the Soviet bloc as a whole was incapable of providing the kind of economic and technical aid that Africa most needed. The Soviet military intervention in Afghanistan was criticized by all but three African governments, while its interference in Poland was widely commented on. The Cubans appeared eager to reduce their military role, and there was some criticism of what was felt to be a lowering of the quality of experts provided by Havana.

Social and Economic Conditions. The international economic recession, worldwide inflationary pressures, and the continuing rise in the price of energy and other imports continued to play havoc with the foreign trade balances of the majority of African countries, resulting in greater indebtedness to Western financial institutions and a slowdown in local development programs. Stark

economic disaster faced much of the continent. Adebayo Adedeji, executive secretary of the UN Economic Commission for Africa (ECA), reported that the inhabitants of the poorest African countries were as badly off in the early 1980s as they had been throughout the 1970s. He could foresee no improvement in the $10 billion trade deficit registered by the non-oil-producing African countries. These nations had registered a real per capita income increase of only 1% during the 1970s, well below the annual population growth of about 3%.

A report by the UN-sponsored World Food Council showed that 60 million Africans, almost one-fifth of the continent's total population, faced prolonged hunger in the 1980s. According to the UN Food and Agriculture Organization, grain imports by black African countries had almost tripled in the last two decades. This grim economic picture had obvious implications for the continent's future political stability as well as for its future relations with the developed world. It explained the impatience of African leaders over the West's failure to follow up the Brandt Commission report (1980), which had clearly demonstrated the close interrelationship between the economies of the major Western industrial nations and those of the third world. (COLIN LEGUM)

See also Dependent States; articles on the various political units.

WHAT IT MEANS TO STARVE

by Liv Ullmann

In 1980 UNICEF—the United Nations Children's Fund—appointed the internationally acclaimed actress Liv Ullmann as its "goodwill ambassador." Ullmann undertook the task with wholehearted dedication, devoting much of her time and talent to drawing attention to the special needs and problems of children in the less developed countries. In December 1980 she visited the famine-afflicted countries of the Horn of Africa and was profoundly affected by what she saw there: "I came back from my trip to the Horn of Africa to a hotel room in Kenya and was met by the radio: 'Jingle bells, jingle bells, jingle all the way, Oh what fun it is to ride in a one-horse open sleigh.' And I wondered about the little four-year-old naked figure I saw collecting food in his little can at the health station in a refugee camp, the little body walking away, the tiny little behind wrinkled as an old man, and I wondered if he was still alive, and how his Christmas would be. So I wrote a story, about the fundamental gift I would wish for him: Peace." With Liv Ullmann's permission we reproduce that story here:

Once upon a time there was a 14-year-old girl who wrote in her diary: "I believe that deep down all human beings are really good." Her name was Anne Frank and she ended her life some months later in a concentration camp during World War II. I used to believe in these words—I used to say that we must prove this 14-year-old right: "that deep down all human beings are really good."

And I traveled in the world and saw the victims of poverty and drought and man-made disasters, met children who smiled in trust to a stranger within a refugee camp, and I struggled to maintain belief that if we just reached out to each other in *love* we would find the kindness *even* within those who were the abusers of these homeless children who took your hand and gave you of their heart.

And then I came to the Horn of Africa and I finally lost trust in the words of Anne Frank. I do not believe any more that "all human beings are good." It is with sadness I lose this illusion, but after hearing the testament of the innocent victims of man's cruelty I have no right to hide behind the beauty and innocent words of a 14-year-old. You are *wrong,* Anne Frank, and I am sorry you died in vain, that we did not learn a thing from the tragedies of World

War II. Your sisters and brothers here in Africa are but some of the millions who have been abused by man-made catastrophe since your diary was written. They are the shocking proof that evil is very much part of our world. Though the world *need* not be evil, it is only evil when we *allow* evil to exist. Therefore, I accuse indifference—indifference is the silence with which we must not meet war. Indifference is the enemy of peace. Indifference toward the victims, toward their future—which, in the end, is also our future.

Better then to believe the words of Martin Luther King, the great leader of a nonviolent action for human rights: "We shall overcome!" Believe these words when we see the women of Africa hold their children up to you, pleading for their lives. Believe these words when a woman clasps her empty breasts which can no more keep the milk for the little baby, sucking and sucking in vain. Or the old man who points to his blind eyes, because his right to decent food had been taken away from him a long time ago. The children who put their hands on their big bellies to show that it hurts to be hungry. The young man pressing his wooden leg angrily into the dust—amputated by a bullet that tore his leg apart. A family showing the little wooden bowl, which when filled with food is their *whole* meal that day for *all* of them—however many family members there are. And then there are those who had to flee in such a panic from their homes that they did not even *have* a wooden bowl to put the ration of water and food in. The mother who gave life to her child under a tree and next day was found and brought to a refugee camp where the child is to grow up with no knowledge of its father or a home, with a harsh welcome to the world—which is a bed of stone and sand and no roof or walls to shelter it, from the first months of its life.

Liv Ullmann with children in Ethiopia.

ARILD VOLLAN—UNICEF

The people in the Horn of Africa are brothers and sisters. They live so close to each other and should be allowed to live in peace. The world community has to meet their suffering with obligation and responsibility, and their war with a demand for *peace*. They are not to be drowned in our tears and our pity, but sheltered with the understanding and compassion we show our *own* family, because their future is our future—*they* are *you* and *me*. Too many people in the countries of Africa have been deprived of the basic elements of life: water and crops and a home. Though still the men, women, and children move in the dust with grace and with dignity, creating inspired love and songs which they willingly share.

God created Ethiopia, Djibouti, Somalia in a desert, but out of the sand grew a people of flowers, giving new meaning to the words of Martin Luther King: "We shall overcome!"

You and I must not let them down.

Hunger in the Horn of Africa
by Victoria Brittain

Uncounted thousands of people have died of hunger in the Horn of Africa in the last two years. Neither governments nor international aid agencies can control the waves of people who have moved across the borders of Uganda, Sudan, Ethiopia, Somalia, and Djibouti in flight from drought and war. Of an estimated five million refugees in all Africa, probably half are in the Horn or the countries bordering it.

Drought is an old and well-known enemy of people here, many of whom are nomads who have traditionally crossed national boundaries with their flocks. Every six or seven years when the drought struck parts of this area, the nomads reduced its impact by moving on. Emergency relief efforts by governments, churches, and international agencies have been enough to save most people except when the droughts have been on an immense scale, like the great Sahel drought of the early 1970s, or deliberately hidden by the responsible government, like the Welo famine that began the downfall of Emperor Haile Selassie of Ethiopia.

But the last two years in the Horn of Africa have defeated the aid givers and the various national governments because the drought's effect has been compounded by war. The Ogaden war between Ethiopia and Somali guerrillas has not only spawned refugees but has also caused the slaughter of huge herds of camels and the destruction of thousands of acres of grain. The Ethiopian Army has similarly destroyed the livelihood of thousands of peasant families in southern and western Ethiopia in its attempts to stamp out resistance to the central authority in Addis Ababa. In northern Ethiopia, in Eritrea and Tigre, civil war smolders on after 20 and 6 years, respectively. Resources of men and money no longer go into agriculture, but into war. In Somalia the situation is even worse. The country's fragile administration and its four million people living in extreme poverty have been swamped by over one million refugees. Any one of Somalia's refugee camps tells the story of famine. Rows and rows of makeshift huts of sticks and paper house skeletal families. Listless children line up for UNICEF supplementary feeding programs. Dedicated European and Somali doctors sit in the dust under the blazing sun as lines of women, children, and old men show them the symptoms of hunger-related diseases.

In most of the refugee camps in the Horn of Africa there is a daily or weekly ration of porridge, rice, corn (maize), or cow peas. On such a diet people stay alive, but evidence of vitamin and protein deficiencies jumps to the eye. Often, particularly in Somalia, water is chronically short, and dehydrated children are a common sight. If there is water it is often dirty and a potential disease carrier. As the camps grow, it becomes increasingly difficult too to find firewood nearby to boil water and cook the daily ration. The lack of records in all camps, the extreme logistical difficulties of transport to the more remote ones, and the frequent poor coordination by the UN agencies have often meant periods of no food at all and dozens of deaths a day in many camps.

An enormous commitment of qualified administrators from the Sudanese government has led to better organization of the half-million or so Eritreans and Ethiopians in the camps in the eastern Sudan. Some camps grow part of their own food, and from others the refugees go out to work on the country's big new agricultural schemes. Nowhere do the refugees say they have enough food, but in eastern Sudan they do not die of starvation.

In southern Sudan, where communications are as difficult as in Somalia and the few tracks disappear in the rainy season, more than 100,000 Ugandans have fled in several waves over the border from fighting in the remote West Nile province of their own country. Again war has disrupted planting patterns, and harvests have been stolen by soldiers. The cattle raiding which has been a traditional way of life among neighbouring tribes in northeast Uganda's Karamoja Province, southern Sudan, and northern Kenya's Turkana district has also contributed to the pattern of famine. Since former Ugandan president Idi Amin's soldiers broke open the armoury at Moroto as they fled north from the Tanzanian Army in April 1979, thousands of machine guns and rifles have been freely available for sale or barter from Zaire to Ethiopia. Cattle have been killed by the thousands in raids as well as by the drought. Even the small amount of agriculture practiced in previous years has become virtually impossible because of the insecurity still reigning more than two years after Amin's fall.

Even without war and without chronic drought, famine is growing inexorably in this part of Africa. Thus Kenya, previously an exporter of corn, has had to turn to the U.S. for food shipments to keep its 15 million people fed.

Victoria Brittain was until recently East African correspondent for The Guardian, London. *She is now in the paper's foreign department.*

Agriculture and Food Supplies

World agricultural and food production increased in 1981, led by recovery in U.S. and Canadian output from the 1980 drought. Most of the less developed countries of Asia and Latin America shared in the growth, but the Soviet Union experienced poor grain harvests for the third year in a row. Aggregate food production in the less developed nations of Africa continued to grow more slowly than population. The United States in April 1981 ended its embargo on the exportation of various agricultural products to the U.S.S.R., but the question of trade sanctions was again raised at the end of the year because of political turmoil in Poland.

Although world supplies of coarse grains and oilseeds became more ample in 1981, world stocks of wheat by the end of 1981–82 were expected to remain, as a percentage of utilization, at a 20-year low. Short-term world food security continued to be heavily dependent upon the next season's harvests. The United Nations Food and Agriculture Organization (FAO) reported that "man-made disasters were placing a greater strain upon international emergency food resources than were natural causes."

Another impasse was reached in efforts to draft an international grain reserve agreement when the U.S., supported by other leading exporting countries, announced opposition to international control or coordination of national actions involving stocks of grain. A new food import financing facility was inaugurated, and the 1980 Food Aid Convention was extended for two years.

Production Indexes. After two years of stagnation, world food and agricultural output (excluding China) began expanding again in 1981, both increasing about 2.75%, according to indexes prepared by the Economic Research Service of the U.S. Department of Agriculture (USDA). Agricultural production was up nearly 4% in the developed countries, largely because of the recovery in farm output in North America from the drought-reduced level of 1980. Agricultural output failed to grow in the centrally planned economies, where recovery in Eastern European production to 1979 levels was offset by the third straight year of smaller Soviet harvests.

In the less developed countries, total agricultural production increased about 3.5%. The East Asian, South Asian, and Latin-American regions all achieved increases of approximately 5%, but output failed to grow in West Asia and Africa. Output leveled off in the largest African countries, while a sharp decline in Moroccan production, because of drought, helped to offset increases elsewhere in Africa. A continuing decline in Iranian production largely offset gains by other countries in the West Asian region.

Although world food production per capita increased about 1%, it remained below the levels achieved in 1977–79. Total food production grew at about the same 3.5% rate in 1981 in both the developed and less developed countries, but faster population growth in the latter translated into a 1.1% increase in per capita food production there, compared with 2.8% in the developed countries. Per capita food output fell nearly 0.5% in the centrally planned countries.

Per capita production gains were strongest and most widely distributed among the less developed countries of East Asia and Latin America. South Asia also achieved an improvement based on a

A mild winter and early summer rains resulted in enormous wheat crops in the northwestern United States. Fields on this farm in Oregon produced double their normal yield.

UPI

World Production and Trade of Principal Grains (in 000 metric tons)

	Wheat Production 1961–65 average	Wheat Production 1980	Wheat Imports−/Exports+ 1977–80 average	Barley Production 1961–65 average	Barley Production 1980	Barley Imports−/Exports+ 1977–80 average	Oats Production 1961–65 average	Oats Production 1980	Oats Imports−/Exports+ 1977–80 average	Rye Production 1961–65 average	Rye Production 1980	Rye Imports−/Exports+ 1977–80 average	Corn (Maize) Production 1961–65 average	Corn (Maize) Production 1980	Corn (Maize) Imports−/Exports+ 1977–80 average	Rice Production 1961–65 average	Rice Production 1980	Rice Imports−/Exports+ 1977–80 average
World total	254576	445123	−70608[1] +71711[1]	98474	162327	−13820[1] +14058[1]	47775	42667	−1387[1] +1466[1]	33849	27324	−760[1] +756[1]	216429	390549	−66155[1] +67658[1]	254711	399225	−10573[1] +10858[1]
Algeria	1254	1301	−1439	476	791	−c320	28	c110	−11[1]	—	—	—	4	c6[2]	−171	7	c1[2]	−14[1]
Argentina	7541	7830	+4001	679	238	+48	676	501	+166	422	178	+13	4984	6410	+5203	193	178	−4 +106
Australia	8222	10800	+9929	978	2890	+2052	1172	1260	+337	11	c17	−1[1]	176	127	−3[1] +21	136	613	−1[1] +312
Austria	704	1201	−2 +138	563	1515	−17 +16	322	316	−11	393	383	—	197	1293	−23 +1[1]	—	—	−44
Bangladesh	37	c1200	−1120	15	13[2]	−1[1]	—	—	—	—	—	—	4	c2[2]	—	15048	20990	−c260
Belgium	826	c850	−1093[3] +551[3]	485	c790	−1207[3] +546[3]	389	c107	−68[3] +12[3]	120	c40	−15[3] +7[3]	2	c37[2]	−2423[3] +1124[3]	—	—	−138[3] +67[3]
Brazil	574	2614	−3765	26	98[2]	−32	20	71	−29	17	12	—	10112	20377	−1097 +362	6123	9746	−248 +147
Bulgaria	2213	3839	−202 +344	694	c1280	−91 +12	141	c60	—	58	c20	—	1601	c2500	−365 +71	37	c65[2]	−9[1] +1[1]
Burma	38	41[2]	—	—	—	—	—	—	—	—	—	—	58	c78[2]	+10	7786	13317	+c730
Canada	15364	19131	+14427	3860	11041	+3264	6075	3028	+172	319	448	+279	1073	5462	−750 +357	—	—	−82
Chile	1082	966	−808	74	105	+2	89	173	−2[1] +1[1]	7	10	—	204	405	−213	85	181[2]	−17 +15[1]
China	22200	54155	−c8830	c5700	c4800	−480	c1600	c1000	—	c1500	c2000	—	c22500	c30000	−3580 +c40	c86000	c134000	−c110 +c1550
Colombia	118	38[2]	−406	106	72	−81	—	c5[2]	−9[1]	—	—	—	826	813	−122	576	1892	−7[1] +88
Czechoslovakia	1779	c5100	−476	1556	c3900	−118 +31	792	c450	−2[1]	897	c585	−10[1]	474	c700	−862	—	—	−78
Denmark	535	648	−31 +158	3506	6098	−103 +637	713	160	−22 +3	380	198	−4[1] +81	—	—	−250	—	—	−12 +2
Egypt	1459	c1796	−3825	137	c107	−1[1]	—	—	—	—	—	—	1913	c3230	−690	1845	c2348	+140
Ethiopia	540	c469	−237	628	c772	−11[1]	5	c14	—	141	c120	—	743	c1144	—	—	—	−1[1]
Finland	448	c284	−177 +31[1]	400	c1534	−15 +121	828	c1680	+66	141	c120	−34	—	—	−3[1]	—	—	−14
France	12495	23668	−490 +7386	6594	11758	−164 +3535	2583	1927	−1[1] +250	367	405	−4[1] +74	2760	9219	−834 +2411	120	c45[2]	−266 +43
Germany, East	1357	c3600	−c850 +c56	1291	c3528	−c940 +c156	850	c570	−c58 +c95	1741	c1900	−c43 +c50	3	c2[2]	−c1340	—	—	−44
Germany, West	4607	8156	−1236 +719	3462	8826	−1254 +240	2185	2658	−212 +18	3031	2098	−70 +166	55	672	−2768 +200	—	—	−171 +46
Greece	1765	2931	+77	248	949	−59	143	87	—	19	6	—	239	1223	−1078	88	78	+18[1]
Hungary	2020	c6048	−2[1] +676	970	c926	−124 +9	108	c70	−7	271	c130	−5[1] +5[1]	3350	c6575	−141 +171	36	c48[2]	−26
India	11191	31564	−390 +358	2590	1616	+8[1]	—	—	—	—	—	—	4593	c6400	−18[1]	52733	c83000	−83 +324
Indonesia	—	—	−952	—	—	—	—	—	—	—	—	—	2804	c3600	−44 +13	12396	c28680	−1937
Iran	2873	c6000	−c1310	792	c1100	−c500	—	—	—	—	—	—	24	c57[2]	−c360	851	c1150	−c480
Iraq	849	c1300	−c1370	851	c575	−c220	—	—	—	—	—	—	2	c85[2]	−c110	142	c220	−320
Ireland	343	c235	−211 +29	575	c1370	−38 +187	357	c96	−13	1	c1[2]	—	—	—	−224 +1[1]	—	—	−3[1]
Italy	8857	9291	−3156 +24	276	958	−1387 +6[1]	545	456	−148 +1[1]	87	36	−3	3633	6493	−3584 +12	612	911	−180 +467
Japan	1332	583	−5712	1380	c385	−1540	145	c10	−174	2	c1	−79	96	c5[2]	−10960	16444	12819	−34 +348
Kenya	122	c210	−47	15	c75[2]	−2[1] +1[1]	2	c7	—	—	—	—	1110	c1450	−81 +38	14	43[2]	+1[1]
Korea, South	170	42[2]	−1798	1148	811	−111	—	—	—	18	c3	−1[1]	26	100[2]	−2059	4809	c6000	−302 +27[1]
Malaysia	—	—	−453	—	—	—	—	—	−5[1]	—	—	—	8	c30[2]	−470 +1[1]	1140	2129	−268
Mexico	1672	2645	−726 +17	175	505	−75 +17[1]	76	c75	—	—	—	—	7369	11081	−1829	314	462	+21[1]
Morocco	1516	c1811	−c1540	1514	c2212	−19[1]	18	c33	—	2	c2	—	405	c333	−90	20	c22[2]	—
Netherlands, The	606	c882	−1416 +606	390	c258	−362 +164	421	c94	−38 +53	312	c39	−48 +10	—	c5	−3520 +1176	—	—	−158 +92
New Zealand	248	325	−26 +5[1]	98	295	+53	34	64	—	—	c1	—	16	187	+37	—	—	−7[1]
Nigeria	16	c21[2]	−c870	—	—	—	—	—	—	—	—	—	997	c1550	−84	207	c725	−c460
Norway	19	c77[2]	−320 +2[1]	440	c670	−48	126	c400	+24[1]	3	5	−45	—	—	−66	—	—	−7
Pakistan	4153	10805	−c1140	118	118	+14[1]	—	—	—	—	—	—	514	c963	+1[1]	1824	4595	+1023
Peru	150	85	−770	185	c150	−27	4	c1	−6[1]	1	c1	—	490	425	−236 +1[1]	324	423	−107
Philippines	—	—	−c680	—	—	—	—	—	−3[1]	—	—	—	1305	3117	−98	3957	c7431	−10[1] +94
Poland	2988	c4176	−2825 +18[1]	1368	3420	−1577 +7[1]	2641	2245	−107 +2[1]	7466	6566	−248	20	187[2]	−1983	—	—	−78
Portugal	562	377	−675	61	43	−47[1]	87	88	−11[1]	177	127	−15[1]	617	468	−1970	167	155	−82
Romania	4321	c6417	−c630 +c940	415	c2400	−c210 +c10[1]	154	c50	−c13[1]	95	c50	—	5853	c11180	−c740 +c780	40	c65	−c52
South Africa	834	1470	−1[1] +122	40	141[2]	+c32	107	78	−5[1] +5[1]	10	5	−1[1]	5248	10230	−30[1] +2542	2	c3[2]	−120 +1[1]
Spain	4365	5901	−240 +4	1959	8561	−142 +2[1]	447	664	+2[1]	385	292	−2[1]	1101	2297	−4346 +2[1]	386	433	+61
Sweden	909	1291	−25 +496	1167	2486	−3[1] +184	1304	1685	−6[1] +191	142	c241	+86	—	—	−34	—	—	−23
Switzerland	355	403	−348	102	201	−428	40	48	−143	52	41	−13	14	108	−249	—	—	−27
Syria	1093	2229	−100 +8[1]	649	1587	−2[1] +42[1]	2	c2	—	—	—	—	7	c68[2]	−70	1	—	−98
Thailand	—	—	−133	—	—	—	—	—	—	—	—	—	816	c3150	+1911	11267	c18000	+2538
Turkey	8585	17455	−2[1] +918	3447	c5500	+134	495	350	—	734	580	+26	950	1150	—	222	224[2]	−25
U.S.S.R.	64207	98100	−c9520 +c1900	20318	c44500	+c940 +c400	6052	c14200	−c157 +c15	15093	c10200	−184	13122	c9700	−c10900 +c150	390	2800	−c540 +c35
United Kingdom	3520	8145	−3060 +306	6670	10350	−440 +1109	1541	645	−45 +6	21	24	−23 +1[1]	—	1[2]	−3435 +24	—	—	−207 +53
United States	33040	64492	−11 +31764	8676	7806	−146 +1096	13848	6642	−20 +101	828	413	−2 +58	95561	168855	−44 +53254	3084	6580	−1[1] +2483
Uruguay	465	c300	−44 +23[1]	28	c55[2]	−4[1] +1[1]	66	c20	−1[1] +1[1]	—	—	—	148	71[2]	−21[1] +7[1]	67	289	+132
Venezuela	1	1[2]	−770	—	—	—	—	—	—	—	—	−6	477	c584	−600 +1[1]	136	681	+44
Yugoslavia	3599	5078	−c535 +24	557	c650	−32	343	c295	−1[1]	169	c84	—	5618	9106	−c300 +c190	23	34[2]	−16[1]

Note: (—) indicates quantity nil or negligible. (c) indicates provisional or estimated. [1] 1977–79 average. [2] 1979. [3] Belgium-Luxembourg economic union.

Sources: *FAO Monthly Bulletin of Statistics; FAO Production Yearbook 1979; FAO Trade Yearbook 1979.*

(M. C. MacDONALD)

bumper harvest in Pakistan and increased Indian output. In both West Asia and Africa per capita food output fell for the third year in a row. African per capita food production was 15% lower than a decade earlier.

Grains. World grain production in 1981–82 was expected (in December) to rise above the trend of the past 20 years after 2 years of subnormal harvests. Most of the increase was the result of an estimated 3.5% rise in yield over the 1.99 metric tons per hectare (1 ha = 2.47 ac) achieved in 1980–81; harvested area was likely to be only 4 million ha larger than the 720 million ha of that year. U.S. cereal grain output increased sharply, and strong production gains were also reported for such other major grain exporters as Canada and Australia. Western Europe experienced a disappointing grain harvest, as did the Soviet Union for the third straight year. The concentration of production increases in exporting countries supported a moderate expansion in grain trade, with the U.S.S.R., Western Europe, and India recording the largest growth in imports.

Soviet imports of wheat and coarse grains were forecast to reach 42 million tons (valued at nearly $7 billion) in 1981–82, compared with 15.1 million, 30.5 million, and 34 million, respectively, in 1978–79, 1979–80, and 1980–81. On April 24, 1981, U.S. Pres. Ronald Reagan lifted the partial U.S. embargo on the export to the Soviet Union of grains, animal feeds, meat, dairy products, and phosphates that Pres. Jimmy Carter had imposed in January 1980 in response to the Soviet invasion of Afghanistan. The ban was never applied to the eight million tons of wheat and coarse grains that the U.S. was committed to supply under a five-year agreement with the U.S.S.R.

That agreement was to expire on Sept. 30, 1981, but it was extended for one year by mutual agreement in June 1981. The U.S. then offered to make an additional three million tons each of corn and wheat available beyond the eight million limit before the end of the agreement's fifth year. Consultations that concluded on Oct. 1, 1981, resulted in an offer to make 15 million tons of grain available during the extension year at whatever proportion of wheat and coarse grain was preferred by the Soviets beyond the agreement's 8 million-ton limit. The U.S.S.R. reentered the U.S. market in July 1981 and had purchased about 11.9 million tons of grain by mid-November, 10.4 million of which was to be delivered under the agreement's extension. The Canadian government announced on May 26, 1981, that Canada had agreed to supply the U.S.S.R. with at least 25 million tons of wheat and feed grains over the succeeding five years.

In late December 1981 President Reagan suspended various nonagricultural U.S. exports to the Soviet Union in response to the formation of a military government in Poland. U.S. agricultural exports were not suspended, although the United States indefinitely put off plans for a meeting later in the year to consider extension of the U.S.-U.S.S.R. grain agreement beyond Sept. 30, 1981. Earlier in December Reagan signed into law a new farm bill that included a provision requiring the government to compensate farmers should the U.S. government alone single out agricultural exports for embargo. It required that the government compensate farmers for the difference between market prices and 100% of parity for lost sales, a provision that was likely to be extremely costly.

Total world grain production was expected in 1981–82 to exceed total utilization for the first time

Table I. Indexes of World Agricultural and Food Production
1969–71 = 100

Region or country	Total agricultural production						Total food production						Per capita food production					
	1976	1977	1978	1979	1980	1981[1]	1976	1977	1978	1979	1980	1981[1]	1976	1977	1978	1979	1980	1981[1]
Developed countries	109	112	116	119	117	122	109	113	117	119	118	122	103	106	109	111	109	112
United States	113	118	118	124	118	132	113	117	119	125	119	132	107	111	112	116	110	120
Canada	113	116	119	112	118	128	117	119	122	115	121	132	108	109	110	103	107	115
Western Europe	107	109	115	118	123	120	107	109	116	118	123	120	103	105	111	114	118	115
European Community	104	108	114	118	121	120	104	107	113	117	121	120	101	104	110	113	117	116
Japan	97	106	105	104	94	97	97	106	105	104	94	96	90	97	95	94	84	85
Oceania	113	112	120	114	107	112	122	120	130	121	112	117	109	107	114	105	96	99
South Africa	113	122	125	123	128	140	116	124	127	124	130	143	99	104	104	99	101	109
Centrally planned economies	118	118	125	120	117	117	117	117	125	118	115	115	111	110	117	110	105	105
U.S.S.R.	116	116	124	117	116	114	115	114	123	114	110	109	109	106	115	105	101	99
Eastern Europe	121	121	126	124	121	124	121	122	127	125	122	125	116	116	120	117	114	116
Less developed countries	117	122	127	125	129	133	119	123	128	127	130	135	103	104	106	102	103	104
East Asia[2]	129	133	140	142	144	152	132	136	142	145	146	156	115	116	119	119	118	123
Indonesia	120	123	133	137	147	150	123	126	137	140	150	155	108	108	115	116	121	123
South Korea	146	157	161	169	148	168	145	155	160	169	148	168	130	137	139	144	125	139
West Malaysia	132	132	128	148	153	154	136	141	132	171	185	192	117	118	106	137	145	147
Philippines	133	133	135	130	134	142	134	135	137	132	136	143	115	112	111	104	105	108
Thailand	133	135	160	145	161	172	143	146	172	151	168	180	122	121	140	120	131	136
South Asia	110	119	124	118	121	127	111	120	125	118	122	127	97	103	105	97	98	100
Bangladesh	103	113	115	114	125	127	105	116	116	115	129	132	90	97	94	91	99	99
India	110	120	126	117	122	127	110	120	126	117	121	127	97	104	106	97	99	101
Pakistan	106	119	113	128	128	139	116	126	123	132	134	144	97	102	97	101	99	104
West Asia	136	135	141	139	140	140	137	136	143	141	143	142	117	112	115	110	109	105
Iran	154	152	161	149	135	125	158	155	165	153	140	129	134	128	133	119	106	95
Turkey	127	128	132	132	133	136	126	128	132	133	133	138	109	107	108	107	104	105
Africa[3]	108	107	111	112	115	115	110	108	112	113	116	116	93	89	90	88	87	85
Egypt	109	109	113	118	122	122	117	116	120	124	126	127	102	99	100	100	99	97
Ethiopia	78	74	72	74	75	75	73	68	66	68	70	69	62	56	53	53	53	51
Nigeria	110	109	112	115	115	115	110	110	112	113	115	115	91	88	87	85	84	81
Morocco	113	95	118	120	122	97	113	94	118	120	121	96	94	76	93	92	90	69
Latin America	122	127	132	135	140	147	126	129	134	138	143	150	108	108	110	111	112	114
Argentina	119	121	135	138	128	137	120	121	135	140	130	141	111	110	121	124	113	120
Brazil	130	141	138	145	162	172	145	150	145	151	172	176	125	127	120	123	137	137
Colombia	107	116	141	149	158	164	128	127	144	151	161	165	110	108	119	124	129	129
Mexico	117	121	129	127	136	141	121	123	132	131	140	146	99	98	101	97	101	102
Venezuela	123	140	146	158	160	162	125	145	148	161	164	167	102	115	114	120	118	117
World[4]	114	117	122	121	121	124	114	117	122	121	121	124	102	103	106	103	101	102

[1]Preliminary.   [2]Excludes Japan.   [3]Excludes South Africa.   [4]Excludes China and some small countries and islands.
Source: USDA, Economic Research Service, International Economics Division, December 1981.

Table II. World Cereal Supply and Distribution
In 000,000 metric tons

	1978–79	1979–80	1980–81	1981–82[1]
Production				
Wheat	447	422	439	449
Coarse grains	754	740	727	767
Rice, milled	259	254	266	275
Total	1,460	1,416	1,432	1,491
Utilization				
Wheat	430	444	444	449
Coarse grains	747	741	739	747
Rice, milled	255	257	266	274
Total	1,432	1,442	1,449	1,470
Exports				
Wheat	72	86	94	102
Coarse grains	90	101	105	108
Rice, milled	12	12	13	12
Total	174	199	212	222
Ending stocks				
Wheat	101	79	75	74
Coarse grains	91	90	77	97
Rice, milled	28	25	24	26
Total	220	194	176	197
Stocks as % utilization				
Wheat	23.5%	17.9%	16.8%	16.5%
Coarse grains	12.2%	12.1%	10.5%	13.0%
Rice, milled	11.2%	9.6%	9.2%	9.5%
Total	15.4%	13.4%	12.1%	13.2%

[1]Preliminary.
Source: USDA, Foreign Agricultural Service, December 1981.

since 1978–79, permitting a modest rebuilding of cereal stocks. Stocks, as a percentage of utilization, had fallen to the lowest level in 20 years at the end of 1980–81. The increase was likely to be confined almost entirely to coarse grains, leaving wheat stocks, as a percentage of consumption, at their 20-year low.

Based on a nearly completed world wheat harvest, output of wheat was expected to recover strongly in 1981–82. Since the area harvested barely exceeded the nearly 236 million ha in 1980–81, most of the increase came from an estimated 2% rise in yield per hectare over the 1.86 metric tons recorded in 1980–81. Production increases were largest in the major wheat-exporting countries. U.S. wheat production was estimated to be more than 10 million tons higher than the 64.5 million grown in 1980–81, while Canada and Australia were each forecast to increase output by about 5 million tons. Both China and India were expected to show recovery from reduced 1980–81 production levels. Wheat production fell the most in the U.S.S.R., down 10 million tons from 98.2 million in 1980–81. A nearly 10 million-ton increase in U.S. wheat exports from the 41.9 million shipped in 1980–81 was forecast to help push world trade in wheat to a record high in 1981–82 and to support a modest increase in total wheat consumption. Soviet wheat imports were expected to exceed the 16 million tons bought in 1980–81 by about 3 million. India purchased about 3 million tons for delivery in 1981–82 in order to rebuild stocks depleted by the small 1980–81 harvest.

Because wheat production and consumption were expected to about equal each other in 1981–82, wheat stocks were not expected to grow. However, the combination of increased wheat utilization and exports in the U.S. was expected to reduce the U.S. share of world wheat stocks from nearly 57% to about 50% by the end of 1981–82.

A strong increase in world rice production in 1981–82 was forecast based on an estimated 2.5% increase in yields over the 2.76 tons per hectare recorded for 1980–81 and a small rise in harvested area from the 143 million ha of that year. Some of the largest gains in output were forecast for countries that are frequently large rice importers, such as Indonesia and South Korea, thus contributing to an overall reduction in import demand.

Chinese rice production was forecast to rise 3 million tons above the 95 million in 1980–81 despite a reduction in areas planted to rice for the fifth year in a row. Large rice harvests were also in prospect in the two largest exporting countries, Thailand and the U.S. Rice consumption was not expected to grow as rapidly as output, with the result that stocks were forecast to increase modestly during 1981–82.

A 47 million-ton recovery in U.S. coarse grain production from the drought-reduced harvest of 1980–81 was expected to push world coarse grain output to a record high in 1981–82. Average yields around the world were forecast to rise 5% above the figure of 2.13 tons per hectare in 1980–81 on an area only a little larger than the 341 million ha harvested then. Production fell for the third year in a row in the U.S.S.R., and the Western European harvest was also smaller. Southern Hemisphere harvests of coarse grains were forecast to be down in early 1982 in the exporting countries of Argentina and South Africa, although Australian crop prospects were improved over 1980–81.

Almost all of the traditional exporters—particularly Argentina—were expected to ship more coarse grain in 1981–82. The U.S., however, was likely to fall about 2 million tons short of the 72.4 million exported in 1980–81. Soviet coarse grain imports were expected to total about 23 million tons, compared with 9.9 million, 18.4 million, and 18 million, respectively, in 1978–79, 1979–80, and 1980–81.

World utilization of coarse grains, held down by tight supplies in 1980–81, was expected to rebound in 1981–82, largely because of expanded use in the U.S. However, dampened demand for livestock products because of sluggish economic growth in the developed countries was restraining coarse grain use and contributing to a large buildup in stocks. The U.S. was expected to account for the entire 20 million-ton increase in world coarse grain stocks forecast for 1981–82.

Cassava. World cassava production rose an estimated (in August) 3.2% in 1981 to the caloric energy equivalent of about 45 million tons of grain, according to the FAO. Nearly all of the crop

Table III. World Cassava Production
In 000,000 metric tons (root equivalent)

Region	1979	1980[1]	1981[2]
Far East	42.2	43.8	46.4
China	2.7	3.2	4.0
India	6.1	6.5	6.0
Indonesia	13.8	13.3	13.4
Thailand	12.1	13.5	16.0
Africa	45.1	46.7	48.0
Nigeria	10.5	11.0	11.0
Tanzania	4.6	4.6	4.6
Zaire	12.0	12.5	13.0
Latin America	31.2	31.6	31.6
Brazil	24.9	24.6	24.5
Total	118.5	122.1	126.0

[1]Preliminary.
[2]Estimated.
Source: FAO, Food Outlook, August 1981.

PASTEURIZED PROCESS
AMERICAN CHEESE

SIX 5-POUND CARTONS
GROSS WT. 32 LBS.
PLANT NUMBER 49-64
1980

MONTH AND YEAR

Millions of pounds of
surplus butter, milk, and
cheese accumulated in
warehouses in the U.S.
as a result of govern-
ment price-support
programs.

is consumed as food in Africa, but in the Far East more than one-third is processed into more concentrated feed or flour for export, and another 20% is used in the countries where it is grown as feed or to produce starch, alcohol, and other industrial products.

The FAO estimated that world trade in cassava rose at least 12% in 1981, with Thailand, which accounts for nearly 90% of the total, shipping about 5.8 million tons (product weight) of the 6.5 million total. The European Economic Community (EEC), which has an informal agreement limiting cassava imports from Thailand to 5.5 million tons in 1981, imported a total of about 5.3 million tons for feed use. Corn gluten meal was becoming increasingly competitive with cassava-oilseed compounds for use in EEC feed rations.

Protein Meal and Vegetable Oil. The estimated (in December) 9.4% increase in world oilseed production in 1981–82 over the 159.8 million tons harvested a year earlier largely reflected a nearly 19% recovery in U.S. output from drought-reduced levels. Production outside the United States (62% of the world total)—including forecast Southern Hemisphere crops to be harvested in 1982—was estimated to increase less than 5%. The largest increase was for soybeans, forecast at 11% above the 80.9 million tons produced in 1980–81 but below the record output of 93.6 million recorded in 1979–80. The 1981–82 soybean crush was expected to total 76 million tons, 6.8% above 1981, and soybean stocks were forecast to rise nearly 11% from the 16.5 million tons held at the end of 1980–81; the latter figure reflected a decline of nearly 8% during that year.

Prices for soybeans and soy meal peaked in November 1980 at $363 and $335 per ton (Rotterdam), respectively, following the poor U.S. oilseed harvests, but they began to decline as 1980–81 Southern Hemisphere crops were harvested. The recovery in U.S. output in 1981 forced those prices

down to $254 and $228, respectively, by November 1981, the lowest since April–May 1980.

The reduced supplies and high prices in 1980–81 resulted in a 2.6% reduction in total consumption of high-protein meal to about 87 million tons (44% protein content equivalent) in that year, but the easing of supplies in 1981–82 was expected to result in about a 4.7% increase in consumption. The EEC and the U.S. were responsible for most of the slowdown in the consumption of meal, with the slow expansion of livestock numbers in both regions a major restraint.

World trade in soybeans declined in 1980–81, largely because of reduced soybean availabilities in the United States and smaller imports by the EEC. But trade in soybean meal increased in 1980–81 as Brazil took up the slack in reduced U.S. availabilities and imports by the EEC rose, partly to supplement the increased use of cassava in feed

Table IV. World Oilseed Products and Selected Crops
In 000,000 metric tons

Region and product	1979–80	1980–81	1981–82
Selected Northern Hemisphere crops			
U.S. soybeans	61.7	48.8	56.5
Chinese soybeans	7.5	7.9	8.1
U.S. sunflower seed	1.8	1.7	2.1
U.S.S.R. sunflower seed	5.3	4.7	4.8
U.S. cottonseed	5.2	4.1	5.6
U.S.S.R. cottonseed	4.5	5.1	5.0
Chinese cottonseed	4.4	5.4	5.8
Chinese rapeseed	2.4	2.4	3.8
Indian rapeseed	1.4	2.2	2.2
Canadian rapeseed	3.4	2.5	1.8
Indian peanuts	5.8	5.7	6.2
U.S. peanuts	1.8	1.0	1.8
Selected Southern Hemisphere crops			
Brazilian soybeans	15.1	15.5	15.2
Argentine soybeans	3.7	3.5	4.3
Malay palm oil	2.4	2.7	3.0
World production[1]			
Total fats and oils	58.9	56.7	59.3
Edible vegetable oils	41.0	39.2	42.0
High-protein meals[2]	95.6	85.5	93.7

[1]Processing potential from crops in year indicated.
[2]44% protein content equivalent.
Source: USDA, Foreign Agricultural Service, June and December 1981.

Agriculture and Food Supplies

WIDE WORLD

Icicles hanging from Florida oranges after a record-shattering January chill mock farmers' efforts to reduce frost damage with water sprays.

The cyclical growth in cattle numbers (including buffalo) that began in 1980 continued. The U.S. accounted for most of the increase, rising 3% to 118.5 million head, as beef and veal production grew nearly as rapidly. Herds contracted in Argentina, Australia, and the EEC, and in Eastern Europe; output of beef and veal also fell in those regions, except in Argentina. The Soviet Union appeared to maintain its cattle inventory at about 115 million head and to expand output of beef and veal 0.4% to 6.7 million tons despite three consecutive years of poor grain and forage crops. The Polish herd was reduced 5%, the third year of decline, and meat production fell 15% to about 685,000 tons (carcass weight).

The largest decline in hog inventories was in the United States—down 5% from 64.5 million head in 1980—where pork output also fell about 5.5% to 7.1 million tons because of unprofitable feed-cost margins. The reduction in U.S. hog numbers was largely offset by gains elsewhere, particularly in South America and parts of Asia. Eastern Europe also registered a reduction in pork production because of a nearly 19% decline in Poland resulting from a shortage of feed. The U.S.S.R. managed a small increase in pork output.

Poultry production increased in 1981 in nearly all of the major producing countries throughout the world except Canada and Japan. U.S. output was about 5.6% above the 6.6 million tons in 1980. Production was stimulated by strong import demand in the Middle East and North Africa and also by poultry's favourable competitive price position relative to red meat. Soviet poultry imports rose sharply, supported by policies to encourage both production and consumption of poultry to take pressure off high-cost red meat supplies.

Dairy Products. The growth of fluid milk production in 36 major producing countries was estimated in December to have slowed to about 0.5% in 1981. A shortage of feed supplies or forage reduced output in the U.S.S.R. and Poland, while poor pasture conditions hurt production in Australia and New Zealand. The strong expansion in U.S. dairy output continued, although at a slower rate than in 1980, and contributed to a buildup in stocks of milk products that sparked controversy over the level of U.S. dairy-support programs. Although milk output per cow was up in the EEC, policies to reduce herd numbers were successful in slowing the growth in total production. The strong rise in Indian milk output from both cows and water buffaloes continued, thanks to improved breeding, animal health, and forage production programs.

Dairy-support programs in the two largest milk-producing areas, the EEC and the United States, continued to generate more milk than was consumed directly or in the form of manufactured dairy products. In addition, overall consumption of butter and cheese fell nearly 1.5% in the major producing countries as a group, although cheese consumption did rise in both the EEC and the United States. Consequently, world stocks of major dairy products all increased during 1981: butter (5%) to 686,000 tons, cheese (9%) to 1,251,000, and nonfat dry milk (13%) to 945,000.

rations. Soviet imports of soy meal increased substantially. In 1981–82 trade in soybeans was expected to expand, but soy meal exports could contract. A shortage of foreign exchange in Eastern Europe could restrict soy meal imports there.

The decline in production of vegetable oils in 1980–81 was less than that for protein meal. World utilization of all fats and oils fell only 2.1% from 1979–80 to about 56.6 million tons in 1980–81 and was forecast to increase at least 4% in 1981–82.

Meat. The growth in total meat production in 54 major meat-producing countries was estimated as of December to have slowed in 1981. The strong expansion in poultry output continued, pork production fell for the first time in four years, and the decline in output of beef and veal almost leveled off. Poultry's greater feed efficiency and lower price relative to red meats gave it an advantage in much of the world.

Table V. Total Meat Production and Livestock Numbers in Major Producing Countries[1]

In 000,000 metric tons (carcass weight) and 000,000 head

Product	1978	1979	1980	1981
Meat production				
Beef and veal	42.5	40.9	40.6	40.5
Pork	34.2	36.5	37.5	36.9
Lamb, mutton, goat	4.4	4.4	4.5	4.5
Poultry	18.6	19.9	20.8	21.8
Livestock numbers				
Cattle and buffalo	936.5	937.1	942.3	946.7
Hogs	416.4	431.3	426.3	426.0
Sheep	707.9	722.4	721.7	724.0

[1]Includes all but a few countries in the Western Hemisphere, Europe, Turkey, Israel, Morocco, South Africa, Oceania, Japan, India, South Korea, Taiwan, and Philippines, except no livestock numbers for Morocco and South Africa. Livestock numbers are as of the year's end.
Source: USDA, Foreign Agricultural Service, December 1981.

Table VI. World Milk Production[1]
In 000,000 metric tons

Region	1979	1980	1981
North America	70.6	73.1	75.2
United States	56.0	58.3	60.0
South America	18.3	18.6	18.9
Brazil	10.1	10.3	10.5
Western Europe	128.9	131.3	133.5
EEC	104.8	107.7	108.7
France	33.4	35.1	35.4
West Germany	23.9	24.9	25.0
Italy	11.2	11.7	11.6
Netherlands, The	11.7	12.0	12.5
United Kingdom	15.9	16.0	16.0
Other Western Europe	24.0	23.6	24.8
Eastern Europe and U.S.S.R.	131.5	129.0	126.1
Poland	17.3	17.1	16.4
U.S.S.R.	93.3	90.6	88.0
India	28.0	29.0	30.0
Australia and New Zealand[2]	12.4	12.4	11.9
Japan and South Africa	8.7	8.9	8.8
Total	398.4	402.3	404.4

[1]Based on 36 major producing countries; production is very small or data are not available for most less developed countries.
[2]Year ending June 30 for Australia and May 31 for New Zealand.
Source: USDA, Foreign Agricultural Service, December 1981.

Inasmuch as the EEC was more successful than the U.S. in slowing milk production—as well as in exporting substantial quantities of dairy products (with the help of export subsidies)—the U.S. contributed most to the stock buildup, largely in the form of government-owned stocks. Indeed, during 1981 EEC stocks of butter and cheese both declined and those of nonfat dry milk stabilized. By contrast, U.S. stocks of those products rose 41, 57, and 53%, respectively, by the end of 1981. At the year's end the U.S. share of total stocks in the major producing countries was 28% for butter, 39% for cheese, and 43% for nonfat dry milk.

In an attempt to reduce stocks, the U.S. sold 30,000 tons of butter to Poland in the first half of 1981 and in August sold 100,000 tons more (about one-half of the government-held stock) to New Zealand at below prevailing market prices for delivery through mid-1982. New Zealand intended to process and market the butter as butter oil, with the understanding that no U.S. butter would be sold to the U.S.S.R. The U.S. agreed to refrain from selling butter to the Soviet Union until July 1982, except for emergency food relief.

Sugar. World sugar prices fell sharply in 1981 in response to expectations of a large harvest in 1981–82. Although sugar use was expected (in November) to exceed the 89 million tons consumed in 1980–81 by about 3 million tons, sugar stocks were forecast to rise to about 25 million tons, compared with an estimated 21.3 million at the end of 1980–81. The largest increases in production were expected to be in the EEC (especially in France and West Germany), Eastern Europe, and India. An aggressive export policy by the EEC, which was not a member of the International Sugar Agreement (ISA), in the form of increased export "restitution" payments on refined sugar of up to the equivalent of U.S. 13 cents per pound, contributed to the downward pressure on prices of raw sugar.

Exporter members of the ISA were unrestricted by export quotas, and nonmembers faced no prohibitions on shipments to importer members after March 1980, when the ISA "prevailing price" (indicator price) moved above the ISA's then upper trigger point of 13 cents per pound. The price

peaked in October 1980 at an average of 40.5 cents per pound and did not fall back into the agreement's 16–23-cent target range (agreed to in November 1980) until early March 1981. By mid-September, however, the price had fallen below the lower trigger point, reaching 11.5 cents per pound in mid-November.

As prices fell, restrictions on sugar imports from nonmembers were reinstituted, as were export quotas, which were cut by the maximum 15% in September 1981. In addition, the fee that is applied to the ISA's stock financing fund on all sugar moving between members was increased on July 1 from 50 cents to $1.65 per ton. By July 1, 1982, ISA exporter members would be obligated to rebuild ISA reserves, which had been drawn down during 1980, by accumulating 40% of targeted reserves, or about one million tons. The reimposition of export quotas probably had little effect on prices in 1981 because exporters were permitted, under the ISA, to export a quantity equal to that which would have been allowed for all of 1981.

Table VII. World Production of Centrifugal (Freed from Liquid) Sugar
In 000,000 metric tons raw value

Region	1979–80	1980–81	1981–82[1]
North America and Caribbean	17.7	17.6	18.8
United States	5.2	5.4	5.8
Cuba	6.5	6.4	6.8
Mexico	2.8	2.5	2.7
South America	11.6	13.1	13.6
Argentina	1.4	1.7	1.6
Brazil	7.0	8.1	8.5
Europe	20.3	19.6	22.7
Western Europe	14.8	14.8	16.9
EEC	13.1	12.8	14.7
France	4.3	4.2	5.1
West Germany	3.1	3.0	3.4
Italy	1.7	1.9	2.1
Eastern Europe	5.5	4.7	5.8
U.S.S.R.	7.8	6.9	7.1
Africa	6.5	6.3	7.0
South Africa	2.2	1.7	2.0
Asia	16.8	19.5	22.6
China	2.5	3.1	3.4
India	5.2	6.5	8.2
Indonesia	1.3	1.4	1.5
Philippines	2.3	2.4	2.5
Thailand	1.1	1.6	2.2
Oceania	3.4	3.8	4.0
Australia	3.0	3.4	3.6
Total	84.2	86.7	95.8

[1]Preliminary.
Source: USDA, Foreign Agricultural Service, November 1981.

The Council of the International Sugar Organization agreed to extend the ISA, which would have expired at the end of 1982, for one year. The extension retained the ISA's current price band and avoided, for the moment, difficult questions about how to improve the agreement. The council did, however, form a working party charged with exploring the EEC's possible future adherence.

Coffee. World coffee production was forecast, as of October, to climb sharply in 1981–82, with exportable production (harvested production less domestic consumption in producing countries) of green coffee estimated to be 18% above the 1980–81 output of 63.3 million bags (one bag=60 kg [132 lb]). Brazilian output may have been up 50%, largely because many of the coffee trees replanted following the devastating Brazilian frost in 1975 were reaching optimum productivity. The frost that struck Brazil in July 1981 had little effect on its 1981–82 harvest, but it was expected to reduce the

Table VIII. World Green Coffee Production

In 000 60-kg bags

Region	1979–80	1980–81	1981–82
North America	15,246	14,874	15,008
Costa Rica	1,507	2,038	1,875
El Salvador	3,122	2,376	2,214
Guatemala	2,647	2,450	2,600
Honduras	1,140	1,380	1,500
Mexico	3,600	3,650	3,850
South America	38,765	39,385	51,167
Brazil	22,000	21,500	32,500
Colombia	12,712	14,000	14,500
Ecuador	1,584	1,362	1,525
Africa	18,374	19,862	19,388
Cameroon	1,658	1,750	1,790
Ethiopia	3,088	3,100	3,200
Ivory Coast	4,120	5,333	4,666
Kenya	1,625	1,503	1,587
Uganda	2,082	2,000	1,900
Asia and Oceania	9,455	9,556	10,021
India	2,600	2,175	2,250
Indonesia	4,803	5,162	5,420
Total	81,840	83,677	95,584

Source: USDA, Foreign Agricultural Service, October 1981.

potential 1982–83 crop—forecast earlier at 27 million–30.5 million bags—by 15 million–18 million bags.

Because of the large 1981–82 crop, however, world coffee stocks were forecast to be 13.6 million bags larger at the beginning of 1982–83 than the 31.8 million held a year earlier. A plan was proposed to invest the equivalent of $700 million in replantings in Brazil. These efforts were on a smaller scale than those following the 1975 frost, and no further drive was expected to shift production farther north in Brazil into less frost-prone areas.

On Sept. 25, 1981, the International Coffee Council put a new export quota system into effect beginning Oct. 1, 1981, for the 1981–82 coffee year. The new International Coffee Agreement resembled the old by its establishment of a global quota—distributed proportionately among exporting members—that is cut or expanded as prices rise or fall in order to hold coffee prices within an agreed-upon price band. Some differences were that the 1981–82 agreement attempted to defend a price ceiling of $1.45 per pound, compared with $1.55 per pound for the 1980–81 pact; the size of individual cuts or increases was reduced from 1.4 million to 1 million bags; the number of the cuts or increases that could be imposed automatically was increased from 3 to 4; a 15-day-moving-average composite indicator price was substituted for the former 20-day average; and the time that a price had to remain at a particular level to trigger a cut or increase was reduced from 20 to 15 days. The floor price under the agreement remained at $1.15. The new global quota was set at 56 million bags, compared with an initial quota of 57.4 million in 1980–81.

The agreement's indicator price rose from a 1980 low of $1.16 per pound in November 1980 to a peak of $1.30 per pound in January 1981, fell to about 90 cents in June, when a large 1981–82 harvest appeared likely, and recovered to about $1.17 in October. The upward trend late in the year reflected the Brazilian freeze and triggered a one million-bag increase in the global export quota.

The U.S. imported close to one-third of all the coffee exported in the world. According to a survey sponsored by the International Coffee Organiza-

tion in 1981, Americans consumed an average of 1.92 cups of coffee a day. U.S. per capita consumption of coffee had fallen nearly 40% since 1962, and the percentage of the population that drinks coffee had declined from about 75 to 56%. Thus, total U.S. coffee consumption was no higher than it had been in 1950 despite a 45% increase in population. The average coffee drinker now took just under 3.5 cups a day. In 1981 about one-third of the U.S. population drank tea, compared with one quarter in 1962.

Cocoa. The continuing strong upward trend in cocoa production by the Ivory Coast was expected to contribute to a bumper cocoa harvest in 1981–82. Although the cocoa bean grind in 1982 was forecast to be about 3% higher than the 1,564,000 tons ground in 1981, stocks of cocoa beans were expected to rise by about 105,000 tons during 1981–82. This compared with an estimated 83,000-ton increase in 1980–81 and would be the fifth consecutive annual increase.

The downward slide in cocoa bean prices that began in 1979 continued in 1981, as the New York futures price (average of the nearest three months) fell from 92 cents per pound at the end of 1980 to a five-year low of 70 cents in June 1981. The decline in prices began to bring about adjustments in the producing countries. The Ivory Coast—with an annual increase in production that averaged more than 12% during the last five years so that by 1981 it accounted for one quarter of world output—planned to reduce new plantings by 60% annually. Nevertheless, recent planting already done there and in Brazil and Malaysia was likely to ensure ample world supplies well into the 1980s.

Following the provisional implementation of the new International Cocoa Agreement (ICCA) on Aug. 1, 1981, prices rose to $1.01 per pound in September; at that time the ICCA's Buffer Stock Fund began to be drawn upon to purchase cocoa in an attempt to reach the agreement's minimum price objective of $1.10 per pound. Nevertheless, prices declined in October and November 1981, making it apparent that the fund would need to be augmented by new financial resources in addition to the $225 million it held at the end of September 1981 if even a fall-back objective of $1.06 per pound was to be maintained.

The Council of the ICCA approved extension to March 31, 1982, of the deadline for ratification of the agreement. That action and the provisional im-

Table IX. World Cocoa Bean Production

In 000 metric tons

Region	1979–80	1980–81	1981–82[1]
North and Central America	90	90	97
South America	447	495	487
Brazil	296	352	345
Ecuador	95	83	80
Africa	1,030	998	1,053
Cameroon	124	118	120
Ghana	296	260	265
Ivory Coast[2]	379	405	445
Nigeria	175	159	164
Asia and Oceania	81	82	95
Malaysia	37	40	50
Total	1,647	1,664	1,732

[1]Forecast.
[2]Includes some cocoa marketed from Ghana.
Source: USDA, Foreign Agricultural Service, October 1981.

Crop dusters sprayed orchards in California in July in an attempt to halt a Mediterranean fruit fly infestation. The image of the fruit fly (pictured above) is enlarged; the actual wingspan is less than one-half inch.

plementation of the ICCA were made necessary by the fact that an insufficient number of exporting and importing nations had ratified it. Both the world's largest cocoa producer (Ivory Coast) and largest importer (U.S.) had so far opposed joining the ICCA.

Cotton. World cotton production rebounded sharply in 1981, largely because of an estimated 40% increase in U.S. output from the drastically reduced level of 1980. Although cotton use in 1981–82 throughout the world was expected to exceed the 65.6 million bales (216 kg [480 lb] each) consumed in 1980–81 by about 2%, excess production was still expected to push world cotton stocks by the end of 1981–82 about 3.7 million bales higher than the 22.3 million held at the beginning of the marketing year. At nearly 40% of annual cotton consumption, stocks would be at their highest level since 1974–75.

World cotton prices (Outlook "A" Index) climbed to an average monthly peak of 100.6 cents per pound in September 1980, based on knowledge of the small 1980 cotton harvest, and remained strong into the first months of 1981. They began to weaken a little around April as it became apparent that slow economic growth around the world was dampening demand. Prices weakened further during the summer as the prospects of a large 1981 harvest became clearer, and they fell below 75 cents per pound in the fall (according to the New "A" Index that replaced the Outlook "A" Index in August). The widespread uncertainty about the prospects for economic recovery was producing similar uncertainty about the prospects for cotton demand in 1982.

The increased price competitiveness of cotton relative to man-made fibres had not yet had much effect on the price of the latter as 1981 drew to a close. The Multi-Fibre Arrangement (MFA), which attempted to regulate world trade in textiles and apparel, was scheduled to expire at the end of 1981. In September 1981 the General Agreement on Tariffs and Trade (GATT) Textiles Committee began a new series of meetings in Geneva with the aim of renewing the MFA. The negotiations proved difficult, especially as regards demands for liberalized access for textiles of less developed countries to the markets of industrialized nations.

INTERNATIONAL FOOD SECURITY

Grain Reserves. The International Wheat Council (IWC), the governing body of the International Wheat Agreement (IWA), announced in December 1981 that efforts to develop an "alternative ap-

Table X. World Cotton Production
In 000,000 480-lb bales

Region	1979	1980	1981
North and Central America	17.3	13.9	18.1
Mexico	1.5	1.6	1.5
United States	14.6	11.1	15.6
South America	4.9	4.8	4.8
Brazil	2.6	2.8	2.7
Europe	0.8	0.8	0.9
U.S.S.R.	13.1	14.3	13.9
Africa	5.3	5.3	5.4
Egypt	2.2	2.4	2.4
Asia and Oceania	24.3	26.3	28.0
China	10.1	12.4	13.3
India	6.1	6.1	6.4
Pakistan	3.4	3.3	3.6
Turkey	2.2	2.2	2.3
Total	65.6	65.4	71.0

Source: USDA, Foreign Agricultural Service, June and December 1981.

proach" to establishing a new Wheat Trade Convention (wTC) were unsuccessful. The iwc was not able to arrive at a pact acceptable to both exporters and importers.

A new wTC had been widely advocated as the primary international means for achieving market stability in cereal trade and for improving world food security by assuring the access of countries to food supplies in times of shortage. The search for an alternative began after a UN-sponsored negotiating conference in February 1979 failed to agree upon a wTC after extensive preliminary negotiations in the iwc and elsewhere that dated back to 1975. The approach that was rejected at that time spelled out in concrete terms the specific actions that nations were obligated to take—such as acquisition or release of reserve stocks—when a price indicator reached a specified trigger point.

The alternative approach also centred on the international coordination of the acquisition and release of nationally held reserve stocks and on special provisions to assist less developed countries in meeting their reserve stock obligations. The new approach, however, relied much more heavily upon consultations to achieve coordination and gave nations greater discretion in interpreting their more general commitments than did the older, more rigid proposal.

The most fundamental opposition to the alternative approach appeared to come from the leading exporting countries. The iwc had reported at its July 1981 meeting that "most delegations indicated their support for the proposals currently under consideration" but that some delegations "had conceptual difficulties with the proposals and could not support them." The U.S. delegation voiced opposition to any international control or coordination of grain reserves and advocated a market-oriented approach to world food security and reserve stocks. The U.S. had earlier urged at a meeting of the World Food Council that other nations begin to establish their own reserve programs and explore more market-oriented approaches to the operation of reserve policies.

The U.S. opposition to international coordina-tion—as opposed to international control—of national stock operations represented a major departure by the new administration of Pres. Ronald Reagan from the policies of previous administrations. However, the administration of Pres. Jimmy Carter had also given signs of backing away from support for a broadly based food security system comprised of an elaborate set of rules and automatic mechanisms. The usDA's under secretary for international affairs and commodity programs had advocated in November 1980 that future wheat negotiations should be limited to those countries "that count in world trade and who contribute to its instability"—the United States, Canada, the eec, Australia, and Argentina as exporters and Japan, the U.S.S.R., Mexico, Brazil, the eec, China, Eastern Europe, and one or two others as importers. He would put the burden of organizing, operating, and paying for world food security on those nations that most use and benefit from trade. He argued that the system should operate on a consultative basis that both allowed and caused the major trading countries "to act in the appropriate direction as needed." He advised the development of stockholding capacity in a large number of countries to be managed "solely on criteria relating to their own needs and conditions."

Although the iwc in December urged a continuing search to strengthen the iwa and to establish an agreed-upon basis for its renewal, the specific steps proposed did not go beyond improved monitoring of market conditions, strengthening of existing consultative procedures, increased analysis of the medium-term outlook for wheat, and a comprehensive evaluation of the stockholding policies and practices of members. The iwa of 1971—which had no economic provisions but provided a consultative mechanism—was to expire June 30, 1981, but was extended until June 30, 1983, by action of the iwc in March 1981.

Food Financing Facility. The International Monetary Fund (iMF) in May 1981 created an integrated Compensatory Financing Facility (cFF) designed to benefit less developed, food-deficit countries whose balances of payments are tem-

Angry Italian farmers drove their tractors through the streets of Rome in April to protest European Economic Community policies that they felt were biased against them.

A giant dehydrating
plant in Colorado is ca-
pable of processing up
to 30 tons of alfalfa per
hour. Alfalfa is highly
prized as a feed by cat-
tle growers.

porarily strained by steep increases in cereal import costs resulting from either a domestic crop
shortfall or a rise in the price of imported grain.
The facility was not intended to deal with chronic
food shortages and balance of payments problems.

Before May the CFF provided financing to member countries in the form of short-term loans,
primarily to offset shortfalls in export earnings.
The new procedure gave a country the option of
taking account of the net effect of both shortfalls in
export earnings and excess cereal imports in determining the level of borrowings from the facility.

Malawi in September 1981 became the first
country to draw upon the facility. In the absence
of the integrated CFF it would have been ineligible
to borrow because its export earnings in 1981 were
$5.9 million above trend (a five-year geometric av-
erage centred on 1981, using forecast earnings for
1982 and 1983). However, because its cereal imports were $16.5 million in excess of trend (five-
year arithmetic average) in the 1981 marketing
year because of poor crops, Malawi was authorized
to borrow $10.6 million; this amount was the net
foreign exchange shortfall (cereal import excess
minus export earning surplus). Had Malawi also
experienced a shortfall in export earnings, it could
have borrowed an amount equal to the cereal import excess plus the export earning shortfall. A
country could borrow an amount equal to up to
100% of its IMF quota for both excess cereal imports
and a shortfall in export earnings as long as the
combined total did not exceed 125% of the quota.
The loan to Malawi was to be repaid in quarterly
installments over five years, at a 6¼% interest
rate, with a three-year grace period.

The new procedure gave some countries additional flexibility in determining the combination

of domestic stocks and financial capacity to import
that they can use to assure steady food supplies. It
also provided a partial means for coping with fluctuations in food import bills that result from increasing world price variability. The International
Food Policy Research Institute estimated that
world price variability accounted for 59% of the
fluctuation in the food import bills of less developed countries in the 1970s, compared with 12%
in the 1960s. The procedure represented a compromise, however, between the need to assure less
developed countries of access to food and the desire
to maintain IMF liquidity without greatly increasing the financial resources that member countries
devote to the Fund. In the absence of effective policies to reduce world cereal price variability, a potential steep rise in world cereal prices, especially
if combined with widespread or repeated poor harvests in less developed countries, could easily and
quickly push most such countries to their 125%
quota limit.

Food Aid. Total shipments of food aid in cereals
fell for the second year in a row in 1980–81 to about
900,000 tons below the most recent high of 9.5
million tons in 1978–79. This was 1.4 million below
the yet-to-be-achieved 10 million-ton aid target
first set at the 1974 World Food Conference. The
extent of the forecast recovery in cereal aid in 1981–
82 was uncertain since actual shipments have usually fallen short of preliminary estimates of allocations. A parallel decline was also registered for non-
cereal aid, mainly dairy products and fats and oils.

The Food Aid Committee of the IWC in March
1981 adopted a protocol to extend the Food Aid
Convention of 1980 for two years. The convention,
which expires June 30, 1983, includes pledges by
donor countries to provide minimum contribu-

Agriculture and Food Supplies

CATHERINE LEROY—GAMMA/LIAISON

Food shortages in Poland forced customers to wait for hours in long lines.

tions of food aid totaling the equivalent of 7.6 million tons of wheat in the form of cereals or cash.

Low-income (below $650 per capita in 1979) food-deficit countries continued to be the recipients of about 80% of all food aid. The proportion that such aid represents of the total cereal imports of those countries declined, according to the FAO, from 26% in 1976–77 to 18% in 1980–81. In most cases the decline resulted from total import requirements increasing more rapidly than food aid imports.

In 1975–76 Bangladesh, India, Egypt, and Pakistan—each receiving about one million tons or more of food aid—composed the list of countries receiving three-fifths of all cereal food aid. By 1979–80 Egypt had become the largest recipient (1,764,000 tons), Bangladesh was still a major beneficiary (1,480,000), and Indonesia had joined the list (831,000). Pakistan (146,000) was no longer included, and aid to India had fallen almost one million tons to 344,000, making room on the list for South Korea (265,000), Portugal (267,000), the Sudan (212,000), and Vietnam (184,000).

Pledges by donors to the World Food Program (WFP) for 1981–82 totaled $730 million as of October 1981, short of the $1 billion target. Pledges for 1979–80 had fallen $133 million short of the $950 million target. However, contributions in 1981 to the International Emergency Food Reserve (IEFR), administered by the WFP, exceeded the 500,000-ton target for the first time, reaching 540,000 tons of cereals, compared with 391,000 in 1980. Efforts, primarily by less developed countries, to convert the IEFR into a permanent, legally binding convention were unsuccessful.

Of the 415,000 tons of cereals and 37,000 tons of other products, valued at $166 million, devoted to meeting food emergencies from WFP and IEFR resources for 1981 (through November 20), 75% was used to help refugees, displaced persons, and victims of war and civil disorder. Victims of natural disasters were the beneficiaries of the remaining 25%. African countries covered by the FAO's appeal for assistance in November 1980, Kampuchea (Cambodia), and refugees from Afghanistan received aid specially earmarked by donors in 1980 and 1981.

Table XI. Shipments of Food Aid in Cereals
In 000,000 metric ton grain equivalent

Country	average 1976–77, 1978–79	1979–80	1980–81[1]	1981–82[2]
Argentina	28	38	50	35
Australia	265	318	403	445
Austria	0	0	5	20
Canada	932	730	600	600
China	28	25	25	n.a.
EEC	1,221	1,205	1,300	1,900
Finland	30	14	20	20
India	132	80	51	n.a.
Japan	178	688	567	550
Norway	10	37	40	30
OPEC Special Fund	0	0	0	14
Saudi Arabia	9	10	31	10
Spain	0	0	20	20
Sweden	110	98	90	90
Switzerland	32	32	27	27
Turkey	13	5	15	n.a.
United States	6,125	5,418	5,141	5,300
World Food Program[3]	64	22	13	50
Others	94	270	166	166
Total	9,269	8,990	8,564	9,277

[1]Partly estimated.
[2]Allocations, some estimated.
[3]Purchases only.
Source: FAO, *Food Outlook*, December 1981.

FOREIGN ASSISTANCE TO AGRICULTURE

Although official commitments of external assistance to agriculture—broadly defined to include rural infrastructure, agro-industries, fertilizer production, and regional river-basin projects—increased modestly in 1980 in nominal terms, inflation caused a fall in real terms for the second year in a row. Agriculture in the least developed countries (per capita income under $680), however, received $1.5 billion in concessional capital commitments, 30% more than in 1979. Nevertheless, their share of such aid going to all less developed countries rose to only 18–19%.

Although multilateral agencies, such as the World Bank, increased their commitments to agriculture as bilateral commitments fell, they experienced increased difficulty in obtaining donor support. For instance, financial support appeared to be weakening for the World Bank's International Development Association, which provides loans on soft terms—40% to agriculture and rural development in fiscal 1980—to the poorest nations. The U.S. stretched out its $3.2 billion pledged replenishment to the agency from three years to five—in effect a cut—and Congress could prove reluctant to appropriate all of that. Other countries also indicated plans to cut their contributions.

The proposed $1,270,000,000 replenishment of the International Fund for Agricultural Development (IFAD), a UN agency created following the 1974 World Food Conference, to finance its continued operation through 1983 was endangered by a dispute between the industrialized countries and the Organization of Petroleum Exporting Countries (OPEC) over their respective shares as 1981 ended. The original $1 billion of capital, $567 million from industrial and $435 million from OPEC countries, was all committed to projects aimed primarily at helping small farmers in poor countries. The Reagan administration cut the earlier proposed U.S. contribution, and OPEC countered with its own reduction; this was followed, in turn, by congressional action that appeared to postpone any likely U.S. contribution at least until fiscal 1983. Although some European nations had proposed increasing their contributions to offset

the U.S. cut, OPEC said it would not consider the question until its June 1982 meeting.

(RICHARD M. KENNEDY)

See also Environment; Fisheries; Food Processing; Gardening; Industrial Review: *Alcoholic Beverages; Textiles; Tobacco.*
[451.B.1.c; 534.E; 731; 10/37.C]

Albania

A people's republic in the western Balkan Peninsula, Albania is on the Adriatic Sea, bordered by Greece and Yugoslavia. Area: 28,748 sq km (11,100 sq mi). Pop. (1980 est.): 2,734,000. Cap. and largest city: Tirana (pop., 1978 est., 198,000). Language: Albanian. Religion: officially atheist; historically Muslim, Orthodox, and Roman Catholic communities. First secretary of the Albanian (Communist) Party of Labour in 1981, Enver Hoxha; chairman of the Presidium of the People's Assembly (president), Haxhi Leshi; chairman of the Council of Ministers (premier) until December 18, Mehmet Shehu.

Albania's relations with Yugoslavia, always frosty, became hostile in 1981 as a result of the situation in the province of Kosovo, in the Yugoslav republic of Serbia. Kosovo, lying directly northeast of the border with Albania, had a population of 1.6 million, four-fifths of whom were ethnic Albanians. In March Albanian students at the University of Pristina in Pristina, the chief town

Albania

ALBANIA

Education. (1973–74) Primary, pupils 569,600, teachers 22,686; secondary, pupils 32,900, teachers (1971–72) 1,318; vocational and teacher training, pupils 69,700, teachers (1971–72) 1,712; higher (1971–72), students 28,668, teaching staff 1,153.

Finance. Monetary unit: lek, with (June 30, 1981) an official exchange rate of 3.3 leks to U.S. $1 (6.4 leks = £1 sterling) and a noncommercial rate of 7 leks to U.S. $1 (13.5 leks = £1 sterling). Budget (1980 est.): revenue 8 billion leks; expenditure 7,950,000,000 leks.

Foreign Trade. (1979) Imports *c.* 900 million leks; exports *c.* 1 billion leks. Import sources: Czechoslovakia *c.* 12%; Yugoslavia *c.* 12%; China *c.* 10%; Italy *c.* 8%; Poland 8%; West Germany *c.* 7%. Export destinations: Czechoslovakia *c.* 11%; Yugoslavia *c.* 10%; Italy *c.* 10%; China *c.* 9%; Poland *c.* 7%; West Germany *c.* 7%. Main exports (1964; latest available): fuels, minerals, and metals (including crude oil, bitumen, chrome ore, iron ore, and copper) 54%; foodstuffs (including vegetables and fruit) 23%; raw materials (including tobacco and wool) 17%.

Transport and Communications. Roads (1971) 5,500 km. Motor vehicles in use (1970): passenger *c.* 3,500; commercial (including buses) *c.* 11,200. Railways: (1979) 330 km; traffic (1971) 291 million passenger-km, freight 188 million net ton-km. Shipping (1980): merchant vessels 100 gross tons and over 20; gross tonnage 56,127. Shipping traffic (1975): goods loaded *c.* 2.8 million metric tons, unloaded *c.* 760,000 metric tons. Telephones (Dec. 1965) 13,991. Radio receivers (Dec. 1977) 200,000. Television receivers (Dec. 1977) 4,500.

Agriculture. Production (in 000; metric tons; 1979): corn *c.* 320; wheat *c.* 420; oats *c.* 28; potatoes *c.* 132; sugar, raw value *c.* 40; sunflower seed *c.* 26; olives *c.* 50; grapes *c.* 60; tobacco *c.* 14; cotton, lint *c.* 7. Livestock (in 000; 1979): sheep *c.* 1,163; cattle *c.* 474; pigs *c.* 120; goats *c.* 665; poultry *c.* 2,376.

Industry. Production (in 000; metric tons; 1978): crude oil *c.* 2,800; lignite *c.* 1,020; petroleum products *c.* 2,735; chrome ore (oxide content) *c.* 390; copper ore (metal content) *c.* 11; nickel ore (metal content) *c.* 8; fertilizers (nutrient content) *c.* 80; cement *c.* 800; electricity (kw-hr) *c.* 2,350,000.

Table XII. Official Commitments of External Assistance to Agriculture in Less Developed Countries[1]
In $000,000

Commitments	1977	1978	1979	1980[2]
Total				
Multilateral	4,028	5,193	5,263	6,402
Bilateral	3,113	3,838	4,816	4,114
Current prices	7,141	9,031	10,079	10,516
1975 prices[3]	6,551	7,225	7,048	6,656
Concessional				
Multilateral	1,633	2,390	2,653	3,397
Bilateral	2,933	3,444	4,495	4,049
Current prices	4,566	5,834	7,148	7,446
1975 prices[3]	4,189	4,667	4,998	4,713
Nonconcessional				
Multilateral	2,395	2,803	2,610	3,005
Bilateral	180	394	321	65
Current prices	2,575	3,197	2,931	3,070
1975 prices[3]	2,362	2,558	2,050	1,943

[1]Excludes commitments by centrally planned countries.
[2]Preliminary.
[3]Deflated by the UN unit-value index of exports of manufactured goods.
Sources: OECD and FAO, November 1981.

Aircraft:
see Aerial Sports; Defense; Industrial Review; Transportation

Air Forces:
see Defense

of Kosovo, started a series of demonstrations demanding separation of the province from Serbia and its establishment as the seventh Yugoslav republic. At the eighth congress of the Albanian Party of Labour in November, First Secretary Enver Hoxha supported these demands.

In May the Yugoslav interior minister, Gen. Franjo Herljevic, disclosed that there was evidence of direct links between the leaders of the Kosovo troubles and the Albanian government. As a consequence, Yugoslavia canceled cultural exchange programs with Albania.

On May 24 two bombs exploded at the Yugoslav embassy in Tirana. Yugoslavia protested the "provocation," but Albania denied any involvement in the incident. Mehmet Shehu, premier since 1954, died on December 18 (*see* OBITUARIES).

(K. M. SMOGORZEWSKI)

Algeria

Algeria

A republic on the north coast of Africa, Algeria is bounded by Morocco, Western Sahara, Mauritania, Mali, Niger, Libya, and Tunisia. Area: 2,-381,741 sq km (919,595 sq mi). Pop. (1979 est.): 19,129,000. Cap. and largest city: Algiers (pop., 1978 est., 1,998,000). Language: Arabic, Berber, French. Religion: Muslim 99%; Roman Catholic 0.3%. President in 1981, Col. Chadli Bendjedid; premier, Mohamed Ben Ahmed Abdelghani.

Algeria was primarily engaged in domestic consolidation during 1981. At the National Liberation Front (FLN) Central Committee meeting in July, Pres. Chadli Bendjedid's opponents in the succession struggle, Abdel Aziz Bouteflika and Mohamed Salah Yahiaoui, were expelled from the FLN Political Bureau. Despite the government's determination to root out corruption and the arrest of several party officials on corruption charges, the public remained unconvinced. Management cadres were demoralized by purges and austerity policies introduced in late 1980, and strikes occurred in January 1981 as inflation topped 20%.

Although the first anniversary of the Tizi-

Ouzou riots passed without incident, the frustration of the Berber minority continued to smolder. In May dissident intellectuals formed an association to preserve popular Algerian culture. The FLN Central Committee's June resolution on cultural policy satisfied no one. While paying lip service to popular Algerian culture, it reaffirmed the dominance of Arabic and the Middle East in national cultural life. Violent incidents in Algerian universities in May and June brought the growing pro-Arabic fundamentalist movement into confrontation with Berberist groups.

The January budgetary law showed that petroleum receipts would provide two-thirds of national income, even more than in previous years. Negotiations with the El Paso Co. of Houston, Texas, over natural gas prices finally collapsed in February, with the U.S. company writing off its investment. Oil sales were disappointing. Despite the world oil glut, Algeria refused to drop its price, proposing instead to barter imports against crude oil sales. Nonetheless, the government pushed ahead with the ambitious 1980–84 plan. The 1981 budget emphasized social spending and consumer goods industries.

The advent of a Socialist government in Paris brought renewed warmth to relations with France. The visit of French Foreign Minister Claude Cheysson to Algiers in August was followed in the autumn by a visit from Pres. François Mitterrand. Algeria renewed relations with the U.S.S.R. in June when President Bendjedid made his first visit to Moscow. At the same time, the country remained open to friendship with the West, particularly the U.S., despite disappointment with the U.S. response to Algerian help in resolving the Iran hostage crisis at the beginning of the year.

The major event in foreign affairs was President Bendjedid's tour of 11 African nations in April. Algeria also stated its support for African liberation movements and its opposition to the proposed fusion of Libya and Chad. Diplomatic support for the Popular Front for the Liberation of Saguia el Hamra and Río de Oro (Polisario Front) in the Western Sahara continued. (GEORGE JOFFÉ)

U.S. Deputy Secretary of State Warren Christopher (left) and Algerian Foreign Minister Mohamed Ben Yahia signed an agreement in Algiers in January that resulted in the release of the U.S. hostages, who had been held in Iran for 444 days.

Alcoholic Beverages:
see Industrial Review

Education. (1980–81) Primary, pupils 3,918,827, teachers 88,481; secondary, pupils 999,937, teachers 38,845; vocational, pupils 12,903, teachers 1,168; teacher training, students 13,315, teachers 1,124; higher (1978–79; universities only), students 51,510, teaching staff 6,421.

Finance. Monetary unit: dinar, with (Sept. 21, 1981) a free rate of 4.15 dinars to U.S. $1 (7.70 dinars = £1 sterling). Gold and other reserves (June 1981) U.S. $3,654,000,000. Budget (1980 est.): revenue 50,830,000,000 dinars; expenditure 27,780,000,000 dinars (excludes 23,120,000,000 dinars development expenditure). Money supply (Dec. 1980) 83,219,000,000 dinars.

Foreign Trade. (1980) Imports c. 36,840,000,000 dinars; exports 47,618,000,000 dinars. Import sources (1978): France 18%; West Germany 18%; Italy 11%; Japan 9%; U.S. 7%; Spain 5%. Export destinations (1978): U.S. 51%; West Germany 14%; France 11%; Italy 7%. Main exports: crude oil 87%; petroleum products 5%.

Transport and Communications. Roads (1976) 78,500 km. Motor vehicles in use (1978): passenger 396,800; commercial (including buses) 206,500. Railways (1978): 3,890 km; traffic 1,452,000,000 passenger-km, freight 2,016,000,000 net ton-km. Air traffic (1980): c. 2,300,000,000 passenger-km; freight c. 13 million net ton-km. Shipping (1980): merchant vessels 100 gross tons and over 130; gross tonnage 1,218,621. Shipping traffic (1978): goods loaded 49,840,000 metric tons, unloaded 13.5 million metric tons. Telephones (Jan. 1979) 346,400. Radio receivers (Dec. 1976) 3 million. Television receivers (Dec. 1977) 560,000.

Agriculture. Production (in 000; metric tons; 1980): wheat 1,301; barley 791; oats c. 110; potatoes c. 500; tomatoes c. 187; onions c. 114; dates c. 180; oranges 305; mandarin oranges and tangerines c. 146; watermelons (1979) c. 150; olives c. 140; wine c. 260. Livestock (in 000; 1979): sheep c. 10,900; goats c. 2,600; cattle c. 1,313; asses c. 500; horses c. 150; camels c. 140; chickens c. 16,970.

Industry. Production (in 000; metric tons; 1979): iron ore (53–55% metal content) 2,870; phosphate rock (1978) c. 997; crude oil (1980) 47,418; natural gas (cu m; 1979) 25,939,000; petroleum products (1978) c. 4,800; fertilizers (nutrient content; 1979–80) nitrogenous 21, phosphate c. 56; cement 3,770; crude steel (1978) 178; electricity (excluding most industrial production; kw-hr; 1980) c. 5,500,000.

Andorra

An independent co-principality of Europe, Andorra is in the Pyrenees Mountains between Spain and France. Area: 468 sq km (181 sq mi). Pop. (1980): 33,900. Cap.: Andorra la Vella (commune pop., 1980, 13,400). Language: Catalan (official), French, Spanish. Religion: predominantly Roman Catholic. Co-princes: the president of the French Republic and the bishop of Urgel, Spain, represented by their *veguers* (provosts) and *batlles* (prosecutors). An elected Council General of 28 members elects the first syndic; in 1981, Estanislau Sangrà Font.

Control of the two radio stations on Andorran territory was a matter of dispute between the Council General and the co-princes in 1981. A protocol signed in 1961 between the principality and the French and Spanish companies controlling, respectively, Sud-Radio and Radio Andorra had given the companies the right to operate the stations for 20 years, after which they would revert to the principality. In May 1981 the Council warned that the concession would not be renewed and submitted a new draft protocol to the co-princes.

When the French and Spanish governments insisted on modification of the draft, the General Council ordered both transmitters to suspend

Education. (1979–80) Primary, pupils 4,711, teachers 305; secondary, pupils (1979–80) 2,134; teachers (1974–75) 120.

Finance and Trade. Monetary units: French franc and Spanish peseta. Budget (1979 est.) balanced at 3,209,000,000 pesetas. Foreign trade (1979): imports from France Fr 933,809,000 (U.S. $219.6 million), from Spain 8,568,945,000 pesetas (U.S. $127.7 million); exports to France Fr 22,201,000 (U.S. $5.2 million), to Spain 269,730,000 pesetas (U.S. $4 million). Tourism (1977) 6.7 million visitors.

Communications. Telephones (Dec. 1978) 11,700. Radio receivers (Dec. 1977) 7,000. Television receivers (Dec. 1977) 3,000.

Agriculture. Production: cereals, potatoes, tobacco, wool. Livestock (in 000; 1978): sheep c. 12; cattle c. 4.

Andorra

broadcasting and threatened to resign as a body if the new protocol was not adopted. Andorrans believed the French co-prince, then Pres. Valéry Giscard d'Estaing, was responsible for the deadlock. Following Giscard's defeat in the French elections, the Council petitioned the new co-prince, Pres. François Mitterrand, for a just settlement of the dispute and the granting of a truly democratic constitution for Andorra. In late 1981 the two transmitters were still off the air.

(K. M. SMOGORZEWSKI)

Angola

Angola

Located on the west coast of southern Africa, Angola is bounded by Zaire, Zambia, South West Africa/Namibia, and the Atlantic Ocean. The small exclave of Cabinda, a province of Angola, is bounded by the Congo and Zaire. Area: 1,246,700 sq km (481,353 sq mi). Pop. (1980 est.): 6,759,000. Cap. and largest city: Luanda (pop., 1979 est., 475,300). Language: Bantu languages (predominant), Portuguese (official), and some Khoisan dialects. Religion: traditional beliefs 45%; Roman Catholicism 43%; Protestantism 12%. President in 1981, José Eduardo dos Santos.

In December 1980 an extraordinary meeting of the ruling Popular Movement for the Liberation of Angola (MPLA) had been held to consider the country's failure to meet the economic targets set in 1977 (viz., to achieve pre-independence production levels) and to make plans for the next five years. It was agreed that some of the aims had been unrealistic but that failure to achieve them was due chiefly to poor organization. The main lines of development were reaffirmed, but greater emphasis was to be placed on encouraging small farmers to grow more than they needed for their own consumption by making other goods more readily available for purchase. By this means it was hoped to make the country self-sufficient in food and to stamp out the black market. Defense was also to be made a priority. As a step toward achieving greater efficiency in government, a number of Cabinet changes took place on March 20, 1981, affecting the Ministries of Agriculture, Education, Planning, and Internal Trade. Various junior posts also changed hands.

Development in the southern region of the country was intermittently affected by raids carried out by South African troops, ostensibly in pursuit of

American Literature: see Literature

Anglican Communion: see Religion

guerrillas belonging to the South West Africa People's Organization (SWAPO) who were said to have attacked targets in Namibia. A particularly sustained attack by South African ground and air forces, continuing throughout much of August, led the Angolan government to order a general mobilization. Pres. José Eduardo dos Santos appealed to UN Secretary-General Kurt Waldheim for help, indicating that if it were not forthcoming he might have to call on friendly countries for assistance. France, West Germany, Britain, and Canada condemned South Africa's action.

The South Africans withdrew in September. They claimed to have cleared SWAPO bases from a 144-km (90-mi)-wide strip of Angolan territory along the Namibian border, and they certainly struck a severe blow at Angola's antiaircraft radar and missile defenses. They also claimed to have killed Soviet soldiers operating alongside Angolan troops who had assisted the SWAPO guerrillas and to have captured one Soviet sergeant major. Angola protested that Soviet troops, though present in Angola to assist with Soviet equipment, had not been involved in any fighting.

U.S. distrust of the activities of the U.S.S.R. and its Cuban allies in Angola led to some tension in relations between Angola and the U.S. In January Gen. Alexander Haig, then Pres. Ronald Reagan's nominee for the post of U.S. secretary of state, said that the U.S. could not recognize the Angolan government as long as up to 20,000 Cuban troops remained in the country. President dos Santos's presence at the 26th congress of the Communist Party of the Soviet Union in February did little to change the U.S. administration's view. In Septem-

ber the U.S. Senate, acting on the administration's initiative, voted to repeal a ban on government aid to Jonas Savimbi's National Union for the Total Independence of Angola (UNITA) guerrillas. This measure required the assent of the U.S. House of Representatives before it could become effective, and in the meantime Savimbi claimed to have financial backing from Saudi Arabia, Qatar, Morocco, Senegal, and Ivory Coast. Savimbi visited the U.S. late in the year.

Despite the U.S. administration's hostility, the U.S. Export-Import Bank granted credits of $85 million in July to finance an offshore oil development project, to be run jointly by a subsidiary of Gulf Oil and Sonangol, Angola's state-run oil company. Also in July, President dos Santos attended a meeting of the year-old Southern African Development Coordination Conference in Salisbury, Zimbabwe. The conference called on leaders of the principal industrial countries, meeting simultaneously in Ottawa, to take account of the needs of poorer nations. (KENNETH INGHAM)

Antarctica

International Activities. The third International Symposium on Antarctic Glaciology, sponsored by the Scientific Committee on Antarctic Research, was held at the Institute of Polar Studies, Ohio State University, in September 1981. This was the first Antarctic glaciology symposium in 13 years. At the 11th Consultative Meeting of the Antarctic Treaty nations, held in Buenos Aires, Arg., in July, the representatives decided to hold a special consultative meeting to draft an international regime for the development of Antarctic mineral resources. Five nations—Australia, Chile, Japan, South Africa, and the U.S.S.R.—had ratified the Convention on the Conservation of Antarctic Marine Resources. Three additional ratifications were required before the convention would come into effect. Uruguay became the 22nd nation to accede to the Antarctic Treaty.

National Programs. ARGENTINA. A glacier inventory was completed on Vega, James Ross, and surrounding islands. In cooperation with the French, several ice cores, including a 155-m (508-ft) core from the ice dome, were taken on James Ross Island. Biweekly commercial flights between Río Gallegos, Arg., and Auckland, N.Z., via the sub-Antarctic were begun. The Argentine Air Force announced plans to make Vicecomodoro Marambio Base on Seymour Island an intercontinental air terminal for commercial flights.

AUSTRALIA. Rebuilding of the bases at Casey, Davis, and Mawson began, with completion of the project expected in 1989–90. Headquarters for all Australian activities in Antarctica were being consolidated in Kingston, Tasmania, making the Hobart area an international centre for Antarctic and marine research. Glaciologic field research dominated Australia's Antarctic program, which included radio echo-sounding on the Law Dome in East Antarctica.

CHILE. A new base, Chiloe, was established in the Graham Mountain Range of the Antarctic

---

ANGOLA

Education. (1977) Primary, pupils 1,026,291, teachers 25,000; secondary and vocational, pupils 105,868, teachers (1972–73) 4,393; teacher training (1972–73), students 3,-388, teachers 330; higher (1978; university only), students 3,146, teaching staff 293.

Finance and Trade. Monetary unit: kwanza, with a free rate (Sept. 21, 1981) of 33.95 kwanzas to U.S. $1 (62.94 kwanzas = £1 sterling). Budget (1974 est.): revenue 23,-540,000,000 kwanzas; expenditure 19,475,000,000 kwanzas. Foreign trade (1979): imports 28,093,000,000 kwanzas; exports 39,531,000,000 kwanzas. Import sources: South Africa c. 12%; Portugal c. 12%; U.S. c. 9%; West Germany c. 8%; U.K. c. 7%; Sweden c. 6%. Export destinations: The Bahamas c. 45%; U.S. c. 20%; U.S. Virgin Islands c. 8%; U.K. c. 6%. Main exports: crude oil 68%; coffee 14%; diamonds 11%; petroleum products 6%.

Transport and Communications. Roads (1974) 72,323 km. Motor vehicles in use (1978): passenger 143,100; commercial (including buses) 42,600. Railways: (1977) c. 2,315 km; traffic (1974) 418 million passenger-km, freight 5,461,-000,000 net ton-km. Air traffic (1980): c. 553 million passenger-km; freight c. 21 million net ton-km. Shipping (1980): merchant vessels 100 gross tons and over 35; gross tonnage 65,667. Shipping traffic (1976): goods loaded c. 6,250,000 metric tons, unloaded c. 1.5 million metric tons. Telephones (Jan. 1979) 29,400. Radio receivers (Dec. 1977) 118,000. Television receivers (Dec. 1980) c. 2,000.

Agriculture. Production (in 000; metric tons; 1980): corn c. 320; cassava (1979) c. 1,800; sweet potatoes (1979) c. 180; dry beans c. 42; bananas c. 300; citrus fruit (1979) c. 80; palm kernels c. 12; palm oil c. 40; coffee c. 40; cotton, lint c. 11; sisal c. 20; fish catch (1979) 106; timber (cu m; 1979) c. 8,559. Livestock (in 000; 1979): cattle c. 3,120; sheep c. 220; goats c. 930; pigs c. 380.

Industry. Production (in 000; metric tons; 1978): cement c. 600; diamonds (metric carats; 1979) 841; crude oil (1980) c. 7,400; petroleum products c. 940; electricity (kw-hr) c. 1,360,000.

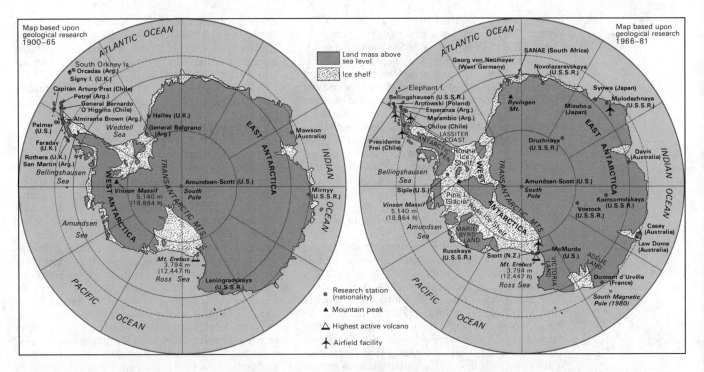

Land mass above sea level
Ice shelf

● Research station (nationality)
▲ Mountain peak
△ Highest active volcano
✈ Airfield facility

Peninsula, where a 4,000-m (13,120-ft) airstrip was being constructed. Chile now had 12 permanent and temporary bases in Antarctica. Construction workers also lengthened the airstrip at Teniente Marsh on King George Island to 1,200 m (3,900 ft).

EAST GERMANY. Scientists from East Germany had been active in Antarctic research for more than 20 years, primarily as members of the Soviet Antarctic expeditions. During 1980–81 East German scientists conducted research at Novolazarevskaya, Druzhnaya, and Bellingshausen stations and aboard marine biology research ships in the Scotia and Weddell seas.

FRANCE. Glaciologic fieldwork continued during a multiyear traverse along the flow line from Dome C in East Antarctica toward the French base at Dumont d'Urville on the coast. A French-U.S. katabatic (downslope) wind study continued in coastal Adélie Land with the building of two automatic weather stations 100 km (62 mi) and 200 km (125 mi) from the coast. Four additional weather stations on 20-m (66-ft) towers were also installed. The data were transmitted to France via the ARGOS satellite system.

JAPAN. Most glaciologic research of the Japanese Antarctic Research Expedition was conducted under the auspices of POLEX-South. Ice sheet and ice shelf studies near Mizuho and Syowa stations were carried out, as were aerial surveys of ice along the Soya Coast and near the Yamato and Sør Rondane mountains. Several ice cores were drilled, one to a depth of 143 m (470 ft) at Mizuho Station. A marine geophysics program, begun in the Bellingshausen Sea from the ship "Hakurei-Maru," was to be expanded to the Weddell and Ross seas in future years.

NEW ZEALAND. The rebuilding of Scott Base, designed to more than triple the size of the station, passed the halfway mark. Geologic work on the

relationship of the mountain ranges to the huge Ross embayment continued along the North Victoria Land coast from Cape Adare to the Transantarctic Mountains. Drilling into the Ross Sea bottom continued from an annual ice platform, and marine life research was expanded with possible commercial implications for the future.

NORWAY. During 1980–81 Norwegian scientists joined the Scott Polar Research Institute (U.K.) to study icebergs in the Scotia Sea from HMS "Endurance." Automatic weather stations were established on three large icebergs.

POLAND. Biological programs continued at Arctowski Station on King George Island, but the overall size of the Polish research program was reduced for reasons of economy. The emphasis was to be shifted from large-scale summer programs to small teams occupying Arctowski on a rotating basis.

SOUTH AFRICA. Geologic, glaciologic, and atmospheric research continued at SANAE Base. A long-term study of the southern ocean lithosphere was begun.

UNITED KINGDOM. Research activities were again concentrated in the Antarctic Peninsula region, but the British Antarctic Survey used a Twin Otter with an airborne radio echo sounder to fly ten profiles, including several northward from the Ellsworth Mountains, the least known area of West Antarctica. Using a doppler radar positioning system, the flights discovered evidence of a subglacial trough some 1,000 m (3,280 ft) below sea level that links the Weddell and Amundsen seas via the Pine Island Glacier. As part of the Glaciology of the Antarctic Peninsula (GAP) project, an 83-m (272-ft) ice core was taken from the southern plateau of the peninsula. GAP is an effort to derive a 1,000-year climatic record for the peninsula from evidence of impurities in ice cores. The three-man Trans Globe Expedition successful-

Recent geological studies indicate that the land mass of Antarctica is smaller than had previously been believed. As the map to the right indicates, some of what had been thought to be land mass turned out upon further investigation to be ice shelf.

ly completed a trek from the winter camp on Ryvingen Mountain to Scott Base via the South Pole. The 2,900-km (1,800-mi) journey took 66 days.

U.S.S.R. The 26th Soviet Antarctic Expedition involved some 1,400 men and women, with eight ships used to resupply the seven permanent Soviet stations and do marine research. A second summer scientific base was established on the Ronne Ice Shelf near the Lassiter Coast. About 300 scientists and technicians wintered over in 1981. The Moscow to Molodezhnaya Station air route was used again, and multiengine jet transports would begin using this route in the near future. Glaciologic traverses continued in East Antarctica. The borehole at Vostok Station was extended to 1,475 m (4,835 ft), and a second deep borehole was begun at Komsomolskaya.

UNITED STATES. Major research efforts during 1980–81 included studies of Mt. Erebus, at Siple Station, FIBEX (First International Biological Experiment), and glaciologic studies at the South Pole. U.S., New Zealand, and Japanese scientists established three seismic stations on the Mt. Erebus volcano to improve monitoring of its internal activity. One unexpected result was the observation of earthquakes, indicating that Antarctica is active tectonically. At Siple Station radio signals were sent from the 21-km (13-mi) antenna along the magnetic field line that returns to Earth in Roberval, Que. Several rockets and high-altitude balloons were launched to measure the effects of the radio signals, which caused an aurora in Quebec. Scientists on board the research vessel "Melville" discovered a school of some ten million tons of krill near Elephant Island, the largest swarm of sea animals ever seen. The astronomy program at the South Pole continued in cooperation with Swedish scientists.

WEST GERMANY. Frustrated by heavy ice conditions, the West German Antarctic Expedition did not build its planned Filchner Station on the Filchner/Ronne Ice Shelf. Instead, participating scientists built Georg von Neumayer Station on the Ekström Ice Shelf at Atka Iceport. Glaciologic studies at Neumayer began, and helicopter-borne scientists visited the Filchner site to remeasure accumulation stakes left in 1979–80.

(PETER J. ANDERSON)

Anthropology

Perhaps the most important Neanderthal discovery since the early 20th century was announced in late 1980. Known as St. Cesaire, the new Neanderthal was discovered in 1979 at the site of Saint-Césaire in Charente-Maritime, France. Although the fossil is fragmentary, it is indisputably a classic Neanderthal, sharing with others of this group the distinctive forward projecting face, large nasal aperture, and large curving brow-ridges. However, it is of more recent age than other known European Neanderthals and is associated with a different archaeological industry, one that in the past was thought to have been produced only by anatomically modern *Homo sapiens*. Both of these factors focused renewed attention on the controversy surrounding the transition from Neanderthal man to anatomically modern man in Europe. Did Neanderthal man give rise to anatomically modern man through gradual evolutionary change, or did modern man evolve elsewhere and immigrate to Europe?

Before the discovery of St. Cesaire, the known Neanderthal remains dated to perhaps 55,000 BP (before present) and were associated with the Mousterian stone tool industries. These industries are characterized by tools made mostly on flakes and probably struck using stone hammers. Although a continuous archaeological record existed from this time on, there were no other known human fossils until approximately 31,000 to 32,000 BP. These later fossils were anatomically modern in appearance and were associated with an entirely

Bones belonging to *Australopithecus,* an ancient hominid who lived two million years ago, were discovered in Romania. These fossils are the first of their kind to be found in Europe.

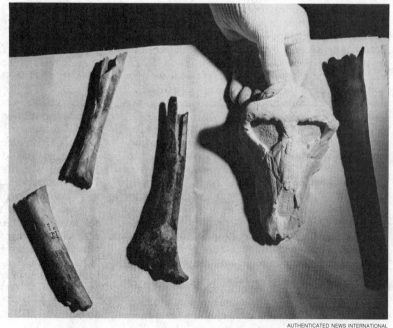

different stone tool industry, the Aurignacian, an Upper Paleolithic industry characterized by tools made on distinctive long flakes (blades), probably struck off using antler punches. Some anthropologists felt that the 20,000 years separating Neanderthal man from anatomically modern man would have been sufficient for the transition to have taken place by gradual evolutionary change. The difference in tool traditions was most often cited as the reason for the change. Under the untested assumption that the Mousterian industry was less efficient, the transition to more efficient tools was seen as taking the pressure off the use of the teeth as tools. This resulted in a decrease in the size of the teeth and in the forward projection of the face, producing the modern human cranial form.

With the discovery of the St. Cesaire Neanderthal, however, there is no longer sufficient time for such a postulated gradual change. The St. Cesaire Neanderthal dates to between 34,000 and 31,000 BP. In addition, its clear association with an Upper Paleolithic tool industry also takes away the explanation for the change. This one fossil has seriously weakened if not completely undermined the hypothesis that Neanderthal man was the direct ancestor of anatomically modern man in Europe.

But what is the evidence for the immigration of modern human populations into Europe during this period? The St. Cesaire Neanderthal is associated with a type of Upper Paleolithic tool industry known as the Chatelperronian, which is different from the Aurignacian. For many years French archaeologists have suggested that this industry is a local outgrowth from the western European Mousterian, while the Aurignacian is an intrusive culture. Although this offers suggestive evidence to support the immigration hypothesis, there is little unambiguous evidence that the Aurignacian complex appears earlier in central Europe than in France. It is significant, however, that human fossils of modern appearance are known from the Near East at Skhul and Jebel Qafzeh in Israel.

When different human populations come into contact, interbreeding occurs, and there is no reason to believe that this was not the case when the populations of modern appearance came into contact with the Neanderthals. Recently found human fossils from Vindija Cave in Croatia, Yugos., may document this interbreeding. In this stratified cave site, fragmentary remains have been found associated with both the Mousterian and the Aurignacian stone tool industries. Although there are only a few specimens associated with the Aurignacian industry, they have been interpreted to show the same morphology as the Mousterian-associated specimens. Both are within the range of Neanderthal variation, but they give the impression of being nearer to the early modern European condition than most other European Neanderthals.

Although this population appears to show a mixture of Neanderthal and modern features, later European Upper Paleolithic fossils are completely modern in appearance. About 35,000 BP, shortly before the appearance in western Europe of both the Aurignacian and Chatelperronian tool cultures, there was a warm interval in the last ice age.

Before this time, when Neanderthal man was the sole occupant of western Europe, the continental ice sheet extended far south into Europe and, together with ice sheets spreading from the Alps, virtually cut off western Europe from areas to the east. Because Neanderthal had been isolated, it is possible that the modern immigrant populations were carrying diseases to which Neanderthal was not immune. It is equally possible that the immigrant population was more effective at hunting animals or gathering food. In either case, the immigrant population would have increased rapidly while the Neanderthal population declined. If this happened, even though interbreeding occurred, the Neanderthal features would rapidly be lost.

The St. Cesaire discovery helps to eliminate the probability of an in situ evolution of modern man in Europe, but it does not answer the ultimate question of the origin of anatomically modern man

Anthropologists at Harvard and Johns Hopkins universities used scanning electron microscopy to compare cut marks found on fossil animal bone from a hominid-occupied site in Kenya (bottom) with marks made on modern bone by a variety of processes, including slicing with a stone tool (top) and gnawing by animals. Their study gave evidence of hominid butchering activity in the region at least 1.5 million years ago.

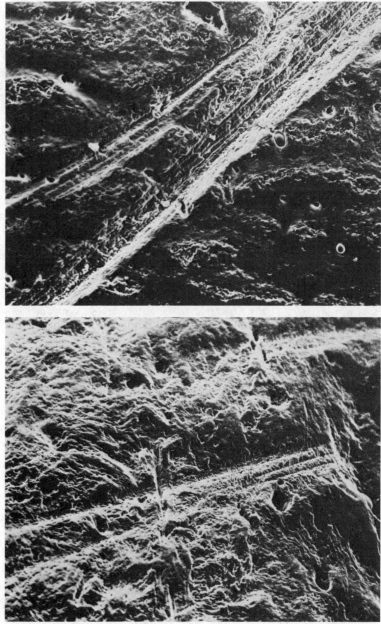

PHOTOS, RICHARD POTTS AND PAT SHIPMAN

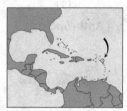

Antigua and Barbuda

elsewhere in the world. Along with the presence of anatomically modern forms in Israel at about 50,-000 BP, fossils of anatomically modern appearance are found in Africa dating from this time (Border Cave, on the Mozambique-South Africa border, 48,000 BP) and possibly much earlier (Omo, Ethiopia, 130,000 BP; Klasies River, South Africa, 90,-000 BP). They are also found in China and in Borneo at about 40,000 BP.

Understanding of the appearance of modern man is hampered by the fragmentary and, in some cases, poorly dated fossil record, as well as by insufficient understanding of the process of evolution in general and the specific causes of modern human morphology in particular. There are no convincing adaptive reasons why the robust morphology of man's earlier ancestors gave rise to the more lightly built human morphology. It is not even known whether this transition occurred in one small area or was a broader phenomenon.

This uncertainty has led to a closer examination of the source populations from which anatomically modern Homo sapiens would have evolved, fossils that lived during the Middle Pleistocene, between 700,000 and 180,000 BP. For many years primary knowledge of the fossils from this time period came from the Far East—Peking man in China and Java man in Java. These are the fossils upon which the taxonomic group Homo erectus is defined. However, with the discovery of many more fossils of Middle Pleistocene age in Africa and Europe, the existence of Homo erectus as a homogeneous taxon spread widely across the Old World has come into question. Recent analyses have suggested marked differences in details of cranial morphology between the Asian, African, and European populations. Although these studies are still in their infancy, it has been suggested that the European Middle Pleistocene hominids are so different from their Far Eastern counterparts that they should not be included in the taxon Homo erectus at all, but in Homo sapiens, albeit a primitive form that led to Neanderthal man. It has also been suggested that the African Middle Pleistocene fossils may be more closely related to the European forms than to the Far Eastern forms, belonging to Homo sapiens rather than to Homo erectus.

Although much work remains to be done, this information suggests that evolution may not have been proceeding in a homogenous fashion across the Old World. In Java, particularly, Homo erectus features are found in the comparatively recent Solo fossils of perhaps 100,000 BP, while in Europe populations were evolving throughout the Middle Pleistocene toward the classic Neanderthal descendants. At present the earliest dates for the appearance of anatomically modern morphology are from Africa.

The evolution of anatomically modern human morphology may have occurred in a relatively small area from an already distinct geographic race of Middle Pleistocene early man, and on present paleontological evidence this area would be Africa. It must be remembered that the last 100,000-year period was the time of the last ice age, and the fluctuating temperature and associated changes in ecological zones would have provided the optimum circumstances for population movement across large geographic zones. This could be related not only to the spread of modern man into Europe to replace Neanderthal man but also to his spread throughout the Old World and into Australia and the New World.   (LESLIE C. AIELLO)

See also Archaeology.
[411; 10/36.B]

Antigua and Barbuda

An independent state and a member of the Commonwealth, Antigua and Barbuda comprises the islands of Antigua (280 sq km), Barbuda (161 sq km), and Redonda (uninhabited, 1 sq km) and lies in the eastern Caribbean approximately 60 km north of Guadeloupe. Total area: 442 sq km (171 sq mi). Pop. (1981 est.): 76,000. Cap.: Saint John's (pop., 1977 est., 24,600). Language: English. Religion: Church of England (predominant), other Protestant sects, and Roman Catholic. Queen, Elizabeth II; governor-general in 1981, Sir Wilfred E. Jacobs; prime minister, Vere Cornwall Bird.

On Nov. 1, 1981, nearly a year after a lengthy and sometimes acrimonious constitutional conference in London in December 1980, the British associated state of Antigua finally achieved independence as Antigua and Barbuda. The new nation's prime minister was Vere Cornwall Bird (*see* BIOGRAPHIES). The main source of disagreement related to Antigua's island ward of Barbuda. Barbudans, who alleged years of economic neglect by Antigua, expressed particular concern over the future of their unique land tenure system and over future control of the police. The Antiguan government, however, successfully argued that these were internal issues and should be discussed separately.

In economic terms Antigua was among the best prepared of the islands of the eastern Caribbean for independence. It had a buoyant tourist industry, a small but expanding manufacturing sector, inflation in 1980 of 16%, unemployment at 19%, and an annual growth rate in 1979 of 7.8%.

The government pursued policies slightly to the right of centre and placed heavy emphasis on strong regional relations. In particular, Antigua was at the forefront of moves to establish the new subregional grouping, the Organization of East Caribbean States. The government also maintained close relations with the U.S., Britain, Canada, and Venezuela.   (DAVID A. JESSOP)

ANTIGUA

Education. (1976–77) Primary, pupils 13,285, teachers 477; secondary, pupils 6,458, teachers 271; vocational, pupils 153, teachers 21; teacher training, students 89, teachers 9.

Finance and Trade. Monetary unit: East Caribbean dollar, with (Sept. 21, 1981) an official rate of ECar$2.70 to U.S. $1 (free rate of ECar$5.01 = £1 sterling). Budget (1980): revenue ECar$62 million; expenditure ECar$69 million. Foreign trade (1977 est.): imports ECar$110 million; exports ECar$35 million. Import sources (1975): U.K. 19%; U.S. 19%; Trinidad and Tobago 11%; The Bahamas 11%; Venezuela 9%; Iran 7%; Canada 5%. Export destinations (1975): bunkers 57%; U.S. 10%; Guyana 5%. Main export (1975): petroleum products 87%.

Archaeology

Eastern Hemisphere. No spectacular archaeological discoveries in the Old World were reported during 1981. The year's spectacles—to the embarrassment of real archaeologists—were both media events. A highly popular movie, *Raiders of the Lost Ark*, reached a new high level of the ridiculous in its portrayal of archaeological fieldwork. And public confusion over the borderline between archaeology and paleoanthropology was apparent in the media coverage of *Lucy*, a best-selling book about some early African fossil hominid bones.

For understandable reasons, there was no archaeological news from Iran. In the U.S. archaeologists braced for the effects of Pres. Ronald Reagan's cutbacks in federal funding to universities and museums. In Israel ultra-Orthodox zealots did their best to disrupt excavations in Jerusalem because the bones of Jewish ancestors might be disturbed. Before his death, Egyptian Pres. Anwar as-Sadat was reportedly giving serious thought to the reburial (with full state honours) of the mummies of ancient Egyptian pharaohs now in the Cairo museum.

PLEISTOCENE PREHISTORY. In fact, very early artifacts were being found in east Africa, some in contexts suggesting that they were probably the work of australopithecine hominids. Stone core and flake tools found in excavations on an apparent campsite in the Hadar region of Ethiopia were dated to 2.5 million–2.7 million years ago. A microscopic study of animal bones recovered from sites in Olduvai Gorge (Tanzania) and Koobi Fora (Kenya), of about 1.6 million years ago, revealed the cut marks of ancient butchering tools.

An important summary account of work in the loess deposits of Tadzhikistan, Soviet Central Asia, appeared in *Scientific American* (Dec. 1980). Two sites, Lakhuti I and Karatau, yielded a sequence of buried soils, some containing tools. The earliest tools—choppers and retouched flakes—came at the very base of the Pleistocene (identified as about one million years ago). Excavations on the middle Rissian terraces at Tares, in the Dordogne, France, yielded a rich collection of Mousterian side scrapers. Another open-air French site, Tanneron in the Alpes-Maritimes, had an important variety of Aurignacian II flint tools. For the first time, paleolithic cave art, in the form of engravings of animals, was found in England. The find, in Herefordshire, was dated to about 15,000 BC. At the El Juyo Cave near Santander in northern Spain, University of Chicago workers found what was described as the oldest known religious shrine. The sanctuary contained a stone head and altar-like slab dating to about 14,000 years ago.

Work in Egypt's Western Desert, especially in the Wadi Kubbaniya, resulted in the recovery of important late Pleistocene artifacts. However, claims for the cultivation of cereals as early as 18,-000 years ago were being treated with skepticism.

NEAR EAST. An important new source of current archaeological information on the area appeared: the *Lettre d'Information Européenne Archéologie Orientale*, published by the Centre de Recherches Archéologiques-Valbonne of the Centre Nationale de Recherches Scientifiques, France. It was announced that the considerable proceeds of the very successful traveling exhibition of treasures from the tomb of Tutankhamen would be used for renovation of the Egyptian Museum at Cairo. There was little to report, as yet, on the year's work by the long-range research teams in Egypt, such as the Oriental Institute of Chicago's Luxor expedition, which was concentrating on the copying of reliefs on the great temples. President Sadat's death appeared to have had no effect on archaeological work.

An impressive number of excavations were being carried out in Israel, many as locally staffed salvage operations. The Hebrew University's impressive exposures on the eastern slope of the City of David area in Jerusalem uncovered late Iron Age II structures built over an earlier ramp. It was these excavations that aroused the anger of the Orthodox Jews. At Tell Dan, in the far north, the excavations by Hebrew Union College of Cincinnati, Ohio, were concentrating on clearing early 2nd-millennium BC fortifications. A French team excavated at two Natufian (10th–8th millennium BC) sites. A British team continued its excavations at Tell Nebi Mend (ancient Kadesh) in Syria. Several French expeditions were also at work in Syria, one at an important coastal site, Ras el Bassit. A Yale University expedition did more clearance at Tell Leilan in northeast Syria, once a walled Assyrian capital city.

In Turkey there was considerable activity in the Euphrates salvage area (which would be flooded when new dams were completed), as well as on the Anatolian plateau and to the west. In the Malatya salvage region, an Istanbul University team uncovered important new evidence of the northern Ubaid complex, with a number of clay bullae (seals), at Dagirmen Tepe. At Kurban Huyuk in the Urfa salvage region, an Oriental Institute excavation exposed a fine sequence of 3rd- and 2nd-millennium BC buildings. Outside the salvage region, the joint Istanbul-Chicago-Karlsruhe team continued to clear the remarkable 8th-millennium BC architecture at the early village site of Cayonu. The University of Ankara excavations at Kultepe, Masat, and Acemhoyuk, mainly 2nd millennium BC, were continued, as were the extraordinary end-4th–early-3rd-millennium BC exposures of Alba Palmieri of Rome University at Malatya-Arslantepe.

GRECO-ROMAN REGIONS. In Greece itself, there was still considerable concern over the effects of industrial air pollution on the monuments. The Greek antiquities service denied, however, that the palace of Knossos on Crete was in a state of decay. To complicate matters further, an earthquake in February 1981 did substantial damage in several parts of Greece; one corner of the Parthenon was cracked, and a number of vases in the Athens museum were broken. After a five-year break, excavations were resumed on the Athenian Agora. In November the American School of Classical Studies announced the discovery of the foundation of the Painted Stoa, which had been a gath-

An Orthodox Jew watches as excavation continues at a sit_ known as the City of David in Jerusalem. The excavation aroused anger on the part of ultra-Orthodox Jews in Israel, who believe the site to be a cemetery and, therefore, not to be disturbed.

ering place for philosophers. Stoicism took its name from the building, where its founder, Zeno, often lectured. On Crete a new Minoan site of importance, Anemospilia, yielded a freestanding shrine and also the suggestion of human sacrifice.

A limestone slab with a sundial was found by French archaeologists in a city founded by Alexander the Great in Afghanistan. The American Schools of Oriental Research was affiliated with some 17 field projects in Israel, Jordan, Syria, and Cyprus in the summer of 1981; most of them concerned the Greco-Roman and later ranges of time. At Pella of the Decapolis, Jordan, more exposures of building remains—both domestic and monumental—were made, and another mosaic was found. In Turkey long-range work at Sardis (U.S.), Ephesus (Austrian), and Pergamon (West German) continued. The British journal *Current Archaeology* (No. 75) contained a "Round-up 1980" of clearances of Roman remains in Britain.

LATE PREHISTORIC EUROPE. A series of radiocarbon age determinations on later Pleistocene "mesolithic" and "neolithic" contexts in Romania, reported in the *American Journal of Archaeology* (85:483), was especially noteworthy since few such determinations were available from southeastern Europe. An impressive exposure of a "mesolithic" village, with traces of round huts, was made at the site of Mount Sandel in the northernmost part of Ireland. It yielded evidence of the life of hunter-collectors of c. 7000 BC. In Switzerland the remains of a lakeside village site were

being recovered by scuba-diving archaeologists in full view of downtown Zürich.

ASIA AND AFRICA. Radiocarbon assays on materials from cemeteries of 5000 to 2000 BC were reported by Chinese archaeologists as showing a gradual increase in the prominence of males, perhaps associated with the intensification of cultivation. Evidence of social rank was also suggested by the contents of certain rich graves. These, however, did include females as well as males. At the great underground vault near Xian, Shaanxi Province (Sian, Shansi Province), more of the life-size terra-cotta horses, chariots, and soldiers of the emperor Ch'in Shih Huang Ti (220 BC) were being cleared. In the sea off Nagasaki, the remains of the emperor Kublai Khan's fleet, which attempted to invade Japan, were being found.

A series of radiocarbon assays fixed the age of the rock art in the Wonderwerk Cave, South Africa, at at least 10,000 years ago. In *Scientific American* (Feb. 1981), Thurstan Shaw presented a useful analysis of the Nok terra-cotta figures of Nigeria, which date to about 2,500 years ago.

(ROBERT J. BRAIDWOOD)

Western Hemisphere. An unprecedented amount of archaeological fieldwork occurred throughout the New World in 1981. Despite federal budget cuts and a faltering economy, at least 5,000 projects were conducted in the U.S., the overwhelming majority of them mandated by historic preservation and environmental protection requirements.

HISTORICAL ARCHAEOLOGY. During 1981 more historic sites were investigated than ever before, and several research themes emerged; they included the study of colonial, urban, and industrial sites, as well as those associated with ethnic and minority groups. The St. Augustine project at St. Augustine, Fla., directed by Kathleen Deagan of Florida State University, explored locations of at least six late-16th-century households. Funded by Florida State University, the National Endowment for the Humanities, and the St. Augustine Restoration Foundation, the research focused on the emergence and development of the Hispanic-American cultural tradition over a 300-year period.

In Canada James Tuck, Memorial University of Newfoundland, directed an investigation of a 16th-century Basque whaling station on Saddle Island, Red Bay, Labrador, funded by the Social Sciences and Humanities Research Council of Canada. Domestic deposits spanning the period 1815–55 were unearthed at two Spanish-period sites in California, the Ontiveros Adobe in Los Angeles County (Greenwood and Associates under a grant from the National Endowment for the Humanities), and the Cooper-Molera Adobe in Monterey County (California Department of Parks and Recreation).

On the plantation known as Flowerdew Hundred on the James River in Virginia, James Deetz, University of California, Berkeley, initiated a multiyear research project to study the evolution of the plantation from the early 17th century to the present. Sponsored by the Flowerdew Hundred Foundation and University Research Expeditions, the investigation in its first year uncovered remains of several 17th- and 18th-century buildings. A long-term program of archaeological research within Alexandria, Va., was continued by the city's Archaeological Research Center under the direction of Pamela Cressey.

Late 19th-century interethnic relations figured strongly in projects undertaken at mining sites in Nevada and California. Donald Hardesty, University of Nevada, Reno, directing investigations within the Cortez Mining District in central Nevada, obtained preliminary information on Paiute, Chinese, Mexican, and Italian occupation of this silver-mining locality. In California James Deetz, University of California, Berkeley, continued work at Somersville, a late 19th-century coal-mining town in Contra Costa County.

TECHNICAL STUDIES. Utilizing uranium series analysis, which measures the decay rate of uranium absorbed by bone from surrounding soil shortly after burial, James L. Bischoff and Robert J. Rosenbauer, U.S. Geological Survey, Menlo Park, Calif., reported in *Science* that they had obtained ages of 11,000 and 8,300 years, respectively, for human skeletal remains from the Del Mar and Sunnyvale sites in California. These remains had been dated several years earlier by amino acid racemization at 48,000 and 70,000 years, respectively, creating controversy because of the implication that anatomically modern humans appeared in North America considerably earlier than in Europe and the Near East. The new results were consistent with the geologic and archaeological contexts of the two finds.

A study of archaeological obsidian in Alaska under the direction of Larry Haskin, Washington University, St. Louis, Mo., identified 12 distinct sources for the material, only three of which were known. Obsidian from unknown sources was clustered at sites along the Alaska Range, implying that as yet undiscovered quarries are present there. Luis Hurtada de Mendoza, San José, Costa Rica, reported a hydration rate for obsidian derived from the Chimaltenango source in the Central Highlands of Guatemala, thus complementing the already known rate for obsidian from the El Chayal source and expanding the potential for accurate dating of sites in the region.

A study of the skeletal remains of more than 600 individuals from sites along the Georgia coast, divided about equally between earlier hunters and gatherers (c. 2200 BC–AD 1150) and later corn farmers (c. AD 1150–1550), was reported by Clark S. Larsen, American Museum of Natural History. The agricultural population showed a significant increase in the frequency of dental caries, probably associated with a high carbohydrate diet, and of nonspecific skeletal infections, presumably reflecting an increase in infectious diseases as larger numbers of people followed a more sedentary

The oldest intact Ark of the Covenant was discovered in the ruins of a synagogue in Upper Galilee by archaeologists who dated the ark's antiquity to be between AD 250 and 306. The ark is a chest kept in synagogues to hold the law of God.

UPI

life-style. On the other hand, there was less osteoarthritis, a finding related to less severe demands made on the body by farming.

David S. Weaver, Wake Forest (Winston-Salem, N.C.) University, reported a similar study of juvenile skeletons from Casas Grandes in the state of Chihuahua, Mexico. A burial population from the Medio period (c. AD 1060–1340), a time of larger populations and more densely populated villages, showed more indications of infectious diseases than did a population from the earlier Viejo period (c. AD 700–1060). Although increased dependence upon maize was postulated for the Medio period, an expected increase in porotic hyperostosis, resulting from lower animal fat intake, was not observed.

MESOAMERICA. Don S. Rice, University of Chicago, and Prudence M. Rice, University of Florida, reported on an extensive dry-laid-stone wall of Maya origin near Lake Macanché in El Petén department, Guatemala. The wall, which measured up to 4 m (13 ft) in height and extended intermittently for a distance of about 1.4 km (0.87 mi) around a small plateau overlooking the lake, was far beyond the capabilities of the small population, estimated at about 75, that resided within its confines. It was believed to have been built during the Late Preclassic period (c. 450 BC–AD 250) by residents of the larger Lake Macanché region to protect the local elites and/or as a temporary refuge for the area's residents.

Norman Hammond, Rutgers University, reported on investigations at Cuello, Belize, designed to provide data on Classic Maya florescence. The Early and Middle Formative populations of about 250 persons per square kilometre (0.386 sq mi) at the site rose to more than 1,000 per square kilometre during the Late Formative period, an increase that was accompanied by more complex ceremonial structures and more widespread canal networks and raised field farming complexes. Data from Finca Santa Leticia in western El Salvador, reported by Arthur A. Demarest, Harvard University, documented the occurrence in the Maya area of massive, low-relief boulder sculptures during the Late Preclassic period. However, the possibility remained that the sculptural style was part of a long tradition that originated with the Olmecs.

Also in El Salvador, Stanley Boggs, Instituto del Patrimonio Cultural, directed excavations at El Chapernalito on the Gulf of Fonseca, a site that served as a port during the Classic and Postclassic periods. Bronze ornamental artifacts from Costa Rica and Panama were recovered, as was polychrome pottery from Honduras and elsewhere in El Salvador. Boggs also conducted investigations in eastern El Salvador within the inundation area of the San Lorenzo Dam on the Lempa River.

SOUTH AMERICA. A survey and excavation project in the Paute River Valley of southern highland Ecuador, directed by Karen Olsen Bruhns, San Francisco State University, and Norman Hammond, Rutgers University, yielded information on exchange relationships between the Amazonian lowlands, the interior highland valleys, and the Pacific Coast. John Hyslop, in work sponsored by the Institute of Andean Research, New York,

concluded fieldwork focusing on the Inca road system. More than 2,000 km (1,240 mi) of Inca roads were studied.

In northwest Argentina, Rodolfo Raffino, Hector Lahitte, and Horacio Calandra, Universidad Nacional de la Plata, conducted a computer study of pre-Hispanic architecture as evidenced in archaeological sites in an effort to shed light on urbanization processes in the area. Juan Schobinger, Universidad Nacional de Cuyo, investigated four prehistoric petroglyph (rock carving) zones in San Juan Province, Argentina, as well as a large group of petroglyphs in Valle Hermoso in Mendoza Province.   (DAVID A. FREDRICKSON)

See also Anthropology.
[723.G.8.e; 10/41.B.2.a.ii]

Architecture

The art of architecture, more than ever in 1981, encompassed not only the design and form of buildings but also the entire built environment, with considerations ranging from energy and preservation to social research, city planning, and building technology. The annual convention of the American Institute of Architects (AIA), held in Minneapolis, Minn., in May, focused on design and energy. Seeing energy-conscious design as a major challenge in the final decades of the 20th century, architects realized that this aspect of their art had the potential to change the characteristics of the built environment. As architects responded positively to the increasing demands for energy-conscious design, new forms would inevitably emerge and a new design syntax would be created. The theme of the convention was "A Line on Design and Energy."

At least three distinct approaches to design and form could be traced in 1981. Many new projects could be fitted into one of these, and some even combined elements of all three. One was a continuation of the trend toward historical allusion. Renewed interest in preservation encouraged designers to consider how new and old might best blend. Coupled with this historicism was the adaptation of new buildings to harmonize with vernacular styles of architecture. Thus, housing could be low-rise with sloping roofs and traditional brick or timber construction. Courtyards and private open areas were developed as integral parts of the overall design. Massive masonry construction not only would save energy but could also create a style of its own.

A second strand of design theory continued to favour the new neoclassicism or neo-International Style (also called neomodernism), a mode of design in which the forms established by architectural pioneers of the 1920s and 1930s, in particular Le Corbusier, are readapted. Leading architects of this persuasion included Richard Meier and Gwathmey Siegel of New York. References to the International Style of modern architecture, especially readaptation of its formal elements such as flat, white surfaces, cleanly incised windows, and interplay of formal geometric elements, are characteristic of this design ethic. It was not confined to

Archery:
see Target Sports

the U.S. Italian architect Giovanni di Domenico designed a cultural centre at San Salvo, near Chieti, Italy, in a Corbusian formalist mode. The design comprised an isolated rectangular block with a semicylindrical apse. The pure volumes were interrupted and defined by galleries and ramps.

A third strand of design theory produced the sort of architecture sometimes called high tech, in which the technological aspects of the building create and dictate the characteristics of the architecture. Such buildings, often identifiable by their brightly coloured tubing, sheet metal and pipes, and use of industrial materials such as corrugated iron, were exemplified in the work of British architects Richard Rogers & Partners and Foster Associates. (Rogers was co-architect of the Beaubourg Centre in Paris.)

Awards. In October 1980 the first presentations of the new Aga Khan Award for Architecture in modern Islamic society were made in Lahore, Pakistan, to 15 winning projects selected from some 200 nominations. The award was to be distributed every three years to projects completed at least two years before submission; the prize fund of $500,000 was to be shared among the winners. The rationale behind the award was to value and preserve the traditional quality of Islamic architecture while recognizing the requirements of technology and 20th-century social factors. Design quality remained significant but was not the prime consideration.

The importance of extra-design factors was illustrated by the project in Jakarta, Indonesia, which received an award less for its visual impact than for its social benefits. The Kampung Improvement

Program was sponsored by the municipal government of Jakarta to create access roads and sewage and drainage systems in an already densely populated settlement without disturbing the existing structures. The cultural and social fabric was left intact, yet at a cost of only $60 per head the quality of life was greatly improved.

Another project recognized by the Aga Khan Award was an agricultural school at Nianing, Senegal, which utilized a prototype design structure based on narrow roof vaults. This scheme, designed by UNESCO, could be adapted for use in other countries where similar conditions prevailed. Natural ventilation and energy conservation were important aspects of this and most of the winning designs.

Progressive Architecture's 1981 awards included a first prize for urban design and planning to Steven K. Peterson for his University Avenue project in Ithaca, N.Y. This hillside development comprised housing, a theatre, a hotel, and an auditorium and was situated on a site linking the town of Ithaca and Cornell University.

The influential U.S. firm of Skidmore, Owings & Merrill received two awards for planning projects and one for architectural design. One planning award went to the scheme for revitalizing the downtown area of Providence, R.I. This development, around the state capitol, was planned to utilize land made available through the removal of railroad tracks. The other planning award was for the firm's master plan for a new town in Saudi Arabia—Yanbu New Community, near the existing town of Yanbu on the Red Sea. The town was designed to house 150,000 people and was geared

Hugh Newell Jacobsen designed this house in Pennsylvania in imitation of the traditional way of adding living space. The gable edges and the largest gable end are glazed, permitting more light to enter the dwelling.

HUGH NEWELL JACOBSEN; PHOTO. ROBERT LAUTMAN

to petrochemical production and shipping. The functions provided for by the designers included residential accommodations and commercial, social, and educational and religious buildings.

Skidmore, Owings & Merrill received an award for architectural design for New Jidda International Airport in Jidda, Saudi Arabia. The project comprised the airport terminal and support complex, which consisted of two identical roofed halves separated by a landscaped central mall. The support area was covered by semiconical fabric roofs, like tents, which provided shelter while allowing the air to circulate. The fabric roofs were stretched and formed by radial cables, and the whole design gave a feeling of openness and flexibility highly appropriate to the environment. The project showed how traditional and vernacular building forms could be reinterpreted using modern technology.

Reorganization changed the emphasis of the Royal Institute of British Architects (RIBA) awards for architecture for 1981. Rather than being "architects' awards for architects," the awards became a means of giving fine buildings the public recognition they were considered to merit. New rules required that eligible buildings must have been completed between two and seven years before submission in order that they might settle into their surroundings and be realistically assessed from a functional point of view. For the first time, members of the public as well as architects were invited to nominate buildings.

Arup Associates received the two awards for 1981. More than those of many firms, their buildings seemed to grow directly out of the needs of the individual commission, and there was no one label that accurately described their designs. For example, the Sir Thomas White building at St. John's College, University of Oxford, was an uncompromisingly modern structure that nevertheless, through its materials, forms, and varied skyline, blended in beautifully with its historic neighbourhood. The structure itself, of white precast-concrete frame with solid service towers and staircases alternating with glazed areas between, was modern. Yet the organization of the spaces was traditional: the general configuration with rooms grouped around staircases followed the ancient Oxford and Cambridge precedent. The L-shaped plan formed an open courtyard.

The second RIBA award to Arup Associates was for their administrative headquarters for the Corporation of Lloyd's at Chatham, Kent, England. Of this building it was said that its principal achievement was "the high quality of its working environment, which is more like a new university than an insurance brokers. The architects have succeeded in humanizing the office world." The form chosen for the site on the River Medway was a three-story stepped-back structure of slate and brick featuring sloping roofs and overhanging eaves to give shelter to the windows. The building appeared to grow out of its site in a fashion similar to much of the early work of Frank Lloyd Wright, and the use of traditional materials gave a warm and human feel to it.

The senior partner of Arup Associates, Sir Phil-ip Dowson, received the RIBA Royal Gold Medal for 1981. Sir Nikolaus Pevsner, the eminent architectural historian and author of *The Buildings of England*, was chosen to receive an AIA medal recognizing "recorders of architectural accomplishments." The 1981 AIA Gold Medal was awarded to Josep Lluis Sert.

Educational and Cultural Buildings. Historicist and vernacular design could be clearly seen in the new building for Robinson College, University of Cambridge, by architects Gillespie, Kidd & Coia. Faced with the problem of designing a modern Cambridge college on a small, central site, the architects seemed to take inspiration from the castle form. The approach was over a ramp reminiscent of a drawbridge through a main entrance that conjured up a towered gatehouse. The jagged skyline brought to mind battlements, and the enclosed interior space defined by the building called up a castlelike image. It was significant that the historical prototype was vernacular and not monumental or classical. Materials were traditional. The beautifully detailed brickwork, which required more than 1,250,000 handmade bricks, was punctuated by jagged, triangular, greenhouse-type windows that defined interior spaces, in particular the library and chapel. The height of the building was restricted by planners, and the interior court area was like an urban street.

Too apparent for some critics were the historical references in James Stirling's proposed design for an extension to the Tate Gallery in London. Stirling's neoclassically inspired Clore Gallery, set sideways to the main 19th-century Tate Gallery, was intended to provide space to house Britain's collection of paintings by the 19th-century landscape artist J. M. W. Turner and was to be paid for by the Clore Foundation. The design would complement the existing architecture, and the various architectural references to the past, including stucco panels ranging in colour from ochre to red and a cutaway entrance portico topped by an arched window, were justified as inspired by English country-house architecture. In the traditional English country house, according to Stirling, additions over the centuries were built to harmonize with existing buildings but at the same time to maintain their own identities. Such was his ambition for the Tate.

The architectural firm of Shepley, Bulfinch, Richardson & Abbott received praise for its addition to the Walters Art Gallery in Baltimore, Md. The design problems were similar to those posed by the Tate Gallery extension: how to harmonize a turn-of-the-century building of Beaux-Arts design with a modern addition providing additional gallery space. The solution at Baltimore involved building a square block with a raised basement and two top floors set back. Exterior gallery walls of glass were shielded by an ingenious outer layer of concrete screens. Cornices, moldings, and other horizontal elements of the new building were carefully aligned to match up with the old to create a highly successful visual relationship. The setback of the top two floors allowed natural light to penetrate the exhibition space through skylights, solving in a new way the old problem of how to

FAY JONES & ASSOCIATES; PHOTOS, HURSLEY & LARK, LITTLE ROCK, ARKANSAS

A clever arrangement of lattices was used in the design of a chapel in the Ozark Mountains of Arkansas. The architects were Fay Jones & Associates.

provide natural light in a multistory gallery. The concrete screens allowed natural light to enter indirectly, thus protecting valuable objects from the direct light of the Sun and also helping to conserve energy. Although it covered roughly the same site area as the original gallery, the new building provided far more exhibition space.

The Herreshoff Yachting Museum at Bristol, R.I., provides 2,000 sq m (21,500 sq ft) of exhibition space for historic wooden boats and yachts. Architect Evan L. Schwartz, who received a *Progressive Architecture* award for this design, created a building consisting essentially of two wedge-shaped forms intersecting at the entrance point with a cylindrical projection at one end. The interior made use of wood to harmonize with the exhibits, and a colonnaded facade faced the waterfront. The Herreshoff boatworks formerly occupied the site, and references to this previous use could be found in the fine detailing and soaring forms of the new structure. The interior of the museum featured a progressive increase in height and length of bay to allow increasingly larger boats to be accommodated. The construction was of timber trusses supported by tubular steel columns, and the east and west facades were clad in stained vertical cedar siding with exterior columns and beams painted yellow.

In this building all the various trends currently fashionable in architectural design could be seen: neomodernism in the use of basic geometric forms such as the wedge and half cylinder; vernacular references to the old boatyard in the use of natural wood and exploitation of site; the historical feeling of the colonnade; and the high-tech use of primary colour to emphasize exterior structural features.

Public, Commercial, and Industrial Buildings. In Washington, D.C., the Pennsylvania Avenue Development Corporation gave preliminary approval for an office, hotel, and apartment complex to be built opposite the National Gallery of Art. The architect for the scheme, which was to cost approximately $112 million, was Leo A. Daly. On the site diagonally opposite the National Gallery of Art's east wing, the Canadian government planned to build a new chancellery, for which it was sponsoring a design competition.

Among the most controversial of recent designs was that for the Portland Public Service Building in Portland, Ore. Architect Michael Graves (*see* BIOGRAPHIES) won a competition with a 17-story structure that featured the classical skyscraper tripartite division of base, shaft, and capital. The green-coloured base made a visual connection to the park faced by one side of the building. The shaft was a cream-coloured concrete box with small square windows; the light colour contrasted with the base and the two terra-cotta pilasters supporting a large keystone that capped the building.

In June the *RIBA Journal* devoted an issue to architecture for industry, pointing out that many of the most innovative English designs of the last few years had been in this field. In 1981 only some 38% of factory buildings were designed by architects,

©ARUP ASSOCIATES, LONDON

Arup Associates received an award for the design of the Sir Thomas White building at St. John's College, University of Oxford.

as compared with about 70% of buildings in general. Industrial units, however, were being treated more seriously by both architects and clients. Architects could provide help to clients with such concerns as energy, costs, maintenance, and future expansion.

Two contrasting events pointed up the importance of how well modern buildings last and continue to serve the purpose for which they were designed. On the one hand, the AIA cited Ludwig Mies van der Rohe's last single-family residential design, the Farnsworth House in Plano, Ill., to receive its Twenty-Five Year Award, which recognizes architecture of enduring significance. The house remains "a masterpiece of architecture, as elegant in 1980 as in 1950."

On the other hand, a prefabricated housing project of 1972 designed by architect Paul Rudolph was to be demolished. The decision to do so was made in September 1980 by the U.S. Department of Housing and Urban Development (HUD). Oriental Gardens was a 148-unit project near New Haven, Conn. Construction was originally funded by HUD, but financial problems plagued it from the start. One reason given for the severe roof leaks and penetration of cold air that led to the decision to demolish was that insufficient maintenance funds had been provided from the outset. No permanent solution seemed viable for the severe leakage problems, and by the time demolition became inevitable, one-third of the apartments in the project had been voluntarily abandoned.

Marcel Breuer, one of the pioneers of modern furniture design and architecture, died in New York City in July, and Jack Coia, until his retirement senior partner of Gillespie, Kidd & Coia, died in Glasgow, Scotland, in August (see OBITUARIES).　　　　(SANDRA MILLIKIN)

See also Engineering Projects; Historic Preservation; Industrial Review.
[626.A.1–5; 626.C]

Arctic Regions

Alaska. In May 1981 U.S. Secretary of the Interior James Watt (*see* BIOGRAPHIES) announced plans to open up nearly 130 million ac (53 million ha) of federal land in Alaska to possible oil and gas leasing, the first onshore leasing program for public lands in Alaska in 15 years. Almost all of the newly opened land lies south of the Brooks Range.

In a related development Alaska leaders signed a cooperative policy statement with Watt to implement the Alaska Lands Act. The agreement appeared to settle some problems but at the same time possibly led to future legal battles on other fronts. Among the terms of the pact, Watt accelerated the timetable for oil and gas studies of the Arctic National Wildlife Refuge, rejected a U.S.-Canadian treaty to protect the migrating Porcupine herd of caribou in northeast Alaska, and ruled that no additional wilderness reviews would be conducted on Alaska's Bureau of Land Management lands.

In April the journal *Alaska* reported that the Inupiat Eskimos on Alaska's North Slope were seeking to halt oil exploration in the Beaufort Sea. They claimed sovereign jurisdiction over the Beaufort Sea because they had not given up their offshore rights beyond the three-mile limit under the 1971 Alaska Native Claims Settlement Act.

After bitter legislative and court battles, 330 km (205 mi) of the Haul Road (officially designated the Dalton Highway), Alaska's only road access north of the Arctic Circle, were officially opened for public use between June 1 and September 1. Construction of the approximately 670-km (416-mi)-long highway, which stretches from the Elliott Highway near Livengood to Prudhoe Bay on the Arctic Ocean, was begun in 1974 to provide access for construction of the Trans-Alaska oil pipeline.

North of Dietrich the road, the most heavily traveled of all gravel-surfaced highways in Alaska, remained restricted to residents of the area and to industrial-permit holders whose use of it exceeded 2,000 vehicles per month in the summer.

In mid-May the U.S. Coast Guard's icebreaker-research vessel "Polar Sea" finally drifted free of the Arctic ice near Point Barrow, Alaska, after being trapped for the winter. Its unsuccessful attempt to reach Prudhoe Bay was part of a seven-year study to determine if it would be commercially feasible to develop tanker shipping lanes through the Arctic Ocean.

Toward the end of the year a major roadblock to the construction of the Alaska Highway gas pipeline was overcome. The pipeline would link the gas reserves of Prudhoe Bay, Alaska (which contain about 10% of U.S. reserves), to the lower 48 states and could provide up to 5% of U.S. natural gas requirements toward the end of the century. In October U.S. Pres. Ronald Reagan sent Congress a package of changes to existing law that would enable construction of the proposed $25 billion, 7,-700-km (4,800-mi) pipeline. Later in the year Congress approved the legislation, key provisions of which would enable gas customers to be billed for part or all of the cost of a multibillion-dollar gas-processing plant, the main Alaska pipeline segment, and a Canadian segment even before the pipeline system was ready to ship any gas to the lower 48 states of the U.S. However, some doubt was being expressed by financial experts that the pipeline would ever be built because of the high cost of the project.

In May an 80-year goal for the people of Skagway, Alaska, was realized when the Klondike Highway was dedicated. The highway runs from Skagway to its juncture with the Alaska highway just 20 km (12.5 mi) south of Whitehorse, Yukon. It represented Skagway's first road link with Canada and the southern U.S. and was expected to be a boon to Yukon tourism.

Canada. In January it was announced that about 300 Yukon Indians over the age of 60 would benefit from a financial program to be established in advance of settlement of the Yukon Indian land claims. The Canadian federal government approved payment of $600,000 per year, retroactive to July 1, 1980, to the Indians. The funds were considered an interest-free loan to the Indians that would be repaid out of the eventual total settlement.

In July the construction of an oil pipeline running 870 km (540 mi) from Norman Wells, N.W.T., to Zama, Alta., was approved by the Canadian government. According to the project schedule, the 32.39-cm (12.75-in)-diameter pipeline would come into operation in 1985. The pipeline was designed to deliver 28,300 bbl of oil and natural gas liquids a day into the Canadian crude-oil pipeline grid at the Zama connection point.

In October Panarctic Oils Ltd. announced that it was stepping up its exploration in the Arctic Islands and expected to double, from three to six, the number of drilling rigs operating during the 1981–82 winter season. Two important factors influencing the expansion of activities were the discovery of considerable oil potential near Lougheed Island and at several locations in the King Christian-Ellef Ringnes Islands area and the exploration incentives contained in the national energy plan established earlier in the year by the Canadian government.

For the sixth consecutive year exploration offshore for oil and gas was resumed in the Beaufort Sea. The results of five seasons of drilling operations by Dome Petroleum Ltd., one of the largest exploration companies, totaled four oil and gas discoveries. The 1981 program anticipated the completion of five wells previously started and the drilling of three or more additional wells.

In July a comprehensive northern land use policy was approved by the minister of Indian and northern affairs. The formal planning system was designed to improve management of land resources in the North and to resolve conflicting interests of the resource users—native people, developers, conservationists, and others—in the Northwest Territories and the Yukon. Attention was to be focused on such priority areas as the Mackenzie Valley, North Yukon, and Lancaster Sound.

The Dene Languages Study, submitted in the Northwest Territories legislature in February, stated that both representational government and the cultural survival of the original peoples of the central Arctic and Mackenzie River valley depend on a strong commitment to preservation of the native Indian languages. Other educational issues being addressed in the two-year study included the fact that the region's educational system does not realistically meet the needs of residents who are unlikely to go outside the communities for their higher education, and the need for adult education programs.

In June a Yukon-based company, Canadian Satellite Communications Inc., received a license to provide radio and television broadcasts via satellite to hundreds of thousands of households in remote and underserved communities throughout northern Canada. English, French, and native-language programs were to be beamed via Canada's Anik-B satellite.

The best cross-country skiers in the world gathered in Whitehorse, Yukon, in March for the first World Cup finals ever held outside Europe. Twelve nations competed, and more than 100 athletes were attracted to the event.

The Soviet North. In April the U.S.S.R. issued a statement indicating that it intended to stop whaling on a large scale and that some of its factory ships already were being converted to fish-processing. In 1981 the U.S.S.R. and Japan were the only two countries engaged in large-scale commercial whaling, accounting for about 70% of the whales caught under the International Whaling Commission's quota system.

The May issue of *Soviet News and Views* reported that a new Soviet research station, SP-25, was being established on the drifting Arctic Ocean ice north of Wrangel Island, approximately 965 km (600 mi) from the mainland.

(KENNETH DE LA BARRE)

See also Environment.

Areas:
see Demography; *see
also the individual
country articles*

Argentina

Argentina

The federal republic of Argentina occupies the southeastern section of South America and is bounded by Chile, Bolivia, Paraguay, Brazil, Uruguay, and the Atlantic Ocean. It is the second-largest Latin-American country, after Brazil, with an area of 2,758,829 sq km (1,065,189 sq mi). Pop. (1980): 27,862,800. Cap. and largest city: Buenos Aires (pop., 1980, 2,908,000). Language: Spanish. Religion: Roman Catholic 92%. Presidents in 1981, Lieut. Gen. Jorge Rafael Videla, Gen. Roberto Eduardo Viola from March 29, and, from December 22, Lieut. Gen. Leopoldo Galtieri.

Gen. Roberto Eduardo Viola assumed the military presidency of Argentina on March 29, 1981, at the completion of Gen. Jorge Videla's term of office. On November 20, however, the government announced that he was stepping aside temporarily for reasons of health, and on December 11 he was removed from office by the three-man military junta. Lieut. Gen. Leopoldo Galtieri, the army commander and one of the members of the junta, was sworn in as president on December 22.

Shortly after taking office, President Viola appointed a new treasury and finance minister, Lorenzo Sigaut, to deal with the serious economic problems that had accumulated under the previous minister, José Martínez de Hoz. These included persistent inflation, capital flight, and a high level of industrial bankruptcies. Initial measures included two devaluations of the peso against the U.S. dollar of about 30% each in March and June (following an earlier devaluation of 10% in February), the setting up of a dual exchange rate system, and more restrictive borrowing and trade regulations. A $600 million loan was arranged by international banks to help the country reschedule some of its debt after the devaluation of the peso. On August 21 the industry minister, Eduardo Oxenford, resigned because of disagreements over industrial protection policies.

At the beginning of his three-year term, it was thought that President Viola would speed up the process of returning to some form of civilian government by 1984. This belief was encouraged by his meetings with prominent politicians and the release on July 6 of former president Isabel Martínez de Perón, who had spent five years under house arrest. She immediately left for Madrid; in September an investigative council called for her arrest on charges of using public money for personal purposes.

However, these moves toward recognizing the political opposition were, it seemed, belied when Gen. Albano Harguindeguy, former minister of the interior, implied in September that the next president would again be appointed by the military. President Viola later remarked that no decision had yet been made about the process to be adopted in 1984, but that the armed forces' plans stated objectives, not a timetable, for a return to democracy. Two retired members of the armed forces who had criticized the government were put under house arrest for ten days: Adm. Emilio Massera, a former member of the junta, and former president Juan Carlos Onganía.

A general strike called by leaders of the Confederación General del Trabajo (CGT) on July 22 was heeded by only 20% of all workers, but leaders of the strike were temporarily detained. In September the CGT issued a demand for higher wages, an end to unemployment, and a return to democratic rule. In November more than 10,000 people attended an outdoor mass in Buenos Aires to protest unemployment.

Among other notable political events was the disclosure that the notorious secret Italian Masonic lodge Propaganda Due (P-2) had members in Argentina; José López Rega, a former social welfare minister under the Peronist regime, and Gen. Carlos Suárez Mason, the president of the state oil company, were implicated. P-2 was accused of various illegal activities in Italy, and the Italian government fell in May when it was revealed that some officials were members. Ricardo Balbín, the longtime leader of Argentina's radical movement, died on September 9 in La Plata; he was elected to Congress in 1946, and during his career he ran for president, unsuccessfully, four times. Also in September, Adolfo Pérez Esquivel, winner of the 1980 Nobel Peace Prize and an advocate of human rights, was denied the right to renew his passport for travel to Mexico. In October Argen-

ARGENTINA
Education. (1979) Primary, pupils 4,003,670, teachers 224,673; secondary and vocational, pupils 1,295,815, teachers 178,681; higher, students 479,799, teaching staff 45,179.

Finance. Monetary unit: peso, with (Sept. 21, 1981) a free financial rate of 7,078 pesos to U.S. $1 (13,123 pesos = £1 sterling). Gold and other reserves (May 1981) U.S. $4,289,000,000. Budget (1980 est.): revenue 33,459,000,000,000 pesos; expenditure 37,248,000,000,000 pesos. Gross national product (1978) 51,902,000,000,000 pesos. Money supply (Dec. 1980) 36,155,000,000,000 pesos. Cost of living (Buenos Aires; 1975 = 100; June 1981) 40,796.

Foreign Trade. (1979) Imports 9,125,000,000,000 pesos; exports 10,282,000,000,000 pesos. Import sources: U.S. 21%; Brazil 10%; West Germany 9%; Japan 5%; Italy 5%;. Export destinations: Brazil 11%; The Netherlands 10%; Italy 8%; U.S. 7%; West Germany 6%; Spain 5%; U.S.S.R. 5%; Japan 5%. Main exports: meat 15%; corn 8%; wheat 7%; hides and skins 6%; machinery c. 5%.

Transport and Communications. Roads (1978) 207,630 km. Motor vehicles in use (1978): passenger 2,866,000; commercial (including buses) 1,244,000. Railways: (1978) c. 34,600 km; traffic (1979) 12,058,-000,000 passenger-km, freight 10,947,000,000 net ton-km. Air traffic (1980): c. 7,935,000,000 passenger-km; freight c. 199 million net ton-km. Shipping (1980): merchant vessels 100 gross tons and over 537; gross tonnage 2,546,305. Shipping traffic (1979): goods loaded 24,624,000 metric tons, unloaded 11,148,000 metric tons. Telephones (Jan. 1979) 2,659,900. Radio receivers (Dec. 1977) c. 10 million. Television receivers (Dec. 1979) c. 5.5 million.

Agriculture. Production (in 000; metric tons; 1980): wheat 7,830; corn 6,410; sorghum 2,960; millet 188; barley 238; oats 501; rice 178; potatoes 1,-568; sugar, raw value c. 1,710; linseed c. 512; soybeans 3,240; sunflower seed c. 1,505; tomatoes

546; oranges 762; lemons 370; apples 958; wine c. 2,300; tobacco 64; cotton, lint 146; cheese c. 247; wool, clean c. 85; beef and veal c. 2,923; fish catch (1979) 566; quebracho extract (1979) 105. Livestock (in 000; June 1980): cattle c. 56,000; sheep c. 33,000; pigs c. 3,800; goats c. 3,058; horses (1979) c. 3,000; chickens c. 35,400.

Industry. Fuel and power (in 000; metric tons; 1980): crude oil 25,199; natural gas (cu m) 9,490,000; coal 391; electricity (excluding most industrial production; kw-hr) 35,730,000. Production (in 000; metric tons; 1980): cement 7,125; crude steel 2,404; cotton yarn (1979) 92; man-made fibres (1979) 66; petroleum products (1978) 23,186; plastics and resins 149; sulfuric acid c. 250; newsprint (1979) 102; other paper (1978) 709; passenger cars (including assembly; units) 221; commercial vehicles (including assembly; units) 61. Merchant vessels launched (100 gross tons and over; 1980) 64,800 gross tons.

FRANKEN—SYGMA

Lieut. Gen. Jorge Rafael Videla (left) was replaced by Gen. Roberto Eduardo Viola (right) as president of Argentina on March 29 amid growing economic difficulties in that country.

tina boycotted the presentation of Columbia University's Maria Moors Cabot awards for journalists who further U.S.-Latin-American understanding because one of the prizes went to Jacobo Timerman (*see* BIOGRAPHIES). Timerman, an exiled Argentine publisher, had accused the Argentine government of gross violations of human rights.

On the international front the Vatican continued its efforts to solve the Beagle Channel dispute between Chile and Argentina, with the Roman Catholic churches of both countries campaigning for an early, nonmilitary solution. Relations with the United States improved when U.S. Pres. Ronald Reagan took office. Lieutenant General Galtieri, then commander in chief of the Army, spent two weeks in the U.S. at the invitation of Gen. Edward Meyer, his U.S. counterpart, and Foreign Minister Oscar Camilión visited Washington in September.

Relations with the U.K. continued to be strained by the Falkland Islands dispute. U.K. Foreign Secretary Lord Carrington was understood to have told Camilión that Britain would support the right of the islanders to determine their own future. Argentina had earlier dismissed a proposal from the islanders to freeze sovereignty negotiations for 25 years. Argentina's relations with the U.S.S.R. improved significantly in 1981; the Soviet Union agreed to buy a major percentage of Argentine grain and beef over the next five years, while Argentina sought nuclear and hydroelectric cooperation with the U.S.S.R.

The balance of payments showed a change in reserves from $4.4 billion in favour in 1979 to a deficit of $2.8 billion in 1980. This was related to a large increase in import payments coupled with declining export receipts, large outflows for tourism, and interest payments on the foreign debt. The rate of real economic growth declined from 6.8% in 1979 to 1.1% in 1980. Inflation, which had dropped in 1980 to 87.6%, was expected to show a rate of increase of 130% for 1981.

(BARBARA WIJNGAARD)

Art Exhibitions

Just as it had begun to seem that ideas and subjects for large, lavish art exhibitions might finally be exhausted, attention turned to shows focusing on the art of non-Western and primitive cultures. The largest and most lavish such exhibitions in 1981 were devoted to the art of the Far East and Africa. Perhaps gallery-goers were tiring of mammoth retrospectives on European and American artists. Or had they all been done? More likely the large Oriental exhibitions were in the nature of public relations exercises, representing efforts by governments to increase knowledge of cultures generally less well studied in the West. Such a goal might justify the expenditure of huge sums of money on traveling exhibitions; however, organizing museums wishing to mount large loan exhibitions remained constrained to some extent by budgetary pressures and the ever increasing costs of travel and insurance.

Together with the new focus on the art of China, Japan, and Africa, there was increasing interest in primitive and folk art of all periods and cultures—including, in the U.S., naïve and primitive painting and the art of the American Indian. The influence of China and Japan on Western art of the modern period was a point of great interest, especially in the U.S.

"The Great Bronze Age of China: An Exhibition from the People's Republic of China," which opened at New York City's Metropolitan Museum of Art in 1980, was certainly one of the most significant and impressive exhibitions of non-Western art seen in the West for a long time. Lent by the Chinese government, it consisted of about 100 bronze, jade, and terra-cotta objects, all discovered within the last 30 years. Included in the show were a group of terra-cotta cavalry figures, part of an "army" of 7,000 men found in the tomb of the emperor Ch'in Shih Huang Ti, which one critic

Armies:
see Defense

Art:
see Architecture; Art Exhibitions; Art Sales; Dance; Literature; Museums; Theatre

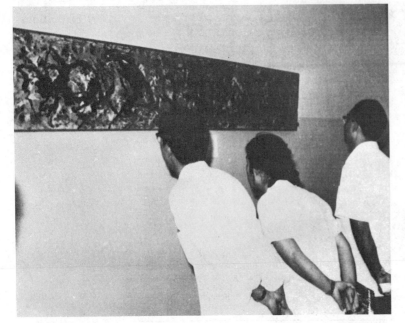

Chinese viewers in Beijing gazed intently at a Jackson Pollock painting, part of an exhibition of American art shown in the Chinese capital in September. The exhibition was assembled by the Museum of Fine Arts in Boston.

Two bronze statues of Greek warriors, found in the Mediterranean off the Italian coast, went on display in Italy after extensive restoration had been accomplished by Florentine experts. The statues are believed to be the work of Phidias, a 5th-century BC Greek sculptor.

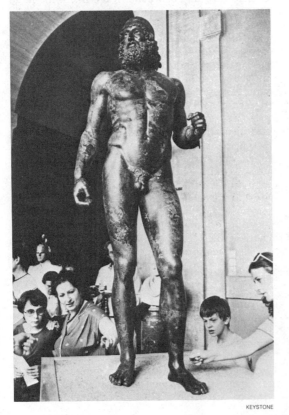

called "the greatest archaeological discovery of our time." After appearing at the Field Museum of Natural History in Chicago in the fall of 1980, the exhibition was on view at the Kimbell Art Museum, Fort Worth, Texas, at the turn of the year and then traveled to the Los Angeles County Museum of Art and to the Museum of Fine Arts in Boston.

In exchange, the Museum of Fine Arts organized the first exhibition of American art to travel to China in more than 30 years. Mounted at the request of the U.S. government's International Communication Agency, it included 70 paintings ranging in date from Colonial times to the present. The opening in Beijing (Peking) was almost canceled when Chinese officials demanded the removal of 13 modern abstract works, but the matter was resolved after a weekend of intense negotiations.

The largest exhibition of Chinese painting ever shown in the U.S. was on view in Kansas City, Mo., and Cleveland, Ohio; later it was to travel to the National Museum in Tokyo. Entitled "Eight Dynasties of Chinese Painting: The Collections of the Nelson Gallery–Atkins Museum, Kansas City, and the Cleveland Museum of Art," the show was drawn from the impressive resources of these two museums. It formed a striking reminder of the great richness of material on this subject to be found in U.S. collections.

"The Great Japan Exhibition: Art of the Edo Period 1600–1868," organized jointly by the Royal Academy of Art, London, and the Japan Foundation, opened in London in October 1981. The exhibition was closed for a week over the Christmas period to allow new exhibits to be installed. Objects of the Edo period were displayed in a setting designed by a Japanese architect and intended to show the origins of modern Japanese art, a genre that was somewhat more familiar to people in the West.

A slightly later period was the subject of "Imperial Japan: The Art of the Meiji Era (1868–1912)." Organized for the Herbert F. Johnson Museum of Art at Cornell University, Ithaca, N.Y., this exhibition was also seen at Portland, Ore. During the Meiji period enormous quantities of Japanese lacquerware were exported to the West, and the art of the era had a profound influence on American art of the early 20th century. However, this was the first comprehensive exhibition devoted to the subject to be shown in the U.S. since 1904.

"One Thousand Years of Japanese Art (650–1650)" was the first of a series of exhibitions planned by the Japan House Gallery in New York City to portray the history of Japanese art through examples from American public collections. The U.S. possessed the greatest concentration of Japanese art in any country outside Japan, with particularly fine collections in museums at Cleveland; Boston; Washington, D.C.; New York City; Chicago; Seattle, Wash.; and Honolulu.

Genre paintings from the Kyusei Atami Art Museum in Japan were shown at the Los Angeles County Museum of Art and also at the Honolulu Academy of Arts. The exhibition, "Japanese Genre Paintings from the Kyusei Atami Art Museum," celebrated the centenary of the birth of the founder of that museum, Mokichi Okada. It was the first time a substantial portion of the collection had been shown in the U.S.

African art was also the subject of some impressive exhibitions. "Treasures of Ancient Nigeria," organized by the Detroit Institute of Arts and also seen at the Calgary (Alta.) Museum and the Metropolitan Museum of Art, was the first comprehensive exhibition of Nigerian art to be shown in the U.S. Among the objects on display, all of which were lent by the government of Nigeria,

The Whitney Museum of American Art in New York City mounted a large exhibition of works by U.S. painter Edward Hopper at the Hayward Gallery, London. "Early Sunday Morning" (1930) was part of the exhibit, also seen in Amsterdam, Düsseldorf, Chicago, and San Francisco.

were terra-cotta sculptures dating from the 5th century BC that compared favourably in quality with Greek sculpture of the same date. There were also some fine sculptured heads from Nok cultures, discovered within the last 40 years and never before exhibited outside Nigeria. Clearly, art lovers could expect to learn more about this interesting and relatively little-known subject in years to come as discoveries continued to be made and more attention was devoted to the art of Africa south of the Sahara.

In "African Majesty," shown at the Art Gallery of Ontario in Toronto, one of the most important private collections of African art in North America was cataloged and exhibited in its entirety for the first time. There were 59 carvings on display from the Barbara and Murray Frum Collection, built up in just over ten years and rich in works from Cameroon and the Congo. This was yet another example of the growing interest in primitive arts, especially those of Africa, Oceania, and ancient America. "Art from Africa," shown in London at the Commonwealth Institute in the early spring, was an exhibition of more than 300 works of contemporary African art. Works from such non-Commonwealth countries as Ethiopia, Zaire, and Upper Volta were shown along with works from Commonwealth countries, including Ghana, Kenya, Nigeria, Uganda, and Zambia. Prior to its London showing, the exhibition had been seen in Berlin; Stockholm; Frankfurt, West Germany; and Amsterdam.

A charming exhibition entitled "Hawaii: The Royal Isles" was shown at several U.S. museums during the winter. Drawn from the Bernice P. Bishop Museum, Honolulu, and comprising more than 300 objects, it included examples of the art of the islands around the time of Captain Cook's arrival in 1778. Among the pieces was an extraordinary carved wooden idol dating from about 1825. Prehistory was the theme of "The Gauls: Celtic

Antiquities from France," shown at the British Museum, London, in the spring. It was the fullest view ever seen in Britain of the art of the Iron Age in France. Most of the objects had been found in tombs, and they included weapons, jewelry, and pottery. Many had been lent by French museums, among them the Musée des Antiquités Nationales, Saint-Germain-en-Laye.

Few classical bronzes have survived from antiquity, so the discovery off the Ionian coast of Calabria, Italy, in 1972 of two over-life-size bearded, nude male figures from 5th-century Greece was an event of major importance. These two bronzes went on show in Florence for a short period in 1981 after extensive restoration had been completed. The public's response was overwhelming, causing the show to be extended by popular

"The Golden Age of Naples," an exhibit of 18th-century paintings, drawings, and art objects, was shown at the Detroit Institute of Arts in August.

Art Exhibitions

(Left to right) Richard Oldenberg, director of the Museum of Modern Art, posed with Spanish Ambassador José Lladó, Spanish Cultural Minister Iñigo Cavero, and Javier Tussell, director general of Spain's National Artistic Patrimony, in September in front of Pablo Picasso's "Guernica" before the painting was packed for shipment to Spain. Picasso had ordered the painting not to be returned to Spain until Spain had achieved a democratic government.

demand. The sculptures, named the Riace Bronzes, were of the highest quality. The showing at the Florence Archaeological Museum was permitted by the town of Reggio di Calabria, which owned the sculptures under Italian law, as a tribute to the Florentine craftsmen who carried out the restoration. Eventually it was hoped the sculptures would be on permanent display in Reggio, and research was to be undertaken by art experts from that city to document the history of these fine classical works from the Periclean Age.

Since its opening in 1977, the Centre National d'Art et de Culture Georges Pompidou (the Beaubourg) in Paris had mounted a series of five gigantic shows of 20th-century art designed to show the importance of France in the evolution of modern art. The last of these, "Paris–Paris: Créations en France 1937–1957," was on display during the summer. It covered the period from the 1937 Paris Exhibition through World War II and beyond and was divided into 40 sections on such diverse aspects of the arts as painting, literature, music, architecture, politics, and fashion. Léger, Matisse, Bonnard, Braque, and Picasso were among the artists represented. An earlier show, "Les Réalismes entre Révolution et Réaction: 1919–1939," was devoted to realism in art. A large space was given over to works by little-known German artists, and there were also areas showing English, Spanish, and American facets of the movement. Paintings, drawings, sculpture, architecture, photography, film, posters, and applied arts were all on display.

A number of important shows featured American themes, including the first important exhibition of American art ever shown in the Vatican. "A Mirror of Creation: 150 Years of American Nature Painting," organized by the Friends of American Art in Religion and shown late in 1980, comprised 56 paintings, each by a different artist. In exchange the Vatican planned to send a large selection from its collection to the U.S. in 1983 for exhibition in New York City, Chicago, and San Francisco. The 180 works to be sent would range in age from antiquity to the present.

In 1969 a collection of more than 2,000 works by the American realist painter Edward Hopper was bequeathed to the Whitney Museum of American Art, New York City. Though well known in the U.S., Hopper's work had not been seen previously in Europe. "Edward Hopper: The Art and the Artist," organized by the Whitney and shown at the Hayward Gallery, London, gave British viewers a chance to learn about and assess this artist's work. The works were drawn from public and private collections, including that of the Whitney. Some interesting studies for a number of Hopper's better-known paintings were included. The show was also seen in Amsterdam; Düsseldorf, West Germany; Chicago; and San Francisco.

The Los Angeles County Museum of Art celebrated the city's bicentennial with a large two-part exhibition devoted to the art of Los Angeles. The first part, on art in the 1960s, included works by native Californian artists as well as artists from elsewhere who worked in southern California. Representative works by Ed Ruscha, Richard Diebenkorn, and David Hockney were among the exhibits. The second part of the show, called "L.A.: 1981," displayed works by 15 Los Angeles artists, including some pieces created especially for the exhibition.

Dutch art of the 17th century was the subject of

two important exhibitions in the U.S. "Gods, Saints and Heroes: Dutch Painting in the Age of Rembrandt," devoted to historical and biblical subjects, was on view at the National Gallery of Art, Washington, D.C., and the Detroit Institute of Arts. The second show, "Dutch 17th Century Portraiture—The Golden Age," was mounted at the Ringling Museum, Sarasota, Fla., and included drawings, prints, and decorative arts. Especially notable was a set of tiles in naïve designs showing members of the House of Orange. A comprehensive retrospective of 20th-century Israeli art was shown at the Jewish Museum in New York City. Entitled "Artists of Israel: 1920–1980," it included works by Yaacov Agam, Mordecai Arden, and Reuven Rubin.

"Masterpieces of Medieval Painting: The Art of Illumination," shown at the Pierpont Morgan Library in New York City, was drawn from the library's own collection of medieval and Renaissance manuscripts, one of the greatest in the world with more than 1,000 illuminated manuscripts. The exhibition was arranged to celebrate the completion of a project making available some 1,200 slide and microfiche reproductions of the library's treasures.

The new print galleries at the Metropolitan Museum of Art opened with an exhibition called "The Painterly Print: Monotypes from the 17th to the 20th Century," which was later shown at Boston. A monotype is the simplest form of printmaking: the artist inks or paints a surface (glass, metal, or stone) and prints directly onto paper, pulling only one print. Blake and Degas were two artists who favoured the medium.

The Anderson Collection of Art Nouveau was shown at the Sainsbury Centre for Visual Arts at the University of East Anglia, Norwich, England. This collection, formed by Sir Colin and Lady Anderson and given to the university in 1978, included furniture by Gallé, glass and jewelry by

Lalique, furniture by Majorelle, and glass by Tiffany. A much-criticized exhibition at the Royal Academy, London, was "A New Spirit in Painting," a mixed bag of modern paintings by 38 artists, including Picasso, Hockney, Lucian Freud, and Andy Warhol, with a bias toward various forms of realism. In Madrid the Buen Retiro organized a large-scale exhibition devoted to work by the English sculptor Henry Moore, shown at the Palacio Velázquez and the Palacio de Cristal in the summer. In a departure from the usual scheme, the works were arranged thematically rather than chronologically, with sections devoted to such Moore themes as "mother and child" and "reclining figure."

The National Gallery of Art in London continued its series of shows called "The Artist's Eye," in which a contemporary artist selected certain works from the gallery's collection to form a small exhibition. The last artist in the series was Hockney, whose choices included Vermeer's "Young Woman Standing at a Virginal," Piero della Francesca's "Baptism," Van Gogh's "Sunflowers," and Degas's "Woman Drying Her Hair." In addition, Hockney painted a picture showing a friend of his viewing the four pictures. This painting, called "Looking at Pictures on a Screen," was the first picture seen by visitors entering the gallery. Another interesting small exhibition at the gallery, "Second Sight No. 3," compared and contrasted two paintings with the same title by different artists: one version of "The Watering Place" by Rubens and another version by Gainsborough.

In the autumn "Picasso's Picassos: An Exhibition from the Musée Picasso, Paris," shown at the Hayward Gallery, set an attendance record for a British Arts Council exhibition. The works, chosen from those in Picasso's estate, were bound for the Musée Picasso, due to open in Paris in 1983. The biggest display of Italian Renaissance art seen

"The Poor Poet," an oil by Carl Spitzweg, was one of 150 works of 19th-century German painters on display in the Metropolitan Museum of Art in New York City in May.

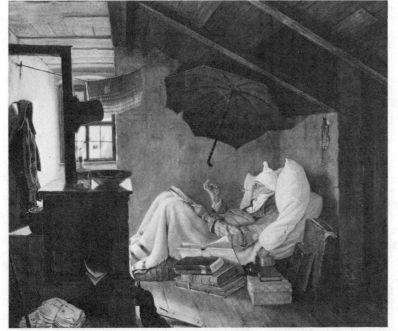

outside Italy for half a century opened in London at the Victoria and Albert Museum in November. Entitled "Splendours of the Gonzaga," the show was mounted in cooperation with the Italian government as part of the Anglo-Italian cultural agreement and contained more than 300 works.

Finally, the University of Arizona Museum of Art at Tucson held an unusual show devoted to four forged works of art. Previously attributed to Kandinsky, Franz Marc, Lyonel Feininger, and Degas, the forgeries were among a group of paintings donated to the museum by a Baltimore, Md., businessman in the mid–1970s. The forged works were exhibited next to documents relating the researches that had led to their discovery. The originals were shown in reproduction so that viewers could learn by comparing the real and the fake.

(SANDRA MILLIKIN)

[631.D.1.b]

Art Sales

Market Trends. The worldwide recession made 1980–81 a difficult season for the art market. Buyers in all fields became more selective, and while items of outstanding distinction found buyers without difficulty, more routine works often went unsold at auction. The very bottom of the market, where prices of $500 or less are paid for pretty curiosities, remained relatively strong.

For most of the year the market in the U.S. was more buoyant than in Europe, but in the summer of 1981 the strong dollar proved a deterrent to foreign buyers and New York auctions suffered. After a century of collecting, however, the U.S. internal market was expanding. Turnovers of Sotheby's and Christie's New York auction rooms both increased by about 30%. In Europe the most severely affected area was West Germany, where recession sapped the confidence of collectors and trade appeared to dry up.

Art Sales. Sales from aristocratic British collections provided two of the sensations of the year. In December 1980 Lord Coke, son of the 6th earl of Leicester, sent a 36-page Leonardo da Vinci manuscript for sale at Christie's in London. A collection of notes on water and cosmology embellished with drawings, it was the last Leonardo manuscript still in private hands. Armand Hammer, chairman of Occidental Petroleum, paid £2.2 million to secure it. He announced his intention to exhibit it widely and bequeath it to the Los Angeles County Museum.

On April 10, 1981, Christie's offered for sale a Poussin from the collection of the duke of Devonshire, "The Holy Family with the Infant St. John." The duke had hoped to secure at least £2 million to endow a charitable trust for the upkeep of Chatsworth, his family home in Derbyshire, but the picture failed to meet the reserve price. However, it was sold to the dealers Wildenstein & Co. immediately after the auction for £1,650,000 and subsequently was purchased jointly from Wildenstein by two U.S. galleries.

In contrast, the year's major offerings in the modern field brought buoyant prices. At the end of March, 28 Surrealist paintings from the Edward James collection were sold by Christie's in London for £1.7 million when only £1 million had been expected. Salvador Dali's "Le Sommeil" of 1937 became the most expensive work by a living artist ever sold at auction when Alexander Iolas, a Greek dealer, purchased it for £360,000. In May 1981 Sotheby's in New York auctioned a self-portrait painted by Picasso in the spring of 1901 for $5.3 million, an auction record price for any 20th-century painting. In 1975 the same painting had sold for only £283,500.

In virtually every collecting field a few items of outstanding quality achieved new high price levels. In October 1980, at the sale of the Leonard Linton collection of astronomical instruments in Paris, a planispheric astrolabe of 1556 bearing the

Seventeenth-century French artist Nicolas Poussin's painting "The Holy Family with the Infant St. John" was sold by the duke of Devonshire for £1,650,000. The painting was sold in order to provide funds for the upkeep of Chatsworth, the duke's home in Derbyshire.

KEYSTONE

arms of Mary I of England and her husband, Philip II of Spain, sold for Fr 1.2 million. Sales of the superb Edward T. Chow collection of Chinese ceramics in November and December 1980 and May 1981 included two 15th-century Doucai chicken cups at HK$4.8 million and HK$3.8 million. In April 1981 a medieval tapestry frieze woven in Switzerland around 1468–76 and depicting "Wildleute auf der Jagd" ("Wild Men Hunting") sold at Sotheby's in London for £550,000. A magnificent Louis XVI desk and *cartonnier* made for the duc de Choiseul was sold for Fr 5 million by Sotheby's in Monte Carlo in June. One of the finest known sets of silver apostle spoons, dating from the reign of Henry VIII, was sold at Christie's for £120,000 and subsequently purchased by the British Museum.

High prices for 19th- and early 20th-century American paintings were a feature of the year. In December 1980 the $300,000 paid for Georgia O'-Keeffe's "Spring 1948" and $260,000 for William Merritt Chase's "Sunny Day at Shinnecock Bay" were among a number of new auction record prices for individual artists at Sotheby's in New York. Running against the general recessionary trend were the buoyant results of Impressionist and modern painting sales in late 1980 and early 1981. A late Renoir nude, "Baigneuse debout," went for £820,000 (an auction record) at Christie's in London in March, and Edvard Munch's "Two People" (1908) made £700,000 at Sotheby's. In May New York took over, with a Degas portrait of "Eugène Manet" going for $2.2 million and Van Gogh's "Mas à Sainte-Maries" for $2.1 million, both at Christie's. Francis Bacon's triptych painted in 1971 in memory of his friend George Dyer made $350,000, the highest price on record for a living British painter.

By the time the major summer sales began in London, however, the tide had turned; 27% of Christie's sale on June 29 was unsold, as was 40% of Sotheby's sale on June 30. The late summer sales of Old Master paintings were even more disastrous, though there had already been rumblings of trouble in New York in June. Even major works failed to find buyers; a Goya portrait remained unsold at £900,000.

A number of old sagas were concluded during the year. A Bernini marble bust of Pope Gregory XV — it had passed unrecognized through a Christie's South Kensington sale at £85 two years before — fetched £120,000 at Sotheby's in December 1980. International dealers Thomas Agnew & Sons were acquitted of a charge of entering into an illegal bidding agreement with two other dealers; their purchase of an Algardi bust for £165,000 at Christie's in 1979 was ruled to be legal. The proposed sale of the bust to the Metropolitan Museum of Art, New York City, fell through, however, since a three-month delay in issuing an export license allowed the Manchester City Art Gallery to raise the purchase price.

Book Sales. The effect of the recession on book sales was less marked than on art and antiques. Nevertheless, auction prices were unpredictable and irregular, though the few rare and important books that came up for sale were hotly contested.

A self-portrait by Pablo Picasso brought $5.3 million in May at Sotheby's in New York. The price was the highest ever paid for a 20th-century painting.

The most sensational event of the year was the purchase for £700,000 by H. P. Kraus of a 12th-century illuminated manuscript, a *Sacramentary* written and illuminated at Otto Beuren Abbey, near Augsburg, West Germany. The price set a resounding new record for a Western illuminated manuscript.

A new development came with Sotheby's sale of single leaves and miniatures from illuminated manuscripts in London in July. The connection between illumination and painting, long overlooked, was grasped on this occasion, as art dealers and collectors joined the bidding. Rainer Zietz, a West German art dealer, paid £4,500 for six illuminated fragments from the Bible of Conradin of Hohenstaufen (Italy, 1260–68). Prices for Indian miniatures rose strongly. Colnaghi's set a new auction record price for a Pahari miniature: £25,000 for "An excited wife greeting Krishna," an illustration to the *Rasamanjari* (Basohli, c. 1665), at Sotheby's in April.

Prices for modern first editions were still modest enough to attract private collectors. A first edition of Hemingway's *In Our Time*, inscribed by the author to his friend Edward J. O'Brien, made £1,900 at Sotheby's in July. An international stir was caused in December 1980 by the sale of the Codrington family papers, chronicling the history of slavery and the West Indies over three centuries, with particular reference to Antigua. They were purchased by a private collector for £106,000 against strong competition from the government of Antigua, whose citizens had raised a large fund to help with the purchase.

The distinguished library of English literary works formed by Marjorie Wiggin Prescott and her father, Albert Wiggin, was dispersed by Christie's in New York in February. It included a

first folio of Shakespeare at $210,000 and the typescript of Oscar Wilde's *The Importance of Being Earnest* at $90,000. Sotheby's in London completed the dispersal of the great Honeyman collection of scientific books in November 1980 and May 1981. Rhäticus's *De Libris Revolutionum* of 1541, a summary of Copernicus's heliocentric theory, sold for £75,000 in November. (GERALDINE NORMAN)

Astronomy

Solar System. On Aug. 25, 1981, the U.S. space probe Voyager 2 raced past Saturn, photographing its rings and moons and the planet itself, measuring its magnetic fields, and sampling its local cosmic-ray environment. Following the spectacular discoveries and success of the Voyager 1 encounter with Saturn in November 1980, Voyager 2 produced a host of new surprises. The cloud-enshrouded planet was found to have a temperature of only −185°C (−300°F) at a depth of 40 km (25 mi) below the cloud tops, with winds raging at 1,600 km/h (1,000 mph). The cause of the bands of equatorial winds, which move four times faster than those found on Jupiter, the solar system's largest planet, remained a mystery. Like Jupiter, Saturn was found to radiate more heat than it receives from the Sun, just about what is expected from the settling of helium in the planet's strong gravitational field.

The moons of Saturn each provided at least one surprise. Titan, once thought to be the largest satellite in the solar system, was found to take second place to Jupiter's Ganymede. Nonetheless, its nitrogen atmosphere presented a chilling image of a world on which liquid-nitrogen rain collects as vast seas at the poles, an inhospitable welcome for a place previously thought the most likely in the solar system to harbour extraterrestrial life. Rhea, Saturn's second largest satellite, showed some large craterless regions, possibly due to an era of "resurfacing" in its past. Enceladus presented a surprisingly lightly cratered, fresh surface with almost 100% reflectivity. The battered face of Dione is overlain with what seemed to be wisps of frozen water. Mimas, nearest of Saturn's major satellites, showed a huge crater 130 km (80 mi) across, about one-third the size of the entire object.

Perhaps most intriguing and mysterious were the observations of Saturn's rings. Rather than consisting of the handful of rings visible from Earth, the major ring system seemed to comprise hundreds or thousands of narrow ringlets. The F-ring, farthest out and only discovered by Pioneer 11 in 1979, did not show evidence of the braiding of its component ringlets seen by Voyager 1. This phenomenon had defied explanation although electromagnetic forces were thought to play a role in shaping them. The particles of this ring (as well as of the D- and E-rings) appeared to be dust-sized. By contrast the objects making up the C-ring are typically one metre (three feet) across. Perhaps what remained most disturbing were the spokelike structures seen pointing away from the planet and cutting across the rings. Whether these are a physical feature of the rings, an electrically in-

duced light-scattering effect, or some other phenomenon was unclear.

Despite its spectacular success the flight of Voyager 2 past Saturn marked the end of an era in U.S. planetary exploration. With the exception of Voyager's encounters with Uranus and Neptune in 1986 and 1989, the few such American projects under way for the 1980s faced imminent cancellation. Thus, the story of planetary exploration moved from a futurist's dream to a historian's recollection in less than a decade.

Stars. Stars are known to exist in a wide range of sizes, colours, and luminosities, but during the year the limits of stellar properties were greatly extended. In January Joseph P. Cassinelli, John S. Mathis, and Blair P. Savage of the University of Wisconsin at Madison reported the discovery of a star with a mass 3,000 times that of the Sun. The star, listed as R136a, is located in the centre of the Tarantula Nebula in the Large Magellanic Cloud, a satellite galaxy of the Milky Way. Observations made with the International Ultraviolet Explorer satellite indicated that it is ten times hotter than the Sun, 100 times larger in radius, and an incredible 100 million times greater in luminosity—as bright as a small galaxy. In addition to providing the energy source for radiation from the surrounding nebula, it also appeared to be ejecting matter equivalent to a solar mass every century. If it is indeed a single object, it is by far the largest, most luminous star thus far discovered.

Astronomers I. Neill Reid of the University of Edinburgh in Scotland and Gerard Gilmore of the Royal Observatory in Edinburgh reported that a star with the undistinguished name RG0050-2722 in the constellation Sculptor and lying some 75 light-years from the Earth is the dimmest, least massive star known. This object appeared to have only about one half the Sun's surface temperature, a fortieth of its mass, a hundredth of its radius, and a mere millionth of its luminosity. Interestingly, for many years theoretical astrophysicists had

Voyager 2's cameras captured the intriguing visage of Enceladus as the probe passed within 119,000 km (74,000 mi) of the Saturnian moon on August 25.

WIDE WORLD

postulated a lower limit to the size of an object that can exist as a nuclear burning star, one with just about these observed properties.

For sheer novelty the object SS433 must hold the current record. It first drew astronomers' attention about three years earlier when its spectrum in visible light indicated that it consists of at least three separate components: one that is relatively stable and is presumably the underlying star and two others that appeared to move back and forth. Kinematic models suggested that the object is a star spewing out two jets of radiating material in opposite directions at about one-fourth light speed.

New observations both confirmed and extended this picture. Using the Einstein Observatory X-ray satellite, Frederick Seward and colleagues from the Harvard-Smithsonian Center for Astrophysics detected directly the X-ray emission from beams extending from SS433 over a degree across the sky, along the direction of the bulge in the surrounding supernova remnant, W50. At much lower observing energies and spatial scales, R. M. Hjellming and K. J. Johnston used the Very Large Array radio telescope in New Mexico to observe SS433 throughout the year. Detecting structure on scales of one arc-second, they found a corkscrewlike pattern whose changing appearance also implied that the object ejects plasma, which then spirals away. Despite all the new observational material, the actual ejection mechanism still confounded theorists.

Quasars. Although the true nature of quasars (quasi-stellar objects, or QSO's) was still enigmatic, new radio observations made during the year increased astronomers' knowledge, if not their understanding, of the properties of these objects. Quasars usually appear starlike to optical telescopes with resolutions of perhaps one arc-second, but worldwide networks of radio telescopes making very long baseline interferometer (VLBI) observations of quasars can study their structure with resolution in the thousandths of an arc-second. A group at the California Institute of Technology headed by T. J. Pearson used such a VLBI network to follow the apparent motion of a radio-emitting jet as it leaves the presumed centre of 3C 273, one of the nearest and brightest quasars. If its motion is interpreted as a real velocity transverse to the line of sight from the Earth, the jet appears to be moving away from the centre at ten times the speed of light (c). But is such a velocity, which would seem to violate Einstein's special theory of relativity, real or just an illusion?

Over the past decade two other quasars (3C 279 and 3C 345) and one galaxy (3C 120) showed evidence for such "superluminal" outbursts. In 1981 VLBI observations made by R. W. Porcas of the Max Planck Institute for Radioastronomy in Bonn, West Germany, found a fourth quasar, 3C 179, exhibiting superluminal expansion at an apparent velocity of more than seven times c. Late in the year a fifth quasar, NRAO 140, also appeared to have superluminal ejecta. One popular explanation for this behaviour, the so-called Christmas tree model whereby independent plasma blobs "light up" sequentially to give the appearance of motion faster than c, seemed ruled out, since it predicts equal numbers of objects moving toward

Fine details of Saturn's atmospheric circulation were imaged on August 23 by Voyager 2 from a distance of 2.3 million km (1.4 million mi). The large spot may be a layer of dark cloud showing through a hole in the planet's upper cloud deck.

or away from the central object. The spate of new data favoured a model involving beams or jets of matter spewed out almost along the line of sight to the Earth. This arrangement produces the illusion of motion faster than c.

Cosmology. Despite the successes of the big bang model of the universe in accounting for its apparent expansion and initially fiery state, serious problems remained. Given the symmetry in the laws of physics, why is the universe made almost entirely of matter and very little antimatter? Will the universe expand forever, or will it collapse back on itself? Given that the speed of light is the limiting speed for the propagation of all phenomena, why does the universe appear so uniform today when, in the past, different parts of it could not influence each other and thus smooth out any initial fluctuations?

All of these questions were examined during the year in a many-pronged attack motivated by recent advances in elementary-particle physics. Theories that attempt to unify the fundamental forces of nature on a subatomic level propose that a mere 10^{-35} seconds after the initial explosion the present-day symmetry in the physical laws was broken, resulting in a small excess of matter over antimatter, with the remainder of the antimatter subsequently annihilating with matter to produce the observed microwave background radiation. Soviet nuclear physicist Andrey D. Sakharov, as well as Y. B. Zeldovitch of the Space Research Institute in Moscow, suggested that such a "phase transition" in the early universe might produce small-scale fluctuations that could lead ultimately to the formation of galaxies. At the same time, these considerations also lead to the description of a relatively uniform universe on large scales. The simplest unified theories suggest that in early times there might also have existed very massive neutrinos, electrically neutral particles usually taken to have zero rest mass. A. De Rujula of the Massachusetts Institute of Technology and Sheldon Glashow of Harvard proposed that such massive neutrinos should be unstable, decaying to

Association Football:
see Football

Astronautics:
see Space Exploration

produce a present-day ultraviolet background field, which could already have been detected.

One new observation directly bearing on cosmological problems came from Stephen P. Boughn, Edward S. Cheng, and David T. Wilkinson of Princeton University. They reported not only a small dipole anisotropy (variance in a measured value depending on the direction of measurement) in the relic radiation from the Big Bang related to the net motion of the Earth through the cosmos, but a small residual quadrupole one as well. If confirmed, this observation would mean that the universe is not as perfectly and mysteriously uniform as had heretofore been believed.

Other evidence for nonuniformity came from Robert P. Kirshner of the University of Michigan and co-workers, who described what appeared to be an immense void in the distribution of galaxies that is five times the size of any previously known. Their observations in the direction of the constellation Boötes showed stretches of 360 million to 540 million light-years in which brighter galaxies (down to magnitude 17) were seen much less frequently than expected. Although a gap of this size challenged theorists for adequate explanation, it was not sufficiently large to undermine the assumption of an overall uniformity in the present-day universe.   (KENNETH BRECHER)

See also Earth Sciences; Space Exploration.
[131.A.1.b and d; 131.A.3.c; 131.E.; 132.D.3; 133.C.3.b]

Australia

A federal parliamentary state and a member of the Commonwealth, Australia occupies the smallest continent and, with the island state of Tasmania, is the sixth largest country in the world. Area: 7,682,300 sq km (2,966,200 sq mi). Pop. (1981 est.): 14,720,300. Cap.: Canberra (metro. pop., 1980 est., 245,500). Largest city: Sydney (metro. pop., 1980 est., 3,231,700). Language: English. Religion (1981): Church of England 27.7%; Roman Catholic 25.7%; Methodist 7.3%; Presbyterian 6.6%; Lutheran 1.4%; Baptist 1.3%; other Christian 8.6%; Jewish 0.4%; Muslim 0.3%. Queen, Elizabeth II; governor-general in 1981, Sir Zelman Cowen; prime minister, Malcolm Fraser.

Domestic Affairs. During 1981 Prime Minister Malcolm Fraser consolidated his position after a shaky period in which he was attacked by a member of his Cabinet, Andrew Peacock (*see* BIOGRAPHIES). Peacock subsequently resigned, and thereafter Fraser faced no challenge to his authority as he successfully directed the attention of Australians away from the problems of unemployment and toward such issues as interest rates and inflation. Despite problems of illness, Fraser made considerable headway in 1981 in his attempts to present a more likable and acceptable image to Australian voters. This was especially necessary because he had lost ground politically after a decision to cut public expenditures severely and to reduce the economic power of the states. The decision resulted from a review of Commonwealth functions by a committee of senior Cabinet ministers in which they described areas where unneces-

sary or unduly costly public sector activities could be eliminated. The drastic pruning of the public sector by the "Razor Gang," in line with the government's beliefs that "big government" was not in the national interest, put Fraser in a difficult position from which he tried to extricate himself by a popular gesture. (*See* Special Report.)

Fraser's opportunity came when public opinion was outraged to find that the Cabinet had accepted a salary increase of 20% for federal members of Parliament. The deputy prime minister, Douglas Anthony, leader of the National Country Party, presided over the Cabinet meeting that accepted the pay raise, which Liberal Party politicians argued was the result of an application to a salaries tribunal similar in form to that offered other wage earners in Australia through the Conciliation and Arbitration Commission. Anthony and his pro-acceptance group claimed that only higher salaries would attract the right sort of person into Parliament. The acceptance of the parliamentary salaries tribunal ruling was a matter for bipartisan approval, and the Australian Labor Party (ALP) was prepared to go along with it. Only the Australian Democrats opposed the salary increase, their leader, Don Chipp, pointing out that the nation's leaders ought to set an example on wage restraint.

Fraser was furious at the pay increases, and members of his party told the press he had "gone like a terrier" at the Cabinet, berating them not only for accepting the offer but also for announcing it while he was overseas. Fraser eventually was able to persuade the government leaders to forgo the increase, and he then told the delighted voters that the government believed that if the parliamentarians' example of restraint could be followed throughout the community "we would be able to grab inflation by the throat." In his most shining hour Fraser added that the inflationary threats posed by excessive wage increases were so serious that the parliamentary salary raises (which, if accepted, would have taken Fraser's own salary to A$111,250 a year) should be substantially reduced. Restraint and responsibility on the part of all sections of the community were, he concluded, essential if progress was to continue strongly in Australia.

The ALP attempted to gain some ground in June, when the federal executive began a campaign to persuade the Australian electorate that they were "democratic socialists," similar to the progressive parties in Europe. Left-wingers on the executive insisted, however, that the ultimate aim of the ALP, as defined in 1923, ought to remain "the democratic socialization of industry, distribution, and exchange, to the extent necessary to eliminate exploitation and other anti-social features in these fields."

The government in 1981 once again changed the basis of Australia's health system by requiring potential patients in government hospitals to be insured either with private health insurance companies or with the government agency, or else face the consequences of heavy bills in the event they needed hospital treatment. The new scheme, effective from September 1, exempted two million holders of pensioner benefit cards, the unem-

Australia

Athletics:
see articles on the various sports

ployed, and refugees and migrants in their first six months in Australia, but it was expected to result in the closing of some Aboriginal and women's health care shelters. Critics claimed that the changes would merely add to the cost of health care to consumers and benefited only those who provided the health services and ran the insurance companies.

The government also faced strong criticism of its handling of Aboriginal affairs by a group of visiting clergymen from the World Council of Churches (WCC). The WCC pointed to the great gap between Aboriginal and non-Aboriginal living standards. They were particularly critical of the policies of the premier of Queensland, Johannes Bjelke-Petersen, and foreshadowed activity by Amnesty International in Australia on behalf of Aboriginals. Bjelke-Petersen responded by accusing Amnesty of indulging in a "ridiculous" smear campaign against Queensland by referring to some state legislation as repressive and against human rights. He also forbade members of the Queensland Aboriginal and Islanders Affairs Department to talk to WCC delegates.

The government decided in 1981 to establish Trans Australia Airlines (TAA), the government-owned public airline, as a private company. The decision was part of the major overhaul of Australia's domestic aviation policy. The ALP opposed what it described as the dismemberment of TAA, saying that the airline belonged to the Australian people and that there was no need to dispose of it.

TAA's general manager predicted that the airline would be set up as a private company along the same lines as Queensland and Northern Territory Aerial Services (Qantas). Qantas, although a private firm, was wholly owned by the government, to which, in years of profit, it paid dividends. TAA on the other hand was a statutory authority run by a commission instead of a board of directors.

The Economy. In a far-reaching and major decision in 1981, the Australian Conciliation and Arbitration Commission decided to end the system of national wage indexation begun in 1975. Under this system all wages in the nation were adjusted each quarter to reflect changes in the consumer price index. The president of the commission, Sir John Moore, said that the commitment of the participants was not strong enough to sustain the continued operation of indexation.

The government continued to face pressure from the labour unions for the acceptance of a 35-hour week. In April Fraser threatened Imperial Chemical Industries (Australia) with retaliation if the company agreed with the Federated Ironworkers Association's demands for a 35-hour week. Fraser said he would begin an investigation into tariff protection for the chemical industry if ICI did not stop the negotiations. ICI responded to this by threatening to cancel its plans for expansion in Australia, including a A$400 million project at Botany, New South Wales. A showdown was narrowly averted after the chairman of ICI Australia, Milton Bridgland, flew to Canberra for talks with

Melbourne was host nation to the Commonwealth heads of government meeting in October. The session brought together leaders of developed and less developed nations.

the prime minister, the minister for industry and commerce, Sir Philip Lynch, and the then minister for industrial relations, Andrew Peacock. After the discussions the government agreed not to refer the chemical industry to the Industries Assistance Commission, and Bridgland said that he was disturbed at the prospect of a reduction in working hours at ICI.

A similar conflict occurred when the state government of Victoria decided to increase the price of electricity it charged to Aluminum Co. of America (Alcoa). Alcoa said that it might have to consider stopping a proposed A$400 million development at Portland, Victoria, unless the state government could guarantee that the company could expect a long-term electric power supply at rates that enabled it to be competitive in the international marketplace.

The Australian economy was affected by a massive inflow of foreign capital. In the financial year ended June 1981, A$6,033,000,000 in foreign investment funds poured into Australia, A$4,765,000,000 more than in the previous year. The inflow helped create a A$1,142,000,000 balance of payments surplus. Consequent appreciation of the currency led to speculation that the government might be forced to revalue rather than continue with its policy of letting the dollar float upward. In addition, the overseas funds flowing into Australia resulted in an excess of available finance, to which the government responded in June by increasing the interest rate on tap funds to 14.5%, with obvious damage to Australian home buyers, manufacturers, small businesses, and consumer borrowers. (Tap funds, generally government securities, are offered for sale continuously and have no limit on the amount that can be purchased.) There was strong pressure on Fraser to do as little as possible about the capital inflow, and he was particularly urged not to cut tariffs. According to the Metal Trades Industry Association, such cuts would lead to serious economic and social problems, including increased unemployment, especially in the car and apparel industries.

Strikes continued to plague Australia in 1981, often as a result of what trade unionists considered too rigid interpretation of the wage indexation guidelines by the Conciliation and Arbitration Commission. For two weeks in June technicians employed by Telecom, the state-owned telecommunications agency, struck, and the numbers of telephone, telex, and computer data lines were progressively reduced because no one was repairing broken equipment. The Cabinet spent more than 12 hours discussing the Telecom dispute, which threatened to stop all telecommunications in Australia, and finally agreed to withdraw its opposition to a proposed settlement. This involved the Cabinet in having to agree to payments to the technicians over and above the wage indexation guidelines. Other major strikes included those by transport workers, dockers, and technicians in the Australian Broadcasting Commission; the last-named stopped international telecasts of cricket matches between England and Australia.

Federal Treasurer John Howard submitted the 1981 budget in August. Howard largely ignored the problem of unemployment and depicted the budget as an essential part of the government's strategy for containing wage and price inflation while at the same time trying to ease pressure on interest rates. The latter reached record levels during the year as the total demand for money in the community exceeded the supply. The budget strategy relied upon a 2.5% increase in sales tax on goods previously exempted (clothing, footwear, building materials, and books) and similar rises in other existing sales taxes in order to mop up any excess liquidity in the community.

The government sought to end the 1981–82 financial year with a deficit of A$146 million, compared with a deficit of A$1,127,000,000 in 1980–81. Among minor adjustments, the government raised the prices of potable spirits and imported beer and wine by 2.5% and increased the departure tax for those leaving Australia from A$10 to A$20. The cost of health service prescriptions was also raised to A$3.20 per item, and an export duty of A$1 per metric ton was extended to include steaming as well as coking coal. On the credit side, family allowances were increased for big families, and unemployment benefits were increased for those aged 18 years and over.

Howard predicted that the inflation rate would

rise from 8.8 to 10.75% in 1981–82. He expected total income-tax revenue from individuals to rise by 18.9% to A$811 million; a major share of the total revenue of A$40,862,000,000 was to be spent on defense, scheduled to rise by 16.3% to A$4,122,000,000. By comparison, expenditures on social security and welfare were estimated to rise by 14.5% to A$11,357,000,000 and outlays on education by 11.1% to A$3,255,000,000.

Foreign Affairs. It was a difficult year for Australian foreign policy makers, who faced the problems associated with a new administration in the U.S., a deteriorating relationship with New Zealand as the result of a South African rugby tour, and the question of whether or not to contribute to a peacekeeping force in the Sinai, to be established when Israel withdrew from that territory in the spring of 1982. The most important priority was given to establishing good relations with the United States.

The Australian foreign minister, Anthony Street, visited Washington, D.C., in March to meet and talk with his U.S. counterpart, Alexander Haig, so as to explore likely changes in U.S. foreign policy under Pres. Ronald Reagan. The Australian government expected that it would have to adapt to a more assertive U.S. foreign policy, one that would feature a more resolute opposition to the Soviet Union. While recognizing that in major ways Australia and the U.S. had converging interests, Street pointed out that Australians lived in a different part of the world, were a middle power and nonnuclear state, had different economic priorities, and were shaped in some way by membership in the Commonwealth. Nevertheless, the U.S. was Australia's second most important trading partner (after Japan) and its major supplier of defense equipment.

The most concrete example of Fraser-Reagan cooperation was the agreement by Australia to a U.S. request that it be allowed to use Darwin as an air base for B-52 bombers (perhaps in some circumstances armed with nuclear weapons). This reopened the question of likely nuclear targets in Australia, a matter on which the ALP and the government strongly disagreed. The year marked the 30th anniversary of the signing of the ANZUS treaty, which linked Australia, New Zealand, and the U.S. in a defense alliance. That alliance would be undermined, argued the government, should the ALP withdraw its bipartisan support for it by criticizing the use made of U.S. facilities in Australia. The ALP leader, William Hayden, asked Street how the government could claim that the U.S. would inform it of any intent to carry nuclear weapons on B-52s using Darwin, especially since the U.S. refused to supply such information to allies who were at least as important as Australia, such as West Germany and Japan.

Australian-U.S. relations were further complicated by the premature disclosure by Secretary Haig that plans were well advanced for Australia to participate in a Sinai peacekeeping force, a suggestion ridiculed by the ALP on the grounds that the Australian military forces were too small and too weak to be dissipated around the globe. Trade relations suffered a blow when ship-

SYDNEY MORNING HERALD, JOHN FAIRFAX & SONS LTD.

ments of "beef" to the U.S. were found to be adulterated with horse and kangaroo meat.

Relations with New Zealand, the third side of the ANZUS triangle, were poor in 1981 as a result of New Zealand's insistence that the South Africans should be permitted to play rugby in New Zealand. Australia responded by condemning apartheid, South Africa's policy of racial separation, by warning New Zealand that it might be banned from the Commonwealth Games due to be staged in Brisbane, and by refusing the South African rugby players transit rights through Australia.

Relations between the two nations were further strained by the decision of the Australian government to require New Zealanders entering Australia after trans-Tasman flights to carry passports. Before July 1981 New Zealanders had been able to enter Australia without passports, a situation that the minister of immigration and ethnic affairs, Ian McPhee, regarded as unsatisfactory. McPhee said that the new passport requirements had been instituted to help discourage terrorists, drug traffickers, child abductors, and others engaged in illegal activities from entering Australia through New Zealand. Stricter immigration rules were also implemented with the intention of stopping "back door migration" by visitors overstaying their visas.

The Australian government was particularly eager to participate in informal and less structured consultation on a global level. In this regard Australia's status as host nation to the Commonwealth heads of government meeting in Melbourne in October 1981 provided an opportunity for bringing together the leaders of developed and less developed nations.   (A. R. G. GRIFFITHS)

See also Dependent States.

Police officers maintained control as unemployed workers staged a protest rally in Australia. Continuous strikes were staged during the year while the government struggled with wage increase demands and inflation.

AUSTRALIA'S NEW FEDERALISM

by A. R. G. Griffiths

The separate states of Australia surrendered most of their sovereign rights in 1901 when that nation became a federation. For only 18 of the next 80 years was government in the hands of the Australian Labor Party. For much of the time, including almost all of the period after World War II, Australia was governed by a succession of conservative prime ministers. Malcolm Fraser, elected in 1975 after the last Labor government, led by Gough Whitlam, was defeated, conceived a strategy to ensure continuance of Liberal Party (*i.e.*, conservative) domination when he invented and christened "the New Federalism."

The New Federalism was a deliberate attempt to get away from the policies of the Whitlam era, when it appeared to the conservatives that government consisted of giving large grants to the states in return for control of their activities. Believing that "big government" was not in the national interest, Fraser set out to reduce its size through the elimination of unnecessary or unduly costly public-sector activities. His philosophy was that activities could be transferred to the states and the funds to carry out the new programs provided through a policy of federal-state income tax sharing.

Fraser argued that centralization of power in the federal government had led to unnecessary duplication, that each sphere of government should make decisions on matters appropriate to that sphere, and that decisions ought not to be enforced by the use of financial power. By 1981, however, Sir Charles Court, the Liberal premier of Western Australia, complained that Fraser's New Federalism amounted to "financial dictation, in a style that other countries call guided democracy."

The "Razor Gang." The main instrument of the Fraser government's policy to develop the New Federalism was a committee established in November 1980 to review Commonwealth functions. The committee was quickly christened the "Razor Gang," a name that proved apt when its report, published in April 1981, outlined a plan to cut

---

A. R. G. Griffiths is a senior lecturer in history at the Flinders University of South Australia.

A$560 million from the government's expenditure program. Much of the saving was expected from the loss of 17,000 jobs in public employment, as the Razor Gang decided that existing staff levels were too high for taxpayers to support in the 1980s.

Fraser's aim was to end the growth of government and the centralization of political power in Canberra, and he proposed to do it by selling some Commonwealth enterprises to the private sector. In his view traditional federal monopolies should not be able to use their privileged position to compete with private enterprise in circumstances where no public benefit could be discerned. He argued that a free enterprise system based on market influences and decentralized control gave consumers greater influence through their spending decisions; the more government intervened by means of regulations and subsidies to change the impact of consumers' decisions, the more control of the economy passed from the many to the few.

Naturally, the public servants about to be sacked or redeployed did not see the benefits of the government's attempts to redress the balance between the public and private sectors. Commonwealth assets scheduled for sale included a government clothing factory in Melbourne; an ordnance factory in Bendigo; the Commonwealth wool testing authority; a shopping mall in Canberra; and all land, property, and stockholdings designated surplus. Fraser also proposed to abolish the Prices Justification Tribunal and to sell domestic airline terminals, and he raised the possibility of the sale of the two government airlines, Qantas and TAA.

The leader of the opposition, William Hayden, speaking on behalf of those about to lose their jobs, described the Razor Gang's decisions as "wholesale slaughter." He considered it a "grotesque program" in which Fraser had begun a massive liquidation sale of Australia's national assets. Hayden claimed that profitable state-run enterprises were being handed over to private businessmen and real estate developers. The government's guiding principle, he maintained, was: if there's a profit in it, hand it over to your friends in business, and if there's a burden in it, hand it over to the states.

Certainly the states saw it that way. To make matters worse, in June the Commonwealth proposed an alteration in the balance of revenue sharing between the larger and smaller states. The government expected to reduce the amount of tax revenue it would give to the states to conduct their affairs. It also altered the proportion of tax reimbursement. The basis of the plan was a 900-page report issued after two years of investigation by Justice Rae Else-Mitchell of the Commonwealth Grants Commission. Else-Mitchell's report aimed to achieve "fiscal

Controversy over government funding of the states swirled around Australian Prime Minister Malcolm Fraser (left) and Federal Treasurer John Howard (right) when news of the funding scheme was leaked to the press.

equalization" among the states; its main thrust was that federal funding to the states with the smallest populations—South Australia, Western Australia, and Tasmania—would be reduced.

Hard on the heels of the Razor Gang's report, the state premiers were rocked by a revelation that the federal government had kept funds from them. The *Melbourne Sun* newspaper published a story revealing that the Commonwealth had been prepared to give the states an extra 1% in revenue, or A$70 million, if they had insisted on it at the annual meeting between state and federal leaders held to divide income-tax revenue among them. The state premiers were furious at being tricked and were also aghast that Prime Minister Fraser and Federal Treasurer John Howard had leaked the story of their victory to the press. When he heard of the deception, the premier of South Australia, David Tonkin, said that he expected the treasurer's resignation and a check to his state from the federal government, and the other premiers agreed with his attitude. However, Fraser and Howard refused to disgorge the extra A$70 million.

Secession Threat. Perhaps the most interesting effect of the power struggle between the states and the federal government was the degree to which the state premiers were prepared to use their influence in the Senate. The Senate was designed by the constitution-makers to protect the interests of the smaller and less powerful states, with the intention of ensuring forever that populous New South Wales and Victoria in the southeast did not grow prosperous at the expense of, for example, Queensland and Western Australia. By the 1980s, however, the resources boom had resulted in a change in the economic balance of Australia, as the huge mineral and energy fuel deposits in the north and west meant that the citizens of Perth and Brisbane were subsidizing their more numerous but less productive southeastern cousins in Sydney and Melbourne.

In this new situation, Sir Charles Court threatened the Fraser government that if he did not get his own way Western Australia would consider seceding from the Commonwealth. Speaking on the national radio network in June, he pointed out that Western Australia had come close to seceding in the 1930s and added that if Fraser's New Federalism got any worse, the demand for secession would be renewed. Court reassured his listeners that personally he was not a secessionist, but at the same time he acknowledged the sincerity of people who were reverting back to the thinking of the 1930s. He stressed that the situation in Western Australia was now so changed that the installation of U.S. military and naval bases on Western Australia's coastline meant that a foreign power would in all possibility deal with Western Australia rather than with the federal government.

Lessons for President Reagan? Fraser was not dismayed or worried by threats that the whole future of the Commonwealth of Australia was being undermined by his New Federalism. He believed that his style of leadership, involving smaller government, tighter control of spending, and incentives for private enterprise, was paying off in a way that was being recognized throughout the world. He said that U.S. Pres. Ronald Reagan was seeking to give effect to an economic philosophy similar to the one that the Australian Liberal-National Country Party had introduced to Australia after 1975, adding that there was great enthusiasm in the U.S. for what Australia had achieved in the last few years. Australia, he claimed, was widely regarded as having led the way in showing that a reversal in the growth of government was essential to the restoration of economic strength.

Austria

Austria

A republic of central Europe, Austria is bounded by West Germany, Czechoslovakia, Hungary, Yugoslavia, Italy, Switzerland, and Liechtenstein. Area: 83,853 sq km (32,376 sq mi). Pop. (1981 prelim.): 7,546,200. Cap. and largest city: Vienna (pop., 1981 prelim., 1,504,200). Language: German. Religion (1979): Roman Catholic 88%. President in 1981, Rudolf Kirchschläger; chancellor, Bruno Kreisky.

The resignation of Hannes Androsch as vice-chancellor and finance minister gave rise to changes in Chancellor Bruno Kreisky's Austrian Socialist Party (SPÖ) government in January 1981. Androsch (who in January was appointed chairman of Austria's largest commercial bank, the Creditanstalt-Bankverein) was succeeded as finance minister by Herbert Salcher, formerly minister for health and the environment, and as vice-chancellor by the former minister for education, Fred Sinowatz. New Cabinet members were Kurt Steyrer, who replaced Salcher as health minister, and Hans Seidel, formerly head of the Institute for Economic Research, appointed state secretary to assist Salcher.

Androsch's resignation resulted from criticism, by the opposition and from within his own party, of his conduct in financial deals that linked his name with irregularities currently under investigation in connection with the construction of Vienna's new general hospital. During the year Parliament considered a 3,000-page report submitted by a commission of inquiry, and legal proceedings began against some individuals and firms involved.

The influx of refugees into Austria increased dramatically in 1981. Two-thirds of the 17,000 who sought political asylum in September were Poles.

A wounded victim is assisted after two Arab terrorists attacked a synagogue in Vienna on August 29. Two people were killed and about 20 others were wounded, including two policemen.

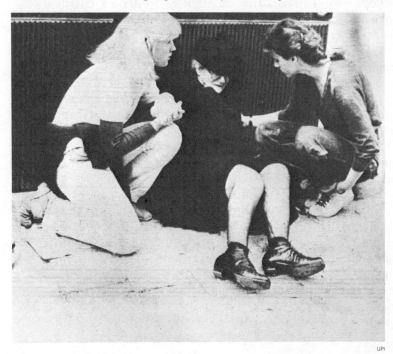

UPI

AUSTRIA

Education. (1980–81) Primary, pupils 401,396, teachers (1979–80) 26,369; secondary, pupils 549,061, teachers (1979–80) 45,213; vocational (1979–80), pupils 387,952, teachers 20,832; teacher training (1979–80), students 7,431, teachers 742; higher (1979–80), students 123,463, teaching staff 11,792.

Finance. Monetary unit: schilling, with (Sept. 21, 1981) a free rate of 15.71 schillings to U.S. $1 (29.12 schillings = £1 sterling). Gold and other reserves (June 1981) U.S. $5,073,000,000. Budget (1979 actual): revenue 189,780,000,000 schillings; expenditure 221.3 billion schillings. Gross national product (1980) 979.4 billion schillings. Money supply (May 1981) 143,910,000,000 schillings. Cost of living (1975 = 100; June 1981) 137.8.

Foreign Trade. (1980) Imports 316 billion schillings; exports 226,170,000,000 schillings. Import sources: EEC 62% (West Germany 41%, Italy 9%); Switzerland 5%. Export destinations: EEC 54% (West Germany 31%, Italy 11%); Switzerland 8%. Main exports: machinery 23%; iron and steel 10%; chemicals 9%; textile yarns and fabrics 6%; timber 6%; metal manufactures 5%; paper and board 5%. Tourism (1979): visitors 12,875,000; gross receipts U.S. $5,571,000,000.

Transport and Communications. Roads (1979) 106,679 km (including 876 km expressways). Motor vehicles in use (1979): passenger 2,138,700; commercial 172,500. Railways: (1979) 6,487 km; traffic (1980) 7,427,000,000 passenger-km, freight 11,040,000,000 net ton-km. Air traffic (1980): 1,120,000,000 passenger-km; freight 14.6 million net ton-km. Navigable inland waterways in regular use (1979) 358 km. Shipping (1980): merchant vessels 100 gross tons and over 13; gross tonnage 88,784. Telephones (Dec. 1978) 2,617,600. Radio licenses (Dec. 1978) 2,287,000. Television licenses (Dec. 1978) 2,121,000.

Agriculture. Production (in 000; metric tons; 1980): wheat 1,201; barley 1,515; rye 383; oats 316; corn 1,293; potatoes 1,386; sugar, raw value c. 435; apples c. 230; wine 268; meat c. 611; timber (cu m; 1979) 14,386. Livestock (in 000; Dec. 1979): cattle 2,548; sheep 195; pigs 4,003; chickens c. 14,496.

Industry. Fuel and power (in 000; metric tons; 1980): lignite 2,880; crude oil 1,476; natural gas (cu m) c. 1,920,000; manufactured gas (cu m) 640,000; electricity (kw-hr) 41,950,000 (66% hydroelectric in 1977). Production (in 000; metric tons; 1980): iron ore (31% metal content) 3,200; pig iron 3,486; crude steel 5,092; magnesite (1979) 1,104; aluminum 125; copper 43; zinc 26; cement 5,456; newsprint 176; other paper (1979) 1,394; petroleum products (1979) 9,814; plastics and resins 488; fertilizers (nutrient content; 1979–80) nitrogenous c. 275, phosphate c. 98; man-made fibres (1978) 138.

Refugee camps were filled to overflowing, and hotels, schools, and barracks were used as emergency shelters. Most of the refugees hoped to proceed to other countries, primarily the U.S., Canada, and Australia.

In February the Austrian embassy in Santiago, Chile, was occupied by opponents of the Chilean regime. About the same time, Austria's honorary consul in Bilbao, Spain, was kidnapped by Basque separatists, but he was later released. In July opponents of the Islamic revolutionary regime in Iran stormed the Iranian embassy in Vienna; nine people were wounded in the subsequent action to clear the building.

Kreisky's efforts toward mediation in the Middle East conflict brought terrorist violence to Vienna. On May 1 Heinz Nittel, a Socialist city councillor, was murdered. At the end of July two Arabs were arrested for attempting to smuggle weapons into Austria. Ghasi Hussain, official representative of the Palestine Liberation Organization (PLO) in Austria, allegedly involved in these affairs, was required to leave the country. PLO leader Yasir Arafat denied any connection be-

tween the PLO and the weapon smuggling or between it and an alleged plan to assassinate Kreisky and Egyptian Pres. Anwar as-Sadat, who were to have met in Salzburg. Sadat's visit was canceled. Shortly afterward there was a bomb attack against the Israeli embassy in Vienna, and at the end of August Arab terrorists attacked a Viennese synagogue, killing 2 persons and wounding about 20.

Relations with Czechoslovakia became strained in July as the result of an espionage affair. Josef Hodic had entered Austria in 1977 seeking political asylum as a signatory of the Czechoslovak dissidents' Charter 77, but after two years he disappeared. Later he reappeared in Prague, where he was feted as a member of the Czechoslovak secret service whose mission had been to infiltrate dissident circles in the West. The sale of 57 tanks to Argentina in June was strenuously opposed by Austrian pacifists, who demanded that the constitutional prohibition on the sale of weapons to warring nations be extended to include countries that violate human rights.

The international recession began to affect Austria in 1981; unemployment and inflation both rose, although the economic policies that had maintained relative stability in recent years were continued. Provisional results of the 1981 census put the number of inhabitants at 7,546,200, an increase of 90,000 over 1971. The population of Vienna was now 1,504,200, a drop of 110,000 from 1971. (ELFRIEDE DIRNBACHER)

Bahamas, The

A member of the Commonwealth, The Bahamas comprises an archipelago of about 700 islands in the North Atlantic Ocean just southeast of the United States. Area: 13,864 sq km (5,353 sq mi). Pop. (1981 est.): 235,000. Cap. and largest city: Nassau (urban area pop., 1979 est., 138,500). Language: English (official). Religion (1970): Baptist 28.8%; Anglican 22.7%; Roman Catholic 22.5%; Methodist 7.3%; Saints of God and Church of God 6%; others and no religion 12.7%. Queen, Elizabeth II; governor-general in 1981, Sir Gerald Cash; prime minister, Lynden O. Pindling.

During 1981 the Bahamian government met with little success in tackling rising unemployment, revitalizing flagging economic development, and expanding the social services—aims outlined by Finance Minister Arthur D. Hanna in presenting a budget totaling $336.4 million. In February Prime Minister Lynden O. Pindling paid an official visit to Mexico, where it was agreed that The Bahamas would receive oil at preferential rates from the joint Venezuelan-Mexican regional oil facility.

Negotiations on a new rental agreement for existing U.S. military facilities on the islands continued, with the U.S. offering assistance to upgrade the Bahamian defense force and coast guard service. For The Bahamas such an arrangement was seen as essential following a substantial increase in the level of drug trafficking and criminal activity in the Out Islands.

In contrast to The Bahamas' usual low-key ap-

The Bahamas

proach to regional and international affairs, relations with Haiti sank to a new low following the violent expulsion and repatriation of illegal Haitian immigrants. In retaliation, the Haitian government announced that all Bahamians wishing to visit Haiti must obtain visas in advance.

By late 1981 the fugitive U.S. financier Robert Vesco had left The Bahamas for an unknown destination. The government had sought his deportation. (DAVID A. JESSOP)

Bahrain

An independent monarchy (emirate), Bahrain consists of a group of islands in the Persian Gulf, lying between the Qatar Peninsula and Saudi Arabia. Total area: 669 sq km (258 sq mi). Pop. (1981): 358,900. Cap.: Manama (pop., 1980 est., 150,000). Language: Arabic (official), Persian. Religion (1980): Muslim 95%, of which 50% are Shi'ah Muslim; Christian 4%; others 1%. Emir in 1981, Isa ibn Sulman al-Khalifah; prime minister, Khalifah ibn Sulman al-Khalifah.

Tensions resulting from Bahrain's division between Shi'ah Muslims, numbering half the native population, and Sunni Muslims, who dominate politically, eased considerably in 1981. In Decem-

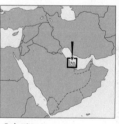

Bahrain

ber 1980 the government released several Shi'ah detainees, including former National Assembly member Muhsen Marhoun, who had been held since the assembly was suspended in 1975. Sympathy among the Shi'ah for an Iranian-style government in Bahrain appeared to be much diminished because of the increasing violence in Iran.

Bahrain moved closer to the other Gulf monarchies, Saudi Arabia, Kuwait, Qatar, Oman, and the United Arab Emirates, through the establishment of the Gulf Cooperation Council in March. An aluminum rolling mill, to be owned by a number of Gulf states, was planned. Bahrain was also chosen as the site for a Gulf university.

On the domestic front, the country continued to develop its role as an offshore banking centre; 63 offshore banking units (OBU's) were operational by September. The Bahrain Monetary Agency announced plans for a commodity trading enclave and played a major part in raising finance from the OBU's for a Gulf petrochemicals venture. The most important domestic event was the signing of a $555 million contract with the Dutch Ballast Nedam group to build a causeway link to Saudi Arabia.

(JOHN WHELAN)

Bangladesh

Bangladesh

An independent republic and member of the Commonwealth, Bangladesh is bordered by India on the west, north, and east, by Burma in the southeast, and by the Bay of Bengal in the south. Area: 143,998 sq km (55,598 sq mi). Pop. (1981): 89,940,-000. Cap. and largest city: Dacca (pop., 1979 est., 2.5 million). Language: Bengali. Religion: Muslim 85%, with Hindu, Christian, and Buddhist minorities. Presidents in 1981, Maj. Gen. Ziaur Rahman and, from May 30, Abdus Sattar; prime minister, Shah Azizur Rahman.

The assassination of Pres. Ziaur Rahman (*see* OBITUARIES) in Chittagong on May 30, 1981, sent a shock wave through Bangladesh. Vice-Pres. Abdus Sattar (*see* BIOGRAPHIES), who took over the administration on Zia's death, brought order swiftly with the help of the army chief of staff,

In Bangladesh millions attended the funeral services on June 2 of their assassinated leader Ziaur Rahman.

WIDE WORLD

BANGLADESH

Education. (1978) Primary, pupils 8,312,011, teachers 187,078; secondary, pupils (1977) 2,213,068, teachers (1976) 98,965; vocational, pupils (1977) 393,000, teachers (1975) 906; teacher training, students 9,070, teachers (1973) 631; higher (1977), students 181,756, teaching staff 13,110.

Finance. Monetary unit: taka, with (Sept. 21, 1981) a free rate of 18.70 taka to U.S. $1 (34.65 taka = £1 sterling). Gold and other reserves (June 1981) U.S. $234 million. Budget (1980–81 est.): revenue 22,951,000,000 taka; expenditure 14,080,000,000 taka (excludes development budget 27 billion taka). Gross domestic product (1979–80) 163,320,000,000 taka. Money supply (April 1981) 19,523,-000,000 taka. Cost of living (1975 = 100; April 1981) 157.1.

Foreign Trade. (1980) Imports 37,460,000,000 taka; exports 11,728,000,000 taka. Import sources (1979): Japan 13%; U.S. 13%; U.K. 7%; West Germany 6%; Australia 5%; Singapore 5%; China 5%; India 5%. Export destinations (1979): U.S. 14%; U.S.S.R. 8%; U.K. 8%; Italy 7%; Japan 7%; Pakistan 5%. Main exports (1979): jute fabrics 27%; jute bags and sacks 21%; jute 20%; leather 13%; fish 7%; tea 5%.

Transport and Communications. Roads (main; 1978) c. 6,240 km. Motor vehicles in use (1978): passenger 24,-600; commercial 10,100. Railways: (1978) 2,874 km; traffic (1979–80) 5,119,000,000 passenger-km, freight (1976–77) 722 million net ton-km. Navigable waterways (1979) c. 8,000 km. Air traffic (1980): 1,179,000,000 passenger-km; freight c. 20 million net ton-km. Shipping (1980): merchant vessels 100 gross tons and over 179; gross tonnage 353,-586. Shipping traffic (1978–79): goods loaded 1,042,000 metric tons, unloaded 5.3 million metric tons. Telephones (Jan. 1979) 102,300. Radio receivers (Dec. 1977) 500,000. Television receivers (Dec. 1977) 36,000.

Agriculture. Production (in 000; metric tons; 1980): rice 20,990; wheat c. 1,200; potatoes c. 950; sweet potatoes (1979) 795; sugar, raw value (1979) c. 439; onions c. 140; mangoes c. 215; bananas c. 605; pineapples c. 142; rapeseed c. 142; tea c. 39; tobacco c. 44; jute 830; meat c. 315; fish catch (1979) c. 640; timber (cu m; 1979) c. 10,345. Livestock (in 000; 1980): cattle c. 32,248; buffalo c. 1,558; sheep c. 1,061; goats c. 11,500; chickens c. 71,500.

Industry. Production (in 000; metric tons; 1980): cement 352; crude steel (1978–79) 126; natural gas (cu m) 1,296,000; petroleum products (1978–79) 1,032; fertilizers (nutrient content; 1979–80) nitrogenous 166, phosphate 33%; jute fabrics (1978–79) 509; cotton yarn 45; newsprint 39; other paper (1978–79) 39; electricity (kw-hr; 1979) c. 2,600,000.

Lieut. Gen. H. M. Ershad, and promised new presidential elections within 180 days as provided for in the constitution. The new government proclaimed a state of emergency and suspended fundamental rights, though political parties were free to hold meetings.

The short-lived Chittagong rebellion was led by Zia's one-time colleague and a former freedom fighter, Maj. Gen. Mohammad Abdul Manzoor, who was captured two days after the coup attempt and killed in a gun battle. His close aides in the plot were arrested, and subsequently 12 of them were sentenced to death by a court-martial.

Although Sattar, Ershad, and Prime Minister Shah Azizur Rahman governed the country with comparative ease in the aftermath of Zia's murder, fears of another army coup were freely mentioned in political circles. Sattar appointed three separate commissions of inquiry to untangle the events and motives that had led to the killing of Zia. A White Paper issued by the government on August 4 gave the background to Manzoor's coup and also touched on the findings of the court-martial, which had taken place in secret; this was done partly to satisfy the opposition, which had demanded an open trial. The execution on September

23 of the 12 convicted officers was violently protested by opposition parties.

Some 30 candidates contested the presidential election, which was held on November 15, but the principal contenders were Sattar, candidate of the Bangladesh Nationalist Party, a heterogeneous grouping founded by Zia in 1978, and Kamal Hossain of the Bangladesh Awami League, the party of the late Sheikh Mujibur Rahman, first leader of Bangladesh. In the event, Sattar won easily with 66% of the votes cast, although Hossain charged that there had been widespread fraud. After the election it was revealed that some army officers had considered a military takeover; they had been dissuaded when a secret poll showed that Sattar, whom they had planned to install at the head of a military government, would be the almost certain winner if the election was held.

Before his death Zia made several trips abroad and traveled widely in Bangladesh by helicopter to feel the pulse of the rural masses. During a trip to France he signed a nuclear cooperation agreement under which France was to help set up a $400 million nuclear power plant in Roopur, northern Bangladesh. Foreign aid continued to play a major role in sustaining the economy. Loans totaling about $75 million were sanctioned by the Asian Development Bank during the year for such projects as irrigation, hydroelectric power, and oil exploration. The Bangladesh Aid Consortium increased its allocation for the coming year from $1.3 billion to $1,630,000,000. After years of shortages there was a temporary glut of food-grain stocks as a result of a record harvest of 14.8 million metric tons in 1980.

While relations with China and the U.S. remained friendly, those with India and the U.S.S.R. showed signs of strain. The Soviets were upset when the Dacca government sent back a cargo of electronic equipment, along with two Soviet diplomats who were charged with smuggling in the equipment for espionage purposes. With India, differences mounted over the sovereignty of New Moore Island in the Bay of Bengal and the demarcation of a maritime boundary, while the dispute over the sharing of the Ganges River waters continued to evade a solution. India had put its flag on New Moore and stationed a naval vessel in the vicinity, a situation that led to anti-Indian demonstrations in Dacca. However, a visit to India in September by the Bangladesh foreign minister, Shamsul Huq, brought an improvement in relations. (GOVINDAN UNNY)

Barbados

The parliamentary state of Barbados is a member of the Commonwealth and occupies the most easterly island in the southern Caribbean Sea. Area: 430 sq km (166 sq mi). Pop. (1980 prelim.): 249,000; 91% Negro, 4% white, 4% mixed. Cap. and largest city: Bridgetown (pop., 1980 prelim., 7,600). Language: English. Religion: Anglican 53%; Methodist 9%; Roman Catholic 4%; Moravian 2%. Queen, Elizabeth II; governor-general in 1981, Sir Deighton Lisle Ward; prime minister, J. M. G. Adams.

BARBADOS

Education. (1978–79) Primary, pupils 35,555, teachers (1977–78) 1,227; secondary, pupils 25,888; vocational, pupils 1,822; secondary and vocational, teachers (1977–78) 1,517; higher (university only), students 1,380, teaching staff 270.

Finance and Trade. Monetary unit: Barbados dollar, with (Sept. 21, 1981) an official rate of Bar$2.01 to U.S. $1 (free rate of Bar$3.73 = £1 sterling). Budget (1979–80 actual): revenue Bar$376.7 million; expenditure Bar$395.9 million. Cost of living (1975 = 100; May 1981) 187.7. Foreign trade (1980): imports Bar$1,049,100,000; exports Bar$455.4 million. Import sources (1979): U.S. 32%; U.K. 16%; Trinidad and Tobago c. 10%; Canada 8%. Export destinations (1979): U.S. 36%; U.K. 13%; Trinidad and Tobago c. 12%; Canada 5%. Main exports (1979): electrical equipment c. 22%; sugar 19%; clothing c. 16%; petroleum products 9%; chemicals 7%. Tourism (1979): visitors 371,000; gross receipts U.S. $184 million.

Agriculture. Production (in 000; metric tons; 1979): corn c. 2; sweet potatoes c. 1; sugar, raw value c. 117.

Barbados

In general elections held in June 1981, Prime Minister J. M. G. ("Tom") Adams and his ruling Barbados Labour Party (BLP) were returned for a second term of office, but with a reduced majority. (*See* POLITICAL PARTIES.)

Though the island's economy remained more buoyant than those of its near neighbours, a downturn began around midyear. Adams introduced a popular budget in March which provided tax cuts and increased social benefits. In September, however, a further budget levied new taxes. Gross domestic product had risen by 22.8% in 1980, but this rate of growth was not sustained in 1981 because of a reduction in tourism and failure to reach sugar production targets.

Relations with Grenada sank to a new low when Adams and Prime Minister Maurice Bishop argued publicly. In contrast, relations with Trinidad and Tobago strengthened. Barbados was host to Carifesta, the regional arts festival. The island received international attention when Britain's "great train robber," Ronald Biggs, was taken there after being kidnapped in Brazil. Britain's request for his extradition was refused, and he was released.

(DAVID A. JESSOP)

Baseball

The 1981 season was perhaps the most traumatic in major league baseball history. A long-simmering quarrel between the players and management resulted in a midsummer strike that lasted seven weeks. When play resumed, the sport had lost not only vast revenues but also continuity—a vital aspect of its attractiveness. Analysts theorized that the so-called national pastime had not endured a more tarnished period since the Black Sox scandal of 1919, when several members of the Chicago White Sox were found to have accepted payoffs to lose World Series games.

World Series. If normal baseball interest existed anyplace, it probably was in Los Angeles, where fans celebrated their Dodgers' first world championship since 1965. The Dodgers captured the World Series by defeating the New York Yankees, four games to two, in a gallant comeback performance.

Los Angeles Dodgers whooped it up after winning the World Series four games to two over the New York Yankees. In the centre, Steve Yeager gives a bear hug to relief pitcher Steve Howe. Steve Garvey is at the left, Derrel Thomas at right.

Los Angeles lost the opener in Yankee Stadium 5–3 on October 20, thanks to excellent performances by New York pitchers Ron Guidry and Rich Gossage and the defensive work of third baseman Graig Nettles. The favoured Yankees also won the second game 3–0, again primarily because of pitchers Tommy John and Gossage.

But when the Series moved to Los Angeles, its complexion changed drastically. On October 23 the Dodgers prevailed 5–4 behind Fernando Valenzuela (*see* BIOGRAPHIES), a rookie left-hander who was the most colourful personality of the season. Valenzuela, a 20-year-old from Mexico, struggled repeatedly but pitched a complete game. "He was like a sharp poker player bluffing his way through some bad hands," said Los Angeles manager

Tom Lasorda. "His win was the turning point in the Series."

Indeed, the next afternoon, the Dodgers evened the best-of-seven set at two victories each with an 8–7 triumph after trailing 4–0. This 3-hour 32-minute contest was one of the most entertaining, if not well-executed, games in Series annals.

Game five on October 25 was more skillful. Jerry Reuss hurled a five-hitter, and Pedro Guerrero and Steve Yeager clubbed back-to-back seventh inning home runs as the Dodgers prevailed 2–1. The Yankees hoped that the return to New York would cure their problems, but the Dodgers, losers of six straight games in Yankee Stadium, ended that streak and the Series with an easy 9–2 conquest on October 28.

Third baseman Ron Cey, who was beaned by a Gossage pitch in the fifth game and suffered a concussion, singled home the winning run in the sixth contest. Cey shared most valuable player honours for the Series with teammates Yeager and Guerrero, though Los Angeles first baseman Steve Garvey led both teams in hitting with .417.

Meanwhile, Dave Winfield, whose ten-year, $21 million contract was the richest in team sports history, closed his first season as a Yankee with only one hit in 22 Series at bats. George Frazier, a Yankee relief pitcher, became the first three-game loser since Claude Williams, one of the eight wrongdoers on the 1919 White Sox. Bob Lemon, the Yankee manager, was criticized for his Series strategies, and Yankee owner George Steinbrenner pledged wholesale changes for the ballclub during the off-season. Steinbrenner issued an apology to the city of New York and Yankee fans everywhere for failing to win the annual classic.

"But the Yankees didn't lose this Series, we won it," stressed Lasorda. "I've never seen a club which had such character. We were faced with adversity all season, and we never gave up."

Regular Season and Play-offs. Indeed, the Dodgers' season had been rife with drama. They won the National League pennant over the Montreal Expos, three games to two, when Rick Monday hit a tie-breaking home run to give Los An-

Final Major League Standings, 1981

AMERICAN LEAGUE

East Division—First half				East Division—Second half			
Club	W.	L.	Pct.	G.B.	Club	W.	L.	Pct.	G.B.
New York	34	22	.607	...	Milwaukee	31	22	.585	...
Baltimore	31	23	.574	2	Boston	29	23	.558	1½
Milwaukee	31	25	.554	3	Detroit	29	23	.558	1½
Detroit	31	26	.544	3½	Baltimore	28	23	.549	2
Boston	30	26	.536	4	Cleveland	26	27	.491	5
Cleveland	26	24	.520	5	New York	25	26	.490	5
Toronto	16	42	.276	19	Toronto	21	27	.438	7½

West Division—First half				West Division—Second half			
Club	W.	L.	Pct.	G.B.	Club	W.	L.	Pct.	G.B.
Oakland	37	23	.617	...	Kansas City	30	23	.566	...
Texas	33	22	.600	1½	Oakland	27	22	.551	1
Chicago	31	22	.585	2½	Texas	24	26	.480	4½
California	31	29	.517	6	Minnesota	24	29	.453	6
Kansas City	20	30	.400	12	Seattle	23	29	.442	6½
Seattle	21	36	.368	14½	Chicago	23	30	.434	7
Minnesota	17	39	.304	18	California	20	30	.400	8½

NATIONAL LEAGUE

East Division—First half				East Division—Second half			
Club	W.	L.	Pct.	G.B.	Club	W.	L.	Pct.	G.B.
Philadelphia	34	21	.618	...	Montreal	30	23	.566	...
St. Louis	30	20	.600	1½	St. Louis	29	23	.558	½
Montreal	30	25	.545	4	Philadelphia	25	27	.481	4½
Pittsburgh	25	23	.521	5½	New York	24	28	.462	5½
New York	17	34	.333	15	Chicago	23	28	.451	6
Chicago	15	37	.288	17½	Pittsburgh	21	33	.389	9½

West Division—First half				West Division—Second half			
Club	W.	L.	Pct.	G.B.	Club	W.	L.	Pct.	G.B.
Los Angeles	36	21	.632	...	Houston	33	20	.623	...
Cincinnati	35	21	.625	½	Cincinnati	31	21	.596	1½
Houston	28	29	.491	4	San Francisco	29	23	.558	3½
Atlanta	25	29	.463	9½	Los Angeles	27	26	.509	6
San Francisco	27	32	.458	10	Atlanta	25	27	.481	7½
San Diego	23	33	.411	12½	San Diego	18	36	.333	15½

geles a 2–1 victory in the final game; at one time they had trailed in the best-three-out-of-five series two games to one. In the earlier play-off series between division leaders in the pre- and post-strike halves of the season (a device designed to revive lagging fan interest), Los Angeles dropped the first two games and then won the next three to beat Houston for the National League West Division crown. The Expos had subdued the defending world champion Philadelphia Phillies three games to two to win the National League East.

The Yankees, American League East Division titlists, took the pennant with relative ease, beating the Oakland A's three games to none. But, earlier, the Yankees had had to go five games before outlasting the Milwaukee Brewers for the East Division championship. The A's, conversely, swept the Kansas City Royals three games to none for the American League West honours.

Batting champion of the National League was Bill Madlock of Pittsburgh with an average of .341. Mike Schmidt of the Phillies hit the most home runs, 31, and batted in the most runs, 91. The league's leading pitchers were Tom Seaver of Cincinnati with a 14–2 record and Steve Carlton of Philadelphia with 13–4. In the American League Carney Lansford of Boston won the batting championship with .336. Eddie Murray of Baltimore batted in the most runs with 78 and shared the home-run title, at 22, with Dwight Evans of Boston, Bobby Grich of California, and Tony Armas of Oakland. Pete Vuckovich of Milwaukee led the pitchers with a 14–4 record.

To an unprecedented extent the postseason awards were dominated by pitchers. The Cy Young awards for best pitchers were won by Valenzuela for the National League and Rollie Fingers of Milwaukee for the American. Fingers was

also named the American League's most valuable player, the first relief pitcher ever to be so honoured. Valenzuela won the National League rookie-of-the-year award and became the first player ever to win that prize and the Cy Young award in the same year. He also was the third Dodger pitcher in a row to win the rookie-of-the-year honours, following Rick Sutcliffe in 1979 and Steve Howe in 1980. Rookie of the year in the American League was Yankee pitcher Dave Righetti. Philadelphia third baseman Mike Schmidt became the only nonpitcher to win an award when he was named the National League's most valuable player. Manager of the year in the American League for the second straight season was Billy Martin of the Oakland A's. The National League winner was Whitey Herzog of the St. Louis Cardinals.

Players' Strike. Though opposing factions agreed on only one point—that it should not happen—a baseball strike began on June 12. The 650 members of the Major League Baseball Players Association called the strike, forfeiting paychecks for principle. The walkout lasted 49 days, causing economic and emotional strife, not to mention the cancellation of 713 regularly scheduled games.

The players, whose salaries averaged about $175,000 a year, estimated total losses of approximately $4 million per week. Dave Winfield, the highest paid player, lost almost $400,000.

The owners, who had feared such a possibility since players staged a 13-day walkout in 1972, took out strike insurance before the season began. By paying premiums totaling $2 million, they received payments of about $44 million before a settlement was finally reached on July 31 during marathon negotiations in New York City. The owners' policy was due to expire in several days, shortly before the season resumed on August 10.

"The owners loaded up on insurance for a strike they say we caused," said Marvin Miller (see Biographies), head of the Players Association. "Then, after weeks of throwing our proposals in the wastebasket, they magically reach a solution minutes before their insurance is due to expire. It is obvious who caused this strike, and it was not us. The owners didn't want to solve this strike, they wanted to win it."

Ray Grebey, chief negotiator for the owners, dismissed Miller's claims as "pure rhetoric." But baseball commissioner Bowie Kuhn summarized public opinion when he stated, "We cannot ever let this happen again."

The issue of compensation was the main cause of the dispute. Owners of the 26 franchises claimed that ballplayers represent long-term investments and that when an athlete leaves a team as a free agent, that team should receive compensation from the receiving team as a salve. Players contended that they should enjoy the freedom of movement granted to other workers in society. If, for instance, a secretary switches from Company A to Company B, Company B is not obligated to supply Company A with money or an equal employee.

The peace treaty eventually was a compromise, though most observers concluded that the players

On June 10 the Phillies' Pete Rose got his 3,630th career hit to tie Stan Musial's National League record. Rose subsequently raised his total to 3,697.

WIDE WORLD

UPI

Ray Grebey, bargaining agent for the major league baseball owners, flashed a big smile on July 31 after an agreement to end the 49-day baseball strike was concluded.

sacrificed little but their salaries during the seven-week brouhaha. The settlement provided that only eight ranking free agents (Type A) would require professional compensation during 1981 and only nine for each of the next two years until 1984, when the negotiated agreement would expire. All other free-agent players seeking a change of team would be able to transfer with no strings attached.

(ROBERT WILLIAM VERDI)

Latin America. Professional organized baseball in Mexico continued in 1981 to suffer its most severe crisis ever. The crisis was mostly political. Differences among club owners and players' associations had finally erupted into open struggle in 1980.

Mexican Pres. José López Portillo, an avid baseball fan, had tried to put an end to the chaos in 1980. Representatives of the various contending parties were invited to meet at the presidential residence. Although at first some progress was made in the attempts to prevent the splitting of the Mexican League, no final agreement was reached. As a result three independent leagues vied for the fans' attention during the 1981 summer season.

The Mexican League continued to offer the highest level of play, and the final best-of-seven championship series proved to be a thriller. The Mexico City Red Devils at first posted two victories against the Reynosa Broncos, but the Broncos fought back and took a three-to-two lead. Mexico City then won the last two games and the series. The Yaquis of Ciudad Obregón won the pennant of the Mexican Pacific League. In the new National League the Puebla 450 Angels defeated the Durango Scorpions in a hard-fought final series.

In the 1980 winter Caribbean leagues the Escogido Lions won the championship in the Dominican Republic. In Venezuela, where the level of baseball had greatly improved during the past few years, the Caracas Lions reclaimed possession of a title that had often been theirs in the past. The Bayamón Cowboys surprised their rivals with an unprecedented show of strength to win the Puerto Rican championship. Farther south, the Tegucigalpa Green Sox won an exciting pennant race

in the Honduran League. Ballplaying in Honduras, according to some commentators, was becoming outstanding by Central American standards. (SERGIO SARMIENTO)

Japan. The Yomiuri Giants of Tokyo beat the Nippon Ham Fighters of Tokyo four games to two in the best-of-seven Japan Series to win the national championship for the first time in eight years and bring their total number of titles to 16. The four victories were achieved by two pitchers, Takashi Nishimoto and Suguru Egawa. Infielder Tatsunori Hara hit two home runs, tying a Series record for a rookie.

In the Central League the Giants took the lead early in the season and won the league championship by a wide margin. Cited for this achievement were the newly appointed manager, Motoshi Fujita, head coach Shigeru Makino, and assistant manager Sadaharu Oh. Among the pitchers worthy of note were Egawa, who had 20 wins against 6 losses, Nishimoto, and relief specialist Mitsuo Sumi. Outstanding hitters included Toshio Shinozuka, who ranked second in the league with .357, infielder Kiyoshi Nakahata, rookie Hara, and former major leaguer Roy White.

Infielder Taira Fujita of the Hanshin Tigers of Osaka won the Central League batting championship with .358, his first title in 16 years of playing. Koji Yamamoto of the Hiroshima Toyo Carp captured both the home-run and runs-batted-in titles with 43 and 103, respectively. The most valuable player award was given to Egawa.

In the Pacific League the Nippon Ham Fighters, the second-half winner, beat the first-half champion Lotte Orions of Kawasaki three wins against one loss and a tie. The Ham Fighters were led by a powerful pitching staff. Shigeki Mashiba recorded a 15–0 mark, while Noriaki Okabe had an earned-run-average of 2.70 and Yutaka Enatsu had 28 saves in relief. Designated hitter Tony Solaita of the Nankai Hawks of Osaka won both the home-run and the runs-batted-in crowns with 44 and 108, respectively. Hiromitsu Ochiai of the Orions won the batting title with .326, and Hiromitsu Kadot of the Nankai Hawks shared the home-run title with Solaita. Enatsu was the league's most valuable player. (RYUSAKU HASEGAWA)

Basketball

United States. PROFESSIONAL. The Boston Celtics, a consistent star of the National Basketball Association, became a supernova once again in the 1980–81 season. But not even the glow generated by the Celtics' 14th NBA championship could dispel gloomy clouds hanging over the league. Attendance was down, reflecting economic conditions across the country, and television ratings remained unspectacular, indicating that professional basketball was failing to live up to its self-styled image as "the sport of the '80s."

Far from the rosy optimism that spawned such slogans, the situation was serious enough for speculation as to whether the NBA would survive the 1980s in its present form. Caught in the transition period between free network and pay cable

television, the league was in a state of flux, with salaries escalating faster than revenues. Despite expansion to Dallas, bringing NBA membership to 23 teams, the long-range outlook was pessimistic.

In Philadelphia it was closer to total frustration. The 76ers, playing confident, aggressive basketball, took a three-games-to-one lead over Boston in the best-of-seven Eastern Conference final play-off. Because the heavily favoured Los Angeles Lakers had been ousted by Houston in a stunning Western Conference upset, the 76ers appeared to have reservations in the throne room. Instead, the Celtics made an incredible comeback to capture the series with three straight victories, advancing to the championship round. The prevailing mood among depressed Philadelphia fans was to accuse the 76ers of a colossal choke-up, and owner Fitz Dixon showed his opinion by selling the club for $12 million to health-food tycoon Harold Katz.

By contrast, with the emergence of superstar Larry Bird the Celtics foresaw another era like the one when their green-clad legion sacked and pillaged the NBA for 8 straight titles and 11 in 13 years, a dynasty that began in 1956.

Still, the notion that hauling another world championship flag into Boston Garden's rafters was automatic proved a trifle premature. The Houston Rockets, lightly regarded because they had lost 13 straight times to Boston, put up tenacious resistance in the final round before succumbing, four games to two. Paced by 6-ft 10-in centre Moses Malone and 5-ft 8-in guard Calvin Murphy, the Rockets made their presence felt.

Given absolutely no chance in their first-round play-off against the mighty Lakers, the upstart Rockets knocked Kareem Abdul-Jabbar and company off the championship perch with a dazzling mixture of rebounding and defense. They rubbed salt in the wound by winning the decisive game before a disbelieving crowd in Los Angeles, thereby making the Lakers the 12th straight defending champion failing to repeat since Boston took two straight NBA crowns in 1968 and 1969.

COLLEGE. It was appropriate that Bobby Knight's Indiana University team swept to the top of the collegiate basketball heap with a convincing 63–50 National Collegiate Athletic Association (NCAA) tournament victory over North Carolina in Philadelphia's Spectrum. The Hoosiers' coach was one of the few with courage to speak about the impending crisis in athletics. "We play for too much," Knight said of the $360,000 share pocketed by each of the final four NCAA meet survivors from the expanded 48-team field. "There's too much temptation. A lot of dishonest college presidents, administrators, coaches, and alumni are willing to believe that the end justifies the means. The fact that we are playing for so much money now directly affects the level of recruiting irregularities." (See FOOTBALL: *Special Report.*)

As if to underscore Knight's fears, another "fix" scandal arose when five persons, including a former Boston College player, were convicted of involvement in a point-shaving scheme. The object was to control the point spread, on which gamblers usually bet, by deliberately missing shots or making mistakes.

WIDE WORLD

Houston Rockets' Mike Dunleavy (centre) got rid of the ball to a teammate after he was blocked by Boston Celtics' Larry Bird (right). The action occurred in the fourth game of the NBA championship play-off, which the Celtics later won.

Such practices almost sounded the death knell of college basketball as a major sport in the 1950s, but the image gradually was repaired. For the most part that was made possible by the image on television screens, with nationwide exposure bringing on a basketball boom that produced multimillion-dollar contracts from the networks. Besides enriching the coffers of the NCAA and its member schools, the revival brought fans streaming into college gyms and fieldhouses throughout the U.S.

From a competitive standpoint the 1980–81 season was a highly successful one. Fierce struggles for supremacy in such major leagues as the Big Ten and Atlantic Coast Conference (ACC) held the fans' attention from November until the tourney showdown on March 30. Not surprisingly, it all led up to Big Ten champion Indiana squaring off against North Carolina of the ACC in the final.

The independent ranks, topped by DePaul of Chicago and Notre Dame, also were well represented in the NCAA meet. DePaul was ranked first in the nation through most of the season but fell victim for the second straight year to a stunning first-round tourney upset. A last-second basket by unheralded St. Joseph of Philadelphia toppled the Blue Demons.

The same fate befell highly touted Oregon State and defending NCAA champion Louisville. When survivors of the four regionals gathered in the Spectrum, the ACC had two representatives, Virginia and North Carolina, to vie with Louisiana State of the Southeastern Conference and Indiana.

Reversing two earlier defeats, North Carolina conquered Virginia's 7-ft 4-in tower of talent, Ralph Sampson, in the all-ACC semifinal, 78–65. Knight's Hoosiers exploded in the second half to rout Louisiana State 67–49.

In the national championship game North Carolina took an early lead but eventually was worn down by the patterned precision at which Knight's teams excel. Indiana took the lead on a

Belgium

WIDE WORLD

Indiana's Isiah Thomas (11) was the leading scorer with 23 points as Indiana defeated North Carolina 63–50 to win the NCAA championship in March.

Belgium

Beer:
see Industrial Review

long shot just before halftime and steadily drew away on the wings of the tournament's most valuable player, Isiah Thomas. The brilliant sophomore, playing his last game for Indiana before accepting a $2.5 million contract from the NBA Detroit Pistons, paced all scorers with 23 points.

In women's basketball, the All-America tandem of Pam Kelly and Janice Lawrence paced Louisiana Tech to a perfect 34–0 season. It was capped by a 79–59 victory over Tennessee in the final of the Association of Intercollegiate Athletics for Women (AIAW) Tournament.

The rapid growth of big-time women's college basketball was spurred by two developments. The NCAA planned to stage a rival tournament in 1981–82, hoping to displace the AIAW meet as the showcase for top teams. Meanwhile, recruiting for talented players reached a frenzied pitch, almost reminiscent of the scramble for men by colleges seeking national recognition.

Cream of the 1980–81 high-school crop was 5-ft 10-in Linda Page from Dobbins Tech in Philadelphia. She scored 100 points in a high-school game, breaking Wilt Chamberlain's record, and chose to attend North Carolina State.

(ROBERT G. LOGAN)

World Amateur. The eighth Asian Basketball Championship for Women was contested in Hong Kong during September 1980. The South Koreans were in a class by themselves; their two nearest rivals were China, whom South Korea beat 101–68, and Japan, whom they defeated 109–54. Final places were: (1) South Korea; (2) China; (3) Japan; (4) Malaysia; (5) Thailand; (6) Hong Kong. In the 17th European Championship for Women, played in Yugoslavia during September 1980, Eastern European teams took the first five places. The Soviet Union won all its games, defeating Poland 95–49 in the final. The real battle was for the silver medal between Poland and Yugoslavia; at halftime the score was Poland 39, Yugoslavia 38, and at the final whistle Poland was 7 points ahead. Final

standings were: (1) Soviet Union; (2) Poland; (3) Yugoslavia; (4) Czechoslovakia; (5) Bulgaria.

The 22nd European Championship for Men was contested in Czechoslovakia during May–June 1981. Preliminary tournaments were divided into two groups, Group A playing in Bratislava and Group B in Havirov. Qualifying in Bratislava were Spain and Czechoslovakia and in Havirov, the Soviet Union and Yugoslavia. The finals were played in Prague before capacity crowds. The determination of the Soviet Union team to wipe out the humiliation of a mere bronze medal at the Moscow Olympic Games in 1980 was evident; they won all nine of their games. The Soviets met Yugoslavia twice, once in the preliminaries, where they won 108–88, and again in the final, where they were easy winners, 84–67. This victory won them their 13th European championship.

In 1977 Maccabi Tel Aviv (Israel) won its first European Club Championship for Men, and in 1981 it repeated that success. The final was played in Strasbourg, France, during April between Maccabi and Sinudyne of Bologna, Italy; with just nine seconds to go Maccabi scored the winning basket for an 80–79 victory. In the European Club Championship for Women the Soviet club TT Daugawa from Riga beat Crvena Zvezda of Belgrade, Yugos., 83–65, to win the title for the 17th time.

(K. K. MITCHELL)

Belgium

A constitutional monarchy on the North Sea coast of Europe, the Benelux country of Belgium is bordered by The Netherlands, West Germany, Luxembourg, and France. Area: 30,521 sq km (11,784 sq mi). Pop. (1981 est.): 9,863,400. Cap. and largest urban area: Brussels (pop., 1981 est., metro. area, 1,000,200; commune 141,900). Language: Dutch, French, and German. Religion: predominantly Roman Catholic. King, Baudouin I; prime ministers in 1981, Wilfried Martens, Mark Eyskens from April 6, and, from December 17, Martens.

In early 1981 Belgium's budgetary problems and rising unemployment continued to haunt the fourth government of Prime Minister Wilfried Martens. The prime minister pinned high hopes on the national labour conference called in support of his scheme for wage restraint. When the trade unions rejected the proposals, Parliament tacked a rider onto the bill stating that the legally imposed wage restraint would be lifted if similar, voluntary measures were arranged. On February 13 employers and trade unions reached such an agreement.

The budgetary situation caused tension within the government. The Social Christians insisted on severe cuts in public expenditure, while the Socialists demanded increased taxation on company profits and on higher incomes. In March agreement was reached on cuts amounting to BFr 33 billion and on the floating of a special crisis loan. However, Socialists refused to reduce social benefits or to change the wage indexation system whereby wages were tied to the cost of living.

Meanwhile, the Belgian franc came under strong pressure, and Martens proposed more strin-

Members of the European Commission gathered for an opening session on January 6 in Brussels. The biggest task was to settle budgetary conflicts with some of the members.

gent measures: a complete overhaul of the indexation system, a price and wage freeze, and wage cuts of 10% in enterprises receiving government aid. Confronting the leaders of all major parties as well as the top figures of all social and economic groups on April 1, King Baudouin stressed that the country was fighting for its economic survival, its prosperity, and its place in the world. The National Bank of Belgium raised the prime rate (official interest rate) by a massive 3%, relieving pressure on the franc. However, the Socialists rejected the Martens plan, and the prime minister resigned.

Mark Eyskens, the finance minister, was asked to form a new government. Forsaking protracted negotiations, he retained the government coalition and its program. The government introduced measures that allowed lower benefit contributions by industry, but it imposed hefty increases in the value-added tax, as well as an 8% luxury tax. Nevertheless, budget matters plagued the Eyskens government. The deficit in the 1981 budget, initially fixed at BFr 90 billion, climbed to BFr 220 billion.

In the event, a crisis in the steel industry precipitated the government's resignation after only five months in office. The Cabinet was unable to reach agreement over the question of granting government aid to the newly merged Cockerill-Sambre steel plant.

General elections on November 8 brought no quick solution, since the three major parties—Social Christian, Socialist, and Liberal—emerged with an almost equal number of seats. (*See* POLITICAL PARTIES.) Greatest gains went to the Liberals, who thus expected a share of power. On December 17, after one month of negotiations, King Baudouin swore in Martens, a Social Christian, as prime minister of a centre-right coalition of Social Christians and Liberals. Martens sought emergency powers to implement sweeping economic changes.

Tension between the two major language communities (Dutch and French) erupted repeatedly

BELGIUM

Education. (1979–80) Primary, pupils 877,138, teachers (1977–78) 46,484; secondary, pupils 562,610; vocational, pupils 287,848; secondary and vocational, teachers (1967–68) 88,030; teacher training, pupils 23,773; higher, pupils 164,459, teaching staff (university level) c. 8,700.

Finance. Monetary unit: Belgian franc, with (Sept. 21, 1981) a free commercial rate of BFr 36.42 to U.S. $1 (BFr 67.52= £1 sterling) and a free financial rate of BFr 40.10 to U.S. $1 (BFr 74.35 = £1 sterling). Gold and other reserves (June 1981) U.S. $7,465,000,000. Budget (1980 actual): revenue BFr 1,012,400,000,000; expenditure BFr 1,313,100,000,000. Gross national product (1980) BFr 3,473,000,000,000. Money supply (March 1981) BFr 798 billion. Cost of living (1975 = 100; June 1981) 144.6.

Foreign Trade. (Belgium-Luxembourg economic union; 1980) Imports BFr 2,096,100,000,000; exports BFr 1,886,-100,000,000. Import sources: EEC 63% (West Germany 20%, The Netherlands 16%, France 14%, U.K. 8%); U.S. 8%; Saudi Arabia 6%. Export destinations: EEC 71% (West Germany 21%, France 19%, The Netherlands 15%, U.K. 8%, Italy 6%). Main exports: chemicals 12%; machinery 11%; motor vehicles 10%; iron and steel 10%; food 8%; petroleum products 8%; precious stones 6%; textile yarns and fabrics 6%; nonferrous metals 5%.

Transport and Communications. Roads (1979) c. 125,-000 km (including 1,177 km expressways). Motor vehicles in use (1979): passenger 3,076,600; commercial 258,600. Railways: (1979) 3,978 km; traffic (1980) 6,935,000,000 passenger-km, freight 7,990,000,000 net ton-km. Air traffic (1980): 4,852,000,000 passenger-km; freight 405.8 million net ton-km. Navigable inland waterways in regular use (1979) 1,509 km. Shipping (1980): merchant vessels 100 gross tons and over 290; gross tonnage 1,809,829. Shipping traffic (1979): goods loaded 37,981,000 metric tons, unloaded 65,556,000 metric tons. Telephones (Jan. 1979) 3,270,900. Radio licenses (Dec. 1979) 4,450,900. Television licenses (Dec. 1979) 2,924,800.

Agriculture. Production (in 000; metric tons; 1980): wheat c. 850; barley c. 790; oats c. 107; potatoes c. 1,200; tomatoes c. 100; apples c. 280; sugar, raw value c. 900; milk c. 3,860; pork c. 720; beef and veal c. 270; fish catch (1979) 47. Livestock (in 000; Dec. 1979): cattle 2,894; pigs 4,987; sheep 84; horses 37; chickens c. 27,500.

Industry. Fuel and power (in 000; 1980): coal (metric tons) 6,323; manufactured gas (cu m) 2,020,000; electricity (kw-hr) 53,643,000. Production (in 000; metric tons; 1980): pig iron 9,849; crude steel 12,337; copper 526; lead 128; tin 5; zinc 249; sulfuric acid 2,148; plastics and resins 1,821; fertilizers (nutrient content; 1979–80) nitrogenous c. 750, phosphate c. 500; cement 7,481; newsprint 101; other paper (1979) 789; cotton yarn 57; cotton fabrics 50; wool yarn 80; woolen fabrics 36; man-made fibres (1979) 64. Merchant vessels launched (100 gross tons and over; 1980) 415,000 gross tons.

during 1981, and in this area the Cockerill-Sambre plant once again figured large. The government had invited the General Savings Bank to float a loan for the merged company, situated in (French-speaking) Wallonia; lobbies in (Dutch-speaking) Flanders objected that Flemish money deposited with the bank would be drained into a bottomless pit. Statements by three French-speaking Socialist ministers regarding the status of Voeren (Fourons), long the subject of controversy between the two language communities, underlined the fact that the 1980 reform of the state structures was still incomplete. It did not offer a solution for the Brussels region or for the bilingual communes.

(JAN R. ENGELS)

Prime Minister George Cadle Price of Belize presided over ceremonies when that new nation became independent on September 21.

Belize

Belize

A parliamentary state on the eastern coast of Central America and a member of the Commonwealth, Belize is bounded on the north by Mexico, west and south by Guatemala, and east by the Caribbean Sea. Area: 22,965 sq km (8,867 sq mi). Pop. (1981 est.): 146,000. Cap.: Belmopan (pop., 1980 est., 4,500). Largest city: Belize City (pop., 1980 est., 42,200). Language: English, Spanish, and native Creole dialects. Religion: Roman Catholic, Anglican, and Methodist. Queen, Elizabeth II; governor-general in 1981, Minita Gordon; prime minister, George Cadle Price.

Belize, Great Britain's last colony on the American mainland, achieved independence on Sept. 21, 1981. However, Guatemala's claim to Belize, dating back to a dispute over an 1859 treaty, complicated negotiations throughout the year. On March 11 representatives from Belize, Great Britain, and Guatemala signed an agreement paving the way for Belize's independence. Even though specific territorial concessions were offered at that time to Guatemala as part of a settlement of its claim, further talks collapsed, and on September 7 Guatemala broke off diplomatic relations with Britain, closed its two consulates in Belize, and ordered the closing of Britain's consulate in Guatemala City. Nevertheless, the progress toward independence continued, and at the ceremonies on September 21 Prince and Princess Michael of Kent represented Queen Elizabeth II.

Belize has a parliamentary government consisting of a Cabinet of Ministers and a National Assembly that is comprised of an 8-seat appointed Senate and an 18-seat elected House of Representatives. The People's United Party (PUP) is the

majority force with 13 seats in the House and is headed by Prime Minister George Cadle Price (*see* BIOGRAPHIES). Elections are held every five years.

Mexico opened diplomatic relations with Belize by appointing Pedro Gonzales Rubis as its ambassador to the new nation, and the U.S. promised to upgrade its consulate general to an embassy. Also, the Caribbean Development Bank approved a $750,000 loan for hotel construction in Belmopan.

Prime Minister Price attended his first UN General Assembly session on September 25, at which time Belize became the 156th member of the international organization. With independence also came membership in the Commonwealth. Until the Guatemalan land dispute was resolved, however, Belize would not be admitted to membership in the Organization of American States.

(INES T. BAPTIST)

Benin

A republic of West Africa, Benin is located north of the Gulf of Guinea and is bounded by Togo, Upper Volta, Niger, and Nigeria. Area: 112,600 sq km (43,475 sq mi). Pop. (1981 est.): 3,641,000, mainly Dahomean and allied tribes. Cap.: Porto-Novo (pop., 1980 est., 123,000). Largest city: Cotonou (pop., 1980 est., 215,000). Language: French and local dialects. Religion: mainly animist, with Christian and Muslim minorities. President in 1981, Col. Ahmed Kerekou.

The most noteworthy political event of 1981 in Benin was the release in April of three former heads of state who had been kept under house arrest since the coup of Oct. 26, 1972, that had brought Pres. Ahmed Kerekou to power. The three were Justin Timotin Ahomadegbé, Sourou Migan Apithy, and Hubert Maga—all members of the former Presidential Council. Of the three only

Benin

BELIZE

Education. (1979–80) Primary, pupils 35,628, teachers 1,310; secondary, pupils 6,131, teachers 470; vocational, pupils 672; teacher training, pupils 144; higher, students (1978–79) 580, teaching staff (1977–78) 20.

Finance and Trade. Monetary unit: Belize dollar, with (Sept. 21, 1981) an official rate of Bel$2=U.S. $1 (free rate of Bel$3.71=£1 sterling). Budget (1979 est.): revenue Bel$62.6 million; expenditure Bel$52.3 million. Foreign trade (1978): imports Bel$210 million; exports Bel$161 million. Import sources (1977): U.S. 42%; U.K. 15%. Export destinations (1977): U.S. 47%; U.K. 44%. Main exports: sugar 38%; clothing 15%; fish 5%.

Ahomadegbé stayed in Benin; Maga went to France and Apithy to the Ivory Coast.

Foreign relations centred upon two events: the first conference of ministers of culture of French-speaking countries, held in Cotonou on September 18–19, and President Kerekou's first official visit to France later that month (September 22–24). The visit marked the normalization of relations that had been strained since the 1977 attack by mercenaries on Cotonou airport, allegedly masterminded by French soldier of fortune Bob Denard. The aim of that abortive operation had been to overthrow President Kerekou's military regime.

(PHILIPPE DECRAENE)

Bhutan

A monarchy situated in the eastern Himalayas, Bhutan is bounded by China and India. Area: 46,-100 sq km (17,800 sq mi). Pop. (1981 est.): 1,174,-000, including Bhutia 60%, Nepalese 25%, and 15% tribal peoples. Official cap.: Thimphu (pop., approximately 10,000). Administrative cap.: Paro (population unavailable). Language: Dzongkha (official). Religion: approximately 75% Buddhist, 25% Hindu. Druk gyalpo (king) in 1981, Jigme Singye Wangchuk.

Bhutan's fifth five-year plan (1981–86), worked out in consultation with Indian planning experts, envisaged a total outlay of Rs 2,740,000,000, more than three times the fourth plan projection of Rs 880 million. During a visit to Thimphu in June 1981, Indian Foreign Minister P. V. Narasimha

Rao pledged the same proportion of aid from India as for the fourth plan, when Indian assistance totaled Rs 700 million. The new plan sought to promote self-sufficiency in agricultural and livestock products, industries based on local manpower, and training. Deputy Planning Minister Dasho Lam Penjor visited Vienna in April to try to convince economics ministers of advanced countries to contribute liberally to Bhutan's development.

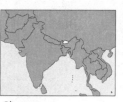

Bhutan

In line with the policy of expanding foreign representation, a new embassy had been opened in Dacca, Bangladesh, in October 1980. A trade pact was signed with Bangladesh, which agreed to make arrangements for the export of Bhutanese minerals and agricultural and forest products, most of which currently passed through Indian ports.   (GOVINDAN UNNY)

Billiard Games

Billiards. Winning the 36th world three-cushion championship was made easier for Ludo Dielis of Belgium when his fellow Belgian Raymond Ceulemans, the 1980 champion, did not defend his title in Cairo, Egypt, in February. This made the six-day, 12-man tournament a contest between Dielis and perennial contender Nobuaki Kobayashi of Japan. Both entered the final match with 10–0 records. Playing a masterful safety game, Dielis took a 47–22 lead before Kobayashi had an opportunity to respond in kind with runs of 6 and 10. Despite a final average of 1.426 balls per inning, Kobayashi lost to Dielis 60–46 in 50 innings. Representing the United States were American Billiard Association champion George Ashby, who placed sixth with a 1.011 average, and Harry Sims, who finished seventh with an 0.0841 average.

In June many of the same players participated in the World Cup two-man team championships in the Mexican resort town of Toluca. A mixture of violent hailstorms, military bands, electrical blackouts, Latin hospitality, and dizziness caused by lack of oxygen at the town's 2,745-m (9,000-ft) altitude made the event memorable to all. Comprising the six teams were Ashby and Frank Torres of the U.S., Edigio Vierat and Richard Bitalis of France, Luis Martínez and Luis Doyharzabal of Argentina, Kobayashi and Junichi Komori of Japan, Ceulemans and Dielis of Belgium, and the hosts, Gilberto Avalos and Carlos Barraza of Mexico. On the first day of play Japan took the lead with Kobayashi's 1.818 average, followed by Belgium with a 1.363 by Ceulemans. On the seventh day Komori strengthened Japan's position with an almost perfect game against Ceulemans. On the last day he repeated the performance by triumphing over Dielis, thus handily winning the championship for Japan. The Belgians were second, France was third, and the United States was fourth.

Pocket Billiards. The third All-American League championships, sponsored by the Billiard Congress of America for eight-ball teams, were held in Las Vegas, Nev., in June. Sixty-three men's and women's teams participated, representing more than 50 leagues from all regions of the U.S.

Bicycling: see Cycling

COURTESY, BILLIARDS DIGEST; PHOTO, MICHAEL PANOZZO

Danny DiLiberto won the BCA national eight-ball championship in tournament play at Las Vegas, Nevada, in September.

The quality of the competition became evident early, when the Wheeler Dealer men's team from Tulsa, Okla., soundly thrashed the two-time defending champions, the Tam O'Shanters from Colorado Springs, Colo. This dropped the Tams into the losers' bracket, where in the final three days of the tournament they had to play back-to-back matches and win every match in order to have a chance to defend their title. This they did, eventually gaining a berth in the finals. Defeating the Maxine's men's team from Fort Worth, Texas, they faced the Wheel Inn five from Billings, Mont., for the 1981 championship. Wheel Inn won the first round of the two-out-of-three match. In the second the Tams began showing the championship form of the past two years and tied the contest with a sparkling performance by team captain Charlie Shootman. In the deciding round Shootman fired two back-to-back runs of the table to retrieve the crown from the grasp of the contenders with the help of teammates Scott Smith, Keith Woestehoss, Gary Gross, Jim Gravil, Tony Cisneros, Don Bautista, and Chuck Cantrell.

The women's division of the All-American appeared to be a two-team race from the beginning, between Gordy's Club from Sacramento, Calif., and the defending champions, Burt's Girls of Colorado Springs. That expectation appeared short-lived when the two were forced to play each other in the second round. The defending champions lost that contest and moved to the losers' bracket. For two days Gordy's Club moved through the field undefeated, only to discover that Burt's Girls had done the same. The two teams thus met in the finals to decide the 1981 title. This time, Burt's Girls proved their stature by defeating the contenders the necessary two times to retain the championship for another year. Members of the team were captain Barb Campbell, Esther Durand, Patti Murphy, Lois Cross, Jane Bartram, Shereen Strong, and Vicki Gallimore.

The Billiard Congress of America's fifth national eight-ball (singles) championships were held in

September at Las Vegas. A total of 81 men and 41 women were on hand to determine the nation's top players; all had won local tournaments that involved more than 5,000 contestants. In the first two days of play the men's division was pared down to six flight winners, including defending champion Nick Varner of Owensboro, Ky., Danny DiLiberto of New York City, Emeroy Skenadore of Las Vegas, Doug Smith of Gosport, Ind., Emmett Martinez of Houston, Texas, and Howard Vickery of Reynoldsburg, Ohio.

An immediate upset occurred when Vickery put champion Nick Varner into the losers' bracket, where he was forced to defeat Smith, Skenadore, Martinez, and eventually Vickery to defend his title in the championship match with DiLiberto, who had been undefeated thus far. The title match required 12 games before either had won the required 7. At the end of eight games the match was tied at four each. In the ninth game DiLiberto broke (the triangular rack) and ran out. He also won the tenth, when Varner left a ball on the lip of a pocket. In the 11th game Varner broke and ran out but was still two games short of victory. DiLiberto, needing to win only one more game, broke, dropping two balls on the shot. He then pocketed the remaining balls to win the match and the national championship.

In the women's division the competition progressed through three separate flights, with the winners (and championship finalists) being Sherry Lively of Fairfield, Wash., Sue Warnes of Renton, Wash., and Belinda Campos of Austin, Texas. Of the trio, Warnes was the first to be eliminated. In the championship match emotions got the best of Lively. Normally an accomplished player, she fouled twice and scratched once, permitting the more experienced Campos to take over. Taking full advantage, Campos won 7–4 to gain her first national title. (ROBERT E. GOODWIN)

Bolivia

A landlocked republic in central South America, Bolivia is bordered by Brazil, Paraguay, Argentina, Chile, and Peru. Area: 1,098,581 sq km (424,-165 sq mi). Pop. (1981 est.): 5,718,000, of whom more than 50% are Indian. Judicial cap.: Sucre (pop., 1979, 66,300). Administrative cap. and largest city: La Paz (pop., 1979, 696,800). Language: Spanish 78%, Quechua 15%, Aymara 7%. Religion (1979 est.): Roman Catholic 93.8%. Presidents in 1981, Maj. Gen. Luis García Meza Tejada until August 4 and, from September 4, Gen. Celso Torrelio Villa.

Gen. Luis García Meza clung to power as president of Bolivia and head of the governing military junta until August 1981, despite repeated coup attempts, a burgeoning economic crisis, foreign debt renegotiations, and the international isolation of his regime—at first for overthrowing the democratically elected government of Pres. Lydia Gueiler Tejada in July 1980 and for the ensuing repression, later because of alleged links with international drug rings. A fifth coup attempt led by Generals Alberto Natusch Busch (briefly president

Bolivia

Biographies:
see People of the Year

Biological Sciences:
see Life Sciences

Birth Statistics:
see Demography

Boating:
see Rowing; Sailing; Water Sports

Bobsledding:
see Winter Sports

in 1979) and Lucio Añez Rivero (former army commander in chief) came near to success, but it left the garrisons in Santa Cruz and La Paz, the respective bases of the rebels and the government, on the brink of civil war.

The two sides agreed upon mediation by the Roman Catholic Church, with the result that García Meza resigned on August 4 (as he had promised to do earlier) and handed power back to the military junta. A month later, after prolonged negotiations, the junta elected one of its members, army commander Gen. Celso Torrelio Villa (*see* BIOGRAPHIES), as president. A source within the military who took part in the negotiations said that García Meza, who was still living in the presidential palace at the time, had chosen his friend Torrelio as his successor. Despite this friendship, Torrelio had the public image of a young, efficient officer without ties to drug dealers; his rise in 1981 had been meteoric, starting with his appointment in February as minister of the interior, replacing Col. Luis Arce Gómez (discredited by the U.S. Drug Enforcement Administration), and his later appointment as army commander in chief. On September 8 President Torrelio named his Cabinet, which contained only six new appointments. Among these was Gonzalo Romero, a leader of the Bolivian Socialist Falange Party, named as foreign minister.

Civilians took little part in the events in August–September, despite immense potential support for an uprising against the García Meza regime and the call for a supporting general strike by the banned labour confederation, the Central Obrera Boliviana. Supporting strikes and demonstrations took place at Santa Cruz, but the La Paz government was able to prevent news of the disorders from being widely disseminated. Despite government claims that no political prisoners were being held, the Roman Catholic Church alleged in October that repression of political opponents had increased under Torrelio's regime.

The confrontation between La Paz and Santa Cruz was based on a legacy of frustration and disillusion; the central government had usurped and channeled into other regions scarce resources that were either earmarked for or produced in Santa Cruz. The new government announced plans to relax the curfew, in effect since July 1980; to hold elections; and to return the country to constitutional normality within three years—dependent, however, upon the political conduct of the Bolivian people. (MICHAEL WOOLLER)

Botswana

A landlocked republic of southern Africa and a member of the Commonwealth, Botswana is bounded by South Africa, a part of Bophuthatswana, South West Africa/Namibia, Zambia, and Zimbabwe. Area: 581,700 sq km (224,600 sq mi). Pop. (1981 prelim.): 936,000, almost 99% African. Cap. and largest city: Gaborone (pop., 1981 prelim., 59,000). Language: English (official) and Setswana. Religion: Christian 60%; animist. President in 1981, Quett Masire.

Though economic progress was tempered by the effects of world recession in 1981, nevertheless the pula in March was revalued for the third time in five years. Developments in the meat industry included the opening at Lobatse of a new cannery and tannery and in Gaborone of a foot-and-mouth vaccine factory; a second cannery at Maun was in the planning stage. The European Economic Community agreed in June to resume importing beef from Botswana; it had purchased none since February 1980, when foot-and-mouth disease broke out.

On the mineral front the future of coal mining looked bright. Shell Coal Botswana announced plans to develop a large mine in the area between

Botswana

Morupule and Serowe. This, it was hoped, would enable Botswana to enter the coal export market by the end of the decade. Work continued on the new diamond mine at Jwaneng, which was scheduled to open in 1982.

Substantial aid commitments were made during the year, many from Arab countries. Donors promised $45 million for the construction of the new international airport at Gaborone. Botswana purchased arms from the U.S.S.R., and in October it was reported that Soviet military advisers had arrived in the country.   (GUY ARNOLD)

Bowling

Tenpin Bowling. WORLD. All three zones of the Fédération Internationale des Quilleurs (FIQ), the world amateur bowling organization, held championship tournaments in 1980–81. The Asian and European zones also staged junior championships, and there was the Cup of Europe for teams and individuals. The year ended with the tenpin tournament at World Games I and the World Cup (see below). FIQ acceptance of Ethiopia and Greece increased national member federations to 65.

In the eighth American Zone championships, held in Winnipeg, Man., in July 1981, U.S. players captured six of the ten first-place medals, leaving three to the host country and one to Mexico. In the masters play-off finals for the individual crown, Barbara Walker of the U.S. defeated Mexico's Edda de Boneta in the women's division 356–348, and Bob Puttick of Canada beat Steve Fehr of the U.S. in the men's 454–431.

The Asian Zone conducted its sixth championships in Adelaide, Australia, in November 1980. In the women's division, Australia and Japan shared the gold medals. In the masters final playoff match, Alice Roser of Australia defeated Japan's Mitsuyo Yonemasu 372–370. The host team cap-

tured four gold medals in the men's division, and South Korea gained one. In the men's final play-off match, Eric Thompson of Australia beat Ringo Wang of Malaysia 390–381.

The European Zone held its sixth championships in Frankfurt am Main, West Germany, in June 1981. The West German team took only one first place, the other winning countries being Belgium (2), The Netherlands (2), Sweden, Italy, and Finland. In the masters final play-off for women, Yvonne Berndt of Sweden beat Jette Hansen of Denmark 347–322. In the men's division, Arne Svein Strøm of Norway defeated Heinrich König of West Germany 474–396.

The World Games I of the non-Olympic sports took place in Santa Clara, Calif., in July 1981. The tenpin tournament allowed each nation to enter only one man and one woman bowler, who bowled singles in a double elimination format and mixed doubles. It was the first time that this format had been tried in an official FIQ event. Ruth Guerster and Chris Batson of Australia won the mixed doubles title, and Liliane Gregori of France was the winner of the women's singles. In the men's final, Ernst Berndt of Austria upset Arne Strøm of Norway 398–390, but because each man had lost one match in the double elimination format, there was a roll-off of one additional game which Strøm won 224–170. In the first World Cup ever held in the U.S., in New York City, in November, the winners were Robert Worrall (U.S.) and Pauline Smith (U.K.).

(YRJÖ SARAHETE)

UNITED STATES. Earl Anthony of Dublin, Calif., a left-hander with a medium-speed delivery, regained his dominant position in U.S. professional bowling in 1981, despite a significant trend toward hard-throwing right-handers. With only a handful of events remaining on the Professional Bowlers Association (PBA) schedule, the 43-year-old Anthony, bowler of the year from 1974 through 1976, had earned the most prize money, $143,135, and had won the most tournament championships, four. Other contenders for 1981 honours included Marshall Holman, Medford, Ore., with prize money of $119,685, and Tom Baker, Buffalo, N.Y., with $100,535. Holman and Baker each won three PBA titles. Wayne Webb of Rehoboth, Mass., 1980 bowler of the year, did not appear likely to retain his title.

In the American Bowling Congress (ABC) tournament in Memphis, Tenn., one of the standouts was Bill Lillard of Houston, Texas, an ABC Hall of Fame member now competing as a nonprofessional. He took third place in the all-events with a nine-game total of 2,085 and fourth place in singles with 749. Lillard was bowler of the year in 1956. The ABC Regular Division champions were: team, Strachota's Milshore Bowl, Milwaukee, Wis., 3,188; singles, Rob Vital, Lancaster, Pa., 780; doubles (tie), Jim Kontos, Munster, Ind., and Al Burder, Chicago, 1,362, and Bob Blaney and Ted Hannahs, Cambridge, Ohio, 1,362; all-events, Rod Toft, St. Paul, Minn., 2,107. The ABC Masters tournament, in Memphis, Tenn., was captured by Randy Lightfoot of St. Charles, Mo.

Katsuko Sugimoto of Tokyo, who in 1972

Grim determination appeared on the face of Randy Lightfoot as he rolled his way to the championship in the American Bowling Congress Masters tournament held in Memphis in May.

WIDE WORLD

switched her preference from basketball to bowling, won the Avon/Women's International Bowling Congress (WIBC) Queens meet in Baltimore, Md. The 35-year-old Sugimoto, a professional bowler, received $15,745 for her victory. In the Open Division of the WIBC tournament the champions were: team, Earl Anthony's Dublin Bowl, Dublin, Calif., 2,963; singles, Virginia Norton, Southgate, Calif., 672; doubles, Nikki Gianulias, Vallejo, Calif., and Donna Adamek, Duarte, Calif., 1,305; all-events, Virginia Norton, 1,905. In Division I of the tournament the winners included: team, Gibson Specialty Co., Waterloo, Iowa, 2,796; singles, Dorothy Batey, East Orange, N.J., 651; doubles, Jen Gue, New Castle, Del., and Jo Ann Scott, Wilmington, Del., 1,181; all-events, Ferol Streib, Leavenworth, Wash., 1,738.

Duckpins. In the U.S. National Duckpin Bowling Congress national tournament the winners were: men's singles, Bart Matteson, East Taunton, Mass., 568; men's doubles, Thomas T. Bohara, Sr., and Len Gdula, Norwich, Conn., 1,037; men's team, Legion Major No. 3, Cranston, R.I., 2,200; women's singles, Pat Smith, Warwick, R.I., 523; women's doubles, Carol Deshong, Riverside, R.I., and Anne Mello, Rehoboth, Mass., 913.

(JOHN J. ARCHIBALD)

Lawn Bowls. The women's bowls world championships of 1981, held at Willowdale, North York, Ont., attracted contestants from 17 countries and were won by England. Champions of the events were: singles, Norma Shaw (England); pairs, Eileen Bell and Nan Allely (Ireland); triples, Hong Kong; and fours, England.

Bill Mosely of South Africa won the Kodak International Masters at Worthing, England, beating David McGill of Scotland in the final. David Bryant from England won the world indoor bowls championship at Coatbridge, Scotland, for the third successive year.

The second world championships for blind bowlers (in two categories, totally blind and partially blind) were staged at the Belgrave Club, Leicester, England. Australia, England, Indonesia, Scotland, South Africa, Wales, and Zimbabwe entered teams. In the first category Des Chandler (Zimbabwe) and Kathleen Bonnett (England) captured gold medals in singles, and Lyndsey Lacas and Ivor Singer (Zimbabwe) won the mixed pairs competition; in the second, singles gold medalists were George Arnold (Scotland) and Delina Marx (South Africa).

(C. M. JONES)

Brazil

A federal republic in eastern South America, Brazil is bounded by the Atlantic Ocean and all the countries of South America except Ecuador and Chile. Area: 8,512,000 sq km (3,286,500 sq mi). Pop. (1980 prelim.): 119,098,900. Principal cities (pop., 1980 prelim.): Brasília (cap.; federal district) 411,305; São Paulo 12,588,400; Rio de Janeiro 9,019,000. Language: Portuguese. Religion: Roman Catholic 90.3%. President in 1981, Gen. João Baptista de Oliveira Figueiredo.

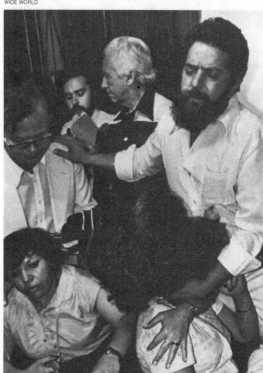

Luis Ignacio da Silva (right), president of the Brazilian Party of the Workers, comforts his family after being sentenced on November 19 to three and a half years in prison. The labour leader had been convicted by a military tribunal of inciting an illegal strike in 1980.

Domestic Affairs. Since his inauguration on March 15, 1979, Pres. João Baptista de Oliveira Figueiredo had adhered to his promise to return Brazil gradually to a democratic regime, thus continuing the policy of former president Ernesto Geisel. This policy became known as *abertura*, the opening or broadening of the people's participation in the political process. During 1981 Figueiredo's accomplishments included the amnesty and restoration of political rights to those who had lost them under the provisions of the emergency Institutional Act number 5 (AI-5) adopted in 1968, the reorganization of the national political party system (adopted in 1965) with provision for the establishment of new parties (five had announced their organization since 1979), the postponement for two years of municipal elections (previously scheduled for Nov. 15, 1980), and the relaxation of the strict prior censorship of the press.

Two other measures were insistently demanded by political leaders: the reform of the electoral system and an overhauling of the 1967 constitution, which had been adopted after the 1964 revolution. The existing electoral system was criticized because of its provisions for the indirect election of state governors and some of the federal senators, as well as of the national president and vice-president. There was also a strong demand for the abolition of the restrictions that had been imposed on candidates for public office regarding the campaign propaganda they could broadcast over radio and television.

When it was organized early in 1980, the government-sponsored Social Democratic Party (PDS) declared itself in favour of a reform of the existing constitution in order to permit the alternation of

Brazil

Boxing:
see Combat Sports

the parties in power, the political autonomy of the state and local governments, and the direct election of all elective officials. Later in 1980 the Congress adopted (and the president sanctioned) legislation providing for the direct election of municipal officers (mayors, vice-mayors, and assembly members), of state governors, and of all federal senators. Thus, at the general elections scheduled for Nov. 15, 1982, all members of the federal Congress and state and municipal officers would be elected directly by voters for the first time since 1967.

The indirect election (by an electoral college) of the national president and vice-president was to continue at least until the constitutional reform planned for 1983.

Considerable unrest was observed throughout the country owing to the constant rise in the prices for all commodities, the laying off of more than

200,000 industrial workers, and bomb explosions at various places attributed to extreme rightists in the military. On Aug. 6, 1981, the resignation of the influential political leader Gen. Golbery do Couto e Silva, allegedly for health reasons, was announced. As a member of the presidential Cabinet and close friend of President Figueiredo, he had consistently advocated the return to a democratic regime.

President Figueiredo retired from office for 53 days following a heart attack but resumed his duties on November 12. During his illness Vice-Pres. Aureliano Chaves served as acting president.

The Economy. The struggle against rampant inflation continued to be the most important problem facing the nation. It was estimated that inflation reached a rate of 94% during the 12-month period from June 1979 to May 1980. By August 1980 it was estimated at 99.2%, and by the middle of 1981 it was said to be running at a rate of more than 120%. The highest rate before had been 91.9% at the time of the revolution of 1964.

One of the major causes of the high rate of inflation was the greatly increased cost of imported oil. Brazil was believed to have spent more than $11 billion for imported oil during 1980. As a consequence, the government had to use part of its foreign exchange reserves to pay for the unfavourable balance of trade. The situation was aggravated by the total of the country's foreign debt, estimated at $55 billion–$60 billion in 1981. Brazil during the year had to pay large sums for interest and amortization.

In an effort to improve the situation, steps were taken to cut government expenditures, reduce imports, and prohibit the hiring of new employees by government departments and government-sponsored corporations. The replacement of oil with other energy sources was actively promoted, including the use of alcohol produced from sugarcane. An increase in exports was also encouraged, a situation that was somewhat improved by the discovery of large amounts of gold in Serra Pelada in the interior of the state of Pará.

Foreign Affairs. The administration continued to promote foreign trade and services through diplomacy. An agreement was signed with Iraq providing for close cooperation in the development of Iraq's nuclear energy program. Petrobrás, Brazil's oil-monopoly corporation, also maintained an agreement with the Iraqi National Oil Company for cooperation in oil prospecting in Iraq.

On July 15 a comprehensive trade agreement with the Soviet Union was announced. It provided, among other things, for the U.S.S.R. to increase its purchases of Brazilian products, especially soybeans, soybean oil, and other agricultural goods, in exchange for the sale to Brazil of approximately 20,000 bbl of oil a day and electrical equipment for the nation's hydroelectric development program. It was estimated that the total value of this five-year agreement would be about $6 billion.

Canadian Prime Minister Pierre Trudeau visited Brazil as an official guest early in 1981. President Figueiredo accepted an invitation to visit Canada in the near future. (RAUL D'EÇA)

BRAZIL

Education. (1978) Primary, pupils, 21,473,100, teachers 854,813; secondary, vocational, and teacher training, pupils 2,519,122, teachers 184,767; higher (1979–80), students 1,311,799, teaching staff 108,821.

Finance. Monetary unit: cruzeiro, with a free rate (Sept. 21, 1981) of 105.85 cruzeiros to U.S. $1 (196.25 cruzeiros = £1 sterling). Gold and other reserves (June 1981) U.S. $5,281,000,000. Budget (1980 actual): revenue 1,219,418,-000,000 cruzeiros; expenditure 1,217,383,000,000 cruzeiros. Gross national product (1979) 5,619,400,000,000 cruzeiros. Money supply (May 1981) 1,421,330,000,000 cruzeiros. Cost of living (São Paulo; 1975 = 100; June 1981) 1,539.8.

Foreign Trade. (1980) Imports 1,278,000,000,000 cruzeiros; exports 1,041,000,000,000 cruzeiros. Import sources (1979): U.S. 18%; Iraq 14%; Saudi Arabia 10%; West Germany 7%; Japan 6%; Argentina 5%. Export destinations (1979): U.S. 19%; West Germany 7%; The Netherlands 7%; Japan 6%; Argentina 5%; U.K. 5%; Italy 5%. Main exports (1979): coffee 15%; soybeans and products 11%; machinery 10%; iron ore 8%; cocoa 6%; iron and steel 5%; motor vehicles 5%.

Transport and Communications. Roads (1979) 1,384,-423 km. Motor vehicles in use (1979): passenger 8,238,200; commercial 926,300. Railways: (1979) c. 31,120 km; traffic (1978) 11,952,000,000 passenger-km, freight 63,979,-000,000 net ton-km. Air traffic (1980): 15,572,000,000 passenger-km; freight c. 610 million net ton-km. Shipping (1980): merchant vessels 100 gross tons and over 607; gross tonnage 4,533,633. Shipping traffic (1979): goods loaded 98,010,000 metric tons, unloaded 75,328,000 metric tons. Telephones (Dec. 1978) 5,733,000. Radio receivers (Dec. 1975) 16,980,000. Television receivers (Dec. 1977) 11 million.

Agriculture. Production (in 000; metric tons; 1980): wheat c. 2,614; corn 20,377; rice 9,746; cassava (1979) 24,935; potatoes 1,932; sweet potatoes (1979) c. 1,516; sugar, raw value c. 8,300; tomatoes c. 1,611; dry beans 1,975; soybeans c. 15,128; bananas 6,773; oranges 8,948; coffee 1,067; cocoa c. 294; cotton, lint c. 578; sisal 254; tobacco 410; rubber c. 25; beef and veal c. 2,150; pork c. 850; fish catch (1979) c. 843; timber (cu m; 1979) c. 212,-727. Livestock (in 000; 1980): cattle c. 93,000; pigs c. 36,-800; sheep c. 18,500; goats c. 7,400; horses (1979) c. 6,000; chickens c. 484,000.

Industry. Fuel and power (in 000; metric tons; 1980): crude oil 9,118; coal (1979) c. 4,640; natural gas (cu m) c. 2,870,000; manufactured gas (cu m; 1979) c. 510,000; electricity (kw-hr; 1979) 124,673,000 (93% hydroelectric in 1977). Production (in 000; metric tons; 1980): cement 27,-185; pig iron 12,484; crude steel 15,249; iron ore (68% metal content; 1978) 103,896; bauxite (1979) c. 2,400; manganese ore (1978) 2,744; gold (troy oz; 1978) c. 300; wood pulp (1978) 1,977; paper (1978) 2,668; fertilizers (nutrient content; 1979–80) nitrogenous 288, phosphate 1,306; passenger cars (including assembly units; 1979) 553; commercial vehicles (units; 1979) 575. Merchant vessels launched (100 gross tons and over; 1980) 625,000 gross tons.

Brazilian Literature: see Literature

Bulgaria

A people's republic of Europe, Bulgaria is situated on the eastern Balkan Peninsula along the Black Sea, bordered by Romania, Yugoslavia, Greece, and Turkey. Area: 110,912 sq km (42,823 sq mi). Pop. (1981 est.): 9,059,000, including 85.3% Bulgarians (but excluding some 210,000 Macedonians classified as Bulgarian according to official statistics), 8.5% Turks, 2.6% Gypsies, and 2.5% Macedonians. Cap. and largest city: Sofia (pop., 1979 est., 1,031,600). Language: chiefly Bulgarian. Religion: official sources classify 35.5% of the population as religious, although this figure is suspect since the regime promotes atheism. Of those who practice religion, it is estimated that 85% are Bulgarian Orthodox, 13% Muslim, 0.8% Jewish, 0.7% Roman Catholic, and 0.5% Protestant, Gregorian-Armenian, and others. General secretary of the Bulgarian Communist Party and chairman of the State Council in 1981, Todor Zhivkov; chairmen of the Council of Ministers (premiers), Stanko Todorov and, from June 16, Grisha Filipov.

The 12th congress of the Bulgarian Communist

BULGARIA

Education. (1979–80) Primary, pupils 70,114, teachers 3,636; secondary, pupils 1,146,074, teachers 54,459; vocational, pupils 228,138, teachers 18,846; teacher training, pupils 9,082, teachers 686; higher, students 67,097, teaching staff 10,353.

Finance. Monetary unit: lev, with (Sept. 21, 1981) a free exchange rate of 0.95 leva to U.S. $1 (1.76 lev = £1 sterling). Budget (1980 est.): revenue 13,187,000,000 leva; expenditure 13,167,000,000 leva.

Foreign Trade. (1980) Imports 8,283,000,000 leva; exports 8,901,000,000 leva. Main import sources: U.S.S.R. 57%; East Germany 7%; West Germany 5%. Main export destinations: U.S.S.R. 50%; East Germany 5%. Main exports (1979): machinery 37%; tobacco and cigarettes 8%; transport equipment 8%; chemicals 7%; fruit and vegetables 6%. Tourism: visitors (1979) 5,120,000; gross receipts (1975) U.S. $230 million.

Transport and Communications. Roads (1979) 36,304 km (including 107 km expressways). Motor vehicles in use (1978): passenger c. 480,000; commercial (including buses) c. 110,000. Railways: (1979) 4,341 km; traffic (1980) c. 6,950,000,000 passenger-km, freight 17,681,000,000 net ton-km. Air traffic (1980): c. 775 million passenger-km; freight c. 10 million net ton-km. Navigable inland waterways (1973) 471 km. Shipping (1980): merchant vessels 100 gross tons and over 192; gross tonnage 1,233,303. Telephones (Jan. 1979) 1,032,100. Radio licenses (Dec. 1979) 2,176,000. Television licenses (Dec. 1979) 1,634,000.

Agriculture. Production (in 000; metric tons; 1980): wheat 3,839; corn c. 2,500; barley c. 1,280; potatoes c. 440; sunflower seed c. 415; tomatoes c. 820; grapes c. 980; apples c. 290; tobacco c. 160; meat c. 633. Livestock (in 000; Jan. 1980): sheep 10,536; cattle 1,787; goats 433; pigs 3,830; horses (1979) 124; asses (1979) 340; chickens 39,164.

Industry. Fuel and power (in 000; metric tons; 1980): lignite 29,950; coal 273; crude oil 280; natural gas (cu m; 1979) 32,300; electricity (kw-hr) 34,385,000. Production (in 000; metric tons; 1980): cement 5,359; iron ore (33% metal content; 1979) 2,100; manganese ore (metal content; 1979) 12; copper ore (metal content; 1979) 58; lead ore (metal content; 1979) 116; zinc ore (1978) 88; pig iron (1979) 1,501; crude steel 2,566; sulfuric acid 859; nitric acid (1978) 862; soda ash (1978) 1,268; fertilizers (nutrient content; 1979) nitrogenous 677, phosphate 282; cotton yarn (1979) 85; cotton fabrics (m; 1979) 347,000; wool yarn (1979) 34; woolen fabrics (m; 1979) 34,000. Merchant vessels launched (100 gross tons and over; 1980) 206,000 gross tons.

Party was held in Sofia from March 31 to April 4, 1981. In his opening speech, First Secretary Todor Zhivkov announced that national income had doubled during the previous decade. Summarizing the achievements of the seventh five-year plan (1976–80), however, Zhivkov noted that targets had not been reached; national income rose 36% instead of the planned 45%, and industrial production grew by 40%, not the planned 50%. Bulgaria's foreign debt at the end of 1980 stood at some $5 billion.

Introducing the eighth five-year plan (1981–85), Zhivkov declared that Bulgaria would increase its participation in the Council for Mutual Economic Assistance (Comecon) but would also continue to encourage economic relations with capitalist countries. He called for the role of trade unions in economic activity to be strengthened.

Zhivkov, who was 70 in September, was reelected party leader and granted the additional title of general secretary. The 12-member Politburo was reduced by the death of Lyudmila Zhivkova, minister for cultural affairs and daughter of Zhivkov (*see* OBITUARIES).

A new National Assembly was elected on June 7. Zhivkov was reelected chairman of the State Council. Stanko Todorov, appointed president of the National Assembly, was replaced as chairman of the Council of Ministers by Grisha Filipov, a Politburo member.   (K. M. SMOGORZEWSKI)

Bulgaria

Burma

A republic of Southeast Asia, Burma is bordered by Bangladesh, India, China, Laos, Thailand, the Bay of Bengal, and the Andaman Sea. Area: 676,577 sq km (261,288 sq mi). Pop. (1981 est.): 36,166,000. Cap. and largest city: Rangoon (pop., 1980 est., 2,186,000). Language: Burmese. Religion (1977): Buddhist 80%. Chairmen of the State Council in 1981, U Ne Win and, from November 9, U San Yu; prime minister, U Maung Maung Kha.

U Ne Win's announcement in August 1981 that he was stepping down from the chairmanship of the State Council at the end of his four-year term in November brought an element of uncertainty to Burma. The move was not expected to pose major problems to the government, as Ne Win was to retain his commanding role as chairman of the ruling Burma Socialist Program Party (BSPP) although he was 70 years old and in poor health. U San Yu, a retired army general and close associate of Ne Win, took office as president on November 9, having been chosen by the newly elected Parliament. U Maung Maung Kha remained as prime minister at the head of a new Cabinet.

An estimated 3,000–4,000 politicians, intellectuals, and insurgents were rehabilitated in the months following the announcement of amnesty by Ne Win in 1980. Some 1,400 rebels surrendered during the amnesty, among them insurgent leader Yan Naing, who returned from exile in Thailand.

The economy underwent no major change in 1981, although food production maintained the slight improvement of the previous year and foreign aid commitments increased. The U.S. government signed a $30 million economic assistance

Burma

BURMA

Education. (1978–79) Primary, pupils 3,731,160, teachers 84,593; secondary, pupils 924,739, teachers 31,433; vocational, pupils 9,576, teachers 786; teacher training, students 5,163, teachers 367; higher, students 112,671, teaching staff 3,922.

Finance. Monetary unit: kyat, with (Sept. 21, 1981) a free rate of 6.40 kyats to U.S. $1 (11.86 kyats = £1 sterling). Gold and other reserves (June 1981) U.S. $274 million. Budget (1980–81 est.): revenue 24,968,000,000 kyats; expenditure 27,104,000,000 kyats.

Foreign Trade. (1980) Imports 2,337,000,000 kyats; exports 3,123,000,000 kyats. Import sources (1978): Japan 31%; U.S. 12%; U.K. 9%; West Germany 6%; Singapore 6%; China 5%. Export destinations (1978): Bangladesh 14%; Switzerland 12%; Singapore 10%; Hong Kong 10%; Sri Lanka 10%; U.S. 9%; Japan 9%; Indonesia 9%. Main exports: rice 39%; teak 24%.

Transport and Communications. Roads (1977) 22,402 km. Motor vehicles in use (1978): passenger c. 33,000; commercial (including buses) c. 41,500. Railways: (1978) 4,473 km; traffic (1979–80) c. 3,760,000,000 passenger-km, freight c. 600 million net ton-km. Air traffic (1980): c. 218 million passenger-km; freight c. 1.6 million net ton-km. Shipping (1980): merchant vessels 100 gross tons and over 90; gross tonnage 87,519. Telephones (Jan. 1978) 32,600. Radio licenses (Dec. 1977) 693,000.

Agriculture. Production (in 000; metric tons; 1980): rice 13,317; dry beans c. 185; onions c. 107; plantains (1979) c. 425; sesame seed c. 210; peanuts c. 394; cotton, lint c. 17; jute c. 87; tobacco c. 52; rubber c. 15; fish catch (1979) 565; timber (cu m; 1979) c. 25,303. Livestock (in 000; March 1980): cattle c. 7,702; buffalo c. 1,803; pigs c. 2,280; goats c. 577; sheep c. 217; chickens c. 17,420.

Industry. Production (in 000; metric tons; 1980): cement c. 370; crude oil (1979) c. 1,550; natural gas (cu m; 1979–80) 360; electricity (excluding most industrial production; kw-hr) c. 1,170,000; lead concentrates (metal content; 1979–80) 5.7; zinc concentrates (metal content) 5.5; tin concentrates (metal content) 0.8; tungsten concentrates (oxide content; 1979–80) 0.6; nitrogenous fertilizers (nutrient content; 1979–80) 58; cotton yarn 14.

agreement with Burma in October, the first substantial U.S. aid since 1966. The Asian Development Bank sanctioned a total of $75 million in loans for various projects. (GOVINDAN UNNY)

Burundi

Burundi

Cameroon

Cambodia:
see Kampuchea

A republic of eastern Africa, Burundi is bordered by Zaire, Rwanda, and Tanzania. Area: 27,834 sq km (10,747 sq mi). Pop. (1979): 4,110,000, mainly Hutu, Tutsi, and Twa. Cap. and largest city: Bujumbura (pop., 1979, 151,000). Language: Rundi and French. Religion: Roman Catholic 60%; animist 30%; Protestant 8%; Muslim 2%. President in 1981, Col. Jean-Baptiste Bagaza.

During 1981 the government continued attempts to diversify Burundi's economy, which was increasingly disrupted by transportation problems. A peat development project funded by the U.S. and Ireland aimed to develop the country's considerable peat potential and thus reduce fuel imports.

In a referendum held in November, voters approved a new constitution. The document designated the Union for National Progress as the only legal political party and its head (currently Pres. Jean-Baptiste Bagaza) as the sole candidate for president. Elections were to be held in the near future.

The old railway from Kigoma to Dar es Salaam, Tanzania, was the subject of a report in January,

BURUNDI

Education. (1978–79) Primary, pupils 146,467, teachers 4,445; secondary, pupils 6,753, teachers (1977–78) 425; vocational, pupils 1,623, teachers (1975–76) 192; teacher training, students 6,322, teachers 355; higher (university level), students 1,710, teaching staff 130.

Finance. Monetary unit: Burundi franc, with (Sept. 21, 1981) an official rate of BurFr 90 to U.S. $1 (free rate of BurFr 161.60 = £1 sterling). Gold and other reserves (June 1981) U.S. $70 million. Budget (1980 actual): revenue BurFr 11,452,300,000; expenditure BurFr 13,051,100,000.

Foreign Trade. (1980) Imports BurFr 15,109,000,000; exports BurFr 5,861,000,000. Import sources (1979): Belgium-Luxembourg 11%; Japan 6%; France 5%; West Germany 5%. Export destinations (1979): U.S. c. 33%; Belgium-Luxembourg c. 16%; West Germany c. 14%; China c. 7%. Main export: coffee 89%.

Agriculture. Production (in 000; metric tons; 1980): sorghum c. 120; corn c. 140; cassava (1979) c. 942; potatoes (1979) c. 233; sweet potatoes (1979) c. 943; dry beans c. 173; bananas c. 985; coffee c. 20; tea c. 2; cotton, lint c. 2. Livestock (in 000; Dec. 1979): cattle c. 836; sheep c. 336; goats c. 585; pigs c. 51.

which showed that goods sometimes took more than a year to arrive in Burundi by this route. The railway handled less than one-quarter of Burundi's freight requirements, which averaged 12,000 metric tons a month. The remainder was routed through Mombasa, Kenya. The runway at Bujumbura was being extended to accommodate jumbo jets. (GUY ARNOLD)

Cameroon

A republic of west Africa on the Gulf of Guinea, Cameroon borders on Nigeria, Chad, the Central African Republic, the Congo, Gabon, and Equatorial Guinea. Area: 465,054 sq km (179,558

CAMEROON

Education. (1978–79) Primary, pupils 1,254,065, teachers 25,248; secondary, pupils 147,073, teachers 5,112; vocational, pupils 45,051, teachers 1,804; teacher training, students 1,677, teachers 168; higher, students 10,060, teaching staff (1977–78) 439.

Finance. Monetary unit: CFA franc, with (Sept. 21, 1981) a parity of CFA Fr 50 to the French franc and a free rate of CFA Fr 265 to U.S. $1 (CFA Fr 491 = £1 sterling). Budget (total; 1980–81 est.) balanced at CFA Fr 246 billion.

Foreign Trade. (1980) Imports CFA Fr 338 billion; exports CFA Fr 291 billion. Import sources (1979): France 44%; West Germany 8%; U.S. 6%; Italy 5%. Export destinations (1979): France 25%; The Netherlands 21%; U.S. 21%; Italy 7%. Main exports (1979): coffee 25%; cocoa and products 24%; crude oil 23%; timber 9%.

Transport and Communications. Roads (1975) 43,500 km. Motor vehicles in use (1978): passenger 58,600; commercial (including buses) 37,600. Railways: (1978) c. 1,320 km; traffic (1980) 230 million passenger-km, freight 610 million net ton-km. Air traffic (1980): c. 477 million passenger-km; freight c. 29 million net ton-km. Shipping (1980): merchant vessels 100 gross tons and over 44; gross tonnage 62,080. Telephones (June 1973) 22,000. Radio receivers (Dec. 1977) 240,000.

Agriculture. Production (in 000; metric tons; 1980): corn c. 490; millet c. 400; sweet potatoes (1979) c. 173; cassava (1979) c. 864; bananas c. 97; plantains (1979) c. 955; peanuts c. 299; coffee c. 102; cocoa c. 110; palm kernels c. 47; palm oil c. 82; rubber c. 17; cotton, lint c. 30; timber (cu m; 1979) c. 9,782. Livestock (in 000; 1979): cattle c. 3,027; pigs c. 806; sheep c. 2,211; goats c. 1,720; chickens c. 10,352.

Industry. Production (in 000; metric tons; 1979): crude oil c. 1,500; cement (1977) 278; aluminum 53; electricity (kw-hr; 1980) c. 1,340,000.

sq mi). Pop. (1981 est.): 8,646,000. Cap.: Yaoundé (pop., 1976, 313,700). Largest city: Douala (pop., 1976, 458,400). Language: English and French (official), Bantu, Sudanic. Religion: mainly animist, with Roman Catholic (25.5%), Protestant, independent Christian, and Muslim minorities. President in 1981, Ahmadou Ahidjo; prime minister, Paul Biya.

Apart from some minor agitation on the Yaoundé university campus in February, Pres. Ahmadou Ahidjo's regime encountered no domestic difficulties during the year. Relations with Nigeria and the continuing troubles in Chad, however, were matters of concern. Five Nigerian soldiers were killed in a frontier clash in May. Wider conflict was avoided by Togo's mediation.

Honouring its predecessor's undertakings, the new French government gave immediate diplomatic and military support to Cameroon in the Nigerian dispute. France also helped to evacuate Cameroonian nationals expelled from Gabon in May following riots at a football match in Douala. In September President Ahidjo was received in Paris by Pres. François Mitterrand.

Economic growth accelerated. Petroleum production was estimated to exceed four million metric tons in 1981.   (PHILIPPE DECRAENE)

Canada

Canada is a federal parliamentary state and member of the Commonwealth covering North America north of conterminous United States and east of Alaska. Area: 9,976,139 sq km (3,851,809 sq mi). Pop. (1981 est.): 24,213,000, including (1971) British 44.6%; French 28.7%; other European 23%; Indian and Eskimo 1.4%. Cap.: Ottawa (metro pop., 1980 est., 753,300). Largest cities: Toronto (metro pop., 1980 est., 2,883,100); Montreal (metro pop., 1980 est., 2,827,300). Language (mother tongue; 1976): English 61%; French 26%; others 13%. Religion (1971): Roman Catholic 46%; Protestant 42%. Queen, Elizabeth II; governor-general in 1981, Edward R. Schreyer; prime minister, Pierre Elliott Trudeau.

Domestic Affairs. The year was dominated by two subjects: the constitution and the state of the economy. Prime Minister Pierre Elliott Trudeau pressed ahead with his effort to enact a "made-in-Canada" constitution containing a sweeping charter of rights and freedoms. The policies of his government designed to give direction to an uncertain economy were less decisive. The effect of unprecedented interest rates, high inflation, and worrying unemployment brought criticism from labour, consumers, and homeowners. In spite of these difficulties, Trudeau's position as the head of a majority party in the early years of its term was unchallenged.

The main document in Canada's constitution, the British North America (BNA) Act, was largely written by Canadians but was passed into law by the British Parliament in 1867 while Canada was still a colony. Over the years, the BNA Act was amended many times by the British Parliament acting on the request of the Canadian Parliament.

This arrangement, which suggests the continuance of a colonial status, came to be seen as inappropriate for a sovereign Canada. From 1927 on many attempts were made to define an amending process acceptable to the federal government and the provinces, but all failed to achieve consensus.

In October 1980 Prime Minister Trudeau decided to take the matter into his own hands. He dramatically brought forward a resolution requesting the British Parliament to declare the BNA Act a Canadian act (patriation) and to make it amendable in Canada by a process involving action by the federal legislature and the consent of a majority of the provinces, arranged in regions. A charter of rights, guaranteeing fundamental freedoms to be respected across Canada, was an essential part of the proposal.

Condemned as a unilateral move that did violence to the customary practices of the Canadian federation, Trudeau's proposals were sent for study to a 25-member special committee drawn from the two houses of Parliament. The committee's report, issued on February 13, suggested 65 changes but maintained the essential features of the plan. The opposition New Democratic Party (NDP), with most of its electoral seats in the West, secured a modification confirming provincial control over natural resources. This point gained, it announced its support of Trudeau's proposals. The Progressive Conservatives, under Joseph ("Joe") Clark, fought the measure with a two-week-long filibuster in the Commons in which some 60 points of order were raised. An interparty agreement was finally reached on April 8. More important, the prime minister bowed to Conservative demands that the constitutional resolution be referred to the Supreme Court of Canada.

Of the ten provinces, Ontario and New Brunswick threw their weight behind Trudeau, while six others decided to test the legality of the measure in the courts. The resulting judicial decisions were mixed. The first, from the Manitoba Court of Appeal on February 3, was a 3–2 verdict that upheld the right of the federal government to amend the Canadian constitution unilaterally. On March 31

Canada

Canadian Prime Minister Pierre Elliott Trudeau (left) and other members of Parliament applaud Justice Minister Jean Chrétien after his speech in February at the opening of debate on a Canadian constitution.

Quebec Premier René Lévesque and his wife gave a victory salute to crowds after scoring a large election victory in April.

the Newfoundland Court of Appeal ruled unanimously that Ottawa could not change the constitution without the consent of the provinces. Finally, on April 15, the Quebec Court of Appeal, in a 4–1 decision, stated that Ottawa did not require provincial agreement to send its proposed changes to London. In the end, the three provincial decisions were referred to the Supreme Court.

The eight provinces opposed to Trudeau's constitutional changes met in Ottawa on April 16 to unveil an alternative package. It promised simple patriation with an amending formula that would allow a province to opt out of proposed changes by a majority vote of its legislature. Trudeau and his justice minister, Jean Chrétien, denounced the premiers' plan as "a victory for those who want to move Canada slowly toward disintegration."

Finally, on September 28, the eagerly awaited decision from the Supreme Court was announced. The justices ruled 7–2 that the federal Parliament had the legal power to ask London to patriate the BNA Act. At the same time, they decided, 6–3, that provincial consent was, by convention, necessary for major constitutional change. The distinction between law and convention is not an easy one to

apply, and both parties claimed the judgment as a victory. In a legal sense Trudeau had won, but morally the provinces had been upheld.

Uncertainty and renewed activity followed the court's ruling. Trudeau agreed to a final meeting with the provincial premiers, to be held in Ottawa beginning November 2. For the first two days there seemed no chance of agreement, but on November 5 a compromise emerged. It provided for simple patriation of the BNA Act, together with an amending process based on that suggested by the eight provinces on April 16: constitutional change by approval of the federal Parliament and two-thirds of the provinces (7) containing at least 50% of the national population. The charter of rights was accepted with an important modification: certain parts of it could be overridden within individual provinces by "notwithstanding clauses" passed by their legislatures and renewed every five years. Mobility rights in employment could also be set aside in provinces where job levels were below the national average.

Although Trudeau conceded some valued features of his original plan, his flexibility did not go far enough to satisfy Premier René Lévesque of

CANADA

Education. (1980–81 prelim.) Primary, pupils 3,341,053; secondary, pupils 1,758,021; primary and secondary, teachers 272,271; higher, students 643,-430, teaching staff 53,758.

Finance. Monetary unit: Canadian dollar, with (Sept. 21, 1981) a free rate of Can$1.19 to U.S. $1 (Can$2.21 = £1 sterling). Gold and other reserves (June 1981) U.S. $3,055,000,000. Budget (1980–81 actual): revenue Can$59.9 billion; expenditure Can$67,260,000,000. Gross national product (1980) Can$288.1 billion. Money supply (April 1981) Can$33,370,000,000. Cost of living (1975 = 100; June 1981) 171.

Foreign Trade. (1980) Imports Can$73,057,-000,000; exports Can$79,003,000,000. Import sources: U.S. 70%; Japan 4%. Export destinations: U.S. 63%; Japan 6%. Main exports: motor vehicles 15%; machinery 10%; cereals 7%; crude oil and products 6%; natural gas 6%; nonferrous metals 6%; metal ores 6%; chemicals 6%; wood pulp 5%; newsprint 5%; timber 5%. Tourism (1979) visitors 12,267,000; gross receipts U.S. $2,007,000,000.

Transport and Communications. Roads (1976) 884,273 km. Motor vehicles in use (1978): passenger 9,745,000; commercial 2,717,800. Railways (1979): 67,563 km; traffic 2,760,000,000 passenger-km, freight 221,920,000,000 net ton-km. Air traffic (1980): c. 36,169,000,000 passenger-km; freight 762.2 million net ton-km. Shipping (1980): merchant vessels 100 gross tons and over 1,324; gross tonnage 3,180,126. Shipping traffic (includes Great Lakes and St. Lawrence traffic; 1979): goods loaded 134,639,-000 metric tons, unloaded 67,414,000 metric tons. Telephones (Dec. 1978) 15,059,400. Radio receivers (Dec. 1977) 24.3 million. Television receivers (Dec. 1977) 10 million.

Agriculture. Production (in 000; metric tons; 1980): wheat 19,131; barley 11,041; oats 3,028; rye 448; corn 5,462; potatoes c. 2,523; tomatoes c. 443; apples 500; rapeseed c. 2,430; linseed c. 503; soybeans 653; tobacco c. 113; beef and veal 975; fish catch (1979) 1,332; timber (cu m; 1979) c. 160,348. Livestock (in 000; Dec. 1979): cattle 12,403; sheep 481; pigs 9,688; horses (1978) c. 350; chickens 80,-358.

Industry. Labour force (June 1980) 11,828,000. Unemployment (Dec. 1980) 7.1%. Index of industrial production (1975 = 100; 1980) 116. Fuel and power (in 000; metric tons; 1980): coal 30,581; lignite 5,971; crude oil 70,405; natural gas (cu m) 74,710,-000; electricity (kw-hr) 366,677,000 (69% hydroelectric in 1979 and 8% nuclear in 1977). Metal and mineral production (in 000; metric tons; 1980): iron ore (shipments; 61% metal content) 49,811; crude steel 15,891; copper ore (metal content) 710; nickel ore (metal content; 1978) 130; zinc ore (metal content) 1,059; lead ore (metal content) 297; aluminum (exports; 1979) 860; uranium ore (metal content; 1979) 6.7; asbestos (1978) 1,380; gold (troy oz) 1,-580; silver (troy oz) c. 34,000. Other production (in 000; metric tons; 1980): cement 10,349; wood pulp (1979) 19,530; newsprint 8,625; other paper and paperboard (1977) 3,986; sulfuric acid (1979) 3,686; plastics and resins (1978) c. 1,300; synthetic rubber 251; fertilizers (nutrient value; 1979–80) nitrogenous c. 1,675, phosphate c. 685, potash c. 7,063; passenger cars (units) 847; commercial vehicles (units) 527. Dwelling units completed (1980) 176,000. Merchant vessels launched (100 gross tons and over; 1980) 75,000 gross tons.

Quebec. Alone among the provinces, Quebec rejected the agreement, fearing it would undermine the hope of making Quebec a unilingual (French) community while removing the safeguard it had always claimed of an absolute veto over constitutional change. Trudeau pressed ahead with the resolution, finally securing its passage in the House of Commons by a vote of 246–24 on December 2. Members from all three parties supported the accord establishing a new constitution which, by year's end, had been sent to London for final approval by the British Parliament.

Joe Clark, leader of the Progressive Conservative Party since 1976 and prime minister during the short-lived Conservative administration of June 1979–March 1980, received the support of only 66% of party delegates attending a convention in Ottawa on February 27. His poor showing reflected unhappiness among party members over his part in the 1980 electoral defeat, as well as the feeling that he should be replaced by a leader with stronger personal appeal.

The governing Liberal Party held onto three of five vacant Commons seats in 1981, saw a Quebec riding remain with the Conservatives, and lost a supposedly safe seat in Toronto to the NDP. The results of the by-elections left party standings in the 282-seat House of Commons as follows: Liberals 147; Progressive Conservatives 102; NDP 33.

Four provinces went to the polls in 1981. The most important contest was in Quebec, where Premier Lévesque led his separatist Parti Québécois (PQ) back into office on April 13. In spite of having lost 11 consecutive by-elections in its first four and a half years of power, the PQ won 80 of the 122 seats in the assembly, a gain of 13 from its previous standing. The Liberals took the remaining 42 seats. Lévesque dropped his goal of sovereignty-association for the election, campaigning instead on his party's record of competent, honest government. Ontario gave its 38-year-old Conservative administration, led by William Davis (see BIOGRAPHIES) since 1971, a majority position in an election on March 19. The Conservatives captured 70 seats in the legislature, their opponents 55. The victory reflected voter confidence in the middle ground position occupied by the Davis government. Nova Scotia had a general election on October 6, when Premier John Buchanan's Con-

servative government, seeking a stronger mandate, won 38 of the 52 seats in the legislature. In office since September 1978, the Buchanan government capitalized on the optimism regarding offshore resource development in the Atlantic area. An election in Manitoba on November 17 saw Premier Sterling Lyon's four-year-old Conservative administration soundly defeated by the NDP under Howard Pawley. The NDP captured 33 of the 57 seats in the legislature, the Conservatives 24. The Lyon government probably fell because of voter unhappiness over the depressed state of Manitoba's economy.

The Economy. The economy expanded with surprising strength in the first two quarters of 1981, then subsided and stagnated for the rest of the year. Gross national product was expected to reach Can\$324.1 billion on an annual basis, representing a rate of real growth over the year of about 3.5%. Exports were generally strong, as were retail sales and business investment. There was much public concern about high interest rates. The Bank of Canada's lending rate, based on the interest paid in the weekly auction of treasury bills, topped 21% in late August, a record for Canada, then declined sharply by November. The effect of high loan rates was felt over the entire economy, choking demand and dealing a devastating blow to the housing market. On August 4 the Canadian dollar fell to 80.4 U.S. cents, the lowest in 50 years. For most of 1981 it hovered between this figure and 84 U.S. cents. Inflation continued at the highest point since the years immediately after World War II, running around 13%. The unemployment rates also recalled 1945 figures, standing at 8.3% overall in October but with considerable variation across the country.

The most encouraging economic news was the resolution of the one-and-a-half-year stalemate between the federal government and the province of Alberta over oil prices and the sharing of petroleum revenues. An agreement signed in Ottawa on September 1 by Trudeau and Premier Peter Lougheed (see BIOGRAPHIES) of Alberta gave Alberta most of what it had wanted: a price close to the world level for new oil and a large share of energy revenues. Over the next five years Canadian consumers would pay an additional \$32 billion for oil, with both Alberta and Ottawa taking more

Plans for an economic summit conference to be held in Ottawa in July were discussed at a meeting between Canadian Prime Minister Pierre Elliott Trudeau (left) and French Pres. François Mitterrand.

WIDE WORLD

in taxes and royalties. The industry's share of income was to be reduced, but because of a two-tier, old-new oil pricing agreement, it would actually receive more income than before. Ottawa agreed to drop, at least temporarily, a controversial export tax on natural gas, and both governments promised to work toward the start-up of new projects to recover petroleum from the oil sands of northern Alberta.

The Trudeau government's continued reliance on high interest rates and a tough fiscal policy to combat inflation was revealed in Finance Minister Allan MacEachen's budget on November 12. MacEachen promised to reduce the federal deficit from its current $13.3 billion figure to $10.5 billion in 1982–83 by cutting federal transfer payments to the provinces and other expenditures. The budget closed or changed 11 personal tax loopholes while lowering federal tax rates slightly. It gave help to homeowners facing high mortgage renewal charges and to farmers in distress because of the high cost of borrowing. It contained no measures affecting future U.S. investment in Canada, nor were there policies directed at the problem of growing unemployment.

Foreign Affairs. The most important event of the year for Canada was the economic summit conference, held at a large resort hotel on the edge of the Laurentian Mountains about 64 km (40 mi) east of Ottawa. The seventh in the series that began in France in 1975, the conference on July 20 and 21 was attended by the leaders of the seven major industrial democracies and the president of the Commission of the European Communities. Trudeau devoted considerable effort before the meeting to ensuring a thorough discussion of North-South issues: food supplies, trade rules, international financial arrangements, energy, commodity markets. The result was a tentative commitment to explore the possibility of global negotiations on these issues. To prepare the ground for consideration of the rich nation-poor nation agenda, Trudeau made three trips across the Atlantic and two to Washington before the July summit.

In August Trudeau and his three sons visited East Africa on a combined official trip and holiday. The prime minister addressed a UN Conference on New and Renewable Sources of Energy in Kenya, promising $40 million in additional Canadian funds to support research into energy sources for less developed countries. From September 30 to October 7 he was in Melbourne, Australia, for the Commonwealth heads of government meeting. Finally, on October 22 and 23, he traveled to Cancún, Mexico, for the 22-nation International Meeting on Co-operation and Development, called in an attempt to ease tensions building up in the international system over perceived economic injustices. On the eve of the meeting Trudeau's efforts to promote the North-South dialogue were recognized when he was invited to share the chairmanship of the conference with Pres. José López Portillo of Mexico in the absence, through illness, of Chancellor Bruno Kreisky of Austria.

In other developments, Canada sold a second Candu nuclear reactor to Romania for electrical power generation, reached an agreement with Cuba on compensation to Canadians who lost assets in that country following the Castro revolution in 1959, received Japan's agreement that auto exports to Canada would be voluntarily reduced by 6% during the 1981–82 fiscal year, and concluded a major grain sale to the Soviet Union (25 million metric tons over five years).

A number of irritations, some of them deriving from Canada's nationalistic energy and investment policies, disturbed the relationship with the U.S. in 1981. The Trudeau government's national energy policy, unveiled in 1980, sought to increase the current 25% Canadian control of the country's oil and gas industry to 50% by 1990 and provided incentives for Canadian companies in the exploration and development of energy sources. During the year there were several takeovers of U.S. oil companies by Canadian firms in pursuit of this goal. (*See* Special Report.)

U.S. officials labeled the Canadian policies unfair and discriminatory, and a number of proposals for retaliation were studied in Congress. These included prohibiting Canadian companies from participating in mineral leases on U.S. federal land and requiring Canadian companies taking over U.S. companies to abide by the same Federal Reserve Board margin rules as U.S. corporations. In July Finance Minister MacEachen asked Canadian chartered banks to restrict the availability of funds for foreign takeovers to their Canadian customers.

Canada's response to the U.S. criticism was to deny that the changes in the rules for investment were discriminatory. No U.S. firms were being nationalized or forced to sell their Canadian assets. Canada wished to correct an untenable situation in which the degree of foreign control over vital sectors of its economy was far more than the U.S. would have tolerated.

Fisheries were another area of disagreement in 1981. Two linked treaties, signed in 1979 for the management of fish stocks and the definition of maritime boundaries in the Georges Bank and Gulf of Maine areas on the Atlantic coast, were uncoupled by the U.S. The first was withdrawn by the Reagan administration; the second was approved in the Senate on April 29, sending the boundary dispute to binding arbitration by a panel of the World Court. Conservation of the valuable fish stocks in the Gulf of Maine, threatened by overfishing, remained an urgent problem.

Acid rain pollution, the result of emissions of sulfur dioxide into the atmosphere, constituted an acute environmental problem for the two countries. Responsibility was shared equally, and there were calls in each country for tougher action to control emissions.

Pres. Ronald Reagan made his first state visit outside the U.S. to Ottawa on March 10 and 11, where he discussed bilateral issues such as fisheries and pollution with Prime Minister Trudeau. The North American Aerospace Defense Command (Norad) was renewed on this occasion for an additional five years. Its new name (Aerospace in place of Air) reflected the fact that it now watched the skies for missiles and satellites as well as for enemy aircraft. (D. M. L. FARR)

THE RAGING ENERGY WAR

by Peter Ward

When Canada's energy minister, Marc Lalonde, had his national energy policy introduced in Parliament on Oct. 28, 1980, he put in train a series of events that would dominate the economic and political life of the nation throughout 1981 and possibly for several decades. So sweeping were the aims of Lalonde's blueprint for Canada's energy future that Price-Waterhouse, one of Canada's leading chartered accountant firms, said in a detailed analysis: "The overall program is mammoth both in terms of dollars and in its impact on Canada's energy industries. It represents a very substantial change in the tax and regulatory climate of the oil and gas sector and will affect Canadians in every walk of life for years to come."

Lalonde's energy policy put the federal government almost on a war footing with the energy-producing provinces, the oil companies, and the new administration of Pres. Ronald Reagan in the U.S. It caused the exodus of billions of investment dollars from Canada, the departure of thousands of petroleum industry experts, and the flight of hundreds of oil- and gas-exploration rigs. It also increased Canadian control over the crucial oil industry, traditionally dominated by foreign interests, and vastly strengthened the power of the central government in Ottawa at the expense of the provincial governments. It sent the stalled Canadian economy into a tailspin, contributed to a dramatic reduction in the value of the Canadian dollar, and helped push the interest rate banks charged their best customers to a record 22.75%, while other interest rates rose correspondingly.

Oil Politics, Canadian Style. The energy policy was aimed at giving Canadians control of a domestic oil and gas industry that was 71% owned by foreign interests, bringing energy self-sufficiency to Canada by 1990, and establishing an energy pricing scale that would enlarge the federal share of revenue from oil and natural gas. By Canadian constitutional law, resources belong to the provinces. Escalation of en-

Peter Ward operates Ward News Services Canada in the Parliamentary Press Gallery, Ottawa.

ergy prices during the 1970s had created a bonanza for the provinces with oil and gas resources, dramatically changing Canada's regional wealth patterns in favour of the western petroleum-rich provinces of Alberta, British Columbia, and Saskatchewan. The central government, controlled politically by the two populous provinces of Ontario and Quebec, sought through the national energy policy to increase central control over the economy. But the western provinces were suspicious of the federal claim that such actions would be in the overall Canadian interest.

Taxation and incentive provisions of the energy policy were designed to encourage exploration for new oil and natural gas in areas controlled solely by the federal government—the Yukon and Northwest territories and seabed regions offshore. In these federal areas, the national oil company, Petro-Canada, automatically obtained a 25% interest in any petroleum finds, and there was no bothersome conflict with provincial governments over revenue sharing. The federal share of revenue from all oil and gas production was to be increased considerably. Canadian-controlled companies would get a far better tax break than foreign-controlled companies.

Alberta, the chief energy-producing province, reacted with anger and muscle, warning Ottawa that the new energy policy would destroy the industry in Alberta. It also claimed that the federal government had no right to impose the tax on exported natural gas that had been proposed as part of the new policy and was shortly enacted into law. Alberta Premier Peter Lougheed decreed that his province would cut back oil production by 180,000 bbl a day in three stages, as a protest. Lougheed also refused to give the necessary approval to begin construction of two plants for extracting heavy oil from tar sands.

Ottawa had long insisted on keeping the price of oil in Canada lower than the world price—Can$18.75 per barrel, as opposed to Can$40 per barrel on the world market. Canada imports roughly 400,000 bbl of foreign oil daily, and the federal government pays a subsidy to make up the difference. Alberta's production cutbacks meant that Canada had to import more oil and pay heavier subsidies. Oil taxes were imposed to raise money for the subsidies, and additional taxes were put on oil to pay for government takeovers of foreign oil interests. By the fall of 1981, the effective Canadian price of oil was more than Can$28 a barrel.

Politically, high-priced oil proved dangerous for Prime Minister Pierre Elliott Trudeau, whose Liberal Party had defeated Joe Clark's Conservative government in February 1980 largely on the basis of a promise to keep oil prices down. Trudeau claimed that Lalonde's energy policy would meet that

On September 1 a news conference was called to announce an agreement on the pricing of Canadian oil; (from left) Alberta Energy Minister Merv Leitch, Alberta Premier Peter Lougheed, Prime Minister Pierre Trudeau, and federal Energy Minister Marc Lalonde.

pledge, benefiting the energy-consuming provinces of Ontario and Quebec the most.

An Economy in Retreat. The fight between east and west, producers and consumers, pinched the revenue of the oil and gas industry so badly that in the first nine months of 1981, 200 oil-exploration rigs left Canada to drill in the U.S., where controls were being dismantled. Foreign-controlled oil companies—most of them U.S.—were being forced to sell to Canadians at fire-sale prices because they faced much more onerous taxation schedules than Canadian-owned companies.

In the year following announcement of the national energy policy, an estimated Can$14 billion was spent buying out foreign-controlled oil companies. The lion's share of the new controlling interest went to Petro-Canada, and critics began to charge that Lalonde's program was really a drive to give the federal government—not just Canadians—control of the industry. At the same time, Washington, upset at the punishment U.S. investors were taking, began to threaten retaliatory action. By Sept. 1, 1981, 35% of the oil and gas industry was Canadian-controlled, and Lalonde said that 50% Canadian control could easily be achieved by 1985.

Before long, however, the slowdown in the Alberta-Saskatchewan-British Columbia oil and gas industry began to pinch Ontario and Quebec deeply, just as Premier Lougheed had predicted. Jobs in the vital service and drilling-equipment industries were being sacrificed to the federal program, and criticism mounted.

The cost to Canada's economy grew almost by the week. Dollars that might have been used for new investment went to buy control of foreign companies or fled the country. Massive Canadian schemes, like the two Alberta oil sands plants, were scrapped or postponed. The Canadian dollar plunged to 80.4 U.S. cents, its lowest value in 50 years, and interest rates hit record highs, virtually halting the housing and construction industry. Canada ran its foreign reserves to a record low defending its troubled dollar. Inflation reached 13%.

A Skirmish, Not the War. In the face of these developments, Trudeau came under increasing pressure from within his own Liberal Party to modify his policies. On Aug. 17, 1981, Liberals lost two key by-elections called to fill vacant parliamentary seats —one to the Conservatives and one to the left-wing New Democrats. Gallup Polls indicated that Trudeau would be defeated if he had to face an election. Circumstances and politics had given Alberta an extremely strong bargaining position.

On September 1, after more than a year of sporadic bargaining, Ottawa capitulated to Alberta's oil and gas pricing demands, accepting the dictum that Canadian energy prices must move more rapidly toward world prices. The five-and-a-quarter-year pricing agreement that resulted would pour rivers of revenue into the coffers of Ottawa, Alberta, and the oil industry and cost Canadian consumers Can$212.8 billion. Alberta also forced the federal government to modify some of the discriminatory measures against petroleum companies exploring in provincial, rather than federal, lands. But Alberta won only a preliminary battle, not the war.

Ottawa appeared to have no intention of retreating from its basic goal of greater federal control over the oil and gas industry. Indeed, indications were that the Trudeau government intended to expand its influence in other sectors of the economy as well. Several announcements of programs to promote economic nationalism were made late in 1981. The national energy policy, which caused considerable hardship to all Canadians during 1981, could be merely the leading edge of a series of policies designed to give the central government far greater control over the entire Canadian economy.

Cape Verde

An independent African republic, Cape Verde is located in the Atlantic Ocean about 620 km (385 mi) off the west coast of Africa. Area: 4,033 sq km (1,557 sq mi). Pop. (1980 prelim.): 296,100. Cap. and largest city: Praia (pop., 1980 prelim., 36,600). Language: Portuguese. Religion: 91% Roman Catholic. President in 1981, Aristide Pereira; premier, Pedro Pires.

The government of Cape Verde condemned the coup that took place in Guinea-Bissau in November 1980, and the policy of unity between the two countries was abandoned. On Jan. 19, 1981, Cape Verde decided to leave the joint African Party for the Independence of Guinea-Bissau and Cape Verde (PAIGC) and form its own African Party for the Independence of Cape Verde (PAICV). In February the National Assembly approved a new constitution that formalized the split from Guinea-Bissau. It also returned Pres. Aristide Pereira for another term of office.

The economy continued its slow recovery. The 1981 budget set aside $84 million for investment, with transport and communications receiving the highest priority. Almost two-thirds of investment funds came from overseas. Emigration was down to one-third of pre-independence levels. Unemployment figures fell, and the food supply improved. Emphasis was placed on the development of agriculture and on fishing, which accounted for 70% of export earnings.

Although 1981 was dominated by the break with Guinea-Bissau, the two countries, together with Mali, joined forces to oppose the establishment of a defense pact by the Economic Community of West African States (ECOWAS).

(GUY ARNOLD)

CAPE VERDE
Education. (1978–79) Primary, pupils 46,539, teachers 1,431; secondary, pupils 6,607, teachers 220; vocational, pupils 474, teachers (1977–78) 43; teacher training (1977–78), pupils 198, teachers (1976–77) 32.

Finance and Trade. Monetary unit: Cape Verde escudo, with (June 30, 1981) a free rate of 50 escudos to U.S. $1 (96.50 escudos = £1 sterling). Budget (1979 est.) balanced at 1,327,000,000 escudos. Foreign trade (1976): imports 911.4 million escudos; exports 48,030,000 escudos (excluding transit trade). Import sources: Portugal 58%; The Netherlands 5%. Export destinations: Portugal 63%; Angola 14%; Zaire 5%; U.K. 5%. Main exports: fish 29% (including shellfish 16%); bananas 19%; salt 9%.

Transport. Shipping traffic (1977): goods loaded 27,000 metric tons, unloaded 195,000 metric tons.

Central African Republic

The landlocked Central African Republic is bounded by Chad, the Sudan, the Congo, Zaire, and Cameroon. Area: 622,436 sq km (240,324 sq mi). Pop. (1980 est.): 2,362,400. Cap. and largest city: Bangui (pop., 1979 est., 362,700). Language: French (official), local dialects. Religion: animist 60%; Christian 35%; Muslim 5%. President until Sept. 1, 1981, David Dacko; premiers, Jean-Pierre

Pres. David Dacko, who was elected to a new term in March, was overthrown in September after a state of siege had been declared.

Lebouder and, from April 4 until September 1, Simon Narcisse Bozanga; head of state and chairman of the Military Committee of National Recovery from September 1, Gen. André Kolingba.

On Sept. 1, 1981, Gen. André Kolingba (*see* BIOGRAPHIES) replaced Pres. David Dacko as head of state and set up a Military Committee of National Recovery. Circumstances surrounding the bloodless takeover were confused, but it seemed to have been achieved with Dacko's acquiescence, perhaps at his request. It put an end to political tension that had been mounting throughout the year. French forces stationed in the country since the deposition of the former emperor, Bokassa I, were not involved.

CENTRAL AFRICAN REPUBLIC
Education. (1977–78) Primary, pupils 241,201, teachers 3,690; secondary, pupils 46,084, teachers 462; vocational, pupils 2,523, teachers 128; teacher training (1976–77), students 522, teachers 47; higher, students 972, teaching staff 185.

Finance. Monetary unit: CFA franc, with (Sept. 21, 1981) a parity of CFA Fr 50 to the French franc and a free rate of CFA Fr 265 to U.S. $1 (CFA Fr 491 = £1 sterling). Budget (total; 1980 est.) balanced at CFA Fr 25,447,000,000.

Foreign Trade. (1979) Imports CFA Fr 14,816,000,000; exports CFA Fr 16,937,000,000. Import sources: France 63%; U.S. 5%. Export destinations: France 46%; Belgium-Luxembourg 21%; Israel 11%; U.S. 8%. Main exports: diamonds 44%; coffee 25%; timber 12%; cotton 7%.

Agriculture. Production (in 000; metric tons; 1980): millet *c.* 50; corn (1979) *c.* 40; sweet potatoes (1979) *c.* 60; cassava (1979) *c.* 940; peanuts *c.* 127; bananas *c.* 78; plantains (1979) *c.* 63; coffee *c.* 11; cotton, lint *c.* 14. Livestock (in 000; 1979): cattle *c.* 670; pigs *c.* 128; sheep *c.* 80; goats *c.* 780; chickens *c.* 1,433.

Industry. Production (in 000; 1978): electricity (kw-hr) 60,000; diamonds (metric carats) 284; cotton fabrics (m) 3,000.

Cape Verde

Central African Republic

Catholic Church: *see* Religion

Cave Exploration: *see* Speleology

Census Data: *see* Demography; *see also the individual country articles; U.S. census data beginning on page 142*

Following a referendum in February that gave approval to a French-type presidential constitution, elections on March 15 had narrowly confirmed Dacko as president with 50.23% of the votes. Violent demonstrations after the election led to the proclamation of a state of siege, which was not lifted until August 16. On April 4 Simon Narcisse Bozanga replaced Jean-Pierre Lebouder as premier. Following an announcement on May 9 that legislative and municipal elections would be deferred until 1982, the political situation deteriorated progressively, with strikes and further violence occurring against a background of economic crisis.

On January 24 six associates of Bokassa were executed. Bokassa himself, sentenced to death in absentia on Dec. 24, 1980, was living in the Ivory Coast. His former palace was featured as a tourist attraction. (PHILIPPE DECRAENE)

Chad

Refugees fled from Chad into Cameroon after a bloody civil war intensified in Chad in February.

Chad

A landlocked republic of central Africa, Chad is bounded by Libya, the Sudan, the Central African Republic, Cameroon, Nigeria, and Niger. Area: 1,284,000 sq km (495,755 sq mi). Pop. (1981 est.): 4,636,000, including Saras, other Africans, and Arabs. Cap. and largest city: N'Djamena (pop., 1979 est., 303,000). Language: French (official). Religion: Muslim 45%; animist 45%; Christian 10%. President in 1981, Goukouni Oueddei.

In a new swing of the pendulum in Chad's continuing internal conflict, Libyan troops brought in at Pres. Goukouni Oueddei's request in December 1980 were withdrawn, again at his request, in November 1981. In a reverse movement the Armed Forces of the North of Hissen Habré, which had retreated into Sudan in December 1980, reoccupied all the important towns in eastern Chad in November 1981.

ARTAULT—GAMMA/LIAISON

CHAD

Education. (1976–77) Primary, pupils 210,882, teachers c. 2,610; secondary, pupils 18,382, teachers 590; vocational, pupils 649, teachers (1965–66) 30; teacher training, students 549, teachers (1973–74) 26; higher, students 758, teaching staff 62.

Finance. Monetary unit: CFA franc, with (Sept. 21, 1981) a parity of CFA Fr 50 to the French franc and a free rate of CFA Fr 265 to U.S. $1 (CFA Fr 491 = £1 sterling). Budget (total; 1978 est.) balanced at CFA Fr 17,084,000,000.

Foreign Trade. (1976) Imports CFA Fr 28,111,000,000; exports CFA Fr 14,861,000,000. Import sources (1976): France 46%; Nigeria c. 22%; Cameroon c. 5%; Netherlands Antilles c. 5%. Export destinations (1976): Nigeria c. 19%; Japan c. 14%; France c. 13%; West Germany c. 13%; Spain c. 11%. Main exports (1975): cotton 66%; petroleum products 8%; beef and veal 7%.

Agriculture. Production (in 000; metric tons; 1980): millet c. 600; sweet potatoes (1979) c. 34; cassava (1979) c. 180; peanuts c. 85; beans, dry c. 40; dates c. 25; mangoes c. 30; cotton, lint c. 46; meat c. 50; fish catch (1979) c. 115. Livestock (in 000; 1979): horses c. 154; asses c. 271; camels c. 410; cattle c. 4,070; sheep c. 2,278; goats c. 2,278.

On January 6, following a visit by Oueddei to Tripoli, Chad and Libya announced their intention to unite. Though in N'Djamena the significance of this was played down, France immediately condemned the agreement as "revealing ambitions that menace African security." The French military presence in central Africa was reinforced, with men and matériel being sent to the Central African Republic and aircraft to Gabon. At a meeting of 12 heads of state of the Organization of African Unity (OAU) at Lomé, Togo, on January 14, Nigeria, despite its opposition to French African policy, took the lead in condemning the proposed union.

In the face of concerted African disapproval, Libya on several occasions expressed its willingness to leave Chad, but it was not until early November that the withdrawal was completed. Several factors may have influenced Libya's decision: the wish to end involvement in what had become less a conflict between Chad's Muslim northern and black southern regions and more a struggle between northern political factions; the need for an improved Libyan image at the 1982 OAU summit conference in Tripoli; and the new French government's decision to give full logistic and other aid to Oueddei's Transitional Government of National Union (GUNT). Whatever the reason, at the Franco-African summit in Paris on November 3–4, Libya's withdrawal was seen as a victory for France and its African partners. However, despite the arrival of an OAU peacekeeping force composed of troops from Nigeria, Senegal, and Zaire, the threat of continued civil war remained. Habré resumed his offensive and Acyl Ahmat, the GUNT foreign minister, openly opposed Oueddei. (PHILIPPE DECRAENE)

Chemistry

Ingenious organic syntheses, development of an all-plastic battery, and increasing automation in laboratory operations were among noteworthy features of 1981. Chemists also played a role in developing alternative sources of energy, in better

understanding how fluoride prevents tooth decay, and in ensuring the safety of the space shuttle "Columbia" after its historic first landing.

Organic Chemistry. Recognition of a fundamental advance in understanding how compounds react led to the award of the 1981 Nobel Prize for Chemistry in October to Roald Hoffmann of Cornell University, Ithaca, N.Y., and Kenichi Fukui of Kyoto University in Japan (*see* NOBEL PRIZES). Their independent theories of the way in which electronic orbitals around atomic nuclei overlap and interact have allowed organic chemists to design new syntheses and make accurate predictions of reaction outcomes. Among recent syntheses that benefited from these fundamental theories was that of the naturally occurring antileukemic agent maytansine (1), regarded by some as the most complex natural product to be synthesized after vitamin B_{12}. Another was of aklavinone, a key portion of another anticancer agent, aclacinomycin A. Yoshito Kishi and his group at Harvard played a key role in the final stages of a 50-man project leading to an ingenious synthesis for the well-known antibiotic erythromycin. This work had been started by Nobel laureate Robert B. Woodward (d. 1979), Hoffmann's collaborator in the famous Woodward-Hoffmann theory.

Research progressed on other chemicals with pharmaceutical applications, and syntheses were increasingly supplemented by techniques involving enzymes, microorganisms, cell cultures, or genetic engineering. Announcements came from Merck Sharp and Dohme, West Point, Pa., of the development of a new class of drugs for curing hypertension; from Beecham Pharmaceuticals, in the U.K., of an exciting antibiotic called Augmentin, based on ampicillin; and from the Wellcome

A breakthrough in polymer chemistry led to the development of a rechargeable plastic battery that developers say can deliver more energy per unit weight than conventional lead-acid storage batteries.

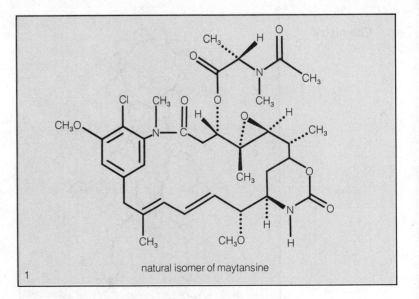

natural isomer of maytansine

1

Research Laboratory, London, of 4'6-dichloroflavan, claimed to be the most potent antiviral compound yet reported and to have great potential for treating the common cold.

Organic chemists from West Germany and the U.S. made news by overturning the textbook rule that there are only 20 kinds of amino acids in the proteins of living organisms. Two previously unknown amino acids were discovered: one, from animal ribonucleoprotein, called amino citric acid (2) and the other, from bacteria, known as β-carboxyaspartic acid (3). The biological functions of these new discoveries, how they are made in cells, and their distribution in living systems would be keen topics of future biochemical research. Among structurally interesting compounds found were tetraphenyl squaramidine, amusingly nicknamed the "man-on-the-Moon molecule" (4), and spiropentene, a molecular bow tie (5).

Polymer science also surged forward on many fronts. One new polymer was employed as an adhesive for an insulating blanket on space probes, and another was used as a membrane to replace the skin of badly burned patients. Also of interest was the highly novel synthesis of polyhydroxybutyrate by Imperial Chemical Industries, Ltd. (ICI) in England, based on a bacterial fermentation process, which opened the way to an alternative to oil-derived plastics. Perhaps most

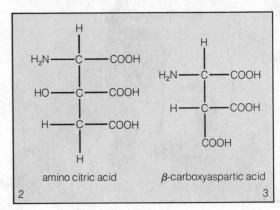

amino citric acid   β-carboxyaspartic acid

2   3

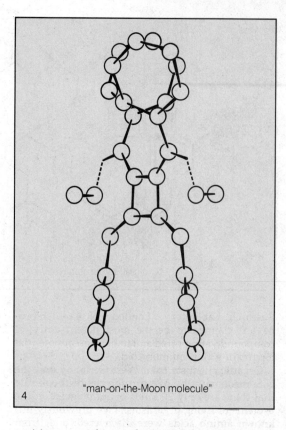

"man-on-the-Moon molecule"

4

Scientists at Bell Laboratories investigated a liquid-junction solar cell that can convert 11.5% of the sunlight striking it into electricity, making it competitive with single-crystal solid-state devices commonly in use.

exciting were the revolutionary developments in the field of "organic metals," polymers selectively made impure (doped) to give them some of the electrical properties of metals. The simple organic polymer polyacetylene was the key component of the first plastic battery. Designed by Alan G. MacDiarmid and Alan J. Heeger at the University of Pennsylvania, the rechargeable battery was made from two oppositely charged doped polyacetylene films in a suitable electrolyte (*e.g.*, tetrabutyl-ammonium perchlorate in propylene carbonate) and could generate as much as 3.7 volts and 20 milliamperes per square centimetre of film. Experts believed that such lightweight nonmetallic batteries

would be ideal for powering electric automobiles or in homes for storing off-peak electricity for later use.

Inorganic Chemistry. Inorganic complexes attracted increased interest from medical scientists. In the field of medical imaging, for example, radiologists were using injections of a complex of radioactive thallium-201 to provide information on the living heart, but this element had several drawbacks, including expense and low photon energy. A new material, developed by researchers at the University of Cincinnati and the U.S. Food and Drug Administration's Bureau of Radiological Health, is a water-soluble and nontoxic complex of the artificial element technetium. Like its thallium predecessor the new complex accumulates in heart tissue, emitting gamma rays that can be used to construct a diagnostically useful image of the heart.

Water retained its attraction for scientists as they sought to understand more of its structure, chemistry, solvent properties, and its role in living systems. A new theory of water structure, proposed by Martyn Symons at the University of Leicester in the U.K., gave persuading nonmathematical evidence that the so-called anomalous behaviour of water was something that could be expected and predicted. A physicist from the same university, John Enderby, together with collaborators at the University of Bristol, used one of the most intense neutron sources in the world to resolve a controversy about water that had been debated since the 19th century. The question was whether the ions of sodium (Na^+) and chlorine (Cl^-) that form when common salt ($NaCl$) is dissolved in water affect each other in solution. The researchers used the neutron diffraction patterns of salt solutions to show that water molecules clustered around the charged ions, insulating them from each other and making them essentially independent entities. The work should lead to a much-simplified theory of solutions.

The investigation of reaction mechanisms gained impetus, especially in the field of organometallic chemistry. Of more practical importance, however, was a study by Dhanpat Rai and collaborators at Pacific Northwest Laboratory in Washington State, who explained how solutions containing compounds of plutonium-238 and -239 could change chemically over several months, becoming more corrosive and more capable of degrading and leaching through nuclear waste containers.

Work by Gobinda C. Maiti and Friedemann Freund of the University of Cologne, West Germany, on the bonelike minerals hydroxyapatite and hydroxyfluoroapatite gave clues to the mechanism by which fluoride ions in the latter act as a barrier to acid attack. Their study could lead to a better understanding of the way in which fluoride reduces tooth decay.

Physical Chemistry. Interest in photochemistry, particularly with respect to solar energy, blossomed during the year. Adam Heller and Barry Miller of Bell Laboratories, Murray Hill, N.J., made headlines with specially developed photocathodes that could generate electricity from

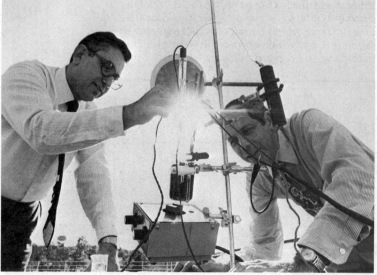

COURTESY, BELL LABORATORIES

sunlight with an efficiency of 11.5%. Research groups in Western Europe announced successes in decomposing water into its elements with light; among them were those from the Institut le Bel, Strasbourg, France, and the École Polytechnique Fédérale in Lausanne, Switz. Leading the Swiss group was Michael Grätzel, who later in the year reported a sunlight-driven system to split hydrogen sulfide, a process that could provide a handy alternative to present expensive and inadequate methods of removing this gas from oil refinery emissions and industrial effluents.

Spectroscopy, the study of electromagnetic radiation absorbed or emitted by matter, maintained its central role as an invaluable tool not only in chemistry but in astronomy, physics, and biology as well. Infrared spectra provided the cornerstone for a highly controversial theory by Fred Hoyle and Chandra Wickramasinghe of University College, Cardiff, Wales, who proposed that the spectra pointed to the existence of such biologically produced molecules as cellulose in the dust grains that litter interstellar space. From this conclusion and other studies they further speculated that living cells first arose in space. Support for the possibility of molecules of life in space also came from Mayo Greenberg of the University of Leiden in The Netherlands, who simulated in his laboratory the passage of a frozen mixture of simple interstellar gases near a star and confirmed the existence of complex molecules in the final product. Despite these studies, researchers were still having no success in finding glycine, the most primitive amino acid, in the space between the stars.

Many techniques previously used by chemists alone gained ground in the life sciences. Nuclear magnetic resonance (NMR) spectroscopy, for example, was finding increasing success in the study of proteins. Eric Oldfield at the University of Illinois, Urbana-Champaign, oriented samples in a magnetic field to help in the study of the structure and dynamics of such proteins as myoglobin. The technique provided information previously impossible to obtain even by X-ray crystallography.

Other noteworthy topics were the discovery of superconducting organic crystals that could be promising alternatives to metal alloys, the successful engineering of a system of oscillating chemical reactions that mirrored many biological activities, and the revelation that the magnetic field of simple stirring devices commonly used by chemists could affect the products of certain polymerization reactions.

Analytical Chemistry. Increasingly stringent regulations relating to foods, drugs, energy use,

pollution control, and worker safety continued to stimulate interest in new analytical methods, instruments, and techniques, as witnessed by the 17,000-strong attendance at the Pittsburgh Conference on Analytical Chemistry and Applied Spectroscopy held in Atlantic City, N.J., in March.

Computers became more commonplace in automating sampling of test materials, running analyses, and processing results. New programs were developed for training analysts at the console, matching analytical results to data banks of spectra on known compounds, and helping users resolve instrument faults. One major analytical-instrument manufacturer announced a computerized system for managing all laboratory operations, from organizing the workloads on instruments to producing reports, doing the bookkeeping, and advising when instruments need maintenance.

Mass spectrometry enjoyed a renaissance as it evolved to cope with an expanding range of analytical problems and increasingly large molecules, especially biomolecules. In one study Ronald D. Macfarlane and Catherine J. McNeal of Texas A&M University, College Station, used mass spectrometry to characterize an 18-base-long nucleotide sequence in DNA. Reflecting recent emphasis on methods in which the ionization of the sample is less vigorous, a new technique for mass spectrometry called fast atom bombardment, developed by Michael Barber and co-workers of the University of Manchester in England, generated much excitement throughout the analytical world. Unlike previous methods, this technique could be applied to nonvolatile samples and was used successfully for analyzing drugs and complex biological materials.

Among notable studies performed by analytical chemists were the month-long investigation by the U.S. Department of Justice laboratories to analyze China White, a deadly synthetic substitute for heroin, and efforts by Israeli chemists in unraveling the mechanism by which the Dead Sea Scrolls had partly deteriorated. One analysis was watched by millions of television viewers worldwide on April 14. Within seconds of the landing of the U.S. space shuttle "Columbia," a space-suited group of analysts began using a specially developed mobile infrared analyzer to check the orbiter for potentially explosive fumes. Less than ten minutes later the homecoming celebrations began in safety. (GORDON WILKINSON)

See also Materials Sciences; Nobel Prizes.
[111.A.1.e; 121.B.1.e; 122.A.6; 122.E.1.u; 123.D,G,H; 124.D.4.b; 321.B.3.a.i; 723.F.4]

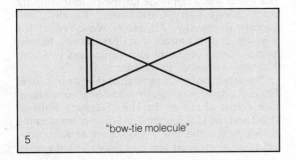

"bow-tie molecule"

5

Chess

The year 1981 was dominated by the rivalry between the world champion, Anatoly Karpov, and his challenger, Viktor Korchnoi. As prelude to their contest, Korchnoi in late 1980 and early 1981 defeated Robert Hübner of West Germany in the final match of the Candidates series at Merano, Italy, 4½–3½. During the same period Ralf Akesson (Sweden) won the European junior championship at Groningen, Neth. In the 48th Soviet cham-

pionship, Lev Psakhis and Aleksandr Beljavsky tied for first place. The Swedish grand master Ulf Andersson won the Hastings International Tournament.

In February Karpov won the Chess Oscar for the seventh time. Korchnoi was ranked second and Harry Kasparov of the U.S.S.R., third. The play-off for the British championship was won by John Nunn, who defeated William Hartston in a match in London. An intercontinental tournament at Mar del Plata, Arg., was won by Europe, which defeated the Americas 19½–12½. The first international tournament to be held in China was won by Robert Bellin of the U.K. ahead of I. M. Liang of China. Korchnoi was first at the Banco di Roma tournament, 2½ points ahead of the field. In March Mikhail Tal of the Soviet Union won the Keres Memorial Tournament in Tallinn, Estonia. Lubomir Kavalek of the U.S. was first in a tournament at Brasília, Brazil. Oxford won the university match against Cambridge 6–2. Kavalek won a competition at Bochum, West Germany, in March–April, and Psakhis was first at Sarajevo, Yugos.

Korchnoi had an outstanding victory at Bad Kissingen, West Germany, in a tournament extending from April into May, with 9 points out of 10, 3 points ahead of the field. Not to be outdone, Karpov, playing at Moscow in the strongest tournament of the year, finished first 1½ points ahead of the 18-year-old Kasparov, Lev Polugayevsky, and Vassily Smyslov, who finished in a three-way tie for second. Later in the year Karpov suffered one of his rare semifailures when he tied for second in a tournament with Lajos Portisch of Hungary, one-half point behind Jan Timman of The Netherlands.

Tal shared first prize with fellow countryman Oleg Romanishin at Lvov, U.S.S.R., in June. Boris Gulko of the Soviet Union, who had disappeared from the chess scene when he applied for an exit visa to go to Israel, resurfaced in June by winning a strong Moscow championship tournament one point ahead of Soviet champion Psakhis. A strong Hungarian championship tournament resulted in

Politics were as important as chess when world champion Anatoly Karpov (left) of the U.S.S.R. successfully defended his title against Soviet defector Viktor Korchnoi in Merano, Italy, in November.

WIDE WORLD

18th and Last Game of the World Championship Match at Merano, Italy, 1981

Ruy Lopez

White A. Karpov	Black V. Korchnoi	White A. Karpov	Black V. Korchnoi
1 P–K4	P–K4	22 P–K6	PxP
2 N–KB3	N–QB3	23 P–B6	N–K4
3 B–N5	P–QR3	24 RxP	R–B1
4 B–R4	N–B3	25 QR–QB1	RxR
5 0–0	NxP (a)	26 RxR	R–Q1 (i)
6 P–Q4	P–QN4	27 P–R3	P–R3
7 B–N3	P–Q4	28 R–R7	N–B5
8 PxP	B–K3	29 B–N6	R–N1
9 QN–Q2	N–B4	30 B–B5 (j)	BxB ch (k)
10 P–B3	P–Q5	31 NxB	PxP
11 BxB	NxB	32 P–QN4	R–Q1
12 PxP	QNxQP	33 RxP	K–B2
13 P–QR4 (b)	B–K2 (c)	34 R–R7 ch	K–N3
14 NxN	NxN (d)	35 R–Q7	R–K1
15 N–K4 (e)	N–K3	36 P–R6	R–QR1
16 B–K3	0–0	37 R–QN7	K–B4 (1)
17 P–B4 (f)	QxQ	38 RxP	K–K4
18 KRxQ	KR–N1 (g)	39 R–N7	K–Q4
19 R–Q7	B–B1	40 R–KB7	P–B4
20 P–B5	N–Q1	41 R–B6	P–K4
21 P–R5 (h)	N–B3	and Black resigns.	

(a) The Open Defense with which Korchnoi has often achieved successes against Karpov. The challenger knows this variation like the back of his hand and is the author of the relevant section on the Ruy Lopez in the *Encyclopedia of the Openings*. The defense suits, or should suit, Korchnoi well since he is the master of the delayed counterattack. (b) A new and powerful move that makes the whole variation suspect for Black. In the 16th game he played 13. N–K4, B–K2; 14. B–K3, but then after 14 ..., N–KB4 Black had fully equalized. The new move attacks and weakens Black's Queenside pawn formation before he has time to castle and bring his Rooks into cooperation. (c) The obvious move; but since Black seems in dire trouble from now on it would have been better to have abandoned the QR file and played 13 ..., R–QN1 when he still is not without difficulties after 14. PxP, PxP; 15. N–K4, but has quite a playable game. (d) He cannot play 14 ..., QxN because of 15. PxP, winning a pawn. (e) Threatening 16. PxP, when Black must weaken his pawn structure further by 16 ..., NxP since 16 ..., PxP; 17. RxR, wins the Knight. (f) A powerful thrust that not only foreshadows a Kingside attack but forces Black's pieces into awkward and passive positions on the back rank. Note the difference between White's active Kingside and Black's passive Queenside pawn position. (g) A typical Korchnoi counterplay idea, but it does not work here and better seems 18 ..., KR–Q1. (h) Or he could have forced the win by 21. RxBP, PxP; 22. B–Q4, R–N1; 23. R–Q1, QR–N1; 24. B–R7, QR–N2; 25. R–B8. (i) Or 26 ..., N–N6; 27. P–B7 ch, K–R1; 28. B–B5 with a win for White very much as in the game. (j) Playing with deadly accuracy; after 30. Rx–, NxNP; Black has counterchances. (k) If instead 30 ..., NxNP; 31.B–Q4. (l) 37 ..., N–Q3 is met by 38. R–N6.

a tie between Lajos Portisch and Ivan Farago. Wulfgang Uhlmann of East Germany was first in the East German tournament at Halle. A three-way tie for first place occurred at Dortmund, West Germany, among Gennadi Kuzmin of the U.S.S.R., Jonathan Speelman of the U.K., and Lubomir Ftacnik of Czechoslovakia.

Korchnoi's fine tournament results came to an end at a double-round tournament at Las Palmas, Spain, where he tied for third with Yasser Seirawan of the U.S. Timman was first. Another poor result for Korchnoi was his third place at Baden-Baden, West Germany, in July.

The U.S. championship at South Bend, Ind., was also the zonal tournament for the 1984 world championship. Walter Browne and Seirawan tied for first and thus qualified for the interzonal round. But there was a triple tie for the third qualifying place among Larry Christiansen, Kavalek, and Sammy Reshevsky. All games were tied in the play-off, and this meant that Christiansen, having beaten Reshevsky in the tournament and tied with Kavalek, advanced to the interzonal.

The world under-26 team championship, held at Graz, Austria, was won by a powerful Soviet team two points ahead of the U.K. Hungary finished third and the U.S. fourth. The Soviet team won the title through the fine performance of Kasparov, who had eight wins and two draws in ten games.

The culmination of the year's chess events was the world championship match between Karpov and Korchnoi, which had originally been scheduled to start at Merano, Italy, in September. But in an effort to secure the release of Korchnoi's family from the Soviet Union, World Chess Federation Pres. Fredrik Olafsson decided that it should start a month later in order to allow time for negotiations to take place for such a release. Karpov protested against this delay, and in the end a compromise was reached by which play would start on October 1. Korchnoi's start was disastrous. He lost three out of the first four games and, though he did make some sort of comeback, he never really seemed to have a chance of saving the match. In the end Karpov won 6–2 with 10 draws, one of the most crushing victories in the history of world championship matches.

In December Maya Chiburdanidze of the Soviet Union held her compatriot Nana Aleksandriya to an 8–8 tie in matches in Borzhomi and Tbilisi, U.S.S.R., to retain the world's championship.

(HARRY GOLOMBEK)

Chile

A republic extending along the southern Pacific coast of South America, Chile has an area of 756,626 sq km (292,135 sq mi), not including its Antarctic claim. It is bounded by Argentina, Bolivia, and Peru. Pop. (1981 est.): 11,297,000. Cap. and largest city: Santiago (metro. pop., 1980 est., 3,853,300). Language: Spanish. Religion: predominantly Roman Catholic. President in 1981, Maj. Gen. Augusto Pinochet Ugarte.

On March 11, 1981, Chile's new constitution, which had been approved by plebiscite in September 1980, was brought into effect. Pres. Augusto Pinochet Ugarte was sworn in for an additional eight-year term of office with an option to serve a subsequent eight-year term, although he had stated that he would not do this. A Cabinet reshuffle took place at the end of December 1980, and the changes, in particular of José Pinera to minister of

mines, were widely interpreted as a sign of the president's continued resolve to promote a market economy within the country. In a speech given at the inauguration of the constitution, the president stressed his desire to carry out reforms in the following seven broad areas: labour unions, social security, education, health, the judiciary, agriculture, and administration.

In the first three cases the government's new legislation had already been enacted. The Labour Plan of 1979, which allowed collective bargaining at an individual plant and strikes for a period of up to 60 days (after which workers were assumed to have dismissed themselves), led to considerable labour unrest. About 10,000 workers at the El Teniente copper mine went on strike on April 22 after management had offered them a 2% pay increase; they were obliged to return to work 59 days later and to accept the management's offer. In November 1980 a decree was issued making all employees directly responsible for social security contributions from March 1, 1981. (*See* SOCIAL SECURITY AND WELFARE SERVICES.)

Within the framework of encouraging the establishment of private universities, a decree came into force in January which limited courses offered in the eight state universities to 12 main vocational areas. Philosophy, journalism, and sociology were downgraded to nonuniversity level, and political activity within universities was banned. Before a new private university could be established, it had to be judged to constitute no threat to national security. A group of students occupied the UNESCO headquarters in Santiago to protest the government's educational policy and also the arrest of student leader Patricia Torres.

The Chilean government continued to strengthen its relations abroad. In February the U.S. lifted its ban on Export-Import Bank financing for exports to Chile and invited the Chilean Navy to participate in a joint exercise. In June South Africa appointed its first resident ambassador in Santiago.

The long-standing and often acute dispute with Argentina over the three islands Picton, Lennox,

Chile

Pres. Augusto Pinochet Ugarte of Chile read the oath of office during his inauguration on March 11 for eight more years of power.

UPI

and Nueva, to the south of the Beagle Channel, had subsided following Chile's acceptance of the proposal by Pope John Paul II to mediate the conflict. In March, however, Argentina announced that the proposals were unacceptable. The dispute resumed, and there were a number of border incidents in which one country accused the other of espionage. Full diplomatic relations with Peru were restored on April 10, and it was hoped that this new rapprochement between the two countries would restore good relations within the Intergovernmental Council of Copper Exporting Countries (CIPEC).

Repression continued during 1981 with no sign of any political liberalization. A state of emergency had been in force in Chile since the 1973 coup; in March Pinochet declared a "state of danger," which empowered him to carry out arrests, restrict labour-union activity and the freedom of the press, and expel dissidents from the country. These powers, extended on September 11 for a further six months, were widely used by Pinochet. For example, ten unionists were arrested following a petition made to the government in June demanding a 30% increase in the minimum wage to $250 per month, respect for human rights, and greater protection for Chilean industry from for-

eign imports; later all but two of the ten were released.

The case of the unionists was taken up by a number of politicians. Their involvement was the formal justification given for the sudden arrest and deportation of four major opposition figures in August. They were Jaime Castillo, a prominent Christian Democrat and president of Chile's two-year-old human rights commission; two former Cabinet ministers, Carlos Briones and Orlando Cantuarias; and former senator Alberto Jérez. All had been members of Salvador Allende's government (1970–73).

Evidence of both physical and psychological torture was produced in an Amnesty International report published in July. The United Nations passed a resolution expressing grave concern at the "deterioration of the human rights situation in Chile." A representative was appointed to investigate the plight of political prisoners; at the time of the announcement some 50 Chilean prisoners were on hunger strike.

In January Chile's top military court found three officers innocent of any involvement in the 1976 murder in Washington, D.C., of Orlando Letelier, a Chilean diplomat in exile and a strong critic of the Pinochet regime. In Washington a new trial was ordered in April for two Cubans, Guillermo Novo Sampol and Alvin Ross Díaz, charged with the murder of Letelier. They had been convicted of the crime in 1979, but that decision was later overturned on the grounds that the trial judge had erred in admitting testimony from "government informants" who were prisoners in the same jail as the Cubans.

During 1980 the gross domestic product grew by 6.5%, lower than the average rate of 7.5% between 1976 and 1979. Official forecasts for 1981 estimated that growth would remain steady at its 1980 level. The inflation rate fell from 38.9% in 1979 to 31.2% in 1980 and was expected to continue to decline. However, difficulties were experienced in the external sector. The overall balance showed a surplus of $1,244,000,000 in 1980, but it was expected to be severely reduced by the end of 1981. This was mainly because of the widening deficit in the trade account. The main explanations for the trade deficit were thought to be the overvaluation of the Chilean currency in relation to others and low world copper prices. (LUCY BLACKBURN)

CHILE

Education. (1980) Primary, pupils 2,332,566, teachers 66,354; secondary, pupils 422,856, teachers 24,387; vocational, pupils 211,112, teachers (1979) 11,029; higher, students 127,446, teaching staff (1975) 11,419.

Finance. Monetary unit: peso, with (Sept. 21, 1981) an official rate of 39 pesos to U.S. $1 (free rate of 72.31 pesos = £1 sterling). Gold and other reserves (June 1981) U.S. $3,317,000,000. Budget (1979 actual): revenue 256,-374,000,000 pesos; expenditure 225,888,000,000 pesos. Gross national product (1979) 736,870,000,000 pesos. Money supply (Dec. 1980) 78,874,000,000 pesos. Cost of living (Santiago; 1975 = 100; June 1981) 1,802.

Foreign Trade. (1980) Imports U.S. $5,821,000,000; exports U.S. $4,818,000,000. Import sources (1979): U.S. 23%; Brazil 9%; Iran 8%; Japan 8%; West Germany 6%. Export destinations (1979): West Germany 16%; Japan 11%; U.S. 11%; Brazil 10%; Argentina 7%; U.K. 6%; Italy 5%. Main exports: copper 46%; metal ores c. 10%.

Transport and Communications. Roads (1979) 76,677 km. Motor vehicles in use (1979): passenger 379,200; commercial 180,700. Railways: (1976) 10,819 km; traffic (1980) 1,377,000,000 passenger-km, freight 1,521,000,000 net ton-km. Air traffic (1980): 1,875,000,000 passenger-km; freight 103.9 million net ton-km. Shipping (1980): merchant vessels 100 gross tons and over 172; gross tonnage 614,425. Telephones (Jan. 1979) 531,100. Radio receivers (Dec. 1977) c. 2 million. Television receivers (Dec. 1976) 710,000.

Agriculture. Production (in 000; metric tons; 1980): wheat 966; barley 105; oats 173; corn 405; rice (1979) 181; potatoes 903; rapeseed 73; dry beans 84; tomatoes c. 155; sugar, raw value (1979) 104; apples c. 195; wine c. 570; wool, clean c. 10; beef and veal c. 180; fish catch (1979) 2,633; timber (cu m; 1979) 11,560. Livestock (in 000; 1980): cattle 3,664; sheep (1979) 5,952; goats (1979) c. 600; pigs c. 1,000; horses c. 450; poultry (1979) c. 22,000.

Industry. Production (in 000; metric tons; 1980): coal 751; crude oil c. 1,500; natural gas (cu m; 1979) 5,732,000; petroleum products (1978) 4,810; electricity (kw-hr; 1979) 10,940,000; iron ore (61% metal content) 10,314; pig iron 662; crude steel (ingots) 743; copper ore (metal content) 1,052; copper 687; nitrate of soda (1979) 621; manganese ore (metal content; 1979) 8.9; sulfur (1978) 32; iodine (1979) 2.4; molybdenum concentrates (metal content; 1979) 13.6; gold (troy oz; 1979) 111; silver (troy oz; 1979) 8,733; cement 1,583; nitrogenous fertilizers (1979–80) 94; newsprint 130; other paper (1978) 162; fish meal (1977) 244.

China

The most populous country in the world and the third largest in area, China is bounded by the U.S.S.R., Mongolia, North Korea, Vietnam, Laos, Burma, India, Bhutan, Nepal, Pakistan, and Afghanistan and also by the Sea of Japan, the Yellow Sea, and the East and South China seas. From 1949 the country has been divided into the People's Republic of China (Communist) on the mainland and on Hainan and other islands, and the Republic of China (Nationalist) on Taiwan. (*See* TAIWAN.) Area: 9,561,000 sq km (3,691,521 sq mi), including Tibet and excluding Taiwan. Population of the People's Republic (1981 est.): 982,550,000. Capital:

China

Beijing (Peking; metro. pop., 1980 est., 9,029,000). Largest city: Shanghai (metro. pop., 1979 est., 11 million). Language: Chinese (varieties of the Beijing dialect predominate). Chairman of the Permanent Standing Committee of the National People's Congress (nominal chief of state) in 1981, Ye Jianying (Yeh Chien-ying); chairmen of the Communist Party, Hua Guofeng (Hua Kuo-feng) and, from June 29, Hu Yaobang (Hu Yao-pang); premier, Zhao Ziyang (Chao Tzu-yang).

Convocation of the much-delayed sixth plenum of the 11th Chinese Communist Party congress proved to be the most significant event of 1981. It signaled the achievement of consensus within the hierarchy on two controversial but vital questions: the official view of Mao Zedong's (Mao Tse-tung's) place in history; and the forced resignation of Hua Guofeng (Hua Kuo-feng) as chairman of the party. The plenary session formally named Hu Yaobang (Hu Yao-pang; *see* BIOGRAPHIES), a protégé of Deng Xiaoping (Teng Hsiao-p'ing; *see* BIOGRAPHIES), as chairman in place of Hua, Mao's hand-picked successor. It also issued an official document summing up the 32 years of Communist control in China and including an important assessment of Mao's rule. Mao's early contributions as founder of the Chinese Communist state were said to "far outweigh his later mistakes." His worst mistake was declared to have been the Cultural Revolution of 1966–76, which "led to domestic turmoil and brought catastrophe to the party, the state and the whole people."

On July 1, in his first speech to the nation as party chairman, Hu emphasized the importance of collective leadership and warned against a personality cult as practiced by Mao. The speech marked the triumph of the pragmatist leadership under Deng, the country's de facto leader, who had placed economic growth and modernization ahead of Marxist ideology and Mao's "Thought" on the class struggle.

While the pragmatist leadership repudiated Mao's basic principles and policies and succeeded in eliminating Mao's leftist followers, including the "gang of four" headed by his widow, it repeatedly emphasized the importance of adhering to fundamental principles: "upholding the socialist road, the people's democratic dictatorship [*i.e.*, the dictatorship of the proletariat], the leadership of the Communist Party, and Marxism-Leninism and Mao Zedong Thought." The sixth plenum resolution on the history of the party declared: "Any word or deed which denies or undermines these four principles cannot be tolerated." On the other hand, the pragmatist leadership adopted a policy of liberalization toward intellectuals, writers, artists, and both traditional and Western cultural values. It also turned to the West for assistance with the Four Modernizations: agriculture, industry, science and technology, and defense.

On June 14, about two weeks before the formal session of the sixth plenum, U.S. Secretary of State Alexander M. Haig, accompanied by dozens of experts from the U.S. State and Defense departments, arrived in Beijing (Peking) for three days of intensive talks with Foreign Minister Huang Hua, Deng, and others on military and intelligence matters. At the conclusion of the talks, both sides stressed the importance of Sino-U.S. cooperation in meeting serious threats to world peace and tranquillity. Before leaving Beijing, Haig declared that the U.S. was preparing to sell arms and military technology to China and also to ease export controls on sophisticated technology, thus placing China in a different category from the Soviet Union. At the same time, it was officially admitted that for a year China and the U.S. had operated a listening post in China's Xinjiang Uygur (Sinkiang Uighur) Autonomous Region to monitor Soviet missile tests. As China and the U.S. established closer ties, China was being encouraged to play a part in the global balance of power against its former Communist allies.

On the eve of the People's Republic's national day on October 1, Premier Zhao Ziyang (Chao

(Left) The new premier of China, Zhao Ziyang, at a news conference after a visit to the Philippines in August. (Right) Newly elected Communist Party Chairman Hu Yaobang took office in June.

PHOTOS, UPI

被告人

The widow of Mao Zedong, Jiang Qing, sat in the dock when the trial of the "gang of four" began in November 1980. On Jan. 25, 1981, she received a suspended death sentence.

Tzu-yang) stated that Beijing's repeated guarantee of Taiwan's autonomy after reunification was a serious and sincere effort to reunite the country. The following day Ye Jianying (Yeh Chien-ying), the ceremonial head of state, declared that the Communist Party was willing to negotiate with the Nationalists on a basis of equality and to accept them in top posts in the Communist government.

Domestic Affairs. Less than a month after Mao's death on Sept. 9, 1976, Hua, then chairman of the party and premier, had arrested four members of the Politburo who were closely identified with the Cultural Revolution: Mao's widow, Jiang Qing (Chiang Ch'ing); Zhang Chunqiao (Chang Ch'un-ch'iao); Yao Wenyuan (Yao Wen-yüan); and Wang Hongwen (Wang Hung-wen). The arrest of this so-called gang of four paved the way for the rehabilitation of many victims of the Cultural Revolution, notably Deng and Hu. The trial of the gang of four and six other defendants on charges of treason was intended to further discredit the Cultural Revolution, as well as to demonstrate China's new legal codes. The show trial before a special tribunal began in November 1980, but the convictions were not announced until Jan. 25, 1981. Jiang Qing and Zhang received suspended death sentences; Wang was given life imprisonment; and Yao was sentenced to 20 years. Defiant to the last, Mao's widow declared before her sentencing that she did everything on Mao's orders and that "when you vilify me, you are vilifying Chairman Mao and the Cultural Revolution. . . ."

Hua's authority as party chairman had been undercut when Hu was made general secretary of the Central Committee, in charge of running the party on a day-to-day basis, and in September 1980 Hua had relinquished the post of premier to Zhao. Reportedly, there was growing opposition to the efforts of Deng and his associates to force Hua's resignation from the party chairmanship as well. However, with most of Mao's close associates ei-

ther dead or disgraced, the People's Liberation Army was the only power base that could effectively oppose Deng. Late in November 1980, Hua agreed to give up the chairmanship of the party's Military Commission, and Deng assumed the responsibility. In December a working conference of the Central Committee was held to pressure Hua to resign formally, but Hua refused to attend. This delayed the sixth plenum, originally scheduled for the same month, and considerable backstage bargaining and maneuvering were necessary before it could be convened.

The sixth plenum finally held its formal session June 27–29. It "unanimously approved" Hua's resignation as chairman of the Central Committee and the Military Commission but made him a second vice-chairman of the Central Committee. Hu and Zhao, Deng's close and trusted associates, were elected chairman and first vice-chairman of the Central Committee, respectively. Deng formally assumed the chairmanship of the Military Commission. Under his leadership, military maneuvers were conducted in late September to demonstrate the importance of military modernization, and Deng addressed the commanders and troops on the need for military obedience to party directives.

In accordance with the decision of the plenary session, the elite standing committee of the 26-member Politburo was composed of seven members ranked in the following order: Hu, Ye, Deng, Zhao, Le Xiannian (Li Hsien-nien), Chen Yun (Ch'en Yün), and Hua. The election of Premier Zhao to be senior vice-chairman of the Central Committee and a member of the standing committee further solidified Deng's control.

The resolution on "certain questions in the history" of the Chinese Communist Party since 1949, "unanimously adopted" by the plenary session, was the product of months of debate by top leaders and cadres. In realistically assessing the historical

role played by Mao, it formally criticized his Cultural Revolution but praised him as a revolutionary hero and a "respected and beloved great leader and teacher." While his policies and programs were repudiated, Mao's Thought, defined as "Marxism-Leninism applied and developed in China," was upheld. The long document constituted a party platform affirming the new leadership's goal of modernizing China systematically and in stages without resorting to unrealistic campaigns or violent actions.

Nevertheless, the pragmatic policy of the new leadership still faced opposition from some cadres, especially those still in power who had joined the party during the Cultural Revolution and benefited from it. From outside the party, youth associations and underground publications also criticized Deng's four fundamental principles. The central leadership moved to crack down on critics among the intelligentsia who had enjoyed freedom of expression under Deng's initial liberalization. At a special conference in July, called by the party's propaganda department, both Deng and Hu declared that open and organized criticism in opposition to the party leadership and the socialist system would not be permissible. Late in August editorials in the official press attacked "bourgeois liberalism," indicating that strict limits on open dissent and freedom of speech would be enforced.

The Economy. The policy of economic retrenchment continued, and further readjustments were made in the national economic plan. The ambitious and unrealistic ten-year plan of heavy industrial development and capital construction originally put forward by the new leadership had been drastically modified. Instead, emphasis was being placed on readjustment, reconstruction, consolidation, and improvement of the economy, mainly by giving priority to agriculture and light industry. To revitalize sluggish agriculture and industry, a measure of autonomy had been introduced in communes and factories. Bonuses and material incentives to workers and farmers were being provided, private plots of peasants were enlarged, and self-employed peddlers and craftsmen had reappeared. At the opening of the fourth session of the National People's Congress (the nominal parliament) on November 30, Premier Zhao outlined the policy of economic readjustment and reform, looking toward a more consumer-oriented mixed economy, expansion of foreign trade, and greater individual motivation.

Because of the need for foreign capital, technology, equipment, and expertise during the period of economic readjustment, China adopted an "open door" policy of expanding foreign trade and imports of technical equipment. China began to accept both governmental and nongovernmental foreign loans, and in 1981 more agreements on joint ventures with foreign firms were signed by Chinese central and local governments. These activities were reflected in the trade figures. The total value of China's imports and exports rose about 23% from $29,570,000,000 in 1979 to $38,198,-000 in 1980.

In July the State Planning Commission announced China's sixth five-year plan (1981–85), along with a ten-year program to streamline the economic system. High priority was given to consumer goods. In 1980 production of consumer goods in general continued to increase appreciably, while such items as television sets, radios, and cameras registered especially large gains.

Despite these gains, the Four Modernizations progressed slowly. Budget deficits, inflation, and unemployment, plus the lack of an industrial infrastructure, capital, and trained technical personnel, continued to plague the economy. The prolonged drought in the north and disastrous flooding along the central and upper Chang Jiang (Yangtze River) compelled China to abandon Mao's policy of national self-reliance and ask for

The Chinese government has begun experimenting with free enterprise, allowing people to sell whatever they can make at home. A cyclist balances an enormous load of baskets on his bicycle.

UPI

international assistance. In March the International Monetary Fund approved a new loan of $550 million, and in June the World Bank announced the approval of its first loan, amounting to $200 million.

Grain production in 1980 totaled 318,220,000 metric tons, a decline of 13,893,000 tons from 1979. The need for more grain imports was expected. Under a four-year agreement (1980–84) with the U.S., China had agreed to buy at least 6 million–8 million tons of wheat and corn annually.

Foreign Affairs. Under the new leadership, Chinese foreign policy had assumed a more pragmatic and outlooking posture. While soliciting the support of socialist countries and identifying its interests with those of the third world, China considered Soviet hegemonism rather than capitalist imperialism to be the major threat to world peace and security. Accordingly, it also moved to consolidate its ties with Japan and the Western industrialized countries. The heavy buildup of Soviet troops on China's border, the Soviet military presence in the Pacific and South Asia, and Soviet support of Vietnamese expansion in Indo-

china made China fearful of Soviet-Vietnamese encirclement and drew it closer to the U.S.

Since the resumption of diplomatic relations between China and the U.S. on Jan. 1, 1979, there had been frequent exchanges of official missions and delegations on various subjects. On Sept. 5, 1981, China and the U.S. signed a new agreement to broaden cultural exchange programs for 1982–83. In 1980 Sino-U.S. trade rose to $4.9 billion, double that of the previous year, and in the first quarter of 1981 it increased nearly 60%. U.S. exports to China in the first quarter of 1981 amounted to $1.2 billion, up 53% from the same period in 1980, while China's exports rose 84% to $379 million. According to U.S. Pres. Ronald Reagan's report on East-West trade, China had replaced the Soviet Union as the most active Communist trading partner of the U.S.

The Reagan administration came into office in January reiterating its desire to improve relations with the Chinese Nationalists on Taiwan. Under the terms of the Taiwan Relations Act, which provides that the U.S. will supply whatever arms are necessary to enable Taiwan to maintain a self-defense capability, Taiwan had requested the purchase of advanced jet fighters. Beijing, however, regarded the act as contravening the joint Sino-U.S. communiqué of December 1978, which provided that the U.S. would recognize Beijing and not Taiwan as the sole government of China. Beijing viewed arms sales as official deals between governments. Furthermore, it feared that U.S. arms would bolster Taipei's determination not to accept Beijing's proposals for reunification.

During a White House meeting with the Chinese ambassador, Chai Zemin (Ch'ai Tse-min), on March 19, President Reagan gave personal assurances of Washington's intention to live up to and enlarge upon the normalization agreement. At about the same time, former president Gerald R. Ford, visiting Beijing as President Reagan's envoy, said he was confident that differences between China and the U.S. could and would be resolved. Former president Jimmy Carter toured China in August as an invited guest of the Chinese government, receiving a hero's welcome in Beijing as the negotiator of normalization. On August 27 he emphasized that the future of Taiwan was a matter for the Chinese alone to resolve.

Secretary of State Haig's visit to Beijing and his announcement of the U.S. decision to sell arms to China gave a new momentum to Sino-U.S. relations, although Haig also declared that no specific request for arms had been received from China and that each application would be reviewed on a case-by-case basis after consultation with Congress and America's allies. Responding to Soviet accusations that the U.S. and China were forming a conspiracy of aggression and imperialism, Haig on June 28 stated that the U.S. would not permit Moscow to have a veto over Sino-U.S. relations. Concerning a renewed attack on the Reagan administration by Beijing over the Taiwan issue, Haig said he hoped that a decision on selling advanced fighters to Taiwan would be based on the island's genuine needs and that he saw no need for an immediate decision.

CHINA

Education. (1979–80) Primary, pupils 146,270,000, teachers (1964–65) c. 2.6 million; secondary, pupils 65 million; vocational, pupils 888,000; higher, students 850,000.

Finance. Monetary unit: yuan, with (Sept. 21, 1981) a market rate of 1.71 yuan to U.S. $1 (3.17 yuan = £1 sterling). Gold and other reserves (Dec. 1978 est.) U.S. $4.5 billion. Budget (1981 est.) balanced at 97.6 billion yuan. Total industrial and agricultural output (1980; at 1970 prices) 661.9 billion yuan.

Foreign Trade. (1980) Imports 29.2 billion yuan; exports 27.2 billion yuan. Import sources: Japan c. 26%; U.S. c. 21%; Hong Kong c. 7%; West Germany 6%. Export destinations: Japan c. 24%; Hong Kong c. 22%; U.S. c. 6%. Main exports: textile yarns and fabrics c. 15%; crude oil c. 10%; cereals c. 9%; meat and fish c. 9%; fruit and vegetables c. 5%; clothing c. 5%.

Transport and Communications. Roads (1978) 890,000 km. Motor vehicles in use (1978): passenger c. 50,000; commercial c. 710,000. Railways: (1978) c. 50,000 km; traffic (1980) 138,300,000,000 passenger-km, freight 571,700,000,000 net ton-km. Air traffic (1980): c. 4,000,000,000 passenger-km; freight 140.6 million net ton-km. Inland waterways (including Chang Jiang [Yangtze River]; 1978) 136,000 km. Shipping (1980): merchant vessels 100 gross tons and over 955; gross tonnage 6,873,608. Telephones (Dec. 1977) c. 5 million. Radio receivers (Dec. 1977) c. 45 million. Television receivers (Dec. 1977) c. 1 million.

Agriculture. Production (in 000; metric tons; 1980): rice c. 134,000; corn c. 30,000; wheat c. 54,155; barley c. 4,800; millet c. 5,500; sorghum c. 7,500; potatoes c. 12,500; soybeans 7,880; peanuts 3,600; rapeseed 2,384; sugar, raw value c. 3,500; tobacco c. 1,000; tea 304; cotton, lint 2,707; jute c. 1,100; cow's milk 1,141; beef, pork, and mutton 12,055; fish catch (1979) 4,054; timber (cu m) c. 212,000. Livestock (in 000; 1980): horses c. 6,500; asses c. 11,500; cattle c. 64,000; buffalo c. 30,000; sheep c. 102,000; goats c. 80,000; pigs c. 320,000; chickens c. 800,000.

Industry. Fuel and power (in 000; metric tons; 1980): coal (including lignite) 620,000; crude oil 105,950; natural gas (cu m) 14,270,000; electricity (kw-hr) 300,600,000. Production (in 000; metric tons; 1980): iron ore (metal content) c. 41,000; pig iron 38,020; crude steel 37,120; bauxite c. 2,400; aluminum c. 400; copper c. 300; lead c. 200; zinc c. 200; magnesite c. 1,000; manganese ore c. 1,000; tungsten concentrates (oxide content) c. 12; cement 79,860; sulfuric acid 7,640; plastics 898; fertilizers (nutrient content) nitrogenous 9,990, phosphate 2,310; soda ash 1,613; caustic soda 1,923; cotton yarn 2,930; cotton fabrics (sq m) 12,800,000; man-made fibres 450; paper 5,350; motor vehicles (units) 222.

Documents setting up a cultural exchange program were signed in September by U.S. International Communication Agency Director Charles Z. Wick (left) and Chinese Minister for Cultural Affairs Huang Zhen.

Relations between China and The Netherlands suffered a setback when the Dutch government approved the sale of two submarines to Taiwan. Beijing decided to recall its ambassador to The Netherlands and asked The Hague to do the same. From May 5 diplomatic relations between the two countries were downgraded to the level of chargé d'affaires.

The Sino-Japanese relationship remained cordial despite China's economic retrenchment, which involved the cancellation of Japanese contracts for several industrial projects. On February 11 Japan warned China bluntly that cancellation of billions of dollars of contracts would erode trust between the two countries, but the next day China accepted blame for the cancellations and promised to compensate companies involved according to international practice. Two major projects, a steel complex and a petrochemical plant, were reactivated in the autumn.

Relations with the U.S.S.R. worsened, and the prolonged boundary negotiations over Zhenbao (Chen-Pao) Island (Damasky in Russian) became deadlocked. China repeatedly attacked the Soviet policy of military and political expansion. At the 36th UN General Assembly on September 23, Vice-Foreign Minister Zhang Wenjin (Chang Wen-chin) denounced the Soviet invasion of Afghanistan and the Soviet-backed Vietnamese invasion of Kampuchea (Cambodia).

The 1979 frontier war between China and Vietnam remained unsettled, and new border clashes took place in May, June, and August. China lodged a strong protest against Vietnamese armed intrusions in the border areas of Guangxi Zhuang (Kwangsi Chuang) Autonomous Region and Yunnan Province. While maintaining a hard-line attitude toward Vietnam, China took more conciliatory and friendly positions toward the members of the Association of Southeast Asian Nations (ASEAN), and it supported ASEAN's proposal "to establish a free, peaceful and neutral Southeast Asia." In February and August Premier Zhao visited Southeast Asia to strengthen friendly ties with Thailand and Burma in particular and to assure members of ASEAN that China's relations with the Communist parties of those countries were "main-

ly political and moral." At a UN-sponsored international conference on Kampuchea, held July 13–17 and boycotted by Vietnam and the Soviet-bloc countries, a resolution was adopted unanimously calling for the withdrawal of Vietnamese troops from Kampuchea. In a compromise with China, which continued to support the Khmer Rouge (Pol Pot) guerrillas, the resolution did not call for disarmament of all Kampuchean factions as originally proposed by ASEAN. (*See* SOUTHEAST ASIAN AFFAIRS.) (HUNG-TI CHU)

Colombia

A republic in northwestern South America, Colombia is bordered by Panama, Venezuela, Brazil, Peru, and Ecuador and has coasts on both the Caribbean Sea and the Pacific Ocean. Area: 1,141,-748 sq km (440,831 sq mi). Pop. (1981 est.): 26,729,200. Cap. and largest city: Bogotá (pop., 1981 est., 4,486,200). Language: Spanish. Religion: Roman Catholic (96%). President in 1981, Julio César Turbay Ayala.

Colombia

The government of Colombia was dismissed on March 5, 1981, the second time this had occurred since Pres. Julio Turbay Ayala took office. The action was taken to permit ministers who wished to register as candidates to be relieved of their official duties prior to the congressional elections scheduled for May 1982. President Turbay made several Cabinet changes, but the balance between Liberals and Conservatives was maintained.

At the Liberal Party convention in Medellín on September 19, former president Alfonso López Michelsen was nominated as the party's candidate in the 1982 presidential election. He was the last of four Liberals to announce his candidacy in a campaign marked by bitter arguments that threatened party unity. President Turbay, himself a Liberal, noted that disunited parties could not effectively oppose the forces that were trying to foment civil war in Colombia.

This reference to the active guerrilla movements came when the leader of the left-wing movement M-19, Jaime Bateman Cayón, was pursuing his own presidential campaign. M-19's public image

The body of Chester Bitterman, a U.S. Bible translator, lies beside a bus in Bogotá, where he was shot to death by guerrillas on March 7. He had been kidnapped by the guerrillas in January.

was seriously harmed, and its forces split, when on March 7 a breakaway faction was accused of the shooting of Chester Bitterman, a U.S. Bible translator working for the U.S.-based Summer Institute of Linguistics (SIL). Bitterman had been kidnapped in January on suspicion of being an agent for the U.S. Central Intelligence Agency (CIA). The SIL

refused to accede to demands by leftist guerrillas that it leave Colombia.

In March the president offered to M-19 a limited amnesty, lasting until July 20. This was answered with increased violence; only 12 guerrillas surrendered. Subsequent anti-insurgency offensives by the Army encountered reunited resistance from M-19, the Colombian Revolutionary Armed Forces, and other groups. In an interview given in July to two Bogotá journalists kidnapped expressly for that purpose, Bateman insisted that the 1982 elections would be disrupted if his candidacy was blocked by the Army.

On March 23 Colombia severed diplomatic relations with Cuba on the grounds that Cuba was training Colombian guerrillas. A further anti-Communist stance was taken in April when President Turbay canceled a visit to Moscow and Beijing (Peking). In March the novelist Gabriel García Márquez left Colombia for Mexico City following rumours, later denied, that he was to be interrogated regarding his possible involvement with M-19. President Turbay paid a visit to Brazil in September.

In April the Inter-American Human Rights Commission of the Organization of American States reported its findings that the Colombian government and armed forces were not guilty of using torture on guerrilla suspects. This was in sharp contrast to the findings of two Amnesty International reports published during 1980.

In 1981 Colombia's gross domestic product was expected to grow at 3–4%, compared with 4% in 1980. An increase of 26.5% in the national minimum wage was derided by the labour unions, which pointed out that the rate of inflation was 24.5% in 1980 and 30% in 1981. International reserves remained high, at approximately $5 billion, while for the second consecutive year the balance of payments was in deficit owing to reduced coffee income and large imports of capital goods and oil. In May Colombia became a member of the General Agreement on Tariffs and Trade (GATT). Electricity rationing was enforced in January, but foreign loans and contracts were signed for four new hydroelectric projects.   (JOHN B. H. BOX)

COLOMBIA

Education. (1978) Primary, pupils 4,265,598, teachers 131,214; secondary (1977), pupils 1,187,148, teachers 56,-402; vocational (1977), pupils 348,590, teachers 18,316; teacher training (1977), students 80,373, teachers 5,024; higher, students 274,893, teaching staff 25,708.

Finance. Monetary unit: peso, with (Sept. 21, 1981) a free rate of 55.76 pesos to U.S. $1 (103.37 pesos = £1 sterling). Gold and other reserves (June 1981) U.S. $4,734,-000,000. Budget (1979 revised actual): revenue 148,334,-000,000 pesos; expenditure 143,354,000,000 pesos. Gross domestic product (1980) 1,547,870,000,000 pesos. Money supply (Dec. 1980) 213,150,000,000 pesos. Cost of living (Bogotá; 1975 = 100; May 1981) 371.9.

Foreign Trade. Imports (1980): U.S. $4,739,000,000; exports U.S. $3,916,000,000. Import sources (1978): U.S. 35%; Japan 10%; West Germany 7%. Export destinations (1978): U.S. 29%; West Germany 21%; Venezuela 8%; The Netherlands 7%. Main exports (1978): coffee 66%; textile yarns and fabrics 6%. Tourism (1978): visitors 826,-000; gross receipts U.S. $329 million.

Transport and Communications. Roads (1979) 65,129 km. Motor vehicles in use (1979): passenger 509,000; commercial 94,800. Railways: (1978) 2,912 km; traffic (1979) 322 million passenger-km, freight 1,128,000,000 net ton-km. Air traffic (1980): c. 4,189,000,000 passenger-km; freight c. 155 million net ton-km. Shipping (1980): merchant vessels 100 gross tons and over 69; gross tonnage 283,457. Telephones (Jan. 1979) 1,445,000. Radio receivers (Dec. 1977) 2,930,000. Television receivers (Dec. 1977) 1,850,000.

Agriculture. Production (in 000; metric tons; 1980): corn 813; rice 1,892; sorghum 409; potatoes 2,038; cassava (1979) 2,081; soybeans 155; cabbages (1979) 449; onions 278; tomatoes 245; bananas c. 1,200; plantains (1979) 2,-236; sugar, raw value 1,230; palm oil 70; coffee c. 738; tobacco 52; cotton, lint c. 101; beef and veal c. 608; timber (cu m; 1979) 42,022. Livestock (in 000; Dec. 1979): cattle 24,545; sheep 2,440; pigs c. 2,030; goats 644; horses (1979) c. 1,644; chickens c. 33,000.

Industry. Production (in 000; metric tons; 1979): crude oil 6,410; natural gas (cu m; 1979) c. 2,410,000; coal (1978) c. 4,000; electricity (kw-hr; 1979) c. 18,000,000; iron ore (metal content) 370; crude steel (1980) 263; gold (troy oz) 268; emeralds (carats; 1973) 109; salt (1978) 620; cement 4,260; caustic soda 24; fertilizers (nutrient content; 1979–80) nitrogenous 57, phosphate c. 45; paper (1978) c. 350.

Combat Sports

Boxing. World Boxing Council (WBC) champion Larry Holmes (U.S.) continued to dominate the heavyweight scene. Three championship victories in 1981 against Trevor Berbick (Canada), Leon Spinks (U.S.—a former world champion), and Renaldo Snipes (U.S.) brought his record to 39 wins in 39 fights. Mike Weaver (U.S.) retained the World Boxing Association (WBA) heavyweight championship by outpointing James Tillis (U.S.). Interest was raised by the progress of Gerry Cooney (U.S.), who knocked out Ken Norton in one round to remain unbeaten in 25 contests with 21 opponents stopped. Cooney was due to face Holmes for the WBC title in 1982 in what was expected to be the richest prizefight in history. Former champion Joe Frazier returned from a five-year retirement to fight Jumbo Cummings; the ten-round bout ended in a draw. In his second comeback effort, three-time former champion Muhammad Ali (U.S.) lost again, this time to Trevor Berbick in a unanimous ten-round decision.

There was little activity in the cruiserweight division of 182 lb (82.6 kg), introduced by the WBC in 1980. Carlos de León (Puerto Rico) remained champion; the WBA had no titleholder in this division. Matthew Saad Muhammad (U.S.) continued as WBC light-heavyweight champion most of the year, with wins against Vonzell Johnson (U.S.), Murray Sutherland (U.S.), and Jerry Martin (U.S.), but lost the title in December to Dwight Braxton (U.S.), who knocked him out. Mike Spinks (U.S.), former Olympic champion and brother of Leon, became WBA light-heavyweight champion, outpointing Eddie Mustafa Muhammad (U.S.). In his first defense Spinks stopped Vonzell Johnson in seven rounds.

Marvin Hagler (U.S.) continued as undisputed middleweight champion, recognized by both the WBC and WBA. Hagler halted Fulgencio Obelmejías (Venezuela) in eight rounds and Vito Antuofermo (U.S.) in four and outpointed Mustafa Hamsho (Syria). Wilfred Benítez (Puerto Rico) took the WBC junior middleweight crown from Maurice Hope (England). Benítez thus continued to add to his remarkable record. He had become the youngest-ever world champion by winning the junior welterweight title at 17, then became the youngest welterweight champion at 20, and finally became the youngest junior middleweight champion at 22. Sugar Ray Leonard, the WBC welterweight champion, won the WBA junior middleweight title by halting Ayub Kalule (Uganda) in nine rounds, but he later gave it up in order to keep the title he took from Thomas Hearns (U.S.), WBA welterweight titleholder, for the undisputed welterweight championship. Tadashi Mihara (Japan) then became WBA junior middleweight champion, outpointing Rocky Fratto (U.S.). Hearns stopped Pablo Báez (Dominican Republic) in four rounds to retain the WBA welterweight title, having earlier in the year defended it successfully against Randy Shields (U.S.) in 13 rounds. In the most exciting fight of 1981 Leonard stopped Hearns in the 14th round at Las Vegas, Nev., in September to become WBC and WBA welterweight champion. Leonard's $10 million share of the purse increased his earnings to $50 million since turning professional in 1977.

Saoul Mamby (U.S.) kept the WBC junior welterweight championship, outpointing Jo Kimpuani and Thomas Americo (Indon.). Aaron Pryor (U.S.) retained the WBA version by stopping Lennox Blackmoore (Guyana) in two rounds.

Alexis Argüello (Nicaragua) joined the ranks of the superchampions when he outpointed Jim Watt (Scotland) to win the WBC lightweight crown in London. Like Benítez, Argüello had thus held world titles in three separate weight classes, the others being the WBA featherweight in 1974 and the WBC junior lightweight in 1978. After his victory over Watt, Argüello defeated Ray Mancini (U.S.), bringing his total of world title contests at three different weights to 17 with only one defeat. The WBA lightweight championship changed hands twice. Hilmer Kenty (U.S.) was outpointed by Sean O'Grady (U.S.). O'Grady was ordered to defend against Claude Noel (Trinidad), but he declined and was stripped of the title, a decision upheld by a federal court. Noel then beat Rodolfo Gonzalez (Mexico) to win the vacant championship but later lost the title to Arturo Frías (U.S.).

The WBC junior lightweight championship changed hands twice. Cornelius Boza-Edwards (Uganda) gained it from Rafael Limón (Mexico) and retained it against Bobby Chacon (U.S.). Boza-Edwards was then beaten by Rolando Navarette (Phil.). Sammy Serrano (Puerto Rico) regained the WBA junior lightweight crown from Yasutsune Uehara (Japan). The Japanese fighter had taken the title from him in 1980.

Salvador Sánchez (Mexico) retained the WBC featherweight championship three times, stopping Roberto Castañón (Spain) in 10 rounds, Wilfredo Gómez (Puerto Rico), the WBC junior

One of the year's most celebrated boxing matches, between Sugar Ray Leonard and Thomas Hearns, took place in Las Vegas, Nevada, in September. Leonard (right) was declared winner when the referee stopped the fight in the 14th round.

UPI

Table I. Boxing Champions

as of Dec. 31, 1981

Division	World	Europe	Commonwealth	Britain
Heavyweight	Larry Holmes, U.S.* Mike Weaver, U.S.†	Lucien Rodriguez, France	Trevor Berbick, Canada	Neville Meade, Wales
Cruiserweight	Carlos de León, Puerto Rico*	...	...	...
Light heavyweight	Dwight Braxton, U.S.* Mike Spinks, U.S.†	Rudi Koopmans, The Netherlands	Lottie Mwale, Zambia	vacant
Middleweight	Marvin Hagler, U.S.*†	Tony Sibson, England	Tony Sibson, England	Roy Gumbs, England
Junior middleweight	Wilfred Benítez, Puerto Rico* Tadashi Mihara, Japan†	Luigi Minchillo, Italy	Herol Graham, England	Herol Graham, England
Welterweight	Sugar Ray Leonard, U.S.*†	Jørgen Hansen, Denmark	Colin Jones, Wales	Colin Jones, Wales
Junior welterweight	Saoul Mamby, U.S.* Aaron Pryor, U.S.†	Clinton McKenzie, England	Obisia Nwankpa, Nigeria	Clinton McKenzie, England
Lightweight	Alexis Argüello, Nicaragua* Arturo Frías, U.S.†	Giuseppe Gibilisco, Italy	Barry Michael, Australia	Ray Cattouse, England
Junior lightweight	Rolando Navarette, Philippines* Sammy Serrano, Puerto Rico†	Carlos Hernández, Spain	Johnny Aba, Papua New Guinea	...
Featherweight	Salvador Sánchez, Mexico* Eusebio Pedroza, Panama†	Salvatore Melluzzo, Italy	Azumah Nelson, Nigeria	Pat Cowdell, England
Junior featherweight	Wilfredo Gómez, Puerto Rico* Sergio Palma, Argentina†	...	...	...
Bantamweight	Lupe Pintor, Mexico* Jeff Chandler, U.S.†	Valerio Nati, Italy	Paul Ferreri, Australia	John Feeney, England
Super flyweight	Chul-Ho Kim, South Korea* Rafael Pedroza, Panama†	...	...	...
Flyweight	Antonio Avelar, Mexico* Juan Herrera, Mexico†	Charlie Magri, England	Steven Muchoki (Kenya)	vacant
Junior flyweight	Hilario Zapata, Panama* Katsuo Tokashiki, Japan†	...	...	...

*World Boxing Council champion.   †World Boxing Association champion.

featherweight champion, in 8, and Pat Cowdell (England) in a 15-round split decision. Eusebio Pedroza (Panama) also twice defended the WBA featherweight crown, stopping Patrick Ford (Guyana) in 13 rounds and Carlos Pinango (Venezuela) in 7. This was his 12th defense, a record for the featherweight division. Wilfredo Gómez continued as WBC junior featherweight champion, having failed to take the featherweight title from Sánchez. Sergio Palma (Arg.) retained the WBA junior featherweight championship, defeating Leonardo Cruz (Dominican Republic), Ricardo Cardona (Colombia), and Vilchit Muangroi-Et (Thailand).

Lupe Pintor (Mexico) continued to dominate the WBC bantamweight division as he defeated José Uziga (Arg.) in 15 rounds, Jovito Rengifo (Venezuela) in 8, and Hurricane Teru (Japan) in 15. Jeff Chandler (U.S.) also made three successful defenses of the WBA bantamweight title, outpointing Jorge Luján (Panama), drawing with Eijiro Murata (Japan), and stopping Julian Solís (Puerto Rico) in seven rounds.

Chul-Ho Kim (South Korea) won the WBC super flyweight title from Rafael Orono (Venezuela) in 13 rounds and retained it in 13 against Willie Jensen (U.S.), in 15 against Jiro Watanabe (Japan), and in 9 against Ryotetsu Muruyama. The WBA super flyweight championship was won by Gustavo Ballas (Arg.), but Ballas then lost it to Rafael Pedroza (Panama). The WBC flyweight championship was won by Antonio Avelar (Mexico), who knocked out Shoji Oguma (Japan) in seven rounds in Japan and then went to South Korea to knock out former WBA champion Tae-Shik Kim (South Korea) in two. The WBA flyweight title changed hands three times. Santos Laciar (Arg.) beat Peter Mathebula (South Africa) in 7 rounds before losing to Luis Ibarra (Panama) over 15. Ibarra was then knocked out in 11 by Juan Herrera (Mexico). Hilario Zapata (Panama) held the WBC junior flyweight crown, stopping Joey Olivio (U.S.) in 13 rounds and outpointing Rudy Crawford (Nicaragua). The WBA version changed hands three times,

Pedro Flores (Mexico) stopping Yoko Gushiken (Japan) in 12 rounds, Hwan-Jin Kim (South Korea) halting Flores in 13, and Katsuo Tokashiki (Japan) defeating Kim on points.

In Europe Lucien Rodriguez (France) outpointed Luis Felipe Rodríguez (Spain) to take the heavyweight title, which had become vacant when John L. Gardner (England) retired. Rudi Koopmans (Neth.) retained the light-heavyweight title by stopping Hocine Tafer (France) and Fed Serres (Luxembourg). Tony Sibson (England) kept the middleweight championship with victories against Andoni Amana (Spain), Alan Minter (England), and Nicola Cirelli (Italy).

Luigi Minchillo (Italy) took the European junior middleweight title from Louis Acaries (France). Earlier in the year Acaries had taken the crown from Marijan Benes (Yugos.). Jørgen Hansen (Den.) remained welterweight champion by beating Richard Rodriguez (France) and Hans Henrik Palm (Den.). The junior welterweight championship was won by Antonio Guinaldo (Spain), who knocked out Giuseppe Martinese (Italy) and André Holyk (France). Guinaldo then lost the title to Clinton McKenzie (England). Giuseppe Gibilisco (Italy) won the lightweight title from Charlie Nash (Ireland) and retained it against José Luis Heredia (Spain). Carlos Hernández (Spain) kept the junior lightweight championship, beating Alain Le Fol (France) and Carlos Miguel Rodríguez (Spain). Salvatore Melluzzo (Italy) won the vacant featherweight crown, outpointing Laurent Grimbert (France) in seven rounds. Valerio Nati (Italy) gained the vacant bantamweight title by outpointing Juan Francisco Rodríguez (Spain) and retained it by beating Vincente Rodríguez (Spain), John Feeney (England), and Jean-Jacques Souris (France). Charlie Magri (England) retained the flyweight title.

In the Commonwealth Berbick won the vacant heavyweight championship by halting Conroy Nelson (Canada) in two rounds. Colin Jones (Wales) won the vacant welterweight crown, stopping Mark Harris (Guyana), while Barry

Colonies:
 see Dependent States

Table II. World Wrestling Champions, 1981

Weight class	Freestyle	Greco-Roman
48 kg (105.5 lb)	S. Kornilaev, U.S.S.R.	Z. Ushkempirov, U.S.S.R.
52 kg (114.5 lb)	T. Asakura, Japan	V. Blagidze, U.S.S.R.
57 kg (125.5 lb)	S. Beloglazov, U.S.S.R.	P. Passarelli, W. Germany
62 kg (136.5 lb)	S. Sterev, Bulgaria	I. Toth, Hungary
68 kg (149.5 lb)	S. Absaidov, U.S.S.R.	G. Ermilov, U.S.S.R.
74 kg (163 lb)	M. Knosp, W. Germany	A. Kudriavzev, U.S.S.R.
82 kg (180.5 lb)	C. Campbell, U.S.	G. Korban, U.S.S.R.
90 kg (198 lb)	S. Oganesyan, U.S.S.R.	I. Kanygin, U.S.S.R.
100 kg (220 lb)	R. Gehrke, E. Germany	M. Saladze, U.S.S.R.
100+ kg	S. Hasimikov, U.S.S.R.	R. Memisevic, Yugos.

Michael (Australia) took the lightweight championship from Langton Tinago (Zimbabwe) and retained it against Dave McCabe (Scotland). Azumah Nelson (Nigeria) gained the vacant featherweight title, stopping Brian Roberts (Australia). Paul Ferreri (Australia) won the bantamweight title, and Steve Muchoki (Kenya) retained the flyweight crown. (FRANK BUTLER)

Wrestling. The top wrestling tournament in the world in 1981 was the freestyle world championships held in Skopje, Yugos., on Aug. 28–31, 1981. The Soviet Union was again the team champion with 42 points, while Bulgaria finished second with 33 points and the U.S. third with 28.

The Greco-Roman championship tournament took place in Oslo, Norway, on August 28–31. The Soviet Union continued its domination of this sport with 49 points; Hungary placed second with 23 points, and Finland was third with 21.

The University of Iowa continued its domination of the U.S. National Collegiate Athletic Association Championships, which were held at Princeton, N.J., March 12–14. Iowa's point total was 129.75. The University of Oklahoma was second with 100.25 points, and Iowa State University finished third with a total of 84.75 points. (MARVIN G. HESS)

Fencing. The Soviet Union, a power in fencing in recent years, continued to demonstrate its strength in the world championships held at Clermont-Ferrand in France in 1981. The Soviets captured four of the eight gold medals and two bronzes in outpointing a large international field.

The continued resurgence of Hungary as a world power was one of the more significant developments during the ten-day competition. Hungary garnered two gold medals, one silver, and two bronzes. Noteworthy too was a performance by Luan Juji in the women's foil to give China its first silver medal in the history of the international classic. Only in recent years had China evinced interest in the championships.

France, a strong performer in the 1980 Olympic Games at Moscow, with four gold medals, was shut out on its own soil. Its best showings were fourth places in the men's foil and women's foil. The United States, never a top contender in international fencing, emerged with an 8th place in men's foil and 11th places in sabre and épée.

The only individual to repeat for a gold medal victory was Vladimir Smirnov. The Soviet star, who had triumphed in the 1980 Olympics after a fence-off with two rivals, had less difficulty this time. In women's foil Cornelia Hanisch, a seasoned world performer, gave West Germany its only victory. Noteworthy too was the success by Poland's Mariusz Wodke in sabre for that nation's only first place. The three other victories by the Soviet Union were in the team competitions in men's foil, women's foil, and épée. The remaining individual event, the épée, was captured by Hungary's Zoltan Szekely; Hungary also triumphed in team sabre.

Noticeable was a stricter adherence to the rules by officials, a trend that was becoming increasingly evident in the sport. In the foil team event, for example, a Frenchman was penalized three times, thereby forfeiting three winning touches to lose the bout. The infraction by the French fencer was "covering the target area with his hands." In one final round robin bout, the Hungarian competitor Gerevitch was penalized for "not trying."

(MICHAEL STRAUSS)

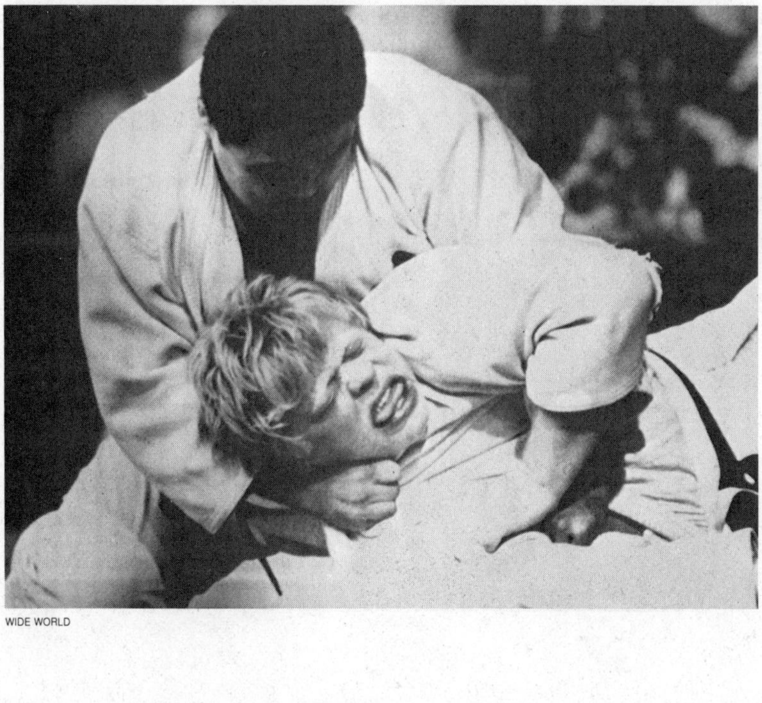

Fun and games at the judo championship. Yashuhiro Yamashita of Japan put a stranglehold on Wojciech Resco of Poland and went on to win the open category at the World Judo Championships in Maastricht, The Netherlands, in September.

WIDE WORLD

Judo. Japan reasserted its dominance in judo in 1981 by winning half of the eight golds at stake in the 11th World Judo Championships (WJC) in Maastricht, Neth., in early September and seven of the eight golds in the International Judo Tournament in Tokyo in November. Yashuhiro Yamashita, the 26-year-old, 135-kg world judo champion, won golds in both the heavyweight and open events of the WJC, took the heavyweight title in the Tokyo meet (he did not compete in the open), and captured first place in the All-Japan Judo Championships for an unprecedented fifth time. Other gold medalists in the world championships included: light-heavyweight Tamiz Khubuluri (U.S.S.R.), middleweight Bernard Tchoullouyan (France), light-middleweight Neil Adams (U.K.), lightweight Chong Hak Park (South Korea), welterweight Katsuhiko Kashiwazaki (Japan), and bantamweight Yasuhiko Moriwake (Japan).

Japan also dominated the Asian Judo Championships in Jakarta, Indon., in July by winning 13 of the 16 men's and women's events. A young Japanese team came out on top in the Paris International Tournament in early 1981 by grabbing four first places to three for France. At the second Pacific Judo Championships in February, the Japanese men won five of the eight golds, and the Japanese women took three. The Japanese women won only one silver in the first Women's World Judo Championships, which the Europeans dominated. On the eve of the world championships, the International Judo Federation announced it would start issuing certificates recognizing rankings in judo proficiency. Japan condemned the step and said it threatened to split the judo world, apparently because it challenged the long-time supremacy of the Kodokan School of Judo.

Karate. It was an active year in karate, both in Japan and abroad, with the holding of the first World Games in midsummer and the All-Japan All-Styles Tournament in December. Japan won three of the seven gold medals and Britain two in the first World Games at Santa Clara, Calif., in July. Masayuki Naito won the 60-kg class, Zenichi Ono took the 65-kg title, and Osamu Kamikado captured the 80-kg category. Victor Charles and Cecil Hackett of Great Britain won the open and 70-kg classes, respectively. Other *kumite* (free fighting) winners were L. Kotezebue of The Netherlands in the heavyweight category and Lin Chin-ming of Taiwan in the 75-kg class. Both golds in the *kata* (prescribed forms) competition went to Japanese—Keiji Okada for the men and Reiko Okamura for the women. Some 200 *karateka* from 16 nations took part. In the All-Japan All-Styles Tournament in mid-December, Seiji Nishimura and Hisao Murase finished first and second, respectively. Both are *Wado-kai* specialists and had dominated Japanese karate for several years. In the women's *kumite* competition, Sonoko Tanka of *Joshinmen* style was first and Hiromi Kawashima second. In an all-military tournament in July Japan's Ground, Air, and Maritime Self-Defense Force (GSDF) teams came in 1-2-3, but a "Good Fight Prize" was awarded to both the "A" and "B" teams of the U.S. Seisaku Udaka of the GSDF won the individual contest with a *jodan-zuki* punch against Katsunori Sumiyoshi. The Japan Self-Defense Forces held its own tourney at the same time. Iruma ASDF Base got the nod over Komatsu ASDF Base on points after a 2–2 tie. At the September National Athletic Meet in Shiga Prefecture, Hsiao Murase of Tokyo won the open competition for the fourth year in a row. The finalists of the two previous years in the National Kokushin-kai Tournament fought it out again, with Keiji Sanpei beating Makoto Nakamura for the second straight time in their three-year rivalry.

Sumo. In 1981 33-year-old *yokozuna* (grand champion) Wajima retired, along with *ozeki* (champions) Takanohana and Masuiyama. Their departure was balanced out by the dramatic emergence of a new sumo hero, 25-year-old Chiyonofuji ("Chiyo"). The handsome, muscular *rikishi* (sumo wrestler) leaped from the third-highest rank of *sekiwake* in January to the very pinnacle of the ancient sport by midyear, becoming the 58th *yokozuna* in sumo history. Meanwhile, the great Kitanoumi ("Kita"), a 28-year-old *yokozuna*, failed for the first time since 1977 to win at least half of the six annual 15-day *basho* (tournaments) and,

The Fighting Spirit award at the Nagoya Sumo Tournament in Japan in July went to Takamiyama (Hawaiian-born Jesse Kuhaulua; right). Asashio (left) received the Outstanding Performance award.

WIDE WORLD

because of a knee injury, withdrew from a tournament for the first time in his 15-year career. But Kita still managed to collect the year's best win-loss record—69–15 with 6 absences—to gain Rikishi of the Year honours for the seventh straight year. His two *yusho* (tournament victories) gave him a total of 22, only 10 short of retired *yokuzuna* Taiho's all-time mark. Wakanohana, the third *yokozuna*, had a disastrous year because of physical and psychological problems. He dropped out of the second and third *basho*, skipped the fourth altogether, and then missed the sixth following a hip operation.

Hawaiian-born Takamiyama, now a Japanese citizen, pulled out on the second day of the Aki *basho* in September with a sprained ankle, thus closing the book on his all-time mark for most consecutive bouts at 1,426. Up to that time, Jesse (as he was affectionately known) had not missed a single bout because of injury, illness, or any other reason since entering sumo in March 1964.

Chiyonofuji, rather slightly built at 5 ft 11 in and 250 lb, thrilled millions of sumo fans by upsetting 365-lb Kitanoumi in the play-off of the Hatsu *basho* in January to capture the first of his tourney titles. The victory earned him promotion to *ozeki*. But Kita roared back in the Haru *basho* in March by walking off with the Emperor's Cup with a 13–2 record. Chiyo was second with 11–4. Kita continued his dominance in May in the Natsu *basho*, defeating Chiyo in the final bout to take his 22nd *yusho* with an excellent 14–1 mark, while Chiyo was runner-up again with 13–2. But Chiyonofuji had the smell of *yokozuna* in his nostrils and overpowered Kita in the climactic finale to win the Nagoya *basho* in July with a 14–1 record, thus ensuring his promotion to *yokozuna*. Kita was second at 13–2. *Sekiwake* Kotokaze overcame a repeated injury to his knee to grab the *yusho* of the Aki *basho* in September with a 12–3 mark. Chiyo pulled out with a sprained ankle on the third day, and Kita faltered badly to end up 10–5. In the final Kyushu *basho* in November, Chiyonofuji came back strong to win the title with a 12–3 mark in a play-off with 385-lb Komusubi Asashio after Kitanoumi withdrew with a knee injury on the eighth day.

Kendo. Unlike judo and karate, activity in kendo in 1981 was confined to key tournaments as Japan prepared for the 1982 World Kendo Championships in São Paulo, Brazil. As usual, the year's most prestigious tournament was the December All-Japan Kendo Championships for men. The title went to Yuji Takada of the Tokyo Metropolitan Police Department, who defeated Kajiya Kosaka with *men* (helmet) and *do* (side) strikes. A Tokai University senior, Mizue Morita, emerged victorious among 56 competitors, beating Nagako Kawazoe in the final match by a *men* strike to win the All-Japan Women's Kendo Championships in Osaka in May. The National Men's Team Championships, held on the same day at the same venue, was an all-Kyushu affair as the Kagoshima Prefecture team won the title for the second consecutive year by edging the Miyazaki Prefecture team 3–2. In the 1981 All-Japan Police Tournament, one of the year's major kendo events, Hiroyuki Tsukamoto of the Tokyo Metropolitan

Police Department scored *men* and *kote* (forearm) points to defeat Y. Ishihara and capture first place at the Budokan in June. Tochigi Prefecture won the team event in the All-Japan Teacher's Tournament in Akita in August, while Nippon Unso (Japan Transport Co.) took the top prize in the All-Japan Industrial Championships in September at the Budokan. (ANDREW M. ADAMS)

Commonwealth of Nations

The Commonwealth heads of government meeting in Melbourne, Australia (Sept. 30–Oct. 7, 1981), both overshadowed and reflected the Commonwealth's activities in development, decolonization, and democracy. Of the 45 members only Dominica and the three special members—Tuvalu, Nauru, and St. Vincent and the Grenadines—were absent. The attendance of 30 heads of state set a new record.

There were 13 new faces at Melbourne, including the prime ministers of the three new member countries: Robert Mugabe of Zimbabwe, Walter Lini of Vanuatu, and Belize's George Price (*see* BIOGRAPHIES). During the two years since the last meeting, Sir Seretse Khama of Botswana (d. 1980) and Eric Williams (*see* OBITUARIES) of Trinidad and Tobago had died; Bangladesh's Pres. Ziaur Rahman (*see* OBITUARIES) was assassinated in May. Milton Obote, Uganda's president and the first African leader to be ousted by bullet and returned, if shakily, by ballot, was absent, as was Sir Dawda Jawara, after the abortive July coup in The Gambia.

Common concern and support were demonstrated in the consideration of problems from every region. Guyana and Belize asked for help against Venezuelan and Guatemalan claims on their territory. Canada discussed the patriation of its constitution (at the time only changeable by British act of Parliament) and consulted Caribbean

Leaders of the Commonwealth nations gathered for eight days of meetings in Melbourne, Australia (Sept. 30–Oct. 7).

UPI

members on the development of the Caribbean Community. Both Singapore's Lee Kuan Yew and the U.K.'s Margaret Thatcher voiced Commonwealth opposition to Soviet expansion in Asia, while Indira Gandhi of India, concerned with Indian Ocean neutrality and military aid to Pakistan, criticized the latter's proposed reentry into the Commonwealth.

For the first time the Pacific island governments set forth an organized view to the conference, particularly in relation to seabed control and the law of the sea. New Zealand with its large Polynesian population emerged as leader of the South Pacific Forum. African nations concentrated on the issues of South Africa and South West Africa/Namibia.

The meeting focused generally on the potential of the Commonwealth for diminishing poverty and conflict. The Melbourne Declaration, supported by specific policies on agriculture and free trade, provided a consensus for the seven Commonwealth representatives to take to the October North-South summit meeting in Mexico.

British official aid reached £1,000 million for the first time, while over half of the International Development Association's £550 million in loans went to Commonwealth nations. The Commonwealth Development Corporation in 1980 undertook 31 new projects worth £80 million.

The Food and Agriculture Organization reported a decline in food and agricultural production in Africa. While the FAO emphasized drought and debt as primary causes, the World Bank report also condemned inefficiency and corruption. The Commonwealth conference pinpointed the inability of African nations to relate political to economic reality; for example, their call for economic sanctions against South Africa was contradicted by their increasing trade with and dependence upon that country.   (MOLLY MORTIMER)

See also articles on the various political units.
[972.A.1.a]

Comoros

Comoros

An island state lying in the Indian Ocean off the east coast of Africa between Mozambique and Madagascar, the Comoros in 1980 administratively comprised three main islands, Grande Comore (Ngazídja), Moheli (Mohali), and Anjouan (Dzouani); the fourth island of the archipelago, Mayotte, continued to be a de facto dependency of France. Area: 1,792 sq km (692 sq mi). Pop. (1980 prelim., excluding Mayotte): 347,000. Cap. and largest city: Moroni (pop., 1980 prelim., 20,000), on Grande Comore. Language: Comorian (which is allied to Swahili), Arabic, and French. Religion: Islam (official). President in 1981, Ahmed Abdallah; premier, Salim Ben Ali.

The International Federation for the Rights of Man and Amnesty International expressed concern in 1981 over the conditions under which supporters of the previous Comoran regime were being held without trial. Disquiet increased in November when Abdallah Mouzaoir, foreign minister under former president Ali Soilih and now considered leader of the opposition, was ar-

COMOROS
Education. (1980–81) Primary, pupils 59,709, teachers 1,292; secondary, pupils 13,528, teachers 434; vocational, students 196, teachers 18; teacher training, students 131, teachers 9.
Finance and Trade. Monetary unit: CFA franc, with (Sept. 21, 1981) a parity of CFA Fr 50 to the French franc and a free rate of CFA Fr 265 to U.S. $1 (CFA Fr 491 = £1 sterling). Budget (1979 est.) balanced at c. CFA Fr 3.2 billion. Foreign trade: imports (1977) CFA Fr 4,055,000,000; exports (1978) CFA Fr 2,105,000,000. Import sources: France 41%; Madagascar 20%; Pakistan 8%; Kenya c. 5%; China 5%. Export destinations (1977): France 65%; U.S. 21%; Madagascar 5%. Main exports: vanilla 35%; essential oils 30%; cloves 22%; copra 10%.

rested on his return to Moroni from abroad.

Reports of an attempted coup in February were denied by the government. Despite opposition efforts to destabilize the regime and isolate it from the new Socialist government in France, Pres. Ahmed Abdallah was twice received by French Pres. François Mitterrand in Paris, in October and November. Although Abdallah offered not to oppose the French military presence on the island of Mayotte (still a de facto French dependency) should the island be reintegrated with the Comoros, this problem remained in suspense. The inhabitants of Mayotte were generally opposed to reintegration under the presidency of Abdallah, a native of Anjouan.   (PHILIPPE DECRAENE)

Computers

The transition of the personal computer from a hobbyist's compulsion to a productivity tool for professionals, managers, and very small businesses became evident during 1981. Industry giant IBM Corp. capped that trend by introducing its first personal computer system. IBM chose to distribute its new product not only through its usual sales channels and computer stores but also through such general retailers as Sears, Roebuck and Co.

Technology. Besides IBM's new system, the Star 8010 professional work station of the Xerox Corp. was a spectacular offering of a personal computer designed to be used in the workplace. Although the work station, which is a type of personal computer and an important component of the "office of the future," was not yet being adopted in great numbers by major companies, the Star's enthusiastic reception was an indication that the business community recognized that it must improve the productivity of white collar workers —professionals and managers—if U.S. business was to remain competitive in world commerce.

The giants of the computer industry responded to the need for companies to improve productivity among white collar workers. Major mainframe companies such as Burroughs Corp. and Honeywell Inc. introduced their first "office automation" systems. By the mid-1980s such systems were expected to allow data processing, word processing, electronic mail, and voice and video applications to operate off the same device. A network using a broadband cable, which permits the transmission

of voice, data, and video, is the mechanism that would permit these systems to communicate among one another and also with various central host facilities.

The increasing power of the microprocessor, a computer on a chip, was a key factor in permitting the sophisticated tasks described above to be accomplished on small machines. During the year a 16-bit microprocessor of Motorola, Inc. became available to the public. Previously, the 8-bit microprocessor had been standard. Also, Intel Corp. announced its advances in building a 32-bit microprocessor, called a micromainframe. Although the size of a desk-top computer, it was designed to pack the power of a mainframe on three chips. (A bit in a computer system is the smallest increment of usable data, expressed in machine language as a 0 or 1; a 32-bit microprocessor can handle that many bits simultaneously.)

The race to produce very-large-scale integrated (VLSI) circuits continued, with the Japanese creating a 256K-bit memory chip. (A K-bit equals 1,024 bits.) IBM announced that it had successfully created a 288K-bit memory chip, the largest ever built; although smaller than the size of a fingernail, it could hold the equivalent of 20 typewritten, double-spaced manuscript pages. Extensive commercial production of these VLSI chips remained several years in the future.

Business. Despite the technological strides made by the semiconductor industry during the year, a nose dive took place on the business side. This downturn was all the more dramatic because the preceding five years had been prosperous ones for semiconductor vendors.

The supply of 16K-bit and 64K-bit memory devices outstripped the demand, and prices for certain memory devices fell in some cases by a factor of ten. The glut of devices on the market was fueled by intense price and production competition from Japanese vendors.

While the economic news was bad in the semiconductor industry, most computer system and software vendors had healthy revenue growth rates during the year. However, a slowdown in the economy in Europe resulted in a decline of orders for many U.S.-based firms. This, along with high interest rates and the strengthening of the dollar on world money markets, reduced the profitability of many computer companies. Some suppliers of small business systems experienced reduced volume as small firms deferred the acquisition of computer equipment because of high interest rates.

On the whole, the computer industry was expected to earn more than $60 billion in revenue for 1981, an average growth of about 12%, according to some data processing market researchers. But some segments of the industry, such as office automation, personal computers, superminicomputer systems, and software packages, were growing at annual revenue rates of 30 to 40%, while the expensive general-purpose units (mainframes) were growing at a rate of only about 5% annually.

One of the best selling items on the market in 1981 was the 32-bit minicomputer, known popularly as a supermini. Most major minicomputer makers and IBM brought out versions of these machines in various sizes during the year. The superminis started a revolution in the minicomputer industry, which for the past decade had been built on 16-bit architecture. By 1981 the 32-bit mini was on its way to replacing the 16-bit model. The primary advantage of superminis is that they can directly access about 16 megabytes (128 million bits) of memory, compared with traditional minicomputers that access 64 kilobytes (512,000 bits) of memory, too little for the new complex software programs.

On the software side of the industry, at least three major packaged software firms—Management Science America, Inc., Pansophic Systems, Inc., and Software AG of North America, Inc.—made their first public stock offerings. The ability

With their versatility increasing and their prices falling, home computers were becoming big business in the U.S. A potential customer looks at a small home computer in an exhibit.

COURTESY, IBM CORP.

Supermarket checkout lines began to move faster in the U.S. as scanners linked to computers came into more widespread use. The scanners "read" specially marked codes printed on grocery cans and boxes.

of software companies to raise public equity capital during 1981 resulted from the recognition that packaged software computer programs could be used with little modification by many different customers.

Applications. Perhaps the most startling manifestations of computer technology during the year were the two flights of the U.S. space shuttle "Columbia" in April and November. The specially designed battery of five redundant AP-101 computers aboard the craft were 40 times faster, had 5 times more memory capacity, and carried 8 times more memory instructions than the onboard data processing units aboard the Apollo 11, the spacecraft that landed on the Moon in 1969. It was, in fact, the lack of synchronization among those five computers that caused the two-day delay in the launch of the first flight. The flights were monitored by the largest assortment of computer systems ever assembled for a U.S. space mission.

While the "Columbia" captured the imagination of the public, computers were also tirelessly working back on Earth at a wide range of tasks. One of the most notable was the attempt to link the clues associated with the series of child killings that haunted Atlanta, Ga.

The accelerating rate at which computers were proliferating within organizations caused some consternation about their compatibility, that is, whether they would be able to communicate with one another and whether the programs written for one vendor's machine would be portable to another vendor's product. Some positive moves toward standardization took place in 1981. In particular, it appeared that most microcomputers were using an operating system named CP/M as a standard. Moreover, IBM's adoption of the X.25 communications protocol during the year was an indication that this protocol would be the standard one for public data networks.

Besides compatibility, U.S. computer makers, still the dominant force in the world computer markets, were keenly watching the inroads made

by the Japanese. By the end of the year all major Japanese computer companies had announced that they would be producing very large mainframe systems and also made clear their plans to be a dominant force in the personal and desk-top computer markets, particularly in the U.S.

Moreover, surfacing during the year was a report initiated by Japan's Ministry of International Trade and Industry. It outlined the Japanese industry's commitment to creating a so-called fifth-generation computer that would break away from the architecture now used. Such a machine, called a knowledge information processing system, would be designed with a high degree of artificial intelligence (the ability of the machine to solve problems) and would allow users to communicate with it through natural language patterns.

(MARCIA A. BLUMENTHAL)

[735.D; 10/23.A.6–7]

Congo

A people's republic of equatorial Africa, the Congo is bounded by Gabon, Cameroon, the Central African Republic, Zaire, Angola, and the Atlantic Ocean. Area: 342,000 sq km (132,047 sq mi). Pop. (1981 est.): 1,577,000, mainly Bantu. Cap. and largest city: Brazzaville (pop., 1977 est., 310,000). Language: French (official) and Bantu dialects. Religion (1977 est.): Roman Catholic 40.5%; Protestant 9.6%; Muslim 2.9%; animist 47%. President in 1981, Col. Denis Sassou-Nguesso; premier, Col. Louis Sylvain Ngoma.

Relations between the Congo and the U.S.S.R. became strained during 1981, notwithstanding the Congo's support of Soviet policy in Afghanistan and the signing of a cooperation agreement between the two countries in Moscow on May 13. During Pres. Denis Sassou-Nguesso's visit to Moscow in May, he refused to accept another military base in addition to the one at Pointe-Noire, the port through which, since 1975, Cubans and Sovi-

Congo

CONGO

Education. (1978–79) Primary, pupils 358,761, teachers 6,832; secondary, pupils 138,525, teachers 3,099; vocational, pupils 9,633, teachers 505; teacher training, students 1,228, teachers 102; higher, students (1977–78) 3,642, teaching staff (1975–76) 165.

Finance. Monetary unit: CFA franc, with (Sept. 21, 1981) a parity of CFA Fr 50 to the French franc and a free rate of CFA Fr 265 to U.S. $1 (CFA Fr 491 = £1 sterling). Budget (1980 est.) balanced at CFA Fr 119,126,000,000.

Foreign Trade. (1978) Imports CFA Fr 58,860,000,000; exports CFA Fr 31,160,000,000. Import sources: France 50%; Italy 6%; West Germany 5%; U.S. 5%. Export destinations: Italy 31%; France 24%; Spain 8%; The Netherlands 6%; Chile 6%; Belgium-Luxembourg 5%. Main exports (1977): crude oil 54%; timber 13%; food 9%; chemical fertilizer 7%; manganese ore 5%.

Transport and Communications. Roads (all-weather; 1977) 8,246 km. Motor vehicles in use (1977): passenger 13,250; commercial 3,700. Railways: (1977) 803 km; traffic (1979) 286 million passenger-km, freight 470 million net ton-km. Air traffic (including apportionment of Air Afrique; 1980): c. 197 million passenger-km; freight c. 19.3 million net ton-km. Telephones (Jan. 1978) c. 12,000. Radio receivers (Dec. 1977) 88,000. Television receivers (Dec. 1977) 3,500.

Agriculture. Production (in 000; metric tons; 1979): cassava c. 542; sweet potatoes c. 26; peanuts c. 18; sugar, raw value c. 27; bananas c. 26; plantains c. 33; coffee c. 3; cocoa c. 4; palm oil c. 7; tobacco c. 1. Livestock (in 000; 1979): cattle c. 71; sheep c. 66; goats 119; pigs 49; chickens c. 1,000.

Industry. Production (in 000; metric tons; 1978): cement 61; crude oil (1980) c. 2,650; lead concentrates (metal content) c. 2.5; zinc ore (metal content) 4.8; potash fertilizers (nutrient content; 1977–78) c. 81; electricity (kw-hr) c. 126,000.

ets had passed on their way to Angola. In contrast, the president visited France in July and received the French minister for cooperation and development in Brazzaville in October.

Divisions in the ruling Congo Labour Party, the country's sole political party, continued between those who advocated exclusive cooperation with Moscow and those who proposed strong overtures to the West. The economy made rapid progress thanks to increased petroleum output, which topped four million metric tons in 1981.

(PHILIPPE DECRAENE)

Consumerism

By 1981 the scope of the consumer movement had widened considerably since its beginnings, when it was primarily occupied with prices and quality of goods. Now included were such areas of concern as environmental protection, energy conservation, health, safety, and education.

International Cooperation. Typifying this trend, consumer organizations from the industrialized lands in 1981 followed the pattern established in the 1970s and continued to help fellow consumers in the less developed countries. The tenth International Consumer Congress, gathering in The Hague, Neth., in June, discussed this cooperation. The theme of the congress, "Consumers in a Shrinking World," pinpointed the influence that the Western way of life and pattern of consumption exercised on societies of the third world, which in turn needed to be protected from the undesirable aspects of that influence.

Attended by well over 300 delegates, the congress, which was organized by the International Organization of Consumers Unions (IOCU), welcomed the announcement of plans for launching a sort of consumer "Interpol" that would not only serve as a citizens' network for exchanging information but would also be a tool for action and a basis for local, national, and international campaigns against hazardous products. This project was supported by a grant from the Dutch government, it was announced at the congress, and was given high priority because of the dangerous dumping in the third world of food, goods, and medicines that had been rejected in the industrialized lands. To counteract and put a stop to such practices, IOCU hoped to publicize details of the exporting and importing of dangerous products and technologies.

As long ago as 1975 IOCU had published a report on the availability and use of the drug clioquinol in 34 countries in Asia. The survey then found great inconsistencies in the instructions and warnings about the use of the drug, not only as between different brands but also for the same brand in different countries. The intervening years brought no improvement in the situation, and IOCU undertook to distribute worldwide a leaflet published by a London-based action research group, Social Audit, in which doctors were asked not to prescribe clioquinol. The leaflet reminded readers that although clioquinol was banned in many developed countries, it was still sold extensively in more than 100 other nations. Clioquinol was by no means the only suspect drug, and following a teach-in on drugs organized by IOCU in Penang, Malaysia, in late 1980, the beginnings were established of a network of people who could research the marketing techniques, effectiveness, and safety—or lack of it—of dangerous drugs.

In May 1981 representatives of nongovernmental organizations from 27 countries concluded a three-day conference, organized by a West German coalition of development action groups, by

A new artificial sweetener, aspartame, was introduced to the public during the year. The sweetener had received final approval by the U.S. Food and Drug Administration in July.

WIDE WORLD

forming a Health Action International, aimed at combating the "ill-treatment of consumers by multinational drug companies." The delegates discussed a wide range of issues and were strongly critical of the high-pressure marketing and promotional methods of multinational drug firms, their large profits, and the provision of irrelevant and inappropriate drugs, especially in less developed countries. A spokesman for the conference said that in recent years the pharmaceutical industry had blocked the World Health Organization's essential drugs program and other initiatives meant to control the international trade in hazardous drugs.

Food problems facing consumers were the subject of a European Economic Community (EEC) forum, "Towards Community Food Policy," held in West Berlin in January. Of the pledges given at the 1974 World Food Conference, none had come to fruition, and the situation had deteriorated: every day some 50,000 were dying of starvation, food production in the less developed countries was not keeping pace with increase in population, and food shortages were serious in 31 less developed lands. Also, in several countries traditional staple foods were being displaced by Western fashions in foodstuffs—white rice, white sugar, and white flour were absorbed into local cultures to the detriment of nutritional standards.

Another issue that continued to be of great concern to consumer organizations was the promotion of powdered milks and breast-milk substitutes in the less developed countries, which had led to a decline in breast-feeding and an increase in infant disease, malnutrition, and death. An eight-nation study by the IOCU Regional Office for Asia and the Pacific revealed more than 100 examples of inappropriate marketing policies. In May 1981, as a result of pressure from consumer and other action groups, the World Health Assembly was asked to adopt as a recommendation a draft International Code that represented the minimum requirements for the framing of national regulations for the promotion of breast-milk substitutes. This code was approved by a vote of 118–1, with the U.S. casting the only dissenting vote. Japan, Argentina, and South Korea abstained.

National Legislation. The U.S. government in 1981 began to move away from the consumerism movement that had been in force since the mid-1960s. Pres. Ronald Reagan attempted to abolish the Consumer Product Safety Commission. He was not able to accomplish this, but in 1981 the commission received a small budget that forced it to curtail many of its projects; these included investigations into the safety of riding mowers, snowblowers, and electric clothes dryers and the screening of products for carcinogens. The commission was able to enforce the ban on urea-formaldehyde foam insulation and to establish flammability standards for upholstered furniture and safety standards for chain saws. Virginia Knauer, head of the federal Office of Consumer Affairs, said that although the 1981 budget cuts were intended to make federal agencies "leaner and meaner," the Reagan administration would not abandon consumerism.

The Reagan administration took a strong position on the future of the Federal Trade Commission with a proposal to reduce the FTC staff by 40% by 1986. The FTC abandoned its aggressive policy of issuing broad rules affecting entire industries and reverted to its former practice of bringing lawsuits against companies on a case-by-case basis.

A new low-calorie sweetener called aspartame was approved by the U.S. Food and Drug Administration during the year. Aspartame was the result of an intensive search for an alternative to saccharin that had been under way since cyclamates were banned in 1970. Saccharin has been a candidate for removal from the market since 1977 as a potential cancer-causing agent. The government had allowed the product to remain on grocers' shelves with health warnings on the label. Aspartame was derived from two amino acids found naturally in food, aspartic acid and phenylalanine. This sugar substitute would be used in products such as cold breakfast cereals, coffee and tea, powdered soft drinks, desserts, topping mixes, and chewing gum. Aspartame is unstable at high temperatures, and therefore could not be used in baking.

An order issued by the FTC in September 1981 required American Home Products to have scientific support behind claims for Anacin and its other analgesic products. The order required analgesics containing aspirin to disclose that aspirin is the pain-reliever whenever performance claims for the products are made.

In Nigeria the government brought into force a comprehensive bill setting guidelines for water pollution, sewage, and solid-waste disposal. Sweden introduced regulations to protect water from pollution by vessels and updated existing regulations on environmentally dangerous wastes and the clearing up of oil spills. The U.K. Office of Fair Trading recommended measures to give consumers greater protection against used-car dealers.

Cigarette and tobacco advertising received critical examination: in Belgium and The Netherlands cigarette packages now had to carry a health warning, and in Portugal tobacco advertising was banned on television and radio. In the U.K. the government and the tobacco industry reached agreement on a new code of advertising practice; new warnings appeared on cigarette packets, and the companies undertook to reduce their poster advertising by 30% over the next two years. In Hong Kong publication of the Consumer Council's test results on cigarettes started much public discussion on smoking, and the government set up a Working Group on Cigarette Smoking.

In China, as state planning gave way to the law of the marketplace, the government adopted new measures to curb growing trade malpractices. Some factories were caught illegally raising prices or reducing the quality of their products, and peddlers were reverting to stuffing poultry with sand or vegetable hearts with rotten leaves to increase their weight.

(ISOLA VAN DEN HOVEN; EDWARD MARK MAZZE)

See also Economy, World; Industrial Review: *Advertising.*
[532.B.3; 534.H.5; 534.K]

Contract Bridge

A significant development in 1981 was the emergence of China, made a member of the World Bridge Federation (WBF) in 1980, as an active world bridge participant. In May WBF Pres. Jaime Ortiz-Patino led a WBF group to China at the invitation of the Chinese Bridge Association. They were received by and played bridge with Chinese leader Deng Xiaoping (Teng Hsiao-p'ing), a much better than average player. In October the International Bridge Press Association named Deng as the bridge personality of the year for "distinguished service to world bridge."

For the first time the Bermuda Bowl and the Venice Cup were held together as the respective

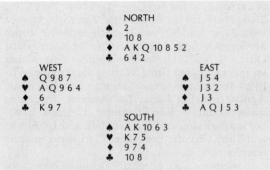

```
                    NORTH
                    ♠ 2
                    ♥ 10 8
                    ♦ A K Q 10 8 5 2
                    ♣ 6 4 2
      WEST                          EAST
      ♠ Q 9 8 7                     ♠ J 5 4
      ♥ A Q 9 6 4                   ♥ J 3 2
      ♦ 6                           ♦ J 3
      ♣ K 9 7                       ♣ A Q J 5 3
                    SOUTH
                    ♠ A K 10 6 3
                    ♥ K 7 5
                    ♦ 9 7 4
                    ♣ 10 8
```

Dealer West, Love All.
Bidding in the Open Room:

West	North	East	South
J. Solodar	Masood Salim	R. Levin	Zia Mahmood
2 ♦	Pass	2 ♥	Pass
Pass	3 ♦	3 ♥	Pass
Pass	4 ♦		

Two diamonds was a multipurpose bid requiring a conventional response of two hearts on most hands. West, with a weak-two opening, passed. After a trump lead, declarer was able to discard a heart loser from hand and make his contract for a score of 130.
Bidding in the Closed Room:

West	North	East	South
Muneer Ataulah	J. Meckstroth	Jan-E-Alam Fazli	E. Rodwell
1 ♥	3 ♥	Double	3 no trumps
Pass	Pass	Double	Pass
Pass	Redouble		

Meckstroth's bid of three hearts showed a solid suit and invited partner to convert to three no trumps if he guarded the other three suits. Rodwell accepted the invitation, and Meckstroth's double confirmed the solidity of his diamond suit. Although the redouble made it clear that one suit was out against him, Rodwell decided to stand his ground and hope that West could not find the killing lead.

Muneer, on lead, fingered alternately the two black sevens and finally settled for the spade—and that gave declarer the first nine tricks and a score of 750. Had he led the club seven, the defense could have taken the first ten tricks for a score of 2,200. Thus, the U.S. gained 12 IMP where it might have lost 20. There was a middle course available for Muneer. The bidding made it certain that the heart king was with declarer, and a low heart lead was therefore excluded. It was equally clear that partner held one black suit strongly. With five spades headed by the ace-king he might have ventured a bid of three spades: he would have been less likely to introduce a club suit at the four level. That argued for a club lead, but the more certain line was to lead the ace of hearts and see what advice his partner could offer. In the event his partner would have played the two, a low card, suggesting a switch to the lower-ranking suit. That line would have produced a score of 600 for Pakistan, a good deal less than the 2,200 that might have been but a good deal better than the minus 750 that was.

open and women's world championships. The tournament took place in Port Chester, N.Y., in late October. In the Venice Cup, Australia, Brazil, Great Britain, Venezuela, and the U.S. played three round-robin tournaments to produce the two finalists. Early in the competition the U.S. emerged as a certain qualifier. In the contest for the other finalist, Great Britain edged out Brazil. In the final the British team was always in control, eventually winning 160–122.

In the Bermuda Bowl, Argentina, Australia, Great Britain, Indonesia, Pakistan, Poland, and the U.S. played two round robins to determine the four semifinalists. Once again the issue was determined on the very last board when Argentina edged out Great Britain to join the U.S., Pakistan, and Poland. In the semifinal round Pakistan beat Argentina, while the U.S. outplayed Poland to claim the other place.

For the first half of the 96-deal final the scores were close, Pakistan leading by 3 international match points (IMP) at the end of the 48th board. The U.S. gained 56 points in the next 16 boards, but shortly thereafter Pakistan had a chance to come back into contention with what proved to be the most dramatic board of the tournament. (See box.)

That hand was the last chance for the Pakistan team, and the final score, in favour of the U.S., was 271–182. For the second successive time the winning team was made up of a sponsor and five professionals. The sponsor was 67-year-old Bud Reinhold. His teammates were Jeff Meckstroth and Eric Rodwell, Bobby Levin and Russ Arnold, and John Solodar, with Tom Sanders as nonplaying captain.   (HAROLD FRANKLIN)

[452.C.3.a.i]

In a closed-room bridge tournament match in Port Chester, N.Y., players sit at a table divided by a wide screen to prevent them from conveying hand signals to their partners. (From left) Tim Seres, Australia; Eduardo Scanavino, Argentina; Richard Cummings, Australia; Hector Camberos, Argentina.

Costa Rica

A Central American republic, Costa Rica lies between Nicaragua and Panama and has coastlines on the Caribbean Sea and the Pacific Ocean. Area: 50,898 sq km (19,652 sq mi). Pop. (1981 est.): 2,-276,700, including white and mestizo 98%. Cap.

Costa Rica

Cost of Living:
see Economy, World

Council for Mutual
Economic Assis-
tance:
see Economy, World

COSTA RICA

Education. (1980) Primary, pupils 347,708, teachers 10,-536; secondary, pupils 103,579, teachers 4,263; vocational, pupils 30,229, teachers 2,056; higher, students (1977) 38,-629, teaching staff (1973) 1,967.

Finance. Monetary unit: colón, with (Sept. 21, 1981) a free rate of 19.87 colones to U.S. $1 (36.83 colones = £1 sterling). Gold and other reserves (June 1981) U.S. $183 million. Budget (1979 actual): revenue 4,344,000,000 colones; expenditure 6,653,900,000 colones. Gross national product (1980) 39,612,000,000 colones. Money supply (April 1981) 8,515,000,000 colones. Cost of living (San José; 1975 = 100; May 1981) 187.1.

Foreign Trade. (1980) Imports 13,103,000,000 colones; exports 8,722,000,000 colones. Import sources (1979): U.S. 30%; Japan 12%; Netherlands Antilles 9%; El Salvador 5%; Guatemala 6%; West Germany 5%. Export destinations (1979): U.S. 37%; West Germany 12%; Guatemala 7%; El Salvador 5%. Main exports: coffee 24%; bananas 20%; beef 7%. Tourism (1978): visitors 340,000; gross receipts U.S. $71 million.

Transport and Communications. Roads (1976) 25,339 km (including 665 km of Pan-American Highway). Motor vehicles in use (1978): passenger *c.* 62,300; commercial (including buses) *c.* 65,900. Railways: (1979) *c.* 980 km ; traffic (main only; 1974) 81 million passenger-km, freight 14 million net ton-km. Air traffic (1980): *c.* 495 million passenger-km; freight *c.* 23.5 million net ton-km. Telephones (Jan. 1979) 175,400. Radio receivers (Dec. 1977) *c.* 400,000. Television receivers (Dec. 1977) *c.* 160,000.

Agriculture. Production (in 000; metric tons; 1980): sorghum *c.* 40; corn (1979) 86; rice (1979) *c.* 214; potatoes (1979) *c.* 24; bananas *c.* 1,187; oranges *c.* 75; sugar, raw value (1979) *c.* 195; coffee *c.* 113; cocoa *c.* 9; palm oil *c.* 25. Livestock (in 000; 1979): cattle *c.* 2,071; horses *c.* 112; pigs *c.* 226; chickens *c.* 5,600.

Industry. Production (in 000; metric tons; 1978): cement 426; petroleum products 392; nitrogenous fertilizers (1979–80) *c.* 36; electricity (kw-hr; 1979) 1,940,000 (76% hydroelectric in 1977).

and largest city: San José (metro. pop., 1981 est., 843,800). Language: Spanish. Religion: predominantly Roman Catholic. President in 1981, Rodrigo Carazo Odio.

Traditionally a stable country, Costa Rica faced severe economic problems during 1981, and confidence in Pres. Rodrigo Carazo Odio's Partido de Unidad administration was at a low ebb. At home the rate of inflation had risen from 13.5% in 1979 to 17.8% in 1980, and a rate approaching 40% was projected for 1981. Abroad, Costa Rica was finding difficulty in fulfilling its debt obligations. In May the government sold about three-quarters of the central bank's gold reserves, valued at approximately $50 million, and in September it announced its decision to reschedule the $2.4 billion public external debt.

The International Monetary Fund (IMF) formally agreed to a loan on June 17, following six months of negotiations. The loan amounted to $330 million over a three-year period, as well as 30 million SDR's to compensate for a shortfall in coffee exports. Later in the year, however, there were fears that the loan might be jeopardized because the terms of the agreement had not been met.

Diplomatic relations with Cuba, reestablished in 1977, were broken off in May 1981. Two terrorist bombings in San José in March and a congressional committee report on arms smuggling aroused fears that Costa Rica could not escape involvement in the unrest afflicting Central America. A number of political exiles were deported after the bombings, which were attributed to foreign leftists. (LUCY BLACKBURN)

Court Games

Handball. Fred Lewis of Tucson, Ariz., won his sixth U.S. National Open handball title in 1981 by defeating defending champion Naty Alvarado of Los Angeles, 10–21, 21–2, 11–1, at the Charlie Club in Palatine, Ill. The upset win was Lewis's third of the season on the Spalding professional handball tour. Alvarado remained the top-ranked player in the world by virtue of his six wins on the Spalding tour during the season.

In the finals of the U.S. Handball Association open doubles competition, Jack Roberts (Cambridge, Mass.) and partner Tom Kopatich (Milwaukee, Wis.) defeated Jim Vandenbos and Jim Barnett, both of Long Beach, Calif., 15–21, 21–15, 11–7. In masters play for men over 40, Pat Kirby of Tucson defeated Ted Gewertz of New York City, 21–6, 21–15, for the singles title, and Kirby teamed with New York's Fred Munsch to defeat Bruce McCormick and Roger Nickels of Cincinnati, Ohio, 21–5, 21–11, for the doubles title. Other winners included Craig Work of Burlington, Vt., in golden masters singles (for men over 50); Arnie Aguilar and Del Mora, Los Angeles, in golden masters doubles; Ken Schneider, Chicago, in super masters singles (men over 60); and Irv Simon and Tony Chavez, Los Angeles, in super masters doubles.

In women's play Rosemary Bellini of New York City defeated Rosanna Ettinger of Long Beach,

U.S. women's national volleyball team defeated Japan at Northwestern University in Evanston, Ill., during a U.S. tour by Japan in September.

Fred Lewis (centre) of Tucson, Ariz., won his sixth U.S. National Open handball title by defeating defending champion Naty Alvarado of Los Angeles in Palatine, Ill.

21–3, 21–4, for her second straight national open title. Bellini teamed with Sue Oakleaf of Austin, Texas, to win the doubles crown, defeating Allison Roberts and Gloria Motal of Houston, Texas, 21–19, 21–15.

Lake Forest (Ill.) College and the University of Texas (Austin) tied for the national intercollegiate title at the University of Colorado at Boulder. Bob Martin of Lake Forest defeated Steve Stanisich of Montana Tech., 21–17, 21–4, for the A singles title. For Stanisich, a senior, this was his fourth consecutive runner-up finish in national intercollegiate competition. Sue Oakleaf from Texas A&M won the women's title, defeating Cathy Meyer of the University of Texas, 21–4, 21–8.

(TERRY CHARLES MUCK)

Volleyball. The year 1981 was a relatively quiet one for volleyball insofar as major international championships were concerned, a normal situation for a year following the Olympic Games. Only the World Cup, organized during November in Japan, was of major significance.

In the Bi-Annual North Central and Caribbean American Championship (Norceca), the U.S. women were the winners for the first time in the tournament's 14-year history. To accomplish that feat the U.S. women defeated defending world champion Cuba both during the preliminary round of play and in the championship match. The U.S. men at Norceca were narrowly defeated by Cuba, the match going the full five games and the final game being decided by two points. By winning the tournament the U.S. women and the Cuban men qualified for the World Cup.

In dual competition the U.S. men entertained Brazil and defeated the Olympic veteran visitors five matches to four. During a visit to Japan the U.S. men dropped five close matches and then, on returning with the Japanese to the U.S., defeated the visitors three matches to one to win the first Friendship Cup.

The U.S. women defeated the Olympic gold medalist U.S.S.R., Olympic silver medalist East Germany, and Olympic bronze medalist Bulgaria to win the Rostok Invitational in East Germany during June. Visiting Japan in July, the U.S. captured three of five matches with the host team and then traveled to Bulgaria, where it finished second in the Varna Summer Invitational behind the Soviet Union. Japan visited the U.S. in September, and each team won four matches.

In the women's World Cup, held in Osaka, Japan, in November, the Chinese team defeated the United States and Japan, both by three games to two, to emerge as the victor. China was undefeated throughout the tournament. The victory, China's first in the World Cup event, set off enthusiastic demonstrations in Beijing (Peking). Previously, China's chief claim to fame in international sports had been in table tennis.

(ALBERT M. MONACO, JR.)

Jai Alai. The 1981 U.S. amateur jai alai championships were played at the Miami, Fla., jai alai fronton on August 2. The tournament was dominated by Billy Schofill of Miami, who won the frontcourt championship at the age of 15 to match Joey Cornblit as the youngest ever to gain the title. Schofill scored 96 points and was followed by Danny Schwartz with 88 and Scott Kessler with 59. First place in the backcourt competition went to 17-year-old Raymond Duran with 80 points, followed by Dennis Barquin with 75 and Teddy Griffin with 71.

Frontcourters Schofill and Schwartz and backcourters Duran and Barquin were named as the U.S. team for the world tournament at Biarritz, France. The competition took place during the first week of September 1981. After defeating Mexico 40–29 and Spain 40–37, the U.S. lost 40–38 to finish the tournament in second place. France won the championship, defeating Spain 40–26, Mexico 40–32, and the U.S. 40–38 and 40–29. Spain finished in third place by defeating Mexico 40–28. The 1982 world championships were scheduled to be played in Mexico City in September. Meanwhile, the U.S. amateur jai alai association submitted a protest of the tournament to the world amateur jai alai association, charging that France had entered professional players in the amateur championship.

(ROBERT H. GROSSBERG)

Cricket

The 1980–81 test match season began with a series between Pakistan and West Indies, with the latter winning the one match and the other three drawn. The West Indian fast bowlers, S. T. Clarke, C. E. H. Croft, M. D. Marshall, and J. Garner, created problems for Pakistan. I. V. A. Richards was the outstanding batsman for West Indies, and for Pakistan Javed Miandad was a fine leader and batsman, helped by Wasim Raja and Imram Khan, the leading all-rounder.

Australia easily won the first two tests in its series against New Zealand and tied the third. For Australia the veteran K. D. Walters batted well, as did G. M. Wood, G. S. Chappell, and R. W. Marsh. D. K. Lillee twice took five or more wickets, and leg-spinner J. D. Higgs twice took four. For New Zealand the captain, G. P. Howarth, set an example with the bat, supported by J. M. Parker, J. V. Coney, and R. J. Hadlee, who also took 19 wickets.

Australia won the first match in a series against India, thanks chiefly to 204 by G. S. Chappell and the bowling of Lillee, Higgs, and L. S. Pascoe. In the drawn second contest K. J. Hughes made 213 and Wood 125 for Australia, and S. M. Patal scored 174 and C. P. S. Chauhan 97 for India. India won the final match, with G. R. Viswanath scoring 114, Chauhan 85, and S. M. Gavaskar 70. For Australia A. R. Border made 124, and Lillee took four wickets in each innings. In Australia's second innings K. Dev took 5 for 28.

New Zealand won its first test against India, and the other two were drawn largely because of rain. Howarth made 137 not out, and Hadlee and B. L. Cairns were in form with the ball. In the second test J. F. Reid made a first century (123 not out). In the third J. G. Wright made 110, Reid 74, and Coney 65, and offspinner J. G. Bracewell took 9 wickets.

England under Ian Botham (*see* Biographies)

was overwhelmed in its first test match against West Indies. D. L. Haynes (96), C. G. Greenidge (84), C. H. Lloyd (64), and Roberts (50 not out) led the West Indian batting, and English offspinner J. E. Emburey took 5 for 124. For England only G. Boycott and D. I. Gower batted successfully against Croft (5 for 40). The second test against Guyana was canceled because its government refused to allow R. D. Jackman (a replacement for the injured R. G. D. Willis) to play because of his association with South African cricket. During the third test England's morale was shattered by the sudden death of K. Barrington (*see* Obituaries), its coach and former test batsman. West Indies won with the persistent fast bowling of M. A. Holding, A. M. E. Roberts, Croft, and Garner along with a fine batting side led by Lloyd. Croft took 4 for 39, and Lloyd and Richards made centuries; there was some brave batting by G. A. Gooch (116) and Gower (54) for England. In the fourth test, for West Indies Richards scored 114, E. H. Mattis 71, Greenidge 63, Lloyd 58, and Holding 58 not out. For England P. Willey (102 not out), Boycott (104 not out), and Gooch (83) ensured a draw. Croft took 6 for 74. In the drawn fifth test Gooch (153) and Gower (154) again batted well, though Holding, the fastest bowler, took 5 for 56. For West Indies Lloyd made 95, H. A. Gomes 90 not out, Haynes 84, and Greenidge 62.

In an incredible and exciting test series against Australia, England won three matches to one with two drawn. In the first test England led by six runs in the first innings (M. W. Gatting 52) but was then bowled out by Lillee (5 for 46) and T. M. Alderman (5 for 62) and lost. In the drawn second Gatting made 59 and Willey 82, and in the second innings Gower 89 and Boycott 60. For Australia Border made 64, and in the second innings Wood 62 not out. Best bowler for Australia was G. F. Lawson (7 for 81). At the end of the match Botham, who had lost his form, resigned England's captaincy, and the veteran J. M. Brearley was brought back. Not only was Brearley a superb tactician but

Test	Host country and its scores		Visiting country and its scores		Result
		Test Series Results, October 1980–September 1981			
1st	Pakistan	369 and 156 for 7 wkt	West Indies	297	Match drawn
2nd	Pakistan	176 and 145	West Indies	235 and 242	West Indies won by 156 runs
3rd	Pakistan	128 and 204 for 9 wkt	West Indies	169	Match drawn
4th	Pakistan	166	West Indies	249 and 116 for 5 wkt	Match drawn
1st	Australia	305 and 63 for 0 wkt	New Zealand	225 and 142	Australia won by 10 wkt
2nd	Australia	265 and 55 for 2 wkt	New Zealand	196 and 121	Australia won by 8 wkt
3rd	Australia	321 and 188	New Zealand	317 and 128 for 6 wkt	Match drawn
1st	Australia	406	India	201 and 201	Australia won by an innings and 4 runs
2nd	Australia	528 and 221 for 7 wkt dec	India	419 and 135 for 8 wkt	Match drawn
3rd	Australia	419 and 83	India	237 and 324	India won by 59 runs
1st	New Zealand	375 and 100	India	223 and 190	New Zealand won by 62 runs
2nd	New Zealand	286 for 5 wkt	India	255	Match drawn
3rd	New Zealand	366 and 95 for 5 wkt	India	238 and 284	Match drawn
1st	West Indies	426 for 9 wkt dec	England	178 and 169	West Indies won by an innings and 79 runs
2nd	Match canceled				
3rd	West Indies	265 and 379 for 7 wkt dec	England	122 and 224	West Indies won by 298 runs
4th	West Indies	468 for 9 wkt dec	England	271 and 234 for 3 dec	Match drawn
5th	West Indies	422	England	285 and 302 for 6 dec	Match drawn
1st	England	185 and 125	Australia	179 and 132 for 6 wkt	Australia won by 4 wkt
2nd	England	311 and 265 for 8 wkt dec	Australia	345 and 90 for 4 wkt	Match drawn
3rd	England	174 and 356	Australia	401 for 9 wkt dec and 111	England won by 18 runs
4th	England	189 and 219	Australia	258 and 121	England won by 29 runs
5th	England	231 and 404	Australia	130 and 402	England won by 103 runs
6th	England	314 and 261 for 7 wkt	Australia	352 and 344 for 9 wkt dec	Match drawn

Botham, relieved of the cares of captaincy, won the series for England with two marvelous centuries and superb bowling.

England won the third test after an astonishing turn of fortune. Australia made 401 for 9, J. H. Dyson (102), Hughes (89), G. N. Yallop (58), and Botham 6 for 95. England was bowled out for 174, Lillee, Alderman, and Lawson sharing the wickets and Botham making 50. England then lost its first five wickets for 105 when Botham came in. Two more wickets fell, and England was still 92 behind when Dilley joined Botham. They added 117, and the last two wickets added 104 before England was all out for 356 (Botham 149 not out after an amazing display of powerful hitting). Alderman took 6 for 135. Australia then collapsed against Willis (8 for 43). In the fourth test, won by England, Brearley and Gatting batted best for England, Hughes and Border for Australia. Alderman took 5 for 42 and slow left-arm R. J. Bright 5 for 68, and for England Emburey took 4 for 43. Botham took the last five wickets and one run in only 28 balls to win the match for England. The fifth was won by England because of another remarkable century by Botham. For England C. J. Tavare made 69 and 78, A. P. E. Knott 59, and Emburey 57; Botham's 118 included 6 sixes. In Australia's reply Border and Yallop made centuries. With the test series safely won England drew the sixth match, despite great bowling by Lillee (11 for 159), Border's second consecutive not-out century, and a first century by D. M. Wellham. For England Botham took 6 for 125, Knott made 70 not out, Gatting 56, and Brearley 51.

The English county championship was won by Nottinghamshire after a close race with Sussex. Somerset won the Benson and Hedges competition by seven wickets from Surrey, and in the NatWest Trophy (replacing the Gillette Cup) Derbyshire beat Northamptonshire, after a tie, on fewer wickets lost. The John Player League was won by Essex.

Western Australia won the Sheffield Shield. In New Zealand Auckland won the Shell Trophy. In the West Indies Combined Islands won the Shell Shield. In South Africa Natal won the Currie Cup and Transvaal the Datsun Shield. In Pakistan Rawalpindi won the Patron's Trophy and in India West Zone won the Duleep Trophy.

(REX ALSTON)

Crime and Law Enforcement

Violent Crime. TERRORISM. In a year during which Egypt's Pres. Anwar as-Sadat (*see* OBITUARIES) was assassinated and the president of the United States and the pope survived near-fatal attempts on their lives, the increasing vulnerability of world leaders to attack by terrorists and other deranged assassins became a matter of international concern. Early in October Sadat was assassinated in Cairo by a group of men in military uniform who attacked his reviewing stand with grenades and automatic weapons during a military parade. At least five other persons were killed and more

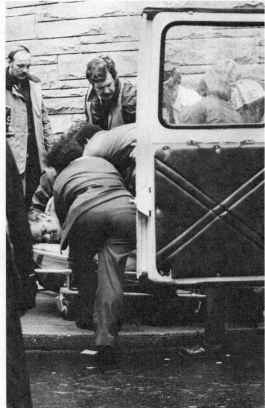

White House Press Secretary James Brady is taken to an ambulance on a stretcher after he was struck in the head by a bullet on March 30 during an assassination attempt on Pres. Ronald Reagan outside a hotel in Washington, D.C.

than two dozen were wounded in the incident. Official blame was placed upon Muslim religious extremists, although a number of groups based in Lebanon and other Middle Eastern countries claimed responsibility. (*See* EGYPT.)

On March 30 U.S. Pres. Ronald Reagan, his press secretary, James Brady, and two law enforcement officers were caught in a fusillade of bullets and seriously wounded as the president and his aides left a Washington, D.C., hotel. A suspect, John W. Hinckley, Jr., was arrested at the scene. A 25-year-old drifter from a wealthy Colorado family, Hinckley seemed to have acted from a bizarre desire to impress a teenage film star he had never met. In September his lawyers indicated they would claim he was insane at the time.

Pope John Paul II was severely wounded on May 13 when a would-be assassin shot him as he rode through a cheering crowd in Vatican City's St. Peter's Square. The attack on the pontiff, which provoked a worldwide outpouring of grief and horror, was carried out by Mehmet Ali Agca, 23, a Turkish right-wing terrorist apprehended at the scene. Agca, who had escaped from a Turkish prison in November 1979, had been sentenced to death in absentia in Turkey for murdering the editor of a liberal Istanbul newspaper. Tried in an Italian court under terms of the Lateran Treaty between Italy and the Vatican, he was sentenced to life imprisonment, the maximum penalty under local law, for shooting the pope and two women tourists who were also injured in the attack. Agca's motives remained obscure. The judges who presided at his trial said they were certain he was part of an

Crime and Law Enforcement

Pope John Paul II was wounded by gunshots fired by a Turkish terrorist on May 13.

international terrorist conspiracy, but they had no evidence as to the possible identity of his fellow conspirators.

In the wake of these attacks, many countries began to review the security around their leaders. In the U.K. the need for such a review was reinforced in June when Marcus Sarjeant, 17, fired a number of blank rounds from a replica pistol near Queen Elizabeth II as she rode at the head of a parade of troops down the Mall in London. Sarjeant, who said he wanted to assassinate the queen to become world famous, was subsequently sentenced to five years' imprisonment.

Tightened security did little to protect the leaders of strife-torn Iran from a wave of political assassinations. In late August the country's newly elected president, Mohammad Ali Raja'i, and the prime minister, Mohammad Javad Bahonar, were killed by an explosion in the prime minister's office in central Teheran. Barely two months earlier a massive bomb explosion at the headquarters of the ruling Islamic Republican Party had killed more than 70 senior officials, including Iran's second most powerful leader, the Ayatollah Mohammad Beheshti. (*See* IRAN.)

Terrorist violence spawned by conflicts in the Middle East spilled over into other countries. In August, in one of a number of attacks in Europe aimed at Jews, two Arab terrorists assaulted worshipers outside Vienna's main synagogue, killing 2 persons and injuring about 20. In the same month, Muhammad Daoud (code-named Abu Daoud), the suspected mastermind behind the massacre of Israeli athletes at the 1972 Olympics in Munich, West Germany, was shot and critically wounded in a Warsaw hotel. This followed the slaying in June of another Palestinian leader, Naim Khader, who was gunned down in Brussels. The Palestine Liberation Organization accused the Israeli secret service of both attacks.

A West German terrorist group, the Red Army Faction, claimed responsibility for an August bombing attack upon U.S. Air Force headquarters at Ramstein in which 20 persons, 18 of them U.S. soldiers, were injured. The same group was

thought to have been involved in the attempted assassination in September of the commander of U.S. forces in Europe, Gen. Frederick Kroesen, who, however, escaped serious injury. The incidents renewed concern among West Germans about a resurgence of ultraleft terrorist activity.

A $1.6 million robbery of a Brink's armoured truck in Rockland County, N.Y., in October led to the arrest of Katherine Boudin of the Weather Underground and several other persons wanted in connection with radical activities a decade earlier. Law enforcement authorities suspected that this and other crimes might have been committed by a coalition of radical groups thought to have been dormant since the 1960s.

Some of the rumours surrounding the 1963 assassination of U.S. Pres. John Kennedy may have been put to rest when the body of his presumed assassin, Lee Harvey Oswald, was exhumed. A team of pathologists examined the remains and certified that they were indeed those of Oswald. A British writer had alleged that the body was actually that of a Soviet agent who had assumed Oswald's identity.

MURDER AND OTHER VIOLENCE. In the U.S. a new administration pledged to wage war against violent crime came to office at a time when the nation's two major statistical series on crime, the FBI's *Uniform Crime Reports* (UCR), based on offenses reported to the police, and the Census Bureau's *National Crime Survey* (NCS), compiled from interviews with crime victims, gave divergent pictures. The UCR showed a 13% rise in the number of violent offenses in 1980 as compared with 1979, while the NCS revealed no significant increase. Some criminologists suggested that the homicide rate would be a more accurate indicator of violent crime. In 1962 the homicide rate in the U.S. stood at about 4.5 per 100,000 residents, while in 1981 it was well over 10 per 100,000.

The terror that had gripped Atlanta, Ga., as, one after another, 28 black children and young adults were found murdered, began to abate when police finally arrested a suspect in June. Wayne Williams, 23, a free-lance photographer, was in-

dicted for just two of the murders, but authorities believed he might be connected with as many as 13 others. Meanwhile, all the murders continued to be investigated by a special police task force.

Another reign of terror, in northern England, ended in early January. After one of the longest (over five years) and most costly (more than £3.4 million [$8 million]) manhunt in British history, police arrested the country's most wanted criminal, the "Yorkshire Ripper." The Ripper proved to be Peter Sutcliffe, a 35-year-old truck driver from the West Yorkshire town of Bradford. The Ripper's vicious attacks on women, many of them prostitutes, had begun in July 1975. In May Sutcliffe pleaded guilty to 7 counts of attempted murder but not guilty to 13 counts of murder on grounds of diminished responsibility. The trial judge refused to accept the diminished responsibility plea, and a jury subsequently convicted Sutcliffe on all the murder counts. He was sentenced to life imprisonment.

In a sensational three-month trial in White Plains, N.Y., Jean Harris, 57, former headmistress of an exclusive school for girls in Virginia, was convicted of killing Herman Tarnower, 69, originator of the popular Scarsdale Diet. Harris admitted shooting Tarnower, her lover of 14 years, but claimed that she had only wished to kill herself and that Tarnower died trying to save her. The jury, however, agreed with the prosecution, which suggested that the March 1980 killing was murder motivated by jealousy over Tarnower's affair with his assistant. Harris was sentenced to 15 years, the minimum period permitted under New York law.

In August Mark David Chapman received a prison term of 20 years after pleading guilty to the 1980 murder of John Lennon, formerly one of the Beatles rock group. Chapman's guilty plea was made over the objections of his lawyer, who insisted that his client was not mentally competent.

Nonviolent Crime. POLITICAL CRIME. The conviction in early May of veteran U.S. senator Harrison A. Williams, Jr., of New Jersey on charges of bribery and conspiracy ended the trials of seven

A bomb exploded near U.S. Air Force headquarters in Ramstein, West Germany, on August 31, wounding 20 persons, 18 of whom were U.S. soldiers. The bomb was said to have been planted by West German terrorists.

members of Congress spawned by the U.S. Justice Department's controversial Abscam operation. Named for a fake company, Abdul Enterprises Ltd., used as a front in the operation, Abscam had involved FBI agents posing as wealthy Arabs or their representatives seeking political favours. Williams, the first U.S. senator convicted of criminal charges while in office since 1920, appealed, as did the defendants convicted in the earlier trials.

In a civil suit in Maryland, former U.S. vice-president Spiro Agnew was ordered to repay the state of Maryland almost $250,000, representing kickbacks of $147,500, plus interest, received when he was governor of Maryland and vice-president. Agnew had resigned the vice-presidency in October 1973 after pleading no contest to a charge of income tax evasion and paying a fine of $10,000, thus avoiding any criminal prosecution. He appealed the civil court's verdict.

WHITE COLLAR CRIME AND THEFT. A major international security firm, Burns, projected that

On October 6 a group of men in military uniforms attacked the presidential reviewing stand during a military parade in Cairo. Pres. Anwar as-Sadat and at least five others were killed and more than two dozen were wounded.

Britain's longest and most costly manhunt ended in early January when police arrested the "Yorkshire Ripper," Peter Sutcliffe (draped with blanket).

losses from computer crimes in the U.S. in 1981 would amount to between $1.2 billion and $1.8 billion and that only 15% of the estimated 1,800 to 2,700 crimes of this type would be detected. In February the Wells Fargo Bank of San Francisco announced that it had been the victim of a $21.3 million embezzlement involving manipulation of the electronic transfer of funds between various accounts at different Los Angeles branches of the bank. The fraud was believed to have been masterminded by a bank employee, L. Benjamin Lewis, who temporarily disappeared after being interrogated by bank investigators. Indicted in connection with the case was boxing impresario Harold J. Smith (also known as Ross Eugene Fields), who, with Lewis, had been a board member of Muhammad Ali Professional Sports Inc. (The boxer Muhammad Ali was not involved.)

In West Germany the Max Planck Institute

released a report indicating that known losses from business crime—fraud, breach of trust, tax evasion, and similar offenses—had increased from $1,730,000,000 in 1975 to $2,680,000,000 in 1978; unsolved cases could raise the total to as much as $20 billion for 1978. One such crime, involving a major building scandal, caused serious political problems for the West Berlin government early in 1981. Bautechnik KG, a Berlin-based construction firm, had received more than DM 132 million ($60 million) in bank loans guaranteed by the West Berlin government. Portions of the loan (at least DM 26 million [$12 million]), which were to have been used to finance construction projects in the Middle East, were allegedly paid as bribes or taken by the firm's owner, Dietrich Garski. Leaving the West Berlin government to pick up the bill, Garski was believed to have fled to the Caribbean.

Moscow sources revealed in January that the Soviet KGB (political police) had exposed a major icon-smuggling operation involving Soviet citizens, foreign diplomats, and dealers in West Berlin. The operation was first uncovered late in 1979 when Soviet border officials found icons and other rare religious art objects, valued at more than $100,000, hidden in the luggage of a diplomat's wife. Soviet authorities were said to have jailed the Soviet members of the smuggling organization.

Law Enforcement. President Reagan chose the annual meeting of the International Association of Chiefs of Police, held in New Orleans, La., in September, for his first major speech on crime since taking office. The president introduced a tough law and order manifesto that included changing bail laws to keep dangerous suspects off the streets pending trial, modifying the "exclusionary rule" that prohibits the use by courts of evidence obtained illegally by police, and legislation requiring offenders to pay restitution to their victims. Many of these proposals were based on recommendations made in August by the Attorney General's Task Force on Violent Crime. Other recommendations that seemed less likely to gain administration sup-

Sen. Harrison A. Williams, Jr., of New Jersey, and his wife, Jeanette, arrive at court in May. He was convicted on nine counts of bribery and conspiracy stemming from the FBI's Abscam operation.

port were the appropriation of substantial additional resources for federal law enforcement agencies—improbable in a time of stringent budget cutting—and strengthening of the Gun Control Act of 1968. Gun-control advocates had made little headway in Congress in the face of intense lobbying by such groups as the National Rifle Association, and President Reagan maintained his opposition to gun control even after the attempt on his life.

The Washington, D.C.-based Police Foundation, an independent law enforcement "think-tank," evaluated major changes that had occurred in U.S. policing since Pres. Lyndon Johnson's Commission on Law Enforcement and Administration of Justice called for sweeping reforms in 1967. It found marked improvements in the training of police personnel; a growing recognition by both police and the public that variations in police strategy had little effect on crime rates; and a dramatic increase in the number of minority persons joining law enforcement agencies. Between 1967 and 1977, the proportion of minorities in the nation's police forces rose from 4 to 10% and the proportion of women from 0.1 to 3%.

Britain's police forces came under scrutiny as the country experienced its worst street rioting in more than a century. (See UNITED KINGDOM.) In his report to the government on the riots, Lord Scarman, a retired senior judge, called for the hiring of more minority policemen, longer training periods for officers, and better liaison between police and local communities. Currently there were only about 100 minority officers in the 25,000-strong London Metropolitan Police and only 4 among the 5,000 police in Liverpool, scene of the fiercest rioting.

The British government ordered an official inquiry into police handling of the Yorkshire Ripper case. In hindsight, the police appeared to have missed a number of clues pointing toward Sutcliffe. He was eventually apprehended not by detectives working on the case but because two

Wayne Williams (handcuffed) is taken to court on June 21 for a preliminary hearing on charges of killing one of the 28 black youths found murdered in Atlanta, Ga.

officers observed him in a red light district sitting in a parked car with a stolen license plate.

In August the Canadian government released the long-awaited report of a royal commission, headed by Mr. Justice David McDonald, on the security activities of the Royal Canadian Mounted Police (RCMP). The report was severely critical of the Mounties, who were found to have engaged in numerous illegal break-ins, wiretaps, and other unlawful acts in pursuit of evidence against suspected radicals. Most of these acts occurred during the early 1970s, when there was substantial public unrest associated with separatism in Quebec. The government announced that it would implement immediately a principal recommendation of the commission: that the RCMP no longer combine police and security/intelligence functions. Instead, a new civilian-controlled internal security service would be established.

In India Prime Minister Indira Gandhi condemned in Parliament the reported blinding of more than 30 suspected criminals by police in Bi-

Members of the Attorney General's Task Force on Violent Crime made recommendations to federal law enforcement agencies in an effort to curb crime in the U.S.

har state. The blindings were believed to have been committed by police in order to obtain confessions. The prime minister ordered the equivalent of about $1,000 paid to each of the victims, most of whom were still in jail awaiting trial.

A meeting of the International Panel on Police Research held in London during March reviewed studies being conducted into the criminal investigation process. Many police forces in the U.S. and Canada were already using research-based screening devices to decide which cases of reported burglary should be followed up by detectives.

(DUNCAN CHAPPELL)

See also Prisons and Penology.
[522.C.6; 543.A.5; 552.C and F; 737.B; 10/36.C.5.a]

Cuba

Cuba

The socialist republic of Cuba occupies the largest island in the Greater Antilles of the West Indies. Area: 110,922 sq km (42,827 sq mi), including several thousand small islands and cays. Pop. (1980 est.): 9,739,900, including (1953) white 72.8%; mestizo 14.5%; Negro 12.4%. Cap. and largest city: Havana (pop., 1980 est., 2,003,600). Language: Spanish. Religion: Roman Catholic (42%). President of the Councils of State and Ministers in 1981, Fidel Castro Ruz.

Political stability in Cuba was maintained during 1981, but little economic progress was made apart from improvements in productivity. Pres. Fidel Castro's position as Cuba's unchallenged leader was confirmed when he was reelected first secretary of the Cuban Communist Party at its second congress in December 1980.

Although elected to the chair of the nonaligned movement in September 1979, Cuba was unsuccessful in convincing the movement of its neutral attitudes. At the end of 1980, as it had done a year before, Cuba declared its candidacy for the Latin-American seat in the election of nonpermanent

Crops:
see Agriculture and Food Supplies

Mexican Pres. José López Portillo (right) and Cuban Pres. Fidel Castro exchanged warm greetings when the two leaders met on the island of Cozumel, Mexico, for two days of private talks in August.

CUBA

Education. (1979–80) Primary, pupils 1,550,323, teachers 77,063; secondary, pupils 825,852, teachers 60,553; vocational, pupils 214,615, teachers 15,018; teacher training, students 109,905, teachers 6,078; higher, students 143,461, teaching staff 10,736.

Finance. Monetary unit: peso, with (Sept. 21, 1981) a free rate of 0.73 peso to U.S. $1 (1.34 pesos = £1 sterling). Budget (1980 est.): revenue 7,584,000,000 pesos; expenditure 7,581,000,000 pesos. Gross national product (1979 est.) U.S. $13.9 billion.

Foreign Trade. (1978) Imports 3,558,000,000 pesos; exports 3,417,000,000 pesos. Import sources (1977): U.S.S.R. 54%; Japan 8%; Canada 6%; Spain 5%. Export destinations (1977): U.S.S.R. 71%. Main exports (1976): sugar 87%; nickel, copper, and chromium ores 6%.

Transport and Communications. Roads (1978) c. 31,-200 km. Motor vehicles in use (1976): passenger c. 80,000; commercial (including buses) c. 40,000. Railways (1979): 14,873 km; traffic 1,637,000,000 passenger-km, freight 1,-899,000,000 net ton-km. Air traffic (1980): c. 932 million passenger-km; freight c. 11.1 million net ton-km. Shipping (1980): merchant vessels 100 gross tons and over 405; gross tonnage 881,260. Telephones (Jan. 1978) 321,000. Radio receivers (Dec. 1978) c. 2,110,000.Television receivers (Dec. 1978) c. 805,000.

Agriculture. Production (in 000; metric tons; 1980): rice c. 500; cassava (1979) c. 320; sweet potatoes (1979) c. 307; tomatoes c. 165; sugar, raw value c. 6,787; bananas c. 147; oranges c. 185; coffee c. 27; tobacco c. 10; jute c. 5; beef and veal c. 147; fish catch (1979) 154. Livestock (in 000; 1980): cattle c. 5,900; pigs c. 1,950; sheep c. 355; goats c. 99; horses (1979) c. 847; chickens c. 25,000.

Industry. Production (in 000; metric tons; 1979): crude oil 288; natural gas (cu m) 17,531; petroleum products c. 6,190; electricity (kw-hr) c. 8,084,000; copper ore (metal content) 2.8; chrome ore (oxide content) c. 9.8; nickel ore (metal content) c. 38; salt 122; paper (1978) c. 123; sulfuric acid 297; fertilizers (nutrient content; 1979–80) nitrogenous 131, phosphate c. 15; cement 2,613; crude steel 328; cotton yarn 22; cotton fabrics (sq m) 146,600.

members to the UN Security Council. Once again, however, the candidacy was withdrawn because of lack of support, and Cuba backed the successful candidate, Panama.

Cuba's presence in Africa continued. About 35,-000 military personnel were stationed in the region, mainly in Angola and Ethiopia, and large numbers of doctors, civilian technicians, and teachers were also employed there. This presence, along with Havana's growing involvement in Central America and the Caribbean, especially Nicaragua and Grenada, contributed to worsening relations with the U.S. Pres. Ronald Reagan's administration was particularly concerned about alleged Cuban support for left-wing guerrillas in El Salvador. The U.S. claimed to possess evidence that arms were reaching El Salvador from Cuba via third countries. Castro denied the charges.

In his speech on July 26, the 28th anniversary of the start of the Cuban revolution, Castro dwelt at length on what he described as U.S. attempts to sabotage the Cuban economy and challenged Washington to define its policy on the Central Intelligence Agency (CIA) and its methods. In September Wayne Smith, head of the U.S. interests section in Havana, was recalled to the U.S. for consultations; it was considered possible that the status of the section would be reduced and that Smith, a moderate and an appointee of former president Jimmy Carter, would be replaced. In August U.S. Secretary of State Alexander Haig stated that the trade embargo established in the early 1960s would be maintained and that further

restrictions on business dealings with Cuba were under review.

In July Washington considered whether to return some 3,000 refugees with criminal records or who were considered otherwise undesirable to Cuba or to remove them to the U.S. naval base at Guantánamo in southeastern Cuba. These were some of the estimated 125,000 Cubans who had emigrated to the U.S. between April and September 1980, with encouragement from the Castro government. The Havana authorities were thought unlikely to accept their return.

Relations between Cuba and Mexico remained cordial during 1981. Castro met Pres. José López Portillo on the island of Cozumel, Mexico, in August. Discussions centred on plans for the North-South summit conference of rich and poor countries held at Cancún, Mexico, in October. Castro announced during the meeting that Cuba had been excluded from the summit as a condition of President Reagan's attendance, and he absolved Mexico from responsibility for the exclusion. The fact that he was able to make the announcement at this point was seen as a public gesture of friendship by the Mexicans. Early in 1981 the two countries signed a comprehensive oil and gas agreement that included plans for oil exploration in Cuba, expansion of a refinery in Havana, construction of a new propane gas plant, and the sale of 10,000 metric tons of propane to Cuba.

An agreement signed with the U.S.S.R. in late 1980 provided for a 50% increase in bilateral trade in the period 1981–85 and for joint planning of Cuban economic policy up to 1990. The five-year plan for 1981–85 was published at the end of 1980. Its principal objective was real growth averaging 5% a year, to be achieved mainly by increasing industrial development. The plan also aimed to introduce decentralization in economic management, to provide incentives for labour productivity, and to bring a gradual end to rationing of some consumer goods.

Official figures showed that economic growth fell from 9.6% in 1978 to 3% in 1980, and preliminary estimates placed it at 3.9% in 1981. The slackening was attributed mainly to energy shortages and transport bottlenecks. Agricultural production growth fell from 7.7% in 1978 to 4% in 1980, largely because of diseases affecting sugar and tobacco crops. The 1980–81 sugar crop was approximately 8 million metric tons, compared with 6.8 million tons in 1979–80 and 8 million in 1978–79. Efforts to improve productivity enjoyed some success during 1981. In the first six months of the year, record industrial output levels were achieved with a decrease of 215,000 workers, and the sugar industry shed 30,000 from its work force. In an effort to reinforce the tourist revival of recent years, the government negotiated with three foreign consortia to establish joint ventures to build hotels and to install infrastructure facilities necessary for tourism on several islands.

Manuel Lleo Urrutia, who had been the first president of revolutionary Cuba but later broke with the Castro regime, died on July 4 in New York City (see OBITUARIES).

(ROBIN CHAPMAN)

Cycling

European riders dominated the 1981 world cycling championships in Czechoslovakia and accounted for all but 3 of the 18 titles. East Germany entered riders in only seven events and won five gold medals, including a fourth successive victory in the 1,000-m time trial for 25-year-old Lothar Thoms, the 1980 Olympic Games champion in that event. The track program was held in Brno, where Sergey Kopylov became the Soviet Union's first winner of the men's amateur sprint in 16 years. Earlier in the season in Moscow, Kopylov had set a new world record of 10.369 sec for a flying-start 200 m. The men's amateur road race, in Prague, also was won by the Soviet Union for the first time, with rider Andrey Vedernikov. Koichi Nakano of Japan won the men's professional sprint championship for the fifth consecutive year, and Danny Clark of Australia retained the professional Keirin title.

Sheila Young-Ochowicz, an Olympic and world speed-skating champion from the U.S., returned from a four-year break to complete a hat trick of victories in the women's sprint. Her previous wins were in 1973 and 1976. The women's road race produced the youngest world champion in cycling history, 16-year-old Ute Enzenauer of West Germany. New ground was also broken in the men's amateur team time trial, won by East Germany's quartet at an average speed of more than 50 km/h, the highest recorded over a full 100 km.

French cyclist Bernard Hinault won the Tour de France in July, his third time in four years.

Curling:
see Winter Sports

1981 Cycling Champions

Event	Winner	Country
WORLD AMATEUR CHAMPIONS—TRACK		
Men		
Sprint	S. Kopylov	U.S.S.R.
Tandem sprint	I. Kucirek and	Czechoslovakia
	P. Martinek	
Individual pursuit	D. Macha	East Germany
Team pursuit	D. Macha, B. Dittert	East Germany
	A. Grosser, V. Winkler	
1,000-m time trial	L. Thoms	East Germany
50-km points	L. Haueisen	East Germany
50-km motor-paced	M. Pronk	The Netherlands
Women		
Sprint	S. Young-Ochowicz	U.S.
Individual pursuit	N. Kibardina	U.S.S.R.
WORLD PROFESSIONAL CHAMPIONS—TRACK		
Sprint	K. Nakano	Japan
Individual pursuit	A. Bondue	France
50-km points	U. Freuler	Switzerland
One-hour motor-paced	R. Kos	The Netherlands
Keirin	D. Clark	Australia
WORLD AMATEUR CHAMPION—ROAD		
Men		
Individual road race	A. Vedernikov	U.S.S.R.
100 km team time trial	F. Boden, B. Drogan,	East Germany
	M. Kommer, O. Ludwig	
Women		
Individual road race	U. Enzenauer	West Germany
WORLD PROFESSIONAL CHAMPION—ROAD		
Individual road race	F. Maertens	Belgium
WORLD CHAMPIONS—CYCLO-CROSS		
Amateur	M. Fisera	Czechoslovakia
Professional	H. Stamsnijder	The Netherlands
MAJOR PROFESSIONAL ROAD-RACE WINNERS		
Het Volk	J. Raas	The Netherlands
Milan–San Remo	A. De Wolf	Belgium
Amstel Gold	B. Hinault	France
Paris–Roubaix	B. Hinault	France
Ghent–Wevelgem	J. Raas	The Netherlands
Flèche Wallone	D. Willems	Belgium
Liège–Bastogne–Liège	J. Van de Velde	The Netherlands
Tour of Flanders	H. Kuiper	The Netherlands
Grand Prix of Frankfurt	J. Jacobs	Belgium
Paris–Nice	S. Roche	Ireland
Bordeaux–Paris	H. Van Springel	Belgium
Tour de France	B. Hinault	France
Tour of Italy	G. Battaglin	Italy
Tour of Switzerland	B. Breu	Switzerland
Dunkirk Four-day	B. Oosterbosch	The Netherlands
Dauphine Libéré	B. Hinault	France
Tour of Britain*	S. Krivocheev	U.S.S.R.
Warsaw–Berlin–Prague*	S. Zagretdinov	U.S.S.R.
Tour de l'Avenir†	P. Simon	France
Tour of Spain	G. Battaglin	Italy

*Amateur.
†Mixed professional/amateur.

Bernard Hinault of France and Belgium's Freddy Maertens were the outstanding figures of the professional road race season. Hinault won the Tour de France for the third time in four years and by the fourth widest margin in the event's 68-race history. He also came close to defending his world title successfully, finishing third in Prague to Maertens, previously champion in 1976. Earlier, Maertens had won five stages of the Tour de France to end a three-year run without a major success. Phil Anderson became the first Australian to wear the Yellow Jersey of tour leader, for one day, and for the first time the field included a U.S. rider, Jonathan ("Jacques") Boyer.

(JOHN R. WILKINSON)

Cyprus

An island republic and a member of the Commonwealth, Cyprus is in the eastern Mediterranean. Area: 9,251 sq km (3,572 sq mi). Pop. (1980 est.): 628,500–662,000, including (1973) Greeks 78.2%; Turks 18.2%; others 3.6%. Cap. and largest city: Nicosia (pop., 1980 est., 161,000). Official popula-

Cyprus

CYPRUS

Education. Greek schools (1980–81): primary, pupils 48,701, teachers 2,183; secondary, pupils 41,794, teachers 2,408; vocational, pupils 5,805, teachers 502; teacher training, students 117, teachers 16; higher, students 1,823, teaching staff 175. Turkish schools (1978–79): primary, pupils 18,353, teachers 610; secondary, pupils 10,524, teachers 531; vocational, pupils 1,434, teachers 175; teacher training, students 37, teachers 4.

Finance. Monetary unit: Cyprus pound, with (Sept. 21, 1981) a free rate of C£0.43 to U.S. $1 (C£0.80 = £1 sterling). The Turkish lira is also in use in North Cyprus (Turkish Federated State). Gold and other reserves (June 1981) U.S. $327 million. Budget (1980 est.): revenue C£142.4 million; expenditure C£131 million. Excludes budget of Turkish Federated State (1980–81 est.) balanced at 3,404,000,000 Turkish liras.

Foreign Trade. (South only; 1980) Imports C£424 million; exports C£188 million. Import sources: U.K. 15%; Italy 11%; Iraq 10%; West Germany 8%; Japan 7%; Greece 7%; U.S. 6%. Export destinations: U.K. 21%; Lebanon 10%; Libya 8%; Saudi Arabia 8%; Syria 7%. Main exports: clothing 18%; potatoes 8%; footwear 7%; wine and spirits 6%; citrus fruit 5%. Tourism (1979): South, visitors 297,-000, gross receipts U.S. $141 million; North, visitors 109,-000.

Transport and Communications. Roads (1978) 9,866 km. Motor vehicles in use (1979): passenger 86,200; commercial 19,800. Air traffic (1980): 798 million passenger-km; freight 19.8 million net ton-km. Shipping (1980): merchant vessels 100 gross tons and over 688; gross tonnage 2,091,089. Telephones (Jan. 1979) 92,600. Radio receivers (Dec. 1977) 212,000. Television licenses (Dec. 1977) 68,-000.

Agriculture. Production (in 000; metric tons; 1980): barley c. 85; wheat (1979) 34; potatoes (1979) c. 197; grapes c. 215; oranges c. 104; grapefruit (1979) c. 70; lemons c. 29; olives c. 25. Livestock (in 000; 1979): sheep c. 495; cattle c. 38; pigs c. 198; goats c. 459.

Industry. Production (in 000; metric tons; 1979): asbestos c. 38; iron pyrites (exports) 141; copper ore (exports; metal content) c. 2.4; chromium ore (oxide content) c. 6.9; petroleum products (1978) 446; cement (1980) 1,234; electricity (kw-hr; 1980) 1,035,000.

tion estimates may not take into account the extensive internal migration or the recent and reportedly extensive Turkish immigration and Greek emigration. Language: Greek and Turkish. Religion: Greek Orthodox 77%; Muslim 18%. President in 1981, Spyros Kyprianou.

The first parliamentary elections in Cyprus since 1976—and the first since the death of Archbishop Makarios III in 1977—were held in May 1981. The results caused dramatic changes in the House of Representatives. The pro-Western Democratic Rally Party of Glafkos Clerides, which had had no representation in Parliament for several years, gained 12 seats, as did the Communist-backed AKEL Party. The Socialist EDEK Party secured three seats, leaving eight for the ruling centre-right Democratic Party of Pres. Spyros Kyprianou. (Of 50 seats in Parliament, 15 were left vacant pending the return of the Turkish-Cypriot members.) Despite predictions of a greater defeat for the president's party, his personal standing and political strength increased, and he retained the balance of power.

There were occasions during the year when the chances of a breakthrough in talks between the island's Greek and Turkish communities looked promising. In August the Turkish Cypriots suddenly announced their intention to put forward proposals on how they envisaged the territorial and constitutional future of the island. However, the Greek Cypriots said these did not even form a

basis for negotiations. A short time later the weekly sessions of the intercommunal talks held under UN auspices in Nicosia became deadlocked and ceased.

In an effort to break the deadlock, UN Secretary-General Kurt Waldheim and his local representative, Hugo Gobbi, drew up their own evaluation of the Cyprus situation. Its contents so angered the Greek Cypriots that they considered refusing to discuss it. But the international implications of ignoring a UN appraisal were considered too serious, and instead they submitted their objections. The Turkish Cypriots also made their objections known.

The accession to power in Greece of Socialist Prime Minister Andreas Papandreou had major implications for Cyprus. He vowed to take a much tougher line with the military regime ruling Turkey, and Greece's relations with the Cyprus government were immediately strengthened.

On the economic front, tourism continued to be the main foreign-currency earner. Oil prices were the chief cause of inflation, which rose above the 1980 level of 13.5%. Wage increases averaged more than 20%. Exports grew by about 16%, with the Middle East replacing Europe as the major market. Negotiations over Cyprus's associate membership in the European Communities were held up by the latter's reluctance to take any final steps until the EC could be certain that both parties would benefit. To increase foreign earnings, the government announced fresh incentives for foreign firms wishing to use the island as an offshore base. These included duty-free cars and office equipment. Work began on construction of an international airport in Paphos. (CHRIS DRAKE)

Czechoslovakia

A federal socialist republic of central Europe, Czechoslovakia lies between Poland, the U.S.S.R., Hungary, Austria, and East and West Germany. Area: 127,881 sq km (49,375 sq mi). Pop. (1980): 15,276,800, including Czech 64.3%; Slovak 30.5%; other 5.2%. Cap. and largest city: Prague (pop., 1980, 1,182,900). Language: Czech and Slovak (official). General secretary of the Communist Party of Czechoslovakia and president in 1981, Gustav Husak; federal premier, Lubomir Strougal.

As in previous years, Czechoslovakia's overriding concern during 1981 was the poor performance of the economy, a problem exacerbated by developments in neighbouring Poland. The leadership had no answer to these difficulties, reluctant as it was to introduce wide-ranging reforms. Hence it resorted to the well-tried and not especially fruitful method of making small adjustments to the existing, rather conservative system of economic management and to exhortations. The results were meagre.

Official spokesmen made it clear on a number of occasions that growth targets for the 1980s would be on the low side. The guidelines for the 1981–85 five-year plan were an indication of the economic future facing the country. Growth targets were scaled down to an expected average annual growth

rate of 2.8%, with the likely consequence that investment and consumption would stagnate.

Economic results for 1980 and for the first six months of 1981 bore out these pessimistic analyses. The 1980 figures showed that even the scaled-down plan targets could not be reached. For example, the target for national income growth in 1980 had originally been set at 3.7%; it was scaled down unannounced during the year to around 3.4%, and the actual fulfillment figure was 3%. Growth in industrial production was 3.2%, also below target. No figure was published for the increase in real wages, but it was thought to have been small. The January–June 1981 results were no better: real wages were up by only 1.3%, and the other indicators reflected a picture of stagnation. The harvest was indifferent. The grain target of 11,060,000 tons was underfulfilled by over 1 million tons. It was estimated that in 1981 around one-fifth of the country's meat consumption was derived from Western agricultural imports.

Czechoslovakia faced a bleak situation on the energy front as well. The days of cheap Soviet oil had gone. The price of Soviet crude rose by 40% between 1980 and 1981, and purchases were reduced, leading the country's planners to place renewed reliance on coal. However, three-quarters of Czechoslovakia's 123 million metric tons of coal was brown coal and lignite, of rather poor quality in terms of energy value. The costs of extracting hard coal were rising as pits were worked out and shafts had to be sunk deeper and deeper. There were repeated complaints from the Ostrava basin, the centre of the hard-coal area, of declining output resulting from inadequate investment, poor safety measures, and some dissatisfaction in the labour force. Miners objected to excessive demands for overtime work, inadequate consumer goods supplies, and the constant breakdown of inferior machinery.

The situation in the Ostrava basin was all the more serious by reason of its proximity to Poland — geologically it was an extension of the Silesian coalfield — and the fact that it could receive Polish television. As a result the population of the Ostrava was well informed about developments in Poland and about the success of Polish miners in abolishing weekend shifts. There had been unconfirmed rumours in October 1980 of work stoppages in the area, and Communist Party General Secretary Gustav Husak had paid a surprise visit to Ostrava in November 1980 in an attempt to calm the situation.

Under the impact of the Polish events, the Czechoslovak authorities somewhat reluctantly moved to upgrade the role of the officially controlled trade unions. It was made clear to the population that there could be no question of establishing an independent trade union on the lines of Poland's Solidarity, but at both the Slovak and the Czechoslovak party congresses, in the spring of 1981, speakers commented on the need for improving the protection of workers' interests. The chairman of the trade union movement, Karel Hoffmann, promised that the unions would be more active in representing workers' rights on issues such as safety, overtime, and industrial dis-

Czechoslovakia

UPI

Soviet Pres. Leonid Brezhnev (left), attending the 16th congress of the Communist Party of Czechoslovakia in April in Prague, is greeted by Czechoslovakian Pres. Gustav Husak.

CZECHOSLOVAKIA

Education. (1979–80) Primary, pupils 1,875,000, teachers 90,368; secondary, pupils 140,355, teachers 8,591; vocational (1978–79), pupils 209,860, teachers 16,175; teacher training (1978–79), pupils 12,387, teachers 825; higher, students 190,571, teaching staff 17,863.

Finance. Monetary unit: koruna, with (Sept. 21, 1981) a commercial rate of 5.88 koruny to U.S. $1 (10.90 koruny = £1 sterling) and a tourist rate of 9.91 koruny to U.S. $1 (18.38 koruny = £1 sterling). Budget (1979 est.) balanced at 285.7 billion koruny. Net material product (1979) $456 billion koruny.

Foreign Trade. (1980) Imports 81,540,000,000 koruny; exports 80,163,000,000 koruny. Import sources: U.S.S.R. 36%; East Germany 10%; Poland 8%; Hungary 6%; West Germany 5%. Export destinations: U.S.S.R. 36%; East Germany 9%; Poland 8%; West Germany 7%; Hungary 5%. Main exports (1979): machinery 44%; iron and steel 9%; motor vehicles 8%; chemicals 6%; textiles 6%.

Transport and Communications. Roads (1974) 145,455 km (including 79 km expressways). Motor vehicles in use (1979): passenger 1,976,700; commercial 324,800. Railways (1979): 13,142 km (including 2,989 km electrified); traffic 18,160,000,000 passenger-km, freight (1980) 72,640,000,000 net ton-km. Air traffic (1980): 1,540,000,-000 passenger-km; freight 14.6 million net ton-km. Navigable inland waterways (1979) c. 480 km. Shipping (1980): merchant vessels 100 gross tons and over 19; gross tonnage 155,319. Telephones (Dec. 1979) 3,073,000. Radio licenses (Dec. 1979) 3,799,000. Television licenses (Dec. 1979) 4,-092,000.

Agriculture. Production (in 000; metric tons; 1980): wheat c. 5,100; barley c. 3,900; oats c. 450; rye c. 585; corn c. 700; potatoes c. 3,700; sugar, raw value c. 810; grapes c. 223; apples c. 200; beef and veal c. 380; pork c. 805; timber (cu m; 1979) 18,324. Livestock (in 000; Jan. 1980): cattle 4,915; pigs 7,588; sheep 875; chickens 46,473.

Industry. Index of industrial production (1975 = 100; 1980) 125. Fuel and power (in 000; metric tons; 1980): coal 28,198; brown coal 94,897; crude oil 96; petroleum products (1978) 17,278; natural gas (cu m) c. 600,000; manufactured gas (cu m) 7,740,000; electricity (kw-hr) 72,820,000. Production (in 000; metric tons; 1980): iron ore (26% metal content) 1,928; pig iron 9,992; crude steel 15,223; magnesite (1975) 2,885; cement 10,546; sulfuric acid 1,287; plastics and resins 894; caustic soda 326; fertilizers (nutrient content; 1979) nitrogenous c. 650, phosphate c. 358; cotton yarn 135; cotton fabrics (m) 614,000; woolen fabrics (m) 59,000; man-made fibres 142; paper (1979) 861; passenger cars (units) 184; commercial vehicles (units) 88. Dwelling units completed (1980) 128,000.

Dams:
see Engineering Projects

eases. On the other hand, the leadership was evidently unwilling to make serious concessions in the area of labour relations. One of the attempted economic remedies was a tightening of the work norms, despite the comment from one official that the measure would not be received with enthusiasm everywhere.

The party congresses proved to be largely ceremonial. There were no personnel or policy changes of any significance, and the stress was on maintaining the status quo. A number of personnel changes in party and state offices were made after the general elections in June, with the aim of improving the economy. It was clear that a section of the leadership was not unwilling to try pragmatic measures, but it was prevented from introducing them by the hard-liners. Opening the party congress in Prague on April 6, Husak reaffirmed his support for the Soviet viewpoint that the protection of socialism concerned all socialist states.

The hard-liners dominated policy toward the opposition. The Charter 77 movement was under considerable pressure and to some extent retreated from the public arena. Emphasis was on *samizdat* (unofficial literature), pop music, and religious activism, the last attracting marked official disfavour. In May 1981 there was a major crackdown on the opposition. After two French citizens had been arrested for trying to bring a duplicator and printed materials into Czechoslovakia, at least 36 people were interrogated by the police and 16 of them, including some of the more prominent members of the opposition still at liberty, were held pending investigation. They were charged with subversion, and the scene was set for a major trial. Rudolf Battek, a former member of Parliament (1968–69), was tried in July for subversion and given a sentence of seven and a half years, the stiffest in a political trial since the 1950s. The sentence was reduced by two years on appeal.

(GEORGE SCHÖPFLIN)

Dance

United States. *Tchaikovsky Festival,* produced by the New York City Ballet (NYCB) from June 4 to 14 at the New York State Theater, constituted a major event on the U.S. ballet scene in 1981. During the ten-day festival more than 20 ballets were given, half new and half from the troupe's regular repertory. George Balanchine, artistic director of the NYCB, had asked for the equivalent of an "ice palace," and that is what Philip Johnson and John Burgee, the architects who conceived and produced the set, provided. Lighting effects that could alter the appearance of the setting for each ballet were planned by Ronald Bates.

New works for the *Tchaikovsky Festival* included wholly new choreography by Balanchine for *Mozartiana,* a work he had previously prepared in different versions for other companies, and for *Adagio Lamentoso* (the fourth movement of the Pathétique Symphony); *Piano Pieces,* choreographed by Jerome Robbins; Peter Martins's *Capriccio Italien* (seen earlier in a workshop student performance) and *Symphony No. 1;* and other pieces by John Taras, Jacques d'Amboise, and Joseph Duell.

In the fall the NYCB opened its 75th New York engagement with repertory before moving into its annual season of *Nutcracker* performances (more than 900 since the Balanchine production premiered in 1954). Earlier in the year Martins choreographed a new (and plotless) *Suite from Histoire du Soldat* (music by Stravinsky).

The American Ballet Theatre (ABT), continuing under the artistic direction of Mikhail Barysh-

nikov (*see* BIOGRAPHIES), who had assumed the post in the fall of 1980, presented in December 1981 at Kennedy Center in Washington, D.C., the world premiere of *The Wild Boy,* with choreography by Britain's Kenneth MacMillan and music by Gordon Crosse. Natalia Makarova and Baryshnikov starred in it. Also in December ABT presented for the first time Balanchine's *Bourrée Fantasque,* to music by Emmanuel Chabrier. The ballet was originally created for the NYCB in 1949. Earlier, a fund-raising gala for the Joffrey had been held at the Metropolitan Opera House during which President and Mrs. Ronald Reagan saw their son, Ron Reagan (a member of Joffrey II), dance.

For its spring-summer season at New York's Metropolitan Opera House, Baryshnikov and his dancers featured his all-Petipa program (seen first in late 1980 at the Kennedy Center) and his partly restaged *Swan Lake* and *Giselle.* He and Cynthia Gregory danced the leading roles in Balanchine's *Prodigal Son* together for the first time. Another new work was Cho San Goh's *Configurations* to the music of Samuel Barber, with Baryshnikov heading the cast. During the year Gelsey Kirkland and Patrick Bissell, both principal dancers, were dismissed from the company for tardiness, missing rehearsals, and other infractions.

In October the Joffrey Ballet marked its 25th anniversary with a season at the New York City Center. Highlighted were the world premiere of Gerald Arpino's *Light Rain* (with music by Douglas Adams and Russ Gauthier) and the Joffrey's first productions of John Cranko's *The Taming of the Shrew* and Jiri Kylian's *Transfigured Night.* Guest appearances in *The Taming of the Shrew* were made by the Stuttgart Ballet's Marcia Haydée and Rich-

The Netherlands Dance Theatre under the direction of Jiri Kylian gave outstanding performances during the year.

MARTHA SWOPE

ALEXANDER KONKOV—TASS/SOVFOTO

Amanda McKerrow of the U.S. won a gold medal in the Moscow International Ballet Competition in June.

ard Cragun, for whom the ballet was originally created in 1969.

In the late winter and spring the Brooklyn Academy of Music completed its "Ballet America" series with performances by the Houston Ballet, featuring its full-length production of *Papillon*; the Cleveland (Ohio) Ballet, highlighting Dennis Nahat's *Quicksilver* and Kurt Jooss's classic antiwar *The Green Table*; the Ohio Ballet; and the Pennsylvania Ballet. Nearby, the Brooklyn Center for the Performing Arts at Brooklyn College completed its "Tribute to American Dance" series with performances by the Atlanta (Ga.) Ballet, the nation's oldest regional ballet troupe, and by the Oakland (Calif.) Ballet; the latter featured revivals of Michel Fokine's *Scheherazade*, Eugene Loring's *Billy the Kid*, and Ron Guidi's *Gallops and Kisses*. Later in the year in its home city, the Oakland Ballet staged a revival of Bronislava Nijinska's historic *Les Noces* (Stravinsky).

The Dance Theatre of Harlem offered a revival of *Scheherazade*, staged by Frederic Franklin, and a production of Glen Tetley's *The Greening*. Franklin's staging of *Swan Lake* (Act II) was also in the repertory, along with a revival of Geoffrey Holder's *Bele*.

Among the many ballet troupes headquartered outside New York City that produced new works were the Houston Ballet with its full-length *Peer Gynt*, choreographed by Ronald Hynd to the music of Grieg and with scenery and costumes by Peter Farmer, and the Pittsburgh (Pa.) Ballet Theatre with Patrick Frantz's new choreography for Ravel's *Daphnis and Chloe* with orchestra and a chorus of 80 singers. The Pittsburgh company also honoured U.S. choreographers with a program of ballets consisting of Agnes de Mille's *Rodeo*, William Dollar's *The Combat*, and Ruth Page's *The Merry Widow*. The Tulsa (Okla.) Ballet Theatre

mounted a *Coppélia* based on that performed for years by the Ballet Russe de Monte Carlo, and the Boston Ballet offered a new four-act *Swan Lake* with 19th-century period sets and costumes by Julia Trevelyan Oman.

In the field of modern dance an outstanding event was "New Dance USA Festival," a series of concerts and conferences focusing upon the experiments of the movement referred to as "post-modern dance." Twenty-seven choreographers, along with critics and reporters, attended the event, held at the Walker Art Center in Minneapolis, Minn. This new variety of modern dance was also stressed in a series called "The Next Wave: New Masters at the Brooklyn Academy of Music," a series that included in its dance section performances by Trisha Brown and Laura Dean. Among other exponents of "post-modern" to perform in various theatres and studios throughout the year were David Gordon, Douglas Dunn, Kei Takei, Jim Self, Karole Armitage, Dana Reitz, Rosalind Newman, Kenneth Rinker, and Lucinda Childs.

Dancers and choreographers representing the more established forms of modern dance included Martha Graham, Merce Cunningham, Paul Taylor, Anna Sokolow, and May O'Donnell. Graham, at 87 the matriarch of modern dance in the U.S., created a new work called *Acts of Light*, to music of Carl Nielsen. New Cunningham creations were *10's with Shoes* (music by Martin Kalve) and *Channels Inserts* (David Tudor music). Taylor's premieres included *Arden Court* (William Boyce music) and *House of Cards* (set to Darius Milhaud's *La Création du Monde*). A gala benefit performance for the Taylor troupe featured Rudolf Nureyev and Baryshnikov dancing together for the first time.

The Alvin Ailey American Dance Theater produced *Phases* (choreography by Ailey to music of Pharoah Sanders, Donald Byrd, and Max Roach); *Treading* (choreography by Elisa Monte to music by Steve Reich); and *The River* (choreographed by Ailey to music by Duke Ellington), restaged for modern dancers from its original ballet format. The José Limón Dance Company featured *The Kitchen Table*, a new work by one of its principal dancers, Bill Cratty, and *Sonata* (Bach), choreographed by the troupe's director, Carla Maxwell.

Twyla Tharp brought her company to Broadway for a four-week engagement at the Winter Garden Theatre. The major production was Tharp's full-length *The Catherine Wheel*, to music of David Byrne. Other major creations were *Uncle Edgar Dyed His Hair Red* and *Short Stories*. The Nikolais Dance Theater's major new work was *The Mechanical Organ*, with choreography, music, and design by Alwin Nikolais.

The 1981 *Dance Magazine* awards were given to Sir Anton Dolin (knighted during the year), Selma Jeanne Cohen, Twyla Tharp, and Stanley Williams. The Capezio Dance Award, with a $5,000 prize, was presented to Dorothy Alexander, founder of the Atlanta Ballet and a pioneer in the regional ballet movement. (WALTER TERRY)

Europe. Celebrations of the 50th anniversary of Britain's Royal Ballet took several forms. On the anniversary date (May 5, 1981) Lesley Collier and Stephen Jefferies led *The Sleeping Beauty* at Covent

Garden, where three later special performances were also given of excerpts from the company's other ballets, past and present. An illustrated history of the company by Alexander Bland, incorporating year-by-year documentation of all works performed, was published under the title *The Royal Ballet: The First Fifty Years*.

These events were supplemented by the staging of MacMillan's *Isadora*, a two-act production ostensibly based on the life of the U.S. dancer Isadora Duncan (1878–1927), with commissioned music by Richard Rodney Bennett and designs by Barry Kay. The title role was a double portrait by ballerina Merle Park and actress Mary Miller (the latter speaking lines from Duncan's memoirs). As an often lurid theatrical spectacle, it divided both public and critics as to the success of its form and choreographic content.

Sadler's Wells Royal Ballet shared the Covent Garden stage as part of the anniversary and in its own theatre gave further attention to fostering emergent choreographic talent with a program featuring new works by five dancers from the two royal companies. Those by David Bintley (*Night Moves*) and Michael Corder (*Three Pictures*) made the biggest impression, and the former, to music by Benjamin Britten, was taken into the repertory. A new *Swan Lake* production by the company's director, Peter Wright, was added in November.

To mark the centennial year of composer Bela Bartok, London Festival Ballet collaborated with the English National Opera to produce his two original ballets and one opera as a triple bill for the first time in London. Geoffrey Cauley's new version of *The Wooden Prince* had overtones of Oriental mime-drama, and after Tetley withdrew from creating a new *Miraculous Mandarin*, it was staged in a reproduction of Flemming Flindt's earlier version for the Royal Danish Ballet. The triple bill as a whole proved more musically demanding than theatrically cogent.

An active year for Ballet Rambert was marked by the appointment in April of Robert North as artistic director. An American from Charleston, S.C., and previously associate director and choreographer with the London Contemporary Dance Theatre, he retained Richard Alston as resident choreographer. Alston created a new *Rite of Spring* to the four-hand piano version Stravinsky first published, and Christopher Bruce created *Ghost Dances*, to South American folk music, an effective poetic tribute to victims of oppression.

Both the Rambert company and Scottish Ballet visited Italy for the Venice International Dance Festival, and the Scottish company became the first in Britain to mount a work by the choreographer most in demand throughout Europe, the Czechoslovak-born Jiri Kylian (*see* below). His *Symphony in D* (to Haydn music), first staged for the Netherlands Dance Theatre in 1976, enriched a season of new works in Scotland, of which *All the Sun Long*, by company dancer Garry Trinder to Bartok music, signaled a developing talent.

London Contemporary Dance Theatre appeared at the Edinburgh Festival for the first time with *Dances of Love and Death*, a two-act production by artistic director Robert Cohan, with commissioned music by Carl Davis and player-piano studies by Conlon Nancarrow. It depicted love and death through figures of classical myth and popular legend, from Pluto/Persephone to Marilyn Monroe, in five linked choreographic poems. The Edinburgh Festival was also host to two U.S. companies. The San Francisco Ballet made its first appearance in Western Europe with a classically based repertory consisting of co-director Michael

The Hamburg Ballet performed Bach's *St. Matthew Passion* June 21–28 in West Germany. U.S.-born John Neumeier choreographed and directed the ballet.

Smuin's three-act *Romeo and Juliet* (Prokofiev) and 12 shorter works by Smuin, co-director Lew Christensen, and others.

Among several U.S. visitors to London, Dance Theatre of Harlem achieved a popular success with its classical repertory at Covent Garden, while the modern dance presentations of the Merce Cunningham and Twyla Tharp troupes, also from New York City, were more variably received at Sadler's Wells. Controversy also arose during debut seasons given by Australia's Sydney Dance Company, directed by Graeme Murphy, and West Germany's Tanz-Forum from Cologne, directed by Jochen Ulrich.

Also new from the U.S. was the Boston Ballet, which participated in the so-called Nureyev Festival at the London Coliseum with only their production of *Swan Lake*, a version that afforded little reason for crossing the Atlantic. They followed a visit to the same theatre by West Germany's Stuttgart Ballet, which was welcomed more for its dancing than for its repertory, although there was an enthusiastic response to *Forgotten Land*, created earlier in the year by Kylian to the music of Britten's *Sinfonia da Requiem*.

Kylian was widely sought after by other companies besides continuing his internationally successful direction (since 1976) of the Netherlands Dance Theatre. His choreographic talent combined an inventive blend of classical and modern technique in movement with a poetic imagination and acute musical sensibility. As well as contributing works to the Scottish, Stuttgart, and Frankfurt companies in 1981, his choreography was the subject of a triple bill by the Swedish Royal Ballet at Stockholm.

The Swedish company appointed a new director, former dancer Gunilla Roempke, and added

Elie Chaib and Susan McGuire give a dynamic and modern performance in Paul Taylor's *Arden Court.*

Danish Literature:
see Literature

Deaths:
see Demography; *see also obituaries of prominent persons who died in 1981 listed under* People of the Year

MacMillan's *Manon* (nonoperatic Massenet) to its repertory, as the Norwegian National Ballet did Tetley's *The Tempest* (Nordheim). The Royal Danish Ballet turned for its new works to Alvin Ailey of the U.S., Hans van Manen and Rudi van Dantzig of The Netherlands, and the U.S.-born John Neumeier, director of the Hamburg Ballet, who staged his 1977 version of *A Midsummer Night's Dream* to a mixture of Mendelssohn and electro-acoustic music. For his own Hamburg company Neumeier sought to harness Bach's *St. Matthew Passion* as the basis of an ambitious ballet production, which was considered to be only partially successful. At West Berlin's Deutsche Oper, the Soviet-born Valery Panov equally ambitiously attempted a balletic digest of Tolstoy's *War and Peace.* Taken also to New York City and Washington, D.C., it was thought to be stronger on theatrical impact than on choreographic content.

No less ambitious was the full-length *Schema* by Nikolais for the Paris Opéra Ballet, where, under Rosella Hightower's direction, the dancers divided into three companies: one resident, a second on tour, and a third devoted to more experimental works. A new version of *La Fille mal gardée* by Basel's Heinz Spoerli for the Paris company suffered a first-night postponement after bales of hay in the stage decor caused a skin infection among the dancers.

In Switzerland Spoerli's ongoing classical work at Basel and Patricia Neary's Balanchine-oriented repertory at Zürich contrasted with the mixed classical and modern choreographic style of Argentine-born Oscar Araiz at Geneva. Following his first programs, which included versions of *Pulcinella* and *Le Baiser de la fée,* Araiz created *Tango,* a successful full-length celebration (in association with music by Atilio Stampone) of the Argentine tango as a basis for theatre dance.

Further resurgence of dance interest in Italy brought Nureyev to stage *Romeo and Juliet* at La Scala, Milan, with himself and Carla Fracci; in it Dame Margot Fonteyn returned to the stage as Lady Capulet. In Rome Pierre Lacotte from Paris created a new version of the 19th-century *Marco Spada* (Auber), with Nureyev dancing the title role. The U.S.-born Carolyn Carlson left Paris to set up a new modern-dance company in Venice, and a new touring company, Aterballetto, was founded in Reggio Emilia.

Italy was also visited by the Jacobson Ballet from Leningrad, never previously seen outside the U.S.S.R., performing works by Leonid Jacobson (1904–75), a formative influence in Soviet ballet. Within the U.S.S.R. Moscow's Bolshoi Ballet and its director, Yuri Grigorovich, were the subject of an unprecedented attack for alleged conservatism in a book of essays by Vadim Gayevsky, *Divertissement—The Fate of Classical Ballet.* Some copies went into circulation before the authorities called in the remainder.

Lydia Lopokova and Felia Dobrovska, stars of Diaghilev's Ballets Russes, died during the year, as did Sigurd Leeder, a pioneer of European modern dance (*see* OBITUARIES). (NOËL GOODWIN)

See also Music; Theatre.

Defense

Symbolized by the October 6 assassination of Egyptian Pres. Anwar as-Sadat, international instability was increasing in 1981, largely as the result of four interconnected factors. Two were familiar: Soviet expansionism, directly and by means of proxies such as the Cubans and Vietnamese; and local and regional instabilities, notably but not exclusively in the Middle East. Compounding these were two factors prevalent during the cold war (1947–62) and now reemerging: domestic problems in the Soviet Union's Eastern European empire, most apparent in Poland but also evident in the Soviet Union itself; and a new U.S. determination to contain Soviet expansionism while protecting U.S. and allied interests against regional instabilities. Taken together, these four factors suggested that the use of force on the international scene was and would continue to be on the rise.

It was difficult to find any continent where local wars were not being fought and where Soviet intervention was not in evidence. In Southeast Asia the Vietnamese continued to fight their own counterinsurgency war against Chinese-supported Kampucheans (Cambodians), using, according to well-documented reports, chemical/biological weapons (CBW). In the Middle East the stalemated Iran-Iraq war continued at a low level, the Camp David peace process between Egypt and Israel appeared to be at a standstill, and Libya persisted in its efforts to destabilize its neighbours. In Africa increased Soviet support for the South West Africa People's Organization guerrillas was being countered by South African military action against their bases in Angola. In Latin America the Cubans were finding targets of opportunity among the unstable Central American and Caribbean countries, especially Nicaragua and El Salvador. In Eastern Europe Poland's domestic revolution threatened the political authority of the Communist Party, leading to the imposition of martial law by the Polish government. (*See* POLAND.) In Western Europe the growing neutralist movement was taking on anti-U.S. overtones.

At the strategic nuclear level, the Soviet buildup continued, complemented by increases in theatre nuclear forces (TNF). The new U.S. administration was trying to counter this bid for nuclear superiority, but it had to overcome years of neglect in the defense area. The absence of any strategic arms control limitation talks (SALT) agreement (with SALT II unratified) symbolized the end of a decade of détente and arms control.

Overall, these events pointed up two conflicting trends. The Soviets appeared to be trying to maximize their gains before the new U.S. containment policy took effect (assuming they could not reverse it). And the U.S. was thus compelled to demonstrate its willingness to uphold containment by military means where necessary. Again symbolically, the shooting down of two Libyan fighters by U.S. planes over the Gulf of Sidra in August marked a new U.S. willingness to use force.

But neither superpower could completely control regional and local developments, and these could pull them into increased confrontation. This was particularly true in the Middle East, where the oil-producing countries combined vast natural assets with negligible military forces and domestic instability. Historically, such a combination had always tempted potential aggressors, especially when, like the Soviets, they were neighbours. Moreover, though the Soviets had created the most powerful military machine in history, they were experiencing significant domestic social and economic problems. Traditionally, military successes abroad have provided a diversion from domestic difficulties—exacerbated, in this case, by the Soviets' inability to consolidate their conquest of Afghanistan. This interpretation might be overly pessimistic, but it seemed borne out by the year's events in defense.

UNITED STATES

On taking office in January, Pres. Ronald Reagan moved quickly to increase the U.S. budget authority for defense to $226.3 billion, compared with former president Jimmy Carter's $195.7 billion proposal. Although these figures seemed large, especially when other programs were being cut in an effort to balance the budget, 1980 defense expenditure amounted to only 5.5% of the gross domestic product (GDP), compared with 12–14% of gross national product (GNP) for the Soviet Union. The administration's goal was to increase defense spending gradually to 6.9% of GNP by fiscal 1984, but even this was probably insufficient to meet the country's security commitments.

Historically, U.S. defense spending dropped to 5% of GNP after World War II, rose to 13.9% during the Korean War, leveled off at about 8% under Pres. Dwight D. Eisenhower, and increased to 10.3% under Pres. John Kennedy. During the Vietnam war it ran at roughly 8% excluding the costs of the war, but these were massive. U.S. forces other than those fighting in Vietnam were run down, and replacement of aging equipment was delayed from the late 1960s on. The U.S., therefore, had to make up the deficiencies caused by years of

The issue of U.S. defense parity with the U.S.S.R. was a major one during the year. Defense Secretary Caspar Weinberger describes classes of Soviet ships at a news conference after the release of a Pentagon study entitled "Soviet Military Power."

UPI

Table I. U.S./NATO–Soviet Strategic and Theatre Nuclear Balance, July 1981

Weapons systems	Range (km)	Payload[1] (000 lb)	Warheads, yield[2]	CEP[3]	Speed (Mach)	Number deployed
UNITED STATES Strategic Forces						
Intercontinental ballistic missiles						1,052
Titan II	15,000	7.5	1 x 9 mt	0.5	...	52
Minuteman II	11,300	1–1.5	1 x 1–2 mt	0.4	...	450
Minuteman III	13,000	1.5–2	3 x 350 kt	0.12–0.7	...	550
Submarine-launched ballistic missiles (in 36 nuclear submarines)						584
Polaris A-3	4,600	1	3 x 200 kt	0.5	...	64
Poseidon C-3	4,600	2–3	10 x 50 kt or 14 x 50 kt	0.15	...	336
Trident C-4	7,400	3+	8 x 100 kt	c. 0.15	...	184
Manned bombers						376
B-52D	9,900	60	...	...	0.95	75
B-52G/H	12,000	70	...	...	0.95	241
	16,000			...	0.95	
FB-111A	4,700	37.5	...	...	2.5	60
U.S./NATO Long-range Theatre Nuclear Forces[4] (Total: 436 weapons, 218 delivery systems)						
Medium/short-range ballistic missiles						
U.S. Pershing I	720	...	kt	...	...	108
Manned bombers						218
U.S. F-111A/E	4,700	28	2	...	2.5	220[5]
U.K. Vulcan B-2	6,400	21	2	...	0.95	48
BRITAIN (Strategic Nuclear Forces only)						
Submarine-launched ballistic missiles (in 4 nuclear submarines)						
Polaris A-3	4,600	1	3 x 200 kt	0.5	...	64
FRANCE (Strategic and LRTNF)[6]						
Submarine-launched ballistic missiles (in 5 nuclear submarines)						
MSBS M-20	3,000	...	1 x mt	...	...	80
Intermediate-range ballistic missiles (IRBM)						
SSBS S-3	3,000	...	1 x mt	...	...	18
Manned bombers						63
Mirage IVA	3,200	16	2 x mt	...	2.2	33
Mirage IIIE	2,400	19	2 x mt	...	1.8	30
SOVIET UNION Strategic Forces						
Intercontinental ballistic missiles						1,398+
SS-11 Mod 1	10,500	1.5–2	1 x 2 mt	0.3–0.5	...	580
Mod 3			3 x 100–300 kt			
SS-13 Savage	10,000	1	1 x 1 mt	0.7	...	60
SS-16	9,300	2	3 x 150 kt	0.3	...	...
SS-17 Mod 1	10,000	6	4 x 900 kt	(1,500')	...	150
Mod 2			1 x 5 mt			
SS-18 Mod 1	10,500	16–20	1 x 18–25 mt	0.2–0.34	...	308
Mod 2	9,300	16–20	8 x 2 mt	(600')		
Mod 3	10,500	16–20	1 x mt	(600')		
SS-19 Mod 1	11,000	7	6 x 550 kt	(850')	...	300
Mod 2	10,200	7	1 x 5 mt			
Submarine-launched ballistic missiles (in 69 nuclear plus 15 diesel submarines)						989
SS-N-5 Serb	1,120	1.5	1 x 1–2 mt	1–2	...	57
SS-N-6 Mod 1,2	2,400	1.5	1 x 1–2 mt	1	...	165
Mod 3	3,000	1.5	2 x 3 kt			288
SS-N-8	8,000	1.5	1 x 1 mt	0.5	...	291
SS-NX-17	5,000	3+	1 x 1 mt	0.2–0.3	...	12
SS-N-18	8,000	5+	3 x 1–2 mt	...	...	176
Manned bombers						150
Tu-95 Bear	12,800	40	...	...	0.78	105
Mya-4 Bison	11,200	20	...	...	0.87	45
Soviet LRTNF (Total: 1,800 weapons, 990 delivery systems)						
Variable/intermediate/medium-range ballistic missiles (V/I/MRBM)						860
SS-4 Sandal	1,900	...	1 x mt	...	...	340
SS-5 Skean	4,100	...	1 x 1 mt	...	...	40
SS-20 Mod 1	5,000	1.2	1 x 1.5 mt	...	...	500–
Mod 2	5,600		3 x 150 kt			756[7]
Mod 3	7,400		1 x 50 kt			(230)
Short-range ballistic missiles (SRBM) and sea-launched cruise missiles (SLCM)[8]						
SS-12/22 SRBM	1,000	...	mt	...	...	c.500
SS-N-12 SLCM	3,700	...	2 x kt/mt	...	...	c.100
Manned bombers[9]						880
Tu-16 Badger	6,400	20	2	...	0.8	580
Tu-22 Blinder	2,250	12	2	...	1.5	165
Tu-22M/26 Backfire	8,000	17.5	4	...	2.5	135

[1] Payload refers to a missile's throw weight or a bomber's weapons load.

[2] For MIRV and MRV the figure to the left of the multiplication sign gives the number of warheads and the figure to the right is the yield per warhead. For bombers, weapons per bomber are given.

[3] Circular Error Probable: the radius (in nautical miles) of a circle within which at least half of the missile warheads aimed at a specific target will fall.

[4] LRTNF systems are missiles with ranges or aircraft with unrefueled combat radii such that Soviet systems can unambiguously hit targets in Western Europe. Combat radii are about one quarter or less of the range.

[5] Total deployed worldwide, including FB-111A; 170 is the inventory normally based in Europe, or within striking range of Europe.

[6] French nuclear forces are controlled and targeted independently of NATO.

[7] Total deployed against both NATO and China theatres; two-thirds are thought to be deployed against NATO.

[8] Although not classified as Soviet LRTNF, Soviet SRBM and SLCM could hit targets in Western Europe and are therefore shown for illustrative purposes.

[9] Total deployed worldwide. Of these, about half are allocated to Soviet Naval Aviation (some 270 Tu-16, 40 Tu-22 and 70 Tu-26). Two-thirds of the remaining strike bombers and ASM carriers are considered deployed against NATO.

Sources: International Institute for Strategic Studies, *The Military Balance 1981–1982*; and *Aviation Week and Space Technology*. Figures for Soviet forces, especially LRTNF can only be estimates.

---

cumulative disinvestment in existing forces while, at the same time, providing for long-overdue re-equipment across the board. This meant procurement at uneconomically high rates and inevitable supply bottlenecks.

Compounding these problems were the high costs of the all-volunteer force (AVF). With a 2,049,100-strong AVF (167,760 women), personnel and related costs accounted for some 24% of the total defense budget. Even so, there were grave doubts about the educational level of the force, its racial composition (about 40% nonwhite) relative to the general population, and its ability to retain skilled technical personnel. However, President Reagan argued, probably correctly, that reintroducing a peacetime draft would be politically and socially divisive.

The first Reagan defense budget emphasized general preparedness of U.S. conventional forces, including adequate levels of supplies and logistic support. In keeping with the traditional strategy of the U.S. as a maritime power, the Navy was to be rebuilt to a 600-ship level, with 15 carrier battle groups. Strategic nuclear forces (SNF) were to be modernized with the purchase of 100 B-1B bombers, accelerated deployment of the Trident I (C-4) submarine-launched ballistic missile (SLBM) on the new Ohio-class ballistic missile submarines (SSBN's) and the 31 Lafayette-class SSBN's, increased deployment of air-launched cruise missiles (ALCM's) in B-52G/H bombers, and deployment of sea-launched cruise missiles (SLCM's) on a variety of surface and submarine platforms.

These programs failed, however, to address the near-total vulnerability of the land-based leg of the U.S. deterrent triad (air-, land-, and sea-based missiles); Soviet land-based intercontinental ballistic missiles (ICBM's) now had sufficient accuracy and throw weight (payload) to destroy the U.S. Minuteman II and III ICBM's in their fixed silos. The U.S. Air Force solution to this problem, accepted by most strategic analysts, was a multiple protective shelter (MPS) system in which each ICBM would be provided with more than one silo, forcing the Soviets to attack every silo since they could not know which were empty. The Carter administration had approved deployment of 200 new MX ICBM's in 4,600 MPS, although the precise form of basing mode was changed several times in the face of opposition from Utah and Nevada, the areas chosen for the MPS system.

President Reagan's proposed SNF modernization, announced in October, scrapped MPS in favour of deploying the MX in existing ICBM silos. However, the silos were admittedly vulnerable to a Soviet attack, and proposed superhardening could not make them invulnerable. Defending them with the low-altitude defense system (LOADS) antiballistic missile (ABM) system was sound in principle, but LOADS would not be available for some years, was of uncertain effectiveness, and would certainly be inadequate to defend fixed silos, although it would be very effective in conjunction with an MPS system. Further changes in MX deployment seemed likely. Existing U.S. strategic forces are shown in Table I; the 75 B–52D bombers were being retired as obsolete.

In terms of conventional warfare, attention was focused on the U.S. capability for intervention in the Persian Gulf. The Rapid Deployment Force (RDF) was a paper concept, and the actual forces available for deployment in the area had to be drawn from the regular services. It seemed unlikely that the U.S. could deploy more than token forces in the Gulf (2,000–20,000 men without heavy equipment), possibly adequate as a symbolic deterrent but not as a fighting force.

The U.S. had a one-and-a-half-ocean navy trying to cover three oceans, the Atlantic, the Mediterranean, and the Pacific. Its core remained the carrier battle group (one or two attack carriers with 70–95 aircraft each, plus escorts), but only 12 carriers were equipped with regular air wings. Of these, three were nuclear powered and four others were relatively modern; hence the decision to order two new nuclear-powered carriers in addition to the Nimitz-class "Carl Vinson" (CVN 70) scheduled for commissioning in 1982. Deployment of the F-14A Tomcat fighter/fighter-bomber continued, with 374 F-14's currently operational. Prolonged flight testing of the F-18 Hornet fighter-bomber apparently indicated that its many defects could be rectified.

Major surface combatants for carrier escort, antisubmarine warfare (ASW), and landing support included 9 nuclear-powered guided weapons (GW) cruisers, 18 GW cruisers, 39 GW and 43 gun/ASW destroyers, and 20 GW and 58 gun frigates. Missiles carried included Standard (SM-1) and Harpoon surface-to-surface missiles (SSM's) and Standard (SA-1), Aegis (SM-2), Talos, Sea Sparrow, Tartar, and Terrier surface-to-air missiles (SAM's). Two battleships, the "Iowa" and "New Jersey," were being reactivated. The submarine force was almost wholly nuclear powered. The 67 amphibious warfare ships included five Tarawa-class general assault ships (LHA's) and seven Iwo Jima-class helicopter landing platforms (LPH) carrying a mix of helicopters and the AV-8A vertical/short take-off and landing (V/STOL) fighter-bomber, developed from the British Harrier. The Marine Corps had 188,100 men organized into three large divisions, each with an integral air wing but with relatively light armour.

The 558,000-strong Air Force had some 3,200 combat aircraft, including 774 F-4 Phantoms, 358 F-15 Eagle fighters, and 150 F-16 fighter-bombers. The airborne warning and control system (AWACS) was deployed in 22 E-3A Sentry aircraft. Token air defense of North America was offered by 108 F-106A Delta Dart and Air National Guard fighters. Canada contributed 54 CF-101 Voodoo fighters to the North American Aerospace Defense Command (Norad).

The Army, with 775,000 personnel, was organized into four armoured, six mechanized, four infantry, one airmobile, and one airborne division, plus smaller supporting and special units. Its 11,400 tanks included 150 of the new M-1 Abrams, and the approximately 20,000 armoured fighting vehicles (AFV's) included M-577 and M-113 armoured personnel carriers (APC's) and the first of the new M-2 (infantry) and M-3 (cavalry) mechanized infantry combat vehicles (MICV's). Artil-

UPI

The USS "Ohio" joined the U.S. fleet on November 11 in a ceremony at Groton, Connecticut, led by Vice-President George Bush. The "Ohio" is the largest and most powerful of U.S. submarines.

lery pieces comprised roughly 2,500 105- and 155-mm towed guns/howitzers, 4,000 105-, 155-, and 203-mm self-propelled howitzers, 6,200 TOW antitank guided weapons (ATGW), and 10,400 Dragon ATGW launchers. Army deployment remained oriented toward the defense of NATO-Europe, with 219,729 personnel in Europe, mostly in the 7th Army. Other major deployments were 30,000 men in South Korea, one understrength infantry division in Hawaii, and one infantry brigade each in Alaska and Panama. The Strategic Reserve consisted of one mechanized and one airborne division plus one armoured and one air cavalry brigade.

Overall, these were impressive forces. Quantitatively, however, they were grossly inferior to those of the Soviet Union, and even qualitatively the U.S. had lost most of its earlier advantage. This was particularly true in terms of currently deployed forces; the newest U.S. systems were technically superior on a one-to-one basis, but this could not offset Soviet superiority in deployed forces equipped with only slightly inferior weapons.

U.S.S.R.

After more than a decade of "arms control" and détente, the momentum of the Soviet military buildup remained unchanged. This was best indicated by the Soviets' continued allocation of roughly the same high percentage of GNP to defense, estimated by the West at 12–15% with some estimates going as high as 18%. Particularly disturbing were the cumulative effects of the Soviets' massive investment in military forces and their failure to reduce defense spending during détente, contrary to the assumptions of U.S. and other

Western policymakers. Objectively, Soviet security did not require such large and expensive military forces, especially given the disproportionate burden defense spending imposed on the Soviet economy. The inescapable conclusion was that the Soviets felt subjectively insecure and that they believed these forces to be usable for political games.

The sheer size of the Soviet forces was impressive: 3,673,000 personnel plus 560,000 paramilitary forces. At the strategic nuclear level, the Soviets had or were close to superiority and at the theatre nuclear level, they were certainly superior to both NATO-Europe and China. In both theatres their conventional and chemical forces were probably sufficient to ensure victory. With their naval and air units, the Soviets, with their Cuban surrogates, could—and did—project power anywhere in the world.

Soviet SNF and long-range TNF are summarized in Table I, but this underestimates the Soviets' advantage. Essentially, the Soviets, using less than half their forces, could destroy virtually all of the U.S. land-based ICBM force, perhaps two-thirds of the U.S. bomber force, and about a third of the U.S. submarine force. The remaining U.S. forces could be less than those required for mutual and assured destruction and much less than those needed to defend the U.S. allies. The latest Soviet missiles were as accurate as any U.S. missile and were married to a much greater throw weight. The argument that inherently unknowable bias factors affecting operational missile flights in wartime over the North Pole made it impossible to reproduce test accuracies was untrue. These factors were known and could be compensated.

Similarly, the obvious Soviet advantage in static TNF indicators underestimates their real advantages in a dynamic exchange. NATO estimates had assumed that each mobile SS-20 intermediate-range ballistic missile (IRBM) launcher had only one SS-20 missile available, but it had become clear that two missiles were almost certainly available for each launcher, a figure that could rise to four or five. Furthermore, this doubling or tripling of the SS-20 threat to NATO-Europe, now comprising some 24 launcher sites, 252 launchers, 756 missiles, and 2,268 warheads (plus swing systems

totaling 45 launchers, 135 missiles, and 405 warheads), had obscured the Soviet medium-range TNF buildup. The SS-23 (190–350-km range [1 km = 0.621 mi]; 1 kiloton-range warhead) was replacing the 410 Scud short-range ballistic missiles (SRBM's); the SS-22 (540–1,000-km range; kiloton-range warhead) was replacing the 65 SS-12 SRBM's; and the SS-21 (65–120-km range) was replacing the 482 FROG-7 SRBM's. Such medium-range TNF could strike significant targets in Western Europe and made any limits on SS-20s meaningless.

Soviet ICBM improvements consisted of continued deployment of the SS-17 and SS-19 and upgrading of the older SS-11s to SS-19s to provide greater targeting flexibility. Several new types of ICBM were under development. Significant changes in the Soviet SLBM force included the fitting out of the giant Typhoon-class SSBN, displacing some 30,000 tons (compared with 18,700 tons for the U.S. Ohio-class SSBN) and carrying 20 new SS-NX-20 SLBM's with multiple independently targeted reentry vehicles (MIRV). Intelligence reassessments had raised the number of D-III-class SSBN's to 11. These and other changes gave the Soviets a provisional total of 989 SLBM's in 84 SSBN's. Soviet strategic bombers included 105 elderly Tu-95 Bears, 45 Mya-4 Bisons, and 65–70 Tu-22M Backfires, with an equal number of Backfires in naval aviation. There was some uncertainty over the exact number of Backfires since the earlier Backfire A appeared to have been withdrawn for modification.

The Soviet Army remained the most powerful in the world, with 1,825,000 personnel, 55,000 tanks, 62,000 AFV's, and some 20,000 artillery pieces, forming 46 tank, 119 motor rifle, and 8 airborne divisions. Soviet divisions had fewer men but more tanks than their U.S. equivalents. The new T-80 tank was being tested, the PT-76 light tank was being phased out in favour of the BMP MICV, and the old BTR-50/60 APC was being replaced by the BTR-70 and the BMP MICV. Deployment remained nominally constant, in terms of divisions, but each of these divisions was much more powerful than it had been a decade earlier. Eastern Europe remained the centre of Soviet military power, with 30 Category 1 (three-quarters to full strength) divisions, including 15 tank and 15 motor rifle. A further 67 divisions, half in Category 1 or 2 (half to three-quarters strength), were in the European U.S.S.R. military districts, and 24 divisions (1 tank, 21 motor rifle, 2 airborne), most in Category 3 (one-quarter strength), were in the southern U.S.S.R. but were available for use against the Persian Gulf. On the Sino-Soviet border, half the 46 divisions were in Category 1 or 2.

Over 85,000 men were in Afghanistan. Casualties there were thought to have totaled some 20,000–30,000 since the 1979 invasion. Despite the Soviets' lavish use of helicopter gunships and—apparently—illegal chemical weapons (CW), they seemed unable to control the countryside or even all of the capital. Major deployments elsewhere included 2,600 troops in Cuba, 1,750 in Libya, 1,000 in Iraq, 2,500 in Syria, 1,500 in Yemen (Aden), 500 in Yemen (San'a'), and 4,500 in Vietnam. There were smaller detachments stationed in An-

The Boeing Aerospace Co. displayed its first full-production air-launched cruise missile in November. The missile is the first of 705 that Boeing was to build for the U.S. Air Force.

gola, Kampuchea, Mali, Mauritania, Mozambique, and the Seychelles.

The Navy continued its steady expansion, to 443,000 personnel with 294 major surface combat ships, 259 cruise-missile and attack submarines (99 nuclear, 160 diesel), 755 combat aircraft, and 245 helicopters. Of the surface ships, the most impressive remained the 25,000-ton Kirov-class nuclear missile cruiser, with 20 SS-N-19 ssm's, 10 SA-N-6 and 4 SA-N-4 sam's, and 4 SS-N-14 asw missile launchers, all with multiple reloads. Two Kiev-class carriers were deployed and two more were nearing completion. The Soviets appeared to be developing, from the Kiev class, a nuclear-powered attack carrier of about 60,000 tons with an air wing of 60 aircraft. New cruisers to be constructed were of a large, conventionally powered, multipurpose GW-cruiser design, displacing 11,000 to 13,000 tons and equipped with sam's, ssm's, and improved command and control capabilities; the first was building in the Black Sea. Two new destroyer types appeared. The 7,000–8,000-ton "Sovremenny" DDG, designed primarily for surface warfare, was the first major Soviet combatant deployed since 1970 that did not have significant asw capability. The 8,000–9,000-ton "Udaloy" was designed for asw, with eight asw missiles and two helicopters.

Soviet naval aviation provided integrated reconnaissance, air/ship strike, antisubmarine, and general aviation support. Amphibious warfare capabilities were now second only to those of the U.S.; the new 13,000-ton Ivan Rogov amphibious assault vessel (one deployed, more building) carried 550 naval infantry, three hovercraft, and helicopters. The Soviet submarine fleet was notable for having the world's fastest attack boat, the Alfa-class nuclear submarine (ssn), as well as 47 cruise-missile submarines. The new Oscar-class nuclear-powered guided missile submarine (ssGN) carried 20 to 24 slcm's and the Papa-class carried 10, while the other 45 ssGN's carried 8 missiles each. There were also 22 diesel guided missile submarines (ssG's), each with four missiles. These ssGN's and ssG's would be particularly effective in a coordinated attack within range of Soviet air bases.

The 475,000-strong Soviet Air Force had some 5,300 combat aircraft and 2,550 armed helicopters, providing a significant offensive deep-interdiction capability built up in the last decade. Most of the 1,700 counter-air fighters would soon be improved MiG-23 Flogger B's (1,300 deployed), replacing the remaining 400 MiG-21 Fishbed c/d/f's. The Soviet stress on air defense was in striking contrast to the attitudes of the U.S. and Canada, at least until very recently. The Air Defense Force had 2,500 aircraft, and over 10,000 sam's were deployed in some 1,-200 sites. The older SA-2/3 and SA-5 were being supplemented by the SA-10, with increased low-altitude capabilities against manned aircraft and cruise missiles. The SA-5 and SA-10 also had some abm capability, supplementing the 32 abm 1B Galosh abm's deployed around Moscow. A ten-site Try Add system of abm-associated control radars was being installed. Passive civil defense included two major shelter programs, down to the city level, to protect the Communist Party leadership.

UPI

The U.S.S.R.'s latest battle cruiser, the 25,000-ton "Kirov," made her trial run in the Baltic Sea. The "Kirov" is the biggest nuclear missile cruiser to be built by any country.

NATO

Thirty-two years after the alliance was founded, the central problem for NATO-Europe was still the impossibility of mounting a prolonged conventional defense of Western Europe against a Soviet attack. Thus Europe's independence still depended, in the last analysis, on the U.S. president's willingness to use U.S. strategic nuclear forces in its defense. Paradoxically, in the face of the Soviet buildup of forces targeted on NATO-Europe, an increasing segment of European public opinion was adopting a neutralist position, arguing that if U.S. and NATO nuclear weapons were removed from Europe, the chances of a Soviet attack would be lessened. However illogical, this movement had become a major political factor, threatening NATO's ability to implement its 1979 TNF modernization decision.

NATO's TNF modernization was designed partially to offset the massive Soviet TNF buildup in both long-range and medium/mid-range TNF (see TABLE I) by deploying, between 1983 and 1988, 108 Pershing II medium-range ballistic missiles (MRBM's) and 464 U.S.-operated ground-launched cruise missiles (GLCM's). All Pershing II's were to be deployed in West Germany, replacing Pershing I SRBM's, while the cruise missiles were to be sited in Britain, Belgium, The Netherlands, Italy, and West Germany. However, Belgium and The Netherlands had only accepted deployment in principle and now seemed likely to withdraw. There was also a serious possibility that West Germany would follow suit, despite Chancellor Helmut Schmidt's strong support of the NATO decision. Antinuclear, neutralist, and nationalistic sentiments had surfaced within his own party, and they were also strong in Scandinavia, the Benelux countries, and among British left-wingers. Taking advantage of the situation, the Soviets were urging a moratorium on further TNF modernization, which would leave their own modernized TNF in

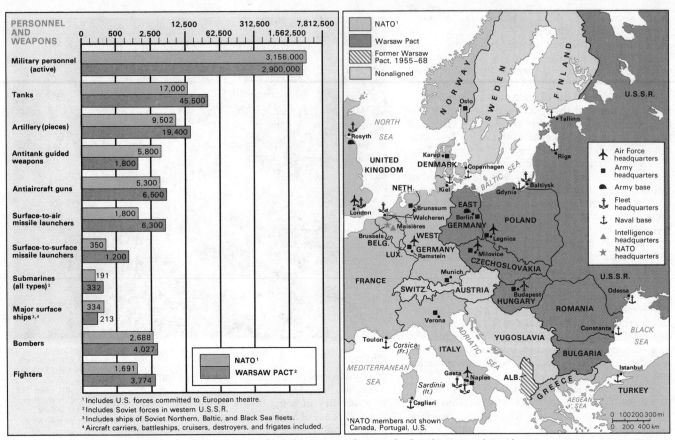

Conventional military power of NATO and Warsaw Pact forces as distributed in Europe during the year.

place while stopping NATO's offsetting modernization before it began.

NATO was thus experiencing the worst crisis since its founding, with influential voices in the U.S. arguing that the U.S. should abandon NATO-Europe to its fate if it was no longer prepared to defend itself. These political problems adversely affected NATO's efforts to address—via its 1978 Long Term Defense Program—its very real military problems. These were inadequate conventional forces, virtually nonexistent chemical forces, and very limited battlefield TNF. The momentum of the Soviet and Warsaw Pact buildup over the past decade meant that NATO was actually worse off, in relative terms, than in 1971.

The key problem was that, on the crucial Central Front (from Norway to southern Germany), the Soviets could concentrate sufficient forces to break through NATO's conventional defenses within a week to ten days. Static force comparisons probably underestimated the Soviets' advantage, since their forces were standardized with those of the Warsaw Pact and could be reinforced more quickly than NATO forces anytime up to 20–30 days after mobilization. However, even the crude figures emphasized NATO's inferiority: 10,356 tanks to some 17,000 Soviet tanks, plus reserves; the equivalent of some 59 divisions to 119 for the U.S.S.R./Warsaw Pact.

WARSAW PACT

The upheaval in Poland underlined the Soviets' inability to deal with political and economic fer- ment within their Eastern European empire. Consequently, the political reliability of the Warsaw Pact allies' military forces was at its lowest in many years. Paradoxically, this increased NATO's security problems. NATO could not gamble that the Pact armies would not fight alongside the Soviets. At the same time, the Soviets had to strengthen their own forces in case the Pact armies did not support them. This also enabled the Soviets to maintain a credible threat of military intervention against unacceptable internal changes within Eastern Europe.

Whether the Soviets could continue to abstain from direct military intervention in Poland remained an open question at year's end. Clearly they preferred that the Polish government—now an essentially military government under Gen. Wojciech Jaruzelski—deal with the matter itself, presumably with covert Soviet support. Overt intervention could have a high price, not only politically but because the Polish Army was an integral part of the Polish nation and would almost certainly fight to defend it.

Other than those of the U.S.S.R., Poland's armed forces were the largest in the Warsaw Pact, totaling 319,500 personnel (605,000 reserves) plus 72,-000 in paramilitary forces and 200,000 in the active Citizens Militia. The 210,000-strong Army was well equipped and trained, with a highly professional officer corps. It fielded five armoured, eight mechanized, one airborne, and one amphibious assault division with 3,400 T-54/55 tanks and 5,500 MICV/APC's. The Air Force of 87,000 had 705 com-

bat aircraft, mostly older types but including 35 newer Su-20 fighter-bombers, while the 22,500-strong coast defense Navy, with 4 W-class submarines, 1 Kotlin-class destroyer, and 30 fast attack craft, would be useful against Soviet landings from the Baltic. From the Soviet viewpoint, these were significant forces, astride the lines of communication with Soviet forces in East Germany.

Any Soviet intervention might therefore require assistance from East Germany, although this would certainly guarantee Polish resistance against the traditional Prussian enemy. East German forces totaled 167,000 personnel, including an army of 113,000 comprising two tank and four motor rifle divisions with 1,500 T-54/55 and T-72 medium tanks (1,600 more in storage), 700 BMP MICV's, and 1,000 APC's. The 38,000-strong East German Air Force had 35 MiG-17 and 12 MiG-23 fighter-bombers, and the Navy of 16,000 included 2 frigates and 64 fast attack craft. Overseas deployment reflected East Germany's new role as a Soviet proxy in Algeria, Angola (800 personnel), Ethiopia, Libya (1,600), Mozambique, Yemen (Aden), and Syria.

Czechoslovakia's numerically large armed forces —194,000 personnel— were of questionable combat value. The Army had 140,000 personnel and 3,420 medium tanks, and the Air Force of 54,000 had 471 combat aircraft. Hungary's 101,000-strong forces included an army of 80,000 with 1,230 medium tanks and an air force of 21,000 with 115 fighters. The more independent Romanians had armed forces totaling 184,500 personnel, comprising an army of 140,000 with 1,800 medium tanks and an air force of 34,000 with 240 fighters and 70 fighter-bombers. Significantly, Warsaw Pact defense spending remained relatively high compared with that for NATO-Europe: 4% of GNP for Czechoslovakia, 6.1% for East Germany, 3.2% for Poland, 2.3% for Hungary, but only 1.3% for Romania.

UNITED KINGDOM

Defense spending as a percentage of GDP remained high (5.1%), closest to the U.S. figure among the major members of NATO-Europe. However, because Britain's GDP was low, actual spending amounted to only about $27,770,000,000. Britain's decision to modernize and expand its independent nuclear deterrent with the purchase of Trident SLBM's from the U.S. meant that other elements of its forces had to be reduced, notably the Royal Navy. The Tridents were to be carried in four or five new British-built SSBN's. Details of the new Chevaline reentry vehicles for Britain's existing 64 Polaris A-3 SLBM's (in four SSBN's) remained unclear, but they could increase the number of multiple reentry vehicles (MRV) per missile from three with 200-kiloton yields to six. It also seemed likely that Britain would purchase the superior Trident II D-5 SLBM, currently under development, rather than the Trident I, which would make Britain's nuclear deterrent extremely powerful and credible.

Despite reductions, the Royal Navy remained the third largest in the world, with 74,687 personnel, 62 major surface combatants, and 28 attack submarines (12 SSN and 16 diesel). Its primary mission was to protect the Atlantic sea-lanes against Soviet surface, submarine, and air attacks. The first of three Invincible-class ASW light carriers was deployed, while the elderly carrier "Hermes" was being retired. The 176,248-strong Army was oriented toward the defense of NATO-Europe. Equipment included 900 Chieftain heavy tanks and 2,998 APC's. Deployment overseas included 9,128 personnel in Northern Ireland, 55,000 in the British Army of the Rhine (BAOR), and 7,100 in Hong Kong. The 92,701-strong Royal Air Force had some 700 combat aircraft.

FRANCE

France's defense spending and policy remained surprisingly consistent under its new Socialist president, François Mitterrand. It would increase its already considerable cooperation with NATO without rejoining NATO's military command structure and it would maintain the independent French nuclear deterrent, including a French neutron bomb. French nuclear strategy, however, had returned to the stress on massive retaliation characteristic of Charles de Gaulle, in contrast to Valéry Giscard d'Estaing's emphasis on graduated response. Ironically, in light of NATO's bitter debate on TNF modernization, Mitterrand proved a hard-liner, stressing the need for a major military response to the Soviet TNF buildup.

The French defense budget of $21,230,000,000 represented 3.9% of GDP. The core of the nuclear strike force consisted of five SSBN's, each with 16 M-20 missiles (3,000-km range, 1 × 1-megaton warhead); these were to be replaced by the M-4, with a greater range and 3 × 200 kiloton MIRV. A sixth submarine was building, a seventh ordered, and an eighth authorized. Supplementing these were 18 S-2/3 IRBM's (3,000-km range, 1 × 150-kiloton warhead) and 33 Mirage IVA strategic bombers. Tactical and theatre forces included some 45 Jaguars and 30 Mirage III's, plus 36 Super Étendard carrier-borne fighter-bombers and 42 Pluton SSM's (120-km range, 15–25 kiloton warhead). Other aircraft in the 103,460-strong Air Force, which had 460 combat aircraft, included 30 Mirage IIIC and 105 Mirage F-1C interceptors in the Air Defense Command. The Mirage F-1 series and Mirage 2000 series fighter/strike/reconnaissance aircraft were replacing the Mirage III series.

The Army of 321,320 comprised eight armoured, four motor rifle, one alpine, one airborne, and one parachute division, with 1,114 AMX-30 medium tanks, 600 AMX-10P MICV's, and 1,540 AMX-13 VTT and 900 VAB APC's. Three armoured divisions (48,500 men) were deployed in West Germany and 2,700 men in Berlin, as well as 16,400 in France's overseas dependencies and 23,000 elsewhere in Africa and the Middle East. The 69,600-strong Navy had 44 major surface combat vessels, including 2 Clemenceau-class carriers and 21 diesel submarines.

WEST GERMANY

West Germany's defense spending had dropped to 3.2% of GDP, but it still totaled $20,170,000,000. Armed forces strength totaled 495,000 personnel,

Table II. Approximate Strengths of Regular Armed Forces of the World

Country	Military personnel in 000s			Warships [1]			Jet aircraft [3]		Tanks [4]	Defense expenditure as % of GNP
	Army	Navy	Air Force	Aircraft carriers/ cruisers	Submarines [2]	Destroyers/ frigates	Bombers and fighter- bombers	Fighters/ recon- nais- sance		
I. NATO [5]										
Belgium	65.0	4.4	20.1	—	—	4 FFG	90 FB	36, 18 R	389	3.3
Canada	13.0	5.5	15.3	—	3	4 DDG, 19 FF	—	138	114	1.7
Denmark	19.3	5.7	7.6	—	6 C	4 FFG	60 FB	40, 16 R	180	2.4
France [6]	321.3	69.6	103.5	2 CV, 1 CVH, 1 CG	21, 5 SSBN	20 DDG, 11 FFG, 9 FF	33 SB, 291 FB	165, 45 R, 42 MR	1,114	3.9
Germany, West	335.2	36.5	106.0	—	24 C	7 DDG, 2 DD, 6 FF	402 FB	60, 87 R, 19 MR	3,787	3.2
Greece	150.0	19.0	24.5	—	10	16 DD, 6 FF	141 FB	81, 22 R, 12 MR	1,390	5.1
Italy	225.0	42.0	69.0	1 CVH, 2 CAH	9	4 DDG, 1 DD, 4 FFG, 8 FF	162 FB	72, 24 R, 14 MR	1,750	2.4
Luxembourg	0.7	—	—	—	—	—	—	—	—	1.0
Netherlands, The	67.0	16.8	19.0	—	6	2 DDG, 3 DD, 10 FFG	90 FB	36, 18 R, 17 MR	811	3.4
Norway	18.0	9.0	10.0	—	15 C	5 FFG	70 FB	16, 3 R, 7 MR	116	2.9
Portugal	47.0	13.4	10.5	—	3	17 FF	51 FB	4 R	57	3.8
Turkey	470.0	46.0	53.0	—	14	14 DD, 2 FF	250 FB	32, 43 R	3,500	4.2
United Kingdom	176.2	74.7 [7]	92.7	2 CVH	16, 12 SSN, 4 SSBN	14 DDG, 46 FFG	48 SB, 60 B, 140 FB	112, 60 R, 28 MR	900	5.1
United States	775.0	716.1 [7]	558.0	3 CVN, 11 CV, 9 CGN, 18 CG, 5 LHA, 7 LPH, 14 LPD, 33 LSD/T	5, 79 SSN, 36 SSBN	39 DDG, 43 DD, 20 FFG, 58 FF	376 SB, 252 B, 2,199 FB	1,020, 191 R, 453 MR	11,975	5.5
II. WARSAW PACT										
Bulgaria	105.0	10.0	34.0	—	2	2 FFG	84 FB	140, 24 R	1,860	3.4
Czechoslovakia	140.0	—	54.0	—	—	—	164 FB	252, 55 R	3,420	4.0
Germany, East	113.0	16.0	38.0	—	—	2 FFG	47 FB	300, 12 R	1,500	6.1
Hungary	80.0	—	21.0	—	—	—	—	130	1,230	2.3
Poland	210.0	22.5	87.0	—	4	1 DDG	220 FB	430, 55 R, 10 MR	3,430	3.2
Romania	140.0	10.5	34.0	—	—	—	70 FB	240, 18 R	1,800	1.3
U.S.S.R.	1,825.0	443.0 [7]	1,455.0 [8]	2 CV, 2 CVH, 1 CGN, 25 CG, 11 CA	138, 52 SSN, 69 SSBN, 15 SSB, 47 SSGN, 22 SSG	41 DDG, 32 DD, 72 FFG, 108 FF	150 SB, 880 B, 2,735 FB	4,200, 899 R, 290 MR	55,000	12–14
III. OTHER EUROPEAN										
Albania	30.0	3.0	10.0	—	3	—	—	100	100	...
Austria	46.0	—	4.3	—	—	—	34 FB	—	220	1.2
Finland	34.4	2.5	3.0	—	—	1 FF	—	40	...	1.5
Ireland	12.4	0.9	0.7	—	—	—	—	—	—	...
Spain	255.0	49.0 [7]	38.0	1 CV	8	12 DD, 9 FFG, 7 FF	41 FB	110, 17 R, 6 MR	700	...
Sweden [9]	44.5/700.0	10.0	9.8	—	12	3 DDG	119 FB	198, 54 R	670	3.2
Switzerland [9]	10.5/580.0	—	8.0/45.0	—	—	—	239 FB	103, 25 R	805	...
Yugoslavia	190.0	17.5 [7]	45.0	—	7	1 FFG	142 FB	126, 35 R	1,300	...
IV. MIDDLE EAST AND MEDITERRANEAN; SUB-SAHARAN AFRICA; LATIN AMERICA [10]										
Algeria	90.0	4.0	7.0	—	—	1 FFG	13 B, 114 FB	105, 10 R, 12 MR	650	...
Egypt	235.0	20.0	112.0	—	9	5 DD, 3 FF	16 B, 255 FB	160, 17 R	1,660	...
Iran [11]	150.0	10.0 [7]	35.0	—	—	3 DDG, 4 FFG	354 FB	77, 14 R, 2 MR	1,410	...
Iraq [11]	210.0	4.2	38.0	—	—	—	17 B, 167 FB	151	2,600	...
Israel [9]	135.0/450.0	9.0/10.0	28.0/37.0	—	3	—	424 FB	28 R	3,500	23.2
Jordan	60.0	0.3	7.2	—	—	—	32 FB	32	516	...
Kuwait	10.0	0.5	1.9	—	—	—	30 FB	20	240	...
Lebanon [12]	22.3	0.3	1.3	—	—	—	—	—	—	...
Libya [13]	45.0	5.0	5.0	—	4	1 FFG	9 B, 159 FB	197, 13 R	2,700	...
Morocco	107.0	5.0	8.0	—	—	—	42 FB	—	180	6.7
Oman	11.5	1.0	2.0	—	—	—	20 FB	—	18	...
Qatar	9.0	0.4	0.3	—	—	—	—	8	24	...
Saudi Arabia	35.0	2.2	14.5	—	—	—	65 FB	15	630	...
Sudan	68.0	1.5	1.5	—	—	—	44 FB	—	197	...
Syria	170.0	2.5	50.0	—	—	2 FF	191 FB	225, 2 R	3,700	13.1
Tunisia	24.0	2.6	2.0	—	—	1 FF	—	—	12	...
United Arab Emirates	40.0	1.0	1.5	—	—	—	10 FB	30	75	...
Yemen, North	30.0	0.6	1.5	—	—	—	—	65	714	...
Yemen, South	22.0	1.0	1.3	—	—	—	8 B, 74 FB	36	375	...
Angola [14]	30.0	1.5	1.5	—	—	—	40 FB	1 MR	235	...
Ethiopia [15]	225.0	1.5	3.5	—	—	—	94 FB	—	790	...
Kenya	12.0	0.7	2.1	—	—	—	12 FB	—	36	...

rising to 1,250,000 on mobilization. The Army of 335,200 had completed its reorganization into 6 armoured (17 brigades), 4 armoured infantry (15 brigades), 1 mountain, and 1 airborne division (3 brigades). Equipment included 150 new Leopard 2 and 2,437 Leopard 1 medium tanks, plus 1,200 elderly M-48A2/A2G2 tanks, 2,136 Marder MICV's, and 4,270 APC's. Tactical nuclear forces operated by West Germany, with U.S.-controlled nuclear warheads, comprised 72 Pershing I SSM's (720-km range, kiloton-yield warhead) and 26 Lance SSM's (110-km range, kiloton-range warhead).

The Air Force had 106,000 personnel and 479 combat aircraft, but it was handicapped by economic constraints on introduction of the Tornado multirole combat aircraft to replace the 144 obsolete F-104G Starfighter fighter-bombers. SAM's included 216 Nike Hercules, many with nuclear warheads, and 216 improved Hawk launchers. The 36,500-strong Navy, oriented to operation in the Baltic, had 24 coastal submarines, 7 modern GW/ASW destroyers, and 6 frigates, and the Naval Air Arm had 112 combat planes including 66 F-104G fighter-bombers. Overall, the size and efficiency of West Germany's military forces were impressive, but the emergence of major domestic opposition to NATO's TNF modernization and, indeed, to any defense effort had exacerbated the difficulties of defense funding in a period of economic stagnation.

ARMS CONTROL AND DISARMAMENT

The prospects for technically effective, meaningful arms control declined sharply with the discovery that the Soviets had violated the 1925 Geneva

Country	Military personnel in 000s			Warships [1]			Jet aircraft [3]		Tanks [4]	Defense expenditure as % of GNP
	Army	Navy	Air Force	Aircraft carriers/ cruisers	Submarines [2]	Destroyers/ frigates	Bombers and fighter-bombers	Fighters/ recon-naissance		
Madagascar	18.0	0.7 [7]	0.9	—	—	—	12 FB	—		...
Mozambique [16]	25.0	0.7	1.0	—	—	—	35 FB	—	300	...
Nigeria	140.0	6.0	10.0	—	—	1 FF	12 FB	6	65	...
Somalia	60.0	0.6	2.0	—	—	—	3 B, 9 FB	17	190	...
South Africa [9]	76.0/404.5	6.4 [7]	10.3	—	3	3 FF	12 B, 32 FB	30, 11 R, 25 MR	310	...
Tanzania	43.0	0.9	1.0	—	—	—	—	24	30	...
Zaire	18.5	1.5	2.1	—	—	—	—	10	—	...
Zimbabwe	33.0	—	1.0	—	—	—	5 B, 14 FB	—	20	...
Argentina	130.0	36.0 [7]	19.5	1 CV, 1 CA	4	5 DDG, 4 DD	9 B, 137 FB	19, 20 R, 5 MR	185	...
Brazil	182.8	47.0 [7]	42.8	1 CV	7	4 DDG, 8 DD, 6 FFG	38 FB	17, 28 MR	25	0.7
Chile	53.0	24.0 [7]	15.0	3 CA	3	2 DDG, 4 DD, 2 FFG, 3 FF	38 FB	8, 8 MR	120	...
Colombia	57.0	9.2 [7]	3.8	—	2	2 DD, 2 FF	—	12, 4 R	...	...
Cuba	200.0	11.0	16.0	—	3	—	42 FB	133	710	8.5
El Salvador	9.0	0.1	0.8	—	—	—	—	—	—	...
Mexico	95.0	20.0 [7]	4.5	—	—	2 DD, 6 FF	—	14 MR	—	...
Nicaragua	5.0	0.2	1.5	—	—	—	—	—	3	...
Peru	75.0	15.0 [7]	40.0	1 CG, 2 CA	9	2 DDG, 2 DD, 2 FFG	32 B, 60 FB	11 MR	510	...
Venezuela	27.0	9.0 [7]	4.8	—	3	2 DD, 4 FF	20 B, 16 FB	36, 1 R	142	2.3
V. FAR EAST AND OCEANIA [10]										
Afghanistan [17]	35.0	—	8.0	—	—	—	20 B, 60 FB	20	1,200	...
Australia	32.9	17.3	22.4	1 CV	6	3 DDG, 8 FF	24 FB	48, 14 R, 36 MR	73	3.0 [5]
Bangladesh	70.0	4.0	3.0	—	—	2 FF	16 FB	3	30	...
Burma	163.0	7.0 [7]	9.0	—	—	2 FF	—	—	25	...
China	3,900.0	360.0 [7]	490.0	—	102, 2 SSN, 1 SSB	15 DDG, 12 FFG, 5 FF	90 SB, 800 B, 500 FB	4,600, 130 R	11,000	...
India	944.0	47.0	113.0	1 CV, 1 CA	8	2 DD, 24 FF	50 B, 184 FB	380, 8 R, 13 MR	2,120	3.8
Indonesia	195.0	52.0 [7]	26.0	—	4	10 FF	14 FB	16, 24 MR	—	...
Japan	155.0	44.0	44.0	—	14	18 DDG, 16 DD, 12 FFG, 4 FF	64 FB	225, 16 R, 120 MR	830	0.9
Korea, North	700.0	31.0	51.0	—	19	4 FF	90 B, 370 FB	240	2,500	...
Korea, South	520.0	49.0 [7]	32.6	—	—	10 DD, 7 FF	268 FB	54, 12 R, 20 MR	860	5.7
Laos	46.0	1.7	8.0	—	—	—	—	10	—	...
Malaysia	90.0	6.0	6.0	—	—	2 FF	19 FB	3 MR	—	...
Mongolia	30.0	—	3.1	—	—	—	—	12	130	...
New Zealand	5.7	2.8	4.4	—	—	4 FFG	9 FB	5 MR	—	1.8
Pakistan	420.0	13.0	17.6	—	6	8 DD	11 B, 55 FB	144, 10 R, 3 MR	1,285	2.0
Philippines	70.0	26.0 [7]	16.8	—	—	8 FF	20 FB	22, 1 MR	—	2.0
Singapore	35.0	3.0	4.0	—	—	—	53 FB	21, 8 R	—	6.1
Taiwan	349.0 [7]	35.0	67.0	—	2	15 DDG, 7 DD, 11 FF	334 FB	21, 4 R, 27 MR	200	...
Thailand	160.0	35.0 [7]	43.1	—	—	6 FF	14 FB	36, 7 R, 22 MR	50	...
Vietnam	1,000.0	4.0	25.0	—	—	3 FF	10 B, 295 FB	180	1,900	...

Note: Data exclude paramilitary, security, and irregular forces. Naval data exclude vessels of less than 100 tons standard displacement. Figures are for July 1981.
[1] Aircraft carrier (CV); helicopter carrier (CVH); general purpose amphibious assault ship (LHA); amphibious transport dock (LPD); amphibious assault ship (helicopter) (LPH); dock/tank landing ship (LSD/T); heavy cruiser (CA); guided missile cruiser (CG); helicopter cruiser (CAH); destroyer (DD); guided missile destroyer (DDG); frigate (FF); guided missile frigate (FFG); N denotes nuclear powered.
[2] Nuclear powered attack submarine (SSN); ballistic missile submarine (SSB); guided (cruise) missile submarine (SSG); coastal (C); N denotes nuclear powered.
[3] Bombers (B), fighter-bombers (FB), strategic bombers (SB), reconnaissance fighters (R); maritime reconnaissance (MR) data include jet combat aircraft from all services including naval and air defense. MR also includes propeller driven ASW and ECM aircraft; data exclude light strike/counter-insurgency (COIN) aircraft.
[4] Main battle tanks (MBT), medium and heavy, 31 tons and over.
[5] Defense expenditure calculated as percentage of gross domestic product (GDP).
[6] French forces were withdrawn from NATO in 1966, but France remains a member of NATO.
[7] Includes marines.
[8] Figure includes the Strategic Rocket Forces (385,000) and the Air Defense Force (550,000), both separate services, plus the Long-Range Air Force (45,000).
[9] Second figure is fully mobilized strength.
[10] Sections IV and V list only those states with significant military forces.
[11] Iranian figures refer to pre-revolutionary situation. Iraqi figures before Iran-Iraq war. War losses uncertain.
[12] Figures approximate, given Lebanon's civil war and division.
[13] Some advanced Libyan aircraft maintained and manned by Soviet/Warsaw Pact crews.
[14] Plus 19,000 Cubans and 2,500 East Germans serving with Angolan forces.
[15] Ethiopia also has 14,000 Cuban plus other Soviet bloc troops.
[16] Plus Cuban, Warsaw Pact, and Chinese advisers and technicians in Mozambique.
[17] Figures approximate, given civil war in Afghanistan. Exclude Soviet and Warsaw Pact advisers and/or troops.

Sources: International Institute for Strategic Studies, 23 Tavistock Street, London, *The Military Balance 1981–1982, Strategic Survey 1980–1981.*

Protocol and the 1972 treaty banning the use, respectively, of chemical weapons (CW) and biological weapons (BW). This had long been suspected, but in November 1981 the U.S. announced that it had incontestable proof from soil and plant samples that mycotoxins and other CBW had been and were being used in Indochina. Use of CW by the Soviets in Afghanistan was also reported, although absolute proof was still awaited. Mycotoxins were a Soviet invention: dead biological agents that did not multiply and whose use could therefore be controlled, they killed their victims by destroying the stomach and lungs.

The possibility of arms control had been based on the assumption that national technical means (NTM) of verification had improved to the point where gross violations of agreements could be detected, while the Soviet stake in arms-control agreements guaranteed their observance. However, it was now clear that the Soviets had not only used CBW against unprotected guerrilla fighters and civilians but had also engaged in the manufacture of BW. In 1979 an apparently accidental large-scale release of anthrax germs — a particularly virulent BW agent — had taken several thousand lives in Sverdlovsk. The Soviet violation of two of the more significant arms-control treaties — including one observed throughout World War II — was even more disturbing because it had been done for relatively marginal gains. Manufacturing BW would not give the Soviets any significant military advantage. Use of mycotoxin and asphyxiating (possibly nerve) gases in Indochina and Afghanistan could yield only slight returns in those frustrating counterinsurgency campaigns.

Future arms-control agreements with the Sovi-

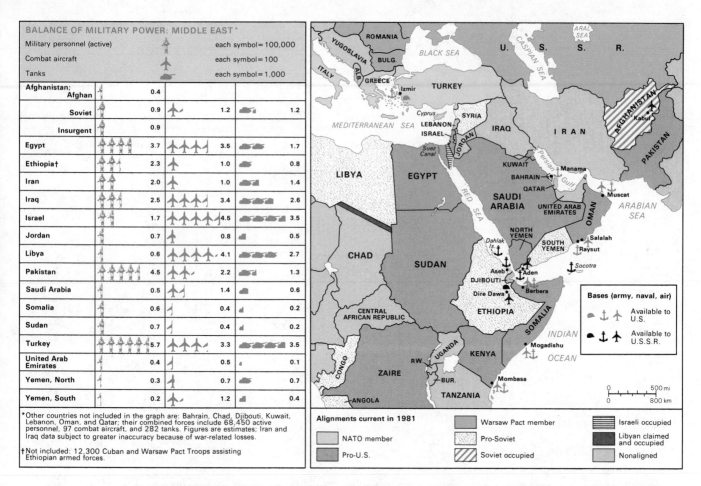

ets would thus have to include rigorous verification provisions, but NTM were unlikely to be adequate unless supplemented by on-site inspection. Under these circumstances, the future for SALT and TALT (theatre arms limitation talks) seemed poor. The U.S. and the U.S.S.R. had agreed to continue unilaterally to observe the provisions of the 1972 SALT agreements (expired in 1977) and the unratified 1979 SALT II treaty pending clarification of SALT's status. The Soviets, however, had already exceeded their SALT I limits of 950 SLBM's in 62 modern SSBN's and were maintaining a total of strategic delivery vehicles above their SALT II level of 2,250. Also, the protocol limiting U.S. cruise missiles and mobile missile deployment, which the Soviets had always insisted was an integral part of SALT II, would expire at the end of 1981.

The Reagan administration was committed to seeking effective strategic arms control through what it called strategic arms reduction talks (START). Also, shortly before the opening of U.S.-Soviet talks on TNF limitation, Reagan proposed, in a nationally televised speech, that the Soviets dismantle their SS-20s, SS-4s, and SS-5s in exchange for cancellation of Pershing and cruise missile deployment in Europe. However, the Soviets rejected the offer, and the outlook for TALT, which began on November 30 in Geneva, was not bright. All of these developments cast doubts on continuation of the 1972 ABM treaty after the 1982 review conference. The treaty limited each superpower to possession of one ABM site, with 100 ABM launch-ers and associated radars, but the Soviets had developed significant additional capabilities and the U.S. wished to defend its ICBM's with ABM's. Thus a major U.S. debate on ABM was likely in 1982.

Negotiations continued on CW limitations, despite the evidence of Soviet usage, and on a comprehensive (nuclear) test ban (CTB) treaty. Implementation of the 1968 Non-Proliferation Treaty remained a continuing problem for the United States and its allies. Israel's attack on Iraq's Osirak reactor suggested that this might become an increasingly attractive option for countries whose enemies were on the verge of acquiring a nuclear capability.

MIDDLE EAST

The Iran-Iraq war that began in September 1980 remained stalemated at a relatively low level of intensity, but the drain on both combatants' resources and manpower was creating domestic problems. If these led to major political upheavals, the entire strategic balance in the Middle East could be changed. Given the continuing power struggles in Iran, such an outcome seemed more likely there, raising the spectre of Soviet intervention to seize Iran's oil fields. The fragility of any Middle East power balance was underlined by the assassination of President Sadat, although U.S. support for his successor, Hosni Mubarak, was immediately exhibited by the airlifting of U.S. troops to Egypt for the exercise Operation Bright Star. The extent to which security, for states in the

area, was seen to depend on military force was illustrated by Israel's strike on Iraq's reactor and its attempts to prevent the U.S. sale of five AWACS aircraft to Saudi Arabia.

The effective Israeli-Egyptian-U.S. alliance gave Israel and Egypt superiority over their Palestinian, Syrian, and Iraqi opponents to the east, but on their western flank Libya's Col. Muammar al-Qaddafi was becoming an increasing—and increasingly unpredictable—threat. The Libyan armed forces totaled 55,000 personnel, including an army of 45,000 with 2,600 T-54/55/62/72 and 100 Lion (Leopard I) tanks, 600 armoured cars, 250 BMP MICV's, and 1,100 APC's of various types. It seemed unlikely that the Libyan Army could operate all this equipment, not to mention the considerable additional stockpiles built up by the Soviets, who were using Libya as their Middle East arms depot. They were also supplying pilots for Libya's 5,000-strong Air Force, which had 408 combat aircraft, mostly Soviet. The Libyan intervention force in neighbouring Chad was withdrawn in November, but during the year strikes had been launched against Sudan.

The Sudanese Army of 68,000 could offer only limited opposition, but Egypt's 367,000-strong armed forces provided formidable support. Following Sadat's break with the U.S.S.R., an effort had been made to replace Soviet equipment with Western supplies or reconstruct it with Western materials. Active holdings of Soviet types, some one-third of the total, included about 850 T-54/55 and 750 T-62 medium tanks, 2,750 APC's, and 1,500 artillery pieces. The Western replacements, mostly U.S. and French, included M-60A3 medium tanks (60 operational, 251 ordered) and M-113A2 APC's (50 operational, 1,000 ordered). The Air Defense Command of 85,000 had 160 MiG-21MF/U interceptors, about one-third of them operational, but the 27,000-strong Air Force had effective modern fighter-bombers. The 20,000-strong Navy included five destroyers. Egypt's defense budget totaled $2,170,000,000.

Israel's armed forces remained the most effective in the area and perhaps in the world, with 172,000 personnel, rising to 400,000 within 24 hours of mobilization. But the cost was high, with defense spending amounting to $7,340,000,000, or some 23.3% of GNP (hyperinflation made these figures approximate). The Army of 135,000 (450,000 on mobilization) had 3,500 medium tanks, 4,000 AFV's, over 4,000 APC's, and more than 1,000 artillery pieces of 105-mm to 203-mm calibre, both towed and self-propelled. The 28,000-strong Air Force (37,000 on mobilization) had 602 combat aircraft, the newest types being 25 F/TF-15 Eagles and 53 F-16A/B's. The Navy of 9,000 (10,000 on mobilization) was built around 22 fast attack craft and 2 Aliya-class corvettes, all with mixes of Harpoon and Gabriel SSM's.

The main threat to Israel remained Soviet-backed Syria, with armed forces totaling 225,500 personnel and defense spending of $2,390,000,000 (13.1% of GNP). The Army of 170,000 had 3,700 medium tanks and some 1,800 APC's, plus about 2,300 of 122-mm to 180-mm artillery pieces and 1,300 ATGW's. The Air Force, with 50,000 person-

nel, had 448 combat aircraft; modern types included 64 MiG-23BM Flogger F, 26 Su-20, and 16 Su-7 fighter-bombers, 230 MiG-21PF/MF interceptors, and 25 Soviet-piloted MiG-25 Foxbats. With 25,000 troops in Lebanon, Syria effectively controlled that country north of the Litani River. Lebanon's Army of 22,250 was only an infantry force. Jordan's 67,500-strong armed forces were significant chiefly because of their professionalism.

Losses in the Iraq-Iran war and low serviceability of the remaining equipment made estimates of their force strengths difficult. Based on prewar figures, Iraq's forces totaled 252,250 personnel including an army of 210,000 with 2,350 T-54/55/62 medium tanks and 2,000 AFV's and an air force of 38,000 with 335 combat aircraft. Iran's forces of 195,000 included an army of 150,000 with some 1,400 medium tanks and 700 AFV's. Its 35,000-strong air force had some 100 serviceable combat aircraft. The remaining Gulf states were essentially unable to protect themselves.

SOUTH, EAST, AND SOUTHEAST ASIA

The conflict between India and Pakistan, dating from their independence, had become limited to the political and cultural arenas, although the likelihood that Pakistan might explode a nuclear device raised the possibility of a preemptive Indian strike on Pakistan's nuclear facilities. India, increasingly leaning toward the Soviet Union, had the third largest armed force in Asia, with 1,104,000 personnel and defense spending of $116 billion (3.8% of GNP). The 944,000-strong Army was equipped with 170 new Soviet T-72, 1,000 Vijayanta, and 950 T-54/55 medium tanks and 700 APC's, while the Air Force of 113,000 had 614 com-

On November 14 the largest U.S. military exercise in the Middle East since World War II began in Egypt; 5,000 U.S. troops took part, with the cooperation of Somalia, Oman, the Sudan, and Egypt.

UPI

285

Defense

bat aircraft; modern types included 16 Jaguar GR-1, 10 MiG-23BM/UM, 50 Su-7BM/KU, and 50 HF-24 Marut fighter-bombers. Pakistan's concentration on its relatively defensible border with India left few forces to protect the Afghanistan frontier. Pakistan's armed forces totaled 450,600, defense spending amounted to $1,540,000,000, and the Army of 420,000 had some 1,285 medium tanks and 550 M-113 APC's. The 17,600-strong Air Force had 220 combat aircraft, but modern types were scarce; U.S. F-16s were on order. Afghanistan's armed forces normally totaled 43,000, but there were constant defections to the anti-Soviet guerrillas. The latter were estimated at roughly 20,000.

China's forces remained the largest in the world quantitatively, but they were poorly equipped. The U.S., along with other Western suppliers, had agreed to sell modern arms to China. However, the defense budget had been reduced by an estimated 20%, and at 6–8% of GNP, even this represented a real burden. China's nuclear forces remained small, vulnerable, and barely adequate for minimum deterrence. Deployment of the liquid-fueled CSS-4 ICBM (13,000-km range; 5–10 megaton warhead) might have started. Other nuclear delivery systems available included 4 CSS-3 ICBM's, 65–85 CSS-2 IRBM's and 50 CSS-1 MRBM's, as well as 90 elderly B-6s (Tu-16s), 550 light bombers, and 500 fighter-bombers. Other aircraft in the 490,000-strong Air Force were comparable to obsolete Soviet types. The Army of 3.9 million personnel had 118 infantry divisions and 85 divisions in local forces but only 11 tank divisions and 40 field artillery divisions. Equipment included 11,000 tanks, mainly Soviet T-34s and T-54s and Chinese-produced T-59s and T-69s. The Navy was limited to coastal defense. Clearly, modernizing these forces would be a lengthy and expensive business.

Vietnam's armed forces totaled 1,029,000, including an army of 1 million (51 divisions) with 1,900 tanks and an air force of 25,000 with 485 combat aircraft. The 200,000 Vietnamese troops in Kampuchea and 40,000 in Laos were being opposed by nationalist forces. North Korea's armed forces totaled 782,000 personnel, mainly in the 700,000-strong Army. Equipment included 2,500 tanks (mostly T-54/55/62) and 4,100 artillery pieces. The Air Force of 51,000 had 700 combat aircraft. The South Korean forces, with 601,600 personnel, included an army of 520,000 with 860 medium tanks and 2,000 artillery pieces and an air force of 32,600 with 378 combat aircraft, notably 228 F-5A/B/E fighter-bombers. Taiwan's 310,000-strong Army and 67,000-strong Air Force with 386 combat aircraft constituted no threat to the mainland. Japan's defense spending remained at only 0.9% of GNP ($975.7 billion), and significant sectors of U.S. opinion were becoming increasingly critical of what they regarded as Japan's free ride in defense. The Japanese Navy of 44,000 personnel had only 34 destroyers, mostly GW/ASW vessels with helicopters, plus 16 GW/ASW frigates and 14 submarines. The Naval Air Arm of 12,000 was equipped with 120 combat aircraft and 70 ASW helicopters. The Army, with 155,000 personnel, had 830 medium tanks, and the Air Force of 44,000 had 350 combat aircraft.

AFRICA SOUTH OF THE SAHARA

The problems posed by Soviet-proxy interventions in Africa were becoming increasingly serious. In Ethiopia, with armed forces totaling 230,000 personnel and 790 medium tanks, 11,000 Cubans and 1,300 Warsaw Pact troops were operating sophisticated equipment. Angola was host to 19,000 Cuban and 2,500 East German troops, and others were in Mozambique. Soviet advisers were present in all three countries. The South Africans announced the capture of a Soviet sergeant and the killing of two Soviet lieutenant colonels during a strike against Namibian guerrillas in Angola.

In a continent characterized by political and economic instability and with indigenous forces of only minimal effectiveness, even modest Cuban and Warsaw Pact forces, if unopposed, could continue to yield the Soviets disproportionately large gains. South Africa remained the regional superpower, with armed forces totaling 92,700 (404,500 on mobilization) plus 90,000 commandos and 35,500 South African Police, both paramilitary formations. A separate South West Africa Territory Force was under South African control. Army equipment included 250 Centurion/Olifant tanks and 1,450 APC's, while modern combat aircraft included 46 Mirage F-1AZ/CZ and 27 Mirage IIICZ/RZ/BZ fighter-bomber/reconnaissance aircraft plus 96 Impala I/II counterinsurgency aircraft. Defense spending amounted to $2,560,000,000. South Africa's nuclear weapons status remained ambiguous. So did the nature of the possible nuclear test detected in 1979, although additional circumstantial evidence indicated that the incident was indeed a nuclear test, and informed speculation suggested that it was of a joint South African-Israeli device.

LATIN AMERICA

Growing intervention by the Soviet Union's Cuban proxies had become a major threat to regional stability. Pro-Soviet elements in the postrevolutionary government of Nicaragua were becoming dominant, providing Cuba with a base from which to export advisers and Soviet arms throughout the region. Given that most of the region's governments were authoritarian, in varying degrees, it was inevitable that significant revolutionary groups would arise. These turned to the Soviets and Cubans for support just as the governments turned to the U.S., creating the danger of superpower confrontation. The potential Soviet/Cuban gains from relatively modest investments of manpower and equipment were considerable since, historically, one or two reliable and efficient regiments (2,000–3,000 men) had been sufficient to seize power.

Although the armed forces of the area looked large on paper (*see* Table II), they were basically internal security forces of limited reliability spread over large areas. Thus Cuba's 227,000-strong armed forces (35,250 deployed outside Latin America) provided a significant pro-Soviet lever.

(ROBIN RANGER)

See also Space Exploration.
[535.B.5.c.ii; 544.B.5–6; 736]

U.S. MILITARY POLICY: PERFORMANCE OR PROMISE?

by Robin Ranger

As U.S. Pres. Ronald Reagan approached the end of his first year in office, the overall impression of many observers was that his administration's external policies still lacked the coherence of its domestic policies. The new president and his advisers were clearly committed to selective containment of the Soviet Union, combined with the buildup of U.S. and allied forces needed to implement this policy. In principle, this policy clearly recognized the reality of a Soviet political-military threat of unprecedented proportions and the unavoidable necessity of balancing Soviet power.

Policy Problems. The inherent difficulties of translating these principles into practice had been compounded by the administration's decision to dispense with almost all the president's campaign advisers, representing most of the conservative analytical and political communities. In addition, a conscious effort was being made to lessen the role of the president's assistant for national security affairs (for most of the year, Richard V. Allen) and the National Security Council (NSC) staff, but no serious attempt was made to fill the resultant gap in the machinery for making and executing external policy. Secretary of State Alexander Haig (*see* BIOGRAPHIES) attempted, but failed, to become foreign policy overlord in the tradition of Dean Acheson and Henry Kissinger. His chief rival, Secretary of Defense Caspar Weinberger (*see* BIOGRAPHIES), was also trying to attain the dominant position, with equal lack of success. Although an able manager, Weinberger was handicapped by lack of knowledge of the very complex defense field—a deficiency shared by his deputy secretary, Frank Carlucci.

The absence of clear central direction exacerbated the problems of changing entrenched bureaucratic policies—and policymakers—built up over 10 or 20

Robin Ranger is visiting associate professor, Defense and Strategic Studies Program, at the University of Southern California, and an associate professor in the Department of Political Science, St. Francis Xavier University, Antigonish, Nova Scotia.

years of détente and emphasis on arms control. These problems were symbolized by the difference between the assistant secretary of state for European affairs, Lawrence Eagleburger, one of the few career State Department officials on whom Kissinger had relied and a supporter of his now largely discredited policies, and Richard Perle, the assistant secretary of defense for international planning. Perle had been chief defense adviser to Sen. Henry M. Jackson (Dem., Wash.) during the latter's long, and ultimately successful, fight against Kissinger's policies.

The Policy Gap. The result was extraordinary confusion, particularly evident in four crucial fields: the rebuilding of U.S. strategic and theatre nuclear forces (TNF); U.S. relations with NATO-Europe; strategic and theatre nuclear arms-control negotiations; and Latin America.

In each case, the broad policy seemed unarguable: giving the U.S. adequate nuclear forces and a more realistic and credible doctrine for their use; educating neutralist elements in NATO-Europe on the realities of the Soviet military buildup and insisting that the 1979 TNF modernization decisions stand; engaging in theatre/intermediate nuclear force (T/INF) arms-control negotiations while preparing for strategic arms reduction talks (START); and checking Soviet/Cuban expansion in Latin America. But in each instance the policies were developed and implemented so uncertainly, with so many internal arguments and so many internal contradictions, that neither America's allies nor its Soviet opponents were clear as to what the new policies were, what principles they were based on, and how far they would be taken.

Thus it was plain that placing intercontinental ballistic missiles in superhardened silos was unrealistic, and the U.S. Senate refused to fund this plan. But how was the MX missile to be based, and was it to be defended with antiballistic missiles, requiring abrogation of the 1972 ABM treaty? Did the administration believe that meaningful arms control was both desirable and negotiable or (more likely) only desirable? What would be its approach to arms-control agreements in terms of reductions sought plus verification and to compliance policies? How great was the threat to established governments in Latin America from indigenous revolutionaries, the Soviets, and the Cubans, and how were these threats to be contained?

Ultimately, these questions could only be resolved by the president himself, but Reagan seemed reluctant to act. He preferred to rely on team players, with Cabinet secretaries given considerable autonomy to implement the general policy directions of the president and Cabinet. This approach appeared to work well domestically but badly externally; the

West Germans staged many protests against the positioning of nuclear weapons in their country and other nations of Western Europe. This protest took place in April in Bonn.

issues were too complex and the time available to solve them was too short.

The continued rivalry between Secretaries Haig and Weinberger and the grossly overblown affair of Allen's acceptance of token gifts from Japanese journalists were symptomatic of the underlying problem of unworkable defense and foreign policy machinery. Its defects were exacerbated by the lack of experience in these areas of the president's three closest advisers, James Baker, Michael Deaver, and Edwin Meese, who were concerned more with the process and appearance of defense policymaking than with its substance.

A Confused Image. Overall, it was difficult to say whether the U.S. was more or less secure after the first year of the Reagan administration. It was certainly moving to meet a serious Soviet threat, but so hesitantly as to get the worst of all worlds. To the Soviets, the U.S. now appeared as an outright opponent against whom the strongest measures would be justified. Yet the administration's defense spending was clearly inadequate to meet possible Soviet moves against, for example, Poland or the Persian Gulf. Its planned increases lacked any coherent overall strategic framework, amounting instead to a little bit more of everything.

The Reagan administration had so far failed to answer the crucial questions of what forces the U.S. needed, for which missions, protecting which clearly identified U.S. interests, and when. It also left such increases as there were vulnerable to elimination by the Congress. Ironically, however, this inadequate and uncoordinated increase in U.S. defense forces had created an impression among U.S. allies that it was the U.S., not the U.S.S.R., that was the expansionist military superpower seeking confrontation. This perception, skillfully fostered by a massive Soviet propaganda campaign, was widespread, especially in the crucial areas of NATO-Europe and Japan.

President Reagan was seen in liberal NATO-Europe circles as a cold-warrior because he had a habit of being disarmingly candid about the Soviet threat and the resultant need for Western countermeasures. The allies, on the other hand, still clung to the fading hopes for détente and arms control. The furor over the president's suggestion that a limited nuclear exchange in Europe would not necessarily lead to an all-out strategic nuclear war illustrated these perceptual differences. What he said was self-evident, but it was an issue that liberal Europeans wanted to avoid, so they criticized the president for raising it.

The episode highlighted the deepening divisions within NATO. A coalition of liberals, anti-nuclear-power groups, and churchmen had emerged in Britain, Belgium, Denmark, The Netherlands, Norway, and West Germany, opposing increases in NATO's defenses, notably in TNF. Essentially they argued for a neutral Europe, despite the likelihood that it would inevitably come under Soviet control. However unrealistic, this movement posed an unprecedented threat to NATO, and it represented a frightening willingness to surrender in the face of the Soviet nuclear threat. However, it also reflected the underlying reality that Western Europeans in general, and West Germany in particular, had a far larger economic, political, and personal stake in détente between the two halves of Europe than had the U.S. Hence the European hope that the intra-European détente could be preserved despite the collapse of the superpower détente.

Here, as elsewhere, what happened in Poland might well be decisive. Direct or indirect Soviet intervention on a large scale, especially if met by armed Polish resistance, could mark the start of a second cold war as sharply as the Soviet and German invasion of Poland marked the start of World War II. In the absence of such a watershed, the Reagan administration showed little sign of changing its course: the pursuit of a defense policy sound in principle but confused and uncertain in execution.

Demography

With the world population exceeding 4,500,000,-000 in 1981, there was growing concern over related population problems. The widely distributed "Global 2000 Report to the President," prepared by the U.S. Council on Environmental Quality and the Department of State, concluded that environmental, natural resource, and population stresses were intensifying and that by the year 2000, when the population could exceed 6,000,000,000, the world would be "more crowded, more polluted . . . and more vulnerable to disruption than the world we live in now." Coincidentally, the UN Food and Agriculture Organization revised its data on the world's undernourished population, estimating that some 450 million persons (one of every ten on Earth) are undernourished. The world refugee problem also assumed new dimensions; some estimates put this group at 16 million. (See REFUGEES.) The World Bank, in its annual development report, stated that the gap between the richest and poorest nations was widening and would continue to widen even more in the 1980s.

In June a report by the UN Fund for Population Activities stated that the world's population could stabilize at 10,500,000,000 in 30 years, depending on the success of campaigns to limit population growth. The UN projections ranged from 8,-000,000,000 to 14,000,000,000 persons on Earth by 2110.

Birth Statistics. An estimated 3,598,000 births occurred in the U.S. in 1980, almost 4% more than in 1979 and 14% above the low point of 1975. At 16.2 births per 1,000 population, the birthrate was 3% higher than in 1979 (15.8) and the highest since 1971. The fertility rate was 69.2 live births per 1,-000 women 15–44 years of age, about 2% higher than in 1979 and 5% above the low point of 65.8 in 1976. According to the National Center for Health Statistics, the increases were related to continued growth in the number of women of childbearing age as well as in the rate of childbearing. The upward trend continued into 1981. For the 12-month period ended June 1981, there were 3,628,000 births and a rate of 15.9 per 1,000 population, 2.3% above the corresponding period in 1980. The fertility rate also rose, to 68.1 per 1,000 women 15–44, compared with 67.3 for the period ended June 1980.

There was a wide difference in birthrates between the developed (16 per 1,000 population) and less developed countries (38 per 1,000, excluding China). Regional rates ranged from 13 in northern Europe to 49 in western Africa.

According to final data for 1979, there were 597,-800 births to unmarried women in the U.S. in that year, 10% more than in 1978. Of these, 263,000, or 44%, were to white mothers and 315,800, or 53%, to black mothers. Ninety-four of every 1,000 live white births and 547 of every 1,000 live black births were to unwed mothers. Almost half of the babies were born to mothers 15–19 years old.

Death Statistics. Provisional figures indicated that 1,986,000 deaths occurred in the U.S. in 1980, 2.3% more than in 1979. The rate of 8.9 deaths per

1,000 population, although slightly higher than for 1979, represented relative stability. Between 1975 and 1980 the rate had ranged between 8.7 and 8.9. Also, the increase in 1980 was attributed to influenza epidemics, which were absent in 1979; the rate for pneumonia and influenza rose 18%. Other causes with increased rates were diseases of the heart 3.6%; malignant neoplasms 1.5%; chronic obstructive pulmonary diseases 10.1%; homicide and legal intervention 8%; and nephritis, nephrotic syndrome, and nephrosis 6.8%.

The increase in the death rate was reflected in data by race and sex. The white rate rose 2.3% in 1980, from 8.8 per 1,000 population to 9, and the

continued on page 293

Table I. Birthrates and Death Rates per 1,000 Population and Infant Mortality per 1,000 Live Births in Selected Countries, 1980*

	Registered			Estimated		
Country	Birth-rate	Death rate	Infant mortality	Birth-rate	Death rate	Infant mortality
Africa						
Algeria	39.1[1]	8.0[1]	20.5[1]	42.0–47.0[2]	13.0–14.0[2]	127.0[1]
Egypt	41.0[1]	11.0[1]	73.5[1]	41.0–42.0[2]	12.0[2]	92.0[1]
Gabon	...	...	...	35.2[3]	20.9[3]	229.0[4]
Ghana	...	...	...	43.0–47.0[2]	12.0–13.0[2]	156.0[3]
Kenya	20.0[5]	51.4[6]	...	52.0–54.0[2]	12.0[2]	83.0[7]
Libya[8]	43.6	5.6	44.5	47.0–48.0	13.0	...
Mauritius	27.5	7.2	32.9	28.0[1]	7.0[1]	34.0[1]
Nigeria	...	...	...	48.0–51.0[2]	17.0–19.0[2]	178.0[8]
South Africa	...	...	...	35.0–37.0[9]	12.0–13.0[9]	93.0–101.0[10]
Zaire	...	...	...	43.0–46.0[2]	15.0–19.0[2]	165.0–177.0[11]
Zambia	...	...	...	47.0–50.0[9]	16.0–18.0[9]	127.0–160.0[12]
Asia						
Bangladesh	45.0[1]	17.6[1]	13.2[1]	41.5	16.5	125.0
China[1]	24.0	9.0	50.0	...	...	...
India	34.3[6]	15.0[6]	134.0[6]	33.2[9]	14.1[9]	...
Indonesia[1]	...	...	...	40.0	20.0	137.0
Israel[1]	24.6	6.9	16.0	...	...	...
Japan[1]	13.7	6.2	7.4	14.2	6.0	7.9
Kuwait[7]	41.5	4.8	39.1	...	...	...
Pakistan	42.6	13.0	113.0	...	...	...
Philippines	30.3[5]	6.9[5]	56.9[5]	31.8[1]	8.4[1]	58.0[1]
Singapore	17.3	5.2	11.7	17.3[1]	5.3[1]	13.2[9]
Turkey	33.0[1]	11.0[1]	125.0[13]	39.6[14]	14.6[14]	153.0[14]
Vietnam	40.1[1]	17.1[1]	130.0[1]	41.0[15]	19.8[15]	...
Yemen (San'a')[15]	48.7	19.8	...	48.7	26.4	...
Europe						
Austria	12.0	12.2	13.9	...	...	...
Czechoslovakia	16.2	12.1	16.6	...	...	...
France[1]	14.2	10.1	10.1	...	...	...
Germany, East[1]	14.0	13.9	12.9	...	...	...
Germany, West	10.0	11.5	14.7	...	...	...
Hungary	13.9	13.6	23.1	...	...	...
Ireland[1]	21.5	9.7	12.4	...	...	...
Italy	11.2	9.7	14.3	...	...	...
Poland[9]	19.0	9.3	22.5	...	...	...
Spain[9]	16.1	7.8	15.1	...	...	...
Sweden	11.7	11.0	6.7	...	...	...
Switzerland[1]	11.3	9.0	8.5	...	...	...
United Kingdom[1]	13.1	12.1	12.9	...	...	...
North America						
Canada[1]	15.5	7.1	12.0	...	...	...
Costa Rica[1]	29.2	4.2	24.2	...	...	...
Dominican Republic	32.4[1]	4.4[1]	37.2[1]	42.0[15]	10.7[15]	...
El Salvador[1]	39.2	7.4	42.2	...	...	...
Grenada[1]	24.5	6.8	15.4	...	...	...
Mexico	34.0[9]	6.0[9]	44.1[9]	42.0[15]	...	...
Nicaragua	43.3[1]	12.2[1]	121.0[1]	48.3[15]	13.9[15]	...
Panama[1]	28.0	4.4	24.9	...	6.9	...
United States	16.2	8.9	12.5	...	...	...
Oceania						
Australia[9]	15.7	...	...	15.7	7.6	12.2
New Caledonia[9]	...	...	...	26.5	6.7	30.2
New Zealand[9]	16.8	4.3	18.0	16.4	8.2	75.4
Papua New Guinea[1]	42.1	...	114.0	15.0	15.4	...
Vanuatu[1]	45.0	47.0	...	...	...	...
South America						
Argentina[9]	25.2	8.9	40.8	...	...	...
Brazil[14]	37.1	8.8	170.0	...	...	...
Chile[1]	21.5	6.8	37.9	...	...	...
Ecuador	29.5[9]	7.1[9]	70.9[9]	...	12.1[14]	...
French Guiana[7]	24.5	7.6	32.8	...	...	...
Peru[9]	27.5	8.1	70.3	41.0	13.6	...
Uruguay	18.6	10.6	37.4	...	...	...
Venezuela[1]	35.6	5.5	33.1	36.2	7.1	...
U.S.S.R.	18.2[1]	10.1[1]	28.0[9]	...	...	...

* Both registered and estimated rates are shown only for countries with incomplete registered rates.
[1]1979. [2]1981. [3]1975–80. [4]1960–61. [5]1976. [6]1973. [7]1977. [8]1965–66. [9]1978. [10]1970. [11]1955–57. [12]1969. [13]1967. [14]1970–75. [15]1950.

Sources: United Nations, *Population and Vital Statistics Report*; U.S. Department of Commerce, *World Population 1979: Summary*; Far Eastern Economic Review, *Asia Yearbook 1981*; United Nations, Economic Commission for Africa, *Population Growth in Africa 1970–2000*; various national publications.

Table II. World Populations and Areas[1]

Country	AREA AND POPULATION: MIDYEAR 1980 Area in sq km	Total population	Persons per sq km	POPULATION AT MOST RECENT CENSUS Date of census	Total population	% Male	% Female	% Urban	Age distribution (%)[2] 0–14	15–29	30–44	45–59	60–74	75+
AFRICA														
Algeria	2,381,741	18,594,000	7.8	1977	17,422,000	49.7	50.3	40.6	47.9	25.4	12.7	8.2	4.5	1.3
Angola	1,246,700	6,759,000	5.4	1970	5,620,001	52.1	47.9	14.2	41.7	23.2	17.0	7.4	3.8	1.0
Benin	112,600	3,567,000	31.7	1979	3,338,240	47.9	52.1	14.2	49.0	——39.4——			——11.6——	
Botswana	581,700	819,000	1.4	1981	936,600	...	...	...	...	...	...	...	...	...
British Indian Ocean Territory	60	...	...			...	...	...	...	...	...	...	...	...
Burundi	27,834	4,512,000	162.1	1979	4,110,000	...	...	...	...	...	...	...	...	...
Cameroon	465,054	8,444,000	18.2	1976	7,661,000	49.9	50.1	28.5	42.2	26.4	16.5	9.7	——5.2——	
Cape Verde	4,033	296,000	73.4	1980	296,093	...	...	...	...	...	...	...	...	...
Central African Republic	622,436	2,362,000	3.8	1975	2,088,000	...	...	34.8	...	...	...	...	...	...
Chad	1,284,000	4,524,000	3.5	1975	4,029,917	47.7	52.3	16.0	40.6	28.3	17.2	9.5	——4.4——	
Comoros[3]	1,792	347,000	193.6	1980	347,000	50.1	49.9	33.4	...	...	...	...	...	...
Congo	342,000	1,537,000	4.5	1974	1,300,120	48.5	51.5	37.8	...	...	...	...	...	...
Djibouti	23,200	315,000	13.6	1961	81,200	...	...	57.4	...	...	...	...	...	...
Egypt	997,667	41,955,000	42.1	1976	38,228,180	51.0	49.0	43.9	31.6	——65.5——			——2.9——	
Equatorial Guinea	28,051	363,000	12.9	1965	254,684	50.0	50.0	47.6	...	...	...	...	...	...
Ethiopia	1,223,000	31,065,000	25.4	1970	24,068,800	50.7	49.3	9.7	43.5	27.0	16.3	8.8	3.7	0.7
French Southern and Antarctic Lands	7,366	...	...			...	...	...	...	...	...	...	...	...
Gabon	267,667	1,356,000	5.1	1970	950,009	47.9	52.1	31.8	35.4	19.1	22.3	16.4	——6.5——	
Gambia, The	10,690	601,000	56.2	1973	493,499	51.0	49.0	15.0	41.3	——44.1——			——14.6——	
Ghana	238,533	11,542,000	48.4	1970	8,559,313	49.6	50.4	28.9	46.9	24.4	15.8	7.5	3.8	1.6
Guinea	245,857	5,014,000	20.4	1972	5,143,284	...	...	...	43.1	——56.9——				
Guinea-Bissau	36,125	792,000	21.9	1979	777,214	48.2	51.8	...	...	...	...	...	...	...
Ivory Coast	322,463	8,245,000	25.6	1975	6,671,827	52.0	48.0	31.8	44.6	——55.4——				
Kenya	580,367	16,402,000	28.3	1979	15,322,000	...	...	12.6	53.5	——46.5——				
Lesotho	30,352	1,339,000	44.1	1976	1,216,815	51.7	48.3	...	...	...	...	...	...	...
Liberia	97,790	1,873,000	19.2	1974	1,503,368	50.5	49.5	29.1	40.9	26.7	17.7	8.8	4.6	1.3
Libya	1,749,000	3,250,000	1.9	1973	2,249,237	53.0	47.0	59.8	44.3	22.2	15.4	8.2	4.0	1.6
Madagascar	587,041	8,714,000	14.8	1975	7,603,790	50.0	50.0	16.3	44.4	25.7	14.2	10.0	4.6	1.1
Malawi	118,484	5,968,000	50.4	1977	5,561,821	48.1	51.9	8.3	...	...	...	...	...	...
Mali	1,240,192	6,646,000	5.4	1976	6,394,918	49.1	50.9	16.7	47.3	22.2	17.2	8.8	——3.8——	
Mauritania	1,030,700	1,634,000	1.6	1976	1,419,939	...	...	21.9	...	...	...	...	...	...
Mauritius	2,040	959,000	470.1	1972	826,199	50.0	50.0	42.9	40.3	28.6	14.5	11.0	4.9	0.7
Mayotte	378	50,000	132.3	1978	47,246	49.9	50.1	53.3	50.2	23.4	13.9	7.0	3.8	1.7
Morocco	458,730	20,242,000	44.1	1971	15,379,259	50.1	49.9	35.4	46.2	22.4	16.0	8.3	5.3	1.8
Mozambique	799,380	12,375,000	15.5	1980	12,130,000	48.7	51.3	...	...	...	...	...	...	...
Niger	1,189,000	5,305,000	4.5	1977	5,098,427	49.3	50.7	11.8	...	...	...	...	...	...
Nigeria	923,800	77,082,000	83.4	1963[4]	55,670,055	50.5	49.5	16.1	43.0	31.9	16.5	5.1	2.5	1.0
Réunion	2,512	491,000	195.5	1974	476,675	48.5	51.5	43.0	42.6	25.8	15.6	10.0	4.8	1.2
Rwanda	26,338	5,130,000	194.8	1978	4,819,317	48.8	51.2	4.3	——60.0——			——40.0——		
St. Helena & Ascension Islands	412	5,000	12.6	1976	5,866	52.0	48.0	29.4	34.2	27.7	16.3	10.8	8.4	2.6
São Tomé & Príncipe	964	85,000	88.2	1970	73,631	50.3	49.7	25.0	...	...	...	...	...	...
Senegal	196,722	5,661,000	28.8	1976	4,907,507	49.2	50.8	29.6	42.5	27.3	17.2	8.6	3.7	0.1
Seychelles	444	63,000	141.9	1977	61,898	50.4	49.6	37.1	39.7	26.3	14.0	10.8	6.9	2.2
Sierra Leone	71,740	3,474,000	48.4	1974	2,729,479	54.1	45.9	...	36.7	27.2	19.4	9.0	——7.6——	
Somalia	638,000	3,645,000	5.7	1975	3,253,024	...	...	15.0	...	...	...	...	...	...
South Africa	1,133,759	25,083,000	22.1	1980	23,771,970	...	...	...	...	...	...	...	...	...
Bophuthatswana[5]	40,430	1,268,000	31.4	1970	903,883	46.9	53.1	14.2	50.7	22.9	11.3	——13.1——		2.0
Ciskei[5]	8,300	720,000	86.7	1980	635,631	...	...	...	...	...	...	...	...	...
Transkei[5]	41,002	2,263,000	55.2	1970	1,745,992	41.2	58.8	3.2	46.4	22.8	14.1	——15.3——		1.2
Venda[5]	7,184	358,000	49.8	1970	265,129	38.8	61.2	0.2	48.1	22.7	13.7	6.4	7.6	1.5
South West Africa/Namibia	824,268	989,000	1.2	1970	761,562	50.8	49.2	24.9	...	...	...	...	...	...
Sudan	2,503,890	1,621,000	0.6	1973	14,819,000[6]	50.4	49.6	...	46.7	——48.4——			——4.9——	
Swaziland	17,364	547,000	31.5	1976	494,534	45.6	54.4	15.2	47.7	25.2	13.7	7.9	3.7	1.7
Tanzania	945,050	18,618,000	19.7	1978	17,551,925	49.2	50.8	...	...	...	...	...	...	...
Togo	56,785	2,505,000	44.1	1970	1,953,778	48.1	51.9	...	49.8	21.5	15.1	8.0	3.6	2.0
Tunisia	154,530	6,367,000	41.2	1975	5,588,209	50.8	49.2	49.0	43.7	25.6	14.7	10.0	4.9	0.9
Uganda	241,139	12,600,000	52.3	1980	12,630,076	...	...	...	...	...	...	...	...	...
Upper Volta	274,200	235,000	0.9	1975	5,638,203	50.2	49.8	9.0	47.4	21.1	16.1	9.3	——6.1——	
Western Sahara	266,769	135,000	0.5	1970	76,425	57.5	42.5	45.3	42.9	27.2	16.3	7.4	4.4	1.8
Zaire	2,344,885	28,291,000	12.1	1976	25,568,640	48.5	51.5	...	——52.8——			——47.2——		
Zambia	752,614	5,680,000	7.5	1980	5,679,808	...	...	43.0	...	...	...	...	...	...
Zimbabwe	390,759	7,360,000	18.8	1969	5,099,350	50.3	49.7	16.8	47.2	25.4	15.7	8.4	——3.3——	
Total AFRICA	30,217,883	448,042,000	14.8											
ANTARCTICA total	14,244,900	[7]	—	—	—					—			—	
ASIA														
Afghanistan	652,090	15,523,000	23.8	1979	13,051,358[8]	51.4	48.6	15.1	44.5	26.9	15.8	8.6	3.6	0.6
Bahrain	669	383,000	572.5	1981	358,857	58.6	41.4	...	...	...	...	...	...	...
Bangladesh	143,998	88,678,000	615.8	1981	87,052,024	51.5	48.5	...	...	...	...	...	...	...
Bhutan	46,100	1,174,000	25.5	1969	931,514	...	...	...	...	...	...	...	...	...
Brunei	5,765	191,000	33.1	1971	136,256	53.4	46.6	63.6	43.4	28.0	15.7	8.1	3.9	0.9
Burma	676,577	35,289,000	52.2	1973	28,885,867	49.7	50.3	...	40.5	——53.4——			——6.0——	
China	9,561,000	971,000,000	101.6	1953	574,205,940	51.8	48.2	13.3	35.9	25.1	18.8	12.9	6.3	1.0
Cyprus	9,251	629,000	68.0	1976	612,851	50.6	49.4	...	25.4	29.0	17.9	13.4	10.8	3.5
Hong Kong	1,050	5,068,000	4,826.7	1976	4,420,390	51.0	49.0	...	30.0	30.2	15.4	14.9	7.3	1.7
India	3,287,782	663,596,000	201.8	1981	683,810,051	51.7	48.3	...	...	...	...	...	...	...
Indonesia	1,919,443	147,380,000	76.8	1980	147,490,298	49.0	51.0	22.3	40.8	27.0	16.4	10.2	4.5	1.1
Iran	1,648,000	37,695,000	22.9	1976	33,708,744	51.5	48.5	47.0	44.5	25.2	14.8	10.1	3.8	1.0
Iraq	437,522	13,084,000	29.9	1977	12,029,700	51.7	48.3	...	...	...	...	...	...	...
Israel	20,700	3,878,000	187.3	1972	3,147,683	50.3	49.7	85.3	32.6	26.9	15.6	13.6	9.2	2.0
Japan	377,682	116,960,000	309.7	1980	117,057,485	49.2	50.8	...	23.6	21.5	24.2	17.9	9.7	3.1
Jordan	95,396	2,290,000	24.0	1979	2,152,273	52.3	47.7	60.0	...	...	...	...	...	...
Kampuchea	181,035	4,839,000	26.7	1962	5,728,771	50.0	50.0	10.3	43.8	24.9	16.8	9.8	4.1	0.6
Korea, North	121,929	17,914,000	146.9	—	—	—								
Korea, South	98,966	37,449,000	378.4	1975	34,678,972	50.0	50.0	48.4	38.0	28.2	17.9	10.2	4.6	1.0
Kuwait	16,918	1,356,000	80.2	1975	994,837	54.7	45.3	85.9	31.3	60.0	43.0	16.8	——9.0——	

Table II. World Populations and Areas[1] *(Continued)*

Country	AREA AND POPULATION: MIDYEAR 1980			POPULATION AT MOST RECENT CENSUS					Age distribution (%)[2]					
	Area in sq km	Total population	Persons per sq km	Date of census	Total population	% Male	% Female	% Urban	0–14	15–29	30–44	45–59	60–74	75+
Laos	236,800	3,721,000	15.7	—	—	—	—	—	...	...	...	...	...	...
Lebanon	10,230	3,161,000	309.0	1970	2,126,325	50.8	49.2	60.1	42.6	23.8	16.7	9.1	—7.7—	
Macau	16	274,000	17,125.0	1981	276,673	...	...	...	...	...	...	...	...	...
Malaysia	329,747	13,923,000	42.2	1980	13,435,588	50.2	49.8	...	...	...	...	...	...	...
Maldives	298	145,000	486.6	1978	142,832	52.6	47.4	20.7	...	...	...	...	...	...
Mongolia	1,566,500	1,669,000	1.1	1979	1,594,800	50.1	49.9	51.2	...	...	...	...	...	...
Nepal	145,391	14,180,000	97.5	1981	14,179,301	50.3	49.7	...	...	...	...	...	...	...
Oman	300,000	891,000	3.0	—	—	—	—	—	—	—	—	—	—	—
Pakistan	796,095	82,441,000	103.6	1981	83,700,000	—	—	—	—	—	—	—	—	—
Philippines	300,000	47,914,000	159.7	1975	42,070,660	50.6	49.4	31.6	44.0	28.0	14.9	8.4	3.9	0.8
Qatar	11,400	260,000	22.8	—	—	—	—	—	—	—	—	—	—	—
Saudi Arabia	2,240,000	8,367,000	3.7	1974	7,012,642	...	49.0	100.0	27.0	34.7	19.8	11.3	5.9	1.3
Singapore	618	2,391,000	3,868.9	1980	2,413,945	51.0	49.0	100.0	27.0	34.7	19.8	11.3	5.9	1.3
Sri Lanka	65,610	14,871,000	226.7	1971	12,689,897	51.3	48.7	22.4	39.3	27.8	15.9	10.5	5.2	1.3
Syria	185,179	8,979,000	48.5	1970	6,304,685	51.3	48.7	43.5	49.3	22.4	14.3	7.5	4.8	1.7
Taiwan	36,002	17,704,000	491.8	1980	17,970,821	...	...	...	...	...	...	...	...	...
Thailand	542,373	46,455,000	85.7	1977	44,035,129	50.4	49.6	...	...	...	...	...	...	...
Turkey	779,452	45,218,000	58.0	1980	45,217,556	...	...	...	...	...	...	...	...	...
United Arab Emirates	77,700	891,000	11.5	1981	1,043,225	69.0	31.0	80.9	...	...	...	...	...	...
Vietnam	329,465	52,299,000	158.7	1979	52,741,766	48.5	51.5	19.2	...	...	...	...	...	...
Yemen (Aden)	338,100	1,859,000	5.5	1973	1,590,275	49.5	50.4	33.3	47.3	20.8	15.8	8.6	—6.6—	
Yemen (San'a')	200,000	5,212,000	26.1	1975	5,237,893	47.6	52.4	8.2	47.0	20.0	17.0	10.0	4.5	1.5
Total ASIA[9,10]	44,642,079	2,606,614,000	58.4											
EUROPE														
Albania	28,748	2,734,000	95.1	1979	2,591,000	...	...	...	...	...	...	...	...	...
Andorra	468	34,000	72.6	1980	33,900	47.0	53.0	...	...	...	...	...	...	...
Austria	83,853	7,482,000	89.2	1971	7,456,403	47.0	53.0	51.9	24.4	20.5	18.3	16.5	15.5	4.8
Belgium	30,521	9,855,000	322.9	1970	9,650,944	48.9	51.1	...	23.5	21.0	19.4	17.1	14.4	4.6
Bulgaria	110,912	8,850,000	79.8	1975	8,727,771	49.9	50.1	58.0	21.8	22.4	20.6	18.6	13.0	3.4
Channel Islands	194	130,000	670.1	1981	133,000	48.1	51.9	...	...	—60.0—			—15.9—	
Czechoslovakia	127,881	15,277,000	119.5	1980	15,276,799	...	...	59.4	24.1	—60.0—			—15.9—	
Denmark	43,080	5,126,000	119.0	1976	5,072,516	49.5	50.5	82.6	22.4	22.5	19.4	16.8	13.8	5.1
Faeroe Islands	1,399	43,000	30.7	1977	41,969	...	...	...	...	...	...	...	...	...
Finland	337,032	4,771,000	14.2	1979	4,771,292	48.3	51.7	...	20.5	24.7	21.6	16.9	12.3	4.0
France	544,000	53,752,000	98.8	1975	52,655,802	48.9	51.1	70.0	22.6	24.4	17.8	16.2	13.3	5.6
Germany, East	108,328	16,750,000	154.6	1971	17,068,318	46.1	53.9	73.8	23.3	19.9	20.1	14.7	16.9	5.1
Germany, West	248,667	61,566,000	247.6	1979	61,439,400	47.7	52.3	...	16.8	23.1	20.1	18.3	13.8	7.9
Gibraltar	6	29,000	4,833.3	1970	26,833	48.1	51.9	91.9	22.9	22.7	21.1	18.7	11.2	3.4
Greece	131,990	9,308,000	70.5	1981	9,706,687	...	...	...	...	...	...	...	...	...
Hungary	93,033	10,710,000	115.1	1980	10,709,536	48.5	51.5	53.2	21.7	—61.4—			—16.9—	
Iceland	103,000	227,000	2.2	1970	204,930	50.6	49.4	...	32.3	25.1	16.4	13.7	9.0	3.5
Ireland	70,285	3,431,000	48.8	1979	3,368,217	50.3	49.7	...	...	...	...	...	...	...
Isle of Man	572	64,000	111.9	1976	61,723	47.5	52.5	51.8	20.5	19.1	15.6	17.3	20.2	7.3
Italy	301,263	56,999,000	189.2	1971	54,136,547	48.9	51.1	...	24.4	21.2	20.7	17.0	12.8	3.9
Jan Mayen	373	—	—	1973	37	...	...	—	...	...	...	...	...	...
Liechtenstein	160	25,000	156.3	1970	21,350	49.7	50.3	...	27.9	27.1	18.6	14.5	9.3	2.6
Luxembourg	2,586	364,000	140.8	1979	363,166	...	...	...	...	...	...	...	...	...
Malta	320	344,000	1,075.0	1967	314,216	47.9	52.1	94.3	29.8	25.9	17.6	13.8	10.2	2.7
Monaco	1.9	26,000	13,684.2	1975	25,029	45.2	54.8	100.0	12.9	17.5	18.4	20.9	21.2	9.1
Netherlands, The	41,160	14,091,000	342.3	1971	13,060,115	49.9	50.1	54.9	27.2	24.6	17.9	15.6	10.9	3.7
Norway	323,895	4,082,000	12.6	1980	4,092,340	...	...	...	...	...	...	...	...	...
Poland	312,683	35,382,000	113.2	1978	35,061,500	...	...	...	...	...	...	...	...	...
Portugal	91,985	9,856,000	107.1	1981	9,784,201	...	...	...	...	...	...	...	...	...
Romania	237,500	22,100,000	93.0	1977	21,657,569	49.3	50.7	47.8	25.7	23.7	19.6	17.2	10.9	3.0
San Marino	61	21,000	349.2	1976	20,284	50.4	49.6	...	24.4	23.0	19.9	17.4	11.4	3.9
Spain	504,750	37,272,000	73.8	1970	34,032,801	48.9	51.1	54.7	27.8	22.0	19.9	16.1	10.8	3.4
Svalbard	62,050	—	—	1974	3,472	...	...	...	...	...	...	...	...	...
Sweden	449,964	8,314,000	18.5	1975	8,208,544	49.7	50.3	82.7	20.7	21.3	18.8	18.1	15.4	5.7
Switzerland	41,293	6,310,000	152.8	1980	6,365,383	...	...	...	...	...	...	...	...	...
United Kingdom	244,035	55,945,000	229.2	1981	55,671,000	48.6	51.4	...	...	...	...	...	...	...
Vatican City	.44	1,000	2,272.7	—	—	—	—	—	—	—	—	—	—	—
Yugoslavia	255,804	22,328,000	87.3	1971	20,522,972	49.1	50.9	38.6	27.2	24.6	22.7	13.5	9.8	2.2
Total EUROPE[10]	10,504,953	679,728,000	64.7											
NORTH AMERICA														
Anguilla	91	7,000	76.9	1974	6,519	...	...	...	...	24.2	12.0	...	...	...
Antigua and Barbuda	440	75,000	170.5	1970	64,794	47.2	52.8	33.7	44.0	24.3	16.8	11.7	—8.0—	
Bahamas, The	13,864	234,000	16.9	1970	168,812	49.6	50.4	71.4	43.6	24.3	16.8	9.8	4.4	1.1
Barbados	430	249,000	579.1	1980	248,983	47.6	52.4	...	29.9	32.6	14.1	11.9	10.4	3.4
Belize	22,965	141,000	6.1	1970	119,934	50.6	49.4	54.4	49.3	22.5	13.0	8.7	5.0	1.5
Bermuda	46	54,000	1,173.9	1980	54,050	48.8	51.2	...	22.7	27.5	22.2	15.7	9.0	2.9
British Virgin Islands	153	13,000	85.0	1970	10,484	53.0	47.0	21.9	39.0	29.1	14.7	10.0	5.1	1.9
Canada	9,976,139	23,936,000	2.4	1976	22,992,604	49.8	50.2	75.5	25.6	28.3	18.4	15.1	9.3	3.3
Cayman Islands	264	17,000	64.4	1979	16,677	...	...	...	...	...	...	...	...	...
Costa Rica	50,898	2,232,000	43.9	1973	1,871,780	50.1	49.9	40.6	43.3	27.0	14.2	8.4	4.4	2.7
Cuba	110,922	9,740,000	87.8	1970	8,569,121	51.3	48.7	60.3	27.0	25.0	16.9	12.1	6.8	2.2
Dominica	772	90,000	116.6	1970	69,549	47.4	52.6	46.2	49.1	21.2	11.2	10.0	6.3	2.2
Dominican Republic	48,442	5,400,000	1,114.7	1970	4,006,405	50.4	49.6	40.0	47.2	24.8	15.2	7.8	3.8	1.2
El Salvador	21,041	4,801,000	228.2	1971	3,554,648	49.6	50.4	39.4	46.2	25.1	15.2	8.2	4.3	1.0
Greenland	2,175,600	50,000	.02	1976	49,630	54.1	45.9	74.7	...	...	...	...	...	...

Table II. World Populations and Areas[1] (Continued)

Country	AREA AND POPULATION: MIDYEAR 1980			POPULATION AT MOST RECENT CENSUS					Age distribution (%)[2]					
	Area in sq km	Total population	Persons per sq km	Date of census	Total population	% Male	% Female	% Urban	0–14	15–29	30–44	45–59	60–74	75+
Grenada	345	110,000	318.8	1970	92,775	46.2	53.8	25.3	47.1	23.0	11.6	9.4	6.6	2.2
Guadeloupe	1,705	320,000	187.7	1974	324,500	...	...	41.9	41.2	22.8	14.3	10.4	5.3	1.7
Guatemala	108,889	7,262,000	66.7	1981	6,043,559	49.9	50.1	...	...	...	...	...	...	...
Haiti	27,750	5,009,000	180.5	1981	4,329,991	48.2	51.8	20.4	41.5	25.8	16.5	9.5	5.0	1.7
Honduras	112,088	3,691,000	32.9	1974	2,656,948	49.5	50.5	37.5	48.1	25.8	13.9	7.8	3.6	0.9
Jamaica	10,991	2,192,000	199.4	1980	2,176,762	49.4	50.6	...	36.7	29.8	12.9	10.1	—10.6—	
Martinique	1,079	312,000	289.2	1974	324,832	48.2	51.8	55.6	39.5	25.0	14.2	11.8	7.3	2.2
Mexico	1,958,201	67,382,600	34.4	1980	67,382,581	49.4	50.6	...	42.9	27.6	14.9	8.5	—5.9—	
Montserrat	102	12,000	117.6	1980	11,606	48.1	51.9	54.1	31.5	—————68.5—————				
Netherlands Antilles	993	247,000	248.7	1972	223,196	48.8	51.2	...	38.0	26.7	16.7	10.3	6.4	1.8
Nicaragua	128,875	2,732,000	21.2	1971	1,877,972	48.3	51.7	48.0	48.1	25.6	14.1	7.4	3.6	1.1
Panama	77,082	1,825,000	23.7	1980	1,824,796	50.5	49.5	...	39.4	27.7	16.4	9.5	5.2	1.8
Puerto Rico	8,897	3,186,000	358.1	1980	3,187,566	...	...	...	...	...	...	...	...	...
St. Christopher-Nevis	269	50,000	185.9	1970	44,884	46.8	53.2	31.7	37.9	20.6	9.8	12.1	10.7	8.9
St. Lucia	622	130,000	209.0	1970	99,806	47.2	52.8	36.9	49.6	21.3	11.6	9.8	5.5	2.2
St. Pierre & Miquelon	242	6,000	24.8	1974	5,840	49.4	50.6	...	33.8	24.7	18.0	12.9	—10.5—	
St. Vincent & the Grenadines	388	120,000	309.3	1970	86,314	47.3	52.7	...	51.2	21.7	11.0	8.8	—7.2—	
Trinidad and Tobago	5,128	1,060,000	206.7	1980	1,059,825	49.8	50.2	...	...	...	...	...	...	...
Turks and Caicos Islands	500	7,000	14.0	1970	5,558	47.4	52.6	—	47.1	20.4	12.6	11.1	7.0	2.5
United States	9,363,123	226,505,000	24.2	1980	226,504,825	48.6	51.4	73.7	22.6	27.4	19.1	15.2	11.3	4.4
Virgin Islands (U.S.)	345	95,000	275.4	1980	95,214	60.5	39.5	18.4	...	...	...	...	...	...
Total NORTH AMERICA	24,229,681	369,292,000	15.2											
OCEANIA														
American Samoa	199	32,000	160.8	1980	32,395	...	...	...	...	...	...	...	...	...
Australia	7,682,300	14,518,000	1.9	1976	13,915,500	50.0	50.0	86.0	27.2	25.5	18.3	15.7	9.8	3.2
Canton and Enderbury Islands	70	—	—	1970	—	—	—	—	...	...	...	...	...	...
Christmas Island	135	3,000	22.2	1981	2,871	66.8	33.2	...	25.9	26.4	35.8	10.8	—1.1—	
Cocos Islands	14	500	35.7	1981	555	53.7	46.3	...	27.4	28.3	27.2	11.2	—6.0—	
Cook Islands	241	19,000	78.8	1976	18,128	51.3	48.7	...	49.8	22.1	12.9	9.2	4.9	1.2
Fiji	18,272	630,000	34.5	1976	588,068	50.5	49.5	37.2	41.1	29.8	16.2	8.8	3.3	0.8
French Polynesia	4,182	155,000	37.1	1977	137,382	52.5	47.5	39.7	42.0	27.2	17.0	8.9	4.0	0.8
Guam	549	120,000	218.6	1980	105,821	...	...	...	...	...	...	...	...	...
Johnston Island	3	1,000	333.3	1970	1,007	...	...	0	...	...	...	...	...	...
Kiribati	690	59,000	85.5	1978	56,452	...	...	...	...	...	...	...	...	...
Midway Islands	5	2,000	400.0	1970	2,220	...	...	0	...	...	...	...	...	...
Nauru	21	8,000	381.0	1977	7,254	52.1	47.9	0	44.2	33.1	11.4	8.5	—2.8—	
New Caledonia	19,079	140,000	7.3	1976	133,233	52.0	48.0	42.1	38.6	26.3	18.6	10.4	4.9	1.2
New Zealand	269,057	3,148,000	11.7	1981	3,167,357	...	...	83.6	...	...	...	...	...	...
Niue	259	3,000	11.6	1976	3,843	50.2	49.8	24.8	46.2	23.8	13.6	7.9	5.8	2.6
Norfolk Island	35	2,000	57.1	1981	1,849	...	...	0	...	...	...	...	...	...
Pacific Islands, Trust Territory of the	1,880	137,000	72.9	1973	114,973	51.7	48.3	43.9	46.2	25.8	12.7	9.1	—5.9—	
Papua New Guinea	462,840	3,007,000	6.5	1980	3,006,799	52.3	47.6	13.1	...	...	...	...	...	...
Pitcairn Island	4	63	15.8	1979	61	...	...	0	...	...	...	...	...	...
Solomon Islands	27,556	228,000	8.3	1976	196,823	52.2	47.8	...	47.8	24.1	14.5	8.4	3.6	1.3
Tokelau	10	2,000	200.0	1976	1,575	...	...	...	...	...	...	...	...	...
Tonga	750	96,000	128.0	1976	90,085	51.1	48.9	20.3	44.2	26.0	14.7	9.5	4.0	1.6
Tuvalu	26	7,000	269.2	1979	7,400	...	...	...	...	...	...	...	...	...
Vanuatu	12,190	118,000	9.7	1979	112,596	53.1	46.9	13.3	45.1	27.4	14.9	7.7	3.3	1.6
Wake Island	8	2,000	250.0	1970	1,647	...	...	...	...	...	...	...	...	...
Wallis and Futuna	255	9,000	35.3	1976	9,192	50.0	50.0	...	46.6	23.6	14.0	9.9	5.1	0.8
Western Samoa	2,849	156,000	54.8	1976	151,983	51.7	48.3	21.1	48.2	26.0	12.6	8.7	3.5	1.0
Total OCEANIA	8,503,479	22,602,000	2.7											
SOUTH AMERICA														
Argentina	2,758,829	27,863,000	10.1	1980	27,862,771	49.2	50.8	...	...	...	...	...	...	...
Bolivia	1,098,581	5,570,000	5.1	1976	4,613,486	49.1	50.9	41.7	41.5	27.0	15.4	9.8	4.6	1.7
Brazil	8,512,000	123,032,000	1.4	1980	119,098,992	49.7	50.3	67.6	...	...	...	...	...	...
Chile	756,626	11,104,000	14.7	1970	8,884,768	48.8	51.2	75.1	39.0	25.5	16.6	10.4	5.6	2.9
Colombia	1,141,748	27,326,000	23.9	1973	22,915,229	48.6	51.4	63.6	44.1	27.3	14.9	8.5	4.1	1.0
Ecuador	281,334	8,354,000	29.7	1974	6,521,710	50.1	49.9	41.3	44.6	26.5	14.7	8.4	4.6	1.3
Falkland Islands	16,265	2,000	0.1	1972	1,957	55.2	44.8	44.7	26.7	22.4	—————51.9—————			
French Guiana	90,000	64,000	0.7	1974	55,125	52.1	47.9	76.5	37.9	27.7	16.7	10.7	5.5	1.5
Guyana	215,000	884,000	4.1	1970	699,848	49.7	50.3	33.3	47.1	25.1	13.4	9.0	4.4	1.0
Paraguay	406,752	3,067,000	7.5	1972	2,433,399	49.6	50.4	37.4	44.7	25.6	14.4	9.2	4.6	1.5
Peru	1,285,215	17,780,000	13.8	1972	13,538,208	50.0	50.0	59.6	43.9	25.8	15.6	8.7	—5.9—	
Suriname	163,820	352,000	2.1	1980	352,041	49.2	50.8	...	39.1	—————60.9—————				
Uruguay	176,215	2,897,000	16.4	1975	2,782,000	49.0	51.0	83.0	27.0	22.6	19.2	16.9	10.8	3.5
Venezuela	912,050	13,913,000	15.3	1971	10,721,522	50.1	49.9	73.1	45.0	26.9	14.9	8.5	3.7	1.0
Total SOUTH AMERICA	17,814,435	242,208,000	13.6											
U.S.S.R.[9]	22,402,200	266,542,000	11.9	1979	262,400,000	46.6	53.4	62.4	...	...	...	...	...	...
in Asia[9]	16,831,100	69,413,000	4.1											
in Europe[9]	5,571,100	196,129,000	35.2											
TOTAL WORLD[11]	150,157,410	4,368,486,000	29.1											

[1]Any presentation of population data must include data of varying reliability. This table provides published and unpublished data about the latest census (or comparable demographic survey) and the most recent or reliable midyear 1979 population estimates for the countries of the world. Census figures are only a body of estimates and samples of varying reliability whose quality depends on the completeness of the enumeration. Some countries tabulate only persons actually present, while others include those legally resident, but actually outside the country, on census day. Population estimates are subject to continual correction and revision; their reliability depends on: number of years elapsed since a census control was established, completeness of birth and death registration, international migration data, etc.

[2]Data for persons of unknown age excluded, so percentages may not add to 100.0.

[3]Excludes Mayotte, shown separately.

[4]A census was taken in Nigeria in 1973, but the results were officially repudiated.

[5]Transkei received its independence from South Africa on Oct. 26, 1976; Bophuthatswana on Dec. 6, 1977; Venda on Sept. 13, 1979; Ciskei on Dec. 4, 1981. All are Bantu homeland states whose independence is not internationally recognized.

[6]Sudan census excludes three southern autonomous provinces.

[7]May reach a total of 2,000 persons of all nationalities during the summer.

[8]Excludes nomadic population.

[9]Includes 18,130 sq km of Iraq-Saudi Arabia neutral zone.

[10]Asia and Europe continent totals include corresponding portions of U.S.S.R.

[11]Area of Antarctica excluded in calculating world density.

continued from page 289

nonwhite rate rose 5.1%, from 7.8 to 8.2. The total male rate increased 3.1% (9.7 to 10) and the female rate almost 4% (7.6 to 7.9). Age-specific death rates declined for infants under one year and increased at ages 65 and over. The rates for other age groups remained about the same.

For the 12 months ended June 1981, the number of deaths was over two million and the rate was 8.8 per 1,000 population. These data were higher than for the corresponding period of the previous year. The major causes of death in the U.S. in 1980 were:

Cause of death	Estimated rate per 100,000 population
1. Diseases of the heart	343.0
2. Malignant neoplasms	186.3
3. Cerebrovascular diseases	76.6
4. Accidents	47.9
5. Chronic obstructive pulmonary diseases	25.1
6. Pneumonia and influenza	23.7
7. Diabetes mellitus	15.4
8. Chronic liver disease and cirrhosis	14.1
9. Atherosclerosis	13.4
10. Suicide	12.7
11. Homicide and legal intervention	11.3
12. Conditions in the prenatal period	10.1
13. Nephritis, nephrotic syndrome, and nephrosis	7.8
14. Congenital anomalies	6.2
15. Septicemia	4.1

Of the total, diseases of the heart accounted for 38%, cancer for 21%, and stroke for 9%; together, they were responsible for 68% of all deaths.

The world death rate was estimated at 11 per 1,000 population, with the rate for less developed countries averaging around 14 per 1,000 and that for the developed areas around 9 per 1,000.

Expectation of Life. In 1980, for the first time since 1968, the estimated average length of life for the total U.S. population showed a decline from the previous year. The expectation of life at birth was 73.6 years, compared with 73.8 years in 1979. This small variation was observed for both sexes and for both the white and nonwhite populations. Past differentials remained constant. Women had a higher life expectancy than men (7.7 years) and white persons had a higher life expectancy than nonwhite persons (4.7 years). The average life expectancy at birth for men was 69.8 years and for women, 77.5 years. For white men it was 70.5 years; for white women, 78.1 years; for nonwhite men, 65.3 years; and for nonwhite women, 74 years. Recent estimates of life expectancy in the world ranged from 39 years in Ethiopia to 76 years in Iceland; the world average was about 62 years.

Infant and Maternal Mortality. There were an estimated 45,000 deaths to infants under one year of age in the U.S. in 1980, the same as in 1979. The infant mortality rate of 12.5 deaths per 1,000 live births was 4% below that for 1979 and the lowest ever computed for the U.S. The significant decline in infant mortality over the last 50 years was associated with the saving of babies in the first month of life. In the 1930s the neonatal death rate was over 30 deaths to infants under 28 days old, and in 1980 it was 8.4. The infant mortality rate continued to decline in 1981. For the 12-month period ended in June, the rate was 12.2 infant deaths per 1,000 live births, compared with 12.8 for the corresponding period ended June 1980.

The 1980 rate of 6.7 infant deaths per 1,000 live births in Sweden was the lowest in the world. This contrasted with estimates of over 200 for some countries of western Africa. In 1981 the Soviet Union acknowledged that Soviet infant mortality rates, not publicly reported after 1974, had remained relatively high. A low rate of 22.9 in 1971 was followed by a rise to 27.7 in 1974. From 1978 the official rate had been about 28, although some analysts considered it to be higher.

Marriage and Divorce Statistics. An estimated 2,413,000 marriages took place in the U.S. in 1980, 82,000, or 3.5%, more than in 1979 and the highest annual total on record. The 1980 marriage rate was 10.9 per 1,000 population, an increase of 2% over 1979; this rate had increased each year since 1977.

According to final statistics for 1979, almost two-thirds of the brides married for the first time, about one-third were divorcees, and about 5%

Table III. Life Expectancy at Birth, in Years, for Selected Countries

Country	Period	Male	Female
Africa			
Burundi	1975–80[1]	43.3	45.3
Egypt	1975–80[1]	53.6	56.1
Ivory Coast	1975–80[1]	44.4	47.6
Kenya	1979[1]	47.0	51.0
Nigeria	1975–80[1]	45.9	49.2
Swaziland	1975–80[1]	44.3	47.5
Asia			
China	1980	68.0	68.0
Hong Kong	1976	69.6	76.4
India	1961–70	47.1	45.6
Indonesia	1975–80[1]	48.7	51.3
Israel[2]	1978	71.9	75.6
Japan	1979	73.4	78.9
Kuwait	1975–80[1]	67.3	71.6
Pakistan	1975–80[1]	51.9	51.7
Taiwan	1979	69.4	74.5
Thailand	1975–80[1]	57.6	63.0
Europe			
Albania	1979	69.0	69.0
Austria	1976	68.1	75.1
Belgium	1976	68.6	75.1
Czechoslovakia	1977	67.0	74.1
Denmark	1978–79	71.3	77.4
Finland	1978	68.5	77.1
France	1978	69.9	78.0
Germany, East	1978	68.8	74.7
Germany, West	1976–78	69.0	75.6
Greece	1970–72	70.1	73.6
Hungary	1979	66.7	73.6
Iceland	1977–78	73.4	79.3
Italy	1978	67.0	73.1
Netherlands, The	1978	71.9	78.5
Norway	1978–79	72.3	78.7
Poland	1975–76	67.4	75.1
Romania	1976–78	67.4	72.1
Spain	1975	70.4	76.2
Sweden	1979	72.5	78.7
Switzerland	1968–73	70.3	76.2
United Kingdom	1976–78	69.8	75.9
Yugoslavia	1977	67.6	72.6
North America			
Canada	1971	69.3	76.4
Martinique	1975–80[1]	66.6	72.0
Mexico	1970	60.1	64.0
Panama	1970	64.3	67.5
Puerto Rico	1976	74.0	74.0
Trinidad and Tobago	1970	64.1	68.1
United States	1980	69.8	77.5
Oceania			
Australia	1977	69.9	76.8
New Zealand	1975–77	69.4	75.9
South America[1]			
Argentina	1969–71	61.9	69.7
Brazil	1960–70	57.6	61.1
Chile	1970–75	59.5	65.7
Peru	1975–80[1]	55.1	58.0
Suriname	1975–80[1]	64.8	69.8
Uruguay	1975–80[1]	66.3	72.8
Venezuela	1975	65.0	69.7
U.S.S.R.	1971–72	64.0	74.0

[1] Projection.
[2] Jewish population only.
Sources: United Nations, *World Population Trends and Prospects by Country, 1950–2000: Summary report of the 1978 assessment*; official country sources.

Denmark

were widows. Fewer grooms than brides were previously single, and more were previously divorced. The increase in the divorce rates during the 1970s had an effect on remarriages. Between 1970 and 1979, the proportion of brides who were remarrying after divorce rose from 17 to 25% and of grooms, from 18 to 27%.

The median age at marriage in 1979 was 23.4 years for brides and 25.8 years for grooms. These figures were higher by 1.7 years for brides and 2.2 years for grooms than those for 1970. In part, the increase in median age reflected the fact that there were proportionally more remarriages among the marriages. The average age at first marriage in 1979 was 21.6 years for brides and 23.4 years for grooms; on average, the partners were one year older than in 1970. A reverse trend occurred with remarriages, however; the median ages were 31.9 years for brides and 35.3 years for grooms, a drop of 1.4 years for brides and 2.2 years for grooms since 1970. The median age of divorced persons remarrying was 30.8 years for brides and 33.9 years for grooms; for those previously widowed it was 55.2 years for brides and 61.7 years for grooms.

The annual number of divorces rose between 1979 and 1980, with an estimated 1,182,000 divorces granted in 1980, the highest number ever recorded in the U.S. This represented 67% more divorces than in 1970 and three times as many as in 1960. The divorce rate of 5.3 per 1,000 population in 1980 was the same as that of 1979, but it was more than double that of 1960. Divorces continued to rise during the first half of 1981, and for the 12-month period ended in June about 1,199,000 divorces had been recorded with a rate of 5.3 per 1,000 population.

Marriages that ended in divorce in 1979 lasted somewhat longer than those that ended in any other year in the 1970s; the median duration of marriages was 6.8 years. The increase in divorce was accompanied by an increase in the number of children involved, to an estimated 1,181,000 under 18 years of age. This figure had more than doubled in 16 years (562,000 in 1963) and more than tripled in 22 years (379,000 in 1957). A record high 18.9 children per 1,000 total children under 18 in the population had divorced parents. The number of children per divorce declined somewhat in 1979 to an average of one child per couple. In the peak year of 1964, this figure had been 1.4.

Censuses and Surveys. The U.S. Census Bureau's count of April 1, 1980, was 226,504,825, as compared with 203,302,031 in 1970, an increase of 11.4% in the decade. (*See* Feature Article: *The Changing Face of America.*) The census of China was postponed until 1982.

The UN Statistical Office reported that concern over the migration of millions of persons, including refugees, had created an interest in improving international migration statistics. Countries were increasingly interested in knowing where their migrant populations had settled, and UN projects included reports on immigrants by country of birth and emigration statistics.

The World Health Survey was being developed by the U.S. Centers for Disease Control with the cooperation of the UN, the World Health Organi-

zation, and the countries to be studied. Various surveys measuring morbidity and mortality, disease distribution, and health resources would be under way in 1982.   (ANDERS S. LUNDE)

[338.F.5.b; 525.A; 10/36.C.5.d]

Denmark

A constitutional monarchy of north central Europe lying between the North and Baltic seas, Denmark includes the Jutland Peninsula and 100 inhabited islands in the Kattegat and Skagerrak straits. Area (excluding Faeroe Islands and Greenland): 43,080 sq km (16,633 sq mi). Pop. (1981 est.): 5,132,500. Cap. and largest city: Copenhagen (pop., 1980 est., 654,400). Language: Danish. Religion: predominantly Lutheran. Queen, Margrethe II; prime minister in 1981, Anker Jørgensen.

Danish politics were again dominated by economic problems during 1981. Unemployment figures were rising; in the autumn more than 260,-000 people were out of work. The balance of payments deficit proved intractable; the budget for 1982, reflecting the internal economic difficulties, forecast a deficit of between 40 billion and 50 bil-

---

DENMARK

Education. (1979–80) Primary, pupils 448,370; teachers 40,261; secondary, pupils 61,757, teachers 44,642; vocational, pupils 223,831, teachers (1974–75) 5,290; teacher training, students 23,626, teachers (1978–79) 502; higher, students 81,352, teaching staff (1978–79) 6,713.

Finance. Monetary unit: Danish krone, with (Sept. 21, 1981) a free rate of 7.04 kroner to U.S. $1 (13.06 kroner = £1 sterling). Gold and other reserves (June 1981) U.S. $2,804,000,000. Budget (1980 est.): revenue 108,220,000,-000 kroner; expenditure 118,874,000,000 kroner. Gross domestic product (1980) 374,280,000,000 kroner. Money supply (Dec. 1980) 82,550,000,000 kroner. Cost of living (1975 = 100; May 1981) 182.3.

Foreign Trade. (1980) Imports 108,895,000,000 kroner; exports 94,359,000,000 kroner. Import sources: EEC 49% (West Germany 18%, U.K. 12%, The Netherlands 7%); Sweden 13%; U.S. 6%. Export destinations: EEC 50% (West Germany 19%, U.K. 14%, France 5%, Italy 5%); Sweden 13%; Norway 6%. Main exports: machinery 20%; meat 14%; chemicals 8%; dairy products 5%; fish 5%. Tourism: visitors (1976) 16,232,000; gross receipts (1979) U.S. $1,312,000,000.

Transport and Communications. Roads (1979) 68,194 km (including 464 km expressways). Motor vehicles in use (1979): passenger 1,423,400; commercial 264,000. Railways: (1979) 2,944 km; traffic (1978–79) 1,990,000,000 passenger-km, freight 1,790,000,000 net ton-km. Air traffic (including apportionment of international operations of Scandinavian Airlines System; 1980): 3,043,000,000 passenger-km; freight 128.5 million net ton-km. Shipping (1980): merchant vessels 100 gross tons and over 1,253; gross tonnage 5,390,365. Shipping traffic (1980): goods loaded 7,758,000 metric tons, unloaded 35,567,000 metric tons. Telephones (including Faeroe Islands and Greenland; Jan. 1979) 2,935,100. Radio licenses (Dec. 1979) 1,906,000. Television licenses (Dec. 1979) 1,815,000.

Agriculture. Production (in 000; metric tons; 1980): wheat 648; barley 6,098; oats 160; rye 198; potatoes 850; rutabagas (swedes; 1979) 929; sugar, raw value c. 455; apples c. 126; rapeseed c. 149; butter 114; cheese c. 221; pork 953; beef and veal 245; fish catch (1979) 1,738. Livestock (in 000; July 1980): cattle c. 2,944; pigs 9,527; sheep (1979) 55; chickens (1979) c. 14,570.

Industry. Production (in 000; metric tons; 1980): crude steel 734; cement (1979) 2,409; fertilizers (nutrient content; 1979–80) nitrogenous 130, phosphate 115; plastics and resins (1976) 145; crude oil c. 350; petroleum products (1978) c. 7,540; manufactured gas (cu m; 1979) c. 317,000; electricity (kw-hr) 25,162,000. Merchant vessels launched (100 gross tons and over; 1980) 225,000 gross tons.

lion kroner. Inflation rose by 7.4% during the first nine months of 1981. However, in June 1981—for the first time since November 1958—the balance of trade showed a surplus.

Exports of manufactured goods rose, and Denmark's competitiveness improved. This was brought about by pressure to control costs, particularly wages, which in real purchasing power had declined by some 8% during the preceding two years. The 1981 harvest was above average. Nevertheless, forecasts for the current account deficit (foreign) were altered from 52 billion kroner to some 60 billion kroner in the autumn.

The Social Democrat government of October 1979, maintained by an unofficial coalition with the Radical Liberals, the Centre Democrats, and the Christian People's Party, had difficulty maintaining its narrow majority in the Folketing (parliament). The coalition commanded 90 of the total of 179 seats. In January Prime Minister Anker Jørgensen increased his Cabinet from 17 to 20 members.

Attempts to reduce unemployment received top priority. A "job-creation" plan was proposed by the minister for labour, under which industries engaging people who had been unemployed for a long time would receive a government subsidy to offset the cost of the new employees' wages. This subsidy would in part be saved by the consequent reduction in unemployment payments. One argument against the scheme was that employers would dismiss workers and then hire subsidized labour to replace them.

The lack of investment in industry caused widespread concern. For banks, savings banks, and insurance companies the most attractive form of investment was the government bond, which had an effective rate of interest of about 20% per annum. In an attempt to divert some of these funds to industry, the government proposed to tax the interest. The necessary political majority to approve the idea could not be achieved, however. On November 12 Prime Minister Jørgensen submitted to the Folketing a bill that would order public and private pension plans to reinvest in industry and agriculture about $425 million earned in interest on government bonds. In the vote on the bill the six Centre Democrats abandoned the government coalition, and the government consequently was defeated and fell. Jørgensen called for general elections to be held on December 8.

In the elections the Social Democrats lost 9 seats in the Folketing, winning only 59. The leftist Socialist People's Party gained 9 seats for a total of 20, and the Centre Democrats increased their share by 9 for a total of 15. (*See* POLITICAL PARTIES.) Jørgensen announced that he would resign as prime minister, but on December 22 he accepted the request of Queen Margrethe to try to form a new government. He presented a new minority Social Democrat Cabinet to the queen on December 31.

Whereas, on the whole, settlements in the labour market were reached without industrial action, in the autumn the postal services were severely disrupted by a strike. Worst hit was Copenhagen, where more than half a million letters were delayed daily. Postal workers maintained that they were unable to cope with the volume of mail because of staff shortages.

Discussion of a Scandinavian "nuclear-free zone" continued, particularly on the left wing of Danish politics. Nevertheless, it seemed that Denmark's role within NATO was supported by a solid majority in the Folketing and, according to opinion polls, in the country as well.

(STENER AARSDAL)

See also Dependent States.

Dependent States

In 1981 two dependent states, Belize and Antigua, both British dependencies in the Caribbean, were granted independence. (*See* BELIZE; ANTIGUA AND BARBUDA.)

continued on page 299

Pro-independence saboteurs in Puerto Rico blew up nine jet fighter planes at the Muñiz Air National Guard base in San Juan in January.

WIDE WORLD

Dentistry:
see Health and Disease

ANTARCTIC

Claims on the continent of Antarctica and all islands south of 60° S remain in status quo according to the Antarctic Treaty, to which 19 nations are signatory. Formal claims within the treaty area include the following: Australian Antarctic Territory, the mainland portion of French Southern and Antarctic Lands (Terre Adélie), Ross Dependency claimed by New Zealand, Queen Maud Land and Peter I Island claimed by Norway, and British Antarctic Territory, some parts of which are claimed by Argentina and Chile. No claims have been recognized as final under international law.

AUSTRALIA

CHRISTMAS ISLAND

Christmas Island, an external territory, is situated in the Indian Ocean 1,410 km NW of Australia. Area: 135 sq km (52 sq mi). Pop. (1980 est.): 3,200. Main settlement: Flying Fish Cove and the Settlement (pop., 1978 est., 1,400).

COCOS (KEELING) ISLANDS

Cocos (Keeling) Islands is an external territory located in the Indian Ocean 3,685 km W of Darwin, Australia. Area: 14 sq km (5.5 sq mi). Pop. (1980 est.): 487.

NORFOLK ISLAND

Norfolk Island, an external territory, is located in the Pacific Ocean 1,720 km NE of Sydney, Australia. Area: 35 sq km (13 sq mi). Pop. (1979 est.): 2,200. Cap. (de facto): Kingston.

DENMARK

FAEROE ISLANDS

The Faeroes, an integral part of the Danish realm, are a self-governing group of islands in the North Atlantic about 580 km W of Norway. Area: 1,399 sq km (540 sq mi). Pop. (1980 est.): 43,300. Cap.: Thorshavn (pop., 1980 est., 13,700).

Education. (1979–80) Primary, pupils 6,025; secondary, pupils 2,597; primary and secondary, teachers (1977–78) 466; vocational, pupils (1978–79) 1,304, teachers (1966–67) 88; teacher training, students 113, teachers (1966–67) 12; higher, students 49.

Finance and Trade. Monetary unit: Faeroese krone, at par with the Danish krone, with (Sept. 21, 1981) a free rate of 7.04 kroner to U.S. $1 (13.06 kroner = £1 sterling). Budget (1979–80 est.): revenue 515,752,000 kroner; expenditure 514,893,000 kroner. Foreign trade (1980): imports 1,235,000,000 kroner; exports 1,058,000,000 kroner. Import sources (1979): Denmark 72%; Norway 10%; U.K. 6%. Export destinations (1979): Denmark 24%; U.K. 19%; U.S. 14%; France 8%; Italy 8%; Spain 7%; West Germany 9%. Main exports (1979): fish 80%; ships 8%; fish meal 6%.

Transport. Shipping (1980): merchant vessels 100 gross tons and over 185; gross tonnage 66,085.

Agriculture and Industry. Fish catch (1979) 267,000 metric tons. Livestock (in 000; 1979): sheep c. 72; cattle c. 2. Electricity production (1978 –79) 136 million kw-hr.

GREENLAND (Kalâtdlit-Nunât)

An integral part of the Danish realm, Greenland, the largest island in the world, lies mostly within the Arctic Circle. Area: 2,175,600 sq km (840,000 sq mi), 84% of which is covered by ice cap. Pop. (1980 est.): 49,800. Cap.: Godthaab (Nûk; pop., 1980 est., 9,600).

Education. (1979–80) Primary, pupils 8,695; secondary, pupils 3,566; primary and secondary, teachers 744; vocational, pupils (1980–81) 660, teachers 53; teacher training, students 100, teachers 27; higher, students 450.

Finance and Trade. Monetary unit: Danish krone. Budget (1978 est.): revenue 132 million kroner; expenditure 122 million kroner. Foreign trade (1980): imports 1,846,000,000 kroner; exports 1,168,000,000 kroner. Import sources (1979): Denmark 80%; The Netherlands 5%. Export destinations (1979): Denmark 42%; France 17%; West Germany 10%; Finland 8%; U.S. 8%; Brazil 5%. Main exports: fish 55%; lead ore 22%; zinc ore 16%.

Agriculture. Fish catch (1979) 83,000 metric tons. Livestock (in 000; 1979): sheep 18; reindeer 2.

Industry. Production (in 000; metric tons; 1978): lead ore (metal content) 36; zinc ore (metal content) 90; electricity (kw-hr) 154,000.

FRANCE

FRENCH GUIANA

French Guiana is an overseas département situated between Brazil and Suriname on the northeast coast of South America. Area: 90,000 sq km (34,750 sq mi). Pop. (1981 est.): 66,600. Cap.: Cayenne (pop., 1978 est., 32,900).

Education. (1979–80) Primary, pupils 12,920, teachers 429; secondary, pupils 6,706, vocational, pupils 562; secondary and vocational, teachers 432; teacher training, students (1978–79) 39.

Finance and Trade. Monetary unit: French (metropolitan) franc, with (Sept. 21, 1981) a free rate of Fr 5.29 to U.S. $1 (Fr 9.81 = £1 sterling). Budget (total; 1980 est.) balanced at Fr 391 million. Foreign trade (1980): imports Fr 1,077,710,000; exports Fr 105,390,000. Import sources (1979): France 63%; Trinidad and Tobago 15%; U.S. 5%. Export destinations (1979): France 35%; U.S. 21%; Japan 12%; Martinique 8%; Portugal 7%; Venezuela 7%. Main exports (1979): shrimp 30%; timber 23%; instruments 12%; machinery 8%; aircraft 7%.

FRENCH POLYNESIA

An overseas territory, French Polynesia consists of islands scattered over a large area of the south central Pacific Ocean. Area of inhabited islands: 4,182 sq km (1,615 sq mi). Pop. (1981 est.): 160,000. Cap.: Papeete, Tahiti (pop., 1977, 65,600).

Education. (1979–80) Primary, pupils 38,964, teachers 1,687; secondary, pupils 9,613, teachers 610; vocational, pupils 2,757, teachers 214; teacher training, students 225, teachers 20.

Finance and Trade. Monetary unit: CFP franc, with (Sept. 21, 1981) a parity of CFP Fr 18.18 to the French franc and a free rate of CFP Fr 96 to U.S. $1 (CFP Fr 178 = £1 sterling). Budget (1978) balanced at CFP Fr 13.5 billion. Foreign trade (1979): imports CFP Fr 36,705,000,000 (52% from France, 18% from U.S., 5% from West Germany in 1978); exports CFP Fr 2,215,000,000 (83% to France, 7% to Italy in 1978). Main exports (1978): nuclear material c. 65%; coconut oil 11%; instruments 8%. Tourism: visitors (1979) 101,000; gross receipts (1977) U.S. $51 million.

GUADELOUPE

The overseas département of Guadeloupe, together with its dependencies, is in the eastern Caribbean between Antigua to the north and Dominica to the south. Area: 1,705 sq km (658 sq mi). Pop. (1979 est.): 319,000. Cap.: Basse-Terre (pop., 1977 est., 15,800).

Education. (1978–79) Primary, pupils 55,202, teachers 2,139; secondary and vocational, pupils 48,329, teachers 2,602; higher, students 1,645.

Finance and Trade. Monetary unit: French (metropolitan) franc. Budget (total; 1977 est.) balanced at Fr 1,199,000,000. Cost of living (Basse-Terre; 1975 = 100; April 1981) 176. Foreign trade (1980): imports Fr 2,872,690,000 (72% from France, 5% from U.S. in 1979); exports Fr 446,090,000 (73% to France, 15% to Martinique, 5% to U.K. in 1979). Main exports (1979): bananas 38%; sugar 34%; wheat meal and flour 7%; rum c. 7%.

MARTINIQUE

The Caribbean island of Martinique, an overseas département, lies 39 km N of St. Lucia and about 50 km SE of Dominica. Area: 1,079 sq km (417 sq mi). Pop. (1979 est.): 311,900. Cap.: Fort-de-France (pop., 1974, 98,800).

Education. (1979–80) Primary, pupils 70,406, teachers 3,345; secondary and vocational, pupils 49,929, teachers 2,993; higher, students 1,475, teaching staff 77.

Finance and Trade. Monetary unit: French (metropolitan) franc. Budget (1977 est.): revenue Fr 594 million; expenditure Fr 531 million. Cost of living (Fort-de-France; 1975 = 100; Feb. 1981) 183. Foreign trade (1980): imports Fr 3,276,000,000; exports Fr 592 million. Import sources (1979): France 63%; Venezuela 11%. Export destinations (1979): France 52%; Guadeloupe 30%; Italy 12%. Main exports (1979): bananas 44%; petroleum products 25%; rum c. 12%.

MAYOTTE

An African island dependency of France that was formerly a part of the Comoros, Mayotte lies in the Indian Ocean off the east coast of Africa. Area: 378 sq km (146 sq mi). Pop. (1980 est.): 50,400. Cap.: Dzaoudzi (pop., 1978, 4,100).

Education. (1979–80) Primary, pupils 9,118, teachers 231; secondary, pupils 637, teachers 34; vocational (1978–79), pupils 62.

Finance and Trade. Monetary unit: French (metropolitan) franc. Budget (1980 est.) balanced at Fr 197 million. Foreign trade (1979): imports Fr 24.7 million; exports Fr 6.6 million. Import sources: Réunion 27%; France 27%, Pakistan 16%; Kenya 14%. Export destination: France 100%. Main exports: ylang-ylang 56%; copra 26%; coffee 9%; vanilla 8%.

NEW CALEDONIA

The overseas territory of New Caledonia, together with its dependencies, is in the South Pacific 1,210 km E of Australia. Area: 19,079 sq km (7,366 sq mi). Pop. (1980 est.): 139,600. Cap.: Nouméa (pop., 1976, 56,100).

Education. (1979–80) Primary, pupils 33,939, teachers 1,450; secondary, pupils 8,660, teachers 557; vocational, pupils 3,038, teachers 275; higher, students 396, teaching staff 60.

Finance and Trade. Monetary unit: CFP franc. Budget (1979 est.) balanced at CFP Fr 17,163,-000,000. Foreign trade (1979): imports CFP Fr 27,791,000,000; exports CFP Fr 27,905,000,000. Import sources: France 41%; Bahrain 12%; Australia 11%. Export destinations: France 57%; Japan 20%; U.S. 13%. Main exports: ferroalloys 60%; nickel ores 14%; nickel 13%.

RÉUNION

The overseas département of Réunion is located in the Indian Ocean about 720 km E of Madagascar and 180 km SW of Mauritius. Area: 2,512 sq km (970 sq mi). Pop. (1981 est.): 535,400. Cap.: Saint-Denis (pop., 1981 est., 115,700).

Education. (1980–81) Primary, pupils 125,300, teachers (1979–80) 4,392; secondary and vocational, pupils 63,800, teachers (1979–80) 3,111; higher (university only), students 2,334, teaching staff (1979–80) 63.

Finance and Trade. Monetary unit: French (metropolitan) franc. Budget (1978 est.) balanced at Fr 3,573,000,000. Cost of living (Saint-Denis; 1975 = 100; April 1981) 168.2. Foreign trade (1979): imports Fr 3,305,010,000; exports Fr 549,140,000. Import sources: France 63%; South Africa 6%; Bahrain 5%. Export destinations: France 74%; U.K. 11%; Italy 5%. Main exports: sugar 81%; essential oils 6%.

SAINT PIERRE AND MIQUELON

The self-governing overseas département of Saint Pierre and Miquelon is located about 20 km off the south coast of Newfoundland. Area: 242 sq km (93 sq mi). Pop. (1980 est.): 6,300. Cap.: Saint Pierre, Saint Pierre (pop., 1980 est., 5,600).

Education. (1980–81) Primary, pupils 738, teachers 59; secondary, pupils 527; vocational, pupils 221; secondary and vocational, teachers 61.

Finance and Trade. Monetary unit: French (metropolitan) franc. Budget (1979 est.) balanced at Fr 31.5 million. Foreign trade (1979): imports Fr 148 million; exports Fr 19 million. Import sources (1976): Canada 64%; France 27%. Export destinations (1976): ship's bunkers and stores 53%; Canada 30%; U.S. 13%. Main exports (1974): petroleum products 53%; cattle 30%; fish 12%.

WALLIS AND FUTUNA

Wallis and Futuna, an overseas territory, lies in the South Pacific west of Western Samoa. Area: 255 sq km (98 sq mi). Pop. (1981 est.): 9,000. Cap.: Mata Utu, Uvea (pop., 1976, 558).

NETHERLANDS, THE

NETHERLANDS ANTILLES

The Netherlands Antilles, a self-governing integral part of the Netherlands realm, consists of an island

group near the Venezuelan coast and another group to the north near St. Kitts-Nevis-Anguilla. Area: 993 sq km (383 sq mi). Pop. (1979 est.): 246,500. Cap.: Willemstad, Curaçao (pop., 1970 est., 50,000).

Education. (1973–74) Primary, pupils 38,170, teachers 1,492; secondary and vocational, pupils 12,104, teachers 631; higher (university only), students c. 150, teaching staff c. 15.

Finance. Monetary unit: Netherlands Antilles guilder or florin, with (Sept. 21, 1981) a par value of 1.80 Netherlands Antilles guilders to U.S. $1 (free rate of 3.32 Netherlands Antilles guilders = £1 sterling). Budget (1979 actual): revenue 213 million Netherlands Antilles guilders; expenditure 256 million Netherlands Antilles guilders. Cost of living (Aruba, Bonaire, and Curaçao; 1975 = 100; March 1981) 168.8

Foreign Trade. (1977) Imports 5,631,000,000 Netherlands Antilles guilders; exports 4,764,000,000 Netherlands Antilles guilders. Import sources: Venezuela 61%; Nigeria 11%; U.S. 8%. Export destinations: U.S. 49%; Nigeria 11%; Ecuador 5%. Main exports: petroleum products 89%; crude oil 7%. Tourism (1977): visitors 396,000; gross receipts U.S. $207 million.

Transport and Communications. Roads (1972) 1,150 km. Motor vehicles in use (1978): passenger c. 50,900; commercial c. 8,500 Shipping traffic (1976): goods loaded c. 31.1 million metric tons, unloaded c. 38 million metric tons. Telephones (Jan. 1979) 50,000. Radio receivers (Dec. 1977) 175,000. Television receivers (Dec. 1977) c. 38,000.

Industry. Production (in 000; metric tons; 1978): petroleum products c. 26,900; phosphate rock 81; salt c. 400; electricity (kw-hr) c. 1,750,000.

NEW ZEALAND
COOK ISLANDS
The self-governing territory of the Cook Islands consists of several islands in the southern Pacific Ocean scattered over an area of about 2.2 million sq km. Area: 241 sq km (93 sq mi). Pop. (1980 est.): 19,200. Seat of government: Rarotonga Island (pop., 1976, 9,800).

Education. (1977) Primary, pupils 4,962; secondary, pupils 2,210; primary and secondary, teachers (1975) 360; teacher training, students 48.

Finance and Trade. Monetary unit: Cook Islands dollar, at par with the New Zealand dollar, with (Sept. 21, 1981) a free rate of CI$1.16 to U.S. $1 (CI$2.22 = £1 sterling). Budget (1978–79 est.): revenue CI$13,849,000; expenditure CI$15,034,000. Foreign trade (1980): imports CI$23,610,000 (62% from New Zealand, 11% from Japan, 6% from Australia, 5% from U.S. in 1978); exports CI$4,190,000 (99% to New Zealand in 1977). Main exports: clothing 30%; copra 12%; bananas 11%; citrus juice 10%; pineapple juice 9%; pearl shell 8%.

NIUE
The self-governing territory of Niue is situated in the Pacific Ocean about 2,400 km NE of New Zealand. Area: 259 sq km (100 sq mi). Pop. (1981 est.): 3,400. Capital: Alofi (pop., 1979, 960).

Education. (1980) Primary, pupils 666, teachers 45; secondary, pupils 397, teachers 25.

Finance and Trade. Monetary unit: New Zealand dollar. Budget (1979–80): revenue NZ$4,078,000 (excluding New Zealand subsidy of NZ$2.8 million); expenditure NZ$4,013,000. Foreign trade (1979): imports NZ$2,087,000 (80% from New Zealand); exports NZ$373,000 (98% to New Zealand). Main exports (1978): passion fruit 36%; copra 16%; plaited ware 12%; limes, fresh and juice 9%; honey 9%.

TOKELAU
The territory of Tokelau lies in the South Pacific about 1,130 km N of Niue and 3,380 km NE of New Zealand. Area: 10 sq km (4 sq mi). Pop. (1980 est.): 1,600.

NORWAY
JAN MAYEN
The island of Jan Mayen, a Norwegian dependency, lies within the Arctic Circle between Greenland and northern Norway. Area: 373 sq km (144 sq mi). Pop. (1973 est.): 37.

SVALBARD
A group of islands and a Norwegian dependency, Svalbard is located within the Arctic Circle to the north of Norway. Area: 62,050 sq km (23,957 sq mi). Pop. (1980 est.): 3,600.

PORTUGAL
MACAU
The overseas territory of Macau is situated on the mainland coast of China 60 km W of Hong Kong. Area: 16 sq km (6 sq mi). Pop. (1981 prelim.): 276,700.

Education. (1979–80) Primary, pupils 33,334, teachers 732; secondary, pupils 13,034, teachers 619; vocational, pupils 2,261, teachers 67.

Finance and Trade. Monetary unit: patacá, with (Sept. 21, 1981) a free rate of 6.17 patacás to U.S. $1 (11.43 patacás = £1 sterling). Budget (1980 est.) balanced at 303 million patacás. Foreign trade (1979): imports 1,817,900,000 patacás; exports 2,014,300,000 patacás. Import sources: Hong Kong 51%; China 29%; Japan 6%. Export destinations: U.S. 23%; West Germany 17%; France 16%; Hong Kong 13%; U.K. 8%; Italy 5%. Main exports: clothing 81%; textile yarns and fabrics 7%.

Transport. Shipping traffic (1979): goods loaded 781,000 metric tons, unloaded 566,000 metric tons.

SOUTH WEST AFRICA/NAMIBIA
South West Africa has been a UN territory since 1966, when the General Assembly terminated South Africa's mandate over the country, renamed Namibia by the UN. South Africa considers the UN resolution illegal. Area: 824,268 sq km (318,251 sq mi). Pop. (1981 est.): 1,038,000. National cap.: Windhoek (pop., 1975 est., 77,400). Summer cap.: Swakopmund (pop., 1975 est., 13,700).

Education. Primary, secondary, and vocational, pupils (1980) 228,287, teachers (1978) 5,388.

Finance and Trade. Monetary unit: South African rand, with (Sept. 21, 1981) a free rate of R 0.93 to U.S. $1 (R 1.73 = £1 sterling). Budget (total; 1978–79 est.): revenue R 378 million; expenditure R 374 million. Foreign trade (included in the South African customs union; 1978 est.): imports c. R 500 million (c. 80% from South Africa in 1972); exports c. R 850 million (c. 50% to South Africa in 1972). Main exports: diamonds c. 50%; uranium c. 25%; cattle and meat c. 10%; karakul pelts c. 5%; fish c. 5%.

Agriculture. Production (in 000; metric tons; 1979): corn c. 15; millet c. 20; beef and veal c. 101; sheep and goat meat c. 26; fish catch 327. Livestock (in 000; 1979): cattle c. 3,000; sheep c. 5,150; goats c. 2,150; horses c. 45; asses c. 66.

Industry. Production (in 000; metric tons; 1978): copper ore (metal content) c. 50; lead ore (metal content) 39; zinc ore (metal content) 37; tin concentrates (metal content) c. 0.8; vanadium ore (metal content) c. 0.8; uranium (1979) 4.5; diamonds (metric carats) 1,898; salt c. 220; electricity (kw-hr; 1963) 188,000.

UNITED KINGDOM
ANGUILLA
Formally a part of the associated state of St. Kitts-Nevis-Anguilla, the island of Anguilla comprises a separate administrative entity, having received a constitution separating its government from that of St. Kitts-Nevis-Anguilla in 1976. Area: 91 sq km (35 sq mi). Pop. (1977 est.): 6,500.

Education. (1979) Primary, pupils 1,610, teachers 68; secondary, pupils 450, teachers 20.

Finance and Trade. Monetary unit: East Caribbean dollar, with (Sept. 21, 1981) an official rate of ECar$2.70 to U.S. $1 (free rate of ECar$5.01 = £1 sterling). Budget (1978 est.) balanced at ECar$4.3 million (including U.K. grant of ECar$1.3 million). Foreign trade (1976 est.) exports c. ECar$1 million. Main export destinations: Trinidad and Tobago c. 40%; Puerto Rico c. 30%; Guadeloupe c. 14%; U.S. Virgin Islands c. 10%. Main exports: salt c. 40%; lobster c. 36%; livestock c. 14%.

BERMUDA
The colony of Bermuda lies in the western Atlantic about 920 km E of Cape Hatteras, North Carolina.

Area: 46 sq km (18 sq mi). Pop. (1980): 54,000. Cap.: Hamilton, Great Bermuda (pop., 1980, 1,600).

Education. (1977–78) Primary, pupils 6,466, teachers 319; secondary, pupils 5,269, teachers 404; vocational (1974–75), pupils 510, teachers 49.

Finance and Trade. Monetary unit: Bermuda dollar, at par with the U.S. dollar (free rate, at Sept. 21, 1981, of Ber$1.85 = £1 sterling). Budget (1980–81 est.): revenue Ber$111.7 million; expenditure Ber$115.8 million. Foreign trade (1979): imports Ber$234 million; exports Ber$31.3 million. Import sources: U.S. 49%; Netherlands Antilles 16%; U.K. 12%; Canada 6%. Export destinations: bunkers 51%; U.S. 14%; Spain 9%; Netherlands Antilles 5%. Main exports: petroleum products 55%; drugs and medicines 24%; aircraft supplies 5%. Tourism (1979) 599,000; gross receipts (1978) U.S. $195 million.

Transport. Roads (1979) c. 240 km. Motor vehicles in use (1978): passenger 13,300; commercial (including buses) 2,300. Shipping (1980): merchant vessels 100 gross tons and over 114; gross tonnage 1,723,682.

BRITISH INDIAN OCEAN TERRITORY
Located in the western Indian Ocean, this colony consists of the islands of the Chagos Archipelago. Area: 60 sq km (23 sq mi). No permanent civilian population remains. Administrative headquarters: Victoria, Seychelles.

BRITISH VIRGIN ISLANDS
The colony of the British Virgin Islands is located in the Caribbean to the east of the U.S. Virgin Islands. Area: 153 sq km (59 sq mi). Pop. (1981 est.): 13,000. Cap.: Road Town, Tortola (pop., 1973 est., 3,500).

Education. (1978–79) Primary, pupils 2,251, teachers 109; secondary and vocational, pupils 814, teachers (1975–76) 48.

Finance and Trade. Monetary unit: U.S. dollar (free rate, at Sept. 21, 1981, of U.S. $1.85 = £1 sterling). Budget (1980 est.): revenue U.S. $9,811,000; expenditure U.S. $11.3 million. Foreign trade (1978): imports U.S. $19.8 million; exports U.S. $706,000. Import sources (1976): U.S. 28%; Puerto Rico 24%; U.K. 15%; U.S. Virgin Islands 12%; Trinidad and Tobago 11%. Export destinations (1974): U.S. Virgin Islands 53%; Anguilla 22%; St. Martin (Guadeloupe) 9%; U.K. 5%. Main exports (mainly reexports; 1974): motor vehicles 16%; timber 14%; beverages 10%; fish 7%; iron and steel 6%; machinery 6%. Tourism: visitors (1979) 133,800; gross receipts (1978) U.S. $24 million.

BRUNEI
Brunei, a protected sultanate, is located on the north coast of the island of Borneo, surrounded on its landward side by the Malaysian state of Sarawak. Area: 5,765 sq km (2,226 sq mi). Pop. (1980 est.): 213,000. Cap.: Bandar Seri Begawan (pop., 1978 est., 70,000).

Education. (1978) Primary, pupils 33,053, teachers 1,996; secondary, pupils 15,571, teachers 987; vocational, pupils 306, teachers 85; teacher training, students 533, teachers 66.

Finance and Trade. Monetary unit: Brunei dollar, with (Sept. 21, 1981) a free rate of Br$2.11 to U.S. $1 (Br$3.91 = £1 sterling). Budget (1980 est.): revenue Br$4.5 billion; expenditure Br$1.2 million. Foreign trade (1980): imports Br$1,230,600,000; exports Br$9,852,940,000. Import sources (1979): Japan 26%; Singapore 21%; U.S. 17%; U.K. 10%. Export destinations (1979): Japan 71%; U.S. 8%; Singapore 6%. Main exports (1978): crude oil 62%; natural gas 31%.

Agriculture. Production (in 000; metric tons; 1979): rice c. 7; cassava c. 3; bananas c. 2; pineapples c. 2. Livestock (in 000; 1979): buffalo c. 14; cattle c. 3; pigs c. 13; chickens c. 1,041.

Industry. Production (in 000; 1978): crude oil (metric tons) c. 11,900; natural gas (cu m) 10,277,000; petroleum products (metric tons; 1978) 107; electricity (kw-hr; 1978) c. 362,000.

CAYMAN ISLANDS
The colony of the Cayman Islands lies in the Caribbean about 270 km NW of Jamaica. Area: 264 sq km (102 sq mi). Pop. (1980 est.): 17,000. Cap.: George Town, Grand Cayman (pop., 1980 prelim., 7,600).

Education. (1979–80) Primary, pupils 2,109, teachers 112; secondary, pupils 1,446, teachers 134; vocational, pupils 119, teachers 8.

Finance and Trade. Monetary unit: Cayman Islands dollar, with (Sept. 21, 1981) an official rate of CayI\$0.83 to U.S. \$1 (free rate of CayI\$1.54 = £1 sterling). Budget (1979 est.): revenue CayI\$21 million; expenditure CayI\$16.7 million. Foreign trade (1978): imports CayI\$42 million; exports CayI\$2,-860,000,000. Most trade is with the U.S. (about two-thirds) and Jamaica. Main export (1976): turtle products 98%. Tourism (1979): visitors 100,600; gross receipts U.S. \$27 million.

Shipping. (1980) Merchant vessels 100 gross tons and over 200; gross tonnage 256,715.

FALKLAND ISLANDS

The colony of the Falkland Islands and dependencies is situated in the South Atlantic about 800 km NE of Cape Horn. Area: 16,265 sq km (6,280 sq mi). Pop. (1980 est.): 1,800. Cap.: Stanley (pop., 1978 est., 1,100).

Education. (1978–79) Primary, pupils 219, teachers 29; secondary, pupils 98, teachers 14.

Finance and Trade. Monetary unit: Falkland Island pound, at par with the pound sterling, with (Sept. 21, 1981) a free rate of U.S. \$1.85 = Fl£1. Budget (excluding dependencies; 1980–81 est.): revenue Fl£2,213,000; expenditure Fl£2,284,000. Foreign trade (1978): imports Fl£1,448,000 (86% from U.K. in 1975); exports Fl£2,502,000 (100% to U.K. in 1975). Main export (1976): wool 83%.

GIBRALTAR

Gibraltar, a self-governing colony, is a small peninsula that juts into the Mediterranean from southwestern Spain. Area: 5.80 sq km (2.25 sq mi). Pop. (1980 est.): 29,800.

Education. (1979–80) Primary, pupils 2,705, teachers 147; secondary, pupils 1,771, teachers 128; vocational, pupils 40, teachers 23.

Finance and Trade. Monetary unit: Gibraltar pound, at par with the pound sterling. Budget (1978–79 est.): revenue Gib£26,588,000; expenditure Gib£27,838,000. Foreign trade (1979): imports Gib£55,519,000 (64% from U.K.); reexports Gib£19,453,000 (31% to EEC, 16% to U.K. in 1971). Main reexports: petroleum products 76%; tobacco and manufactures 20%; wines and spirits 6%. Tourism (1979) 148,000 visitors.

Transport. Shipping traffic (1979): goods loaded 9,000 metric tons, unloaded 307,000 metric tons.

GUERNSEY

Located 50 km W of Normandy, France, Guernsey, together with its small island dependencies, is a crown dependency. Area: 78 sq km (30 sq mi). Pop. (1976): 54,400. Cap.: St. Peter Port (pop., 1976, 17,000).

Education. (1979–80) Primary and secondary, pupils 9,400, teachers 524.

Finance and Trade. Monetary unit: Guernsey pound, at par with the pound sterling. Budget (1979): revenue £37,098,000; expenditure £30,-966,000. Foreign trade (1979): imports £150 million; exports £110 million. Main source and destination: U.K. Main exports (1979): manufactures c. 62%; tomatoes c. 21%; flowers and fern c. 11%. Tourism (1979): visitors c. 305,000; gross receipts U.S. \$85 million.

HONG KONG

The colony of Hong Kong lies on the southeastern coast of China about 60 km E of Macau and 130 km SE of Canton. Area: 1,050 sq km (405 sq mi). Pop. (1981 prelim.): 5,108,000. Cap.: Victoria (pop., 1976, 501,700).

Education. (1979–80) Primary, pupils 544,673, teachers 17,929; secondary, pupils 446,187; vocational, pupils 10,913; secondary and vocational, teachers 15,291; teacher training, students 1,099, teachers 188; higher, students 26,862, teaching staff 2,490.

Finance. Monetary unit: Hong Kong dollar, with (Sept. 21, 1981) a free rate of HK\$5.98 to U.S. \$1 (HK\$11.09 = £1 sterling). Budget (1979–80 est.): revenue HK\$15.6 billion; expenditure HK\$14.4 billion.

Foreign Trade. (1980) Imports HK\$11,843,-000,000; exports HK\$98,419,000,000. Import

sources: Japan 23%; China 20%; U.S. 12%; Taiwan 7%; Singapore 7%; U.K. 5%. Export destinations: U.S. 26%; West Germany 8%; U.K. 8%; China 6%; Japan 5%. Main exports: clothing 25%; textile yarns and fabrics 9%; watches and clocks 9%; electrical equipment 7%; telecommunications apparatus 6%; plastic toys and dolls, etc. 6%; nonelectrical machinery 5%. Tourism (1980): visitors 2.3 million; gross receipts U.S. \$1,320,000,000.

Transport and Communications. Roads (1979) 1,147 km. Motor vehicles in use (1979): passenger c. 175,000; commercial 61,700. Railways (1979): 50 km; traffic 442 million passenger-km, freight 69 million net ton-km. Shipping (1980): merchant vessels 100 gross tons and over 187; gross tonnage 1,-717,230. Shipping traffic (1980): goods loaded 8,939,000 metric tons, unloaded 24,623,000 metric tons. Telephones (Dec. 1979) c. 1,520,000. Radio receivers (Dec. 1977) 2,510,000. Television receivers (Dec. 1979) c. 1,035,000.

ISLE OF MAN

The Isle of Man, a crown dependency, lies in the Irish Sea approximately 55 km from both Northern Ireland and the coast of northwestern England. Area: 572 sq km (221 sq mi). Pop. (1980 est.): 64,-000. Cap.: Douglas (pop., 1976, 20,300).

Education. (1979–80) Primary, pupils 5,890; secondary, pupils 5,158; vocational, pupils 3,044.

Finance and Trade. Monetary unit: Isle of Man pound, at par with the pound sterling. Budget (1980–81 est.): revenue £58.3 million; expenditure £50.9 million. Foreign trade included with the United Kingdom. Main exports: fish, beef and lamb, livestock, potatoes. Tourism (1980) c. 564,000 visitors.

JERSEY

The island of Jersey, a crown dependency, is located about 30 km W of Normandy, France. Area: 117 sq km (45 sq mi). Pop. (1976): 74,500. Cap.: St. Helier (pop., 1976, 25,100).

Education. (1979) Primary, pupils 4,675; secondary, pupils 4,460; primary and secondary (1976–77), teachers 670.

Finance. Monetary unit: Jersey pound, at par with the pound sterling. Budget (1979): revenue £84,699,000; expenditure £67,920,000.

Foreign Trade. (1980) Imports £230,895,000 (85% from U.K.); exports £89,930,000 (67% to U.K.). Main exports: fruit and vegetables 16%; motor vehicles 11%; telecommunications apparatus 10%; works of art 6%; aircraft 6%; knitted fabrics 6%; jewelry 6%; tea 5%; musical instruments 5%; clothing 5%. Tourism (1979): visitors 1,285,000; gross receipts U.S. \$244 million.

MONTSERRAT

The colony of Montserrat is located in the Caribbean between Antigua, 43 km NE, and Guadeloupe, 60 km SE. Area: 102 sq km (40 sq mi). Pop. (1980 prelim.): 11,600. Cap.: Plymouth (pop., 1980 prelim., 1,600).

Education. (1978–79) Primary, pupils 2,144, teachers (1977–78) 110; secondary, pupils 850, teachers (1977–78) 48; vocational, pupils 55, teachers (1977–78) 8.

Finance and Trade. Monetary unit: East Caribbean dollar. Budget (total; 1979 est.): revenue ECar\$14,916,000; expenditure ECar\$15,710,000. Foreign trade (1979): imports ECar\$30 million; exports ECar\$2.1 million. Import sources (1978): U.K. 33%; U.S. 23%; Trinidad and Tobago 9%; Canada 5%. Export destinations (1978): U.S. 54%; Trinidad and Tobago 7%; Antigua 5%. Main exports (domestic only; 1978): postage stamps 31%; electronic apparatus 30%; food 15%; sand 8%; fishhooks 6%; hot peppers 5%.

PITCAIRN ISLAND

The colony of Pitcairn Island is in the central South Pacific, 5,150 km NE of New Zealand and 2,170 km SE of Tahiti. Area: 4.53 sq km (1.75 sq mi). Pop. (1980 est.): 63, all of whom live in the de facto capital, Adamstown.

ST. HELENA

The colony of St. Helena, including its dependencies of Ascension Island and the Tristan da Cunha island group, is spread over a wide area of the At-

lantic off the southwestern coast of Africa. Area: 412 sq km (159 sq mi). Pop. (1980 est.): 5,200. Cap.: Jamestown (pop., 1978 est., 1,500).

Education. (1978–79) Primary, pupils 831, teachers (1977–78) 42; secondary, pupils 561, teachers (1977–78) 38; vocational, pupils 16, teachers (1977 –78) 3; teacher training, students 6.

Finance and Trade. Monetary unit: St. Helena pound, at par with the pound sterling which is also used. Budget (1979–80 est.): revenue St.H£4,-227,000; expenditure St.H£4,326,000. Foreign trade (1979–80): imports St.H£1,835,000 (52% from U.K., 36% from South Africa, 5% from Ghana in 1976–77); exports nil.

ST. KITTS-NEVIS

This associated state consists of the islands of St. Kitts and Nevis (Anguilla received a separate constitution in 1976). Area: 269 sq km (104 sq mi). Pop. (1980 prelim.): 44,400. Cap.: Basseterre, St. Kitts (pop., 1980 prelim., 14,700).

Education. (1979–80) Primary, pupils 6,477, teachers 266; secondary, pupils 6,919, teachers 374; vocational, pupils 160, teachers 21; teacher training, students 39, teachers 9.

Finance and Trade. Monetary unit: East Caribbean dollar. Budget (1979 est.): revenue ECar\$31.3 million; expenditure ECar\$36.4 million. Foreign trade (1979): imports ECar\$86.6 million; exports ECar\$45.5 million. Import sources (1975): U.S. 29%; U.K. 20%; Trinidad and Tobago 10%; Canada 7%; The Netherlands 5%; Japan 5%. Export destinations (1975): U.S. 51%; U.K. 42%. Main exports (1975): sugar 61%; television sets and parts 34%.

TURKS AND CAICOS ISLANDS

The colony of the Turks and Caicos Islands is situated in the Atlantic southeast of The Bahamas. Area: 500 sq km (193 sq mi). Pop. (1980 est.): 7,000. Seat of government: Grand Turk Island (pop., 1977 est., 2,900).

Education. (1978–79) Primary, pupils 1,849, teachers 90; secondary, pupils 708, teachers 38.

Finance and Trade. Monetary unit: U.S. dollar. Budget (1979–80 rev. est.): revenue U.S. \$5,-843,000; expenditure U.S. \$5,548,000. Foreign trade (1979): imports U.S. \$9,240,000; exports c. \$U.S. 81.8 million. Main exports: crayfish c. 68%; conch meat c. 29%.

UNITED STATES

AMERICAN SAMOA

Located to the east of Western Samoa in the South Pacific, the unincorporated territory of American Samoa is approximately 2,600 km NE of the northern tip of New Zealand. Area: 199 sq km (77 sq mi). Pop. (1980 prelim.): 32,400. Cap.: Pago Pago (pop., 1980 est., 2,600).

Education. (1979–80) Primary, pupils 6,680, teachers 355; secondary, pupils 2,911, teachers 175; vocational, pupils 45, teachers 4; teacher training, pupils 256, teachers 6; higher, students 472, teaching staff 54.

Finance and Trade. Monetary unit: U.S. dollar. Budget (1979 est.) balanced at \$44.3 million (including U.S. grants of \$36 million). Foreign trade (1977–78): imports (excluding fish for canneries) \$73 million (73% from U.S., 12% from Japan, 6% from New Zealand); exports \$104 million (99% to U.S. in 1976–77). Main export: canned tuna 93%.

GUAM

Guam, an organized unincorporated territory, is located in the Pacific Ocean about 9,700 km SW of San Francisco and 2,400 km E of Manila. Area: 549 sq km (212 sq mi). Pop. (1981 est.): 124,000. Cap.: Agana (pop., 1974 est., 2,500).

Education. (1979–80) Primary, pupils 18,180, teachers (1976–77) c. 770; secondary and vocational, pupils 13,434, teachers c. 570; higher (university), students 3,448, teaching staff (1971–72) c. 140.

Finance and Trade. Monetary unit: U.S. dollar. Budget (1978–79 est.): revenue \$204.9 million; expenditure \$197 million. Foreign trade (1978–79): imports \$446 million (32% from U.S., 7% from Japan); exports \$44 million (49% to U.S. Trust Territories, 26% to U.S., 16% to Taiwan). Main exports: petroleum products, 38%; copra, watches, clothing. Tourism: visitors (1979) 264,000; gross receipts U.S. \$132 million.

Agriculture and Industry. Production (in 000; metric tons; 1979): copra c. 1; eggs 1; fish catch 0.22; petroleum products (1978) c. 1,410; electricity (kw-hr; 1978) c. 1,060,000.

PUERTO RICO

Puerto Rico, a self-governing associated commonwealth, lies about 1,400 km SE of the Florida coast. Area: 8,897 sq km (3,435 sq mi). Pop. (1980 prelim.): 3,186,100. Cap.: San Juan (pop., 1980 prelim., mun., 422,700).

Education. (1979–80) Primary, pupils 432,012, teachers 15,308; secondary, pupils 341,716, teachers 13,676; vocational, pupils 57,863, teachers 2,600; higher, students 130,105, teaching staff 3,300.

Finance. Monetary unit: U.S. dollar. Budget (1978–79 actual): revenue $3,712,000,000; expenditure $3,165,000,000. Gross domestic product (1979–80) $13,916,000,000. Cost of living (1975 = 100; March 1981) 140.6.

Foreign Trade. (1979–80) Imports $8,638,-000,000 (71% from U.S., 8% from Venezuela in 1978–79); exports $6,942,000,000 (85% to U.S.). Main exports (1974–75): chemicals 25%; petroleum products 14%; clothing 11%; machinery 11%; fish 8%. Tourism (1978–79): visitors 1,662,000; gross receipts U.S. $565 million.

Transport and Communications. Roads (paved; 1978) 12,343 km. Motor vehicles in use (1978): passenger 793,800; commercial 135,900. Railways (1977) 96 km. Telephones (Jan. 1979) 604,300. Radio receivers (Dec. 1976) 1,765,000. Television receivers (Dec. 1977) 535,000.

Agriculture. Production (in 000; metric tons; 1980): sugar, raw value c. 164; pineapples 36; bananas 102; oranges 31; coffee 12; tobacco (1979) 2; milk 407; meat (1979) 76. Livestock (in 000; Jan. 1979): cattle 532; pigs 246; chickens 6,568.

Industry. Production (in 000; metric tons; 1979): cement 1,327; beer (hl) 736; rum (hl; 1977) c. 600; petroleum products (1978) c. 12,530; electricity (kw-hr) c. 14,500,000.

TRUST TERRITORY OF THE PACIFIC ISLANDS

The Trust Territory islands, numbering more than 2,000, are scattered over 7,750,000 sq km in the Pacific Ocean from 720 km E of the Philippines to just west of the International Date Line. Separate administrative actions within the Trust Territory have, since 1978, created four new administrative entities that are to form the framework for local government upon cessation of the UN trusteeship: the Commonwealth of the Northern Mariana Islands (1978); the Federated States of Micronesia (Yap, Ponape, Kosrae, and Truk; 1979); the Marshall Islands (1979); and the Republic of Palau (early 1981). The government of the Trust Territory will not, however, cease to exist until the UN permits its dissolution, subject to referendums. Area: 1,880 sq km (726 sq mi). Pop. (1980): 133,800. Seat of government: Saipan Island (pop., 1973 census, 12,-400).

Education. (1978–79) Primary, pupils 31,297, teachers 1,485; secondary, pupils 7,990, teachers 509; vocational (1976–77), pupils 257, teachers (1973–74) 13; higher, students 581, teaching staff (1977–78) 55.

Finance and Trade. Monetary unit: U.S. dollar. Budget (1979–80 est.): revenue $124.6 million (including U.S. grant of $112.7 million); expenditure $109.4 million. Foreign trade (1977–78): imports $39 million (35% from U.S., c. 25% from Japan, 6% from Australia in 1976–77); exports $19 million (54% to Japan in 1972). Main exports: coconut oil 57%; fish 27%; copra 11%.

VIRGIN ISLANDS

The Virgin Islands of the United States is an organized unincorporated territory located about 60 km E of Puerto Rico. Area: 345 sq km (133 sq mi). Pop. (1980 prelim.): 95,200. Cap.: Charlotte Amalie, St. Thomas (pop., 1980 prelim., 11,700).

Education. (1979–80) Primary, pupils 20,191, teachers 861; secondary, pupils 12,134, teachers 612; vocational, pupils 3,738, teachers 103; higher, students 584, teaching staff 86.

Finance. Monetary unit: U.S. dollar. Budget (1979–80 est.): revenue $189 million; expenditure $162 million.

Foreign Trade. (1979) Imports $3,766,000,000; exports $3,093,000,000. Import sources (1978): Iran 46%; U.S. c. 12%; Libya 11%; Nigeria 9%; United Arab Emirates 8%; Angola 6%. Export destinations (1978): U.S. 92%. Main exports (1978): petroleum products 91%; chemicals 6%. Tourism (1979): visitors 1.2 million; gross receipts U.S. $333 million.

continued from page 295

Europe and the Atlantic. Greenland, granted a degree of home rule in May 1979, remained, on the whole, bound by the international terms and treaties into which Denmark entered. Nevertheless, it was agreed that Greenlanders themselves should decide the question of the island's continued membership in the European Communities, and to this end it was announced that a referendum would be held in February 1982. Most of the islanders were expected to vote to leave the EC. However, toward the end of 1981 it emerged that Greenland could not expect automatically to remain an associate member of the EC if it voted to give up full membership. This new pressure, it was thought, might influence some voters to change their minds.

Discussions on the future status of Gibraltar seemed no closer. The Lisbon agreement (April 1980) between the U.K. and Spain had determined that negotiations would begin at the same time that Spain lifted its blockade of Gibraltar. However, the border remained closed throughout the year. The stalemate was underlined by an amendment to a nationality bill passing through the U.K. Parliament, which allowed Gibraltarians to retain full British citizen rights, and by Spanish protests over the prince of Wales's visit to the Rock.

The British decision to withdraw the protection of HMS "Endurance," together with the new U.K. nationality bill and proposed talks with Argentina, increased fears of abandonment in the Falkland Islands. This occurred despite continued British assertions of sovereignty and protests by the British Foreign and Commonwealth Office over the presence of Argentine oil tenders within the Falklands' 200-mi (322-km) economic zone. Clear indications that the islands had valuable oil and fish reserves weakened claims that the cost of lengthening the airstrip was prohibitive.

The Isle of Man Parliament voted in July to seek from the U.K. recognition as a fully self-governing territory, with the U.K. remaining responsible only for foreign affairs and defense.

Although Saint-Pierre and Miquelon supported French Pres. Valéry Giscard d'Estaing in his unsuccessful bid for reelection in May, Socialist candidates were elected to represent two of the island's constituencies. In November there was a strike by civil servants.

Caribbean. During the year two of the remaining British dependencies in the Caribbean achieved independence: Belize on September 21 and Antigua and Barbuda on November 1.

In the associated state of St. Kitts-Nevis, the vociferous political debate between the ruling coalition (of the People's Movement Party and the Nevis Reformation Party) and the opposition continued, but it was dampened somewhat by high bonuses paid to workers in the economically vital but opposition-controlled sugar industry. The number of tourists to the island increased steadily following the inclusion of St. Kitts in the regular schedules of two airlines providing direct jet services to North America. Toward the year's end, a major political row occurred when the government of Premier Kennedy Simmonds requested the replacement of Gov. Sir Probyn Innis. The move followed Sir Probyn's refusal to sign into law certain bills which, though passed by the legislature, had been challenged in the courts by the opposition Labour Party. At about the same time, the government announced that it would downgrade the island's defense force to a paramilitary corps.

In Montserrat the right-of-centre administration of Chief Minister John Osborne continued to pursue policies aimed at achieving self-sufficiency with the ultimate goal of independence. Generally, the economy remained buoyant, though in Sep-

The Modern History of Micronesia

The island groups comprising the Trust Territory of the Pacific Islands include high volcanic islands and low atolls formed from eroded volcanoes fringed by coral reefs. Located in the western Pacific Ocean, the Trust Territory consists of 96 islands with an area of 1,779 sq km (687 sq mi).

Settled about 3,500 years ago by the Micronesian peoples, the islands were first colonized by Spain in 1668. After the loss of its Pacific colonies, Spain sold the islands to Germany between 1885 and 1899. Japan occupied the islands in 1914 and was granted a League of Nations mandate to govern them in 1920. Fortified heavily by the Japanese prior to World War II, the islands were occupied after bitter fighting by the U.S. during 1944. The United Nations granted a trusteeship mandate to the U.S. in 1947.

After seven years of administration by the U.S. Navy, the islands were placed under the jurisdiction of the Department of the Interior and governed by a high commissioner appointed by the U.S. president. The islanders were granted the right to elect local governments. Between 1946 and 1958 Bikini and Eniwetok atolls in the Marshall Islands district were the site of nuclear weapons tests. Their populations were removed first to Rongelap, later to Kwajalein, and finally to Kili Atoll. In the 1970s the islanders petitioned for a return to their home atolls, but testing for residual radiation delayed the move.

In 1968 a three-branch government patterned on the U.S. federal government was created in the territory under the authority of the high commissioner. During 1973–74 the Congress of Micronesia adopted guidelines for a constitutional convention that would lead to independence. Regional differences led to a division of the islands into four constituencies when the proposed constitution was voted on in 1978. The Kosrae, Ponape, Truk, and Yap districts approved it and formed the Federated States of Micronesia. Of the districts that rejected the constitution, the Northern Marianas chose commonwealth status with the U.S. in 1978. The Marshall Islands voted for an independent constitution in 1979. Palau, after two unsuccessful attempts, approved a constitution as the Republic of Palau (Belau) in November 1980. In mid-1981 a fifth state, Faichuk, was created in the Federated States of Micronesia when eight municipalities in the western part of Truk lagoon seceded from Truk State.

Pres. Jimmy Carter set early 1981 as the date of independence for the territory, but the delay in constitutional conventions and the change in U.S. administrations led to postponement of the final UN-sponsored referendum and independence.

tember agriculture suffered a major setback because of damage caused by unusually heavy rains. The relative political harmony of the country was upset in midyear by an apparently ill-judged decision to introduce a newspaper act which, by requiring a substantial deposit from any person or company wishing to publish, would have closed down virtually all publications. Following a local, regional, and international outcry, Chief Minister Osborne announced that he intended to reconsider the legislation.

General elections held in November 1980 produced an overwhelming victory for the opposition, the right-of-centre People's National Party led by Norman Sanders, in the Turks and Caicos Islands. As a result, the islands no longer sought independence. Work on the basic infrastructure for a Club Méditerannée complex began, but not without criticism from a U.K. parliamentary committee on foreign affairs, which questioned the use of British aid funds for the project.

The British Virgin Islands continued their steady tourist-based economic development. An agreement to explore for minerals, including copper, was signed with Noranda Mines of Canada. In the Cayman Islands visitor arrivals continued to show steady growth. Government expenditure for fiscal year 1981–82 was budgeted to increase 53% to $49.6 million. Emphasis was placed on developing the infrastructure in Cayman Brac and Little Cayman.

In early 1981 Bermuda's economy suffered a major setback following a three-and-a-half-week-long strike by blue-collar workers, supported by workers in the hotel industry. During and after the strike, tourist arrivals fell substantially, and by midyear they were 10% below 1980 figures. The government introduced a tough budget that levied sizable tax increases on almost all Bermudians. In late 1981 Premier David Gibbons paid an official visit to China.

In the French presidential election, the French départements of Martinique, Guadeloupe, and French Guiana voted overwhelmingly for President Giscard. During the campaign, the Groupe de libération armée, which wanted full independence for Guadeloupe and Martinique, claimed responsibility for a number of bomb explosions both in the départements and in Paris. A number of persons were arrested and taken to France but were released following Pres. François Mitterrand's election. The new French government indicated that the Caribbean départements would remain as part of France but that greater economic autonomy would be encouraged.

Movement toward the independence of Netherlands Antilles was slow. At a conference in The Hague in April, it was agreed that the existing federal structures should be loosened and each island given more autonomy to determine economic policy. In October the Dutch government agreed provisionally to the independence of Aruba.

On January 12 nine U.S. fighter planes were destroyed and two others were damaged by bombs at the Muñiz Air National Guard base near San Juan, P.R. Responsibility was claimed by the Macheteros, a pro-independence group that had been among those claiming responsibility for the December 1979 attack on a bus carrying U.S. Navy personnel. Recession in the U.S. severely affected

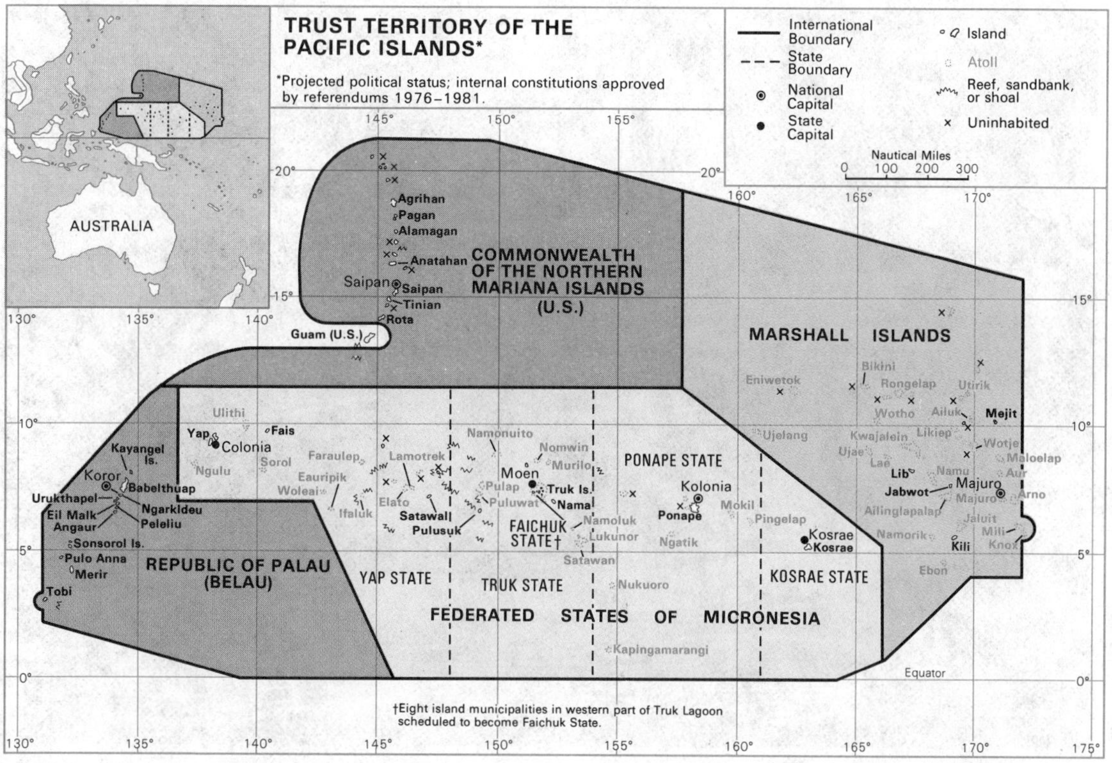

TRUST TERRITORY OF THE PACIFIC ISLANDS*

*Projected political status; internal constitutions approved by referendums 1976–1981.

International Boundary
State Boundary
National Capital
State Capital
Island
Atoll
Reef, sandbank, or shoal
Uninhabited

Nautical Miles
0 100 200 300

†Eight island municipalities in western part of Truk Lagoon scheduled to become Faichuk State.

the Puerto Rican economy. In the spring the Puerto Rican planning board projected growth of real gross national product in fiscal 1981 at between 0.1 and 1.8%, the lowest since the 1973–75 recession. Officials were highly critical of the Reagan administration's planned cuts in welfare and nutritional programs on which the island was heavily dependent; the Puerto Rican food stamp program alone had grown to about $1.1 billion a year. After heated debate in Congress, conversion of nutritional programs for Puerto Rico into a block grant was postponed until July 1, 1982. In late March and early April, Gov. Carlos Romero Barceló made a tour of Western Europe, the first such trip ever undertaken by a Puerto Rican governor.

Africa. The problem of South West Africa/ Namibia continued unresolved throughout 1981. A succession of meetings were convened to discuss the territory and to attempt to implement the UN formula for Namibian independence. At the UN-sponsored Geneva conference in January, UN Secretary-General Kurt Waldheim appealed for a cease-fire agreement which would allow a transitional process to begin. A South African delegation attended the conference, as did one from the South West Africa People's Organization (SWAPO), which had been recognized by the UN General Assembly as the "sole legitimate representative of the Namibian people." However, this recognition of SWAPO proved the major stumbling block. The territory's internal parties, of which the Democratic Turnhalle Alliance (DTA) was the most important, claimed that recognition proved the UN was not impartial and therefore could not oversee the proposed cease-fire and elections.

In May the contact group of five Western nations —the U.S., the U.K., France, Canada, and West Germany—met in Rome, where they agreed to attempt to incorporate constitutional guarantees for minorities into the UN peace plan for Namibia. The U.S.-backed initiative was aimed at allaying South African fears for the future of DTA supporters in an independent Namibia. The proposals were drawn up and approved by the contact group in September.

At first the new initiative did little to repair the fragile relations between the contact group and the black African "front-line" states. Earlier, the U.S., the U.K., and France vetoed a UN Security Council resolution, proposed by the front-line states, to impose sanctions against South Africa. In May a meeting called jointly by the UN and the Organization of African Unity (OAU), which the contact-group nations did not attend, voiced virtually unanimous support for a resolution calling for an embargo on economic and military cooperation with South Africa. However, Angola announced its tentative approval of the Western proposals when details were made known in September.

The OAU peace proposals for a resolution of the Western Sahara issue were advanced further during the year. Morocco, which claimed the territory, reached an agreement with Libya, a major supporter of the Popular Front for the Liberation of Saguia el Hamra and Río de Oro (Polisario Front) and its struggle to achieve the territory's independence as the Saharan Arab Democratic Republic. The OAU convened a committee to mediate among the various parties, and in the end Morocco agreed to the OAU proposals. These involved a cease-fire in the area, allowing a joint OAU and UN peacekeeping force to oversee an interim administration while a referendum on the territory's future status was held.

UPI

Hong Kong marine police patrol nearby waters in an effort to halt refugees from China who had fled their homeland in fear of an impending earthquake.

Indian Ocean. In Mayotte, the island in the Comoros group that remained dependent on France by its own choice, the question of the island's status dominated politics. Pres. Ahmed Abdallah of the Comoros refused to give up his aim of reuniting Mayotte with the other islands.

The island of Diego Garcia in the Chagos Archipelago retained minimal U.K. Foreign and Commonwealth Office administration in the form of a naval presence, although the U.S. military presence on the island was much greater. In June a delegation from Mauritius arrived in London to represent the people of Diego Garcia, who had been removed from the island in 1966 to make room for the U.S. military bases. Its object was to discuss compensation for the evacuation with the British government, but the two sides failed to reach agreement. The U.K. offered £1.5 million, while the Diego Garcians had asked for £8 million.

Pacific. With Pres. Ronald Reagan's election in the U.S., the date for terminating the Trust Territory of the Pacific Islands was postponed. The draft compact on future political status, signed by the U.S. with three of the four island groups—the Federated States of Micronesia, the Republic of Palau, and the Marshall Islands—in the last days of Pres. Jimmy Carter's administration, was held for review. The draft had provided for each of these three entities to become self-governing in free association with the U.S., for substantial financial assistance, and for continued military activity. In May these Micronesian governments and the fourth island group—the Commonwealth of the Northern Marianas—appeared before the Trusteeship Council of the UN, where they called on the U.S. to reopen negotiations on the compact

and its subsidiary agreements and for an early termination of the trusteeship.

Talks were resumed in October, with the main areas of discussion being future financial assistance, the period during which the U.S. could exercise a strategic denial over the islands, and future military use. The U.S., determined to retain enough control to prevent foreign encroachment, insisted on retaining exclusive use of military installations on the islands. The Micronesians claimed that the U.S., having created an economy dependent on rising expectations and having destroyed the traditional subsistence economy, should provide generous aid during a transitional period. At about the same time, a press leak revealed U.S. intentions to build a Trident submarine base in Palau despite that country's "nuclear-free" constitution. (*See* Sidebar.)

In March the people of Bikini Island, one of the Marshall Islands, sued the U.S. for $450 million as compensation for the effects of nuclear testing in the 1940s and 1950s. Pres. Amata Kabua of the Marshall Islands found few supporters when, in September, he suggested that Japan should use the already polluted Bikini and Eniwetok atolls for nuclear-waste disposal instead of dumping nuclear waste in the ocean adjacent to the Marianas as planned.

In February Pope John Paul II visited Guam on his way to Japan. Guam and the Virgin Islands both retained a strong U.S. military presence.

France's Pacific possessions moved against the national trend in the French presidential elections of April–May. In the second round of voting, Wallis and Futuna voted 97.7% for Giscard; in New Caledonia, where independentists supported Mitterrand, Giscard won 65.5% of the vote; and in

French Polynesia, 76.7% voted for Giscard. This latter result was unusual in that the autonomist majority in the Territorial Assembly campaigned for Giscard rather than Mitterrand, who favoured a change in France's colonial relationships. More than 1,000 people—2% of those who voted—rejected both candidates and "wrote in" a vote for independence. With pro-independence groups calling for a boycott, turnout was a low 63% of registered voters.

All major political parties in French Polynesia supported a policy of full internal self-government. The vice-president of the government council made a case for this in Paris in July, but no redirection of policy was announced. Nuclear testing at Moruroa was suspended by the new French government but was resumed in August after a review. Henri Emmanuelli, French minister for overseas départements and territories, visited French Polynesia and Wallis and Futuna in August.

In New Caledonia the independence movement drew increasing support from the region. In August the South Pacific Forum called for independence for New Caledonia and appointed Fiji's prime minister, Sir Kamisese Mara, to lead a delegation to Paris to make representations to the French government. In the same month, Emmanuelli called for an end to social inequality, a redistribution of land, and a reduction of white power before independence for New Caledonia could be contemplated. Tension increased in September after the assassination of independentist Pierre Declercq by a young French settler. Declercq, though a Frenchman, had served as secretary-general of the Union Calédonienne, New Caledonia's major pro-independence party, which was supported by the indigenous Melanesians.

Albert Henry, former premier of the Cook Islands, died in Rarotonga in January (see OBITUARIES). Henry's nephew, Geoffrey, was elected leader of the Cook Islands Party—defeating Henry's son, Tupui—and thus remained leader of the opposition. The government of Premier Sir Thomas David (knighted during 1981) used its two-thirds majority to amend the constitution. The Legislative Assembly was to become the Parliament; the premier was to become the prime minister; the parliamentary term was to be extended from four years to five, thus making the next elections due in 1983; and, in an attempt to end the "fly-in" voting scandal that had caused Henry's downfall in 1978, the Cook Islanders living overseas were to form a new, separate electorate. At 24,000, the overseas population outnumbered the 22,000 who remained in the islands.

East Asia. Brunei was scheduled to gain complete independence at the end of 1983. In the meantime, the U.K. remained responsible for defense and external affairs. In February 1981 it was announced that Brunei had applied for, and had been granted, special membership in the Commonwealth.

(PHILIPPE DECRAENE; DAVID A. JESSOP; BARRIE MACDONALD; MOLLY MORTIMER)

See also African Affairs; Commonwealth of Nations; United Nations.

Djibouti

Djibouti

An independent republic in northeastern Africa, Djibouti is bordered by Ethiopia, Somalia, and the Gulf of Aden. Area: 23,200 sq km (8,900 sq mi). Pop. (1980 est., excluding refugees): 315,000, most of whom are Cushitic Afars or Somali Issas; there are smaller Arabic and European communities. Capital: Djibouti (pop., 1980 est., 200,000). Language: Arabic and French (official); Saho-Afar and Somali are spoken in their respective communities. Religion: predominantly Muslim. President in 1981, Hassan Gouled Aptidon; premier, Barkat Gourat Hamadou.

Pres. Hassan Gouled Aptidon was reelected unopposed on June 12, with 84.58% of the votes cast. Premier Barkat Gourat Hamadou's government, after resigning on June 30, returned to office on July 7 with some minor changes.

In August two former premiers, Abdallah Kamil and Ahmed Dini, founded the Djibouti People's Party in Paris. On their return to Djibouti on September 7, both were arrested, together with 11 of their supporters. Kamil and five others were released on October 25. Meanwhile, on October 19, the National Assembly declared Djibouti a one-party state.

President Gouled sought to develop relations with France, the former colonial power, with the Arab states, and with Ethiopia. Cooperation with France, which maintained its biggest African military base at Djibouti, was close; in November Gouled attended the Franco-African summit meeting in Paris. Among the Arab states, Saudi Arabia was the major donor of aid to Djibouti. In March, on the occasion of a visit by Gouled to Addis Ababa, a treaty of friendship and cooperation was concluded with Ethiopia.   (PHILIPPE DECRAENE)

DJIBOUTI

Education. (1980–81) Primary, pupils 16,841, teachers 375; secondary, pupils 3,812, teachers 174; vocational, pupils 1,279, teachers 88; teacher training, students 65, teachers 11; higher, students 150.

Finance. Monetary unit: Djibouti franc, with (Sept. 21, 1981) a par value of DjFr 178.16 to U.S. $1 (free rate of DjFr 330 = £1 sterling). Budget (1980 est.) balanced at DjFr 12,120,000,000.

Foreign Trade. (1977) Imports DjFr 18,506,000,000; exports DjFr 3,381,000,000. Import sources: France 55%; U.K. 6%; Japan 6%; Ethiopia 5%. Export destination: France 74%. Main exports (most trade is transit): cattle *c.* 7%.

Dominica

Dominica

A republic within the Commonwealth, Dominica, an island of the Lesser Antilles in the Caribbean Sea, lies between Guadeloupe to the north and Martinique to the south. Area: 772 sq km (300 sq mi). Pop. (1981 est.): 80,000. Cap.: Roseau (pop., 1981 est., 20,000). President in 1981, Aurelius Marie; prime minister, Eugenia Charles.

Following a crisis in Dominica's Defence Force in late December 1980, it was revealed that the

Ten U.S. citizens were arrested by federal agents in April and charged with attempting to invade and overthrow the government of Dominica.

Three people were killed when a further coup attempt was foiled in December. Those involved were also reported to be allies of John.

Prime Minister Charles pursued a policy of encouraging private investment, but the island's weak economic base did little to attract overseas investors. Charles criticized Grenada's left-wing policies, which she claimed had caused the U.S. government to abandon a $4 million line of credit for all eastern Caribbean islands.

Dominica announced a record ECar$143.7 million budget, ECar$85.9 million of which was to be spent on capital projects. (DAVID A. JESSOP)

Dominican Republic

Covering the eastern two-thirds of the Caribbean island of Hispaniola, the Dominican Republic is separated from Haiti, which occupies the western third, by a rugged mountain range. Area: 48,442 sq km (18,704 sq mi). Pop. (1980 est.): 5,431,000, including mulatto 75%; white 15%; Negro 10%. Cap. and largest city: Santo Domingo (pop., 1979 est., 1,103,400). Language: Spanish. Religion: mainly Roman Catholic (95%), with Protestant and Jewish minorities. President in 1981, Antonio Guzmán Fernández.

During 1981 a sharp increase in strikes and demonstrations was met with violence by the Dominican Republic's security forces. Several people were killed, and their deaths brought a wave of indignation and opposition to Pres. Antonio Guzmán Fernández. The government's claim that the strikes were politically motivated received lit-

situation was linked to a plot to overthrow the government. As 1981 progressed it emerged that North American mercenaries had been employed to act jointly with local politicians and members of the Defence Force to seize power. With French, U.S., and British assistance, the government arrested and charged a number of people, among them former prime minister Patrick John. The Defence Force was disbanded, and Prime Minister Eugenia Charles sought further security assistance, principally from the U.S. Ten mercenaries, some of them linked to the Ku Klux Klan, were arrested by U.S. authorities as they attempted to launch an invasion of Dominica from Louisiana.

DOMINICA
Education. (1978–79) Primary, pupils 16,540, teachers 887; secondary, pupils 6,343, teachers c. 300; vocational, pupils 386, teachers 25; teacher training, students 50, teachers 141.
Finance and Trade. Monetary unit: East Caribbean dollar, with (Sept. 21, 1981) an official rate of ECar$2.70 to U.S. $1 (free rate of ECar$5.01 = £1 sterling). Budget (1976–77 est.): revenue ECar$21,554,000; expenditure ECar$28,611,-000. Foreign trade (1978): imports ECar$76.8 million; exports ECar$42.9 million. Import sources: U.K. 27%; U.S. 15%; St. Lucia 7%; Trinidad and Tobago 7%; Canada 5%. Export destinations: U.K. 67%; Barbados 5%. Main exports: bananas 58%; soap 12%; coconut oil 5%; grapefruit 5%.

Dominican Republic

DOMINICAN REPUBLIC
Education. (1975–76) Primary, pupils 903,521, teachers 17,932; secondary, pupils 136,570, teachers c. 4,417; vocational, pupils 5,326, teachers c. 299; teacher training, students 1,353, teachers c. 49; higher (universities only), students (1976–77) 44,725, teaching staff 1,435.
Finance. Monetary unit: peso, at parity with the U.S. dollar, with a free rate (Sept. 21, 1981) of 1.85 pesos to £1 sterling. Gold and other reserves (June 1981) U.S. $197 million. Budget (1979 actual): revenue 745.6 million pesos; expenditure 973.9 million pesos. Gross national product (1979) 5,321,400,000 pesos. Money supply (May 1981) 608.8 million pesos. Cost of living (Santo Domingo; 1975 = 100; April 1981) 169.9.
Foreign Trade. (1980) Imports 1,639,600,000 pesos; exports 961.9 million pesos. Import sources (1979): U.S. 42%; Venezuela 18%; Netherlands Antilles 7%; Japan 7%. Export destinations (1979): U.S. 53%; Switzerland 15%; Puerto Rico 6%; Venezuela 6%; The Netherlands 5%. Main exports: sugar 32%; gold and alloys 27%; ferronickel 11%; coffee 8%; cocoa 5%.
Transport and Communications. Roads (1980) 17,659 km. Motor vehicles in use (1980): passenger 115,300; commercial 77,221. Railways (1979) c. 590 km. Telephones (Jan. 1980) 155,400. Radio receivers (Dec. 1977) 210,000. Television receivers (Dec. 1978) c. 385,000.
Agriculture. Production (in 000; metric tons; 1980): rice c. 413; sweet potatoes (1979) c. 80; cassava (1979) c. 160; sugar, raw value c. 1,100; dry beans c. 43; tomatoes c. 160; peanuts c. 69; oranges c. 72; avocados (1979) c. 137; mangoes c. 172; bananas c. 320; plantains (1979) c. 550; cocoa c. 27; coffee c. 57; tobacco c. 44. Livestock (in 000; June 1979): cattle 2,826; sheep 22; pigs c. 700; goats 294; horses 197; chickens c. 8,000.
Industry. Production (in 000; metric tons; 1980): cement 1,014; bauxite 510; nickel ore (1979) 25; gold (troy oz) 370; silver (troy oz; 1979) 2,259; petroleum products (1978) c. 1,750; electricity (kw-hr; 1979) c. 2,820,000.

tle credence; the strikers called for an end to the public-sector wage freeze as inflation rose to an unofficial level of 30%.

Political maneuvering increased as the 1982 presidential election approached. President Guzmán was not seeking reelection as the Partido Revolucionario Dominicano candidate; the nomination was won by Salvador Jorge Blanco, who opposed Guzmán in 1978. Joaquín Balaguer, president in the 1960s and 1970s, received the Partido Reformista nomination despite serious questions about his health and age.

In October the Dominican Republic failed to obtain special status as a sugar supplier to the U.S. The U.S. decision to place a tariff on sugar imports was expected to harm the Dominican Republic's economy at a time when prices for gold and coffee exports were also falling and the trade deficit was becoming acute.   (SARAH CAMERON)

Earth Sciences

GEOLOGY AND GEOCHEMISTRY

In honour of the centenary of the Geological Society of America in 1988, work was under way to publish some 20 volumes synthesizing the geology, geochemistry, geophysics, and mineral resources of the North American plate. Many scientists were collaborating to make maps and cross sections of the geology and structure of selected portions of the crust from continents right out to the ocean margins. This kind of cooperation illustrated a trend for the earth sciences to organize into interdisciplinary consortia, a trend fostered

by the new international Lithosphere Program, which was approved for the 1980s. Funding of the consortia programs would be more costly than the small science proposals of the past. The National Science Foundation reported in 1981 that research support, in real dollars, was not able to keep up with expanding U.S. research proposals.

Cocorp is a good example of a successful consortium program, with geophysical approaches solving geological problems. The project began in 1975 with application of the petroleum industry's exploration technique of seismic reflection profiling to study the deep crust and upper mantle. During the past seven years the project made profiles at 11 sites, from New England to the Rocky Mountains, mapping geological structures to depths as great as 50 km (30 mi). According to a recent report, comparison of data from all sites suggests that evolution of the continents is characterized not by lateral accretion of sedimentary rocks along continental margins but by thrusting and deposition of seafloor sediments onto the continents. The large-scale thin thrust sheets mapped in several mountain ranges were interpreted as a consequence of the stacking and shuffling of thin horizontal sheets of crustal material following the closure of an ocean basin and continental collision. Profiles for the southern Appalachian Mountains revealed layers of sedimentary material beneath an overthrust sheet of older, deformed crustal rocks. There was speculation that undiscovered deposits of oil and gas exist in the deep sedimentary layers, whose presence had been previously unsuspected.

If continental collision is followed by partial subduction of one continent beneath another, then the thin-skin thrusting of the near-surface sedi-

305

Earth Sciences

KEYSTONE

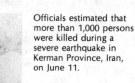

Officials estimated that more than 1,000 persons were killed during a severe earthquake in Kerman Province, Iran, on June 11.

Drama:
see Motion Pictures; Theatre

Dress:
see Fashion and Dress

Earthquakes:
see Earth Sciences

mentary rocks may be associated with the formation of continental crust of double thickness. Evidence from geology, mineralogy, thermodynamics, and experimental geochemistry combined recently to confirm that crustal doubling does occur. Granulites are metamorphosed rocks formed at great depths and subsequently elevated to the surface. Thermodynamic measurements made in the laboratory on the granulite minerals recently were formulated into a "geobarometer" for estimating depths of formation. Application of this geobarometer to granulites from four continents gave results indicting pressures of about eight kilobars, corresponding to a depth of burial of 35 km (22 mi). The granulites include rocks that could only have been formed as sediments on continental shelves, and continental collision followed by crustal doubling is the only plausible mechanism for burying such rocks by the thickness of the continental crust. Distribution of granulite terranes in continental interiors therefore may indicate earlier sites of continental collision, similar to the Himalayas of today.

The evolution of continents involves not only the reorganization of crustal material following continental collision but also the emplacement of new material from the Earth's interior as basaltic lava, most abundantly from the oceanic spreading centres, and as andesitic lava and granitic batholiths in or near continental margins. According to recent reviews of the geochemistry of andesites and batholiths, and of the experimentally determined high-pressure phase relationships of the known igneous rocks and their inferred sources at depth, the rocks are formed by complex, multistage processes involving material from more than one source rock. Still unresolved questions include the proportions of the magmas that are derived from the mantle and from preexisting continental crust and how these proportions have varied through time.

It has long been believed that the Earth's upper mantle is composed of peridotite and that basaltic magma is formed when this source rock is heated sufficiently to cause partial melting. This view was challenged by a proposal that within the peridotite there exists another layer of rock, eclogite, between the known seismic discontinuities at 220 km (136 mi) and 670 km (415 mi) depth. It was suggested that this layer formed early in the Earth's history when heat from meteoric bombardment melted the outer part of the Earth completely. As the magma cooled, crystal settling of garnet, pyroxene, and olivine produced the eclogite. Eclogite has the same composition as basalt, and according to the new hypothesis mid-ocean ridge basalts are produced by complete remelting of the eclogite, rather than by partial melting of peridotite, and are later returned to the Earth's interior via subduction zones. High pressure then converts the basalt into eclogite, which is so dense that it sinks further and settles into the perched eclogite layer within the mantle. This layer is a rock reservoir with geochemistry distinct from that of the peridotite above and below it, and the geochemistry of various basalts can be explained in terms of their derivation from these complementary reservoirs. This proposal would require careful reevaluation of geochemical data on trace elements and isotopes.

A team of U.K. and U.S. geologists continued their survey of the tectonic history of Antarctica with techniques that included aerial traverses with aircraft carrying magnetic and radar detection equipment. The radar beam penetrates the ice and is reflected by the rock surface below. Most igneous rocks are readily distinguished from sedimentary rocks by their magnetic properties. Recent results indicated that the Dufek intrusion of mafic rocks is much larger than previously thought. The igneous complex covers about 50,000 sq km (19,000 sq mi) and is exceeded in size only by the Bushveld Complex of South Africa, which is a rich source of minerals including platinum and chromium. The enormous volume of basaltic magma that differentiated to produce the Bushveld Complex rose from the Earth's mantle about 2,000,000,000 years ago, whereas the Dufek intrusion was emplaced fairly recently, as Antarctica separated from Africa 170 million years ago during breakup of the supercontinent of Gondwana.

Results published from the Deep Sea Drilling Project's exploration of the Blake Bahama Basin revealed that the early spreading rate of the North Atlantic Ocean was 3.76 cm (1.48 in) per year, almost twice the previously accepted rate of 2 cm (0.8 in) per year. The new rate is based on the age of the sediments covering the basaltic ocean basement, which at 155 million years are the oldest sediments yet recovered in the program. The hole, which was the second deepest ever drilled, reached 1,666.5 m (5,467 ft) below the abyssal seafloor under 4,970 m (16,300 ft) of water. These results showed that the major spreading associated with the beginning of the modern Atlantic Ocean occurred perhaps 20 million years later than previously thought, coinciding with the stratigraphic record of rapid widespread marine transgressions (spread of the sea over land areas) around the North Atlantic. The transgressions can be explained by abrupt subsidence of the rifted ocean margins, together with a worldwide rise in sea level caused by the fast-spreading North Atlantic Ridge. (See *Geophysics*, below.)

Scientists with the Greenland Ice Sheet Program recently completed drilling through 2,037 m (6,683 ft) of ice to bedrock. The ice core represents a time span of about 100,000 years. Study of the ratios of oxygen isotopes in the ice and of the bubbles of air trapped in the ice provides information about the Earth's prehistoric temperature and atmosphere. These studies reveal variations in global climate, which are used for projections on future climates. The geochemistry of dust particles within the ice provides information about volcanic activity vigorous enough to throw ash high into the atmosphere for distribution around the globe.

The high-resolution photographs returned by the U.S. space probe Voyager 2 provided a closer look at the geology of Saturn's moons than did Voyager 1. Tethys has the largest crater seen in the Saturnian system, about 400 km (250 mi) in diameter, and a canyon cutting across 270° of its surface. The canyon may have formed when frozen

water melted and froze again, splitting the surface as the ice expanded. Much of Enceladus is smoother than Saturn's other heavily cratered moons, indicating the occurrence of some process that erased the scars of the primordial bombardment. A small group of craters appears to have been cut in half by wind action. There is, in addition, much evidence for tectonic activity. A great fault system includes two faults offset by a third.

Between the rocky cores and atmospheres of hydrogen and helium of the outer giant planets there is believed to be a mantle, or "ice" layer, composed of water, ammonia, and methane. High-velocity particles fired into these materials in recent laboratory experiments produced shock waves, with results indicating that at the pressures and temperatures believed to exist in the mantles of Uranus and Neptune, the methane would dissociate into carbon and hydrogen. The carbon could form diamond crystals. Carbon amounts to an estimated 17% of the mass of Uranus and Neptune, and the prospect that this quantity of diamonds could sink down to form a dense layer on a rocky core is very intriguing.

A champion for the hypothesis that vast quantities of methane exist within the Earth's mantle maintained that the gas must have formed during accretion of the Earth from the solar nebula and argued that these deposits could be tapped and used as a vast energy source. Few geologists believed that conditions in the mantle are favourable for trapping vast deposits of methane, but the search continued for nonbiologically produced methane leaking through cracks and fissures in the crust. (PETER JOHN WYLLIE)

[133.C.3.b–d; 214.B.1.c; 214.B.1.e.ii; 241.D; 241.F–G]

GEOPHYSICS

Although no great earthquakes (magnitude 8.0 or greater) occurred in 1981, several large shocks were destructive. Two major earthquakes spaced less than two months apart rocked the Kerman region in southeastern Iran: one, of magnitude 6.8, on June 11 and the second, of magnitude 7.3, on July 28. Together they left more than 2,500 dead and many thousands homeless. Other destructive earthquakes included a shock in west Irian Province, Indonesia, on January 19, which resulted in more than 300 deaths and 1,000 injuries; one on January 23 in Sichuan (Szechwan) Province, China, which killed 150 and did extensive damage; and one on September 2 in northeastern Kashmir, which killed more than 200 persons. Additionally, beginning in February a series of small shocks occurred in Greece and resulted in at least 20 deaths.

The sociological repercussions of earthquake prediction were illustrated dramatically during the year. In May 1980 two U.S. government scientists, a seismologist and an expert in rock mechanics, predicted a sequence of increasingly large earthquakes culminating in the largest shock of the century in mid-September of 1981. All of them were to occur off the coast of Peru within 100–200 km (60–120 mi) of Lima. The assertiveness and persistence of their claims caused such concern in Lima that the Peruvian government asked the U.S. Geological Survey to convene its National Earth-

quake Prediction Evaluation Council. In January 1981 the council met to discuss a specific prediction for the first time since its formation and, after hearing two days of testimony by the two forecasters, concluded that the methodology and the predictions were essentially without merit. Subsequent events proved the council correct. A sequence of unique shocks that should have begun in June never materialized, and by late 1981 the area had exhibited only a normal level of activity. Nevertheless, apprehension in Peru was only partially assuaged by the official pronouncement of the council.

A phenomenon under surveillance since 1974 as a possible precursor of a large earthquake is the Palmdale Bulge in California. Annual fluctuation in elevation of as much as 200 mm (nearly 8 in) had been noted as far back as 1961. This astonishing movement naturally alerted seismologists, who subsequently made observations and measurements in the area for several years. No significant seismicity was correlated with the changes in elevation, and recent government and university studies noted the likelihood that large errors had been made in measurements. Thus the uplift may be smaller and less ominous than first thought.

Volcanic activity continued at a high level, although no major eruptions occurred. Mt. St. Helens remained active, behaving in a rather predictable manner and providing an excellent volcanological laboratory. The lava dome that had formed in the crater continued to grow, accompanied by minor explosions, tephra (solid matter) ejections, and lava intrusions. Other volcanoes active during the year were Pavlof in Alaska, Krafla and Hekla in Iceland, Etna in Sicily, Piton de la Fournaise on Réunion Island, Erebus in Antarctica, Semeru in Java, and Tarumai in Japan.

Major studies continued in the fields of geodesy, geodynamics, geomagnetism, plate tectonics, and the structure of the Earth's interior. With the advent of satellite geodesy, the Earth's gravitational field and the shape of the geoid could be determined with much greater accuracy. A recent re-

A technician monitors earthquakes in the vicinity of Mt. St. Helens, which began erupting again in April.

WIDE WORLD

port by a team of British scientists gave the latest and most accurate dimensions of the "pear-shaped" Earth. The conventional spheroidal profile is flattened so that the polar radii are 1/298.25 shorter than the equatorial radius. The new profile varies from the conventional in that the north polar radius is about 28 m (92 ft) shorter than that of the conventional spheroid profile. In addition, the radii from the Equator to about 60° S are longer and from the Equator to about 45° N are shorter than those of the regular spheroid. Gaps in the previous data were provided by the Soviet satellites Cosmos 248 and Cosmos 273. An accuracy of about 50 cm (20 in) was claimed for this model up to latitudes of 86°.

The U.S. National Science Foundation combined its proposed Ocean Margin Drilling Program with its very productive 14-year-old Deep Sea Drilling Project. But plans to replace the drilling ship "Glomar Challenger" with the larger, more powerful ex-salvage vessel "Glomar Explorer" tottered late in the year when a consortium of oil companies withdrew financial support. Meanwhile, the "Glomar Challenger" continued its mission with the launch of Leg 76 in the Gulf of Mexico in October 1980. Two holes were drilled, one on the Blake Outer Ridge, a feature that extends southeast like a spur from the continental shelf off northern Florida, and the other in the North American Basin at the latitude of central Florida. The first hole was drilled to learn more about a previously discovered seismic reflector and the second to explore a known magnetic anomaly zone.

Finally Leg 77, comprising eight holes at six sites, was completed in the Gulf of Mexico. Evidence of drowned carbonate platforms and thick talus deposits were found. Potential oil-source beds deposited between 120 million and 100 million years ago also were discovered. The objective of the cruise was to test the concepts of the evolution of the Gulf, which is believed by some scientists to have originated by seafloor spreading in the same manner as the North Atlantic Basin. Drilling on Leg 77 confirmed this view to a degree but revealed some unexpected detail that would force changes in the model. (RUTLAGE J. BRAZEE)

[211.B; 212.D.4; 213.B; 241.G.3]

HYDROLOGY

A prolonged drought and consequent water shortage plagued a large part of the U.S. from September 1980 to April 1981. The combined flow of that nation's "big five" rivers—the Mississippi, St. Lawrence, Ohio, Columbia, and Missouri—was 12% below normal in 1981. Streamflow, lake levels, and shallow groundwater levels approached or reached record lows in many regions of the Northeast and South. Drought-emergency delarations were issued by the governors of Pennsylvania, New Jersey, and New York, and several communities in New Jersey, Pennsylvania, and Connecticut experienced water-supply shortages and placed restrictions on water use. In late 1980 the saltwater front in the estuarine section of the Delaware River migrated upstream to a point only 2.4 km (1.5 mi) downstream from Camden, N.J., and threatened saltwater contamination of the city's water supply. In southern and central Florida many lakes, wells, and streams were reported at or near their lowest levels. In central Florida sinkholes suddenly appeared because of declining groundwater levels.

During the year several symposia concentrated on topics of current hydrologic interest. The Geological Society of America held a symposium in Cincinnati, Ohio, on subsurface hydrology, hydrology of disposal sites for high-level nuclear wastes, and regional hydrology. An international conference on hydrology and the scientific bases

A bulging lava dome in the crater of Mt. St. Helens was photographed in September.

WIDE WORLD

As underground water was pumped from deep watertables in Florida, sinkholes resulted. This one swallowed a house and several vehicles.

for management of water resources was convened by UNESCO and the World Meteorological Organization in Paris. The conference, which was attended by representatives of 100 nations, evaluated progress and laid further plans for UNESCO's International Hydrological Program. Water utilities, industry, consultants, federal and state organizations, and universities jointly sponsored a symposium in Washington, D.C., entitled "Water Reuse in the Future." This conference was held because of current interest in policy, regulations on water-quality standards, and health effects relating to wastewater discharges. Its program emphasized water recycling, pollution control, and water policy.

The U.S. Geological Survey recently established a National Water-Use Information Program to complement existing data on the availability and quality of that nation's water resources. Its computerized National Water-Use Data System had the participation of 49 states and would contain information for 12 categories of use summarized by counties within each state and by river basins. The program would aid in defining how much fresh and saline surface water and groundwater is withdrawn and for what purposes, how much water is consumed, and how much water is returned.

Two Canadian-U.S. Great Lakes study boards completed their assignments. The International Lake Erie Regulation Study Board finished an investigation of the possibility of partial regulation of the water level of Lake Erie and concluded that it would not be economically feasible. The International Great Lakes Diversions and Consumptive Uses Study Board studied the effect that water use would have on the water levels of the lakes, the

flow in the connecting channels, and the St. Lawrence River. It concluded that future consumption would be considerably greater than had been estimated previously.　　　　(JOHN E. MOORE)

[222.A.2.b; 222.D.; 355.D.5.a.ii; 355.D.5.d.iii]

METEOROLOGY

Beginning in the 1960s the civilized world annually spent more than $2 billion evaluating, reporting, predicting, modifying, and researching weather and climate and related atmospheric entities. A total of 154 countries operated national meteorological services. More than 10,000 weather stations made observations or measurements at least four times every day and telecommunicated the data to mapping and analysis centres. Added to these were the hundreds of thousands of climatological observers who recorded air temperatures and precipitation and reported weekly or monthly by mail. Hundreds of ships at sea, aircraft in flight, and radar and radiosonde stations reported their observations, and orbiting satellites telemetered viable atmospheric data. This vast global system was designed to give comprehensive knowledge of atmosphere and weather with its kaleidoscopic variations, information needed for man's multitude of pursuits.

National regions of the worldwide system were operated and administered by individual governments, whereas overall cooperation and coordination were the responsibility of the UN World Meteorological Organization (WMO) in Geneva. In all but a few of the 149 member nations and five member territories of WMO, daily weather reporting and forecasting services were functions of government, and in many there were laws pro-

hibiting these services by private parties. By contrast the U.S. and Canada, among a few, encouraged active work outside government in all branches of meteorology.

In 1981 the Soviet Union's hydrometeorological establishment was the world's largest, but in overall development and use of meteorology throughout the economic and social structure, the U.S. was foremost. The American Meteorological Society (AMS) with its many professional meetings and projects including workshops every year was an aggressive promoter. The research initiative and scientific qualifications of the faculties of more than 30 major U.S. universities provided world leadership in the atmospheric and geophysical sciences. In the U.S. some 300 consulting meteorologists certified by the AMS and about 250 radio and TV broadcasters encouraged public awareness of meteorology in all of its aspects.

Fewer destructive weather events occurred in 1981 than in most years. Rainfall was deficient in many localities and in a few large regions, but droughts other than in normally arid lands were more tolerable than in the past. Freakish exceptions were those in Florida, where brushfires in the dry Everglades fed spreading blazes for weeks and dehydration in the limestone substructure caused sinking of upper layers of soil in a few places and made huge sinkholes. Low waters in rivers led to water-use restrictions in several states and contamination of drinking water locally in central Virginia. More serious were acid rains over large sections in Canada and New England downwind from the greater Detroit and Pittsburgh industrial factories, whose airborne emissions were believed to acidify lakes and land soil, thereby killing fish and plant life.

New evidence of impending damage to the protective ozone layer in the upper atmosphere was found in research by the U.S. National Aeronautics and Space Administration; other studies confirmed an increase in carbon dioxide in the air. Both ozone and carbon dioxide are vital to the Earth's present climate and weather, and their quantities are critical. How subtle changes in these gases might affect life was yet another unknown

among complex meteorological problems that needed to be solved.

Another anomaly of 1981 was the Janus-like influence of the Bermuda high on the consequences of hurricanes for North American coastal regions. The Azores-Bermuda semipermanent area of high barometric pressure did not extend westward as far as usual. This development enabled hurricanes to curve northward into the open Atlantic before reaching the U.S. East Coast. Consequently, even though these tropical cyclones were more numerous than in most years, they caused little damage. Their seaward paths, however, deprived the eastern U.S. of the rainfall usually brought by storms from the tropics. In addition, the curtailed Bermuda high failed to produce the usual warm, humid summer winds, thus giving much of the eastern U.S. the mildest August in many years. Cyclone Norma in October was an exception. It brought torrential rains to northern Mexico and Texas. Destructive floods engulfed buildings and resulted in loss of life after 40–50 cm (15–20 in) of rain fell within a few days.

In the Far East typhoons also were fewer than in most years. Two severe ones, however, hit Japan during the summer.   (F. W. REICHELDERFER)

[224.B.3.b; 224.C.1 and 4; 224.D.2.c.iii]

OCEANOGRAPHY

From April through July 1981, U.S. scientists from six universities and government laboratories studied a 100-km (60-mi) stretch of the Pacific coastal ocean between California's Point Reyes and Punta Arenas. An array of moorings anchored at depths from a few tens of metres near the coast to about 130 metres (400 feet) at a distance of 40 km (25 mi) from the coast supported current meters, temperature and pressure recorders, and surface-wind gauges during those four months. Meanwhile, ships crisscrossing the region measured temperature, salinity, and surface currents, and aircraft tracked surface floats (to outline surface flow) and measured near-surface winds and surface temperature. Radar studies of the way in which currents move waves were carried out to improve the mapping of surface currents, and infrared images

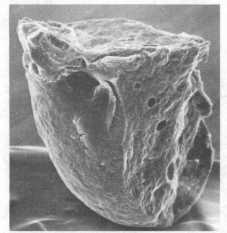 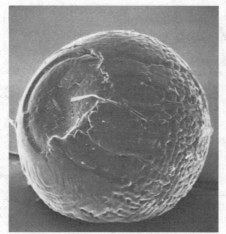 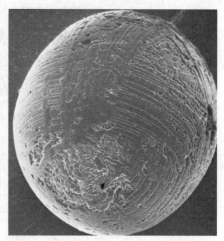

of the sea surface (which map sea-surface temperatures) were gathered from satellites.

The experiment was scheduled for a time when winds along the California coast generally blow toward the Equator. Because of the Earth's rotation, these winds move surface waters offshore so that deep waters must upwell at the coast. The upwelled water is high in nutrients, making the region rich in life and marine resources. One aim of this Coastal Ocean Dynamics Experiment (CODE) was to learn what part of the observed upwelling is due to local winds and what part is due to other factors, as well as which patterns of wind and nearshore current are well correlated and which are not. The fieldwork also tested new instruments and measurement techniques.

At the end of the year most of the data were still under analysis, but several new facts emerged early. Offshore surface winds over the CODE array are distributed in such complicated spatial patterns that simple coastal observations of the wind may give a very misleading picture of the winds that actually drive the sea. Satellite-obtained infrared images of the CODE region showed long streamers of cold water and fronts (regions across which temperature changes abruptly) extending seaward from very near the coast out well beyond the CODE area. Surface floats tracked by aircraft showed that strong currents are associated with these features of the surface temperature field. It thus can be concluded that satellite images tell a great deal about how water, nutrients, and pollutants leave the coastal ocean and enter the deep sea. Full results of this study were expected in 1982.

According to the theory of plate tectonics, seafloor crust is extruded from mid-ocean ridges and spreads laterally as a global system of surprisingly rigid crustal plates. In the early 1970s scientists realized that the depth to which a point on the seafloor has sunk since extrusion depends only on its age, the time since extrusion. The reason is that crustal material cools as it spreads and therefore contracts. Consequently, the amount of heat conducted upward through the crust should be greatest at the ridges, the centres of spreading, and should decrease away from them. In fact, however, conductive heat flow is quite low at spreading centres. The discrepancy indicated that heat must

be carried out of mid-ocean ridges by seawater, which percolates through the overlying sediments into the crustal material, is heated, and then rises at spreading centres, where it returns to the ocean through hot-water vents. In recent years such vents were discovered directly along the East Pacific Rise, a spreading centre west of South America. During 1981, scientists continued to study hydrothermal vents in the Pacific. Their observations, as well as further analysis of earlier observations, led to new conclusions regarding the importance of these vents and of the hydrothermal circulation for the oceans.

Hydrothermal vents are evidently major sources of helium (He). The fact that helium from the Earth's mantle is some ten times richer in the isotope ^{3}He than is atmospheric helium makes it possible to trace, by isotopic analysis of water samples, the path taken by mantle-produced helium as it moves through the Pacific away from the East Pacific Rise. Very high concentrations of ^{3}He were found just over the rise, evidently indicating the existence of as yet undiscovered systems of vents. These high concentrations extend more than 2,000 km (1,200 mi) to the west of the rise (as far as measurements were made) but scarcely at all to the east. This pattern provides a clear indication of the flow of the ocean at the depth (2,000–3,000 m, or 6,600–9,800 ft) at which the ^{3}He is concentrated. Extension of such studies into other oceans could yield unique information on mid-depth and deep-ocean circulation.

Observations during the year along the East Pacific Rise provided further examples of communities of bottom-living marine organisms (such as giant clams, crabs, and tube worms) that apparently obtain their nutrients ultimately from the mineral-rich water coming from the vents. It was suggested that leaching of the metals from the crust, which occurs as water percolates through it, followed by discharge of this water into the sea is a major source of some of the metals found in seawater as well as an important process in the deposition of metal ores in earlier geologic times.

(MYRL C. HENDERSHOTT)

[223.C; 241.G.3; 723.G.4.b; 738.B]

See also Disasters; Energy; Life Sciences; Mining and Quarrying; Space Exploration; Speleology.

Seafloor sediments contain quantities of microscopic iron and stony spherules (centre and right) that according to conventional theory originate as molten droplets shed from meteors entering the Earth's atmosphere. A recent British study, which compared their shape, texture, and composition with those of meteorites, including the crust fragment at left, concluded instead that the spherules first form in space in the asteroid belt from "sparks" thrown off when asteroids collide. The particles eventually rain down on the Earth as part of the general dust in interplanetary space.

312

Economy, World

Although economic growth in the large developed countries of the Organization for Economic Cooperation and Development (OECD) was only 1.3% during 1980, by the end of that year there were some tentative signs of a gentle acceleration in the underlying trend. Coupled with still high levels of inflation, this encouraged most OECD governments to formulate their economic strategies for 1981 on the basis of continued tight monetary policies. Confirmed monetarists such as British Prime Minister Margaret Thatcher needed little encouragement to do this, but other governments took the view that the anticipated recovery in demand not only reinforced the need for tough anti-inflationary policies but also, perhaps even more important, made them politically more acceptable.

By the end of 1981, however, it was clear that earlier expectations of an acceleration in growth were largely misplaced. Although there were significant differences among the countries, by late spring the "recovery" appeared to have run out of steam. Thus, in the U.S. the first quarter's remarkably buoyant growth was followed by a drop in gross national product (GNP), while in Japan official concern over the weakness of domestic demand led in March to the appearance of a modest package of measures supporting business. Nevertheless, although most governments made some policy adjustments to deal with the weaker than expected trend, the outcome for the whole OECD for

CHART 1

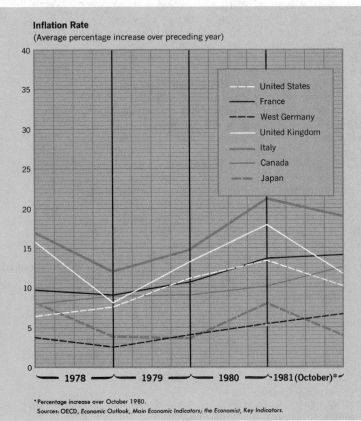

Inflation Rate
(Average percentage increase over preceding year)

*Percentage increase over October 1980.
Sources: OECD, Economic Outlook, Main Economic Indicators; the Economist, Key Indicators.

Table I. Real Gross Domestic Products of Selected OECD Countries
% change, seasonally adjusted at annual rates

Country	Average 1969–79	1979	1980	1981*
Canada	4.2	3.4	1.2	2.50†
France	4.0	3.2	1.3	...
West Germany	3.2	4.6	1.8	−1.25†
Italy	3.3	2.9	0.1	−0.75†
Japan	5.4	5.5	4.2	3.50†
United Kingdom	2.2	0.9	−1.8	−1.50†
United States	2.9	2.4	−0.2	25.00†
Total major countries	3.5	3.4	1.2	1.25†
Australia	4.6	4.4	2.7	5.75
Austria	4.3	5.1	3.6	−0.75
Belgium	3.5	2.4	1.4	−0.50
Denmark	2.8	3.5	−1.0	...
Finland	3.7	7.2	5.3	2.25
Greece	5.3	3.8	0.6	1.00
Ireland	3.9	1.9	1.0	1.75
Netherlands, The	3.5	2.2	0.8	−0.50
New Zealand	2.9	1.0	2.7	2.75
Norway	4.5	4.5	3.7	0.50
Spain	4.1	0.8	1.7	2.00
Sweden	2.3	4.0	1.4	0.75
Switzerland	1.4	2.2	3.2	1.50
Total OECD countries	4.3	3.3	1.3	1.25†

*Estimate. †GNP.
Sources: Adapted from OECD, Economic Outlook, July 1981; National Institute of Economic Review; EIU estimates.

1981 was estimated to be a gross domestic product (GDP) gain of only 1.3%, the same as in the previous year. Inflation, however, recorded a further slowdown from 12.8% to some 11%, although it was not clear whether this was the result of the policies pursued or the gradual fading away of the effects of the 1979 oil price shock. The level of unemployment, however, rose everywhere. In the first half of 1981 the OECD total stood at more than 23.5 million, compared with 22.5 million in the second half of 1980, and the latest available figures suggested that the corresponding figure in the second half of 1981 was approximately 25 million.

Although most countries looked upon a further cutback in inflation as their major task, there were some significant differences in the policies pursued. As in the preceding year, on the deflationary (but none too successful) extreme stood Britain's Thatcher, who was joined by the newly elected Pres. Ronald Reagan of the U.S. when he unveiled his economic package in March. By contrast, the least deflationary position was adopted by the Japanese authorities, who became increasingly concerned with the weakness of domestic demand. Somewhere in the middle were West Germany's policymakers, while, in the case of France, a reasonably strict monetary approach gave way to Keynesian policies halfway through the year, following the election of François Mitterrand to the presidency and the subsequent election of a Socialist government.

In view of the different positions adopted by governments, it was not surprising that economic growth rates varied widely from country to country. As in 1980, the United Kingdom was heading for the largest drop in the volume of GDP, although, rather uncharacteristically, West Germany's estimated fall of 1% was not far behind. Italy, Austria, and The Netherlands were also thought to have had negative growth rates, but France, which started off poorly but became more buoyant as Mitterrand's policies were developed, was es-

Leaders of the major industrialized democracies posed for an official photograph during an economic conference, held at the Chateau Montebello near Ottawa in July.

timated to have recorded a growth of 1–1.5%. In the U.S. the likely outcome for the year was a GDP growth of 2%, largely the consequence of the good growth of the first few months of the year and in sharp contrast to the increasingly recessionary trend that developed late in the year as a result of President Reagan's monetarist policies. Once again, the Japanese economy outperformed that of most other OECD countries with a GDP gain of some 4–4.5%. In spite of this, Japan managed a significant drop in inflation from 8 to 5%. Although this was surpassed in the U.K., where consumer prices rose by some 12% as against 18% in the preceding year, a number of other countries, such as France and West Germany, failed to record any slowdown. In the U.S. it was estimated that the rate of inflation for 1981 would be 10.5%, compared with 13.5% in the preceding year.

During 1981 most OECD countries attempted to weaken inflationary tendencies by restrictive monetary policies and a reduction in budget deficits. Thus, with the exception of Japan, where the already low discount rate of 7.25% was reduced by one percentage point in March, interest rates were generally high. In the U.S. the Federal Reserve Board (Fed) raised the discount rate in May and ensured that prime rates were high, at times even hitting the 20% mark, until the final few months of the year. Partly in response to the U.S. example, both West Germany and the United Kingdom felt compelled to pursue a relatively high interest rate policy for much of 1981, although by the end of the year rates in those countries were on a gently falling trend. Coupled with high interest rates was a general reduction in the target growth of the money supply, although—largely because of difficulties of accurate measurement and interpretation

—the use of monetary aggregates for economic policymaking and control came in for growing criticism.

The other major strand in official policies was the desire to reduce budget deficits by cutting back public expenditure and raising extra revenue. Virtually all governments formulated their policies on this basis, and nearly all of them seemed likely to miss their targets by a significant margin. Once again Japan was the exception, not because it managed to balance the budget—on the contrary it faced a large deficit that was a source of growing concern to the authorities—but because it accepted the belief that the deficit could not be significantly reduced in the short term. In most other countries, however, performance in this field came as a disappointment. In the U.K. the government felt it necessary to levy additional taxation but still failed to reach its targets; in West Germany the revised budget deficit for 1981 was well above the previous year's figure; and in the U.S. even President Reagan's new package provided for a smaller reduction in taxation and a larger deficit than originally estimated. Once again, therefore, governments overestimated their ability to reduce the size and scope of their bureaucracies, and in some countries, notably the U.K., policymakers seemed oblivious to the fact that deflation causes higher unemployment, which leads in turn to greatly increased spending on social welfare.

The year under review witnessed sharp movements in exchange rates, which introduced additional complications for most governments. The outstanding feature of the year was the sharp recovery in the value of the U.S. dollar. Partly because of the level of U.S. interest rates, the effective rate of the dollar against a representative basket of

major currencies rose from 94 in 1980 to about 109 in 1981, the highest level since the current index was started in 1975. The U.S. dollar did particularly well against European currencies such as the Deutsche Mark, the French franc, the Dutch guilder, the pound sterling, and even the Swiss franc. Although the performance of those countries against one another varied, the trend of exchange rates was a major problem for most of them, especially given their commitment to cut back inflation. The effective rate of sterling fell from 96.1 in 1980 to some 90, although this was not altogether unwelcome since, by improving the competitiveness of British exports, it strengthened export demand and helped to take some of the slack generated by the government's deflationary policies. Sweden devalued the krona by 10% in September, and France, facing considerable uncertainty on the foreign exchange markets as a result of the policies announced by the new Socialist government, was forced to devalue the franc by 8.8% against the mark in the autumn. In Japan a steady weakening in the value of the yen took place during the year; this was largely responsible for a spectacular upsurge in exports and renewed complaints about Japan's aggressive trade policies.

On the foreign trade and payments front most OECD countries did better than in 1980. Relatively sluggish demand, coupled with the high price of oil, had a depressive effect on their imports. At the same time, because of the weakening of their currencies (except in the U.S.) and the growing import demand coming from oil-producing countries, exports rose strongly, with the result that the net foreign trade position recorded a significant improvement from the previous year. This was carried through into the current account, and at the end of 1981 the current account deficit for the OECD, which was estimated at some $70 billion for 1980, had been cut back to $30 billion–$40 billion. Once again the most spectacular turnaround was recorded by Japan, which managed to transform an $11 billion deficit into a surplus of some $6 billion–$7 billion. The U.S. seemed to have achieved a somewhat larger surplus than the $4 billion recorded in 1980, while in the U.K. the outcome appeared to be a surplus of $9 billion as against $7 billion the year before. All other major OECD countries were likely to have registered current account deficits for 1981, although all but Italy improved on the previous year.

The less developed countries turned in a fairly poor performance in 1981. Although only partial figures were available at the year's end, the indications were that economic growth slowed to about 4%. Non-oil producing countries were affected by the weakness of primary commodity prices, while the oil producers faced a greatly reduced demand for oil in the wake of the 1979 price increase. Although some price stabilization measures were introduced, these were expected to be only partially successful. In the non-oil less developed countries the 1981 inflation rate was anticipated at 28%, although oil producers were expected to do significantly better. By and large, oil producers achieved a strong external trade and payments position despite weaker demand for oil, but the external balances of the non-oil nations deteriorated, with an estimated deficit of $100 billion.

NATIONAL ECONOMIC POLICIES

Developed Market Economies. UNITED STATES. The year 1981 witnessed the unveiling of a radical approach to economic management in the U.S. by the newly elected President Reagan. In many ways the president's strategy was likened to the equally radical economic policy adopted two years earlier by Prime Minister Thatcher. The aim of the policy was to revitalize the U.S. economy with a combination of large tax cuts and lower public spending, reinforced by tight restrictions on monetary growth. Thus, the simultaneous goals of the new administration were a reduction in the inflation rate and a boost to economic output. The intrinsic contradiction in these twin goals, which was glossed over by the promoters of the program, became acutely evident later in the year. As 1981 drew to a close, the prospects of a balanced budget by 1984 vanished, as did the last remaining illusions that the recession would be brief and would be followed by a vigorous rebound early in 1982. The onset of the steep recession was greeted with a mixed reaction both in the U.S. and abroad. That it enabled the high interest rates to fall was good news, but a downswing in the world's largest economy when the rest of the world was hoping for a stronger international environment to assist in their own economic recovery was, without doubt, bad news.

The surprising burst of activity in the second half of 1980, which reversed the previous sharp

CHART 2

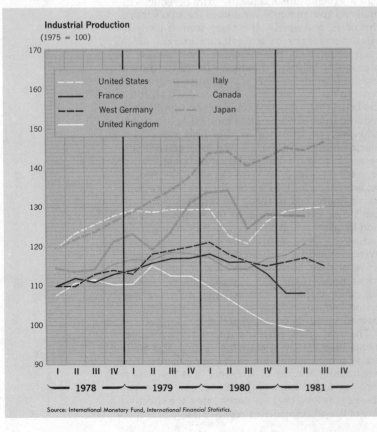

Industrial Production
(1975 = 100)

United States
France
West Germany
United Kingdom
Italy
Canada
Japan

1978 1979 1980 1981

Source: International Monetary Fund, *International Financial Statistics.*

mini-recession, continued into 1981. The rise in real GNP in the first quarter was an astonishing 8.4%, which was much faster than in the previous two quarters (3.8 and 2.4%, respectively). Most of the unexpected strength came from higher consumer expenditures and increased exports. However, as financially overextended consumers reduced their savings ratios to a level much lower than usual, the economy weakened. The economic statistics for the second quarter, issued in August, confirmed the pessimistic message of the leading indicators. The loss in momentum was quite substantial, and GNP fell by 1.6% in real terms. A steep fall in the sales of durable goods, automobiles in particular; a decline in the housing market; weakening exports; and a lower level of government purchases were the main causes.

In spite of a slight recovery in consumer spending, the downward trend continued into the third quarter. Although the rate of decline of real GNP was less steep at 0.6%, a number of features, such as falling employment, sluggish consumer demand, and lower industrial output, indicated that it was premature to regard this as a harbinger of recovery. Persistently high interest rates, which resulted from the Fed's tight monetary policy aimed at curbing inflation, was seen by many economic observers as a major cause of the deepening recession. The final quarter was expected to show a decline of 4–5% in real GNP. Thus, overall real economic growth during 1981 was likely to be no more than 2%. More significantly, the downswing was predicted to continue into the next year.

Employment was on a rising trend through the autumn and winter of 1980–81, but it reached a plateau in the spring and went into reverse in the summer. The official unemployment rate, seasonally adjusted, was 7.3% in February, March, and April, compared with 7.5% during the previous November. In May 1981 it rose to 7.6%, but after a dip in the summer it shot up to reach 8.9% in December; at such a rate the number out of work totaled about nine million. The winter peak was widely expected to touch 9.5% as the recession deepened.

The inflation rate buckled under the combined weight of a persistent limitation of money supply and the gathering forces of a full-blown recession. Consumer prices rose at an annual rate of 9.6% during the first quarter but slowed appreciably to 7.4% in the second. However, the improvement came to a temporary halt during the late summer as the record interest rates added to housing costs and increased business costs. This, to some extent, was counterbalanced by the lower cost of imports, thanks to the strength of the dollar. By October the downward trend was resumed. The month-to-month increase was only 0.4%, and it was accompanied by the cheerful news of an 8% drop in the durable goods index. Other measures of inflation, such as the GNP implicit price deflator, also followed a downward trend, enabling the policymakers to claim, with some justification, that the prospects for a sustained slower inflation had been greatly improved.

The monetary policy of the Fed was directed toward bringing inflation down from an annual

WIDE WORLD

rate of about 9–10% in late 1980 to somewhere in the region of 7.5% in 1981 through restrictions in money supply. Accordingly, the target ranges for the expansion of money aggregates were tightened from 3.5–6% to 3.5–5.5% for M1A (currency plus demand deposits) and from 4–6.5% to 3–6.5% for M1B (M1A plus "other checkable deposits such as negotiable orders of withdrawal"). Against this background of tighter money supply targets and buoyant economic conditions, in the beginning of 1981 money growth expanded below the target range, enabling short-term interest rates to fall from the dizzy heights of the previous November and December. The Federal Funds rate, for instance, dropped from nearly 21 to 17%. However, the overall cautious attitude of the Fed changed aggressively in May when it became clear that monetary expansion was accelerating rapidly. The discount rate was raised from 13 to 14% in order to discourage bank borrowing. This triggered an upward climb in interest rates, taking the prime rate to over 20% in a space of six weeks.

During the summer and early autumn the Fed kept the monetary reins tight, partly to demonstrate its determination to keep the inflationary pressures at bay, while President Reagan steadily retreated from his pledge of reducing the budget deficit to zero by 1984. The Fed's other concern was to avoid volatile interest rates as in 1980. Not surprisingly, it came under growing criticism from economic and financial observers for being too rigid and keeping interest rates unnecessarily high when the money supply growth during the summer and early autumn expanded well below the lower end of the target range. Moderating inflation and the deepening recession strengthened the case of the critics.

Eventually, interest rates started their descent in October when the Fed eased the pressure on the financial markets by supplying extra funds to the credit system. This did not, however, indicate a departure from the basic counterinflationary stance; the Fed was simply compensating for the earlier undershooting of some of the monetary aggregates. In December the discount rate was down

Rumours in October that the French franc was about to be devalued brought crowds of Parisians and tourists to currency exchanges.

Table II. Percentage Changes in Consumer Prices in Selected OECD Countries

Country	Average 1961–70	Average 1971–76	1978	1979	1980	Latest month* 1981
Canada	2.7	7.5	9.0	9.1	21.2	12.6
France	4.0	9.0	9.1	10.8	13.6	14.1
West Germany	2.7	5.6	2.7	4.1	5.5	6.7
Italy	3.9	13.1	12.1	14.8	10.1	19.0
Japan	5.8	10.7	3.8	3.6	8.0	4.0
United Kingdom	4.1	13.9	8.3	13.4	18.0	11.7
United States	2.8	6.6	7.7	11.3	13.5	10.2
Australia	2.5	10.8	7.9	9.1	9.9	9.0
Austria	3.6	7.0	3.6	3.7	6.4	7.0
Belgium	3.0	8.3	4.5	4.5	6.6	7.8
Denmark	5.9	9.5	10.0	9.6	12.3	12.0
Finland	5.0	12.2	7.8	7.5	11.6	11.4
Greece	2.1	12.4	12.6	19.0	24.9	23.7
Iceland	11.9	26.5	44.9	44.1	57.5	49.7
Ireland	4.8	14.0	7.6	13.3	18.2	20.1
Luxembourg	2.6	7.5	3.1	4.5	6.3	9.4
Netherlands, The	4.1	8.3	4.1	4.2	6.5	7.5
New Zealand	3.8	11.3	12.0	13.8	17.1	15.5
Norway	4.5	8.6	8.1	4.8	10.9	13.5
Portugal	3.9	17.6	22.6	23.6	16.6	23.6
Spain	6.0	14.6	19.8	15.7	15.5	14.1
Sweden	4.0	8.8	10.0	7.2	13.7	11.3
Switzerland	3.3	5.9	1.1	3.6	4.0	7.5
Turkey	5.9	19.5	61.9	63.5	94.3	33.0
Total OECD countries	3.4	8.6	7.7	9.9	12.8	10.8

*Twelve-month rate of change (not directly comparable with annual changes).
Sources: OECD, *Economic Outlook*, July 1981; OECD, *Main Economic Indicators*; The Economist, *Key Indicators*.

to 12% and the prime rate to 15½%. Nevertheless, many economic analysts took the view that, if the Fed strictly adhered to its newly announced target for monetary expansion of 2½–5½% during 1982, economic growth would remain sluggish. The upswing expected in the second half of 1982 would quickly lead to higher interest rates than those experienced in 1981, choking off economic recovery before it had a chance to gather momentum.

While monetary policy was in the front line of day-to-day economic management in the fight against inflation, fiscal policy aimed at shifting the economic growth rate to a higher level in the medium term while maintaining an overall restrictive stance. The economic program of President Reagan announced in March had the following four basic components: a stringent budgetary policy, an incentive taxation policy, a regulatory reform program, and support for the counterinflationary policy of the Fed. By far the most radical aspect of the program was a proposed 30% reduction in personal income tax rates over the next three years (10% in each year) starting in July 1981. As part of the tax reform package a more generous depreciation allowance for business investment was proposed. The rationale of the tax reforms was that they would provide a greater incentive for individuals to work, save, and invest. Similarly, the business sector would respond by increasing output to meet the higher demand.

The other major strand of the program was a sharp decline in the growth of federal spending with a view to achieving a balanced budget in fiscal 1984. This entailed reducing the fiscal 1981–82 deficit to $45 billion and that of 1982–83 to $22.9 billion. Although defense spending was scheduled to rise, proposed spending reductions elsewhere were spread widely, affecting all classes of society —except the "truly needy"—and all sectors of the economy.

The impact of the program during fiscal 1981 (ended September 1981) was marginal, partly be-

cause of the nature of the budgetary process in the U.S. and partly because the personal tax cuts in 1981 were delayed until October (originally July). Furthermore, the proposed 10% cut was reduced to 5%. The net effect during 1981–82 was a modest $6 billion stimulus, mostly through tax cuts that were not fully matched by expenditure savings.

Having skillfully engineered the passage of his spending and tax cuts through Congress, President Reagan then encountered a credibility crisis on the financial markets. The budget arithmetic, which, when simplified, provided for $90 billion of additional defense spending over the next three years plus $280 billion in tax cuts, matched by only $130 billion in spending cuts, did not augur well for a balanced budget by 1984. The markets feared that higher deficits would cause interest rates to stay high and that in consequence economic growth would be sluggish. The possibility of further spending cuts or reversal of the tax cuts already enacted was thought to be highly unlikely. Therefore, panic set in, and the Dow Jones industrial average, which stood at 950 in early August, fell headlong to 840—the lowest level in 16 months —in a space of four weeks, dragging down the other major stock markets with it.

The ad hoc nature of the additional $16 billion spending cuts proposed by the president to bring the 1981–82 deficit back on target failed initially to impress the markets. In the autumn, however, as the economy rapidly slid into a recession and interest rates fell, the financial markets' concern about the size of the budget deficit subsided. They appeared to be reconciled to the view that even if the projected deficit for 1981–82 were $60 billion, a realistic estimate, as a proportion of GNP it was less than half the peak levels of 1975 and 1976, when it reached 5%. Also, because of the recession a wider budget deficit was thought to be more suitable than further spending cuts.

JAPAN. The Japanese economy performed somewhat unevenly in 1980 and, although the year as a whole recorded a volume growth of some 4%, the final quarter produced a disappointing gain of only 0.5%. Not surprisingly, 1981 began on a note of uncertainty with business circles predicting growth that was below the projections suggested by the government. Nearly 12 months later, and on the basis of still incomplete figures, it seemed that much of the initial skepticism by businessmen was justified. This was only partly because the volume of GDP was heading for a smaller annual gain than originally forecast by the authorities (4–4.5% as against 5.3% for fiscal 1981); another, and potentially more worrying, variance from plan was to be found in the source and composition of the increase in GDP.

Thus, at the start of the year official expectations were that the strength of domestic demand would be the major expansionary force in the economy, with external demand providing little more than a marginal stimulus. However, with some figures for the first nine months available, it seemed that most principal components of domestic demand remained sluggish and that it was only the unexpectedly rapid growth of exports that produced a respectable gain in GDP. Thus, in late 1981 it was

estimated that, of the anticipated gain in GDP of 4.5%, about two-thirds would be produced by the external sector. This was regarded as an unsatisfactory outcome, largely because the inevitable consequence was a huge increase in Japan's trade and external payments surplus that threatened to spark off another "trade war" with its major trading partners. On the credit side, however, wages remained well under control, with the "spring wage offensive" yielding an average increase of 7.5% (compared with 7% in 1980), and there was a further slowdown in the rate of inflation.

During 1980 wholesale prices were still affected by the large increase in oil prices and rose by 13%, but even on the basis of some unfavourable assumptions for the closing months, 1981 was unlikely to have yielded more than an average gain of 4%. Similarly, a cautious estimate on the basis of the available figures was for retail price inflation of 5% for the entire year, compared with nearly 8% in 1980. Thus, while the year's performance could not be regarded as entirely satisfactory, Japan remained true to form in that it outperformed most comparable developed countries as well as the OECD group as a whole.

Unlike Britain, where the authorities started off the year by putting more deflation into an already deflated economy, Japan attempted to boost the level of domestic activity. Reacting to the somewhat weak keynote of late 1980, the authorities announced another, seven-point, business-stimulating package in March 1981. The most important feature of this was a reduction in the Bank of Japan's discount rate from 7.25 to 6.25%, the third cut in nine months. Coupled with this was a reduction in the bank's reserve requirement ratio and a significant easing of the limits placed on the volume of lending by commercial banks. At the same time a substantial proportion of the public works planned for fiscal 1981 were brought forward into the first half of the year, and the lending activities of the government's Housing Finance Corporation were stepped up in an attempt to assist the small building companies.

By early summer it looked as if the measures, and the resulting improvement in business confidence, were having the desired effect. Mining/ manufacturing production, which remained on a plateau between January and April and went into a sharp reverse in May, picked up strongly in June and the following months. The index of producers' shipments was also pointing in an upward direction, and the level of inventories, which was rising quite sharply only a few months earlier, was registering a falling trend. All in all, demand appeared to be getting stronger and, despite the less than buoyant note of construction starts and retail sales, the Ministry of International Trade and Industry declared that the "recession" was at an end.

In the light of this and similarly optimistic assessments the publication of the GDP figures for the April–June quarter came as something of a disappointment. Although the annualized gain was 5%, which represented a marginal improvement over the preceding three months, the detailed figures pointed to a sustained weakness in the domestic sector. Thus, private consumption grew

by only 0.5%, and plant and equipment investment recorded a decline for the first time since the end of 1976. Public spending was also sluggish, with the result that domestic demand managed only a 1.5% annualized increase. As in the preceding quarter, the main impetus came from foreign trade: exports rose at an annual rate of some 32%. The main reason for the upsurge in overseas shipments was the sizable decline in the external value of the yen (from an average of 203 yen to the dollar in the final quarter of 1980 to 226 yen in the second quarter of 1981), which was caused by the strength of the dollar and low Japanese interest rates and could not be resisted by the Bank of Japan's moderate interventions. The main impact on imports was the weakness of domestic demand, although the rise in import costs also had a dampening effect. The overall result was a balance of trade surplus of nearly $5 billion in the quarter. This, coming in the wake of surpluses of $2 billion and $3.7 billion in the two previous quarters, caused further tension between Japan and its trading partners and laid Japan open to the charge of causing disruption in specific markets and of maintaining a rapid economic growth at the expense of other countries.

Exports seemed to be set for further strong growth, and domestic demand appeared to be sluggish in the early part of the second half of 1981. Early figures suggested that the third quarter would yield another very large trade surplus,

CHART 3

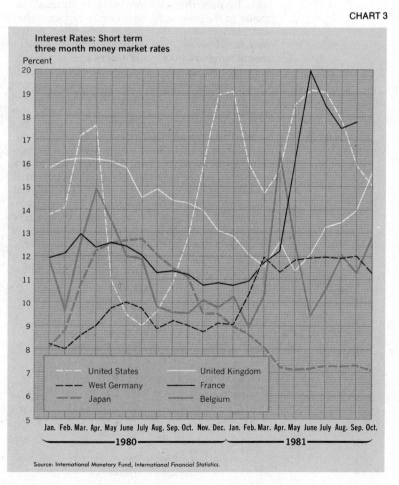

Interest Rates: Short term three month money market rates

Percent

United States • United Kingdom • West Germany • France • Japan • Belgium

Jan. Feb. Mar. Apr. May June July Aug. Sep. Oct. Nov. Dec. Jan. Feb. Mar. Apr. May June July Aug. Sep. Oct.

1980 — 1981

Source: International Monetary Fund, International Financial Statistics.

while most short-term forward indicators of foreign trade performance suggested that this trend would continue into 1982. On the domestic front, however, there were no easily discernible signs of an early upswing. Retail sales in the third quarter appeared to be weak; indications of construction activity remained dull; and the trend of machinery orders, usually regarded as a good indication of investment activities, continued largely flat.

UNITED KINGDOM. During 1981 the British economy laboured under the twin handicap of a world recession that was deeper than anticipated and a relentlessly deflationary policy pursued by the government. As a result the volume of GDP was estimated to have fallen by 1.5–2%, repeating the rather sorry performance of the previous year. Industrial output, which tumbled by 6.5% in 1980, was believed to have recorded another decline of some 5% and was at its lowest level in ten years. Unemployment rose rapidly, from an average of 6.8% of the labour force in 1980 to over 10% in 1981; by October 1981 the unemployment rate stood at 11.3%, equivalent to more than 2.7 million people. This high, virtually unprecedented level of joblessness was widely blamed for the outbreak of large-scale rioting in several cities during the summer.

On the credit side a further modest reduction in inflation took place during the year, with the 12-month increase in the index of retail prices falling from 15.1% in December 1980 to 11.7% in October 1981. In part this represented a traditional response to the deepening recession, a response that was reinforced by the gradual slowdown in the increase of wage rates as the growing level of unemployment forced trade unions to accept lower wage settlements. Thus, while at the beginning of the year the 12-month rise in wage rates was running at nearly 14%, by September 1981 the corresponding figure stood at 8.6%. Also during the year there was some improvement in output per man in industry, although because of the continuing reluctance of business to invest in new machinery there were fears that this was just a temporary response to the recession rather than a long-lasting structural improvement. The external trade and payments position could not be assessed with any certainty since, as a result of selective strike action by civil servants, the appropriate figures were not collected for much of the year.

As the year opened, the economy was already on a steady downward curve with all the indica-

tions promising a deepening of the recession. In spite of this there was nothing to suggest that the government's targets for a slowdown in monetary growth and a reduction in public spending and the borrowing requirement were being achieved. On the contrary, there was growing evidence that, inasmuch as the government's deflationary strategy aggravated the recession, it raised the cost of financing unemployment and made it increasingly difficult to reduce public expenditure, which was one of the main reasons for adopting a deflationary approach in the first place. Nevertheless, the government refused to relax its stance. On the contrary, in March the chancellor of the Exchequer submitted a highly deflationary budget. The effect of it was to increase both direct and indirect personal taxation, to reduce the real value of a range of social security benefits, and to levy additional taxes on some of the few remaining profitable areas of business, namely banks and oil companies. To counter this the chancellor announced a reduction in the Bank of England lending rate from 14% to 12% and handed back a fraction of the extra taxation in the form of stock relief to industry and some special concessions for large energy users and small companies. Although these moves resulted in a slight reduction in industry's financial burden, this benefit was more than offset by the inevitable weakening of demand resulting from the large increase in personal taxation.

Not surprisingly, the budget did not do very much for business confidence. Industry continued to reduce its labour force and to cut back inventory, with the result that both industrial production and GDP recorded a decline in the second quarter. By the middle of the year, however, there was some evidence that stocks of goods were down to more acceptable levels and that an increasing proportion of demand was being met from production rather than inventories. Furthermore, partly because of the reduction in the minimum lending rate in March, sterling became weaker; through its effect on the overseas competitiveness of U.K. manufacturers, this was beginning to exert a positive influence on export demand. These factors combined to produce an increase in industrial output in June and again in September.

Although the government was quick to seize upon the increase as evidence that recovery was just around the corner, a more dispassionate interpretation suggested that while the recession was, at long last, bottoming out, there was little prospect of a significant upturn in the economy in the short term. In fact, as the economy moved into the final quarter of the year, there was growing concern that the modest stimulus inherent in the end of the destocking process would be offset by the weakness of private consumption—weakness that resulted from the decline in personal disposable incomes in the wake of the budget and the slowdown in wage increases. Furthermore, partly because of the movement of world money rates, British interest rates were allowed to move up in early October, with base rates of the leading banks rising from 14 to 16% in a few days. The inevitable effect was to increase corporate financing costs, and there was evidence that by the final quarter of

Table III. Total Employment in Selected Countries
1975=100

Country	1978	1979	1980	1981 First quarter	1981 Second quarter	1981 Third quarter
Australia	102	104	107	108	109	...
Canada	107	112	115	114	119	122
France	97	96	99	94	93	93
West Germany	100	101	102	101	101	...
Italy	102	103	105	105	105	106
Japan	104	105	106	104	108	108
Sweden	101	103	104*	103	104	106
United Kingdom	100	101	99	94	94	...
United States	111	114	115	114	117	117

*Partially estimated.
Source: OECD, *Main Economic Indicators.*

the year this was becoming a significant problem for many firms. In early December, however, rates were on a downward trend again.

Other disappointing developments in the latter part of the year included an apparent change in the downward trend of inflation and renewed evidence that, despite the chancellor's deflationary budget, government public spending targets were being missed by a wide margin. Inflation, as measured by the index of retail prices, was on a steadily downward curve until July, but each of the following three months registered a modest increase. This was mainly the result of the weakening in the external value of sterling.

Reacting to the failure of his strategy to achieve his public spending and related objectives, the chancellor decided to prescribe a further dose of the same medicine in December. The principal features of this mini-budget were an increase in personal taxation by means of higher national insurance contributions, an increase in public health charges and public housing rents, and a further erosion of the real value of social security benefits.

In conclusion, 1981 was a year of failure, failure in economic management and in stopping, or even slowing down, the downward slide of the economy. Living standards fell and social tensions were greatly accentuated. Against this there was a small decline in the rate of inflation, greater realism in wage bargaining, and an increase in efficiency, although there were fears that some of these hard-won gains would prove to be temporary.

WEST GERMANY. The West German economic recession during 1981 proved to be more severe and longer lasting than seemed possible in the summer of 1980, when the economy finally ran out of steam. A 2.75% decline registered in the GNP during the second half of 1980 set the tone for the opening months of 1981. The economy continued to fall during the first six months, registering a decline of 1.3%. However, a mild, export-led swing materialized in the closing months of the year. In spite of this turnaround, GNP was widely expected to have declined at least 1% for the year as a whole, giving West Germany its first annual negative economic growth since 1975.

Private consumption, all types of construction activity, and fixed business investment were among the weakest components of demand. In the opening months of the year overseas demand could have been included in the list, but thanks to the improved competitiveness of German products arising from the sharp fall in the value of the Deutsche Mark, exports rose strongly. The weak demand was mirrored by industrial production and retail sales trends. Industrial production in the first half of the year declined by 2.5%. Hardest hit were consumer goods industries, particularly textiles, but recovery in overseas demand enabled manufacturers of machinery and electrical equipment to maintain production at the same levels as in 1980. Retail sales slumped by 3% during the first six months and remained depressed throughout the remainder of the year.

Given the decline in demand and output, it was not surprising that unemployment became a major

Saudi Arabian oil minister Sheikh Ahmad Zaki Yamani (centre) and his aides were all smiles when the OPEC ministers met in Geneva in May. The Saudis agreed to raise the price of their oil if other exporting countries would lower their prices nearer to the Saudis' price.

political and economic problem during the year. Although the actual number of jobless (nonseasonally adjusted) appeared to drop from a winter peak of 1.3 million in January 1981 to 1.1 million by April, this masked a deteriorating underlying trend, on a seasonally adjusted basis, which showed a rise in the unemployment rate from 4.5 to 5%. At the same time the number of workers on short time hit a six-year peak. By midsummer the actual number of unemployed rose to 1,240,000, and by November it exceeded the previous winter's peak, reaching 1,490,000 for an unemployment rate of 6.4%. In some heavily populated industrial regions unemployment exceeded 7.5%, a level not seen since 1952. As the year drew to a close, the trend was still pointing upward, lending support to forecasts of 1.5 million out of work during the 1981–82 winter.

The unresponsiveness of inflation to the government's tight monetary policy gave rise to concern throughout the year. Although the upward trend inherited from the second half of 1980 was to some extent counterbalanced by moderate wage increases, the sharp decline in the value of the mark fueled a rise in import prices. Higher interest rates and a rise in unit labour costs, owing to lower output, also added to the inflationary pressures. The government's original aim was to bring the inflation rate down to 4.5% from the 5.5% experienced in 1980. In the event, however, it was forced to revise its forecast up to 5.5%; the actual rate was expected to be about 6%.

Not for the first time, West Germany's success in export markets helped ward off a deeper recession. The recovery became evident during the second quarter, when the previous quarter's small trade deficit was turned into a massive DM 6.5 billion surplus (total for 1980 DM 8.9 billion). Although the improvement was aided by a decline in imports, the role of the competitive advantage regained through the sharp depreciation of the mark and lower wage settlements was much in evidence. The current account deficit, however, was somewhat slow to respond to the underlying

strengthening trend. Indeed, the deficit during the first half was marginally worse than that recorded in the first half of 1980. Nevertheless, the deficit for the full year was expected to be somewhat below the 1980 deficit of DM 29.8 billion.

The main burden of economic policy during 1981, as in the previous year, was concerned with promoting price stability and a reduction in the current account deficit. To achieve these objectives, the government held public spending and money supply on a tight rein and actively intervened in the currency markets to protect the value of the mark. The 1981 budget originally proposed a modest spending rise of 4%, which was below the estimated increase in revenue. Coupled with a sharp cutback in the capital expenditure program, the planned deficit at DM 27.4 billion was marginally above the 1980 result. However, under the impact of the recession, which reduced tax revenues and increased social benefit payments, the government was forced to revise its expected deficit to about DM 34.3 billion. Thus, the impact of fiscal policy during 1981 was expected to be positive although the original intention was to have a broadly neutral stance.

FRANCE. As a result of the victory of Francois Mitterrand in the presidential election in May, the French economy came under a new management committed to radical reform, largely inspired by socialist and Keynesian principles. The expansionist approach of the new government appeared to have met with some success in checking the decline of the economy, at least in the short term. GNP, having declined and/or stagnated for several quarters, rose by 1.2% in the second quarter and by 0.4% in the third. This trend appeared to have been maintained in the final quarter, enabling GNP for the year as a whole to register an increase of 1%—marginally down from the previous year.

The quality of the growth, however, was somewhat unsatisfactory as it appeared to have been based on a recovery of household consumption, which, in turn, was stimulated by pre-election wage increases and by the increase in social allowances and higher minimum wages introduced by the new administration in June. Industrial production, on the other hand, remained stagnant during the first half of the year, at a level that was 8.5% lower than during the corresponding period of 1980. The automobile industry was particularly badly affected, but steel and nonferrous metals also suffered large declines. Manufacturing as a whole declined by an alarming 15%, and the fall would have been even larger had it not been for a comparatively good performance by the electrical industries. The construction sector, too, suffered severely in the opening months of the year but staged a good recovery from the summer onward. A modest recovery in industrial output was evident in the closing months of the year but, given the low base figure, it was not significant enough to have a positive impact on the economy.

Reflecting the downward trend in production, unemployment rose steadily throughout the year. Although until June the actual (nonseasonally adjusted) number of unemployed declined slightly, the underlying seasonally adjusted trend was upward. Having stood at 1,660,000 in March (adjusted basis), it jumped to 1,720,000 in April and climbed to 1,850,000 in July. It was expected to reach two million by the end of the year. The fight against unemployment was the government's number one priority, and so its rise caused acute embarrassment. The problem was made all the more difficult not only by structural changes that led to a labour shakeout on a large scale but also by an increasing labour force.

Under the impact of the recession, inflation in the early part of the year remained on a downward trend. In the summer, however, it began to rise and by the autumn appeared to be poised for an upsurge. Taking fright, the government reluctantly introduced direct price controls. The reversal of the earlier favourable trend was brought about by a number of factors. Chief among these was an increase in the minimum wage, which, in turn, affected other wages through a gradual restoration of the differentials. Another major factor was the fall in the value of the franc and the rise in interest rates aimed at defending the currency. Given that the expansionary stance of the government's policy was inherently inflationary, the 8.8% devaluation against the mark in October would have given the already accelerating inflation rate a sharp upward thrust and blown the government's economic strategy widely off course. Thus, control of inflation assumed higher priority, although the finance minister's announced goal of bringing the rate of inflation down from 14 to 10% was greeted with huge skepticism.

The trade deficit reflected the overall trend in household consumption and inflation quite closely. In the early part of the year the deficit had narrowed, enabling the exports-to-imports ratio to reach 95.7%; this was the best performance since December 1979. By July, however, the improvement evaporated, and the adjusted deficit at Fr 6,115,000,000 in that month was the worst in a year. The recovery in consumption in the latter part of the year, which, as discussed, was not accompanied by a rise in production, helped bring in imports. Unlike other countries, France was expected to end the year with only a modest improvement in its external deficit.

Until the change in government the main thrust of France's economic policy was control of inflation while providing a mild stimulus to demand. The fight against inflation, as in previous years, was approached through a steadily tightened monetary policy. In practice this meant setting a lower target for money supply growth than in previous years, 10% compared with actual growth of 11.6 and 13.4% in 1980 and 1979, respectively. This was accompanied by a squeeze on liquidity and fairly high interest rates. However, until the first week in May French interest rates were relatively moderate. Then, as the franc plummeted on the panic-stricken foreign exchanges following Mitterrand's presidential victory, the discount rate was raised by 2½% on May 11. By the beginning of June the domestic money market rates reached 22%, outpacing even the dollar and the Italian lira Eurocurrency rates. The rise in interest rates was accompanied by new exchange control regulations

aimed at preventing the flight of capital and dampening speculation. It was not until the autumn that confidence gradually returned (and not before an 8.8% devaluation against the mark), enabling interest rates to come down to around 15%.

The fiscal policy stance was moderately mild in that it allowed for a slightly faster growth in government expenditure than income. As it was an election year, a somewhat larger budget deficit than that of the previous year was judged to be appropriate. The new regime thus inherited a gently rising budget deficit that was heading for an equivalent of 2.5–3% of the GDP. Fulfilling its election pledges, the incoming government announced a number of measures designed to boost the economy coupled with an ambitious job creation plan in the public sector. Undeterred by the possible inflationary aspects of the 1981 stimulus, the government in August announced the 1982 budget, designed for a larger deficit of Fr 95 billion. This served to underline President Mitterrand's commitment to Keynesian principles of spending his way out of the recession, an approach largely out of favour in the other major OECD countries.

Developing Countries. In spite of a discouraging global environment characterized by widespread recession, persistent high inflation rates, high and volatile interest rates, sluggish world trade, and weak commodity prices, the developing countries as a group once again succeeded in achieving significantly higher economic growth rates than the developed nations. However, other aspects of their economies, such as inflation rates and balance of payments deficits, worsened sig-

nificantly, adding to their already considerable economic management difficulties.

PRODUCTION. The developing countries as a whole achieved a growth rate of 4.6% during 1960 according to World Bank estimates. Although this represented a noticeable slowdown from the previous year (5.2%) and the long-term average of 1966–76 (6.1%), at first glance it appeared to be satisfactory because it was still well above the growth rates of the industrialized countries. But viewed in the context of low-base income levels and fairly rapid population growth, the progress was not entirely satisfactory. In fact, the overall increase in per capita income was only 2.3% in 1980, and in many regions and individual countries it was negative. The general slowdown in economic output was expected to continue in 1981, resulting in an annual growth rate in the region of 4%.

The overall growth rate masked vast regional and other variations. Countries at the lower end of the middle-income scale were badly affected by the decline in the prices of primary products, while semi-industrial exporters of manufactured products escaped fairly lightly. Regionally, Africa south of the Sahara (excluding South Africa) registered a decline in per capita income. The poor performance of South Korea reduced the average growth rate in East Asia and the Pacific. By contrast, Latin-American and Caribbean countries continued to expand rapidly, as did some of the North African and Middle Eastern nations.

The fortunes of most oil-exporting countries took a turn for the worse during the latter part of 1980 and early 1981. Under the impact of lower international demand for oil and a consequent softening in oil prices, economic activity weakened. According to International Monetary Fund (IMF) estimates the GDP of these countries declined by 3% in 1980. However, since oil production plays such a dominant role in the economies of these countries, it is not altogether surprising that the non-oil sector was not affected to the same extent and managed to show a 4% rise in 1980.

CONSUMER PRICES. The rapid rise in the inflation rates of non-oil developing countries, much in evidence in 1979, accelerated during 1980 to reach 32%. Only a modest slowdown to 28% was expected during 1981. The causes of higher inflation were quite familiar: increased import prices and expansionary financial policies that gave rise to large budgetary deficits. IMF sources attributed the easing of inflationary pressures during 1981 to the

Table VII. Industrial Production in Eastern Europe
1975 = 100

Country	1976	1977	1978	1979	1980
Bulgaria	107	114	122	128	134
Czechoslovakia	106	112	117	121	125
East Germany	106	111	116	121	127
Hungary	105	112	117	120	118
Poland	110	117	122	126	125
Romania	...	...	...	...	...
U.S.S.R.	105	111	116	120	124

Source: UN, *Monthly Bulletin of Statistics.*

Table VIII. Foreign Trade of Eastern Europe
In $000,000

Country	Exports			Imports		
	1978	1979	1980	1978	1979	1980
Bulgaria	7,448	8,869	10,372	7,617	8,514	9,650
Czechoslovakia	12,322	13,198	14,891	12,560	14,262	15,148
East Germany	13,267	15,063	17,312	14,572	16,214	19,082
Hungary	6,350	7,938	8,677	7,898	8,674	9,235
Poland	13,361	16,233	16,998	15,121	17,488	18,871
Romania	8,077	9,724	12,230	8,910	10,916	13,201
U.S.S.R.	52,176	64,762	76,481	50,546	57,773	68,523

Source: UN, *Monthly Bulletin of Statistics.*

adoption of various stabilization programs that attempted to contain domestic demand and shift more resources to exports.

The oil-exporting countries also were not immune to the higher inflationary forces during 1980, as was demonstrated by a 1½ percentage point rise to 13% from the previous year's figure. However, at this level it was well below the inflation rates in non-oil countries. As in other parts of the world, the acceleration in the inflation rate was not expected to continue in 1981 owing to the adoption of more cautious demand management policies. Furthermore, lower inflation rates among the industrial countries were expected to have a beneficial impact since a large proportion of the imports of oil-exporting countries originate in industrial countries.

TRADE POSITION. Coincidental with the expansionary policies followed by the non-oil countries, their trade positions deteriorated sharply in 1980. Two other factors were also at play: higher import prices and lower demand for their exports. The latter was of course entirely due to the recession in industrial countries. This also led to a marked weakening in prices of primary products, causing the terms of trade of the non-oil developing countries to deteriorate further. Thus, despite a cutback in the volume of imports, the combined current account deficit of non-oil countries widened to more than $80 billion in 1980, compared with $58 billion in 1979. The deficit was expected to reach

$100 billion in 1981. The oil exporters, on the other hand, moved to a surplus of $112 billion in 1980 from virtually an equilibrium position two years earlier.

The financing of such a large deficit became a major burden on the developing countries, necessitating a reduction in official reserves and recourse to short-term credit. There was also increased borrowing from official sources, including international development agencies.

Centrally Planned Economies. The 35th plenary session of the Council for Mutual Economic Assistance (CMEA or Comecon) was held in Sofia, Bulg., on July 2–4, 1981. The Council session is the most important activity of the CMEA, but its powers are largely undefined. It makes recommendations, and it establishes the main directions of its activities, but it is up to the governments of member countries to implement them. It should be noted, however, that the existence of CMEA is based on political rather than economic considerations and that the main political force behind it is the Soviet Union. The final communiqué was issued in Sofia two days after the end of the meeting, and it seemed that the Council session decided to leave the main issues facing the CMEA countries to the governments concerned. (As of 1981, the CMEA consisted of ten full member countries: the Soviet Union, Bulgaria, Czechoslovakia, East Germany, Hungary, Mongolia, Poland, Romania, Vietnam, and Cuba. Yugoslavia had a "limited participation status," while Afghanistan, Angola, Ethiopia, Laos, Mozambique, and Yemen (Aden) had observer status.)

In a concluding speech delivered at the session, Bulgarian Premier Grisha Filipov claimed that the session had "made a great contribution to defining the main trends of cooperation in the 1980s." According to Filipov, delegates formulated aims and methods of cooperation in production, planning, and scientific-technical cooperation. The Bulgarian premier added that delegates reached "an absolute identity of views on most of the subjects discussed." It was not clear, however, what subjects were discussed and what agreements were reached. The communiqué issued by the CMEA secretariat gave the impression that the session was uneventful and that the delegates concentrated their efforts on reviewing the achievements of the "Comprehensive Program," which was agreed upon ten years earlier at the 25th Council session. This program was directed toward achieving three main aims: bilateral and multilateral economic and technical cooperation; long-term targets; and joint

Table IX. Output of Basic Industrial Products in Eastern Europe, 1980
In 000 metric tons except for natural gas and electric power

Country	Anthracite (hard coal)	Lignite (brown coal)	Natural gas (000,000 cu m)	Crude petroleum	Electric power (000,000 kw-hr)	Steel	Sulfuric acid	Cement
Bulgaria	276	29,796	...	276	34,836	2,568	859.2	5,369
Czechoslovakia	28,200	94,896	19,740	96	72,600	15,228	1,287.6	10,478
East Germany	...	258,000	...	...	98,796	7,308	...	...
Hungary	3,060	23,436	231,408	2,028	23,868	3,768	590.4	4,656
Poland	193,116	36,864	219,540	324	121,860	19,488	2,964.0	18,444
Romania	8,100	27,096	...	...	67,500	...	...	15,600
U.S.S.R.	492,996	159,996	15,168,480	603,000	1,295,004	147,996	23,028.0	124,800

Source: UN, *Monthly Bulletin of Statistics.*

investments. While the communiqué claimed that the "Comprehensive Program" had "raised cooperation within the community to a qualitatively new level," it provided no indication as to the future plans of the organization or the possible solution to the problems that had emerged since the last session was held in Prague, Czech., in 1980.

The main problem that confronted all the CMEA member countries was the virtual collapse of the Polish economy. This affected both the planning and the economic performance of other CMEA countries, especially those that depended on deliveries of Polish coal and other raw materials and on Polish machinery and industrial equipment. Another problem that deeply affected the CMEA countries was a general shortage of fuels and energy. The Soviet Union, the main supplier of crude oil to all European CMEA countries, was unwilling to increase deliveries of that fuel, while Poland was unable to fulfill its obligation to deliver coal.

In spite of all these major issues, the final communiqué published after the 35th CMEA session did not contain anything that would indicate their existence. It was also characteristic that the communiqué contained no reference whatsoever to the economic and political crisis in Poland. It was well known, however, that in 1980 Poland failed to fulfill its planned deliveries of coal, coke, sulfur, machinery, industrial equipment, and consumer goods to its CMEA partners. It was also known that the Soviet Union and other CMEA countries had given considerable economic aid to Poland. This aid, however, was given on an ad hoc and bilateral basis, and nothing indicated that Poland's CMEA partners were considering some form of multilateral cooperation in order to help that nation stabilize its economy.

It was clear that the Polish crisis, both political and economic, was of such magnitude that the Council session found itself unable to tackle it. Many political commentators believed that delegates at the Sofia session reached an agreement to defer major decisions until a summit meeting scheduled to be held in the near future.

There were also other problems that required joint action. In the short term the CMEA countries needed to formulate the Coordinated Plan for Multilateral Integration Measures. This plan was to be implemented during the five years beginning in 1981. It had been expected that the plan would be approved at the previous Council session in June 1980. When that did not happen, it was to be submitted to the 35th session. There was no indication, however, that the plan was even mentioned during the debates in Sofia.

It should be noted that all CMEA member countries were going through a period of economic difficulties on a scale never before experienced in the 32-year history of the organization. A number of factors contributed to these difficulties, including drastic shortages of energy supplies, stagnating labour productivity, and widespread harvest failures over many years. These factors required an examination of CMEA aims and activities, another reason why many countries wanted a summit conference.

The Soviet leader, Leonid Brezhnev, spoke of a summit conference at the 26th congress of the Soviet Communist Party in February 1981. The Czechoslovak leader, Gustav Husak, took up Brezhnev's suggestion at the Czechoslovak Party congress a few weeks later. It seemed, however, that in the final analysis the Soviet leaders had adopted a wait-and-see attitude and that the proposed meeting was indefinitely postponed. This meant that urgent problems facing the CMEA countries were being ignored. This was a dangerous situation because many of those countries had to introduce formal or virtual rationing of food and to curtail their economic plans. According to estimates of the UN Economic Commission for Europe, Eastern European countries might owe the West more than $80 billion by the end of 1981.

INTERNATIONAL TRADE

The world recession that threatened throughout 1980 had its effects on world trade in 1981. Although GNP in the OECD area probably expanded in 1981, total world trade was unlikely to have risen by more than 1%, with trade in manufactured goods increasing by a little more than that but offset by a fall in oil exports and by a sagging

CHART 4

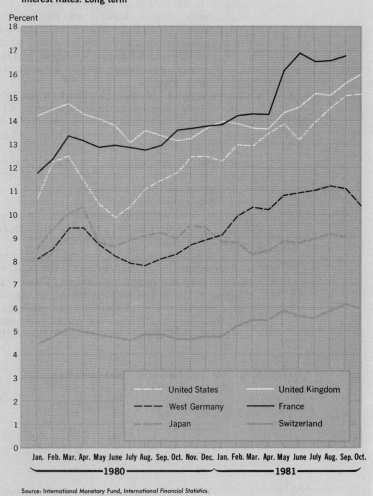

Interest Rates: Long term

Percent

Legend: United States, United Kingdom, West Germany, France, Japan, Switzerland

Jan. Feb. Mar. Apr. May June July Aug. Sep. Oct. Nov. Dec. Jan. Feb. Mar. Apr. May June July Aug. Sep. Oct.

1980 — 1981

Source: International Monetary Fund, *International Financial Statistics*.

market in raw materials. Imports into the OECD area fell by about 2% in 1981, while exports from OECD countries rose. The difference can be accounted for by the fall in exports from the Organization of Petroleum Exporting Countries (OPEC) and the expansion of imports in those countries, while the non-oil developing countries expanded both their import and export volumes.

Trade in 1980 and 1981 was reacting to the 1979 oil price crisis in a way similar to the pattern after the 1973 price crisis. Then OECD countries first of all found their external accounts plunging into deficit, but as a recession hit, their external positions improved dramatically, yielding a trade surplus in 1975. In particular, the seven largest industrial countries (U.S., U.K., Japan, West Germany, France, Canada, and Italy) moved back into substantial surplus at the expense of non-oil developing countries and of the smaller industrial nations. This time, however, the oil-induced recession was not so marked, and the volume of trade did not plunge as it had in 1975. The big seven improved their trade balances overall but were still in deficit; while the lesser industrial nations remained in overall deficit, their situation did not deteriorate substantially. The difference was that this time the OECD (responsible for 85% of world oil consumption) cut its demand for oil more drastically in the face of higher prices. Demand for oil fell by 8% in the period 1973–75, but for the period 1979–81 demand was estimated to have decreased by 13%; in terms of oil usage per unit of economic output, the decrease was much larger. OPEC oil exports suffered, therefore, and the OECD countries were better able to keep up the level of other imports.

Conversely, the position generated for the non-oil developing countries became even worse. The debts incurred by those countries since 1973 required considerable sums to service them and by 1981 accounted for an increasing proportion of their export receipts and other income. Higher oil prices, together with an inability to cut oil consumption significantly, caused the import bills of those nations to remain high. Their exports of raw materials were adversely affected by the slowdown in world economic activity, and their external positions thus deteriorated further.

This difficult international trading situation led to a strengthening of tacit protectionist policies, especially by the industrial nations. They were faced with the problems of adapting to rapidly changing patterns of production and trade and were unwilling to allow market forces to proceed unfettered when unemployment was high and ris-

ing in most countries. Thus, Japan's successful automobile producers found entry to several of their major markets restricted in 1981. The U.K., France, and Italy had already enforced or agreed upon some form of restriction on Japanese cars; the U.S. authorities coerced the Japanese into a substantial reduction in deliveries, and Canada soon followed suit. West Germany, alarmed at the rapid growth of Japan's market share, obtained an agreement limiting that growth.

These moves merely turned Japanese attention to other markets, competing there against the U.S. and European makers. Similar pressures arose in the U.S. to limit the alleged dumping of steel by European manufacturers and to tax what were considered to be subsidized lamb imports. Dissatisfaction of footwear producers in the European Economic Community (EEC) with the expansion of imports from outside the Community and general criticism of the EEC's policy of restricting agricultural trade were further examples of this.

Symbolic of the divergence of opinion on freer trade between the industrial nations and the newly developing economies was the negotiation of the new Multi-Fibre Arrangement to replace those signed in 1974 and 1978. This agreement regulates trade in textiles and clothing, and there were signs that the existing agreement would be replaced by something even more restrictive on exports from the developing nations to, especially, Europe. (*See* Special Report.)

Industrialized Nations. Whereas in the period from 1978 to 1980 it had been the seven major industrialized nations that had borne the brunt of the turnaround in trade in the OECD area, the reverse happened in 1981. As in the period following the 1973 oil crisis, contraction of the seven major economies halted import growth and enabled them to cut their overall trade deficit from $33 billion in 1980 to an estimated $12 billion in 1981. The other industrial nations also cut their trade deficit, but by only $5 billion to $37 billion. This left these countries (Australia, New Zealand, and Western Europe except for the U.K., France, West Germany, and Italy) having to bear deficits on current account that were relatively high in comparison with total GNP, while most of the big seven countries improved their external position relative to GNP, the exceptions being France, Italy, and probably Canada.

The advent of the Reagan administration at the beginning of 1981 and the radical economic policies pursued by it had not yet boosted the U.S. economy as of the end of the year. After a rapid rise in the first quarter of 1981, the economy bumped

Table XI. Soviet Crude Petroleum and Products Supplied to Eastern Europe

In 000 rubles

Country	1979	1980
Bulgaria	920,236	1,061,006
Czechoslovakia	1,077,804	1,162,706
East Germany	1,036,629	1,420,757
Hungary	817,963	755,355
Poland	1,109,255	1,277,917
Romania	39,551	210,540

Source: U.S.S.R. Foreign Trade Statistics/Moscow.

Table X. Soviet Trade with Eastern European Countries

In 000,000 rubles, current prices

Country	Exports 1978	Exports 1979	Exports 1980	Imports 1978	Imports 1979	Imports 1980
Bulgaria	3,144.4	3,312.7	3,660.2	2,997.4	3,173.7	3,438.9
Czechoslovakia	3,002.0	3,362.9	3,648.1	3,058.6	3,183.4	3,535.9
East Germany	3,982.0	4,216.5	4,873.4	3,711.2	3,917.0	4,326.6
Hungary	2,396.4	2,741.3	2,981.6	2,429.9	2,413.8	2,756.6
Poland	3,449.6	3,837.5	4,405.9	3,600.0	3,717.5	3,596.1
Romania	971.3	1,077.8	1,350.3	979.0	1,067.8	1,441.2

Source: U.S.S.R. Foreign Trade Statistics/Moscow.

World leaders from 22 nations gathered in Cancún, Mexico, in October for a North–South economic conference. The discussions were prolonged, but there were few positive results.

along for the remainder of the year. Despite this, imports improved in volume through the year, while U.S. exporters became less competitive. The effective exchange rate of the dollar rose by over 8% in the first half of 1981 compared with the second half of 1980, and unit labour costs rose by 9–10% in 1981. This had the effect of raising manufactured export prices by 10%, in contrast to the decline in such prices (expressed in dollars) in other major industrialized nations. Most sectors of the U.S. export trade experienced difficulty in maintaining high volumes in 1981, the exception being agriculture. Farm exports rose strongly throughout the year despite the higher value of the dollar and the increased competition from Argentina and Brazil in grain markets, especially to the Soviet Union. Exports of raw materials fell as the world recession tightened. Despite the trend toward greater usage of coal as a replacement for oil, U.S. exports of energy and energy-related products also fell in the wake of weakening world economic activity.

Despite the unfavourable world trade picture, Japanese exporters made yet further gains. After an 18% increase in export volume in 1980, there was a further rise of 8% in Japanese exports in 1981. Because Japanese exports are so concentrated in manufactures, this led to further inroads into major industrial markets throughout the world. There were difficulties, however; most major automobile markets in North America and Europe imposed restrictions or had "orderly marketing agreements" that restricted the penetration of Japanese cars into their domestic markets. Machine tools were a source of friction between Japan and the EEC countries. But the overall impact was in all sectors of manufacturing trade, and the restrictions on cars and other goods merely led the Japanese to seek (successfully) markets in Latin America, the Middle East, and Africa. Their efforts were aided by a currency that remained low against the dollar because of relatively low interest rates in Japan. In addition, the willingness of labour to accept low wage increases enabled the rise in unit labour costs to remain well below the OECD average. Stagnating domestic demand also held back inflation and at the same time provided little impetus for imports. Indeed, Japan's success in boosting exports while its import trade remained dull caused considerable resentment in the indus-

trialized world and led to calls for further restrictions on Japanese exports. The result of this excellent trade performance was that the trade surplus topped $20 billion in 1981; this could mean a current account surplus of $6 billion, a massive turnaround from the $10.7 billion deficit in 1980.

The West German authorities in 1981 pursued a policy designed to keep inflation down and bolster the value of the mark against the dollar. Because of high interest rates in the U.S. and a $16 billion deficit on current account in 1980 (a $25 billion turnaround from two years earlier), the mark came under increasing pressure against the dollar. This had adverse effects on the trade balance; for example, although oil imports were down by about 20%, the higher prices for oil and the fact that because it was priced in dollars, each barrel became even more costly in terms of marks led to a rise of some 10% in the mark cost of oil imports. Nevertheless, the strategy of squeezing the economy to reduce the demand for imports, and the effect of the mark's depreciation on competitiveness, caused West Germany's performance to be much better in the second half of 1981. There was a record trade surplus in October, for example, and the deficit on invisibles was declining. Exports to other industrialized countries, especially to other EEC nations, were adversely affected by the recession in those countries. But West German exports performed well in OPEC markets and in the major non-oil developing countries.

French exports performed reasonably well in an unfavourable environment, and the depreciation of the franc that began in April and eventually resulted in a realignment of parities within the EMS helped to keep them competitive. But with the West German market (which took 15% of French exports in 1980) faltering, even the expansion of trade with third world countries could not do more than help bring about a volume rise of only 2% in 1981. At the same time, despite poor domestic growth, imports fell only slightly, while there was a significant adverse movement in the terms of trade, particularly in energy prices. The result was a continued deficit on trade, which was estimated at more than $10 billion in 1981.

The British trade picture was obscured by the strike among the civil servants who process statistics; thus, data on the period March–August were delayed. But based on information that was pub-

lished, exports held up relatively well, considering the fact that the high level of the pound in the second half of 1980 and the first half of 1981 gave great concern to exporters. They considered that retaining competitiveness would be impossible with such an overvalued exchange rate, given the U.K.'s poor performance in containing unit labour costs. At the same time, imports also remained firm despite the continuing fall in domestic output, and in so doing they reflected the loss of competitiveness of British industry. Nevertheless, the U.K. trade account remained firmly in the black, which, together with the usual surplus on invisibles, meant that the current account was estimated to have reached $9 billion.

Italy suffered badly from the increased cost of energy, which represented 25% of its import bill. Besides higher oil prices, the devaluation of the lira pushed the effective rate of exchange down by nearly 9%, while the fall against the dollar was 25%. This helped export volumes to hold up relatively well, while the level of imports fell. Italy's trade deficit for 1981 was estimated at $17 billion, with a current account deficit nearer $12 billion.

The relatively buoyant market for imports in the U.S. helped sustain exports from Canada. While the demand for Canadian manufactures was boosted in this way, the general recession worldwide held back the expansion of trade in foodstuffs and raw materials, which account for 30% of Canada's export trade. Energy exports were affected by the general reduction in energy consumption. A relatively buoyant domestic economy helped to sustain imports; indeed, among the big seven industrialized countries Canada maintained the fastest rate of growth of imports in 1981. Despite this the trade balance remained firmly in surplus, estimated at $5 billion for the year.

For the other industrialized nations the year in most cases was one marked by merely a steadying or small improvement of the trade position after the adverse movements of 1980. The Netherlands improved its trade performance, while that of Australia deteriorated because the growth of imports grew strongly as economic activity prospered. Spain's relatively good export performance benefited from the depreciation of the peseta in 1980 and early 1981 but did not compensate for the adverse movements in terms of trade in both 1980 and 1981.

Developing Countries. For the oil-exporting nations there was a fall in those exports, and their non-oil trade also suffered as world demand for raw materials stagnated. Import growth, on the other hand, was rapid, at about 15%, following a similar rise in 1980. In the "high absorber" nations, such as Nigeria and Venezuela, large populations and requirements for development led to expenditures of most of their export revenues on imports and invisible items, leaving them with only a small surplus or even a deficit on current account. For those countries the fall in oil exports meant that total exports rose little, if at all, and thus there was reduced leeway for import growth. The "low absorbers" included Saudi Arabia, which improved its share of overall world oil trade markedly during 1980; this group generally was able to maintain oil revenues and keep imports expanding at a high rate, probably double that of the "high absorbers." For the year as a whole the trade surplus for the OPEC countries was probably about $150 billion, some $20 billion less than in 1980. For the "low absorbers" the trade surplus was probably the same as in 1980, while the "high absorbers" suffered a marked decline in their trade surplus and, with a further deterioration in their deficit in invisibles, moved to a position of near balance on current account.

The non-oil developing countries probably suffered a further $10 billion deterioration in their trade deficit from the 1980 level of $45 billion. Again, the bulk of this deterioration fell upon those nations that did not have large indigenous energy resources and also on those that were not rapidly industrializing and thus generating the exports to pay for their import bills. This group included most of Africa, much of Central and South America, and the East Asian countries. Their main export goods were commodities, the demand for which fell off in 1981 as industrial activity declined in the OECD area. Prices of commodities also fell rapidly, with food commodities down 25% from a year earlier by the end of 1981 and declines of 15% for fibres and 10% for metals.

For the rapidly industrializing developing economies there was a slowdown in the rate of growth of their exports, but nevertheless they continued to expand relatively quickly. Import growth was held back by the need to keep trade deficits within the limits that could be financed by net capital inflows, since overall this group ran a trade and current account deficit of some $10 billion–$15 billion in 1981. For those developing countries with some domestic energy resources, the effect of the oil price rise on their external accounts was strong. Indeed, for countries such as Mexico that increased their oil exports there was greater leeway to expand their import trade.

Table XII. Current Balances of Payments

In $000,000,000

Country	1975	1976	1977	1978	1979	1980	1981*
Canada	−4.7	−3.9	−4.1	−4.4	−4.4	−1.7	−6
France	+0.1	−5.9	−3.0	+3.8	+1.2	−7.9	−1
West Germany	+3.6	+3.6	+4.0	+9.5	−5.5	−16.0	−11
Italy	−0.6	−2.9	+2.5	+9.1	+5.1	−10.1	−11
Japan	−0.7	+3.7	+10.9	+17.6	−8.8	−10.8	+7
United Kingdom	−3.7	−1.5	−0.4	+1.2	−3.0	+6.6	+9
United States	+18.3	+4.5	−14.1	−14.2	+1.4	+3.7	+5
OECD total	+2.0	−16.8	−23.8	+15.0	−31.0	−74.4	−35
Other developed countries	−4.9	−2.8	−1.7	−0.1	−0.7	−0.8	−6
Centrally planned economies*	−6.9	−2.2	+2.1	+1.0	+4.9	+7.2	+4
Oil exporting countries*	+45.0	+43.7	+41.5	+14.8	+71.0	+139.0	+119
Other less developed countries*	−35.2	−21.8	−18.1	−30.7	−44.2	−71.0	−83
at 1975 prices†							
OECD total	+2.0	−16.8	−21.8	+12.0	−21.7	−47.1	−23
Other developed countries	−4.9	−2.8	−1.6	−0.1	−0.5	−0.5	−4
Centrally planned economies*	−6.9	−2.2	+1.9	+0.8	+3.4	+4.6	+3
Oil exporting countries*	+45.0	+43.7	+38.1	+11.8	+49.7	+88.0	+79
Other less developed countries*	−35.2	−21.8	−16.6	−24.6	−30.9	−44.9	−55

*Estimate.
†In terms of export prices of manufactured goods.
Sources: International Monetary Fund, *International Financial Statistics*;
UN, *Monthly Bulletin of Statistics*; national sources.

CHART 5

Centrally Planned Economies. Despite the reduction of U.S. exports to the Soviet Union after the latter's intervention in Afghanistan, trade with the U.S.S.R. and other centrally planned economies continued to increase at a normal pace. The U.S. and Japanese curb on trade was not matched by the Europeans, who continued to push their goods aggressively in those markets. Trade in grain with the Soviet Union was a major casualty of the U.S. restrictions, but this was easily circumvented by the Soviets in two ways. First, they imported more grain from other major producers, including Argentina and other South American nations. Second, they imported more meat, thus reducing their requirements for grain that would have been used for animal feed. Nevertheless, the trade restrictions, plus the disruptions to trade from Poland's political and economic difficulties and from China's cutback in orders from the West as its development program was drastically revised, led to a slowdown in import growth in those economies. President Reagan lifted the restriction on U.S. grain exports to the U.S.S.R. in April.   (EIU)

INTERNATIONAL EXCHANGE AND PAYMENTS

In 1981 the most important issues in international economic relations were found among the industrial countries, in contrast to most of the preceding ten years when relations between the developed and developing countries were dominant. In particular, the effects of internal monetary policies in one country on the economies of others explain much of the economic history of 1981. It was not that the linkages among countries were stronger than in the past, but the international effects of interest rates or other credit conditions were more direct and immediate than those of government spending or tax policies, which operate on trade only indirectly and after a certain time lag. The general switch in recent years to managing domestic economies by means of restrictive monetary policies had, therefore, increased the international sensitivity to domestic policies. Greater use of monetary controls, whatever its benefits or costs on the domestic side, thus created new questions in international economic relations; there were not yet any international or national policy instruments to deal with them nor was there any tradition of generally accepted limits on a country's behaviour.

In 1981 the most important influence was the move by the U.S. to strict monetary control, made even tighter by its combination with stimulative fiscal policy. The effect of this on the rest of the world was made more severe by the simultaneous ending of the previous administration's policy of direct intervention in the exchange markets, in particular of the policy of building up holdings of foreign exchange. This meant that the effects on the dollar exchange rate of the high interest rates required by domestic policy were not mitigated by any U.S. purchases of other countries' currencies.

The rise in U.S. interest rates had an upward influence on those of most other industrial countries because the latter were unwilling to accept the full amount of the outflow of capital and conse-

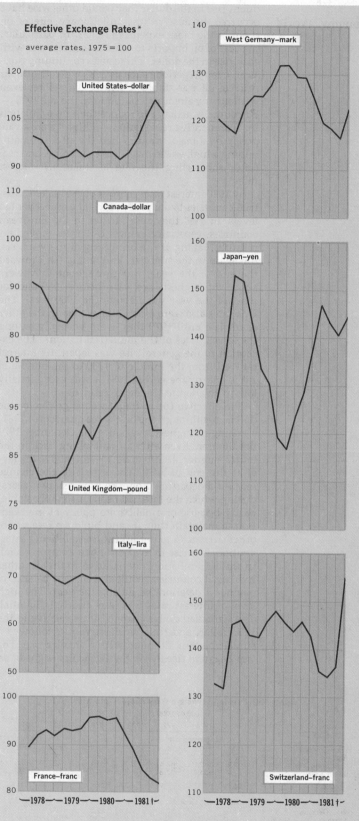

Effective Exchange Rates*

average rates, 1975 = 100

* Measure of a currency's value relative to a weighted average of
   the values of the currencies of the country's trading partners.
† Fourth quarter figures for 1981 are estimated.

Source: International Monetary Fund, *International Financial Statistics.*

quent rise in the dollar that would otherwise have occurred because of the inflationary effects on them of the more expensive dollar. In particular, the cost of oil imports to other countries rises with each rise in the dollar. This causes continuing pressure, even in periods such as 1981 when the dollar price of oil was stable or falling. Therefore, even without any attempts—as found in the late 1970s—by countries actually to reduce their own inflation by "competitive revaluation," a high interest rate policy by a major country had the effect of maintaining a high world level of both nominal and real (after subtracting the rate of inflation) interest rates.

By 1980 interest rates in most of the major industrial countries had already reached unprecedented levels. In 1981 they rose further in the European countries, especially France. U.S. rates moved erratically, falling at the beginning of the year, rising again in the summer, and falling back toward the end of the year, but throughout they were above the highest level seen before 1980 and for most of the year were above the 1980 level. The U.S. rates also were much higher than in the other countries; until 1979 they were normally among the lowest rates of the industrial nations. The exception to the general rise was Japan. Its interest rate fell from the middle of 1980 to the middle of 1981, and by the end of 1981 it was exceptionally low in relation to the other countries.

The effective (or average) exchange rate of the dollar rose through the first three quarters of 1981, reaching its highest level since the December 1971 devaluation. Even after a small falling back in the fourth quarter, it remained 10–15% above the level at the end of 1980. The extent of the change marked a departure from the previous two years, during which the rate had been reasonably stable, partly because of a deliberate policy of intervention to maintain the rate and build up reserves of other currencies to permit future stabilizing intervention. The rise in 1981 did not accompany a fall in the U.S. inflation rate relative to that in other industrial countries, while the current balance of payments deteriorated during the year. The high level of interest rates was thus clearly influential. The Canadian dollar changed little relative to the U.S. dollar, and thus its effective rate followed a similar pattern although with a smaller rise. The yen began to rise in 1980 with the first signs of an

improvement in Japan's current balance, although this did not move into surplus until the second quarter of 1981. The rate, however, changed little during 1981. This must, of course, be partly because the large rise, about a quarter, between the beginning of 1980 and the beginning of 1981 was considered sufficient, but the rate was also probably influenced by the declining Japanese interest rates. The relatively steady effective rate during 1981 consisted of a fall against the dollar and a rise against the European currencies.

The pound sterling fell back during 1981 from its high level at the end of 1980, although it then had a small recovery at the end of the year. British interest rates, which have traditionally been at least 2–3 percentage points higher than U.S. rates, fell below them at the end of 1980 and remained lower, although relative rates were raised at the end of the summer in order to prevent a further fall in the exchange rate. Because the exchange rate had risen through 1980, the change in the rate on average between 1980 and 1981 was held to almost zero. The Swiss franc, like the other currencies, declined against the dollar in the first part of 1981, but it later recovered to about its level at the end of 1980; the resulting rise against the other European currencies meant that its effective level had risen. Its average for the year was probably slightly (2–3%) below the 1980 level.

The Deutsche Mark began to decline in 1980 as it became clear that the move into current deficit in 1979 was not, as had been thought in West Germany, temporary, and it continued to fall in the first three quarters of 1981. At the beginning of October there was a revaluation of the mark within the EMS; the West German balance was clearly improving by that time, and inflation there was lower than in the other members. This improvement against the other European currencies, combined with the falling back of the dollar, raised the mark's effective rate to nearly its level at the end of 1980, but the average for the year was still about 7% below that of 1980. The French franc and the lira followed the same pattern because of their links to the mark, since the franc was not revalued in October and the lira was devalued in March and October, they had larger falls, of 11 and 13%, for the year. The principal change in 1981 was thus the realignment between the dollar and the EMS European currencies, with the other European currencies on balance changing little and the yen maintaining its 1980 rise.

In its current form, of an association of currencies that were already closely linked by their countries' trading patterns and extensive use of the mark, the EMS by 1981 had survived three years. There remained, however, unresolved difficulties in the relationships of its member currencies. Stability (or at least expected stability) among members' exchange rates could lead to flows of capital based on relative interest rates. If, as was probable, this meant flows from countries with low inflation to those with high inflation, it could lead to pressure on relative exchange rates in a perverse direction. This problem seemed to have contributed to pressure on the mark and, therefore, to the high level of West German interest rates since the

Table XIII. Foreign Investment by Major Countries

In $000,000,000

Country	1974	1975	1976	1977	1978	1979	1980	1981*
				Long-term capital flows				
West Germany	−2.4	−7.4	−0.6	−5.6	−1.5	+5.9	+3.8	+8
Japan	−3.9	−0.3	−1.0	−3.2	−12.4	−12.6	+2.4	−7
United Kingdom	+6.7	+2.2	+2.9	+6.5	−6.1	−5.1	−10.3	−14
United States	−7.4	−21.4	−21.2	−17.6	−14.3	−15.6	−13.8	−18
Total	−7.0	−26.9	−19.9	−19.9	−34.3	−27.4	−17.9	−31
				Net interest, dividends, and profits				
West Germany	+0.4	+1.0	+1.3	+0.2	+2.5	+2.5	+1.8	−1
Japan	−0.5	−0.3	−0.2	+0.1	+0.9	+2.0	+0.9	0
United Kingdom	+3.3	+1.7	+2.5	+0.2	+1.1	+1.8	−0.1	+1
United States	+15.5	+12.8	+16.0	+18.0	+21.4	+33.5	+32.8	+36
Total	+18.7	+15.2	+19.6	+18.4	+26.0	+39.7	+35.3	+36

*Estimate.
Source: National sources.

second half of 1980. In 1981, although it might still have raised West German rates relative to those of the other European currencies, the influence of U.S. rates was probably more important.

There was little change in the pattern of the current balances of the major areas in 1981. (In looking at all dollar values for 1980–81 it is important to remember that one effect of the rise in the value of the dollar was that average world prices measured in dollars actually fell in 1981, by about 2–3% for all trade prices and perhaps 4–5% for world manufactured exports; this is the customary price index used in converting international values to "real" terms.) The industrial countries as a group were able to reduce their deficit by cutting imports and increasing exports (their export prices fell more than their import prices), but the improvement was not as rapid as after the first oil price rise in 1974. In 1975 the real price of oil fell, giving the industrial countries a large improvement in their terms of trade, but in 1981 it rose 15–20%.

Among the developed countries, all improved their balances in 1981 except for Canada and Italy. (The U.K. figure was uncertain because a strike prevented publication of half the year's data.) The largest improvement was by Japan, and the U.S. had one of the smallest. The change in the current balance of the developed countries was less than in their trade balance ($40 billion, compared with $50 billion). Although the U.S. increased its surplus on services, largely because of a recovery of its earnings on direct investment from their exceptionally low level in 1980, and France had little change, the other countries all experienced significant declines in their earnings (or rises in net spending) on these nontrade current items. For Canada this was because of higher deficits on interest payments and travel. For West Germany the traditional surplus on interest payments moved into deficit, the result of the recent rise of capital inflows, and there was an increase in contributions to the EEC budget. Its net deficit on tourism, however, did not appear to have had its usual rise. Japan also had a reduction in its net interest income, while Italy appeared to have suffered lower tourism income.

The balance of the oil exporters fell in 1981 in spite of the continued improvement in their terms of trade; this only just balanced their 15–20% rise in import volume, while the volume of their exports again fell sharply. Even adjusted for inflation, however, the size of their surplus, and therefore of the financing problem for the rest of the world, remained higher than in 1974 after the first oil price rise. The deficits of the other developing countries remained correspondingly large with both the volume and the prices of their exports depressed by a lack of demand in the industrial countries. Their total deficit had increased in each of the last four years, with the worst rises occurring in the Asian countries that had little oil of their own and rapidly growing economies. The balance of the centrally planned economies appeared to have deteriorated in 1981 after being sustained in recent years by the rising value of Soviet oil exports.

In 1981 the major industrial countries returned to their normal role as large suppliers of long-term capital to the rest of the world. Japan in particular moved back into deficit from its temporary surplus in 1980, caused by the inflow of large amounts of capital from the oil producers after the relaxation of Japanese capital controls, although the outflow was still less than in the late 1970s. The increase in inflows into West Germany in 1981, as in 1980, came principally from OPEC. The outflow from the U.K. was exceptionally high in the first half of the year, apparently for interest-rate and exchange-rate reasons; even if these became less influential in the second half, the outflow for the year was likely to have risen substantially.

The situation in the U.S. was rather uncertain because estimates of its borrowing on the Euro-credit markets suggested that this rose sharply in July. This rise accounted for much of the total increase in the value of international borrowing in 1981. Some other OECD countries in deficit increased their borrowing, notably Canada, but in general there appeared to have been only a small rise. Borrowing by France, Italy, Japan, Spain, and Sweden remained high, however, in spite of improvements in some of their current balances.

The apparently large use of their international reserves was an arithmetic result of the rise in the value of the dollar and consequent fall in the dollar value of reserves held in other currencies. In terms of an average currency unit (such as the Special Drawing Right of the IMF), the value was almost unchanged. After allowing for this, there was significant use of reserves by Belgium, Canada, Denmark, France, Italy, and the U.K.

In spite of their growing deficits, the centrally planned economies reduced their borrowing on international markets, and the oil-exporting countries were also again able to cut their borrowing. There was a significant increase in lending by the oil exporters to the other developing countries, restoring the total value to the 1979 level, but most of both the rise and the fall could be explained by one country, Mexico. The Latin-American countries and South Korea continued to be the most important borrowers, although borrowing rose in both Hong Kong and India. There was an increase in IMF lending to those countries.

It was clear that after a prolonged period of deficits, for which no immediate end could be seen, some official lender of last resort was necessary. The number of countries that had been compelled to seek rescheduling of their commercial loans and which, therefore, were unlikely to be immediately eligible for further such borrowing continued to rise in 1981 among both the developing and the centrally planned economies. With World Bank lending almost unchanged from 1980 (when it was $11.5 billion), and also with reductions in the real value of the aid programs of individual developed countries, there was no obvious alternative to increasing IMF lending. The increase in this was not only larger than the $1 billion rise that occurred in 1974 but also was different in both direction and kind. Nearly all the lending following the first oil price rise went to the industrial countries; all of the last increase in the last two years went to the developing countries and the centrally planned economies.

(SHEILA A. B. PAGE)

PRESSURES FOR PROTECTIONISM

by Paul Cheeseright

Increasingly in 1981, political leaders in the Western world, grappling with recession and growing unemployment, were finding it harder to ward off pressures for the protection of their domestic industries. The liberal trading system seemed to be under greater threat than at any time since the end of World War II.

Bending the Rules. Though full of imperfections, the liberal trading system is based on the principle of equal treatment for all countries, without discrimination by some against the exports of others. It is embodied in the disciplines of the General Agreement on Tariffs and Trade (GATT), first drawn up in 1947 and later modified to promote greater freedom for the movement of goods. But in 1981 the international trading community was forcefully reminded that the principle of equal treatment was being progressively eroded. Pressure from the U.S. on Japan to restrain the export of its motor vehicles, followed by demands from countries in the European Economic Community (EEC) for analogous treatment, showed that major exporters could be cowed into holding back sales for fear of setting off stronger protectionist pressures. Bilateral trade flows were being throttled, even in some cases where they appeared to be given the opportunity to flow more easily. The U.S., for example, lifted import quotas on footwear from South Korea and Taiwan as an indication of its commitment to free trade, but the suppliers immediately responded by declaring restraints on their sales.

Direct assaults on the GATT rules have been few. "That there has not been open violence to the rules is partly explained by the increasing resort to privately agreed, and officially tolerated if not promoted, restraints of trade and competition," the GATT secretariat commented in its annual study of international trade. "Developments in such important industrial sectors as steel, automobiles, synthetic fibres, and perhaps other petrochemicals exemplify this tendency."

Paul Cheeseright is world trade editor of the Financial Times, *London.*

In a period of general expansion in the world economy, such moves might have been less noticeable. Indeed, in the years before the oil crisis of 1973–74, when the trading system was more liberal than it had ever been, limited protection existed, but it had been contained. The agricultural protectionism of the EEC and Australia's protection of its car and footwear industries were cases in point. The signal difference between the early 1970s and the early 1980s was the emergence of Japan as a major force on the world markets and, in its wake, of a group of newly industrializing countries—Taiwan, South Korea, Singapore, Brazil. Their pressure on the domestic markets of the traditional Western trading powers and the additional competition they posed to Western exports raised serious problems of economic adjustment. But the fluctuations of the world economy since 1973, with recession, limited recovery, and then recession again, made the adjustment difficult to manage. Governments have manifestly felt they could not do it without some bending of the trading rules within which the expansion of world trade had taken place during 1947–73.

Growing Tensions. "The key to maintaining an open trading system is for each industrial country to come to grips domestically with the opportunity which adjusting to a challenging international environment involves," the World Bank said in August 1981. In the absence of rapid internal changes in the depressed economies of the West, however, tensions between the industrial and less developed countries emerged strongly during 1981. This was

U.S. shoe manufacturers claimed that they were suffering losses as a result of large imports of shoes from South Korea and Taiwan.

IRA WYMAN—THE NEW YORK TIMES

clearly marked in the early stages of renegotiation of the Multi-Fibre Arrangement (MFA), which controls international textile trading. Originally, the MFA (due to expire at year's end) was conceived as a means of permitting orderly expansion of textile exports from the less developed countries and, at the same time, orderly contraction of higher priced textile industries in the developed world. In fact, from the mid-1970s onward the MFA had become increasingly restrictive. By the fall of 1981 it was clear that the less developed countries would not readily accept a regime that permitted industrial countries to impose strict quotas on third world exports, on a country-by-country basis, while refusing willingly to accept reciprocal restrictions that would endanger their own large employment stake in textiles.

More was involved than a simple clash between rich and poor nations, however. From the point of view of the industrialized countries, the adaptation of the trading system to absorb the newcomers of the 1970s and early 1980s should include the progressive opening of the newcomers' domestic markets to Western manufactured goods. Trading has to be reciprocal, as Pres. Ronald Reagan's administration in the U.S. continually argued. This was at the bottom of the running dispute between the U.S., the EEC, and Japan, the three major trading powers around which the international trading system pivots. Japan, which weathered the recession better than its rivals, was managing to penetrate the U.S. and EEC markets for a relatively narrow range of products—automobiles and electronics, for example. At the same time, the U.S. and the EEC were complaining that the Japanese market was not as open as it should be, as the rising Japanese trade surplus indicated. The pressures on Japan built to a peak in mid-1981, resulting not only in Japan's agreement to hold back some exports but also in a conscious effort on the part of the Japanese to guide potential foreign suppliers through the thickets of their notoriously complicated distribution system.

How Committed? Three efforts to deal with these running disputes surfaced during the year. The first was the commitment to an open trading system made at the July summit of the seven leading industrialized powers in Ottawa, Ont. Without such a commitment, conscientiously applied, the system would be in jeopardy. "An international trade system based on rules cannot be effective unless the few large trading countries support it by their national policies," the GATT secretariat noted. The second was the intention of the U.S., the EEC, and Japan to meet in an attempt to forestall future friction. Any move that would ease tension was welcome, but there was a lurking fear that any attempt to coordinate trading policy without sufficient consideration

J. P. LAFFONT—SYGMA

A clerk stands beside a display of calculators in Tokyo. Japan has become a major force in the manufacturing and export of electronic calculators.

of the interests of smaller powers would of itself create new tensions.

The third concerned the fear that adjustments in the European economies would not take place quickly enough to permit the growth of new high technology industries in the face of Japanese competition, given Japan's lead in some electronic fields and in robotics. Various proposals for dealing with the situation were circulated, but all had in common a desire to change the trading rules, especially where they concern the use of safeguards to prevent injury to domestic industry. By the late summer of 1981 the British government was considering how to promote changes that would give international legality to unilateral safeguards against Japanese exports. It was suggested that the thrust of these had not been envisaged when the GATT was drawn up, and some observers doubted that the trading system could withstand them.

Both the strength of the commitment to open trading and the desire to change the rules would be evident when the 86 nations that had signed the GATT held a ministerial conference in 1982. The conference was being called because it was widely felt that the GATT system would not work without additional political impetus. It would be the first ministerial conference since 1973, when the last major round of multilateral trade negotiations began in Tokyo. The meeting would be timely. "No government is really 'protection-minded'; on the contrary, all continue to resist protectionist pressures," the GATT secretariat said. "Nonetheless, governments do give ground to pressure now and then; the trend is on the whole in one direction, and clearly unsustainable for long."

Ecuador

Ecuador

A republic on the west coast of South America, Ecuador is bounded by Colombia, Peru, and the Pacific Ocean. Area: 281,334 sq km (108,624 sq mi), including the Galápagos Islands (7,976 sq km), which is an insular province. Pop. (1981 est.): 8,644,000. Cap.: Quito (pop., 1980 est., 807,700). Largest city: Guayaquil (pop., 1980 est., 1,-116,300). Language: Spanish, but Indians speak Quechuan and Jivaroan. Religion: predominantly Roman Catholic. Presidents in 1981, Jaime Roldós Aguilera to May 24 and Osvaldo Hurtado Larrea.

A new outbreak of the long-standing border dispute with Peru at the beginning of 1981 had the effect of consolidating the popularity of Pres. Jaime Roldós Aguilera (*see* OBITUARIES). The government took advantage of the situation to carry out a long-postponed increase in the domestic price of gasoline and to diffuse the threat of a general strike called to protest the rise in the cost of living.

On May 24 an airplane crash claimed the lives of President Roldós and his wife, the minister of defense and his wife, and several military officials. Although investigations by both the Ecuadorian and U.S. air forces concluded that the crash resulted from pilot error in bad weather, Congress ordered a new inquiry into the incident after allegations of sabotage were made. The presidency was immediately assumed by Vice-Pres. Osvaldo Hurtado Larrea, leader of Democracia Popular, the Christian Democrat grouping. Hurtado had been responsible for drawing up the national development plan in 1980. He faced the same political problems as his predecessor in dealing with Congress and was forced to fight to procure a government majority.

The economy foundered in the face of declining world market prices for Ecuador's major export commodities, principally oil. The national budget was based on an average price of $36 a barrel, but

Crowds lined the streets in Quito in May as the body of Pres. Jaime Roldós Aguilera was taken into the national palace to lie in state.

UPI

by midyear the price had fallen to $32. A current account deficit was expected as exports fell and the trade surplus narrowed. Imports also declined (though at a slower rate than exports), reflecting sluggishness in the domestic economy.

(SARAH CAMERON)

Education

Education reflected the troubles of the world economy in 1981. In most advanced industrial countries it was a year of continued contraction of educational services, in some cases provoking vigorous if not indeed violent demonstrations. Nonetheless, there were those who argued that educational institutions would benefit from being pared down and brought into line with economic realities. In a few countries—notably France—political changes resulted in some measure of expansion. In general, however, governments were examining their educational establishments with a view toward cutting back, and what was left of the excesses of the 1960s came under critical scrutiny.

One of the fashions of the 1960s, "participation," especially by parents, retained much of its hold. In England and Wales an Education Act was passed providing for more active "school governors" in every type of school, and in Scotland a system of "schools councils" with parent involvement was sustained. There were some exceptions, however. Northern Ireland's attempts to institute a system of school government ran into sectarian troubles as Roman Catholics and Protestants dis-

agreed strongly over how the schools should be run. In Quebec the plan to create councils—called *conseils d'orientation*—in every school, with sweeping powers that included determining the school's character, setting its educational aims, and evaluating them, encountered persistent opposition from the powerful teachers' union. In Australia a survey, commissioned by the federal government, showed that as many as 80% of parents did not want to become involved in the schools at all.

The biennial meeting of European ministers of education, held in Portugal, concentrated on preschooling and the transition to primary school. A number of differences of opinion were apparent. The Belgians, for example, were extending compulsory education downward to age five while the West Germans were firmly committed to voluntary preschooling. Uppermost in the ministers' minds, however, were escalating youth unemployment and shrinking educational budgets. Education of the handicapped received considerable international attention, and there was a good deal of discussion in several European countries concerning the merits of "mainstreaming," or integrating the disabled into ordinary schools. An international conference on the subject was held in Wales in September.

Primary and Secondary Education. In the U.S. Ronald Reagan's election to the presidency set in motion a revolution in the federal role in education, involving sweeping reversals of policies dating back to Pres. Lyndon Johnson's Great Society programs of the 1960s. Opponents charged that the poor, minorities, and women would suffer from the various procedural changes and a 25% cut in federal education spending. The cornerstone of the Reagan policy was to provide education money to the states in the form of block grants, leaving to the states much of the determination of how funds were to be spent. Forty-four programs previously administered through federally controlled "categorical" grants and contracts would be converted into large block-grant programs, one for $3.5 billion in fiscal 1982, the second for $4.4 billion in the 1982–83 school year.

Among the programs being questioned by feder-al officials was bilingual education. Some $1 billion had been spent on bilingual programs designed to help non-English-speaking students study school subjects in their native tongues while mastering English. A new federal report, however, concluded that the programs were based on false assumptions and that many of the students in districts with bilingual programs were affected as much by poverty and other factors as by linguistic difficulties. The report also drew attention to rising costs and a shortage of thousands of bilingual teachers. Hispanic groups charged that the study was biased. The new secretary of education, Terrel H. Bell, indicated that local and state education officials, not the federal government, should determine how best to help students master English. He dropped some federal regulations but worked to keep funds for bilingual education separate from the block grants. Officials in Austin, Texas, claimed that children in bilingual programs fell somewhat further behind in school subjects than their Spanish-speaking counterparts in regular classes. Meanwhile, the Supreme Court agreed to review efforts by the state of Texas to avoid court-ordered responsibility for educating the children of illegal aliens, most of them Spanish-speaking.

In keeping with Reagan's campaign promise to abolish the Department of Education, Secretary Bell submitted four options to the president concerning the future of his agency, none of which retained its Cabinet-level status. He also announced a series of moves to simplify state applications for federal funds and state reporting on how such moneys were being spent. By this means and by eliminating many federal regulations affecting local and state education agencies, he claimed that thousands of pages of paperwork would be eliminated and millions of dollars saved. Threats to withhold federal funds from local districts because of noncompliance in civil rights and other matters were soft-pedaled.

In a similar vein, the Civil Rights Office of the Department of Justice changed its tactics, putting the emphasis on negotiation with local districts to obtain desired changes. Pressure on Chicago, one of the nation's largest school districts, was relaxed

Jay Sommer, a teacher from New Rochelle, N.Y., was congratulated at a White House ceremony by Nancy Reagan on being elected 1981 National Teacher of the Year. The annual event is sponsored by the Encyclopaedia Britannica companies, *Good Housekeeping* magazine, and the Council of Chief State School Officers.

MARY ANNE FACKELMAN—THE WHITE HOUSE

Ecumenical Movement:
see Religion

KEYSTONE

Headmistress Sheila Greenfield walks with students on the opening day of classes at Lagan College, Belfast. The school was the only one in Northern Ireland to place Protestant and Roman Catholic children in the same classes.

as Justice Department officials agreed to a plan proposed by the city's board of education that used approaches other than mandatory busing to promote desegregation. Previously, Justice Department lawyers had criticized Chicago for not providing mandatory measures as a backup in case voluntary programs failed to produce sufficient racial mixing. The department also said it would not appeal a court order dismissing an earlier department suit to force cross-district busing between Houston, Texas, and suburban school districts. In testimony before a House committee, a department spokesman said Justice planned to concentrate on specific schools where there was evidence of intentional segregation rather than trying to desegregate entire districts. The attorney general announced that he would seek creative ways to encourage desegregation, as, for example, college scholarships for those who voluntarily attended desegregated schools.

In other desegregation developments, a federal judge in Seattle, Wash., held that voters had the right to rescind a voluntary desegregation plan adopted by three school districts; the Supreme Court agreed to review the case. The high court also said that it would review a 1979 state constitutional amendment designed to curb a court-ordered busing plan in Los Angeles, the nation's second-largest school district. The amendment was upheld by the state supreme court in March, effectively ending the most ambitious court-ordered busing program in the 25 years since the landmark desegregation decision in *Brown* v. *Board of Education of Topeka*. Commenting on some 400 busing plans effected over the past several years, the Justice Department's chief civil rights official said that busing had not been successful. Instead, he advocated upgrading predominantly black schools while removing any remaining barriers that prevented blacks from attending the schools of their

choice. A different view was put forward in a federally sponsored seven-year study, which claimed that integration aids minority students and that busing produces no harmful results.

Enrollment in U.S. schools approached 57.5 million in 1981; nearly 3.3 million teachers were employed, as well as about 300,000 superintendents, principals, and other administrators. Continuing the trend started in 1969, elementary enrollments fell from 31.4 million in 1980 to 31 million in 1981. However, moderate increases were expected by the mid-1980s. High school enrollments fell from 14.9 million to 14.4 million, and the decline was expected to continue throughout the decade. Expenditures for education at all levels were projected at $198 billion for 1981–82, compared with $181 billion in the previous year. Of that amount, $127 billion was for elementary and secondary schools and $71 billion for colleges and universities. Public schools and colleges were expected to spend $161 billion and private institutions, $37 billion. The federal government contributed 10% of the total; the state share was 39%, and the local share was 25%. The remainder came from various sources such as tuition, endowment earnings, and private contributions.

There were fewer teacher strikes than usual in the U.S. at the beginning of the 1981–82 school year, although Philadelphia's 21,000-member teachers' union conducted a strike that ran on for several weeks. The issues were layoffs and wage freezes. In Boston more than 5,000 teachers threatened to strike over layoffs and delays in implementing a scheduled 7.5% pay raise. Job prospects for teachers would be brighter as elementary school enrollments rose in the mid-1980s, according to the National Center for Education Statistics. The National Education Association projected the greatest teacher surpluses in the Northeast, Middle Atlantic, and Great Lakes states.

In Western Europe developments in France aroused the greatest interest as the country's first Socialist government since World War II took office under Pres. François Mitterrand. Education was not a prominent issue in the presidential campaign, but it came to the fore during the campaign for the National Assembly. One major issue involved the long-standing dispute over the privileged position of private (mainly Roman Catholic) schools, which took in some 16% of all French school pupils. The new minister of education, Alain Savary, hoped to avoid a "school war" by finding a solution through negotiations, but it was clear that sooner or later he would have to grapple with the problem of bringing state-subsidized private education into the public sector.

The most tangible action of the new government was to create about 7,000 new jobs in primary and secondary schools, in addition to the 2,400 planned by the previous government. France, like other countries in the West, had falling school enrollments—some 40,000 fewer children in 1981 than in 1980. Hence, the creation of these new jobs, plus another 17,000 posts promised for 1982, should go far toward reducing classroom overcrowding. The additional manpower was to be applied chiefly to "priority education zones," including areas of cultural deprivation and those with large immigrant populations.

In West Germany there were widespread protests against cutbacks in education. According to the main teachers' union, some 20,000 teachers were unemployed, while an additional 150,000 teachers would be needed to bring the pupil-teacher ratio down from the 1981 figure of 20 to 1 to the 15 to 1 that the teachers considered desirable. The city of Hesse witnessed a parents' strike, and in Eschenstruth parents established their own alternative primary school after a mathematics teacher was let go by the local authority. In Sweden cutbacks carried out by the Conservative minister of education (later replaced in a government change) sparked immediate protests; the children in 90 Stockholm schools went on a one-day strike. Teachers in Australia resorted to industrial action in February and March to protest growing constraints on the education budget, although the federal government insisted that real spending had increased. As in France, protests were also directed against state funding of private schools.

In the U.S., where the Constitution mandated strict separation of church and state, the Supreme Court planned to review a ten-year-old policy of the Internal Revenue Service under which tax-exempt status was denied to private schools charged with practicing discrimination based on race or religion. Challengers claimed the IRS had no right to interfere with the religious views and practices of private schools. James Coleman, the sociologist whose controversial 1966 study of segregated and desegregated schools had had a major effect on federal policy, unleashed another controversy when he claimed that parochial and other private high schools are more effective than comparable public schools. In the largest federally funded investigation of nonpublic high schools ever undertaken (58,728 students in 1,016 high schools), Coleman claimed to have found that private and parochial schools provide better education and are more effective in helping minority children learn. The report, funded by the National Center for Education Statistics, was challenged on policy grounds (for example, because it might detract from efforts to improve public schools) and for its research methodology. Private school advocates, on the other hand, saw it as ammunition in their fight to obtain tuition tax credits for parents who send their children to nonpublic schools. President Reagan had endorsed tuition tax credits during his campaign.

Students at Schaumburg (Ill.) Christian School listen to an instructor in a class on "Successful Christian Living." Fundamentalist religious schools were increasing rapidly in the U.S.

JOSE MORE—© CHICAGO TRIBUNE, 1981

World Education

Most recent official data

Country	1st level (primary)			General 2nd level (secondary)			Vocational 2nd level			3rd level (higher)			Literacy	
	Students (full-time)	Teachers (full-time)	Total schools	Students (full-time)	Teachers (full-time)	Total schools	Students (full-time)	Teachers (full-time)	Total schools	Students (full-time)	Teachers (full-time)	Total schools	% of population	Over age
Afghanistan	942,787	30,518	3,417	92,391	6,530	317	19,364[1]	1,295[1]	28	11,367	1,012	29	16.2	15
Algeria	3,918,827	88,481	9,263[2]	999,937	38,845	1,128[2]	26,218[1]	2,292[1]	71[2]	51,510	6,421	...	26.4	15
Angola	1,026,291	25,000	5,585	105,868[3]	4,393[3]	177	3,388[4]	330[4]	73	3,146	293	1	30.0	15
Argentina	4,003,670	224,673	20,590	1,295,815[3]	178,681[3]	1,679	...	...	3,718	479,799	45,179	521	92.6	15
Australia	1,884,094	91,279	8,153	1,100,468[3]	85,340[3]	1,526	870,972	9,564	...	322,622	58,407	561[1,3]	98.5	...
Austria	401,396	26,369	3,466	549,061	45,213	2,023	395,383[1]	21,572[1]	1,146[1]	123,463	11,792	37	98.0	15
Bahrain	48,672	2,826	112	22,141	929	20	2,147[1]	211[1]	5[1]	4,059	125	2	40.2	15
Bangladesh	8,312,011	187,078	40,313	2,213,068	98,965	9,304	402,070[1]	1,537[1]	122[1]	181,756	13,110	700	22.2	15
Bolivia	949,446	38,737	...	128,081[3]	7,143[1,3]	...	17,000[4]	270[4]	80	55,315	2,624	16	39.8	15
Botswana	171,914	5,316	415	18,325	844	38	3,050[1]	318[1]	25[1]	928	113	1	22.0	15
Brazil	21,473,100	854,813	186,009	2,519,122[1,3]	168,336[1,3]	9,323	...	...	...	1,311,799	108,821	...	83.0	15
Bulgaria	70,114	3,636	831	1,146,074	54,459	2,780	228,138	18,846	520	76,179	11,039	44	95.0	8
Burma	3,731,160	84,593	21,999	924,739	31,433	1,848	14,379[1]	1,153[1]	70[1]	112,671	3,922	23	68.3	8
Cameroon	1,254,065	25,248	4,721	147,073	5,112	301	46,728[1]	1,972[1]	164[1]	10,060	439	10	12.0	...
Canada	3,341,053	272,271[3]	...	1,758,021	...	...	...	...	...	643,430	53,758	66	95.6	14
Chile	2,332,566	66,354	7,861	422,856	24,387	593	211,112	4,176	236	127,446	11,419	15	90.7	10
China	146,270,000	2,600,000	900,000	65,000,000	...	160,000	880,000[1]	...	2,000[1]	850,000	...	598	95.0	15
Colombia	4,265,598	131,214	32,230	1,187,148	56,402	3,252	428,963[1]	23,340[1]	932[1]	274,893	25,708	70	98.5	15
Congo	358,761	6,832	...	138,525	3,099	...	10,861[1]	607[1]	...	3,642	165	2	28.8	...
Costa Rica	347,708	10,536	2,951	103,579	4,263	167	30,229	2,056	74	38,629	1,967	5	84.7	15
Cuba	1,550,323	77,063	13,319	825,852	60,553	1,024	224,520[1]	21,096[1]	462[1]	143,461	10,736	28	98.0	...
Cyprus	48,701	2,183	443	41,794	2,408	82	5,922	518	9	1,823	175	13	89.0	15
Czechoslovakia	1,875,000	90,368	8,860	140,380	8,591	339	222,247[1]	17,000[1]	585[1]	190,571	17,863	42	99.5	15
Denmark	448,370	40,261	2,263	61,757	44,642	2,516	247,457[1]	5,792[1]	271	81,352	6,713	358	100.0	15
Ecuador	1,427,627	39,747	10,655	435,056	24,120	990	55,161[1]	6,140[1]	221	274,968	11,998	30	79.0	10
Egypt	4,287,124	127,021	10,297	1,990,383	67,562	2,402	533,259[1]	32,726[1]	448[1]	550,171	23,390	12	45.7	10
El Salvador	858,811	16,563	3,103	72,898[3]	2,844[3]	161	1,069[4]	25[4]	91[4]	31,351	1,809	14	49.0	15
Fiji	129,300	4,209	644	35,054	1,662	124	3,063[1]	242[1]	31[1]	1,448	150	1	79.0	15
Finland	406,921	25,142	4,297	345,603	19,549	1,056	100,438[1]	13,173[1]	541	122,825	5,841	20	100.0	15
France	5,405,056	230,634	54,044	3,844,733	300,145	10,611[3]	1,253,666	58,771	231[4]	859,646	41,978	82	100.0	7
Germany, East	1,320,500	114,622[3]	12,014[2]	1,102,862	12,014	5,599	462,236	16,259	...	298,633	...	289	100.0	15
Germany, West	5,044,200	495,300	23,393[5]	3,729,700	...	...	2,665,900	77,600	9,632	1,044,200	114,000	3,079	99.0	15
Greece	922,698	35,750	9,593	585,130	26,921	2,162	125,039	...	1,991	126,244	6,705	144	86.0	15
Guatemala	709,018	21,060	6,010	145,770[1,3]	8,604[1,3]	493	...	...	...	29,234	1,934	5	36.7	15
Honduras	555,871	13,670	5,088	119,080[3]	2,766[3]	211	1,628[4]	139[4]	14	21,386	1,228	3	59.5	10
Hong Kong	544,673	17,929	838	10,913	...	25	446,181	15,291[2]	396	27,961	2,678	24	80.9	15
Hungary	1,162,000	75,422	4,214	...	...	251[1]	203,000	15,460	282	64,000	13,890	48	98.2	15
India	72,947,804	1,276,446	477,037	26,435,894	1,581,263	155,193	421,028[1]	14,024	2,045[1]	4,296,242	235,822	9,805	34.2	15
Indonesia	21,123,482	676,236	92,499	3,517,319	206,504	9,307	546,126[1]	40,995[1]	3,879[1]	195,994	36,426	306	64.0	15
Iran	4,403,106	154,577	40,197	2,370,341	91,960	7,667	314,135[1]	13,029[1]	950[1]	175,675	13,952	244	36.1	15
Iraq	2,459,870	87,148	10,560	781,766	25,254	1,579	68,674[1]	4,212[1]	155[1]	89,197	5,207	62	52	15
Ireland	565,742	19,651	3,508	288,926	17,881	830	6,666	206	56	38,890	3,594	58	100.0	15
Israel	645,095	35,066	2,088	84,416	6,220	342	78,743	8,517	371	37,724	13,981	55	93.4	14
Italy	4,584,300	278,044	29,762	3,545,298	309,933	31,524	1,687,949[1]	148,296[1]	4,911[1]	756,922	43,120	67	94.0	15
Ivory Coast	894,184	18,704	2,697	144,605	3,423	83,456	22,437	620	12[4]	20,087	368	2	20.0	15
Japan	11,924,706	473,957	25,004	9,982,110[2]	506,198[2]	16,029	9,982,110	506,198	...	2,240,991	125,535	1,036	100.0	15
Jordan	448,411	13,898	1,095	238,763	11,267	1,333	9,880	641	44	27,526	1,178	31	60.0	15
Kampuchea	350,000[5]	7,500[5]	1,333	...	...	...	...	...	...	...	...	...	36.1	...
Kenya	2,977,000	89,773	8,896	368,000[3]	12,696[3]	1,486[3]	377,000	13,368[1]	2[4]	5,837	892	20	40.0	15
Korea, South	5,586,494	122,727	6,517	3,580,258	87,974	2,955	827,579	25,573	621	734,900	23,750	232	88.5	13
Kuwait	145,626	7,722	224	167,253	14,032	281	3,461[1]	582[1]	6[1]	12,391	1,020	...	59.6	15
Laos	451,800	14,218	5,893	72,600	2,494	...	7,814[1]	591[1]	27[1]	1,684	152	3	60.0	15
Lebanon	380,695	32,901[5]	2,319	232,255	32,901[5]	257	7,133[1]	1,059[1]	159[1]	78,628	2,313	13	88.0	15
Lesotho	228,523	4,233	1,081	17,732	621	60	1,780[1]	142[1]	11	847	95	9	56.5	15
Liberia	192,185	4,567	843	45,668	2,713	275	1,778[1]	101[1]	6[1]	3,789	190	3	21.5	15
Libya	600,747	28,229	2,150	196,079	12,915	861	35,402[1]	3,000[1]	106[1]	15,018	1,340	19	52.4	15
Luxembourg	30,112	1,998	541	8,801	1,801[3]	3059	15,903[1]	1,801	...	284	172	2	100.0	15
Malawi	675,740	11,115	2,371	15,079	707	61	2,040[1]	174[1]	13[1]	1,153	128	4	16.5	15
Malaysia	2,033,803	73,881	6,461	1,102,908	48,199	970	17,424	1,430	37	57,139	5,569	34	60.8	10
Mali	293,227	6,877	...	64,491	8,915	...	4,870[1]	666[1]	...	4,216	450	...	2.2	...
Mauritius	123,666	6,177	257	80,881	3,075	148	721[1]	61[1]	3[1]	98	76	1	61.6	12
Mexico	13,604,476	334,146	62,511	3,375,026	193,448	8,449	524,852[1]	36,222[1]	2,688[1]	610,840	52,294	223	86.7	15
Morocco	2,331,000	55,303	2,498	826,500	31,794	644	20,766[1]	847[4]	...	80,345	2,558	19	22.2	...
Mozambique	1,387,000	...	...	104,000	...	...	...	...	...	804	164	...	7.0	...
Nepal	1,012,530	23,395	7,275	342,929	11,630	...	236,643[1]	809[1]	871	31,942	1,980	55	12.5	15
Netherlands, The	1,470,097	64,881	9,632	823,594	53,955	1,525	561,279[1]	48,000[1]	1,859[1]	278,654	28,600	364	100.0	15
New Zealand	506,602	20,402	2,569	226,346	13,527	396	145,075	2,216	21	57,141	3,682	15	100.0	15
Nicaragua	472,167	13,318	4,421	120,522	3,145[3]	259	19,221[1]	3,200[1]	81[1]	34,710	1,052	4	87.0	15
Nigeria	11,457,772	287,040	36,287	1,159,404	19,409	2,906	329,841[1]	19,059[1]	426[1]	101,210	5,019	53	25.0	15
Norway	593,579	31,719	3,021	178,514[3]	14,204[3]	1,419[3]	12,734[4]	1,049[4]	...	40,643	3,648	134	100.0	15
Pakistan	7,090,000	139,300	53,162	1,996,000	115,600	8,204	46,361[1]	3,558[1]	406[1]	349,259	19,878	554	26.7	10
Panama	337,726	12,361	2,306	130,496	5,971	188	40,777[1]	6,019[1]	118	40,369	1,959	2	82.0	10
Papua New Guinea	288,287	9,280	2,077	37,068	1,599	99	5,949[1]	419[1]	97	2,224	374	3	30.4	10
Paraguay	504,377	18,038	2,799	110,095[3]	9,830[3]	731	...	...	24	25,232	1,984	...	79.7	10
Peru	3,584,300	77,844	20,126	1,119,000[3]	37,383[3]	284	...	...	...	278,700	13,468	58	76.0	15
Philippines	8,056,013	274,205	33,180	2,941,210	104,657[3]	2,445[2]	182,196	...	284[2]	946,860	41,384	...	83.4	15
Poland	4,167,313	201,712	12,394[2]	345,214	23,016	871[2]	1,328,655[1]	74,548[1]	6,274[2]	388,443	54,681	91	98.0	15
Portugal	1,777,868	58,652	...	417,112	13,272	...	88,257[1]	9,590[1]	...	79,592	8,111	96	71.0	...
Puerto Rico	432,012	15,308	1,725	142,836	6,051	203	57,863	2,600	124	130,105	3,300	27	90.5	14
Romania	3,289,108	153,568	14,487	1,030,120	50,201	1,837[1,3]	178,595[1]	4,190[1]	...	192,546	14,500	44	100.0	8
Rwanda	515,712	8,161	1,606	13,799[1,3]	820[1,3]	56	...	...	...	975	184	4	25.0	15
Saudi Arabia	752,977	40,779	2,711	265,256	20,046	749	22,162[1]	2,245[1]	88	43,897	3,964	17	25.0	...
Senegal	346,585	8,186	140	78,384	1,758	89	14,090[1]	820[1]	124[1]	9,454	900	130	45.6	14
Singapore	296,608	11,267	351	170,316	8,019	135	14,871[1]	1,106[1]	16	20,183	1,753	4	77.9	10
South Africa	4,480,493	164,149[1,3,5]	2,511[5]	1,225,153	...	...	29,591	...	153	218,275	16,708	106	89.0	...
Soviet Union	34,400,000	2,638,000[5]	147,000[5]	9,900,000	...	...	4,612,000	229,700	8,704	5,235,500	345,000	883	100.0	15
Spain	6,896,227	224,704	216,637	1,055,788	63,645	2,425	515,119	33,583	2,037	634,950	36,578	114	90.1	15
Sri Lanka	1,975,749	138,488[5]	3,588	1,159,967	...	5,501	8,897[1]	1,771[1]	25[4]	13,154	2,498	...	82.0	...
Sudan	1,358,193	38,881	5,729	835,322	17,072	1,477	16,662[1]	1,325[1]	60[1]	24,109	1,963	17	68.6	10
Suriname	75,139	2,803	285	29,790	1,854	96	1,275	148	4	2,353	155	2	65.0	15
Sweden	556,481	129,969[3,5]	4,923	486,852	...	...	103,485	...	...	155,352	...	...	100.0	...
Syria	1,407,223	46,132	7,435	552,677	25,945	1,230	36,309[1]	4,073[1]	74	96,040	1,332	3	46.6	10
Taiwan	2,222,595	68,627	2,401	1,598,028	69,280[3]	1,011	...	...	178	342,528	16,495	104	85.9	15
Thailand	6,848,121	283,204	32,956	1,503,646	66,965	2,249	244,277[1]	34,934[1]	309	169,639	29,667	12	81.8	10
Togo	421,436	7,251	1,199	105,770	2,328	112	9,201[1]	347	23	2,777	236	2	54.9	14
Tunisia	1,024,537	26,207	2,469	184,084	15,075[3]	202	57,824[1]	128[4]	...	25,602	2,236	...	50.0	...
Turkey	5,562,315	187,027	40,383	1,591,615	65,262	2,933	507,045[1]	27,846[1]	563[1]	313,517	19,700	81	54.7	6
Uganda	1,208,915	34,213	4,022	21,280	2,838	198	13,310[1]	676[1]	44[1]	5,494	587	4	44.0	15
United Arab Emirates	88,167	5,136	244	31,138	2,736	68	422	83	4	125,209	8,343	318	...	...
United Kingdom	5,535,082	241,607	27,098	4,785,520	290,359[3]	5,570	...	...	61	322,722	42,300	106	100.0	15
United States	24,254,359	1,192,131	105,424[5]	16,684,925	1,001,794[3]	...	...	...	...	11,500,000	820,000	3,046	100.0	15
Uruguay	325,888	13,821	2,307	151,962	13,980	259	46,268[1]	4,541[1]	105	39,392	3,263	1	93.9	15
Venezuela	2,378,601	91,384	12,753	787,032	47,137[1,3]	1,447	61,535	...	...	282,075	23,449	68	84.9	15
Western Samoa	42,073	1,458	153	9,719	458	39	473[1]	41[1]	4	425	53	6	98.3	10
Yugoslavia	1,427,769	57,335	13,119	1,912,231	127,906[1,3]	5,905	501,557[1]	41,206[1]	1,630[1]	285,431	18,178	349	83.5	15
Zaire	3,818,934	80,481	5,924	458,776	14,483[1,3]	2,511	184,899[1]	...	...	21,021	2,550	36	35.0	...
Zambia	985,528	19,441	2,786	88,842	3,669	125	8,711[1]	819[1]	26[1]	3,773	412	1	40.7	15
Zimbabwe	1,235,994	33,516	2,559	74,321	4,110	...	9,532[1]	536[1]	...	4,563	483	...	34.3	15

[1]Includes teacher training. [2]Public schools only. [3]Includes vocational. [4]Teacher training only. [5]Data for primary include secondary. [6]Includes preprimary education.

For the second time since 1968, scores on the Scholastic Aptitude Test (SAT), widely used in the U.S. for college entrance, did not decline. The stabilization of the scores was attributed to tougher standards in the schools and to more serious attitudes on the part of both students and parents. In several countries standards of attainment were surveyed, in line with the growing demand for more accountability by the schools. In Australia a national survey of attainment in the three R's among 10–14-year-olds indicated that there had been a slight improvement since 1975. Girls did better than boys at reading and writing. In England and Wales the first report produced by the Assessment of Performance Unit attempted to assess reading skills at age 11. Not surprisingly, pupils with an affluent background did considerably better than their poorer fellows.

Also in England and Wales, data were being gathered for a major report on the teaching of mathematics. The evidence there and elsewhere seemed to indicate that the 1960s reform of the mathematics curriculum had gone too far. In France, for example, *le maths moderne* was promoted by publishers and seemed to have the backing of international authorities and such organizations as UNESCO. In-service training for teachers was inadequate, however, and the new concepts were ineffectually applied. This, plus the association in the public mind of new math with school reform and student unrest, led to some disillusionment and dwindling interest.

The political convulsions in Poland affected education. The battle between the independent trade union Solidarity and the Ministry of Education led to the establishment of a "national coordinating commission of educational workers on the teaching of history in primary and secondary schools." This group, which soon identified the teaching of history as a burning issue, demanded that study of the Christian tradition in Europe be included in the school syllabus and that official guidelines on the interpretation of history be dropped.

In Spain, still emerging from a long period of educational neglect under the Franco regime, the Ministry of Education proposed to replace the three-year middle school and one-year pre-university period with four years of secondary school broken into two cycles of two years each, the first providing for a general curriculum and the second divided into academic and technical streams. The main objective was to increase opportunities for developing technical skills.

At a conference on the future of education in Zimbabwe, held in Salisbury in September, a key paper was delivered by Edmund Garwe, director of primary education. He foresaw an educational system consisting of three stages: one covering ages three to five, followed by primary and secondary education, which together would last nine years. He spoke strongly against selective secondary schools and argued that pupils should go on to some form of higher education at age 15. He also believed that cumulative records or profiles should be used to evaluate students rather than examination results alone. Farther south, in South Africa, periodic boycotts of schools by black pupils were reported, sometimes accompanied by violence. It was estimated that some 1.5 million black pupils attended schools in white areas and 2 million were in all-black schools in nonindependent homelands. There were no official statistics for the number of black pupils in the "independent" homelands.

Resistance in black Africa to what was seen as white influence on education was demonstrated in Kenya, where a strong reaction was reported against the new math. Similar reactions were also being reported in developed countries (*see* above), but in Kenya the new math appeared to have entered the curriculum as a result of U.S., British, and Canadian influence. Kenyan teachers also objected to attempts by the U.S. Agency for International Development and the Association of Education Development to introduce the teaching of English by radio.

Progress in the oil-rich states was uneven. Besides the inevitable problems of overrapid expansion, the Arab countries faced the need to reconcile demand for islamization with the secular requirements of education. The United Arab Emirates had increased its education budget from $17 million in 1973 to some $300 million in 1981, but 95% of the state's 6,300 teachers had had to be recruited from such countries as Egypt and Jordan, and there were continued reports of severe disciplinary problems. The first graduates of al-Ain University, opened in 1977, were described as having attained a level no higher than that of English school leavers at the Advanced level. In Venezuela an estimated $12 billion had been invested in education since 1974, but a report to the government by Meir Merhav, a former Israeli planning minister and UN official, stated that more than 30% of the country's labour force had had no education beyond the third grade and that about 15% were illiterate.

In India the fourth survey carried out by the National Council for Educational Research and Training reported that one in three primary schools in India had only one teacher. Only 38% of children enrolled in the lower primary schools were girls. The average pupil-teacher ratio in lower primary schools was 41 to 1, and in secondary schools it was 18 to 1. There were reports that outcastes (Harijans) were underrepresented, particularly at the higher stages of education.

Higher Education. Universities in a number of Western countries faced serious retrenchment, either because of cuts in government funding or because prospective students opted to enter the job market. In Italy, for example, the number of young people seeking to enter the universities in 1980–81 was only 73% of what it had been the previous year. In Denmark only half as many students went on to higher education as had been the case in 1974. The Conservative government in the U.K. announced that the university system would be reduced 15% by 1983. The vice-chancellors (principals of universities) estimated that this would reduce a young person's chances of going to a university by one in seven. Complete tenure for university teachers in Britain came under attack as a system of short-term contracts was proposed by the university authorities.

In the U.S. the Reagan administration's budget cutbacks included tightening the eligibility requirements for federally guaranteed student loans. Students wishing to take out such loans would be subject to a "needs test" if they came from families with incomes above $30,000. In addition, limits were placed on other student-aid programs, and schedules for the repayment of student loans were made more stringent. Proponents of the cutbacks claimed the student loan program had been abused, citing wealthy families who had applied for the low-interest loans and put the money into short-term, high-yield investments. At the same time, with college expenses rising 13–14% for the 1981–82 academic year, supporting children in college was becoming increasingly difficult for the middle class. According to a survey conducted by the College Scholarship Service, total expenses (tuition and fees, room and board, books, transportation, and personal expenses) would average $6,885 per year at private four-year colleges and $3,873 at public colleges in 1981–82. At some prestigious East Coast schools, annual expenses topped $11,000.

Despite the escalating costs, enrollment in institutions of higher education in the U.S. continued to rise moderately, reaching an all-time high of 12.1 million in 1980–81. Although the number of 18-year-olds in the population had been declining for two years, the number of college freshmen was increasing, and thousands of applicants had difficulty in finding places. However, a slight declining trend was predicted for the 1980s. The Census Bureau estimated that the number of people in the U.S. 25 years old or older with college degrees had doubled since 1960. Job opportunities for 1981 college graduates were good, according to the College Placement Council. Engineering graduates fared best, and there was a 25% increase in job opportunities for those with master's degrees in science, math, and other technical categories. The increase was chiefly in the private sector, while civil service job opportunities were moderate to low. Liberal arts graduates continued to earn significantly less than their counterparts in technical fields.

In Australia the Fraser government's stringent economic policies began to bite hard on higher education in 1981. The Australian Tertiary Education Commission produced figures to show that since 1974 the proportion of all young people proceeding directly from secondary to higher education had declined by one-fifth, representing a substantial reversal of the previous trend. Teacher education, especially, appeared to suffer. In April Prime Minister Malcolm Fraser told Parliament that 30 colleges of education would have to merge with other institutions or have their funds cut off in 1982. Despite this retrenchment, the government's financial policies appeared to have widespread public support.

Political changes in Europe inevitably brought some changes at the higher education level. In France half the rectors of the universities (who also had administrative responsibilities for schools) were dismissed for political reasons following the election of the Socialist government. In Ireland the new Fine Gael government under Garret FitzGerald, which took office in June, had promised greater support for the Irish universities. The number of full-time students in "third-level" colleges was to be raised from the current 38,800 to 45,000 in 1985 and 65,000 by 1990; four regional technical colleges were promised for the Greater Dublin area; and additional technical colleges were to be established in areas of growing population. Once in office, however, the government announced that the state of public finances was worse than anticipated and that some of the more attractive election promises would have to be delayed. Among European Economic Community countries, Ireland had the highest proportion of population under 15 years of age (31%, compared with an EEC average of 22%), the highest birthrate, and the lowest percentage of young people in higher education.

The West German advisory body on higher education, the Wissenschaftsrat (Science Council), recommended expansion of the *Fachhochschulen* (colleges of advanced vocational education). These colleges provided a narrower but more intensive type of education than the universities, with the course of study lasting three and a half to four years, as compared with university courses of at least six years. *Fachhochschulen* were also smaller than universities, averaging between 1,000 and 3,000 students, and teaching was done in smaller groups. The Science Council noted that these institutions tended to attract a higher proportion of young people from working-class families.

The development of "long-distance learning" via radio and television continued to attract worldwide interest. In Britain, which had pioneered the "Open University" concept, it was estimated that some 100,000 students had received direct help with home studies from the Open University and 45,000 mature students had obtained a degree through the OU. Other countries showing an interest were Finland and Japan, although both had well-developed systems of higher education. The Japanese hoped to attract some 30,000 students to their "University of the Air," which was to be operated mainly by radio. The government's plans were opposed by the Socialists on the grounds that they could lead to greater government control over education.

Saudi Arabia continued to expand higher education. The third five-year plan, due to end in 1985, put particular emphasis on "saudization." By the end of the plan period, it was expected that there would be 69,000 students, 59,000 of them Saudis. China was to receive a World Bank loan of $100 million for higher education. In addition, a $100 million credit was promised by the International Development Association. The Chinese announced a goal of 4 million graduates and 2.2 million university students by 1990. Since 1977 some 2,700 Chinese postgraduate students had gone abroad to study in 41 foreign countries, the majority of them in the U.S., the U.K., France, and West Germany.

South Africa's National Manpower Commission proposed that blacks be allowed to study at white universities and technical institutions, but the government, which had consistently opposed ra-

cial mixing in higher education, pressed ahead with plans to establish separate "township colleges" for urban Africans. In Zimbabwe differences of opinion emerged over the role of the university in Salisbury. Prime Minister Robert Mugabe argued that the university should be African-minded with a socialist orientation; others contended that it should not become the tool of the state. (JOEL L. BURDIN; TUDOR DAVID)

See also Libraries; Motion Pictures.

Egypt

A republic of northeast Africa, Egypt is bounded by Israel, Sudan, Libya, the Mediterranean Sea, and the Red Sea. Area: 997,667 sq km (385,201 sq mi). Pop. (1981 est.): 43 million. Cap. and largest city: Cairo (pop., 1979 est., 5,399,000). Language: Arabic. Religion (1976): Muslim 94%, according to official figures; non-Muslims, however, may be undercounted. President and prime minister in 1981, Anwar as-Sadat until October 6; president from October 14 and prime minister from October 7, Hosni Mubarak.

The assassination of Pres. Anwar as-Sadat (*see* OBITUARIES) on Oct. 6, 1981, brought to a head international concern about the stability of Egypt. Sadat was shot during a military parade, an annual event marking Egypt's successful campaigns during the Egypt-Israeli war of 1973. He was taking the salute at the parade when a group of men in military uniform fired submachine guns and threw hand grenades into the reviewing stand where he stood. Four people were accused by the state of the assassination of Sadat, and 20 others were accused of complicity in the killing. The state

asked for the death penalty at the trial, which opened on November 21. The chief accused was Lieut. Khalid Ahmad Shawqi al-Istanbuli of the artillery corps, but 11 of the accused were college teachers and students. In a series of measures against individuals believed to be involved in the anti-Sadat movement, property and assets belonging to some prominent exiles, including Lieut. Gen. Sa'd ash-Shazli, a former Egyptian Army chief of staff, were confiscated on November 15. In December the interior minister, Muhammad Nawabi Ismail, announced that 2,500 persons had been detained since the assassination.

Egypt

In the months before his assassination, Sadat had divided his time between promoting peace in the Middle East abroad and facing increasing sectarian strife within his own country. He visited France in February and Britain in August, on both occasions exploring ways in which the Europeans might possibly mediate between the Israelis and the Palestinians. The European Communities 1980 Venice declaration on the Middle East had been welcomed by Sadat since it recognized the rights of the Palestinians to self-determination, an issue on which the Camp David peace process had made no progress. At home increasing tension between Muslim fundamentalists and Christians seriously scarred Egypt's reputation for domestic stability; street rioting in Cairo in June left at least 17 dead and more than 50 injured. The unrest culminated in a severe nationwide security crackdown in September. More than 1,500 people—in the main Muslim fundamentalists, Coptic Christians, and leading opposition figures—were arrested.

In the aftermath of the assassination, fear of a broadly based conspiracy involving popular support from fundamentalist Muslim groups such as

The body of Egyptian Pres. Anwar as-Sadat was carried on a caisson for burial in a crypt under the Tomb of the Unknown Soldier in Cairo on October 10.

EL KOUSSY—GAMMA/LIAISON

Members of the Muslim Brotherhood were rounded up in Egypt and jailed during a government crackdown on dissidents in October.

Al Takfir wal Hijra proved unfounded. Hosni Mubarak (*see* BIOGRAPHIES), vice-president at the time of the shooting, was immediately nominated as Sadat's successor. He moved rapidly after his inauguration to tone down some of the rhetoric of the Sadat years. Mubarak released first 31 and later 17 leading Egyptians from among those arrested in

September. It was predicted in Cairo in late 1981 that the Coptic patriarch Shenuda III might soon be reinstated. During the September purges he had been stripped of his official secular status as head of the Coptic Church, though remaining its spiritual head.

President Mubarak remained totally committed to completing the Camp David agreements for achieving peace in the Middle East. Under these accords the return of the Sinai Peninsula by the Israelis to Egypt was scheduled to be completed on April 25, 1982. Only then was it likely that Egypt would adopt a hard line toward Israel. Mubarak, it was suggested, might then act to improve relations with certain moderate Arab nations. Egypt denounced Israel's annexation of the Golan Heights, but Mubarak denied that it represented a slap at Egypt.

After the initial nervousness following the assassination, most European and other Western countries moved quickly to support Mubarak. The Japanese announced a new aid package for the Suez Canal in November, and in a show of strength and support the U.S. lent two AWACS (airborne warning and control system) aircraft to monitor any possible threat from Libya. The U.S. then carried out its planned military exercises, code-named "Bright Star '82," which involved U.S., Egyptian, Sudanese, and Omani troops. A bilateral investment agreement with the U.S. was scheduled to be signed in 1982.

Though Egypt was naturally anxious to avoid being classified as a puppet of the West, a further strengthening of its relationship with Washington seemed inevitable. The growing commitment was to be emphasized in 1982 by the presence of U.S. combat troops in Sinai as part of the proposed multinational peacekeeping and observation force that was scheduled to patrol there after Israel's withdrawal. U.S. support was, however, also expressed in late 1981 with the conclusion of the first-ever U.S. mixed-credit financing deal involving the U.S. Agency for International Development and the U.S. Export-Import Bank. The credit was extended for the purchase of turbines for the Aswan II power station.

EGYPT

Education. (1978–79) Primary, pupils 4,287,124, teachers 127,021; secondary, pupils 1,990,383, teachers 67,562; vocational, pupils 492,664, teachers 29,353; teacher training, students 40,595, teachers 3,373; higher (1977–78), students 550,171, teaching staff 23,390.

Finance. Monetary unit: Egyptian pound, with (Sept. 21, 1981) an official rate of E£0.70 to U.S. $1 (free rate of E£1.30 = £1 sterling). Gold and other reserves (June 1981) U.S. $776 million. Budget (total; 1979 est.): revenue E£10,249 million; expenditure E£12,929 million. Gross national product (1979) E£13,260 million. Money supply (June 1981) E£5,288 million. Cost of living (1975 = 100; Feb. 1981) 194.

Foreign Trade. (1980) Imports E£3,402 million; exports E£2,132 million. Import sources (1979): U.S. 18%; West Germany 11%; Italy 8%; France 8%; U.K. 7%; Japan 5%. Export destinations (1979): Italy 27%; U.S.S.R. 8%; The Netherlands 8%; West Germany 5%; U.K. 5%; Japan 5%. Main exports (1979): crude oil 31%; cotton 21%; cotton yarn and fabrics 13%; petroleum products 11%; fruit and vegetables 7%; aluminum 5%.

Transport and Communications. Roads (1979) 28,910 km. Motor vehicles in use: passenger (1980) 325,500; commercial (including buses; 1979) 114,700. Railways: (1980) c. 4,882 km; traffic (1978) 9,290,000,000 passenger-km, freight 2,302,000,000 net ton-km. Air traffic (1980): 2,870,-000,000 passenger-km; freight 30.9 million net ton-km. Shipping (1980): merchant vessels 100 gross tons and over 278; gross tonnage 555,786. Telephones (Jan. 1975) 503,-200. Radio receivers (Dec. 1977) 5,275,000. Television receivers (Dec. 1977) 1 million.

Agriculture. Production (in 000; metric tons; 1980): wheat c. 1,796; barley c. 107; millet c. 643; corn c. 3,230; rice c. 2,348; potatoes c. 1,157; sugar, raw value 662; tomatoes c. 2,571; onions c. 567; dry broad beans (1979) 236; watermelons (1979) c. 1,344; dates c. 418; oranges c. 1,092; grapes c. 280; cotton, lint c. 530; cheese c. 243; beef and buffalo meat c. 243. Livestock (in 000; 1979): cattle 1,954; buffalo 2,321; sheep 1,679; goats 1,427; asses 1,672; camels 105; chickens 27,292.

Industry. Production (in 000; metric tons; 1980): cement 3,014; iron ore (50% metal content; 1979) 1,440; crude oil 29,446; natural gas (cu m) 2,190,000; petroleum products (1978) 11,252; sulfuric acid (1978) 235; fertilizers (nutrient content; 1979–80) nitrogenous 264, phosphate c. 93; salt (1978) 755; cotton yarn 231; cotton fabrics (m) 632,000; electricity (kw-hr; 1978) c. 14,500,000.

Mubarak's political strategy was aimed at stressing continuity in the government at Cabinet level, but after the "honeymoon" period was over he was expected to make Cabinet changes. He received a grim economic inheritance, particularly with regard to the heavy burden of government subsidies on food and other commodities. Subsidies were costing the government 11% of gross national product, and the figure was expected to rise to 28% in the financial year ending in June 1982. It was politically difficult for the government to alter the subsidy system on food and basic commodities, but a steady reduction was expected by most outside observers, including the International Monetary Fund. The IMF was a persuasive influence, since it was considering providing a standby facility to the value of 600 million special drawing rights ($670 million) to Egypt in order to help meet a budget deficit.

Mubarak was also expected to come under pressure to improve the so-called open-door trade policy that was introduced by Sadat in 1974. Foreign banks in Cairo, although many reported good profits on their operations, maintained that there had been little benefit to the economy as a result of al-infitah ("opening-up"). Banks had profited from letter-of-credit business, but very little direct investment in local enterprises had taken place. One effect of the open-door policy had been to encourage the importing of goods that could have been made in Egypt. Banks said that they needed time, given conditions in Egypt, to evaluate political and credit risks.

Tighter monetary controls were announced in September following a 20% devaluation of the Egyptian pound in August. Banks were no longer able to accept cash deposits in foreign currencies without proofs that the money had been imported legally. The central bank hoped that this move would help reduce pressure on the black-market dollar price, which was reckoned to be helping to fuel an inflation rate of 25–30% annually.

The economy's four principal revenue earners were tolls from the Suez Canal, remittances from Egyptians working abroad, tourism, and, most important of all, sales of crude oil. Altogether, these sources brought in $9 billion a year. Future production prospects for crude oil appeared good; there was general optimism that additional offshore deposits, particularly of gas, remained to be discovered. Despite the slack world demand for oil, there was no shortage of interest in Egyptian crude. In the financial year ending June 1982 a total of more than $3 billion was expected from crude-oil sales. The exciting finds of 1981 were in the Red Sea near Hurghada, a beach resort area, by the U.S. Mobil Oil Corp. A group comprising West Germany's Deminex, British Petroleum, and Royal Dutch Shell made another find north of the Mobil discovery.

It was thought possible that Mubarak would prove more hesitant than his predecessor in committing Egypt to a single source of military equipment. He was expected to favour diversification away from dependence on the U.S. France seemed the most likely alternative supplier.

(JOHN WHELAN)

El Salvador

El Salvador

A republic on the Pacific coast of Central America and the smallest country on the isthmus, El Salvador is bounded on the west by Guatemala and on the north and east by Honduras. Area: 21,041 sq km (8,124 sq mi). Pop. (1981 est.): 4,942,000. Cap. and largest city: San Salvador (pop., 1980 est., 433,000). Language: Spanish. Religion: Roman Catholic (1979) 91.1%. President of the civilian-military junta in 1981, José Napoleón Duarte.

The civil war in El Salvador intensified in 1981, with guerrilla and counterinsurgency activity spreading into the northern departments of Morazán, Chalatenango, and Cabañas. The appointment of Pres. José Napoleón Duarte (see BIOGRAPHIES), a leading Christian Democrat and member of the ruling junta, and the dismissal of Col. Adolfo Arnoldo Majano Ramos, the most moderate member of the junta, in December 1980 did little to reduce right-wing activity, which was increasingly directed not only against the left but also against the junta. In the same month the Frente Farabundo Martí para la Liberación Nacional (FMLN), military wing of the leftist Frente Democrático Revolucionario (FDR), had announced a renewed offensive against the junta.

The polarization between left and right led to strife that resulted in the deaths of some 22,000 people during the year following the 1979 coup. The situation severely undermined the credibility of the junta, especially its proposals to hold elections to approve a new constitution in March 1982 and to return to civilian government a year later.

The main support for the junta, besides that from the right wing of the Christian Democrats and the military, came from U.S. Pres. Ronald Reagan. U.S. military and economic aid contributions increased; figures published in March showed that

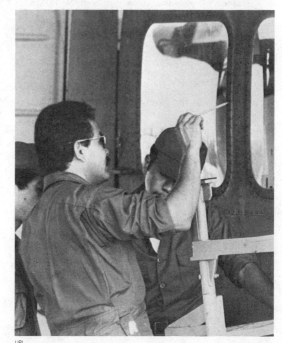

A U.S. military adviser (left) instructs El Salvador Army personnel in the repair of U.S. helicopters that had been provided to the Salvadoran government. The helicopters were being used against guerrillas in El Salvador.

UPI

Eire:
see Ireland

Electrical Industries:
see Energy; Industrial Review

Electronics:
see Computers; Industrial Review

the U.S., up to that time, had sent a total of $35.4 million in military assistance and $125 million in economic aid. At the diplomatic level, Robert E. White was dismissed in February from his post as U.S. ambassador to El Salvador and replaced two months later by a hard-liner, Deane R. Hinton. Later in the year, however, there were signs that President Reagan was putting more emphasis on a political rather than a military solution. In September the U.S. Senate insisted that aid from the U.S. should remain dependent upon a satisfactory report twice a year on human rights within El Salvador. President Reagan expressed his official support for the proposed 1982 elections. U.S. aid to Nicaragua was suspended in an attempt to halt the supply of arms to left-wing guerrilla groups; it was claimed that arms from Cuba were reaching El Salvador through that country.

Attempts by the Socialist International and by other countries to mediate the conflict failed. In August France and Mexico issued a joint declaration to the UN Security Council; as a prelude to free and fair elections they recommended negotiations between the junta and the leftist coalition (FDR and FMLN) and a "restructuring" of the armed forces. This proposal was rejected by the junta, criticized by the U.S., and condemned by a group of nine Latin-American nations comprising Argentina, Bolivia, Chile, Colombia, Guatemala, Honduras, Paraguay, Dominican Republic, and Venezuela. Only Cuba, Nicaragua, Panama, and The Netherlands expressed their support. The UN General Assembly passed a resolution on December 16 calling on the junta to open negotiations with the guerrillas before elections were held.

EL SALVADOR

Education. (1978) Primary, pupils 858,811, teachers (1976) 16,563; secondary and vocational, pupils 72,898, teachers (1975) 2,844; teacher training (1977), students 1,-069, teachers (1975) 25; higher, students 31,351, teaching staff (1977) 1,809.

Finance. Monetary unit: colón, with (Sept. 21, 1981) a par value of 2.50 colones to U.S. $1 (free rate of 4.63 colones = £1 sterling). Gold and other reserves (June 1981) U.S. $108 million. Budget (1980 actual): revenue 1,028,900,000 colones; expenditure 1,422,400,000 colones. Gross national product (1980) 8,550,000,000 colones. Money supply (May 1981) 1,417,200,000 colones. Cost of living (1975 = 100; June 1981) 212.6.

Foreign Trade. (1980) Imports 2,415,200,000 colones; exports 2,417,000,000 colones. Import sources (1979): U.S. 29%; Guatemala 18%; Venezuela 8%; Japan 8%; Costa Rica 5%; West Germany 5%. Export destinations (1979): U.S. 27%; West Germany 20%; Guatemala 16%; The Netherlands 9%; Costa Rica 6%; Japan 6%. Main exports: coffee 54%; cotton 9%; textile yarns and fabrics c. 9%; chemicals c. 6%.

Transport and Communications. Roads (1976) 11,005 km. Motor vehicles in use (1977): passenger 70,100; commercial (including buses) 35,500. Railways: (1978) 602 km; traffic (1980) c. 26 million passenger-km, freight 57 million net ton-km. Air traffic (1980): c. 178 million passenger-km; freight c. 13 million net ton-km. Telephones (Jan. 1978) 70,400. Radio receivers (1977) 1,415,000. Television receivers (1977) 148,000.

Agriculture. Production (in 000; metric tons; 1980): corn 537; sorghum c. 177; dry beans c. 47; sugar, raw value 207; bananas (1979) c. 55; oranges c. 97; coffee c. 126; cotton, lint 69. Livestock (in 000; 1979): cattle 1,368; pigs 560; horses c. 89; chickens c. 6,000.

Industry. Production (in 000; metric tons; 1978): cement 520; petroleum products c. 706; fertilizers (nutrient content; 1979–80) nitrogenous c. 15, phosphate c. 2; cotton yarn (1977) 6.4; electricity (kw-hr; 1979) c. 1,580,000.

Employment:
see Economy, World

The widespread political unrest and terrorist attacks resulted in severe disruption of the economy, both in agriculture and in the small but once dynamic industrial sector. Guerrilla kidnappings of businessmen, arson of crops, and sabotage of the country's hydroelectric and geothermal power generators continued throughout 1981. On October 15 guerrillas destroyed Golden Bridge, the most important bridge across the Lempa River, thus severely disrupting communications with the eastern third of the country. Coffee growers reduced sowing for the 1982 crop because of fears that the junta intended to implement the second stage of the agrarian reform, in which properties between 100 and 500 ha (240–1,200 ac) would be converted to peasants' cooperatives.

Gross domestic product in 1980 was estimated to have declined by 6% and was expected to decline still further in 1981. The balance of trade for 1980 also showed a marked deterioration, with exports falling by 20% to $967 million and imports increasing by 13% to $1,107,000,000. From February 1981 all imports considered nonessential were prohibited and certain others, including basic foods and medicines, required prior deposit by the importer of twice the goods' value with the central bank.

(LUCY BLACKBURN)

Energy

As in the previous year, the dominant events on the energy scene during 1981 took place in the international oil markets. The Organization of Petroleum Exporting Countries (OPEC) began the year with a continuation of its series of price increases. These increases reflected the continuing fundamental disagreement within OPEC over pricing strategy. Saudi Arabia, the world's leading exporter, held to its long-standing position that there should be a uniform base price for all OPEC oil and that any increase should be moderate. It raised its price by only $2, to $32 a barrel. The price "hawks," such as Libya and Nigeria, disagreed. With prices already higher than that of Saudi Arabia, they announced increases to levels of $37–$41 a barrel. Non-OPEC exporters, such as Mexico and the United Kingdom, followed suit with price increases of their own.

These actions were taken in the face of the worldwide oversupply of oil that had developed during 1980 and had filled inventories to overflowing. As the year progressed, the strain that these circumstances placed on the market could no longer be borne, and in April the first break came when Ecuador and Mexico reduced the prices of their less desirable crude oils. Buyers throughout the world then began to reduce their purchases of high-priced oil, and Saudi Arabia announced that it would continue to maintain its level of production at its lower price, thus intensifying the supply-demand imbalance.

The OPEC dispute remained unresolved at the organization's semiannual meeting in May. Saudi Arabia refused to raise its price or cut production, and the others refused to lower their prices despite the decline in sales. In June the Mexican national

oil company cut the price of its best grade of oil by $4, an action that was promptly disavowed by the government and that cost the director of the company his job. North Sea and other exporters then followed with their own price cuts. During the summer, buyers continued to cut back on their purchases from all sellers except Saudi Arabia, and Mexico's six-week attempt to restore half of the $4 price cut was fruitless. With the decline in sales, some OPEC members for the first time in many years experienced a substantial reduction in oil revenues.

In August a special meeting of OPEC was convened at the behest of the price hawks, who attempted to obtain agreement on a unified price above the Saudi level along with a Saudi production cutback. The Saudis refused to raise their price, and the impasse continued. Nigeria cut its price by $4, and Algeria and Libya attempted to maintain their $40 price by offering to barter oil for other products. World demand continued to decline, however, and storage levels remained so high that a record number of idle tankers were used for floating storage.

Agreement was finally reached at a second meeting, held at the end of October. Saudi Arabia raised its price to $34, and the other OPEC members agreed that this price would be the benchmark from which to establish quality differentials. It was further agreed that there would be no increase in this price throughout 1982 and that Saudi Arabia would reduce its production by any amount necessary to maintain the price at the agreed-on level.

Domestic prices of crude oil and products followed the course of the international market in most countries. In January U.S. Pres. Ronald Reagan eliminated the controls that had governed oil prices since 1971. The result was a prompt rise in crude oil prices to world market levels and a sharp increase in product prices. The effect of world oversupply was soon felt in the U.S., however. Both crude and product prices began to sag. Gasoline stocks reached record levels, and the U.S. public experienced the forgotten joy of price wars at some filling stations. Continued sluggish demand

also had a severe effect on refining. Many small refineries went out of business, and some large ones in both the U.S. and Europe were closed. The level of refinery operations in the U.S. industry sank to an all-time low, with some 50 refineries shut down completely.

The major discovery news of the year was the confirmation of a new oil province in the Grand Banks area off Newfoundland. The Hibernia field, discovered in 1980, was shown to be larger than all but 2 of the 33 oil fields in the North Sea, and a second large field was discovered 37 km (23 mi) to the southeast. Elsewhere in the Atlantic the disappointing succession of dry holes in the Baltimore Canyon area off New Jersey continued, and several of the companies involved relinquished their leases. Offsetting this was the beginning of drilling in July in the waters of Georges Bank, off New England, after many years of legal and political delays. In the Canadian Arctic, 13 years of perseverance finally paid off with the discovery of an indicated giant oil field off Lougheed Island. All previous Arctic island discoveries had been of natural gas. On the Kola Peninsula, near the Barents Sea west of Murmansk, the Soviet Union continued drilling its very deep well. Having broken the previous world record for depth in 1980, the well reached a new depth of 10,636 m (34,895 ft). Drilling was being pursued to the target depth of 15,000 m (49,212 ft).

Among other noteworthy events concerning oil, the U.S. began buying Mexican oil for storage in its strategic petroleum reserve. Greece joined the ranks of the world's oil-producing nations with the beginning of production from its Prinos field in the Aegean Sea, eight years after discovery. The Soviet Union set a world record for production by a single country with a level of 12.2 million bbl a day in March. A terminal capable of handling two-thirds of British North Sea oil production began operation in May at Sullom Voe, in the Shetland Islands. Its capacity of 1.4 million bbl a day made it Europe's largest. The U.S. acquired its first deepwater port capable of accommodating supertankers with the unloading of the first cargo of crude oil at a facility 30 km (19 mi) off the Louisiana coast

China's first high flux nuclear reactor went into operation in Beijing (Peking) in April.

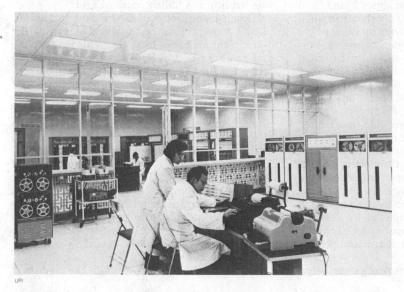

in 33 m (110 ft) of water. Tankers moor at a buoy, and the oil is pumped by undersea pipeline to storage onshore.

Several events regarding natural gas deserve mention. In Massachusetts unusually severe cold weather in January caused the declaration of an emergency and forced a limitation on gas use. In May the U.S. Supreme Court declared unconstitutional a use tax imposed by Louisiana on gas produced in the federal waters of the Gulf of Mexico and transported through the state. For the long term there was favourable news: the U.S. Geological Survey raised its estimate of undiscovered gas resources. Together with discovered reserves, the indicated future U.S. supply of natural gas was equivalent to 51 times the production in 1979. Construction began on the first U.S. portion of the pipeline that would eventually carry gas from the giant Prudhoe Bay field on Alaska's north coast through Canada to consumers in the lower 48 states, and deliveries of gas from Alberta to southern California began through a completed Canadian portion of the pipeline. A giant gas field with potential reserves of 200,000,000,000 cu m (7 trillion cu ft), equivalent to four years of Canada's total consumption, was discovered in Alberta south of Edmonton. In Europe financing was arranged for a massive gas pipeline project to transport gas from Siberian fields to countries in Western Europe.

The major event with regard to coal was a 72-day miners' strike in the U.S. from March until June, the second longest in the industry's history. Stockpiling by large users, such as the electric utility industry, averted any adverse effects on the U.S. economy; as the strike went on, however, European consumers of U.S. coal became increasingly nervous because of the decline in supplies from Poland associated with the political and social unrest in that country. In June a ten-year moratorium on the leasing of federal coal lands ended with the issuance of the first lease in Wyoming under a new long-term program of the Bureau of Land Management.

A large power outage in the western U.S. had a highly unusual cause. A flash fire in a dump ionized the air around transmission lines 23 m (75 ft) above the ground and momentarily short-circuited them. The result was a seven-hour blackout of the entire state of Utah and neighbouring areas of Wyoming and Idaho. The state of Alaska inaugurated a $5 billion, five-year program for the development of hydroelectric power plants, using revenues received from taxes on oil operations within the state. Canada licensed the first exportation of uninterruptible electric power to the United States, covering 1,200 Mw of capacity for a period of ten years. In the English Channel, construction began on a new link between the electric grids of Britain and France. The direct-current cable would be buried in the seafloor, in contrast to the existing cable, which was laid on the bottom and subject to frequent damage. When completed in 1984 the new link would increase the capacity for electricity interchange between the two countries by more than 12 times.

China celebrated the beginning of power deliv-

ery from the first hydroelectric project on the Chang Jiang (Yangtze River) and the successful diversion of the river from its main channel into tunnels to allow completion of the main dam. The Gezhouba project was located at the mouth of the Chang Jiang gorges, 5 km (3.1 mi) upstream from Yichang (I-ch'ang) in Hubei (Hupeh) Province. Begun in 1971, the project was scheduled for completion in 1986. In France the new Socialist government reduced the number of new nuclear plants to be built as it moved to slow down the development of that country's nuclear power industry. President Reagan announced a new program to revive the moribund nuclear power industry in the United States by rescinding the ban on the reprocessing of nuclear fuel that had been instituted by the previous administration and by speeding up the regulatory and licensing process for new plants. Nuclear projects under construction continued to be canceled, however, in the face of the inflation-induced escalation of costs, persistent high interest rates, and lagging growth in the consumption of electricity.

In the field of unconventional energy the world's first "multimegawatt wind farm" was dedicated at a site in the state of Washington. The "farm," consisting of three large wind turbines of 2.5-Mw capacity each, was part of the government program to develop wind energy. The output from the turbines fed into the Bonneville Power Administration grid. Elsewhere in the U.S. other projects under the wind energy development program suffered setbacks; large machines were damaged or collapsed because of structural failures under high wind conditions.

Two large solar power installations began operation on a commercial basis during the year. In Texas a solar collector 20 m (65 ft) in diameter, the world's largest, produced 10 kw of electricity, the first ever generated from solar-produced steam. At Adrane, Italy, a one-Mw plant employed a different technique. Solar rays were concentrated on a boiler atop a 55-m (180-ft) tower by means of 182 Sun-tracking mirrors. With a heat storage system of molten salt, the plant could operate for half an hour when clouds covered the Sun. The output was fed into the Italian national grid.

Hawaii inaugurated its first geothermal power plant. Located at Puna on the island of Hawaii, the 3-Mw plant fed to the local grid. This was also the first geothermal project to tap the energy of an active volcano (Mt. Kilauea). In North Dakota construction was begun on the first commercial-scale coal gasification plant in the U.S. When completed, the plant would convert 14,000 tons of lignite per day into 3,537,500 cu m (125 million cu ft) of methane, the principal constituent of natural gas. Gaz de France, the French national gas company, announced that it would build Europe's first demonstration coal gasification plant at Le Havre. Scheduled for completion in 1985, the plant was designed to produce 283 million cu m (10,000,000,-000 cu ft) of industrial gas per year from 330,000 tons of coal; the ultimate intention was to gasify more than three million tons of coal a year to produce high-quality gas by 1990.

(BRUCE C. NETSCHERT)

COAL

In *Energy in a Finite World* (1981), a study of global energy systems as a whole, the International Institute for Applied Systems Analysis concluded that coal production, after growing slowly to the end of the century, would need to expand rapidly thereafter in order to meet the demand for synthetic fuels. Taking global energy consumption in 1975 as 8.2 terawatt years (one Tw-yr [1,000,000,000 kw-yr] = 1.1×10^9 metric tons of coal equivalent), the institute considered two scenarios for the year 2030: a consumption high reaching 36 Tw-yr and a low of 23 Tw-yr (*see* TABLE).

This outlook indicated probable coal requirements of from 7,000,000,000 to 13,000,000,000 metric tons in 2030, depending on which scenario best suited the actual conditions. About 56% of these amounts would be required for conversion to synthetic fuels. The researchers concluded that the world was going to have to rely on coal—particularly for producing liquid fuels—to an ever increasing extent for at least the next half century. The world market would tend to become dominated by the U.S.S.R., the U.S., and China, each of which had resources greater than those of other coal-producing nations. It would be necessary to develop both the technical and institutional facilities to handle coal as it replaced oil as the world's principal fossil fuel. For the longer term the researchers believed that nonfossil fuel technologies would penetrate the primary energy market as oil and gas reserves dwindled.

Turning back to the more recent situation, 1980—despite the world recession—saw a further increase in world coal output. The West German *Statistik der Kohlenwirtschaft* put world output for 1980 at 2,829,-600,000 metric tons, thus continuing the long-term upward trend. The rise above the previous year was only 1.45%, however, compared with the previous year's increase of about 6%. The largest contributors remained the U.S., China, and the U.S.S.R. Increases were reported from the U.S., South Africa, India, and the U.K., but there were small declines in the U.S.S.R., China, and Poland. (All production figures given below are in metric tons.)

Global Primary Energy by Source
In terawatt years per year

Primary source	Base year 1975	High scenario 2000	High scenario 2030	Low scenario 2000	Low scenario 2030
Oil	3.83	5.89	6.83	4.75	5.02
Gas	1.51	3.11	5.97	2.53	3.47
Coal	2.26	4.94	11.98	3.92	6.45
Light water reactor	0.12	1.70	3.21	1.27	1.89
Fast breeder reactor	0	0.04	4.88	0.02	3.28
Hydroelectricity	0.50	0.83	1.46	0.83	1.46
Solar	0	0.10	0.49	0.09	0.30
Other	0	0.22	0.81	0.17	0.52
Total[1]	8.21	16.84	35.65	13.59	22.39

[1]Columns may not sum to totals because of rounding.
Source: International Institute for Applied Systems Analysis, *Energy in a Finite World* (1981).

For lignite and brown coal the world figure was 965,345,000 tons, also a small increase (1.3%) over the previous year and again representing a slowing down of growth compared with the previous year's increase of 3.4%. More than 71% of the world's output came from Europe, and the largest production by far was in East Germany with almost 27% of the world total. The oil "glut" during 1981 and the accompanying reductions in oil prices were seen as transient features, and there was general confidence that demand for coal would continue to increase. Ulf Lantzke, executive director of the International Energy Agency, urged efforts to maintain a stable international situation in order to encourage the huge investments necessary for new mines and other facilities.

The political troubles in Poland had an important effect on the world coal scene. For the first time in many years Poland's coal production fell—from 203 million tons in 1979 to 193 million in the following year—with serious repercussions on the nation's economy. Coal exports from Poland, which in 1979 provided one quarter of all world coal exports, correspondingly fell from 41.3 million tons in 1979 to an estimated 31.3 million in 1980. V. J. Calarco of Chase Manhattan Bank expected them to fall further to 20.4 million tons in 1981 and then start to recover. This decline contributed to difficulties for coal importers in 1981, while another cause was bottlenecks in ports. Overall, Calarco saw the trade in bituminous coal as rising from a world total of 228.8 million tons in 1979 to an estimated 244.5 million tons in 1980 and forecast 247.3 million tons for 1981 and 270.9 million tons for 1982. Between 1980 and 1982 a decline was expected in shipments of metallurgical coal, but a continuing small increase was forecast in steam coal trade. The most significant growth in export volume was due from Australia, where the total quantities exported were expected to rise from 42.1 million tons in 1980 to 58.5 million tons two years later. Over the same period the U.S. was also likely to increase its total coal exports from 83.5 million to 92.7 million tons.

MARINE FUEL. The U.S. Department of Energy reported that the use of coal-fired steam turbines for bulk carriers would save up to 28% of operating costs, taking into account capital costs and increased maintenance and labour costs. A study commissioned by the department with the

The world's first experimental coal gasification plant went into operation in Schenectady, N.Y., in September. The plant first gasifies the coal, cleans it of impurities, then burns it to produce electricity with less air pollution.

Energy

Argonne National Laboratories resulted in a recommendation that every effort should be made to implement the use of coal as a primary alternative to fuel oil for marine vessels. Financial incentives should be provided to assist development of port bunkering facilities for coal and coal-slurry systems. For both marine and general industrial uses there was growing interest in the coal-slurry systems (in oil and/or water) as a halfway house giving partial replacement of oil by coal while allowing the use of oil-handling and oil-burning equipment. Early trials with such systems foundered because the coal settled in pipes and interfered with the working of valves. More recent work on fine dispersion of coal into oil (with or without water) appeared to have overcome these difficulties.

Extensive trials reported at the third International Symposium on Coal-Oil Mixture Combustion indicated that mixtures with up to 50% coal could be satisfactorily stored, pumped, transported in tankers, and burned in oil burners, with only slight modification of conditions. The calorific value of the mixes was closer to that of oil than that of coal. In the U.K., British Petroleum was completing a plant at West Thurrock that was due to start producing, from the end of 1981, up to 100,000 tons a year of high-stability emulsion for extensive user trials in its own and its customers' boiler plants. Shell Oil Co. undertook trials on injecting such mixtures into blast furnaces, as well as normal boiler trials.

CONVERSION. In several major coal-producing countries there was growing activity with regard to coal conversion to gas and to liquid synthetic fuels. South Africa was completing Sasol 3, which, along with the two earlier Sasol plants, used Lurgi coal gasification followed by reaction of the gases. The three Sasol plants together were designed to convert 33 million tons of coal a year to gasoline, waxes, solvents, and other products, based on the availability of exceptionally cheap coal. West Germany planned to start building a ten-ton-a-day pilot plant for coal liquefaction for the U.S.S.R. in the Moscow coal basin as a forerunner of much larger production plants. In West Germany itself plans were going ahead for the country's first commercial gasification plant, due to become operational by 1984 and to convert two million tons of lignite a year by 1987. The Netherlands company, Gasunie, planned a two-million-ton-a-year gasification plant at Eemshaven for commissioning in 1985. The U.K. was also setting up a pilot plant to make oil from coal and was even examining ways of converting coal in the seam by, among other means, using microorganisms supplied with extra nutrients. The organisms would feed on the coal and thus transform it into gas and liquid.

The situation in the U.S., which had the largest synthetic fuel research, development, and demonstration program in the world, remained confused. There was considerable opposition in President Reagan's administration to financing the program, and a House of Representatives subcommittee voted to cut the funding very severely.

Yet a feasibility study was authorized for a coal-to-methanol plant, which, if further endorsed, would cost many billions of dollars. The uncertainty was likely to hinder the U.S. in achieving a leading role in those technologies that would grow in importance as oil increased in price and became scarcer. (ISRAEL BERKOVITCH)

ELECTRICITY

The electrical power industry could be said to have reached its centennial in 1981, but there was little official recognition of this landmark in technological history. In 1881 Joseph Swan in England achieved the first commercial manufacture of filament lamps; Thomas Edison was building his first two power stations, one in London and the other in New York City (they came into operation the following year); the first public supply of electricity was switched on in the small English town of Godalming; and the British House of Commons, a New York City factory, and ships, trains, and theatre stages were lit by electricity.

Lighting continued to be the mainstay of the industry, and research and development had continued throughout the years, especially in the laboratories of the world's five largest lamp manufacturers. An early Swan lamp produced two lumens of light intensity per watt of electrical power. By 1981 the figure for white-light sources had reached 90 lumens per watt with metal-halide lamps. Monochromatic low-pressure sodium luminaires reached 170 lumens per watt. The limit for tungsten-filament lamps was reckoned to be about 50 lumens per watt, but this had not yet been achieved even in the latest tungsten-halogen lamps. Work continued on lamps at the lower extreme of size, namely, lamps for calcula-

tors, computers, and visual displays. Solid-state lasers were coming into use for fibre-optics communications.

Although electricity is the most versatile form of energy, it is not a primary source; it must be created, and it was in the generation of electricity that there was most activity. Conceptually, the simplest means of generation is the chemical cell, and there was considerable and continuing development in the design of rechargeable cells or batteries. This was due to the greatly increased interest—a feature of the year's international exhibitions and conferences—in electric road vehicles, of which there were 40,000 in the U.K. alone. It was estimated that in the next two decades there could be some 34 million electric vehicles on U.S. roads. In May the first electric vehicle made under the sponsorship of the U.S. Department of Energy, the ETV-1, was exhibited in London. The batteries used were improved lead-acid accumulators. Gasoline, however, has a power-to-weight ratio about 500 times better than such accumulators. One U.S. company produced a zinc-chloride battery with a power-to-weight ratio about three times better than that of the lead-acid battery. The best so far to reach practical testing in vehicles was the sodium-sulfur battery, which not only had a five-to-one power-to-weight advantage over the lead-acid battery but also occupied only one-third as much space. A British battery manufacturer joined with a research institution to build a pilot plant to develop the technology of this battery and its manufacture and to license it to producers. The company also joined a leading U.S. engineering group in a program, but it was expected to be several years before commercial batteries became available.

Electrical Power Production of Selected Countries, 1980
By source

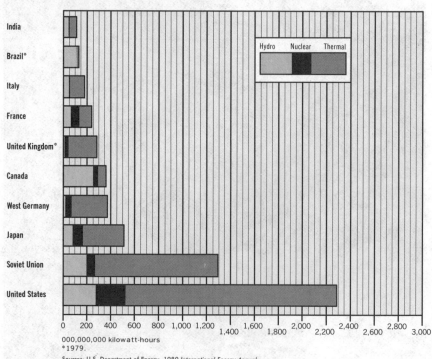

000,000,000 kilowatt-hours
*1979.

Sources: U.S. Department of Energy, 1980 *International Energy Annual*;
United Nations, *Monthly Bulletin of Statistics*; individual country reports.

Most of the world's electrical energy, some 80%, continued to be derived from heat in central power stations, with the other 20% coming from hydroelectric stations. Thermal stations differ only in the way the heat-energy input is created, whether from the burning of combustible materials or from nuclear fission in a reactor. The choice was governed by various considerations, both economic and political. A factor in many vocally democratic countries of the West was the degree of popular opposition to nuclear power, expressed through the lobbying of antinuclear and environmental groups, as in the U.S. and the U.K.; through referenda, as in Austria and Sweden; and through often violent public demonstrations, as in West Germany.

Economically, a major factor in some countries was the declining growth in energy consumption since oil prices began to rise in 1973. This had shattered, however temporarily, the long-term planning of utilities, which was based on an assumed growth rate of about 7% a year. In the U.S. electricity output was currently rising by only 1% a year; in the U.K. consumption fell by 4.5% in 1980–81 and in the first six months of 1981 was down by 4.1% from the comparable period of 1980. In these circumstances there was no demand for the large generating plants for which nuclear energy was best suited, and where additional capacity was needed utilities were more likely to choose small plants using the less intricate and less expensive technology of fossil-fueled generation. In some countries, however, demand for electricity still exceeded supply. This was the case in the Soviet Union, where there were plans for considerable expansion in the production of electricity; it was also true in the less developed countries, which were hungry for electricity.

The fossil fuel on which most interest currently centred was coal. No new oil-fired stations were being planned in the advanced industrial countries. Following the change of government in France, the new minister for energy announced large increases in the subsidy for coal in order to encourage the building of more coal-fired power stations. In Spain a utility in the north opted for two coal-fired stations. Coal-fired stations were also being planned in the U.S. In Britain coal research projects sponsored by the International Energy Agency included the world's first large-scale experimental facility for the use of gas from a pressurized fluidized-bed combustor to operate gas turbines while steam was generated for conventional turbines. This "combined cycle plant," raising efficiency to 42% or more, was operated by the National Coal Board and paid for by West Germany, the U.S., and the U.K.

In the long term the other main source of heat for the generation of electricity seemed likely to be nuclear fission, whatever the current problems. This had already proved itself to be the cheapest source, apart from water power. In the advanced countries it already contributed a considerable percentage of the total electricity generated, even as much as 36% in France on occasion, and this was increasing. Uranium is, of course, a fossil fuel, but the energy density of uranium-235 is some three mil-

lion times that of the best steam coal. Furthermore, the use of fast breeder reactors would create more fuel from the unusable part of natural uranium. Already there was a 600-Mw power station in the Soviet Union based on such a reactor, while France was building a 1,200-Mw station (Super-phénix, at Creys-Malville). The U.K. in 1981 announced plans for a large power station based on the experience with the Prototype Fast Reactor at Dounreay. In the U.S. President Reagan gave the go-ahead for the 350-Mw demonstration fast breeder reactor at Clinch River, Tenn., work on which had been halted by Pres. Jimmy Carter in 1977. West Germany also had plans for a fast breeder reactor at Kalkar. Breeding would greatly extend the useful life of natural uranium.

Eventually, nuclear fusion—inherently safer than fission—might become the preferred source of electrical energy. Research into fusion continued at the European Atomic Energy Community's experimental Joint European Torus project, based in the U.K.

Formerly idealists' dreams, devices using renewable sources of energy to generate electricity emerged into practical, though still experimental, applications during the year. It seemed unlikely that they would make important contributions to bulk sup-

ply in the near future, but such devices could be of immediate benefit to some isolated and small communities.

During the year, solar power stations were in operation in Sicily and Spain, where the two 500-kw generators were driven by steam turbines, the heat for which was supplied by liquids heated by the Sun. In addition, Japan announced that it expected to produce 50 Mw by 1985 by turning solar radiation directly into electricity by means of photovoltaic cells, the price of which was falling rapidly.

Wind was another renewable power source, producing mechanical movement instead of heat. In the U.K. the Central Electricity Generating Board was erecting a 200-kw aerogenerator and was looking for sites for larger ones. There were aerogenerators in Canada, Ireland, and many other countries, including the U.S., where a cluster of aerogenerators with a combined capacity of 7.5 Mw was in operation. Use of the mechanical energy in sea waves and tides was mostly at the small-model stage or was the subject of theoretical studies, although France had had a tidal station in operation for some years.   (C. L. BOLTZ)

In May protesters at the Diablo Canyon nuclear power plant in California attempted to force the closing of the plant, which they said was built on a subterranean vault and constituted a potential health hazard.

WIDE WORLD

NATURAL GAS

World proven natural gas reserves on Jan. 1, 1981, were estimated to be 77,711,000,-000,000 cu m (77,711 billion cu m, or bcm), compared with 74,090 bcm a year earlier. This was double the size of proven reserves in 1970. The U.S.S.R. had 39.2% of the total, OPEC 32.9%, and the U.S. 7.3%.

World commercial production of natural gas in 1980, excluding gas flared or reinjected, was 1,522 bcm, 3 bcm less than in 1979. The largest producers of natural gas were the U.S. (569 bcm), the U.S.S.R. (435 bcm), and The Netherlands (87 bcm). OPEC produced 91 bcm. The world's proven reserves at Jan. 1, 1981, would permit 51 years of commercial production at the 1980 rate.

The volume of gas in international trade continued to grow, to 202 bcm in 1980. The principal exporters of gas by pipeline were the U.S.S.R., which supplied 57 bcm to Eastern and Western Europe, including France for the first time; The Netherlands, supplying 51 bcm to six Western European countries; Norway, exporting 25 bcm, principally to West Germany and the U.K.; and Canada, exporting 23 bcm to the U.S. The international trade in liquefied natural gas (LNG) declined slightly to 32 bcm as Algerian exports of LNG to France, Spain, the U.K., and the U.S. fell following disagreements over pricing. Libyan supplies to Italy and Spain declined slightly. Japan continued to take the lion's share of the international LNG trade, importing 24 bcm from Abu Dhabi, Brunei, Indonesia, and Alaska.

No other countries were involved in LNG trade, although there were several additional importers and exporters expecting deliveries to begin in the next few years. Japan expected to receive supplies of LNG from Australia, Malaysia, and the U.S.S.R. Nigeria and Cameroon were interested in exporting LNG to Europe, although Nigeria's Bonny LNG project might be affected by the withdrawal of one of the members of the consortium developing the LNG industry. In the past Algeria had been the largest exporter of LNG, but it had reduced its exports while trying to obtain a higher price from its customers. The contract for supplying Algerian LNG to Britain, which began in 1964, expired at the end of 1980. Under an interim agreement, British Gas paid Algeria an average of $4.60 per million BTU for nine months, but when this agreement expired at the end of September 1981, another could not be reached and deliveries stopped. Supplies to France suffered intermittent delays, with Algeria demanding higher prices, but Belgium agreed to start imports in late 1982. The Trans-Mediterranean Gas Pipeline to take gas from Algeria to Italy was effectively completed, but deliveries could not start without an agreement on pricing.

In the North Sea, Norway decided to sell gas from the Statfjord and Heimdal fields to a group of Western European utilities rather than to Britain, and a proposed British gas-gathering pipeline was abandoned. By the fall of 1981 the future of the Siberian gas pipeline project seemed assured. The 5,150-km (3,200-mi) pipeline would bring 40 bcm of gas a year from the Yamal Peninsula in Siberia to Western Europe, but there had been fears that it could lead to excessive dependence on imports from the U.S.S.R. in France, West Germany, Austria, The Netherlands, Belgium, and Italy. West German banks arranged financing and contracts were placed for pipeline and compressor equipment, but the complexity of the project and the reported opposition, on strategic grounds, of the U.S. led to considerable delays in negotiations.

Thailand's first gas field, the Erawan field in the Gulf of Thailand, began test production in August 1981. Initially, the gas would be supplied to power stations. There were several other fields to be developed, and the Thai government reversed its previous policy and decided to allow gas exports rather than concentrate on the use of gas within the nation. South Korea began talks on possible supplies of LNG from Thailand. The LNG importing terminal planned in South Korea might also be used for supplies from Indonesia by 1985. South Korea could thus begin to compete with Japan for supplies. Japan agreed in principle to buy LNG from the western coast of Canada starting in 1985, and Qatar offered to sell LNG to Japan from 1987 at a rate of more than 8 bcm a year. The North West Dome gas field dramatically increased Qatar's reserves to 1,848 bcm, a rise of 970 bcm over its proven reserves at the beginning of 1980. Japan, on the other hand, had indigenous reserves of only 15 bcm and produced 2.5 bcm in 1980. Environmental pressures to reduce the use of oil in Japan, particularly in power stations, made it likely that Japan's need for a clean imported fuel would continue to increase.

In the U.S. the arrival of President Reagan's administration intensified the debate about the decontrol of natural gas prices. The 1978 Natural Gas Policy Act was intended to remove most controls from gas prices by 1985, encouraging gas production by allowing prices to rise nearer to the price of oil. Gas producers complained that the act was too complicated and too slow to take effect, hoping that the new administration would be sympathetic to allowing gas prices to rise to free market levels. Gas consumers feared a rapid increase in costs if controls were removed too quickly. The administration seemed reluctant to make a decision that would inevitably offend either producers or consumers.

An unusual use for natural gas was developed in Australia. The world's first ship to use compressed natural gas as a fuel was built for an Adelaide cement company. It was scheduled to be in service by the end of 1981, making a daily run across the St. Vincent Gulf in South Australia. Although compressed natural gas was unlikely to be widely used in ships, some Australian designers were considering LNG as a fuel for bulk carriers taking iron ore to Japan.

(RICHARD J. CASSIDY)

PETROLEUM

Two features distinguished 1981 in the petroleum markets: the determination of Saudi Arabia throughout most of the year to insist on the marker crude price of Arabian light at $32 a barrel; and the persistent decline in consumption, leading to notable reductions on the spot market even below the Saudi Arabian posted price. At a meeting of OPEC in May no satisfactory solution on a reunification of pricing policy was achieved, although a majority of members recommended cutting production by 10%. Disagreements on reconciling Saudi Arabian objectives with those of the majority of OPEC members persisted at the Geneva OPEC conference in August. Meanwhile, amid the controversy over pricing and the reasons for the lack of demand, in the first half of 1981 consumption in West Germany fell by 15.2%, in France 12.9%, in the U.K. 11.5%, in Japan 7%, in Canada 5.9%, and in the U.S. 5.2%, continuing a trend from the previous year. In the same period, production declined by 6% to some 59,961,000 bbl a day, with OPEC production running at 22 million bbl a day at midyear, compared with an average of 26.8 million bbl a day in 1980.

While the consumer was benefiting from the surplus of oil on the market, much of the industry, particularly in Europe, was having a difficult task recovering its costs. Crude oil prices were high in comparison with the returns from realized sales. There was excess refinery capacity; almost half of it was underutilized, with resultant refinery losses. The strength of the dollar, the currency for most crude oil sales, on the foreign exchange markets exacerbated the cost of product sales; these costs were not always adequately recouped in the markets, where government pricing controls were adjusted slowly.

During September and October there were signs of a more realistic adaptation to market forces by a growing number of the producing countries, including Nigeria, Iraq, and Venezuela. At a meeting in Geneva on October 29 OPEC finally agreed on a unified pricing policy based on a new "marker" price of $34 a barrel. The agreement took effect on November 1 and was to remain in force until the end of 1982.

RESERVES. There was a small increase in the total world "published proved" reserves at the end of 1980, 654,900,000,000 bbl, compared with 649,200,000,000 bbl a year earlier. There was a further small rise in the Western Hemisphere share at 16.6% (15% the year before) and a slight decrease in the Middle East share to 55.3% (55.7% in 1979). China's share again remained the same at 3.1%, as did Western Europe's at 3.6%; but the U.S. share at 4.9%, the U.S.S.R.'s at 9.6%, and Africa's at 8.4% all showed minor decreases. Only the Latin-American share rose, from 8.7% in 1979 to 10.6% in 1980, principally because of discoveries in Mexico.

PRODUCTION. World oil production decreased by 4.7% in 1980 in contrast to a 4.1% increase in 1979 and compared with an average 2.4% increase in the five years 1975–80. Output averaged 62,585,000 bbl a day, as against 65,710,000 bbl a day the previous year. The U.S.S.R. remained the biggest single producer with 12,215,000 bbl a day, up by 2.9%, constituting 19.8% of the world total; second was Saudi Arabia, up 4.9% to 9,999,000 bbl a day, 16% of the world total; and third was the U.S., up 0.6% to 8,590,000 bbl a day, 13.9% of the world total. Middle East production as a whole fell by 14.2% (as against an increase of 1.7% in 1979) to 18,750,000 bbl a day. Iran declined by 53.4% to 1,480,000 bbl a

day, compared with 3,175,000 in 1979 and 5,235,000 in 1978, when it was the fourth largest producer; Kuwait dropped by 37.1% to 1,425,000 bbl a day and Iraq by 23.7% to 2,645,000 bbl a day.

African production, too, was down by 9.3% to 6,090,000 bbl a day. Only in Egypt was there a real rise, 14.7% to 635,000 bbl a day, a modest 1% of the world total. Libyan production was down by 14.3% to 1,-790,000 bbl a day, 2.8% of the world total; Algeria's by 14.2% to 1,040,000 bbl a day; and Gabon's by 14% to 2,055,000 bbl a day, 3.3% of the world total. South Asia's production declined by 23.2% to 230,000 bbl a day and Southeast Asia's by 1.2% to 2,120,-000 bbl a day, with Indonesia's down slightly by 0.2% to 1,580,000 bbl a day. Australasia's production dropped by 12.2% to 400,000 bbl a day and Eastern Europe's by 6.2% to 385,000 bbl a day.

Latin-American production was up by 6% at 855,000 bbl a day. Of this, Mexico's share was the greatest, increasing by 31.8% to 2,130,000 bbl a day, 3.5% of the world total, followed by Brazil with 10.4% (185,-000 bbl a day) and Argentina with 4.8% (490,000 bbl a day). In Western Europe, up by 8.3% to 2,560,000 bbl a day, Norway had the largest annual increase, 37.3% to 525,000 bbl a day, but the U.K. remained the largest producer with 1,645,000 bbl a day, up by 3.3% to 2.6% of the world total. French production, though minor, increased by 25% to 30,000 bbl a day, equaling Austria's.

CONSUMPTION. Throughout the world there was a decrease of 3.9% in consumption from 1979 to 61,705,000 bbl a day, compared with a 2% increase over the previous five years. Excluding the U.S.S.R., Eastern Europe, and China, the decrease was greater, 5.2% to 49 million bbl a day.

U.S. consumption declined by 8.8% (2.9% in 1979) to 26.4% of the world total, 16,390,000 bbl a day, compared with a small increase of 0.7% over the previous five years. Total Western Hemisphere consumption declined 6.1% to 22,855,000 bbl a day, with Canada's down by 2.8% and Latin America's up by 3.7%.

Western European consumption was down by 6.5% to 22.7% of the world total at 14,015,000 bbl a day. Only Turkey (up 16.8%), Portugal (4.6%), Spain (3.2%), and Greece (1.2%) showed increases. Otherwise, Denmark was down by 16.7%, the U.K. 14.8%, Sweden 13.4%, West Germany 10.8%, Iceland 10.4%, Ireland 9.2%, and Norway 9.1%. West Germany consumed 2,735,000 bbl a day, 4.4% of the world total, followed by France, 2,295,000 bbl a day, 3.7%; Italy, 1,985,000 bbl a day, 3.3%; the U.K., 1,675,000 bbl a day, 2.7%; and Spain, 1,040,000 bbl a day, 1.7%.

Japan, the third largest consumer at 5,010,000 bbl a day, 8% of the world total, was down by 9.1%; Australasia by 4.1% to 775,000 bbl a day; and China by 3.4% to 1,770,000 bbl a day, 2.9% of the world total. African consumption was up by 9.2% to 1,485,000 bbl a day, 2.4% of the world total; the Middle East by 8.7% to 1,630,000 bbl a day, 2.7%; South Asia by 4.5% to 785,000 bbl a day; and Southeast Asia by 2% to 2,449,000 bbl a day, 4.1%. The U.S.S.R., up by 2.1%, 14.6% of the world total, and Eastern Europe, up by 1.5%, increased consumption to 8,820,000 and 2,115,000 bbl a day, respectively. Middle distillates continued to be the primary petroleum product consumed.

REFINING. In 1980 world refining capacity increased by 2% to 81,715,000 bbl a day, compared with gains of 5.6% in 1979 and 2.8% over the five years preceding 1980.

Oil exploration began in the Baltic Sea as a mutual effort among Poland, East Germany, and the Soviet Union.

KEYSTONE

U.S. capacity rose by 2.7% to 18.4 million bbl a day, at 22.5% the biggest world share; Canadian capacity dropped by 7.1%. In Latin America Argentina's capacity grew by 26.7% to 840,000 bbl a day and Brazil's by 11.9% to 1,035,000 bbl a day; Mexico's remained unchanged at 1,395,000 bbl a day. Total Western Hemisphere capacity, at 29,695,000 bbl a day, rose 2.2% to 36.2% of the world total (35.9% in 1979). In Western Europe there was considerable underutilization of refinery capacity, which decreased slightly by 0.1% to 20,515,000 bbl a day, 28.2% of the world total. West Germany showed a minor increase of 1.7% to 3,095,000 bbl a day, accounting for 3.8% of the world total, and Belgium experienced a minute increase of 0.1% to 1,020,000 bbl a day. Spanish capacity decreased by 3.2%, that of The Netherlands by 2.2%, Italy's by 1.5%, and France's by 1.3%. The capacity of the U.K. was unchanged at 2,460,000 bbl a day.

In the Middle East, Iranian refining capacity increased by 17.4% to 1,225,000 bbl a day, but that of Saudi Arabia dropped by 22% to 495,000 bbl a day, with no significant changes elsewhere. The total Middle East refining capacity increased by 0.9% to 3,570,000 bbl a day. Southeast Asia's capacity, at 3,515,000 bbl a day, increased 4.5% over the previous year, with Singapore's rising to 1,070,000 bbl a day. African capacity rose by 3% to 2,080,000 bbl a day, but the largest increase of all was in South Asia. There the rise of 20.2% to 998,-000 bbl a day was much higher than the previous five-year average of 6.2%. Japanese capacity, 6.9% of the world total, grew by 6.6% to 5,635,000 bbl a day. The refining capacity of the U.S.S.R., Eastern Europe, and China increased by 1.7%, constituting 18.3% of the world total at 14.9 million bbl a day. North America refined the greatest volume of gasolines, 44% of the world total; Western Europe refined the largest portion of middle distillates (36%) and Japan, of fuel oil (37%).

TANKERS. The size of the world tanker fleet declined in 1980 by 3.1% to 324.8 million long tons deadweight (dw). Liberian tonnage dropped by 2.2% to 200.3 million tons dw but retained the largest world share at 30.9% (31.3% in 1979), followed by Japan (9.3%), the U.K. (7.6%), and Norway (7.4%). Tonnage on order at the end of 1980 was 18.4 million tons dw, compared with 16.5 million tons dw in 1979. Tankers of between 205,000 and 285,000 tons dw made up some 43% of world tanker tonnage.

Voyages from the Middle East represented 71% of tanker movements in 1980 (74.5% in 1979), about one-third going to Western Europe and North and West Africa and 12% to Japan. Interarea total oil movements in 1980 fell to 31,935,000 bbl a day from 35,350,000 bbl a day in 1979; of this total, 11,825,000 bbl a day related to Western Europe, 6,735,000 bbl a day to the U.S., and 4,985,000 bbl a day to Japan.

(R. W. FERRIER)

See also Engineering Projects; Industrial Review; Mining and Quarrying; Transportation.
[214.C.4; 721; 724.B.2; 724.C.1-2; 737.A.5]

Engineering Projects

Bridges. Recent dramatic increases in the cost of fuel highlighted the need to cut travel distances and therefore, where appropriate, to build new bridges. Bridges that replace ferries across waterways, especially wide ones such as Tampa Bay, Florida, or, say, the English Channel, would also save fuel since cars and trucks use only between one-third and one-half the fuel that the ferry requires to carry them. Moreover, the bridge also eliminates the time spent loading and unloading the vehicles, which, of course, would also complete the journey much faster than the ferry. Exemplifying such advantages, the Humber Bridge across the Humber estuary on England's east coast, which was opened by Queen Elizabeth II on July 17, 1981, reduced road journeys between towns on opposite sides of the estuary by approximately 95 km (1 km = 0.62 mi). The 1,410-m (1 m = 3.3 ft) main span of this 2.2-km suspension bridge was the world's longest.

The vulnerability of such large structures crossing heavily traveled waterways to damage from ships (the 1980 Tampa Bay disaster, for example) meant that they must be designed to withstand the impact of any accidental collision. Another design factor was the high cost of foundations of bridges in deep water. Lessons learned in building oil platforms on shore and then floating them out for use in deep water might soon be adapted for placing bridge foundations in deep waterways. More thought was also being given by designers to the environmental impact of bridges, both during construction and when in service. Interruption of traffic moving through the construction site could be reduced by the choice of an appropriate bridge type and erection plan. Of still greater significance was the effect of the finished structure on its surroundings. Generally speaking, function and aesthetics are interrelated. What is functionally correct usually looks right, and the experienced designer can achieve aesthetic merit at little extra initial cost.

Though many bridge engineers were engaged in designing new structures for both the industrial and the less developed areas of the world, the majority were concerned with the maintenance of old bridges. In the U.S. four out of ten bridges—some 200,000—were said to be deficient. Approximately 98,000 of these were described by the Federal Highway Administration in a recent report as being "structurally weak or unsound . . . and should be closed or restricted to light vehicles or immediately rehabilitated to prevent further deterioration and collapse." The report described the other 102,000 as functionally obsolete and no longer able to serve present traffic safely. This state of affairs was to be found in most industrialized countries, and a very high expenditure—an estimated $41 billion in the U.S.—would be required to remedy the situation.

At a London symposium of the International Association for Bridge and Structural Engineering in September 1981, J. E. Gordon, professor emeritus of materials science at the University of Reading

The massive main dam at Itaipú, Brazil, will span nearly a mile when completed. The dam will be the world's highest hollow concrete gravity dam and the top hydroelectric energy producer.

(England), observed that "structural engineering has tended to harden into a series of conventions or mystiques which, although they are held with almost religious fervour by the initiated, inevitably become irrelevant in a changing world." The time, he thought, was already in sight when traditional metal and concrete construction would join the steam engine in the filing cabinets of history. In particular, he continued, "Steel is a material which is peculiarly unsuited for carrying compressive loads over long distances: in fact, it is probably one of the worst materials ever conceived for diffuse structures." Gordon was especially critical of the current fashion of metal plate structures. The answer to the quest for a new material was likely to be found in lightweight plastics reinforced with fibreglass. Such materials would necessarily dictate new or at least modified structural forms. The objective must be to eliminate compression, except in very short components, by making greater use wherever possible of tension, which most materials accommodate more readily.

Although the majority of recently built large bridges incorporated new, improved points of detail, no new principles appeared to have been introduced. However, one newly completed bridge was notable for the speed with which it was designed and built. In January 1980 the Almö arch bridge in Sweden was totally demolished when a ship ran into it in a fog. Just 21 months later the new cable-stayed bridge, with a 366-m steel main span, was opened to traffic. The span was sufficient to take the piers and concrete towers behind the high-water line and, therefore, clear of ship-

ping. The cable-stay arrangement was such that, at any time, one stay could be replaced if necessary. (DAVID FISHER)

Buildings. Winners of the 1981 Aga Khan awards for architecture, given for buildings that reveal "understanding and awareness of Muslim cultural traditions," included water towers in Kuwait and the Intercontinental Hotel in Mecca, Saudi Arabia. The water towers were clustered in groups, one group consisting of three white, reinforced-concrete, needle-shaped towers with large spherical water storage tanks, one of which also housed a restaurant; the tanks were clad in blue, white, and turquoise enameled steel. Another, smaller sphere, high up on one tower, contained observation platforms. In another group of six, the tanks took the form of inverted cones on cylindrical shafts. The tanks had varying heights and colouring, and the group provided a shaded area with a small park. At the Intercontinental Hotel the architect made extensive use of tension structures. The cables, struts, and curved suspended surfaces were reminiscent of a Bedouin tent.

The intense construction activity in the Middle East, while producing some exciting engineering, also created some problems. Frequently, contractors failed to appreciate the difficulties of obtaining durable concrete with the materials available. Many instances were coming to light of poor concrete durability because of the use of chemically contaminated aggregates and inferior cement. In some cases buildings became unserviceable within four to five years of completion.

In the field of structural steelwork there was

In mid-November the dome of the Hubert H. Humphrey Metrodome in Minneapolis tore and collapsed under the weight of a foot of snow. The stadium with its inflated fabric dome, completed only a month earlier, was to be the home of the Minnesota sports teams beginning in 1982.

UPI

increasing sophistication in both design and manufacturing techniques. Steel remained the predominant material for large-span roofs, and in multilayer grid construction sections of structure could be prefabricated in the relatively controlled environment of the factory, leaving a minimum of work to be done on site. The new Winter Gardens at Niagara Falls and a large church at Garden Grove, Calif., illustrated the use of glass-clad structural steel in contemporary architecture. Both buildings used light steelwork in the form of grids and trusses to support large plane areas of glass that form large enclosures. The Winter Gardens used clear glass and a shade of rusty red for the steel; the church, in the warmer climate of California, employed reflective glass, to minimize heat gain, and white painted steelwork.

Other methods of enclosing large areas of space included air-supported structures. The development of improved tension materials such as Teflon-coated fibreglass ensured a continuing interest in these soft-skin fabric structures. One recent example of an air-supported roof was that at Dalhousie University at Halifax, Nova Scotia. This took the form of a stainless steel membrane covering an area 91 × 73 m. While a number of ambitious schemes had been proposed, few had been built, and it remained to be seen if air-supported tension structures would begin to displace rigid structures for enclosing large areas.

Work continued on Canada's unfinished Olympic Stadium in Montreal. Its revolutionary design, with a 165-m-high sloping tower to support a retractable roof, had encountered such problems that it had been only partially completed in time for the 1976 Olympic Games. Work resumed in 1979 but stopped again in 1980 when structural defects in the tower base were discovered. Alternatives under consideration included leaving the stadium essentially in its present, partially covered state; completion of the project to the original design; or the use of an alternative roof system not dependent on the defective tower. Whichever scheme was adopted, it appeared unlikely that the stadium would be completed before 1984.

Europe's second tallest building, the 183-m-high National Westminster Tower in London, was completed in 1981. The main load-bearing element was a reinforced-concrete core some 25 m in diameter. The floors were of lightweight concrete on a steel corrugated deck and beam system supported at the exterior on closely spaced columns doubling as window mullions. These columns were supported on three giant cantilevers extending from the central core at about the eighth-floor level, below which there were no floors external to the core. The various site and planning constraints played a part in producing an extended construction period and high cost.

Among buildings of domestic scale, Ton Albert's de Waal house in Utrecht, Neth., was notable. This displayed how brick and concrete, generally used in precise geometric and modular fashion, could also be used with geometric freedom and made almost organic. Concrete-framed, with brick and tile cladding, the house appeared to grow out of the ground with vertical and horizontal curves that were somewhat reminiscent of the work of Antonio Gaudí in Spain.

(GEOFFREY M. PINFOLD)

Dams. To illustrate the advances made in the construction of dams, the Hoover Dam in Nevada established world records when it was completed in 1936, but by 1981 it ranked 18th in height and 20th in the size of its reservoir. In 1976 the Tarbela Dam in Pakistan exceeded the record volume of earth that had been placed in the Fort Peck Dam in Montana in 1940.

Advances in earth-moving equipment technology have improved the feasibility and economic aspects of building earth and rockfill dams that utilize locally available materials. As a result more than 80% of the major dams under construction in 1981 were of the earth and rockfill types.

The centre of activity in dam building by 1981 had shifted to the less developed countries, where water resource development is central to alleviating those nations' problems of food production, water supply, and energy development. Food production was substantially increased with the aid of irrigation by water captured during flood seasons and stored behind dams.

With fossil fuel costs rising, development of hydroelectric projects was selected by some countries as a means of achieving energy independence. For example, Brazil had many such dams under way. Besides their capability of generating large amounts of energy, they also provide water to cities and for irrigation.

In Canada dam sites in remote areas with great energy potentials were being developed. The James Bay Project was expected to provide 10,200 Mw by 1985, to be followed by the Grand Baleine and the Nottaway-Broadback-Rupert schemes.

In China the main channel of the Chang Jiang (Yangtze River) was closed for the Gezhouba Dam, scheduled for completion in 1986. It was to supply 2,715 Mw of power and permit ships of 10,000 deadweight tonnage to pass through locks. All materials and equipment were being furnished from Chinese plants. The 245-m-high Chicoasen Dam was being completed in Mexico. It was designed to provide 2,400 Mw of power. Mexico was allocating more than $8 billion for the development of irrigation-related works.

Dam building was not confined to large countries. Sri Lanka was constructing the 120-m-high Victoria Dam, and Ghana was completing its Kpong project. Nepal was building two dams, with the surplus power to be exported to India.

Elsewhere, innovative British engineers provided the River Thames with a rotating movable barrier or dam to protect London from floods; its cost was more than $1 billion. The 18-m-high gates could be raised in 30 minutes to block any tidal surge that could endanger London.

A special category of dams, built to retain mine waste or tailings, was receiving increased attention following some failures that caused severe loss of life and property. Some of these dams had been built without proper regard for engineering principles or safety. A special committee was established within the International Commission on Large Dams to inventory such dams throughout

Major World Dams Under Construction in 1981[1]

Name of dam	River	Country	Type[2]	Height (m)	Length of crest (m)	Volume content (000 cu m)	Gross reservoir capacity (000 cu m)
Altinkaya	Kizilirmak	Turkey	E, R	195	604	15,310	5,763,000
Amaluza	Paute	Ecuador	A	170	410	1,157	120,000
Atatürk	Euphrates	Turkey	E, R	179	1,700	84,500	48,700,000
Baishan	Songhuajiang	China	G	150	670	1,630	6,215,000
Boruca	Terraba	Costa Rica	E, R	267	700	43,000	14,960,000
Canales	Genil	Spain	E, R	156	340	4,733	7,070,000
Chicoasen	Grijalva	Mexico	E, R	245	584	14,500	1,680,000
Dabaklamm	Dorferbach	Austria	A	220	332	1,000	235,000
Dongjiang	Laishui	China	A	157	438	1,389	8,120,000
Dry Creek	Dry Creek	U.S.	E	110	915	23,000	310,000
El Cajon	Humuya	Honduras	A	226	382	1,480	5,650,000
El M'Jara	Overgha	Morocco	E	87	1,600	25,000	4,000,000
Emborcacao	Paranaíba	Brazil	E, R	158	1,500	24,000	17,600,000
Finstertal	Nederbach	Austria	E, R	150	652	4,500	60,000
Grand Maison	Eau d'Olle	France	E, R	160	550	18,450	140,000
Guavio	Orinoco	Colombia	E, R	250	461	17,000	10,000,000
Guri (Raúl Leoni)	Caroní	Venezuela	E, R, G	162	9,404	55,382	135,000,000
Inguri	Inguri	U.S.S.R.	A	272	680	3,880	1,100,000
Itaipú	Paraná	Brazil/Paraguay	E, R, G	196	7,760	27,000	29,000,000
Itaparica	São Francisco	Brazil	E, R	135	4,500	29,750	12,000,000
Karakaya	Euphrates	Turkey	A, G	180	420	2,000	9,580,000
Kenyir	Trengganu	Malaysia	E, R	150	900	15,900	13,600,000
Kishau	Tons	India	E, R	253	360	NA	2,400,000
La Grande No. 2	La Grande	Canada	E, R	160	2,835	23,000	61,720,000
La Grande No. 3	La Grande	Canada	E, R	100	3,855	22,187	60,020,000
La Grande No. 4	La Grande	Canada	E, R	125	7,243	20,000	19,390,000
Lakhwar	Yamuna	India	G	192	440	2,000	580,000
Lunyangxia	Huanghe	China	G	172	342	1,300	24,700,000
Los Leones	Los Leones	Chile	E	179	510	9,200	106,000
Maqarin	Yarmouk	Jordan	E, R	171	800	14,900	320,000
Menzelet	Ceyhan	Turkey	E, R	150	420	7,000	19,500,000
Mihoesti	Aries	Romania	E, R	242	242	180	6,000
Mosul	Tigris	Iraq	E	100	3,600	36,000	11,100,000
Naramata	Naramata	Japan	E, R	155	587	11,600	90,000
Nurek	Vakhsh	U.S.S.R.	E	300	704	58,901	10,500,000
Oosterschelde	Vense Gat Oosterschelde	The Netherlands	E, G	45	8,400	35,000	2,000,000
Oymapinar	Manavgat	Turkey	A	185	360	575	310,000
Özköy	Gediz	Turkey	E, R	180	420	11,251	940,000
Revelstoke	Columbia	Canada	E, R, G	162	1,615	8,900	5,310,000
Rogun	Vakhsh	U.S.S.R.	E	325	660	75,500	11,600,000
Salvajina	Cauca	Colombia	E, R	154	368	4,000	773,000
São Felix	Tocantis	Brazil	E, R	160	1,950	34,000	50,600,000
Sayano-Shushenskaya	Yenisei	U.S.S.R.	A	242	1,068	9,117	31,300,000
Sterkfontein	Nuwejaarspruit	South Africa	E	93	3,060	19,800	2,693,000
Tehri	Bhagirathi	India	E, R	261	570	25,200	3,539,000
Thein	Ravi	India	E, R	47	878	21,920	3,670,000
Thomson	Thomson	Australia	E, R	165	1,275	13,200	1,100,000
Tokuyama	Ibi	Japan	E, R	161	420	10,600	660,000
Tucurui	Tocantis	Brazil	E, G	85	5,294	36,375	43,000,000
Upper Wainganga	Wainganga	India	E	43	181	NA	50,700,000
Wujiangdu	Wujiang	China	G	165	368	1,930	2,300,000
Yacambu	Yacambu	Venezuela	E	158	107	3,000	427,000
Yacyreta-Apipe	Paraná	Paraguay/Argentina	E, G	41	72,000	81,000	21,000,000
Zillergründl	Ziller	Austria	A	180	505	980	90,000
Major World Dams Completed in 1980 and 1981[1]							
Foz do Areia	Iguaçu	Brazil	E, G, R	153	830	13,700	7,320,000
Gura Apelor Retezat	Riul Mare	Romania	E, R	168	460	9,000	225,000
Hasan Ugurlu	Yesilirmak	Turkey	E, R	175	435	9,042	1,078,000
Itumbiara	Paranaiba	Brazil	E, G	106	6,262	35,600	17,000,000
Sobradinho	São Francisco	Brazil	E, G, R	43	3,900	13,200	34,200,000
Ust-Ilim	Agnara	U.S.S.R.	E, G	105	3,565	8,702	59,300,000

[1] Having a height exceeding 150 m (492 ft); or having a total volume content exceeding 15 million cu m (19.6 million cu yd); or forming a reservoir exceeding 14,800 × 10⁶ cu m capacity (12 million ac-ft).
[2] Type of dam: E = earth; R = rockfill; A = arch; G = gravity.
NA = not available.

(T. W. MERMEL)

the world, review design considerations, and develop safety criteria. In Chile a 179-m-high dam was being built for the sole purpose of retaining mine tailings, utilizing the latest techniques to help improve its safety.

Tidal power was again being revived because of high energy costs. Canada took a first step toward harnessing the Bay of Fundy tides with a $46 million pilot project on the Annapolis River in Nova Scotia. Indians in the area initiated a tidal project that would generate about 12 Mw at Half Moon Cove at Passamaquoddy Bay between New Brunswick and Maine. Alaska's Cove Inlet tidal project was undergoing environmental studies to evaluate its impact on the fishing industry, wildlife, and sedimentation patterns. (T. W. MERMEL)

Roads. Many of the world's developed countries were undergoing significant changes in their road programs and priorities in 1981 as a result of increased fuel costs and reduced tax revenues. In many nations the highway systems built as long as a quarter of a century earlier had already exceeded their expected lives and urgently needed reconstruction. The role of highway maintenance attained new importance, as costs of initial construction rose. Materials for road construction had become scarce and expensive, and highway agencies explored methods of extending the lives of existing roads. Pavement recycling was becoming increasingly popular as a method of reducing costs and conserving scarce material.

The U.S. Interstate Highway System, described as the world's largest public works project, celebrated its 25th anniversary in 1981. Approximately 64,800 km of the system were open to traffic, and an additional 3,600 km were in planning, design, or construction stages. Construction was also approved for the 6.75-km Westway Highway

in New York City, to cost more than $250 million a mile. In Alaska a $200 million upgrading of gravel roads was planned to link the capital of Juneau with the state's interior, 520 km away. Canada's road spending was reduced due to declining investments in many provinces.

Construction of the Darien Gap highway in Colombia and Panama, stalled for several years because of environmental considerations, was progressing slowly, with some sections of the 400-km road already paved. A 1,200-km network of highways was approved by the government of Guatemala; it included the National Ring Road, which would connect the capital city with the Pacific Ocean. The La Paz–Cotapata Highway in Bolivia, crossing the Andes Mountains at points up to 4,530 m and one of the highest paved roads in the world, was almost complete. Chile's North–South Highway, 3,118 km long, was to be reconstructed, and a new 1,100-km road was to be built into the country's previously impenetrable "Wild South."

In the Middle East a contract was awarded for construction of a 25-km causeway carrying a four-lane highway between Saudi Arabia and the island nation of Bahrain. The $140 million General Ahmed Hamdi Tunnel under the Suez Canal was opened to traffic in 1981, the first direct link between the eastern and western Muslim worlds in more than a century. Kuwait was at the midpoint in its $2 billion expressway construction program, and an 800-km road through the desert interior of Oman neared completion.

The Trans-East African Highway Authority was established in 1981 to supervise planning and construction of the 8,200-km highway that would link Cairo, Egypt, with Gabarone, Botswana. Study groups from Spain and Morocco were examining methods of building a road link across the

Strait of Gibraltar. Uganda was rebuilding its 30,000-km road network, which had deteriorated under the regime of Idi Amin.

About 70% of Japan's 7,600-km expressway system was complete in 1981, and Japan's National Highway System totaled approximately 40,000 km. Indonesia was planning a $356 million highway from Jakarta to the interior of Java, while Bangladesh was building a 320-km network of roads in areas having a surplus of food grains. A 542-km section of the Great Northern Highway in Western Australia was opened to traffic in July 1981, part of the road that would eventually link Perth and Darwin.

In Europe Britain planned to spend $720 million on trunk road construction annually, with more than 2,400 km needing to be built or improved. A ring road around Athens, Greece, was designed to include 29 km of depressed or underground sections, at a total cost of over $700 million. Opening of a 220-km section of the motorway linking Paris with Hendaye, on the French-Spanish border, made it possible to drive entirely on expressways from Hamburg, West Germany, or Amsterdam to Bilbao, Spain. The Soviet Union expected to build 80,000 km of new roads by 1985.

(HUGH M. GILLESPIE)

Tunnels. Major tunneling projects being promoted in 1981 included the Channel tunnel between England and France, a tunnel under Bombay Harbour, India, and a tunnel under Oslo Fjord, Norway. Hydraulic rock drills for the drill and blast cycle, hard rock tunneling machines, and slurry shields became established as the key equipment for tunneling projects in the 1980s. Immersed tubes for shallow crossings retained their popularity, and an estimated 60 or more were in use throughout the world. Improved methods for ground freezing to control water increased world-

The Furka tunnel, the world's longest narrow-gauge railway tunnel (15 km; 9.5 mi), was completed in Switzerland in April.

wide applications of this system for underground works.

In Switzerland appropriate ground conditions and increased shortages of skilled labour encouraged contractors to use tunneling machines on three major projects. At the Gubrist Tunnel, forming part of the N20 highway, one of the largest mechanically excavated cross sections in the world was being excavated by a full-face Robbins machine with a diameter of 11.45 m. Precast concrete segments were being used for the primary lining, and an in situ permanent concrete road deck was advanced concurrently with the drive approximately 100 m behind the face. At the Rosenberg Tunnel at St. Gallen four Dosco road headers mounted in a shield were driving the second bore of the 11.3-m-diameter twin road tunnel. Excavating through sandstones and marls, the builders achieved a maximum progress of one meter per hour on the first drive. The third tunnel demonstrating the versatility of modern rock tunneling machines was at Karenzerberg, 50 km south of Zürich. There a single-bore two-lane highway tunnel was being driven through limestone and chalk using a Wirth three-stage tunneling machine that progressively widened the bore from 3.5 m to its full diameter of 11 m.

A long-overdue sharing of practical technology between mining and civil engineering projects was evident worldwide. The largest full-face tunneling machine ever constructed in West Germany began work in a coal mine north of Dortmund. The 6.5-m-diameter, 340-metric ton machine was designed so that steel supports could be installed only 2 m behind the face. At Selby, England, the National Coal Board was carrying out one of the world's largest mining developments. An access drift was successfully driven using a Dosco road header mounted in a shield and lined with spheroidal graphite cast-iron segments. At the end of the drift a 6-m-diameter Robbins full-face tunneling machine was assembled to begin a 13.3-km drive to the main coal production area. It was planned to complete the first 5 km of the roadway by the end of 1982.

Driving continued on the Kan Etsu tunnel, which at a length of 10.9 km would be the longest vehicular tunnel in Japan. Full-face excavation was being carried out by drill and blast methods using hydraulic rock drills. The tunnel was to be one of the first of its kind to employ longitudinal ventilation in conjunction with shafts. Japanese engineers continued to achieve success with slurry moles, and in 1981 their machines were operating in the Americas and, for the first time, in Europe. The world's largest slurry shield, a 10.6-m-diameter machine manufactured in West Germany, began work on the Aurelia railway tunnel in Rome.

Australian engineers claimed a record for sinking what they believed was the world's largest nonarticulated immersed-tube tunnel. Required to carry cooling water to a new power station 100 km north of Sydney, the complete tunnel, 263 m long, was cast as a single four-cell unit that weighed 25,000 metric tons at launching.

(DAVID A. HARRIES)

[733; 734.A]

Environment

As the worldwide recession continued to deepen and unemployment rose in 1981, governments showed signs of reviewing their more extreme environmental policies. In the U.S. Pres. Ronald Reagan's administration saw these policies as needlessly restrictive and as impediments to economic recovery. As the influence of national environmentalist lobbies waned, so did their success in elections. Even in France, where some observers thought the closely contested presidential election had been influenced by the intervention of the "green" candidate, it was doubtful whether the environmentalists secured any genuine modifications of the incoming president's policies. There were some environmental gains at the international level. The most successful of the UN Environment Program enterprises, the program aimed at protecting regional seas, continued to prosper. The International Whaling Commission agreed to quotas that afforded much greater protection to sperm whales. In terms of the urban environment, the year was dominated by urban violence in many European cities, most seriously in Britain.

Environmentalists, and all those who shared her passionate and informed concern for the plight of less developed countries, mourned the death on May 31 of Barbara Ward (Lady Jackson of Lodsworth; see OBITUARIES).

INTERNATIONAL COOPERATION

UN Environment Program. At the 36th session of the UN General Assembly, late in 1980, Mostafa Tolba was elected to continue as UNEP executive director for another year. The UNEP governing council met in Nairobi, Kenya, during May 13–16. In his "state of the environment" report, Tolba emphasized the benefits that less developed countries gain from environmental protection, even when measured in purely economic terms. He proposed to the council a levy on the use of such "international commons" as the oceans, airspace, telecommunications frequencies, and satellite orbits, with the proceeds going to environmental projects in less developed countries.

The proposal was not accepted and, although Sweden suggested an increase in UNEP funding, Britain, France, Canada, and West Germany said they would not increase their contributions. The U.S. delegate, Elizabeth Hoinkes, said her government planned to lower its contribution by $10 million; it was disappointed in UNEP's achievements and felt the annual budget should be reduced from the $120 million proposed by UNEP itself to $65 million. Less developed countries fought hard to keep the budget at the $120 million level, but in the end it was reduced to $77 million. A Swedish proposal for a special fund to finance projects in less developed countries was defeated.

In April UNEP announced that, at a meeting sponsored by the government of Sri Lanka and held in Colombo earlier in the year, Afghanistan, Bangladesh, India, Iran, Maldives, Nepal, Pakistan, and Sri Lanka had signed a declaration estab-

A small child plays in a dump of asbestos scrap in India. The Indian government, like some other third world governments, had failed to recognize asbestos as a health hazard.

lishing a South Asian Cooperative Environment Program; Bhutan and Burma would also be invited to join. The program was to study environmental problems in South Asia and to encourage and support projects. UNEP scientists, meeting late in 1980 at Bilthoven, Neth., called for continued monitoring and research to determine the likelihood of ozone-layer depletion and the consequences of increased penetration of ultraviolet rays from the Sun into the atmosphere.

World Health Organization. At another meeting in Bilthoven, February 9–13, WHO was given global responsibility for devising methods to deal with accidental spills of toxic wastes. The meeting was attended by representatives from 17 countries, UNEP, and the International Labour Office. The WHO Working Group on Guidelines for the Control of Toxic and Other Hazardous Waste held its first session at Garmisch-Partenkirchen, West Germany, March 17–20.

European Communities (EC). On Oct. 10, 1980, the EC had announced new proposals aimed at eliminating disparities in legislation on asbestos in member states. They called for asbestos to be phased out of all uses and replaced where possible, as well as for tighter medical surveillance of workers exposed to it. The proposals distinguished between the more dangerous crocidolite (blue) asbestos, for which they recommended a limit of 0.2 fibres per millilitre of air, and chrysolite (white) asbestos, for which they recommended one fibre per millilitre. By late April 1981 the proposals were running into difficulty because some members of the European Parliament (MEP's) and the parliamentary Public Health Committee felt it was confusing to issue two standards. However, committee members and MEP's disagreed as to which of the two figures should be accepted.

In November 1980 the Council of Ministers approved a proposal to ban the import into the EC member states of shoes and other leather products that had been treated with sperm whale oil.

UN Conference on the Law of the Sea. What was to have been the final session of UNCLOS opened in New York City on March 9, 1981. A week earlier, the U.S. Department of State had announced that it found serious difficulties in the sections of the draft convention that dealt with deep-sea mining. This led to fears that the new U.S. administration would insist on substantial renegotiation, but on March 11 UN Secretary-General Kurt Waldheim stated that all the U.S. required was time to study the draft more deeply. The session was adjourned and opened again in Geneva on August 3. The U.S. objections to the draft were (1) that the proposed International Seabed Authority was to be constituted with a decision-making apparatus that offered inadequate protection for U.S. interests and failed to reflect the position of the U.S. as the world's leading producer and consumer of raw materials; and (2) that the Authority was likely to be unduly restrictive and afforded too few guarantees to potential investors.

Soviet delegate Semyon Kozyrev offered to assist in working out investment protection guarantees. However, the Group of 77 (less developed) nations considered the U.S. attitude to be an attack on the concept that seabed resources are the common property of all mankind, including the landlocked states, and that control over them and benefits from their exploitation should be shared. This view was repeated early in October at the meeting of Commonwealth heads of government in Melbourne, Australia, where island members of the Commonwealth, led by the Solomon Islands, said the U.S. was behaving like a superpower seeking to protect its interests.

By the time the UNCLOS session ended on August 28, the U.S. had become somewhat isolated, and the draft convention was accepted unaltered as the official text. It was agreed that the International Seabed Authority would be based in Jamaica and that the arbitration tribunal would sit in Hamburg, West Germany. UNCLOS was to reconvene on

March 8, 1982, in New York City for a final eight-week session in which details of the convention would be settled. It was hoped that in early September 1982 the convention would be opened for signature in Caracas, Venezuela, where the first UNCLOS working session was held in 1974.

The many delays in approving the convention led to pressure on governments from the mining industry. The U.S. and West Germany passed legislation permitting seabed operations to begin, and Belgium, Italy, The Netherlands, and Britain (whose Deep Sea Mining [Temporary Provisions] Bill was considered in May by a House of Commons committee) contemplated similar legislation.

Marine Environment. Secretary-General Chandrika Srivastava of the International Maritime Consultative Organization announced in Geneva on July 6 that 15 countries, representing half the world's shipping tonnage, were about to ratify a marine pollution convention. In October 1980 a group of scientists met in Kuwait under UNEP auspices to pledge $5 million for a study of the ecology of the Persian Gulf. In this, the world's fastest growing region, UNEP was concerned about pollution from chloralkali works, aluminum smelters, refineries, and oil spills.

In January 1981 the Arab League Educational, Scientific, and Cultural Organization (ALESCO) held its Jidda III conference. Delegates from seven countries bordering on the Red Sea agreed to set up a mutual aid centre to fight pollution, which was said to be increasing rapidly. Domestic sewage, industrial wastes, disturbances caused by dredging, and oil spills were all implicated, and there was a likelihood of further problems resulting from a proposed operation to exploit metalliferous muds.

The latest success for the UNEP Regional Seas Program came on March 24, when a three-year, $4.4 million conservation project for West Africa was adopted at a meeting in Abidjan, Ivory Coast. The agreement followed discussion held late in 1980 at Lomé, Togo, when 13 of the 20 West African coastal states met under UNEP auspices. The

project would give priority to training in coastal management, the creation of facilities for inspecting tankers prior to deballasting, waste control legislation, and environmental assessment.

Discussions began in October in Nairobi that, it was hoped, would lead to an environmental treaty protecting the eastern Indian Ocean and the sea off the East African coast. A seven-man mission, led by Stjepan Keckes, a director of the UNEP Regional Seas Program, planned to visit all the states in the area, from Somalia in the north to Madagascar and Mozambique, prior to a meeting of their representatives.

Scientists and lawyers from more than 20 Caribbean countries met in February at Managua, Nicaragua, where they agreed to a $3.1 million conservation program, beginning with action to prevent oil spills and to improve watershed management. Of 66 projects considered, 25 were regarded as urgent enough to warrant implementation over the next three years. On April 6–8, 23 of the 27 Caribbean states met again, at Montego Bay, Jamaica, to endorse the Caribbean Action Plan under the terms of the Jamaica Accord. Part of the UNEP Regional Seas Program, the plan had a budget target of $8.2 million, to be raised over three years, and included all 66 projects to be coordinated from a headquarters in Jamaica.

Under the terms of the Helsinki Convention for the Protection of the Marine Environment of the Baltic Sea, Finland had special responsibility for dealing with oil spills. Following the publication of a report on the 1979 grounding of the tanker "Antonio Gramsci" in the Gulf of Riga, which was critical of Finnish preparations, the Finnish government decided in October 1980 to start a research and rescue program with a $100,000 budget. Under the convention, responsibility for Soviet waters was given to East Germany because of the time needed for Soviet experts to obtain visas to attend emergency meetings.

Fresh Water. On Nov. 10, 1980, the UN General Assembly had declared that the 1980s were to be the International Drinking Water Supply and

"Aye, lad—she's doomed to sail these waters 'til the end o' time."

LAW OF THE SEA TALKS

ED ASHLEY—THE TOLEDO BLADE

In October members of Friends of the Earth and the Sierra Club appeared in Washington, D.C., to petition for the removal of U.S. Secretary of the Interior James G. Watt. Rafe Pomerance, president of Friends of the Earth, is at the lectern; beside him is Joseph Fontaine, president of the Sierra Club.

Sanitation Decade (IDWSSD), with the aim of bringing clean water and adequate sanitation to everyone by 1990. This would mean providing water supplies for 1,800,000,000 people and sanitation for 2,400,000,000 in a situation that was said to be deteriorating. WHO estimated that poor sanitation caused some 25 million deaths a year. The IDWSSD programs would cost more than $600 billion at 1978 prices, although some experts believed the cost could be reduced substantially if cheaper technologies were used.

Environment ministers from France, Switzerland, West Germany, Luxembourg, and The Netherlands met on Jan. 26, 1981, in The Hague but failed to agree to a French proposal that all five countries contribute to the cost of a plant to extract salt from the Rhine. A counterproposal, to inject excess salt in the ground in Alsace, was rejected by France. It was then proposed that France should transport the salt from its potash mines, by barge or pipeline, to the North Sea for dumping.

Population. A report by Rafael Salas, executive director of the UN Fund for Population Activities, published in mid-June, revised earlier estimates of the future size of the world population. The report gave a low estimate of 8,000,000,000 people by the year 2040, a median estimate of 10,500,000,000 by 2110, and a high estimate of 14,200,000,000 by 2130. The population of Europe should stabilize at 540 million around the year 2030, that of North America at 320 million around 2060, and that of the Soviet Union a little later. The main growth areas would be Africa and southern Asia, and by the year 2110 the industrialized countries would contain 13% of the world's population, as compared with 24% in 1981.

NATIONAL DEVELOPMENTS

"Ecopolitics." In Malaysia on April 9 a law came into force, amending the Societies Act, 1966, that deprived nonpolitical organizations of the right to criticize official policies or to campaign for legislative changes. Directed against Malaysian Friends of the Earth, the Consumers Association of Penang, the Environmental Protection Society of Malaysia, and a number of scientific and intellectual bodies, the law prevented environmentalists from campaigning on environmental issues. In France Brice Lalonde, the ecologist candidate in the presidential election and leader of the largest of the "little" parties, received 1,126,254 votes in the first round of balloting. This represented 3.88% of the votes cast and 3.09% of the total electorate, and although Lalonde was eliminated from the contest, he was fifth in the poll and ahead of former premier Michel Debré.

A proposal by the new U.S. secretary of the interior, James Watt (*see* BIOGRAPHIES), to release federal land for mineral exploitation, starting with 2,400 sq km (600,000 ac) of seabed near Santa Barbara, Calif., enraged environmentalists. A petition opposing the move received 100,000 signatures, and Watt was taken to court by California Gov. Jerry Brown, supported by environmentalists and some Republican groups, in an effort to prevent the sale of leases on 31 tracts. The court ruled in favour of Governor Brown, and in August Watt announced that further oil exploration off the California coast would be delayed for at least two years. Leasing in other offshore areas continued, however, including the Georges Bank off New England, one of the nation's richest fishing grounds. Watt, who removed all the surviving "preser-

vationists" from his department and cut $3 million from environmental programs, was seen by many as an antienvironmental crusader devoted to the interests of ranchers and businessmen. The Sierra Club, which led a petition drive demanding his removal, reported that its membership had risen as a result of opposition to his actions.

British environmentalists lobbied vigorously and vociferously for the Wildlife and Countryside Bill, which would supply a framework for conservation and landscape management in rural areas for many years to come. The bill was enacted in October but some of its provisions would not take effect before 1982.

Urban Problems. The year was marked by more violent disturbances in several European cities. In Switzerland, where young people and police had clashed in Zürich, Lausanne, and Bern in the fall of 1980, violence again broke out in Zürich in March 1981. Young people protesting the closing of the Free Youth Centre in a disused factory broke into the building. Police used tear gas and water cannon against the demonstrators, who retaliated with bricks, gasoline (petrol) bombs, and steel balls. On March 30 it was agreed that the centre would be refurbished at the municipality's expense and reopened. In West Berlin, where there was an acute housing shortage, squatters occupying 117 apartment buildings received support from young people during the election campaign for the city government. On March 12 and over the weekend of March 14–15, rioters wrecked cars, smashed windows, and threw paving stones at the police. They also set fire to the Reichstag building, emulating the incident in 1933 that preceded Hitler's rise to power.

It was in Britain, however, that some of the most serious urban violence occurred. Deteriorating city centres, high unemployment among young people, especially young blacks, and aggressive and insensitive policing were blamed for riots that affected most large cities between April and July. The first was at Brixton, London, on April 9–13, and it was followed by clashes of extreme violence at Finsbury Park, London, on April 20; Southall, London, on July 3; Toxteth, Liverpool, during July 3–8; Wood Green, London, on July 7; Moss Side, Manchester, on July 7–8; and by smaller riots in Leicester, Birmingham, Leeds, and other cities. After the Brixton riot the government ordered an inquiry into the causes. The inquiry was conducted by Lord Scarman, a senior judge, whose report was published in November. (*See* RACE RELATIONS; UNITED KINGDOM.)

On May 20 residents of Centralia, Pa. (population 1,017), voted by 434 to 204 to abandon their homes if necessary in order to allow a fire that had burned in a local coal mine for 20 years to be extinguished. The mine, which once provided most of the town's employment, had been closed years earlier. Some of its galleries had collapsed, causing severe subsidence and consequent structural damage to buildings, while the fire emitted carbon monoxide and other noxious gases.

Nuclear Power. The massive antinuclear demonstrations that took place in several European cities in 1981, though primarily motivated by opposition to the deployment of nuclear weapons in Europe, also attracted support from environmentalist groups and those opposed to the use of nuclear power. Demonstrations in London, Brussels, and Rome on October 24–25 surpassed all previous such gatherings in the number of participants, estimated at between 200,000 and 300,000.

WEST GERMANY. An inquiry opened early in the year into the application by the West German Federal Institute of Physics and Technology in Braunschweig for permission to store spent nuclear fuel at Gorleben, Lower Saxony. On the night of February 2 a demonstration organized by the Social Democratic Party to protest the proposed Brokdorf nuclear power station led to a march by 12,000 to 14,000 people through the streets of Hamburg, and 2,500 police were brought in. A group of 50 to 100 demonstrators wearing helmets and masks stoned police, smashed hotel and shop windows, and wrecked cars; 36 people were injured and about 20 arrested. On the same evening, with the support of the Social Democrat mayor, Hans-Ulrich Klose, Hamburg Social Democrats voted 198–157 to withdraw from the Brokdorf project. (Klose resigned on May 25 because he no longer commanded a parliamentary majority and was replaced, on June 16, by Klaus von Dohnanyi.)

Police used water cannon to combat another demonstration at Brokdorf on February 25. On February 28 there was an even larger demonstration, in which more than 50,000 rioters using steel bolts, stones, gasoline bombs, paint bombs, and flares fought for three hours against more than 10,500 police equipped with helicopters, water cannon, and tear gas; 128 police and an unspecified number of demonstrators were injured, and 240 people were arrested.

FRANCE. A fire in a silo containing spent nuclear fuel at the Cap de la Hague reprocessing plant caused minor internal contamination by cesium-137 on January 7. On May 16 the government announced its approval of a scheme to rebuild the existing plant, install a second, 800-metric-ton-capacity plant alongside it, and build pools to hold up to 4,000 metric tons of waste, together with a workshop for cutting up fuel elements. Environmentalists demanded abandonment of the scheme, but after the election the new government agreed to continue with it.

The ecologists, led by Brice Lalonde, had demanded closing of all of France's 14 nuclear power stations. On June 3 incoming Pres. François Mitterrand said that work on the controversial plant at Plogoff, Brittany, would not be started, and on July 30 the Cabinet decided to halt work at five plants, two of which (Golfech and Cattenom) were in the very early stages. The nuclear energy policy was debated by the National Assembly on October 8, and by a vote of 331–67 it was agreed that the strongly pro-nuclear policy inherited from the previous administration should be continued. However, Premier Pierre Mauroy said work on the five suspended stations would continue only with the consent of the local authorities unless they were deemed essential to the national interest; in that case, the National Assembly would decide.

There were clashes on August 6–7 between pronuclear demonstrators and police. The demonstrators blocked the main Paris–Toulouse and Bordeaux–Sète railway lines and demonstrated in Moselle over the suspension of work at the Golfech and Cattenom 3 and 4 plants. On August 6 police at Cherbourg clashed with antinuclear demonstrators protesting against the arrival of a Japanese ship carrying spent fuel for reprocessing. Despite the many protests and demonstrations at Plogoff during the presidential election campaign, people in the area voted overwhelmingly for pro-nuclear candidates.

UNITED STATES. In September some 3,000 demonstrators, headed by the Abalone Alliance, attempted a peaceful blockade of the Diablo Canyon nuclear power plant in California, hoping to prevent the plant from being charged with fuel and started. The attempt failed, but the start-up was postponed indefinitely when officials of the operating company, the Pacific Gas and Electric Co., announced that two containment domes, identical from the outside but constructed differently inside, had each been built on the site intended for the other. The discovery raised doubts about the ability of some of the piping to withstand a major earthquake in this seismically active area. In November the Nuclear Regulatory Commission suspended the license permitting fuel loading and low-power testing until the plant had undergone seismic tests. The No. 2 reactor at Indian Point, on the Hudson River 65 km (40 mi) from New York City, was closed in October 1980 because of accidental flooding, started again in April 1981, then closed again in October because of vibration in a coolant pump and a suspicion that the plant had leaked mildly radioactive material into the river.

In the aftermath of the 1979 Three Mile Island (Pennsylvania) nuclear plant accident, decontamination operations estimated to cost $1 billion began in September 1981. They involved the filtering and pumping into storage tanks of radioactive water accumulated in the containment building of one of the plant's units.

UNITED KINGDOM. Safety regulations at British Nuclear Fuel (BNF) Ltd.'s reprocessing plant at Windscale, Cumbria, were severely criticized in a report submitted to the Department of Energy by the Health and Safety Executive. The report followed an inquiry instituted in 1979 into radioactive leakages at the plant, which reprocessed nuclear waste from Japan and other countries as well as from Britain's own power plants. In October 1981, some six months after the report was submitted, further leaks occurred at Windscale, details of which were withheld by BNF for four days. This led to an investigation by the Nuclear Fuels Inspectorate into the procedure for releasing information to local communities following nuclear accidents.

Atmospheric Pollution. The U.S. Environmental Protection Agency (EPA) had announced a freeze on the production of chlorofluorocarbons (CFC's) in October 1980. This was believed to imply the setting of quotas for permitted CFC's (used as aerosol propellants). In September 1981, however, the Reagan administration altered the ground rules of the CFC debate. In its proposed amendments to the Clean Air Act, which was due for reauthorization, it required that the EPA base its regulation of CFC's on measurements of atmospheric ozone rather than computer predictions.

At the same time, Donald Heath, a National Aeronautics and Space Administration scientist, announced that the Nimbus 4 and 7 satellites, monitoring atmospheric ozone between 1970 and 1979, had detected a steady decrease of 0.5% a year at an altitude of 40 km (25 mi). In his opinion this could be caused by CFC's. His claim was heavily qualified, however, and the view of other experts was that the situation remained unchanged. Heath's sampling and statistical techniques differed from those most commonly used.

Fears that the Clean Air Act would be undermined seriously were eased somewhat when the administration proposed a set of principles for revision of the act that represented a withdrawal from its former hard line. Thus, for example, scientific data would continue to supply criteria for estimating the effects of pollution on health, rather than cost-benefit analyses as proposed by the budget director, David Stockman. On the other hand, emission standards for automobiles would be changed from one to two grams of nitrogen oxides per mile for cars made during or after 1981, and the regulations forbidding any significant deterioration in air quality, even in regions that currently had no industry, would be relaxed. Environmental groups remained suspicious, and a struggle was expected before Congress acted on the measure, probably in 1982. Opinion polls indicated that the public did not want the act changed significantly.

One of the administration's Clean Air Act proposals was for increased research on acid rain. At the annual meeting of the American Association for the Advancement of Science, held in Toronto, Ont., in January, John Roberts, Canadian minister for science and technology, called on

World's 25 Most Populous Urban Areas[1]

Rank	City and Country	City proper Population	City proper Year	Metropolitan area Population	Metropolitan area Year
1	Tokyo, Japan	8,349,200	1980 census	28,637,000	1980 estimate
2	New York City, U.S.	7,071,000	1980 census	16,120,000	1980 census
3	Osaka, Japan	2,648,200	1980 census	15,527,000	1980 estimate
4	Mexico City, Mexico	9,373,400	1980 census[2]	14,750,200	1979 estimate
5	São Paulo, Brazil	8,584,900	1980 census	12,708,600	1980 census
6	London, U.K.	6,696,000	1981 census[2]	12,074,600	1981 census[2]
7	Cairo, Egypt	5,399,000	1979 estimate	12,000,000	1980 estimate
8	Rhine-Ruhr, West Germany	[3]	[3]	11,777,800	1980 estimate
9	Los Angeles, U.S.	2,966,800	1980 census	11,496,200	1980 census
10	Shanghai, China	5,910,000	1980 estimate	11,320,000	1980 estimate
11	Buenos Aires, Argentina	2,922,900	1980 census	10,796,000	1980 estimate
12	Calcutta, India	[4]	[4]	9,165,700	1981 census[2]
13	Rio de Janeiro, Brazil	5,184,300	1980 census	9,153,500	1980 census
14	Paris, France	2,050,000	1980 estimate	8,765,500	1980 estimate
15	Beijing, China	4,952,000	1980 estimate	8,706,000	1980 estimate
16	Seoul, South Korea	[4]	[4]	8,367,000	1980 census[2]
17	Bombay, India	[4]	[4]	8,202,800	1981 census[2]
18	Moscow, U.S.S.R.	[4]	[4]	8,015,000	1981 estimate
19	Chicago, U.S.	3,005,100	1980 census	7,868,200	1980 census
20	Nagoya, Japan	2,087,900	1980 census	7,461,000	1980 estimate
21	Tianjin, China	3,310,000	1980 estimate	7,390,000	1980 estimate
22	Jakarta, Indonesia	[4]	[4]	6,556,000	1981 estimate
23	Chongqing, China	[4]	[4]	6,000,000	1978 estimate
24	Manila, Philippines	1,538,500	1980 estimate	5,900,600	1979 estimate
25	Philadelphia, U.S.	1,688,200	1980 census	5,548,800	1980 census

[1] Ranked by population of metropolitan area.
[2] Preliminary figures.
[3] An industrial conurbation within which no single central city is identified.
[4] City proper not identified by reporting countries.

the U.S. to curb the emissions of sulfur dioxide that were said to fall as acid rain over the northeastern U.S. and eastern Canada. Relations between the two countries were becoming strained over the issue. However, the effects were said to be most serious in the U.S. itself, especially in the Adirondack Mountains where the naturally acid soils had no buffer to protect them from the additional acid falling in rain and snow.

The Polish Ecological Society, formed in September 1980, campaigned throughout the year against pollution caused by the Skawina aluminum works at Krakow. The Krakow region lies in a hollow where the circulation of air is restricted, and each year it receives an estimated 95,000 tons of dust and 70,000 tons of sulfur dioxide from Nowa Huta to the east and 33,000 tons each of dust and sulfur dioxide from the coal-fired power station and aluminum works that comprise the Skawina complex. About 20 km (12 mi) away, the Niepolomice forest had to be sprayed with lime in the 1970s to counteract the acid rain, and in 1979 gold art treasures in the Wawel Castle museum were found to be corroding. On Jan. 5, 1981, the metallurgy minister, Zbigniew Szalajda, said that ways must be found to increase aluminum output from Poland's other plant at Konin, and on January 7 he announced that the Skawina complex would be closed.

Mayors of five towns near Marseilles, France, received support in the last week in July from Environment Minister Michel Crépeau, who ordered Charbonnages de France to install equipment to reduce sulfur dioxide emissions from the coal-fired power station it was building. The station was to burn Provençal soft brown coal with a 4 to 6% sulfur content, and it would have emitted some 540 tons of sulfur dioxide a day from a chimney 30 m (98 ft) wide at the base and as tall as the Eiffel Tower. Previously, the company had claimed that equipment that could remove sulfur from the coal did not exist.

In May a joint working party from the U.K. Department of the Environment and the Greater London Council reported that, in Britain as a whole, 38 district councils were failing to comply with an EC Council directive on emissions of sulfur dioxide and suspended particulates. The directive was supposed to come into force on April 1, 1983. A further 33 councils might fail to meet the standards, and because the recession led people to burn high-sulfur coal instead of more expensive smokeless fuels, the problem was likely to grow worse. Powers to ban high-sulfur fuels had been vested in the secretary of state for the environment by the Control of Pollution Act, 1974, but they had never been invoked. In at least one borough, Epping, a smoke-control zone approved in 1975 had never been implemented.

To protect the Taj Mahal, the Indian Department of the Environment announced in June that two coal-fired power stations at Agra, about 85 km (50 mi) from New Delhi, were to be closed. In addition, the railway authorities agreed to change from coal to oil fuel in their Agra workshops.

Industrial Wastes. Recession in Brazil provided the rationale for a presidential decree, issued at the insistence of detergent manufacturers, that post-

Residents of the small town of Centralia, Pa., voted in May to abandon their homes if it became necessary in order to fight a coal mine fire that has been burning for 20 years underneath their town.

DAN MILLER—THE NEW YORK TIMES

Environment

Widespread opposition to the Brok-dorf nuclear power plant, under construction near Hamburg, West Germany, broke into violence in late February when police armed with tear gas faced rock-throwing demonstrators.

poned indefinitely the implementation of a ban on nonbiodegradable detergents. The legislation, planned in 1976, had been due to come into force in January 1981. In the state of São Paulo, foaming in the rivers was now chronic.

A report issued in March indicated that the condition of Lake Baikal in the Soviet Union was deteriorating, despite strict antipollution legislation. Factories discharging effluent into rivers that fed the lake were blamed, together with paper mills, ships carrying oil, and the city of Slyudyanka, which discharged raw sewage into the lake.

Delegates at the International Conference on the Effects of Pollution on the Sea, held on Nov. 17–18, 1980, in Tynemouth, England, heard an account of the activities of Riafield Ltd. The company had been engaged in importing toxic wastes from The Netherlands, which were stored in Britain and then reexported to the Far East. After July 1980 the company held no U.K. license for this operation, but while Humberside County Council deliberated on whether to issue a license, other firms issued writs against Riafield for nonpayment of debts. In July 1981 Riafield went out of business. The House of Lords Select Committee on Science and Technology considered the Riafield case in the course of its hearings on toxic waste management. The hearings brought to light several cases of allegedly illegal dumping. The committee's report, published on September 7, criticized both local authorities and the national government, but it declared safe the country's largest disposal site, at Pitsea, Essex; concern over the site had prompted the hearings.

In Canada paint bombs and smoke bombs were thrown through windows of the British Columbia Department of the Environment during protests against the dumping of wastes containing arsenic, mercury, lead, cadmium, copper, iron, and radium-226 into the Pacific. In April it was announced that permission for the dumping had been given to Amax of Canada Ltd., which planned to reopen a molybdenum mine north of Prince Rupert. The wastes would consist of mine tailings, discharged at concentrations many times higher than the max-

imum permitted by the Fisheries Act. Despite the protests, which were supported by the Anglican Church of Canada, the dumping began in May.

Pesticides. From January 1, in accordance with an EC Council directive, the U.K. began phasing out most remaining uses for organochlorine and several mercury-based compounds. Late in 1980 British trade unions had announced their opposition to the manufacture of 2,4,5-T, rejecting the finding of the Advisory Committee on Pesticides that the herbicide was safe. On May 19, 1981, however, manufacturers rejected union appeals to cease production. In the U.S., following discussions with the Dow Chemical Co., it was announced in June that the EPA would probably lift its ban on the use of 2,4,5-T, imposed in 1979.

California Governor Brown's reluctance to authorize aerial spraying of pesticides over populated areas was blamed by growers for the spread of the Mediterranean fruit fly in that state. Imported accidentally, probably around June 1980, the "medfly," a serious horticultural pest, was first identified in Santa Clara County south of San Francisco. An attempt to control the fly by releasing sterilized males imported from Peru failed, apparently because some of the flies were not sterile, and by August 1981 the insect was in the San Joaquin Valley fruit-growing area. Faced with the U.S. Department of Agriculture's threat to quarantine California produce that had not been fumigated, Governor Brown finally ordered helicopter spraying of the relatively mild pesticide malathion to begin on July 14. However, some growers, fearing the possibility of a quarantine, sprayed about 350 ha (850 ac) from four aircraft using the more toxic diphos. The medfly larva can attack about 200 plant species of commercial value. (*See* LIFE SCIENCES: *Entomology*.)   (MICHAEL ALLABY)

WILDLIFE CONSERVATION

In western Europe, January and February 1981 were the worst months ever recorded for the killing of sea birds by oil pollution. On January 1 five tons of dead birds were washed up at Stockholm;

by January 7, 70,000 dead birds had been counted, and a further 11,000 were recovered at Göteborg. The final toll was expected to reach about 100,000. Meanwhile, Danish wildlife protection authorities said they had found nearly 100,000 in the Kattegat, and in Norway two cleansing centres for birds were opened in the Oslo Fjord. Reports reaching the Royal Society for the Protection of Birds indicated that 42,000 birds, dead and dying, had been counted in January on beaches between northwestern France and southern Norway. These included 32,000 killed by an oil spill in the Skagerrak strait between Norway and Denmark, allegedly caused in part by the Greek tanker "Stylis."

In February more than 1,000 murres (auks) and puffins were found oiled off the East Anglian coast of England. At the same time, more than 10,000 oiled sea birds were found on the French, Belgian, Dutch, and West German coasts. It was clear that deliberate discharge of waste fuel oils by ships, contrary to international treaty obligations, was the major cause of the oil pollution.

In February the Species Survival Commission of the International Union for Conservation of Nature (IUCN), meeting in New Delhi, reported the success of Project Tiger, which had saved that splendid animal from extinction. The tiger was common in India during the 19th century but had become rare by the mid-20th. Thanks to the enthusiasm of the Indian central and state governments and to financial aid from the World Wildlife Fund and others, 11 tiger reserves had been established with a total area of 15 sq km (5.8 sq mi).

Efforts to preserve the rhinoceros were less successful. The world's five species of rhinoceros all remained in danger of extermination. A possible exception was the square-lipped (or white) rhinoceros, which was being protected successfully in Natal, South Africa.

In February five tons of walrus tusks, valued at $450,000, were seized by the U.S. Fish and Wildlife Service (FWS), mostly in Alaska. Under U.S. law only Alaskan natives may kill walruses or hold their ivory. Later, disquieting reports were received concerning marine turtle populations. The Atlantic ridley turtle (*Lepidochelys kempi*) had declined from 40,000 to about 400 at its Mexican breeding place, and 100,000 green turtles (*Chelonia mydas*) were being taken annually off the Mexican Pacific coast. On the other hand, a proposal to build a tourist hotel near the main breeding place of the green turtle on Ascension Island in the South Atlantic Ocean had been shelved. On tiny East Island in the Hawaiian National Wildlife Refuge, volunteers from the Fisheries Service and the FWS cleared beaches of debris to make them usable by nesting turtles and by the endangered Hawaiian monk seal (*Monachus schauinslandi*).

Operation Oryx, the attempt to restore the Arabian oryx (*Oryx leucoryx*) to its desert habitat as a wild animal, suffered a setback in April when a young male, one of ten oryx flown from the San Diego (Calif.) Zoo to Oman, died from the bite of a carpet viper. In Jordan the oryx enclosure at Shaumari was enlarged to 15 sq km to accommodate its 15 animals.

Officials in New York State ordered the dropping of lime into lakes to counteract acid rain, which had been rendering lakes in the Adirondack Mountains less capable of supporting life.

More than 10,000 sea birds were found dead on French, Belgian, Dutch, and West German seacoasts as a result of the discharge of waste fuel oil.

André Dupuy, director of Nikolo-Koba National Park, Senegal, reported in May that elephant numbers had fallen from 225 to 170 in 12 months and not a single large tusker survived. The game guards had been engaged in running battles with well-armed ivory poachers, and two of them had been awarded the IUCN medal for courage in defense of wildlife.

During the spring 110 whooping cranes left their winter quarters in the Aransas National Wildlife Sanctuary, Texas, for their breeding grounds in Wood Buffalo National Park, Canada; 17 other whooping cranes were recorded. In 1953, when Freda Davis asked in the journal *ORYX*, "Can the Whooping Crane be Saved?," only about 30 of these cranes had existed.

The International Whaling Commission (IWC) met in Brighton, England, during July 20–25. Backed by the U.S. and by a personal message from Pres. Ronald Reagan, Britain proposed a full moratorium on commercial whaling or, failing that, a ban on all North Atlantic whaling and all hunting of sperm whales, a ban on cruel methods of killing (especially the explosive harpoon), and an extension of the ban on cold grenade harpoons to minke whales. The moratorium and North Atlantic ban proposals were defeated. Kunio Yonizawa, representing Japan, threatened that his country would leave the IWC or exercise its right to object and so ignore any agreement. He also complained that China, Costa Rica, India, Jamaica, Uruguay, Saint Lucia, and Dominica, which had just joined the IWC, were not whaling nations.

By the end of the meeting, zero quotas had been set for sperm whales in the North Atlantic and Antarctic from the end of the 1981 season, and it was agreed to set a Pacific quota to cover Japanese operations at a special meeting in March 1982. From November 1982 the use of the cold harpoon would be banned. The Antarctic quota for minke whales was increased by about 1,000 for the 1982 season.

In January it was announced that, in implementation of the Soviet Union's 1978 pledge to the IWC, the Soviet Far Eastern fishing fleet had ceased whaling in the Pacific. In April the U.S. National Oceanic and Atmospheric Administration signed a two-year agreement with the Alaskan Eskimo Whaling Commission making management of stocks of bowhead whales the responsibility of the Eskimos. The agreement allowed 17 whales to be killed and 32 to be struck (presumed dead but not landed) during the 1981 season, with a further 17 landings permitted on payment of fees of $1,000 to $5,000 per whale. Conservation groups feared that the Eskimos would exceed their quota, bring the bowhead to extinction, and so remove the last environmental objection to oil and gas drilling in the region. From August 2 it became an offense to take any cetacean within U.K. fishery limits.

An unexpected threat had arisen to imperil the Californian gray whale, which has the longest known migration of any whale—summering in the Arctic but breeding in Baja California, Mexico. Once in its breeding ground, it was protected from Japanese whalers by the Mexican government. However, the whales had become a tourist attraction and were being menaced by the disturbances caused by whale watchers.

By October the Convention on International Trade in Endangered Species of Wild Fauna and Flora (CITES) had been ratified by 72 countries. Both the Royal Society for the Prevention of Cruelty to Animals and the Fauna and Flora Preservation Society (FFPS) had been specially concerned in preparing the *Guidelines for the Transport of Live Animals*. Its aim was to reduce the cruelties of the wildlife trade.

Perhaps the most notable work in bird conservation during the year was done on Stewart Island, where the New Zealand Wildlife Service was attempting to save the kakapo (*Strigops habroptilus*) from extermination. Until 1980, only male specimens of this large, nocturnal, flightless, owl-like parrot had been identified in over 70 years. Trained dogs were then used to find kakapo, and radio transmitters were attached to the birds to follow their movements. By these means a nesting female was found on March 18. Up to August 4, 26 kakapo had been banded, and no great sexual disparity in numbers had been proved. Feral cats seemed to be the chief obstacle to kakapo recuperation.

In Great Britain the Wildlife and Countryside Bill gave almost complete protection to all British species of bats. No other country safeguarded its bats to this extent. (C. L. BOYLE)

See also Agriculture and Food Supplies; Energy; Fisheries; Historic Preservation; Life Sciences; Transportation.
[355.D; 525.A.3.g and B.4.f.i; 534.e.2.a; 724.A; 737.C.1]

EARTH'S JUNGLE HERITAGE

by Jon Tinker

How to describe the rain forests of the Amazon basin? A green hell of impenetrable jungle, say some. A verdant lung for the planet, whose trees supply the oxygen keeping the atmosphere breathable, suggest the environmentalists. The empty quarter of Brazil, claim the patriots, which the nation must occupy and exploit. A decade ago, the issues seemed simple: national sovereignty versus global trusteeship; short-term profit against a wise conservation of natural resources. Today, the alternatives are starting to become reconciled. How has this come about?

Rich Green Mantle. Tropical rain forest is the richest ecosystem known to man. In comparison, the great plains of East Africa, with their teeming herds of wildebeest and zebra, are biological deserts. While a hectare (2.47 ac) of the most complex woodland—in the Appalachians, for example—contains at most 20 species of tree, the Amazon rain forest has at least 100 and sometimes 200 tree species per hectare.

This vast expanse of virtually flat land stretching from the Atlantic to the Andes lies mainly in Brazil, spilling over into Bolivia, Peru, Ecuador, Colombia, Venezuela, Guyana, Suriname, and French Guiana. One-third of it has already been deforested, and another 100,000 sq km (38,600 sq mi)—an area bigger than Denmark and Switzerland combined—is felled each year.

The Brazilian government, when it sells off state land to private buyers, prices it *valor da terra nua*—the value of the naked earth—ignoring the worth of the trees which stand there. Ecologically, the concept of *valor da terra nua* is peculiarly inappropriate. In most ecosystems, half or more of the minerals and other nutrients are locked away in the soil. But in the biological hothouse that is a tropical rain for-est, 90% of the nutrients are actively at work in the forest's living plants and animals.

When forest is cleared and the vegetation burned, these nutrients blow away in smoke or wash off in the rains, lost to the soil forever. Not surprisingly, the land that remains is rapidly exhausted by cultivation or cattle ranching, and unless it receives immense and continuing inputs of fertilizers, it can become in a few short years an exhausted, barren wasteland.

Nutrient Cycle. Such an ecological dead end is in dramatic contrast to the ecological ingenuity of Amazonia undisturbed. Caimans, for example, feed on fish swimming up the smaller rivers; the excreta of these small crocodiles then slowly enrich the nutrient-poor lakes fed by the rising streams—lakes to which the fish themselves must go to spawn. And turtles, feeding on aquatic vegetation, similarly pass on their nutrients to carnivorous fish which thrive on a diet of young turtlets.

More remarkable is the very recent discovery that many Amazonian fish feed directly in the forest. From June to November the Amazon rivers inundate 100,000 sq km of floodplain. The fish migrate with the water into the trees, to feed on falling seeds and fruits. Many species (including several relatives of the flesh-eating piranha) have developed specially adapted molars to crush nuts and bloated stomachs to store fat through the drier season when they must return to a nutless river.

Fish are a major source of protein for Amazonians; in the city of Manaus half the protein comes from fish, and the most important commercial species, the tambaqui, is a seed-eater. No forest, no caimans, no turtles—and no fish. Research is beginning to persuade at least some influential Brazilians that the rain forest might be more valuable standing than felled. This conclusion is not wholly a matter of ecological eye-opening, for Brazil is clearly becoming disappointed over its dramatic efforts to colonize the jungle, once seen as the Latin-American

Jon Tinker is director of Earthscan, an agency of the International Institute for Environment and Development.

equivalent of the American West. The Transamazonian Highway, for example, was designed as a 5,000-km (3,100-mi) road from the Atlantic to Peru that would open up the interior for colonization by five million people during the 1970s. Today, the expensive dirt road is flooded in places for half the year, colonized more by the forest than by people.

Pattern for Protection. Even if the benefits of Amazonian deforestation are illusory in the long term, the short-term profits can still be substantial when land is bought cheaply and the newly cleared pasture abandoned after six or seven years. The momentum of attrition in Amazonia is so powerful, and the poverty and land-hunger in Brazil's nearby Northeast Region are so great, that conservationists expect at least another third of the Amazonian rain forest to disappear by the end of the century. So instead of outright opposition to all deforestation, they have been trying to determine just which parts of the forest are most worth saving. Recently they have detected a curious pattern.

During the relatively cold, dry glacial periods of the Pleistocene, a million or so years ago, the Amazon rain forest persisted only in small, isolated fragments. In each of these areas the wildlife evolved rapidly, and when the warm, wet weather returned, the plants and animals of each sanctuary had become different. The new species spread out into the returning rain forest, but the wildlife of what biologists now call "Pleistocene refugia" remained permanently enriched. Clusters of species-richness have been mapped for birds, for butterflies, for reptiles, and for trees. Where all four disciplines pinpoint the same spot on the map, that area takes on a top priority for protection.

Moves by the Amazonian nations toward at least a degree of rain forest conservation, in part through the 1980 Amazon Treaty, have been helped by a realization among agriculturalists that some of the region's soils are markedly less suitable for cultivation than others. Within the rain forest proper, only the floodplain or *várzea*, whose fertile and friable soil is renewed each year by upriver silts, offers real farming potential. The *várzea*, though, is at present largely inaccessible, and Brazil is beginning to look instead to the *cerrado*, drier savannah scrub that covers 1.8 million sq km (700,000 sq mi) surrounding the capital, Brasília. With an initial liming and regular inputs of fertilizer, its acid, nutrient-poor soil grows good crops. Liming is relatively cheap, but nitrates are not. An ideal solution would be to grow leguminous crops such as soybeans, whose roots sustain the *Rhizobium* bacteria that convert nitrogen from the air into nitrates in the soil. Unfortunately, soy refuses to grow on the *cerrado* soils, and the Brazilian Agricultural Research Institution

(EMBRAPA) has discovered the cause: a soil fungus called *Streptomycetes*. This fungus releases the antibiotic streptomycin, which kills the bacteria. Now EMBRAPA is searching for other ways of enhancing the fertility of the *cerrado*, still seen as a better agricultural prospect than rain forest.

Genetic Treasure House. There is growing worldwide interest in the genetic potential of Amazonia. Tea, cocoa, coffee, and rubber all came out of tropical rain forests, and all must ultimately depend on new genetic material from the wild to reinvigorate cultivated strains. For example, West African cocoa breeders have recently introduced greater vigour, high disease resistance, and better productivity by crossing with wild and semiwild strains of the cacao plant from the upper Amazon. The rain forest contains uncounted species whose economic potential is unknown.

Almost any temperate tree species grown in the Amazon would succumb rapidly to attack by plant-eating insects and fungi. Yet rain forest trees thrive there for decades, undoubtedly because their bark contains chemicals that are powerful insecticides and fungicides. "Studies of the relations of insects to tropical barks," suggested botanist Clifford Evans in a recent presidential address to the British Ecological Society, "would provide the basis for a whole new generation of agricultural insecticides."

Peoples of the Forest. If an understanding of Amazonia's genetic treasure house is slowly growing, there is still little awareness of the role the region's native peoples could play in releasing this knowledge. Their scores of unique cultures, in which details of beneficial uses of hundreds of species are passed from one generation to the next, are still being wantonly destroyed, even more rapidly than their physical existence.

The last large Indian tribe in Brazil still following a traditional way of life, the Yanomami, has been decimated in the past few years by measles and other diseases, introduced by road builders and prospectors seeking the newly discovered mineral wealth. One of the companies involved is Rio Doce Mining, whose former chief of security, Col. João Nobre da Veiga, is now president of FUNAI, the Brazilian government agency responsible for protecting the forest Indians.

The shameful neglect—and at times deliberate persecution—of the rain forest Indians is widespread in other Amazonian countries besides Brazil. If ethical arguments carry little weight—and in conflicts between powerful colonists and native peoples they usually have—then perhaps enlightened self-interest may prove more persuasive. For the Amazon's indigenous nations carry in their oral traditions the keys to the region's genetic treasures.

Equatorial Guinea

The African republic of Equatorial Guinea consists of Río Muni, which is bordered by Cameroon on the north, Gabon on the east and south, and the Atlantic Ocean on the west; and the offshore islands of Bioko and Pagalu. Area: 28,051 sq km (10,-831 sq mi). Pop. (1981 est.): 372,000. Cap. and largest city: Malabo, on Bioko (pop., 1974 est., 25,-000). Language: Spanish. President of the Supreme Military Council in 1981, Lieut. Col. Teodoro Obiang Nguema Mbasogo.

In March 1981 Pres. Teodoro Obiang Nguema Mbasogo appointed the first civilian to the Cabinet; he was Emiliano Buale, who was made responsible for agriculture. This was seen as an important step toward demilitarization of the government.

Only days later, on April 10, the government reported a coup attempt. In its aftermath some 150 people, including former ministers, were arrested, and about 40 stood trial. Opponents of the regime suggested that the coup had been arranged by the president in order to undermine the opposition. Three Spanish newspapers were banned temporarily for carrying such suggestions.

During the year the country's economy recovered slowly. Traffic returned to a semblance of normality, and some water and electricity were available in the capital. Cocoa recovered its place as the country's chief source of income, but production was still well below the pre-independence level of 40,000 metric tons annually. In April the International Monetary Fund agreed to a finance facility of 4.7 million SDR's to cover an export earnings shortfall. (GUY ARNOLD)

EQUATORIAL GUINEA

Education. (1973–74) Primary, pupils 35,977, teachers 630; secondary (1975–76), pupils 3,984, teachers 115; vocational (1975–76), pupils 370, teachers 29; teacher training (1975–76), students 169, teachers 21.

Finance and Trade. Monetary unit: epkwele (bipkwele for more than one), with (Sept. 21, 1981) a par value of 2 bipkwele to 1 Spanish peseta (free rate of 184 bipkwele = U.S. $1; 341 bipkwele = £1 sterling). Budget (1981 est.): revenue 1,951,000,000 bipkwele; expenditure 2,025,000,-000 bipkwele. Foreign trade (1980): imports c. 10.1 billion bipkwele; exports c. 3.1 million bipkwele. Import sources: Spain c. 70%; China c. 13%; Tunisia c. 5%. Export destinations: The Netherlands c. 46%; West Germany c. 17%; Senegal c. 16%; Spain c. 10%; Italy c. 6%. Main exports (1975): cocoa c. 60%; coffee c. 30%.

Agriculture. Production (in 000; metric tons; 1979): sweet potatoes c. 33; cassava c. 52; bananas c. 16; cocoa c. 8; coffee c. 6; palm kernels c. 3; palm oil c. 5. Livestock (in 000; 1979): sheep c. 34; cattle c. 4; pigs c. 8; goats c. 8; chickens c. 85.

Equestrian Sports

Thoroughbred Racing and Steeplechasing. UNITED STATES AND CANADA. John Henry, who passed from owner to owner for as little as $1,100 early in his career, won all the annual Eclipse honours for which he was eligible in 1981. The six-year-old son of Ole Bob Bowers-Once Double, by Double Jay, was voted horse of the year, best male turf horse, and best older horse. The gelding received all 191 votes cast for horse of the year, the first time in the 11-year history of Eclipse Award voting that the choice was unanimous.

Jockey Bill Shoemaker, trainer Ron McAnally, and the Dotsam Stable of Dorothy and Sam Rubin of New York City, all part of the implausible success story of John Henry, also won Eclipse Awards. John Henry was responsible for a seventh Eclipse Award, that won by Mrs. Verna Lehmann's Golden Chance Farm of Kentucky as outstanding breeder.

Other Eclipse winners included: two-year-old colt, Deputy Minister; two-year-old filly, Before Dawn; three-year-old colt, Pleasant Colony; three-year-old filly, Wayward Lass; older filly or mare, Relaxing; female turf horse, De La Rose; sprinter, Guilty Conscience; steeplechase, Zaccio. Aside from John Henry, male turf champion in 1980, the only repeat winner was Mrs. Lewis C. Murdock's Zaccio (Lorenzaccio-Delray Dancer, by Chateaugay). He capped his season with victory in the Colonial Cup.

The 50-year-old Shoemaker, who won a special Eclipse Award in 1976, rode John Henry in his final five starts after replacing Laffit Pincay, Jr. While helping John Henry establish two money-earning records—$1,798,030 for a single season and $3,022,810 for a career—Shoemaker himself added to his own standards, which were approaching 9,000 victories and $86 million in purses won. John Henry, the first $3 million horse, broke the career record of $2,781,607 set by Spectacular Bid in 1980 and the single-season mark of $1,148,-800 established by Affirmed in 1979.

John Henry, small and undistinguished in appearance, raced chiefly in California. It was there he suffered his two defeats, finishing fourth in both the Hollywood Gold Cup and the campaign-ending Hollywood Turf Cup. He made two successful forays to Belmont Park and one to Arlington Park to capture the inaugural of the Arlington Million, which carried first-prize money of $600,-000. John Henry annexed five other turf stakes races besides the Million; they were the San Luis Obispo, San Luis Rey, Hollywood Invitational, Sword Dancer, and Oak Tree Invitational. On dirt trails he won the Santa Anita Handicap and the Jockey Club Gold Cup. In three consecutive starts John Henry won the Arlington Million by a nose, the Jockey Club Gold Cup by a head, and the Oak Tree Invitational by a neck. Besides John Henry, McAnally's stakes winners included Super Moment, Seafood, Syncopate, and Happy Guess. They helped his stable accumulate approximately $4 million in earnings.

The Canadian-bred Deputy Minister (Vice Regent-Mint Copy, by Buntys Flight) won eight of nine starts, including seven stakes races, for co-owners D. G. ("Bud") Willmot and Mort and Marjoh Levy. The colt's sole defeat came in the Champagne, where he finished fourth while making his first start in nine weeks because of illness. In his final two races in the U.S., Deputy Minister completed his season with victories in the Laurel Futurity and Young America Stakes.

Equatorial Guinea

Epidemics:
see Health and Disease

Episcopal Church:
see Religion

Calumet Farm's Before Dawn (Raise A Cup-Moonbeam, by Tim Tam) won her first five starts before suffering her only loss when competing against males in the Champagne. She finished second to Timely Writer after starting from the unfavourable number one post position. Her stakes triumphs came in the Fashion, Spinaway, Astarita, and Matron.

Buckland Farm's Pleasant Colony (His Majesty-Sun Colony, by Sunrise Flight) was first in the Wood Memorial, Kentucky Derby, Preakness, and Woodward Stakes and accumulated earnings of $877,415. His chance for winning the Triple Crown was ended when Summing won the Belmont Stakes. Flying Zee Stables' Wayward Lass (Hail the Pirates-Young Mistress, by Third Martini) gained top honours by winning such stakes races as the Mother Goose and the Coaching Club American Oaks, the latter through disqualification of Real Prize.

Ogden Phipps's Relaxing (Buckpasser-Marking Time, by To Market) won four stakes races including two against males, the Assault and Campbell handicaps. She finished third in the Jockey Club Gold Cup, three-quarters of a length back of John Henry. Her other victories came in the Delaware and Ruffian handicaps.

Henryk de Kwiatkowski's De La Rose (Nijinsky II-Rosetta Stone, by Round Table) took seven turf stakes, including the Saranac, Long Branch, and a division of the Hollywood Derby against males. There was no standout sprinter, but Mrs. Richard Davison's Guilty Conscience (Court Ruling-Gracefully, by Gallant Man) was the most consistent. His most important victory came in the Vosburgh.

In the Triple Crown races for Canadian-foaled three-year-olds, Fiddle Dancer Boy won the Queen's Plate, Cadet Corps the Prince of Wales Stakes, and Social Wizard the Breeder's Stakes. Open Call was winner of the Rothmans International, and Regent Miss triumphed in the Canadian Oaks. (JOSEPH C. AGRELLA)

EUROPE AND AUSTRALIA. A harsh spring had a radical effect on racing throughout Europe in 1981. Few of the horses that were prepared, in unhelpful conditions, for the important races of the first part of the season held their form for the rest of the year.

Shergar was the early-season champion in the British Isles. Owned by the Aga Khan and trained by Michael Stoute at Newmarket, this son of Great Nephew won five consecutive races by a total margin of 40 lengths, including the Epsom Derby, Irish Sweeps Derby, and the King George VI and Queen Elizabeth Diamond Stakes. He beat Glint of Gold by ten lengths in the Epsom Derby, the easiest victory recorded in the 202-year history of the race. Shergar ran only once after winning the King George on July 25—in the St. Leger, when he finished a never-dangerous fourth behind Cut Above, a 28–1 chance, Glint of Gold, and Bustomi. He was retired, after syndication in early July, to the Aga Khan's Ballymany Stud in Ireland.

The Aga Khan owned two other top-class three-year-old colts in Akarad and Vayrann, both of which were trained by François Mathet in France. Akarad won the Grand Prix de Saint-Cloud. Vayrann ended a successful year by taking the Champion Stakes, beating the 1980 winner of that race, Cairn Rouge, to give French trainers their only victory in Britain in 1981. (The result of a dope test on Vayrann made it probable that Cairn Rouge would be declared the winner, but no Jockey Club inquiry had been held by year's end.)

Their British counterparts proved much more successful, triumphing in 6 of France's 23 Group One races, starting with Recitation, which added the Poule d'Essai des Poulains to his victory in the 1980 Grand Critérium. Madam Gay, which was also second to Shergar in the King George and third to John Henry in the inaugural running of the Arlington Million, beat the Italian Oaks winner, Val d'Erica, in the Prix de Diane de Revlon (French Oaks). Glint of Gold won the Grand Prix de Paris, Marwell the Prix de l'Abbaye de Long-

Pleasant Colony, with Jorge Velasquez as jockey, was the winner of the Kentucky Derby in Louisville, with a time of 2:02.

WIDE WORLD

champ, and Ardross the Prix Royal-Oak, while Moorestyle gained a repeat success in the Prix de la Fôret. Marwell (July Cup) and Ardross (Ascot Gold Cup) also took Group One races at home.

The biggest European prize of all, the Prix de l'Arc de Triomphe, which had been increased in value by two-thirds, with a winner's share of Fr 2 million, eluded the foreign challengers. Nine of the 24 runners came from either England or Ireland, but only Ardross, which was fifth, reached the first ten. Gold River, ridden by the Hong Kong-based Gary Moore, produced a 53–1 surprise, beating Bikala and April Run in a close finish.

Green Forest, a U.S.-bred colt owned by Mahmoud Fustok, was easily the most successful two-year-old in France, winning the Prix Morny, Prix de la Salamandre, and Grand Critérium. Zino, which he beat in the Salamandre, went on to gain an impressive win in the Critérium de Maisons-Laffitte.

Lester Piggott, who rode 179 winners, was champion jockey in Britain for the tenth time but for only the first time since 1971. He would probably have had to settle for second if Willie Carson, who was in the lead, had not broken his leg at York in mid-August. Yves Saint-Martin, who had been a top jockey in France for more than 20 years, gained his 13th riding championship there.

Two horses that raced with distinction throughout the year were Glint of Gold and To-Agori-Mou. Glint of Gold won five races, including the Derby Italiano, the Preis von Europa, and the Grand Prix de Paris. To-Agori-Mou, which won the English Two Thousand Guineas, was later involved in some struggles with the Irish-trained King's Lake. The two milers were almost equal, but Anglo-Irish pride received a blow when they were both beaten by five lengths by Northjet in the Prix Jacques le Marois at Deauville, France, in August.

Just a Dash, which had already won the Adelaide Cup and South Australian St. Leger, was a convincing winner of Australia's most celebrated race, the Melbourne Cup. Tommy Smith had trained the winners of more than 4,000 races, including all the important ones, but this was only his second success in the Cup. He would probably have been much happier if he could have won it with Kingston Town, but that colt finished 20th. Kingston Town, which was the favourite, had become the first horse ever to earn A$1 million, when winning the George Main Stakes at Randwick on September 26.

In National Hunt racing in Britain, Aldaniti, ridden by Bob Champion, won the Grand National by four lengths from the favourite, Spartan Missile. Only 12 of the 39 runners completed the course. Sea Pigeon won his second consecutive Champion Hurdle. He was trained by M. H. ("Peter") Easterby, who also sent out Little Owl and Night Nurse to take the first two places in the Cheltenham Gold Cup Steeplechase. J. Francome was the National Hunt champion jockey.

(ROBERT W. CARTER)

Harness Racing. In 1981 Fan Hanover became the first filly to win the Little Brown Jug, equaling the record time of 1 min 54.8 sec. She also set a new

Shergar won the Epsom Derby with a ten-length margin, the widest margin since the race was founded. The Aga Khan, the horse's owner, is at right.

world pacing mark for five-eighths-mi tracks when she won a mile at The Meadows in 1 min 55.6 sec and later was named 1981 harness horse of the year. Toy Poodle, 1980 three-year-old filly of the year, in 1981 set world pacing records on mile (1 min 54.4 sec) and five-eighths-mi tracks (1 min 54.6 sec). Two-year-old pacing records were broken on mile tracks, and colt and gelding records were broken on half-mile tracks. Filet Of Sole won the Kentucky Futurity; the gray filly Watering Can won the Horseman and Fair World pace. Tenujin won the Kentucky Pacing Derby for two-year-olds.

The $540,870 World Trotting Derby for three-year-olds at Du Quoin, Ill., was won by Panty Raid, and the $463,000 Sheppard Pace at Yonkers was taken by Icarus Lobell. In the $838,000 Hambletonian, Shiaway St. Pat was the winner, and McKinzie Almahurst took the $1,760,000 Woodrow Wilson two-year-old classic from Lou Todd Hanover and Warren Hanover. Conquered won from Computer and Seahawk Hanover in the $1 million Meadowlands three-year-old pace. French horses dominated the $250,000 Roosevelt International in New York with Idéal du Gazeau winning from Jorky.

In Australian harness racing, five-year-old stallion Popular Alm won the City Tattersalls Golden Mile at Harold Park, Sydney, on Nov. 7, 1981. On November 1 the ten-year-old stallion Pure Steel paced a 1-min 56.9-sec time trial in Perth, Western Australia. The top four-year-old by the end of 1981

Major Thoroughbred Race Winners, 1981

Race	Won by	Jockey	Owner
United States			
Acorn	Heavenly Cause	L. Pincay, Jr.	Ryehill Farm
Alabama	Prismatical	E. Maple	Happy Valley Farm
American Derby	Pocket Zipper	R. Sibille	Mr. and Mrs. Robert F. Bensinger
Arkansas Derby	Bold Ego	J. Lively	Double B Ranch and Dr. Joseph Kidd
Arlington Classic	Fairway Phantom	J. Lively	William H. Floyd
Arlington Million	John Henry	W. Shoemaker	Dotsam Stable
Arlington-Washington Futurity	Lets Dont Fight	J. Lively	Bwamazon Farm
Beldame	Love Sign	W. Shoemaker	Stephen C. Clark, Jr.
Belmont	Summing	G. Martens	Charles T. Wilson, Jr.
Blue Grass	Proud Appeal	J. Fell	Malcolm H. Winfield, Stanley M. Hough, John R. Gaines
Brooklyn	Hechizado	R. Hernandez	Charles E. Schmidt, Jr.
Champagne	Timely Writer	J. Fell	Nitram Stable
Charles H. Strub	Super Moment	F. Toro	Elmendorf Stable
Coaching Club American Oaks	Wayward Lass	C. Asmussen	Flying Zee Stable
Delaware	Relaxing	A. Cordero, Jr.	Ogden Phipps
Flamingo	Tap Shoes	R. Hernandez	Leone J. Peters and Arthur B. Hancock
Florida Derby	Lord Avie	C. McCarron	SKS Stable
Frizette	Proud Lou	D. Beckon	William D. Graham
Futurity	Irish Martini	J. Velasquez	Seymour Cohen
Gulfstream Park	Hurry Up Blue	C. Lopez	Due Process Stable
Hollywood Derby (2 divisions)	De La Rose	E. Maple	Henryk de Kwiatkowski
	Silveyville	D. Winick	Kjell Qvale
Hollywood Gold Cup	Eleven Stitches	S. Hawley	Claudia H. and Morey Mirkin
Hollywood Invitational	John Henry	L. Pincay, Jr.	Dotsam Stable
Hopeful	Timely Writer	R. Danjean	Nitram Stable
Jockey Club Gold Cup	John Henry	W. Shoemaker	Dotsam Stable
Kentucky Derby	Pleasant Colony	J. Velasquez	Buckland Farm
Kentucky Oaks	Heavenly Cause	L. Pincay, Jr.	Ryehill Farm
Ladies	Jameela	A. Cordero, Jr.	Peter Brant
Laurel Futurity	Deputy Minister	D. MacBeth	Centurion Farm and Kinghaven Farms
Man o' War	Galaxy Libra	W. Shoemaker	Louis R. Rowan, Lessee
Marlboro Cup Invitational	Noble Nashua	R. Hernandez	Flying Zee Stable
Matron	Before Dawn	J. Velasquez	Calumet Farm
Metropolitan	Fappiano	A. Cordero, Jr.	John A. Nerud
Monmouth	Amber Pass	C. Asmussen	Entremont
Oak Tree Invitational	John Henry	W. Shoemaker	Dotsam Stable
Preakness	Pleasant Colony	J. Velasquez	Buckland Farm
Ruffian	Relaxing	A. Cordero, Jr.	Ogden Phipps
San Juan Capistrano Invitational	Obraztsovy	P. Valenzuela	W. T. Pascoe III and Brian Sweeney
Santa Anita Derby	Splendid Spruce	D. McHargue	Surf and Turf Stable
Santa Anita	John Henry	L. Pincay, Jr.	Dotsam Stable
Santa Susana	Nell's Briquette	W. Shoemaker	Triple L Stable
Sapling	Out of Hock	D. Brumfield	Charles J. Cella
Selima	Snow Plow	J. L. Kaenel	Joanne Blusiewicz
Sorority	Apalachee Honey	M. Morgan	Muckler Stable
Spinaway	Before Dawn	G. McCarron	Calumet Farm
Spinster	Glorious Song	R. Platts	Frank Stronach and Nelson Bunker Hunt
Suburban	Temperence Hill	D. MacBeth	Loblolly Stable
Swaps	Noble Nashua	L. Pincay, Jr.	Flying Zee Stable
Travers	Willow Hour	E. Maple	Mrs. Marcia W. Schott
Turf Classic	April Run	P. Paquet	Mrs. Bert Firestone
United Nations	Key to Content	G. Martens	Rokeby Stable
Vanity	Track Robbery	P. Valenzuela	Summa Stable
Washington (D.C.) International	Providential II	A. Lequeux	Serge Fradkoff
Whitney	Fio Rito	L. Hulet	Raymond J. LeCesse
Widener	Land of Eire	E. Fires	Mrs. Joseph S. Nash
Wood Memorial	Pleasant Colony	J. Fell	Buckland Farm
Woodward	Pleasant Colony	A. Cordero, Jr.	Buckland Farm
England			
One Thousand Guineas	Fairy Footsteps	L. Piggott	H. H. Joel
Two Thousand Guineas	To-Agori-Mou	G. Starkey	Mrs. A. Muinos
Derby	Shergar	W. R. Swinburn	Aga Khan
Oaks	Blue Wind	L. Piggott	Mrs. B. Firestone
St. Leger	Cut Above	J. Mercer	Sir J. Astor
Coronation Cup	Master Willie	P. Waldron	R. Barnett
Ascot Gold Cup	Ardross	L. Piggott	C. St. George
Eclipse Stakes	Master Willie	P. Waldron	R. Barnett
King George VI and Queen Elizabeth Diamond Stakes	Shergar	W. R. Swinburn	Aga Khan
Sussex Stakes	King's Lake	P. Eddery	J.-P. Binet
Benson & Hedges Gold Cup	Beldale Flutter	P. Eddery	A. Kelly
Champion Stakes	Vayrann	Y. Saint-Martin	Aga Khan
France			
Poule d'Essai des Poulains	Recitation	G. Starkey	A. Bodie
Poule d'Essai des Pouliches	Ukraine Girl	P. Eddery	Mrs. J. Mullion
Prix du Jockey Club	Bikala	S. Gorli	J. Ouaki
Prix de Diane de Revlon	Madam Gay	L. Piggott	G. Kaye
Prix Royal-Oak	Ardross	L. Piggott	C. St. George
Prix Ganay	Argument	A. Lequeux	B. McNall
Prix Lupin	No Lute	P. Eddery	R. Sangster
Grand Prix de Paris	Glint of Gold	J. Matthias	P. Mellon
Grand Prix de Saint-Cloud	Akarad	Y. Saint-Martin	Aga Khan
Prix Vermeille	April Run	P. Paquet	Mrs. B. Firestone
Prix de l'Arc de Triomphe	Gold River	G. W. Moore	J. Wertheimer
Ireland			
Irish Two Thousand Guineas	King's Lake	P. Eddery	J.-P. Binet
Irish One Thousand Guineas	Arctique Royale	G. Curran	J.-P. Binet
Irish Guinness Oaks	Blue Wind	W. Swinburn	Mrs. B. Firestone
Irish Sweeps Derby	Shergar	L. Piggott	Aga Khan
Irish St. Leger	Protection Racket	B. Taylor	S. Fradkoff
Italy			
Derby Italiano	Glint of Gold	J. Matthias	P. Mellon
Gran Premio del Jockey Club	Königsstuhl	P. Alafi	Gestüt Zoppenbroich
West Germany			
Deutsches Derby	Orofino	P. Alafi	Gestüt Zoppenbroich
Grosser Preis von Baden	Pelerin	G. Starkey	Sir P. Oppenheimer
Grosser Preis von Berlin	Lydian	F. Head	Ecurie Aland
Preis von Europa	Glint of Gold	J. Matthias	P. Mellon

was Gundary Flyer, and Indemnity was the leading three-year-old. The Inter-Dominion Pacing championships final at Hobart was won by West Australian four-year-old San Simeon, from Single Again and Ardstraw. The first Galaxy Grand Slams of $40,000 each for two-year-olds were won by Karamea Bella Bella in the fillies' event and Good to Win in the colts'. The Sires Stakes final in New South Wales for $20,000 for colts and fillies, respectively, were won by two-year-olds Happy Toliver and Teramby Princess and three-year-olds Bundanoon and Karmea Melody.

The 1981 New Zealand Cup was taken by Armalight. The great mare Delightful Lady had earlier won all her efforts only to lose form two weeks before the cup. The $35,000 Rowe Memorial Cup for trotters went to No Response, a previous Inter-Dominion winner. Melton Monarch took the $40,000 Great Northern Derby and Amaze the New Zealand Derby.

In European trotting Idéal du Gazeau won the 1981 Prix d'Amérique at Vincennes, Paris. Eléazar won the Prix de France, and Hillion Brillouard the Gran Premio Nazionali at Milan, the Copenhagen Cup, and the Stockholm Solvalla Elitlopp. Express Gaze won both the Oslo Grand Prix and the Preis von Bayern at Munich. In Norway Lin's Royal won the Farris Trophy. Sweden's Pamir Brodde won Norway's Jarlsberg International (beating Lin's Royal). She later finished third in the Roosevelt International. The Swedish championship in Göteborg was won by Darstes F, and the Austrian Trotting Derby was won by Swedish-bred MacDonald. In an international event at The Hague, Jorky beat Finland's Keystone Patriot. A new Finnish record was set by Keystone Patriot at St. Mikkeli, Fin., when he won International Trot over 1,600 m in 1 min 57.2 sec. Billy The Kid of Finland also recorded a fast 1-min 58.2-sec win over 1,600 m. Duvil took the Danish Derby from Dwight Vixi and Frosty Lep. (NOEL SIMPSON)

Show Jumping. Great Britain won the European three-day event championship at Horsens, Den., in September 1981. It was represented by Richard Meade on Kilcashel, Virginia Holgate on Priceless, Elizabeth Purbrick on Peter the Great, and Sue Benson on Gemma Jay. All were successful in the vital speed and endurance phase, scoring a total of 327.15 penalty points. Switzerland (350.4) finished second, Poland (366.50) third, and West Germany (399.45) fourth. The individual championship went to Hans Schmutz (Switz.) on the Dutch-bred Oran, the silver medal to Helmut Rethemeier (West Germany) on Santiago, and the bronze to Brian McSweeney (Ireland) on Inis Meain.

A week later in Munich, honours in the European show jumping championship all went to the host nation; West Germany, represented by Paul Schockemöhle on Deister, Norbert Koof on Fire, Peter Luther on Livius, and Gerd Wiltfang on Roman, won the team gold medal with 11.86 points. Switzerland (21.86) finished second, The Netherlands (26.35) third, and Britain (28.63) fourth. Schockemöhle and Deister, who did not make a mistake throughout the competition, won the individual gold medal with a zero score; Malcolm

Pyrah (Great Britain) was second on Towerlands Anglezarke; and Bruno Candrian (Switz.) was third on Van Gogh.

(PAMELA MACGREGOR-MORRIS)

Polo. England's one-day international spectacular at the Guards Polo Club, Windsor Great Park, drew a crowd of 23,000, the highest attendance for a European polo event since the 1936 Olympic Games. In the main contest South America beat England 7–6. In the supporting match, for the Silver Jubilee Cup, the England II team beat Spain 10–5.

New Zealand won all three test matches against South Africa. Owing to bad weather, the Camacho Cup, between Mexico and the U.S., was not concluded; Mexico won the first game 11–6 and the U.S. the second 9–8. In the World Cup final at Palm Beach, Fla., Boehm-Palm Beach beat the Rolex A&K team 14–8. In the U.S. Open, Boca Raton defeated Rolex A&K 12–11.

In the European polo championship, at the Guards Polo Club, the gold medal went to Hurlingham II and the silver to the European Polo Academy II 6–5. In the British Open, Alex Ebeid's Falcons from Egypt defeated Ronaldo de Lima's La Ipanema team from Brazil 13–3. In the Queens Cup, Cowdray Park beat Stowell Park 7–5. At Sotogrande, Spain, Cadarejo beat Brattas 7–6 for the Gold Cup. In the Australian Open, Kooralbyn defeated Shoalhaven in a tight final 9–8. In the Australian Masters, Shoalhaven easily triumphed over Gil Gil 11–3.   (COLIN J. CROSS)

[452.B.4.h.xvii; 452.B.4.h.xxi; 452.B.5.e]

Ethiopia

A socialist state in northeastern Africa, Ethiopia is bordered by Somalia, Djibouti, Kenya, the Sudan, and the Red Sea. Area: 1,223,600 sq km (472,400 sq mi). Pop. (1980 est.): 31,065,300. Cap. and largest city: Addis Ababa (pop., 1980 est., 1,277,200). Language: Amharic (official) and other tongues. Religion: Ethiopian Orthodox and Muslim, with various minorities. Head of state and chairman of the Provisional Military Administrative Council in 1981, Lieut. Col. Mengistu Haile Mariam.

During 1981 internal political developments in Ethiopia included the promulgation of new regulations concerning the powers and duties of Urban Dwellers Associations (the Kebeles). Elections to Kebele committees were held under new regulations, which involved the Commission to Organize the Party of the Working People of Ethiopia (COPWE) in the selection of candidates. Subsequently the Kebele representatives elected the chief municipal officials from lists of screened candidates judged on the basis of their identification with the Ethiopian revolution.

In February the second plenary meeting of the COPWE Central Committee passed a series of resolutions covering COPWE's responsibilities for providing political guidance pending the formation of the Party of the Working People of Ethiopia. The resolutions covered the need to exert greater efforts to attain "proletarian supremacy" in national affairs, the continuing task of consolidating mass

organizations to provide a foundation for the future party, directives for the general strategy for national development, improvements in government administration, the strengthening of national defense, the promotion of Socialist discipline and control, and directives for the development of education and the social services.

In September more than 500 prisoners were granted amnesty. These included one of ministerial rank, Hapte Selassie Taffessa, detained since 1974, who was returned to his previous post in charge of tourism. On the eve of the anniversary of the deposing of the old monarchy in September 1974, the Provisional Military Administrative Council issued a proclamation setting up control committees and a Special Court of the Working People charged with "stamping out corruption and wastefulness."

The major emphasis of the year, however, was on education. In June the director general of UNESco launched, from Addis Ababa, an international appeal for assistance to the National Literacy Campaign. The aim of the appeal was to raise $90 million over a period of six years to 1987, the target date for the eradication of illiteracy from the country. The national campaign had been launched in June 1979 and by April 1981 had reduced the illiteracy rate to 65%. Parallel to these developments was a great increase in regular education for school-age children. It was estimated that almost 50% of the relevant age group would enroll for primary school during the school year 1981–82. At

Ethiopia

ETHIOPIA

Education. (1978–79) Primary, pupils 1,376,927; secondary and vocational, pupils 326,808; primary, secondary, and vocational, teachers 40,419; teacher training (1973–74), students 3,126, teachers 194; higher, students 13,674, teaching staff (1977–78) 476.

Finance. Monetary unit: birr, with (Sept. 21, 1981) a par value of 2.07 birr to U.S. $1 (free rate of 3.84 birr = £1 sterling). Gold and other reserves (June 1981) U.S. $132 million. Budget (total; 1979–80 est.): revenue 1,971,800,-000 birr; expenditure 2,365,000,000 birr. Gross national product (1979–80) 8,426,000,000 birr. Money supply (June 1981) 1,675,400,000 birr. Cost of living (Addis Ababa; 1975 = 100; June 1981) 222.7.

Foreign Trade. (1980) Imports 1,494,700,000 birr; exports 879.3 million birr. Import sources (1979): Kuwait 15%; U.S. 12%; Japan 10%; West Germany 10%; Italy 10%; U.K. 7%. Export destinations (1979): U.S. 29%; Italy 11%; Saudi Arabia 9%; U.S.S.R. 7%; West Germany 6%; Japan 6%; Djibouti 6%. Main exports: coffee 64%; hides and skins 12%.

Transport and Communications. Roads (1980) 35,937 km. Motor vehicles in use (1980): passenger 38,600; commercial 11,700. Railways: (1979) 988 km; traffic (including Djibouti traffic of Djibouti-Addis Ababa line; excluding Eritrea; 1978–79) 171 million passenger-km, freight 148 million net ton-km. Air traffic (1980): 647 million passenger-km; freight 26.2 million net ton-km. Telephones (Jan. 1980) 83,800. Radio receivers (Dec. 1977) 215,000. Television receivers (Dec. 1978) c. 30,000.

Agriculture. Production (in 000; metric tons; 1980): barley c. 772; wheat c. 469; corn c. 1,144; millet c. 193; sorghum c. 689; potatoes (1979) c. 235; sugar, raw value (1979) c. 168; sesame seed c. 45; chick-peas c. 79; dry peas c. 129; dry broad beans (1979) 236; bananas (1979) c. 74; coffee (1979) c. 193; cotton c. 20. Livestock (in 000; 1980): cattle c. 26,000; sheep c. 23,250; goats c. 17,180; horses c. 1,540; mules (1979) c. 1,446; asses (1979) c. 3,885; camels (1979) c. 966; poultry c. 53,000.

Industry. Production (in 000; metric tons; 1977–78): cement 103; petroleum products c. 640; cotton yarn 7.9; cotton fabrics (sq m) 65,500; electricity (kw-hr) c. 690,000.

Starving women and children wait for food at a refugee camp at Bume.

the time of the 1974 revolution, 93% of the population was illiterate and 18% of primary school-age children attended school.

This progress was made within the program for economic and cultural development. The primary economic objective of the program was to raise the level of productivity in the small modern commercial sector and, most importantly, in agriculture. The latter was to be accomplished by providing services to peasants and by enlarging state farms.

The Central Planning Supreme Council was engaged in the elaboration of a ten-year Perspective Development Plan in which the growth of food production and agriculture was given top priority. To achieve a surplus for capital formation, heavy reliance was placed on the formation of peasant service cooperatives and the creation of Multi-Purpose Peasant Training Centres to disseminate improved technologies. The first of these centres, at Agarfa in the Bale administrative region, was nearing completion.

Ethiopia possessed the highest potential on the continent for hydroelectric and thermal power; although efforts to develop these resources were under way, the country remained heavily dependent upon imported oil. In 1981 the fuel bill was expected to claim almost 70% of export earnings.

An important achievement during the year was the construction of the first bridge across the Baro River at Gambela. It linked routes from the south passing through Jima and Gore with the road being constructed along the north bank of the Baro toward Malakal, Sudan.

A bumper coffee crop for the year was announced. Development of the pastoral areas of the northeast rangelands (Welo region) and the southern rangelands (Sidamo region) continued with financing from international organizations, and the afforestation campaign—launched three years earlier to augment timber supplies and arrest the rapidly spreading erosion on the steep slopes of the highlands—produced significant results.

Ethiopia's diplomatic activities during 1981 ap-

peared to emphasize nonalignment, although there was no doubt about the policy imperative for transition to socialism and continued reliance on Soviet assistance in the military sphere. The head of state, Lieut. Col. Mengistu Haile Mariam, visited Kenya in December 1980 and held several consultations with Sudan and Djibouti. In April 1981 a tripartite consultative meeting of ministers of foreign affairs from Ethiopia, Sudan, and Kenya took place. Djibouti indicated its willingness to join these meetings and, in an attempt to mediate between Ethiopia and Somalia, expressed its wish that Somalia also take part in the future. Later in the year Ethiopia, Libya, and Yemen (Aden) issued a joint declaration pledging mutual assistance and condemning U.S. activity in the Indian Ocean and the Mediterranean.

Ethiopia continued to receive considerable assistance from the West and from international organizations, most significantly from the World Bank, the United Nations Development Program, and the European Economic Community. Sweden, Italy, France, and West Germany stated their willingness to increase aid programs to Ethiopia. In August an agreement was signed on the "accelerated implementation of earlier accords between Ethiopia and the U.S.S.R." Diplomatic contacts with other African countries included the visits of Pres. Siaka Stevens of Sierra Leone and Master Sgt. Samuel Doe, head of state of Liberia. In April Pres. Cvijetin Mijatovic of Yugoslavia visited Ethiopia, and Pres. Gustav Husak of Czechoslovakia participated in the anniversary celebrations in Addis Ababa in September.

European Unity

The European Communities (EC; the European Economic Community [EEC], the European Coal and Steel Community [ECSC], and Euratom) began 1981 with a new member: on January 1 Greece became the tenth nation to join the organization.

The EC also found itself with a newly appointed Commission, the executive body responsible for its day-to-day operation. The new president of the Commission, Gaston Thorn, a former prime minister of Luxembourg, took over from Britain's Roy Jenkins (*see* BIOGRAPHIES), and he quickly acknowledged that the problems facing the EC and the Commission remained dauntingly similar to those encountered under his predecessor.

Before the Commission could begin to confront such problems as the European economic crisis and the promised reform of the EEC budgetary system and its spending policies, Thorn had to achieve a general agreement on the distribution of portfolios among his colleagues. This was finally agreed upon after a protracted and, at times, stormy meeting early in January which involved the intervention of British Prime Minister Margaret Thatcher.

Within a few days Thorn was faced with a new difficulty when Finn Olav Gundelach (*see* OBITUARIES), the experienced Danish commissioner for agriculture and fisheries, died suddenly while attending the European Parliament in Strasbourg, France. After internal consultations, this key post was given to Poul Dalsager, who was at the time Danish minister of agriculture and fisheries.

Economic Affairs. Almost immediately the Commission began to prepare proposals for budgetary and agricultural reform. The aims of the reform were to prevent the prospective exhaustion of the EC's limited budget revenues, to achieve a more satisfactory balance between agricultural and nonagricultural expenditures, and to ensure that in the future no one country would be obliged to pay unacceptably large net contributions to the EC budget. The Commission unveiled its initial reform proposals in June.

The original impetus for reform had been provided by British objections to the scale of its budget payments, which arose largely as a result of the operations of the common agricultural policy (CAP). The CAP traditionally benefited the less efficient agricultural producers by maintaining high prices for their exports, thereby penalizing food-importing countries. However, during the spring and summer it became clear that West Germany, which took over from the U.K. as the major net contributor to the EC following a temporary rearrangement of the budget contributions, also wanted a ceiling on its future payments. The Commission's attempts to reduce the excessive costs of agriculture in the EC budget were made no easier by an agreement among the farm ministers of the member nations. This agreement, reached in March, awarded EC farmers an average 9% price increase and did little to penalize the costly overproduction of foodstuffs; the surplus had to be stockpiled or exported with large subsidies.

However, the pressure imposed by agricultural spending on the Community's financial resources eased a little during 1981. This was mainly because of agricultural problems in the U.S.S.R. and elsewhere, which resulted in increased world demand for food and thus raised prices for certain products. Higher world prices, in turn, meant that the EC was able to dispose of its food surpluses at a lower cost in terms of export subsidy. On two occasions the Commission was able to reimburse funds totaling some £750 million from the CAP. Some of this money was used to finance the EC's social and regional policies, while some was returned to the member governments.

In the months prior to June, when the Commission outlined its reform proposals, it became increasingly clear that negotiations with the governments of Portugal and Spain about their applications for membership in the EC would be affected by the internal debate on reform. This led to some irritation in Spain, where the authorities imputed a certain lack of good faith to the EC for delaying the central negotiations affecting Spain's membership. But the new Socialist government of France insisted that until the Ten reached an agreement about the future of their internal policies, it would be impossible to assess the consequences of enlarging the Community.

When Thorn launched the Commission's proposals, he made it clear that detailed propositions on the CAP or on budgetary contributions had to be seen in a much wider economic and political context. He referred to the need for the European Community to recover momentum in the progression toward greater unity, and in particular to develop a wider range of alternative policies designed to tackle the major economic and social problems facing the continent. As a result, the Commission proposed a series of measures to deter the overproduction of food and also suggested an expansion of the Community's action in the fields of social and regional development, industry, and energy. The initial reaction of the member states was muted; defenders of the CAP objected to what they saw as a threat to the one completely "common" EC policy in operation. The British were satisfied that the Commission recognized the need to limit the U.K.'s budget payments, but there was dissatisfaction in Bonn that West Germany had been given no such assurances and concern among the smaller members that in the future they might lose part of the net receipts drawn from the EC budget at present.

The Commission of the European Communities met in January in Brussels to welcome Greece as its newest member. At right is Georgios Kontogeorgis, the Greek representative, with Italian representative Lorenzo Natali.

The start of the European Council meeting, held in Maastricht, Neth., in March, was marred by demonstrations by West German fishermen and Belgian and Dutch farmers who were protesting Common Market policies.

In March the European Council (made up of the EC heads of government) met in Maastricht, Neth. The meeting was largely preoccupied with the growing economic recession and the relentless rise in unemployment. But while EC governments recognized the social and political dangers in continued high levels of unemployment, particularly among the young, successive meetings of EC ministers during the year produced no clear consensus about what new policies should be introduced. The European Council meeting in London in November again failed to produce agreement on budgetary and agricultural matters, and the controversy was referred back to a further special meeting of foreign ministers.

During April it became clear that the special arrangements administered by the Common Market for dealing with the crisis in the EC steel industry were not sufficient to their purpose. Following protracted negotiations between the Commission, the major steel companies, and the national governments, a new system of partly mandatory and partly voluntary production limits on steel output was agreed upon in June.

The summer months were overshadowed by friction between the Community and Japan concerning Japan's growing trade surplus with the EC and the difficulties reported by European exporters in penetrating the Japanese domestic market. Some of these tensions abated following a visit to EC capitals by Japanese Prime Minister Zenko Suzuki and promises by the Japanese government that it would ensure voluntary restraint by Japanese exporters in key European markets.

During the year there was occasional disagreement over financial policies between the EC and the new administration of Pres. Ronald Reagan in the U.S. Some of the EC governments took particular exception to President Reagan's emphasis on high interest rates as the centrepiece of his administration's monetary strategy to reduce inflation in the U.S. As the year passed, there were growing fears in Europe that high U.S. interest rates would oblige EC governments to follow suit and prolong the recession.

Political Relations. In the area of politics, EC affairs were overshadowed by a series of general elections in the member nations. New governments took office in The Netherlands, Ireland, Belgium, Greece, and Italy; outweighing them all, however, was the election of a Socialist government in France. Although the new government in Paris did not effect any major shift in the content of French policies toward the EC, it did introduce a new and more pro-European tone to French declarations.

A revival of interest in foreign policy cooperation took place during the year. The Council of Ministers agreed in principle during September that arrangements for political cooperation and, in particular, concerted reaction in times of crisis would be improved and strengthened. The West German government wanted to go further and discuss aspects of security and defense, possibly as part of a new treaty aimed at ultimate European union. In the closing months of the year there was much consideration of the project, but some clear reservations were expressed by certain member countries. For example, as a neutral country, Ireland was anxious that defense should not become a matter of EC policy.

On July 1 Britain assumed the presidency of the Council of Ministers from The Netherlands for the second half of the year. U.K. Foreign Secretary Lord Carrington made it clear that foreign policy issues would be given a major priority during the U.K. presidency. In July Lord Carrington tried to interest the Soviet government in EC political proposals for a solution of the conflict in Afghanistan. The proposals, involving a withdrawal of Soviet forces, called for a two-stage conference on the political future of Afghanistan, from which the Afghan government would initially be excluded. The Soviet government insisted that the proposals were "unacceptable."

During the British presidency active discussions continued both within the EC and outside it in an effort to pursue the Community's earlier declaration on the Middle East problem. In June 1980 EC leaders in Venice had stated their broad ideas for

negotiating Palestinian self-determination while guaranteeing Israel's right to exist in secure borders. But the Community felt unable to pursue its initiative pending the outcome of the presidential election in the U.S. and the general election in Israel. The initial response from Israel—and to a lesser extent from the U.S.—was discouraging for the Europeans. The EC governments insisted that they were not trying to undermine the U.S.-sponsored Camp David process, involving Egypt and Israel, but were trying to broaden the base of the peace-making discussions within the region. However, the EC came under increasing pressure from the Arab world, particularly the traditionally pro-Western governments of Jordan and Saudi Arabia, to pursue its Middle East initiative more actively.

One motive for the desire to step up foreign policy coordination appeared to be the wish to exercise a greater collective influence over U.S. policy. During the year there was a marked increase in popular opposition in Europe to the planned deployment of some 600 cruise and Pershing medium-range nuclear missiles. West German Chancellor Helmut Schmidt reflected the unease of a number of EC governments when he responded to the U.S. announcement in August that it would go ahead with the production of enhanced radiation ("neutron") nuclear weapons. The lack of consultation by the U.S. with its European allies was cited by Community foreign ministers in the autumn as a further reason to improve EC foreign policy coordination.

In the closing months of the year the focus of attention again switched to the prospects for agreement on internal policy and financial reform. The pace of negotiations with Portugal and Spain were stepped up to achieve an accession date of 1983 or 1984. However, the outcome of the Greek general election in October, in which a Socialist government came to power, placed a question mark over the future of that most recent member nation within the Community. At the same time, it was accepted that the forthcoming referendum in Greenland (a self-governing part of the Danish realm) on its continued accession to the EC would almost certainly lead to a decision to withdraw.

On the other hand, closer relations developed in 1981 between the EC and another grouping of Western European countries, the European Free Trade Association (EFTA). Some EFTA governments, notably Norway, made known their desire to be consulted more fully on important international political questions discussed by EC foreign ministers. However, the year did not produce any noticeable progress in relations between the EEC and the Soviet-led Council for Mutual Economic Assistance (Comecon).   (JOHN PALMER)

See also Defense; Economy, World.
[534.F.3.b.iv; 971.D.7]

Fashion and Dress

Rather dull at the start and relying mainly on the pantsuit, women's fashion, in the course of 1981, gradually took on a fancy dress aspect. In time it developed a strong case of gold fever, ending the

year in a sunset burst of glitter and razzle-dazzle.

As the year began, the only lift to the winter street look was provided by a few down-stitched garments in bright colours carried over from the winter before. The fur-lined and belted raincoat in a neutral shade of rainproof poplin remained a classic standby, while the traditional olive-green loden coat became a "must" for both men and women. A stitched pleat circled the armhole of the set-in sleeve, and a high box pleat reaching to the shoulder blades, pressed or unpressed according to the wearer, gave ease to the fit. Low-heeled shoes and opaque tights in dark hues were far more popular than boots with this outfit. In an effort to feminize the pantsuit in classic men's suitings, spike-heeled pumps and ruffled blouses became part of the uniform. The pants themselves gained volume at the sides, puffing the hips and slimming the legs in jodhpur fashion.

Once coats were cast off in the spring, pleated skirts of the kilt type gave way to divided skirts or culottes. Hems were definitely up, skimming the knees and clearing the way for bermudas. The latter appeared most frequently in khaki or pure white—both important colours all through the spring and summer. Utility jeans were still around, stone-washed for faster wear and tear and as skintight as ever. Some jeans were dressed up with turquoise cabochons and gold nailheads and worn with frilly blouses instead of shirts.

On the London scene the terrifying look elaborated by the Punks—of fierce individuals with bloodstained T-shirts, porcupine-like hair dyed all colours, and safety pins piercing the cheeks—was completely eradicated. The Chelsea world toppled over and went romantic as pirates took to the gangplank with baroque grace, dressed in velvet with satin sashes and lacy frills and wearing curled and powdered wigs. Still in the tough line of fashion were short, sexy skirts in leather and the "Western Look" with its fringes and high, cuffed boots. In the U.S. it became the "Life on the Ranch" look, country and rugged, exemplified by Pres. and Mrs. Ronald Reagan during their visits to the "western White House" in California.

If the Reagans at leisure epitomized the western country look, the incoming U.S. administration brought to Washington a well-publicized renewal of formality and an emphasis on dressing for the occasion. Nancy Reagan's preferences—for classic styles and bright colours—were noted more carefully than those of any first lady since Jacqueline Kennedy. In Britain it was the new princess of Wales whose clothes claimed attention, and the British were quick to pick up the romantic trend evident in her ruffled taffeta and tulle wedding dress.

French and Italian designers also went ruffle-and-flounce-crazy. Ruffles trimmed everything in sight from necklines to hemlines, shoulder yokes, and cuffs. Ruffled or fluted blouses were a "must" with pants, supplanting the classic mannish shirt. The knee-length skirts of rock'n' roll dresses were formed entirely of ruffles, most frequently in glossy silk taffeta or in black chiffon, transparent tulle, or lace.

The skirt of the summer was the petticoat skirt,

DON HOGAN CHARLES—THE NEW YORK TIMES   UPI

Donna Karan and Louis dell'Olio designed this pleated metallic gold dress for evening (left) for Anne Klein. It was a standout in a year that saw a huge boom in metallic fabrics, leathers, and accessories. Perry Ellis was riding the crest of popularity with loose-fitting, easy designs like this soft pleated skirt with signature handknit sweater.

very full and softly flaring like butterfly wings, made in a sheer fabric like crinkled cotton crepon or cotton poplin. Sometimes knee-length, sometimes descending to just above the ankle, it was cut in three gathered tiers, easy to make and easy to wear. Another summer trend, the underwear look, was apparent in bodices of white gauze or transparent lace, gathered all around the waistline or wrapped. Also displaying an underwear influence was the top cut straight across the chest like an underbodice, trimmed with a wide band of embroidery and with shoulder straps, usually in all-white cotton but not, in this case, transparent.

The summer all-white look was accented with gold accessories on every occasion when a bit of glitter could add a more sophisticated touch: shoes, from open spike-heeled sandals to ballerinas and flat tennis shoes with gold piping and gold lacing; T-shirts, duffle coats, waistcoats, and blazers in gold kid; knitwear with a glint of gold added to the cotton or wool thread; two-piece beach suits made of three triangles of gold Lurex. A huge range of costume jewelry—earrings and necklaces, bracelets, belts, little purses, makeup pouches, even metal suitcases—reflected a golden light.

In the early fall, trousers, jeans, bermudas, and divided skirts were all swept aside in favour of knickers. Gathered below the knee or in the form of loose breeches, knickers had the same overwhelming appeal in all the major fashion centres, particularly among the junior crowd. The daytime version was in small-checked tweed or gray flannel, in leather (with a preference for khaki still

strong), or in fine-ribbed corduroy. For evening and discotheque wear, a more fancy-dress style prevailed, as Little Lord Fauntleroys, page boys, and toreros appeared in tight-fitting suits ready to split at the seams.

Dresses that appeared in the daytime were more like maxi-pullovers, ending well above the knee, in various multiple jacquard designs. Colours were exotic and designs mostly geometric, echoing the traditional Scandinavian, Peruvian, and Scottish patterns. The gold touch was here, too, in more elaborately designed fabrics—often made in China —that combined gold or silver Lurex threads with wool.

The newest separate skirts were the mini, best reserved for juniors and college girls, and the slim, knee-level style that demanded—but did not always get—a lean body and good legs. Rough textures made unheard of matches with gold. Lamé shirts were worn with heavy knit jackets; knee-level skirts in gold kid accompanied tweed jackets; heavy canvas lumberman's jackets got a lift from gold leather trousers and were even seen over knee-length pleated skirts of flimsy gold silk.

The gold fever spread to cosmetics and hair fashions. Lips and cheeks were dusted with gold and khaki, golden sand, gold-tinted copper, gold-dusted orange. "Golden Khaki" was one of the favourite eye shadows in the "Sahara" line presented by Helena Rubinstein. The desert country of the American West inspired an Estée Lauder line with a base called "Colour Wash" and "Bronze Glow" as the best-seller. Cheeks were tinted with irridescent pink and eyelids shaded with bronze to match lips golden-bronzed with "Autumn Bittersweets" from Elizabeth Arden.

Golden-wrapped pigtails and gold-lacquered ornaments kept side hair strands in place, while the remainder was controlled by gold tinsel headbands and hairnets. The new direction in hairstyles was achieved through a natural approach with only very light permanent waving. Most important was the cut. The extremes were the short, curly, boyish cut and the long, spread-over-shoulders, crinkled mass that looked straight out of the jungle and yet, paradoxically, brought to mind something of the false innocence portrayed by the Pre-Raphaelites. But the number-one hairstyle was the medium-length cut with side-brushed fringe, part of the modern romantic charm of the bride of the prince of Wales.

(THELMA SWEETINBURGH)

Men's Fashions. The business suit became even more classic and conservative in style in 1981, its sobriety relieved only by the neatest of stripes. At the same time, country suits were much more "sporty," appearing in colourful and bold checks, sometimes with equally colourful overchecks. These trends were noticeable in North America, most of Europe, and Australia.

Interchangeable separates, while not new, were given a new lease on life on an international scale through promotions by the International Wool Secretariat. The depressed economy and changes in social attitudes accounted for the trend, which involved jackets and trousers, knitwear, blouson tops, belts, ties, and socks in separate colours and

Separates, long a mainstay of womenswear, became increasingly popular for men in 1981. The look was especially suited to the "preppie" fashions in collegiate wear, such as corduroy trousers and cable-pattern sweaters.

patterns that could be alternated for separate occasions. The menswear trade called it the "put together" look; men themselves looked upon it as providing a "do-it-yourself" fashion kit. U.S. fashions—especially jeans and leisure jackets but not headwear—made a bigger impact in Europe. There was also a greater interchange of fashion among European countries, especially those in the European Economic Community.

A strong nautical influence was apparent in both colours and styling; for example, in horizontally striped sports shirts and knitwear and in navy blue and striped blazers. The rolled-up look for sports shirts and sports trousers made its untidy appearance for outdoor wear among the younger age groups. The "grandfather" or collarless shirt with just a white collar band at the neck was another fashion favoured by younger men. The "flowerpot" shape tweed hat helped to keep the hatters in the fashion picture.

Fashion revivals in Britain included the Norfolk jacket and knickerbockers, recalling the outfits favoured by George Bernard Shaw. Prince Charles and his fashion-conscious princess both wore knickerbockers on the royal estates. One of the most exclusive tailors in London, Huntsman of Savile Row, established in 1805, launched its first collection of ready-to-wear suits and coats. They were made by Chester Barrie, internationally known makers of high-quality ready-to-wear clothes for men.   (STANLEY H. COSTIN)

See also Industrial Review: *Furs.*
[451.B.2.b and d. 1; 629.C.1]

Field Hockey and Lacrosse

Field Hockey. At Karachi in January 1981 The Netherlands won the Champions Trophy from Pakistan, titleholders for two years. The final standings were: The Netherlands, Australia, West Germany, Pakistan, Spain, England.

This was the beginning of a number of exchange visits. Australia, Pakistan, West Germany, and The Netherlands took part in quadrangular tournaments at Frankfurt, West Germany, and Amsterdam. Australia emerged unbeaten at Amsterdam and finished third at Frankfurt, where West Germany finished first. Earlier, Poland had visited London and played two matches against England, the first won by England and the second tied. Pakistan and Scotland visited Poland. At Poznan, Scotland lost to Pakistan and Poland, and the Pakistan-Poland game ended in a tie. India's tour of Europe brought the Olympic champions convincing victories. But after winning its first match against The Netherlands, India lost the second.

In August England toured in Australia, winning the international series by two matches to one with two tied. On a short tour of Europe, Malaysia beat Spain but lost to The Netherlands. In October the Hockey Association's annual tournament was played on an artificial surface at Queen's Park Rangers football ground in London. There, England beat West Germany and lost to The Netherlands, while Scotland was beaten badly by both the Germans and the Dutch. Earlier, The Netherlands played West Germany and won easily in Amsterdam. At Warrington, England lost to Spain but avenged the defeat the next day at Preston. Indoors, Scotland won the home countries' championship at Cardiff, Wales, in January, beating England in the final, but England reversed the result in the four nations' tournament at Crystal Palace in London two months later.

In women's hockey England gained the triple crown among the home countries. The big annual match at Wembley was won against Wales and, having also beaten Scotland, England completed its triumph by defeating Ireland at Manchester. In August and September eight nations took part in a tournament organized by the U.S. at Columbus, Ohio, Springfield, Mass., and Philadelphia. Australia beat Great Britain in the final, while the U.S. took third place with a victory over West Germany. Earlier, in the World Cup tournament at Buenos Aires, Arg., West Germany beat The Netherlands in the final.   (SYDNEY E. FRISKIN)

Lacrosse. MEN. Preparation for the World Series scheduled for Baltimore, Md., in mid-June 1982 meant that international visits in 1981 were confined to the juniors. Two U.S. collegiate squads went to the U.K. In the U.S., North Carolina University won its first National Collegiate Athletic Association championship by defeating Johns Hopkins University of Baltimore 14–13 before 22,-100 spectators. Loyola College in Baltimore was the second-division champion, and Hobart College at Geneva, N.Y., took the third division title. The champion club was Long Island (N.Y.) Athletic

Fencing:
see Combat Sports

The underdog North Carolina lacrosse team scored an upset victory in NCAA championship competition against mighty Johns Hopkins. Johns Hopkins had won the previous three tournaments and had dominated the sport since 1891.

Club, which defeated the Mount Washington Club of Baltimore. Jeff Cook of Johns Hopkins received the outstanding college player award. The North defeated the South, 20–18.

In Australia the interstate competition was won by Western Australia, its third win but its first triumph away from home. The award for the "fairest and best" player went to Jeff Kennedy of Western Australia.

In England the North beat the South, and Cheadle was the outstanding club team. Cheadle won the English club championship (Iroquois Cup) by defeating Hampstead and won the North of England senior flags by defeating South Manchester and Wythenshaw; it also won the North of England Senior League. The Southern League and flag winner was Hampstead. The University Cup was won by the University of Sheffield, and Oxford defeated Cambridge in the intervarsity game. The title of "champion county" went to Cheshire.

(CHARLES DENNIS COPPOCK)

WOMEN. In Britain, counties champion Surrey, having beaten Middlesex in the South Counties Tournament, could only manage to tie with them in the hard-fought final of the National Tournament and therefore shared the title. For the first time in nine years the East reserves won the reserves territorial championship, while the North retained its territorial title though the final matches had to be abandoned owing to snow. The National Clubs and Colleges Tournament was won by Pendley.

As usual, England dominated the home internationals, defeating Wales 15–4 and Scotland 7–2 in semiaquatic conditions, but caused a sensation by losing 6–5 to their reserves in a superb match played under floodlights at Crystal Palace. The Celts, a combined team of Scottish and Welsh players, lost 15–4 to England but then beat the England reserves 14–4 before going on a successful tour to the U.S.

The U.S. sent a national team on tour to Australia, where they won two of their three test matches. (MARGARET-LOUISE FRAWLEY)

Fiji

An independent parliamentary state and member of the Commonwealth, Fiji is an island group in the South Pacific Ocean, about 3,200 km E of Australia and 5,200 km S of Hawaii. Area: 18,272 sq km (7,055 sq mi), with two major islands, Viti Levu (10,388 sq km) and Vanua Levu (5,535 sq km), and several hundred smaller islands. Pop. (1981 est.): 636,000, including 50.1% Indian, 44.6% Fijian. Cap. and largest city: Suva (pop., 1978 est., 64,000). Language: English, Fijian, and Hindi. Religion: Christian and Hindu. Queen, Elizabeth II; governor-general in 1981, Ratu Sir George Cakobau; prime minister, Ratu Sir Kamisese Mara.

FIJI

Education. (1979) Primary, pupils 129,300, teachers (1977) 4,209; secondary, pupils 35,054, teachers (1977) 1,662; vocational, pupils 2,445, teachers (1977) 177; teacher training, students 618, teachers (1977) 65; higher, students 1,448, teaching staff 150.

Finance and Trade. Monetary unit: Fiji dollar, with (Sept. 21, 1981) a free rate of F$0.88 to U.S. $1 (F$1.63 = £1 sterling). Budget (1980 est.): revenue F$219.4 million; expenditure F$223.5 million. Foreign trade (1980): imports F$458,740,000; exports F$295,570,000. Import sources: Australia 30%; New Zealand 15%; Japan 14%; Singapore 11%; U.K. 7%; U.S. 7%. Export destinations: U.K. 25%; New Zealand 10%; U.S. 10%; Malaysia 8%; Japan 8%; Australia 7%; Canada 7%. Main exports (1979): sugar 54%; petroleum products 12%; coconut oil 5%; fish 5%. Tourism: visitors (1979) 188,740; gross receipts (1978) U.S. $102 million.

Transport and Communications. Roads (1979) 2,960 km. Motor vehicles in use (1978): passenger cars 19,400; commercial 11,980. Railways (1978) 869 km. Air traffic (1980): c. 241 million passenger-km; freight c. 3.3 million net ton-km. Shipping traffic (1980): goods loaded 730,000 metric tons, unloaded 822,000 metric tons. Telephones (Jan. 1980) 37,500. Radio receivers (Dec. 1977) 308,000.

Agriculture. Production (in 000; metric tons; 1980): sugar, raw value c. 504; rice (1979) c. 33; cassava (1979) c. 93; copra c. 25. Livestock (in 000; 1979): cattle c. 170; pigs c. 18; goats c. 55; horses c. 39; chickens c. 870.

Industry. Production (in 000; 1979): cement (metric tons) 87; gold (troy oz) 32; electricity (kw-hr) 209,000.

Fiji

In January 1981 Prime Minister Sir Kamisese Mara of Fiji reshuffled his Cabinet and created a new energy ministry. The 1981 budget attempted to reduce fuel imports by increasing taxes on gasoline and by placing punitive import duties on large cars.

There was conflict over a pine-harvesting scheme when a U.S. company bypassed the government and won the support of landowners. The government's refusal to deal with the company was one factor in the emergence of a new pro-Fijian (by implication, anti-Indian) political movement led by Ratu Osea Gavidi, the only independent MP.

Fiji agreed to sign the South Pacific Regional Trade and Cooperation Agreement when New Zealand agreed to review its citrus juice import policy. In August the South Pacific Forum decided to send a delegation headed by Mara to Europe to discuss the future in the Pacific of the second Lomé Convention, which governs the European Economic Community's trade and aid relationships with less developed countries. In July Fiji agreed to provide 500 men for the U.S.-proposed Sinai peacekeeping force.　　(BARRIE MACDONALD)

Finland

The republic of Finland is bordered on the north by Norway, on the west by Sweden and the Gulf of Bothnia, on the south by the Gulf of Finland, and on the east by the U.S.S.R. Area: 337,032 sq km (130,129 sq mi). Pop. (1981 est.): 4,792,200. Cap. and largest city: Helsinki (pop., 1981 est., 483,700). Language: Finnish, Swedish. Religion (1980): Lutheran 97.1%; Orthodox 1.2%. President until Oct. 27, 1981, Urho Kaleva Kekkonen; acting president from September 11, Mauno Koivisto; prime ministers, Koivisto and, from September 11, Eino Uusitalo (acting).

The thorny issue of who should eventually succeed Pres. Urho Kaleva Kekkonen occupied the political leaders of Finland throughout 1981. Having celebrated 25 unbroken years in office on March 1, the president fell seriously ill in September with a respiratory infection and resigned on October 27. On September 11 Prime Minister Mauno Koivisto became acting president. Elections for a new president were scheduled for January 1982.

By late 1981 interparty and personal rivalries had crystallized around the presidential question. Koivisto, Social Democratic leader of a four-party centre-left coalition, had built up a strong lead in opinion polls. Others, aware that party backing in the electoral college could be more crucial than popularity, were eager to clip his wings. Twice the Centre Party attempted to break up the government and discredit Koivisto by squabbling over ostensibly minor issues. On April 10, when Kekkonen apparently instructed him to resign because of differences between Communist and other ministers over a social benefits package, Koivisto refused on the grounds that he enjoyed the confidence of Parliament. In September Kekkonen's illness prevented the collapse of a government

deadlocked over the financing of 0.8% of its 1982 budget. In November Koivisto secured the Social Democratic presidential nomination. Among candidates selected to oppose him were Johannes Virolainen of the Centre Party and Harri Holkeri for the Conservatives.

At the 19th congress of the Communist Party of Finland (May 22–24), Chairman Aarne Saarinen, exponent of a national road to socialism, and Vice-Chairman Taisto Sinisalo, leader of the Stalinist wing, kept their jobs, but the extensive turnover of members in the Politburo and Central Committee reflected grass-roots discontent with the decline in effective support for the party. Saarinen later failed to win approval as the party's presidential candidate.

President Kekkonen's proposal for a Nordic zone free of nuclear weapons received a more positive airing in Scandinavia during 1981 than at any time since it was first advanced in 1963. Finnish officials planned to discuss with the U.S.S.R. what Soviet Pres. Leonid Brezhnev meant when he spoke of "possible measures applying to Soviet territory adjoining the proposed zone." Prominent visitors to Finland included Egyptian Foreign Minister Kamal Hassan Ali, who failed to attract a Finnish contribution toward the Sinai peacekeeping force; South Korean Prime Minister Nam Duck Woo, whose interest in trade was overshadowed by

Finland

FINLAND
Education. (1978–79) Primary, pupils 406,921, teachers 25,142; secondary, pupils 345,603, teachers 19,549; vocational, pupils 100,438, teachers 13,102; teacher training, students 745, teachers 71; higher (universities only), students 122,825, teaching staff 5,841.
Finance. Monetary unit: markka, with (Sept. 21, 1981) a free rate of 4.35 markkaa to U.S. $1 (8.07 markkaa = £1 sterling). Gold and other reserves (June 1981) U.S. $1,640,-000,000. Budget (1980 actual): revenue 43,548,000,000 markkaa; expenditure 44,877,000,000 markkaa. Gross national product (1979) 157,160,000,000 markkaa. Money supply (May 1981) 14,634,000,000 markkaa. Cost of living (1975 = 100; June 1981) 187.2.
Foreign Trade. (1980) Imports 58,236,000,000 markkaa; exports 52,871,000,000 markkaa. Import sources: U.S.S.R. 21%; West Germany 13%; Sweden 12%; U.K. 9%; U.S. 6%; Saudi Arabia 5%. Export destinations: U.S.S.R. 18%; Sweden 17%; U.K. 11%; West Germany 11%; France 5%. Main exports: paper 23%; machinery 13%; timber 10%; wood pulp 7%; chemicals 5%; clothing 5%.
Transport and Communications. Roads (1980) 74,960 km (including 208 km expressways). Motor vehicles in use (1980): passenger 1,225,900; commercial 149,150. Railways: (1979) 6,101 km; traffic (1980) 3,216,000,000 passenger-km, freight 8,335,000,000 net ton-km. Air traffic (1980): 2,130,000,000 passenger-km; freight 52.8 million net ton-km. Navigable inland waterways (1979) 6,675 km. Shipping (1980): merchant vessels 100 gross tons and over 354; gross tonnage 2,530,091. Telephones (Jan. 1980) 2,-244,400. Radio receivers (Dec. 1978) c. 2.5 million. Television receivers (Dec. 1977) c. 2,010,000.
Agriculture. Production (in 000; metric tons; 1980): wheat c. 284; barley c. 1,534; oats c. 1,680; rye c. 120; potatoes c. 675; sugar, raw value (1979) 95; rapeseed c. 47; butter c. 76; cheese c. 74; eggs c. 75; meat (1979) 287; fish catch (1979) c. 125; timber (cu m; 1979) 43,885. Livestock (in 000; June 1980): cattle 1,738; sheep 106; pigs 1,410; reindeer (1979) 205; horses 22; poultry 9,376.
Industry. Production (in 000; metric tons; 1980): pig iron 2,020; crude steel 2,508; iron ore (66% metal content) 809; cement 1,788; sulfuric acid 1,020; petroleum products (1978) c. 10,522; plywood (cu m; 1979) 539; cellulose (1979) 4,488; wood pulp (1977) mechanical 1,774, chemical 3,472; newsprint 1,345; other paper and board (1979) 4,216; electricity (kw-hr) 38,530,000; manufactured gas (cu m) c. 25,000.

Finnish concern about his country's human rights record; and Zimbabwean Prime Minister Robert Mugabe, who was likely to obtain further diplomatic and economic support.

In the autumn, political uncertainty was accompanied by a loss of economic momentum caused largely by the recession in Western markets. With the Organization for Economic Cooperation and Development forecasting growth of 2.25% in 1981 and 2% in 1982 (against the 7.2% and 5.3% spurts in the two previous years), it was feared that unemployment would increase again above its 4–5% level. Attempts to curb inflation (officially estimated at 12% for 1981) proved disappointing. A two-year centralized pay settlement was concluded with relatively little friction, though the largest union—the metalworkers—held out for marginally higher increases.

A slump in the sawmills appeared likely to spread to other sectors of wood processing, but metals and engineering were buoyed by huge orders for ships and construction projects from the U.S.S.R. Finland was in the process of wiping out a large deficit in bilateral trade with the U.S.S.R. that developed during 1979–80, stemming from the escalation in energy import prices. In the summer of 1981 the Soviets cut the price of their oil and gas to Finland by 8 and 20%, respectively.

(DONALD FIELDS)

Fisheries

World fisheries in 1981 were not expected to show any marked recovery from the previous year, when the global catch fell by one million metric tons. This was the forecast of the UN Food and Agriculture Organization (FAO), whose statistics for 1980 indicated a world catch of about 70 million metric tons. After nearly five years of restricted foreign access to the fishing grounds of coastal states under the now virtually universal 200-mi exclusive economic zone regime, this was a predictable situation.

Many of the world's big catchers, excluded from their traditional grounds, were being forced to scrap, sell, or negotiate for the right to fish in what were now controlled waters—often in unprofitable circumstances. On the other hand, many of the nations that now exercised control over those waters lacked the means to exploit them; others were nursing them back to health after years of overexploitation by the world's fish-hungry fleets. In some cases, too, fishing operations were restricted by the still punitive price of fuel, which had the effect of making certain established fisheries unprofitable. Everywhere there was a greater awareness of costs, and measures were developed to save fuel, particularly by the use of less energy-intensive fishing methods such as long-lining and gillnetting.

Among the nations most able to benefit from the situation were those of North America, with their ability to restrict activity by foreign fleets, high technical and industrial capability, and low fuel prices. The U.S. and Canada were both building bigger trawlers to fish the now protected northern grounds, particularly for cod, pollack, and shrimp. However, although shrimping was expanding in Oregon, the *Pandalus borealis* shrimp fishery in Alaska was badly affected by a rise in water temperature. Even worse hit was the Gulf of Mexico shrimp industry, where rising fuel costs and falling catches had laid up many boats and forced the shrimp-dependent shipyards to diversify into new designs and conversion work. A number of boats turned to new fisheries such as swordfishing and long-lining.

The tuna fishery was also having problems, as Mexico got tough over 200-mi-limit violations and seized U.S. boats. This brought a U.S. embargo on the importation of Mexican tuna, which hurt Mexico but also cut supplies to California canneries. Invitations by Mexico to set up joint enterprises in Mexican waters were not taken up for fear of loss of control. U.S. tuna interests continued to expand worldwide—to France and Papua New Guinea, for example—and eight 245-ft super tuna seiners were ordered from Italy.

It was a bad year for British Columbia salmon, although farther north Alaska reported excellent returns from hatchery-released salmon. British Columbia's problems were blamed on the activities of larger boats which restricted catches by longshore and river fishermen—particularly the Indian communities. Low prices and reduced catch quotas sparked a one-day protest by fishermen, who blocked the port of Victoria with their boats. Another cause for concern was the effect of acid rain on lakes and rivers, a problem shared with Scandinavia and blamed on the take-up of air pollution from factories and automobile exhausts.

On the Atlantic coast the 200-mi limit had paid off, and cod stocks were said to have recovered. In 1980 they yielded Canadian fishermen 138,000 tons, compared with 79,500 tons in 1977. Nevertheless, owners of large vessels were protesting over the preferential allocation of catch to smaller boats. Considerable activity centred on Newfoundland, where the shrimp catch was increasing and trawling interests had proposed the building of 30 new 150-ft trawlers by South African yards. Newfoundland fishermen were also exploring new fisheries for lumpfish, dogfish, snow crab, and eels.

In Europe prospects of a common fisheries policy within the European Economic Community (EEC) improved in September 1981, when agreement was reached in Brussels on a new marketing system, primarily designed to stabilize prices and provide protection from cheap imports. Previously, lack of a sense of direction had held back planning and investment. In December 1980 agreement had seemed certain, but a last-minute and unexpected veto by France had destroyed hopes once again. The sudden death of the EEC agriculture and fisheries commissioner, Finn Gundelach (*see* OBITUARIES), in January 1981 was also a blow to negotiations. There was disillusionment in Britain when France and The Netherlands were seen to be flouting the EEC ban on herring fishing, imposed as an urgent conservation measure. By summer the EEC had allocated what Britain condemned as an overgenerous catch quota of 145,000 tons, but in

U.S.-born Peter Shayne has pioneered in the development of shrimp farms in Ecuador. By his innovative methods using man-made ponds, he has become the world's largest exporter of farmed shrimp.

Britain, at least, the market had contracted, and much of the first catch went to the fish-meal plant at rock-bottom prices. Scottish fishermen stepped up their demand for unilateral action on conservation.

Also disappointing was the southwest of England mackerel fishery, which for several years had been attracting the giant factory ships of the Soviet bloc and big trawlers and purse seiners from the deep-sea ports. New controls over this multi-thousand-ton fishery had come too late, which was no surprise to local fishermen, now once again able to fish in peace with hand lines from their small boats. During the winter, massive shoals of sprats around southeastern England had been good news for the small trawlers, which had landed direct to Soviet factory vessels. In the North Sea, sprats, together with capelin and sand eel, helped to satisfy the fish-meal plants of Denmark and Norway. Scottish fishermen, now Britain's main suppliers of fresh fish, again staged a stay-in-port protest, this time against massive imports of cheap fish from The Netherlands. However, merchants pointed out that Dutch supplies were reliable, quality was high, fish was graded, and prices were predictable. A later report on the industry confirmed that British fishermen had much to learn about marketing, and there was talk of a £3 million fish-promotion program.

Building subsidies had been withdrawn in Britain to restrict fleet expansion, but owners went abroad where credit was easy and cheap. New steel inshore boats continued to join the fleet, equipped with a staggering array of electronic aids, from fuel consumption calculators to colour screen radars and echo sounders. The microchip was now firmly established in fishing, with computerized sonar displays in Norway, desk-top computers in U.S. tuna boats, and even a vocalizing navigation aid to give course and position when asked. France was placing high priority on fuel economy and commissioned its first sail-assisted tuna troller, but with disappointing results. One shipyard proposed a 100-ft catamaran with auxiliary propulsion by rotating "sail," while smaller catamarans

were finding favour as trawlers and trap boats. France held its second major fishery exhibition at Nantes during the year.

The French tuna industry, largely based on West Africa and Brittany, continued to expand. Building plans included a series of nine tuna superseiners, plus 64 replacement trawlers for the coastal fisheries. Senegal, the French West African base, planned a 250,000-ton-a-year increase for its fisheries, involving $187 million in aid to buy 26 tuna boats and 47 trawlers by 1990. Portugal also entered the tuna business with its first tuna purse seiner. Despite problems of lost fishing grounds, the Spanish fish catch rose in 1980 to 1.4 million metric tons. During 1981 the Mediterranean fleet ended its dispute with Morocco and returned to sea, and the giant Pescanova company set up its first joint venture in Europe as the Eiranova Company, based in Ireland. This was only one of 13 countries in which Spain had joint ventures, involving 10% of its fleet. Spanish fishermen again blockaded the frontier against imported French fish to protest reduced licenses from the EEC to fish Community waters.

Table I. Whaling: 1979–80 Season (Antarctic); 1979 Season (Outside the Antarctic) Number of whales caught								
Area and country	Fin whale	Sei/ Bryde's whale	Hump-back whale	Minke whale	Sperm whale	Killer whale	Total	Percentage assigned under quota agreement[1]
Antarctic pelagic (open sea)								
Japan	–	–	–	3,279	–	–	3,279	40.5
U.S.S.R.	–	–	–	3,879	–	916	4,795	47.9
Brazil	–	–	–	–	–	–	–	11.6
Total	–	–	–	7,158	–	916	8,074	100.0
Outside the Antarctic[2]								
Japan	–	347	–	407	1,502	–	2,256	
U.S.S.R.	–	227	–	–	3,570	–	3,975[3]	
Brazil	–	–	–	738	27	–	765	
Peru	–	300	–	–	742	–	1,042[1]	
Iceland	260	84	–	199	96	–	639	
Greenland	7	–	14	189	–	–	210	
Others	476	84	–	3,922	295	–	4,777	
Total	743	1,042	14	5,455	6,232	–	13,664[3]	

[1]Minke; Antarctic only.
[2]Excluding small whales.
[3]Including 178 gray whales.
Source: The Committee for Whaling Statistics, *International Whaling Statistics*.

The healthiest EEC fishery was that of Ireland, with a sixfold catch increase in 17 years. Norway, on the other hand, had been cutting back its fleet, a program that ended in 1981. The emphasis was now on smaller boats in coastal waters and on providing equipment and expertise to foreign fisheries. The Soviet Union aimed at a 33% increase in the national catch by the end of the current (1981–85) five-year plan, together with increased mariculture and aquaculture activity. Poland, which was having doubts about the practicality of distant-water fishing, was considering a greater involvement in the Baltic.

India's investment in big trawlers was being held back by tougher credits, and its shrimp industry was in trouble with the main buyers, Japan and the U.S. The former had established a united front of buyers to hold down prices, and the U.S. was maintaining a hard line on sanitary and quality control that cost India 40% of its shrimp exports. In Pakistan a $52 million aid program, including a $12 million EEC grant, was aimed at providing 7,000 motorized boats; a $2 million Japanese credit would provide inboard and outboard motors. Bangladesh was planning to raise production from inland waters to 2.6 million metric tons. Increased investment in fisheries was announced by the World Bank during the Southeast Asian Fisheries Conference, and the Asian Development

WIDE WORLD

A U.S. destroyer (centre) dwarfs a Japanese fishing boat (foreground) in the Sea of Japan; in the background is a Soviet cruiser. U.S. warships have been accused of damaging the equipment of Japanese fishing boats.

Bank was also active. A 90-vessel development program in Burma continued, but in many areas of Southeast Asia fuel prices and marketing problems restricted expansion. According to the Southeast Asian Development Corporation, the future was in aquaculture.

Peru again failed to resolve the conflict between the interests of the fish-meal plants and the developing food fish industry, which still lacked both capital and catching power. Each was demanding a greater share of limited stocks of pilchards, and the fisheries minister warned that this fishery could easily suffer the same fate as the disappearing anchoveta. In Chile, however, the catch had been rising and now stood at 3 million metric tons, putting that country in fifth position in the world league.

Australia was taking a tough line with foreign vessels caught in its 200-mi zone, as fish and squid stocks were found to be smaller than had at first been thought. The tuna fishery started the year well, however, with an 11,000-ton catch by April. Prawns from the Gulf of Carpentaria were still the main export earner. In New Zealand the failure of a joint venture with West Germany was blamed on lack of fish, but a venture with the U.S.S.R. paid off, and another was planned with Poland. Japan remained a world fishing force, with a fleet of 412,-000 vessels, but it was also a major fish and shellfish importer. Taiwan's $540 million expansion plan called for 137 new vessels.

Once again, the International Whaling Commission failed to achieve a total ban on whaling, but it did approve a world moratorium on the killing of sperm whales. (*See* ENVIRONMENT.)

(H. S. NOEL)

See also Food Processing.
[731.D.2.a]

Table II. World Fisheries, 1979[1]
In 000 metric tons

Country	Catch		Trade	
	Total	Freshwater	Imports	Exports
Japan	9,966.4	302.6	1,053.6	714.6
U.S.S.R.	9,114.0	992.9	1,096.9	526.2
China	4,054.3	1,067.5	...	91.0
Peru	3,682.4	15.2	0.3	607.8
United States	3,510.8	309.5	1,104.3	355.4
Norway	2,651.6	1.9	61.0	749.4
Chile	2,632.6	...	1.8	478.5
India	2,343.4	880.6	0.3	87.7
South Korea	2,162.5	32.3	53.0	436.9
Denmark	1,738.4	20.0	219.2	658.8
Indonesia	1,731.7	410.4	15.6	56.0
Thailand	1,716.4	146.8	79.9	279.5
Iceland	1,644.8	0.5	1.2	558.6
Philippines	1,476.2	176.5	48.0	376.2
Canada	1,331.9	122.7	84.8	470.8
North Korea	1,330.0	66.0	...	...
Spain	1,205.1	24.5	265.3	210.1
United Kingdom	1,013.5	1.3	784.2	450.8
Vietnam	1,013.5	176.3	...	...
Mexico	874.9	28.2	55.4	55.8
Brazil	843.1	140.2	94.8	29.7
France	732.1	3.2	468.3	129.3
Malaysia	698.1	8.2	121.8	78.1
South Africa	658.7	0.1	16.6	170.8
Ecuador	644.3	...	...	...
Bangladesh	640.0	540.0	...	5.5
Poland	601.1	24.8	235.9	81.5
Argentina	565.9	15.6	9.3	206.9
Burma	565.3	152.5	...	0.2
Nigeria	535.4	259.6	63.1	3.6
Italy	427.2	30.0	416.8	123.4
West Germany	356.2	15.7	838.0	185.3
Tanzania	344.3	259.7	3.7	0.2
South West Africa/ Namibia	327.1	...	...	...
Netherlands, The	323.7	2.4	350.2	322.9
Senegal	308.2	5.5	11.7	62.2
Pakistan	300.4	50.2	0.1	23.7
Morocco	279.9	0.4	...	80.0
Faeroe Islands	266.6	...	0.4	103.8
Portugal	241.9	...	85.4	55.2
Ghana	229.9	45.9	76.6	2.2
East Germany	224.4	18.4	102.0	...
Uganda	223.8	22.4	...	...
Sweden	205.6	13.7	201.5	109.2
Oman	198.0	...	...	...
Other	5,351.3	...	...	...
World	71,286.9	7,480.4 [2]	9,193.5 [2]	9,673.3 [2]

[1] Excludes whaling.
[2] Includes unspecified amounts in Other category.
Source: United Nations Food and Agriculture Organization, *Yearbook of Fishery Statistics*, vol. 48 and 49.

Food Processing

Rising energy costs, the continuing recession, and political pressures against high food prices accelerated many structural changes in food manufacture and distribution. The introduction of microprocessors led to increased automation both in food manufacture and in wholesale and retail distribution systems. This resulted in numerous economies, but it also caused layoffs and the disappearance of many small enterprises. Economic and environmental factors stimulated the utilization of food-industry by-products, necessitating a reappraisal of routine methods of food analysis and law enforcement.

A tighter family budget and health propaganda, supported in some countries by government action, caused discernible changes in food-consumption patterns. There was increased emphasis on low-calorie foods, products with low sugar content, and vegetable fats (margarines). Products containing dietary fibre, especially brown bread, grew in popularity. At the same time, greater leisure and travel had increased interest in unfamiliar foods. Even the habit of eating regular meals was changing in the face of new life-styles and the availability of fast foods, "impulse" foods, and snacks.

Overproduction of many commodities, notably dairy products, heightened competition within the food industry, especially as traditional foods vied for the consumer's attention with products having reduced carbohydrate or fat content, artificial sweeteners, nonnutritive fillers, and spreads with much of the fat replaced by air and water. This situation was in ironic contrast to a sombre warning from the Food and Agriculture Organization that in more than 45 countries agricultural production had not kept pace with population growth and that every African had 10% less to eat than had been the case a decade earlier.

Fruits, Vegetables, and Cereals. A decline of about two million tons in the consumption of tomatoes in the U.S. was blamed on the effects of a recession on the restaurant and fast food industries. Producers initiated research in an effort to find new outlets, and the successful development of a wide range of tomato-based products, including bread, crackers, and chips, was reported. A British company was engaged in a joint venture with a regional electricity-generating board in which waste heat from electrical generating equipment was utilized for fruit and vegetable production under glass. Another British company commissioned a £3 million plant for manufacturing an entirely natural onion concentrate that retained all the flavour components of the onion. Utilization of the lupine as a source of food was reviewed at an international workshop held in Peru. Lupine oil is rich in essential fatty acid, and the seeds yield 40% protein which, however, requires fortification with methionine to improve its nutritional value.

CARE and UNICEF provided funds to equip a Soybean Foods Research Centre in Sri Lanka for training and pilot-plant production of such products as drum-dried soy beverage; fortified infant-weaning food made from full-fat soy flour, rice, and mung beans; and high-protein soy-corn mixture. Soy-based yogurt and ice cream were under development. The U.S. organization INTSOY was cooperating with Peruvian technologists on the development of soy-fortified bread and noodles and on liquid and powdered soy beverages. U.S. corn processors reported that high-fructose corn syrups could now replace sugar in most food-processing operations.

Dairy Products. The advent of the microprocessor had affected all aspects of the dairy industry. A British plant manufacturer, the recipient of the Queen's Award for Technical Achievement, introduced a system that provided for continuous monitoring, automatic start-up, safe routing of product and/or cleaning solution, and fault detection. Manufacturing instructions could be varied by means of a teletape machine, which also provided a timed record of processing throughout the day. Another system, developed by a U.S. company, had interchangeable modules which could handle many levels of complexity. A Swedish company introduced a novel system embracing process control, automatic fault-tracing and reporting, but with simplified circuitry that reduced installation costs and permitted additions to the system without major rewiring. In a flexible Danish system, product routing and processing data for all sections of the plant were displayed on a video monitor, and the operator could control the system manually if necessary.

French dairy technologists were investigating the feasibility of immobilizing the enzyme rennin (rennet) on an inert support so that it could be recovered and reused in the cheese-making process, thereby effecting considerable economies. Scientists in the U.S., Australia, and Switzerland were reportedly studying the application of genetic engineering to the improvement of dairy bacteria. Possibilities included the development of

Grapefruit can be easily damaged using ordinary shipping methods, but this automatic packing machine and a new design for packing the fruit in a chipboard honeycomb will help solve the problem.

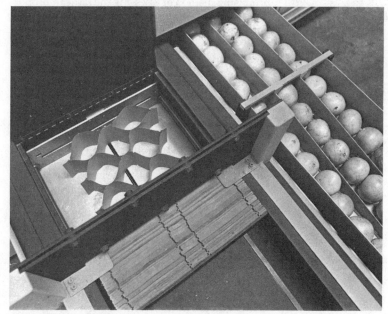

SCIENCE AND EDUCATION ADMINISTRATION—USDA

new types of cheese-making bacteria that would hasten ripening and flavour development, as well as single strains of bacteria combining the characteristics of the two kinds normally used in making yogurt.

Investigators in the U.S., Australia, and Europe continued their efforts to find new uses for surplus skim milk and butterfat. French technologists succeeded in making processed cheese from these products. A new method of making various cheeses of superior keeping quality from skim milk powder and butterfat was developed by a British scientist. Sizable energy savings were claimed, although these did not take into account the energy required to produce the skim milk powder and butter in the first place. Australian and British scientists continued research on the fractionation and modification of milk proteins with a view to developing new products, including meat analogues.

Meat and Seafood. Considerable progress was made in the production of food-quality products from meat wastes. Improved processing equipment had been developed that would accept anything from bone to soft-fat trimmings and produce edible oil, meat emulsion, and pulverized bone. Protein could subsequently be extracted from these products, and the residue could be converted to phosphates suitable for use in cakes, beverages, and icing sugar. Progress was also made in the utilization of blood fractions and rinds. The meat emulsion, protein from bone, rinds, and blood plasma had various uses in sausages, restructured hams and steaks, burgers, and in brine curing.

Some consumers considered that restructured meats were moister, more tender, and more easily sliced than the conventional products. However, there was dispute as to whether some of the recovered protein could rightfully be described as "meat," and it was apparent that these new developments would necessitate a review of the legal specifications for meat products and for labeling. Australian and British technologists developed a promising method of assessing the fat/lean proportions of carcasses and of frozen and fresh meat portions. The meat was scanned electronically as it moved on a conveyor belt, and the data were analyzed by a computer. The resulting readout of the fat/lean ratio was said to be much more accurate than subjective assessments.

An international conference on aquaculture attracted visitors and exhibitors from the U.S., Britain, Belgium, Canada, Ireland, and Norway. Of particular interest were Norwegian technology and the contribution of the British White Fish Authority, which had pioneered marine fish farming. During 1980 Norway's fish farm industry delivered 4,153 metric tons of Atlantic salmon and trout worth £21 million, 21% more than in the previous year. There were also some 420 farms producing oysters and mussels. Scottish fish farmers, with a turnover approaching £20 million, were producing salmon, trout, shellfish, and, more recently, eels, dover sole, turbot, and sea bass.

Aquaculture was reportedly contributing 8–10% of the world catch of fish and crustaceans. China accounted for about half of this total, but India, the U.S.S.R., Japan, the U.S., France, Spain, and Israel had active development programs. Genetic engineering was under study in Scotland and Norway with a view to improving strains of salmon and trout. The UN was assisting China to integrate carp ponds with the growing of mulberry trees for silkworm culture. This was proving to be a very efficient use of land, water, and labour with little capital outlay; moreover, excess mud from the dikes was made into bricks. A shrimp culture project utilizing the Malaysian freshwater prawn was begun in the KwaZulu homeland in South Africa. A Guernsey company successfully completed a seven-year project for rearing shellfish seed on plankton cultured in a seawater lagoon.

New Products. "What constitutes a new product" was debated at an industry seminar, which concluded that genuinely innovative products are exceedingly rare. A British can manufacturer opened new laboratories with provision for some 550 scientists, primarily to assist customers in new product development. U.K. government approval was given to a fungal protein food developed by a British company. Another innovation was a sliceable cured turkey meat product, which fried like bacon. The Royal Commonwealth Society for the Blind announced a £1.5 million plan to prevent blindness due to vitamin A deficiency in Indian children by providing them with fortified lollipops.

Recently introduced new products included "butter-like" margarines; low-sugar jams; low-calorie carbonated citrus fruit juices; flavoured skim milk beverages; low-cholesterol foods; low-salt cereal products and seasonings; a fatless, low-sugar, barley-based breakfast cereal (Denmark); cereal products containing apple and bran (U.K.); a polyunsaturated filled-milk supplement (South Africa); yogurt cake mixes (U.S.); a long-life yogurt beverage (The Netherlands); yogurt dressings (U.K.); sugarless frozen fruit salads (South Africa); bran with date topping (U.K.); and cereal and yogurt bars (West Germany). An anti-caries chewing gum containing dextranase, an enzyme that breaks down the polysaccharide plaque formed on teeth by the action of certain mouth bacteria on sugar, was introduced in Japan.

In Britain and West Germany the observation that a substantial proportion of diabetic food products were being purchased by nondiabetics stimulated further development of these products. The popularity of snack foods accounted for numerous pizza variations, extruded vegetable-protein products, concentrated soups for instant reconstitution, and a new commercial line of once-common home desserts such as bread-and-butter pudding. The surprising success of high-priced "gourmet" foods in the U.S. led to the elevation of many conventional foods to this category by means of innovative packaging. Thus a "gourmet" honey cost $7.99, compared with 69 cents for honey in a conventional package. (H. B. HAWLEY)

See also Agriculture and Food Supplies; Fisheries; Health and Disease; Industrial Review: *Alcoholic Beverages.*

[451.B.1.c.ii; 731.E–H]

Football

Association Football (Soccer). During 1981 most member countries of the Federation of International Football Associations (FIFA) concentrated on qualifying for the World Cup finals, to be held in Spain during June and July 1982. Yet by the beginning of September 1981 only four countries were sure of a place in the 24-team finals. They were Spain (the host country), Argentina (the defending champions), Brazil, and Chile.

Crowd trouble still dogged football matches in 1981, and no real solution was produced; newly erected fences did no more than keep the hooligans off the playing fields. Among other developments, synthetic playing surfaces, pioneered in the U.S., were being introduced into Europe on an experimental basis. In England, Queens Park Rangers, a London club of the Football League's Second Division, installed the first such surface in senior competition.

EUROPEAN CHAMPIONS' CUP. With eight minutes remaining in the final game at Paris on May 27, Alan Kennedy, the Liverpool fullback, chased down the left flank, beat two ill-timed challenges by Real Madrid defenders, and drilled home the ball to win the contest 1–0 and keep the European Champions' Cup in England for the fifth consecutive year. The match was won finally by the team that made the fewest mistakes, as Liverpool's well-organized defensive machine—goalkeeper Ray Clemence in particular—did all that was required to contain the lively Real Madrid forwards. The capacity of the Parc des Princes stadium was limited, and so fewer than 50,000 spectators, little more than Liverpool's average gate, watched the game live, although millions saw it on television.

The match was far from a one-sided affair. Real Madrid coach Vujadin Boskov gambled on English-born Laurie Cunningham to provide some flair down the flanks and in the penalty area. Cunningham and Juan Juanito certainly stretched the capability of the Liverpool rear guard at times, but solid covering by Phil Thompson and Alan Hansen foiled their attempts to beat Clemence. Real Madrid almost scored early in the second half when García Navajas chipped the ball over the defenders, but José Comacho lifted the final shot over Clemence—and the bar. Try as they might, Juanito, Cunningham, and Carlos Santillana never had the same authority as their Liverpool counterparts, and goalkeeper Augustín Rodríguez was in action far more than Clemence. Liverpool thus joined Real Madrid, Ajax of Amsterdam, and West Germany's Bayern Munich as three-time winners of the coveted cup.

EUROPEAN CUP-WINNERS' CUP. Dynamo Tbilisi became the second Soviet team to win a senior European trophy, narrowly defeating the East German cup holders Carl Zeiss Jena 2–1 in Düsseldorf, West Germany, on May 13. The 60,000-capacity Rheinstadion had only 9,000 spectators for the contest, with probably fewer than 200 supporting the winners.

Ascendancy fluctuated back and forth in the opening half, as Otari Gabelia in the Dynamo goal was kept busy turning back efforts from Lutz Lindemann, Jurgen Raab, and Eberhard Vogel. Urged on by midfielder David Kipiani, Dynamo had a free kick booted out of the goal area, and Jena goalkeeper Hans-Ulrich Grapenthin collected a drive from Ramas Shengelia and tipped George Tavadze's shot over the bar. Jena scored first when Gerhardt Hoppe drove in a cross from Vogel after 63 minutes. Tbilisi then stormed back and drew even when Vladimir Gutsayev scored four minutes later, following a break by Shengelia, who outsped the Germans' defense. The Soviet players clearly scented victory and pressed Jena hard. They gained their reward when Kipiani directed a pass into the penalty area for Vitaly Daraselia to latch onto. The latter nimbly eluded three tackles before letting fly with the shot, four minutes before the end of the game, that sent the cup back to Georgia in the southern U.S.S.R. The smallness of the crowd robbed the final of some of the sense of occasion, although the game was beamed on television to 14 countries.

The lack of a crowd had also marked the return leg of West Ham's game with Castille at Upton Park, London. This contest, however, was played behind closed doors because of crowd violence during the first leg in Madrid, when one West Ham fan was killed in a coach accident. The order banning spectators for the second match was made by the Union of European Football Associations (UEFA).

UEFA CUP. Ipswich Town strengthened Britain's near-monopoly of the UEFA Cup by defeating the Dutch entrants AZ '67 Alkmaar over two legs during May 1981. Ironically, perhaps, it was two Dutchmen, Arnold Muhren and Frans Thijssen,

New York Cosmos defender Jeff Durgan goes airborne to try to head off a goal attempt by the Chicago Sting's Karl-Heinz Granitza (12) in the North American Soccer League Soccer Bowl in Toronto. The Chicago team emerged victorious, 1–0, on September 26.

who helped Ipswich to collect the prize. Ipswich's victory was based on a three-goal advantage gained in its own Portman Road stadium on May 6 during the first leg. True to the established format of European two-legged competition, Alkmaar decided to play a defensive game at Ipswich and did so for most of a spirited, flowing contest. But that tactic played into the English club's hands, and a penalty shot by John Wark midway through the first half, along with goals by Thijssen and Paul Mariner in the opening 11 minutes of the second, gave Ipswich its 3–0 victory. Belatedly the Dutch team tried to salvage something by going for goals in the last phase of the game but to no avail, as Kees Kist and "Pier" Tol wasted good chances.

When the return was played a fortnight later in Amsterdam, the scene was set for a tactical encounter of attacking football. The Ipswich players did not fall into the trap of being ultradefensive and sitting on their first-leg advantage, because they knew that any goal they scored in Alkmaar would count double in the event of a tie in the aggregate scores. Within five minutes Thijssen scored to give Ipswich a 4–0 overall advantage, but then Alkmaar started to increase its attacks, with Johnny Metgod pushing forward. This aggressiveness paid off in the form of three goals from Kurt Welzl, Metgod, and Tol, but the not-to-be-denied Wark whipped in a second goal for Ipswich to leave the overall score at 5–3 in Ipswich's favour at halftime. In the second half Ipswich's manager, Bobby Robson, reorganized his defense to cope with the threat of Metgod, and AZ was limited to a single goal from Jos Jonker; thus, Ipswich, though beaten 4–2 in the second leg, triumphed 5–4 overall.

U.K. HOME INTERNATIONAL CHAMPIONSHIP. The traditional end-of-season U.K. home tournament, which in recent years had been played

Table I. Association Football Major Tournaments

Event	Winner	Country
Inter-Continental Cup	Nacional	Uruguay
European Champions' Cup	Liverpool	England
European Cup-Winners' Cup	Dynamo Tbilisi	U.S.S.R.
UEFA Cup	Ipswich Town	England
Libadores Cup (South American Champions' Cup)	Flamengo	Brazil

Table II. Association Football National Champions

Nation	League winners	Cup winners
Albania	Partizan Tirana	Vlaznia
Austria	Austria Wien	Graz AK
Belgium	Anderlecht	Standard Liège
Bulgaria	CSKA Sofia	Trakia Plovdiv
Cyprus	Omonia	Omonia
Czechoslovakia	Banik Ostrava	Dukla Prague
Denmark	KB Copenhagen	Vejle
England	Aston Villa	Tottenham Hotspur
Finland	OPS Oulu	Kotkan TP
France	Saint-Étienne	Bastia
Germany, East	Dynamo Berlin	Lokomotiv Leipzig
Germany, West	Bayern Munich	Eintracht Frankfurt
Greece	Olympiakos	Olympiakos
Hungary	Ferencvaros	Vasas Budapest
Iceland	Valur	Fram
Ireland	Athlone	Dundalk
Italy	Juventus	AS Roma
Luxembourg	Niedercorn	Jeunesse D'Esch
Malta	Hibernians	Floriana
Netherlands, The	AZ '67 Alkmaar	AZ '67 Alkmaar
Northern Ireland	Glentoran	Ballymena
Norway	IK Start	Valengeren
Poland	Widzew Lodz	Legia Warsaw
Portugal	Benfica	Benfica
Romania	Univer Craiova	Univer Craiova
Scotland	Celtic	Rangers
Spain	Real Sociedad	Barcelona
Sweden	Öster Växjö	Kalmar FF
Switzerland	Zürich	Lausanne
Turkey	Trabzonspor	Andaragucu
U.S.S.R.	Dynamo Kiev	Donezk Schachtjor
U.S.	Chicago Sting	
Wales		Swansea
Yugoslavia	Red Star Belgrade	Velez Mostar

within a period of eight or ten days, was thrown into disarray when the English and Welsh football associations refused to play their matches in Belfast, Northern Ireland, because of the danger of violence there. Therefore, only four soccer matches were played. During the first, at Swansea, Wales, the Welsh rattled Scotland and won with a pair of goals in the first half from Ian Walsh, the Crystal Palace forward. Three days later, on May 19 at Hampden Park, Glasgow, the Scots redeemed themselves by beating Northern Ireland by the same score with a goal in each half from London-based players Ray Stewart and Steve Archibald. But the stadium was less than a quarter full for a game that produced its quota of good football.

Wales and England ground out a 0–0 draw at Wembley Stadium in London the following night. Both sides wasted good opportunities to score, and perhaps the fans who stayed away—there were less than 35,000 in the 100,000-capacity stadium—knew a thing or two. In the final match, at the same arena in London, the Scots triumphed over England with a solitary penalty shot by John Robertson (Nottingham Forest) after 64 minutes. The penalty was given when Bryan Robson (West Bromwich) tripped Spurs player Archibald.

NORTH AMERICAN SOCCER LEAGUE. The Chicago Sting won the NASL Soccer Bowl for the first time by defeating the defending champion New York Cosmos on Sept. 26, 1981, in Exhibition Stadium, Toronto, Ont., before a noisy crowd of nearly 37,000. The Sting's narrow victory was by

During competition in a home international rugby championship match at Cardiff, Wales, Wales (dark jerseys) defeated England 21–19.

KEYSTONE

a single goal from Rudy Glenn scored in the "shoot-out" after the teams had finished even following the two seven-and-a-half-minute periods of extra time. Dieter Ferner blocked the Cosmos' final shot by Bob Iarusci, which secured the Bowl for Chicago. Both teams were renowned during the season for their high scoring potential, but the defenses dominated in the title match. The teams had identical records of 23 wins and 9 defeats during the season. Top scorer in the league again was Giorgio Chinaglia of the Cosmos, with 29 goals.

(TREVOR WILLIAMSON)

Rugby. RUGBY UNION. The 1980–81 season featured great activity by touring teams. Also during the period the International Board made changes in the rules that could have a far-reaching effect on the game. The first team to tour was Romania, which played six games in Ireland and England in October 1980. The Romanians won four of their matches, and their holding of Ireland to a draw of 13–13 at Lansdowne Road, Dublin, did much to enhance their growing reputation as a rugby country. At the same time of the year France toured South Africa, winning three of its four games but losing 37–15 to South Africa (the Springboks) at Pretoria. The Springboks had themselves just returned from South America, where they won their two internationals against a South American team 22–13 in Montevideo, Uruguay, and 30–16 in Santiago, Chile.

The New Zealand team, the All Blacks, visited North America, beating the U.S. 53–6 in San Diego, Calif., and Canada 43–10 in Vancouver, B.C., on their way to Wales to mark the centenary of the Welsh Rugby Union. In Wales in October and November the All Blacks won all five of their games, putting on a great display to defeat Wales 23–3 at Cardiff Arms Park.

The home international championship was won by France, which gained the grand slam—beating all four home countries—for only the third time in history. France beat Scotland 16–9 in Paris, Ireland 19–13 in Dublin, and Wales 19–15 in Paris before clinching the championship with a victory of 16–12 over England at Twickenham. England, Scotland, and Wales tied for second, while Ireland, which failed to score even a draw, finished last.

All the countries involved in the international championship went on tour at the end of the European season, with the exception of Wales. France lost both their tests in Australia, the scores being 17–15 and 24–14. England fared better in Argentina, drawing the first of their two tests against the Pumas 19–19 and winning the second 12–6, both in Buenos Aires. Scotland was heavily defeated in New Zealand, losing 11–4 and 40–15. Ireland likewise was beaten 23–15 and 12–10 in South Africa.

Then the Springboks, hounded by political demonstrators, toured New Zealand, winning 11 of their 14 games but losing the test series 2–1. The All Blacks won the first test 14–9 and the Springboks the second 24–12; the All Blacks then triumphed in the third 25–22 thanks to a penalty goal kicked in injury time. The Springboks also encountered political opposition during a tour in September of the U.S., where they defeated regional all-star teams.

The International Board's rules changes were concerned with an attempt to reduce the likelihood of serious injury and to eliminate the pileup. The main burden of the alterations was that it became no longer possible for a player on the ground—even in a sitting position or on one knee—to play the ball in any manner in a ruck-maul situation or after a tackle.

RUGBY LEAGUE. The chief event of 1980–81 was the game's spread to the south of England with the formation of a team at the Fulham soccer club's ground in London. Fulham, placed in the second division of the league, did so well in its first season that it won promotion to the first division. This success inspired the Cardiff City soccer club in Wales to start a Rugby League team for the 1981–82 season, and at the same time another team was formed at Carlisle. Both were placed in the second division.

(DAVID FROST)

U.S. Football. PROFESSIONAL. The San Francisco 49ers climaxed one of the most remarkable comeback seasons in National Football League (NFL) history by defeating the Cincinnati Bengals 26–21 in the Super Bowl on Jan. 24, 1982, in Pontiac, Mich. Led by quarterback Joe Montana, the 49ers took a 20–0 halftime lead over the Bengals and then withstood Cincinnati's second-half rally. Among the highlights of the game was a goal-line stand by the 49ers during which they turned back Cincinnati three times from the one-yard line.

In reaching the Super Bowl for the first time in its history, San Francisco compiled a 13–3 regular-season record, the best in the NFL. This followed seasons of 2–14, 2–14, and 6–10 in 1978–80. In the play-offs the 49ers defeated the New York Giants 38–24 and then won the National Conference championship 28–27 over Dallas on a last-minute pass from Montana to Dwight Clark.

Cincinnati Bengals running back Pete Johnson (46) was stopped just short of the goal line when the San Francisco 49ers beat the Bengals in the Super Bowl at the Silverdome in Pontiac, Michigan, on January 24. The Bengals were thwarted several times before the 49ers goal-line defense.

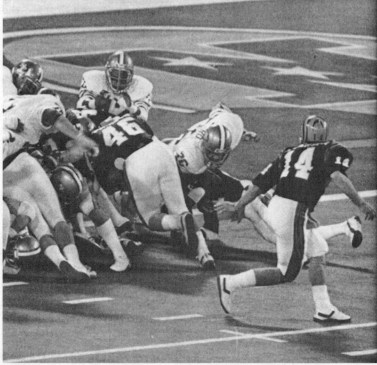

Cincinnati also reached the Super Bowl for the first time as quarterback Ken Anderson (*see* BIOGRAPHIES) led them to a 12–4 season record after 4–12, 4–12, and 6–10 marks the previous three years. The Bengals won their play-off games 28–21 over Buffalo and 27–7 over San Diego.

During the regular season little went according to form. Only 4 of the 13 NFL teams that had winning records in 1980 had them again in 1981. Dallas, Philadelphia, San Diego, and Buffalo were also the only four teams to make repeat appearances in the ten-team Super Bowl tournament.

San Francisco and Cincinnati, which had had two of the NFL's three worst records in 1979, had the best records in the National and American Football conferences (NFC and AFC), respectively, in 1981. San Francisco's last play-off appearance had been in 1972 and Cincinnati's in 1975. The New York Jets reached the play-offs for the first time since 1969, their last winning season. The New York Giants had their first winning season since 1972 and made the play-offs for the first time since 1963. Miami won the AFC East Division and Tampa Bay the NFC Central, both returning to the play-offs after one-year absences.

Neither 1980 Super Bowl team, Oakland or Philadelphia, was among the final eight teams contesting for the 1981 championship. Oakland missed the tournament altogether, and Philadelphia lost to the Giants in the NFC wild-card game between the conference's two best teams that did not win division championships. Wild-card teams came from the same division for the first time, Philadelphia and the Giants from the NFC East and Buffalo and the Jets from the AFC East.

Along with Oakland, which had its first losing season since 1964, the other 1980 play-off teams to fall from grace were Atlanta, Cleveland, Houston, Minnesota, and Los Angeles. Pittsburgh, with an 8–8 record, ended a nine-year streak of winning seasons, and New England's record dropped the furthest, from 10–6 to 2–14.

San Francisco improved the most, going from 6–10 to 13–3, the best record for an NFC team since the conference was born in the NFL's merger with the American Football League in 1970. Winning the NFC West Division, San Francisco had NFL coach of the year Bill Walsh, NFC receiving leader Clark with 85 catches, and NFC passing leader Montana, who had an 88.2 rating based on his percentage of completions, touchdowns, interceptions, and average gain per pass attempt. Montana's .637 completion percentage led the league.

Dallas rookie cornerback Everson Walls, passed over in the draft of college seniors, led the league with 11 interceptions. In light of the league's shifting power structure, the 15th play-off appearance in 16 years by the Cowboys was no less impressive than the other teams' sudden improvement.

New Orleans halfback George Rogers, the first choice in the draft, led the league with a rookie record of 1,674 yd rushing. The total of 15 runners rushing for more than 1,000 yd was three more than ever before. Dallas's Tony Dorsett, who ran for 28 fewer yards than Rogers and ranked second, set a record with his fifth 1,000-yd season in five years. Chuck Muncie of San Diego tied a record

with 19 rushing touchdowns. Earl Campbell of Houston led the AFC in rushing for the fourth consecutive year.

San Diego, at the vanguard of the trend toward more passing yardage, continued to fill the air with footballs as Dan Fouts led the NFL with 33 touchdown passes and 4,802 yd passing, breaking his own record by 385 yd. Kellen Winslow of San Diego led the NFL with 88 catches; he and San Francisco's Clark were the first receivers in 20 years to catch more than 80 passes in two consecutive seasons. San Diego led the league in scoring, total yardage, and passing yards, overcoming its 27th-ranked defense to win the AFC West for the third consecutive year.

Cincinnati, like San Francisco, rose on the shoulders of an outstanding quarterback to win the AFC Central. Ken Anderson led the league with a 98.5 rating and a .021 interception percentage, and his .626 completion percentage led the AFC. Cincinnati's Pat McInally led the NFL with a 45.4-yd punting average.

Passing was not a panacea, though. Denver missed the play-offs in spite of Craig Morton, who ranked second among NFL passers, and Steve Watson, who tied Atlanta's Alfred Jenkins with 13 touchdown catches. Atlanta's record dropped from 12–4 to 7–9 despite Steve Bartkowski, who led the NFC with 30 touchdown passes, and Alfred Jenkins, who added a league-leading 1,358 receiving yards to his touchdown catches. Minnesota led the NFC in passing yardage but lost its last five games.

Philadelphia's defense allowed the fewest points, yards, and passing yards in the NFL. The Jets, paced by defensive end Joe Klecko, led the AFC in total defense and sacks and finished 10–5–1 after losing their first three games.

Detroit's Eddie Murray and Dallas's Rafael Septien shared the scoring lead with 121 points. Stump Mitchell of St. Louis set a kick return record with 1,737 yd, and his teammate Roy Green became the first player since 1957 to catch and intercept passes in the same game, doing it three times. Green Bay's 38-year-old Jan Stenerud broke a 28-year-old record with his .917 field goal percentage, 22 of 24. Alan Page, the only defenseman ever named the NFL's most valuable player, retired after 15 seasons with Minnesota and Chicago.

Average NFL attendance reached 60,000 for the first time. Monday night football had its highest television ratings in 12 years amid speculation that the league's new multiyear television contract for 1982 would be worth more than $1 billion.

COLLEGE. Clemson was the only undefeated major college team in 1981 with a 12–0 record, clinching the national championship by defeating Nebraska 22–15 in the Orange Bowl at Miami, Fla., on New Year's Day 1982. Before Clemson reached the top of the wire-service polls on the final ballot of the regular season, Michigan, Notre Dame, Southern California, Texas, Penn State, and Pittsburgh all had been ranked first. These seven different teams broke the old record of five.

Besides Clemson, the only major teams to avoid at least two defeats were Pittsburgh (11–1), Texas (10–1–1), and Southern Methodist (10–1), which was ineligible for a Bowl appearance and lost the

---

Table III.
NFL Final Standings and Play-offs, 1981

AMERICAN CONFERENCE
Eastern Division

	W	L	T
*Miami	11	4	1
*New York Jets	10	5	1
*Buffalo	10	6	0
Baltimore	2	14	0
New England	2	14	0

Central Division

	W	L	T
*Cincinnati	12	4	0
Pittsburgh	8	8	0
Houston	7	9	0
Cleveland	5	11	0

Western Division

	W	L	T
*San Diego	10	6	0
Denver	10	6	0
Kansas City	9	7	0
Oakland	7	9	0
Seattle	6	10	0

NATIONAL CONFERENCE
Eastern Division

	W	L	T
*Dallas	12	4	0
*Philadelphia	10	6	0
*New York Giants	9	7	0
Washington	8	8	0
St. Louis	7	9	0

Central Division

	W	L	T
*Tampa Bay	9	7	0
Detroit	8	8	0
Green Bay	8	8	0
Minnesota	7	9	0
Chicago	6	10	0

Western Division

	W	L	T
*San Francisco	13	3	0
Atlanta	7	9	0
Los Angeles	6	10	0
New Orleans	4	12	0

*Qualified for play-offs.

Play-offs
Wild-card round
New York Giants 27, Philadelphia 21
Buffalo 31, New York Jets 27

American semifinals
Cincinnati 28, Buffalo 21
San Diego 41, Miami 38

National semifinals
San Francisco 38, New York Giants 24
Dallas 38, Tampa Bay 0

American finals
Cincinnati 27, San Diego 7

National finals
San Francisco 28, Dallas 27

Super Bowl
San Francisco 26, Cincinnati 21

Southwest Conference championship to Texas because it was on probation for recruiting violations. Two other teams in the Associated Press Top 20, Miami of Florida and Arizona State, were on probation, and Clemson was under investigation for similar violations as the year ended.

Alabama lost to Texas 14–12 in the Cotton Bowl, but its coach, Paul ("Bear") Bryant (*see* BIOGRAPHIES), broke Amos Alonzo Stagg's record for college coaching victories with his 315th in the final regular-season game on November 28. In other postseason contests Pittsburgh defeated Georgia 24–20 in the Sugar Bowl, and Michigan triumphed over UCLA 33–14 in the Bluebonnet Bowl.

Iowa had its first winning season in 20 years and made its first trip in 22 years to the Rose Bowl. However, it was defeated there 28–0 by Washington in the first Rose Bowl shutout since 1953. The Big Ten, with Iowa and Ohio State its co-champions, departed from its cloud-of-dust tradition by averaging more passing yards per game than any other conference and shed its "Big Two" subtitle by keeping Ohio State and Michigan out of the Rose Bowl for the first time in 14 years.

Washington survived a Pacific 10 Conference race in which five teams finished within a game of first place. One of them, Southern California, lost to Penn State 26–10 in the Fiesta Bowl, which joined the Rose, Cotton, Sugar, and Orange Bowl games on New Year's Day.

Marcus Allen became the fourth Southern California tailback in 17 years to win the Heisman Trophy, the award for the best college player. Allen set ten major college records and tied one. His 2,342 yd rushing broke the old record by 394 yd, and he also set records with an average of 212.9 yd per game, five consecutive 200-yd games, and 11 200-yd games in his career. During the 1981 season he also led the country with 23 touchdowns.

Allen overshadowed Georgia sophomore Herschel Walker, who ran for 1,891 yd and 20 touchdowns. Georgia's defense ranked third in scoring and second against the run as the Bulldogs tied Alabama for the Southeast Conference.

The unprecedented balance among major teams was attributed partly to the effect of a 1978 rule limiting teams to 95 scholarships, which kept the traditional powers from stockpiling good players on their benches, away from other schools. Television money also contributed to the balance by making it attractive for top-ranked teams of approximately equal strength to play each other.

Nebraska, the Big Eight champion, ranked second in rushing and led the country in pass defense, allowing 100.1 yd per game. Nebraska's David Rimington became only the third junior and the second centre to win the Outland Award for the outstanding college lineman.

Pittsburgh led the country defensively by allowing 224.8 yd and 62.4 rushing yards per game. Pittsburgh also ranked fourth in scoring, and its quarterback, second-ranked Dan Marino, led in touchdown passes with 34.

The top-ranked quarterback, Jim McMahon of 10–2 Brigham Young, finished his college career with 60 passing or total offense records, including 84 touchdowns, a career passing efficiency grade of

Clemson's Frank Magwood catches a pass as Nebraska's Jeff Krejci looks on. Clemson won the Orange Bowl 22–15.

156.9, and 9,723 yd of total offense, which broke the old record by 1,279 yd. McMahon led the country with 272 pass completions, a .643 completion percentage, and a .165 interception percentage.

Iowa punter Reggie Roby's 49.8-yd average set a record, as did Gary Anderson's .947 field-goal percentage for Syracuse. Darrin Nelson of Stanford set an all-purpose yardage record of 6,885 yd rushing, pass receiving, and returning punts and kickoffs.

Canadian Football. The Edmonton Oilers won a record fourth consecutive Canadian Football League (CFL) championship by defeating the Ottawa Rough Riders 26–23 in the Grey Cup game at Montreal on November 22. Dave Cutler's 27-yd field goal with three seconds to play decided the game for Edmonton, which was favoured by 22½ points but trailed 20–1 at halftime. Western Conference champion Edmonton had a 14–1–1 record for the regular season and Ottawa had 5–11, the worst record ever for a CFL finalist.

Quarterback Dieter Brock, of 11–5 Winnipeg, won the CFL outstanding player award for the second year in a row as he led the league with 32 touchdown passes and set a record with 4,796 yd passing. Among his teammates, guard Larry Butler was named outstanding lineman and wide receiver Joe Poplawski outstanding native Canadian player. Winnipeg wide receiver Eugene Goodlow set a record with 100 catches, and kicker Trevor Kennard led the league with 185 points.

Edmonton's award winners were linebacker Danny Ray Kepley, named outstanding defensive player, and quarterback Warren Moon, the passing leader. Saskatchewan had rookie of the year linebacker Vince Goldsmith and receiving yardage leader Joey Walters, with 1,715. Calgary's Jimmy Sykes led in rushing with 1,107 yd.

(KEVIN M. LAMB)

Foreign Aid:
see Economy, World

Foreign Exchange:
see Economy, World

COLLEGES, ATHLETES, AND SCANDAL

by Andrew David

British statesman Benjamin Disraeli once said in a speech before the House of Commons: "A university should be a place of light, of liberty, and of learning." A century later, were he alive and on the other side of the Atlantic, he would no doubt be astonished at the way his counsel is interpreted in many of the major universities of the United States. He would find that for some college students the "place of light" is nothing more than the enormous football stadium that is their playground on autumnal Saturday afternoons, that the "liberty" is the freedom to avoid classes and still receive passing grades, and the "learning" is either nonexistent or limited to the lore of the coach's playbook.

The Business of Winning. Certainly no stock can be put in Grantland Rice's starry-eyed observation: "When the one great scorer comes to write against your name, he marks not that you won or lost but how you played the game"; it is about as appropriate in the universities of the 1980s as Ptolemy's view of an Earth-centred universe. Winning is the name of the game today, and the principal concerns are the team's standing in its conference, its rank from week to week in the AP and UPI polls, and the Bowl game to which it will receive an invitation.

College football (and college basketball as well) is big business. At some major universities football brings in hundreds of thousands of dollars each year in revenue and binds some affluent alumni to the school more tightly than any other single factor. But to achieve and maintain that kind of fiscal bliss, the university must produce a winner or at least it must strive to do so.

To produce teams that win, a university must have exceptionally good players. But the problem all too often is that consummate athletic skills and intellectual prowess do not always coexist in the same person. So to get the young athletes and keep them, schools bend the rules of eligibility that have been set down by the college conferences and the Na-

Andrew David is the author of several books and numerous articles on contemporary affairs.

tional Collegiate Athletic Association (NCAA). Some not only bend the rules but totally distort them.

Not all student-athletes, of course, fall into this category. Many have been quite successful in school and out of it, some becoming Rhodes scholars and Phi Beta Kappa key holders; one college football all-star, Byron White, was appointed to the U.S. Supreme Court, and another, Gerald Ford, served as the nation's president. But many athletes occupy the other end of the scholastic spectrum, and that is where the scandals arise. Some young men are recruited into college without being able to read beyond the fourth-grade level; there have even been cases of functional illiterates attending college on football or basketball scholarships.

How do these student-athletes manage to earn passing grades in courses in otherwise academically respected colleges? There are various ways, and though they are all illegal they are about as commonplace as bootleg whiskey was during the era of Prohibition.

Crackdown on Violators. Many get away with violations, but many do not. Since the NCAA began enforcing athletic rules of conduct in 1952, virtually hundreds of major violations have been cited and acted upon. The university with the dubious distinction of having the most citations is Wichita (Kan.) State, with five during the past three decades. Close behind at four each are Auburn, the University of Oklahoma, Southern Methodist, and Texas A & M. Twenty schools have felt the sting of NCAA censure three times, and 32 others twice. And the schools represent, although not uniformly, all areas of the U.S. Penalties imposed on the censured colleges range from probation to restrictions on recruiting and post-season competition.

Perhaps the most dramatic incident occurred in 1980 when the Pacific Ten conference was reduced to the "Pacific Five," at least as far as post-season or championship play was concerned. Literally half of the Pacific Ten schools (Arizona State, Oregon, Oregon State, UCLA, and Southern California) were punished by their own conference and denied access to all Bowl games (and any revenues from them) because of academic malfeasance. Among the violations were the accepting of bogus credits for athletes from junior colleges or from correspondence or extension courses that were never taken and nonattendance by athletes at courses at their own university—courses for which they received passing grades. *Time* magazine cited the ultimately absurd when it described how one University of Oregon linebacker received full credit for a course in jogging from a community college although he never set one running foot anywhere near that campus. Instead, credit was awarded on the grounds that the

According to legend, the famous Notre Dame coach Knute Rockne (left) played professional football under an assumed name during his college football days.

running he did during football practice at his own school qualified as enough course work.

In one of the most controversial cases in recent years, the Big Ten conference in May placed the University of Illinois on three-year probation, barred the school from participating in any post-season event in any men's sport for two years, and cut off all conference revenue that Illinois would have received for the next two years. The case centred on quarterback David Wilson, who in 1980 set 6 NCAA, 11 Big Ten, and 15 University of Illinois passing records. He became the first quarterback in history to pass for more than 600 yd in one game by totaling 621 yd against Ohio State.

Before the season, however, the Big Ten had ruled that Wilson had only one more year of eligibility (his first year consisted of three plays in one game for a junior college in California before an injury sidelined him) and that he would have to sit out the 1980 season and acquire academic senior status before playing football. Wilson responded with a lawsuit against the NCAA and the Big Ten; the courts granted him an injunction, and he was allowed to play. After the season the Big Ten accused Illinois of backing Wilson in the lawsuit, a charge that the school denied, and of submitting to it an incorrect high school transcript of Wilson's grades. The university admitted the latter charge but maintained that it had been a clerical error that was soon rectified. Subsequently, the courts denied Wilson his bid for another year of eligibility, and he was drafted into the professional National Football League. Relations between Illinois and the Big Ten were strained but later were eased when, in August, the Big Ten reduced the sanctions to a ban of one year on post-season football play and on a share in conference football revenues; other men's sports would not be penalized under the revised sanctions.

An Old Story. Scandals are hardly new to college football. Slush funds and wealthy, overzealous alumni have been around for decades. Over the years there have been the cars that magically materialized for some players, the loans that were never expected to be paid back, the secret bank accounts, the jobs at which athletes never worked but for which they received enviable salaries, and, more recently, the job given to an athlete's father by a generous alumnus.

Even the famous have been involved. Just after World War I many college stars played a little professional football on the side to earn some extra money, even though that was considered the cardinal sin of the day. For example, Knute Rockne played for money under an assumed name for the old Massillon (Ohio) Tigers. And George Gipp, the legend Rockne coached at Notre Dame, also was known to take a different name and participate in various pro games in Illinois, Michigan, and Indiana. In 1922, 16 college stars were caught playing in a professional game in southern Illinois, and the Big Ten declared all of them ineligible for the rest of their college careers.

Today's scandals often have a different set of consequences, however. Some of the young men who are enticed into college for their athletic abilities are led to believe that there will be a lucrative professional career at the end of the line. But few of them make it to the pros, and, instead, many come to an inglorious end with neither that career nor an education, only a one-way ticket back to the city neighbourhoods or small towns from which they came so hopefully four years earlier.

France

France

A republic of Western Europe, France is bounded by the English Channel, Belgium, Luxembourg, West Germany, Switzerland, Italy, the Mediterranean Sea, Monaco, Spain, Andorra, and the Atlantic Ocean. Area: 544,000 sq km (210,040 sq mi), including Corsica. Pop. (1981 est.): 53,957,000. Cap. and largest city: Paris (pop., 1980 est., 2,050,-500). Language: French. Religion: predominantly Roman Catholic. Presidents in 1981, Valéry Giscard d'Estaing and, from May 21, François Mitterrand; premiers, Raymond Barre and, from May 21, Pierre Mauroy.

Domestic Affairs. The year 1981 marked a turning point in the history of modern France. After 23 years during which Charles de Gaulle, Georges Pompidou, and Valéry Giscard d'Estaing had held undisputed power, François Mitterrand (see BIOGRAPHIES) became France's 21st president and its first Socialist president to be elected by universal suffrage. Subsequently, the French people confirmed and expanded their decision in the legislative elections by giving the left a considerable majority in the National Assembly.

With the first round of the presidential election on April 26, the stage was set for a close contest between the two leaders of right and left on the lines of the previous election in 1974. Giscard (28.31%) and François Mitterrand (25.84%) came well ahead of the other eight candidates allowed by the Constitutional Council. The Gaullist candidate, Jacques Chirac, gained 17.99%, while the Communist Party's Georges Marchais finished fourth with 15.34%. The result itself was less surprising than the decline in the Communist vote. Marchais saw his support fall to the lowest level

recorded by the Communists in France since the 1936 Popular Front led by Léon Blum.

As had occurred seven years earlier, the two-hour confrontation on television between Giscard and Mitterrand, held on May 5 in the presence of two independent journalists, was the high point of the presidential election campaign. Afterward, the second round still promised to be close, although unofficial opinion polls at that time gave Mitterrand 51% of the vote. On May 10, according to the official figures released by the Constitutional Council, of 36,398,762 registered voters, the number of votes cast was 31,249,552, of which 30,350,-568 were valid. Of these, Mitterrand gained 15,708,262 (51.76%) and Giscard 14,642,306 (48.24%). The number of abstentions was just over 14%, a little above the 1974 figure.

What might explain this turn of the tide? Among the factors were the world economic crisis, an element of hostility toward the personality of Giscard, and, above all, a massive desire for change. Mitterrand also benefited from the excellent discipline of the Communist electorate, the winning of almost one million votes from Brice Lalonde's Ecologist Party, and the contributions from some who in the first round voted for Chirac. Finally, as a result of the lowering of the voting age, more than two million people under 21 were entitled to vote for president for the first time. All the polls on this topic showed that these young voters were significantly inclined toward the left.

Giscard's personal standing was affected by the continuing controversies of the Bokassa affair and the de Broglie case. In March Giscard finally announced that the diamonds given to him by Bokassa, the former emperor of the Central African Empire, had been sold and the proceeds sent to charities in that country. The investigations into the murder of Prince Jean de Broglie (December

François Mitterrand (right), the new president of France, is escorted by former president Valéry Giscard d'Estaing after swearing-in ceremonies in the Elysée Palace.

1976), however, were not so easily dismissed. An inquiry into the involvement of Michel Poniatowski, former minister of the interior and Giscard's close aide, found that there were no grounds for impeaching Poniatowski; but in November, during the trial of the four charged with the murder, the judge accused him, along with several senior police officers, of withholding evidence.

On May 21 Mitterrand officially took up his post as president of the republic at the Élysée Palace. Before continuing with the traditional round of ceremonial visits to the Arc de Triomphe, the Panthéon, and the Hôtel de Ville, Mitterrand appointed Pierre Mauroy (see BIOGRAPHIES) as premier. The next day Mauroy formed a government reflecting the different tendencies and age groups in the Socialist Party (PS). The resulting Cabinet also included Michel Jobert, leader of the Democratic Movement (MD), and three representatives of the Left Radicals (MRG). There were no Communists, but three new ministries had significant titles — national solidarity, leisure, and the sea — while the Ministry of Foreign Affairs (on the Quay d'Orsay) became the Ministry of Foreign Relations. The Cabinet included six women, compared with three in the outgoing Cabinet, and in all there were 5 ministers of state, 25 ministers, and 12 secretaries of state. This total of 42 ministers was two more than in outgoing premier Raymond Barre's government.

The following were the main officeholders in the new government: premier, Pierre Mauroy (PS); ministers of state: interior and decentralization, Gaston Defferre (PS); national solidarity, Nicole Questiaux (PS; see BIOGRAPHIES); foreign trade, Michel Jobert (MD); planning and development, Michel Rocard (PS); research and technology, Jean-Pierre Chevènement (PS); ministers-delegate to the premier: women's rights, Yvette Roudy (PS); relations with Parliament, André Labarrère (PS); ministers and ministers-delegate: justice, Maurice Faure (MRG); foreign relations, Claude Cheysson (PS; see BIOGRAPHIES); European affairs, André Chandernagor (PS); cooperation, Jean-Pierre Cot (PS); defense, Charles Hernu (PS); economy and finance, Jacques Delors (PS); budget,

Laurent Fabius (PS); education, Alain Savary (PS); agriculture, Edith Cresson (PS); industry, Pierre Joxe (PS); trade and crafts, André Delelis (PS); labour, Jean Auroux (PS); equipment and transport, Louis Mermaz (PS); health, Edmond Hervé (PS); leisure, André Henry (PS); youth and sport, Edwige Avice (PS); culture, Jack Lang (PS); communications, Georges Fillioud (PS); housing, Roger Quilliot (PS); environment, Michel Crépeau (MRG); sea, Louis Le Pensec (PS); postal services, Louis Mexandeau (PS); veterans, Jean Laurain (PS).

Under bills published in the *Journal Officiel* on May 23, the National Assembly was dissolved and the electors called to vote on June 14 and 21. The first round of these legislative elections went well beyond a simple confirmation of the poll on May 10 for President Mitterrand. Despite a decline in the Communist Party (PC) vote, the voters gave the PS, and with it the whole of the left, electoral support without precedent under the Fifth Republic. This ballot filled 156 of the 491 seats, but already the Socialist landslide was evident in the rise of the PS vote from 22.6% in the first round of the 1978 elections to 37.51% in 1981, giving it 9,432,-362 votes out of the total of 25,141,190 cast. On the other hand, the PC was in a precarious situation: despite its 4,065,540 votes, it had lost 6% of the total vote since 1978 and, at 16.17% of the total poll, stood to lose half its seats in the Assembly. The two major parties of the outgoing "majority" (the Gaullist Rassemblement pour la République, or RPR, and the Giscardian Union pour la Démocratie Française, or UDF) had fallen back significantly in comparison with 1978.

The second round of the legislative elections brought a resounding confirmation of the PS victory. The Socialists gained ground throughout the country at the expense of almost all other parties, which, in broad terms, lost half their seats. In the new 491-seat National Assembly, the PS, even without its left-wing allies, emerged with an absolute majority. (See POLITICAL PARTIES.) The next day, in accordance with tradition, Mauroy handed in the resignation of his government to the president, who called on him to form the second

---

Iranian dissidents hijacked a gunboat in Cadiz, Spain, that had been sold to Iran by France. The hijackers returned the boat, which was on its way to join the Iranian Navy, to French waters. After negotiations, France granted the hijackers political asylum.

government in the seven-year presidential term of office.

The new Cabinet met on June 24. Like the previous one, it included five ministers of state, but Nicole Questiaux, though she remained minister of national solidarity, gave up her place as minister of state to the Communist Charles Fiterman, who took over the Ministry of Transport from Louis Mermaz; the latter had been chosen as president of the National Assembly. The three other PC members appointed to the Cabinet were Anicet le Pors (civil service and administrative reform), Jack Ralite (health), and Marcel Rigout (professional training). Pierre Dreyfus (PS), former Renault director, replaced Pierre Joxe in the Ministry of Industry, reinforcing the reformist tendency, and Robert Badinter (PS) took over from Maurice Faure as minister of justice, a move that seemed to foreshadow a rapid abolition of the death penalty.

Thus, 34 years after its exclusion from government, the Communist Party once more had a hand on the reins of power. While it was true that this "historic event" did not alter the fact that the Socialist Party had extensively supplanted the Communist Party as the first party of the left, there were signs of unfavourable reaction outside France, especially in the U.S.

Once the country had given him "the means for action on the broadest base," Mauroy lost no time in getting the promised "reforms" under way as soon as Parliament returned for its extraordinary summer session. Under the president's right of pardon passed on July 14, 4,775 prisoners, most with little time remaining in their sentences, were freed. After three years of arduous negotiations between employers and unions, an agreement was reached on the length of the workweek, 39 hours instead of 40, with a fifth week of paid vacation. But the Communist Confédération Général du Travail (CGT) trade union federation would not sign the agreement.

Changes of previously unprecedented scope

affected some 60 prefectures in a reshuffle that allowed the government to replace most of the prefects. The directors of the nationalized railways and Paris transport systems were also replaced. Next it was the turn of university rectors, half the regional directors of education being moved in favour of others more acceptable to the government. The directors of French broadcasting were also replaced, though the new directors were not considered militant Socialists. At the Foreign Ministry there was the biggest reshuffle since the end of World War II, with noncareer diplomats being brought into key posts. In September the National Assembly by a vote of 329 to 129 passed the whole of the draft bill on decentralization, which was described as the major theme of the presidential term. The aim of this bill was to give increased rights and freedoms to local government.

In this tide of change the National Assembly abolished the death penalty. It also gave massive approval to the government's energy program, which allowed for six new nuclear power plants to be built rather than the nine planned by the previous administration. After 13 days of debate the draft bill on nationalization of industry, another issue around which the left had rallied, was passed on its first reading by a comfortable majority. It affected five major industrial groups—Compagnie Générale d'Électricité, Saint-Gobain-Pont-à-Mousson, Pechiney-Ugine-Kuhlmann, Rhône-Poulenc, and Thomson-Brandt—as well as most of the country's major private banks and two finance companies. However, the terms of compensation for the affected stockholders raised problems.

The draft budget for 1982 showed a deficit of nearly Fr 100 billion, or 2.6% of gross national product; state expenditure was to grow by 27.6% over the original budget for 1981. Bitter conflict was expected over the creation of a tax on wealth, but this did not materialize, and a very limited wealth tax was approved by the Assembly at the end of October. The budget minister announced

that as of October 1 there would be an end to the anonymity that had been allowed in regard to transactions in gold. On October 4 France learned that its currency had been devalued within the European Monetary System.

Despite these measures, the social and economic situation continued to worsen. The annual rate of inflation was approaching 15%, compared with 5.5% in West Germany and 9% in the U.S. At the end of October the number of unemployed passed the two million mark, and the balance of trade over the first nine months of the year showed a deficit of nearly Fr 40 billion. Numerous strikes, particularly in the Renault and Peugeot automobile plants and among government workers, demonstrated union dissatisfaction.

Foreign Affairs. In his first press conference during his term of office, in September, President Mitterrand concentrated on foreign policy, an area held by his predecessors to be the particular preserve of the presidency. He adopted Gaullist accents to declare, clearly and forcefully, "France rejects all interdictions," and to denounce the "double hegemony" of the two superpowers.

On Middle East policy, he declared that Israel had an indefeasible right to exist and that the Palestinians had the same right to build whatever state structures they chose. On the questions of Poland, Afghanistan, and nuclear missiles in Europe, Mitterrand adopted positions very close to those of the U.S., West Germany, and the U.K. In September he visited Saudi Arabia, the country that supplied France with more than half of its oil. The Saudi Arabian plan for peace in the Middle East, according to France, constituted a "useful point of departure" for negotiations.

European affairs were marked chiefly by the sixth Franco-British summit in September, the first since Mitterrand's election to the presidency. It was, however, the fourth time that the president had met Prime Minister Margaret Thatcher. The previous meetings had taken place in June at the European Community summit in Luxembourg, in July at the summit of the major industrialized countries in Canada, and in London on the occasion of Prince Charles's wedding. The atmosphere at those meetings was friendly, and the coincidence of views was especially evident in the field of East-West relations. The two leaders agreed that Western forces had to be in a position to maintain the strategic and tactical balance in relation to the Soviet bloc before discussions could be started with the U.S.S.R. on the disarmament process. In July Mitterrand celebrated the link between France and West Germany with Chancellor Helmut Schmidt, whom he met in Bonn at the 38th Franco-German summit.

On October 18–19, Mitterrand met U.S. Pres. Ronald Reagan in Yorktown, Va., to mark the bicentennial of the battle there in which the French helped the Americans to gain a decisive victory over the British troops in the U.S. war of independence. From Mexico, where he spoke with Pres. José López Portillo, Mitterrand launched a message of hope to all those struggling for freedom in the world. He subsequently took part in the North-South summit at Cancún, Mexico.

The eighth Franco-African summit, the first since Mitterrand took office, was held in France at the start of November. The French expressed a desire to work out a new style of relations with Africa. In December Mitterrand's two-day visit to Algeria was much publicized as marking a new era of friendly relations between the two countries.

(JEAN KNECHT)

See also Dependent States.

Gabon

Gabon

A republic of western equatorial Africa, Gabon is bounded by Equatorial Guinea, Cameroon, the Congo, and the Atlantic Ocean. Area: 267,667 sq km (103,347 sq mi). Pop. (1979 est.): 1.1 million. Cap. and largest city: Libreville (pop., 1978 est., 225,200). Language: French and Bantu dialects. Religion: traditional tribal beliefs; Christian minority. President in 1981, Omar Bongo; premier, Léon Mébiame.

During 1981 some persons close to the previous French administration attempted to create discord between Pres. Omar Bongo and French Pres. François Mitterrand. President Bongo was named in connection with the murder in France in October 1979 of Robert Luong, a Vietnamese who reputedly had been his wife's lover; in September 1981 he denounced what he called the "slanderous campaign against himself and his regime" in the French press.

Nevertheless, relations with France's new Socialist government remained good. At Libreville in August the foundations were laid for France's decision to support Pres. Goukouni Oueddei of Chad in the internal conflict there. Although in September Bongo rejected the proposal to send an inter-

GABON

Education. (1978–79) Primary, pupils 141,569, teachers 3,088; secondary, pupils 20,344, teachers 1,000; vocational, pupils 3,405, teachers 256; teacher training, students 2,008, teachers 108; higher, students 1,247, teaching staff 235.

Finance. Monetary unit: CFA franc, with (Sept. 21, 1981) a parity of CFA Fr 50 to the French franc (free rate of CFA Fr 265 = U.S. $1; CFA Fr 491 = £1 sterling). Budget (1981 est.): revenue CFA Fr 389.5 billion; expenditure CFA Fr 299.9 billion.

Foreign Trade. Imports (1978) c. CFA Fr 139 billion; exports (1979) CFA Fr 368 billion. Import sources: France 55%; U.S. 6%. Export destinations (1978): France 25%; U.S. 20%; Argentina 11%; Brazil 8%; Gibraltar 8%; West Germany 6%; Chile 5%. Main exports (1978): crude oil 72%; manganese ore 10%; uranium and thorium ores 8%; timber 6%.

Transport and Communications. Roads (1979) 7,082 km. Motor vehicles in use (1976): passenger c. 17,400; commercial (including buses) c. 12,700. Railways (1979) c. 185 km. Air traffic (1980): c. 374 million passenger-km; freight c. 27.3 million net ton-km. Telephones (Jan. 1980) 11,600. Radio receivers (Dec. 1977) 95,000. Television receivers (Dec. 1977) 9,000.

Agriculture. Production (in 000; metric tons; 1979): cassava c. 110; corn c. 8; peanuts c. 7; bananas c. 8; plantains c. 63; palm oil c. 3; cocoa c. 4; timber (cu m) c. 2,297. Livestock (in 000; 1979): cattle c. 3; pigs c. 6; sheep c. 100; goats c. 90.

Industry. Production (in 000; metric tons; 1980): crude oil 9,881; natural gas (cu m) 70,000; uranium (1979) 1.1; manganese ore (metal content; 1979) c. 1,000; petroleum products (1978) 1,370; electricity (kw-hr; 1978) 513,000.

Pres. Omar Bongo of Gabon (right) was welcomed by French Pres. François Mitterrand when Bongo visited France in July.

African peacekeeping force to Chad, at the Franco-African summit in Paris on November 3–4 he promised logistic support for the transport of the force's first units. Plans for an economic grouping of 11 central African states, to include Chad, were announced at Libreville in December.

In May relations with Cameroon were clouded by violent demonstrations in Libreville and Port-Gentil against Cameroon nationals, several thousand of whom were evacuated by air with French assistance. The demonstrations were triggered by strife that had occurred when a Gabonese soccer team visited Cameroon.   (PHILIPPE DECRAENE)

The Gambia

Gambia, The

A small republic and member of the Commonwealth, The Gambia extends from the Atlantic Ocean along the lower Gambia River in West Africa and is surrounded by Senegal. Area: 10,690 sq km (4,127 sq mi). Pop. (1981 est.): 618,000, including (1973) Malinke 37.7%; Fulani 16.2%; Wolof 14%; Dyola 8.5%; Soninke 7.8%; others 15.8%. Cap. and largest city: Banjul (pop., 1980 est., 47,700). Language: English (official). Religion: predominantly Muslim. President in 1981, Sir Dawda Jawara.

Economic decline provided the backdrop to the July 1981 coup attempt in The Gambia. As a result

GAMBIA, THE
Education. (1978–79) Primary, pupils 32,196, teachers 1,241; secondary, pupils 7,464, teachers 416; vocational (1977–78), pupils 401, teachers 34; teacher training, students 231, teachers 27.
Finance. Monetary unit: dalasi, with (Sept. 21, 1981) a free rate of 2.16 dalasis to U.S. $1 (par value of 4 dalasis = £1 sterling). Budget (1979–80 est.): revenue 76,531,000 dalasis; expenditure 72,495,000 dalasis.
Foreign Trade. (1980) Imports 282,440,000 dalasis; exports 54,860,000 dalasis. Import sources (1979): U.K. 25%; China 13%; France 9%; West Germany 8%; The Netherlands 6%; U.S. 5%. Export destinations (1979): The Netherlands 22%; U.K. 14%; Italy 14%; Switzerland 13%; France 7%; Portugal 7%; Belgium-Luxembourg 6%. Main exports: peanuts and byproducts 54%.

of adverse weather conditions, the peanut (groundnut) crop—providing 80% of exports—fell to 45,000 metric tons, the lowest harvest in 30 years. At the same time, tourism declined, and gross domestic product fell by an estimated 3.2%.

While Pres. Sir Dawda Jawara (see BIOGRAPHIES) was in the U.K. for the royal wedding, an attempted coup under the leadership of socialist politician Kukli Samba Sanyang was launched on July 30. The president obtained Senegalese military intervention and the rebellion was put down, but not before a number of lives had been lost and The Gambia's reputation for stability had been shattered.

In the aftermath the question of some form of union with Senegal was inevitably raised. President Jawara held talks with Senegal's Pres. Abdou Diouf (see BIOGRAPHIES) in August, and a treaty to form a confederation of the two countries under the name of Senegambia was signed by both presidents on December 17. Each country, however, was to retain its sovereignty.   (GUY ARNOLD)

Gambling

On Oct. 5, 1981, a magistrates' court in Great Britain withdrew the gambling licenses for two of the London casinos owned by the U.S. firm Playboy Enterprises Inc. The court took the action after ruling that the casinos had violated British gaming laws. Playboy, which had operated casinos in the U.K. since 1966, at first planned to appeal but on November 3 announced that it would sell all of its gambling operations in Britain to the British firm Trident Television Ltd. In the fiscal year ended June 30, 1981, Playboy earned pretax profits of $38.8 million from its three London casinos.

Clifford Perlman and his brother Stuart, chairman and vice-chairman, respectively, of Caesar's World Inc., agreed in October to resign so that the firm's Boardwalk Regency Hotel in Atlantic City, N.J., could obtain a casino license. In 1980 the New Jersey Control Commission determined that the two men had ties to organized crime.

Three new casinos opened in Atlantic City during 1981 to bring the total number of legal operations in that city to nine. Although the casinos enjoyed good business during the summer, most expected that 1981 would be the first money-losing year for Atlantic City's gaming industry.

In the largest known lottery payoff, a Manhattan maintenance worker won $5 million in the New York state lottery in November. Despite the recession, state lotteries were growing rapidly, with an estimated $3.6 billion bet during 1981.

Gambling continued during 1981 to be one of the major leisure activities in the United Kingdom. During 1980 nearly £12,000 million was bet, principally on horse and dog racing, football pools, bingo, slot machines, lotteries, and in casinos. The most popular form of gambling in terms of the number of participants was football (soccer) pool betting, on which approximately 15 million people staked some £389 million. Casino gambling, largely attracting the wealthy, declined somewhat in popularity but still accounted for more than half

Victory was sweet as Stu Ungar raked in his winnings after he won the World Series of Poker competition in Las Vegas, Nevada, in May.

the total amount of money staked during the year.

In cash terms the overall level of betting was about the same as for the previous year, but there were considerable variations from one form of gambling to another. Bookmakers, football pools, and gaming machines fared the best, while casino gambling and lotteries both declined considerably. Insofar as casinos are concerned, this may have been attributable in some measure to the high value of sterling and the consequent fall in the popularity of Britain as a tourist attraction.

During 1981 casino gambling continued to give cause for concern to law enforcement authorities. Two major public companies (including Playboy Enterprises) departed from the casino gambling scene in 1981, in each case following police raids that revealed malpractices in the conduct of their London casinos. In all, this resulted in the closing of four London casinos plus one in the provinces and the transfer to new ownership of 3 London and 15 provincial clubs.

In the bingo industry there was some concern over the continuing slight decline in the number of licensed clubs and in the number of persons playing the game. Nevertheless, the amount of money staked continued to rise, the increase being more or less in line with the level of inflation.

(DAVID R. CALHOUN; GBGB)

See also Equestrian Sports.

Games and Toys

The major international toy fairs of 1981 were a disappointment to trade buyers, who found little that was new but saw many basic products that had been refurbished. Clearly, toy manufacturers in the U.S., Europe, and the Far East had similar views about prospects for 1981 and were playing it

safe. A U.S. commentator who visited the Nürnberg (West Germany) International Toy Fair noted that a symptom of European caution was the large number of 1979 U.S. products that had been licensed to European manufacturers eager to cut down on research and development costs by using existing designs. At the New York Toy Fair, too, it was observed that many well-known producers had been content to repackage items that had sold well rather than venture into new fields.

Toy manufacturers suffer more than most from having successful items copied. Nowhere was this more evident than in the case of the Rubik's Cube, without doubt the best-selling toy in the world in 1981. The intriguing puzzle, many millions of which were sold internationally, was the brainchild of a Hungarian professor, Erno Rubik. The inventor sold the design rights to Politechnijka Company of Hungary, after which the firm and Rubik sold manufacturing licenses to a number of toymakers in different parts of the world. Patent rights were applied for in some countries, but this failed to deter manufacturers in the Far East, principally in Taiwan, from turning out cheap copies of the product at the rate of 100,000 a day. Indicative of the widespread interest in Rubik's Cube was the fact that a 13-year-old London schoolboy, Patrick Bossert, wrote a 112-page book entitled *You Can Do the Cube*, which sold 750,000 copies in Britain and Europe. In the U.S. it earned for its author the distinction of being the youngest person ever to have a book included on the *New York Times* paperback best-seller list.

Microprocessor-based toys continued to grow as a category during 1981, but the extraordinary rate of increase experienced in 1979–80 leveled off. The original excess of demand over supply led to considerable overstocking in the U.S. and Europe, and by the end of 1980 consumers could sometimes buy

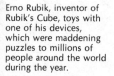

Erno Rubik, inventor of Rubik's Cube, toys with one of his devices, which were maddening puzzles to millions of people around the world during the year.

GYULA TOTH—INTERFOTO MTI/PICTORIAL PARADE

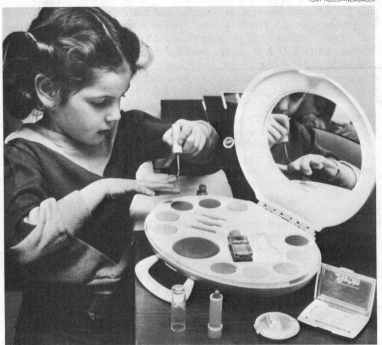

Play cosmetics for young girls were among the year's most popular toys in the U.S.

the British subsidiary of General Mills. On the retail side, in September the world's largest toy shop, Hamleys of Regent Street, London, moved into new premises some two-thirds larger.

The International Committee of Toy Industries, embracing the national toy-manufacturing associations of 11 leading toy-producing countries, held its annual meeting in April in San Diego, Calif. The committee, which monitors impending government safety and other regulations affecting toymaking in all countries, decided to set up a secretariat in London to serve as a focal point for the reception and dissemination of information relevant to the toy industry.

(THEODORE V. THOMAS)

Gardening

Gypsy moths defoliated millions of acres of trees in the U.S. from Maine to Maryland during the spring and summer of 1981, according to the Animal and Plant Health Inspection Service of the U.S. Department of Agriculture (USDA). They also did damage in portions of six previously unaffected states: Arkansas, California, Nebraska, Oregon, Washington, and West Virginia. Six years of testing in Massachusetts, Pennsylvania, and Maryland indicated that use of the insect's own sex pheromone (attractant) effectively reduced mating, but the method was most successful in areas with a low density of moths. Ornamental pine trees in at least 28 states were damaged by pinewood nematodes, which in 1978 killed over eight million pines in Japan. According to USDA nematologists, trees attacked in the spring usually wilt and die by late summer. The appearance of the Mediterranean fruit fly near the major fruit- and vegetable-growing areas of California led to a political struggle over the question of spraying. (See LIFE SCIENCES: *Entomology.*) In Britain damage to apples and pears by starlings and blue tits was unusually severe. The good colour of new apple cultivars and a dry period in late summer were believed to be contributory factors.

Four roses were chosen as All-America Rose Selections for 1982: French Lace, hybridized by William Warriner of Jackson & Perkins, an ivory white floribunda with a light, spicy fragrance; Shreveport, hybridized by Reimer Kordes, Sparrieshoop Holstein, West Germany, a grandiflora with three- to four-inch blooms varying from orange to salmon to coral; Mon Cheri, hybridized by Jack Christensen of Armstrong Nurseries, a hybrid tea bearing deep red blooms in full sunlight with pink highlights in the most shaded areas; and Brandy, a hybrid tea with blooms that age from a rich golden brandy colour to creamy apricot. Brandy was the result of a cross by Herbert Swim with seedlings grown by Armstrong, and the seedling that won the award was picked by Christensen. Swim and Christensen also created a new rose for Armstrong named First Lady Nancy, a light yellow bloom with soft pink borders and highlights, bushes of which were sent to the White House garden.

In Britain the Royal National Rose Society's

electronic toys at bargain-basement rates. The inevitable result was a pause for reassessment by manufacturers, some of whom left the field while others gave less emphasis to it. Electronic toys would undoubtedly continue to grow as a category, but supply and demand would be more in balance than in the two preceding years.

With little girls losing their traditional little-girl interests sooner than their mothers and grandmothers did, and with clothes and records becoming ever more appealing, toymakers strove to evolve products that would capture the female child's interest. They appeared to have found a possible answer with fun makeup and play cosmetics, for at the 1981 New York Toy Fair cosmetics for little girls were in abundance. Fears were expressed about the long-term dangers of skin disease and allergies if the toy cosmetics should prove to be unsafe, but U.S. producers claimed that their products were safe and nontoxic.

In the U.K. the year opened on a sombre note for the toy industry. Twelve months after the demise of Dunbee-Comtex-Marx Ltd., Airfix Industries, which had bank loans of £17 million, failed to convince its bankers that it had reasonable prospects of recovery and in January called in the receivers. Airfix's problems stemmed in large part from its inability to digest its 1971 acquisition of Meccano Ltd., a subsidiary of the failed Lines Bros. The old-fashioned Meccano factory at Liverpool occupied much management time that should have been devoted to other areas of the Airfix group. The factory was finally closed late in 1979, but protracted wranglings with the 900 laid-off employees delayed arrangements that management was making for the production of Meccano products elsewhere. Airfix Industries' toy division was subsequently purchased by General Mills, Inc., and the Airfix, Dinky Toys, and Meccano lines were added to those marketed by Palitoy,

President's International Trophy and a gold medal were awarded to Anna Ford, a deep orange dwarf or short floribunda raised by R. Harkness & Co. Ltd. Chosen for 1982 awards at the Fleuroselect (All Europe) Seed Trials were the geranium Red Elite (Goldsmiths Seeds); two carnations, Telstar Mixed (Takii & Co.) and Scarlet Luminette (Sakata); the gazania Mini Star Yellow (Ernst Benary); the marigolds Yellow Jacket (Denholm) and Hybrida Florence (Royal Sluis); and the zinnia Dasher Scarlet (Bodger Seed Co.). All-America Selections bronze medals were won by the squashes Jerry Golden Acorn and Peter Pan, the zinnias Small World Cherry and Fantastic Light Pink, and the carnation Scarlet Luminette.

The USDA Agricultural Research Service developed a new white potato, Lemhi Russet, said to outyield Russet Burbank, currently the most widely grown potato in the U.S, by 34%. It is also higher in vitamin C, more resistant to malformation, and equally resistant to early blight and *Verticillium* blight. Using breeding material from Scandinavia and Canada, the Scottish Crop Research Institute raised three new black currant cultivars, Ben Lomond, Ben Nevis, and Ben More, which were considered better than those now being grown commercially. Selection was made on the basis of late flowering to escape spring frost, tolerance to low temperatures at flowering time, yield, juice quality, and habit of growth. Growing conditions in Britain during 1981 were highly favourable for the production of giant leeks and onions; a fine-quality onion weighing 3.72 kg (8 lb 3¼ oz) was believed to have broken all records.

Research at the University of Rhode Island's College of Resource Development indicated that it

Research conducted at the University of Rhode Island indicated that New Englanders can grow their own vegetables even during the winter provided they construct a solar greenhouse as shown.

would be feasible for a homeowner even in New England to install a solar greenhouse next to his home to grow vegetables during cold weather. The greenhouse could also store extra heat, probably enough to heat the house until mid-November and from mid-March on. In commercial greenhouses, polycarbonate was being used as a glass substitute. The material is 200 times stronger than glass, provides 33 to 45% better insulation, and is light in weight so that the need for glazing bars and structural members is cut to a minimum. Polycarbonate absorbs infrared rays but not the growth-promoting ultraviolet rays.

(J. G. SCOTT MARSHALL; TOM STEVENSON)

See also Agriculture and Food Supplies; Environment; Life Sciences.
[355.C.2–3; 731.B.1]

German Democratic Republic

A country of central Europe, Germany was partitioned after World War II into the Federal Republic of Germany (Bundesrepublik Deutschland; West Germany) and the German Democratic Republic (Deutsche Demokratische Republik; East Germany), with a special provisional regime for Berlin. East Germany is bordered by the Baltic Sea, Poland, Czechoslovakia, and West Germany. Area: 108,325 sq km (41,825 sq mi). Pop. (1981 est.): 16,759,000. Cap. and largest city: East Berlin (pop., 1980 est., 1,140,300). Language: German. Religion (1969 est.): Protestant 80%; Roman Catholic 10%. General secretary of the Socialist Unity (Communist) Party and chairman of the Council of State in 1981, Erich Honecker; chairman of the Council of Ministers (premier), Willi Stoph.

In 1981 the citizens of East Germany were assured by their leaders that, despite the international economic recession, their living standards would increase. At the conference of the Socialist Unity (Communist) Party in April, Premier Willi Stoph promised that more and better quality consumer goods would be available and that basic food prices and rents would remain low. In fact, East Germany was facing major problems. State subsidies to hold down consumer prices were expected to reach an annual rate of nearly M 300 billion by 1986. Imported energy was using up precious foreign currency. East Germany was called upon to step up financial aid to Poland, and the U.S.S.R. expected the East Germans to make a still bigger contribution to Warsaw Pact defenses.

East Germany's planners decreed that trade with Western countries must be increased in order to pay for the import of new technologies. Western experts, however, believed the chances of a major East German trade expansion were limited; the country's current volume of trade could be maintained only by lowering prices. By concentrating on the bright side, the party leadership was implying to the public that Poland's economic ills would not be allowed to spread to East Germany. The party conference was a demonstration that the East German rulers had the situation well under con-

German Democratic Republic

UPI

During a ceremony marking the 20th anniversary of the Berlin Wall, members of the Italian-German Society placed a wreath at a memorial for Peter Fechter, who was shot and killed trying to escape East Berlin in 1962.

award of an honorary doctorate of law to the visitor for his work "in the cause of peace." However, the West Germans comforted themselves by saying that these were expressions of Japanese regard for the Germans generally.

East Germany weighed in heavily on the side of the Soviet Union in the international debate over medium-range nuclear missiles. The East German case was that the U.S. had been forced to the negotiating table by the pressure of world opinion. The government in East Berlin argued that NATO's concept of a "zero option" on medium-range nuclear weapons in Europe was quite different from most people's understanding of the term. The aim of the U.S. was to cause the Soviet Union to dismantle its land-based SS-4/5 and SS-20 missiles without replacing them, while the U.S. dispensed solely with the planned deployment of land-based Pershing II and cruise missiles in Western Europe. This, said the East Germans, would still leave Western Europe with some 700 U.S. forward-based (*i.e.*, air-launched) systems.

Among East German citizens there was considerable sympathy for the West German peace movement, especially for suggestions that Europe should be declared a nuclear-free zone. In an open letter to Soviet Pres. Leonid Brezhnev during his visit to Bonn in November, the East German dissident Robert Havemann wrote that, 36 years after World War II, it was urgently necessary to conclude peace treaties and withdraw "occupying troops" from both parts of Germany. The position of West Berlin had to be secured, he added, and the superpowers had to guarantee that an aggressive military potential would never again be created in Germany. "How we Germans then solve our own national question would be a matter for us. The solution would certainly not be more frightening than the risk of nuclear war."

Despite the tensions in East-West relations, both German states seemed anxious to stay on reasonably good terms. The long-discussed summit meeting between Honecker and West German Chancellor Helmut Schmidt was held December 11–13 near Biesenthal, East Germany. In a luncheon speech Honecker emphasized that the relationship between the two Germanys would be affected by NATO's nuclear rearmament plans. Schmidt agreed that the two countries had a special role to play in working for peace within their respective alliances

trol. Although they had expressed themselves in favour of a tough line against Polish dissidence, there was very little mention of Poland at the conference.

The East German Communist leader, Erich Honecker, paid a state visit to Japan in May. The invitation, long awaited, proved to be worth waiting for. There was business to be done—Honecker took an impressive shopping list with him—and agreements required signature. More important for Honecker, however, the visit was a political event, representing East Germany's acceptance in the capitalist world. Honecker spent a considerable amount of money in Japan, mostly on heavy industrial plant and technological equipment. The East Germans also bought 10,000 Japanese cars to help fill a gap in deliveries of Soviet models. Trade between the two countries flourished, and the East Germans were probably happy to reduce their dependence on their West German neighbours. On the other side, with memories of the Soviet intervention in Afghanistan fading, Japan was trying to build up trade with the Council for Mutual Economic Assistance (Comecon) countries, and it hoped Honecker would put in a good word with the U.S.S.R. on its behalf. The West Germans were somewhat jealous about Honecker's elaborate reception, and a few eyebrows were raised at the

---

GERMAN DEMOCRATIC REPUBLIC

Education. (1979) Primary, pupils 1,320,500; secondary, pupils 1,102,862; primary and secondary, teachers 114,622; vocational, pupils 462,236, teachers (1978) 16,259; higher (including teacher training), students 298,633.

Finance. Monetary unit: Mark of Deutsche Demokratische Republik, with (Sept. 21, 1981) a free rate of M 2.23 to U.S. $1 (M 4.14 = £1 sterling). Budget (1979 est.): revenue M 140,633,000,000; expenditure M 148,223,000,000. Net material product (at 1975 prices; 1979) M 166.6 billion.

Foreign Trade. (1979) Imports M 56,425,000,-000; exports M 52,420,000,000. Import sources: U.S.S.R. *c.* 36%; Czechoslovakia *c.* 7%; Poland *c.* 7%; West Germany *c.* 6%; Hungary *c.* 6%. Export destinations: U.S.S.R. *c.* 36%; Czechoslovakia *c.* 9%; Poland *c.* 9%; West Germany *c.* 6%; Hungary *c.* 6%.

Main exports (1975): machinery 37%; transport equipment 12% (ships 5%); chemicals; textiles.

Transport and Communications. Roads (1979) *c.* 118,995 km (including 1,675 km autobahns). Motor vehicles in use (1979): passenger 2,532,941; commercial 231,228. Railways: (1979) 14,164 km (including 1,621 km electrified); traffic (1980) 23,120,000,000 passenger-km, freight 56,490,-000,000 net ton-km. Air traffic (1979): 1,848,000,000 passenger-km; freight 67.3 million net ton-km. Navigable inland waterways in regular use (1979) 2,302 km; goods traffic 1,933,000,000 ton-km. Shipping (1980): merchant vessels 100 gross tons and over 451; gross tonnage 1,532,197. Telephones (Jan. 1980) 3,071,500. Radio licenses (Dec. 1978) 6,289,-000. Television licenses (Dec. 1979) 5,634,000.

Agriculture. Production (in 000; metric tons; 1980): wheat *c.* 3,600; barley *c.* 3,528; rye *c.* 1,900; oats *c.* 570; potatoes *c.* 8,568; sugar, raw value *c.* 770; cabbages (1979) 483; rapeseed *c.* 280; apples *c.* 600; pork *c.* 1,152; beef and veal *c.* 385; fish catch (1979) *c.* 224. Livestock (in 000; Dec. 1979): cattle 5,596; sheep 1,979; pigs 12,132; goats 25; poultry 51,444.

Industry. Index of production (1975 = 100; 1980) 127. Production (in 000; metric tons; 1980): lignite 258,000; electricity (kw-hr) 98,800,000; iron ore (39% metal content) 60; pig iron 2,460; crude steel 7,308; cement 12,440; sulfuric acid (1979) 952; petroleum products (1978) 19,455; fertilizers (nutrient content; 1979) nitrogenous 875, phosphate 411, potash 3,395; synthetic rubber (1978) 155; man-made fibres (1978) 291; passenger cars (units) 177; commercial vehicles (units) 37.

but noted their limited ability to influence events. Schmidt also said inter-German relations had been harmed by East German moves to limit the number of West German visitors.

(NORMAN CROSSLAND)

Germany, Federal Republic of

A country of central Europe, Germany was partitioned after World War II into the Federal Republic of Germany (Bundesrepublik Deutschland; West Germany) and the German Democratic Republic (Deutsche Demokratische Republik; East Germany), with a special provisional regime for Berlin. West Germany is bordered by Denmark, The Netherlands, Belgium, Luxembourg, France, Switzerland, Austria, Czechoslovakia, East Germany, and the North Sea. Area: 248,667 sq km (96,011 sq mi). Pop. (1981 est.): 61,658,000. Provisional cap.: Bonn (pop., 1980 est., 287,100). Largest city: Hamburg (pop., 1980 est., 1,648,800). (West Berlin, which is an enclave within East Germany, had a population of 1,898,900 in 1980.) Language: German. Religion (1970): Protestant 49%; Roman Catholic 44.6%; Jewish 0.05%. President in 1981, Karl Carstens; chancellor, Helmut Schmidt.

The international economic recession began to bite hard in West Germany in 1981. Unemployment rose sharply to 1,370,000 by the end of October, and a series of economic measures were introduced to balance the 1982 budget. Although the popularity of Chancellor Helmut Schmidt remained high, the fortunes of his Social Democratic Party (SPD) slumped. The peace movement, campaigning against nuclear missiles, became a major political factor.

Domestic Affairs. From the beginning of 1981, deep dissension within the SPD raised doubts about the stability of Schmidt's coalition government and its chances of survival in the longer term. Disagreements, kept under control by the party's traditional sense of discipline, suddenly burst into the open. Schmidt was at odds with

numerous factions on a range of vital issues, among them the deployment of NATO theatre nuclear weapons, the level of defense spending generally, and the development of atomic energy.

Paradoxically, it was partly the coalition's impressive performance in the 1980 federal elections that brought the discontent to the surface. In October 1980 the electorate voted emphatically for Schmidt's return but showed itself far less enthusiastic about his party. The increase in the coalition's majority was won almost entirely by the junior partner, the Free Democratic Party (FDP). Consequently, the FDP began the new term exercising greater influence on government policy. Some left-wing Social Democrats saw West Germany, under this coalition, knuckling under to the U.S. Schmidt, working in close cooperation with the FDP leader and foreign minister, Hans-Dietrich Genscher, was charged with abandoning party principles.

It was estimated that, of the 218 SPD deputies, about 60 could fairly be described as left wing. They could not, however, be dubbed left wing on all counts. An indication of their influence was provided in January when 24 of them introduced a motion to cut the defense budget by DM 1 billion in favour of development aid. But the left-wing label could not be pinned on all those Social Democrats who were overtly challenging some of the government's policies. Others had misgivings about atomic energy or rejected the idea that West Germany should export Leopard II tanks to Saudi Arabia.

The West Berlin state election on May 10 was a disaster for the SPD. Its share of the poll fell from 42.6 to 38.4% while the FDP's declined from 8.1 to 5.6%. The Christian Democratic Union (CDU) increased its vote from 44.4 to 47.9% and came within two seats of winning an absolute majority—in a city where the SPD had dominated since World War II.

The Berlin campaign was mainly concerned with local issues. The city had an appalling housing shortage, and more than 150 old houses were occupied by squatters; there had been many violent demonstrations, accompanied by a clamour

Federal Republic of Germany

GERMANY, FEDERAL REPUBLIC OF

Education. (1980) Primary, pupils 5,044,200; secondary, pupils 3,729,700; primary and secondary, teachers 495,300; vocational, pupils 2,665,900, teachers 747,600; higher, students 1,044,200, teaching staff (1979) 114,000.

Finance. Monetary unit: Deutsche Mark, with (Sept. 21, 1981) a free rate of DM 2.23 to U.S. $1 (DM 4.14 = £1 sterling). Gold and other reserves (June 1981) U.S. $52,480,000,000. Budget (federal; 1980 actual): revenue DM 199.5 billion; expenditure DM 228,260,000,000. Gross national product (1980) DM 1,491,900,000,000. Money supply (June 1981) DM 233.2 billion. Cost of living (1975 = 100; June 1981) 129.2.

Foreign Trade. (1980) Imports DM 341,260,000,-000; exports DM 350.4 billion. Import sources: EEC 46% (The Netherlands 11%, France 11%, Italy 8%, Belgium-Luxembourg 7%, U.K. 7%); U.S. 8%. Export destinations: EEC 48% (France 13%, The Netherlands 10%, Italy 9%, Belgium-Luxembourg 8%, U.K. 7%); U.S. 6%; Switzerland 6%; Austria 5%. Main exports: machinery 28%; motor vehicles 14%; chemicals 13%; iron and steel 6%; textiles and cloth-

ing 5%. Tourism (1979): visitors 8,940,000; gross receipts U.S. $5,741,000,000.

Transport and Communications. Roads (1979) 482,000 km (including 7,292 km autobahns). Motor vehicles in use (1980): passenger 23,236,100; commercial 1,288,100. Railways: (1979) 31,711 km (including 11,211 km electrified); traffic (1980) 41,355,000,000 passenger-km, freight 65,301,-000,000 net ton-km. Air traffic (1980): 21,056,000,-000 passenger-km; freight 1,584,540,000 net ton-km. Navigable inland waterways in regular use (1979) 4,-329 km; freight traffic 50,987,000,000 ton-km. Shipping (1980): merchant vessels 100 gross tons and over 1,906; gross tonnage 8,355,638. Shipping traffic (1980): goods loaded 35,054,000 metric tons, unloaded 114,031,000 metric tons. Telephones (Jan. 1980) 26,632,300. Radio licenses (Dec. 1979) 21,151,500. Television licenses (1979) 19,421,500.

Agriculture. Production (in 000; metric tons; 1980): wheat 8,156; barley 8,826; oats 2,658; rye 2,-098; potatoes 7,930; sugar, raw value 2,935; apples 1,880; wine c. 399; cow's milk 24,778; butter 576;

cheese 776; beef and veal 1,520; pork 2,726; fish catch (1979) 356. Livestock (in 000; Dec. 1979): cattle 15,050; pigs 22,374; sheep 1,145; horses used in agriculture (1979) 378; chickens 84,932.

Industry. Index of production (1975 = 100; 1980) 118. Unemployment (1980) 3.8%. Fuel and power (in 000; metric tons; 1980): coal 87,145; lignite 129,833; crude oil 4,631; coke (1979) 27,438; electricity (kw-hr) 368,773,000; natural gas (cu m) 18,941,000; manufactured gas (cu m) c. 13,900,000. Production (in 000; metric tons; 1980): iron ore (32% metal content) 1,949; pig iron 34,055; crude steel 43,840; aluminum 1,138; copper 374; lead 301; zinc 512; cement 33,725; sulfuric acid 4,774; newsprint 593; cotton yarn 170; woven cotton fabrics 163; wool yarn 60; man-made fibres 875; petroleum products (1978) c. 98,317; fertilizers (1979–80) nitrogenous 1,476, phosphate 735, potash 2,704; synthetic rubber 409; plastics and resins 6,708; passenger cars (units) 3,513; commercial vehicles (units) 381. Merchant vessels launched (100 gross tons and over; 1980) 461,000 gross tons. New dwelling units completed (1980) 389,000.

for more law and order; environmental problems abounded. But above all, Berliners were registering their rejection of a political party whose reputation had been besmirched by a series of financial scandals. In the wake of one of the most serious of these, governing Mayor Dietrich Stobbe, himself innocent, resigned in January. He was replaced by Hans-Jochen Vogel, the federal minister of justice. Vogel called a midterm election and tried desperately to make up lost ground, but the malaise of the SPD had gone too deep and he had arrived too late. Moreover, he was challenged by a strong CDU candidate, Richard von Weizsäcker.

The Free Democrats, previously the SPD's allies in the city government, did not accept the CDU's invitation to form a coalition, so Weizsäcker set up a minority CDU government, "tolerated" by the FDP. A feature of the Berlin election was the progress made by the Alternative List, a loose grouping of environmentalists, squatters, antimaterialists, commune dwellers, and people described as "positive dropouts." They captured 7.2% of the votes and were represented by nine seats in the new city parliament.

In June another federal politician was dispatched from Bonn to head a state goverment and to repair the crumbling dikes of the SPD. Klaus von Dohnanyi, former minister of state in the Foreign Ministry, was elected mayor of Hamburg in succession to Hans-Ulrich Klose, who resigned after a party dispute over nuclear power. Traditionally, the SPD in Hamburg was right of centre, but under Klose it had developed a strong list to the left. In February a special conference of the Hamburg party voted against the city's collaboration with the neighbouring state of Schleswig-Holstein in building a nuclear power plant at Brokdorf on the Elbe River. Klose resigned when the city's withdrawal from the Brokdorf contract ran into political and legal difficulties.

Although Chancellor Schmidt remained the most popular politician in the country, opinion polls in October showed that his party could expect only 33% of the total vote, compared with 42.9% in the 1980 election. The public standing of the government had not been so low since the closing months of former chancellor Willy Brandt's administration in 1974. The opposition, composed of the CDU and the Bavarian Christian Social Union (CSU), was supported by just over half the electorate.

The coalition survived the hard bargaining over the 1982 budget, but it did not come through the negotiations unscathed. The SPD surrendered more ground than its FDP allies and was forced to accept compromises that angered left-wingers and the trade unions. Federal expenditure in 1982 was fixed at DM 240.8 billion, a modest increase of 4.2% over 1981. New borrowing was pegged at DM 26.5 billion, DM 15 billion less than in 1981. The West Germans would have to tighten their belts, though not to the point of acute discomfort. Children's allotments were cut, social insurance contributions increased, and public-sector pay was reduced by 1%. Additional economies had to be made when it became clear that revenue would still fall far short of expenditure. The bill for unemployment benefits was much higher than envisaged, and the recession meant that income from taxation would be considerably lower.

Until 1981, unemployment, though high by West German standards, had not presented an intolerable social problem. But by the end of 1981 the jobless total was climbing rapidly, firms were closing, and the bankruptcy courts were overworked. Unemployment was expected to peak at 2 million during the winter months and to average 1.6 million in 1982.

The peace movement's campaign against nuclear rearmament, particularly the NATO decision to deploy U.S. medium-range nuclear missiles in Western Europe, gathered momentum during the year. In West Germany the movement fell into three, not always distinct, groups: the environmentalists (the Green Party); the political left, including Communists of various shades; and church followers. A demonstration by about 300,-000 people in Bonn on October 10 proved convincingly that the movement was capable of concerted action. According to an opinion poll taken a few weeks after U.S. Pres. Ronald Reagan's inauguration, 57% of West Germans opposed the deployment of nuclear missiles on their territory. A similar poll taken a few months later found that 53% supported the NATO decision on deployment, coupled with the plan to negotiate an arms-limitation agreement with the U.S.S.R. Some observers believed that the antinuclear movement was a symptom of growing West German patriotism (or nationalism), which was directed against the U.S.

All the established political parties in West Germany worried about losing supporters to the peace campaign. The SPD was to face a crucial party conference in April 1982 at which delegates planned to review their attitude toward the missiles policy. Schmidt threatened to resign should the party reverse its backing for deployment, but there were signs that the conference would postpone a decision to allow time for progress in the arms-control negotiations between the superpowers.

East Germany's most famous spy, Günter Guillaume, whose arrest in 1974 had brought about

French Pres. François Mitterrand (left) met with West German Chancellor Helmut Schmidt during Mitterrand's visit to Bonn in July.

WEREK/KATHERINE YOUNG

Approximately 20,000 angry farmers protested in Bonn against what they felt were insufficient price increases for their crops. Prices for farm commodities were raised by about 10% in the European Economic Community.

Brandt's resignation, was released from prison at the end of September 1981. Guillaume, sentenced to 13 years' imprisonment for treason in 1975, was the centrepiece in a spy swap. Also released by the West Germans was Renate Lutze, a former secretary in the Defense Ministry, who received a six-year sentence for spying in 1979.

West Germany's neo-Nazis could no longer be dismissed as harmless cranks. They were increasingly militant, well armed, and had made so many unpleasant friends abroad that the authorities were beginning to refer to a "neo-Nazi International." In the first half of 1981 they committed 43 acts of violence. The Interior Ministry estimated that nearly 20,000 West Germans belonged to extreme right-wing organizations, mainly the National Democratic Party (NPD), which blossomed in the late 1960s, and a group headed by a Munich publisher, Gerhard Frey, whose weekly *National Zeitung* had a circulation of well over 100,000.

Terrorists who tried to kill the commander in chief of the U.S. Army in Europe, Gen. Frederick Kroesen, on September 15 were thought to be banking on winning sympathizers in a climate of opinion that was increasingly hostile to U.S. defense and foreign policies. An antitank grenade, fired from a hillside at a range of about 200 m (650 ft), hit the general's car as he was being driven to his headquarters in Heidelberg. General Kroesen and his wife were slightly hurt. This was the tenth attack on U.S. military personnel or property in West Germany in 1981. On August 31 a bomb explosion at the U.S. air base at Ramstein injured 20 people. The terrorist organization known as the Red Army Faction (RAF) admitted planting the Ramstein bomb, and the authorities believed the RAF also shot at the general.

Foreign Affairs. The government tried to dispel doubts about West Germany's reliability as a mainstay of NATO. The West Germans were relieved that President Reagan had restored the quality of calculability to U.S. foreign policy after the erratic years of former president Jimmy Carter, but when the contours of that policy became clearer, they did not accept some of the calculations. Above all, they saw a danger that the U.S.—determined to draw level with, if not to surpass, the Soviet Union militarily—could neglect the quest for arms control. Ever conscious of the Soviet divisions on the other side of the demarcation line, the West Germans, while admitting that détente was on its last legs, still cherished the belief that it could be brought back to life.

For this reason, they urged President Reagan to agree to Soviet Pres. Leonid Brezhnev's proposal for a summit meeting of the superpowers. The West Germans wanted theatre nuclear forces to be placed at the top of the agenda, but they also believed that Reagan and Brezhnev should seek agreement on a code of conduct, based on the principle of noninterference, to shape their policies toward the third world.

West Germany, regarded by the Soviets as their main contact in Western Europe and by the U.S. as the most important NATO ally, found itself playing a key role in the superpower relationship. Schmidt preferred to describe the West German role as that of interpreter, and he was called upon to play it during Brezhnev's visit to Bonn, November 22–25. Four days before Brezhnev's arrival, Reagan proposed that if the U.S.S.R. dismantled its SS-20s and other medium-range nuclear missiles, the U.S. would abandon plans to deploy Pershing II and land-based cruise missiles in Western Europe. This "zero option" had always been close to West Germany's heart, and Schmidt warmly welcomed the Reagan speech as a positive approach to the U.S.-Soviet arms-limitation negotiations that started in Geneva on November 30.

The Soviets, however, condemned the offer as a propaganda ploy. Brezhnev insisted during his Bonn visit that the Soviet Union did not possess

superiority in the medium-range nuclear field. He urged reconsideration of the Soviet proposal for a moratorium on the deployment of nuclear missiles, at least during the Geneva negotiations. Schmidt countered that unless the Soviets started to scrap their SS-20s, deployment of U.S. missiles from the end of 1983 was inevitable. At the end of the year West Germany diverged from the U.S. on a major policy matter when it failed to respond to U.S. calls for immediate economic sanctions against Poland and the U.S.S.R. following the imposition of martial law in Poland.

Schmidt's government was in the process of reviewing its arms-export policy, which for many years had more or less followed the principle that West German arms should not be delivered to areas of tension. The chancellor felt that the term area of tension was too restrictive and should be replaced by guidelines that took more account of the national interest and the need to establish — not least in areas of tension — a military balance. West Germany did not intend, however, to become a leading arms seller.

The visit of the chancellor to Saudi Arabia in April was one of his most difficult missions. In Riyadh he had to explain why his government did not find it possible "for the time being" to supply Saudi Arabia with the Leopard II tank and other weapons. The decision was expected to spoil West Germany's chances of major involvement in Saudi Arabia's industrial development.

Nevertheless, Schmidt managed to incur the wrath of the Israelis. In May Israeli Prime Minister Menachem Begin described him as avaricious, heartless, unprincipled, and lacking in human feeling. What appeared to have enraged Begin most was Schmidt's reply to a question, in an interview in Saudi Arabia, about the moral aspect of the West German relationship with Israel. In viewing the Palestinian conflict, said the chancellor, one could not award one side all the morality. "That won't do. And in particular it won't do for a German, living in a divided nation and laying moral claim to the right of self-determination for the German people. One must then recognize the moral claim of the Palestinian people to the right of self-determination."

Schmidt was the first foreign statesman to call on French Pres. François Mitterrand after his election, and Mitterrand visited Bonn in July. On East-West relations and the deployment of U.S. medium-range nuclear missiles, the chancellor and the president found themselves in full agreement. But it was feared in Bonn that the sharp differences between the economic policies of the two countries could place a strain on the relationship between the two countries in European Community affairs.

(NORMAN CROSSLAND)

See also German Democratic Republic.

Ghana

Ghana

A republic of West Africa and member of the Commonwealth, Ghana is on the Gulf of Guinea and is bordered by Ivory Coast, Upper Volta, and Togo. Area: 238,533 sq km (92,098 sq mi). Pop. (1980

GHANA

Education. (1977–78) Primary, pupils 1,245,853, teachers 45,119; secondary, pupils 568,947, teachers 27,464; vocational, pupils 19,684, teachers 990; teacher training, students 3,631, teachers 212; higher (1975–76), students 9,079, teaching staff 1,103.

Finance. Monetary unit: cedi, with (Sept. 21, 1981) a free rate of 2.65 cedis to U.S. $1 (4.92 cedis = £1 sterling). Gold and other reserves (June 1981) U.S. $158 million. Budget (1978–79 est.): revenue 3.2 billion cedis; expenditure 2.9 billion cedis. Gross national product (1977) 11,123,000,000 cedis. Money supply (May 1981) 7,169,600,000 cedis. Cost of living (Accra; 1975 = 100; May 1981) 2,799.

Foreign Trade. (1978) Imports 1,653,000,000 cedis; exports 1,645,000,000 cedis. Import sources: U.K. *c.* 18%; Nigeria *c.* 13%; West Germany *c.* 12%; U.S. *c.* 10%; Switzerland *c.* 6%; Italy *c.* 5%. Export destinations: U.S. *c.* 16%; U.K. *c.* 15%; U.S.S.R. *c.* 11%; The Netherlands *c.* 9%; West Germany *c.* 9%; Japan *c.* 8%. Main exports (1977): cocoa 73%; aluminum 9%; timber 8%.

Transport and Communications. Roads (1979) 32,200 km. Motor vehicles in use (1978): passenger 33,000; commercial (including buses) 27,000. Railways: (1980) 953 km; traffic (1974) 521 million passenger-km, freight 312 million net ton-km. Air traffic (1980): *c.* 324 million passenger-km; freight *c.* 2.8 million net ton-km. Shipping (1980): merchant vessels 100 gross tons and over 104; gross tonnage 250,428. Telephones (Jan. 1980) 68,850. Radio receivers (Dec. 1977) 1,095,000. Television receivers (Dec. 1979) *c.* 55,000.

Agriculture. Production (in 000; metric tons; 1980): corn *c.* 339; cassava (1979) *c.* 1,900; taro (1979) *c.* 1,500; yams (1979) *c.* 900; millet 66; sorghum 106; tomatoes 119; peanuts 92; oranges *c.* 164; cocoa *c.* 255; palm oil *c.* 21; meat (1979) *c.* 88; fish catch (1979) 230; timber (cu m; 1979) *c.* 9,359. Livestock (in 000; 1979): cattle *c.* 930; sheep *c.* 1,650; pigs *c.* 400; goats *c.* 2,000; chickens *c.* 11,500.

Industry. Production (in 000; metric tons; 1979): bauxite 235; petroleum products (1978) *c.* 1,180; gold (troy oz) 370; diamonds (metric carats) 1,500; manganese ore (metal content) *c.* 140; electricity (kw-hr) 4,700,000.

est.): 11,542,300. Cap. and largest city: Accra (pop., 1980 est., 998,800). Language: English (official); local Sudanic dialects: Akan 43.3%, Mole-Dagbani 12.8%, Ewe 14.5%, and Ga-Adange 9.4%. Religion: Christian 43%; Muslim 16%; animist 38%. President until Dec. 31, 1981, Hilla Limann.

On Dec. 31, 1981, former flight lieutenant Jerry Rawlings overthrew the government of Pres. Hilla Limann. In 1979 Rawlings had led a coup against the military government of Lieut. Gen. Fred Akuffo and then retired voluntarily in favour of civilian rule. In a speech over Accra radio, Rawlings claimed that Limann's civilian government had brought Ghana no nearer to a solution for its economic problems.

Presenting the 1981–82 budget in June, the finance minister had reported an inflation rate of 70%, due in the main, he claimed, to the rise in the minimum daily wage from 4 to 12 cedis. (The black market exchange rate was 35 cedis to U.S. $1.) The performance of Ghana's three main exports — cocoa, gold, and timber — was disappointing. Substantial aid was committed, especially by West Germany, the U.S., Japan, Canada, the World Bank and African Development Bank, and the U.K.

In July President Limann obtained promises from two warring tribes in northern Ghana that they would cease hostilities. As many as 1,000 people were said to have died during four months of fighting.

(GUY ARNOLD)

Golf

Honours were more evenly divided than usual in professional golf in the United States in 1981. There was no single outstanding golfer such as Tom Watson, the leading money winner and player of the year from 1977 to 1980, or Jack Nicklaus, who had won the U.S. Open and Professional Golfers' Association (PGA) championships in 1980. Tom Kite won the Palmer Award for the leading money winner, with $375,699, and the Vardon Trophy with a stroke average of 69.80, the second lowest since 1950. Bill Rogers, with victories in the British Open and the World Series of Golf, was player of the year.

Had either Raymond Floyd, who enjoyed his most prosperous year, or Watson won the final tournament of the season at Pensacola, Fla., he would have overtaken Rogers. Had Kite not qualified for the final 36 holes at Pensacola, he also could have been overtaken. Consistency had been the foundation of Kite's career. His one victory in 1981, when he finished in the top ten in all but 5 of the 26 tournaments in which he competed, was only his third in an official PGA event since he turned professional in 1972. Yet his lifetime winnings up to the end of 1981 were $1,319,747. Kite, Floyd, Watson, Bruce Lietzke, and Rogers all won more than $300,000, the first time that five players had reached that figure in one year.

After seven years on the tour Rogers, an engaging Texan, had a reputation for being one of the straightest players. This quality undoubtedly helped him to finish second to David Graham in the U.S. Open at the Merion Golf Club, Ardmore, Pa., and to win the British Open soon afterward at Royal St. George's, Sandwich. He crowned this rare double achievement by holing a birdie putt to beat Kite on the last green in the World Series at Akron, Ohio, and by winning the Texas Open after a sudden-death duel with Ben Crenshaw.

When Jack Nicklaus posted a second round of 65 at Augusta, Ga., and led the Masters by four strokes, it seemed that he was headed for his sixth victory. The next day saw one of the fascinating swings of fortune for which the Masters is famous. At one point Watson gained eight strokes in ten holes on Nicklaus but then slipped back to being even with him. The last round revealed Watson's great competitive spirit. He took an early lead, but when Nicklaus could have closed on him, he saved par at the 13th with a masterly chip, hit a superb four wood that alighted soft as a feather on the 15th green, and protected his two-stroke margin with a great bunker shot on the 17th.

Earlier, Johnny Miller had emerged from comparative shadows, and he confirmed his return to form in the Masters with a final round of 68 that enabled him to tie for second with Nicklaus. In his first Masters Greg Norman of Australia controlled his powerful swing admirably in finishing fourth. It was a memorable Masters from the outset, when Gene Sarazen and Byron Nelson, in their 80th and 70th years, respectively, revived the traditional opening ceremony.

Bill Rogers, a 29-year-old from Texas, won the 1981 British Open and prize money of £25,000, at Sandwich, England, in July.

Without question the finest single round under severe pressure was Graham's closing 67 at Merion. He missed the first fairway by a fraction, but otherwise his drives and approach shots were flawless and he putted superbly on lightning-fast greens. Going into the last round, he was three strokes behind George Burns and one ahead of Rogers. But Burns then had problems with his long game, and only brave scrambling kept him in the competition. Meanwhile, Rogers played his cool, steady game for a 69, but Graham showed no sign of yielding. His four-round total of 273 was seven under par, only a stroke above Nicklaus's record for the Open, and he became the first Australian to win the title. Nicklaus's challenge for a fifth title faded during the last nine holes in the last round; Watson, after a promising start, drifted back into 23rd place, exactly where he finished in the British Open, and Lee Trevino, champion ten years earlier at Merion, missed the 36-hole qualifying cut.

One of the most unexpected results of the year was the victory of Peter Oosterhuis in the Canadian Open at Glen Abbey. It was his first after seven years on the tour and the reward of courage and patience after several lean seasons. No British player had won on the tour since Tony Jacklin in 1972, and all the leading U.S. players were competing.

If Graham's 67 at Merion was the year's classic round, Nicklaus's opening 83 in the British Open was the most startling. The highest score of his first-class career was partly due to anxiety concerning his second son's accident with a car, which was resolved without harm to anyone. Knowing that the exceptional was essential if he was to survive the cut, he produced a great 66 the following morning and qualified. Meanwhile, Rogers was laying the foundation for his victory.

Gibraltar:
see Dependent States

Glass Manufacture:
see Industrial Review

Gliding:
see Aerial Sports

UPI

Pat Bradley of the U.K. was all smiles after she won the U.S. Women's Open in July in LaGrange, Ill.

After an opening 72 Rogers played supremely well for 66 and 67, which gave him a lead of five strokes over Bernhard Langer of West Germany and Mark James of England. The third round was significant because, with Nicklaus out of the running, Ben Crenshaw was the popular favourite of the overseas players. In the previous three Opens he had been second, second, and third, but the strain of striving for victory proved too great. Playing with Rogers, a close friend, on the third day, Crenshaw lost nine strokes to him and was out of contention.

For a moment on the last afternoon Rogers was in danger with a double bogey at the seventh while Ray Floyd, playing ahead of him, had made three birdies, but Rogers kept his composure admirably. After birdies on the ninth and tenth he was almost safe; all conceivable challenge died, even from Floyd, and Langer was the last remote threat. Langer, the only first-class golfer yet to emerge from West Germany, deserved high praise for finishing even with par, four strokes behind Rogers and three ahead of Floyd and James.

It was surprising that so few eminent golfers mounted a lasting challenge to Rogers. The wind was never severe, and if the rough was punishing, the fairways were perfect and the greens moderate in pace. Accuracy was of the essence, and in this Rogers excelled.

Few men have moved from birth as a golfer to major champion as swiftly as Larry Nelson, who discovered the game at a driving range in 1969. A quiet man with a beautifully measured swing, he had become one of the most consistent players in recent years and took command of the PGA championship in Atlanta, Ga., with middle rounds of 66. He led by four strokes over Fuzzy Zoeller going into the last round, and his beautifully straight golf never gave his pursuers much hope of catch-

ing him. Again a major championship had ended without a stirring climax, but the World Series of Golf at Akron was different, with Rogers overtaking Hale Irwin, resisting Kite's fine last round of 67 with a like score, and enriching himself by $100,000.

Langer was the outstanding golfer in Europe until late in the season, when Severiano Ballesteros of Spain recovered form with victories in the Spanish Open and Suntory match play championship at Wentworth, England. Although Langer won only twice, he was frequently in close contention. His official winnings of £81,036 were easily a record; he also finished sixth in the World Series, his first U.S. tournament. Langer impressed everyone by the power and purity of his strokes and his unshakable poise in all situations. Ballesteros hardly surfaced in the major championships but finished the year in fine style. Having won two matches commandingly, he beat Langer in the semifinal at Wentworth and Crenshaw on the last green of a splendid 36-hole final.

At the Ryder Cup match at Walton Heath, England, the U.S. team was among the most powerful ever assembled. Only Crenshaw, Kite, and Lietzke had not won a major championship, but the Europeans led by a point after the first day. Had Floyd not holed two crucial putts at the end of the last match of the day, the U.S. could have been three behind. The reverse spurred them to their finest golf. Of the remaining 20 matches the Europeans won only four, three after the contest had been decided. Nelson, Nicklaus, and Trevino won all their four matches, but Kite produced the most spectacular golf. In his single against Sandy Lyle he was ten under par for 16 holes. Lyle, consistently the best of the European teams, was unfortunate to face such figures. He himself had eight birdies. The Europeans deserved credit that the final margin was not greater than 18½–9½.

The same was true of the British and Irish team, which lost the Walker Cup 15–9 at the Cypress Point course on the Monterey peninsula in California. The Irish players, Ronan Rafferty, the youngest so far to appear in the match, and Philip Walton, aged 17 and 19, respectively, won both their foursomes and Walton one of his singles, while Roger Chapman won three of his matches. At lunch on the final day the U.S. led by only two points, but strength in depth gave the U.S. the edge in the singles. Jodie Mudd, the public links champion, and Joe Rassett were the most effective of the U.S. players.

Bing Crosby would have been proud of his youngest son, Nathaniel, for his stirring achievement in winning the U.S. amateur championship at the Olympic Golf Club in San Francisco. The largest crowds to watch the championship in years saw Crosby recover from three down in his semifinal match and from four down after 28 holes against Brian Lindley in the final. He holed from 20 ft on the 37th. Bob Lewis, runner-up in 1980, was the only player from either Walker Cup team to reach the last eight, and he lost to Lindley in the next round. For the first time, a Frenchman, Philippe Ploujoux, won the British amateur, beating a Chicago golfer, Joel Hirsch, in the final.

In women's competition Pat Bradley survived a tremendous battle with Beth Daniel for a victory in the U.S. Open. Her final round of 66 and total of 279 were records for the championship and gave her the victory by one stroke. During the year Kathy Whitworth became the first woman golfer to pass the $1 million mark in prize money, and she was soon followed by JoAnne Carner and Donna Caponi. The leading money winner for 1981 was Daniel with $206,977. Juli Inkster became the first woman successfully to defend the U.S. amateur title since Betty Jameson in 1940. She finished with two birdies to beat Lindy Goggin of Australia on the last green of the final. Deborah Massey of the U.S. won the British Open, and Belle Robertson, previous loser in three finals, the British amateur championship.   (P. A. WARD-THOMAS)

Greece

A republic of Europe, Greece occupies the southern part of the Balkan Peninsula. Area: 131,990 sq km (50,962 sq mi), of which the mainland accounts for 107,194 sq km. Pop. (1981 prelim.): 9,-706,700. Cap. and largest city: Athens (pop., 1981 prelim., 885,100). Language: Greek. Religion: Orthodox. President in 1981, Konstantinos Karamanlis; prime ministers, Georgios Rallis and, from October 21, Andreas Papandreou.

The victory of the Panhellenic Socialist Movement (Pasok) of Andreas Papandreou (*see* BIOGRAPHIES) in the general elections of Oct. 18, 1981, promised to bring about substantial changes in the internal and external policies that Greece had pursued during five decades of almost uninterrupted conservative rule. (For details of the election results, *see* POLITICAL PARTIES.) With 172 seats out of 300, the Pasok government had a comfortable majority, enough to push through its ambitious program of socialist reforms.

The New Democracy Party, deposed after seven years in power, remained a formidable opponent in Parliament. In December it moved perceptibly to the right with the election of Evangelos Averoff,

a former defense minister, as its leader in place of former prime minister Georgios Rallis. The Greek Communist Party (KKE) not only failed to reach its target of 17% (the percentage required to qualify for the second distribution of seats) but also saw its chance of wielding influence in Parliament evaporate as Pasok was returned with a more than adequate majority. The smaller parties were annihilated by the electoral system and also by the enormous success of Pasok's campaign for change. Pasok derived strength on its right from the splintered centre, as well as from disgruntled voters who wanted a change; on its left it attracted those fringe Communists who opted for Pasok's "Change—Here and Now" rather than the KKE's promise of a more distant paradise.

The results of the Greek elections for the European Parliament, held simultaneously, showed that one out of every five voters who supported Pasok for the national Parliament preferred the small pro-European Communities parties when it came to filling the European seats. This suggested that Pasok's opposition to Greek membership in the EC found less favour among the electorate than its other policies.

Pasok's other policies remained ambiguous for some time. While its basic platform opposed NATO and the U.S. bases in Greece, during the campaign it toned down these positions to attract the less radical floating vote. But the question remained: which policy would Pasok follow when it came to power? In November Parliament approved a government program that called for negotiations leading to phased withdrawal of the U.S. bases, negotiations for better terms for Greece within NATO and the EC, and a referendum on EC membership.

Before the elections, foreign affairs dominated the Greek scene. Perhaps the most important development occurred on January 1, when Greece became the tenth member of the EC. Negotiations on the future of the U.S. bases began in earnest in Athens on January 27. The government of Prime Minister Rallis pressed the U.S. for two main safeguards in exchange for letting the bases remain.

Greece

Andreas Papandreou's Pasok party won a landslide victory in elections held in Greece in October.

Great Britain:
see United Kingdom

UPI

GREECE

Education. (1978–79) Primary, pupils 922,698, teachers 35,750; secondary, pupils 585,130, teachers 26,921; vocational, pupils 125,039; higher, students 126,244, teaching staff 6,705.

Finance. Monetary unit: drachma, with (Sept. 21, 1981) a free rate of 54.84 drachmas to U.S. $1 (101.67 drachmas = £1 sterling). Gold and other reserves (June 1981) U.S. $836 million. Budget (1980 est.): revenue 365,950,000,000 drachmas; expenditure 374,950,000,000 drachmas. Gross national product (1980) 1,779,600,000,000 drachmas. Money supply (March 1981) 295,870,000,000 drachmas. Cost of living (1975 = 100; June 1981) 264.5.

Foreign Trade. (1980) Imports 452,880,000,000 drachmas; exports 223,910,000,000 drachmas. Import sources: EEC 40% (West Germany 14%, Italy 8%, France 6%, U.K. 5%); Japan 11%; Saudi Arabia 7%; Egypt 7%; U.S. 5%. Export destinations: EEC 48% (West Germany 18%, Italy 10%, The Netherlands 6%, France 7%); U.S. 6%; Saudi Arabia 5%. Main exports: petroleum products 16%; fruit and vegetables 15%; textile yarns and fabrics 9%; clothing 8%; chemicals 7%; iron and steel 6%. Tourism (1979): visitors 5,233,000; gross receipts U.S. $1,663,000,000.

Transport and Communications. Roads (1980) 37,132 km (including 91 km expressways). Motor vehicles in use (1980): passenger 877,900; commercial 401,970. Railways (1979): 2,479 km; traffic 1,531,000,000 passenger-km, freight 841 million net ton-km. Air traffic (1980): 5,062,000,000 passenger-km; freight 68,074,000 net ton-km. Shipping (1980): merchant vessels 100 gross tons and over 3,922; gross tonnage 39,471,744. Telephones (Jan. 1980) 2,664,000. Radio receivers (Dec. 1978) c. 3.3 million. Television receivers (Dec. 1978) c. 1.5 million.

Agriculture. Production (in 000; metric tons; 1980): wheat 2,931; barley 949; oats 87; corn 1,223; rice 78; potatoes 954; sugar, raw value (1979) 337; tomatoes 1,666; onions c. 130; watermelons (1979) c. 707; apples 259; oranges 596; lemons 177; peaches (1979) 327; olives c. 1,270; olive oil 281; wine c. 440; raisins 139; tobacco 113; cotton, lint 115. Livestock (in 000; Dec. 1979): sheep c. 8,000; cattle (1978) 975; goats 4,465; pigs (1978) 892; horses (1978) 125; asses (1978) 253; chickens c. 30,181.

Industry. Production (in 000; metric tons; 1979): lignite 23,395; electricity (kw-hr) 20,454,000; petroleum products (1978) 11,306; iron ore (43% metal content) 1,834; bauxite 2,757; aluminum 141; magnesite 1,390; cement 12,064; sulfuric acid 1,061; fertilizers (1979–80) nitrogenous 320, phosphate c. 189; cotton yarn 114. Merchant vessels launched (100 gross tons and over; 1980) 22,000 gross tons.

The first was maintenance of the seven to ten ratio of U.S. military aid to Greece and Turkey, respectively, in order not to upset the balance of power between them. The second was the reiteration of earlier assurances that the U.S. would "actively oppose" any attempt to solve Greek-Turkish differences in the Aegean Sea by military means. Satisfactory formulas on these points were reached, but the Greek military, which was participating in the negotiations, also demanded a one-time grant of expensive, sophisticated weapons. The talks were stalled while repeated Greek ultimatums proved unsuccessful, their credibility eroded by repetition. The negotiations were suspended amicably on June 18 in view of the parliamentary recess and the subsequent elections.

Greek foreign policy continued to be influenced by the obsession that Turkey had expansionist designs on Greece. Hopes that the presence of a military regime in Turkey would facilitate an understanding soon faded. The Rallis government unilaterally lifted most air-traffic restrictions in the Aegean on March 6. However, a massive violation of Greek airspace by Turkish aircraft during a military exercise in early April upset matters, undermining a Greek-Turkish meeting in Athens on April 13 that was scheduled to solve the Aegean airspace problem. The foreign ministers and senior diplomats of the two countries met on several occasions but achieved little, other than to keep the dialogue alive as a hedge against crisis.

Uncertainty over the outcome of the election, along with the diametrically opposed policies of the two main contenders, slowed down the Greek economy, already plagued by a 25% annual inflation rate for the third consecutive year. This was coupled with a continuing dearth of productive investments, despite some quite generous inducements decreed by the government. The balance of payments was affected by the steady devaluation of the drachma against the U.S. dollar (increasing the cost of the oil bill), but the general recession somewhat reduced imports, so the current account deficit remained manageable. There were fears that the election results could affect the country's ability to obtain international credits, given the Socialist government's still undefined program of nationalization.

Benefits from the first year of accession to the European Communities were slow in appearing, but the disadvantages came promptly in the form of higher food prices for consumers. On the whole, Greek farmers seemed to be better off, although inflation, the highest in the EC, eroded their earnings.

Greece suffered from earthquakes throughout 1981. The shock of February 24, which had its epicentre in the Gulf of Corinth, caused unprecedented scenes of panic and chaos in Athens, at least 16 deaths, and extensive damage throughout the area. There were also tremors in Epirus, the Ionian islands, and Crete. Conflagrations depleted Greece's rare forests throughout the summer, and the authorities suspected arson. Many Greeks were inclined to relate the incidents to the series of department-store fires, mainly in Athens, that began just before Christmas 1980 and continued in 1981. The authorities believed they were acts of political terrorism, but no one was apprehended.

(MARIO MODIANO)

Grenada

A parliamentary state within the Commonwealth, Grenada, with its dependency, the Southern Grenadines, is the southernmost of the Windward Islands of the Caribbean Sea, 161 km N of Trinidad. Area: 345 sq km (133 sq mi). Pop. (1981 est.): 120,000, including Negro 84%, mixed 11%, white 1%, and East Indian 3%. Cap.: Saint George's (pop., 1978, 30,813). Language: English. Religion: Roman Catholic 64%; Anglican 22%; Seventh-day Adventist 3%; Methodist 2%. Queen, Elizabeth II; governor-general in 1981, Sir Paul Scoon; prime minister, Maurice Bishop.

Grenada's war of words with the U.S. escalated in 1981. U.S. criticism centred on the construction of a new international airport near Saint George's, which, it was alleged, could be used for Cuban activity in Africa or Latin America. The government, however, argued that the airport was essential to tourism, and the European Economic Com-

Grenada

Greek Orthodox Church: *see* Religion

Greenland: *see* Dependent States

Education. (1978–79) Primary, pupils 24,106, teachers 814; secondary, pupils 6,498, teachers 275; vocational, pupils 384, teachers 28; teacher training, students 450, teachers 29; higher, students 700, teaching staff 137.

Finance and Trade. Monetary unit: East Caribbean dollar, with (Sept. 21, 1981) a par value of ECar$2.70 to U.S. $1 (free rate of ECar$5.01 = £1 sterling). Budget (1980–81 est.) balanced at ECar$103 million. Foreign trade (1979): imports ECar$122.8 million; exports ECar$58.5 million. Import sources: U.K. *c.* 21%; Trinidad and Tobago *c.* 20%. Export destinations: U.K. 40%; West Germany 17%; Belgium-Luxembourg 16%; The Netherlands 11%. Main exports: cocoa 46%; nutmeg 21%; bananas 18%. Tourism (excluding cruise passengers; 1978): visitors 32,300; gross receipts *c.* U.S. $10 million.

munity, despite U.S. pressure, agreed to support the project. In August Grenada suggested that the object of U.S. exercises on the Puerto Rican island of Vieques was to train troops for an invasion. The U.S. emphatically denied this. In June the Grenada government banned all newspapers for a year.

Relations with Cuba, Mexico, Nicaragua, the Middle East, and Eastern Europe became closer as the government tried to offset Western hostility. Britain refused further aid until the island arranged elections and proceeded with the trials of detainees. Relations with right-of-centre Caribbean governments—particularly Barbados—remained strained.

Despite its Marxist principles, the government maintained a mixed economy. Earnings from agriculture were down, but tourism showed signs of improvement. (DAVID A. JESSOP)

Guatemala

A republic of Central America, Guatemala is bounded by Mexico, Belize, Honduras, El Salvador, the Caribbean Sea, and the Pacific Ocean. Area: 108,889 sq km (42,042 sq mi). Pop. (1981 prelim.): 6,043,600. Cap. and largest city:

Education. (1978) Primary, pupils 709,018, teachers 21,-060; secondary, vocational, and teacher training, pupils 145,770, teachers 8,604; higher (1977), students 29,234, teaching staff (1976) 1,934.

Finance. Monetary unit: quetzal, at par with the U.S. dollar (free rate, at Sept. 21, 1981, of 1.85 quetzales to £1 sterling). Gold and other reserves (June 1981) U.S. $295 million. Budget (1980 actual): revenue 754 million quetzales; expenditure 1,116,000,000 quetzales. Gross national product (1979) 6,873,000,000 quetzales. Money supply (June 1981) 874 million quetzales. Cost of living (1975 = 100; April 1981) 182.

Foreign Trade. (1980) Imports (f.o.b.) 1,469,000,000 quetzales; exports 1,545,000,000 quetzales. Import sources (1979): U.S. 32%; El Salvador 11%; Japan 8%; Venezuela 7%; West Germany 7%. Export destinations (1979): U.S. 29%; El Salvador 12%; West Germany 9%; Japan 8%; Costa Rica 6%; China 5%. Main exports: coffee 30%; cotton 11%; chemicals *c.* 8%; textile yarns and fabrics *c.* 5%.

Transport and Communications. Roads (1979) 17,278 km. Motor vehicles in use (1979): passenger 147,500; commercial (including buses) 73,100. Railways: (1980) *c.* 967 km; freight traffic (1976) 117 million net ton-km. Air traffic (1980): 159 million passenger-km; freight 6.4 million net ton-km. Telephones (Jan. 1980) 81,600. Radio licenses (Dec. 1978) *c.* 280,000. Television receivers (Dec. 1977) 150,000.

Agriculture. Production (in 000; metric tons; 1980): corn *c.* 1,058; sugar, raw value *c.* 398; tomatoes *c.* 86; dry beans *c.* 80; bananas *c.* 560; coffee *c.* 156; cotton, lint *c.* 156; tobacco *c.* 8. Livestock (in 000; 1979): sheep 685; cattle *c.* 1,575; pigs 747; chickens *c.* 13,800.

Industry. Production (in 000; metric tons; 1979): cement 556; petroleum products (1978) *c.* 803; electricity (kw-hr) 1,490,000.

Guatemala

Guatemala City (pop., 1981 prelim., 1,307,300). Language: Spanish, with some Indian dialects. Religion: Roman Catholic (1976) 88%. President in 1981, Fernando Romeo Lucas García.

The political situation in Guatemala deteriorated seriously during 1981, giving rise to protests by human rights organizations. In February Amnesty International accused Pres. Fernando Romeo Lucas García's government of directing a program of murder and torture against its political enemies. Guerrilla and counterinsurgency activity spread, and it was estimated that sometimes more than 30 political murders occurred each day.

Guatemalan Indian farmers, who are fighting against what they regard as oppressive government tactics, meet secretly in the central highlands.

KEYSTONE

With the approach of the presidential elections, scheduled for March 1982, tension mounted and electioneering was in full swing. Candidates selected by the eight registered political parties included the official candidate, Angel Aníbal Guevara, who resigned as defense minister in August to represent a coalition of the Partido Revolucionario and the Partido Institucional Democrático; Mario Sandoval Alarcón, former vice-president (1974–78), representing the Movimiento de Liberación Nacional; Gustavo Anzueto Vielman for the Central Auténtica Nacionalista; Roberto Alejos Arzú for the Frente Unidad Nacional; and Alejandro Maldonado Aguirre for the Partido Nacionalista Renovador.

The government's relations with the U.S. administration strengthened; this was demonstrated in June when U.S. Pres. Ronald Reagan agreed to sell Guatemala military vehicles worth $3.2 million. However, relations with the U.K. were at a low ebb because of Britain's decision to grant independence to Belize. Guatemala, which claimed the territory as its own, broke off its remaining diplomatic relations with the U.K. and appealed to the UN not to recognize the new nation; nevertheless, Guatemala pledged not to invade Belize.

(LUCY BLACKBURN)

Guinea

Guinea

Guinea-Bissau

A republic on the west coast of Africa, Guinea is bounded by Guinea-Bissau, Senegal, Mali, Ivory Coast, Liberia, and Sierra Leone. Area: 245,857 sq km (94,926 sq mi). Pop. (1981 UN est.): 5,144,000. Cap. and largest city: Conakry (pop., 1980 est., 763,000). Language: French (official). Religion: mostly Muslim. President in 1981, Ahmed Sékou Touré; premier, Louis Lansana Beavogui.

After more than 20 years in power, Pres. Ahmed Sékou Touré of Guinea was still opposed by a group of his fellow countrymen. On the night of Feb. 20, 1981, he escaped an assassination attempt —the second in nine months—at Conakry airport. The death on September 25 of one of the president's closest associates, Diallo Saifoulaye, was the occasion of three days of national mourning.

Relations with France, under Pres. François Mitterrand as under Pres. Valéry Giscard d'Estaing, were characterized by ambiguity. Abdoulaye Touré, the minister of foreign affairs, was received in Paris on April 20, but nothing was decided about the possibility of an official visit to France by President Touré. The latter was not invited to take part in the Franco-African summit conference in Paris on November 3–4. French concern over the fate of eight political prisoners, married to French women, was probably a factor.

The government announced a ten-year development plan (1981–90) with an annual growth rate target of 10% by 1990. The plan aimed to increase the productivity of land already under cultivation; to exploit further the country's bauxite and aluminum resources; and to develop the embryonic manufacturing sector.   (PHILIPPE DECRAENE)

Guinea-Bissau

An independent African republic, Guinea-Bissau has an Atlantic coastline on the west and borders Senegal on the north and Guinea on the east and south. Area: 36,125 sq km (13,948 sq mi). Pop. (1981 est.): 801,000. Cap. and largest city: Bissau (metro. area pop., 1979, 109,500). President of the Council of the Revolution in 1981, João Bernardo Vieira.

Following the November 1980 coup in which the government of Pres. Luis de Almeida Cabral was overthrown, the Council of the Revolution, with former premier João Bernardo Vieira at its head, held absolute power. Shortly after Vieira claimed that 500 political prisoners had been executed under Cabral's leadership, former security chief André Gomes committed suicide in prison. Rafael Barbosa, the black nationalist leader released from prison during the coup, was later rearrested.

In January 1981 Cape Verde broke from the joint African Party for the Independence of Guinea-Bissau and Cape Verde. In an attempt to repair the rift, the Council reversed its decision to try the Cape Verdean-born Cabral for murder. By October Guinea-Bissau was making overtures toward resuming relations with Cape Verde. It was announced in November that Cabral would be released from prison at year's end.

The provisional government, set up in November 1980, was expanded in February 1981. Several members of Cabral's administration retained ministerial posts. The government appealed for international aid and concentrated on improving economic performance.   (GUY ARNOLD)

Guiana:
see Dependent States; Guyana; Suriname

GUINEA
   Education. (1978–79) Primary, pupils 272,000, teachers 6,413; secondary and vocational, pupils 106,000, teachers 3,700; higher, students 24,000, teachers 650.
   Finance. Monetary unit: syli, with (Sept. 21, 1981) a free rate of 21.28 sylis to U.S. $1 (39.46 sylis = £1 sterling). Budget (total; 1979 est.) balanced at 11,250,000,000 sylis.
   Foreign Trade. (1977) Imports 5,664,000,000 sylis; exports 6,629,000,000 sylis. Import sources: France *c.* 20%; U.S.S.R. *c.* 11%; U.S. *c.* 6%; Italy *c.* 6%. Export destinations: U.S. *c.* 18%; France *c.* 13%; West Germany *c.* 12%; U.S.S.R. *c.* 12%; Spain *c.* 12%; Canada *c.* 7%; Italy *c.* 7%. Main exports (1975–76): bauxite *c.* 57%; alumina *c.* 31%.

GUINEA-BISSAU
   Education. (1977–78) Primary, pupils 85,575, teachers 2,599; secondary, pupils 4,922; vocational, pupils 76; teacher training, students 373; secondary, vocational, and teacher training, teachers 540.
   Finance and Trade. Monetary unit: Guinea-Bissau peso, with (Sept. 21, 1981) a free rate of 37.93 pesos to U.S. $1 (70.33 pesos = £1 sterling). Budget (1979 est.): revenue 890 million pesos; expenditure 1,474,000,000 pesos. Foreign trade (1979): imports *c.* 2,070,000,000 pesos; exports *c.* 480 million pesos. Import sources: Portugal 27%; Sweden 10%; U.S.S.R. 9%; France 9%; Italy 7%; East Germany 6%; West Germany 5%; The Netherlands 5%. Export destinations: Portugal 38%; Angola 23%; Spain 21%; Senegal 6%; U.K. 5%. Main exports (1977): peanuts 60%; fish 19%; copra 12%.
   Agriculture. Production (in 000; metric tons; 1979): rice *c.* 60; plantains *c.* 25; peanuts *c.* 35; palm kernels *c.* 10; palm oil *c.* 5; copra *c.* 5; timber (cu m) *c.* 524. Livestock (in 000; 1979): cattle *c.* 264; pigs *c.* 175; sheep *c.* 73; goats *c.* 183.

Guyana

A republic and member of the Commonwealth, Guyana is situated on the Atlantic Ocean between Venezuela, Brazil, and Suriname. Area: 215,000 sq km (83,000 sq mi). Pop. (1981 est.): 904,000, including (1978) East Indian 50%; African 30%; mixed 10%; Amerindian 5%. Cap. and largest city: Georgetown (pop., 1979 est., 195,000). Language: English (official). Religion (1970): Hindu 37%; Protestant 32%; Roman Catholic 13%. President in 1981, Forbes Burnham; prime minister, Ptolemy Reid.

In 1981 Venezuela decided to pursue its long-standing claim to the potentially mineral-rich Essequibo region, covering some two-thirds of Guyana's territory, rather than renegotiate the Protocol of Port-of-Spain, which provided for a moratorium on the issue until June 1982. Following Pres. Forbes Burnham's visit to Caracas in April, Guyana moved swiftly to mobilize domestic, regional, and world opinion in its favour.

Despite reservations about the internal political scene in Guyana, Caribbean and other nations supported Guyana's moves to counter Venezuela's diplomatic thrust. The U.S., however, maintained a position of strict neutrality. Closer links were established with Cuba, North Korea, Brazil, and Colombia, and late in the year relations with the U.S.S.R. appeared to be improving. However, relations with neighbouring Suriname (also with territorial claims against Guyana) deteriorated. The economy remained severely depressed.

(DAVID A. JESSOP)

GUYANA

Education. (1979–80) Primary, pupils 164,830, teachers 6,021; secondary, pupils 46,595, teachers 2,513; vocational, pupils 3,595, teachers 242; teacher training, pupils 1,052, teachers 106; higher (university only), students 1,889, teaching staff (1975–76) 172.

Finance. Monetary unit: Guyanan dollar, with (Sept. 21, 1981) a par value of Guy$3 to U.S. $1 (free rate of Guy$5.56 = £1 sterling). Budget (total; 1979 est.): revenue Guy$626 million; expenditure Guy$788 million.

Foreign Trade. (1980) Imports Guy$1,084,000,000; exports Guy$984 million. Import sources (1978): Trinidad and Tobago 27%; U.S. 23%; U.K. 22%. Export destinations (1978): U.K. 30%; U.S. 20%; Trinidad and Tobago 7%; Canada 7%; Norway 6%; Jamaica 5%. Main exports: bauxite 37%; sugar 31%; alumina 11%; rice 9%.

Agriculture. Production (in 000; metric tons; 1980): rice c. 313; sugar, raw value c. 300; bananas and plantains c. 26; oranges (1979) c. 12; copra c. 3. Livestock (in 000; 1979): cattle c. 280; sheep c. 113; goats c. 68; pigs c. 132; chickens c. 12,000.

Industry. Production (in 000; metric tons; 1979): bauxite 1,795; alumina 280; diamonds (metric carats) 16; electricity (kw-hr; 1978) 405,000.

Gymnastics and Weight Lifting

Gymnastics. The Soviet Union, as it had done in the 1980 Olympic Games, won both team and individual all-around honours in the 1981 men's and women's world gymnastics championships in

Guyana

Julianne McNamara of Oregon won the all-around competition in the American Cup gymnastics meet held in Texas in March.

Moscow. Yury Korolev of the Soviet Union overtook teammate Bogdan Makuts in the final event to win the men's all-around title. The bronze medal for that event was earned by Koji Gushiken of Japan. Olympic champion Aleksandr Dityatin of the U.S.S.R. abandoned the floor exercises and was not eligible for the all-around final competition. Bart Conner in 11th place finished highest for the U.S.

Olga Bicherova led the Soviet sweep of the three medals in the women's all-around competition, edging out Maria Filatova with a perfect 10 in the vault. Third place went to Olympic champion Yelena Davydova. The three U.S. entrants were Julianne McNamara, tied for 7th; Kathy Johnson, 15th; and Tracee Talavera, 20th.

In the men's team competition the Soviet Union finished first with 588.95 points, followed by Japan with 585.85, China with 583.90, and East Germany with 583.75. The U.S. placed fifth with 577.30. In the women's team event the Soviet Union was first with 389.30 points, while China finished second with 384.60 and East Germany placed third with 382.10. As in the 1979 tourney, the U.S. finished sixth.

In the individual competition Maxi Gnauck of East Germany won three gold medals, retaining her Olympic title on the uneven parallel bars with a perfect 10 score, the only one awarded in the women's individual finals. She also won the balance beam and the vault but had to withdraw from the all-around competition because of an ankle injury in the optional exercises. The outstanding performer in the men's individual finals was Dityatin, who won gold medals on the rings and the parallel

Bart Conner of the University of
Oklahoma was the men's champion
in the American Cup gymnastics
competition in Texas in March.

Anatoly Pisarenko of the
U.S.S.R. won the super-
heavyweight champion-
ship in European
weight-lifting competi-
tion in France in Sep-
tember.

bars. In the men's finals ten perfect 10 scores were awarded by the judges.

Of the 14 gold medals available, the Soviet Union won both men's and women's team and individual all-around, four men's individual titles, and one women's event (Natalya Ilyenko in the floor exercises). The U.S.S.R. also won or shared six silver and two bronze medals. East Germany won four gold medals outright and shared another, while China shared two gold medals and Japan won one.

In the U.S. championships the all-around champions were Jim Hartung and Tracee Talavera, respectively. Anelia Ralenkova of Bulgaria was the 1981 world champion in rhythmic gymnastics as Bulgaria swept the top three places.

It appeared that the men and women from the People's Republic of China would be the number one threat to the supremacy of the U.S.S.R. at the 1984 Olympic Games. Ma Yanhong was fourth in the women's all-around, and Tong Fei also placed fourth in the men's all-around. Romania, whose women had dominated the sport for six years, was rebuilding with a young team, which could mature in the next three years.

Weight Lifting. The world championships in Lille, France, were a repeat of the 1980 Olympic Games weight-lifting competition—a dual meet between the Soviet Union and Bulgaria. Three Olympic champions repeated in 1981. They were Kanybek Osmanoliev of the Soviet Union in the 52-kg class with a total lift of 247.5 kg, Yanko Rusev of Bulgaria in the 75-kg class with a lift of 360 kg, and Yurik Vardanyan of the U.S.S.R. in the 82.5-kg class with a lift of 392.5 kg. The U.S.S.R. retained the team title with 307 points, followed by Bulgaria with 267 and Poland with 177. The U.S. finished tenth with 41 points.

In the ten weight classes the Soviet lifters won five firsts, three seconds, and two thirds. Bulgaria earned four gold medals, two silvers, and three bronzes. Of the 30 medals available, the U.S.S.R.,

Bulgaria, Poland, East Germany, Czechoslovakia, and Cuba won 28. Japan and France each won one third-place medal.

For a post-Olympic year the lifting was extraordinary. The Soviets had champions in the three heaviest weight classes who were competing in their first world tournament. In the 100-kg class Victor Sots lifted 407.5 kg; in the 110-kg class Valery Kravchuk lifted 415 kg; and in the over-110-kg class Anatoly Pisarenko lifted 425 kg.

Blagoi Blagoev of Bulgaria won the 90-kg class with a total of 400 kg, 23 kg greater than the Olympic gold medalist at Moscow. Daniel Nuñez of Cuba had won the 56-kg title in the 1980 Olympics. In the 60-kg class he and Beloslav Manolov of Bulgaria each lifted 302.5 kg, but Manolov was declared the winner because he had a lighter body weight at the weigh-in after the lifting.

The best performance for the U.S. was by superheavyweight Jerry Hannan, who finished sixth with a total lift of 350 kg. Other champions included Anton Kodjabashev of Bulgaria in the 56-kg class with a total lift of 272.5 kg and Joachim Kunz of East Germany in the 67.5-kg class with a total lift of 336.4 kg.　　　(CHARLES ROBERT PAUL, JR.)

[452.B.4.f]

Haiti

The Republic of Haiti occupies the western one-third of the Caribbean island of Hispaniola, which it shares with the Dominican Republic. Area: 27,-750 sq km (10,715 sq mi). Pop. (1980 est.): 5,009,-000, of whom 95% are Negro. Cap. and largest city: Port-au-Prince (pop., 1978 est., 745,800). Language: French (official) and Creole. Religion: Roman Catholic; Voodoo practiced in rural areas. President in 1981, Jean-Claude Duvalier.

In April 1981 Pres. Jean-Claude Duvalier celebrated his tenth year in office. His wife, Michèle Bennett, whom he had married in May 1980, was

HAITI

Education. (1977–78) Primary, pupils 268,460, teachers 8,432; secondary, pupils 55,816, teachers (1976–77) 3,324; vocational (1975–76), pupils 5,356, teachers 747; higher, students 5,196, teaching staff 697.

Finance. Monetary unit: gourde, with (Sept. 21, 1981) a par value of 5 gourdes to U.S. $1 (free rate of 9.27 gourdes = £1 sterling). Gold and other reserves (June 1981) U.S. $12 million. Budget (1978–79 est.) balanced at 473 million gourdes. Cost of living (Port-au-Prince; 1975 = 100; Dec. 1980) 151.5.

Foreign Trade. Imports (1978) 1,103,400,000 gourdes; exports (1979) 927.1 million gourdes. Import sources: U.S. 45%; Netherlands Antilles 10%; Japan 9%; Canada 8%; West Germany 5%. Export destinations (1978): U.S. 59%; France 13%; Italy 7%; Belgium-Luxembourg 6%. Main exports (1976–77): coffee 44%; bauxite 12%; toys and sports goods 10%.

Transport and Communications. Roads (1979) c. 4,-000 km. Motor vehicles in use (1979): passenger 23,900; commercial (including buses) 8,500. Railways (1979) c. 250 km. Telephones (Jan. 1980) 34,900. Radio receivers (Dec. 1978) c. 100,000. Television receivers (Dec. 1978) c. 15,-000.

Agriculture. Production (in 000; metric tons; 1980): rice c. 91; corn (1979) c. 260; sorghum c. 125; sweet potatoes (1979) c. 97; cassava (1979) c. 262; sugar, raw value (1979) c. 65; dry beans c. 45; bananas (1979) c. 53; plantains (1979) c. 198; mangoes c. 326; coffee c. 35; sisal c. 16. Livestock (in 000; 1979): cattle c. 1,000; pigs c. 1,900; goats c. 1,300; sheep c. 87; horses c. 408.

Industry. Production (in 000; metric tons; 1979): cement 240; bauxite (exports) 769; electricity (kw-hr; 1980) c. 350,000.

officially named first lady in May. The announcement ended a power struggle between her and the president's mother, Simone Duvalier. The latter was removed from the presidential palace, and her chief supporters, the most important of whom was the chief of secret police, Luc Desyr, were dismissed from office.

A harder political line prevailed during the year. In January two prominent conservatives, Edouard Berrouet and Edouard Francisque, were appointed ministers of interior and defense and of foreign affairs, respectively. In August the leader of the Christian Democratic Party, Sylvio Claude, and

Thirty-three Haitian refugees drowned when their rickety sailboat was swamped by heavy seas off the Florida coast in October. Thirty-four others were rescued.

UPI

his daughter, Marie-France, were among 24 people given 15-year jail sentences on charges of attempted arson and plotting to overthrow the government.

Little economic progress was made in 1981, mainly as a result of Hurricane Allen, which struck the southern peninsula in August 1980, largely destroying the rice and bean crops and the coffee harvest. Tough import controls were imposed in July after international reserves fell to $9.6 million; this compared with $55 million at the end of 1979. (ROBIN CHAPMAN)

See also Migration, International.

Health and Disease

General Developments. In 1981, as in the previous year, new medical applications of biotechnology appeared to be launching a therapeutic revolution. Several new uses were announced for monoclonal antibodies, substances made by hybrids of antibody-producing cells and cancer cells. Unlike normal cells the hybrids grow and multiply indefinitely in culture. Monoclonal antibodies (so called because they are synthesized by a clone of identical hybrids producing just the one agent) have many potential medical uses by virtue of their capacity to attach themselves to—and thus identify or destroy—cells only of the kind used to stimulate their production. Their first successful use in the treatment of human disease was reported in the *New England Journal of Medicine*. The threatened rejection of a grafted kidney, which established methods had failed to prevent, was aborted by infusion of a monoclonal that reacted with the patient's own immune cells, which had been working against the implanted organ.

Doctors at the Stanford (Calif.) University Medical Center reported a dramatic reduction of cancerous white cells in the blood of leukemia patients within minutes of injecting an appropriate mono-

clonal. Because the antibody did not stop the production of new leukemia cells, effective treatment of the disease probably would require regular, repeated doses. Unfortunately, patients rapidly develop immune responses to material in monoclonal preparations made from hybridized mouse cells (the current technique), making sustained treatment impossible. In the summer, however, it became known that scientists at the University of Glasgow in Scotland, in collaboration with a new firm, Monotech, had succeeded in producing at least one monoclonal using human cells; such an agent might not provoke a rejection reaction.

In May Howard Jones of the Eastern Virginia Medical School announced the first successful implantation of a human test-tube embryo in the U.S. The ovum from the mother was fertilized in the laboratory by the method pioneered by Robert Edwards and Patrick Steptoe in the U.K. The world's first test-tube twins were born at the Queen Victoria Medical Centre in Melbourne, Australia, in June. The Australian workers, based at Monash University, gave the prospective mother hormones that caused her to shed several eggs at a time. These were all fertilized, and two embryos were implanted in the womb to increase the chance for success. The spare embryos were frozen and stored in liquid nitrogen in case the first implantation failed. The technique also allowed the doctors to wait until the mother had recovered from the egg-harvesting operation before undertaking the implantation. This practice did raise ethical problems, however, regarding the eventual fate of the unused embryos, which, according to one of the workers involved, could survive for 400 years. Some thawed and apparently normal embryos also were implanted at Monash, but it was not yet known whether freezing did any damage. A Bioethics Research Centre set up at the university began a study of the implications of test-tube fertilization and frozen embryo storage.

A new fetal surgical technique for hydrocephalus, or water on the brain, was tried successfully for the first time. Hydrocephalus occurs when fluid that normally circulates throughout the brain and spinal cord is blocked. The fluid becomes trapped in brain cavities called ventricles, where it exerts increasing pressure on the developing fetal brain. As a result babies with hydrocephalus may be mentally retarded, experience convulsions, or even die. Early in the year a team led by William Clewell of the University of Colorado Health Sciences Center in Denver inserted a valve in the skull of a 24-week-old fetus with hydrocephalus. The accumulating fluid drained from the brain to the amniotic sac surrounding the fetus. In mid-July the shunt clogged and fluid began building up in the brain, necessitating cesarean delivery of the baby several weeks prematurely. In late 1981 the baby was home and seemed to be doing well.

Another team of doctors, at Brigham and Women's Hospital and Harvard Medical School in Boston, also reported successfully operating on a hydrocephalic fetus in the womb. They inserted a needle through the mother's abdomen and womb wall and into the fetal skull at a point where the fluid was collecting. The procedure eventually was

U.S. Senators Robert Byrd (left) and Patrick Leahy demonstrated the skimpy school lunch proposed by the administration of Pres. Ronald Reagan.

UPI

repeated six times before birth. The baby was born with some mental retardation because the brain was abnormal, but the doctors hoped that the technique could be used to prevent brain damage in babies whose hydrocephalus is due solely to a blockage of the normal drainage channels.

Yet another feat of prenatal treatment was announced by a team from the University of California at San Francisco, who had given large doses of the B vitamin biotin to the mother of a fetus that, because of a rare genetic defect, was unable to remain healthy on normal and natural supplies of the vitamin. The mother was given biotin because a previous child had suffered the same disease, and there was a one-in-four chance this fetus would be affected. The mother gave birth to a child who at the time of the report was a happy five-year-old, normal apart from the need to continue taking biotin. Also at the same university surgeons drained the distended bladder of one of twin fetuses that was suffering from a urinary obstruction, using a catheter inserted through the mother's abdominal wall.

Such reports emphasized the growing importance of prenatal medicine. During the summer the American Medical Association commented that "[work with] the unborn has now reached the stage where the fetus is on the threshold of becoming a patient."

A heart attack usually occurs when a blood clot completely blocks a coronary artery, thus cutting off the blood supply that the artery delivers to the heart. As a result the portion of heart muscle that normally receives blood from the blocked artery dies. During the past year cardiologists in the U.S. enthusiastically began adopting a method of stopping heart attacks that are actually in progress. The technique was developed in 1979 by two West German doctors, Peter Rentrop and Karl Karsh, who found that they could stop a heart attack by threading a catheter into the blocked coronary artery and injecting the enzyme streptokinase, which breaks down the clot. After a streptokinase injection the patient's chest pains disappear and his electrocardiogram looks normal, indicating that the heart is functioning properly. The sooner that the clot is dissolved after a heart attack begins, the better. Although heart attacks generally last 12–24 hours, about 50% of the heart cells that will die in the attack do so in the first few hours.

The U.S. National Heart, Lung, and Blood Institute (NHLBI) started a register of the use of a new technique, pioneered in Switzerland, for relieving obstruction in diseased coronary arteries. This procedure involves threading a balloon-tipped catheter by way of an artery into the diseased heart vessel and then inflating the balloon to stretch the constriction. By August the register, which was designed to facilitate early assessment of the procedure, had more than 1,500 entries.

The year produced the usual crop of additions to the ever lengthening list of everyday materials suspected of being capable of causing cancer. New recruits included red wine, grape juice, tea, parsnips, urea-formaldehyde foam, cutting oils, suntan creams containing bergamot oil, peanut oil in cosmetics, and coffee. Coffee became suspect fol-

Julius Jacobson of Mount Sinai Medical Center, New York City, demonstrates the centre's new hyperbaric chamber. The chamber is used to supply additional oxygen during operations on stroke victims.

lowing a study of patients with cancer of the pancreas in hospitals in Boston and Rhode Island. The investigators had been seeking a possible association between cigarette smoking and the disease but found an unexpected and even stronger link with coffee drinking. They suggested that, although the risk was small, the beverage could be responsible for perhaps half the cases of pancreatic cancer that occur. Much more work was needed before the carcinogenic potential of coffee was either dismissed or confirmed.

In March two leading British epidemiologists, Richard Doll and Richard Peto, lent their support to a suggestion made the previous year that vitamin A protects against cancer. Writing in the science periodical *Nature*, they concluded that a study of the anticancer effects of the vitamin was one of the few lines of research that, in the medium term, stood a chance of reducing overall cancer incidence rates.

In June a U.S. congressional committee made a blistering attack on the way the National Cancer Institute (NCI) had carried out research over the previous ten years. Particular concern was voiced over a $910,000 research grant made to Marc J. Straus of New York Medical College, who received the money in March 1980, 21 months after he had resigned from Boston University School of Medicine because of charges that he had falsified data, changed patients' histories to conform with rules governing drug trials, and failed to obtain the consent of patients for experiments. Although other charges of mismanagement of funds and research projects were made against the institute, perhaps the major difficulty lay in a naïve approach by politicians to the problems involved, as exemplified by a remark reportedly made by one U.S. senator: "We've spent a lot of money on cancer . . . why isn't the cure round the corner a la polio?" Such were signs that the lavish official support and funding enjoyed by U.S. cancer workers since Pres. Richard Nixon declared war on the disease in 1971 were coming to an end. The field of cancer

PHOTOS, JIM POZARIK—GAMMA/LIAISON

A calf named Tennyson was kept alive for 268 days with an artificial heart similar to the one pictured at right. The heart was developed by researchers at the University of Utah School of Medicine.

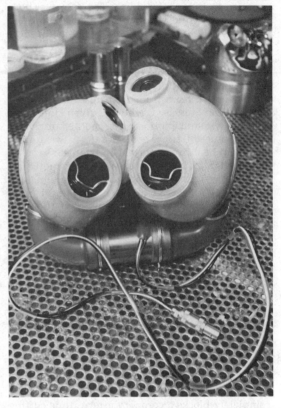

research suffered another blow in the autumn when a brilliant biochemical model of the mechanism of the disease, put forward by Mark Spector, a young researcher at Cornell University, Ithaca, N.Y., was shown to have been based, in part at least, on falsified experimental findings.

What appeared to be a human cancer virus was isolated from patients with a rare form of leukemia that involves mature T lymphocytes, which are cells of the immune system. Robert Gallo and his associates at the NCI, who isolated the virus, found that a few patients with this disease, as well as some of their relatives, had antibodies to the virus, indicating that they had been exposed to it, but that healthy unrelated volunteers did not. Working with a similar, if not identical, virus Yorio Hinuma of Kyoto University in Japan reported that the virus caused normal cells grown in culture to become cancerous. But the leukemia virus clearly is not highly contagious since this form of cancer is so rare. Previously, viruses that cause cancer in animals, including monkeys, had been isolated.

Like most years 1981 was also a year of medical controversies. One involved the link between cholesterol-lowering diets and cancer that had been first suggested a decade earlier. Doctors had reported that men put on cholesterol-lowering diets tended to get cancer, but other scientists subsequently could not confirm this result. Then in the mid-1970s scientists began reporting that those people in various populations who had the lowest serum-cholesterol concentrations sometimes had higher than expected incidences of cancer. For example, in the Framingham Study, a long-term look at the population of Framingham, Mass., sponsored by the NHLBI, it was found that men with cholesterol concentrations below 190 mg (milligrams) per 100 ml (millilitres) of blood had three times the incidence of colon cancer as men with higher cholesterol concentrations. (The average American has a cholesterol concentration of 215 mg per 100 ml of blood.) The question arose: are people who go on cholesterol-lowering diets trading heart disease for cancer?

In May 1981 the NHLBI sponsored a review meeting at which it was concluded that cholesterol-lowering diets to reduce the risk of heart disease do not put people at risk for cancer. Those people whose cholesterol is high enough to put them at risk for heart disease will not be able to lower it to the cancer-risk range. The meaning of the connection between low cholesterol and cancer, however, remained a mystery.

In late 1980 the NCI began a clinical study of the alleged anticancer drug Laetrile. The patients were given not only Laetrile but also the special diet of fresh fruits, vegetables, whole grains, and little meat that was advocated by pro-Laetrile groups. The results of the study showed that Laetrile is not effective. Of 156 patients who were followed, only one showed a partial remission, but after ten weeks even that person had a relapse. Only 54 patients were still alive in May, after eight months of the Laetrile regimen, and cancer had spread in 49 of them. Nonetheless, Robert W. Bradford, president of the Committee for the Freedom of Choice for Cancer Therapy, argued that the study was meaningless because it used the wrong chemical form of Laetrile. Hence, those who wanted to continue believing in the drug were given a reason to do so.

During the summer Spain suffered an outbreak of mass poisioning from olive oil adulterated with industrial rapeseed oil, which had been sold for human consumption by traders seeking a quick profit. There were an estimated 200 deaths, mostly children and old people, and many more were admitted to hospitals. Aniline mixed with the rapeseed oil, which was intended as a lubricant, was thought to be responsible.

Mortality rates in less developed countries, which had been improving dramatically since World War II, were reported to have leveled off such that life expectancy was still less than 50 years. Whereas such communicable diseases as smallpox yielded rapidly to new drugs and medical management, poverty-related diseases like pneumonia, diarrhea, and malnutrition remained, and slow economic improvements were not keeping pace with population increases. According to a publication from the U.S. Overseas Development Council, a private research group, this situation should be tackled by providing expectant mothers with food supplements, monitoring the state of nutrition of underweight infants, teaching the technique of oral rehydration for children with diarrhea, and ensuring the availability of antibiotics for respiratory infections. In the longer term, maximum advantage should be taken of methods already available for improving food production.

Regulation and Legal Matters. The perennial disputes over abortion arose again in the U.S. in 1981, this time with a new twist in the form of a "human life" bill sponsored by Sen. Jesse Helms (Rep., N.C.) and Rep. Henry J. Hyde (Rep., Ill.). The bill would prohibit abortions by defining human life as originating at conception. Fetuses, therefore, would legally be "persons" whose lives would be protected by the 14th Amendment to the Constitution. The purpose of this bill was to overturn the 1973 Supreme Court decision that antiabortion laws violate the constitutional right to privacy.

According to legal scholars the human life bill was unconstitutional because Congress does not have the authority to overturn a Supreme Court decision. Nonetheless, a subcommittee of the Senate Judiciary Committee held hearings at which scientific and religious organizations and social commentators ranging from the National Academy of Sciences to advice columnist Ann Landers expressed opinions on the start of human life. At year's end the fate of the bill remained undecided.

With the new administration of U.S. Pres. Ronald Reagan came a new commissioner of the Food and Drug Administration (FDA), Arthur Hayes, Jr. Hayes demonstrated his stated intention of cutting through regulatory delays by approving aspartame, a low-calorie artificial sweetener made by G. D. Searle & Co. Searle had first won FDA approval for the sweetener in 1974, but that approval was soon withdrawn because of allegations by researcher John Olney of Washington University, St. Louis, Mo., that it might cause nerve-cell and brain damage and possibly brain tumours. In 1980 an FDA panel concluded that aspartame does not cause nerve-cell or brain damage, but it could not rule out the possibility of brain tumours. Hayes argued that the FDA did not have to be convinced that there is zero risk before approving a substance and that the risk from aspartame is not significant. The sweetener was expected to take over about 25% of saccharin's market, primarily in breakfast cereals, chewing gum, powdered beverages, whipped toppings, and gelatin and as a tabletop sweetener. It would not be used in soft drinks because it is not stable during the shelf life of these beverages.

Under Hayes the FDA also approved two new classes of drugs that should benefit a wide variety of patients. One is the calcium antagonists, which would be used to treat heart disease. Recently cardiologists recognized that many patients have chest pains and sometimes even heart attacks because their coronary arteries go into spasms, thereby preventing blood from reaching the heart muscle. The calcium antagonists were the first drugs available to relax these spasms.

The second class of drugs is the new generation of cephalosporins. These drugs are antibiotics, closely resembling penicillin in chemical structure, that are effective against a broad range of microorganisms. For example, they cure penicillin-resistant gonorrhea, bacterial meningitis, urinary tract infections, and many infections acquired in the hospital environment. The new cephalosporins, however, must be injected and so should find their greatest use in hospitals.

In November the FDA approved the drug timolol for use in treating heart attack victims following impressive results for the drug and a related compound in recent studies in the U.S. and Norway. Doctors believed that timolol could sharply reduce the death rate among the thousands of patients who might otherwise succumb to heart disease within two years of their first attack.

In April a U.S. federal district court jury unanimously decided that Bendectin (Debendox in the U.K.), a morning-sickness suppressant, had not been responsible for the birth defects of a six-year-old boy. The parents had been awarded $20,000 at a previous trial to cover medical expenses but had received no part of the $12 million in damages that they had claimed. A retrial had been ordered on appeal because it was held that the plaintiffs were either entitled to damages or, if Bendectin was not to blame, nothing.

Economic Aspects. In keeping with his vow to cut federal spending, President Reagan sharply reduced government funds for social services, including Medicaid, food stamps, and the school lunch program. Cuts in funds for the basic welfare program, Aid to Families with Dependent Children, eliminated nearly 500,000 families from the rolls and reduced benefits for an additional 258,000 families. About 875,000 families were dropped from the food stamp program, and 1.4 million households had their benefits reduced. Reductions in Medicaid benefits varied from state to state. Cuts in federal subsidies for school lunch programs resulted in higher priced lunches. The Reagan administration also attempted to change the requirements for school lunches—by defining ketchup and relish as "vegetables," for example—but backed off after severe public criticism. Many of those who would be hit first by the Reagan cuts were families headed by women who earned some money on their own. They were likely to lose supplemental welfare payments and, more importantly, to be dropped from Medicaid rolls.

In June the *New England Journal of Medicine* stated that U.S. medicine had become too expensive for the public and forecast that during the 1980s

more doctors would be cutting costs, working shorter hours, writing fewer prescriptions, and hospitalizing fewer patients. The Melrose-Wakefield obstetric hospital in Massachusetts, backed by the Blue Cross-Blue Shield health insurance agency, offered new mothers $100 to go home within 24 hours of delivery if fit to do so plus a further $100 to pay for health services not covered by insurance, as well as free home visits from a nurse and five days of help with the housework. Fearful of the increasing costs of medical insurance some U.S. employers began offering workers cash to stay away from their doctors. A Connecticut company announced awards as high as $500 to employees who kept their medical bills below the $775 mark.

In Great Britain the Conservative Party government favoured an expansion of private medicine and declared its intention of examining alternative ways of financing health care, such as the introduction of compulsory health insurance to replace the present method of paying for the National Health Service almost entirely from central funds. The opposition Labour Party, at its annual conference, passed a resolution demanding the abolition of all private medicine, but conference decisions were not binding on any future Labour government.   (DONALD W. GOULD; GINA BARI KOLATA)
[321.C.5; 421.B.2.d.iii; 424.B.1.a; 424.C.1; 424.C.4.b; 424.H; 425.I.2.d–e; 425.J]

MENTAL HEALTH

The rights and management of patients diagnosed as suffering from mental illness attracted as much attention in 1981 as any advance in understanding or treating disorders of the mind.

The British government prepared to introduce a Mental Health Act amendment bill to modify the act of 1959, which, hailed at the time as a humane and enlightened measure, had been harshly criticized within recent years by many, including the European Commission on Human Rights. The new bill was expected to abolish the power of the home secretary to detain mental patients without limit of time (exercised in the case of certain criminals committed to special hospitals by the courts), to give all detained patients the right of appeal to a tribunal, to abolish censorship of mail, and to allow patients to sue members of the staff of mental

hospitals under certain circumstances. The bill also was expected to limit forcible treatment, singling out such procedures as brain surgery, electroconvulsive therapy, and treatment with drugs having potentially serious side effects, and to forbid doctors to undertake such therapy on unwilling patients without support of a second opinion. Nonetheless, mental health reformers remained fearful that the new legislation would not go far enough toward safeguarding the civil liberties of the mentally ill.

In April the British medical journal *Lancet* published an article by Anatoly Koryagin, a Soviet psychiatrist who had worked as a consultant for the Working Commission to Investigate the Use of Psychiatry for Political Purposes. At the time of publication Koryagin was awaiting trial on charges of anti-Soviet agitation. His article related that, on behalf of the commission, he had examined perfectly sane people who had been classified as mentally ill because they said or did things considered anti-Soviet, and it quoted an official state psychiatrist, A. P. Filatova, as saying "No normal person can be opposed to the Workers' and Peasants' State." Of those committed to mental hospitals for political reasons, 70% were classified as "psychopaths" and 30% as "schizophrenics," and most were also described as "paranoid." Many such patients claimed to have received no kind of treatment except when they were judged to have merited punishment; they were then given tranquilizers or insulin shock therapy.

Further evidence was reported on the possible harmful effects of the long-term administration of the benzodiazepines; for example, Valium and Librium. A study at the University of Oxford on rats demonstrated that these tranquilizing agents reduce tolerance to stress, and a human trial conducted at the Institute of Psychiatry in London showed that the results of psychological performance tests improved by 30% after patients receiving therapeutic doses of such drugs had been weaned from their medication. The researchers involved in both experiments said that their results supported earlier claims that these widely used drugs should be given for short periods only.

Yet another possible biochemical basis for schizophrenia was proposed by workers at the University of Alabama and the Veterans Adminis-

Noting that there are 33 million handicapped persons in the U.S., the American Dental Association has begun providing dental services for homebound patients.

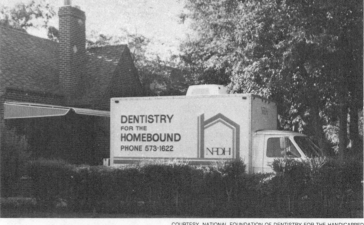

tration Hospital in Augusta, Ga. They suggested that schizophrenic symptoms arise as a result of a genetically determined metabolic fault that results in an accumulation in the brain of a simple organic chemical, formaldehyde. Their theory, published in *Medical Hypotheses*, leads to testable predictions (such as increased levels of formaldehyde in the urine of schizophrenic patients) which, if confirmed, could advance treatment of the disease.

According to a study of 1,124 patients in British hospitals for the mentally handicapped, 10% showed a significant loss of hearing, which is a much higher proportion than in the population at large. In addition, 15 of these poor hearers achieved an IQ score above 70, taking them out of the "mentally handicapped" classification. This find suggested that nearly a thousand British citizens, and many thousands worldwide, could be wrongly placed in mental hospitals because of an unrecognized hearing disability.

A French study of the psychological performance of children with Down's syndrome (mongolism), supported by chromosomal studies, suggested that vitamin supplements—particularly, large doses of the B vitamin folic acid—may bring about a significant improvement in victims of this congenital disease. A larger cooperative study in France and the U.K. was under way.

It has long been conventional wisdom that children do not suffer from true endogenous depression, but the use of diagnostic criteria recently developed by the American Psychiatric Association suggested that there may be more than 40,000 depressed children in the U.S. During the year Lenore Sawyer Radloff of the National Institute of Mental Health, Bethesda, Md., launched a massive epidemiological study aimed at establishing the incidence of depressive symptoms among that nation's children.   (DONALD W. GOULD)
[321.C.4.c.iii; 438.D.1.a; 438.D.2.e]

DENTISTRY

Dental insurance in the U.S. continued to attract new subscribers during 1981, covering 75 million or one in every three Americans. Because prepaid dental care had become an established employee benefit in virtually all major industries, many small businesses were trying to obtain the same popular fringe benefit for their employees. An emerging trend was to continue dental insurance even after the employee or union member had retired.

University of Buffalo (N.Y.) dental scientists discovered that the effectiveness of dental and orthopedic devices may be increased with the use of a technique that "supercleans" their surfaces before implantation. The technique, called radiofrequency glow discharge (RFGD), involves putting the implant into an evacuated chamber containing electrically excited argon gas. The gas sterilizes the implant and "scrubs" its surface of contaminants that may interfere with the body's ability to heal. Because the method results in better adhesion of the implant to surrounding tissue, it may be useful in a variety of implant procedures including hip and knee surgery.

The extent to which saliva bathes the teeth dur-

ing eating may well control the development of cavity-causing acids, suggested dental scientist David C. Abelson of Columbia University in New York City. Results of his recent study indicated that a food that stimulates greater salivary flow may result in diminished acid attack on teeth. His study examined the relative cariogenic (decay-producing) potential of a variety of sugar-containing processed foods to find out which food characteristics might be modified most effectively. Abelson tested 29 food products as well as some components of particular foods (like the filling and icing of a cake) and found that their ability to stimulate salivation when chewed was linked to the amount of sugar they left in the mouth as food for acid-producing bacteria. In relating the effect of saliva flow on acid production for iced chocolate cake, plain chocolate cake, and white bread, Abelson found that "in descending order, the chocolate cake with the icing resulted in a greater amount of acid than the white bread, which in turn produced more than the plain chocolate cake."

Researchers at Boston's Forsyth Dental Center reiterated previous scientific evidence that flossing coupled with proper brushing results in healthier gums. Patients with periodontal, or gum, problems participating in the study were given instructions by demonstration and videotape in the use of waxed, unwaxed, and mint-flavoured dental floss. Special emphasis was placed on removing dental plaque, a major cause of tooth decay and periodontal disease, from spaces between the teeth. Supervised daily flossing lasted for eight weeks, at which time a significant reduction in the rate of periodontal disease was found, according to Ralph R. Lobene, who headed the research team.
          (LOU JOSEPH)
[422.E.1.a.ii; 10/35.C.1]

See also Demography; Life Sciences; Nobel Prizes; Social Security and Welfare Services.

Historic Preservation

Reflecting the continuing and growing concern for the conservation of the man-made and natural environment, 61 nations by late 1981 had deposited an instrument of ratification or acceptance of the

The ancient city of San'a', North Yemen, was the centre of a UNESCO campaign to preserve the unique beauty of classic Yemeni architecture.

1972 International Convention Concerning the Protection of the World Cultural and Natural Heritage. Adherents to the convention since January 1980 included the Central African Republic, Chile, Cuba, Greece, Haiti, Ivory Coast, Mauritania, Portugal, Seychelles, South Yemen, and Sri Lanka. As of September 1980, 85 sites had been inscribed on the World Heritage List; at the last meeting of the World Heritage Committee in Sydney, Australia, in October 1981 an additional 26 sites were inscribed. Among those included were the Medina of Fez (Morocco); Shalimar Gardens (Pakistan); palace and gardens of Fontainebleau (France); Great Barrier Reef (Australia); Speyer Cathedral (West Germany); Niokolo-Koba National Park (Senegal); and Mammoth Cave National Park (U.S.).

With the completion in 1980 of the first of UNESCO's international conservation campaigns—for the preservation of the monuments of Egyptian and Sudanese Nubia—a logical extension of this successful endeavour was being planned in 1981. This was an international campaign to assist in the development of a Nubian Museum in Aswan and a National Museum of Egyptian Antiquities in Cairo. Another UNESCO international campaign, work on which would soon be completed, centred on Borobudur in Indonesia. This huge, square, stone Buddhist monument, measuring 123 m (400 ft) on each side and featuring four terraces, 1,460 bas-reliefs, and 432 statues, was being painstakingly disassembled and reconstructed on stable foundations. Other targets of international historic preservation campaigns that were initiated with resolutions at the September–October 1980 General Conference of UNESCO in Belgrade, Yugos., included Plaza Vieja, Havana (Cuba); Wadi Hadramawt and Shibam (South Yemen); San'a' (North Yemen); Goreme and Istanbul (Turkey); and Paharpur Vihara and Khalifatabad (Bangladesh). A campaign for the preservation of structures at the slave station on the island of Goree, Senegal, and a campaign for four towns in Mauritania were launched by UNESCO Director General

Amadou Mahtar M'Bow in December 1980 and February 1981, respectively.

The less developed countries, particularly those that formerly were possessions of colonial powers, increasingly expressed a desire to retrieve part of their lost heritage. These claims were the basis of a symposium held in London in May 1981 organized by the Commonwealth Arts Association and the Africa Centre. The symposium brought together leading members of the British museum establishment with representatives from museums in the less developed nations and UNESCO. UNESCO's efforts in this area were concentrated on an "Intergovernmental Committee for Promoting the Return of Cultural Property to its Country of Origin or its Restitution in Case of Illicit Appropriation." In recent years both Belgium and The Netherlands had returned objects of art to their former colonies. The Australian Museum Trust also returned objects such as a slit drum to Vanuatu.

The Organization for Museums, Monuments, and Sites in Africa (OMMSA), which was founded in 1978, became operative in 1980. With a secretariat located in Accra, Ghana, OMMSA was concentrating on the training of conservationists. Courses for museum specialists in French-speaking Africa also began in Niamey, Niger, in December 1980. The Rome-based International Centre for the Study of the Preservation and Restoration of Cultural Property continued to have a leading role internationally in the training of conservationists of monuments. Reflecting a growing global concern for the preservation of rock art, the International Council of Monuments and Sites, with headquarters in Paris, established an international committee on this subject, and an International Training Seminar on Rock Art was organized by the Centro Comuno di Studi Preistorici, Capo di Ponte (Brescia), with the support and cooperation of the Italian government and UNESCO. The seminar was conducted at Capo di Ponte during August–September 1981, with the participation of 23 nations.

Within the framework of the Council of Europe's campaign for the "renaissance of the city," prizes for the best films produced to encourage the preservation of historic city centres were awarded in 1981. First place was won by a West German-Italian film, *Sanierung in Siena* ("Restoration in Siena"), by Thomas Sprengel and Cinzia Torrini; the second prize went to the Dutch *What's Happening to Our Cities?*, made by Jan Vrijman; and the third prize to a Belgian film, *Out of Harm's Way*, by Frans de Medts.

A notable two-volume, 1,200-page study of the development of historic preservation in the U.S. was published in 1981 for the Preservation Press of the U.S. National Trust for Historic Preservation. This important historiographic study by Charles B. Hosmer provided a model for nations attempting to inventory and protect their cultural heritage. The two volumes essentially formed the second and third volumes of Hosmer's earlier work, *Presence of the Past: A History of the Preservation Movement in the United States Before Williamsburg.*   (JOHN POPPELIERS)

See also Architecture; Environment; Museums.

Restoration work began on the Sphinx, in Giza, Egypt. The colossal statue has been flaking and crumbling as a result of sandstorms, rain, wind, and pollution.

WIDE WORLD

TOO MUCH PRESERVATION?

by Michael D. Kilian

Rhodes Tavern, in Washington, D.C., the unobtrusive building at the centre of one of U.S. preservationists' biggest controversies, stands virtually abandoned as it awaits a decision on its fate.

Perhaps the most acrimonious debate embroiling Washington, D.C., in recent years has had nothing to do with tax cuts or arms spending. It is over a dilapidated three-story building at 15th and G streets that houses a defunct souvenir shop, a great deal of grime, and not much else.

Built in 1799, Rhodes Tavern is claimed as the oldest extant structure in the city. Adm. George Cockburn, the British commander who burned most of Washington in 1814, reportedly had a leisurely dinner at the Rhodes while his troops were putting the torch to the nearby White House.

At the same time, the Rhodes is demonstrably one of the ugliest buildings in Washington, easily as hideous as the FBI's J. Edgar Hoover Building, long celebrated as Washington's worst. Ardent preservationists want the Rhodes Tavern kept intact come what may and stage enthusiastic protest marches to make their point. Others, including, of course, the developer who owns the property, take one look at the Rhodes's sagging, flaking exterior and ask, simply, "Why?"

Preservation Fever. The United States, among many other civilized societies, has been on a preservation binge in the last decade. There are now some 4,000 groups active in historic preservation in America and, despite the Reagan administration's budget cuts, at least 24 federal agencies are involved as well. Every year 2,200 equivalents of the Rhodes Tavern are added to the Department of the Interior's *National Register of Historic Places*, rendering them essentially immune from the wrecking ball.

But many continue to ask, "Why?" There are no official guidelines that determine absolutely what constitutes the preservable, and probably there should not be. But obviously not everything can be preserved. There would be no room for anything new. The question is: Are we saving the right stuff?

"We really know very little about everything we

Michael D. Kilian is a columnist for the Chicago Tribune *and news commentator on WBBM Radio, Chicago. His books include* Who Runs Chicago? *and* The Valkyrie Project.

want to preserve," says Prof. Richard W. Longstreth, chairman of the Committee on Preservation of the Society of Architectural Historians. "As the scope of our investigation broadens, so it necessitates reexamination of our values."

The principal value accorded historic places, naturally enough, is age. But one man's antiquity can be another's brand spanking new. In Britain almost no effort is made to save the period pieces of the 19th century; the chief concern is for the 13th century. In Greece preservationists are fighting to save the remnants of the 4th century BC from modern pollution. In Egypt the concern is for things from 2000 BC and earlier. The pharaohs would not be impressed with the Rhodes Tavern.

"Significance" is another factor, but "significant" to whom? The first "Chicago School" of architecture, created when architects from all over the U.S. scurried to the city to share in the rebuilding after the 1871 Chicago Fire, produced, among other things, the world's first structural steel skyscrapers and made the names of Dankmar Adler, Louis Sullivan, William Le Baron Jenney, and William Holabird immortal—to other architects. Not too many others remember who they were. But their remaining works in Chicago's Loop, including the gruesome Monadnock Building, are preserved as holy relics—even though to most people they exist simply as structures enclosing all sorts of stationery stores and coffee shops.

Yet, while preserving grotesque, obscure, arcane, and basically uninteresting old office buildings, usually housing third-rate lawyers and strange export-import firms, the city of Chicago blithely knocked down and steamrollered some of the most significant buildings in its history. At the command of the late Mayor Richard J. Daley, never a devotee of Chicago's gangster folklore, the city destroyed the garage on North Clark Street where the St. Valentine's Day Massacre took place, along with author Nelson Algren's favourite saloon, and replaced them with a bland senior citizens' residence. The lakefront Potter Palmer mansion, quintessential symbol of the robber baron ethic that made the city great, was also leveled.

New York City tore down Pennsylvania Station, which was classically beautiful, while preserving Grand Central Terminal, which is not. Presumably, as the longtime railroad gateway to the rest of the country, Grand Central is more significant. But now it serves as the gateway to Amtrak and has been disfigured by the hulking presence of the ugly Pan Am Building just to the north, which probably never will be torn down.

Landmarks in the Red. A problem with many historic landmarks is that they are not economically viable. New York City's Biltmore Hotel, just across the street from Grand Central, was no greater shakes as a hostelry than the nearby Commodore or Roosevelt, but it was favoured by Ivy League and Daisy Chain college men and women as their New York headquarters from the '20s through the '50s. Consequently, it ended up in the literature of F. Scott Fitzgerald, J. D. Salinger, and John Cheever.

When in 1981 the owners of the Biltmore began converting the failing hotel to more profitable use as an office building, the preservationists began clamouring to save the Biltmore music room, Palm Court restaurant, and "under the clock" saloon as national shrines. At the time, the hotel had only 25% occupancy. Declaring something a national shrine does not guarantee it customers, even if it is haunted by Holden Caulfield.

Harry Weese, designer and planner of Washington's Metro subway and one of the world's most respected architects, has long tried to have Chicago's Loop elevated structure made a historic landmark—without success, and logically so. Whatever the "significance" of the noisy, grimy, ugly, graffiti-covered, 19th-century contrivance, the "L"—despite having the highest fares in the nation—is having enough difficulty surviving economically as a rapid transit line let alone as a museum piece.

In 1978 the National Trust for Historic Preservation established an emergency Endangered Properties Fund to rescue structures facing imminent extinction. Its assets are about $2 million, hardly enough to buy a decent mansion nowadays. The Fund was able to save novelist Edith Wharton's estate in Lenox, Mass., from condominium development by buying it for $290,000, and selling it to a Shakespearean theatre group. However, there are few Shakespearean theatre groups about, and even fewer with $290,000 at hand.

Historic and Unhistoric Uses. Some "historic" Quaker Oats grain silos in Akron, Ohio, were recently preserved through conversion into a Hilton Hotel. They now resemble a hotel, not grain silos. The more usual practice is to convert a historic structure or district into restaurants, saloons, and boutiques. So many restaurants, saloons, and boutiques clog what was once John Steinbeck's Cannery Row in Monterey, Calif., that the original is about as recognizable as a fisherman in a three-piece suit.

Some historic sites one hopes will not be restored to their original function. The "Under-the-Hill" riverfront section of Natchez, Miss., is now part of a restoration project. In riverboat days, "Under-the-Hill" was where all of Natchez's brothels were. As though disapproving, the Fates have not been kind to the project. The Mississippi River has washed away all but two streets, and mudslides from the top of the hill keep wiping out buildings.

While the Greeks labour to save the crumbling Parthenon, preservationists in Miami Beach, Fla., are labouring to restore and preserve the area's small, seedy hotels, built in the 1920s and '30s, because of their Art Deco architecture. The city's Art Deco Historic District was entered in the *National Register of Historic Places* in 1979, the youngest historic place on record. New York City's Empire State Building and Chicago's Palmolive Building are magnificent examples of Art Deco at its best. Can the same be said for the Victor Hotel?

An instructive lesson for the Rhodes Tavern preservationists is perhaps to be found in the case of the house that once belonged to Francis Scott Key, author of "The Star Spangled Banner," on Washington's K Street. Though it was a national landmark owned by the National Park Service, the two-story red brick house was dismantled in 1947 to make room for Washington's Whitehurst Freeway, which itself is now being considered for demolition. The parts of the Key house were carefully stored away to be reassembled in another location at a later date. The government never got around to it and, as will happen in even the best of bureaucracies, the Park Service lost the pieces.

A retired Park Service historian said he thinks some of the bricks may be in storage bins under one of the Potomac River bridges, but he's not sure.

And no one cares enough to look and find out.

Honduras

A republic of Central America, Honduras is bounded by Nicaragua, El Salvador, Guatemala, the Caribbean Sea, and the Pacific Ocean. Area: 112,088 sq km (43,277 sq mi). Pop. (1980 est.): 3,-691,000, including 90% mestizo. Cap. and largest city: Tegucigalpa (pop., 1980 est., 444,700). Language: Spanish; some Indian dialects. Religion: Roman Catholic. Provisional president in 1981, Gen. Policarpo Paz García.

Under Honduras's new constitution, elections for the presidency, Congress, and the municipal authorities took place on Nov. 29, 1981. The Liberal Party, which had won the most seats in the 1980 elections to the Constituent Assembly, selected Roberto Suazo Córdova as its presidential candidate; the right-wing National Party candidate was Ricardo Zúñiga. Suazo was the victor with about 54% of the votes, compared with approximately 42% for Zúñiga, and his Liberal Party gained an absolute majority in Congress. The new administration, the country's first civilian government since 1972, would take office on Jan. 27, 1982.

Though a peace treaty with El Salvador had been signed on Oct. 30, 1980, relations deteriorated following Honduras's decision to increase taxes on all regional imports. Border tension resulted from the presence in Honduras of an estimated 40,000 refugees from strife-torn El Salvador. Also, supporters of the late Pres. Anastasio Somoza of Nicaragua continued to use Honduras as a base from which to conduct raids. Nicaragua claimed the Honduran Army was lending active support to the raiders. In an attempt to maintain Honduras as a buffer state within the region, the U.S. increased military aid.   (LUCY BLACKBURN)

Honduras

Hungary

Hungary

A people's republic of central Europe, Hungary is bordered by Czechoslovakia, the U.S.S.R., Romania, Yugoslavia, and Austria. Area: 93,033 sq km (35,920 sq mi). Pop. (1981 est.): 10,711,000, including (1970) Hungarian 95.8%; German 2.1%. Cap. and largest city: Budapest (pop., 1980 prelim., 2,060,000). Language: Magyar 95.8%. Religion (1979): Roman Catholic 61%, most of the remainder Protestant or atheist. First secretary of the Hungarian Socialist Workers' (Communist) Party in 1981, Janos Kadar; chairman of the Presidential Council (chief of state), Pal Losonczi; president of the Council of Ministers (premier), Gyorgy Lazar.

The 25th anniversary of the anti-Soviet uprising in Hungary in October 1956 passed quietly, but it was not completely ignored. Under the supervision of the Hungarian Socialist Workers' Party secretariat, newspaper articles and television programs recalled the demonstrations of 1956 and the street fighting that ensued once the Soviet Army had intervened. The purpose of this coverage

---

HONDURAS

Education. (1979) Primary, pupils 555,871, teachers 13,-670; secondary and vocational, pupils 119,080, teachers 2,766; teacher training, students 1,628, teachers 139; higher (university only), students 21,386, teaching staff 1,228.
Finance. Monetary unit: lempira, with (Sept. 21, 1981) a par value of 2 lempiras to U.S. $1 (free rate of 3.71 lempiras = £1 sterling). Gold and other reserves (June 1981) U.S. $113 million. Budget (1980 actual): revenue 756.6 million lempiras; expenditure 896.8 million lempiras. Gross national product (1980) 4,825,000,000 lempiras. Money supply (June 1981) 633.2 million lempiras. Cost of living (Tegucigalpa; 1975 = 100; Dec. 1980) 158.5.
Foreign Trade. (1980) Imports 2,036,900,000 lempiras; exports 1,612,500,000 lempiras. Import sources (1979): U.S. 44%; Venezuela 8%; Japan 7%; Guatemala 6%. Export destinations (1979): U.S. 54%; West Germany 10%; The Netherlands 8%; Japan 5%. Main exports: bananas 27%; coffee 25%; beef 8%; metal ores c. 6%.
Transport and Communications. Roads (1978) 8,308 km. Motor vehicles in use (1979): passenger 19,800; commercial (including buses) 42,400. Railways (1980) 1,928 km. Air traffic (1980): c. 394 million passenger-km; freight c. 3.5 million net ton-km. Shipping (1980): merchant vessels 100 gross tons and over 124; gross tonnage 213,421. Telephones (Jan. 1980) 27,400. Radio receivers (Dec. 1977) 163,000. Television receivers (Dec. 1977) 48,000.
Agriculture. Production (in 000; metric tons; 1980): corn c. 358; sorghum c. 34; sugar, raw value (1979) c. 169; dry beans c. 38; bananas c. 1,400; plantains (1979) c. 162; oranges c. 28; pineapples c. 32; palm oil c. 12; coffee c. 76; cotton, lint (1979) c. 8; tobacco c. 8; beef and veal (1979) c. 51; timber (cu m; 1979) c. 5,308. Livestock (in 000; 1979): cattle c. 1,800; pigs c. 530; horses c. 149; chickens c. 4,700.
Industry. Production (in 000; metric tons; 1979): cement 288; petroleum products (1978) c. 517; lead ore (metal content) 16; zinc ore (metal content) 20; electricity (kw-hr; 1978) c. 755,000.

HUNGARY

Education. (1980) Primary, pupils 1,162,000, teachers 75,422; secondary, pupils 203,000, teachers 15,460; higher, students 64,000, teaching staff 13,890.
Finance. Monetary unit: forint, with (Oct. 12, 1981) a unified free rate of 33.56 forints to U.S. $1 (62.83 forints = £1 sterling). Budget (1980 est.): revenue 423.5 billion forints; expenditure 428 billion forints. Net material product (1979) 559.5 billion forints.
Foreign Trade. (1980) Imports 299,898,000,000 forints; exports 281,012,000,000 forints. Import sources: U.S.S.R. 28%; West Germany 12%; East Germany 7%; Austria 5%; Czechoslovakia 5%. Export destinations: U.S.S.R. 29%; West Germany 10%; East Germany 7%; Czechoslovakia 6%; Italy 5%. Main exports: machinery 21%; food 19%; motor vehicles 10%; chemicals 9%.
Transport and Communications. Roads (1980) 87,689 km (including 209 km expressways). Motor vehicles in use (1980): passenger 1,021,330; commercial 124,540. Railways: (1979) 7,950 km; traffic (1980) 12,370,000,000 passenger-km, freight 23,868,000,000 net ton-km. Air traffic (1980): c. 998 million passenger-km; freight c. 19 million net ton-km. Inland waterways in regular use (1979) 1,302 km. Telephones (Jan. 1980) 1,186,500. Radio licenses (Dec. 1979) 2,608,000. Television licenses (Dec. 1979) 2,-702,000.
Agriculture. Production (in 000; metric tons; 1980): corn c. 6,575; wheat c. 6,048; barley c. 926; rye c. 130; potatoes c. 1,400; sugar, raw value c. 482; cabbages (1979) c. 250; tomatoes c. 400; onions c. 135; sunflower seed c. 400; rapeseed c. 75; green peas (1979) c. 250; plums (1979) c. 226; apples c. 800; wine c. 565; tobacco c. 22; milk c. 2,530; beef and veal c. 135; pork c. 900. Livestock (in 000; Dec. 1979): cattle 1,950; pigs 8,355; sheep 2,927; horses 126; chickens 64,446.
Industry. Index of production (1975 = 100; 1980) 118. Production (in 000; metric tons; 1980): coal 3,067; lignite 23,431; crude oil 2,031; natural gas (cu m) c. 6,130,000; electricity (kw-hr) 23,876,000; iron ore (24% metal content) 427; pig iron 2,223; crude steel 3,763; bauxite 2,950; aluminum 73; cement 4,660; petroleum products c. 9,400; sulfuric acid 590; fertilizers (1979) nitrogenous 640, phosphate c. 225; cotton yarn 60; man-made fibres 29; commercial vehicles (units) 14.

Hockey:
see Field Hockey and Lacrosse; Ice Hockey

Holland:
see Netherlands, The

Hong Kong:
see Dependent States

Horse Racing:
see Equestrian Sports; Gambling

Horticulture:
see Gardening

Hospitals:
see Health and Disease

Libyan leader Muammar al-Qaddafi (right) was escorted by First Secretary Janos Kadar when Qaddafi visited Budapest in September.

was to explain the events to the young people of Hungary; the Soviet action was described as a "fraternal rescue."

Hungary was the only Soviet-bloc country, apart from Poland itself, to afford any sign of recognition to Solidarity, Poland's independent trade union movement. A letter signed by Sandor Gaspar, a member of the Politburo and general secretary of the state-run Council of Hungarian Trade Unions, was read at Solidarity's first national congress in October. Although reiterating Soviet-bloc criticisms of the movement, the letter expressed a willingness to hold talks with Solidarity leaders. However, the official Hungarian party newspaper rejected the idea of a meeting between Gaspar and Solidarity leader Lech Walesa.

On Dec. 5, 1980, the Presidential Council published a decree amalgamating the Ministries of Heavy Industry, Light Industry, and Metallurgy and Machine Industry into a single Ministry of Industry, to be headed by Lajos Mehes, Politburo member and former first secretary of the Budapest party committee. As a result of this reorganization and another which combined the Ministries of Education and Culture into one Ministry of Cultural Affairs, the Council of Ministers was reduced to 15 members. The new industry ministry supervised the activities of some 1,100 industrial enterprises, most of them state owned, with about 1.3 million workers.

In April 1981 Parliament passed a bill aimed at streamlining the whole process of state administration. Another bill was concerned with the activities of the Hungarian National Bank. According to Matyas Timar, its governor, the bank intended to continue its current investment policy but would attach greater importance to promoting imports that would assist economic growth. Outlining the prospects for further development during the 1981–85 plan, Peter Veress, minister of foreign trade, pointed to the unfavourable effect on the Hungarian economy of world recession and the ever increasing prices of crude petroleum and raw materials. He also complained that protectionist tendencies within the European Economic Community countries had adversely affected Hungarian exports.

Pal Ligeti, a member of the National Planning Office, suggested that the rising cost of energy be combated by reducing imports of crude petroleum and its products from hard-currency countries and increasing reliance on the U.S.S.R. In the summer Rezso Nyers, a former member of the Politburo (1967–75) and chief architect of the 1968 New Economic Mechanism, complained that his reform of the Hungarian system of economic management had been watered down by "negative outside influence" favouring a centrally planned national economy.

Addressing the congress of Hungary's 855,000-member Communist Youth Association in May, party First Secretary Janos Kadar said: "The capitalists are trying to solve the insuperable problems of their social order by stepping up the arms race, but there can be no prospect for mankind other than that of peace and social progress."

The final figures of the January 1980 census revealed that Hungary's population was only 3.8% higher than it had been a decade earlier. One-fifth of the population lived in Budapest.

(K. M. SMOGORZEWSKI)

Ice Hockey

North American. There was talk of a new "dynasty" in the air when, after finishing with the most points in the National Hockey League (NHL), the New York Islanders went on to win their second consecutive Stanley Cup by beating the Minnesota North Stars four games to one. The North Stars, a young team, had inspired parallels to the Islanders of some six years past. Continuing to replenish their ranks, the Islanders started the 1981–82 season with a strong team and hopes for a third consecutive cup, a feat so far accomplished by only two NHL teams, Montreal and Toronto, both of which did it twice.

To create better rivalries and save air fare, the NHL plunged into its first major realignment,

Hydroelectric Power: see Energy; Engineering Projects

Hydrology: see Earth Sciences

redistributing its 21 teams into new, geographically based divisions and conferences. The league governors also created an unbalanced schedule in which the teams within a division play each other eight times. The play-off format was rearranged to produce, in progressive rounds, division winners, conference winners, and, finally, a Stanley Cup winner.

Team Canada, made up of NHL players, was the sad loser in September of the second Canada Cup. In the final of the six-nation tournament, the Soviet Union defeated Canada 8–1. Canada had won the inaugural competition in 1976. It was the Soviet national team's first appearance in North America since it lost the Olympic Games gold medal to the United States at Lake Placid, N.Y., in February 1980.

Among the individual accomplishments during the 1980–81 NHL season was New York Islander Mike Bossy's feat of scoring 50 goals in 50 games to equal Maurice ("Rocket") Richard's milestone.

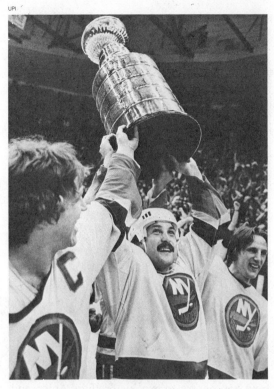

Joyous members of the New York Islanders raise their trophy aloft after winning hockey's Stanley Cup for the second consecutive time by beating the Minnesota North Stars four games to one in championship play.

Bossy went on to score 68 goals in the regular season, tops in the league.

Wayne Gretzky (*see* BIOGRAPHIES), the Edmonton centre who was 20 years old and in his second season, was the league's leading point scorer. He set records for most points (164) and most assists (109), breaking Phil Esposito's previous mark of 152 points. Gretzky was also named the league's most valuable player for the second consecutive year.

Esposito, meanwhile, retired from the game in January after scoring 717 goals during a career in which he played for the Chicago Black Hawks, Boston Bruins, and New York Rangers. His goal total was second only to that of Gordie Howe. Esposito's record of 76 goals in one season remained intact. Bobby Hull failed in his bid to come out of retirement with the New York Rangers.

Bobby Carpenter, a centre, became the highest U.S.-born draft pick in NHL history when Washington chose him third overall in the 1981 draft. A 17-year-old from Peabody, Mass., he honed his hockey skills at St. John's Preparatory School in Danvers, Mass. The first choice in the draft was centre Dale Hawerchuk of Cornwall in the Quebec Junior League, who went to the Winnipeg Jets.

Coaching switches in the NHL included the hiring by the New York Rangers of Herb Brooks, the U.S. 1980 gold-medal Olympic team coach. Brooks promised to bring a more fluid, European style to the Rangers. Montreal signed Los Angeles' Bob Berry as its new coach after being swept out of the preliminary round of the play-offs in three games by the Edmonton Oilers and Gretzky. The young centre set up five goals in the final game of that series.

There was a new look to many teams by virtue of the mass signing of players born outside of

Table I. NHL Final Standings, 1980–81

	Won	Lost	Tied	Goals	Goals against	Pts.
ADAMS DIVISION						
Buffalo	39	20	21	327	250	99
Boston	37	30	13	316	272	87
Minnesota	35	28	17	292	263	87
Quebec	30	32	18	314	318	78
Toronto	28	37	15	322	367	71
NORRIS DIVISION						
Montreal	45	22	13	332	232	103
Los Angeles	43	24	13	337	290	99
Pittsburgh	30	37	13	302	345	73
Hartford	21	41	18	292	372	60
Detroit	19	43	18	252	339	56
PATRICK DIVISION						
Islanders (N.Y.)	48	18	14	355	260	110
Philadelphia	41	24	15	313	249	97
Calgary	39	27	14	329	298	92
Rangers (N.Y.)	30	36	14	312	317	74
Washington	26	36	18	286	317	70
SMYTHE DIVISION						
St. Louis	45	18	17	352	281	107
Chicago	31	33	16	304	315	78
Vancouver	28	32	20	289	301	76
Edmonton	29	35	16	328	327	74
Colorado	22	45	12	258	344	57
Winnipeg	9	57	14	246	400	32

Table II. World Ice Hockey Championships, 1981

	Won	Lost	Tied	Goals	Goals against	Pts.
GROUP A Championship Section						
U.S.S.R.	4	0	2	38	12	10
Sweden	3	2	1	16	26	7
Czechoslovakia	2	2	2	20	22	6
Canada	0	5	1	16	30	1
GROUP A Relegation Section						
United States	4	1	1	35	28	9
Finland	3	1	2	33	21	8
West Germany	3	2	1	40	30	7
Netherlands, The	0	6	0	22	51	0
GROUP B						
Italy	6	0	1	38	18	13
Poland	5	1	1	49	25	11
Switzerland	4	1	2	28	20	10
East Germany	4	2	1	37	25	9
Romania	2	5	0	25	30	4
Norway	2	5	0	21	39	4
Yugoslavia	1	5	1	33	44	3
Japan	1	6	0	18	38	2
GROUP C						
Austria	7	0	0	43	5	14
China	6	1	0	46	14	12
Hungary	4	2	1	38	22	9
Denmark	3	3	1	36	27	7
France	3	4	0	48	36	6
Bulgaria	3	4	0	22	32	6
North Korea	1	6	0	18	66	2
Great Britain	0	7	0	11	60	0

The University of Wisconsin hockey team overcame the University of Minnesota team to win the NCAA hockey crown in March.

North America, mostly from Sweden, Finland, and Czechoslovakia. Among the newcomers was Marian Stastny of Czechoslovakia, who defected from his country to join his brothers Anton and Peter on the Quebec Nordiques. Peter Stastny was the 1980–81 rookie of the year.

Post-season trophy winners in the NHL included Randy Carlyle of Pittsburgh as best defenseman and, for the fourth year in a row, Bob Gainey of Montreal as best defensive forward. Rick Kehoe of Pittsburgh won the Lady Byng Trophy for sportsmanship and high standard of play, and Blake Dunlop of St. Louis took the Masterton Trophy for sportsmanship, perseverance, and dedication to hockey. Coach of the year was Red Berenson of St. Louis, and Butch Goring of the Islanders was named most valuable player in the play-offs. The Vezina Trophy for best goalkeeping was shared by the Montreal Canadien team of Richard Sevigny, Denis Herron, and Michel ("Bunny") Larocque. It was the first time that three goalies had their names on the Vezina in the same year.

The league champion in the Central Hockey League was Salt Lake City, which defeated Wichita four games to three. In the American Hockey League, Adirondack defeated Maine four games to two. (ROBIN CATHY HERMAN)

European and International. A continuing absence of top North American strength in international competitions denied any fair opportunity in the 1980–81 season to assess a true comparison between Europe's best talent and that of leading NHL players. A world cup competition for national club champions, the dream of promoters on either side of the Atlantic for many years, came no nearer to reality yet remained an apparently inevitable likelihood in the not-too-distant future. As a possible alternative, a world league for clubs from the sport's leading nations continued to be discussed unofficially, though the demands of domestic competitions were among difficult factors delaying possible eventual agreement.

The 47th world championships were contested, as usual, in three groups by 24 nations, the eight title contenders competing in Group A during April 12–26 in Göteborg and Stockholm, Sweden. Preliminary round-robin matches resolved which four teams would contest the championship. The other four played to determine which one of them would be relegated to the following year's Group B.

The Soviet Union retained the title with an undefeated performance, though it was held to tie games with Canada and Czechoslovakia. Sweden, although trounced 13–1 by the U.S.S.R., finished runner-up, with Czechoslovakia third and Canada fourth. It was the 17th victory for the Soviets, only two short of the Canadian record number of 19 wins.

The U.S., holder of the 1980 Olympic Games title, was unable to include players involved in the Stanley Cup play-offs but finished fifth above strong Finnish and West German teams. The Netherlands lost all of its six games and dropped back to Group B.

Accredited journalists in attendance selected Peter Lindmark of Sweden as the outstanding goalkeeper in the tournament, Canadian Larry Robinson and Soviet Valerij Vassiliev as the best defensemen, and three more Soviet players, Aleksandr Maltsev, Sergey Kapastin, and Sergey Maharov, as the most successful forwards. Maltsev was the leading scorer, with 13 points from 6 goals and 7 assists.

Italy earned the right to move up to Group A by heading the eight nations in Group B at Val Gardena, Italy, on March 20–29. The teams played each other once and the Italians were chased hard by Poland, Switzerland, and East Germany. At the bottom end Yugoslavia and Japan were demoted to Group C.

In Group C, contested in Beijing (Peking), China, March 6–16, the victor, Austria, and China, which finished runner-up, earned promotion to Group B. North Korea, making its international debut, finished ahead of Great Britain. The latter lost all seven games, underlining the fact that the nation that was world champion in 1936 was still severely handicapped by a dearth of home ice available for training.

The annual senior international tournament for the Izvestia Cup, in Moscow in December 1980, was won by the U.S.S.R. for the 11th time, but only on superior goal difference over the runner-up, Czechoslovakia, and third-place Finland. The U.S. and Canada did not compete.

The European Cup play-offs, patterned after the soccer cup of national league club champions, was contested during August in Innsbruck, Austria, and was won by the Red Army of Moscow. Tappara Tampere from Finland was runner-up, with Slovan Bratislava of Czechoslovakia third and Modo Kempehallen of Sweden fourth. Because some games turned into high-scoring routs, it was suggested that European administrators might copy the North American Allan Cup formula, which permits weaker entries to strengthen their teams.

The world junior (under 21) championship, in

Augsburg, West Germany, was won by Sweden, whose 3–2 defeat of the Soviet defending champions clinched the issue. Finland, which also beat the Soviets, finished second, followed by the U.S.S.R., Czechoslovakia, West Germany, the U.S., Canada, and Austria. (HOWARD BASS)

Iceland

Iceland is an island republic in the North Atlantic Ocean, near the Arctic Circle. Area: 103,000 sq km (39,769 sq mi). Pop. (1981 est.): 229,000. Cap. and largest city: Reykjavik (pop., 1980 est., 83,500). Language: Icelandic. Religion: 97% Lutheran. President in 1981, Vigdís Finnbogadóttir; prime minister, Gunnar Thoroddsen.

The Icelandic economy developed rather favourably in 1981. The growth in real gross national product was about 1%; there was full employment; the current account of the balance of payments was just about in balance; and the inflation rate, above 50% in 1980, declined to about 40% during the year.

At the beginning of 1981 the Icelandic króna was replaced with a new króna. In the new system one new currency unit equaled 100 old units. A package of economic measures, including a price freeze, was implemented at the same time in order to reduce inflation and invest the new currency with some public confidence. It was decided to stop the gradual devaluation of the króna vis-à-vis foreign currencies for several months, and it was agreed that there would be a small cut in the price indexation of wages. This helped bring down domestic inflation in the course of the year.

The pledge to fight inflation was one of the major promises of the coalition government of Prime Minister Gunnar Thoroddsen, which had come to office in February 1980. Composed of members of the left-wing People's Alliance, the Progressive Party (a farmers' party), and a splinter group from the traditionally right-of-centre Independence

ICELAND

Education. (1979–80) Primary, pupils 25,600, teachers (including pre-primary) 3,074; secondary and vocational, pupils 26,500, teachers 1,340; teacher training, pupils (1976–77) 266, teachers (1975–76) 30; higher, students 4,-200, teaching staff 779.

Finance. Monetary unit: new króna (introduced from Jan. 1, 1981, at 1 new króna = 100 old krónur) with (Sept. 21, 1981) a free rate of 7.59 new krónur to U.S. $1 (14.08 new krónur = £1 sterling). Gold and other reserves (June 1981) U.S. $198 million. Budget (1980 est.): revenue 346 billion krónur; expenditure 343 billion krónur. Gross national product (1980) 13,242,000,000 new krónur. Money supply (June 1981) 1,351,000,000 new krónur. Cost of living (Reykjavik; 1975 = 100; May 1981) 800.9.

Foreign Trade. (1980) Imports 4,801,600,000 new krónur; exports 4,459,000,000 new krónur. Import sources: West Germany 10%; U.S.S.R. 10%; U.K. 9%; U.S. 9%; The Netherlands 9%; Denmark 8%; Norway 7%; Sweden 7%. Export destinations: U.S. 22%; U.K. 16%; West Germany 10%; Nigeria 7%; U.S.S.R. 5%; Italy 5%; Portugal 5%. Main exports: fish and products 75%; aluminum 12%.

Transport and Communications. Roads (1980) 11,707 km. Motor vehicles in use (1979): passenger 81,025; commercial 7,873. There are no railways. Air traffic (1980): 1,-295,000,000 passenger-km; freight 23.6 million net ton-km. Shipping (1980): merchant vessels 100 gross tons and over 393; gross tonnage 188,215. Telephones (Jan. 1980) 103,800. Radio licenses (Dec. 1979) 66,500. Television receivers (Dec. 1979) 59,800.

Agriculture. Production (in 000; metric tons; 1979): potatoes 6; hay c. 315; turnips 0.3; milk 132; mutton and lamb 16; fish catch 1,645. Livestock (in 000; Dec. 1979): cattle 57; sheep 797; horses 50; poultry 394.

Industry. Production (in 000): electricity (public supply only; kw-hr; 1980) 3,143,000; aluminum (exports; metric tons; 1979) 71.

Iceland

Party, the left-of-centre coalition continued in power throughout the year.

Iceland was plagued by bad weather in the early part of 1981. On February 16 a heavy storm inflicted much damage in the southern part of the country. Dry weather had earlier limited the potential for the production of hydroelectricity, a situation that lasted for most of the summer and into the autumn.

Three volcanic eruptions took place during the year. The first was near Lake Myvatn in the northeastern part of the country on January 30.

The remains of a U.S. Navy airplane that crashed in 1953 were discovered in October on a glacier in Iceland. A crew of nine had died in the accident.

This was the fourth eruption at that site within 11 months, and a further outbreak of volcanic activity took place in the same region on November 18. The other eruption was of Mt. Hekla in the southwestern part of Iceland on April 9. The three eruptions were brief and caused little damage, since both sites were in uninhabited areas of the country.

Iceland's Pres. Vigdís Finnbogadóttir went on three state visits during the year, to Denmark in January and to Norway and Sweden at the end of October. On the occasion of the visit to Norway, the two countries signed an accord to end their dispute over the use of an area of the sea between Jan Mayen Island and Iceland, in furtherance of an agreement on fishing rights in the same region signed between the two governments in May 1980. Each of the two countries claimed that the disputed area lay within its 200-mi economic zone.

The Icelandic government was engaged in a dispute with the Swiss concern Alusuisse during the year. The latter operated a wholly owned aluminum plant in Iceland, on the proceeds of which it paid income taxes. The Icelandic government contended that the firm had not reported the full extent of its profits and called in an outside auditing firm to investigate. The latter concluded that the firm had indeed underreported its profits by some $16.2 million–$18.5 million during the period 1975–80. (BJÖRN MATTHÍASSON)

India

A federal republic of southern Asia and a member of the Commonwealth, India is situated on a peninsula extending into the Indian Ocean with the Arabian Sea to the west and the Bay of Bengal to the east. It is bounded (east to west) by Burma, Bangladesh, China, Bhutan, Nepal, and Pakistan; Sri Lanka lies just off its southern tip in the Indian Ocean. Area: 3,287,782 sq km (1,269,420 sq mi), including the Pakistani-controlled section of Jammu and Kashmir. Pop. (1981 prelim.): 683,810,100; Indo-Aryans and Dravidians are dominant, with Mongoloid, Negroid, and Australoid admixtures. Cap.: New Delhi (pop., 1971, 301,800). Largest cities: Calcutta (metro pop., 1981 prelim., 9,165,700) and Greater Bombay (metro pop., 1981 prelim., 8,202,800). Language: Hindi and English (official). Religion (1971): Hindu 83%; Muslim 11%; Christian 3%; Sikh 2%; Buddhist 0.7%. President in 1981, N. Sanjiva Reddy; prime minister, Indira Gandhi.

Domestic Affairs. After a succession of eventful, even turbulent, years, 1981 was somewhat placid. There was perceptible improvement in the economy. With the opposition unable to unite, Prime Minister Indira Gandhi continued to dominate the national scene. By-elections to 7 seats in the Lok Sabha (lower house of Parliament) and 23 in state assemblies in June confirmed the dominance of her Congress (I) Party. A notable development was the election of her surviving son, Rajiv Gandhi (*see* BIOGRAPHIES), to Parliament. A repoll was ordered in the Garhwal constituency after charges of unfair practices. Two no-confi-

dence motions against the government were defeated in the Lok Sabha: one on May 8 by 275–90 and the other on September 17 by 294–83. The house revoked a resolution adopted in December 1978 expelling Indira Gandhi.

The state of Assam gradually returned to normal after the disturbances of the year before, but several rounds of talks failed to produce a solution to the vexed problem of foreigners living there, most of them Bengalis from Bangladesh. The ministry of Anwara Taimor lost its majority, and the state was placed under president's rule on June 30. Another state to come under president's rule was Kerala; in October the chief minister, E. K. Nayanar, resigned after Congress (S) (formerly Congress [U]) and the Kerala Congress (Mani Group) withdrew from the coalition state government led by the Communist Party of India (Marxist). President's rule was promulgated in Manipur in February when Rishang Keishing lost his majority, but he succeeded in forming a new Cabinet in June. The chief minister of Maharashtra, A. R. Antulay, came under severe attack when opposition parties charged that he had misused his office to collect

INDIA

Education. (1978–79) Primary, pupils 72,947,804, teachers 1,276,446; secondary, pupils 26,435,894, teachers 1,581,263; vocational, pupils 318,956, teachers (1970–71) 14,024; teacher training, pupils 102,072; higher, students 4,296,242, teaching staff (1975–76) 235,822.

Finance. Monetary unit: rupee, with (Sept. 21, 1981) a free rate of Rs 9.02 to U.S. $1 (Rs 16.72 = £1 sterling). Gold and other reserves (May 1981) U.S. $6,594,000,000. Budget (1980–81 est.): revenue Rs 121,328,000,000; expenditure Rs 133,103,000,000. Gross national product (1978–79) Rs 960.8 billion. Money supply (April 1981) Rs 222.7 billion. Cost of living (1975 = 100; June 1981) 136.8.

Foreign Trade. (1980) Imports Rs 111,050,000,000; exports Rs 63,168,000,000. Import sources (1979–80): U.S. 10%; Iraq 10%; U.S.S.R. 9%; U.K. 8%; West Germany 7%; Iran 7%; Japan 7%. Export destinations (1979–80): U.S. 13%; Japan 10%; U.S.S.R. 10%; U.K. 8%; West Germany 6%. Main exports (1979–80): food 26%; textile yarns and fabrics 15%; clothing 8%; leather 8%; diamonds 7%.

Transport and Communications. Roads (1979) 1,604,110 km. Motor vehicles in use (1979): passenger 1,035,300; commercial 440,200. Railways: (1979) 60,775 km; traffic (1978–79) 192,900,000,000 passenger-km, freight 154,820,000,000 net ton-km. Air traffic (1980): 10,765,000,000 passenger-km; freight 401.4 million net ton-km. Shipping (1980): merchant vessels 100 gross tons and over 616; gross tonnage 5,911,367. Telephones (March 1980) 2,615,100. Radio licenses (Dec. 1978) 19,611,000. Television licenses (Dec. 1979) c. 1,150,000.

Agriculture. Production (in 000; metric tons; 1980): wheat 31,564; rice c. 83,000; barley 1,616; corn c. 6,400; millet c. 9,500; sorghum c. 12,800; potatoes c. 10,500; cassava (1979) 6,053; sugar, raw value c. 4,300; sugar, non-centrifugal (1979) c. 8,200; chick-peas 3,280; mangoes c. 9,500; bananas c. 4,500; cottonseed c. 2,800; rapeseed 1,433; sesame seed c. 530; linseed 270; peanuts c. 6,400; tea c. 590; tobacco c. 400; cotton, lint c. 1,400; jute (including substitutes) c. 1,495; meat c. 873; fish catch (1979) 2,343. Livestock (in 000; 1980): cattle c. 182,500; sheep c. 41,300; pigs c. 10,000; buffalo c. 61,300; goats c. 71,650; poultry c. 146,000.

Industry. Production (in 000; metric tons; 1980): coal 109,102; lignite 4,548; crude oil 9,450; natural gas (cu m) 1,450,000; iron ore (63% metal content) 40,425; pig iron 8,707; crude steel 9,409; bauxite 1,731; aluminum 185; gold (troy oz) 96; manganese ore (metal content; 1979) 610; cement 17,710; cotton yarn 1,058; woven cotton fabrics (m) 7,531,000; man-made fibres 170; petroleum products (1979) 26,364; sulfuric acid 1,976; caustic soda 549; electricity (excluding most industrial production; kw-hr) 107,847,000; passenger cars (units) 48; commercial vehicles (units) 65.

Ice Skating:
see Winter Sports

The first meeting in 20 years between an Indian prime minister and a top Chinese leader took place in June when Chinese Foreign Minister Huang Hua visited Indian Prime Minister Indira Gandhi.

funds. In Rajasthan J. N. Pahadia resigned in July and S. C. Matbur became chief minister.

The Election Commission held that the party led by Indira Gandhi was the real Indian National Congress party. With the election of Sharad Pawar as president in place of Devraj Urs, the other group came to be called Congress (S) instead of Congress (U). The Communist Party of India underwent a split; one of its stalwarts, S. A. Dange, was expelled, and his group formed a separate party.

Strained relations between the executive and the judiciary continued. While the Supreme Court upheld the validity of the National Security Act (adopted in December 1980) and the Essential Services Maintenance Ordinance (of June 1981), it was not happy with the government's policy regarding judicial appointments. The court held extensive hearings on petitions challenging a letter from the law minister to the states which required new high-court judges to give an undertaking expressing willingness to be posted outside their own states. The court also ordered the Bihar state government to release on bail all prisoners who had spent more than five years in jail awaiting trial.

There were minor changes in the union Cabinet. V. C. Shukla (civil supplies) was dropped in August; N. D. Tiwari was made minister of industry and labour; and S. B. Chavan was appointed minister of planning.

A disturbing development was the agitation by Akali activists in Punjab demanding an autonomous state for Sikhs under the name of Khalistan. The murder of a Hindu leader and the hijacking of an Indian Airlines plane to Pakistan in September highlighted the seriousness of the problem. Hindu-Muslim riots occurred in Biharsharif in May and in Hyderabad in July, and there were some disturbances in Aligarh in May. The organized conversion of people of the scheduled castes (former outcastes) to Islam in Tamil Nadu evoked concern and complaints that Middle Eastern money was being used. In March–April students in Gujarat agitated against the reservation of seats in medical colleges for scheduled caste candidates. (*See* RELIGION: *Hinduism.*)

Results of the decennial census were announced in March. The country's population had increased by 24.75% since 1971. The percentage of literacy was 36.17 and the sex ratio, 935 females per 1,000 males. The ten largest cities were: Calcutta 9.1 million; Greater Bombay 8.2 million; Delhi 5.2 million; Madras 4.3 million; Bangalore 2.9 million; Hyderabad and Ahmedabad 2.5 million; Kanpur and Pune 1,780,000; and Nagpur 1.3 million. The capital, New Delhi, marked its 50th anniversary.

India's space program moved forward with three launchings. On June 19 an Indian-built experimental satellite (named Apple) was launched from French Guiana with the help of a French rocket; the Rohini satellite was launched with the help of an Indian-built launch vehicle in May (this satellite burned up before it could complete its mission); and Bhaskara 2 was launched with Soviet help in November. In July it was announced that the country's fifth nuclear power station would be established in Gujarat. A department of ocean development and a commission on new and alternative sources of energy were established.

The year was marred by several accidents and disasters. In April more than 120 people died in a tornado in Orissa; at least 268 lost their lives when a train fell into the Baghmati River in Bihar in June; 84 died in floods in Rajasthan in July; and 110 were killed when a lake burst its banks in Karnataka in October. At least 66 were killed in a fire in a circus tent in Bangalore in February, and over 300 died after drinking illicitly manufactured liquor in the same city in July. In December 45 people died in the Qutab Minar tower, Delhi, when crowds panicked in its narrow staircase.

The Economy. Both agricultural and industrial output rose. Total grain production in the agricultural year ended June 30, 1981, increased by 20 million metric tons over the previous year. There were marked gains in the production of sugar, coal, electricity, cement, fertilizer, and petroleum and in the movement of railway freight. Increased oil production enabled the oil import bill to be reduced by Rs 10 billion, and new petroleum finds were reported. The wholesale price index stood at 284.6 on September 25, compared with 264.1 a year

Indian women demonstrated in Calcutta in January against the constantly rising prices of fuel and food.

earlier; this represented an increase of 7.6%, compared with an inflation rate of 20% in 1980. The money supply in public hands showed a steady decline during the year. National income grew by an estimated 7% in 1980–81.

The government augmented its earnings by means of two substantial raises in the price of petroleum products, one in January and the other in July, and a 15% increase in railway fares and freight rates. The union government's budget for 1981–82 was a comparatively moderate effort in terms of revenue mobilization, with an anticipated addition of Rs 2,710,000,000. Annual receipts for 1981–82 were placed at Rs 143,270,000,000 and expenditure at Rs 152,990,000,000. Including capital receipts of Rs 90,050,000,000 and capital disbursements of Rs 95,720,000,000, the overall deficit was estimated at Rs 15,390,000,000.

The National Development Council approved the sixth economic plan, which envisaged an outlay of Rs 1,722,100,000,000 for development over 1980–85. Several projects were started or approved, among them four superthermal stations and an aluminum plant in Orissa costing Rs 14 billion, to be built with French assistance. The Aid-India Consortium made credit commitments of $3,450,-000,000, and in November India received assurances of aid from the International Monetary Fund worth $5.8 million over 1981–84. An Export-Import Bank was established, and a five-year agreement on trade and economic cooperation was signed with the European Community.

Foreign Affairs. There was considerable anxiety during the year over the decision of U.S. Pres. Ronald Reagan's administration to supply F-16 aircraft to Pakistan. According to Prime Minister Gandhi, this would put Pakistan a generation ahead of India in the air. The foreign ministers of India and Pakistan exchanged visits. Pakistan suggested a "no-war" pact, prompting India to retort that this was an old Indian offer. India negotiated the purchase of Mirage-2000 planes with France, and delivery of the first Anglo-French Jaguar aircraft took place in February. Relations with China improved slowly. The Chinese foreign minister visited India in June, and one of the measures agreed on was to permit Indian pilgrims to visit Mt. Kailas and Lake Manasarowar in Tibet. Five days of talks on the Sino-Indian border dispute in Beijing (Peking) in December produced no results, but the two countries agreed to continue their contacts.

Prime Minister Gandhi undertook five visits abroad: to Switzerland, Kuwait, and the United Arab Emirates in May; to Seychelles and Kenya in August; to Indonesia, Fiji, Tonga, Australia, and the Philippines in September–October; to Romania and Mexico (for the North-South summit conference on development at Cancún) in October; and to Bulgaria, Italy, and France in November. In Australia she attended the conference of Commonwealth heads of government. At Cancún the prime minister met President Reagan, French Pres. François Mitterrand, and Chinese Premier Zhao Ziyang (Chao Tzu-yang). She addressed the UN World Health Organization in Geneva in May, the UN Energy Conference in Nairobi in August, and the UN Food and Agriculture Organization in Rome in November. Pres. Sanjiva Reddy represented the country at the wedding of Prince Charles in London in July.

Among the foreign dignitaries visiting India during 1981 were the prime ministers of Britain, Australia, and Zimbabwe, the king of Bhutan, the presidents of Mexico, West Germany, Kenya, Guinea, Tanzania, and Uganda, the emir of Bahrain, the foreign ministers of France, China, Italy, Kampuchea (Cambodia), and Portugal, and Jeane Kirkpatrick, U.S. ambassador to the UN. There was concern over the racial riots in Britain. India also had misgivings about the British Nationality Bill, which British Prime Minister Margaret Thatcher sought to allay during her visit. A conference of foreign ministers of nonaligned countries was held in New Delhi in February.

(H. Y. SHARADA PRASAD)

Indonesia

A republic of Southeast Asia, Indonesia consists of the major islands of Sumatra, Java, Kalimantan (Indonesian Borneo), Celebes, and Irian Jaya (West New Guinea) and approximately 3,000 smaller islands and islets. Area: 1,919,443 sq km (741,101 sq mi). Pop. (1980): 147,490,300. Area and population figures include former Portuguese Timor. Cap. and largest city: Jakarta (pop., 1980, 6,503,400). Language: Bahasa Indonesia (official); Javanese; Sundanese; Madurese. Religion: mainly Muslim; some Christian, Buddhist, and Hindu. President in 1981, Suharto.

Indonesia attained a degree of political stability and economic prosperity in 1981 unparalleled since the proclamation of independence in 1945. In foreign affairs it moved closer to its neighbours through the Association of Southeast Asian Nations (ASEAN), a regional grouping that included Thailand, Singapore, Malaysia, and the Philippines as well as Indonesia. Despite a global economic recession the Indonesian economy continued to perform well.

Tension was surprisingly absent as more than 70 million people registered for the election in 1982 of a People's Consultative Congress (MPR) to a new, five-year term. The MPR is empowered to elect a president and vice-president and to determine "broad lines of state policy." The general election would be the third under the quasi-military government of President Suharto, a retired four-star general who came to power after an abortive Communist coup in 1965. Under Suharto, Indonesia had enjoyed its longest period of internal peace. Barring a refusal to run, Suharto's reelection to a fourth term was a foregone conclusion. During 1981 the country's three parties, the Indonesian Democratic Party, the Islamic Development Unity Party, and the government-sponsored Functional Groups (Golkar), endorsed Suharto's reelection. Opposition to Suharto had arisen in 1980, but the president partly assuaged his critics by announcing that he favoured going to the people with a referendum after the 1982 elections to determine whether to do away with the practice whereby the government appointed one-third of the members of the MPR from the armed forces. The use of a national referendum would be the first in Indonesia's political history. Suharto's critics were chiefly alarmed at galloping corruption and expressed fear that the president's focus on economic development at the expense of civil liberties might result in a revolution similar to the one that took place in Iran.

In foreign affairs Indonesia continued to denounce the Vietnamese occupation of Kampuchea (Cambodia) and the Soviet Union's occupation of Afghanistan. Indonesia's principal concern was Kampuchea, where instability could unsettle Thailand, Indonesia's ASEAN partner. Thailand borders on Malaysia, which, in turn, has a long border with Indonesia. "With a peaceful Kampuchea," Suharto said in August, "the peace around this zone of ours will grow more stable." Indonesia

Indonesia

and ASEAN called on Vietnam to withdraw from Kampuchea.

Partly because of Vietnam's claims to the continental shelf north of the Natunas—a group of Indonesian islands in the South China Sea—Indonesia in April doubled its defense budget to $800 million. Another reason for the increased military spending was Indonesia's uneasiness over the U.S. decision to sell arms to China. Indonesia was annoyed because the U.S. neither consulted it nor gave it advance warning of the decision.

Indonesia's gross national product continued to increase at about 7% in 1981, making it one of the fastest growing economies in a world wracked by recession. The country's reserves climbed to an unprecedented $10 billion-plus, and rice production continued to grow, soaring from 13 million tons in 1971 to 20 million tons in 1980. For the first time, however, there were signs of labour unrest, including sporadic strikes over wages and other issues.   (ARNOLD C. BRACKMAN)

Industrial Relations

In 1981 the tough economic climate again exercised a dominant influence on industrial relations in many countries. The main preoccupations of labour unions tended to be the continuing high unemployment and the maintenance of their

members' living standards. There was little room for improving real wages or for new social gains.

United Kingdom. In Britain the conflicting views of government and unions underlay the year's most notable industrial relations developments. In the case of the civil service pay claim, the government's imposition of tight cash limits and suspension of the use of pay comparison with the private sector were met by unusually concerted action by the traditionally moderate civil service unions. The unions used mainly selective industrial action—including action to stop the flow of government revenue—to force an increase in the employer's offer. In the end, compromise was reached, though the settlement fell far short of union hopes. The government set up a Committee of Inquiry into Civil Service Pay, under Sir John Megaw.

Debate continued throughout the year about the legal framework of British industrial relations. A government Green Paper on *Trade Union Immunities*, published in January, struck a cautious note, but a number of voices, including many associated with the ruling Conservative Party, called for more legislation. This would include action

against the closed shop, making collective agreements legally binding, reducing the immunities of unions from legal action, and limiting the existing extent of freedom to strike. The appointment in September of Norman Tebbit (*see* BIOGRAPHIES) as secretary of state for employment, replacing James Prior, was widely viewed as heralding a harder line by government with regard to industrial relations legislation. The government stood aside in a confrontation between unions and management at the state-owned BL Ltd. (formerly British Leyland) automobile company. A strike that threatened to close down BL's 32 plants and possibly result in its liquidation was averted in November when workers in 25 plants voted against the union officials' recommendation to reject the company's offer of a 3.8% basic pay increase. The unions had demanded 17.5%.

A judgment in August by the European Court of Human Rights held that the dismissal of three British Rail workers following the introduction of a closed shop was a violation of their human rights.

United States. The U.S. labour movement celebrated its centenary in 1981. (*See* Sidebar.) It was not, however, a happy year for the unions, faced,

---

The Labour Movement—100 Years Later

A handful of dedicated trade unionists met in Pittsburgh, Pa., on Nov. 15, 1881, to form a national labour alliance in order to "elevate trade unionism and obtain for the working classes that respect for their rights, and that reward for their services, to which they are justly entitled." One hundred years later to the day, meeting in New York City, 900 delegates at a biennial convention of the American Federation of Labor–Congress of Industrial Organizations (AFL-CIO) celebrated the centennial of the modern labour movement. Looking back, the AFL-CIO decided that the goals of the founders had been achieved.

The AFL developed in 1886 from the Federation of Organized Trades and Labor Unions (FOTLU), which had been created by 107 delegates to the 1881 convention. They were representatives of unions that included the horse-collar workers, architectural cornice makers, and umbrella and walking-stick makers, all long gone.

Unions were not new in the U.S. in 1881. They had been a part of American life since before the colonies declared themselves independent of Great Britain in 1776. The idea of a national alliance had, in fact, been a goal from the 1830s on.

The new FOTLU set as initial goals legal enforcement of compulsory education of children, an eight-hour workday, abolition of contracting out convicts for private work, the protection of wages by a mechanic's lien law giving workers a prior claim on an employer's assets, the establishment of a federal bureau of labour statistics, and uniform apprenticeship laws. It also called for strict laws requiring safety inspections of mines, factories, and workshops and employer liability for "accidents resulting from their negligence or incompetency."

With the founding of the AFL in 1886, and the election of Samuel Gompers as president, labour began moving along a course of political action to reward friends and deny office to foes. In 1981 the AFL-CIO was following this course with increasing concentration and effort.

The AFL has had its ups and downs during its first century. In the 1930s it weathered a serious division. AFL unions had been set up on a craft basis, but later some demanded the right to organize workers on an industrial union basis, taking in all workers in a plant regardless of the jobs they held. Denied this right by the AFL, rebel unions split off to form the Congress of Industrial Organizations in 1938. The division lasted until a merger in 1955 formed the AFL-CIO, with the AFL's George Meany as president.

By 1981 the AFL-CIO had 102 unions reporting about 15 million members. Its total income amounted to $32,198,739 in fiscal 1981, a figure that would have been far beyond belief—and beyond comprehension—at the founding meeting. Its program in the U.S. at the start of its second hundred years is no longer limited to a concentration on workers' needs—the "more" called for by Samuel Gompers—but now covers civil rights, urban affairs, housing, energy, environmental protection, health and safety, and a wide range of other issues. Its leaders now say it is the spokesman for the poor and others lacking a strong voice.

The AFL-CIO is, at the same time, a changing organization. The ranks of industrial workers are getting thinner, and as a result there has been a decline in membership. But it is expanding in new areas of government employment, the service trades, and white-collar, semiprofessional jobs.

(EDWARD T. TOWNSEND)

U.S. union members and supporters protested Pres. Ronald Reagan's economic and social programs in a Solidarity Day demonstration in Washington, D.C., on September 19.

as they were, with somewhat of a decline in membership in many sectors; with a new government that seemed to them to be whittling away many of the social benefits that they valued; and with tough resistance to claims and in some cases demands for wage cuts by employers. A union-sponsored protest demonstration against government policies in Washington, D.C., on September 19 was supported by some 250,000 people. Revealing of the industrial relations climate was the dismissal in August of nearly 12,000 air traffic controllers who, under the leadership of Robert Poli (*see* BIOGRAPHIES), had struck for shorter hours and higher pay in breach of their obligation as federal employees. After the dismissal the Federal Aviation Administration was successful in keeping air services in operation, albeit with some delays and reductions in service.

Negotiations on a new agreement in the U.S. coal industry broke down in March, and 160,000 mine workers were on strike until June, when they voted to accept a new 40-month contract in which they received an additional $3.60 per hour. A nationwide strike of postal workers was averted in July when the U.S. Postal Service awarded wage increases of 11% over three years. The United Automobile Workers union (1.2 million members) rejoined the American Federation of Labor-Congress of Industrial Organizations (AFL-CIO) on July 1. At its congress in November, the AFL-CIO itself decided to rejoin the International Confederation of Free Trade Unions, which it had left in 1969.

Australia. Disputes, notably in telecommunications, road transport, docks, and the public service, marked a year of disturbance in Australia's industrial relations. A new review procedure adopted by the Commonwealth Conciliation and Arbitration Commission failed to bring order into

wage settlements, and at the end of July the commission decided to abandon, for the time being, the practice of wage indexation introduced in 1975. An Australian trade union campaign for shorter working hours scored a major success in December when employers in the important metal trades conceded a 38-hour week. (*See* AUSTRALIA.)

Continental Western Europe. While in the three countries so far mentioned trade unions were faced with what they regarded as unfriendly governments, in France the year's presidential and legislative elections produced a government that was committed to a wide range of reforms and enjoyed considerable—though not unqualified—union support. The new government acted quickly to improve the national minimum wage and social security benefits. Its further objectives included a shorter workweek; earlier retirement; improved facilities for part-time workers; greater powers for works councils; and an extension of plant-level bargaining. Nationalization measures envisioned worker representation on the boards of designated enterprises. In July the central employer and trade union organizations reached an agreement in principle to shorten the normal workweek to 39 hours and to extend paid vacation time from four to five weeks. The agreement also contained provisions concerning overtime working. Detailed arrangements were left to bargaining at the industry level.

The economic and unemployment problems of Belgium led to a series of long and difficult discussions between government, unions, and employers' organizations. Topics included levels of wage increases, number of working hours per week, and the scale of social security contributions. Mandatory powers of control were taken by the government but were not used, as a central agreement was achieved by unions and employers in the pri-

An armed guard stands by the opening of a mine near Hatfield, Ky., which had been closed by union pickets on April 2. The mine reopened on April 22, and violence and shooting resulted.

vate sector in February. The agreement called for moderation with regard to wage increases and the reduction of weekly working hours, added to which there was an undertaking to refrain from industrial action in support of claims outside the agreement.

A new framework for Danish industrial relations came into operation on March 1, when a renegotiated Basic Agreement between the central union and employer confederations took effect. This new pact strengthened workers' protection against dismissal, revised the concept of managerial rights, and reiterated the fundamental obligation to maintain industrial peace during the lifetime of a collective agreement. Denmark had normally followed a highly centralized form of collective bargaining, with wage agreements being made every two years. In 1975, 1977, and 1979, unions and employers were not able to reach agreement, and the government had found it necessary to intervene. In 1981 the parties decided to decentralize their bargaining to the industry level. Most industries managed to conclude agreements without too much difficulty, but a strike of slaughterhouse workers had to be settled by emergency legislation. There was also a lengthy dispute in the printing industry concerning both pay and the introduction of new technology.

In The Netherlands wage determination continued to arouse disagreement. The government retained powers for the minister of social affairs to limit and even change wage adjustments and in December, after attempts to reach a central wage agreement had failed, decided to continue controls in 1982. An agreement by the unions and employers made within the Foundation of Labour stressed the importance of economic recovery, a more stable price level, and increased profitability for business and industry with a view to improving employment. The agreement also provided for employers and unions to start a joint exploration of the possibilities of reducing unemployment and improving the operation of the labour market.

West Germany continued, overall, to demon-

strate how smoothly and effectively an industrial relations system can work in a major industrialized market economy. Nevertheless, areas of friction were not absent. In 1981, for instance, employers' organizations in the metal industries lodged a complaint against the union IG Metall with the Federal Labour Court about "warning strikes" that had occurred during wage negotiations. Recent union meetings had tended to stress anxieties about unemployment and union dissatisfaction with the extent of co-determination legislation. A new law on co-determination in the mining and iron and steel industries provided that companies engaged in those activities should continue to follow the traditional arrangements for workers' representation on company boards for six years.

In Sweden the wage negotiations went much more smoothly in 1981 than in 1980, though there were appreciable difficulties in reaching settlements for white-collar and supervisory employees. The five-yearly congress of the manual workers' central trade union organization was held in September. The congress stressed its strong support for maintenance of the welfare state and for an integrated approach to economic and social policies. Among other objectives discussed were full employment, particularly action to help youth employment; the struggle against inflation; more equitable distribution of income and wealth; regional development; improving the competitiveness of Swedish industries in the world market; and reducing the country's dependence on oil.

In June the employers' federation, the major unions, and the government in Spain signed a social contract covering, among other things, the limits of wage increases for 1982; pension increases; minimum-wage levels; funding of social security; checkoff of union dues; job creation; and unemployment pay. The agreement, to be monitored and interpreted by a tripartite committee, was to extend until the end of 1982. The levels of wage increases in 1981 had already been effectively set by an agreement in January between the employers' federation and the Socialist General Workers' Union.

Eastern Europe. In Poland the newborn free labour union movement Solidarity soon achieved a number of successes and established itself internationally as the voice of the Polish workers. However, its increasingly political demands eventually proved intolerable to the Communist establishment. In December the government declared martial law and arrested most of the union's leaders, leaving the movement's future in doubt. (*See* Feature Article on page 15; POLAND.)

A papal encyclical, *Laborem Exercens*, published in September, presented a contemporary view from the Roman Catholic Church of the place of work in human life and the proper rights of workers in the organization of economic activity.

(R. O. CLARKE)

The views expressed in this article are the author's and should not be attributed to any organization with which he may be connected.

See also Economy, World; Industrial Review.
[521.B.3; 534.C.1.q; 552.D.3 and F.3.b.ii]

LABOUR'S NEW WEAPON— THE STEVENS STRIKE

by A. H. Raskin

Among the often bloody struggles of organized labour in the United States to win for workers a collective voice in determining their wages and job security, few exceeded in bitterness or drama the 17-year battle that led to the signing on Oct. 19, 1980, of the first union contracts covering cotton mill employees at ten Southern plants of J. P. Stevens & Co., Inc. It was a conflict that involved repeated flouting by Stevens, the country's second largest textile manufacturer, of National Labor Relations Board orders to end unfair labour practices and, on the union side, the development by the Amalgamated Clothing and Textile Workers Union of innovative tactics for using the pooled power of billions of dollars in union-negotiated pension funds to isolate the company from traditional sources of support in the financial community.

The long dispute also involved frequent recourse to the federal courts by the Labor Board and the union, payment by the company of $1.3 million in back wages to workers illegally discharged for union activities, and a $50,000 settlement by Stevens of a suit initiated after union organizers discovered that their hotel room had been "bugged" with electronic listening devices. Actress Sally Field received an Academy Award for her performance in *Norma Rae*, a Hollywood-made film based on the experiences of a Stevens employee fired for union-organizing activities. What gave the battle over unionization of the Stevens textile empire its profound significance for both sides and for the national economy was the company's position as bellwether in an industry that for decades had successfully resisted large-scale union penetration—one that many in organized labour regarded as the pivotal stronghold of antiunionism in the Sun Belt states where population and jobs are growing most rapidly and unions are weakest.

Despite the breakthrough for unionism represented by the contracts at the ten plants in North and

---

Abraham H. Raskin is associate director of the National News Council. He is co-author, with David Dubinsky, of David Dubinsky: A Life with Labor.

South Carolina and Alabama, the extent to which this initial victory would affect the overall balance in either the textile industry or the South remained highly conjectural. Indeed, even at Stevens the union's future was far from clear-cut. The 3,500 workers in the ten unionized plants represented less than 10% of the total Stevens work force of 44,000, and the company vowed to avail itself of every legal weapon at its command to keep the rest of its 84 plants nonunion. A year after the signing of the first pacts, the line against further union inroads was being firmly held both by Stevens and by other textile giants, including Burlington Industries, Inc., the biggest in the field.

New Strategies. For observers, the most interesting aspect of the union campaign at Stevens was the conscious avoidance by the Amalgamated of any reliance on labour's traditional mainstay, the strike, as an instrument for bringing about capitulation by the corporation. This avoidance did not result from any distaste for militancy on the union's part. Rather, it stemmed from the union's recognition that, realistically, its foothold at Stevens was so tenuous that it was much more likely to lose its members there if it called them off the job than it was to bring the company to heel.

The union's search for alternate weapons took two principal forms. One was a worldwide consumer boycott of Stevens products by unions and their sympathizers in church, civil rights, student, and other groups. The other was a so-called corporate campaign that, far beyond anything ever undertaken by labour before, relied on the use of money power to defeat the employer—a reversal of the Marxist stereotype of the wealthy capitalist squashing unions with his bulging bag of gold.

Both of these weapons were added to the union's arsenal in 1976 after the Textile Workers Union of America, which had signed its first union cards at Stevens 13 years earlier, merged with the larger Amalgamated Clothing Workers of America to give extra momentum to its stalled membership drive. At the merger convention George Meany, then president of the parent AFL-CIO, denounced Stevens as the nation's number one labour law violator and pledged that the full resources of the labour movement would be mobilized to bring "this outlaw company" to the bargaining table.

The consumer boycott won expressions of endorsement from city councils in many areas and from hundreds of prominent citizens and organizations all over the globe, but its practical effect was small, principally because only about 30% of Stevens products are sold at retail and few of these carry a Stevens label. The great bulk of the company's customers are hospitals, hotels, industry, and

PHIL JONES—TIME MAGAZINE © 1980 TIME INC.

Jubilant employees of J. P. Stevens & Co. voted to approve a contract with the company after a long-standing dispute.

government agencies, and Stevens's records of sales and profits indicated no great response to the boycott drive by these buyers.

The Corporate Weapon. By contrast, much greater success attended the union's unorthodox attempt to drive a wedge between the huge textile manufacturer and the banks, insurance companies, and industries with which it had ties through interlocking directorates or financial arrangements. This corporate campaign was under the direction of Ray Rogers, a former VISTA volunteer in Appalachia, who was in his mid-30s and whose favourite garb for his forays into Wall Street consisted of T-shirt and jeans.

The first target was the Manufacturers Hanover Trust Co., which had as one of its directors James D. Finley, then chairman of Stevens and chief strategist in its fight against the union. Threats by other unions and religious organizations to withdraw as much as a billion dollars in pension reserves from management by the bank led Finley to quit his directorship in 1978. A letter-writing blizzard initiated by women's groups brought sufficient fear of a boycott of cosmetics and jewelry merchandised by Avon Products, Inc., to cause that firm's chairman, David Mitchell, to resign from the Stevens board.

Plans to enter a union-backed opposition slate in the normally uncontested election of directors of the New York Life Insurance Co. resulted in the abrupt resignation of Finley from the board of that company and the simultaneous departure of New York Life's chairman, R. Manning Brown, from the Stevens board. The textile maker insisted that this only stiffened its resistance, but these affirmations were belied by an announcement late in 1979 that Finley was stepping down as Stevens chairman at age 63, two years before normal retirement. He was replaced by Whitney Stevens, generally viewed as less intractable in union relations.

The final shot in the corporate campaign took the form of a union move in September 1980 to enter two candidates for election to the 22-member board of the Metropolitan Life Insurance Co., holder of nearly $100 million of Stevens's long-term debt. This move, which would have required Metropolitan to spend at least $5 million in election costs, touched off frantic behind-the-scenes conferences involving Richard Shinn, the insurance company's chairman. He met separately with Stevens and Murray H. Finley, president of the Amalgamated. The air was filled with denials that Shinn was exerting any pressure for a settlement, but the negotiations between Stevens and the union quickly came out of the deep freeze and a contract was reached.

A Famous Victory? The one novel feature of the contract was a clause committing the union to refrain from any efforts to force directors off the Stevens board or to cut off the company's access to credit or other forms of financial support. The union also agreed to give up, for a year and a half, its court-granted rights to use Stevens plants, bulletin boards, canteens, and parking lots for organizing purposes. On the positive side, the Amalgamated won grievance and arbitration guarantees and a company pledge to maintain safety and health committees in each plant, made up of equal numbers of union and management appointees. The union members received $3 million in retroactive wage increases, but the new scales were identical with those already in effect in nonunion Stevens plants.

In human terms, the significance of the settlement was perhaps best summarized by Lucy Taylor, a Stevens worker who had been a leader in the union's parallel campaign to win government compensation for brown-lung disease, an occupational hazard that afflicts many cotton mill employees. "The contract is one of the most wonderful things that ever happened to us," she said. "I believe in the union. I believe in people being organized. God meant the people to stick together." Less than a month later, Lucy Taylor died of brown-lung disease.

Industrial Review

After four years of moderate increases, manufacturing production in the advanced industrial countries fell appreciably during 1980 but, because of the continued increase of output in the less industrialized countries, manufacturing activity in the Western world as a whole was only marginally below that of 1979. The centrally planned economies produced more manufactured goods in 1980 than in 1979, but their rate of growth declined.

In the advanced countries the heavy and light industries were about equally affected by weaker demand conditions and by sharp competition from newly industrializing countries. The worst hit were the basic metal industries in the advanced countries, particularly iron and steel, which suffered not only from low investment activity and competition from new producers but also from the trend favouring lighter products. Output of the chemical industry, especially that of basic chemicals, also fell considerably. Industries supplying the building and construction sector were adversely affected by the latter's severe recession. The general stagnation accelerated the long-term decline of the textile and clothing industries in the advanced countries. Almost the only relatively bright spot in

those nations was the food industry, the output of which continued to rise.

All the main components of final demand contributed to the weakening of demand for manufactured products in the advanced countries. Though current consumption by public authorities came close to maintaining its long-term growth trend in 1980, the much more important private consumption of goods and services rose by only about 1% in volume, far below its average rate of almost 4% for the ten years ended in 1979. The growth rate of fixed investment from 1970 to 1979 averaged 3%, while in 1980 it actually declined by approximately 0.5%.

Video discs are handled by technicians using a vacuum in an Indianapolis, Indiana, plant. Video discs have 10,000 grooves per inch (1 in = 2.54 cm), while LP audio records have only 250. Each disc contains 24 mi (38.6 km) of grooves.

UPI

Table I. Index Numbers of Production, Employment, and Productivity in Manufacturing Industries
1975 = 100

Area	Relative importance[1] 1975	1980	Production 1979	1980	Employment 1979	1980	Productivity[2] 1979	1980
World[3]	1,000	1,000	123	123	...	...	...	...
Industrial countries	868	862	123	122	...	...	...	...
Less industrialized countries	132	138	125	128	...	...	...	...
North America[4]	315	321	131	125	...	...	...	...
Canada	27	25	117	114	104	102	113	112
United States	288	296	132	126	115	111	115	114
Latin America[5]	74	76	121	126	...	...	...	...
Brazil	27	32	133	143	...	...	...	...
Argentina	15	11	97	93	...	...	...	...
Mexico	12	13	127	135	127	136	100	99.
Asia[6]	159	178	132	138	...	...	...	...
India	11	11	125	126	115	115	109	110
Japan	109	127	133	143	97	100	137	143
South Korea	...	...	220	216	137	...	161	...
Europe[7]	416	393	116	116	...	...	...	...
Austria	8	8	120	125	97	98	124	128
Belgium	14	13	118	117	...	...	...	...
Denmark	6	6	120	120	101	99	119	121
Finland	6	6	116	125	97	101	120	124
France	80	76	117	117	98	96	119	122
West Germany	115	110	118	118	100	101	118	117
Greece	3	3	128	128	118	119	108	108
Ireland	1	1	138	137	116	114	119	120
Italy	43	46	124	131	104	106	119	124
Netherlands, The	16	15	114	114	90	88	127	130
Norway	6	5	99	100	93	95	106	105
Portugal	4	5	134	143	105	...	128	...
Spain	24	22	114	115	83	78	137	147
Sweden	17	14	98	99	89	89	110	111
Switzerland	13	11	109	107	92	93	118	115
United Kingdom	50	39	104	95	96	96	108	104
Yugoslavia	11	13	134	140	116	...	116	...
Rest of the world[8]	36	32	104	108	...	...	...	...
Oceania	18	16	104	107	...	...	...	...
South Africa	7	6	105	114	101	106	104	108
Centrally planned economies[9]	...	...	126	132	...	...	...	...

[1]The 1975 weights are those applied by the UN Statistical Office; those for 1980 were estimated on the basis of the changes in manufacturing output since 1970 in the various countries.
[2]This is 100 times the production index divided by the employment index, giving a rough indication of changes in output per person employed.
[3]Excluding Albania, Bulgaria, China, Czechoslovakia, East Germany, Hungary, Mongolia, North Korea, Poland, Romania, the U.S.S.R., and Vietnam.
[4]Canada and the United States.
[5]South and Central America (including Mexico) and the Caribbean islands.
[6]Asian Middle East and East and Southeast Asia, including Japan.
[7]Excluding Albania, Bulgaria, Czechoslovakia, East Germany, Hungary, Poland, Romania, and the U.S.S.R.
[8]Africa and Oceania.
[9]These are not included in the above world total and consist of the European countries listed in note 7 above.

Table II. Pattern of Output, 1977–80
Percent change from previous year

	World[1] 1977	1978	1979	1980	Developed countries 1977	1978	1979	1980	Less developed countries 1977	1978	1979	1980	Centrally planned economies 1977	1978	1979	1980
All manufacturing	4	4	5	−0.5	4	4	5	−1	7	6	3	3	7	6	5	5
Heavy industries	5	5	5	−0.5	4	5	5	−1	9	6	4	3	8	7	5	6
Base metals	0	5	6	−5	−1	5	5	−6	8	8	10	4	4	4	1	4
Metal products	5	5	5	1	5	5	5	1	5	7	7	4	9	8	7	7
Building materials, etc.	4	5	4	−0.5	4	5	5	−1	7	6	3	4	5	4	2	4
Chemicals	7	5	5	−2	6	5	7	−3	13	4	0	2	7	6	3	2
Light industries	3	3	3	−0.5	3	2	4	−1	4	5	2	2	6	4	3	3
Food, drink, tobacco	3	4	3	2	3	3	3	2	6	6	2	2	5	3	3	3
Textiles	−1	0.5	4	−2	−2	0	5	−2	1	3	3	0	4	4	2	3
Clothing, footwear	0	0	1	−3	0	−1	1	−4	0	3	2	1	4	4	5	3
Wood products	4	1	4	−2	3	1	3	−3	9	3	5	4	5	4	0	3
Paper, printing	3	4	5	1	3	4	5	1	3	6	7	5	5	4	−2	3

[1]Excluding centrally planned economies.   [2]Excluding China.
Source: UN, *Monthly Bulletin of Statistics*.

Robotic machines are increasingly being used to do the work of human hands. These robots at a car assembly plant in Fenton, Missouri, do welding and other assembly tasks.

The recession in 1980 started in the United States and after some delay spread to Europe. By contrast, early in 1981 the North American economy was back on a moderate growth trend, while Western Europe seemed to be stagnating. Japan avoided the recession but held to a markedly reduced rate of growth. In many countries the government's main aim was to reduce the high rate of inflation—stimulated by a major rise in petroleum prices in 1979–80—by means of deflationary fiscal policies and a squeeze on the supply of money; promoting growth was low on their list of priorities. The depression in the manufacturing sector was an unavoidable outcome of those policies.

Table III. Output per Hour Worked in Manufacturing
1975=100

Country	1974	1976	1977	1978	1979	1980
France	103	112	115	121	129	131
West Germany	96	107	110	113	118	117
Italy	106	109	108	111	122	127
Japan	104	110	115	124	134	142
U.K.	102	105	106	107	109	107
U.S.	98	106	108	110	113	115

Source: National Institute, *Economic Review*.

Table IV. Manufacturing Production in the U.S.S.R. and Eastern Europe[1]
1975=100

Country	1977	1978	1979	1980
Bulgaria[2]	114	122	128	134
Czechoslovakia	112	117	122	126
East Germany[2]	111	116	121	127
Hungary	112	117	121	118
Poland	117	123	126	126
U.S.S.R.	111	117	121	124

[1] Romania not available.
[2] All industries.
Source: UN, *Monthly Bulletin of Statistics*.

Most important in 1980 was the marked fall in the output of U.S. manufacturing industries, exceeding 4%; among the other major countries, Japan achieved a sizable increase, on the order of 7%, as did Italy (5%), while production in West Germany and France remained at 1979 levels. Production fell by 10% in the United Kingdom, where domestic deflation and the high exchange rate of sterling added to difficulties stemming from the already weakened competitive position of the nation's industries. Among the smaller industrial nations, only Austria, Finland, and South Africa registered noteworthy growth rates; in the others output either fell or remained at approximately the same level.

In Latin America the Brazilian and Mexican industries grew at a fast rate, but production in Argentina declined. In Asia, Indian output rose a little, but the rapid growth of South Korean industry, which had more than doubled its output between 1975 and 1979, came to a halt.

The faltering of the growth in output adversely influenced the rate of improvement of productivity. The rates of advance in output per hour worked declined in all major industrial countries, and productivity actually fell in the U.K.

In the U.S.S.R. manufacturing output grew in 1980 at a rate of about 2–3%, not more than about one-half that of the previous two years. Social and political troubles prevented any growth in Poland; output fell in Hungary, mainly as a result of measures aimed at restoring the internal and external equilibrium in the economy. In the other centrally planned Eastern European countries, output grew at about the same rate as in recent years.

(G. F. RAY)

ADVERTISING

The midseason strike of major league baseball players in 1981 resulted in heavy losses of advertising revenue for radio and television stations. Independent stations suffered more than the networks. WPIX-TV, an independent New York station that regularly broadcasts Yankee games, saw its audience cut in half.

The investigation of television advertisements aimed at children, begun in the U.S. in 1978, came to an end in 1981. Proposals had included a ban on commercials aimed at audiences containing a significant proportion of children too young to understand the purpose of the advertisement and a ban on commercials seen by older children for sugared products with dental-health risks. The Federal Trade Commission (FTC), charged with determining whether specific advertisements aimed at children were unfair or deceptive, concluded that it was no longer in the public interest to continue studying the matter. The commission declared that even if it could resolve the issues involved and develop rules, questions would remain about its ability to enforce its decisions.

In a different approach to advertising, Sears, Roebuck and Co. placed its summer 1981 catalog on a video disc and tested this medium in 1,000 consumer homes nationwide. This was Sears's first step in moving toward cable television video-cataloging. Consumers would receive a video catalog, similar to a phonograph record, that could be used with a video-disc player. Instructions and content information would appear on the album jacket.

The U.S. Postal Service was looking into the feasibility of selling advertising space on its trucks, in post office lobbies, and on the covers of stamp booklets. Advertising might also be accepted for the design side of stamps. The Postal Service requested public comment on the subject. It planned to publish a summary of the responses and its own conclusions in 1982.

Morality in the media was a major concern in 1981 as organized groups began calling on concerned citizens to pressure radio and television networks to eliminate obscene material. One such group, the Coalition for Better Television, began monitoring programs for sexual, profane, and violent content in an effort to gather ammunition for a boycott of the sponsors' products. Over 4,000 Coalition volunteers watched prime time TV shows over a three-month period and wrote down examples of obscene material. Owen Butler, chairman of the board of Procter & Gamble, the largest television advertiser in the U.S., responded to the Coalition's concerns by stating that Procter & Gamble was listening to critics who complained about sex and violence on prime time television. Procter & Gamble withdrew sponsorship of 50 programs that it considered objectionable. Meanwhile, the Moral Majority, a leading member of the Coalition, used newspaper advertising to educate people on what it was and what it stood for.

A strike by the Writers Guild of America delayed the start of the fall television season and advertising campaigns tied to it. The issue was whether or not the writers should obtain royalties for programs aimed at the home video market.

Brooke Shields became a controversial figure in advertising when the U.S. Public Health Service rejected posters and television spots, distributed by the American Lung Association, in which she warned of the dangers of smoking. Reagan administration officials contended that her movie roles made her an inappropriate role model for teenagers.

Hospitals began to advertise their services. One Nevada hospital used TV ads to promote its emergency room service and also advertised a special offer making patients eligible to win an expense-paid vacation if they checked in on a Friday or Saturday.

A thousand new low-power neighbourhood television stations using VHF or UHF channels were being planned in the U.S. The Federal Communications Commission (FCC) issued a report in 1981 that recommended opening up the neighbourhood stations to minorities and noncommercial broadcasters who could afford a $50,000 start-up cost. The FCC's proposed rules would make it difficult for the three major television networks to enter this market. The Neighborhood TV Co., financed by Sears, was approved for more than 140 low-power stations. Full-power independent TV stations increased their audience share in 1981 at the expense of the networks, and the independents' advertising revenues rose more than those of network affiliates.

The tax law changes that took effect in the U.S. in October precipitated an avalanche of advertising by banks to attract savers. Banks in major metropolitan areas took out full-page advertisements in newspapers and magazines announcing the new tax-exempt "All Saver" certificates, and direct mail promotions were sent to holders of six-month certificates of deposit informing them that they could convert to the new instruments without penalty. Radio and television were also used to attract investors with offers of merchandise and cash premiums.

Television became a $10 billion-a-year advertising medium in 1980, according to FCC figures. *Advertising Age* reported the top five U.S. advertisers in 1980 as Procter & Gamble, Sears, General Foods, Philip Morris, and K-Mart. General Motors moved from fourth in 1979 to sixth. The 100 largest national advertisers increased their advertising spending in 1980 by 11%, to $13 billion, but 21 companies on the list reduced their expenditures because of overseas competition, inflation, and high interest rates. The U.S. government rose from 28th to 24th place by spending $173 million, an 18% increase over 1979. R. J. Reynolds Industries was the largest spender for magazine and newspaper advertising and outdoor media. Chrysler Corp. was first in spot radio advertising, and Procter & Gamble continued to be the top user of spot and network television.   (EDWARD MARK MAZZE)

AEROSPACE

In the commercial sector of the aerospace industry, the year's principal theme was the appearance of designs for what might become a major market, the 150-seat transport. Barely recognized before January 1981, it was a major discussion topic at the

Sears, Roebuck and Co., the largest U.S. mail-order marketer, began putting its catalog on video discs for in-store and home viewing.

biennial Paris Air Show six months later. Europe's Airbus Industrie unveiled there a model of its proposed A320 contender, while McDonnell Douglas Corp. and Fokker of The Netherlands showed off a representation of the MDF 100, a combination of their respective earlier DC-11 and F-29 projects that had been shelved in order to concentrate on a common airliner. There were reports of a Boeing project designated 7-7, but with so many commitments to other programs that firm would have a hard time launching yet another design.

In September Boeing rolled out its first 767 airliner, the first completely new Western transport in its class in nearly two decades, buoyed up by 173 firm orders and 138 options. Europe's rival to the 767, the A310 derivative of the top-selling A300 Airbus, was due for rollout in March 1982. Its selection by Middle East Airlines in December 1980 upstaged the U.S. aircraft, but Boeing could afford the loss; a few weeks earlier United Airlines had placed with it the largest order ever signed for a commercial transport aircraft. For $3 billion United was to acquire a fleet of 60 757s, a new design slightly smaller than the 767 and seating 170 passengers. The 757 was due to fly in the spring of 1982. In March 1981 Boeing committed itself to the 737-300, a "halfway house" contender for the 150-seater market, developed from the 737 twinjet transport. A number of airlines, mostly in the U.S., were eager for Boeing to modify the top-selling 727 trijet to take a pair of much more efficient engines. In December Lockheed announced that it was ceasing production of the L-1011 Tristar jumbo jet, citing a lack of orders.

In Britain the increasingly tenuous links between the airlines and the U.K. airframe industry were further weakened by the retirement after only 17 years of service of the British Airways' VC-10s, which were being converted into tankers for the Royal Air Force. The Comet IV, which in 1958 narrowly beat a Boeing 707 for the honour

of inaugurating the first transatlantic jet passenger route, made its last flight in commercial service. Nevertheless, the fortunes of British Aerospace (BAe), a giant agglomeration of many famous industrial names, were far from bleak. In February BAe was denationalized, or "privatized," by the sale of 100 million 50-pence shares for £1.50 each. In May the BAe 146, a four-jet short-haul feeder transport seating 80–100, made its appearance, with initial orders for 25.

In France the arrival of a Socialist government signaled a tighter grip by the state on private companies, notably Dassault, and the Paris Air Show revealed some loss of momentum in the normally ebullient French industry as uncertainty took hold. China was building a four-engined transport, the C-10, said to resemble a Boeing 707. In the U.S.S.R., meanwhile, the new Ilyushin Il-86 wide-body airliner began scheduled services, though with old-fashioned, low-bypass engines; the U.S.S.R. was still struggling with high-bypass engine technology, mastered by the West well over a decade earlier.

In June U.S. Pres. Ronald Reagan's task force on flight-deck manning made an important decision: two-pilot crews were adequate to operate the new-generation transports, beginning with the McDonnell Douglas DC-9-80. The argument of the task force, predictably unpopular with pilots' unions, recognized that the new electronic control systems, based on sophisticated computers, multipurpose cathode-ray tube displays, and flight management equipment, could adequately replace the engineer on the flight deck. The engineer thus became an endangered species and would disappear in the 1990s as the navigator did in the 1970s.

Also emerging at the Paris Air Show was the "supercommuter" market with planes of 40–70 seats, a development that most people except the professional analysts had overlooked. The numbers involved were far more modest than those associated with the 150- and 200-seaters, probably amounting to about 1,200–1,800 aircraft by the mid-1980s. With nearly a dozen contenders planned or already flying, some companies

could have a lean time relying on this market. All turboprop-powered, these aircraft might be considered the true replacement for what would remain the most famous transport aircraft of all time, the DC-3. While that 1935 workhorse was still to be seen throughout the world, its founder, Donald W. Douglas, died in February at the age of 88. Shortly afterward another famous aviation personality, John K. Northrop, also died (*see* Obituaries).

The Anglo-French Concorde supersonic transport celebrated its fifth year of service in January. A British Airways claim that it had made a £4 million profit the previous year was challenged by a House of Commons Select Committee, which converted the figure into a £6 million deficit and recommended that steps be taken to remedy the situation. France, too, showed dissatisfaction with its one-time favourite protégé and by autumn was publicly wondering whether the time had not come to end the venture.

Perhaps the most significant military development was the October announcement of President Reagan's choice of nuclear policy for the late 1980s. The U.S. deterrent would comprise 100 "revitalized" Rockwell B-1 bombers (several were flying in the development program when the project was canceled by Pres. Jimmy Carter in 1977), 100 MX land-based missiles, and Trident II missiles for launch by submarines. In Europe the reality of new program costs finally obliged the West German defense minister to protest that his country was no longer prepared to support the multinational TKF 90 program, an attempt by West Germany, Britain, and France to combine their fighter requirements into a common airframe. Britain therefore stepped up its studies for a Jaguar replacement. A more positive development was Britain's decision to cooperate with the U.S. on the AV-8B Advanced Harrier vertical take-off fighter program in preference to building its own version of the plane.

(MICHAEL WILSON)

ALCOHOLIC BEVERAGES

Beer. Estimated world beer production in 1980 was 938 million hectolitres (hl), 3.2% higher than in 1979. Generally low levels of output were recorded in Europe and Asia, but they were offset by advances in Africa and North and South America. The U.S. maintained its position as the world's number one brewer, increasing production over 1979 by 5.7% to 227,756,000 hl, more than one-quarter of the world's beer. West Germany retained second place with 92,-309,000 hl (a 0.7% increase), and the U.K. remained third despite a 3.8% decrease to 64,830,000 hl. The Soviet Union and Japan again ranked fourth and fifth with outputs of 61.3 million hl and 45,535,000 hl, respectively. In 1980 Europe for the first time produced less than half of the world output.

After Europe experienced shortages of hops in 1980, estimates for the 1981 crop indicated an increase of 8.7% to 2,570,000 centners (1 centner=50 kg=110.23 lb); West Germany was expected to provide more than 40% of this increase. Hop picking in England began in the Kent fields in September with indications of a good crop. The commercial use of liquid carbon dioxide hop extract spread worldwide. The

A new commercial twin-jet airliner, the Boeing 767, made its maiden flight in September. The company received orders for 173 of the craft.

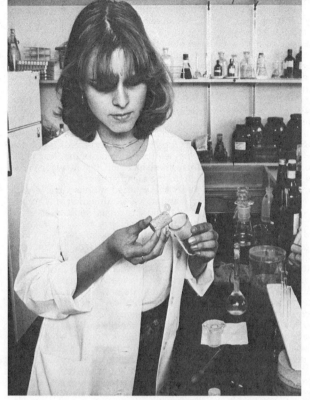

Scientists in Switzerland discovered why some corks were giving an unpleasant taste to wine. A bleaching process gave the corks a bad taste, making even good wine taste bad.

technique, which produced a stable extract free from residual solvent, was developed jointly by the Brewing Research Foundation and the Distillers Company Ltd. in the U.K. The world's first commercial plant, with a nominal capacity of 30,000 centners a year, opened in Australia.

The biennial congress of the European Brewery Convention was held in Copenhagen in 1981. In Britain brewers celebrated the wedding of Prince Charles and Lady Diana Spencer in July with the production of more than 80 commemorative ales and lagers. (MICHAEL D. RIPLEY)

Spirits. Sales of spirits again suffered from the recession in 1981, and in the U.K. there was a dramatic increase in the share taken home at the expense of those bought by the drink in public houses and restaurants. The worldwide trend to light spirits continued, with vodka and white rum brands topping the U.S. sales chart. In West Germany, where rum sales reached a record 7.5 million cases, and in France consumption of dark rum still dominated; dark rum accounted for 90% of the total West German rum market.

Irish cream liqueurs were a major growth area, with many new brands appearing in 1981. North America was the biggest market for this rapidly expanding sector, and the total Irish cream liqueurs market was expected to grow to 2,850,000 cases in 1982. There was also growth in the flavoured spirits sector of the liqueur market, up 27% during 1975–80 to 107 million cases. Within this group the most marked growth over the five-year period was in traditional liqueurs, premixed cocktails, and anisette. West Germany had the greatest increase in consumption of liqueurs.

Scotch whisky continued to dominate the British spirits market with a 50% share, but case sales of 13.4 million in 1980 (worth £1,150 million) were likely to fall to 12.8 million in 1981, dropping for the third year in succession. Scotch could also face a tough time in the U.S., where Canadian brands were doing well, and this prompted Scotch manufacturers to conduct their first generic advertising campaign in the U.S. Latest figures showed the world market for Scotch to be some 77 million cases a year.

"Unfair" duty levels within the European Economic Community (EEC) remained under examination. The prime example, according to U.K. Scotch whisky suppliers, was the higher level of tax put on Scotch in France compared with cognac. The U.K., however, also operated a similar two-tier duty system on wines and beer.

(ANTONY C. WARNER)

Wine. World production of wine in 1981 was estimated at 320 million hl, a decline of nearly 9% from the 1980 total. This was caused mainly by bad climatic conditions

Table V. Estimated Consumption of Beer in Selected Countries
In litres[1] per capita

Country	1978	1979	1980
West Germany	145.6	145.1	145.7
Czechoslovakia	129.0	137.0	137.8
East Germany	130.0	135.0	135.0
Australia[2]	137.6	134.2	134.3
Belgium[3]	125.5	125.8	131.3
Ireland	121.8	122.7	121.76
Denmark	116.89	120.38	121.53
Luxembourg	119.0	111.0	121.0
New Zealand	127.4	118.7	118.0
United Kingdom	121.3	122.1	117.1
Austria	100.9	103.9	101.9
United States	87.4	90.1	92.0
Canada[4]	86.1	84.2	87.6
Netherlands, The	85.18	84.95	86.3
Hungary	86.0	86.0	86.3
Switzerland	68.0	68.2	69.0
Bulgaria	59.0	57.7	...
Finland	54.96	56.18	57.39
Spain	52.1	53.7	54.4
Venezuela	48.7	47.7	50.0
Norway	46.04	45.88	48.28
Sweden	48.9	48.2	47.2
Colombia	42.8	43.6	45.0
France	45.26	45.51	44.31
Yugoslavia	38.7	39.7	44.2

[1] One litre = 1.0567 U.S. quart = 0.8799 imperial quart.
[2] Years ending June 30.
[3] Excluding so-called household beer.
[4] Years ending March 31.

Table VI. Estimated Consumption of Potable Distilled Spirits in Selected Countries
In litres[1] of 100% pure spirit per capita

Country	1978	1979	1980
Luxembourg	5.5	5.8	9.0
Poland	5.6	5.6	6.0
East Germany	4.0	4.3	4.5
Hungary	4.61	4.5	4.5
Czechoslovakia	3.6	3.24	3.52
Canada[2]	3.45	3.51	3.38
U.S.S.R.	3.3	3.3	3.3
United States	3.15	3.1	3.08
West Germany	3.0	3.37	3.07
Spain	3.0	3.0	3.0
Finland	2.82	3.03	2.79
Sweden	2.99	3.03	2.75
Netherlands, The	3.01	3.41	2.71
France[3]	2.46	2.53	2.53
New Zealand	2.0	2.28	2.5
Belgium	2.38	2.26	2.37
Romania	2.2	2.3	2.3
Iceland	2.25	2.35	2.25
Switzerland	2.09	2.04	2.05
Ireland	2.29	2.24	2.04
Yugoslavia	2.6	2.0	...
Cyprus	1.9	1.9	2.0
Bulgaria	2.0	2.0	2.0
Argentina	0.9	1.7	2.0

[1] One litre = 1.0567 U.S. quart = 0.8799 imperial quart.
[2] Years ending March 31.
[3] Including aperitifs.

Table VII. Estimated Consumption of Wine in Selected Countries
In litres[1] per capita

Country	1978	1979	1980
France[2]	96.29	92.8	95.36
Italy	91.0	90.0	93.0
Argentina	82.0	77.0	75.0
Portugal	91.3	80.0	70.0
Spain	70.0	65.0	64.7
Luxembourg	42.7	39.4	48.2
Switzerland[3]	45.5	45.8	47.4
Chile	47.7	46.56	45.0
Greece	42.0	40.5	44.9
Austria[4]	35.0	35.8	35.8
Hungary	33.8	35.0	35.0
Romania	33.1	35.5	28.0
Yugoslavia	26.4	27.3	...
West Germany	24.4	24.3	25.6
Uruguay	25.0	25.0	...
Bulgaria	22.0	22.0	...
Belgium	17.8	20.4	20.6
Australia[4]	14.3	16.5	17.4
Czechoslovakia	17.5	15.5	15.5
U.S.S.R.	14.0	14.0	14.4
Denmark	12.22	13.88	14.0
Netherlands, The	12.18	11.96	12.85
New Zealand	11.5	11.3	11.0
Poland	9.3	9.8	10.1
Cyprus	8.8	9.0	9.8
Sweden	9.06	9.43	9.54

[1] One litre = 1.0567 U.S. quart = 0.8799 imperial quart.
[2] Excluding cider (c. 20 litres per capita annually).
[3] Excluding cider (c. 4.95 litres per capita 1979–80).
[4] Years ending June 30.

Source: Produktschap voor Gedistilleerde Dranken, *Hoeveel alcoholhoudende dranken worden er in de wereld gedronken?*

during September and October in the major producing countries.

In France the 1981 harvest was estimated at 62.7 million hl (69.2 million hl in 1980). Earlier hopes of a higher figure were dashed by September storms and rain that affected all regions. The decline occurred mainly in the table wine sector. For quality wines the harvest was expected to exceed somewhat that of the previous year, with the notable exception that Champagne harvested only some 565,000 hl (716,000 hl in 1980), little more than half the volume needed to replenish stocks. White wines were most affected by shortfalls, the Charente-Maritime harvest being far below expectations. Wines of excellent quality were expected in Anjou-Saumur and Alsace.

Italy's harvest was provisionally estimated at 70 million hl, or some 17% below that of 1980, with the biggest shortfall expected in Emilia-Romagna. Quality was predicted to be good and likely to contribute to higher domestic consumption; increased exports to West Germany and the U.S. might be expected to compensate for France's embargo on imports of Italian wine. In Spain, too, an appreciable drop in production was forecast, the 1981 harvest being estimated at 30 million–33 million hl (43.5 million hl in 1980). In West Germany the 1980 harvest of 4.8 million hl had been the lowest since 1966; that for 1981, though delayed by bad weather and affected by frost, was expected to be better, perhaps 10–20% below the normal 8 million hl. Yugoslavia's production was expected to be lower than average in Macedonia and Serbia and higher elsewhere, with quality good in all regions. Production in the U.S.S.R. was estimated at 30 million–32 million hl.

Preliminary estimates suggested that U.S. production would be about 20% below the final 1980 figure of 18 million hl. South Africa's output—affected by flood in some areas—was estimated at 6.6 million hl and Australia's at 3.7 million hl.

(MARIE-JOSE DESHAYES-CREUILLY)

AUTOMOBILES

While attention in 1980 was focused on the financial woes of the Chrysler Corp., the fact that the entire U.S. auto industry was in trouble became clear in 1981. The U.S. manufacturers did not lose a combined record $4,170,000,000 in 1981 as they did in 1980, but third-quarter losses of nearly $1 billion pointed to the fact that the industry's troubles were not limited to Chrysler and were far from over.

In 1981 the U.S. auto industry was plagued by persistently high interest rates. That made it difficult for car buyers to find new-car loans (the industry estimated that 80% of all new-car purchases are financed). Those rates also made it difficult for new-car dealers to purchase automobiles to have in showrooms for shoppers. Car buyers found 16–16.5% new-car loan rates common, and dealers often were paying 22–23% on loans used to purchase cars for their inventory.

Adding to the interest rate problem in '81 were new-car price increases. In the fall of 1981, as the 1982 models were introduced,

General Motors Corp. raised the price of its cars by 5.8%, or $617, Ford Motor Co. by 4.8%, or $430, Chrysler by 3.7%, or $306, and American Motors Corp. (AMC) by 5.6%, or $473. The average base price of a 1982 model U.S.-made car rose to $8,767, an increase of $911 from the average of $7,856 at the start of the 1981 model year.

Throughout 1981 the domestic producers found themselves offering cash rebates to entice buyers to purchase what was becoming a mounting inventory of unsold cars. In a startling move Chrysler opened the 1982 model year by freezing prices on several subcompact Dodge Omni and Plymouth Horizon and compact Dodge Aries and Plymouth Reliant models at 1981 prices and then offering rebates of from $300 to $1,000. Ford and AMC also introduced rebates as the 1982 models were introduced. Only General Motors differed. Rather than offering rebates, the firm announced that it would reduce the new-car loan rate on automobiles purchased at its dealers and financed through its General Motors Acceptance Corp. subsidiary to 13.8%; at that time most people were paying 16–16.5%. When the 1982 models were introduced, GM reduced the interest rate to 12.9% on selected compact X-body cars such as the Citation, Omega, Phoenix, and Skylark. Another aspect of the rebate situation was the demand by manufacturers that the dealers pay half the rebate amount.

The problems of the auto industry were evident in the sales figures. In the 1981 model year, which extended from Oct. 1, 1980, to Sept. 30, 1981, sales fell 2.1% to 6,644,444 units from the 6,787,846 sold in the 1980 model year. GM sales dropped 4.6% to 4,032,729 units, the lowest since 1975. Ford sales slipped less than 1% to 1,-542,388, while AMC sales were down 11.1% to 145,206 units and those of U.S.-built Volkswagen Rabbits down 16.1% to 159,588 units. Only Chrysler, ironically, experienced a sales gain to 764,535 units, a 17.7% increase.

There also was a shift in market shares with GM falling to 60.7% from 62.3% in the 1980 model year, Ford rising to 23.2% from 22.9%, Chrysler climbing to 11.5% from 9.6%, AMC drifting down to 2.2% from 2.4%, and Volkswagen dropping to 2.4% from 2.8%.

Imports experienced mixed results with sales strong at the outset of the 1981 calendar year and then tapering off near the end as a variety of adverse factors made their presence felt. Among them were government restrictions on the number of Japanese cars that could be exported to the U.S. and the aforementioned high interest rates, which caused even the historically more affluent import buyer to have trouble obtaining credit.

While faltering a bit in sales, imports once again were strong in the annual U.S. Environmental Protection Agency fuel economy ratings for the 1982 model cars. For the fifth straight year the car achieving the best mileage was the subcompact Volkswagen Rabbit powered by a four-cylinder diesel engine. Though the Rabbit is built in the U.S., the EPA categorized it as an import because more than 50% of its components originate in West Germany. The Rabbit's 1982 rating was 45 mi per gallon (mpg) estimated in city driving. The only "true"

domestic car in the EPA's top ten was the mini Chevrolet Chevette powered by a four-cylinder diesel engine and rated at 40 mpg in city driving. The dubious title of least fuel-efficient was given to the limited-production Maserati Quattroporte powered by a V-8 engine and with automatic transmission; it was rated at 8 mpg in city driving.

In 1981 the U.S. National Highway Traffic Safety Administration abandoned the requirement to have air bags or automatic seat belts installed in cars. Auto industry observers had expected the air bag law to be dropped because the Reagan administration had said that it was sympathetic to the manufacturers.

With the mileage ratings came several new cars and a continuation of Detroit's policy to downsize its vehicles to make them more fuel-efficient. One major change announced at the time of the 1982 model introductions was that General Motors no longer would introduce new cars only in the fall but would introduce them at any time when it considered them ready for the market. Thus, its newest cars, the downsized, front-wheel-drive versions of its intermediate A-body cars—the Chevrolet Celebrity, Oldsmobile Cutlass Ciera, Pontiac 6000, and Buick Century—were to be delayed until after Jan. 1, 1982, as were the newly designed sporty Chevrolet Camaro and Pontiac Firebird compacts.

As a result, new models were few at GM in the fall. The mini Chevette added a barebones four-door, high-mileage Scooter to complement the two-door Scooter previously offered, and the two-door midsize Chevrolet Malibu was dropped until its A-body replacement, the Celebrity, would be ready at midyear. The Malibu name was kept on the four-door sedan and wagon models. At Buick the two-door Century was dropped, to appear later as a front-wheel-drive Century model. At the same time the former four-door Century and wagon took the Regal name.

Pontiac dropped full-size cars altogether by discontinuing the Bonneville and Catalina but kept the Bonneville name alive by putting it on the former four-door midsize LeMans model. The new A-body replacement for the LeMans was to be called the 6000. At Oldsmobile the new Cutlass A-body front-wheel-drive model was to be called Ciera. New for the outset of the 1982 model year was a 4.3-l V-6 diesel engine that would be used later as an option in selected front-wheel-drive A-body cars.

The new A-body cars would be shrunk from 108-in (1 in=2.54 cm) wheelbases to the same 105-in wheelbase currently on the X-body compacts. But overall lengths would be about 188 to 189 in, as compared with 181 in on the X-bodies.

Along with the size and weight reductions, GM also planned to offer the Pontiac-built 2.5-l, 4-cylinder engine as standard in all the A-body cars with mileage ratings of about 25 mpg for city driving with automatic transmission. Optional engines would be the 4.3-l V-6 diesel from Oldsmobile and the 2.8-l V-6 built by Chevrolet.

The new so-called F-body cars, Camaro and Firebird, were slated for February 1982 introductions along with two new GM subcompact front-wheel-drive J-cars, the Oldsmobile Firenza and Buick Skyhawk.

Ford Motor Co. Chairman Philip Caldwell unveiled the 1982 Ford Escort sedan at a press conference in August.

In the spring of 1981 GM introduced the first J-cars, the Chevrolet Cavalier, Pontiac J-2000, and Cadillac Cimarron.

GM unveiled an all-new compact-size pickup truck called the S-10 at Chevrolet and the S-15 at GMC. The small (108-in and 118-in wheelbase) versions were aimed at eventually replacing the subcompact (104-in and 117-in wheelbases) LUV truck that GM imported from Isuzu of Japan.

At Ford the subcompact, front-wheel-drive Ford Escort and Mercury Lynx, which were introduced in two-door hatchback and four-door wagon versions in 1981, added four-door hatchbacks for 1982. The compact Ford Fairmont and Mercury Zephyr lines dropped wagons because the compact Ford Granada and Mercury Cougar lines added new wagons in 1982. At Lincoln-Mercury a 108-in-wheelbase luxury car called the Continental was added. It was built on the same platform as the midsize Thunderbird.

Early in 1982 Ford planned to bring out its rival to the new S-10 and S-15 at GM. The new domestically built compact Ford truck would be called Ranger. It eventually would replace the subcompact Courier Ford imported from Toyo Kogyo of Japan. Ford also brought out a new 3.8-l V-6 gasoline engine for use in the Granada, Cougar, Thunderbird, Cougar XR-7, and Continental and in Ford pickup trucks.

Chrysler took the next step in downsizing by bringing out a pair of new front-wheel-drive intermediates called LeBaron, an old name, and Dodge 400, a new one that replaced the old two-door Diplomat. Both were offshoots of the already offered compact K-body cars, the Dodge Aries and Plymouth Reliant. Both were built on 99.9-in wheelbases, stretched a bit from the 99.6 in on the K-bodies, and were 179.7 in long versus 176 in on the K's. Both, too, were

powered by a Chrysler-built 2.2-l four-cylinder engine as standard; a 2.6-l four-cylinder Mitsubishi-built four-cylinder engine with automatic transmission was optional. LeBaron was offered as a two- and four-door model, while the 400 was a two-door only. Both planned to add convertibles eventually, as did the Mustang and Chevrolet Cavalier in 1983.

Chrysler also planned to begin offering a domestically built small truck, to be introduced in mid-1982. Called Rampage, the truck was a conversion of the Dodge Omni 024 car with a cargo bed in back. American Motors had nothing new to offer at the outset of the 1982 model year. Later it said that it would begin importing another subcompact, front-wheel-drive car from its French partner, Renault, to be called Fuego.

Among the other major car producers, Volkswagen replaced the former Dasher model with a car called Quantum, offered in coupe, sedan, and wagon versions and at prices starting at more than $10,000. It also restyled the sporty Scirocco and for the first time made a four-cylinder diesel engine available as an option in its Vanagon wagon/van model.

Toyota restyled its Celica ST and GT sports models along with the top-of-the-line Supra. Nissan (Datsun) for the first time since it began selling cars in the U.S. in 1958 brought out a new car under the Nissan rather than the Datsun name. The new front-wheel-drive Stanza was a replacement for the former 510 model. Honda added a new Civic model called the 1300 FE (for fuel economy). Equipped with a small four-cylinder engine and five-speed manual transmission, it achieved a 41-mpg EPA city driving rating.

The long-awaited DeLorean two-seat gullwing sports coupe appeared in July. The undertaking of former GM executive

John Z. DeLorean had been under development since 1975. Built in Northern Ireland and imported into the U.S., the car had a $25,000 base price with five-speed manual transmission; with automatic transmission, it cost $25,650.

(JAMES L. MATEJA)

BUILDING AND CONSTRUCTION

The sharp drop in home building in the U.S. in 1981 was a major contributor to an overall depression in the construction industry. Home building was experiencing the longest decline since World War II, and the downtrend in the construction industry was in its third year. On a seasonally adjusted annual rate basis, dollar outlays for construction were at an all-time high of $259,049,000,000 in January 1981, and in June they stood at $236,167,000,000. However, viewed in terms of constant dollars (1979 = 100), outlays were $181,987,-000,000 in 1978, $179,265,000,000 in 1979, $160,696,000,000 in 1980, and about $152 billion (preliminary estimate) in 1981.

The slump in construction cut deeply into the nation's economy and led to the bankruptcy of increasing numbers of building contractors. During the first eight months of 1981, there were almost 2,000 reported bankruptcies among general building contractors, 41% more than in the corresponding period of 1980. The unemployment rate in the construction industry in the third quarter of 1981 was 16.3%, more than twice the nation's overall rate of 7.5%. More than 800,000 construction workers were unemployed. In addition, the National Association of Home Builders estimated that 200,000 self-employed workers were out of work. New construction in the public and private sectors was also depressed. In the public sector the decline was most evident in the construction of schools, hospitals, and other public buildings.

The index of prices for construction materials stood at 139 (1977 = 100) in June 1981, 13% above June 1980. With few exceptions, the prices of the major material components of construction registered substantial gains. However, while builders acknowledged the effects of inflation on the price of housing, they believed that by far the biggest factor contributing to the decline in sales was the high interest rates on mortgages, which averaged more than 17% nationally. They noted also that the home-building industry was being hit by a 20% interest rate on billions of dollars of loans on construction and on finished but unsold homes.

A Task Force on Housing Costs of the U.S. Department of Housing and Urban Development reported that the high cost of shelter was not merely a serious problem for millions of American families but often an "insurmountable crisis." In June 1981 the median price of a new home in the U.S. was $71,600, compared with $44,200 in 1976. Prices were highest in the northeast, where the median was $90,700, and lowest in the north central states, with a median of $64,500.

Housing investment in Canada had been

expected to revive in 1981 and 1982 from the low levels of the preceding four years. However, surveys by the Conference Board of Canada, based on consumer sentiment, were gloomy. With most countries experiencing continuing inflation and rising unemployment, the outlook in Western Europe was uncertain. In Great Britain private investment in housing in 1981 was expected to make only modest gains over the low level of 1980, and it was anticipated that public investment would be even lower. Total investment in dwellings was forecast at £2,940 million for 1981 and £3,325 million for 1982, both figures below those for 1979 and 1980.

Construction of housing in France was also at low levels. It was not believed that public and private investment in production would offset the housing investment decline. In West Germany the government's tight monetary policy was expected to contribute to a decline in nonresidential construction and a sharp drop in housing, accompanied by rising unemployment among construction workers. Public investment in housing in Italy was aided by a program to help victims of the 1980 earthquake. In the smaller countries of Western Europe, there were indications that inflation would be curbed somewhat in 1981, but the outlook for building and construction was not good.

The Japanese economy was mixed in 1981. Large companies were investing in plant and equipment because of strong overseas demand for their products, but investment by smaller firms was low. The output of construction materials declined, and home building was down. However, the government had undertaken new programs to stimulate lagging sectors of the economy, and housing was expected to benefit.   (CARTER C. OSTERBIND)

CHEMICALS

High prices for petroleum — needed by the chemical industry for fuel and as a raw material — combined with generally depressed economic conditions were taking their toll on the chemical industry in 1981. Even industries in countries that had previously seemed immune to economic cycles were beginning to feel the pinch.

In the U.S. chemical shipments and profits of chemical companies increased in 1980 and in the first part of 1981. But the increases were the result of inflation and did not reflect the underlying problems accurately. Shipments of chemicals, as reported by the U.S. Department of Commerce, reached $167,101,000,000 in 1980, 8.6% higher than the $153,849,000,000 of chemicals shipped in 1979. In the first half of 1981 shipments totaled $92,867,000,000, 9.9% above the first half of 1980. Profits of U.S. chemical companies in 1980 amounted to $11,219,000,000, according to the U.S. FTC. That was 3% above the $10,896,000,000 earned in 1979.

But chemical production actually fell in 1980 from 1979. The Federal Reserve Board index of chemical production, which averaged 211.8 (1967 = 100) in 1979, dropped to 206.7 in 1980. It later began to rise, however, and averaged 219.7 for the first six months of 1981, on a seasonally adjusted basis.

And the U.S. chemical industry continued to maintain a favourable balance of trade. The U.S. Department of Commerce reported a net export of chemicals of $9,829,000,000 in 1979, on exports of $17,308,000,000 and imports of $7,479,000,000. In 1980 net exports increased 23.7% on exports of $20,740,000,000 and imports of $8,583,000,000. For the first half of 1981 chemical exports were $10,813,000,000 and imports were $4,757,000,000.

Propelled in large measure by high oil prices, chemical prices increased 17.1% in 1980, as the U.S. Department of Labor's index of producer prices for chemicals rose from 222.3 (1967 = 100) in 1979 to 260.3 in 1980. The upward trend continued into 1981; the index rose every month in the first part of the year and reached 291.4 in July.

In the fourth quarter of 1981 the outlook for chemicals was clouded by the general economic conditions in the U.S. and, in particular, by the sharp decline in housing starts and automobile sales. A fall survey of capital spending revealed that chemical companies planned to spend $13,740,000,000 in 1982, only 5% higher than the $13,080,000,000 estimated expenditure for 1981.

The long-term prospects for chemicals in the U.S., however, continued to be bright. Although the industry had reached a state of relative maturity, the expectation was that it would continue to grow at a rate 50% greater than that of the gross national product.

In Japan the chemical industry in 1980 enjoyed a sales increase of about 10% to a total of $77.6 billion. After a slump that began in late 1980, chemical makers looked for a recovery to begin in the second half of 1981. But by early in the fourth quarter the recovery had not materialized.

The situation was unusual because the Japanese chemical industry, which had been accustomed to rapid production increases, was not growing as fast as the economy as a whole. Man-made fibres and fertilizers were problem areas, and demand for polyvinyl chloride was running so far behind supplies that the government allowed makers to form a cartel. Five dye makers were also given permission to band together. In a 1981 survey, Japan's Ministry of International Trade and Industry found that 366 chemical companies planned to devote $3.2 billion to capital expenditures. That represented an increase of 6.4%, only slightly more than the expected 1981 inflation rate of 4%. However, an average growth rate of 4.4% a year through 1985 was projected.

Conoco Inc.'s refinery at Lake Charles, La., was part of the target of a takeover by Du Pont & Co., the largest producer of chemicals in the U.S. Du Pont succeeded in effecting the merger in August.

CHRISTOPHER HARRIS

In West Germany the chemical industry had a record first quarter in 1980, but then a recession set in and the industry had one of its worst years in two decades. Early figures revealed that chemical sales in 1980 increased some 5% to $59.2 billion. But these figures reflected the inflation, and output in real terms declined 4%.

West German chemical companies recorded another good first quarter in 1981. Sales of the three largest chemical companies were 10% higher than they were in 1980. But by midyear the industry had become cautious about the remainder of 1981. The U.S. dollar, which had increased in relation to the mark by 8%, rose an additional 9% through May 1981. On balance, the stronger dollar was good for West German chemical companies, making their exports more competitive in world markets against U.S. exports. It also meant that income from their substantial operations in the U.S. would add more marks to the parent companies' income. On the other hand, the weaker mark also meant that the West German chemical companies were paying more for their imports of crude oil and other raw materials.

Chemical sales in the United Kingdom in 1979 were estimated at $37,745,000,000 by the Organization for Economic Cooperation and Development. Comparable figures for 1980 were not available, but the British Chemical Industries Association's preliminary estimate was that they were $40.7 billion. Chemical output dropped significantly, however, the index of chemical production falling from 119.2 (1975 = 100) in 1979 to 109.1. The downward trend continued into the early part of 1981 and reached 104 in May.

Along with the rest of the economy, the chemical industry in the U.K. was struggling. In addition, it was suffering from a currency that was strong compared with those of West Germany and France, its main chemical competitors in the EEC. But the industry maintained a strong export position, nonetheless. In 1980 it exported an estimated $12,070,000,000 of chemicals, while imports were estimated at $7,-020,000,000. Although the immediate outlook for the U.K. chemical industry was far from bright, there was hope that growth rates would start climbing after 1984 or 1985, when natural gas liquids from North Sea sources became available as chemical feedstocks.

In France the chemical industry was having a difficult time. French chemical sales reached $37 billion in 1980. But investment had been flat for five years, and the labour force, which was estimated at 305,000 in 1978, had fallen to 295,000 by 1981. The new Socialist government under Pres. François Mitterrand was out to change that. In late September the Socialists presented a plan calling for nationalization of 36 banks and 11 major industrial companies. Targeted for takeover were Rhône-Poulenc, the biggest chemical company in the country; Pechiney Ugine Kuhlmann, a chemical and metal producer; and Roussel-Uclaf, a large pharmaceutical company in which a West German firm held a majority interest. If approved, the Socialist plan would give the government control of approximately 60% of French chemical sales.

(DONALD P. BURKE)

ELECTRICAL

A new commitment to research and development characterized the corporate plans of most electrical engineering manufacturers. U.S. and European firms were investing heavily in new technology and expected a new range of products to bring them through the recession. In 1980 Siemens in West Germany plowed back a record DM 3 billion, about 9% of turnover, into research and development. In Britain the General Electric Co. Ltd. spent more than 10% of its £4,129 million turnover on research and development in the year ended March 31, 1981. In the U.S. Westinghouse Electric Corp. spent $186 million in 1980 on in-house research (15% above 1979) and $374 million on sponsored research (14% more than in 1979), a total of 6.5% of the 1980 sales turnover of $8,514,000,000. In addition, in 1980 a record $446 million (41% above 1979) was spent on capital improvements as part of Westinghouse's corporate quality and productivity improvement effort. This expenditure included modernizing existing facilities and introducing advanced manufacturing processes.

General Electric Co. (GE) also increased in-house research and development, by 19% to $760 million, in 1980. Including external funding, GE's total research and development expenditure in 1980 was $1.6 billion, or 6.4% of the 1980 sales turnover of $24,959,000,000. This self-renewal was being accelerated with investments in the construction and acquisition of new laboratories and manufacturing centres to ensure the company's position as a leader in the microelectronics revolution. A total of $2 billion was spent in 1980 to upgrade GE's production facilities.

Varta, the West German battery manufacturer, was convinced that the only firms with a chance of cashing in on any growth in the battery market were those that could afford a large research and development budget. Varta employed 200 researchers and spent about DM 40 million on research, 2.6% of its 1980 turnover of DM 1,530,000,-000.

Microelectronics was the key to growth in electrical equipment product design, and many large Japanese firms were increasing their investments in 1981 in the production of semiconductors and the development of applications for them. In 1980 Hitachi spent 72 billion yen, and it planned to spend 80 billion in 1981; Mitsubishi's investments would climb from 30 billion yen to around 40 billion, and those of Matsushita Electrical Industrial from 47 billion yen in 1980 to 65 billion in 1981.

Japan made considerable inroads in export markets in 1980, taking over second place from the U.S. behind West Germany. The Organization for Economic Cooperation and Development gave exports of electrical equipment in 1980 as: West Germany $10,128,000,000, Japan $7,367,000,000, and the U.S. $6,833,000,000 (the 1979 figures being West Germany $9,573,-000,000, the U.S. $5,789,000,000, and Japan $5,687,000,000). France was fourth in 1980 with $4,828,000,000 in exports, Britain fifth with $4,062,000,000, and Italy sixth with $3,119,000,000.

In 1981 Japan was accused by most other industrialized countries of breaking trade

rules. The European federation of electrical manufacturers' trade associations published a paper which estimated that as much as 90% of Japan's distribution network for electrical and electronic goods was linked to national producers; the Japanese home market was protected by the Electrical Appliance and Material Control Law. In export markets there was intense competition from Japanese firms, "often at prices which defy any economic analysis." It seemed reasonably certain, the federation stated, that in some cases Japanese firms had been able to call upon their government to cover losses resulting from sales at reduced prices.

Microelectronics was finding its way into all types of electrical equipment, including utility switchgear, battery chargers, and electricity load controllers. The most spectacular innovation, which could cause a major revolution in electricity production and supply, was the use of microelectronics to allow electric utilities to provide consumers with spot electricity prices updated every five minutes. This was expected to result in up to 20% savings in the production cost of electricity. The keys to this revolution were the new electronic electricity meters and consumer load control units being developed by manufacturers, principally in the U.S. and Britain.

(T. C. J. COGLE)

FURNITURE

The economic malaise caused by tight consumer credit and high inflation in 1981 dampened the growth of the U.S. furniture industry for the second straight year. The 4% drop in the wholesale value of manufacturers' shipments experienced in 1980 continued through the first half of 1981. Adjusted for inflation, the actual decline was 11.9%, which more nearly reflected the number of units manufactured.

According to the National Association of Furniture Manufacturers, overall industry shipments were off 2% in the first quarter of 1981, compared with the same period a year earlier. Summer and casual furniture fared the worst, with a 15% decline. Furniture continued to be priced below most consumer durables. During all of 1980, the wholesale price index rose 32.9%, while household furniture prices increased 16.1%. U.S. exports of furniture to Europe rose during 1981 to an estimated $370 million. Domestic furniture production in most EEC countries was reported as sluggish.

At the retail level, U.S. home furnishings stores suffered a 1% loss in 1980 as sales fell from $18.6 billion in 1979 to $15.6 billion. Adjusted for inflation, the actual drop was 7.7%. An estimated 1% recovery in the first half of 1981 was attributed to a slight easing of retail credit loan rates during that period. Two key factors that affect home furnishings sales, the number of new homes built and sales of existing homes, were both slowed by high mortgage rates.

The increasing conservatism of the American public was reflected in furniture styles, with 18th-century furniture experiencing a surge of popularity. A second dominant style, known as "Country," was

Americans showed an increased preference in 1981 for high quality 18th century furniture, such as this Sheraton bow front sideboard built in about 1790.

somewhat more casual, with evidences of Colonial American, French, and Italian influences. Brass, which originally gained consumer acceptance for bedroom furniture, was being used for casual pieces, such as end tables, and as a trim on many wood pieces. Rattan moved from the patio and sunroom into the dining and living rooms.

The concept of the modular wall system, originally designed to meet the need for vertical storage space in small modern rooms, was expanded by some manufacturers into the "entertainment centre," a unit housing television, tape deck, stereo, and bar. "Flotation sleep" had gained widespread public acceptance, to the point where an estimated one out of every 20 beds sold was either a waterbed or a combination of water and conventional mattress material. As a result, most bedroom furniture makers were offering a flotation-unit frame as an option with bedroom suites.

There had been a virtual revolution in the sales of unfinished furniture at the retail level. Formerly, most unfinished furniture had been made by small producers from low-cost pine and less expensive hardwood, but the new do-it-yourself buyer demanded a higher-grade product. Oak was most in demand, and many conventional furniture manufacturers were now offering their solid wood furniture to the unfinished furniture market. (ROBERT A. SPELMAN)

FURS

Record interest rates in many parts of the world and the sustained strength of the U.S. dollar against most other important currencies had a major effect on the international fur trade in 1981. On a worldwide basis, fur business in 1981 was about the same or slightly lower than in the previous year, but there was considerable variation among countries.

The important West German market, which traditionally boasted the highest per capita consumption of furs in the world, suffered a severe setback as the economy weakened and the mark fell about 17% against the dollar by May 1981. Conversely, Japan, with its healthy economy and relatively strong yen, enjoyed an excellent fur season. In the U.S. the picture was mixed. The recession curbed spending for luxuries by lower- and middle-income groups but apparently had little effect at the upper-income level.

Early in the year unfavourable exchange rates caused such traditionally early buyers as West Germany, Italy, and Switzerland to limit their participation in the international auctions. Pelt prices fell 5–20% and would have dropped even further if American and Far Eastern buyers had not stepped in with heavy commitments. Prices recovered as the season progressed, however. From a profit standpoint, 1981 was not a good year. Delayed and selective buying, higher overhead costs, and keen competition forced many in the trade to operate on a narrow margin. High interest rates also cut deeply into profits.

Extreme heat and drought in 1980 had caused heavy losses among U.S. herds of both wild and ranched animals. As a result, there were shortages of certain furs in 1981, particularly such wild types as raccoon, coyote, and red fox. Indications at year's end were that supplies would be back to normal in 1982, with the possible exception of muskrat and nutria. West Germany, the main buyer of these items, had refused to pay the 1981 asking prices, and trappers apparently decided that these two furs were not attractive economically. Karakul production would also be down, reflecting consumer apathy. On the other hand, world production of ranched mink for sale in 1982 increased about 6% to a total of 23.3 million pelts. There was also increased farm production of foxes, fitch, and raccoon. (SANDY PARKER)

GLASS

The worldwide economic recession continued to affect the glass industry in 1981. In the U.K. several firms had to curtail production as home and overseas demand fell because of the high value of sterling and high interest rates. One of the casualties of the recession was Whitefriars Glass Ltd., a 300-year-old firm producing handmade crystal glass, which was forced to close down. Other closings included the Webb Corbett factory near Derby, as a result of an economy drive launched by its parent company, the Royal Doulton group; and Wood Brothers, another old firm producing handmade glass. The Triplex Safety Glass Co. Ltd. was adversely affected by the decline in the volume of motor vehicles produced in the U.K. but was relieved by an order from Mitsubishi Motors of Japan to supply annually up to 60,000 heated rear windows to be fitted onto cars offered for sale in Europe.

Despite the recession there were some significant developments and achievements. A laser-based device capable of engraving designs and decorations on crystal ware, claimed to be almost indistinguishable from classical acid etching, was introduced in Czechoslovakia with a reported doubling of productivity. The U.S. space shuttle "Columbia" had more than 70% of its outer surface covered by special silica-fibre tiles. The British television tube manufacturer Mullard Ltd. installed a computerized batch-mixing system at its factory in Simonstone, England. Another British firm, Chance Brothers Ltd., was using a robot gatherer to work on the production of radar cones and screens. The West German firm Nonchtman Bleikristallwerke GmBh introduced a diamond wheel to manufacture hand-cut crystal glassware; this increased productivity and reduced labour costs by up to 50% as well as improving quality. In the medical field Fibrelase 100 was a promising new product developed by Pilkington Brothers Ltd. of the U.K. for the treatment by laser of internal bleeding.

Pilkington, the world's largest flat-glass producer, acquired 80% of the issued share capital of Solec International Inc., a Los Angeles-based manufacturer of photovoltaic cells, panels, and other devices. Guardian Industries of the U.S. was to acquire control of the leading Spanish flat-glass producer, Vidrierase de Llodio (Villosa). Apart from normal flat glass, this company produced double glazing, laminated glass, and nonreflective glass. A new fibre-optics company was to be formed in France in which the major participant would be the Saint-Gobain group, with a 66% share; the remaining 34% would be owned by Corning Glass of the U.S.

The glass packaging industry experienced a gloomy year as it continued to face fierce competition from other forms of packaging materials. A quarter-litre wide-mouth bottle was launched nationally by the British bottlers of Coca-Cola, and in the U.S. Coca-Cola bottlers introduced a new 0.5-litre bottle. The EEC was pressuring Britain to allow importation from the European continent of milk in disposable cartons or plastic containers, and as a result the well-established British tradition of

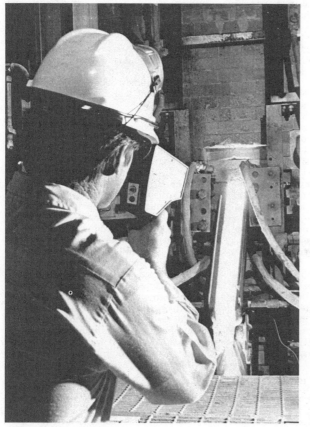

An optical pyrometer that gauges the temperature of molten glass is used by technicians to maintain proper temperature control. Precise temperatures are needed in the production of certain forms of glass designed for special uses.

doorstep delivery of milk in glass bottles was in jeopardy.

In the U.K. glass manufacturers succeeded in establishing a nationwide recycling scheme that would soon be saving the country the equivalent of seven million gallons of oil a year. By the year's end "Bottle Bank" facilities were operating in more than 200 towns and cities, and the prototype of a new smaller-sized glass-recycling machine called the "Bottle Bin" was launched. This would enable glass recycling to be expanded to inner city areas and such locations as public houses, restaurants, and hospitals that are unsuitable for full-size Bottle Banks.   (RAMILA MISTRY)

INSURANCE

Worldwide private insurance sales in 1981 exceeded $450 billion, representing a 20-fold increase in premiums written during the past two decades. The insurance market was divided approximately as follows: life 40%; motor 20%; accident, health, and liability 20%; fire 10%; and other 10%. The four leading insurance countries, the U.S., Japan, West Germany, and the U.K., accounted for three-fourths of the global premium volume.

For the U.K. insurance companies, overcapacity and strong competition in world markets drove rates below the cost of claims and expenses. Although investment gains provided net profits on total premiums of more than £15,000 million, some companies withdrew from unprofitable areas such as Australian general insurance. For the first time, U.K. overseas premiums fell to less than half of total sales.

Lloyd's of London announced record figures in 1981. On 1978 business, which requires a three-year accounting basis, premiums rose 14% to £2,163 million and profits increased 33% to £174 million. Succeeding years, however, appeared to be less profitable and largely dependent on investment income. A new regulatory act to strengthen the powers of self-regulation of the Committee of Lloyd's was being sought. The Insurance Brokers (Registration) Act, which became fully effective in December, limited the use of the term insurance broker to persons or firms under the disciplinary rules of the Registration Council.

U.S. life insurance appeared to be on the brink of the most important product, service, and tax changes in many years. So-called universal life insurance introduced a new combination of annuity and term insurance to compete with traditional "ordinary life" and other policies. The higher and tax-deferred (if current rulings prevailed) interest earnings on the cash values, plus flexibility of premiums, coverage amounts, and withdrawals, could make universal life the major marketing product challenge of the 1980s. The financial services revolution was also well under way, with the trend being toward larger conglomerates such as Prudential-Bache, Shearson-American Express, and INA-Connecticut General that could provide a broad range of insurance, investment, and financial advisory services.

The Economic Recovery Tax Act of 1981 made major insurance and pension tax-planning changes advisable. Lower income and capital gains rates, increased deductions for individual retirement accounts (IRA's) and Keogh pension plans for the self-employed, and substantially reduced estate and gift taxes would be phased in by 1987. Tight money policies caused concern for life insurers as the number of policy loans increased; such loans now amounted to more than $40 billion, or about 9% of assets. Pension assets of life insurers, in contrast, rose by almost 20% to more than $180 billion. Health insurance also grew in volume but was hampered by slow progress in containing health care costs.

Property and liability insurance in the U.S. suffered a $2.5 billion underwriting loss in the first half of 1981 and appeared to be headed for an annual loss exceeding the previous records of more than $4 billion in 1975 and $3 billion in 1980. The losses were attributed to greater price competition, particularly in the commercial insurance markets. However, offsetting investment gains remained high, resulting in overall operating gains for most companies.

Major losses of 1981 included the disastrous collapse of suspended walkways in a Hyatt Regency hotel in Kansas City, Mo., resulting in liability claims in the billions of dollars. There was considerable discussion about the purchase of retroactive coverage to insure the many defendants against their potential losses. Wind and hail losses in Texas and three other states in May caused insured property damage claims of $200 million. Insurers agreed to pay $25 million for property damages resulting from the Three Mile Island (Pa.) nuclear accident in 1979. Losses from the grounding of the $180 million natural-gas tanker "Taurus" near Japan were reduced to $30 million by successful salvage operations.

Among major legislative changes in 1981, a federal Risk Retention Act permitted businesses to group together in writing insurance plans for troublesome product liability exposures. Vermont passed a law permitting the organization of captive insurance companies to compete with Bermudan and other offshore companies. An appeal court upheld the Carnation case verdict, which denied deductions for a captive company insuring only its parent company. Another court decision increased the scope of manufacturers' liability for losses attributed to asbestos. Arson losses continued to plague insurance companies, but a new industry-wide Property Insurance Loss Reporting System was combating fire loss frauds.   (DAVID L. BICKELHAUPT)

IRON AND STEEL

World production of iron and steel in 1980 was 717 million metric tons, a return to the 1978 level after the modest recovery of 1979 and only marginally higher than the level achieved six years earlier. This prolonged stagnation in the overall world situation concealed the disproportionately severe effect on the traditional Western steel-producing countries, which, moreover, had had expensive new production facilities begin operations during those years. The output of a number of newer producers, such as China, Brazil, Mexico, South Korea, and Taiwan, had grown far more during the crisis years than the marginal increase in the world total.

Industrial Review

Overall world production in 1981 was unlikely to be very different from that of 1980. However, South Korea again expanded its output spectacularly. Production in the U.S. was also higher, as it was in the U.K., where the contrast was with the severe effect in 1980 of a three-month strike. On the other hand, many countries were producing less in 1981, including the continental countries of the European Coal and Steel Community (ECSC), Japan, Poland, and Brazil.

The continuing commercial and financial pressures experienced by the steel industry had the widest political repercussions in Europe and in the U.S. In Sweden the steel industry had been badly affected over recent years, and extensive restructuring of firms and of capacity in both the commercial and special steel sectors, designed to meet the changed world market situation, was undertaken with government involvement and financial support. In the European Community the year opened with the Commission's regime of compulsory production quotas, introduced with the unanimous approval of member governments under the ECSC "manifest crisis" provisions, in operation since October 1980. The Commission had been driven to take this extreme step by further severe deterioration in the Community market during the late summer and autumn of 1980, which resulted in a collapse of prices and clearly demonstrated the inadequacy of the Commission's long series of essentially voluntary market support measures to deal with the crisis. The "manifest crisis" measures

achieved some success in at least arresting the market slide and introducing a measure of stability, but as the early months of 1981 went by it became evident that the system had not been operated stringently enough to achieve the desired improvement in prices in the absence of underlying market recovery.

It thus became evident that further measures would be required to succeed the first period of quotas, which had been set to terminate at midyear. The Commission strongly encouraged the producers to agree to voluntary commitments for the second half of the year, and intensive negotiations were held to this end. This eventually proved possible for some products but not for others. The latter included the crucial coil-product sector, where adamant opposition was encountered from one major producer; therefore, the Commission and governments had no choice but to continue compulsory quota arrangements for that sector until mid-1982.

As 1981 drew to a close, there were increasing signs that the market support measures might be working this time in the sense of permitting an increase in prices to more remunerative levels; indeed, consumers were expressing concern about the size of planned increases. Against this background, the Community institutions began reviewing the measures for restraint of imports from outside the ECSC, in order to assess how much strengthening they needed in 1982 to prevent imports from taking undue advantage of what could be a relatively attractive ECSC market. Member governments and the Commission also continued to wrestle with the issue of long-term restructuring of the industry to reduce capacity, their chosen instrument for this

purpose being a revised and strengthened Commission decision intended to phase out all aids to member nations by the end of 1985 and to control them more stringently in the meantime. So involved with the fate of the steel industry had governments become that issues concerning its financing and future brought about the fall of the Belgian government in September. (See BELGIUM.)

In the U.S. the steel industry operated in a stronger economic climate early in 1981, allowing higher utilization of capacity and better financial results; the latter, however, were inadequate for the levels of investment considered necessary to ensure the future. The trigger price system, intended to allow quick identification of imports against which antidumping action could reasonably be taken, had been restored in October 1980. U.S. producers continued to allege that it was ineffective in operation, but it was not until a commercial downturn took place in the U.S. in mid-1981, at a time when imports were rising, that the issue again became politically acute. Then the U.S. government began investigations of the import situation in some products and in November announced the commencement of a number of antidumping investigations. The prospect was clearly for steel's international trade problems to move even nearer the centre of the political stage in 1982.

(TREVOR J. MACDONALD)

MACHINERY AND MACHINE TOOLS

In 1980, the latest year for which data were available, shipments of metal-cutting and metal-forming machine tools by U.S. manufacturers totaled $4.8 billion. Of this total, approximately $3.7 billion represented met-

Table VIII. World Production of Crude Steel
In 000 metric tons

Country	1976	1977	1978	1979	1980	1981 Year to date	No. of months	Percent change 1981/80
World	676,360	675,430	717,230	747,520	717,380	*		
U.S.S.R.	144,810	146,660	151,440	149,000	147,930	49,200	4	− 3.0
U.S.	116,120	113,700	124,310	123,280	101,700	85,900	9	+ 16.3
Japan	107,400	102,410	102,110	111,750	111,400	75,490	9	− 11.3
West Germany	42,410	38,980	41,250	40,040	43,840	31,260	9	− 7.9
Italy	23,460	23,340	24,280	24,250	26,520	18,180	9	− 10.2
France	23,230	22,090	22,840	23,360	23,180	16,060	9	− 12.1
United Kingdom	22,340	20,470	20,370	21,550	11,340	11,470	9	+ 39.2
China†	21,000	23,700	31,780	34,436	37,040	*	9	
Poland	15,640	17,840	19,250	19,200	19,490	8,820	6	− 12.1
Czechoslovakia	14,690	15,050	15,290	14,800	14,930	5,170	4	+ 3.0
Canada	13,290	13,630	14,900	16,080	15,900	11,750	9	− 1.3
Belgium	12,150	11,260	12,600	13,440	12,320	9,030	9	− 8.1
Spain	10,980	11,170	11,340	12,250	12,670	8,500	8	+ 3.4
Romania	10,970	11,460	11,780	12,910	13,180	*		
India	9,360	10,010	10,100	10,130	9,510	7,810	9	+ 9.7
Brazil	9,250	11,250	12,210	13,890	15,310	10,150	9	− 10.6
Australia	7,790	7,340	7,600	8,120	7,590	5,990	9	+ 5.6
South Africa	7,110	7,300	7,900	8,880	9,070	6,830	9	+ 0.8
East Germany	6,740	6,850	6,980	6,960	7,310	3,720	6	+ 2.7
Mexico	5,300	5,600	6,710	7,010	7,100	5,720	9	+ 10.3
Netherlands, The	5,180	4,920	5,580	5,810	5,260	4,290	9	+ 2.6
Sweden	5,140	3,970	4,330	4,730	4,240	2,670	9	− 15.4
Luxembourg	4,570	4,330	4,790	4,950	4,620	2,830	9	− 22.1
Austria	4,480	4,090	4,340	4,920	4,620	3,460	9	− 3.5
Hungary	3,650	3,720	3,880	3,900	3,770	1,580	5	− 6.0
South Korea†	3,520	4,350	4,970	7,610	8,560	7,940	9	+ 23.5
North Korea†	3,000	4,000	5,080	5,400	5,800	*		
Yugoslavia	2,750	3,180	3,460	3,540	3,630	2,950	9	+ 8.2
Bulgaria	2,460	2,590	2,470	2,390	2,570	860	4	+ 6.0
Argentina	2,410	2,680	2,780	3,200	2,680	1,870	9	− 12.7
Turkey	1,970	1,900	2,170	2,340	2,540	1,600	9	+ 6.0
Finland	1,650	2,200	2,330	2,460	2,510	1,760	9	− 4.9
Taiwan	1,630	1,770	3,430	4,250	4,230	2,350	9	− 6.9
Venezuela	940	800	860	1,510	1,820	1,460*	9	− 5.2
Greece	720	760	940	1,000	1,200	*		
Iran	550	1,830	1,300	1,430	1,200	*		

*1980 figures not yet available. †Estimated.
Sources: International Iron and Steel Institute; British Steel Corporation.

Table IX. World Production of Pig Iron and Blast Furnace Ferroalloys
In 000 metric tons

Country	1976	1977	1978	1979	1980
World	484,230	480,760	498,150	519,770	498,940
U.S.S.R.	105,380	107,370	110,700	109,000	108,000
Japan	86,580	85,890	78,590	83,830	87,040
U.S.*	78,810	73,780	79,540	78,900	62,350
West Germany*	31,850	28,980	30,160	35,180	33,670
France*	19,020	18,260	18,500	19,410	18,690
China†	18,000	20,000	26,000	28,000	30,000
United Kingdom	13,870	12,270	11,470	12,930	6,380
Italy	11,630	11,410	11,340	11,330	12,150
Canada	10,030	9,660	10,340	11,080	10,890
Belgium	9,870	8,910	10,130	10,780	9,850
India	9,780	9,800	9,270	8,770	8,510
Czechoslovakia	9,480	9,720	9,940	9,530	9,530
Brazil	8,170	9,380	10,040	11,590	12,680
Poland*	8,040	9,650	11,240	11,100	11,600
Romania	7,650*	7,780	8,160	8,880	8,900
Australia	7,310	6,730	7,280	7,760	6,960
Spain	6,630	6,640	6,250	6,510	6,380
South Africa	5,850	5,810	5,900	7,020	7,200
Netherlands, The	4,270	3,920	4,610	4,810	4,330
Luxembourg	3,760	3,570	3,720	3,800	3,570
Austria	3,320	2,970	3,080	3,700	3,490
North Korea†	3,000	4,000	5,000	5,000	5,400
Sweden	2,950	2,330	2,360	2,910	2,440
East Germany	2,530	2,630	2,560	2,390	2,400
Mexico	2,330	3,000	3,510	3,490	3,630
Hungary	2,220	2,320	2,330	2,370	2,370
South Korea	2,010	2,430	2,740	5,050	5,580
Yugoslavia	1,920	1,930	2,080	2,370	2,440
Turkey	1,680	1,620	1,710	2,300	2,230
Bulgaria	1,550	1,610	1,490	1,450	1,600
Finland	1,330	1,760	1,860	2,040	2,050
Argentina	1,280	1,100	1,440	1,110	1,040
Norway	650	500	550	650	600

*Including ferroalloys.
†Estimated.
Source: International Iron and Steel Institute.

al-cutting machine tools (such as lathes and milling machines) and $1.1 billion represented metal-forming machine tools (such as punch presses and shears).

The U.S. machine tool balance of trade was negative in 1980, the third such year in a row. The U.S. exported machine tools worth about $800 million but imported such equipment worth $1.3 billion. The negative balance in 1980 was about $120 million larger than in 1979. Most of the U.S. machine tool exports were to Canada, Mexico, the United Kingdom, and Japan (in that order), and most of the imports came from Japan, West Germany, the U.K., and Switzerland (in that order). As of 1981 the U.S. imported about 23% of its machine tools.

As of mid-1981 the backlog of orders for U.S. machine tools was about $4 million. With the passage in the U.S. of the Economic Recovery Tax Act of 1981, which provides for more rapid depreciation of capital equipment such as machinery, it was believed that any significant reduction in interest rates would trigger increased purchases of such equipment. Pressure for such purchases existed because of the aging state of machine tools in many plants. (A study indicated that nearly 70% of the machine tools in use in the U.S. were more than ten years old.) This pressure was also increased because of the recognition of the desirability of heightening industrial productivity.

Many advances for improving productivity in the field of machine tools had been made in recent years, including the increased use of numerical control. With this approach, information for producing a particular part is conveyed to the machine tool in numerical form for automatic use by an electronic control system. This system then sends proper signals to the electric or hydraulic motors and other apparatus used for making the part. Although numerical control was first used commercially in the mid-1950s, this type of machine tool still accounted for less than 4% of the total installed in U.S. plants. This percentage seemed likely to increase significantly, however, because of the interest on the part of both government and industry officials in the reindustrialization of the nation.

Another area to benefit from the automation of an increasing number of machine tools was that of inspection. The inspection could be of the in-process variety, in which such measurements as those for proper size are made during the production of a part and corrective adjustments are made as the fabrication of the part progresses. Conversely, the inspection could be done following completion of one part, with corrections to the operation being made as necessary before starting the next part.

(JOHN B. DEAM)

MICROELECTRONICS

During the 1970s there was a dramatic increase in the consumption of dynamic random-access memories (RAM's), and production in 1980 was valued at approximately $1 billion. With the 64-kilobit (1 kilobit = 1,024 bits) dynamic RAM going into volume production, growth was expected to continue; eventually, however, static memories would probably become the high-growth portion of the RAM market. The reasons for this shift included the

rapid increase in the testing cost of dynamic RAM's and the comparatively lower testing cost of static RAM's, the higher level of reliability in static memories, and the lower board cost of static RAM's. By the late 1980s, it was believed, the consumption of static memories in the U.S. would exceed that of dynamic memories.

The microprocessor industry was expected to continue to grow rapidly in the 1980s, with the 16-bit product substantially penetrating the 8-bit market as well as developing its own customers. The 16-bit was expected to compete successfully with the 8-bit microprocessor because its software costs were comparatively lower. An additional reason was the limited memory capability of the 8-bit. Another trend in the microprocessor area was expected to be the increased use of high-level languages such as Pascal and the incorporation of software into firmware. The result would be an explosion of microprocessor-based end products.

In 1980 Japanese-based semiconductor production was 35% of the U.S. level. During the 1980s it was predicted that production would reach 50% of the U.S. output. If production by Japanese companies in the U.S. was included, the total could reach 60% by 1990.

Japanese production was growing at a faster rate than that of the U.S. for several reasons. These included excellent long-term planning by Japanese companies with regard to products and technologies, product specialization, and production geared for competitiveness in the world market.

The number of semiconductor firms in the U.S. that were both business and technical leaders decreased from about 35 in

1970 to about 10 in 1980. By 1990 this number could decline again to perhaps four or five companies. This was the case mainly because of higher capital equipment requirements and higher research and development costs in the U.S. As a result, the leaders in the electronics business were expected to try to achieve improved cost efficiency by expanding their capability for vertical integration, the production and integration of many phases of the business ranging from hardware manufacture to sales of software.

One complex area making use of vertical integration was that of very large-scale integration, entailing not only placing more functions and gates on a chip but also accomplishing the implementation of a system on the chip. If the system is a minicomputer, one of the keys to that system is the operating software. That system can be implemented only by the combined efforts of the system architect, the software specialist, the applications specialist, and the semiconductor designer.

System concepts are far more complex than the design of semiconductors. The driving force for their development is not semiconductor technology but system performance, which, in turn, is driven by the market requirements. Successful vertical integration would produce systems that have an edge in the marketplace and thus achieve the profits to reinvest in semiconductor technology. Firms that could accomplish this integration would become the industry leaders. (HANDEL H. JONES)

Integrated circuit frames are examined by a computer-controlled inspection device at a factory in Pennsylvania. The frames must be accurate to plus or minus two ten-thousandths of an inch.

NUCLEAR INDUSTRY

Presidential elections brightened the prospects of the nuclear industry in the United States but dimmed them a little in France. U.S. Pres. Ronald Reagan, although cutting the energy budget overall by $1.9 billion, made the highest cuts in nonnuclear areas. He declared his administration was in favour of speeding up work on nuclear waste disposal, revival of the Clinch River fast breeder reactor project, and sorting out the nuclear regulatory logjam that had virtually brought the industry to a halt in the United States.

For the first time since the accident at the Three Mile Island nuclear power plant in Pennsylvania in 1979, nuclear generation rose in the U.S., by nearly 8%. The U.S. government agreed to help in meeting the Three Mile Island cleanup bill. Owners of the plant, General Public Utilities, facing bankruptcy over the costs of the accident, filed a $4 billion action against the Nuclear Regulatory Commission (NRC) for its alleged share of the responsibility for the incident as detailed in the Kemeny Commission report. The NRC, meanwhile, announced that the pressure vessels in 13 nuclear units that had been in service for some time might have to be repaired soon because of suspected damage from radiation and heat.

Newly elected Pres. François Mitterrand of France opposed nuclear power during his campaign, but his new Socialist administration canceled only the highly controversial Plogoff project in Brittany; it did halt work on units at five existing sites. The new administration's target was 53,000 Mw

of installed nuclear capacity by 1990 (compared with 66,000 Mw under the previous administration). Violent demonstrations in the Lot et Garonne region and at Cattenom against the suspension of the projects there revealed the strength of pro-nuclear feeling in those areas. Other French developments included the announcement of new sites for fast breeder reactors to follow the Superphenix reactor at Creys-Malville and the signing of a new licensing agreement between the French constructor Framatome and the U.S. reactor vendor Westinghouse Electric Corp.

Toward the end of the year the Mexican state electricity company CFE called for bids for a new project. This was to be a plant generating up to 2,300 Mw, which would probably be built at the existing Laguna Verde nuclear power station site.

Romania placed an order for a second Canadian 600-Mw Candu-type reactor for the Cernavoda site in the Danube River delta. The Canadian nuclear industry also made other strenuous export sales efforts during the year in Mexico, South Korea, and other countries. The provincial government of Ontario announced a speeding up of the construction program on the four 850-Mw units for the Darlington nuclear station.

The Canadian reactor designer Atomic Energy of Canada Ltd. announced in June a new Candu design for a 950-Mw unit that was aimed particularly at export markets. The company also announced development work on a small, simple reactor that was based on the well-tried Slowpoke research reactor widely used in universities and intended for supplying heat to large buildings or building complexes.

Elections in Australia returned the incumbent government to power, allowing

further development of the country's uranium mining plans; these had been threatened by the opposition Labor Party during the campaign. Commissioning of the Ranger mine, potentially the largest uranium mine in the world, reached the first production stage near the end of the year. A major block to the sale of uranium was removed when the government gave permission for the reprocessing of irradiated fuel using Australian uranium, under appropriately agreed-upon safeguards.

The British government's plans to install 15,000 Mw of new plant over the next ten years was sharply criticized by the all-party Select Committee on Energy. It recommended a more step-by-step approach to nuclear power expansion and was critical of the emerging policies on reactor choice, suggesting that the Candu reactor be reexamined in view of its outstanding performance compared with Britain's favoured gas-cooled reactors. The state electricity utility, the Central Electricity Generating Board, applied to the government for consent to build the new Sizewell pressurized water reactor (PWR); this would result in a public inquiry, probably in 1982.

Chancellor Helmut Schmidt of West Germany reaffirmed the need to expand his country's nuclear program. The latest federal energy program called for the installing of 25 Gw of nuclear capacity by 1990 (1 Gw = 1,000,000,000 w). A new company was established to produce a commercial design of a high-temperature reactor for applications in coal gasification and liquefaction. DWK of Hanover received a construction permit for the first German AFR (away-from-reactor) storage facility at Gorleben. It was to be used for the temporary accommodation of 1,500 tons of irradiated fuel.

In the Soviet Union the large new production line for nuclear reactors at the Atommash factory began production after considerable delays over the past few years. A new five-year plan set a target of 24,000–25,000 Mw of new nuclear capacity. Designs for a 1,600-Mw fast breeder reactor were completed, and construction of a thermal plant for combined heat and power was in progress near Odessa. Construction work began on new plants at Zaporozhe, Krymsk, and Khmelnitskaya.

A new agreement between Japan and the U.S. on fast breeder reactor development was extended to cover fuel. The U.S. EBR2 and Fast Flux Test Facility was to be used to test Japanese fuel. The Japanese company, the Power Reactor and Nuclear Fuel Development Corp., produced its first enriched uranium from the pilot centrifuge enrichment plant. Plans for three more boiling water reactors (BWR's) were approved, the first reactors to be approved in Japan since the Three Mile Island accident.

The first Almaraz 930 Mw PWR reached full load in Spain, bringing the total of nuclear units in operation in that nation to four (generating 2,030 Mw). Another 11 were being built, and firm plans existed for 3 more.

The fifth power station in the Indian nuclear program was to be at Kakrapar, near Surat, in Gujarat. It would comprise two 235-Mw Candu-type reactors, and there were plans for an additional two units at the site.

According to statistics (excluding Com-

An atomic reactor that produces radioactive isotopes was completed by technicians in China in April. It was the first such reactor to be built in China.

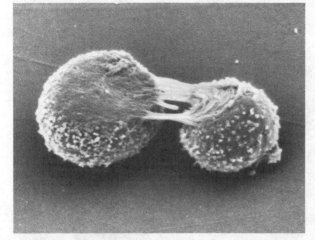

Immunologically active antibody cells are fused with malignant tumour cells. They produce artificially contrived hybrid cells known as monoclonal antibodies, which can be targeted to fight cancer, diseases of the immune system, and other disorders.

munist countries) released for the previous year, 12 new nuclear reactors were commissioned in 1980. The total number of reactors over 150 Mw in service at the beginning of 1981 was 190, with a total generating capacity of 128,682.3 Mw. They included 88 PWR's (70,327 Mw), 54 BWR's (38,683 Mw), 13 pressurized heavy-water reactors (PHWR's; 6,526 Mw), and 26 Magnox (8,-515.3 Mw). Analysis of reactor performance for 1980 published during the year placed three Canadian PHWR's at the top of the charts.   (RICHARD A. KNOX)

PAINTS AND VARNISHES

Europe's paint industry was hard hit by recession in 1981. Output in most countries fell by 4–9%, while sales values stagnated around 1980 levels. Only France appeared to be achieving a real, though modest, advance. In the U.S. the picture was brighter, with volume down only slightly and income about 11% higher than in the previous year. U.S. paint companies were also encouraged by the new climate under the Reagan administration, which was expected to favour a lower level of regulatory activity relating to environmental protection and job safety. Japan's output fell by 7%.

The industry's U.S. and European associations released the results of a three-year mortality study of 17,000 U.S. paint workers, showing that it was slightly safer to make paints than to work in other typical industries. In Europe there were health scares concerning the presence of cadmium and glycol ethers in paints. The industry's view was that these chemicals had been used for decades and only required good housekeeping practices. Lead came under fire again. Having decided to reduce the lead content of gasoline, the British authorities opened discussions with paint makers on formulation trends. The U.S. industry was required to begin medical surveillance of workers.

Work was completed on the first revision of the EEC paints directive. Implementation by member states was set for July 1983, but the situation was still complicated by provisions of the related solvents directive and the sixth amendment to the parent dangerous substances directive. National associations prepared to handle a flood of data on raw materials, while individual companies planned changes in their labeling.

On the technical front, much effort continued to be devoted to compliance with regulations. Development of improved products was also slowed by the recession, and a British conference on powder coatings was postponed. Nevertheless, work on aqueous powder technology progressed. Use of special-purpose coatings was expected to increase 12–16% by 1995.

Economic pressure led to several mergers. In the U.K. the Bestobell engineering group sold its paint interests for £2,-250,000 to the Silver group, while Tube Investment's coatings business went to Donald Macpherson for £2.7 million. In North America Sherwin-Williams, Inmont, and Pratt & Lambert made significant acquisitions. Faced with a stagnant home market, many companies sought growth abroad.   (LIONEL BILEFIELD)

PHARMACEUTICALS

The Reagan administration's emphasis on deregulation began to affect both the U.S. pharmaceutical industry and its primary regulatory agency, the Food and Drug Administration, during 1981. The new FDA commissioner, Arthur Hull Hayes, promised to speed up the process for approving new drugs, and a special panel was formed to make suggestions on how to accelerate the clinical testing process and curtail the considerable burden of paperwork. However, this effort could be thwarted by substantial cuts in funding for the agency's operations.

These cuts had already had a profound effect on inspection, report processing, and other operations of the FDA's regional offices. At one pivotal regional office, in New Jersey (where many food, drug, and cosmetic manufacturers have their headquarters), the number of inspectors had fallen from 75 to fewer than 50. Deregulation also slowed the over-the-counter drug review process. Issuance of individual product monographs was delayed, as was agency compliance with a federal court order mandating that the FDA clarify its plans to speed up handling of so-called Category III (needs more safety or efficacy testing) ingredients. Instructions from the administration to justify new regulations halted, among other agency plans, the formulation of "good manufacturing practice" regulations for injectable drugs and publication of a drug compendium for physicians and pharmacists.

A General Accounting Office report issued late in 1980 confirmed that FDA insistence on maximum safety and efficacy data for new drugs had created a "drug lag" between European countries and the U.S. The report generated support for patent life extension as a way of compensating drug companies for delays in the approval process. However, consideration of such a measure in Congress was slowed by preoccupation with budgetary, tax, and other pressing matters.

The promise of gene-splicing techniques in the development of radically new pharmaceutical entities remained high in 1981, though the emphasis shifted from interferon to insulin, animal drugs, biological blood products, and monoclonal antibodies. Another advance that caught the public's attention was the development of drug implants and skin patches, systems of dispensing drugs at a controlled rate that were pioneered by a California firm known as Alza. Ciba-Geigy introduced a transdermal (through the skin) product to prevent motion sickness by dispensing scopolamine from an externally applied adhesive patch, and Searle brought out a similar product to maintain a therapeutic level of nitroglycerin in heart patients. These developments, plus the introduction of new second- and third-generation antibiotics and beta blockers (to regulate heart rhythm), gave the industry cause for optimism, despite the forthcoming expiration of a series of important drug patents.   (DONALD A. DAVIS)

PLASTICS

The plastics industry during 1981 showed no appreciable recovery from its recent downturn. Especially in Western Europe, growth in tonnage terms was almost nonexistent—although there were one or two materials, notably polypropylene among the commodity plastics and specialties such as polyethylene terephthalate (for the rapidly growing market for soft-drink bottles), whose market growth provided faint glimmers of light in the generally gloomy picture. The decline seemed to have bottomed, however, since there was no general fall below the levels of activity experienced in late 1980.

It was generally accepted that the root cause of the industry's problems remained the enormous excess of manufacturing capacity for the large-tonnage polymers—the polyolefins, polyvinyl chloride (PVC), and polystyrene—exacerbated by the large number of individual producers. In 1981 it at last dawned on them that this was no passing phenomenon and that the traditional response of grimly hanging on to their market shares until better times returned was no longer practical and was, indeed, likely to lead to disaster. Much of the plastics materials manufacturing capacity was either idle or, at best, operating at minimal levels for all or most of the year. It became evident that merely curtailing production was not enough; some producers would have to drop whole product lines, abandon carefully nurtured markets, and perhaps even get out of plastics altogether.

A Harris eight-page web offset press went on-line in the U.S. The press was mainly devoted to book manufacturing.

By year's end it seemed that such radical curtailment was at last under way and that producers had assessed their areas of strength. There also seemed to be a new determination to get prices up to levels at which some profit would be made, even at the expense of market share. European manufacturers also realized that there must inevitably be a tendency for commodity polymer production to move to oil-rich countries, because of the dearth of feedstock resources (despite the North Sea) comparable to those, for instance, of the Middle East.

A product newly significant in the commodity plastics field during the year was linear low-density polyethylene (LLDPE). Major process economies were associated with LLDPE production, especially with regard to energy input, and the new material exhibited attractive properties. For instance, LLDPE film that has been extruded so that it is as much as 50% thinner than conventional LDPE (low-density polyethylene) film might be of equivalent strength. LLDPE established a firm base in the U.S. and aroused much interest in Europe. It seemed certain to replace a large segment of LDPE usage, possibly up to one-third in the U.S. by 1985. Eventually, it might capture as much as 85% of the LDPE market, which in 1981 accounted for over one-fifth of all plastics consumption.

The automotive sector showed reintensified interest in plastics in its search for further production economies and fuel savings through lighter weight. Fiat and Peugeot introduced research vehicles based on

actual production models that demonstrated practical possibilities for extending plastics usage. Another promising area involved greater use of plastics for energy saving through insulation, for example, in rigid PVC window frames.

The value of engineering plastics for high-performance, if low-tonnage, work was dramatically illustrated by the flight of "Solar Challenger," a manned aircraft, from France to England on July 7, 1981. The craft was powered entirely by the Sun's energy. Like the flight of "Gossamer Albatross," which flew from England to France in 1979 relying solely on human power provided by pedaling, this remarkable achievement was made possible only through the use of a variety of high-strength and lightweight plastics, films, and fibres.　　　　(ROBIN C. PENFOLD)

PRINTING

The pace of technological change increased in 1981. Fully electronic pre-press systems, much discussed in the 1970s, had arrived. In addition to the 200 or so major printers and publishers of the world, the smaller reproduction and typesetting houses were coming around to the point of view that all-electronic reproduction and form-making systems could be for them. The first installations, in fact, went not to the big printers with their elaborate technical specifications but to repro trade houses.

Crosfield Electronics of the U.K. led the world in automatic picture-composition installations, but it showed disappointing financial results. An OEM agreement with

Information International Inc. (Triple I) heightened the prospects of digital integration of text and pictures and, down the road, filmless production of the printing form. Joining the all-electronic reproduction systems from Crosfield and West Germany's Dr.-Ing. Rudolf Hell were Dainippon Screen and PDI systems from Japan.

New markets for print were discovered. In the U.S. department and chain stores began to publish their own customer magazines, often with outside advertising and with much use of colour. As more magazines issued demographic editions aimed at specific readership groups, the demand rose for sophisticated bindery systems and microprocessor production controls to effect frequent change of pages without undue paper wastage. At Mid-America Printing in the U.S., Aller Press in Sweden, Burda in West Germany, and Asahi in Japan, highly advanced integrated automatic mailroom operations went into action based on Harris and Wamac lines. Lasergravure went into actual production at Sun Printers in Britain, and in Switzerland Daetwyler continued development of the wraparound gravure printing plate. BASF announced the feasibility of laser exposure of photopolymer plates.

Two new rotogravure press projects were announced that would bring U.S. Motter presses to Europe via the Swiss Bell Engineering Co., and Nebiolo of Italy announced plans to enter this field. A religious group in the U.S. bought its tenth Harris eight-page web press. GMA-Nohab

in Sweden began manufacture of East German-designed Zirkon web-offset presses. TKS newspaper presses from Japan went to Europe via Graphicart of Switzerland. The first Gravoman rotogravure press with individual unit drive went into operation in West Germany. Advertisers were coming to appreciate offset-to-gravure conversion systems, such as Toppan-CH and Lithogravure.

In France Didier, a major web-offset group, entered the rotogravure field. British Gravure Corp. was formed within the British Printing Corp. In Italy effective control of the Rizzoli group went to a finance company. Harris gained impressive web-offset sales in Taiwan and Central America; in the U.S. it obtained the largest order ever made for web-offset presses—over 100 units from Treasure Chest. Consumer acceptance of teletext systems continued to be slow, but inroads were made into office information systems.   (W. PINCUS JASPERT)

RUBBER

The rubber industry in 1981 was undergoing readjustments that resulted in the majority of the tire firms becoming profitable. Cost control in materials, manufacturing, inventory, and labour were primarily responsible. Some small firms registered marked profit improvement. The industrial products and molded goods segment remained troubled. The continued slump in automobile sales was responsible for the considerable decreases in the production of both tires and other rubber products. Michelin of North America, which had been operating at full capacity, was forced to close six of its plants for 14 days to bring inventory under control.

In 1980 the imports of tires from Japan to the U.S. increased by 111% over 1979. Japan exported 14% of its production, while the U.S. exported less than 3%. Michelin became the world's largest producer of tires in 1980 with worldwide sales of $6,-650,000,000.

Tire-fuel efficiency ratings were published by the U.S. Environmental Protection Agency. Reduced rolling resistance tread compounds tend to have relatively poor skid resistance, particularly on wet pavement. Thus, Shell Ltd. and Dunlop Ltd. collaborated on the development and extensive testing of a new polymerized synthetic rubber, reported to provide a 5% fuel saving with no loss of wet or dry traction. It was estimated that a 5% fuel saving would result in savings of 86 million bbl of oil per year in the U.S. Dunlop planned to produce about 60,000 tires using this material in 1981 and a larger quantity in 1982. The polymer, expected to be expensive, was to be made available to all tire makers as soon as suitable amounts were produced. Another factor in reduced rolling resistance was that all U.S. 1982 cars were to have radial tires as standard equipment. Radial tires have significantly lower rolling resistance than bias or cross-ply tires.

The U.S. National Highway Traffic Safety Administration was examining the Uniform Tire Quality Grading Standard for its merit. Much controversy was associated with this standard. Of the major tire makers only Uniroyal Inc. agreed that the testing was valid. The others were attempting to show that errors existed in the basic concepts involved in the testing. However, the U.S. General Services Administration, ten states, and the U.S. Postal System based their tire purchases on the values obtained from the Uniform Tire Quality Grading Standard.

Because of competitive pressures resulting from the supply-demand situation, materials prices did not necessarily reflect costs or inflation. The New York City spot price of natural rubber was 79 cents per pound on Oct. 1, 1980. On Oct. 1, 1981, it was 46¾ cents, a 41% decrease. The list price of the most widely used synthetic rubber, SBR (styrene-butadiene rubber), rose from 60 cents per pound to 70 cents because of increased raw material costs. Widespread

Table X. Natural Rubber Production
In 000 metric tons

Country	1978	1979	1980
Malaysia	1,583	1,600	1,552
Indonesia*	902	905	1,020
Thailand	467	531	501
India	133	147	155
Sri Lanka	156	153	133
China*	75	98	100
Liberia*	78	73	70
Philippines	57	60*	65*
Vietnam*	40	50	50
Nigeria*	58	56	44
Others	206	187	125
Total*	3,755	3,860	3,815

*Estimate, or includes estimate.
Source: The Secretariat of the International Rubber Study Group, *Rubber Statistical Bulletin.*

Table XI. Synthetic Rubber Production
In 000 metric tons

Country	1978	1979	1980
United States	2,662	2,725	2,150
U.S.S.R.*	1,950	2,025	2,040
Japan	1,029	1,107	1,094
France	492	541	511
West Germany	407	418	390
Canada	248	283	253
Italy*	250	270	250
Brazil	206	224	249
United Kingdom	294	278	212
Netherlands, The*	223	238	212
East Germany*	145	165	170
Romania	147	149	155*
Belgium*	124	125	125
Poland	126	130	118
Mexico	80	90*	100*
China*	70	80	90
Spain	86	87	80
Korea	62	60	74
Taiwan	47	85	73
Czechoslovakia	59	59	60*
Australia	44	43	46
South Africa	32	31	38*
Argentina*	34	37	33
Others	93	110	440
Total*	8,910	9,360	8,663

*Estimate, or includes estimate.
Source: The Secretariat of the International Rubber Study Group, *Rubber Statistical Bulletin.*

discounting of the price of SBR existed, however.

While the reduced cost of natural rubber was welcomed by users, the small plantation owners in Malaysia, who produce significant amounts of rubber, were being subsidized by their government. Otherwise they might substitute palm trees for rubber trees because palm trees are more profitable in the short term.

World production of natural rubber in 1980 was estimated at 3,815,000 metric tons, a decrease of 45,000 tons compared with 1979. Production for 1981 was estimated at 3,780,000 tons, a decrease of 35,000 tons from 1980. World production of synthetic rubber was estimated at 8,663,000 metric tons in 1980, a decrease of 697,000 tons from 1979.

World consumption of natural rubber latex (dry basis) in 1980 was estimated at 296,000 metric tons. Statistics on world consumption of synthetic rubber were incomplete, but U.S. consumption was 110,933 metric tons (dry basis) of the styrene-butadiene type. Worldwide consumption of both natural and synthetic rubber was estimated at 12,425,000 metric tons for 1980. The U.S. continued to be the largest single buyer of natural rubber, purchasing 585,000 metric tons in 1981.

Production at a radial auto tire plant in Union City, Tenn., was increased in response to a U.S. requirement that all 1982 automobiles be equipped with gasoline-saving radial tires.

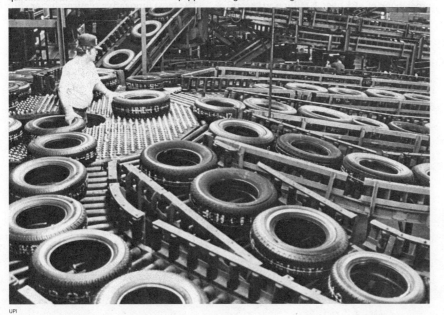

UPI

Industrial Review

Production estimates, by country, are shown in Table X for natural rubber and Table XI for synthetic rubber. Little change in the production of natural rubber by the various countries is noted. However, for synthetic rubber, decreases in production are observed in the more developed countries, while increases have taken place in the less developed nations.

Reclaimed rubber production continued to remain steady, as did consumption of that product. Rubber manufacturers were trying to increase the amount of reclaimed material in their rubber compounds, but even greater effort was being made to promote the use of ground scrap particles as a substitute for some of the rubber. This was being done for cost and conservation reasons. (JAMES R. BEATTY)

SHIPBUILDING

For the second consecutive year there was an increase in the volume of ship tonnage on order in the world's shipyards. At mid-1981 just over 37.5 million gross registered tons (grt) were on order, compared with 32 million grt at mid-1980. The comparable deadweight figures were 74 million and 67 million, respectively. Unfortunately, the high level of overcapacity in shipbuilding remained, largely as a result of the continued financial aid given by some governments to their shipyards, as well as the commissioning of further shipbuilding facilities in South Korea and China. Japan's dominance in the shipbuilding market was confirmed when more than half the orders placed in the 12 months ended June 30, 1981, went to Japanese yards. Of the world tonnage on order, nearly 15 million grt was in Japan. Its nearest competitors were South Korea with 2.7 million grt and Spain with 2.5 million grt.

As prospects for the bulk freight market improved, there was a further increase in the number of bulk carriers on order—a total of 40 million tons deadweight (dw), or 20 million grt, compared with 23.5 million tons dw (8.8 million grt) of tankers. Four million grt of dry-cargo vessels were on order, of which nearly half were containerships. There was continued interest in the Panamax-type bulk carriers—vessels designed to suit the maximum dimensions of the locks in the Panama Canal—principally because of the steady increase in the amount of steaming coal being carried and the large quantities of grain being shipped to the U.S.S.R. and China. Several orders were placed for 200,000-ton-dw bulk carriers for Japanese owners who had charters to move coal from Australia to Japan. The outstanding development in this field was the placing of orders for four 74,000-ton-dw bauxite carriers, each powered by a steam turbine supplied with steam by a coal-fired boiler.

U.S. shipyards still needed more orders if they were to avoid heavy layoffs, but they managed to hold the overall order book at 1 million grt (1.5 million tons dw). There was an urgent need for an official, long-range U.S. merchant navy shipbuilding program; U.S. shipbuilders believed that the nation's security was endangered be-

cause too much reliance was being placed on foreign flagships to carry strategic materials. A feature of the U.S. shipyards' order book was the concentration of highly specialized tonnage, including large liquefied-natural-gas carriers, containerships, and products tankers with deliveries extending well into 1983.

Despite the dramatic political situation in Poland, the country's shipyards continued to supply a large amount of tonnage to other nations; tonnage on order totaled 1.5 million grt. Included in the French shipyards' order book of just over 1 million grt were orders for several passenger ships to be used for cruising. Nearly 90% of the orders placed in Yugoslavian shipyards were for other countries. Shipbuilding in the U.K. declined further during the year and now ranked 11th in terms of the world order book. West Germany's shipyards also continued to feel the effects of recession; the current order book stood at less than 900,-000 grt, with about 50% for export.

World shipbuilding capacity was further increased by China's efforts to become an exporter of ships. Several Hong Kong and Panamanian owners ordered vessels, nearly all bulk carriers, from the China Shipbuilding Corporation, with delivery extending into 1984. The size of the vessels ranged from 15,000 to 50,000 tons dw, and many smaller dry-cargo vessels in the 4,000- to 16,000-ton-dw class were on order. Despite strenuous efforts by the International Maritime Industries Forum, no significant move was made to introduce an internationally agreed-on ship-scrapping program as a solution to the overcapacity problem. (W. D. EWART)

TELECOMMUNICATIONS

In 1981 the telecommunications industry experienced continued technological innovation and regulatory controversy. Of the innovations, advances in semiconductor chips and fibre optics were the most important because of their direct influence on the worldwide telephone network. As usual, events through the year demonstrated that government regulation is as important as technological advance and often tempers its effect.

The most innovative semiconductor chip was a switching device, known as a cross-point array, produced by Mitel Corp. of Kanata, Ont. It switches any of 256 voice or data communications channels (inputs) to any of 256 output channels while replacing 100 medium-scale and small-scale integration-based parts. As a large-scale integration-based part, the switching chip is highly reliable. It promised to revolutionize the techniques used for switching in private branch exchanges and telephone switching offices because it uses so little space and power.

The cross-point array is concerned with electrical logic signals. But optical logic design is equally important when telephone signals are carried on fibre-optic cables and must be switched. This technology received a boost during the year at Bell Telephone Laboratories in Murray Hill, N.J., with the construction of a two-input switch (known as an AND gate) on a semiconductor chip. An electrical output signal from the gate depends on the simultaneous presence of a pair of input light signals at different wavelengths.

		Percentage increase over 1970	Telephones per 100 population			Percentage increase over 1970	Telephones per 100 population
Country	Number of telephones			Country	Number of telephones		
Algeria	422,010	149.4	2.2	Lebanon¹	321,500	67.4	11.2
Argentina	2,759,736	65.0	10.3	Luxembourg	198,905	79.2	54.8
Australia¹	7,396,212	105.5	52.0	Malaysia¹	439,161	144.0	3.2
Austria	2,812,678	110.8	36.6	Mexico	4,532,557	241.4	6.4
Belgium	3,447,697	78.0	35.0	Morocco	227,000	46.8	1.1
Bolivia¹	125,800	235.0	2.6	Netherlands, The	6,852,776	119.6	48.6
Brazil	6,494,000	263.4	5.1	New Zealand	1,729,916	47.7	55.0
Bulgaria¹	1,032,106	149.2	11.7	Nigeria	154,236	89.4	0.2
Canada	15,560,264	...	...	Norway	1,725,678	58.2	42.3
Chile	553,856	59.0	4.9	Pakistan	314,000	62.2	0.3
Colombia	1,524,000	179.2	5.8	Panama	176,477	107.6	9.3
Costa Rica	194,528	213.7	8.9	Peru²	402,459	108.9	2.6
Cyprus	104,268	661.1	16.8	Philippines	519,642	77.0	1.2
Czechoslovakia	3,072,829	62.1	20.1	Poland	3,243,693	84.7	9.1
Denmark	3,144,558	96.5	61.4	Portugal	1,305,580	87.0	13.1
Dominican Republic	155,400	230.6	2.9	Puerto Rico	651,388	115.5	18.5
Ecuador	260,000	175.0	3.3	Romania	1,479,627	236.0	6.7
Egypt¹	486,143	...	1.2	Saudi Arabia	280,491	...	3.3
Finland	2,244,365	106.0	47.1	Singapore	625,130	358.7	26.5
France	22,211,952	173.7	41.4	South Africa	2,662,399	79.6	10.8
East Germany	3,071,515	54.6	18.3	Spain	11,107,624	169.2	29.4
West Germany	26,632,302	113.8	43.4	Sweden	6,407,031	48.8	77.1
Greece	2,664,050	202.4	28.2	Switzerland	4,446,205	56.2	70.4
Hong Kong	1,517,294	202.0	30.2	Syria	236,020	127.6	2.7
Hungary	1,186,526	52.6	11.1	Taiwan	2,566,078	657.3	14.7
India	2,615,075	125.5	0.4	Thailand¹	451,409	235.2	1.0
Indonesia	392,563	115.3	0.2	Tunisia	173,485	151.7	2.9
Iran	730,000	155.0	2.2	Turkey	1,747,854	240.3	3.9
Ireland¹	586,000	104.1	17.3	U.S.S.R.	22,464,000	104.2	8.4
Israel	1,081,480	136.3	28.2	United Kingdom	26,651,384	91.1	47.7
Italy	18,084,996	112.0	31.8	United States	175,505,000	52.3	79.1
Jamaica	117,252	75.9	5.9	Uruguay¹	269,734	30.5	9.6
Japan	55,421,515	139.6	47.6	Venezuela	1,165,016	208.5	8.5
Kenya	168,249	118.5	1.1	Yugoslavia	1,912,883	207.0	8.5
Korea, South	2,898,687	415.7	7.8	Zimbabwe	214,414	...	2.8
Kuwait	191,941	231.0	14.6				

¹1979.
²1978.
Sources: American Telephone and Telegraph Company, *The World's Telephones*, 1970; 1980.

A technician at Bell Laboratories checks new switching equipment that combines microelectronics and photonics. The switching equipment is capable of handling more phone calls at a speedier pace.

While many industrial firms investigated semiconductor chips suitable for switching, others looked into chips suitable for generating and receiving the light signals on fibre-optic telephone lines that carry data as well as voice signals. For example, IBM designed a chip that acts as an optical receiver. It converts light to electrical pulses at megabit-per-second data rates. In fact, IBM's Thomas J. Watson Research Center in Yorktown Heights, N.Y., claimed that the new design can take full advantage of the 200-megabit-per-second (or more) information-carrying capacity of the latest fibre-optic cables.

While this activity was going on in the U.S. and Canada, telecommunications chip and fibre-optics technology did not stand still in Japan. For example, Nippon Telegraph and Telephone Public Corp. built what it claimed was the world's first fibre-optic laser-driven superheterodyne receiver. It tested the receiver both as a 300-MHz analogue device and as a 100-megabit-per-second digital device. With the superheterodyne design a receiver can pick out signals on the optical fibre even if they are only a few megahertz apart in frequency. Thus, more telephone conversations can be put on the fibre.

Much of the world's long-distance voice and data traffic was being carried on Earth satellites. These systems, which retransmit signals from one ground station to another thousands of miles away, continued to be launched throughout the world. Among the most significant was the launch by Satellite Business Systems Corp. of McLean, Va., of two SBS communications satellites. They provided new spectrum space for commercial users to meet the ever increasing demands for telecommunications channels. Seventeen European nations planned to launch several European-manufactured satellites to perform the same functions as the SBS craft.

In 1981 AT&T, the giant of the U.S. telecommunications industry, engaged in its usual rounds with U.S. government agencies. In Congress it failed to win dismissal of the government's antitrust suit. But the Senate moved to consider a new telecommunications act that would permit the firm to enter unregulated markets for telecommunications equipment. This would be done, in one view, through a fully separated subsidiary rather than a spinoff company. Just what AT&T would be allowed to do was complicated by the dozens of government agencies, consumer groups, and trade associations from other segments of the telecommunications industry who wanted their viewpoints to be made known.

Ever anxious to find more uses for the telephone, AT&T extended its influence into the home information market. To the dismay of Canada's Telidon organization, England's Prestel, and France's Antiope, which were already in the business, AT&T announced its own plans for home and business services. It also announced tests to try out its ideas.   (HARVEY J. HINDIN)

TEXTILES

The textile industries of the industrially developed countries continued to experience extreme depression. In the less developed countries, however, new plants were being built to exploit domestically grown cotton wherever possible. The Indian and Indonesian textile industries, in particular, were expanding rapidly, with new projects being launched in both textile manufacture and, in India, textile-machine building.

In South Korea the pace appeared even more rapid, but there the accent was on the establishment of a comprehensive spectrum of more sophisticated products. The Koreans were purchasing know-how for building textile machinery, for making dyestuffs and textile auxiliary chemicals, and even expertise in the design of gar-

ments. They reached agreements not only with jeans manufacturers but also with high-quality French design houses that were prepared to allow their trademarks to be used on the new Korean products.

In the developed countries emphasis shifted from the simpler types of textiles to those offering high-performance properties and requiring complex and precisely controlled manufacturing processes. Examples included such new fibres as the aromatic polyamides (a form of "supernylon"), the immensely strong carbon fibres, and hollow fibres being used for ultrafiltration.

While the number of workers needed in textile manufacture was falling rapidly as a result of automation, low-labour-cost countries could still supply perfectly acceptable fabrics or finished garments to the developed world at prices well below those of locally produced goods. Thus the future of textile industries in the older industrialized countries continued to look bleak.

(PETER LENNOX-KERR)

Wool. Demand for merino wool in 1981 approximately matched available supply, but there was an imbalance for crossbreds. This was related partly to rising production of crossbred types and partly to the effect of recession, especially on carpet wools. Production of merino wool in the 1980–81 season ended June 1981 was 940,000 metric tons. The estimate for 1981–82 was 941,000 tons, which maintained the static or very slightly declining trend of recent years. Crossbred wool production was 1,051,000 tons in 1980–81, continuing a rising trend apparent since 1976–77.

Prices in the merino sector, with Australia the largest producer, were very slightly firmer in the first half of 1981 and eased even more slightly in the closing months. Stocks purchased by the Australian Wool Corporation to support prices were down to 158,000 bales at the end of January 1981, but they rose to 188,000 bales at the end of June and then increased in the new season to more than 300,000 bales toward the end of the year. New Zealand Wool Board stocks rose throughout the 1980–81 season, from 199,000 bales in July 1980 to 343,000 by the end of June 1981. The increase continued in the 1981–82 season, but more slowly owing to the board's flexible buying approach.

Worldwide usage of wool was at a fairly high rate at the beginning of 1981 but declined through the year as a result of recession. This trend was apparent in all the main manufacturing countries except China, where consumption rose to an eight-year high.   (H. M. F. MALLETT)

Cotton. World production of raw cotton in the 1980–81 season was only fractionally below the record output of almost 66 million bales achieved in 1979–80. In China, where yields were noticeably higher than anticipated, output reached a total of 12.5 million bales, an increase of nearly one-quarter over the previous season's level. The average yield per acre, worldwide, was 391 lb.

Preliminary estimates of consumption in the season ended August 1981 suggested that the global total would reach a record 67

million bales. Consumption rose 1.7 million bales in the U.S.S.R., China, and Eastern Europe, but the offtake declined in the U.S. As a result, carry-over stocks were down roughly 1 million bales to 21 million bales, adequate to cover only 3.8 months' consumption at the current rate.

The average price of raw cotton in Liverpool at the beginning of the 1980–81 season was little more than 84 cents per pound, but it moved up rapidly to more than 100 cents by early September 1980, reaching a peak of almost 104 cents. It remained just below 100 cents during the final quarter of the year, but from January 1981 onward it fell, declining to 86.75 cents at the end of the season. The fall persisted into the 1981–82 season, with just over 74½ cents quoted at the end of September 1981.

Further gains in production and consumption were anticipated in the 1981–82 season, again concentrated in the less developed Asian countries and the Communist bloc. (ARTHUR TATTERSALL)

Silk. The amount of raw silk stock (about 9,000 tons and still growing) in the hands of the Japanese Custody Corporation continued to dominate the world silk market in 1981. This circumstance dated back to the oil crisis of 1973, when the hitherto seemingly insatiable demand for silk in Japan came to an abrupt halt. Once a principal exporter, Japan had for some time been unable to satisfy domestic demand from the home crop. Instead, it became a major importer, especially from China, South Korea, and Brazil. To protect the politically influential Japanese silk farmers, the government stepped in and imposed a virtual ban on the import of raw silk. Outside suppliers offered their silk in other forms, such as cocoons and thrown silk, but each loophole was plugged in turn, and Japan remained in self-imposed isolation.

Certain import relaxations were negotiated with both China and Korea in the early years, but it became evident that Japan could no longer be viewed as a potential customer, at least for the time being. Korea reduced its silk output somewhat, while China, to absorb its growing production, developed woven fabrics for export. China now replaced Japan as the world's premier silk producer, with India and the U.S.S.R. in third and fourth places. An estimated three-quarters of the world's silk trade was located in Asia. The previous year's lull in Western demand for raw silk continued into 1981. (PETER W. GADDUM)

Man-Made Fibres. As a result of the depression in the world textile industries, a great deal of surplus plant became available. Some of this was being reengineered into comparatively small production units for fibres with special properties that could be made profitably in relatively small quantities. By contrast, the mass producers of commodity synthetic fibres were building even bigger and more automated plants in order to gain economies of scale.

Carbon fibre was undergoing the explosive growth that nylon had experienced when it was first introduced commercially. This very expensive and sophisticated fibre might reach a state of excess capacity in two

to three years. Researchers were concentrating on more complex synthetics such as the moisture-absorbent acrylics, polyesters that could dye at temperatures below 100° C (212° F), and hollow fibres. The comparatively inexpensive polypropylene fibre, with zero moisture absorption, could be used very effectively in apparel, since it was able to contact the skin and remain dry while perspiration was conducted away from the body and released into an absorbent layer on the exterior of the fabric or garment. This stimulated considerable interest in "thermal underwear," and strenuous efforts were being made to match or better the performance of polypropylene and PVC fibres for this use.

(PETER LENNOX-KERR)

TOBACCO

World tobacco consumption increased in 1981 by about 1.2% and would have risen more had not recession restrained consumer buying in developed countries and leaf shortage kept China's huge market undersupplied. Growers harvested 5,500,000,000 kg (12,100,000,000 lb) of leaf, 2% more than in 1980 but still less than current consumption required. Therefore, stocks of maturing tobacco were at the lowest level since 1975, and prices of superior-quality leaf were buoyant in many markets.

If current trends persisted, production could be lifted back into line with demand without taking land out of food production in hungry countries. This would be possible because the world's average tobacco yields had recently been rising by almost 3.5% a year, notably in the least developed countries. Third world tobacco-growing nations were less sensitive about the "food or tobacco" issue than international bodies such as the World Health Organization and the Food and Agriculture Organization; tobacco remained a uniquely profitable cash crop for many of them, able to generate the capital and provide the farming experience that backward rural economies sorely needed.

In numerous countries, notably in the third world, farmers' views of the previous season's prices determine how much tobacco is planted each year. Interest in controlling production, in an effort to achieve greater price stability, was increasing in countries where governments did not intervene in the market. Manufacturers, used to buying in free markets without commitment, were apprehensive. They had traditionally been reluctant to give long-term purchasing and price guarantees to producing countries, but some were beginning to think that unless they did, their raw material supply could over the long term be less certain than it needed to be.

The smoking and health controversy now reverberated worldwide, but it was largely abstract in the half of the world where daily personal tobacco consumption was far below that of the countries that produced the basic statistics on the health risk. Many low-income countries began to print health warnings on cigarette packs, and antismoking campaigns were commonplace throughout the world. Manufacturers in advanced countries were on the defensive against ever tighter restraints on marketing freedom and penalization of smokers by taxation, smoking bans, and induced

shame. Climates of opinion were being generated in which smoking was considered antisocial. Thus, while manufacturers had established that "buy my brand" advertising did not influence the level of total consumption, governments favoured bans on advertising because they viewed them as articulating society's view that smoking was no longer respectable and sophisticated.

Manufacture of the 4,400,000,000,000 cigarettes, which, despite the controversy, the world would smoke in 1982, was undergoing rapid technological advance. Preparation, blending, and cutting of tobacco were fully automated and under electronic control in many cigarette factories. New machines made and packed cigarettes at a rate of 6,000 a minute, three times faster than had been common ten years earlier, and production speeds were expected to increase to 10,000 a minute within four years. Thus employment in the labour-intensive cigarette business was rapidly shrinking.

(MICHAEL F. BARFORD)

TOURISM

International tourism became a $100 billion industry in 1981. World Tourism Organization (WTO) preliminary estimates revealed a rise from $95.3 billion in receipts in 1980 to almost $106 billion in 1981. International tourist arrivals increased from 279 million in 1980 to 290 million in 1981. Total tourist movements, including domestic travel within national frontiers, were calculated at more than 2,600,000,000 arrivals.

Under the pressures of continuing world inflation, slow economic growth, and high energy prices, development remained slack during the first months of 1981, with operators predicting lower growth than during the previous year. The summer season proved unexpectedly satisfactory, however, with peak occupancies being recorded in popular tourist destinations such as Spain's Costa Blanca and Balearic Islands. West Germany remained the world's leading spender in 1981. The estimated $22 billion of international expenditures by its citizens represented one-fifth of the world total. U.S. expenditures on foreign travel, encouraged by the increased strength of the dollar, headed toward the $12 billion mark. Both British and French tourists spent nearly $7 billion abroad, while expenditures by Japanese overseas travelers were close to $5 billion.

Countries reporting strong growth of incoming tourism during the first half of 1981 were Japan and Portugal (20%), Switzerland (11%), Canada (6%), and Greece (5%). In Italy arrivals showed no change, while slight decreases were noted in Austria, Turkey, and the U.K.

Despite the unfavourable economic climate, a number of tour operators reported good results in 1981. One explanation was the keen competition between destinations, which benefited operators, and the high propensity of vacationers to switch destinations on grounds of price, image, or product quality. Among the 16.5 million holidays spent abroad by citizens of West Germany in 1981, for example, 71% of those booked through agents or operators were to destinations not visited the previous year.

There were further moves to adapt tour-

Table XIV. Major Tourism Earners and
Spenders in 1980
In $000,000

Major spenders	Expenditure
West Germany	$20.8
United States	10.4
United Kingdom	6.4
France	6.0
Netherlands, The	4.6
Japan	4.5
Belgium/Luxembourg	3.3
Austria	3.2
Canada	3.1
Switzerland	2.4
Sweden	2.2
Italy	1.9
Denmark	1.6
Mexico	...
Norway	1.3

Major earners	Receipts
United States	$10.1
Italy	8.9
France	8.2
Spain	7.0
United Kingdom	6.9
West Germany	6.6
Austria	6.4
Switzerland	3.1
Canada	2.3
Belgium/Luxembourg	1.8
Greece	1.7
Netherlands, The	1.6
Mexico	...
Denmark	1.3
Hong Kong	1.1

Source: World Tourism Organization.

Reporting to the wto's fourth General Assembly at Rome in September, Secretary-General Robert C. Lonati noted that world tourist movements had doubled since 1968 and that 50% of travel was now undertaken for holiday, pleasure, or family purposes. Reception capacity worldwide in hotels and similar establishments comprised sleeping accommodations for 17 million and gave employment to between 6 million and 8 million people. Camping sites provided 14 million places.

Twelve countries together accounted for two-thirds of worldwide tourist movements. In those nations an average of one out of every four individuals traveled abroad once a year. International tourism's share of world trade was 4.6% in 1980. More than 600 million wage earners throughout the world enjoyed paid vacations, which could justly be regarded as the mainstay and fount of the holiday and travel market. Looking to the future, wto forecasts for 1990, based upon statistical projections and a survey of its 104 member states, pointed to the following profile for tourism in the 1980s: (1) domestic tourism would constitute the most active segment of world demand; (2) international demand in 1990 should produce between 460 million and 480 million tourist arrivals, representing a 5% growth rate; (3) the world's less developed nations would show a growth rate of double the forecast average, significantly increasing their market share by 1990; and (4) new products, tailor-made to individual needs and with stronger emphasis upon understanding of peoples and cultures, would come to the fore.

At the World Tourism Conference in Manila in September 1980, delegations from 107 states and 91 public and private organizations concerned with tourism had adopted the "Manila Declaration on World Tourism." This recognized tourism in its broadest sense as being an activity essential to the life of nations and the well-being of peoples and producing not only economic but also political, social, cultural, and educational benefits. A salient feature of the Manila declaration, the implementation of which would be debated at a special meeting to be held at Acapulco, Mexico, in August 1982, was equal access to holidays for all, including the world's underprivileged.

(PETER SHACKLEFORD)

WOOD PRODUCTS

A crisis in homebuilding—possibly the worst since World War II—made 1981 a poor year for the U.S. forest products industry. At a time when the housing markets should have been buoyed by the crest of the postwar "baby boom," high interest rates were blamed for keeping all but a fraction of this public out of the running for mortgages.

Since construction is one of the largest markets for forest products, problems in this area overshadowed many of the forest industry's other concerns. One of these was taxation, specifically the need for policies that would encourage landowners to devote their property to the long-term growing of trees. Changes in estate and other tax laws in the U.S. in 1981 were seen as a boost for the estimated four million private individuals who collectively owned almost 60% of the nation's commercial forest land. The

American Tree Farm System, an industry-sponsored program that helps such individuals manage their forests, celebrated its 40th anniversary in 1981.

Another traditional concern of the forest products industry was the productivity of government and private forest lands. A study completed by the U.S. Forest Service in 1981 predicted a loss of 36 million presently forested acres (15 million ha) by the year 2030, a drop of 8%. Reasons included loss of timberland to highway and power line rights-of-way, reservoirs, and urban development and the withdrawal of national forest land through redesignation as wilderness. This decline would have serious implications for future supplies of lumber, plywood, and paper.

The falloff in residential construction kept U.S. lumber shipments overall about 20% below 1979 levels. Softwoods, such as pine and fir, account for almost 80% of the lumber used in construction and manufactured products. Sixty percent of America's softwood lumber is produced in the western states and 30% in the South, while almost all hardwoods (such as oak and walnut) are grown in the eastern U.S. Lumber and plywood mills in both the West and South functioned well below capacity in 1981.

Hardwood lumber production dropped 2% from 1980 levels. Domestic demand for hardwood used in furniture was down, and decreased shipment of goods due to the slowed economy meant less demand for hardwood pallets. Production of oak flooring was up 12% in the first eight months of 1981, reflecting activity in the home improvement sector. The total value of lumber shipments in 1981 was estimated at $5.5 billion.

Consumer demand for paper products is less seriously affected by changes in the economy than construction, and markets for paper and paperboard improved from 1980 levels. Paper production overall was up 25%, and pulp mills operated at nearly 95% of capacity. Production of the many grades of paper used in printing and publishing continued at 1980 levels. Total U.S. paper and paperboard production in 1981 was 66 million tons, 3 million tons more than in 1980.

U.S. softwood plywood exports rose nearly 50% to 53 million sq m (575 million sq ft). Lumber exports, however, dropped about 6% below 1980 figures. Exports to Japan were down about 30% but those to Australia were up 25%, and new markets in Saudi Arabia and Egypt grew in importance. The U.S. exported wood to about 150 countries but was still a net importer, with about 97% coming from Canada. Hardwood and softwood lumber imports together represented about a quarter of total U.S. lumber consumption of 37,000,000,000 bd-ft in 1981, down from 38,500,000,000 bd-ft in 1980.

(JAMES BEEK)

See also Agriculture and Food Supplies; Computers; Consumerism; Economy, World; Energy; Food Processing; Games and Toys; Industrial Relations; Materials Sciences; Mining and Quarrying; Photography; Television and Radio; Transportation.

ism to the high cost of energy. Hotel owners conducted energy audits, installed heat pumps, and experimented with solar heating for pools. But transportation continued to be the principal source of energy consumption for tourists. Globally, automobile transport accounted for two-thirds of arrivals. In this sphere governments relied upon fuel price increases and improvements in fuel economy to achieve savings. At the same time, official encouragement was given to fuel-economic modes of transport such as railways. In September 1981, for example, French Railways inaugurated its new TGV High Speed Train running at speeds of up to 255 km/h (160 mph) on the Paris–Lyon and Paris–Geneva run. Services at regular intervals without supplementary fares were the hallmark of this new intercity service, which, following renewed government interest in a rail-only Channel Tunnel link between Britain and France, promised to be only the beginning of a new European high-speed network. Financial concerns continued, however, to cloud the outlook of the world's airlines. (See TRANSPORTATION: *Aviation*.)

Iran

Iran

An Islamic republic of western Asia, Iran is bounded by the U.S.S.R., Afghanistan, Pakistan, Iraq, and Turkey and the Caspian Sea, the Arabian Sea, and the Persian Gulf. Area: 1,648,000 sq km (636,000 sq mi). Pop. (1981 est.): 39,097,000. Cap. and largest city: Teheran (pop., 1980 est., 6 million). Language: Persian. Religion (1976): Muslim 99%; Christian, Jewish, and Zoroastrian minorities. Presidents in 1981, Abolhassan Bani-Sadr to June 21, Mohammad Ali Raja'i from July 24 to August 30, and Sayyed Ali Khamenei from October 12; prime ministers, Raja'i, Mohammad Javad Bahonar from August 4 to August 30, and Mir Hossein Moussavi from October 29.

The postrevolutionary crisis in Iran continued throughout 1981. Political upheavals in domestic and foreign affairs brought the country to virtual civil war and almost total isolation from the international community. The only relief in a worsening situation was the ending of the confrontation with the U.S. over the hostages taken from the Teheran embassy in 1979. Financial arrangements came to dominate the final agreement between Iran and the U.S. reached in Algiers on January 19. Through the good offices of the Algerian government, the U.S. agreed to the transfer of frozen Iranian assets valued at $11.1 billion, including $2.4 billion in gold and securities from the Federal Reserve, $2.2 billion from home-based U.S. banks, $5.5 billion from holdings of U.S. banks abroad, and $1 billion of other funds. The transfer of assets, managed through the Bank of England, resulted in

the immediate disposal of $2.8 billion to Iran, repayment by Iran of $3.7 billion to cover syndicated loans drawn from U.S. banks, the freezing of $1.4 billion in an escrow account to await settlement of unsyndicated loans outstanding on Iranian account, and allocation of $3.2 billion for possible claims against Iran by U.S. companies. The hostages left Iran on January 20 after 444 days in captivity.

Border warfare with Iraq continued. At the beginning of 1981 the Iraqi Army had occupied a large enclave in Kurdistan around the town of Gasr Shirin and a broad but ill-defined front in Khuzestan including a bridgehead east of the Karun River adjacent to Abadan. Only Khorramshahr fell entirely under Iraqi control, though large portions of the populations of Ahvaz, Susangerd, Dezful, and Abadan left their homes; the number of refugees was estimated at up to 1.5 million. After failing to take Abadan, Iraq began a systematic bombardment that left much of the city and the entire refinery complex in ruins. An Iranian counterattack in January achieved only temporary success. However, it was reported on September 27 that an Iranian drive east of the Karun near Abadan had forced the Iraqis to abandon this zone, while in early December the Iranians claimed to have broken through Iraqi lines near Susangerd.

Iranian air strikes against Iraqi oil installations around Basra in January and Kirkuk during the summer were followed in early October by attacks on Iraqi power stations in the south. Iraqi air strikes against shipping at southern Iranian ports, the oil terminal of Kharg, and the main oil-pumping station at Gurreh succeeded by late 1981 in

Seventy-two people, including Chief Justice Ayatollah Mohammad Beheshti and dozens of members of the Iranian Majlis (parliament), were killed when the headquarters of the Islamic Republican Party was bombed in Teheran in June.

PROUTIERE—SYGMA

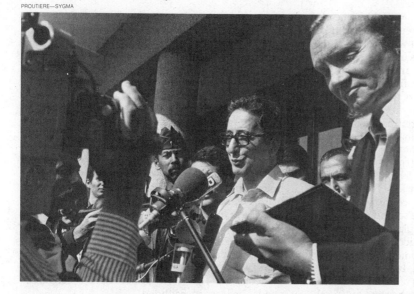

Former Iranian president Abolhassan Bani-Sadr spoke with reporters in Paris on July 29 after escaping from Iran.

halting all but a trickle of oil exports and delaying vital imports. Iranian casualties were estimated at 10,000–20,000 killed by the end of 1981. Nevertheless, peace proposals put forward by the Islamic Conference were all rejected, despite increasing concessions from the Iraqis.

Relations with the U.S.S.R. improved gradually. A trade agreement signed in June provided for increased transit of goods via the Soviet rail system to the Iranian frontier town of Julfa. Mohsadeq Khalkhali, an extreme Islamic fundamentalist judge, visited Muslim centres in the U.S.S.R. in June, and in the second half of the year the wing of the Islamic Republican Party best disposed toward the Soviet Union gained ascendancy in Teheran. This trend was accentuated by Iran's isolation from normal international relations.

In domestic politics, the struggle between the supporters of Pres. Abolhassan Bani-Sadr and followers of the Islamic Republican Party (IRP) erupted into open fighting in March. But the stand against increasing clerical control of the state came too late. On March 11 the IRP-dominated Majlis (parliament) passed legislation permitting the premier to appoint temporary acting ministers, considerably diminishing the powers of the president. Bani-Sadr's advisers were arrested, his newspaper was closed, and his allies in the government were replaced. On June 10 he was dismissed as commander in chief of the armed forces, and on June 21 the Majlis voted to strip him of the presidency. Formal warrants for his arrest were issued. In hiding, he formed an alliance with the Mujaheddin-i Khalq opposition group before fleeing to France in July with the Mujaheddin leader, Massoud Rajavi. The prime minister, Mohammad Ali Raja'i (*see* OBITUARIES), was elected president on July 24, and the Majlis voted in Mohammad Javad Bahonar (*see* OBITUARIES) as prime minister on August 4.

A bomb explosion at the Teheran headquarters of the IRP on June 28 killed 72 persons, including Ayatollah Mohammad Hossein Beheshti (*see* OBITUARIES), the head of the party, four Cabinet ministers, and a number of leading clerics. Arrests and

executions of Mujaheddin supporters failed to halt the violence, and on August 30 an explosion at the office of the prime minister killed both the president and the prime minister. Other members of the administration were assassinated in separate incidents. Hojatoleslam Sayyed Ali Khamenei (*see* BIOGRAPHIES), elected as Iran's third presi-

IRAN

Education. (1978–79) Primary, pupils 4,403,106, teachers (1977–78) 154,577; secondary, pupils 2,370,341, teachers (1977–78) 91,960; vocational, pupils 256,303, teachers (1976–77) 10,041; teacher training, students 57,832, teachers (1977–78) 2,988; higher, students 175,675, teaching staff (1976–77) 13,952.

Finance. Monetary unit: rial, with (Sept. 21, 1981) a free rate of 78.48 rials to U.S. $1 (145.50 rials = £1 sterling). Gold and other reserves (June 1980) U.S. $15,358,000,000. Budget (1980–81 est.): revenue 2,723,000,000,000 rials; expenditure 2,118,000,000,000 rials. Gross national product (1977–78) 5,212,000,000,000 rials. Money supply (Feb. 1981) 2,322,870,000,000 rials. Cost of living (1975 = 100; May 1981) 270.

Foreign Trade. (1980) Imports 863.3 billion rials; exports 963.5 billion rials. Import sources: Japan c. 14%; West Germany c. 14%; U.K. c. 8%; France c. 7%; Italy c. 5%. Export destinations: Japan c. 27%; West Germany c. 12%; Spain c. 7%; Brazil c. 6%; India c. 5%; The Bahamas c. 5%; France c. 5%. Main exports: crude oil 73%; petroleum products 21%.

Transport and Communications. Roads (1980) 63,100 km. Motor vehicles in use (1979): passenger 1,028,400; commercial (including buses) 396,300. Railways: (1979) 4,-604 km; traffic (1976) 3,511,000,000 passenger-km, freight 4,627,000,000 net ton-km. Air traffic (1980): 2,071,000,000 passenger-km; freight 23.4 million net ton-km. Shipping (1980): merchant vessels 100 gross tons and over 229; gross tonnage 1,283,629. Telephones (Jan. 1980) c. 730,-000. Radio receivers (Dec. 1977) 2,125,000. Television receivers (Dec. 1979) 2.1 million.

Agriculture. Production (in 000; metric tons; 1980): wheat c. 6,000; barley c. 1,100; rice c. 1,150; potatoes c. 697; sugar, raw value c. 600; onions c. 273; tomatoes c. 326; watermelons (1979) c. 930; melons (1979) c. 480; dates c. 300; grapes c. 931; apples c. 455; soybeans c. 100; tea c. 29; tobacco c. 15; cotton, lint c. 70. Livestock (in 000; 1980): cattle c. 7,645; sheep c. 32,000; goats c. 13,627; horses c. 350; asses c. 1,800; chickens c. 70,384.

Industry. Production (in 000; metric tons; 1977–78): cement 6,323; coal 900; crude oil (1980) 73,770; natural gas (cu m) 900; petroleum products (1979) c. 36,-700; lead concentrates (metal content; 1978–79) c. 30; chromium ore (oxide content) c. 80; electricity (kw-hr; 1978–79) c. 18,500,000.

dent in October, appointed a new Cabinet headed by Hossein Moussavi. Severe reprisals were taken against the Mujaheddin, and it was estimated that at least 2,150 persons were executed between June 20 and the end of October. Meanwhile, a government in exile was formed by Bani-Sadr and the Mujaheddin. Although rumours that the country's aged and ailing religious leader, Ayatollah Ruhollah Khomeini, would soon retire were denied, during the year he delegated many of his powers to Ayatollah Hussein Ali Montazeri.

Iran's economic plight worsened appreciably. Oil output fluctuated between 500,000 and 1.5 million bbl a day, dropping markedly after an air attack on September 30. The country's financial holdings fell to $2 billion in the second half of 1981, and rigid restrictions were placed on imports, affecting not only consumer goods but also basic foodstuffs and capital equipment. The Bandar Khomeini petrochemical plant, built in association with Mitsui of Japan at a cost of $3.5 billion, was left incomplete and unused. By the close of 1981 the economy was marked by acute inflation, growing unemployment, disinvestment in industry, and shortages of most imported goods.

(KEITH S. MCLACHLAN)

Iraq

Iraq

A republic of southwestern Asia, Iraq is bounded by Turkey, Iran, Kuwait, Saudi Arabia, Jordan, Syria, and the Persian Gulf. Area: 437,522 sq km (168,928 sq mi). Pop. (1981 est.): 13,542,000, including Arabs, Kurds, Turks, Aramaic-speakers, Iranians, and others. Cap. and largest city: Baghdad (pop., 1977, 3,205,600). Language: Arabic. Religion: mainly Muslim, some Christian. President in 1981, Saddam Hussein at-Takriti.

In September 1981 Iraq marked the first anniversary of the start of the war with Iran with a renewed offensive. On September 28, however, a spokesman admitted that the Iraqi Army had been

forced to withdraw to the left bank of the Karun River, which had been crossed triumphantly on Oct. 11, 1980. The reverse emphasized the seesaw pattern of the conflict and the heavy toll of casualties. Despite a year of siege, Iraqi forces had been unable to seize the important oil-refining town of Abadan. With Iranian artillery able to shell Basra, Iraq seemed as far away as ever from its goal of controlling the Shatt al-Arab waterway.

Pres. Saddam Hussein at-Takriti remained firmly in control at home. Estimates of the number of war casualties varied widely, but whatever the exact figure, the impact was minimized. Ostentatious funerals were discouraged, and there were lucrative benefits for war widows and orphans. Life at the front was reported to be relatively easy. Hussein's position was thought to be safe provided he managed to fuel the economy and keep the people fed. Import allocations for major retailers were increased after the war broke out, and there was evidence of increased spending on consumer goods, at least in Baghdad.

By the end of 1981 Iraq's finances were still in reasonable shape. Reserves stood at $15 billion–$20 billion. In April a number of Arab states announced substantial loan commitments: Saudi Arabia granted $6 billion and Kuwait, $2 billion. A "business-as-usual" attitude prevailed in Iraq's dealings with foreign contractors engaged in development projects. Nevertheless, many Western companies preferred to form consortia in order to spread the risk. In Baghdad considerable disapproval was voiced for certain Japanese companies that fled when the war broke out only to return a month or so later. The Iraqis subsequently took a strong line in talks with the Japanese over compensation for delays.

In September 1982 Baghdad would be host to the nonaligned movement's summit conference. In preparation, a massive $8 billion construction program was under way. This was part of a $133.4 billion, five-year development plan (1981–85), in which priority was given to services, transport,

Iraqi prisoners of war, part of an exchange of prisoners between Iran and Iraq in August, are helped to board a plane in Teheran by delegates of the International Committee of the Red Cross.

THIERRY GASSMANN—KEYSTONE

and communications. The plan placed special emphasis on housing, providing electricity and drinking water for all residential areas, building more rural roads, and improving education and health facilities. Transport links were to include an expressway from Baghdad to Turkey and railway lines from Baghdad to Mosul in the north and to Basra and Umm Qasr in the south. A new airport was planned for Mosul. It was hoped that 10 out of every 100 people in Iraq would have a telephone by 1985.

Iraq responded to an Israeli attack on its nuclear reactor near Baghdad on June 7 by securing funds from Saudi Arabia to rebuild the installation. The Osirak-type, French-supplied reactor, which the Israelis claimed had been intended for the production of nuclear weapons, was totally destroyed. On July 20 President Hussein said that Iraq intended to build "two, five, ten nuclear reactors, according to its needs." The French government informed Iraq in August that it would be prepared to rebuild the reactor, although controls to prevent the installation from having military uses would be increased.

Before the war Iraqi crude oil production was running at 3.4 million bbl a day. However, Iranian attacks forced the closing of the Mina-al-Bakr and Khor al-Amaya terminals. A maximum of 900,000 bbl a day was flowing through the Turkish and Syrian pipelines. Iraq's major customers—France, Japan, Italy, and Brazil—were taking only 440,000 bbl a day, less than half of prewar levels.

Despite its problems, Iraq emerged in the first half of 1981 as the biggest spender on development projects in the Arab world. Iraq awarded contracts worth $15.4 billion to foreign and domestic contractors, compared with the $11.3 billion awarded by Saudi Arabia, the second biggest spender. The Mosul dam contract was awarded to a West German-Italian consortium.   (JOHN WHELAN)

Ireland

Ireland

Separated from Great Britain by the North Channel, the Irish Sea, and St. George's Channel, the Republic of Ireland shares its island with Northern Ireland to the northeast. Area: 70,285 sq km (27,137 sq mi), or 84% of the island. Pop. (1981 est.): 3,431,000. Cap. and largest city: Dublin (pop., 1979, 544,600). Language (1971): mostly English; 28% speak English and Irish or Irish only. Religion: 94% Roman Catholic. President in 1981, Patrick J. Hillery; prime ministers, Charles J. Haughey and, from June 30, Garret FitzGerald.

Expectation of a general election dominated the first half of 1981 in Ireland. It seemed inevitable that Charles J. Haughey, who only a year before had succeeded Jack Lynch as prime minister and leader of the Fianna Fail Party, would go to the country in the wake of the government's 1980 by-election victory in Donegal. A sense of urgency was given to this expectation by the state of the economy, which was beset by rising inflation, rising unemployment, greater dependence on foreign borrowing, and falling output.

IRAQ
   Education. (1978–79) Primary, pupils 2,459,870, teachers 87,148; secondary, pupils 781,766, teachers 25,254; vocational, pupils 48,186, teachers 3,273; teacher training, students 20,488, teachers 939; higher, students 89,197, teaching staff 5,207.
   Finance. Monetary unit: Iraqi dinar, with (Sept. 21, 1981) a par value of 0.295 dinar to U.S. $1 (free rate of 0.548 dinar = £1 sterling). Budget (total; 1980 est.) balanced at 14,103,000,000 dinars. Gross domestic product (1977) 5,692,000,000 dinars. Cost of living (1975 = 100; Sept. 1979) 148.4.
   Foreign Trade. (1980) Imports *c.* 4,440,000,000 dinars; exports 7,782,000,000 dinars. Import sources: Japan *c.* 18%; West Germany *c.* 15%; France *c.* 9%; Italy *c.* 8%; U.K. *c.* 6%; U.S. *c.* 6%. Export destinations: France *c.* 18%; Brazil *c.* 15%; Japan *c.* 14%; Italy *c.* 9%; Spain *c.* 5%. Main export: crude oil 99%.
   Transport and Communications. Roads (1975) 9,692 km. Motor vehicles in use (1979): passenger 120,600; commercial (including buses) 129,400. Railways: (1975) 1,990 km; traffic (1976–77) 797 million passenger-km, freight 2,254,000,000 net ton-km. Air traffic (1980): 1,161,000,000 passenger-km; freight 52.7 million net ton-km. Shipping (1980): merchant vessels 100 gross tons and over 142; gross tonnage 1,465,949. Telephones (Jan. 1978) 319,600. Radio receivers (Dec. 1977) 2 million. Television receivers (Dec. 1977) 475,000.
   Agriculture. Production (in 000; metric tons; 1980): wheat *c.* 1,300; barley *c.* 575; rice *c.* 220; cucumbers (1979) *c.* 163; watermelons (1979) *c.* 648; onions *c.* 80; tomatoes *c.* 465; dates *c.* 395; grapes *c.* 427; tobacco *c.* 12; cotton, lint (1979) *c.* 6. Livestock (in 000; 1979): cattle *c.* 2,740; sheep *c.* 11,440; goats *c.* 3,600; camels *c.* 235; asses *c.* 450.
   Industry. Production (in 000; metric tons; 1978): cement *c.* 3,300; crude oil (1980) 129,865; natural gas (cu m; 1980) 1,760,000; petroleum products *c.* 5,500; electricity (kw-hr) *c.* 6,950,000.

IRELAND
   Education. (1979–80) Primary, pupils 565,742, teachers 19,651; secondary, pupils 288,926, teachers 17,881; vocational, pupils 6,666, teachers 206; higher, students 38,890, teaching staff 3,594.
   Finance. Monetary unit: Irish pound (punt), with (Sept. 21, 1981) a free rate of I£0.61 to U.S. $1 (I£1.13 = £1 sterling). Gold and other reserves (June 1981) U.S. $2,145,000,000. Budget (1980 actual): revenue £3,256 million; expenditure £4,541 million. Gross national product (1980) £8,329 million. Money supply (June 1981) £1,657 million. Cost of living (1975 = 100; May 1981) 225.
   Foreign Trade. (1980) Imports £5,419.4 million; exports £4,131.4 million. Import sources: EEC 71% (U.K. 51%, West Germany 7%, France 5%); U.S. 9%. Export destinations: EEC 74% (U.K. 43%, West Germany 10%, France 8%, The Netherlands 5%, Belgium-Luxembourg 5%); U.S. 5%. Main exports: machinery 16%; chemicals 13%; beef and veal 11%; textiles and clothing 8%; dairy products 7%. Tourism (1979): visitors 1,676,000; gross receipts U.S. $384 million.
   Transport and Communications. Roads (1977) 92,294 km. Motor vehicles in use (1980): passenger 734,400; commercial 65,100. Railways (1979): 1,988 km; traffic 1,007,000,000 passenger-km, freight (1980) 580 million net ton-km. Air traffic (1980): 2,049,000,000 passenger-km; freight 91.9 million net ton-km. Shipping (1980): merchant vessels 100 gross tons and over 141; gross tonnage 208,986. Telephones (Jan. 1980) 586,000. Radio receivers (Dec. 1976) 949,000. Television licenses (Dec. 1979) 592,700.
   Agriculture. Production (in 000; metric tons; 1980): barley *c.* 1,370; wheat *c.* 235; oats *c.* 96; potatoes *c.* 990; sugar, raw value (1979) *c.* 192; cabbages (1979) *c.* 170; cow's milk *c.* 4,850; butter 111; cheese *c.* 49; beef and veal *c.* 410; pork *c.* 145; fish catch (1979) 93. Livestock (in 000; June 1980): cattle 6,935; sheep 3,291; pigs *c.* 1,120; horses (1979) *c.* 78; chickens *c.* 8,700.
   Industry. Production (in 000; metric tons; 1980): cement 1,812; coal 59; petroleum products *c.* 2,040; electricity (kw-hr) 10,890,000; manufactured gas (cu m) *c.* 670,000; beer (hl; 1977–78) 4,400; wool fabrics (sq m; 1977) 3,700; rayon, etc., fabrics (sq m; 1977) 49,400; fertilizers (nutrient content; 1979–80) nitrogenous *c.* 102, phosphate *c.* 42.

Three prominent members of the Irish Dail (parliament), Neil Blaney (left), Sile de Valera (centre), and John O'Connell (right), spoke with press representatives in Dublin after returning from Belfast, where they had met with the hunger strikers in Maze Prison.

The pre-election tensions would have been resolved in February but for the wide-ranging effects of a fire in the Stardust Cabaret nightclub in Artane, a suburb of Dublin, in which 48 people died. The disaster occurred in the prime minister's constituency in the early hours of February 14, shortly before the Fianna Fail Party's annual conference, for which he had prepared a pre-election address, was due to start. The conference was canceled, the general election postponed, and the chance of victory for the party in power was lost. In the following months several factors intervened to turn this chance of victory into a narrow defeat.

The first of these factors was the divisive effect of the hunger strike by Irish Republican Army (IRA) prisoners in Northern Ireland. Resumed on March 1, some two months after an earlier fast had been abandoned, the protest was at its height of bitterness and death when the election was finally called. Second, the delay exposed serious deficiencies in economic forecasting, reinforcing the opposition's strong criticism of government prodigality. Third, the main opposition party, Fine Gael, ill-prepared at the beginning of the year, gained time to put together an effective electoral manifesto.

By May 21, when it was announced that the general election would take place on June 11, any element of surprise had vanished. The government's campaign was lacklustre, and there were sharp and even bitter differences of emphasis between the government and opposition camps. Although the two major opposition parties, Fine Gael and the Irish Labour Party, ran separate campaigns, it was assumed that they would form a partnership in power.

The compelling campaign run by Garret Fitz-Gerald (*see* BIOGRAPHIES), the Fine Gael leader, together with the natural shift in support from a government whose policies lacked conviction, resulted in a narrow majority in the Dail (parliament) for the two opposition parties. The results of the June poll were: Fianna Fail 78 seats; Fine Gael 65 seats; Labour 15 seats; independents 8 seats. (Two of the independents were National H-Block/-Armagh Committee candidates, standing in support of the demands of the IRA hunger strikers; both were in prison in Northern Ireland and did not, therefore, take their seats.)

Several major figures in the Labour Party movement, particularly in the trade unions, spoke out strongly against a pact with Fine Gael; where Fine Gael's emphasis during the campaign had been on tax reform, the Labour Party had demanded more jobs and a reduction in inflation. However, differences were finally resolved. At the end of June FitzGerald became prime minister at the head of a precarious Fine Gael-Irish Labour Party coalition government, which was dependent on the support of three independent deputies (members).

Of the two IRA candidates who stood successfully in the general election, one, Kieran Doherty, was on hunger strike and subsequently died. His death in August further exposed the tenuous nature of the new government's majority. Although the general election had been fought on the economy rather than the issue of Northern Ireland, the first few weeks of the new administration were devoted to intense though fruitless efforts to settle the hunger-strike deadlock.

At the same time, a stiff second budget was introduced by Minister for Finance John Bruton, imposing new taxes and foreshadowing a harsh autumn and winter. The government lost one significant vote—for the election of deputy speaker—during the early days of the new Dail, and there were expectations that the coalition would be short-lived. However, a reasonable prospect of stability emerged. Of the six independent deputies who took their seats, one became speaker and three others more or less aligned themselves with the government.

It was a bad year for the economy, made worse by political pressures. The first budget, formulated in expectation of a general election, proved ineffective, as did subsequent economic measures. Pay awards remained high, particularly in the public sector, and the rate of inflation for the year was running at some 20%. Unemployment, which reached a record 122,000 at the beginning of the

year, was still increasing at the time of the election; by the end of September the figure was 127,-000. It was clear that the new administration faced a period of at least 18 months during which it would have to attempt to solve the basic problems.

Though much of the year was overshadowed by the hunger strike of IRA prisoners in the Maze Prison, Belfast, more profound moves were made, by both Haughey and FitzGerald, in the direction of improving Anglo-Irish relations over the issue of Northern Ireland. Institutional studies continued throughout the year, and in the autumn the new prime minister initiated a debate on constitutional change, the main purpose of which was to prepare the ground for further joint moves by London and Dublin on resolving the Northern Ireland impasse. The debate took on a bitter colouring in its early stages. It was, however, an effective way of airing differences, and it served to divert public attention from the economic gloom.

(MAVIS ARNOLD)

See also United Kingdom.

Israel

A republic of the Middle East, Israel is bounded by Lebanon, Syria, Jordan, Egypt, and the Mediterranean Sea. Area (not including territory occupied in the June 1967 war): 20,700 sq km (7,992 sq mi). Pop. (1980 est.): 3,877,700. Cap. and largest city: Jerusalem (pop., 1980 est., 398,200). Language: Hebrew and Arabic. Religion: predominantly Jewish (1979 est., 84%) with Muslim, Christian, and other minorities. President in 1981, Yitzhak Navon; prime minister, Menachem Begin.

As 1981 began, the government of Prime Minister Menachem Begin (*see* BIOGRAPHIES), which in 1977 had ended 30 years of unchallenged Labour Party rule, seemed itself to be running out of steam. With new elections due sometime in the new year, public opinion appeared to have turned against Begin and, even more so, against his government. Two of the government's outstanding

members, Moshe Dayan (*see* OBITUARIES) and Ezer Weizman, had resigned over matters of policy and style, and it was an open secret that a third, Finance Minister Yigael Hurvitz, would follow suit. Moreover, the prime minister would soon be 68 and was not in the best of health. All the omens pointed to an early change in Israel's leadership.

The advent of the new administration in Washington had injected an element of uncertainty into Israeli foreign policy, though Pres. Ronald Reagan was believed to favour more open and direct support for Israeli positions in the peace process with Egypt and in the confrontation with Israel's adversaries, especially the Palestine Liberation Organization (PLO). However, the main problems confronting Begin were domestic. His first opportunity to restore the image of his ailing administration came with the resignation of Finance Minister Hurvitz on January 12. On January 19 Begin appointed as his successor Yoram Aridor, a lawyer and political science graduate.

Aridor's initial measures brought cries of derision from economists and from the opposition, which charged that they were aimed solely at winning votes. Subsidies for food and domestic essentials were increased, and taxes on consumer durables were substantially reduced. When the opposition charged the government with reckless handling of the national finances, it responded by instituting monthly—rather than quarterly—adjustments of wages to the cost of living. The Cabinet approved the budget on February 8. It foresaw expenditures totaling 206 billion shekels, assuming an inflation rate of 120% (it was more) and that the value of the shekel against the U.S. dollar would double during 1981. Within days of the new budget announcements, the country embarked on a spending spree, and the polls began to shift in favour of the government.

But the government was still in trouble when, on February 10, the Knesset (parliament) advanced the parliamentary election date from the year's end to June. Yigael Yadin's Democratic Movement for Change, Begin's most prestigious

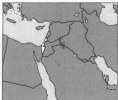

Israel

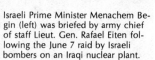

Israeli Prime Minister Menachem Begin (left) was briefed by army chief of staff Lieut. Gen. Rafael Eiten following the June 7 raid by Israeli bombers on an Iraqi nuclear plant.

UPI

coalition partner, dissolved itself on February 18, and Yadin retired from politics. The minister for religious affairs had been charged with committing misdemeanours in office. Only two men in the administration stood out in the public eye: Foreign Minister Itzhak Shamir, Begin's closest colleague, and Ariel Sharon (*see* BIOGRAPHIES), the minister of agriculture. Taking charge of his party's campaign, Begin began an oratorical drive, wooing Israel's underprivileged Oriental communities, championing Israel against its detractors (real and imagined), and skillfully exploiting the split within the opposition Labour Party between Shimon Peres, the elected leader, and former prime minister Yitzhak Rabin. But always his chief target was the "so-called PLO."

Throughout March and April, Israel was engaged in an escalating conflict across the southern border of Lebanon, where PLO raiding parties had established bases. Syrian forces stationed in Lebanon became involved, and the situation was complicated by fighting between Lebanese Muslims and Christians. At this juncture, President Reagan sent a senior U.S. diplomat, Philip Habib (*see* BIOGRAPHIES), to the Middle East with instructions to bring about a cease-fire. Habib succeeded, with Saudi Arabian help. However, the question of Syrian missile batteries installed in Lebanon's Bekka Valley, which the Israelis repeatedly threatened to remove by force, remained dangerously unsolved at year's end.

In the relative calm following the cease-fire, and with the polls showing Likud and Labour almost even, Begin met with Egyptian Pres. Anwar as-Sadat (*see* OBITUARIES) at Ophira (the old Sharm-as-Sheikh) on June 4. The two leaders agreed on formation of a multinational force to police the Sinai after Israel's withdrawal in April 1982, but both clearly wanted to wait until after the election before embarking on any major initiative. Three days later Begin sprang the first of the year's several surprises. In the early hours of June 7, the Israeli Air Force attacked and destroyed an Iraqi nuclear reactor at Daura, 24 km (15 mi) east of Baghdad, which Begin claimed was to be used to make nuclear weapons. It was a precedent that few countries wanted to encourage. The UN Security Council condemned the attack, and the U.S. instituted a punitive delay in the delivery of F-16 planes to Israel. The attack also became a major pre-election topic, but on balance public opinion backed the government.

The election, on June 30, was a cliff-hanger, with the Begin coalition finally scraping home with a single-seat majority (later increased to three). (For detailed results, *see* POLITICAL PARTIES.) Begin had until August 5 to form a government, and he presented his government to the Knesset and the president on August 4. To put together a viable coalition with the National Religious Party and the Orthodox Agudat Israel, he had to make far-reaching concessions to extreme religious demands which were certain to be unpopular with the majority of the population. In

Israeli troops returned to their base by helicopter after they had attacked Palestinian targets in southern Lebanon in February.

UPI

ISRAEL

Education. (1979–80) Primary, pupils 645,095, teachers 35,066; secondary, pupils 84,416, teachers 6,220; vocational, pupils 78,743, teachers 8,517; higher, students 87,-724, teaching staff (1974–75) 13,981.

Finance. Monetary unit: shekel , with (Sept. 21, 1981) a free rate of 13.08 shekels to U.S. $1 (24.25 shekels = £1 sterling). Gold and other reserves (June 1981) U.S. $3,544,-000,000. Budget (1979–80 actual): revenue 27,098,000,000 shekels; expenditure 34,703,000,000 shekels. Gross national product (1980) 99,887,000,000 shekels. Money supply (March 1981) 8,531,000,000 shekels. Cost of living (1975 = 100; June 1981) 2,226.

Foreign Trade. (1980) Imports 41,118,000,000 shekels (excluding military goods); exports 28,389,000,000 shekels. Import sources: U.S. 19%; West Germany 10%; U.K. 8%; Switzerland 8%; Belgium-Luxembourg 5%. Export destinations: U.S. 16%; West Germany 10%; U.K. 8%; Switzerland 6%; France 5%; Italy 5%; Hong Kong 5%. Main exports: diamonds 29%; chemicals 15%; fruit and vegetables 9%; machinery 9%; metal manufactures 7%. Tourism (1979): visitors 1,138,000; gross receipts U.S. $765 million.

Transport and Communications. Roads (1979) 12,160 km. Motor vehicles in use (1980): passenger *c.* 423,000; commercial *c.* 91,000. Railways (1979): 826 km; traffic 222 million passenger-km, freight 768 million net ton-km. Air traffic (1980): *c.* 4,727,000,000 passenger-km; freight 299.1 million net ton-km. Shipping (1980): merchant vessels 100 gross tons and over 56; gross tonnage 450,216. Telephones (Jan. 1980) 1,081,500. Radio receivers (Dec. 1977) 750,000. Television licenses (Dec. 1976) 475,000.

Agriculture. Production (in 000; metric tons; 1980): wheat *c.* 250; potatoes *c.* 172; watermelons (1979) 93; tomatoes 258; onions 32; oranges 855; grapefruit 502; grapes *c.* 78; apples 100; olives 43; bananas *c.* 76; cotton, lint *c.* 78; cheese *c.* 59; poultry meat *c.* 169; fish catch (1979) 27. Livestock (in 000; 1979): cattle *c.* 280; sheep 200; goats *c.* 130; pigs *c.* 93; camels *c.* 11; chickens *c.* 26,200.

Industry. Production (in 000; metric tons; 1980): cement 2,089; crude oil 50; natural gas (cu m) 220,000; phosphate rock (1979) 2,216; petroleum products (1978) *c.* 8,100; sulfuric acid 209; fertilizers (nutrient content; 1979–80) nitrogenous *c.* 77, phosphate *c.* 37, potash 769; paper (1978) 101; electricity (kw-hr; 1979) 12,433,000.

particular, these included strict observance of the Sabbath by all government workers, including those catering to tourists, and massive subsidies for religious institutions. The most significant appointments in the new Cabinet were Sharon as defense minister and the confirmation of Shamir as foreign minister. Aridor was reappointed as finance minister despite some opposition.

Meanwhile, immediately after the election and before the new government was formed, Israel launched a series of preemptive attacks against PLO bases in Lebanon. The reason for the timing remained unclear, although the government claimed that the PLO was preparing to place guns and rockets in strategically significant positions from which they could harass settlements in northern Israel. The attacks culminated on July 17 in a massive air raid on a PLO headquarters and command post in the heart of Muslim Beirut. The targets were substantially destroyed, but civilian casualties were heavy, with estimates ranging from 80 to 300. Once again, usually friendly foreign voices were critical, and the U.S. extended the suspension of deliveries of the F-16s. In Israel also there was considerable criticism, and the government's answers were less convincing than after the attack on the Iraqi reactor.

Two weeks after the formation of the new government, the U.S. lifted the ban on the shipment of military aircraft. A mood of international relaxation was further underlined by a meeting between Begin and Sadat in Alexandria, where progress was made in hastening the normalization process, though the problem of Palestinian autonomy remained unsolved. In this regard, continued support among the European Community countries for a peace initiative that would involve the PLO in the peace process led the Israelis to seek a closer understanding with Washington. Begin visited President Reagan on September 9, at which time the U.S. agreed to purchase $200 million worth of Israeli-produced military equipment. More important, agreement was reached on a strategic cooperation understanding that would allow wide-ranging Israeli-U.S. cooperation in military matters. Not for the first time, however, there had been a failure of communication. Reagan had understood from Begin that Israel would stand aside from the coming congressional debate over the sale of arms, including sophisticated airborne warning and control system (AWACS) radar planes, to Saudi Arabia. But Begin denounced the deal even before flying home and continued to oppose it strongly.

All this was soon overshadowed by the assassination of President Sadat on October 6. However, the smooth transition of power in Egypt impressed the Israelis, as did the evident determination of Pres. Hosni Mubarak (*see* BIOGRAPHIES) to continue with the Camp David peace process. Shortly afterward, tragedy struck again with the death of Dayan.

On October 26, Britain, France, Italy, and The Netherlands announced that they would serve in the multinational force in the Sinai but that this could not be taken to indicate support of the Camp David agreement, a reservation that was unacceptable to Israel. On October 28 the U.S. Senate approved the Saudi arms deal. Despite Israel's opposition to the sale, there was some feeling of relief, since Reagan's defeat on the issue might have provoked an anti-Israeli backlash. Israel now hoped for a more even-handed attitude in Washington, but on October 31 it complained about a marked tilt by the U.S. administration in favour of the peace plan put forward by Saudi Arabia, which Israel found totally unacceptable. (*See* SAUDI ARABIA.) The U.S. did succeed in negotiating a new formula for European participation in the multinational force that was acceptable to Israel, and the Israelis were encouraged by a change of attitude on the part of France, which distanced itself from the European peace initiative. However, the strategic cooperation agreement, which Sharon signed in Washington, fell short of initial U.S. undertakings.

The Saudi plan was rejected at an Arab summit in Fez, Morocco, on November 25, but Begin still felt that the U.S. attitude toward it had been unnecessarily ambivalent. Leaving the hospital, where he had been recovering from a fractured thigh, he pushed through the Knesset legislation that made Israeli law applicable to the Golan Heights, which Israel had captured from the Syrians in 1967. The U.S., the Arabs, and the UN Security Council treated this as tantamount to arbitrary annexation. The Security Council unani-

mously condemned Israel for its action, and on December 18 the U.S. informed Israel that it had suspended the strategic cooperation agreement, canceled arrangements made under its terms, and suspended the purchase of Israeli military equipment. On December 20 Begin met with the U.S. ambassador and later ordered the text of his remarks to be released. They were sharp. The U.S., Begin said, should not treat Israel as if it were a vassal or a banana republic; Washington's repeated breaches of contract raised serious doubts as to its credibility, and he regarded the U.S. suspension of the cooperation agreement as tantamount to cancellation. The U.S. reaction was low keyed, but at year's end there was evident concern in both Washington and Israel over the future of the U.S.-Israeli relationship.   (JON KIMCHE)

See also Middle Eastern Affairs.

Italy

Italy

A republic of southern Europe, Italy occupies the Apennine Peninsula, Sicily, Sardinia, and a number of smaller islands. On the north it borders France, Switzerland, Austria, and Yugoslavia. Area: 301,263 sq km (116,318 sq mi). Pop. (1981 est.): 57,198,000. Cap. and largest city: Rome (pop., 1980 est., 2,911,700). Language: Italian. Religion: predominantly Roman Catholic. President in 1981, Alessandro Pertini; premiers, Arnaldo Forlani until May 26 and, from June 28, Giovanni Spadolini.

An attempt to kill Pope John Paul II (*see* BIOGRAPHIES) in St. Peter's Square in Vatican City on May 13 was the worst terrorist incident in Italy in a year marked by continuing activity by the Red Brigades and other extremist groups. A Turk, Mehmet Ali Agca, was charged and convicted by the Rome Assize Court of the crime. He claimed that he had acted alone, but many Italians supported the view that their country had become the target of a deliberate campaign of destabilization organized from abroad.

A corruption scandal involving hundreds of public servants who were allegedly members of a secret Masonic lodge called P2 (Propaganda Due)

erupted during the early part of the year and brought down the government. In June Giovanni Spadolini (*see* BIOGRAPHIES), leader of the Republican Party, became the first non-Christian Democrat premier in the 35-year history of the Italian republic.

Domestic Affairs. The shooting of the pope took place during an open-air general audience in St. Peter's Square. One bullet passed through the pope's abdomen and then injured a U.S. woman; another bullet injured the pope's right arm and left hand and ricocheted into the crowd, injuring another woman. The pontiff was rushed to Rome's Gemelli Hospital, where an emergency operation was successfully performed. Police arrested Mehmet Ali Agca on the spot and charged him with attempted murder under Italian law. Territorial jurisdiction over St. Peter's Square is shared by the Vatican and Italy under the Lateran Treaty of 1929.

During the trial, evidence was given that Agca, convicted in his own country of the murder of an Istanbul newspaper editor, had already threatened to kill the pope during his visit to Turkey in 1979. No serious attempt was made during the trial to trace possible international connections with the crime. Agca was convicted on the evidence of eyewitnesses present at the shooting and was sentenced to life imprisonment on July 22. Pres. Alessandro Pertini went on public record as saying that he believed Italy was the target of subversion from abroad.

Although police reported a 30% drop in the number of terrorist incidents during the year, which resulted in 21 dead in comparison with 122 deaths the previous year, the activities of the Red Brigades urban guerrillas continued to gain headlines. The terrorists carried out five political kidnappings during the year, including that of the first foreigner to fall into the hands of terrorists in Italy, U.S. Brig. Gen. James Dozier, a senior NATO officer. Other hostages included factory managers, a Neapolitan politician, and the brother of a terrorist who turned state's evidence. Two victims were murdered; at year's end the fate of Dozier was unknown.

More than 100 people were tried and convicted on terrorism charges, and at one trial in Genoa

---

ITALY

Education. (1978–79) Primary, pupils 4,584,300; teachers 278,044; secondary, pupils 3,545,298, teachers 309,933; vocational, pupils 1,469,987, teachers 128,239; teacher training, students 217,962, teachers 20,057; higher (1977–78), students 756,922, teaching staff 43,120.

Finance. Monetary unit: lira, with (Sept. 21, 1981) a free rate of 1,134 lire to U.S. $1 (2,102 lire = £1 sterling). Gold and other reserves (June 1981) U.S. $20,063,000,000. Budget (1980 actual): revenue 91,-052,000,000,000 lire; expenditure 120,546,000,-000,000 lire. Gross national product (1980) 337,-482,000,000,000 lire. Money supply (April 1981) 165,662,000,000,000 lire. Cost of living (1975 = 100; June 1981) 250.3.

Foreign Trade. (1980) Imports 85,390,000,-000,000 lire; exports 66,724,000,000,000 lire. Import sources: EEC 44% (West Germany 17%, France 14%); U.S. 7%; Saudi Arabia 6%. Export destinations: EEC 49% (West Germany 18%, France 15%, U.K. 6%); U.S. 5%. Main exports: machinery 23%; motor vehicles 8%; chemicals 7%; clothing 6%; pe-

troleum products 5%; food 5%; textile yarns and fabrics 5%; iron and steel 5%; footwear 5%. Tourism (1979): visitors 21,918,000; gross receipts U.S. $8,185,000,000.

Transport and Communications. Roads (1980) 293,799 km (including 5,901 km expressways). Motor vehicles in use (1980): passenger c. 17.6 million; commercial c. 1.3 million. Railways: (1976) 19,923 km; traffic (1980) 38,901,000,000 passenger-km, freight 18,268,000,000 net ton-km. Air traffic (1980): 14,096,000,000 passenger-km; freight 542.1 million net ton-km. Shipping (1980): merchant vessels 100 gross tons and over 1,739; gross tonnage 11,095,694. Telephones (Jan. 1980) 18,085,000. Radio receivers (Dec. 1978) 13,401,000. Television licenses (Dec. 1978) 12,868,000.

Agriculture. Production (in 000; metric tons; 1980): wheat 9,291; corn 6,493; barley 958; oats 456; rice 911; potatoes 3,072; sugar, raw value c. 1,892; cabbages (1979) 603; cauliflowers (1979) 595; onions 463; tomatoes 5,023; grapes 12,830; wine 7,900; olives c. 3,124; oranges 1,830; mandarin oranges and

tangerines 355; lemons 802; apples 1,910; pears (1979) 1,030; peaches (1979) 1,230; tobacco 125; cheese 613; beef and veal c. 1,132; pork 1,067; fish catch (1979) 427. Livestock (in 000; Dec. 1979): cattle 8,719; sheep 9,110; pigs 8,807; goats 978; poultry c. 110,000.

Industry. Index of production (1975 = 100; 1980) 130. Unemployment (1980) 7.6%. Fuel and power (in 000; metric tons; 1980): lignite 1,798; crude oil 1,800; natural gas (cu m) 12,530,000; manufactured gas (cu m) 3,560,000; electricity (kw-hr) c. 188,500,-000. Production (in 000; metric tons; 1980): iron ore (44% metal content) 185; pig iron 12,410; crude steel 26,449; aluminum 267; zinc 206; cement 41,770; cotton yarn c. 190; man-made fibres 463; fertilizers (nutrient content; 1979–80) nitrogenous 1,524, phosphate 620, potash 118; sulfuric acid 2,819; plastics and resins 2,464; petroleum products c. 108,000; passenger cars (units) 1,445; commercial vehicles (units) 167. Merchant vessels launched (100 gross tons and over; 1980) 167,000 gross tons. New dwelling units completed (1979) 136,700.

prison sentences totaling 264 years were handed down to more than 30 defendants. The wheels of justice, however, continued to turn slowly, and little progress was recorded in bringing to justice those responsible for previous terrorist crimes, including the Red Brigades murder of former premier Aldo Moro in 1978 and the Bologna railway station massacre of 1980.

One of the worst political scandals in many years came to light with the publication on the orders of a Milan magistrate of 953 names of alleged members of a secret lodge of Freemasons called by its code name P2 and recruited by an Italo-Argentine businessman named Licio Gelli. It is an offense under Italian law for public servants to join secret societies, and there was great embarrassment in political and business circles when it was found that the list included several Cabinet ministers, junior ministers, senior members of the armed forces and of the police, heads of the secret service, diplomats, civil servants, prominent journalists, and bankers. Documents found with the membership list linked P2 with right-wing terrorist activities in the 1960s and 1970s as well as more recent scandals, including an oil tax evasion scandal uncovered in 1980. The subsequent political storm left no alternative to Premier Arnaldo Forlani but to hand in the resignation of his government, which he did on May 26.

Many senior public servants named in the list were suspended from their jobs or transferred, and President Pertini dismissed two members of his personal staff. Gelli himself had fled the country, and a warrant was issued for his arrest on charges of political espionage and currency offenses. He remained a mysterious figure, with connections to almost all of the powerful persons and institutions in Italy.

A new coalition of Christian Democrats, Republicans, Socialists, Social Democrats, and Liberals was sworn in on June 28. The new premier, Giovanni Spadolini, was the first non-Christian Democrat to head a coalition in the history of the Italian republic. His first act was to introduce a bill to dissolve the P2 secret society and to set up a parliamentary commission of inquiry into the affair.

Partial local elections were held on June 21–22. The results showed a 4% swing in favour of the Socialists, mainly at the expense of the ruling Christian Democrats, although the Communist Party also suffered losses.

A referendum on proposals to amend the controversial 1978 abortion law was held in May. A two-thirds majority of the electorate rejected proposals to make abortion either easier or more difficult to obtain. The result was interpreted as a defeat for the Roman Catholic Church, which had campaigned under instructions from the pope for a tightening up or abrogation of the existing law, which permits abortion during the first trimester of pregnancy more or less upon demand.

Reconstruction of the appalling devastation caused by the 1980 earthquake in southern Italy proceeded lethargically, and a year after the quake only half the promised 40,000 prefabricated homes had been built; moreover, because of the lack of

Giovanni Spadolini (left) signs papers confirming him as Italy's new premier in June. Pres. Alessandro Pertini is at right.

basic services, many of those had not been handed over to the homeless. The badly damaged city of Naples, many of its more beautiful monuments and palaces destroyed or trembling on the verge of destruction, was paralyzed by a prolonged local government crisis. More than 200 murders were reported in the city during 1981—an all-time record—as local crime snowballed in an atmosphere of tension, growing poverty, and heavy unemployment.

Police reported 52 kidnappings for ransom during the year. A typical case was that of Giuliano Ravizza, a wealthy fur merchant from Pavia who was kept blindfolded, had plugs in his ears, and was chained to a bed in a mountain hut in southern Italy for 93 days until his family paid a $5 million ransom. A "kidnap" of a different kind caused consternation in Venice, where the bones of St. Lucy, patron saint of opticians, were stolen from a church on November 7. The thieves demanded, unsuccessfully, a ransom of $200,000 from church authorities, who said they would not pay. Police recovered the relics on the saint's feast day, December 13, exactly 1,677 years after her martyrdom in Syracuse, Sicily.

A dramatic accident involving a six-year-old boy, Alfredo Rampi, who fell down a well shaft in the countryside near Rome on June 11, gripped the nation for two days and nights as rescue workers attempted unsuccessfully to haul the boy to the surface. The boy slipped farther down the shaft and was suffocated. It took more than a month to recover his body, and there was widespread criticism of the lack of preparedness in Italy for civil disasters, whatever their scale.

Foreign Relations. NATO foreign ministers meeting in Rome on May 4–5 decided to go ahead with plans to deploy nuclear-tipped cruise and Pershing missiles in Western Europe from 1983 and at the same time to seek nuclear force limitation talks with the Soviet Union. More than 100 of

Italian Literature: see Literature

the missiles were due to be deployed in Italy, and there were protests, encouraged by the Communist Party, against plans for the preparation of a large missile site at Comiso in Sicily.

During the year Italy's Communist Party, with 1.8 million card-carrying members the largest Communist organization in Western Europe and the second largest political party in Italy, reached a new low in its relations with the Soviet Union. Enrico Berlinguer, party secretary, said after the declaration of martial law in Poland that the period of European history that had begun with the Bolshevik Revolution had now come to an end. An unprecedented Communist Party policy statement accused the Soviet Union of using "sledgehammer" tactics against the Poles and said that the Soviet system had developed not into a commonwealth of equals but into an "ideological and military system governed by the logic of power."

The Economy. The lira was devalued twice within the European Monetary System, by 6% in March and by 3% in October, and the dollar/lira exchange rate reached an all-time high of 1,242.5 lire = U.S. $1. The year produced other records, including a huge monthly balance of payments deficit in May of 1,630,000,000,000 lire followed by a record balance of payments surplus in June of 2,300,000,000,000 lire after the imposition of a cash deposit requirement for imports.

In July trading on the Milan stock exchange was suspended for most of a week by the government after a sudden slump in stock prices. The last time that such a dramatic measure had been taken by the government was after a military defeat during World War I.

The growing recession was reflected by an estimated 40% fewer industrial strikes and by a doubling in the total paid to workers from a special government unemployment fund. The annual rate of inflation reached 19%, and zero economic growth was forecast. There was no evidence that the government was able to stem the continuing rise in public expenditure.

Italy's ailing chemical industry received an unexpected boost with an agreement between the Italian state oil company, ENI, and Occidental Petroleum Corp. of the U.S. to set up ENOXY, a $1,-050,000,000 joint venture to operate 60 chemical plants in Italy and 4 coal mines in the eastern U.S.

(DAVID DOUGLAS WILLEY)

Ivory Coast

Ivory Coast

Jamaica

A republic on the Gulf of Guinea, the Ivory Coast is bounded by Liberia, Guinea, Mali, Upper Volta, and Ghana. Area: 322,463 sq km (124,504 sq mi). Pop. (1981 est.): 8,574,800. Cap. and largest city: Abidjan (metro pop., 1981 est., 1,686,100). Language: French (official) and local dialects (Akan 41%, Kru 17%, Voltaic 16%, Malinke 15%, Southern Mande 10%). Religion: animist 65%; Muslim 23%; Christian 12%. President in 1981, Félix Houphouët-Boigny.

There was concern during 1981 over the health of 75-year-old Pres. Félix Houphouët-Boigny. He was obliged to cancel some engagements (includ-

---

IVORY COAST

Education. (1977–78) Primary, pupils 894,184, teachers 18,704; secondary, pupils 144,605, teachers (1976–77) 3,-423; vocational, pupils 22,437, teachers (1974–75) 620; higher (1978–79), students 20,087, teaching staff (1973–74) 368.

Finance. Monetary unit: CFA franc, with (Sept. 21, 1981) a parity of CFA Fr 50 to the French franc (free rate of CFA Fr 265 = U.S. $1; CFA Fr 491 = £1 sterling). Gold and other reserves (June 1981) U.S. $15 million. Budget (total; 1980 est.): revenue CFA Fr 601 billion; expenditure CFA Fr 591 billion. Money supply (Sept. 1980) CFA Fr 415,810,-000,000. Cost of living (Abidjan; 1975 = 100; May 1981) 238.5.

Foreign Trade. (1979) Imports CFA Fr 528,850,000,000; exports CFA Fr 534,850,000,000. Import sources: France 37%; U.S. 7%; Japan 6%; West Germany 5%; Venezuela 5%. Export destinations: France 24%; The Netherlands 17%; U.S. 10%; Italy 8%; West Germany 6%. Main exports: coffee 31%; cocoa and products 28%; timber 16%.

Agriculture. Production (in 000; metric tons; 1980): rice c. 550; corn (1979) c. 275; millet c. 47; yams (1979) c. 1,800; cassava (1979) c. 780; peanuts c. 59; bananas c. 200; plantains (1979) c. 800; pineapples c. 320; palm kernels c. 30; palm oil c. 170; coffee c. 200; cocoa c. 325; cotton, lint 54; rubber c. 22; fish catch (1979) c. 92; timber (cu m; 1979) 11,726. Livestock (in 000; 1979): cattle c. 650; sheep c. 1,150; goats c. 1,200; pigs c. 320; poultry c. 11,000.

Industry. Production (in 000; metric tons; 1978): petroleum products 1,551; cement (1977) 875; cotton yarn c. 7; diamonds (metric carats) c. 25; electricity (kw-hr; 1980) 1,830,000.

---

ing the North-South conference at Cancún, Mexico), but he was present at the Franco-African summit in Paris on November 3–4. Speculation continued as to who might succeed him. One possible indicator was the return to the political scene of former finance minister Henri Konan Bédié, who on Dec. 22, 1980, had replaced Philippe Yacé as president of the National Assembly. The number of possible successors was reduced by the accidental death in January 1981 of the health minister, Jean-Baptiste Mockey. Cabinet changes in February 1981 did not appear to affect the issue.

Houphouët-Boigny was the first African head of state to visit Pres. François Mitterrand after the latter's election. In March, following a raid on a coastal village, Ivory Coast police held 53 suspected smugglers, mostly from Ghana, in a small cell, with the result that 46 of them died of suffocation. Relations with Ghana became strained as a result, but they improved in April after a meeting of the countries' presidents.

Depressed cocoa prices affected Ivory Coast, the world's major producer, which declined to join the new International Cocoa Agreement. In September an oil-prospecting contract was signed with a consortium of U.S., French, and Italian companies.

(PHILIPPE DECRAENE)

Jamaica

A parliamentary state within the Commonwealth, Jamaica is an island in the Caribbean Sea about 145 km (90 mi) S of Cuba. Area: 10,991 sq km (4,244 sq mi). Pop. (1980 est.): 2,183,800, predominantly African and Afro-European, but including European, Chinese, Afro-Chinese, East Indian, Afro-East Indian, and others. Cap. and largest city: Kingston (metro pop., 1980 est., 671,000). Language: English. Religion: Christian, with Angli-

JAMAICA

Education. (1978–79) Primary, pupils 381,293, teachers 7,092; secondary, pupils 240,664, teachers (1976–77) 8,377; vocational (1976–77), pupils 5,321, teachers 355; higher, students 13,556, teaching staff (1973–74) 638.

Finance. Monetary unit: Jamaican dollar, with (Sept. 21, 1981) a par value of Jam$1.78 to U.S. $1 (free rate of Jam$3.30 = £1 sterling). Gold and other reserves (June 1981) U.S. $98 million. Budget (1978–79): revenue Jam$803 million; expenditure Jam$1,114,000,000.

Foreign Trade. (1980) Imports Jam$2,098,700,000; exports Jam$1,718,500,000. Import sources (1979): U.S. 32%; Venezuela 18%; Netherlands Antilles 12%; U.K. 10%; Canada 5%. Export destinations (1979): U.S. 45%; U.K. 19%; Canada 6%; Norway 5%. Main exports: alumina 56%; bauxite 21%; sugar 6%. Tourism (1978): visitors 382,-000; gross receipts U.S. $148 million.

Agriculture. Production (in 000; metric tons; 1980): sugar, raw value c. 269; bananas c. 175; oranges c. 32; grapefruit c. 30; sweet potatoes (1979) c. 22; yams (1979) c. 130; cassava (1979) c. 30; corn (1979) c. 15; copra c. 7. Livestock (in 000; 1979): cattle c. 290; goats c. 370; pigs c. 250; poultry c. 4,100.

Industry. Production (in 000; metric tons; 1979): bauxite 11,574; alumina 2,074; cement (1978) 294; gypsum 58; petroleum products (1978) 724; electricity (kw-hr; 1978) c. 2,124,000.

cans and Baptists in the majority. Queen, Elizabeth II; governor-general in 1981, Florizel Glasspole; prime minister, Edward Seaga.

Jamaica's new government (elected in October 1980) set to work in 1981 to try to rebuild the island's shattered economy. A three-year loan from the International Monetary Fund amounting to some $650 million was announced in April. The island also received substantial grants and loans from the U.S., Britain, Canada, Venezuela, Mexico, and several Western European nations. To emphasize renewed U.S. interest in the Caribbean and Central America, Pres. Ronald Reagan invited Prime Minister Edward Seaga to Washington, the first official visitor after Reagan's inauguration.

Tourism increased, but agriculture and manufacturing remained depressed. While the number of political murders fell, robbery with violence remained at pre-election levels. There was an upsurge in trade union activity. The government maintained, though in a more subdued form, the third world role promoted by former prime minister Michael Manley. Diplomatic relations with Cuba were broken in December.

Jamaican reggae singer Bob Marley died in May (*see* OBITUARIES). (DAVID A. JESSOP)

Japan

A constitutional monarchy in the northwestern Pacific Ocean, Japan is an archipelago composed of four major islands (Hokkaido, Honshu, Kyushu, and Shikoku), the Ryukyus (including Okinawa), and minor adjacent islands. Area: 377,682 sq km (145,824 sq mi). Pop. (1981 est.): 117,810,000. Cap. and largest city: Tokyo (pop., 1980 est., 8,349,000). Language: Japanese. Religion: primarily Shinto and Buddhist; Christian 0.8%. Emperor, Hirohito; prime minister in 1981, Zenko Suzuki.

Domestic Affairs. In December 1980 the Cabinet had completed an austerity budget for fiscal year 1981 (April 1981–March 1982) incorporating

expenditures of 46,790,000,000,000 yen. The budget provided the smallest expansion (9.9%) of outlay in 22 years and the largest tax increase in the country's history. The most controversial item was defense, which, despite a request (and U.S. pressure) for a 9.7% increase, came in at 7.61%, making total defense expenditure equivalent to 0.9% of Japan's gross national product (GNP). The opposition to the ruling Liberal-Democratic Party (LDP) singled out, for comparison, the smaller increase for social welfare (7.6%).

Japan

On March 12 the LDP had to push the budget through the budget committee of the lower house of the Diet without opposition participation in the vote. On March 14 the ruling party acceded to mediation, promising the opposition that it would consider a tax cut in the supplemental accounts, in order to assure passage of the budget in time for the new fiscal year. The LDP then turned to a package of stimulative economic measures designed to shake up the sluggish economy.

In June the number of unemployed totaled 1.2 million, a sharp 20% increase over the figure of a year earlier. Even so, the jobless rate (2.29%) represented a decline from the May level. Japanese real wages rose, reflecting a slowly falling inflation rate. In May the consumer price index for the city (ward) area of Tokyo recorded an increase of 4.8% from the year before to reach 144.6 (1975 = 100). This was the first time in 19 months that the annual inflation rate had been held below the 5% level.

Despite the evidences of stagflation, Japan's economy, led by brisk exports, grew by 5.1% (seasonally adjusted annual rate) during the April–June quarter. Nominal GNP came to 250,085,200,-000,000 yen ($1,087,000,000,000). One research institute estimated the GNP would grow at an average annual rate of 4.5% in real terms (as against 2% in the U.S. and 2.3% in the European Economic Community [EEC]) in the decade to 1990.

To buttress growth, the government on August 25 announced a multifaceted program designed to streamline Japan's bureaucracy and to cut the huge budget deficit. The plan was based on a series of recommendations submitted in July by an ad hoc commission headed by Toshio Doko, former president of the Federation of Economic Organizations (Keidanren). The aims were to cut government spending by more than 400 billion yen over a three-year period beginning April 1981 and to reduce the central administration by about 44,000 employees (5%) over a five-year period beginning in fiscal year 1982. Prime Minister Zenko Suzuki was quoted several times as saying that the future of his government rested on administrative reform.

Suzuki had emerged as the surprise, compromise leader of the LDP in July 1980, after the death of Prime Minister Masayoshi Ohira. Popular support for Suzuki as prime minister had declined in the April–June 1981 period, according to a Kyodo News Service survey, but a poll taken in September showed that the popularity of the Suzuki Cabinet had stabilized at a relatively high 46% of respondents. The ratio of those not supporting, or opposing, Suzuki had declined from 41.2 to 39.4%. Moreover, the LDP as a party was backed by a high

Jai Alai:
see Court Games

Protesters, jammed into small boats, circled the giant U.S. carrier "Midway" when it returned to the U.S. base at Yokosuka on June 5. They were demonstrating against the presence of nuclear weapons in Japanese waters.

ratio of 46.8% of voters, while the support rate for opposition parties dropped to 26.3% The proportion of those who supported no parties, however, rose to 23.3%

On September 21 two small centrist parties, the New Liberal Club (NLC, with 10 members in the lower house) and the Social Democratic Federation (Shaminren, with 3 members), combined to form a 13-member Diet strategy group. At that point the party lineup in the (lower) House of Representatives was as follows: LDP 287; Japan Socialist Party (JSP) 104; Clean Government Party (Komeito) 34; Democratic Socialist Party (DSP) 32; Japan Communist Party (JCP) 29; NLC/Shaminren (Shinjiren) 13; independents 7; vacancies 5 (total, 511). The makeup of the (upper) House of Councillors was: LDP 135; JSP 47; Komeito 26; DSP 12; JCP 12; Shinjiren 4; independents 15; vacancy 1 (total, 252).

In a major Cabinet reorganization in November, only 5 of the 20 members remained in their previous posts. Prime Minister Suzuki identified trade relations as a major problem facing the new Cabinet. Yoshio Sakurauchi was named foreign minister and Shintaro Abe, minister of international trade and industry.

The only important election scheduled in 1981 was held July 5 to fill the 127 seats in the Tokyo Metropolitan Assembly. It was heralded as a midterm assessment by greater Tokyo's eight million voters of the conservative administration of Gov. Shunichi Suzuki, who had won the 1979 gubernatorial election with the backing of the LDP, Komeito, and DSP. Despite the poor performance of the LDP (which dropped from 55 to 52 seats), the

conservative-centrist coalition retained a two-thirds majority in the assembly.

On April 29 Emperor Hirohito observed his 80th birthday, setting a record as the oldest active emperor in the history of the nation. Three of his most noted subjects died during the year. Fusae Ichikawa (see OBITUARIES), 87, a pioneer of Japan's equal rights movement since before World War II, died on February 11. The oldest parliamentarian in either house of the Diet, she had been reelected as an independent to the upper house in June 1980 with almost three million votes, the most received by any of the 50 candidates in the national constituency. In a eulogy, Prime Minister Suzuki called her Japan's "woman prime minister." On September 8 the physicist Hideki Yukawa (see OBITUARIES) died in Kyoto at the age of 74. He had been awarded the Nobel Prize for Physics in 1949 for his theoretical work predicting the existence of mesons, and he later became one of Japan's most prominent leaders of the movement to ban nuclear weapons. Suehiro Nishio (see OBITUARIES), a founder of the JSP and later of the DSP, died October 3 at the age of 90.

During 1981 one of every seven Japanese visited the Kobe Port Island Exposition (called Portopia '81), which ended a 180-day run on September 15. Thirty-seven nations and international organizations participated in the exhibition.

Foreign Affairs. On September 1 the government released what is commonly known as Japan's "Blue Book" on foreign affairs. The report promised that the nation would strive to carry out "comprehensive security measures" in an "increasingly

difficult international situation" marked by Soviet military expansionism. Japan would continue to rely on the U.S.-Japan security treaty, but at the same time it would make an effort to play a significant international role through diplomacy and economic cooperation with less developed nations.

The Tokyo-Washington axis, although it undergirded Prime Minister Suzuki's foreign policy, was subject to significant strains during 1981. The first source of friction was Japan's towering trade surplus vis-à-vis the U.S., specifically that from the export of automobiles. Japan's auto production for the January–June period reached a record 5,645,000 units, maintaining the nation's position as the world's biggest producer. In February it was reported that Japan's exports of four-wheeled vehicles in 1980 had also set a record of almost six million units (a 31% increase over 1979), representing more than half the total output. The U.S. remained the chief market, taking 2,407,000 units (16.1% more than in 1979).

Despite the final report of the Japan-U.S. Economic Relations Group (the "Wise Men's Group"), which was released in January and strongly supported the principle of free trade, the threat of U.S. protectionist legislation rose steadily. In a meeting with Pres. Ronald Reagan in Washington on March 24, Foreign Minister Masayoshi Ito told the new president that an early solution of the bilateral automobile trade issue must be found, preferably before the planned meeting between Reagan and Prime Minister Suzuki. Early in May the minister of international trade and industry, Rokusuke Tanaka, and U.S. trade representative William Brock reached agreement in Tokyo. Japan offered to reduce auto exports to the U.S. in fiscal year 1981 to 1,680,000 units, 7.7% below the 1980 level.

The second source of friction between Tokyo and Washington lay in the two governments' differing views on security and the defense of Japan. When a revised U.S.-Japan security treaty was signed in 1960, Washington assuaged Tokyo's concerns by a provision that "major changes in deployment" of U.S. forces would require "prior consultation." Japanese public opinion remained skeptical, however, and after Okinawa reverted to

Japanese control (1972), governments in Tokyo came to adopt the so-called three nonnuclear principles: Japan would not produce, possess, or allow nuclear arms to be "introduced" into its territory. Many Americans, particularly in the U.S. Congress, tended to link trade friction with what they called Japan's "free ride" in security. With the advent of the Reagan administration, pressure on Tokyo to increase its defense efforts mounted.

On April 9 the Polaris missile-bearing U.S. submarine "George Washington" rammed a Japanese freighter in the East China Sea. The Japanese were incensed over the sub's failure to rescue the 15-man crew (13 were saved by Japanese patrols) and over Washington's delay in notifying Tokyo of the incident. The U.S. Defense Department responded that it was not U.S. policy to reveal the location of nuclear weapons systems. On May 5, just before Suzuki's visit to Washington, U.S. Ambassador Mike Mansfield delivered a preliminary report to Foreign Minister Ito; later the U.S. accepted responsibility and "liability" for the accident.

Prime Minister Suzuki held talks with President Reagan in Washington May 7–8. Back in Tokyo, he came under fire because of discrepancies in the interpretation of the word alliance, used for the first time in the joint communiqué to describe the U.S.-Japanese relationship. On May 16 Foreign Minister Ito announced his resignation and assumed responsibility for the confusion; he was replaced by Sunao Sunoda. The prime minister repeated his earlier assurances that the term alliance lent no new military meaning to the U.S. tie. Foreign Ministry experts, however, maintained that an alliance without military implications was inconceivable.

Meanwhile, in mid-May Edwin O. Reischauer, a former U.S. ambassador to Japan, was widely quoted as citing a long-standing "verbal agreement" between the two countries. The U.S. had respected Japan's "nuclear allergy," Reischauer said, but U.S. ships carrying nuclear arms could enter Japan's territorial waters without prior consultation and, indeed, had called at Japanese ports. After some initial confusion, Prime Minister Suzuki took the position that the former ambassador was in error: passage or port calls would constitute

JAPAN

Education. (1981) Primary, pupils 11,924,706, teachers 473,957; secondary and vocational, pupils 9,982,110, teachers 506,198; higher, students 2,240,991, teaching staff 125,535.

Finance. Monetary unit: yen, with (Sept. 21, 1981) a free rate of 224 yen to U.S. $1 (416 yen = £1 sterling). Gold and other reserves (June 1981) U.S. $28.4 billion. Budget (1980–81 est.) balanced at 42,-589,000,000,000 yen. Gross national product (1980) 235,762,000,000,000 yen. Money supply (June 1981) 71,244,000,000,000 yen. Cost of living (1975 = 100; June 1981) 144.8.

Foreign Trade. (1980) Imports 31,995,000,-000,000 yen; exports 29,383,000,000,000 yen. Import sources: U.S. 17%; Saudi Arabia 14%; Indonesia 9%; United Arab Emirates 6%; Australia 5%. Export destinations: U.S. 25%. Main exports: machinery 27%; motor vehicles 23%; iron and steel 14%; instruments 9%; chemicals 8%; textiles 5%.

Transport and Communications. Roads (1980) 1,113,387 km (including 2,579 km expressways). Motor vehicles in use (1980): passenger 23,659,500;

commercial 13,948,500. Railways: (1979) 26,849 km; traffic (1980) 315,372,000,000 passenger-km, freight 39,585,000,000 net ton-km. Air traffic (1980): c. 51,-217,000,000 passenger-km; freight c. 2,002,000,000 net ton-km. Shipping (1980): merchant vessels 100 gross tons and over 10,568; gross tonnage 40,959,-683. Telephones (March 1980) 55,421,500. Radio receivers (Dec. 1977) 64,979,000. Television licenses (Dec. 1978) 28,394,000.

Agriculture. Production (in 000; metric tons; 1980): rice c. 12,189; wheat c. 583; barley c. 385; potatoes c. 3,200; sweet potatoes (1979) c. 1,400; sugar, raw value c. 749; onions c. 1,170; tomatoes c. 1,026; cabbages (1979) c. 4,170; cucumbers (1979) c. 1,150; aubergines (1979) c. 675; watermelons (1979) c. 1,263; apples c. 844; pears (1979) c. 502; oranges c. 387; mandarin oranges and tangerines c. 3,200; grapes c. 361; tea c. 108; tobacco c. 173; milk c. 6,502; eggs c. 1,999; pork 1,067; timber (cu m; 1979) c. 34,012; fish catch (1979) 9,966. Livestock (in 000; Feb. 1980): cattle c. 4,248; sheep c. 12; pigs c. 9,998; goats c. 71; chickens c. 294,825.

Industry. Index of production (1975 = 100; 1980) 142. Fuel and power (in 000; metric tons; 1980): coal 18,027; crude oil 433; natural gas (cu m) 2,197,000; manufactured gas (cu m) 8,190,000; electricity (kw-hr; 1979–80) 581,440,000. Production (in 000; metric tons; 1980): iron ore (54% metal content) 483; pig iron 88,908; crude steel 111,395; aluminum 1,091; copper 1,014; petroleum products c. 196,000; cement 87,957; cotton yarn 502; woven cotton fabrics (sq m) 2,202,000; man-made fibres 1,832; newsprint 2,674; sulfuric acid 6,777; caustic soda 3,157; plastics and resins 6,422; fertilizers (nutrient content; 1979–80) nitrogenous 1,493, phosphate c. 744; cameras (35 mm; units) 11,802; wrist and pocket watches (units) 86,233; radio receivers (units) 15,343; television receivers (units; 1979) 13,577; passenger cars (units) 7,038; commercial vehicles (units) 4,004. Merchant vessels launched (100 gross tons and over; 1980) 7,308,000 gross tons. New dwelling units started (1980) 1,483,000.

U.S. trade representative William Brock met in Tokyo in May with Japanese Prime Minister Zenko Suzuki to discuss the curtailing of exports of Japanese cars to the U.S. The Japanese agreed to reduce their automobile shipments to the United States.

"introduction" and would require prior consultation. Since the U.S. had never once asked for such permission, Japan continued to trust its ally to abide by Japan's nuclear policy. Nevertheless, public opinion surveys revealed that a majority of Japanese respondents continued to have doubts.

Relations between Tokyo and Moscow continued to be plagued by the "Northern Territories" issue. On February 7 Prime Minister Suzuki, speaking at a rally in Tokyo, stressed that the Soviet failure to return the Kuril Islands, northeast of Hokkaido, to Japan stood in the way of "peaceful and friendly relations" with the Soviets. A similar rally was held at Shimoda, where, 126 years before, a Russo-Japanese treaty had been signed acknowledging that the islands, occupied by the U.S.S.R. since World War II, were Japanese land. Moscow referred to the demonstrations as an "anti-Soviet campaign."

On September 11 Japan and South Korea ended two days of ministerial talks without reaching agreement on Seoul's request for $6 billion in economic aid. Japan stated that it "highly appreciated" South Korea's defense efforts, which contributed to the maintenance of security on the Korean Peninsula. A summit meeting between Prime Minister Suzuki and Pres. Chun Doo Hwan was promised for the future, but the timing remained indefinite.

After Japan normalized relations with the People's Republic of China in 1972 and concluded a peace treaty with that country in 1978, the mainland had seemed to offer Japanese business limitless opportunities. China was experiencing severe setbacks to its modernization program, however, and a sharp falloff in plant exports, the mainstay of Sino-Japanese trade, was the result. (*See* CHINA.)

During June 9–19 Prime Minister Suzuki made a six-nation tour of Western Europe, conferring with (among others) West German Chancellor Helmut Schmidt, U.K. Prime Minister Margaret Thatcher, Arnaldo Forlani, then heading a caretaker government in Italy, and Pres. François Mit-

terrand of France. Suzuki promised actions to ease problems caused by exports of Japanese autos and electronic goods in order to head off protectionist moves in the EEC.

The prime minister met the leaders of these same nations—plus those of Canada and the U.S.—at the summit meeting of advanced industrial democracies, held at Ottawa on July 20–21. On July 28 Suzuki informed his Cabinet that the summit had agreed to promote free trade and to cooperate in solving the North-South problems of development and revitalizing the world economy. The conferees had expressed concern about the Soviet military buildup. Japan, however, had promised only to continue its defense efforts according to its own judgment, on the basis of its own security policy and within the limits of the provision in its constitution renouncing war.

In an unprecedented and historic visit, Pope John Paul II was in Japan February 23–26 on what he called a Christian mission. To the emperor he offered praise of the nation as having a strong moral sense. In Hiroshima and Nagasaki, the pope called for abolition of all nuclear arms.

(ARDATH W. BURKS)

Jordan

A constitutional monarchy in southwest Asia, Jordan is bounded by Syria, Iraq, Saudi Arabia, and Israel. Area (including territory occupied by Israel in the June 1967 war): 95,396 sq km (36,833 sq mi). Pop. (excluding Israeli-occupied West Bank, 1979 prelim.): 2,152,300. Cap. and largest city: Amman (pop., 1979 prelim., 684,600). Language: Arabic. Religion (1973 est.): Muslim 95%; Christian 5%. King, Hussein I; prime minister in 1981, Mudar Badran.

Jordan's staunch support for Iraq in the Iran-Iraq war continued throughout 1981, providing an important stimulus to the economy. Jordan became one of Iraq's major suppliers, almost regardless of price. The war also boosted the transport sector;

Jordan

with the Iraqi Gulf coast exposed to bombing, most imports to Iraq in 1981 were routed through Aqaba, in Jordan, or Kuwait.

King Hussein's visit to the U.S. at the beginning of November somewhat dispelled the chill that had settled over U.S. relations with Jordan during the administration of former president Jimmy Carter. The king was warmly welcomed in Washington; the security of Jordan, Pres. Ronald Reagan stressed, was of critical importance to the U.S. The two leaders emerged from their talks with an agreement to discuss further the question of sales by the U.S. of air-defense systems to Jordan. However, President Reagan's major objective—to involve Jordan in the Camp David initiative toward peace in the Middle East—was not advanced. King Hussein continued to support a solution along the lines of the Saudi Arabian peace plan, which called for the Israelis to withdraw from all territories occupied during the 1967 war. While in Washington, the king confirmed that his country had, for the first time, agreed to buy arms from the U.S.S.R.

The economy continued to rely heavily on remittances by Jordanian expatriates working in oil-rich Persian Gulf countries. In 1980 only about 5,000 workers emigrated, but the level of remittances continued to be high. They had increased from $500 million in 1978 to $800 million in 1980. At home Jordan's economy presented a balanced picture, with high employment figures, annual growth in gross domestic product of about 10%, and a stable financial environment. Inflation, most of it imported, was running at 11% and was expected to be in single figures by the end of 1981.

An ambitious five-year development plan (1981–85), calling for total expenditure of about $10 billion, was approved by the Cabinet in October. Some 61% of investment spending was to be in the public sector and 39% in the private sector. The plan allocated the greatest share of investment to infrastructure development, industrial production, and the provision of social and public services. One of the most ambitious schemes proposed to meet Jordan's long-term water needs by drawing 160 million–250 million cu m (5,600,-

JORDAN
Education. (1979–80) Primary, pupils 448,411, teachers 13,898; secondary, pupils 238,763, teachers 11,267; vocational, pupils 9,880, teachers 641; higher, students 27,526, teaching staff 1,178.
Finance. Monetary unit: Jordanian dinar, with (Sept. 21, 1981) a free rate of 0.33 dinar to U.S. $1 (0.61 dinar = £1 sterling). Gold and other reserves (June 1981) U.S. $1,267,-000,000. Budget (1980 actual): revenue 439 million dinars (including foreign aid and loans of 215 million dinars); expenditure 500 million dinars. Gross national product (1980) 1,073,800,000 dinars. Money supply (June 1981) 696,660,000 dinars. Cost of living (1975 = 100; June 1981) 199.3.
Foreign Trade. (1980) Imports 716,110,000 dinars; exports 171,450,000 dinars. Import sources (1979): Saudi Arabia 13%; West Germany 12%; U.K. 8%; U.S. 7%; Italy 7%; Japan 6%; France 5%. Export destinations: Saudi Arabia 23%; Iraq 15%; Syria 15%; India 7%; Kuwait 5%; Turkey 5%. Main exports (1979): phosphates 22%; vegetables 14%; fruit 8%; chemicals 8%; machinery 5%; aircraft 5%. Tourism (1978): visitors 1,184,000; gross receipts c. U.S. $340 million.
Transport and Communications. Roads (excluding West Bank; 1980) 4,950 km. Motor vehicles in use (1980): passenger 90,400; commercial 27,400. Railways (1979) c. 618 km. Air traffic (1980): 2,607,000,000 passenger-km; freight 81.2 million net ton-km. Telephones (Jan. 1979) 52,400. Radio receivers (Dec. 1977) 532,000. Television licenses (Dec. 1977) 165,000.
Agriculture. Production (in 000; metric tons; 1979): wheat 15; barley 5; tomatoes 172; eggplants c. 64; watermelons c. 28; olives 7; oranges c. 13; lemons c. 9; grapes c. 31. Livestock (in 000; 1979): cattle 33; goats c. 382; sheep c. 875; camels c. 10; asses c. 50; chickens c. 5,846.
Industry. Production (in 000; metric tons; 1979): phosphate rock 2,845; petroleum products 1,423; cement 623; electricity (kw-hr) 901,000.

000,000–8,800,000,000 cu ft) of water a year from the Euphrates River in Iraq. The project was to involve the building of a 650-km (400-mi) pipeline, pumping stations, and associated works at a total cost estimated at $1.5 billion. The emphasis in industrial development shifted toward light manufacturing. Jordan's high fuel bill caused the nation to have a deficit in its balance of trade and thus injected a sense of urgency into efforts to develop alternative energy sources.

Jordan's impressive economic performance was made possible by the large inflow of foreign aid, which, mainly in the form of direct grants from

Jordan's King Hussein (right) was greeted in Moscow by Soviet Pres. Leonid Brezhnev when Hussein visited the Soviet Union in May.

WIDE WORLD

Arab countries, totaled more than $1.3 billion a year. The Baghdad Arab summit conference (November 1978) had produced a commitment to provide Jordan with $1.2 billion a year for ten years. Although there were some delays in carrying out this aid program, by 1981 the deficit had been paid up. This new-found stability in aid payments helped Jordan to increase its public-sector expenditure. Aid commitments made from Arab funds during 1981 included $53 million from the Kuwait Fund for Arab Economic Development, to finance in part the Jordan River irrigation project and the Amman water-supply project, and $176 million from the Iraqi government for development plans. In addition, Jordan's stable economy attracted the attention of pan-Arab investment banks. (JOHN WHELAN)

See also Middle Eastern Affairs.

Kampuchea

Kampuchea

A republic of Southeast Asia, Kampuchea (formerly Cambodia) is the southwest part of the Indochinese Peninsula, on the Gulf of Thailand, bordered by Vietnam, Laos, and Thailand. Area: 181,035 sq km (69,898 sq mi). Pop. (1981): 5,746,-100. It is estimated to comprise: Khmer 93%; Vietnamese 4%; Chinese 3%. Cap.: Phnom Penh (urban area pop., 1981 est., 500,000). Language: Khmer (official) and French. Religion: Buddhist. Secretaries-general of the People's Revolutionary (Communist) Party of Kampuchea in 1981, Pen Sovan from May 29 and, from December 5, Heng Samrin; president of the Council of Ministers (premier) from June 27, Pen Sovan; president of the People's Revolutionary Council and, from June 27, president of the Council of State, Heng Samrin.

Further attempts at consolidation by the Vietnamese-backed government of Pres. Heng Samrin

In a well-orchestrated election, Kampucheans cast ballots for local officials in March. The elections were organized by the Vietnamese-backed administration in Phnom Penh.

WIDE WORLD

Journalism:
see Publishing

Judaism:
see Religion

Judo:
see Combat Sports

and fractious feuding among the resistance forces opposed to it highlighted 1981. The Phnom Penh regime made its intentions clear in March when it announced that elections to a new National Assembly would be held in 20 sectors on the basis of a universal, direct, secret, and mandatory franchise. It explained, however, that only candidates put up by the Kampuchean United Front for National Salvation would be allowed to contest the 117 seats. The election was held on May 1. Radio Hanoi reported that 99% of the country's 3.5 million voters participated and that Heng Samrin was returned with 99.75% of the vote.

In June the new National Assembly adopted a draft constitution and elected the country's collective leadership. Strong man Pen Sovan was named premier, heading a 17-member Council of Ministers. Heng Samrin became head of a seven-member Council of State and thus, automatically, titular head of state and commander in chief.

As part of its consolidation process, the ruling group revealed in May that the official name of its party was the People's Revolutionary Party of Kampuchea. At a 162-delegate congress held in the capital that month, Pen Sovan was named to the powerful post of secretary-general, with Heng Samrin and Hun Sen as the other top party leaders. In a surprise move in December, however, Pen Sovan was replaced as secretary-general by Heng Samrin, allegedly for health reasons.

The moves by the nationalist Communists to entrench themselves in Phnom Penh seemed to make their chief adversary, China, step up its own countermoves. It became clear early in the year that Beijing (Peking) was increasing its military supplies to the Khmer Rouge, Pol Pot's Communist group, which had been driven from power in 1979. In May China formally gave notice that it would give similar aid to all "patriotic" forces in Kampuchea.

That position was seen as part of China's bid to get the former head of state, Prince Norodom Sihanouk, to cooperate with the Khmer Rouge. Sihanouk had maintained that the Vietnamese were preferable to the Khmer Rouge, whom he described as "butchers" because of their genocidal past. But in September, under continuing pressure from China and its allies, Sihanouk traveled to Singapore for a summit with Khieu Samphan, representing the Khmer Rouge, and Son Sann, leader of the staunchly anti-Communist Khmer People's National Liberation Front.

The three sides agreed to form a combined military council and to study the possibility of a coalition government, but it was clear that the participants themselves did not expect much from their agreement. Effective coordination on the military front proved beyond the reach of the summiteers because of their suspicions of one another. Within a month even the semblance of an agreement fell apart. As representatives of the three sides met in Bangkok, Thailand, for their first negotiations, the Khmer Rouge radio denied that the summit had agreed on Son Sann as premier. Earlier, Sihanouk had said that Son Sann was chosen for the premier's post at Khmer Rouge request.

KAMPUCHEA

Education. (1979–80) pupils 515,400, teachers *c.* 12,000 (figures are for Vietnamese-controlled areas of Cambodia).

Finance. Monetary unit: riel, with (end 1980) a reported free rate of 4 new riels to U.S. $1 (10 riels = £1 sterling). Budget (1974 est.): revenue 23 billion old riels; expenditure 71 billion old riels.

Foreign Trade. (1979) Imports *c.* U.S. $150 million; exports *c.* U.S. $2 million. Import sources (1973): U.S. *c.* 69%; Thailand *c.* 11%; Singapore *c.* 5%; Japan *c.* 5%. Export destinations (1973): Hong Kong *c.* 23%; Japan *c.* 22%; Malaysia *c.* 18%; France *c.* 12%; Spain *c.* 10%. Main export (1973): rubber 93%.

Transport and Communications. Roads (1976) *c.* 11,000 km. Motor vehicles in use: passenger (1972) 27,200; commercial (including buses; 1973) 11,000. Railways: (1978) *c.* 600 km; traffic (1973) 54,070,000 passenger-km, freight 9,780,000 net ton-km. Air traffic (1977): 42 million passenger-km; freight 400,000 net ton-km. Inland waterways (including Mekong River; 1979) *c.* 1,400 km. Telephones (Dec. 1975) 71,000. Radio receivers (Dec. 1975) 110,000. Television receivers (Dec. 1977) 35,000.

Agriculture. Production (in 000; metric tons; 1980): rice *c.* 1,000; corn *c.* 50; bananas *c.* 65; oranges (1979) *c.* 20; dry beans (1979) *c.* 12; rubber *c.* 10; tobacco *c.* 5; jute (1979) *c.* 3. Livestock (in 000; 1980): cattle *c.* 810; buffalo *c.* 400; pigs *c.* 600.

Although there was little hope that the resistance would gain momentum with the Chinese-backed Khmer Rouge at its helm, the ousted regime continued to enjoy diplomatic recognition at the UN. In a UN General Assembly vote in September to decide the issue, 77 nations backed the Khmer Rouge, 37 opposed it, and 31 abstained. In December the New China News Agency announced that the Pol Pot regime's Communist Party organization was disbanding, a move some observers saw as an effort to gain respectability. The insurgency, however, was to continue.

(T. J. S. GEORGE)

Kenya

An African republic and a member of the Commonwealth, Kenya is bordered on the north by Sudan and Ethiopia, east by Somalia, south by Tanzania, and west by Uganda. Area: 580,367 sq km (224,081 sq mi), including 11,230 sq km of inland water. Pop. (1981 est.): 16,572,300, including (1969) African 98.1%; Asian 1.5%. Cap. and largest city: Nairobi (pop., 1979 prelim., 835,000). Language: Swahili (official) and English. Religion: Protestant 32.6%; Roman Catholic 17.4%; Muslim 24%; other, mostly indigenous, 26%. President in 1981, Daniel arap Moi.

In January 1981 Pres. Daniel arap Moi of Kenya held discussions with Pres. Milton Obote of Uganda, Pres. Julius Nyerere of Tanzania, and Pres. Kenneth Kaunda of Zambia. As a result of this and several subsequent meetings, the countries of eastern Africa committed themselves to closer cooperation; later in the year Moi, Nyerere, and Obote agreed to open discussions on the distribution of the assets of the former East African Community (a common market formed by the three countries). It was hoped that improving relations might lead to the reopening of the Kenya-Tanzania border.

As chairman of the Organization of African Unity (OAU) from June 1981, President Moi played a prominent role in moves to restore peace in the Western Sahara. In August he chaired an OAU committee set up to find a solution to the conflict. The committee consulted the leaders of Morocco, Algeria, Mauritania, and the Popular Front for the Liberation of Saguia el Hamra and Río de Oro (Polisario Front). They agreed on a program involving a cease-fire and the deployment of an OAU and UN peacekeeping force to support an interim administration that would organize a referendum in the disputed area. In June Moi presided over an OAU summit meeting in Nairobi.

A shortfall in the country's main food crop, corn (maize), led to an agreement under which Kenya received 70,000 tons of corn from the U.S. in February and March. Early in February Kenya's currency was devalued by 5%, and in March a central bank order required all Kenyan citizens with assets abroad to transfer them to Kenya by the end of the year. Meanwhile, the population of Turkana, suffering as a result of prolonged drought, disease, and raids by neighbouring tribes, was sustained by a relief system organized by the European Economic Community. Despite these problems, confidence in Kenya's economy was reflected in the decision of the Hong Kong Trade Development Council to open a new office in Nairobi, its first in Africa, to develop trade with African countries.

In March two Kenyans faced treason charges in connection with an alleged plot to overthrow President Moi. During the preliminary hearing, Charles Njonjo, minister of home and constitutional affairs, was linked with the alleged conspiracy. In his testimony, Njonjo denied any involvement. When the case was heard before the

KENYA

Education. (1978) Primary, pupils 2,977,000, teachers (1977) 89,773; secondary and vocational, pupils 368,000, teachers (1977) 12,696; teacher training, students 9,000, teachers (1977) 672; higher (universities only, 1977), students 5,837, teaching staff 892.

Finance. Monetary unit: Kenyan shilling, with (Sept. 21, 1981) a free rate of KShs 10.15 to U.S. $1 (KShs 18.82 = £1 sterling). Gold and other reserves (June 1981) U.S. $336 million. Budget (1979–80 actual): revenue KShs 12,508,000,000; expenditure KShs 13,839,000,000. Gross national product (1979) KShs 43,887,000,000. Cost of living (Nairobi; 1975 = 100; May 1981) 199.7.

Foreign Trade. (1980) Imports KShs 17,288,000,000; exports KShs 10,276,000,000. Import sources (1979): U.K. 23%; West Germany 11%; Saudi Arabia 8%; Japan 8%; U.S. 6%; Qatar 5%. Export destinations (1979): West Germany 15%; U.K. 14%; Uganda 9%; aircraft and ship stores 8%; Italy 6%. Main exports (1979): coffee 29%; petroleum products 20%; tea 16%; fruit and vegetables 6%; chemicals 5%. Tourism (1978): visitors 360,620; gross receipts U.S. $158 million.

Transport and Communications. Roads (1980) 50,960 km. Motor vehicles in use (1979): passenger 118,035; commercial 111,048. Railways: (1979) 2,645 km; freight traffic (1977) 3,538,000,000 net ton-km. Air traffic (1980): 863 million passenger-km; freight *c.* 20.3 million ton-km. Telephones (Jan. 1980) 168,200. Radio receivers (Dec. 1977) 525,000. Television receivers (Dec. 1977) 60,000.

Agriculture. Production (in 000; metric tons; 1980): corn *c.* 1,450; wheat *c.* 210; millet *c.* 130; potatoes *c.* 360; sweet potatoes (1979) *c.* 340; cassava (1979) *c.* 630; sugar, raw value (1979) *c.* 250; bananas *c.* 135; coffee *c.* 85; tea *c.* 87; sisal 31; cotton, lint *c.* 13; fish catch (1979) 52. Livestock (in 000; 1979): cattle *c.* 10,600; sheep *c.* 4,000; pigs 75; goats *c.* 4,500; camels *c.* 550; chickens *c.* 17,500.

Industry. Production (in 000; metric tons; 1979): cement 970; soda ash (1978) 153; petroleum products *c.* 2,050; electricity (kw-hr) *c.* 1,500,000.

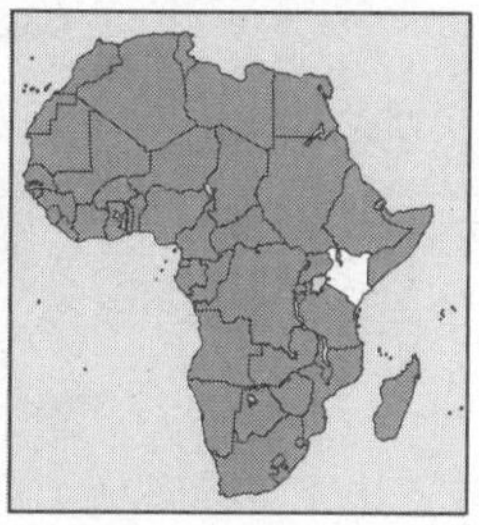

Kenya

Karate:
see Combat Sports

Kashmir:
see India; Pakistan

Kendo:
see Combat Sports

Prime Minister Indira Gandhi of India
was welcomed by Pres. Daniel arap
Moi when Gandhi visited Kenya.

high court in May, the two accused men were acquitted.

In April former vice-president Oginga Odinga was again rejected by the ruling Kenya African National Union party as a by-election candidate. The ban followed Odinga's public statement describing the late Pres. Jomo Kenyatta as a "land grabber." Odinga's failure to be selected provoked widespread anger.

Early in May several hundred physicians in government hospitals went on strike in support of demands for higher pay and better working conditions. Some 20 of them were arrested. Students at the University of Nairobi then demonstrated against the arrests and also condemned the ban on Odinga. Police broke up the demonstration, and on May 18 the university was closed.

Speaking on June 1, Moi said that recent events did not suggest that Kenya had lost direction but only that a few people had been involved in sedition, corruption, and strikes. In an earlier speech in March he condemned the policy of racial separation in South Africa but also stressed that he was far from happy, as an African, with what was going on in the continent at large.

On Dec. 31, 1980, a bomb had exploded in one of Nairobi's leading hotels, killing about 15 people. By the end of 1981 no one had been charged with the crime. (KENNETH INGHAM)

Kiribati

An independent republic in the western Pacific Ocean and a member of the Commonwealth, Kiribati comprises the former Gilbert Islands, Banaba (Ocean Island), the Line Islands, and the Phoenix Islands. Area: 690 sq km (266 sq mi). Pop. (1980 est.): 58,500, including Micronesian 91%, Polynesian 4%, other indigenous 4%, others 1%. Cap.: Bairiki (pop., 1979 est., 1,800) on Tarawa atoll (pop., 1980 est., 22,100). Language: English (official). Religion (1973): Roman Catholic 48%;

Kiribati

Protestant 45%. President (*beriti-tenti*) in 1981, Ieremia Tabai.

In 1981 Kiribati faced worsening economic problems. Prices for copra, the mainstay of the rural economy, continued to fall. Despite an injection of more than A$1 million in an attempt to stabilize prices, payments to growers were reduced. The government also lost support over the dismissal, after a strike, of more than a hundred labourers. The powerful labourers' union called unsuccessfully for an international trade boycott of Kiribati. In May the government was challenged over these and other issues, but a no-confidence motion was defeated by 22 votes to 12.

In April the former inhabitants of Banaba accepted A$10 million from Britain, Australia, and New Zealand as compensation for the phosphate mining of their homeland. Banaba's future remained undecided. The Banabans wished the island to become independent and to exist in free association with Fiji, where many Banabans lived.

In August Pres. Ieremia Tabai attended the South Pacific Forum in Vanuatu. In October he was among the island leaders attending the Commonwealth heads of government meeting in Melbourne, Australia, who secured recognition of the special problems faced by the small countries of Oceania. (BARRIE MACDONALD)

KIRIBATI

Education. (1978) Primary, pupils 13,481, teachers 429; secondary, pupils 873, teachers 92; vocational, pupils 1,- 176, teachers (1977) 28; teacher training, students (1979) 114, teachers (1978) 15.

Finance and Trade. Monetary unit: Australian dollar, with (Sept. 21, 1981) a free rate of A$0.86 to U.S. $1 (A$1.60 = £1 sterling). Budget (1978 est): revenue A$14 million; expenditure A$11 million. Foreign trade (1979): imports A$15,545,000; exports: A$21,028,000. Import sources (1978): Australia 58%; U.K. 8%; New Zealand 8%; Japan 7%; U.S. 6%. Export destinations (1977): Australia 57%; New Zealand 29%; U.K. 13%. Main exports: phosphates 88%; copra 12%.

Industry. Production (in 000): phosphate rock (metric tons; 1979) *c.* 446; electricity (kw-hr; 1978) *c.* 5,000.

Korea

A country of eastern Asia, Korea is bounded by China, the Sea of Japan, the Korea Strait, and the Yellow Sea. It is divided into two parts roughly at the 38th parallel.

The settling in of the Republican Party administration in the U.S. and of Pres. Chun Doo Hwan's government in South Korea seemed to decide the course and temper of events in Korea in 1981. Both put the North Koreans into a belligerent mood, which in turn provoked the South Koreans into equally indignant polemics. The recriminations reached their highest pitch in May and June. Throughout May the North held rallies of college students, industrial workers, military personnel, and the general public. Numerous statements were issued by different segments of society condemning the South and its U.S. backers. The objective of the campaign was to publicize the reasonableness of North Korea's unification policy and to cement unity around Pres. Kim Il Sung and his son, Kim Chong Il, who remained in charge of the Central Committee of the Workers' Party of Korea.

The South Koreans staged their most militant demonstrations against the North in June on the occasion of the 31st anniversary of the start of the Korean War. At a mammoth rally in Seoul, unofficially estimated at 1.5 million to 2 million strong, speeches and placards roundly condemned the North. Effigies of Kim Il Sung and Kim Chong Il were burned. Analysts said that the anniversary was emphasized in 1981 because the authorities wanted the postwar generation to appreciate the agony of the war and understand the reasons for the continuing confrontation with the North.

Republic of Korea (South Korea). Area: 98,966 sq km (38,211 sq mi). Pop. (1980 prelim.): 37,448,-800. Cap. and largest city: Seoul (pop., 1980 pre-lim., 8,366,800). Language: Korean. Religion (1979): Buddhist 38.7%; Christian 19%; Confucian 13.1%; Tonghak (Chondokyo) 3%; other 26.2%. President in 1981, Chun Doo Hwan; prime minister, Nam Duck Woo.

The year opened for South Korea with the announcement that Pres. Chun Doo Hwan was to become the first Asian leader to visit U.S. Pres. Ronald Reagan in Washington, D.C. Chun was known to have long lobbied for such a visit, but the jailing in 1980 of the country's most celebrated political prisoner, Kim Dae Jung, had remained a serious obstacle. In January, soon after South Korea's supreme court confirmed Kim's much-protested death sentence on sedition charges, Chun exercised his presidential prerogative to commute the sentence to life imprisonment. At the same time he officially lifted the martial law that had been decreed in October 1979 following the assassination of Pres. Park Chung Hee.

With the air thus cleared, Chun arrived in the U.S. at the end of January. It was immediately evident that President Reagan's administration was determined to stand unequivocally behind South Korea, with all previous talk of troop withdrawals completely forgotten. A joint statement issued by the two presidents said that they would resume their joint security committee, which last met in the autumn of 1979, economic collaboration, and annual political consultations. Reagan affirmed that "the U.S., as a Pacific power, will seek to ensure the peace and security of the region" while also supporting "the efforts of South Korea to resume a constructive dialogue with North Korea in order to build the framework for peaceful reunification." The statement stressed that the U.S. would sell South Korea all weapons necessary to "strengthen its ability to resist aggression." Amid reports that U.S.-South Korean military cooperation would now reach record levels, a high U.S. Department of State official said that it was neces-

Korea

Seoul's Mayor Park Young Su was exultant when the International Olympic Committee announced in September in Baden-Baden, West Germany, that the South Korean capital had been chosen as the site of the 1988 Olympic Summer Games.

sary to increase military aid to South Korea because the North's forces outnumbered those of the South.

Chun returned to the theme of peace when he called on UN Secretary-General Kurt Waldheim in New York City and asked him to use his good offices to improve relations between the two Koreas. Chun suggested that both countries be admitted to the UN. The otherwise successful visit was marred only by scuffles between opposing groups of Koreans in Los Angeles and by complaints from Korean residents in New York City that they had been pressed by their (Korean) companies to appear with their families at welcoming ceremonies for Chun at the airport.

Chun's image-boosting U.S. visit provided a favourable backdrop to South Korea's presidential elections in February. Voters chose a 5,278-member electoral college, which, in turn, elected the country's president. Under new constitutional provisions the president was to hold office for only one seven-year term. There was never any doubt about the result. Of 17 registered political parties, only 4 fielded candidates for the electoral college and the subsequent presidential vote. Along with Chun's Democratic Justice Party, these were the Democratic Korea Party, the Korean National Party, and the Civil Rights Party. The Democratic Justice Party won an easy victory, gaining 70% of the seats in the college. In the presidential poll that followed, Chun obtained 90.2% of the votes.

To mark his formal inauguration on March 3, Chun announced an amnesty for 5,221 political opponents "to remove the unhappy legacy of the old era." But the list did not include the best-known dissidents; Chun had made it clear that there would be no amnesty for what he called left-wing elements and political outcasts. At the inauguration, Chun warned that there was "no substitute for national security" and then outlined four national goals: a viable democracy, a welfare state, a just society, and innovative education and culture.

After elections in March to the National Assembly, the Democratic Justice Party emerged with 151 seats. Under electoral law no party could hold more than 153 of the total of 276 seats.

The newly inaugurated president gave a clear indication of his priorities when, in June–July, he undertook the first tour by a Korean head of state of the Association of Southeast Asian Nations. He told his hosts of the dawn of a "Great Pacific Age" and how, if North Korea tried any adventurous provocation, it "will be reduced to ashes." But business was the main item on his agenda. In Thailand, Malaysia, and the Philippines, in particular, he sought double-taxation and investment-guarantee treaties and most-favoured-nation status in selected areas of trade.

Having experienced a negative growth rate in 1980, South Korea was well on the way to its accustomed economic buoyancy in 1981. Wage increases were fixed at 10–15% against 30% the previous year. A currency reform was introduced in 1980 with a 20% devaluation of the won followed by a floating of the currency, which resulted in a total devaluation of about 36% for that year. The real growth in gross domestic product for 1981 was expected to be about 4–5%.

Democratic People's Republic of Korea (North Korea). Area: 121,929 sq km (47,077 sq mi). Pop. (1981 est.): 18,348,000. Cap.: Pyongyang (metro. pop., 1976 est., 1.5 million). Language: Korean. Religion: Buddhist; Confucian; Tonghak (Chondokyo). General secretary of the Central Committee of the Workers' (Communist) Party of Korea and president in 1981, Marshal Kim Il Sung; chairman of the Council of Ministers (premier), Li Jong Ok.

Angry international posturings and confident domestic maneuverings characterized North Korea during 1981. Relations with the U.S. became

---

KOREA: Republic

Education. (1980–81) Primary, pupils 5,586,494, teachers 122,727; secondary, pupils 3,580,258, teachers 87,974; vocational, students 827,579, teachers 25,573; higher, students 734,900, teaching staff 23,750.

Finance. Monetary unit: won, with (Sept. 21, 1981) a free rate of 679 won to U.S. $1 (1,259 won = £1 sterling). Gold and other reserves (June 1981) U.S. $2,451,000,000. Budget (1980 actual): revenue 6,833,200,000,000 won; expenditure 6,467,600,000,000 won. Gross national product (1980) 35,031,000,000,000 won. Money supply (June 1981) 3,712,000,000,000 won. Cost of living (1975 = 100; June 1981) 276.1.

Foreign Trade. (1980) Imports 13,548,300,000,000 won; exports 10,636,600,000,000 won. Import sources: Japan 26%; U.S. 22%; Saudi Arabia 15%; Kuwait 8%. Export destinations: U.S. 26%; Japan 17%; Saudi Arabia 5%; West Germany 5%; Hong Kong 5%. Main exports (1979): clothing 19%; textile yarns and fabrics 12%; electrical machinery and equipment 12%; iron and steel 7%; transport equipment 7%; fish 5%; footwear 5%. Tourism (1978): visitors 1,079,000; gross receipts U.S. $408 million.

Transport and Communications. Roads (1980) 46,951 km (including 1,225 km expressways). Motor vehicles in use (1980): passenger 249,100; commercial 226,900. Railways (1980): c. 5,800 km; traffic c. 20,780,000,000 passenger-km, freight 10,548,000,-000 net ton-km. Air traffic (1980): 10,833,000,000 passenger-km; freight 850.3 million net ton-km. Shipping (1980): merchant vessels 100 gross tons and over 1,426; gross tonnage 4,344,114. Telephones (Jan. 1980) 2,898,700. Radio receivers (Dec. 1977) 14,574,000. Television receivers (Dec. 1978) 5,133,000.

Agriculture. Production (in 000; metric tons; 1980): rice c. 6,000; barley 811; potatoes c. 446; sweet potatoes (1979) 1,328; soybeans 216; cabbages (1979) c. 1,034; watermelons (1979) c. 202; onions c. 402; apples 410; oranges c. 146; tobacco 92; fish catch (1979) 2,162. Livestock (in 000; Dec. 1978): cattle 1,651; pigs 1,719; goats 224; chickens 40,753.

Industry. Production (in 000; metric tons; 1980): coal 18,545; iron ore (56% metal content) 488; pig iron 5,685; crude steel 5,789; cement 15,631; tungsten concentrates (oxide content; 1979) 3.4; zinc concentrates 56; gold (troy oz; 1979) 24; silver (troy oz; 1979) 2,278; sulfuric acid 1,683; fertilizers (nutrient content; 1979–80) nitrogenous 838, phosphate 489; petroleum products c. 23,900; man-made fibres 579; electricity (excluding most industrial production; kw-hr) 37,239,000; radio receivers (units; 1979) 4,772; television receivers (units; 1979) 5,867. Merchant vessels launched (100 gross tons and over; 1980) 626,000.

KOREA: People's Democratic Republic

Education. (1976–77) Primary, pupils 2,561,674; secondary and vocational, pupils c. 2 million; primary, secondary, and vocational, teachers c. 100,000; higher, students c. 100,000.

Finance and Trade. Monetary unit: won, with (Sept. 21, 1981) a nominal exchange rate of 0.95 won to U.S. $1 (1.76 won = £1 sterling). Budget (1980 est.) balanced at 18,894,000,000 won. Foreign trade (approximate; 1980): imports c. 2.2 billion won; exports c. 2 billion won. Import sources: China c. 32%; U.S.S.R. c. 20%; Japan c. 17%. Export destinations: China c. 35%; U.S.S.R. c. 22%; Saudi Arabia c. 12%; Japan c. 9%. Main exports (1975): lead and ore c. 30%; zinc and ore c. 20%; magnesite c. 15%; rice c. 6%; cement c. 5%; coal c. 5%; fish c. 5%.

Agriculture. Production (in 000; metric tons; 1980): rice c. 4,800; corn c. 2,200; barley c. 380; millet c. 440; potatoes c. 1,550; sweet potatoes (1979) c. 450; soybeans c. 340; apples c. 460; tobacco c. 45; fish catch (1979) c. 1,330. Livestock (in 000; 1979): cattle c. 925; pigs c. 2,000; sheep c. 285; goats c. 230; chickens c. 17,850.

Industry. Production (in 000; metric tons; 1978): coal c. 45,000; lignite c. 10,500; iron ore (metal content) c. 3,800; pig iron c. 3,300; steel c. 3,200; lead ore c. 105; zinc ore c. 140; magnesite c. 1,500; silver (troy oz) c. 1,600; tungsten concentrates (oxide content) c. 2.7; cement c. 7,000; electricity (kw-hr) c. 32,000,000.

notably acerbic because of Pyongyang's belief that the Reagan administration would pursue a more "vicious" Korean policy. In January the government condemned the policy approach of U.S. Secretary of State Alexander Haig, which it saw as provocative and ill-intentioned. In February North Korea called a meeting of the military armistice commission in Panmunjom to protest the U.S.-South Korean joint military exercise then under way. The annual U.S.-South Korea security consultative meeting was condemned in May as "dangerous war conspiracy."

Outbursts of indignation greeted reports in July that the U.S. had decided to deploy new medium-range nuclear missiles in the South. Official sources described it as "a reckless move to perfect preparations for a nuclear war against the North." For his part, the U.S. military commander in South Korea, Gen. John Wickham, said in July that the North still presented a major threat as it continued "its tactics of harassment, sending armed teams into the South for reconnaissance, subversion, and organization of potential guerrilla networks." But in spite of all the charges and countercharges, Pres. Kim Il Sung used an interview with a Chinese correspondent in April to renew his call for a peace treaty with the U.S.

Nothing of the sound and fury of foreign relations was allowed to affect the controlled tenor of domestic affairs. Elections to the provincial people's assemblies were held in March with what officials described as a 100% turnout of eligible voters and 100% support for the candidates. In all, 3,705 deputies to the provincial people's assemblies and 24,191 to city and county people's assemblies were chosen.

In February the official Central News Agency claimed a significant increase in people's income. The per capita income in 1980, it said, averaged $1,920. In the ten years to 1980, the real income of factory and office workers had grown 2.2 times and that of farmers, 2.3 times. The average life span of North Koreans, compared with pre-liberation times, had lengthened by 35 years to 73 years, the agency said.

The budget for 1981, presented to the Supreme People's Assembly in April, envisioned total expenditure of $11.6 billion, of which military expenditure accounted for 14.7% (South Korean officials argued that actual military spending had to be 30.9% for the North to maintain its existing military power). The budget showed an increase of 7% in revenues over the previous year and a rise of 8.7% in spending. (T. J. S. GEORGE)

Kuwait

An independent constitutional monarchy (emirate), Kuwait is on the northwestern coast of the Persian Gulf between Iraq and Saudi Arabia. Area: 16,918 sq km (6,532 sq mi). Pop. (1981 est.): 1,463,-000. Cap.: Kuwait City (pop., 1980 prelim., 60,400). Largest city: Hawalli (pop., 1980 prelim., 152,300). Language: Arabic. Religion (1975): Muslim 94.9% (of which Sunni 85%; Shi'ah 15%); Christian 4.5%. Emir, Sheikh Jabir al-Ahmad al-

Kuwait

KUWAIT

Education. (1979–80) Primary, pupils 145,626, teachers 7,722; secondary, pupils 167,253, teachers 14,032; vocational, pupils 2,022, teachers 313; teacher training, pupils 1,439, teachers 269; higher (1977–78), students 12,391, teaching staff 1,020.

Finance. Monetary unit: Kuwaiti dinar, with (Sept. 21, 1981) a free rate of 0.28 dinar to U.S. $1 (0.52 dinar = £1 sterling). Gold and other reserves (June 1981) U.S. $4,188,-000,000. Budget (total; 1979–80 actual): revenue 6,-923,000,000 dinars; expenditure 2,147,000,000 dinars. Gross national product (1979–80) 6,663,000,000 dinars. Money supply (June 1981) 1,042,000,000 dinars. Cost of living (1975 = 100; Dec. 1980) 145.5.

Foreign Trade. (1980) Imports (f.o.b.) c. 1,697,000,000 dinars; exports 5,206,900,000 dinars. Import sources (1979): Japan 18%; U.S. 14%; U.K. 10%; West Germany 8%; Italy 6%. Export destinations (1979): Japan 24%; The Netherlands 11%; Italy 9%; South Korea 7%; U.K. 6%; Singapore 5%. Main exports: crude oil 73%; petroleum products 16%.

Transport. Roads (1978) 2,400 km. Motor vehicles in use (1979): passenger 363,300; commercial 125,400. Air traffic (1980): c. 2,114,000,000 passenger-km; freight c. 74.7 million net ton-km. Shipping (1980): merchant vessels 100 gross tons and over 266; gross tonnage 2,529,491.

Industry. Production (in 000; metric tons; 1980): petroleum products c. 26,400; crude oil c. 85,500; natural gas (cu m) 6,895,000; electricity (kw-hr; 1979) 7,200,000.

Jabir as-Sabah; prime minister in 1981, Crown Prince Sheikh Saad al-Abdullah as-Salim as-Sabah.

Kuwait maintained a policy of neutrality in the Iran-Iraq war throughout 1981, despite its accusations that Iran was responsible for an air attack on Kuwaiti oil installations on October 1. The most obvious source of strain was at the Ash-Shu'aybah and Ash-Shuwaykh ports, where transit cargo bound for Iraq caused considerable congestion. Moral support for Iraq, an Arab neighbour, was

Prime Minister Margaret Thatcher of Great Britain met with Kuwait's prime minister, Crown Prince Sheikh Saad, in September. Thatcher and her delegation sought to improve economic and political relations between the two countries.

tempered by a desire to see Iran survive and keep intact a balance of power in the region.

An election of February 23 revived the Kuwait Parliament after a suspension of five years. Conservative tribal leaders emerged as clear winners, increasing their representation to about one-half of the 50 seats. The government of Prime Minister Sheikh Saad resigned on February 24; his new government, formed on March 4, included only one member of Parliament. Women were not included in the 90,000-strong electorate, although an expanded franchise was a major campaign issue.

Kuwait took a leading role in the Gulf Cooperation Council, which it formed in March along with Saudi Arabia, Bahrain, Qatar, Oman, and the United Arab Emirates. It urged that the council's member governments ensure the neutrality of the region by offering recognition to the U.S.S.R. In September Emir Sheikh Jabir visited Turkey, Bulgaria, Hungary, Romania, and Yugoslavia.

Before the October meeting of the Organization of Petroleum Exporting Countries, oil production dropped to about 800,000 bbl a day—well short of the budget requirement of 1,250,000 bbl a day—because of customer resistance to the price. Investment income, however, was expected to rise to $8 billion in 1981. (JOHN WHELAN)

Laos

Laos

A landlocked people's republic of Southeast Asia, Laos is bounded by China, Vietnam, Kampuchea (Cambodia), Thailand, and Burma. Area: 236,800 sq km (91,400 sq mi). Pop. (1981 est.): 3,810,000. Cap. and largest city: Vientiane (pop., 1978 est.: 200,000). Language: Lao (official); French and English. Religion: Buddhist; tribal. President in 1981, Prince Souphanouvong; premier, Kaysone Phomvihan.

LAOS

Education. (1978–79) Primary, pupils 451,800, teachers (1977–78) 14,218; secondary, pupils 72,600, teachers (1977–78) 2,494; vocational (1977–78), pupils 1,623, teachers 205; teacher training (1977–78), students 6,191, teachers 386; higher (university only), students 1,684, teaching staff (1974–75) 152.

Finance. Monetary unit: new kip, with (Sept. 21, 1981) a par value of 10 new kip to U.S. $1 (free rate of 18.54 new kip = £1 sterling). Budget (1981 est.): revenue 930 million new kip (including foreign aid of 1,230,000,000 new kip); expenditure 2,160,000,000 new kip.

Foreign Trade. (1980) Imports U.S. $130.1 million; exports U.S. $30.5 million. Import sources (1974): Thailand 49%; Japan 19%; France 7%; West Germany 7%; U.S. 5%. Export destinations (1974): Thailand 73%; Malaysia 11%; Hong Kong 10%. Main exports (1978): timber 31%; electricity 21%; coffee 12%; tin 9%.

Transport and Communications. Roads (1979) c. 16,-750 km. Motor vehicles in use (1974): passenger 14,100; commercial (including buses) 2,500. Air traffic (1980): c. 7 million passenger-km; freight c. 100,000 net ton-km. Inland waterways (total; 1979) c. 4,600 km. Telephones (Dec. 1973) 5,000. Radio receivers (Dec. 1977) 200,000.

Agriculture. Production (in 000; metric tons; 1979): rice c. 925; corn c. 30; onions c. 31; melons c. 23; oranges c. 19; pineapples c. 30; coffee c. 3; tobacco c. 5; cotton, lint c. 3; timber (cu m) 3,537. Livestock (in 000; 1980): cattle 399; buffalo 756; pigs 843; chickens (1979) c. 18,608.

Industry. Production (1979): tin concentrates (metal content) c. 600 metric tons; electricity c. 840 million kw-hr.

Domestic priorities as well as external problems continued to be governed throughout 1981 by Laos's position as junior partner in the Vietnamese-led Indochina grouping of Laos, Vietnam, and Kampuchea. The country had to cope with military pressure on both its southern and northern borders. On the western boundary shooting incidents involving Laotian and Thai troops occurred along the Mekong River early in February. Thailand accused Laos of violating Thai sovereignty. Two Thai villages were evacuated, and border crossing points near the scene were closed. Laos said that the incidents stemmed from efforts by other countries to destabilize Indochina. Its own troop action, it explained, was in self-defense following Thai attacks on Laotion cargo boats in the Mekong. Both sides agreed that border tension was part of the overall situation in the region.

As if to underline this, Vietnam joined the dispute on behalf of Laos. It charged that Thailand was staging armed provocation against Laos as part of a plot by China and the U.S. against Indochina. It singled out "Chinese expansionists" for special mention and pointed out that the February shellings followed a visit to Thailand by Chinese Premier Zhao Ziyang (Chao Tzu-yang).

China itself was embroiled in several gun battles along the northern border of Laos. At least one incident, in May, was serious enough to be reported in China. The Chinese claimed that Vietnamese disguised as Laotian soldiers had intruded approximately 600 m (655 yd) into China and that one Chinese soldier had been killed in the ensuing clash.

In the midst of its border problems, Laos played a visible diplomatic role in Southeast Asia on behalf of the Indochina group. Foreign Minister Phoune Sipraseuth visited various Southeast Asian leaders in the spring to explore ways of improving relations with the Association of Southeast Asian Nations (ASEAN). He pleaded for mutual consultations, trust, and understanding to achieve "the just interests of all countries in Southeast Asia." But the tour produced no positive results, as Indochina and the ASEAN adopted irreconcilable positions on Kampuchea.

A ray of light was thrown on the whereabouts of Laos's former royal family. Deposed in 1975, former King Savang Vatthana disappeared in 1977. Two of his grandsons escaped across the Mekong into Thailand in early August and sought asylum in the U.S. They told police that the former king, now 73, was detained near the Laos-Vietnam border together with several members of his immediate family.

A study for the International Monetary Fund in mid-1981 noted that real gross domestic product in Laos had increased by an estimated 6% in 1979 but that the economy in 1980 had suffered from low agricultural yields, serious urban unemployment, and severe price distortions. However, in 1981 there were prospects of near self-sufficiency in food grains and increases in timber exports, a major foreign exchange earner. The 1981 budget envisioned a deficit of 1,230,000,000 kip, to be fully financed from external sources.

(T. J. S. GEORGE)

Labour Unions:
see Industrial Relations

Lacrosse:
see Field Hockey and Lacrosse

Latin-American Affairs

The Montevideo Treaty (August 1980), creating the Latin American Integration Association (LAIA or, in its Spanish form, ALADI), entered into force on March 18, 1981. It replaced the Latin American Free Trade Association (LAFTA), which had been in existence since 1960. By May the treaty had been ratified by Argentina, Chile, Colombia, Mexico, Paraguay, and Uruguay. (The other five signatories were Bolivia, Brazil, Ecuador, Peru, and Venezuela.) The basic purposes of LAIA were the promotion and regulation of mutual trade, economic complementation, and the development of economic cooperation aimed at expanding markets. As an alternative to a free-trade area, which had been in operation under LAFTA, the 1980 treaty opted for the establishment of various levels of economic preferences. Among member countries three categories of comparative development were created, with each category receiving a different preferential tariff arrangement. The treaty also allowed for regional or partial agreements, which could be arranged and signed between individual member countries.

The first major negotiating conference of LAIA members was held in 1981 (April 30–May 16). A review was made of the signing and implementation of partial agreements, and negotiations were conducted on lists of exports to be made on preferential terms to other member countries by Bolivia, Ecuador, and Paraguay. A total of 25 partial agreements had been concluded between Andean Group countries (Bolivia, Colombia, Ecuador, Peru, and Venezuela) and non-Andean countries by the end of July. A second negotiating conference took place in Bogotá, Colombia, at the end of the year (November 30–December 15).

In 1981 the Andean Group made limited progress. The heads of state of four member countries —Bolivia's Pres. Luis García Meza was excluded because he was not elected to power by popular vote—held a meeting at Santa Marta, Colombia, in December 1980. It was also attended by the heads of state of Costa Rica, Panama, El Salvador, Honduras, the Dominican Republic, and Spain, and permanent observer status to the Andean Pact was granted to the Dominican Republic, Panama, and Costa Rica. Spain was already an observer, and Panama had been made an associate member in 1979. Bolivia suspended its participation in the Group between December 1980 and May 1981; its decision to reactivate membership was made with a proviso that it would be restricted to participation in economic aspects of integration.

The Andean Commission, the Group's ruling body, met in Sochogata, Colombia, in September, and agreed to stress the consolidation and development of existing free-trade efforts and to play down broader integration goals, such as a common external tariff and integrated industrial development. It was decided to revise the industrial development programs, to reconsider preferential treatment granted to Bolivia and Ecuador, and to tackle the failure of member countries to honour commitments entered into by their representatives. The Commission confirmed its adherence to Decision 24, which regulated foreign investment within the Group's member countries, and decided to study links with LAIA, the European Communities (EC), and the Council for Mutual Economic Assistance (Comecon). The Venezuelan industrialists' association strongly attacked Venezuelan membership in the Group throughout the year, stating that it was against the national interest. This campaign received some support in government quarters. The administration of Pres. Fernando Belaúnde Terry of Peru also expressed considerable reservations about continuing Peru's membership; foreign investment incentives, more generous than those permitted under Decision 24, became law in Peru in 1981.

Efforts to reconstruct the Central American Common Market (CACM) continued throughout the year. The CACM included Costa Rica, El Salvador, Guatemala, Honduras, and Nicaragua. Negotiations took place on a new import tariff for the region. Prospects for CACM's revitalization were enhanced by a peace treaty between El Salvador and Honduras, which was concluded in Lima, Peru, on Oct. 30, 1980. The Honduran segment of the Pan-American Highway was reopened to Salvadoran vehicles and nationals, and the resumption of trade between the two countries was ensured through a bilateral agreement. There was growing concern, however, over the political and social difficulties in Central America, particularly in El Salvador and Guatemala, which observers thought could severely jeopardize the effective functioning of a reconstructed CACM.

The Central American nation of Belize became independent on September 21, ending more than 300 years of British colonial presence on the American mainland. However, because of a long-standing claim to the territory by Guatemala, British troops were to remain stationed there indefinitely to protect the country.

El Salvador Foreign Minister Fidel Chávez Mena (second from right) held a press conference upon returning from a meeting in September with nine other Latin-American countries in Caracas, Venezuela. The Caracas meeting had condemned a joint declaration made by Mexico and France that there be negotiations between the Salvadoran junta and the leftist coalition in El Salvador.

UPI

In July the Bolivian, Paraguayan, and Uruguayan governments formalized the creation of Urupabol, which had been informally established since 1960. The prime aims of Urupabol were to coordinate representation of the three countries in negotiations with international financial institutions such as the World Bank and the Inter-American Development Bank (IDB) and to propose ways of linking the members' road, rail, air, telecommunications, and radio networks. Ministerial meetings were scheduled to take place once a year to decide on strategy, and an executive secretariat was to be established in Asunción, Paraguay.

The policy of U.S. Pres. Ronald Reagan's administration toward Latin America became clear during the year. Top priority was given to improving relations with Mexico, and the presidents of both countries met in Washington, D.C., early in June. It was agreed that two high-level permanent committees, one on trade and one on political aspects of bilateral relations, would be set up and that it was essential that the economies of the Caribbean basin should be strengthened. President Reagan attended the "North-South" summit conference at Cancún, Mexico, in October, along with 21 other heads of state; the economic imbalance between less developed and industrialized countries was discussed.

The second priority of the Reagan administration was Central America and the Caribbean. The U.S. increased both military and economic aid to El Salvador, and aid totals amounted to $144 million and $35 million, respectively, in fiscal 1981. In September the U.S. government outlined an aid program for the Caribbean and Central America; it combined trade, aid, and investment (with emphasis on private investment) and was developed in conjunction with Canada, Mexico, and Venezuela. Third priority was given to strengthening ties with South American countries. In July U.S. delegates to international banks were instructed to support loans to Chile, Argentina, Paraguay, and Uruguay, reversing the policy of former president Jimmy Carter's administration, which had vetoed such loans on human-rights grounds. Since 1977 the U.S. had opposed all loans to Chile and had abstained on international loan proposals for the other three countries.

The U.S. government did not proffer an explicit plan for promoting trade with Latin America. It intended gradually to withdraw tariff privileges for imports to the U.S. from relatively more developed countries, the first two of which in Latin America were Brazil and Mexico.

A ministerial conference was held in Madrid in early November to consider ways of improving commercial, financial, and technological links between Spain and Latin America. It was attended by representatives from 13 Latin-American countries and several international organizations, including the World Bank, the IDB, and the UN Economic Commission for Latin America. Specific attention was devoted to the consequences of Spain's proposed entry into the EC.

The state oil agencies of Brazil, Mexico, and Venezuela reached agreement in October on providing technical assistance to other Latin-American countries for the development of oil resources. The decision was taken at a ministerial meeting of the Latin-American Energy Organization in Caracas, Venezuela. A formal agreement was expected to be signed by the governments of the three countries early in 1982.

There were several other important developments regarding Latin-American external relations. The Vatican presented its proposals for resolving the Beagle Channel dispute to the Argentine and Chilean governments at the end of 1980. Chile accepted the proposals, but Argentina called for further intervention by the Vatican and sent Foreign Minister Oscar Camilión to discuss the dispute with Pope John Paul II. A large-scale trade agreement was signed by Brazil and the U.S.S.R. in July. The Brazilians undertook to purchase 3% of their total import requirement of oil from Soviet sources and to supply soybeans, corn (maize), and cocoa to the U.S.S.R.; the Soviet Union undertook to furnish technical assistance to Brazil for oil exploration, hydroelectric projects, and the diversification of energy supply sources. In August Pres. Luis Herrera Campins of Venezuela visited Brazil and agreed to large-scale joint ventures between the two countries in the field of oil extraction and refining. Work began in October on the 2,700-Mw Yacyretá hydroelectric scheme, a joint project by Argentina and Paraguay on the Paraná River; it was to be the sixth largest project of its kind in the world.

The IDB reported that the gross domestic product of the region grew by 5.4% in 1980 to reach $519.5 billion in 1980 U.S. dollars ($492.7 billion in 1979); income per head in 1980 was $1,507, a rise of 83% in real terms over the 1960 level. At the end of 1980 regional crude oil output amounted to about 2,100,000,000 bbl, 10% higher than in 1979; it accounted for 9.8% of the world's total. Proven oil reserves reached 87,000,000,000 bbl at the end of 1980, as against 74,000,000,000 bbl in 1979; Mexico's share of these reserves rose from 64% in 1979 to 68% in 1980. The region's current account balance of payments deficit grew from $18,704,000,000 in 1979 to $27,328,000,000 in 1980.

(ROBIN CHAPMAN)

See also articles on the various political units.
[971.D.8; 974]

Law

Court Decisions. As in past years, the most important judicial decisions handed down in 1981 emanated from the U.S. Supreme Court. This reflected the fact that the common law system prevalent in the English-speaking world attaches more significance to judicial decisions than does the civil law system applicable in other countries, as well as the fact that the U.S. Constitution vests extraordinary powers in the Supreme Court. Nevertheless, a number of remarkable decisions were also handed down in the civil law countries and in England.

EXECUTIVE POWER. The international crisis precipitated by the seizure of the U.S. embassy in Iran and the capture of its diplomatic personnel in November 1979 induced Pres. Jimmy Carter to is-

UPI

Sandra Day O'Connor was sworn in as the first female justice of the U.S. Supreme Court on September 25. The oath was administered by Chief Justice Warren Burger (left); O'Connor's husband, John, held two family Bibles.

sue an order blocking the removal or transfer of any assets of the government of Iran that were subject to U.S. jurisdiction. Under regulations implementing this order, certain judicial proceedings against the government of Iran were authorized, but no final judgment or decree could be obtained. Pursuant to these regulations, Dames & Moore in 1979 was granted an attachment of Iranian property to satisfy an alleged claim of over $3,436,000.

In January 1981 the hostages were freed by Iran pursuant to an agreement between Iran and the U.S. under which the U.S. promised to release the frozen Iranian assets and to create a tribunal to arbitrate the claims of any U.S. creditors against Iran. President Carter then issued a series of executive orders, one of which nullified any attachment of Iranian assets. Subsequently, Pres. Ronald Reagan ratified this order and, in addition, decreed that all claims subject to arbitration under the agreement with Iran were "suspended" and had no legal effect. Dames & Moore challenged the power of Presidents Carter and Reagan to take these actions.

In *Dames & Moore* v. *Regan*, the Supreme Court upheld the authority of the presidents to carry out the terms of the agreement with Iran. The court underscored the importance of the decision by remarking, "The questions presented by this case touch fundamentally upon the manner in which our Republic is to be governed." Specifically, the court was required to review the sensitive matter of presidential power. In this regard, it reaffirmed earlier statements that the president's power, if any, to issue an order must stem either from the Constitution or from an act of Congress and, in any case, is subject to judicial review.

"When the president acts pursuant to an express or implied authorization from Congress, he exercises not only his powers but also those delegated by Congress. In such a case the executive action would be supported by the strongest of presumptions. . . ." When the president acts in the absence of express congressional authority, a determination must be made whether he has arrogated to himself powers that constitutionally belong to Congress or whether he is simply exercising his own powers or those over which he has concurrent jurisdiction with Congress. In this "zone of twilight," it is also important to recognize that Congress may impliedly delegate authority to the president through "inertia, indifference or quiescence." "Finally, when the President acts in contravention of the will of Congress 'his power is at its lowest ebb,' and the Court can sustain his actions 'only by disabling the Congress from acting upon the subject.' "

The court found that President Carter's actions were expressly authorized by a congressional statute, the International Emergency Economic Powers Act, and thus fell within the first class. President Reagan's actions, however, were found not to have been expressly authorized by this or any other statute, but they did not contravene announced congressional policy and thus fell within the second category. A review of the actions of past presidents in settling claims by Americans against foreign states convinced the court that Congress had impliedly agreed that the president has the power to act as President Reagan did. In this respect, the court pointed out that more than 80 executive agreements settling claims of U.S. nationals against foreign governments had been consummated since 1799 and that Congress had consistently failed to object to them.

SEX DISCRIMINATION. The West German Federal Constitutional Court decided that an unmarried father of a child had no rights to the custody of the child. Against the contention of sex discrimination, the court held that the mother had the exclusive right to custody of the child, but the father was under a duty to pay for his or her maintenance and the child had a right to participate in the father's estate upon his death. The court rejected the claim that these rights and duties conflicted with Art. 6 of the Basic Law, which guarantees protection of the family and the institution of marriage.

The European Court of Justice nullified, on sexual discrimination grounds, a common type of pension plan existing in the U.K. In a case involving Lloyds Bank, the court held that a pension plan

that offers more benefits to male employees than to female employees contravenes Art. 119 of the treaty establishing the European Economic Community (EEC). The nullified plan required employees to contribute to a retirement arrangement but mandated that employers supplement the salaries of men under 25 to make up for their contributions.

In *Rostker* v. *Goldberg*, the U.S. Supreme Court held that the Military Selective Service Act, which authorized the president to require the registration for potential conscription of males only, did not violate the equal protection clause of the U.S. Constitution. Despite the strong reactions of feminists and their opponents, legal scholars tended to agree that the case did not blaze new trails but simply affirmed the traditional power of Congress under the so-called war powers clause of the Constitution.

ABORTION. In *H.L.* v. *Matheson*, the U.S. Supreme Court was called upon to decide whether a Utah statute that required a physician to "notify if possible" the parents of a dependent, unmarried minor girl prior to performing an abortion on the girl violated her constitutional rights. The court held that it did not. The case involved an unmarried 15-year-old girl living with her parents in Utah and dependent on them for support. When she became pregnant, she was advised by her physician that an abortion would be in her best medical interests. The doctor, however, told her that because of the statute he would not perform the operation without first notifying her parents. She then brought an action to declare the statute unconstitutional.

The court held that the girl had a right to decide whether or not she wanted to terminate her pregnancy, and the right to make that decision could not be unconstitutionally burdened. The basic question at issue, therefore, was whether the Utah statute impermissively burdened that decision. While the requirement of notice may inhibit some minors from seeking abortions, the court opined that the parents often will be able to help "a girl of tender years, under emotional stress" to come to a correct decision. Thus the statute plainly serves considerations of family integrity and protection of adolescents. On balance, the court found that these interests had more weight than the possible chilling effect on the abortion decision.

In a decision that surprised some observers, the Constitutional Court of Italy held constitutional a 1978 law permitting abortions on demand for women aged 18 and over. The law also permits abortions for women under 18 with parental consent. In a related matter, the House of Lords, the highest court in the U.K., held that a nurse could perform an abortion under the Abortion Act of 1967 as long as he or she worked under the direction of a registered doctor. The act requires abortions to be done "by a doctor," but the court said this did not mean the doctor had to do it "with his own hands"; he could delegate it in accordance with usual medical procedures.

FREEDOM OF SPEECH. The West German Federal Supreme Court handed down an important decision on press law in 1981. The case involved an action brought by a newspaper publisher, Axel Springer Verlag, against a former employee who had published material about the publisher that had been obtained confidentially. The employee contended that the people had a right to know this information, while the publisher claimed that the law protected editorial confidentiality and the secrets of his publishing empire. The court held for the employee, striking the balance, at least in this case, in favour of "right to know."

This opinion of the West German Federal Supreme Court must be synthesized with another of its decisions handed down in 1981 concerning the right of a prosecutor to seize photographs taken by a newspaper. The photographs, showing "demonstrations," were seized over the newspaper's protest, and as a result several of the demonstrators were identified and arrested. The court ruled that the seizure did not infringe press freedom. It also rejected a contention that the seizure, in effect, abridged the journalist's right to refuse to give evidence of his source of information.

In *Haig* v. *Agee*, the U.S. Supreme Court held that the secretary of state could revoke a citizen's passport on the ground that his activities were damaging to national security. Philip Agee, a former employee of the Central Intelligence Agency, announced a campaign to fight the CIA and undertook to expose CIA agents operating in foreign countries. On the basis of this campaign, the secretary of state revoked Agee's passport. The court, in a divided decision, upheld the revocation, finding that it did not violate Agee's right to freedom of speech. To the extent that revocation of the passport inhibits Agee, it is an inhibition of action, said the court, rather than of speech.

In *Chandler* v. *Florida*, the U.S. Supreme Court was presented with the question whether, consistent with constitutional guarantees, a state may provide for television, radio, and photographic coverage of a criminal trial if the accused makes timely objection to it. The case thus presented a classic confrontation between the right of the public to know and the right of the accused to a fair trial. The court held that a state could constitutionally provide for such coverage, notwithstanding the objections of the defendants.

In so holding, the court upheld the validity of a controversial program developed in Florida for the televising of civil and criminal trials. In its original form, the Florida program required the consent of all parties before a trial could be televised, but it developed that such consent could not usually be obtained. The Florida Supreme Court then revised its rules and established a one-year pilot program, during which the electronic media (and others) were permitted to cover all judicial proceedings in the state without regard to the consent of the participants. The constitutional validity of this program, particularly as it related to criminal trials, was widely debated in legal circles. *Chandler* v. *Florida* seemed to have resolved the debate as far as constitutional requirements are concerned, but the court recognized that there was no requirement that court proceedings be televised and that the Florida Supreme Court had a right to revise the rules under which such televising could occur "or

indeed to bar all broadcast coverage or photography in courtrooms." (*See* Special Report.)

(WILLIAM D. HAWKLAND)

International Law. Violation of territorial sovereignty continued to be a major theme in 1981. Border attacks as a spillover from local wars and unrest seemed to be increasing, with raids on refugee camps or guerrilla bases from Afghanistan into Pakistan, South Africa into Angola, Libya into Sudan via Chad, and Morocco into Mauritania. More premeditated were the air attack by Iran on oil installations in Kuwait and the Israeli bombing of a nuclear research centre in Iraq.

One incident involved violation of territorial waters. In October, during trials of a new Swedish torpedo, a Soviet Whiskey-class submarine was forced by engine trouble to surface in Swedish internal waters in the middle of a restricted military zone. Another submarine penetrated Swedish territorial waters to come to its assistance but was chased away. The first submarine was released some ten days later, after unsuccessful attempts had been made to interrogate its captain. Tests by Swedish divers revealed the presence of uranium on board, probably in a torpedo warhead. This discovery was a serious setback to the Soviet diplomatic campaign to establish a Nordic nuclear-weapon-free zone.

Other incidents occurred on the high seas. In August part of a U.S. naval exercise in the Mediterranean was deliberately situated within the 480-km (300-mi)-wide Gulf of Sidra, claimed by Libya as internal waters under the "historic bays" rule. Two U.S. aircraft were attacked by two Libyan aircraft while they were flying a patrol over the gulf some 95 km (60 mi) off the Libyan coast, but both attackers were shot down. Soon afterward a U.S. reconnaissance aircraft flying over the high seas just outside North Korean territorial waters was the target of a missile launched from within North Korea, which had been claiming an additional 50-mi contiguous military zone. Piracy was reported not only from the Gulf of Thailand, where the "boat people" fleeing Vietnam had long been easy pickings for pirates, but also from Nigeria (in 1980 alone, some 80 Danish ships were attacked in the Lagos roads); the Gulf of Suez; and Singapore, especially the Malacca Strait and the Phillip Channel.

Threats of violence and border disputes occurred throughout Latin America. The Chile-Argentina dispute over the Beagle Channel, which British arbitration and papal mediation had failed to settle, reerupted; Argentina closed its entire land border with Chile and mobilized its troops. A five-day skirmish between Peru and Ecuador arose from a dispute over their border in the Condor Mountains. Venezuela undertook not to go to war over its claim to the Essequibo region, covering some two-thirds of Guyana's territory, when a 12-year moratorium expired in June 1982; however, it forcefully continued to maintain its claim. The British colony of Belize became independent in September without settlement of Guatemala's claims to the whole of its territory.

The status of South West Africa/Namibia continued to be discussed in the UN and elsewhere,

but without significant progress. Libya withdrew its troops from Chad in November; it was intended that they should be replaced by joint forces provided by the Organization of African Unity. The OAU set up a ministerial committee to investigate the border dispute between Cameroon and Nigeria. The separation of Cape Verde from Guinea-Bissau was formalized by Cape Verde's adoption of a new constitution in January. Senegal and The Gambia agreed to merge into a single new state of Senegambia early in 1982.

INTERNATIONAL DISPUTES. Against a background of increasing international lawlessness, there was discernible, surprisingly, a faint trend toward greater use of international adjudication. Through a series of major decisions, the Court of Justice of the European Communities and the European Court of Human Rights consolidated their positions as dominant tribunals in Western Europe. Even the International Court of Justice seemed to be moving slowly toward greater acceptance by states, particularly in boundary disputes. Its hearing of the continental shelf issue between Libya and Tunisia continued with the court's dismissal of Malta's request to intervene and Libya's ratification of a special agreement with Malta to submit their continental shelf disagreement to the court. The court also delivered an advisory opinion on the establishment of a World Health Organization regional office in Egypt.

A judicial board established by the Organization of Arab Petroleum Exporting Countries would have mandatory jurisdiction over disputes between members and optional jurisdiction over other disputes referred to it by consent of the parties. The International Chamber of Commerce and the Comité Maritime International formulated new rules for international maritime arbitration, including a standing 12-member committee to assist in arbitration when the parties to a submitted dispute failed to act. The UN General Assembly, in December 1980, adopted the UN Commission on International Trade Law's conciliation rules, providing parties to commercial contracts with an opportunity to reach an amicable settlement without resort to arbitral or judicial proceedings.

Although the U.S. Supreme Court in July upheld draft registration of men only, women continued to join the all-volunteer army in increasing numbers.

LAFFONT—SYGMA

U.S. fighter-plane officers who shot down two Libyan jets in August held a press conference on their aircraft carrier, the USS "Nimitz."

The dispute between Canada and the U.S.S.R. over damage caused by the disintegration of a Soviet satellite over Canadian territory was settled by an agreement in December 1980, the first such settlement under the 1972 convention on international liability for damage caused by space objects. The dispute between the U.S. and Iran over the detention of U.S. diplomats and the retaliatory freezing of Iranian assets in the U.S. was settled by an agreement, signed in Algiers, to set up a special claims commission. The U.S. action before the International Court of Justice was thereupon withdrawn. U.S. banks were instructed by presidential order to release Iranian assets, and the U.S. Supreme Court held in July that the order was valid. (*See* above.)

MARITIME AFFAIRS. The UN Conference on the Law of the Sea (UNCLOS) continued with its traditional two annual sessions in New York and Geneva. At the beginning of the year, President Reagan withdrew effective U.S. participation in the conference in order to engage in a year-long reassessment of the issues and of the U.S. negotiating position. However, the conference adjourned in August with the expectation that the treaty would be ready for signature at the final session in New York in March–April 1982, whether or not the U.S. took part. The changed U.S. attitude was partly related to deep-sea mining (the issue that had led to the creation of UNCLOS in the first place). Just as states throughout the world adopted the principle of the 200-mi extended economic zone before the conclusion of UNCLOS, so a cautious unilateral movement could be seen regarding exploration of the ocean floor. Britain joined the U.S. and West Germany in enacting interim legislation, and a French bill was making its way through Parliament.

A number of maritime boundary agreements were concluded (Colombia-Venezuela, in the Gulf of Venezuela), came into force (Greece-Italy in November 1980), or were the subject of a conciliation commission report (Iceland-Norway, off Jan Mayen Island). Flags of convenience were again attacked within the UN Conference on Trade and Development at a special meeting in Geneva, but the new Pacific state of Vanuatu passed legislation setting up its own open register for international shipping. A Danish company transferred four of its oil platforms to the Panamanian flag to avoid new Danish safety legislation. Since platforms, once fixed to the seafloor, are not usually regarded as vessels, it was doubtful whether the maneuver would succeed in divesting them of Danish nationality.

An interesting legal situation could have arisen out of the recovery by a British salvage consortium of some £45 million worth of Soviet gold bullion from a British cruiser, HMS "Edinburgh," lying in 250 m (800 ft) of water in the high seas 275 km (170 mi) north of the Soviet port of Murmansk. The insurance for the original World War II loss had been borne by the U.K. and the U.S.S.R. in the proportions 1:2. Property in the gold was claimed by the U.K. and Soviet governments in the same proportions, and no objection was made to the claim, even though the legal status of abandoned wrecks is by no means clear. The salvors kept 45% of the recovered gold by agreement of the two governments.

EUROPE. The Court of Justice of the European Communities started 1981 with a new president, three new judges, and three new advocates general, representing a net increase of two judges and one advocate general. It then proceeded to show the effects of this strengthening by delivering some major judgments that settled or delimited several long-outstanding issues. In particular, it finally held that fisheries jurisdiction had irretrievably passed from the member states to the Community. It also held that free commerce between states took priority over industrial and intellectual property rights as long as the goods being traded had originally been put on the market within the Community with the consent of the holder of the rights. It did not matter that the market value in the place of sale was lower because of compulsory licensing rules (the *GEMA* case on disc recording rights) or even lack of any patent protection at all (*Merck,* on pharmaceuticals marketed in Italy and then imported into The Netherlands).

Controversial drafts of major legislation on trademarks and on the extension of European Economic Community (EEC) antitrust rules to air and sea transport were introduced by the European Commission. Extraterritorial claims made by U.S. courts and agencies relating to European shipping were settled in the autumn, but in a surprise move a U.S. senator introduced a bill to give protection against EEC attempts to exercise extraterritorial jurisdiction in the U.S.

The Council of Europe opened for signature an important convention on automatic processing of personal data that could be of great significance for international trade in data. The European Court of Human Rights delivered strong judgments on the trade union closed shop, professional discipline of dissident doctors, compulsory detention of mental patients, and the rights of homosexuals.

(NEVILLE MARCH HUNNINGS)

See also Crime and Law Enforcement; United Nations.

Law Enforcement:
see Crime and Law Enforcement

Lawn Bowls:
see Bowling

Lawn Tennis:
see Tennis

TELEVISION IN THE COURTROOM

by Geoffrey R. Stone

For more than 50 years, lawyers, judges, social scientists, journalists, and broadcasters have wrestled with the issue of photographic, radio, and television coverage of judicial proceedings. Indeed, as early as 1927 a state court upheld the criminal contempt convictions of several newspaper reporters who had violated a court-ordered ban on in-court photography. Spurred by the overbearing news media coverage of the Lindbergh kidnapping trial, the American Bar Association in 1937 adopted Canon 35 of its Canons of Judicial Ethics. This canon banned all news cameras from judicial proceedings and was later amended to prohibit radio and television coverage as well. In 1972 the Canons of Judicial Ethics were replaced by the Code of Judicial Conduct and Canon 35 was superseded by Canon 3A(7).

Advantages of Canon 3A(7). Although recognizing the potential value of electronic and photographic coverage of trials as a means of educating and informing the public, supporters of Canon 3A(7) maintain that prohibition of such coverage is necessary to protect both the right to a fair trial and the right to privacy. With respect to the fair trial concern, supporters of the canon contend that the very presence of photographic and broadcasting equipment tends to distract the participants and to undermine the essential dignity and decorum of the proceedings. The potential psychological effects of such coverage are thought to be especially pernicious. For example, a witness's knowledge that he is being observed by a vast audience may affect his testimony in incalculable ways. He may become self-conscious and fall victim to stage fright. Alternatively, he may crave the limelight and become cocky and self-important. Judges and attorneys might also be affected. Judges up for reelection might be tempted to posture and to act "judicial" for the electorate, and attorneys eager to establish their reputations might use the media exposure as a windfall opportunity for free advertising—at the expense of their clients' interests.

There is also a danger of prejudicial publicity. As

Geoffrey R. Stone is professor of law at the University of Chicago and the author of numerous articles on constitutional law.

a general rule courts prohibit prospective witnesses from hearing the testimony of other witnesses before they testify themselves. But the broadcasting of trial proceedings can effectively undermine this rule, for prospective witnesses may be exposed to televised broadcasts of other witnesses' testimony. Similarly, there is concern that, unless they are sequestered, jurors might be exposed to televised excerpts of the trial. Taken out of context, such excerpts might distort the jurors' perceptions and recollections of the proceedings.

Finally, supporters of Canon 3A(7) point to an asserted conflict between television coverage of trials and the right to privacy. The defendant, for example, has a right not to have his fate decided in a circus atmosphere, and he has a legitimate interest in not having his reaction to every turn in his trial broadcast into every home in the community as if he were merely a character on some midday soap opera. Other trial participants may also have powerful claims to privacy. Victims of sexual crimes, for example, may have a legitimate desire for at least relative anonymity, and confidential informants have an obvious need to keep their identities secret.

Challenges to the Rule. Because of these varied concerns, Canon 3A(7) was adopted by the federal government and virtually every state within a few years of its promulgation. A few states, however, permitted television, radio, and photographic coverage of judicial proceedings at the discretion of the presiding judge. The U.S. Supreme Court considered the constitutionality of this approach in its 1965 decision in *Estes* v. *Texas*. Billie Sol Estes, a Texas financier and close friend of Presidents John Kennedy and Lyndon Johnson, was charged with swindling and embezzlement. Because of the national interest in the case, the trial judge, over Estes's objection, permitted photographic and broadcast coverage of the proceedings. At least a dozen cameramen were present at the pretrial hearing, causing confusion and some disruption. Coverage of the trial, however, was more restrained. Although almost the entire trial was filmed and recorded, live television coverage was limited to the prosecution's closing arguments and announcement of the jury's verdict. The U.S. Supreme Court, in a 5–4 decision, held that radio, television, and photographic coverage of the proceedings unleashed subtle psychological forces upon jurors, witnesses, and lawyers which inherently distorted the judicial process and thus deprived Estes of his constitutional right to a fair trial.

Despite *Estes*, a growing number of states since the mid-1970s have decided to permit at least limited electronic and photographic coverage of judicial proceedings. In August 1978 the National Confer-

Television cameras are now permitted in courtrooms in most U.S. states.

ence of Chief Judges recommended that Canon 3A(7) be amended to permit the supervisory court of each state to allow media coverage of judicial proceedings. Critics of the canon maintain that technological advances have eliminated the problem of physical disruption and that the psychological effects of such coverage had in the past been largely exaggerated. Problems of prejudicial publicity, they argue, can be handled by such traditional safeguards as the juror's oath, instructions to witnesses not to watch television, and the voir dire examination (preliminary scrutiny to determine competence or bias) of jurors. And although conceding the legitimacy of the privacy concerns, critics of the canon contend that such concerns can be dealt with effectively on a case-by-case basis.

These arguments have been effective. Although the American Bar Association refused in 1979 to revise Canon 3A(7), by early 1981 a majority of states had decided to permit television, radio, and photographic coverage of their judicial proceedings, and several other states were in the process of reexamining their policies.

The Florida rule is typical. Florida permits no more than one television camera, one still photographer, and one audio system in a proceeding. A schedule of approved equipment establishes permissible sound and light standards. Media personnel must remain within designated areas. The presiding judge is authorized to exclude electronic or photographic coverage of a particular participant upon a finding "that such coverage will have a substantial effect upon the particular individual which would be

qualitatively different from coverage by other types of media."

In its 1981 decision in *Chandler* v. *Florida*, the Supreme Court addressed the constitutionality of the Florida rule. *Chandler* involved a prosecution for burglary. Because the defendants were policemen, the case generated considerable public attention. Over the objection of the defendants, the trial judge permitted the trial to be televised, recorded, and photographed in accordance with the Florida rule. In a unanimous decision, the Supreme Court interpreted *Estes* narrowly and rejected the defendants' contention that the media coverage had violated their constitutional rights to a fair trial. Citing technological advances that had been made since *Estes*, the restrictions imposed by the Florida rule, and the interest of the states in experimenting with novel trial procedures, the court held that only upon a showing of specific, demonstrable prejudice to the defendant would such coverage constitute a denial of due process.

The Supreme Court in *Chandler* has thus opened the door to further experimentation. The fundamental issue, however, remains unresolved. Is the interest in informing and educating the public through broadcast coverage of criminal trials sufficiently weighty to justify the risk, emphasized by the court in *Estes* and discounted in *Chandler*, that such experimentation might cause inherent, perhaps critical but nonetheless unprovable, prejudice to a criminal defendant whose liberty may be the price of the experiment? The free press—fair trial debate will no doubt continue.

Lebanon

A republic of the Middle East, Lebanon is bounded by Syria, Israel, and the Mediterranean Sea. Area: 10,230 sq km (3,950 sq mi). Pop. (1981 est.): 3,238,-000. Cap. and largest city: Beirut (metro. pop., 1975 est., 1,172,000). The populations of both Lebanon and its capital city, Beirut, are thought to have declined since the outbreak of civil war in 1974, but reliable figures are not available. Language: Arabic predominates; Armenian-, Kurdish-, and French-speaking minorities. Religion: available estimates show Christians comprising variously from 40 to 55% of the population and Muslims from 45 to 60%; there is a Druze minority. President in 1981, Elias Sarkis; prime minister, Shafiq al-Wazzan.

In 1981 Lebanon endured some of the worst guerrilla fighting since the 19-month civil war of 1975–76. Israeli attacks on Beirut and fierce clashes between Syrian troops belonging to the Arab Deterrent Force (ADF) and right-wing Christian (Phalangist) irregulars also increased the death toll. It was estimated that 2,100 persons were killed during the year.

On March 22 the Israeli Army chief of staff, Gen. Rafael Eitan, set the tone for the summer, predicting a "war of attrition" if Palestinian efforts to infiltrate Israeli- and Christian-held areas in the south of Lebanon were not abandoned. At a meeting with Gen. William Callaghan, commander of the 6,000-strong UN Interim Force in Lebanon (UNIFIL), on March 18, the commander of Israel's northern forces, Gen. Avigdor Ben-Gal, rejected a demand that Israel withdraw from southern Lebanon. On March 16 the Israeli-backed Christian militia, led by Maj. Saad Haddad, shelled the village of Qantara, killing three Nigerian UNIFIL soldiers.

Israeli attacks were stepped up in the succeeding months. On March 31 a raid by naval commandos on Palestinian positions near Tyre led to eight deaths. On April 1 a force crossed by land and raided the village of Tulin, policed by Nigerians and Lebanese. The moves in the south triggered bitter fighting in the north, between Syrian ADF troops and the Phalangists and between rival Christian groups. The port of Beirut was shelled in April, but east Beirut bore the brunt of the violence. A series of cease-fire announcements, including one in April by the foreign ministers of Kuwait, Saudi Arabia, and Syria, had little effect.

Worse was to follow in July with the escalation of Israeli air strikes on Palestine Liberation Organization (PLO) targets. Air raids on July 17–20 destroyed at least five bridges across the Litani and Zahrani rivers. Air raids on Beirut on July 17 reportedly killed 300 people and wounded more than 500. A cease-fire between Israel and the Palestinians was concluded on July 24, with the U.S. Middle East negotiator, Philip Habib (see BIOGRAPHIES), the UN, and Saudi Arabia acting as intermediaries between the two parties. Five days later, however, Palestinian guerrillas attacked a bus in Israel, wounding four people. On October 1 a car packed with explosives blew up outside the PLO office in Beirut, killing over 80 people, and more than 20 died when an explosion destroyed the Iraqi embassy on December 15. The PLO chairman, Yasir Arafat, made political capital out of the fighting, claiming that it would convince U.S. Pres. Ronald Reagan that the "PLO exists." Syria demanded that Beirut be protected by a ring of surface-to-air missiles, thereby further raising tension. Haddad renounced the cease-fire on November 13, and for a time his forces besieged some 1,150 military and civilian UN personnel in their southern Lebanon headquarters.

The domestic consequences for Lebanon were also severe. On July 22 the Israelis bombed the pipeline that brought crude oil from Saudi Arabia to the Zahrani refinery in the south, causing severe disruption of the economy and rapidly escalating fuel prices. In the aftermath of the attack, Prime Minister Shafiq al-Wazzan called for an enhanced role for UNIFIL. Libya's offer of $2 billion in military assistance to Lebanon was not taken seriously in Beirut, but France's offer of an $86 million

Lebanon

Soldiers moved through the streets of Beirut during fighting in April. Battles between Syrian troops and Christian militiamen caused many casualties.

Huge clouds of black smoke arose after Israeli planes attacked an oil refinery near Zahrani, Lebanon, in July.

military purchase loan was welcomed by Wazzan on August 8.

In the face of these problems, the work of the Council for Reconstruction and Development (CDR) became increasingly difficult. Rehabilitation work started in the south, but the CDR laboured under many handicaps quite apart from the endemic violence. The CDR maintained that, of the $2 billion pledged at the Arab summit in Tunisia in November 1979, only $206 million had materialized in the first 18 months of the five-year period. Reconstruction aid from other sources had totaled

$460 million. A hopeful prospect for Lebanon was the European Community agreement in October to provide $54.6 million in grants and loans for projects to be identified by the CDR.

(JOHN WHELAN)

Lesotho

A constitutional monarchy of southern Africa and a member of the Commonwealth, Lesotho forms an enclave within the republic of South Africa, bordering the Republic of Transkei to the southeast. Area: 30,352 sq km (11,716 sq mi). Pop. (1981 est.): 1,373,000. Cap. and largest city: Maseru (pop., 1976 prelim., 14,700). Language: English and Southern Sotho (official). Religion: Roman Catholic 38.7%; Lesotho Evangelical Church 24.3%; Anglican 10.4%; other Christian 8.4%; non-Christian 18.2%. Chief of state in 1981, King Moshoeshoe II; prime minister, Chief Leabua Jonathan.

On July 31, 1981, Lesotho made a strong protest to South Africa, claiming that a mortar attack on a gasoline supply depot near Maseru had been launched from South African territory. A number of bomb outrages in Maseru in September were

LEBANON

Education. (1977–78) Primary, pupils 380,695; secondary, pupils 232,255; primary and secondary (1972–73), teachers 32,901; vocational (1972–73), pupils 3,898, teachers (1970–71) 508; teacher training (1972–73), students 3,235, teachers (1971–72) 551; higher, students (1978–79) 78,628, teaching staff (1972–73) 2,313.

Finance. Monetary unit: Lebanese pound, with (Sept. 21, 1981) a free rate of L£4.67 to U.S. $1 (L£8.66 = £1 sterling). Gold and other reserves (June 1981) U.S. $1,713,000,000. Budget (1980 rev. est.): revenue L£3,026 million; expenditure L£4,544 million.

Foreign Trade. (1980) Imports c. L£11,133 million; exports c. L£2,811 million. Import sources: Italy c. 12%; Saudi Arabia c. 9%; France c. 9%; U.S. c. 8%; West Germany c. 6%; Romania c. 6%; Japan c. 5%. Export destinations: Saudi Arabia c. 32%; Syria c. 9%; Kuwait c. 7%; Switzerland c. 5%; Jordan c. 5%; United Arab Emirates c. 5%. Main exports (1977): financial papers and stamps 21%; food, drink, and tobacco 17%; chemicals 11%; machinery 9%; metals 8%; textiles and clothing 7%.

Transport and Communications. Roads (1979) c. 7,100 km. Motor vehicles in use (1978): passenger 282,400; commercial 28,600. Railways: (1979) 417 km; traffic (1974) 2 million passenger-km, freight 42 million net ton-km. Air traffic (1980): c. 1,571,000,000 passenger-km; freight c. 540 million net ton-km. Shipping (1980): vessels 100 gross tons and over 203; gross tonnage 267,787. Telephones (Dec. 1978) 231,000. Radio receivers (Dec. 1976) 1.6 million. Television receivers (Dec. 1977) 450,000.

Agriculture. Production (in 000; metric tons; 1979): potatoes c. 112; wheat c. 40; tomatoes c. 80; grapes c. 135; olives c. 15; bananas c. 18; oranges c. 225; lemons c. 65; apples c. 135; tobacco c. 5. Livestock (in 000; 1979): cattle c. 84; goats c. 340; sheep c. 242; chickens c. 6,900.

Industry. Production (in 000; metric tons; 1978): cement c. 1,200; petroleum products c. 2,150; electricity (kw-hr) c. 1,700,000.

LESOTHO

Education. (1978) Primary, pupils 228,523, teachers (1976) 4,233; secondary, pupils 17,732, teachers (1976) 621; vocational, pupils 945, teachers (1976) 103; teacher training, students 835, teachers (1976) 39; higher (university), students 847, teaching staff (1976) 95.

Finance and Trade. Monetary unit: loti (plural maloti), at par with the South African rand, with (Sept. 21, 1981) a free rate of 0.93 loti to U.S. $1 (1.73 maloti = £1 sterling). Budget (1978–79 est.): revenue 77,443,000 maloti; expenditure 50,532,000 maloti (excludes development expenditure of 87.7 million maloti). Foreign trade (1978): imports 237 million maloti; exports 27.7 million maloti. Main exports (1977): wool 21%; mohair 16%; diamonds 10%. Most trade is with South Africa.

Agriculture. Production (in 000; metric tons; 1979): corn 129; wheat 30; sorghum 69; dry peas c. 7; wool c. 1.3. Livestock (in 000; 1979): cattle c. 550; goats c. 730; sheep c. 1,300.

Lesotho

attributed to the Lesotho Liberation Army (LLA), the military wing of the underground Basotho Congress Party. At the same time, several known critics of the government disappeared. The aim of the LLA was to force Chief Leabua Jonathan to hold democratic elections.

Lesotho signed an agreement with the U.K. on the promotion and protection of investment. A factory to produce hessian bags was established at Maputsoe, an area earmarked by the government for development. A Lesotho promotion mission visited West Germany. The consultancy contract for the new international airport at Thota-Moli was awarded to Dalcanda International of Canada.

Lesotho remained heavily dependent on foreign aid. During the year aid commitments were made by West Germany, Sweden, Canada, the U.K., and the European Investment Bank. South Africa promised a loan for agricultural development.

(GUY ARNOLD)

Liberia

A republic on the west coast of Africa, Liberia is bordered by Sierra Leone, Guinea, and Ivory Coast. Area: 97,790 sq km (37,757 sq mi). Pop. (1981 est.): 1,926,000. Cap. and largest city: Monrovia (pop., 1978 est., 229,300). Language: English (official) and tribal dialects. Religion: mainly animist. Head of state and chairman of the People's Redemption Council in 1981, Master Sgt. Samuel K. Doe.

In the year following the coup that brought him to power, Master Sgt. Samuel K. Doe insisted that there was to be no change of ideology in Liberia. After the most serious of several alleged plots against the People's Redemption Council, the

LIBERIA

Education. (1978) Primary, pupils 192,185, teachers 4,-567; secondary, pupils 45,668, teachers 2,713; vocational, pupils 1,181, teachers (1976) 63; teacher training, students 597, teachers 38; higher, students (1980) 3,789, teaching staff (1978) *c.* 190.

Finance. Monetary unit: Liberian dollar, at par with the U.S. dollar, with a free rate (Sept. 21, 1981) of L$1.85 = £1 sterling. Budget (total; 1979–80 actual): revenue L$202 million; expenditure L$281 million.

Foreign Trade. (1980) Imports L$534,660,000; exports L$600,560,000. Import sources (1979): U.S. 24%; West Germany 11%; Saudi Arabia 10%; U.K. 8%; The Netherlands 7%; Japan 7%; Canada 5%. Export destinations (1979): West Germany 26%; U.S. 20%; France 11%; Italy 10%; Belgium-Luxembourg 9%; The Netherlands 7%. Main exports (1979): iron ore 54%; rubber 16%; timber 11%; diamonds 7%; coffee 5%.

Transport and Communications. Roads (1979) 9,973 km. Motor vehicles in use (1979): passenger 13,070; commercial 8,999. Railways (1979) 490 km. Shipping (1980): merchant vessels 100 gross tons and over 2,401 (mostly owned by U.S. and other foreign interests); gross tonnage 80,285,176. Telephones (Jan. 1980) 7,740. Radio receivers (Dec. 1977) 274,000. Television receivers (Dec. 1977) 10,-000.

Agriculture. Production (in 000; metric tons; 1980): rice 243; cassava (1979) *c.* 180; bananas (1979) *c.* 69; palm kernels *c.* 7; palm oil *c.* 27; rubber *c.* 75; cocoa *c.* 4; coffee *c.* 12; timber (cu m; 1979) 4,814. Livestock (in 000; 1979): cattle *c.* 38; sheep *c.* 190; goats *c.* 190; pigs *c.* 100.

Industry. Production (in 000; metric tons; 1978): petroleum products *c.* 540; cement 132; iron ore (68% metal content; 1979) 19,870; diamonds (metric carats) 308; electricity (kw-hr) *c.* 890,000.

deputy head of state, Thomas Weh Syen, was executed in August. Although some political prisoners were freed, a student leader and several journalists were imprisoned for two weeks in July. All government ministers were made army officers, and Doe was appointed commander in chief of the Liberian armed forces. Doe promised a return to civilian rule in 1985.

In an effort to alleviate economic problems, a scheme was launched obliging all salaried employees to purchase government bonds. Overseas debts amounting to $700 million were rescheduled at the end of 1980. Oil imports cost $90 million annually. The price of rice, a major factor in the coup, was increased by 20% in a crisis budget presented in July. The U.S. granted substantial aid, and the European Economic Community allocated some $40 million over five years.

The Doe regime gradually won acceptance in Africa. The Libyans set up a people's bureau in Monrovia in March but were ordered to close it in May; at the same time, the U.S.S.R. was ordered to reduce the size of its mission. In contrast, 100 U.S. soldiers arrived during April to train with the Liberian Army. In June Doe attended the Organization of African Unity summit in Nairobi, Kenya.

(GUY ARNOLD)

Liberia

Libraries

The pressure on library and information services to reduce costs or operate on no-growth budgets continued in 1981, reflecting the recession and the general state of the world's economy. Efforts were, therefore, concentrated on protecting budgets and the quality and level of services. Resolution of the latter problem was not, however, helped by the increase in the prices of books and journals. This was particularly true of those published in the less developed countries, where price increases due to inflation coincided with libraries' reduced purchasing powers.

Shortage of money in individual institutions encouraged improved cooperation and resource sharing at local, national, regional, and international levels. At the local level, moves toward further development of corporate acquisition policies and the usage of libraries by nonmembers increased. At the international level, through the International Federation of Library Associations (IFLA) and with UNESCO's support, preparations continued for a Conference on the Universal Availability of Publications—a program to complement the Universal Bibliographic Control program—scheduled for Paris in May 1982.

It was at the regional level, however, that interest in cooperation increased most noticeably. This was nowhere better exemplified than in an examination of the regional conferences organized in 1981 and of their themes. The International Association of Technological University Libraries considered the topic of "Libraries and the Communication Process." Delegates to the fifth Conference of Southeast Asian Librarians, meeting in Kuala Lumpur, Malaysia, addressed themselves to "Access to Information." The Seminar on

Familiar library card catalogs were giving way to computers as the U.S. Library of Congress was in the process of converting to electronic cataloging.

the Acquisition of Latin American Library Materials considered "Latin American Economic Issues: Information Needs and Information Sources."

In the English-speaking Western Hemisphere, library and information workers indicated a growing concern for the principles that underlie the operational activities of library and information services—namely, the storage and delivery to users of documents and data. Such activities were exemplified by concern for freedom of information where, as in Canada and the U.K., governments were being pressed to review policies affecting data protection and the right to privacy of the individual. Concern for the protection of the users from poor standards of service and the inadequate provision of information was demonstrated by work to produce codes of conduct for professional librarians and information scientists, although, it should be stressed, these efforts met with some opposition and controversy.

Publication of *North-South: A Programme for Survival: Report of the Independent Commission on International Development Issues* and the UNESCO report *Many Voices, One World* encouraged consideration of the differences that existed between the information-poor and the information-rich. UNESCO member nations debated their requirements from the organization's Medium Term Program for 1985–89 and particularly from the General Information Program components, with special concern in some European countries to ensure that maximum assistance was provided to the "South" to develop its national library and information infrastructures. Plans for the development of such infrastructures advanced in The Netherlands, where the Library Council produced a program for future development. Similar concerns were apparent in the U.K., where Paul Channon, the new minister for arts and libraries, indicated the government's willingness to consider an enhanced role in the development of the nation's library and information infrastructure.

Deliberations continued, nationally and internationally, on the subject of copyright. Both in Australia and in the U.K., where the government

issued a consultative Green Paper, librarians and publishers, from different positions, considered the issues involved. Public Lending Right continued to operate in some of the Scandinavian countries and in West Germany, and some U.K. authors benefited from it for the first time. Although differences existed between authors and publishers and librarians, economic constraints tended to unite the professions, as they did the different elements of the library and information science professions. This was best exemplified by a meeting between the IFLA, the International Documentation Federation, and the International Council of Archives.   (RUSSELL BOWDEN)

Recession and inflation were powerful forces acting on U.S. libraries in 1981; the prices of library materials and most things bought by libraries kept climbing, and income sources shrank. Libraries responded in many ways, seeking more private funds, raising user charges or instituting them for the first time, supplementing paid staff with volunteers, redeploying staff members, and cutting back on many services. In some areas (California and Massachusetts, for example) libraries were caught in taxpayer revolts, but wherever they were able to go directly to the voters for funding, they tended to be well supported.

Library cooperation held new promise of reducing the costs of services, and a wide consensus on the need for cooperation among all types of libraries motivated experiments and investigations aimed at the sharing of resources and assets by public, academic, school, and special libraries. At the same time, a countercurrent leading away from the long-honoured concept of larger units of service developed, and more libraries began thinking of a future in which networks and automation would open a new era of local autonomy.

Automation of library functions spread rapidly, with many libraries moving on from automated circulation to on-line catalogs and acquisitions systems. The new microcomputers spurred a wave of interest and were the subjects of considerable experimentation at the year's end.

There was a sharp decrease in the number of

librarians being graduated from accredited library schools and a continuing decrease in the percentage of professionals on library staffs. At the same time, however, the need was expressed for more highly qualified librarians to provide the increasingly sophisticated services.

In their recasting of efforts to observe priorities, U.S. libraries showed continued determination to provide service to the disadvantaged of all kinds. For example, despite their cost, ramps and Kurzweil reading machines were becoming common sights in academic and public libraries.

(KARL NYREN)

[441.C.2.d; 613.D.1.a; 735.H]

Libya

A socialist country on the north coast of Africa, Libya is bounded by the Mediterranean Sea, Egypt, the Sudan, Tunisia, Algeria, Niger, and Chad. Area: 1,749,000 sq km (675,000 sq mi). Pop. (1980 est.): 3,250,000. Cap. and largest city: Tripoli (pop., 1980 est., 994,000). Language: Arabic. Religion: predominantly Muslim. Chief of state in 1981, Col. Muammar al-Qaddafi; secretary-general of the General People's Congress, Muhammad az-Zaruq Rajab.

The steady annual increase in oil revenues, a feature of the Libyan economy in the 1970s, did not continue in 1981. Libya's production, which had equaled that of Saudi Arabia in 1969, the year of Libya's revolution, had already fallen to one-quarter of Saudi production in the early 1970s. In 1981 it shrank sharply to less than one-third of the two million bbl a day regarded as necessary to finance Libya's ambitious development programs. In December Libya lowered the price of its oil by up to $1.20 a barrel.

The development programs were detailed in the five-year plan (1981–85), which showed that the productive sectors of agriculture and industry were to be supported strongly in accordance with the regime's socialist principles of central planning and investment. Success in infrastructure investment continued to be recorded, but the goal of self-sufficiency in food and improved industrial production remained elusive. Water shortages in coastal tracts led to the announcement of plans to build water pipelines to convey the southern fossil water resources to the coast.

The change in Libya's economic circumstances largely explained a marked shift in the policy of Col. Muammar al-Qaddafi (*see* BIOGRAPHIES) toward some North African and Middle Eastern monarchs who had previously drawn his fierce disapproval. King Hassan II of Morocco was happy to find that the Libyan leader had ceased for a time to support the forces of the Popular Front for the Liberation of Saguia el Hamra and Río de Oro (Polisario Front) in the Western Sahara. Qaddafi also visited the Gulf states, and diplomatic relations with Saudi Arabia were resumed in December. Relations with Tunisia continued to improve despite an important case heard by the International Court of Justice in September–October, which dealt with the division of territorial waters and the offshore economic zone between Tunisia and Libya. Oil resources were the main concern of both parties.

Libya remained close to the other confrontationist state, Syria, and in general accord with Algeria, although Algeria saw Libya's altered attitude to the Western Sahara as delaying that territory's movement toward independence. A conference of the heads of state of Libya, Yemen (Aden), and Ethiopia, all of which had cordial relations with the U.S.S.R., was held in Aden in August.

The two major friends of Israel—Egypt and the U.S.—were opposed loudly by Colonel Qaddafi. In August two Libyan jets were shot down by better equipped U.S. Navy planes that were taking part in naval exercises provocatively close to Libyan territorial waters in the Gulf of Sidra. The air battle itself was said to have occurred 95 km (60 mi) off the Libyan coast. Libya claimed a 19-km (12-mi) territorial limit except in the Gulf of Sidra, where the limit runs 19 km (12 mi) north of a baseline drawn across the mouth of the Gulf. The U.S. recognized only a 4.25-km (3-mi) limit off the Libyan coast. Relations deteriorated further in December when the U.S. announced it had information that a Libyan-trained team of assassins had arrived in North America on a mission to kill Pres. Ronald Reagan. Although Qaddafi vigorously denied the report, President Reagan invalidated U.S. passports for travel to Libya and urged all Americans in that country to return home. Muddying the situation were stories that surfaced during the year concerning U.S. citizens working for Qaddafi, among them former Central Intelligence Agency officers who illegally obtained explosives for Libya and helped to train Libyan terrorists. The assassi-

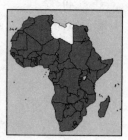

Libya

Libyan leader Muammar al-Qaddafi (left) received a warm greeting from United Arab Emirates Pres. Sheikh Zaid ibn Sultan an-Nahayan when Qaddafi arrived in Abu Dhabi for a visit in August.

UPI

nation of Egypt's Pres. Anwar as-Sadat (*see* Obituaries) in October was marked by rejoicing in Tripoli.

Libya's military involvement in Chad continued to provoke strong criticism from many African nations. On January 6 it was announced that the two countries intended to merge; however, the merger did not take place, and by November the situation had so altered that the Chadian leader requested the Libyan troops to leave his country, which they did on November 5. (J. A. ALLAN)

Liechtenstein

A constitutional monarchy between Switzerland and Austria, Liechtenstein is united with Switzerland by a customs and monetary union. Area: 160 sq km (62 sq mi). Pop. (1980 est.): 25,200. Cap. and largest city: Vaduz (pop., 1980 est., 4,600). Language: German. Religion (1979): Roman Catholic 88%. Sovereign prince, Francis Joseph II; chief of government in 1981, Hans Brunhart.

The Liechtenstein royal family's private fortune, believed to be well in excess of $500 million and thus among the largest in Europe, had since 1970 been administered by the Prince of Liechtenstein Foundation, headed by Crown Prince Hans Adam. Following a decision by 75-year-old Prince Francis Joseph II that the family's financial interests should be further internationalized, a Swedish banker, Christian Norgren, was appointed in May 1981 as executive head of the foundation

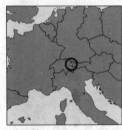

Liechtenstein

and chairman of the family Bank of Liechtenstein. Norgren was formerly chief executive of the Deutsch-Skandinavische Bank in West Germany.

The family fortune was already internationally based. However, according to Crown Prince Hans Adam, the foundation would seek to increase its North American interests. Its main asset continued to be an extensive art collection that included works by Rubens, Van Dyck, and Rembrandt.

Prince Hans Adam and his wife, Princess Marie, were guests at the wedding of Charles, prince of Wales, and Lady Diana Spencer in July.

(K. M. SMOGORZEWSKI)

Life Sciences

Studies of interactions between different species of living organisms and between species and their environment permeated much of biological research in 1981. Scientists charted the evolving relationship between populations of rabbits and a deadly virus, uncovered a role for Amazonian fish in the seed dispersal of trees, increased their understanding of the effects of pollution on oceanic life, and found evidence of natural gene transfer between a small marine fish and its symbiotic bacteria. Scientific and political controversy over an infestation of the Mediterranean fruit fly in California orchards spotlighted the need for better pest management strategies.

ZOOLOGY

New insights into old theories, advances in technology, and long-term research projects contributed to the discoveries made in 1981 in zoology.

Results of research in biochemical genetics indicated that there are many more species of animals than previously thought. A technique known as starch gel electrophoresis permits investigators to measure isozyme variation in tissues. Patterns of isozymes (chemically distinct enzymes having the same function) are considered to be an expression of particular alleles (gene alternatives) at given genetic loci in an individual; hence the term biochemical genetics. The technique has proven invaluable in addressing certain questions about population genetics. Using electrophoresis, Anthony A. Echelle of Oklahoma State University and Doyle T. Mosier of Texas Memorial Museum discovered an all-female species of fish along the Texas Gulf Coast. Fewer than a dozen species of all-female fish are known. Although abundant, the unisexual species had gone undetected in previous taxonomic studies because it closely resembles two

bisexual species in the vicinity. The allelic patterns clearly reveal that three species are present. The investigators concluded that similarities in form and structure (morphology) may often preclude detection of species, which can be distinguished on the basis of such electrophoretic studies. Richard Highton of the University of Maryland likewise concluded that the salamander genus *Plethodon* has several morphologically similar species that are distinguishable only when electrophoresis is used to reveal the allelic patterns.

Long-term, in-depth research continued on the effect of worldwide pollution from pesticides, industrial by-products, urban wastes, and other sources. Reports on the synergistic and interactive properties of man-produced environmental contaminants revealed far-reaching consequences for animal life histories. The environmental problems associated with DDT may be even more persistent than previously thought. D. Michael Fry and C. Kuehler Toone of the University of California reported that the excessively high ratio of female to male sea gulls noted recently in the Channel Islands off southern California is a consequence of abnormal embryonic development following DDT contamination. Laboratory studies revealed that DDT levels prevalent on the southern California coast in the 1950s and 1960s were sufficient to suppress male development during the embryonic stages and to result in abnormal feminization.

The federal Centers for Disease Control in Atlanta, Ga., reported an unsuspected synergism between one of the polybrominated biphenyls (PBB's) and sunlight. When exposed to natural light the PBB compound, previously considered nonpathogenic, transforms to another compound that can cause skin abnormalities in rabbits. Research at the Savannah River Ecology Laboratory in South Carolina revealed a similar phenomenon in a polyaromatic hydrocarbon (PAH). Sunlight degrades the PAH to a compound toxic to sunfish. PAH compounds are fossil-fuel by-products.

In another study Z. S. Dolinsky of the State University of New York and associates examined the interaction between the effects of lead and a common parasite in mice. They discovered that mice infected with the parasite and given high doses of lead were less severely affected by the parasite than were mice without lead. These and other recent findings emphasized the subtle and highly intricate relationships between environmental conditions and the effect on animals.

Among exciting recent discoveries was the identification of the fossil remains of what is the largest known bird. This condorlike bird from Argentina had a wingspan of 8 m (25 ft) and was named the giant teratorn, *Argentavis magnificens.*

Magnetic material consisting at least partly of the iron oxide magnetite was discovered to be associated with sensory tissue in the heads of dolphins. The scientists who made the find suggested that the material may be used in the detection of magnetic fields, perhaps for navigational purposes. Although magnetic material had been reported in certain birds, fish, insects, and bacteria this was the first known occurrence in a mammal.

Several advances in understanding evolutionary principles were made at the basic research level as controversy continued about the rate of evolution. Saltationists assert that species evolve as a consequence of major abrupt changes in anatomy or physiology. Gradualists, holding the more traditional view, consider that organic evolution is a slow, orderly process. Punctuated evolution, an intermediate view originally proposed by Stephen J. Gould and Niles Eldredge of Harvard University and the American Museum of Natural History, respectively, holds that species normally undergo minor changes and adaptations but evolve rapidly and speciate during certain periods. John E. Cronin of Harvard and colleagues challenged punctuated evolution by using human fossils as evidence for gradualism. According to them, fossil evidence reveals gradual changes in more than 40 morphological characters of humans. This result, they claimed, demonstrates an orderly and directional process with none of the discontinuities of punctuated evolution. By contrast, Peter C. Williamson of Harvard found support for punctuated evolution from a study of an extensive record of mollusk fossils from a Kenyan lake. He reported that these animals remained unchanged for long periods and then underwent brief, rapid speciation during a period of environmental stress.

A 180-million-year-old jawbone of a mouse-sized mammal was discovered in Arizona. The fossil remnant (about 1.3 cm; 0.5 in) is believed to be of a new variety and to represent one of the earliest stages of mammalian evolution.

WIDE WORLD

Life Insurance:
see Industrial Review

Coevolution, the process by which organisms and species mutually affect the evolution of each other, also received considerable attention. Simon Levin and David Pimentel of Cornell University examined the relationship between the myxomatosis virus, which causes a fatal disease of rabbits, and their hosts in Australia. In 1950 myxomatosis killed virtually 100% of infected rabbits within two weeks. Because of the short life expectancy of the rabbit host, the chance for the virus to spread to other hosts was reduced. By 1964 no infected rabbits died within two weeks, and most survived more than a month. In one explanation for this changing host-disease relationship the investigators invoked group selection, a highly controversial concept which contends that natural selection acts upon groups or populations rather than individuals. In this case natural selection favoured less virulent viruses because the rapid reduction in the host population that occurred under a high-virulence system was detrimental to continued survival of the viral population.

Another example of coevolution, reported by James E. Lloyd of the University of Florida, involves species-specific codes in fireflies. Female and male fireflies locate each other in darkness by intricate query-and-response lighting patterns. A synthesis of Lloyd's long-term studies revealed that females of some species of fireflies mimic the patterns of other species. Unwitting males, attracted by the false signals, subsequently are devoured by the females. This aggressive mimicry system was revealed to be even more complex in that males of some species have evolved countermeasures to combat such deceit. By flashing false signals of their own while flying, the males provoke the predatory females into sending answering flashes and revealing their true species identity.

Yet another example of coevolution was reported by Michael Goulding of the National Research Institute for Amazonia, Nanaus, Brazil, who found that seed dispersal of certain trees in the Amazon River system was dependent on several species of fish. The fish invade flooded swamp forests, ingest fruits and nuts, and later defecate the viable seeds, sometimes great distances from the parent tree. Such findings supported the opinion of many biologists that natural ecosystems are more complex and intricately interwoven than had been thought previously.

In consideration of high environmental complexity, Peter Van Voris and associates from Oak Ridge (Tenn.) National Laboratory used experimental ecosystems to test and reinforce the longstanding and controversial axiom that an ecosystem's stability is directly related to its species diversity and functional complexity. Using the heavy metal cadmium as an environmental stressor (stress-inducing agent), they measured the response and recovery of a series of systems differing in complexity. Their results revealed that many species considered to be of little or no consequence may be critical in maintaining diversity and complexity and, therefore, the stability of the entire system. (J. WHITFIELD GIBBONS)

[242.B.2.xiv; 312.C.3.b; 312.D; 337.A.2.c.iii; 338.D.3.b.iii; 355.D.5.d.i; 10/34.B.6.d]

Entomology. A heavy infestation of the Mediterranean fruit fly, a costly horticultural pest, in California orchards caused a major political and environmental controversy in the U.S. in 1981. This highly fertile insect lays eggs on a wide variety of fruit and vegetables, within which its maggots develop. Possible control measures include stripping trees of fruit and localized spraying from the ground using a mixture of chemical bait and the insecticide malathion, aerial spraying of large areas with the mixture, and release of sterile males (to inseminate females with ineffective sperm). An early attempt to contain the problem with "sterile" insects, some of which apparently were fertile, was blamed for spreading the infestation.

Environmentalists and urban groups vigorously opposed and succeeded in delaying wholesale spraying, but because there was insufficient manpower to carry out local treatments rapidly enough over the large area already affected, the pest continued to spread. In July, under threats of a federal statewide quarantine and of interstate and international embargoes on millions of dollars worth of California produce unless effective eradication measures were taken, Gov. Edmund G. Brown, Jr., ordered helicopter spraying of several hundred square kilometres of central California. Subsequent discoveries of flies ever farther from the original infestation area prompted additional aerial spraying.

Eradication of pest species is rarely accomplished, however, and in the U.K. the Royal Society meanwhile had been debating integrated pest management, the strategy of maintaining established pest populations at economically acceptable levels using as many techniques as are necessary to ensure against failure of any one. Speakers at a two-day symposium on the topic warned of a limited period of usefulness for any one chemical pesticide if pests became selected for resistance to it. Julius Menn of Zoecon Corp. of California pointed out that in the early 1980s it cost as much as $15 million to develop a new insecticide and that the time taken to have it registered had risen from six years in 1970 to nine by 1978. Brian Croft of the Pesticide Research Center, Michigan State University, advocated alternating insecticides to confound insects' adaptation processes.

Central to the concept of pest management was the restriction of pesticide use to exactly when and where required, and Trevor Lewis of Rothamsted Experimental Station in England pointed out that this meant adequate pest forecasting. He cited Japan as having 11,000 pest watchers, who used some 2,000 pest detection sites and reported regularly to a central control. Few countries had such a comprehensive system. Even when information was gathered and analyzed, there were insufficient means to pass on advice to growers, many of whom still decide intuitively when to use pesticides. Lewis believed that a computerized advisory system that farmers could tap via visual display units was needed.

Such data-based management systems, which would require sophisticated programming to deal efficiently with input from pest scouts, was the subject of a special report by G. C. Brown and his

Ornithologists the world over were excited by the news that Jared Diamond (left), while exploring a mountainous area in Indonesian New Guinea, had seen a pair of yellow-fronted gardener bowerbirds. Previous expeditions had been unable to find the birds, known only from three skins procured in the 1890s.

associates at the University of Kentucky and Michigan State University. In Indiana, county agents had terminal access to a central computer. Other states used punch cards or optical scanning of specially designed questionnaire forms or cards. For some pests computer programs provided forecasts of crop/pest status that were updated continuously as information flowed in. Data on other pests were stored for research. Farmers received both immediate information from the scouts and computer forecasts via extension agents.

Most entomologists accept the evolutionary derivation of insect wings from paranotal lobes, which are lateral extensions of the thorax possessed by fossils of some Paleozoic insects, but the function of the lobes themselves remained an intriguing question. They have been supposed to have covered the gills of amphibious species, aided the concealment of insects from predators, helped aerial dispersal of small forms, or acted as sexual displays. Matthew M. Douglas of Boston University presented a new hypothesis, this time backed by experimental evidence, that the ancestral lobes were used for thermoregulation.

Many cold-blooded animals bask to increase their body temperature without metabolic cost, thereby increasing locomotory efficiency, and in insects the thorax contains the main locomotory muscles. Douglas took the bodies of a conveniently shaped butterfly, cut the wings to resemble those of a presumed preflight ancestor and showed that, given the irradiance of a temperate summer day and an ambient temperature of 22.5° C (72° F), a lobe five millimetres by three millimetres in close contact with the body increased thoracic temperature as much as 20.8° C (37.4° F), whereas a wingless body rose by only 13.4° C (24.1° F). Wing stubs that were longer than ten millimetres were of no further thermoregulatory value, but at this length they would have aided escape by gliding. Since it had been shown recently that paranotal lobes were primitively articulated, the

evolution of flight thereafter was not difficult to envisage. (PETER W. MILES)
[321.E.2.a; 731.A.5]

Ornithology. A ten-year study by two U.S. ornithologists of more than 500 Mexican jays living in six groups in Arizona enabled them to work out family relationships among the birds. Stable social units were found that included grandparents, uncles, aunts, and cousins as well as parents, brothers, and sisters. The social units are discrete, and although only the older birds may actually nest, all birds in the unit help in feeding the young and in driving intruders from the unit's territory. The apparent altruism of those that help the true parents with rearing duties might be explained by the "selfish gene" theory, by which natural selection operates not on individuals of a species but on genes that are represented in more than one individual. Alternatively, it may be that helpers benefit from "rehearsing" a role that they later will play themselves.

A number of species of rare birds have been brought into captivity in order to rescue them from extinction, breed them, and later return a surplus to the wild. One, the Hawaiian goose or nene, actually went through the entire cycle and was returned to its native habitat on high volcanic slopes with initial success. In their recent book devoted to the biology and conservation of this goose, Andrew Berger and Janet Kear argued that breeding wild animals in captivity in order to rescue species is neither a desirable nor a sufficient step; it is beset with problems and should be opted for only as a desperate last measure.

Among the species of wild birds whose eggs are exploited by humans for food, the only one that yields more than a million eggs a year is the sooty tern. Overexploitation was known to have caused the bird's decline in some colonies. At perhaps the best known location, Bird Island in the Seychelles, numbers returned to 395,000 pairs (despite the arrival of rats in 1967), having declined from a mil-

lion pairs at the beginning of the century to 18,000 pairs in 1955.

It was estimated that by 1981, nearly a century after the very first bird-song recording had been made, about 100,000 recordings of 5,000 bird species (of the 9,000 known to be living) were held in 50 libraries. In addition, the voices of 2,500 birds had been published on about 1,100 phonograph records and tapes between 1910 and 1980. The uses of these recordings were many and varied: in field and laboratory identification; in studies of bird behaviour, development, learning ability, heredity, and taxonomy; and in pest control. The most pressing task, as one ornithological sound specialist pointed out at a 1981 bio-acoustics meeting, was to register as soon as possible the voices of many tropical species—particularly those in lowland rain forests—which probably would be extinct before the turn of the century.

A new species of bird, a screech owl, was recently discovered in Peru. It was named the cloud-forest screech owl (*Otus marshalli*).

A major publishing event was the appearance of a completely new edition of Roger Tory Peterson's legendary *Field Guide to the Birds* (of eastern and central North America), history's best-selling bird book. The second volume of *The Birds of the Western Palearctic* (Europe, North Africa, and the Middle East), the most comprehensive ornithological reference work ever begun in any language, also appeared during the year. It covered diurnal birds of prey, game birds, rails, cranes, and bustards.

(JEFFERY BOSWALL)

[313.J.6.h and l; 342.C.1.c]

MARINE BIOLOGY

The first marine biological laboratories were established around 1880. A centennial review in the journal associated with the Stazione Zoologica di Napoli (Zoological Station of Naples, Italy) documented the historical development of marine biology through observations by seafarers, oceanographic expeditions, establishment of marine stations, field research aided by diving, remote-controlled equipment, and underwater experiments. Cooperation with related disciplines led toward bridging gaps in knowledge, development of marine ecological theory, and a greater understanding of the complexity of marine ecosystems.

The sea-surface microlayer (the ocean's upper one millimetre or less) is the habitat for neuston, a community with higher densities of microalgae and bacteria than occur a few centimetres deeper; larval fish, crustaceans, and mollusks also concentrate in the neuston layer. It was reported that naturally occurring phytoneuston finally could be duplicated in laboratory tanks for experimental studies; for example, for following the biological transfer of pollutants through the air-water interface.

The Adriatic is a small, oceanographically unique sea that accepts drainage from the Po, one of the most polluted rivers in Europe. Increased pollution coincided with unusual blooms of nannoplankton (the smallest of planktonic organisms) beginning about 1968 and nearly anoxic (oxygen-depleted) bottom conditions beginning in 1977. That metal pollution might be influencing primary production in contaminated seas was suggested by studies indicating that carbon fixation in coastal phytoplankton is inhibited by copper concentrations in the range of 1–2.5 micrograms per litre, well below the levels reported in some regions around Britain, for example. Copper and chlorine together are discharged in small quantities in power station effluents; there, likewise, they lead to reduction of biomass and diversity in phytoplankton, and thermal conditions in summer even further reduce biomass.

Considerable attention had been focused recently on factors responsible for damaging coral reefs, but few studies had considered the process of recovery. In a review of documented recoveries following disturbances and infestation by the crown-of-thorns starfish (*Acanthaster*) all suggested that at least several decades were required for recovery by recolonization with settlement of coral larvae.

The external layer of mucus on fish offers disease

"Evolution's been good to me."

resistance and also had been assumed to reduce friction drag during swimming. The latter function was confirmed in the laboratory by studying velocity profiles over rainbow trout and wax models of trout.

Many sea anemones (Actiniaria) are found attached to gastropod shells inhabited by hermit crabs. The hermit crab *Pagurus prideauxi* need never change its shell when in association with the cloak anemone *Adamsia palliata*, which wraps around the crab's abdomen and secretes a chitinous cuticle over the small mollusk shell initially occupied by the crab. New work demonstrated the high sophistication of such shell formation by some deep-sea mutualistic anemones, explaining why the coiled shell (carcinoecium) secreted by the Pacific sea anemone *Stylobates aeneus* was originally described as a new genus and species of trochid gastropod.

Mucus secreted by the foot of a crawling gastropod mollusk functions primarily for lubrication, but in some species such mucus laid in trails can be detected and followed by the same individual for navigation purposes. In a number of forms, including *Onchidium verruculatum* studied recently on rocky shores in Kuwait, animals placed on trails could distinguish the directions toward or away from "home," providing evidence that the mucous trails are polarized. The mechanisms of polarization and its detection were as yet unknown. (ERNEST NAYLOR)

[313.G.2.c; 313.G.4.a; 313.I.1.b; 354.B.2 and 5]

BOTANY

Included among the plant growth regulators is the simple gaseous hydrocarbon ethylene (C_2H_4). Since its recognition as a growth regulator, ethylene has been implicated as playing a role in a variety of phenomena including fruit ripening and elongation of stems, roots, and leaves.

Ethylene is synthesized in the living plant from the sulfur-containing amino acid methionine, which is converted to S-adenosylmethionine (SAM). In ripening fruit and in pea stem sections treated with the plant growth regulator auxin, SAM interacts with the enzyme 1-aminocyclopropane-1-carboxylate synthase (ACC synthase) to form 1-aminocyclopropane-1-carboxylic acid (ACC). The latter is ultimately converted to ethylene by an, as yet, unidentified enzyme or enzymes.

In recent experiments conducted with green fruit of the tomato (*Lycopersicon esculentum*) it was demonstrated that wounding of the pericarp (fruit wall) resulted in a substantial increase in ACC and ethylene production as well as in a rapid enhancement in ACC synthase activity. When wounded pericarp was incubated in the presence of aminoethoxyvinylglycine (AVG), a powerful inhibitor of ACC synthase and ethylene synthesis, within one hour ethylene production was strongly reduced. A similar inhibition in ethylene formation resulted when wounded pericarp was maintained for two hours in the presence of the protein synthesis inhibitor cycloheximide. Consequently it was concluded that in wounded pericarp of tomato, as in ripening fruit and auxin-treated pea stem sections,

ACC is also an intermediate in the pathway of ethylene synthesis. The observed increase in ethylene production in the wounded tissue was ascribed to enhanced ACC synthase activity. Because in the presence of cycloheximide ethylene production was dramatically curtailed, it was suggested that ethylene formation is regulated at the level of ACC synthase and that, in response to wounding, de novo synthesis of the enzyme may occur.

In a subsequent investigation with intact tomato fruit it was shown that the rate of ethylene formation increased during ripening and then decreased as the fruit became ripe. Similar results were obtained with "whole" disks (disks 11.5 mm [about a half inch] in diameter and 3 mm in thickness) and "wounded" disks (disks of the same size cut into 12 sectors) that were excised from the pericarp of tomatoes in different stages of ripening, with wounded pericarp exhibiting the highest rates of ethylene production. Although 20 hours following excision the rate of ethylene formation in whole disks from ripe fruit was lower than in whole disks removed from fruit in a number of stages of ripening, the ACC content and ACC synthase activity of disks from ripe fruit were unexpectedly high. Because it was also found that in the presence of cycloheximide the ACC content in wounded pericarp from green and ripening tomatoes remained constant while the rate of ethylene synthesis declined, it was concluded that ACC is not a limiting factor in ethylene synthesis. In view of the fact that wounded pericarp disks excised from tomatoes in several stages of ripening contained comparable amounts of ACC but exhibited significantly different rates of ethylene formation, it was suggested that during ripening there is regulation of the conversion of ACC to ethylene. The regulatory mechanism, however, remained to be elucidated in future investigations.

According to the Cholodny-Went hypothesis, the geotropic response in shoots (upward bending of horizontally oriented stems) is caused by a gravity-induced redistribution of the plant growth regulator auxin in such a way that more auxin accumulates on the lower than the upper side of the stem. The higher concentration of auxin causes the cells on the lower side to elongate more than those on the upper. Consequently the stem bends upward.

Since its formulation in the 1920s, the Cholodny-Went hypothesis has been widely accepted. There exists a body of evidence, however, that is inconsistent with this explanation. For example, it was demonstrated that the amount of auxin that accumulates on the lower side of the stem is too small to cause the observed differences in growth. In addition, auxin redistribution was shown to occur too slowly in the stem to cause geotropic curvature.

Recently ethylene was implicated in the geotropic response. From stems of cocklebur (*Xanthium strumarium*), tomato, and castor bean (*Ricinus communis*), all leaves were removed except the youngest fully expanded one. When these stems were horizontally positioned and treated with inhibitors of ethylene synthesis (cobaltous ion and AVG) and inhibitors of ethylene action (silver ion

and carbon dioxide), the rate of geotropic bending was delayed, in some cases by as much as 12 hours. Although the evidence was circumstantial at best, it led to the suggestion that the geotropic response in dicot stems laid on their sides is caused by an ethylene inhibition of the cells on the top of the stem. (LIVIJA KENT)

[321.B.9.d; 338.D.3; 338.D.5.a; 341.A.1.a]

MOLECULAR BIOLOGY

Natural Gene Transfer. The ponyfish (*Leiognathus equulus*) is a small marine fish found in Indonesian waters. It is luminescent, and in a unique fashion. Virtually all luminescent creatures emit light most actively in the dark and do so in order to be seen. The firefly, for example, luminesces in the dark to attract a mate, while the anglerfish luminesces to attract prey. In contrast, the ponyfish luminesces during the day, and it does so to avoid being seen.

To a deeper swimming predator a small fish swimming close to the surface of the sunlit sea appears in silhouette against the bright surface. One way for this fish to decrease its visibility would be to have a white ventral surface, a commonly used strategy. A better way to escape detection would be to actually emit light from the ventral surface, in an attempt to more nearly match the luminosity of the watery ceiling. This is the remarkable camouflage of the ponyfish.

The light emitted by the ponyfish is not actually made by the fish but by a bacterium, *Photobacter leiognathi*, which lives as a symbiont in a special gland in the belly of the fish. This intimate symbiosis has been in effect for a long time, long enough to have allowed the fish to evolve a special gland in which to house the bacterium. If one wanted to discover an example of gene transfer from a higher to a lower organism, the ponyfish-bacterium symbiosis would be a good place to look.

Transfer of genetic information from higher organisms into bacteria is currently a major preoccupation of genetic engineers. Implantation of human genes into bacteria by recombinant DNA technology is being vigorously pursued because it promises new knowledge of genetic mechanisms at the molecular level as well as such practical benefits as abundant and inexpensive supplies of human insulin, interferons, and other proteins. Some practitioners of genetic engineering have been disquieted because of the feeling that they were doing something "unnatural," the consequences of which could not be anticipated. They would be greatly reassured to know that gene transfer from higher to lower organisms had already occurred in nature. A gene product needed alike by bacteria and by higher organisms, yet taking a distinct form in each, would be a convenient marker of such a gene transfer. The enzyme superoxide dismutase is such a gene product.

The superoxide radical (O_2^-) is a common product of the reduction of molecular oxygen, and it is dangerously reactive. When it is generated within living things, it threatens their integrity and defenses are necessary. The superoxide dismutases efficiently scavenge O_2^- by catalyzing the reaction $O_2^- + O_2^- + 2H^+ \rightarrow H_2O_2 + O_2$, and in so doing they provide the needed defense. As an important component of the biological defense against oxygen toxicity, superoxide dismutases would not be needed in a world without oxygen; they must have evolved concomitant with the oxygenation of the biosphere. This gradual oxygenation was caused by the advent of cyanobacteria (blue-green algae), capable of true photosynthesis. It imposed a common and a stringent selection pressure upon a variety of life for which oxygen was deadly. Under such conditions parallel solutions to the common problem would be favoured, and several kinds of superoxide dismutases might be evolved.

Biologists currently do find three distinct types of superoxide dismutases in the living world. One of these contains both copper and zinc at its active sites and is found in the cytoplasm of eucaryotic (nucleated) cells. The second type contains manganese, and the third type contains iron. The manganese and the iron enzymes are characteristic of procaryotes (primitive, non-nucleated cells) and have been shown to be related to each other in an evolutionary sense. The copper:zinc enzymes represent an independent line of evolution and are unrelated to the manganese or to the iron enzymes. Eucaryotes contain subcellular organelles, called mitochondria, that are thought to have evolved from a procaryote living symbiotically within a proto-eucaryotic cell. It is fascinating, and entirely consistent with this theory, that mitochondria contain a manganese superoxide dismutase very similar to that found in procaryotes and unrelated to that found in cytoplasm that surrounds the mitochondria.

Procaryotes do not contain the copper:zinc superoxide dismutase. This statement is certainly valid for the dozens of varieties of bacteria thus far examined—but it is not valid for *P. leiognathi*. Symbiotic *P. leiognathi* was shown by A. M. Michelson and co-workers at the Institute de Biologie Physico-Chimique, Fondation Edmond de Rothschild, Paris, to contain a copper:zinc superoxide dismutase in addition to the iron enzyme one might expect to find in a bacterium. It appears that *P. leiognathi* contains this eucaryotic type of superoxide dismutase because of a gene transfer from the ponyfish. Many species of luminescent bacteria are closely related to *P. leiognathi*, but these are free-living rather than symbiotic, and none of them contains the copper:zinc enzyme.

Copper:zinc superoxide dismutases have been isolated from numerous species of fungi, plants, fish, birds, and mammals and from *P. leiognathi*, and the amino-acid compositions of these enzymes have been determined. All enzymes are composed of amino acids polymerized into long strands, which then coil and fold into compact structures. There are 20 different amino acids used in the construction of enzymes, and their specific sequence determines the final structure and the properties of each enzyme. During the course of evolution of a particular enzyme, changes in its amino-acid composition occur. The more closely related two enzymes are, the more nearly identical their amino-acid sequences and their compositions.

Although sequence information is more discriminating than gross amino-acid composition, it is more difficult to obtain. Because changes in se-

quence are accompanied by changes in composition, it is possible to study the relatedness of different enzymes by comparing only their amino-acid compositions. Indeed, a computer program has been developed to facilitate such comparisons, and it was applied by Joseph P. Martin of Rice University, Houston, Texas, to a comparison of all known superoxide dismutases.

In the first level of this analysis the computer reviewed the amino-acid compositions of approximately 60 different superoxide dismutases. It correctly clustered all copper:zinc enzymes into one group, all manganese enzymes into a second group, and all iron enzymes into a third group. Moreover, this computer analysis recognized that the manganese and the iron groups were related to each other, but not to the copper:zinc group. From gross amino-acid compositions the computer thus was able to derive conclusions in full accord with those already reached from knowledge of amino-acid sequences and of metal contents. This result provided confidence in the analytic program being used.

In the final level of analysis the computer was fed only the amino-acid compositions of copper:zinc superoxide dismutases, and it separated them into three subgroups. The first of these was made up of the enzymes derived from fungi and plants. The second was composed of the mammalian and the bird copper:zinc enzymes. The third encompassed the enzymes from fish and from *P. leiognathi*. This close relationship between the fish and the *P. leiognathi* enzymes could hardly be an accident. Coupled with the anomaly of a copper:zinc superoxide dismutase in a bacterium, it indicates that there was a gene transfer from the host ponyfish to its bacterial symbiont. Amino-acid sequence analyses, which would buttress this conclusion, were under way in 1981 in the laboratory of Howard M. Steinman of the Albert Einstein College of Medicine in New York City.

This first clear case of a eucaryote-to-procaryote gene transfer indicates that the achievements of recombinant DNA technology are not entirely unprecedented. Undoubtedly other examples of natural gene transfers will come to light. Furthermore, since only those gene transfers that confer a selective advantage have been retained, existing cases reflect only a minuscule fraction of those that have occurred.   (IRWIN FRIDOVICH)

Gene Cloning. Many important recent advances in biology and medicine have been made possible by the availability of purified genes. These genes are excised from their normal site of residence in the chromosomes of their species of origin and inserted in a bacterial host. Growth of such bacteria in the laboratory leads to the production of very large amounts of a single gene, which can be purified and analyzed. How is this accomplished?

The genes of an organism are made up of DNA, a long double-stranded molecule. Each strand of DNA is a linear polymer of four components, the deoxyribonucleotide bases, which are represented by the letters A, G, C, and T. The information in DNA resides in the specific sequence of these four bases. One strand of the DNA is complementary to

Figure 1

—A-A-C-T-A-T-G-G-A-T-C-C-A-A-A-A-T—
—T-T-G-A-T-A-C-C-T-A-G-G-T-T-T-T-A—

the other, such that A is always opposite T and G is always opposite C; the sequence in one strand thus can specify that in the other. For example, a short stretch of double-stranded DNA might have the sequence shown in Figure 1. The strands are held together by hydrogen-bonded base pairs between A and T and between G and C.

A gene is a segment of DNA that codes for the synthesis of a specific protein. An average gene in a bacterium contains about 1,000 base pairs of DNA; *i.e.*, it is one kilobase pair (kbp) in length. The whole genome, or genetic endowment, of the commonly studied bacterium *Escherichia coli* contains approximately 4,000 genes and thus is 4,000 kbp (four million base pairs) in length. By contrast, the fruit fly *Drosophila melanogaster* has a genome length of approximately 150,000 kbp, and a human cell genome is about three million kilobase pairs long. How can one purify a single gene, representing a specific DNA sequence of a few thousand base pairs, from a genome containing such a large collection of possible sequences?

Several parallel developments in molecular genetics have made such feats possible and collectively are often called recombinant DNA technology. One development was the discovery of restriction endonucleases, enzymes that recognize specific base sequences in DNA and cleave (or nick) the DNA strands in a specific manner at or near the recognition sequence. For example, the restriction endonuclease Bam H1 recognizes the six-base-pair sequence GGATCC and cleaves the DNA strand between the two G's. In double-stranded DNA, because of base-pair complementarity, Bam H1 cleaves both strands in a staggered fashion to leave a four-base-pair overlap. *See* Figure 2.

An important feature of this event is that the ends generated by this type of enzyme are complementary and can re-form the original base-pair structure; such ends are often referred to as mutually cohesive, or "sticky," ends. Once the ends pair up, or anneal, the nick originally introduced by the endonuclease can be sealed by another enzyme, called DNA ligase. Because each cohesive end generated by Bam H1 is identical, any two fragments made by this enzyme can be linked together whether or not they were neighbours in the original DNA molecule—and in fact whether or not they came from the same species of organism. By 1981 scientists knew of more than 100 restriction enzymes similar to Bam H1, but with different recognition sequences.

Given these capabilities, how can one then identify the DNA fragment containing the gene of interest, separate it from the myriad other DNA

Figure 2

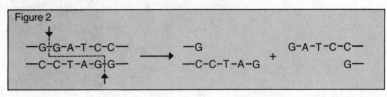

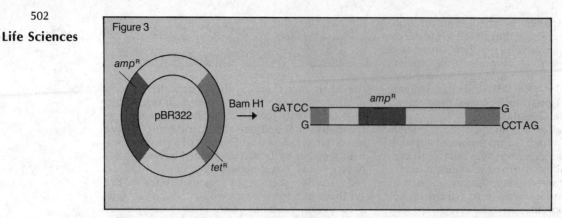

Figure 3

fragments, and generate useful quantities of it? These tasks are achieved by another development of molecular genetics, molecular cloning of DNA. Most DNA sequences are cloned in a bacterial host such as *E. coli* by means of cloning vectors, either viruses that parasitize the cells or plasmids that grow within the cells.

Plasmids are small, circular DNA molecules that exist in bacterial cells as self-replicating entities separate from the normal bacterial host chromosome. Those useful for cloning have certain common characteristics, including the presence of genes that impart resistance to antibiotics. One of the most widely used cloning vectors is the *E. coli* plasmid pBR322, itself a product of recombinant DNA technology. It carries two genes that confer drug resistance upon its host bacteria: the *tet*^{R} gene for tetracycline and the *amp*^{R} gene for ampicillin. It also has single sites that are cut by several restriction endonucleases, strategically located in the *tet*^{R} or *amp*^{R} gene. The following two-phase scheme illustrates how pBR322 might be used to clone and identify specific genes from *Drosophila*.

The initial phase consists of the construction of gene banks or libraries. First, many molecules of pBR322 in a test tube are cut with Bam H1 to yield linear molecules with sticky ends (*see* Figure 3).

Second, *Drosophila* total DNA in a separate test tube is cut with Bam H1 to yield a population of linear molecules, all with Bam H1 sticky ends, representing the entire genome (*see* Figure 4).

Third, the two populations of DNA are mixed together. The sticky ends anneal to re-form double stranded DNA's, which are then sealed together with DNA ligase. One possible combination of the DNA fragments results in the insertion of a piece of *Drosophila* DNA into the *tet*^{R} gene (*see* Figure 5). This new hybrid molecule still has an intact *amp*^{R} gene but an interrupted, and therefore inactivated, *tet*^{R} gene. Bacteria containing this plasmid are

thus ampicillin-resistant but tetracycline-sensitive. Other possible rejoining of DNA's could result in re-forming of original pBR322 (no *Drosophila* insert, thus *tet*^{R} gene still active), or in *Drosophila-Drosophila* combinations (which would not replicate in *E. coli*).

Fourth, from the population of rejoined molecules must now be selected the desired hybrids. To do this, *E. coli* cells are treated with calcium to make them capable of assimilating DNA and then mixed with the ligated DNA population. After allowing time for DNA uptake, the bacteria are grown on nutrient-covered Petri plates in the presence of ampicillin; only those bacteria containing a viable plasmid with an intact *amp*^{R} gene will grow. The cells are diluted so that less than 1,000 grow per Petri plate. Each single cell gives rise to a colony of identical cells that after about 24 hours is easily visible to the naked eye. Each colony of bacteria is a clone of cells harbouring a single plasmid with a functional *amp*^{R} gene.

To distinguish those colonies with *Drosophila* DNA inserted in the *tet*^{R} gene from normal pBR322, an exact imprint of the colonies on the plate is made and transferred (replica plated) to another Petri plate of agar containing tetracycline. The normal pBR322-containing bacteria will grow on the second plate; the cells containing the hybrid plasmid will not because the inserted DNA has inactivated the *tet*^{R} gene. These tetracycline-sensitive colonies, identified from their positions back on the original plate, in fact represent clones, each of which carries a different fragment of *Drosophila* DNA. If enough hybrid plasmids have been constructed, the desired gene is cloned in one of the many colonies that are ampicillin-resistant but tetracyline-sensitive. This collection of colonies is referred to as a library or a bank of cloned DNA fragments from *Drosophila*.

The second phase of the process involves screen-

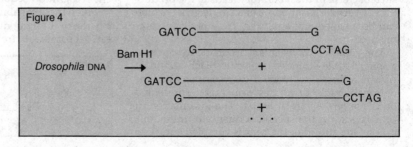

Figure 4

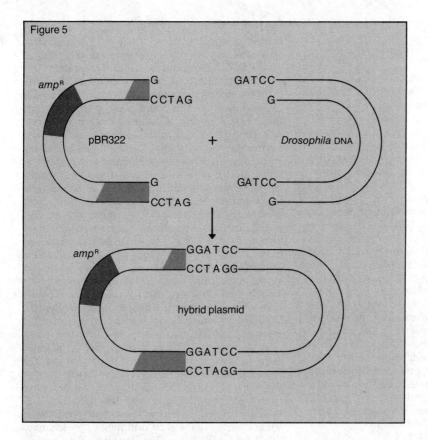

Figure 5

ing the library to identify the gene of interest. Suppose, for instance, that one wants to identify the genes coding for the histones (small ubiquitous proteins that are an integral structural component of chromosomes). Recall how proteins are synthesized. The nucleotide sequence of histone gene DNA is transcribed into a single strand of a closely related molecule called messenger RNA (mRNA). This mRNA is then used as a template on which the linear sequence of amino acids that make up the protein molecule is assembled by the cell's protein-synthesis machinery.

Because histones are made by cells in large amounts, scientists have been able to purify the mRNA's for the histone proteins. Since the base sequence of an mRNA molecule is complementary to the DNA from which it was transcribed, the ability of mRNA to form base pairs specifically with its DNA complement can be used to identify the histone genes in the genomic library.

First, histone mRNA is labeled with a radioactive isotope to make it a hybridization probe.

Second, the colonies in the library are treated so that the mRNA probe can hybridize with its DNA complement carried in a hybrid plasmid. In a technique called colony hybridization, an exact replica of the original colonies is imprinted once again, this time on a piece of special filter paper that fits the Petri plate. The paper is then placed on another Petri plate, and the colonies are allowed to grow up again. Next, the paper is chemically treated to break open the cells, to cause the base-paired strands to come apart, and to affix the DNA to the paper exactly in the position of the original colony. The paper with attached DNA is then immersed in

a solution of the radioactive probe mRNA under conditions that cause the RNA to hybridize to its DNA complement. Finally the paper is washed and dried and exposed to photographic film. Radioactivity from the colonies to which the mRNA hybridized darkens the film, thereby identifying the colonies containing the histone genes.

To study one of the genes, a colony is picked from the master plate and grown in large culture flasks to generate large amounts of the specific plasmid. The DNA is then isolated, and the cloned gene, now chemically homogeneous and highly purified, can be easily analyzed.

Work with cloned genes has revealed fundamental differences in the organization of genes from bacteria and genes from higher organisms, has helped to explain the complex formation of antibody molecules in the immune response, and has allowed inroads in understanding details of regulation of gene expression in higher organisms. On the practical side, engineering cloned genes into bacteria will allow production of inexpensive human proteins such as insulin and interferon. Genetic engineering also recently led to the production of a new vaccine against foot-and-mouth disease. Health care will be altered dramatically by gene cloning, as will the field of agriculture, where improvements in disease resistance, crop yields, and many other areas can be anticipated. Properly applied, the new genetics will have a dramatic positive influence on human lives.

(ARNO GREENLEAF)

[241.B.3; 312.A.3; 321.B.3 and 5; 321.B.7; 323.E; 339.C; 352.B.2.c]

See also Earth Sciences; Environment.

504

Literature

The 1981 Nobel Prize for Literature was awarded to Elias Canetti (*see* NOBEL PRIZES). A Londoner for much of his life but generally referred to as a Bulgarian, he seemed almost a walking compendium of international literature. Born in 1905, he was brought up as a Sephardic Jew speaking Ladino, but German became his principal language for writing. It was thus appropriate that his success should be celebrated in England by the BBC with a talk by an Indian, a long-standing admirer of Canetti, Salman Rushdie, who himself won the Booker Prize for fiction in 1981. In comparing Canetti with such Germanic writers as Robert Musil and Thomas Mann, Rushdie remarked that Canetti's novel, *Auto da Fé* (*Die Blendung*), was written in "a black, ironic, and perhaps peculiarly German tone of voice." It was for *Auto da Fé* and for his memoir, *The Tongue Set Free*, that Canetti was awarded the prize. He was also the author of several plays, including *The Numbered*, a drama about a world in which people know the dates of their deaths—and are measured and assessed by those dates rather than by their birthdays. His bleak study *Crowds and Power*, a poetic essay in sociology, was reexamined. Canetti was an unusual choice for the Nobel Prize, since his work was not obviously marked by the "idealism" that generally recommends the prizewinners.

Comparing Canetti's work with that of other Nobel Prize winners, John Bayley, Warton professor of English literature at Oxford, drew an analogy with Kipling, claiming that Canetti had a similar gift for familiarizing out-of-the-way places. But he found a more timely comparison and contrast with the work of the 1980 Nobel winner, Czeslaw Milosz, another "subtle analyst and historian of national fixations and complexities." Milosz's record of a Polish-Lithuanian childhood, *The Issa Valley*, Bayley said, should be enjoyed together with Canetti's record of life in Austria, Bulgaria, England, and Switzerland. "The fact that two such remarkable writers as Milosz and Canetti should have won [the Nobel Prize] in recent years almost makes one believe in the prize as an award to literature."

Elias Canetti, winner of the 1981 Nobel Prize for Literature

HORST TAPPE—CAMERA PRESS

ENGLISH

United Kingdom. It was generally agreed that 1981 was not a very distinguished year for the production of original writing. The state of the economy prompted a cautious approach. Publishers were among those businesses that attempted to "slim down": fewer books were published; and there was a feeling of "depression" in the air. It was time to look abroad, to bring back reports from overseas, to publish translations of foreign work. The attention of publishers and critics was not restricted to the usual three overseas sources—the U.S., the dissidents of the Soviet world, and the successor states of the British Empire. Some good work from Africa was published—and Edward Blishen's interesting memoir, *Shaky Relations*, provided a neat comment on the prevailing mood, since the ambiguous title referred to the conflicts between English and African literatures as well as to his "shaky relations" with his own kinfolk and their English insularity. There were also several important translations from French, German, Japanese, and Spanish, which attracted more admiration than native English work.

Traditional, established enterprises continued majestically. Perhaps the most important was the latest installment of the great *Dictionary of National Biography* (1961–70), founded by Sir Leslie Stephen (father of Virginia Woolf) and now edited by E. T. Williams and C. S. Nicholls. Another reminder of a more heroic age was an unfinished, posthumous work by C. P. Snow, *The Physicists*. Sir Charles, novelist, scientist, and administrator, strove during his lifetime to bridge the gap between the "two cultures" of science and the arts. In *The Physicists* he offered a history of modern physics through biographies of the most distinguished scientists in this field, from Rutherford to Dirac. Mark Girouard took readers further back with *The Return to Camelot: Chivalry and the English Gentleman*, a study of the Victorian attempt to revive the spirit of medieval chivalry and the effects of this attempt on later generations.

Among travelers' reports, the most highly praised was *Among the Believers*, a study of Islam by the Trinidadian writer V. S. Naipaul, who was becoming the principal literary expert on the third world. "His finest non-fiction to date," wrote the poet D. J. Enright. *Old Glory* was a report on the Mississippi by the young English playwright Jonathan Raban, recording his voyage along that river, alone in a small boat, and his encounters with the people who live by its banks. Even in the department of religious thought, a resistance to insularity was prominent. In his memoir, *Part of a Journey, 1977–79*, Philip Toynbee (*see* OBITUARIES) described his spiritual and practical attempts to blend the merits of Christianity and Far Eastern faiths.

In poetry, the word "Martianism" came into use, through the verse of Craig Raine and his associates, presenting a vision of life on Earth as seen by a visiting Martian. It was noticed that "Martianism" is an anagram for Martin Amis, one of Raine's associates. Other poets were occupied with producing translations of classic plays, generally for the National Theatre. It was not surprising that

one of the few noteworthy original plays was called *Translations*; written by Brian Friel, it told of the shaky relations between the English and native Irish in the last century. In the first volume of his collected plays, the novelist John Symonds, author of *The Guardian of the Threshold*, added an incisive preface about the failings of British drama since the death of Shaw, in which he criticized the fashions of thoughtless leftism, the Theatre of the Absurd, and the Theatre of Cruelty.

FICTION. The Booker Prize for fiction was won by Salman Rushdie, an Indian brought up in England. The prize (founded by a British sugar-making firm from the West Indies) was always intended to assist writers from the Commonwealth. Rushdie's success was generally welcomed. He was 34, and *Midnight's Children* was only his second novel. It is the story of a young man born at the stroke of midnight, when British India was emancipated and divided into two nations; the account of his life blossoms into something of an "epic" of modern India.

Rushdie's nearest rival was D. M. Thomas, whose novel *The White Hotel* began with what seemed to be a pornographic fantasy and turned out to be the outpourings of a patient of Freud. She is a singer, suffering from hysteria, shortly after World War II. History and psychology were neatly blended in this skillfully contrived work, but it was not much admired in England until it had been acclaimed in the U.S., where Freudian, post-Freudian, and anti-Freudian essays were more readily appreciated.

The most interesting fiction published came from abroad, whether in English or translation. Africa retained its fascination. (*See* Special Report.) A new British humorist, William Boyd, presented an informed and entertaining novel, *A Good Man in Africa*, about a keen English booby in a lightly disguised version of Nigeria. From South Africa, Nadine Gordimer published one of her sad novels about her nation's plight. *July's People* is about whites protected by their black servant after the forthcoming black revolution. In no less sombre a mood, the veteran Alan Paton discussed South Africa in his ironically titled novel *Ah! But Your Land Is Beautiful*.

The most distinguished translation of the year was Terence Kilmartin's revised version of Proust's *À la Recherche du Temps Perdu*. It was agreed that Kilmartin had retained the virtues of C. K. Scott-Moncrieff's celebrated translation while correcting its errors and purifying its purple prose and Edwardian unctuousness.

Against this, new British fiction seemed rather frail and bleak, like a dying craft passing from father to son. Piers Paul Read, son of poet and writer Sir Herbert Read, wrote *The Villa Golitsyn*, about decadent bourgeoisie in the south of France. Martin Amis, son of Kingsley Amis, wrote *Other People*, about a young woman trying to find her lost memory in a place like Hell. Ian McEwan, a young and fashionable novelist of squalor, wrote *The Comfort of Strangers*, about decadent bourgeoisie in a place like Venice. Brian Moore, an inventive Irish-Canadian living in the U.S., published *The Temptation of Eileen Hughes*, about a well-to-do

PHOTOGRAPH © 1982 JILL KREMENTZ

V. S. Naipaul

Irish ménage-à-trois in London. Marghanita Laski, of the Arts Council literature panel, remarked that "literary novels" seemed to be the least well liked of the art forms the Council sponsored.

However, one first novel, *A Separate Development* by Christopher Hope, was highly praised for its blend of humour and indignation, and it was awarded the David Higham Prize for Fiction. "One of the funniest tragedies I have read since *Catch 22*," said one critic. William Boyd said it was "rich in lovingly evoked detail and character, and a profound political indictment." Hardly necessary to add that it was about South Africa.

Among the writers who died in 1981 were novelists Enid Bagnold, A. J. Cronin, David Garnett, Rayner Heppenstall, Pamela Hansford Johnson, Robin Maugham, Gwyn Thomas, and Alec Waugh (*see* OBITUARIES).

LIVES AND LETTERS. *The Dictionary of National Biography* (1961–70), mentioned above, was the most important contribution in this field. A similar scholarly confidence was apparent in the steady progression of series of volumes of letters by classic writers—from Cowper to Dickens, from Byron (a concluding volume) to Bentham (quite early in the series, the latest being a most interesting record of the years in which he was developing his "panopticon" principle for penitentiaries and other institutions). There were many contributions to the biographies of favourite subjects—plenty of Churchilliana, another Auden, a new account of the Douglas family from which the scandalous Lord Alfred sprang....

In the field of Churchilliana, the most impressive volume was *Winston Churchill: The Wilderness Years* by Martin Gilbert, who had already covered the prewar period in one massive volume—"and an even more massive supplementary volume of his biography of Churchill, the major biographical venture of our time." Such was the judgment of Robert Rhodes James, the Conservative member of Parliament for Cambridge and himself the author

JERRY BAUER

Salman Rushdie

of *Churchill: A Study in Failure, 1900–1939*. Gilbert's new book was something more than a summary of his earlier work, since he was committed to whole-heartedly arguing the case for Churchill's policies.

At the opposite extreme, a strong example of the denunciatory school of biography was Edward Crankshaw's life of Bismarck, in which he traced the lineaments of Nazism. Then there was John Carey's denunciation of the great poet John Donne, which was seen as a personal attack and was itself denounced by Sir William Empson. The once-popular playwright John Osborne published an autobiography called *A Better Class of Person*, displaying his well-known command of invective and lack of self-control; in it he denounced practically everybody, especially his own mother. It was so repellent that it was serialized in the Sunday papers. Dorothy L. Sayers's illegitimate child and her treatment of him attracted new attention to this Christian apologist and detective-story writer. Sir Harold Nicolson's homosexuality was the attraction in the biography of him by James Lees-Milne. A similar journalistic prurience drew attention to a clumsy but interesting biography of H. H. Munro ("Saki") by a probing American, A. J. Langguth. However, certain first-rate Christian poets received sympathetic biographies despite their supposed sexual lapses, among them Alice Meynell of the 1890s, Edith Sitwell of the 1920s, and W. H. Auden of the 1930s.

POETRY. The Society of Authors was responsible for the presentation of several awards. The Hawthornden Prize, for writers under 41, went to Christopher Reid, a poet (and critic) of peculiarly delicate and surrealistic humour—though he would rather call himself a subrealist and direct the critics' attention toward the "Martian" work of his friend Craig Raine. Roy Fisher and Robert Garioch were among the recipients of the Cholmondeley awards for poetry. Fisher's best-known poem was early Martian, since it concerned "the last rabbit in England," visited by eager tourists and their families traveling down the motorways. D. J. Enright (who edited the *Oxford Book of Contemporary Verse*, published in 1980) was one of the recipients of a traveling scholarship; he

was already well traveled, much of his verse and fiction referring to his sojourn in Malaysia. After publication of his sad, witty, and high-principled collected poems, Enright was awarded the Queen's Gold Medal for Poetry.

Among anthologies was *The Faber Book of Useful Verse*, full of mnemonics and other practical material. Much more serious was the *New Oxford Book of Christian Verse*, edited by the poet Donald Davie. This should be seen as a supplement to the old *Oxford Book of Christian Verse*, edited by Lord David Cecil. Where Lord David was a touch defensive, Davie was militant. The anthology indicated progress from the antireligious consensus about literary values that had been so dominant in the 20th century. (D. A. N. JONES)

United States. FICTION. A perennial exercise in futility is the attempt to make sense of American literature at a time when little about the nation itself smacks of unity or coherence. A survey of the year's books does reveal, however, the pervasive influence of feminism, even as the Equal Rights Amendment threatened to founder. Many writers of both sexes emerged from the 1970s confused about what roles, if any, females and males may legitimately assume. Perhaps more than anything else, that concern and uncertainty have acted to narrow the novelist's vision so that a work like Robert Stone's *A Flag for Sunrise* may seem panoramic by comparison.

Stone's third novel was often and aptly likened to the political thrillers of Joseph Conrad. *A Flag for Sunrise* featured U.S. Central Intelligence Agency (CIA) agents, revolutionaries, and missionaries in an imaginary Central American country called Tecan. An anthropology professor named Frank Holliwell is induced by a former CIA colleague to investigate reports of odd goings-on that might threaten U.S. interests there. Holliwell encounters a religiously wayward priest, a politically and sexually wayward nun, and cruel local authorities, while into this miasma wanders a homicidal drug freak named Pablo who is helping a U.S. couple run guns to Tecan revolutionaries. With its superbly structured plot and colourful characters, the novel could be read for narrative and suspense alone. But Stone also gave the main characters private struggles of conscience or personal belief that, taken together, comprise an effective guide to the spiritual and political uncertainty of the U.S. in the post-Vietnam era.

In *Rabbit Is Rich*, John Updike's third novel in the series containing *Rabbit, Run* (1960) and *Rabbit Redux* (1971), the character of Harry C. ("Rabbit") Angstrom embodies a mundane, domestic brand of those turn-of-the-decade anxieties that Stone has writ large. The year is 1979 and Rabbit is 46 and prospering as part owner of a Toyota dealership, but he worries that things everywhere are falling apart, moons over ghosts from his past, and wrestles with his own sexual Hydra: his son has got a girl pregnant and needs the job currently held by Rabbit's best salesman, who used to sleep with Rabbit's wife. The sexual complications and explicitness of the books have grown with the permissiveness of the times, and Updike has maintained his role as ironic if grim chronicler of mores.

In a sequel to *The Ghost Writer* (1979), Philip Roth continued the fortunes of his neatly autobiographical character, Newark-born Nathan Zuckerman. *Zuckerman Unbound* finds Nathan uncomfortable with the succès de scandale and profitable reception of his novel *Carnovsky* (read *Portnoy's Complaint*). Though he is accused of vulgarity and of betraying friends and his heritage, Nathan is often more troubled by the perquisites he does not rush to exploit and the expectations he does not feel obliged to fulfill. The novel was delightful for letting art hold a mirror up to art and as a vehicle for Roth's undiminished wit.

Rounding out the year's bumper crop of sequels was *Reinhart's Women*, by Thomas Berger, the fourth novel in the author's Reinhart series. A large, sententious German-American, Carlo Reinhart at 54 is a chef on a local television cooking show in Ohio valiantly coping with the more trying manifestations of women's rights among family and neighbouring females. Akin to *Rabbit Is Rich* in its ironic targets, Berger's novel seemed more enjoyable because Reinhart is more a survivor than a succumber.

A highly regarded short-story writer, Leonard Michaels, assembled seven talkative, hungry men in his first novel, *The Men's Club*. A kind of pop psychotherapist leads the men on a long night of self-revelation that deals mainly with the women in their lives. The conversation of these representatives of the first generation to be fully confronted and dislocated by feminism is loud with pain and confusion. Their appetites make raiding the refrigerator an essential rite; their liberating camaraderie leaves the house a mess. Treating the men with terse comic irony, Michaels evoked sympathy in a context dangerously close to a college fraternity house or locker room.

Stylistic variation and challenge, though less in vogue than in the previous decade, was well represented. *Darconville's Cat* by Alexander Theroux was a tale of love lost and revenge plotted. In various narrative forms and with a dazzling richness of vocabulary, the author wittily and abstrusely explored Art, Life, Reality, and other capitalizable verities. Russell Hoban's *Riddley Walker* moved outside the common lexicon to create a world 2,000 years hence and transformed by nuclear disaster in our time to a primitive civilization left with only the shards of the present technology. The novel's difficulty was also its reward, namely, adapting to and reveling in what the author called "a worn-down, broken-apart kind of English." For fans, *Cities of the Red Night* by William S. Burroughs was a welcome return to and an updating of the underground terrain introduced in his *Naked Lunch* (1959).

Two novelists reappeared following financially and critically successful outings. The extraordinary excitement surrounding *The World According to Garp* (1978) did not recur with John Irving's *The Hotel New Hampshire*, however much it relied on the familiar quirks of the earlier novel. The story followed life among the members of an eccentric family to whom a certain amount of sex and violence happens while they inhabit three different dwellings with the same name as the title.

Robert Stone

Mary Gordon's literary debut in *Final Payments* (1978) aroused great expectations for this young writer, and these were mostly fulfilled in *The Company of Women*. The second novel resembled the first in its Catholic elements, its strong heroine, and its theme of sacrifice. A girl, raised among five single working women who have banded around a conservative priest, takes a stab at freedom but returns to the little congregation to bear her illegitimate child and establish a maturer independence. Though still capable of the mawkish or facile turns that marred her first book, Gordon retained her standing as a talented, intelligent writer.

Another second novel of 1981 confirmed the author's promise in the first. Lisa Alther followed *Kinflicks* (1976) with *Original Sins*, an old-fashioned novel that records the fates of five Southern children as they grow up together and go their separate ways. The author controls a spacious, complex plot while forming an insightful picture of people and a region—the South—in flux.

Toni Morrison, whose *Song of Solomon* (1977) won a National Book Critics Circle Award, described in *Tar Baby* an improbable love affair between two socially distant blacks on a Caribbean island. Written in prose as graceful as it is energetic, the novel measured the quality of freedom and bondage in a society that thinks it has already taken care of those old problems. In *Angel of Light*, Joyce Carol Oates updated the Greek tale of the house of Atreus through the vengeful desires of a brother and sister who believe that their politically well-placed father, an apparent suicide, was murdered. The author, ever competent and resourceful, relied too much on newspaper-headline material for interest and on adjectives for an almost smothering prose style. Oates also published *Con-*

traries: Essays, a collection of seven critical essays on literary topics. *Household Saints*, by Francine Prose, drew wittily on the happenstance of life to give a lustrous portrait of two generations in an Italian-American family.

Among the year's literary debuts were three outstanding works. In *Saving Grace*, Celia Gittelson displayed considerable imagination and humour in creating a Roman Catholic pope who runs away from the burdens of the office. Ted Mooney took a number of risks in *Easy Travel to Other Planets*, both in stepping several years into the future for a setting that demanded appropriately dislocated sensibilities and in working through important themes no less compelling for the dislocation. And Joanne Meschery's *In a High Place* was a welcome reminder that traditional novels are often the most engaging, as she described a single woman's struggle to make a home for herself and her family in a small, initially hostile town.

As if in conscious rebuttal to the ever diminishing number of markets for the genre, collections of short stories appeared in abundance. Noteworthy among them were: *Sixty Stories*, a grand retrospective of the work of the entertainingly and irritatingly unconventional Donald Barthelme; *Liars in Love*, by Richard Yates; *What We Talk About When We Talk About Love*, by Raymond Carver; *Listen, Listen*, by Kate Wilhelm, a writer of stunning and thoughtful science fiction; *The Lone Pilgrim*, by Laurie Colwin; and two generous collections by Southern writers, *The Stories of Elizabeth Spencer*, which contained 33 tales from four decades of work, and *The Collected Stories of Caroline Gordon*, which had 24 offerings.

In popular fiction the year's blockbuster came from James Clavell. With a national audience still warm from the 12-hour television production of *Shogun* (1975), he brought out *Noble House*, the fourth novel in his Asian saga. Limited in time to one week in Hong Kong in 1963, the story is nonetheless an expansive (1,206 pages) and complex blend of corporate and international intrigue, in which the ongoing struggle for business power between Asians and British is complicated by the addition of two ambitious Americans. In addition, Clavell published a modestly sized juvenile entitled *The Children's Story*; it was an apocalyptic parable expressing the author's concerns about America's patriotic failings.

The year's pop fiction also included one highly praised newcomer and a number of familiar names. With *Gorky Park*, Martin Cruz Smith garnered critical and popular kudos for creating a believable Moscow detective and a wholly original and intelligent thriller set mainly in the Soviet Union. Joseph Wambaugh set his latest Los Angeles police procedural, *The Glitter Dome*, amid the tinsel of Hollywood and Beverly Hills. The Florida-based Travis McGee made his 19th appearance in John D. MacDonald's *Free Fall in Crimson*.

HISTORY, BIOGRAPHY, AND BELLES LETTRES. Dumas Malone completed his exhaustive 40-year effort on Thomas Jefferson with *The Sage of Monticello*, the sixth and final volume of *Jefferson and His Time*. Theodore Roosevelt's early life, from the ages of 10 to 28, was covered with splendid detail in

Mornings on Horseback, by David McCullough. A more recent and controversial president was the subject of Fawn Brodie's *Richard Nixon: The Shaping of His Character*, an intriguing study that leaned a good deal on the questionable precepts of psychobiography. In *Jefferson Davis Gets His Citizenship Back*, Robert Penn Warren combined biography and memoir; Warren also presented his most recent poetic works in *Rumor Verified: Poems 1979–1980*.

Past and current writers for *The New Yorker* were represented with *Selected Letters of James Thurber*, edited by Helen Thurber and Edward Weeks; *The Last Laugh* by S. J. Perelman, which included uncollected pieces and autobiographical fragments; *Poems and Sketches of E. B. White*; and *Whatever Is Moving* by Howard Moss, a gathering of essays, reviews, and literary profiles by the magazine's poetry editor.

More than 600 letters written by a man very secretive about his correspondence were revealed in *Ernest Hemingway: Selected Letters 1917–1961*, edited by Carlos Baker. And Nobel laureate Isaac Bashevis Singer recalled his arrival from Poland in America during the 1930s in *Lost in America*.

Other noteworthy books in the category of belles lettres included: *From Bauhaus to Our House*, Tom Wolfe's idiosyncratic denunciation of modern architecture; *The Language of Clothes*, in which Alison Lurie turned her novelistic talents to exploring sartorial fads and fashions; and *Philosophical Explanations*, Harvard University philosophy professor Robert Nozick's sensible guide through some of his field's most basic and often-ignored questions.

Toni Morrison

© THOMAS VICTOR

And in *Mrs. Harris: The Death of the Scarsdale Diet Doctor*, Diana Trilling applied a fine intelligence to a sensational murder trial and drew from it both its fascinating detail and its more serious implications for American culture.

The number of books directly related to women or born out of feminism demands separate treatment. Betty Friedan, author of one of the movement's key works, *The Feminine Mystique*, caused a considerable stir with *The Second Stage*. In it she suggested that a "feminist mystique" had come to replace the earlier one with a new set of liberation-seeking constraints and that these were forcing women to deny themselves the human pleasures of home and family. Something of a counterargument to Friedan's could be found in Colette Dowling's *The Cinderella Complex: Women's Hidden Fear of Independence*, which had as its thesis that "personal, psychological dependency . . . is the chief force holding women down today."

In *Pornography and Silence: Culture's Revenge Against Nature*, Susan Griffin argued well, if at times stridently, against the sexual exploitation of women, tracing its surface and subtle dangers to males' sadistic impulses. On what seemed another side of that coin, Shere Hite followed up the success of *The Hite Report* (1976) on female sexuality with *The Hite Report on Male Sexuality*, but her analysis of the proclivities and insecurities men revealed drew almost exclusively on feminist tenets. And in the first study of its kind Helen Rogan provided an informed report and thoughtful analysis in *Mixed Company: Women in the Modern Army*, which attributed most of military women's difficulties not to the traditional physical shortcomings of their sex but to male prejudice, insecurity, and inefficiency.

POETRY. It was a good year for the poetic muse. *The Collected Poems: Sylvia Plath*, edited by Ted Hughes, included 224 poems in chronological order. Gregory Corso published his first collection in 11 years, *Herald of the Autochthonic Spirit*, and another figure from the Beat Generation, Lawrence Ferlinghetti, published *Endless Life: Selected Poems*, chosen from his past 25 years of writing. Gilbert Sorrentino offered his own preferences from his work in *Selected Poems 1958–1980*, and he published a diverting if strained neofictional novel, *Crystal Vision*. Also worthy of note were *One for the Rose* by Philip Levine, *Landfall* by David Wagoner, and *The Red Coal* by Gerald Stern.

(JEFFREY BURKE)

Canada. Among the most interesting first novels of the year was *Obasan* by Joy Kogawa, which recounts the experiences of a Japanese family that is evicted from its home in Vancouver and interned in concentration camps in the interior of British Columbia and Alberta during World War II. It is a story of silences etched in a prose fine enough to cut both ways. A sharp tongue translating for a sharper eye is also characteristic of Margaret Atwood, whose fifth novel, *Bodily Harm*, dissects the existence of a young journalist fleeing Toronto for the Caribbean in a futile attempt to escape herself. Timothy Findley's protagonist in *Famous Last Words* shares no such illusion of escape as he fights to absolve as a witness a writer sucked

© THOMAS VICTOR

Margaret Atwood

into the intellectual and conscious evil of fascism by attempting to manipulate it.

In Aritha Van Herk's *The Tent Peg* the heroine, J. L., cook for a team of nine male geologists in the Arctic, soon becomes, as the only woman, Woman as archetype, fount of feminine wisdom or feminist didacticism; this leads to some stark action under the Arctic stars peppered with tendentious moralizing. By contrast, Doris Anderson takes the conflict between family and career into the workplace in *Rough Layout*, about the struggles of a young woman to become editor of a national women's magazine. Robertson Davies, delving below the seemingly serene surface of a small university town in *The Rebel Angels*, hauls up many a lively or grotesque passion and holds it, dripping and writhing, before our eyes. And in *Flowers of Darkness*, Matt Cohen, founder of the fictional small Ontario town of Salem, also dips down where emotions seethe like eels, displaying his catch in his own dry style. Feelings are also powerful in *High Crimes* by William Deverell, a complex exposé of the intrigue-riddled and double-crossed course of the world's largest cache of marijuana en route from South America to Newfoundland.

Audrey Thomas's latest collection, *Real Mothers*, misses no nuance of that title phrase, while Sean Virgo warns his readers that his book is a collection of *White Lies and Other Fictions*. In *Home Truths: Selected Canadian Stories*, Mavis Gallant, long-time resident abroad, demonstrates that distance has not dissipated her ability to see her country and its people clearly. The stories in *Death Suite* by Leon Rooke are orchestrated into a complex ballet of the *extraordinaire* and the ordinary. Anthologies of re-

gional work included *Manitoba Stories*, edited by Joan Parr, and *Sundogs: Stories from Saskatchewan*, edited by Robert Kroetsch.

Several retrospective collections were among the highlights of the year in Canadian poetry. They included the *Collected Poems of Raymond Souster, Volume Two, 1955–62*, in which, using subtle poetic effects, the author creates an ambience of deceptive simplicity around his musings on life and death; *The Collected Poems of F. R. Scott*, by a noted jurist and irreverent recorder of human trials and errors; and *Cross-Section: Poems 1940–80* by Louis Dudek, which includes both previously unpublished work and some of his best, and best-known, earlier poems. Collections of new work included Margaret Atwood's *True Stories*, a chiaroscuro of meticulously accurate descriptions of torture and acutely crafted visions of love. P. K. Page's first collection since 1974, *Evening Dance of the Grey Flies*, describes a landscape of twilight calm under the advancing stroke of night's wing. In contrast, Gwen Hauser's *Gophers and Swans* is a shout of protest on a hot day, like a fist plunged into a haunted pond. Stephen Scobie's *A Grand Memory For Forgetting* collects poems defined as much by what they leave out as by what they include. An even greater mobility of play is achieved in Scobie's collaboration with Douglas Barbour in *The Pirates of Pen's Chance: Homolinguistic Translations*. Scobie and Barbour were also editors of the year's most untypical anthology, *The Maple Laugh Forever: An Anthology of Canadian Comic Poetry*.

(ELIZABETH WOODS)

FRENCH

France. Although Valérie Valère, at 19, achieved startling success with her second novel, *Obsession blanche*, most of the year's rewards went to such veterans as Lucien Bodard, who won the Prix Goncourt with *Anne-Marie*, a semiautobiographical novel dominated by the personality of his mother. China, where the author lived until the age of ten, persisted as a vivid memory in the background of this account of his first experience of France. Though a popular choice, it seemed an odd one for a prize usually awarded as an encouragement to younger writers. The Prix Renaudot was awarded to Michel del Castillo's *La Nuit de Décret*, in which a Spanish detective gradually discovers in the personality of his boss a sinister image of the police mentality and a reflection of his country's recent history. Other former prizewinners confirmed their reputations: Patrick Modiano with *Une Jeunesse*, Conrad Detrez with *Le Draguer de Dieu*, and Didier Decoin, whose *L'Enfant de la mer de Chine* showed that he was still on the side of justice and the angels: it was as unobjectionable, and about as stimulating, as a hamburger and French fries.

The system of literary awards was slightly tarnished by the revelation that "Émile Ajar," winner of the 1975 Goncourt, had in reality been a pseudonym of the late Romain Gary. The other literary scandal of the year was more sad than farcical: in April Françoise Sagan's *Le Chien couchant* was withdrawn after a charge of plagiarism, though she had acknowledged her debt to a short story in Jean Hougron's *La vieille Femme* (1965).

Even in experimental fiction the Old Guard predominated. Claude Simon's *Les Géorgiques* was an impressive achievement, setting the violence of three wars against the unchanging rhythm of the seasons and the monotonous labour of the fields, "the same vines, the same hedges to trim, the same fences to inspect, the same towns to besiege, the same rivers to be crossed or defended." The symphonic structure of the novel mirrored this cyclical theme, and Simon's prose, with its parentheses and interweaving of narratives, made no concessions to traditional notions of chronology. Another target of the New Novel, the convention of character, was attacked in Jean Cayrol's *L'Homme dans le rétroviseur*, and Alain Robbe-Grillet in *Djinn* wove a science-fiction story into the framework of a structural grammar. Philippe Sollers did his best to fan the controversy around *Paradis*, dismissing most of his fellow writers as hopelessly out of touch with the audiovisual era. He may have had a case: whatever its intention, a competent conventional novel such as Michel Déon's *Un Déjeuner de soleil* made the literary world of the past 50 years, against which it was set, seem depressingly contrived and superficial.

Myth and the power of the imagination were explored by Michel Tournier in *Gaspard, Melchior et Balthazar* and Jean Raspail in *Moi, Antoine de Tounens, Roi de Patagonie*, but the mainstream of fiction held its course through the familiar territory of family relationships. Irène Monesi (*La Voie lactée*) took a boy's search for his absent father as the standpoint for a study of parental feelings, while Claire Gallois's heroine was torn between her roles as wife, mother, mistress, and friend in

Lucien Bodard

Le Coeur en quatre. The suppression of women by the family and by society was a continuing theme in novels, while historical works such as Régine Pernoud's *La Femme au temps des cathédrales* and Georges Duby's *Le Chevalier, la femme et le prêtre* reexamined the status of women in the Middle Ages, a period that held extraordinary appeal for the popular imagination. In this climate of sociological inquiry, love had to struggle against external pressures like those on the Arab man and Jewish girl in Muriel Cerf's novel *Une passion* or the aging painter and young girl in François Nourissier's *L'Empire des nuages*.

There were several interesting volumes of poetry. Jacques Roubaud's *Dors*, preceded by an essay on the spoken word, showed the poet's respect for formal constraints and his erudition, also displayed in *Merlin l'enchanteur*, a further retelling of Arthurian legend in collaboration with Florence Delay. Jean Cayrol carried on with his *Poésie-Journal*; Alain Bosquet examined the tragic impermanence of things in *Poèmes, deux* and *Sonnets pour une fin de siècle*; and a selection from the work of the Breton poet Charles le Quintrec appeared in *La Lumière et l'argile*. The death of the poet and singer Georges Brassens (see OBITUARIES) deprived France of a delightful and irreverent personality who had brought poetry to a vast audience.

It was a good year for literary studies. After the appearance, late in 1980, of the first volume of Hubert Juin's biography of Victor Hugo came Pierre Petitfils on Paul Verlaine, Pierre Gascar on Gérard de Nerval, and Elisabeth de Fontenay on Denis Diderot. The late Jean-Paul Sartre, already in his lifetime the subject of a major scholarly industry in France, Britain, and the U.S., was recalled in Olivier Todd's *Un Fils rebelle* and Jeanette Colombel's *Sartre ou le parti de vivre*, while many forthcoming books, periodicals, and conferences on his work were announced. The fifth volume of Marcel Proust's letters appeared, as well as correspondence by Albert Camus, Jean Cocteau, and Jules-Amédée Barbey d'Aurevilly. Julien Gracq's essays, *En lisant, en écrivant*, displayed a fine sensibility and contained many insights, especially into 19th-century literature.

The vogue for history produced some highly readable biographies, including the third volume of Roger Peyrefitte's study of Alexander the Great and Jean Jacquart's *François 1er*. Marcel Arland and José Cabanis published memoirs or journals and, to counteract the depressing effect of Michel Déon's fictional literary biography, there was the late Marcel Pagnol's *Confidences*, an amusing and affectionate record of literary and theatrical circles in the 1920s and 1930s. (ROBIN BUSS)

Canada. Two novels in particular aroused considerable interest during 1981 among readers and critics alike, *Le Canard de bois* by Louis Caron and *Le Matou* by Yves Beauchemin. In *Le Canard de bois*, events unfold in a rural setting and reflect simultaneously the years just preceding World War II and the difficult period of the Patriote Party in 1836–37. *Le Matou*, however, takes place in the late 1970s in the modern urban setting of the Plateau Mont-Royal area of Montreal.

The episodic content of the two works also dif-

fers. In Caron's book the story alternates between discoveries of life made by Bruno Bellerose — a woodcutter and the son of a farmer — and the participation of one of his ancestors, Hyacinthe, in the patriotic demonstrations organized in the 1830s by a group of parishioners in Port St.-François. Beauchemin's story, however, is dispersed among a multitude of events unfolding for the most part in Montreal but also in Quebec, Florida, and other places.

The ideologies of the two novels contrast with one another. *Le Canard de bois* defends traditional values of Quebec society, while *Le Matou* stands firmly fixed in a modern context: a society of consumerism centred on the idea of economic success.

Apart from these differences, however, the two novels have one point in common, the desire for autonomy. Bruno desires to be liberated from paternal authority and from his apprenticeship to maturity; Hyacinthe's desire takes the form of a refusal to submit to the English regime (a refusal for which he pays with exile). In *Le Matou* the goal is economic autonomy for the character Florent.

A bit drier to read, but quite captivating, is *Chroniques souterraines* by Lise Harou. By writing in fragments, the content and length of which vary, the author succeeds in expressing the rending of a woman torn between her love for her husband, her children, and her male and female lovers and her thoughts on the feminine condition.

Notable in the category of essays is *Le journal piégé ou l'art de trafiquer l'information* by Pierre Berthiaume. It demonstrates how the myth of The Printed Text, a form of The Word As Law, can overwhelm journalists and readers.

(ROBERT SAINT-AMOUR)

GERMAN

The most important publications of the year in German literature concerned an earlier generation of writers: two volumes of Bertolt Brecht's correspondence, autobiographical writings of Alfred Döblin, and diaries (*Siebzig verweht*) of the octogenarian Ernst Jünger. Nor could the award of the Nobel Prize to Elias Canetti be counted as recognition of contemporary German literature. Canetti was 76 and, although writing in German, had lived in London since 1938. *Die Fackel im Ohr*, the second volume of his autobiography, was nonetheless a considerable success with critics and the public and afforded fascinating glimpses of the Frankfurt of the inflation years, Vienna in the late 1920s, and the genesis of Canetti's novel *Die Blendung*. (See NOBEL PRIZES.)

Autobiography was indeed the contemporary fashion; self-contemplation seemed one way of coming to terms with the hostile political and economic climate. One of the year's literary debates revolved around the accusation that writers and intellectuals were not involving themselves actively enough with the burning issues of the day: nuclear weapons, ecology, the alienation of young people. Besides Canetti's, autobiographical works appeared from Heinrich Böll, Thomas Bernhard, Luise Rinser, Eva Zeller, and Cristoph Meckel. Of special interest was Friedrich Dürrenmatt's *Stoffe*, an account not only of the dramatist's early life and

encounters but also, more importantly, of the development of the fictions into which he crystallizes his experiences and ideas.

A number of interesting autobiographically based works appeared by writers either living in East Germany but unable to publish there or who had recently left. These included Einar Schleef's *Gertrud*; Monika Maron's *Flugasche*, which highlighted industrial pollution in Bitterfield and the official suppression of this scandal; and Gert Neumann's *Elf Uhr*.

Peter Weiss completed *Die Ästhetik des Widerstands*, a history of socialist resistance to fascism that became a vast essay-novel on the relation between art and politics. Its reception ranged between total rejection and unstinting praise. The schematic character-drawing and the uncompromising treatment of ideas made it a "difficult" work; nevertheless, its breadth of canvas and the ambitiousness of its theme made it a major publication. More fashionable was the tendency to the miniature, the segment rather than the whole, the reflective snapshot suffused with an all-pervasive melancholy. Fine examples of the genre were Botho Strauss's *Paare, Passanten* and Jürgen Becker's *Erzählen bis Ostende*. Günter Kunert's *Verspätete Monologe* was the most pessimistic of all; he saw no hope for humanity East or West and traced the mechanisms of repression and terror back to 18th-century rationalism.

Frustrated intellectuals featured prominently in fiction. The librarian heroine of Angelika Mechtel's *Die andere Hälfte der Welt* resigns under the pressures from a small town that dislikes her including even moderately left-wing writers on the shelves; the student-teacher hero of Sten Nadolny's *Netzkarte* tries to escape from conformism by crisscrossing Germany by rail; the mathematics student of Franz Mechsner's *Vorwärtsruckwärts* finds his political commitment thwarted by the authorities, while his intellectuality frustrates the spontaneity in the personal relationships he desires. In a complementary vein two novels took conformists as their heroes: Klaus Konjetzky's *Am anderen Ende des Tages* painted the ironic picture of a student failure whose social connections enable him to survive beyond his deserts, while F. C. Delius's *Ein Held der inneren Sicherheit* brilliantly satirized the mentality and language of the industrialists' lobby—his hero is ghostwriter to the kidnapped head of the employers' organization.

More direct social criticism was to be found in a number of works that portrayed people on the margin of society, exploited, shunned, or ignored. Ludwig Fels in his *Ein Unding der Liebe* showed the hindside of affluence through an incompetent, unlovable cook's assistant for whom competitive society can have no time or sympathy. Austrian Ingrid Puganigg had a remarkable debut: her *Fasnacht* described a grotesque partnership between a woman disfigured by a dog bite and a dwarf 25 years her senior in which they find temporary refuge from a hostile, inquisitive, or apathetic environment.

Diametrically opposed to all these works, Peter Handke's *Kindergeschichte* turned its back on the babble of society and its interpreters. In his search for the "secret of the world," no less, he described the "eternal Myth" of the father and daughter relationship in language that equally eschewed the banalities of the mass media. Urs Widmer, another modern Romantic, sought the reality behind reality, whether it be in Frankfurt or the Alps, in his imaginative *Das enge Land*.

In East Germany the most important publications were collected essays and speeches by Anna Seghers and Hermann Kant (*Zu den Unterlagen*). Manfred Pieske's novel *Schnauzer* was reckoned to be his best so far but remained a conventional account of an individual's development into a responsible socialist; similarly, Bernhard Seeger's *Der Harmonikaspieler*, a historical-social novel of a rural community's conversion from Nazi terror to socialist justice, barely strayed from well-trodden paths. Two shorter works were of greater interest; Max Walter Schulz's *Die Fliegerin* included an excellently handled account of a brief encounter between a German soldier and a female Soviet pilot during the closing stages of World War II, and Uwe Saeger's *Warten auf Schnee*, on the ups and downs of a schoolteacher philanderer, was remarkable especially for its unusually frank eroticism. (J. H. REID)

SCANDINAVIAN

Denmark. Over the past few years portraits of women had characterized Danish fiction. In 1981, however, authors of both sexes turned to the problems of middle age, often in men. In *Gårs fortræd*, Martha Christensen portrayed a man's career and pinpointed the decisive moments in his life. In *In genting*, Keld Belert sought human qualities in a man responsible for the breakdown of his marriage. Tage Skou Hansen in *Over stregen* continued his novels based on the character of Holger Mikkelsen by showing him at the age of 56 embarking on an affair with a young adherent of women's liberation. Dea Trier Mørch's *Den indre by* (1980) was an extension of *Vinterbørn*, showing the demands made on those who seek to combine family life with outside activities and politics. Jette Drewsen in *Midtvejsfester* (1980) was concerned with an unsentimental portrayal of three middle-aged unmarried mothers. In *Det sorte hul* (1980), Klaus Rifbjerg told of a 46-year-old man who suddenly loses touch with his marriage and begins to behave in an unwonted fashion.

Anders Bodelsen, well established as the writer of intellectual thrillers, published *Borte Borte*, a psychological thriller based on everyday reality, with overtones of unemployment, recession, and blackmail. On the lighter side was Knud Thomsen's *Klokken fra Makedonien*, while subtle aphoristic reflections characterized Villy Sørensen's *Vejrdage*.

A prolonged period of illness prompted Vagn Steen to reflect on his life and the sense of fear that infected it in the poems in *52år*. After a silence of six years, Ivan Malinowski returned with some carefully composed poems evaluating the modern world in *Vinterens hjerte* (1980). A new name to emerge was that of Bo Green Jensen, whose *Requiem og messe* (1980) was an artistic and compelling requiem for the 1970s. In *Virkelighedens farver*

(1980), Uffe Harder confirmed his position as a delicate and sensitive poet more concerned with his art than with discussing problems.

From the Faeroes came William Heinesen's *Her skal danses* (1980), stories about a mythological Torshavn (the islands' capital), which might well rank among the author's best. Greenland was represented by Thomas Frederiksen's *Grønlandske dagbogsblade*, already translated into 14 languages, a lyrical and unsophisticated description of a Greenland hunter's life, past and present.

(W. GLYN JONES)

Norway. Several of the year's novels had action located outside Norway. Finn Carling's *Visirene* stood out, with its handful of tourists seeking an escape from personal traumatic experiences at a holiday resort in Sri Lanka. With burlesque humour Terje Stigen placed his hero in *Blindgjengeren* in the service of Hitler's Institute for Racial Hygiene, with the task of impregnating German war widows and grass widows in order to produce high-quality Aryan offspring. Italy gave atmosphere to Marie Takvam's *Brevet frå Alexandria*, a penetrating analysis of the sexual anxieties of a middle-aged woman. New York City formed the backdrop to Jon Michelet's humorous and refreshing thriller *Den gule djevelens by*.

Other novels described pre-welfare-state Norway. Johannes Heggland's *Brød fra havet. Anna Gyria* was set in a fishing community in mid-19th-century western Norway. In powerful language and with convincing realism it told of the hardships, tender love, and subsequent disillusionment of the young heroine. The revolutionary development of Norwegian whaling in the second half of the 19th century was dealt with by Karin Bang in *Jutøy 2. Jag etter vind*. Much Norwegian social history from the beginning of the 20th century was contained in Erling Pedersen's *Din plass på jorda. Anna og Johan 1908–1928*.

The devastating consequences of excesses of loveless sex was the theme of Gunnar Lunde's best novel to date, *Klovnens store kjærlighet*, with a "hero" kept as a supplier of sex to an emancipated businesswoman. Female emancipation of an extreme kind was dealt with by Ketil Bjørnstad in *Bingo! eller: En Dyd Av Nodvendighet*, in which a young man tries to trace his mother, who had run away from a secure marriage, only to find that she had joined an international terrorist movement. The painful breakup of a close mother-son relationship was the theme of Dag Sundby's *Orions sverd*.

The pain of love, the meaning of life, and the nature of poetry were central themes in the poems in Stein Mehren's *Den usynlige regnbuen*. Annemarta Borgen's *Deg* was an intimate biography of the writer Johan Borgen (d. 1979), drawing heavily on private letters. A major scholarly event was Daniel Haakonsen's richly illustrated *Henrik Ibsen— mennesket og kunstneren*, a storehouse of pictorial information about Ibsen and the staging of his plays throughout the world.

(TORBJØRN STØVERUD)

Sweden. An undogmatic literary climate prevailed during the year in Sweden. Sven Lindqvist, once a leading exponent of the committed school, published *En älskares dagbok*, a confessional memoir of his love, ever since boyhood, of the beautiful girl destined after many complications to become his wife; and Sara Lidman, who abandoned fiction altogether for a decade during the heyday of the protest movements, delighted admirers of her powerful narrative gifts with *Nabots sten*, the third part of a chronicle charting the struggles against bureaucracy and financial exploitation of a small northern community of vividly presented individuals.

Sven Delblanc published *Samuels bok*, the story of his grandfather's vain efforts to become ordained in late-19th-century Sweden on the basis of theological studies in the U.S.; Delblanc produced a moving work of fiction based on diaries and letters, which like Lidman's book spoke out powerfully, although not didactically, on behalf of all those who cannot work the system and instead become its victims. Among first novels Per Odensten's *Gheel. De galnas stad* met with critical acclaim. The narrative, technically rather difficult to follow, concerned a fictive Swedish counterpart to the Belgian town of Gheel, a community for the insane, offering its denizens human dignity and security and the chance to follow the teachings of Emanuel Swedenborg, an 18th-century Swedish theologian and mystic.

The big event of the year was the publication, 60 years after his death, of the first two of the 75 planned volumes of the official and definitive collected works of August Strindberg, an enterprise of vast scholarly effort and government funding. The same was true of the new translation of the New Testament that the Swedish Bible Commission presented after a decade of work by theologians, philologists, and poets. Feminists published *Kvinnornas litteraturhistoria*, not in fact as its title implied a literary history of women writers but essays by and about this category.

The septuagenarian poet Karl Vennberg published the richly varied *Bilder I–XXVI*, with his characteristic amalgam of irony and pellucid imagery; Goran Sonnevi published *Små klanger; en röst*, deeply serious poems about the human struggle for freedom and justice in the face of the power structures of language and society, written in a spare, ascetic, yet powerfully expressive diction; and Eva Runefelt's third collection, *Augusti*, confirmed her gift for tactile, sensory verse.

(KARIN PETHERICK)

ITALIAN

Despite rising book prices and a considerable contraction in the market, 1981 was an interesting year for literature in Italy. No new ground was broken, but production in the established fields was as abundant and varied as ever and generally of good quality. The most successful novel was *Il nome della rosa* by Umberto Eco. It was a "learned" thriller set in medieval Italy in an abbey where religious and political interests, heresy and orthodoxy, and lust and superstition combine to produce a sequence of mysterious deaths that an English monk is called upon to explain. Particularly intriguing was Eco's clever mixture of invention and accurate historical detail. Also ostensibly his-

torical was the setting of Enzo Siciliano's *La principessa e l'antiquario*, though in this case, history served as a pretext to explore subtly the psychology of a young man who, while investigating the disappearance of a northern princess in 18th-century Rome, is gradually destroyed by his increasing awareness of himself and the evil ways of the world. The initiation of an adolescent into adulthood in Fascist Italy was the theme of Paolo Volponi's *Il lanciatore di giavellotto*. More specifically religious, rather than psychological, was Giorgio Saviane's *Getsèmani*, where the sacrifice of Christ is reenacted to explain the meaning and value of human suffering in the modern world.

While hardly any work of fiction focused on the country's social and political situation, the switch toward personal, often autobiographical, exploration continued unabated. Memory novels were much in evidence. In *Althènopis*, Fabrizia Ramondino masterfully interwove the exemplary story of her family and of her relationship with her mother during and after World War II. A feminist theme was also at the centre of Anna Banti's clearly autobiographical *Il grido lacerante*, the story of a woman who sacrifices her own ambitions for love of her husband and continues to live with her own unresolved dilemma even after his death.

The discovery of the year was the Sicilian Gesualdo Bufalino, whose first novel, *Diceria dell'untore*, deservedly attracted much attention from critics and readers alike. It was a work of consummate literary skill in which lyricism constantly breaks to the surface as the narrator looks back to a period of his life spent in a sanatorium and the theme of sickness and death unfolds. Curiously similar in plot and theme, though different in style, was *La veranda* by Sebastiano Satta, a novel written more than 50 years earlier but not published until 1981 after the death of its author. Among other distinguished novels, but lighter in tone and inspiration, were the amusing *Zio Cardellino* by Luciano De Crescenzo, the story of the metamorphosis into a goldfinch of an executive working for a multinational corporation, and Piero Chiara's elegant *Vedrò Singapore?*, in which the writer's favourite characters return to enact their lives of contented misfits on the stage of provincial Italy in the early 1930s. Giorgio Manganelli's *Amore* escaped classification, being neither novel nor essay nor autobiographical confession but a coherent *poème en prose* about love as an idea that ultimately cannot be grasped or understood.

As witty and imaginative as a work of fiction was *Trans-Pacific Express*, a collection of essays by Alberto Arbasino on his recent travels and experiences in the Far East. The general climate of uncertainty and fear encouraged some writers to produce "consolation books," such as *La fortuna di vivere* by Vittorio Buttafava, a collection of meditations, aphorisms, short pieces of narrative, and variations on the notion that life after all is not a bad thing. Finally, of considerable importance for recent Italian history was *Diari 1976–1979* by the politician and skilled writer Giulio Andreotti, covering effectively in concise note form the years of the "historic compromise" and of terrorism up to the murder of Aldo Moro.

Poetry was overshadowed by the death of Eugenio Montale (*see* OBITUARIES). A few months earlier his collected verse, *L'opera in versi*, was published in a beautiful single volume edited by R. Bettarini and G. Contini. Under the general title of *Altri versi*, the volume included Montale's latest lyrics (1978–80) and a substantial group of poems composed over the last 60 years that were previously unpublished or not included in the poet's major collections. Other important new collections were the refreshing *Poesie del sabato* by the 82-year-old Carlo Betocchi, confirming again his status as a brilliant and unclassifiable outsider in the poetic tradition of 20th-century Italy; *Geometria del disordine* by Maria Luisa Spaziani; and *Il ristorante dei morti* by Giovanni Giudici. Amelia Rosselli offered a good overview of her poetic development with *Primi scritti 1952–1965* and her latest much-praised long poem *Impromptu*. (LINO PERTILE)

SPANISH

Spain. In Spain 1981 was something of a boom year for the publishing industry. Millions of copies of "instant" books purporting to explain the political crisis flooded the country in the weeks following the foiled coup of February 23. The first and perhaps the best of them was *Los últimos días de un presidente* by José Oneto, director of *Cambio-16*, an influential newsmagazine. And politics was behind yet another best-seller, Alfredo Kindelán's documented memoirs, *La verdad de mis relaciones con Franco*.

On the more literary side one of the year's most ambitious endeavours was that of an otherwise staid publisher, Cátedra. This house, known mostly for its scholarly editions of modern classics and reference works, commissioned a series of new novels from major authors and merchandised them in mass editions of 300,000-plus copies designed to sell at a fraction of the price of a standard novel. The works that opened the new series, Alfonso Grosso's *Con flores a María* and Fernando Savater's *Caronte aguarda*, were enthusiastically received by critics and the general public. Not surprisingly, a similar mass-marketing technique was employed by another publisher, Bruguera, which filled Spain's bookstores and other outlets during the summer with huge stacks of Gabriel García Márquez's latest novella, *Crónica de una muerte anunciada*. Other new novels by established writers such as José María Guelbenzú (*El río de la luna*) and the Chilean José Donoso (*El jardín de al lado*) enjoyed a more usual kind of success with readers and critics. Another of the year's more memorable novels was futuristic and feminist: Rosa Montero's *La función delta* tells the story of a liberated woman of 30 in the year 2000.

A feminist point of view was winning in verse as well, with the Adonais Prize going to Blanca Andrea, a previously unknown university student, for her striking account *De una niña de provincias que vino a vivir en un Chagall*. Also noteworthy were new volumes of poetry by Concha Lagos (*Teoría de la inseguridad*), Vicente Presa (*Teoría de los límites*), Pablo Virumbrales (*Cancionero del vaso*), and Antonio Abad (*Misericor de mí*). (RENÉ DE COSTA)

Latin America. Latin-American fiction in 1981 was characterized by works that were shorter than many of the extensive and even monumental novels previously published by the same novelists. Carlos Fuentes's *Agua quemada* and Gabriel García Márquez's *Crónica de una muerte anunciada* were important short novels that suggested this trend. Other renowned novelists who published during the year included Gustavo Alvarez Gardeazábal (*Los míos*), José Donoso (*El jardín de al lado*), Manuel Puig (*Maldición eterna a quienes lean estas páginas*), and Mario Vargas Llosa (*La guerra del fin del mundo*).

The Casa de las Américas Prizes for 1981 were as follows: *Itzam Na* by Arturo Arias (novel); *Imitación de la vida* by Luis Rogelio Nogueras (poetry); *Huelga* by Albio Paz Hernández (theatre); *Las culturas populares en el capitalismo* by Néstor García Canclini (essay). The Premio de Novela Plaza y Janés in Colombia was awarded by Virgilio Cuesta to Manuel Giraldo for *Conciertos del desconcierto* (first prize) and Alvarez Gardeazábal's *Los míos* (second prize). Jorge Luis Borges was given yet another prize in his distinguished career, the Premio Ollín Yoliztli, awarded by Pres. José López Portillo in Mexico.

The works that drew most attention from critics in Mexico were Fuentes's *Agua quemada*, José Emilio Pacheco's *Las batallas en el desierto*, and Ignacio Solares's *El árbol del deseo*. *Agua quemada* is a volume of four stories, some of them reminiscent of Fuentes's writing in the late 1950s and early 1960s. Pacheco's book deals nostalgically with the young author's school days. Solares continued to create fiction concerned with the connections between dreams and reality in *El árbol del deseo*. Other novels published in Mexico in 1981 were Jaime del Palacio's *Parejas*, Luis Casas Velasco's *Death Show*, Silvia Molina's *Ascención Tun*, Luis Zapata's *De pétalos perennes*, Roberto Páramo's *El corazón en la mesa*, Carlos Montemayor's *Mal de piedra*, and Carlos Eduardo Turón's *Sobre esta piedra*. Gerardo María Touissant was acclaimed for his first volume of stories, *Fábrica de conciencias descompuestas*.

Gabriel García Márquez's *Crónica de una muerte anunciada*, in the tradition of the detective novel, was highly publicized and commented upon in the author's native Colombia and throughout Latin America. Nevertheless, Alvarez Gardeazábal's *Los míos*, also highly acclaimed in Colombia, was quite likely the most significant aesthetic accomplishment in Colombia in 1981. Like much recent Latin-American fiction, *Los míos* deals with the traditional aristocracy. Two other important novels in Colombia were Rafael Humberto Moreno Durán's *El toque de Diana* and Manuel Giraldo's *Conciertos del desconcierto*. Mario Escobar Velásquez's *Un hombre llamado Todero*, his second novel, appeared in late 1980.

Chileans continued writing with both a domestic perspective and that of the writer in exile. José Donoso's *El jardín de al lado*, about a young couple's experiences in Spain, treats the problem of the sense of rootlessness experienced by living outside one's homeland. *El museo de cera* by Jorge Edwards takes place in an unidentified Latin-American country. The ambience is aristocratic; the protagonist is a marquis. Jorge Marchant Lezcano's *La Bea-*

triz Ovalle deals with contemporary Chile's aristocracy. Two works awarded prizes in Chile were *Dónde estás, Constanza*, a novel by José Luis Rosasco, and *El círculo dramático*, stories by Antonio Montero Abt. Ariel Dorfman wrote and published *Viudas* abroad.

Argentina's Manuel Puig also continued to write and publish abroad. His novel *Maldición eterna a quienes lean estas páginas* is an extensive dialogue between two characters in a New York City setting. Given the number of writers publishing abroad, it was not surprising that Ediciones del Norte in New Hampshire began to publish fine editions of Latin-American fiction. Such was the case of the Argentine Mario Szichman's *A las 20:25 la señora entró en la inmortalidad*, a superb novel dealing with the Jewish community's history and experience in Buenos Aires. Other Argentine works were Marta Traba's *Conversación al sur* and the critic Noé Jitrik's *Ritual* (stories).

Two Uruguayan writers living abroad published prizewinning novels: Carlos Martínez Moreno's *El color que el infierno me escondiera* (Premio Proceso-Nueva Imagen) and Antonio Larreta's *Volaverunt* (Premio Planeta). After a hiatus of several years Reynaldo Arenas of Cuba and Salvador Garmendia of Venezuela published novels: *La vieja Rosa* and *El único lugar posible*, respectively. One of the most ambitious and unique creations of the year was Edmundo Desnoe's *Los dispositivos en la flor*, a personal anthology of some 500 pages of Cuban literature since the revolution.

(RAYMOND L. WILLIAMS)

PORTUGUESE

Portugal. The April revolution of 1974 continued to haunt Portuguese fiction of the 1980s. The joys and anxieties of inner liberation and political emancipation, the deceptive mood that comes in the sequence and as a consequence of events that seem to be governed by a wicked fate, were the main lines pursued in José de Almeida Faria's novel *Lusitânia*, the final part of a trilogy chronicling a landowning family from the South. By adopting the epistolary device that was so fashionable with the authors of the Enlightenment, Almeida Faria succeeded admirably in presenting a narrative from many and different points of view, preserving at the same time a detachment that enhanced the objectivity of his tale. The compactness and the strict economy of the narrative, within a variety of styles, were literary achievements that owed a great deal to an original structure. For *Lusitânia* was a novel written on a musical pattern. Neatly divided into three movements that attain dramatic intensity without ever reaching a crescendo, it pursues the constant theme that "time is evil." This statement made by one of its characters is modulated by many voices, gaining a polyphonic quality.

A similar concern with the unpredictability of national destiny also pervaded *O Mosteiro*, a novel by Agustina Bessa Luís. In contrast to the directness of the message conveyed by Almeida Faria's title, Bessa Luís expressed in her own title the allegorical meaning of her story. The old monastery that is having its history written by one of the

Gabriel García Márquez

novel's characters has been throughout the centuries the property of the same aristocratic family. Converted eventually, and after many vicissitudes, into a home for the mentally sick, it houses the political follies of a nation, standing then as a symbol for Portugal.

Two major events in poetry were the publication of Herberto Helder's *Poesia Toda* and A. Pinheiro Torre's *O Ressentimento dum Ocidental*. By taking up some of the themes of the 19th-century poet Cesário Verde, Pinheiro Torres voices eloquently the anguish against the mental siege that has weighed so heavily on Portugal and gives vent to his anger in a vigorous and tempered tone. The eminent novelist and poet Carlos de Oliveira died on July 1, 1981. (L. S. REBELO)

Brazil. The year 1981 was the centenary of the birth of Alfonso Henriques de Lima Barreto (1881–1920); Maria Zilda Cury's *Um mulato no reino de Jambom* was the most interesting new study of his works. Several evaluations of José Lins do Rêgo's fiction appeared. Heloísa Toller Gomes's *O poder rural na ficção* is a provocative comparison of rural society in Lins do Rêgo's and William Faulkner's works. Cassiano Nunes continued his pioneering efforts in studying writers' correspondence with an analysis of Monteiro Lobato's letters, while James Amado prepared an edition of Graciliano Ramos's letters in cooperation with the author's widow.

Although many publishing houses continued to suffer financial difficulties and questions arose about the orientation of their activities, production in all genres flourished. The years of military rule and the recent liberalization remained important themes in fiction. Antônio Callado's moving novel *Sempreviva* became an instant best-seller; it recounts the epoch of torture and self-evaluation through which Brazilians have passed. Roberto Drummond's *Sangue de Coca-Cola* is a violent satire on the political liberalization. In *O mulo* Darcy Ribeiro presents a "coronel" of the interior whose deathbed confession is a penetrating view of an almost junglelike existence and one that evokes the masterpieces of Guimarães Rosa. Other important novels included a posthumously published work by Marques Rebelo; an autobiographical novel by Lya Luft about the life of German immigrants to southern Brazil, and a political novel about the 1932 revolution by Afonso Schmidt.

Felicidade clandestina, a collection of stories by the late Clarice Lispector, once again takes the reader into her unique world of real unreality; an interpretive biography of Lispector by Olga Borelli also appeared. Other volumes of short fiction were by Dalton Trevisan, Lygia Fagundes Telles, and João Ubaldo Ribeiro. The New Discovery Prize for Short Fiction was won by João Gilberto Noll.

Carlos Drummond de Andrade wrote a new volume of poetry, *A paixão medida*. In addition, Affonso Romano de Sant'Anna published a study of Drummond's works. João Cabral de Melo Neto's *A escola das faces* invokes Brazil's northeast, while Adélia Prado's *Terra de Santa Cruz* has a mystical orientation. Mário da Silva Brito produced several volumes of poetry, and Pedro Nava began to edit his memoirs. (IRWIN STERN)

RUSSIAN

Soviet Literature. The year's novels included many with political themes. Typical was Aleksandr Chakovsky's *Victory*, in which the problems of the contemporary struggle for international détente were featured against the background of experience of the first years after World War II. Frequently, the political novel was based on dynamic detective intrigue, with professional politicians, diplomats, journalists, and intelligence agents among the characters.

Historical novels were also popular. A number of them commemorated the 600th anniversary of the battle of Kulikovo Pole. They included *The Moscow Sovereigns* by D. Balashov, featuring the establishment of Russian statehood; and *The Kulikovo Field* by V. Vozovikov, *Redemption* by V. Lebedev, and *Dmitri Donskoy* by Yury Loshchits, all portraying the people's struggle against the Tatar-Mongolian invaders.

A number of writers who had made their literary debuts in the 1970s and had now reached professional maturity produced novels that met with considerable success. Among these were Leonid Bezhin's *Metro Turgenevskaya*, Sergey Yesin's *Lit up by a Small Searchlight*, and Vladimir Gusev's *Spasskoe-Lutovinovo*. Gusev's novel centred on the lot of a young scientist determined to find "a place in the Sun" by hook or by crook. The characters in Yesin's and Bezhin's books were also members of the "intellectual professions"—actors, artists, scholars, journalists.

Probably the biggest popular success of the period under review was Daniil Granin's novel *The Painting*. There was not a shade of sensationalism in either the style or substance of this quiet and circumstantial narration of the daily round of a small, out-of-the-way Soviet town. The main character is the mayor of the town, in love with it and doing his best to safeguard a beautiful spot designated as a future factory site. He pins great hopes on a painting he has brought from Moscow that shows the beauty of the very spot that the factory designers propose to destroy. The painting makes the characters of the book see their town in a new light and reflect on the past and the future, elaborately intertwined. Thus Granin succeeds in demonstrating the impact of art on human souls.

Another best-seller was Yury Bondarev's *The Choice*. His main character, Vasiliev, an artist, seems to possess everything his stars could offer: talent, recognition, prestige in society, a good family, and the wife he loves. Yet what seemed to be a well-established home turns out to be uncertain and shaky in many ways. His wife has not forgotten her early passion for another man; the daughter of whom he was so fond had a great misfortune; a friend of his youthful years turns out to be an entirely different sort of man, foreign to him. Complex moral problems, which do not always find a uniform solution in the novel, make up the main ideological message of this work.

The seventh Congress of Soviet Writers, held during June 30–July 4, was an important event in the literary year. Also significant was the 15th All-Union Pushkin Festival of Poetry. (SERGEY CHUPRININ)

Expatriate Russian Literature. Several interesting titles appeared in the West during 1981. In London they included Vladimir Voinovich's *Pretender to the Throne*, a sequel to his earlier satirical novel recounting the adventures of Private Ivan Chonkin; Lev Kopelev's *The Education of a True Believer*; and a collection of letters by the 19th-century Russian philosopher Konstantin Leontiev to his contemporary Vasily Rozanov. It was the first time the letters had been published anywhere and represented something of a coup for the publisher, Nina Karsov.

In the U.S., Ardis published Josif Oleshkovsky's satirical novel *Ruka* ("The Hand") and a collection of short stories by Yevgeny Popov, one of the Moscow writers involved with the suppressed literary almanac *Metropol* in 1979. In Switzerland *L'age d'homme* brought out a political treatise by Aleksandr Zinoviev, *Komunism kak realnost* ("Communism as Reality"), and *Life and Fate* by the late Vasily Grossman. Considered lost for many years, the manuscript of Grossman's novel on microfilm was sent mysteriously to Efim Etkind, a Russian literary scholar living in Paris.

Writing in *Index on Censorship* about *Life and Fate*, Robert Chandler pointed out that the author had been an officially accepted writer who published novels and stories during the '30s and worked through World War II as a front-line correspondent for *Red Star*. "In 1952 he published a novel. . . about the Russian victory at Stalingrad, *For a Just Cause*. . . a thoroughly orthodox, patriotic, and Socialist Realist book. Nevertheless, it was heavily criticized in the press. *Life and Fate* is, in a sense, a continuation. . . . Artistically, however, . . . it is written in an entirely different spirit. . . . Grossman completed this epic work in 1962 and sent off the text to a perfectly orthodox Soviet literary journal. Its editors promptly contacted the KGB." KGB officers visited Grossman and confiscated all copies of his manuscript, as well as his rough drafts, sheets of carbon paper, and typing ribbons. He died a year and a half later.

In his review of Kopelev's book, Edward Crankshaw said in *The Observer* that it made "almost unbearable reading." "For here is the witness of a one-time persecutor. As a young man, a true believer, he was active and zealous in the collectivization of the early 1930s. . . . But this persecutor himself became a victim (he spent years in the camps). . . who believes his punishment was both deserved and beneficial . . . because his own incarceration prevented him from participating in 'still newer villainies and deceits.' "

Voinovich and Kopelev had been deprived of their Soviet citizenship and were living abroad. In the Soviet Union the Ukrainian writer and journalist Vyacheslav Chornovil, who had spent all but 18 months of the past 14 years in labour camps or exile, was charged with attempted rape a short time before he was due for release and sentenced to five more years' imprisonment. Anatoly Marchenko, whose *My Testimony* provided the first detailed account of Soviet labour camps after Stalin's death, was arrested for the fifth time in March and, in September, sentenced to ten years in a labour camp.   (GEORGE THEINER)

EASTERN EUROPEAN LITERATURE

The Nobel Prize for Literature again went to an Eastern European writer, this time to a Bulgarian Jew living in Britain, Elias Canetti, the sixth émigré author to be thus honoured. The 1980 laureate, Czeslaw Milosz, was able to visit his native Poland for the first time in almost 30 years, following the Nobel Prize ceremony in Stockholm. He was given a hero's welcome by his fellow countrymen, whom the authorities had kept in ignorance of his work for three decades. It was altogether a bumper year for literary prizes. Two exiled Czechoslovak writers, Milan Kundera and Josef Skvorecky, received the Commonwealth award in the U.S. and the Neustadt International Prize in West Germany, respectively. Another West German prize went to Lev Kopelev, a Soviet author living in Munich.

Jaroslav Seifert, Czechoslovakia's greatest living poet, celebrated his 80th birthday in September. Two of his verse collections, *The Plague Column* and *Umbrella from Piccadilly*, which hitherto had appeared only abroad and in Czechoslovak *samizdat* editions, came out in Prague; however, the poet's charming memoirs remained unpublished. After receiving a telegram of congratulations from Pres. Gustav Husak, Seifert was visited by plainclothesmen, who wanted him to publish a "thank you" message to Husak. Seifert refused, since he intended to put out a more general acknowledgment thanking all his well-wishers. No Prague newspaper would print this, however, and the incident led to a worsening of the poet's already frail health.

Two books by the Hungarian author Gyorgy Konrad appeared in the West: his third novel, *Der Komplize* ("The Accomplice"), in West Germany and *Az autonómia kisértése: Kelet-nyugati utigondolatok 1977–79* ("The Temptation of Autonomy: East-West Travel Thoughts 1977–79") by Magyar Füzetek in Paris. "The book is courageous," wrote a reviewer in *World Literature Today*. "It could certainly not be published in Hungary at present."

The great Romanian playwright I. L. Caragiale was also the author of many pieces of prose fiction, 11 of which appeared in *Schite si povestiri* ("Sketches and Stories"), a bilingual collection by Eric Tappe, professor of Romanian studies at the University of London. In Bucharest the Romanian Academy published a *Dictionary of Romanian Literature from the Beginning to 1900*, the most comprehensive work of its kind to date, with a total of 1,311 entries.

The year brought unprecedented if short-lived freedom to the writers and publishers of Poland. Not only were the works of Milosz appearing there for the first time since his "defection" in the early 1950s but another distinguished author, 76-year-old Julian Stryjkowski, was able to tell an interviewer in London in May, "I don't think there is now any Polish writer who can't publish with the official publishing houses. They all have the green light."

Stryjkowski's semiautobiographical novel *Wielki strach* ("The Great Terror"), which had come out earlier in the unofficial literary quarterly *Zapis*, was the first literary treatment in Poland of the events of September 1939, when the country was

Aleksandr Zinoviev

invaded by both Soviet and German forces. Another personal record of life in Poland—in this case during the period immediately following the death of Stalin—appeared in the West: Leopold Tyrmand's *Diary 1954*. The author had been one of his country's most popular novelists until the late 1960s, when he went to the U.S. A collection of essays by the poet Stanislaw Baranczak, who was at last able to take up his long-deferred appointment at Harvard University, was published in Paris by the Instytut Literacki. Jerzy Andrzejewski's novel *Miazga* ("Pulp"), hitherto available only in *samizdat* editions from the unofficial publishing house NOWA, was brought out in London by the Polonia Book Fund, which for years had published censored Polish and Soviet works. The death in November of its founder and director, Andrew Stypulkowski, was a great loss to the cause of free literature.

Many writers and other intellectuals were among the thousands interned when the Polish government imposed martial law in December. Although news was difficult to obtain at year's end, it was reliably reported that the renowned film director Andrzej Wajda and the historian Adam Michnik were among those detained. The name of Miroslaw Chojecki, the director of NOWA, appeared on a list of detainees issued by the authorities, but Chojecki was in the U.S. at the time and thus escaped arrest. (GEORGE THEINER)

JEWISH

Hebrew. During 1981 the veteran poet A. Hillel returned to active publication with his collection *Devareiy*. The senior poets Gavriel Preil, Avot Yeshurun, and S. Shalom also published new poetry collections, as did Yehuda Amichai (*Shalva gedola, she'elot uteshuvot*) and Meir Wieseltier (*Motsa el hayam*). New poets included Robert Whitehill, from the U.S., and the Israelis Peretz Banai, Esther Ettinger, and Yosef Yehezkel. Other collections of note were published by Aharon Shabtai, Mordecai Geldman, Hannah Barzilai, Batsheva Sharif, Michal Senunit, and Menachem Ben. Poets mourned in 1981 were Uri Zvi Greenberg, Hebrew literature's most skillful and dramatic expressionistic poet, and Yonatan Ratosh, the founder of the Canaanite movement.

Prose collections included short stories by Hanoch Bartov, Uzi Behar, and Shulamit Hareven, with volumes of note by Amalia Kahana-Carmon (*Himurim gevohim*), Y. Ben-Ner (*Erets rehoka*), and Shlomo Abyu (*Enkat madregot*). Among published novelists were Benjamin Tammuz (*Minotaur*), Aharon Megged (*Masa be'av*), and H. Gouri (*Hahakira: Sefer Re'u'el*). Most popular were *Notsot* by Hayim Be'er, *Shavua betashah* by A. Almog, and *Jabotinsky va'ani* by Yitzhak Oren.

Other interesting works included a volume of essays by A. B. Yehoshua; the collection *Shirei Tel-Aviv* edited by D. Hertz and O. Rabin; diary entries by Avraham Shlonsky; and literary notebooks for *Hahayim Kemashal* by P. Sadeh.

(WARREN BARGAD)

Yiddish. Several leading writers published works about various Jewish communities throughout the world. *Life Goes On* is Yoysef Burg's description of a shtetl in Bukovina. Moise Held's collection of stories, *From the Red Bridge into the World*, is set in the U.S.S.R. during the early 1940s and later in Romania. Khaim Maltinsky's *The Moscow Trial of the Birobidzhaners* details the arrest and trial of those accused of nationalism, their sentencing, and their experiences in the gulags. Alexander Lizen provides sympathetic portraits of Jews in the Ukraine during the civil war period and again during World War II in his newest collection, *Nokhemke Esreg*. Jewish life in France is the theme of Benyumin Schlevin's collection *An Unhappy Disposition*.

Avrom Sutzkever, His Poetry and Prose by Itskhak Janosowicz is a contribution to criticism about Israel's leading Yiddish poet. Yakov Zvi Shargel's *Springs Around the Tent* analyzes the work of Yiddish writers in Israel. Reference materials were enriched by the publication of the eighth and final volume of *The Lexicon of Modern Yiddish Literature* and by Khaim Leyb Fuks's *Biographical Dictionary of Hebrew and Yiddish Writers* in Canada.

Mordkhe Tsanin concluded his five-volume historical opus with *The Jordan Falls into the Dead Sea*, dealing with the Holocaust and the establishment of the nation of Israel. Leyb Kurland's novel *A Narrow Bridge* reflects on contemporary issues in Israeli life. Yehuda Elberg's *Tales* recast a number of Hasidic stories in modern idiom. Four noteworthy collections of poetry appeared: Mordkhe Husid's philosophical *Dust and Eternity*; Beyle Schaechter-Gottesman's modernist collection, *Dawn*; and M. M. Shaffir's two finely crafted volumes, *Four Ells of Solitude* and *To Find a Moment of Peace*.

The Holocaust remained a major leitmotiv in the writing of poets and novelists. Meir Yelin's *The Mirages of Jogger Oscar Frik* describes the psychic evolution of an alienated Hungarian Jew who is assigned to liquidate the inhabitants of the Kovno ghetto. Josef Goldkorn's *Unbelievable and Yet . . .* consists of compelling reportage about his encounters with survivors.

(THOMAS E. BIRD; ELIAS SCHULMAN)

CHINESE

China. In 1981 China experienced a growing demand by its writers and intellectuals for greater freedom. The nation continued to stress its commitment to "let a hundred flowers bloom and a hundred schools of thought contend," but Chinese leaders were revealing an increasing wariness in regard to Western influence and "bourgeois liberalism," which they believed were sweeping the country. A campaign of criticism and self-criticism against writers described as "pernicious" and "erroneous" was launched on the grounds that their works propagated "pessimism, nihilism, and ultra-individualism" and opposed "the leadership of the party." Those who "hold that creation is solely the expression of writers and artists" and those who crave "absolute freedom and extreme individualistic rights" were denounced. While stressing that the current campaign would not lead to the sweeping repression of the past, when hundreds of writers were persecuted, the Chinese authorities found it necessary to condemn Bai Hua's

(Pai Hua's) screenplay *Bitter Love* and Sun Jingxuan's (Sun Ching-hsüan's) poem "A Spectre Haunts the Land of China," both of which seemingly reveal their authors' doubts about the Communist rule and leadership. Both writers published self-criticisms after extensive attacks from literary and political authorities.

Another movement launched in 1981 was a campaign against pure lyric poetry and abstract works. Highly personal poetry was viewed by official critics as representing an "unhealthy" tendency. Several literary journals published articles on the necessity of literature and art following the party's line and direction.

While the new crackdown had a dampening effect on writers and artists, there was no indication that China would impose the absolute uniformity in literary and artistic works that had been ordained during the Cultural Revolution (1966–76). In early December Hu Qiaomu (Hu Ch'iaomu), a leading ideologist, reflected the party's policy by reaffirming that literature and art must "serve the people and socialism." He also struck a conciliatory note, however, by adding that writers who deviated from the party line but who repented of such errors would not be penalized.

Despite the current campaigns, Chinese writers continued to produce satirical and realistic works revealing China's social conditions and political reality. Attacks on corruption, inefficiency, selfishness, incompetence, and privileges enjoyed by high officials and their families were popular themes. Stories and novels written with biting humour and ironic twists gained popularity. Love had also become an increasingly favoured subject. Works reflecting these recent trends include Zhang Jie's (Chang Chieh's) stories on love, Dong Luoshan's (Tung Lo-shan's) works on intellectuals, and Jiang Zilong's (Chiang Tze-lung's) stories on cadres and bureaucrats.

Taiwan. As in 1980, Taiwan witnessed the publication of few notable literary works in 1981. Established writers were unusually inactive, and few promising young writers emerged. Interest in serious literary works among readers seemed to have declined, and even literary contests failed to produce notable works.

Several Taiwan writers residing abroad, however, produced works that attracted considerable attention. Among them were Chang Hsi-kuo, who was the first Taiwan author to publish science fiction; Liu Ta-jen, whose novel *The Plankton Community* vividly reflects the life of Chinese intellectuals in Taiwan in the 1960s; and Ch'en Jo-hsi, whose story "We Went to Reno" and other pieces reveal the agony of Chinese students in the U.S. during the turbulent years of the Cultural Revolution. (WINSTON L. Y. YANG; NATHAN MAO)

JAPANESE

For Japanese literature 1981 could be characterized as a relatively quiet, inconspicuous year. It had been rumoured that Yasushi Inoue, author of the novel *Roof-tiles of Tempyô*, was among the most promising candidates for the Nobel Prize for Literature, and many journalists rushed to his house on the day that the prize was announced. However,

this expectation did not materialize. The most remarkable best-seller of the year was not a novel but a touching memoir of the girlhood of television actress Tetsuko Kuroyanagi. She was expelled from a grade school as an incorrigible dreamer-idler but fortunately came across a broad-minded, sympathetic teacher and could enjoy her school life in another institution. The book sold almost a million copies within a year. Its great success probably was due to the fact that it provided the Japanese public with an emotional outlet for their vague dissatisfaction with the great amount of emphasis upon grades and examinations in most schools.

Of course, Japanese novelists were not inactive. Yasushi Inoue's *Hangakubo's Testament* was an impressive historical novel dealing with Sen-no Rikyu, legendary master of the tea ceremony of the 16th century, who apparently fell into disfavour with the military dictator and killed himself in a mystifying way. Hisashi Inoue's *Kiri-Kiri People* was a hilarious novel that sold quite well in spite of its length. The tone was comical, but the central idea was serious social criticism of the post-World War II Japan of economic prosperity. "Kiri-kiri" people were Japanese hillbillies who decided to secede from Japan and create an independent state of their own. Their brave experiment was a failure, but the implied criticism of various "dirty" aspects of contemporary Japan was both funny and biting.

As for young authors, there were three remarkable books. Wahei Tatematsu described postwar scenes in a provincial town with refreshing vigour in *City of Joy*, trying to develop a new picture of Japan at that time from the point of view of the generation that was then very young. Kyoko Hayashi, a woman novelist who survived the atomic bomb in Nagasaki, wrote a novel of social protest, *As If Nothing Happened.* In it she followed the later careers of several of her own classmates after the war, and her emphasis was on both the sufferings of those survivors and the responses to them on the part of the Japanese who did not experience "the Bomb." Although not fully integrated as a novel, *As If Nothing Happened* remained a moving and sharp testament. Rie Yoshiyuki's *Little Lady* was a charming collection of short stories dealing with reminiscences of the narrator's favourite cat (already dead), an effective mixture of poetic fantasy and physical sense.

There were several remarkable books of biography and literary criticism. Kenkichi Yamamoto's *Forms and Soul: Roots of Japanese Beauty* was highly suggestive in tracing the psychic shades of Japanese imagination through various examples, both literary and artistic. Shinroku Komatsu's *Attracted by Vision of Beauty* contained a series of sensitive comments on the Japanese writers who had committed suicide. Toru Haga's *Gennai Hiraga* was a readable biography of a Japanese eccentric of the 18th century, rich in vivid episodes and remarkable for its far-reaching perspective on the international intellectual scene of that period.

(SHOICHI SAEKI)

See also Art Sales; Libraries; Nobel Prizes; Publishing.
[621]

THE AFRICAN MUSE
by Gerald Moore

Whether because of the conditions of literary production within the continent or because of the temptations that entice budding writers to accept political or academic dignities, Africa remains very short of professional writers. Too many careers still follow a falling trajectory from a couple of early successes toward silence. Nevertheless, although relatively few new writers who appear to have a serious and continuing engagement with literature have emerged since the mid-1970s, some of the continent's major writers have added significantly to their achievements.

Cameroon, Nigeria. In Cameroon, Mongo Beti, after a long interval following his anticolonial satires of 1954–60, published two novels in 1974. *Remember Ruben* is a work of epic scope and imaginative range. Embracing the colonial period, the war years 1939–45, the anticolonial wars that followed, and the struggle of Ruben um Nyobe and his party to internationalize the Cameroonian fight for independence, it culminates in the stage-managed transfer of power in 1958–60 and the ensuing civil war. *Perpétue* is a different but complementary work, focusing closely on the tragic fate of the heroine whose life and purity are sacrificed to the rampant materialism of the new black elite. In 1979 Beti published a sequel to *Remember Ruben, La Ruine presque cocasse d'un polichinelle*, but compared with its majestic predecessor, it proved disappointingly thin and uninventive.

Nigeria's output of written work is such that it prompts examination as a national literature. Wole Soyinka's profound study of an African civilization in decline, *Death and the King's Horseman* (1975), contains some of his most vivid dramatic poetry, though some critics felt that the play's verbal richness conceals a certain ideological weakness. Its black nationalism seems occasionally to beg the question, for the white man here is surely the instrument of change rather than its cause. Africa could

not have entered the 20th century unscathed by its secularism and materialism. Another Nigerian depicter of pre-colonial values, Elechi Amadi, is content to stick to the task of narration, showing his culture in action but refusing to comment on it. His 1978 novel, *The Slave,* for all its classical beauty and symmetry, moved toward a new raciness in its rendering of African speech that was refreshing after the proverb-laden solemnity of so much African fictional dialogue.

Among the most prolific of the younger Nigerian writers are Kole Omotoso and Femi Osofisan. Both have a preference for local publication and for writing plays and short novels, which are more marketable in Africa and reach a wider audience. Omotoso's novel *Sacrifice* (1974) is a moving defense of feminine dignity and love against the prevailing selfishness and greed of the young. Osofisan, who is primarily a dramatist, has a flair for reworking myths or historical events to make a contemporary point, evident in his use of the Moremi myth in *Morountodun* (1979) and the reign of the 18th-century Oyo king Abiodun in *The Chattering and the Song* (1976). Both writers represent a new mood of public engagement in Nigerian literature, which extends to their publishing activities and criticism and their determination to use their writing to raise political consciousness.

Southern Africa. A rejection of literary self-indulgence, a determination to see the pen as just one instrument in the struggle for liberation, can be seen also in the new poetry pouring out of Angola and South Africa. In Angola the foundations were laid by such major poets of the older generation as António Jacinto and the late Agostinho Neto, his country's first president (d. 1979). But their work was often that of prophecy and the call to action, whereas much of the new poetry is full of bitterness and grief for comrades fallen in the struggle.

A similar urgency, grief, and anger stamp the new black poets of South Africa. The first announcement of the new mood was Oswald Mtshali's *Sounds of a Cowhide Drum* (1971). Since then a whole generation of young poets has arisen, adding a new tone

Gerald Moore is dean of arts at the University of Jos in Nigeria. His books include Twelve African Writers, Wole Soyinka, *and* Modern Poetry from Africa.

to South African literature. Most prominent of these are Sipho Sepamla and Wally Serote. Serote's poetry anatomizes the pain of his situation but also announces action: "I do not know where I have been/ To have fear so strong like a whirlwind (will it be that brief?)/ But Brother,/ I know I'm coming."

One of South Africa's best known prose writers, Alex La Guma, also showed a new direction with his fine portrayal of the obscure underground resistance worker Beukes in *In the Fog of the Season's End* (1972). He followed this with an explosive short novel of racial murder and revenge on the veld, *Time of the Butcherbird* (1979). Mention should also be made of Bessie Head, one of Africa's most original and powerful women writers, now settled in Botswana. Her novel *A Question of Power* (1973) is a haunting study of a mind passing through madness and gradually rebuilding a kind of stability and a fragmentary happiness.

Farther north, in Malawi, a new poetic talent appeared in 1981 with the publication of Jack Mapenje's *Chameleons and Gods*. Mapenje's poetry is economical and full of ironic humour, as in his "Poem for 1979" (the International Year of the Child): "Today no poet sufficiently asks why dying children/ Stare or throw bombs . . . / The year of the child must make no difference then/ Where tadpoles are never allowed to grow into frogs."

Eastern Africa. The early 1970s saw the beginning of an interesting popular literature in Kenya where, for example, Meja Mwangi's proletarian heroes (*Going Down River Road*, 1976) inhabit a world of poverty and hunger, far from the angst of exile or of the educated "been-to" (one who has lived long overseas and returned). But Kenyan literature is still dominated by the genius of Ngugi wa Thiong'o, whose epic novel *Petals of Blood* (1977) did for Kenyan historical experience something of what Beti did for Cameroon in *Remember Ruben*. In 1976 Ngugi co-authored a powerful political drama, *The Trial of Dedan Kimathi*, which prepared the way for his more recent works written in his native Kikuyu language. This direction, pioneered by the Ugandan poet Okot p'Bitek, is one that other African writers must be expected increasingly to follow: to compose first in one's own mother tongue and later to widen one's audience through an English (or French) translation.

The question of language choice leads to mention of the outstanding Somali novelist Nuruddin Farah, who surprisingly writes in English. Having grown up with both Somali and Arabic as mother tongues, Farah was educated mainly in Italian and only came to English through university studies in India. His English has a distinctive flavour deriving, perhaps, from its closeness to Somali dialogue. His most im-

pressive achievement to date is *Sweet and Sour Milk* (1979), a terrifying depiction of a totalitarian society through which the hero makes a sad odyssey in quest of the truth about his brother's murder. Writing of a society in which the status of women is particularly depressed, Farah displays a deep imaginative sympathy with their plight.

Ghana, Francophone Africa. The recent literature of Angola and South Africa, so closely welded to action and to a deeply rooted political movement, makes some of the earlier literature of bourgeois black nationalism look like attitudinizing and breast-beating in a void. The Ghanaian novelist Ayi Kwei Armah came close to this in his third book, *Why Are We So Blest?* (1974), and did not altogether avoid it in his more ambitious *Two Thousand Seasons* (1973), in which he attempted to encompass African history within the microcosm of a fictional plot. But with the publication of *The Healers* in 1978, Armah raised his reputation to new heights. The hero of this novel, Densu, represents a lone idea struggling against a corrupt system (the structure of the novel here closely resembles Soyinka's *Season of Anomy* of 1973). However, Armah lends a special dimension to this struggle by relating it to the Ashanti war of 1874 and the unholy alliance subsequently established between the local chiefs and the alien conquerors. This historical consciousness is much more effective than the rather diffuse effect of *Two Thousand Seasons,* where the subject matter tends to be crushed under the weight of abstraction.

In Francophone Africa generally there has been a slackening in the flow of fiction and poetry that ran so strongly from the early 1950s to the early 1970s. The eminent Sembene Ousmane of Senegal, who for some years turned his back on fiction in favour of the more immediate art of the film, has, however, produced an impressive new novel in two volumes, *Le Dernier de l'Empire*. A deeply felt feminist novel, *Une si longue lettre*, by a new Senegalese woman writer, Mariama Ba, also appeared in 1981. The Congolese poet Tchicaya U Tamsi remains as prolific as ever, with three volumes of poetry and several plays published during the 1970s; these include, notably, the verse drama *Le Zulu* (presented at the 1976 Avignon Festival) and the lyric collection *La Veste d'intérieur* (1977). Although not living by his pen, U Tamsi thus joins the lonely example of Léopold Senghor (president of Senegal, 1960–80, and originator, with the West Indian Aimé Césaire, of the concept of *négritude*) in having produced a real oeuvre in which the development of his art can be traced over three decades.

Bibliographical information on the works cited above will be found in the author's *Twelve African Writers* (1980) and in Lewis Nkosi's *Tasks and Masks* (1981).

Luxembourg

Madagascar

Luxembourg

A constitutional monarchy, the Benelux country of Luxembourg is bounded on the east by West Germany, on the south by France, and on the west and north by Belgium. Area: 2,586 sq km (999 sq mi). Pop. (1981 est.): 365,000. Cap. and largest city: Luxembourg (pop., 1979 est., 79,600). Language: French, German, Luxembourgian. Religion: Roman Catholic 97%. Grand duke, Jean; prime minister in 1981, Pierre Werner.

In September the government of Luxembourg threatened to bring the European Parliament before the European Court of Justice "for attempting to exclude Luxembourg as one of the official sites for its meetings." This unprecedented action represented a desperate attempt to retain Luxembourg, along with Strasbourg, France, as one of the two official meeting places of the Parliament.

In July the European Parliament had voted to exclude Luxembourg and concentrate its plenary sessions in Strasbourg, while reserving Brussels for meetings of its committees. In the past the Parliament had met in Luxembourg on two occasions a year, and its secretariat was based there.

The work of some 14,000 people in the city of Luxembourg was linked to such European institutions as the European Investment Bank, the Court of Justice, and the European Statistical Office. A large proportion of them would, however, be expected to move to either Strasbourg or Brussels if the resolution were endorsed by the Council of Ministers of the European Communities.

On February 14 Crown Prince Henri of Luxembourg married María Teresa Mestre, a Swiss commoner of Cuban origin. The princess gave birth to a son on November 11.   (K. M. SMOGORZEWSKI)

LUXEMBOURG

Education. (1979–80) Primary, pupils 30,112, teachers (1978–79) 1,998; secondary, pupils 8,801; vocational, pupils 15,769; secondary and vocational, teachers (1975–76) 1,801; teacher training, students, 134; higher, students 284, teaching staff (1977–78), 172.

Finance. Monetary unit: Luxembourg franc, at par with the Belgian franc, with (Sept. 21, 1981) a free rate of LFr 36.42 to U.S. $1 (LFr 67.52 = £1 sterling). Budget (1981 est.): revenue LFr 49,746,000,000; expenditure LFr 51,157,-000,000. Gross domestic product (1978) LFr 106,570,000,-000. Cost of living (1975 = 100; June 1981) 145.2.

Foreign Trade: *see* BELGIUM.

Transport and Communications. Roads (1980) 5,094 km (including 44 km expressways). Motor vehicles in use (1979): passenger 162,800; commercial 10,800. Railways: (1979) 270 km; traffic (1980) 299 million passenger-km, freight 662 million net ton-km. Air traffic (1980): *c.* 55 million passenger-km; freight *c.* 200,000 net ton-km. Telephones (Jan. 1980) 198,900. Radio receivers (Dec. 1979) *c.* 182,000. Television receivers (Dec. 1979) 105,000.

Agriculture. Production (in 000; metric tons; 1979): barley 75; wheat 29; oats 30; potatoes 33; wine *c.* 6. Livestock (in 000; May 1979): cattle 224; pigs 85; poultry 157.

Industry. Production (in 000; metric tons; 1980): iron ore (29% metal content) 562; pig iron 3,569; crude steel 4,618; electricity (kw-hr) 1,114,000.

Madagascar

Madagascar occupies the island of the same name and minor adjacent islands in the Indian Ocean off the southeast coast of Africa. Area: 587,041 sq km (226,658 sq mi). Pop. (1980 est.): 8,714,000. Cap. and largest city: Antananarivo (pop., 1980 est., 547,100). Language: Malagasy (national) and French (official). Religion: animist 54%; Roman Catholic 21%; Protestant 18%; Muslim 7%. President in 1981, Didier Ratsiraka; prime minister, Lieut. Col. Désiré Rakotoarijaona.

Pres. Didier Ratsiraka faced difficulties at home during 1981, although in March Monja Jaona, elderly leader of the dissident Madagascar National Independence Movement, realigned himself with the sole authorized political grouping, the National Front for the Defense of the Revolution. Placed under house arrest in November 1980, Jaona was set free in March.

At that time Jaona denied any responsibility for disturbances that had taken place on February 3 and 4 in Antananarivo. Confrontations between schoolchildren and students and the police had left 6 dead and some 50 people injured. The situation had been considered serious enough for the government to impose a curfew, which was not lifted until June 26, the 21st anniversary of Madagascar's independence. In November further incidents, less serious this time, flared up in Antananarivo; for two days police clashed with opposition party militants attending a congress in the city.

President Ratsiraka obtained significant aid for the economy in May, when representatives of the 11 Club of Paris nations agreed to consolidate Madagascar's external debt; repayment was to take place over nine years, with a four-year grace period. In September the president visited Moscow and Paris, where he was received by Pres. François Mitterrand of France on September 30. The dispute with France over the Glorieuses Archipelago and other islands in the Indian Ocean and the Mozambique Channel seemed to be moving toward settlement through the establishment of a condominium.   (PHILIPPE DECRAENE)

Crown Prince Henri of Luxembourg led his bride, the former María Teresa Mestre of Switzerland, down the aisle after their marriage on February 14.

UPI

MADAGASCAR

Education. (1978) Primary, pupils 1,311,000, teachers 23,937; secondary, pupils (1976) 114,468, teachers (1975) 5,088; vocational, pupils (1976) 7,000, teachers (1973) 879; teacher training (1973), students 993, teachers 63; higher (1976), students 11,711, teaching staff 941.

Finance. Monetary unit: Malagasy franc, at par with the CFA franc, with (Sept. 21, 1981) a parity of MalFr 50 to the French franc (free rates of MalFr 265 = U.S. $1 and MalFr 491 = £1 sterling). Gold and other reserves (March 1980) U.S. $1.9 million. Budget (1980 est.): revenue MalFr 236 billion; expenditure MalFr 278 billion.

Foreign Trade. (1979) Imports MalFr 135,320,000,000; exports MalFr 83,830,000,000. Import sources: France 32%; U.S. 11%; West Germany 9%; Iraq 7%; Japan 6%; China 5%. Export destinations: France 26%; U.S. 15%; Indonesia 13%; West Germany 8%; Algeria 5%; Japan 5%. Main exports: coffee 45%; cloves 18%.

Transport and Communications. Roads (1979) 27,556 km. Motor vehicles in use (1979): passenger *c.* 57,000; commercial (including buses) *c.* 50,000. Railways: (1978) 1,035 km; traffic (1979) 300 million passenger-km, freight 210 million net ton-km. Air traffic (1980): *c.* 310 million passenger-km; freight *c.* 20.1 million net ton-km. Shipping (1980): merchant vessels 100 gross tons and over 56; gross tonnage 91,211. Telephones (Jan. 1978) 28,700. Radio receivers (Dec. 1977) 1,020,000. Television receivers (Dec. 1977) 12,000.

Agriculture. Production (in 000; metric tons; 1980): rice *c.* 2,327; corn (1979) *c.* 100; cassava (1979) *c.* 1,348; sweet potatoes (1979) *c.* 340; potatoes (1979) *c.* 134; mangoes *c.* 144; dry beans 55; bananas 240; oranges *c.* 86; pineapples *c.* 58; peanuts 28; sugar, raw value (1979) *c.* 113; coffee 80; cotton 12; tobacco *c.* 4; sisal 19; beef and veal *c.* 119; fish catch (1979) 54. Livestock (in 000; Dec. 1979): cattle *c.* 8,800; sheep *c.* 660; pigs *c.* 570; goats (1978) *c.* 1,583; chickens (1978) *c.* 14,082.

MALAWI

Education. (1977–78) Primary, pupils 675,740, teachers 11,115; secondary, pupils 15,079, teachers 707; vocational (1976–77), pupils 685, teachers 88; teacher training, students (1976–77) 1,355, teachers 86; higher, students 1,153, teaching staff (1976–77) 128.

Finance. Monetary unit: kwacha, with (Sept. 21, 1981) a free rate of 0.89 kwacha to U.S. $1 (1.66 kwacha = £1 sterling). Gold and other reserves (June 1981) U.S. $90 million. Budget (1980 actual): revenue 199 million kwacha; expenditure 302 million kwacha.

Foreign Trade. (1980) Imports 356.2 million kwacha; exports 239.2 million kwacha. Import sources (1979): South Africa 42%; U.K. 19%; Japan 9%; West Germany 5%. Export destinations (1979): U.K. 41%; West Germany 10%; The Netherlands 9%; U.S. 8%; South Africa 5%. Main exports: tobacco 44%; sugar 15%; tea 12%; peanuts 7%.

Transport and Communications. Roads (main; 1980) 10,772 km. Motor vehicles in use (1980): passenger 11,800; commercial 13,300. Railways (1980): 768 km; traffic 80 million passenger-km, freight 241 million net ton-km. Air traffic (1980): 68 million passenger-km; freight 1 million net ton-km. Telephones (Jan. 1980) 28,800. Radio receivers (Dec. 1976) 130,000.

Agriculture. Production (in 000; metric tons; 1980): corn *c.* 1,100; cassava (1979) *c.* 80; sorghum *c.* 120; sugar, raw value (1979) 109; peanuts *c.* 170; tea *c.* 32; tobacco *c.* 58; cotton, lint (1979) *c.* 10. Livestock (in 000; 1979): cattle 790; sheep *c.* 140; goats *c.* 860; pigs 174; poultry *c.* 8,000.

Malawi

Malawi

A republic and member of the Commonwealth in east central Africa, Malawi is bounded by Tanzania, Mozambique, and Zambia. Area: 118,484 sq km (45,747 sq mi). Pop. (1981 est.): 6,370,000. Cap.: Lilongwe (pop., 1977, 98,700). Largest city: Blantyre (pop., 1977, 219,000). Language: English (official) and Chichewa (national). Religion: Christian 33%; remainder, predominantly traditional beliefs. President in 1981, Hastings Kamuzu Banda.

Stabilization of Malawi's economy was Pres. Hastings Kamuzu Banda's main concern during 1981. Despite its growing output of hydroelectric power, Malawi could not escape the effects of rising petroleum prices. A sharp decline in the balance of payments occasioned a report early in 1981 that government bodies had overspent seriously and that some members of ministries had been guilty of misappropriation and fraud.

The president reshuffled his Cabinet in an attempt to effect some improvement. In January he transferred Lewis Chimango from the Ministry of Finance to the Ministry of Local Government and replaced him by Chaziya Phiri, formerly minister of health. A month later the president created a new Ministry of Housing. He also reorganized his own Ministry of Agriculture and Natural Resources, appointing John Chiwewe to the Cabinet as minister for forestry and natural resources. Significant progress was made by the National Seed Company of Malawi, set up in 1978 with the aim of making the country self-sufficient in seed for agricultural crops. (KENNETH INGHAM)

Malaysia

A federation within the Commonwealth comprising the 11 states of the former Federation of Malaya, Sabah, Sarawak, and the federal territory of Kuala Lumpur, Malaysia is a federal constitutional monarchy situated in Southeast Asia at the southern end of the Malay Peninsula (excluding Singapore) and on the northern part of the island of Borneo. Area: 329,747 sq km (127,316 sq mi). Pop. (1980 prelim.): 13,435,600, including (1980 est.) Malays 47.1%, Chinese 32.7%, Indians 9.6%, and Dayaks 3.7%. Cap. and largest city: Kuala Lumpur (metro pop., 1980 UN est., 1,081,000). Language: Malay (official). Religion: Malays are Muslim; Indians mainly Hindu; Chinese mainly Buddhist, Confucian, and Taoist; indigenous population of Sabah and Sarawak (est.), 47% animist, 38% Muslim, and 15% Christian. Supreme head of state in 1981, with the title of *yang di-pertuan agong,* Tuanku Sultan Haji Ahmad Shah al-Musta'in Billah ibni al-Marhum Sultan Abu Bakar Ri'ayatuddin al-Mu'adzam Shah; prime ministers, Datuk Hussein bin Onn and, from July 16, Datuk Seri Mahathir bin Mohamad.

On May 15, 1981, Prime Minister Datuk Hussein bin Onn, who had undergone coronary bypass surgery in February, announced his intention to resign as president of the United Malays National Organization (UMNO) and as prime minister for reasons of health. The UMNO party elections took place in June. Datuk Seri Mahathir bin Mohamad (*see* BIOGRAPHIES), deputy president of UMNO as well as deputy prime minister, was elected president without opposition. The election for deputy president was won by Datuk Musa Hitam, a UMNO vice-president and minister for education. These elections within the dominant party of the ruling National Front coalition settled the succession to offices of state. On July 16 Mahathir was

Malaysia

Magazines:
see Publishing

Maldives

sworn in as prime minister. He appointed Datuk Musa deputy prime minister and minister for home affairs.

Controversy arose over an attempt to secure a royal pardon for Datuk Harun Idris, former chief minister of the state of Selangor, who was serving a prison sentence for corruption and criminal breach of trust. Datuk Harun stood successfully for one of the posts of vice-president in the UMNO elections. On August 1, two days after 21 political detainees had been released from prison, Datuk Harun received a remission of sentence and was set free. He was permitted to take up his UMNO office as the result of a special dispensation granted by the Home Ministry.

In April an amendment was passed to the 1966 Societies Act: in a contentious provision, any club, society, or association was required to register as either political or nonpolitical. Any nonpolitical body commenting on government policy would risk deregistration. An amendment to Article 150 of the constitution empowered the supreme head of state to declare a state of emergency if he felt that a threat was posed to public security.

In January the government announced the return to Malaysia from China of Musa Ahmad, chairman of the proscribed Malayan Communist Party. Although he had been in exile for more than 20 years and was only a figurehead, his return and subsequent confession on television represented a major propaganda coup. Abdul Samad Ismail, former managing editor of the *New Straits Times*, who

had been detained since June 1976, was released in February. In July the government expelled three Soviet diplomats on charges of espionage. Siddiq Mohamed Ghouse, political secretary for several years to Mahathir (then prime minister-designate), was arrested on similar charges.

In September it was announced that the office of the Palestine Liberation Organization had been accorded full diplomatic status. Mahathir declined to attend the meeting of Commonwealth heads of government in Australia. In October he instructed government bodies to show a definite preference for non-British firms when awarding contracts.

In March Datuk Abdul Rahman Yakub resigned as chief minister of Sarawak to assume the ceremonial office of head of state. He was succeeded by his nephew Datuk Amar Haji Abdul Taib Mahmud. In the same month elections to the state assembly in Sabah were won overwhelmingly by the incumbent Sabah People's Union (Berjaya Party).   (MICHAEL LEIFER)

Maldives

Maldives, a republic in the Indian Ocean consisting of about two thousand small islands, lies southwest of the southern tip of India. Area: 298 sq km (115 sq mi). Pop. (1981 est.): 152,000. Cap.: Male (pop., 1978, 29,600). Language: Divehi. Religion: Muslim. President in 1981, Maumoon Abdul Gayoom.

One of the world's poorest countries and dependent on fishing for three-quarters of its income, the Maldives continued to import almost everything in 1981. Nonetheless, the government announced an ambitious development program based on tourism and international assistance. Foreign aid accounted for about 10% of gross national product despite the Maldives' refusal to rent out Gan Island as a base to either the U.S. or the U.S.S.R. Repercussions of the 1980 coup attempt continued; former president Ibrahim Nasir was to be tried in absentia for attempting to overthrow the government.

The Maldives looked to the Arab world in particular for aid, and in March 1981 the Islamic Development Bank agreed to provide an additional loan, bringing IDB loans to the islands to a total of $13 million. An international business complex was planned for Gan, while £1.5 million was allocated to make Gan airport fully operational.

MALAYSIA

Education. (1981) Primary, pupils 2,033,803, teachers 73,881; secondary, pupils 1,102,908, teachers 48,199; vocational, pupils 17,424, teachers 1,430; higher (including teacher-training colleges), students 57,139, teaching staff 5,569.

Finance. Monetary unit: ringgit, with (Sept. 21, 1981) a free rate of 2.32 ringgits to U.S. $1 (4.30 ringgits = £1 sterling). Gold and other reserves (June 1981) U.S. $4,046,-000,000. Budget (1980 actual): revenue 13,511,000,000 ringgits; expenditure 18,933,000,000 ringgits. Gross national product (1980) 49,633,000,000 ringgits. Money supply (March 1981) 10,120,000,000 ringgits. Cost of living (Peninsular Malaysia; 1975 = 100; May 1981) 135.7.

Foreign Trade. (1980) Imports 23,539,000,000 ringgits; exports 28,201,000,000 ringgits. Import sources: Japan 23%; U.S. 15%; Singapore 12%; Saudi Arabia 6%; Australia 5%; West Germany 5%; U.K. 5%. Export destinations: Japan 23%; Singapore 19%; U.S. 16%; The Netherlands 6%. Main exports: crude oil 24%; rubber 16%; timber 14%; palm oil 9%; tin 9%; thermionic valves and tubes *c.* 8%.

Transport and Communications. Roads (1979) *c.* 29,-800 km. Motor vehicles in use (1979): passenger *c.* 690,-000; commercial *c.* 154,000. Railways (1980): *c.* 2,292 km; traffic (Peninsular Malaysia only; including Singapore) 1,-587,000,000 passenger-km, freight 1,196,000,000 net ton-km. Air traffic (1980): 4,076,000,000 passenger-km; freight 116.7 million net ton-km. Shipping (1980): merchant vessels 100 gross tons and over 221; gross tonnage 702,145. Telephones (Jan. 1979) 439,200. Radio receivers (Dec. 1977) 1.5 million. Television licenses (Dec. 1979) 819,000.

Agriculture. Production (in 000; metric tons; 1980): rice 2,129; rubber *c.* 1,600; copra *c.* 231; palm oil 2,575; tea *c.* 3; bananas *c.* 455; pineapples 203; pepper (Sarawak only; 1979) 36; tobacco *c.* 10; meat (1979) *c.* 167; fish catch (1979) 698; timber (cu m; 1979) *c.* 43,205. Livestock (in 000; Dec. 1978): cattle *c.* 430; buffalo *c.* 293; pigs *c.* 1,171; goats *c.* 380; sheep *c.* 46; chickens *c.* 49,201.

Industry. Production (in 000; metric tons; 1980): cement 2,349; tin concentrates (metal content) 61; bauxite 921; iron ore (56% metal content) 371; crude oil 13,156; petroleum products (Sarawak only; 1979) 705; electricity (kw-hr) 8,974,000.

MALDIVES

Education. (1979) Primary, pupils 17,583, teachers 590; secondary, pupils 3,885, teachers 105; vocational, students 30, teachers 8; teacher training, students 20, teachers 4.

Finance and Trade. Monetary unit: Maldivian rupee, with (June 30, 1981) an official rate of MRs 3.93 to U.S. $1 (MRs 7.64 = £1 sterling) and a free rate of MRs 7.50 to U.S. $1 (MRs 14.57 = £1 sterling). Budget (1979): revenue MRs 16.4 million; expenditure MRs 39.5 million. Foreign trade (1979): imports MRs 86.6 million; exports MRs 23 million. Main import sources: India *c.* 25%; West Germany *c.* 15%; Japan *c.* 14%; Sri Lanka *c.* 11%; Burma *c.* 7%; Pakistan *c.* 7%. Main export destinations: Japan *c.* 44%; Sri Lanka *c.* 14%; Switzerland *c.* 14%; Mauritius *c.* 12%. Main exports: fresh fish 56%; dried salt fish 36%.

Tourism, however, remained the major hope; in 1980 a total of 42,000 tourists came to the islands, compared with only 919 in 1972.

During the year diplomatic relations were established with a number of countries, including Oman, Saudi Arabia, Sudan, and Mali. Pres. Maumoon Abdul Gayoom visited Singapore, and in September agreements covering extradition and cooperation in education, science, and culture were made with Sri Lanka.   (GUY ARNOLD)

Mali

A republic of West Africa, Mali is bordered by Algeria, Niger, Upper Volta, Ivory Coast, Guinea, Senegal, and Mauritania. Area: 1,240,192 sq km (478,841 sq mi). Pop. (1981 est.): 6,833,000. Cap. and largest city: Bamako (pop., 1980 est., 440,000). Language: French (official); Hamito-Semitic and various tribal dialects. Religion: Muslim 65%; animist 30%; Christian 5%. President in 1981, Gen. Moussa Traoré.

Mali was one of the West African states most anxious to keep its distance from the Soviet Union and to maintain close relations with France. Accordingly, following the November 1980 inauguration of an airport at Mopti built with Soviet aid, the Malian leadership decided it was time to turn its back on the East. In October Guy Penne, counselor on African affairs to French Pres. François Mitterrand, visited Mali with assurances of France's goodwill. Although opposed by some member states, including Upper Volta (in conflict with Mali over a frontier dispute), agreement on Mali's reintegration into the West African Monetary Union was reached in the autumn.

Pres. Moussa Traoré had thwarted an attempted coup on Dec. 30–31, 1980, and in March 1981 three of those involved were sentenced to death, one in absentia. Further social unrest surfaced in May. In July President Traoré granted clemency to teachers and students involved in the previous year's agitation.   (PHILIPPE DECRAENE)

Mali

Malta

Malta

The Republic of Malta, a member of the Commonwealth, comprises the islands of Malta, Gozo, and Comino in the Mediterranean Sea between Sicily and Tunisia. Area: 320 sq km (124 sq mi), including Malta, Gozo, and Comino. Pop. (1980 est.): 344,000. Cap.: Valletta (pop., 1979 est., 14,000). Largest city: Sliema (pop., 1979 est., 20,100). Language: Maltese and English. Religion: mainly Roman Catholic. President in 1981, Anton Buttigieg; prime minister, Dom Mintoff.

Elections on Dec. 12, 1981, returned the Malta Labour Party, led by Prime Minister Dom Mintoff, to power for its third five-year term. In September the budget for 1982 was approved with an estimated expenditure of M£220.5 million.

Malta's dispute with Libya remained unresolved. Libya ratified the 1976 agreement to refer the continental shelf dispute to the International Court of Justice, but added a sentence restricting oil exploration to which Malta could not agree. Malta accused Libya of frustrating oil exploration in order to maintain economic dominance over the island. Later, Libya suspended the importation of Maltese products.

In January Soviet merchant shipping was granted the use of the former NATO oil depot on the island. The Malta government declared that Malta was a neutral state pursuing a policy of nonalignment and refusing to participate in any military alliance. In October the U.S.S.R. signed an agreement with Malta pledging to support the island's neutral status, and it appointed the first full-time ambassador to Malta. They also established air services and trade agreements.

Support for Malta's neutrality was sought from the United States. Pres. Ronald Reagan said that the U.S. government respected Malta's choice, but it could not offer a guarantee of its neutral status.

(ALBERT GANADO)

MALI

Education. (1978–79) Primary, pupils 293,227, teachers 6,877; secondary, pupils (1977–78) 64,491, teachers (1976–77) 8,915; vocational, pupils (1976–77) 2,609, teachers 540; teacher training, students (1977–78) 2,261, teachers (1974–75) 126; higher (1977–78), students 4,216, teaching staff 450.

Finance. Monetary unit: Mali franc, with (Sept. 21, 1981) a par value of MFr 100 to the French franc and a free rate of MFr 529 to U.S. $1 (MFr 981 = £1 sterling). Budget (1980 est.) balanced at MFr 78 billion.

Foreign Trade. (1980) Imports MFr 176.3 billion; exports MFr 74.2 billion. Import sources (1977): France 38%; Ivory Coast 19%; Senegal 8%; West Germany 7%; China 5%. Export destinations (1977): France 29%; Ivory Coast 14%; U.K. 14%; China 12%; Japan 7%; The Netherlands 6%; West Germany 6%. Main exports (1977): cotton 57%; peanuts and oil 17%; livestock 12%; cereals 5%.

Agriculture. Production (in 000; metric tons; 1980): millet and sorghum c. 750; rice (1979) 177; corn (1979) c. 60; peanuts c. 183; sweet potatoes (1979) c. 37; cassava (1979) c. 40; cottonseed c. 80; cotton, lint c. 50; beef and veal (1979) c. 47; mutton and goat meat (1979) c. 46; fish catch c. 100. Livestock (in 000; 1979): cattle c. 4,459; sheep c. 6,067; goats c. 5,757; camels c. 208; horses c. 180; asses c. 489.

MALTA

Education. (1978–79) Primary, pupils 32,218, teachers 1,411; secondary, pupils 22,907, teachers 1,510; vocational, pupils 4,395, teachers 481; higher, students 1,592, teaching staff 149.

Finance. Monetary unit: Maltese pound, with (Sept. 21, 1981) a free rate of M£0.39 = U.S. $1 (M£0.72 = £1 sterling). Gold and other reserves (June 1981) U.S. $909 million. Budget (total; 1981 est.): revenue M£219 million; expenditure M£220 million.

Foreign Trade. (1980) Imports M£323,740,000; exports M£166,720,000. Import sources: Italy 24%; U.K. 22%; West Germany 14%; U.S. 6%. Export destinations: West Germany 31%; U.K. 20%; Libya 7%; The Netherlands 7%; Italy 6%; Belgium-Luxembourg 6%; ship and aircraft stores 6%. Main exports: clothing 41%; machinery 11%; instruments 5%; printed matter 5%; petroleum products 5%. Tourism (1979): visitors 618,300; gross receipts U.S. $213 million.

Transport and Communications. Roads (1979) 1,286 km. Motor vehicles in use (1979): passenger 66,200; commercial 13,800. There are no railways. Air traffic (1980): 602 million passenger-km; freight 4.5 million net ton-km. Shipping (1980): merchant vessels 100 gross tons and over 60; gross tonnage 132,861. Shipping traffic (1979): goods loaded 120,000 metric tons, unloaded 1,050,000 metric tons. Telephones (Dec. 1979) 77,300. Radio receivers (Dec. 1977) 85,000. Television licenses (Dec. 1979) 71,000.

Manufacturing:
see Economy, World; Industrial Review

Marine Biology:
see Life Sciences

Materials Sciences

Ceramics. One of the key events of the past year for ceramists was the long-awaited testing of the thermal protection tiles on the first flight of the space shuttle in April. Although some of the tiles on the orbital-maneuvering-system engine pods were lost and about 300 points of damage appeared on the surfaces of the shuttle's tiles, probably sustained during the ascent phase of the flight, the "Columbia" reentered safely with only minor tile degradation. Only one of the areas of surface damage grew significantly during reentry as a result of melting of the internal silica fibres, and few of the tiles, aside from those near the nose-gear and main landing-gear doors, shrank very much.

Though the current generation of reusable tiles thus was shown to be suitable for the basic shuttle task, NASA had already developed a stronger, less dense, and more impact-resistant tile material for future versions of the shuttle. The new material, called fibrous refractory composite insulation, is a mixture of high-purity silica fibres similar to those used in the current tiles and aluminum borosilicate fibres, Nextel 312, made by the 3M Co., St. Paul, Minn. It was quite likely that the new tile would be used extensively on the third and fourth orbiting vehicles to be built. The next step might well be an advanced flexible, reusable surface-insulation blanket consisting of a high-purity silica-fibre felt sandwiched and stitched between face sheets of silica-glass cloth. This new blanket material was being considered for the troublesome orbiter-maneuvering-system pod areas of the "Columbia" in upcoming flights and might replace many of the tiles on the upper wings and fuselage of the third shuttle vehicle, the "Discovery," to be introduced in 1983.

Ceramics also surfaced as an important filter material for diesel engines. Although diesels have many economic advantages, many of them also have rather high exhaust particulate levels. In fact, many diesel engines in the U.S. would not meet that nation's 1985 emission standards of 0.125 g/km (0.2 g/mi) without some form of filter. Corning Glass Works, Corning, N.Y., recently announced the development of a ceramic honeycomb filter with walls of controlled porosity. The exhaust gases flow through the porous walls, but soot particles are filtered out. To prevent soot from accumulating and clogging the filter, the filter is regenerated by adjusting the temperature and oxygen concentration within the filter to consume the particles.

Ceramic reinforcements, especially silicon carbide fibres and whiskers, received a great deal more attention as a result of continuing advances in their use in metal-matrix composites. In this case the extremely high strength and modulus of elasticity of the ceramic in fibre or whisker form are used to reinforce a matrix of aluminum or titanium alloy. The result is a strong, stiff, lightweight composite with a blend of attractive properties.

In 1981 silicon carbide fibres were being produced by a variety of processes. Avco Corp., with

What is believed to be the largest microwave oven in the world was completed by Thermex, Inc. of Santa Clara, California. The 30-kw oven will be used to process plastics.

UPI

headquarters in Greenwich, Conn., produced continuous filaments with a tensile strength above 4,100 megapascals (MPa; 600,000 psi) and a modulus of 414,000 MPa (60 million psi) by chemical vapour deposition and employed them in reinforced aluminum composites that were stronger than many steels at less than half their weight. The Exxon Corp. pursued a novel route to discrete silicon carbide whiskers of high length-to-diameter ratio, beginning with the silicon and carbon contained in scrap rice hulls. Millions of kilograms of these hulls are left over every year in the U.S. in the processing of rice for the consumer market. Exxon expected a production capacity of 4,540 kg (10,000 lb) of reinforced aluminum and magnesium matrix composites in 1981 and anticipated capacities of 113,500 kg (250,000 lb) by 1983 and 3.4 million kg (7.5 million lb) per year by 1987.

In the field of ceramic processing D. Lynn Johnson of Northwestern University, Evanston, Ill., reported a startling ability to sinter some ceramic materials from their initial consolidated powder state to their fired, almost fully dense final state in seconds or minutes rather than hours. Working specifically with beta-alumina tubes, which are needed as solid electrolytes in sodium-sulfur batteries, he showed that thin-walled tubes could be sintered by passing them rapidly through an ionized plasma generated in an argon gas chamber by a 5-MHz induction generator. Whereas conventional firing of these tubes required 15 minutes at about 1,600° C (2,900° F) to achieve densification followed by about an hour at 1,450° C (2,640° F) to obtain important compositional transformations, the same results were achieved within 30 seconds in the plasma. In addition to economic advantages over conventional processing routes, the plasma sintering approach yields a much finer grain structure that suggests performance and property advantages for many applications.

(NORMAN M. TALLAN)

[721.B.8.a.ii; 724.C.5]

Metallurgy. During 1981 developments in metallurgy were strongly directed by energy considerations. Falling productivity, environmental protection, and decreasing research and development funding were other areas of concern. The basic research that often leads to widespread innovation seemed to be especially restrained financially. An exception was the study of surface phenomena, which influence every facet of metallurgy from crushing of ore to the outcome of finished products. This field was benefiting from the powerful surface-analysis techniques that had become available during the past few years.

Extractive metallurgy continued profiting from mathematical modeling to optimize processes, on-stream analytical equipment, and computer control to maintain the desired operation. For example, in upgrading taconite iron ore in one plant, four grinding lines were able to do the work of five after constant automatic monitoring and full computer control was established. Modern microcomputers on line in the plant kept the capital cost reasonable. Fine grinding, which is very energy consuming, was showing improved efficiency through changes, such as in mill-liner shape,

A unique, new protective device for detecting corrosive alkali metals in coal-derived gaseous synthetic fuels has been developed at the General Electric Research and Development Center in Schenectady, N.Y.

based on experience and shrewd guesswork rather than on rigorous design calculations.

In the early 1980s the most energy-efficient aluminum smelters used about six kilowatt-hours of electricity to produce a pound of metal, which seemed to be about the lower limit for processes in widespread use. Commercial use of the more efficient chloride process still required solution of some scale-up problems. Experiments in Japan with an aluminum blast furnace, coal as the reducing agent, and clay containing 30% aluminum oxide as the ore yielded an aluminum-silicon alloy while keeping energy consumption low. Problems remained for producing aluminum from the alloy and obtaining refractories to withstand the 2,000° C (3,600° F) furnace temperature.

Hot isostatic pressing (HIP), originally developed for compacting and sintering parts from powdered metals, was being used for improving the strength and reliability of casting for aerospace use. Under heat and pressure many strength-reducing defects present in casting will heal. Because castings can be made closer to final shape than forgings, much material and machining time is saved. A remaining problem was the satisfactory elimination of surface defects, which the pressure fluid used in HIP fills rather than closes.

The efficient molten salt bath process for producing a wear-resistant surface on such parts as automotive gears was reviving. A new hardening bath contained much less cyanide than previously used formulas and employed a special salt bath quench that destroyed any cyanide carried from the first bath, thus eliminating the environmental problem of toxic fumes.

Superalloy-based composites for very high temperature use approached commercial application. A nickel-base superalloy strengthened with an yt-

trium oxide dispersion had a rupture strength at 1,100° C (2,000° F) that was significantly higher than that of the conventional alloy, although at 760° C (1,400° F) its strength was lowered. Such properties as oxidation resistance were unaffected. Tungsten-fibre-strengthened superalloys also were being developed. Strength at 1,100° C for these materials was reported to be as much as four times that of the matrix alloy, although there was little improvement in strength at lower temperatures. (DONALD F. CLIFTON)

See also Industrial Review: *Glass; Iron and Steel; Machinery and Machine Tools;* Mining and Quarrying. [724.C.3; 725.B]

Mathematics

Following a year of celebrating the successful classification of the finite simple groups in 1980—a rare and monumental achievement—mathematics research reverted in 1981 to the normal pace of small progress on numerous fronts.

Among the many problems that were solved, one result shed some light on a major unsolved problem in the theory of computation, to determine which problems have times of solution that grow exponentially with the size of the problem, and which do not. The former problems—called NP complete—quickly get out of range of even modern computers, so it is useful to know in advance whether a problem is in this class.

In 1981 Hendric W. Lenstra, Jr., of the University of Amsterdam showed that a certain class of integer programming problems does not exhibit the much-feared pattern of exponential growth. Integer programming problems are widely used in business and industry in assignment and classification problems; they are termed "integer" programs because of the requirement that the solution be in whole numbers, as it must be when the solution represents numbers of people assigned to different jobs.

Although Lenstra's result neither shows nor suggests that all integer programming problems are solvable in polynomial time (the moderate alternative to exponential growth), it does represent a significant and, in some respects, surprising solution to part of the main problem. It is somewhat parallel to Soviet mathematician Leonid G. Khachian's famous 1979 proof that the common problem of linear programming—in which solutions are not restricted to whole numbers—can be solved in polynomial time.

Two other results of 1981 serve not so much to surprise as to confirm old conjectures. In the Soviet Union G. T. Igorychez of the Kirensky Institute of Physics proved a conjecture made in 1926 by the Dutch algebraist B. L. van der Waerden concerning an optimization property of square matrices.

A square matrix is an array of numbers n rows deep by n columns across. Van der Waerden examined the behaviour of the permanent of such matrices, a number calculated by forming all possible products of elements selected one from every row and column and then adding them together. Permanents of matrices are important in combinatorial mathematics, where they can help count the ways in which objects can be arranged.

As the values of a matrix change, the size of its permanent also changes. Van der Waerden discovered that the minimum value of the permanent is achieved when every element in the matrix has the same value, namely $1/n$. He never was able to prove this observation, however. In 1961 Morris Newman and Marvin Marcus of the University of California at Santa Barbara proved an important special case of the van der Waerden conjecture, but it took 20 more years to complete the proof. The missing ingredient—discovered and effectively applied by Igorychez—is an obscure pair of inequalities published in 1938 by another Soviet mathematician, A. D. Aleksandrov.

The other long-standing conjecture resolved in 1981 concerns the behaviour of the sums of trigonometric functions—the sine and cosine wave-

The brightest high school math students came from 27 countries around the world to compete in the 1981 International Mathematical Olympiad held at Georgetown University in Washington, D.C., in July. The U.S. team, with 314 points out of a possible 336, emerged the leader, followed by West Germany and Great Britain.

by two points. The two-day exam, prepared by an international committee, consisted of six challenging problems from school mathematics (*see* box), three problems to be done each day in 4½ hours. Four of the U.S. contestants achieved perfect scores, a record. (LYNN ARTHUR STEEN)

1981 International Mathematical Olympiad

1. *P* is a point inside a given triangle *ABC*. *D, E, F* are the feet of the perpendiculars from *P* to the lines *BC, CA, AB*, respectively. Find all *P* for which

$$\frac{BC}{PD} + \frac{CA}{PE} + \frac{AB}{PF}$$

is least.

2. Let $1 \leqq r \leqq n$ and consider all subsets of *r* elements of the set $\{1, 2, \ldots, n\}$. Also consider the least number in each of these subsets. $F(n, r)$ denotes the arithmetic mean of these least numbers; prove that

$$F(n, r) = \frac{n + 1}{r + 1}$$

3. Determine the maximum of $m^2 + n^2$, where *m* and *n* are integers satisfying $m, n \in \{1, 2, \ldots, 1981\}$ and $(n^2 - mn - m^2)^2 = 1$.

4. (a) For which values of $n > 2$ is there a set of *n* consecutive positive integers such that the largest number in the set is a divisor of the least common multiple of the remaining $n - 1$ numbers?

(b) For which values of $n > 2$ is there exactly one set having the stated property?

5. Three congruent circles have a common point *O* and lie inside a given triangle. Each circle touches a pair of sides of the triangle. Prove that the incentre and the circumcentre of the triangle and the point *O* are collinear.

6. The function $f(x, y)$ satisfies
   (1) $f(0, y) = y + 1$,
   (2) $f(x + 1, 0) = f(x, 1)$,
   (3) $f(x + 1, y + 1) = f(x, f(x + 1, y))$
for all non-negative integers *x, y*. Determine $f(4, 1981)$.

---

forms of which all complex waves are formed. In 1948 British mathematician John E. Littlewood observed that these superimposed waves could never completely cancel; as ever more were added there would be an inevitable slow growth in the overall magnitude of the resulting wave.

In 1959 Paul Cohen of Stanford University nearly proved Littlewood's conjecture, but his result was not quite as sharp as Littlewood's original formulation. Recently Brent Smith of Illinois State University, Louis Pigno of Kansas State University, and O. Carruth McGehee of Louisiana State University finally verified the original conjecture. They used no new methods but only clever applications of a traditional mathematician's tool — the Cauchy-Schwarz inequality taught to every undergraduate mathematics major.

In July 1981 the International Mathematical Olympiad was held in Washington, D.C., the first time it had been held in the Western Hemisphere. Competing in this 22nd annual competition were 185 high school students from 27 countries. For only the second time in five years the U.S. team captured first place, edging out West Germany

Mauritania

Mauritania

The Islamic Republic of Mauritania is on the Atlantic coast of West Africa, adjoining Western Sahara, Algeria, Mali, and Senegal. Area: 1,030,700 sq km (398,000 sq mi). Pop. (1981 est.): 1,682,000. Cap.: Nouakchott (pop., 1977, 135,000). (Data above refer to Mauritania as constituted prior to the purported division of Spanish Sahara between Mauritania and Morocco.) Language: Arabic, French. Religion: Muslim. President of the Military Committee for National Salvation in 1981, Lieut. Col. Mohamed Khouna Ould Haidalla; premiers, Sid Ahmed Ould Bneijara and, from April 25, Lieut. Col. Maaouya Ould Sidi Ahmed Taya.

Mauritania accused Morocco of involvement in an attempted coup on March 16, 1981, alleging that a commando that was to have assassinated Lieut. Col. Mohamed Khouna Ould Haidalla, president of the Military Committee for National Salvation, had arrived in Nouakchott from Marrakech via Paris and Dakar, Senegal. Diplomatic relations with Morocco were suspended until June 28. Four officers implicated in the affair were executed in March.

The civilian government set up on Dec. 12, 1980, was replaced on April 25 by a largely military Cabinet headed by Lieut. Col. Maaouya Ould Sidi Ahmed Taya as premier and defense minister. The Western Saharan conflict continued to dominate the country's affairs. Morocco repeatedly accused Mauritania of being a rear base for the Popular Front for the Liberation of Saguia el Hamra and Río de Oro (Polisario Front), while Mauritania accused Morocco of encouraging subversive activity against it. In April Mauritania was said to be considering confederation with the Saharan Arab Democratic Republic, the Polisario-sponsored "government" of Western Sahara. In August the London-based Anti-Slavery Society reported that there were 100,000 slaves in Mauritania.

(PHILIPPE DECRAENE)

MAURITANIA

Education. (1978–79) Primary, pupils 82,408, teachers (1977–78) 1,765; secondary, pupils 11,957, teachers (1977–78) 389; vocational, pupils (1974–75) 1,591, teachers (1973–74) *c.* 117; higher, pupils 477, teaching staff 110.

Finance. Monetary unit: ouguiya, with (Sept. 21, 1981) a free rate of 55.43 ouguiya = U.S. $1 (102.76 ouguiya = £1 sterling). Gold and other reserves (June 1981) U.S. $115 million. Budget (1979 est.) balanced at 10,726,000,000 ouguiya.

Foreign Trade. (1980) Imports 13,119,000,000 ouguiya; exports 8,916,000,000 ouguiya. Import sources: France *c.* 34%; Spain *c.* 9%; Belgium-Luxembourg *c.* 8%; The Netherlands *c.* 7%; U.S. *c.* 7%; West Germany *c.* 5%. Export destinations: France *c.* 29%; Italy *c.* 19%; Japan *c.* 9%; Belgium-Luxembourg *c.* 9%; U.K. *c.* 8%; West Germany *c.* 8%; Spain *c.* 7%. Main exports: iron ore 78%; fish 22%.

Mauritius

Mauritius

Mexico

The parliamentary state of Mauritius, a member of the Commonwealth, lies about 800 km E of Madagascar in the Indian Ocean; it includes the island dependencies of Rodrigues, Agalega, and Cargados Carajos. Area: 2,040 sq km (787.5 sq mi). Pop. (1980 est.): 969,900, including (1977) Indian 69.3%; Creole (mixed French and African) 28%; others 2.7%. Cap. and largest city: Port Louis (pop., 1980 est., 147,400). Language: English (official); French has official standing for certain legislative and judicial purposes, and Creole is the lingua franca. Religion (1974 est.): Hindu 51%; Christian 30%; Muslim 16%; Buddhist 3%. Queen, Elizabeth II; governor-general in 1981, Sir Dayendranath Burrenchobay; prime minister, Sir Seewoosagur Ramgoolam.

Mauritius continued to suffer during 1981 from the effects of Cyclone Claudette, which destroyed 30% of the 1980 crop. Spiraling labour costs meant that Mauritius had become, comparatively, a high-cost sugar producer, and a new slump in world sugar prices in March 1981 compounded the balance of trade deficit. Manufacturing industries remained of marginal importance to exports.

The government embarked on a program of agricultural diversification with the object of reducing food imports, which accounted for 25% of all imports in 1980. It was hoped that inherent difficulties, such as the shortage of suitable land and poor irrigation, could be overcome by encouraging the use of high-yield seeds and fertilizers and offering grants to farmers.

At the end of March the Mauritius Militant Movement, which held more seats in Parliament than any other single party, formed an alliance with a new left-wing group, the Mauritius Socialist Party. The alliance was expected to pose a strong challenge to Prime Minister Sir Seewoosagur Ramgoolam's coalition government in the next elections. In December Mauritius accused Seychelles Pres. France-Albert René of trying to overthrow the Mauritian government.

(GUY ARNOLD)

MAURITIUS

Education. (1980) Primary, pupils 123,666, teachers 6,-177; secondary, pupils 80,881, teachers 3,075; vocational, pupils 295, teachers 38; teacher training, students 426, teachers 23; higher (university only), students 98, teaching staff 76.

Finance and Trade. Monetary unit: Mauritian rupee, with (Sept. 21, 1981) a free rate of MauRs 8.50 to U.S. $1 (MauRs 15.75 = £1 sterling). Gold and other reserves (June 1981) U.S. $31 million. Budget (1980–81 est.): revenue MauRs 2.2 billion; expenditure MauRs 2,294,000,000. Foreign trade (1980): imports MauRs 4,381,100,000; exports MauRs 3,300,100,000. Import sources (1979): South Africa 14%; U.K. 14%; France 9%; Bahrain 8%; Australia 5%; Japan 5%; India 5%. Export destinations (1979): U.K. 64%; U.S. 12%; France 11%. Main exports (1979): sugar 68%; clothing 15%. Tourism (1979): visitors 128,400; gross receipts c. U.S. $47 million.

Agriculture. Production (in 000; metric tons; 1980): sugar, raw value c. 504; bananas (1979) c. 9; tea c. 5; tobacco c. 1; milk (1979) c. 23. Livestock (in 000; 1979): cattle c. 56; pigs c. 6; sheep c. 4; goats c. 70; chickens c. 1,400.

Mexico

A federal republic of Middle America, Mexico is bounded by the Pacific Ocean, the Gulf of Mexico, the U.S., Belize, and Guatemala. Area: 1,972,546 sq km (761,604 sq mi). Pop. (1980 prelim.): 67,382,600, including about 55% mestizo and 29% Indian. Cap. and largest city: Mexico City (pop., federal district, 1980 prelim., 9,373,400; metro. area, 1979 est., 14.7 million). Language: Spanish. Religion (1980): Roman Catholic 89.4%; Protestant (including Evangelical) 3.6%; Jewish 0.1%; others 6.9%. President in 1981, José López Portillo.

Oil continued to play a major role in the Mexican economy and politics in 1981. Contrary to the government's program for balanced growth of the economy, the contribution of oil exports rose to over 70% of the total in the first quarter of the year, while non-oil exports declined and the deficit on the trade balance rose to double that of the same period in 1980. This generated serious repercussions when, late in the first half of the year, high world stocks of oil caused a drop in demand. On June 1 Jorge Díaz Serrano, director of Petróleos Mexicanos (Pemex), the state oil company, announced a $4 cut in the price of Mexican oil in response to market forces. His action proved unacceptable to the government, partly because it meant a reduction of an estimated $2 billion–$3 billion in expected revenue. Díaz Serrano resigned and was replaced by Julio Rodolfo Moctezuma Cid.

In July negotiations began for a $2 increase in the oil price, but France, India, Yugoslavia, Sweden, the Philippines, and a number of U.S. oil companies temporarily canceled their orders. The government took a number of measures to offset the negative effect of the loss in oil income on the economy. These included a 4% cut in public expenditure and tariff controls on 85% of all imported goods. In December the domestic price of gasoline was raised 115%.

In his annual state of the nation address on September 1, the last before the 1982 presidential election, Pres. José López Portillo was able to announce that, after the depression of June and July, Mexico's list of oil clients had been broadened, and orders of 1,250,000 bbl a day were guaranteed until the end of the year. The president said that average daily production in 1981 was 2,350,-000 bbl a day and that Mexico's proven reserves, increased to 72,000,000,000 bbl, had moved from sixth to fourth largest in the world. From the June average price of $30.60 per barrel, the benchmark price rose first to $31.25 and then, in November, to $31.75.

Foreign activities related to oil included Pemex's acquisition of a majority shareholding in the Spanish Petronor oil refinery in Bilbao in January; later in the year Spain increased its purchases of oil to 230,000 bbl a day. Also in January, Mexico agreed to prospect for oil off the coast of China. Assistance to Cuba in its exploration for oil, first announced in January, was reaffirmed in May during a visit by Secretary of Foreign Affairs Jorge Castañeda de

A condemnation of the neutron bomb was stressed by Mexican Pres. José López Portillo when he delivered his fifth state of the union address in September.

la Rosa to Moscow. Cuba was also to receive 10,000 metric tons of liquefied natural gas from Mexico in 1981. Bilateral agreements concerning the sale of oil in return for trade, technology, and investment were signed during the year with Canada, Japan, Brazil, West Germany, and Sweden.

On two occasions López Portillo had talks with Pres. Ronald Reagan of the U.S. The first, on January 5, before the latter's inauguration, was an introductory meeting held at the Mexico-U.S. border. On June 8–9 López Portillo went to Camp David, Md., where he and Reagan discussed the regional political situation and established a bilateral commission for trade. Presidents Reagan and López Portillo met informally while attending the dedication of the presidential museum of former U.S. president Gerald Ford in Grand Rapids, Mich., and Reagan returned to Mexico on October 22–23 for the North-South development summit in Cancún, at which Mexico played host to the leaders of 22 countries. Relations between Mexico and

the U.S. improved as a result of these meetings, although there were still areas of tension, including the continuing flow of illegal immigrants into the U.S. from Mexico.

Mexico was critical of U.S. policy toward El Salvador. At the end of August, having resolved a disagreement over oil supplies, Mexico and France declared that they recognized the left-wing guerrilla organizations in El Salvador as a "representative political force." The U.S. and Venezuela, both of whom supported the ruling junta, condemned the joint statement. At the same time, the U.S. disapproved of Mexico's strong links with Nicaragua and Cuba. In July an agricultural aid agreement was signed between Mexico and Nicaragua; in August López Portillo met Pres. Fidel Castro to discuss Cuba's exclusion from the Cancún summit.

On September 25 López Portillo named the minister for planning and the budget, Miguel de la Madrid Hurtado, as the official Partido Revolucionario Institucional (PRI) candidate for the 1982

MEXICO

Education. (1978–79) Primary, pupils 13,604,476, teachers 334,146; secondary, pupils 3,375,026, teachers 193,448; vocational, pupils 347,614, teachers 24,942; teacher training, students 177,238, teachers 11,280; higher (1977–78), students 610,840, teaching staff 52,294.

Finance. Monetary unit: peso, with (Sept. 21, 1981) a free rate of 24.94 pesos to U.S. $1 (46.23 pesos = £1 sterling). Gold and other reserves (March 1981) U.S. $3,177,000,000. Budget (total; 1981 est.) balanced at 2,333,000,000,000 pesos. Gross domestic product (1979) 2,767,000,000,000 pesos. Money supply (Dec. 1980) 508.7 billion pesos. Cost of living (1975 = 100; June 1981) 330.4.

Foreign Trade. (1980) Imports 446,970,000,000 pesos; exports 357,520,000,000 pesos. Import sources: U.S. 66%; Japan 5%; West Germany 5%. Export destinations: U.S. 63%; Spain 7%. Main exports: crude oil 60%; machinery and transport

equipment c. 5%. Tourism (1979): visitors 4,135,000; gross receipts U.S. $1,422,000,000.

Transport and Communications. Roads (1980) 213,192 km (including 978 km expressways). Motor vehicles in use (1980): passenger 4,031,970; commercial 1,534,100. Railways: (main; 1978) 20,288 km; traffic (1979) 5,450,000,000 passenger-km, freight 36,740,000,000 net ton-km. Air traffic (1980): c. 13,-870,000,000 passenger-km; freight c. 136 million net ton-km. Shipping (1980): merchant vessels 100 gross tons and over 361; gross tonnage 1,006,417. Telephones (1980) 4,532,600. Radio receivers (1978) 17,514,000. Television receivers (1977) 5,480,000.

Agriculture. Production (in 000; metric tons; 1980): corn 11,081; wheat 2,645; barley 505; sorghum 4,677; rice 462; potatoes c. 902; sugar, raw value c. 2,950; dry beans 1,130; soybeans 299; tomatoes c. 1,420; bananas 1,515; oranges c. 1,630; lemons 504; cottonseed 534; coffee c. 222; tobacco

c. 72; cotton, lint 340; beef and veal c. 594; pork c. 490; fish catch (1979) 875. Livestock (in 000; Dec. 1979): cattle 31,094; sheep 7,318; pigs 13,222; goats 7,185; horses (1978) 6,447; mules (1978) 3,207; asses (1978) 3,233; chickens c. 152,000.

Industry. Production (in 000; metric tons; 1980): crude oil 96,960; coal (1978) c. 7,100; natural gas (cu m) 32,350,000; electricity (kw-hr; 1979) 59,410,000; cement 16,263; iron ore (metal content) 4,048; pig iron c. 5,150; crude steel c. 6,980; sulfur (1979) 2,390; petroleum products c. 48,100; sulfuric acid 2,064; fertilizers (nutrient content; 1979–80) nitrogenous 642, phosphate 227; aluminum 41; copper 84; lead 132; zinc 137; manganese ore (metal content; 1979) c. 180; gold (troy oz) 190; silver (troy oz) 51,280; woven cotton fabrics 66; man-made fibres (1978) 204; radio receivers (units; 1978) 1,126; television receivers (units; 1978) 767; passenger cars (units) 312; commercial vehicles (units) 132.

Miguel de la Madrid Hurtado (right)
was generally expected to be the victor in the presidential elections to be
held in July 1982.

presidential election. The nomination did not receive full support from all sections of the ruling
PRI. In October Javier García Paniagua resigned as
the party's president, a post to which he had been
appointed on March 19. His dissatisfaction was
echoed by members of Mexico's labour movement.

One of de la Madrid's intended policies was the
elimination of corruption. In 1981 the governor of
the state of Coahuila, Oscar Flores Tapia, resigned
following accusations that his administration was
corrupt; a congressional committee subsequently
recommended his impeachment.

At the end of September riots broke out in the
city of Nezahualcóyotl on the northeastern edge of
Mexico City. Several hundred people were injured
and 70 were arrested in the disturbances, which
were in protest against a fare increase by private
bus companies. Immediately after the Cancún
summit an earthquake registering 6.5–7.1 on the
Richter scale struck central Mexico. Few casualties
were reported, but there was some damage to services in the capital.   (JOHN B. H. BOX)

Middle Eastern Affairs

The assassination of Egypt's Pres. Anwar as-Sadat
(*see* OBITUARIES) on Oct. 6, 1981, momentarily
halted the peace process between Egypt and Israel
and the search for a settlement of Palestinian
claims for autonomy. Yet 1981 was also the year
when Saudi Arabia's Crown Prince Fahd threw
the weight of the Arab world's richest country
behind a new search for a solution in the Middle
East. The eight-point Fahd plan gained support
from other members of the Gulf Cooperation
Council (GCC) and was placed on the agenda of the
Arab summit meeting in Fez, Morocco, on
November 25. (*See* SAUDI ARABIA.)

Elsewhere in the Middle East, Iran and Iraq continued fighting in the conflict that had erupted in
September 1980 and in which no other country in
the region became directly involved. Saudi Arabia's plan to buy AWACS (airborne warning and

Microbiology:
see Life Sciences

Microelectronics:
see Computers; In-
dustrial Review

control system) aircraft from the United States appeared likely to go ahead after the U.S. Senate voted by a narrow margin on October 28 to approve
the sale.

Arab-Israeli Relations. Saudi Arabia's peace
plan announced on August 8 was welcomed more
for its acceptance of Israel's right to exist within
secure boundaries than for any other point. It was
also seen as an Arab initiative to a problem in
which the U.S. or international mediators were
regarded as brokers. Almost all its points, including the implicit allusion to Israel's right to exist,
had been made before in United Nations resolutions supported by Arab countries. These included
withdrawal of Israel from all Arab territory occupied in 1967, the dismantling of Israeli settlements
built on such territory, and the establishment of
an independent Palestinian nation with East
Jerusalem as its capital. The new proposal was that
the UN assume control of the West Bank (of the
Jordan River) and Gaza Strip for a transitional
period not exceeding a few months before they
were returned to Arab control.

Initial reactions to the Fahd proposals were varied. Some Arab nations, including Jordan, Morocco, Tunisia, Sudan, Yemen (San'a'), and members
of the GCC welcomed the Saudi initiative. The GCC,
however, agreed at its meeting in Riyadh, Saudi
Arabia, on November 11 that Saudi Arabia should
propose the plan individually at Fez; it was believed that Kuwait, the second most influential
state in the six-country GCC grouping, blocked a
move to have the plan adopted as a joint proposal
of the organization. Of the radical Arab countries,
Iraq and Libya at first opposed the move. Palestine
Liberation Organization (PLO) chairman Yasir
Arafat gave the plan qualified support despite the
fact that it failed to name the PLO, referring only
to the establishment of an independent Palestinian
state with East Jerusalem as its capital. Radical PLO
elements opposed the plan.

The Arab summit at Fez in November resulted
in a setback for the Fahd peace plan, although
there was growing evidence in the days after the

abrupt end to the summit on November 25 that the Saudis were recovering some of their lost prestige. It had become apparent on the day before the summit opened that the Fez meeting would not rubber-stamp the Fahd proposals in order to allow them to go to the UN. Heads of state from countries opposed to the Fahd document sent junior representatives; Syria, for example, was represented by its foreign minister. Some countries, notably Iraq, Algeria, and Libya, failed to attend.

In a hurried late-night meeting, King Hassan II of Morocco, as sponsor of the meeting, met with the Saudis and King Hussein of Jordan. It was agreed to suspend the meeting rather than allow divisions to come into the open. King Hassan used the absence of heads of state as the pretext for suspending the meeting and said that it would be reconvened in three months. This was changed on November 27 to an announcement that the meeting would reconvene in six months—after the date agreed upon for Israeli withdrawal from the Sinai Peninsula under the Camp David accords.

It was thought that the six months would give the Saudis more time to apply pressure on their moderate allies in the Gulf as well as to involve Syria and the PLO. There were also encouraging signs of private support from Iraq and Algeria. The Iraqis badly needed help from Saudi Arabia because of reversals in the war with Iran. Algeria was believed to have stayed away from Fez because of a quarrel with Morocco over the Western Sahara issue rather than any strong opposition to the peace proposals. Arafat had by this time firmly attached himself to the Fahd proposals—another

source of encouragement to Riyadh. Although Arafat was under attack from other segments of the PLO leadership, his charisma counted for a great deal. The maverick remained Libya, whose leader, Col. Muammar al-Qaddafi (*see* BIOGRAPHIES), was outspokenly critical of the Fahd plan. Providing Qaddafi remained isolated, his opposition was not expected to count for much.

Israel totally rejected the Fahd plan, although an Israeli parliamentary delegation conceded after a meeting in Washington, D.C., in November that the implicit recognition of their nation was a positive move. Israel also repeated its rejection of the 1980 Venice declaration of the European Communities (EC), which called for involvement of the PLO in the peace process. Essentially, any peace plan that entailed the creation of a Palestinian state in the West Bank and Gaza following an Israeli withdrawal was rejected by the government of Prime Minister Menachem Begin (*see* BIOGRAPHIES). In this policy, following the 1981 elections in Israel, Begin was supported not only by the 61 members of the ruling coalition in the Knesset (parliament) but also by many members of the opposition Labour Party. Following the assassination of President Sadat, attitudes in Israel hardened, with many more Israelis questioning the wisdom of completing the planned withdrawal from the Sinai by April 25, 1982.

In the West U.S. Secretary of State Alexander Haig said on November 12 that the U.S. could not accept the Saudi plan, although he acknowledged that it contained positive elements. He said that it was "unacceptable" for an Arab nation to be creat-

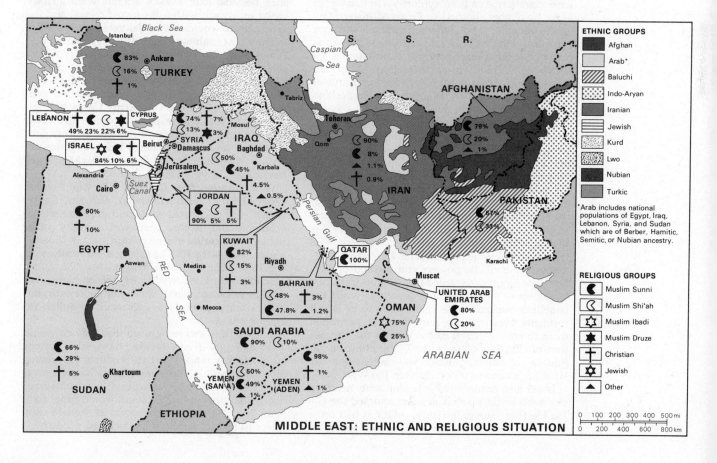

MIDDLE EAST: ETHNIC AND RELIGIOUS SITUATION

ETHNIC GROUPS
- Afghan
- Arab*
- Baluchi
- Indo-Aryan
- Iranian
- Jewish
- Kurd
- Lwo
- Nubian
- Turkic

*Arab includes national populations of Egypt, Iraq, Lebanon, Syria, and Sudan which are of Berber, Hamitic, Semitic, or Nubian ancestry.

RELIGIOUS GROUPS
- Muslim Sunni
- Muslim Shi'ah
- Muslim Ibadi
- Muslim Druze
- Christian
- Jewish
- Other

Leaders from the Arab world met in Taif, Saudi Arabia, in January to discuss issues confronting the Muslim world, including the war between Iran and Iraq.

ed with East Jerusalem as its capital. European sympathy with the Fahd plan, particularly as expressed by U.K. Foreign Secretary Lord Carrington in his capacity as president of the EC Council of Ministers, angered the U.S. administration.

Fiji, Colombia, and Uruguay had agreed to join the Sinai peacekeeping force, but at issue was the participation of Britain, Italy, France, and The Netherlands. In Israel Prime Minister Begin said that he would veto the participation of European nations that remained committed to the 1980 Venice declaration. At a press conference in London in early November, both U.K. Prime Minister Margaret Thatcher and Italian Premier Giovanni Spadolini said that they considered that participation in the Sinai force was not inconsistent with support for the Venice declaration. After the December visit to Israel of French Foreign Minister Claude Cheysson, France's support for the declaration appeared to be in doubt.

Following the installation of Egypt's new president, Hosni Mubarak (see BIOGRAPHIES), attempts were made to reopen talks on Palestinian autonomy between Egypt and Israel. On November 12 Mubarak met the Israeli ministerial delegation to the talks in Cairo. Israeli Interior Minister Youssef Burg then reaffirmed his country's position that the Camp David accords constituted "the only solid base to reach peace in the Middle East." This viewpoint was repeated later by Mubarak. The talks centred on the proposals for a Palestinian autonomy council, its powers and method of election. The Egyptians wanted Palestinians from East Jerusalem to participate in the voting, while the Israelis considered those Palestinians to be Israeli residents even though they had not permitted them to vote in Israeli elections since the annexation of East Jerusalem in 1967. The difficulty in finding common ground was intensified by Israeli crackdowns on civilians in the West Bank.

Israel also exacerbated relations with much of the Arab world when it in effect annexed the Golan Heights, Syrian territory, which it had occupied since the 1967 war. An earlier source of

contention was the destruction by Israeli planes of a French-built nuclear reactor in Iraq; Israel argued that the facility would be used for arming Iraq with nuclear weapons.

AWACS Sale. U.S. Pres. Ronald Reagan's victory in the Senate vote on the $8.5 billion sale of AWACS surveillance aircraft to Saudi Arabia was unexpected. The 52–48 vote was a defeat for the Israeli lobby, whose resolve had been stiffened by visits from leading Israeli politicians to the U.S. The sale was expected, in fact, to make little difference because four AWACS aircraft were already based in Riyadh with full support crews, and the extra planes would not be delivered until 1985.

The AWACS sale was originally proposed by U.S. Pres. Jimmy Carter but became a key part of Reagan's policy to strengthen the defenses of pro-Western Arab Gulf nations. Oman received U.S. military assistance through a construction program managed by the U.S. Army Corps of Engineers, and the Reagan administration also made offers of sales of military equipment to other Gulf states. In November a massive U.S. war games exercise, "Operation Bright Star," involved practice landings in Egypt, Oman, and Somalia.

Gulf Cooperation Council. The GCC, which grouped Saudi Arabia, Kuwait, Bahrain, Qatar, Oman, and the United Arab Emirates in a regional economic and defense pact, was formally established at a meeting of foreign ministers in Muscat, Oman, on March 10. The first heads-of-state meeting took place in Abu Dhabi on May 26, and a second meeting followed in Riyadh on November 11. The GCC's secretariat was based in Riyadh, but the secretary-general was a Kuwaiti, Abdullah Yacoub Bishara.

Although it was recognized that the GCC would have difficulty in coordinating its member nations on many key issues, particularly over oil production and pricing, there was also satisfaction over progress in a number of areas. It was considered likely that in 1982 the GCC states would adopt common food standards for imports as well as measures to protect locally manufactured goods.

STAYSKAL—© 1981 CHICAGO TRIBUNE

"I lost track . . . is it their turn to
retaliate or ours?"

The Gulf War. The attack on a crude-oil gathering centre in Kuwait on October 1, which Kuwait blamed on Iran, sparked fears of Iranian aggression against a neutral neighbour. Kuwait was, however, providing Iraq with financial aid as well as allowing it to use Kuwaiti ports for transshipment of cargo. The attack, in the Umm al-Aish area about 40 km (25 mi) south of the Iraqi border, was the fourth by Iranian aircraft since the war started in September 1980. In an acrimonious exchange with Iran in November, Saudi Arabia warned that it would not tolerate attacks on its borders or any more misbehaviour by Iranian pilgrims to Mecca.

The fighting between Iran and Iraq continued throughout 1981, confirming fears expressed at the start of the conflict that the Gulf region would have to live for some time with the spectre of instability in its northern sector since the best that could be achieved would be an armed truce between the combatants. The balance in the war during 1981 reflected Iranian gains, including the lifting of the siege of Abadan and the recapture of other Iranian towns from the Iraqis.

Arab International Finance. Arab financiers continued their drive to diversify holdings in the West. The Kuwait Petroleum Corporation, Kuwait's state-owned oil company, made a successful takeover bid for the oil-drilling and exploration group Santa Fe International Corp. in October. The takeover raised fears among U.S. pro-Israeli lobbies about the extent of Arab holdings in the U.S. Under an agreement with Saudi Arabia and Kuwait, the U.S. Department of the Treasury promised not to reveal in detail the volume of investments in the U.S. held by those two nations. Arab banks increased their share of Euromarket syndications, accounting for just under 10% of the underwriting. They also broadened their holdings in European banks with the decision by the National Bank of Kuwait to buy 50% of the Paris-based Frab Bank International. In October the Arab Insurance Group opened in Bahrain with a capital base authorized at $3 billion.

(JOHN WHELAN)

See also Energy; articles on the various political units. [978.B]

Migration, International

Migration on a global scale continued unabated during 1981. Escaping from unemployment or persecution, sometimes from both simultaneously, groups of would-be immigrants faced danger, privation, and hostility in their search for security. Unfortunately for many, their countries of destination in Europe and North America were experiencing economic recession and hence sought to limit new additions to the population.

The U.S. Department of Justice issued a statement in July on proposed immigration and refugee policy in which it recognized that a clear policy on the issue was long overdue; legislation and enforcement procedures were inadequate, particularly with regard to illegal immigrants and mass requests for asylum. Pres. Ronald Reagan's administration, advised by a Cabinet-level task force, recommended ways to strengthen the existing Immigration and Nationality Act, passed in 1952 and amended in 1965 and 1976.

According to the Department of Justice, immigrants, both legal and illegal, were entering the country in greater numbers than at any time since the early 1900s. During 1980 more than 800,000 persons entered the U.S., largely because of the Cuban and Haitian refugee admissions program. In addition, the U.S. Bureau of the Census estimated that 3.5 million to 6 million people were in the country illegally, 1 million–1.5 million of whom entered in 1980. The influx of illegal Haitian immigrants into southern Florida continued to pose a serious problem in 1981. On September 29, in a move aimed mainly at Haitians, President Reagan authorized the Coast Guard to intercept and turn back vessels on the high seas suspected of carrying illegal immigrants. A month later, when 33 Haitians drowned after their small boat capsized a mile off the Florida coast, the authorities claimed to have found evidence that they had been brought most of the way from Haiti by organized smugglers.

On Oct. 31, 1980, Canada's employment and immigration minister, Lloyd Axworthy, introduced

UPI

Illegal Haitian immigrants to the U.S.
began being deported from the
Miami airport in June.

a report in the House of Commons providing for an intake of 130,000 to 140,000 immigrants during 1981, including 16,000 government-assisted refugees. Moves to change the basis of Canada's immigration levels from an annual to a medium-term planning cycle of three years were also announced. Figures for the first quarter of 1981 showed that Britain (4,426) once again headed the list of countries of origin, followed by Vietnam (2,460), the U.S. (2,285), and India (1,457). The total number of immigrants from all countries entering Canada during this period was 26,519. In 1980 immigrants totaled 142,439.

In Britain immigration continued to be a linchpin in the political doctrine of right-wing extremists. On March 28, speaking to Young Conservatives at Ashton-under-Lyne, Enoch Powell predicted that civil war would be the inevitable result of the growth of Britain's black population. Tory Action, a private backbench "immigration group" consisting of approximately 20 Conservative members of Parliament, was formed in April to press for a "more vigorous program of immigrant repatriation." Under sec. 29 of the Immigration Act 1971, people could be assisted by the government to return to their country of origin. In 1980, 126 persons were repatriated at a cost of £69,003. Meanwhile, a report on Britain's immigration rules, drawn up by the Legal Affairs Committee of the European Communities and approved by the European Parliament in March 1981, concluded that the rules might contravene the European Convention on Human Rights since they restricted the ability of women settled and living in Britain to bring in husbands or fiancés. In 1980 immigrants accepted for settlement in Britain totaled 69,920, 33,170 of whom were from "new" Commonwealth countries (*i.e.*, excluding Australia, Canada, and New Zealand) and Pakistan.

Immigration was an issue in the French presidential election. Georges Marchais, secretary-general of the French Communist Party and a candidate for the presidency, led a demonstration on January 10 in support of the mayor and council of Vitry, a Paris suburb, who had ransacked a hostel for Malian workers on Dec. 24, 1980. Marchais later said that it was inadmissible to allow immigrant workers into France at a time when there were already two million unemployed.

Australia continued to be a popular destination for immigrants: 94,500 took up permanent residence there in the year ended March 31, 1980, compared with 72,236 in the previous year. Britain was the main source country. South Africa reported a marked increase in British immigrants in 1981; it was also the destination of many white emigrants from Zimbabwe (13,000 in the first seven months of 1981, representing a 50% increase over the corresponding period of 1980).

(STUART BENTLEY)

See also Refugees.
[525.A.1.c]

Mining and Quarrying

Instead of making plans for new mines, plant modernization, or technological advances, the mining and quarrying industry in 1981 was embattled in corporate takeover bids. The depressed state of metal prices, which persisted from the previous year, and the high cost of money accounted for the lack of interest in building. But the financial community nonetheless focused on mining shares because of their low price/earnings ratio.

Industry Developments. The takeovers and attempted takeovers were changing the character of the mining industry in the United States. Standard Oil Co. of Ohio (Sohio) made a successful bid for Kennecott Corp., which cost the oil firm about $1,770,000,000, but Amax Inc. directors turned down the $4 billion offer by Standard Oil Co. of California to acquire the 80% of Amax not already

owned by the oil company. The French government company, Elf Aquitaine, gained control of Texasgulf Inc., and the British company Consolidated Gold Fields Ltd. continued to acquire shares in Newmont Mining Corp. Mining industry executives were concerned that the expertise and dedication to engage in mining, built up over generations, would be diluted or dispersed by these corporate giants to the detriment of national security.

In recent years Canadian officials at both the national and provincial levels had encouraged local ownership of energy and mineral resources, causing some U.S. natural resource companies to divest themselves of their Canadian holdings, either fully or partially. In 1981 a notable turnabout occurred when Seagram Co. of Canada, having sold its Canadian oil and gas interests in 1980 for $2.3 billion, began looking for new investments in natural resources in a more favourable area. Through its U.S. subsidiary, Joseph E. Seagram & Sons, Inc., unsuccessful acquisition offers were made to shareholders of two U.S. companies, St. Joe Minerals Corp. and Conoco Inc. The unsolicited offer of $45 per share of St. Joe, worth $2 billion, was balked when that company reached a merger agreement with Fluor Corp. This transaction was significant to the mining industry because, as discussed above, it represented another case in which the business of the purchasing firm was unrelated to mining. In its effort for a share of Conoco, Seagram was outbid by Du Pont.

Inhibiting development plans in the minerals industry were regulations regarding environmental and health and safety matters. To bring new mines into compliance with these rules was often costly and time-consuming. In addition, there was uncertainty as to whether or not complying with current regulations would be recognized as compliance in the future. Industry leaders often had to decide how far they should go in modifying an old facility before giving up on it and building a new one.

At the end of May the United Mine Workers signed an agreement with the Bituminous Coal Operators Association for a 40-month period during which wages and benefits would rise about 38%. The 160,000 UMW members were on strike for 72 days, which cost the average worker about $6,000 in wages. The UMW has struck for every contract since 1964. Coal output by union workers had been declining; in 1981 it was 44% of total U.S. coal production as compared with 70% in 1974.

Early in 1981 Kennecott Corp., the largest U.S. copper producer, sold a one-third interest in its Chino Mines Division, situated near Silver City, N.M., to Mitsubishi Corp. of Japan. The purpose of the sale was to enable Kennecott to expand capacity from 59,000 metric tons per year of copper to 100,000 tons and to modernize the old facilities. It was anticipated that such modernization would reduce the cost of producing copper by about one-third of the current selling price. In addition, the new plant, in which the Mitsubishi smelting process probably would be employed, could be operated within environmental quality tolerances. Kennecott had been short of investment capital

UPI

Thousands of coal miners gathered in Washington, D.C., in March to protest the Reagan administration's proposal to reduce federal support of the black lung disability program.

and plagued with high operating costs and costly environmental problems, and these circumstances combined to trigger the sale. Mitsubishi paid Kennecott $116 million for a one-third interest in the new operating company, Chino Mines Co., and promised to pay for one-third of the expansion costs, estimated at $400 million. Ironically, less than three months later, thanks to being taken over by Sohio, Kennecott was bankrolled for major improvements at its two other large divisions: Ray Mines in Arizona and Utah Copper.

The White Pine Copper Co., White Pine, Mich., began development of an electrolytic copper refinery that would cost approximately $72 million. Copper from this area of the Upper Peninsula of Michigan is noted for containing silver, nine ounces per ton, in the blister copper. Recently, it was determined that it would be cost effective for the company to add a refinery to produce electrolytic copper in various shapes and recover the silver as a by-product.

Typical of new Nevada gold mines was the Pinson, which came into production early in the year. The project had first come under study in 1974 by a trio of small companies, of which the Canadian firm of Rayrock Resources Ltd. was the manager. Repeated evaluations kept the project on hold because the gold content, about one-eighth of an ounce per ton, did not make mining the ore economically feasible. However, in 1978, when the price of gold reached $200 per ounce, it was decided to go ahead. Mill construction began early in 1980, and the 900-ton-per-day facility, utilizing

Mining and Quarrying

A gold-mining dredge that was built in 1938 was resurrected and put back to work in the Klondike region of Canada. Increases in gold prices over recent years have revived interest in gold prospecting.

the modern carbon-in-pulp technology, was completed in 11 months at a cost of $18.8 million. Annual gold production was estimated to be 45,000 oz, which at a gold price of $500 per ounce would pay off the facility in 18 months as well as providing $2 million for heap leaching facilities for "low grade" ore. Mining was by conventional surface methods.

Union Oil Co. of California began the first phase of a major oil shale project at Parachute Creek in Colorado. Shale was to be mined underground by the room-and-pillar method at the rate of 11,340 metric tons per day and then would be retorted with a yield of 10,000 bbl per day of shale oil. Union also planned to construct a facility that

would make a product of a better grade than conventional crude oil. The facility was scheduled to be started up in 1983, and the objective was to produce 50,000 bbl per day.

In late August Gulf Resources & Chemical Corp. made the decision to close the Bunker Hill lead, zinc, and silver mine and smelter at Kellogg, Idaho. In operation for 94 years, Bunker Hill had produced 35 million tons of ore. The mine and smelter complex employed 2,100 workers directly, but the mine closing was expected to eliminate an additional 3,000 to 5,000 jobs in the community of 15,000 residents. In 1980, with a silver price of $20 per ounce, the unit had made a good profit. But in 1981 the price fell to $9 per ounce, and the profit disappeared.

Amax of Canada reopened the Kitsault molybdenum mine, located at Alice Arm, 140 km (87 mi) NE of Prince Rupert, B.C. The open-pit mine was expected to produce about 11,000 tons of ore per day, which would yield up to 4,500 tons per day of molybdenum disulfide. The estimated cost of the project, including mine, concentrator, housing, and recreation and shopping facilities, was about $150 million. Kennecott opened the mine in 1968 at a capacity about half that of Amax, but the operation was never profitable and Kennecott took a $25 million write-off. Amax purchased the property in 1973 for about $2.5 million. One problem that had plagued Kennecott was the high lead content of the concentrate, but Amax planned to overcome this difficulty by adding a leaching circuit to the concentrator.

The Kitsault project was criticized by environmentalists, and the question of a full public inquiry was raised several times. But the British Columbia government, after thorough review, concluded that the permits to develop and operate had been prudently issued. Amax had spent five years on environmental studies and had prepared 35 reports. Nevertheless, there were further objections regarding disposal of tailings in the sea and the land rights of the Nishga Indians. These were resolved by including Nishga Indians in a program that Amax was offering in order to allay the environmentalists' suspicions.

In February the Peruvian government enacted new legislation expected to revitalize that nation's mining investments. The principal improvement was the gradual abolition of the 17.5% ad valorem (17.5% of the value of the goods as stated on the invoice) export levy introduced in 1976. In addition, the export marketing monopoly of Minero Peru Commercial was abolished, and special tax concessions for new developments were given to encourage the opening of mineral properties.

In other South American developments, the outlook for mining in Chile was favourable. There was, however, a delay on various projects such as the huge Exxon Los Bronces copper expansion because of uncertainty about the status of foreign ownership of mineral rights and leases under the new mining law enacted in September 1980. In addition, inflation of the peso exceeded that of the dollar, and thus Chile's policy of maintaining a fixed exchange rate was a deterrent to investment.

(JOHN V. BEALL)

Indexes of Production, Mining, and Mineral Commodities

(1975=100)

	1976	1977	1978	1979	1980	1981 I	1981 II
Mining (total)							
World[1]	107.8	112.5	112.6	117.2	114.4	114.6	...
Centrally planned economies[2]	104.4	108.4	112.0	115.1	116.2	120.1	119.7
Developed market economies[3]	102.7	108.3	112.3	119.2	124.1	130.3	123.6
Less developed market economies[4]	111.8	116.3	113.1	116.9	108.4	104.0	...
Coal							
World[1]	100.7	101.8	101.0	106.1	109.5	113.6	...
Centrally planned economies[2]	102.0	104.2	105.8	107.6	106.7	106.3	106.8
Developed market economies[3]	99.5	99.9	97.2	104.9	110.9	116.6	95.9
Less developed market economies[4]	103.2	106.3	107.8	109.9	118.9	148.1	...
Petroleum							
World[1]	110.0	115.6	116.2	120.4	115.7	115.0	...
Centrally planned economies[2]	106.9	112.2	118.2	122.2	125.4	130.4	129.4
Developed market economies[3]	104.2	115.3	126.1	134.0	142.5	155.9	147.5
Less developed market economies[4]	112.0	116.2	113.3	116.6	107.1	101.8	...
Metals							
World[1]	102.5	103.7	101.6	104.1	105.7	104.5	...
Centrally planned economies[2]	101.7	102.9	103.6	104.9	111.1	113.1	112.5
Developed market economies[3]	102.0	101.7	97.7	100.8	99.4	97.8	102.4
Less developed market economies[4]	103.9	107.9	106.8	109.2	112.5	109.4	...
Manufacturing (total)	108.2	113.3	118.6	124.1	125.0	126.3	...

[1] Excluding Albania, China, North Korea, Vietnam.
[2] Bulgaria, Czechoslovakia, East Germany, Hungary, Poland, Romania, U.S.S.R.
[3] North America, Europe (except centrally planned), Australia, Israel, Japan, New Zealand, South Africa.
[4] Caribbean, Central and South America, Africa (except South Africa), Asian Middle East, East and Southeast Asia (except Israel and Japan).
Source: UN, *Monthly Bulletin of Statistics* (November 1981).

Production. The overall world mining production index calculated by the United Nations (*see* Table) showed a decline of about 2.4% during 1980 and little tendency toward recovery during the first quarter of 1981 except in the coal sector of the less developed countries. There were many reasons for this: development capital being tied up in financial operations unrelated to production, continued high energy costs, and projections indicating a low growth in demand during the 1980s for many commodities.

Worldwide, of a group of 73 mineral commodities for which reasonably complete information was available, only 31 showed growth during 1980; 40 indicated net losses as compared with production levels of 1979; and 2 were about the same as in the previous year. Those showing growth included a few major metals (aluminum and bauxite, titanium, tungsten, and zinc), but more nonmetals (diamond, garnet, nitrogen, potash, pumice, and sulfur). Most of the major metals, even such strategic metals as chromium, showed losses against 1979. Minerals and metals useful in electronic applications, such as cadmium, indium, mercury, mica, rhenium, selenium, and tellurium, generally declined, with indium and rhenium the only exceptions.

Commodities useful in chemical applications, such as rock phosphate, potash, sulfur, salt, and barite, all showed growth during 1980. However, metals used similarly did less well, losses being registered by antimony, bismuth, and lithium.

Gemstones utilized as jewels did poorly (diamonds being the exception), while gems in industrial applications fared better, garnet showing nearly a 30% growth over 1979. Of minerals used in insulating or refractory applications, only vermiculite registered a gain in 1980, although losses were not major. Metals utilized in the steel industry showed mixed results; the major components, iron, nickel, manganese, vanadium, and chromium all declined, while the lesser metallurgical metals, such as tantalum, molybdenum, and columbium, rose.

In the United States, the value of mining output in 1980 rose only slightly over 1979, totaling about $24,802,000,000 (valued at some $240 billion after processing). This was a gain of 3.5% in terms of current prices but a loss if inflation is taken into account. Of a group of 21 metal commodities 10 gained, 10 lost, and 1 remained the same in terms of quantitative output. Of a group of 47 nonmetallic commodities only 14 showed increases, while 32 declined. The strongest growth was shown by secondary (recovered) refinery silver (84%), barite (28%), secondary refinery gold (24%), uranium (for nonenergy uses; 21%), and zinc (20%). The greatest declines occurred in secondary tin (−39%), secondary nickel (−30%), bromine and iron castings (both −25%), and fluorspar (−21%).

A single-mine production record was established in February 1981, when the Bingham Canyon mine of the Kennecott Corp. moved 579,255 metric tons of ore during a single day.

Aluminum. World production of bauxite, the primary ore of aluminum, was estimated to have risen by only about 2.5% during 1980, from 87,676,000 metric tons to 89,933,000 tons, according to the U.S. Bureau of Mines. This was, however, an additional advance over the strong 9.8% growth of the previous year. The major producers were little changed, with Australia, Guinea, and Jamaica accounting together for almost 60% of the world total; Australia produced about half of this, with some 27,189,000 tons, followed by Guinea 13,780,000 tons, and Jamaica 12,261,000. Of the middle-rank producers only Brazil showed a strong increase, rising 66% to an estimated 3,970,000 tons. Output of alumina (aluminum oxide, the concentrated intermediate stage in the production of aluminum metal) rose somewhat more strongly, by some 6.2% to 32,983,000 tons; Australia, with more than a fifth of this (7,247,000 tons), was the leader, although the U.S., with a 5.6% rise against Australia's 2.3% loss, gained ground, reaching a new high of 6,810,000 tons. Production of aluminum metal remained almost level, rising by only 0.2% to about 31,418,000 tons (excluding China). The U.S. was the major producer, with about 4,650,000 tons, followed, probably, by the Soviet Union, at about 1.8 million tons, and Canada and Japan, both slightly above 1 million tons. Worldwide declines in the output of the automobile, appliance, and construction industries kept demand weak, with U.S. plant closings reducing domestic operations to 80% of capacity by late 1981.

Antimony. World mine production was estimated to have declined somewhat during 1980, falling from about 73,000 metric tons in 1979 to about 70,000. The major producers were Bolivia with 12,622 metric tons, a 24% decline from 1979 levels, and South Africa with about 10,000 tons. Production levels in Communist (centrally planned) economies were speculative, but China was believed to exceed 10,000 tons and the Soviet Union to exceed 6,000.

Cement. World production of cement was thought to amount to about 760 million metric tons in 1980, a decline of some 5.7% from the record production levels of 1979 but still the second best year ever. The Soviet Union was the world leader with about 125 million tons, followed by Japan at 88.9 million, China at 79,860,000, and the U.S. at 69,590,000. Middle-range producers (20 million to 60 million tons) showed no important changes in output levels; these countries were Italy 41,850,000, West Germany 34,250,000, France 29.1 million, Spain 28 million, and Brazil 27.2 million. U.S. consumption declined by about 10% as a consequence of continuing weakness in the construction industry and civil engineering projects.

Chromite. Production worldwide rose by only about 2.1% during 1980, reaching 9,730,000 metric tons as against 9,535,000 the previous year. South Africa accounted for more than a third of this, with 3.4 million tons, followed, according to U.S. Bureau of Mines estimates, by the Soviet Union at 2,450,000 tons and Albania at 1,080,000.

Copper. World mine production of copper was estimated to have declined during 1980, mostly as a result of strikes in the U.S., the major producer. Total production amounted to some 7,654,000 metric tons, down about 1.1% from the previous year. The U.S. accounted for 1,168,000 tons, off almost 20% from the 1979 level of 1,440,000 tons. The other major producers were Chile 1,072,000 tons, the Soviet Union estimated at about 920,000 tons, Canada 708,000, Zambia 610,000, Zaire 426,000, and Peru 366,000. Blister copper production (smelter output) was slightly above 1979 levels, and the output of refined metal was also higher although detailed data were unavailable. An October 1981 meeting of the Intergovernmental Council of Copper Exporting States (CIPEC) in Paris expressed concern over fluctuating market prices but produced no program of concerted action, although agreeing that producer-consumer agreements were a means of stabilizing markets. Production levels in the U.S. through September 1981 rose about 28%, indicating some recovery from 1980 levels, and total output was expected to exceed 1,430,000 tons for the year.

Gold. World production of gold was estimated to have remained virtually unchanged from 1979, output in 1980 reaching an estimated 1,328 metric tons. South Africa, the major producer, accounted for just over 50% of this, despite a slight (4.2%) decline to a total of 674 tons. The Soviet Union was probably second with an output of about 258 tons, followed by China, perhaps in excess of 50 tons, Canada with 48 tons, and the U.S. with 30.6 tons. The strong gold prices worldwide during 1980 gave South Africa a 78% increase in the value of gold sales over 1979 and provided the country an 8% growth rate in real terms for the year. The decline of the same prices to the $400 level in 1981, however, led the 1981–82 budget forecasts to anticipate 40% reductions in tax revenues from the gold mines.

Iron. Mine production of iron ore fell by an estimated 6.6% during 1980, reaching an estimated total of 828 million metric tons as compared with 886.8 million the previous year. The Soviet Union enlarged its share of world production by attaining a slight gain from 238.2 million tons to 240 million, about 29% of the total. Australia again replaced the U.S. as the second-leading producer with 95,534,000 tons, a gain of more than 10% over 1979, while the U.S. fell to fourth place, dropping from 85.5 million to only about 68.9 million. This decline amounted to about 20% and fol-

lowed a similar drop in demand from the steel industry, the primary consumer. Brazil retained its third-place position with virtually the same production as in 1979, about 85.8 million tons. Other major producers included China, with about 72 million tons, Canada 50,866,000, and India 41 million. The 3.2% drop in world production of pig iron was largely attributable to the U.S. decline, but the similarly beset iron and steel industries of the European Coal and Steel Community also registered a 6.7% drop, producing just over 100 million tons in 1980. The largest single producing country was the Soviet Union with about 127 million metric tons, a strong 5.8% gain; other major producers included Japan, with 96.8 million tons, based almost entirely on imported ores, the U.S. with about 69 million tons, and China 38 million. In the depressed U.S. market, however, partial results for 1981 indicated production levels about 9% above comparable 1980 results, while shipments were up 11%, and consumption of iron ore rose 13%.

Lead. World mine production of lead was estimated to have fallen off somewhat during 1980, declining 4.6% to an estimated total of 3,353,000 metric tons. The major producing country was the U.S. with 550,952 metric tons, up 4.8% over the previous year. Other leading producing countries included Australia, at 390,000 tons, off 6.3% from the previous year; Canada, 274,000 tons, off more than 13% from 1979; Peru, replacing Mexico as the fourth-leading country with 178,000 tons and the only leading producer besides the U.S. to have shown growth; and Mexico, off more than 16% to a total of about 145,500 tons. In the U.S. production of refined lead was almost identical with ore totals, at 550,000 tons, off 4.9% from 1979. Consumption of lead in the U.S., about 28% of world usage, declined by about 17% during the year, reflecting continuing reductions in automotive applications such as batteries and gasoline additives.

Magnesium. Production in 1980 of magnesite, the principal ore of magnesium, amounted to an estimated 2.9 million metric tons, virtually unchanged from the previous year. The two leading producers were China and the Soviet Union, both estimated at about 550,000 to 560,000 metric tons. World production of magnesium metal was believed to have risen by about 5.1% during 1980, reaching an estimated total of about 319,000 tons. The U.S. was the leading producer, with about 48% of the world total, utilizing brines or dolomites to produce approximately 154,000 tons. The Soviet Union was thought to be the second leading producer at about 75,000 tons, and Norway third at about 50,000.

Manganese. World mine production of manganese in 1980 fell off slightly from the previous year. Production totaled about 22,-950,000 metric tons according to preliminary data from the U.S. Bureau of Mines. About half of this was produced in the Soviet Union, some 10,250,000 tons; about half of the remainder came from South Africa, with 5,711,000 tons, up 10.2% from 1979 following a 24% gain in that year over 1978. Other major producers were Gabon 2,136,000 tons, Australia 1,961,000, India 1,645,000, and Brazil 1,230,000. The U.S. National Oceanic and Atmospheric Administration issued an environmental impact statement in September 1981 pursuant to the 1980 Deep Seabed Hard Mineral Resources Act, providing assessments of the effect of deep seabed mining of the oceans for manganese nodules.

Mercury. Estimated mine production of mercury in 1980 amounted to 190,200 34.5-kg (76-lb) flasks, off about 1.5% from the previous year. The Soviet Union was probably the leading producer, at about 62,000 flasks, followed by Spain at about 48,000 flasks. The United States' production of 33,200 flasks, representing an 11% gain over 1979, ranked third; Algerian production probably amounted to about 30,000 to 33,000 flasks. Projections of minimal growth in mercury consumption through 1990 left producers with only mine closings and sales restrictions as feasible means of stabilizing world prices, both methods being adopted during 1980–81.

Molybdenum. Production worldwide of molybdenum was estimated to have risen in 1980 for the fifth year in a row, reaching a total of 108,000 metric tons, up 3.8% from 1979. About 63% of this originated in the U.S., its 68,350 tons providing most of the world increase. The only other major producers were Chile 13,340 tons, Canada 12,198 tons, and the Soviet Union, with an estimated 10,400 tons. Mine production for the first time since 1972, however, exceeded demand, and with the planned completion of new mines worldwide during 1981–85, it was anticipated that profitability during the 1980s would depend on continued growth of demand.

Nickel. World mine production of nickel rose by nearly 12% in 1980, reaching 771,000 metric tons as compared with only 683,000 in 1979. This total, however, only allowed producers to recover production levels of the mid-1970s, lost in the steep declines of 1978 and 1979. Most of this new production was in Canada, where strikes and other labour actions had previously limited output. Canadian production in 1980 amounted to 195,000 tons, a 54% gain over the 126,500 tons of 1979. The Soviet Union was estimated to have produced about 154,000 tons, excluding utilization of Cuban ores. The French Pacific territory of New Caledonia was third at 87,800 tons, followed by Australia 69,723 tons, Indonesia with perhaps 37,000 tons, and the Philippines 25,382 tons. Cuban

and South African production may have amounted to about 25,000 to 30,000 tons each, but detailed information was not available. Smelter production of nickel also recovered and, indeed, surpassed previous production levels, attaining an output of about 754,000 tons, up 9.9% over 1979 and 24.1% over 1978. The two major producers were the Soviet Union and Canada, with about 174,000 and 145,000 tons, respectively; they accounted for about 42% of the world total. Japan was displaced to third position by the return of Canadian production but attained a total of 104,000, based on imported supplies. Other major producers included the United States 40,100 tons, Australia 32,850, New Caledonia 32,580, and Norway 31,000.

Platinum-Group Metals. World production of platinum-group metals (platinum, iridium, palladium, osmium, rhodium, and ruthenium) was estimated to have risen by about 1.2%. Most of this slight increase was estimated to have occurred in South Africa, the world leader at 3,250,000 troy ounces, constituting approximately 48% of total world production of 6,740,000 oz. The Soviet Union was thought to be the second leading producer with 3.2 million oz. The only other important producer was Canada; its 404,585 oz regained production levels of 1977 lost during 1978–79 because the bulk of Canadian production originates as a by-product of nickel mining, then in the midst of labour disputes.

Silver. World mine production of silver fell slightly during 1980, off about 1.3% against 1979 for a total of approximately 340 million troy ounces, or about 10,930 metric tons. The two largest producers were Mexico, with 1,473 metric tons, down about 4.2% from the previous year, and the Soviet Union, with an estimated 1,430 tons; other producing nations were Peru 1,245 tons, Canada 1,037 tons, the U.S. 995 tons, Australia 996 tons, and Poland 766 tons.

Tin. Estimated world production of tin during 1980 declined by about 2.3% to approximately 250,000 metric tons. The major producers were Malaysia 61,404 tons, off about 2.6%, Thailand 45,986 tons, the Soviet Union at about 34,000, Indonesia 30,465, Bolivia 18,620, and China about 16,500. There were no important changes in production levels as most leading producers belonged to the International Tin Agreement (ITA), under which they voluntarily limited production in the interests of international price stability. The October 1981 meeting in Kuala Lumpur, Malaysia, of the fifth World Conference on Tin concentrated on issues connected with production and marketing (particularly of new resources) but paid little attention to manufacturing or consumption of the metal. Negotiations connected with the start of the sixth ITA on July 1, 1982, continued.

Titanium. World production of titanium sponge grew by about 13% during 1980, attaining an estimated total of 61,300 metric tons. Japan was the leading sponge producer for which data were available with about 18,000 tons, U.S. data being withheld for reasons of confidentiality. Production of the Soviet Union was estimated at about 37,000 tons. In the production of titanium concentrates Australia continued to lead in all categories, which included ilmenite, rutile, and zircon.

Tungsten. World mine production rose by about 13% during 1980 to an estimated total of 53,300 metric tons, up from 47,000 the previous year. Major producers included China, for which only estimated data were available, at about 15,000 tons, and the Soviet Union at 8,700 tons; the most important non-Communist producers were Canada with 4,650 tons, up 43% from 1979, Bolivia at 3,435 tons, Australia 3,332 tons, and the U.S. 2,754 tons.

Zinc. Production of zinc rose during 1980 but by only about 1% according to preliminary estimates by the U.S. Bureau of Mines. The world total was about 6,060,000 metric tons, the leading producers of which were Canada 894,575 tons, down slightly from 1979; the Soviet Union, about 760,000 tons; Australia 486,369 tons; Peru 429,007; the U.S. 312,956; and Mexico 238,231. In the U.S. plans announced for the opening of new facilities in New York and Missouri and for the redevelopment of existing facilities during 1981–84 were expected to add 40,000 tons per year to present capacity.   (WILLIAM A. CLEVELAND)

See also Earth Sciences; Energy; Industrial Review: *Iron and Steel;* Materials Sciences.

[724.B.1; 724.C.3]

Monaco

A sovereign principality on the northern Mediterranean coast, Monaco is bounded on land by the French département of Alpes-Maritimes. Area: 1.90 sq km (0.73 sq mi). Pop. (1981 est.): 26,000. Language: French. Religion: predominantly Roman Catholic. Chief of state, Prince Rainier III; ministers of state in 1981, André Saint-Mleux and, from July, Jean Herly.

Monaco

With only three strings to its economic bow—industry, real estate, and gambling—Monaco was concentrating its efforts on tourism in general and on the convention trade in particular. In 1980, 156 congresses brought in more than 38,000 visitors. The proportion of U.S. tourists fell from 34% of the total in 1979 to 18% in 1980. The balance included mainly French, Italian, British, and West German visitors. Reflecting economic trends worldwide, apartment prices in Monaco had doubled to around Fr 12,000 per square metre in three years.

In May 1981 Prince Rainier and Princess Grace were present at the graduation ceremony at Amherst (Mass.) College, where their son Prince Albert received his diploma. Princess Grace attended the wedding of Charles, prince of Wales, and Lady Diana Spencer in London on July 29.

(K. M. SMOGORZEWSKI)

Mongolia

A people's republic of Asia lying between the U.S.S.R. and China, Mongolia occupies the geographic area known as Outer Mongolia. Area: 1,-566,500 sq km (604,800 sq mi). Pop. (1981 est.): 1,685,400. Cap. and largest city: Ulan Bator (pop., 1981 est., 435,400). Language: Khalkha Mongolian. Religion: Lamaistic Buddhism. First secretary of the Mongolian People's Revolutionary (Communist) Party in 1981 and chairman of the Presidium of the Great People's Hural, Yumzhagiyen Tseden-

bal; chairman of the Council of Ministers (premier), Zhambyn Batmunkh.

At the 18th congress of the Mongolian People's Revolutionary Party (MPRP) in Ulan Bator in May 1981, Yumzhagiyen Tsedenbal was reelected first secretary. In his report to the congress he forecast a rise in real income of 10–12% during the seventh five-year plan (1981–85). Industry's share of total production had risen to 60% during the previous five years. In general elections in June, the official MPRP candidates gained 99.9% of the votes.

In June Marshal Dmitry Ustinov, the Soviet defense minister, inspected Mongolian and Soviet army units positioned along the Mongolian-Chinese border. During his visit he accused China of trying to undermine the unity of the socialist states. In early August Tsedenbal met Soviet leader Leonid Brezhnev in the Crimea. Brezhnev expressed support for Tsedenbal's proposal for a convention on mutual nonaggression among Asian and Pacific countries.

Jugderdemidiyn Gurragcha of Mongolia accompanied a Soviet cosmonaut in the spacecraft Soyuz 39, which docked with the Salyut 6 space station on March 23. (K. M. SMOGORZEWSKI)

Mongolia

Morocco

A constitutional monarchy of northwestern Africa, on the Atlantic Ocean and the Mediterranean Sea, Morocco is bordered by Algeria and Western Sahara. Area: 458,730 sq km (177,117 sq mi). Pop. (1981 est.): 20,970,000. Cap.: Rabat (pop., 1979 est., 768,500). Largest city: Casablanca (pop., 1979 est., 2,220,600). (Data above refer to Morocco as constituted prior to the purported division of Western Sahara between Morocco and Mauritania and the subsequent Moroccan occupation of the Mauritanian zone [1979]). Language: Arabic (official); with Berber, French, and Spanish minorities. Religion: Muslim. King, Hassan II; prime minister in 1981, Maati Bouabid.

Events in Morocco in 1981 were again dominated by the continuing war with the Popular Front for the Liberation of Saguia el Hamra and Río de Oro (Polisario Front) in the Western Sahara. A defensive wall was constructed by Morocco from the Jebel Ouarkziz in southern Morocco to Cape Bujdur on the coast of the Western Sahara to protect economically significant regions from Polisario attacks.

The government poured development aid into the Western Sahara and attempted to integrate the region with Morocco. In May, by-elections for the Moroccan Parliament were held for the first time in Dakhla, Western Sahara. The Saharan Arab Democratic Republic, Western Sahara's government-in-exile founded by Polisario five years earlier, was recognized by more than 40 nations, including a majority of African countries. During the Organization of African Unity (OAU) summit in Nairobi, Kenya, in June, King Hassan II agreed to a referendum in the Western Sahara, and further OAU proposals on the nature of the referendum were accepted in August. Just before the June summit diplomatic relations with Libya, broken

Morocco

Missiles:
see Defense

Molecular Biology:
see Life Sciences

Monetary Policy:
see Economy, World

Money and Banking:
see Economy, World

Mormons:
see Religion

Morocco

At a preliminary meeting in Fez, Arab foreign ministers prepare for the annual Arab League summit. The summit, which broke down within hours over Saudi Arabia's Middle East peace plan, was suspended for six months.

MOROCCO

Education. (1981) Primary, pupils 2,331,000, teachers 55,303; secondary, pupils 826,500, teachers (1979–80) 31,-794; vocational, pupils 10,020; teacher training (1979–80), students 10,746, teachers 847; higher, students 80,345, teaching staff 2,558.

Finance. Monetary unit: dirham, with (Sept. 21, 1981) a free rate of 5.27 dirhams to U.S. $1 (9.77 dirhams = £1 sterling). Gold and other reserves (June 1981) U.S. $151 million. Budget (total; 1981 est.): revenue 31.8 billion dirhams; expenditure 34.8 billion dirhams. Gross national product (1980) 71.3 billion dirhams. Money supply (May 1981) 25,723,000,000 dirhams. Cost of living (1975 = 100; March 1981) 172.3.

Foreign Trade. (1980) Imports 16,792,000,000 dirhams; exports 9,756,000,000 dirhams. Main import sources: France 25%; Iraq 9%; Spain 8%; Saudi Arabia 8%; U.S. 6%; West Germany 6%; Italy 6%. Main export destinations: France 25%; West Germany 8%; The Netherlands 6%; Spain 6%; Italy 6%; U.S.S.R. 5%; Belgium-Luxembourg 5%. Main exports: phosphates 31%; fruit and vegetables 21%; phosphoric acid 8%; nonferrous metal ores 6%; textile yarns 5%; fish 5%; clothing 5%. Tourism: visitors (1979) 1,549,000; gross receipts (1977) U.S. $375 million.

Transport and Communications. Roads (1980) 57,634 km. Motor vehicles in use (1979): passenger 413,700; commercial 157,500. Railways: (1978) 1,756 km; traffic (1979) 803 million passenger-km, freight 3,854,000,000 net ton-km. Air traffic (1980): 1,868,000,000 passenger-km; freight 26.5 million net ton-km. Shipping (1980): merchant vessels 100 gross tons and over 145; gross tonnage 359,552. Telephones (Jan. 1980) 227,000. Radio receivers (Dec. 1977) 1.6 million. Television licenses (Dec. 1977) 597,000.

Agriculture. Production (in 000; metric tons; 1980): wheat c. 1,811; barley c. 2,212; corn c. 333; potatoes c. 390; sugar, raw value c. 360; tomatoes c. 420; grapes c. 250; oranges c. 720; mandarin oranges and tangerines c. 267; olives c. 300; dates c. 104; fish catch (1979) 280. Livestock (in 000; 1980): sheep c. 16,100; goats c. 6,070; cattle (1979) c. 3,650; horses (1979) c. 320; mules (1979) c. 380; asses (1979) c. 1,350; camels (1979) c. 220; poultry c. 24,000.

Industry. Production (in 000; metric tons; 1980): coal 680; crude oil c. 48; petroleum products c. 4,400; electricity (excluding most industrial production; kw-hr) 4,460,000; cement 3,600; iron ore (55–60% metal content) 80; phosphate rock (1979) 20,031; copper concentrates (metal content) 24; lead concentrates (metal content) 172; manganese ore (metal content; 1979) c. 78; zinc concentrates (metal content) 13.

off in 1980, were restored at Libyan request. Despite moves toward peace, fighting in the disputed area intensified later in the year. After Polisario forces attacked the Moroccan garrison at Guelta Zemmour in October, Morocco requested military assistance from the U.S.

Although the position of France's new Socialist government on the Sahara, formally one of neutrality, represented a shift toward the Algerian stance, good relations with France continued. Mauritania accused Morocco of involvement in an attempted coup against its government in March.

Morocco's economic position became increasingly serious, despite substantial aid from Saudi Arabia, the Gulf states, and Iraq. The World Bank, reporting that one-third of Moroccans lived in "absolute poverty," offered a $1 billion loan. Phosphate revenue—one-third of total export earnings—had not recovered from the 1976 collapse in world prices. Agricultural production grew by only 2% as drought severely damaged the 1981 harvest.

In May the government announced cuts in subsidies on staple foods, causing price rises of more than 70%. Faced with protests by political parties and strikes by trade unions, the government halved the increases. Nonetheless, strikes continued, culminating in violent riots in Casablanca on June 20 in which about 100 persons died. The protests were led by the Democratic Labour Confederation and by the major opposition party, the Socialist Union of Popular Forces (USFP). In late August the USFP criticized the king for endangering Moroccan control of the Western Sahara by conceding to the OAU on the proposed referendum. The party leader, Abderrahim Bouabid, was sentenced to a year in prison in September, despite nationwide and international protests.

(GEORGE JOFFÉ)

Motion Pictures

English-Speaking Cinema. UNITED STATES. The extreme shifts of Hollywood's economic philosophies are traditional. The last few years had demonstrated a growing faith in the multimillion-dollar picture, and the faith had seemed to pay off in a series of vastly profitable enterprises such as *Star Wars* and *Superman*. In 1981 the faith was shaken by several box-office disasters. Michael Cimino's epic of the old West, *Heaven's Gate*, defied repeated attempts to give it dramatic form and public appeal, and John Schlesinger's *Honky-Tonk Freeway* obscured the point of what should have been a modest social comedy in the extravagance of a $30 million production. Even the public's taste for nostalgic revisits to childhood heroes proved to be satiable, with the financial (and admittedly artistic) failure of William Franklin's *The Legend of the Lone Ranger*.

The universal yearning for tales of childhood innocence and nostalgia seemed, all the same, persistent; and two of the big-budget films of the year that did achieve vast profitability were Richard Lester's sequel to the earlier success, *Superman II*, and the Steven Spielberg-George Lucas production *Raiders of the Lost Ark*. The latter returned to the stuff of schoolboy adventure yarns in the Edgar Rice Burroughs manner, with a story of the hero's race against Nazi villains to discover the lost Ark of the Covenant.

One of the most lucrative movies of 1981 was *Raiders of the Lost Ark,* an old-fashioned adventure yarn in which hero Indiana Jones (Harrison Ford) faces a series of encounters with picturesque villains.

© 1981 LUCASFILM, LTD.—SYGMA

At the other end of the economic scale modestly budgeted horror films seemed to promise much surer returns, appealing irresistibly to a large teenage market, and a profusion of such films, mostly of slight quality or imagination, appeared during the year. Old successes led to such sequels as *Halloween II* and *Friday the 13th Part II*. Ingenuity was mostly expended on finding new locations for horror scenes—the seaside (Jeffrey Bloom's *Blood Beach*), a high school (Frank Laloggia's *Fear No Evil*), and a carnival show (Tobe Hooper's *The Fun House*).

The genres most favoured by more adult audiences seemed to be the crime film and the romantic comedy. Among the most distinguished crime pictures was Sidney Lumet's *Prince of the City*, a darkly realist study, closely based on fact, about the experiences and demoralization of a policeman who had turned federal informer to expose the corruption of his colleagues. Michael Mann's *Thief* was an interesting and stylish portrait of a professional criminal (played by James Caan), as serious and conscientious about his job as any other kind of craftsman. Daniel Petrie's *Fort Apache, The Bronx*, again, allegedly, closely based on actuality, painted an even more dispirited picture of the fight against crime, both outside and inside a Bronx police station.

A classic crime story already adapted twice for the cinema, James M. Cain's 1934 novel *The Postman Always Rings Twice*, was filmed by Bob Rafelson. Although Rafelson was able to treat the sexual content of the story with greater fidelity than his predecessors, the world of Cain, with its special mixture of sexual passion and murder, seemed more successfully captured in an original scenario, Lawrence Kasdan's *Body Heat*. A crime story that aimed primarily to explore a new field for the cinema—the higher executive echelons of the Roman Catholic church—was Ulu Grosbard's *True Confessions*, adapted by John Gregory Dunne, with his wife, Joan Didion, from his own novel. Robert De Niro played a worldly priest and Robert Duvall his policeman brother—men whose worlds collide embarrassingly as a result of a sordid murder case (again based on real events, of the 1940s).

Among the year's romantic comedies, one of the most successful was *Rich and Famous*, a second remake of John Van Druten's 1940 stage success *Old Acquaintance*. Directed by the octogenarian George Cukor, it was notable for the performances of Candice Bergen and Jacqueline Bisset. Peter Bogdanovich's *They All Laughed*, a deft romantic comedy about assorted couplings, was a welcome return to form for this director. Alan Alda's *The Four Seasons* revealed two middle-aged married couples reassessing their relationships after the breakup of the marriage of a third couple.

Comedy of a broader sort was represented by *Arthur*, written and directed by a fledgling director, Steve Gordon, and starring Dudley Moore and Liza Minnelli, and by Ivan Reitman's army farce *Stripes* starring Bill Murray; both were financially successful. Mel Brooks's *History of the World, Part I* exemplified the most extravagant and ribald aspects of the director's style, with a series of episodes set in various historical periods from the

Motion Pictures

Meryl Streep was widely acclaimed for her portrayal of the enigmatic Sarah in *The French Lieutenant's Woman*, based on the novel by John Fowles.

Stone Age to the French Revolution. The comedy rested on the confrontation of period settings and situations with the speech and psychology of modern Jewish New York City. Something of the same method inspired *Caveman*, a distinct curiosity among comedies using almost no dialogue, with Ringo Starr as an indomitable prehistoric inventor, pitting brain against the brawn of his fellow men. A promising new director, Albert Brooks, clearly set out in the tracks of Woody Allen. His second feature film as writer-director-star, *A Modern Romance*, was an imperfect but intermittently original comedy about a film editor torn between saving his love affair and saving a terrible film.

The blackest and bleakest comedy of the year was perhaps Blake Edwards's *S.O.B.*, a portrait of Hollywood at its least lovable, seen as a collection of crooks and charlatans all dedicated to the task of saving a hopeless musical film by the injection of pornographic episodes. The most eccentric piece of black comedy, though, was John Waters's *Polyester*, which introduced a system of "smellies" as an extra attraction to its bizarre soap opera story.

Hollywood promised a new vogue for screen biographies of the more revelatory type. *Mommie Dearest* was based on the horrific revelations of Joan Crawford's adopted daughter, about the nightmares of home life with the great star (played, with astonishing resemblance, by Faye Dunaway). *Chanel Solitaire*, a somewhat fanciful re-creation of the life of the great fashion designer (portrayed by Marie-France Pisier), exploited the U.S. fascination with French chic.

Interest in future worlds seemed somewhat on the decline, though Peter Hyams's *Outland* projected to a science fiction future the *High Noon* plot about a man singlehandedly fighting the corrup-

tion of a community. By contrast, in *Atlantic City* Louis Malle evoked the past and vividly depicted the present of a town in transition.

Released late in the year were two ambitious film sagas dealing with the early years of this century. In *Reds* Warren Beatty directed and starred in the story of John Reed, journalist and chronicler of the Bolshevik Revolution. Milos Forman's *Ragtime*, based on the novel by E. L. Doctorow, depicts the ferment of pre-World War I society in and near New York City. James Cagney returned from two decades of retirement to appear in the film. Other late releases of note included Sydney Pollack's *Absence of Malice*, about abuses of investigative journalism; Louis Malle's unusual *My Dinner with André*, consisting almost entirely of a 1½-hour dinner conversation between two articulate men; and Mark Rydell's *On Golden Pond*, most notable as a vehicle for Henry Fonda and Katharine Hepburn, co-starring for the first time in their long careers. From Brazil came Hector Babenco's *Pixote*, a drama about street children filmed on location in the slums of that nation's large cities.

Notable documentaries of the year included Connie Fields's *The Life and Times of Rosie the Riveter*, looking back, through reminiscences and old films, at the realities of women in wartime industry; and Murray Lerner's record of Isaac Stern's tour of a China long deprived of Western cultural contacts, *From Mao to Mozart: Isaac Stern in China*.

Among those who died in 1981 were actors Richard Boone, Melvyn Douglas, William Holden, Natalie Wood, and Robert Montgomery; directors William Wyler and Norman Taurog; and writer Paddy Chayefsky (*see* OBITUARIES).

At the annual awards ceremony of the Academy of Motion Picture Arts and Sciences in Hollywood, Robert Redford's first film in the role of director, *Ordinary People*, won Oscars for best film, best director, best supporting actor (Timothy Hutton), and best screenplay from another source (Alvin Sargent from the novel by Judith Guest). Robert De Niro was judged best actor for his role in *Raging Bull*, directed by Martin Scorsese (*see* BIOGRAPHIES), which also received an editing award (Thelma Schoomaker). Sissy Spacek was best actress, for Michael Apted's *Coal Miner's Daughter*. The best supporting actress was Mary Steenburgen in *Melvin and Howard*, for which Bo Goldman received the award for best original screenplay. Roman Polanski's *Tess* received awards for best cinematography (Ghislain Cloquet and Geoffrey Unsworth) and best art direction (Pierre Guffroy and Jack Stephens). The best foreign-language film was the Soviet Union's *Moscow Does Not Believe in Tears*.

GREAT BRITAIN. The major commercial and critical success of the year was Karel Reisz's *The French Lieutenant's Woman*, adapted by Harold Pinter from John Fowles's novel. The adaptation adopted a film-within-a-film device to parallel Fowles's experiments in commentating a Victorian anecdote with 20th-century hindsights. The film was especially memorable for the performance of Meryl Streep in the title role. Almost comparable success was achieved by the first feature film directed by Hugh Hudson, *Chariots of Fire*, based on

the successes of two notable British runners at the Paris Olympic Games of 1924.

Even at its most debased and infantile, the series of James Bond thrillers maintained its hold on the popular audience, with John Glen's *For Your Eyes Only*. Otherwise the production of commercial entertainment pictures appeared to have dwindled still further. Terry Gilliam's *Time Bandits* applied the Monty Python style of comedy to a mythical tale of travel through time and the battle between good and evil. *The Great Muppet Caper* was a sequel that did not achieve the same success as the original film version of the popular television puppet show.

Doris Lessing's novels inspired two low-budget films. David Gladwell's *Memoirs of a Survivor* was an attempt, more courageous than successful, to convey the vision of a future Britain of urban breakdown and decay. Michael Raeburn's *The Grass Is Singing*, co-produced with Sweden and Zanzibar, emerged as a cliché-prone, old-fashioned melodrama of white colonists succumbing to the alien and unsympathetic climate of Africa. More interesting literary exercises were Christopher Miles's re-creation of the last years of D. H. Lawrence, *Priest of Love*, and James Ivory's *Quartet*, an intelligent if low-pitched attempt to adapt a novel by Jean Rhys. The most interesting work continued to appear in areas of low-budget, often independently financed production. Ken Loach's *Looks and Smiles*, shot in Sheffield with nonprofessional actors, vividly showed the plight of the young unemployed.

IRELAND. With its own National Film Studios, Ireland was battling to establish an identity as a film-producing country. The most notable demonstration was certainly John Boorman's imaginative, magical evocation of the Arthurian legend, *Excalibur*. Other Irish feature films were Tommy McArdle's *It's Handy When People Don't Die*, a saga

Peter Weir, one of Australia's new wave of directors, presented *Gallipoli,* the story of a friendship between Mel Gibson (left) and Mark Lee (right), two young Australians caught up in World War I.

PHOTO TRENDS

of the fight for Irish independence in the 18th century, hampered by a lack of expository skill, and Joe Comerford's *Traveller*, a "road" film about a contemporary young couple's exploration of Ireland and its people.

AUSTRALIA. Peter Weir's *Gallipoli*, an "intimate epic," was Australia's most ambitious production to date. It told of the trauma of the young Australian nation encountering its first war, from the viewpoint of two young men of different backgrounds and dispositions, caught in the tragedy of the Dardanelles campaign in World War I. Other notable films of the year were John Duigan's *Winter of Our Dreams*, a compassionate study of a young, drug-addicted prostitute, and Donald Crombie's *The Killing of Angel Street*, a strong drama about corruption in a large-scale construction development.

NEW ZEALAND. Following the example of Australia, the government Film Commission continued to make determined attempts to develop feature production in the country. The best film of the year was Roger Donaldson's *Smash Palace*, a drama of escalating tension between a separated couple fighting for possession of their small daughter. In a very different tone was Michael Black's original and visually ravishing *Pictures*, based on the true story of Alfred Burton, a photographer whose studies of the life of native Australians led him into conflict with the bigoted mid-19th-century colonial establishment.

CANADA. Canadian producers continued to find a profitable speciality in low-budget, extravagantly nasty horror pictures such as Joe Dante's werewolf story *The Howling* and John Dunning's *My Bloody Valentine*. The most successful among them was David Cronenberg's science-fiction horror story about extraterrestrial invaders, *Scanners*. More substantial English-language productions were Ralph Thomas's *Ticket to Heaven*, a thriller about a young teacher who falls under the influence of a Moonie-like cult, which won the top award at the Taormina Festival, and Donald Shebib's charming comedy of ordinary working life, *Heartaches*. The major French-Canadian production of the year was Gilles Calre's *Les Plouffes*, a four-hour saga of a family on the eve of World War II, which had already been the subject of a best-selling novel and popular radio and television shows.

Western Europe. FRANCE. French commercial production continued to favour light romance and police thrillers. Among the best of them was Alain Corneau's *Le Choix des armes*, the story of the parallel rivalries between an old and young policeman and an old and young crook. A growing fashion for adapting dramatic classics to the screen resulted in Roger Coggio's dynamic and cinematic version of *Les Fourberies de Scapin*. One of the best films of the year was Eric Rohmer's *La Femme de l'aviateur*, described as the first of a series of "Plays and Proverbs" in homage to Alfred de Musset, with whose plays the film shared the charm and whimsicality of its pattern of intrigues within the emotional entanglements of everyday people.

Among the newer French directors, Bertrand Tavernier filmed *Coup de torchon*, a drama about French colonial Africa in the years preceding

Annual Cinema Attendance[1]

Country	Total in 000	Per capita
Afghanistan	10,000	0.6
Albania	9,000	4.1
Algeria	41,500	2.3
Angola	3,700	0.6
Argentina	65,600	2.5
Australia	32,000	2.6
Austria	17,500	2.3
Bahrain	2,000	8.0
Barbados	1,100	4.5
Belgium	23,300	2.3
Bolivia	3,200	0.9
Brazil	208,300	1.8
Bulgaria	112,000	12.7
Burma	222,500	7.2
Cameroon	6,500	1.0
Canada	82,300	3.5
Chad	24,200	5.7
Chile	19,400	1.8
Colombia	96,000	4.0
Cuba	81,000	8.2
Cyprus	6,100	9.5
Czechoslovakia	82,500	5.3
Denmark	17,000	3.3
Dominican Republic	6,800	1.5
Ecuador	38,700	5.6
Egypt	70,000	1.9
El Salvador	15,400	3.4
Finland	10,000	2.1
France	177,900	3.3
Germany, East	80,800	4.8
Germany, West	124,200	2.0
Ghana	1,000	0.1
Greece	34,200	3.6
Grenada	1,000	9.1
Guatemala	7,200	1.1
Guyana	10,200	12.5
Haiti	5,700	1.2
Hong Kong	60,200	13.3
Hungary	61,000	5.7
Iceland	2,500	11.3
India	2,260,000	3.8
Indonesia	123,600	0.8
Iran	25,000	0.7
Iraq	8,300	0.6
Ireland	38,000	13.0
Israel	22,000	6.1
Italy	372,300	6.5
Ivory Coast	9,000	1.2
Japan	165,200	1.5
Jordan	14,000	4.8
Kampuchea	20,000	3.1
Kenya	6,000	0.4
Korea, South	65,000	1.7
Kuwait	4,500	4.5
Lebanon	49,700	18.0
Liberia	1,900	1.2
Libya	15,500	6.0
Luxembourg	1,100	3.2
Macau	2,272	9.1
Madagascar	2,900	0.4
Malaysia	34,000	2.7
Mali	2,500	0.5
Malta	3,100	9.3
Martinique	2,100	6.0
Mauritius	17,500	19.3
Mexico	262,400	4.1
Mongolia	15,300	9.7
Morocco	35,800	1.9
Mozambique	3,200	0.4
Netherlands, The	23,800	1.7
New Zealand	14,100	4.5
Nicaragua	7,700	7.7
Norway	18,000	3.8
Pakistan	195,000	3.0
Philippines	318,000	7.5
Poland	107,900	3.0
Portugal	32,700	3.2
Puerto Rico	6,800	2.2
Romania	178,600	8.8
Senegal	3,800	0.7
Singapore	44,800	19.4
Somalia	4,700	1.7
South Africa	67,000	2.5
Spain	220,100	6.0
Sri Lanka	65,500	4.7
Sudan	11,000	0.7
Sweden	25,000	3.0
Switzerland	23,000	3.6
Syria	42,000	5.6
Taiwan	216,000	12.5
Tanzania	3,000	0.2
Thailand	71,000	1.6
Trinidad and Tobago	8,400	8.0
Tunisia	8,800	1.5
Turkey	246,700	6.7
Uganda	1,600	0.1
U.S.S.R.	4,080,000	15.8
United Kingdom	112,000	2.0
United States	1,300,000	5.9
Upper Volta	1,000	0.2
Venezuela	33,000	2.6
Vietnam	288,200	6.0
Yemen (Aden)	5,600	1.0
Yugoslavia	69,200	3.1
Zaire	1,600	0.1
Zambia	1,600	0.3

[1]Countries having over one million annual attendance.

World War II; Christian de Chalonge's *Malevil* was a spectacular and melodramatic speculation of the effects on individual lives of a nuclear bomb attack; and Bertrand Blier's *Beau-père* was a comedy about a young girl who seduces her mother's lover after her mother's death. René Clair and Abel Gance, both outstanding figures in the history of the French cinema, died during the year (*see* OBITUARIES).

WEST GERMANY. Directors were increasingly preoccupied with the memory of the Third Reich. Wolfgang Petersen's *The Boat*, the most costly German production since World War II, was based on a best-selling autobiography about life in a German submarine and, as the first nonhostile study of Germans at war, aroused considerable controversy. Rainer Werner Fassbinder's *Lili Marleen* was a superficial melodrama vaguely based on the career of the singer Anna Andersen. Other movies adopted more personal approaches to the period: *Raindrops*, the first film of Michael Hoffman and Harry Raymon, was based on the experiences of Raymon's family as German Jews in the 1930s. Jeanine Meerapfel's *Malou* was also clearly semiautobiographical in describing a woman's search for the memory of her mother, a German who had married a Jew.

More recent history was the concern of Fassbinder's *Lola*, a satire on civic corruption during West Germany's reconstruction period of the 1950s, and of Margarethe von Trotta's *The German Sisters*, about two women reacting variously to the political ferment of 1968. Von Trotta was the first woman to win the Grand Prix of the Venice Film Festival since Leni Riefenstahl, with *Olympia* (1938). Von Trotta's husband, Volker Schlöndorff, adapted Nicolas Born's best-selling novel *Die Fälschung*, about the doubts of conscience of a war correspondent working in Lebanon in the 1970s. Other films were toughly contemporary in theme. Ulrich Edel's *We Children from Bahnhof Zoo* was a harrowing account of two early teenagers destroyed by drugs. Frank Ripploh's *Taxi Zum Klo* was a cheerful, casual autobiographical sketch of a homosexual life and relationship.

ITALY. The most considerable productions of the year were Francesco Rosi's *Tre fratelli*, which used the catalyst of a family funeral reunion for a wide-ranging analysis of contemporary Italian sentiment and malaise, and Bernardo Bertolucci's *Tragedia di un uomo ridiculo*, an eventually somewhat nebulous essay on psychological reaction to terrorism — in this case the kidnapping of the son of a small businessman. One of the most ambitious films of the year was Liliana Cavani's meretricious adaptation of Curzio Malaparte's novel about Naples just after the defeat of Italy in World War II, *La pelle*.

A revival of comedies was evident in the work of several talented young comedian-directors: Maurizio Nichetti, with his second feature, *Ho fatto splash*; Carlo Verdone with *Bianco, rosso e verdone*; and Massimo Troisi with *Ricomincio da tre*. A comedy of a different style, Sergio Citti's *Il minestrone* was a droll, endearing fable about the efforts of two hungry men to find food in a society that does not readily feed its needy.

SWITZERLAND. From German Switzerland came a remarkable debut in Markus Imhoof's *Das Boot ist Voll*, which offered an unfamiliar picture of the role of the neutral Swiss in World War II. The story told of the reaction of a village community to a group of Jewish concentration camp escapees, who are eventually dutifully handed back over the German border to certain death.

SCANDINAVIA. Sweden was host to Dusan Makaveyev, who had been almost inactive since his final Yugoslav film, *W.R.-Mysteries of the Organism*. Something of the old anarchy remained in his *Montenegro, or Pigs and Pearls*, a black comedy about the fatal effects that ensue when the bored wife of a U.S. businessman falls in with a group of crazy emigré Serbs. Another notable Swedish production, Kay Pollak's *Children's Island* was a sharp, touching, unsentimental picture of a lonely child bearing up bravely against the continual disappointments he meets in adults. In Norway Anja Breien made *Witch Hunt*, finding modern parallels in the persecution of an independent-minded woman of the 17th century. Laila Mikkelson's *Little Ida* was another tale of unmerited suffering, based on Marit Paulsen's memories of childhood as the daughter of a woman who had consorted with a soldier of the German occupation forces during World War II and was consequently rejected by the community.

Eastern Europe. U.S.S.R. The major release of the year was Elem Klimov's *Agonia*, shelved for six years and finally permitted after reediting. This historic epic about the influence of the monk Rasputin on the Russian royal family dealt with an era hitherto prohibited in Soviet cinema. Another of the few major talents still at work in Soviet films, Gleb Panfilov, adapted a play by the rural writer Aleksandr Vampilov: a finely observed study, within a unity of time and place, of the people of a deprived Siberian village. A survivor of the great days of revolutionary filmmaking, Sergey Yutkevich, returned to his old theme of Lenin's biography with *Lenin in Paris*, a piece of hagiography retrieved by the director's grace and urbanity. New evidence of a more lively filmmaking activity

Both a sentimental and an artistic success, *On Golden Pond* teamed Katharine Hepburn and Henry Fonda for the first time in their long careers. Jane Fonda played the couple's daughter.

PHOTO TRENDS

in the Eastern republics of the U.S.S.R. was provided by an enchanting period comedy from Armenia, Henrik Malyan's *A Slap in the Face*, about the bigotry and hypocrisy of a small town around 1915. The director Mark Donskoi died in March (*see* OBITUARIES).

POLAND. The events of 1980–81 and the spirit of the nation's independent labour union Solidarity had been anticipated by the Polish cinema. During the year they were reflected in a remarkable way. The processes of the new political situation were vividly recorded in the documentaries *Workers 80* and *Peasants 81*. The first masterwork to come out of the new Poland was Andrzej Wajda's *Man of Iron* (winner of the Golden Palm at Cannes), an epic of the Gdansk shipyards from the strikes to the signing of the accord between Solidarity and the government.

In the new atmosphere films previously banned, such as Jerzy Skolimowski's *Hands Up* (1967) and Janusz Kijowski's study of the processes of suppression, *Indeks* (1977), were brought to light. Historical periods previously forbidden were the subject of new films. The period of resistance against tsarist Russia culminating in the 1905 Revolution (which had uncomfortable parallels with more recent Soviet-Polish history) was treated in Agnieszka Holland's *Fever* and Edward Zebrowski's *In Broad Daylight*. Stalinist indoctrination was the subject of Wojciech Maczewski's harrowing, technically excellent *Creeps*.

HUNGARY. The outstanding film of the year was Istvan Szabo's *Mephisto*. Based on Klaus Mann's novel, it was a fictionalized portrait of Mann's brother-in-law, Gustav Gründgens, the most gifted director and star of the stage and screen in Nazi Germany. Szabo's finely staged film enlarged Mann's view to a profound analysis of the dilemma of the artist working under a corrupt totalitarianism. Miklos Jancso, the star director of Hungarian cinema, made his first film inside the studio, *The Tyrant's Heart, or Boccaccio in Hungary*.

Asia. JAPAN. Two films stood out from the undifferentiated, assembly-line production of most Japanese cinema. Shoehi Imamura's *Eijanaika* was a sprawling and episodic portrait of Japan in 1867, a period of transition when a new popular movement was coming into prominence. Imamura did not hesitate to draw modern parallels. In direct contrast, Oguri Kohei's first feature film, *Muddy River*, was a gentle, finely observed account of a small boy's awakening to the hard facts of adult life during the 1950s.

TAIWAN. Pai Ching-Hu's *The Coldest Winter in Peking* attracted redoubled attention after it was banned in Hong Kong in the cause of good relations with China. The rambling story related the sufferings of a young, foreign-educated Chinese during the years of China's Cultural Revolution.

INDIA. The major award of the New Delhi Film Festival went to *Cry of the Wounded*, the first motion picture directed by Govind Nihalani, the cameraman of Shyam Benegal's films. It was a strong drama about the fight of a young lawyer against a corrupt and insuperable political establishment. Another new director, Kahan Mehta, made a hardly less ferocious attack upon the injus-

tices of authoritarianism with *A Folk Tale*, a Brechtian fable about a king and his capricious fairy-tale management of his kingdom. Of established directors, Mrinal Sen had greater success with *In Search of Famine*—a sharp, satirically edged story of a film company on location in a remote village—than with his elaborate, effortfully poetic study in personal nostalgia, *Kaleidoscope*.

Africa. Filmmaking activity erupted in several African nations in 1981. From Nigeria Ola Balogun's *Cry Freedom!* was the story of a guerrilla-led uprising against white colonists. In the Ivory Coast *Djelli*, directed by Fadika Kramo-Lancine, recounted the efforts of an educated young couple to break with tribal traditions. From the Congo Jan-Michel Tchissoukou's *The Chapel* described the insensitive and miscalculated efforts of a 1930s missionary to impose Christianity in the countryside. From Botswana came a delirious comedy, Jamie Uys's *The Gods Must be Crazy*, about the far-reaching effects of a Coca-Cola bottle dropped in the bush by a passing aircraft. In marked contrast to these modestly budgeted productions was *Omar Mukhtar*, a Libyan co-production with Britain, directed by Mustapha Akkad and recounting the story of the Bedouin who led the resistance to Mussolini in 1929–31.   (DAVID ROBINSON)

Nontheatrical Motion Pictures. Two U.S. films were winners at the prestigious International Industrial Film Festival, held at Turin, Italy, in 1981. They were *Shipbuilding: The Trades That Make It Happen*, produced by Tim Hickman (Image and Sound Productions) for Newport News Shipbuilding, and *Farewell Etaoin Shrdlu* by David Loeb Weiss for the *New York Times*, also an American Film Festival category winner. *The Hawk and John McNeely*, made by Hugh Morton for Piedmont Airlines, took first prize in the Real Life Adventure Film Competition at Cortina d'Ampezzo in Italy.

At the Sofia (Bulg.) Architectural Festival a Cor-

The Hawk and John McNeely took first prize in the Real Life Adventure Film Competition. It was filmed on 1,830-m (6,000-ft) Grandfather Mountain in the Blue Ridge Mountains and starred a red-tailed hawk.

HUGH MORTON—HOPE REPORTS, INC.

poration for Public Broadcasting motion picture, *A Place to Be: The Construction of the East Wing of the National Gallery* by Charles Guggenheim, captured first place. An educational subject, *The Little Prince* by Will Vinton (Billy Budd Films), won the Danzante De Oro Trophy at the Heusca Festival of Short Films (Spain).

An amateur film, *Le Plan Americain* (*The American Shot*), made by Steven M. Wasserstein for the Women's Interart Center, swept four awards including the grand prize at Velden (Austria) plus one of two top honours at the Melbourne (Australia) Amateur Festival. Another winner at Melbourne was *One*, a 1979 New York University student film by Mark Tarnawsky and Robert Just.

(THOMAS W. HOPE)

See also Photography; Television and Radio.
[623; 735.G.2]

Motor Sports

Grand Prix Racing. During the 1981 season of international Formula One racing, the organizers, in order to reduce cornering speeds, banned ground-effect skirts, but they were forestalled by manufacturers' mechanical ploys. The drivers' world championship was in contention until the very last round, at Las Vegas, Nev., when it was clinched by Nelson Piquet of Brazil.

The season opened at Kyalami, South Africa, but some of the leading teams were absent in protest against the host nation's racial policies, and there was a shortage of proper racing tires. Carlos Reutemann of Argentina won in a Williams-Cosworth, from Piquet (Brabham) and Elio de Angelis of Italy in a Lotus. Racing became serious at Long Beach, Calif., in the U.S. Grand Prix (West). Panic over the temporary withdrawal of Goodyear Tire & Rubber Co. was met by a supply of Michelin tires. Colin Chapman's British-designed "twin-chassis" Lotus 88 was declared invalid in its attempt to overcome the "skirts" ban. Out of 24 starters only 8 finished, the winner being the reigning world champion, Alan Jones (Australia), in a Wil-

liams, with his teammate Reutemann second and Piquet's Brabham third; Jones made the fastest lap, at 144.66 km/h. In the Brazilian Grand Prix at Rio de Janeiro, Reutemann won for Williams, followed by Jones in the other Williams car and Ricardo Patrese of Italy in an Arrow. The fastest lap was driven by Marc Surer (Switz.) in an Ensign, at 158.453 km/h.

At Buenos Aires for the Argentine Grand Prix, the Brabham team introduced for the BT49C a hydropneumatic suspension system that allowed them to "cheat" the rules and that was soon being copied. It worked as Piquet won from Reutemann with Alain Prost's (France) turbocharged Renault third. Piquet had the fastest lap at 204.066 km/h.

The European events began at Imola for the San Marino Grand Prix, won by Piquet after a smooth drive for Brabham, with Patrese second and Reutemann third. The fastest lap was driven by Gilles Villeneuve of Canada in a Ferrari, at 167.9 km/h. The Belgian Grand Prix at Zolder followed, won by Reutemann in a Williams from Jacques Laffite (France) in a Ligier JS17-Matra. Reutemann drove the fastest lap, at 184.192 km/h. At the Monaco Grand Prix, Jones drove the fastest lap at 136.311 km/h before he was overtaken by Villeneuve's Ferrari. Piquet crashed, and only 7 of the original 20 finished. Jones was second and Laffite's Talbot third. In a turbocharged V6-cylinder Ferrari, Villeneuve won the Spanish Grand Prix, at Jarama, from Laffite; John Watson of the U.K. placed third in a McLaren. Jones had the fastest lap at 153.998 km/h.

In the French Grand Prix at the Dijon-Prenois circuit, Goodyear reentered the tire competition. Prost in the French Renault RE32 won, with Watson second and Piquet third; the results were decided on the addition of times, as the race had been stopped when rain deluged the course and then restarted. Prost drove the fastest lap, at 197.859 km/h. The British Grand Prix, held at Silverstone, was won by Watson from Reutemann and Laffite; of the field of 24 only 8 were running at the end. René Arnoux (France) made fastest lap for Renault, at 226.29 km/h. At the German Grand Prix at Hockenheim, Piquet won from Prost and Laffite. The best lap was accomplished by Jones, at 217.371 km/h. Laffite's Talbot won from Arnoux at the Austrian Grand Prix with Piquet's Brabham third; the winner had the fastest lap, at 219.124 km/h. At the Dutch Grand Prix at Zandvoort, Prost led Piquet and Jones over the finish, the only 3 out of 24 to go the whole distance. Jones drove the fastest lap, at 187.061 km/h. At Monza the Italian Grand Prix was won by Prost's Renault, from Jones and Reutemann, after Reutemann had made the fastest lap, at 214.092 km/h.

The scene then shifted to North America, with the championship still undecided. The Canadian Grand Prix was contested under appallingly wet conditions at Montreal, where Laffite won for Talbot and Watson and Villeneuve finished second and third. Watson had the fastest lap at 145.019 km/h. The final event was over a parking lot circuit at Las Vegas. The intense duel for the drivers' championship did not materialize because Reutemann was delayed with mechanical maladies and

For the first time in four years, someone from Great Britain, John Watson of Ulster, won the British Grand Prix. He powered his way to victory in a McLaren car.

CENTRAL PRESS/PICTORIAL PARADE

Piquet elected to coast to a fifth-place finish; Jones won from Prost, with Bruno Giacomelli (Italy) driving an Alfa Romeo V12 home in third place. The fastest lap was made by Didier Pironi in a Ferrari, at 163.929 km/h.

Rallies and Other Races. The Monte Carlo Rally was won by a Renault 5 Turbo. The new turbocharged four-wheel drive Audi Quattro won the Swedish Rally, and the Portuguese Rally went to a Fiat 131 Abarth. The African Safari Rally was marred by protests over the results, but the Datsun Violets were convincing champions. At the Acropolis Rally in Greece a Ford Escort won. A Ford Escort RS won the Castrol 5 event in South Africa. The Codasur Rally in the U.S. was won by Talbot and the Brazilian Rally by Ford. Finland's Thousand Lakes Rally was won by an Escort RS. At San Remo, Michèle Mouton, with Fabrizia Pons as co-driver, won in an Audi Quattro, the first woman to win a world championship rally. The Cyprus Rally went to a Mitsubishi Lancer. A Datsun won the Bomdama Rally in Japan. The Lombard RAC Rally around Britain was a convincing success for Finnish and Swedish drivers. It was easily won by Hannu Mikkola and Arne Hertz in an Audi Quattro. The world champion rally driver of 1981 was Vatenen, and the manufacturers' world rally championship went to Talbot. The Le Mans 24-hour race, marred by a crash that caused the death of a race marshal, was won by Derek Bell of the U.K. and Jacky Ickx of Belgium in a Porsche 936-81.   (WILLIAM C. BODDY)

U.S. Racing. The richest and most traditional race in the U.S., the Indianapolis 500, produced the most bizarre occurrence in automobile racing in 1981 and perhaps in the modern era when the naming of the official winner was delayed for at least five months and perhaps longer. Some 16 hours after the finish Bobby Unser, who had apparently finished first, was penalized one lap for passing illegally under a caution flag, and the victory was awarded to Mario Andretti, whose STP Wildcat Cosworth Ford V8 had finished second. But the Unser team protested, requesting an impartial review board. That board in mid-October reversed the decision of the sanctioning United States Auto Club (USAC) and gave the victory back to Unser, who, however, was fined $40,000 and board costs for his infraction. Andretti thereupon appealed to the Auto Competition Committee for the U.S., the country's representative to the International Auto Federation (FIA). At the year's end the appeal was pending.

If Andretti's appeal was rejected, Unser would have his third Indianapolis 500 victory and some $262,000. Andretti would collect $168,000, and Australian Vern Schuppan, who finished a lap back in third place, some $100,000. The time of the race was 3 hours 35 minutes 47.08 seconds, an average speed of 139.084 mph.

The Indianapolis 500 emphasized the continuing split in this area of competition between Indianapolis Motor Speedway and USAC on one side and most of the name drivers and Championship Auto Racing Team (CART) on the other. The fact that USAC ran only one other race in its Gold Crown series (won by A. J. Foyt at Pocono, Pa.,

Formula One Grand Prix Race Results, 1981

Race	Driver	Car	Average speed
South African	C. Reutemann	Williams FWO7B	180.74 km/h
U.S. West	A. Jones	Williams FWO7B	140.979 km/h
Brazilian	C. Reutemann	Williams FWO7C	155.450 km/h
Argentine	N. Piquet	Brabham BT49C	200.63 km/h
San Marino	N. Piquet	Brabham BT49C	162.87 km/h
Belgian	C. Reutemann	Williams FWO7C	180.445 km/h
Monaco	G. Villeneuve	Ferrari 126CK	132.03 km/h
Spanish	G. Villeneuve	Ferrari 126CK	149.07 km/h
French	A. Prost	Renault RE32	190.36 km/h
British	J. Watson	McLaren MP4	221.509 km/h
German	N. Piquet	Brabham BT49C	213.294 km/h
Austrian	J. Laffite	Talbot JS17	215.698 km/h
Dutch	A. Prost	Renault RE34	183.002 km/h
Italian	A. Prost	Renault RE34	209.0 km/h
Canadian	J. Lafitte	Talbot JS17	137.2 km/h
Las Vegas	A. Jones	Williams FWO7C	157.554 km/h

WORLD DRIVERS' CHAMPIONSHIP: Piquet, 50 pt; Reutemann, 49 pt; Jones, 46 pt.
CONSTRUCTORS' WORLD CHAMPIONSHIP: Williams-Cosworth-Ford, 95 pt; Brabham-Cosworth-Ford, 61 pt; Renault-Turbo, 54 pt.

over a star-depleted field) while CART had a sponsor and completed a successful 11-race series would seem to indicate the winner. But the future remained unclear because the Indianapolis event dominates this competition.

Rick Mears, driving a Gould PC-9B Cosworth, was CART's champion. He won six events, including the three road races at Mexico City, Watkins Glen, N.Y., and Riverside, Calif. Bill Alsup was runner-up to Mears.

Meanwhile, other types of auto racing enjoyed banner seasons. Geoff Brabham, son of former world champion Jack Brabham, won the Sports Car Club of America's (SCCA's) Can-Am road racing series in a VDS 001 Chevrolet. Italy's Teo Fabi, who won the most events at four, finished second.

For the first time in five years the National Association for Stock Car Auto Racing (NASCAR) changed the size of the cars to smaller models in the $7.2 million Winston Cup stock car series, and the public responded by making 1981 the most successful season in the history of the organization. A season-long battle for the championship between Bobby Allison and Darrell Waltrip was resolved in favour of Waltrip when he won 4 straight late in the season, bringing his season total to 12 victories against 5 for Allison. Waltrip earned $693,342 in his Junior Johnson-prepared Buick, while Allison won $644,311. But Waltrip failed in each of the stock car classics. Richard Petty won the Daytona 500, Allison the Charlotte World 600, and Neil Bonnett the Darlington Southern 500.

In the 24-Hour Pepsi Challenge at Daytona Beach, Fla., a Porsche Twin Turbo driven by Brian Redman, Bobby Rahal, and Bob Garretson managed to hang on to defeat another Porsche driven by Derek Bell, Bob Akin, and Craig Siebert. In the Coca Cola 12 Hours at Sebring, Fla., the winner again was a Porsche Turbo, driven by Hurley Haywood, Bruce Leven, and Al Holbert. Redman, of Australia, driving 13 of 17 events in either a Porsche or a Lola-Chevrolet, won the Camel GT season crown, of which Daytona and Sebring are part.   (ROBERT J. FENDELL)

Motorcycles. Something of an upset occurred in the world 500-cc road-race series when three-time champion Kenny Roberts (U.S.) finished third. The new champion was Italy's Marco Luc-

chinelli, riding a Suzuki, with another Suzuki rider, Randy Mamola (U.S.), second. Roberts and Barry Sheene (U.K., fourth) were Yamaha riders. Other world champions were West German Anton Mang (Kawasaki) in the 250-cc and 350-cc categories; Angel Nieto (Minarelli) of Spain, 125-cc; and Rolf Biland (Yamaha) of Switzerland, in the sidecar.

In the Isle of Man Tourist Trophy racing notable winners were Mick Grant (senior), Steve Tonkin (junior), New Zealander Graeme Crosby (classic), and Jock Taylor (sidecar); Crosby won the Mallory Park Race of the Year. The 11th annual Transatlantic Trophy series between the U.S. and Great Britain was won by the British team, captained by Sheene.

The world speedway championship was won by 24-year-old Californian Bruce Penhall. The 56th International Six Days' Enduro (enduro being a new word, for 1981, in place of the traditional "trial"), held on Elba, was dominated by Italy, which won the main contests for trophy and vase, with West Germany runner-up in both. The world trials championship went to a 19-year-old Frenchman, Gilles Burgat, who earlier had won the Scottish Six Days' Trial.

André Malherbe of Belgium became 500-cc world motocross champion, while his Honda teammate, Graham Noyce, finished second. Neil Hudson (Yamaha) was the 250-cc champion, and Harry Everts (Belgium), riding a Suzuki, triumphed in the 125-cc class. Tom O'Mara, Donnie Hansen, Danny LaPorte, and Chuck Sun won both the main motocross team events, the Trophée des Nations and the Motocross des Nations, for the U.S. Mike Hailwood, winner of ten world motorcycle championships, died in March (*see* OBITUARIES).   (CYRIL J. AYTON)

See also Water Sports.
[452.B.4.c]

Mountaineering

Activity by foreign expeditions in China increased considerably during the 1980–81 intermonsoon climbing season. As in Nepal, Japanese expeditions outnumbered all others. A U.S. party failed on Gongga in the Daxue Shan in Sichuan (Szechwan) Province after the 1980 monsoon, and one member of the group was lost. Eight members of a Japanese expedition attempting Gongga before the 1981 monsoon also died, and a British Army party failed on Jiazi in the same range.

Sigunian was climbed by a Japanese party. In Qinghai (Tsinghai) Province a Japanese expedition made the first ascent of Anyemaqen in 1981. The most important mountaineering event in China during the year, however, was the conquest of Kongur in Xinjiang Uygur (Sinkiang Uighur) Autonomous Region by a British expedition; on a later Japanese attempt, all three of the summit party disappeared. Other ascents in this region, all by Japanese groups, were Kongur Tiube, Muztagata north peak, and Bogda Ola.

In Tibet Austrians made the third ascent of Xixabangma in 1980, and Reinhold Messner climbed

Motorboating:
see Water Sports

Motor Industry:
see Industrial Review

UPI

Nine handicapped climbers were part of a group that made it to the summit of Washington's Mt. Rainier in July. Kirk J. Adams (right) of Snohomish, Washington, who has been blind since the age of five, is led by a guide.

its west face in 1981. A U.S. expedition attempted the east face of Everest but failed to find a feasible route. China announced that the Xinjiang Uygur region sides of the main Karakorum peaks—K2 (called Mt. Qogir by the Chinese), Gasherbrum I and II, and Broad Peak—would be open to foreign expeditions beginning in 1982.

In Nepal the Ministry of Tourism added a number of virgin peaks to the list of mountains available for expeditions. Some of the peaks on the list had always been available for joint Nepalese-foreign expeditions, with the proviso that the Nepalese members be endorsed by the Nepal Mountaineering Association (NMA) after being chosen. New rules made consultation with the NMA obligatory before a choice was made, and the NMA also demanded involvement from the beginning in the planning, organization, and execution of future expeditions.

On Everest unsuccessful attempts were made during the winter on the west ridge direct (British) and the normal South Col route (Japanese). After the monsoon a joint Nepalese-Italian expedition also failed on the South Col route, but it was completed by a U.S. expedition in 1981. A Japanese attempt on the west ridge failed. Solo ascents of Lhotse by the west face, by the leader of a Bulgarian expedition, and Makalu by the northwest ridge, by an Austrian climber, both without oxygen, were especially noteworthy. A West German expedition put 15 members on the summit of Manaslu via the northeast face, also without oxygen.   (JOHN NEILL)

Mozambique

An independent African state, the People's Republic of Mozambique is located on the southeast coast of Africa, bounded by the Indian Ocean, Tanzania, Malawi, Zambia, Zimbabwe, South Africa, and Swaziland. Area: 799,380 sq km (308,-642 sq mi). Pop. (1980 prelim.): 12,130,000. Cap. and largest city: Maputo (pop., 1980 prelim., 755,-300). Language: Portuguese (official); Bantu languages predominate. Religion: traditional beliefs 65%, Christian about 21%, Muslim 10%, with Hindu, Buddhist, and Jewish minorities. President in 1981, Samora Machel.

Faced with a serious, continuing trade deficit in 1981, the Mozambique government did not hesitate to seek assistance from non-Communist Western European countries, including the former colonial power, Portugal. In 1980 an agreement had been signed with Portugal under which Mozambique was to receive financial help to the value of $100 million to enable the country to purchase Portuguese goods and services. Of that sum, $30 million was to be spent on consumer goods; the remainder was to be used to purchase equipment and services that would enable Portugal to reestablish its trading position in Mozambique.

As a result of the part played by Pres. Samora Machel in the achievement of Zimbabwe's independence, relations with Britain were also greatly improved. Foreign Minister Joaquim Chissano visited London in January with the aim of expanding trade and economic links with Britain. In March Britain granted financial assistance for improving the railway track in the vicinity of the Zimbabwe border. Zimbabwe was eager to make more extensive use of rail links with the coast through Mozambique, especially through the port of Beira, in order to reduce its dependence on the South African railway system. During 1981, however, the Mozambique route was subject to harassment by guerrillas of the Mozambican National Resistance (MNR), who were believed to be supported by South Africa.

South African troops themselves raided Mozambique in January, claiming that their targets were houses in a Maputo suburb occupied by members of the African National Congress, a guerrilla organization banned in South Africa. This was the first attack of its kind launched by South Africa against Mozambique, and it was strongly denounced by the government and by neighbouring countries. The U.S.S.R., through its ambassador in Maputo, offered to help Mozambique in the event of further South African raids, an offer that was underscored by a visit of Soviet warships to Beira and Maputo.

During the raid, eight Mozambique Army officers were alleged to have ordered their troops not to resist the South Africans. Those men, President Machel said, would be charged with treason and corruption. In July two of their number, Fernandes Baptista and Jossias Dlakhama, both former lieutenant colonels, escaped from custody. It was then revealed that Baptista, who had been a

Mozambique

member of the Frelimo Party Central Committee and of the Popular Assembly, was believed to have been spying for the U.S. Central Intelligence Agency.

In April guerrillas struck a major blow at the Cabora Bassa hydroelectric installation, which supplied 10% of South Africa's electricity; the power supply was cut off completely for a time. This was followed in June by fierce fighting in the north between guerrillas and Frelimo troops. Hundreds of refugees crossed the border into Zimbabwe with stories of rough treatment at the hands of both factions. To check the guerrilla activity, the government adopted a policy of creating fortified villages on the pattern developed in Zimbabwe during the fighting that preceded independence. In November Machel ordered his security services purged of men guilty of mistreating the public on the pretext of maintaining order.

In July Machel met Prime Minister Robert Mugabe of Zimbabwe to discuss the problem of the refugees and to try to formulate plans to control the guerrillas. Mozambique and Zimbabwe had signed a defense agreement in January.

(KENNETH INGHAM)

Museums

New museum projects made headlines in 1981. They ranged from entirely new museums that had not yet formed collections or built premises to major or minor additions to existing institutions. In addition, a number of important acquisitions were made, and new items went on display.

New Museums. The National Building Museum, a private museum devoted to U.S. building arts and technology, urban planning, and landscape, was founded in Washington, D.C. It would

The Whitney Museum of American Art of New York City opened its first suburban satellite branch in Stamford, Conn., in July.

eventually organize exhibitions and provide programs for radio and television as well as compile a historical and technical data archive on U.S. architecture. The museum occupied a 19th-century building. Also in Washington the National Capitol Planning Commission approved a plan by the Smithsonian Institution to construct a $50 million underground complex that would ultimately house two new museums—the Museum of African Art and an Eastern art collection that would form an extension to the Freer Gallery of Art.

The San Antonio (Texas) Museum of Art opened in the spring. Housed in the late 19th-century former Lone Star Brewery, the $7.2 million project was administered by the San Antonio Museum Association and focused on the arts of the Americas, with special sections devoted to the art of the American Indian and Spanish colonial, pre-Columbian, and Mexican folk art. Texas artists were, of course, well represented. The inaugural show at the museum was devoted to contemporary American realism.

In mid-July the new west wing of the Museum of Fine Arts in Boston, Mass., opened. Designed by architect I. M. Pei, it provided 7,500 sq m (80,-000 sq ft) of space for galleries, an auditorium, offices, shops, and a restaurant. It was part of a $22 million program that was to include the installation of a climate-control system and renovation of the original building, dating from 1909.

The new headquarters for the Asia Society opened in April in New York City. The eight-story building on Park Avenue cost $16.6 million and replaced the former Asia House Gallery. The architect, Edward Larrabee Barnes, provided in his design for a total of 500 sq m (5,600 sq ft) of exhibition space, an auditorium, a book shop, and seminar rooms. The ground-floor gallery was to house temporary exhibitions, and the second-floor galleries the society's permanent collection. Works from the permanent collection were to be rotated so that over a period of two years the public would be able to see the entire collection.

At the Metropolitan Museum of Art in New York City, the first phase of the Far Eastern Collections' reinstallation was completed. The new Chinese Garden Court and the Ming Furniture Room represented the first permanent cultural exchange between the U.S. and China.

New facilities were begun in Raleigh, N.C., for the North Carolina Museum of Art. In a 66-ha (164-ac) park, the structure was expected to cost $15,750,000, of which $10,750,000 would come from the state. Local funding in Akron, Ohio, raised $4.5 million for the renovation of a 19th-century U.S. Post Office as the new home of the Akron Art Museum. In Houston, Texas, plans were announced for a permanent museum building to house one of the largest private U.S. collections, that of Domenique and the late John de Menil.

Plans were announced by the Vancouver (B.C.) Art Gallery for a move to a historic downtown building late in 1982. The new headquarters was to be in a former 1910 courthouse, and a $16.1 million renovation program would provide four times the existing amount of exhibition space, as well as the usual ancillary facilities.

The new Museum for Contemporary Art in Basel, Switz., was housed in a renovated paper mill. This new facility went some way toward remedying the dearth of contemporary art in Swiss public collections. A branch of the Kunstmuseum Basel, the new gallery was devoted entirely to art from the late 1950s to the present. Contemporary art was also to be shown in a new museum in Los Angeles, scheduled for completion in 1983.

Several new galleries opened in the new wing of the British Museum in London. The Room of Latin and Greek Inscription was the first in a series of sculpture and inscription galleries to be opened to the public. On display were 23 Greek and 17 Latin inscriptions on stone drawn from a collection of several thousand held by the museum.

In Egypt part of the $16 million profit made by the Tutankhamen exhibition's tour of the U.S., Canada, the U.K., and West Germany was to be used for a variety of museum projects. The Coptic Museum and the Egyptian Museum in Cairo were to be renovated, and a museum and orientation centre were to be built at Saqqarah, site of the ancient Step Pyramid. Other possible projects included a Nubian museum at Aswan and a new museum for the Sinai.

The Whitney Museum of American Art in New York City opened its first suburban "satellite" in Stamford, Conn. The new branch was housed in the headquarters of Champion International Corp. and represented a joint project between Champion and the Whitney, with the corporation providing financing and accommodations and the museum providing staff. This was the second branch of the Whitney; the third was expected to open in 1982 in midtown Manhattan.

New Acquisitions. The Princes Gate Collection went on view in London at the Courtauld Institute Galleries. This fine collection, formed by Count Antoine Seilern (d. 1978), was particularly rich in Italian and Flemish Old Master paintings and drawings, with fine works by Giovanni Battista Tiepolo and Rubens. The collection was be-

The British Museum unveiled its renovated Egyptian Sculpture Gallery in September. The gallery was originally opened in 1834.

queathed to the University of London and went on public view in July for the first time. Sixty major examples of Chinese painting and calligraphy from the collection of John M. Crawford, Jr., were promised to the Metropolitan Museum of Art. The works ranged from the 11th to the 18th century.

Two California institutions, the J. Paul Getty Museum and the Norton Simon Foundation, jointly purchased Nicolas Poussin's "The Holy Family with the Infant St. John." Attempts to raise sufficient funds to prevent its export from Britain were unsuccessful. The painting was to be shared by the two galleries and exhibited alternately at each. Another example of museum-sharing was begun by the Peabody Museum at Harvard University. After three years of preliminary planning, portions of its undisplayed ethnographic and archaeological collection were to be loaned to nine other museums in a long-term collection-sharing program.

The Corning Glass Center at Corning, N.Y., was to receive the most complete collection of English cameo glass of the 19th century ever formed. The collection of Dr. and Mrs. Leonard Rakow was put together over more than 25 years. In the spring of 1982 the museum planned to mount a comprehensive exhibition of cameo glass, with ancient examples compared and contrasted with items from the Rakow collection.

Picasso's "Guernica" was at last returned to Spain from the Museum of Modern Art in New York City, where it had been on loan from the artist for many years. The painting was to hang in the Casón del Buen Retiro, an annex of the Prado in Madrid.

A Chicago collector, Muriel K. S. Newman, would substantially increase the contemporary holdings of the Metropolitan Museum of Art with her future bequest of paintings and sculpture worth more than $12 million. Other significant acquisitions included a mural-sized 1899 work by Edouard Vuillard, "Landscape: Window Overlooking the Woods," at the Art Institute of Chicago.   (JOSHUA B. KIND; SANDRA MILLIKIN)

See also Art Exhibitions; Art Sales.
[613.D.1.5]

Music

Classical. As worldwide recession bit ever deeper, events in 1981 only served to confirm the general slowing of activity in the music business noted in 1979 and 1980.

SYMPHONIC MUSIC. With people like Mehta, Solti, and Giulini still in charge of the major U.S. orchestras, earthshaking changes were not to be expected and indeed did not transpire. In New York City the popular and likable Zubin Mehta retained his post as principal of the city's Philharmonic Orchestra despite continuous critical sniping and a constant stream of album releases so cool and uncontroversial that they arguably served only to burden further an already glutted market. A reading of Brahms's *Double Concerto*, featuring Mehta in partnership with violinist Pinchas Zukerman and cellist Lynn Harrell (subsequently recorded for Columbia CBS), provided a yardstick example of Mehta's lacklustre approach, as did his account of the same composer's Fourth Symphony.

Sir Georg Solti continued to force the Chicago Symphony Orchestra through various hoops, Seiji Ozawa and Sir Colin Davis shared indifferent honours with Eric Leinsdorf at Boston, and Carlo Maria Giulini continued what appeared more than ever to be an ecclesiastical pilgrimage through the great European classics in Los Angeles. In Boston it was especially disturbing to find the usually reliable Ozawa falling so far off form that a launch-pad-bound performance of Gustav Holst's suite *The Planets* sank effortlessly into a black hole exclusively of its own making. The best playing that Bostonians heard during 1981 came paradoxically from the city's Symphony Orchestra players in their off-duty manifestation as the Boston Pops, now firmly in the capable and often exciting hands of movie-maestro John Williams. For the rest, it was left to out-of-the-mainstream orchestras to provide the fireworks. Eduardo Mata, once again burnishing his reputation as both a concert and recording conductor, turned in a series of above-average performances with the Dallas Symphony Orchestra that recalled the best of the orchestra's palmy days under Donald Johanos.

Elsewhere, there were few changes to report. Superstar Herbert von Karajan retained control of Berlin's legendary Philharmonic Orchestra despite recurring health problems; Daniel Barenboim seemed firmly at the helm at the Paris Orchestra after some stormy scenes in the past; and only Sir Georg Solti positively stepped down, relinquishing his position as principal of the London Philharmonic Orchestra to East German maestro Klaus Tennstedt. According to one disgruntled pundit,

A symphony composed by Wolfgang Amadeus Mozart at the age of nine was discovered among private papers in West Germany. Pictured is Mozart's inscription for the violin part.

this change was for the worse, but others saw it as a move in the right direction, given Solti's importation to Europe of a Chicago Symphony-style brashness and insensitivity.

Also in London, a flurry of last-minute diplomatic activity prevented Gennadi Rozhdestvensky's removal as principal of the BBC house orchestra. Rozhdestvensky's Soviet masters had planned to terminate his contract and shuttle him pawnlike to another posting, but he now seemed assured of at least another season's work with the orchestra that he had made his own. This was also good news given the choice of his announced successor, the musicianly but uninteresting John Pritchard. Rozhdestvensky's conducting was certainly the high point in an otherwise strangely disappointing series of summer Promenade concerts at London's Royal Albert Hall (an Elgar *Violin Concerto* with Itzhak Perlman was outstanding). The back-to-normal stance of the BBC, the concerts' sponsor, following the previous season's strike-riddled fiasco was inconveniently compromised by publication of a critical attack on the corporation's running of the "Proms" by a much-respected former linchpin of the BBC's music department, composer Robert Simpson.

In Liverpool, David Atherton, principal conductor of the city's Philharmonic Orchestra, fell out with his players and reportedly almost found himself displaced in a palace coup by controversial Israeli maestro Pinchas Steinberg. By contrast, the young Simon Rattle (*see* BIOGRAPHIES) continued his reign with the City of Birmingham Symphony Orchestra in pursuit of the greatness still confidently being predicted for him. As the year progressed Rattle consolidated his reputation as one of the world's most promising younger conductors, a

tag he reputedly disliked but, at age 26, perhaps found inevitable. With Bernard Haitink continuing to preside over the Concertgebouw Orchestra of Amsterdam, James Loughran still content to split his time between Manchester's Hallé Orchestra and the Bamberg Symphony Orchestra in West Germany, and Jean-Claude Casadesus firmly in charge of France's lively if occasionally raw-sounding New Philharmonic Orchestra, it was indeed a case of status quo.

OPERA. As it was with symphonic music in 1981, so was it also with opera. The previous year's strike that had threatened to liquidate New York City's Metropolitan Opera was resolved at the 11th hour, but this led only to a penny-plain snippet of a 1980–81 season in which concert performances of a handful of warhorses tarnished rather than polished the Met's reputation. Notable among exceptions to the general dullness was the triple bill comprising Satie's *Parade*, Poulenc's *Les Mamelles de Tirésias*, and Ravel's *L'Enfant et les sortilèges*, for which the Met's artistic director, John Dexter, British artist David Hockney, and French conductor Manuel Rosenthal shared the honours. Happily, the Met's 1981–82 season opened enthusiastically and on schedule with a restaged production of Bellini's *Norma*, with management, orchestra, and performers all reporting welcome relief from the oppressive tensions of a year earlier.

In the U.K., standards at the Royal Opera House, Covent Garden, continued to waver alarmingly. The company's managers, after just staving off a serious attempt by the Greater London Council to terminate the opera's local-government grant (but still facing possible cuts in its 1982 Arts Council grant), launched an ill-starred production of Mozart's *Don Giovanni* under the baton of house conductor Sir Colin Davis. As so often happened, the best opera in the U.K. was to be found at the English National Opera at the London Coliseum (last season's disastrous *Fidelio* notwithstanding) and in the provinces. In particular, the Welsh National Opera, in Cardiff, thrived; "the most ambitious, most successful of our regional companies . . . it can even surpass anything found in London," eulogized the *Daily Telegraph*. Its exciting mix of productions included English-language editions of Beethoven's *Fidelio*, Verdi's *The Force of Destiny*, Janacek's *The Cunning Little Vixen*, and Mozart's *The Magic Flute*.

Glyndebourne Festival Opera wound its gilded way through the cold and wet English summer, and the controversial Patrice Chéreau-Pierre Boulez *Ring* cycle at that international shrine of Wagnerdom, the Bayreuth Festspielhaus, came at last to an end, although it was preserved on some excitingly engineered digital records taped live during the penultimate run.

Sad news for opera lovers came in August with the death of veteran Austrian conductor Karl Böhm (*see* OBITUARIES). A friend of Richard Strauss and Bruno Walter, Böhm had suffered a stroke in March during the film recording of Strauss's *Elektra* and never fully recovered. His memorial took the form of recently taped readings (for DG) of Schubert's Ninth Symphony and Beethoven's Ninth Symphony. Other losses to music

were conductors Karl Richter and Kyril Kondrashin; composers Kazimierz Serocki, Tadeusz Baird, and Seppo Nummi; pianists Hephzibah Menuhin and Ivor Newton; violinist Daisy Kennedy; and singer Olive Gilbert. (*See* OBITUARIES.)

ALBUMS AND CASSETTES. In 1981 the smaller companies again trounced the big names and increased, often dramatically, their share of a market that otherwise continued to fall or lie fallow in the face of adverse economic factors. Prominent among important releases in this small-is-beautiful category were a boxed set of Frederick Delius rarities conducted by the composer's amanuensis, Eric Fenby (Unicorn); Haydn's 14 "Morzin" symphonies, played on early instruments (Saga); a series of instrumental and vocal works by Maltese-born composer Charles Camilleri (Bedivere); clarinet quintets by Arthur Somervell and Gordon Jacob (Hyperion); and orchestral and instrumental selections from Sir Hamilton Harty, Nicholas Maw, and Nicola LeFanu (all Chandos).

The big recording companies seemed generally less intent on beating new paths than in boosting the much-vaunted digital recording system, a valid option given the rising sales of both digital products and the excellent new metal-particle tape cassettes, but one that showed occasional signs of blowing up in company moguls' faces. Various authorities began to question the more extravagant claims for digital technology, and some listeners felt let down by a spate of technically spectacular recordings of otherwise undistinguished and even substandard performances. What case, it was asked increasingly during the year, could really be made for an album of Tchaikovsky's *1812 Overture* so "realistically" encoded that the cannon shots at the end would rupture any normal speaker system, or for a recording of Carl Orff's bubbly *Carmina Burana* that emerged as musically flat as last night's beer?

Fortunately, the brand leaders did release some interesting material during the year. Particularly worthwhile albums included first recordings of Sir Michael Tippett's Fourth Symphony and *King Priam* (both London Decca), Weinberger's *Schwanda the Bagpiper* and Mussorgsky's *Salammbo* (both

Columbia CBS), Martinu's *The Greek Passion* (Supraphon), and Elgar's *The Light of Life* (Angel EMI). A number of complete cycles also were given decent treatments: the Haydn *Lieder* (Philips), Karl Amadeus Hartmann's eight symphonies and *Gesangsszene* (Wergo), the orchestral music of Carl Ruggles (Columbia CBS), Janacek's chamber music (London Decca), and the integral Rachmaninoff and Copland piano music (both Columbia CBS).

Tape cassettes, too, fared better during 1981 than hitherto, technical advances being matched by many more simultaneous releases with the disc equivalent. Disc quality improved steadily because pressing plants were able to spend more time on quality control now that volume demand had slackened. Once again Philips, DG, Columbia CBS, and EMI (though not EMI's U.S. and French arms, Angel and Pathé-Marconi) led the field, with London Decca (now pressing with Philips, in The Netherlands) and a mass of smaller companies in hot pursuit. Raspberry of the year went to RCA: whenever RCA did deign to release a classical product, the result, unless it hailed from West Germany, was invariably so poorly pressed and presented that collectors began to question RCA's commitment to continuing its already scaled-down operation.

Digital recording came in for something of a battering during 1981 but by general consent emerged vindicated. In other branches of the art the arrival of Toshiba's ADRES and JVC's Super ANRS systems, potential serious rivals to the Dolby-B noise-reduction decoder long available to cassette and tape-deck buffs, had to be noted. So did the introduction, to almost unanimous acclaim and following some 20 years of active research, of Acoustical Quad's ESL 63 electrostatic speaker system. Despite a hefty price tag, demand was such that by the fall Quad's Huntingdon factory in England was working overtime to catch up with backlogged orders.

(MOZELLE A. MOSHANSKY)

Jazz. It was once again striking that on the rare occasions during the year when the outside world considered jazz music to be newsworthy, veneration of the ancient was more in evidence than celebration of the new. The climax to an orgy of

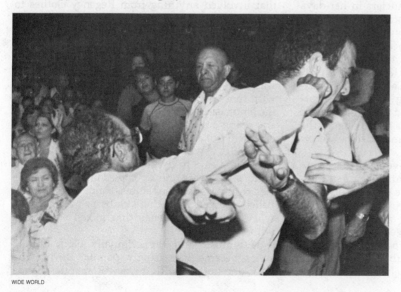

Most of the audience applauded but a few tempers flared when the Israel Philharmonic, with Zubin Mehta conducting, performed music by Richard Wagner in Tel Aviv on October 15. The music of Wagner, a Nazi favourite, had been banned in Israel since 1939.

WIDE WORLD

retrospective rapture came in December with the Kennedy Center Honors gala in Washington, D.C. Count Basie, 77 years old and laughingly fighting the inroads of arthritis from a wheelchair, led his orchestra in a typically spirited performance and finally could claim officially to have inherited the crown of Grand Old Man of Jazz, which had lain unworn since the death of Duke Ellington in 1974. Basie had less command of the muscles of his hands than in former days, but as his style had always depended as much on timing as on dexterity, vestiges of his classic style remained apparent to the discerning ear.

One curiosity of the year received less notice than its aesthetic merits deserved: a rare attempt at jazz program music by the pianist Oscar Peterson, who composed the orchestral work *Royal Wedding Suite* to mark the nuptials of Prince Charles of Great Britain. This work varied from full orchestral effects to small-group interludes, from traditional big-band jazz to Elgarian overtones, and from conventional instrumentation to the neologisms of electronic innovation. More to the point was the success with which Peterson interjected into his orchestral ruminations some spirited jazz flourishes.

Of all the deaths in the jazz world during the year, few could have evoked more happy memories of a carefree style than that of trumpeter Bill Coleman. Many people had first been introduced to Coleman's playing through his recordings in the 1930s with Thomas "Fats" Waller or through the many recordings he made, with Django Reinhardt and others, in the course of what was virtually self-imposed exile in Europe. Coleman's was an unusually buoyant style, bubbling with felicities, and remained a classic example of the jazz that preceded the new wave of the early postwar years.

One of Coleman's contemporaries, pianist Mary Lou Williams (*see* OBITUARIES), also died during the year. She had enjoyed a very different career, attempting to remain abreast and at times even ahead of the latest theories. Her later works, sometimes orchestrally conceived and occasionally abstruse, bore no relation to her earlier rolling style that had first impressed jazz fanciers in her days with the Andy Kirk band. Associations of a different kind again were evoked by the death of guitarist Oscar Moore, who had once been so brilliant a member of the Nat Cole Trio. Another death was that of William "Cozy" Cole (*see* OBITUARIES), drummer with such bands as Cab Calloway, Benny Goodman, Louis Armstrong, and Jack Teagarden. Cole would be remembered as one of the very few drummers whose style was formulated in the premodern era but who still managed to be acceptable to the newer players.

Other casualties included several of the eccentrics of the music world, including Carmen Mastren, the first and virtually the only harpist ever to capture the jazz imagination; Eddie Sauter (*see* OBITUARIES), an orchestrator of great brilliance whose work occasionally betrayed his jazz years as a trumpeter with the Red Norvo and Benny Goodman bands; and Lawrence "Snub" Mosley, a trombonist who pioneered the lonely art of the slide saxophone, a device so bizarre that he billed himself as "The Man With the Funny Horn." Another gifted performer to die during the year was vocalist Helen Humes (*see* OBITUARIES), who first came to fame with the Count Basie band in the late 1930s and who went on to establish herself as one of the most effective female singers following in the wake of Billie Holiday, Ella Fitzgerald, and Sarah Vaughan.

Three other deaths during the year were perhaps not epoch-making in themselves but pointed out a stark lesson for the jazz historian. These concerned trumpeter William "Cat" Anderson, clarinetist and saxophonist Russell Procope (*see* OBITUARIES), and trumpeter Louis Metcalf. The common denominator linking the three men was their long association with the Duke Ellington Orchestra. Ellington's was the most important big band in the evolution of jazz, and it is a sad fact that it was also the one orchestra that would prove to be inimitable. For Ellington was the only orchestrator in the field who wrote not so much for instruments as for individual instrumentalists. Consequently, as his great featured soloists have died, so has any prospect that his orchestral grandeur would survive his death. Anderson in particular was vital to Ellington's later method; without Anderson's stratospheric effects at hand, Ellington would never have composed some of his more spectacular and whimsical sketches.

(BENNY GREEN)

Popular. Two songs summed up the divisions that emerged in British pop music during 1981, both reflecting in different ways youthful attitudes toward society. "Ghost Town" by The Specials, a best-seller at the time of the inner-city rioting in the summer, was a slinky, wailing, mournful song lamenting the closure of factories and clubs in a provincial town. It was a song of despair rather than of anger or rebellion, and the multiracial band that recorded it split up soon after its success. The second song, massively popular with younger audiences, was "Prince Charming" by Adam and the Ants, a band that emerged in the furious punk era in 1976–77 but went on to become teenage idols by marketing a fantastic, escapist image and style that involved anything from Regency clothes to tribal warpaint. The message of "Prince Charming" was that "ridicule is nothing to be scared of."

The British music scene was fragmented between such realism and all-out escapism during the year, and on the whole escapism won out. It was easy to compare the music and the fashions with those of the Depression era in the 1930s, for the emphasis was on "dance music," dressing up, and going out to clubs. The year started with the emergence of a group initially known as the "new Romantics," who met at their own clubs where they were safe to dress up; their ever changing exotic styles were quickly copied and commercialized through the major stores. Bands like Spandau Ballet emerged from these clubs to become best-sellers with dance songs that mixed electronics with "white soul."

Soul music and the originally black "funk" styles became increasingly popular during the year, and not just with the new Romantics. Bands

like Dexy's Midnight Runners provided their own, white version of black America's 1960s soul sounds, while Linx, a band started by two black Londoners, was successful with its mixture of "pop funk."

The fragmented British scene was also enlivened by whole series of bands working to widen the range of electronic and synthesizer-based music. The most commercially successful of these, Ultravox, notched up an impressive list of hit singles during the year by mixing the atmospheric qualities of electronic music with strong melodies and the sheer power of a rock band. Other synthesizer-based bands produced more limited, tinkling dance tunes (many of them surprisingly popular), though the Liverpool-based band Orchestral Manoeuvres in the Dark showed the continuing potential of electronic music with their third album, *Architecture and Morality*, which mixed a melodic use of synthesizers with light, witty lyrics and decidedly nonmechanical-sounding vocals. Gary Numan, one of the first artists to popularize such electronic music, albeit in a theatrical, dehumanized form, meanwhile announced his (doubtless temporary) retirement from live performance.

If all the different forms of dance music, electronics, and funk were confusing to an outsider, so too were the regional differences in British pop music that became evident during the year. With the surprising breakup of The Specials, there was less musical attention to their home town of Coventry. Instead, it was the turn of Liverpool to enjoy a continuing musical renaissance, with the emergence of more good bands than at any time since the Beatles era in the early 1960s. But there was no one "Liverpool sound."

Sheffield also enjoyed an unexpected bout of musical success, thanks to the electronic pop and dance music of The Human League and their more sophisticated offshoot Heaven 17, who managed to mix a political message in with the dance rhythms. In London, along with the new Romantic styles, musical fashion ranged from the good-natured, sophisticated mixture of music hall and ballads of the group Madness to the more intense, personal ballads of The Sound, who emerged as one of the best London bands of the year. The capital's favourite antiheroes from the punk era, The Clash, returned from the U.S. for a week-long series of concerts that showed how they had assimilated other influences, from reggae to jazz, but remained one of the most uncompromisingly impressive British bands of the past decade.

Soloists who had emerged in the post-punk era and become established artists followed their own quirky interests during the year. Joe Jackson recorded and toured with a band playing big-band jazz from the 1940s, Ian Drury deserted the East End to record in the West Indies with distinguished reggae musicians, while Elvis Costello took his band to Nashville, Tenn., where they recorded a successful but unexpected album of American country music standards.

Some British enthusiasts remarked with amusement that punk had suddenly emerged on the West Coast five years after it swept through Britain. But there were also notable American achieve-

UPI

ments during the year, particularly the performances of Bruce Springsteen (*see* BIOGRAPHIES). During a U.K. visit this stirring, emotional beat balladeer gave what were surely the best live shows of the year. He played his lengthy set at such large halls as London's Wembley Arena and left the audience with the impression that they had been watching him in some small intimate club, such were his energy and powers of projection.

Britain repaid the compliment later in the year when the Rolling Stones gave their first U.S. concerts in three years and had the biggest commercial success of their 19-year-long career. During the three-month tour they were seen by two million people. The group's new album, *Tattoo You*, released just before the tour, showed a return to their early gutsy rhythm-and-blues style and was considered to be their best recording in ten years. Another reminder of things past came in September, when an estimated 500,000 people crowded New York's Central Park for the reunion concert of Paul Simon and Art Garfunkel, the first time the two had appeared together in 11 years.

In February Simon had been host at the Grammy awards ceremony, which returned to New York after five years in Los Angeles. Christopher Cross dominated the awards with four: for record of the year and song of the year with "Sailing," for album of the year with *Christopher Cross*, and for new artist. Among the other winners were Kenny Loggins, male pop vocal; Bette Midler, female pop vocal; George Jones (*see* BIOGRAPHIES), male country vocal; Anne Murray, female country vocal; George Benson, male rhythm and blues vocal; and Stephanie Mills, female rhythm and blues vocal. Winners in the rock category included Billy Joel, male vocal; Pat Benatar, female vocal; Bob Seger and the Silver Bullet Band, group vocal; and the Police, instrumental.

One major rock-music tragedy occurred during the year: Bob Marley, the Jamaican who popularized the island's reggae music worldwide, died in May (*see* OBITUARIES).   (ROBIN DENSELOW)

See also Dance; Motion Pictures; Television and Radio; Theatre.

[624.D–J]

Mick Jagger, leader of the Rolling Stones, performs at Madison Square Garden in New York City during one of the concerts on the group's first U.S. tour since 1978. It was reported that ticket scalpers were getting $500 for a pair of $15 tickets.

BONANZA IN COUNTRY MUSIC

by William Ivey

Just as denim trousers were once representative of the farmer, country music was thought to be primarily Southern entertainment with only a few devotees in rural pockets of the rest of the United States. These attitudes have changed considerably, and in 1981 not only were designer denim jeans popular throughout the nation but country music had crossed the Mason-Dixon line to prime-time television and New York supper clubs.

Country music is a form of American popular music that developed in the southeastern United States in the late 19th and early 20th centuries. Though historically associated with the folk music of rural whites in states such as Kentucky, North and South Carolina, Tennessee, and West Virginia, and once referred to in a derogatory manner as "hillbilly" music, it is drawn from several sources, including Anglo-American folk music, 19th-century popular music, and the blues of rural blacks.

These elements were found in combination by the record-company talent scouts who first recorded rural Southern musicians in the early 1920s. The scouts traveled in the South and cut discs on location or brought musicians to urban centres to conduct recording sessions. These records were then marketed to a rural audience. Their success revealed the commercial value of Southern white music. The fiddle solo "Sallie Goodin" by "Eck" Robertson, recorded in June 1922, is considered to be the first country music recording.

Early instruments employed in country music included the fiddle, banjo, and mandolin. More recently, acoustic and amplified guitars and the steel guitar have given the music a distinctive sound.

Country music has been a commercial music form from its inception. It is performed by professional musicians. Regional and cultural performing styles have influenced one another, and the sound of individual substyles has changed over time. Innovations in recording technology, the development of radio and television, and changes in the ways of

marketing recordings have all had an impact upon the sound of country music.

Identifiable substyles of country music have emerged:

Western Swing combines country music repertory and instrumentation with those of big-band jazz. The style, first recorded in the middle 1930s, is associated with such southwestern musicians as Bob Wills and Milton Brown.

Bluegrass music is a string-band style that developed just after World War II. Bluegrass instrumentation includes fiddle, five-string banjo, mandolin, guitar, and string bass. Vocals are high-pitched, and instrumentals are fast-paced. Performers such as Earl Scruggs and Bill Monroe are associated with the development of bluegrass.

Honky-tonk music developed in the working-class bars of Texas and Alabama in the late 1940s and early 1950s. It emphasized singing and employed few instrumental selections. Songs were frequently about real-life situations of work and love and sometimes told about the suffering that followed immoral behaviour. Hank Williams, Sr., was a leading honky-tonk singer and songwriter.

Rockabilly emerged in the mid-1950s. Representing a combination of country music and the blues, it paved the way for the success enjoyed by rock 'n' roll. Elvis Presley, Carl Perkins, and Jerry Lee Lewis were important rockabilly performers.

The Nashville Sound recording style integrated such pop music recording techniques as violin sections and background vocal groups into country music. Jim Reeves, Eddy Arnold, and Patsy Cline were among the singers who performed in this style.

In whatever style they are performed, country songs utilize realistic language and present real-life situations. Early country songs often told stories of events, and many songs were religious in content. Today the influence of the strict Protestant faith of Southern mountain people survives in secular songs that present a moral or lesson.

Since it was first recorded, country music has interacted with other forms of music. However, since the early 1950s country music has had a marked and

---

William Ivey is Director of the Country Music Foundation in Nashville, Tenn.

(Left) Barbara Mandrell was named Entertainer of the Year by the Country Music Association; George Jones and Dolly Parton also were honoured. (Right) Willie Nelson, long a favourite among fans of country music, derives his sound from traditional country styles.

increasing influence on the larger popular music scene. Such Hank Williams songs as "Cold, Cold, Heart" and "Your Cheatin' Heart" became pop hits in the early 1950s. A decade later Roger Miller's "King of the Road" successfully "crossed over" from the country to the pop field. In 1969 Johnny Cash's "Boy Named Sue" became a crossover hit, and by the early 1970s recordings by country singers were regularly aired on pop radio stations and purchased by pop music fans.

In recent years country music has accounted for a growing percentage of all records sold. In 1978, 10.2% of all recordings sold in the United States were country. That percentage rose to 11.9% in 1979 and to 14.3% in 1980.

Media other than recordings supported this growing country influence. In 1961 there were 81 radio stations in the U.S. programming country music full time, and by 1980 that number had grown to 1,534. During recent years "Hee Haw," "The Johnny Cash Show," and "The Glen Campbell Goodtime Hour" have presented country material on network television in prime time. In 1978 the Public Broadcasting Service began the annual televising of an evening "Grand Ole Opry" show; thus, more than 50 years after the "Opry" first was broadcast on radio, the show appeared in its entirety on prime-time television. Films such as the Loretta Lynn biography *Coal Miner's Daughter*, Willie Nelson's *Honeysuckle Rose,* and *Urban Cowboy* introduced country mu-

sic and country performers to the moviegoing audience in 1980 and 1981.

During the 1970s there emerged major new country entertainers who gave definition to contemporary country music. Ronnie Milsap, Crystal Gayle, Barbara Mandrell, Eddie Rabbitt, and Kenny Rogers all perform in a style that combines elements of pop and country music in a manner that appeals to a large audience. Songs that deal with the everyday experiences of adults along with the use of such country instrumentation as the pedal steel guitar link the work of these singers to the country mainstream. However, the vocal style and some of the instrumentation have much in common with pop. The work of these singers has contributed much to the contemporary acceptance of country.

In 1980 and 1981 country music drawn from styles current in the 1950s gained significantly in popularity. Willie Nelson, Waylon Jennings, and Merle Haggard performed in a honky-tonk manner little influenced by pop music. Ricky Skaggs and Emmylou Harris were successful in emulating bluegrass and other styles that link country music with its roots. Increasing media exposure, the desire of the popular music audience for songs that deal with adult themes, the vigour of historical country styles, and the blending of pop and country performance styles achieved by some contemporary country singers have combined to give country music the largest audience it has ever enjoyed.

Nauru

Nauru

An island republic within the Commonwealth, Nauru lies in the Pacific Ocean about 1,900 km (1,200 mi) E of New Guinea. Area: 21 sq km (8 sq mi). Pop. (1981 census): 8,000, including Nauruan 57%; Pacific Islanders 26%; Chinese 9%; European 8%. Capital: Yaren. Language: Nauruan and English. Religion (Nauruans only): Protestant 60%; Roman Catholic 33%. President in 1981, Hammer DeRoburt.

Pres. Hammer DeRoburt began 1981 confidently, celebrating his 25th year since being elected head chief of Nauru. On Dec. 9, 1980, he had been chosen unopposed for a further term as president.

Air Nauru celebrated its tenth anniversary in 1981. President DeRoburt, as minister responsible for aviation, recognized that only the rich income from phosphate deposits enabled the republic to continue to run its airline at an annual loss of A$15 million, about one-quarter of the national budget. DeRoburt maintained that Air Nauru had helped to relieve the tremendous isolation associated with Pacific Island life.

Prosperity, however, was accompanied by the growth of a number of environmental problems associated with increased urbanization. Critics claimed the government was not working quickly enough to stop the relative decline in the islands' quality of life caused by phosphate dust precipitation, growing litter, an unwanted dog problem, lack of street lighting, and health problems posed by the dumping of toxic waste material from a calcination plant. (A. R. G. GRIFFITHS)

NAURU
Education. (1978) Primary, pupils 1,500; secondary, pupils 600; primary and secondary, teachers 129; vocational, pupils 61, teachers 4; teacher training (1977), students 6, teacher 1.
Finance and Trade. Monetary unit: Australian dollar, with (Sept. 21, 1981) a free rate of A$0.86 to U.S. $1 (A$1.60 = £1 sterling). Budget (1978–79 est.): revenue A$40.6 million; expenditure A$33.6 million. Foreign trade (1975–76): imports A$13.8 million (c. 58% from Australia, c. 30% from The Netherlands in 1974); exports A$37.3 million (c. 51% to Australia, c. 41% to New Zealand, c. 5% to Japan). Main export: phosphate c. 100%.
Industry. Production (in 000): phosphate rock (exports; metric tons; 1978–79) 1,828; electricity (kw-hr; 1978) 26,-000.

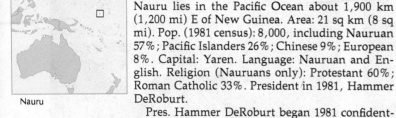

Nepal

Nepal

A constitutional monarchy of Asia, Nepal is in the Himalayas between India and the Tibetan Autonomous Region of China. Area: 145,391 sq km (56,136 sq mi). Pop. (1980 est.): 14,180,000. Cap. and largest city: Kathmandu (pop., 1976 est., 171,-400). Language: Nepali (official) 52.5%; also Bihari (including Maithili and Bhojpuri) 18.5%, Tamang 4.8%, Tharu 4.3%, and Newari 3.9%. Religion (1971): Hindu 89.4%; Buddhist 7.5%. King, Birendra Bir Bikram Shah Deva; prime minister in 1981, Surya Bahadur Thapa.

In the general election held in May 1981 under

NEPAL
Education. (1979–80) Primary, pupils 1,012,530, teachers (1977) 23,395; secondary, pupils 342,929, teachers (1977) 11,630; vocational (1977), pupils 20,875, teachers 594; teacher training (1977), students 2,768, teachers 215; higher, students 31,942, teaching staff (1977) 1,980.
Finance. Monetary unit: Nepalese rupee, with (Sept. 21, 1981) a par value of NRs 13.20 to U.S. $1 (free rate of NRs 24.47 = £1 sterling). Gold and other reserves (June 1981) U.S. $192 million. Budget (total; 1979–80 actual): revenue NRs 1,860,000,000 (excludes foreign aid of NRs 806 million); expenditure NRs 3,471,000,000.
Foreign Trade. (1980) Imports NRs 4,107,300,000; exports NRs 964.2 million. Import sources (1979–80): India 51%; Japan c. 12%. Export destinations (1979–80): India 42%; West Germany c. 8%; Japan c. 7%; Bangladesh c. 6%; U.S. c. 6%. Main exports (1974–75): jute goods c. 33%; raw jute c. 13%; curio goods c. 11%; jute cuttings c. 7%. Tourism: visitors (1978) 156,000; gross receipts U.S. $28 million.
Agriculture. Production (in 000; metric tons; 1980): rice c. 2,440; corn c. 700; wheat c. 440; millet c. 150; potatoes c. 305; jute c. 46; tobacco c. 6; buffalo milk c. 480; cow's milk c. 220. Livestock (in 000; 1980): cattle c. 6,900; buffalo c. 4,200; pigs c. 355; sheep (1979) c. 2,360; goats (1979) c. 2,480; poultry (1979) c. 21,500.

the new constitution, more than 7.8 million of Nepal's 8 million voters went to the polls to elect 111 members to the 140-seat National Assembly. (One member was returned unopposed and 28 were appointed by the king.) All major democratic groups, as well as the banned Communist Party, boycotted the poll. One surprising aspect was the victory of 70 "independent" candidates who had actively campaigned for the party system rejected in the 1980 referendum. Prime Minister Surya Bahadur Thapa was chosen to continue in office. His 22-member Cabinet, the first elected one in the 21-year history of the partyless panchayat system, included one woman.

By the end of the assembly's first session three months later, there were signs of simmering discontent among students and politicians who felt an assumption of broad leadership by the king and a new period of reconciliation would be necessary. The economic situation showed no improvement over the previous year, with stagnant agricultural production, mounting trade deficits with India and other countries, and shortfalls in revenue and expenditure. (GOVINDAN UNNY)

Netherlands, The

A kingdom of northwest Europe on the North Sea, The Netherlands, a Benelux country, is bounded by Belgium on the south and West Germany on the east. Area: 41,160 sq km (15,892 sq mi). Pop. (1981 est.): 14,208,600. Cap. and largest city: Amsterdam (pop., 1981 est., 712,300). Seat of government: The Hague (pop., 1981 est., 456,700). Language: Dutch. Religion (1971): Roman Catholic 40.4%; Dutch Reformed 23.5%; no religion 23.6%; Reformed Churches 9.4%. Queen, Beatrix; prime minister in 1981, Andreas van Agt.

On April 28, 1981, the president of The Netherlands Bank, Jelle Zijlstra, presented the 1980 annual report. The contents were gloomy; the rate of inflation rose from 4.5 to 6.5% and the government's financial deficit increased from 5.6 to 7.5%.

NETHERLANDS, THE

Education. (1979–80) Primary, pupils 1,470,097, teachers 64,881; secondary, pupils 823,594, teachers 53,955; vocational, pupils 553,775, teachers 47,000; teacher training, students 7,504, teachers 1,000; higher, students 278,654, teaching staff 28,600.

Finance. Monetary unit: guilder, with (Sept. 21, 1981) a free rate of 2.48 guilders to U.S. $1 (4.59 guilders = £1 sterling). Gold and other reserves (June 1981) U.S. $10,647,000,000. Budget (1980 actual): revenue 115.4 billion guilders; expenditure 125.9 billion guilders. Gross national product (1980) 317.4 billion guilders. Money supply (May 1981) 71,080,000,000 guilders. Cost of living (1975 = 100; June 1981) 142.

Foreign Trade. (1980) Imports 155,180,000,000 guilders; exports 146,760,000,000 guilders. Import sources: EEC 53% (West Germany 22%, Belgium-Luxembourg 12%, U.K. 8%, France 7%); U.S. 9%; Saudi Arabia 6%. Export destinations: EEC 71% (West Germany 30%, Belgium-Luxembourg 15%, France 11%, U.K. 8%, Italy 6%). Main exports: food 17%; chemicals 15%; petroleum products 14%; machinery 13%; natural gas 7%. Tourism (1979): visitors 2,750,000; gross receipts U.S. $1,325,000,000.

Transport and Communications. Roads (1977) 107,355 km (including 1,661 km expressways). Motor vehicles in use (1979): passenger 4.1 million; commercial 327,000. Railways: (1979) 2,880 km (including 1,759 km electrified); traffic (1980) 8,926,000,000 passenger-km, freight 3,468,000,000 net ton-km. Air traffic (1980): 14,643,000,000 passenger-km; freight 995.5 million net ton-km. Navigable inland waterways (1979) 4,340 km; freight traffic 33,472,000,000 ton-km. Shipping (1980): merchant vessels 100 gross tons and over 1,263; gross tonnage 5,723,845. Shipping traffic (1979): goods loaded 84,529,000 metric tons, unloaded 274,278,000 metric tons. Telephones (Jan. 1980) 6,852,800. Radio receivers (Dec. 1977) 8.5 million. Television receivers (Dec. 1977) 4.5 million.

Agriculture. Production (in 000; metric tons; 1980): wheat c. 882; barley c. 258; oats c. 94; rye c. 39; potatoes 6,267; tomatoes 395; onions 445; sugar, raw value 951; cabbages (1979) 238; cucumbers (1979) 385; carrots (1979) 135; apples 470; rapeseed c. 29; milk c. 11,800; butter 181; cheese 448; eggs c. 537; beef and veal c. 410; pork c. 1,160; fish catch (1979) 324. Livestock (in 000; May 1980): cattle c. 5,054; pigs c. 9,746; sheep c. 745; chickens c. 79,226.

Industry. Index of production (1975 = 100; 1980) 113. Production (in 000; metric tons; 1980): crude oil 1,281; natural gas (cu m) 87,270,000; manufactured gas (cu m) 1,020,000; electricity (kw-hr) 64,810,000; pig iron 4,330; crude steel 5,309; aluminum 309; cement 3,744; petroleum products c. 51,700; sulfuric acid 1,759; plastics and resins 1,976; fertilizers (nutrient content; 1979–80) nitrogenous c. 1,500, phosphate c. 360; newsprint 177. Merchant vessels launched (100 gross tons and over; 1980) 125,000 gross tons. New dwelling units (1980) 116,400.

In order to reduce inflation, Zijlstra advised, wage settlements should be kept in check for a number of years.

On May 26 national elections for the 150-seat lower house of Parliament took place. During the election campaign it became evident that the main political parties had different opinions about the future composition of the Cabinet. The Christian Democratic Appeal (CDA) did not declare itself in favour of a particular coalition, but the Liberal Party (VVD) wanted a national Cabinet based on the support of all the main political parties. The Socialist Party (PVDA) wanted a left-wing Cabinet, but the Democratic Party (D'66) was in favour of a Cabinet based on the support of the CDA, the PVDA, and itself.

The results of the voting surprised most of the politicians. The PVDA suffered the heaviest losses (from 53 to 44 seats), and D'66 made the greatest gains (up from 8 to 17 seats). The VVD lost two, leaving it with 26 seats, and the CDA one, giving it a total of 48 seats. The Cabinet of Prime Minister Andreas van Agt, based on a Christian Democrat-Liberal coalition, had lost its slender majority, so a new coalition had to be made. On September 11 the CDA, the PVDA, and D'66 reached a satisfactory agreement on policies and individuals, and the new Cabinet was sworn in by Queen Beatrix.

The main points of friction during the formation of the coalition were the respective positions of Andreas van Agt (CDA) and Joop den Uyl (PVDA); the allowable financial deficit of the government; and the employment program, aimed at combating unemployment. The CDA, which had emerged from the elections as the biggest single party, wanted van Agt as prime minister. The PVDA wanted den Uyl in that position as a symbol of a new, progressive policy. The personalities of the two politicians were quite different, and relations between them had always been a source of strain. Ultimately, the three parties agreed on van Agt as prime minister, with den Uyl as minister of social affairs. Jan Terlouw, the leader of D'66, became minister of economic affairs. The parties also reached agreement on the questions of the government deficit and the employment program.

However, before the Cabinet presented the lower house with the outlines of its policy and an account of the coalition, a Cabinet crisis broke out. The CDA and D'66 members of the Cabinet refused to accept the proposals of the PVDA members regarding the financing of the employment program. Thanks to the work of two well-known socialist economists, who acted as mediators, the three parties reached agreement again. On November 16 the Cabinet was ready to present itself to Parliament.

On November 21 some 400,000 people marched through Amsterdam in what was described as the largest demonstration ever held in The Netherlands. The demonstration protested against the deployment of any new nuclear weapons in Europe and called on the Dutch government to reverse its decision to approve NATO plans to modernize theatre nuclear weapons. Representatives from the PVDA and D'66 took part in the rally, but official government policy did not support its aims. Government policy continued to take the view that a decision on the deployment of new missiles was dependent on the outcome of East-West negotiations on disarmament and control of nuclear weapons. (DICK BOONSTRA)

See also Dependent States.

Activists opposed to nuclear energy staged a demonstration of the "victims of a nuclear pile accident" in The Netherlands in February. The protesters were seeking the closure of a nuclear power station.

KEYSTONE

New Zealand

New Zealand

New Zealand, a parliamentary state and member of the Commonwealth, is in the South Pacific Ocean, separated from southeastern Australia by the Tasman Sea. The country consists of North and South islands and Stewart, Chatham, and other minor islands. Area: 269,057 sq km (103,883 sq mi). Pop. (1981 est.): 3,117,000. Cap.: Wellington (pop., 1981 prelim., 134,700). Largest city: Christchurch (pop., 1981 prelim., 164,300). Largest urban area: Auckland (pop., 1981 prelim., 144,600). Language: English (official), Maori. Religion (1976): Church of England 35%; Presbyterian 22%; Roman Catholic 16%. Queen, Elizabeth II; governor-general in 1981, Sir David Stuart Beattie; prime minister, Robert David Muldoon.

New Zealand's National Party government, led by Prime Minister Robert Muldoon, appeared to be more threatened by the rising star of Social Credit than by the opposition Labour Party as the general election of Nov. 28, 1981, approached. Battling rising inflation and pitting industrial expansion plans against enervating unemployment, National feared a tight finish in which the third party might hold the balance of power.

The closeness of the election was evidenced by

NEW ZEALAND

Education. (1980) Primary, pupils 506,602, teachers 20,-402; secondary, pupils 226,346, teachers 13,527; vocational, pupils 145,075, teachers 2,216; higher, students 57,141, teaching staff 3,682.

Finance. Monetary unit: New Zealand dollar, with (Sept. 21, 1981) a free rate of NZ$1.16 to U.S. $1 (NZ$2.22 = £1 sterling). Gold and other reserves (June 1981) U.S. $361 million. Budget (1979–80 est.): revenue NZ$6,560,000,-000; expenditure NZ$7,587,000,000. Gross national product (1979–80) NZ$20,441,000,000. Money supply (June 1981) NZ$2,697,200,000. Cost of living (1975 = 100; 2nd quarter 1981) 225.7.

Foreign Trade. (1980) Imports NZ$5,615,900,000; exports NZ$5,568,500,000. Import sources: Australia 19%; U.S. 14%; Japan 14%; U.K. 12%; Singapore 6%; Saudi Arabia 6%. Export destinations: U.S. 14%; U.K. 14%; Australia 13%; Japan 13%. Main exports (1979–80): wool 18%; dairy products 13%; lamb and mutton 11%; beef and veal 10%. Tourism (1979): visitors 432,400; gross receipts U.S. $191 million.

Transport and Communications. Roads (1980) 93,353 km. Motor vehicles in use (1980): passenger 1,307,300; commercial 247,700. Railways (1979): 4,543 km; traffic (1980) 414 million passenger-km, freight 3,184,000,000 net ton-km. Air traffic (1980): 5,725,000,000 passenger-km; freight 193.3 million net ton-km. Shipping (1980): merchant vessels 100 gross tons and over 122; gross tonnage 263,543. Telephones (Jan. 1980) 1,729,900. Radio receivers (Dec. 1977) 2,725,000. Television licenses (Dec. 1980) 891,081.

Agriculture. Production (in 000; metric tons; 1980): wheat 325; barley 295; oats 64; corn 187; potatoes (1979) c. 280; dry peas c. 59; tomatoes c. 43; wine c. 44; apples 201; milk c. 6,770; butter 249; cheese 100; wool 252; sheepskins (1979) c. 109; mutton and lamb 559; beef and veal c. 470; fish catch (1979) 110; timber (cu m; 1979) c. 9,003. Livestock (in 000; June 1980): cattle 8,165; sheep 68,765; pigs c. 540; chickens c. 6,400.

Industry. Production (in 000; metric tons; 1980): coal 1,924; lignite 196; crude oil 330; natural gas (cu m) 1,183,-000; manufactured gas (cu m) 55,000; electricity (excluding most industrial production; kw-hr) 22,011,000; cement 719; aluminum (1979) 154; petroleum products (1979) 2,-812; phosphate fertilizers (1979–80) c. 410; wood pulp 1,142; paper 684.

the fact that initially a "hung" Parliament resulted (National 46; Labour 44; Social Credit 2); after recounts and absentee votes had been taken into account, National finally won a slender majority of two. (See POLITICAL PARTIES.) Social Credit had rested its case on the personal appeal of its leader, Bruce Beetham, and some common-sense policies. Labour had provided a comprehensive alternative program, faintly tinged with socialist solutions, and relied less than at the last election on the charisma of its leader, Wallace Rowling.

Growth or the promise of it had been National's major election concern. Plans to convert natural gas through methanol to gasoline were aimed at making New Zealand 30% self-sufficient in gasoline by 1987, which would result in foreign exchange savings of NZ$170 million annually. But Mobil Oil Corp., the company behind the project, declined to commit itself until after the election.

A 5% general cost-of-living increase in wages in May was followed by renegotiations that promised an 11% rise; this was expected to nudge inflation up to 15–17% in 1982. An economic research institute predicted real growth of gross domestic product at 3.5% and a NZ$1.5 billion external debt in 1982–83.

New Zealand was deeply divided by the issues surrounding the tour of South African rugby union football players in the summer. The tour was opposed by a significant proportion of New Zealanders, who preferred isolation of South Africans as the best means of campaigning against the republic's racial separation policies. Tour supporters argued that some contact provided the best way of influencing South Africans on the issue.

When tour opponents forced their way into the stadium at Hamilton and caused a game to be canceled, rugby fans turned on the demonstrators and began a more violent, potentially explosive, phase of the confrontations. Police adopted riot gear and paramilitary operations to ensure that a legal sporting program continued, and the factions were kept apart. Demonstrators never rivaled match-goers in numbers, but they created siege conditions around the playing fields, and the last international match was flour-bombed by a protester in an airplane. The government insisted that under the 1977 Commonwealth Gleneagles Agreement and its own preelection promises it could not deny its sportsmen and women contact with South Africans, and in October, at the Commonwealth heads of government meeting in Melbourne, Australia, Muldoon challenged delegates to prove otherwise. Some would have liked to have seen the same force used to persuade the Rugby Union not to accept the tour.

In other developments during the year, passports were introduced between New Zealand and Australia in an attempt to curb the movement of criminals; a public information bill was put aside until 1982; the government suffered some injury from an inquiry report on a land loan to a minister's son-in-law; and eight Air New Zealand executives were routinely suspended in the aftermath of the 1979 airliner disaster in Antarctica.

(JOHN A. KELLEHER)

See also Dependent States.

Nicaragua

The largest country of Central America, Nicaragua is a republic bounded by Honduras, Costa Rica, the Caribbean Sea, and the Pacific Ocean. Area: 128,875 sq km (49,759 sq mi). Pop. (1981 est.): 2,-465,000. Cap. and largest city: Managua (pop., 1978 est., 517,700). Language: Spanish. Religion: Roman Catholic. In 1981 the nation was governed by a five-member (after March 5 a three-member) Junta of the Government of National Reconstruction.

During 1981 the Sandinista National Liberation Front government consolidated the position it had held in Nicaragua since the overthrow of the late Gen. Anastasio Somoza in 1979. However, the revolutionary regime faced increasing problems. The U.S. administration of Pres. Ronald Reagan announced in April that it had suspended economic aid to Nicaragua; this was expected to have serious effects on a country that was heavily dependent on financial assistance from abroad for reconstruction and development.

Relations with the U.S. suffered another setback because of publicized reports early in the year that some 600 Nicaraguan exiles hostile to the government were undergoing military training in Florida. Nicaragua asked the U.S. government to condemn the exiles' activities. U.S. Secretary of State Alexander Haig replied that the training was not illegal unless it could be shown to be part of a plan to invade a friendly country. The U.S., on the other hand, accused the Nicaraguan government

of delivering arms to the El Salvador guerrillas and condemned Nicaragua's own military buildup. The Sandinistas denied that they were still shipping weapons to El Salvador and said that they considered the buildup necessary because of the U.S. support given to their enemies in the region.

Repeated tension on the border with Honduras flared up again in October. The government called for a civilian and military mobilization in response to what it saw as a threat of invasion from Honduras, where some 4,000 former Nicaraguan national guardsmen fled after the revolution.

In March it was reported that the ruling junta had reduced its membership from five to three. Outgoing members Arturo Cruz Porras and Moisés Hassán Morales were appointed ambassador to the U.S. and president of the Council of State, respectively.

Nicaragua's gross domestic product (GDP) grew by 10.7% in 1980, as compared with a fall of 26% in 1979. The junta's latest development plan forecast a GDP increase of 18.5% for 1981.

(MARTA BEKERMAN DE FAINBOIM)

Nicaragua

Niger

Niger

A republic of north central Africa, Niger is bounded by Algeria, Libya, Chad, Nigeria, Benin, Upper Volta, and Mali. Area: 1,189,000 sq km (459,100 sq mi). Pop. (1981 est.): 5,466,000, including (1972 est.) Hausa 53.7%; Zerma and Songhai 23.6%; Fulani 10.6%; Beriberi-Manga 9.1%; Tuareg 3%. Cap. and largest city: Niamey (pop., 1977, 225,300). Language: French (official) and Sudanic dialects. Religion: Muslim 85%; animist 14.5%; Christian 0.5%. Chief of state and president of the Supreme Military Council in 1981, Col. Seyni Kountché.

Ministerial changes in February and August 1981 reinforced Pres. Seyni Kountché's personal authority over the governing Supreme Military

---

NICARAGUA

Education. (1980–81) Primary, pupils 472,167, teachers 13,318; secondary, pupils 120,522; vocational, pupils 16,-661; secondary and vocational, teachers (1977) *c.* 3,145; teacher training, students 2,560, teachers (1974) 55; higher, students 34,710, teaching staff (1976) 1,052.

Finance. Monetary unit: córdoba, with (Sept. 21, 1981) a par value of 10.05 córdobas to U.S. $1 (free rate of 18.63 córdobas = £1 sterling). Budget (1979 est.): revenue 1,751,000,000 córdobas; expenditure 2,925,000,000 córdobas. Gross domestic product (1979) 13,409,000,000 córdobas. Money supply (Dec. 1980) 4,704,300,000 córdobas. Cost of living (Managua; 1975 = 100; March 1981) 274.6.

Foreign Trade. (1980) Imports 8,916,500,000 córdobas; exports 4,526,800,000 córdobas. Import sources (1979): U.S. 25%; Venezuela 18%; Costa Rica 11%; Guatemala 10%; El Salvador 6%. Export destinations (1979): U.S. 32%; China 11%; West Germany 10%; Costa Rica 7%; Japan 5%; The Netherlands 5%; Belgium-Luxembourg 5%. Main exports (1979): coffee 28%; cotton 24%; meat 17%; chemicals *c.* 6%.

Transport and Communications. Roads (1978) 18,197 km. Motor vehicles in use (1979): passenger 37,700; commercial (including buses) *c.* 30,100. Railways: (1979) 373 km; traffic (1978) 17 million passenger-km, freight 10 million net ton-km. Air traffic (1980): *c.* 76 million passenger-km; freight *c.* 1.4 million net ton-km. Telephones (Jan. 1980) 57,900. Radio receivers (Dec. 1977) 600,000. Television receivers (Dec. 1979) *c.* 170,000.

Agriculture. Production (in 000; metric tons; 1980): corn *c.* 229; rice (1979) *c.* 21; sorghum *c.* 73; dry beans *c.* 50; sugar, raw value (1979) *c.* 223; bananas *c.* 160; oranges *c.* 52; cottonseed *c.* 37; coffee *c.* 55; cotton, lint *c.* 21. Livestock (in 000; 1979): cattle *c.* 2,846; pigs *c.* 725; horses *c.* 280; chickens *c.* 4,620.

Industry. Production (in 000; metric tons; 1978): petroleum products *c.* 560; cement 161; gold (exports; troy oz; 1980) 48; electricity (kw-hr) *c.* 1,180,000.

NIGER

Education. (1978–79) Primary, pupils 187,251, teachers (1977–78) 4,215; secondary (1977–78), pupils 21,944, teachers 831; vocational (1977–78), pupils 333, teachers 34; teacher training (1977–78), students 1,225, teachers 48; higher (1977–78), students 782, teaching staff 340.

Finance. Monetary unit: CFA franc, with (Sept. 21, 1981) a par value of CFA Fr 50 to the French franc (free rate of CFA Fr 265 = U.S. $1; CFA Fr 491 = £1 sterling). Gold and other reserves (June 1981) U.S. $140 million. Budget (1979 –80 est.) balanced at CFA Fr 72.1 billion.

Foreign Trade. (1980) Imports *c.* CFA Fr 111 billion; exports *c.* CFA Fr 97 billion. Import sources: France *c.* 45%; West Germany *c.* 8%; Libya *c.* 7%; Ivory Coast *c.* 7%. Export destinations: France *c.* 74%; West Germany *c.* 16%; Sweden *c.* 5%. Main exports (1977): uranium 74%; fruit and vegetables 10%; livestock 9%.

Transport and Communications. Roads (1980) 8,219 km. Motor vehicles in use (1980): passenger 25,800; commercial 4,400. There are no railways. Inland waterway (Niger River; 1979) *c.* 300 km. Telephones (Jan. 1977) 8,100. Radio receivers (Dec. 1971) 150,000.

Agriculture. Production (in 000; metric tons; 1980): millet 1,371; sorghum 380; rice (1979) 24; cassava (1979) *c.* 210; onions *c.* 100; peanuts *c.* 100; goat's milk *c.* 135. Livestock (in 000; 1979): cattle *c.* 2,995; sheep *c.* 2,500; goats *c.* 6,400; camels *c.* 330.

Industry. Production (in 000; metric tons; 1979): uranium 3.6; tin concentrates (metal content) *c.* 0.1; cement (1978) *c.* 37; electricity (kw-hr; 1978) *c.* 45,000.

Council. Kountché's main preoccupation during the year was Libya's involvement in Chad. His reaction to the proposed union of the two was to expel Libya's diplomatic representatives. Previously, Libyan chief of state Muammar al-Qaddafi's criticism of Niger had triggered anti-Libyan demonstrations in Niamey. Kountché maintained close relations with France, which in January reinforced its contingent of military advisers in Niger. In July and again in November Kountché was received in Paris by Pres. François Mitterrand.

Niger's economy was threatened by the falling price of uranium on the French market over the year, from Fr 490 per kilogram to Fr 400 (as against Fr 330 on the international spot market). Niger supplied more than 20% of France's uranium requirements.   (PHILIPPE DECRAENE)

Nigeria

A republic and a member of the Commonwealth, Nigeria is located in Africa north of the Gulf of Guinea, bounded by Benin, Niger, Chad, and Cameroon. Area: 923,800 sq km (356,700 sq mi). Nigeria's total population is extremely uncertain; in 1979 estimates ranged from 77 million to 104 million, with official Nigerian figures falling toward the middle of that range; principal ethnic groups were Hausa 21%; Yoruba 20%; Ibo 17%;

Nigeria

NIGERIA

Education. (1979–80) Primary, pupils 11,457,772, teachers (1978–79) 287,040; secondary, pupils (1978–79) 1,159,404, teachers (1973–74) 19,409; vocational, pupils 45,095, teachers (1973–74) 1,120; teacher training, students 234,680, teachers (1973–74) 2,360; higher, students (1978–79) 101,210, teaching staff (1975–76) 5,019.

Finance. Monetary unit: naira, with (Sept. 21, 1981) a free rate of 0.66 naira to U.S. $1 (1.23 naira = £1 sterling). Gold and other reserves (June 1981) U.S. $8,638,000,000. Federal budget (1979–80): revenue 8,805,000,000 naira; expenditure 9,510,000,000 naira (including 6,610,000,000 naira capital expenditure). Gross domestic product (1978–79) 28,737,000,000 naira. Money supply (April 1981) 8,948,400,000 naira. Cost of living (1975 = 100; June 1980) 194.8.

Foreign Trade. (1980) Imports (f.o.b.) c. 8,147,000,000 naira; exports 14,689,000,000 naira. Import sources: U.K. c. 19%; West Germany c. 12%; Japan c. 10%; France c. 9%; U.S. c. 8%; The Netherlands c. 6%; Italy c. 5%. Export destinations: U.S. c. 43%; West Germany c. 12%; The Netherlands c. 11%; France c. 11%. Main export: crude oil 95%.

Transport and Communications. Roads (1980) 107,990 km. Motor vehicles in use (1980): passenger 215,-400; commercial 33,100. Railways: (1978) 3,505 km; traffic (1974–75) 785 million passenger-km, freight 972 million net ton-km. Air traffic (1980): c. 1,877,000,000 passenger-km; freight c. 11.1 million net ton-km. Shipping (1980): merchant vessels 100 gross tons and over 116; gross tonnage 498,202. Telephones (June 1980) 154,200. Radio receivers (Dec. 1977) 5,250,000. Television receivers (Dec. 1977) 450,000.

Agriculture. Production (in 000; metric tons; 1980): millet c. 3,200; sorghum c. 3,800; corn c. 1,550; rice c. 725; sweet potatoes (1979) c. 230; yams (1979) c. 15,000; cassava (1979) c. 11,500; tomatoes c. 400; peanuts c. 570; palm oil c. 675; cocoa c. 175; cotton, lint c. 30; rubber c. 60; fish catch (1979) 535. Livestock (in 000; 1980): cattle c. 12,300; sheep c. 11,700; goats c. 24,000; pigs c. 1,100; poultry c. 120,000.

Industry. Production (in 000; metric tons; 1980): crude oil 102,209; natural gas (cu m) c. 1,070,000; cement (1978) 1,541; tin concentrates (metal content) 2.5; petroleum products (1978) 2,833; electricity (kw-hr; 1979) c. 5,200,-000.

Fulani 9%. Cap.: Lagos (metro. pop., 1980 est., 4.1 million). Largest city: Ibadan (metro. pop., 1980 est., 6 million). Language: English (official), Hausa, Yoruba, and Ibo. Religion (1963): Muslim 47%; Christian 34%. President in 1981, Alhaji Shehu Shagari.

For Nigeria 1981 began on a gloomy note. Riots in Kano during the last two weeks of December 1980, in which at least 200 people were killed, were reported to have involved members of a fundamentalist Muslim sect, foreign agents, and other antigovernment factions. In July further riots in Kano, in which four people died, arose because of a dispute between the traditional emir of the state and the elected governor, a member of the small, radical People's Redemption Party (PRP), and two people died in riots following the PRP convention in December. The incident highlighted the problems that the government faced in its attempts to implement the two-year-old constitution and to devolve power to Nigeria's 19 states.

A further controversy, in the state of Kaduna, increased pressure on the already shaky coalition between the National Party of Nigeria (NPN) and the Nigerian People's Party (NPP). The PRP governor of Kaduna had been unable to pass legislation through the NPN-dominated state assembly since the 1979 elections; the NPN then resolved the crisis by impeaching the governor. In protest the NPP formally quit the coalition in July, leaving the NPN to carry on a minority government.

Nigeria's Pres. Alhaji Shehu Shagari paid a state visit to London in March, and U.K. Foreign Secretary Lord Carrington journeyed to Lagos in February. Nigeria attempted to persuade Britain to alter its policy toward South Africa, but Lord Carrington reiterated Britain's claim that sanctions against South Africa would not work. The president did not succeed, either, in changing British policies concerning South West Africa/Namibia.

Nigeria continued its leadership of the Economic Community of West African States. An incident on May 16 on the Nigeria-Cameroon border, in which five Nigerian soldiers were killed, led to concern that a new area of tension was emerging. The incident was discussed at the Organization of African Unity summit conference in June.

The year opened with an annual budget forecast of 14,750,000,000 naira, with an increase in both capital and recurrent expenditure. The fourth national development plan (1981–85), outlined in January, envisioned total expenditure of 82 billion naira (as against 43 billion naira for the third plan). Emphasis was placed on the need to maintain existing infrastructure: 6.6 billion naira was to be spent on the upkeep of roads, airports, and ports. The president, acknowledging the failure of the agricultural sector to reach production targets, recommended increased aid to small farmers, who produced 90% of agricultural output; while food demand increased at 3.5% annually, current production was rising by only 1%, risking the dangerous deficit of 5.5 million tons by 1985.

Problems of financing the fourth plan were increased by declining oil production and revenue. Nigeria, dependent upon oil for more than 90% of export earnings and government revenues, experi-

enced a fall in production from 2,090,000 bbl a day in January 1981 to 640,000 bbl a day in August. In December measures to discourage imports were announced, and the 1982 budget was cut back by 10%. Exchange reserves declined from 5 billion naira in February to 2 billion naira in July.

National celebrations on October 1 to celebrate 21 years of independence included amnesty for Gen. Yakubu Gowon and 14 prisoners convicted after the 1976 coup attempt. The rejoicing was marred, however, when in the same month the Supreme Court declared invalid the controversial 1981 Revenue Allocation bill, which provided 58.5% of total revenue to the federal government, 31.5% to the states, and 10% to local government. The decision entailed a return to the 1978 allocations of 75% for the federal government, 22% for the states, and 3% for local units. The verdict, though a triumph for legal independence, was feared by many to be economically unsound.

(MOLLY MORTIMER)

Norway

A constitutional monarchy of northern Europe, Norway is bordered by Sweden, Finland, and the U.S.S.R.; its coastlines are on the Skagerrak, the North Sea, the Norwegian Sea, and the Arctic Ocean. Area: 323,895 sq km (125,057 sq mi), excluding the Svalbard Archipelago, 62,048 sq km, and Jan Mayen Island, 373 sq km. Pop. (1981 est.): 4,099,900. Cap. and largest city: Oslo (pop., 1981 est., 451,000). Language: Norwegian. Religion: Lutheran (94%). King, Olav V; prime ministers in 1981, Odvar Nordli until February 4, Gro Harlem Brundtland until October 14, and, from October 14, Kåre Isaachsen Willoch.

In February 1981 ailing Prime Minister Odvar Nordli was replaced as head of Norway's minority Labour government by Gro Harlem Brundtland, deputy chairman of the Labour Party and former environment minister. Norway's first woman prime minister, she was also the first middle-class academic ever to lead a Labour Cabinet.

Brundtland took over the premiership only seven months before the parliamentary elections, at a time when her party was divided on many issues and opinion polls were showing widespread public dissatisfaction with the Labour government's performance. Under her firm leadership the government bettered its rating in the public opinion polls, and party unity improved.

There was too much ground to be made up, however, and many Norwegians felt the need for a change after eight years of Labour rule. As was widely expected, the Conservatives and their parliamentary allies, the Centre and Christian People's parties, won a clear majority in the elections on September 13–14. (For tabulated results, *see* POLITICAL PARTIES.) A month later, after the Storting (parliament) had assembled, a minority Conservative government took over under the leadership of Kåre Isaachsen Willoch (*see* BIOGRAPHIES). It was Norway's first all-Conservative administration in more than 50 years.

On the economic front, oil and gas production

Prime Minister Gro Harlem Brundtland (right) held office for only seven months before she was succeeded by Conservative Party leader Kåre Willoch (left) following elections in September. Willoch, who was unable to arrange a coalition with allied parties, formed Norway's first all-Conservative minority government in over half a century.

from Norway's continental shelf stopped rising in 1981, causing stagnation in the country's economic growth for the first time since World War II. The gross national product rose by only 0.1% from 1980 to 1981. Petroleum output leveled off, sooner than

NORWAY

Education. (1979–80) Primary, pupils 593,579, teachers 31,719; secondary and vocational, pupils 178,514, teachers 14,204; teacher training, students 12,734, teachers 1,049; higher, students 40,643, teaching staff 3,648.

Finance. Monetary unit: Norwegian krone, with (Sept. 21, 1981) a free rate of 5.80 kroner to U.S. $1 (10.74 kroner = £1 sterling). Gold and other reserves (June 1981) U.S. $6,259,000,000. Budget (1981 est.): revenue 100,520,000,000 kroner; expenditure 104,742,000,000 kroner. Gross national product (1980) 273.7 billion kroner. Money supply (May 1981) 46,740,000,000 kroner. Cost of living (1975 = 100; June 1981) 170.

Foreign Trade. (1980) Imports 83,747,000,000 kroner; exports 91,332,000,000 kroner. Import sources: Sweden 17%; U.K. 15%; West Germany 14%; U.S. 8%; Denmark 6%. Export destinations: U.K. 41%; West Germany 17%; Sweden 9%. Main exports: crude oil 31%; natural gas 14%; machinery 6%; chemicals 6%; aluminum 5%.

Transport and Communications. Roads (1980) 81,718 km (including 56 km expressways). Motor vehicles in use (1980): passenger 1,233,600; commercial 152,500. Railways: (1979) 4,239 km (including 2,440 km electrified); traffic (1980) 2,380,000,000 passenger-km, freight 3,080,000,000 net ton-km. Air traffic (including Norwegian apportionment of international operations of Scandinavian Airlines System; 1980): c. 4,068,000,000 passenger-km; freight c. 136 million net ton-km. Shipping (1980): merchant vessels 100 gross tons and over 2,501; gross tonnage 22,007,490. Shipping traffic (1980): goods loaded 37,185,000 metric tons, unloaded 22,554,000 metric tons. Telephones (Dec. 1979) 1,725,100. Radio licenses (Dec. 1977) 1,313,000. Television licenses (Dec. 1979) 1,173,100.

Agriculture. Production (in 000; metric tons; 1980): barley c. 670; oats c. 400; potatoes c. 568; apples c. 40; milk (1979) c. 1,878; cheese 69; beef and veal (1979) c. 72; pork (1979) c. 81; timber (cu m; 1979) 8,082; fish catch (1979) 2,652. Livestock (in 000; June 1979): cattle 971; sheep 1,919; pigs 711; goats c. 74; chickens c. 3,744.

Industry. Fuel and power (in 000; metric tons; 1980): crude oil 24,407; coal (Svalbard mines; Norwegian operated only) 284; natural gas (cu m) 25,124,000; manufactured gas (cu m) 13,000; electricity (kw-hr) 83,985,000. Production (in 000; metric tons; 1980): iron ore (65% metal content) 3,807; pig iron 1,429; crude steel 867; aluminum 652; copper 26; zinc 79; cement 2,092; petroleum products c. 7,800; sulfuric acid 354; fertilizers (nutrient content; 1979–80) nitrogenous 452, phosphate 146; fish meal (1978) 331; wood pulp (1978) mechanical 791, chemical 666; newsprint 588; other paper (1978) 657. Merchant vessels launched (100 gross tons and over; 1980) 315,000 gross tons. New dwelling units completed (1980) 38,100.

Norway

Nobel Prizes:
see People of the Year

Norwegian Literature:
see Literature

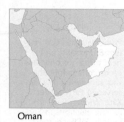

Oman

Pakistan

expected, because production from Norway's Ekofisk field began declining more rapidly than forecast, having reached its peak in 1980. This fall was offset by increased production from the Norwegian portion of the Statfjord field. There were fears, however, that the real value of Norway's oil and gas could fall in 1982 if the world oil glut should continue.

The budget for 1982, presented by the minority Labour government just before its resignation in October, indicated that Norwegians could expect no increase in living standards during the coming year. It provided for increases in the income tax and many indirect taxes in order to offset concessions on company taxation approved earlier in the year. Some substantial increases were proposed in charges for a wide range of public services. Public spending was held at about the previous year's level, in real terms. The new Conservative government proposed some modest changes in the budget, in line with tax-cut promises made during the election campaign.

Norwegians continued to enjoy virtually full employment and a higher standard of living than most of their neighbours, although the world recession adversely affected some export industries. In the summer the Storting approved several large offshore development projects that were expected to generate hundreds of new jobs over the next four to five years. The package included an 843-km (524-mi) undersea pipeline to link the Statfjord field with the continent, and development of two additional fields on the Norwegian shelf.

The excess of demand in the economy led to inflation at a rate of about 14% during the first nine months of 1981 and, consequently, to strong pressure from wage earners for pay increases to keep pace. In a number of important industries the Labour government ordered compulsory arbitration of wage disputes. Resentment over the government's tactics led to an unusually high number of wildcat strikes. In August, to prevent a round of pay increases in the autumn, the Labour government ordered a virtual price freeze, to extend until the end of the year, and temporarily lowered income tax rates. (FAY GJESTER)

See also Dependent States.

Oman

An independent sultanate, Oman occupies the southeastern part of the Arabian Peninsula and is bounded by the United Arab Emirates, Saudi Arabia, Yemen (Aden), the Gulf of Oman, and the Arabian Sea. A small part of the country lies to the north and is separated from the rest of Oman by the United Arab Emirates. Area: 300,000 sq km (120,000 sq mi). Pop. (1981 est.): 919,000; for planning purposes the government of Oman uses an estimate of 1.5 million. No census has ever been taken. Cap.: Muscat (pop., 1973 est., 15,000). Largest city: Matrah (pop., 1973 est., 18,000). Language: Arabic. Religion: Muslim (of which Ibadi 75%; Sunni 25%). Sultan and prime minister in 1981, Qabus ibn Sa'id.

Sultan Qabus ibn Sa'id of Oman fulfilled a 1980 pledge by appointing a 45-member advisory council in October 1981. Its president, former labour and social affairs minister Khalfan Nasir al-Wahaibi, said that the council would apply a "second mind" to government thinking at its four annual meetings.

Qabus, who planned a state visit to the U.K. in March 1982, was a founder member of the six-nation Gulf Cooperation Council inaugurated in March 1981. In view of its poor relations with Yemen (Aden), Oman wished to convince its Gulf neighbours of the need for cooperation in matters of security. A military-access agreement concluded with the U.S. in 1980 was implemented when the U.S. began improving military facilities on Masirah Island and other air bases.

It was thought that lower oil prices in 1982 could lead Oman to revise an ambitious five-year plan begun in January 1981. The spending target of over $21 billion was to be paid for by crude-oil exports of about 330,000 bbl a day and earnings from a copper-ore project. The Qabus University proposed by the sultan in his 1980 national-day address as a gift to the nation was expected to proceed, but it was resited from Nazwa to Rusail in the capital. Also at Rusail, a light-industry zone was planned, to create more revenue-earning enterprises. Oman's biggest trading partners in 1981 were Japan and the U.K. (JOHN WHELAN)

Pakistan

A federal republic, Pakistan is bordered on the south by the Arabian Sea, on the west by Afghanistan and Iran, on the north by China, and on the east by India. Area: 796,095 sq km (307,374 sq mi), excluding the Pakistani-controlled section of Jammu and Kashmir. Pop. (1981 prelim.): 83.7 million. Cap.: Islamabad (pop., 1972, 77,300). Largest city: Karachi (metro. area pop., 1980 est., 5,005,000). Language: Urdu and English. Religion: Muslim 97% (of which Sunni 70%; Shi'ah 30%); Hindu 1.6%; Christian 1.4%. President in 1981, Gen. Mohammad Zia-ul-Haq.

The martial law regime, in power since July 1977, further strengthened its hold on Pakistan on March 24, 1981, when the chief martial law administrator and president, Mohammad Zia-ul-

PAKISTAN

Education. (1979–80) Primary, pupils 7,090,000, teachers 139,300; secondary, pupils 1,996,000, teachers 115,-600; higher, students 349,259, teaching staff 19,878.

Finance. Monetary unit: Pakistan rupee, with (Sept. 21, 1981) a par value of PakRs 9.90 to U.S. $1 (free rate of PakRs 18.35 = £1 sterling). Gold and other reserves (June 1981) U.S. $1,133,000,000. Budget (1980–81 est.) balanced at PakRs 37,181,000,000. Gross national product (1979–80) PakRs 253,710,000,000. Money supply (June 1981) PakRs 72,734,000,000. Cost of living (1975 = 100; June 1981) 172.

Foreign Trade. (1980) Imports PakRs 52,968,000,000; exports PakRs 25,923,000,000. Import sources (1979–80): Japan 12%; U.S. 11%; Kuwait 10%; Saudi Arabia 7%; U.K. 6%; West Germany 5%; France 5%. Export destinations (1979–80): Hong Kong 8%; Japan 8%; China 6%; United Arab Emirates 6%; West Germany 6%; Saudi Arabia 5%; U.S. 5%; U.K. 5%. Main exports (1979–80): rice 18%; cotton 14%; cotton fabrics 10%; carpet 9%; cotton yarn 9%; petroleum products 7%; leather 5%.

Transport and Communications. Roads (1980) 87,069 km. Motor vehicles in use (1980): passenger 135,700; commercial 36,100. Railways: (1980) 8,815 km; traffic (1979–80) 16,510,000,000 passenger-km, freight 9,370,000,000 net ton-km. Air traffic (1980): 5,696,000,000 passenger-km; freight 241.3 million net ton-km. Shipping (1980): merchant vessels 100 gross tons and over 84; gross tonnage 478,019. Telephones (Jan. 1980) 314,000. Radio receivers (Dec. 1977) 5 million. Television receivers (Dec. 1977) 625,000.

Agriculture. Production (in 000; metric tons; 1980): wheat 10,805; corn c. 963; rice 4,595; millet c. 330; sorghum c. 280; potatoes c. 395; sugar, raw value 625; sugar, noncentrifugal (1979) c. 1,700; chick-peas 313; onions c. 390; rapeseed 247; cottonseed c. 1,400; mangoes c. 560; dates c. 205; oranges c. 515; tobacco c. 70; cotton, lint c. 700; beef and buffalo meat 344; mutton and goat meat 313; fish catch (1979) 300. Livestock (in 000; 1980): cattle 15,-038; buffalo 11,547; sheep 26,239; goats 30,203; camels (1979) c. 830; chickens 56,672.

Industry. Production (in 000; metric tons; 1980): cement 3,503; crude oil 484; coal and lignite 1,695; natural gas (cu m) 8,140,000; petroleum products (1978) c. 3,940; electricity (excluding most industrial production; kw-hr) 16,148,000; sulfuric acid 56; caustic soda 40; soda ash (1979–80) 79; nitrogenous fertilizers (nutrient content; 1979–80) 399; cotton yarn 368; woven cotton fabrics (sq m) 355,000.

Hostages were released from a Pakistani airliner in Damascus, Syria, in March after the Pakistan government released 54 political prisoners as demanded by the hijackers.

Haq, promulgated a provisional constitution order that came into force at once. It envisaged a government set up under martial law for an unspecified interim period. The order was promulgated because the constitution of 1973 (suspended in 1977) had not provided for the imposition of martial law, and the legality of the regime had been challenged in the courts. A month earlier the authorities had arrested several opposition politicians who had led a campaign to restore democracy.

The order conferred unfettered powers on the president through Art. 16, which read: "The president as well as chief martial law administrator shall have and shall be deemed always to have had the power to amend the constitution." The order also declared void any court judgments dealing with the legality of the martial law regime and provided for a nominated Federal Advisory Council, which was established in December. President Zia said the 350-member council would have no decision-making powers.

A Pakistan International Airlines aircraft was hijacked to Kabul, Afghanistan, on March 2. Al Zulfikar, an organization led by Murtaza Ali Bhutto, son of the executed former president Zulfikar Ali Bhutto, claimed responsibility. The hijackers shot and fatally wounded a passenger, Tariq

Rahim, a Pakistani diplomat. Some passengers were released, but negotiations faltered and the aircraft was flown to Damascus, Syria. Finally, the Pakistan government released 54 political prisoners in response to the hijackers' demands, and on March 14 the passengers and crew were set free. Granted temporary refuge by the Syrian authorities, the hijackers later returned to Kabul.

On the economic front, there was an improvement in agricultural production. The economy maintained a growth rate of about 5%. A World Bank release, announcing assistance pledged by donors at a meeting held in Paris in June, "appreciated the positive economic progress made by Pakistan during the last year." Assistance worth $1,170,000,000 for 1981–82 was pledged at the meeting. In view of the heavy economic burden caused by the influx of Afghan refugees, the bank promised an additional $110 million. A conservative estimate put the number of Afghan refugees in Pakistan by mid-1981 at over two million.

The security situation stemming from the Soviet military intervention in Afghanistan continued to influence foreign relations. The principal development in this area was the emerging military relationship between Pakistan and the U.S. It was disclosed in June that the two countries had agreed on a six-year program of economic assistance and credits for military sales, including F-16 fighter planes. The package was worth approximately $3 billion. Foreign Minister Agha Shahi declared, in clarification, that "Pakistan accepts no obligation which affects in any manner whatsoever its commitment to the principles and purposes of the nonaligned movement and the Organization of the Islamic Conference." However, the introduction of more sophisticated arms further soured Pakistan's relations with India.

Reports persisted that Pakistan proposed to explode a nuclear device soon, despite repeated assertions by President Zia that the country had no intention of manufacturing a nuclear bomb and that its nuclear development was meant only for

peaceful purposes. The budget for 1981–82 showed that Pakistan was to spend $56.3 million on its nuclear development projects. In 1980–81 the projects—a nuclear power plant and a nuclear reprocessing plant that would provide its fuel—were allotted $40 million, though actual expenditure was $49 million.   (GOVINDAN UNNY)

Panama

Papua New Guinea

Panama

A republic of Central America, Panama is bounded by the Caribbean Sea, Colombia, the Pacific Ocean, and Costa Rica. Area: 77,082 sq km (29,762 sq mi). Pop. (1980): 1,824,800. Cap. and largest city: Panama City (pop., 1980, 386,400). Language: Spanish. Religion (1979 est.): Roman Catholic 87%. President in 1981, Aristides Royo.

Panamanians were pleased to see ships passing through the Panama Canal in record numbers, but ship captains were irritated by the necessity of waiting in long lines for their turn to enter the channel. The costs of operating the canal were much larger than the income. A further disappointment was the slow rate at which Panamanians attained higher posts in the canal administration.

At the end of 1980 Panama successfully mounted a campaign for a seat on the UN Security Council, motivated in part by suspicions of the course that then U.S. President-elect Ronald Reagan might adopt toward Panama and the canal. When Cuba, supported by Panama's strong man, Omar Torrijos Herrera (*see* OBITUARIES), failed to gain the seat, that country threw its support to Panama. About six months later Torrijos was killed in a plane crash near Penonomé. Col. Florençio Flórez Aguilar was chosen to succeed him as commander of the National Guard, but the general staff of the Guard was inclined to assume some of the functions that Flórez might have expected to exercise.

Relations between Panama and Colombia improved when they ratified a treaty in which the former granted free transit of the canal, to take effect some time in the future. On the other hand, Panama displayed nervousness about the Cuban

Mourners lined the streets of Panama City during the funeral of Gen. Omar Torrijos Herrera, who died in an airplane crash on July 31.

presence in Nicaragua. Torrijos refused to attend an anniversary celebration of the Sandinista victory there. Panama was host to an international conference of Socialist parties which met to promote mediation in El Salvador.

In June and July a number of clashes between students and police occurred, triggered by the depressed economy and high prices. Higher oil prices and the flight of capital prompted attempts to renegotiate foreign debts. A glimmer of improvement appeared in the form of a small loan from the Inter-American Development Bank, destined to go to small farmers for banana-cacao cultivation.

(ALMON R. WRIGHT)

Papua New Guinea

Papua New Guinea is an independent parliamentary state and a member of the Commonwealth. It is situated in the southwest Pacific and comprises the eastern part of the island of New Guinea, the islands of the Bismarck, Trobriand, Woodlark, Louisiade, and D'Entrecasteaux groups, and parts of the Solomon Islands, including Bougainville. It is separated from Australia by the Torres Strait. Area: 462,840 sq km (178,704 sq mi). Pop. (1980 prelim.): 3,006,800. Cap. and largest city: Port Moresby (pop., 1980 prelim., 116,900). Language: English, Hiri or Police Motu (a Melanesian pidgin), and Pisin (also called Pidgin English or Neo-Melanesian) are official, although the latter is the most widely spoken. Religion (1966): Roman Catholic 31.2%; Lutheran 27.3%; indigenous 7%. Queen, Elizabeth II; governor-general in 1981, Sir Tore Lokoloko; prime minister, Sir Julius Chan.

Papua New Guinea's prime minister, Sir Julius

RANDY TAYLOR—SYGMA

PAPUA NEW GUINEA

Education. (1980) Primary, pupils 288,287, teachers 9,-280; secondary, pupils 37,068, teachers 1,559; vocational, pupils 3,992, teachers 261; teacher training, students 1,957, teachers 158; higher, students 2,224, teaching staff 374.

Finance. Monetary unit: kina, with (Sept. 21, 1981) a free rate of 0.68 kina to U.S. $1 (1.26 kinas = £1 sterling). Gold and other reserves (June 1981) U.S. $291 million. Budget (1980 est.): revenue 624.3 million kinas; expenditure 623.5 million kinas.

Foreign Trade. Imports (1979) 643 million kinas; exports (1980) 756.5 million kinas. Import sources (1979): Australia c. 49%; Japan c. 16%; Singapore c. 13%. Export destinations (1979): Japan 34%; West Germany 25%; Australia 8%; U.K. 6%; U.S. 6%. Main exports: copper concentrates 41%; coffee 16%; cocoa 6%; coconut products 5%; timber c. 5%.

Transport. Roads (1977) 17,241 km. Motor vehicles in use (1979): passenger c. 21,600; commercial (including buses) c. 27,800. There are no railways. Air traffic (1980): 520 million passenger-km; freight c. 10.2 million net ton-km. Shipping (1980): merchant vessels 100 gross tons and over 76; gross tonnage 24,904.

Agriculture. Production (in 000; metric tons; 1980): bananas c. 916; cassava (1979) c. 92; taro (1979) c. 230; yams (1979) c. 180; palm oil c. 84; cocoa 30; coffee c. 50; copra 140; tea c. 8; rubber c. 4; timber (cu m; 1979) c. 6,611. Livestock (in 000; 1979): cattle c. 136; pigs c. 1,388; goats c. 15; chickens c. 1,105.

Industry. Production (in 000; 1979): copper ore (metal content; metric tons) 171; silver (troy oz) c. 1,450; gold (troy oz) c. 630; electricity (kw-hr; 1978–79) 1,215,000.

PARAGUAY

Education. (1980) Primary, pupils 504,377, teachers 18,-038; secondary and vocational, pupils 110,095, teachers 9,830; higher, students 25,232, teaching staff 1,984.

Finance. Monetary unit: guaraní, with (Sept. 21, 1981) a par value of 126 guaranis to U.S. $1 (free rate of 234 guaranis = £1 sterling). Gold and other reserves (June 1981) U.S. $801 million. Budget (1980 est.): revenue 54,-496,000,000 guaranis; expenditure 53,494,000,000 guaranis. Gross national product (1979) 428 billion guaranis. Money supply (June 1981) 65,803,000,000 guaranis. Cost of living (Asunción; 1975 = 100; April 1981) 223.9

Foreign Trade. (1980) Imports 77,452,000,000 guaranis; exports 39,087,000,000 guaranis. Import sources: Brazil 24%; Argentina 22%; U.S. 10%; Japan 8%; Algeria 8%; West Germany 7%; U.K. 6%. Export destinations: Argentina 24%; West Germany 12%; Brazil 12%; Switzerland 10%; The Netherlands 6%; U.S. 5%. Main exports: cotton 34%; timber 21%; soybeans 14%; vegetable oils 6%.

Transport and Communications. Roads (1980) c. 15,-000 km. Motor vehicles in use (1979): passenger c. 32,100; commercial (including buses) c. 23,100. Railways: (1978) 498 km; traffic (1977) 23 million passenger-km, freight 17 million net ton-km. Air traffic (1980): c. 262 million passenger-km; freight c. 2.8 million net ton-km. Navigable inland waterways (including Paraguay-Paraná River system; 1979) c. 3,000 km. Telephones (Jan. 1977) 41,600. Radio receivers (Dec. 1977) 187,000. Television receivers (Dec. 1977) 55,000.

Agriculture. Production (in 000; metric tons; 1980): corn c. 600; cassava (1979) c. 1,494; sweet potatoes (1979) c. 124; soybeans c. 600; dry beans 65; sugar, raw value (1979) c. 69; tomatoes c. 57; oranges c. 220; bananas c. 300; palm kernels c. 16; tobacco c. 14; cottonseed c. 146; cotton, lint c. 77; beef and veal (1979) c. 62. Livestock (in 000; 1979): cattle 5,203; sheep 423; pigs 1,273; horses 334; chickens 12,471.

Industry. Production (in 000; metric tons; 1979): petroleum products (1978) c. 225; cement 155; cotton yarn (1978) 91; electricity (kw-hr) 772,000.

Paraguay

Peru

Chan, gave diplomatic priority in 1981 to maintaining good relations with Indonesia and Australia. He visited both nations during the year and obtained assurances from President Suharto that Indonesia did not wish to interfere in the affairs of its neighbours.

Chan appointed four new Cabinet ministers in March. The new team faced immediate problems when security officers discovered a plot to smuggle weapons from Papua New Guinea into the neighbouring Indonesian province of Irian Jaya.

Depressed commodity prices and relatively low production of Bougainville copper led to speculation that the International Monetary Fund might consider taking over the Papua New Guinea economy. Speaking at a symposium on energy and equity in the third world in July, former prime minister Michael Somare said that Australia had left Papua New Guinea unprepared to face the "brutal economic realities" of dependence on petroleum-based fuels. He criticized the Chan government for opposing expenditure on alternative forms of energy.   (A. R. G. GRIFFITHS)

Paraguay

A landlocked republic of South America, Paraguay is bounded by Brazil, Argentina, and Bolivia. Area: 406,752 sq km (157,048 sq mi). Pop. (1981 est.): 3,158,000. Cap. and largest city: Asunción (metro. pop., 1979 est., 673,200). Language: Spanish (official), though Guaraní is understood by more than 90% of the population. Religion: Roman Catholic (official). President in 1981, Gen. Alfredo Stroessner.

Opposition to Gen. Alfredo Stroessner's regime continued in 1981, amid public allegations of government corruption and inefficiency. The opposition coalition, the Acuerdo Nacional, which in-cluded the Partido Liberal Radical Auténtico, Partido Demócrata Cristiano (PDC), Partido Revolucionario Febrerista, and the Movimiento Popular Colorado, denounced the increasing violations of human rights that followed the assassination of Nicaragua's former president, Anastasio Somoza, in Asunción in September 1980. PDC leader Luis Alfonso Resk was deported in June 1981 after supporting a Venezuelan condemnation of Stroessner's regime. In August the country's Roman Catholic bishops published a statement criticizing the regime's rigidity and intolerance. There was international concern over the fate of the Toba-Maskoy Indians, forcibly evicted from their ancestral homelands in the Chaco in January.

At its 14th congress, in March, the Confederación Paraguaya de Trabajadores (trade union confederation), controlled by the ruling Partido Colorado since 1958, faced a growing struggle between pro-government *continuistas* and reform-oriented *aperturistas*. Paraguay's gross domestic product rose by 11.4% in 1980 as the result of an economic boom based on massive investment in hydroelectric projects.

(MARTA BEKERMAN DE FAINBOIM)

Peru

A republic on the west coast of South America, Peru is bounded by Ecuador, Colombia, Brazil, Bolivia, Chile, and the Pacific Ocean. Area: 1,285,-215 sq km (496,224 sq mi). Pop. (1980 est.): 17,780,000, including approximately 52% whites

Paper and Pulp:
see Industrial Review

Parachuting:
see Aerial Sports

Penology:
see Prisons and Penology

Pentecostal Churches:
see Religion

Petroleum:
see Energy

Pharmaceutical Industry:
see Industrial Review

PERU

Education. (1979) Primary, pupils 3,584,300, teachers (1978) 77,844; secondary and vocational, pupils 1,119,000, teachers (1978) 37,383; higher, students 278,700, teaching staff (1978) 13,468.

Finance. Monetary unit: sol, with (Sept. 21, 1981) a free rate of 430 soles to U.S. $1 (796 soles = £1 sterling). Gold and other reserves (Feb. 1981) U.S. $1,816,000,000. Budget (1981 est.): revenue 1,634,000,000,000 soles; expenditure 1,859,000,000,000 soles. Gross national product (1980) 4,-860,800,000,000 soles. Money supply (Dec. 1980) 713 billion soles. Cost of living (Lima; 1975 = 100; June 1981) 1,326.7.

Foreign Trade. (1979) Imports 490,850,000,000 soles; exports 805,820,000,000 soles. Import sources: U.S. *c.* 34%; Italy *c.* 16%; West Germany *c.* 8%; Japan *c.* 7%. Export destinations: U.S. *c.* 32%; Japan *c.* 13%. Main exports: copper 19%; lead 8%; coffee 7%; silver 7%; fish meal 7%; zinc 5%.

Transport and Communications. Roads (1976) 56,940 km. Motor vehicles in use (1979): passenger *c.* 312,000; commercial (including buses) *c.* 160,700. Railways: (1978) 2,494 km; traffic (1976) 528 million passenger-km, freight (1977) 612 million net ton-km. Air traffic (1980): 1,974,-000,000 passenger-km; freight *c.* 40.7 million net ton-km. Shipping (1980): merchant vessels 100 gross tons and over 698; gross tonnage 740,510. Telephones (Jan. 1978) 402,-500. Radio receivers (Dec. 1977) 2.2 million. Television receivers (Dec. 1977) 825,000.

Agriculture. Production (in 000; metric tons; 1980): rice 423; corn 425; wheat 85; barley *c.* 150; potatoes 1,480; sweet potatoes (1979) *c.* 166; cassava (1979) *c.* 416; sugar, raw value 550; onions *c.* 175; oranges *c.* 172; lemons *c.* 84; coffee *c.* 100; cotton, lint *c.* 98; fish catch (1979) 3,682. Livestock (in 000; 1980): cattle 3,837; sheep *c.* 14,473; pigs 2,150; goats *c.* 2,000; horses (1979) *c.* 648; poultry *c.* 37,-000.

Industry. Production (in 000; metric tons; 1978): cement 2,058; crude oil (1980) 9,654; natural gas (cu m) *c.* 1,140,000; iron ore (metal content; 1979) 2,170; pig iron 246; crude steel 377; copper (1980) 232; lead (1979) 85; zinc (1979) 69; tungsten concentrates (oxide content; 1979) *c.* 0.6; gold (troy oz; 1980) *c.* 160; silver (troy oz; 1980) *c.* 40,500; fish meal (1977) 497; petroleum products *c.* 6,080; electricity (kw-hr) *c.* 8,875,000.

and mestizos and 46% Indians. Cap. and largest city: Lima (metro. area pop., 1978 est., 4,376,100). Language: Spanish and Quechua are official; Indians also speak Aymara. Religion: Roman Catholic. President in 1981, Fernando Belaúnde Terry; prime minister, Manuel Ulloa Elías.

The sporadically recurring frontier dispute between Peru and Ecuador flared up at the beginning of 1981. Ecuador claimed that a Peruvian military helicopter had fired on an Ecuadorian border outpost in an unmarked area of the frontier. Peru claimed that Ecuadorian troops had occupied three deserted Peruvian outposts. Mediation in the dispute was entrusted to Argentina, Brazil, Chile, and the U.S., the four guarantor countries of the 1942 Protocol of Rio de Janeiro, which had settled a ten-day border war between Peru and Ecuador in 1941.

During the crisis (which ended April 2, when the frontier was reopened) Peruvian Pres. Fernando Belaúnde Terry received the full backing of all political parties and was able to use the ensuing nationalistic fervour temporarily to diffuse domestic social and political pressures. Social problems soon reemerged, however, on the rising tide of inflation, which at the end of July was running at an annual rate of 81%. Strikes for higher wages and better working conditions continued among steelworkers, mineworkers, state-employed physicians, and bank employees, although several calls by the labour unions for general strikes were largely ineffectual.

A wave of terrorist bombings that began in mid-1980 continued into 1981, and a stringent antiterrorist law—criticized by the opposition as endangering civil liberties—was enacted in March. A supposedly Maoist group known as Sendero Luminoso claimed responsibility for most of the attacks on electricity pylons, railways, and other infrastructural installations. A series of bombings in August on U.S. private and government property, including the U.S. embassy, caused thousands of dollars worth of damage; it was speculated that the attacks were the work of narcotics traffickers attempting to slow down a U.S.-assisted program against cocaine production. Interior Minister José Maria de la Jara resigned in October after a student demonstrator died in police custody.

In May Prime Minister Manuel Ulloa Elías presented a 1981–85 public investment program for consideration by the World Bank consultative group meeting in Paris. The plan included a list of 88 projects to be started by the end of 1983 with a total investment of $11.5 billion, of which $4.9 billion would be provided through external financing. Of the total, 40% would be allocated to the productive sectors (with priority for agriculture), 35% to infrastructure (priority for tourism), and 25% to the social services (priority for education). The program was favourably received.

Under special powers granted for six months to the executive by Congress in December 1980, the government issued a package of 110 legislative decrees in mid-June 1981, designed to reorganize the administration inherited from the military dictatorship. The principal decrees concerned tax reform, state companies, and mining. The goods and services tax was replaced by a value-added tax; new tax scales for individuals and companies were introduced; 27 state companies were converted into limited liability companies; and the state development finance company, Cofide, was restructured.

After the rapid improvement of the Peruvian economy in 1979–80, a significant deterioration in public finances occurred in 1981, largely because of an increase in imports and lower world prices for Peru's major export commodities such as copper, lead, silver, zinc, and other minerals. The trade deficit for the year was expected to be approximately $300 million, leading to a current account deficit of $1.5 billion and an overall deficit of $780 million. Public sector borrowing was to be increased to prevent development projects from falling behind schedule, despite already burdensome debt servicing requirements that amounted to nearly 50% of export receipts.

(SARAH CAMERON)

Philately and Numismatics

Stamps. Despite the continuing world recession, very rare philatelic items held their value. Trade in less rare stamps and postal history slumped, however, and values no longer increased to match inflation, especially in the U.K. and the U.S.

Even so, many famous collections sold well at auction. The demand for good Australian material was demonstrated by the sales of the J. R. Boker collection of Australian states for £452,133 and of the J. B. Williamson Australian Commonwealth collection for £120,871. Both sales were held in London, by Harmers and Sotheby's, respectively. At Robson Lowe's in London, a used first day (May 6, 1840) 2*d* Mulready letter sheet made a record £3,-750. Two unusual sales were those of the E. F. Hugen collection of Victorian stamp boxes and letter scales (Phillips, London) and the George T. Turner philatelic library (Roger Koerber, Southfield, Mich.), each the largest of its kind in the world.

A growing interest in forgeries for study was shown by realizations of £3,100 for a Verona postal forgery of the 1850 Lombardy-Venetia 15-centesimi red; £2,100 for a complete set of the 1933 Falkland Island "Centenary" in blocks of four with a forged Port Stanley cancellation; and £525 for a "Sperati" die proof of the 1913 Australia £2 Kangaroo, all in London sales. At the first New York sale of Robson Lowe (now the philatelic division of Christie's International), the outstanding lot was a complete imperforate sheet of the U.S. 1912–21 five-cent carmine error of colour ($32,000).

The omnibus issue for the wedding of Prince Charles and Lady Diana Spencer, issued throughout the Commonwealth and by a few non-Commonwealth countries, created a short-term boom, largely caused by speculative buying. However, most philatelists were unhappy about the expensive issues from many small Caribbean and Pacific islands and from privately owned islands with no genuine postal service. A more restrained worldwide omnibus issue promoting the UN International Year of the Disabled received good support from collectors.

The major International Philatelic Federation-sponsored exhibition was WIPA 81, held in Vienna, May 22–31. The main awards were: Grand Prix d'Honneur, Antonio Perpina (Spain) for classical Spanish issues; Grand Prix National, Emil Capellaro (West Germany) for Lombardi and Venetia; and Grand Prix International, Ryohei Ishikawa (Japan) for U.S. 1947–69. At the British Philatelic Federation congress held in Guernsey, Channel Islands, new signatories to the Roll of Distinguished Philatelists were Horst Aisslinger (West Germany), Giulio Bolaffi (Italy), James T. DeVoss (U.S.), and Harold W. Fisher (U.K.). The Philatelic Congress medal was awarded to Alfred J. Branston of Chelmsford, England, and the Lichtenstein Medal of the Collectors Club of New York to Barbara R. Mueller of Jefferson, Wis.

Leslie S. Wheeler was elected president of the Royal Philatelic Society, London, in succession to A. Ronald Butler. After 88 years, Stanley Gibbons (now owned by Esselte of Sweden) moved from its Victorian shop at 391 Strand, London, to a modern open-plan shop at 399 Strand. The reorganization of the Gibbons general stamp catalog into 22 volumes was completed under the editorship of James Negus. In June the London International Stamp Centre opened in Covent Garden.

(KENNETH F. CHAPMAN)

UPI

A display of some of the world's rarest stamps from 30 countries was shown at the philatelic fair in Stuttgart, West Germany, in April.

Coins. The event of greatest importance to coin collectors in 1981 may well have been the decision of the U.S. Congress to change the common cent from the current 95% copper alloy to copper-plated zinc containing only 2.4% copper. The Treasury planned to have a supply of these coins ready for release early in 1982.

Other numismatic activities of the U.S. government included the Bureau of Engraving and Printing's instigation of the sale of 16- and 32-note sheets of $1 paper money; the sale through local post offices of the 1981 gold bullion medals, a one-ounce depicting humorist Mark Twain and a half-ounce portraying the author Willa Cather; issuance of a congressional medal marking Canadian Ambassador Kenneth Taylor's efforts in helping six U.S. diplomatic personnel to escape from Iran; and congressional debate relative to issuing a silver dollar commemorating the 250th anniversary of George Washington's birth and several coins in support of the Olympic program.

The wedding of Prince Charles and Lady Diana Spencer prompted the most numerous issue of related coins. In addition to the wedding crown of Great Britain, 16 Commonwealth nations struck sterling silver coins marking the marriage.

The Reagan administration brought new faces into most U.S. departments concerned with coins, medals, and paper money. As treasurer of the United States, Angela M. Buchanan headed both the Bureau of the Mint and the Bureau of Engraving and Printing. Donna Pope became director of the U.S. Mint, and Elizabeth Jones, chief engraver of the U.S. Mint. Jones was the 12th chief engraver and the first woman to serve in that position.

Uncertain business and economic conditions had adverse effects on coin collecting, especially as an investment. Although the market for desirable collector items continued to be good, there was a noticeable decline in the prices of great rarities that are usually bought by investors rather than by true collectors.

Many countries issued new coins during the year, some being especially struck for collectors,

others for regular circulation. Andorra released a silver thaler dated 1980. Canada commemorated the centennial of approval to construct the Trans-Canada railway with a silver dollar and the adoption of "O Canada" as the country's national anthem with a $100 gold coin, both dated 1981. Colombia issued a 1980 one-ounce gold 30,000-peso coin to commemorate the 150th anniversary of Simon Bolívar's death. Equatorial Guinea issued gold and silver coins marking the 1979 visit of the Spanish king and queen. Finland honoured its 80-year-old president, Urho Kekkonen, in 1980 with a silver 50-markkaa coin. The first Soviet-Hungarian space flight was commemorated with a 100-forint Hungarian coin in 1980. The Isle of Man issued four coins in observance of the 60th birthday of Prince Philip.

Important medals issued during the year included the official observance of the inauguration of U.S. Pres. Ronald Reagan and several unofficial ones; a Jewish-American Hall of Fame medal honouring Rebecca Gratz; Australian gold and silver medals marking Skylab's return to Earth over Australia in July 1979; and the Corner Brook, Newfoundland, Chamber of Commerce silver jubilee "trade dollar" depicting a Newfoundland dog.

(GLENN B. SMEDLEY)

[452.D.2.b; 725.B.4.g]

Philippines

Philippines

Situated in the western Pacific Ocean off the southeast coast of Asia, the Republic of the Philippines consists of an archipelago of about 7,100 islands. Area: 300,000 sq km (115,800 sq mi). Pop. (1980): 47,914,000. Cap. and largest city: Manila (pop., metro. area, 1979 est., 5,900,600). Language: Pilipino and English are the official languages. Pilipino, the national language, is based on a local language called Tagalog and is spoken by 55.2% of

Philippine Pres. Ferdinand E. Marcos announced in January that he was lifting martial law, which had been in effect for more than eight years.

UPI

the population but only by 23.8% as a mother tongue. English is spoken by 44.7% of the population but only by 0.04% as a mother tongue. Other important languages spoken as mother tongues include Cebuano 24.4%, Ilocano 11.1%, Hiligaynon 8%, Bicol 7%; others 25.7%. Religion (1970): Roman Catholic 85%; Muslim 4.3%; Aglipayan 3.9%; Protestant 3.1%; others 2.4%. President in 1981, Ferdinand E. Marcos; prime ministers, Marcos and, from April 8, Cesar Virata.

Ferdinand E. Marcos began a new six-year term as president of the Philippines on June 30, 1981. In one of a series of political and economic changes instituted during the year, he named Finance Minister Cesar Virata (see BIOGRAPHIES) to succeed him as prime minister, a post that Marcos had also held since 1978.

The changes began on January 17 with the lifting of martial law after eight years and four months. Marcos turned over legislative power to the National Assembly, released 341 political prisoners, and said he would no longer rule by decree. A plebiscite on April 7 gave 79% approval to various constitutional changes. The 1973 constitution had abandoned the old U.S.-style presidential system and established a parliamentary form of government, but the new changes created a "Philippine-style" presidential system. It gave strong powers to the president but provided for a Cabinet to handle daily governmental business. In the presidential election on June 16, Marcos won

88% of the vote against token opponents after the main opposition groups decided not to contest the election.

Marcos's inauguration was attended by a number of dignitaries, including Prime Ministers Lee Kuan Yew of Singapore and Prem Tinsulanond of Thailand. Vice-Pres. George Bush, representing the U.S., told Marcos that "We love your adherence to democratic principles and democratic processes." Opposition groups and exiles bitterly criticized Bush's remarks.

When the presidential election results were announced, Marcos said he would restructure the government to "make it deal more effectively with peace and order problems and to eliminate corrupt elements in the bureaucracy." Named to work with Virata, a technocrat who had been a senior government official since 1970, were Deputy Prime Minister José Rono, a politician, and a Cabinet of mostly nonpolitical experts.

The first budget announced by the new government, for 1982, shifted from the 1981 emphasis on basic necessities like food, shelter, and education to encouragement of rural enterprise and resource exploitation. Earlier, the government introduced a plan to use subsidies to improve food production and consumption, encourage better nutritional habits, and raise the average daily calorie intake from 1,800 to 2,030. Credit was tightened after a financial panic and the collapse of some companies. The government worked closely with experts from the World Bank and the International Monetary Fund to try to overcome problems caused by a large foreign exchange deficit—made worse by dependence on imported fuel for 80% of the country's energy needs.

One of the worst government losses of the nine-year struggle against Muslim separatists in the southern Philippines occurred February 12 when an estimated 119 troops were killed on Pata Island. A separate guerrilla force, the Communist New People's Army, was blamed for a grenade explosion at the Davao City cathedral on Easter that killed at least 13 persons. The NPA, operating in many parts of the country, was considered a greater long-term threat by the Army than the Muslims in the south. Since martial law began in 1972 and the two rebellions grew, the armed forces had expanded from 60,000 to 200,000 men.

Pope John Paul II made a five-day visit to the Philippines beginning February 17. He emphasized that human dignity and rights should not be subjugated to the state.   (HENRY S. BRADSHER)

Photography

The technology of photography advanced significantly during 1981, a year in which its growth as a worldwide industry and market was erratic and limited, reflecting international economic problems of inflation, devaluation, and high interest rates. As an art form it continued as a serious concern of cultural institutions, galleries, critics, publishers, academia, and private collectors, although prices at auction and in galleries showed signs of retrenchment from the unprecedented highs of the preceding year.

Photo Equipment. The continuing meld of electronics with conventional silver-based image-making technology was emphasized in August when Sony Corp. of Japan introduced in Tokyo a prototype of a single-lens-reflex (SLR) camera in which film was replaced with a CCD (charge-coupled device) imager that recorded 50 individual colour frames on a magnetic disk for reproduction on a television screen. Not shown but promised was a hard-copy device that would produce colour prints of the magnetically captured image.

Sony's system, called the Mavica (an acronym for magnetic video camera), was scheduled to go on sale in Japan 18–24 months after the date of the announcement and in the U.S. shortly thereafter. In appearance it was about the same size and

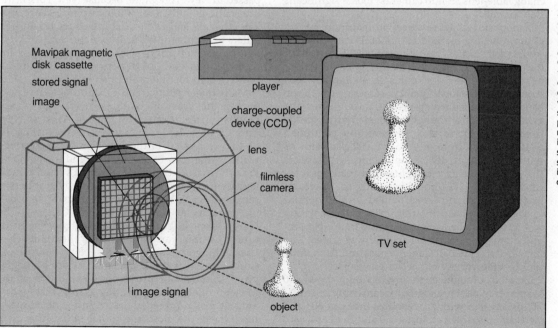

Mavipak magnetic
disk cassette

stored signal

image

charge-coupled
device (CCD)

lens

filmless
camera

player

image signal

object

TV set

An ingenious filmless camera for still pictures, called the Mavica, was introduced in prototype during the year by Sony Corp. Camera optics focus the subject image onto a light-sensitive charge-coupled device, which converts it into a string of electrical impulses for storage on a magnetic disk. The disk is then inserted into a special player that instantly reproduces the image in colour on an ordinary television set.

weight as a conventional 35-mm SLR but with the lens offset to one side. The prototype model shown accepted three bayonet-mounted lenses, a 25-mm $f/2$, 50-mm $f/1.4$, and 16–64-mm $f/1.4$ zoom. The CCD imaging screen was said to have an exposure index equivalent to 200 and to include 570 horizontal by 490 vertical "pixels," or image elements. Shutter speeds ranged from 1/60 to 1/2,000 sec on the automatic setting, and the camera also could be connected to a videocassette recorder for recording continuous motion. The Mavipac magnetic recording disk measured $60 \times 56 \times 3$ mm (about 2¼ in square and ⅛ in thick), weighed eight grams (little more than ¼ oz), and yielded a horizontal resolution superior to current home video cameras.

Although Sony's announcement raised questions as to the image quality the Mavica can deliver and its appeal to consumers accustomed to conventional silver imaging, it stimulated interest among photojournalists because its electronic images could be transmitted over telephone lines immediately and directly from location to home office. Overall, the camera was a landmark in photographic technology and seemed likely to serve as a catalyst for future developments.

Pentax introduced the first production-model autofocus 35-mm interchangeable-lens SLR, the MEF, which was a modification of the Pentax ME Super. A built-in, passive, solid-state image-detection system, activated by lightly pressing the shutter-release button, analyzed the light falling on a focus sensor on the mirror-box floor. The viewfinder was provided with a central autofocus aiming ring as well as with conventional split-image/microprism focusing. When the autofocus device was used, light-emitting diodes in the viewing area indicated when best focus was achieved. With a Pentax AF 35–70-mm $f/2.8$ lens, which incorporated a servomotor, the autofocus system drove the lens to focus on the area included within the aiming ring. Thus autofocusing, which had become commonplace on compact, noninterchangeable-lens 35-mm cameras, took a significant step forward.

Canon moved aggressively to maintain its top position among manufacturers of 35-mm cameras (with a total monthly production of 200,000 units). It introduced the New F-1, a redesigned version of its top-of-the-line F-1 35-mm SLR. A ruggedly constructed professional-quality camera, the basic New F-1 provided match-needle, through-the-lens metering, electronically controlled shutter speeds from 8 to 1/90 sec and mechanically controlled shutter speeds from 1/90 to 1/2,000 sec with or without batteries. By changing focusing screens the user had a choice of light-meter readings: centre-weighted, 12% limited area, or spot. Aperture-priority automation was provided with an optional viewfinder head. Shutter-priority automation was obtained when an optional five-frame-per-second motor drive or power winder was added. The New F-1 accepted all Canon lenses and flash units plus a wide variety of special accessories.

Polaroid brought forth an ultra-high-speed 600 system of instant photography consisting of an SX-70 instant film with an exposure index of 600 and two cameras, the Autofocus 660 and the Land 640,

both of which incorporated a unique built-in electronic flash system. The flash unit, powered by the Polapulse battery contained within the film pack, automatically provided proportional fill-in flash for normal levels of brightness and full flash for low-light situations.

Ilford introduced Cibachrome-A II, an amateur version of its newest positive (slide-to-print) colour material. Based on the relatively stable dye-bleach process of previous Cibachrome, the new colour print product was modified to reduce contrast by a self-masking process and to provide purer colours. It was available with a high-gloss surface and a pearl surface on an RC (resin-coated) base and required a new P-30 processing kit.

Kodak unveiled a novel Ektaflex colour printing system based on its PR-10 instant technology, which eliminated the need for precise temperature control and multiple processing solutions. A sheet of Ektaflex colour negative material was exposed in the conventional way and then inserted in an Ektaflex Model A Printmaker filled with a developing solution. By manually turning a crank, the user laminated the negative to a sheet of positive image-receiving paper. The resulting sandwich was ejected from the Printmaker and developed automatically in daylight in six to ten minutes. Negative and positive were then separated to provide the finished colour print. A positive Ektaflex material for making prints from colour slides was expected to be introduced shortly.

Cultural Trends. Despite an uncertain economy, there was no major collapse of prices for photographic prints at galleries and major auctions during the year, although some rollback was evident. An Ansel Adams "Moonrise, Hernandez, New Mexico," a bellwether of print prices for contemporary work, was withdrawn from a New York auction when the minimum acceptable bid was not achieved.

A "full-disclosure" law relating to the sale of multiple art prints (including photographs) was passed in New York State. Because New York is the international hub of the photographic and art markets, the law had wide-reaching effect. It required sellers to document the source, date, authenticity, and number of prints sold. Although the law increased paperwork for dealers, most felt it to be a positive step for themselves and collectors.

Many major photographic exhibitions were held during the year, including a display of photographs of rural France by Eugène Atget at New York City's Museum of Modern Art, revealing little-known aspects of that Parisian photographer's work; "American Photographers and the National Parks," a visual tribute to America's natural heritage by early and contemporary photographers; a retrospective of William Kline's innovative urban photography at New York's Light Gallery; "The New Vision: 40 Years of Photography at the Institute of Design," an exploration of the influence of Laszlo Moholy-Nagy and his New Bauhaus in Chicago, also at the Light; and "Before Photography," a small but provocative exhibition at the Museum of Modern Art, suggesting that photographic vision preceded the invention of the medium. One of the most interesting publications was

Camera Lucida, by the late Roland Barthes, noted French critic, in which he explored the function of photography as art and communication.

The Erna and Victor Hasselblad Foundation, a $4-million, not-for-profit institution in Göteborg, Sweden, gave its second annual awards in photography. Approximately $387,000 in grants went to nine institutions and individuals in Sweden, Scotland, Israel, and the U.S. for photographic research. A gold medal and $20,000 prize were awarded to Ansel Adams for his contributions to photography. The 39th Pictures of the Year awards, co-sponsored by the University of Missouri School of Journalism, the National Press Photographers Association, and Nikon, Inc., named George Wedding of the *San Jose* (Calif.) *Mercury-News* as Newspaper Photographer of the Year and Jim Brandenburg of *National Geographic* as Magazine Photographer of the Year; its World Understanding Award went to Bryce Flynn of the *Providence* (R.I.) *Journal* for "Warren's Guardian Angel," a photographic essay on a mother's love for her severely handicapped son.

The year's Pulitzer Prize for spot news photography went to Larry C. Price of the *Fort Worth* (Texas) *Star-Telegram* and for feature photography to Taro N. Yamasaki of the *Detroit Free Press.* Photographer Roger A. Werth of the *Longview* (Wash.) *Daily News* also received a Pulitzer for general local coverage of the eruption of Mt. St. Helens. The World Press Photo competition's Picture of the Year award was given to Michael Wells, a British photographer working for *Life* magazine, for a close-up of the hand of a starving Tanzanian child. Eugene Richards, a free-lance photographer associated with Magnum, received a $10,000 grant from the W. Eugene Smith Memorial Fund for humanistic photography. Richards was working on a photographic essay on emergency medical treatment.   (ARTHUR GOLDSMITH)

See also Motion Pictures.
[628.D; 735.G.1]

Physics

Laser-Generated Ultrasound. In 1981 the application of physical principles to the subject of nondestructive testing (NDT) continued its growth toward becoming a major field of study. In particular, increase in both the number of nuclear power stations and the size and location of chemical storage and processing plants, coupled with general public interest in safety margins, was lending considerable weight to NDT development. A short review of the complete range of NDT techniques available would be impossible; instead, this discussion concentrates on one technique that developed rapidly during the past year and that combines two branches of physics that are themselves of great interest.

A standard way of searching for faults, flaws, or defects in components that are opaque to visible light is to use ultrasound, sound above the audible frequency limit. Conventionally, ultrasound is generated by transducers clamped to the component under test, and ultrasonic echoes from defects

are detected by the same transducers or others arrayed around the component. Obviously, this approach is difficult if the component is chemically corrosive, radioactive, very hot, or simply in a physically inaccessible situation. Consequently, much work was being focused on the generation of ultrasound by alternative methods. It had been known almost since discovery of the laser that an intense pulse of laser radiation will generate ultrasound when it strikes an opaque solid. Until recently the technique had not been well enough understood to allow it to be used most effectively.

The major advantage of laser-produced ultrasound is that the equipment can be remote from the material under study, some metres away if required. In such an application remote generation would be rather limited without parallel techniques for remote detection, a development also recently accomplished by means of the laser. Reflection of a portion of a helium, neon, or argon laser beam from the surface of the sample is combined with reflection of the remainder from a reference mirror. The interference produced between these two beams, a modified Michelson interferometer, varies as the test surface moves owing to the ultrasonic waves generated within it. As of 1981 available resolution allowed detection of surface displacements of the order of 100 picometres (10^{-10} metres).

When a pulse of laser radiation falls on a metal surface, all three possible acoustic modes are produced. Both longitudinal (compressional) and shear (transverse) waves propagate in the bulk of the material, and surface waves are generated on the sample surface. A portion of the surface-wave energy is propagated as a longitudinal wave, while a much larger fraction is channeled into a Rayleigh wave, which gives an elliptical retrograde motion to surface particles.

Two generation regimes were identified, one in which the laser only has sufficient energy per pulse to heat the sample surface by a few tens of degrees Celsius and a second in which the laser is sufficiently intense to form a plasma (a gas of nega-

Workers assemble a large streamer chamber —a particle-track recording device—for use in proton-antiproton colliding beam experiments at CERN's Super Proton Synchrotron in Geneva. The chamber, which can make visible particle tracks several metres long, should aid high-energy physicists in the search for exotic events.

CERN

tively charged electrons and positively charged ions) by vaporizing surface material. In the former case, shear bulk waves and Rayleigh surface waves predominate, whereas the longitudinal waves that are produced propagate in a cone about 60° to the normal to the surface. This form of generation may be ideal for testing a whole range of weld structures in metals in which access to the weld has to be from the side.

In the latter case, longitudinal waves are generated preferentially and radiate into the material normal to the surface. This mode, therefore, approximates the pistonlike output of a conventional ultrasonic transducer. It was demonstrated that coating the component—for example, with a thin layer of oil—enhances the amplitude of the ultrasound produced. Several laboratories demonstrated quite conclusively the capability of laser ultrasonic generation and detection for remote NDT in real situations.

Solid-State Theory. A theoretical approach known as renormalization-group theory recently was applied to two problems in solid-state physics and proved outstandingly successful in both cases. In these fields of research experimental and theoretical work demands such high quality that disagreement of the order of 1% can lead to theories being criticized and even totally rejected.

The first of the two problems involves the Kondo effect observed in dilute ferromagnetic alloys. The Kondo effect was first modeled satisfactorily by Jun Kondo of the University of Tokyo in 1964 and thereafter became the centre of much controversy, attention, and experimental and theoretical investigation. It is well known that the electrical resistivity of metals decreases as temperature is decreased. However, in alloys made of a minute amount of magnetic impurity dissolved in a nonmagnetic host (*e.g.*, less than one atom of iron in 10,000 of copper), at very low temperatures—typically a few degrees above absolute zero (0 K)—resistivity reaches a minimum and then rises again upon further cooling. The effect has been attributed to the influence of the magnetic impurity on the conduction electrons in the host metal. At high temperatures coupling between the conduction electrons in the metal and the impurity is very weak, whereas at much lower temperatures there is an exchange interaction between the impurity and surrounding electrons. (This exchange interaction is similar to that responsible for ferromagnetism in such magnetic materials as iron, cobalt, and nickel.)

The high- and low-temperature behaviour of Kondo systems had been well known for some time, but a mathematical understanding of the intermediate region remained elusive until renormalization-group techniques recently permitted some exact calculations, for example, of the magnetization curve of a Kondo system at zero temperature. The Kondo behaviour for a particular host-impurity system can be described in terms of an effective temperature, the Kondo temperature. The new formula for the Kondo temperature obtained from the calculations was in very good agreement with earlier work and boded well for the future. In fact, the method soon was extended

to evaluate the temperature dependence of the specific heat of a Kondo system. The next major goal for theorists would be calculation of a formula to describe the resistivity itself.

The second success for renormalization-group theory relates to the study of phase changes. Examples of great interest to physicists at the present time include transitions in materials between normal and superconducting states and between paramagnetic and ferromagnetic states. If one measures a thermodynamic variable such as magnetic susceptibility, specific heat, or ultrasonic attenuation through such a phase change, one finds that the thermodynamic variable diverges at the critical point as $(T - T_c)^\gamma$, in which T_c is the critical temperature (for example, 0° C [32° F] for the ice-water phase change) and γ is a critical index for the thermodynamic variable. The critical index of the power law is different for different thermodynamic variables.

The values of γ can be calculated theoretically by two techniques. One is the renormalization-group method, whereas the second involves a series expansion. For example, magnetic susceptibility can be expanded in an infinite series in powers of the exchange interaction energy divided by the temperature. γ can be calculated exactly from this infinite series. Computer limitations recently were stretched so that the first 21 terms of the series could be evaluated, allowing very reliable estimates of γ to be obtained. Earlier results involving only 15 terms yielded values of γ that were at least 1% less than those obtained by renormalization-group methods, which were in almost perfect agreement with experiment. The new series expansion lost the erroneous 1%, and all values for γ for magnetic susceptibility agreed to within three parts in a thousand. Consequently, it is clear that the original renormalization-group theory was correct and experimental results reliable.

High-Energy Physics. The physics community continued actively debating the nature of the most fundamental of particles, the quarks, which were believed to be the building blocks of protons, neutrons, and certain other formerly "elementary" entities. The theoretical approaches that describe electromagnetism require the exchange of photons between particles that interact electromagnetically; in other words, photons are the field quanta that mediate the electromagnetic force between particles. In a similar manner field quanta must exist for the quarks, and these are known in the picturesque language of the particle physicist as gluons. Moreover, gluons should be able to exist transiently in groups of two and three, completely independent of quarks; these groups have been given the name glueballs or gluonia. In 1981 several investigators pointed to evidence from high-energy experiments in the U.S. and West Germany that suggested the existence of glueballs, but their arguments were far from persuasive. Other physicists would be working to advance their own opposing points of view until further experiments were conducted. (S. B. PALMER)

See also Nobel Prizes.
[111.H; 124.A.5.c; 124.G.1.a and b; 127.C.5; 128.A.2.b; 733.A.4.b.iii]

Poland

A people's republic of eastern Europe, Poland is bordered by the Baltic Sea, the U.S.S.R., Czechoslovakia, and East Germany. Area: 312,683 sq km (120,727 sq mi). Pop. (1981 est.): 35,746,000. Cap. and largest city: Warsaw (pop., 1980 est., 1,576,-600). Language: Polish. Religion: predominantly Roman Catholic. First secretaries of the Polish United Workers' (Communist) Party in 1981, Stanislaw Kania and, from October 18, Gen. Wojciech Jaruzelski; chairman of the Council of State, Henryk Jablonski; chairmen of the Council of Ministers (premiers), Jozef Pinkowski and, from February 9, General Jaruzelski.

During 1981 the Polish crisis became even more dramatic than it had been in 1980, as the continuing revolt by Polish workers succeeded in badly shaking the Polish United Workers' (Communist) Party (PUWP). On the one hand the Soviet Union urged PUWP leaders to restore "the leading role of the party in the state," while on the other hand First Secretary Stanislaw Kania faced the fact that one million of the 2.9 million PUWP members had joined the 9.5-million-strong independent trade union Solidarnosc (Solidarity). The Polish farmers won official recognition for their independent trade union, Rural Solidarity, in May.

On Feb. 9, 1981, Premier Jozef Pinkowski was dismissed and was replaced on February 11 by Gen. Wojciech Jaruzelski (see BIOGRAPHIES), minister of defense. Never before in the socialist countries had a superior officer on active service been called in to serve as head of government. The following day Jaruzelski dropped two deputy premiers and six ministers and offered their portfolios to new nominees.

Kania and Jaruzelski attended the 26th congress of the Communist Party of the Soviet Union (CPSU) in Moscow in February. In his speech Kania assured the congress that Poland would remain "a socialist state, . . . and an inseparable link in the Socialist community." Back in Warsaw, Jaruzelski on June 12 replaced another deputy premier and four Cabinet ministers.

Stefan Cardinal Wyszynski (see OBITUARIES), archbishop of Gniezno and Warsaw and primate of Poland, died on May 28, plunging the nation into deep mourning. On July 7 Pope John Paul II appointed Jozef Glemp (see BIOGRAPHIES), the bishop of Warmia, as archbishop of both Polish metropolitan sees and thus the new Polish primate.

In June the Central Committee of the PUWP received a strongly worded letter from that of the CPSU. The Soviets complained that their "friendly warnings . . . were not taken into consideration, and were even ignored." The letter went on, "If the worst were to happen, and the enemies of socialism seize power . . . who could then guarantee the independence, sovereignty, and borders of Poland as a state? Nobody."

Nevertheless, the ninth (extraordinary) PUWP congress went ahead as planned on July 14. For the first time the 1,964 delegates were freely elected by secret ballot with multiple candidacies. The congress elected the Central Committee, enlarged from 143 to 200 members, and only one-tenth of the outgoing body was reelected. The congress also

Little was left to buy in Polish supermarkets after food shortages and rampant hoarding emptied the shelves.

Poland

POLAND

Education. (1980–81) Primary, pupils 4,167,313, teachers 201,712; secondary, pupils 345,214, teachers 23,016; vocational and teacher training, pupils 1,328,655, teachers 74,548; higher, students 388,443, teaching staff 54,681.

Finance. Monetary unit: zloty, with (Sept. 21, 1981) a commercial and tourist rate of 35.30 zlotys to U.S. $1 (65.44 zlotys = £1 sterling). Budget (total; 1979 est.): revenue 1,150,400,000,000 zlotys; expenditure 1,109,600,000,000 zlotys. Net material product (1979) 1,935,400,000,000 zlotys.

Foreign Trade. (1980) Imports 57,630,000,000 exchange zlotys; exports 51,915,000,000 exchange zlotys. Import sources: U.S.S.R. 33%; West Germany 7%; East Germany 7%; Czechoslovakia 6%. Export destinations: U.S.S.R. 31%; West Germany 8%; East Germany 7%; Czechoslovakia 7%. Main exports (1979): machinery 39%; coal 11%; transport equipment 9%; chemicals 7%; food 6%.

Transport and Communications. Roads (1980) 298,512 km (including 139 km expressways). Motor vehicles in use (1980): passenger 2,383,000; commercial 617,800. Railways: (1979) 24,415 km (including 6,687 km electrified); traffic (1980) 46,325,-000,000 passenger-km, freight 134,736,000,000 net ton-km. Air traffic (1980): 2,232,000,000 passenger-km; freight 18,793,000 net ton-km. Navigable inland waterways in regular use (1979) 2,878 km. Shipping (1980): merchant vessels 100 gross tons and over 842; gross tonnage 3,639,078. Telephones (Dec. 1979) 3,243,700. Radio licenses (Dec. 1979) 8,555,-000. Television licenses (Dec. 1979) 7,708,000.

Agriculture. Production (in 000; metric tons; 1980): wheat c. 4,176; rye 6,566; barley 3,420; oats 2,245; potatoes c. 25,000; sugar, raw value c. 1,250; rapeseed c. 564; cabbages (1979) c. 1,902; onions c. 350; tomatoes c. 200; carrots (1979) c. 619; cucumbers (1979) c. 232; apples c. 600; tobacco c. 85; butter 252; cheese c. 371; hen's eggs c. 491; beef and veal c. 700; pork c. 1,700; fish catch (1979) 601; timber (cu m; 1979) 20,296. Livestock (in 000; June 1980): cattle c. 12,685; pigs c. 21,326; sheep c. 4,207; horses

(1979) 1,856; chickens (adult birds) 79,292.

Industry. Index of industrial production (1975 = 100; 1980) 125. Fuel and power (in 000; metric tons; 1980): coal 193,121; brown coal 36,866; coke (1979) 19,324; crude oil 320; natural gas (cu m) 6,330,000; manufactured gas (cu m; 1979) 7,793,000; electricity (kw-hr) 121,862,000. Production (in 000; metric tons; 1980): cement 18,444; iron ore (30% metal content; 1979) 250; pig iron 11,902; crude steel 19,484; aluminum (1979) 96; copper (1979) 336; lead (1979) 84; zinc (1979) 209; petroleum products (1978) c. 15,-500; sulfuric acid 2,964; plastics and resins 667; fertilizers (nutrient content; 1979) nitrogenous 1,376, phosphate 931; cotton yarn 217; wool yarn 106; man-made fibres 244; cotton fabrics (m) 883,000; woolen fabrics (m) 106,000; passenger cars (units) 351; commercial vehicles (units) 60. Merchant vessels launched (100 gross tons and over; 1980) 393,-000 gross tons. New dwelling units completed (1979) 284,200.

Political Parties

WIDE WORLD

Party leader Wojciech Jaruzelski of Poland took over a shattered economy in October after the ouster of Stanislaw Kania. He had to deal with labour unrest and shortages of food and other supplies.

limited the period of service of top officials to two terms; furthermore, it decided that the Central Committee was empowered to recall the party's first secretary. These restrictions were unique in the countries of the Soviet bloc. Though Kania was bitterly criticized by a few hard-liners, he was reelected first secretary.

Kania and Jaruzelski were received by Soviet leader Leonid Brezhnev in the Crimea on August 14. While the Polish leaders explained to their host that, considering the economic and political situation in Poland, they saw their priority as being to rally all patriotic forces for the sake of national salvation, Brezhnev insisted that Polish Communists must above all aim to strengthen their party.

On the eve of the opening on September 5, at Oliwa near Gdansk, of the first national congress of Solidarity, Kania declared that the PUWP and the Polish government were striving for close collaboration with all social and national movements that were not opposing socialism. On September 11 Boris Aristov, the Soviet ambassador in Warsaw, called on Kania and Jaruzelski, drawing their attention to the fact that at the Gdansk congress "counterrevolutionary forces are conducting with impunity an unbridled campaign of lies and slander against the U.S.S.R." Convinced that Soviet criticism was directed mainly against him, on October 18 Kania resigned as first secretary. The Central Committee accepted his resignation and elected Jaruzelski.

Archbishop Glemp and Solidarity leader Lech Walesa had an unprecedented two-hour meeting with Jaruzelski on November 4 concerning creation of a Council of National Understanding. In mid-November talks were held between the leaders of the government and Solidarity. The government appealed for cooperation but instead the conflict intensified. On December 2 policemen supported by Army units forcibly broke up a strike of fire-fighter cadets in Warsaw, and on December 6 the government charged the leaders of Solidarity with breaking a previous agreement to negotiate for a national accord.

Meeting in Gdansk on December 12, Solidarity

leaders proposed a nationwide referendum on establishing a non-Communist government and defining Poland's military relationship with the Soviet Union if the government did not agree to a series of union demands by the end of the year. These demands included access to the mass media and free and democratic elections to local councils in the provinces.

On December 13 the government struck back. In a nationwide radio address, General Jaruzelski imposed martial law on the nation, maintaining that a strict regime was necessary to save Poland from catastrophe and civil war. Public gatherings, demonstrations, and strikes were banned, and a news blackout was imposed on both internal and external communications. Leaders of Solidarity reacted to the martial law by urging a nationwide strike. This did not materialize, but there were scattered work stoppages, especially in the coal mines; at least seven miners were killed in clashes with the Army and police at Katowice. According to Polish television some Solidarity leaders were to undergo trial for trying to resist the martial law orders, and Walesa was reportedly detained at a country house near Warsaw. On December 24, however, Jaruzelski said that there would still be a place for independent labour unions in Poland.

The Soviet Union expressed approval of Jaruzelski's action but denied any responsibility for the imposition of martial law. The U.S. reacted by imposing economic sanctions against Poland to remain in force as long as martial law continued. For an extended discussion of the Polish situation, *see* Feature Article: *"Not a single Polish problem can be solved by violence."*　　　　　(K. M. SMOGORZEWSKI)

Political Parties

The following table is a general world guide to political parties. All countries that were independent on Dec. 31, 1981, are included; there are a number for which no analysis of political activities can be given. Parties are included in most instances only if represented in parliaments (in the lower house in bicameral legislatures); the figures in the last column indicate the number of seats obtained in the last general election (figures in parentheses are those of the penultimate one). The date of the most recent election follows the name of the country.

The code letters in the affiliation column show the relative political position of the parties within each country; there is, therefore, no entry in this column for single-party states. There are obvious difficulties involved in labeling parties within the political spectrum of a given country. The key chosen is as follows: F-fascist; ER-extreme right; R-right; CR-centre right; C-centre; L-non-Marxist left; SD-social democratic; S-socialist; EL-extreme left; and K-Communist.

The percentages in the column "Voting strength" indicate proportions of the valid votes cast for the respective parties, or the number of registered voters who went to the polls in single-party states.

[541.D.2]

Police:
see Crime and Law Enforcement

COUNTRY AND NAME OF PARTY	Affiliation	Voting strength (%)	Parliamentary representation
Afghanistan			
Pro-Soviet government since April 27, 1978	—	—	—
Albania (November 1978)			
Albanian Labour (Communist)	—	99.9	250 (250)
Algeria (February 1977)			
National Liberation Front	—	99.95	261
Angola (August 1980)			
Movimento Popular de Libertaçao de Angola (MPLA)	—	—	203
Antigua and Barbuda (April 1980)			
Antigua Labour Party	C	59.0	13 (11)
Progressive Labour Movement	L	...	3 (5)
Independents		...	1 (1)
Argentina			
Military junta since March 24, 1976	—	—	—
Australia (November 1980)			
National Country	R	8.7	20 (19)
Liberal	C	37.5	54 (67)
Australian Labor	L	45.4	51 (38)
Other	—	1.9	0 (0)
Austria (May 1979)			
Freiheitliche Partei Österreichs	R	6.06	11 (10)
Österreichische Volkspartei	C	41.90	77 (80)
Sozialistische Partei Österreichs	SD	51.03	95 (93)
Bahamas, The (July 1977)			
Progressive Liberal Party	CR	55.0	30 (30)
Bahamian Democratic Party	L	...	5 (8)
Free National Movement	L	...	2 —
Bahrain			
Emirate, no parties	—	—	—
Bangladesh (February 1979)			
Jatiyabadi Dal (Nationalist Party)	R	49.0	207
Awami League	CR	...	40
Muslim League	C	...	20
Jatiya Samajtantrik Dal (National Socialist)	L	...	9
Others	—	...	24
Barbados (June 1981)			
Democratic Labour	C	47.1	10 (7)
Barbados Labour	L	52.2	17 (17)
Belgium (November 1981)			
Vlaams Blok	ER	...	1 (1)
Volksunie	R	...	20 (14)
Front Démocratique Francophone/ Rassemblement Wallon	R	...	8 (15)
Parti Libéral {Flemish	CR	...	28 (22)
{Wallon	CR	...	24 (15)
Parti Social-Chrétien {Flemish	C	...	43 (57)
{Wallon	C	...	18 (25)
Parti Socialiste Belge {Flemish	SD	...	26 (26)
{Wallon	SD	...	35 (32)
Parti Communiste	K	...	2 (4)
Others	—	...	7 (1)
Belize (November 1979)			
United Democratic Party	R	46.8	5 (6)
People's United Party	C	51.8	13 (12)
Benin (November 1979)			
People's Revolutionary Party	—	—	336
Bhutan			
A monarchy without parties	—	—	—
Bolivia			
Military junta since July 17, 1980	—	—	—
Botswana (October 1979)			
Botswana Democratic Party	C	...	29 (27)
Botswana People's Party	L	...	1 (2)
Botswana National Front	EL	...	2 (2)
Brazil (November 1978)			
Aliança Renovadora Nacional (ARENA)	CR	...	231 (199)
Movimento Democrático Brasileiro (MDB)	L	...	189 (165)
Bulgaria (June 1981)			
Fatherland Front {Bulgarian Communist Party / Bulgarian Agrarian Union / No party affiliation}	—	99.9	{271 / 99 / 30} 400 (400)
Burma (October 1981)			
Burma Socialist Program Party	—	99.0	464 (464)
Burundi (October 1974)			
Tutsi ethnic minority government	—	—	—
Cameroon (May 1978)			
Cameroonian National Union	—	99.98	120 (120)
Canada (February 1980)			
Social Credit	R	1.9	0 (6)
Progressive Conservative	CR	33.0	103 (136)
Liberal	C	43.9	147 (114)
New Democratic	L	19.8	32 (26)
Cape Verde (December 1980)			
African Party for the Independence of Guinea-Bissau and Cape Verde	—	93.0	—
Central African Republic			
Military Committee of National Recovery took power on Sept. 1, 1981	—	...	—
Chad			
Military government since 1975	—	—	—
Chile			
Military junta since Sept. 11, 1973	—	—	—
China, People's Republic of (February 1978)			
Communist (Kungchantang) National People's Congress	—	...	3,500
Colombia (February 1978)			
Partido Conservador	R	...	86 (66)
Partido Liberal	C	...	109 (113)
Unión Nacional de Oposición	L	...	4 (20)
Comoros (December 1974)			
Single party rule from Aug. 3, 1975	—	—	—
Congo (July 1979)			
Parti Congolais du Travail	—	—	115
Costa Rica (February 1978)			
Partido de Liberación Nacional	R	...	25 (27)
Partido de Unidad	C	...	27 (16)
Three left-wing parties	L	...	5 (8)
Cuba (November 1976)			
Partido Comunista Cubano	—	...	481
Cyprus			
Greek Zone: (May 1981):			
Democratic Rally	R	31.89	12
Democratic Party	CR	19.50	8
Socialist Party (EDEK)	S	8.17	3
Communist Party (AKEL)	K	32.79	12
Turkish Zone (June 1981):			
National Unity Party	—	42.6	18 (30)
Socialist Salvation Party	—	28.6	13 (6)
Republican Turkish Party	—	15.1	6 (2)
Democratic People's Party	—	8.1	2 (0)
Turkish Union Party	—	5.5	1 (0)
Czechoslovakia (June 1981)			
National Front	—	99.5	200 (200)
Denmark (December 1981)			
Conservative	R	14.4	26 (22)
Liberal Democratic (Venstre)	CR	11.3	21 (23)
Christian People's	CR	2.3	4 (5)
Progress	C	8.9	16 (20)
Radical Liberal (Radikale Venstre)	C	5.1	9 (10)
Centre Democrats	C	8.3	15 (6)
Social Democrats	SD	32.9	59 (69)
Socialist People's	EL	11.3	20 (11)
Left Socialists	EL	2.6	5 (6)
Others	—	...	4 (2)
Djibouti (October 1981)			
Rassemblement Populaire pour le Progrès declared only official party	—	—	—
Dominica (July 1980)			
Freedom Party	C	...	17 (3)
Labour Party	L	...	2 (16)
Independents	—	...	2 (2)
Dominican Republic (May 1978)			
Partido Reformista	C	...	42 (86)
Partido Revolucionario	SD	...	49 ...
Others	—	...	... (5)
Ecuador (April 1979, figures incomplete)			
Partido Conservador	R	...	10
Concentración de Fuerzas Populares	C	...	30
Izquierda Democrática	L	...	14
Unión Democrática Popular	EL	...	3
Egypt (November 1976)			
Arab Socialist Union	—	...	350
El Salvador			
Provisional military government since Oct. 15, 1979	—	—	—
Equatorial Guinea			
Provisional military government since Aug. 3, 1979	—	—	—
Ethiopia			
Military government since 1974	—	—	—
Fiji (September 1977)			
Alliance Party (mainly Fijian)	—	...	36 (24)
National Federation (mainly Indian)	—	...	15 (26)
Others	—	...	1 (2)
Finland (March 1979)			
National Coalition Party (Conservative)	R	21.7	47 (35)
Swedish People's	R	4.3	10 (10)
Centre Party (ex-Agrarian)	C	17.4	36 (39)
Liberal	C	3.7	4 (9)
Christian League	C	4.8	9 (9)
Rural	L	4.6	7 (2)
Social Democratic	SD	24.0	52 (54)
People's Democratic League (Communist)	K	17.9	35 (40)
Others	—	1.75	0 (2)
France (June 1981)			
Centre-Right:			
Gaullists (Rassemblement pour la République)	R	...	83 (148)
Giscardians (Union pour la Démocratie Française)	CR	...	64 (137)
Other	—	...	11 (6)
Union of Left:			
Parti Radical	L	...	14 (10)
Parti Socialiste	SD	...	269 (103)
Parti Communiste	K	...	44 (86)
Others	—	...	6 (1)
Gabon (February 1973)			
Parti Démocratique Gabonais	—	...	70
Gambia, The (April 1977)			
People's Progressive Party	C	...	29 (28)
United Party	L	...	2 (3)
German Democratic Republic (June 1981)			
National Front (Sozialistische Einheitspartei and others)	—	99.2	500 (500)
Germany, Federal Republic of (October 1980)			
Christlich-Demokratische Union	R	34.2	174 (190)
Christlich-Soziale Union	R	10.3	52 (53)
Freie Demokratische Partei	C	10.6	53 (39)
Sozialdemokratische Partei Deutschlands	SD	42.9	218 (214)
The Green (Ecology) Party		1.5	0
Ghana			
Military dictatorship since Dec. 31, 1981	—	—	—
Greece (October 1981)			
Progressive Party	R	1.7	0 (5)
New Democracy Party	CR	35.9	115 (172)
Panhellenic Socialist Movement (Pasok)	SD	48.1	172 (93)
Greek Communist Party	K	10.9	13 (11)
Others	—	2.3	0 (19)
Grenada			
People's Revolutionary Government since March 13, 1979	—	...	—
Guatemala (March 1978)			
Movimiento de Liberación Nacional	CR	...	20
Partido Institucional Democrático	CR	...	17
Partido Demócrata Cristiano	C	...	7
Partido Revolucionario	L	...	14
Others	—	...	3
Guinea (December 1974)			
Parti Démocratique de Guinée	—	100.0	150
Guinea-Bissau			
Governed by the Council of the Revolution since Nov. 14, 1980	—	—	—

COUNTRY AND NAME OF PARTY	Affiliation	Voting strength (%)	Parliamentary representation
Guyana (December 1980)			
People's National Congress	—	...	(37)
People's Progressive Party	—	...	(14)
Others	—	...	(2)
Haiti			
Presidential dictatorship since 1957	—	—	—
Honduras (November 1981)			
Partido Nacional	R	42.0	34 (33)
Partido Liberal	CR	54.0	44 (35)
Partido de Innovación y Unidad	C	2.5	3 (3)
Partido Demócrata Cristiano	C	1.5	1 (0)
Hungary (June 1975)			
Patriotic People's Front	—	97.6	352
Iceland (December 1979)			
Independence (Conservative)	R	35.4	21 (20)
Progressive (Farmers' Party)	C	24.9	17 (12)
Social Democratic	SD	17.4	10 (14)
People's Alliance	K	19.7	11 (14)
Independent	—	...	1 (0)
India (January 1980)			
Congress (I) and allied parties:			
Congress (I)	C	...	351
Dravida Munnetra Kazhagam	R	...	16
Lok Dal (Janata secular)	—	...	41
Three smaller parties	—	...	7
Opposition:			
Janata (People's) Party	C	...	32 (295)
Congress (Urs)	C	...	13 (150)
Communist Party of India (Marxist)	K	...	35 (22)
Communist Party of India (pro-Soviet)	K	...	10 (7)
Anna Dravida Munnetra Kazhagam	R	...	2 (19)
Akali Dal (Sikh Party)	C	...	1 (9)
Six small parties	—	...	11
Independents	—	...	6
Indonesia (May 1977)			
Golkar (Functional Groups)	—	62.1	232 (236)
Islamic Development Unity Party	—	29.3	99 (94)
Partai Demokrasi Indonesia (merger of five nationalist and Christian parties)	—	8.6	29 (30)
Iran (May 1980)			
Islamic Republican Party	R	...	150
Islamic National Party	CR	...	80
Independents	—	...	40
Iraq			
Military and Ba'ath Party governments since 1958	—	...	...
Ireland (June 1981)			
Fianna Fail (Sons of Destiny)	C	45.5	78 (84)
Fine Gael (United Ireland)	C	36.5	65 (43)
Irish Labour Party	L	9.9	15 (17)
Sinn Fein (We Ourselves)	—	...	1 (0)
Others	—	...	7 (4)
Israel (June 1981)			
Likud	R	37.1	48 (43)
National Religious	CR	4.9	6 (12)
Agudat Israel	C	3.7	4 (4)
Labour Alignment	SD	36.6	47 (32)
Democratic Front (Communist)	K	3.4	4 (5)
Others	—	...	11 (24)
Italy (June 1979)			
Movimento Sociale Italiano	F	5.3	30 (35)
Partito Liberale Italiano	CR	1.9	9 (5)
Democrazia Cristiana	C	38.3	262 (262)
Partito Repubblicano Italiano	C	3.0	16 (14)
Partito Social-Democratico Italiano	L	3.8	20 (15)
Partito Socialista Italiano	SD	9.8	62 (57)
Partito d'Unità Proletaria	EL	1.4	6 (6)
Partito Radicale	EL	3.4	18 (4)
Partito Comunista Italiano	K	30.4	201 (228)
Südtiroler Volkspartei	—	0.6	4 (3)
Others	—	2.1	2 (1)
Ivory Coast (October 1980)			
Parti Démocratique de la Côte d'Ivoire	—	99.9	100
Jamaica (October 1980)			
Jamaica Labour Party	L	57.0	51 (12)
People's National Party	SD	43.0	9 (48)
Japan (June 1980)			
Liberal-Democratic	R	...	284 (258)
Komeito (Clean Government)	CR	...	33 (57)
Democratic-Socialist	SD	...	32 (35)
Socialist	S	...	107 (107)
Communist	K	...	29 (39)
Independents and others	—	...	26 (25)
Jordan			
Royal government, no parties	—	—	60
Kampuchea (May 1981)			
Kampuchean United Front for National Salvation (Vietnamese-backed)	—	99.0	117
Kenya (November 1979)			
Kenya African National Union (158 elected, 12 nominated, 2 ex-officio)	—	...	172 (158)
Kiribati (ex. Gilbert Islands, July 1979)			
House of Assembly	—	...	35
Korea, North (November 1977)			
Korean Workers' (Communist) Party	—	100.0	579
Korea, South (March 1981)			
Korean National	CR	...	25
Democratic Justice	C	...	151
Democratic Korea	L	...	81
Democratic Socialist	S	...	2
Others	—	...	17
Kuwait (February 1981)			
Princely government with elected Parliament, no parties	—	—	30
Laos, People's Democratic Republic of			
Lao People's Revolutionary Party	—	...	...
Lebanon (April 1972)			
Maronites (Roman Catholics)	—	...	30
Sunni Muslims	—	...	20
Shi'ite Muslims	—	...	19
Greek Orthodox	—	...	11
Druzes (Muslim sect)	—	...	6
Melchites (Greek Catholics)	—	...	6
Armenian Orthodox	—	...	4
Other Christian	—	...	2
Armenian Catholics	—	...	1
Lesotho			
Constitution suspended Jan. 30, 1970	—	...	—
Liberia			
People's Redemption Council since April 1980	—	—	—
Libya			
Military government since Sept. 1, 1969	—	—	—
Liechtenstein (February 1978)			
Vaterländische Union	CR	...	8 (7)
Fortschrittliche Bürgerpartei	C	...	7 (8)
Luxembourg (June 1979)			
Parti Chrétien Social	CR	34.5	24 (18)
Parti Libéral	C	21.3	15 (14)
Parti Ouvrier Socialiste	SD	24.3	14 (17)
Parti Social Démocratique	S	6.0	2 (5)
Parti Communiste Luxembourgeois	K	5.8	2 (5)
Independents	—	...	2 (0)
Madagascar (June 1977)			
Avant-garde de la Révolution Malgache	C	...	112
Parti du Congrès de l'Indépendance	L	...	16
Others	—	...	9
Malawi (June 1978)			
Malawi Congress Party	—	...	87
Malaysia (July 1978)			
Barisan Nasional	—	...	131 (120)
Democratic Action Party (mainly Chinese)	L	...	16 (9)
Party Islam	—	...	5 (14)
Maldives (February 1975)			
Presidential rule since 1975	—	—	—
Mali			
Military government since Nov. 19, 1968	—	—	—
Malta (December 1981)			
Nationalist Party	R	...	31 (31)
Labour Party	SD	...	34 (34)
Mauritania			
Military government since April 25, 1981	—	—	—
Mauritius (December 1976)			
Independence Party (Indian-dominated)	C	...	28 (39)
Parti Mauricien Social-Démocrate	L	...	8 (23)
Mauritius Militant Movement	K	...	34
Mexico (July 1979)			
Partido Demócrata Mexicano	R	2.1	10
Partido Revolucionario Institucional	CR	68.3	296
Partido Acción Nacional	C	11.1	43
Partido Auténtico de la Revolución Mexicana	L	2.2	12
Partido Socialista de los Trabajadores	L	2.3	10
Partido Popular Socialista	S	2.8	11
Partido Comunista Mexicano	K	5.1	18
Monaco (January 1978)			
Union Nationale et Démocratique	—	...	18 (17)
Mongolia (June 1981)			
Mongolian People's Revolutionary Party	—	99.9	354 (354)
Morocco (June 1977)			
Independents (pro-government)	CR	44.7	141 (159)
Popular Movement (rural)	CR	12.4	44 (60)
Istiqlal (Independence)	C	21.6	49 (8)
National Union of Popular Forces	L	14.6	16 (1)
Others	—	...	14 (12)
Mozambique (December 1977)			
Frente da Libertação do Moçambique (Frelimo)	—	...	210
Nauru (November 1977)			
Nauru Party (Dowiyogo)	—	...	9
Opposition Party (DeRoburt)	—	...	8
Independent	—	...	1
Nepal (May 1981)			
140-member Parliament, 112 elected and 28 appointed by the King; no parties	—	—	—
Netherlands, The (May 1981)			
Christian Democratic Appeal (Anti-Revolutionaire Partij, Christelijk-Historische Unie, and Katholieke Volkspartij)	CR	30.8	48 (49)
Boerenpartij (Farmers' Party)	CR	0.2	0 (1)
Volkspartij voor Vrijheid en Democratie	C	17.3	26 (28)
Democrats 1966	C	11.1	17 (8)
Radical Political Party	L	2.0	3 (3)
Partij van de Arbeid	SD	28.3	44 (53)
Communistische Partij van Nederland	K	2.1	3 (2)
Four other parties	—	...	9 (6)
New Zealand (November 1981)			
National (Conservative)	CR	...	47 (51)
Labour Party	L	...	43 (40)
Social Credit	C	...	2 (1)
Nicaragua			
Provisional government since July 20, 1979	—	...	—
Niger			
Military government since April 17, 1974	—	—	—
Nigeria (July–August 1979)			
National Party of Nigeria	—	...	168
Unity Party of Nigeria	—	...	111
Nigerian People's Party	—	...	79
Great Nigeria People's Party	—	...	48
People's Redemption Party	—	...	49
Norway (September 1981)			
Høyre (Conservative)	R	...	54 (41)
Kristelig Folkeparti	CR	...	15 (22)
Senterpartiet (Agrarian)	C	...	10 (12)
Venstre (Liberal)	C	...	2 (2)
Party of Progress	C	...	4 (0)
Arbeiderpartiet (Labour)	SD	...	66 (76)
Sosialistisk Venstreparti (Socialist Left)	S	...	4 (2)

COUNTRY AND NAME OF PARTY	Affiliation	Voting strength (%)	Parliamentary representation
Oman			
Independent sultanate, no parties	—	—	—
Pakistan			
Military government since July 5, 1977	—	—	—
Panama (August 1978)			
National Union Assembly	—	...	505
Papua New Guinea (June–July 1977)			
Pangu Party	—	...	39 (22)
United Party (chief opposition)	—	...	38 (34)
People's Progress Party	—	...	18 (12)
National Party	—	...	3 (10)
Country Party	—	...	1 —
Papua Besena	—	...	5 (2)
Other	—	...	5 —
Paraguay (February 1977)			
Partido Colorado (A. Stroessner)	R	69.0	...
Opposition parties	—	31.0	...
Peru (May 1980)			
Acción Popular	—	...	98
Alianza Popular Revolucionaria Americana	—	...	58
Popular Christian Party	—	...	10
Others	—	...	14
Philippines			
Martial law lifted Jan. 17, 1981	—	—	—
Poland (March 1980)			
Front of National Unity — Communists	—	99.0	261
Peasants			113
Democrats			37 — 460 (460)
Non-party			49
Portugal (October 1980)			
Democratic Alliance	R	47.1	136 (128)
Republican and Socialist Front	SD	28.0	75 (74)
United People's Alliance	K	16.9	41 (47)
Popular Democratic Union	K	...	1 (1)
Qatar			
Independent emirate, no parties	—	—	—
Romania (March 1980)			
Social Democracy and Unity Front	—	98.5	369 (349)
Rwanda (July 1975)			
National Revolutionary Development Movement	—	—	—
Saint Lucia (July 1979)			
United Workers' Party	C	...	5
St. Lucia Labour Party	S	...	12
Saint Vincent and the Grenadines (December 1979)			
St. Vincent Labour Party	—	...	11
New Democratic Party	—	...	2
San Marino (May 1980)			
Communist coalition — Partito Comunista		56.0	16
Partito Social Democratico			9
Partito Socialista Unitario			8
Christian Democrats		40.0	26
Independent		...	1
São Tomé and Príncipe (1975)			
Movimento Libertaçao	—	—	—
Saudi Arabia			
Royal government, no parties	—	—	—
Senegal (February 1978)			
Parti Socialiste	CR	82.5	83
Parti Démocratique Sénégalais	L	17.1	17
Seychelles			
People's Progressive Front (alone in power after the June 5, 1977, coup)	—	—	—
Sierra Leone (June 1978)			
All People's Congress	CR	...	85 (70)
Singapore (December 1980)			
People's Action Party	CR	75.5	75 (69)
Solomon Islands			
Independent Group	C	...	...
National Democratic Party	L	...	...
Somalia (December 1979)			
Somalian Revolutionary Socialist Party	—	...	171
South Africa (April 1981)			
Herstigte Nasionale Partij	ER	13.8	0 (0)
National Conservative Party	R	—	0 —
National Party	R	56.1	131 (134)
South Africa Party	CR	—	— (3)
New Republic Party	C	7.7	8 (10)
Progressive Federal Party	L	19.1	26 (17)
Others	—	...	0 (0)
Spain (March 1979)			
Coalición Democrática	R	5.0	9 (16)
Unión Centro Democrático	CR	34.0	168 (165)
Partido Socialista Obrero Español	SD	29.0	121 (118)
Partido Comunista Español	K	10.0	23 (20)
Catalans (two parties)	—	...	9 (13)
Basques (three parties)	—	...	12 (9)
Others	—	...	8 (9)
Sri Lanka (July 1977)			
United National Party	R	...	139 (19)
Freedom Party	C	...	8 (91)
Tamil United Liberation Front	C	...	17 (12)
Communists and others	—	...	2 (44)
Sudan			
National assemblies dissolved on Oct. 5, 1981, pending future elections	—	—	—
Suriname			
National Military Council since Feb. 25, 1980	—	—	—
Swaziland			
Royal government, no parties	—	—	—
Sweden (September 1979)			
Moderata Samlingspartiet	R	20.4	73 (55)
Centerpartiet	CR	18.2	64 (86)
Folkpartiet (Liberal)	C	10.6	38 (39)
Socialdemokratiska Arbetarepartiet	SD	43.5	154 (152)
Vänsterpartiet Kommunisterna	K	5.6	20 (17)
Switzerland (October 1979)			
Christian Democrats (Conservative)	R	...	44 (46)
Republican Movement	R	...	3 (6)
National Action (V. Ochen)			
Evangelical People's	R	...	3 (3)
Swiss People's (ex-Middle Class)	CR	...	23 (21)
Radical Democrats (Freisinnig)	C	...	51 (47)
League of Independents	C	...	8 (11)
Liberal Democrats	L	...	8 (6)
Social Democrats	SD	...	51 (55)
Socialist Autonomous	EL	...	3 (1)
Communist (Partei der Arbeit)	K	...	3 (4)
Others	—	...	3 (0)
Syria (November 1981)			
National Progressive Front	—	...	195 (159)
Others	—	...	0 (36)
Taiwan (Republic of China)			
Nationalist (Kuomintang)	—	...	773
Tanzania (October 1980)			
Tanganyika African National Union	C	...	111 (218)
Zanzibar Afro-Shirazi (nominated)	L	...	40 (52)
Thailand (April 1979)			
Social Action Party	—	...	82
Thai Nationalist Party	—	...	38
Democratic Party	—	...	32
Thai People's Party	—	...	32
Serithan (Socialist) Party	—	...	21
Others	—	...	96
Togo (December 1979)			
Rassemblement du Peuple Togolais	—	96.0	67
Tonga (May 1981)			
Legislative Assembly (partially elected)	—	—	21
Trinidad and Tobago (November 1981)			
People's National Movement	C	...	26 (24)
Organization for National Reconstruction	—	...	0 —
National Alliance:			
United Labour Front	L	...	8 (10)
Democratic Action Congress	EL	...	2 (2)
Tunisia (November 1981)			
National Front (led by the Parti Socialiste Destourien)	—	94.6	136 (121)
Turkey			
National Security Council since Sept. 12, 1980; 160-member Consultative Assembly appointed and political parties abolished on Oct. 15, 1981	—	—	—
Tuvalu (September 1981)			
No political parties	—	...	...
Uganda (December 1980)			
Uganda People's Congress Party	—	...	68
Democratic Party	—	...	48
Union of Soviet Socialist Republics (March 1979)			
Communist Party of the Soviet Union	—	99.99	1,500 (767)
United Arab Emirates			
Federal government of seven emirates	—	—	—
United Kingdom (May 1979)			
Conservative	R	43.9	339 (276)
Liberal	C	13.8	11 (13)
Labour	L	36.9	268 (319)
Communist	K	...	0 (0)
Scottish National Party	—	...	2 (11)
Plaid Cymru (Welsh Nationalists)	—	...	2 (3)
Ulster Unionists (four groups)	—	...	10 (10)
Others	—	...	3 (3)
United States (November 1980)			
Republican	CR	...	192 (159)
Democratic	C	...	242 (276)
Independent		...	1 (0)
Upper Volta			
Military Committee of Recovery for National Progress since Nov. 25, 1980	—	—	—
Uruguay			
Rule by Council of State from 1973	—	—	—
Vanuatu (New Hebrides) (November 1979)			
Vanuaaku Pati	C	...	26
Others	—	...	13
Venezuela (December 1978)			
COPEI (Social Christians)	CR	...	88 (64)
Acción Democrática	L	...	88 (102)
Movimiento al Socialismo	SD	...	11 (9)
Movimiento Electoral del Pueblo	S	...	3 (8)
Movimiento Institucional Revolucionario	EL	...	4 (2)
Partido Comunista Venezuelano	K	...	1 (2)
Vietnam, Socialist Republic of (April 1981)			
Communist Party	—	...	...
Yemen, People's Democratic Republic of			
National Liberation Front	—	—	—
Yemen Arab Republic			
Military government since 1974	—	—	—
Yugoslavia (May 1978)			
Communist-controlled Federal Chamber	—	...	220
Zaire (October 1977)			
Legislative Council of the Mouvement Populaire de la Révolution	—	...	268
Zambia (December 1973)			
United National Independence Party	—	80.0	125
Zimbabwe (February–March 1980)			
Zimbabwe African National Union	—	63.0	57
Zimbabwe African People's Union	—	24.0	20
United African National Council	—	8.0	3
Rhodesian Front (Europeans)	—		20

(K. M. SMOGORZEWSKI)

Portugal

Portugal

A republic of southwestern Europe, Portugal shares the Iberian Peninsula with Spain. Area: 91,-985 sq km (35,516 sq mi), including the Azores (2,247 sq km) and Madeira (794 sq km). Pop. (1981 prelim.): 9,784,200, excluding about 550,000 refugees (mostly from Africa). Cap. and largest city: Lisbon (pop., 1981 prelim., 812,400). Language: Portuguese. Religion: Roman Catholic. President in 1981, Gen. António dos Santos Ramalho Eanes; premier, Francisco Pinto Balsemão.

After general elections in October 1980, in which Portugal's ruling Democratic Alliance (AD) coalition increased its majority, there was a delay in the announcement of a new Cabinet. Certain members of the premier's Social Democratic Party (PSD) refused to serve under his leadership, and there were disagreements over the distribution of portfolios among the component parties of the coalition. Premier Francisco Pinto Balsemão (*see* BIOGRAPHIES) was finally able to have his Cabinet confirmed by Pres. António Ramalho Eanes on Jan. 9, 1981. It contained ten new ministers and three new portfolios (European integration, administrative reforms, and quality of life). The incoming government presented its program to the Assembly on January 16, and debate was completed six days later. At that time the program was approved by 133 votes to 97.

Introducing his program, Balsemão pledged a larger role for the private sector in industry as well as a reduction in state ownership. The civil service was to be modernized, become fully professional, and be made free of party patronage. Constitutional reform would be one major task for the government, and others included accession to the European Communities (EC) and continuing membership in NATO. Efforts would also be directed at increasing exports, assisting agriculture, and boosting energy, tourism, transport, and housing projects.

Francisco Pinto Balsemão (left) was sworn in as premier of Portugal in January. At right is Portuguese Pres. António Ramalho Eanes.

UPI

Even as the incoming administration was taking office, there were predictions of a short life for the government despite the premier's declaration that he intended to form a government that would serve its full four-year term. Tension in the PSD was not long in emerging. The premier was attacked by the right wing of his party for not pursuing Francisco Sá Carneiro's policy of confrontation with President Eanes. (Former premier Sá Carneiro died in a plane crash in December 1980.) However, Balsemão was able to win endorsement of his leadership from a majority of delegates and qualified support for his policy from the PSD.

The Socialist Party (PSP) leader, Mário Soares, was meanwhile facing complaints from his party, owing in part to his withdrawal of support from Eanes during the 1980 presidential election. Other factors contributing to his unpopularity were the persistent electoral decline of the party, which was blamed on overconcentration of power in the leader's hands, and the fact that Soares opposed an alliance with smaller parties to the left of the Socialists in order to retain the possible future option of a coalition with the PSD. Nevertheless, by the time of the PSP congress in May, Soares had garnered enough votes to defeat his left-wing critics.

For the fourth time in a year the Council of the Revolution, led by President Eanes, in July vetoed a bill to allow the reentry of private capital into banking and insurance, a key AD measure. In response Minister of Social Affairs Carlos Macedo resigned, causing a Cabinet crisis. In August the powerful confederation of Portuguese farmers withdrew its support from the premier because of the government policy of returning collectively owned farmland to its previous owners. Thus Balsemão's isolation deepened, making a Cabinet reshuffle more difficult.

Eurico de Melo, former minister of the interior, Aníbal Cavaco Silva, former minister of finance, and Freitas do Amaral, leader of the Democratic Social Centre (CDS), all refused posts in a remodeled Cabinet that would have marked a shift to the right in the AD. Angered by continued attacks from within his own party, led by Helena Roseta, and by statements from do Amaral that he had lost confidence in Sá Carneiro's successor, Balsemão summoned a meeting of the PSD political commission in early August. The result of a vote of confidence—37 for, 15 against, and 2 abstentions—was regarded by Balsemão as inconclusive; he resigned as premier on August 10, though retaining the PSD leadership.

President Eanes accepted the resignation, but the anti-Balsemão faction in the AD was unable to propose an acceptable substitute. High-level meetings within the various component parties of the AD followed, with the result that on August 16 Balsemão was asked by the PSD and AD leadership to withdraw his resignation and stay on; a motion of confidence was resoundingly passed by the PSD —58 for, 1 against, and 3 abstentions. On August 22 it was announced that do Amaral had agreed to serve as deputy premier and minister of defense in the new Cabinet; Ribeiro Telles, leader of the Popular Monarchist Party, also accepted a Cabinet post, in charge of the new quality of life ministry. By September 1 Balsemão had his new Cabinet prepared, and three days later it was sworn in. The number of ministers was reduced from 17 to 14; Fernandes Salgueiro, an economist, became minister for finance and planning, but only after demanding a free hand to deal with Portugal's worsening economic situation.

The incoming Cabinet's program was debated on September 14. It sought to strengthen the market economy and bring about those structural changes needed if Portugal was to benefit from joining the EC. Within this general framework the government's main priorities were to provide housing for thousands living in illegal shanty dwellings, to develop a more aggressive export policy, to modernize the backward agricultural sector, and to strengthen municipal and regional local government.

To add to the political difficulties of the Balsemão administration, economic factors were negative as well. With the strong U.S. dollar adding to inflation, high interest rates made servicing of the public debt more costly. Meanwhile, a prolonged drought inflated the energy bill and, coupled with forest fires, added enormously to the already high costs of food and raw materials. The social climate

was marred by public-service strikes in protest against a prices and incomes policy that sought to contain wages below annual inflation rates.

(MICHAEL WOOLLER)

See also Dependent States.

Prisons and Penology

Crime rates continued to rise in most countries in 1981, particularly among the growing number of unemployed youth. Although the trends in offenses known to the police did not precisely reflect the trends in the number of persons found guilty, almost everywhere the latter rose to stretch the financial, physical, and manpower resources of penal systems and, in particular, of prisons. The situation was almost as difficult for the staff as it was for the inmates. In March 1981, for the first time in any country, Italian prison governors went on strike. An additional reason there was the alleged unresponsiveness of the centralized prison administration. A prolonged industrial dispute between uniformed prison staff and the Home Office in England and Wales was ostensibly about money, but the aloofness of headquarters personnel also played a part, as did the cramped conditions and physical decay of many old prison buildings.

Ironically, the dispute in Britain resulted in improved conditions; the officers decided not to admit new prisoners and, consequently, overcrowding was reduced. In this situation the courts im-

Picketers marched outside the Indiana State Prison protesting the scheduled execution of convicted murderer Steven Judy. The execution took place on March 9, as scheduled.

WIDE WORLD

Flames leaped through a building at
the Marquette State Prison in Michigan after inmates had rioted
there in May.

posed fewer custodial sentences on the less dangerous offenders. But the temporary easing of the
situation stopped almost as soon as the dispute was
over. By the beginning of July the prison population was at a new record level. The subsequent
serious street disturbances in a number of British
cities required special emergency accommodations
to deal with an increased number of prisoners. In
December Home Secretary William Whitelaw introduced a bill in Parliament that included plans
for two new prisons and proposed a system of early
release for short-term prisoners in order to ease
overcrowding. In France 5,000 such prisoners had
been granted an amnesty for the same reason, and
in Alabama a federal judge in July ordered the
release of 400 state inmates to relieve the crowded
conditions. The U.S. Supreme Court upheld the
ruling, and eventually 222 were freed.

The most dramatic escape of the year was made
by helicopter by two men who managed to outwit
the sophisticated security system of the fairly new
maximum security prison at Fleury-Mérogis near
Paris. Belgians were surprised that three men got
out of the brand-new jail at Lantin, near Liège.
Incidents such as that in which officers were taken
hostage by inmates at Gazzi in Sicily occurred in
many prisons. Disturbances took place in several
state prisons in the U.S.; riots in Michigan resulted
in injuries to inmates and staff. Sometimes tensions could be eased by conjugal visits, as at the
Parchman, Miss., state prison; or by having men
and women prisoners living together, as at Ringe
prison in Denmark, where that experiment had
successfully completed its fifth year. But prisoners
and staff were also capable of at least intermittent
unity of purpose. At Pontoise in France 70 prisoners joined the staff in a hunger strike to protest the
disciplining of three staff members.

In the U.S. many death sentences were pronounced, and in the Indiana State Prison Steven
Judy was executed on March 9. In France, as a
result of some sensational murder trials, there had
again been fierce public debate about the death
penalty. Several death sentences were actually pronounced, but none was carried out.

The world recession put fresh emphasis on the
cost-effectiveness of penal methods. It became essential to get value for money. For example, treatment in the community for nondangerous
offenders was cheaper and no less effective than
putting them inside a prison. Also, the practice of
creating probation "packages" increased. These
combined probation with education, job training,
and, perhaps, a condition of residing at a hostel.
Because resources were so expensive, hard looks
were taken at how probation officers actually spent
their time and the funds that were used for paying
for their accommodations and working costs. The
state of Virginia, for example, had strict operating
criteria, including carefully spelled-out standards
for supervision of offenders that probation officers
were expected to follow. Noncompliance with
minimum requirements had to be justified.

There had been a move away from indetermi-
nate sentences, with their many inequities. This
had occurred particularly in some states of the U.S.
Unfortunately, the result quite frequently was
longer fixed sentences, leading, in turn, to even
greater pressures on prison space. Something had
to give, and in some cases discretion was exercised
elsewhere in the system, for example, through
plea-bargaining by lawyers.

When a particular penal administration was actually willing to spend more public funds on prisons, there was often opposition from the public. In
March the justice minister of Hessen in West Germany proposed a major program of prison building to ease the considerable overcrowding.
Working against the proposal were various citizens' groups. The enormous cost of building new
institutions was compared with the relative cheap-
ness, flexibility, and variety of community-based
programs. But in August in the U.S., a committee
headed by former attorney general Griffin Bell
nevertheless recommended an increase in prison
building to house violent offenders, the abolition
of parole in federal cases, a tightening of bail laws,
the pretrial detention of suspects considered dangerous, a limitation of habeas corpus petitions,
and some tightening of gun-control laws.

Economic stringency made policymakers look more closely at early crime prevention. A mass of research had shown that no one penal method was particularly good at reducing the overall rate of relapse into crime. A study of children, parents, and crime in an inner-city area showed that lax parents were seven times more likely to have delinquent children than were parents who exercised more careful control. This raised the question as to whether more "parent-craft" should be taught in school. There was also evidence that crime rates in a street or housing development within the same area could vary considerably because of the presence, or absence, of a tiny number of highly criminal youths.

The role of the police in preventing crime has long been studied and examined. In July Pauline Morris and Kevin Heal published a synthesis of major research on an international level into the subject. The undertaking proved to be complex. For example, a special police drive in one area might not necessarily prevent or control crime overall but might merely displace it elsewhere. However, the development of "situational" policing, which linked the plotting of precisely where a certain sort of criminal activity was liable to occur with a planned attempt by the police to involve the local community appropriately in crime prevention, sometimes provided a systemic and optimistic approach. Much depended on the values current in a particular local community and how they coincided with those held by the police. There was some evidence that police work made no greater impact on crime than the penal system made on recidivism.

It did not follow, in the view of most observers, that the police and the penal system ought to be at least partially disbanded, as radical critics suggested. What was required was a concentration of efforts in those specific areas where the greatest impact could be made, together with an accurate selection of the most appropriate method backed by the necessary finances. In this way, penal and preventive measures could operate as efficiently and cost-effectively as possible.

(HUGH J. KLARE)

See also Crime and Law Enforcement; Law.
[521.C.3.a; 543.A.5.a; 10/36.C.5.b]

Publishing

The announcement in December 1981 that the *New York Daily News* was up for sale was a fitting postscript to the year's developments in Western newspaper publishing. In an unfavourable economic climate, closures and changes of ownership punctuated frenzied competition to boost sales.

There was no easing of other perennial pressures on independent journalism. Not unexpectedly, a clamp on the media was one of the first acts of the Polish government when finally it turned on the independent trade union Solidarity. In Brazil a woman journalist was jailed for violating the country's press laws. In Yugoslavia journalists were among hundreds purged from their jobs and the Communist Party in a crackdown on unrest in the

province of Kosovo. The military regime in Turkey remained in conflict with the country's outspoken press, and constant warnings were backed up by arrests. In South Africa black newspapers were forced to close and black journalists were banned. The British government, after dispelling earlier hopes of freer publication of official information, passed a new law on contempt of court that made this important area of reporting more difficult.

Within UNESCO, debate continued on the "new world information order," called for mainly by third world countries. In June an International Program for the Development of Communications was inaugurated under the direction of a 35-nation governing council.

Newspapers. One of the more bizarre years in the history of Britain's national press started with two major changes of ownership. The long crisis of Times Newspapers Ltd., following the decision by Lord Thomson and his board to sell or close the money-losing group, was resolved by its sale to Rupert Murdoch's (*see* BIOGRAPHIES) News International Ltd. The sale was contested by several other groups, and the decision was greeted by calls for government action under antimonopoly legislation. Murdoch fought off the challenges and emerged as controller (in addition to his extensive Australian and U.S. media interests) of the serious *The Times* and *The Sunday Times*, as well as his racy *Sun* and *News of the World*. Rapid management changes ensued, including the transfer of Harold Evans (*see* BIOGRAPHIES) to edit *The Times* (William Rees-Mogg having already stated he would resign when a sale was concluded) and the promotion of Frank Giles from deputy editor to succeed Evans at *The Sunday Times*.

The end of February brought the control of *The Observer*, Britain's other long-established serious Sunday newspaper, to the Scottish-based publishing house of George Outram. This excited concern on two fronts: the speed with which the California-based Atlantic Richfield Co., which had "rescued" the paper only four years earlier, had tired of its losses, estimated at $20 million over the period; and the possible clash of interests between editorial independence and the new owner, effectively Roland ("Tiny") Rowland, whose international conglomerate, Lonrho Ltd., controlled Outram. In July, however, after a Monopolies Commission inquiry, and with the establishment of a new board charged with protecting the public interest, *The Observer* passed to Rowland.

Rowland immediately announced a plan to launch a new evening newspaper in London, which had had only one evening newspaper since the merger of the *Evening News* and *Evening Standard* into the *New Standard* a year earlier. By year's end Rowland's plan seemed no nearer fruition, but there had been the announcement of a new national Sunday newspaper; with a launch date of May 2, 1982, the *Mail on Sunday* would be a sister to Associated Newspapers Ltd.'s *Daily Mail*.

This apparent enthusiasm for owning newspapers and starting new ones was in marked contrast with the actual state of the industry. In November the Newspaper Publishers' Association predicted an overall profit for 1981 of £8 million on a turn-

World Daily Newspapers and Circulation, 1979–80[1]

Location	Daily newspapers	Circulation per 1,000 population	Location	Daily newspapers	Circulation per 1,000 population
AFRICA			**ASIA**		
Algeria	5	26	Afghanistan	17	11
Angola	2	85	Bangladesh	31	6
Benin	1	3	Burma	7	24
Botswana	1	23	China	392	...
Cameroon	1	6	Cyprus	13	96
Central African Republic	1	...	Hong Kong	51	350
Chad	3	...	India	992	...
Congo	5	36	Indonesia	172	...
Egypt	10	102	Iran	28	25
Equatorial Guinea	2	...	Iraq	5	21
Ethiopia	3	2	Israel	25	156
Gabon	2	24	Japan	180	396
Ghana	4	35	Jordan	6	58
Guinea	1	2	Kampuchea	17	10
Guinea-Bissau	1	2	Korea, North	11	...
Ivory Coast	1	4	Korea, South	37	133
Kenya	3	12	Kuwait	8	322
Lesotho	3	24	Laos	3	...
Liberia	3	6	Lebanon	38	177
Libya	3	22	Macau	6	28
Madagascar	7	5	Malaysia	36	139
Malawi	2	6	Mongolia	2	101
Mali	2	...	Nepal	29	...
Mauritius	12	94	Pakistan	106	...
Morocco	10	13	Philippines	18	25
Mozambique	3	...	Saudi Arabia	12	28
Niger	1	0.2	Singapore	12	356
Nigeria	23	8	Sri Lanka	14	25
Réunion	3	65	Syria	7	8
Senegal	1	6	Taiwan	31	171
Seychelles	2	79	Thailand	31	50
Sierra Leone	2	...	Turkey	450	...
Somalia	2	...	Vietnam	5	11
South Africa	25	60	Yemen (Aden)	4	...
Sudan	4	7	Yemen (San'a')	2	...
Tanzania	2	9	Total	2,798	
Togo	2	4			
Tunisia	5	22			
Uganda	1	2			
Upper Volta	3	...	**EUROPE**		
Zaire	6	2	Albania	2	54
Zambia	4	43	Austria	31	412
Zimbabwe	2	16	Belgium	39	418
Total	179		Bulgaria	16	214
			Czechoslovakia	30	286
			Denmark	49	367
			Finland	57	517
			France	157	214
NORTH AMERICA			Germany, East	39	514
Antigua	2	146	Germany, West	411	404
Bahamas, The	3	140	Gilbraltar	2	488
Barbados	1	130	Greece	106	113
Belize	2	60	Hungary	29	275
Bermuda	1	203	Iceland	6	567
Canada	119	218	Ireland	10	246
Costa Rica	5	109	Italy	80	123
Cuba	16	...	Liechtenstein	2	533
Dominican Republic	10	45	Luxembourg	5	321
El Salvador	11	...	Malta	5	...
Guadeloupe	1	121	Netherlands, The	95	315
Guatemala	9	25	Norway	83	440
Haiti	6	30	Poland	47	351
Honduras	7	67	Portugal	30	62
Jamaica	3	53	Romania	35	145
Martinique	1	143	Spain	143	116
Mexico	256	...	Sweden	113	584
Netherlands Antilles	7	200	Switzerland	97	233
Nicaragua	8	89	U.S.S.R.	686	396
Panama	6	75	United Kingdom	130	251
Puerto Rico	5	159	Vatican City	1	70
Trinidad and Tobago	4	175	Yugoslavia	28	101
United States	1,745	282	Total	2,564	
Virgin Islands (U.S.)	4	178			
Total	2,232				
			OCEANIA		
			American Samoa	2	325
SOUTH AMERICA			Australia	70	370
Argentina	176	...	Cook Islands	1	83
Bolivia	13	46	Fiji	3	108
Brazil	328	...	French Polynesia	4	98
Chile	47	...	Guam	1	156
Colombia	40	...	New Caledonia	2	131
Ecuador	29	49	New Zealand	33	240
French Guiana	1	21	Niue	1	60
Guyana	3	2	Papua New Guinea	1	8
Paraguay	5	40	Total	118	
Peru	34	66			
Suriname	7	91			
Uruguay	30	39			
Venezuela	54	178			
Total	767				

[1]Only newspapers issued four or more times weekly are included.
Sources: UNESCO, *Statistical Yearbook, 1980*; *Editor and Publisher International Year Book* (1981); *Europa Year Book 1981, A World Survey*; various country publications.

over of £900 million, pointed to a 4.2% drop in sales from the first half of 1980, and revealed that newsprint manufacturers had been asked to reduce exchange-rate-inflated prices immediately to keep some papers in business. All the major provincial newspaper chains reported poor results, numerous titles were closed or merged, and in November Thomson Regional Newspapers announced a retrenchment plan implying 500 lost jobs. At the same time, Murdoch announced that the Times Newspapers group was losing at a rate of £13 million a year, despite the previous management's traumatic efforts at cost cutting.

It was in this climate that the "bingo war" was started in June by Lord Matthews's *Daily Star*. The *Sun* and the *Daily Mirror* quickly followed suit, and by autumn the *Daily Express*, the *Daily Mail*, and all their associated Sunday papers were involved. Bingo cards were distributed by mail or house-to-house delivery, and a selection of numbers was printed in the paper daily, with increasingly huge cash prizes for the first reader who could match the numbers with those on his or her card. Total prize money soon ran into millions of pounds, on top of the expensive distribution system. By year's end sales figures of the popular newspapers were being wildly distorted as people bought copies of several papers just for the game. It was hard to see how the craze could be kept going, but no easier to see who would be first to pull out.

Italy suffered a national one-day newspaper strike in November as journalists expressed sympathy with colleagues hit by layoff and closure plans of the money-losing Rizzoli group, publishers of *Il Corriere della Sera* and other papers. The closures followed legislation passed earlier in the year that made the availability of state subsidies subject to compliance with regulations restricting monopoly ownership of newspapers and periodicals. The P2 Freemasons' lodge scandal that brought down the Italian government in May had repercussions in newspaper publishing: Angelo Rizzoli was named as being on the P2 list, as was *Il Corriere della Sera*'s editor, Franco Di Bella, who stepped down in June. In West Germany *Die Welt*, prestige daily of Axel Springer's publishing empire, was losing around $15 million annually, and stringent economies were planned. Peter Bönishch, editor of *Die Welt* since 1979 but thought to be too liberal for Springer's liking, was replaced in March by a three-member directorate.

(PETER FIDDICK)

After years of growth in both prosperity and prestige, the U.S. newspaper industry endured a number of setbacks in 1981. For the first time in seven years, total daily circulation declined, from 62,223,040 in 1980 to 62,201,840 (−0.3%), according to the 1981 *Editor & Publisher International Year Book*. Morning circulation rose by 2.9% over the previous year's all-time high to 29,414,036, but evening circulation dropped 2.6% to 32,787,804, the lowest in more than two decades. The total number of daily newspapers fell by 18, to 1,745.

Much of that decline was accounted for by mergers, notably the consolidation of ten small dailies in the Chicago area. But the reduction also reflect-

ed one of the most enduring trends on the newspaper scene, the decline of the evening newspaper. Though most U.S. dailies were still published in the afternoon (1,388, as compared with only 387 published in the morning), evening dailies, especially those in large cities, were losing readers to the suburbs, where delivery through afternoon rush-hour traffic grew increasingly difficult, and to the growing popularity of evening television newcasts. Four evening papers switched to morning delivery, and six others began issuing editions around the clock.

The year's most stunning "death in the afternoon" was the disappearance of the *Washington Star*, which ceased publication after years of declining fortunes. The *Star* had gained a reprieve in 1978, when it was purchased by Time Inc. The firm invested $85 million in a rescue operation, but after 3½ years the *Star*'s daily circulation had slipped from 349,000 to 323,000 and the rival *Washington Post*'s share of the local advertising market remained a formidable 75%.

Only two weeks after the *Star* fell, another major daily came close to suffering the same fate. The *Bulletin*, for years the dominant paper in Philadelphia, announced that it would cease publication. Despite the addition of morning editions and an infusion of cash from its new owner, the Charter Co., the *Bulletin* had lost $31.2 million since 1979. A few days before the *Bulletin* was to close, however, the paper's union employees accepted a management proposal to save $5 million a year in labour costs. In return, Charter agreed to spend another $30 million to keep the paper afloat.

Among other notable evening casualties was the morning *New York Daily News*'s year-old evening offshoot, *Tonight*. That venture was intended to halt the *News*'s huge circulation loss (from 2.3 million to 1.9 million since 1975) and add "upscale" middle-class readers to the paper's traditional blue-collar base. But *Tonight*'s circulation, projected at 300,000, never rose much beyond the 95,000 copies it was selling at the end. In December the parent Chicago Tribune Co. announced that it was seeking a buyer for the *News*.

The year was marked by major embarrassment for two of the nation's most important dailies. Janet Cooke, a young staff member of the *Washington Post*, was awarded a Pulitzer Prize for feature writing for her sensational article about "Jimmy," an otherwise unnamed eight-year-old heroin addict. Shortly after the prize was announced, Cooke admitted that she had fabricated the story and that the boy did not exist. She resigned, and the *Post* returned the award and apologized to its readers in an editorial. Less than a month later, Michael Daly, a columnist for the *New York Daily News*, resigned after it was found that he had invented at least some details in a column about British soldiers in Northern Ireland.

Aside from the Cooke affair, the 1981 Pulitzer Prize awards were uncharacteristically free of controversy. The Gold Medal for Public Service went to the *Charlotte* (N.C.) *Observer* for a series of articles on brown lung disease among textile workers. The prize for criticism went to Jonathan Yardley for his book reviews in the *Washington Star*. The

Washington, D.C., was left with one major daily newspaper after the *Washington Star* ceased publication in August.

award for international coverage went to Shirley Christian of the *Miami Herald* for her reporting from Central America. The *New York Times*, which had won more Pulitzers than any other paper, added two more for John Crewdson's account of U.S. immigration problems and for Dave Anderson's commentary on sports. After the *Washington Post* returned Cooke's feature writing award, it was given to Teresa Carpenter of New York City's *Village Voice*. (DONALD MORRISON)

Magazines. In a year dominated by economic factors, the most prominent failure among British magazines could not be attributed to the recession. In April Sir James Goldsmith closed his weekly news magazine, *Now!*, after barely 18 months of existence. The French-based entrepreneur had made several attempts to buy a base in the British press before launching the magazine that was to be for Great Britain what *Time* and *Newsweek* were for the U.S. and his own *L'Express* was for France. Defying those who said that nationwide daily newspapers and television in the U.K. made conditions different, he proclaimed a target circulation of 350,000, launched the magazine at around 250,000, and saw it slide steadily down in spite of the high pay and professionalism of the staff.

In France Goldsmith's activities as proprietor focused on support for Pres. Valéry Giscard d'Estaing in the year's presidential election campaign. In January he refused to let an edition of *Now!* sell in France with an article critical of Giscard. In May, when *L'Express* appeared with an unflattering cover drawing of Giscard, Goldsmith fired editor Olivier Todd.

Science Magazines

Although the National Science Foundation predicted that Americans were headed toward virtual scientific and technological illiteracy, magazine publishers bet against the odds. Between 1979 and 1981 a new popular technology or science magazine appeared in the U.S. almost every six months on the average and more were promised. The reason for the new wave was success. Scientific magazines like *Psychology Today* and *Smithsonian* had proved lucrative and popular, and publishers were guessing readers wanted more.

They were probably right, for as the U.S. and other developed countries moved from an industrial to a technological/service society there was more need for people conversant with science and technology. Beyond the pragmatic were the millions who simply enjoyed scientific TV programs and computer games.

In 1981 the leading "objective-science" title remained *Scientific American*, established in 1845 and boasting 700,000-plus readers. Despite elaborate illustration and some down-to-earth material, it has been a difficult magazine for the average layperson to read. Filling the comprehension gap were the magazines directed to readers who wanted the facts free of technicalities. Here the leader was *Science 81*. Established in 1979 by the American Association for the Advancement of Science, it had a circulation of 465,000. Also popular were

The Sciences, with a more modest 50,000 circulation, and the highly regarded *Science News*, with a circulation of 175,000.

Another type was the more journalistic, easy-to-understand magazine with a focus on recent scientific discoveries and moderately sensational findings. Time Inc.'s 1980 entry here was *Discover*, which followed the news format, featured excellent illustration, and sold to 506,000 readers. Yet a third type comprised titles that claimed some objectivity but essentially stressed the future, the sensational, and the world of science fiction. The leader was *Omni*, the 1978 brainchild of the publisher of *Penthouse*, with a circulation of more than 800,000. Finally there were the technology and specialized magazines, which ranged from the theoretical *Technology Review*, published by MIT since 1899, to the new *Technology*, *Technology Illustrated*, and *High Technology*, whose readers were laypersons involved with practical interests, and to specialty titles like *Microcomputing*, established in 1980.

As a reminder, although there has been a sudden burst of scientific titles, many popular ones have been around for years: *Astronomy* (1973), *Archaeology* (1948), *Audubon Magazine* (1899), *Natural History* (1900), and *Science* (1880), to name some major ones.

(WILLIAM A. KATZ)

In France and England two magazines founded on very different principles from those of Goldsmith—equal salary for all staff members—suffered extended closedowns in 1981, though for different reasons. In Paris *Libération*, founded as a left-wing, cooperatively run publication in 1973, decided that it needed a rethink and took the admirably honest step of going off the streets. It returned on May 14 after a 12-week break, smaller in format and crisper in style and apparently determined to attract a wider public. In London the staff of *Time Out* wanted to continue their equal-pay policy counter to the wishes of owner and founder Tony Elliott. The journalists struck and then were locked out; ultimately no compromise could be found. With a circulation of some 80,000, *Time Out* had been one of the successes of the 1970s, selling as a remarkably comprehensive weekly guide to events in London with a front section of radically inclined features. Its extended absence resulted in a battle between three magazines where there had been one; most of the staff of *Time Out* started their own *City Limits*, allowing Elliott to start again, while another new contender, *Event*, began under record tycoon Richard Branson.

The *Sunday Express* and the *News of the World* newspapers each launched a colour magazine supplement, a move viewed with suspicion by the magazine business proper, with despair by delivery boys and girls (there were five such magazines every Sunday), and with doubt even in newspaper circles, in which it was felt that part of the gain in revenue from colour advertising was at the ex-

pense of the parent papers' regular black-and-white advertisements.

Index on Censorship, a forum for writers unable to publish in their own countries, celebrated its 50th issue and tenth year in November.

(PETER FIDDICK)

Cable television, computers, and magazines became joint partners in 1981, continuing a phenomenon of the late 1970s. *Reader's Digest* purchased the information-game database SOURCE and began marketing the home computer service as it would a popular magazine. *Playboy* and *Penthouse* announced plans to produce cable versions of their titles, and the television cable service USA Network, which developed out of a general magazine format, reported wide acceptance of its approach.

The natural extension of this three-way partnership was likely to be the on-line periodical. Through such home information systems as teletext or viewdata, readers could call up what they wanted to view on the TV screen. (*See* TELEVISION AND RADIO: *Special Report.*) Another version of this personalized interest approach was offered by *Games*, which produced separate inserts for interests of various readers. A puzzle insert might go to one group of readers, a science fiction game to another group. The inserts were sorted from the magazine's circulation lists by computer.

Several titles introduced in 1981 reflected the increased involvement of readers and publishers with the new information technology. *Software* featured articles on the influence of automation on business policies and decisions. *Data Sources*, cast-

ing a wider net, was directed toward anyone interested in information on the newest data processing and communications equipment. The Institute of Electrical and Electronics Engineers (IEEE) Computer Society began publishing two new technical journals, *IEEE Micro* on microcomputing and *IEEE Computer Graphics and Applications.* The new entry likely to have the greatest effect was *Electronic Learning,* a classroom magazine to be issued by Scholastic Inc. and intended for a wide readership in elementary and secondary schools.

In the precarious financial world of magazine publishing, women's magazines continued to flourish, showing annual reader gains of 4–35%. The leader in 1981 was *Self,* a Conde Nast title started in 1979 and directed to the average woman, regardless of age or income. Its pages of advertisement jumped from 520 in the first year to about 800. Among the year's promising new entries were *Spring,* a health-oriented publication; *Every Woman,* for the independent single; and *Woman's World,* the first weekly women's magazine in the U.S.

Several periodicals had their troubles during the year. The editorial staff of *Quest* refused to publish an article by the magazine's founder and then quit, forcing the successful title to be sold. The scholarly *Marxist Perspectives* closed because, despite excellent contributors, the staff could not agree on ideology. *The Atlantic* was the centre of a lawsuit, its new owner claiming that the old owner had not revealed the true state of the magazine's finances. Nevertheless, after a near death in 1979–80, *The Atlantic* became a booming success. The largest libel award of the year was assessed against *Penthouse* when a U.S. federal jury awarded $26.5 million in damages to a former Miss Wyoming for a story about her in the publication. The decision was being appealed.

A soggy U.S. economy dominated the publishing financial scene in 1981, and glorious hopes of 41% increases in advertising revenues over two years dwindled toward a less exciting 10–12% rise. At the same time, publishers reported drops of as much as one-third in both single and subscription sales. Coupled with the mid-1981 jump in second-class mail rates and increasing costs for paper and labour, magazines looked to higher cover prices. The average cost of a single issue of a popular title rose to $1.50 in 1981 from 63 cents in 1970. In terms of annual subscriptions, the cost was $156 for the average chemistry or physics journal in 1981, compared with $8.50 for a children's magazine.

(WILLIAM A. KATZ)

Books. The 1981 Frankfurt (West Germany) Book Fair, held October 14–19, was a rather quiet affair, with fewer spectacular auctions than in previous years, but many companies were nevertheless delighted with the amount of business that emerged. For U.K. publishers this reflected the improvement in the industry's fortunes over the past 12 months. Although world recession still posed a major problem, there was amelioration in interest rates, and a more realistic level of the pound sterling, particularly in relation to the U.S. dollar, provided the renewed competitiveness in export markets necessary to move sales. By the end of 1981

ELECTRONIC LEARNING

THE MAGAZINE FOR EDUCATORS OF THE 80'S

Shopping for Technology
EL's Guide for Educators

- The How-To's of Electronic Teaching
- Making Your Computer Skills Pay Off
- New Life for Video Technology

PREMIER ISSUE

One of the newest entries on the U.S. magazine publishing scene was *Electronic Learning,* aimed at educators in elementary and secondary schools; the publisher was Scholastic Inc.

many publishers turned in considerably improved results and had developed more optimistic and confident attitudes. Hardest hit were trade publishing and mass-market paperbacks, but even in those fields some publishing houses achieved encouraging figures. Educational publishers, particularly those with strong English-language teaching and export interests, generally performed better.

Overall, the problems of 1980 had created a slimmer, tougher, and more competitive U.K. publishing industry. Total sales of British books in 1980 were reported at £646 million, an increase of 11% over the 1979 figure of £580 million. Exports accounted for £310 million of the total, an increase of about 7% over the previous year.

The Whitford report on copyright, published during the year, did not go as far as some educational publishers had hoped, but it nevertheless gave indications of tougher attitudes toward photocopying in schools and educational institutions. Indications at year's end, however, were that the government would postpone taking action on the report's recommendations.

Schoolbook piracy in Nigeria contributed notably to the international book piracy problem, becoming of as much concern as the more traditional piracy centres in Southeast Asia and the Indian subcontinent. Legal proceedings were instituted against book pirates in Singapore, and British publishers also took action in India, Jordan, Hong Kong, and Greece. Chinese publishing authorities continued to examine international copyright conventions amid growing optimism that their accession might not be far distant. Several other countries also were considering accession or were revising or redrafting existing legislation. Numerous instances of market infringements (the sale of

editions in markets for which no distribution rights had been granted) were countered with a series of legal actions to protect these market rights.

A growing number of less developed countries experienced severe difficulties in providing sufficient books for even their most basic educational requirements. Rising oil prices reduced available finance for book or materials purchases, and foreign exchange facilities were frequently uncertain. Consequently, basic book supplies depended increasingly on aid money.

Although the third biennial Moscow International Book Fair, held September 3–8, was boycotted by the Association of American Publishers, it reportedly produced contracts worth some $125 million. Time-Life Books, among a group of U.S. publishers who disregarded the boycott, was said to have signed contracts covering 200 titles.

(ANTHONY A. READ)

Economic woes, both national and worldwide, were reflected in the stagnant state of U.S. book sales in 1981. Although the publishing industry topped an estimated $7 billion in 1980 on sales of more than 1,800,000,000 books (a dollar increase of 11% over 1979), unit sales, or the actual number of books sold, rose by only 3% over 1979. This pattern of modest dollar growth on small unit increases continued through the first half of 1981. The Association of American Publishers estimated book sales through May 1981 at nearly $2.4 billion on sales of some 635 million books. Those figures represented an 8.7% increase in dollar volume over the same period in 1980 but a rise of only 0.2% in unit sales. In another analysis the Book Industry Study Group estimated an 11% growth in dollar sales during the first six months of 1981 on an increase of 1.5% in unit sales over a comparable period in 1980. (Exact accounting of publishing sales statistics is made difficult by the fractured nature of the industry and by the standard practice of allowing returns of unsold books.)

Recognizing that booksellers were confronted with similar difficulties, many publishers announced radical new discount, shipping, and returns policies that would allow bookstores to increase their margin of profit by passing along some costs to the consumer. These adjusted policies represented the first fundamental changes in many years in the way the publishing industry sells its books.

During the 1970s many formerly independent publishing houses were acquired by investment-minded conglomerates including Gulf & Western, MCA, Warner Communications, CBS, ABC, and Time Inc. This concentration of publishing power was most notable in the trade, or general book, publishing field, where it was estimated that by 1981 the nine largest companies accounted for 50% of sales. This intense concentration was the cause for much heated debate over the control of editorial decision making. Many writers and editors feared that a new and overriding emphasis on commercially successful books would stifle publication of serious, scholarly, and literary books, which are often less profitable. A flurry of changes in key editorial offices at several prominent houses,

accompanied by cutbacks in publishing programs and staff layoffs at others, was offered as evidence in support of these misgivings.

The first antitrust suit brought against a publishing conglomerate was settled when CBS Inc. agreed to sell off Popular Library, a small paperback operation. Under the terms, CBS was permitted to retain Fawcett Books, another larger paperback operation, along with several other book and magazine publishing interests it held.

There were two notable transfers of publishing firms during 1981, although neither one involved an independent house. In the first, William Morrow & Co. was acquired by the Hearst Corp. from the SFN Companies for more than $25 million. Hearst, a large communications conglomerate, already owned Avon Books, a publisher of paperbacks, and Arbor House, a hardcover operation, in addition to its extensive holdings in newspapers, television, and magazines. In the other exchange, the 129-year-old firm of Dutton was sold by its Dutch owners, Elsevier NDU, on a tentative basis to a New York information company whose directors subsequently rejected the sale. Dutton was later sold to the Dyson-Kissner-Moran Corp., a private investment firm, for a price reported to be less than $2 million. Ironically, this figure was less than the amount that paperback publisher Pocket Books had paid to Dutton for reprint rights to *The Hotel New Hampshire,* a bestselling novel by John Irving.

The lull on the previously overheated paperback auction scene offered another indication of the caution and belt-tightening among publishers. Besides the sale of Irving's novel, some of the prominent paperback deals reportedly involving more than a million dollars were for a biography of Elizabeth Taylor, a book about Elvis Presley, a novel by Thomas Harris, and a novel by Cynthia Freeman. In a nonpaperback deal Simon & Schuster paid celebrity astronomer Carl Sagan, author of *Cosmos,* the sum of $2 million for the rights to an unwritten first novel about contact with beings from another planet. The single largest deal in dollar value was the sale by St. Martin's Press of the paperback, book-club, and condensation rights to *The Lord God Made Them All* for a combined total of more than $3.5 million. The book was the fourth in a series of best-sellers by British veterinarian James Herriott (*see* BIOGRAPHIES). Most authors, however, were not so fortunate. As a survey of American writers showed, the median salary was $4,775, and 25% of those surveyed made less than $1,000 from their writing.

On top of its other problems, the publishing industry was confronted by a potentially devastating tax ruling. In 1980 the Supreme Court had handed down a decision against the Thor Power Tool Co. that had the effect of disallowing depreciation of stock in inventories for tax purposes. Threatened with large increases in their tax bills, many publishers reported that they were faced with the prospect of destroying thousands of backlist books that they could no longer afford to warehouse. Several attempts at legislative relief had been rejected in 1980, and yet another attempt was under consideration by Congress at the end of 1981.

The new strength of the conservatives in Washington mirrored a nationwide grass-roots movement that was evidenced by the strength of such groups as the Moral Majority. As one effect librarians around the nation experienced an alarming increase in demands for the removal of certain books and materials from school and public libraries. This new wave of attempted book bannings was the most powerful of its kind since the landmark court decisions in favour of *Lady Chatterly's Lover* and *Tropic of Cancer* more than 20 years earlier. In addition to such perennial targets of censorship as *The Catcher in the Rye*, many of the books being questioned dealt with American history, feminism, and racial attitudes. Examples were *365 Days*, a nonfiction account of a medic's Vietnam experiences; *Run, Shelley, Run*, a novel about juvenile runaways; and *The Magician*, a novel by Sol Stein. The Supreme Court agreed to hear arguments in a case involving a Long Island, N.Y., community where censored books included *Slaughterhouse Five, The Naked Ape, Down These Mean Streets, Soul on Ice, The Fixer*, and a collection of black writing edited by Langston Hughes.

Fundamentalists in other sections of the country revived the debate over the teaching of evolutionary theory, with potentially damaging possibilities for publishers of science and other textbooks. Several states passed or were considering laws directing schools to teach biblical creationism along with scientific evolutionary theory, thus requiring all science and biology textbooks used in those states to be revised to include a creationist view of human origins. At year's end challenges to the constitutionality of these laws were before the courts. (KENNETH C. DAVIS)

See also Literature.
[441.D; 543.A.4.e]

Qatar

An independent monarchy (emirate) on the west coast of the Persian Gulf, Qatar occupies a desert peninsula east of Bahrain, with Saudi Arabia and the United Arab Emirates bordering it on the south. Area: 11,400 sq km (4,400 sq mi). Pop. (1981 est.): 220,000. Capital: Doha (pop., 1981 est., 190,-000). Language: Arabic. Religion: Muslim. Emir and prime minister in 1981, Sheikh Khalifah ibn Hamad ath-Thani.

Qatar's commitment to closer ties with five other Gulf monarchies—Bahrain, Kuwait, Oman, Saudi Arabia, and the United Arab Emirates—was evident in its membership in the Gulf Cooperation Council, formed in March 1981. Emir Sheikh Khalifah ibn Hamad ath-Thani, a consistent advocate of closer Gulf ties, urged the formation of a Gulf common market and a monetary union, both long-term policies adopted by the council.

The government celebrated the tenth anniversary of independence in September with every evidence of stability at home and the respect of friends abroad. A decision was pending on the choice of joint venture partners for development of the North West Dome gas field, the first phase of which was likely to cost at least $4 billion. Among

Qatar

the 13 Organization of Petroleum Exporting Countries (OPEC) members, only Gabon and Ecuador produced less oil than Qatar; in 1981 output was reduced to 360,000 bbl a day. With the end of its oil reserves in sight, Qatar was looking toward its abundant reserves of gas for further revenue.

Attempts to diversify the economy were concentrated on the Umm Said industrial zone, 46 km (30 mi) south of Doha, the site of fertilizer and petrochemical plants, refineries, and the Gulf's first direct reduction steel plant. In February the emir opened the latest project, the Qatar Petrochemical Company's low-density polyethylene plant. Plans for the future included stimulating investment in light industry and encouraging development in places other than Doha. (JOHN WHELAN)

Race Relations

An aspect of race relations that claimed attention in 1981 concerned the status and rights of indigenous peoples in various regions of the world colonized from Europe in past centuries, notably the American Indians and the Australian Aborigines. In Europe itself worsening economic conditions, which generally affected immigrant ethnic minorities disproportionately, led to racially accented civil disturbances in some countries, and there was a continuance of neo-Fascist and other racist activity by groups such as the National Front in Britain and the National Democrats in West Germany.

Great Britain. The London Institute of Race Relations, in its *Annual Report 1980–81*, stated that "we have warned repeatedly about the unprecedented level of racist violence on the streets and the continual pressures put on black people—not the least of which is having constantly to prove, in any encounter with officialdom, their right even to be in Britain." The level of unprovoked assaults on minority ethnic groups received Home Office recognition in a study published on Nov. 17, 1981. A two-month survey of police records in 13 areas during the summer found 2,630 crimes involving 2,851 victims; in 25% (713) of these crimes there was found to be a racist motive where the victim and the alleged offender were of different ethnic

groups. In these, Asian victimization was 50 times greater than for white people, and the rate for black people was more than 36 times greater.

An earlier Home Office study published on August 20 on the progress of ethnic minority groups over the past 20 years confirmed continuing discrimination. It noted that despite its proscription by law in the Race Relations Act 1976, discrimination continued in housing, employment, and the provision of goods and services, "particularly against minorities perceived as 'coloured'."

Rioting occurred in more than 30 of Britain's towns and inner city areas during the year. Evidence did not indicate that they were race riots as such, those involved in the violent confrontations with police being predominantly unemployed youth who were both white and black. A special police operation code-named "Swamp 81" was mounted on April 6 in Brixton, south London, "to combat street crime"; more than 1,000 people were stopped and questioned there in the first four days. This heavy-handed operation was later held responsible for the angry resentment that erupted in the area on April 10–12. Nazi-inspired "skinhead" youths provided the spark for the next major outbreak of disorder, which took place in Southall, west London, on July 3–4; Asian youths burned down the Hamborough public house after skinheads there had assaulted an Indian woman. The biggest confrontation, however, took place in Toxteth, Liverpool, on July 3–7. In Moss Side, Manchester, on July 8 youths apparently answered police taunts by looting and holding the police at bay with gasoline bombs.

Government response to the riots was twofold. Home Secretary William Whitelaw announced on April 13 that an inquiry conducted by Lord Scarman would examine the serious disorder in Brixton and make recommendations (Scarman himself widened the terms of reference to include the "background"). Then on July 16 the home secretary announced that Michael Heseltine (*see* BIOGRAPHIES), the secretary of state for the environment, would visit Liverpool to study the city's problems.

Lord Scarman's report was published on November 25. It contained implicit criticism of policing methods, recommended a coordinated social policy to combat inner city decline, and drew attention to the special problems and needs of ethnic minorities. In conclusion it stated that "racial disadvantage is a fact of current British life."

The British Nationality Act 1981 became law in October. It created three new types of citizen, namely, citizen of U.K. and colonies; citizen of the British dependent territories; and British overseas citizen. There was widespread criticism of the act during its passage. The Legal Affairs Committee of the European Parliament said on July 6 that it created statelessness and conflicted with European Community law on citizens' freedom of movement. On April 2 the parliamentary Home Affairs Committee concluded that it would create 210,000 stateless British overseas citizens in, for example, Malaysia (130,000) and India (39,000). In London on April 5 a 15,000-strong demonstration was organized by the Campaign Against Racist Laws.

The Commission for Racial Equality (established in 1977) was severely criticized by the Home Affairs Committee in December. The committee's report called the commission ineffective and recommended changes in its structure and the scope of its operations.

Australia. The living conditions and rights of Australia's Aborigine peoples were recurrent themes of discussion in the media and among federal and state politicians during 1981. The first land rights agreement between Aborigine people and the state of South Australia was signed at Itjinpiri in November. State Premier David Tonkin handed a certificate to leaders of the Pitjantatjara people granting them inalienable freehold title to 102,000 sq km (40,000 sq mi), about one-tenth of the state's area. Up to 3,000 Aborigines living in neighbouring areas of the Northern Territories, Western Australia, and South Australia had their traditional lands restored, and similar action was proposed in Queensland and New South Wales.

Earlier in the year a World Council of Churches (wcc) delegation expressed serious concern about the condition of Aborigines in Australia and said that there was a lack of political commitment to solving their problems. The wcc repeated the accusation in a detailed report released in August, which was especially critical of conditions in Queensland and Western Australia. Queensland Premier Johannes Bjelke-Petersen characterized the report as "part of a concerted plan to bring black people to the fore."

North America. Canada's minister of state for multiculturalism, James Fleming, announced in November that his department's budget would be increased by $1.5 million and that three programs would deal with the problem of racism: a research unit to examine causes of racial intolerance; a comprehensive program of public education; and a national symposium to find ways in which the country's legal framework could respond to incidents of racial discrimination and harassment. "Racism is an insult to the spirit of Canada," said Fleming.

Proposals to patriate the Canadian constitution,

State court judge Richard L. Lee accompanies three students to court in Alexandria, La., to show cause in a contempt hearing. He had been escorting the students to Buckeye High School in defiance of a federal district judge's order that had assigned them to attend a different school as part of a desegregation plan.

WIDE WORLD

enshrined in the British North America Act 1867, led Canadian Indians to suspect that their treaty rights might be endangered. "Life for Canada's Indians is very hard with high unemployment and a high suicide rate," said Chief Soloman Sanderson, a Canadian Indian leader. "We want real control over our affairs." However, in December an application by the Association of Indians of Alberta for judicial review of their case in the English courts, in order to stop or influence the patriation process, was refused.

American Indians marched to the UN European office in Geneva on September 15, demanding a permanent seat at the UN. Criticism was also aimed at Pres. Ronald Reagan for suppressing those in the U.S. who demanded land rights.

Southern Africa. Speaking in October, Oscar Dhlomo, minister of education and culture in the KwaZulu Cabinet and secretary-general of the Inkatha movement representing 300,000 blacks, rejected the "independent" status the South African government planned for the Zulu people. Dhlomo said that if the choice lay between being "a foreigner and constitutional beggar (as fake independence implies) or a revolutionary, the latter is a respectable choice." Chief Gatsha Buthelezi reportedly told Piet Koornhof (*see* Biographies), South Africa's minister of cooperation and development, that if Pretoria tried to force independence at the point of a gun "then I will reply with a gun."

On November 4 South Africa's 800,000 Indians boycotted the election for a seat on the 45-member advisory South African Indian Council in protest against the government's apartheid policy. A nationwide poll of only 10.5% was recorded. Shelters of illegal black African squatters at Nyanga near Cape Town were destroyed by police in August; tear gas and dogs were used, and the area was blockaded to prevent food from reaching the squatters. Opposition member of Parliament Helen Suzman accused the government of letting the squatters "starve or freeze." The Department of Cooperation and Development arrested about 2,000 and deported them to the Transkei, their legal homeland. However, the Transkei refused to accept them and sent them back.

A large majority of voters in the wealthy white Cape Town suburb of Constantia supported desegregation of the area in a plebiscite organized by opposition MP Roger Hulley on November 5. Prime Minister P.W. Botha responded to the event on November 8 by calling it "transparent political antics." He assured National Party MP's that "I am not prepared to scrap the Group Areas Act. If that is going to be done it will have to be done by another prime minister."

In another challenge to one of apartheid's cornerstones, the Mixed Marriages Act which prohibits interracial marriages, the General Assembly of the Presbyterian Church of Southern Africa voted in favour of marrying couples of different races. Press reports in the Afrikaans newspaper *Beeld* on October 23 quoted prominent theologian Johan Heyns as saying that interracial marriages were not prohibited by Scripture. Botha was believed to have been referring to the Mixed Marriages and immorality acts, when, on accession to office in

1978, he said that he was not prepared to tolerate laws that insulted people. Nevertheless, about 300 people a year were charged under the Immorality Act. Former British Conservative Prime Minister Edward Heath, speaking in Johannesburg on August 31, warned that the West would not stand in strategic alliance with South Africa "as long as she pursues a system [which] is profoundly insulting to the rights of the overwhelming majority of its people."

In Zimbabwe it was announced in August that private community schools, used as a means of continuing whites-only education in an officially desegregated society, would be closed by the government at the end of the month. Addressing a political rally in November, Prime Minister Robert Mugabe said that the country's whites had not changed their racial attitudes since the end of white rule. He warned employers who insisted on referring to him as the "kaffir" prime minister that they would be deported.   (STUART BENTLEY)

[522.B]

Anti-apartheid demonstrators protested the appearance of Springbok, the South African rugby team, in Auckland, N.Z., in September.

Racket Games

Badminton. In July 1981 Santa Clara, Calif., was the site for the first World Games for Non-Olympic Sports. It was a major event in badminton because the World Badminton Federation had rejoined the International Badminton Federation in May. Because China had only recently joined the federation, it was allotted only one entry in each category. Though the Chinese lacked experience, they were highly regarded. Even so, no one expected them to be the sensations of the tournament.

Chen Changjie (China), competing in his first world tournament, met Frost Hansen, veteran from Denmark, in the men's singles final. Chen lost the first game but rallied to take the next two. The victory gave him the gold medal.

The women's singles final pitted Hwang Sun Ae (South Korea), winner of four gold medals in the prestigious All-England 1981 championships,

against Zhang Ailing (China). Hwang won the first game and was leading 6–1 in the second when Zhang made a spectacular comeback to tie the match 1–1. The third game reached 9–9 before Zhang pulled ahead to win the match and the women's title.

The men's doubles team of Sun Zhian and Yao Ximing (China) met European champions Thomas Kihlstrom and Stefan Karlsson (Sweden) for the championship. The Chinese emerged victorious 2–1. The finals of the women's doubles was also decided in three games. Liu Xia and Zhang Ailing (China) defeated Nora Perry and Jane Webster (England), the reigning All-England champions, to capture the gold medal.

The best single-day attendance at Santa Clara was 1,100. Had the event been staged in Japan, England, or Indonesia, the spectators would have numbered about 13,000 each day. The World Games was expected to be a biennial affair.

Though U.S. players had not attained world-class standards, there was growing interest in the sport, and the U.S. Badminton Association took heart from the fact that its membership increased about 17% during the year. The closed U.S. national championships would be long remembered by Chris and Utami Kinard of Pasadena, Calif. They became only the second husband and wife to win the individual singles crowns in the same year.

(C. R. ELI)

Squash Rackets. During the 1980–81 season the decision to abandon amateur status took effect. An early casualty was the British amateur championship, first played in 1922; its place was taken by a new competition for amateurs organized by the Jesters Club. The tournament, which offered no prize money and was of a lower calibre than in the past, was won by T. O'Connor of South Africa.

News of the year included the rapid rise of 17-year-old Jahangir Khan (Pak.), whose world ranking rose from 26th in 1980 to second in 1981. In the final of the British Open championship, however, Geoffrey Hunt (Australia), the current champion and seven times winner of the event, defeated Khan. J. G. A. Lyon (England) won the Open Veterans championship (45 and over), while the ageless Hashim Khan, who admitted to being 68, won his fourth successive Open Vintage championship (55 and over). Hunt also won the South African Open, beating G. Briars (England). In the International Squash Rackets Federation championships, Pakistan won the team event and S. Bowditch (Australia) the individual title. England won the European team championship.

The North American Open was won for the 13th time by Sharif Khan, son of Hashim Khan. The U.S. amateur championship went to M. Alger (U.S.), who in the final beat J. Gillespie (Canada). The Canadian softball was won by D. Whittaker and the handball by Gillespie. Stuart Davenport (N.Z.) became the World Junior champion.

Women's squash centred on the decision of Heather McKay (Australia) to retire from competitive squash after dominating the game for 29 years. In the final of the women's World championship, Rhonda Thorne (Australia) faced her compatriot Vicky Hoffman, the top seed and holder of the British Women's Open championship. Thorne won 8–9, 9–4, 9–5, 7–9, 9–7. (JOHN H. HORRY)

Rackets. John Prenn, the reigning titleholder, won the British Open singles championship for the third time, beating Willie Boone at Queen's Club, London, in April. Boone had regained the amateur singles title from Prenn in January. Boone and Randall Crawley won the new British Open doubles championship, defeating Charles Hue Williams and Prenn at Queen's Club in May; they also retained the amateur doubles title against the same opponents.

Prenn won the Canadian amateur singles title in Montreal in February, besting Willie Surtees, the world champion. Norwood Cripps regained the British professional championship from Terry Whatley, and James Male won the public schools singles championship in December 1980.

Real Tennis. Howard Angus, lacking practice because of an eye injury, lost all his titles in 1981. Chris Ronaldson, professional at Hampton Court, won the world championship from Angus at Queen's Club, London, in April. He retained the British Open singles, the Scottish Open singles, the Unigate world invitation singles, the British professional singles, and won the U.S. professional singles. In the world championship Ronaldson conquered Frank Willis, the former British professional champion, and Barry Toates, the U.S. contender, in two eliminating matches. In the championship match Angus tore a calf muscle during the third set and was forced to retire, thereby giving the victory to Ronaldson.

Alan Lovell won the amateur singles championship by defeating Angus in the final at Queen's Club in March. Later Lovell won the Marylebone Cricket Club gold racket at Lord's, again triumphing over Angus, who had held both this and the amateur singles for 15 years. Lovell and Norwood Cripps preserved their unbeaten record in doubles. They won the British Open doubles championship, the world invitation doubles, and the Scottish Open doubles. (CHRISTINA WOOD)

Racquetball. The 1981 Pro-Am racquetball championships were decided in June during a tournament held in Tempe, Ariz. Marty Hogan of San Diego, Calif., won his fourth consecutive professional title. All other matches involved amateurs. In men's singles competitions, Ed Andrews won the open, Gary Lusk the veteran (age 30+), Jay Schwartz the senior (age 35+), and Charles Garfinkel the veteran senior (age 40+). The masters (age 45+) was won by Myron Roderick, the veteran masters (age 50+) by Frank Leydens, the golden masters (age 55+) by Fred Zitzer, and the veteran golden masters by Luzell Wilde. Five doubles championships were also decided. Ken Garrigus and Keith Fleming won the open, Mike Romano and Gary Lusk the veteran, Ron Starkman and Robert Carson the senior, Bud Muehleisen and Myron Roderick the masters, and Leslie Skelton and Burt Morrow the golden masters.

In women's competition Liz Alvarado captured the open, Linda Liau the singles (30+ and 35+), and Geri McDonald the singles (40+ and 45+). The open doubles title was won by Liz Alvarado and Brenda Young. (ROBERT W. KENDLER)

Refugees

In 1981, for the second time since its establishment in 1951, the Office of the UN High Commissioner for Refugees (UNHCR) was awarded the Nobel Prize for Peace. (*See* NOBEL PRIZES.) During the year eight more nations became parties to the 1951 Convention or the 1967 Protocol Relating to the Status of Refugees, bringing the total number of countries acceding to these major international legal instruments to 91.

The work of UNHCR continued to be dominated by massive relief operations. In Pakistan and the Horn of Africa, the two areas with the largest concentrations of refugees in the world, durable solutions remained beyond reach. Elsewhere, a significant number of refugees were helped to return to their countries of origin, while thousands were either integrated locally in countries of first asylum or resettled abroad.

An estimated half of the world's refugees were located in Africa. In Somalia, where destitute Ethiopian refugees and displaced persons continued to arrive, difficulties were compounded by drought in the early part of the year followed by excessive rains and flooding in April and May. In Sudan the number of refugees rose to some 500,000 by mid-1981 and included persons of Ethiopian, Ugandan, Chadian, and Zairian origin. Assistance was also required by Ugandans fleeing to Zaire and by refugees from Chad in Cameroon, Nigeria, and the Central African Republic. In Angola, Namibian refugees were again at the mercy of military attacks by South African forces.

More positive developments occurred in other refugee situations in Africa. In 1981 UNHCR wound up an operation providing for the initial settlement and rehabilitation of 660,000 Zimbabweans, both returning refugees and persons who had been displaced within Zimbabwe as a result of the war. In Ethiopia the returnee movement gained momentum during the year. On October 1 a voluntary repatriation operation to Chad was launched by UNHCR. The problems resulting from the presence of some five million refugees and displaced persons in Africa were the focus of considerable public attention in 1981, thanks in part to the International Conference on Assistance to Refugees in Africa, held in Geneva in April and attended by the representatives of some 100 governments. Some $572 million was pledged during the conference.

Afghan refugees in Pakistan formed one of the largest concentrations of displaced persons anywhere. By mid-1981 Pakistani authorities estimated their number to be two million. Their steady influx necessitated periodic revisions of financial targets and a third special appeal for resources in June. While the emphasis by necessity remained on relief assistance, efforts were made to promote income-generating activities, notably in agriculture, carpet weaving, and the manufacture of handicrafts. A vocational training project was also established.

After reaching a peak in 1979 with some 205,000 arrivals throughout the region, the influx of Viet-

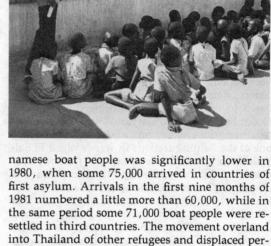

The Office of the UN High Commissioner for Refugees was awarded the 1981 Nobel Prize for Peace for its various activities in aiding refugees such as these small children in Zimbabwe.

namese boat people was significantly lower in 1980, when some 75,000 arrived in countries of first asylum. Arrivals in the first nine months of 1981 numbered a little more than 60,000, while in the same period some 71,000 boat people were resettled in third countries. The movement overland into Thailand of other refugees and displaced persons, mainly from Laos, continued in 1980 with the arrival of some 43,000 persons. Some 20,000 more arrived during the first nine months of 1981. More than 90,000 of these overland cases were resettled overseas in 1980 and more than 30,000 between January 1 and September 30 of 1981. Since 1977 UNHCR had assisted in the resettlement of more than 700,000 Indochinese refugees. Among them, by the end of September 1981, were some 12,000 persons who had left Vietnam for countries of resettlement.

Because of a large-scale exodus from El Salvador the total refugee population in Latin America grew considerably in 1980 and during the first nine months of 1981. Financial requirements for UNHCR's 1981 operations to aid Salvadoran refugees in Central America totaled some $10 million. In the absence of prospects for an early return home of the refugees, UNHCR's efforts in the area aimed to facilitate some degree of self-sufficiency for them, mainly through projects in the agricultural sector. (UNHCR)

See also Migration, International.

Religion

On Feb. 25, 1981, Pope John Paul II, speaking in Hiroshima, Japan, at the site where the first atomic bomb fell in 1945, made the most impassioned speech of his papacy, an appeal for world peace. "Let us take a solemn decision now that war will

never be tolerated or fought as a means of resolving differences," the pontiff pleaded. "Let us replace violence and hate with confidence and caring."

On March 31, however, a would-be assassin shot and wounded the president of the United States. And on May 13, as he was being driven into St. Peter's Square in Vatican City for one of his popular Wednesday audiences, John Paul himself became the victim of the violence he deplored when he was shot in the abdomen by a Turkish terrorist, Mehmet Ali Agca. Neither of these two assassination attempts was successful, but in October the president of Egypt, Anwar as-Sadat, was assassinated while reviewing a military parade. Many blamed conservative "Muslim fanatics" for the attack. A few weeks before his death, Sadat had tried to quell dissent in his country by closing numerous mosques and imposing restrictions on Coptic Christians. (See *Eastern Non-Chalcedonian Churches*, below.)

In a variety of ways, in a variety of places, religion and violence were intertwined in 1981. As the year began, members of the Maryknoll religious orders, Roman Catholic missionary organizations based in the U.S., were mourning the deaths in December 1980 of two Maryknoll nuns, murdered, together with another nun and a lay worker, by one of the fighting factions in war-ravaged El Salvador. On July 28 Stanley Rother, a Catholic missionary priest, was killed in the rectory near his church in Guatemala. The worldwide fear of violent attacks on prominent figures was so great that when the Dalai Lama, the gentle Buddhist monk exiled from his Tibetan home, toured the U.S. for six weeks, he was under heavy guard at all public appearances.

Violence, often connected with religion, continued to sweep through Iran. Under the regime's interpretation of Islamic law, numerous "enemies of the state" were executed. Among the major targets were members of the Baha'i sect, which grew out of 19th-century Islam but was regarded as heretical by leaders of the dominant faith. Violence answered violence, and much of the ruling Islamic Republican Party's leadership died in bombing attacks. (See *Islam*, below.)

Many religious leaders shared Pope John Paul's "intolerance" of war, but their ways of expressing it differed. The antiwar, antinuclear movement in Western Europe was instigated, in part, by activists driven by religious convictions. In the U.S. a number of religious leaders criticized the Reagan administration for sending weapons and advisers to El Salvador, for approving the building of the neutron bomb, and for greatly enlarging the defense budget. Veteran activists Philip F. Berrigan, a former Roman Catholic priest, and his brother, Father Daniel Berrigan, were sentenced to three to ten years in jail for their participation in an antinuclear protest and break-in at a General Electric plant in King of Prussia, Pa.

Antiwar sentiment also was registered by a coalition of Christians drawn from the ranks of traditional "peace churches," liberal wings of mainline Protestantism, and the small but influential Sojourners community in Washington. In its New Abolitionist Covenant, the coalition stated:

"Christian acceptance of nuclear weapons has brought us to a crisis of faith. The nuclear threat is not just a political issue. . . . It is a question that challenges our worship of God and our commitment to Jesus Christ." Nor was opposition to what was perceived as a revival of militarism confined to "nonestablishment" sectors of the religious community. Roman Catholic Archbishop Raymond Hunthausen of Seattle, Wash., attracted national attention in July when he called nuclear arms "demonic weapons which threaten all life on Earth" and called for citizens to withhold part of their federal income taxes as a protest. By November the Catholic Church in the U.S. was being called a "peace church." At the annual meeting of the National Conference of Catholic Bishops in Washington, D.C., Archbishop John Roach of St. Paul-Minneapolis, the conference president, devoted the heart of his "state of the church" speech to a denunciation of nuclear war. Two weeks earlier, Roach's immediate predecessor, Archbishop John R. Quinn of San Francisco, had asserted that traditional Catholic teaching on "just war" is anachronistic in the age of nuclear warfare.

At the same time, the U.S. administration's increased defense budget drew strong support from some conservative religious leaders. Most conspicuous and vocal were members of the so-called New Christian Right, especially fundamentalist preachers like the Rev. Jerry Falwell of Lynchburg, Va., and the Rev. James Robison of Fort Worth, Texas. In one of its pamphlets, the Moral Majority, one of the most prominent New Christian Right groups, stated: "We believe that a strong national defense is the best deterrent to war. We therefore support the efforts of President Reagan to regain our position of military preparedness. . . ." Closer to the middle of the road, there emerged a cluster of religious thinkers who, specifically in relation to the dispute over U.S. policy in El Salvador, took issue with Reagan's liberal critics without aligning themselves with the New Right. In this cluster were such well-known Christian writers as sociologist Peter L. Berger; Lutheran theologian Richard Neuhaus, a onetime leader of the anti-Vietnam war movement; and Michael Novak, a Roman Catholic theologian and former speechwriter for George McGovern, liberal hero of the 1972 presidential campaign.

Religious opinion in the U.S. was divided not only on war and peace issues but on other aspects of national policy as well. After the January inauguration of President Reagan, leaders of organized religion were required to stake out new positions. Ostracized from the Oval Office at the White House during the Nixon administration, leaders of the National Council of Churches again discovered they were on the outside looking in. That was not too surprising. At its May meeting, the NCC's governing board said it was in "fundamental disagreement" with the administration over its "survival of the fittest" economic and military policies. The U.S. hierarchy of the Roman Catholic Church had a more complicated relationship with the White House. Catholic leaders banked on the administration to support their stands against abortion and favouring tuition tax credits for parents with chil-

dren in nonpublic schools. Simultaneously, the hierarchy criticized the administration for budget cuts that "would fall most heavily on the poor." Generally, the new president received his strongest support from the New Christian Right, moderate evangelicals, and conservative segments of the Catholic and Orthodox churches and mainline Protestant denominations.

Throughout the year, the activities of militant religious conservatives and the backlash against them dominated the headlines on news stories about religion. After celebrating its victories in the 1980 elections, the New Christian Right turned its attention to the fights against pornography, abortion, and homosexuality and for prayers in the public schools and "cleaning up the airwaves." The moral crusaders, particularly the Rev. Donald E. Wildmon's Coalition for Better Television, claimed a major victory in the spring when Procter & Gamble, television's largest advertiser, announced it would not advertise on programs regarded as containing excessive sex, violence, and profanity. Other victory celebrations were staged after the Arkansas and Louisiana legislatures passed laws favoured by "scientific creationists," who argued that public schools should teach "the biblical view of creation" as well as the Darwinian theory of evolution.

These activities generated strong counterattacks. Civil libertarians filed suits in Louisiana and Arkansas challenging the constitutionality of the new laws that required teaching creation theory in the schools. In Arkansas a ruling was expected early in January 1982. Newspaper and magazine columns were filled with warnings about "absolutist" threats to First Amendment rights to freedom of speech and religion. Addressing freshmen at the start of the fall term, A. Bartlett Giamatti, president of Yale University, accused the Moral Majority and similar groups of engaging in a "radical assault" on the nation's values: "Angry at change, rigid in the application of chauvinistic slogans, absolutistic in morality, they threaten . . . whoever dares to disagree with their authoritarian positions." A Moral Majority spokesman countered by accusing Giamatti of practicing "liberal demagoguery."

Despite such attacks from the heart of the Establishment, grass-roots conservative movements continued to grow and to form institutions that embodied their views. *Phi Delta Kappan*, a journal for professional educators, reported that "the most rapidly growing segment of American elementary and secondary education is that of Protestant fundamentalist schools." One evangelical leader claimed that Protestant evangelical schools were growing at the rate of three a day, though he admitted that many were quite small. A concurrent development was the establishment of independent fundamentalist congregations that, according to the *New York Times*, might constitute "10 per cent of all the churches in the U.S."

The voices of religious conservatives continued to dominate television and radio's "electronic church," but during the year representatives of more moderate religious bodies made serious efforts to gain access to U.S. airwaves. The U.S.

Catholic Conference activated its National Catholic Telecommunications Network in an effort to get Catholic programs on cable and conventional television stations from coast to coast.

In early autumn two federal investigations of church officials led to new debates over church-state issues. In Chicago the *Chicago Sun-Times* published a series of stories revealing that John Cardinal Cody, leader of the nation's largest Roman Catholic archdiocese, was being investigated by a federal grand jury to determine whether he had diverted large sums of tax-exempt church funds to a lifelong friend. For months Cardinal Cody refused to turn over documents subpoenaed by the government and declined to answer the allegations. Meanwhile, a federal grand jury in New York indicted the Rev. Sun Myung Moon, the Korean-born head of the controversial Unification Church, on charges that he had filed false income tax returns.

A mixture of piety and politics was a global phenomenon. In Italy voters overwhelmingly rejected a Catholic Church-supported motion to rescind a law permitting women over 18 to have free abortions in state hospitals if two doctors agreed. (See *Roman Catholic Church*, below.) In Israel Orthodox Jewish religious parties gained new leverage in national decision-making following the close election in June. Prime Minister Menachem Begin's Likud bloc edged out the Labour Alignment by 48 seats to 47 in the Knesset, but Begin could not form a new coalition government without the support of the religious parties. This development upset many Jews inside and outside of Israel, especially representatives of the Reform and Conservative movements, who had long objected to exclusive Orthodox control over Jewish religious life in the Jewish state. (See *Judaism*, below.)

In Communist Poland, where the Roman Catholic Church still commanded the loyalty of millions despite the atheistic dogmas of the Marxist state, the church took on the difficult task of remaining in dialogue with both the government and the independent labour union, Solidarity. In the midst of a year of social unrest, Stefan Cardinal Wyszynski, primate of Poland and symbol of the church's resistance to Communist restrictions on religious life, died at the age of 79. His successor, Archbishop Jozef Glemp, vowed to continue the policies of his formidable predecessor. In China religious leaders rejoiced as the government relaxed many of its restrictions on the freedom to worship. Thousands of Buddhist temples and numerous Christian churches and Muslim mosques were reopened, leading one religious leader to speak of a "far-reaching religious revival" in China.

Obviously, not all religious developments during the year were politically oriented. New technology had led to dramatic developments in medical theory and practice, and the attention of many of the world's foremost religious thinkers was focused on complex questions in the field of biomedical ethics: When does life begin? What signals the precise moment when death occurs? Ethicists insisted that the question "What is possible?" always must be paired with the question "What is right?"

(ROY LARSON)

PROTESTANT CHURCHES

Anglican Communion. The year opened on a note of tantalizing hope over prospects for seven British and Iranian Anglicans held in Iran on suspicion of spying. The archbishop of Canterbury's special envoy, Terry Waite, had been allowed to visit the detainees, and in London on January 1 he said the revolutionary authorities had exonerated all of them and had told him they would be freed soon. Eight weeks later Waite brought the three British missionaries back to England, having been assured that the four Iranian Anglicans had also been released. Whether the tiny church in Iran was managing to survive remained unknown to the outside world.

In the spring in Washington, D.C., the chief bishops of Anglicanism held another of their recently instituted primates' meetings where, appropriately, they wrestled with the issue of authority in the church. Anglican authority, they agreed, was "dispersed," but they also felt that they had "a special obligation to . . . practice collegiality in a divided Church." Among other actions, the primates pledged to work for multilateral disarmament and to seek to influence those who shaped nuclear policy.

The Church of England had long had one of the strictest marriage disciplines in the world, refusing a church wedding to anyone who had been divorced; with church opinion evenly divided, repeated attempts at reform had foundered. In July, however, the General Synod suddenly and surprisingly declared by large majorities that there were circumstances in which divorced persons could be married in church after all. Because of the legal and administrative machinery involved, it was likely to be some time before this would be put into practice.

After 12 years of searching for common ground, the Anglican-Roman Catholic International Commission (ARCIC) held a final meeting at St. George's House, Windsor, England, at the end of August. Their report first had to go to the leaders of the two churches, so the statement made after the meeting said little about its content. However, it did indicate that the report contained material already agreed on concerning the Eucharist, ministry, and authority, plus new material elucidating the agreed statement on authority.

Members of the fifth Anglican Consultative Council, held immediately afterward in Newcastle upon Tyne, had to content themselves with discussing how Anglicanism might respond to the report when it did appear. The outcome was that General Synods throughout the world would be asked to debate whether the report was consonant with Anglican faith and if it offered a sufficient basis for taking the next concrete step toward reconciliation. The council also invited the Lutheran World Federation to establish a joint working group to assess what had been achieved thus far by regional talks between Anglicans and Lutherans.

(SUSAN YOUNG)

Baptist Churches. The most singular event among U.S. Baptists in 1981 was the holding of a national gathering of a major Baptist denomination outside the continental U.S. During June 24–27, 2,700 registered delegates and visitors from the approximately 6,000 American Baptist Churches in the U.S.A. (formerly Northern Baptists) met in San Juan, P.R., at the invitation of the small but vigorous Puerto Rican Baptist Churches. The convention, which initiated a Spanish-English bilingual program, was consistent with recent developments in the ABC, USA indicating a cultural moderation and increasing awareness of minorities within the denomination.

The largest Protestant group in the U.S., the Southern Baptist Convention, met in June in Los Angeles, where the preoccupation if not the official agenda was to ward off an attempt by moderates to remove from office the incumbent president, Bailey Smith (*see* BIOGRAPHIES). During his first year as president, Smith had created a furor by some ill-considered anti-Semitic remarks, but the real issue in Los Angeles was the hard line Smith took on biblical inerrancy. A corollary to that inerrancy position was a political movement to remove from seminary faculties any teachers who might not take such a literal and legalistic view of the Scriptures. The sometime president of SBC-related Baylor University, Abner McCall, was presented to the 13,000 "messengers" as a "Lincoln who can preserve this Baptist union." The conservatives mustered a 61% majority for Smith, but the opposition felt that their candidate made a good enough showing to remove any suggestion of a mandate.

The largest of the black Baptist groups in the U.S., the National Baptist Convention, U.S.A., Inc., led since 1953 by Joseph H. Jackson, met in Detroit September 8–13 to celebrate its 101st year. Plans were made for investing $500,000 raised since 1980. Jackson claimed this was the first time any religious organization had entered into such an investment venture. At its annual meeting in St. Louis, Mo., the smaller but more assertive black denomination, the Progressive National Baptist Convention, Inc., approved a resolution calling the Moral Majority, led by another Baptist, Jerry Falwell, "antipoor and antiblack."

In Eastern Europe "unregistered Baptists," as compared with the officially accepted Baptist group, continued to be persecuted. By contrast, Baptists in Nagaland, India, were increasing their missionary outreach. One tribal grouping—the Angamis—appointed 19 new missionaries.

(NORMAN R. DE PUY)

Christian Church (Disciples of Christ). In 1981, 13 years after moving from a loose association of churches to a more formal structure in the U.S. and Canada, the 1.2 million-member Christian Church (Disciples of Christ) formalized its overseas mission philosophy. Some 7,000 church members in General Assembly overwhelmingly endorsed overseas policies emphasizing ecumenical commitment, support of self-governing foreign churches, and identification with the poor and oppressed.

The assembled Disciples also took steps to guard against another Jim Jones (the minister who led his Disciples-related People's Temple in a mass suicide in Guyana in 1978). Henceforth, ministers would have to meet mental, physical, emotional, and moral standards to maintain relationship to the church, and ministers serving outside the country would come under the jurisdiction of the General Board rather than a regional commission. However, the anticredal Disciples carefully sidestepped any action that would pass judgment on the fitness of congregations to remain a part of the church.

Disciples celebrated the 150th anniversary of the 1832 meeting in Lexington, Ky., that brought the movements led by Alexander Campbell and Barton W. Stone together in a single body seeking Christian unity through restoration of a simple New Testament faith. British Disciples of Christ underscored the church's historic quest for unity by becoming a part of the United Reformed Church in Great Britain on September 26. (ROBERT LOUIS FRIEDLY)

Archbishop of Canterbury Robert Runcie (right centre) presided over a week-long meeting of Anglican primates in Washington, D.C.

UPI

Churches of Christ. Media efforts to spread the cause of Christ formed the main thrust among Churches of Christ in 1981. The Christian Broadcasting Corporation purchased land in Anchor Point, Alaska, where it planned to construct a 250,000-w radio transmitter that would reach most of Asia and Eastern Europe. *La Vos Eterna*, with a circulation of 50,000 monthly, celebrated 18 years of publication to Latin-American countries.

The World Mission Information Bank's 1981 directory listed 732 workers in the mission field, making Churches of Christ ninth among U.S. religious groups. Growth was exceptional in several African nations. In Uganda, left without American evangelists since 1972, the church grew from two to six congregations, despite government persecution. The church in Kenya had grown from 18 to 96 congregations in seven years. The largest school for training evangelists, the Sunset School of Preaching in Lubbock, Texas, added a school of Slavic studies and a similar program in Chinese.

Campus ministries at the Universities of Florida, Colorado, and Southern Colorado reported over 100 conversions each among students. The largest single Sunday contribution for any religious group, $2,213,000, was given by the Central Church in Amarillo, Texas.   (M. NORVEL YOUNG)

Church of Christ, Scientist. Several thousand church members from around the world gathered in Boston in early June 1981 for reports of church progress during the preceding year. Keynote speaker Hal M. Friesen, chairman of the Christian Science Board of Directors, noted the world's great need for "visible and active brotherhood."

Other church officers reported a strong, debt-free financial condition, increased activity to correct misconceptions about Christian Science, and continuing legisla-

tive acceptance of the right to rely on Christian Science for healing. Syndication of the *Christian Science Monitor* news services in both broadcast and print media continued to grow. A *Monitor* endowment fund, started in 1978, was increasing steadily. Mrs. Berthe S. Girardin, a Christian Science practitioner from Paris, was named church president for 1981–82.

(ALLISON W. PHINNEY)

Church of Jesus Christ of Latter-day Saints. The church's First Presidency issued three statements decrying international tensions and the nuclear arms race. In their last statement they opposed multiple-protective-shelter deployment of the MX missile, which the Carter administration had proposed for basing in Utah and Nevada.

A document was discovered in early 1981 that contained an 1844 blessing by church founder Joseph Smith, designating his young son Joseph III as a successor. At the time of the elder Smith's murder later in 1844, leadership passed to the Council of Twelve Apostles, led by Brigham Young, and Joseph III later accepted the presidency of the dissident Reorganized Church of Jesus Christ of Latter Day Saints. While the discovery revived interest in the historical development of succession in church leadership, it had little effect on the relationship between the two churches. The document was presented to the Reorganized Church in exchange for a rare copy of an early church publication.

In July Gordon B. Hinckley, a member of the Council of Twelve, was added to the First Presidency as a third counselor to church president Spencer W. Kimball. This was seen as an effort to compensate for the effects of advancing age on other members of the First Presidency, all of whom were now in their 80s.

Growth outside the U.S. was underlined by the creation in June of the first stakes (dioceses) in Italy and Portugal. In view of the rising costs of temple and chapel construction and of markedly increased church welfare aid in 1979–80, systematic efforts were made to reduce costs of church programs and to reemphasize family preparation for emergencies.

(LEONARD J. ARRINGTON)

Jehovah's Witnesses. An international body of Christians who endeavour to follow closely the life-style and teachings of Jesus Christ as set forth in the Gospels, Jehovah's Witnesses believe the proclamation of the message of the kingdom of God was the principal work performed by Jesus when on Earth. In their efforts to imitate that "model," they have devoted more than 300 million hours annually in recent years to house-to-house visitations to interest people in the message of the Bible. This work has been carried on in 205 countries and territories.

Over the years, Jehovah's Witnesses have distributed nearly eight billion Bibles and Bible-related publications in more than 160 languages. During the summer of 1981 the organization released a revised edition of the *New World Translation of the Holy Scriptures* at 100 "Kingdom Loyalty" district conventions throughout the U.S., bringing total distribution of this modern English Bible to 34 million.

Jehovah's Witnesses define the kingdom of God as a heavenly government to be made up of 144,000 persons who will "rule as kings over the earth" with Jesus Christ. The rest of humankind who receive salvation will "inherit the Earth" and transform it into an everlasting paradise.

(FREDERICK W. FRANZ)

Lutheran Churches. In 1981 Lutherans were between major anniversaries. The 450th anniversary of the Augsburg Confession, basic statement of the Lutheran theological position, was widely celebrated in 1980. The 500th anniversary of the birth of Martin Luther would occur in 1983. Most of the sites associated with Luther's life are in East Germany, and in 1981 the Communist state announced its own plans to remember Luther in 1983. Recent improvements in church-state relations there continued, though not without some tensions. The 1981 meeting of the Central Committee of the World Council of Churches (WCC) was held in Dresden, headquarters of the Evangelical Lutheran Church of Saxony. The 11-day gathering was a major opportunity for the Saxon church and other East German Christians to witness to their life and work.

Much of the attention during the 1980 commemoration of the Augsburg Confession was on Lutheran-Roman Catholic relationships. Meeting in Finland in August 1981, the Executive Committee of the Lutheran World Federation (LWF) urged greater "reception" of the results of nearly two decades of official Lutheran-Roman Catholic theological dialogue and called for consideration of "practical steps" to implement conclusions reached by the theologians. Theological dialogues with other Christian traditions continued, including

A historian of the Reorganized Church of Jesus Christ of Latter Day Saints, Richard P. Howard (left), holds an 1844 manuscript written by Joseph Smith, Jr., the founder of the Mormon Church. With him is Earl E. Olson, a Mormon church official.

UPI

the first meeting of the international Lutheran-Eastern Orthodox commission. In the U.S. reports were released urging Lutherans and Episcopalians to grant each other official recognition.

A major international Lutheran preoccupation continued to be independence for Namibia, where the largest portion of the population was Lutheran. The LWF Executive Committee reiterated previous calls for action on the subject. Efforts to loosen church-state ties in mostly Lutheran Scandinavia continued, especially in Norway and Sweden. However, resistance to change for a variety of reasons surfaced during the year.

About two-thirds of Lutheranism in the U.S. and Canada continued efforts to unite into one denomination in each country. National conventions of the three U.S. Lutheran bodies involved were to vote simultaneously on the principle in September 1982. A favourable vote was expected, after which a committee would work out details over several years. On the other hand, the denomination accounting for most of the other third of North American Lutheran membership, the Lutheran Church-Missouri Synod, terminated official fellowship with the American Lutheran Church in protest against what the synod considered false teaching and practice in the ALC.

(TOM DORRIS)

Methodist Churches. The 14th World Methodist Council (WMC) and Conference met in Honolulu in July 1981, when 3,500 delegates from 93 countries discussed important religious, social, and economic problems under the general theme "Gathered into One." Significantly, the Social and International Affairs Committee was enlarged, given an increased budget, and accorded a more important place in the affairs of the Council.

Typical resolutions called upon Methodist churches everywhere to "identify with and sustain the struggle of the world's poor for justice"; condemned the policy of apartheid in South Africa; and commended the Methodist Church in Southern Africa for its stand against apartheid laws. One of the two Methodist Peace Awards went to the Rev. Abel Hendricks for his courageous work in South Africa.

The dangers of the arms race were brought to the attention of the members in the opening address by the chairman, Kenneth Greet, president of the British Conference, and a resolution was passed calling upon member churches to "urge their governments and the other nations of the world with the utmost urgency to outlaw production and use of nuclear armaments." Lord Soper, a former president of the British Conference, received the second Methodist Peace Award in recognition of his work for peace and disarmament over more than half a century.

An ambitious and far-reaching program of evangelism was outlined by Sir Alan Walker of Australia. It proposed a ten-point plan of "Mission to the Eighties," which involved setting up an Institute of Evangelism to train pastors and laypersons through a multiracial faculty. Already

there were encouraging signs of growth, particularly in Korea and parts of Africa.

Publication of the report of the WMC-Roman Catholic joint commission, which included a section entitled "Towards an agreed statement on the Holy Spirit" and a report on "Christian Moral Decisions," was another step forward in ecumenical relations. A report on conversations with the Lutheran World Federation was also received.

Biship William Cannon from Georgia was installed as chairman of the Executive Committee for the next quinquennium. The new president of the World Federation of Methodist Women was Oknah Kim Lah of South Korea. In the U.S. the United Methodist Church appointed Marjorie Matthews of Wisconsin as the first woman bishop in the Methodist Church.

(PETER H. BOLT)

Pentecostal Churches. During 1981 the American Pentecostal denominations increased their identification with the growing forces of evangelicalism. The American Festival of Evangelism, which convened in Kansas City, Mo., in July, was chaired by Thomas F. Zimmerman of the Assemblies of God, and the National Association of Evangelicals elected its second Pentecostal president, Bishop J. Floyd Williams of the Pentecostal Holiness Church.

For the first time, a Pentecostal was named to the U.S. Cabinet: James Watt (see BIOGRAPHIES), secretary of the interior. A lay member of the Assemblies of God, Watt created controversy when his theology of the second coming of Christ surfaced in testimony before a congressional committee.

M. E. Nichols, president of the International Church of the Foursquare Gospel and chairman of the Pentecostal Fellowship of North America, died in March. The Pentecostal Holiness Church's quadrennial conference elected a new bishop, Leon Stewart of Roanoke, Va. Stewart achieved election despite the fact that he was legally blind. Zimmerman was reelected to head the Assemblies of God, while Nathaniel A. Urshan was returned to the office of general superintendent of the United Pentecostal Church.

Rapid growth was reported among various Pentecostal groups. The Assemblies of God reported the organization of 593 new congregations in the U.S. in the previous two years. The International Church of the Foursquare Gospel reported 463 new mission churches overseas and 339,778 converts in 1980. In 1981 U.S. membership in the Pentecostal Holiness Church passed 100,000.

(VINSON SYNAN)

Presbyterian, Reformed, and Congregational Churches. Preparations for the next General Council of the World Alliance of Reformed Churches (WARC), to be held in Ottawa during Aug. 17–27, 1982, dominated the activity of the WARC's Geneva-centred staff. Over and above its statutory and organizational functions, the General Council was planned first of all as a festival of faith for representatives of the 149 (since August 1981) member churches from all continents.

The last General Council, held in Nairobi, Kenya, in 1970, marked the merger of the former Reformed World Alliance with the International Congregational Council into the present WARC. The next General

Council, due in 1977, was suppressed for financial reasons and replaced by a more limited "centennial colloquium" in St. Andrews, Scotland.

Some 700 delegates and consultants were expected to take part in the Ottawa General Council sessions. The theme, "Thine is the Kingdom, the Power and the Glory," was divided into three subthemes with theological, political, and ecological emphases: (1) the people of the Covenant and the mission of the Kingdom; (2) the power of grace and the graceless powers; and (3) the theatre of glory and a threatened creation's hope.

Both the Caribbean and North American Area Council and the European Area Council of the WARC held their area committee meetings, in Mississauga, Ont., in February 1981 and in Belfast, Northern Ireland, in September, respectively. The WARC was represented at meetings connected with the Madrid (Spain) review conference of the 1975 Helsinki Conference on Security and Cooperation in Europe, thus demonstrating its constant interest and participation in the field of human rights.

Bilateral dialogues between the Reformed and the Anglican, Lutheran, Orthodox, and Roman Catholic churches continued in 1981. However, in the trilateral colloquium of Lutheran, Reformed, and Roman Catholic churches on the theology of interconfessional marriages, the participants recognized that before further progress could be made the question of "mutual recognition of the churches" had to be reexamined.

The question of "the community of women and men in the Church" (the title of an ecumenical study organized by the World Council of Churches) ranked high among the concerns of WARC's member churches.

(ALDO COMBA)

Religious Society of Friends. In March 1981 Mexican Friends welcomed participants to the fourth Mission and Service Gathering at Ciudad Victoria. These occasions are important in fostering unity between Friends' "churches" that emphasize evangelism and the more liberal and traditional branches of the Society, whose faith is more indirectly expressed in concerns for peace and human rights. A more intimate occasion was the Quaker Family Gathering at Gwatt, Switz., in July, which brought together some 150 British and other European Friends.

Among American Friends there was anxiety that the policies of President Reagan's administration would lead to a "less compassionate society." Australian Friends, long concerned over the treatment of the Aboriginal people, invited Friends worldwide to try to influence international opinion in the Aborigines' favour.

Peace, as always, was a major focus for Quaker effort. Particularly in Europe, Friends joined in protests against theatre nuclear weapons and the neutron bomb. An invitation from the Northern Friends Peace Board brought a delegation from the Soviet Peace Committee to the north of England and London. A personal initiative of an 80-year-old woman Friend led to the well-publicized visits of British "Mothers for Peace" to the U.S. and the U.S.S.R.

(DAVID FIRTH)

Salvation Army. Gen. Arnold Brown, the Salvation Army's international leader since 1977, retired in December 1981. Meet-

ing in London in October, the Army's High Council elected Jarl Wahlström to succeed him as the Army's 12th general. During his last year in office, General Brown traveled to a number of countries. He visited, with much difficulty, the small but vital representation in Cuba and became the first general to visit Iceland.

Salvationists everywhere again devoted their energies to relieving suffering and showing their Christian concern in a practical way. Refugee programs continued in Hong Kong and central Africa, medical teams continued to operate in Thailand, and Army relief teams worked to relieve the devastation that followed the 1980 earthquake in southern Italy, where the Army hoped to build 600 homes. *The Young Soldier*, the Army's children's newspaper with a weekly circulation of 200,000, celebrated its centenary in 1981.

In August the Army withdrew its formal membership in the wcc. This followed some years of disagreement with the wcc's policy of financial support for black nationalism in southern Africa, which the Army felt endangered its operational freedom in the region.   (MICHAEL H. WILLIAMS)

Seventh-day Adventist Church. During 1981 the church maintained work in 190 countries and territories, and appropriations to maintain this outreach totaled $142,161,000. Sabbath school membership climbed to well beyond four million. More than 110,000 converts were added in Latin America, and a new seminary was opened with campuses in Brazil and Argentina. Approximately 7,000 people in 22 locations in the U.S. participated in a one-day Bible teleseminar broadcast live via satellite.

Because of doctrinal differences, about 20 pastors and teachers either resigned or were removed from their posts. One small congregation in Texas separated from the denomination. A North American pastor charged that Ellen G. White, one of the church's founders, was a plagiarist. However, the charge was refuted by Diller, Ramik and Wight, Ltd., a Washington, D.C., law firm specializing in copyrights.

In July a Seventh-day Adventist physician-turned-real-estate-developer, who had borrowed large sums from denominational organizations during the past 15 years, filed for bankruptcy in Los Angeles. The denomination's auditors reported that loans outstanding totaled $17,873,424, plus interest due of $3,137,313. It was not known how much of the money, if any, might be recovered.

(KENNETH H. WOOD)

Unitarian (Universalist) Churches. Three major annual Unitarian general assemblies were held during 1981. The Canadian Unitarian Council, meeting May 15–17 in Victoria, B.C., attracted over 300 persons, double the usual attendance. The same number attended the General Assembly of the Unitarian and Free Christian Churches of Great Britain, in Newcastle upon Tyne, April 13–16. The British conference passed resolutions on prison reform; causes, effects, and injustices in the poverty situation; and the U.K.'s Law Against Blasphemy, which was described as "neither relevant to our age nor conducive to good relationships."

The General Assembly of the Unitarian Universalist Association (UUA), covering

the North American continent, met in Philadelphia, June 12–18, to examine the theme "An Urban Experience." Approximately 1,500 delegates, friends, and overseas visitors were in attendance. Eugene Pickett and Sandra Mitchell were reelected to four-year terms as president and moderator, respectively. General resolutions were passed on ending the arms race, alternative sources of energy, opposition to biochemical warfare, the UN, civil rights and the Ku Klux Klan, home health care, and (by petition) El Salvador. Not approved for the final agenda in a parish poll were resolutions on peace in the Middle East, reform of the U.S. Criminal Code, Indian rights, Martin Luther King's birthday, and strategy for survival.

As of 1981, 12% of all settled ministers in the UUA were women. The Annual Fund for the programs and operating expenses of the UUA raised slightly over 10% more than in 1980. Representatives from 20 countries and five continents gathered during July 24–31 at the Leeuwenhorst Congress Centre, near Leiden, Neth., for the triennial congress of the International Association for Religious Freedom. Since 1978 study commissions had been preparing a framework for discussions on "The Tide of Religion."   (JOHN NICHOLLS BOOTH)

The United Church of Canada. In common with many North American mainline churches, the United Church experienced declining membership in the 1970s and early 1980s. However, the decline from 1979 to 1980 (the latest statistics available) was only 0.4%, the smallest since 1968, the year of union with the Canadian branch of the Evangelical United Brethren Church. Overall membership in the United Church increased in five of the regional conferences and at the end of 1980 stood at 903,302.

Some other indicators gave grounds for optimism: average weekly attendance rose slightly to 389,492; the number of Sunday schools increased 2.3% to 3,622; and overall giving to national funds was up by approximately 11.6%. However, the Mission and Service Fund—the main funding for home and overseas undertakings—fell $204,273 short of its $20.6 million goal, and officials were worried because contributions were not keeping up with inflation.

Despite the difficult financial situation, church leaders were exploring the feasibility of a $50 million campaign for new church development. Construction of new church buildings had been negligible since the mid-'60s, and since that time there had been dramatic population increases in Newfoundland and western Canada because of the expansion of resource industries. Regionalism as practiced by the United Church was also under review. A major concern was relieving tensions between eastern and western Canada.

"These Things We Share," the first United Church television special, was broadcast Sept. 20–26, 1981, on stations reaching 68% of member households. The one-hour program portrayed faith-styles of United Church members from Newfoundland to Vancouver Island. A task force with a full-time staff member was appointed during the year to consider a number of issues relating to the church's attitude toward and treatment of women.

(NORMAN K. VALE)

United Church of Christ. A vigorous program known as New Initiatives in Church Development was winning the commitment and contributions of church members throughout the United Church of Christ. Administered by the United Church Board for Homeland Ministries, with funds raised through efforts of the church's Stewardship Council, the program had already provided support for 33% of new church starts throughout the U.S.

Delegates to the 13th General Synod, held in Rochester, N.Y., June 27–July 1, 1981, voted to name peace and family life as two priorities of the church for a four-year period. Church-wide programming, based on the goals of the two priorities, was being prepared by two task forces. In a special service of thanksgiving, the Synod celebrated the freedom and vindication of the "Wilmington Ten," following a favourable action on their case by a panel of U.S. Circuit Court judges in 1980. For nearly ten years the church had worked to free Ben Chavis, a UCC staff member, and nine young people of Wilmington, N.C., who had been arrested in a racial incident in 1971.

The most spirited moment at the General Synod was easily the vote in which the United Church of Christ responded warmly and with commitment to *Kirchengemeinshaft* (church fellowship or full communion), voted in the spring of 1980 by the Synods of the Church of the Union in East and West Germany. Through the vote, the churches on two continents committed themselves to work together in missions of peace and justice, recognized each other's ministries, and would join each other in the celebration of the sacraments as they had opportunity. Reelected at the Synod to four-year terms were Avery D. Post, president, and Charles H. Lockyear, director of finance and treasurer. Helen I. Barnhill of Milwaukee, Wis., was elected moderator of the Synod for the 1981–83 biennium.

(AVERY D. POST)

[827.D; 827.G.3; 827.H; 827.J.3]

ROMAN CATHOLIC CHURCH

At 5:19 PM on May 13, 1981, shots echoed round St. Peter's Square. Pope John Paul II (*see* BIOGRAPHIES) had been hit. He was rushed to the Gemelli Hospital and operated on for nearly five hours. The following Sunday, in a broadcast on Vatican Radio, he said that he had forgiven "the brother who attacked me." With a relapse, the convalescence took three and a half months.

Until the shooting, the hyperactive pope had dominated the life of the church, at least in the sense of grabbing the headlines. In January he received a delegation from the Polish independent labour union, Solidarity, led by Lech Walesa. Although his language was prudent, it was evident that he welcomed the creation of Solidarity. In his third encyclical, *Laborem Exercens* ("On Human Work"), he seemed to be echoing Solidarity positions when he said that unions should have a social rather than a political role and presented co-ownership and profit-sharing as the path to industrial peace.

In February John Paul set off on a 40,000-km (25,000-mi) round-the-world trip. Martial law had been abolished in the Philippines shortly before his visit. In Manila he beatified 16 of the martyrs who had sailed from the Philippines to Japan in the 17th century. If the pope's welcome in the Philippines was ecstatic, the Japanese were puzzled and curious about their guest. At Hiroshima John Paul appealed for peace in one of his most eloquent sermons so far. One disappointing feature of the Asia journey was that the pope's attempt to improve relations with China seemed to have failed. The contradictory responses to his broadcast to China from Manila left everyone confused. "It is very difficult to understand Chinese," remarked Agostino Cardinal Casaroli, the Vatican secretary of state.

In the spring John Paul was heavily involved in the Italian abortion referendum. Voters had a choice between maintaining Law 194, which permitted abortions in certain cases, or replacing it with a more liberal law or with a more stringent law (the "pro-life proposal"). The "lay" political parties objected to this papal intervention in the internal affairs of Italy, but John Paul replied that this was a moral issue on which he could not remain silent. The referendum was held on May 18, the Monday after the assassination attempt, with the result that the existing moderate law remained in force. Despite so much papal and episcopal exhortation, 67.9% of Italians voted against the pro-life proposal.

Another attempt at intervention, indirect this time, took place in April. Father John Magee, an Ulsterman and the pope's English-language secretary, was sent on

what the pope called "a good will mission" to see Bobby Sands, on hunger strike in the Maze Prison in Northern Ireland. Father Magee never said whether his real purpose was to dissuade or to comfort Sands, who died a few days later.

The shooting prevented the pope from going to Lourdes in June for a Eucharistic Congress. It also meant that a planned visit to Switzerland was postponed. But it did not stop him from appearing on the balcony of St. Peter's on Pentecost, June 7, when the 1,600th anniversary of the Council of Constantinople was celebrated with Orthodox leaders present. There was a simultaneous celebration by the Orthodox in Istanbul with Roman Catholic participation. The St. Peter's ceremony was the most important ecumenical event of the year since the pope, in his homily, omitted the controversial *filioque* clause (stating that the Holy Spirit proceeds from the Son as well as the Father) from his reading of the creed. It was a sizable olive branch to the Orthodox churches.

Among administrative changes during the year, Jean-Marie Lustiger (*see* BIOGRAPHIES), a convert from Judaism, was appointed archbishop of Paris and Jozef Glemp (*see* BIOGRAPHIES) succeeded Stefan Cardinal Wyszynski (*see* OBITUARIES) as archbishop of Warsaw and Gniezno and primate of Poland. The most surprising change in personnel came in October. Father Pedro Arrupe, superior general of the Jesuits, had a stroke on August 7 that left him partially paralyzed and, for a time, speechless. Following normal procedure, he and his assistants appointed a "vicar general," Father Vincent O'Keefe, a New Yorker. But Pope John Paul removed the vicar general and instituted a newly devised office of "Personal Delegate of the Holy Father to the Society of Jesus." The

John Cardinal Cody of Chicago makes his first public appearance after a Chicago newspaper published allegations in September that he had misappropriated church funds and given them to a lifelong friend.

man appointed to this office, moreover, was 80-year-old Father Paolo Dezza, an almost blind Italian. It appeared that the pope was trying to take control over the world's 26,000 Jesuits, whose political commitment in Latin America had caused offense.

One of the most important meetings of the year passed almost unnoticed. It concerned what was expected to be the final revision of the new code of canon law. What the code would have to say about "priests in politics" could have a bearing on Father Dan Berrigan, in prison for his part in a break-in at a Pennsylvania nuclear missile plant. What it might say on marriage annulment would be of great interest to U.S. canon lawyers, who had been accused by some in the Vatican of granting annulments too easily. Meanwhile, local bishops continued to take strong stands on controversial issues. In January Archbishop James Hickey of Washington, D.C., met President Reagan in a vain attempt to dissuade him from resuming military aid to El Salvador, where three U.S. sisters and a lay church worker had been killed late in 1980.

On September 3 the Anglican-Roman Catholic International Commission submitted its final report to the respective authorities of the two churches. Some believed that John Paul would respond to it favourably during his visit to Britain, planned for May 1982. (*See* VATICAN CITY STATE.)

(PETER HEBBLETHWAITE)
[827.C; 827.G.2; 827.J.2]

THE ORTHODOX CHURCH

Two major problems stood at the centre of preparations for an eventual pan-Orthodox Great Council: the issue of Christian unity and the internal problem of overlapping Orthodox jurisdictions in the Western world. An official theological dialogue began with Rome, and a subcommittee meeting was held in Venice, Italy, in May, but it was somewhat clouded by the Vatican's attitudes—which many Orthodox considered as contradictory—toward the Eastern-rite Catholics (or "uniats").

On the one hand, answering a protest by Patriarch Pimen of Moscow, Pope John Paul II, in February, wrote to the Russian primate that no official approval was given

Roman Catholic faithful wept for joy in St. Peter's Square, Vatican City, as Pope John Paul II recited a prayer from his hospital bed following an assassination attempt in May.

to the decisions of a Ukrainian-Catholic synod held in Rome in November 1980, which condemned the return of Eastern-rite Ukrainians to Orthodoxy in Lvov (1946). On the other hand, the pope personally addressed the same Ukrainian synod and praised the Union of Brest (1596), at which the Ukrainians broke with their mother church of Constantinople to join Rome. Criticism of the "uniat" policies of Rome was also voiced in Greece, and some circles, particularly the monastic communities on Mt. Athos, disapproved of the dialogue itself under current conditions. Thus, sad events of past history seemed still to weigh heavily in the debates.

The Orthodox were critical of the radical feminist trends dominating the program on "the relations between women and men" in the wcc. This criticism was particularly vociferous at the wcc Consultation at Sheffield, England (July 1981) and the Central Committee meeting at Dresden (August). However, the Orthodox churches had not remained totally immune to the woman's movement. In November 1980 the All-American Council of the Orthodox Church in America, the highest administrative body of that church, gave full voting rights to women in its midst.

The action seemed to reflect the basic Orthodox position on full equality of men and women on the level of the laity—a significant fact, since in Orthodoxy the entire laity, and not only the male clergy, possesses responsibility for the faith and structure of the church. A special Pan-Orthodox Consultation, meeting in Sofia, Bulg., in May, complained about the policies that were dominant, in that and other areas, within the wcc, reaffirmed unity of faith as the main goal of ecumenism, and demanded a stronger voice for the Orthodox in wcc's activities.

The problem of overlapping jurisdictions linked to ethnic mother churches was a major point on the agenda of the future council. Numerous debates on the issue were being held. The church of Romania expressed itself in favour of temporarily preserving the ethnic structures. In the U.S., however, the autocephalous Orthodox Church in America and the Antiochian Archdiocese, currently dependent on a patriarch residing in Damascus, Syria, announced plans for organic administrative unity.

On February 16 the Metropolitan Diodoros of Hierapolis, previously residing in Amman, Jordan, was elected new Greek Orthodox patriarch of Jerusalem.

(JOHN MEYENDORFF)

EASTERN NON-CHALCEDONIAN CHURCHES

The year was critical for the Coptic Church in Egypt, the largest single Christian group in the Middle East, numbering more than six million. Representatives of the church had long complained about repeated and violent attacks by Muslim extremists against churches and communities and had accused Egyptian authorities of deliberate failure in protecting Christian lives and property. Observers speculated that the Egyptian government, criticized for its peace policies, was not unhappy seeing Muslim wrath directed at others than itself.

As disturbances mounted, a police crackdown finally came in early September. However, it was directed not only against Muslim fanatics but also against the Copts. The highly respected Coptic patriarch, Shenuda III, was accused of fomenting sectarian strife, "deprived of state recognition," and forced to retire to a desert monastery. In fact, no evidence of Christian violence against Muslims ever came forth, whereas, as late as September 4, a large Muslim crowd stoned the Coptic patriarchate in Cairo. In the absence of the patriarch, the church was governed temporarily by a synod of five bishops. When President Sadat was shot in October one of the bishops, who was seated near him, was also killed.

(JOHN MEYENDORFF)

[827.B; 827.G.1; 827.J.1]

Primate Metropolitan Philaret of the Russian Orthodox Church of Outside Russia canonized Tsar Nicholas II and 30,000 others killed during the Russian Revolution, in New York City in October.

UPI

JUDAISM

The sea change in U.S. politics climaxed by the 1980 elections swept across American Judaism. On theological grounds and for religious purposes, Jews moved to organize themselves at both right and left. Rabbi Seymour Siegel of the Jewish Theological Seminary founded the American Jewish Forum to investigate "in an academic way the relationship between Jewish traditional thought and conservative political ideologies." At the other pole, the New Jewish Agenda was established to advance a liberal position in society. The founders invoked the concept of *tikun olam*, "repair of the world." The Agenda's position included endorsing "the Palestinians' right to national self-determination, including the right to create a Palestinian state."

The position of the New Jewish Agenda turned out to be representative of the views of older and better known Jewish groups. The World Jewish Congress, under the leadership of Edgar Bronfman, a Canadian Jewish businessman, published a two-year study on "The Implications of Israel-Arab Peace for World Jewry." The document expressed the view that there are increasing strains in the relationship between the Diaspora and the State of Israel. The wjc criticized the religious monopoly exercised by the Orthodox rabbinate in Israel; Israel's settlement policies in the West Bank and Gaza; and the materialism that had hastened "the erosion of old ideals and Jewish values." Further, it rejected "the classic Zionist ideology which denigrates the prospects for a secure or meaningful Jewish existence in the diaspora and which conceives of diaspora existence as living in exile."

In response, Leon Dulzin, chairman of the World Zionist Organization, pointed out that the World Jewish Congress does not compete with his organization. A more telling comment came from Leonard Fein, editor of *Moment*, who noted that, while "the World Jewish Congress seeks to be a parliament of the Jewish people, it behaves as if it were the House of Lords alone." It lacked representation from the three most vigorous constituencies of Judaism in the Diaspora: no rabbi, no professor of Jewish studies, no representative of the recent Jewish resurgence in America. It even lacked significant representation of those under 50. "The report," Fein said, ". . . seeks to judge Jewish life without the impediment of ideological commitment—and without the benefit of ideological perspective."

On behalf of the wjc, others noted that it had undertaken major work in the preservation of the Jewish heritage. It set up a Heritage Committee, under the leadership of Doris Brickner, to seek out, preserve, and restore important Jewish sites of art and religion in the Diaspora. The Roman catacombs, for example, dating from the 2nd through the 4th centuries AD, include vast Jewish burial areas, containing inscriptions and symbols from a time when Jews formed 10% of the Roman population. Most of these catacombs had never been restored and opened for public view. The wjc Heritage Committee in 1980 undertook the work of digging out and displaying them,

and other projects in Italy as well as in Egypt, France, and elsewhere were planned. The success of such a project would go a long way toward meeting criticism of the Congress in the aftermath of its attack on Israeli life and politics.

Meanwhile, Gary Rosenblatt, writing in the *Baltimore Jewish Times*, reviewed the story of another project in Jewish cultural renaissance, the Institute for Jewish Life, founded in 1970 in Boston. At that time a small, articulate group of young Jews confronted the organized Jewish community with the demand that organized Jewry become more Jewish and take Judaism more seriously. In response, the general assembly of the Council of Jewish Federations founded the Institute for Jewish Life, and a wealthy Ohio businessman, Gordon Zacks, even demanded that $100 million be invested in the project. The funds ultimately available to the Institute came to less than $250,000 a year, but the principal problem was not financial; it was the difficulty of coming up with a proposal that was agreeable to all factions and also workable and effective. In the end the Institute came to nothing and closed its doors. Rosenblatt's account wrote the epitaph for the decade of disappointment that came to a close in 1980. Whether projects such as the Heritage Committee would signal greater success in the 1980s could not be discerned as 1981 ended. (JACOB NEUSNER)
[826]

BUDDHISM

Although there was no single traumatic event in 1981, the unstable political situations, unhealthy economies, and growing discontent in various parts of Asia gave much anxiety to Buddhists. The killing of 8,000 Buddhist tribesmen by Muslims in Bangladesh made Buddhists everywhere apprehensive. Understandably, the 13th Conference of the World Fellowship of Buddhists (WFB), held in the autumn of 1980 in Thailand, gave as much attention to social, economic, and political problems as to doctrinal issues. No one was optimistic about the future of "institutional" Buddhism in Kampuchea (Cambodia), Laos, or Vietnam, although it might be difficult to eradicate the "cultural" Buddhism that was so deeply embedded in the social and mental fabric of the populace. Also of great concern to the WFB was the slow progress of the project to restore the Buddha's birthplace in Lumbini, Nepal. On the other hand, restoration of the world's largest Buddhist monument, Borobudur in Java, was expected to be completed in 1982.

Events in China provided grounds for cautious optimism. Historic temples were repaired, the Buddhist Association of China resumed various activities, and the Institute for Research on World Religions of the Chinese Academy of Social Sciences published some books and journals on Buddhism. In 1980 the prestigious Drepend monastery in Tibet was authorized to accept 20 new novices for the first time since 1959. Whether or not the Dalai Lama would be invited to return to Tibet, however, was not certain. In Japan, where both old and

new Buddhist groups were extremely sensitive to the issues of war and nuclear disarmament, a small offshoot of Nichiren Buddhism sponsored a World Assembly of Religious Workers for General and Nuclear Disarmament, held in April 1981.

Buddhism continued to arouse the religious, cultural, and scholarly interests of Westerners. The Foundation for the Promotion of Buddhism was reported to have donated 100,000 copies of *The Teaching of Buddha*, the Buddhist counterpart of the Gideon Bible, to hotels in Europe. The film *The Life of Buddha* received a certificate of merit at the 1980 International Film Festival in Chicago. One of the most active new groups, Nichiren Shoshu/Soka Gakkai, sponsored a gala Grand Peace Cultural Festival at Rosemont, Ill., in July 1981. Among summer seminars on Buddhist studies held during 1981 was one at Harvard, sponsored by the American Institute of Buddhist Studies, which featured the Dalai Lama as the main lecturer.
(JOSEPH M. KITAGAWA)
[824]

HINDUISM

Perhaps the single most important issue for Hinduism in 1981 was actually centuries old: conversion from Hinduism. In February 800 Harijans (noncaste Hindus) publicly converted to Islam in Meenakshipuram, a small village in the state of Tamil Nadu, claiming that they sought relief from oppression by caste Hindus. However, local caste Hindus and some religious and political leaders alleged that the converts had been bribed with money from oil-rich Arab states. An inquiry by the state government revealed no coercion or bribery, but charges of foreign intrigue persisted throughout the year. The Rashtriya Swayamsevak Sangh (RSS), a militant Hindu group, called for a constitutional ban on religious conversion.

The Meenakshipuram conversion focused attention anew on the plight of India's 210 million Harijans. The Indian constitution proscribes any discrimination on the basis of caste, and by law a certain number of scholarships, jobs in education and government, and other privileges are "reserved" for Harijans. Harijan groups complained that the legal guarantees were not being enforced by the government and were constantly being violated by caste Hindus. In Kanpur, 25,000 Harijans threatened to renounce Hinduism for Islam, Buddhism, or Christianity on Independence Day (August 15) as a protest against the violation of their rights, even though this would cost them the special privileges promised by the reservation system.

The response of caste Hindus was negative and sometimes led to communal violence. In January 10,000 Brahmins in Madras demonstrated against what they alleged were the efforts of Harijans to destroy orthodox religious life and against the reservation system. In February caste Hindu medical students and junior physicians in the state of Gujarat began agitation against the reservation system, leading to weeks of turmoil that included bloody clashes between Harijans and caste Hindus in and around Ahmadabad.

By contrast, throughout the year thousands of caste Hindus flocked to a temple in

Kerala state to receive the blessings of a Harijan holy man believed to be possessed by the god Subrahmanya. The continuing vitality of religious practice in Hinduism was demonstrated in other ways. At the ancient holy place of Deogarh, more than a million pilgrims worshiped Shiva at the Baidyanathdnom temple in July. A solar eclipse on July 31 brought about 500,000 worshipers to Kurukshetra, traditional site of the composition of the *Bhagavad-gita*, for sacrifice and purifying bathing.

The fifth World Sanskrit Conference in Varanasi (Banaras) in October brought together 150 scholars from 42 countries to discuss aspects of Sanskrit language and literature. Of special significance for Hinduism was the consideration of new methods of reconstructing and analyzing sacred texts. (H. PATRICK SULLIVAN)
[823]

ISLAM

The year began with the release of the hostages from the U.S. embassy by Iran, but this did not end political tensions and violence in Iran and other Muslim countries. Of serious and long-ranging consequence for Iran were the deaths of 72 high-ranking leaders in June, including Ayatollah Mohammad Hossein Beheshti (see OBITUARIES), head of the ruling fundamentalist group, in a terrorist bombing. Arrests and killings appeared to be everyday occurrences in Iran, with announced executions becoming commonplace. (See IRAN.)

In October Egypt's Pres. Anwar as-Sadat (see OBITUARIES) was killed while reviewing a military parade; the assassins were linked to an extremist group, and the assassination may have been connected with Egypt's increasingly evident religious troubles. (See EGYPT; *Eastern Non-Chalcedonian Churches*, above.) Muslim extremist groups continued to be active in Egypt and elsewhere. Violence between the Christian and Muslim communities in Lebanon persisted, while in Turkey internal disturbances, mainly political in nature, occasionally took on a religious colouring. In Syria there was evidence of growing friction between the top military and political leaders, who were Alawites, and more conservative Muslim groups.

In January Nigeria broke off diplomatic relations with Libya, charging that Libya had fomented riots among Nigerian Muslims; Libya denied any involvement. (See NIGERIA.) A growing number of Cham Muslims from Kampuchea were turning up in refugee camps; they constituted a relatively small proportion of Southeast Asian refugees, but their presence could no longer be ignored. Increased contact with China was allowing outsiders a new view of that country's Muslims. Estimated to number between 60 million and 100 million, they had become the objects of Soviet-supported propaganda efforts. Some mosques were being reopened, and some religious objects were becoming increasingly available.

In late January the Islamic Conference held in Saudi Arabia brought together leaders of 37 Muslim nations and the Palestine Liberation Organization. The agenda was taken up by political and diplomatic matters. Social changes in Saudi Arabia had promoted searching discussion, resulting in some legal changes. Of recent concern

In many villages in India Harijans (noncaste Hindus) are converting from the Hindu religion to the Muslim religion in an attempt to avoid oppression from higher Hindu castes.

Differing procedures are followed even within the same religion. Quite reliable religious statistics are available on the mission fields, for Buddhism, Islam, and Hinduism as well as Christianity. In areas where a religion has been dominant for centuries (*i.e.*, Europe for Christianity, India for Hinduism), official figures usually report whole populations as adherents, although the decline of religious observance and the rise of antireligious ideologies calls this casual procedure into question. Although Albania is the only officially atheist state, the 20th century has produced a number of governments hostile to all traditional religions. It is difficult if not impossible to get reliable religious statistics on the peoples they control.

The traditional listing of religions, used by scholars since the comparative study of religions became an academic discipline, makes no provision for several religions now numerous and influential: *e.g.*, Baha'i, Cao Dai, Jainism, Ch'ondokyo, and cults such as the Unification Church. Nor does the traditional table make a place for Marxism, which functions in some ways like a state church. Finally, each year brings reports of new genocides and refugee movements that change the map of religious adherence, as well as the movements of large numbers seeking better living conditions. Muslim Turks residing for decades as "guest workers" in West Germany change the religious colour of that nation, and at some point, perhaps with the coming of the third generation, several hundred thousand Muslims will be counted in the statistics for Europe, an area once considered overwhelmingly Christian.

The reader is advised to reflect carefully upon the statistics reported and to refer to articles discussing the different countries and religions when pursuing the subject in depth.

(FRANKLIN H. LITTELL)

was the soaring divorce rate, brought on by the strains of westernization, especially the increase in the number of working women. In April religious leaders ruled that a woman could unveil her face to her betrothed after their formal engagement, a change generally welcomed by younger and better educated Saudis but resisted by older and more conservative persons.

Formation of a Muslim international bank was announced during the year. Based in London and called the First Interest-Free Finance Consortium (FIFC), it began seeking funds from Islamic countries. Because of the Islamic prohibition against ordinary bank interest, the Consortium was organized to provide an equity participation basis for its members in which, as in other shareholding associations, profits and losses could be apportioned.

(REUBEN W. SMITH)

[828]

WORLD CHURCH MEMBERSHIP

Reckoning religious adherence is a precarious exercise. Different religions and even different Christian churches vary widely in their theories and methods of counting and reporting. Some simply depend on government population figures; for others "numbering the people" is blocked by religious law. Some number only adults or heads of families; others count children, servants, and retainers. Where religious liberty obtains, some count contributors; others estimate communicants or constituents.

Estimated Membership of the Principal Religions of the World

Religions	North America[1]	South America	Europe[2]	Asia[3]	Africa	Oceania[4]	World
Total Christian	238,028,500	174,112,000	340,780,400	95,787,240	130,917,000	18,158,000	997,783,140
Roman Catholic	133,889,000	161,489,000	177,187,300	55,027,000	48,024,500	4,445,000	580,061,800
Eastern Orthodox	4,782,000	514,000	53,035,600	2,328,000	13,106,000 [5]	409,000	74,174,600
Protestant[6]	99,357,500	12,109,000	110,557,500	38,432,240	69,786,500 [7]	13,304,000	343,546,740
Jewish[8]	6,295,340	585,800	4,057,120	3,492,860	176,900	76,500	14,684,520
Muslim[8]	386,200	254,000	15,945,000	429,766,000	145,714,700	92,000	592,157,900
Zoroastrian	2,750	2,600	12,000	257,000	700	1,000	276,050
Shinto[9]	60,000	90,000	—	58,003,000	1,200	—	58,154,200
Taoist	16,000	10,000	—	30,260,000	—	—	30,286,000
Confucian	97,100	70,000	—	153,887,500	1,500	24,000	154,080,100
Buddhist[10]	197,250	194,450	194,500	255,741,000	25,000	35,000	256,387,200
Hindu[11]	96,500	852,000	425,000	478,073,000	1,379,800	415,000	481,241,300
Totals	245,179,640	176,170,850	361,414,020	1,505,267,600	278,216,800	18,801,500	2,585,050,410
Population[12]	376,000,000	251,000,000	754,000,000	2,607,000,000	483,000,000	23,000,000	4,495,000,000

[1] Includes Central America and the West Indies.
[2] Includes the U.S.S.R. and other countries with established Marxist ideology where religious adherence is difficult to estimate.
[3] Includes areas in which persons have traditionally enrolled in several religions, as well as mainland China with a Marxist establishment.
[4] Includes Australia and New Zealand as well as islands of the South Pacific.
[5] Includes Coptic Christians, of restricted status in Egypt and in a precarious situation under the military junta in Ethiopia.
[6] Protestant statistics vary widely in terms of reference. Many large denominations count only adults as full members; their statistics are not comparable to those of ethnic religions or churches counting all constituents of all ages including infants.
[7] Including a great proliferation of new sects and cults among African Christians.
[8] The chief base of Islam is still ethnic, although missionary work is now carried on in Europe and America (viz., "Black Muslims"). In countries where Islam is established, minority religions are frequently persecuted and accurate statistics are rare.
[9] A Japanese ethnic religion, Shinto declined markedly after the Japanese emperor surrendered his claim to divinity (1947) but has recently staged a revival in cultic participation in the homeland. Shinto does not transplant well or survive easily outside Japan.
[10] Buddhism has produced several renewal movements in the last century which have gained adherents in Europe and America. In Asia too it has made rapid gains in some areas in recent years. Under persecution it has shown greater staying power than Taoism or Confucianism. It also transplants better.
[11] Hinduism's strength in India has been enhanced by nationalism, a phenomenon also observable in the world of Islam. Modern Hinduism has developed several renewal movements that have won adherents in Europe and America.
[12] United Nations, Department of International Economic and Social Affairs; data refer to midyear 1981.

(FRANKLIN H. LITTELL)

RELIGIOUS GROWTH IN A NEW AREA

by Martin E. Marty

Sometime in the 1980s an event of immeasurable importance to world religion will occur. According to the best computer analyses and statistical hunches, for the first time in 2,000 years Christianity, the globe's largest communion, will have more adherents in the Southern Hemisphere than in the Northern. A trend in that direction has been clearly established. David Barrett, an expert on church growth, reported that in the typical year 1978, while European and North American churches lost 2,750,-000 members, churches in black Africa grew by 6 million—16,000 per day! Nor is Christianity alone in experiencing growth in the world's southern regions. In 1960 every seventh person alive was claimed by Islam. By 1980 every fifth person was part of the Islamic population, and much of the expansion had taken place in Indonesia and sub-Saharan Africa.

Fifty years ago a conservative Roman Catholic, Hilaire Belloc, could virtually equate Christianity with "Europe," including America. Today, Northern Hemispheric Christians are learning to watch for their religious news south of the Equator. Thus when leaders of three of the four major Lutheran bodies in the U.S. protested their government's actions concerning South West Africa/Namibia, there were questions as to why Lutherans cared. Issues of justice aside, they cared because their faith, once largely centred in Germany and Scandinavia, was now the church of 600,000 of Namibia's 1.1 million people.

The Burgeoning South. Assumptions of continuing church growth in Africa were based on the hope that regimes in the continent's new nations would not be unstable or repressive. There were reasons for concern, but the signs were mixed. When Robert Mugabe, an avowed Marxist, came to power in Zimbabwe, displacing Methodist bishop Abel Muzorewa as black governmental leader, many feared that he would suppress religion. His early actions gave

Martin E. Marty is Fairfax M. Cone distinguished service professor at the University of Chicago and associate editor of The Christian Century.

encouragement to Christians and other believers. When Catholic Archbishop Emmanuel Milingo and Christian Council leader Zingsley Mwenda expressed fears that Zambia was moving toward antireligious socialism of a Marxist-Leninist sort, Pres. Kenneth Kaunda, an active Methodist, had to go out of his way to reassure them. In Malawi, H. Kamuzu Banda's government persecuted the community of 30,000 Jehovah's Witnesses, who in 1967 refused to join his Malawi Congress Party. Many fled to Zambia and Mozambique but later returned to Malawi, which has a Christian majority and a significant Muslim minority.

The tension in South Africa is compounded by the fact that the ruling Nationalist Party has a strong religious base in the Dutch Reformed Church and uses this base to bolster its policy of apartheid or racial discrimination. Yet the black movements and their white supporters are also organized largely along religious lines. Christian novelist Alan Paton is pessimistic about the future because, he says, white South African church people are "psychologically incapable" of moving toward compromise and reconciliation with blacks.

The strong Christian presence in Africa has changed the outlook of ecumenical organizations. Pope John Paul II, like Paul VI before him, has shown special concern and affection for African Catholicism. Protestants have tried to learn to come to terms with native practices that some Africans carried over into Christianity. Missionaries once tried to do away with polygamy immediately. Now all but the more fundamentalist groups are more patient.

Contrary to many assumptions, the day of the missionary from the Northern Hemisphere is not over. Missions Advanced Research and Communication Center (MARC) surprised itself and those who use its data when it found that in 1979, 53,494 American Protestant missionaries were working overseas. This compared with 37,677 four years earlier and amounted to a growth rate of almost 10% per year. Most of these missionaries had headed southward. Most also were from the conservative, not the mainline churches.

Most of the Muslim and Christian growth in Africa results from the drastic population growth among the poor of the Southern Hemisphere. Many become members of fiery Pentecostal churches inspired by self-starting "prophets." Yet in the course of time, according to church historian Adrian Hastings, these groups frequently turn more "churchly" and staid.

Another area of rapid religious expansion is the largely Islamic island nation of Indonesia, whose 150 million people are experiencing growth in population and in conversions to the faith. What is more, Indonesia, like many other Muslim nations, is undergoing a resurgence of hard-line fundamentalism that resists modernization, thus creating serious problems for the government. From time to time conflict breaks out between those who hold to the islands' traditional faiths, Muslims and the Christian minority, and antireligious Marxists.

The exceptions to the explosive religious trends in the Southern Hemisphere are Australia and New Zealand, settled by Europeans who displaced the native religions but were themselves semisecularized. Religious fervour has been less noticeable there than in other parts of the South, although such U.S.-based faiths as the Latter-day Saints, Jehovah's Witnesses, and the Seventh-day Adventists have experienced significant growth.

Latin America: Changing Roles. Latin America is something of a special case. For almost 500 years it has had an enormous Catholic presence alongside and blended with native faiths. In 1981 the small Jewish community of Argentina made world news when journalist Jacobo Timerman (see BIOGRAPHIES) toured Israel and the U.S. promoting his book *Prisoner Without a Name, Cell Without a Number.* While Timerman admitted that some of the torture he and other Jews experienced at the hands of the rightist government was politically inspired, he claimed that it was especially vicious because repression was focused in anti-Semitism. This charge divided the Argentine Jewish community: some were highly adapted to the general culture, others wished to remain less visible, and still others agreed with Timerman. Statistically, Judaism was not a major faith in the hemisphere. Of a world population of 15 million Jews, only 500,000 were in all of South America, 165,000 in all of Africa, and 75,000 in Oceania.

The eyes of the Northern Hemisphere's believers have been directed chiefly to Latin-American Catholicism. Yet Pentecostal-type Protestantism has made swift advances. Curiously, many Pentecostals support governments that Catholicism, long identified with the existing order, has criticized. Thus, in Chile, Pentecostals have given support to the ruling junta

of Pres. Augusto Pinochet Ugarte. The junta returns the favour out of fear of a Catholic leadership that still identifies with the government Pinochet and his supporters overthrew.

Despite a shortage of priests and the discouragement of priests-in-politics by Pope John Paul II, Catholic leadership today often sides with the oppressed against old elites of wealth, learning, and power. New forms of church life are developing. In Brazil there are 50,000 *communidades eclesiais de base* or "base communities." These lay-led clusters of believers pursue social forms that affirm their historic faith but allow them to organize independently of institutions that strike them as overly traditional or supportive of government. Advocates call them "the church born of the people." The Brazilian Bishops' Conference has tried to encourage them while remaining alert to the possibility that they could become too independent.

Along with "base communities," the South American churches have also presented the religious world with a form of thought known as "liberation theology." To its critics, the term sounds suspiciously Marxist, but advocates claim that they draw impetus chiefly from the Bible, where, they say, God always sides with the poor and the oppressed and topples the rich and powerful. While Christian identification with guerrilla movements or revolutionary forces that would do the toppling has made news chiefly in Central America, particularly Nicaragua and El Salvador, these forces are present in Latin nations south of the Equator as well.

A Shifting Focus. As Muslims, Jews, and Christians in the Northern Hemisphere become ever more aware of Southern Hemispheric trauma and triumph, they find their own consciousness and their symbols changing. More and more the Christians of the North have people of the South as heroes. Thus Mother Teresa of Calcutta, India (technically in the Northern Hemisphere but identifying with the South), has become one of the most admired Christians in the world. Blacks see in the late Steve Biko a South African martyr to the black Christian cause. Pastor Beyers Naudé, a banned white minister in the same nation, is a model for European and American Christians. Dom Helder Câmara has come to be admired—or despised, depending upon one's political and spiritual outlook—in the Christianity of the North because of his high-risk identification with the Brazilian poor.

This change in the locales where one finds heroes and saints is but a sign of a shift that marks world religion as a whole in the 1980s. Religious news is being made in the Southern Hemisphere. The North must awaken to this fact, for the repercussions will shape world history.

Rodeo

As 1981 was drawing to a close, hundreds of cowboys were looking forward to the richest rodeo competition in the history of the sport. It would be the World Cup Rodeo, scheduled to be held in January 1982 in Sydney and Melbourne, Australia. One million dollars in prize money was guaranteed. The World Cup had been organized by a group of Australian businessmen who wanted to initiate a rodeo with so much prize money it would attract cowboys and cowgirls from around the world. The contest was sanctioned by the Australian Rough Riders Association, New Zealand Rough Riders Association, the Professional Rodeo Cowboys Association (PRCA) in the U.S., and the Canadian Professional Rodeo Association (CPRA).

The PRCA, oldest and largest rodeo association, had another record year in terms of prize money in 1981. Cowboys won more than $10 million at 642 rodeos in North America, including the National Finals, held in Oklahoma City in December. World championships are determined on the basis of total money won in the season, including the National Finals Rodeo, which had a record of $618,000 at stake for 1981. World all-around champion for 1981 was Jimmie Cooper of Monument, N.M., who competed in calf roping, steer wrestling, and team roping and won $105,862 in the arena during the year. Cooper won the title by a mere $47, beating his cousin, Roy Cooper of Durant, Okla., who finished runner-up for the prestigious crown. But Roy Cooper did win the calf roping world championship with $94,476 in winnings. Other reigning PRCA world champions included J. C. Trujillo of Steamboat Springs, Colo., $76,140 in bareback riding; Brad Gjermundson of Marshall, N.D., $64,409 in saddle bronc riding; Don Gay of Mesquite, Texas, $63,908 in bull riding; Byron Walker of Ennis, Texas, $65,245 in steer wrestling; Walt Woodard of Stockton, Calif.,

and Doyle Gellerman of Oakdale, Calif., who won $48,818 each in team roping; and Arnold Felts of Mutual, Okla., $36,121 in steer roping. Lynn McKenzie of Shreveport, La., won the barrel racing title of the Women's Professional Rodeo Association.

Tom Eirikson of Innisfail, Alta., won his second straight all-around crown in the CPRA with $19,836. Eirikson competed in calf roping, steer wrestling, and saddle bronc riding.

In the International Rodeo Association, Dan Dailey of Franklin, Tenn., had his fifth all-around title assured with more than $50,000 in winnings as the IRA prepared for its annual International Finals Rodeo, held each January in Tulsa, Okla. Dailey had proved to be one of the most versatile cowboys in the history of rodeo, competing in six events while most rodeo cowboys specialize in only one or two.

The ranks of professional rodeo continued to swell as youth rodeo gained in popularity. At the National High School Rodeo Association (NHSRA) finals in Douglas, Wyo., during the summer, 1,200 qualifiers competed for year-end awards. Tommy Todd of Bell City, La., and Nancy Rea of Tom, Okla., won the all-around championships. In the American Junior Rodeo Association finals at Snyder, Texas, senior all-around winners included Jinita Williams of Hobbs, N.M., and Gene Baker of Tuscola, Texas.

The 1981 all-around champs in the National Intercollegiate Rodeo Association (NIRA) were George Mesimer of the University of Tennessee at Martin and Sabrina Pike of Southeastern Oklahoma State at Durant.

The Sixth Annual Indian National Finals Rodeo was held in Albuquerque, N.M., in November. Top Indian rodeo contestants from throughout the country vied for championships during four days of competition. The all-around title went to Jerry Small, a Northern Cheyenne from Busby, Mont. Small, who competed in three events, also won the championship in 1977.   (RANDALL E. WITTE)

Jimmie Cooper, of Monument, New Mexico, shows the form that made him the new world all-around champion for 1981.

Romania

A socialist republic on the Balkan Peninsula in southeastern Europe, Romania is bordered by the U.S.S.R., the Black Sea, Bulgaria, Yugoslavia, and Hungary. Area: 237,500 sq km (91,700 sq mi). Pop. (1981 est.): 22,302,000, including (1977) Romanian 88.1%; Hungarian 7.9%; German 1.6%. Cap. and largest city: Bucharest (pop., 1979 est., 1,850,800). Religion: Romanian Orthodox 70%; Greek Orthodox 10%. General secretary of the Romanian Communist Party, president of the republic, and president of the State Council in 1981, Nicolae Ceausescu; chairman of the Council of Ministers (premier), Ilie Verdet.

Romania's economic and social troubles became serious in 1981. With the aim of achieving self-sufficiency in energy in 1990, Romania was spending huge sums on developing energy sources, including nuclear power. Although self-sufficient in crude petroleum ten years earlier, Romania by 1981 was importing roughly one-third of its oil, mainly from Arab countries and partly from the U.S.S.R. Oil prospecting was under way off the Black Sea coast, and the excavation of the Danube-Black Sea canal, started in 1971, was expected to be completed in 1982. But these important and necessary public works could not be undertaken without importing special machinery and equipment from the West. By mid-1981 Romania's debt to the West amounted to $10 billion–$14 billion.

Western credit was obtained mainly on a short-term basis with high interest rates. According to the Romanian Finance Ministry, the Bucharest government did not aim to reschedule its debts but wanted instead to spread out its short-term obligations to Western banks. The only country of the Soviet bloc belonging to the International Monetary Fund, Romania received a three-year standby credit of $1.5 billion from the IMF in 1981.

Romania's economic problems were aggravated by poor harvests. To offset the shortage of hard currency, exports of meat and other food products

Romania

had to be increased, and the consequent food shortages affected the morale of a work force already disenchanted by years of hard work and low living standards. A series of antigovernment incidents occurred in the autumn of 1981: the police

C. BONAZZA—IMAPRESS/PICTORIAL PARADE

Romanians were finding it necessary to stand in line for hours in order to buy bread. There were shortages of many food items during the year.

station of Motru was burned; a strike was called in the Danube port of Giurgiu; and a helicopter taking Pres. Nicolae Ceausescu to the Jiu Valley mining region was stoned. Ceausescu introduced bread and cereal rationing in October, with heavy fines for profiteering and hoarding. Top-level Cabinet changes affecting several senior officials, carried out by Ceausescu in March, September, and November, were attributed to the worsening economic situation.

During 1981 relations between Romania and the other countries of the Soviet bloc eased significantly. In April Gheorghe Pana, a member of the Executive Political Committee of the Romanian Communist Party, visited East Berlin where he spoke of the need to strengthen cooperation between the Communist parties of Romania and East Germany. In May Pres. Gustav Husak of Czechoslovakia received Ceausescu in Prague. On July 31 Ceausescu met Soviet Pres. Leonid Brezhnev in the Crimea, and during their talks he asked the Soviet leader for an increased supply of crude petroleum. Nevertheless, Romanian-Polish relations remained friendly. The Romanian press, alone among those of Eastern Europe, ignored the warning letter that the Soviet Communist Party Central Committee sent to the Polish party leadership on June 5.

Pres. Karl Carstens of West Germany arrived in Romania on October 26 for a five-day state visit. Originally planned for April, the visit was postponed by Bonn because Ceausescu declined to grant Carstens's request to visit German minorities in the Transylvania and Banat areas. Later, Ceausescu changed his mind, and Carstens talked to the representatives of some 310,000 Saxons and Swabians whose forefathers had settled in what is now Romania during the 13th century. The majority of this German-speaking population wished to emigrate, and in 1980 the Romanian government had allowed 16,000 Germans to return to West Germany. In an interview given to the West German newspaper *Die Zeit*, President Ceausescu explained that only those Romanian citizens of German nationality who had "close

relatives" in West Germany would be allowed to emigrate.

Ceausescu personally led a Romanian movement in support of a nuclear-free Europe. A mass rally for this cause took place in Bucharest on December 5.   (K. M. SMOGORZEWSKI)

Rowing

The Soviet Union displaced East Germany as the leading nation in world rowing in 1981. Although East Germany dominated the junior championships in Sofia, Bulg., its men's and women's teams in the world championships in Munich, West Germany, failed to win any medals in eights and had to yield to the Soviet oarsmen on overall performance. Twenty-three nations won medals in the four world-class competitions.

The Soviet Union won 7 of the 14 titles in the men's and women's classes, while East Germany could only manage 4. The other world title winners were Italy and West Germany in men's events and Romania in the women's competition. Eleven nations won medals in the men's events, seven in the women's, and four in both. East Germany started well in men's competition by defeating the U.S. and the Soviet Union in coxed fours and then Finland and Norway in double sculls. The Soviet Union won the coxless pairs from The Netherlands and Italy and then the coxless fours from Switzerland and East Germany. Using a sliding rigger boat of a new design, Peter Michael Kolbe scored an effortless victory for West Germany in single sculls, with East Germany and the U.S. second and third. Italy won its gold medal in coxed pairs from East Germany with Great Britain taking the bronze. East Germany won its third gold medal in quadruple sculls ahead of the Soviet Union and France.

The closest race did not occur until the final of the eights, after four of the contestants had qualified with only 0.76 sec separating their times. The Soviet Union and Great Britain qualified directly as heat winners, leaving the six other entries to row another heat to qualify for the remaining

The first woman to take part in the University Boat Race led her crew to victory as Oxford defeated Cambridge in April. Sue Brown led the Oxford crew over the four-mile course in a little over 18 minutes.

UPI

places. The U.S. was the winner over East Germany, West Germany, and Czechoslovakia, in that order; the four boats were less than a length apart at the finish. The final was not quite so close. The Soviet Union won the gold medal from Great Britain by 2.01 sec with the U.S. third, 1.82 sec behind.

Racing for the women's titles was much closer. East Germany was only 0.27 sec faster than Canada in coxless pairs, and Sanda Toma of Romania held off Beryl Mitchell of Great Britain by 1.12 sec to retain her single sculls title. The Soviet Union won the coxed fours, double sculls, and eights by nearly 3 sec but was held to a 1.82-sec margin of victory by East Germany in the quadruple sculls.

Australia, Denmark, Italy, and the U.S. were the gold medal winners in the lightweight championships, in which four other countries shared the medals. East Germany won all eight gold medals in the boys' junior championships, with ten other nations sharing the remaining medals. In the girls' events East Germany (2), Romania (2), Bulgaria, and the Soviet Union were the title winners.

In England the U.S. won three open trophies in eights at the Henley Royal Regatta: the University of Washington collected the Ladies Plate; Holy Spirit High School captured the Princess Elizabeth Cup; and the Charles River Rowing Association took the Thames Cup. A joint crew from RV Ingelheim and Ulmer and RC Donau, both of West Germany, became the first winners of the Queen Mother Cup (quadruple sculls), and Hanlan Boat Club of Canada triumphed in the Wyfold Cup (coxless fours). The 142-year-old regatta admitted women to competition for the first time, but only by invitation. They raced in two experimental events, won by the 1980 Rowing Club of the U.S. (coxed fours) and Adanac Boat Club, Canada (double sculls). Oxford won the 127th University Boat Race by eight lengths, steered by Susan Brown, the first woman to take part in the historic series, in which Cambridge now led 68–58.

(KEITH OSBORNE)

Rwanda

A republic in eastern Africa and former traditional kingdom whose origins may be traced back to the 15th century, Rwanda is bordered by Zaire, Uganda, Tanzania, and Burundi. Area: 26,338 sq km (10,169 sq mi). Pop. (1981 est.): 5,256,000, including (1970) Hutu 90%; Tutsi 9%; and Twa 1%. Cap. and largest city: Kigali (pop., 1981 est., 156,650). Language (official): French and Kinyarwanda. Religion: Roman Catholic 45%; Protestant 10%; Muslim 1%; remainder mostly animist. President in 1981, Maj. Gen. Juvénal Habyarimana.

Early in 1981, when Pres. Juvénal Habyarimana addressed the third party congress of the National Revolutionary Development Movement, he announced that Rwanda was to acquire a legislative assembly. This was in accordance with the terms of the constitution, which had been approved by referendum in December 1978. In March the president reshuffled his Cabinet, retaining the tasks of head of government and defense himself and splitting the education ministry into two parts, one

RWANDA
Education. (1978–79) Primary, pupils 515,712, teachers (1976–77) 8,161; secondary, vocational, and teacher training, pupils 13,799, teachers (1976–77) 820; higher, students 975, teaching staff (1976–77) 184.
Finance. Monetary unit: Rwanda franc, with (Sept. 21, 1981) a par value of RwFr 92.84 to U.S. $1 (free rate of RwFr 172.13 = £1 sterling). Gold and other reserves (June 1981) U.S. $169 million. Budget (1979 est.) balanced at RwFr 9,214,000,000.
Foreign Trade. Imports (1979) RwFr 17,856,000,000; exports (1980) RwFr 6,709,000,000. Import sources: Belgium-Luxembourg 17%; Japan 10%; West Germany 10%; Kenya 8%; Iran 8%; France 7%; China 5%. Export destinations (1979): U.S. c. 28%; West Germany c. 22%; Spain c. 8%; Belgium-Luxembourg c. 7%; U.K. 6%; Kenya c. 6%; Yugoslavia c. 5%. Main exports: coffee 55%; tea 18%; tin 8%.
Agriculture. Production (in 000; metric tons; 1980): sorghum c. 170; corn (1979) c. 72; potatoes c. 221; sweet potatoes (1979) c. 842; cassava (1979) c. 460; dry beans c. 176; dry peas c. 46; pumpkins (1979) c. 62; plantains (1979) c. 2,127; coffee c. 14; tea c. 5. Livestock (in 000; July 1979): cattle c. 640; sheep c. 257; goats c. 786; pigs c. 83.

Rwanda

dealing with school education and the other with higher education and scientific research.

Rwanda continued to fall short of self-sufficiency in food production. Its already dense population was augmented by thousands of refugees. The main emphasis for the national economy was upon the development of roads and bridges and improvements to rural communications. A 30-kv high-tension line was to be installed from Ruhengeri to Gisenyi to link the latter to the national electric grid.

West Germany provided aid for the construction of an 1,800-kw hydroelectric power station near Gisenyi. During the year France increased its capital in the Banque Rwandaise from $4.4 million to $10.8 million. (GUY ARNOLD)

Sailing

At the beginning of 1981 a new Bruce Farr-designed boat (helmsman, Peter Blake) won overall honours in the Sydney–Hobart classic. Many of the small yachts were frustrated by light winds at the end of the race. A month later in the Caribbean, the Southern Ocean Racing Conference series got under way. This series was important not only as an indicator for new yacht designs but also as the selection trials for the U.S. Admiral's Cup team. The competition was keen, but two of the yachts initially selected for the U.S. team were found to have large rating discrepancies. This led to the final selection of other U.S. yachts—"Stars and Stripes," "Intuition," and "Scaramouche." The rating discrepancy, which involved alterations in ballast and freeboard measurements when in sailing trim, led to more checks by the measurers before the Admiral's Cup and several of the ton cup series. For the Half-Ton Cup a French yacht was not accepted by the measurers.

The two-man transatlantic race proved that the multihulled boats had reached a new peak in design. For years they had been faster than the monohulls off the wind, but by 1981 they could match them to windward even in heavy weather. "Brittany Ferries GB," sailed by Chay Blyth and Robert

611
Sailing

Rubber:
see Industrial Review
Rugby Football:
see Football
Russia:
see Union of Soviet Socialist Republics
Russian Literature:
see Literature
Sabah:
see Malaysia

"Victory," captained by Philip Crebbin, succeeded in winning the Admiral's Cup for Britain in a race held in the English Channel.

"Yeoman XXIII," "Victory," and "Dragon" (sailed by Robin Aisher, Philip Crebbin, and Brian Saffery-Cooper, respectively), after a disastrous first race set the pace in the second with first and second places by "Victory" and "Yeoman." During these two races the U.S., West German, and Irish yachts were achieving consistent performances. The British consolidated their position in the Channel race and third inshore races with "Victory" and "Yeoman" again finishing among the leaders. Thus, the British team set out on the Fastnet race in a strong position.

The first three-quarters of that event were sailed in reasonable winds of force 3 to 4. But as the bigger yachts approached the Bishop Rock on their return from the Fastnet, a massive calm settled in. For 12 or more hours an ever increasing armada of yachts gathered in the calm off the Bishop Rock. When some wind arrived, it was still very light, and "Victory," which thus far had been the outstanding yacht of the series, demonstrated how with an alert crew a yacht could be kept going. It was second boat to finish over the line at Plymouth, only 2 hours behind the 80-ft "Kialoa." Because of its handicap, "Victory" dropped to 15th place, but with an 11th place for "Dragon" and a 25th for "Yeoman," Britain won the Admiral's Cup. Best boat in the series was the New Zealand yacht "Swuzzlebubble," one point better than "Victory." (ADRIAN JARDINE)

[452.B.4.a.ii]

James, was a trimaran designed by John Shuttleworth. It broke the east-to-west transatlantic race record of 17 days 23 hours, finishing in 14 days 13 hours 54 minutes. Its best day's run was about 300 mi. It was followed home by the French catamaran "Elf Aquitaine." This catamaran then broke the west-to-east record by more than 5 hours on its return trip to Europe in 9 days 10 hours 6½ minutes.

In the Admiral's Cup, the main offshore series of the year, very light winds in the Solent made a mockery of the first race. However, in general the conditions were good, and the favourite teams ended up on top. The British team, consisting of

Saint Lucia

A parliamentary democracy and a member of the Commonwealth, St. Lucia, the second largest of the Windward Islands in the eastern Caribbean, is situated 32 km NE of St. Vincent and 40 km S of Martinique. Area: 622 sq km (240 sq mi). Pop. (1979 est.): 130,000, predominantly of African descent. Cap. and largest city: Castries (pop., 1979 est., 45,000). Language: English and a local French dialect. Religion (1970): Roman Catholic 91%, Anglican 3%, Seventh-day Adventist 2%, others 4%. Queen, Elizabeth II; governor-general in 1981, Boswell Williams (acting); prime ministers, Allan Louisy and, from May 4, Winston Francis Cenac.

The early part of 1981 saw a renewal of the power struggle between factions of the ruling St. Lucia Labour Party; a central issue was the challenge to

World Class Boat Champions

Class	Winner
Albacore	Jon Webb (U.K.)
International canoe	Max Tollquist (Sweden)
Europe (women)	Marit Söderström (Sweden)
Fireball	Philip Morrison (U.K.)
Flying Dutchman	Albert Batzill (West Germany)
505	Etham Bixby (U.S.)
470	David Barnes (New Zealand)
International 14	Frank McLaughlin (Canada)
Hornet	Gordon Lucas (Australia)
International Moth	David Iszatt (U.K.)
Optimist	Guido Tavelli (Argentina)
Sailboard World Cup	Hervé Borde (France)
Six-metre	Lawrie Smith (U.K.)
Snipe	Jeff Lenhart (U.S.)
Soling	Vincent Brun (Brazil)
Solo	Rob Van Ooyen (Neth.)
Sunfish	Dave Chapin (U.S.)
Tornado	Randy Smyth (U.S.)

YACHT CUP SERIES

2-ton	"Hitch Hiker"	Peter Briggs (Australia)
1-ton	"Justine III"	Frank Woods (Ireland)
¾-ton	"Soldier Blue"	I.B. Andersen (Sweden)
½-ton	"King One"	Paul Elvstrom (France)
¼-ton	"Lacydon Protis"	Bruno Trouble (France)
Mini-ton	"Gullisara"	Tiziano Nava (Italy)
Micro-ton	"Saumon Futé"	Paul Lucas (France)
Seahorse maxi	"Antares"	Philippe Briand (France)

Saint Lucia

ST. LUCIA

Education. (1978–79) Primary, pupils 30,295, teachers 863; secondary, pupils 4,584, teachers 173; vocational, pupils 169, teachers 24; teacher training, students 125, teachers 11.

Finance and Trade. Monetary unit: East Caribbean dollar, with (Sept. 21, 1981) a par value of ECar$2.70 to U.S. $1 (free rate of ECar$5.01 = £1 sterling). Budget (1977–78 est.) revenue ECar$50,596,000; expenditure ECar$51,120,-000. Foreign trade (1978): imports ECar$223.6 million; exports ECar$72.3 million. Import sources: U.S. 36%; U.K. 19%; Trinidad and Tobago 10%; Japan 5%. Export destinations: U.K. 49%; Barbados 9%; Trinidad and Tobago 8%; Dominica 6%; St. Vincent 6%; Jamaica 6%. Main exports: bananas 45%; cardboard boxes 11%; beverages 8%; coconut oil 7%. Tourism (including cruise passengers; 1978) 107,000 visitors.

the leadership of Prime Minister Allan Louisy by Deputy Prime Minister George Odlum. In April Louisy resigned after failing to win approval for his budget. The governor-general, in a surprise move, appointed Winston Francis Cenac (*see* Biographies), a former attorney general, as Louisy's successor. Odlum and two other former ministers launched the new, left-wing Progressive Labour Party.

The island's economy, once buoyant, suffered as a result of this political unrest. Tourism fell to half its 1978 level. Loss of confidence by investors caused industry to decline, though the banana plantations continued their slow recovery from the hurricane damage of 1980. Later in the year, relative calm was restored. Although internal problems were paramount, St. Lucia was instrumental in bringing into being the Organization of East Caribbean States. (DAVID A. JESSOP)

Saint Vincent and the Grenadines

A constitutional monarchy within the Commonwealth, St. Vincent and the Grenadines (islands of the Lesser Antilles in the Caribbean Sea) lies southwest of St. Lucia and west of Barbados. Area (including Grenadines): 388 sq km (150 sq mi). Pop. (1979 est.): 119,900, predominantly of African descent. Cap. and largest city: Kingstown (pop., 1978 est., 22,800). Language: English (official). Religion (1970): Anglican 47%; Methodist 28%; Roman Catholic 13%. Queen, Elizabeth II; governor-general in 1981, Sir Sydney Gun-Munro; prime minister, Milton Cato.

Hudson Tannis, acting prime minister while Milton Cato was abroad, announced on Aug. 4, 1981, that a plot to overthrow the government had been uncovered. However, no arrests were made, and the statement, never expanded, became the subject of considerable criticism.

When water workers went on strike, causing fresh water supplies to run out, the government announced plans to introduce legislation that would redefine essential services and give the police wide powers of search and arrest. The effect of the proposals was to unify the opposition and trade unions against the government. However, the dispute was settled, and the bills lapsed when Parliament went into recess.

Exports of bananas, the economy's mainstay, re-

mained low as a result of hurricane damage in previous years. St. Vincent received a loan of 1.3 million SDR's from the International Monetary Fund. St. Vincent joined the Organization of East Caribbean States. (DAVID A. JESSOP)

Saint Vincent and the Grenadines

San Marino

A small republic, San Marino is an enclave in northeastern Italy, 8 km (5 mi) SW of Rimini. Area: 61 sq km (24 sq mi). Pop. (1981 est.): 21,500. Cap. and largest city: San Marino (metro. pop., 1981 est., 8,600). Language: Italian. Religion: Roman Catholic. The country is governed by two *capitani reggenti*, or co-regents, appointed every six months by a Grand and General Council. Executive power rests with three secretaries of state: foreign and political affairs, internal affairs, and economic affairs. In 1981 the positions were filled, respectively, by Giordano Bruno Reffi, Alvaro Selva, and Emilio della Balda.

San Marino

The most important news of 1981 from San Marino, Western Europe's only Communist-controlled country, was that a woman was elected as joint head of state for the first time in the country's 1,680-year history. In the middle of March the Grand and General Council of the republic elected the two joint *capitani reggenti*, or co-regents, who took office for a term of six months from April 1. Maria Lea Pedini-Angelini, a 27-year-old ministerial secretary, was elected along with Gastone Pasolini. Pedini-Angelini was a Socialist and Pasolini was a Communist.

São Tomé and Príncipe

The coalition government of San Marino, first formed after the general election held in May 1978, continued in office. Power was in the hands of a left-wing three-party coalition composed of 16 Communists, 8 Socialists, and 9 Social Democrats. In opposition to the government were 26 Christian Democrats and 1 independent.

(K. M. SMOGORZEWSKI)

São Tomé and Príncipe

An independent African state, the Democratic Republic of São Tomé and Príncipe comprises two main islands and several smaller islets that straddle the Equator in the Gulf of Guinea, off the west coast of Africa. Area: 964 sq km (372 sq mi), of which São Tomé, the larger island, comprises 854 sq km. Pop. (1981 est.): 86,000. Cap. and largest city: São Tomé (pop., 1977 est., 20,000). Language: Portuguese. Religion: mainly Roman Catholic. President in 1981, Manuel Pinto da Costa.

In July 1981, on the sixth anniversary of São Tomé and Príncipe's independence, the former premier, Miguel Trovoada, was released from

prison. He had been detained for nearly two years, accused of economic sabotage and failure to reveal a plot against the president. The nation continued to express interest in forming links with the West; late in 1980 the São Tomé minister of industries, trade, and fisheries, Carlos Gomes, visited London to attract investment. Although relations with Angola were good, those with neighbouring Gabon were somewhat difficult.

Aid was provided by the European Economic Community to assist the fishing industry, while the Organization of Petroleum Exporting Countries gave $1 million in support of the balance of payments. Agriculture, accounting for the livelihood of more than one-third of the total population, was accorded the highest priority for development. Green banana production was increased by 50%, to 3,000 metric tons. Cocoa production, which had fallen to only 4,000 metric tons after the departure of the Portuguese, increased to double that figure. A major effort was made to exploit the rich tuna fishing grounds, but there was resistance by fishermen to joining cooperatives. (GUY ARNOLD)

Saudi Arabia

Saudi Arabia

A monarchy occupying four-fifths of the Arabian Peninsula, Saudi Arabia has an area of 2,240,000 sq km (865,000 sq mi). Pop. (1981 est.): 8,631,000. Cap. and largest city: Riyadh (pop., 1980 est., 1,044,000). Language: Arabic. Religion: Muslim, predominantly Sunni; Shi'ah minority in Eastern Province. King and prime minister in 1981, Khalid.

In August 1981 Saudi Arabia published the Fahd plan for a Middle East peace settlement. Under this plan: (1) Israel would withdraw from all Arab territory occupied in 1967, including Arab Jerusalem (East Jerusalem); (2) Israeli settlements built on Arab land after 1967 would be dismantled; (3) all religions would be guaranteed freedom of worship in holy places; (4) the right of the Palestinian Arabs to return to their homes, and compensation for those who wished to stay away, would be affirmed; (5) the West Bank and the Gaza Strip would have a transitional period under the UN, not to exceed several months; (6) an independent Palestinian state would be set up with East Jerusalem as its capital; (7) all states in the region should be able to live in peace; and (8) the UN or member states of the UN would guarantee the carrying out of these principles.

Crown Prince Fahd put the weight of his personal relationships with world statesmen behind the initiative. Although the move was startling in that it brought Saudi Arabia out of its isolation from pan-Arab politics, it became clear that even the Saudi Arabians with their enormous financial and religious influence would not solve the peace question at a stroke. The November Arab summit meeting in Fez, Morocco, broke up in disarray over the proposals, and Arab discussion of the plan was postponed for six months.

Greater success attended Saudi Arabia's pursuit of its avowed policy of maintaining a unified pricing system for crude oil within the context of the Organization of Petroleum Exporting Countries (OPEC). At the October OPEC meeting in Geneva, Saudi Arabia carried the day with its bottom-line price of U.S. $34 a barrel for Arabian light crude. The meeting, at which price differentials were agreed on and OPEC renewed its commitment to price unity, was followed by a cut in Saudi output from 9.6 million to 8.5 million bbl a day. This was the kingdom's preferred output ceiling, but it had been consistently exceeded since 1979. Saudi Arabia won another victory at the December OPEC meeting in Abu Dhabi, when crude oil prices were further trimmed to bring them into line with the price of Arabian light crude.

While Oil Minister Sheikh Ahmad Zaki Yamani warned that crude oil supply and demand on the world markets could be in balance by the spring of 1982, there was no doubt that Saudi Arabia's moderate voice and power as a producer had prevailed in OPEC counsels. Sheikh Yamani announced that

A U.S. AWACS plane soars over Riyadh, Saudi Arabia. In October the U.S. Senate approved an agreement to sell the sophisticated radar planes and other military equipment to Saudi Arabia.

his country would be prepared to cut production still further in order to defend the $34 price, but he also stressed that it would use the threat of increased production if other OPEC members strayed beyond the agreed price differentials.

A source of reassurance to the Saudi Arabians was U.S. Pres. Ronald Reagan's victory over the sale of five Boeing airborne warning and control system (AWACS) aircraft to the kingdom. In October the U.S. Senate voted by a slim majority to approve the $8.5 billion sale. It had been regarded by Saudi Arabia as a crucial test of U.S. friendship. Israel had vigorously opposed the sale of such sophisticated equipment to an Arab country. In acid remarks, Israeli spokesmen referred to the Saudi regime as one of "corrupt princes."

This was not, however, the way Saudi Arabia was regarded in 1981 by international organizations. In an accord with the International Monetary Fund in the spring, Saudi Arabia agreed to provide the IMF with 4 billion special drawing rights ($4.7 billion) over the next two to three years. The increased quotas put the kingdom in sixth place in the IMF hierarchy. Later an agreement was reached with the World Bank.

The first year of Saudi Arabia's five-year development plan, announced in May 1980, resulted in greater emphasis on industrialization. The Saudis were aiming for a share of at least 6% in the world market for petrochemicals and refined products by the 1990s. Within the Gulf region, Saudi Arabia was preparing to play a greater coordinating role through the Gulf Cooperation Council (GCC), a regional economic and defense cooperation pact, established in March, which grouped the kingdom with Kuwait, Bahrain, Qatar, Oman, and the United Arab Emirates. During the year Saudi Arabia made renewed commitments to pan-Gulf industrial projects in Bahrain and elsewhere. An agreement for construction of a causeway linking Bahrain and Saudi Arabia, a project that had been the subject of deliberation for some time, was signed in the summer.

On December 23 the Saudi government announced its full support for Syria in the dispute over Israel's annexation of the Golan Heights. At the same time, a scheduled visit to the U.S. by Prince Fahd was postponed "because of current Middle East developments . . . and the international situation." An agreement ending a nearly 60-year border dispute with Iraq was signed on December 27. On December 31 it was announced that diplomatic relations with Libya were being resumed after a 14-month break.

In April Margaret Thatcher became the first British prime minister to visit Saudi Arabia. A major object of her visit was to interest the Saudi Arabians in buying British arms. Crown Prince Fahd urged her to take the initiative in European attempts to involve the Palestinians in Middle East peace negotiations. West German Chancellor Helmut Schmidt visited the kingdom in the same month, when he communicated his government's strong opposition to the sale of West German Leopard II tanks to the Saudis.

A growth rate of 15% a year was being recorded by the Saudi economy as the kingdom demonstrated its ability to absorb huge public spending. The 1981–82 budget was larger than expected, with total spending fixed at the equivalent of $86 billion, 42% above the 1980–81 figure. Defense spending, at $25 billion, received the biggest share of the budget. The sharp increase in expenditure suggested that over the period of the current plan (1980–85) total spending could exceed 1,000 billion riyals ($292,397,000,000).

Despite the high level of spending, inflation was restricted to an annual rate of less than 10%. Early in 1981 the riyal was devalued in stages in order to avoid loss of confidence on the foreign exchange markets. High domestic rates of interest persisted nevertheless, reflecting trends in international capital markets.

Of major projects completed in 1981, the Jidda International Airport, which became fully operational in April, was the most spectacular. Also completed was a 1,200-km (746-mi) crude oil pipeline that ran from east to west, linking the oil fields

of Buqayq in the Eastern Province to the export terminal on the Red Sea at Yanbu. Supplies started flowing through the pipeline on July 1, 1981. A parallel gas line, to provide fuel supplies for Yanbu's new industrial complexes, was under construction.

The twin industrial cities of Yanbu and Jubail, on the Gulf coast, were undergoing rapid development. In May Japanese companies headed by Mitsubishi signed an accord for an important petrochemical venture. This was a particularly important boost for the Saudi Basic Industries Corporation (Sabic). Because Mitsui of Japan had suffered serious setbacks on a petrochemical venture at Bandar Khomeini, Iran, corporate investors in Tokyo were nervous about heavy commitments of this sort in the Gulf. Two other agreements for petrochemical ventures were signed in 1981, bringing to seven the total number of major projects agreed to by Sabic. Foreign investors were being encouraged by an incentive in the form of crude oil supplies, offered in proportion to the amount of investment involved. Sabic was evaluating a number of other proposals for petrochemical projects and intended to announce its decisions in 1982.

Several other major oil industry projects were under consideration, some of which seemed likely to be started in 1982. Approval was given for a crude oil pipeline linking the Upper Gulf with the Red Sea. A more tentative proposal was for a pipeline from Ras at-Tannurah to the Oman border; such a scheme would mean that tankers loading Saudi crude oil would not have to navigate the strategic Strait of Hormuz. A more immediate plan involved construction of a strategic reserve for crude oil in the al-Hijaz Mountains, east of Yanbu.

The move to give more weight to local businesses continued in 1981. Early in the year a policy of awarding contracts for all road and bridge construction to local companies was announced, but it was implemented only in the case of small- and medium-sized projects. This was part of a wider move to discriminate in favour of local companies first and joint ventures second. The saudization of the banking sector was expected to be completed in 1982, when the last three foreign banks operating in the kingdom were to be merged into a new commercial bank.   (JOHN WHELAN)

Senegal

Senegal

A republic of West Africa, Senegal is bounded by Mauritania, Mali, Guinea, and Guinea-Bissau and by the Atlantic Ocean. The independent nation of The Gambia forms an enclave within the country. Area: 196,722 sq km (75,955 sq mi). Pop. (1981 est.): 5,811,000. Cap. and largest city: Dakar (pop., 1978 est., 914,500). Language: French (official); Wolof 29%; Serer 17%; Peulh 17%; Diola 8%; Bambara 6%; other tribal dialects. Religion: Muslim 86%; Christian 5%; animist 9%. President in 1981, Abdou Diouf; premier, Habib Thiam.

Senegal's new president, Abdou Diouf (*see* BIOGRAPHIES), was sworn in on Jan. 1, 1981. He was succeeded as premier by Habib Thiam and on

Seychelles

January 15 was named secretary-general of the ruling Parti Socialiste.

The most notable innovation in domestic politics under President Diouf was a constitutional amendment, adopted by the National Assembly on April 24, removing restrictions on the formation of political parties (limited to four under former president Léopold Sédar Senghor). A number of small parties, mostly extreme left-wing, were formed, as well as the Rassemblement National Démocratique of Sheikh Anta Diop, expected to become the leading opposition party. The Parti Démocratique Sénégalais (PDS) of Abdoulaye Wade, which as one of the four permitted parties had previously constituted the parliamentary opposition, suffered a setback; following resignations it no longer had the 15 deputies necessary for recognition as a parliamentary group with representation in the office of the National Assembly. In September a number of PDS members were arrested on suspicion of subversive activities.

Senegal's relations with France were reinforced by visits to Paris by Premier Thiam (in June) and by President Diouf, who attended the Franco-African summit there on November 3–4. On July 31, for the second time in less than a year, Senegalese troops intervened in The Gambia at the request of Gambian Pres. Sir Dawda Jawara (*see* BIOGRAPHIES; GAMBIA, THE). On December 17 Presidents Diouf and Jawara signed an agreement on the confederation of their two countries under the name of Senegambia.   (PHILIPPE DECRAENE)

Seychelles

A republic and a member of the Commonwealth in the Indian Ocean consisting of 89 islands, Seychelles lies 1,450 km from the coast of East Africa. Area: 444 sq km (171 sq mi), 166 sq km of which includes the islands of Farquhar, Desroches, and Aldabra. Pop. (1981 est.): 64,000, including Creole 94%, French 5%, English 1%. Cap.: Victoria, on Mahé (pop., 1977, 23,000). Language: English and French are official, creole patois is also spoken. Religion: Roman Catholic 90%; Anglican 8%. President in 1981, France-Albert René.

An attempt by some 50 mercenaries to overthrow Pres. France-Albert René was foiled in late November. The Seychelles government accused South Africa of involvement in the abortive coup, which it claimed had been mounted on be-

Sierra Leone

half of former president James Mancham. The mercenaries arrived at Victoria airport on November 25 disguised as rugby players. They were detected, however, and during the subsequent gun battle, 44 of them hijacked an Indian airliner and flew to Durban, South Africa, where 5 were arrested on kidnapping charges and the rest were freed. Among those arrested was Mike Hoare, who had gained notoriety as a mercenary leader in the Congo (Kinshasa; now Zaire) in the 1960s. Seychelles said it had captured five mercenaries and that three others were still at large.

The 1981 budget revealed a fall in private-sector activity in Seychelles, compensated in part by an expansion in the public sector. The budget allowed a major rise in education expenditure, from 17.2 to 27.2%. In January China agreed to low-interest terms for a loan to finance a new high school on Mahé. (GUY ARNOLD)

Sierra Leone

A republic within the Commonwealth, Sierra Leone is a West African state on the Atlantic coast between Guinea and Liberia. Area: 71,740 sq km (27,699 sq mi). Pop. (1981 est.): 3,571,000, including (1979) Mende and Temne tribes 60%; other tribes 39.5%; non-African 0.4%. Cap. and largest city: Freetown (pop., 1974, 314,340). Language: English (official); tribal dialects. Religion: animist 54%, Muslim 40%, Christian 6%. President in 1981, Siaka Stevens.

In his capacity as chairman of the Organization of African Unity until June, Pres. Siaka Stevens was occupied with African affairs during much of 1981. In October he announced his intention to resign as president following the general election early in 1982. During the year three Cabinet ministers were arrested in a scandal involving fraudulent payments to nonexistent companies.

As a result of President Stevens's official visit to Britain in 1980, the U.K. pledged aid to Sierra Leone worth £3.5 million in June. The World Bank provided a loan of $12 million for agricultural projects. Awarded a substantial grant from Japan, the fishing industry purchased a fleet of 17 vessels. The Magbass sugar mill was opened.

Generally, however, it was a difficult economic year. In real terms, gross domestic product for 1980–81 showed a growth of only 1%. A fall in investment was partly responsible, but produc-

tion of important minerals and crops was also disappointing. A three-year austerity program introduced in March followed an International Monetary Fund loan agreement. In August a general strike forced the government to reduce and control the price of rice. (GUY ARNOLD)

Singapore

Singapore, a republic within the Commonwealth, occupies a group of islands, the largest of which is Singapore, at the southern extremity of the Malay Peninsula. Area: 618 sq km (239 sq mi). Pop. (1981 est.): 2,443,300, including (1980) 76.9% Chinese, 14.6% Malays, and 6.4% Indians. Language: official languages are English, Malay, Mandarin Chinese, and Tamil. Religion: Malays are Muslim; Chinese, mainly Buddhist; Indians, mainly Hindu. Presidents in 1981, Benjamin Henry Sheares to May 12, Yeoh Ghim Seng (acting) from May 12 to October 24, and Chengara Veetil Devan Nair from October 24; prime minister, Lee Kuan Yew.

Cabinet reshuffles in January and April 1981 served to highlight the process of political self-renewal initiated by Singapore's Prime Minister Lee Kuan Yew. Four senior ministers relinquished office, including two founder members of the ruling People's Action Party, Toh Chin Chye and Jek Yeun Thong. Communications and Labour Minister Ong Teng Cheong assumed the post of chairman of the ruling party. In May Pres. Benjamin Henry Sheares died of a cerebral hemorrhage at the age of 73. Speaker of the Parliament Yeoh Ghim Seng served as acting president until, in October, Chengara Veetil Devan Nair was elected to the office.

In June the government released three men who had been held for alleged Communist activities. Two had been detained since 1963 under the Internal Security Act without charge or trial. In February a court discharged 15 crew members of the state airline who had pleaded guilty to charges of illegally working exactly to regulations and thereby causing a slowdown; their union, the Sin-

Singapore

SINGAPORE

Education. (1980) Primary, pupils 296,608, teachers 11,-267; secondary, pupils 170,316, teachers 8,019; vocational, pupils 12,543, teachers 912; teacher training, students 2,-328, teachers 194; higher, students 20,183, teaching staff 1,753.

Finance. Monetary unit: Singapore dollar, with (Sept. 21, 1981) a free rate of Sing$2.11 to U.S. $1 (Sing$3.91 = £1 sterling). Gold and other reserves (May 1981) U.S. $6,670,000,000. Budget (1980–81 est.) balanced at Sing$4,113,000,000. Gross national product (1979) Sing$19,451,000,000. Money supply (May 1981) Sing $7,013,000,000. Cost of living (1975 = 100; June 1981) 129.3.

Foreign Trade. (1980) Imports Sing$51,355,000,000; exports Sing$41,458,000,000. Import sources: Japan 18%; U.S. 14%; Malaysia 14%; Saudi Arabia 12%; Kuwait 6%. Export destinations: Malaysia 15%; U.S. 13%; Japan 8%; Hong Kong 8%. Main exports: petroleum products 29%; machinery 22%; rubber 8%; ship and aircraft fuel 6%; food 5%. Tourism (1979): visitors 2,247,100; gross receipts U.S. $515 million.

Transport and Communications. Roads (1980) 2,314 km. Motor vehicles in use (1980): passenger 164,500; commercial 78,000. Railways (1980) 38 km (for traffic *see* Malaysia). Air traffic (1980): 14,719,000,000 passenger-km; freight *c.* 634 million net ton-km. Shipping (1980): merchant vessels 100 gross tons and over 988; gross tonnage 7,664,229. Shipping traffic (1980): goods loaded 32,943,-000 metric tons, unloaded 49,346,000 metric tons. Telephones (Dec. 1980) 702,000. Radio licenses (Dec. 1980) 459,100. Television licenses (Dec. 1980) 396,800.

gapore Airlines Pilots' Association, was fined for taking illegal industrial action. The union was subsequently deregistered and a new union formed in which foreigners could only be associate members and were prohibited from holding office. In July the new Changi Airport was officially opened; it had cost £250 million and could handle ten million passengers per year.

During the visit of China's Premier Zhao Ziyang (Chao Tzu-yang) in August, Prime Minister Lee Kuan Yew indulged in blunt talking. China's government, he said, would have to make up its mind about priorities in Southeast Asia. It could not continue to enjoy friendly relations with the majority of the countries of the region and yet reserve the right to intervene in their affairs through insurgency movements. Nonetheless, Singapore agreed to exchange trade representatives with China.

In a surprise by-election result in November, the Workers' Party became the first opposition party in 13 years to win a seat in Parliament.

(MICHAEL LEIFER)

Social Security and Welfare Services

The economic recovery announced for 1981 failed to materialize in most countries, and by the end of the year the outlook was clearly one of increased unemployment. The wish to restrain public expenditure and to reduce budget deficits continued to dominate economic policy-making. In this climate, social expenditure was under considerable pressure, especially as some other types of government spending (*e.g.,* military expenditure) were maintained or increased. Social security benefits suffered, and there were indications that in practice certain social services were cut back even more

sharply. Rising unemployment led to greater expenditure on social security benefits while at the same time tending to reduce revenue from social security contributions or payroll taxes. The search was on for new sources of finance.

International Developments in Social Security. In the U.S. social security reform was one of the main preoccupations of Pres. Ronald Reagan's administration. A plan announced in May, designed to save about $7.9 billion in fiscal year 1982, would have lowered benefits for those retiring before age 65, postponed the next cost-of-living adjustment for three months, and mandated future adjustments once a year in September rather than twice a year as had been planned. The plan would also have phased out the earnings test for retirees aged 65–72, although this measure was designed not to save money but to encourage older workers to remain active longer. The plan met with significant opposition and was dropped, but the administration maintained that changes in the system were inevitable. (See *U.S. Developments,* below.)

In West Germany the budget package announced in September 1981 contained substantial cuts in social security. Family allowances were reduced by 17%, and cuts were made in certain benefits concerning the relocation and retraining of the unemployed. The budget was badly received within the ranks of the Social Democratic Party and clearly put a strain on its coalition partnership with the Free Democratic Party, at whose insistence the cuts were allegedly made.

Restrictive measures introduced in Sweden in January marked something of a break with the continuous improvement in social benefits that had been a hallmark of Swedish policy under the Social Democrats. Benefits under the partial pensions scheme would amount to 50% rather than 65% of earnings loss, though the benefits of those awarded a partial pension prior to 1981 were unaffected. Furthermore, a reduction in the real value of benefits would result from the exclusion of rises in indirect taxes, customs duties, and energy prices from the index used to adjust payments.

In many cases, social security cuts were supported by the argument that the state was doing too much for the individual. This ideology was reflected in the new pension system introduced in Chile on May 1. The administration of pensions was turned over to commercial enterprises; pensions would be determined on a money-purchase basis, which meant that the system was essentially nothing more than an individual savings plan; and the system would be funded rather than pay-as-you-go, creating a massive volume of investable funds but also exposing workers' savings to the risks of currency depreciation. Employees with coverage under the existing social insurance system could choose to retain it, but those who began employment after the end of 1982 would have to be "insured" under the new arrangement. Employers would no longer have to contribute to the cost of pensions, which would be entirely borne by workers. Furthermore, the employers' contributions to family allowances and unemployment compensation were abolished, and these benefits would be financed from general revenue.

"When he promised us a safety net, I didn't know we were gonna use it like this!"

In a number of countries, measures were being taken to shore up the finances of social security schemes, which had been severely undermined by high unemployment. Belgium, for example, passed a law in June providing for a 23% rise in the contribution ceiling in January 1982, over and above any rise due to normal indexation. The new government in Ireland planned to introduce legislation that would abolish the contribution ceiling entirely. In Poland, where improved social security provisions figured prominently in the agreements signed in August 1980, the contribution payable by socialized enterprises was raised on Jan. 1, 1981, from 20 to 25% of payroll. Conversely, contributions were reduced in some cases in order to cut employers' labour costs: Finland abolished the contribution for family allowances; Belgium lowered employers' contributions for manual workers by over 6 percentage points; and France reduced employers' contributions for the low paid in order to cover half of the cost resulting from the decision to raise the minimum wage by 10%.

Women continued to suffer disproportionately from the effects of the recession; not only were women workers more likely to lose their jobs than men (reflecting their lower job security), but in the home they were subjected to greater strain as a result of cutbacks in social services such as old people's homes and day-care facilities. Nevertheless, there were certain legislative and judicial developments aimed at reducing sex discrimination. Two British women who sued Lloyds Bank Ltd.

won an important victory at the European Court of Justice in March. The bank's pension scheme required employee contributions for male, but not female, bank clerks under age 25, and to compensate for the resulting reduction in take-home pay, male clerks under 25 received 5% more gross pay. The judge ruled that this arrangement fell within Art. 119 of the Treaty of Rome, which states that men and women should receive equal pay for equal work. However, the ruling did not challenge discriminatory features in statutory as distinct from occupational pension schemes.

In Austria the social security law was amended so that widowers would receive survivors' benefits on the same basis as widows. For financial reasons, the new legislation would be implemented in stages.

One country, France, challenged the prevailing economic orthodoxy by embarking on an ambitious plan to stem unemployment and improve the living standards of the less-well-off. Better social security benefits and social services were an important part of the government's strategy. On July 1 family allowances were raised by 25%, and the minimum pension was increased by 20%, bringing it up to 58% of the minimum wage, which was itself raised by 10%. A further increase on Jan. 1, 1982, would make the minimum pension equal to 60% of the minimum wage.

The government proposed to lower the age at which a full pension was awarded from 65 to 60 and make it possible for a worker to draw a pension after around 40 years in covered employment; the latter measure would help to correct the injustice resulting from the fact that manual workers contribute longest to the system but, because of their comparatively low life expectancy on retirement, derive the least benefit from it. It was also proposed that pre-pensions currently available to workers aged 60 be extended to workers aged 55 and over, provided the employer contracted with the authorities to replace workers who chose to retire. Finally, the government was committed to restoring to insured persons majority representation on the management boards of social security institutions. Implementation of these reforms would constitute the most far-reaching change in the French social security system since the 1940s.

(ROGER A. BEATTIE)

U.S. Developments. Social welfare policy in the U.S. underwent the most revolutionary changes in nearly half a century in 1981 as the Reagan administration pushed through its program to reduce federal spending. Federal assistance for the poor was reduced by $25 billion in the fiscal 1982 budget that took effect Oct. 1, 1981, and programs that had been expanding since New Deal days began to shrink. At the same time, the country's basic social welfare philosophy was altered. Emphasis was shifted from helping all relatively poor persons to helping only the most destitute, and much of the responsibility for carrying out programs was transferred from Washington to the state level. Reduced funds and tighter eligibility requirements meant that millions of Americans would lose welfare payments, food stamps, school lunch subsidies, public service jobs, and other

Maximum Welfare Benefits: State-by-State Comparisons

Maximum monthly benefit for a family of one adult and three children under Aid to Families with Dependent Children

	July 1970	July 1980	Oct. 1981
Ala.	$ 81	$148	$148
Alaska	375	514	634
Ariz.	167	244	244
Ark.	100	188	144
Calif.	221	563	601
Colo.	235	375	379
Conn.	330	553	581
Del.	187	312	312
D.C.	238	349	349
Fla.	134	230	230
Ga.	133	193	216
Hawaii	263	546	546
Idaho	242	367	345
Ill.	282	350	368
Ind.	150	315	315
Iowa	243	419	419
Kan.	244	390	399
Ky.	187	235	235
La.	109	213	213
Me.	168	352	378
Md.	196	326	326
Mass.	314	444	445
Mich.*	263	501	525
Minn.	299	486	520
Miss.	70	120	120
Mo.	130	290	290
Mont.	228	331	331
Neb.	200	370	420
Nev.	143	314	288
N.H.	294	392	392
N.J.	347	414	414
N.M.	182	267	281
N.Y.*	336	563	599
N.C.	158	210	210
N.D.	261	408	408
Ohio	200	327	327
Okla.	185	349	349
Ore.	225	569	409
Pa.	313	395	395
R.I.	263	389	420
S.C.	103	158	158
S.D.	300	361	361
Tenn.	129	148	148
Texas	179	140	141
Utah	212	429	438
Vt.	304	552	566
Va.	261	360	360
Wash.	303	536	501
W.Va.	138	249	249
Wis.	217	529	563
Wyo.	227	340	340

*Amounts shown are for the highest-paying counties in Michigan and New York (Wayne and Suffolk, respectively).

Source: Congressional Research Service.

benefits. Hardest hit would be families with annual incomes in the $6,500 to $17,000 range.

While stressing the need to reduce federal expenditure in order to revive the economy, supporters of the new policy argued that, even with the cutbacks, federal assistance would continue to provide a "safety net" for the poorest of the poor. Opponents contended that the budget cuts would deprive the poor of basic necessities and that, over time, the new emphasis on the very poor would seriously erode social programs. The cuts came at a time when the ranks of the nation's poor were growing. In 1980, 29.3 million Americans, or 13% of the population, lived below the poverty level ($8,414 for a nonfarm family of four). In 1979 the figure was 26.1 million, or 11.7%.

The restructured social policy was evident in two major programs, food assistance and welfare. The food stamp budget was sliced by about $1.7 billion in fiscal 1982, and eligibility requirements were tightened to remove 1.1 million of the 22.6 million stamp recipients. Those no longer eligible included families with incomes above 130% of the poverty level, people living in boarding houses, and households with a member on strike. Benefits for those who continued to receive food stamps would not keep up with rising food costs. Another food program, school lunches, was similarly trimmed. The poorest children would continue to receive free lunches, but costs would rise for all others and schools would be allowed to serve smaller portions.

Nearly one out of five families on welfare would have benefits reduced as a result of new regulations for Aid to Families with Dependent Children (AFDC). The maximum income that a welfare family could have was lowered, as was the amount of assets it could possess. Benefits to students over 18 were eliminated, and states would be allowed to reduce benefits to families that received food stamps or housing subsidies. States would also be able to require community service work of some recipients in exchange for assistance. The stringent

Residents of a nursing home staged a protest in front of the Massachusetts state house against proposed cutbacks in funds for senior citizens.

new rules were expected to end benefits entirely for about 408,000 of the 3.6 million welfare families and reduce them for 279,000 more. The welfare cutbacks were expected to save the federal government $6 billion and states $5 billion over the next five years.

Ironically, no major changes were made in the biggest entitlement program of all, Social Security. Some relatively small cutbacks were enacted, among them elimination of the lump-sum death benefit in most cases, phasing out of student benefits for higher education, and dropping of the $122-a-month minimum benefit for persons who retire after Dec. 31, 1981. But despite dire warnings from several sources that the Social Security system was in trouble, all attempts at significant reform failed. Faced with public and congressional opposition, President Reagan withdrew his proposal for broad cuts in benefits. An attempt to raise the retirement age from 65 to 67 was defeated in a House of Representatives committee. Instead, Congress passed a stopgap measure that reallocated funds within the Social Security system to tide it over while a presidential commission and lawmakers sought a long-term solution. Meanwhile, Social Security taxes, which rose steeply in 1981, were due to go up again. On Jan. 1, 1982, the tax rate for employees and employers would be 6.7% on the first $32,400 of earnings, compared with 6.65% on the first $29,700 in 1981.

The first round of budget cuts affected several other social programs. The Community Services Administration was abolished, and its grants to local community action agencies for specific social services were cut 25% and converted into block grants that would be administered by the states. Federal Medicaid payments to the states were reduced from $18.5 billion to $17.4 billion. Aged and disabled persons receiving Medicare would have to pay more themselves as the deductible for hospital care rose from $204 to $256 in 1982. Funding for Title XX of the Social Security Act, which provides federal grants to the states for such services as day care, foster care, and family planning, was cut by 25%.

The public service jobs portion of the Comprehensive Employment and Training Act (CETA) was abolished, and funding for job training was reduced. The extra 13 weeks of extended unemployment benefits, which previously supplemented the 26 weeks of regular benefits, were eliminated. Federal housing subsidies were cut by 40%, to $17.5 billion for fiscal 1982. The program that provides grants to help welfare and other low-income families pay their energy bills was converted into a block grant and reduced by $400 million. The Legal Services Corporation, which provides legal assistance to the poor in civil cases, survived despite administration opposition, but funding was greatly reduced. Furthermore, the retrenchment might not be over, since the administration, late in the year, announced that another round of massive budget cuts would be necessary.

(DAVID M. MAZIE)

See also Education; Health and Disease; Industrial Review: *Insurance*.
[522.D; 535.B.3.e; 552.D.1]

UPI

VIOLENCE AGAINST CHILDREN

by Anne Harris Cohn

The year 1981 was marred by an increase in the number of headlines dealing with violence against children: "6 children die in fire, mother cited"; "Adoptive mother of four gets 9 to 30 years in child murder"; "Housing authority police report hours-old baby was thrown 18 floors to its death; mother charged." Drawing the most public attention were those concerning the murders of some 28 black children and youths in Atlanta, Ga., a tragedy that led the *New York Times* to comment editorially: "All too often children bear the brunt of the sickness and cruelty in our society and are the most defenseless." (*See* CRIME AND LAW ENFORCEMENT.) Despite a decade of unparalleled judicial and legislative efforts to define children's rights and to protect children from violence, statistics suggested that children were becoming increasingly vulnerable at the hands of adults.

Extent of the Problem. Homicide rates for those under age 25 have nearly tripled in the U.S. in the last 20 years; of the 20,591 murders recorded by the FBI in 1979, children were the victims in 2,746, or 13.3%, of the cases. Given that the national crime information centre does not keep statistics on crimes against children under 12, and many youth murders are unreported, it is estimated that more than 4,000 children are murdered each year. Young men and boys (under 20) are the most frequent victims. At the first National Conference for Family Violence Researchers, held in 1981, it was reported that sexual abuse of children is far more widespread than earlier research had indicated. One study suggests that one out of every four adolescent girls is sexually molested, usually by a relative or friend of the family. During 1981 more children were involved in divorce than ever before, and more than 100,000 children were kidnapped by one of their own parents in a custody dispute. Excluding these children and habitual runaways, more than 50,000 children

were reported missing. Suicide rates for young people have risen by 75% since 1976 and more than 300% since 1960. But perhaps most distressing of all is the noticeable increase in the number of deaths due to child abuse and neglect—an increase that cannot be accounted for by improved reporting and recording alone.

The problem was first brought to public attention in 1961 by dramatic media coverage of the "battered child syndrome," a term coined by C. Henry Kempe, founder of the National Center for the Prevention and Treatment of Child Abuse and Neglect in Denver, Colo. By the end of the 1960s every state had a law mandating the reporting of child abuse; all states strengthened these laws during the 1970s, bringing them into agreement with federal guidelines. Also significant in this regard was the launching in 1976 of a continuing national public awareness campaign sponsored jointly by the National Committee for Prevention of Child Abuse, a private organization, and the Advertising Council. By 1981 every state had established a "hot line" facility to receive child abuse reports on a 24-hour basis. There were indications, however, that the rise in reporting attributable to these factors might be leveling off. The annual studies of the American Humane Association (AHA), which began recording reported cases of child abuse and neglect in the U.S. in 1973, show that the number of such reports almost doubled between 1976 and 1980 but rose only 9% from 1979 to 1980. The ratio of abuse to neglect cases (1:2) remained constant, and although the number of emotional and sexual abuse cases reported continued to increase, the proportion of those cases that were substantiated (40–45%) had not changed significantly, suggesting that reports were stabilizing.

In 1980 the AHA recorded 775,000 officially reported cases of child abuse and neglect. A recent national study conducted by the National Institute of Mental Health estimated that more than 14 out of every 100 children in the U.S.—6.5 million in total—are subject to violent acts each year within their

---

Anne Harris Cohn is executive director of the National Committee for Prevention of Child Abuse and author of An Approach to Preventing Child Abuse.

families and that 1.7 million of these are seriously abused. A federal government study, released in 1981, concludes that each year at least 10.5 of every 1,000 children under 18 are abused or neglected by parents or guardians (652,000 children); very likely the actual number is at least one million.

Victims and Perpetrators. While extremely violent crime is most prevalent among boys and young men aged 12 to 19, violence cuts across all age groups, with the type of violence varying by age and sex. For example, very young children are more susceptible to physical abuse while older children suffer emotional abuse, educational neglect, sexual abuse, and self-inflicted violence. Some children, regardless of age, are more vulnerable than others. A child who is excessively difficult or more demanding—for example, a colicky baby or a child with severe learning disabilities, or a child who is different in some respect, such as an unwanted child—is at greater risk.

Violence against children within the home is seldom attributable to a psychosis or character disorder suffered by the abuser. Most often the perpetrator is a person who is overwhelmed by life circumstances and who reacts to stress by striking out. Usually there is a pattern of violence within the family, including difficult or stressful relationships among the adults and experiences with parent-child violence dating back to the adults' own childhoods. The perpetrator also usually exhibits a lack of knowledge about child development, unrealistic expectations of children, a low self-image, and social isolation from other adults.

Most often (62% of the time) the perpetrator is a woman because of the greater amount of time spent with children. While violence within the home cuts across all income, ethnic, and cultural groups, statistics continue to confirm that close to half of the reported cases of child abuse occur in families on public assistance, suggesting overrepresentation of families from lower income groups. Nonwhites also continue to be overrepresented relative to their proportion in the general population. However, one metropolitan survey released in 1981 indicates that child abuse cases in suburban areas may be underreported by as much as 800%.

Efforts to Respond. Organized efforts to respond to child abuse can be traced to 1874, when church workers found that Mary Ellen, a New York City child, had been chained to her bed by her guardians and repeatedly beaten. Because there was no precedent allowing for legal intervention in a case of child abuse, they were able to remove Mary Ellen from her home only on the grounds that cruelty to animals was illegal and Mary Ellen was a member of the animal kingdom. Thereafter, Societies for the Pre-

vention of Cruelty to Children were organized in the U.S. and elsewhere. In 1912 the U.S. Children's Bureau was established, and in 1935, with the passage of the Social Security Act, government grants became available for the protection and care of homeless, dependent, and neglected children. The Social Security Amendments of 1962 required each state to make child welfare services available to all children, including the abused child.

In 1974 the U.S. Congress passed the Child Abuse Prevention and Treatment Act, which established a National Center on Child Abuse and Neglect. The definition of child abuse in that act—the physical or mental injury, sexual abuse, negligent treatment or maltreatment of a child under the age of 18 by a person responsible for the child's welfare—was amended in 1978 to include sexual exploitation such as child pornography. In 1981 the Reagan administration proposed letting the act expire and including funds to combat child abuse in a program of block grants to the states. Alarmed at the prospect of losing the federal focus on violence against children, concerned individuals and organizations banded together for the first time in the National Child Abuse Coalition to fight for continuation of the federal child abuse program. In July Congress voted to continue the program, albeit with diminished funding. Federal budget cutbacks were also forcing a contraction of state social services.

Meanwhile, there has been continued growth in the number of private services, which recent studies suggest are often the most cost-effective approaches to treatment. Among the most well known are Parents Anonymous (established in 1970), a national self-help organization for abusive parents, and Parents United (established in 1971), a self-help organization for sexual abusers and their families. In 1981 the National Center on Child Abuse and Neglect identified more than 150 help or counseling hot lines in the U.S., and lay-counseling programs that link abusive parents with a neighbour or friendly visitor were also growing in number. Increased emphasis on prevention sparked the growth of community-based prevention programs such as neighbourhood support groups, crisis nurseries, parent education courses, and perinatal-bonding programs to get new parents off to a good start. The National Committee for Prevention of Child Abuse, founded in 1972, had established statewide coalitions of concerned citizens in close to half of the states by the end of 1981. Outside the U.S., the third International Conference on Child Abuse held during 1981 in Amsterdam was especially notable for the expanded representation from third world countries, reflecting the growing international concern over violence against children.

Solomon Islands

The Solomon Islands is an independent parliamentary state and member of the Commonwealth. The nation comprises a 1,450-km chain of islands and atolls in the western Pacific Ocean. Area: 27,556 sq km (10,640 sq mi). Pop. (1981 est.): 235,400 (Melanesian, 93.8%; Polynesian, 4%; Gilbertese 1.4%; others 1.3%). Cap. and largest city: Honiara (pop., 1981 est., 19,200). Language: English (official), Pidgin (lingua franca), and some 90 local languages and dialects. Religion (1976): Anglican 34%; Roman Catholic 19%; South Sea Evangelical 17%; other Protestant 25%; traditional 5%. Queen, Elizabeth II; governor-general in 1981, Baddeley Devesi; prime ministers, Peter Kenilorea and, from August 31, Solomon Mamaloni.

On Aug. 21, 1981, Prime Minister Peter Kenilorea, who led the Solomon Islands to independence in 1978, resigned. In the subsequent balloting, Solomon Mamaloni emerged as leader of a coalition of his own People's Alliance Party, the National Democratic Party, and independents.

Mamaloni soon made headlines when he said that the Solomon Islands was receiving insufficient aid and might seek new donors, including the U.S.S.R. Subsequently, however, he reaffirmed his country's commitment to its neighbours and to the traditional donors—Britain, Australia, and New Zealand. Earlier, the South Pacific Forum had rejected a Soviet offer to conduct fisheries and seabed research in the Solomon Islands and adjacent countries and, instead, had accepted a similar offer by Australia, New Zealand, and the U.S.

After taking office in 1980, Kenilorea's coalition government had considered replacing Queen Elizabeth II as titular head of state with a "ceremonial president." The government came under attack in May 1981 when several thousand trade unionists marched in support of tripling the minimum wage. (BARRIE MACDONALD)

Solomon Islands

Somalia

SOLOMON ISLANDS
   Education. (1980–81) Primary, pupils 28,870, teachers 1,148; secondary, pupils 3,547, teachers 196; vocational, pupils 367, teachers 37; teacher training, students 116, teachers 24.
   Finance and Trade. Monetary unit: Solomon Islands dollar, with (Sept. 21, 1981) a free value of SI$0.89 to U.S. $1 (SI$1.65 = £1 sterling). Budget (total; 1979): revenue SI$22.4 million (excluding SI$9.4 million U.K. aid); expenditure SI$37.3 million. Foreign trade (1978): imports SI$30.9 million; exports SI$30.6 million. Import sources: Australia 33%; Japan 13%; U.K. 10%; Singapore 10%; New Zealand 6%. Export destinations: Japan 24%; U.K. 20%; Singapore 10%; The Netherlands 10%; Western Samoa 6%; U.S. 6%. Main exports: copra 25%; timber 23%; fish 22%; palm oil 15%.

Somalia

A republic of northeast Africa, the Somali Democratic Republic, or Somalia, is bounded by the Gulf of Aden, the Indian Ocean, Kenya, Ethiopia, and Djibouti. Area: 638,000 sq km (246,300 sq mi). Pop. (1981 est.): 3,752,000, mainly Hamitic, with

Arabic and other admixtures. Cap. and largest city: Mogadishu (pop., 1980 UN est., 377,000). Language: Somali spoken by a great majority (Arabic also official). Religion: predominantly Muslim. President of the Supreme Revolutionary Council in 1981, Maj. Gen. Muhammad Siyad Barrah.

Pres. Muhammad Siyad Barrah's regime held onto power during 1981 under increasingly heavy pressures. The military Supreme Revolutionary Council (SRC) continued to govern, and the recently elected People's Assembly was still in abeyance. In April President Barrah dismissed ten members of the SRC, including former close associates.

Overshadowing all other problems was that of the refugees. Driven by war and drought from the Ogaden province of Ethiopia, where Somali secessionist guerrillas were still fighting, they were estimated by the government to number 1 million–1.5 million, or between one-quarter and one-third of Somalia's population. Most were ethnic Somalis, and at least three-quarters were women and children. Early in the year the situation appeared desperate, but repeated appeals from the Somali government, the joint conference of the Organization of African Unity (OAU), and the UN High Commissioner for Refugees (UNHCR) in April were followed by increases in aid. At the end of September UNHCR reported that food supplies to the refugee camps were adequate.

The population as a whole was hit by drought in the earlier part of the year, followed by excessive rains and heavy flooding. Despite a good harvest some months later, the government's objective of attaining self-sufficiency in food receded. Soaring inflation was aggravated by oil shortages. In July the government, backed by an International Monetary Fund credit, launched an economic stabilization program and devalued the Somali shilling by 50%.

Clan and ethnic loyalties complicated the situation. The Ethiopian-based Somali Salvation Front,

SOMALIA
   Education. (1978–79) Primary, pupils 56,798, teachers 4,014; secondary, pupils 3,361, teachers 731; vocational, pupils 1,098, teachers 333; teacher training, students 902, teachers 162; higher (1977–78), students 299.
   Finance. Monetary unit: Somali shilling, with (Sept. 21, 1981) a par value of 12.59 Somali shillings to U.S. $1 (free rate of 23.34 Somali shillings = £1 sterling). Gold and other reserves (June 1981) U.S. $14 million. Budget (total; 1980 est.): revenue 1,935,000,000 Somali shillings; expenditure 2,479,000,000 Somali shillings. Cost of living (Mogadishu; 1975 = 100; June 1981) 402.3.
   Foreign Trade. (1980) Imports 1,734,100,000 Somali shillings; exports 887.8 million Somali shillings. Import sources (1978): Italy 30%; West Germany 11%; U.K 10%; The Netherlands 5%; Iraq 5%; Kenya 5%. Export destinations (1978): Saudi Arabia 86%; Italy 8%. Main exports: livestock 80%; bananas 6%.
   Transport and Communications. Roads (1977) 18,803 km. Motor vehicles in use (1977): passenger 4,200; commercial (including buses) 5,700. There are no railways. Air traffic (1980): c. 140 million passenger-km; freight c. 500,000 net ton-km. Shipping (1980): merchant vessels 100 gross tons and over 22; gross tonnage 45,553. Telephones (Jan. 1971) c. 5,000. Radio receivers (Dec. 1977) 75,000.
   Agriculture. Production (in 000; metric tons; 1980): sorghum c. 110; corn (1979) c. 80; cassava (1979) c. 31; sesame seed c. 26; sugar, raw value (1979) c. 30; bananas c. 78; goat's milk c. 284. Livestock (in 000; 1979): cattle c. 3,800; sheep c. 10,000; goats c. 16,000; camels c. 5,400.

Soil Conservation:
see Environment

© HARRY BENSON

A U.S. physician, Mark Jacobson, carries a starving child to a feeding centre in Somalia. He was one of a number of foreign doctors who were attempting to alleviate disease and famine in that country.

with Ethiopian and Libyan support, made cross-border raids and claimed responsibility for bomb explosions in Mogadishu. Of the guerrilla groups fighting against Ethiopia in the Ogaden, the Western Somali Liberation Front aimed to unite the Ogaden with Somalia, while the Western Somali Liberation Movement wanted it to be an independent state. Meanwhile, another group attempted to organize the continual *shifta* ("bandit") raids among the Somalis of northern Kenya into a regular secessionist movement.

President Barrah himself, persuaded by his new ally, the U.S., drew back from the territorial claims that had long bedeviled Somalia's relations with its neighbours. At the OAU summit meeting in June, he renounced any claim to territory in Kenya, and the Somali and Kenyan governments later agreed to joint border patrols to control the *shifta*. Relations with Ethiopia remained tense, however, although Somalia no longer officially backed the Ogaden secessionists. Relations with Libya were severed in August.

The $40 million worth of defensive military equipment promised by the U.S. in 1980 in return for the use of Somali ports and airfields still had not arrived by the end of 1981. In November, however, the first contingent of U.S. troops arrived at the Berbera naval base.   (VIRGINIA R. LULING)

See also African Affairs: *Special Report.*

South Africa

The Republic. Occupying the southern tip of Africa, South Africa is bounded by South West Africa/Namibia, Botswana, Zimbabwe, Mozambique, and Swaziland and by the Atlantic and Indian oceans on the west and east. South Africa

South Africa

entirely surrounds Lesotho and partially surrounds the four former Bantu homelands of Transkei (independent Oct. 26, 1976), Bophuthatswana (independent Dec. 6, 1977), Venda (independent Sept. 13, 1979), and Ciskei (independent Dec. 4, 1981), although the independence of the latter four is not recognized by the international community. Walvis Bay, part of Cape Province since 1910 but administered as part of South West Africa since 1922, was returned to the direct control of Cape Province on Sept. 1, 1977. Area (including Walvis Bay but excluding the four former homelands): 1,-125,459 sq km (435,868 sq mi). Pop. (1980 prelim.): 23,772,000 (excluding the four homelands), including black (Bantu) 67%, white 19%, Coloured 11%, Asian 3%. Executive cap.: Pretoria (pop., 1980 prelim., 528,000); judicial cap.: Bloemfontein (pop., 1978 est., 174,500); legislative cap.: Cape Town (pop., 1978 est., 892,200). Largest city: Johannesburg (pop., 1980 prelim., 1,536,000). Language: Afrikaans and English (official); Bantu languages predominate. Religion: mainly Christian. State president in 1981, Marais Viljoen; prime minister, P. W. Botha.

DOMESTIC AFFAIRS. The parliamentary session was interrupted early in 1981 by the government decision to hold a general election ahead of the due date, with the object of testing the electorate's opinion on the policy of change pursued by the ruling National Party (NP). The election, both parliamentary and provincial, took place at the end of April. It resulted in the return to power of the ruling party, with a somewhat reduced majority. (*See* POLITICAL PARTIES.)

There was a considerable stay-away vote, as well as evidence of a marked swing to the Progressive Federal Party (PFP), the official opposition, and to the right-wing Herstigte Nasionale Partij (HNP) of Jaap Marais (*see* BIOGRAPHIES). The number of PFP seats rose from 18 to 27, including one caucus-elected member, with four gained in Cape Province and five in Natal. The New Republic Party (NRP) won one seat in the Cape and seven in Natal. The HNP won no seats but polled a considerably increased number of votes (14%), particularly in the Transvaal. In the provinces the NP retained control of the Cape, the Transvaal, and the Orange Free State, while the NRP remained in control of Natal.

Prime Minister P. W. Botha (*see* BIOGRAPHIES) claimed that, despite some loss of support, the government had obtained a clear-cut majority for its declared policies and for the direction in which it had embarked: working for a new constitutional structure in consultation with the different national groups and for a "constellation of states" in southern Africa. He emphasized afresh the importance of group self-determination and of regional development within an overall system that would safeguard the common interests of all groups and areas. He stressed the role that the newly formed President's Council, consisting of white, Coloured, and Asian representatives, would play in formulating constitutional and other proposals for consideration by the government.

Opposition quarters, however, maintained that the outcome of the election would create a dilemma

for Botha, caught between the need to satisfy the expectations of his more liberal followers and the need to placate conservative elements being wooed by the HNP and other rightist movements. This situation, it was argued, would lead to a slowing down of the process of change and possibly to the shedding of some of its aspects. The NP Transvaal leader and minister of state administration and of statistics, A. P. Teeurnicht, known for his conservative leanings, openly voiced reservations on such matters as labour legislation, mixed sport, and the admission of nonwhites to certain white schools.

In September an alliance of several right-wing and ultraconservative splinter groups, styling itself the Aksie Red Blanke Suid-Africa (Action to Save White South Africa), was formed under the aegis of C. P. Mulder. The HNP refused to join but agreed to be associated with a rightist effort to support whites who were opposed to a UN settlement in South West Africa/Namibia.

Members of right-wing and underground white movements were sentenced on charges of violence and terrorism against academics and others whom they accused of helping to undermine white supremacy by collaborating with blacks. At the other extreme, the banned African National Congress (ANC) and other agents were held responsible for various acts of sabotage, committed chiefly on the Witwatersrand, in Natal, the Cape, and Ciskei. After one incident a number of arrests were made, and in the subsequent trials the death penalty was imposed in a few instances. In the context of race relations generally, numbers of people of all races were detained, usually without trial, under the security laws. Disturbances, police raids, and detentions in black and Coloured townships on the Rand marked the fifth anniversary of the Soweto school riots that had occurred in June 1976.

The recurring problems of large-scale illegal and uncontrolled squatting in the cities by black migrants from the homelands and rural areas were again highlighted by the plight of Nyanga, a squatter settlement in the Cape Peninsula. When ordered to move by the Ministry of Cooperation and Development, headed by Piet Koornhof (*see* BIOGRAPHIES), the squatters refused on the plea that they had nowhere to go in the bitter midwinter conditions. The shelters were demolished, over

The chief South African delegate to the UN, Jacobus Adriaan Eksteen (right), was unsuccessful in preventing the ejection of South Africa from a UN General Assembly session in September. Many of the members objected to South Africa's continued rule over South West Africa/Namibia.

2,000 people were rounded up, and about half were sent back to Transkei, where most of them were from. Some were allowed to return to fetch children and possessions they had left behind. Efforts by others to make their way back were halted by roadblocks. Finally, the government agreed to permit those who had worked in the area before the demolition to settle in the peninsula legally, and the principle of providing for "controlled squatting" was accepted.

Bound up with the whole issue was the problem of providing more adequate housing and facilities for the urban black population generally, subject to the fact that the western Cape was officially considered to be an area primarily reserved for the Coloured people, with limited room for blacks. In a move to ameliorate the housing situation in black urban areas, legislation was adopted enabling

---

SOUTH AFRICA

Education. (1981) Primary, pupils 4,480,493; secondary, pupils 1,225,153; vocational, pupils 29,591; primary, secondary, and vocational, teachers 164,149; higher, students 218,275, teaching staff 16,-708.

Finance. Monetary unit: rand, with (Sept. 21, 1981) a free rate of R 0.93 to U.S. $1 (R 1.73 = £1 sterling). Gold and other reserves (June 1981) U.S. $1,231,000,000. Budget (1980 actual): revenue R 12,-495,000,000; expenditure R 13,726,000,000. Gross national product (1980) R 59,851,000,000. Money supply (June 1981) R 9,685,000,000. Cost of living (1975 = 100; June 1981) 198.4.

Foreign Trade. (South Africa Customs Union; 1980) Imports R 14,919,000,000; exports R 19,981,-000,000. Import sources (26% are unspecified): U.S. 14%; West Germany 13%; U.K. 12%; Japan 10%. Export destinations (48% are unspecified): U.S. 8%; U.K. 7%; Japan 6%; Switzerland 6%. Main exports:

gold specie 51%; food 9%; gold coin 7%; diamonds 6%; iron and steel 5%; nonferrous metals and ores 5%.

Transport and Communications. Roads (1980) 183,502 km. Motor vehicles in use (1980): passenger *c.* 2,456,000; commercial *c.* 911,000. Railways: (1980) 20,685 km; freight traffic (including Namibia; 1979–80) 96,770,000,000 net ton-km. Air traffic (1980): *c.* 8,920,000,000 passenger-km; freight 272.3 million net ton-km. Shipping (1980): merchant vessels 100 gross tons and over 291; gross tonnage 728,-926. Telephones (March 1980) 2,662,400. Radio receivers (Dec. 1977) 2.5 million. Television receivers (Dec. 1978) *c.* 1,250,000.

Agriculture. Production (in 000; metric tons; 1980): corn 10,230; wheat 1,470; sorghum 577; potatoes *c.* 650; tomatoes 270; sugar, raw value *c.* 1,622; peanuts 345; sunflower seed 332; oranges 550; grapefruit 100; pineapples 208; apples *c.* 380;

grapes *c.* 1,140; tobacco 38; cotton, lint 52; wool *c.* 63; milk *c.* 2,500; meat *c.* 1,061; fish catch (1979) 659. Livestock (in 000; June 1980): cattle 12,575; sheep 31,641; pigs 1,317; goats *c.* 5,320; horses (1979) *c.* 225; chickens *c.* 30,000.

Industry. Index of manufacturing production (1975 = 100; 1980) 127. Fuel and power (in 000; 1979): coal (metric tons) 103,460; manufactured gas (cu m; 1977) *c.* 3,500,000; electricity (kw-hr) 92,410,-000. Production (in 000; metric tons; 1979): cement 6,420; iron ore (60–65% metal content) 31,565; pig iron (1980) 7,204; crude steel (1980) 8,819; copper (1980) 154; chrome ore (oxide content) 1,570; manganese ore (metal content) 2,107; uranium 4.8; gold (troy oz; 1980) 21,670; diamonds (metric carats) 8,-392; asbestos 247; petroleum products (1978) *c.* 12,-700; fertilizers (nutrient content; 1979–80) nitrogenous *c.* 433, phosphate *c.* 444; newsprint (1978) 240; fish meal (including Namibia; 1977) 176.

In June students fled tear gas fired by South African police after violence erupted outside a memorial service commemorating the fifth anniversary of the Soweto race riots.

white employers and township developers to own land in black townships on a 99-year leasehold basis and build houses there with the help of building loans.

At the insistence of the President's Council, the government appointed a committee to make recommendations on the working of the Group Areas Act and various other apartheid measures, but without affecting the policy of separate areas for separate population groups. This followed a public outcry over the eviction of many Coloured and Indian tenants who occupied flats in Johannesburg "white" areas in contravention of the provisions of the Group Areas Act. The tenants claimed this was the result of a serious shortage of suitable accommodation in their own areas. In some cases tenants were convicted and given suspended sentences.

Radical changes in the South African educational system were proposed in a wide-ranging report embodying the findings of an investigation conducted by the Human Sciences Research Council with the help of a multiracial team of experts. The recommendations aimed at achieving an educational structure of equal quality for all population groups. Key proposals were the establishment of a single department of education for all races under one minister and the admission of students of all races to state schools and other institutions under defined conditions. The government accepted many of the detailed subsidiary recommendations, but it withheld support for the basic recommendations and adhered to the principle of separate ethnic education.

FOREIGN RELATIONS. The future of South West Africa/Namibia remained a cardinal issue in South African foreign relations. After the UN-sponsored all-party Geneva conference in January failed to reach an agreement, negotiations continued behind the scenes between South Africa and the Western contact group (the U.S., the U.K., France, West Germany, and Canada) in an effort to devise an acceptable settlement within the framework of UN resolution 435.

Formal negotiations were resumed in October when a Western delegation visited South Africa and other African countries concerned. The delegation submitted proposals envisaging the establishment of a unitary sovereign state in Namibia under a constituent assembly representing all parties, to be elected by universal and equal suffrage in a UN-supervised election. Provision was made for a legislature, an executive, and an independent judiciary with testing powers on the U.S. model. Entrenched in the constitution would be a bill of rights on the lines of the UN Declaration of Human Rights, enforceable by the courts and free from all discrimination. The proposals formed the first phase of the settlement plan. The second was to deal with the machinery for a free and fair election, and the third with implementation of the plan as a whole.

While the talks leading up to these proposals were in progress, South Africa launched a massive military operation in Angola aimed at destroying bases of the South West Africa People's Organization (SWAPO). A UN Security Council resolution condemning the operation and demanding reparations for Angola was vetoed by the U.S. Angola claimed South Africa was aiding the National Union for the Total Independence of Angola (UNITA) guerrilla movement, headed by Jonas Savimbi, and justified the presence of Cubans and Eastern Europeans in the country on these and other grounds.

Early in the year South African forces raided an ANC camp near Maputo, Mozambique, which they claimed harboured anti-South African terrorists. Botswana reported occasional border incidents, and Lesotho accused South Africa of helping dissidents there—a charge denied by Pretoria. The preferential trade pact with Zimbabwe, in force since 1954, was terminated by South Africa.

Attention was focused on South Africa's participation in world sport and entertainment by the publication of a blacklist compiled by UN and third world sources. It named sportsmen and artists from many countries who had ties with South Africa and called for their ostracism from organized sport and the theatre.

THE ECONOMY. Presenting the postelection interim budget on August 12, Minister of Finance O. P. F. Horwood emphasized that it was essentially a budget of consolidation and adjustment: consolidation of the economic gains achieved during the upward cyclical phase in 1980, and adjustment to the adverse effect on the economy of the prevailing world recessionary trends, high interest rates in the U.S. and elsewhere, the appreciation of the U.S. dollar, and the decline in the price of gold. Excessive monetary expansion in the private sector was curbed by a succession of interest rate hikes and restrictions on bank-loan credit.

An anticipated deficit of R 2.7 billion in the current account was met largely by borrowing and by relatively small tax increases. On the expenditure side, the largest single item was defense, which rose from R 1,890,000,000 to an estimated R 2,465,000,000. With the decline in the gold price, there was a deficit in the balance of payments and a drop in the reserves. Borrowings abroad in the first quarter totaled R 727 million.

Frankly admitting that the white population was no longer able to provide the skills and higher-level technical manpower required in a developing industrial society, Minister of Manpower S. P. Botha actively promoted training facilities for black workers. A national training board and a manpower training fund were established to serve all races while maintaining the principle of separate institutions. Growing numbers of black apprentices were registered; wage gaps were narrowed for similar work in many industries; and job reservation based on race was almost entirely abolished. In the case of the mining industry, where the statutory colour bar still existed, the government declared its willingness in principle to lift the barrier to black advancement, provided that white mine workers' jobs were safeguarded and that it had the cooperation of the white trade unions, traditional opponents of any relaxation of the colour bar in key areas of the industry.

There was a wave of unrest and strikes among black workers in a number of industries. In some cases union officials and strikers were arrested on charges of incitement and violating the Riotous Assemblies Act. Unemployment among blacks was rife, and a scheme for training or retraining the workless was launched.

Bophuthatswana. The republic of Bophuthatswana consists of six discontinuous, landlocked geographic units, one of which borders Botswana on the northwest; it is otherwise entirely surrounded by South Africa. Area: 40,430 sq km (15,610 sq mi). Pop (1981 est.): 1,328,600, including 99.6% Bantu, of whom Tswana 69.8%, Northern Sotho 7.5%. Cap.: Mmabatho. Largest city: Ga-Rankuwa (pop., 1980 prelim., 48,300). Language (official): Central Tswana, English, Afrikaans. Religion: predominantly Christian (Methodist, Lutheran, Anglican, and Bantu Christian churches). President in 1981, Lucas Mangope.

The consolidation of the disjointed territorial units dividing the country since independence continued to be a major issue in relations with the South African government. Pres. Lucas Mangope emphasized that there could be no question of his supporting the concept of a constellation of states, as proposed by South Africa, without a settlement of the land issue.

Under its National Development Corporation, Bophuthatswana maintained a steady flow of capital investment into a variety of new and existing industries, vacation hotels, and an international airport. A multiracial university was opened in September with more than 500 students. In the same month a gang of about 20 terrorists attacked the Mahopane police station near the South African border, killing three people.

Ciskei. Bordering the Indian Ocean in the south and surrounded on land by South Africa, Ciskei is separated by a narrow corridor of land from Transkei to the east. Area: 8,300 sq km (3,200 sq mi). Pop. (1981 est.): 1,250,000, including Bantu 99.4%, of whom 97% are Xhosa. Cap.: Bisho (pop., 1970 est., 4,800). Largest city: Mdantsane (pop., 1975 est., 98,300). Language: Xhosa (official); English may be used for official purposes. Religion: predominantly Christian (Methodist, Lutheran, Anglican, and Bantu Christian churches). President in 1981, Lennox Sebe.

The republic of Ciskei became independent under an act passed by the South African Parliament in October 1981, with effect from December 4. Its exact boundaries were left for final negotiation after independence. A strip of land along the Kei River remained in dispute with Transkei.

Bophuthatswana

BOPHUTHATSWANA

Education. Primary (1976), pupils 326,826, teachers 5,329; secondary (1976), pupils 58,930, teachers 1,568; vocational (1973), students 471, teachers 37; teacher training, students (1976) 3,035; higher, students (1973) 167.

Finance and Trade. Monetary unit: South African rand, with (Sept. 21, 1981) a free rate of R 0.93 to U.S. $1 (R 1.73 = £1 sterling). Budget (1980–81) balanced at R 300 million. Foreign trade included in South Africa.

Ciskei

CISKEI

Education. (1974) Primary, pupils 188,441, teachers 3,363; secondary, pupils 13,807, teachers 565; vocational, pupils 320; teacher training, students 1,572.

Finance and Trade. Monetary unit: South African rand. Budget (1975–76) balanced at R 64.2 million. Most trade is with South Africa.

TRANSKEI

Education. (1978) Primary, pupils 647,985, teachers 12,627; secondary, pupils 33,636, teachers 1,179; vocational, pupils 908, teachers 59; teacher training, students 3,034, teachers 126; higher, students 503, teaching staff 96.

Finance and Trade. Monetary unit: South African rand. Budget (total; 1979–80 est.): revenue R 260 million; expenditure R 297 million. Most trade is with South Africa.

Transkei

VENDA

Education. (1978) Primary, pupils 107,711, teachers 2,300; secondary, pupils 23,466, teachers 555; vocational, pupils 323; teacher training, students 674.

Finance and Trade. Monetary unit: South African rand. Budget (1980–81) balanced at R 70.3 million. Most trade is with South Africa.

Venda

Ciskei was the first black homeland to opt for independence by way of a referendum. As a prelude to independence, Pres. Lennox Sebe laid down a package of preconditions chiefly designed to protect the rights of Ciskeians living and working in South Africa. Most of the points were embodied in a bilateral convention that guaranteed the position of Ciskeian citizens within South Africa and assured them of protection as South African nationals when traveling abroad. The white inhabitants of King William's Town voted against its incorporation in Ciskei. The city, an important commercial centre, remained an enclave, with a corridor to the port of East London. A new capital was sited near King William's Town and named Bisho, the original Xhosa name for the area.

Transkei. Bordering the Indian Ocean and surrounded on land by South Africa, Transkei comprises three discontinuous geographic units, two of which are landlocked. Area: 41,002 sq km (15,-831 sq mi). Pop. (1981 est.): 2.8 million including (1970) Bantu 99%, of whom 95% were Xhosa. Cap. and largest city: Umtata (pop., 1978 est., 30,000). Language: Xhosa (official); English and Sesotho may be used for official purposes. Religion: Christian 65.8%, of which Methodist 25.2%; non-Christian 13.8%; 20.4% unspecified. President in 1981, Kaiser Daliwonga Matanzima; prime minister, George Matanzima.

At the fifth anniversary of independence, a general election resulted in the return of the ruling National Independence Party with an overwhelming majority. Pres. Kaiser Matanzima announced that he would retire as president in February 1982. While restoring relations with South Africa after a temporary diplomatic rift, Prime Minister George Matanzima joined the president of Bophuthatswana in criticizing South Africa's constellation of states policy. He opposed Ciskei's move toward independence and urged a union of Xhosas north and south of the Kei River. Under a standing agreement, Transkei received some R 250 million from South Africa. The republic sought ties with several Western countries, and a Transkei delegation established economic relations with Taiwan.

Venda. The independent republic of Venda comprises two geographic units in extreme northeastern South Africa separated by a narrow corridor belonging to its eastern neighbour, the Gazankulu homeland. Area: 7,184 sq km (2,448 sq mi). Pop. (1979 est.): 449,000, including (1970) 90% Venda, 6% Shangaan, and 3% Northern Sotho. Cap.: Thohoyandou. Largest town: Makearela (pop., 1976 est., 1,972). Language (official): Venda, English, and Afrikaans. Religion: traditional religions predominate; Christian minority. President in 1981, Patrick Mphephu.

A government-appointed commission found that the traditional system of communal land tenure was hampering economic development. It recommended modification of the system to allow for the gradual extension of private ownership of land or of leasehold by negotiation with the tribal authorities. Relations with South Africa were good, and the Venda National Force cooperated with South Africa in combating possible guerrilla

threats. In October a police post at Sibasa, the former capital, suffered an attack that left two policemen dead. Since independence Venda had obtained a total of R 172 million in grants. Plans were being made for an ethnic university.

(LOUIS HOTZ)

See also Dependent States.

Southeast Asian Affairs

There was a marked increase in big-power interest in Southeast Asia during 1981, much of it centred around the continuing Vietnamese occupation of Kampuchea (Cambodia) and the efforts by the region's non-Communist nations to contain what they perceived as Vietnamese expansionism. China, Japan, and the U.S. joined in the maneuvers while Hanoi and Moscow stubbornly held their line in Indochina. The result was a diplomatic-military stalemate amid a growing feeling that the region had become part of a renewed East-West cold war.

The situation began developing in early January when the new Japanese prime minister, Zenko Suzuki, undertook a tour of Southeast Asia as his first overseas priority. This was immediately seen as a new departure. Previously Japan had confined itself to a purely economic role in the region. It accounted for 30% of the Association of Southeast Asian Nations' (ASEAN's) total trade. Now Tokyo was publicly serving notice that it was

A frightened-looking Khmer Rouge soldier appeared out of the bush during battles that erupted between Khmer Rouge forces and troops of the Kampuchean (Cambodian) government along the border of Thailand.

KEYSTONE

Thai soldiers set up military positions along the Mekong River near the border town of Nong Khai in February as fighting continued between Laotian and Thai forces.

ready to take a political and security role in the region as well.

The Suzuki visit produced mixed reactions. Malaysians and Filipinos made pointed remarks about lack of access to Japanese markets. Indonesians expressed reservations about Japanese military resurgence. Singapore was concerned primarily with learning from the Japanese economic miracle, while Thailand was preoccupied with the Indochinese crisis on its border. Suzuki said what Southeast Asia most wanted to hear: that Japan was "committed never to become a military power" and that the Kampuchean tragedy was "the result of military intervention by Vietnam." He offered various aid packages to his hosts, as well as a network of training centres to be set up in each of the five ASEAN nations.

No sooner had the Japanese prime minister returned home than Chinese Premier Zhao Ziyang (Chao Tzu-yang) began an official visit to Burma and Thailand. Zhao took what he clearly intended to be significant steps toward winning Southeast Asian support for Chinese policies. He appeared to soften Chinese insistence on backing the deposed Pol Pot regime in Kampuchea, which Southeast Asian governments found an embarrassment because of its past record of genocide. He said Beijing (Peking) would bless efforts to unite all anti-Vietnamese groups in Kampuchea under the leadership of a prominent non-Communist, a position ASEAN had been advocating. In Bangkok Zhao declared that Beijing would not allow its ties with the Communist parties of the region to harm relations between China and the region's countries.

Many Southeast Asian leaders found that statement somewhat supercilious, and some of them gave it another look when Zhao made a second swing through the region in August. Mincing no words, Singapore Prime Minister Lee Kuan Yew said that Southeast Asian countries needed neither Communism nor Communist parties to bring a better life to their people. Even more pointedly, Malaysian Foreign Minister Ghazali Shafie said he could not accept Zhao's explanations for Beijing's continued relations with the outlawed Communist Party of Malaya.

It was apparent that many Southeast Asian governments wanted a security umbrella that would not have a Communist state like China as one of its props. Lee Kuan Yew said in January that the U.S. and Japan should develop their military reach and striking power in Southeast Asia in the interest of "peace and stability" in the region. That sentiment fitted in with the strategy of the new U.S. administration. Visiting the region in July, U.S. Secretary of State Alexander Haig, referring to pleas for assistance by Lee and Philippine Pres. Ferdinand Marcos, said, "You can be confident that there is a new America, an America that understands you." He identified "the greatest threat to the interests, prosperity and well-being of the peoples of Southeast Asia" as "the policies of Vietnam" and pledged all-round commitment to helping non-Communist Southeast Asian countries.

The Soviets and their Indochinese allies lost no time in countering what they saw as a concerted plan to undermine their position. Early in the year Moscow began accusing the Southeast Asian countries of ganging up with China, Japan, and the U.S. in a grand anti-Soviet alliance. China's real motive, it said, was "hegemonistic" influence in the region, while Japan's objective was to make Southeast Asia economically dependent on itself and the industrialized West. Hanoi turned on Zhao, characterizing his visit to Burma and Thailand as an attempt "to fish in troubled waters."

For all the powers vying for influence in the region, the proposal for a UN-sponsored international conference on Kampuchea turned into a prestige issue. In April Soviet Deputy Foreign Minister Nikolai Firyubin visited Malaysia and Thailand in an effort to convince them that the conference would constitute unacceptable interference in Kampuchea's internal affairs. Rather, he supported the Indochinese proposal for a regional dialogue between ASEAN's five countries and Indochina's three (Vietnam, Laos, and Kampuchea). ASEAN rejected the suggestion on the grounds that, as Thai Deputy Foreign Minister Arun Bhanupongse put it, such an arrangement would be tantamount to pitting Indochina against ASEAN.

Declarations by the pro-Soviet states that they

would not participate in a UN conference or accept its recommendations only intensified ASEAN support for the idea. However, the conference itself, held in New York City in mid-July with 93 nations attending, proved an anticlimax. Five days of deliberation produced only a nominal agreement. China and the ASEAN countries, united in their opposition to Vietnam, took different positions on a fundamental issue: ASEAN wanted all Kampucheans, including Pol Pot's Khmer Rouge, to be disarmed, but China was not prepared to stop its military supplies to the Pol Pot guerrillas. Former Kampuchean head of state Norodom Sihanouk summed up the conference by saying that it "succeeded only in pouring a bit more oil on the fire consuming my country and its people." Though generally disappointed, the Southeast Asian governments remained convinced that they must continue to exert pressure on Vietnam until it withdrew from Kampuchea. They also continued efforts to form a coalition of anti-Vietnamese forces. In November plans put forward by Singapore were approved by Sihanouk and by former Kampuchean premier Son Sann; the Khmer Rouge agreed to consider the proposals. The breakthrough followed months of deadlock among the three parties.

In April Sri Lanka's prime minister, Ranasinghe Premadasa, stated that his country was seeking membership in ASEAN. This caused embarrassment in ASEAN capitals in view of the unwritten understanding that the ASEAN region comprised only the five existing members, the three Indochina states, and Burma. The only addition to membership currently in the cards was Brunei, which was expected to be admitted when its last colonial links with Britain were severed in 1983. It was generally thought that Sri Lanka's hopes were generated by the close economic links it had recently developed with Singapore. However, the proposal made no headway either in ASEAN or Sri Lanka itself.

By midyear there were fears that Southeast Asia might again be swamped under a new surge of "boat people" fleeing Vietnam. The UN High Commissioner for Refugees reported that more than 10,000 refugees arrived in various East and Southeast Asian ports in April, double the rate of arrivals during the first three months of the year. By July the total had risen to 40,000, the bulk of them landing in Malaysia and Thailand. Among them were the familiar groups—ethnic Chinese (who formed the majority of the exodus in 1979) complaining of discrimination and South Vietnamese opposed to Communism. But the new wave also included people who were apparently seeking an escape from growing food shortages and rising inflation, as well as from the military draft. The ASEAN countries reacted by erecting barriers against the new arrivals and accusing Vietnam of forcing its people out.

A note of warning about future economic problems for ASEAN was sounded by Singapore. In an official statement in February, it pointed to deteriorating world economic conditions and said: "There will be growing unemployment in the industrialized countries where our markets lie. We

must expect even more stringent measures by some of them as they act to put their and the global economy right." But, according to Boonchu Rojansthien, one of the region's best known banker-economists, ASEAN as a group was not geared to meet such a situation. In February, when he was a deputy prime minister of Thailand, Boonchu pointed out that ASEAN had used a great deal of political rhetoric but made no progress toward achieving "even the very first level" of economic integration. "Without radical changes," he added, "I do not foresee any more progress in the 1980s than in the 1970s."   (T. J. S. GEORGE)

See also articles on the various countries.

[976.B]

Space Exploration

During a year generally marked by gloom and low morale, the U.S. National Aeronautics and Space Administration (NASA) achieved two technological triumphs in 1981. The space shuttle "Columbia" made a highly successful maiden flight in April and repeated the feat in November. However, the space agency had little else about which to cheer. With the advent of the administration of U.S. Pres. Ronald Reagan, it was evident that the agency would fare no better than it had during the preceding presidencies of Jimmy Carter, Gerald Ford, and Richard Nixon. A new NASA administrator, James M. Beggs, and his deputy, Hans Mark, were both confirmed by the U.S. Senate, but because of tight budgets they appeared destined to be caretakers rather than leaders. The one note of optimism shown by NASA during the year was the assignment of 19 new astronauts, who had spent a year in training, bringing the total to 79. NASA's European counterpart and collaborator in developing the space transportation system, the European Space Agency (ESA), announced that it had gained a new member; Ireland joined the organization, and Norway and Austria became associate members.

Manned Flight. The Soviet Salyut 6-Progress 11 space station gained a new crew on Nov. 28, 1980. Launched the day before in the T-3 spacecraft, the crew consisted of Lieut. Col. Leonid Kizim, Oleg Makarov, and Gennadiy Strekalov. Strekalov, a veteran of 20 years in the Soviet space program, had worked as a metalsmith on Sputnik 1, launched in 1957.

The crew set up a gas laser to make holograms of crystal growth processes under weightless conditions and performed maintenance on Salyut to prepare it for future tasks. The T-3 returned to Earth on December 10 with several experiments from the Salyut for analysis on the ground. The Progress 11 unmanned spacecraft reentered the atmosphere on December 11. In preparation for another period of manned occupancy, the unmanned Progress 12 docked with Salyut 6 on Jan. 26, 1981. It delivered fuel and other consumables and was detached from the space station on March 19. Soyuz T-4, with Vladimir V. Kovalenok and Viktor P. Savinykh aboard, was launched on March 12 and docked with Salyut two days later.

The two men unloaded the Progress 12 and began a series of biomedical experiments. On March 23 the two were joined by Vladimir Dzhanibekov and Mongolian cosmonaut Jugderdemidyin Gurragcha, who had been launched in Soyuz 39 on the previous day.

The two new cosmonauts assisted in the biomedical experiments and in the operation of the space station until they returned to Earth on March 30. On May 14 Leonid Popov and Dumitru Prunariu, a Romanian, were launched in Soyuz 40, and they joined Kovalenok and Savinykh at Salyut on the following day. They carried on the work of Dzhanibekov and Gurragcha and operated special detectors in Earth resources and space environmental studies. They returned to Earth on May 22.

After 75 days Kovalenok and Savinykh left the Salyut 6 and landed on Earth on May 26. The Soviets then announced that there would be no more manned space flights for several months. In China Wang Zhuanshan (Wang Chuan-shan), secretary general of the China Space Research Society, announced that his nation would not be launching astronauts until after the 1980s.

Launch Vehicles. After a frustrating two-day delay, the U.S. space shuttle "Columbia" lifted off on its maiden voyage on April 12 from the Kennedy Space Center at Cape Canaveral, Fla. It was piloted by veteran astronaut John Young, commander of Apollo 16 when it landed on the Moon in 1972. His co-pilot was Robert Crippen, who had never flown in space although he had been an astronaut for 15 years.

The basic objective of the mission was to prove the flightworthiness and reliability of the orbiter in delivering men into orbit and returning them to Earth, but it was also designed to verify the combined systems performance of all elements of the space shuttle. Once launched, the "Columbia" performed as its designers and builders had predicted and went smoothly into orbit. The vehicle lofted approximately 5% more than expected, a deviation that could have caused some problems in case of an aborted mission. This condition was largely offset, however, because the liquid-propellant engines produced slightly greater thrust than expected. The only other problems were the loss of or damage to 164 of the approximately 31,000 heat-protective tiles on various parts of the orbiter and trouble with the communications link among the five computers aboard the orbiter.

Concern over the loss of tiles led to an attempt to photograph the underside of the orbiter during the mission using U.S. Air Force cameras at Malibar, Fla., and Maui, Hawaii. These efforts were unsuccessful, but pictures made by an Air Force KH-11 reconnaissance satellite showed that there was no damage that could cause trouble upon reentry. "Columbia" landed at Edwards Air Force Base in California on April 14 as planned and without incident. Both solid-propellant motor cases were recovered for refurbishment and later reuse.

In summing up the mission, Neil B. Hutchinson, flight director at the Johnson Space Center in Houston, Texas, said, "Having simulated for years, practicing every malfunction we could

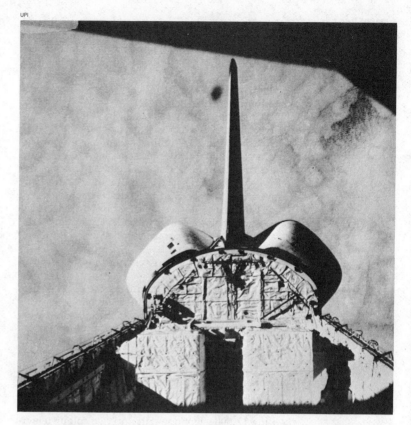

UPI

possibly dream up, I just kept waiting for something to go wrong and nothing did. We took this brand-new vehicle that's never been in the air, ran it through its paces, and it performed absolutely admirably."

After an eight-day postponement because of impaired auxiliary power units that operated the oil hydraulic system, "Columbia" was launched for its second mission from Cape Canaveral on November 12. Piloted by Joe Engle and Richard Truly, both making their first space flights, the orbiter again performed successfully though the mission was shortened because of a malfunctioning fuel cell. The astronauts tested the craft's 15-m (50-ft) remote-controlled mechanical arm and photographed lightning flashes from orbit. In contrast with the first mission, only 12 of the heat-protective tiles were damaged and none was lost. Engle and Truly successfully landed "Columbia" at Edwards Air Force Base on November 14. A third flight was planned for March 1982.

Elsewhere during the year the initial attempt to launch the privately financed, unmanned Percheron space vehicle from Matagorda Island, off the Texas coast, ended in disaster as the vehicle exploded on lift-off. However, the third test flight of ESA's Ariane launch vehicle on June 19 from the ESA launch centre at Kourou, French Guiana, was a complete success and moved that vehicle into a more competitive position in relation to other launch vehicles.

During 1981 the U.S. Department of Defense estimated that the giant launch vehicle currently under development by the Soviet Union had a payload capability ranging from 177,000 to 206,000 kg (390,000 to 455,000 lb). If this was true,

A view of the cloud-covered Earth from the U.S. space shuttle "Columbia" was provided in April. The photograph (above) was taken from the cargo bay window on the flight deck and shows the cargo area of the shuttle as well as several areas of missing tiles on the pods housing the spacecraft's maneuvering engines.

the vehicle would exceed greatly the capability of the Saturn V vehicle developed for the Apollo space program, which had a low-Earth orbital capability of only 127,000 kg (280,000 lb). Possible payloads for the Soviet vehicle included large manned space stations and very heavy, high-energy-beam space weapons.

Unmanned Satellites. Late in 1981 the U.S. Congress expressed criticism of a proposed sale by the U.S. of some $79 million worth of communications satellites and related technology to the Arab Satellite Communications Organization for the three-satellite Arabsat system. In view of this congressional disapproval, the sale was canceled.

Also during the year France announced that it was undertaking studies to adapt its Spot Earth resources satellite for conversion to a military reconnaissance satellite. The proposed satellite would operate in a Sun-synchronous, near-polar orbit.

Most launching activity during the year consisted of communications satellites. On Nov. 15, 1980, the U.S. launched the first SBS (Satellite Business Systems) satellite. Placed in a geosynchronous orbit, it was developed to provide business data channels to commercial users such as computer services firms, insurance companies, and automotive and electronics manufacturers. A second SBS was launched on Sept. 24, 1981. The first in a series of improved Intelsat 5 satellites, capable of handling 12,000 telephone calls and two colour-television channels simultaneously, was launched on Dec. 6, 1980. A second satellite was put into orbit on May 23, 1981, bringing to 12 the number of satellites owned and operated by the International Telecommunications Satellite Organization, which handles about two-thirds of the world's overseas communications traffic.

The international cooperative space program of the U.S.S.R. continued on February 6 with the launch of Intercosmos 21. The scientific satellite contained experiments from Hungary, Romania, Czechoslovakia, and East Germany. Studies were

made of the oceans and of Earth's surface. Later in the year the Soviet Union and France collaborated in equipping and launching the Arcad 3 satellite on September 21. It was designed to gather data on the magnetosphere in the polar regions.

The U.S. Explorer series of scientific satellites gained two spacecraft when Dynamics Explorer A and B were launched together August 3. Their mission was to study the interactions between the magnetosphere and the ionosphere. Also, the Solar Mesosphere Explorer was launched on October 6 to study the production of ozone in the mesosphere.

Probes. On October 30 the U.S.S.R. launched Venera 13. The probe was expected to arrive at Venus in March 1982 and attempt a soft landing.

As analysis of data from the U.S. Pioneer Venus probe continued, scientists became convinced that the extremely hot surface temperature of the planet, 482° C (900° F), is due to an atmospheric greenhouse effect, in which radiation arriving from the Sun is trapped by gases in the planet's atmosphere and not reflected back into space. Other data from the probe suggested that the atmosphere of Venus received much higher quantities of several elements from the Sun than did Earth during the evolution of the solar system. Gases found there included argon-36, krypton, and xenon.

Data from Voyager 1 indicated that Saturn's moon Titan has a diameter of 5,117 km (3,180 mi). Its atmosphere extends about ten times higher above its surface than does that of Earth, and the pressure at the surface is 1.5 times that on Earth. The temperature at the surface of Titan is about −181.7° C (−295° F), and the atmospheric density at the surface is some five times as great as that at the Earth's surface.

Even though Voyager 1 had long since left Saturn, the data gathered by it provided project scientists with much information, especially concerning the structure of the planet's rings. Two so-called shepherding satellites were discovered in Saturn's F ring. Early in 1981 NASA made the decision to target Voyager 2 for Uranus after its en-

Soviet cosmonaut Leonid Popov (left) and Romanian cosmonaut Dumitru Prunariu autographed their descent module after they returned to Earth from a successful space mission in May.

Major Satellites and Space Probes Launched Oct. 1, 1980–Sept. 30, 1981

Name/country/ launch vehicle/ scientific designation	Launch date, lifetime*	Physical characteristics				Experiments	Orbital elements			
		Weight in kg†	Shape	Diam- eter in m†	Length or height in m†		Perigee in km†	Apogee in km†	Period (min)	Inclination to Equator (degrees)
Raduga 7/U.S.S.R./D le/ 1980-081A	10/5/80	5,000 (11,023)	cylinder	2 (6.56)	5 (16.4)	Communications satellite	35,921 (22,320)	35,963 (22,346)	1,444	0.4
Fleetsatcom 4/U.S./Atlas Centaur/1980-087A	10/31/80	1,884 (4,154)	hexagon with two panels	2.4 (7.87)	1.3 (4.27)	Military communications satellite	35,534 (22,080)	36,036 (22,392)	1,436	2.3
SBS 1/U.S./Delta/ 1980-091A	11/15/80	1,060 (2,337)	cylinder with parabolic antenna	2.2 (7.22)	6.7 (21.98)	Business communications satellite; first in a projected series	35,771 (22,227)	35,800 (22,245)	1,436.1	0.1
Molniya-1 (48)/U.S.S.R./ A lle/1980-092A	11/16/80	1,000 (2,205)	cylinder with cone and six solar panels	1.6 (5.25)	3.4 (11.15)	Communications satellite	640 (398)	40,651 (25,259)	736	62.8
Soyuz-T (3)/U.S.S.R./A ll/ 1980-094A	11/27/80 12/10/80	7,000 (15,432)	cone and cylinder	2.7 (8.86)	7.5 (24.61)	Ferried crew of three to Salyut 6 space station	255 (158)	260 (162)	89.6	51.6
Intelsat 5 (F-2)/U.S./Atlas Centaur/1980-098A	12/6/80	1,928 (4,251)	cube with two antennas	‡	‡	Communications satellite	35,639 (22,145)	35,734 (22,204)	1,431	0.8
Prognoz 8/U.S.S.R./A lle/ 1980-103A	12/25/80	985 (2,172)	‡	1.8 (5.91)	‡	Solar-magnetospheric research satellite	550 (342)	199,000 (123,653)	5,689	65
Ekran 6/U.S.S.R./D le/ 1980-104A	12/26/80	2,000 (4,409)	cylinder with two panels	2 (6.56)	5 (16.4)	Television relay communications satellite	35,844 (22,272)	35,844 (22,272)	1,439	0.1
Molniya-3 (14)/U.S.S.R./ A lle/1981-002A	1/9/81	2,000 (4,409)	cylinder with conical end and six solar cell panels	1.6 (5.25)	4.2 (13.78)	Communications satellite	485 (301)	40,784 (25,342)	736	62.5
Progress 12/U.S.S.R./A ll/ 1981-007A	1/24/81 3/20/81	7,000 (15,432)	sphere and cone	2.2 (7.22)	8 (26.25)	Resupplied Salyut 6 space station	188 (117)	299 (186)	89.1	51.6
Molniya-1 (49)/U.S.S.R./ A lle/1981-009A	1/30/81	1,800 (3,968)	cylinder with cone and six solar panels	1.6 (5.25)	5 (16.4)	Communications satellite	464 (288)	40,801 (25,353)	736	62.8
Intercosmos 21/U.S.S.R./C l/ 1981-011A	2/6/81	550 (1,213)	octagonal ellipsoid	1.5 (4.92)	2 (6.56)	Studies of oceans and land areas	475 (295)	520 (323)	94.5	74
Kiku 3 (ETS-4)/Japan/N-2/ 1981-012A	2/11/81	640 (1,411)	cylinder	2.1 (6.89)	2.8 (9.19)	Engineering experiments including plasma engine	231 (144)	35,654 (22,154)	629.1	28.4
Astro 1 (Hinoturi)/Japan/ Mu-3s/1981-017A	2/21/81	‡	cylinder	‡	‡	X-ray telescope	571 (355)	637 (396)	96.8	31.4
Comstar 4/U.S./Atlas Centaur/1981-018A	2/21/81	1,516 (3,342)	cylinder	2.4 (7.87)	6.1 (20.01)	Communications satellite; last in series of four	35,778 (22,231)	35,797 (22,243)	1,436	0.1
Soyuz-T (4)/U.S.S.R./A ll/ 1981-023A	3/12/81 5/26/81	7,000 (15,432)	sphere and cylinder with two panels	2.2 (7.22)	7 (22.97)	Ferried crew to Salyut 6 space station	250 (155)	331 (206)	90.1	51.6
Soyuz 39/U.S.S.R./A ll/ 1981-029A	3/22/81 5/30/81	6,500 (14,330)	sphere and cylinder	2.2 (7.22)	7.5 (24.61)	Ferried crew to Salyut 6 space station	195 (121)	260 (162)	89.1	51.7
Molniya-3 (15)/U.S.S.R./ A lle/1981-030A	3/24/81	2,000 (4,409)	cylinder with cone and six panels	1.6 (5.25)	4.2 (13.78)	Communications satellite	641 (398)	40,655 (25,262)	736	62.8
STS 1 ("Columbia")/U.S./ Space Shuttle/1981-034A	4/12/81 4/14/81	2,041,200 (4,500,076)	delta with two solid boosters and cylindrical tank	23.8 (78.08)	56.14 (184.19)	Initial flight test of space shuttle	238 (148)	250 (155)	89.4	40.4
Cosmos 1267/U.S.S.R./ Proton/1981-039A	4/24/81	15,000 (33,069)	cylinder and panels	4 (13.12)	15 (49.21)	New Soviet spacecraft capable of unmanned docking with Salyut 6 space station	254 (158)	268 (167)	89.7	51.6
Soyuz 40/U.S.S.R./A ll/ 1981-042A	5/14/81 5/22/81	6,500 (14,330)	sphere and cylinder	2.2 (7.22)	7.5 (24.61)	Ferried crew to Salyut 6 space station	260 (162)	307 (191)	90.1	51.6
Meteor-2 (7)/U.S.S.R./A l/ 1981-043A	5/14/81	2,750 (6,063)	cylinder with two panels	1.5 (4.92)	5 (16.4)	Meteorological satellite	850 (528)	880 (547)	102.3	81.3
GOES 5/U.S./Atlas F/ 1981-049A	5/22/81	243 (536)	cylinder	1.9 (6.23)	2.6 (8.53)	Observations of Earth's weather and natural resources	35,771 (22,227)	35,775 (22,242)	1,435.9	0.3
Intelsat 5B/U.S./Atlas Centaur 1981-050A	5/23/81	1,928 (4,251)	cube with two antennas	‡	‡	Communications satellite	35,776 (22,230)	35,779 (22,244)	1,436.2	0.3
Rohini 2/India/SLV-3/ 1981-051A	5/31/81 6/8/81	38 (84)	spheriod	0.5 (1.64)	0.5 (1.64)	Scientific satellite with Earth-imaging system; launched primarily to check out SLV vehicle	187 (116)	418 (260)	90.6	46.3
Molniya-3 (16)/U.S.S.R./ A lle/1981-054A	6/9/81	1,500 (3,307)	cylinder with cone and six panels	1.6 (5.25)	4.2 (13.78)	Communications satellite	569 (354)	39,783 (24,720)	717.7	62.9
Meteosat 2/ESA/Ariane/ 1981-057A	6/19/81	700 (1,543)	cylinder	2.1 (6.89)	3.2 (10.5)	Meteorological satellite	35,779 (22,232)	35,797 (22,243)	1,436.2	0.9
Apple/India/Ariane/ 1981-057B	6/19/81	670 (1,477)	cylinder with two panels	1.2 (3.94)	1.2 (3.94)	Experimental communications satellite	35,582 (22,110)	36,012 (22,377)	1,436.7	1.1
CAT 3/France/Ariane/ 1981-057C	6/19/81	266 (586)	cylinder	‡	‡	Instruments to permit orbit calculation by ground station	229 (142)	35,880 (22,295)	630	10.2
NOAA 7/U.S./Atlas E/ 1981-059A	6/23/81	723 (1,594)	cube with three panels	1 (3.28)	1.2 (3.94)	Meteorological satellite	838 (521)	860 (534)	102	98.8
Molniya-1 (50)/U.S.S.R./ A lle/1981-060A	6/24/81	1,000 (2,205)	cylinder with cone and six panels	1.5 (4.92)	3.4 (11.15)	Military communications satellite	611 (380)	39,740 (24,693)	717.7	62.8
Ekran 7/U.S.S.R./D le/ 1981-061A	6/25/81	‡	cylinder with two panels	‡	‡	Communications satellite	35,582 (22,110)	35,989 (22,363)	1,436.1	0.1
Meteor-1 (31)/U.S.S.R./ A l/1981-065A	7/10/81	2,750 (6,063)	cylinder with two panels	1.5 (4.92)	5 (16.4)	Meteorological satellite	609 (378)	666 (414)	97.5	97.9
Iskra/U.S.S.R./A l/ 1981-065B	7/10/81	‡	‡	‡	‡	‡	(625) (388)	(664) (413)	97.6	97.9
Meteor-Priorda/U.S.S.R./ A l/1981-065C	7/10/81	‡	cylinder with two panels	‡	‡	New Earth resources satellite	625 (388)	664 (413)	97.6	97.9
Cosmos 1283/U.S.S.R./‡/ 1981-067A	7/17/81 7/31/81	‡	‡	‡	‡	Earth resources satellite	180 (112)	260 (162)	88.9	82.3
Dynamics Explorer A/U.S./ Delta/1981-070A	8/3/81	403 (888)	cylinder	‡	‡	Studies of ionosphere and magnetosphere	558 (347)	23,296 (14,475)	410	89.9
Dynamics Explorer B/U.S./ Delta/1981-070B	8/3/81	415 (915)	‡	‡	‡	Studies of ionosphere and magnetosphere	294 (183)	952 (592)	97.6	90
Fleetsatcom 5/U.S./Atlas Centaur/1981-073A	8/6/81	1,860 (4,101)	hexagon with two panels	2.4 (7.87)	1.3 (4.27)	Last of five in series of communications satellites	34,777 (21,609)	36,803 (22,868)	1,436.3	0.3
GMS 2/Japan/N-2/ 1981-076A	8/10/81	‡	cylinder with two parabolic antennas	‡	‡	Geostationary meteorological satellite	796 (495)	897 (557)	101.9	81.2
China 9/China/CSL-2/ 1981-093A	9/19/81 9/26/81	‡	‡	‡	‡	‡	240 (149)	1,610 (1,000)	‡	59.5
China 10/China/CSL-2/ 1981-093B	9/19/81	‡	‡	‡	‡	‡	240 (149)	1,610 (1,000)	‡	59.5
China 11/China/CSL-2/ 1981-093D	9/19/81	‡	‡	‡	‡	‡	240 (149)	1,610 (1,000)	‡	59.5
Arcad 3/U.S.S.R./France/‡/ 1981-094A	9/21/81	1,000 (2,205)	cylinder with eight solar panels	‡	‡	Studies of Earth's magnetosphere at upper latitudes	380 (236)	1,920 (1,193)	108.2	82.6
SBS 2/U.S./Delta/ 1981-096A	9/24/81	1,060 (2,337)	cylinder with parabolic antenna	2.2 (7.22)	6.7 (21.98)	Business communications satellite	36,806 (22,870)	36,806 (22,870)	‡	‡

*All dates are in universal time (UT).   †English units in parentheses: weight in pounds, dimensions in feet, apogee and perigee in statute miles.   ‡Not available.   (MITCHELL R. SHARPE)

UPI

The European Space Agency's launch vehicle, Ariane, had a successful test flight in June from Kourou, French Guiana.

Spain

A constitutional monarchy of southwest Europe, Spain is bounded by Portugal, with which it shares the Iberian Peninsula, and by France. Area: 504,750 sq km (194,885 sq mi), including the Balearic and Canary islands. Pop. (1981 est.): 37,547,-000, including the Balearics and Canaries. Cap. and largest city: Madrid (pop., 1981 est., 3,-267,500). Language: Spanish. Religion: Roman Catholic. King, Juan Carlos I; premiers in 1981, Adolfo Suárez González and, from February 25, Leopoldo Calvo Sotelo y Bustelo.

Premier Adolfo Suárez González started 1981 under pressure, as Spain's ruling Unión Centro Democrático (UCD) coalition threatened to disintegrate over the issues of terrorism in the Basque region, regional autonomy, and more liberal divorce laws. On January 29 Suárez resigned as premier and leader of the UCD. In a television broadcast he stated that he did not wish Spain's new democracy to become "once again a parenthesis in the history of Spain." Leopoldo Calvo Sotelo y Bustelo (*see* BIOGRAPHIES), the second vice-premier, was selected by the UCD executive committee to replace him, despite opposition from the Christian Democrat section.

Calvo Sotelo was nominated as premier on February 10 but was unable to muster the required overall majority in the 350-member Cortes (parliament). The deputies therefore reassembled on February 23 for a plenary session to hold a second vote on Calvo Sotelo's candidacy. As they were in the process of voting, armed Civil Guards led by Lieut. Col. Antonio Tejero Molina broke into the Cortes, took members of the lower house hostage, and announced that a "competent military authority" (thought to be Gen. Alfonso Armada Comyn, deputy chief of staff of the Army) would arrive shortly to begin the process of setting up a new government. Meanwhile, Lieut. Gen. Jaime Milans del Bosch declared a state of emergency in the name of the king in the military region of Valencia and sent tanks into the streets.

King Juan Carlos I (*see* BIOGRAPHIES) reacted to the takeover by convening the Council of the Joint Chiefs of Staff and forming the secretaries and undersecretaries of state into a temporary government. The heads of the military regions were then ordered to stand firm behind the crown, and troops and police were confined to their quarters. The king personally prevailed on Lieutenant General Milans del Bosch to withdraw his troops from Valencia. After prolonged negotiations and the intervention of General Armada and the head of the Civil Guard, Tejero was persuaded to surrender and placed under arrest. Both Lieutenant General Milans del Bosch and General Armada were relieved of their posts. In the aftermath the king warned politicians to avoid antagonizing the armed forces. Calvo Sotelo was finally endorsed as premier by 186 votes to 158. His new Cabinet contained no military representative.

King Juan Carlos received a mixed welcome during his February 3–5 visit to the Basque region.

counter with Saturn. In February Voyager 2 entered the magnetosphere of Jupiter for the second time, and on August 25 it made its closest approach to Saturn, passing 101,386 km (63,000 mi) above the planet's cloud tops.

Despite a balky sensor platform that malfunctioned while the probe was behind Saturn, the Voyager 2 mission was pronounced highly successful. Photographs of the ring system showed that there was a "kinky" ring within the Encke division similar to the "braided" strands of the F ring discovered by Voyager 1. After examining pictures of the planetary ring system, scientists placed the estimated number of rings about Saturn in the thousands. Other photographs showed that Saturn's moon Tethys has a crater some 400 km (250 mi) in diameter and 16 km (10 mi) deep, the largest observed in the Saturnian system.

Other photographs from Voyager 2 showed in greater detail than those of Voyager 1 the turbulence and complex dynamics of the Saturnian atmosphere. Finally, Voyager 2 discovered a doughnut-shaped region of plasma surrounding the planet centred on the orbits of Rhea and Dione. In commenting on the temperature of the ring, S. M. Drimigis, of Johns Hopkins Applied Physics Laboratory, said, "These temperatures are about 300 times hotter than the solar corona."

(MITCHELL R. SHARPE)

See also Astronomy; Defense; Earth Sciences; Industrial Review: *Aerospace* and *Telecommunications;* Television and Radio.

Spain

Curious onlookers watched as authorities removed bodies from an automobile that had been bombed in Madrid in May. The automobile had contained a military aide to King Juan Carlos and several officers. Three persons died in the blast.

The day after his visit ended, the kidnapped chief engineer of the Lemóniz nuclear power station was found murdered; the military wing of the Euzkadi ta Azkatasuna (ETA) claimed responsibility. The death in police custody of José Arregui Izaguirre, a Basque militant, resulted in top-level resignations from the police. On February 28 ETA's political wing announced an indefinite and unconditional cease-fire. In reply, the military wing stepped up its campaign of murdering high-ranking police and military officers in an attempt to provoke a military coup. By April 1 a law was passed making it an offense to advocate terrorism or support the overthrow of democracy. Legislation to allow the government to declare states of alarm, emergency, and siege was rushed through by April 24.

While visiting West Germany in April, Calvo Sotelo announced that Spain was seeking to accelerate its entry into NATO. The opposition Socialist Party, however, proposed that the question of

NATO entry be postponed until after the 1983 elections or made the subject of a national referendum. Negotiations on Spain's accession to the European Communities (EC) remained blocked. France continued to advocate that the EC complete its own internal negotiations on the common agricultural policy before the problem of Spanish accession was addressed.

A wages pact signed by unions, employers, and the government in early June provided the backing for economic policy up to the end of 1982. A 9–11% private-sector wage increase was agreed on, allowing an extra 150 billion pesetas to be invested in the public sector. In return, the government promised to create 350,000 jobs and to ensure that the record unemployment rate of nearly 13% did not worsen significantly. Under consideration was a framework for regional autonomy based on the Enterría Report, which advised greater central control of the regions, a slowdown in the pace of devolution, and parity among the 16 autonomous

SPAIN

Education. (1979–80) Primary, pupils 6,896,027, teachers 224,704; secondary, pupils 1,055,788, teachers 63,645; vocational, pupils 515,119, teachers 33,583; higher, students 634,950, teachers 36,518.

Finance. Monetary unit: peseta, with (Sept. 21, 1981) a free rate of 92.07 pesetas to U.S. $1 (170.70 pesetas = £1 sterling). Gold and other reserves (June 1981) U.S. $11,016,000,000. Budget (1980 actual): revenue 2,148,000,000,000 pesetas; expenditure 2,352,000,000,000 pesetas. Gross domestic product (1979) 13,144,000,000,000 pesetas. Money supply (June 1981) 4,035,000,000,000 pesetas. Cost of living (1975 = 100; June 1981) 258.8.

Foreign Trade. (1980) Imports 2,450,700,000,000 pesetas; exports 1,493,200,000,000 pesetas. Import sources: EEC 31% (France 8%, West Germany 8%, Italy 5%, U.K. 5%); U.S. 13%; Saudi Arabia 9%; Iraq 5%. Export destinations: EEC 50% (France 17%, West Germany 10%, Italy 8%, U.K. 7%); U.S. 6%. Main exports: machinery 13%; motor vehicles 11%; fruit and vegetables 10%; iron and steel 9%; chemicals 7%; textiles and clothing 5%. Tourism

(1979): visitors 38,902,000; receipts U.S. $6,-484,000,000.

Transport and Communications. Roads (including rural paths; 1980) 237,904 km (including 2,008 km expressways). Motor vehicles in use (1980): passenger 7,556,500; commercial 1,338,300. Railways (1979): 15,344 km (including 5,691 km electrified); traffic 17,151,000,000 passenger-km, freight 10,912,-000,000 net ton-km. Air traffic (1980): 15,517,000,-000 passenger-km; freight 417.6 million net ton-km. Shipping (1980): merchant vessels 100 gross tons and over 2,767; gross tonnage 8,112,245. Telephones (1979) 11,107,600. Radio receivers (1976) 9.3 million. Television receivers (1976) 7,425,000.

Agriculture. Production (in 000; metric tons; 1980): wheat 5,901; barley 8,561; oats 664; rye 292; corn 2,297; rice 433; potatoes 5,742; sugar, raw value c. 949; tomatoes 2,173; onions 914; cabbages (1979) c. 538; melons (1979) 705; watermelons (1979) 520; apples 911; pears (1979) 480; peaches (1979) 395; oranges 1,741; mandarin oranges and tangerines 993; lemons 359; sunflower seed 488; bananas 464; olives

c. 2,435; olive oil 488; wine 4,243; tobacco c. 30; cotton, lint 45; cow's milk c. 5,996; eggs c. 649; meat 2,410; fish catch (1979) 1,205. Livestock (in 000; 1980): cattle 4,679; pigs 10,715; sheep 14,547; goats c. 2,100; horses (1979) c. 260; mules (1979) c. 257; asses (1979) c. 238; chickens c. 53,500.

Industry. Index of industrial production (1975 = 100; 1980) 117. Fuel and power (in 000; metric tons; 1980): coal 12,733; lignite 15,704; crude oil c. 1,220; manufactured gas (cu m) c. 1,570,000; electricity (kw-hr) 110,194,000. Production (in 000; metric tons; 1980): cement 28,008; iron ore (50% metal content) 8,865; pig iron 6,723; crude steel 12,553; aluminum (1979) 254; copper (1979) 166; zinc (1979) 186; petroleum products (1978) c. 44,620; sulfuric acid (1979) c. 2,906; fertilizers (nutrient content; 1979–80) nitrogenous 950, phosphate c. 478, potash 669; cotton yarn (1977) 82; wool yarn (1977) 35; man-made fibres (1978) 251; passenger cars (units) 1,024; commercial vehicles (units) 151. Merchant vessels launched (100 gross tons and over; 1980) 510,000 gross tons.

The Helsinki Accords Review Conference

The second follow-up meeting to review the 1975 Helsinki Conference on Security and Cooperation in Europe (CSCE) started in Madrid on Nov. 11, 1980, and was adjourned for three months at the end of July 1981. After a further session (October 27–December 18), the meeting recessed again until Feb. 9, 1982. At the first follow-up meeting, held in Belgrade, Yugos., in 1977–78, provisions on human rights and fundamental freedoms under Principle VII of the 1975 Helsinki Final Act formed the centre of debate. The Madrid meeting tackled the same issues in its first phase, but security issues remained at the top of the agenda thereafter.

The main arguments were about a conference on disarmament in Europe (CDE) and the so-called confidence-building measures (CBM). Under some pressure from its Western European allies, the U.S. agreed to the proposal, first put forward by France in January 1978, for a European disarmament conference. The Soviet Union showed keen interest, but disagreement arose over modalities. The Soviet Union and its allies wanted a mandate for the conference to be held in 1982. The Western side insisted that there should be a first phase that would set out a substantive framework for the CBM's to cover troop movements on the European continent.

There was disagreement about the area to be covered by CBM's. On the basis of the definitions in the Helsinki Final Act, the Soviet leadership was under no obligation to report troop movements unless they took place in the 250-km (155-mi) zone along the western frontier of the Soviet Union. In Western Europe, however, all major military movements, including those of the U.S. and Canadian armies, had to be reported. In Madrid the Western side proposed a zone that would cover the whole continent of Europe from the Atlantic to the Urals and also the "adjoining sea area and air space . . . in so far as the activities of forces operating there are an integral part of notifiable acts [*i.e.*, maneuvers] on the continent." The Soviet side counterproposed a CBM zone covering the whole of the European continent with adjoining sea and air areas of "corresponding width." According to the Western side this was ambiguous and could be interpreted to cover an area stretching as far west as Philadelphia.

During 1981 the Soviet Union continued its repressive measures against various groups of dissidents. As the meeting entered its final phase, little hope was held out for any agreement in this sphere, but there was held to be some possibility of agreement on the CBM's because of the Soviet side's wish for a conference to promote its "peace campaign" in Europe. However, the Polish military takeover, strongly condemned by the Western side before the meeting adjourned on December 18, created a new impasse.

(K. V. CVIIC)

---

areas to be established by 1983. The Basque and Catalan communities reacted negatively. A liberal divorce law was passed in June.

During the May–November period 12,522 people were affected by a mysterious disease and over 200 people died. Symptoms included respiratory complaints, rashes, and blindness. Finally, a laboratory in Valencia connected the illness with the consumption of adulterated rapeseed oil being sold as "olive oil." The cooking oil scandal involved the ministries of agriculture, commerce, health, and labour.

Iberia remained in the grip of the worst drought in a century. Harvests of cereals and olive oil were estimated to be 40% below 1980 figures, and 1.3 million people had drinking water for only a few hours a day.

Rifts in the UCD widened during the year. In protest against what was seen as a swing to the right, the 16 parliamentary representatives of the Social Democrat wing left the UCD in November to form the Democratic Action (AD) Party, together with defectors from the Socialist Party. However, they continued to cooperate with the government to avoid provoking an early crisis. In the same month Suárez announced his intention to resign from the party. Four right-wingers also left to join the right-wing Alianza Popular after disagreement with the Cabinet over policies on devolution and the divorce bill. Calvo Sotelo reshuffled his Cabinet in early December in an attempt to reunite the UCD.

(MICHAEL WOOLLER)

Socialists and Communists conducted active campaigns which included wall posters against the proposed entrance of Spain into NATO.

WIDE WORLD

Speleology

In 1981 explorers continued to discover new passages in many of the world's longest and deepest caves. The longest of all, the combined Mammoth Cave and Flint Ridge system in Kentucky, was extended to 361.6 km (224.7 mi), and additional passages were being mapped. The length of the Optimisticheskaya cave in the U.S.S.R. was confirmed as 142.4 km (88.5 mi), making it the second longest. The third longest cave, the Hölloch in Switzerland, was also lengthened, to 139.8

km (86.9 mi). A new entrance into this cave allowed the frequently flooded old entrance passage to be avoided. In South Dakota, Jewel Cave reached 107.2 km (66.6 mi) with the survey still in progress, making this cave the fourth longest.

The deepest cave became significantly deeper. The two caves Gouffre Jean Bernard and Aven B21, joined under the name Réseau de Foillis, were further explored in February by a French expedition led by Pierre Rias. Underground camps were set up at depths of 500 m (1,640 ft) and 900 m (2,953 ft), and the end of the cave was reached at a sump 1,455 m (4,774 ft) deep. Exploration led by Jean-François Pernette in the Sima de las Puertas de Illamina (BU56) in the Spanish Pyrenees reached a depth of 1,338 m (4,390 ft). Deeper than the Pierre Saint-Martin in the French Pyrenees, it became the second deepest cave in the world. A revised survey of the Pierre Saint-Martin system reduced its overall depth to 1,321 m (4,334 ft). This resulted from an improved surface survey between the top and bottom entrances. It was now the third deepest in the world. The fourth deepest became the Snezhnaya cave (U.S.S.R.), where a depth of 1,280 m (4,199 ft) was claimed. Sistema Huautla in Mexico remained in fifth place although its depth increased slightly to 1,240 m (4,067 ft). A new and higher entrance to the French Gouffre Berger increased its total depth to 1,198 m (3,930 ft), thus placing it sixth.

A Franco-Spanish team, led by Jean-François Pernette, explored the recently discovered Sima Uquerdi (BU56) in Spain, close to the French border at Pierre Saint-Martin. A depth of 1,195 m (3,921 ft) was reached, with the cave still continuing. The explorers had to stop at the top of a deep rift owing to lack of equipment. In northern Spain a connection discovered between Avenc B15 and the Fuente de Escuain gave a vertical depth to the combined system, renamed Sistema Badalona, of 1,130 m (3,707 ft). It became the world's eighth deepest, while a revised survey of the Schneeloch (Austria) reduced it to ninth, at 1,101 m (3,612 ft). Tenth was the Gouffre Mirolda in France.

The 1980–81 British expedition to Mulu in Sarawak, Borneo, found some 70 km (43.5 mi) of new cave passages. One discovery was the Sarawak Chamber in Nasib Bagus Cave. Measuring nearly 700 m (2,297 ft) long by more than 300 m (984 ft) wide and 70 m (230 ft) high, this was by far the largest known cave in the world.　　(T. R. SHAW)

Sri Lanka

An Asian republic and member of the Commonwealth, Sri Lanka (Ceylon) occupies an island in the Indian Ocean off the southeast coast of peninsular India. Area: 65,610 sq km (25,332 sq mi). Pop. (1981): 14,859,300, including (1978) Sinhalese about 73%; Tamil 19%; Moors 7%. Cap. and largest city: Colombo (pop., 1978 est., 624,000). Language: Sinhalese (official), Tamil, English. Religion (1971): Buddhist 67%; Hindu 18%; Christian 8%; Muslim 7%. President in 1981, Junius Richard Jayawardene; prime minister, Ranasinghe Premadasa.

Recurring racial tension between Sri Lanka's Sinhalese and Tamil communities erupted into violence during 1981. The most serious wave of clashes occurred during the second week of August, taking a heavy toll of casualties (no official estimates were released) and damage to property. Pres. Junius Richard Jayawardene used emergency powers more than once to curb riots. Leaders of the Tamil United Liberation Front (TULF) continued their demands for a separate homeland for the Tamil minority. In September the government appointed a high-level committee of Cabinet ministers and TULF leaders to try to resolve the racial problems and to look into the development of the island's poorer areas.

The economy failed to make headway despite government measures to attract private investment and improve public sector performance. Government expenditure was slashed by 10%. Nationalized tea, rubber, and coconut plantations, the mainstays of the economy, operated at a loss. Tea production suffered work stoppages during the racial riots. The budget for 1981 showed a massive deficit of SLRs 15 billion. Increased taxes on tobacco and liquor and a 10% surcharge on income tax covered only a fraction of the total deficit.

Aid totaling some $830 million was pledged by the 14-nation Sri Lanka Aid Consortium, which met in Tokyo in June. The government pressed ahead with the ambitious Mahaweli River basin development project. The trade agreement with China was renewed for another year, with China agreeing to provide 80,000 metric tons of rice in exchange for 20,000 metric tons of rubber.

(GOVINDAN UNNY)

SRI LANKA

Education. (1979) Primary, pupils 1,975,749; secondary, pupils 1,159,967; primary and secondary, teachers 138,488; vocational (1976), pupils 4,778, teachers 1,239; teacher training, students 4,119, teachers 532; higher (1976), students 13,154, teaching staff 2,498.

Finance. Monetary unit: Sri Lanka rupee, with (Sept. 21, 1981) a free rate of SLRs 19.72 to U.S. $1 (SLRs 36.57 = £1 sterling). Gold and other reserves (June 1981) U.S. $223 million. Budget (1980 actual): revenue SLRs 14,068,-000,000; expenditure SLRs 28,841,000,000. Gross national product (1980) SLRs 68,096,000,000. Money supply (June 1981) SLRs 8,986,000,000. Cost of living (Colombo; 1975 = 100; May 1981) 186.9.

Foreign Trade. (1980) Imports SLRs 33,360,000,000; exports SLRs 17,799,000,000. Import sources: Japan 13%; Saudi Arabia 10%; U.K. 9%; Iraq 6%; Iran 6%; India 5%. Export destinations: U.S. 11%; U.K. 7%; West Germany 5%; China 5%. Main exports: tea 36%; rubber 15%; clothing 10%; petroleum products 6%.

Transport and Communications. Roads (1978) 24,911 km. Motor vehicles in use (1979): passenger 114,500; commercial 51,700. Railways (1980): c. 1,453 km; traffic c. 3,-660,000,000 passenger-km, freight 165 million net ton-km. Air traffic (1980): c. 691 million passenger-km; freight c. 9.8 million net ton-km. Telephones (Jan. 1978) 74,200. Radio receivers (Dec. 1977) 1 million.

Agriculture. Production (in 000; metric tons; 1980): rice 2,120; cassava (1979) c. 590; sweet potatoes (1979) c. 130; onions c. 67; mangoes c. 58; lemons c. 55; pineapples c. 95; copra c. 126; tea c. 191; coffee c. 10; rubber c. 155; fish catch (1979) 166. Livestock (in 000; June 1979): cattle 1,-623; buffalo 844; sheep 24; goats 461; pigs 49; chickens 5,882.

Industry. Production (in 000; metric tons; 1980): cement c. 650; salt (1979) 123; graphite (exports; 1979) 9.5; petroleum products (1979) c. 1,270; cotton yarn (1979) 8.5; electricity (kw-hr) 1,670,000.

Sri Lanka

Squash Rackets:
see Racket Games

Stamp Collecting:
see Philately and Numismatics

Steel Industry:
see Industrial Review

Stock Exchanges

Despite worldwide recession, record high unemployment rates, unsettling political developments, and turmoil in international currency markets, many of the world's major stock market indexes staged broad-based advances in 1981. In countries where economic activity and stock-market prices moved in opposite directions, equity prices were generally anticipating future changes in economic and business conditions. Of 17 major stock price indexes, 10 were higher at the end of 1981 than at the end of 1980 (TABLE I).

The failure of the global economy to emerge from the recession that hit Western Europe in late 1979 was mainly due to the pursuit of restrictive monetary and fiscal policies by virtually all major industrialized nations in order to restrain inflationary pressures. The resulting sky-high interest rates discouraged capital investment and darkened the prospects for reducing the highest unemployment levels since the depression of the 1930s. Moreover, high inflationary expectations remained prevalent, which meant that any effort by major industrial countries to stimulate economic activity would touch off renewed inflation, since substantially higher demand tends to be quickly translated into higher prices.

However, some negative economic news is positive for an economy in which the main problem is controlling inflation. Investors know that once inflation begins to subside, interest rates will drop and that once the back of inflationary expectations is broken, the path is cleared for accelerated declines in inflation and interest rates.

As 1981 came to a close, equity investors appeared to be anticipating lower inflation and interest rates, as well as a recovery in stock prices after the recession ended. Yet the outlook for the world economy was clouded by uncertainties over the effects that high interest rates combined with weak economic activity would have on the major industrialized nations. In summary, the ability of the global economy to make the difficult transition from a period of high inflation and sluggish growth to a period of stable and less inflationary growth would largely determine whether the 1981 bullishness of investors toward equity securities was justified.   (ROBERT H. TRIGG)

United States. Stock market performance in the U.S. in 1981 was the most disappointing to investors since 1974, as the markets trended downward on most of the significant indicators. The Dow Jones industrial average of 30 blue-chip stocks closed the year at 875, off 9.4% for the year and its lowest year-end level since 1977. Standard & Poor's 500-stock index, the broadest measure of major U.S. corporations, dropped 9.6%. An estimated $135 billion in equity values was eroded for companies traded on the major stock exchanges and on Nasdaq, the over-the-counter electronic trading system. The effect of the economic recession, with its declining orders for durable goods, sagging productivity, excessive inventories, poor housing industry performance, and record low auto sales, was felt throughout the securities markets. Securities Industry Association surveys indicated a sharp drop in foreign purchases of U.S. stocks. The number of major companies omitting dividends rose sharply to 198, up 23.7% from 1980 and the most since 1975. Major stock brokerage firms skipped the usual year-end bonuses as stock market volume fell in the second half of the year.

Increased merger activity provided spectacular gains on selected issues during a year that set a record for large mergers. According to W. T. Grimm & Co., mergers were up 27% over the previous year. The dollar volume of such transactions totaled $82.6 billion, far exceeding the record $44.3 billion for all of 1980. The acquisition of Conoco Inc. by E. I. Du Pont de Nemours & Co. was the biggest takeover in U.S. business history, with the largest chemical company paying $7.5 billion for the ninth largest oil company.

The principal factors underlying the bearish market were economic. The recession began in July according to the National Bureau of Economic Research, the arbiter in such matters, and spread rapidly throughout the economy. U.S. unemployment reached 8.9% in December. Housing starts

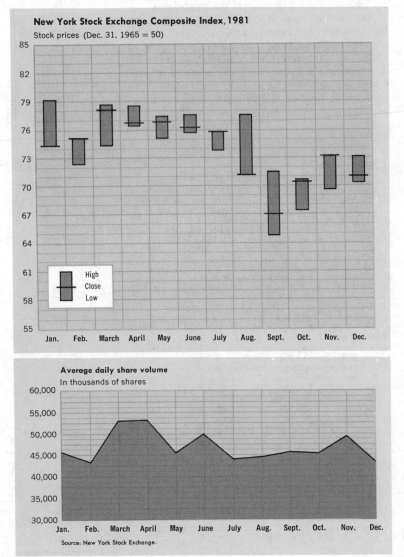

New York Stock Exchange Composite Index, 1981

Stock prices (Dec. 31, 1965 = 50)

Jan. Feb. March April May June July Aug. Sept. Oct. Nov. Dec.

High
Close
Low

Average daily share volume
In thousands of shares

Jan. Feb. March April May June July Aug. Sept. Oct. Nov. Dec.

Source: New York Stock Exchange.

fell sharply from an annualized level of 1.6 million units in January to 871,000 by November; auto production fell to the lowest level since 1961. The Index of Leading Indicators dropped steadily throughout most of the year, from 136 in January to 127 by December.

The Dow Jones industrial averages displayed a roller-coaster pattern, starting at 970 in January, dipping to 932 in February, climbing to 1,015 in March, achieving the year's high of 1,024 in April, and dropping to 850 between June and September. The index ended the year at 875. All of the component indexes of the Dow Jones averages were off for the year. Dividend yields on the 30 Dow Jones blue-chip stocks averaged 6.46% in November, compared with a 13.16% average yield on Barron's best-grade corporate bonds.

Interest rates remained at high levels during 1981 as the Federal Reserve Board acted throughout the year to curb the growth in the money supply within its target range of 3.5 to 6% in order to combat inflation. The actual growth rate was only 3%. The prime rate, which rose to a historic high in December 1980 at 21.5%, declined to 17% in April 1981 and then rose to 20.5% during the summer before declining to 15.75% by the year's end. Money market funds maintained their popularity because of their high short-term yields, and their total assets grew by $111.4 billion.

The volume of trading on the New York Stock Exchange (NYSE) during 1981 was 11,853,740,659 shares, up 4% from the 1980 figure of 11,352,293,-531. This slight gain compared with the 39% growth in volume recorded in 1980. The most active stocks were IBM Corp. with a turnover of 1,-329,659,100 shares, Exxon Corp. 115,818,000, Sony Corp. 105,281,000, AT&T 103,857,200, Mobil Corp. 92,195,100, Texaco Inc. 91,964,000, General Motors Corp. 85,350,900, and Sears, Roebuck and Co. 80,459,600. Bond sales on the NYSE totaled $5,733,071,000 in 1981, up 10% from the volume of $5,190,304,000 the year before. Block trades of more than 10,000 shares, an indicator of institutional activity, rose to about 35% of the total volume on the exchange. On Jan. 7, 1981, Joseph Granville (see BIOGRAPHIES), a leading investment adviser, triggered a massive sell-off in the market with a record volume of 92,881,420 shares and a price drop of 23.80 on the Dow industrials as a result of his midnight warning to his subscribers to "sell everything."

Three securities firms collapsed in 1981, including John Muir & Co., a leader in "hot new issues." A major concern was the potential invasion of the investment banking field by banks and insurance companies as a response to the successful development of money market instruments by the brokerage firm Merrill Lynch, Pierce, Fenner & Smith Inc. Dean Witter Reynolds Organization Inc. merged with Sears, Roebuck and Co. to create the largest financial services empire in the U.S. American Express Co. acquired Shearson, Loeb Rhoades Inc., and Prudential Insurance Co. of America bought Bache Group Inc. Morgan Stanley & Co., the largest underwriter of securities issues in 1981, reported $11,910,000,000 of securities underwritten as either sole manager or lead manager, an

all-time record. The entire volume of underwritings for the year was $57.7 billion.

A number of significant innovations were introduced in 1981 including debt-equity swaps and zero-coupon bonds. A debt-equity swap permitted a company to exchange treasury stock for outstanding debt, thereby improving the debt-equity ratio on its balance sheet. The zero-coupon bonds were offered at deep discounts from face value to be redeemed at full face amount at maturity, thereby locking in the effective interest rate and providing protection against early call.

Table I. Selected Major World Stock Price Indexes*

Country	1981 range† High	1981 range† Low	Year-end close 1980	Year-end close 1981	Percent change
Australia	737	546	716	596	−17
Austria	66	54	67	57	−15
Belgium	87	70	84	87	+ 4
Denmark	123	96	96	119	+24
France	113	77	112	92	−18
West Germany	749	666	684	675	− 1
Hong Kong	1,810	1,114	1,474	1,406	− 5
Italy	292	166	172	195	+13
Japan	8,019	6,957	7,063	7,682	+ 9
Netherlands, The	97	79	85	85	...
Norway	146	110	120	126	+ 5
Singapore	973	615	661	781	+18
South Africa	709	537	594	701	+18
Spain	146	100	100	124	+24
Sweden	660	404	423	613	+45
Switzerland	304	243	299	259	−13
United Kingdom	597	446	475	530	+12

*Index numbers are rounded and limited to countries for which at least 12 months' data were available on a weekly basis.
†Based on the daily closing price.

Table II. U.S. Stock Market Prices

Month	Railroads (10 stocks) 1981	Railroads (10 stocks) 1980	Industrials (400 stocks) 1981	Industrials (400 stocks) 1980	Public utilities (40 stocks) 1981	Public utilities (40 stocks) 1980	Composite (500 stocks) 1981	Composite (500 stocks) 1980
January	102.31	58.64	151.06	124.72	52.01	50.26	132.97	110.87
February	97.69	69.61	145.70	130.91	49.81	49.04	128.40	115.34
March	101.32	63.39	151.03	118.73	50.36	45.40	133.19	104.69
April	103.25	59.46	152.29	115.57	50.96	48.37	134.43	102.97
May	94.77	61.12	149.06	120.80	50.37	50.63	131.73	107.69
June	90.91	65.44	148.70	128.80	52.15	52.48	132.28	114.55
July	92.55	70.79	145.30	135.23	52.28	52.82	129.13	119.83
August	91.12	73.90	145.95	140.18	54.06	51.18	129.63	123.50
September	78.81	80.64	132.67	143.73	51.01	51.10	118.27	126.49
October	83.83	90.82	133.98	148.36	51.41	51.49	119.80	130.22
November	...	106.28	...	155.08	...	52.08	...	135.65
December	...	106.74	...	162.19	...	51.66	...	133.48

Sources: U.S. Department of Commerce, *Survey of Current Business;* Board of Governors of the Federal Reserve System, *Federal Reserve Bulletin.* Prices are Standard & Poor's monthly averages of daily closing prices, with 1941–43 = 10.

Table III. U.S. Government Long-Term Bond Yields

Month	Yield (%) 1981	Yield (%) 1980	Month	Yield (%) 1981	Yield (%) 1980
January	11.65	10.03	July	13.05	9.83
February	12.23	11.55	August	13.61	10.53
March	12.15	11.87	September	14.14	10.94
April	12.62	10.83	October	14.13	11.20
May	12.96	9.82	November	...	11.83
June	12.39	9.40	December	...	11.89

Source: U.S. Department of Commerce, *Survey of Current Business.* Yields are for U.S. Treasury bonds that are taxable and due or callable in ten years or more.

Table IV. U.S. Corporate Bond Prices and Yields
Average price in dollars per $100 bond

Month	Average 1981	Average 1980	Yield (%) 1981	Yield (%) 1980	Month	Average 1981	Average 1980	Yield (%) 1981	Yield (%) 1980
January	38.0	44.0	12.81	11.09	July	33.0	45.5	14.38	11.07
February	36.1	37.8	13.35	12.38	August	31.8	42.1	14.89	11.64
March	36.5	37.3	13.33	12.96	September	29.9	41.1	15.49	12.02
April	34.5	41.0	13.88	12.04	October	30.0	39.7	15.40	12.31
May	32.9	45.7	14.32	10.99	November	...	37.8	...	12.97
June	35.1	47.4	13.75	10.58	December	...	37.2	...	13.21

Source: U.S. Department of Commerce, *Survey of Current Business.* Average prices are based on Standard & Poor's composite index of A1 + issues. Yields are based on Moody's Aaa domestic corporate bond index.

640

Stock Exchanges

Volume of trading on the American Stock Exchange (Amex) in 1981 was 1,343,525,000 shares, down 17% from the 1980 figure of 1,625,790,000. Of the 957 issues traded, 424 advanced, 521 declined, and 12 were unchanged over the year. This contrasted with the 1980 figures, in which there were 600 advances and only 369 declines. Bond sales on the Amex were also off sharply with a year-to-year drop of 15%.

The over-the-counter markets recorded record activity levels as volume hit 7,640,811,342 shares on the Nasdaq system in 1981, compared with 6,-547,983,023 in 1980 and only 3,560,058,254 in 1979. Nasdaq, a nationwide electronic system in which 3,700 stocks are quoted by members of the National Association of Securities Dealers, raised its listing requirements.

Mutual funds staged a comeback in 1981, with common stock mutual funds achieving record net sales of $1.2 billion, compared with $222 million in 1980. The leading companies in the portfolios of those institutional investors were IBM, AT&T, Schlumberger Ltd., Exxon, and Philip Morris, Inc.

The Standard & Poor composite index of NYSE stocks exhibited the same patterns as did the Dow Jones. From a level of near 400 at the beginning of the year it fluctuated between 125 and 135 until August, when it dropped sharply to a low of about 112 before rising to 125 and closing the year at that level. The composite monthly average (TABLE II) was 132.97 in January 1981, up 20% from the corresponding figure of 1980. It dipped in February to 128.40, recovered in March and April, and then slid to 129.63 in August before a decline in September to a level of 118.27. The high for the year was 138.12; the low was 112.77; and the final figure was 122.55. The 400 stocks in the industrials sector of the index also moved irregularly downward during 1981, with a high of 157.02, a low of 125.93, and a close of 137.12 for a year-to-year drop of 17.33%. Public utilities fared somewhat better, as those stocks traded within a narrow range with a yearly high of 55.73 and a low of 48.96, closing at 52.98 for a year-to-year gain of 0.53%. Railroad stocks were more volatile. In January the index averaged 102.31, 74% above the corresponding level of 1980, then, following an irregular pattern with a high of 103.25 in April, these prices fell throughout most of the year.

Yields on U.S. government long-term bonds (TABLE III) rose from 11.65% in January to 12.23% in February, 13.05% in July, and 14.14% in September. The same upward movement was shown in the Bond Buyers' Average Index of Municipal Bonds; its yield of 9.8% at the beginning of the year rose unevenly to a peak of 13.2% in early September. Short-term issues had declining yields, by contrast, with the discount rate on 13-week and 26-week Treasury bills falling sharply in the fourth quarter of 1981. From a level of 15.5% in early September, they declined to 12.5% in November and closed the year at 10.5%. U.S. corporate bond (TABLE IV) prices reflected the rising yields, and the average declined from 38 in January to 30 in October. Yields rose from 12.81% in January to 13.35% in February and 14.32% by May. In September the record level of 15.49% was established. Yields were well above prior-year figures for every month of 1981.

The options markets were increasingly active in 1981 as financial futures contracts changed hands at record levels. The largest number of contracts traded on one day on one market was established by Treasury bonds on the Chicago Board of Trade. High interest rates were the underlying force in 1981 for the growth of financial futures trading as contrasted with the more traditional commodity trades, which declined in volume. As the cost of money increased, companies without a history of futures trading began to use the financial instruments to hedge. Options trading activity was up on all of the exchanges, and many new contract proposals were approved during the year. The Chicago Board of Trade voted to approve a proposed electronic linkup with the New York Fu-

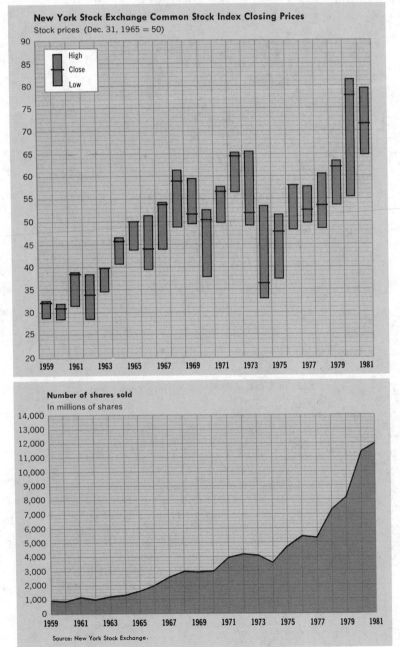

New York Stock Exchange Common Stock Index Closing Prices

Stock prices (Dec. 31, 1965 = 50)

High
Close
Low

Number of shares sold

In millions of shares

Source: New York Stock Exchange.

tures Exchange, the trading arm of the NYSE. The Philadelphia Stock Exchange offered to trade options on five foreign currencies; the Amex proposed trading options on certificates of deposit and on certain promissory notes; and the Pacific Stock Exchange sought to trade options on gold coin securities.

The Securities and Exchange Commission (SEC) and the Commodity Futures Trading Commission (CFTC) settled their conflict over which agency should oversee trading in a vast array of proposed nonstock options, stock-index futures contracts, and options on futures contracts. Their informal agreement gave the SEC exclusive authority over most options on nonstock securities; the CFTC gained control over options on futures contracts for the securities. The SEC approved NYSE and Amex proposals to trade options contracts on 13-week Treasury bills with principal amounts of $200,000 and $1 million and to list options contracts on 26-week Treasury bills with principal amounts of $100,000 and $150,000. The commission also approved an NYSE proposal to trade options on Treasury bonds and notes with principal amounts of $20,000 and $100,000.

Canada. The Canadian recession was felt in the second half of 1981, as industrial production fell month after month in the face of tight money and unemployment hit a record level of 8.6% in December, the highest figure in 35 years. While the gross national product (GNP) rose during the year, the real gains were small after accounting for the inflation factor. Interest rates were high, and a bearish mood prevailed in the stock markets. The Conference Board expressed concern about poor economic performance as a result of high interest rates, continuing double-digit inflation, a weak U.S. economy, and growing emphasis on restraint in government spending. Monetary policy was extremely tight. Short-term rates were below the levels of 1980, but long-term rates rose. Canada 90-day treasury bills ended the year at 15%, compared with 17% a year earlier. Bellwether bonds such as the Canada 10% 1984's yielded 15.15%, compared with 12.77% a year earlier, and Canada 10¼% 2004's yielded 15.50%, contrasted with 12.71% in 1980. The prime rate, which started the year at 18%, climbed to a record 22.75% in early August but closed 1981 at 16.5%, the lowest level in more than a year.

The Toronto Stock Exchange recorded a poor performance in 1981, well behind the gains of the previous year. Share prices dropped sharply, and both volume and value were down. The market, as measured by its broadly based composite index of 300 stocks, fell 14% in 1981, closing at 1,954.24. Volume totaled 1,520,000,000 shares, down 28% from 1980, while the value of trading was Can$25 billion, down from the record Can$29.3 billion a year earlier. The major factor affecting the Toronto exchange in 1981 was the continuing high level of interest rates. All of the major indexes of stocks were down except for electrical and electronics, up 47.07%; property management and investment, up 61.10%; and tobacco, up 24.70%. Large losses were reflected in transportation equipment, down 41.62%; metal mines, off 39.55%; gold, off 36.38%;

and cable television, down 38.79%. The Montreal Stock Exchange agreed with the European Options Exchange in Amsterdam to establish a joint gold options market. The Montreal exchange would operate the market in Canada, and the European Options Exchange would do so in Europe. Options bought on one exchange could be sold on the other. Later, other options classes on commodities of an international nature would be added.

The Investment Dealers Association of Canada recorded 1981 as a year of positive developments, with employment up to 20,000 from the prior year's level of 18,500 and with the belief that there were substantial cash funds waiting for an opportunity to reenter the market. This viewpoint conflicted with the attitudes expressed in a poll of Canadian businessmen, who expected higher unemployment and a deterioration of overall economic performance by the end of the year.

(IRVING PFEFFER)

Western Europe. Stock markets in the four largest European economies recorded mixed results in 1981. Italy and the United Kingdom experienced gains of 13 and 12%, respectively. In contrast, France posted a decline of 18%, and West Germany ended the year down 1%. Among the remaining European stock markets, higher prices prevailed in Sweden, Denmark, Spain, Norway, and Belgium. On the bearish side were Austria and Switzerland, while in The Netherlands prices showed no change.

The stock market in Italy not only had the best relative performance among Europe's largest economies in 1981, but it was also the most volatile. Prices on the Milan Stock Exchange at the end of December were 13% higher than at the beginning of the year. A strong rally began in January

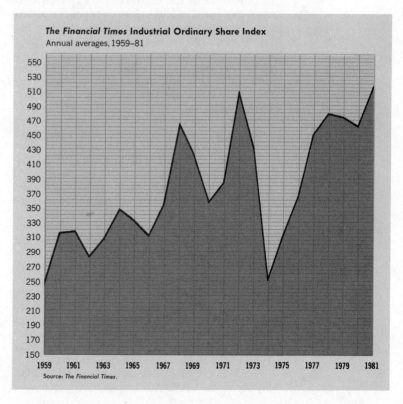

The Financial Times Industrial Ordinary Share Index
Annual averages, 1959–81

Source: The Financial Times.

and accelerated over the next five months. On June 3 stock prices were nearly 70% above the 1980 close. This increase was triggered by a financial and political climate replete with uncertainty and fears of runaway inflation. As a result investors flocked to the stock market as a means of protecting savings against an inflation rate that in March was 18% higher than a year earlier. Moreover, the collapse of Italy's 41st post-World War II government near the end of May was viewed as causing more delay in rejuvenating the stagnant Italian economy and attacking inflation.

However, the speculative fever was substantially reduced when equity investors were required to settle transactions in three days instead of the month permitted in the past. From June 3 to July 24 equity values fell by 43%. A resumption of the rally following a slight easing of the settlement rules caused equity prices to retrace more than one-half of the previous losses by the end of August before profit takers gained the upper hand. From that point until mid-October the market plunged another 23%. The subsequent rebound was relatively moderate (11%) despite an improved political climate following the formation of a new coalition government in July and its announced intention to achieve a 15% inflation rate for 1982. Stock prices finished nearly 33% below the year's high and 17% above the low.

In Great Britain the *Financial Times* index of 30 industrial issues traded on the London Stock Exchange rose for the second year in a row. From the end of 1980 to the end of 1981 stock prices on average jumped 12%, and the index recorded an all-time high on April 30, surpassing the previous peak set on May 4, 1979.

Throughout 1981 the British economy continued to deteriorate as the Conservative Party government continued its anti-inflationary policies aimed at curbing government expenditures, reducing the public sector borrowing requirement, and keeping a close rein on the nation's money supply. As a result the economic recession that began in mid-1979 was sharper and steeper than in other Western nations. Unemployment during 1981 reached its highest level since the 1930s. However, the government's deflationary policies led to a sharp recovery in investor confidence and widespread hope that the recession would soon end.

In addition, the rate of decline of industrial output slowed appreciably as the year progressed, suggesting that the recession might have bottomed out. The government's September announcement that it would keep public sector wage increases to 4%, coupled with the decline in wage settlements in the private sector, further reinforced investor beliefs that future gains in productivity would be spectacular. Expectations of economic recovery and a significant reversal of a grim economic picture were also fueled by the British government's proposed 1982 legislative program, which reaffirmed anti-inflationary policies as the nation's highest priority, as well as by economic predictions that the country's worst recession since World War II would end within months.

Stock prices in France took a beating in 1981. Equity values fell sharply in January but recovered all of the loss by the end of March. Investors, nevertheless, became disheartened by news of a deep drop in industrial output, which pointed to a widening of the recession that had begun in the last quarter of 1979, and by signs that Pres. Valéry Giscard d'Estaing's bid for reelection was in jeopardy. When Socialist leader François Mitterrand emerged victorious in the May 10 presidential runoff election, thus ending 23 years of conservative rule in France, heavy selling took place. By mid-June equity values had fallen nearly 30% from their level the day before the election.

Subsequently, the Mitterrand government announced plans to nationalize 11 of the nation's largest industrial firms along with the remaining privately owned banks and insurance companies. Terms of the government's compensation for stockholders, however, were much more favourable than expected, and an August rally to correct the market's oversold condition continued through September. Following that advance, the general index of share prices on the Paris Bourse traded between a high of 98 and a low of 86 from September through December. In an attempt to buoy investor confidence, Mitterrand pledged no further nationalization of publicly owned companies for at least five years. Stock prices at the end of December were 18% lower than at the end of 1980 but 19% above the June lows.

In West Germany the stock market drifted within a relatively narrow range throughout 1981 and ended the year at about the same level as the 1980 close. The Commerzbank index of 60 issues traded on the Frankfurt Stock Exchange reached its 1981 high on July 3; the low was set on February 16.

After a hesitant start stock prices followed the downward trend that had been in force since January 1979. The bearish attitude of investors reflected the country's worst economic performance since the recovery after World War II. Equity selling picked up in July, when it became evident that West Germany's economy would remain in recession at least until 1982. From July 4 to October 31, share prices slipped 10%. Industrial output was expected to decline during the year as a whole. Unemployment in November rose to 6.4% of the labour force, the highest rate in 28 years. This relatively poor economic performance was aggravated by the increased value of the U.S. dollar against the Deutsche Mark in foreign exchange markets. The weakness of the mark against the dollar meant that more marks were required to pay for dollar-denominated imports, thus feeding inflation and forcing a restrictive monetary policy. At the first sign of solid strength in the Deutsche Mark, the West German Central Bank in October reduced its interest rate to commercial banks for borrowing on securities, the first such cut since January 1979. It appeared, however, that it would take more than the potentially bullish consequences of an ease in monetary policy to drive up stock prices, which finished the year not far from the levels recorded in October but almost 34% below the all-time highs set on Sept. 5, 1960.

Sweden experienced a strong stock market for the second year in a row. After a modest decline in January, average share prices on the Stockholm

Exchange moved steadily higher until the end of April, when prices began to advance much faster. In May and June stock prices jumped 9 and 9½%, respectively. By August 10 prices had surged 63% above the January lows. The technical correction that followed caused stock prices to backtrack almost 18% before the rally resumed in early October. The ensuing rebound recovered nearly all of these losses and kept the bullish trend intact. For 1981 as a whole the gain in equity value amounted to 45%, the best performance among the 17 major stock price indexes.

The stock market in Spain was also a star performer in 1981. The price index of shares traded on the Madrid Stock Exchange was up 24% after rising 6% in 1980. The rally appeared to be an extension of the upward trend established in April 1980 and a reversal of the long decline in equity prices that had begun in 1974. The rise in equity values occurred following the political violence that led to the selection of Leopoldo Calvo Sotelo (see BIOGRAPHIES) as premier after an attempted coup by right-wing military forces. Deep resentment over double-digit inflation and rising unemployment reportedly played a part in the attempted coup. Thus, spirited rallies in the stock market were touched off when the new government announced an easing of regulations in order to spur investments, and a wage agreement was concluded between the country's principal unions and the national employers' confederation, which guaranteed wage restraint in 1982. After stock prices peaked in late September, they moved gradually lower until November, when the decline accelerated following the resignation of 17 members from Premier Calvo Sotelo's party and the outbreak of social unrest among disenchanted farm workers. As a result stock prices ended the year 15% below the peak recorded in September.

Other Countries. Stock markets in Japan and South Africa followed a bullish pattern. The index of 225 issues traded on the Tokyo Stock Exchange jumped 9% in 1981 to its highest level ever recorded. Extending the bull market that began near the end of 1977, stock prices began rising sharply in March and by the end of June were up over 9%. Despite the 1980 oil price increases of the Organization of Petroleum Exporting Countries, which produced inflationary pressures and hurt economic growth, the Japanese economy turned in the best performance of the major industrial countries. Much of the country's success could be attributed to maintaining productivity gains at a rate higher than wage increases and to restricting the growth of the money supply.

The Nikkei Dow Jones average of leading industrial stocks pierced the 8,000 level for the first time in mid-August, but increased credit requirements on share purchases triggered a sharp reaction. By the end of October equity values had fallen 7%. News that the government planned to stimulate lagging industries and that the Bank of Japan had lowered its discount rate to 5½ from 6½% to encourage domestic activity set the stage for a rebound. Consequently, as 1981 came to a close the Tokyo stock market was headed higher.

In South Africa the *Rand Daily Mail* index of industrial shares traded on the Johannesburg Stock Exchange also climbed to a record high. From the end of 1980 to the end of 1981 the index gained 18%. This strong performance occurred despite the country's problems with race relations and border tensions. South Africa's inflation-adjusted growth of GNP was among the highest in the world, and the dividend rate on equity securities grew at an annual rate of 20%. This exceeded the 16% inflation rate and thus provided investors with a real gain after inflation.

The influence of worldwide recession and social unrest was especially apparent in the Australian stock market. Average share prices on the Sydney Stock Exchange dipped 17% from year-end 1980 to year-end 1981, while the retreat in the All Ordinaries Index from its record high set in October 1980 to the October 1981 low amounted to 48%. This reflected the general decline in world demand for raw materials and precious metals, a result of lower economic activity and the trend toward energy conservation. In addition, labour turbulence in coal, wool, and several service industries raised doubts among major foreign buyers about the reliability of Australia as a source of supply for natural resources and threatened to drive up costs, making the country less competitive internationally.

Commodity Markets. Sharply lower prices generally prevailed in international commodity markets during 1981. *The Economist*'s commodity price indicator, which measures spot prices in terms of the U.S. dollar for 29 internationally traded commodities, fell 20% from the end of 1980 to mid-December 1981. Major factors underlying the weakness in overall commodity prices included the slowdown in real growth of the economies of the developed nations, record high interest rates, a strong U.S. dollar, lower oil prices, and decelerating inflation.

The four major components of *The Economist*'s index of commodity prices all declined in 1981. The average price level of foodstuffs plunged 23%, fibres 20%, industrial materials 13%, and metals 3%. Relatively high interest rates played a major role in keeping down prices of key agricultural commodities, since they discourage inventory replenishment and encourage farmers to sell products rather than store them. The softness in nonfood commodity prices reflected an unwinding of inflationary expectations. Weakening world trade and the strength in the U.S. dollar tended to drive European countries to raise interest rates, thereby hindering demand for raw materials and metals in particular.

The price of gold, an inflation bellwether, fell below $400 an ounce in July for the first time since 1979. At the end of 1980 gold closed in the London market at $589.50 an ounce. By March 5 the price had dropped to $457 before a rally pushed it to $547.25 on March 27. After the price of gold fell below the $400 level, it rebounded and traded between $464 and $395 for the rest of the year. At the end of December the London gold quotation settled at $400, a net decline of 32% for 1981 as a whole.   (ROBERT H. TRIGG)

See also Economy, World.
[534.D.3.g.i]

Strikes:
see Industrial Relations

Sudan

Suriname

Sudan

A republic of northeast Africa, the Sudan is bounded by Egypt, the Red Sea, Ethiopia, Kenya, Uganda, Zaire, the Central African Republic, Chad, and Libya. Area: 2,503,890 sq km (966,757 sq mi). Pop. (1981 est.): 18,895,000, including Arabs in the north and Negroes in the south. Cap. and largest city: Khartoum (pop., 1980 est., 1,621,000). Language: Arabic, various tribal languages in the south. Religion: Muslim (66%) mainly in the north; predominantly animist (29%) with Christian minority (5%) in the south. President and prime minister in 1981, Gen. Gaafar Nimeiry.

Efforts to rejuvenate the Sudan's economy continued in 1981, with a marked lack of success, against a background of growing fear of aggression by Libya. Tension began with Libya's military intervention in Chad, the Sudan's western neighbour, and intensified when the Sudan restored full diplomatic relations with Egypt.

In June an explosion in the Chad embassy in Khartoum was attributed to Libya. A few days later Pres. Gaafar Nimeiry, with three other African presidents, accused Libya's Col. Muammar al-Qaddafi (see BIOGRAPHIES) of gross interference in the affairs of member states of the Organization of African Unity. In September the government claimed that Libyan planes had bombed several border towns, and Egypt successfully appealed for U.S. assistance in protecting the frontiers of the Sudan and Egypt. The assassination of Egypt's Pres. Anwar as-Sadat (see OBITUARIES) on October 6 was a serious blow to the Sudan.

In March the government forestalled a military coup, backed, Nimeiry claimed, by Syria and the U.S.S.R. The huge influx of refugees from Chad led the government to impose strict measures to prevent the stirring up of discontent.

On October 5 Nimeiry dissolved the National People's Assembly in the north and called for elections in the near future to a Parliament reduced by more than half and with many of its powers transferred to five regional assemblies. The Southern Region People's Assembly was also dissolved, and elections were scheduled within six months. On November 9 the president dismissed his Cabinet, simultaneously devaluing the currency by 12.5% and increasing taxes.   (KENNETH INGHAM)

Suriname

A republic of northern South America, Suriname is bounded by Guyana, Brazil, French Guiana, and the Atlantic Ocean. Area: 181,455 sq km (70,060 sq mi). Pop. (1980 prelim.): 352,000, including (1971) Hindustanis 37%, Creoles 30.8%, Indonesians 15.3%, Bush Negroes 10.3%, Amerindians 2.6%. Cap. and largest city: Paramaribo (pop., 1980 prelim., 67,700). Language: Dutch (official); English and Sranan (a creole) are lingua francas; Hindi, Javanese, Chinese, and various Amerindian languages are used within individual ethnic communities. Religion: predominantly Hindu, Christian, and Muslim. President and prime minister in 1981, Hendrick R. Chin A Sen.

SUDAN

Education. (1978–79) Primary, pupils 1,358,193, teachers 38,881; secondary, pupils 335,322, teachers 17,072; vocational, pupils 11,784, teachers 602; teacher training, students 4,878, teachers 723; higher, students (1977–78) 24,109, teaching staff (1976–77) 1,963.

Finance. Monetary unit: Sudanese pound, with (Sept. 21, 1981) a par value for a commercial rate of Sud£0.50 to U.S. $1 (free rate of Sud£0.93 = £1 sterling) and a par value for other transactions of Sud£0.80 to U.S. $1 (free rate of Sud£1.48 = £1 sterling). Gold and other reserves (June 1981) U.S. $33 million. Budget (total; 1980–81 est.): revenue Sud£1,006 million; expenditure Sud£1,347 million. Gross national product (1977–78) Sud£2,868 million. Money supply (June 1981) Sud£1,254.8 million. Cost of living (1975 = 100; Dec. 1980) 248.5.

Foreign Trade. (1980) Imports Sud£788,190,000; exports Sud£271,340,000. Import sources (1979): U.K. 16%; West Germany 14%; U.S. 8%; Italy 7%; Belgium-Luxembourg 6%; France 6%; Japan 5%; China 5%. Export destinations (1979): China 16%; Italy 11%; Saudi Arabia 11%; Japan 7%; U.S.S.R. 6%; Yugoslavia 6%. Main exports: cotton 45%; food c. 17%; sesame 9%; gum arabic 7%.

Transport and Communications. Roads (1980) c. 48,000 km (mainly tracks, including c. 2,000 km asphalted). Motor vehicles in use (1979): passenger c. 35,000; commercial (including buses) c. 37,000. Railways: (1980) c. 5,500 km; freight traffic (1973–74) 2,324,000,000 net ton-km. Air traffic (1980): c. 710 million passenger-km; freight c. 12.5 million net ton-km. Inland navigable waterways (1979) c. 4,100 km. Telephones (Jan. 1980) 63,000. Radio receivers (Dec. 1977) 1.4 million. Television receivers (Dec. 1977) 100,000.

Agriculture. Production (in 000; metric tons; 1980): wheat 231; millet c. 450; sorghum c. 2,200; sesame seed c. 200; cottonseed c. 200; peanuts c. 810; sugar, raw value (1979) c. 130; dates c. 113; cotton, lint c. 114; cow's milk c. 940; goat's milk c. 387; beef and veal 208; mutton and goat meat c. 126; timber (cu m; 1979) c. 33,432. Livestock (in 000; 1980): cattle 18,354; sheep c. 17,800; goats c. 12,570; camels (1979) c. 2,500; asses (1979) c. 680; chickens c. 27,000.

Industry. Production (in 000; metric tons; 1978): petroleum products c. 1,010; electricity (kw-hr) 911,000; salt 72; cement c. 140.

SURINAME

Education. (1980–81) Primary, pupils 75,139, teachers 2,803; secondary, pupils 29,790, teachers 1,854; vocational (1978–79), pupils 4,394, teachers 249; teacher training, students 1,275, teachers 148; higher, students 2,353, teaching staff 155.

Finance. Monetary unit: Suriname guilder, with (Sept. 21, 1981) a par value of 1.785 Suriname guilders to U.S. $1 (free rate of 3.31 Suriname guilders = £1 sterling). Gold and other reserves (June 1981) U.S. $215 million. Budget (1978 est.): revenue 623 million Suriname guilders; expenditure 650 million Suriname guilders.

Foreign Trade. (1979) Imports 734 million Suriname guilders; exports 793 million Suriname guilders. Import sources (1977): U.S. 31%; The Netherlands 21%; Trinidad and Tobago 14%; Japan 7%. Export destinations (1977): U.S. 41%; The Netherlands 24%; Norway 8%; U.K. 7%; Japan 5%. Main exports: alumina 42%; aluminum 16%; bauxite 13%.

Transport and Communications. Roads (1977) c. 2,500 km. Motor vehicles in use (1979): passenger c. 22,800; commercial (including buses) c. 8,900. Railways (1980) 167 km. Navigable inland waterways (1979) c. 1,500 km. Telephones (Jan. 1980) 21,300. Radio receivers (Dec. 1977) 182,000. Television receivers (Dec. 1977) 39,000.

Agriculture. Production (in 000; metric tons; 1980): rice c. 240; oranges (1979) c. 11; grapefruit c. 7; bananas c. 35; palm kernels c. 24; sugar, raw value (1979) c. 12. Livestock (in 000; 1979): cattle c. 27; pigs c. 19; goats c. 5; chickens c. 1,038.

Industry. Production (in 000; metric tons; 1979): bauxite 4,769; alumina 1,312; aluminum 54; electricity (kw-hr) 1,529,000 (86% hydroelectric in 1977).

Sumo:
see Combat Sports

Surfing:
see Water Sports

During 1981 the political situation in Suriname remained confused, with the direction of social, economic, and foreign policies in dispute between the National Military Council (NMC), headed by Sgt. Maj. Daysi Bouterse, and Pres. Hendrick R. Chin A Sen's civilian government. Bouterse was known to favour a revolutionary socialist course. In March a Cuban trade delegation visited Paramaribo, and it was reported that full diplomatic relations with Cuba would be established. Also in March, the government defeated an attempted coup led by Sgt. Maj. Willem Hawker, who had taken part in the 1980 coup. Late in the year there were reports of the impending removal of President Chin A Sen by the NMC and of the formation of a Revolutionary People's Front.

Relations with The Netherlands remained tense, with discussions on the allocation of Dutch grant aid proceeding at a slow pace. It was announced that plans for building a Dutch-financed hydroelectric plant and bauxite smelter were to be dropped. (DICK BOONSTRA)

Swaziland

A landlocked monarchy of southern Africa and a member of the Commonwealth, Swaziland is bounded by South Africa and Mozambique. Area: 17,364 sq km (6,704 sq mi). Pop. (1981 est.): 572,000. Cap. and largest city: Mbabane (pop., 1976 census, 23,100). Language: English and siSwati (official). Religion: Christian 60%; animist 40%. King, Sobhuza II; prime minister in 1981, Prince Mandabala Fred Dlamini.

Swaziland celebrated the diamond jubilee of King Sobhuza II (see BIOGRAPHIES) on Sept. 4, 1981. The festivities, to which 22 heads of state were invited, also marked 13 years of stable progress since independence was achieved in 1968. Proof of Swaziland's remarkably balanced economy, coal exports began to replace those of iron ore, which had ceased in 1980, while sugar, wood pulp, asbestos, citrus fruits, and tourism also provided important contributions to the economy.

SWAZILAND
    Education. (1980) Primary, pupils 112,019, teachers 3,-278; secondary, pupils 23,198, teachers 1,292; vocational, pupils 1,109, teachers 105; higher, students 1,403, teaching staff 139.
    Finance and Trade. Monetary unit: lilangeni (plural emalangeni), at par with the South African rand, with (Sept. 21, 1981) a free rate of 0.93 lilangeni to U.S. $1 (1.73 emalangeni = £1 sterling). Budget (1980–81 est.): revenue 145 million emalangeni; expenditure 85 million emalangeni (excludes capital expenditure of 123 million emalangeni). Foreign trade (1979): imports 299 million emalangeni; exports 185 million emalangeni. Import sources (1977): South Africa 96%. Export destinations (1977): U.K. 33%; South Africa 20%. Main exports: sugar 35%; wood pulp 14%; asbestos 9%; citrus and canned fruit 9%.
    Agriculture. Production (in 000; metric tons; 1979): corn c. 55; rice c. 5; potatoes c. 6; sugar, raw value (1980) c. 330; pineapples c. 20; cotton, lint c. 6; timber (cu m) c. 2,588. Livestock (in 000; 1979): cattle c. 650; sheep c. 33; pigs c. 22; goats c. 265.
    Industry. Production (in 000; metric tons; 1978): coal 166; iron ore (metal content) 624; asbestos 37; electricity (kw-hr) 281,000.

The Royal Swaziland Sugar Corporation opened its Simunye sugar mill at Lusothi in 1980; supported by a 9,000-ha (22,500-ac) sugarcane estate, it was expected to produce, by 1982, 120,000 metric tons of raw sugar, about one-third of Swaziland's total output in 1980. The estate employed 3,000 workers and the new mill an additional 360. A major hydroelectric project in the Ezulwini valley was announced. To be financed in part by the World Bank and the African Development Bank, the project involved damming the Little Usutu River, thus creating a reservoir of 20 million cu m (26 million cu yd). The plant was expected to provide additional power capacity of 20,000 kv; it was part of a long-term program to reduce dependence upon imported power. From August 21 to September 7, Swaziland was host to an international trade fair. (GUY ARNOLD)

Swaziland

Sweden

A constitutional monarchy of northern Europe lying on the eastern side of the Scandinavian Peninsula, Sweden has common borders with Finland and Norway. Area: 449,964 sq km (173,732 sq mi). Pop. (1981 est.): 8,317,900. Cap. and largest city: Stockholm (pop., 1981 est., 647,200). Language: Swedish, with some Finnish and Lapp in the north. Religion: predominantly Lutheran. King, Carl XVI Gustaf; prime minister in 1981, Thorbjörn Fälldin.

In 1981 Sweden found itself at the centre of a remarkable international incident. On October 27 a U.S.S.R. Whisky-class submarine 137 went aground on rocks deep inside Swedish territorial waters in a military area eight nautical miles (14 km) from the main southern naval base, Karlskrona. What was at first a huge joke at the expense of the Soviet Navy assumed more sinister aspects when it was revealed that Swedish naval experts who had examined the submarine believed it to be carrying nuclear warheads. This possibility deeply alarmed a small neutral nation and brought home to its population the uncomfortable facts of life in the nuclear age.

The submarine's captain blamed the whole affair on a "navigational error." This remained the official Soviet line throughout, but it was never accepted by the Swedish government. The submarine was kept under armed guard as "clarification" was sought from the Soviet Union concerning radioactivity detected by Swedish naval experts in the region of the torpedo tubes. When no clarification was forthcoming, the Swedes announced their belief that the submarine was armed with nuclear weapons. On November 6, Whisky 137 was towed back to international waters.

The incident was expected to cloud relations between the two countries for many years and to dent severely the credibility of Moscow's support for a zone free of nuclear weapons in the Nordic area. Prime Minister Thorbjörn Fälldin described it as a "flagrant violation" of Swedish neutrality. The U.S.S.R., which did not admit that there were nuclear weapons on the submarine, in turn accused Sweden of espionage.

Sweden

Education. (1979–80) Primary, pupils 556,481; secondary, pupils 486,852; vocational, pupils 103,485; primary, secondary, and vocational, teachers 129,969; higher (including teacher training), students 155,352.

Finance. Monetary unit: krona, with (Sept. 21, 1981) a free rate of 5.44 kronor to U.S. $1 (10.09 kronor = £1 sterling). Gold and other reserves (June 1981) U.S. $4,058,000,000. Budget (total; 1980–81 est.): revenue 155,459,000,000 kronor; expenditure 209,277,000,000 kronor. Gross national product (1979) 431,140,000,000 kronor. Money supply (Dec. 1979) 65,750,000,000 kronor. Cost of living (1975 = 100; June 1981) 183.9.

Foreign Trade. (1980) Imports 141,332,000,000 kronor; exports 130,777,000,000 kronor. Import sources: West Germany 17%; U.K. 12%; U.S. 7%; Finland 7%; Denmark 6%; Norway 5%; Saudi Arabia 5%. Export destinations: West Germany 12%; U.K. 10%; Norway 10%; Denmark 8%; Finland 6%; France 6%; U.S. 5%; The Netherlands 5%. Main exports: machinery 26%; motor vehicles 12%; paper 10%; iron and steel 7%; chemicals 5%; wood pulp 5%.

Transport and Communications. Roads (1980) 129,018 km (including 850 km expressways). Motor vehicles in use (1980): passenger 2,882,960; commercial 181,570. Railways: (1979) 12,010 km (including 7,583 km electrified); traffic (1980) 6,841,000,000 passenger-km, freight 15,627,000,000 net ton-km. Air traffic (including Swedish apportionment of operations of Scandinavian Airlines System; 1980): 5,-342,000,000 passenger-km; freight 190.9 million net ton-km. Shipping (1980): merchant vessels 100 gross tons and over 700; gross tonnage 4,233,977. Telephones (Dec. 1979) 6,407,000. Radio receivers (Dec. 1977) 8.3 million. Television licenses (Dec. 1979) 3,103,200.

Agriculture. Production (in 000; metric tons; 1980): wheat 1,291; barley 2,486; oats 1,685; rye c. 241; potatoes 1,153; sugar, raw value 327; rapeseed c. 356; apples c. 85; milk c. 3,475; butter c. 65; cheese c. 100; beef and veal c. 154; pork c. 317; fish catch (1979) 206; timber (cu m; 1979) 60,916. Livestock (in 000; June 1980): cattle c. 1,923; sheep (1979) c. 384; pigs c. 2,710; chickens (1979) c. 11,650.

Industry. Index of industrial production (1975 = 100; 1980) 99. Production (in 000; metric tons; 1980): cement 2,524; electricity (kw-hr) 93,570,000 (59% hydroelectric in 1977); iron ore (60–65% metal content) 27,183; pig iron 2,436; crude steel 4,235; aluminum 97; petroleum products c. 17,600; sulfuric acid (1979) 764; wood pulp (1979) 8,400; newsprint 1,534; other paper (1979) 4,797; passenger cars (units) 256. Merchant vessels launched (100 gross tons and over; 1980) 326,000 gross tons. New dwelling units completed (1980) 52,800.

In the wake of the incident, faith in the effectiveness of Sweden's policy of armed neutrality was badly shaken. Although there had been almost unanimous applause in the West for the tough stand taken by the government, the uncomfortable fact remained that the submarine had spent 12 hours aground before being spotted. One immediate result of the affair was a demand from all of Sweden's political parties for increased defense spending on submarine-detection vessels and equipment. Another was a series of angry demonstrations against the Soviet Union.

At the start of the year the protests had all been against the U.S. for its involvement in El Salvador. One of these, held in a snowstorm and attended by several thousand Swedes, had the distinction of being the largest anti-U.S. demonstration since the days of the war in Vietnam.

International political discontent became subordinate to the domestic scene in May, when the Conservative Party walked out of the Centre-Liberal-Conservative coalition government. This precipitated a three-week-long crisis that coincided with a major labour dispute involving 17,000 white-collar workers, which, in turn, threatened to escalate into massive industrial action similar to the wave of strikes and lockouts that had paralyzed Sweden in April–May 1980. Industrial peace was saved at the last minute, as was Prime Minister Fälldin, who announced that he would remain as head of a minority coalition government comprising his own Centre Party and the Liberals.

The issue that split the three-party government —a package of income-tax reforms—remained a major bone of contention, but it was Sweden's economic crisis that dominated government policy, forcing cuts in public spending and, in September, the devaluation of the krona by 10%. Devaluation was aimed at stimulating exports. It was accompanied by a price freeze and a reduction of value-added tax from a record high 23.46% to 20% in a bid to hold down inflation.

As the government's difficulties increased, so did the popularity of the Social Democrats, who entered the 1982 election year well ahead in all public opinion polls. However, the government's tough handling of the submarine crisis greatly improved its standing, and polls showed that the Communists could lose their parliamentary representation as a result of the affair. As the year ended, the Swedish Navy reported increased recruitment as a result of its new advertising campaign, "Whiskey on the rocks—it's something we don't want." (CHRIS MOSEY)

A Soviet submarine ran aground in territorial waters off Sweden in October. The 67-m (220-ft) craft was held for several days before Swedish officials allowed it to be towed into open waters and released.

Swedish Literature:
see Literature

Swimming

Competitive swimming in the year after the 1980 Olympic Games was expected to suffer a post-Olympic letdown but certainly not the decline that did occur, as evidenced by the meagre number of new world records set. Though the United States selected a national team to compete against the Soviet Union in September, even this traditional rivalry failed to provide the incentive for outstanding performances. Men and women swimmers set ten world records, but two were in events not contested in the 1980 Olympics, four were the effort of East Germany's Olympic champion Ute

Geweniger, and two were by Mary T. Meagher of the U.S.

The first world record of 1981 was set immediately after the U.S. national indoor championships at the University of Texas on April 3 during special time trials. Rowdy Gaines of Auburn (Ala.) University, in his final effort before retiring, clocked 49.36 sec in the 100-m freestyle to erase the oldest world mark in the books, 49.44 sec set in August 1976 by Jonty Skinner. The second world mark was in the men's 100-m butterfly. William Paulus of Fort Worth, Texas, was timed in 53.81 sec, lowering the previous standard of 54.15 sec by Sweden's Par Arvidsson in the same pool a year earlier.

Alex Baumann of Sudbury, Ont., competing for Canada against West Germany and the U.S.S.R. in Heidelberg, West Germany, on July 29, swam the 200-m individual medley in 2 min 2.78 sec to break the record of 2 min 3.24 sec set by William Barrett of the U.S. in 1980. In that tournament West Germany upset the Soviets, winning by two points over Canada with the U.S.S.R. a distant third.

In the 200-m butterfly Craig Beardsley of Harrington Park, N.J., cut 0.2 sec off his 1980 record as he swam the event in 1 min 58.01 sec on August 22 in Kiev during a dual meet between the U.S. and the U.S.S.R. In this tournament the U.S. defeated the Soviet Union, the women winning 10 out of 14 events to score 104 points to 60 and the men 10 out of 15 races for a total of 99 points to 81. It was the fourth meeting between the two nations in the last decade, and the Soviets had yet to score a victory.

East Germany's Ute Geweniger firmly established herself as successor to 1976 Olympic and world champion Kornelia Ender, also from East Germany. On three occasions Geweniger lowered her own world standard of 1 min 10.11 sec for the 100-m breaststroke, set in the 1980 Olympic Games. On April 21 at Gera, East Germany, swimming against the Soviet Union, she was timed in 1 min 9.52 sec. On July 2 at East Berlin she again set a new record of 1 min 9.39 sec. And finally on September 8 at the European championships in Split, Yugos., she climaxed the season with a time of 1 min 8.60 sec. At the East Berlin meet Geweniger swam the 200-m individual medley in 2 min 11.73 sec, erasing the mark of 2 min 13 sec set by teammate Petra Schneider in the 1980 Olympics.

Mary T. Meagher of Louisville, Ky., continued where she left off in 1980. At the U.S. national championships at Brown Deer, Wis., the 5 ft 7 in, 128-lb schoolgirl lowered her 100-m and 200-m butterfly records with clockings of 2 min 5.96 sec on August 13 for the longer event and 57.93 sec three days later for the 100 m. Aside from these two records, the championships were conspicuously devoid of times of merit.

Two multinational international swimming events were noteworthy. From July 19 to 30 the XI World University Games were staged at Bucharest, Rom. In swimming the U.S., led by Jill Sterkel, won 16 gold medals to 10 for the second-place Soviet Union. Sterkel, of Hacienda Heights, Calif., won the 100-m and 200-m freestyle and the 100-m butterfly and swam on to win the 400-m freestyle and medley relays to gain five gold medals. The XV

World Swimming Records Set in 1981			
Event	Name	Country	Time
MEN			
100-m freestyle	Rowdy Gaines	U.S.	49.36 sec
100-m butterfly	William Paulus	U.S.	53.81 sec
200-m butterfly	Craig Beardsley	U.S.	1 min 58.01 sec
200-m individual medley	Alex Baumann	Canada	2 min 2.78 sec
WOMEN			
100-m breaststroke	Ute Geweniger	E. Ger.	1 min 9.52 sec
100-m breaststroke	Ute Geweniger	E. Ger.	1 min 9.39 sec
100-m breaststroke	Ute Geweniger	E. Ger.	1 min 8.60 sec
100-m butterfly	Mary T. Meagher	U.S.	57.93 sec
200-m butterfly	Mary T. Meagher	U.S.	2 min 5.96 sec
200-m individual medley	Ute Geweniger	E. Ger.	2 min 11.73 sec

European Championships at Split, held September 5–12, featured a record 798 competitors (379 swimming, 280 water polo, 66 diving, and 73 synchronized swimming) representing 27 nations. East Germany's women won every gold medal and all but three silvers in the 14 swimming events. Geweniger won four golds and one silver plus another gold for swimming on the winning medley relay. The East Germans won the swimming championship with 696 points, followed by the Soviet Union with 679, West Germany 503, Sweden 420, and Great Britain 392 for the top five.

On August 21–23 at Brown Deer, a U.S. junior national team defeated a Soviet junior team, the women winning by 105 to 59 and the men 107 to 73. The outstanding performer was 15-year-old Sabrina Sagehorn of Pleasant Hill, Calif., who captured the four women's freestyle events at distances from 200 m to 1,500 m.

The U.S. Olympic Committee sponsored the National Sports Festival II at Syracuse, N.Y., on July 24–25. Approximately 2,600 U.S. athletes competed in various Olympic sports, and they were grouped in four regional teams, West, Midwest, East, and South. In the swimming competition West won with 422 points, followed by Midwest 357, East 285, and South 267.

Diving. The Fédération Internationale de Natation Amateur, the world governing organization for amateur aquatics, conducted the II Cup Diving Championship June 12–14 in Mexico City. The U.S.S.R. and East Germany were not present. China swept all but one event, giving notice that it would be a definite contender for medals in the 1984 Olympics. Li Hong Ping won the men's platform, followed by Mexico's Carlos Giron and Bruce Kimball of the U.S. Giron won the 3-m springboard, edging 1976 Olympic silver medalist Greg Louganis of the U.S. In women's competition Shi Meiqin won the springboard and teammate Chen Xiaoxia the platform. Megar Neyer of the U.S. and Valerie MacFarlane of Australia finished second and third in the springboard, while in the platform Mexico's Guadalupe Canseco and Wendy Wyland of the U.S. trailed the winner.

The U.S. national outdoor championships took place at Mission Viejo, Calif., August 11–15. Louganis of Mission Viejo won both the 1-m and 3-m springboard, and Kimball, from Ann Arbor, Mich., triumphed in the platform. Kelly McCormick of Long Beach, Calif., and Megan Neyer of Mission Viejo won the women's 1-m and 3-m

WIDE WORLD

East Germany's Ute Geweniger raised her arms in victory after setting a new world record of 1 min 8.60 sec in the women's 100-m breaststroke in the finals of the European swimming championships in Yugoslavia in September.

springboard events, respectively. Debbie Rush of Columbus, Ohio, was the platform winner.

At the World University Games China won three of the four events. Li Yi Hua and Chen Xiaoxia won the women's springboard and platform events. In men's competition Soviet diver Sergey Kuzmin won the springboard and China's Li Hong Ping the platform. The Soviet Union won three of the four events in the European championships. In men's competition Aleksandr Portnov won the springboard and David Ambartsumian the platform. East Germany's Katrin Zipperling won the women's platform to prevent a Soviet sweep, as Zhanna Tsirulnikova took the springboard. (ALBERT SCHOENFIELD)

Switzerland

A federal republic in west central Europe consisting of a confederation of 23 cantons (three of which are demi-cantons), Switzerland is bounded by West Germany, Austria, Liechtenstein, Italy, and France. Area: 41,293 sq km (15,943 sq mi). Pop. (1980): 6,365,400. Cap.: Bern (pop., 1980, 145,300). Largest city: Zürich (pop., 1980, 369,500). Language (1970): German 65%; French 18%; Italian 12%; Romansh 1%. Religion (1970): Roman Catholic 49.4%; Protestant 47.7%. President in 1981, Kurt Furgler.

Switzerland in 1981 once again offered a picture of relative stability. Regional, cantonal, and communal interests and activities asserted themselves against the pressure of centralizing tendencies and made it difficult, if not impossible, to obtain a

Switzerland

national consensus on some issues, such as abortion. While there were four already in operation, construction of new nuclear power plants prompted agitated debate.

There were three federal plebiscites. In April all the cantons voted against the mostly left-wing-inspired initiative proposing broader rights for the more than 100,000 foreign seasonal workers in Switzerland. In June more than 60% of the voters approved the introduction of measures specifying male and female equality of legal and economic rights. On November 29 a plebiscite approved the latest government-proposed plan to improve the federal budget, which was expected in 1982 to attain the record deficit of SFr 1,120,000,000. The government hoped to reduce this figure by at least several hundred million Swiss francs by means of a comprehensive revision of taxes and a redistribution of financial claims and responsibilities among the cantons and the confederation.

Proposals for the revised federal constitution elaborated by a team of experts were submitted for comments and counterproposals to all organizations and institutions concerned. The Federal Council was expected to announce its position during 1982, though Kurt Furgler, head of the Department of Justice and Police and guiding spirit of the revision, proposed that a totally new—not merely revised—constitution be drawn up.

One of the vexing problems remained the exact interpretation of the constitutional "permanent neutrality" in light of the forthcoming campaign and plebiscite on Switzerland's accession to the UN. The federal government asked the Parliament to agree to Switzerland's joining the UN provided guarantees could be obtained in favour of certain implications, considered inalienable, of the principle of neutrality. While parliamentary approval was expected, final approval would require a majority vote in a national referendum, and according to some unofficial polls only one out of three Swiss citizens was prepared to approve full membership in the UN.

As a result of the economies imposed in the 1982 budget, Swiss governmental aid to less developed countries was expected to fall short of the planned 0.35% of gross national product (GNP). The overall economic situation remained stable. In terms of GNP and individual living standards, Switzerland continued to figure among the world's most privileged countries. Employment remained all but full. The one industry suffering in 1981 was watchmaking, but some promising efforts to counter strong foreign competition were made. Although the balance of trade showed a record excess of imports over exports, the balance of payments remained favourable and the Swiss franc was strong. The only serious concern was the threat of inflation, with the rate increasing steadily each month so that it exceeded 7% in late autumn.

Expenditure for national defense remained the first item in the federal budget, with 21.3% of the total. Great importance was attached to the acquisition of new defensive weapons, military training, and the construction of antinuclear civil protection shelters.

Clashes between police and young people came

SWITZERLAND

Education. (1979–80) Primary, pupils 506,100, teachers (excluding craft teachers; 1961–62) 23,761; secondary, pupils 427,900, teachers (full time; 1961–62) 6,583; vocational, pupils 215,400; teacher training, students 8,600; higher, students 74,200, teaching staff (universities and equivalent institutions only; 1977–78) 5,911.

Finance. Monetary unit: Swiss franc, with (Sept. 21, 1981) a free rate of SFr 1.91 to U.S. $1 (SFr 3.54 = £1 sterling). Gold and other reserves (June 1981) U.S. $15,495,000,000. Budget (1980 actual): revenue SFr 16,456,000,000; expenditure SFr 16,474,000,000. Gross national product (1979) SFr 164.6 billion. Money supply (June 1981) SFr 70,010,000,000. Cost of living (1975 = 100; June 1981) 119.2.

Foreign Trade. (1980) Imports SFr 60.9 billion; exports SFr 49.6 billion. Import sources: EEC 67% (West Germany 28%, France 12%, Italy 10%, U.K. 8%); U.S. 7%. Export destinations: EEC 51% (West Germany 20%, France 9%, Italy 8%, U.K. 6%); U.S. 7%; Austria 5%. Main exports: machinery 31%; chemicals 19%; precious metals and stones 8%; watches and clocks 7%; textile yarns and fabrics 5%; instruments, etc. (excluding watches and clocks) 5%. Tourism (1979): visitors 7,608,000; gross receipts U.S. $2,568,000,000.

Transport and Communications. Roads (1980) 64,029 km (including 876 km expressways). Motor vehicles in use (1980): passenger 2,246,800; commercial 169,400. Railways: (1978) 4,975 km (including 4,946 km electrified); traffic (1980) 8,485,000,000 passenger-km, freight 7,485,000,000 net ton-km. Air traffic (1980): 10,831,000,000 passenger-km; freight 453.2 million net ton-km. Shipping (1980): merchant vessels 100 gross tons and over 35; gross tonnage 310,775. Telephones (Dec. 1979) 4,446,200. Radio licenses (Dec. 1979) 2,209,800. Television licenses (Dec. 1979) 1,937,400.

Agriculture. Production (in 000; metric tons; 1980): wheat 403; barley 201; oats 48; corn 108; potatoes 864; rapeseed 34; apples 342; pears (1979) 148; sugar, raw value (1979) 108; wine c. 84; milk 3,616; butter 35; cheese 123; beef and veal 173; pork 288. Livestock (in 000; April 1980): cattle 2,031; sheep 353; pigs 2,205; chickens (1979) 6,337.

Industry. Index of industrial production (1975 = 100; 1980) 108. Production (in 000; metric tons; 1979): aluminum 83; cement 3,934; petroleum products c. 4,500; manmade fibres (1978) 83; cigarettes (units) 29,282,000; watches (exports; units) c. 33,700; manufactured gas (cu m) 53,000; electricity (kw-hr; 1980) 46,626,000.

SYRIA

Syria

Education. (1979–80) Primary, pupils 1,407,223, teachers 46,132; secondary, pupils 552,677, teachers 25,945; vocational, pupils 25,945, teachers 3,085; teacher training, students 10,364, teachers 988; higher, students 96,040, teaching staff (universities only; 1975–76) 1,332.

Finance. Monetary unit: Syrian pound, with (Sept. 21, 1981) a par value of S£3.925 to U.S. $1 (free rate of S£7.28 = £1 sterling). Gold and other reserves (Dec. 1980) U.S. $360 million. Budget (total; 1981 est.) balanced at S£30,480 million. Gross domestic product (1979) S£35,887 million. Money supply (Dec. 1980) S£21,854 million. Cost of living (Damascus; 1975 = 100; April 1981) 191.

Foreign Trade. (1980) Imports S£16,187 million; exports S£8,273 million. Import sources (1979): Iraq 15%; Italy 13%; West Germany 9%; Romania 6%; France 6%. Export destinations (1979): Italy 26%; France 18%; U.S. 10%; Greece 8%; Romania 6%; U.S.S.R. 5%. Main exports: crude oil 63%; cotton 8%; fruit and vegetables c. 5%.

Transport and Communications. Roads (1976) c. 16,339 km. Motor vehicles in use (1978): passenger 65,400; commercial 81,400. Railways: (1976) 1,672 km; traffic (1979) 410 million passenger-km, freight 450 million net ton-km. Air traffic (1980): 948 million passenger-km; freight 16.2 million net ton-km. Telephones (Jan. 1980) 236,000. Radio receivers (Dec. 1978) 1,792,000. Television receivers (Dec. 1978) 454,000.

Agriculture. Production (in 000; metric tons; 1980): wheat 2,229; barley 1,587; potatoes (1979) c. 201; pumpkins (1979) c. 148; cucumbers (1979) c. 196; tomatoes c. 460; onions c. 160; watermelons (1979) c. 616; melons (1979) c. 212; grapes c. 288; olives c. 320; cottonseed c. 196; cotton, lint c. 127. Livestock (in 000; 1980): sheep c. 8,800; goats c. 1,000; cattle (1979) c. 705; horses (1979) c. 51; asses (1979) c. 270; chickens c. 18,000.

Industry. Production (in 000; metric tons; 1979): cement 1,850; crude oil (1980) 8,498; natural gas (cu m) c. 200,000; petroleum products c. 9,000; cotton yarn 13; phosphate rock 1,169; electricity (kw-hr) 3,420,000.

to a head at the end of March, as protesters sought the reopening of an autonomous youth centre in Zürich that had been closed by the authorities in September 1980. The city government conceded the protesters' demands.

On December 9 the federal Parliament elected the Zürich radical Fritz Honegger to succeed Kurt Furgler as president of the confederation in 1982. Because of the large number of items still pending on the agenda, a supplementary extraordinary session was scheduled for the beginning of 1982.

(MELANIE STAERK)

Syria

A republic in southwestern Asia on the Mediterranean Sea, Syria is bordered by Turkey, Iraq, Jordan, Israel, and Lebanon. Area: 185,179 sq km (71,498 sq mi). Pop. (1980 est.): 8,979,000. Cap. and largest city: Damascus (pop., 1980 est., 1,200,200). Language: Arabic (official); also Kurdish, Armenian, Turkish, Circassian, and Syriac. Religion: predominantly (over 80%) Muslim. President in 1981, Gen. Hafez al-Assad; premier, Abdul Rauf al-Kasm.

Syria's involvement in Lebanon and military posturing toward Israel in 1981 were accompanied by a worsening economic crisis at home. Closer military and economic cooperation with the U.S.S.R. was sought by Pres. Hafez al-Assad's government. The ill health of Premier Abdul Rauf al-Kasm prompted fears that his largely technocratic Cabinet would disintegrate. When reports of his illness were gaining wide currency in August, the favourite to replace him was Muhammad Abu Diab, a member of the Ba'ath Party's national committee. In August the People's Council approved the fifth five-year plan (1981–85), and on August 17 the council was dissolved pending new elections. As anticipated, the National Progressive Front (NPF), led by the ruling Ba'ath Party, won all 195 seats in the elections on November 10. The deputies, who included 99 workers' representatives, were elected for a four-year term of office.

Sporadic acts of terrorism continued to reveal the potential for political instability in Syria. On August 17 an explosion killed three people in the premier's office, although it was attributed to "an air-conditioning equipment short circuit." During the year the Muslim Brotherhood, an extremist organization, was blamed for several acts of violence, including a car-bomb explosion that killed 90 people in Damascus on November 29.

President Assad continued to lead Syria in opposition to compromise with Israel. Diplomatic contact was maintained, however, with Saudi Arabia over the Middle East peace proposals made by Crown Prince Fahd. Deputy Premier and Foreign Minister Abdul-Halim Khaddam visited Riyadh before the November Arab summit in Fez,

Morocco, for talks with Saudi Foreign Minister Prince Saud al-Faisal. Initial Syrian opposition to the Fahd plan, which included recognition of Israel's right to exist, was somewhat muted; Syria was dependent on Saudi aid. On December 14 the Israeli Knesset voted to annex the Golan Heights, Syrian territory captured during the 1967 war. The move, apart from further increasing tension between the two countries and provoking worldwide criticism, hardened Syrian opposition to the Fahd peace plan.

Defense Minister Gen. Moustapha Tlas visited Moscow on September 17 seeking new supplies of Soviet weapons. His visit followed Syrian concern about Israel's defense agreements with the U.S. Syria had signed a friendship treaty with the Soviet Union in October 1980. In July 1981 major Soviet naval exercises were accompanied by a mock landing in Syria of about 800 Soviet marines. At the military talks Syria asked for more MiG-25 jet fighters and T-72 tanks. It was reported that Syria also asked for an improved version of the MiG-23, which would match Israel's U.S.-built F-15 jet fighters. A wider economic agreement signed in Moscow on May 14 included an undertaking by the Soviet Union to lend Syria 40 million rubles ($49.5 million) to finance five railway projects. From the Soviet point of view, friendship with Syria was designed to counter Iraq's growing links with Western countries and to give the U.S.S.R. a bulwark in the eastern Mediterranean.

The broad outlines of the five-year plan were published in August. The plan aimed to cut Syria's balance of payments deficit and to increase its gross national product by an average of 8.5% a year. A total of 460,000 new jobs were to be created. Annual growth in exports was to be 6.5%, with imports growing at only 3.4%.

Of the total investment, about 17%, S£17,200 million ($4,354,000,000), was to be applied to agriculture. Ba'athist Party ideology had always favoured large investment. Few details were announced about specific projects despite the fact that the official starting date for the plan was Jan. 1, 1981. By 1985 Syria expected to cease exporting oil; production in 1980 was thought to have been only 8.5 million metric tons. Dependence on Arab aid — particularly from the conservative regime in Saudi Arabia — was likely to increase, posing difficult problems of adjustment for Syria.

(JOHN WHELAN)

Table Tennis

In April 1981 Novi Sad, Yugos., played host to participants in the 36th biennial world table tennis championships. China captured both the Swaythling Cup, symbol of supremacy in the men's team competition, and the Marcel Corbillon Cup, given to the victorious women's team. In the men's team competition, Hungary finished second to China. Others, in order of finish, were Japan, Czechoslovakia, and France. In the women's team play, South Korea was runner-up to China. Next in order were North Korea, the Soviet Union, and West Germany.

Xie Saike of the People's Republic of China was the winner of the men's crown at the U.S. Open table tennis championships held at Princeton, N.J., in June.

The finals of all the individual championships featured Chinese athletes. Guo Yuehua defeated Cai Zhenhua for the men's singles crown. In the men's doubles Cai Zhenhua and Li Zhenshi triumphed over Guo Yuehua and Xie Saike. The women's singles title went to Tong Ling, who defeated Cao Yanhua in a five-set match. In the women's doubles, Cao Yanhua and Zhang Deying subdued Tong Ling and Bu Qijuan in three straight sets. The mixed doubles was won by Xie Saike and Huang Junqun.

During the world championships the Congress of the International Table Tennis Federation admitted Angola, Congo, and Zimbabwe to membership, thereby bringing the total number of affiliated associations to 125. The Congress also granted Japan the right to organize the world championships in 1983; Sweden would have that privilege in 1985.

The second World Cup competition featuring the world's top 16 men players got under way in Kuala Lumpur, Malaysia, on July 30. Prize money totaled $40,000. In the finals, Tibor Klampar (Hung.) dropped the first two sets to Xie Saike (China), then made an exciting comeback by winning the next three sets.

The European top 12 players tournament began on February 6 in Miskolc, Hung. The final standings in the men's division showed Klampar at the head of the list. Next in order were Stellan Bengtsson (Sweden), Dragutin Surbek (Yugos.), Josef

1981 World Rankings

MEN	WOMEN
1. Guo Yuehua (China)	1. Tong Ling (China)
2. Cai Zhenhua (China)	2. Cao Yanhua (China)
3. Xie Saike (China)	3. Zhang Deying (China)
4. Tibor Klampar (Hungary)	4. Lee Soo Ja (South Korea)
5. Dragutin Surbek (Yugoslavia)	5. Qi Baoxiang (China)
6. Stellan Bengtsson (Sweden)	6. Pak Yong Sun (North Korea)
7. Shi Zhihao (China)	7. Bu Qijuan (China)
8. Desmond Douglas (England)	8. Huang Junqun (China)
9. Wang Huiyuan (China)	9. Valentina Popova (U.S.S.R.)
10. Istvan Jonyer (Hungary)	10. Li Song Suk (North Korea)

Dvoracek (Czech.), and Jacques Secretin (France). In the women's competition Jill Hammersley (England) finished first, followed by Bettine Vriesekoop (Neth.), Valentina Popova (U.S.S.R.), Judit Magos (Hung.), and Ilona Uhlikova (Czech.).

The Latin-American best 16 players tournament was held in Mexico from February 27 to March 1. In the final standings, Aristides Franca (Brazil) was first, followed by Gustavo Patino (Arg.) and Betancourt (Cuba).

The European League winners for 1980–81 were: Hungary in the Superdivision, Poland in Division 1, Denmark in Division 2, and Scotland in Division 3.

On October 1 the International Olympic Committee decided that table tennis would be an Olympic event beginning in 1988.

In late December 1980 the 21st South American championships were decided in Puerto Montt, Chile. Brazil not only won both the men's and women's team titles but took home the men's singles title as well when Ricardo Inokuchi defeated fellow countryman Aristides Nascimiento. The women's singles championship was won by H. J. Kim (Arg.). The Colombian team of J. Ríos and V. Suaza emerged victorious in the men's doubles, and Andrade and Murgan of Chile took the women's doubles. Díaz and Ramos (Chile) won the mixed doubles.

The sixth All African championships, also played in late December 1980, were held in Dakar, Senegal. Nigeria won all the titles except the women's singles.　　(ARTHUR KINGSLEY VINT)

Taiwan

Taiwan, which consists of the islands of Taiwan (Western conventional Formosa) and Quemoy and other surrounding islands, is the seat of the Republic of China (Nationalist China). It is north of the Philippines, southwest of Japan, and east of Hong Kong. The island of Taiwan has an area of 35,779 sq km (13,814 sq mi); including its 77 outlying islands (14 in the Taiwan group and 63 in the Pescadores group), the area of Taiwan totals 36,002 sq km (13,900 sq mi). Pop. (1981 est.): 17,982,-

200. Area and pop. exclude the Quemoy and Matsu groups, which are administered as an occupied part of Fukien Province. Their combined area is about 160 sq km; their population at the end of 1979 was 63,800. Cap. and largest city: Taipei (pop., 1981 est., 2,252,700). Language: Mandarin Chinese (official). President in 1981, Chiang Ching-kuo; president of the Executive Yuan (premier), Sun Yün-suan.

Taiwan

On Oct. 10, 1981, the Nationalist government, in its 32nd year in exile on Taiwan, celebrated the 70th anniversary of the 1911 Revolution with a full-scale military parade to demonstrate its spirit of self-reliance and determination. Only 22 nations, half of them in Central and South America, still recognized the Republic of China as the government of China.

Taiwan's remarkable economic growth and steady political progress continued. The December 1980 supplementary elections had sent dozens of new and younger representatives to the Legislative Yuan and the National Assembly. In the executive branch of government, more Taiwanese had been appointed as Cabinet ministers, and their representation at all levels of government had increased notably.

The economy of Taiwan was approaching the status of a developed country; per capita income, at more than $2,000, was ten times that of the Chinese mainland. Economic growth depended largely on foreign trade. In 1980 two-way trade rose 27.9% over 1979 to $39.4 billion; imports increased 33.5% to $19,710,000,000, and exports rose 22.7% to $19,760,000,000. Industrial products accounted for 90.8% of exports. The U.S. remained Taiwan's largest export market.

In 1981 Taiwan established close trade relations with several Western European countries. The Netherlands, which sold two submarines to Taiwan, opened its Council for Trade Promotion in Taipei in January. It was followed by Belgium, West Germany, Britain, Spain, and Austria, all of which established trade offices in Taiwan to handle trade, cultural exchanges, visas, and other affairs.

The Taiwan Relations Act of 1979, which committed the U.S. to providing Taiwan with defen-

The Republic of China (Nationalist) celebrated the 70th anniversary of the 1911 Revolution with an elaborate ceremony attended by 250,000 people in Taipei on October 10.

Tanzania

sive arms, had been the basis of Washington-Taipei relations since the U.S. withdrew formal recognition from the Nationalist government. The People's Republic had protested strongly against continued sales of U.S. weapons to Taiwan, while Taipei was seeking to purchase advanced U.S. jet fighters. U.S. Secretary of State Alexander Haig's announcement in Beijing (Peking) in June of the U.S. decision to lift restrictions on arms sales to the People's Republic brought expressions of concern from Taipei. At a press conference held on June 16, U.S. Pres. Ronald Reagan reiterated his intention to implement the Taiwan Relations Act fully. Meanwhile, the Beijing government warned that if the Reagan administration continued its support of Taiwan, "normal relations between China and the United States . . . will certainly be gravely impaired."

Beijing had shifted its strategy for obtaining the "liberation of Taiwan," but the Nationalists regarded the Communist regime's new peace campaign as an attempt to absorb Taiwan politically, since it could not be done militarily. Beijing's suggestion that the two sides open talks and establish post, shipping, and direct commercial links was rejected by Pres. Chiang Ching-kuo on January 12. On September 30, the eve of the 32nd anniversary of the People's Republic, Ye Jianying (Yeh Chien-ying), nominal head of the Beijing regime, issued a nine-point plan that included a guarantee of Taiwan's autonomy after unification, with re-

tention of its economic and social systems and its armed forces. Beijing also suggested exchanges of trade offices and scientific knowledge. The Nationalists immediately rejected all these proposals.

On October 1 the Communist Party newspaper *People's Daily* appealed directly to Chiang to consider seriously Beijing's proposal for reunification based on power sharing. The following day, however, Premier Sun Yün-suan called it a smokescreen to conceal factional struggles and discontent on the mainland and to promote discord among the Nationalists. In a renewed appeal on the eve of the October 10 holiday, Hu Yaobang (Hu Yao-pang), chairman of the Chinese Communist Party, invited Chiang, Sun, and other high officials to visit the mainland, but the appeal and invitations were ignored.　(HUNG-TI CHU)

Tanzania

This republic, an East African member of the Commonwealth, consists of two parts: Tanganyika, on the Indian Ocean, bordered by Kenya, Uganda, Rwanda, Burundi, Zaire, Zambia, Malawi, and Mozambique; and Zanzibar, just off the coast, including Zanzibar Island, Pemba Island, and small islets. Total area of the united republic: 945,050 sq km (364,886 sq mi). Total pop. (1981 est.): 18,511,000, including 98.9% African and 0.7% Indo-Pakistani. Cap. and largest city: Dar es Salaam (pop., 1978 est., 860,000) in Tanganyika. Language: English and Swahili. Religion (1967): traditional beliefs 34.6%; Christian 30.6%; Muslim 30.5%. President in 1981, Julius Nyerere; prime minister, Cleopa David Msuya.

As part of a drive against inefficiency and corruption, it was announced on Jan. 16, 1981, that over 100 civil servants had been suspended from their duties and several leading businessmen had been arrested. A week later Pres. Julius Nyerere dismissed Augustine Mwingira from his two posts as minister of communications and transport and chairman of the Air Tanzania Corporation on the grounds that he had mismanaged the affairs of ATC. He was replaced as minister by Ibrahim Kaduma, whose own post of minister of trade was then given to Ali Mchumo. On February 5 Nyerere appealed in a broadcast for public support in his anticorruption campaign.

Four years after the enactment of legislation to prevent profiteering in the medical field and to ensure adequate and inexpensive medical care for as many persons as possible, steps were finally taken in June to require all doctors to work at a fixed salary for the government or for an organization approved by the government. All private hospitals and clinics were to be taken over by the government or by approved organizations.

Relations with Kenya seemed likely to improve when, on January 17, Nyerere met the presidents of Kenya, Uganda, and Zambia in Kampala, Uganda. The four chiefs of state affirmed their intention of promoting trade and other forms of cooperation in eastern Africa. The Tanzania-Kenya border remained closed, but at a later meeting in Nairobi, Kenya, it was agreed that discus-

TAIWAN

Education. (1980–81) Primary, pupils 2,222,595, teachers 68,627; secondary and vocational, pupils 1,598,028, teachers 69,280; higher, students 342,528, teaching staff 16,495.

Finance. Monetary unit: new Taiwan dollar, with (Sept. 21, 1981) an official rate of NT$36 to U.S. $1 (free rate of NT$66.74 = £1 sterling). Budget (total 1979–80 actual): revenue NT$367,337,000,000; expenditure NT$346,-212,000,000. Gross national product (1980) NT$1,449,-400,000,000. Money supply (March 1981) NT$288,-951,000,000. Cost of living (1975 = 100; March 1981) 172.1.

Foreign Trade. (1980) Imports NT$711.4 billion; exports NT$712.2 billion. Import sources: U.S. 24%; Japan 13%; Kuwait 11%; Saudi Arabia 7%. Export destinations: U.S. 34%; Japan 11%; Hong Kong 8%; West Germany 5%. Main exports: machinery 22% (including telecommunications apparatus 10%); clothing 12%; textile yarns and fabrics 9%; food 9%; footwear 7%; toys and sports goods 5%.

Transport and Communications. Roads (1980) 17,448 km. Motor vehicles in use (1980): passenger 425,400; commercial 236,700. Railways (1980): 3,700 km; traffic 7,971,-000,000 passenger-km, freight 2,716,000,000 net ton-km. Air traffic (1980): 7,489,000,000 passenger-km; freight 1,-031,400,000 net ton-km. Shipping (1980): merchant vessels 100 gross tons and over 497; gross tonnage 2,039,123. Telephones (Dec. 1980) 2,322,800. Radio licenses (Dec. 1976) 1,493,100. Television receivers (Dec. 1979) 3,248,-000.

Agriculture. Production (in 000; metric tons; 1980): rice 2,354; sweet potatoes 1,055; cassava (1979) 226; sugar, raw value 830; citrus fruit 374; bananas 214; pineapples 229; tea 24; tobacco (1979) 21; pork c. 630; fish catch 936. Livestock (in 000; Dec. 1980): cattle 134; pigs 4,820; goats and sheep 184; chickens 41,394.

Industry. Production (in 000; metric tons; 1980): coal 2,574; crude oil (1979) c. 196; natural gas (cu m; 1979) 1,721,000; electricity (kw-hr; 1979) 40,679,000; cement 14,062; crude steel (1979) 1,570; sulfuric acid (1979) 777; plastics and resins (1979) 407; petroleum products (1979) 13,944; cotton yarn 171; man-made fibres 633; paper and board (1979) 1,316; radio receivers (units; 1979) 8,720; television receivers (units) 6,061.

sions would take place to settle the dispute over the allocation of funds of the former East African Community. It was this dispute that had created the problems leading to the border closing. In December, however, Tanzania refused to sign an agreement that proposed the setting up of an 18-nation preferential trade area. In September Nyerere visited Pres. François Mitterrand of France.

The withdrawal of the remaining Tanzanian troops from Uganda began on May 1, after Pres. Milton Obote stated that the maintenance of internal order in Uganda was now a matter for the police. Tanzania agreed to leave 1,000 police to assist Uganda. The Tanzanian troops had arrived in Uganda in April 1979 and completed their withdrawal at the end of June 1981. In that time, 620 soldiers had lost their lives, and the enterprise had cost Tanzania an estimated $500 million. No doubt recollecting his own moral dilemma in intervening in Uganda, Nyerere in August gave strong support to the Senegalese military intervention in The Gambia to put down an attempted coup.

In May Nyerere met the presidents of Rwanda, Burundi, and Uganda in Burundi to discuss means of improving the transport system between Rwanda and Burundi and the coast. The two countries, particularly Rwanda, had relied heavily on goods brought through Uganda and Kenya. Years of unrest in Uganda had disrupted the flow of imports, however, and it was hoped that improvements in the Tanzanian railway system might relieve the situation.   (KENNETH INGHAM)

TANZANIA

Education. (1976–77) Primary, pupils 2,274,167, teachers 46,274; secondary, pupils 61,178, teachers 3,192; vocational, pupils 833, teachers 119; teacher training, pupils 9,741, teachers 666; higher, students 2,260, teaching staff 459.

Finance. Monetary unit: Tanzanian shilling, with (Sept. 21, 1981) a free rate of TShs 8.01 to U.S. $1 (TShs 14.85 = £1 sterling). Gold and other reserves (June 1981) U.S. $36 million. Budget (1979–80 est.): revenue TShs 7,788,000,-000; expenditure TShs 7,468,000,000 (excludes development expenditure of TShs 7,186,000,000). Gross national product (1979) TShs 37,583,000,000. Money supply (March 1981) TShs 13,226,000,000. Cost of living (1975 = 100; 1st quarter 1981) 227.5.

Foreign Trade. (1980) Imports TShs 10,308,000,000; exports TShs 4,166,000,000. Import sources (1978): U.K. 19%; Japan 11%; West Germany 11%; The Netherlands 7%; Italy 6%. Export destinations (1978): U.K. 21%; West Germany 15%; U.S. 11%; The Netherlands 5%; Italy 5%. Main exports (1978): coffee 36%; cotton 12%; fruit and vegetables 9%; diamonds 6%; tobacco 6%; sisal 6%; tea 5%.

Transport and Communications. Roads (1980) 45,631 km. Motor vehicles in use (1979): passenger 42,200; commercial (including buses) 51,100. Railways (1978) 3,682 km. Air traffic (1980): 284 million passenger-km; freight c. 2.4 million net ton-km. Telephones (Jan. 1978) 74,300. Radio receivers (Dec. 1977) 310,000. Television receivers (Dec. 1978) c. 8,800.

Agriculture. Production (in 000; metric tons; 1980): corn c. 800; millet c. 160; sorghum c. 220; rice c. 180; sweet potatoes (1979) c. 330; cassava (1979) c. 4,300; sugar, raw value (1979) c. 130; dry beans c. 150; mangoes c. 175; bananas c. 780; cashew nuts (1979) c. 58; coffee 52; tea c. 17; tobacco 18; cotton, lint 51; sisal 115; meat (1979) c. 198; fish catch (1979) 344; timber (cu m; 1979) 33,015. Livestock (in 000; 1980): sheep c. 3,790; goats c. 5,686; cattle (1979) c. 15,300; chickens c. 21,050.

Industry. Production (in 000; metric tons; 1978): cement 272; salt 29; diamonds (metric carats) 293; petroleum products c. 650; electricity (kw-hr; 1979) c. 734,000.

Target Sports

Archery. During 1981 archery continued to increase in popularity throughout the world. Only three nations had participated in the conference at Lwow, Poland, in 1931 that established the International Archery Federation (FITA). By comparison, 42 nations attended the 1981 FITA conference in Punta Ala, Italy. Archery was contested in the Olympic Games of 1900, 1904, 1908, and 1920. It was then dropped from the schedule but was added again in 1972.

The number of persons hunting with bows and arrows in the U.S. in 1981 was estimated to be more than 1,750,000. The four leading states in issuing such hunting licenses for the 1980–81 seasons were Pennsylvania (276,225), Michigan (172,925), Wisconsin (155,386), and New York (80,492). Those hunting with bows and arrows in 1931 were probably fewer than 500.

In the 1981 archery world championships, Natalia Boutousova of the U.S.S.R. won the women's title with a score of 2,514. Kyosii Laasonen of Finland was the men's champion with 2,541. In the U.S. tournament the winners were Rick McKinney of Phoenix, Ariz., with 2,565 points, and Debbie Metzger of Lancaster, Pa., with 2,576. McKinney also won the U.S. indoor championships with 1,-167 points out of a possible 1,200, and Ruth Rowe took the women's competition with 1,135.

(CLAYTON B. SHENK)

[452.B.4.h.i]

Shooting. Eleven nations participated in the third Confederation of the Americas championships at Rio de Janerio and São Paulo in Brazil. Two new world records were set. Two more were set at the Running Game Target championships in Buenos Aires, Arg. Other 1981 International Shooting Union events of note included the European championships and the Benito Juárez competitions in Mexico. The U.S. rifle and pistol championships were held at Camp Perry, Ohio.

TRAP AND SKEET. Matt Dryke of the U.S. set a new world record of 200 straight international skeet targets at São Paulo. This bettered by one target a long-standing individual score. The U.S. team followed Dryke's lead to set a team world record score of 593 out of a possible 600. The team from Colombia finished second with a score of 560, and Brazil placed third with 554.

RIFLES. The U.S. team fired a 60-shot prone-position score of 2,361 at Rio de Janeiro to set a new free rifle 300-m world record. Lones Wigger of the U.S. set a new world record individual standard rifle 300-m three-position score of 580. A standard rifle 50-m three-position women's record score of 592 was fired at Titograd, Yugos., by M. Helbig of East Germany.

With the small-bore rifle, F. Rettkowski of East Germany fired a 40-shot standing score of 386 to set a new 50-m record. The Soviet team fired a record 40-shot kneeling score of 1,577 and a record 60-shot prone score of 2,391. On the 50-m running game target, the U.S.S.R. team scored 2,346 for a 60-shot "normal runs" record. J. Sokolov of the U.S.S.R.

fired a record individual score of 595. At the Buenos Aires world championships the Soviet team set a 40-shot "mixed runs" record of 1,550. An individual record of 391 was fired by Rudnitzki of the U.S.S.R. An air rifle record score of 1,497 for 40-shot normal runs at 10 m was fired by the U.S.S.R. team at Athens. G. Maloukhine of the U.S.S.R. fired an individual record of 389.

At the U.S. national championships at Camp Perry, the national high-power rifle championship was won by David Boyd with a score of 2,369-78X. In the small-bore rifle competition Mary Stidworthy won the prone event with a 6,391-530X. The prone metallic-sight championship was won by Ernest Vande Zande with a 3,193-236X. Lones Wigger was the three-position small-bore rifle champion with a score of 2,086.

HANDGUNS. At the rapid-fire pistol matches in Yugoslavia, the Soviet Union set a record team score of 2,382. An individual record of 599 was fired by I. Puzyrev of the Soviet team. The Soviets set another record of 2,358 for centre-fire pistol at 25 m. At Athens the Soviet team set a record 10-m air pistol team score of 2,306. An individual record score of 582 was posted in that event by V. Tourla of the U.S.S.R. The U.S. national pistol champion was Joseph Pascarella, who fired a score of 2,651-134X. At the U.S. international shooting championships, held in June at Phoenix, Ariz., Darius Young of Canada won the standard pistol, free pistol, and centre-fire pistol events. Also at that tournament Terry Howard and Audrey Grosch, both of the U.S., were the men's and women's clay pigeon champions.   (ROBERT N. SEARS)

[452.B.4.e]

Television and Radio

Television and radio service was available in some form in all major nations in 1981. Approximately 830 million radio sets were in use, of which about 457.5 million, or 55%, were in the United States. Television sets numbered about 436 million, of which 170 million, or 39%, were in the U.S.

The Soviet Union, with 80 million television sets, ranked next and Japan was third with 28.5 million, according to estimates published in the 1981 *Broadcasting Yearbook*. Other *Broadcasting* estimates included West Germany, 20.6 million; United Kingdom, 19.5 million; France, 17.6 million; Brazil, 16.5 million; Italy, 12.9 million; Canada, 11 million; Spain, 8.4 million; Poland, 7 million; Mexico, 6 million; East Germany, 5.2 million; The Netherlands, 5.1 million; Australia, 5 million; and Argentina, 4.5 million.

Approximately 7,830 television stations were operating or being built throughout the world. Some 2,200 were in the Far East, 2,110 in Western Europe, 1,176 in the U.S., 920 in Eastern Europe, 180 in South America, 105 in Mexico, 96 in Canada, and 45 in Africa. Radio stations numbered about 16,100; most were amplitude modulation (AM) stations, but the percentage of frequency modulation (FM) outlets was growing. In the U.S. there were 9,451 radio stations, of which 4,699 were FM.

Organization of Services. News coverage of major events was almost routinely exchanged via communications satellites among broadcasting organizations throughout the world. Among the most widely seen were U.S. Pres. Ronald Reagan's inauguration on January 20 and, on the same day, the release of U.S. hostages from Iran; events surrounding attempts on the lives of President Reagan in March and of Pope John Paul II in May; the successful launch and return of the U.S. space shuttle "Columbia" in April and again in November; and the assassination of Pres. Anwar as-Sadat of Egypt in October.

In the U.S., President Reagan's policy of deregulation was felt by both broadcasters and cable television operators. Congress enacted legislation that lengthened broadcast license terms from three years under the old system to seven years for radio stations and five years for television stations. The new law also authorized the U.S. Federal Communications Commission (FCC), the communications regulatory agency, to use lotteries rather than time-consuming hearings to resolve competition among equally qualified applicants for new licenses. And legislation was moving through Congress, though not without opposition, to make radio license terms indefinite and to eliminate requirements of all broadcasters that they devote at least certain amounts of time to news and public affairs programs, formally ascertain community needs, and heed certain guidelines as to the amount of time devoted to commercials. The main beneficiaries of this bill would be television broadcasters; early in the year the FCC removed many of these restraints as they applied to radio stations. Radio broadcasters—and the FCC—also won an important court victory in March when the U.S. Supreme Court upheld the commission's right to leave entertainment to the discretion of the station licensee and the play of the marketplace without being compelled to hear and pass upon complaints from listeners disgruntled by a station's decision to change its programming format.

For cable television, deregulation became a virtual fact when the U.S. Court of Appeals in New York upheld, in June, the 1980 FCC order removing the last regulations that the cable industry considered restrictive. These regulations had limited the number of broadcast signals a cable operator might carry and had protected television stations against cable systems' use of syndicated programs to which the stations held local exhibition rights. In August the FCC granted a waiver of its ban on network ownership of cable systems, granting CBS permission to acquire a system or systems serving no more than 90,000 subscribers or 0.5% of all U.S. cable subscribers, whichever number was smaller, and also indicated that other networks would receive similar waivers "upon the submission of comparable showings."

Competition between broadcasters and cable operators intensified in 1981. Scores of new companies, many with backing and direction by some of the largest broadcasters, were formed to provide programming for the fast-growing cable industry and for the still-emerging home videocassette and video-disc fields. (*See* Special Report.)

Questions about the use of direct broadcast satellites (DBS's), which broadcast programs directly from communications satellites to homes, caused concern over the ultimate fate of conventional ground-based intermediaries, particularly television stations. In April the FCC accepted the Communications Satellite Corporation's (Comsat's) application for authority to operate a three-channel, direct-to-home pay-television service. By July, when it cut off further bids, 12 others had been received. The FCC then opened two proceedings, one to prepare U.S. policy for an international DBS conference to be held in 1983 and the other to formulate a domestic DBS policy.

The U.S. Corporation for Public Broadcasting, operating under a system of government and private financing, began to feel the effects of the Reagan administration's cutbacks in federal spending. Congress passed legislation extending the CPB's life through 1986 but providing for a reduction in federal funding from $172 million in 1982 to $137 million in 1983 and to no more than $130 million a year for the 1984–86 period. This reduction intensified the efforts of the Public Broadcasting Service (PBS), the CPB's programming unit, to find new sources of financing.

Public broadcasting, technically a noncommercial service, moved closer to commercial status during the year. The FCC amended its rules to permit public stations to show the logos and identify the product lines of program underwriters. Stations also were authorized to promote goods and services on the air—if they first determined that the public interest would be served.

On Dec. 28, 1980, the U.K. Independent Broadcasting Authority (IBA) announced the names of the Independent Television (ITV) program companies that had won eight-year contracts in a redistribution of franchises in the country's 14 IBA regions and for a new national breakfast-time service. The breakfast-time contract was awarded to TV-AM, a consortium put together by David Frost and headed by Peter Jay, former British ambassador in Washington, D.C. It was to start broadcasting in May 1983.

The British Broadcasting Corporation's (BBC's) royal charter was renewed, with alterations, for 15 years ending 1996. A new Article 3 allowed the BBC (with Home Office prior approval in some cases) to exploit new cable and satellite technology to commercial advantage. The BBC failed, however, in its attempt to persuade the government to raise the colour TV license fee from £34 annually (fixed in November 1979) to £50. The government would go no higher than £46, fixed for a three-year period as of December 2. Consequently, the BBC would have to cut some of its services. In the long term the BBC hoped, under its new charter, to get at least 10–20% of its budget from pay cable and satellites and from video cassettes and discs.

The U.K. got its first real taste of pay television (or subscription TV) in the fall when the two-year cable experiments approved by Home Secretary William Whitelaw made their first transmissions. Five companies were authorized to provide pay-television services in 11 areas. The services consisted exclusively of feature films; according to Home

Office rules the films had to be at least one year old, and all "X"-certificate films (unsuitable for the young) had to be shown after 10 PM. All the cable companies expected to lose money during the two-year experiment, but they hoped for profits in the long-term future.

In France a committee on broadcasting appointed by the new Socialist government reported to the ministers of culture and of communications. It proposed, as expected, a radical reform of the national structure of broadcasting set up by former president Valéry Giscard d'Estaing in 1974. The committee, chaired by Pierre Moinot, recommended three new controlling bodies: an interministerial committee chaired by the premier; a council of nine members nominated by the president and several senior state bodies; and a Conseil National de la Radiotélévision consisting of about 60 members drawn from the political parties, labour unions, consumer groups, cultural organizations, etc.

In Italy the onward march of private television and radio was checked by a Constitutional Court ruling that Radiotelevisione Italiana (RAI), the public broadcasting organization, had an absolute monopoly of national broadcasting and that the private stations could not form networks on a national or even a regional basis. The court was responding to an injunction brought by RAI against Rizzoli's Channel Europe.

In Australia the Dix Committee on the Australian Broadcasting Commission, reporting to the federal Parliament in June, recommended major changes in the ABC's structure and aims. The existing commission and general manager would be replaced by a seven-member National Broadcasting Organization functioning as a board of directors and headed by a director general. There would also be a National Broadcasting Consultative Council with about 20 members representing different sectors of Australian society.

Programming. For the second year in a row the start of the new prime-time season in the U.S. was

Hundreds of top figures in the entertainment industry joined a strike by the Writers Guild of America against major television producers and the networks in June. (Left to right) Richard Brooks, Bo Goldman, Gore Vidal, and Billy Wilder took part in the 13-week strike.

delayed by a strike. The Writers Guild of America, like the actors' unions in 1980, was on strike against the networks and major producers during the summer while formulas governing payments for future use of programs in the so-called new technologies were developed. The 13-week work stoppage delayed the new prime-time season from its usual mid-September premiere. Instead, the networks introduced new programs as they became available, some starting as early as October 5 but others beginning as late as January 1982.

In preparing for the new season, the networks canceled almost two dozen series that had failed to maintain consistently high ratings and announced plans to bring in 24 to replace them. A distinguishing feature of the new shows was a reduced focus on sex. Some said that this resulted from a threatened boycott by the Coalition for Better Television in protest against sex, violence, and profanity on TV. Others, including the networks, said that television was merely responding, as it always did, to shifts in the public mood. In any case, so-called jiggle programming lost some of its most often criticized but highly popular representatives in the cancellation of such shows as "Charlie's Angels" and "Vega$." Violent programs, however, remained numerous, with law and order the dominant theme of several new entries, including "Today's FBI," "Strike Force," and "Code Red."

CBS, first in the prime-time ratings during the 1980–81 season, brought in a situation comedy called "Mr. Merlin," a one-hour Walt Disney anthology, and four new one-hour dramas. The latter included "Simon & Simon," about a pair of private detectives; "Shannon," about a plainclothes detective; "Jessica Novak," about a young TV news reporter; and "Falcon Crest," about a contemporary family of wine growers embroiled in power struggles and beset by mysterious secrets. ABC, second to CBS in the 1980–81 prime-time ratings, called up the "Code Red," "The Fall Guy," "Today's FBI," and "Strike Force" adventure series; "King's Crossing," a family drama; "Open All Night," a comedy centring on the operator of a 24-hour food market; "Maggie," a comedy about a harried housewife; and "Best of the West," a comedy set in the

old West. NBC's new entries relied in many cases upon long-established stars, including Mickey Rooney, Tony Randall, James Garner, and James Arness, who had starred as Matt Dillon in the "Gunsmoke" series during its 20-year run. Other new NBC series were "Father Murphy," a drama spun off from the highly popular "Little House on the Prairie" series; "Lewis and Clark," about a New Yorker running a country-music club in Texas; "Gimme a Break," about a housekeeper for a widowed police captain and his children; "Chicago Story," a drama; and "The Powers of Matthew Star," about a 16-year-old boy possessing seemingly magical powers.

Even before the new season opened, there were signs that the old program mortality rule—that two out of three new series fail to survive into a second season—would again prove valid. NBC announced in August that "One of the Boys" and "Chicago Story" were being removed from the schedule and reserved for later use, being replaced by "The Nashville Palace," a country-music show that itself was canceled in November, and "Cassie & Co.," which would not start until early 1982. ABC deferred the opening of "King's Crossing" until midseason, replacing it with "Darkroom," a terror-suspense drama.

Networks and stations continued to tone down programming for children. New informational segments were introduced into Saturday- and Sunday-morning schedules, and efforts to curtail violence and minimize racial and sexual stereotypes were continued. In weekday programming, game shows and soap operas remained dominant.

In the 33rd annual Emmy awards, the Academy of Television Arts and Sciences chose the critically acclaimed but low-rated "Hill Street Blues" as the year's outstanding drama series. The series and the artists associated with it received a total of eight Emmys, the most ever awarded to a regular weekly show. "Taxi" was named the outstanding comedy series for the third year in a row and also picked up Emmys in five other categories. "Playing for Time," a high-rated 1980 drama that had become controversial because its lead actress, Vanessa Redgrave, an outspoken Palestine Liberation Or-

"Hill Street Blues" won a record eight Emmy awards in 1981, including one for star Daniel J. Travanti (right).

NBC PHOTO

ganization supporter, was cast as a Jewish inmate in a Nazi death camp, was named the best drama special of the year, and Redgrave won the Emmy for best lead actress in a limited series or special. Shown in 1980, "Shogun," a 12-hour dramatization of the James Clavell novel of feudal Japan, had been one of the highest rated programs in television history, and it was chosen as the year's outstanding limited series. "Life Is a Circus, Charlie Brown" was named the outstanding animated program, and "Donahue and Kids," featuring Phil Donahue, won the award for outstanding children's program. "Live from Studio 8H: An Evening of Jerome Robbins' Ballets with Members of the New York City Ballet" was designated the outstanding classical program in the performing arts.

Emmys for lead actor and actress in a drama series went to Daniel J. Travanti and Barbara Babcock, both of "Hill Street Blues," and for lead actor and actress in a comedy series to Judd Hirsch of "Taxi" and Isabel Sanford of "The Jeffersons." "Lily: Sold Out," starring Lily Tomlin, was named the outstanding variety, music, or comedy program. Supporting actor and actress Emmys went to Danny De Vito of "Taxi" and Eileen Brennan of "Private Benjamin" in the comedy, variety, or music series category; to Michael Conrad of "Hill Street Blues" and Nancy Marchand of "Lou Grant" for drama series; and to David Warner of "Masada" and Jane Alexander of "Playing for Time" for limited series or special.

In international competition, Emmys were presented by the International Council of the National Academy of Television Arts and Sciences to "A Town Like Alice" (by Mariner Films/Channel 7 Australia) in the drama category; "Chartres Pour L'Enfer" (France's TF1) for documentaries; "Sweeney Todd: Scenes from the Making of a Musical" (London Weekend Television) for performing arts; and "Vinicius Para Criancas/Arco de Noe" (Brazil's TV Globo) for popular arts.

Sports remained among the most popular and expensive forms of programming. Professional and college football and major league baseball were again the biggest drawing cards, but basketball, tennis, golf, and, to a lesser extent, ice hockey and soccer also attracted partisan audiences. *Broadcasting* estimated that TV and radio networks and stations paid $210,158,410 for broadcast rights to professional and college football games, about 1.4% more than in 1980, and $89,975,000 for major league baseball games, some 12% more than the year before. However, the schedules of many stations were disrupted by the major league players' strike that eliminated much of the season.

Music and news remained the basic format in radio, and both elements gained impetus from a variety of new radio network services launched during the year. A *Broadcasting* survey of the ten highest rated stations in each of the top 50 markets found that 30.9% of the stations specialized in contemporary, or currently popular, music; 11.7% played "beautiful music"; 11.5%, album-oriented rock music; 9.7%, country music; and 9.5%, so-called middle-of-the-road music. News or news and talk was featured by 9.7% of the stations.

PBS officials believed that they had "crossed a

Tony Randall and Kaleena Kiff starred in the TV series "Love, Sidney."

major threshold" when ratings indicated in 1981 that more than half of all U.S. homes, representing some 75 million persons, watched public television at least once a week. The average PBS prime-time program had a rating of about 2, though some specials scored as high as 16. Major new program plans included a nationwide service "for adults who want to continue their education after finishing high school," involving more than 100 PBS stations and an estimated 500 universities and colleges.

The most widely watched television program of 1981 was undoubtedly the wedding of the prince of Wales and Lady Diana Spencer on July 29. In the U.K. it was watched by 39 million people, and 74 other countries took a live feed to bring the worldwide audience up to 750 million people (BBC figures). The BBC, which supplied sound and picture to most overseas broadcasters, used 60 cameras, and ITV used 40. Independent crews fielded about 20.

Two programs became famous for not being seen at all. The 1981 Dimbleby Lecture, the BBC's most prestigious program of its kind, was finally scrapped by the BBC after a public row over the man who had been invited to give it. E. P. Thompson, a noted historian who had become best known for his support of the European Campaign for Nuclear Disarmament, was invited to speak by the program producer only to have the invitation denied by senior officials. The BBC's reputation suffered among both its friends and its critics.

The same sort of confusion was evident when the BBC decided not to transmit its coverage of a boxing match between Alan Minter and Tony Sibson on the grounds that Minter's trunks bore the name of a sponsor, Daf Trucks. It was widely considered that the BBC was being arbitrary in its rejection of Minter's modest advertising since it

was accepting much more blatant advertising from the sponsors of other sports.

These were only two of a number of editorial judgments by both BBC and ITV that were labeled censorship. In February the BBC's director general intervened at the last moment in two "Panorama" programs about the British security services. He insisted on several cuts, allegedly under government pressure. In June the IBA asked Granada's "World in Action" to make a 27-second cut in "The Propaganda War," about Northern Ireland. After some discussion, Granada decided to withdraw the film altogether rather than implicitly recognize the IBA's claim to act as editor.

As in previous years, the outstanding British drama series were mostly adaptations of novels and biographies. One of the most memorable, and certainly the most publicized, was John Mortimer's adaptation for ITV of Evelyn Waugh's *Brideshead Revisited* (Granada). This lavish £4.5 million, 11-part series was produced with an extremely detailed, loyal adherence to Waugh's 1945 story of a young man's involvement with an aristocratic old Roman Catholic family. It starred Jeremy Irons, Anthony Andrews, and Diana Quick, as well as Laurence Olivier, Claire Bloom, Stephane Audran, John Gielgud, and Mona Washbourne. The result was a series of considerable beauty and style.

The BBC competed with "The Borgias," which started the same week, and "Tenko." "The Borgias" was a swashbuckling account of the Borgia family's villainous control of the papacy at the end of the 15th century. Described as "papal bull" by one critic, it started with a scene of a naked blonde in the pope's bed and maintained these irresistible attractions over ten episodes. "Tenko" was very different: an account of a group of women who had been trapped in Singapore during World War II and captured by the Japanese. Their story was quietly told but attracted a considerable audience.

Other notable series based on novels were Trevor Griffiths's adaptation of D. H. Lawrence's *Sons and Lovers* (BBC) and Christopher Hampton's of Malcolm Bradbury's *The History Man* (BBC). Several stage plays were also adapted, including Ibsen's *Hedda Gabler* (BBC) by John Osborne (with Diana Rigg as a marvelous Hedda), Arthur Miller's *The Crucible* (BBC), and Chekhov's *The Cherry Orchard* (BBC) in an outstanding new interpretation by Trevor Griffiths.

In France the election of a Socialist president and Parliament created tremendous expectations of reform. Both television and radio immediately became more open and outspoken; the direct telephone line between the Élysée Palace (home of the president) and the newsrooms was disconnected. Numerous organizations, from *Le Monde* to a group headed by the mayor of Paris, started to broadcast local radio programs, which were illegal, in the hope of new legislation. Perhaps the most dramatic event was the transmission of Marcel Ophüls's film *Le Chagrin et le Pitié* (*The Sorrow and the Pity*), about French collaboration with Nazis during the war; it had never before been televised in the ten years since it had been made.

In West Germany the series "Death of a Student," telling of the attempt of a boy to overcome his feelings of rejection and of his suicide by jumping in front of a train, was widely blamed for encouraging at least four students to kill themselves and for not offering any "solutions" to similar circumstances that result in 800 young West Germans killing themselves each year.

In Poland the consolidation of Solidarity, the independent labour union, as a national force led to some changes in television and radio services. Several sessions of the Sejm (parliament) were broadcast live without breaks. Local stations spent more time on local issues, and local programs were lengthened; but the two national television services cut back on imported Western programs and thus on overall broadcasting time.

In Australia the increasing concern over television violence led the Senate Standing Committee on Education and the Arts to propose a public inquiry and government guidelines. It also recommended a total ban on weekday early morning television during the school year and a ban on advertisements during programs designed for preschool children. One of the hits of the year was "A Town Like Alice" (Seven Network), based on Neville Shute's novel set in World War II. The large cast, headed by Helen Morse, Bryan Brown, and Gordon Jackson, performed excellently under David Steven's direction.

The year's Prix Italia was marred by dissension among the drama jurors. Most abstained from the final voting, and when "Jackpot" (Swedish Broadcasting), a gentle story of the black market, was announced as the winner, the British delegation walked out. The other winners were more convincing. The documentary prize was won by "The Day After Trinity" (PBS), a perceptive, humane account of the invention of the atomic bomb. The music prize was won by "At the Haunted End of the Day" (London Weekend Television), Tony Palmer's review of composer Sir William Walton; it was the LWT team's second prize in as many years.　　　　(RUFUS W. CRATER; JOHN HOWKINS;
SOL J. TAISHOFF)

Amateur Radio. The number of amateur radio operators continued to increase in 1981. The American Radio Relay League, the leading organization of amateur ("ham") radio operators, estimated that there were 403,680 licensed operators in the U.S. on Sept. 30, 1981, an increase of about 6% in 12 months. Throughout the world, licensed amateur radio operators numbered more than 1.2 million, with Japan's 400,000-plus representing the largest national concentration in the world.

Ham operators provided vital services when normal communications links were down. Networks of amateur radio operators, for instance, continued for several months to provide information on the fates of victims of the earthquakes that struck northern Africa and Italy in November 1980. A ham operator also picked up word of the release of the U.S. hostages by Iran in January before the official announcement.

　　　　(RUFUS W. CRATER; SOL J. TAISHOFF)

See also Industrial Review: *Advertising;* and *Telecommunications;* Motion Pictures; Music.
[613.D.4.6; 735.I.4–5]

REVOLUTION ON THE SMALL SCREEN

by David Lachenbruch

For the 34 years from 1947 to 1980 it simply was called television or, more affectionately, TV—a squarish box with a screen that obediently relayed to viewers everything the networks and program syndicators prescribed, and that was about all. When nothing was worth watching, the eye of Cyclops stared out lifeless and gray.

Although it really was a gradual process, in 1981 the television set seemed suddenly to have kicked off the traces and effected an abrupt and revolutionary transition from a single-purpose machine to a universal motion-sound-and-colour display system of almost limitless potential, destined to become a true home visual-communications centre and window on the world. In fact, its transformation is so all-encompassing that it is even getting a new name: the home video terminal. Its original function, to fish programs out of the air, is now but one of its many uses.

What Else Is On? The most successful nonbroadcast source of video has been cable TV, tracing its roots to early community antenna systems that piped broadcast signals through wire to poor reception areas. Today, cable systems carry both network and nonnetwork programs from a wide variety of sources, often offering 30 channels or more; newer systems can provide literally hundreds of channels.

Nearly 22 million U.S. homes, or more than 27% of the country's TV-equipped households, received video from the cable as of mid-1981, and the number was growing. Almost half also subscribed to pay cable, which provides special programming—so far mostly recent movies—for an extra fee, either on a monthly basis or for a specific charge per program.

Among all countries Canada had the highest density of cable TV penetration; in the fall of 1981 more than 4.4 million homes were wired, or approximately 57% of all TV-equipped households. Cable was attracting heavy attention in Europe, but because

---

David Lachenbruch is editorial director of Television Digest *and a regular contributor to* TV Guide. *His books include* Videocassette Recorders: The Complete Home Guide *and* Color Television—A Look Inside.

strong government control of broadcasting tended virtually to eliminate privately owned cable systems in most countries, wired TV was still in its infancy there. In 1981 Japan was experimenting with various forms of cable, particularly in the so-called new towns, but had few systems in regular operation.

The abrupt change from scarcity to abundance of channels has given rise to many new cable "networks" and program services, including all-news channels, music channels, channels of programs catering to women, all-sports services, and cultural networks. In the U.S. these services, as well as the pay cable networks, are distributed nationally by space satellite.

Available to viewers currently beyond the reach of cable who wish to see recent movies, premium sports events, and other special programming is a new broadcast service called subscription TV. This system requires the user to lease a TV-attached electronic converter in the home to decipher a scrambled signal that is unintelligible to nonsubscribers.

Videotapes to Vegetables. A rapidly growing phenomenon of the new video age is the home video recorder. Although sales started slowly in 1975, they rapidly picked up steam, and by the end of 1981 considerably more than three million recorders were in place in American homes. This versatile machine can record and store programs from the air or from cable TV for later viewing. It also can play purchased or rented prerecorded tape cassettes or, in portable form with an accessory colour camera, make instant electronic home movies for playback through a TV set or video terminal.

The ease with which video recorders can tape TV programs sent over the air or by cable raises new copyright problems. In October 1981 a U.S. court of appeals, reversing a lower court decision, ruled that such home taping constitutes copyright infringement. As the year ended the decision was being appealed, and recorder makers were seeking legislation in Congress to give home videotaping the same exempt status as home audio recording.

Perhaps the first major product to be rendered obsolete by the video recorder is the home movie system. The mere threat of electronic home movies has already caused a slump in sales of 8-mm film equipment. Although a portable recorder and camera are far bulkier than an 8-mm camera, several electronics manufacturers have demonstrated prototypes of camera-recorder combinations that are quite compact. These are expected to be on the market within the next few years.

Still in its infancy is the video-disc system, which plays see-and-hear records through the family TV set in much the same way as a phonograph plays audio discs. Two systems were on the market in

1981, with a third scheduled for 1982. Unfortunately, discs designed for one system will not work on players designed for either of the others.

Another popular add-on is the home video game, a device of continually increasing sophistication that can duplicate many of the exciting effects of arcade games or plunge the viewer into more intellectual pursuits like chess and backgammon. Close to five million of these devices were in use in the United States by the end of 1981.

Waiting in the wings is the home computer, the grown-up offspring of the video game. Although most purchasers of home computers today buy for either hobby or small-business purposes, the computer is destined to occupy a major place in the average American home of the near future as a part of the home video terminal. Its potential uses are almost infinite—from such simple tasks as keeping track of the family finances and working out diets and recipes to controlling the energy efficiency of all the appliances in a household. Computers can be linked via telephone or cable TV lines, thereby extending their capabilities tremendously.

A number of computer-dependent services to feed programming to the home video terminal are in their beginnings or being tested. These include videotex, a generic name for various systems that let the home viewer call up written and graphic material on the screen on demand; security protection for homes via cable TV; two-way cable systems that let viewers express opinions or order merchandise and services; and even home electronic mail.

Videotex, already in regular operation in the U.K., West Germany, and other European countries and undergoing testing in the U.S., covers two major new services that promise to increase vastly the utility of the home video terminal. The more common form is expected to be teletext, which can provide a variety of information—airline schedules, sports results, stock prices, theatre and concert schedules, school-closing information, traffic conditions, and more—at the push of a button. The other variation of videotex is viewdata, a two-way system with access to millions of items of information from computers throughout the world for a fee. The price of green peppers at the local supermarket, the value of tin production in Bolivia in 1860, or the relative efficiencies of various home insulating materials all can be answered on request.

Home electronics manufacturers are beginning to respond to the demands of the transition from television to video. All major TV set makers now are offering high-quality projection sets with screens averaging a metre and a half (four to six feet) in diagonal measurement for viewing movies and sports in life-sized dimensions.

Another step now in progress is the development of a new form for the TV set itself: "component" or "modular" video. This involves the separation of the video system into individual components, as are the more sophisticated stereo sound systems. The basic building block is the screen unit, or monitor, using either a giant-screen projector or a conventional tube, to which may be attached various input devices such as a broadcast TV tuner, cable TV input, video recorder, disc player, computer, or even a satellite receiver. For high-quality sound, a separate audio amplifier can be used.

Changing More than Channels. All of these radical changes in home entertainment and communication are bound to have far-reaching effects, many of which can only be guessed today. Despite assurances to the contrary, "free" network television, although remaining for the foreseeable future the true "mass market" medium, can be expected to change as pay cable and subscription TV gain the capacity to outbid it for important entertainment events.

In the longer term the video revolution is expected to influence life-styles profoundly. Whole new industries will be spawned, and existing ones that fail to adapt will disappear. Although the home movie industry may have been the first to feel it, this revolution eventually will change the nature of many far larger businesses. Publishing, for example, will be strongly affected. Videotex may well be the primary means for distributing newspapers in the future. Magazines and reference books may become widely available in see-and-hear format on videodisc, which can intermix still pictures, text, motion, and sound. As the home video terminal takes on more aspects of the communicating computer, it will substitute increasingly for actual human presence; banking, visits to libraries, shopping, and even education and office work one day may become at-home activities.

As more and more homes are connected to centralized computers by cable, it is only natural that "Big Brother" aspects should cause increasing concern. Unauthorized intrusion is a chilling spectre of the video-computer age, and this problem undoubtedly will require new privacy laws. Such problems have been met before and are difficult, but presumably they are not insurmountable.

In a few years much of the world will be bidding farewell to the "idiot box" that sat so stoically in the corner. The video age has arrived, and the new home terminal is coming under increasing control of the viewer-participant, promising an almost limitless choice of entertainment, information, and education, along with new forms of communication and possibly a cultural revolution. Perhaps it should be called the "genius box."

Tennis

Growth in tennis continued in 1981 with increased spectator attendance at the leading events, with the maintenance of high earnings by the leading players, and with undiminished commercial sponsorship. A problem arose, however, in administration. World Championship Tennis (WCT), a Dallas-based commercial organization, canceled its agreement with the Men's International Professional Tennis Council (MIPTC) and arranged its 1982 circuit of men's tournaments independently of the Grand Prix.

For the first time in the history of the game the racket was defined. At its annual general meeting in July 1981 the International Tennis Federation ruled that the hitting surface of the racket must consist of strings alternately interlaced or bonded where they cross and that the frame, including the handle, should not be longer than 32 in (81.3 cm) or the strung surface exceed 15½ × 11½ in (39.4 × 29.2 cm). The rule also decreed that there be no attached objects or protrusions and no devices making change of shape possible. The innovation followed a temporary ban on double-strung rackets two years earlier, the introduction of which was believed to threaten to change the character of tennis. The ball had been a subject of the rules from the earliest days.

The Davis Cup, the international men's national team championship, was sponsored commercially for the first time. A Japanese electronics corporation gave prize money in excess of $1 million. The winning nation received $200,000 and the runner-up $100,000. The least successful nations received $1,000.

Problems of bad court behaviour occupied administrators and held public interest. John McEnroe (U.S.) aroused widespread controversy during the Wimbledon tournament when his abrasive complaints about line decisions and the efficiency of officials were heard and seen around the world on television. In accordance with the disciplinary code of the Grand Prix, the Wimbledon Management Committee fined McEnroe three sums of $750 and asked the MIPTC to penalize him $10,000 for "aggravated behaviour." The MIPTC responded with a reduced fine of $5,000. Another result of McEnroe's actions was the refusal of the All England Club, joint administrators of the Wimbledon championships with the British Lawn Tennis Association, to elect him an honorary club member after his championship success, a distinction normally bestowed as a matter of course.

Men's Competition. The keynote of the year in men's tennis was the rivalry between McEnroe and Björn Borg (Sweden). McEnroe reversed their former positions and emerged as clearly the better of the two players.

At the beginning of the year the leading contender for the Australian championships in Melbourne was Guillermo Vilas (Arg.). He lost in the semifinal, while Ivan Lendl (Czech.), the most improved player of 1980, lost in the second round. Brian Teacher (U.S.) won the title.

The enfant terrible of tennis, John McEnroe, captured the men's singles championship at Wimbledon in June.

At Madison Square Garden, New York City, in January the Volvo Grand Prix Masters' Tournament brought Borg, McEnroe, and Lendl into the same field, along with five other qualifiers. Borg beat McEnroe 6–4, 6–7, 7–6 in a round-robin match, and McEnroe did not qualify for the final stages. Borg then defeated Jimmy Connors (U.S.) 6–4, 6–7, 6–4 in the semifinal and Lendl in the final 6–4, 6–2, 6–2.

Subsequently, Borg played fewer tournaments than in former years. McEnroe easily won the WCT finals in Dallas, Texas. José-Luis Clerc (Arg.) won the Italian championship in Rome. In the semifinal he beat Lendl 3–6, 7–5, 6–0, 6–2 and then went on to defeat Victor Pecci (Paraguay) 6–3, 6–4, 6–0 in the final.

Borg won the French championship in Paris for the fourth time in four years and for the sixth time in all, an unprecedented achievement on both counts. Lendl beat McEnroe 6–4, 6–4, 7–5 in the quarterfinals. In the semifinals Lendl beat Clerc 3–6, 6–4, 4–6, 7–6, 6–2, and Borg beat Pecci 6–4, 6–4, 7–5. Borg's victory in the final against Lendl was by 6–1, 4–6, 6–2, 3–6, 6–1.

In the Wimbledon championships Borg won five rounds without the loss of a set and then recovered to win a semifinal against Connors 0–6, 4–6, 6–3, 6–0, 6–4. McEnroe, though twice taken to four sets, reached the final without danger. His opening match against Tom Gullikson (U.S.) was the first that caused acrimony between him and the officials. The Borg v. McEnroe final did not reach the exceptional standard of the 1980 final between the same men. It was won by McEnroe 4–6, 7–6, 7–6, 6–4. This was Borg's first defeat at Wimbledon since 1975; he had won 41 singles matches and 5 championships in a row, a record never previously equaled.

McEnroe carried his brilliant left-handed invin-

The tennis Federation Cup was won by the U.S. team in Tokyo in November. The happy victors (left to right) are Kathy Jordan, Andrea Jaeger, Chris Evert Lloyd, and Rosie Casals.

cibility to the U.S. Open championships at Flushing Meadow in New York City. In the semifinals he won a tough match against a fellow New Yorker, Vitas Gerulaitis, 5–7, 6–3, 6–2, 4–6, 6–3. Borg beat Connors in the other semifinal 6–2, 7–5, 6–4. In the final McEnroe beat Borg 4–6, 6–2, 6–4, 6–3 to win the title for the third successive year, a feat never performed at the U.S. Open by a man and last achieved by W. T. Tilden (U.S.), when the title was the U.S. National championships, with six successive wins from 1920 to 1925. The 1981 competition was the centennial tournament for the U.S., the first having been held at Newport, R.I., in 1881.

In men's doubles McEnroe and Peter Fleming (U.S.) were the best pair, winning both the Wimbledon and U.S. Open championships. On a slower shale surface Heinz Gunthardt (Switz.) and Balazs Taroczy (Hungary) won the French championship and the German title as well.

The Nations Cup, a team competition organized by the Association of Tennis Professionals, was held at Düsseldorf, West Germany. Czechoslovakia (Lendl and Tomas Smid) beat Australia (Peter McNamara and Paul McNamee) 2–1 in the final.

Under its new format, the Davis Cup tournament was staged for the 70th time. In the zonal competitions, India, Chile, the U.S.S.R., and Spain won the Eastern, American, and European B and A zones, respectively, to qualify for the main event in 1982. Of the four top-seeded nations, Italy lost to Great Britain in the first round, played indoors at Brighton, England. In the second round Argentina beat Romania 3–2 in Romania; Great Britain defeated New Zealand 4–1 on an indoor court at Christchurch; Australia beat Sweden 3–1 in Bästad; and the U.S. triumphed over Czechoslovakia 4–1 at Flushing Meadow.

Argentina and the U.S. qualified for the final. The former did so for the first time with an overwhelming 5–0 defeat of Great Britain in Buenos Aires. Neither José-Luis Clerc nor Guillermo Vilas lost a set. The U.S. defeated Australia in Portland,

Ore., 5–0 to make its 52nd appearance in the title contest. In the finals, which were played indoors at Cincinnati, Ohio, McEnroe defeated Vilas, and Clerc beat Roscoe Tanner in the opening round of singles. McEnroe and Fleming won the doubles in five sets from Vilas and Clerc, and McEnroe clinched the title for the U.S. by beating Clerc in five sets.

Women's Competition. The top honours in women's tennis were well dispersed. At the Australian championships, held in Melbourne, Hana Mandlikova (Czech.) beat Wendy Turnbull (Australia) 6–0, 7–5 in the final. Turnbull had defeated Martina Navratilova, the favourite, in the semifinal 6–4, 7–5. Navratilova in 1981 changed her citizenship from Czechoslovak to U.S. by naturalization.

Tracy Austin (U.S.), one of eight qualifiers, won the Colgate Series championship, the climax of the 1980 International Series, at Landover, Md., in January. In the final she beat 15-year-old Andrea Jaeger (U.S.) 6–2, 6–2.

Navratilova reasserted herself during the Avon Circuit, the indoor series. In the final of the concluding tournament in March at Madison Square Garden, she beat Jaeger 6–3, 7–6. Chris Evert Lloyd (U.S.) revived her hard-court skills in the Italian championships at Perugia. In the final she defeated Virginia Ruzici (Romania) 6–1, 6–2.

Mandlikova won the French title in Paris. Sylvia Hanika (West Germany) beat Navratilova in the quarterfinals. In the semifinals Mandlikova defeated Evert Lloyd 7–5, 6–4, and Hanika beat Jaeger 4–6, 6–1, 6–4. Mandlikova's final win against Hanika was 6–2, 6–4.

Evert Lloyd won the Wimbledon title for the third time. Pam Shriver (U.S.) beat Austin in the quarterfinals 7–5, 6–4. Mandlikova defeated Navratilova 7–5, 4–6, 6–1, and Evert Lloyd triumphed over Shriver 6–3, 6–1 in the semifinals. Evert Lloyd won the final against Mandlikova 6–2, 6–2 to become champion without the loss of a set, the easiest win since 1967.

Austin reached the final of the U.S. Open championships at Flushing Meadow without losing a set. Evert Lloyd won a quarterfinal against Mandlikova 6–1, 6–3 but then lost to Navratilova in the semifinals 7–5, 4–6, 6–4. In the final Austin beat Navratilova 1–6, 7–6, 7–6 to regain the title she had won in 1979.

In doubles Navratilova won the Australian title with Betsey Negelsen (U.S.) and Wimbledon with Shriver. On the slower shale courts Ros Fairbank and Tanya Harford (South Africa) won the French and German championships. Kathy Jordan and Anne Smith (U.S.) reasserted their form of 1980 and won the U.S. Open title.

The Wightman Cup was staged indoors in Chicago in July. The U.S. (Austin, Evert Lloyd, Jaeger, Shriver, Rosemary Casals) beat Great Britain (Virginia Wade, Sue Barker, Anne Hobbs, Glynis Coles, Jo Durie) 7–0 and lost no sets. It was Wade's 17th successive Wightman contest.

The Federation Cup tournament took place in Tokyo in November. The U.S. (Evert Lloyd, Jaeger, Jordan, and Casals) won for the sixth year in succession and for the tenth time in all. As in the previous two years, the U.S. women lost neither a singles nor a doubles match in any round. In the semifinals the U.S. beat Switzerland, and Great Britain defeated Australia. For Britain Wade uniquely participated for the 15th successive year and played her 95th match.   (LANCE TINGAY)

Thailand

A constitutional monarchy of Southeast Asia, Thailand is bordered by Burma, Laos, Kampuchea (Cambodia), Malaysia, the Andaman Sea, and the Gulf of Thailand. Area: 542,373 sq km (209,411 sq mi). Pop. (1980 est.): 46,455,000. Cap. and largest city: Bangkok (pop., 1980 est., 4,999,500). Language: Thai. Religion (1970): Buddhist 95.3%; Muslim 3.8%. King, Bhumibol Adulyadej; prime minister in 1981, Gen. Prem Tinsulanond.

The year 1981 was a turbulent one for Thailand. An abortive military coup tarnished the image of the Army, and serious economic problems led to devaluation of the national currency, previously considered one of the stablest in the world. If Prime Minister Prem Tinsulanond remained in office, it was because his personal reputation for incorruptibility remained unsullied and he continued to enjoy the full backing of King Bhumibol.

Ironically, the abortive coup was sparked by a corruption scandal. In February information was leaked indicating that large-scale payoffs were involved in a deal to obtain 60,000 bbl of oil a day from Saudi Arabia. This led to the resignation of the deputy industry minister, Visit Tansacha. During the parliamentary furor over the case, Prem came under attack for "weakness" in dealing with the problem. Bickering among the parties constituting Prem's coalition came to a head in March, when the Democratic Party pulled out of the government en masse. Deputy Prime Minister Thanat Khoman led the walkout, along with two deputy interior ministers and a deputy minister of education.

The uncertainties that followed were apparently seen by some sections of the Army as a call to action. Some so-called Young Turks had already been angered by Prem's decision in October 1980 to amend the law and extend his term as commander in chief beyond the mandatory retirement age of 60. According to Army sources, these officers began plotting a coup as soon as they heard of Prem's plans. Chief among them were three colonels who, needing a prestigious senior leader to head the coup, first asked Prem himself. On his refusal, they found a leader in Deputy Army Chief Gen. Sant Chitpatima. On April 1 they took control of some government buildings under the name of the Revolutionary Council.

The coup never gained momentum. Prem received widespread popular sympathy when he went to the palace, was received in a long audience by the royal family, and, the next morning, helicoptered with the king and queen to Korat in the northeast, his stronghold when he was a field commander. The following day, Prem sent several thousand troops into Bangkok, closed the airport, and seized radio and television stations. There was almost no resistance, although one soldier and one civilian were killed in an isolated shootout. Thailand's 14th coup since the establishment of constitutional rule in 1932 ended 56 hours after it started. Prem dismissed Sant and 11 commanders, and

Thailand

THAILAND

Education. (1978–79) Primary, pupils 6,848,121, teachers 283,204; secondary, pupils 1,503,646, teachers 66,965; vocational, pupils 221,411, teachers 28,894; teacher training, students 22,866, teachers 6,040; higher, students 169,639, teaching staff 29,667.

Finance. Monetary unit: baht, with (Sept. 21, 1981) a free rate of 22.76 baht to U.S. $1 (42.20 baht = £1 sterling). Gold and other reserves (June 1981) U.S. $1,522,000,000. Budget (1980 actual): revenue 95,294,000,000 baht; expenditure 121,204,000,000 baht. Gross national product (1980) 659,330,000,000 baht. Money supply (Feb. 1981) 73.3 billion baht. Cost of living (1975 = 100; June 1981) 180.

Foreign Trade. (1980) Imports 188,686,000,000 baht; exports 133,197,000,000 baht. Import sources (1979): Japan 26%; U.S. 16%; Saudi Arabia 6%; West Germany 5%; Singapore 5%. Export destinations (1979): Japan 21%; The Netherlands 11%; U.S. 11%; Singapore 9%; Hong Kong 5%. Main exports: rice 15%; tapioca 11%; rubber 9%; tin 9%; corn 5%. Tourism (1979): visitors 1,591,000; gross receipts U.S. $550 million.

Transport and Communications. Roads (1980) 67,660 km. Motor vehicles in use (1980): passenger 397,900; commercial c. 451,900. Railways: (1980) c. 3,765 km; traffic (1979) 7,030,000,000 passenger-km, freight 2,740,000,000 net ton-km. Air traffic (1980): c. 6,276,000,000 passenger-km; freight c. 247.2 million net ton-km. Shipping (1980): merchant vessels 100 gross tons and over 153; gross tonnage 391,456. Telephones (Sept. 1979) 451,400. Radio receivers (Dec. 1979) 5.9 million. Television receivers (Dec. 1979) 1 million.

Agriculture. Production (in 000; metric tons; 1980): rice c. 18,000; corn c. 3,150; sweet potatoes (1979) c. 350; sorghum c. 350; cassava (1979) c. 12,500; dry beans c. 275; soybeans c. 105; peanuts c. 130; sugar, raw value c. 1,086; pineapples c. 1,500; bananas c. 2,164; tobacco c. 86; rubber c. 510; cotton, lint c. 49; jute and kenaf c. 251; meat c. 627; fish catch (1979) 1,716; timber (cu m; 1979) 37,421. Livestock (in 000; 1980): cattle c. 5,000; buffalo c. 6,250; pigs c. 5,547; chickens c. 70,000.

Industry. Production (in 000; metric tons; 1980): cement c. 5,350; lignite 1,426; petroleum products (1978) c. 7,980; tin concentrates (metal content) 46; lead concentrates 25; manganese ore (metal content; 1979) 8; sulfuric acid (1979) 48; electricity (kw-hr; 1979) 14,067,000.

Sant fled to Burma. A mood of reconciliation followed, however, mainly because the rebels were widely seen as essentially reform-minded. A royal amnesty was granted to 52 of them in May and to the rest in June. After 80 days in Burma, Sant returned home to a warm welcome.

The political atmosphere heated up again in August, when former prime minister Kriangsak Chamanand began what was considered a bid to win back his lost office by contesting a by-election in Roi-et, the northeastern provincial capital. Another former prime minister, Kukrit Pramoj, plunged into the fray in support of Boonlert Lertpricha, candidate of Kukrit's own Social Action Party. Following an acrimonious campaign, Kriangsak won by a landslide, but he made no significant move afterward to propel himself to power.

Global recession, high U.S. interest rates, and higher agricultural yields in other countries played havoc with Thailand's balance of trade in the first half of the year. Commerce Minister Chuan Leekpai estimated the deficit at 34 billion baht ($1.7 billion). In July the government broke with monetary history by devaluing the baht by 8.7% against the dollar. This was in addition to a 1% devaluation announced in May.

(T. J. S. GEORGE)

Theatre

Paul Channon, succeeding Norman St. John Stevas as Britain's arts minister, persuaded the Treasury to give earlier notice to the Arts Council of the government grant earmarked for all the arts. The 1980–81 grant of £80 million was to be raised to £86 million for 1981–82, an increase of 7.5%, or a drop of 2% in real terms. Closings included the Old Vic and the Open Space. The National Theatre (NT) earned approximately £4.5 million against a subsidy of £6 million, while the Royal Shakespeare Company (RSC) showed a negligible loss on costs of just over £6.5 million and attained a record income of £1.2 million from paying patrons. The RSC complained, yet again, that the Arts Council promise of £2.5 million for 1981–82 was inadequate when compared with £5.5 million to the NT.

Two of the year's major developments were the unveiling of the Barbican Centre in the City of London, to which the RSC would move in March 1982, and the successful London International Festival of Theatre (LIFT), in which ten, mostly "fringe," groups from Brazil, Britain, France, West Germany, The Netherlands, Japan, Malaysia, Peru, and Poland took part. LIFT was a small-scale successor to the World Theatre Seasons staged by the RSC and Sir Peter Daubeny during 1964–75.

Reduced subsidies affected theatres in West Germany. A broken promise to build a new theatre in Bremen provoked the resignation of Frank-Patrick Steckel, the city theatre's chief director. Hans-Peter Doll, head of the Württemberg State Theatre, refused to renew his contract beyond 1984 as a protest against cuts. In France, however, Jack Lang, cultural minister in the new government, announced an immediate boost of 20% in subsidies to all theatres, to be followed by another in 1982 of up to 75% in deserving cases.

Great Britain and Ireland. Several of the year's 25 or so new NT productions (including the West End transfers of *Early Days* and *The Crucible*, as well as a twofold transfer of *Amadeus* to London's West End and to Broadway) were given Society of West End Theatre (SWET) awards. The directing award went to Peter Wood for *On the Razzle*, adapted by Tom Stoppard from a Johann Nestroy comedy after a "try-out" at the Edinburgh Festival; those for the best actor and actress in a revival to Daniel Massey in *Man and Superman* and Margaret Tyzack in *Who's Afraid of Virginia Woolf?*; and that for the best design to Carl Toms for *The Provok'd Wife*, invited to Paris by the Comédie Française. Outstanding at the NT were *Translations* by Brian Friel (first seen at the Hampstead Theatre); Michael Bogdanov's colourful productions of *The Mayor of Zalamea* (transferred from the Cottesloe to the Olivier), *The Hypochondriac* starring Daniel Massey, and three one-woman plays by Dario Fo; Peter Gill's productions of *A Month in the Country*, *Much Ado About Nothing*, and *Don Juan* with Nigel Terry; John Dexter's of *The Shoemaker's Holiday*; and, above all, *The Oresteia*, with music by Harrison Birtwistle, planned by Peter Hall for many years and only now realized with an all-male cast of 16 playing in masks. Two oddities were Michael Rudman's staging of *Measure for Measure* in a Caribbean setting and Arnold Wesker's of his own semihistorically inspired *Caritas*, about the spiritual trials of a medieval nun.

Michael Bogdanov returned to the RSC for a boisterous version of *The Knight of the Burning Pestle*, one of 20 new productions at the Aldwych and the Warehouse that included ten transfers from Stratford. Among these were a modern-dress *Merchant of Venice* with David Suchet; *Timon of Athens* with Richard Pascoe; the tragicomic satire *The Suicide* by Nikolai Erdman; *As You Like It*, notable for Sinead Cusack's Rosalind; and *Troilus and Cressida*, in which Carol Royle made an outstanding debut. Both Cusack and Royle made their marks again, the former in *The Maid's Tragedy* and the latter opposite Michael Pennington in *Hamlet*, staged by John Barton as a play within a play. Heading the list of new plays at the Warehouse was the late C. P. Taylor's anti-Nazi *Good*, which won Joe Melia the SWET supporting actor award. At the Aldwych, Aleksandr Solzhenitsyn's flawed Soviet drama set in a gulag camp, *The Love-Girl and the Innocent*, directed by Clifford Williams with decor by Ralph Koltai, was memorable.

Two ambitious works were selected by Bernard Miles (*see* BIOGRAPHIES) to reopen the rebuilt Mermaid: *Eastward Ho!* and Mark Medoff's *Children of a Lesser God*. The latter not only received the SWET award for play of the year but also won for its two stars, the Englishman Trevor Eve and his deaf-mute U.S. partner, Elizabeth Quinn, the awards for best actor and actress of the year in a new play. At London's grant-aided theatres the increasingly long list of revivals and new works included: at the Round House, *Waiting for Godot* and *The Misan-*

thrope, from The Manchester Royal Exchange; at the Young Vic, *King Lear* and *The Winter's Tale*; at the Greenwich, *Another Country* by Julian Mitchell and *Present Laughter*, in which Gwen Watford won the SWET award as supporting actress to Donald Sinden. First works by Jim Morris and Kevin Mandry were seen at the Tricycle; by Tony Marchant at the Theatre Royal, Stratford East, where the irreverent antiestablishment spoofs *Chorus Girls* by Barry Keeffe and *A Short, Sharp Shock* by Howard Brenton aroused mild protests; by Dusty Hughes, Sarah Daniels, and Natasha Morgan at the Royal Court; and by Chris Hawes at the ICA. Transfers included *Steaming* from Stratford East, a first play by Nell Dunn, which won the SWET best comedy award; the nostalgic musical *The Mitford Girls* from Chichester; Alan Ayckbourn's musical *Suburban Strains* from Scarborough; Mike Leigh's farcical *Goose Pimples* from Hampstead; Richard Crane's *Brothers Karamazov* from Edinburgh and Brighton; Claire Luckham's *Trafford Tanzi* from Edinburgh and Birmingham; Fo's *Can't Pay? Won't Pay!* from the Half Moon; and Helene Hanff's *84 Charing Cross Road* from Salisbury.

U.S. imports included English productions of *All My Sons*, *Chapter Two*, and Mike Weller's *Loose Ends*, and several musicals, mostly with English casts: *The Sound of Music*, *They're Playing Our Song*, *Barnum*, *The Best Little Whorehouse in Texas*, and *One Mo' Time*. Michael Crawford (*Barnum*) and Carlin Glynn (*The Best Little Whorehouse*) won the SWET awards for best actor and best actress in a musical. Despite stiff opposition the SWET best musical award went to Andrew Lloyd Webber's *Cats*, the spectacular all-British multimedia show designed around the poems of T. S. Eliot and staged by Trevor Nunn and Gillian Lynne. The SWET best comedy award was won by Rowan Atkinson for his one-man show and that for the most promising newcomer to Alice Krige in *Arms and the Man*. Other light fare included John Wells's ministerial spoof *Anyone for Denis?* and *Her Royal Highness*, in which Royce Ryton and Ray Cooney made harmless fun of the prince and princess of Wales. The SWET award for "services to the theatre" went to 79-year-old Sir Ralph Richardson.

The Abbey Theatre in Dublin put on *Scenes from an Album*, William Trevor's first full-length play, about 300 years of a British settler's family in Ulster, staged by Joe Dowling; a new work by Martin Boylan; and Ray McAnally's production of *All My Sons*. Highlights of the 23rd Dublin Festival at the Abbey were Tom Stoppard's *Night and Day* and the world premieres of *Gaeilgeoiri* by Antoine O'Flatharta and Neil Donnelly's *The Silver Dollar Boys*, an anti-British jape, at the Peacock.

France, Belgium, The Netherlands, and Italy.
French Pres. François Mitterrand's first official act was to open the Jean Vilar Exhibition during the Avignon Festival. The new artistic director, Bernard Faivre d'Arcier, invited Daniel Mesguich and the U.S. director Stuart Seide to stage, respectively, *King Lear* and *Andromaque* alongside the Manfred Karge and Matthias Langhoff production of *Marie-Woyzeck* from Bochum. The annual Critics' Prize for the best foreign production was won by Peter Stein's *The Oresteia* from West Berlin; for the

DONALD COOPER—BLACK STAR

An 8½-hour play, the Royal Shakespeare Company's *The Life and Adventures of Nicholas Nickleby*, which cost theatregoers $100 per ticket, opened on Broadway in October.

best native production by Peter Brook's *The Cherry Orchard*; for the best new play by the Théâtre du Compagnol's collectively mounted *Le Bal*, a history of France seen through ballroom dancers' eyes; and for the best actor by Philippe Clevenot in Bernard Sobel's production of *Edward II* at Gennevilliers. The imprisoned Czechoslovak writer Vaclav Havel was awarded the Prix de Plaisir, while the Georges Lerminier Prize was won by Patrice Chéreau for his production at the Théâtre National Populaire in Lyon of *Peer Gynt*, starring Gérard Désarthe. This was transferred to the Théâtre de la Ville, where Lucian Pintilie's staging of *The Wild Duck* was also outstanding.

The Comédie Française, under Jacques Toja, staged a record number of plays at its two Paris houses, on tour, and abroad. Corneille's *Sertorius* was revived after a gap of 175 years. Other classical dramatists to receive new productions included Molière (a triple bill staged by Maurice Béjart), de Musset, and Marivaux. Among recent works were Artaud's *The Cenci*; Camus's *Caligula*; *The Madwoman of Chaillot* with Annie Ducaux; *The Lady from Maxime's*; *La Locandiera* with Catherine Hiegel; *The Seagull*, directed by Otomar Krejca, in which Nina was played by Ludmila Mikael; and Henri Ronse's staging of Jean Audureau's *There's a Marvellously Strong Man in Memphis*, featuring Tania Torrens as "Ma" Barker, at the Odéon.

At the Théâtre de l'Est Parisien, Guy Rétoré presented plays by Machiavelli, Marivaux, Ionesco, and Fo; an adaptation of *Le Bourgeois Gentilhomme* made by Jérôme Savary and his "Magic Circus"; and a co-production with the Belgian Théâtre de l'Atelier of Brecht's *Peak Heads and Round Heads*. Jean-Louis Barrault and his dismantled Orsay auditorium moved into the Rond Point, which he unveiled with a collage on love starring Anny Duperey and *Happy Days* with Madeleine Renaud, followed by Simone Benmussa's dramatization of Tolstoy's *The Death of Ivan Ilyitch* and Edna O'Brien's *Virginia* with Catherine Sellers.

During the autumn Paris Festival the Pompidou

Centre was one of several theatres celebrating Samuel Beckett's 75th birthday, with Rick Cluchey in *Krapp's Last Tape* and three novelties staged by Alan Schneider and imported from the U.S., *Eh Joe, Ohio Impromptu,* and *Rockaby,* starring Helen Gary Bishop. Joe Chaikin's one-man Beckett show, *Texts,* already seen at the London Riverside, also went to Paris. New plays in the private sector were *Sacrilèges* by Eduardo Manet; *Exercises in Style* by Raymond Queneau; *The Eponine Garden* by Maria Pacôme; *Doublages* by Jean-Paul Wenzel; Jean Anouilh's 45th play, the satirical *The Navel,* starring Bernard Blier; and *We Dine in Bed* by Marc Camoletti.

At the Belgian National Theatre, Jacques Huisman's staging of *Amadeus* rivaled in popularity Bernard de Coster's of *Cyrano de Bergerac* starring Jean-Claude Frison. At the Atelier the director Armand Delcampe, Andrey in Chekhov's *Three Sisters,* reappeared in Beckett's *Endgame.* The Rideau gave Strindberg's *Dreamplay* and a new work by Patrick Bonté. Glasgow Citizens' distinguished themselves at the Holland Festival with their newly staged *The Massacre at Paris* by Marlowe, as well as with *Chinchilla* and *A Waste of Times.* All three also visited West Germany, while their production of *Battlefield* was the first play by Carlo Goldoni to be done at the Venice Festival by a foreign company.

At Santacangelo, the site of Italy's newest festival, the Akroama from Sardinia presented *Mariella,* adapted from *The Match Seller.* Shortly before he died, Giorgio de Lullo (*see* OBITUARIES) revived Luchino Visconti's vision of *La Locandiera* with the Romolo Valli Free Theatre Group. Successful tours were given by Vittorio Gassman's company in *Othello,* Giorgio Albertazzi's in *Enrico IV,* Paolo Stoppa's in *The Miser,* and Rossella Falk's in *Applause.* Notable productions included Giancarlo Sbragia's of *The Rules of the Game* at the Arti and Luigi Squarzina's of *Heartbreak House* at the Eliseo, both in Rome, and Fo's adaptation of John Gay's *Beggar's Opera* as *The Scoffer's Opera* in Turin.

Switzerland, East and West Germany, and Austria. François Rochaix staged *Henry IV* at Carouge with Jean Bruno as Falstaff. Gerd Heinz, manager-elect of the Schauspielhaus, staged *Twelfth Night* for the Zürich Festival, where the Habimah Theatre's *A Simple Story,* adapted from Nobel Prize winner Shmuel Agnon's novella of that name, was also seen. Other productions there included Werner Düggelin's of the world premiere of Thomas Hürlimann's *Grandfather and Stepbrother,* a critique of pro-Nazis in wartime Switzerland. In Basel, Hansjörg Schneider's *Tell the Archer* dealt with received historical beliefs and Heinrich Henkel's *Quiet, Ronnie!* with the generation gap.

The spring Theatre Meeting in West Berlin was mostly notable for the Stein *Oresteia,* which later inaugurated the Schaubühne's home in Erich Mendelssohn's gutted 1928 movie theatre together with Nigel Williams's *Class Enemy,* reset in Berlin's Kreutzberg district. The Festwochen theme of Prussianism resulted in plays by and about Heinrich von Kleist and in two musicals on Prussian themes, past and present. The East Berlin Festtage invited a company from Rostock with Claus Hem-

mel's *The Prussians Are Coming,* the Estonian Academic Theatre from Tallinn, and a company from Schwerin with *The 7th Cross* by Bärbel Jaksch and Heiner Maass. The same couple adapted Alfred Döblin's spectacular *Alexanderplatz* for the Volksbühne, where Istvan Iglodi staged his rock version of *Twelfth Night,* earlier seen in Budapest. *Lulu* at the West Berlin Schiller starred Angelica Domröse, formerly of the Deutsches, which she had left with her husband, Hilmar Thate, for the West.

Among notable productions in West Germany were Ingmar Bergman's swan-song threesome in Munich (before resigning after a dispute with the Residenz Theatre), comprising *Miss Julie* (later taken to Stockholm), *A Doll's House,* and his own *Scenes from Married Life.* Ariane Mnouchkine's adaptation of Klaus Mann's *Mephisto* was seen in several theatres, though not without protest from actors who had known the real-life Mephisto, Gustav Gründgens, and who sprang to his defense. Cologne followed the example of the second Summer Festival in Stuttgart by putting on its First International Festival, to be held every two years, with London's NT and the premiere of Robert Wilson's *The Man in the Raincoat.*

Besides the German-language premiere of Max Frisch's *Triptyque* and Adolf Dresen's farewell production of a Gorky play at the Burg, Viennese theatregoers saw the world premieres at the Akademie of the banned plays of Czechoslovak writers Pavel Kohout, Pavel Landovsky, and Vaclav Havel, as well as Peter Weiss's *The Investigation* at the Burg's newly opened Third Stage. Thomas Bernhard's *On Target* received its world premiere at the Salzburg Festival.

Eastern Europe, Scandinavia, and Israel. Moscow productions included *Sashka* and Yevgeny Yevtushenko's *Berry Fields* at the Mossoviet and Aleksey Arbuzov's *Recollections,* staged by Anatoly Efros, at the Malaya Bronnaya. The Moscow Art produced Andrey Voznesensky's *Juno and Perchance,* adapted from the love story of a 19th-century Russian visitor to San Francisco (*Story Under Full Sail*), with rock music by Aleksey Rubnikov; *The Way* by Anatoly Remez, about the assassination of a tsar; and Mark Rozovsky's *Father and Son.* In Warsaw prizes were won by Tadeusz Kantor, Jerzy Grzegorzewski, and Kazimierz Dejmek, new head of the Polski, where he directed the world premiere of Slawomir Mrozek's *The Ambassador.* Roman Polanski, partnered by Tadeusz Lomnicki, staged and played the title role in *Amadeus* at the Na Woli. In Krakow, Krystyna Skuszanka directed *The Lord God's Brother* by Karol Woytyla (Pope John Paul II), which had Chmielowski, the painter-turned-monk, as hero. *The Government Inspector,* staged by Jerzy Jarocki, was the bicentenary production at the Krakow Stary. In Yugoslavia *The Karamazovs* by Dusan Jovanovic, though banned in Belgrade, was seen at the Novi Sad Festival. Ivan Vazov's *Under the Yoke,* staged by Filip Filipov, was the National Theatre's contribution to the 13th centenary of the foundation of Bulgaria. Highlights of the year in Budapest were *I, Claudius,* staged by Istvan Iglodi at the Castle Theatre, and the two parts of *Henry IV,* staged by Gabor Zsambeki with Ferenc Kallai as Falstaff, and Yuri Liub-

imov's unorthodox production of *The Threepenny Opera*, both at the National.

Stockholm was host for the second time to the World Strindberg Symposium, when delegates saw, at the City Theatre, Jan Håkansson's unusual production of *The Father*, designed by Gunilla Palmstjerna-Weiss (designer of Bergman's *Miss Julie*), and at the Royal Dramatic, a dozen plays by or about the dramatist. In Norway visiting directors included Krystyna Skuszanka (*The Seagull*) and Stavros Doufexis (*Lysistrata*). P. O. Enquist's symbolic drama *From the Life of the Earthworms*, about Hans Andersen, had its world premiere at the Copenhagen Royal Theatre's new Third Stage. In Helsinki Eugen Terttula's production of *Amadeus*, Radu Penciulescu's of *Timon of Athens*, and Patrick Drake's of *Bent*, all at the National, and Ralf Långbacka's of *Peer Gynt* at the City Theatre were all noteworthy.

The seventh Congress of the International Association of Theatre Critics in Tel Aviv allowed critics from 26 countries and 4 continents to discuss the problems of the "New Audience" and to see how these were being tackled in Israel. The growth of a vast fringe activity was noted together with many native dramas, often performed before new immigrants with no theatrical traditions, in outlying areas, in new cultural centres, schools, clubs, and army camps.   (OSSIA TRILLING)

United States and Canada. Theatre is both a reflection and a product of its society. In the U.S., theatre in 1981 was shaped by strained national economics. Ticket prices and production costs rose to record peaks. One new Broadway musical cost $4 million to produce. Several shows increased ticket prices to $50. Amazingly, audiences were not discouraged.

Federal aid to the arts, declining in recent years, plummeted as U.S. Pres. Ronald Reagan slashed subsidies. One result was a crisis for five major institutional theatres in New York City. The American Place Theater and The Circle in the Square were forced to curtail their schedules, the former to the brink of extinction. The adventurous Chelsea Theatre Center and the prestigious BAM Repertory Company actually did close because of funding withdrawal. Even Joseph Papp's celebrated New York Shakespeare Festival drastically reduced its activities. Were it not for profitably transferring a deliciously quirky revival of *The Pirates of Penzance* to Broadway, the festival might have been undone by its own giant budget.

Because the Vivian Beaumont Theatre in Lincoln Center was closed for season-long renovations, New York was left with virtually no professional classical theatre. Such a fact, for a world-class city, was astonishing.

Economic crisis usually brings out the conservative in people, but that was not its effect on Broadway. During the year some of the nation's oldest established stage names went down in flames. Edward Albee's adaptation of Vladimir Nabokov's *Lolita* played a mere eight performances. The musical theatre's perennial prizewinners, songwriter Stephen Sondheim and director Harold Prince, suffered their first disaster when *Merrily We Roll Along* flopped. Even Neil Simon, the most popular playwright in the history of Western theatre, endured a humiliating rejection as *Fools* was forced to shut down after only four weeks of performances.

Nor was any conservative comfort found in musical revivals, which had been thriving on Broadway during the previous few seasons. New productions of *My Fair Lady*, *Fiddler on the Roof*, and *Camelot* were unenthusiastically received. Paradoxically, audiences seemed just as bored with the new musicals. *Woman of the Year*, based on the Katharine Hepburn-Spencer Tracy movie, was a hit but largely because of its popular star, Lauren Bacall. Most of the musical shows that did succeed were new ones that used old music: *Sophisticated Ladies*, for example, was built around the songs of Duke Ellington. The success of *Pirates of Penzance* was due in great part to the sassy but faithful treatment of the Gilbert and Sullivan score. The year's Tony award for the best musical was given to *42nd*

Crimes of the Heart won a Pulitzer Prize for playwright Beth Henley after it opened in New York in the fall season. The leading players (left to right) are Mary Beth Hurt, Lizbeth Mackay, and Mia Dillon.

Street, another show that used familiar songs, these from the 1930s motion picture on which the production was based.

Economic pressures forced Broadway producers to seek low-risk plays that had already been tested at regional theatres. This also reduced production costs through the sharing of expenses by the commercial producer and the nonprofit theatre, although certain legalities had to be respected so that institutional tax exemptions were not compromised. Any compromising of artistic integrity seemed of less concern, however, as these regional theatres eagerly presented plays with commercial, Broadway potential. Government subsidies being at a minimum, many regional theatres felt forced to court the income from a New York hit.

Crimes of the Heart became the first Pulitzer Prize play to originate at a regional, nonprofit theatre, the Actors Theatre of Louisville, Ky. From there, Beth Henley's nostalgic comedy, a minor work, went on to an off-Broadway production that won it the coveted prize. Only then was it taken to Broadway. Also coming to Broadway after regional premieres were Joanna Glass's *To Grandmother's House We Go* (from New Haven's Long Wharf Theatre), Tom Griffin's *Einstein and the Polar Bear* (Hartford Stage Company), Bill C. Davis's *Mass Appeal* (Manhattan Theatre Club), and Jules Feiffer's *Grown Ups* (American Repertory Theatre at Harvard). None of the last four, however, proved to have the size or the polish that "Broadway" connotes.

The biggest events of New York's theatre year did have that muscle. They were *Nicholas Nickleby* and *Dreamgirls*, two productions that would have enhanced any season, although never in stage history had the cost of theatre-making and theatre-going reached such levels. For *Nicholas Nickleby* was presented at a cost of nearly $1 million, which would have been doubled had it originated in the U.S. As for *Dreamgirls*, the musical arrived on Broadway with a $4 million price tag, twice the previous record. Tickets for the 8½-hour two-part *Nickleby* were priced at $100. The whole play could be seen on consecutive evenings or, for the hardy, on one long day, matinee and evening. *Dreamgirls* was comparatively cheap at $40 a ticket, which had become the standard upper limit along Broadway.

A production of the U.K.'s Royal Shakespeare Company, *Nicholas Nickleby* was of course adapted from the Charles Dickens novel. Like so much of Dickens's work, it is the story of a young man's struggle to survive the hardships, inequities, and meanness of London's slums. After many travails, the hero's decency and virtue earn him the rewards of happiness and wealth. Less a dramatization by David Edgar than a theatricalization by co-directors Trevor Nunn and John Caird, the play had few exchanges between characters. More often, the plot was advanced through recitations to the audience as the large cast played an even larger number of characters.

Freely based on the popular singing group the Supremes, *Dreamgirls* traced the emergence of black popular music into the white marketplace through homogenization and commercialization of

the "soul" quality. Although its story elements were melodramatic and its music too weak for it to be a great show, *Dreamgirls* was a glittering production with an artistic spine, providing Broadway with the hit musical every season craves.

Off Broadway had lain relatively dormant in recent years because its own high costs and ticket prices were too close to those of Broadway. But in 1981 the rise in Broadway costs and prices resulted in a comparative bargain situation off Broadway. Economical and discriminating playgoers were motivated to look for alternatives to Broadway, and a number of off-Broadway productions caught their fancies. These included the off-beat, entirely musical *March of the Falsettos*; a spoof of Roman Catholic education, *Sister Mary Ignatius Explains It All For You*; and the plays *Cloud 9* and *Key Exchange*. These offered the adventurous theatre that had originally popularized off-Broadway and marked the healthiest trend in the 1981 U.S. theatre season.

Farther north on the continent, signs were less healthy because mainstream Canadian theatre is governmentally subsidized, and Canada's money squeeze was as suffocating as was that of the U.S. Both of the nation's major theatres, the Stratford (Ont.) Festival and the Shaw Festival in Niagara-On-The-Lake, Ont., were on shaky ground financially.

Shaky for the well-established Shakespearean institution meant a $1 million deficit and attendance dropping from the usual 90–95% of capacity to below 80%. Perhaps Stratford's conservative audience missed the production of a major tragedy or chronicle play, for on the main Festival Theatre stage were *The Comedy of Errors*, *The Taming of the Shrew*, and *Coriolanus*.

Farther east the Shaw Festival had a deficit of only $100,000, though it was a much smaller enterprise than Stratford. Distressing, for a Shaw Festival, was the unenthusiastic audience for plays of its namesake, including *Saint Joan*, *In Good King Charles's Golden Days*, and the one-act rarity *Man of Destiny*. The festival's hit was, of all things, an obscure British period farce, *Tons of Money*, co-written by Will Evans and the pseudonymous "Valentine." (MARTIN GOTTFRIED)

See also Dance; Music.

[622]

Togo

A West African republic on the Bight of Benin, Togo is bordered by Ghana, Upper Volta, and Benin. Area: 56,785 sq km (21,925 sq mi). Pop. (1981 est.): 2,784,000. Cap. and largest city: Lomé (pop., 1980 est., 283,000). Language: French (official). Religion: animist 60%; Muslim 7.5%; and Christian 25%. President in 1981, Gen. Gnassingbe Eyadema.

Pres. Gnassingbe Eyadema's eagerness to play an active role in the search for a settlement of Chad's internal conflict was undiminished in 1981, despite the failure of the previous year's efforts. On January 14, soon after Chad and Libya had announced their intention to unite, he was

Togo

Theology:
see Religion

Timber:
see Industrial Review

Tobacco:
see Industrial Review

Tobogganing:
see Winter Sports

TOGO

Education. (1977–78) Primary, pupils 421,436, teachers 7,251; secondary (1978–79), pupils 105,770, teachers 2,328; vocational (1978–79), pupils 8,723, teachers 326; teacher training (1978–79), students 478, teachers 21; higher (1976–77), students 2,777, teaching staff (university only; 1975–76) 236.

Finance. Monetary unit: CFA franc, with (Sept. 21, 1981) a par value of CFA Fr 50 to the French franc (free rate of CFA Fr 265 to U.S. $1; CFA Fr 491 = £1 sterling). Budget (1981 est.) balanced at CFA Fr 70.7 billion.

Foreign Trade. (1979) Imports CFA Fr 110,208,000,000; exports CFA Fr 46,432,000,000. Import sources (1978): France 34%; Switzerland 10%; U.K. 10%; West Germany 9%; The Netherlands 6%; U.S. 5%. Export destinations (1978): The Netherlands 31%; France 14%; West Germany 8%; U.S. 8%; Yugoslavia 6%; Poland 6%. Main exports: phosphates 47%; cocoa 16%; coffee 13%.

host to a meeting at Lomé of 12 heads of state of the Organization of African Unity (OAU), at which the merger was condemned. At the Franco-African summit conference in Paris on November 3–4, he pledged Togo's participation in the peacekeeping force to be sent to Chad by the OAU.

Despite allegations of violations of human rights in Togo by the Paris-based Mouvement Togolais pour la Démocratie, Franco-Togolese relations remained good. President Eyadema received Guy Penne, adviser on African affairs to the French presidency, in September, and was himself received by Pres. François Mitterrand in Paris in November. In September-October Eyadema paid official visits to China and North Korea.

Togo's economy, weighed down by a mounting foreign debt burden, suffered further in 1981 from falling world demand for its exports, particularly phosphates. (PHILIPPE DECRAENE)

Tonga

An independent monarchy and member of the Commonwealth, Tonga is an island group in the Pacific Ocean east of Fiji. Area: 750 sq km (290 sq mi). Pop. (1981 est.): 97,800, 98% of whom are Tongan. Cap. and largest city: Nukualofa (pop., 1976, 18,300). Language: English and Tongan. Religion (1976): Free Wesleyan 47%; Roman Catholic 16%; Free Church of Tonga 14%; Mormon 9%; Church of Tonga 9%; other 5%. King, Taufa'ahau Tupou IV; prime minister in 1981, Prince Fatafehi Tu'ipelehake.

In May 1981 elections to fill the seven "people's" seats in the Legislative Assembly resulted in the

TONGA

Education. (1978–79) Primary, pupils 19,744, teachers 818; secondary, pupils 12,563, teachers 666; vocational, pupils 280, teachers 19; teacher training, students 134, teachers 9.

Finance and Trade. Monetary unit: pa'anga, with (Sept. 21, 1981) a free rate of 0.86 pa'anga to U.S. $1 (1.60 pa'anga = £1 sterling). Budget (1980–81 est.): revenue 11,915,-000 pa'anga; expenditure 11,899,000 pa'anga. Foreign trade (1980): imports 30,134,000 pa'anga; exports 6,630,-000 pa'anga. Import sources: New Zealand 38%; Australia 31%; U.S. 6%; Japan 6%; Fiji 5%. Export destinations: Australia 36%; New Zealand 34%; U.S. 14%. Main exports: coconut oil 46%; desiccated coconut 10%; bananas 6%.

defeat of four sitting members, including the first woman commoner to sit in that body. The election results generally reflected a move toward conservative, traditional members. In July the new Parliament agreed that some of its proceedings might be broadcast. There was an important break with the past when Baron Tuita announced that his former tenants on the island of Niuafo'ou would be given absolute title to their lands.

A scheme under which passports would have been issued to non-Tongan "protected persons" in return for a payment of $10,000 for the lease of one acre of worthless land was announced in March. The scheme was withdrawn by the Privy Council a month later. In February diplomatic relations were established with Israel.

In December 1980 an interisland ferry sank with the loss of 11 lives; at the time, it was carrying nearly four times its legal limit of passengers. In May 1981 a tornado, the fourth in a year, caused damage estimated at $100,000 in Nukualofa.

(BARRIE MACDONALD)

Tonga

Track and Field Sports

In a season that may be remembered as the "year of the mile," the world's track and field athletes were not as productive as in the Olympic Games year of 1980. This was as expected because post-Olympic competition generally produces a lower level of achievement. In 1981, however, there was the aura of excitement surrounding competition in the mile run to help compensate for the normal letdown.

Men's International Competition. Fourteen new world records highlighted the year in men's track and field. The most outstanding achievements were in the pole vault and the mile run, regarded by most as the sport's glamour event.

Sebastian Coe enjoyed a spectacular year, bettering world standards four times. He cut large amounts of time off the records for the 800 m and 1,000 m, but it was his achievements in the mile that caught the imagination of the public. And, as in 1980, the young Briton received a strong competitive push from his countryman Steve Ovett.

When the year began, the world mile record of 3 min 48.8 sec belonged to Ovett, who in 1980 had bettered Coe's mark of the previous year. Coe's first mile of 1981 took care of that as he raced to a 3 min 48.53 sec clocking at Zürich, Switz., on August 19. But the record lasted only a week. On August 26 at Koblenz, West Germany, Ovett took the record away from Coe for a second time as he ran the distance in 3 min 48.40 sec. Coe responded even more quickly, allowing his rival to hold the honour for just two days. On August 28 at Brussels, Coe sliced more than a second off Ovett's new standard with a time of 3 min 47.33 sec.

It was the first time that the mile record had been broken three times in one year. And the excitement was not limited to Coe and Ovett. By the end of the year 21 of the 29 fastest times ever achieved in the mile had been made in 1981. Coe and Ovett each owned three of the top seven times. Ovett now had run 6 of the 17 fastest miles.

Tourism:
see Industrial Review

Toys:
see Games and Toys

Coe's first success occurred on June 10 at Florence, Italy. There he surprised even himself with his fine early-season form by lowering his own world 800-m standard to 1 min 41.72 sec. A month later, on July 11, he returned to the famed Bislett Stadium track in Oslo where he had set international records at 800 m, 1,000 m, and one mile. This time he attacked his 1,000-m figure and chopped off more than a second, recording a time of 2 min 12.18 sec. He finished his competitive season with an easy 800-m win in the World Cup at Rome.

Ovett was limited to the one world record in the mile, but he came close in the "metric mile," the 1,500-m run. He went after his own world best of 3 min 31.36 sec several times, coming within 0.21 and 0.59 sec. He also easily won the event in the World Cup competition.

Two other current and one former record holders also set new marks during the year. Most notable was Henry Rono, the Kenyan who established four world records in 1978 but then appeared to have lost most of his magic. Late in 1981, after three years without either a record or a major victory, Rono began to produce impressive clockings. He finished the year with a new 5,000-m standard of 13 min 6.20 sec, achieved September 13 at Narvik, Norway.

A somewhat similar comeback was achieved by Renaldo Nehemiah of the United States. A record breaker in 1979, Nehemiah was a bit slower in 1980 and was injured and out of action for much of the 1981 season. But by August 19 he was able to join Coe as a record breaker at the Zürich Weltklasse meet, where Nehemiah scored his third world mark by running the 110-m hurdles in 12.93 sec.

The pole vault produced as much action as the mile, and one of the three record breakers was

Britain's Sebastian Coe (6) set a new world record in the 1,000-m race in Oslo in July. His time was 2 min 12.18 sec.

France's Thierry Vigneron, who in 1980 had set two world records in the event. In 1981 he became the first vaulter ever to clear 19 ft (5.79 m), bettering that milepost by one-quarter inch on June 20. But six days later Vladimir Polyakov of the Soviet Union vaulted 5.81 m (19 ft ¾ in). And on August 2 at Irkutsk, U.S.S.R., Konstantin Volkov, coached by his father, made 5.84 m (19 ft 2 in). Thus a new pole vault record had been set eight times in the last two years.

Controversy surrounded the two discus record throws by Ben Plucknett of the U.S. The 300-lb (136-kg) giant spun the discus 71.20 m (233 ft 7 in) on May 16 at Modesto, Calif., and 72.34 m (237 ft 4 in) on July 7 at Stockholm. But he would not be given credit for the records because it was announced after his second mark that he had failed a doping test during a competition in New Zealand in January. The tests, which are administered at all major meets, showed that Plucknett had used an anabolic steroid. It was common knowledge that such steroids are used by almost all throwers and by many other athletes, who usually quit taking them far enough in advance of competition to escape detection. Plucknett's penalty was suspension from amateur track and field and loss of his records.

Asia gained its only current world records when Toshihiko Seko of Japan accounted for two seldom-run long-distance marks at Christchurch, N.Z., March 22. He covered 25,000 m in 1 hr 13 min 55.8 sec and 30,000 m in 1 hr 29 min 18.8 sec.

In team competition Europe won the third running of the World Cup, scoring 147 points to 130 for East Germany and 127 for the United States in men's competition. East Germany won the European Cup and completely dominated the European junior championships, in which no team scores are kept. In the latter the East Germans won 22 of 38 events, both men's and women's, and set five world junior records.

Indoors, the European championships at Grenoble, France, on February 21–22 produced two record-breaking performances. (There are no official world records in indoor competition.) Vigneron vaulted 5.71 m (18 ft 8¾ in) for his second new mark of the indoor season, and Shamil Abbyasov of the U.S.S.R. triple jumped 17.30 m (56 ft 9¼ in). West Germany's Hartmut Weber ran the 400 m in 45.96 sec and Coe did the 800 m in 1 min 46.0 sec.

Women's International Competition. Record-breaking activity was greatly reduced among the women in 1981. Although not confirmed by the countries involved, it was apparent that the two powerhouses of the sport, East Germany and the Soviet Union, were taking it easy after dominant performances in 1980.

Whereas 20 new marks had been achieved in 1980, only two world records were set in 1981. The most noteworthy was the 71.88-m (235-ft 10-in) javelin toss by 18-year-old Antoaneta Todorova of Bulgaria. The other record was in the mile, a distance not nearly as popular among women as among men. The time of 4 min 20.89 sec was achieved by Lyudmila Veselkova of the Soviet Union.

But even while apparently operating somewhat

UPI

Table I. World 1981 Outdoor Records—Men

Event	Competitor, country, date	Performance
800 m	Sebastian Coe, U.K., June 10	1 min 41.72 sec
1,000 m	Sebastian Coe, U.K., July 11	2 min 12.18 sec
One mile	Sebastian Coe, U.K., August 19	3 min 48.53 sec
	Steve Ovett, U.K., August 26	3 min 48.40 sec
	Sebastian Coe, U.K., August 28	3 min 47.33 sec
5,000 m	Henry Rono, Kenya, September 13	13 min 6.20 sec
25,000 m	Toshihiko Seko, Japan, March 22	1 hr 13 min 55.8 sec
30,000 m	Toshihiko Seko, Japan, March 22	1 hr 29 min 18.8 sec
110-m hurdles	Renaldo Nehemiah, U.S., August 19	12.93 sec
Pole vault	Thierry Vigneron, France, June 20	5.80 m (19 ft ¼ in)
	Vladimir Polyakov, U.S.S.R., June 26	5.81 m (19 ft ¾ in)
	Konstantin Volkov, U.S.S.R., August 2	5.84 m (19 ft 2 in)
Discus*	Ben Plucknett, U.S., May 16	71.20 m (233 ft 7 in)
	Ben Plucknett, U.S., July 7	72.34 m (237 ft 4 in)

*Both marks were disallowed after Plucknett was suspended by the governing body.

Table II. World 1981 Outdoor Records—Women

Event	Competitor, country, date	Performance
One mile	Lyudmila Veselkova, U.S.S.R., September 12	4 min 20.89 sec
Javelin	Antoaneta Todorova, Bulgaria, August 15	71.88 m (235 ft 10 in)

under wraps, the East German women won both the World Cup and European Cup competitions. And they made their nation's future look good by nearly sweeping the European junior contest.

European women accounted for five indoor world bests. Jarmila Kratochvilova of Czechoslovakia emerged as a star after nearly a decade of relative obscurity by running the 200 m in 22.76 sec and the 400 m in 49.64 sec indoors. Outdoors, she missed the world 400-m mark by 0.01 sec. Other new indoor marks were set by Marita Koch of East Germany with 7.10 sec for 60 m, Zofia Bielczyk of Poland with 6.74 sec for the 50-m hurdles, and Karin Hanel of West Germany with 6.77 m (22 ft 2½ in) in the long jump.

U.S. Competition. As elsewhere, the mile was the big event for U.S. runners. Steve Scott, the country's foremost miler, was the overall star performer in 1981.

During the season Scott set five U.S. and one world record. Most significant were his new national standards in the mile and 1,500 m, set at the expense of Jim Ryun, the last U.S. holder of world marks in those events. Scott ran the 1,500 m in 3 min 31.96 sec and the mile in 3 min 49.68 sec. And in a rare try at a longer distance he ran 3,000 m in 7 min 36.69 sec, fastest ever by a U.S. competitor and third fastest of all time.

Indoors, Scott scored national bests of 3 min 36.0 sec for the 1,500 m and 3 min 51.8 sec for the mile. His world record was set in the little-run 2,000 m with a time of 4 min 58.6 sec.

In September a mile-long road race, down Fifth Avenue in New York City before several hundred thousand spectators, produced additional excitement. It was won by Sidney Maree, a South African seeking U.S. citizenship, in a time of 3 min 47.52 sec. Though very close to Coe's record of 3 min 47.33 sec, it was not acceptable as an official mark because it was run on a road rather than a track.

In addition to Scott, six other U.S. men set national bests. Plucknett would get credit for his 71.20 m (233 ft 7 in) performance although denied the world mark, and Nehemiah's 12.93-sec world record hurdle time was of course also a U.S. best. Brian Oldfield, who put the shot 22.86 m (75 ft) as a professional, scored with his best effort since regaining his amateur standing, 22.02 m (72 ft 3 in). Another veteran, former world record holder Dwight Stones, who had been suspended for accepting prize money, came back after two bad years to regain the national record with a high jump of 2.31 m (7 ft 7 in). The oldest U.S. record, dating back to 1967, fell to Dave McKenzie when he powered the hammer 72.30 m (237 ft 2 in). And Willie Banks broke the triple jump figure four times and tied it once. His best was 17.56 m (57 ft 7½ in).

Indoors, the most noted achievement was, once again, in the mile. Eamonn Coghlan of Ireland, a regular competitor in the U.S., established world 1,500-m and mile bests of 3 min 35.6 sec and 3 min 50.6 sec, respectively. Other world indoor bests during the year included 5.61 sec for 50 m by James Sanford, 6.04 sec for 60 yd by Stanley Floyd, 33.33 sec for 300 m by Cliff Wiley, 2 min 4.9 sec for 1,000 yd by Don Paige, 12 min 56.2 sec for three miles and 13 min 20.4 sec for 5,000 m by Suleiman Nyambui, 8.49 m (27 ft 10¼ in) in the long jump by Carl Lewis, and 17.31 m (56 ft 9½ in) in the triple jump by Keith Connor. U.S. indoor bests were earned by Banks with 17.20 m (56 ft 5¼ in) in the triple jump, Jeff Woodard with 2.33 m (7 ft 7¾ in) in the high jump, and Alberto Salazar with 12 min 56.6 sec in the three mile and 13 min 22.6 sec in the 5,000 m.

Sidney Maree of South Africa breaks the tape in a mile-long race down New York City's Fifth Avenue in September. His winning time, 3 min 47.52 sec, was not accepted as an official mark because the race was run on a road rather than a track.

UPI

U.S. women, who lost their only world record when Mary Decker's mile mark was surpassed, accounted for three new national marks. Evelyn Ashford, who won both sprints in the World Cup, ran 11.02 sec, second best time ever for 100 m. And with Alice Brown, Jeanette Bolden, and Florence Griffith she shared the national 4 x 100-m relay record of 42.82 sec. Pam Spencer twice bettered the high-jump standard with a top of 1.97 m (6 ft 5½ in).

In indoor women's competition the U.S. achieved world bests when Alice Brown dashed 60 yd in 6.62 sec and Merlene Ottey, a Jamaican doing most of her running in the U.S., sped 300 m in 35.83 sec. National records fell to Jeannette Bolden with 6.13 sec for 50 m and 7.21 sec for 60 m, Joni Huntley with 1.95 m (6 ft 4¾ in) in the high jump, and Carol Lewis (sister of sprint and long-jump champion Carl Lewis) with 6.59 m (21 ft 7½ in) in the long jump.

In men's team competition the University of Texas at El Paso won the National Collegiate Athletic Association championships for the third time in a row, and the Athletic Attic won the national championships of the Athletic Congress. Outstanding in the NCAA meet was Carl Lewis of the University of Houston, who won both the 100 m and the long jump. Texas at El Paso also won the NCAA indoor tournament. In women's competition Tennessee won the Association of Intercollegiate Athletics for Women outdoor meet, and Virginia captured the indoor title. In dual competition against the U.S.S.R. at Leningrad in July, the U.S. men triumphed 118–105 and the Soviet women won 99–60.

Marathon Running and Cross Country. For the first time in history two world records fell in a single marathon race as Alberto Salazar and Allison Roe won the men's and women's divisions of the New York City Marathon on October 25. Salazar, a recent graduate of the University of Oregon and the defending champion, had a time of 2 hr 8 min 13 sec, fastest ever for the 42,195-m (26-mi 385-yd) course. It was only his second marathon. Roe, from New Zealand, finished in 2 hr 25 min 29 sec to produce the fourth consecutive women's world record in this race. Grete Waitz, who had won the previous three runs in record time, was forced to drop out with an injury.

The Boston Marathon on April 20 was won in a race record time of 2 hr 9 min 26 sec by Toshihiko Seko of Japan. The women's champion also set a race record, Roe winning in 2 hr 26 min 46 sec.

In cross country Craig Virgin of the U.S. retained his International Cross Country Championships at Madrid on March 28, running 12,000 m in 35 min 5 sec. Waitz won her fourth title in a row, taking 14 min 7 sec to cover 4,500 m. Ethiopia won the men's title; the U.S.S.R. the women's; and the U.S. the men's junior championship. Matthews Motshwarateau of South Africa led the University of Texas at El Paso to another NCAA win, while the first NCAA cross-country championships for women were won by Betty Springs of North Carolina State with Virginia taking the team title. Dorthe Rasmussen led her team at Iowa State to AIAW individual and team wins. (BERT NELSON)

Transportation

A number of developments marked 1981 as an eventful year for transportation. The longest road bridge span was opened; the first reusable space vehicle flew twice; the world railway speed record was raised considerably; and perhaps the most opulent airport yet was opened at Jidda, Saudi Arabia. The importance of transportation in the U.S. economy could be gauged by the size of the 50 largest transport operators there. With more than one million employees, they had operating revenues exceeding $85 billion—all this in the country where the private automobile (excluded from these figures) was said to be king.

The year was also marked by some tragic accidents. In India a train fell from a bridge into a river, killing at least 268 people, and a DC-9 charter aircraft crashed in Corsica, killing 174 passengers. (See DISASTERS.) (DAVID BAYLISS)

AVIATION

As 1981 drew to a close, it appeared that the year would be even worse year financially for the world air transport industry than 1980, when losses were the highest since records began in 1947. Traffic had been forecast to increase about 4.5% over 1980, according to the International Air Transport Association (IATA), but it was doubtful that that figure would be achieved.

IATA's member airlines, which accounted for 76% of international capacity (U.S.S.R. excluded), increased their total operating revenue in 1980 by 23%, to $60 billion. Their operating costs, however, rose by 25% to $61.8 billion. Taking nonoperating items into account, their loss was almost $1.1 billion. These results were partly a reflection of the inability to maintain the load factor trends of recent years in international scheduled transport. (The load factor is the ratio, expressed as a percentage, between total capacity and actual utilization.) In 1980 the average passenger load factor slipped to about 61% from more than 63% in 1979, while the average weight load factor dropped to 57% from 59% the previous year. These load factors were high when viewed against historical patterns; the problem was that with costs rising sharply and the revenue yield per metric ton-kilometre rising only slowly, the break-even load factor stood at a high level.

The unit cost/yield relationship was not expected to alter much during 1981, according to IATA director general Knut Hammarskjöld, suggesting that international scheduled services had to be 60% full to cover operating costs, more than 62% full to cover interest charges as well, and more than 67% full to cover all financial targets. Toward the end of 1981 it appeared that these figures were unlikely to be achieved. Unit costs of IATA member airlines in 1981 were estimated by the association at 43.7 cents per available ton-kilometre, compared with 42.4 cents in the previous year. Fuel remained the fastest rising element in total unit operating cost; in 1980 it already represented more than 27% of the total.

UPI

New York's Kennedy International Airport was jammed with passengers awaiting flights during the second day of a strike by U.S. air traffic controllers in August.

Traffic on IATA members' international scheduled services during the first half of 1981 revealed a meagre 4% growth for both passengers and freight. For world airline scheduled operations as a whole (U.S.S.R. included), the total number of passengers in 1980 was 734 million, a decrease of 0.5% from the previous year. Total scheduled passenger-kilometres rose 1.9% to 1,071,000,000,000, but available scheduled passenger-kilometres rose 7.1% to 1,709,000,000,000. Freight scheduled ton-kilometres rose 3.9% to 29,000,000,000. Charter traffic fell sharply in 1980 (by 11.6%), accounting during the year for only 9% of total passenger-kilometres. World total passenger-kilometres in 1980 totaled 1,178,000,000,000, a 0.5% increase over 1979.

The condition of the U.S. airline industry was no better than that of IATA (U.S. airlines in 1980 carried 35% of total world scheduled passenger traffic, according to the International Civil Aviation Organization). During the first eight months of 1981 the 29 most important U.S. airlines carried 191.1 million passengers, a decrease of 6.9% from the corresponding period of 1980. The combined figure, however, obscured important trends in the industry arising largely from the deregulation of recent years. While the traffic of the 12 major U.S. airlines was decreasing in 1981 (by 7% in September, for example), the traffic of the "nonmajor" airlines was increasing beyond all expectations— 35% in September.

Though still small, the nonmajor airlines' market share was growing rapidly; it amounted to 5.2% in September 1980 and 6.9% a year later. At one time many observers believed that after deregulation large airlines would tend to swallow smaller ones, but in practice the opposite was occurring. For example, Texas International gained control of Continental, and Air Florida, growing very rapidly, was bidding for Western. During the year, moreover, executives from nonmajor airlines took over management of two of the more troubled major airlines, Braniff and Pan American. One outward sign of this was that Pan Am, not previously noted as a low-fare carrier, introduced new unrestricted discount fares.

A shadow cast over U.S. air transport throughout the latter part of 1981 was the strike of some 13,000 air traffic controllers, members of the Professional Air Traffic Controllers Organization (PATCO), which began on August 3. It was met by prompt and uncompromising action by the U.S. administration, which dismissed the strikers on grounds that as civil servants their action was illegal. The Federal Aviation Administration (FAA) managed to maintain air traffic service at a reduced level by using nonstriking personnel and by reemploying retired controllers, taking on military personnel, and instituting a major training program for new entrants. Capacity restrictions were imposed on the airway system, but against many expectations it continued to function well..

(DAVID WOOLLEY)

SHIPPING AND PORTS

With available tonnage continuing to exceed demand, there was a reluctance to invest in new ships. Consequently, tonnage of the world merchant fleet at mid-1981, at 420 million gross registered tons (grt) or 691 million tons deadweight (dw), was less than 2% over the mid-1980 total. The increase was fairly evenly shared by tankers, ore and bulk carriers, and general cargo ships. The total tonnages in the different categories were oil tankers 175 million grt, ore and bulk carriers 83 million grt, bulk/oil carriers 26 million grt, general cargo vessels 82 million grt, chemical tankers and gas carriers 10 million grt, and containerships 11 million grt.

There was no change in the overall position of the leaders in the world fleet table, with Liberia in first place with 80 million tons grt, followed by Japan with 47 million, Greece with 39 million, and the U.K. with 27 million tons grt. The poor state of the tanker and dry freight markets was reflected in the increase in laid-up tonnage, which rose to about 20 million tons dw early in 1981.

Major port improvements continued throughout the year with the emphasis on better deepwater facilities for the handling of coal and ore cargoes. In South Korea new coal berths were being built at Inchon, Ulsan, and Mokopo, and Japan as-

World Transportation

Country	Railways Route length in 000 km	Railways Traffic Passenger in 000,000 pass.-km	Railways Traffic Freight in 000,000 net ton-km	Road length in 000 km	Vehicles in use Passenger in 000	Vehicles in use Commercial in 000	Merchant shipping Number of vessels	Merchant shipping Gross reg. tons in 000	Air traffic Total km flown in 000,000	Air traffic Passenger in 000,000 pass.-km	Air traffic Freight in 000,000 net ton-km
EUROPE											
Austria	6.5	7,427	11,040	106.7	2,138.7	172.5	13	89	22.0	1,120	14.6
Belgium	4.0	6,935	7,990	c. 125.0	3,076.6	258.6	290	1,810	54.8	4,852	405.8
Bulgaria	4.3	c. 6,950	17,681	36.3	c. 480.0[1]	c. 110.0[1]	192	1,233	c. 12.7	c. 775	c. 10.0
Cyprus	—	—	—	9.9[1]	86.2	19.8	688	2,091	9.5	798	19.8
Czechoslovakia	13.1	18,160	72,640	145.5[1]	1,976.7	324.8	19	155	24.7	1,540	14.6
Denmark	2.9	1,990	1,790	68.2	1,423.4	264.0	1,253	5,390	c. 33.0[2]	3,043[2]	128.5[2]
Finland	6.1	3,216	8,335	75.0	1,225.9	149.1	354	2,530	35.5	2,130	52.8
France	34.0	54,500	69,468	803.0	19,130.0	2,457.0	1,241	11,925	276.3	34,130	2,092.9
Germany, East	14.2	23,120	56,490	c. 119.0	2,532.9	231.2	451	1,532	34.5	1,848	67.3
Germany, West	31.7	41,355	65,301	482.0	23,236.1	1,288.1	1,906	8,356	196.2	21,056	1,584.5
Greece	2.5	1,531	841	37.1	877.9	402.0	3,922	39,472	40.1	5,062	68.1
Hungary	7.9	12,370	23,868	87.7	1,021.3	124.5	22	75	c. 15.5	c. 998	c. 19.0
Ireland	2.0	1,007	580	92.3[1]	734.4	65.1	141	209	21.9	2,049	91.9
Italy	19.9[1]	38,901	18,268	293.8	c. 17,600.0	c. 1,300.0	1,739	11,096	139.5	14,096	542.1
Netherlands, The	2.9	8,926	3,468	107.4[1]	4,100.0	327.0	1,263	5,724	108.8	14,643	995.5
Norway	4.2	2,380	3,080	81.7	1,233.6	152.5	2,501	22,007	c. 58.1[2]	c. 4,068[2]	c. 136.0[2]
Poland	24.4	46,325	134,736	298.5	2,383.0	617.8	842	3,639	35.1	2,232	18.8
Portugal	3.6	6,078	999	51.7	995.4	63.4	350	1,356	39.2	3,459	c. 111.1
Romania	11.1[1]	22,724	76,031	c. 95.0[1]	c. 235.0	c. 125.0	317	1,856	19.7	1,209	12.3
Spain	15.3	17,151	10,912	237.9	7,556.5	1,338.3	2,767	8,112	164.3	15,517	417.6
Sweden	12.0	6,841	15,627	129.0	2,883.0	181.6	700	4,234	66.2[2]	5,342[2]	190.9[2]
Switzerland	5.0[1]	8,485	7,485	64.0	2,246.8	169.4	35	311	97.8	10,831	453.2
U.S.S.R.	234.2	335,300	3,349,300	1,426.7	c. 8,250.0	c. 7,250.0	8,279	23,444	...	160,299	c. 3,083.0
United Kingdom	18.1	31,700[3]	17,640[3]	376.0	c. 15,440.0	c. 1,804.0	3,181	27,135	384.3	50,046	1,369.0
Yugoslavia	9.4	10,274	24,993	129.5	1,863.2	129.4	486	2,467	c. 34.8	c. 2,984	c. 41.7
ASIA											
Bangladesh	2.9[1]	5,119	722[1]	c. 6.2[1]	24.6[1]	10.1[1]	179	354	11.8	1,179	c. 20.0
Burma	4.5[1]	c. 3,760	c. 600	22.4[1]	c. 33.0[1]	c. 41.5[1]	90	88	c. 6.1	c. 218	c. 1.6
Cambodia	c. 0.6[1]	54[1]	10[1]	c. 11.0[1]	27.2[1]	c. 11.0[1]	3	4	.08[1]	42[1]	0.4[1]
China	c. 50.0[1]	138,300	571,700	890.0[1]	c. 50.0[1]	c. 710.0[1]	955	6,874	c. 46.5	c. 4,000	140.6
India	60.8	192,900	154,820	1,604.1	1,035.3	440.2	616	5,911	84.8	10,765	401.4
Indonesia	6.9	5,981	1,016	128.9	577.3	383.6	1,180	1,412	88.4	5,907	c. 129.0
Iran	4.6	3,511[1]	4,627[1]	63.1	1,028.4	396.3	229	1,284	15.6	2,071	23.4
Iraq	2.0[1]	797[1]	2,254[1]	9.7[1]	120.6	129.4	142	1,466	12.6	1,161	52.7
Israel	0.8	222	768	12.2	c. 423.0	c. 91.0	56	450	c. 30.2	c. 4,727	299.1
Japan	26.8	315,372	39,585	1,113.4	23,659.5	13,948.5	10,568	40,960	c. 364.8	c. 51,217	c. 2,002.0
Korea, South	c. 5.8	c. 20,780	10,548	47.0	249.1	226.9	1,426	4,344	60.7	10,833	850.3
Malaysia	c. 2.3	1,587[4]	1,196[4]	c. 29.8	c. 690.0	c. 154.0	221	702	40.9	4,076	116.7
Pakistan	8.8	16,510	9,370	87.1	135.7	36.1	84	478	49.7	5,696	241.3
Philippines	c. 1.9	417	36	127.1	c. 468.6	c. 370.2	723	1,928	42.4	5,959	155.1
Saudi Arabia	0.7	94[1]	125[1]	47.7	630.8	522.2	214	1,590	91.3	9,938	c. 174.6
Syria	1.7[1]	410	450	c. 16.3[1]	65.4[1]	81.4[1]	44	39	10.5	948	16.2
Taiwan	3.7	7,971	2,716	17.5	425.4	236.7	497	2,039	34.1[1]	7,489	1,031.4
Thailand	c. 3.8	7,030	2,740	67.7	c. 397.9	c. 451.9	153	391	c. 41.8	c. 6,276	c. 247.2
Turkey	8.1[1]	6,014	5,030	232.2	658.7	309.8	508	1,455	c. 14.5	c. 1,103	c. 13.7
Vietnam	c. 2.5	...	...	347.2	c. 100.0[1]	c. 200.0[1]	93	241	c. 0.1	c. 3	c. 0.1
AFRICA											
Algeria	3.9[1]	1,452[1]	2,016[1]	78.5[1]	396.8[1]	206.5[1]	130	1,219	c. 27.9	c. 2,300	c. 13.0
Congo	0.8[1]	286	470	8.2[1]	13.2[1]	3.7[1]	15	7	c. 2.9[5]	c. 197[5]	c. 19.3[5]
Egypt	c. 4.9	9,290[1]	2,302[1]	28.9	325.5	114.7	278	556	30.5	2,870	30.9
Ethiopia	1.0	171[6]	148[6]	35.9	38.6	11.7	17	24	10.5	647	26.2
Gabon	c. 0.2	...	...	7.1	c. 17.4[1]	c. 12.7[1]	14	77	c. 6.4	c. 374	c. 27.3
Ghana	1.0	521[1]	312[1]	32.2	33.0[1]	27.0[1]	104	250	c. 4.3	c. 324	c. 2.8
Ivory Coast	0.6[1]	1,274[1,7]	533[1,7]	45.2[1]	115.3	72.3	70	186	c. 2.8[5]	c. 215[5]	c. 18.6[5]
Kenya	2.6	...	3,538[1]	51.0	118.0	111.0	19	17	11.6	863	c. 20.3
Liberia	0.5	...	4,396[1]	10.0	13.1	9.0	2,401	80,285	c. 1.5	c. 17	c. 0.1
Libya	—	—	—	c. 20.0[1]	c. 360.0[1]	c. 237.0[1]	96	890	c. 11.7	c. 1,101	c. 17.0
Malawi	0.8	80	241	10.8	11.8	13.3	—	—	2.0	68	1.0
Morocco	1.8[1]	803	3,854	57.6	413.7	157.5	145	360	20.5	1,868	26.5
Nigeria	3.5[1]	785[1]	972[1]	108.0	215.4	33.1	116	498	c. 24.2	c. 1,877	c. 11.1
Senegal	1.2	180[1]	164[1]	13.9	72.9[1]	20.2[1]	87	34	c. 3.2[5]	c. 196[5]	c. 18.4[5]
Somalia	—	—	—	18.8[1]	4.2[1]	5.7[1]	22	46	c. 3.5	c. 140	c. 0.5
South Africa	20.7	...	96,770[8]	183.5	c. 2,456.0	c. 911.0	291	729	c. 67.3	c. 8,920	272.3
Sudan	c. 5.5	...	2,324[1]	c. 48.0	c. 35.0	c. 37.0	21	105	c. 10.5	c. 710	c. 12.5
Tanzania	3.7	...	...	45.6	42.2	51.1	32	56	7.5	284	c. 2.4
Tunisia	2.0	862	1,709	17.8	120.6	97.7	43	131	c. 13.6	c. 1,241	12.5
Uganda	1.3	...	...	27.9	26.0	5.4	1	6	c. 3.7	c. 120	c. 3.2
Zaire	5.3	467[1]	2,203[1]	c 145.0	c. 94.2	c. 85.5	33	92	c. 10.0	c. 834	c. 34.9
Zambia	2.2	320[1]	897[1]	36.4	c. 103.5	c. 65.5	—	—	10.5	467	47.5
Zimbabwe	3.5	...	5,842	c. 80.0	c. 175.0	c. 70.0	—	—	4.1	210	2.3
NORTH AND CENTRAL AMERICA											
Canada	67.6	2,760	221,920	884.3[1]	9,745.0[1]	2,717.8[1]	1,324	3,180	c. 337.8	c. 36,169	762.2
Costa Rica	c. 1.0	81[1]	14[1]	25.3[1]	c. 62.3[1]	c. 65.9[1]	26	20	c. 8.4	c. 495	c. 23.5
Cuba	14.9	1,637	1,899	c. 31.2[1]	c. 80.0[1]	c. 40.0[1]	405	881	c. 14.7	c. 932	c. 11.1
El Salvador	0.6[1]	c. 26[1]	57[1]	11.0[1]	70.1[1]	35.5[1]	4	1	c. 3.9	c. 178	c. 13.0
Guatemala	c. 1.0	...	117[1]	17.3	147.5	73.1	6	14	3.7	159	6.4
Honduras	1.9	174[1]	3[1]	8.3[1]	19.8	42.4	124	213	c. 6.8	c. 394	c. 3.5
Mexico	20.3	5,450	36,740	213.2	4,032.0	1,534.1	361	1,006	c. 157.4	c. 13,870	c. 136.0
Nicaragua	0.4	17[1]	10[1]	18.2[1]	c. 37.7	c. 30.1	17	16	c. 1.6	c. 76	c. 1.4
Panama	0.7	...	...	8.6	97.3	25.8	4,090	24,191	c. 6.7	c. 414	c. 3.7
United States	306.6[1]	18,191[9]	1,485,920	6,303.8	120,248.0	33,349.7	5,579	18,464	4,413.4	c. 409,066	c. 10,540.0
SOUTH AMERICA											
Argentina	c. 34.6	12,058	10,947	207.6[1]	c. 2,866.0[1]	c. 1,244.0[1]	537	2,546	c. 93.5	c. 7,935	c. 199.0
Bolivia	3.9	395[1]	579[1]	38.2[1]	35.9	50.3	2	15	c. 13.5	c. 1,342	c. 38.4
Brazil	c. 31.1	11,952[1]	63,979[1]	1,384.4	8,238.2	926.3	607	4,534	203.4	15,572	c. 610.0
Chile	10.8[1]	1,377	1,521	76.7	379.2	180.7	172	614	24.7	1,875	103.9
Colombia	2.9[1]	322	1,128	65.1	509.0	94.8	69	283	c. 44.7	c. 4,189	c. 155.0
Ecuador	c. 1.2[1]	65[1]	34[1]	35.5[1]	c. 66.1[1]	c. 137.4[1]	86	275	c. 20.4	c. 916	c. 34.6
Paraguay	0.5[1]	23[1]	17[1]	c. 15.0	c. 32.1	c. 23.1	27	23	c. 4.3	c. 262	c. 2.8
Peru	2.5[1]	528[1]	612[1]	56.9[1]	c. 312.0	c. 160.7	698	741	24.6	1,974	c. 40.7
Uruguay	3.0	494[1]	303[1]	25.0[1]	c. 168.0	c. 92.0	72	198	c. 4.3	c. 178	c. 1.0
Venezuela	c. 0.4	42[1]	15[1]	61.8	1,390.0	639.5	225	849	c. 64.6	c. 4,318	c. 152.7
OCEANIA											
Australia	39.7[10]	...	32,030[1]	816.8[1]	c. 5,898.0	c. 1,462.0	497	1,643	198.9	25,506	515.6
New Zealand	4.5	414	3,184	93.4	1,307.3	247.7	122	264	c. 52.1	5,725	193.3

Note: Data are for 1979 or 1980 unless otherwise indicated. (—) indicates nil or negligible; (...) indicates not known; (c.) indicates provisional or estimated.
[1] Data given are the most recent available. [2] Including apportionment of traffic of Scandinavian Airlines System. [3] Excluding Northern Ireland. [4] Peninsular Malaysia only; including Singapore. [5] Including apportionment of traffic of Air Afrique. [6] Including Djibouti traffic. [7] Including Upper Volta traffic. [8] Including Namibia traffic. [9] Class 1 railways only. [10] State system only.

Sources: UN, *Statistical Yearbook 1978, Monthly Bulletin of Statistics, Annual Bulletin of Transport Statistics for Europe 1979;* Lloyd's Register of Shipping, *Statistical Tables 1980;* International Road Federation, *World Road Statistics 1976–80;* International Civil Aviation Organization, *Civil Aviation Statistics of the World 1980.* (M. C. MacDONALD)

sisted China with the development of a 20 million-ton-a-year coal wharf at Qinhuangdao (Ch'in-huang-tao). New coal ports were approved for Tarahan in southern Sumatra and at Surabaya to the west of Java, Indonesia. At the Soviet port of Yuzhny a new fully mechanized facility was built for the handling of coal and ore.

In Europe work was in progress on extensive additional facilities at Rotterdam and Antwerp. In the U.S. there was a dramatic change in the traditional federal role of providing full direct funding for congressionally authorized dredging projects, but it was doubtful that the decision to make the ports financially responsible for their own dredging would encourage expansion where it was most needed.

With the greater depth of water now available in the Suez Canal, larger vessels made use of the waterway, and in May the 350,771-ton-dw "World Symphony" transited the canal southbound in ballast. Northbound vessels with a beam of 42 m (140 ft) were accepted with a draft of 15 m (50 ft) when fully loaded. For the Panama Canal the most important development was the decision to undertake a joint U.S.-Japanese study into the feasibility of a new sea-level canal located some 130 km (1 km=0.621 mi) to the south of the existing waterway.   (W. D. EWART)

FREIGHT AND PIPELINES

The European Community agreed during the year on a maximum weight of 40 metric tons for large semitrailer trucks. This was less than the existing maximum in some member nations (for example, The Netherlands) and much less than in some U.S. states. In the U.K. a careful investigation recommended a maximum weight of 44 metric tons, but the government decided on 40.

On the water, tanker operations were still suffering from the restricted oil market, and demand for very large crude carriers fell off. The dry cargo market was more buoyant, especially in grain and coal, and long waits in line were experienced at Newcastle (Australia). The inland waterway network in the U.S. also relied on grain and coal for its traffic and benefited accordingly.

The railway scene was mixed, with Conrail wanting to lay off 21,000 workers from its 55,000-km, $4 billion-a-year system. British Railways benefited from increased carrying of coal, and in India four operations were introduced to feed coal to power stations. The general expansion of rail networks (see *Intercity Rail,* below) was commonly designed to serve the movement of goods rather than people.

Major pipeline developments and proposals were generally associated with the continuing discoveries of oil and gas in remote parts of the world. The two biggest projects were in Alaska and in the Soviet Union, where a 5,150-km line was to be built to carry 40,000,000,000 cu m of gas from Yamal Peninsula to the European network. This would be similar in length to the Orenburg line and reflected the scale of the 9,500-km-per-year Soviet gas pipeline program. In the U.S. there were 28 major pipelines planned to connect parts of Washington State, Wyoming, Minnesota, and

Texas. Major oil and gas pipeline openings included Shegdun to Yanbu (Saudi Arabia; 1,175 km), Kirkuk to Dartzel (Turkey; 1,000 km), and Saint-Lazare to Beynes (France; 370 km). The Far North Liquids and Associated Gas System network neared completion in the North Sea and was to be extended to gather gas from the Magnus, Thistle, and Murchisan fields. Also in the North Sea, a Norwegian gas-gathering network was started, and the Brent and Ninion pipelines were connected to the new Sullom Voe terminal in the Shetland Isles. The major slurry pipeline proposed in 1981 was a 2,400-km coal slurry line connecting the Appalachians and the Illinois Basin. If completed, the $3 billion project would be over five times as large as the existing biggest (Black Mesa) system.

ROADS AND TRAFFIC

During 1981 the world's roads carried about 7.5×10^{12} vehicle-miles of traffic. The 65,000-km Trans-Asian system, first conceived in 1959, was taking shape with a number of key routes 95% completed. The major remaining gaps were in Burma. The Pan-American network had been under way since 1929, and this north–south route from Alaska to Argentina was now complete except for the 400-km Darien Gap in Panama. Two major gaps remained in the 19,000-km Western Asian network.

In Europe the toll road network totaled more than 11,000 km (80% in Italy and France) and the West German autoroutes, 15,000 km. A number of new major roads and links were opened; these included the Bilbao to Zaragoza motorway in Spain, the route from Milan to the Swiss border, Autoroute 26 (North Sea to the South of France), and the Paris–Brittany autoroute. Important links outside Europe included the La Paz–Catapota Highway in South America, rising to almost 4,550 m (15,000 ft) above sea level, a tunnel linking Africa and Asia beneath the southern end of the Suez Canal, a tunnel through the Andes Mountains linking Chile and Argentina, and the parkway between Singapore and its new airport at Changi.

This 192-m (630-ft) ore carrier was christened in Cleveland, Ohio, in July. The boat will make runs on Lake Erie and the Cuyahoga River carrying 19,500 tons of iron ore pellets.

UPI

The "Tijuana Trolley" carries 18,000 persons a day from San Diego, California, to the Mexican border. The German-built cars were paid for from state sales and gasoline tax funds and have no ticket sellers or conductors.

The Pennsylvania Turnpike—forerunner of the U.S. Interstate Highway System—was now 40 years old and showing signs of its age, having carried 2,300,000,000 travelers. Signs of age were also to be seen elsewhere, with the first section of Britain's M1 motorway having to be renewed after only 20 years.

Urban road building was blossoming in third world cities, particularly in the Arab countries and the wealthier nations in the Far East and South America. Work started in 1981 on what was probably the world's most expensive superhighway. Connecting the Lincoln and Battery tunnels in New York City, it was estimated to cost $400 million per mile.

INTERCITY RAIL

The most spectacular event of the year was the initiation of the new Train de Grande Vitesse (TGV) service between Paris and southeastern France. The fleet of handsome orange trains provided a high-class, high-speed service to Lyon and to Geneva, and one modified train set a new railway speed record of 380 km/h (235 mph). The previous standard of 331 km/h (205 mph) was set by French National Railways in 1955. British and Soviet high-speed trains also entered regular service during the year between London and Glasgow and Moscow and Leningrad, respectively.

In the U.S. Amtrak's losses were approaching $1 billion annually. Amtrak introduced the high-speed tilting Light Rail Comfortable (LRC). Tilting trains had been used in the U.S. before World War II and in 1981 were also operating in Canada, Italy, Sweden, Spain, and the U.K. Japanese National Railways had its $13 billion debt written off, and the government grant to British Railways was increased because of the effects of the sluggish economy on usage.

During 1976–80 $24 billion was invested in the Soviet Union's railways, and the new five-year plan proposed an even higher level. In China 14 new lines totaling more than 3,000 km were under

construction, and other lines were being electrified. In 30 years freight traffic had increased tenfold and passenger traffic fivefold on China's railways.

Other developments included the introduction of a coast-to-coast "roadrailer" service in the U.S. Road rail vehicles could be used to form railway trains or as individual road semitrailers. Electronic interlocking was being tried on the Japanese and Dutch railways. A number of new rail links were opened, probably the most significant being the 525-km standard-gauge line from Tarcoala to Alice Springs in Australia.

URBAN MASS TRANSIT

The most pressing problem for urban mass transit systems in industrialized countries was the squeeze on public expenditure arising from governments' attempts to tackle the economic recession.

During 1981 extensions to existing subway systems were completed or under way in many parts of the world, including Canada (Montreal and Toronto), France (Lyon and Paris), Japan (Kobe, Osaka, and Tokyo), Mexico (Mexico City), Spain (Madrid), U.S.S.R. (Tashkent), U.K. (Tyne and Wear), U.S. (Atlanta, Ga., and Washington, D.C.), and West Germany (Munich, Nürnberg, and West Berlin). New systems began operating in Lille, France (an automated light system); Fukuaka and Kyoto, Japan; and Yerevan, U.S.S.R. The first stage of the Melbourne (Australia) rail loop was opened. Work started on the Belo Horizonte (Brazil) system and the Beijing (Peking) loop line, and $800 million of extensions to the New York City subway were under way. The latest U.S. city to propose a mass transit system was Houston, Texas. Suburban rail extensions were completed in Stuttgart and Munich in West Germany, and double tracking of the Kowloon–Canton Railway in China was well under way.

Strong interest continued in modern tramway (streetcar) and light rail systems. In the U.S.S.R. a

new system was opened at Krivai Rog; in the U.S. San Diego acquired a 26-km system, and in Canada a 13-km line opened in Calgary. An important innovation tried in both the U.K. and the U.S. was the Light Rail (diesel) Vehicle, developed by British Railways using a Leyland bus body.

Interest in new bus technology concentrated on trolley and hybrid buses for urban use. Over the last decade 1,000 new trolley buses had been delivered in North America, and new hybrid and guided buses were undergoing trials in West Germany. Gas turbine coaches underwent trials on long-distance routes in the U.S., and although there seemed to be a prospect of these competing with diesel vehicles on steady-speed expressway journeys, their potential for urban operations was limited. (DAVID BAYLISS)

See also Energy; Engineering Projects; Environment; Industrial Review: *Aerospace*; *Automobiles*.
[725.C.3; 734; 737.A.3]

Trinidad and Tobago

A republic and a member of the Commonwealth, Trinidad and Tobago consists of two islands off the coast of Venezuela, north of the Orinoco River delta. Area: 5,128 sq km (1,980 sq mi). Pop. (1981 est.): 1,176,000, including (1970) Negro 43%; East Indian 40%; mixed 14%. Cap. and largest city: Port-of-Spain (pop., 1976 est., 47,300). Language: English (official), Hindi, French, Spanish. Religion (1970): Christian 64%; Hindu 25%; Muslim 6%. President in 1981, Sir Ellis Clarke; prime ministers, Eric Williams to March 29 and, from March 30, George Chambers.

Contrary to previous predictions, the death of Prime Minister Eric Williams (*see* OBITUARIES) after 25 years in office did not bring chaos to Trini-

Trinidad and Tobago

dad and Tobago. When Williams died on March 29, 1981, there was an orderly changeover, and George Chambers (*see* BIOGRAPHIES) was appointed prime minister.

The ruling People's National Movement (PNM) government was endorsed at a general election on November 9 after a hard-fought campaign. In spite of a strong challenge by the Organization for National Reconstruction (ONR), led by Karl Hudson-Phillips, the PNM was returned with an increased majority of 26 out of 36 seats. The National Alliance, a group of three opposition parties, won all the remaining seats; the ONR, despite wide electoral support, took none.

Trinidad remained the Caribbean's richest nation with a balance of payments surplus of TT$1.5 billion in 1980 and reserves of TT$7 billion in mid-1981. But the optimism that led to tax cuts early in the year was tempered later; the rate of inflation was higher than the 1980 level of 18.7%, and the non-oil deficit on trade was rising faster than the increase in surpluses on oil and gas.

Although Trinidad maintained its low profile in the Caribbean, the appointment of Chambers brought optimism that the republic might play a more influential regional role. During the year programs of economic cooperation with Barbados were further developed. (DAVID A. JESSOP)

Tunisia

A republic of North Africa lying on the Mediterranean Sea, Tunisia is bounded by Algeria and Libya. Area: 154,530 sq km (52,664 sq mi). Pop. (1981 est.): 6,554,000. Cap. and largest city: Tunis (pop., 1975 census, city proper 550,404; 1978 est., governorate 1,030,400). Language: Arabic (official). Religion: Muslim; Jewish and Christian minorities. President in 1981, Habib Bourguiba; prime minister, Mohammed Mzali.

Tunisia

The year was marked by a continuance of liberalization policies by the ruling Parti Socialiste Destourien (PSD), leading to Tunisia's first multiparty legislative elections under Habib Bourguiba's presidency. The pace of liberalization had increased after the government reshuffle of Dec. 3, 1980, when previously disaffected PSD members were given ministerial posts. Amnesty was granted in January 1981 to 959 trade unionists who had already been released from detention; in February to all members of the Mouvement de l'Unité Populaire (MUP) with the exception of its exiled founder and leader, Ahmed Ben Salah; and in December to Habib Achour, former leader of the Union Générale des Travailleurs de Tunisie (UGTT), who, though released from prison in 1979, had remained under house arrest.

In April, at an extraordinary congress of the PSD, President Bourguiba approved the introduction of party pluralism. This was followed on July 18 by official recognition of the Tunisian Communist Party (PCT), outlawed since 1963. Unrest continued, however, despite the government's efforts and despite divisions within the MUP, a faction of which rejected Ben Salah's leadership. In February there was student agitation and in March a strike

TRINIDAD AND TOBAGO
Education. (1978–79) Primary, pupils 181,863, teachers (1975–76) 6,471; secondary, pupils 87,301, teachers (1975–76) 1,631; vocational, pupils 4,200, teachers (1975–76) 114; higher (1975–76), students 4,940, teaching staff *c.* 500.
Finance and Trade. Monetary unit: Trinidad and Tobago dollar, with (Sept. 21, 1981) a par value of TT$2.40 to U.S. $1 (free rate of TT$4.45 = £1 sterling). Gold and other reserves (June 1981) U.S. $2,706,000,000. Budget (1980 est.) balanced at TT$5,059,600,000. Foreign trade (1980): imports TT$7,585,500,000; exports TT$9,562,800,000. Import sources: Saudi Arabia 31%; U.S. 26%; U.K. 10%; Japan 7%. Export destinations: U.S. 57%; The Netherlands 6%. Main exports (1979): petroleum products 54%; crude oil 38%.
Transport and Communications. Roads (1977) 7,100 km. Motor vehicles in use (1979): passenger *c.* 131,300; commercial (including buses) *c.* 33,100. There are no railways in operation. Air traffic (1980): 1,505,000,000 passenger-km; freight 18.3 million net ton-km. Telephones (Jan. 1978) 74,900. Radio receivers (Dec. 1977) 275,000. Television receivers (Dec. 1977) 125,000.
Agriculture. Production (in 000; metric tons; 1980): sugar, raw value *c.* 114; rice (1979) 22; tomatoes *c.* 10; grapefruit *c.* 6; copra *c.* 8; coffee *c.* 4; cocoa *c.* 4. Livestock (in 000; 1979): cattle *c.* 77; pigs *c.* 58; goats *c.* 45; poultry *c.* 7,200.
Industry. Production (in 000; metric tons; 1980): crude oil 10,983; natural gas (cu m) *c.* 2,400,000; petroleum products *c.* 10,960; cement 182; nitrogenous fertilizers (nutrient content; 1979–80) *c.* 41; electricity (kw-hr; 1979) 1,820,000.

of transportation workers. In July the activities of Islamic fundamentalists of the Mouvement de la Tendance Islamique led to the arrest of 78 persons. On September 4 all but two were sentenced to prison for terms of up to 11 years.

The election, held on November 1, was contested by a National Front alliance of the PSD and UGTT and by three opposition parties (Mouvement des Démocrates Socialistes, the PCT, and the breakaway faction of the MUP), as well as by some independent candidates. The result was a complete victory for the National Front, which won all 136 parliamentary seats with 94.6% of the vote—an outcome greeted with some skepticism by the opposition.

Relations with Libya had been strained since the previous year's raid on Gafsa in southern Tunisia; in January, at Tunisia's invitation, the Libyan foreign minister visited Tunis for conciliatory talks. Arms purchases and defense agreements were discussed during the visits of Prime Minister Mohammed Mzali to Paris in February and of French Foreign Minister Claude Cheysson and Defense Minister Charles Hernu to Tunis in July and August, respectively; in November Tunisia bought three missile-carrying patrol boats from France. The U.S. also offered military aid, and in November a joint U.S.-Tunisian Military Commission was set up. In February the Inter-African Socialist Organization held its inaugural conference in Tunis.　　　　　　　　　(PHILIPPE DECRAENE)

TUNISIA

Education. (1979–80) Primary, pupils 1,024,537, teachers 26,207; secondary, pupils 184,084; vocational, pupils 54,233; secondary and vocational, teachers 15,075; teacher training, students 3,591, teachers (1978–79) 128; higher, students 25,602, teaching staff 2,236.

Finance. Monetary unit: Tunisian dinar, with (Sept. 21, 1981) a free rate of 0.50 dinar to U.S. $1 (0.92 dinar = £1 sterling). Gold and other reserves (June 1981) U.S. $476 million. Budget (1980 est.): revenue 752 million dinars; expenditure 537 million dinars (excludes 215 million dinars capital expenditure). Gross domestic product (1980) 3,471,000,000 dinars. Money supply (May 1981) 959,770,000 dinars. Cost of living (Tunis; 1975 = 100; May 1981) 148.7.

Foreign Trade. (1980) Imports 1,433,170,000 dinars; exports 891,410,000 dinars. Import sources (1979): France 26%; Italy 13%; West Germany 10%; U.S. 6%; Greece 6%. Export destinations: Italy 20%; France 19%; Greece 16%; West Germany 10%; U.S. 9%. Main exports (1979): crude oil 45%; clothing 16%; phosphates and products 10%; olive oil 6%; food 5%. Tourism (1979): visitors 1,356,000; gross receipts U.S. $525 million.

Transport and Communications. Roads (main; 1979) 17,762 km. Motor vehicles in use (1979): passenger 120,600; commercial 97,700. Railways (1980): 2,013 km; traffic 862 million passenger-km, freight 1,709,000,000 net ton-km. Air traffic (1980): c. 1,241,000,000 passenger-km; freight 12.5 million net ton-km. Telephones (Jan. 1980) 173,500. Radio receivers (Dec. 1979) c. 1 million. Television receivers (Dec. 1979) 255,700.

Agriculture. Production (in 000; metric tons; 1980): wheat 869; barley 296; potatoes (1979) 120; tomatoes c. 280; watermelons (1979) c. 160; grapes 135; dates 58; olives 837; oranges 88. Livestock (in 000; 1979): sheep c. 3,625; cattle c. 910; goats c. 950; camels c. 221; poultry c. 15,778.

Industry. Production (in 000; metric tons; 1980): crude oil 5,626; natural gas (cu m) 360,000; cement 1,779; iron ore (53% metal content) 389; pig iron 152; crude steel 177; phosphate rock (1979) 4,184; phosphate fertilizers (1979–80) c. 298; petroleum products c. 1,800; sulfuric acid 1,336; electricity (excluding most industrial production; kw-hr) 2,432,000.

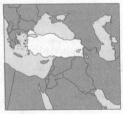

Turkey

Turkey

A republic of southeastern Europe and Asia Minor, Turkey is bounded by the Aegean Sea, the Black Sea, the U.S.S.R., Iran, Iraq, Syria, the Mediterranean Sea, Greece, and Bulgaria. Area: 779,452 sq km (300,948 sq mi), including 23,698 sq km in Europe. Pop. (1981 est.): 46,248,500. Cap.: Ankara (pop., 1980 prelim., 2,203,700). Largest city: Istanbul (pop., 1980 prelim., 2,853,500). Language: Turkish (official), Kurdish and Arabic minorities. Religion: predominantly Muslim. Head of state in 1981, Gen. Kenan Evren; prime minister, Bulent Ulusu.

The high command of the Turkish armed forces, which had constituted itself as the National Security Council and seized power in September 1980, achieved a large measure of success in restoring law and order in 1981. In the areas where martial law was declared, there had been 3,710 political

TURKEY

Education. (1978–79) Primary, pupils 5,562,315, teachers 187,027; secondary, pupils 1,591,615, teachers 65,262; vocational, pupils 482,980, teachers 25,845; teacher training, students 24,065, teachers 2,001; higher, students 313,517, teaching staff 19,700.

Finance. Monetary unit: Turkish lira, with (Sept. 21, 1981) a free rate of 118.74 liras to U.S. $1 (220.15 liras = £1 sterling). Gold and other reserves (June 1981) U.S. $1,014,000,000. Budget (1980–81 est.): revenue 706,687,000,000 liras; expenditure 756,687,000,000 liras. Gross national product (1980) 4,494,270,000,000 liras. Money supply (Sept. 1979) 389.2 billion liras. Cost of living (1975 = 100; June 1981) 1,037.

Foreign Trade. (1980) Imports 592,114,000,000 liras; exports 220,093,000,000 liras. Import sources: Iraq 14%; West Germany 13%; Libya 7%; U.S. 6%; France 5%; Iran 5%; Switzerland 5%; U.K. 5%. Export destinations: West Germany 21%; Italy 8%; U.S.S.R. 6%; France 6%; U.S. 5%. Main exports (1979): fruit and vegetables 34%; textile yarns and fabrics 14%; cotton 10%; tobacco 8%; cereals 5%; fertilizers 5%. Tourism (1979): visitors 1,524,000; gross receipts U.S. $281 million.

Transport and Communications. Roads (1979) 232,162 km (including 189 km expressways). Motor vehicles in use (1979): passenger 658,700; commercial 309,800. Railways: (1978) 8,139 km; traffic (1980) 6,014,000,000 passenger-km, freight 5,030,000,000 net ton-km. Air traffic (1980): c. 1,103,000,000 passenger-km; freight c. 13.7 million net ton-km. Shipping (1980): merchant vessels 100 gross tons and over 508; gross tonnage 1,454,838. Telephones (Dec. 1979) 1,086,800. Radio licenses (Dec. 1979) 4,280,000. Television licenses (Dec. 1979) 3,108,000.

Agriculture. Production (in 000; metric tons; 1980): wheat 17,455; barley c. 5,500; corn 1,150; rye 580; oats 350; potatoes 3,300; tomatoes 3,500; onions 900; sugar, raw value c. 1,000; sunflower seed 650; cottonseed 783; chick-peas 250; dry beans 160; cabbages (1979) c. 566; pumpkins (1979) c. 350; watermelons (1979) c. 4,000; cucumbers (1979) c. 450; oranges 692; lemons 200; apples 1,100; grapes 3,350; raisins c. 353; olives 1,050; tea 120; tobacco 230; cotton, lint 460. Livestock (in 000; Dec. 1979): cattle 15,567; sheep 46,026; buffalo 1,040; goats 18,775; horses (1978) 812; asses (1978) 1,371; chickens 53,709.

Industry. Fuel and power (in 000; metric tons; 1980): crude oil 2,328; coal 3,600; lignite 9,504; electricity (kw-hr) 23,280,000. Production (in 000; metric tons; 1980): cement 13,794; iron ore (55–60% metal content; 1979) 1,960; pig iron (1979) 2,020; crude steel 1,713; petroleum products (1978) c. 12,870; sulfuric acid 154; fertilizers (nutrient content; 1979–80) nitrogenous c. 354, phosphate c. 285; bauxite 522; chrome ore (oxide content; 1979) c. 201; cotton yarn c. 120; man-made fibres (1978) 87.

murders in the 21 months before the military takeover. By contrast, the toll in the entire country during the year after the takeover was 282. The Army seized large quantities of illegal arms, and over 43,000 people were detained (official figures), some 30,000 of whom were still in prison at the beginning of November. Ten convicted terrorists were hanged.

Political party activity was suspended and political parties were dissolved. Bans were also imposed periodically on books and newspapers. The military leaders tightened their grip on the official media (broadcasting and news agencies) and also on the administration in general. These measures drew some protest in the West. Western economic aid was also slightly affected, although $940 million was pledged in May at a meeting of the Organization for Economic Cooperation and Development.

The National Security Council announced measures looking toward a return to parliamentary democracy. On October 15 a 160-member nominated Consultative Assembly, selected from among 11,000 nonparty applicants, was inaugurated in Ankara. Together with the National Security Council, it formed a Constituent Assembly that would devise a new constitution and submit it to referendum. On October 27 the Constituent Assembly elected as its president Sadi Irmak, an elderly independent statesman. Irmak was criticized for saying that the constitution-making would take about two years. In December, however, plans to hold a referendum in November 1982 and general elections in 1983 were announced.

The economy showed some improvement. Consumer prices, which had risen by 94% in 1980, increased by only 34% in the year following the takeover. Exports rose from about $3 billion in 1980 to an estimated $4 billion-plus in 1981. Imports also rose, however, and the deficit was covered by increased remittances from emigrant workers and by foreign aid. The gross national product, which had fallen marginally in 1979 and 1980, was expected to show modest growth in 1981, although this did not prevent an increase in unemployment.

In foreign affairs, the military leaders pursued a cautious pro-Western policy, combined with studied neutrality in the Iran-Iraq war (which brought additional trade to Turkey) and with efforts to improve relations with the Arab countries, particularly Saudi Arabia. No objection was made to Greece's return to the military structure of NATO, and after Andreas Papandreou came to power in Greece, Prime Minister Bulent Ulusu expressed hopes of establishing friendly relations with him. During a July visit to Ankara by the Turkish Cypriot leader, Rauf Denktash, proposals were elaborated for the settlement of the Cyprus dispute. They were presented at the intercommunal talks in Nicosia in August but were coolly received by the Greek Cypriots. (*See* CYPRUS.)

Terrorism, checked at home, presented problems abroad. Attacks by Armenian terrorists on Turkish diplomats continued, bringing the death toll to 19 since 1973 and culminating in the seizure of the Turkish consulate in Paris on September 25. The attack on Pope John Paul II by the fugitive

IMAPRESS/PICTORIAL PARADE

Turkish terrorist Mehmet Ali Agca, who had been sentenced to death for the murder of a prominent Turkish newspaper editor, was condemned by the head of state, Gen. Kenan Evren. General Evren called on all friendly countries to cease harbouring Turkish terrorists.   (ANDREW MANGO)

After holding over 20 hostages for more than 14 hours in the Turkish consulate in Paris in September, a group of Armenian terrorists gave themselves up under the condition that they be granted political asylum. They had previously demanded freedom of Armenian political prisoners held captive in Turkey. One consulate guard was killed and two other people were wounded.

Tuvalu

A constitutional monarchy within the Commonwealth comprising nine main islands and their associated islets and reefs, Tuvalu is located in the western Pacific Ocean just south of the Equator and west of the International Date Line. Area: 26 sq km (10 sq mi). Pop. (1979): 7,400, mostly Polynesians. Cap.: Funafuti (pop., 1979, 2,200). Queen, Elizabeth II; governor-general in 1981, Penitala Fiatau Teo; prime ministers, Toaripi Lauti and, from September 8, Tomasi Puapua.

After a general election on Sept. 8, 1981, Prime Minister Toaripi Lauti of Tuvalu was defeated in a parliamentary leadership ballot. Given the nature of Tuvaluan politics, the government as such was not on trial during the elections; there were no political parties, and there was little discussion of national issues. In the small island constituencies, each with only a few hundred voters, kin affiliations were politically decisive, and members were judged by their success in delivering employment and services.

The former ministers were vulnerable on a number of grounds. They faced continuing embarrassment over the government's investments with a U.S. property speculator, and the government's

TUVALU
Education. (1979) Primary, pupils 1,298, teachers (1977) 48; secondary, pupils 236, teachers (1977) 12.
Finance and Trade. Monetary unit: Australian dollar, with (Sept. 21, 1981) a free rate of A$0.86 to U.S. $1 (A$1.60 = £1 sterling). Budget (1980 est.) balanced at A$2.3 million (including U.K. aid of A$750,000). Foreign trade (1979): imports A$1,850,800; exports A$560,000. Main exports: postage stamps c. 54%; copra c. 42%.

Tuvalu

development and budget targets were not met. Tuvalu's new prime minister, Tomasi Puapua, had been a member of the opposition for four years, and most of the new Cabinet ministers had parliamentary experience.

The economy continued to struggle. Development projects were concentrated on infrastructure; no revenue earner to match philately emerged, though the economy was expected to receive a boost from remittances when employment for Tuvaluan merchant seamen was found.

(BARRIE MACDONALD)

Uganda

Uganda

A republic and a member of the Commonwealth, Uganda is bounded by Sudan, Zaire, Rwanda, Tanzania, and Kenya. Area: 241,139 sq km (93,104 sq mi), including 44,081 sq km of inland water. Pop. (1981 est.): 13,012,000, virtually all of whom are African. Cap. and largest city: Kampala (pop., 1980 prelim., 458,000). Language: English (official), Bantu, Nilotic, Nilo-Hamitic, and Sudanic. Religion: Christian 63%, Muslim 6%, traditional beliefs. President in 1981, Milton Obote; prime minister, Erifasi Otema Allimadi.

When Pres. Milton Obote took office in December 1980, Uganda's economy was in a desperate state and its population was disoriented by years of insecurity and corruption. In January 1981 measures were introduced to try to control the black market but with indifferent results.

There were fears of a serious breakdown in law and order in the middle of the year following the withdrawal of the Tanzanian Army, which had helped to overthrow former president Idi Amin in 1979. Uganda's own army lacked training, and ac-

cusations of excesses and mutinies among its undisciplined troops were frequently made by missionaries as well as by overt critics of the government. Internal security was disturbed throughout the year by a series of bomb attacks on police stations and army bases, particularly in the Kampala area. An underground group calling itself the Uganda Freedom Movement (UFM) claimed responsibility for these attacks. The aim of the movement was said to be to overthrow Obote's government by force, but the main opposition party, the Democratic Party, though critical of Obote's policies, agreed to participate in parliamentary government. In northwestern Uganda fighting took place between supporters of Amin and government troops. There were reports of reprisals by the troops against villagers accused of sympathizing with the pro-Amin guerrillas.

In spite of these difficulties, improvements in the economy were evident. The reestablishment of links with Kenya eased transport problems and allowed coffee exports to be stepped up, while a loan of £15 million from Kenya paid for port and storage charges on imports that had been held up in Mombasa. On May 1 Obote offered considerably higher prices to farmers for their coffee and cotton crops in the hope of increasing output. (The years of insecurity under Amin had resulted in serious underproduction of coffee, in particular.) The UFM called on farmers not to sell to the state-owned marketing organization and threatened to rescind any contracts made between farmers and the government if it gained power.

Undeterred by this opposition and acting on the advice of the International Monetary Fund (IMF), Obote in June devalued the country's currency to about one-tenth of its former rate and said that in the future the Uganda shilling would be allowed to find its own level. His budget, too, left the prices of most commodities free from control. Foreign aid was beginning to have an effect upon the government's efforts to rehabilitate agriculture and restore communications, and in Kampala items such as salt, sugar, and soap—long in short supply—began to reappear, though at high prices.

The cautious support being proffered by Western nations was further evidenced in October when the IMF announced its intention to organize a donors' conference to raise financial aid for Uganda. During 1979 and 1980 the IMF had withheld support from Uganda because of the prevailing corruption. However, the efforts to ease the famine in the northeastern district of Karamoja were once more threatened by renewed violence in the middle of the year.

In July 1,420 former Ugandan soldiers who had served under Amin were released from Luzira prison near Kampala, where they had been kept since Amin's overthrow for fear that their release might add to the internal problems of the country. No charges had been brought against them, and an equal number remained in prison. Another echo of Amin's rule was heard in October when Amin's British-born adviser, Robert Astles, was tried for murder. Astles was acquitted, but he remained in custody and was expected to face further charges.

(KENNETH INGHAM)

Unemployment:
see Economy, World;
Social Security and
Welfare Services

UGANDA

Education. (State aided; 1979) Primary, pupils 1,-208,915, teachers 34,213; secondary, pupils 21,280, teachers 2,838; vocational, pupils 4,075, teachers 274; teacher training, students 9,235, teachers 402; higher, students 5,-494, teaching staff 587.

Finance and Trade. Monetary unit: Uganda shilling, with (Sept. 21, 1981) a free rate of UShs 78.20 to U.S. $1 (UShs 145 = £1 sterling). Budget (1980–81 est.): revenue UShs 5 billion; expenditure UShs 6.8 billion. Foreign trade: imports (1978) UShs 1,963,000,000; exports (1979) UShs 3,182,000,000. Import sources: Kenya 28%; U.K. 17%; West Germany 13%; Japan 8%; Italy 7%; India 6%. Export destinations (1978): U.S. c. 21%; U.K. c. 16%; France c. 10%; Japan c. 9%; Spain c. 7%; Turkey c. 6%. Main export: coffee 98%.

Transport and Communications. Roads (1979) 27,901 km. Motor vehicles in use (1979): passenger 26,000; commercial 5,400. Railways (1979) 1,286 km. Air traffic (1980): c. 120 million passenger-km; freight c. 3.2 million net ton-km. Telephones (Jan. 1980) c. 46,400. Radio receivers (Dec. 1977) 250,000. Television receivers (Dec. 1977) 81,-000.

Agriculture. Production (in 000; metric tons; 1980): millet c. 500; sorghum c. 400; corn (1979) c. 500; sweet potatoes (1979) c. 689; cassava (1979) c. 1,250; peanuts c. 200; dry beans c. 180; bananas c. 374; coffee c. 120; tea c. 13; cotton, lint c. 5; meat (1979) c. 148; fish catch (1979) c. 224; timber (cu m; 1979) c. 5,616. Livestock (in 000; 1979): cattle c. 5,367; sheep c. 1,068; goats c. 2,144; pigs c. 225; chickens c. 13,100.

Industry. Production (in 000; metric tons; 1978): cement 44; copper ore (metal content) 1.3; tungsten concentrates (oxide content) c. 0.14; electricity (kw-hr) 630,000.

Union of Soviet Socialist Republics

The Union of Soviet Socialist Republics is a federal state covering parts of eastern Europe and northern and central Asia. Area: 22,402,200 sq km (8,-649,500 sq mi). Pop. (1981 est.): 266.6 million, including (1979) Russians 52%; Ukrainians 16%; Uzbeks 5%; Belorussians 4%; Kazakhs 3%. Cap. and largest city: Moscow (pop., 1981 est., 8,015,-000). Language: officially Russian, but many others are spoken. Religion: about 40 religions are represented in the U.S.S.R., the major ones being Christian and Islam. General secretary of the Communist Party of the Soviet Union and chairman of the Presidium of the Supreme Soviet (president) in 1981, Leonid Ilich Brezhnev; chairman of the Council of Ministers (premier), Nikolay A. Tikhonov.

Domestic Affairs. The leaders of the Soviet Union found 1981 an even more troublesome year than 1980. The weather was again unkind, drought during the spring and summer being followed by a wet autumn during which Typhoon Phyllis battered the Soviet Far East mercilessly and caused extensive damage. This was a major factor in producing the third harvest failure in a row, making food a highly sought-after commodity.

The chief internal event was the 26th party congress, which convened between February 23 and March 3. The first surprise was the fact that only the opening minutes of Leonid Brezhnev's keynote speech were carried live by Soviet television. An announcer read the rest of the speech, but it was later discovered that nothing was wrong with Brezhnev's health. The triumphal tone of the previous congress in 1976 was missing. The international situation of the Soviet Union had deteriorated sharply after the invasion of Afghanistan in December 1979, and the increasing defense expenditure of the West came as an unpleasant surprise.

U.S. Pres. Ronald Reagan was blamed for the worsening of Soviet-U.S. relations even though he had only just taken office. Nevertheless, Brezhnev proposed a meeting with Reagan, maintaining that experience had shown that "top level sessions" were decisive in improving relations.

With regard to the economy, Brezhnev was critical of the lack of coordination among industrial ministries and the slow rise in labour productivity. The reform of economic administration, which should have been ready for the congress, was not mentioned. Evidently its complexity was greater than anticipated. Brezhnev praised the role of private farm plots in the feeding of the nation and encouraged private producers to grow even more. He revealed that a new party political program was being prepared. It was urgently required because the existing one, adopted in 1961, averred that the U.S.S.R. would pass U.S. per capita output in 1970 and that by 1980 the Soviet people would be living under communism, a condition in which there would be a surplus of goods of all kinds.

The speakers who followed Brezhnev did not fail to praise him, and in this regard he was accorded greater reverence than in 1976. The Azerbaijan party secretary led the others by mentioning Brezhnev 13 times; in 1976 the largest number of references to him in a speech was eight. He was called a "fighter for peace" and an "indefatigable champion of world peace," new appellations compared with 1976.

The new Central Committee (CC) voted in at the end of the congress was "elected," whereas at the previous congress it had been "unanimously elected." This might mean that some of the proposed candidates were not elected. In order for this to happen, half of the delegates would have to vote against the candidate. The new CC was larger than before, with 319 full and 151 candidate members, but 82% of the full members were reelected. Over half of the new full members were Russian, thus adding to the Russian dominance of the Central Committee. By the end of 1981 Russians ac-

Union of Soviet Socialist Republics

During September motorists lined up at Moscow gasoline stations in anticipation of price hikes. The increases doubled the price of gasoline to as much as $2.20 per U.S. gallon.

counted for 68% of the members, while the proportion of Ukrainians declined to 14% and that of Belorussians to 2%. Of the new full members, 42 were from the Communist Party bureaucracy and 21 from the government; there were also 11 workers and peasants, 5 from the armed forces, and 3 from the security force (KGB).

For the first time at a party congress, no personnel changes were made in the Secretariat and the Politburo, revealing the extraordinary stability at the top party levels. The same could not be said of local party secretaries or government officials. Before the congress was convened, many ministers were changed and the party secretary in Moldavia, Ivan Bodyul, was made a deputy prime minister of the U.S.S.R. Corruption led to many changes in the western Ukraine. In Kolomiya, for instance, the party secretary and the town soviet chairman were sacked and expelled from the party for bribery and corruption.

Many death sentences were passed for war crimes. In Smolensk oblast, for example, four men were executed for offenses committed in 1943. The most startling murder was that of Sultan Ibraimov, the prime minister of Kirgiziya, in December 1980 while he was asleep in a sanatorium. Also in Kirgiziya two men were shot for hijacking a truck carrying 2,500 bottles of vodka and killing the driver. The Soviet press was quite frank about the prevalence of bribery and corruption in the party and state apparatus. For example, in Azerbaijan the director of the social security office for industrial enterprises diverted cars meant for invalids to healthy people. He was well paid by the recipients, becoming a millionaire with two flats, a country house, an orange grove, and 34 kg (75 lb) of gold. An enterprising Central Asian sold diplomas and acquired 3 cars, 74 suits, and 149 pairs of shoes.

The private plot was given a boost in a party and government decree in January when credits were promised to producers, and young calves were even to be given to workers free of charge if they agreed to raise them. Nevertheless, the impact of this new policy was hardly felt in 1981. President

Reagan removed the U.S. grain embargo and extended the agreement whereby the U.S.S.R. could purchase eight million metric tons without the permission of the U.S. government. The Soviet Union was expected to import 18 million tons of U.S. grain, a large proportion of the 45 million tons it needed because of the harvest shortfall.

The main reason why demand for food in the Soviet Union far exceeded supply was the cheap food policy that had been pursued by the government. Whereas incomes had doubled over the last 20 years, food prices had remained more or less stable. Prices paid to farmers rose sharply, giving rise to a huge subsidy of some $30 billion annually. More and more food was being distributed privately or held back in stores for special customers at increased prices. The state, of course, only received the official price.

In order to cut gasoline consumption, prices were doubled in September as part of a package that included the biggest price increases in three years. Vodka and cigarette prices went up by about a quarter, and furniture, fine jewelry, cut glass, and carpet prices increased by 25–30%. Despite rumours, the price of bread and other staple foodstuffs remained the same. This had to be regarded as a political and not an economic decision. The unrest in Poland and previous experience, such as the 1962 riots in Novocherkassk which followed food price rises, were evidently heeded. Just before the price increases were announced, wage rises were awarded to miners. Underground workers received a 27% increase, opencut workers 24%, and others employed in mining 19%.

The 1979 census revealed that the proportion of Russians in the Soviet population had dropped to 52.4% and that the annual increase in the population was almost entirely non-Russian. To remedy this situation a pro-natal policy, comparable to that in operation in Hungary and East Germany, was adopted. Pregnant women would now receive a year's paid leave with an option of an additional six months of unpaid leave with their job guaranteed. The allowance was 35 rubles per month with more in the more inhospitable parts of the Russian

---

U.S.S.R.

Education. (1980–81) Primary, pupils 34.4 million; secondary, pupils 9.9 million; primary and secondary, teachers 2,638,000; vocational and teacher training, students 4,612,000, teachers (1978–79) 229,700; higher, students 5,235,500, teaching staff (1978–79) 345,000.

Finance. Monetary unit: ruble, with (Sept. 21, 1981) a free rate of 0.71 ruble to U.S. $1 (1.32 rubles = £1 sterling). Budget (1981 est.) balanced at 271.4 billion rubles.

Foreign Trade. (1980) Imports 44,465,000,000 rubles; exports 49,656,000,000 rubles. Import sources: Eastern Europe 43% (East Germany 10%, Poland 8%, Czechoslovakia 8%, Bulgaria 8%, Hungary 6%); West Germany 7%. Export destinations: Eastern Europe 43% (East Germany 10%, Poland 9%, Bulgaria 8%, Czechoslovakia 7%, Hungary 6%); West Germany 6%; Cuba 5%; France 5%. Main exports: crude oil and products 36%; machinery 11%; natural gas 7%; transport equipment 5%; iron and steel 5%.

Transport and Communications. Roads (1979) 1,426,700 km. Motor vehicles in use (1979): passenger c. 8,250,000; commercial (including buses) c. 7,259,000. Railways (1979): 234,200 km (including

93,100 km industrial); traffic 335,300,000,000 passenger-km, freight 3,349,300,000,000 net ton-km. Air traffic (1980): 160,299,000,000 passenger-km; freight c. 3,083,000,000 net ton-km. Navigable inland waterways (1979) 143,200 km; freight traffic 232,700,000,000 ton-km. Shipping (1980): merchant vessels 100 gross tons and over 8,279; gross tonnage 23,443,534. Telephones (Jan. 1980) 22,464,000. Radio receivers (Dec. 1975) 122.5 million. Television receivers (Dec. 1979) c. 60 million.

Agriculture. Production (in 000; metric tons; 1980): wheat 98,100; barley c. 44,500; oats c. 14,200; rye c. 10,200; corn c. 9,700; rice 2,800; millet c. 2,000; potatoes 66,900; sugar, raw value c. 7,600; tomatoes c. 6,210; watermelons (1979) c. 3,400; apples c. 7,200; sunflower seed 4,650; cottonseed c. 6,600; linseed c. 260; soybeans c. 470; dry peas c. 4,900; wine c. 2,940; tea c. 125; tobacco c. 305; cotton, lint c. 3,200; flax fibres (1979) c. 311; wool 277; hen's eggs 3,724; milk c. 90,200; butter c. 1,350; meat c. 15,000; fish catch (1979) 9,114; timber (cu m; 1979) c. 361,400. Livestock (in 000; Jan. 1980): cattle 115,100; pigs 73,898; sheep 143,599; goats 5,824; horses (1979) c. 5,700; chickens c. 941,664.

Industry. Index of production (1975 = 100; 1980) 124. Fuel and power (in 000; metric tons; 1980): coal and lignite 716,000; crude oil 603,000; natural gas (cu m) 435,000,000; manufactured gas (cu m; 1979) 37,270,000; electricity (kw-hr) 1,295,000,000. Production (in 000; metric tons; 1980): cement 124,800; iron ore (60% metal content) 246,000; pig iron (1979) c. 123,000; steel 148,000; aluminum (1979) c. 2,400; copper (1979) c. 1,170; lead (1979) c. 780; zinc (1979) c. 1,085; magnesite (1979) c. 1,950; manganese ore (metal content) 1979) c. 3,300; tungsten concentrates (oxide content; 1979) c. 11; gold (troy oz) c. 8,300; silver (troy oz) c. 46,000; sulfuric acid 23,000; caustic soda 2,800; plastics and resins 3,500; fertilizers (nutrient content; 1979) nitrogenous 9,074, phosphate 5,930, potash 6,635; newsprint (1979) 1,420; other paper and board (1979) 11,310; manmade fibres (1979) 1,131; cotton fabrics (sq m; 1979) 6,977,000; woolen fabrics (sq m; 1979) 774,000; rayon and acetate fabrics (sq m; 1979) 1,724,000; passenger cars (units) 1,327; commercial vehicles (units) 780. New dwelling units completed (1978) 2,125,000.

Federation. There were nine million families in the U.S.S.R. in 1981 headed by women, and allowances for each child up to the age of 16 rose from 5 to 20 rubles in December. (The free exchange rate was 0.71 ruble = U.S. $1.)

Pensions also rose. Pensions in a family with a breadwinner rose to 28–38 rubles per month. The total cost of the increases was estimated at 2.5 billion rubles a year. They affected 4.5 million families with children under 16 and about 14 million pensioners.

A major change in nationalities policy was announced by Brezhnev at the 26th party congress. He promised that all nonindigenous nationalities in the Russian Federation and in other republics would get their own schools, newspapers, and cultural life. Previously, these were only received by Russians outside the Russian Federation. The new move appeared to be aimed at increasing labour mobility in the Soviet Union. Over the period 1981–85 the work force was expected to increase by 3.3 million and during the years 1986–90 by even less. Since the labour surplus was mainly in Central Asia, the planners realized that they would have to attract Muslim workers to Slavic areas.

Between February and September, on average, four political arrests or trials took place in the Soviet Union every week. At least 48 individuals were arrested, and 80 (most of whom had been arrested previously) were sentenced at 54 political trials throughout the nation. The numbers might in fact be higher since information about all cases might not have reached the West. It was clear that a purge of public dissenters, involving religious, humanitarian, nationalist, cultural, and political protest, was under way. Since 1979 more than 500 dissidents had been arrested. The KGB employed a low-key approach in order to silence all criticism and protest gradually, seeking to avoid provoking large-scale demonstrations such as had occurred in Estonia, Lithuania, and Georgia. The average sentence was five years, but harsher penalties of up to 15 years were handed out in the Ukraine. About 10% of the defendants recanted in return for lighter sentences. A recent study estimated that at least 40% of the political prisoners in Soviet labour camps and jails were Ukrainian. Feelings were particularly strong in the Western Ukraine, a region that only became part of the republic in 1940.

Also during the year Raisa Rudenko of Kiev was arrested and accused of distributing the well-known unofficial journal of human rights, the *Chronicle of Current Events*. She was the wife of Mykola Rudenko, the leader of the Ukrainian Helsinki monitoring group, who was sentenced to 12 years in prison or exile in 1977. A prominent Soviet dissident, Anatoly Marchenko, a founder of the Helsinki human rights group in Moscow, was sentenced to ten years in a strict-regime labour camp and a further five years in internal exile for "anti-Soviet agitation and propaganda." In Estonia Mart Niklus and Yuri Kukk were sentenced to ten years in a special-regime camp and an additional five years of internal exile for defending Estonian national rights. The latter also protested against the Soviet invasion of Afghanistan and went on a hunger strike; he died in March.

British Foreign Secretary Lord Carrington (right) urged Soviet withdrawal from Afghanistan during a Moscow meeting in July with Soviet Foreign Minister Andrey Gromyko.

Sentences handed out to Armenians were especially severe. Ishkhan Mkrtchyan, one of the members of the League of Young Armenians, was tried for creating an "anti-Soviet organization." One of the goals of the League was independence for Armenia, which is permitted by the Soviet constitution but not in practice. He was given seven years in prison and five years of internal exile but escaped while en route to prison, a rare occurrence in the U.S.S.R.

Those who applied to emigrate often suffered harassment. For instance, Sofia Baazova, aged 71, a leading scientist in Georgia, was attacked and had to have 12 stitches inserted in a head wound. She recognized her attacker, the son of a KGB officer and a Georgian high court judge, but the case was dropped for "lack of evidence." All the members of the Working Commission for the Investigation of the Use of Psychiatry for Political Purposes had been arrested and sentenced by late 1981. One of its members, Anatoly Koryagin, who was serving a 12-year sentence, appealed to his colleagues throughout the world to expel the Soviet Union from the World Psychiatric Association. Pastor Pyotr Rumachik, vice-president of the unregistered Baptist Council of Churches, was sentenced to five years in a strict-regime camp. Nikolay Baraksha, a Baptist, was forcibly incarcerated in a psychiatric hospital in Rostov-on-Don. The number of Baptists arrested during the year exceeded 100 for the first time since 1976.

Andrey Sakharov, winner of the 1975 Nobel Prize for Peace, and his wife, Yelena, began a hunger strike on November 22 in protest against the refusal of the Soviet authorities to grant the wife of Sakharov's stepson an exit visa to the U.S. When the visa was granted, the Sakharovs ended their fast. The most prominent defectors during the year were Maxim Shostakovich, an orchestra conductor, and his son Dmitry, a pianist.

An extremely revealing analysis of the political

WIDE WORLD

Dignitaries at the Soviet Communist Party congress in Moscow in February included, from left in front row: Stanislaw Kania, then Polish party chief; Le Duan, party leader of Vietnam; and Pres. Fidel Castro of Cuba. In second row, from left: Premier Willi Stoph of East Germany; Gen. Wojciech Jaruzelski, then Polish premier; and Gus Hall, head of the U.S. Communist Party.

cynicism and spiritual malaise prevalent among Soviet youth was published by Viktor Chebrikov, a deputy head of the KGB. He accused the West of using concepts such as religion, nationalism, and political liberalism to undermine the faith of the younger generation in orthodox Soviet Communism. He suggested that the foundations of the Soviet state were being undermined by bourgeois ideology, political apathy, nihilism, consumerism, and the pervasive view that life was better in the West. He confirmed that foreign nationalist organizations of Lithuanians, Ukrainians, and Armenians were exerting a powerful influence within the U.S.S.R. Alcoholism also continued to be a serious problem.

It became much more difficult for Jews, Armenians, and Germans to emigrate from the Soviet Union during the year. Whereas in 1980 approximately 21,500 Jews left, in 1981 emigration averaged just over 1,000 a month. A determined campaign was conducted against the teaching of Hebrew, but an estimated 60 private teachers and 1,000 students were studying Hebrew in Moscow alone.

The Economy. It was another disappointing year for the Soviet economy. Gross national product was expected to grow only 3% in 1981, with industry achieving a 3.4% increase instead of the planned 4.1%. The steel, coal, and cement industries failed to fulfill their goals. Overall labour productivity rose 2.6% instead of the desired 3.6%.

The grain harvest was unlikely to exceed 175 million metric tons, as compared with the target for the 1981–85 plan period of 239 million tons annually. Food had become "politically and economically the central problem of the five-year plan," according to Brezhnev. A special Central Committee meeting was to be convened to deal with agriculture, during which priority was to be given to grain and fodder production. The envisioned 13% rise in agricultural output over the years 1981–85 appeared to be too ambitious, despite a huge investment of 190 billion rubles ($280 billion). Meat production, for example, was officially stated to be the same during the first half of 1981 as in the corresponding period of 1980. A Ministry of Fruit and Vegetable Production was established in

December 1980 to supervise those crops.

A contract to bring Siberian natural gas to Western Europe was signed with the West German firm Ruhrgas in November. West Germany agreed to take 10.5 billion cu m annually for 25 years, and eventually 40 billion cu m were to be exported to Western Europe each year. For the first time West Berlin was included in a Soviet-West German gas deal; it was to take 700 million cu m annually.

Foreign Affairs. Brezhnev's first visit to a Western nation since the invasion of Afghanistan took place in November when he went to West Germany. The talks were dominated by arms control. The defeat of Valéry Giscard d'Estaing in the French presidential election caused West German Chancellor Helmut Schmidt to become the Western leader with the closest ties to the Soviet Union. The new French president, François Mitterrand, was openly critical of Soviet arms spending and the treatment of dissidents. However, the French Communist Party (PCF) threw off its Eurocommunist garb and again became a loyal supporter of the Soviet Union.

Soviet-U.S. relations, of course, dominated the world scene. Judging by the repeated appeals for arms control by Brezhnev and Soviet Foreign Minister Andrey Gromyko, the Soviet Union needed such a development. This was connected to the increasingly onerous burden of defense expenditure on the Soviet economy. But throughout the year mistrust and mutual recriminations characterized exchanges between the U.S. and the Soviet Union on arms and other subjects. The atmosphere was made even more frigid by the occasionally contradictory statements issued by the U.S. secretaries of state and defense. In November, however, President Reagan, prompted by Chancellor Schmidt, launched an initiative that was called the "zero option." The U.S. promised not to deploy Pershing II and cruise missiles in Western Europe if the U.S.S.R. would remove its new mobile triple-headed SS-20 missiles and the older SS-4s and SS-5s. Arms control talks between the U.S. and the U.S.S.R. began in Geneva on November 30.

The other serious unsolved problem was Poland. In June the Communist Party of the Soviet Union sent the Polish United Workers' Party a stiff letter,

but this had little effect and in September the Soviet party and government sent the Polish party and government another missive. The Soviets pointed out that they had warned the Poles to restrain the independent labour union Solidarity in March, April, June, and August. They also provided Poland with $1.5 billion to sustain its economy, but by midyear Poland's debts had had to be rescheduled. When the Polish Army cracked down on Solidarity in December and imposed martial law, the Soviet Union welcomed the development but also denied any active role in it. President Reagan, however, declared that "the Soviet Union bears a heavy and direct responsibility for the repression in Poland," and the U.S. imposed trade sanctions on the U.S.S.R. on December 29.

In Afghanistan matters continued to go badly, with mounting Soviet casualties being admitted. In the UN in November a motion calling for Soviet withdrawal from Afghanistan was passed by 116 votes to 23 with 12 abstentions, revealing that Soviet efforts to legitimize Babrak Karmal's regime had failed.

In the Middle East the assassination of Egyptian Pres. Anwar as-Sadat in October held out hope for the U.S.S.R. of gaining greater influence in Egypt. Such influence was then at a low ebb due to the expulsion of the Soviet ambassador and six diplomats in September. The Soviet military presence in Yemen (Aden) and Ethiopia was consolidated by military pacts. Jordan bought arms worth $200 million, thus improving the Soviet Union's relations with King Hussein even further. In October the Moscow office of the Palestine Liberation Organization was accorded full diplomatic status. The Congo signed a treaty of friendship and cooperation with the U.S.S.R. in May. In Angola Sgt. Maj. Nikolay Pestretsov was captured by South African forces, and other Soviet nationals were killed in raids in the southeast.

China continued to be a thorn in the flesh for the Soviet Union. Sino-U.S. military cooperation worried Moscow and led to accusations that China was merely a pawn in the hands of the U.S. In other developments Viktor Lazin became the first Soviet diplomat to be expelled from Britain since 1971. A Soviet submarine ran aground well inside Swedish territorial waters on October 27 and was only released on November 6. The incident caused the U.S.S.R. considerable embarrassment, the more so since the Swedes did not accept the official Soviet explanation of the incident.

(MARTIN MCCAULEY)

United Arab Emirates

Consisting of Abu Dhabi, Ajman, Dubai, Fujairah, Ras al-Khaimah, Sharjah, and Umm al-Qaiwain, the United Arab Emirates is located on the eastern Arabian Peninsula. Area: 77,700 sq km (30,000 sq mi). Pop. (1981 est.): 1,040,300, including Arab 42%, South Asian 50% (predominantly Iranian, Indian, and Pakistani), others 8% (mostly Europeans and East Asians). Cap.: Abu Dhabi town (pop., 1975, 95,000). Language: Arabic. Religion: Muslim. President in 1981, Sheikh Zaid ibn

United Arab Emirates

UNITED ARAB EMIRATES
Education. (1979–80) Primary, pupils 88,617, teachers 5,136; secondary, pupils 31,138, teachers 2,736; vocational, pupils 422, teachers 83; higher, students 2,516, teaching staff 344.
Finance. Monetary unit: dirham, with (Sept. 21, 1981) a free rate of 3.63 dirhams to U.S. $1 (6.73 dirhams = £1 sterling). Gold and other reserves (June 1981) U.S. $2,305,-000,000. Budget (federal; 1980 est.) balanced at 15,972,-000,000 dirhams.
Foreign Trade. (1980) Imports 32,425,000,000 dirhams; exports 76,884,000,000 dirhams. Import sources (1979): Japan 17%; U.K. 16%; U.S. 13%; West Germany 8%; Bahrain 7%; France 5%. Export destinations (1979): Japan c. 24%; U.S. c. 14%; France c. 8%; Netherlands Antilles c. 8%; West Germany c. 8%. Main export: crude oil 94%.
Industry. Production (in 000; metric tons; 1980): crude oil 84,194; petroleum products (1978) 523; natural gas (cu m) 7,981,000; electricity (Abu Dhabi only; kw-hr; 1978) 3,759,000.

Sultan an-Nahayan; prime minister, Sheikh Rashid ibn Said al-Maktum.

Political unity in the United Arab Emirates became stronger in 1981 although death removed two of the seven emirs. Sheikh Rashid ibn Humaid of Ajman died on September 6 and Sheikh Rashid ibn Ahmed of Umm al-Qaiwain on February 21. They were succeeded by their sons, Sheikh Humaid and Sheikh Rashid, respectively. Illness dogged Sheikh Rashid of Dubai, prime minister of the federation; his eldest son, Sheikh Maktum, became crown prince. Sheikh Zaid was reelected president of the federation in November.

The federation's currency board finally became the central bank in December 1980. In line with decisions agreed upon by the Organization of Petroleum Exporting Countries, Abu Dhabi trimmed oil production, although Dubai kept its output unchanged. Total production was about 1.5 million bbl a day. Sharjah announced an oil discovery that, when fully developed, could yield 80,000 bbl a day.

The federation's first development plan was drafted with an allocation of $46.6 billion over five years. Industry and agriculture in the non-oil-producing emirates were to be given priority. Nevertheless, the most ambitious projects continued to take place in Abu Dhabi; the state-owned Abu Dhabi National Oil Company was developing a $20 billion industrial zone at Ruwais. Cooperation with other Gulf states through the Gulf Cooperation Council, formed in February, was symbolized by the first heads of state meeting in Abu Dhabi in May.

(JOHN WHELAN)

United Kingdom

A constitutional monarchy in northwestern Europe and member of the Commonwealth, the United Kingdom comprises the island of Great Britain (England, Scotland, and Wales) and Northern Ireland, together with many small islands. Area: 244,035 sq km (94,222 sq mi), including 3,084 sq km of inland water but excluding the crown dependencies of the Channel Islands and Isle of Man. Pop. (1981 prelim.): 55,671,000. Cap. and largest city: London (Greater London pop., 1981 prelim., 6,696,000). Language: English; some

United Kingdom

Welsh and Gaelic also are used. Religion: mainly Protestant, with Catholic, Muslim, and Jewish minorities, in that order. Queen, Elizabeth II; prime minister in 1981, Margaret Thatcher.

Domestic Affairs. The year 1981 was one of political change in Britain. At the beginning of the year British politics were conducted within a two-party system. That is to say, they were conducted on the assumption that either the Conservative Party or the Labour Party would form the next government. The Liberal Party might achieve a flourish of midterm protest, but nobody supposed that it could win enough seats in the House of Commons to take power. By the end of the year, however, the political map of Britain looked very different. The Social Democratic Party (SDP) had risen from nowhere to dominate the scene, at least temporarily, with a series of impressive by-election performances. Britain thus had what looked remarkably like a three- or multiparty system of politics. (*See* Sidebar.)

These political developments took place against a sombre economic background and a continuing struggle to rectify the weaknesses of British industry. The year marked the halfway point of the Conservative Party government of Prime Minister Margaret Thatcher (*see* BIOGRAPHIES). Some of her own supporters grew impatient for results from her attempt to subject the ailing British economy to the discipline of market forces. (*See* Feature Article: *Monetarism—Neither Kill nor Cure.*) Unemployment continued to rise, although it did not quite reach the predicted three-million mark, and it was in the context of economic decline and increasing social tensions that Britons watched aghast as their inner cities leaped into flames while rioting youths, both black and white, looted and smashed. In April there were riots in Brixton, an

inner London neighbourhood with a large population of West Indian origin, and in July there followed many disturbances, the chief of which were in Liverpool, Manchester, and London. Lord Scarman submitted a report on the incidents in November. (*See* RACE RELATIONS.)

The misfortunes of the Labour Party tended to dominate the political scene. The 1980 Labour Party conference had voted in favour of electing the party leader by a wider franchise than the members of Parliament (MP's). The object of a special conference in January 1981 was to agree on the exact composition of the electoral college. Party leader Michael Foot, though he preferred the old system, was prepared to bow to the wishes of the constituency (local) Labour parties and the trade unions. He hoped to see the establishment of an electoral college that would leave MP's with 50% of the votes. A great deal of maneuvering resulted in a college in which the trade unions had 40% of the votes while MP's and local parties had 30% each. This was an open defeat for the parliamentary leadership. More important, it was a radical constitutional departure from the principle of representative parliamentary democracy. The declared aim of the reformers, whose champion was Tony Benn, was to make MP's accountable to the party members and beholden to the policy decisions of the annual conference. It was for this reason that a group of right-wing Labour Party MP's, led by the "gang of four" (Roy Jenkins [*see* BIOGRAPHIES], Shirley Williams, David Owen, and William Rodgers), set up the Council for Social Democracy within days of the January conference; two months later the final break from the Labour Party took place when the Social Democratic Party was launched.

The crisis in the Labour Party deepened in April when Benn declared himself a candidate for the deputy leadership of the party, an office held by Denis Healey (*see* BIOGRAPHIES), the defeated right-wing candidate in the November 1980 leadership contest. Benn's challenge condemned the party to a summer of intense ideological debate and personal rivalry that was seldom for long out of the headlines. Healey started as favourite to win, but it soon became apparent that the "Bennites" had made some organizational inroads into the trade union power structures as well as having captured the great bulk of the constituency Labour parties. Healey won in the end, but by such a narrow majority that the main effect of the contest, fought out in full view in the new electoral college, was to advertise the strength of the left and Benn. The latter captured half of the Labour movement, which was then totally and—or so it seemed to many—irrevocably split.

Foot hoped to be able to reunite the torn party around a shadow Cabinet that could include both Benn and Healey despite the sharp policy differences between them about nuclear weapons and the degree of Socialist intervention in the economy. Benn, however, resolutely refused to compromise. He insisted that as a member of the shadow Cabinet he would feel bound by the policy decisions of the party conference and not by the collective decisions of his parliamentary colleagues.

On May 31, the final day of a month-long march from Liverpool to London, an estimated 100,000 persons joined in a "People's March for Jobs." Unemployment had reached a postwar record in the U.K. of 2.5 million.

UPI

In the end Foot was obliged reluctantly to disown him. As a result, Benn failed to win election to the shadow Cabinet, although the extent of his vote showed that support for him was growing even in the Parliamentary Labour Party and in spite of Fort's disapproval.

The disarray of the Labour Party was of huge benefit to the government. Thatcher began the year with a minor reshuffle of her Cabinet. Francis Pym was removed from the Ministry of Defence, where he had been resisting spending cuts, and made leader of the House of Commons. To make way for him there, the colourful Norman St. John Stevas was sacked from the Cabinet altogether. By the week of the budget in March, however, the new Cabinet was in open disarray. Senior ministers made no secret of their dismay over the deflationary impact of Chancellor of the Exchequer Sir Geoffrey Howe's tax measures and of their indignation over the lack of Cabinet consultation about the government's economic strategy. The roots of the trouble lay in the public expenditure review of the previous autumn, when an alliance of spending ministers and "wets" (so dubbed contemptuously by the prime minister) had defeated the Treasury and the prime minister herself. In the budget the latter took their revenge and taxed back the money that the Cabinet had refused to cut from spending programs.

The theory behind the budget was that by giving continued priority to the countering of inflation and by holding to the government's financial targets, interest rates would be brought down, enabling growth in the economy to resume. The budget's critics pointed to the still-deepening recession, to rising unemployment, and to the plight of manufacturing industry, whose cries for help had reached a pre-budget crescendo. Whether or not Howe's strategy might have succeeded soon became a hypothetical question as world interest rates rose sharply. At a crucial Cabinet meeting in July the prime minister and the chancellor found themselves isolated. Not only the "wets" but also ministers previously loyal or sympathetic to the government's strategy refused to countenance further cuts on the scale proposed by the Treasury.

KEYSTONE

Four former Labour Cabinet ministers (from left: William Rodgers, Shirley Williams, Roy Jenkins, and David Owen) met in January to form the Council for Social Democracy. In March the council announced the creation of the Social Democratic Party.

After the parliamentary summer recess, the prime minister partially purged her Cabinet. Three Cabinet ministers—Sir Ian Gilmour, Lord Soames, and Mark Carlisle—were sacked; but the most important change involved the reluctant move by James Prior, a chief critic of Thatcher's economic policy, who became secretary of state for Northern Ireland. The vacant seat at the Department of Employment was filled by Norman Tebbit (see BIOGRAPHIES), opening the way to the tougher line toward the trade unions favoured by the prime minister. The message was clear: there was to be no change in direction.

The argument burst into the open once more in October at a remarkable Conservative Party conference in Blackpool. While the prime minister basked in the adulation of the predominantly right-wing delegates, a succession of her critics and colleagues assailed her policies. Among Cabinet ministers who expressed themselves in favour of at least a rethinking of current policy was Secretary of State for the Environment Michael Hesel-

Emergence of a New Political Force in Britain

The Social Democratic Party (SDP) was born on March 26, 1981. Its conception, however, was less easily dated. In a television lecture in the autumn of 1979, Roy Jenkins (see BIOGRAPHIES), former Labour Party Cabinet minister, spoke of the need to strengthen what he called the "radical centre." In the summer of 1980, as the Labour Party continued on its leftward path, three leading pro-European right-wingers—David Owen, William Rodgers, and Shirley Williams, all former Labour Cabinet ministers—issued what amounted to a manifesto for a breakaway. Their resolve was strengthened by a rancorous Labour Party conference that October, dominated by the left, followed by the defeat of the right-wing candidate Denis Healey and the election of Michael Foot to the leadership of the Labour Party.

At the end of January 1981 the Labour Party's special conference at Wembley confirmed the dethroning of the parliamentary Labour party. Jenkins, Owen, Rodgers, and Williams were ready the next day with a statement of intent and principle which they dubbed the Limehouse Declaration— it was issued from Owen's riverside residence in London's East End—and the countdown to the launching of a new political party had begun.

It was a formidable and hazardous enterprise. The British political system is hostile to third parties. However, the success of SDP was instant and astonishing. In early March, 12 members of Parliament resigned the Labour Party whip in readiness

for the formation of the new party on March 26; by December 1 the SDP parliamentary representation had grown to 25, including one defector from the Conservative Party. Its membership by the end of the year had soared to more than 70,000.

Most important of all, the desire of a large section of the public for an alternative to the choice between Conservative or Labour translated itself from opinion-poll findings into real votes. In July Jenkins, daring to fight a by-election in the Labour stronghold of Warrington, scored what he proclaimed a "moral victory" with a remarkable 42% of the vote. (The winning Labour Party candidate gained 48%.) A Liberal Party candidate with SDP backing romped to victory in the London suburb of Croydon North West. Finally, in November Williams won an election in the Conservative stronghold of Crosby on the outskirts of Liverpool. Within eight months of the March launching the SDP was in command of the support of some 40% of the electorate, according to opinion polls.

In September the SDP entered into an alliance with the Liberal Party, and in the following weeks a deal was worked out that was designed to give each party a roughly fair share not only of the total seats but also of the winnable seats at a general election. A major difficulty facing the new party was its lack of coherent policy. During its first months this plainly had not troubled the voters, but it was a line of attack for the two established parties that might prove more damaging in time.

tine (see BIOGRAPHIES). The spectacle was of a Cabinet in open revolt. Thatcher, characteristically, made an unrepentant and uncompromising speech at the end of the conference, and there was even some speculation about how long she might survive as leader of her party, although few could envision her removal except by means of a lost election.

When the new Cabinet met, it was plain that there was no majority for the cuts necessary to uphold the Treasury's strategy for another year. Of £7 billion in economies originally deemed necessary, only about £2 billion could be achieved. The prime minister this time bowed to the wind.

Industry continued to suffer the effects of the world recession and—or so the government's critics contended—the economic consequences of Thatcher's policy. By November, when the chancellor announced a package of further measures including the cuts that the Cabinet had managed to approve, unemployment was at more than 11%, compared with under 9% a year previously, inflation was down but not into single figures as the government had planned and hoped, and production, although at last showing some signs of revival, was still 7% below its level at the time Thatcher took office. Manufacturing, hardest hit by the recession, was down more than 13% from the fourth quarter of the previous year.

Ministers spent a good deal of their time throughout the year struggling with the problems

of the nationalized industries. In February the government backed hastily away from a confrontation with the coal miners, who were prepared to strike against the proposed closing of 23 pits in a streamlining program put forward by the National Coal Board. The ministers made no bones about their decision: it was a tactical retreat in the face of superior force. In spite of its free-market philosophy, the government made huge subsidies to the British Steel Corporation, British Leyland (BL), and other losing public enterprises. The losses of British Rail became more of a headache as the year went on. BL for a while basked in the success of its tough-minded chairman, Sir Michael Edwardes, in facing down strike threats by appeals to the company's employees over the heads of their union representatives. By the end of the year, however, production was halted by a prolonged stoppage over tea breaks.

Another matter of concern to the government was the growing strength of the antinuclear movement. The phenomenon was common to most of Western Europe and the cause of much concern to U.S. Pres. Ronald Reagan's administration. In Britain it took the form of a revival of the Campaign for Nuclear Disarmament (CND), which in October staged a rally in London on the scale of its famous Aldermaston marches of the early 1960s. Public opinion, according to the polls, continued to oppose unilateral nuclear disarmament (the policy of the Labour Party, the Trades Union Con-

gress, and CND); but it became opposed to the locating of cruise missiles in Britain under NATO auspices and also to the replacement of the British Polaris submarine missile system by the Trident I. Some doubt was cast upon the feasibility of this enterprise when the U.S. decided to develop instead the Trident II, an even more costly and sophisticated system. The British government made defense cuts, chiefly in the Royal Navy, in the hope of retaining funding for the nuclear program.

The happiest event of the year was the marriage on July 29 of the prince of Wales, Prince Charles, to Lady Diana Spencer (*see* BIOGRAPHIES). The British, as ever, rose to the royal occasion; this one was an example of superb stage management as well as of genuine public rejoicing. The marriage in St. Paul's Cathedral, London, and the state procession to and from Buckingham Palace were seen on television around the world.

Foreign Affairs. In 1981 Britain once again was involved in a delicate balancing act between attempting to reestablish particular links with the U.S. while at the same time continuing diplomatic moves on behalf of the European Community (EC). This effort was notably difficult during the last half of the year when Britain assumed the presidency of the EC Council of Ministers.

Prime Minister Thatcher was the first European head of government to meet President Reagan after his inauguration. At their meeting in Washington, D.C., on February 25–28 the two leaders reached remarkable agreement on almost every point, from pursuit of monetarist economic strategies within their respective countries to the paramountcy of resisting Soviet "encroachment" in the world at large. Thatcher expressed her willingness to involve British troops in a rapid deployment force (RDF) to counter emergency situations, particularly in the Persian Gulf area. Concerned to clarify EC policy on Middle Eastern affairs, she stressed that the Community's 1980 Venice declaration was designed to complement rather than compete with the Camp David accords.

The Persian Gulf countries themselves did not express the same enthusiasm for the RDF, as Thatcher found out when she visited the region in April. Hoping to interest Saudi Arabia in British armaments, she instead found the Gulf kingdom concerned about the level of superpower rivalry in the region, of which the RDF was seen as the latest manifestation. Saudi Arabia pressed the British prime minister to promote the cause of Palestinian autonomy in the Middle East among EC and other Western nations. After the Saudi Arabian proposals for peace in the Middle East were announced in August, U.K. Foreign Secretary Lord Carrington discussed with Crown Prince Fahd the role that the EC might play in bringing about a comprehensive solution. However, attempts to involve the Palestine Liberation Organization in peace talks further estranged Israel, and U.S. Secretary of State Alexander Haig was openly critical of Carrington's intervention.

Relations with France, too, began with a warm accord between Thatcher and Pres. François Mitterrand when they met in London in September. The differences in policy between Socialist France and Conservative Britain did not prevent the two leaders from reaching close agreement on East-West relations and nuclear-missile policy. Plans to deploy U.S. medium-range weapons in Europe, they agreed, were an integral part of the process by which arms-limitation negotiations would come about. Disagreements remained, however, over the EC budget and Middle Eastern policy.

During 1981 two British dependencies achieved independence, Belize on September 21 and Antigua and Barbuda on November 1. The question of Belize's independence caused a diplomatic rift between Britain and Guatemala, which claimed the territory as its own, but last-minute negotiations secured a promise from Guatemala that it would respect Belize's territorial integrity.

Northern Ireland. The year was a bad one for Northern Ireland. In February the Rev. Ian Paisley, leader of the Democratic Unionist Party, took to what he called the "Carson trail" in protest against the December 1980 summit meeting in

Riots broke out in London and its suburbs during the nights of July 10 and 11. Crowds clashed with police, looted, stole, and set cars on fire. More than 250 arrests were made and over 100 persons were injured.

The prince and princess of Wales passed through the Strand approaching Trafalgar Square after their wedding at St. Paul's Cathedral in London on July 29.

Dublin between the British and Irish governments. Paisley, in imitation of Sir Edward Carson's campaign against the 1912 bill for Irish independence, collected 40,000 signatures—or so it was claimed—for his covenant and marched 500 men, masked and carrying firearms certificates, up an Antrim hillside in the dead of night for the benefit of the press. These ominous shenanigans were taken more seriously when they were repeated in November, following a further London-Dublin summit meeting, and this time in the midst of a new wave of murder and violence in which one of the victims was the Rev. Robert Bradford, MP (*see* OBITUARIES).

Earlier in the year the conflict in Northern Ireland had been dominated by the hunger strikes at the Maze Prison in Belfast. The hunger strike began on March 1 following the failure of the previous year's campaign to obtain political status for prisoners who were members of the Irish Republican Army (IRA). The death of the hunger-strike leader, Bobby Sands (*see* OBITUARIES), on May 5 set off a wave of revulsion and anger among Catholic Irish on both sides of the border and in the U.S. and elsewhere. As the hunger strikes continued, they threatened to undermine the good relations between London and Dublin, relations that were important not only for political reasons but also because of their role in promoting border security. Ten hunger strikers died before the protest was ended on October 3, chiefly as a result of intervention by the men's families and the Roman Catholic Church. The British government allowed some improvements in the prison regime, but these fell well short of the strikers' demands.

At their meeting in early November, Thatcher and Prime Minister Garret FitzGerald (*see* BIOGRAPHIES) of Ireland cemented their two countries' relationship by institutionalizing the biannual summit meeting, by setting up an Anglo-Irish intergovernmental council, and by outlining some areas for closer cooperation. Such arrangements were common between partners within the EC, but because of the Northern Ireland problem they took on a somewhat greater symbolic significance.

Paisley used the occasion to whip up suspicions of a British sellout to Dublin. There was no sign of any such move; what was becoming clear, however, was that Britain was growing increasingly reluctant to interpret its constitutional guarantee to the Protestant majority in Northern Ireland as a carte blanche veto on political or diplomatic developments deemed to be in the wider interest of the U.K. The IRA, after the ending of the hunger strike, extended its terrorist campaign to the U.K. mainland once more. A nail-bomb explosion outside a Chelsea army barracks in London on October 10 killed two civilians and wounded 40, including some troops. A bomb in Oxford Street, London, killed a police bomb-disposal expert, and another car bomb severely injured the commandant-general of the Royal Marines, Sir Steuart Pringle. (PETER JENKINS)

See also Commonwealth of Nations; Dependent States; Ireland.

United Nations

As usual, all the world's problems appeared on the agenda of the United Nations and its specialized agencies during 1981. Those which Secretary-General Kurt Waldheim singled out for attention in his annual report in September included renewed East-West strains, the arms race, a deadlock in efforts to promote economic development, and the increasing toll of terrorism. Africa and the Middle East probably occupied most of the delegates' time, but at the year's end the difficulties of electing a secretary-general almost overshadowed the organization's other concerns.

Secretary-General. Waldheim announced on September 10 that if the Security Council (which must nominate a secretary-general) and the General Assembly (which votes on the nominee) wished him to serve another term, he would consider it "a duty and an honour" to accept. His second five-year term was to conclude at the end of 1981.

His principal rival for the post was Salim A. Salim, foreign minister of Tanzania, who had the support of the Organization of African Unity

(OAU). Inconclusive balloting in the Security Council through November revealed the U.S. casting a veto against Salim and China blocking Waldheim. At the urging of Olara A. Otunnu (Uganda), the Council's president for December, both Waldheim and Salim withdrew as candidates. On December 11 the Council chose Javier Pérez de Cuéllar (Peru) as secretary-general. One of seven candidates, Pérez de Cuéllar received ten votes, including those of four of the five permanent members of the Council (the U.S.S.R. reportedly abstained). On December 15 the Assembly elected Pérez de Cuéllar by acclamation to a five-year term. In acknowledging his election, the secretary-general-elect said he would "reactivate the political role of the secretary-general," staying abreast of events and not being dragged along by them. Pérez de Cuéllar, 61, was a former head of the Peruvian delegation to the UN and served as undersecretary-general for two years. He was Waldheim's special representative in Cyprus in 1976 and more recently had attempted to persuade the U.S.S.R. to withdraw from Afghanistan.

Southern Africa. Hardly a week passed during the year when Namibia, formerly South West Africa, did not preoccupy some UN group. The organization sought ways to establish a lasting cease-fire in the area, to conduct UN-supervised elections that would lead to Namibia's independence, and to put an end there to South Africa's policies of apartheid (racial separation). A reconvened 35th General Assembly on March 6 called urgently (125–0, with 13 abstentions) upon the Security Council to impose comprehensive sanctions against South Africa in order to compel it to end an occupation of Namibia that the International Court of Justice had declared in 1971 to be illegal. In another vote (114–0–22) the Assembly condemned South Africa for maneuvering to transfer power to "illegitimate groups subservient to its interests" rather than to the South West Africa People's Organization (SWAPO), which the General Assembly considered the "sole and authentic representative" of the Namibians. Western nations abstained from this vote, but U.S. delegate Jeane Kirkpatrick (*see* BIOGRAPHIES) explained that the "contact group" of five Western countries (Canada, France, West Germany, the U.K., and the U.S.), which had devised the plan that the Security Council approved for settling the problem in 1978, remained committed to securing a peaceful, internationally recognized settlement. They believed, however, that Assembly resolutions did not contribute to that end. The five reiterated their commitment in joint statements (April 14 and May 3) but also endorsed an initiative by the administration of U.S. Pres. Ronald Reagan to provide constitutional political and property guarantees for the white minority in Namibia after independence. The Assembly called twice more for sanctions, in emergency session (September 4–14) by a vote of 117–0–25 and in October during the 36th Assembly (121–19–6).

The Security Council met several times at the request of African nations to consider imposing sanctions against South Africa, an effort that failed because France, the U.K., and the U.S. vetoed the

After his election in December as the fifth UN secretary-general, Javier Pérez de Cuéllar of Peru spoke to the General Assembly. He stressed his support of third world demands for better distribution of the world's wealth.

plans on the grounds that sanctions would frustrate ongoing negotiations. An International Conference on Sanctions against South Africa, jointly sponsored by the OAU, with Tanzania's Salim as president, adopted by acclamation a 15-page "Paris Declaration" on May 27. It called for a stronger arms embargo against South Africa; an end to all military and nuclear collaboration with that nation; an effective oil embargo; an elimination of purchases and marketing of South African gold and other minerals; and an effort to deny to South Africa electronic equipment, machinery, and chemicals.

On June 5 the Council for Namibia accused the U.S. of "providing assistance to Angolan traitor groups in the service of the Pretoria regime" and of flagrantly interfering in the internal affairs of Angola. On August 27 the Security Council heard Angola charge South Africa with aggression. South Africa, however, contended that it was moving only against SWAPO attacks from Angolan territory that aimed at taking over the Namibian government by force. Virtually all Council members condemned South Africa's actions and supported Angola's demands that South Africa withdraw immediately and unconditionally from Angola and pay for damage done. A draft resolution formally condemning South Africa was vetoed by the U.S., however, because the draft did not condemn recourse to violence from all quarters.

North Africa. A Moroccan-Mauritanian controversy about the Western Sahara and several disputes involving Libya figured prominently on the UN agenda during 1981. Mauritania complained in late March of Morocco's alleged efforts to destabilize its government despite its professed determination to stay neutral in the war in the Western Sahara between Morocco and the Popular Front for the Liberation of Saguia el Hamra and Río de Oro (Polisario Front). Morocco promptly denied the charges and later objected to discus-

International Year of Disabled Persons

The United Nations General Assembly in 1976 announced that 1981 would be the International Year of Disabled Persons (IYDP). In the resolution proclaiming the Year, the Assembly established five major objectives. These included: "Helping disabled persons in their physical and psychological adjustment to society; promoting all national and international efforts to provide disabled persons in their physical and psychological adjustment to society; promoting all national and international efforts to provide disabled persons with proper assistance, training, care and guidance, to make available opportunities for suitable work and to ensure their full integration in society; encouraging study and research projects designed to facilitate the practical participation of disabled persons in daily life, for example, by improving their access to public buildings and transportation systems; educating and informing the public of the rights of disabled persons to participate in and contribute to various aspects of economic, social and political life; [and] promoting effective measures for the prevention of disability and for the rehabilitation of disabled persons."

The UN noted that disabilities are more prevalent than is generally believed. About 10% of the population of any country suffers from some kind of disabling affliction. Most common are physical impairment, chronic illness, mental retardation, and sensory disabilities.

A secretariat established at Geneva within the UN Department of International Economic and Social Affairs organized preparations for the IYDP. It helped member governments of the UN with their national efforts and cooperated with other interested international agencies, including the International Labour Organization, UNESCO, and the World Health Organization. A former government minister from Zaire, Zala Lusibu N'Kanza, was appointed chairman of the secretariat.

During 1980 the secretariat issued declarations on the rights of deaf-blind and disabled persons. It also scheduled regional seminars and technical meetings to be held in 1981 at Addis Ababa, Ethiopia; Baghdad, Iraq; Santiago, Chile; and Bangkok, Thailand. An advisory committee consisting of representatives from 23 member nations of the UN met and urged national organizations to plan, coordinate, and execute activities that would support the objectives of the Year. In June 1980 approximately 3,500 delegates attended the World Congress of Rehabilitation International in Winnipeg, Man. One of the sessions of the congress dealt with the IYDP; members of national committees and international organizations met to coordinate plans. In December 1980 the General Assembly recommended that disabled persons themselves should be encouraged to participate in the activities of the Year.

Among the major conferences that took place during 1981 was the third European Regional Conference of Rehabilitation International, held at Vienna in April. Main topics discussed during the meeting were prevention and medical rehabilitation as a task of social medicine and the situation of disabled persons in the framework of education and vocational training systems. Also in April a conference in Kuwait dealt with social, medical, and legislative concerns of the disabled. In Tokyo an international athletic and occupational skills tournament for the disabled took place in October.

sions in the UN decolonization committee about the Western Sahara because, it maintained, the people there had freely chosen to "rejoin Morocco" after Spain withdrew as a colonial power in 1976.

Since 1976 Libya and Malta had been disputing about rights to drill for oil over the continental shelf in the Mediterranean. Malta maintained that Libya had employed delaying tactics in order to keep the controversy from coming before the International Court of Justice, to which the two nations agreed in principle in 1976 to refer the dispute. Malta also claimed that Libya had constantly threatened to resort to force. The Security Council took up the question on July 30, and the Council president appealed to both parties to show moderation.

Sudan and Libya each complained of aggressive actions by the other in September and October. Both the U.S. and Libya informed the Security Council on August 20 about an air clash over the Mediterranean on the previous day, but neither asked for any UN action. (*See* LIBYA.)

Middle East. Disputes involving Iran, Iraq, Israel, and Lebanon all figured in UN proceedings during the year. The secretary-general's special representative, Olof Palme, visited both Baghdad and Teheran in late January, in February, and in June, trying to settle the conflict between Iran and Iraq. He formulated the issues underlying the conflict, outlined elements of an honourable and durable settlement, and reported that, while both countries held firmly to their positions on key issues, prospects for a political solution existed.

Iraq complained on June 8 to the Security Council that on the preceding day Israel had carried out a "premeditated act of aggression" in bombing a nuclear plant near Baghdad. Israel replied that it had acted to avert a "mortal danger" to its people from the Iraqi reactor, which it maintained had been designed to produce nuclear bombs for use against Israel. The Israelis said that they destroyed the reactor because it would become operational shortly and could not have been bombed afterward without causing lethal radioactive fallout that would have hurt tens of thousands of innocent people. Sigvard Eklund, director general of the International Atomic Energy Agency (IAEA) in Vienna, said on June 9 that the Israeli attack was "a serious development with far-reaching implications." On June 12 he said that the IAEA had inspected the Iraqi reactors and found no evidence of any prohibited activity. On June 12 the IAEA board

condemned the Israeli attack and affirmed confidence in its safeguard system. The Security Council on June 19 condemned the Israeli attack unanimously, called on Israel to refrain from such acts or from threatening them in the future, and called for "appropriate redress" for the damage Iraq had suffered. The 36th Assembly also condemned Israel in several resolutions later in the year.

On December 14 Israel decided to apply its civil law, jurisdiction, and administration to the Golan Heights, in effect ending its military occupation and incorporating the area into Israel. Syria immediately asked the Security Council to meet, and on December 17 the Council unanimously labeled the Israeli move legally "null and void" and "without international legal effect" and demanded that Israel rescind its action "forthwith." It threatened "appropriate measures" if Israel did not comply.

Violence flared up in and around the area of operations of the UN Interim Force in Lebanon (UNIFIL) several times during the year. Unarmed UN observers reported in January and November that they were being harassed and even besieged by the "de facto forces," an Israeli-backed Lebanese Christian militia of about 1,500 men commanded by Maj. Saad Haddad. The Security Council president expressed deep shock and outrage on March 20 at the repeated attacks on UNIFIL. Renewed outbreaks of violence in southern Lebanon in April prompted Waldheim to dispatch Undersecretary-General Brian Urquhart to the area, where he met with Israeli and Syrian leaders in efforts to restore order.

The Security Council met twice in July to consider Lebanese complaints that Israel had attacked civilian centres in Beirut and Israeli charges that "terrorists" of the Palestine Liberation Organization were operating from Lebanon and indiscriminately shelling civilian centres in the north of Israel. On July 17 the Council president urgently appealed for an immediate end to "all armed attacks." On July 24, thanks to UN efforts and those of U.S. envoy Philip Habib (*see* BIOGRAPHIES), a cease-fire was established, and on July 21 the Council unanimously affirmed its commitment to Lebanese sovereignty, independence, and territorial integrity. Waldheim expressed gratification "that all concerned have responded positively to the appeal of the Security Council" and hoped that the cycle of violence would cease. He admitted to being tempted to withdraw UNIFIL from Lebanon because of the harassment it received, but he told the Council that he was convinced that removing UNIFIL would only lead to still greater violence. The Council consequently extended UNIFIL's mandate for six months on June 19 and again in December. Nonetheless, in November, the de facto forces placed UNIFIL under siege, and Habib returned to the area to try to reestablish the cease-fire.

Kampuchea. An International Conference on Kampuchea (Cambodia) met in New York City July 13–17 to attempt to arrange for "foreign" (*i.e.*, Vietnamese) troops to withdraw from Kampuchea; for free UN-supervised elections; and for guarantees for Kampuchean independence. Although 93

UPI

nations attended, negotiations between the contending parties did not take place because both the U.S.S.R. and Vietnam boycotted the meeting. The conference did establish a seven-nation committee (later enlarged to nine) to maintain contact with the parties to the conflict. On October 21 the General Assembly endorsed (100–25–19) the conference's call for negotiations. The U.S.S.R. and Vietnam rejected the resolution as illegal interference in Kampuchean internal affairs. The Assembly allowed Democratic Kampuchea to take a seat despite reports by the UN Human Rights Commission that the Pol Pot government had practiced genocide and over Soviet and Vietnamese objections that the seat should go to the Heng Samrin regime which actually ruled the country.

Other Matters. The decolonization committee on August 20 reaffirmed the right of the people of Puerto Rico to self-determination and independence and recommended that the General Assembly take up the issue in 1982. On December 1 the UN accepted the report, but statements by the Assembly president and others stressed that adoption by consensus did not mean that the Assembly actually approved of every word in the document.

The Conference on the Law of the Sea met in Geneva in August and settled the long-standing question of how to delimit maritime boundaries between nations having opposite or adjacent coasts. The U.S. threatened not to sign the nearly completed treaty, but Tommy T. B. Koh of Singapore, president of the conference, said in September that if the U.S. decided not to sign it risked having its seabed mining firms "sucked away" by the Europeans and Japanese because banks were unlikely to lend money to any companies attempting to conduct projects that fell outside the treaty's rules.

UN membership increased to 157 when the General Assembly, acting on Security Council recommendations, admitted Vanuatu, the former Territory of the New Hebrides (September 15);

Soviet Ambassador to the UN Oleg Troyanovsky casts his ballot to elect a president of the UN General Assembly; Ismat Kittani was chosen for 1982.

Belize, the former British Honduras (September 25); and Antigua and Barbuda, a former British colony (November 11).

On November 18 the General Assembly called (116–23–12) for foreign troops to leave Afghanistan. Approximately 85,000 Soviet soldiers were reportedly there to bolster the local government.

On October 14 the Office of the UN High Commissioner for Refugees received the Nobel Prize for Peace because of its extensive and valuable work on behalf of refugees throughout the world. The Office received a first Nobel Prize in 1954 for its work in resettling European refugees. The citation for 1981 referred to the "veritable flood of human catastrophe and suffering" experienced by refugees from Vietnam, Afghanistan, and Ethiopia, among other places. (See REFUGEES.)

(RICHARD N. SWIFT)

United States

United States

The United States of America is a federal republic composed of 50 states, 49 of which are in North America and one of which consists of the Hawaiian Islands. Area: 9,363,123 sq km (3,615,122 sq mi), including 202,711 sq km of inland water but excluding the 156,192 sq km of the Great Lakes that lie within U.S. boundaries. Pop. (1981 est.): 229,805,000, including 83.2% white and 11.7% black. Language: English. Religion (1980 est.): Protestant 72.8 million; Roman Catholic 49.8 million; Jewish 5.9 million; Orthodox 3.8 million. Cap.: Washington, D.C. (pop., 1980, 637,600). Largest city: New York (pop., 1980, 7,071,000). Presidents in 1981, Jimmy Carter and, from January 20, Ronald Reagan.

In his inaugural address on Jan. 20, 1981, newly elected Pres. Ronald Reagan (see BIOGRAPHIES) called for the beginning of "an era of national renewal," declaring that "We have every right to dream heroic dreams." The new president asserted that "we're not, as some would have us believe,

doomed to an inevitable decline. I do not believe in a fate that will fall on us no matter what we do. I do believe in a fate that will fall on us if we do nothing."

Repeating a familiar phrase from his election campaign, Reagan said: "Government is not the solution to our problem. Government is the problem." His solution, also familiar from the campaign, was "to curb the size and influence of the federal establishment." He explained that it was not his aim "to do away with government" but rather to make it work.

But the Reagan inaugural, said to be the most expensive in the nation's history, was not the biggest news event of the day. January 20 also was the date of the release of the 52 remaining U.S. hostages in Iran after 444 days of captivity. They were freed and flown to a U.S. Air Force base in Wiesbaden, West Germany, after the U.S. and Iran had signed an agreement resolving the long dispute.

The major element of the accord was the return to Iran of $11 billion in Iranian assets frozen by the U.S. following the seizure of the hostages and the U.S. embassy in Teheran in November 1979. Under the agreement signed by U.S. Deputy Secretary of State Warren Christopher (see BIOGRAPHIES) and Executive State Minister Behzad Nabavi of Iran, the U.S. immediately sent $8 billion to the Bank of England. Total Iranian assets consisted of $2.2 billion in Iranian deposits in home-based U.S. banks, $5.5 billion in overseas branches of U.S. banks, $2.4 billion in gold and securities that Iran had deposited in the Federal Reserve Bank in New York City, and $1 billion of other funds.

About $3.7 billion of the $11 billion was to be returned to the U.S. Federal Reserve Bank to pay off loans made to Iran by major U.S. banks. Another $1.4 billion was to be deposited in an escrow account to pay off other U.S. bank loans. An additional $4 billion in Iranian assets deposited in the U.S. would not be returned to Iran because of pending claims against those funds in U.S. courts.

UNITED STATES

Education. (1980–81; public schools only) Primary and preprimary, pupils 24,254,359, teachers 1,-192,131; secondary and vocational, pupils 16,-684,925, teachers 1,001,794; higher (includes teacher training colleges), students (1979–80) 11.5 million, teaching staff 820,000.

Finance. Monetary unit: U.S. dollar, with (Sept. 21, 1981) a free rate of U.S. $1.85 to £1 sterling. Gold and other reserves (June 1981) $29.1 billion. Federal budget (1981–82 est.): revenue $650.3 billion; expenditure $695.3 billion. Gross national product (1980) $2,626,100,000,000. Money supply (March 1981) $360 billion. Cost of living (1975 = 100; June 1981): 168.3.

Foreign Trade. (1980) Imports $253 billion; exports (excluding military aid exports of $160 million) $220,550,000,000. Import sources: Canada 17%; Japan 13%; Mexico 5%; Saudi Arabia 5%; West Germany 5%; Nigeria 5%. Export destinations: Canada 16%; Japan 9%; Mexico 7%; U.K. 6%; West Germany 5%. Main exports: machinery 25%; chemicals 9%; cereals 8%; motor vehicles 7%; aircraft 5%. Tourism (1979): visitors 20 million; gross receipts U.S. $10,012,000,000.

Transport and Communications. Roads (1979) 6,303,770 km (including 88,641 km expressways).

Motor vehicles in use (1979): passenger 120,248,000; commercial 33,349,700. Railways: (1978) 306,603 km; traffic (class I railways only; 1979) 18,191,000,-000 passenger km, freight 1,485,920,000,000 net ton-km. Air traffic (1980): c. 409,066,000,000 passenger-km (including domestic services c. 326,427,000,000 passenger-km); freight c. 10,540,000,000 net ton-km (including domestic services c. 6,660,000,000 net ton-km). Inland waterways (1979) 41,099 km; freight traffic (1978) 1,493,631,000,000 ton-km. Shipping (1980): merchant vessels 100 gross tons and over 5,579; gross tonnage 18,464,271. Shipping traffic (1979): goods loaded 325,982,000 metric tons, unloaded 547,555,000 metric tons. Telephones (Jan. 1980) 182,558,000. Radio receivers (Dec. 1978) c. 450 million. Television receivers (Dec. 1978) c. 150 million.

Agriculture. Production (in 000; metric tons; 1980): corn 168,855; wheat 64,492; barley 7,806; oats 6,642; rye 413; rice 6,580; sorghum 14,936; sugar, raw value 5,207; potatoes 13,653; soybeans 49,454; dry beans 1,184; cabbages (1979) 1,508; onions 1,-609; tomatoes 6,753; apples 3,949; oranges 10,740; grapefruit 2,709; peaches (1979) 1,500; grapes 5,059; peanuts 1,042; sunflower seed 1,726; linseed 206; cottonseed 3,955; cotton, lint 2,422; tobacco 804;

butter 518; cheese 2,096; hen's eggs 4,111; beef and veal 10,002; pork 7,535; fish catch (1979) 3,511; timber (cu m; 1979) c. 345,314. Livestock (in 000; Jan. 1980): cattle 111,192; sheep 12,687; pigs 67,353; horses (1979) c. 10,024; chickens 400,585.

Industry. Index of production (1975 = 100; 1980) 125; mining 118; manufacturing 126; electricity, gas, and water 116; construction 107. Unemployment (1980) 7.1%. Fuel and power (in 000; metric tons; 1980): coal and lignite 757,880; crude oil 424,191; natural gas (cu m) 546,200,000; manufactured gas (cu m; 1979) c. 23,600,000; electricity (kw-hr) c. 2,370,-000,000. Production (in 000; metric tons; 1980): iron ore (61% metal content) 70,407; pig iron 62,343; crude steel 100,806; cement (shipments) 64,528; newsprint 4,239; other paper 50,668; petroleum products (1979) c. 675,000; caustic soda 11,324; plastics and resins 12,417; man-made fibres 3,913; synthetic rubber 2,009; fertilizers (including Puerto Rico; nutrient content; 1979–80) nitrogenous 11,180; phosphate 9,083; potash 2,097; passenger cars (units) 6,400; commercial vehicles (units) 1,668. Merchant vessels launched (100 gross tons and over; 1980) 547,000 gross tons. New dwelling units started (1980) 1,299,000.

The U.S. and Iran further agreed to the establishment of a nine-member International Arbitral Tribunal "for the purpose of deciding claims of nationals of the United States against Iran and claims of nationals of Iran against the United States and any counterclaim which arises out of the same contract. . . ." Moreover, the U.S. agreed to (1) end trade sanctions against Iran; (2) locate and freeze the U.S. assets of the late Shah Mohammad Reza Pahlavi; and (3) not to intervene in Iran's internal affairs.

As for the hostages themselves, they were welcomed in Wiesbaden on January 21 by former president Jimmy Carter, acting in President Reagan's behalf. Reagan honoured the group at a White House reception on January 27 following a motorcade through Washington that was viewed by more than 200,000 people. In subsequent days parades and other welcome-home celebrations took place in New York and other cities.

Foreign Affairs. Resolution of the hostage crisis on Reagan's first day in office freed the new administration of one of the nation's most difficult recent problems in foreign relations. On February 24 Reagan signed an executive order implementing the agreement that the Carter administration had negotiated with Iran, and on July 2 the U.S. Supreme Court unanimously upheld presidential authority to reach such an accord. The Iranian situation thereafter ceased to be of pressing concern to U.S. foreign policy makers.

But other problems were not long in emerging. For six months the administration was embroiled in controversy over its decision, announced in April, to sell Saudi Arabia billions of dollars worth of arms, including five airborne warning and control system (AWACS) electronic surveillance aircraft. Israeli Prime Minister Menachem Begin (*see* BIOGRAPHIES) immediately protested the planned sale, claiming that such sophisticated weapons in Saudi hands would endanger peace in the Middle East and jeopardize Israel's security.

The climax of the AWACS debate came in October, and at first it seemed that opponents of the sale had succeeded in killing it. On October 14 the House of Representatives rejected the arms deal by a vote of 301 to 111, and on the following day the Senate Foreign Relations Committee endorsed a resolution of disapproval of the AWACS sale by a vote of 9 to 8. The administration's last hope of salvaging the sale thus lay in the full Senate, since by law only the concurrent opposition of both houses of Congress could block it. After a round of intensive lobbying by Reagan, the Senate on October 28 voted 52 to 48 to let the sale proceed. The Senate vote represented a personal triumph for the president, whose administration had seemed to be facing its first major foreign policy defeat.

The White House scored a foreign policy victory of another sort on August 19, when a pair of U.S. Navy F-14 jet fighters shot down two attacking Soviet-built Libyan S-22s about 95 km (60 mi) from the Libyan coast. The attack occurred in the northern part of the Gulf of Sidra, all of which was claimed by Libya as part of its territorial waters. The U.S., however, regarded the area as international waters.

Reagan defended the U.S. action, and government officials informally confirmed that the naval maneuvers were planned in the gulf to show that the U.S. would not honour Libya's claims concerning the high seas. "We decided it was time to recognize what are the international waters and behave accordingly," Reagan said. But the president denied that the exercises were intended to create an incident or to destabilize the government of Col. Muammar al-Qaddafi (*see* BIOGRAPHIES).

Relations with Libya took an even more ominous turn as the year drew to a close. Reagan said on December 7 that "we have the evidence" that Qaddafi had sent assassination teams to the U.S. to murder top-ranking government officials. It was also disclosed that the White House was planning some form of economic sanctions against Libya.

U.S.-Israeli relations, already strained by the battle over the AWACS sale to Saudi Arabia, were subjected to further stress after Israeli warplanes carried out a surprise attack on June 7 against the Osirak nuclear reactor near Baghdad in Iraq and destroyed the structure. The U.S. State Department condemned the attack, "the unprecedented character of which cannot but seriously add to the already tense situation in the area."

To stress its displeasure the administration sus-

Members of Congress and news media representatives examine an AWACS surveillance aircraft at Andrews Air Force Base in Maryland.

UPI

After a long battle, the tax-cut package called for by Pres. Ronald Reagan was passed by the Senate on August 3. Celebrating the passage are (left to right) Sen. Russell Long (Dem., La.), Sen. Howard Baker (Rep., Tenn.), Sen. Robert Byrd (Dem., W.Va.), and Sen. Robert Dole (Rep., Kan.).

pended delivery of F-16 fighter planes to Israel pending a review to determine whether the raid had violated a 1952 agreement under which Israel was supposed to use U.S.-supplied equipment solely for defensive purposes. The suspension was lifted on August 17. In announcing the resumption of deliveries, U.S. Secretary of State Alexander Haig (see BIOGRAPHIES) said "it wasn't necessary to make a legal or juridical decision" as to whether Israel had violated the 1952 agreement. Another disagreement with Israel arose in December after Begin announced that Israel was, in effect, annexing the Golan Heights, Syrian territory that Israel had occupied since the 1967 war. The U.S. voted with the rest of the UN Security Council when it declared the annexation "null and void" and told Israel to rescind its decision.

Another area of U.S. concern in the Middle East in 1981 was strife-torn Lebanon. Reagan dispatched special envoy Philip Habib (see BIOGRAPHIES) on a mission to Beirut, Jerusalem, and Damascus in May in an attempt to ease the crisis between Syria and Israel stemming from Syria's deployment of surface-to-air missiles in Lebanon. The chief results of Habib's mediation efforts were separate cease-fire agreements by Israel and the Palestine Liberation Organization on July 24 that virtually ended fighting along the Israeli-Lebanese border. The United Nations and the Saudi Arabian government also acted as intermediaries in arranging the agreements.

The Reagan administration's dealings with the Soviet Union began with controversy when the president remarked during an informal interview with five reporters on February 2 that the Soviets wanted "world domination through world rule of Communist states." Two days later, the Soviet government newspaper *Izvestia* responded by accusing Reagan of "heaping the crudest opprobrium on the Soviet Union." However, the *Izvestia* article was careful to moderate its pronouncements, saying it was too early to "hurry with final conclusions." Similarly, Reagan said in the February 2 interview that he did not think the Soviets "would make a reckless move, risking a confrontation with the United States." He also said nuclear arms limitation talks could begin "at any time."

Fulfilling a campaign pledge, Reagan on April 24 ended the 15-month-old partial embargo on grain sales to the Soviet Union. The ban had been invoked by President Carter on Jan. 4, 1980, in response to the Soviet intervention in Afghanistan. Reagan said his decision to allow grain shipments to resume did not lessen the administration's determination to stop Soviet "acts of aggression wherever they take place."

In a speech on November 18 Reagan offered to abandon the planned deployment of 572 Pershing II and land-based cruise missiles in Europe in 1983 in exchange for a Soviet agreement to dismantle its medium-range missiles aimed at Western Europe. The Soviets had urged discussions to achieve "mutually acceptable accord on radical reductions of medium-range nuclear arms in Europe." These were the opening negotiating positions of the two countries in their bilateral theatre-nuclear-weapons-control talks that opened November 30 in Geneva.

Reagan's offer and the opening of the Geneva talks helped to quiet the increasing criticism in Western Europe of U.S. security policy. The antinuclear movement in Europe had gained impetus from remarks made by Reagan at a White House briefing on October 16 with a group of newspaper editors. One editor, referring to "some of the people in Europe. . .afraid they may wind up as kind of proxy victims in a war between us and the Soviet Union," questioned the president as to whether he thought there could be a limited exchange of nuclear weapons between the two superpowers or whether such an exchange "would simply escalate inevitably." Reagan answered, "I don't honestly know," but added that, given a "stalemate situation" in weaponry, "I could see where you could have the exchange of tactical weapons against troops in the field without it bringing either one of the major powers to pushing the button." Reagan's remarks were widely viewed in Europe as a reflection of U.S. indifference to Europe's fate in the event of nuclear war.

On December 13 the government of Poland issued a decree of martial law and suspended operations of the nation's independent trade union Solidarity. Polish troops and police took to the streets to enforce the decree. On December 17 Reagan charged the Soviet Union with responsibility for the military crackdown and later announced imposition of a series of economic sanctions against Poland until the martial law was lifted.

In the Western Hemisphere the administration's leading preoccupation in 1981 was the tiny Central American country of El Salvador. The U.S. Department of State on February 23 issued a report which, it claimed, provided "definitive evidence" that the leftist rebels in El Salvador had received arms and training from several Communist countries, principally Cuba. The report held that Cuba and the Soviet Union had mounted a "well-coordinated, covert effort" to topple El Salvador's ruling civilian-military junta. On March 2 the U.S. expanded its military assistance to El Salvador by sending 20 additional military advisers there and granting $25 million in new aid to its army to control the left-wing guerrillas.

However, in a policy statement on July 16, the administration committed itself to a political rather than a military solution to the Salvadoran conflict and backed free elections in that country. Speaking before the World Affairs Council, a private foreign policy discussion group, Thomas Enders, assistant secretary of state for Inter-American affairs, said the administration's views were that "only a genuinely pluralistic approach can enable a profoundly divided society to live with itself without violent convulsions, gradually overcoming its differences." The statement omitted previous administration references to the Salvadoran war that had depicted it mainly as an arena of Soviet-U.S. conflict.

President Reagan traveled to Mexico in October to discuss economic cooperation between the industrialized countries of the North and the less developed nations of the South. The leaders of the 8 industrialized and 14 less developed countries present at the conference in Cancún did not issue an official communiqué at the conclusion of their talks, but a general summary of the conference proceedings signified that the leaders had agreed to move toward "global negotiations" in order to assist poor nations. In a speech at the opening session of the conference, Reagan stressed the virtues of free enterprise in improving living standards in poor countries. "History demonstrates that time and time again, in place after place, economic growth and human progress make their greatest strides in countries that encourage economic freedom," the president declared. In December Congress authorized spending $5.7 billion on foreign aid in fiscal 1982 and 1983.

Domestic Affairs. Reagan had been scheduled to visit Mexico in April, but that trip was postponed after he was shot in the chest by a single gunman outside the Washington Hilton Hotel on March 30. The president was rushed to nearby George Washington University Hospital, where he underwent two hours of surgery. Reagan's press secretary, James S. Brady, was critically wounded in the attack, and two security officers were also injured. The assailant, identified as John W. Hinckley, Jr., 25, of Evergreen, Colo., was arrested at the scene after having fired as many as six bullets from a .22-calibre revolver, the type known as a "Saturday-night special." He was identified as a college dropout and a loner with a history of psychiatric problems.

Returning to the White House on April 11, Reagan concentrated on winning approval for his economic program, the main goals of which were strengthening the military and reducing the federal government's role in the economy. To achieve these ends the president called for across-the-board cuts in individual income taxes and sharp reductions in nondefense federal spending.

After weeks of often bitter debate, the House and Senate passed the president's tax-cut bill on July 29, giving him his most important legislative victory of the year. The bill's basic provision cut individual income tax rates by 25% over 33 months, starting Oct. 1, 1981. It also improved business depreciation write-offs and provided incentives to encourage personal savings. The mea-

© 1981 HERBLOCK. THE WASHINGTON POST

"Good work, Jesse—save that government aid for us folks who are truly needy."

sure, the largest tax-cut bill in the nation's history, would reduce taxes by nearly $750 billion over the next five years.

Though relishing his victory, Reagan cautioned against anticipating an instant recovery of the economy "from its present moribund condition." He added that "over a nine- to 12-month period . . . I think you'll see it really pick up speed."

The president's caution, it turned out, was justified. Even as he signed the tax-cut bill into law, the nation's economy was sliding into recession. But Reagan avoided using the term until October 18, when in response to a reporter's question he acknowledged that the country was in "a light, and I hope short, recession." Murray Weidenbaum, chairman of the president's Council of Economic Advisers, also conceded that "the economy has entered what can be called a recession," adding that "several more months of poor economic statistics are a likely probability."

Although the slump was felt in nearly all sectors of the economy, the housing and automobile industries were especially hard hit. Interest rates on long-term, fixed-rate mortgages climbed to as high as 18% or more, pricing millions of would-be homeowners out of the housing market. Moreover, many savings and loan associations stopped writing fixed-rate mortgages altogether; instead, they began offering home buyers a wide variety of variable-rate mortgages. Consumer uncertainty about variable-rate financing tended to depress the housing market still further.

High interest rates also were a factor in holding down sales of new U.S.-made automobiles. But potential buyers objected mainly to high sticker prices, which in many cases approached or exceeded $10,000 for nonluxury models. As U.S. car sales lagged, the effects were felt by the steel, rubber,

and other industries heavily dependent on the automakers in Detroit.

By year's end the unemployment rate had climbed to approximately 8.9%. Weidenbaum and Secretary of Commerce Malcolm Baldrige both predicted that joblessness could reach 9% of the nation's labour force before the recession had run its course.

The combination of rising unemployment and budget cutbacks in long-standing social programs led to increasingly strained relations between the Reagan administration and leaders of organized labour. To dramatize the discontent of unionized workers, the AFL-CIO staged a large Solidarity Day rally that drew an estimated 260,000 participants to Washington, D.C., on September 19. The ranks of union protesters were enlarged by groups representing women, minorities, the elderly, and the poor.

But perhaps the most notable development on the labour front in 1981 was the strike staged on August 3 by the 15,000-member Professional Air Traffic Controllers Organization (PATCO), one of the few unions to have endorsed Reagan's candidacy in the 1980 presidential election. The strike brought quick retaliation from the government. Reagan told the controllers that they would be fired if the walkout persisted past August 4.

The president also barred negotiations while the strike was on, saying: "You can't sit and negotiate with a union that is in violation of the law." The strike was in fact illegal, since the controllers were federal employees who worked for the Federal Aviation Administration. Most controllers ignored the government's back-to-work ultimatum, and those who did so received dismissal notices starting August 5. The strike had the effect of reducing air traffic to about 75% of normal levels as well as causing delays of many scheduled flights. Meanwhile, PATCO was decertified and the government began hiring and training new controllers to replace those who had been dismissed.

A 72-day strike by miners in the eastern coal fields ended June 6 with the ratification of a new 40-month contract. The miners lost about $710 million in wages during the walkout, the second-longest in the industry's history. But since coal stockpiles were huge at the outset of the strike, the effect on the national economy was judged to be slight.

More important to the nation's sports fans than the air controllers' and coal miners' walkouts was the 49-day strike by major league baseball players. It was the longest strike in the history of U.S. professional sports and caused the cancellation of 713 games, or about one-third of the 1981 major league season. As a result, major league cities lost hundreds of millions of dollars in business revenue that baseball games ordinarily generate.

The White House was repeatedly embarrassed in 1981 by squabbles among and apparent improprieties by top administration officials. While testifying before a House Foreign Affairs subcommittee on March 24, for example, Secretary of State Haig said he was "not totally satisfied" with the administration's procedures for formulating foreign policy. He also expressed "a lack of enthusiasm" about press reports that Vice-Pres. George Bush would be put in charge of the administration's "crisis management" team. Within hours of Haig's testimony Bush was, in fact, named to that post.

Haig's outspokenness again landed him in trouble after the assassination attempt on President Reagan. In a televised announcement while the president was undergoing surgery, Haig declared: "As of now, I am in control here in the White House, pending return of the vice-president, and in close touch with him." Nervous, his voice trembling with emotion at times, Haig said the "helm" of office had not been transferred to Bush. He added that "There are absolutely no alert measures that are necessary at this time, or contemplated."

The controversy created by Haig's remarks and demeanour eventually died down. But then, on November 3, he publicly accused a top White House aide of starting a "guerrilla campaign" against him to attack his authority and his position as secretary of state. Although Haig did not reveal identities in his accusation, speculation involved Richard Allen, the president's assistant for national security affairs. Both men publicly denied any disagreement.

Allen, too, was soon to become a centre of controversy. The White House admitted on November 13 that he had received $1,000 in cash from a Japanese magazine for helping to set up an interview with Nancy Reagan, the president's wife, the day after the inauguration. The White House announcement came after a report on the affair by a Japanese newspaper.

Discomfiting as the Allen disclosures were to the White House, a published magazine interview with Budget Director David Stockman (see BIOGRAPHIES) was far more damaging politically. In the interview, which appeared in the December issue of *Atlantic Monthly*, Stockman made a variety of critical statements. He expressed doubt that the administration's economic program would work. He foresaw huge deficits, not the balanced budget that had been promised. He said the "supply-side economics" that the administration has espoused was just a new name for old "trickle-down" policies favouring the rich. In fact, Stockman said, the administration's key tax-cut program was a "Trojan horse" to bring down the top income-tax rate. The rest of the program was "secondary," he said.

Obviously angry, President Reagan called Stockman to the White House. At the meeting Stockman offered his resignation, but Reagan refused it. The budget director—the member of the administration most closely identified with its economic policies—expressed thanks for "this second chance to get on with the job."

But Stockman's prediction of huge budget deficits evidently was well founded. In early December, Reagan's economic advisers told him that the federal budget deficit in the fiscal year that began October 1 would reach $109 billion—far more than the $43.1 billion that the president had expected less than three months earlier. In addition, the advisers said that the deficit would climb to $152 billion in fiscal 1983 and to $162 billion in 1984.

Reagan got his first chance to fill a vacancy on

UPI

Long lines at the Detroit Employment Security Office in March reflected the high unemployment rate in Michigan.

the Supreme Court after Justice Potter Stewart announced his retirement in June. To take his place, the president nominated Judge Sandra Day O'Connor (*see* BIOGRAPHIES) of the Arizona Court of Appeals. O'Connor, whose nomination was unanimously confirmed by the Senate on September 21, thus became the first woman justice in Supreme Court history.

Two off-year gubernatorial elections, in Virginia and New Jersey, were widely viewed as referenda on the Reagan administration's performance. The results produced a standoff. In Virginia, Democrat Charles Robb soundly defeated his Republican opponent, J. Marshall Coleman. In an extremely close race in New Jersey, Republican Thomas Kean emerged as the winner over Democrat James Florio.

To carry out his pledge to strengthen the nation's defense capability, Reagan made a number of decisions involving controversial weapons systems. For instance, he ordered full production of neutron warheads for the Lance missile. The decision reversed the Carter administration policy, formulated in 1978, of producing individual parts of neutron weapons but deferring their assemblage and distribution.

On October 2 Reagan announced his proposal for modernizing and reinforcing the U.S. strategic nuclear arsenal. In dealing with the hotly debated MX missile issue, he advocated canceling all plans for the mobile basing system in Utah and Nevada that had been suggested by former president Carter. Instead, he proposed that 100 MX missiles be built, 36 of them to be deployed in existing, stationary Titan missile silos beginning in 1986.

Reagan also advanced the building of 100 B-1 long-range bombers, originally planned to supersede the aging B-52s but canceled by Carter because of their potential vulnerability to Soviet radar detection. The radar-resistant, so-called "Stealth" bomber would also be designed for use by the mid–1990s. (*See* DEFENSE: *Special Report.*)

The nation's space program got a lift when the space shuttle "Columbia," the world's first reusable spacecraft, was launched successfully from Cape Canaveral, Fla., on April 12. After 36 orbits and 54 hours in space, the craft made a perfect landing on a dry lake bed at Edwards Air Force Base in the Mojave Desert in California on April 14. A second orbital flight by "Columbia" in November also was completed successfully.

One of the worst hotel disasters in U.S. history occurred July 17, when two aerial walkways in the Kansas City, Mo., Hyatt Regency Hotel collapsed into the lobby, killing 113 people and injuring 190 others. The sudden tragedy struck shortly after 7 PM during the hotel's weekly "tea dance" when some 1,500 people were present.

Wayne B. Williams, a 23-year-old black freelance photographer, was arrested on June 21 and later indicted for the murder of two of 28 black children and young adults killed in the Atlanta, Ga., area in a 22-month-long series of deaths and disappearances. Williams was charged with two counts of criminal homicide in the slaying of Nathaniel Cater, 27, and Jimmy Ray Payne, 21.

Three members of the Weather Underground, a radical group responsible for terrorist bombings during the Vietnam war, were among four suspects arrested on October 20 near Nyack, N.Y., after an abortive armoured truck robbery and gun battle that left two police officers and one Brink's guard dead. The best-known suspect was Kathy Boudin, a radical activist and Weather Underground leader who had been wanted by authorities for more than 11 years in connection with a 1970 bomb explosion in New York City that accidentally killed three persons. Also arrested were Judith Clark and David Joseph Gilbert, both members of the radical group. The fourth suspect was Samuel Brown, who reportedly had a 23-year record of arrests and convictions for various offenses.

(RICHARD L. WORSNOP)

See also Dependent States.

UNITED STATES STATISTICAL SUPPLEMENT
DEVELOPMENTS IN THE STATES IN 1981

In his inaugural address on Jan. 20, 1981, U.S. Pres. Ronald Reagan initiated a historic year in federal-state relations, an attempt to reverse the recent trend of power from the state capitals to Washington, D.C. The change turned out to be exactly what state governors and legislators had long been clamouring for: loosening of federal control over billions of dollars in U.S. tax money being returned to the states, and the replacement of categorical aid programs administered by Washington bureaucrats with new all-inclusive block grants, to be spent within broad guidelines at state discretion.

Unfortunately, states also found that the changes were exacting a heavy price. Although candidate Reagan had promised that program control would be turned over to states "along with the funding sources to pay for them," no revenue-raising authority accompanied the new order. In fact, the nine block grant programs enacted by Congress during 1981 carried overall 25% funding reductions, with the promise of still more cuts to come. Federal tax cuts and tight money policies translated into still less revenue for hard-pressed states. At the year's end, Georgia Gov. George Busbee, a Democrat, charged that Reagan's policies had caused "disarray and chaos" in state budgets, and even Republican Gov. Richard Snelling of Vermont called for a halt in further intragovernmental spending cuts.

During 1981 state governments approved the biggest tax increases in ten years even while undergoing the political agonies of congressional reapportionment and legislative redistricting. Environmentalists were encouraged by renewed interest in beverage container deposit legislation, but hopes for the Equal Rights and D.C. Voting Rights amendments faded. With energy prices flat during 1981, several states considered easing the 55 mph speed limit. Already-crowded state prisons became more so, with the situation approaching crisis proportions in some areas.

Forty-nine states (all except Kentucky) held regular legislative sessions during 1981. A record 32 states staged one or more special sessions as well, often to address reapportionment and federal block grant problems.

Party Strengths. Although no legislatures changed hands during 1981 elections, Republicans took control of two chambers after internal maneuvering. Rural Democrats in the Alaska House of Representatives, dissatisfied with budget appropriations, established the Bush League in June and joined with Republicans and Libertarians to elect new Republican-dominated leadership. In Washington State Sen. Peter von Reichbauer changed his party affiliation from Democrat to Republican in January, reversing a 25–24 Democratic advantage.

Democrats went to court in Illinois to prevent still another similar loss. Taking advantage of the absence of two Democrats, Republican Gov. James Thompson ruled January 15 that only a simple majority of senators present and voting was necessary to elect Senate leadership, and Republican

Sen. David Shapiro was named Senate president in a 29–28 vote. The Illinois Supreme Court ordered a new election, however, and Democrat Philip Rock was finally named president on February 17.

The addition of the Alaska House and Washington Senate meant that Republicans controlled both legislative chambers in 16 states, while Democrats dominated both bodies in 28. All states were solidly Democratic except Alaska, Arizona, Colorado, Idaho, Indiana, Iowa, Kansas, Montana, New Hampshire, North Dakota, Pennsylvania, South Dakota, Utah, Vermont, Washington, and Wyoming (where Republicans had a majority in both houses); Delaware, Illinois, Maine, New York, and Ohio (where each party controlled one chamber); and Nebraska (a nonpartisan, one-house legislature).

Two governorships changed hands in November. Democrats regained the statehouse in Virginia, but Republicans recaptured the governorship in New Jersey by a razor-thin margin of fewer than 2,000 votes. That left the prospective gubernatorial lineup for 1982 at 27 Democrats and 23 Republicans.

Government Structures and Powers. Regular ten-year reapportionment of both congressional and state legislative districts occupied many state legislatures during 1981, accompanied by a predictable decibel level of political outcries. Population shifts from Democrat-heavy states in the Northeast to Republican-dominated Sunbelt states were expected to increase the number of safe GOP U.S. House seats by a dozen or more, but maneuvering by Democratic state legislatures held the final result down to an estimated Republican gain of only three or four, according to most observers. By the year's end all eligible states except Kansas, Kentucky, Maine, Massachusetts, Montana, and New York had redistricted their legislatures, although several plans had been nullified at least temporarily by court injunctions.

Kentucky voters turned down a proposed state constitutional amendment that would have allowed top elected officials to succeed themselves. After the New Jersey Supreme Court upheld the constitutionality of the governor's pocket veto, state voters eliminated it in November balloting. The relocation of Alaska's capital from Juneau to Willow, a new town near Anchorage, was due to undergo a final test in the November 1982 election. The move was approved in principle in 1974, but voters in 1982 would be asked to okay a $1.5 billion bond issue to finance the project.

Arkansas, Kentucky, and New Hampshire revamped and consolidated major state agencies during the year. California applied termination provisions to state-mandated local programs after six years. North Carolina decided to ask voter approval of four-year terms for legislators in the 1982 election.

Government Relations. President Reagan's "New Federalism" dominated intragovernmental relations during 1981, with state officials developing a love-hate relationship with the new administration's

policy mix of increased authority and reduced revenues flowing out of Washington. Although one U.S. Treasury official suggested that the cuts in federal income and business taxes effectively improved state revenue prospects by leaving more money in taxpayers' pockets, several legislators stated that the federal tax action was illusory because many U.S. spending cuts would have to be offset by state spending increases.

Under the federal budget reconciliation bill nine major block grants to states were established, drawing together federal funding from 57 categorical programs. The federal funding level for the nine was authorized at $7.5 billion, a full 25% reduction from anticipated 1982 levels. States were given the option of taking charge of seven grants on October 1 or at the start of a later fiscal quarter, with two more available in late 1982, but even federally administered programs were reduced by one-quarter. Virtually all states took over the social services and low-income energy block grants immediately, and most also assumed control of community services, preventive health and health services, alcohol, drug, and mental health services, maternal and child health services, and community development block grants as well.

Although a presidential initiative in September for a further 8% reduction in state aid was largely blocked by Congress, the administration's austerity budget promised further reductions in future state assistance. Nonetheless, despite transitional pains, a noticeable easing in some federal-state tensions was evident during 1981. The so-called Sagebrush Rebellion, the resistance by states to federal land policies within their borders, quieted down. Although Nevada and Arizona approved new resolutions calling for court action when federal public land use "impairs state sovereignty," Colorado and South Dakota governors vetoed similar bills and legislators turned the proposition down in Idaho, Montana, and Washington. Significantly, despite federal budget deficit projections far higher than anticipated, no new state joined the 30 that had previously called for a U.S. constitutional convention to require a balanced federal budget; 34 states are required.

Idaho and Oregon became the first states to share truck safety regulations, each agreeing to honour the other's inspection records. And state officials were heartened by the July appointment of a former state legislator and judge, Sandra Day O'Connor (*see* BIOGRAPHIES), to the U.S. Supreme Court.

Finance and Taxes. With federal revenues reduced and obligations rising faster than income, 30 state governments were forced to raise taxes by more than $2.5 billion during 1981, the largest tax increase in ten years. Syndicated columnist Neal Pierce, an expert on federalism, estimated that state and local governments absorbed one-third of the federal budget cuts approved in 1981 even though they accounted for less than 17% of federal obligational authority. The national economic picture affected state finances in several adverse

ways: many state business taxes were tied to federal levies, and so federal tax reductions automatically reduced state collections; the federal government's tight money policies drove borrowing costs up; some tax and fiscal policies made state bonds less attractive, also increasing borrowing costs; and national recession increased necessary social spending while reducing tax revenue. Said economist Walter Heller: "State and local governments are reeling from multiple blows."

A study by the Council of State Governments indicated that since 35 of the 45 states with a corporate income tax based it on federal revenues, the 1981 federal business tax cut would cost states $8.8 billion annually by the full effective date of the legislation in 1986. Citizens for Tax Justice reported that the overall revenue loss for states from all federal legislation in 1981 would range from $15 billion to $27.5 billion a year, depending upon economic circumstances.

The economic hardships forced many states to reduce spending, with unemployment-ridden Michigan, Oregon, and Ohio undergoing major cutbacks. State employees were often angered in the process. A majority of Minnesota state workers went on strike for 22 days starting July 20 to protest what they termed inadequate pay raises. Four-fifths of New Hampshire's 10,000 state workers reported in sick June 23–24 after the legislature reduced Gov. Hugh Gallen's pay increase promise. Massachusetts and New Jersey also experienced public employee work stoppages.

The Tax Foundation reported that general sales taxes were increased permanently during the year in West Virginia and temporarily in Minnesota, Nevada, and Ohio. The District of Columbia and 24 states increased motor fuel tax rates in reaction to declining gasoline usage and lower tax collections that threatened road repair efforts.

Figures accumulated in 1981 showed that state revenue from all sources totaled $277 billion during the 1980 fiscal year, an increase of 12.1% over the preceding 12 months. General revenue (excluding state liquor and state insurance trust revenue) was $233.6 billion, up 12.3%. Total state expenditures rose 14.7% to $257.8 billion, creating a surplus of $19.2 billion for the year. General expenditures, not including outlays of the liquor stores and insurance trust systems, amounted to $228.2 billion, up 13.8% for the year. Of general revenue, 59.4% came from state taxes and licenses; 12.9% from charges and miscellaneous revenue, including educational tuition; and 27.7% from intergovernmental revenue (mostly from the federal government).

The largest state outlay was $87.9 billion for education, of which $27.9 billion went to state colleges and universities and $52.7 billion to local public schools. Other major expenditures were $44.2 billion for public welfare, $25 billion for highways, and $17.9 billion for health and hospitals.

Ethics. Former Tennessee Gov. Ray Blanton, relieved of office in early 1979 amid charges that his administration was selling prison commutations, was convicted of conspiracy, extortion, and mail fraud by a federal jury June 9. Convicted in the same trial, which involved the alleged sale of state liquor licenses, were two former Blanton aides, James M. Allen and Clyde Ed Hood, Jr. Blanton was later sentenced to three years in prison but remained free pending appeal. In a separate action two other Blanton aides, legal counsel T. Ed-

ward Sisk and state highway patrol Lieut. Charles F. Taylor, pleaded guilty to conspiracy charges and were sentenced to five years in prison.

Two former Maryland chief executives made headlines during 1981. Marvin Mandel had his three-year mail fraud and racketeering sentence commuted by President Reagan on December 20 after serving 19 months in prison. And a Maryland judge ruled that Spiro Agnew owed the state treasury $147,500 plus $101,235 interest for kickbacks he took while governor and U.S. vice-president.

Ramifications of a bid-rigging scandal across the South continued to spread. Tennessee tightened its laws against such practices; North Carolina recovered $4.5 million from six companies accused of collusion in 130 paving contract jobs from 1975 to 1980; and Oklahoma's legislature staged a special session after 24 county commissioners resigned amid road scandal allegations. Both Illinois and Mississippi tightened open meetings laws, and Ohio authorities discovered upward of $430,000 in embezzled funds in a special audit of state accounts.

Education. Arkansas and Louisiana startled the national scientific community by requiring that public school instruction in the evolution theory of human life be balanced by equal attention to the "instantaneous or scientific creation" theory, a literal interpretation of biblical teachings.

State efforts to attack unequal funding between rich and poor school districts received legislative and judicial attention. The Kansas legislature took steps to equalize school financing across the state, and courts in Georgia and New York declared their states' financing systems, based on local property tax revenues, to be unconstitutional.

As federal funding assistance was cut back during 1981 and various state tax limitation measures took effect, many hard-pressed states looked for alternative sources of funding for education. The problem was expected to ease, however, since demographic studies predicted that school enrollments nationwide would drop over the next five years. In a District of Columbia referendum in November, tax limitation advocates mounted a major voter test of a new concept, the granting of $1,200 in local tuition tax credits for families who send children to private schools. Opponents charged that the measure would emasculate an already-troubled public school system, and it was defeated by a seven-to-one margin.

The national trend away from mandatory busing to advance integration goals, a trend highlighted by federal government withdrawal from new busing proposals, was especially noticeable during 1981. Both Dallas and Los Angeles ended their mandatory busing programs, the Los Angeles decision coming after the state Supreme Court upheld a law permitting busing only when intentional segregation of students by authorities had been proved.

Health and Welfare. Buffeted by revenue problems, several states struggled with measures to contain health costs. Missouri trimmed its Medicaid program, and both Delaware and Michigan tightened their regulation of insurance carriers, establishing cost ceiling goals.

Alabama joined ten other states in enacting a "right to die." This legislation set conditions under which a terminally ill patient can refuse further medical assistance.

Abortion. Court and legislative battles over the limits of permissible abortion regulation continued in states nationwide during 1981. Federal appellate courts prohibited a 24-hour waiting period required by a South Dakota law and voided a 48-hour wait stipulated in a similar Nebraska law. A North Dakota statute prohibiting the use of state funds to any agency performing, referring, or encouraging an abortion was also struck down as overly vague and violative of free speech guarantees.

Antiabortionists received some encouragement from a U.S. Supreme Court ruling on April 27 that allowed states to prohibit abortion outside hospitals after the first trimester of pregnancy. Nebraska and Rhode Island approved new laws limiting the use of public funds for abortions and requiring that parents of minors seeking them be notified. A prohibition against the use of state Medicaid funding for abortion was vetoed by the Michigan governor.

Drugs. A campaign to decriminalize possession of small amounts of marijuana was stalled during the year, with no new states reducing penalties for personal use of the drug; however, Colorado, Connecticut, New York, and Vermont joined 11 states that had previously legalized the use of marijuana for medical purposes. Other states moved to discourage trafficking in marijuana, with North Carolina banning so-called head shops and Arkansas, Georgia, Kansas, Maine, Montana, North Dakota, Oklahoma, and Texas outlawing the sale or use of drug paraphernalia. Several states stipulated stiffer criminal sentences for drug dealing, and Texas approved a law allowing state police to wiretap suspected drug dealers after obtaining a court order.

In other significant drug regulatory actions, Arkansas, Colorado, Connecticut, Delaware, Indiana, Kansas, Maryland, and South Dakota prohibited the sale of "look-alike" drugs, imitation amphetamines blamed for numerous drug overdoses. Controversy continued to mount over dimethyl sulfoxide (DMSO), a skin-penetrating by-product of wood-pulp and paper manufacturing that some researchers call "the aspirin of the 1980s" for its pain-killing and medicinal properties. In the face of federal refusal to permit the general use of DMSO on humans, seven states (Florida, Louisiana, Montana, Oklahoma, Oregon, Texas, and Washington) approved special laws allowing physicians to prescribe it, and Oregon moved to take over regulation of the drug from the federal Food and Drug Administration.

Law and Justice. Although gun-control legislation made little progress during 1981, several states markedly increased penalties for crimes committed with a firearm. Alabama, Indiana, New Jersey, and West Virginia stiffened gun-aided crime penalties; Connecticut raised the minimum jail sentence for such offenses from one year to five and provided a one-year term for merely carrying a gun without a permit.

In other criminal law action Arkansas, Hawaii, and Vermont toughened laws governing crime by juveniles, expanding circumstances under which youths could be tried as adults. Colorado increased penalties for crime against the elderly. Minnesota and Montana made computer crime a new offense. Alabama and New Jersey joined New York in outlawing fraternity hazing. Connecticut, Maine, and New Hampshire 701

toughened their laws against drunk driving, with Maine mandating a two-day jail sentence for any conviction of driving while intoxicated.

Death penalty laws in Massachusetts, Ohio, and Oregon were declared unconstitutional, and a capital punishment bill was vetoed for the third consecutive year by the Kansas governor. But Alabama and Ohio voted in new death penalty laws, bringing to 35 the number of states providing for capital punishment. Even so, only one prisoner—convicted murderer-rapist Steven Judy of Indiana—was put to death during the year, with delays over legal appeals keeping more than 700 prisoners on death row in states throughout the nation.

The U.S. Supreme Court affirmed a Florida law allowing photographing and televising of criminal trials even over the objection of the defendant; at the year's end some type of photographic coverage was allowed in 31 state judicial systems and was pending in five others.

Gambling. Although no new state enacted a major gambling initiative during 1981, North Dakota, Pennsylvania, and West Virginia legalized charitable bingo and similar games. Iowa toughened its bingo rules to require that three-quarters of all proceeds must go to charity.

In a year marked by budget shortfalls, a report on state lottery revenues gained national attention. The 13 state games of chance produced $2.1 billion in gross revenue during the fiscal year, the U.S. Census Bureau estimated, with more than one-half of the profits going for state purposes. The District of Columbia planned to start the nation's 14th lottery in 1982.

Environment. After two years of no action, the national drive to require significant deposits on beverage containers sprang to life again in 1981, with Delaware and Massachusetts becoming the seventh and eighth states to approve "bottle bills." The Massachusetts measure was approved over a veto by Gov. Edward J. King, who said it would cost $100 million a year to enforce. A Michigan study released during the year concluded that highway litter had been halved by that state's 1979 bottle law. In other legislation Kansas banned disposable pull-tab cans after mid-1983, and Hawaii repealed its never-enforced 1977 prohibition against plastic containers.

Assistance to Vietnam veterans exposed to the chemical defoliant Agent Orange was voted by legislatures in California, Maryland, New Jersey, New York, and Texas. New measures designed to preserve cropland and open space were approved in Delaware and Pennsylvania. Arizona enacted a new law to prevent environmentalists from harassing hunters. California, later joined by Alaska, Oregon, and Massachusetts, sued the U.S. Department of the Interior for allegedly mismanaging the nation's natural resources, particularly in allowing offshore oil and gas exploration in environmentally fragile areas.

California was also the centre of the year's biggest environmental story, an invasion of crop-destroying Mediterranean fruit flies that wreaked heavy agricultural and political damage. After an infestation was discovered in northern California in January, Gov. Jerry Brown was accused of reacting too slowly and with insufficient force. Although the fly infestation was eventually controlled, California spent $100 million in checking and spraying 49 sq m (79 sq km) and had its vulnerable produce temporarily quarantined in Japan, Alabama, Florida, Mississippi, South Carolina, and Texas.

Energy. Amid claims that a few energy-rich states were abusing their favoured position at the expense of the rest of the country, several legal disputes over permissible taxation levels reached the U.S. Supreme Court, with mixed results. The court upheld a challenge by eight states to Louisiana's tax on offshore natural gas, ruling that the levy obstructed interstate commerce and violated federal preemption of interstate gas regulation. Louisiana was ordered to repay $600 million in taxes and interest collected on the tax since 1979.

But the high court rejected a legal suit aimed at Montana's 30% severance tax on coal, brought by four states and utility companies. Some 32 states gained approximately $4 billion annually in severance tax revenue, but Montana's levy was the highest. Following the court ruling, several congressmen promised to introduce in 1982 legislation to stipulate federal ceilings on severance taxes, perhaps at the 12.5% level, and the Montana legislature appropriated $500,000 to fight it.

Nuclear power problems continued to bubble in various states. Following huge cost overruns on nuclear plant projects, Washington voters in November approved an initiative that required statewide ballot approval for future major public energy construction. California, backed by 29 states, won a U.S. Supreme Court ruling that validated its temporary ban on nuclear plant construction. The federal government had claimed exclusive control over nuclear licensing.

Several states made progress in energy exploration and revenues. Massachusetts approved oil and gas exploration in the Georges Bank off Cape Cod; Alabama accepted a $400 million bid for exploration rights in Mobile Bay; New York took a look for oil and gas in Allegheny State Park; and Alaska was awarded the bulk of $23 million in revenues from oil and gas leases on federal wildlife refuges within the state.

Equal Rights. Reflecting a national conservative mood, proposed U.S. constitutional amendments to guarantee equality made little progress during the year. For the fourth consecutive year no additional state ratified the Equal Rights Amendment, designed to ban sex discrimination.

Although ERA supporters promised an intense lobbying effort to get the final three necessary state endorsements (for a total of 38) in 1982, an Idaho federal judge dealt those plans an apparently fatal blow at the year's end. Judge Marion Callister ruled on December 23 that Congress had acted illegally in extending the ratification deadline from 1979 to June 30, 1982, and that five states that had nullified their previous endorsements of the measure (Idaho, Kentucky, Nebraska, South Dakota, and Tennessee) must be removed from the ratification list. ERA advocates planned to appeal to the U.S. Supreme Court.

Another amendment, this one providing District of Columbia citizens with authority to elect two U.S. senators and a representative, also ran out of steam during 1981. Only one state, Oregon, ratified that measure, bringing the approval total to ten.

With the Reagan administration taking a conciliatory line, many states moved to settle their differences with the federal government concerning the desegregation of colleges and universities. Florida, North Carolina, and Pennsylvania reached agreement with the U.S. Department of Health and Human Services, ending a threatened funding cutoff, and Alabama, Delaware, Kentucky, Maryland, Ohio, South Carolina, Texas, and West Virginia moved toward settlement of their problems. Georgia outlawed employment discrimination against the physically handicapped; California ordered a study to ensure comparable pay among women and men in state employment; South Dakota banned sexual harassment in state jobs; and Maryland made sexual harassment a minor criminal offense.

Prisons. With new inmates arriving at record rates, state penal facilities continued during the year to suffer from overcrowding, prisoner unrest, and legal challenges. According to a U.S. Justice Department survey, approximately 19,000 prisoners were added to state prison totals during the first six months of 1981, a record 12.8% growth rate that pushed the U.S. prison population near a record 350,000. At midyear 24 states were under court order to relieve overcrowding in their prisons, and legal challenges over conditions in ten more states were pending.

The inmate influx was due largely to new state laws that required mandatory minimum prison sentences for certain offenses, plus a general toughening or abolition of parole policies nationwide. For the most part hard-pressed state legislatures did not match the prison population boom with new construction of penal facilities.

An Alabama federal judge twice ordered the early release of state prisoners, the first such rulings in U.S. history, and a Texas judge directed that state to bring its entire prison system, the largest in the U.S., up to minimum health and safety standards. However, the U.S. Supreme Court took some pressure off state penal administrators by allowing Ohio, in a landmark ruling, to house two prisoners in cells constructed for one, provided that other institution facilities were adequate.

Two states, Michigan and Iowa, reacted to excessive prison populations by approving novel laws to roll back sentences. The measures allowed state officials to declare a state of emergency, review all sentences of inmates nearing parole, and reduce prison time for property offenders by 90 days if necessary. The first such emergency was declared in May in Michigan, where voters had earlier overwhelmingly rejected a state funding proposition for four new 550-bed prisons.

Consumer Protection. Responding to allegations of illegality and sharp dealing, Connecticut, Ohio, Rhode Island, South Carolina, and Tennessee approved the licensing and regulation of precious metal dealers. The new laws typically required a holding period for material purchased by the dealers in order to discourage the resale or melting down of stolen goods. Reflecting another national trend, Kansas, Minnesota, and North Carolina joined Rhode Island and Tennessee in requiring special passenger restraints for small children in motor vehicles.

A few months after unruly crowd conditions resulted in the death of 11 persons at a Cincinnati rock concert, Ohio in 1981 became the first state to ban unreserved or "festival" seating at public events. The law is effective whenever 3,000 or more seats are offered for sale.

(DAVID C. BECKWITH)

AREA AND POPULATION

Area and Population of the States

State	AREA in sq mi Total	Inland water[1]	POPULATION (000) 1970 census[2]	1980 census	Percent change 1970–80
Alabama	51,609	901	3,444	3,890	12.9
Alaska	589,757	20,157	303	400	32.0
Arizona	113,909	492	1,775	2,718	53.1
Arkansas	53,104	1,159	1,923	2,286	18.9
California	158,693	2,332	19,971	23,669	18.5
Colorado	104,247	481	2,210	2,889	30.7
Connecticut	5,009	147	3,032	3,108	2.5
Delaware	2,057	75	548	595	8.6
Dist. of Columbia	67	6	757	638	−15.7
Florida	58,560	4,470	6,791	9,740	43.4
Georgia	58,876	803	4,588	5,464	19.1
Hawaii	6,450	25	770	965	25.3
Idaho	83,557	880	713	944	32.4
Illinois	56,400	652	11,110	11,418	2.8
Indiana	36,291	194	5,195	5,490	5.7
Iowa	56,290	349	2,825	2,913	3.1
Kansas	82,264	477	2,249	2,363	5.1
Kentucky	40,395	745	3,221	3,661	13.7
Louisiana	48,523	3,593	3,645	4,204	15.3
Maine	33,215	2,295	994	1,125	13.2
Maryland	10,577	686	3,924	4,216	7.4
Massachusetts	8,257	431	5,689	5,737	0.8
Michigan	58,216	1,399	8,882	9,258	4.2
Minnesota	84,068	4,779	3,806	4,077	7.1
Mississippi	47,716	420	2,217	2,521	13.7
Missouri	69,686	691	4,678	4,917	5.1
Montana	147,138	1,551	694	787	13.4
Nebraska	77,227	744	1,485	1,570	5.7
Nevada	110,540	651	489	799	63.4
New Hampshire	9,304	277	738	921	24.8
New Jersey	7,836	315	7,171	7,364	2.7
New Mexico	121,666	254	1,017	1,300	27.8
New York	49,576	1,745	18,241	17,557	−3.8
North Carolina	52,586	3,788	5,084	5,874	15.5
North Dakota	70,665	1,392	618	653	5.7
Ohio	41,222	247	10,657	10,797	1.3
Oklahoma	69,919	1,137	2,559	3,025	18.2
Oregon	96,981	797	2,092	2,633	25.9
Pennsylvania	45,333	367	11,801	11,867	0.6
Rhode Island	1,214	165	950	947	−0.3
South Carolina	31,055	830	2,591	3,119	20.4
South Dakota	77,047	1,092	666	690	3.6
Tennessee	42,244	916	3,926	4,591	16.9
Texas	267,338	5,204	11,199	14,228	27.1
Utah	84,916	2,820	1,059	1,461	38.0
Vermont	9,609	342	445	511	14.8
Virginia	40,817	1,037	4,651	5,346	14.9
Washington	68,192	1,622	3,413	4,130	21.0
West Virginia	24,181	111	1,744	1,950	11.8
Wisconsin	56,154	1,690	4,418	4,705	6.5
Wyoming	97,914	711	332	471	41.8
TOTAL U.S.	3,618,467	78,444	203,302[3]	226,505[3]	11.4

[1] Excludes the Great Lakes and coastal waters.
[2] Corrected.
[3] State figures do not add to total given because of rounding.
  Source: U.S. Department of Commerce, Bureau of the Census, *Current Population Reports*.

Largest Metropolitan Areas[1]

Name	Population 1970 census[2]	1980 census	Percent change 1970–80	Land area in sq mi	Density per sq mi 1980
New York-Newark-Jersey City SCSA	17,035,270	16,120,023	−5.4	4,846	3,326
New York City	9,973,716	9,119,737	−8.6	1,384	6,589
Nassau-Suffolk	2,555,868	2,605,813	2.0	1,218	2,139
Newark	2,057,468	1,965,304	−4.5	1,008	1,950
New Brunswick-Perth Amboy-Sayreville	583,813	595,893	2.1	312	1,910
Jersey City	607,839	556,972	−8.4	47	11,850
Long Branch-Asbury Park	461,849	503,173	8.9	476	1,057
Paterson-Clifton-Passaic	460,782	447,585	−2.9	192	2,331
Stamford	206,340	198,854	−3.6	121	1,643
Norwalk	127,595	126,692	−0.7	88	1,440
Los Angeles-Long Beach-Anaheim SCSA	9,980,859	11,496,206	15.2	34,007	338
Los Angeles-Long Beach	7,041,980	7,477,657	6.2	4,069	1,838
Anaheim-Santa Ana-Garden Grove	1,421,233	1,931,570	35.9	782	2,470
Riverside-San Bernardino-Ontario	1,139,149	1,557,080	36.7	27,293	57
Oxnard-Simi Valley-Ventura	378,497	529,899	40.0	1,863	284
Chicago-Gary-Kenosha SCSA	7,726,039	7,868,246	1.8	4,929	1,596
Chicago	6,974,755	7,102,328	1.8	3,719	1,910
Gary-Hammond-East Chicago	633,367	642,781	1.5	938	685
Kenosha	117,917	123,137	4.4	272	453
Philadelphia-Wilmington-Trenton SCSA	5,627,719	5,548,789	−1.4	4,946	1,122
Philadelphia	4,824,110	4,716,818	−2.2	3,553	1,328
Wilmington	499,493	524,108	4.9	1,165	450
Trenton	304,116	307,863	1.2	228	1,350
San Francisco-Oakland-San Jose SCSA	4,630,576	5,182,021	11.9	6,994	741
San Francisco-Oakland	3,109,249	3,252,721	4.6	2,480	1,312
San Jose	1,065,313	1,295,071	21.6	1,300	996
Vallejo-Fairfield-Napa	251,129	334,402	33.2	1,610	208
Santa Rosa	204,885	299,827	46.3	1,604	187
Detroit-Ann Arbor SCSA	4,669,154	4,617,510	−1.1	4,627	998
Detroit	4,435,051	4,352,762	−1.9	3,916	1,112
Ann Arbor	234,103	264,748	13.1	711	372
Boston-Lawrence-Lowell SCSA	3,526,349	3,448,122	−2.2	1,855	1,859
Boston	2,899,101	2,763,357	−4.7	1,232	2,243
Lawrence-Haverhill	258,564	281,981	9.1	307	919
Lowell	218,268	233,410	6.9	179	1,304
Brockton	150,416	169,374	12.6	137	1,236
Houston-Galveston SCSA	2,169,128	3,101,940	43.0	7,193	431
Houston	1,999,316	2,905,350	45.3	6,794	428
Galveston-Texas City	169,812	195,940	15.4	399	491
Washington, D.C.	2,926,119	3,060,240	4.6	2,815	1,087
Dallas-Fort Worth	2,377,623	2,974,878	25.1	8,360	356
Cleveland-Akron-Lorain SCSA	2,999,811	2,833,957	−5.5	2,917	972
Cleveland	2,063,729	1,898,720	−8.0	1,519	1,250
Akron	679,239	660,328	−2.8	903	731
Lorain-Elyria	256,843	274,909	7.0	495	555
Miami-Fort Lauderdale SCSA	1,887,892	2,640,022	39.8	3,261	810
Miami	1,267,792	1,625,979	28.3	2,042	796
Fort Lauderdale-Hollywood	620,100	1,014,043	63.5	1,219	832
St. Louis	2,410,884	2,355,276	−2.3	4,935	477
Pittsburgh	2,401,362	2,263,894	−5.7	3,049	743
Baltimore	2,071,016	2,174,023	5.0	2,259	962
Minneapolis-St. Paul	1,965,391	2,114,256	7.6	4,647	455
Seattle-Tacoma SCSA	1,836,949	2,092,408	13.9	5,902	355
Seattle-Everett	1,424,605	1,606,765	12.8	4,226	380
Tacoma	412,344	485,643	17.8	1,676	290
Atlanta	1,595,517	2,029,618	27.2	4,326	469
San Diego	1,357,854	1,861,846	37.1	4,261	437
Cincinnati-Hamilton SCSA	1,613,414	1,660,190	2.9	2,620	634
Cincinnati	1,387,207	1,401,403	1.0	2,149	653
Hamilton-Middletown	226,207	258,787	14.4	471	549

[1] Standard Metropolitan Statistical Area, SMSA, unless otherwise indicated; SCSA is a Standard Consolidated Statistical Area and combines two or more contiguous SMSA's.
[2] Revised.
Sources: U.S. Dept. of Commerce, Bureau of the Census, *1980 Census of Population and Housing Advance Reports; State and Metropolitan Area Data Book 1979*.

Population Change

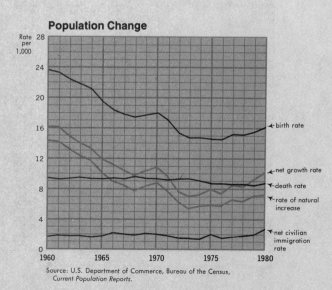

Source: U.S. Department of Commerce, Bureau of the Census, *Current Population Reports*.

Marriage and Divorce Rates

*Includes annulments.

Source: U.S. Department of Health and Human Services, Public Health Service, *Monthly Vital Statistics Report*.

Church Membership

Religious body	Total clergy	Inclusive membership
Baptist bodies		
American Baptist Association	5,700	1,500,000
American Baptist Churches in the U.S.A.	8,600	1,600,521
Baptist General Conference	1,216	133,385
Baptist Missionary Association of America	2,500	224,533
Conservative Baptist Association of America	…	225,000
Free Will Baptists	2,837	227,888
General Baptists (General Association of)	1,349	74,159
National Baptist Convention of America	28,754	2,668,799
National Baptist Convention, U.S.A., Inc.	27,500	5,500,000
National Primitive Baptist Convention	636	250,000
Primitive Baptists	…	72,000
Progressive National Baptist Convention	863	521,692
Regular Baptist Churches, General Assn. of	…	243,000
Southern Baptist Convention	56,200	13,600,126
United Free Will Baptist Church	915	100,000
Buddhist Churches of America	108	60,000
Christian and Missionary Alliance	1,686	189,710
Christian Congregation	1,275	89,379
Church of God (Anderson, Ind.)	3,025	176,429
Church of the Brethren	1,909	170,839
Church of the Nazarene	7,841	484,276
Churches of Christ—Christian Churches		
Christian Church (Disciples of Christ)	6,626	1,177,984
Christian Churches and Churches of Christ	8,074	1,063,254
Churches of Christ	…	1,600,000
Community Churches, National Council of	…	190,000
Congregational Christian Churches, Natl. Assn. of	720	104,000
Eastern churches		
American Carpatho-Russian Orth. Greek Catholic Ch.	68	100,000
Antiochian Orthodox Christian Archdiocese of N. Am.	132	152,000
Armenian Apostolic Church of America	34	125,000
Armenian Church of America, Diocese of the (including Diocese of California)	61	450,000
Bulgarian Eastern Orthodox Church	11	86,000
Coptic Orthodox Church	25	100,000
Greek Orthodox Archdiocese of N. and S. America	655	1,950,000
Orthodox Church in America	531	1,000,000
Russian Orth. Ch. in the U.S.A., Patriarchal Parishes of	60	51,500
Russian Orthodox Church Outside Russia	168	55,000
Serbian Eastern Orth. Ch. for the U.S.A. and Canada	64	65,000
Ukrainian Orthodox Church in the U.S.A.	131	87,745
Episcopal Church	12,672	2,786,004
Evangelical Covenant Church of America	803	77,737
Evangelical Free Church of America	1,218	77,592
Friends United Meeting	581	60,745
Independent Fundamental Churches of America	1,366	120,446
Jehovah's Witnesses	none	565,309
Jews	5,300	5,920,000
Latter Day Saints (Mormons)		
Church of Jesus Christ of Latter-day Saints	25,075	2,811,000
Reorganized Church of Jesus Christ of L.D.S.	16,574	190,087
Lutherans		
American Lutheran Church	7,018	2,353,229
Evangelical Lutheran Churches, Association of	680	107,782
Lutheran Church in America	8,257	2,923,260
Lutheran Church—Missouri Synod	7,296	2,625,650
Wisconsin Evangelical Lutheran Synod	1,290	407,043
Mennonite Church	2,509	99,511
Methodists		
African Methodist Episcopal Church	6,170	2,050,000
African Methodist Episcopal Zion Church	6,766	1,134,176
Christian Methodist Episcopal Church	2,877	786,707
Free Methodist Church of North America	1,637	67,394
United Methodist Church	36,283	9,584,711
Wesleyan Church	2,343	103,160
Moravian Church in America	238	53,781
North American Old Roman Catholic Church	140	61,263
Old Order Amish Church	2,151	80,250
Pentecostals		
Apostolic Overcoming Holy Church of God	350	75,000
Assemblies of God	23,246	1,732,371
Church of God	2,737	75,890
Church of God (Cleveland, Tenn.)	9,676	435,012
Church of God in Christ	6,000	425,000
Church of God in Christ, International	1,502	501,000
Church of God of Prophecy	…	72,977
Full Gospel Fellowship of Ch. and Min., Intl.	931	59,100
International Church of the Foursquare Gospel	2,690	89,215
Pentecostal Church of God	1,574	113,000
Pentecostal Holiness Church	2,889	86,103
United Pentecostal Church, International	5,063	465,000
Plymouth Brethren	400	98,000
Polish National Catholic Church of America	141	282,411
Presbyterians		
Cumberland Presbyterian Church	704	96,553
Presbyterian Church in America	728	90,991
Presbyterian Church in the U.S.	5,631	838,485
United Presbyterian Church in the U.S.A.	14,222	2,423,601
Reformed bodies		
Christian Reformed Church	961	213,995
Reformed Church in America	1,467	345,532
Roman Catholic Church	58,845	50,449,842
Salvation Army	5,167	417,359
Seventh-day Adventist Church	4,266	571,141
Triumph the Church and Kingdom of God in Christ	1,375	54,307
Unitarian Universalist Association	942	139,052
United Church of Christ	9,870	1,736,244

Table includes churches reporting a membership of 50,000 or more and represents the latest information available.
Source: National Council of Churches, *Yearbook of American and Canadian Churches*, 1982.

(CONSTANT H. JACQUET)

THE ECONOMY

Gross National Product and National Income

in billions of dollars

Item	1965[1]	1970[1]	1980	1981[2]
GROSS NATIONAL PRODUCT	688.1	982.4	2,626.1	2,881.6
By type of expenditure				
Personal consumption expenditures	430.2	618.8	1,672.8	1,831.0
Durable goods	62.8	84.9	211.9	227.0
Nondurable goods	188.6	264.7	675.7	734.6
Services	178.7	269.1	785.2	869.4
Gross private domestic investment	112.0	140.8	395.3	455.8
Fixed investment	102.5	137.0	401.2	434.6
Changes in business inventories	9.5	3.8	−5.9	21.2
Net exports of goods and services	7.6	3.9	23.3	17.7
Exports	39.5	62.5	339.8	364.5
Imports	32.0	58.5	316.5	346.8
Government purchases of goods and services	138.4	218.9	534.7	577.1
Federal	67.3	95.6	198.9	219.4
State and local	71.1	123.2	335.8	357.7
By major type of product				
Goods output	336.6	456.2	1,130.4	1,252.6
Durable goods	133.6	170.8	458.6	514.5
Nondurable goods	203.1	285.4	671.9	738.1
Services	272.7	424.6	1,229.6	1,344.3
Structures	78.8	101.6	266.0	284.6
NATIONAL INCOME	566.0	798.4	2,121.4	2,316.5
By type of income				
Compensation of employees	396.5	609.2	1,596.5	1,751.2
Proprietors' income	56.7	65.1	130.6	134.1
Rental income of persons	17.1	18.6	31.8	33.3
Corporate profits	77.1	67.9	182.7	187.0
Net interest	18.5	37.5	179.8	210.8
By industry division[3]				
Agriculture, forestry, and fisheries	20.4	24.5	62.8	65.8
Mining and construction	35.9	51.6	145.4	155.1
Manufacturing	170.4	215.4	527.2	586.3
Nondurable goods	65.4	88.1	215.7	231.4
Durable goods	105.0	127.3	311.5	354.9
Transportation	23.1	30.3	80.0	85.3
Communications and public utilities	22.9	32.5	94.4	105.6
Wholesale and retail trade	84.7	122.2	313.8	348.6
Finance, insurance, and real estate	64.0	92.6	290.8	309.9
Services	64.1	103.3	314.8	348.7
Government and government enterprises	75.4	127.4	301.7	325.3
Other	4.7	4.6	…	…

[1] Revised.   [2] Second quarter, seasonally adjusted at annual rates.
[3] Without capital consumption adjustment.
Source: U.S. Department of Commerce, Bureau of Economic Analysis, *Survey of Current Business.*

Personal Income Per Capita

State	1950	1960[1]	1970[1]	1980
Alabama	$ 880	$1,510	$2,892	$ 7,488
Alaska	2,384	2,743	4,638	12,790
Arizona	1,330	1,994	3,614	8,791
Arkansas	825	1,358	2,791	7,268
California	1,852	2,711	4,423	10,938
Colorado	1,487	2,247	3,838	10,025
Connecticut	1,875	2,838	4,871	11,720
Delaware	2,132	2,735	4,468	10,339
District of Columbia	2,221	2,823	4,644	12,039
Florida	1,281	1,965	3,698	8,996
Georgia	1,034	1,644	3,300	8,073
Hawaii	1,386	2,289	4,599	10,101
Idaho	1,295	1,811	3,243	8,056
Illinois	1,825	2,616	4,446	10,521
Indiana	1,512	2,149	3,709	8,936
Iowa	1,485	1,960	3,643	9,358
Kansas	1,443	2,084	3,725	9,983
Kentucky	981	1,576	3,076	7,613
Louisiana	1,120	1,649	3,023	8,458
Maine	1,186	1,835	3,250	7,925
Maryland	1,602	2,320	4,267	10,460
Massachusetts	1,633	2,435	4,276	10,125
Michigan	1,701	2,326	4,041	9,950
Minnesota	1,410	2,064	3,819	9,724
Mississippi	755	1,196	2,547	6,580
Missouri	1,431	2,091	3,654	8,982
Montana	1,622	1,983	3,395	8,536
Nebraska	1,490	2,009	3,657	9,365
Nevada	2,018	2,791	4,583	10,727
New Hampshire	1,323	2,160	3,720	9,131
New Jersey	1,834	2,700	4,684	10,924
New Mexico	1,177	1,814	3,045	7,841
New York	1,873	2,703	4,605	10,260
North Carolina	1,037	1,577	3,200	7,819
North Dakota	1,263	1,681	3,077	8,747
Ohio	1,620	2,322	3,949	9,462
Oklahoma	1,143	1,850	3,341	9,116
Oregon	1,620	2,194	3,677	9,317
Pennsylvania	1,541	2,239	3,879	9,434
Rhode Island	1,605	2,186	3,878	9,444
South Carolina	893	1,394	2,951	7,266
South Dakota	1,242	1,758	3,108	7,806
Tennessee	994	1,576	3,079	7,720
Texas	1,349	1,894	3,507	9,545
Utah	1,309	1,954	3,169	7,649
Vermont	1,121	1,864	3,447	7,827
Virginia	1,228	1,884	3,677	9,392
Washington	1,674	2,354	3,997	10,309
West Virginia	1,065	1,592	3,038	7,800
Wisconsin	1,477	2,178	3,712	9,348
Wyoming	1,668	2,210	3,672	10,898
United States	1,496	2,201	3,893	9,521

[1] Revised.
Source: U.S. Department of Commerce, Bureau of Economic Analysis, *Survey of Current Business.*

Average Employee Earnings

September figures

Industry	HOURLY 1980	HOURLY 1981[1]	WEEKLY 1980	WEEKLY 1981[1]
MANUFACTURING				
Durable goods				
Lumber and wood products	$6.76	$7.16	$265.67	$272.80
Furniture and fixtures	5.59	6.00	214.10	225.60
Stone, clay, and glass products	7.69	8.53	316.06	346.32
Primary metal industries	9.96	11.25	397.40	456.75
Fabricated metal products	7.63	8.33	309.02	329.04
Nonelectrical machinery	8.21	8.98	336.61	361.89
Electrical equipment and supplies	7.12	7.79	282.66	308.48
Transportation equipment	9.54	10.41	388.28	414.32
Instruments and related products	6.91	7.61	277.09	307.44
Nondurable goods				
Food and kindred products	6.94	7.57	279.68	301.29
Tobacco manufactures	7.53	8.71	287.65	349.27
Textile mill products	5.25	5.68	208.95	221.52
Apparel and related products	4.69	5.05	165.09	177.76
Paper and allied products	8.06	8.92	340.94	386.24
Printing and publishing	7.73	8.39	287.56	314.63
Chemicals and allied products	8.47	9.38	349.81	396.77
Petroleum and coal products	10.33	11.48	448.32	505.12
Rubber and plastics products	6.72	7.40	270.82	294.52
Leather and leather products	4.62	5.07	167.71	183.03
NONMANUFACTURING				
Metal mining	10.55	12.12	423.06	489.65
Coal mining	10.95	12.34	444.57	517.05
Oil and gas extraction	8.75	9.51	396.38	431.75
Contract construction	10.18	11.01	386.84	393.06
Local and suburban transportation	6.97	7.38	272.53	291.51
Electric, gas, and sanitary services	9.12	10.12	379.39	418.97
Wholesale trade	7.07	7.71	272.20	296.84
Retail trade	4.95	5.36	149.49	161.87
Hotels, tourist courts, and motels[2]	4.51	4.88	137.10	148.35
Banking	5.04	5.43	181.94	196.57

[1] Preliminary. [2] Excludes tips. Source: U.S. Dept. of Labor, Bureau of Labor Statistics, *Employment and Earnings*.

Unemployment Trends

quarterly averages, seasonally adjusted

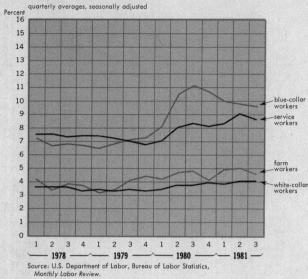

Source: U.S. Department of Labor, Bureau of Labor Statistics, *Monthly Labor Review*.

Value of Agricultural Products, with Fisheries, 1980

in thousands of dollars

State	PRINCIPAL CROPS Corn (grain)	Hay	Soybeans	Wheat	Tobacco	Cotton (lint)	Potatoes	LIVESTOCK AND PRODUCTS Cattle, calves	Hogs, pigs	Sheep, lambs	Milk[1]	Eggs[2]	Chickens[2]	FISHERIES[3]
Alabama	53,217	56,190	252,000	21,880	1,108	105,336	8,560	317,487	125,749	[4]	88,020	180,837	7,467	25,575
Alaska	...	107,100	...	70,940	...	497,112	7,018	473	299	[5]	2,244	440	90	560,603
Arizona	15.400	107,100	...	70,940	...	497,112	7,018	407,538	24,400	9,822	139,435	4,096	61	...
Arkansas	3,730	56,166	609,000	118,408	...	167,400	...	376,222	86,546	...	100,575	209,727	13,454	...
California	145,800	711,712	...	363,390	...	1,239,840	157,590	1,055,606	29,410	41,100	1,779,289	370,165	8,349	323,393
Colorado	304,912	188,370	...	400,730	...	...	63,581	1,062,091	58,437	39,834	123,466	21,267	611	...
Connecticut	...	12,432	...	...	37,073	...	3,605	15,306	2,205	253	85,763	65,678	1,135	4,675
Delaware	50,976	2,540	45,240	4,212	...	...	8,527	4,256	5,459	[4]	17,100	7,360	392	1,969
Florida	52,414	36,432	79,948	...	29,422	3,257	36,217	425,057	51,317	[4]	320,424	117,194	3,069	124,834
Georgia	204,750	43,056	209,292	72,270	1,154,217	32,529	...	254,426	233,768	[4]	191,380	303,928	14,310	20,061
Hawaii	...	...	...	...	...	...	...	30,491	8,563	[4]	27,542	14,005	242	11,870
Idaho	15,745	276,885	...	346,479	...	...	345,202	482,848	15,391	23,697	239,429	8,080	217	20
Illinois	3,783,519	179,679	2,664,925	297,672	...	...	2,567	620,163	1,011,175	6,366	327,660	55,959	1,272	1,103
Indiana	2,140,224	119,232	1,300,860	212,905	25,475	...	8,448	372,322	618,403	3,874	287,300	164,517	4,281	112
Iowa	4,974,200	442,035	2,693,126	13,460	...	...	1,739	1,813,300	2,149,597	15,506	517,608	69,873	2,185	900
Kansas	437,100	260,145	203,363	1,638,000	...	...	...	1,811,855	284,409	8,162	178,318	15,764	1,496	39
Kentucky	424,760	160,380	312,800	53,226	667,906	...	...	485,624	173,935	937	284,032	23,048	808	...
Louisiana	4,830	30,600	587,423	7,129	104	165,984	1,000	190,944	14,868	182	142,727	30,646	1,505	177,994
Maine	...	22,444	...	...	...	...	139,776	14,686	3,081	476	94,557	104,741	3,486	92,697
Maryland	184,320	35,250	81,432	14,375	31,537	...	2,723	66,469	29,904	548	207,480	20,320	752	44,658
Massachusetts	...	19,092	...	...	14,895	...	6,657	10,849	6,072	273	80,569	20,239	332	178,602
Michigan	852,150	161,448	250,800	132,000	...	...	62,749	226,718	128,138	5,058	658,028	58,360	1,833	4,822
Minnesota	2,013,429	441,130	1,264,256	420,627	...	...	74,867	827,179	765,878	10,285	1,182,340	83,178	1,075	2,128
Mississippi	8,131	52,000	523,600	32,550	...	422,832	[4]	282,829	47,120	[4]	113,563	90,684	4,237	26,601
Missouri	411,413	290,550	1,161,300	333,788	8,354	62,200	...	1,071,627	595,004	5,095	363,526	64,484	4,227	220
Montana	2,131	271,050	...	500,773	...	...	13,800	618,406	28,513	12,511	39,830	8,146	159	...
Nebraska	2,142,425	393,107	432,765	431,585	...	...	14,664	1,845,080	548,059	5,833	167,005	27,881	553	28
Nevada	...	99,098	...	7,740	...	...	16,796	125,724	1,403	3,154	27,813	75	2	...
New Hampshire	...	13,651	...	...	...	...	438	9,750	1,445	300	48,337	11,027	495	5,182
New Jersey	28,196	17,978	28,984	7,396	...	...	16,334	18,449	4,143	261	66,923	13,485	545	49,879
New Mexico	26,733	90,948	...	38,850	...	40,320	3,699	413,028	9,372	9,224	84,032	18,900	275	...
New York	254,588	326,966	3,511	23,400	...	...	90,409	199,802	16,036	1,880	1,431,949	74,444	2,031	45,058
North Carolina	373,480	38,480	299,922	42,525	1,120,826	20,074	13,276	153,082	319,457	178	230,787	175,364	16,696	68,784
North Dakota	54,665	186,406	28,875	829,626	32,595	...	87,808	518,960	34,684	7,319	107,026	2,460	225	111
Ohio	1,542,450	206,310	1,137,024	278,590	...	...	14,426	339,981	261,641	12,926	562,455	95,264	2,964	3,351
Oklahoma	21,000	162,050	25,200	770,250	...	81,907	...	1,490,332	46,931	2,672	152,847	43,698	1,645	...
Oregon	4,431	235,780	...	309,600	...	...	87,177	311,559	18,494	12,467	157,581	28,019	710	55,748
Pennsylvania	379,200	263,466	19,940	37,925	16,380	...	35,530	310,500	92,942	3,371	1,179,245	180,668	16,831	312
Rhode Island	...	1,332	...	...	...	...	6,256	1,056	938	...	6,660	5,138	152	46,143
South Carolina	88,992	23,718	191,520	25,574	174,549	28,929	...	98,246	77,215	[4]	79,315	75,835	1,889	20,448
South Dakota	402,270	332,258	157,157	274,062	...	...	4,502	1,162,852	271,415	39,547	207,457	13,378	371	340
Tennessee	108,000	80,262	404,558	49,875	176,539	75,264	1,490	330,728	163,980	295	298,501	45,294	2,048	...
Texas	444,600	352,960	118,503	487,500	...	1,120,973	27,849	3,379,405	113,374	56,674	508,048	167,226	4,648	153,880
Utah	5,625	138,915	...	34,658	...	...	5,892	163,161	6,158	20,281	129,813	16,987	250	...
Vermont	...	55,818	...	...	...	...	1,152	39,210	4,035	392	307,855	7,050	105	...
Virginia	117,810	108,129	74,115	41,270	159,262	79	13,244	316,945	104,336	6,609	265,867	54,248	2,429	84,993
Washington	44,556	241,500	...	640,880	...	...	184,527	311,142	18,214	2,456	382,754	53,095	916	85,511
West Virginia	17,035	57,643	...	1,368	4,502	...	...	80,754	12,833	3,974	47,005	8,369	364	15
Wisconsin	1,184,560	489,255	91,476	16,805	28,431	...	139,200	647,176	244,972	4,848	2,825,157	36,658	1,272	5,901
Wyoming	11,485	130,425	...	32,472	...	...	11,524	342,016	4,073	23,121	16,764	482	20	...
TOTAL U.S.	23,335,452	8,022,373	15,252,915	9,436,765	2,683,175	4,064,474	1,720,381	25,453,709	8,873,816	401,761	16,883,401	3,267,781	134,481	2,237,202

[1] Farm value. [2] Gross income, Dec. 1, 1979–Nov. 30, 1980. [3] Preliminary. [4] Estimates discontinued. [5] Deficit.
Sources: U.S. Department of Agriculture, Statistical Reporting Service, Crop Reporting Board, *Crop Values, Meat Animals, Milk, Poultry*; U.S. Department of Commerce, National Oceanic and Atmospheric Administration, National Marine Fisheries Service, *Fisheries of the United States, 1980*.

Income by Industrial Source, 1980

State and region	SOURCES OF PERSONAL INCOME: Total personal income	Farm income	Govt. income disbursements: Federal	Govt. income disbursements: State, local	Private nonfarm income	SOURCES OF LABOUR AND PROPRIETORS' INCOME % OF TOTAL: Total	Farms	Mining	Construction	Mfg.	Wholesale, retail trade	Finance, insurance, real estate	Transportation, communications, public util.	Service	Govt.	Other
United States	$2,162,936	$31,980	$84,400	$177,147	$1,320,475	$1,614,002	%2.0	%1.8	%5.8	%25.8	%16.6	%6.1	%7.7	%17.7	%16.2	%0.3
New England	125,100	457	3,190	9,420	77,756	90,825	0.5	0.1	4.4	32.1	15.8	6.6	5.9	20.1	13.9	0.6
Maine	8,940	109	488	704	5,013	6,315	1.7	[1]	6.0	28.8	15.9	4.1	6.0	17.0	18.9	1.6
New Hampshire	8,429	16	210	574	5,030	5,829	0.3	0.1	6.8	34.0	16.8	5.2	5.5	17.4	13.4	0.5
Vermont	4,013	123	95	343	2,388	2,950	4.2	[1]	5.8	30.7	14.9	4.3	6.2	18.1	14.9	0.9
Massachusetts	58,232	102	1,435	4,883	43,029	43,131	0.2	[1]	3.8	29.5	16.1	6.6	6.5	22.2	14.6	0.5
Rhode Island	8,975	10	293	710	5,205	6,217	0.2	[1]	4.2	32.8	15.8	5.8	4.6	20.0	16.1	0.5
Connecticut	36,510	97	670	2,206	23,409	26,383	0.4	0.3	4.5	36.7	15.4	8.0	5.2	18.3	10.9	0.3
Mideast	431,671	1,920	18,351	35,842	264,472	320,586	0.6	0.6	4.3	25.7	15.6	7.4	8.1	20.5	16.9	0.3
New York	180,646	624	3,818	16,746	113,221	134,410	0.5	0.2	3.4	22.9	16.0	10.4	8.7	22.3	15.3	0.3
New Jersey	80,724	151	1,952	6,170	47,221	55,493	0.3	0.1	4.6	29.6	17.4	5.3	8.9	18.8	14.6	0.4
Pennsylvania	112,220	838	2,914	7,717	71,378	82,847	1.0	1.8	5.1	33.6	15.0	5.2	7.6	17.6	12.8	0.3
Delaware	6,172	92	190	521	4,062	4,866	1.9	[1]	5.9	39.9	13.0	4.3	5.5	14.5	14.6	0.4
Maryland	44,210	216	3,722	3,678	21,823	29,439	0.7	0.2	6.6	16.8	17.1	5.7	6.6	20.7	25.1	0.5
District of Columbia	7,699	—	5,753	1,009	6,768	13,530	—	[1]	2.0	2.9	6.3	5.1	5.3	27.7	50.0	0.7
Great Lakes	408,455	5,077	7,926	31,073	263,017	307,093	1.6	0.8	5.2	35.6	15.9	5.3	6.9	15.7	12.7	0.3
Michigan	92,339	650	1,357	7,954	59,423	69,385	0.9	0.5	4.4	40.2	14.4	4.3	5.8	15.8	13.4	0.3
Ohio	102,410	811	2,238	7,135	67,566	77,750	1.0	1.1	5.3	37.4	15.6	4.6	7.1	15.6	12.1	0.4
Indiana	49,177	878	939	3,336	32,463	37,716	2.3	0.8	5.9	39.2	15.2	4.6	6.9	13.2	11.6	0.3
Illinois	120,434	1,409	2,667	9,003	76,542	89,622	1.6	1.0	5.5	29.0	17.6	7.1	7.9	16.9	13.0	0.4
Wisconsin	44,095	1,329	625	3,645	27,022	32,620	4.1	0.2	5.1	35.5	15.4	5.0	6.4	15.0	13.1	0.2
Plains	160,862	6,014	4,753	12,796	111,867	117,881	5.1	1.2	6.1	23.5	18.2	5.8	9.0	15.9	14.9	0.3
Minnesota	39,744	1,289	719	3,458	24,844	30,309	4.2	1.5	6.1	25.2	18.4	6.0	8.0	16.4	13.8	0.4
Iowa	27,328	1,192	419	2,211	15,297	19,118	6.2	0.3	6.2	27.6	18.0	5.8	7.1	14.6	13.8	0.4
Missouri	44,273	1,179	1,585	3,112	27,553	33,428	3.5	0.6	5.5	25.6	17.7	5.7	10.3	16.7	14.0	0.4
North Dakota	5,723	334	321	461	2,919	4,035	8.3	4.9	8.8	6.5	20.7	5.3	10.0	15.6	19.4	0.5
South Dakota	5,408	287	291	453	2,618	3,649	7.9	1.8	6.5	11.7	20.6	5.5	8.1	17.0	20.4	0.5
Nebraska	14,738	726	566	1,316	8,064	10,672	6.8	0.4	6.0	16.4	19.2	7.1	10.8	15.5	17.6	0.2
Kansas	23,648	1,007	855	1,785	13,023	16,670	6.0	2.5	6.2	22.8	17.0	5.3	9.0	14.9	15.8	0.5
Southeast	428,822	7,369	22,831	35,614	250,116	315,929	2.3	2.6	6.5	23.6	16.8	5.2	8.1	15.8	18.5	0.6
Virginia	50,333	279	5,926	3,870	25,809	35,884	0.8	1.8	6.1	19.7	14.9	4.9	7.2	17.0	27.3	0.3
West Virginia	15,243	45	336	1,293	9,545	11,218	0.4	16.8	6.6	23.3	13.7	3.2	8.8	12.4	14.5	0.3
Kentucky	27,939	624	1,217	2,162	16,800	20,803	3.0	7.9	5.9	25.9	14.9	4.2	7.9	13.7	16.2	0.4
Tennessee	35,525	373	1,734	2,977	22,259	27,342	1.4	0.8	5.2	29.8	17.0	5.1	7.2	15.9	17.2	0.4
North Carolina	46,043	1,277	2,047	4,165	28,783	36,273	3.5	0.3	5.2	33.1	15.6	4.4	6.9	13.5	17.1	0.4
South Carolina	22,726	264	1,528	2,144	3,658	17,594	1.5	0.2	6.9	34.0	14.2	4.2	6.4	11.8	20.8	0.0
Georgia	44,217	649	2,570	3,932	27,736	34,887	1.9	0.4	5.2	23.5	19.4	5.8	9.9	14.8	18.6	0.5
Florida	88,675	1,539	3,186	6,487	47,011	58,223	2.6	0.4	7.8	13.6	20.0	7.4	8.8	21.7	16.6	1.1
Alabama	29,199	517	1,812	2,584	16,875	21,787	2.4	2.3	5.8	28.5	15.2	4.5	7.4	13.3	20.1	0.5
Mississippi	16,626	573	873	1,560	9,378	12,384	4.6	2.0	6.1	26.0	15.9	4.5	7.1	13.5	19.6	0.7
Louisiana	35,645	416	1,049	3,182	23,080	27,726	1.5	8.4	10.3	17.0	16.9	4.6	10.1	15.5	15.3	0.4
Arkansas	16,651	813	554	1,259	9,182	11,808	6.9	1.1	6.1	26.9	16.2	4.6	8.1	14.1	15.3	0.7
Southwest	197,961	3,380	8,555	15,477	124,799	152,211	2.2	6.6	8.0	19.1	18.2	5.7	7.9	16.0	15.8	0.5
Oklahoma	27,645	615	1,360	2,162	16,189	20,328	3.0	9.4	6.2	18.2	16.8	5.0	8.4	15.0	17.3	0.7
Texas	136,146	2,133	5,308	9,998	89,216	106,654	2.0	6.3	8.1	20.2	18.9	5.8	7.9	15.8	14.3	0.7
New Mexico	10,219	207	797	1,217	5,464	7,685	2.7	10.1	7.4	7.2	15.5	4.3	8.5	17.6	26.2	0.5
Arizona	23,951	425	1,090	2,099	13,930	17,543	2.4	3.3	9.0	18.0	16.8	6.2	7.0	18.1	18.2	1.0
Rocky Mountain	59,742	1,297	3,188	5,337	36,090	45,912	2.8	5.0	7.8	15.3	17.1	5.7	9.0	16.6	18.6	2.1
Montana	6,732	146	326	618	3,613	4,702	3.1	5.2	8.0	10.5	19.0	5.2	11.6	16.9	20.0	0.5
Idaho	7,626	521	327	639	4,119	5,607	9.3	2.0	7.3	17.8	16.8	4.8	7.8	16.0	17.2	1.0
Wyoming	5,152	107	197	490	3,289	4,084	2.6	24.9	11.4	4.8	14.1	3.4	10.2	11.3	16.8	0.5
Colorado	29,029	453	1,555	2,555	18,067	22,630	2.0	4.9	7.3	16.6	17.3	6.7	8.6	17.9	18.1	0.6
Utah	11,203	70	783	1,034	7,002	8,890	0.7	5.6	7.7	18.0	17.0	5.2	8.9	16.0	20.4	0.5
Far West	335,412	6,229	13,429	29,809	201,725	251,193	2.5	0.6	6.1	22.1	16.8	6.7	7.2	20.0	17.2	0.8
Washington	42,677	803	2,044	3,859	25,076	31,783	2.5	0.3	7.6	23.5	17.0	5.7	7.2	16.6	18.6	1.0
Oregon	24,587	430	659	2,299	15,272	18,660	2.3	0.3	6.9	24.7	18.8	6.2	7.9	16.2	15.8	0.9
Nevada	8,597	55	352	721	5,661	6,789	0.8	1.9	9.5	5.4	15.0	4.9	8.0	38.3	15.8	0.4
California	259,551	4,940	10,375	22,930	155,716	193,962	2.5	0.7	5.7	22.2	16.7	6.8	7.2	20.3	17.2	0.7
Alaska	5,136	6	711	896	3,192	4,804	0.1	6.3	9.9	7.7	11.5	3.7	12.5	13.9	33.4	1.0
Hawaii	9,775	231	1,465	883	4,990	7,568	3.0	[1]	7.3	5.4	15.9	7.2	9.3	20.4	31.0	0.5

Dollar figures in millions. Percentages may not add to 100.0 because of rounding.
[1] Less than 0.05%.
Source: U.S. Department of Commerce, Bureau of Economic Analysis, *Survey of Current Business*.

Farms and Farm Income

State	Number of farms 1981 [1,2]	Land in farms 1981 in 000 acres [1,2]	CASH RECEIPTS, 1980, IN $000: Farm marketings: Total [3]	Crops [3]	Livestock and products
Alabama	58,000	12,600	1,839,152	698,633	1,140,519
Alaska	380	1,520 [4]	11,534	7,458	4,076
Arizona	7,100	38,800	1,712,639	929,935	782,704
Arkansas	59,000	16,500	3,030,148	1,573,125	1,457,023
California	80,000	33,800	13,465,276	9,316,683	4,148,593
Colorado	26,500	36,500	3,160,061	940,139	2,219,922
Connecticut	4,100	490	296,229	123,819	172,410
Delaware	3,500	650	332,834	96,329	236,505
Florida	39,000	13,300	3,804,289	2,848,352	955,937
Georgia	59,000	15,500	2,683,817	1,180,507	1,503,310
Hawaii	4,300	1,965	439,343	358,023	81,320
Idaho	24,200	15,400	1,982,417	1,130,904	851,513
Illinois	105,000	28,800	7,745,988	5,433,558	2,312,430
Indiana	87,000	16,800	4,417,078	2,755,322	1,661,756
Iowa	118,000	33,800	9,930,190	4,442,832	5,487,358
Kansas	74,000	48,300	5,895,892	2,534,131	3,361,761
Kentucky	101,000	14,500	2,671,007	1,326,157	1,344,850
Louisiana	37,000	10,100	1,666,555	1,208,476	458,079
Maine	8,300	1,615	424,915	125,001	299,914
Maryland	17,500	2,800	897,883	283,271	614,612
Massachusetts	5,800	680	308,524	182,952	125,572
Michigan	65,000	11,400	2,655,292	1,536,473	1,118,819
Minnesota	105,000	30,000	6,274,207	2,970,241	3,303,966
Mississippi	55,000	14,600	2,167,491	1,275,694	891,797
Missouri	119,000	31,500	4,093,678	1,912,376	2,181,302
Montana	23,900	62,100	1,414,447	667,607	746,840
Nebraska	64,000	47,600	6,094,519	2,524,237	3,570,282
Nevada	2,900	8,990	232,453	74,662	157,791
New Hampshire	3,600	545	98,456	26,112	72,344
New Jersey	9,100	1,000	431,053	308,742	122,311
New Mexico	13,600	46,700	1,144,951	269,073	875,878
New York	48,000	9,200	2,403,850	699,940	1,703,910
North Carolina	93,000	11,700	3,620,466	2,184,217	1,436,249
North Dakota	40,000	41,700	2,474,368	1,692,946	781,422
Ohio	94,000	16,300	3,683,808	2,327,698	1,356,110
Oklahoma	72,000	34,600	3,218,563	1,071,533	2,147,030
Oregon	35,000	18,100	1,593,849	1,056,515	537,334
Pennsylvania	62,000	9,000	2,661,393	741,836	1,919,557
Rhode Island	860	75	32,509	19,191	13,318
South Carolina	34,000	6,400	1,071,629	658,414	413,215
South Dakota	38,000	45,000	2,590,896	800,858	1,790,038
Tennessee	96,000	13,600	1,736,772	852,091	884,681
Texas	186,000	138,800	8,995,038	3,806,986	5,188,052
Utah	13,000	12,600	522,153	138,207	383,946
Vermont	7,900	1,740	378,477	25,592	352,885
Virginia	58,000	9,800	1,458,536	509,077	949,459
Washington	39,000	16,100	2,673,535	1,826,652	846,883
West Virginia	20,000	4,200	236,710	64,339	172,371
Wisconsin	93,000	18,600	4,668,613	925,397	3,743,216
Wyoming	9,200	35,000	649,612	125,285	524,327
TOTAL U.S.	2,418,740	1,041,370	135,993,095	68,587,598	67,405,497

[1] Preliminary. [2] Places with annual sales of agricultural products of $1,000 or more. [3] Excludes Commodity Credit Corporation loans.
[4] Exclusive of grazing land leased from the U.S. Government, Alaska farmland totals about 70,000 acres.
Source: U.S. Department of Agriculture, Statistical Reporting Service and Economic Research Service.

Principal Minerals, Production and Value, 1979

State	Principal nonfuel minerals, in order of value	Value ($000)	% of U.S. total prod.	Crude Petroleum Production (000 bbl)	Crude Petroleum Value ($000)	Natural Gas Production (000,000 cu ft)	Natural Gas Value ($000)	Coal[1] Production (000 ST)	Coal[1] Value ($000)
Alabama	Cement, stone, lime, clays	$336,367	1.40	19,161	$286,281	85,815	$174,977	23,873	...
Alaska	Sand and gravel, stone, gold, gem stones	123,419	.51	511,335	5,493,596	220,754	114,351	706	...
Arizona	Copper, molybdenum, cement, silver	2,490,481	10.39	472	3,913	247	102	11,389	...
Arkansas	Bromine, cement, stone, sand and gravel	302,622	1.26	18,869	277,940	109,452	104,964	521	...
California	Cement, sand and gravel, boron, stone	1,769,675	7.38	352,268	4,438,577	248,206	423,191	...	...
Colorado	Molybdenum, cement, sand and gravel, vanadium	826,098	3.44	32,324	424,737	191,239	269,647	18,135	...
Connecticut	Stone, sand and gravel, feldspar, lime	69,236	.28	...	...	...	...	...	...
Delaware	Sand and gravel, magnesium compounds, clay	3,290	...	...	...	...	...	...	...
Florida	Phosphate rock, stone, cement, sand and gravel	1,269,271	5.29	47,168	616,486	50,190	78,899	...	...
Georgia	Clays, stone, cement, sand and gravel	698,690	2.91	...	...	...	...	50	...
Hawaii	Cement, stone, sand and gravel, pumice	63,904	.26	...	...	...	...	...	...
Idaho	Silver, phosphate rock, lead, zinc	437,885	1.82	...	...	...	...	...	...
Illinois	Stone, sand and gravel, cement, lime	478,405	1.99	21,793	511,978	1,585	2,949	59,507	...
Indiana	Cement, stone, sand and gravel, lime	326,086	1.36	4,715	111,085	350	369	27,502	...
Iowa	Cement, stone, sand and gravel, gypsum	277,901	1.15	...	...	...	...	724	...
Kansas	Cement, salt, stone, sand and gravel	263,392	1.09	56,995	1,253,894	797,762	603,108	857	...
Kentucky	Stone, lime, cement, sand and gravel	207,927	.86	5,514	124,506	59,520	56,365	149,836	...
Louisiana	Sulfur, salt, sand and gravel, cement	455,276	1.89	489,687	5,582,432	7,266,217	8,100,795	...	...
Maine	Sand and gravel, cement, stone, gem stones	45,910	.19	...	...	...	...	...	...
Maryland	Stone, cement, sand and gravel, clays	192,962	.80	...	...	28	29	2,717	...
Massachusetts	Stone, sand and gravel, lime, clays	92,546	.38	...	...	...	...	...	...
Michigan	Iron ore, cement, sand and gravel, magnesium compounds	1,506,476	6.28	34,862	520,832	159,731	277,932	...	...
Minnesota	Iron ore, sand and gravel, stone, lime	2,067,990	8.62	...	...	...	...	...	...
Mississippi	Sand and gravel, cement, clays, magnesium compounds	107,689	.44	37,327	520,708	144,077	230,523	...	...
Missouri	Lead, cement, stone, lime	1,159,835	4.83	91	2,216	...	...	6,487	...
Montana	Copper, silver, cement, sand and gravel	291,287	1.21	29,957	371,181	53,888	65,258	32,147	...
Nebraska	Cement, sand and gravel, stone, lime	99,181	.41	6,068	101,673	3,208	2,727	...	...
Nevada	Gold, barite sand and gravel, diatomite	238,150	.99	1,235	14,202	...	...	...	...
New Hampshire	Sand and gravel, stone, clays, gem stones	23,258	.09	...	...	...	...	...	...
New Jersey	Stone, sand and gravel, zinc, titanium concentrate	151,689	.63	...	...	...	...	...	...
New Mexico	Copper, potassium salts, molybdenum, sand and gravel	694,448	2.89	79,649	1,119,861	1,181,363	1,613,742	15,037	...
New York	Cement, stone, salt, sand and gravel	453,710	1.89	855	20,332	15,500	19,623	...	...
North Carolina	Stone, phosphate rock, sand and gravel, cement	340,411	1.42	...	...	...	...	...	...
North Dakota	Sand and gravel, salt, lime, clays	21,234	.08	30,914	371,000	18,468	23,639	14,963[2]	...
Ohio	Stone, lime, sand and gravel, cement	607,320	2.53	11,953	269,129	123,431	222,824	43,495	...
Oklahoma	Cement, stone, sand and gravel, helium	201,022	.84	143,642	2,158,526	1,835,366	2,062,951	4,782	...
Oregon	Stone, sand and gravel, cement, nickel	165,207	.68	...	...	2	4	...	...
Pennsylvania	Cement, stone, lime, sand and gravel	722,614	3.01	2,874	69,235	96,313	127,711	89,167	...
Rhode Island	Sand and gravel, stone, gem stones	7,886	.03	...	...	...	...	...	...
South Carolina	Cement, stone, sand and gravel, clays	201,711	.84	...	...	...	...	...	...
South Dakota	Gold, cement, stone, sand and gravel	148,686	.62	846	21,387	914	1,926	...	...
Tennessee	Stone, cement, sand and gravel, clays	385,744	1.60	614	12,440	941	1,600	9,303	...
Texas	Cement, sulfur, stone, sand and gravel	1,406,168	5.86	1,018,094	12,848,346	7,174,623	8,850,782	26,634[2]	...
Utah	Copper, gold, molybdenum, cement	753,384	3.14	27,728	316,376	58,605	41,961	11,834	...
Vermont	Stone, asbestos, sand and gravel, talc	54,136	.22	...	...	...	...	...	...
Virginia	Stone, cement, lime, sand and gravel	309,765	1.29	4	92	8,544	14,365	37,038	...
Washington	Cement, sand and gravel, stone, lime	224,948	.93	...	...	...	...	5,050	...
West Virginia	Stone, sand and gravel, cement, salt	118,595	.49	2,406	67,368	150,505	158,030	112,381	...
Wisconsin	Sand and gravel, stone, iron ore, lime	179,682	.74	...	...	...	...	...	...
Wyoming	Sodium carbonate, clays, iron ore, stone	590,176	2.46	131,890	1,121,063	414,416	468,290	71,823	...
TOTAL U.S.		$23,964,000	100.00	3,121,310	$39,051,332	20,471,260	$24,113,634	781,134	...

[1] Bituminous coal, unless otherwise noted.   [2] Lignite only.
Sources: U.S. Department of the Interior, *Minerals Yearbook*; Department of Energy.

Services

Kind of service	NUMBER OF SERVICES 1977	NUMBER OF SERVICES 1978	NUMBER OF EMPLOYEES[1] 1977	NUMBER OF EMPLOYEES[1] 1978
Hotels and other lodging places	45,399	43,307	915,178	997,295
Hotels, tourist courts, and motels	35,109	33,693	859,001	936,011
Rooming and boarding houses	3,579	3,200	30,168	31,508
Camps and trailering parks	3,939	3,706	15,499	17,426
Sporting and recreational camps	2,267	2,115	9,749	11,229
Personal services	162,161	157,535	901,047	947,337
Laundry, cleaning, garment services	44,462	42,508	357,102	368,357
Photographic studios, portrait	6,105	5,809	32,066	33,443
Beauty shops	71,311	69,006	280,645	296,175
Barber shops	11,029	10,304	27,620	28,357
Shoe repair and hat cleaning shops	2,935	2,530	6,994	7,071
Funeral service and crematories	14,733	14,389	71,209	71,782
Miscellaneous personal services	11,023	12,191	123,563	139,017
Business services	145,005	146,801	2,307,384	2,599,088
Advertising	10,203	10,132	120,024	124,778
Credit reporting and collection	5,741	5,640	61,492	63,754
Mailing, reproduction, stenographic	12,297	12,349	95,067	107,456
Building services	23,901	23,472	408,157	466,512
Employment agencies	7,091	7,514	76,084	99,420
Temporary help supply services	3,570	3,969	293,728	348,169
Computer and data processing services	9,109	10,036	199,177	221,980
Research and development laboratories	2,013	2,108	75,929	88,429
Management and public relations	23,095	23,733	240,838	281,415
Detective and protective services	6,312	6,204	268,684	287,380
Equipment rental and leasing	11,002	11,230	85,134	94,205
Photofinishing laboratories	2,478	2,444	60,683	65,447
Auto repair, services, and garages	97,327	97,635	477,370	525,450
Automobile rentals, without drivers	7,386	7,928	76,910	81,502
Automobile parking	7,153	6,808	33,709	36,062
Automotive repair shops	73,970	74,147	305,447	337,141
Automotive services, except repair	8,374	8,243	59,473	68,040
Car washes	5,564	5,359	44,901	49,329
Miscellaneous repair services	49,483	47,807	254,140	280,363
Radio and television repair	9,079	8,306	38,114	38,849
Motion pictures	15,034	14,663	180,933	193,892
Motion picture production	3,529	3,597	55,495	69,855
Motion picture distribution	1,129	1,096	15,940	14,082
Motion picture theatres	10,217	9,808	108,862	109,102
Amusement and recreation services	46,842	45,404	585,304	659,407
Producers, orchestras, entertainers	6,451	6,258	67,497	79,550
Bowling and billiard establishments	7,843	7,512	106,476	114,554
Racing, including track operation	1,781	1,697	37,664	39,285
Public golf courses	2,153	2,038	14,733	14,247
Amusement parks	564	515	32,058	43,584
Membership sports, recreation clubs	9,415	9,187	143,652	152,325
Health services	283,274	288,460	4,339,178	4,734,389
Physicians' offices	132,546	135,164	601,354	659,153
Dentists' offices	80,588	81,712	273,980	313,945
Osteopathic physicians' offices	4,547	4,663	16,024	17,978
Chiropractors' offices	7,231	7,626	14,127	17,583
Optometrists' offices	11,013	11,168	27,514	32,194
Nursing and personal care facilities	12,316	12,258	793,769	870,602
Hospitals	5,414	5,350	2,283,859	2,439,947
Medical and dental laboratories	10,442	10,436	90,035	95,622
Outpatient care facilities	7,704	8,052	126,697	154,049
Legal services	91,942	92,437	392,481	437,412
Educational services	25,994	25,025	992,019	1,154,213
Elementary and secondary schools	13,461	13,047	295,441	317,593
Colleges and universities	2,438	2,397	576,196	697,299
Libraries and information centres	1,599	1,327	12,691	12,479
Correspondence and vocational schools	3,039	2,907	46,082	48,742
Social services	52,322	53,174	764,310	891,356
Residential care	7,645	7,937	172,098	190,241
Museums, botanical, zoological gardens	1,063	1,016	22,588	24,119
Membership organizations	137,891	135,588	1,100,716	1,232,200
Business associations	12,398	12,173	73,130	75,265
Professional organizations	3,958	3,881	36,410	37,810
Labour organizations	22,189	21,507	170,102	186,145
Civic and social organizations	34,182	33,055	266,076	295,297
Political organizations	1,137	1,365	4,160	6,255
Religious organizations	56,712	56,430	482,159	556,879
Miscellaneous services	75,257	77,260	670,425	751,019
Engineering, architectural services	32,520	33,679	369,706	414,285
Noncommercial research organizations	2,398	2,399	52,144	58,490
Accounting, auditing and bookkeeping	37,109	37,967	233,487	261,297
TOTAL[2]	1,233,652	1,230,879	14,059,994	15,567,801

[1] Mid-March pay period.   [2] Includes administrative and auxiliary businesses not shown separately.
Source: U.S. Department of Commerce, Bureau of the Census, *County Business Patterns 1977 and 1978*.

Principal Manufactures, 1977

monetary figures in millions of dollars

Industry	Employees (000)	Cost of labour [1]	Cost of materials	Value of shipments	Value added by mfg.
Food and kindred products	1,520	$18,544	$136,964	$192,912	$56,062
Meat products	309	3,702	. . .	46,276	7,478
Dairy products	154	1,939	. . .	26,010	5,648
Preserved fruits and vegetables	235	2,336	. . .	20,333	7,685
Grain mill products	113	1,576	. . .	22,344	6,626
Beverages	195	2,849	. . .	23,329	9,901
Tobacco products	61	751	4,730	9,051	4,334
Textile mill products	876	7,881	24,753	40,551	16,105
Apparel and other textile products	1,334	9,659	20,866	40,245	19,671
Lumber and wood products	692	7,425	23,919	39,919	16,223
Furniture and fixtures	464	4,448	8,187	16,978	8,922
Paper and allied products	629	8,943	30,148	52,086	22,171
Printing and publishing	1,092	14,025	17,795	49,716	31,980
Chemicals and allied products	880	13,839	62,294	118,154	56,721
Industrial chemicals	110	1,847	. . .	12,845	6,487
Plastics materials and synthetics	157	2,471	. . .	20,064	7,843
Drugs	156	2,460	. . .	14,248	9,940
Soap, cleaners, and toilet goods	112	1,526	. . .	16,331	9,407
Paints, allied products	61	883	. . .	6,630	2,821
Agricultural chemicals	54	784	. . .	9,932	3,808
Petroleum and coal products	147	2,696	81,655	97,453	16,378
Rubber, misc. plastics products	721	8,536	20,218	39,553	19,740
Leather and leather products	243	1,860	3,933	7,607	3,719
Stone, clay, and glass products	614	7,943	16,445	35,477	19,130
Primary metal industries	1,114	18,745	66,171	103,179	37,568
Blast furnace, basic steel products	530	10,086	. . .	50,582	18,318
Iron, steel foundries	222	3,329	. . .	10,830	6,237
Primary nonferrous metals	57	1,032	. . .	10,660	3,619
Nonferrous drawing and rolling	177	2,640	. . .	22,227	5,902
Nonferrous foundries	82	1,044	. . .	3,826	1,960
Fabricated metal products	1,556	21,036	45,385	90,024	45,512
Ordnance and accessories	70	992	. . .	2,641	1,737

Industry	Employees (000)	Cost of labour [1]	Cost of materials	Value of shipments	Value added by mfg.
Machinery, except electrical	2,083	$30,558	$56,532	$122,188	$67,223
Engines and turbines	130	2,238	. . .	10,426	4,960
Farm and garden machinery	151	2,197	. . .	11,857	5,490
Construction and related mach.	333	5,097	. . .	23,682	11,836
Metalworking machinery	298	4,514	. . .	13,283	8,747
Special industry machinery	185	2,616	. . .	9,128	5,271
General industrial machinery	314	4,451	. . .	16,542	9,673
Service industry machines	192	2,516	. . .	12,416	5,963
Office, computing machines	259	3,949	. . .	16,842	9,921
Electric and electronic equipment	1,723	22,544	39,370	88,433	50,366
Electric distributing equip.	115	1,431	. . .	5,772	3,336
Electrical industrial apparatus	198	2,543	. . .	9,591	5,614
Household appliances	162	1,898	. . .	10,737	5,276
Electric lighting, wiring equip.	165	1,925	. . .	8,357	4,741
Radio, TV receiving equipment	98	1,097	. . .	6,913	3,078
Communication equipment	459	6,995	. . .	22,744	14,130
Electronic components, access.	374	4,557	. . .	15,390	9,260
Transportation equipment	1,768	30,674	103,490	166,954	64,291
Motor vehicles and equipment	876	16,038	. . .	117,747	37,023
Aircraft and parts	431	7,621	. . .	25,867	14,732
Ship, boat building, repairing	220	2,940	. . .	8,318	4,681
Railroad equipment	56	889	. . .	4,278	1,883
Guided missiles, space vehicles	120	2,427	. . .	6,599	4,422
Instruments and related products	559	7,520	10,504	28,898	18,762
Measuring, controlling devices	200	2,666	. . .	7,910	5,242
Medical instruments and supplies	114	1,319	. . .	5,217	3,262
Photographic equipment and supplies	112	1,900	. . .	9,947	6,732
Miscellaneous manufacturing industries	441	4,406	9,061	19,151	10,291
All establishments, including administrative and auxiliary	19,590	264,013	782,418	1,358,526	585,166

[1] Payroll only.   Source: U.S. Department of Commerce, *Census of Manufactures, 1977*.

Business Activity

Category of activity	WHOLESALING				RETAILING				SERVICES			
	1960	1965	1970	1977	1960	1965	1970	1977	1960	1965	1970	1977
Number of businesses (in 000)												
Sole proprietorships	306	265	274	307	1,548	1,554	1,689	1,862	1,966	2,208	2,507	3,303
Active partnerships	41	32	30	29	238	202	170	164	159	169	176	227
Active corporations	117	147	166	228 [1]	217	288	351	417 [1]	121	188	281	473 [1]
Business receipts (in $000,000)												
Sole proprietorships	17,061	17,934	21,556	33,499	65,439	77,760	89,315	123,595	23,256	29,789	40,869	67,791
Active partnerships	12,712	10,879	11,325	16,624	24,787	23,244	23,546	31,983	9,281	12,442	18,791	37,788
Active corporations	130,637	171,414	234,885	572,364 [1]	125,787	183,925	274,808	527,571 [1]	22,106	36,547	66,460	146,817 [1]
Net profit (less loss; in $000,000)												
Sole proprietorships	1,305	1,483	1,806	2,548	3,869	5,019	5,767	6,880	8,060	11,008	15,063	22,516
Active partnerships	587	548	557	755	1,612	1,654	1,603	1,870	3,056	4,402	6,189	9,245
Active corporations	2,130	3,288	4,441	15,769 [1]	2,225	4,052	5,217	10,367 [1]	849	1,505	1,199	4,185 [1]

Data refer to accounting periods ending between July 1 of year shown and June 30 of following year.   [1] 1976.
Source: U.S. Department of the Treasury, Internal Revenue Service, *Statistics of Income: Business Income Tax Returns* and *Corporation Income Tax Returns*.

Retail Sales

in millions of dollars

Kind of business	1960	1965	1970	1980
Durable goods stores [1]	70,560	94,186	114,288	297,926
Automotive group	39,579	56,884	64,966	167,017
Passenger car, other automotive dealers	37,038	53,484	59,388	148,799
Tire, battery, accessory dealers	2,541	3,400	5,578	18,218
Furniture and appliance group	10,591	13,352	17,778	43,918
Furniture, home furnishings stores	. . .	. . .	10,483	26,228
Household appliance, TV, radio stores	. . .	. . .	6,073	13,190
Building materials, hardware, farm equipment group	11,222	12,388	20,494	48,210
Lumberyards, building materials dealers	8,567	9,731	11,995	33,682
Hardware stores	2,655	2,657	3,351	7,743
Nondurable goods stores [1]	148,969	189,942	261,239	658,729
Apparel group	13,631	15,765	19,810	44,487
Men's, boys' wear stores	2,644	. . .	4,630	8,025
Women's apparel, accessory stores	5,295	. . .	7,582	16,991
Family clothing stores	. . .	. . .	3,360	9,127
Shoe stores	2,437	. . .	3,501	8,040
Drug and proprietary stores	7,538	9,186	13,352	31,557
Eating and drinking places	16,146	20,201	29,689	86,612
Food group	54,023	64,016	86,114	217,511
Grocery stores	48,610	. . .	79,756	202,065
Meat and fish markets	. . .	. . .	2,244	. . .
Bakeries	. . .	. . .	1,303	3,138
Gasoline service stations	17,588	20,611	27,994	94,470
General merchandise group	. . .	42,299	61,320	116,287
Department stores and dry goods general merchandise stores	. . .	. . .	45,000	107,431
Variety stores	. . .	. . .	6,959	8,856
Liquor stores	4,893	5,674	7,980	16,556
TOTAL	219,529	284,128	375,527	956,655

[1] Includes some kinds of business not shown separately.
Source: U.S. Department of Commerce, Bureau of the Census, *Monthly Retail Trade* and *Revised Monthly Retail Sales and Inventories (1971–80)*, Bureau of Economic Analysis, *1975 Business Statistics*.

Sales of Merchant Wholesalers

in millions of dollars

Kind of business	1960	1965	1970	1980
Durable goods [1]	56,803	82,861	111,970	438,439
Motor vehicles, automotive equipment	7,883	12,140	19,482	81,629
Electrical goods	8,660	12,681	16,667	46,436
Furniture, home furnishings	2,910	3,777	5,199	15,580
Hardware, plumbing, heating equipment	6,422	8,413	10,858	27,623
Lumber, construction supplies	6,680	9,765	10,863	33,245
Machinery, equipment, supplies	14,287	20,561	27,638	129,048
Metals, metalwork (except scrap)	5,708	9,162	13,647	. . .
Scrap, waste materials	3,296	4,789	6,040	16,327
Nondurable goods [1]	80,477	104,470	135,029	605,447
Groceries and related products	27,661	38,068	53,411	149,889
Beer, wine, distilled alcoholic beverages	7,424	9,464	13,332	31,697
Drugs, chemicals, allied products	5,370	7,180	9,135	13,051
Tobacco, tobacco products	4,164	5,014	6,232	10,998
Dry goods, apparel	6,675	8,804	10,577	25,790
Paper, paper products	4,153	5,612	7,679	21,643
Farm products	11,683	13,711	16,837	120,224
Other nondurable goods	13,346	16,966	22,632	69,939
TOTAL	137,281	187,331	246,999	1,043,886

[1] Includes some kinds of business not shown separately.
Source: U.S. Dept. of Commerce, Bureau of the Census, Current Business Reports, *Revised Monthly Wholesale Trade: Sales and Inventories (1973–1980)*.

Commercial Banks[1]

December 31, 1980

State	Number of banks	Total assets or liabilities $000,000	SELECTED ASSETS ($000,000) Loans	Investments[2]	Reserves, cash, and bank balances	SELECTED LIABILITIES ($000,000) Deposits Total	Demand	Time, savings	Capital accounts
Ala.	317	16,859	8,431	5,013	1,922	14,089	4,699	9,361	1,453
Alaska	12	2,251	1,017	652	272	1,757	781	976	198
Ariz.	24	13,354	7,901	2,828	1,793	11,376	3,843	7,491	823
Ark.	260	11,090	5,798	3,152	1,047	9,498	2,843	6,555	943
Calif.	281	237,971	140,316	22,308	47,087	192,609	44,983	92,354	10,814
Colo.	322	16,145	8,889	2,907	2,669	13,391	5,867	7,521	1,227
Conn.	64	13,950	7,839	2,537	2,393	11,559	4,660	6,554	863
Del.	18	3,685	1,788	1,084	432	2,903	1,044	1,859	268
D.C.	17	8,648	4,403	1,650	1,931	6,977	2,782	2,793	554
Fla.	557	48,004	21,289	14,107	7,860	40,537	16,901	23,308	3,497
Ga.	435	23,266	11,609	5,012	3,695	18,894	8,499	10,056	1,798
Hawaii	9	5,381	3,385	997	623	4,792	1,431	3,055	347
Idaho	26	5,106	2,798	1,132	676	4,262	1,288	2,974	360
Ill.	1,253	141,157	77,754	25,673	24,390	109,217	25,638	55,459	8,169
Ind.	405	32,724	16,437	9,261	3,819	27,113	7,531	19,152	2,440
Iowa	651	21,744	11,052	6,003	2,105	18,485	4,996	13,472	1,748
Kan.	619	16,598	8,066	5,011	1,584	14,078	4,504	9,574	1,394
Ky.	344	19,440	9,840	5,041	2,077	16,089	5,611	10,418	1,579
La.	269	24,945	12,251	6,937	3,045	21,195	7,845	13,299	1,946
Maine	41	3,465	1,898	923	370	2,895	784	2,112	255
Md.	102	16,546	9,596	3,126	2,232	13,772	4,860	8,411	1,178
Mass.	138	36,205	17,668	6,996	7,704	27,772	8,754	12,872	1,939
Mich.	375	53,388	29,325	12,655	7,546	43,359	10,663	31,047	3,665
Minn.	760	31,790	16,697	7,623	4,102	25,463	7,243	17,144	2,260
Miss.	177	11,467	5,822	3,370	1,180	9,797	3,083	6,709	880
Mo.	725	34,874	16,661	8,760	4,748	27,386	9,922	17,075	2,522
Mont.	163	5,317	2,883	1,379	552	4,622	1,311	3,311	426
Neb.	457	11,502	5,905	2,701	1,334	9,582	3,296	6,286	960
Nev.	9	3,761	2,150	845	502	3,199	1,340	1,859	303
N.H.	75	3,298	2,012	657	368	2,890	696	2,193	248
N.J.	169	36,126	18,891	9,376	4,646	30,340	10,172	19,850	2,474
N.M.	89	6,107	3,097	1,443	725	5,273	1,798	3,475	459
N.Y.	214	461,595	250,035	44,945	115,090	347,656	89,971	82,931	21,248
N.C.	79	25,555	12,371	5,121	4,827	20,193	6,583	11,435	1,774
N.D.	175	4,628	2,484	1,344	394	4,088	1,116	2,972	401
Ohio	384	56,268	27,866	15,072	7,731	43,716	12,917	29,486	6,120
Okla.	495	22,837	11,273	5,882	2,913	19,379	7,250	12,043	1,739
Ore.	77	12,957	7,671	2,357	1,609	10,574	3,224	7,236	908
Pa.	355	89,471	47,749	20,122	13,555	71,139	18,270	44,558	6,503
R.I.	14	6,969	3,982	1,407	835	5,487	1,169	3,967	412
S.C.	85	7,635	3,677	2,218	975	6,325	3,030	3,295	648
S.D.	152	5,084	2,882	1,356	451	4,535	1,055	3,480	406
Tenn.	350	23,803	12,333	6,072	3,091	19,875	6,057	13,740	1,785
Texas	1,467	118,879	59,171	25,005	21,375	97,476	36,180	53,275	8,313
Utah	76	6,744	3,738	1,219	1,084	5,686	1,966	3,669	510
Vt.	28	2,401	1,543	493	236	2,166	462	1,704	172
Va.	229	24,194	13,770	5,527	2,578	20,216	6,108	14,033	1,819
Wash.	100	23,638	14,316	2,858	3,842	18,747	5,835	11,467	1,493
W.Va.	237	10,315	4,986	3,393	775	8,620	2,195	6,425	892
Wis.	635	26,801	14,977	6,735	2,565	22,058	6,061	15,584	2,022
Wyo.	102	3,450	1,745	898	374	3,035	1,073	1,961	294
TOTAL[3]	14,430	1,855,688	992,415	334,445	331,909	1,481,161	431,539	755,610	114,150

[1] Detail may not add to total given due to rounding; excludes noninsured banks.
[2] Includes investment securities and trading account securities.
[3] Includes Guam and Puerto Rico bank statistics, not itemized in this table.
Source: Federal Deposit Insurance Corporation, *1980 Bank Operating Statistics.*

Life Insurance, 1980

Number of policies in 000s; value in $000,000

State	Total: Number of policies	Total: Value	Ordinary: Number of policies	Ordinary: Value	Group: Number of certificates	Group: Value	Industrial: Number of policies	Industrial: Value	Credit[1]: Number of policies	Credit[1]: Value
Ala.	12,331	$55,483	2,201	$28,284	1,811	$20,995	6,651	$2,756	1,668	$3,448
Alaska	615	7,421	138	3,099	306	4,092	10	3	161	227
Ariz.	4,867	38,384	1,639	22,096	1,434	13,587	179	131	1,615	2,570
Ark.	2,777	24,319	1,043	12,987	790	9,601	391	218	553	1,513
Calif.	30,699	355,377	10,812	178,036	12,108	164,020	1,705	1,218	6,074	12,103
Colo.	4,873	52,090	1,838	27,941	1,711	21,362	238	161	1,086	2,626
Conn.	5,908	62,466	2,358	28,662	2,140	31,410	239	203	1,171	2,191
Del.	1,598	12,992	477	5,016	390	7,206	210	146	521	624
D.C.	2,504	22,242	422	4,968	1,259	16,463	459	276	364	535
Fla.	16,441	127,830	5,759	71,396	3,863	47,166	3,352	2,335	3,467	6,933
Ga.	12,814	88,207	3,923	44,842	2,706	36,079	3,721	2,462	2,464	4,824
Hawaii	1,771	18,792	612	10,347	746	7,457	5	2	408	986
Idaho	1,359	12,610	522	6,952	527	4,842	23	15	287	801
Ill.	22,198	207,706	9,253	103,136	6,824	95,166	2,827	1,996	3,294	7,408
Ind.	10,305	87,510	4,230	44,183	2,786	38,010	1,475	978	1,814	4,339
Iowa	5,023	48,038	2,593	28,001	1,467	17,617	210	129	753	2,291
Kan.	4,253	38,891	1,915	22,916	1,219	13,745	288	179	831	2,051
Ky.	6,324	44,378	2,352	22,376	1,400	18,601	1,252	706	1,320	2,695
La.	9,801	63,328	2,388	33,734	2,112	23,712	3,535	2,096	1,766	3,786
Maine	1,792	13,598	711	7,020	590	5,728	69	52	422	798
Md.	7,926	66,229	2,964	34,607	1,935	27,699	1,638	985	1,389	2,938
Mass.	9,151	89,271	3,869	41,756	2,934	43,997	663	469	1,685	3,049
Mich.	16,711	163,320	5,544	60,406	6,277	95,268	1,755	1,169	3,135	6,477
Minn.	6,538	68,181	2,577	33,288	2,674	32,258	213	145	1,074	2,490
Miss.	4,076	27,800	1,007	14,247	1,011	10,704	748	448	1,310	2,401
Mo.	8,733	75,215	3,717	37,474	2,510	33,891	1,093	696	1,413	3,154
Mont.	1,140	10,300	445	6,125	395	3,468	22	12	278	695
Neb.	2,744	27,053	1,425	16,750	758	9,048	109	68	452	1,187
Nev.	1,484	14,119	326	5,427	504	6,431	10	7	644	2,254
N.H.	1,608	14,255	693	7,565	489	5,890	81	66	345	734
N.J.	12,236	134,332	5,389	64,055	3,723	64,953	1,257	1,080	1,867	4,244
N.M.	1,881	17,133	607	8,324	589	7,543	86	55	599	1,211
N.Y.	26,888	281,051	10,916	126,788	8,131	141,463	1,657	1,214	6,184	11,586
N.C.	12,578	82,922	4,396	42,395	2,570	34,069	2,997	1,626	2,615	4,832
N.D.	1,040	10,483	469	6,325	335	3,425	4	3	232	730
Ohio	20,517	180,332	8,249	87,897	5,763	82,136	2,903	1,999	3,602	8,300
Okla.	4,383	42,835	1,780	23,760	1,250	16,580	352	217	1,001	2,278
Ore.	3,393	38,200	1,202	17,544	1,434	19,013	75	48	682	1,595
Pa.	23,935	184,431	9,903	91,410	6,037	81,095	3,839	2,613	4,156	9,313
R.I.	1,951	15,945	773	8,141	745	7,210	147	102	286	492
S.C.	7,781	43,020	2,658	22,080	1,621	17,259	2,298	1,410	1,204	2,271
S.D.	1,029	9,763	544	6,330	271	2,841	4	3	210	589
Tenn.	9,480	66,672	2,837	32,109	2,574	29,011	2,227	1,281	1,842	4,271
Texas	25,207	226,148	8,866	121,671	6,992	89,427	3,165	2,038	6,184	13,012
Utah	2,200	18,887	698	10,617	947	6,941	85	45	470	1,284
Vt.	817	6,660	354	3,682	241	2,606	30	23	192	349
Va.	10,606	83,293	3,582	41,251	2,552	37,048	2,304	1,375	2,168	3,619
Wash.	5,522	58,909	1,980	29,637	2,282	26,938	145	85	1,115	2,249
W.Va.	3,307	22,880	1,062	10,401	883	10,441	536	339	826	1,699
Wis.	7,835	72,759	3,418	38,493	2,921	31,212	421	307	1,075	2,747
Wyo.	676	6,978	275	3,927	225	2,631	4	4	172	416
TOTAL U.S.	401,626	$3,541,038	147,711	$1,760,474	117,762	$1,579,355	57,707	$35,994	78,446	$165,215

[1] Life insurance on loans of ten years' or less duration.
Source: Institute of Life Insurance, *Life Insurance Fact Book '81.*

Savings and Loan Associations

Dec. 31, 1980[1]

State	Number of assns.	Total assets ($000,000)	Per capita assets
Alabama	58	$5,012	$1,288
Alaska	5	411	1,027
Arizona	18	6,570	2,417
Arkansas	75	4,502	1,970
California	195	120,532	5,092
Colorado	46	10,007	3,464
Connecticut	39	4,417	1,421
Delaware	18	270	455
District of Columbia	14	5,050	7,916
Florida	130	53,372	5,480
Georgia	97	11,147	2,040
Guam	2	70	592
Hawaii	8	4,263	4,418
Idaho	12	1,042	1,104
Illinois	370	46,159	4,043
Indiana	161	10,421	1,898
Iowa	73	7,235	2,484
Kansas	79	7,332	3,103
Kentucky	102	5,986	1,635
Louisiana	131	8,528	2,029
Maine	19	693	616
Maryland	188	10,707	2,540
Massachusetts	154	8,385	1,461
Michigan	63	18,426	1,990
Minnesota	56	10,637	2,609
Mississippi	59	2,975	1,180
Missouri	110	16,149	3,284
Montana	15	1,128	1,433
Nebraska	39	5,457	3,476
Nevada	8	2,444	3,059
New Hampshire	17	1,151	1,250
New Jersey	207	25,209	3,423
New Mexico	34	2,616	2,013
New York	115	27,719	1,579
North Carolina	194	12,315	2,097
North Dakota	11	2,426	3,715
Ohio	384	40,602	3,760
Oklahoma	55	5,854	1,935
Oregon	33	7,129	2,708
Pennsylvania	358	24,941	2,102
Puerto Rico	12	2,302	640
Rhode Island	5	770	813
South Carolina	75	6,473	2,075
South Dakota	19	1,135	1,645
Tennessee	99	7,425	1,617
Texas	320	35,303	2,481
Utah	15	4,263	2,918
Vermont	7	246	481
Virginia	84	9,701	1,815
Washington	48	9,709	2,351
West Virginia	32	1,621	831
Wisconsin	108	12,689	2,697
Wyoming	12	1,029	2,185
TOTAL U.S.	4,613	$629,829	$2,759

[1] Preliminary. Components do not add to totals because of differences in reporting dates and accounting systems.
Source: U.S. League of Savings Associations, *'81 Savings and Loan Sourcebook.*

GOVERNMENT AND POLITICS

The National Executive

December 21, 1981

Department, bureau, or office	Executive official and official title

PRESIDENT OF THE UNITED STATES — Ronald Reagan
Vice-President — George Bush

EXECUTIVE OFFICE OF THE PRESIDENT
Assistant to the President — Richard V. Allen
Martin Anderson
James A. Baker III, chief of staff
Elizabeth Hanford Dole
Max L. Friedersdorf
David R. Gergen
Edwin L. Harper
E. Pendleton James
Franklyn C. Nofziger
Richard Salisbury Williamson
Press Secretary to the President — James Scott Brady
Counsel to the President — Fred F. Fielding
Counselor to the President — Edwin Meese III
Special Assistant to the President — Richard Smith Beal
Office of Management and Budget — David A. Stockman, director
Council of Economic Advisers — Murray L. Weidenbaum, chairman
National Security Council — [1]
Central Intelligence Agency — William J. Casey, director
Office of Policy Development — Edwin J. Gray, director
Office of the United States
  Trade Representative — William E. Brock, trade representative
Council on Environmental Quality — A. Alan Hill, chairman
Office of Science and Technology Policy — George A. Keyworth II, director
Office of Administration — John Rogers, director

DEPARTMENT OF STATE — Alexander M. Haig, Jr., secretary
William P. Clark, deputy secretary
Political Affairs — Walter J. Stoessel, Jr., undersecretary
Economic Affairs — Myer Rashish, undersecretary
Security Assistance, Science, and
  Technology — James L. Buckley, undersecretary
Management — Richard T. Kennedy, undersecretary
Counselor of the Department — Robert C. McFarlane
Congressional Relations — Richard Fairbanks, asst. secretary
Permanent Mission to the Organization
  of American States — Gale W. McGee, permanent representative
Mission to the United Nations — Jeane J. Kirkpatrick, representative
African Affairs — Chester A. Crocker, asst. secretary
European Affairs — Lawrence S. Eagleburger, asst. secretary
East Asian and Pacific Affairs — John H. Holdridge, asst. secretary
Inter-American Affairs — Thomas O. Enders, asst. secretary
Near Eastern and South Asian Affairs — Nicholas A. Veliotes, asst. secretary
Administration — Thomas M. Tracy, asst. secretary
International Organization Affairs — Elliott Abrams, asst. secretary
Consular Affairs — Diego C. Asencio, asst. secretary
International Narcotics Matters — Joseph H. Linnemann, asst. secretary

DEPARTMENT OF THE TREASURY — Donald T. Regan, secretary
R. T. McNamar, deputy secretary
Monetary Affairs — Beryl W. Sprinkel, undersecretary
Tax and Economic Affairs — Norman B. Ture, undersecretary
Comptroller of the Currency — Tad Conover, comptroller
Bur. of Government Financial Operations — William E. Douglas, commissioner
U.S. Customs Service — William von Raab, commissioner
Bureau of Engraving and Printing — Harry R. Clements, director
Bureau of the Mint — Donna Pope, director
Bureau of the Public Debt — H. J. Hintgen, commissioner
Internal Revenue Service — Roscoe L. Egger, commissioner
Office of the Treasurer — Angela Buchanan, treasurer
Savings Bond Division — Angela Buchanan, national director
U.S. Secret Service — John R. Simpson, director
Federal Law Enforcement Training Center — Arthur F. Brandstatter, director

DEPARTMENT OF DEFENSE — Caspar W. Weinberger, secretary
Frank C. Carlucci, deputy secretary
Joint Chiefs of Staff — Gen. David C. Jones, USAF, chairman
  Chief of Staff, Army — Gen. Edward C. Meyer, USA
  Chief of Naval Operations — Adm. Thomas B. Hayward, USN
  Chief of Staff, Air Force — Gen. Lew Allen, Jr., USAF
  Commandant of the Marine Corps — Gen. Robert H. Barrow, USMC
Department of the Army — John O. Marsh, Jr., secretary
Department of the Navy — John F. Lehman, Jr., secretary
Department of the Air Force — Verne Orr, secretary

DEPARTMENT OF JUSTICE
Attorney General — William French Smith
Solicitor General — Rex E. Lee
Community Relations Service — Gilbert G. Pompa, director
Law Enforcement Assistance Admin. — George H. Bohlinger III, administrator (acting)
Antitrust Division — William F. Baxter, asst. attorney general
Civil Division — Thomas S. Martin, asst. attorney general
Civil Rights Division — James P. Turner, asst. attorney general
Criminal Division — D. Lowell Jensen, asst. attorney general
Land and Natural Resources Division — Carol E. Dinkins, asst. attorney general
Tax Division — John F. Murray, asst. attorney general
Justice Management Division — Kevin D. Rooney, asst. attorney general
Federal Bureau of Investigation — William H. Webster, director
Bureau of Prisons — Norman A. Carlson, director
Immigration and Naturalization Service — Doris M. Meissner, commissioner (acting)
Drug Enforcement Administration — Peter B. Bensinger, administrator
U.S. Marshals Service — William E. Hall, director

DEPARTMENT OF THE INTERIOR — James G. Watt, secretary
Donald P. Hodel, undersecretary
Territorial and International Affairs — Pedro A. Sanjuan, asst. secretary
Fish and Wildlife and Parks — G. Ray Arnett, asst. secretary
  National Park Service — Russell E. Dickenson, director
  Fish and Wildlife Service — Robert A. Jantzen, director

Energy and Minerals — Daniel N. Miller, asst. secretary
  Office of Minerals Policy and
    Research Analysis — Robert L. Adams, director (acting)
  Geological Survey — Dallas L. Peck, director
  Bureau of Mines — Robert C. Horton, director
  Office of Surface Mining Reclamation
    and Enforcement — James R. Harris, director
Land and Water Resources — Garrey E. Carruthers, asst. secretary
  Bureau of Reclamation — Robert N. Broadbent, commissioner
  Bureau of Land Management — Robert F. Burford, director
  Office of Water Research and Technology — Gary D. Cobb, director
Indian Affairs — Kenneth L. Smith, asst. secretary

DEPARTMENT OF AGRICULTURE — John R. Block, secretary
Richard E. Lyng, deputy secretary
Small Community and Rural Development — Frank W. Naylor, Jr., undersecretary
  Rural Electrification Administration — Harold V. Hunter, administrator
  Farmers Home Administration — Charles W. Shuman, administrator
Marketing and Transportation Services — C. W. McMillen, asst. secretary
  Agricultural Marketing Service — Mildred Thymian, administrator
International Affairs and Commodity
  Programs — Seeley G. Lodwick, undersecretary
  Commodity Credit Corporation — Seeley G. Lodwick, president
Natural Resources and Environment — John B. Crowell, asst. secretary
  Forest Service — R. Max Peterson, chief
  Soil Conservation Service — Norman A. Berg, chief
Economics, Policy Analysis, and Budget — William G. Lesher, asst. secretary
  Economics and Statistics Service — Kenneth R. Farrell, administrator
Food and Consumer Services — Mary C. Jarratt, asst. secretary

DEPARTMENT OF COMMERCE — Malcolm Baldrige, secretary
Joseph R. Wright, Jr., deputy secretary
International Trade — Lionel Olmer, undersecretary
Trade Administration — Lawrence J. Brady, asst. secretary
Economic Affairs — Robert G. Dederick, asst. secretary
  Chief Economist — Robert Ortner
  Bureau of the Census — Bruce K. Chapman, director
  Bureau of Economic Analysis — George Jaszi, director
  National Bureau of Standards — Ernest Ambler, director
  Patent and Trademark Office — Gerald J. Mossinghoff, commissioner
Travel and Tourism — Peter McCoy, undersecretary (designate)
National Oceanic and Atmospheric
  Administration — John V. Byrne

DEPARTMENT OF LABOR — Raymond J. Donovan, secretary
Malcolm Lovell, undersecretary
Administration and Management — Alfred M. Zuck, asst. secretary
Employment and Training — Albert Angrisani, asst. secretary
Labor-Management Relations — Donald L. Dotson, asst. secretary
Occupational Safety and Health — Thorne G. Auchter, asst. secretary
Veterans Employment — William C. Plowden, asst. secretary
Labor Statistics — Janet L. Norwood, commissioner
Mine Safety and Health — Ford B. Ford, asst. secretary

**DEPARTMENT OF HEALTH AND HUMAN
SERVICES** — Richard S. Schweiker, secretary
David B. Swoap, undersecretary
Office of Human Development Services — Dorcas R. Hardy, asst. secretary
Public Health Service — Edward N. Brandt, M.D., asst. secretary
  Food and Drug Administration — Arthur Hull Hayes, Jr., M.D., commissioner
  National Institutes of Health — Thomas E. Malone, M.D., director (acting)
  Health Resources Administration — Robert Graham, administrator (acting)
  Health Services Administration — John H. Kelso, administrator
  Centers for Disease Control — William H. Foege, director
  Alcohol, Drug Abuse, and Mental
    Health Administration — William E. Mayer, M.D., administrator
Health Care Financing Administration — Carolyne K. Davis, administrator
Social Security Administration — John A. Svahn, commissioner

**DEPARTMENT OF HOUSING
AND URBAN DEVELOPMENT** — Samuel R. Pierce, Jr., secretary
Donald I. Hovde, undersecretary
Community Planning and Development — Stephen J. Bollinger, asst. secretary
Federal Housing Commissioner — Philip D. Winn, asst. secretary
Fair Housing and Equal Opportunity — Antonio Monroig, asst. secretary
Policy Development and Research — E. S. Savas, asst. secretary

DEPARTMENT OF TRANSPORTATION — Andrew L. Lewis, Jr., secretary
Darrell M. Trent, deputy secretary
United States Coast Guard — Adm. John B. Hayes, USCG, commandant
Federal Aviation Administration — J. Lynn Helms, administrator
Federal Highway Administration — Ray A. Barnhart, Jr., administrator
National Highway Traffic Safety
  Administration — Raymond A. Peck, Jr., administrator
Federal Railroad Administration — Robert W. Blanchette, administrator
Urban Mass Transportation Admin. — Arthur E. Teele, Jr., administrator
Maritime Affairs — Samuel B. Nemirow, asst. secretary
  St. Lawrence Seaway Development Corp. — David W. Oberlin, administrator
Research and Special Programs
  Administration — Howard Dugoff, administrator

DEPARTMENT OF ENERGY — James B. Edwards, secretary
Guy W. Fiske, undersecretary
Federal Energy Regulatory Commission — Charles M. Butler III, chairman
General Counsel — R. Tenney Johnson
Nuclear Energy — Shelby T. Brewer, asst. secretary

DEPARTMENT OF EDUCATION — Terrel H. Bell, secretary
William C. Clohan, Jr., undersecretary
Private Education — Charles O'Malley, asst. secretary (acting)
Educational Research and Improvement — Donald Senese, asst. secretary

[1] Council comprised of the President of the United States and certain other members.

Senate January 1982

State, name, and party	Term expires
Ala.—Heflin, Howell (D)	1985
Denton, Jeremiah (R)	1987
Alaska—Stevens, Ted (R)	1985
Murkowski, Frank H. (R)	1987
Ariz.—Goldwater, Barry M. (R)	1987
DeConcini, Dennis (D)	1983
Ark.—Bumpers, Dale (D)	1987
Pryor, David (D)	1985
Calif.—Cranston, Alan (D)	1987
Hayakawa, S. I. (R)	1983
Colo.—Hart, Gary W. (D)	1987
Armstrong, William L. (R)	1985
Conn.—Weicker, Lowell P., Jr. (R)	1983
Dodd, Christopher J. (D)	1987
Del.—Roth, William V., Jr. (R)	1983
Biden, Joseph R., Jr. (D)	1985
Fla.—Chiles, Lawton M. (D)	1983
Hawkins, Paula (R)	1987
Ga.—Nunn, Samuel A. (D)	1985
Mattingly, Mack (R)	1987
Hawaii—Inouye, Daniel K. (D)	1987
Matsunaga, Spark M. (D)	1983
Idaho—McClure, James A. (R)	1985
Symms, Steven D. (R)	1987
Ill.—Percy, Charles H. (R)	1985
Dixon, Alan J. (D)	1987
Ind.—Lugar, Richard G. (R)	1983
Quayle, Dan (R)	1987
Iowa—Jepsen, Roger W. (R)	1985
Grassley, Charles E. (R)	1987
Kan.—Dole, Robert J. (R)	1987
Kassebaum, Nancy Landon (R)	1985
Ky.—Huddleston, Walter (D)	1985
Ford, Wendell H. (D)	1987
La.—Long, Russell B. (D)	1987
Johnston, J. Bennett, Jr. (D)	1985
Maine—Cohen, William S. (R)	1985
Mitchell, George J. (D)	1983
Md.—Mathias, Charles, Jr. (R)	1987
Sarbanes, Paul S. (D)	1983
Mass.—Kennedy, Edward M. (D)	1983
Tsongas, Paul E. (D)	1985
Mich.—Riegle, Donald W., Jr. (D)	1983
Levin, Carl (D)	1985
Minn.—Durenberger, David (R)	1983
Boschwitz, Rudy (R)	1985
Miss.—Stennis, John C. (D)	1983
Cochran, Thad (R)	1985
Mo.—Eagleton, Thomas F. (D)	1987
Danforth, John C. (R)	1983
Mont.—Melcher, John (D)	1983
Baucus, Max (D)	1985
Neb.—Zorinsky, Edward (D)	1983
Exon, J. James (D)	1985
Nev.—Cannon, Howard W. (D)	1983
Laxalt, Paul (R)	1987
N.H.—Humphrey, Gordon J. (R)	1985
Rudman, Warren (R)	1987
N.J.—Williams, Harrison A. (D)	1983
Bradley, Bill (D)	1985
N.M.—Domenici, Pete V. (R)	1985
Schmitt, Harrison H. (R)	1983
N.Y.—Moynihan, Daniel P. (D)	1983
D'Amato, Alfonse M. (R)	1987
N.C.—Helms, Jesse A. (R)	1985
East, John P. (R)	1987
N.D.—Burdick, Quentin N. (D)	1983
Andrews, Mark (R)	1987
Ohio—Glenn, John H., Jr. (D)	1987
Metzenbaum, Howard M. (D)	1983
Okla.—Boren, David L. (D)	1985
Nickles, Don (R)	1987
Ore.—Hatfield, Mark O. (R)	1985
Packwood, Robert W. (R)	1987
Pa.—Heinz, H. John, III (R)	1983
Specter, Arlen (R)	1987
R.I.—Pell, Claiborne (D)	1985
Chafee, John H. (R)	1983
S.C.—Thurmond, Strom (R)	1985
Hollings, Ernest F. (D)	1987
S.D.—Pressler, Larry (R)	1985
Abdnor, James (R)	1987
Tenn.—Baker, Howard H., Jr. (R)	1985
Sasser, James R. (D)	1983
Texas—Tower, John G. (R)	1985
Bentsen, Lloyd M. (D)	1983
Utah—Garn, Jake (R)	1987
Hatch, Orrin G. (R)	1983
Vt.—Stafford, Robert T. (R)	1983
Leahy, Patrick J. (D)	1987
Va.—Byrd, Harry F., Jr. (I)	1983
Warner, John W. (R)	1985
Wash.—Jackson, Henry M. (D)	1983
Gorton, Slade (R)	1987
W.Va.—Randolph, Jennings (D)	1985
Byrd, Robert C. (D)	1983
Wis.—Proxmire, William (D)	1983
Kasten, Robert W., Jr. (R)	1987
Wyo.—Wallop, Malcolm (R)	1983
Simpson, Alan K. (R)	1985

Supreme Court

Chief Justice Warren Earl Burger (appointed 1969)

Associate Justices (year appointed)

William J. Brennan, Jr.	(1956)	Lewis F. Powell, Jr.	(1972)
Byron R. White	(1962)	William H. Rehnquist	(1972)
Thurgood Marshall	(1967)	John Paul Stevens	(1975)
Harry A. Blackmun	(1970)	Sandra Day O'Connor	(1981)

House of Representatives

membership at the opening of the second session of the 97th Congress in January 1982

State, district, name, party

Ala.—1. Edwards, Jack (R)
2. Dickinson, William L. (R)
3. Nichols, William (D)
4. Bevill, Tom (D)
5. Flippo, Ronnie G. (D)
6. Smith, Albert L., Jr. (R)
7. Shelby, Richard C. (D)
Alaska—Young, Don (R)
Ariz.—1. Rhodes, John J. (R)
2. Udall, Morris K. (D)
3. Stump, Bob (D)
4. Rudd, Eldon D. (R)
Ark.—1. Alexander, Bill (D)
2. Bethune, Ed (R)
3. Hammerschmidt, J. P. (R)
4. Anthony, Beryl F. (D)
Calif.—1. Chappie, Eugene A. (R)
2. Clausen, Don H. (R)
3. Matsui, Robert T. (D)
4. Fazio, Vic (D)
5. Burton, John L. (D)
6. Burton, Phillip (D)
7. Miller, George, III (D)
8. Dellums, Ronald V. (D)
9. Stark, Fortney H. (D)
10. Edwards, Don (D)
11. Lantos, Tom (D)
12. McCloskey, Paul N., Jr. (R)
13. Mineta, Norman Y. (D)
14. Shumway, Norman D. (R)
15. Coelho, Tony (D)
16. Panetta, Leon E. (D)
17. Pashayan, Charles, Jr. (R)
18. Thomas, William (R)
19. Lagomarsino, Robert J. (R)
20. Goldwater, Barry M., Jr. (R)
21. Fiedler, Bobbi (R)
22. Moorhead, Carlos J. (R)
23. Beilenson, Anthony C. (D)
24. Waxman, Henry A. (D)
25. Roybal, Edward R. (D)
26. Rousselot, John H. (R)
27. Dornan, Robert K. (R)
28. Dixon, Julian C. (D)
29. Hawkins, Augustus F. (D)
30. Danielson, George E. (D)
31. Dymally, Mervyn M. (D)
32. Anderson, Glenn M. (D)
33. Grisham, Wayne (R)
34. Lungren, Daniel E. (R)
35. Dreier, David (R)
36. Brown, George E., Jr. (D)
37. Lewis, Jerry (R)
38. Patterson, Jerry M. (D)
39. Dannemeyer, W. E. (R)
40. Badham, Robert E. (R)
41. Lowery, Bill (R)
42. Hunter, Duncan L. (R)
43. Burgener, Clair W. (R)
Colo.—1. Schroeder, Patricia (D)
2. Wirth, Timothy E. (D)
3. Kogovsek, Ray (D)
4. Brown, Hank (R)
5. Kramer, Ken (R)
Conn.—1. Kennelly, Barbara B. (D)
2. Gejdenson, Samuel (D)
3. DeNardis, Lawrence J. (R)
4. McKinney, Stewart B. (R)
5. Ratchford, William R. (D)
6. Moffett, Toby (D)
Del.—Evans, Thomas, Jr. (R)
Fla.—1. Hutto, Earl D. (D)
2. Fuqua, Don (D)
3. Bennett, Charles E. (D)
4. Chappell, William, Jr. (D)
5. McCollom, Bill (R)
6. Young, C. William (R)
7. Gibbons, Sam (D)
8. Ireland, Andrew P. (D)
9. Nelson, Bill (D)
10. Bafalis, L. A. (R)
11. Mica, Dan (D)
12. Shaw, Clay (R)
13. Lehman, William (D)
14. Pepper, Claude (D)
15. Fascell, Dante B. (D)
Ga.—1. Ginn, R. B. (D)
2. Hatcher, Charles F. (D)
3. Brinkley, Jack (D)
4. Levitas, Elliott H. (D)
5. Fowler, Wyche, Jr. (D)
6. Gingrich, Newt (R)
7. McDonald, Lawrence P. (D)
8. Evans, Billy Lee (D)
9. Jenkins, Edgar L. (D)
10. Barnard, Doug (D)
Hawaii—1. Heftel, Cecil (D)
2. Akaka, Daniel (D)
Idaho—1. Craig, Larry (R)
2. Hansen, George V. (R)

State, district, name, party

Ill.—1. Washington, Harold (D)
2. Savage, Gus (D)
3. Russo, Martin A. (D)
4. Derwinski, Edward J. (R)
5. Fary, John G. (D)
6. Hyde, Henry J. (R)
7. Collins, Cardiss (D)
8. Rostenkowski, Dan (D)
9. Yates, Sidney R. (D)
10. Porter, John E. (R)
11. Annunzio, Frank (D)
12. Crane, Philip M. (R)
13. McClory, Robert (R)
14. Erlenborn, J. N. (R)
15. Corcoran, Tom (R)
16. Martin, Lynn M. (R)
17. O'Brien, G. M. (R)
18. Michel, Robert H. (R)
19. Railsback, Thomas F. (R)
20. Findley, Paul (R)
21. Madigan, E. R. (R)
22. Crane, Daniel B. (R)
23. Price, Melvin (D)
24. Simon, Paul (D)
Ind.—1. Benjamin, Adam (D)
2. Fithian, Floyd J. (D)
3. Hiler, John P. (R)
4. Coats, Daniel R. (R)
5. Hillis, Elwood H. (R)
6. Evans, David W. (D)
7. Myers, John (R)
8. Deckard, H. Joel (R)
9. Hamilton, L. H. (D)
10. Sharp, Philip R. (D)
11. Jacobs, Andrew, Jr. (D)
Iowa—1. Leach, James (R)
2. Tauke, Tom (R)
3. Evans, Cooper (R)
4. Smith, Neal (D)
5. Harkin, Tom (D)
6. Bedell, Berkley (D)
Kan.—1. Roberts, Pat (R)
2. Jeffries, Jim (R)
3. Winn, Larry, Jr. (R)
4. Glickman, Dan (D)
5. Whittaker, Robert (R)
Ky.—1. Hubbard, Carroll, Jr. (D)
2. Natcher, William H. (D)
3. Mazzoli, Romano L. (D)
4. Snyder, Gene (R)
5. Rogers, Harold (R)
6. Hopkins, Larry J. (R)
7. Perkins, Carl D. (D)
La.—1. Livingston, Bob (R)
2. Boggs, Lindy (D)
3. Tauzin, William J. (D)
4. Roemer, Buddy (D)
5. Huckaby, Jerry (D)
6. Moore, W. Henson, III (R)
7. Breaux, John B. (D)
8. Long, Gillis W. (D)
Maine—1. Emery, David F. (R)
2. Snowe, Olympia J. (R)
Md.—1. Dyson, Roy (D)
2. Long, Clarence D. (D)
3. Mikulski, Barbara A. (D)
4. Holt, Marjorie S. (R)
5. Hoyer, Steny H. (D)
6. Byron, Beverly (D)
7. Mitchell, Parren J. (D)
8. Barnes, Michael D. (D)
Mass.—1. Conte, Silvio O. (R)
2. Boland, Edward P. (D)
3. Early, Joseph D. (D)
4. Frank, Barney (D)
5. Shannon, James M. (D)
6. Mavroules, Nicholas (D)
7. Markey, Edward J. (D)
8. O'Neill, Thomas P., Jr. (D)
9. Moakley, Joe (D)
10. Heckler, Margaret (R)
11. Donnelly, Brian J. (D)
12. Studds, Gerry E. (D)
Mich.—1. Conyers, John, Jr. (D)
2. Pursell, Carl D. (R)
3. Wolpe, Howard (D)
4. Siljander, Mark D. (R)
5. Sawyer, Harold S. (R)
6. Dunn, Jim (R)
7. Kildee, Dale E. (D)
8. Traxler, Bob (D)
9. Vander Jagt, Guy (R)
10. Albosta, Donald J. (D)
11. Davis, Robert W. (R)
12. Bonior, David E. (D)
13. Crockett, George W. (D)
14. Hertel, Dennis M. (D)
15. Ford, William D. (D)
16. Dingell, John D. (D)
17. Brodhead, William M. (D)
18. Blanchard, James J. (D)
19. Broomfield, William S. (R)
Minn.—1. Erdahl, Arlen (R)
2. Hagedorn, Tom (R)
3. Frenzel, William (R)
4. Vento, Bruce F. (D)
5. Sabo, Martin Olav (D)
6. Weber, Vin (R)
7. Stangeland, Arlan (R)
8. Oberstar, James L. (D)
Miss.—1. Whitten, Jamie L. (D)
2. Bowen, David R. (D)

State, district, name, party

3. Montgomery, G. V. (D)
4. Dowdy, Wayne (D)
5. Lott, Trent (R)
Mo.—1. Clay, William (D)
2. Young, Robert A. (D)
3. Gephardt, Richard A. (D)
4. Skelton, Ike (D)
5. Bolling, Richard (D)
6. Coleman, E. Thomas (R)
7. Taylor, Gene (R)
8. Bailey, Wendell (R)
9. Volkmer, Harold L. (D)
10. Emerson, William (R)
Mont.—1. Williams, Pat (D)
2. Marlenee, Ron (R)
Neb.—1. Bereuter, D. K. (R)
2. Daub, Harold (R)
3. Smith, Virginia (R)
Nev.—Santini, James (D)
N.H.—1. D'Amours, Norman (D)
2. Gregg, Judd (R)
N.J.—1. Florio, James J. (D)
2. Hughes, William J. (D)
3. Howard, James J. (D)
4. Smith, Christopher (R)
5. Fenwick, Millicent (R)
6. Forsythe, Edwin B. (R)
7. Roukema, Marge (R)
8. Roe, Robert A. (D)
9. Hollenbeck, Harold C. (R)
10. Rodino, Peter W., Jr. (D)
11. Minish, Joseph G. (D)
12. Rinaldo, Matthew J. (R)
13. Courter, James A. (R)
14. Guarini, Frank J. (D)
15. Dwyer, Bernard J. (D)
N.M.—1. Lujan, Manuel, Jr. (R)
2. Skeen, Joseph (R)
N.Y.—1. Carney, William (C-R)
2. Downey, Thomas J. (D)
3. Carman, Gregory W. (R)
4. Lent, Norman F. (R)
5. McGrath, Raymond J. (R)
6. LeBoutillier, John (R)
7. Addabbo, Joseph P. (D)
8. Rosenthal, Benjamin S. (D)
9. Ferraro, Geraldine (D)
10. Biaggi, Mario (D)
11. Scheuer, James H. (D)
12. Chisholm, Shirley (D)
13. Solarz, Stephen J. (D)
14. Richmond, Frederick W. (D)
15. Zeferetti, Leo C. (D)
16. Schumer, Charles E. (D)
17. Molinari, Guy V. (R)
18. Green, S. William (R)
19. Rangel, Charles B. (D)
20. Weiss, Theodore S. (D)
21. Garcia, Robert (D)
22. Bingham, J. B. (D)
23. Peyser, Peter A. (D)
24. Ottinger, Richard L. (D)
25. Fish, Hamilton, Jr. (R)
26. Gilman, B. A. (R)
27. McHugh, Matthew F. (D)
28. Stratton, Samuel S. (D)
29. Solomon, Gerald (R)
30. Martin, David (R)
31. Mitchell, D. J. (R)
32. Wortley, George (R)
33. Lee, Gary A. (R)
34. Horton, Frank J. (R)
35. Conable, B. B., Jr. (R)
36. LaFalce, John J. (D)
37. Nowak, Henry J. (D)
38. Kemp, Jack F. (R)
39. Lundine, Stanley N. (D)
N.C.—1. Jones, Walter B. (D)
2. Fountain, L. H. (D)
3. Whitley, Charles (D)
4. Andrews, Ike F. (D)
5. Neal, Stephen L. (D)
6. Johnston, Eugene (R)
7. Rose, C. G., III (D)
8. Hefner, Bill (D)
9. Martin, James G. (R)
10. Broyhill, James T. (R)
11. Hendon, William M. (R)
N.D.—Dorgan, Byron L. (D)
Ohio—1. Gradison, Willis D. (R)
2. Luken, Thomas A. (D)
3. Hall, Tony P. (D)
4. Oxley, Michael G. (R)
5. Latta, Delbert L. (R)
6. McEwen, Robert (R)
7. Brown, Clarence J. (R)
8. Kindness, Thomas N. (R)
9. Weber, Ed (R)
10. Miller, Clarence E. (R)
11. Stanton, J. William (R)
12. Shamansky, Robert (D)
13. Pease, Donald J. (D)
14. Seiberling, John F., Jr. (D)
15. Wylie, Chalmers P. (R)
16. Regula, Ralph S. (R)
17. Ashbrook, John M. (R)
18. Applegate, Douglas (D)
19. Williams, Lyle (R)
20. Oakar, Mary Rose (D)
21. Stokes, Louis (D)
22. Eckart, Dennis E. (D)
23. Mottl, Ronald M. (D)

State, district, name, party

Okla.—1. Jones, James R. (D)
2. Synar, Mike (D)
3. Watkins, Wes (D)
4. McCurdy, Dave (D)
5. Edwards, Mickey (R)
6. English, Glenn (D)
Ore.—1. AuCoin, Les (D)
2. Smith, Denny (R)
3. Wyden, Ron (D)
4. Weaver, James (D)
Pa.—1. Foglietta, Thomas (D)
2. Gray, William H., III (D)
3. Smith, Joseph F. (D)
4. Dougherty, C. F. (R)
5. Schulze, Richard T. (R)
6. Yatron, Gus (D)
7. Edgar, Robert W. (D)
8. Coyne, James K. (R)
9. Shuster, E. G. (R)
10. McDade, Joseph M. (R)
11. Nelligan, James (R)
12. Murtha, John P. (D)
13. Coughlin, R. L. (R)
14. Coyne, William J. (D)
15. Ritter, Donald L. (R)
16. Walker, Robert S. (R)
17. Ertel, Allen E. (D)
18. Walgren, Doug (D)
19. Goodling, William F. (R)
20. Gaydos, Joseph (D)
21. Bailey, Don (D)
22. Murphy, Austin J. (D)
23. Clinger, William F., Jr. (R)
24. Marks, Marc L. (R)
25. Atkinson, Eugene V. (R)
R.I.—1. St. Germain, Fernand (D)
2. Schneider, Claudine (R)
S.C.—1. Hartnett, Thomas F. (R)
2. Spence, Floyd D. (R)
3. Derrick, Butler C., Jr. (D)
4. Campbell, Carroll A., Jr. (R)
5. Holland, Kenneth L. (D)
6. Napier, John L. (R)
S.D.—1. Daschle, Thomas A. (D)
2. Roberts, Clint (R)
Tenn.—1. Quillen, James H. (R)
2. Duncan, John J. (R)
3. Lloyd Bouquard, Marilyn (D)
4. Gore, Albert, Jr. (D)
5. Boner, Bill (D)
6. Beard, Robin L., Jr. (R)
7. Jones, Edward (D)
8. Ford, Harold E. (D)
Texas—1. Hall, Sam B. (D)
2. Wilson, Charles (D)
3. Collins, James M. (R)
4. Hall, Ralph M. (D)
5. Mattox, Jim (D)
6. Gramm, Phil (D)
7. Archer, William R. (R)
8. Fields, Jack (R)
9. Brooks, Jack (D)
10. Pickle, J. J. (D)
11. Leath, J. Marvin (D)
12. Wright, James C., Jr. (D)
13. Hightower, Jack (D)
14. Patman, William N. (D)
15. de la Garza, E. (D)
16. White, Richard C. (D)
17. Stenholm, Charles W. (D)
18. Leland, Mickey (D)
19. Hance, Kent (D)
20. Gonzalez, Henry B. (D)
21. Loeffler, Tom (R)
22. Paul, Ron (R)
23. Kazen, Abraham, Jr. (D)
24. Frost, Martin (D)
Utah—1. Hansen, James V. (R)
2. Marriott, Dan (R)
Vt.—Jeffords, James M. (R)
Va.—1. Trible, Paul S. (R)
2. Whitehurst, G. W. (R)
3. Bliley, Thomas J. (R)
4. Daniel, Robert W. (R)
5. Daniel, Dan (D)
6. Butler, M. Caldwell (R)
7. Robinson, J. Kenneth (R)
8. Parris, Stanford E. (R)
9. Wampler, William C. (R)
10. Wolf, Frank R. (R)
Wash.—1. Pritchard, Joel (R)
2. Swift, Al (D)
3. Bonker, Don (D)
4. Morrison, Sid (R)
5. Foley, Thomas S. (D)
6. Dicks, Norman D. (D)
7. Lowry, Mike (D)
W.Va.—1. Mollohan, R. H. (D)
2. Benedict, Cleve (R)
3. Staton, Mick (R)
4. Rahall, Nick J. (D)
Wis.—1. Aspin, Leslie (D)
2. Kastenmeier, Robert W. (D)
3. Gunderson, Steven (R)
4. Zablocki, Clement J. (D)
5. Reuss, Henry S. (D)
6. Petri, Thomas E. (R)
7. Obey, David R. (D)
8. Roth, Tobias A. (R)
9. Sensenbrenner, F. J. (R)
Wyo.—Cheney, Richard (R)

The Federal Administrative Budget

in millions of dollars; fiscal years ending Sept. 30

Source and function	1980 actual	1981 estimate	1982 estimate
BUDGET RECEIPTS	$520,000	$607,500	$711,800
Individual income taxes	244,100	284,000	331,700
Corporation income taxes	64,600	66,000	64,600
Excise taxes	24,300	44,400	69,600
Social insurance taxes and contributions	160,700	184,800	214,700
Estate and gift taxes	6,400	6,900	7,700
Customs duties	7,200	7,400	7,800
Miscellaneous receipts	12,700	13,900	15,700
BUDGET EXPENDITURES	579,600	662,700	739,300
National defense	135,900	161,100	184,400
Department of Defense military functions	132,800	157,600	180,000
Atomic energy defense activities	2,900	3,600	4,500
Defense-related activities	100	−100	−100
International affairs	10,700	11,300	12,200
Conduct of foreign affairs	1,400	1,500	1,800
Foreign economic and financial assistance	5,600	6,700	7,000
Foreign information and exchange activities	500	600	600
International financial programs	2,400	1,800	2,100
Military assistance	900	900	600
General science, space, and technology	5,700	6,300	7,600
Agriculture	4,800	1,100	4,800
Farm income stabilization	3,500	−500	3,100
Agricultural research and services	1,400	1,600	1,700
Natural resources and environment	13,800	14,100	14,000
Water resources	4,300	4,500	4,600
Conservation and land management	2,300	2,600	2,400
Recreational resources	1,700	1,700	1,700
Pollution control and abatement	5,500	5,500	5,800
Other natural resources	1,400	1,600	1,800
Energy	6,300	8,700	12,000
Energy supply	4,600	5,700	6,200
Energy conservation	600	800	1,100
Commerce and housing credit	7,800	3,500	8,100
Mortgage credit and thrift insurance	3,700	−200	1,400
Payment to the Postal Service	1,700	1,300	1,100
Other advancement and regulation	2,400	2,300	5,600
Transportation	21,100	24,100	21,600
Air transportation	3,800	4,000	4,200
Water transportation	2,200	2,900	2,800
Ground transportation	15,100	17,100	14,500
Other transportation	100	100	100
Community and regional development	10,100	11,100	9,100
Community development	4,900	5,100	5,300
Area and regional development	$3,200	$2,800	$2,900
Disaster relief and insurance	2,000	3,300	900
Education, training, employment, and social services	30,800	31,800	34,500
Elementary, secondary, and vocational education	6,700	6,900	7,400
Higher education	5,700	6,500	6,900
Research and general education aids	1,400	1,500	1,500
Training and employment	10,300	9,900	11,000
Social services	6,100	6,300	7,100
Health	58,200	66,000	74,600
Health care services	53,000	60,600	69,000
Health research and education	4,100	4,400	4,400
Consumer and occupational health and safety	1,000	1,100	1,200
Income security	193,100	231,600	255,000
General retirement and disability insurance	123,700	145,500	167,300
Federal employee retirement and disability	14,700	17,600	19,900
Unemployment compensation	18,000	26,100	21,900
Public assistance and other income supplements	36,700	42,400	46,000
Veterans benefits and services	21,200	22,600	24,500
Income security for veterans	11,700	13,100	14,500
Veterans education, training, and rehabilitation	2,300	2,000	1,600
Hospital and medical care for veterans	6,500	6,900	7,700
Other veterans benefits and services	700	700	700
Administration of justice	4,600	4,800	4,900
Federal law enforcement activities	2,200	2,400	2,500
Federal litigative and judicial activities	1,300	1,500	1,600
Federal correctional activities	300	400	400
Criminal justice assistance	700	500	400
General government	4,500	5,200	5,200
Legislative functions	1,000	1,200	1,200
Central fiscal operations	2,500	2,800	3,000
General property and records management	400	600	500
Other general government	600	600	500
General purpose fiscal assistance	8,600	6,900	6,900
Interest	64,500	80,400	89,900
Allowances for contingencies, civilian agency pay raises	—	—	1,900
Undistributed offsetting receipts	−21,900	−27,800	−31,900
Employer share, employee retirement	−5,800	−6,600	−6,800
Interest received by trust funds	−12,000	−13,400	−15,200
Rents and royalties on the Outer Continental Shelf	−4,100	−7,800	−9,900

Source: Executive Office of the President, Office of Management and Budget, *The United States Budget in Brief: Fiscal Year 1982.*

State Government Revenue, Expenditure, and Debt

1980 in thousands of dollars

	GENERAL REVENUE						GENERAL EXPENDITURE[1]					DEBT		
		State taxes												
State	Total	Total	General sales	Income[2]	Intergovernmental	Charges & misc.	Total	Education	Highways	Public welfare	Hospitals	Total	Issued 1980[3]	Retired 1980[3]
Ala.	3,633,716	1,856,789	577,089	396,570	1,252,576	524,351	2,542,717	852,986	329,685	540,759	236,283	1,032,338	30,794	51,865
Alaska	3,011,436	1,437,607	—	100,481	380,637	1,193,192	1,590,449	364,136	173,526	114,448	11,288	1,544,554	258,084	51,056
Ariz.	2,566,150	1,684,399	814,588	287,498	577,616	324,135	1,406,293	505,749	271,127	147,795	80,446	94,007	—	2,163
Ark.	2,102,719	1,160,767	371,825	316,644	723,598	218,354	1,368,498	340,570	303,644	317,911	82,755	362,579	125,409	7,306
Calif.	29,603,059	19,366,696	6,695,242	6,463,736	7,257,017	2,979,346	14,067,025	3,537,133	1,161,699	3,598,830	851,670	8,361,705	1,097,785	385,462
Colo.	2,791,974	1,490,898	537,379	461,325	781,549	519,527	1,632,838	606,905	272,815	210,050	137,976	460,497	56,545	26,035
Conn.	3,110,767	1,839,678	802,950	100,953	815,919	455,170	2,285,973	404,127	225,972	603,456	212,312	3,879,197	505,950	203,058
Del.	892,558	515,715	—	235,763	206,657	170,186	630,499	185,734	85,535	97,996	28,669	1,044,499	257,473	68,805
Fla.	7,303,596	4,804,298	2,252,113	—	1,790,579	708,719	4,079,189	800,820	818,175	704,884	307,213	2,626,926	52,110	96,166
Ga.	4,583,376	2,728,961	931,976	872,073	1,427,845	426,570	2,960,442	708,327	598,990	694,868	227,097	1,404,635	114,000	80,076
Hawaii	1,636,835	998,383	498,293	311,404	373,608	264,844	1,503,822	559,207	97,484	229,392	80,496	1,864,213	250,001	86,959
Idaho	917,331	490,346	137,114	159,138	284,566	142,419	607,701	152,177	109,366	112,706	17,108	327,334	111,160	8,312
Ill.	11,045,235	7,073,077	2,379,123	1,900,676	2,869,941	1,102,217	7,228,245	1,403,461	1,095,794	2,457,552	414,024	6,277,201	874,446	271,393
Ind.	4,322,869	2,695,759	1,331,594	556,709	898,400	728,710	2,642,843	964,219	434,092	430,449	197,410	607,581	29,115	25,966
Iowa	2,957,634	1,746,828	502,055	602,385	781,538	429,268	1,958,990	550,501	338,332	491,696	192,970	380,999	15,775	7,529
Kan.	2,161,779	1,269,671	418,389	336,061	587,664	304,444	1,501,762	380,410	335,736	365,876	120,974	438,137	—	21,007
Ky.	3,743,692	2,144,941	607,604	505,832	1,100,282	498,469	3,206,641	710,437	881,972	637,301	149,534	3,035,267	315,730	90,951
La.	4,792,318	2,397,215	739,347	247,438	1,304,273	1,090,830	3,147,922	708,958	565,182	639,025	337,794	2,977,031	480,363	111,499
Maine	1,178,755	619,160	214,113	142,689	411,739	147,856	839,322	150,162	146,453	258,100	29,766	730,266	84,335	45,216
Md.	4,833,162	2,760,818	712,815	1,097,009	1,164,803	907,541	3,308,131	671,105	448,572	749,060	358,480	3,502,248	475,132	204,018
Mass.	6,748,678	3,927,303	745,996	1,860,033	2,097,467	723,908	4,598,435	573,656	348,639	1,754,825	292,286	5,784,878	734,140	334,445
Mich.	10,277,168	5,947,650	1,706,728	1,916,626	2,816,792	1,512,726	6,934,437	1,734,238	556,179	2,500,234	523,930	2,916,082	614,258	147,197
Minn.	5,253,033	3,202,581	650,138	1,262,697	1,274,458	775,994	2,829,226	781,808	418,651	558,242	249,569	2,069,902	348,452	162,120
Miss.	2,482,408	1,257,932	671,086	150,296	929,212	295,264	1,603,707	393,033	285,690	384,680	113,952	815,045	13,000	40,079
Mo.	3,670,190	2,094,540	792,290	603,319	1,156,044	419,606	2,528,225	560,613	444,336	648,368	235,470	1,017,862	303,189	10,387
Mont.	945,678	435,751	—	135,012	370,572	139,355	633,053	117,807	179,457	93,957	25,690	309,533	169,100	6,566
Neb.	1,419,516	816,767	277,014	235,821	389,420	213,329	928,459	270,364	191,653	173,278	79,833	199,341	150,000	3,331
Nev.	829,112	476,604	182,925	—	241,219	111,289	551,316	126,711	143,514	69,784	17,528	527,969	163,309	7,199
N.H.	672,172	267,495	—	10,474	255,892	148,785	597,587	134,052	120,417	132,551	33,983	899,050	157,546	31,858
N.J.	7,147,524	4,265,830	1,180,267	1,004,781	1,186,391	1,025,303	4,231,011	870,507	374,251	865,131	415,261	6,526,797	1,022,798	167,104
N.M.	1,984,036	926,048	402,909	46,846	438,166	619,822	1,067,608	308,528	193,240	161,577	75,552	707,783	236,435	33,317
N.Y.	22,051,223	12,716,772	2,844,869	5,780,045	7,373,613	1,960,838	11,091,746	2,169,325	988,295	1,596,824	1,414,682	23,640,088	2,476,448	1,264,053
N.C.	5,369,967	3,215,348	693,564	1,180,507	1,561,501	593,118	3,312,088	917,933	589,754	632,586	279,562	1,265,720	219,156	60,438
N.D.	907,133	371,861	124,012	53,346	246,633	288,639	636,782	166,986	111,355	79,882	32,574	219,276	97,102	8,618
Ohio	8,230,517	4,766,665	1,445,788	1,039,728	2,235,588	1,228,264	5,558,786	1,487,656	616,840	1,342,195	528,631	4,014,977	651,171	388,240
Okla.	3,135,059	1,776,044	317,578	361,895	797,599	561,416	2,067,552	602,376	265,973	544,364	160,263	1,525,740	69,565	55,242
Ore.	3,079,327	1,455,352	—	867,976	952,828	671,147	2,107,415	463,051	285,872	452,369	135,783	4,886,286	1,192,640	110,318
Pa.	11,277,432	7,240,808	1,995,829	1,671,842	2,854,579	1,182,045	6,774,450	1,235,465	702,396	2,422,175	610,729	6,347,873	207,785	339,485
R.I.	1,186,593	550,787	169,061	153,912	358,799	277,007	966,902	200,170	51,977	282,962	96,385	1,463,092	335,505	63,313
S.C.	2,905,665	1,678,049	576,489	494,789	849,619	377,997	2,017,679	696,309	228,285	354,749	185,230	1,937,234	280,975	68,015
S.D.	703,253	270,518	147,171	—	269,558	163,177	590,564	128,887	139,093	101,238	21,313	714,274	153,500	15,835
Tenn.	3,571,842	1,886,992	982,251	30,800	1,241,306	443,544	2,568,893	732,463	459,443	568,967	164,781	1,405,948	107,825	57,072
Texas	11,926,955	6,758,706	2,536,805	—	2,917,195	2,251,054	7,356,142	2,175,206	1,672,969	1,455,431	620,021	2,468,627	230,542	93,267
Utah	1,557,722	785,755	324,744	265,327	505,902	266,065	1,137,973	374,259	209,474	181,266	77,813	537,074	161,775	17,749
Vt.	630,156	266,317	40,836	83,182	245,133	118,706	497,097	130,286	64,026	95,417	21,121	654,159	158,237	33,803
Va.	5,034,342	2,743,325	595,060	1,103,006	1,391,394	899,623	3,650,073	949,788	787,559	556,876	388,187	1,926,291	250,690	59,749
Wash.	4,830,772	2,917,445	1,625,006	—	1,236,987	676,340	3,254,134	1,053,386	501,917	782,128	144,198	1,600,407	141,442	67,319
W.Va.	2,177,916	1,219,492	598,512	252,362	712,959	245,465	1,729,857	314,163	576,526	249,257	76,122	1,816,478	243,475	63,884
Wis.	5,596,130	3,366,310	853,863	1,430,475	1,533,017	696,803	2,931,209	924,099	322,672	756,047	166,193	2,445,967	249,800	129,791
Wyo.	801,644	388,125	163,134	—	245,829	167,690	456,702	100,352	136,628	42,560	16,208	362,895	150,000	3,175
TOTAL	233,592,124	137,075,178	43,167,534	37,089,481	64,326,479	32,190,467	143,718,410	35,250,601	20,661,232	33,242,074	11,277,115	121,957,862	16,424,067	5,687,811

Fiscal year ending June 30, 1980, except Alabama, September 30; New York, March 31; and Texas, August 31. [1] Direct only, intergovernmental excluded. [2] Includes individual and corporation. [3] Long term only. Source: U.S. Department of Commerce, Bureau of the Census, *Governmental Finances in 1979–80.*

EDUCATION

Public Elementary and Secondary Schools

Fall 1980 estimates

State	ENROLLMENT[1] Elementary	ENROLLMENT[1] Secondary	INSTRUCTIONAL STAFF Total[2]	Principals and supervisors	Teachers, elementary	Teachers, secondary	TEACHERS' AVERAGE ANNUAL SALARIES Elementary	Secondary	STUDENT-TEACHER RATIO Elementary	Secondary	Expenditure per pupil
Alabama	389,964	354,687	43,230	2,000	21,970	19,260	$14,624	$15,750	17.7	18.4	$1,516
Alaska	49,017	38,490	6,043	276	2,819	2,405	28,854	29,279	17.3	16.0	4,731
Arizona	356,000	157,000	29,500	1,190	18,140	8,060	16,980	17,700	19.6	19.5	2,323
Arkansas	240,399	207,301	26,897	1,403	11,803	12,308	12,900	13,630	20.4	16.8	1,525
California	2,689,396[3]	1,365,852[3]	195,006	9,841	104,609	70,925	19,400	20,480	25.7	19.3	2,477
Colorado	311,000	235,000	33,396	1,614	13,269	13,888	16,945	17,850	23.4	16.9	2,261
Connecticut	362,684	184,578	38,775	2,245	20,350	13,500	17,250	17,675	17.8	13.6	2,715
Delaware	48,612	50,791	6,800	415	2,605	3,304	16,955	17,470	18.7	15.4	2,889
District of Columbia	55,233	44,816	6,164	362	3,108	2,130	23,000	22,710	17.8	21.0	3,291
Florida	1,052,000	470,000	90,500	4,750	42,000	36,250	15,796	15,295	25.0	13.0	2,170
Georgia	655,900	412,800	59,070	2,530	34,300	22,240	15,180	15,851	19.1	18.6	1,787
Hawaii	87,669	77,112	9,157	352	4,688	3,221	22,017	20,891	18.7	23.9	2,350
Idaho	113,034	90,213	11,067	598	5,274	4,664	14,790	15,470	21.4	19.3	...
Illinois	1,335,569	644,952	117,717	6,375	70,079	35,638	18,722	20,734	19.0	18.0	2,586
Indiana	551,493	502,008	61,053	4,236	26,930	26,845	17,603	18,506	20.5	18.7	1,901
Iowa	281,565	252,973	35,310	1,310	15,370	17,060	15,480	16,720	18.3	14.8	2,457
Kansas	237,455	175,108	29,370	1,600	14,300	11,900	15,046	15,075	16.6	14.7	2,531
Kentucky	431,500	238,500	37,890	2,150	21,643	11,757	15,130	16,460	19.9	20.3	1,854
Louisiana	550,000	240,000	46,750	2,150	23,660	19,040	14,686	15,300	23.2	10.1	1,811
Maine	151,200	71,000	11,333	1,040	7,040	3,160	13,233	14,843	21.4	22.5	2,025
Maryland	364,188	386,000	46,999	3,220	18,550	22,553	19,151	19,380	19.6	17.1	2,598
Massachusetts	716,360	302,417	94,335	5,368	28,497	37,321	18,488	18,867	25.1	8.1	2,780
Michigan	963,912	907,000	93,476	6,800	41,876	38,650	21,040	21,400	23.0	23.5	...
Minnesota	370,742	380,455	49,100	2,050	20,550	23,150	17,400	18,650	18.0	16.4	2,581
Mississippi	262,819	209,481	29,460	1,643	14,465	11,835	12,740	13,260	18.2	17.7	1,688
Missouri	567,198	277,450	56,129	3,139	24,764	24,036	14,895	15,488	22.9	11.5	...
Montana	103,600	51,400	10,260	380	5,090	4,160	14,830	16,100	20.3	12.4	2,392
Nebraska	154,389	126,317	20,291	1,072	9,294	8,667	14,212	15,575	16.6	14.6	2,248
Nevada	78,300	71,200	8,061	392	3,568	3,512	17,048	17,167	21.9	20.3	1,922
New Hampshire	99,864	69,720	10,729	623	4,972	4,385	12,521	13,432	20.0	15.9	1,857
New Jersey	774,380	474,620	91,862	6,000	45,349	31,513	18,026	18,702	17.0	15.0	3,019
New Mexico	146,004	125,327	16,383	711	7,025	7,737	15,480	15,950	20.8	17.0	2,045
New York	1,404,960	1,450,790	192,400	13,100	74,000	95,300	20,300	20,500	18.9	15.2	3,120
North Carolina	792,686	349,013	63,070	3,907	34,605	20,738	15,662	16,185	22.9	16.8	1,905
North Dakota	76,318	40,098	8,074	405	4,217	2,902	13,720	14,076	18.0	13.8	1,915
Ohio	1,169,500	802,500	116,820	6,260	54,130	45,210	15,700	16,800	21.6	17.7	1,985
Oklahoma	328,000	250,000	38,156	2,096	18,030	16,350	14,350	14,970	18.2	15.3	1,091
Oregon	283,267	182,223	29,974	2,133	14,641	10,418	17,164	18,029	19.3	17.5	2,767
Pennsylvania	941,700	968,100	123,300	5,400	50,370	59,130	17,360	17,970	18.7	16.4	2,436
Rhode Island	73,311	71,515	10,655	586	4,572	4,623	19,294	19,410	16.0	15.5	2,736
South Carolina	423,029	191,601	36,350	1,960	19,580	12,210	13,610	14,530	21.3	15.7	1,667
South Dakota	86,100	42,252	9,165	495	5,307	2,802	13,450	13,990	16.2	15.0	1,884
Tennessee	516,013	336,901	47,934	2,633	25,559	15,767	14,917	15,141	20.2	21.4	1,719
Texas	1,591,500	1,301,500	185,960	13,629	88,220	74,915	14,801	15,560	18.0	17.4	1,682
Utah	201,340	141,545	16,568	845	8,700	6,078	16,088	17,361	23.1	23.3	1,681
Vermont	50,460	44,928	8,330	890	3,400	3,250	12,561	13,472	14.8	13.8	1,870
Virginia	622,217	388,154	66,490	3,740	34,155	24,045	14,244	15,726	18.2	16.1	1,971
Washington	397,245	359,338	41,490	3,030	20,280	15,410	20,289	21,246	19.6	23.3	2,566
West Virginia	230,973	153,025	25,120	1,683	12,532	9,649	14,294	15,136	18.4	15.9	...
Wisconsin	458,355	374,489	56,200	2,350	28,600	25,250	16,295	17,266	16.0	14.8	2,485
Wyoming	55,919	42,385	7,065	453	3,276	3,074	18,057	19,422	17.0	13.8	2,290
TOTAL U.S.	24,254,359	16,684,925	2,505,234	143,430	1,192,131	1,001,795	$16,879	$17,725	20.3	16.6	$2,228

[1] Kindergartens included in elementary schools; junior high schools in secondary schools. [2] Includes librarians, guidance, health and psychological personnel, and related educational workers. [3] Junior high students included in elementary figures.
Source: National Education Association Research, *Estimates of School Statistics, 1980–81* (Copyright 1981. All rights reserved. Used by permission).

Universities and Colleges

state statistics

State	NUMBER OF INSTITUTIONS 1979–1980 Total	Public	Enrollment[1,2] fall 1979	EARNED DEGREES CONFERRED 1977–1978 Bachelor's and first professional	Master's except first professional	Doctor's
Alabama	57	36	159,784	16,100	6,948	269
Alaska	16	12	20,052	357	160	3
Arizona	25	17	188,976	9,486	4,432	403
Arkansas	34	19	74,701	6,522	2,167	108
California	263	135	1,698,668	84,274	39,960	3,642
Colorado	44	28	156,100	14,480	6,065	679
Connecticut	49	24	156,067	13,433	6,687	530
Delaware	10	6	32,308	2,997	495	75
District of Columbia	17	1	87,855	6,727	8,033	511
Florida	79	37	395,233	27,770	10,704	1,321
Georgia	73	34	178,017	16,351	8,802	563
Hawaii	12	9	47,204	3,679	1,171	129
Idaho	9	6	40,661	2,877	759	59
Illinois	155	63	612,916	43,451	22,066	1,874
Indiana	66	24	228,397	23,607	10,973	1,015
Iowa	60	22	132,599	13,199	4,062	515
Kansas	52	29	133,300	11,621	4,305	480
Kentucky	41	9	135,179	11,226	6,279	242
Louisiana	32	20	153,812	15,307	5,766	319
Maine	27	11	42,912	4,679	674	41
Maryland	54	32	218,745	16,453	6,303	578
Massachusetts	116	33	396,267	38,434	17,881	1,952
Michigan	96	45	503,839	36,279	18,159	1,338
Minnesota	65	30	193,830	18,185	5,008	501
Mississippi	45	27	100,272	8,784	3,978	269
Missouri	85	28	222,046	21,818	10,324	593
Montana	13	9	31,906	3,577	700	49
Nebraska	30	16	86,446	7,657	2,696	206
Nevada	6	5	35,935	1,543	479	18
New Hampshire	24	10	42,112	6,177	1,059	52
New Jersey	63	31	312,460	25,086	9,356	713
New Mexico	19	16	56,189	4,620	2,419	155
New York	296	82	970,168	85,209	40,706	3,399
North Carolina	126	73	269,065	23,792	7,024	742
North Dakota	16	11	31,904	3,436	584	47
Ohio	131	60	463,548	40,407	16,057	1,603
Oklahoma	44	29	152,683	12,744	4,744	390
Oregon	44	21	154,597	10,329	4,351	331
Pennsylvania	177	61	481,347	53,514	17,278	1,645
Rhode Island	13	3	64,435	6,859	1,652	188
South Carolina	60	33	131,459	11,343	4,182	198
South Dakota	19	8	31,294	3,750	782	50
Tennessee	76	23	199,654	17,801	2,224	513
Texas	149	95	676,047	52,306	20,362	1,502
Utah	14	9	90,398	8,589	2,614	357
Vermont	21	6	29,550	3,768	1,363	32
Virginia	71	39	270,559	20,709	6,901	538
Washington	49	33	303,469	16,139	4,926	453
West Virginia	28	17	81,335	7,638	2,547	117
Wisconsin	63	30	255,907	21,347	6,328	757
Wyoming	8	8	19,490	1,359	473	58
TOTAL U.S.	3,142	1,465	11,541,697	917,895	377,270	32,122

Excludes service academies. [1] Excludes non-degree-credit students. [2] Preliminary.
Source: U.S. Department of Health, Education and Welfare, National Center for Education Statistics, *Digest of Education Statistics* and *Education Directory*.

Universities and Colleges, 1980–81[1]

Selected four-year schools

Institution	Location	Year founded	Total students[2]	Total faculty[3]	Bound library volumes
ALABAMA					
Alabama A. & M. U.	Normal	1875	4,306	328	147,600
Alabama State U.	Montgomery	1874	4,096	179	180,952
Auburn U.	Auburn	1856	18,603	1,076	1,125,000
Birmingham-Southern	Birmingham	1856	1,475	130	137,200
Jacksonville State U.	Jacksonville	1883	7,222	305	415,300
Troy State U.	Troy	1887	8,560	414	233,600
Tuskegee Institute	Tuskegee Institute	1881	3,736	319	230,000
U. of Alabama	University	1831	16,388	930	1,132,500
U. of South Alabama	Mobile	1963	8,762	462	209,000
ALASKA					
U. of Alaska	Fairbanks	1917	3,489	355	500,000
ARIZONA					
Arizona State U.	Tempe	1885	38,075	1,343	2,000,000
Northern Arizona U.	Flagstaff	1899	13,000	1,200	1,000,000
U. of Arizona	Tucson	1885	34,206	1,709	1,444,500
ARKANSAS					
Arkansas State U.	State University	1909	7,448	310[4]	546,000
U. of Arkansas	Fayetteville	1871	15,156	864	821,100
U. of A. at Little Rock	Little Rock	1927	9,909	529	300,000
U. of Central Arkansas	Conway	1907	5,739	299	294,000
CALIFORNIA					
California Inst. of Tech.	Pasadena	1891	1,700	381	370,000
Cal. Polytech. State U.	San Luis Obispo	1901	16,200	1,300	555,000
Cal. State Polytech. U.	Pomona	1938	14,800	800	340,000
Cal. State U., Chico	Chico	1887	13,853	790	556,300
Cal. State U., Dominguez Hills	Dominguez Hills	1960	7,000	270	241,600
Cal. State U., Fresno	Fresno	1911	16,775	990	600,000
Cal. State U., Fullerton	Fullerton	1957	26,895	1,324	500,000
Cal. State U., Hayward	Hayward	1957	10,666	584	614,200
Cal. State U., Long Beach	Long Beach	1949	31,239	1,242	738,000
Cal. State U., Los Angeles	Los Angeles	1947	25,600	1,400	748,000
Cal. State U., Northridge	Northridge	1958	28,441	1,500	600,000
Cal. State U., Sacramento	Sacramento	1947	22,190	909[4]	715,200
Golden Gate U.	San Francisco	1901	10,211	1,139	200,000
Humboldt State U.	Arcata	1913	7,500	402	244,000
Loyola Marymount U.	Los Angeles	1911	5,047	328	190,000
Occidental	Los Angeles	1887	1,703	151	340,000
San Francisco State U.	San Francisco	1899	23,586	1,858	508,600
San Jose State U.	San Jose	1857	22,963	1,808	730,000
Sonoma State U.	Rohnert Park	1960	5,621	390	287,000
Stanford U.	Stanford	1885	13,592	1,705	4,577,800
U. of C., Berkeley	Berkeley	1868	28,500	3,100	5,750,000
U. of C., Davis	Davis	1905	17,550	902	1,600,000
U. of C., Irvine	Irvine	1960	10,033	580	930,000
U. of C., Los Angeles	Los Angeles	1919	30,180	3,100	4,230,000
U. of C., Riverside	Riverside	1868	4,500	320	980,000
U. of C., San Diego	La Jolla	1912	9,432	805	1,370,000
U. of C., Santa Barbara	Santa Barbara	1944	14,250	1,051	1,370,000
U. of C., Santa Cruz	Santa Cruz	1965	5,953	350	610,000
U. of the Pacific	Stockton	1851	6,004	371	560,000
U. of San Francisco	San Francisco	1855	6,500	250	57,600
U. of Santa Clara	Santa Clara	1851	6,651	402	411,000
U. of Southern California	Los Angeles	1880	27,563	2,700	1,650,000
COLORADO					
Colorado	Colorado Springs	1874	1,923	212	298,700
Colorado School of Mines	Golden	1874	2,939	191	158,000
Colorado State U.	Fort Collins	1870	18,651	982	1,287,300
Metropolitan State	Denver	1963	15,324	758	350,000
U. S. Air Force Academy	USAF Academy	1954	4,544	530	500,000
U. of Colorado	Boulder	1876	21,878	1,162	1,750,000
U. of Denver	Denver	1864	8,136	460	842,800
U. of Northern Colorado	Greeley	1889	10,870	620	500,000
U. of Southern Colorado	Pueblo	1933	5,637	293	300,000
CONNECTICUT					
Central Connecticut State	New Britain	1849	12,407	629	344,400
Southern Connecticut State	New Haven	1893	10,846	664	385,600
Trinity	Hartford	1823	1,812	134[4]	660,000
U. S. Coast Guard Acad.	New London	1876	1,125	114	125,000
U. of Bridgeport	Bridgeport	1927	6,733	515	311,800
U. of Connecticut	Storrs	1881	21,650	1,544	1,476,700
U. of Hartford	West Hartford	1877	7,100	615	280,000
Wesleyan U.	Middletown	1831	2,522	275	805,000
Western Connecticut State	Danbury	1903	5,700	310	150,000
Yale U.	New Haven	1701	10,054	1,712	7,402,000
DELAWARE					
Delaware State	Dover	1891	2,124	146	128,400
U. of Delaware	Newark	1833	18,997	798	1,700,000
DISTRICT OF COLUMBIA					
American U.	Washington	1893	12,382	634	511,000
Catholic U. of America	Washington	1887	7,400	533	900,000
George Washington U.	Washington	1821	21,719	3,230	1,122,700
Georgetown U.	Washington	1789	5,584	537	983,000
Howard U.	Washington	1867	11,748	1,922	1,012,500
FLORIDA					
Florida A. & M. U.	Tallahassee	1887	5,191	372	294,200
Florida State U.	Tallahassee	1857	21,461	1,379	1,509,100
Rollins	Winter Park	1885	3,316	348	196,000
U. of Central Florida	Orlando	1963	13,365	482	350,000
U. of Florida	Gainesville	1853	26,625	2,527[4]	2,700,000
U. of Miami	Coral Gables	1925	17,105	1,327	1,322,500
U. of South Florida	Tampa	1960	20,778	1,191	523,400
GEORGIA					
Atlanta U.	Atlanta	1865	1,255	140	326,400
Augusta	Augusta	1925	3,713	174	267,900
Emory U.	Atlanta	1836	7,420	1,113	1,637,500
Georgia	Milledgeville	1889	3,369	153	140,200
Georgia Inst. of Tech.	Atlanta	1885	11,261	762	1,000,000
Georgia Southern	Statesboro	1906	6,800	360	600,000
Georgia State U.	Atlanta	1913	20,333	863	678,500
Mercer U.	Macon	1833	3,500	126	240,000
Morehouse[5]	Atlanta	1867	1,756	112[4]	298,500
Oglethorpe U.	Atlanta	1835	1,175	50	185,200
Spelman[6]	Atlanta	1881	1,252	114	60,000
U. of Georgia	Athens	1785	25,662	1,418	2,062,500
HAWAII					
Brigham Young U.-Hawaii	Laie	1955	1,945	119	116,000
U. of Hawaii	Honolulu	1907	20,175	1,595	1,810,300
IDAHO					
Boise State U.	Boise	1932	11,004	344	250,000
Idaho State U.	Pocatello	1901	10,747	436	260,200
U. of Idaho	Moscow	1889	8,998	715	528,600
ILLINOIS					
Augustana	Rock Island	1860	2,420	158	245,000
Bradley U.	Peoria	1897	5,467	575	320,000
Chicago State U.	Chicago	1869	7,441	371	229,000
Concordia Teachers	River Forest	1864	1,194	84	127,000
De Paul U.	Chicago	1898	13,356	722	428,200
Eastern Illinois U.	Charleston	1895	10,374	546	419,000
Illinois Inst. of Tech.	Chicago	1892	7,056	1,042	849,000
Illinois State U.	Normal	1857	19,479	1,013	884,600
Knox	Galesburg	1837	982	84[4]	201,200
Lake Forest	Lake Forest	1857	1,144	84	180,000
Loyola U. of Chicago	Chicago	1870	8,080	1,385	796,000
Northeastern Ill. U.	Chicago	1867	10,045	394	381,000
Northern Illinois U.	De Kalb	1895	25,256	1,249	1,000,000
Northwestern U.	Evanston	1851	15,224	1,704	2,806,300
Southern Illinois U.	Carbondale	1869	23,991	1,656	1,561,300
SIU at Edwardsville	Edwardsville	1965	10,609	687	706,100
U. of Chicago	Chicago	1891	9,182	1,051	4,441,300
U. of Illinois	Urbana	1867	36,285	5,442	5,936,800
U. of I. at Chicago Circle	Chicago	1965	20,600	2,199	747,600
Western Illinois U.	Macomb	1899	12,007	700	496,600
Wheaton	Wheaton	1860	2,521	180	255,000
INDIANA					
Ball State U.	Muncie	1918	18,430	1,008	1,006,900
Butler U.	Indianapolis	1855	4,000	315	300,000
De Pauw U.	Greencastle	1837	2,503	206	373,200
Indiana State U.	Terre Haute	1865	10,700	690	844,900
Indiana U.	Bloomington	1820	32,366	3,798	1,400,900
Purdue U.	West Lafayette	1869	32,797	1,354[4]	1,475,500
U. of Evansville	Evansville	1854	4,756	235	190,000
U. of Notre Dame du Lac	Notre Dame	1842	8,750	749	1,419,400
Valparaiso U.	Valparaiso	1859	4,467	332	230,000
IOWA					
Coe	Cedar Rapids	1851	1,448	113	157,000
Drake U.	Des Moines	1881	6,627	384	400,000
Grinnell	Grinnell	1846	1,243	120	250,000
Iowa State U.	Ames	1858	24,202	2,024	1,414,000
U. of Iowa	Iowa City	1847	26,464	1,577	2,356,100
U. of Northern Iowa	Cedar Falls	1876	10,954	669	540,500
KANSAS					
Emporia State U.	Emporia	1863	6,411	300	664,800
Kansas State U.	Manhattan	1863	19,982	1,544	900,000
U. of Kansas	Lawrence	1866	24,466	1,296[4]	1,855,100
Wichita State U.	Wichita	1895	16,954	540	658,600
KENTUCKY					
Berea	Berea	1855	1,587	142	230,000
Eastern Kentucky U.	Richmond	1906	14,081	719	500,000
Kentucky State U.	Frankfort	1886	2,403	127	218,900
Murray State U.	Murray	1922	7,722	400	353,200
U. of Kentucky	Lexington	1865	23,047	1,487	1,800,000
U. of Louisville	Louisville	1798	20,059	1,332	905,500
Western Kentucky U.	Bowling Green	1907	13,002	727	500,000
LOUISIANA					
Grambling State U.	Grambling	1901	3,928	234	30,000
Louisiana State U.	Baton Rouge	1860	29,323	1,223	1,543,000
Louisiana Tech. U.	Ruston	1894	10,905	445	261,900
Northeast Louisiana U.	Monroe	1931	11,300	393	689,000
Northwestern State U.	Natchitoches	1884	11,344	...	350,000
Southern U.	Baton Rouge	1880	9,337	520	325,400
Tulane U.	New Orleans	1834	9,633	799	1,200,000
U. of Southwestern La.	Lafayette	1898	15,493	1,219	479,300
MAINE					
Bates	Lewiston	1864	1,430	238	325,000
Bowdoin	Brunswick	1794	1,373	114	610,000
Colby	Waterville	1813	1,714	135	239,800
U. of Maine, Farmington	Farmington	1864	1,700	110	86,400
U. of Maine at Orono	Orono	1865	11,574	596	544,400
U. of Southern Maine	Portland	1878	8,203	327	287,800
MARYLAND					
Goucher[6]	Towson	1885	1,054	97	197,100
Johns Hopkins U.	Baltimore	1876	7,999	751	1,865,200
Morgan State U.	Baltimore	1867	4,600	350	519,200
Towson State U.	Baltimore	1866	15,107	801	371,000
U.S. Naval Academy	Annapolis	1845	4,400	600	500,000
U. of Maryland	College Park	1807	36,905	1,942	2,000,000
MASSACHUSETTS					
Amherst	Amherst	1821	1,584	174	565,900
Boston	Chestnut Hill	1863	14,445	686[4]	900,000
Boston U.	Boston	1869	28,707	2,513	1,314,700
Brandeis U.	Waltham	1948	3,457	419	759,000
Clark U.	Worcester	1887	2,619	299	399,800
Harvard U.	Cambridge	1636	19,322	5,170	10,000,000
Holy Cross	Worcester	1843	2,504	194	375,000
Mass. Inst. of Tech.	Cambridge	1861	9,365	1,031	1,844,500
Mt. Holyoke[6]	South Hadley	1837	1,913	211	461,000
Northeastern U.	Boston	1898	40,568	2,674	464,000
Radcliffe[6]	Cambridge	1879	2,315	...	...
Salem State	Salem	1854	8,351	274	131,200
Simmons[6]	Boston	1899	2,803	250	200,000

Institution	Location	Year founded	Total students[2]	Total faculty[3]	Bound library volumes
Smith	Northampton	1871	2,566	260	887,500
Tufts U.	Medford	1852	4,350	990	530,000
U. of Lowell	Lowell	1894	9,000	551	300,000
U. of Massachusetts	Amherst	1863	24,737	1,204	1,806,000
Wellesley[6]	Wellesley	1870	2,147	290	600,000
Wheaton[6]	Norton	1834	1,230	131	250,000
Williams	Williamstown	1793	2,029	179	520,000
MICHIGAN					
Albion	Albion	1835	1,876	120	225,000
Central Michigan U.	Mt. Pleasant	1892	16,477	730	673,600
Eastern Michigan U.	Ypsilanti	1849	18,435	886	627,400
Ferris State	Big Rapids	1884	11,261	585	190,000
Hope	Holland	1866	2,458	180	190,000
Michigan State U.	East Lansing	1855	44,887	2,619	2,600,000
Michigan Tech. U.	Houghton	1885	7,779	517	532,000
Northern Michigan U.	Marquette	1899	8,746	353	362,700
U. of Detroit	Detroit	1877	6,375	445	514,000
U. of Michigan	Ann Arbor	1817	35,670	2,550	5,234,400
Wayne State U.	Detroit	1868	33,408	2,336	1,839,400
Western Michigan U.	Kalamazoo	1903	20,269	1,013	438,100
MINNESOTA					
Carleton	Northfield	1866	1,850	187	278,000
Concordia	Moorhead	1891	2,586	187	255,000
Gustavus Adolphus	St. Peter	1862	2,314	176	190,700
Hamline U.	St. Paul	1854	1,863	108	262,000
Macalester	St. Paul	1874	1,730	161	250,000
Mankato State U.	Mankato	1867	12,004	614	545,600
Moorhead State U.	Moorhead	1885	8,004	282[4]	261,600
St. Catherine[6]	St. Paul	1905	2,427	120	200,000
St. Cloud State U.	St. Cloud	1869	11,600	484[4]	477,300
St. John's U.[5]	Collegeville	1857	2,002	150	400,000
St. Olaf	Northfield	1874	3,035	270	322,600
St. Thomas	St. Paul	1885	4,681	265	3,800,000
U. of Minnesota	Minneapolis	1851	47,350	6,214	173,500
Winona State U.	Winona	1858	5,130	245	
MISSISSIPPI					
Alcorn State U.	Lorman	1871	4,540	300	138,000
Jackson State U.	Jackson	1877	7,099	364[4]	335,300
Mississippi	Clinton	1826	3,800	177	224,000
Mississippi U. for Women	Columbus	1884	2,307	160	304,100
Mississippi State U.	Mississippi State	1878	11,409	559	712,200
U. of Mississippi	University	1848	9,539	480	542,100
U. of Southern Mississippi	Hattiesburg	1910	10,414	549[4]	1,125,000
MISSOURI					
Central Missouri State U.	Warrensburg	1871	10,300	500	600,000
Northeast Missouri State U.	Kirksville	1867	6,649	344	240,200
St. Louis U.	St. Louis	1818	7,521	964	789,000
Southeast Missouri State U.	Cape Girardeau	1873	9,100	410	250,000
Southwest Missouri State U.	Springfield	1906	14,833	671	373,600
U. of Missouri-Columbia	Columbia	1839	24,579	1,003	2,068,800
U. of Missouri-Kansas City	Kansas City	1929	10,931	614	562,800
U. of Missouri-Rolla	Rolla	1870	7,039	517	300,000
U. of Missouri-St. Louis	St. Louis	1963	11,882	582	383,100
Washington U.	St. Louis	1853	10,691	2,261	1,500,000
MONTANA					
Montana State U.	Bozeman	1893	10,109	743	600,000
U. of Montana	Missoula	1893	8,884	404	711,700
NEBRASKA					
Creighton U.	Omaha	1878	5,766	964	457,900
U. of Nebraska	Lincoln	1869	24,786	2,267	1,494,000
U. of Nebraska at Omaha	Omaha	1908	15,000	425	363,000
NEVADA					
U. of Nevada-Las Vegas	Las Vegas	1951	8,140	305[4]	406,300
U. of Nevada-Reno	Reno	1864	9,137	400	680,300
NEW HAMPSHIRE					
Dartmouth	Hanover	1769	4,700	430	1,000,000
U. of New Hampshire	Durham	1866	12,474	553	794,300
NEW JERSEY					
Glassboro State	Glassboro	1923	10,100	454	362,000
Jersey City State	Jersey City	1927	7,050	533	315,000
Kean Col. of N. J.	Union	1855	13,748	449	200,000
Montclair State	Upper Montclair	1908	15,000	500	318,800
Princeton U.	Princeton	1746	5,939	695	3,000,000
Rider	Lawrenceville	1865	5,699	293	332,100
Rutgers State U.	New Brunswick	1766	33,760	2,034	1,532,200
Seton Hall U.	South Orange	1856	9,902	568	300,000
Stevens Inst. of Tech.	Hoboken	1870	3,057	168	103,500
Trenton State	Trenton	1855	10,500	429	400,000
Upsala	East Orange	1893	1,570	116	145,000
William Patterson	Wayne	1855	11,997	393	283,000
NEW MEXICO					
New Mexico State U.	Las Cruces	1888	12,411	920	610,000
U. of New Mexico	Albuquerque	1889	22,902	1,364	1,043,900
NEW YORK					
Adelphi U.	Garden City	1896	11,500	4,000	350,800
Alfred U.	Alfred	1836	2,323	194	235,000
Canisius	Buffalo	1870	4,070	248	210,000
City U. of New York					
Bernard M. Baruch	New York	1919	14,592	796	263,100
Brooklyn	Brooklyn	1930	14,622	1,182	781,000
City	New York	1847	15,508	1,080	1,000,000
Herbert H. Lehman	Bronx	1931	9,247	624	430,000
Hunter	New York	1870	17,509	560	450,000
Queens	Flushing	1937	20,507	1,296	450,000
Staten Island	Staten Island	1955	2,291	101	165,000
York	Jamaica	1966	4,000	166[4]	153,500
Colgate U.	Hamilton	1819	2,625	165	350,000
Columbia U.	New York	1754	15,311	4,000	5,000,000
Barnard[6]	New York	1889	2,550	200	150,000
Teachers	New York	1887	5,200	150	450,000
Cornell U.	Ithaca	1865	17,066	1,863	4,000,000
Elmira	Elmira	1855	2,698	187	134,300
Fordham U.	Bronx	1841	14,990	810	2,160,000
Hamilton	Clinton	1812	1,600	132	353,800
Hofstra U.	Hempstead	1935	10,948	729	855,000
Ithaca	Ithaca	1892	5,362	414	270,000
Juilliard School	New York	1905	1,000	150	50,000
Long Island U.	Greenvale	1926	7,459	789	650,000
Manhattan	Bronx	1853	5,027	359	220,000
Marymount[6]	Tarrytown	1907	1,112	83	104,500
New School for Soc. Res.	New York	1919	27,000	1,500	175,000
New York U.	New York	1831	31,570	3,624	2,613,700
Niagara U.	Niagara University	1856	3,954	276	216,000
Polytechnic Inst. of N.Y.	Brooklyn	1854	4,606	217	251,500
Pratt Inst.	Brooklyn	1887	4,171	491	211,500
Rensselaer Polytech. Inst.	Troy	1824	6,495	402	500,000
Rochester Inst. of Tech.	Rochester	1829	13,265	993	190,800
St. Bonaventure U.	St. Bonaventure	1856	2,590	160	207,800
St. John's U.	Jamaica	1870	16,128	878	838,500
St. Lawrence U.	Canton	1856	2,513	174	295,000
State U. of N.Y. at Albany	Albany	1844	16,128	830	970,000
SUNY at Buffalo	Buffalo	1846	27,412	1,819	2,003,900
SUNY at Stony Brook	Stony Brook	1957	14,252	829	1,093,600
State U. Colleges					
Brockport	Brockport	1836	8,100	433	372,500
Buffalo	Buffalo	1867	21,759	556	408,400
Cortland	Cortland	1868	6,080	362	225,000
Fredonia	Fredonia	1867	5,262	284	313,600
Geneseo	Geneseo	1867	5,540	309	348,900
New Paltz	New Paltz	1828	6,902	399	345,800
Oneonta	Oneonta	1889	6,204	341	350,000
Oswego	Oswego	1861	7,615	722	400,000
Plattsburgh	Plattsburgh	1889	6,155	375	230,800
Potsdam	Potsdam	1816	4,678	316	250,000
Syracuse U.	Syracuse	1870	19,098	1,366	4,406,400
U.S. Merchant Marine Acad.	Kings Point	1943	1,076	83	100,000
U.S. Military Academy	West Point	1802	4,492	550	400,000
U. of Rochester	Rochester	1850	8,632	1,256	1,941,700
Vassar	Poughkeepsie	1861	2,250	228	500,000
Wagner	Staten Island	1883	2,350	158	260,000
Yeshiva U.	New York	1886	4,281	2,486	850,000
NORTH CAROLINA					
Appalachian State U.	Boone	1899	8,500	550	406,700
Catawba	Salisbury	1851	979	57	180,000
Davidson	Davidson	1837	1,376	203	270,000
Duke U.	Durham	1838	9,740	1,400	3,319,600
East Carolina U.	Greenville	1907	13,264	674	600,400
Lenoir-Rhyne	Hickory	1891	1,386	117	113,000
N. Carolina A. & T. St. U.	Greensboro	1891	5,467	367	294,500
N. Carolina State U.	Raleigh	1887	21,225	1,064	1,000,000
U. of N.C. at Chapel Hill	Chapel Hill	1789	21,575	1,999	2,722,800
U. of N.C. at Greensboro	Greensboro	1891	10,201	633	1,250,000
Wake Forest U.	Winston-Salem	1834	4,601	924	781,500
Western Carolina U.	Cullowhee	1889	6,366	352	313,800
NORTH DAKOTA					
North Dakota State U.	Fargo	1890	8,742	415[4]	352,400
U. of North Dakota	Grand Forks	1883	10,531	800	874,600
OHIO					
Antioch	Yellow Springs	1852	1,000	75	240,000
Bowling Green State U.	Bowling Green	1910	17,079	785	694,000
Case Western Reserve U.	Cleveland	1826	7,869	1,700	1,576,000
Cleveland State U.	Cleveland	1964	19,103	714	480,000
Denison U.	Granville	1831	2,060	184	248,000
John Carroll U.	Cleveland	1886	3,950	275	300,000
Kent State U.	Kent	1910	25,000	800	1,500,000
Kenyon	Gambier	1824	1,451	145	260,000
Marietta	Marietta	1835	1,333	93	255,100
Miami U.	Oxford	1809	17,865	762	988,000
Oberlin	Oberlin	1833	2,818	226	789,300
Ohio State U.	Columbus	1870	52,682	2,306	3,615,100
Ohio U.	Athens	1804	13,850	836	1,315,000
U. of Akron	Akron	1870	25,820	1,450	1,282,900
U. of Cincinnati	Cincinnati	1819	37,936	2,245	1,500,000
U. of Dayton	Dayton	1850	10,252	537	690,000
U. of Toledo	Toledo	1872	20,270	914	670,300
Wooster	Wooster	1866	1,800	145	270,600
Xavier U.	Cincinnati	1831	6,643	200	208,000
Youngstown State U.	Youngstown	1908	15,664	761	455,500
OKLAHOMA					
Central State U.	Edmond	1890	12,763	415	604,700
Oklahoma State U.	Stillwater	1890	22,709	1,560	1,280,100
U. of Oklahoma	Norman	1890	21,850	900	1,717,300
U. of Tulsa	Tulsa	1894	6,382	417	1,000,000
OREGON					
Lewis and Clark	Portland	1867	2,476	167	199,200
Oregon State U.	Corvallis	1868	17,460	1,601	910,200
Portland State U.	Portland	1955	16,730	699	600,500
Reed	Portland	1909	1,130	116	283,000
U. of Oregon	Eugene	1872	16,916	1,000	1,504,000
PENNSYLVANIA					
Allegheny	Meadville	1815	1,904	130	290,000
Bryn Mawr	Bryn Mawr	1885	1,722	175	561,900
Bucknell U.	Lewisburg	1846	3,200	311	400,000
Carnegie-Mellon U.	Pittsburgh	1900	5,836	432	604,100
Dickinson	Carlisle	1773	1,776	122	312,000
Drexel U.	Philadelphia	1891	12,902	338	425,000
Duquesne U.	Pittsburgh	1878	6,637	580	450,600
Edinboro State	Edinboro	1857	5,600	396	337,000
Franklin and Marshall	Lancaster	1787	2,066	154	185,000
Gettysburg	Gettysburg	1832	1,956	166	255,000
Indiana U. of Pa.	Indiana	1875	12,174	680	510,000
Juniata	Huntingdon	1876	1,307	94	200,000
Lafayette	Easton	1826	2,413	185	360,000
La Salle	Philadelphia	1863	7,164	363	350,000
Lehigh U.	Bethlehem	1865	6,350	412	750,000
Moravian	Bethlehem	1742	1,355	85	141,000
Muhlenberg	Allentown	1848	2,308	124	177,900

Universities and Colleges (continued)

Selected four-year schools

Institution	Location	Year founded	Total students[2]	Total faculty[3]	Bound library volumes
Pennsylvania State U.	University Park	1855	36,138	1,565	1,597,200
St. Joseph's	Philadelphia	1851	5,578	280	192,000
Slippery Rock State	Slippery Rock	1889	6,299	365	420,300
Susquehanna U.	Selinsgrove	1858	1,829	115	120,000
Swarthmore	Swarthmore	1864	1,315	141	467,900
Temple U.	Philadelphia	1884	33,158	2,601	1,600,000
U. of Pennsylvania	Philadelphia	1740	22,611	6,298	2,950,000
U. of Pittsburgh	Pittsburgh	1787	29,315	2,600	2,268,300
Ursinus	Collegeville	1869	2,031	162	140,000
Villanova U.	Villanova	1842	7,848	512	453,000
West Chester State	West Chester	1812	8,600	1,963	385,000
PUERTO RICO					
Inter American U.	San Juan	1912	28,725	1,125	260,000
U. of Puerto Rico	Río Piedras	1903	50,492	2,722	2,156,600
RHODE ISLAND					
Brown U.	Providence	1764	6,943	493	1,709,300
Rhode Island	Providence	1854	9,177	375	275,000
U. of Rhode Island	Kingston	1892	10,853	800	650,000
SOUTH CAROLINA					
The Citadel[5]	Charleston	1842	3,363	159	367,000
Clemson U.	Clemson	1889	11,748	901	880,000
Furman U.	Greenville	1826	3,194	159	264,000
U. of South Carolina	Columbia	1801	25,671	1,171[4]	1,833,700
SOUTH DAKOTA					
South Dakota State U.	Brookings	1881	7,167	487	324,100
U. of South Dakota	Vermillion	1882	6,220	496	322,100
TENNESSEE					
Fisk U.	Nashville	1867	1,101	87	186,200
Memphis State U.	Memphis	1909	20,784	798	795,800
Middle Tennessee State U.	Murfreesboro	1911	10,931	511	439,600
Tennessee State U.	Nashville	1912	10,880	450	445,053
Tennessee Tech. U.	Cookeville	1915	7,777	632	287,800
U. of Tennessee	Knoxville	1794	30,282	1,719	1,392,000
Vanderbilt U.	Nashville	1873	8,874	2,120	1,439,300
TEXAS					
Austin	Sherman	1849	1,130	113	176,200
Baylor U.	Waco	1845	10,263	1,398	915,100
East Texas State U.	Commerce	1889	8,752	365[4]	550,000
Hardin-Simmons U.	Abilene	1891	2,049	122	160,400
Lamar U.	Beaumont	1923	11,331	621	619,000
North Texas State U.	Denton	1890	17,158	1,152	1,316,900
Prairie View A. & M.	Prairie View	1876	4,800	292	195,700
Rice U.	Houston	1891	3,600	473	1,000,000
Sam Houston State U.	Huntsville	1879	10,290	403	639,300
Southern Methodist U.	Dallas	1911	8,923	595	1,700,000
Southwest Texas State U.	San Marcos	1899	15,282	637[4]	717,100
Stephen F. Austin State U.	Nacogdoches	1923	10,768	541	415,000
Texas A. & I. U.	Kingsville	1925	6,060	237	400,600
Texas A. & M. U.	College Station	1876	31,331	1,615	700,000
Texas Christian U.	Fort Worth	1873	6,558	527	600,000
Texas Southern U.	Houston	1947	9,500	427	270,000
Texas Tech. U.	Lubbock	1923	23,129	1,386	1,250,000
U. of Houston	Houston	1927	30,692	2,413	1,100,000
U. of Texas at Arlington	Arlington	1895	20,166	1,016	750,000

Institution	Location	Year founded	Total students[2]	Total faculty[3]	Bound library volumes
U. of Texas at Austin	Austin	1881	48,145	1,985[4]	4,702,100
U. of Texas at El Paso	El Paso	1913	15,748	666	780,000
West Texas State U.	Canyon	1909	6,693	273	686,600
UTAH					
Brigham Young U.	Provo	1875	25,000	1,481	1,040,000
U. of Utah	Salt Lake City	1850	21,880	1,350	1,500,000
Utah State U.	Logan	1888	9,608[4]	475[4]	805,500
Weber State	Ogden	1889	10,065	450	255,200
VERMONT					
Bennington	Bennington	1925	640	73	85,000
Middlebury	Middlebury	1800	1,900	171	440,300
U. of Vermont	Burlington	1791	11,110	1,131	1,000,000
VIRGINIA					
James Madison U.	Harrisonburg	1908	8,970	518	293,000
Old Dominion U.	Norfolk	1930	14,000	650	500,000
U. of Richmond	Richmond	1830	4,110	329	278,800
U. of Virginia	Charlottesville	1819	16,452	1,627	2,391,600
Virginia Commonwealth U.	Richmond	1838	19,428	2,016	541,683
Virginia Military Inst.[5]	Lexington	1839	1,347	133	264,500
Va. Polytech. Inst. & State U.	Blacksburg	1872	18,698	1,467	1,300,000
Washington & Lee U.[5]	Lexington	1749	1,667	182	340,900
William & Mary	Williamsburg	1693	6,520	481	825,300
WASHINGTON					
Central Washington U.	Ellensburg	1891	7,551	419	300,000
Eastern Washington U.	Cheney	1890	7,469	373	354,000
Gonzaga U.	Spokane	1887	3,404	247	293,400
U. of Washington	Seattle	1861	36,636	2,500	4,000,000
Washington State U.	Pullman	1890	17,048	1,108	1,266,000
Western Washington U.	Bellingham	1893	10,616	512	391,900
Whitman	Walla Walla	1859	1,242	91	272,700
WEST VIRGINIA					
Bethany	Bethany	1840	862	79	141,000
Marshall U.	Huntington	1837	11,857	535	345,500
West Virginia U.	Morgantown	1867	21,265	2,043	994,800
WISCONSIN					
Beloit	Beloit	1846	1,056	89	251,300
Lawrence U.	Appleton	1847	1,141	110	236,000
Marquette U.	Milwaukee	1881	13,932	850	700,000
St. Norbert	De Pere	1898	1,733	122	133,300
U. of W.-Eau Claire	Eau Claire	1916	10,629	660	559,500
U. of W.-Green Bay	Green Bay	1965	3,842	242	350,900
U. of W.-La Crosse	La Crosse	1909	9,000	455	480,000
U. of W.-Madison	Madison	1848	41,349	1,457	3,631,700
U. of W.-Milwaukee	Milwaukee	1956	26,663	1,683	1,300,000
U. of W.-Oshkosh	Oshkosh	1871	10,368	550	292,200
U. of W.-Platteville	Platteville	1866	4,713	354	375,000
U. of W.-River Falls	River Falls	1874	5,600	272	199,900
U. of W.-Stevens Point	Stevens Point	1894	9,251	437	512,000
U. of W.-Stout	Menomonie	1893	7,413	335[4]	172,000
U. of W.-Superior	Superior	1896	2,281	135	216,300
U. of W.-Whitewater	Whitewater	1868	10,207	461[4]	286,300
WYOMING					
U. of Wyoming	Laramie	1886	9,200	850	900,000

[1] Latest data available; coeducational unless otherwise indicated.   [2] Total includes part-time students.   [3] Total includes part-time or full-time equivalent faculty.
[4] Total includes full-time equivalent only.   [5] Men's school.   [6] Women's school.

LIVING CONDITIONS

Health Personnel and Facilities

State	Physicians Dec. 31, 1978[1]	Dentists 1979	Registered Nurses[2]	Hospital facilities 1979 Hospitals	Hospital facilities 1979 Beds	Nursing homes 1978 Facilities	Nursing homes 1978 Beds
Alabama	4,554	1,314	10,235	147	25,345	204	19,246
Alaska	460	232	2,030	26	1,691	12	1,108
Arizona	4,918	1,173	12,383	80	11,720	84	6,823
Arkansas	2,610	714	5,033	96	12,746	179	16,561
California	52,194	14,052	103,385	608	114,354	3,500[2]	138,219[2]
Colorado	5,600	1,701	15,515	99	15,026	190	19,228
Connecticut	7,705	2,194	23,612	66	18,444	286	20,189
Delaware	972	265	4,389	15	4,220	27	2,484
District of Columbia	3,491	587	5,545	17	8,563	70[2]	2,873[2]
Florida	18,353	4,323	38,398	251	56,496	346	34,422
Georgia	7,259	2,167	17,423	189	31,082	278	29,768
Hawaii	1,808	599	4,117	27	3,888	148	3,315
Idaho	1,010	459	2,352	51	3,749	48	4,381
Illinois	20,628	5,999	60,806	285	73,535	557	61,487
Indiana	6,993	2,234	21,481	134	32,335	476	41,010
Iowa	3,635	1,396	11,812	141	21,476	488	33,910
Kansas	3,618	1,080	12,655	164	18,399	283	19,842
Kentucky	4,699	1,490	11,734	121	18,581	237	17,551
Louisiana	5,955	1,586	11,524	158	25,149	133	13,885
Maine	1,752	489	7,440	52	7,089	353	10,733
Maryland	10,390	2,591	22,462	84	25,175	183	19,322
Massachusetts	14,985	3,983	56,567	186	44,458	829	51,175
Michigan	14,290	4,772	46,681	239	50,255	563	60,238
Minnesota	7,676	2,429	23,638	183	30,632	495	44,350
Mississippi	2,571	763	6,288	116	16,483	96	10,162
Missouri	7,839	2,303	18,823	164	34,767	824	40,588

State	Physicians Dec. 31, 1978[1]	Dentists 1979	Registered Nurses[2]	Hospital facilities 1979 Hospitals	Hospital facilities 1979 Beds	Nursing homes 1978 Facilities	Nursing homes 1978 Beds
Montana	1,024	442	4,429	67	5,322	67	4,320
Nebraska	2,338	931	9,798	109	11,905	214	16,586
Nevada	925	340	2,564	25	3,252	29	1,686
New Hampshire	1,542	465	7,044	33	4,680	96	6,583
New Jersey	13,820	4,706	51,061	135	43,743	487	37,528
New Mexico	1,869	511	4,077	54	6,104	43	2,640
New York	47,021	12,611	125,794	358	131,440	1,027[2]	104,523[2]
North Carolina	8,428	2,175	21,366	159	33,374	722[2]	24,614[2]
North Dakota	825	312	3,653	60	5,920	79	5,080
Ohio	17,325	5,064	57,052	239	63,575	669	52,007
Oklahoma	3,650	1,192	8,698	142	17,575	222	17,223
Oregon	4,546	1,685	11,382	85	11,628	184	11,663
Pennsylvania	22,149	6,272	96,414	314	86,360	609	79,888
Rhode Island	1,967	509	6,638	21	6,158	112	7,981
South Carolina	3,873	1,130	10,187	89	16,877	161	9,427
South Dakota	723	286	3,852	69	5,594	138	8,647
Tennessee	6,808	2,034	12,051	167	31,371	245	18,461
Texas	20,143	5,757	40,372	568	80,083	966	92,574
Utah	2,225	853	4,531	41	5,121	72	4,386
Vermont	1,075	270	4,521	19	2,941	214	4,981
Virginia	8,653	2,599	23,935	134	31,859	330	21,008
Washington	6,981	2,611	21,953	125	15,959	504	34,909
West Virginia	2,565	703	7,314	78	14,105	125	6,089
Wisconsin	7,271	2,654	23,318	167	28,714	490	51,138
Wyoming	479	216	1,922	31	2,531	28	1,982
TOTAL U.S.	404,190	117,223	1,127,657	6,988	1,371,849	18,722	1,348,794

[1] Non-federal only.   [2] Latest data available.   Sources: *Physician Distribution and Medical Licensure in the U.S., 1978*, Dept. of Statistical Analysis, Center for Health Services Research and Development, American Medical Association, Chicago, 1980; American Dental Association, *Distribution of Dentists in the United States by State, Region, District, and County, 1979*; American Nurses' Association; American Hospital Association, *Hospital Statistics, 1980 Edition*; U.S. Dept. of Health, Education, and Welfare, Public Health Service.

Crime Rates per 100,000 Population

State or metropolitan area	VIOLENT CRIME										PROPERTY CRIME							
	Total		Murder		Rape		Robbery		Assault		Total		Burglary		Larceny		Auto theft	
	1975	1980	1975	1980	1975	1980	1975	1980	1975	1980	1975	1980	1975	1980	1975	1980	1975	1980
Alabama	392.9	448.5	**16.0**	13.2	20.4	30.0	123.0	132.1	233.5	273.2	3,079.6	4,485.1	1,163.8	1,526.7	1,645.5	2,642.2	270.3	316.2
Alaska	539.8	479.6	12.2	9.7	44.6	62.5	129.5	90.0	353.4	317.4	5,656.8	5,730.1	1,214.5	1,385.8	3,522.4	3,727.7	919.9	617.0
Arizona	547.8	650.9	8.6	10.3	35.5	45.2	170.0	193.6	338.8	401.8	**7,793.7**	7,519.9	**2,529.9**	2,155.4	**4,747.7**	**4,891.2**	516.1	473.3
Arkansas	348.3	335.2	10.1	9.2	25.9	26.7	87.6	80.9	244.7	218.4	3,191.9	3,475.9	1,077.1	1,119.0	1,947.0	2,169.8	167.8	187.1
California	665.4	893.6	10.4	14.5	41.6	58.2	282.4	384.2	321.0	436.7	6,549.2	6,939.5	2,217.3	2,316.5	3,703.7	3,880.0	628.2	742.9
Colorado	463.1	528.6	7.4	6.9	41.5	52.5	174.1	160.1	240.1	309.2	6,212.4	6,804.9	2,001.2	2,030.8	3,744.0	4,325.8	467.2	448.3
Connecticut	268.4	412.5	3.9	4.7	12.4	21.6	131.5	218.0	120.6	168.1	4,688.6	5,469.2	1,512.6	1,700.6	2,603.6	3,089.6	572.4	678.9
Delaware	392.1	474.8	7.3	6.9	18.1	24.2	157.2	137.0	209.5	306.7	6,276.2	6,301.8	1,826.3	1,630.5	3,926.9	4,216.2	523.0	455.1
Florida	688.5	983.5	13.5	14.5	35.7	56.9	239.7	355.5	**399.6**	**556.6**	7,032.7	7,418.4	2,349.6	2,506.8	4,240.4	4,434.2	442.6	477.5
Georgia	459.0	555.3	14.4	13.8	25.4	44.3	166.5	197.6	252.6	299.7	4,167.0	5,048.3	1,580.7	1,699.2	2,248.5	2,976.6	337.7	372.4
Hawaii	218.4	299.5	7.7	8.7	24.7	34.7	127.6	190.2	58.3	65.8	5,808.2	7,182.8	1,826.8	1,847.5	3,457.7	4,723.2	523.7	612.1
Idaho	203.7	313.4	5.2	3.1	16.1	22.4	42.0	46.8	140.4	241.1	3,937.4	4,468.8	1,063.0	1,238.9	2,651.3	2,993.0	223.0	236.9
Illinois	549.7	494.3	10.6	10.6	25.7	26.9	276.2	217.0	237.2	239.8	4,832.3	4,781.0	1,291.1	1,242.7	3,030.0	3,039.3	511.1	498.9
Indiana	332.8	377.8	8.5	8.9	24.3	33.1	156.8	141.4	143.3	194.5	4,578.6	4,552.5	1,376.4	1,313.3	2,813.9	2,807.1	388.3	432.2
Iowa	140.7	200.4	2.5	2.2	10.3	14.3	53.5	54.9	74.4	129.0	3,768.0	4,546.4	818.5	1,079.5	2,719.8	3,219.1	229.7	247.8
Kansas	278.2	389.3	5.4	6.9	17.2	31.5	92.8	113.1	162.8	237.8	4,468.8	4,989.5	1,369.5	1,521.4	2,862.8	3,196.4	236.4	271.7
Kentucky	264.0	266.7	10.2	8.8	15.4	19.2	103.2	95.2	135.3	143.5	3,000.3	3,167.1	962.8	1,040.8	1,774.2	1,875.5	263.4	250.7
Louisiana	478.4	665.0	12.6	15.7	23.7	44.5	153.1	197.0	289.0	407.8	3,645.0	4,788.8	1,114.6	1,523.9	2,191.8	2,888.4	338.5	376.5
Maine	219.5	193.4	2.8	2.8	10.4	12.9	36.4	30.8	169.8	146.8	3,740.1	4,174.2	1,361.5	1,182.8	2,167.9	2,772.3	210.8	219.1
Maryland	709.8	852.4	10.7	9.5	31.5	40.1	344.2	392.7	323.4	410.1	5,197.7	5,777.7	1,413.2	1,698.0	3,267.6	3,629.2	516.9	450.5
Massachusetts	442.6	601.3	4.2	4.1	19.2	27.3	227.0	235.5	192.2	334.4	5,635.3	5,477.8	1,712.5	1,740.4	2,351.7	2,685.8	**1,571.1**	**1,051.6**
Michigan	685.7	639.5	11.9	10.2	38.1	46.6	353.1	244.0	282.7	338.6	6,114.6	6,036.4	1,891.8	1,741.3	3,572.9	3,710.2	649.9	584.9
Minnesota	207.0	227.8	3.3	2.6	18.6	23.2	103.6	99.1	81.4	102.9	4,091.7	4,571.7	1,193.1	1,246.0	2,516.1	3,029.9	382.5	295.9
Mississippi	315.9	341.9	13.9	14.5	16.5	24.6	54.6	81.0	230.9	221.7	2,094.8	3,075.2	784.2	1,179.1	1,181.3	1,717.8	129.3	178.4
Missouri	493.8	554.5	10.6	11.1	25.2	32.6	244.7	223.6	213.3	287.2	4,904.0	4,878.6	1,512.6	1,668.9	2,924.7	2,795.1	466.7	414.6
Montana	189.6	222.6	5.2	4.0	14.3	21.0	41.4	34.0	128.6	163.6	3,999.3	4,801.9	875.1	950.6	2,814.8	3,529.6	309.4	321.7
Nebraska	257.8	224.6	4.3	4.4	19.2	23.2	90.4	82.2	143.9	114.7	3,356.2	4,080.6	760.2	915.4	2,365.0	2,921.6	231.0	243.6
Nevada	678.7	912.6	13.0	**20.0**	**47.1**	**67.2**	302.5	460.6	316.0	364.9	7,474.2	**7,941.4**	2,447.1	**2,906.7**	4,517.1	4,356.3	510.0	678.4
New Hampshire	99.8	179.8	2.9	2.5	8.7	17.3	28.9	42.0	59.3	118.0	3,246.8	4,499.8	853.1	1,312.9	2,135.7	2,877.0	258.1	309.9
New Jersey	413.0	604.4	6.8	6.9	18.9	30.7	222.6	303.7	164.6	263.0	4,731.3	5,797.0	1,521.2	1,878.2	2,672.5	3,189.3	537.7	729.5
New Mexico	534.8	615.0	13.3	13.1	41.0	43.3	126.7	127.9	353.8	430.7	5,304.6	5,364.1	1,728.7	1,492.5	3,258.8	3,521.0	317.2	350.6
New York	**856.4**	**1,029.5**	11.0	12.7	28.1	30.9	**516.0**	**641.3**	301.3	344.6	4,779.3	5,882.0	1,666.6	2,061.6	2,471.0	3,060.4	641.7	759.9
North Carolina	436.5	455.0	12.4	10.6	16.2	22.7	82.2	82.3	325.6	339.4	3,380.3	4,185.5	1,285.1	1,422.9	1,909.2	2,546.4	186.0	216.1
North Dakota	53.1	54.0	0.8	1.2	5.8	9.5	14.3	7.7	32.1	35.6	2,284.1	2,909.7	539.2	488.3	1,614.3	2,242.2	130.6	179.2
Ohio	408.0	498.3	8.1	8.1	25.3	34.3	220.0	223.7	154.6	232.2	4,506.4	4,933.1	1,271.4	1,466.3	2,808.6	3,040.1	426.4	426.7
Oklahoma	303.3	419.5	9.4	10.0	27.2	36.3	90.2	104.9	176.5	268.4	4,274.8	4,633.4	1,551.8	1,692.7	2,375.0	2,520.6	348.0	420.2
Oregon	438.5	490.4	6.2	5.1	32.6	41.5	130.3	152.4	269.4	291.4	6,313.7	6,196.5	1,911.6	1,748.4	3,935.9	4,087.8	466.2	360.3
Pennsylvania	329.2	363.9	6.8	6.8	17.4	23.0	168.6	177.9	136.5	156.1	3,020.3	3,372.4	983.3	1,038.5	1,670.0	1,915.5	367.0	418.3
Rhode Island	302.3	408.5	3.0	4.4	10.9	17.1	95.9	118.6	192.4	268.3	5,341.5	5,524.1	1,446.3	1,716.3	2,878.4	2,964.3	1,016.8	843.6
South Carolina	511.4	660.0	14.7	11.4	26.5	37.5	110.9	118.1	359.3	493.0	4,130.1	4,779.2	1,714.2	1,670.0	2,156.3	2,803.2	259.6	306.0
South Dakota	205.3	126.8	3.7	0.7	16.5	12.5	31.0	20.1	154.0	93.6	2,533.7	3,116.3	667.8	692.5	1,698.0	2,255.2	167.9	168.6
Tennessee	397.0	458.1	11.4	10.8	26.1	37.4	166.8	180.6	192.6	229.4	3,873.5	4,039.8	1,379.3	1,501.5	2,129.5	2,175.2	364.7	363.1
Texas	390.6	550.3	13.4	16.9	28.0	47.3	164.1	208.5	185.2	277.6	5,016.5	5,592.7	1,665.6	1,853.2	2,963.7	3,181.4	387.2	558.1
Utah	231.8	303.3	2.7	3.8	20.9	27.7	79.0	80.2	129.2	191.7	4,880.8	5,577.3	1,187.8	1,321.9	3,372.6	3,931.8	320.5	323.6
Vermont	95.1	178.8	2.1	2.2	14.6	29.1	15.7	38.9	62.6	108.5	3,386.0	4,809.7	1,100.0	1,526.7	2,112.1	2,988.1	173.9	294.9
Virginia	380.9	307.2	11.5	8.6	24.0	27.4	138.5	120.1	206.9	151.1	4,165.6	4,312.8	1,165.7	1,202.6	2,730.7	2,882.3	269.2	227.9
Washington	390.8	464.3	5.7	5.5	32.7	52.7	124.0	135.1	228.4	271.0	5,750.1	6,450.7	1,723.1	1,862.2	3,641.6	4,192.9	385.4	395.6
West Virginia	161.7	183.7	7.4	7.1	9.3	15.8	45.5	48.5	99.5	112.2	1,946.1	2,367.9	591.0	738.5	1,228.7	1,429.8	126.4	199.7
Wisconsin	151.8	182.6	3.3	2.9	10.6	14.9	73.4	70.7	64.5	94.1	3,823.9	4,616.0	918.5	1,079.4	2,665.4	3,291.4	239.9	245.2
Wyoming	204.3	392.6	10.2	6.2	17.1	28.6	49.5	44.4	127.5	313.5	3,951.6	4,593.8	863.4	903.7	2,810.7	3,344.9	277.5	345.2
Baltimore	965.2	1,161.6	14.8	12.5	36.1	43.9	492.1	546.7	422.2	**558.4**	5,641.2	6,311.4	1,542.4	1,833.7	3,474.8	3,966.3	624.0	511.5
Boston	544.5	726.9	5.3	5.2	22.9	29.0	308.0	337.8	208.4	354.8	5,910.7	5,766.4	1,693.3	1,695.3	2,315.8	2,720.3	**1,901.6**	**1,350.8**
Chicago	693.7	585.0	13.9	14.5	31.2	30.0	374.7	293.7	273.8	246.8	5,449.0	5,136.8	1,359.9	1,241.3	3,406.5	3,206.5	682.7	689.1
Dallas	490.4	751.9	15.3	18.1	36.9	62.8	212.7	289.4	225.4	381.5	7,040.0	7,518.8	2,086.5	2,335.7	**4,479.6**	**4,600.6**	473.9	582.5
Detroit	993.7	859.6	17.9	16.1	48.7	53.9	604.2	408.7	323.0	380.9	6,922.1	6,722.8	2,095.1	1,981.4	3,728.2	3,774.0	1,098.8	967.3
Houston	508.7	718.8	**19.1**	**27.6**	34.0	65.9	326.7	426.9	128.8	198.4	5,634.4	6,181.3	1,947.5	2,319.5	2,947.3	2,652.6	739.6	1,209.3
Los Angeles	927.1	1,339.6	14.3	23.3	**51.2**	**75.4**	421.2	628.0	440.3	612.9	6,274.4	7,079.1	**2,332.9**	2,602.5	3,078.6	3,371.7	863.0	1,104.9
Minneapolis	337.8	361.3	4.8	3.4	27.7	35.0	180.3	176.9	125.1	146.1	5,350.0	5,775.7	1,571.2	1,635.8	3,202.1	3,743.7	576.7	396.2
Newark	613.7	999.9	9.1	11.2	26.1	50.0	349.6	550.2	228.8	388.6	4,808.0	5,990.5	1,545.9	2,032.4	2,610.1	3,007.7	651.9	950.3
New York	**1,423.2**	**1,710.6**	18.0	21.0	41.9	43.3	**889.4**	**1,139.7**	**473.9**	506.6	5,544.1	7,242.3	2,081.0	**2,660.7**	2,514.0	3,369.2	949.1	1,212.4
Philadelphia	508.7	637.9	12.0	12.1	26.1	36.4	284.7	334.7	185.9	254.8	3,781.1	4,719.8	1,240.2	1,442.6	1,959.4	2,575.6	581.5	701.6
Pittsburgh	356.5	381.8	5.6	4.5	17.4	25.2	182.4	200.9	151.0	151.3	2,933.1	3,103.5	900.5	991.2	1,552.1	1,581.9	480.6	530.4
St. Louis	719.7	765.7	16.1	15.2	35.6	37.8	385.2	340.2	282.8	372.5	6,383.3	5,722.3	2,019.0	1,953.7	3,612.1	3,184.0	752.2	584.6
San Francisco	758.9	1,004.6	12.4	11.7	48.5	64.0	396.5	520.6	301.5	408.2	**7,293.3**	**7,536.0**	2,315.7	2,267.5	4,283.7	4,571.2	693.9	697.3
Washington, D.C.	749.3	802.8	12.0	10.7	41.4	44.8	473.6	490.2	222.2	257.0	5,527.9	6,136.1	1,431.2	1,767.6	3,608.2	3,911.8	488.5	456.7

Boldface: highest rate among states or listed metropolitan areas. Source: U.S. Department of Justice, Federal Bureau of Investigation, *Uniform Crime Reports*.

TRANSPORTATION AND TRADE

Transportation

State	Road and street mi[1] 1981	Motor vehicles in 000s, 1980[2]			Railroad mileage 1979[3]	Airports 1979[4]	Pipeline mileage 1980[5]
		Total	Auto-mobiles	Trucks and buses			
Ala.	87,327	2,954	2,115	839	4,497	156	19,539
Alaska	10,041	255	156	99	550	734	1,186
Ariz.	75,214	1,866	1,325	541	1,865	210	16,569
Ark.	75,449	1,553	1,017	536	2,749	167	18,033
Calif.	180,693	16,801	12,852	3,949	6,977	819	79,625
Colo.	82,558	2,395	1,764	631	3,413	301	22,670
Conn.	19,384	2,240	2,060	180	664	106	6,733
Del.	5,233	404	326	78	269	35	1,336
D.C.	1,102	257	238	19	52	18	1,157
Fla.	97,153	7,911	6,429	1,482	3,698	458	13,835
Ga.	104,556	3,865	3,038	827	5,471	283	24,693
Hawaii	4,493	580	516	64	...	54	587
Idaho	67,502	810	479	331	2,567	194	4,177
Ill.	136,671	8,779	7,534	1,245	11,167	891	53,205
Ind.	91,469	3,922	2,941	981	5,896	325	28,335
Iowa	112,071	2,380	1,755	625	5,805	258	17,899
Kan.	138,536	2,354	1,393	961	6,699	374	36,793
Ky.	69,321	2,660	1,833	827	3,572	112	19,939
La.	56,058	2,792	1,976	816	3,452	291	41,816
Maine	21,925	722	531	191	1,727	160	395
Md.	29,091	2,872	2,373	499	1,054	144	8,704
Mass.	33,777	3,802	3,325	477	1,462	137	16,717
Mich.	117,236	6,563	5,241	1,322	4,411	413	44,016
Minn.	135,143	3,471	2,459	1,012	6,983	468	16,730
Miss.	70,039	1,547	1,166	381	3,161	165	17,838
Mo.	118,482	3,324	2,454	870	5,902	374	21,695
Mont.	71,710	958	588	370	4,660	177	8,822
Neb.	96,387	1,246	874	372	4,903	319	14,087
Nev.	43,385	578	422	156	1,564	119	3,554
N.H.	14,355	655	543	112	617	52	1,154
N.J.	33,810	4,835	4,324	511	1,576	266	22,838
N.M.	75,351	1,061	680	381	1,964	145	24,349
N.Y.	109,441	8,216	7,162	1,054	4,582	482	41,396
N.C.	93,020	4,662	3,492	1,170	3,640	271	11,846
N.D.	106,511	630	366	264	5,121	221	2,854
Ohio	111,095	7,510	6,254	1,256	7,320	586	52,667
Okla.	109,775	2,759	1,845	914	3,860	292	37,132
Ore.	129,515	2,155	1,513	642	2,957	308	9,709
Pa.	117,634	6,895	5,811	1,084	7,248	684	52,344
R.I.	6,517	592	514	78	143	20	2,374
S.C.	62,460	2,016	1,542	474	2,772	127	9,910
S.D.	83,077	606	374	232	2,829	153	2,609
Tenn.	83,851	3,103	2,373	730	3,136	155	16,292
Texas	267,543	10,219	7,389	2,830	13,304	1,332	119,141
Utah	49,749	1,009	686	323	1,659	100	7,909
Vt.	14,066	339	260	79	384	61	404
Va.	66,060	3,581	3,060	521	3,511	256	11,219
Wash.	88,840	3,261	2,310	951	5,340	365	11,576
W.Va.	37,426	1,365	970	395	3,513	76	22,033
Wis.	107,051	3,208	2,530	678	5,653	382	21,923
Wyo.	36,234	491	289	202	1,985	97	7,795
TOTAL	3,955,387	159,029	123,467	35,562	188,304	14,693	1,050,159

[1] Includes federally controlled roads. [2] Estimated registration, excluding military. Detail may not add to totals because of rounding. [3] Class I and II line-haul only. [4] Public and private. [5] Gas utility industry miles only. Sources: ICC; Dept. of Transportation, FAA, FHWA; Dept. of Energy; Motor Vehicles Manufacturers Assn.

Communications Facilities

State	Post Offices Oct. 21, 1981	Telephones Jan. 1, 1980 Total	Telephones Jan. 1, 1980 Residential	Commercial Broadcast Stations 1979 Radio AM	Commercial Broadcast Stations 1979 Radio FM	Commercial Broadcast Stations 1979 TV	Public TV stations 1980	Newspapers Daily Number	Newspapers Daily Circulation	Newspapers Weekly [1] Number	Newspapers Weekly [1] Circulation	Newspapers Sunday Number	Newspapers Sunday Circulation
Alabama	613	2,528,060	1,934,496	140	74	17	9	28	744,714	118	534,993	21	685,383
Alaska	189	235,529	143,000	22	11	7	4	8	107,291	13	30,560	1	58,532
Arizona	210	1,969,767	1,453,135	61	31	13	2	19	621,184	57	221,183	8	570,281
Arkansas	621	1,436,655	1,085,156	90	54	9	5	33	479,522	120	360,159	17	481,599
California	1,109	20,164,330	14,335,528	232	204	54	13	122	6,013,791	451	5,549,713	50	5,568,875
Colorado	406	2,318,023	1,647,659	72	51	12	2	27	902,290	121	490,496	10	926,995
Connecticut	243	2,652,000	1,976,657	39	25	5	5	25	906,918	55	754,390	7	677,065
Delaware	55	519,808	379,774	10	7	—	3	156,308	14	105,371	2	139,455
District of Columbia	1	1,090,982	518,574	7	9	5	1	2	913,989	...	...	2	1,124,607
Florida	459	7,750,650	5,786,906	199	115	31	9	52	2,633,386	142	948,152	33	2,717,426
Georgia	630	4,088,760	3,032,114	186	90	19	11	36	1,037,049	203	1,174,407	15	1,011,528
Hawaii	77	684,959	455,796	26	7	10	2	7	237,749	4	107,178	2	219,616
Idaho	256	691,261	508,889	44	23	8	3	14	209,326	59	132,399	7	190,256
Illinois	1,263	10,097,304	7,553,863	127	132	23	4	77	2,838,519	699	3,804,450	24	2,795,859
Indiana	751	4,135,253	3,155,596	86	95	20	8	78	1,631,373	183	621,242	18	1,190,390
Iowa	950	2,277,914	1,715,713	76	75	13	8	41	884,087	366	812,469	9	742,768
Kansas	686	1,923,591	1,452,386	59	45	12	2	48	596,796	244	515,863	18	487,076
Kentucky	1,215	2,307,052	1,751,662	121	87	11	14	27	756,512	143	613,257	11	602,255
Louisiana	527	2,879,180	2,186,616	95	64	15	7	25	811,847	103	613,371	14	806,130
Maine	491	793,039	612,666	37	33	7	5	9	289,769	33	130,214	1	118,298
Maryland	425	3,514,629	2,634,858	50	37	6	4	14	702,829	75	872,430	4	648,930
Massachusetts	424	4,550,934	3,319,531	66	39	12	3	48	2,023,834	143	994,918	9	1,483,018
Michigan	854	7,244,774	5,514,554	128	117	24	7	52	2,447,531	277	2,306,123	15	2,360,899
Minnesota	854	3,130,455	2,306,604	93	69	12	5	30	1,018,579	432	1,953,522	11	1,016,849
Mississippi	459	1,535,738	1,186,035	106	72	10	8	25	398,429	99	313,083	13	319,537
Missouri	958	3,798,260	2,853,777	111	78	24	4	53	1,548,126	281	1,610,438	18	1,149,397
Montana	361	604,030	440,220	45	24	12	—	11	196,945	73	150,057	8	198,209
Nebraska	544	1,297,235	963,994	49	37	14	9	19	486,639	207	470,826	6	411,225
Nevada	90	745,419	505,064	22	12	8	1	9	222,044	16	44,880	5	220,697
New Hampshire	239	700,873	530,122	28	15	2	5	9	195,953	24	174,720	2	77,744
New Jersey	519	6,522,910	4,856,879	39	34	5	4	27	1,693,135	199	2,032,396	16	1,591,759
New Mexico	326	860,829	597,756	57	29	9	3	20	273,048	26	193,465	14	250,638
New York	1,625	12,990,694	9,461,938	161	119	30	12	79	7,884,889	415	2,494,621	33	5,995,335
North Carolina	773	4,109,771	3,102,437	211	88	19	9	55	1,377,846	128	560,565	24	1,131,121
North Dakota	439	564,294	412,921	26	10	11	3	10	195,615	93	184,729	3	106,662
Ohio	1,073	8,011,597	6,080,981	123	128	24	14	95	3,289,847	260	1,856,642	28	2,532,017
Oklahoma	620	2,331,300	1,715,890	67	53	12	4	54	837,856	196	390,201	44	861,937
Oregon	345	1,995,342	1,435,229	80	35	12	4	21	702,463	95	585,424	6	618,093
Pennsylvania	1,774	9,741,444	7,398,997	177	124	27	9	101	3,857,446	232	1,652,002	19	3,088,454
Rhode Island	55	711,880	535,376	15	7	2	1	7	315,712	16	99,092	2	238,970
South Carolina	388	2,075,750	1,557,771	108	56	11	8	20	603,020	72	272,362	8	497,385
South Dakota	403	517,391	384,848	33	18	11	8	12	173,564	152	198,827	4	125,525
Tennessee	564	3,190,991	2,418,100	158	50	19	5	31	1,080,701	129	606,901	16	1,004,275
Texas	1,487	10,802,632	7,772,739	289	197	58	11	118	3,438,913	523	1,598,863	97	3,934,811
Utah	209	1,042,347	774,376	35	20	4	2	6	277,823	52	188,322	5	273,954
Vermont	284	363,557	267,652	19	12	2	4	8	117,627	20	59,880	3	75,969
Virginia	885	3,824,367	2,844,384	137	72	16	7	35	1,091,490	95	616,088	15	854,387
Washington	460	3,198,078	2,203,575	92	47	14	5	26	1,187,265	138	1,189,431	16	1,103,252
West Virginia	1,008	1,118,425	860,277	63	34	9	3	25	471,139	75	282,165	9	391,950
Wisconsin	775	3,490,228	2,598,229	102	92	17	8	36	1,222,040	250	777,116	10	926,842
Wyoming	165	374,656	261,832	30	10	5	—	10	97,072	33	97,556	3	63,938
TOTAL U.S.	30,037	175,505,000	129,583,132	4,449	2,997	732	284	1,745	62,201,840	7,954	42,347,512	736	54,676,173

[1] Excluding District of Columbia; data for Sept. 30, 1978.   Sources: U.S. Postal Service; Federal Communications Commission; American Telephone and Telegraph Co.; The Editor & Publisher Co., Inc., *International Year Book, 1981* (Copyright 1981. All rights reserved. Used by permission.); National Newspaper Association; Corporation for Public Broadcasting.

Major Trading Partners, by Value

in millions of dollars

Country	EXPORTS 1975	EXPORTS 1980	IMPORTS 1975	IMPORTS 1980
North America	30,100	56,738	30,771	64,281
Canada	21,785	35,395	21,913	41,459
Mexico	5,160	15,145	3,060	12,580
South America	8,808	17,380	7,340	14,389
Argentina	628	2,625	218	741
Brazil	3,062	4,344	1,465	3,715
Chile	533	1,354	138	515
Colombia	643	1,736	593	1,241
Peru	896	1,172	402	1,386
Venezuela	2,243	4,573	3,730	5,307
Europe	33,117	71,376	21,727	48,039
Belgium and Luxembourg	2,442	6,661	1,191	1,914
France	3,031	7,485	2,190	5,265
Germany, West	5,267	10,960	5,394	11,693
Italy	2,867	5,511	2,401	4,325
Netherlands, The	4,194	8,669	1,087	1,913
Spain	2,164	3,179	833	1,220
Sweden	925	1,767	877	1,617
Switzerland	1,180	3,781	968	2,803
United Kingdom	4,787	12,694	3,855	9,842
U.S.S.R.	1,835	1,513	255	454
Asia	28,913	62,041	28,434	80,851
Hong Kong	809	2,686	1,576	4,739
India	1,290	1,689	548	1,098
Indonesia	810	1,545	2,296	5,217
Iran	3,244	23	2,207	472
Israel	1,551	2,045	313	950
Japan	9,570	20,790	11,282	30,714
Korea, South	1,762	4,685	1,416	4,147
Malaysia	393	1,337	766	2,577
Philippines	832	1,999	760	1,730
Saudi Arabia	1,502	5,769	2,732	12,648
Singapore	994	3,033	539	1,921
Taiwan	1,659	4,337	1,940	6,854
Oceania	2,340	4,876	1,513	3,392
Australia	1,815	4,093	1,152	2,509
Africa	4,266	7,187	8,684	33,871
Algeria	632	542	1,359	6,577
Nigeria	536	1,150	3,396	11,105
South Africa	1,302	2,464	847	3,321
TOTAL	108,113	220,786	98,503	244,871

Source: U.S. Department of Commerce, International Trade Administration, *Overseas Business Reports.*

Major Commodities Traded

in millions of dollars

Item	1977	1978	1979	1980
TOTAL EXPORTS [1]	121,293	143,766	182,025	220,786
Agricultural commodities				
Grains and preparations	8,755	11,634	14,450	18,079
Soybeans	4,393	5,210	5,708	5,883
Cotton, including linters, wastes	1,899	2,302	3,047	3,929
Nonagricultural commodities				
Ores and scrap metals	1,290	1,839	3,325	4,518
Coal, coke, and briquettes	2,655	2,046	3,394	4,621
Chemicals	10,812	12,623	17,306	20,740
Machinery	32,630	38,105	45,914	57,263
Agricultural machines, tractors, parts	1,584	1,337	1,685	3,442
Electrical apparatus	3,264	4,359	5,671	7,763
Transport equipment	730	1,188	1,391	1,756
Civilian aircraft and parts	17,619	21,163	24,577	27,366
Paper manufactures	2,747	3,616	6,177	8,256
Metal manufactures	1,517	1,597	1,967	2,831
Iron and steel mill products	2,608	1,646	2,227	2,998
Yarn, fabrics, and clothing	1,970	2,225	3,189	3,632
Other exports	26,820	32,876	41,997	47,709
TOTAL IMPORTS [1]	150,390	174,762	209,458	244,871
Agricultural commodities				
Meat and preparations	1,276	1,856	2,539	2,346
Fish	2,056	2,212	2,639	2,612
Coffee	3,910	3,728	3,820	3,872
Sugar	1,076	723	974	1,988
Nonagricultural commodities				
Ores and scrap metal	2,732	2,813	3,249	3,696
Petroleum, crude	36,526	34,885	49,361	62,112
Petroleum products	7,846	6,886	9,753	15,525
Chemicals	4,970	6,430	7,479	8,583
Machinery	18,836	24,752	28,530	32,286
Transport equipment	17,571	22,838	25,148	28,260
Automobiles, new	10,623	13,646	14,812	16,775
Iron and steel mill products	5,302	6,681	6,764	6,686
Nonferrous metals	3,380	4,367	4,678	5,183
Textiles other than clothing	1,736	2,200	2,216	2,493
Other imports	32,550	40,745	47,496	52,454

[1] Includes Virgin Islands.
Source: U.S. Department of Commerce, International Trade Administration, *Overseas Business Reports.*

Upper Volta

A republic of West Africa, Upper Volta is bordered by Mali, Niger, Benin, Togo, Ghana, and Ivory Coast. Area: 274,200 sq km (105,900 sq mi). Pop. (1981 est.): 6,251,000. Cap. and largest city: Ouagadougou (pop., 1980 est., 235,000). Language: French (official). Religion: animist 49.8%; Muslim 16.6%; Roman Catholic 8.3%. President of the Military Committee of Recovery for National Progress and premier in 1981, Col. Saye Zerbo.

The ruling Military Committee of Recovery for National Progress headed by Col. Saye Zerbo (*see* BIOGRAPHIES), which had come to power after a bloodless coup in November 1980, announced its plans for Upper Volta's economy at the 1981 May Day rally. The program envisaged a controlled and planned economy and included grants to peasants and plans for agrarian reform. During the year the military rulers hardened their attitude toward the trade unions; on November 1 the right to strike was withheld "until further notice."

Upper Volta continued to be heavily dependent on foreign aid. Relations with France, its most important source of economic aid, remained preferential. Guy Penne, adviser on African affairs to Pres. François Mitterrand, visited Ouagadougou in October. Zerbo attended the Franco-African summit conference in Paris in November.

(PHILIPPE DECRAENE)

Upper Volta

Gen. Gregorio Conrado Alvarez Armelino took the oath of office as president of Uruguay on September 1.

March. Nevertheless, it took 21 officers of the junta four days of debate to reach agreement. Alvarez's plans for gradual political liberalization made him unpopular among hard-line generals.

A new act set out the rules for Alvarez's period

UPPER VOLTA

Education. (1978–79) Primary, pupils 170,791, teachers 3,263; secondary, pupils 17,401, teachers 926; vocational, pupils 2,259, teachers 144; teacher training, students 238, teachers 43; higher, students 1,281, teaching staff (1977–78) 93.

Finance. Monetary unit: CFA franc, with (Sept. 21, 1981) a par value of CFA Fr 50 to the French franc (free rate of CFA Fr 265 = U.S. $1; CFA Fr 491 = £1 sterling). Budget (1981 est.) balanced at CFA Fr 46.2 billion.

Foreign Trade. (1980) Imports CFA Fr 75,610,000,000; exports CFA Fr 19,070,000,000. Import sources (1978): France 40%; U.S. 12%; Ivory Coast 11%; Belgium-Luxembourg 5%. Export destinations (1978): Ivory Coast 43%; France 16%; West Germany 12%; U.K. 12%; China 5%. Main exports (1977): cotton 40%; livestock 29%; oilseeds and nuts 14%.

Uruguay

A republic of South America, Uruguay is on the Atlantic Ocean and is bounded by Brazil and Argentina. Area: 176,215 sq km (68,037 sq mi). Pop. (1980 est.): 2,897,400, including (1961) white 89%; mestizo 10%. Cap. and largest city: Montevideo (pop., 1980 est., 1,260,600). Language: Spanish. Religion: mainly Roman Catholic. Presidents in 1981, Aparicio Méndez and, from September 1, Gen. Gregorio Conrado Alvarez Armelino.

Gen. Gregorio Conrado Alvarez (*see* BIOGRAPHIES), former head of the Army, was chosen as the transitional president of Uruguay in August 1981. His road to office was effectively cleared when a number of his military opponents were implicated in a gambling scandal, uncovered in

---

URUGUAY

Education. (1978) Primary, pupils 325,888, teachers 13,-821; secondary, pupils 151,962, teachers (1976) *c.* 13,980; vocational (1976), pupils 42,271, teachers *c.* 4,200; teacher training, students (1975) 3,997, teachers (1973) 341; higher (1977), students 39,392, teaching staff 3,263.

Finance. Monetary unit: new peso, with (Sept. 21, 1981) a free rate of 11.06 new pesos to U.S. $1 (20.50 new pesos = £1 sterling). Gold and other reserves (June 1981) U.S. $790 million. Budget (total; 1979 actual): revenue 12,185,-000,000 new pesos; expenditure 11,612,000,000 new pesos. Gross national product (1980) 89,493,000,000 new pesos. Cost of living: (Montevideo; 1975 = 100; June 1981) 1,236.

Foreign Trade. (1980) Imports U.S. $1,727,300,000; exports U.S. $1,058,500,000. Import sources (1979): Argentina 17%; Brazil 15%; U.S. 10%; Iraq 8%; West Germany 8%; Venezuela 6%. Export destinations (1979): Brazil 23%; West Germany 16%; Argentina 12%; U.S. 11%; The Netherlands 7%. Main exports (1979): clothing 15%; wool 14%; meat 14%; fish 9%; rice 8%; leather 6%.

Transport and Communications. Roads (1977) 24,954 km. Motor vehicles in use (1979): passenger *c.* 168,000; commercial (including buses) *c.* 92,000. Railways: (1980) 3,016 km; traffic (1978) 494 million passenger-km, freight 303 million net ton-km. Air traffic (1980): *c.* 178 million passenger-km; freight *c.* 1 million net ton-km. Shipping (1980): merchant vessels 100 gross tons and over 72; gross tonnage 198,478. Telephones (Jan. 1978) 268,000. Radio receivers (Dec. 1977) 1,625,000. Television receivers (Dec. 1977) 360,000.

Agriculture. Production (in 000; metric tons; 1980): wheat *c.* 300; corn (1979) 71; rice 289; sorghum 84; potatoes (1979) 135; sweet potatoes *c.* 85; sugar, raw value (1979) *c.* 82; linseed 65; sunflower seed 48; apples 33; oranges *c.* 38; grapes 80; wool *c.* 48; beef and veal *c.* 330. Livestock (in 000; May 1980): cattle 10,952; sheep (1979) *c.* 18,690; pigs *c.* 450; horses (1979) *c.* 525; chickens (1979) *c.* 7,575.

Industry. Production (in 000; metric tons; 1979): cement 681; petroleum products *c.* 1,960; crude steel (1978) 9; electricity (kw-hr) 2,749,000.

Uruguay

Universities:
see Education

Urban Mass Transit:
see Transportation

in office: the presidential term was shortened to three and a half years; the Council of State was enlarged to 35 members and given wider powers; and eight councillors were to be chosen by traditional political parties, the remainder being appointed by the president. Interior Minister Gen. Yamandú Trinidad made it clear that political exiles and left-wingers would continue to be excluded from the slow return to "authoritarian democracy." General elections were planned for November 1984, with a civilian administration taking office in March 1985. The fate of 1,500 political prisoners and 15,000 people without political rights remained to be resolved; the military offered to judge each case on its merits.

(MICHAEL WOOLLER)

Vanuatu

The republic of Vanuatu, a member of the Commonwealth, comprises 12 main islands, the largest of which are Espíritu Santo, Malekula, Efate, Ambrym, Aoba, and Tanna, and some 60 smaller ones in the southwest Pacific Ocean, forming a chain some 800 km (500 mi) in length. Area: 12,190 sq km (4,707 sq mi). Pop. (1981 est.): 120,000, predominantly Melanesian. Cap. and largest city: Vila, on Efate Island (pop., 1979 prelim., 15,100). Language: Bislama, a Melanesian pidgin (national); French and English (official). Religion: Presbyterian 40%, Roman Catholic 16%, Anglican 14%, other Christian 15%, animist 15%. President in 1981, George Sokomanu; prime minister, the Rev. Walter Lini.

Vanuatu's first full year of independence was marked by continuing difficulties in its relationship with France. In January Barak Sopé, Vanuatu's acting foreign minister, was refused entry to New Caledonia because of his support for the "Kanak" independence movement there. In retaliation, Vanuatu expelled the French ambassador. France subsequently refused to sign an aid agreement and, later, deferred aid payments.

Because of administrative difficulties and uncertainties over aid, development targets proved elusive. Some progress was made, however, in

Vanuatu

Vatican City State

VANUATU
  Education. (1977) Primary, pupils 21,161, teachers 839; secondary, pupils 1,791, teachers (1976) 96; vocational, pupils 775, teachers 50; teacher training, students 113, teachers (1976) 12.
  Finance. Monetary unit: Vatu (formerly New Hebridean franc),with (Sept. 21, 1981) a free rate of 81 Vatu = U.S. $1 (Vatu 150 = £1 sterling). The Australian dollar is also in use, but is being phased out. Budget (1980 est.): revenue c. Vatu 1,520,000,000 (excludes c. Vatu 1,162,000,000 grants from France and United Kingdom); expenditure Vatu 2,682,000,000.
  Foreign Trade. (1980) Imports Vatu 4,284,000,000; exports 1,946,000,000 Vatu. Import sources (1978): Australia c. 39%; France c. 12%; Japan c. 11%; New Caledonia c. 7%; New Zealand c. 5%. Export destinations (1978): U.S. 34%; France 33%; Singapore 11%; The Netherlands 8%; Japan 5%. Main exports (1978): copra 43%; fish 36%; cocoa 7%; meat 6%.
  Agriculture. Production (in 000; metric tons; 1979): bananas c. 1; copra c. 49; cocoa c. 1; fish catch c. 8. Livestock (in 000; 1979): cattle c. 97; pigs c. 65; chickens c. 140.

U.S.S.R.:
see Union of Soviet Socialist Republics

Venda:
see South Africa

extending Vanuatu's tax-haven facilities; a "flag-of-convenience" shipping register was established.

Military ties with Papua New Guinea were strengthened when that country undertook the training of police for the Vanuatu Mobile Force. In August Vanuatu was host to the meeting of the South Pacific Forum, during which Prime Minister Walter Lini led demands for New Caledonia's independence. The Forum also endorsed the rejection of a Soviet Union offer to conduct research in the waters around Vanuatu and the Solomon Islands. In September Vanuatu joined the UN.

(BARRIE MACDONALD)

Vatican City State

This independent sovereignty is surrounded by but is not part of Rome. As a state with territorial limits, it is properly distinguished from the Holy See, which constitutes the worldwide administrative and legislative body for the Roman Catholic Church. The area of Vatican City is 44 ha (108.8 ac). Pop. (1978 est.): 729. As sovereign pontiff, John Paul II is the chief of state. Vatican City is administered by a pontifical commission of five cardinals headed by the secretary of state, in 1981 Agostino Cardinal Casaroli.

The assassination attempt on Pope John Paul II (*see* BIOGRAPHIES) on May 13, 1981, overshadowed the affairs of the Vatican for nearly half the year. Not until October 7 did the pope resume his general audiences in St. Peter's Square. Before the attack on his life the pope had received, among

Mehmet Ali Agca, a Turkish right-wing terrorist accused of an assassination attempt on Pope John Paul II, was led away to prison after his arrest in May.

GIANNI GIANSANTI—SYGMA

others, Lech Walesa, leader of the independent Polish trade union Solidarity, Pres. Valéry Giscard d'Estaing of France, King Juan Carlos and Queen Sophia of Spain, and U.S. Secretary of State Alexander Haig.

Msgr. John Magee, one of the papal secretaries, was sent to Northern Ireland in an unsuccessful attempt to persuade Bobby Sands (*see* OBITUARIES), an imprisoned Irish Republican Army member, to abandon his hunger strike. In March the secretary of state, Agostino Cardinal Casaroli, met Farouk al-Kaddumi of the Palestine Liberation Organization. In September the pope received Chancellor Helmut Schmidt of West Germany, as well as the Argentine foreign minister, Oscar Camilión, who discussed the Beagle Channel dispute.

Bishop Paul Marcinkus was appointed governor of Vatican City State. Vatican diplomats were warned to envisage retirement at 70 (rather than 75) and not to expect posts in the Roman Curia, the Vatican's administrative body.

(MAX BERGERRE)

See also Religion: *Roman Catholic Church.*

Venezuela

A republic of northern South America, Venezuela is bounded by Colombia, Brazil, Guyana, and the Caribbean Sea. Area: 912,050 sq km (352,144 sq mi). Pop. (1981 est.): 14,313,400, including mestizo 69%; white 20%; Negro 9%; Indian 2%. Cap. and largest city: Caracas (metro area pop., 1981 est., 3,041,000). Language: Spanish. Religion: predominantly Roman Catholic. President in 1981, Luis Herrera Campins.

The popularity of Venezuela's Pres. Luis Herrera Campins remained very low in 1981 as the economy entered its third year of recession; criticisms of his policies came from all quarters. Results published by the central bank in September showed that in 1980 the gross domestic product had declined by 1.2% while inflation rose by 20%, and there were no signs of revival in 1981. Construction stagnated, commerce declined, manufacturing suffered production problems, and torrential rains damaged crops and forced higher food imports. Industrialists and labour unions alike called for less stringent monetary policies and increased government spending to reactivate demand.

Money flowed out of the country as investors took advantage of higher interest rates abroad. The government was forced to take action when capital flight reached over $100 million a day. In August the central bank announced a restructuring of the monetary system and an end to the low fixed interest rates that had lasted for 40 years. Investors cautiously repatriated some of their funds in September as domestic interest rates responded to market forces.

The balance of payments in 1980 showed considerable improvement on the current account, rising to a surplus of over $4 billion. This was largely the result of oil-price increases agreed to by the Organization of Petroleum Exporting Countries (OPEC); Venezuela received 75% more for its oil exports despite a fall in sales. In 1981, however, the posi-

VENEZUELA

Education. (1978–79) Primary, pupils 2,378,601, teachers (including preprimary) 91,384; secondary, pupils 787,032; vocational, pupils (1977–78) 36,750; teacher training, pupils (1977–78) 24,785; secondary, vocational, and teacher training, teachers (1977–78) 47,137; higher, students 282,075, teaching staff 23,449.

Finance. Monetary unit: bolívar, with (Sept. 21, 1981) a par value of 4.29 bolivares to U.S. $1 (free rate of 7.96 bolivares = £1 sterling). Gold and other reserves (June 1981) U.S. $9,374,000,000. Budget (1980 actual): revenue 62,697,000,000 bolivares; expenditure 64,636,000,000 bolivares. Gross national product (1979) 210 billion bolivares. Money supply (March 1981) 52,434,000,000 bolivares. Cost of living (Caracas; 1975 = 100; June 1981) 197.

Foreign Trade. (1980) Imports c. 49 billion bolivares; exports 79,212,000,000 bolivares. Import sources (1979): U.S. 46%; Japan 8%; West Germany 7%. Export destinations (1979): U.S. 37%; Netherlands Antilles 22%; Canada 10%. Main exports: crude oil 65%; petroleum products 31%.

Transport and Communications. Roads (1979) 61,826 km. Motor vehicles in use (1979): passenger 1,390,000; commercial (including buses) 639,500. Railways: (1980) c. 448 km; traffic (1971) 42 million passenger-km, freight 15 million net ton-km. Air traffic (1980): c. 4,318,000,000 passenger-km; freight c. 152.7 million net ton-km. Shipping (1980): merchant vessels 100 gross tons and over 225; gross tonnage 848,540. Telephones (Jan. 1980) 1,165,000. Radio receivers (Dec. 1977) 5,273,000. Television receivers (Dec. 1978) c. 1,710,000.

Agriculture. Production (in 000; metric tons; 1980): corn c. 584; rice 681; sorghum c. 596; potatoes c. 247; cassava (1979) 350; sugar, raw value c. 371; tomatoes c. 136; sesame seed c. 52; bananas c. 985; oranges c. 370; coffee c. 66; cocoa c. 17; tobacco c. 21; cotton, lint c. 15; beef and veal c. 337. Livestock (in 000; 1980): cattle 10,607; pigs 2,230; sheep c. 344; goats c. 1,368; horses (1979) c. 474; asses (1979) c. 455; poultry c. 45,100.

Industry. Production (in 000; metric tons; 1980): crude oil 114,400; natural gas (cu m) 16,535,000; petroleum products (1979) c. 52,000; iron ore (64% metal content) 15,873; crude steel 2,000; cement (1978) 3,550; gold (troy oz; 1979) 14; diamonds (metric carats; 1978) 763; electricity (kw-hr; 1978) 25,625,000.

Venezuela

tion showed signs of deteriorating. Oil revenues fell by 6% because of the world oil glut and the downward pressure on oil prices, although the current account was still expected to be in surplus. Oil exports accounted for 95% of Venezuela's total export earnings. At 2 million bbl a day, production to the end of September was 4% below the same period in 1980, while exports fell 8% to 1.7 million

U.S. President and Mrs. Ronald Reagan greeted Venezuelan President and Mrs. Luis Herrera Campins when they visited Washington, D.C., in November.

WIDE WORLD

bbl a day. For political reasons President Herrera consistently refused to raise domestic oil prices, despite the fact that they had not changed in 20 years and were heavily subsidized.

At the end of August the president unveiled the long-awaited sixth national development plan. It had undergone months of revision to take account of lower revenue estimates resulting from the fall in oil prices. Gross fixed investment was set at just under $150 billion for 1981–85, 23% of which was allocated to housing, education, and health. A program of industrial expansion envisaged investment in a coal-mining project in the state of Zulia and in thermoelectric, petrochemical, and aluminum plants. Investment in the oil industry was cut. The government's borrowing requirement was estimated at over $4 billion, but this was expected to double if Congress approved additional expenditure proposals.

In 1981 Venezuela and Mexico renewed their agreement whereby certain Caribbean and Central American countries received oil at preferential prices, despite their differences of opinion over other foreign policy issues. In particular, the joint declaration by France and Mexico in August, in which the two countries recognized El Salvador's guerrilla movement as a legitimate political force, was angrily received in Caracas, where the government actively supported its fellow Christian Democrat regime in El Salvador. On a state visit to Washington in November, President Herrera warned the U.S. against intervention in Nicaragua or in Central America generally.

The border dispute with Guyana over the Essequibo region flared up again in 1981. Venezuela refused to renew the agreement by which the dispute had been put on ice for 12 years (until June 1982). Venezuela also contested plans by international development agencies to lend money to Guyana for the construction of a hydroelectric plant in the disputed area.

Former president Rómulo Betancourt (*see* OBITUARIES) died in New York City on September 28 and was deeply mourned by the Venezuelan people.   (SARAH CAMERON)

Veterinary Science

A revolutionary advance was made in the development of veterinary vaccines using genetic manipulation—or DNA recombination—technology. The U.S. Department of Agriculture's Plum Island (New York) Animal Disease Center, in collaboration with the biotechnology company Genentech, produced a completely safe vaccine against the international scourge of cattle, foot-and-mouth disease (FMD). Unlike conventional vaccines, which employ the whole virus, the vaccine utilized only a segment of the FMD virus and thus carried no risk of causing accidental vaccine-induced disease in inoculated animals. The new vaccine was effective against only one strain of FMD, but it was expected that the same techniques could be used to produce a vaccine effective against all strains.

The use of myeloma (bone cancer) cells to produce large quantities of antibody against disease was likely to have important applications in prophylactic therapy and in diagnosis. The technique, developed at the U.K. Medical Research Council's Laboratory of Molecular Biology, consists of fusing antibody-producing cells from an immunized animal with myeloma cells. This gives rise to a hybridoma that grows rapidly, yielding large quantities of the antibody which can then be harvested.

A "test-tube" calf was born at the University of Pennsylvania's School of Veterinary Medicine in June 1981. Benjamin Brackett and his team succeeded in fertilizing an egg obtained from a cow and placed in a tissue culture dish with sperm from a bull. After incubation, the resulting embryo was placed in the oviduct of a second cow, which, after a normal pregnancy, gave birth to the calf. The technique could have implications for animal-breeding schemes, adding a further dimension to the embryo-transfer techniques already widely practiced.

The discovery of considerable amounts of hormone residue in canned baby food in Italy caused

In a rare occurrence, a Holstein cow gave birth to a gaur, a wild ox native to India, at the Bronx Zoo. The event was only the second time in which an interspecies embryo transfer had resulted in a successful birth. Scientists speculated that the process could make it possible to save endangered species.

concern throughout Europe. Veal used in the food had come from calves illegally injected with the hormone stilbestrol to promote growth. Enough of the hormone remained in the food after processing to create the risk that infants consuming it would be affected. There were immediate moves to ban the use of all hormone products in livestock in member states of the European Economic Community (EEC). This would have affected not only livestock farming but also many types of veterinary usage of hormone products. For example, planned breeding programs using hormonal products to time the onset of estrus (heat), which had come to play a useful role in farm management, would not have been permitted. Veterinary scientists argued that growth promotants were harmless unless improperly used. After much debate, the EEC decided to ban two groups of drugs, stilbenes and thyrostatics, while permitting the use of the natural hormones estradiol, progesterone, and testosterone and two synthetics, trenbolone and zeranol, for growth and for veterinary purposes. However, the European Commission was to investigate their safety.

Tapeworms in dogs are virtually harmless to the dog but can cause harmful hydatid cysts in sheep, to which they are transmitted via feces deposited on grass. Humans eating infected meat can also suffer illness or even death. A campaign to eradicate the tapeworm *Echinococcus granulosus* by treating dogs with praziquantel proved successful in two sheep-farming areas in Wales where hydatidosis was prevalent. (EDWARD BODEN)

[353.C]

Vietnam

The Socialist Republic of Vietnam is a southeast Asian state bordered in the north by China, in the west by Laos and Kampuchea (Cambodia), and in the south and east by the South China Sea. Area: 329,465 sq km (127,207 sq mi). Pop. (1981 est.): 55,053,000. Capital: Hanoi (pop., 1979, 2,570,900). Largest city: Ho Chi Minh City (pop., 1979, 3,420,000). Language: Vietnamese, French, English. Religion: Buddhist, animist, Confucian, Christian (Roman Catholic), Hoa Hao and Cao Dai religious sects. Secretary-general of the Communist Party in 1981, Le Duan; acting president to July 4 and, from that date, chairman of the National Assembly, Nguyen Huu Tho; chairman of the State Council from July 4, Truong Chinh; premier, Pham Van Dong.

China's hostility and the continuing strength of Kampuchean resistance combined to make 1981 yet another lost year for Vietnam. The national leadership showed no sign of bowing to international pressure, either diplomatic or military. Instead, it spent a good deal of time and energy reorganizing the domestic leadership structure. Some observers said this was meant to ensure greater cohesion at the top, while others thought it was the result of serious differences of opinion among senior leaders.

The first signs of government reorganization surfaced in January with a reshuffling of the eco-

nomic portfolios. In February there was another round of changes, again involving ministries dealing directly with the economy; new men were put in charge of the State Commission for Prices, the State Bank, and the Ministry of Labour. It was clear that the government was making an all-out attempt to cope with what threatened to become the worst food crisis since the end of the Indochinese war in 1975.

Natural disasters the previous year, the devastation wrought in the northern region by the Chinese military incursion in 1979, and the debilitating war in Kampuchea had brought the Vietnamese economy to its lowest point in years. At the time of the ministerial changes, it was not made clear whether the government had devised new policy initiatives. By midyear, however, Western visitors noted some significant shifts in emphasis and a consequent improvement in the overall situation.

The most important new initiative appeared to be increased "material incentives" to production, presumably with a view to raising output as well as the returns of labour. There were also reports of a step-up in the pace of collectivization, especially in the southern delta. According to some Western and Southeast Asian political sources, this was a major factor behind the increased flow of refugees out of Vietnam in the middle of the year. (*See* SOUTHEAST ASIAN AFFAIRS.) Nevertheless, some Western visitors reported (without statistics) that the food situation at midyear—though still bleak—was better than a year earlier.

The structural changes did not stop with a reorganization of the economic portfolios. The country went through the process of giving itself a new constitution. The precise objective of the exercise

VIETNAM

Education. (1977–78) Primary, pupils 7,784,587, teachers 227,984; secondary, pupils 3,301,145, teachers 129,183; vocational (1980–81), pupils 131,000, teachers 12,160; teacher training, pupils 42,583, teachers (1976–77) 2,336; higher (1980–81), students 148,600, teaching staff 16,400.

Finance. Monetary unit: dong, with (Sept. 21, 1981) a free rate of 2.16 dong to U.S. $1 (4.01 dong = £1 sterling). Budget (1979 est.) balanced at 10.5 billion dong.

Foreign Trade. (1980) Imports *c.* U.S. $1.4 billion; exports *c.* U.S. $1.1 billion. Import sources: U.S.S.R. *c.* 18%; Romania *c.* 11%; Japan *c.* 9%; India *c.* 7%; France *c.* 5%. Export destinations: U.S.S.R. *c.* 65%; Romania *c.* 5%; Poland *c.* 5%. Main exports (1974): clothing *c.* 10%; fish *c.* 10%; rubber *c.* 10%; coal *c.* 5%; beverages *c.* 5%.

Transport and Communications. Roads (1980) 347,243 km. Motor vehicles in use (1976): passenger *c.* 100,000; commercial (including buses) *c.* 200,000. Railways (1980) *c.* 2,510 km. Navigable waterways (1980) *c.* 6,000 km. Shipping (1980): merchant vessels 100 gross tons and over 93; gross tonnage 240,900. Telephones (South only; Dec. 1973) 47,000. Radio receivers (Dec. 1978) *c.* 5 million. Television receivers (Dec. 1978) *c.* 2 million.

Agriculture. Production (in 000; metric tons; 1980): rice *c.* 10,000; sweet potatoes (1979) *c.* 2,400; cassava (1979) *c.* 3,800; bananas *c.* 540; tea (1979) *c.* 21; coffee (1979) *c.* 15; tobacco *c.* 22; jute *c.* 30; rubber *c.* 57; pork *c.* 415; fish catch (1979) *c.* 1,010; timber (cu m; 1979) *c.* 63,095. Livestock (in 000; 1979): cattle *c.* 1,600; buffalo *c.* 2,350; pigs *c.* 9,300; chickens *c.* 57,300; ducks *c.* 30,300.

Industry. Production (in 000; metric tons; 1978): coal *c.* 6,000; cement (1977) 845; salt *c.* 375; phosphate rock *c.* 1,500; fertilizers (nutrient content; 1979–80) nitrogenous *c.* 40, phosphate *c.* 30; electricity (kw-hr) *c.* 3,420,000.

Vietnam

was unclear, since the new charter merely underlined the established principle that "the party rules and the state manages." Elections to the National Assembly, held on April 26 under the new constitution, produced no surprises. Veteran theoretician and reigning Assembly chief Truong Chinh was elected chairman of the powerful new State Council, which had powers to pass legislation when the Assembly was not sitting. The elections left Pham Van Dong undisturbed as premier and Le Duan as secretary-general of the Communist Party and therefore the country's top leader.

All the domestic revamping seemed to have little or no effect on the diplomatic-military imbroglio in which Hanoi had been caught as a result of its Kampuchea policy. China hardly tried to conceal its considered policy of "bleeding" Vietnam through constant military pressure along the common border and full military assistance to Pol Pot's Khmer Rouge guerrillas, battling Hanoi's forces in Kampuchea. Former Kampuchean head of state Prince Norodom Sihanouk said in France in September that China might even unleash a second border war with Vietnam if it thought the Khmer Rouge bands were losing ground.

The Sino-Vietnamese border remained tense, with minor but frequent incidents. The most serious confrontation took place in May, when China accused Vietnam of mounting the biggest border incursion since the 1979 war. More than 150 Vietnamese were killed, Beijing (Peking) said. Amid mutual recriminations and official protests, China even ordered the evacuation of its civilian population from some border regions. The crisis passed, but Beijing (Peking) had proved that it could turn the heat on Hanoi at any given moment.

Vietnam's main battlefront was still the Thailand-Kampuchea border. It had become clear that the Khmer Rouge forces were receiving aid and comfort from Thailand and that the movement of Chinese arms to the guerrillas was being facilitated by Thai officials. Hanoi kept up a constant barrage of angry protests against Thailand's role, accusing it of violating Kampuchean territory and providing sanctuaries from which Pol Pot's guerrillas could carry out "banditry and sabotage against the reconstruction efforts" in Kampuchea. In February Hanoi sent a letter to the UN charging that Thai artillery had shelled Kampuchea 515 times in January and that on 76 of those occasions the objective was to provide cover for guerrilla raids.

The military preoccupations in Laos and Kampuchea clearly stretched Vietnam's capacity to its limits. In July there were reports that Vietnamese troop strength in Kampuchea had declined from 200,000 to 170,000 because of the need to reinforce defenses along the Chinese border, the difficulty in replacing casualties, and desertions.

Vietnam's diplomatic efforts to break out of the military impasse were unsuccessful. In January it was host to a foreign ministers' meeting of the three Indochina states in Ho Chi Minh City. The meeting proposed a regional conference of the Indochina states and the five members of the Association of Southeast Asian Nations (ASEAN) to discuss "problems of common interest" and sign a "treaty of peace and stability in Southeast Asia."

However, ASEAN paid scant attention to the proposals. In December, in what observers saw as a hopeful gesture toward the U.S., four American veterans of the Vietnam war were invited to Vietnam, where they discussed such issues as the fate of U.S. servicemen missing in action and the effects of chemical defoliants used during the war.

The Vietnamese currency underwent a partial devaluation in July, from an official tourist rate of four dong to the U.S. dollar to nine to the dollar. The nontourist official rate remained at 2.7 dong to the dollar.   (T. J. S. GEORGE)

Water Sports

Motorboating. Defending champion Dean Chenoweth of Tallahassee, Fla., turned back all challengers to win his fourth unlimited hydroplane national championship and fourth American Power Boat Association (APBA) Gold Cup in 1981. Chenoweth and the Rolls-Royce Griffon-powered "Miss Budweiser" hydroplane opened the 1981 season with convincing wins in the Champion Spark Plug Regatta on June 7 in Miami, Fla., and the Stroh/Spirit of Detroit Regatta on June 28 in Detroit. Following another Chenoweth victory in the Indiana Governor's Cup in Madison on July 5, Bill Muncey and his "Atlas Van Lines" ended the "Miss Budweiser" streak at three with a win in the Thunder on the Ohio race on July 12 in Evansville, Ind.

Lee ("Chip") Hanauer in "The Squire Shop" earned a thrilling come-from-behind victory in the Columbia Cup on July 26 in Tri-Cities, Wash., before Chenoweth returned to the winner's circle at the Sea Galley-APBA Gold Cup on August 9 in Seattle, Wash. The rest of the season belonged to Chenoweth, as the 43-year-old veteran swept to victory in the Circus Thunderboat Regatta in San Diego, Calif., on September 20 and the Union of International Motorboating World Championship on October 18 in Acapulco, Mexico. The $175,000 world championship was the richest race in the history of powerboat competition and the first unlimited hydroplane event in Mexico. It cost the racing world dearly, however, as defending world champion Bill Muncey, the most successful driver in the history of the sport, was killed when his boat lifted off the water and flipped over backward while leading in the first lap of the championship heat. In his 31-year career the 52-year-old Muncey (see OBITUARIES) had won more than 60 races.

The 1981 offshore racing season belonged to Betty Cook of Newport Beach, Calif., and Paul Clauser of Fort Lauderdale, Fla. Cook earned her third APBA offshore national championship in four years, piloting her 38-ft "Michelob Light" deep vee-hull craft to victories in the Sutphen International on May 30 at Cape Coral, Fla., the Stroh Light Challenge on June 24 at Detroit, and the Coral Gables Challenge Cup on August 8 at Saugatuck, Mich.

Clauser was the only other double winner on the offshore circuit, driving his 41-ft catamaran "Satisfaction" to victories in the Benihana Grand Prix on July 15 at Point Pleasant, N.J., and the Harbour

British offshore power-boat racing champion Ted Toleman set a new world offshore speed record of 156.8 km/h (97.4 mph) on September 25, off Southampton, England.

Towne/Harmsworth Trophy Race on October 3 near Dania, Fla. The Dania victory coupled with a third-place finish in the Needles Trophy Race on August 30 at Needles, England, gave Clauser the Harmsworth Trophy. Rookie drivers Jerry Kilpatrick in "Apache" and Eddie Trotta in "Rampage" scored their first national series triumphs with wins in the Grand Bahama 200 and Bacardi Trophy Race, respectively. (JOHN H. LOVE)

River Sports. At the U.S. national flat-water championships, held in August at Jasonville, Ind., Theresa DiMarino won the women's single kayak events, Matt Streib the men's single kayak 1,000-m race, and Bruce Barton the 10,000-m kayak race. The two-man kayak events were taken by David Gilman and Terry White. Bruce and Barry Merritt won the two-man canoe races.

At the world flat-water championships, held in Nottingham, England, the team from East Germany won first place overall. Birgit Fischer won three of the seven gold medals that went to that nation. The U.S.S.R. team finished second, with 1980 Olympic champion Vladimir Parfenovitch gaining three of the six Soviet gold medals.

In white-water racing Tom McGowan won the men's kayak race at the U.S. national slalom championships, held in August in Wausau, Wis. Linda Harrison won the women's kayaking, and David Hearn was the men's single canoe champion.

Richard Fox of Great Britain won the men's slalom kayaking at the world championships, held at Bala, Wales, in July. Ulrike Deppe of West Germany was the women's champion. The four canoeing events were all won by competitors from the United States: Jon Lugbill was the men's single canoe champion, Michael and Steven Garvis were the two-man canoe champions, and Fritz Haller and Elizabeth Hayman won the mixed canoe class; Lugbill then joined his brother Ron and David Hearn to win the team title. Overall, in both slalom and wildwater events, the French team was first, followed by the U.S. (ERIC LEAPER)

Water Skiing. For the first time in 12 years the men's world overall water skiing title returned to the U.S. in 1981. Sammy Duval of Greenville, S.C., broke the victory string of skiers from Canada, Venezuela, and Great Britain by winning the overall title, the most coveted of all water ski titles, in the 17th biennial World Water Ski Championships in September at Thorpe Water Park near London. Karin Roberge of Orlando, Fla., who, like Duval, was skiing in her first world tournament, won the women's overall title.

Three of the gold medals in individual events also were won by U.S. skiers. Cory Pickos of Eagle Lake, Fla., won the figures with a top run of 9,020 points, the best score ever in world competition. Deena Brush of East Sacramento, Calif., topped the women jumpers with a leap of 39.60 m; Cindy Todd of Pierson, Fla., won the slalom with a two-round total of 57¾ buoys. Todd's final-round performance of 1¼ buoys on an 11.25-m line was a new U.S. record, but it was topped by Sue Fieldhouse of Australia, who set a new world record of 1½ buoys at 11.25 m. Fieldhouse was third in the final standings, behind Roberge.

Andy Mapple of Great Britain won the men's slalom title with a total of 66¾ buoys. His teammate, Mike Hazelwood, won the jumping gold with a leap of 57.90 m, well off his pending world record of 60 m set earlier in the season. Ana Maria Carrasco of Venezuela won the women's figures with a two-round total of 12,750 points, although the defending champion, Natalia Rumjantseva of the Soviet Union, had the best single-round score with 6,660 points. She finished second in the standings. U.S. skiers won the team title for the 17th consecutive time, scoring 8,520 points to 7,777 for Australia and 7,666 for Great Britain. (THOMAS C. HARDMAN)

Surfing. The winter surf on the north shore of Oahu for the 1980–81 season was the best in years with more than 60 days of consistently excellent conditions. A recent study of surf swells of 7 ft (2.1

Western Samoa

m) or more in various places on the globe indicated that the average Hawaiian peak season has swells of that size 36.6% of the time, South Africa 11.9%, and Australia only 6.4%. Based on this study, it is interesting to note that in the 1980 men's division of the International Professional Surfers competitions Australia placed three contenders in the first five positions: Mark Richards finished first, Wayne Bartholomew fourth, and Cheyne Horan fifth. Dane Kealoha of Hawaii placed second, and South Africa's Shaun Tomson was third. In the women's division, however, Hawaii's incomparable Margo Oberg placed first with teammate Lynne Boyer second.   (JACK C. FLANAGAN)

Water Polo. Major international competition is usually rare in post-Olympic years, but 1981 was an exception, as several important tournaments were held. The first took place in Long Beach, Calif., as the U.S. was host to the second Fédération Internationale de Natation Amateur (FINA) Cup. The Soviet Union captured the gold medal with an undefeated record, beating second-place Yugoslavia 8–3 and third-place Cuba 11–6. Following Cuba, in order, were the U.S., Spain, Hungary, Australia, and Bulgaria.

The largest field ever, 19 teams, competed in the European Championships held in Split, Yugos. Eight teams played in the first division, with West Germany finishing on top with a 6–1–0 record. The Soviet Union placed second, followed by Hungary, Yugoslavia, Spain, and Italy.

In the first World Junior Championships ever held, Italy was host to 15 teams from around the world. The Soviet Union took home the crown as Cuba, although playing the Soviets to an 11–11 tie, finished second. Hungary and Italy were forced into a penalty throw shoot-off before the Hungarians were awarded the bronze medal.

In the World University Games in Bucharest, Rom., the Cuban student team captured the prize, followed by the U.S., Romania, and the Soviet Union. In the second FINA Cup for women, Canada won the gold medal over Australia, The Netherlands, New Zealand, and the U.S.

(WILLIAM ENSIGN FRADY)

Western Samoa

A constitutional monarchy and member of the Commonwealth, Western Samoa is an island group in the South Pacific Ocean, about 2,600 km E of New Zealand and 3,500 km S of Hawaii. Area: 2,849 sq km (1,100 sq mi), with two major islands, Savai'i (1,813 sq km) and Upolu (1,036 sq km), and seven smaller islands. Pop. (1980 est.): 155,800. Cap. and largest city: Apia (pop., 1980, 33,400). Language: Samoan and English. Religion (1976): Congregational 50%; Roman Catholic 22%; Methodist 16%; others 12%. Head of state (*O le Ao o le Malo*) in 1981, Malietoa Tanumafili II; prime minister, Tupuola Efi.

Although it was embattled for much of the year, the government of Prime Minister Tupuola Efi continued to survive with a majority of one in the Legislative Assembly. Some senior Health Department officials had to resign after the alleged misuse of $250,000 was uncovered, and the government faced serious economic problems with exports all but coming to a standstill and inflation for the year ended July 1981 running at 25%. The economy continued to depend heavily on remittances from Samoans working abroad.

In 1980 public servants had sought a 30% pay increase and then agreed to a government offer of a staged 22.5% increase. This was cut in the December 1980 budget, and in April 1981, 4,000 public servants struck in protest. After three months they returned to work when a commission of inquiry recommended increases ranging from 5 to 36%, with the greatest raises going to the lowest paid.

As of 1981 only Samoan *matai* (titled heads of families) could vote for 45 of the 47 parliamentary members. (The other two members represented non-Samoan—mainly European—voters.) Proposals that would have given the vote (but not the right to seek election) to all adults were heavily defeated in the assembly.

Western Samoa established its first national park with New Zealand aid and launched a major forestry project with aid from New Zealand and the Asian Development Bank. It also became a signatory to the second Lomé Convention governing the European Economic Community's trade with, and assistance to, less developed countries.

(BARRIE MACDONALD)

Yugoslav goalie Milorad Krivokapic blocked a U.S. shot in the FINA Cup water polo competition in California in May. The U.S. and Yugoslav teams played to a 7–7 tie.

GEORGE TIEDEMANN—SPORTS ILLUSTRATED

WESTERN SAMOA

Education. (1979) Primary, pupils 42,073, teachers 1,458; secondary, pupils 9,719, teachers 458; vocational, pupils 252, teachers 27; teacher training, students 221, teachers 14; higher (1978), students 425, teaching staff 53.

Finance and Trade. Monetary unit: tala, with (Sept. 21, 1981) a free rate of 1.07 tala to U.S. $1 (1.99 tala = £1 sterling). Budget (1980 est.): revenue 31.4 million tala; expenditure 22.7 million tala. Foreign trade: imports (1979) 60,946,000 tala; exports (1980) 15,835,000 tala. Import sources: New Zealand 25%; West Germany 20%; Australia 17%; Japan 11%; U.S. 9%; Singapore 6%. Export destinations (1979): West Germany 27%; New Zealand 24%; The Netherlands 22%; U.S. 9%; American Samoa 7%. Main exports: copra 53%; cocoa 20%.

Winter Sports

Wider interest in the leading sports on snow and ice during 1981 was stimulated by the lavish news media exposure of the preceding season's Winter Olympics. Significantly, the winter sports vacation business expanded at Alpine, Scandinavian, and Rocky Mountain resorts despite below-average snow conditions and the worldwide economic recession; the latter had adversely affected the summer vacation trade.

Skiing. A new ski fastening developed in Sweden was claimed to reduce the risk of broken legs on slalom runs. Whereas conventional bindings release only when skiers fall forward or sideways, the new fastening loosens when they fall backward—perhaps the most frequent skiing accident. The temporary use of a shorter ski to accelerate the progress of beginners became more widespread, as did plastic ski slopes and grass (roller) skiing for practicing technique away from the snow.

ALPINE RACING. Phil Mahre became the first U.S. skier to win the Alpine World Cup when the 15th series of races ended on March 29 at Laax, Switz. Needing to finish at least third in the final giant slalom, he achieved second place to overtake Ingemar Stenmark of Sweden in the final standings. At the end, Mahre's convincing all-round ability had earned him 266 points, 6 more than Stenmark, the slalom specialist who skied only a single downhill, at Kitzbühel, Austria, in January —the first he had ever entered in World Cup competition.

Aleksandr Zhirov, the highest placed Soviet skier in World Cup history, finished third in the competition, which comprised 31 events at 20 venues in ten countries on three continents. In fourth place was Mahre's twin brother, Steve. Stenmark

headed both the slalom and giant slalom lists, while Harti Weirather of Austria was the most successful in downhill.

Marie-Theres Nadig gained the women's title comfortably from her Swiss compatriot Erika Hess, who set a record of six straight slalom wins to edge out the third-place finisher, defending champion Hanni Wenzel of Liechtenstein. Wenzel was hampered by early-season injury. Nadig was the best downhiller and Hess the top slalom scorer, while Tamara McKinney was the giant slalom front-runner, the first U.S. woman in 12 years to lead in one of the World Cup disciplines. Boosted by the performances of its women, Switzerland won the concurrently decided Nations' Cup, ending a run of eight Austrian successes. Austria, whose men were again the best, this time was overall runner-up, with the U.S. third.

André Arnold of Austria decisively won the North American circuit's professional men's title for a fourth successive year. Hans Hinterseer was runner-up to his compatriot for the second time, and Paco Ochoa of Spain finished third. Toril Forland from Norway recaptured the women's crown from the defending champion, Jocelyne Perillat of France. Viki Flekenstein of the U.S. finished third.

NORDIC EVENTS. The second official Nordic World Cup series, contested at ten locations in nine countries, ended in Soviet victories for Aleksandr Zavjalov in the men's cross-country events and for Raïsa Smetanina in the women's. The men's silver and bronze medals went to Norwegians Oddvar Braa and Ove Aunli. The women's runner-up was Ove's sister, Berit Aunli, with Kvetoslava Jeriova third for Czechoslovakia.

The World Cup jump title was won by Armin Kogler of Austria, narrowly edging out the Norwegian runner-up, Roger Ruud, after a see-sawing season of inconsistent finishes by the leaders. Third was Horst Bulau, a promising young

The winners of the World Cup women's giant slalom in Colorado were (left to right) Wanda Bieler (third place) of Italy, Tamara McKinney (first) of the U.S., and Erika Hess (second) of Switzerland.

WIDE WORLD

Canadian. The Nations' Cup victor was Austria, with Norway second and Finland third.

Finnish and East German ski-shooters took the major honours in the biathlon events, organized by the Union Internationale de Pentathlon Moderne et Biathlon (UIPMB). In the world biathlon championships, at Lahti, Fin., on February 10–15, Heikki Ikola won for the host country in the 20 km. Frank Ulrich of East Germany placed second, with another Finn, Erkki Antila, third. Ulrich won the 10 km, with Antila runner-up. Finishing third in the event was Yvon Mongel, who thus became the highest placed Frenchman in the history of senior international biathlon championships, indicative of appreciable French progress in recent seasons. By contrast, Soviet competitors began to lose their previous domination. East Germany won the 4 × 10-km team relay, with West Germany second and the U.S.S.R. third. Biathlon's own World Cup series, decided over 20-km and 10-km races at five meetings in five countries, ended with Ulrich a decisive winner, followed by Anatoly Albyabjev of the U.S.S.R. and Kjell Sobak of Norway.

The eighth annual Finlandia ski marathon, over a 75-km cross-country course from Hameenlinna to Lahti, was contested by 9,670 racers, including 803 foreigners, but Finns took the first three places. Matti Kuosko won, followed by Heikki Rapatti. Pauli Siitonen, seeking a sixth successive victory, ended third.

Jari Puikkonnen of Finland won the sixth world ski-flying championship, at Oberstdorf, West Germany, on March 1. Armin Kogler, the defending champion, was runner-up, with Tom Levorstad from Norway third.

OTHER EVENTS. In the eighth biennial world skibob championships, at Lungötz, Austria, on February 1–7, Robert Mühlberger of West Germany retained the men's title. The silver medal went to Hans Irausek of Austria and the bronze to another West German, Anton Feistl. Alana Hanouskova from Czechoslovakia became the new women's champion. A West German, Rosalinde Lehner, was runner-up, with Andrea Dobler of Austria third.

Ice Skating. An increase in the number of international competitions during 1981 enabled more people to see the stars in live action as well as on television. This helped influence more to take up the sport for recreation, and the number of indoor rinks continued to grow in most areas, particularly in North America, Japan, China, and Western Europe. Increasing numbers of skaters practiced ice dancing, but fewer persevered with the more physically demanding pairs competition.

A plastic blade support, replacing the conventional metal stanchion, was a feature of some new skate designs, lightening the weight and trimming the cost by reducing the overall amount of steel required. Most leading performers, however, continued to use the chromium-plated steel skate.

FIGURE SKATING. New winners emerged in all four events of the world championships, contested by 116 skaters from 24 nations on March 3–7 at Hartford, Conn. The meeting was sponsored, ironically, by the insurance company that had paid the $11 million cost of rebuilding the Coli-seum rink's roof, damaged by ice and snow three years earlier. A victory for the host nation in the men's competition raised the rafters in a more welcome way when the diminutive Scott Hamilton — 5 ft 3 in tall — became the sixth U.S. skater to acquire the crown since it was first contested in 1896.

Hamilton, who had taken up the sport at the age of nine as therapy for Shwachman's disease, ranked third before the final free skating, but four great triple jumps punctuated by well-varied spins and intricate linking footwork earned 5.9 out of a possible 6 for technical merit from six of the nine judges, despite a fluky tumble during a simple turn. He overhauled his compatriot David Santee, who finished runner-up ahead of Igor Bobrin of the Soviet Union.

Brian Orser, sixth for Canada, became the second skater to accomplish a triple axel jump in a world championship, emulating the awesome feat of his fellow Canadian Vern Taylor in 1978. Robert Wagenhoffer (U.S.) achieved a quadruple toe loop jump during practice but did not attempt it in competition.

Denise Biellmann became the first Swiss skater to take the women's title. This gracefully athletic performer had practiced acrobatics for nine years to develop her now famous and unique spin, drawing her free leg back and upward until clutching her skate high above her head. This proved the trump card enabling her to overtake the U.S. runner-up, Elaine Zayak, a petite dynamo of only 15 who landed six triple jumps and seemed certain to become a future champion. Claudia Kristofics-Binder from Austria, who had led in the figures, narrowly outscored Britain's Debbie Cottrill for third place.

The pairs title went comfortably to the Soviet husband and wife team of Igor Lisovsky and Irina Vorobieva. Tassilo Thierbach recovered well from a two-month-old knee operation to end runner-up for East Germany with partner Sabine Baess. The West Germans Andreas Nischwitz and Christina Riegel snatched the bronze from the Soviet title defenders, Sergey Shakhrai and Marina Tcherkasova, this time humbled in fourth place.

The ice dance victory for Britain by Christopher Dean and Jayne Torvill was only the second non-Soviet success in 12 years in this event; the British pair defeated the respected Andrey Minekov and Irina Moiseyeva, victors twice previously but this time runners-up. Third place went to Andrey Bukin and Natalia Bestemianova of the U.S.S.R. The British couple was considered by many to be technically the best-ever performers in this branch of skating.

In the first season with a controversial new scoring system, better free skaters and free dancers had an unprecedented advantage over specialists in compulsory figures, the former being favoured in tie-break decisions when total points were equal. This ruling denied third place in ice dancing to Michael Seibert and Judy Blumberg of the U.S.

SPEED SKATING. Amund Sjøbrend of Norway became the new men's world champion in Oslo on February 14–15. His compatriots Kay Arne Stenshjemmet and Jan Egil Storholt finished second and third. In the four events, Stenshjemmet

won the 500 m, Sjøbrend the 1,500 m, Piet Kleine of The Netherlands the 5,000 m, and Sergey Berezin of the U.S.S.R. the 10,000 m.

Natalia Petruseva of the U.S.S.R. retained the women's title in Quebec City on February 7–8. Karin Enke of East Germany was runner-up, and Sarah Docter of the U.S. finished third. Petruseva was first in the 500 m and 1,000 m, Enke winning the 1,500 m and Olga Pleshkova of the U.S.S.R. the 3,000 m. In the separate world sprint championships, contested at Grenoble, France, on February 21–22, Norway's Frode Rønning gained the men's title, followed by two Soviet racers, Sergey Khlebnikov and Anatoly Medennikov. The women's title was retained by Enke, with Tatiana Tarasova of the U.S.S.R. second and Petruseva third.

Two world men's records were achieved during the season. Yevgeny Kulikov of the U.S.S.R. lowered the 500-m sprint to 36.91 sec at Medeo, U.S.S.R., and Canada's Gaetan Boucher reduced the 1,000 m to 1 min 13.39 sec in Davos, Switz. Every major women's record was broken, all at Medeo. Petruseva clocked new times of 1 min 20.81 sec for the 1,000 m and 2 min 5.39 sec for the 1,500 m. Two East Germans, Christa Rothenburger and Gaby Schönbrunn, covered 500 m in 40.18 sec and 3,000 m in 4 min 21.70 sec, respectively.

Eleven countries sent 39 men and 32 women to compete in the first world short track championships (for indoor rinks) at Meudon, France, on April 4–5. The men's and women's overall titles were won by Benoit Baril (Canada) and Miyoshi Kato (Japan), respectively.

Bobsledding. East German sleds, each driven by Bernhard Germeshausen and braked by Hans Jurgen Gerhardt, won both titles in the 48th world championships in February at Cortina d'Ampezzo, Italy. In the two-man event they avenged their 1980 Olympic defeat by Erich Scharer and Josef Benz of Switzerland, who finished third behind another East German sled steered by Horst Schönau and braked by Andreas Kirchner. Germeshausen's aggregate time for the four descents was less than a second faster than Schönau's.

In the event for four-man crews Germeshausen won his second gold medal by a more comfortable margin of 2.22 sec over the Swiss runner-up, Hans Hiltebrand. Scharer gained his second bronze by steering another Swiss sled into third place. The results were overshadowed by the death of the U.S. driver Jim Morgan when his four-man sled overturned near the finish after rounding the final curve at an estimated speed of 150 km/h (93 mph). The other U.S. foursome had withdrawn the previous day after an accident on the same curve.

Tobogganing. Sergey Danilin of the Soviet Union captured the men's title in the 27th world luge championships at Hammarstrand, Sweden, on February 7–8, followed by an East German, Michael Walter, and an Italian, Ernst Haspinger. Melitta Sollmann of East Germany regained the women's crown she had previously held in 1979, with her compatriot Bettina Schmidt runner-up and Vera Zozoula of the U.S.S.R. third. The doubles title went to the East German brothers Bernd and Ulrich Hahn.

WIDE WORLD

Scott Hamilton of Denver, Colo., captured the gold medal at the Skate America competition at Lake Placid, N.Y., in October. He outpointed 11 other competitors.

Swiss riders monopolized the medals in both the classic events for skeleton tobogganists on the Cresta Run at St.-Moritz, Switz. Franco Gansser won the 72nd Grand National over the full course on February 14, with Patrick Latscha runner-up and Nico Baracchi third. The 58th Curzon Cup, over a shorter distance on January 17–18, was won for the fourth successive time by Poldi Berchtold, the track record holder, with Baracchi second and Gansser third.

Curling. Swiss curling appropriately celebrated its 100th anniversary with a victory in the 23rd men's world championship for the Air Canada Silver Broom, at the Thompson Arena in London, Ont., on March 23–29. The winning rink, from Lausanne, was skipped by Jurg Tanner and also included Jurg Hornisberger, Patrick Loertscher, and Tanner's 53-year-old father, Franz. They beat Bud Somerville's U.S. rink 2–1 in a closely contested final.

Somerville skipped his rink from third position, with Bob Nichols throwing the skip rocks; Bob Christian and Bob Buchanan completed the team. Switzerland reached the final after defeating Kerry Burtnyk's Canadian rink 7–4. In the other semifinal Somerville beat the Norway team skipped by Kristian Soerum, who was competing in his sixth successive championship. Other nations competing were Sweden, Scotland, France, West Germany, Italy, and Denmark. The oldest curler participating in the championship was the French skip, Gérard Alazet, 66.

The third women's world championship, sponsored by the Royal Bank of Scotland at Perth, Scot-

land, on March 16–21, was won for the first time by Sweden. Skipped by Elisabeth Högstrum and also including Karin Sjögren, Birgitta Sewick, and Carina Olsson, Sweden beat Canada (skipped by Susan Seitz) 7–2 in the final. Norway finished third.

In the seventh world junior championship, sponsored by Uniroyal at Mégève, France, on March 7–14, Scotland, represented by a rink from Stranraer skipped by Peter Wilson, retained the title. Canada (skip, Denis Marchand) was runner-up.   (HOWARD BASS)

See also Ice Hockey.
[452.B.4.g-h]

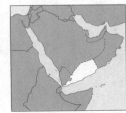

People's Democratic
Republic of Yemen

Yemen, People's Democratic Republic of

A people's republic in the southern coastal region of the Arabian Peninsula, Yemen (Aden; South Yemen) is bordered by Yemen (San'a'), Saudi Arabia, and Oman. Area: 338,100 sq km (130,541 sq mi). Pop. (1981 est.): 1,943,000. Cap. and largest city: Aden (pop., 1980 est., 343,000). Language: Arabic. Religion: predominantly Muslim. Chairman of the Presidium of the Supreme People's Council and prime minister in 1981, Ali Nasir Muhammad Husani.

Chief of state Ali Nasir Muhammad Husani moved toward pro-Soviet policies in early 1981, less than one year after taking office in South Yemen. The late-1980 emphasis on economic liberalization for merchants all but disappeared in 1981. Friendship treaties were signed with Bulgaria and Czechoslovakia, and in August a tripartite alliance

was signed with Libya and Ethiopia, placing South Yemen firmly in the radical Arab camp.

In October 1980 a policy shift in South Yemen resulted in increased support for the National Democratic Front (NDF) antigovernment rebels in Yemen (San'a'; North Yemen). Nevertheless, the NDF suffered military defeats during 1981. When Pres. Ali Abdullah Saleh of North Yemen visited Aden in December, "reunification" of the Yemens was discussed.

Western economic assistance to South Yemen

The Egyptian press reported in February that 1,200 Cuban troops had passed through the Suez Canal and landed in South Yemen.

KEYSTONE

continued despite the Marxist profile of the government. A Japanese-built power station was due to open in February 1982, while Australians were helping with road construction. Oil exploration by Italian and Soviet geologists continued, and a 250-room hotel in Aden was being built with Bulgarian assistance. (JOHN WHELAN)

Yemen Arab Republic

A republic situated in the southwestern coastal region of the Arabian Peninsula, Yemen (San'a'; North Yemen) is bounded by Yemen (Aden), Saudi Arabia, and the Red Sea. Area: 200,000 sq km (77,200 sq mi). Pop. (1981 est.): 5,305,000. Cap. and largest city: San'a' (pop., 1980 est., 210,000). Language: Arabic. Religion: Muslim. President in 1981, Col. Ali Abdullah Saleh; premier, Abdel Karim al-Iriani.

Pres. Ali Abdullah Saleh faced crumbling security in North Yemen during 1981. Bitter fighting erupted in August between government forces and rebels of the opposition National Democratic Front (NDF). The NDF forces, backed by Yemen (Aden; South Yemen), made a determined

Yemen Arab Republic

attempt to seize the town of Ibb, but they were repulsed by heavily armed government forces. A cease-fire agreement was reached in November.

In December Saleh visited Aden to discuss reunification, the first such visit there by a president from North Yemen. In October Saleh visited Moscow, where he apparently succeeded in rescheduling military loans worth more than $400 million. High military spending coupled with widespread tax evasion and smuggling reduced the government's revenue sources.

Contractors and banks reported difficulty in receiving payments from the government. The second five-year plan, to be published in 1982, was expected once again to be dependent on Arab aid. Oil exploration continued, but results were disappointing. Earnings from cotton and coffee declined because farmers found more profit in growing the narcotic leaf qat for domestic consumption.

(JOHN WHELAN)

YEMEN ARAB REPUBLIC

Education. (1976–77) Primary, pupils 221,482, teachers (1975–76) 6,604; secondary, pupils 24,873, teachers (1975–76) c. 1,172; vocational, pupils 503, teachers (1975–76) 60; teacher training, students 1,650, teachers (1975–76) 113; higher, students (1977–78) 4,058, teaching staff (1973–74) 58.

Finance and Trade. Monetary unit: rial, with (Sept. 21, 1981) a par value of 4.56 rials to U.S. $1 (free rate of 8.46 rials = £1 sterling). Budget (1980–81 est.): revenue 4,435,000,000 rials; expenditure 6,806,000,000 rials. Foreign trade (1979): imports 6,804,000,000 rials; exports 61,700,000 rials. Import sources: Saudi Arabia 19%; Japan 10%; France 10%; U.K. 8%; West Germany 7%; Italy 6%; Singapore 5%; China 5%. Export destinations: Yemen (Aden) 49%; Saudi Arabia 23%; Italy 7%. Main exports (1977): cotton 49%; coffee 17%; hides and skins 12%.

Agriculture. Production (in 000; metric tons; 1980): barley c. 56; corn (1979) c. 90; wheat (1979) c. 100; sorghum c. 686; potatoes (1979) c. 106; grapes c. (1979) 45; dates c. 83; coffee c. 4; tobacco (1979) c. 4; cotton, lint c. 1. Livestock (in 000; 1979): cattle c. 950; sheep c. 3,700; goats c. 7,800; camels c. 106; asses c. 716.

Yugoslavia

A federal socialist republic, Yugoslavia is bordered by Italy, Austria, Hungary, Romania, Bulgaria, Greece, Albania, and the Adriatic Sea. Area: 255,804 sq km (98,766 sq mi). Pop. (1981 est.): 22,451,000. Cap. and largest city: Belgrade (pop., 1980 UN est., 976,000). Language: Serbo-Croatian, Slovenian, Macedonian, and Albanian. Religion (1953): Orthodox 41%; Roman Catholic 32%; Muslim 12%. Presidents of the Presidium of the League of Communists in 1981, Lazar Mojsov and, from October, Dusan Dragosavac; presidents of the collective Presidency, Cvijetin Mijatovic and, from May 15, Sergej Kraigher; president of the Federal Executive Council (premier), Veselin Djuranovic.

Yugoslavia maintained its traditional nonaligned stance between East and West during 1981. Sergej Kraigher, the president of the collective Presidency, attended the North-South summit in Cancún, Mexico, in October. However, Yugoslavia's role and importance in the nonaligned grouping showed signs of diminishing in the wake of President Tito's death in May 1980 and the eruption of new conflicts such as the Iraq-Iran war.

Yugoslavia

YUGOSLAVIA

Education. (1978–79) Primary, pupils 1,427,769, teachers 57,335; secondary, pupils 1,912,231; vocational, pupils 487,171; teacher training, pupils 14,386; secondary, vocational, and teacher training, teachers 127,906; higher, students 285,431, teaching staff 18,178.

Finance. Monetary unit: dinar, with (Sept. 21, 1981) a free rate of 37.21 dinars to U.S. $1 (68.98 dinars = £1 sterling). Gold and other reserves (June 1981) U.S. $1,511,000,000. Budget (federal; 1980 est.) balanced at 132.3 billion dinars. Gross material product (1979) 1,165,000,000 dinars. Money supply (May 1981) 515.5 billion dinars. Cost of living (1975 = 100; June 1981) 320.1.

Foreign Trade. (1980) Imports 376.3 billion dinars; exports 226.7 billion dinars. Import sources: U.S.S.R. 18%; West Germany 17%; Italy 7%; U.S. 7%; Iraq 6%. Export destinations: U.S.S.R. 28%; Italy 9%; West Germany 9%; Czechoslovakia 5%. Main exports: machinery 18%; chemicals 11%; transport equipment 10%; food 9%; textiles and clothing 9%;

footwear 5%; nonferrous metals 5%. Tourism (1979): visitors 5,966,000; gross receipts U.S. $1 billion.

Transport and Communications. Roads (1979) 129,455 km (including 285 km expressways). Motor vehicles in use (1979): passenger 1,863,200; commercial 129,400. Railways: (1979) 9,381 km; traffic (1980) 10,274,000,000 passenger-km, freight 24,993,000,000 net ton-km. Air traffic (1980): c. 2,984,000,000 passenger-km; freight c. 41.7 million net ton-km. Shipping (1980): merchant vessels 100 gross tons and over 486; gross tonnage 2,466,574. Telephones (Dec. 1979) 1,913,000. Radio licenses (Dec. 1979) 4,634,000. Television licenses (Dec. 1979) 4,189,000.

Agriculture. Production (in 000; metric tons; 1980): wheat 5,078; barley c. 650; oats c. 295; corn 9,106; potatoes 2,387; sunflower seed c. 306; sugar, raw value c. 805; onions c. 280; tomatoes c. 470; cabbages (1979) c. 700; chilies and peppers (1979) c. 340; watermelons (1979) c. 575; plums (1979) c.

516; apples c. 447; wine c. 687; tobacco 56; beef and veal c. 347; pork c. 710; timber (cu m; 1979) c. 15,898. Livestock (in 000; Jan. 1980): cattle c. 5,436; sheep c. 7,354; pigs c. 7,502; horses c. 617; chickens c. 63,055.

Industry. Fuel and power (in 000; metric tons; 1980): coal 391; lignite 45,446; crude oil 4,224; natural gas (cu m) 1,820,000; manufactured gas (cu m; 1979) c. 240,000; electricity (kw-hr) 59,339,000. Production (in 000; metric tons; 1980): cement 9,315; iron ore (35% metal content) 4,539; pig iron 2,677; crude steel 2,437; magnesite (1979) 293; bauxite 3,111; aluminum 184; copper 131; lead 102; zinc 85; petroleum products c. 15,400; sulfuric acid 1,196; plastics and resins 434; cotton yarn 117; wool yarn 54; man-made fibres (1978) 101; wood pulp (1978) c. 610; newsprint 51; other paper (1979) c. 780; television receivers (units; 1979) 599; passenger cars (units; 1979) 187; commercial vehicles (units) 64. Merchant vessels launched (100 gross tons and over; 1980) 123,000 gross tons.

The first nuclear power plant in Yugoslavia began test operations in November. The plant is located in Krsko.

Relations with Bulgaria cooled during the year. According to the Yugoslavs, recent events indicated an indirect renewal of Bulgaria's past aspirations to the republic of Macedonia. In response, they canceled various traditional frontier meetings between local populations on both sides. On August 30 a Bulgarian national was shot and killed on the Yugoslav side of the border by Yugoslav border guards. The incident led to sharp recriminations, but relations subsequently improved, and in October Yugoslavia and Bulgaria signed several trade and cooperation agreements.

Yugoslavia's relations with Albania deteriorated

sharply in the wake of riots in Kosovo, the largely Albanian-inhabited autonomous province in the republic of Serbia bordering on Albania. In May senior Yugoslav representatives accused Albania of involvement in the riots. Albania repeatedly denied this but expressed its concern for Kosovo. Yugoslavia canceled all agreements for cultural and scientific exchanges, as well as the 1980 agreement to build a rail link connecting Albania with the European railway system. In November Albania accused Yugoslavia of jamming its television and radio broadcasts in order to prevent them from being received in Kosovo.

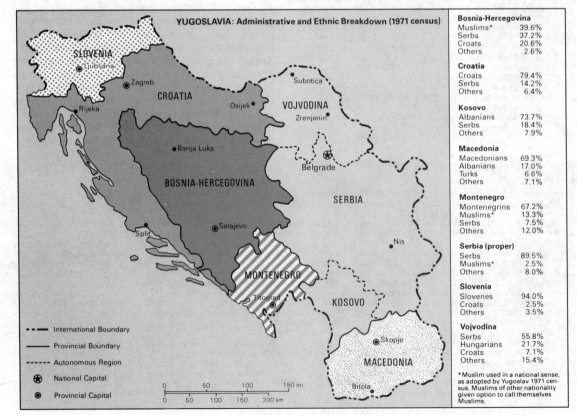

YUGOSLAVIA: Administrative and Ethnic Breakdown (1971 census)

| International Boundary |
| Provincial Boundary |
| Autonomous Region |
| National Capital |
| Provincial Capital |

Bosnia-Hercegovina
Muslims*	39.6%
Serbs	37.2%
Croats	20.6%
Others	2.6%

Croatia
Croats	79.4%
Serbs	14.2%
Others	6.4%

Kosovo
Albanians	73.7%
Serbs	18.4%
Others	7.9%

Macedonia
Macedonians	69.3%
Albanians	17.0%
Turks	6.6%
Others	7.1%

Montenegro
Montenegrins	67.2%
Muslims*	13.3%
Serbs	7.5%
Others	12.0%

Serbia (proper)
Serbs	89.5%
Muslims*	2.5%
Others	8.0%

Slovenia
Slovenes	94.0%
Croats	2.5%
Others	3.5%

Vojvodina
Serbs	55.8%
Hungarians	21.7%
Croats	7.1%
Others	15.4%

*Muslim used in a national sense, as adopted by Yugoslav 1971 census. Muslims of other nationality given option to call themselves Muslims.

Demonstrations broke out among the students of the University of Pristina, the capital of Kosovo, on March 11. Much larger demonstrations, involving students, school pupils, industrial workers, and farmers, occurred in the March-May period and were put down with the aid of police and army reinforcements. According to the Albanian press, tanks, armoured cars, and helicopters were also used. Official figures stated that 11 died and 57 were injured during one week of disturbances. Yugoslav authorities rejected the main demand of the demonstrators: that Kosovo be upgraded to the status of a federal republic.

On May 5 Mahmut Bakali, leader of the League of Communists in Kosovo, was dismissed, marking the start of a purge of the province's party officials, government, and university. Nearly 30 Kosovo Albanians were sentenced to prison terms of up to 15 years for their part in the spring disturbances. In November a special meeting of the League of Communists Central Committee heard that "enemy activity" in Kosovo continued.

In January several Roman Catholic bishops were accused of keeping alive the cult of Alojzije Cardinal Stepinac, who had been sentenced to 16 years' imprisonment in 1946. Croatian dissident Gen. Franjo Tudjman was sentenced to three years' imprisonment for publishing "hostile interviews" abroad. Vlado Gotovac, a Croatian poet, received a two-year sentence. Marko Veselica, a professor of economics, was sentenced to 11 years, and Gojko Djogo, a Serbian poet accused of having insulted Tito in his poetry, to two years.

In 1981 Yugoslavia's debt reached $20 billion; debt service charges were $2.5 billion, or 3% of national income. Yugoslav exports were 19% higher and imports 10% higher in the January–September 1981 period than in the corresponding period of 1980. For the first time in years, trade with the Council for Mutual Economic Assistance countries accounted for more than 50% of total Yugoslav external trade. Exports to the non-Communist world were 3% lower and imports 12% higher in January-September than in the same period of 1980. (K. F. CVIIC)

Zaire

A republic of equatorial Africa, Zaire is bounded by the Central African Republic, Sudan, Uganda, Rwanda, Burundi, Tanzania, Zambia, Angola, Congo, and the Atlantic Ocean. Area: 2,344,885 sq km (905,365 sq mi). Pop. (1980 est.): 28,291,000. Cap. and largest city: Kinshasa (pop., 1979 est., 2,242,300). Language: French; Bantu dialects. Religion: animist approximately 50%; Christian 43%. President in 1981, Mobutu Sese Seko; prime ministers, Nguza Karl-I-Bond and, from April 23, N'singa Udjuu.

The economic stabilization program launched in Zaire with the support of the International Monetary Fund (IMF) in 1980 began to show results in 1981. The government deficit for 1980 fell well within the limit permitted by the IMF, and inflation was reduced from 80 to 50%. The external debt remained at about $5 billion, however, and there

ZAIRE

Education. (1977–78) Primary, pupils 3,818,934, teachers (1972–73) 80,481; secondary, pupils c. 458,776; vocational, pupils c. 84,995; teacher training, students c. 99,904; secondary, vocational, and teacher training, teachers (1973–74) 14,483; higher, students (1974–75) 21,021, teaching staff 2,550.

Finance. Monetary unit: zaire, with (Sept. 21, 1981) a free rate of 5.42 zaires to U.S. $1 (10.04 zaires = £1 sterling). Gold and other reserves (June 1981) U.S. $76 million. Budget (1978 actual): revenue 740 million zaires; expenditure 1,506,000,000 zaires. Gross national product (1978) 5,336,000,000 zaires. Money supply (May 1981) 3,413,500,000 zaires. Cost of living (Kinshasa; 1975 = 100; May 1981) 1,685.

Foreign Trade. (1980) Imports 2,327,800,000 zaires; exports 4,553,800,000 zaires. Import sources: Belgium-Luxembourg c. 16%; West Germany c. 10%; U.S. c. 10%; South Africa c. 9%; France c. 8%; Brazil c. 7%; Zimbabwe c. 6%. Export destinations: Angola c. 22%; U.S. c. 13%; Mozambique c. 10%; India c. 9%; France c. 6%; Italy c. 5%; Belgium-Luxembourg c. 5%. Main exports: copper 43%; cobalt 21%; coffee 10%.

Transport and Communications. Roads (1979) c. 145,000 km. Motor vehicles in use (1979): passenger c. 94,200; commercial (including buses) c. 85,500. Railways: (1979) 5,254 km; traffic (1976) 467 million passenger-km, freight 2,203,000,000 net ton-km. Air traffic (1980): c. 834 million passenger-km; freight c. 34.9 million net ton-km. Shipping (1980): merchant vessels 100 gross tons and over 33; gross tonnage 91,894. Inland waterways (including Zaire River; 1980) c. 14,000 km. Telephones (Jan. 1980) 30,300. Radio receivers (Dec. 1977) 125,000. Television receivers (Dec. 1977) 8,000.

Agriculture. Production (in 000; metric tons; 1980): rice c. 230; corn c. 500; sweet potatoes (1979) c. 300; cassava (1979) c. 12,000; peanuts c. 323; palm kernels c. 74; palm oil c. 180; mangoes c. 174; pineapples c. 154; bananas c. 312; oranges c. 155; coffee c. 88; rubber c. 20; cotton, lint c. 17; meat (1979) c. 180; fish catch (1979) 115; timber (cu m; 1979) c. 10,009. Livestock (in 000; 1979): cattle c. 1,144; sheep c. 779; goats c. 2,783; pigs c. 753; poultry c. 12,411.

Industry. Production (in 000; metric tons; 1979): copper ore (metal content) 400; zinc ore (metal content) 73; manganese ore (metal content) 10; cobalt ore (metal content) 14; gold (troy oz) 73; silver (troy oz) 3,592; diamonds (metric carats) 11,225; crude oil (1980) 1,023; coal (1978) 105; petroleum products (1978) 183; sulfuric acid (1978) 138; cement (1978) 468; electricity (kw-hr; 1978) c. 3,957,000.

was still an acute shortage of foreign exchange. This threatened the effective maintenance of communications because the nation could not afford spare parts and technical assistance; this, in turn, adversely affected the transportation of the two main exchange earners, copper and cobalt.

Hopes of help from Western companies were at first tentative because expert opinion held that it would be some time before conditions were suitable for economic expansion. In June, however, the IMF authorized a loan of 912 million special drawing rights ($1,060,000,000), the largest to that date to any African country, to support economic adjustment during the period 1981–83. The object of the loan was to enable Zaire to reduce inflation still further and to improve the nation's balance of payments. As a first step, the currency was devalued. The Executive Council at first set aside $50 million and later $20 million more to pay for essential imports and raw materials and spare parts for industry and agriculture.

Romanian officials visiting Kinshasa promised to send technical assistance, tools, and seeds to revive the joint Zaire-Romanian agricultural company. Its main object was to teach the production of basic foodstuffs in the hope of reducing dependence on imported food. The Chinese deputy

Zaire

Zambia

minister for external cultural relations visited Zaire and discussed a cultural exchange program, while other visitors included members of a Soviet youth delegation. The election of Pres. François Mitterrand of France led Pres. Mobutu Sese Seko to call for a reappraisal of Franco-African relations.

While the prospect of external financial aid was in the balance, Sozacom, the state-controlled mineral marketing agency, opened negotiations with a number of companies with a view to selling diamonds outside the Central Selling Organization (cso) of the Anglo-South African diamond group De Beers. Discussions aimed at negotiating a new marketing agreement with De Beers broke down, and Zaire proceeded to sell independently to three European companies. In September the cso accepted defeat and closed its market in Tshikapa. One consequence of the new arrangement was that, because customers paid in cash immediately, the cash flow to Miba, the most important mine, improved. Encouraged by the experiment, Miba claimed that it would be able to double its output within a few years. This prospect depended upon the availability of financial aid to support plans for underground mining because the alluvial deposits were almost exhausted.

In February Mobutu reshuffled his Cabinet, bringing Bomboko Lokumba to the fore once again as state commissioner for foreign affairs and international cooperation and also as deputy prime minister; foreign minister in the 1960s, Bomboko had been accused after accusations of plotting against the president in the 1970s. In October, however, Mobutu dismissed Bomboko as part of another Cabinet reshuffle. In April Prime Minister Nguza Karl-I-Bond, while on a visit to Brussels, wrote to the president announcing his resignation. He also published a pamphlet calling on the people of Zaire to overthrow the president. Mobutu then threatened to break off diplomatic relations with Belgium if that country did not curb the subversive activities of Zairian exiles. Belgium responded by condemning the exiles' attacks on Mobutu and by summoning Nguza to the Ministry of Justice, where he was ordered to stop his political activities. Nguza, however, later insisted that he would continue to criticize the Zairian government and would be prepared to campaign as a candidate if elections were held. Nguza was succeeded as prime minister by N' singa Udjuu.

Some weeks later Zairian demonstrators surrounded President Mobutu's house in Brussels, protesting the release from a Belgian prison of the former governor of Shaba Province. Mobutu countered by suing the group for trespass and damage to property. Nguza attempted to enlist U.S. support for his campaign by releasing a document said to have been prepared by the Zairian Parliament and alleging misappropriation of over $150 million in funds by the president, but the attempt met with a rebuff when the U.S. Department of State reaffirmed its support for Mobutu. Belgian Minister of Foreign Affairs Charles-Ferdinand Nothomb visited Zaire in July; in a broadcast over Zaire Radio he stressed Belgium's desire for good relations with Zaire but at the same time emphasized his nation's commitments to freedom of speech.

In Zaire itself there was criticism of the government from Roman Catholic bishops, who published a document denouncing the decadence and misery that prevailed in the country and the corruption in courts, hospitals, and schools. They also cited cases of kidnapping, arbitrary arrests, and torture by officials.

External political relations were mainly directed toward the stabilization of the situation in Angola. In June the foreign minister called upon the U.S. not to resume aid to antigovernment forces in Angola because of the harmful consequences that internal disruption in Angola would have for Zaire.

(KENNETH INGHAM)

Zambia

A republic and a member of the Commonwealth, Zambia is bounded by Tanzania, Malawi, Mozambique, Zimbabwe, South West Africa/Namibia, Angola, and Zaire. Area: 752,614 sq km (290,586 sq mi). Pop. (1980 prelim.): 5,679,800, about 99% of whom are Africans. Cap. and largest city: Lusaka (pop., 1980 prelim., 538,500). Language: English and Bantu. Religion: predominantly animist, with Roman Catholic (21%), Protestant, Hindu, and Muslim minorities. President in 1981, Kenneth Kaunda; prime ministers, Daniel Lisulo and, from February 18, Nalumino Mundia.

The Zambian government's failure to meet economic targets caused increasing unrest during 1981. Against this background, the growing political strength of the trade union movement presented a serious challenge to the ruling United National Independence Party (UNIP). On January

ZAMBIA

Education. (1979) Primary, pupils 985,528, teachers (1977) 19,441; secondary (1978), pupils 88,842, teachers 3,669; vocational, pupils 5,284, teachers (1977) 510; teacher training, students (1978) 3,427, teachers (1977) 319; higher, students (1978) 3,773, teaching staff (1976) 412.

Finance. Monetary unit: kwacha, with (Sept. 21, 1981) a free rate of 0.87 kwacha to U.S. $1 (1.61 kwachas = £1 sterling). Gold and other reserves (June 1981) U.S. $69 million. Budget (1979 actual): revenue 596.9 million kwachas; expenditure 770.9 million kwachas. Gross domestic product (1979) 2,524,000,000 kwachas. Cost of living (1975 = 100; June 1981) 232.8.

Foreign Trade. (1979) Imports 595.4 million kwachas; exports 1,091,000,000 kwachas. Import sources: U.K. 26%; Saudi Arabia c. 18%; South Africa 11%; U.S. 9%; West Germany 8%. Export destinations: Japan 19%; France c. 15%; U.K. 13%; U.S. 10%; West Germany 9%; Italy c. 8%; India 6%. Main export: copper 83%.

Transport and Communications. Roads (1979) 36,415 km. Motor vehicles in use (1979): passenger c. 103,500; commercial (including buses) c. 65,500. Railways (1980) 2,189 km (including 892 km of the 1,870-km Tanzam railway). Air traffic (1980): 467 million passenger-km; freight 47.5 million net ton-km. Telephones (Jan. 1980) 60,500. Radio receivers (Dec. 1978) c. 125,000. Television receivers (Dec. 1978) c. 60,000.

Agriculture. Production (in 000; metric tons; 1980): corn c. 800; cassava (1979) c. 175; millet c. 60; sorghum c. 35; peanuts c. 80; sugar, raw value (1979) c. 105; tobacco c. 5. Livestock (in 000; 1979): cattle c. 1,800; sheep c. 51; goats c. 300; pigs c. 180; poultry c. 14,000.

Industry. Production (in 000; metric tons; 1979): coal 599; copper ore (metal content; 1980) 736; lead ore (metal content; 1980) 12; zinc ore (metal content; 1980) 37; petroleum products (1978) c. 850; cement 300; electricity (kw-hr) 8,770,000.

20 copper-belt miners began an eight-day strike in protest against the expulsion of 17 trade-union leaders from UNIP for allegedly meddling in politics. Another strike of copper workers broke out while the president was paying a state visit to Zimbabwe in July. Four senior trade unionists and a businessman were arrested for inciting illegal strikes; in October one trade unionist was released, and a truce was reached between the unions and the government.

In February Pres. Kenneth Kaunda promoted Humphrey Mulemba to the post of secretary-general of UNIP, the second most important office in the country, and Nalumino Mundia replaced Daniel Lisulo as prime minister. In June security police uncovered a plot against Kaunda with the backing, it was claimed, of South African mercenaries.

(KENNETH INGHAM)

Zimbabwe

A republic in eastern Africa and member of the Commonwealth, Zimbabwe is bounded by Zambia, Mozambique, South Africa, and Botswana. Area: 390,759 sq km (150,873 sq mi). Pop. (1981 est.): 7.6 million, of whom 96% are African and 4% white. Cap. and largest city: Salisbury (urban area pop., 1980 est., 654,000). Language: English (official) and various Bantu languages (1969 census, Shona 71%, Ndebele 15%). Religion: predominantly traditional tribal beliefs; Christian minority. President in 1981, the Rev. Canaan Banana; prime minister, Robert Mugabe.

In spite of tension among political parties, both black and white, and intermittent strained relations with South Africa, during 1981 the government maintained its objectives of uniting Zimbabwe and of expanding the economy. In February control of the country's five main newspapers, previously in the hands of South African interests, was taken over by the Zimbabwe Mass Media Trust. The government said that it was committed to freedom of the press and considered that South African control was an infringement of Zimbabwean independence and had been responsible for misrepresentations in the press. At the end of June the takeover was completed by the creation of the Zimbabwe Inter-Africa News Agency. During the year Prime Minister Robert Mugabe announced his wish to introduce a one-party state "when the people give their consent."

Joshua Nkomo, leader of the Patriotic Front's Zimbabwe African People's Union (ZAPU [PF]) and at the time minister of home affairs, attacked the decision to transfer control of the press to the trust when it was first announced in January, claiming that it would make the press the mouthpiece of Mugabe's Patriotic Front party, the Zimbabwe African National Union (ZANU [PF]). Only a few days later, on January 10, Nkomo was demoted and offered the post of public service minister in a Cabinet reshuffle. At the same time, Edgar Tekere, minister of manpower planning and development, was dropped; Tekere, acquitted a month earlier on a charge of murdering a farm manager, retained the important office of secretary-general

of ZANU (PF) until August, when he was dismissed for constant criticism of the government. Nkomo, meantime, protested his demotion and finally agreed to become minister without portfolio with special responsibilities regarding security matters.

Against this background of uncertainty about Nkomo's future, there were clashes early in February between different factions of the Zimbabwe Army stationed near Bulawayo and near Gwelo. The fighting soon involved as yet undisbanded guerrillas in the vicinity of Bulawayo, and it was several days before Nkomo was able to persuade those of his Zimbabwe People's Revolutionary Army (Zipra) followers who had taken part to lay down their arms; by that time more than 200 people had lost their lives. The fighting was a reflection of the difficulties experienced in integrating former guerrillas of the Zipra and the Zimbabwe African National Liberation Army sections of the Patriotic Front into a united national force.

Meanwhile, on February 17 a plan was set in motion to disarm the guerrillas. Zipra members, however, feared that any such action would weaken Nkomo's authority and enhance the power of Mugabe's party. Nonetheless, the campaign to disarm the guerrillas was successfully completed in May. About one-fifth of Zimbabwe's budget was devoted to the maintenance of the armed forces; in June, therefore, it was decided to halve the size of the Army by providing incentives to soldiers to return to civilian life.

Progress was made on a number of other fronts, though not without setbacks. By the beginning of February the drive to make secondary education

Zimbabwe

Prime Minister Robert Mugabe of Zimbabwe made his first official visit to Europe in September and met with the press in Copenhagen.

WIDE WORLD

ZIMBABWE

Education. (1981) Primary, pupils 1,235,994, teachers 33,516; secondary, pupils 74,321, teachers 4,110; vocational (including part-time), pupils 6,048, teachers (1979) 278; teacher training, students 3,484, teachers (1979) 258; higher (1979), students 4,563, teaching staff 483.

Finance. Monetary unit: Zimbabwe dollar, with (Sept. 21, 1981) a free rate of Z$0.71 to U.S. $1 (Z$1.31 = £1 sterling). Budget (1980–81 est.): revenue Z$863 million; expenditure Z$1,227,000,000. Gross national product (1979) Z$2,583,000,000.

Foreign Trade. (1980) Imports Z$811.9 million; exports Z$898.5 million. Import sources (1965): U.K. 30%; South Africa 23%; U.S. 7%; Japan 6%. Export destinations (1965): Zambia 25%; U.K. 22%; South Africa 10%; West Germany 9%; Malawi 5%; Japan 5%. Main exports (1978): food 17%; tobacco 17%; iron and steel 12%; asbestos 9%; gold 8%; cotton 7%; nickel 6%.

Transport and Communications. Roads (1979) c. 80,-000 km. Motor vehicles in use (1979): passenger c. 175,-000; commercial (including buses) c. 70,000. Railways: (1979) 3,470 km; freight traffic (1980) 5,842,000,000 net ton-km. Telephones (June 1980) 214,400. Radio licenses (June 1980) 214,400. Television licenses (June 1980) 74,-300.

Agriculture. Production (in 000; metric tons; 1980): corn c. 1,600; millet c. 180; wheat (1979) c. 100; sugar, raw value c. 300; peanuts c. 84; tobacco 114; cotton, lint c. 61; beef and veal (1979) c. 125. Livestock (in 000; 1979): cattle c. 5,000; sheep c. 754; goats c. 2,061; pigs c. 218.

Industry. Production (in 000; metric tons; 1980): coal 3,134; cement 460; asbestos (1979) 260; chrome ore (1979) 542; iron ore (metal content) 1,622; tin concentrates (metal content) 0.9; nickel ore (metal content; 1979) 15; gold (troy oz) 367; electricity (kw-hr) 4,542,000.

more widely available was under way. Teachers were recruited in Britain and Australia, and programs of internal training for local teachers were started. Late in February Bernard Chidzero, minister of economic planning, announced a new economic program, which, it was hoped, would lead to the establishment of an egalitarian and socialist society under democratic conditions. The policy envisioned an investment of $4 billion within a three-year period; one major aim was the resettlement of black peasant farmers on land acquired from European owners. The government also intended to become involved in major industries—particularly mining—to an extent to be determined by mutual agreement between the government and the present owners and in the light of national priorities.

In March a conference on reconstruction and development took place in Salisbury. It was attended by delegates from 45 countries who were asked by Mugabe to contribute $1.2 billion toward the rehabilitation of Zimbabwe. About 70% of this amount was offered during the conference, and among those countries that responded were Britain, the U.S., Canada, West Germany, France, Sweden, Australia, Norway, and Denmark, together with the World Bank and UN Development Program. Notable absentees were the Communist countries of Eastern Europe, though later in the year North Korea provided equipment and military advisers for the Army. In May Mugabe visited China for discussions on South African relations and Soviet influence in Africa. He also traveled to Japan, India, and Pakistan. In August it was agreed that China would cooperate with Zimbabwe in a number of joint ventures in mining, agriculture, and light industry.

Zimbabwe's second budget since independence was made public in July when Finance Minister Enos Nkala announced sharp increases in taxes on gasoline and on all foods except milk, meat, and bread. His aim was to increase government spending by 37%.

At the beginning of March it was recognized that there would be a record corn crop, the result of timely rainfall and the encouragement given by the government to farmers to grow corn after Zimbabwe had been forced to import some of the country's staple food crop from South Africa in 1980. The government increased the price offered to growers from Z$85 to Z$120 per metric ton. The cost to consumers, however, was held at Z$60 per ton, involving the government in the payment of considerable subsidies to the growers. The tobacco crop was the best since 1965.

The success of the farmers was, however, offset by the difficulty experienced in exporting corn and tobacco. This was mainly due to a shortage of railway locomotives, a situation made more acute in March by South Africa's withdrawal of 24 locomotives that had been operating in Zimbabwe. They were returned in November, but in the meantime supplies of corn that could have found a ready market in the famine-stricken areas of Somalia, Uganda, and Kenya were held up until assistance came from Mozambique and Botswana.

South Africa struck a further blow to Zimbabwe by scrapping the preferential trade agreement between the two countries. In July the supply of diesel fuel to retailers was cut by one-fifth owing to delays in transport through South Africa. This, in turn, seriously disrupted the activities of farmers, and the government set as its target the achievement of independence from oil imports through South Africa by the end of the year. In August the South African government ordered the expulsion of all Zimbabwean workers who had arrived in the country since 1958. This was the result, in part, of South Africa's own unemployment problem but also of its government's hostility toward Mugabe. The prime minister frankly admitted that because of his country's economic dependence upon South Africa, it would be impossible to take part in any scheme of economic sanctions against the republic. In December, reacting to a bomb attack on the ZANU (PF) headquarters in Salisbury in which at least six persons died, Mugabe announced that his government might be forced to harden its attitude toward dissident whites.　　　　(KENNETH INGHAM)

See also Feature Article: *Struggling for Nationhood: The Birth of Zimbabwe.*

Zoology:
see Life Sciences

Zoos and Botanical Gardens

Zoos. During 1981 some of the legislation needed to curb the accelerating rate of extinction among the world's animal and plant species and reduce the destruction of habitats was promulgated, including a number of international and national laws relating to the keeping of animals in captivi-

Chia-Chia, a giant panda, whom it was hoped would mate with Ling-Ling, a female panda at the National Zoo, Washington, D.C., returned home to the London Zoo in June. The sign that greeted him indicated that he had tried but failed.

ty. At the third conference of the parties to the Convention on International Trade in Endangered Species of Wild Fauna and Flora, which met in New Delhi, India, during February 25–March 8, 50 of the 67 signatory countries, 8 international groups, 10 nonmember countries, and 72 nongovernmental organizations were represented, and many controversial issues were debated. Included in the important decisions of particular relevance to zoos were: the adoption of guidelines for the more humane transportation of live animals; a possible acceptable definition of ranching operations; and the production of forgery-proof documents to accompany shipments of wildlife and its products.

In the U.S. important amendments to the Lacey Act were proposed to reduce deliberate violations of foreign and domestic wildlife laws. In Britain Parliament enacted legislation, which, for the first time, made compulsory the licensing of all zoos; the granting of licenses was dependent on regular inspections. In the U.S.S.R. a new law on "the protection and utilization of the animal world" came into effect in January. It contained the important provision that, "If an international treaty to which the U.S.S.R. is a party establishes rules other than those contained in Soviet legislation on the protection and utilization of the animal world, the rules of the international treaty shall apply."

The ups and downs of the married lives of giant pandas once again made the headlines. It was announced from Beijing (Peking) that, following artificial insemination, twin pandas were born in September, though only one survived. A cub was born in Chapultepec Park Zoo, Mexico City, and,

for the first time outside China, was progressing well and being reared by the mother. In Washington, D.C., a much-publicized arranged marriage between the visiting male from the London Zoo and the resident female ended without the hoped-for consummation. Artificial insemination of London Zoo's female panda, Ching Ching, failed to induce pregnancy.

Throughout the world more and more emphasis was being given in zoos to long-term breeding programs and to manipulative techniques in reproduction. In Memphis, Tenn., the first successful artificial insemination of a gorilla resulted in a birth; though the baby gorilla died after only a few days, it was still probably the only primate other than man to be conceived using frozen semen. In New York important progress was reported when four embryos of gaur (*Bos gaurus*, the Indian wild ox) were transferred to domestic cows. One embryo survived full term, and the resultant calf was being reared by the host parent.

Noteworthy births included second-generation Toco toucans, bred at San Antonio (Texas) Zoo; the first emperor penguins born in captivity, in Sea World, San Diego, Calif.; a second birth of a freshwater dolphin in Jaya Ancol Oceanarium, Jakarta, Indonesia; 24 gharials (*Gavialis gangeticus*) hatched in Nandakana Biological Park, Orissa, India, after a male was loaned from Frankfurt (West Germany) Zoo.

The total population of the Przewalski horse in 1981 was only about 330, all in captivity in about 70 collections. Until 1981 no wild horses had been seen since 1968, but a report from China suggested that small numbers might still be found in the northern region of Xinjiang Uygur (Sinkiang Uighur). This raised the exciting possibility of new blood being found for the inbred captive population. Certainly cooperation was needed to reduce the problems of inbreeding, and a welcome example was given when three mares from San Diego, Calif., were sent in May to rendezvous with a stallion in Prague, Czech. It was hoped that the mares would be impregnated before their return to California. (P. J. OLNEY)

The new Alpine House at the Royal Botanic Gardens at Kew was officially opened in April.

The Mombasa pavilion, which features an African atmosphere, was opened to the public at the San Diego Wild Animal Park in February. The pavilion provides dining facilities for 325 people.

Botanical Gardens. The International Association of Botanic Gardens held its ninth general meeting and conference in Sydney, Australia, during August 1981. The various papers presented indicated a growing preoccupation with the problems of nature conservation.

Worldwide efforts to protect threatened plant species were spearheaded by the Threatened Plants Committee (TPC) of the International Union for Conservation of Nature and Natural Resources. The TPC's secretariat, based at the Royal Botanic Gardens, Kew, England, reported that botanical gardens throughout the world were seeking membership in the Botanic Garden Conservation Coordinating Body, indicating their awareness of the increasing importance of collaboration among establishments in different regions.

An essential need had improved proceedings for the international exchange of seeds and plants, with greater exploitation of the possibilities offered by electronic data processing in collating the necessary information. Particularly pressing problems calling for further research were the long-term storage of seeds and the cultivation of wild orchids from seed. The existing stock of naturally occurring plants in all continents and countries had to be assessed so that it could be determined which species were most threatened; then it could be ascertained which threatened species were already held in collections, with a likelihood of survival. It was considered important that botanical gardens should in the future give special attention to the species to be found in their own regions. At a meeting of environmental authorities and botanical garden heads in Bad Windsheim, West Germany, agreement was reached and procedures were established for the possible transference of threatened species to suitable new habitats.

While botanical gardens possessed considerable expertise in the cultivation of rare plants, collaboration in concerted moves toward conservation would tax their resources considerably. Probably only the larger, better equipped establishments with adequate personnel would be able to make an effective contribution. Many of the smaller, less up-to-date gardens already had pressing day-to-day problems to contend with, lack of adequate space and insufficient funds being the most common. Meanwhile, the plundering of natural resources was rising to dangerous levels everywhere. With these considerations in mind, there arose the idea of centralizing comprehensive protective collections in climatically favourable areas where saving energy would not be a primary consideration. For example, in the Mediterranean region and in the Canary Islands there were ideal locations for such projects.

At the Royal Botanic Gardens at Kew the new Alpine House was officially opened in April 1981. This remarkable greenhouse, 14 m (46 ft) square, had a pyramidal roof and was unusually well ventilated, being surrounded by a water channel to increase humidity. A refrigerated central bench enabled the cultivation of varieties of high mountain plants that require cool rooting conditions.

(JOHANNES APEL)

See also Environment; Gardening.
[355.C.6]

CONTRIBUTORS

Names of contributors to the Britannica Book of the Year *with the articles written by them.*
The arrangement is alphabetical by last name.

AARSDAL, STENER. Economic and Political Journalist, *Borsen,* Copenhagen.
Denmark

ADAMS, ANDREW M. Free-lance Foreign Correspondent; Editor and Publisher, *Sumo World* magazine. Author of *Ninja: The Invisible Assassins; Born to Die: The Cherry Blossom Squadrons.* Co-author of *Sumo History and Yokozuna Profiles; Japan Sports Guide.*
Combat Sports: *Judo; Karate; Kendo; Sumo*

AGRELLA, JOSEPH C. Correspondent, *Blood-Horse* magazine; former Turf Editor, *Chicago Sun-Times.* Co-author of *Ten Commandments for Professional Handicapping; American Race Horses.*
Equestrian Sports: *Thoroughbred Racing and Steeplechasing (in part)*

AIELLO, LESLIE C. Lecturer, Department of Anthropology, University College, London.
Anthropology

ALLABY, MICHAEL. Free-lance Writer and Lecturer. Author of *The Eco-Activists; Who Will Eat?; Inventing Tomorrow; World Food Resources.* Co-author of *A Blueprint for Survival; Home Farm.* Editor of *The Survival Handbook; Dictionary of the Environment.*
Environment *(in part)*

ALLAN, J. A. Lecturer in Geography, School of Oriental and African Studies, University of London.
Biographies *(in part);* **Libya**

ALSTON, REX. Broadcaster and Journalist; retired BBC Commentator. Author of *Taking the Air; Over to Rex Alston; Test Commentary; Watching Cricket.*
Biographies *(in part);* **Cricket**

ANDERSON, PETER J. Assistant Director, Institute of Polar Studies, Ohio State University, Columbus.
Antarctic

APEL, JOHANNES. Curator, Botanic Garden, University of Hamburg. Author of *Gärtnerisch-Botanische Briefe.*
Zoos and Botanical Gardens: *Botanical Gardens*

ARCHIBALD, JOHN J. Feature Writer, *St. Louis Post-Dispatch.* Author of *Bowling for Boys and Girls.*
Bowling: *Tenpin Bowling (in part); Duckpins*

ARNOLD, GUY. Free-lance Writer. Author of *Modern Nigeria; Kenyatta and the Politics of Kenya; The Last Bunker; Britain's Oil; Aid in Africa.*
Botswana: Burundi; Cape Verde; Equatorial Guinea; Gambia, The; Ghana; Guinea-Bissau; Lesotho; Liberia; Maldives; Mauritius; Rwanda; São Tomé and Príncipe; Seychelles; Sierra Leone; Swaziland

ARNOLD, MAVIS. Free-lance Journalist, Dublin.
Biographies *(in part);* **Ireland**

ARRINGTON, LEONARD J. Church Historian, Church of Jesus Christ of Latter-day Saints. Author of *Great Basin Kingdom; An Economic History of the Latter-day Saints; Building the City of God: Community and Cooperation Among the Mormons; The Mormon Experience: A History of the Latter-day Saints.*
Religion: *Church of Jesus Christ of Latter-day Saints*

AYTON, CYRIL J. Editor, *Motorcycle Sport,* London.
Motor Sports: *Motorcycles*

BAPTIST, INES T. Administrative Assistant, Encyclopædia Britannica, Yearbooks.
Belize

BARFORD, MICHAEL F. Editor and Director, *World Tobacco,* London.
Industrial Review: *Tobacco*

BARGAD, WARREN. Milton D. Ratner Professor of Hebrew Literature and Dean, Spertus College of Judaica, Chicago. Author of *Hayim Hazaz: Novelist of Ideas; Anthology of Israeli Poetry.*
Literature: *Hebrew*

BASS, HOWARD. Journalist and Broadcaster. Editor, *Winter Sports,* 1948–69. Winter Sports Correspondent, *Daily Telegraph* and *Sunday Telegraph,* London; *Evening Standard,* London; *Toronto Star,* Toronto; *Canadian Skater,* Ottawa; *Skating,* Boston; *Ski Racing,* Denver; *Ski,* London. Author of *The Sense in Sport; The Magic of Skiing; International Encyclopaedia of Winter Sports; Let's Go Skating.* Co-author of *Skating for Gold.*
Ice Hockey: *European and International;* **Winter Sports**

BAYLISS, DAVID. Chief Transport Planner, Greater London Council. Co-author of *Developing Patterns of Urbanization; Uses of Economics.* Advisory Editor of *Models in Urban and Regional Planning.*
Transportation *(in part)*

BEALL, JOHN V. Sales Manager, Davy McKee Corp. Author of sections 1 and 34, *Mining Engineering Handbook.* Frequent Contributor to *Mining Engineering.*
Mining and Quarrying *(in part)*

BEATTIE, ROGER A. Member of Secretariat, International Social Security Association, Geneva.
Social Security and Welfare Services *(in part)*

BEATTY, JAMES R. Research Fellow, B. F. Goodrich Research and Development Center, Brecksville, Ohio. Co-author of *Concepts in Compounding; Physical Testing of Elastomers and Polymers in Applied Polymer Science.*
Industrial Review: *Rubber*

BECKWITH, DAVID C. National Economic Correspondent, *Time* magazine, Washington, D.C.
United States Statistical Supplement: *Developments in the States in 1981*

BEEK, JAMES. Editorial Director, American Forest Institute.
Industrial Review: *Wood Products*

BENTLEY, STUART. Principal Lecturer in Sociology, Sheffield City Polytechnic, England. Co-author of *Work, Race, and Immigration.*
Migration, International; Race Relations

BERGERRE, MAX. Vatican Affairs Correspondent, *La Vie Catholique,* Paris.
Vatican City State

BERKOVITCH, ISRAEL. Free-lance Writer and Consultant. Author of *Coal on the Switchback; Coal: Energy and Chemical Storehouse.*
Energy: *Coal*

BICKELHAUPT, DAVID L. Professor of Insurance and Finance, College of Administrative Science, Ohio State University, Columbus. Author of *Transition to Multiple-Line Insurance Companies; General Insurance* (10th ed.).
Industrial Review: *Insurance*

BILEFIELD, LIONEL. Technical Journalist.
Industrial Review: *Paints and Varnishes*

BIRD, THOMAS E. Assistant Director, Yiddish Program, Queens College, City University of New York; Chairman, Yiddish Section, Modern Language Association of America. Contributor to *Lexicon of Modern Yiddish Literature.*
Literature: *Yiddish (in part)*

BLACKBURN, LUCY. Economist, Group Economics Department, Lloyds Bank Ltd., London.
Biographies *(in part);* **Chile; Costa Rica; El Salvador; Guatemala; Honduras**

BLUMENTHAL, MARCIA A. Senior Editor, Computer Industry, *Computerworld.*
Computers

BODDY, WILLIAM C. Editor, *Motor Sport.* Full Member, Guild of Motoring Writers. Author of *The History of Brooklands Motor Course; The World's Land Speed Record; Continental Sports Cars; The Bugatti Story; History of Montlhéry.*
Motor Sports: *Grand Prix Racing; Rallies and Other Races*

BODEN, EDWARD. Editor, *The Veterinary Record;* Executive Editor, *Research in Veterinary Science.*
Veterinary Science

BOLT, PETER H. Secretary, British Committee, World Methodist Council. Author of *A Way of Loving.*
Religion: *Methodist Churches*

BOLTZ, C. L. Free-lance Industrial Writer, London.
Energy: *Electricity*

BOONSTRA, DICK. Assistant Professor, Department of Political Science, Free University, Amsterdam.
Netherlands, The; Suriname

BOOTH, JOHN NICHOLLS. Lecturer and Writer; Co-founder, Japan Free Religious Association; Senior Pastor of a number of U.S. churches. Author of *The Quest for Preaching Power; Introducing Unitarian Universalism.*
Religion: *Unitarian (Universalist) Churches*

BOSWALL, JEFFERY. Producer of Sound and Television Programs, BBC Natural History Unit, Bristol, England.
Life Sciences: *Ornithology*

BOTHELL, JOAN N. Free-lance Writer and Editor; former Staff Writer, Encyclopædia Britannica.
Biographies (*in part*)

BOWDEN, RUSSELL. Deputy Secretary-General, Library Association, U.K.
Libraries (*in part*)

BOX, JOHN B. H. Free-lance Writer and Researcher on Latin America and Iberia.
Colombia; Mexico

BOYLE, C. L. Lieutenant Colonel, R.A. (retired). Chairman, Survival Service Commission, International Union for Conservation of Nature and Natural Resources, 1958–63; Secretary, Fauna Preservation Society, London, 1950–63.
Environment (*in part*)

BRACKMAN, ARNOLD C. Asian Affairs Specialist. Author of *Indonesian Communism: A History; Southeast Asia's Second Front: The Power Struggle in the Malay Archipelago; The Communist Collapse in Indonesia; The Last Emperor.*
Indonesia

BRADSHER, HENRY S. Foreign Affairs Writer.
Philippines

BRAIDWOOD, ROBERT J. Professor Emeritus of Old World Prehistory, the Oriental Institute and the Department of Anthropology, University of Chicago. Author of *Prehistoric Men; Archeologists and What They Do.*
Archaeology: *Eastern Hemisphere*

BRAZEE, RUTLAGE J. Manager of Engineering Seismology, Alexandria Laboratories, Teledyne Geotech, Alexandria, Va.
Earth Sciences: *Geophysics*

BRECHER, KENNETH. Professor of Astronomy and Physics, Boston University. Co-author and co-editor of *Astronomy of the Ancients; High Energy Astrophysics and Its Relation to Elementary Particle Physics.*
Astronomy

BRITTAIN, VICTORIA. Formerly East African Correspondent, *The Guardian;* presently with the paper's foreign department.
African Affairs: *Special Report* (*in part*)

BRITTAN, SAMUEL. Assistant Editor and Chief Economic Columnist, *Financial Times,* London. Author of *How to End the Monetarist Controversy; Capitalism and the Permissive Society.*
Feature Article: *Monetarism — Neither Kill Nor Cure*

BRUNO, HAL. Director of Political Coverage, ABC News, Washington, D.C.
Biographies (*in part*)

BURDIN, JOEL L. Professor of Educational Administration, Ohio University, Athens, Ohio. Co-author of *A Reader's Guide to the Comprehensive Models for Pre-*paring Elementary Teachers; Elementary School Curriculum and Instruction.*
Education (*in part*)

BURKE, DONALD P. Executive Editor, *Chemical Week,* New York City.
Industrial Review: *Chemicals*

BURKE, JEFFREY. Former Book Columnist, *Harper's Magazine;* Contributor, *New York Times Book Review.*
Literature: *United States*

BURKS, ARDATH W. Emeritus Professor of Asian Studies, Rutgers University, New Brunswick, N.J. Author of *The Government of Japan; East Asia: China, Korea, Japan; Japan: Portrait of a Postindustrial Power.*
Japan

BUSS, ROBIN. Lecturer in French, Woolwich College of Further Education, London.
Literature: *French* (*in part*)

BUTLER, FRANK. Sports Editor, *News of the World,* London. Author of *A History of Boxing in Britain.*
Combat Sports: *Boxing*

CALHOUN, DAVID R. Editor, Encyclopædia Britannica, Yearbooks.
Gambling (*in part*)

CAMERON, SARAH. Economist, Group Economics Department, Lloyds Bank Ltd., London.
Dominican Republic; Ecuador; Peru; Venezuela

CARTER, ROBERT W. Free-lance Journalist, London. Author of numerous newspaper and magazine articles.
Equestrian Sports: *Thoroughbred Racing and Steeplechasing* (*in part*)

CASSIDY, RICHARD J. Senior Public Relations Officer, British Gas Corporation. Author of *Gas: Natural Energy.*
Energy: *Natural Gas*

CASSIDY, VICTOR M. Senior Editor, *Specifying Engineer* magazine, Chicago.
Biographies (*in part*)

CATER, S. DOUGLASS, JR. Senior Fellow, Aspen Institute for Humanistic Studies, Washington, D.C. Author of *The Fourth Branch of Government; Power in Washington.*
Feature Article: *Letter from Washington*

CHAPMAN, KENNETH F. Former Editor, *Stamp Collecting* and *Philatelic Magazine;* Philatelic Correspondent, *The Times,* London. Author of *Good Stamp Collecting; Commonwealth Stamp Collecting.*
Philately and Numismatics: *Stamps*

CHAPMAN, ROBIN. Senior Economist, Group Economics Department, Lloyds Bank Ltd., London.
Cuba; Haiti; Latin-American Affairs

CHAPPELL, DUNCAN. Professor, Department of Criminology, Simon Fraser University, Vancouver, B.C. Co-author of *The Police and the Public in Australia and New Zealand.* Co-editor of *The Australian Criminal Justice System* (1st and 2nd ed.); *Violence and Criminal Justice; Forcible Rape: the Crime, the Victim and the Offender.*
Crime and Law Enforcement

CHEESERIGHT, PAUL. World Trade Editor, *Financial Times,* London.
Economy, World: *Special Report*

CHU, HUNG-TI. Expert in Far Eastern Affairs; Former International Civil Servant and University Professor.
China; Taiwan

CHUPRININ, SERGEY. Journalist, Novosti Press Agency, Moscow.
Literature: *Russian* (*in part*)

CLARKE, R. O. Principal Administrator, Social Affairs and Industrial Relations Division, Organization for Economic Cooperation and Development, Paris.
Industrial Relations

CLEVELAND, WILLIAM A. Geography Editor, *Encyclopædia Britannica* and Britannica Yearbooks.
Mining and Quarrying (*in part*)

CLIFTON, DONALD F. Professor of Metallurgy, University of Idaho.
Materials Sciences: *Metallurgy*

CLOUD, STANLEY W. Free-lance Writer; formerly Managing Editor, *Washington* (D.C.) *Star.*
Biographies (*in part*)

COGLE, T. C. J. Editor, *Electrical Review,* London.
Industrial Review: *Electrical*

COHN, ANNE HARRIS. Executive Director, National Committee for Prevention of Child Abuse, Chicago. Author of *An Approach to Preventing Child Abuse.*
Social Security and Welfare Services: *Special Report*

COMBA, ALDO. Executive Secretary, Department of Cooperation and Witness, World Alliance of Reformed Churches; former President, Federation of Protestant Churches in Italy. Author of *Le Parabole di Gesù.*
Religion: *Presbyterian, Reformed, and Congregational Churches*

COPPOCK, CHARLES DENNIS. Vice-President, English Lacrosse Union. Author of "Men's Lacrosse" in *The Oxford Companion to Sports and Games.*
Field Hockey and Lacrosse: *Lacrosse* (*in part*)

COSTIN, STANLEY H. British Correspondent, *Herrenjournal International* and *Men's Wear, Australasia.* Council of Management Member, British Men's Fashion Association Ltd. Former President, Men's Fashion Writers International.
Fashion and Dress (*in part*)

CRATER, RUFUS W. Chief Correspondent, *Broadcasting,* New York City.
Television and Radio (*in part*)

CROSS, COLIN J. Editor, *The Polo Times;* U.K. Chairman, European Polo Academy.
Equestrian Sports: *Polo*

CROSSLAND, NORMAN. Bonn Correspondent, *The Economist.*
Biographies (*in part*); **German Democratic Republic; Germany, Federal Republic of**

CVIIC, K. F. Leader Writer and East European Specialist, *The Economist,* London.
Spain (*sidebar*); **Yugoslavia**

DAVID, ANDREW. Author of several books and numerous articles on contemporary affairs.
Football: *Special Report*

DAVID, TUDOR. Managing Editor, *Education,* London.
Education (*in part*)

DAVIS, DONALD A. Editor, *Drug & Cosmetic Industry* and *Cosmetic Insider's Report*, New York City. Contributor to *The Science and Technology of Aerosol Packaging; Advances in Cosmetic Technology.*
Industrial Review: *Pharmaceuticals*

DAVIS, KENNETH C. Free-lance Writer, currently at work on a history of the paperback in America.
Publishing: *Books (in part)*

DEAM, JOHN B. Technical Director, National Machine Tool Builders Association, McLean, Va. Author of *The Synthesis of Common Digital Subsystems.*
Industrial Review: *Machinery and Machine Tools*

d'EÇA, RAUL. Retired from foreign service with U.S. Information Service. Co-author of *Latin American History.*
Brazil

de COSTA, RENÉ. Professor of Spanish Literature, University of Chicago. Author of *The Poetry of Pablo Neruda; En pos de Huidobro.*
Literature: *Spanish (in part)*

DECRAENE, PHILIPPE. Member of editorial staff, *Le Monde,* Paris. Former Editor in Chief, *Revue française d'Études politiques africaines.* Author of *Le Panafricanisme; Tableau des Partis Politiques Africains; Lettres de l'Afrique Atlantique; L'expérience socialiste Somalienne; Le Mali.*
Benin; Biographies (in part); **Cameroon; Central African Republic; Chad; Comoros; Congo; Dependent States** (in part); **Djibouti; Gabon; Guinea; Ivory Coast; Madagascar; Mali; Mauritania; Niger; Senegal; Togo; Tunisia; Upper Volta**

de FAINBOIM, MARTA BEKERMAN. Economist, Group Economics Department, Lloyds Bank Ltd., London.
Nicaragua; Paraguay

de la BARRE, KENNETH. Director, Katimavik, Montreal.
Arctic Regions

DENSELOW, ROBIN. Rock Music Critic, *The Guardian,* London; Current Affairs Producer, BBC Television. Co-author of *The Electric Muse.*
Music: *Popular*

DE PUY, NORMAN R. Minister, First Baptist Church, Newton Centre, Mass.; Columnist, *American Baptist* magazine. Author of *The Bible Alive; Help in Understanding Theology.*
Religion: *Baptist Churches*

DESHAYES-CREUILLY, MARIE-JOSE. Head of Documentation Services, International Vine and Wine Office, Paris.
Industrial Review: *Alcoholic Beverages (in part)*

DIRNBACHER, ELFRIEDE. Austrian Civil Servant.
Austria

DORRIS, TOM. Editor, Ecumenical Press Service, Geneva. Author of several periodical articles on religion, education, and medicine.
Religion: *Lutheran Churches*

DRAKE, CHRIS. Managing Director, MEMO: Middle East Media Operations, Nicosia, Cyprus.
Cyprus

EIU. The Economist Intelligence Unit, London.
Economy, World (in part)

ELI, C. R. Executive Director, U.S. Badminton Association.
Racket Games: *Badminton*

ENGELS, JAN R. Editor, *Vooruitgang* (Bimonthly of the Centre Paul Hymans, liberal study and documentation centre), Brussels.
Belgium

EWART, W. D. Editor and Director, *Fairplay International Shipping Weekly,* London. Author of *Marine Engines; Atomic Submarines; Hydrofoils and Hovercraft; Building a Ship.* Editor of *World Atlas of Shipping.*
Industrial Review: *Shipbuilding;* **Transportation** (in part)

FARR, D. M. L. Professor of History and Director, Paterson Centre for International Programs, Carleton University, Ottawa. Co-author of *The Canadian Experience.*
Canada

FENDELL, ROBERT J. Auto Editor, *Science & Mechanics;* Auto Contributor, *Gentlemen's Quarterly.* Author of *The New Era Car Book and Auto Survival Guide; How to Make Your Car Last Forever.* Co-author of *Encyclopedia of Motor Racing Greats.*
Motor Sports: *U.S. Racing*

FERRIER, R. W. Group Historian and Archivist, British Petroleum Company Ltd., London.
Energy: *Petroleum*

FIDDICK, PETER. Specialist Writer, *The Guardian,* London.
Publishing: *Newspapers (in part); Magazines (in part)*

FIELDS, DONALD. Helsinki Correspondent, BBC, *The Guardian,* and *The Sunday Times,* London.
Finland

FIRTH, DAVID. Editor, *The Friend,* London; formerly Editor, *Quaker Monthly,* London.
Religion: *Religious Society of Friends*

FISHER, DAVID. Civil Engineer, Freeman Fox & Partners, London; formerly Executive Editor, *Engineering,* London.
Engineering Projects: *Bridges*

FLANAGAN, JACK C. Travel Counselor.
Water Sports: *Surfing*

FRADY, WILLIAM ENSIGN, III. Editor, *Water Polo Scoreboard,* Newport Beach, Calif.
Water Sports: *Water Polo*

FRANKLIN, HAROLD. Editor, *English Bridge Quarterly.* Bridge Correspondent, *Yorkshire Post; Yorkshire Evening Post.* Broadcaster. Author of *Best of Bridge on the Air.*
Contract Bridge

FRANZ, FREDERICK W. President, Watch Tower Bible and Tract Society of Pennsylvania.
Religion: *Jehovah's Witnesses*

FRAWLEY, MARGARET-LOUISE. Retired Press Officer, All-England Women's Lacrosse Association.
Field Hockey and Lacrosse: *Lacrosse (in part)*

FREDRICKSON, DAVID A. Professor of Anthropology, Sonoma State University, Rohnert Park, Calif.
Archaeology: *Western Hemisphere*

FRIDOVICH, IRWIN. James B. Duke Professor of Biochemistry, Duke University Medical Center, Durham, N.C. Contributor to *Oxidase and Redox Systems; Molecular Mechanisms of Oxygen Activation.*
Life Sciences: *Molecular Biology (in part)*

FRIEDLY, ROBERT LOUIS. Executive Director, Office of Communication, Christian Church (Disciples of Christ), Indianapolis, Ind.
Religion: *Disciples of Christ*

FRISKIN, SYDNEY E. Hockey Correspondent, *The Times,* London.
Field Hockey and Lacrosse: *Field Hockey*

FROST, DAVID. Rugby Union Correspondent, *The Guardian,* London.
Football: *Rugby*

GADDUM, PETER W. Chairman, H. T. Gaddum and Company Ltd., Silk Merchants, Macclesfield, Cheshire, England. Honorary President, International Silk Association, Lyons. Author of *Silk—How and Where It Is Produced.*
Industrial Review: *Textiles (in part)*

GANADO, ALBERT. Lawyer, Malta.
Malta

GBGB. Gaming Board of Great Britain.
Gambling (in part)

GEORGE, T. J. S. Editor, *Asiaweek,* Hong Kong. Author of *Krishna Menon: A Biography; Lee Kuan Yew's Singapore; Revolt in Mindanao.*
Kampuchea; Korea; Laos; Southeast Asian Affairs; Thailand; Vietnam

GIBBONS, J. WHITFIELD. Associate Ecologist, Savannah River Ecology Laboratory, University of Georgia.
Life Sciences: *Zoology*

GILLESPIE, HUGH M. Director of Communications, International Road Federation, Washington, D.C.
Engineering Projects: *Roads*

GJESTER, FAY. Oslo Correspondent, *Financial Times,* London.
Biographies (in part); **Norway**

GOLDSMITH, ARTHUR. Editorial Director, *Popular Photography* and *Camera Arts,* New York City. Author of *The Photography Game; The Nude in Photography; The Camera and Its Images.* Co-author of *The Eye of Eisenstaedt.*
Photography

GOLOMBEK, HARRY. British Chess Champion, 1947, 1949, and 1955. Chess Correspondent, *The Times,* London. Author of *Penguin Handbook of the Game of Chess; A History of Chess.*
Chess

GOODWIN, NOËL. Associate Editor, *Dance & Dancers;* U.K. Dance Correspondent, *International Herald Tribune,* Paris, and *Ballet News,* New York City. Author of *A Ballet for Scotland;* editor of Royal Ballet and Royal Opera yearbooks for 1978, 1979, and 1980. Contributor to the *Encyclopædia Britannica* (15th ed.).
Dance (in part)

GOODWIN, R. M. Free-lance Writer, London.
Biographies (in part)

GOODWIN, ROBERT E. Formerly Executive Director, Billiard Congress of America; Managing Director, Billiard and Bowling Institute of America.
Billiard Games

GOTTFRIED, MARTIN. Drama Critic, *Saturday Review*, New York City. Author of *A Theater Divided*; *Opening Nights*; *Broadway Musicals*.
Theatre (*in part*)

GOULD, DONALD W. Medical Writer and Broadcaster, U.K.
Health and Disease: *Overview* (*in part*); *Mental Health*

GREEN, BENNY. Record Reviewer, BBC. Author of *Blame It on My Youth*; *58 Minutes to London*; *Jazz Decade*; *Drums in My Ears*; *Shaw's Champions*. Contributor to *Encyclopedia of Jazz*.
Music: *Jazz*

GREENLEAF, ARNO. Assistant Professor, Department of Biochemistry, Duke University Medical Center, Durham, N.C.
Life Sciences: *Molecular Biology* (*in part*)

GRIFFITHS, A. R. G. Senior Lecturer in History, Flinders University of South Australia. Author of *Contemporary Australia*.
Australia; Australia: *Special Report*; **Biographies** (*in part*); **Nauru; Papua New Guinea**

GROSSBERG, ROBERT H. Executive Director, U.S. Amateur Jai Alai Players Association, Miami, Fla.
Court Games: *Jai Alai*

HARDMAN, THOMAS C. Editor and Publisher, *The Water Skier*, American Water Ski Association. Co-author of *Let's Go Water Skiing*.
Water Sports: *Water Skiing*

HARRIES, DAVID A. Director, Tarmac International Ltd., London.
Engineering Projects: *Tunnels*

HASEGAWA, RYUSAKU. Editor, TBS-Britannica Co., Ltd., Tokyo.
Baseball (*in part*)

HAWKLAND, WILLIAM D. Chancellor and Professor of Law, Louisiana State University, Baton Rouge. Author of *Sales and Bulk Sales Under the Uniform Commercial Code*; *Cases on Bills and Notes*; *Transactional Guide of the Uniform Commercial Code*; *Cases on Sales and Security*.
Law: *Court Decisions*

HAWLEY, H. B. Specialist, Human Nutrition and Food Science, Switzerland.
Food Processing

HEBBLETHWAITE, PETER. Rome Correspondent, *National Catholic Reporter*, Kansas City, Mo. Author of *The Council Fathers and Atheism*; *The Runaway Church*; *Christian-Marxist Dialogue and Beyond*; *The Year of Three Popes*; *The New Inquisition?*
Biographies (*in part*); **Religion:** *Roman Catholic Church*

HENDERSHOTT, MYRL C. Professor of Oceanography, Scripps Institution of Oceanography, La Jolla, Calif.
Earth Sciences: *Oceanography*

HERMAN, ROBIN CATHY. Reporter, *New York Times*.
Ice Hockey: *North American*

HESS, MARVIN G. Executive Vice-President, National Wrestling Coaches Association, Salt Lake City, Utah.
Combat Sports: *Wrestling*

HINDIN, HARVEY J. Communications Editor, *Electronics* magazine, New York City. Author of numerous articles on electronics and mathematics.
Industrial Review: *Telecommunications*

HOPE, THOMAS W. President, Hope Reports, Inc. Rochester, N.Y. Author of *Hope Reports AV-USA*; *Hope Reports Education and Media*; *Hope Reports Perspective*.
Motion Pictures (*in part*)

HORRY, JOHN H. Former Secretary, International Squash Rackets Federation. Contributor to *The Oxford Companion to Sports and Games*.
Racket Games: *Squash Rackets*

HOTZ, LOUIS. Former Editorial Writer, *Johannesburg* (S.Af.) *Star*. Co-author and contributor to *The Jews in South Africa*.
Biographies (*in part*); **South Africa**

HOWKINS, JOHN. Editor, *InterMedia*, International Institute of Communications, London. Author of *Understanding Television*; *Mass Communications in China*.
Television and Radio (*in part*)

HUNNINGS, NEVILLE MARCH. Editorial Director, European Law Centre Ltd., London. Editor, *Common Market Law Reports*; *European Commercial Cases*. Author of *Film Censors and the Law*. Co-editor of *Legal Problems of an Enlarged European Community*.
Law: *International Law*

INGHAM, KENNETH. Professor of History, University of Bristol, England. Author of *Reformers in India*; *A History of East Africa*.
Angola; Kenya; Malawi; Mozambique; Sudan; Tanzania; Uganda; Zaire; Zambia; Zimbabwe

IVEY, WILLIAM. Director, Country Music Foundation, Nashville, Tenn.
Music: *Special Report*

JACQUET, CONSTANT H. Staff Associate for Information Services, Office of Research, Evaluation and Planning, National Council of Churches. Editor of *Yearbook of American and Canadian Churches*.
United States Statistical Supplement: *Church Membership table*

JARDINE, ADRIAN. Company Director. Member, Guild of Yachting Writers.
Sailing

JASPERT, W. PINCUS. Technical Editorial Consultant. European Editor, North American Publishing Company, Philadelphia. Member, Inter-Comprint Planning Committee; Member, Society of Photographic Engineers and Scientists; Life Member, *Eurographic Press*. Author of *State of the Art*. Editor of *Encyclopaedia of Type Faces*.
Industrial Review: *Printing*

JENKINS, PETER. Policy Editor and Political Columnist, *The Guardian*, London.
United Kingdom

JESSOP, DAVID A. Editor, *Caribbean Chronicle* and *Insight*. Consultant on Caribbean affairs.
Antigua and Barbuda; Bahamas, The; Barbados; Biographies (*in part*); **Dependent States** (*in part*); **Dominica; Grenada; Guyana; Jamaica; Saint Lucia; Saint Vincent and the Grenadines; Trinidad and Tobago**

JOFFÉ, GEORGE. Journalist and Writer on North African Affairs.
Algeria; Morocco

JONES, C. M. Consultant, *World Bowls*; Editor, *Tennis*. Member, British Society of Sports Psychology; Associate Member, British Association of National Coaches. Player-Captain, Great Britain's Britannia Cup tennis team (1979–81). Author of *Winning Bowls*; *How to Become a Champion*; numerous books on tennis. Co-author of *Tackle Bowls My Way*; *Bryant on Bowls*.
Bowling: *Lawn Bowls*

JONES, D. A. N. Assistant Editor, *The Listener*, London.
Literature: *Introduction*; *United Kingdom*

JONES, HANDEL H. President, Gnostic Concepts, Inc., Menlo Park, Calif.
Industrial Review: *Microelectronics*

JONES, W. GLYN. Professor of Scandinavian Studies, University of Newcastle upon Tyne, England. Author of *Johannes Jørgensens modne år*; *Johannes Jørgensen*; *William Heinesen*; *Færø og kosmos*; *Danish: A Grammar and Exercises*.
Literature: *Danish*

JOSEPH, LOU. Senior Science Writer, Hill and Knowlton, Chicago. Author of *A Doctor Discusses Allergy: Facts and Fiction*; *Natural Childbirth*; *Diabetes*; *Childrens' Colds*.
Health and Disease: *Dentistry*

KATZ, WILLIAM A. Professor, School of Library Science, State University of New York, Albany. Author of *Magazines for Libraries* (3rd ed.); *Magazine Selection*.
Publishing: *Magazines* (*in part*)

KELLEHER, JOHN A. Group Relations Editor, INL (newspapers), Wellington, N.Z.
New Zealand

KENDLER, ROBERT W. President, United States Racquetball Association.
Racket Games: *Racquetball*.

KENNEDY, RICHARD M. Agricultural Economist, International Economics Division of the Economic Research Service, U.S. Department of Agriculture.
Agriculture and Food Supplies

KENT, LIVIJA. Associate Professor, Botany Department, University of Massachusetts.
Life Sciences: *Botany*

KILIAN, MICHAEL D. Columnist, *Chicago Tribune*; News Commentator, WBBM Radio, Chicago. Captain, U.S. Air Force Civil Air Patrol. Author of *Who Runs Chicago?*; *The Valkyrie Project*.
Aerial Sports; Historic Preservation: *Special Report*

KILLHEFFER, JOHN V. Associate Editor, *Encyclopædia Britannica*.
Nobel Prizes (*in part*)

KIMCHE, JON. Editor, *Afro-Asian Affairs*, London. Author of *There Could Have Been Peace: The Untold Story of Why We Failed With Palestine and Again with Israel; Seven Fallen Pillars; Second Arab Awakening*.
Biographies (*in part*); **Israel**

KIND, JOSHUA B. Associate Professor of Art History, Northern Illinois University, De Kalb. Author of *Rouault; Naive Art in Illinois 1830–1976; Geometry as Abstract Art: The Third Generation*.
Museums (*in part*)

KITAGAWA, JOSEPH M. Professor of History of Religions, Divinity School, University of Chicago. Author of *Religions of the East; Religion in Japanese History*.
Religion: *Buddhism*

KLARE, HUGH J. Chairman, Gloucestershire Probation Training Committee, England. Secretary, Howard League for Penal Reform 1950–71. Author of *People in Prison*. Regular Contributor to *Justice of the Peace*.
Prisons and Penology

KNECHT, JEAN. Formerly Assistant Foreign Editor, *Le Monde*, Paris; formerly Permanent Correspondent in Washington and Vice-President of the Association de la Presse Diplomatique Française.
Biographies (*in part*); **France**

KNOX, RICHARD A. Senior Public Affairs Officer, Atomic Energy of Canada Limited Engineering Company; formerly Editor, *Nuclear Engineering International*, London. Author of *Experiments in Astronomy for Amateurs; Foundations of Astronomy*.
Industrial Review: *Nuclear Industry*

KOLATA, GINA BARI. Writer, *Science* magazine, Washington, D.C. Co-author of *The High Blood Pressure Book; Combatting the Number One Killer*.
Health and Disease: *Overview* (*in part*)

KOPPER, PHILIP. Author and Free-lance Journalist, Washington, D.C.
Biographies (*in part*); **Nobel Prizes** (*in part*)

KUNKLER, JULIE. Picture Editor, Encyclopædia Britannica, *Yearbook of Science and the Future*.
Biographies (*in part*)

LACHENBRUCH, DAVID. Editorial Director, *Television Digest*; regular contributor to *TV Guide*. Author of *Videocassette Recorders. The Complete Home Guide; Color Television—A Look Inside*.
Television and Radio: *Special Report*

LAMB, KEVIN M. Sports Writer, *Chicago Sun-Times*.
Biographies (*in part*); **Football:** *U.S. Football; Canadian Football*

LARSON, ROY. Religion Editor, *Chicago Sun-Times*.
Religion: *Introduction*

LEAPER, ERIC. Executive Director, National Organization for River Sports, Colorado Springs, Colo.
Water Sports: *River Sports*

LEGUM, COLIN. Associate Editor, *The Observer*; Editor, *Middle East Contemporary Survey* and *Africa Contemporary Record*, London. Author of *Must We Lose Africa?; Congo Disaster; Pan-Africanism: A Political Guide; South Africa: Crisis for the West*.
African Affairs; Biographies (*in part*)

LEIFER, MICHAEL. Reader in International Relations, London School of Economics and Political Science. Author of *Dilemmas of Statehood in Southeast Asia*.
Biographies (*in part*); **Malaysia; Singapore**

LENNOX-KERR, PETER. Editor, *High Performance Textiles*; European Editor, *Textile World*. Author of *The World Fibres Book*. Editor of *Nonwovens '71*; Publisher of *OE-Report* and *WP-Report*, New Mills, England.
Industrial Review: *Textiles* (*in part*)

LITTELL, FRANKLIN H. Professor of Religion, Temple University, Philadelphia, Pa. Co-editor of *Weltkirchenlexikon*; Author of *Macmillan Atlas History of Christianity*.
Religion: *World Church Membership*

LOGAN, ROBERT G. Sportswriter, *Chicago Tribune*. Author of *The Bulls and Chicago—A Stormy Affair*.
Basketball (*in part*)

LOVE, JOHN H. Executive Director, American Power Boat Association, East Detroit, Mich. Editor, *Propeller*, a publication of the APBA.
Water Sports: *Motorboating*

LULING, VIRGINIA R. Social Anthropologist.
Somalia

LUNDE, ANDERS S. Consultant; Adjunct Professor, Department of Biostatistics, University of North Carolina. Author of *The Person-Number Systems of Sweden, Norway, Denmark and Israel*.
Demography

McCAULEY, MARTIN. Lecturer in Russian and Soviet Institutions, School of Slavonic and East European Studies, University of London. Author of *Khrushchev and the Development of Soviet Agriculture: The Virgin Land Programme 1953–1964; Marxism-Leninism in the German Democratic Republic; The Stalin File*. Editor of *The Russian Revolution and the Soviet State 1917–1921; Communist Power in Europe 1944–1949*.
Union of Soviet Socialist Republics

MACDONALD, BARRIE. Senior Lecturer in History, Massey University, Palmerston North, N.Z. Author of several articles on the history and politics of Pacific islands.
Dependent States (*in part*); **Fiji; Kiribati; Solomon Islands; Tonga; Tuvalu; Vanuatu; Western Samoa**

MacDONALD, M. C. Director, World Economics Ltd., London.
Agriculture and Food Supplies: *grain table;* **Transportation:** *table;* statistical sections of articles on the various countries

MACDONALD, TREVOR J. Manager, International Affairs, British Steel Corporation.
Industrial Review: *Iron and Steel*

MACGREGOR-MORRIS, PAMELA. Equestrian Correspondent, *The Times* and *Horse and Hound*, London. Author of books on equestrian topics.
Equestrian Sports: *Show Jumping*

McLACHLAN, KEITH S. Senior Lecturer, School of Oriental and African Studies, University of London.
Iran

MALLETT, H. M. F. Editor, *Wool Record Weekly Market Report*, Bradford, England.
Industrial Review: *Textiles* (*in part*)

MANGO, ANDREW. Orientalist and Broadcaster.
Turkey

MAO, NATHAN. Professor of Chinese Studies, Seton Hall University, South Orange, N.J. Author of *Modern Chinese Fiction; Pa Chin*.
Literature: *Chinese* (*in part*)

MARSHALL, J. G. SCOTT. Horticultural Consultant.
Gardening (*in part*)

MARTY, MARTIN E. Fairfax M. Cone Distinguished Service Professor, University of Chicago; Associate Editor, *The Christian Century*. Author of *Righteous Empire; A Nation of Behavers*.
Religion: *Special Report*

MATEJA, JAMES L. Auto Editor and Financial Reporter, *Chicago Tribune*.
Industrial Review: *Automobiles*

MATTHÍASSON, BJÖRN. Economist, European Free Trade Association, Geneva.
Iceland

MAZIE, DAVID M. Associate of Carl T. Rowan, syndicated columnist. Free-lance Writer.
Social Security and Welfare Services (*in part*)

MAZZE, EDWARD MARK. Dean and Professor of Marketing, School of Business Administration, Temple University, Philadelphia. Author of *Personal Selling: Choice Against Chance; Introduction to Marketing: Readings in the Discipline*.
Consumerism (*in part*); **Industrial Review:** *Advertising*

MERMEL, T. W. Consultant; formerly Chairman, Committee on World Register of Dams, International Commission on Large Dams. Author of *Register of Dams in the United States*.
Engineering Projects: *Dams; Dams table*

MEYENDORFF, JOHN. Professor of Church History and Patristics, St. Vladimir's Orthodox Theological Seminary; Professor of History, Fordham University, New York City. Author of *Christ in Eastern Christian Thought; Byzantine Theology; Byzantium and the Rise of Russia*.
Religion: *The Orthodox Church; Eastern Non-Chalcedonian Churches*

MILES, PETER W. Dean of Agricultural Science, University of Adelaide, Australia.
Life Sciences: *Entomology*

MILLIKIN, SANDRA. Architectural Historian.
Architecture; Art Exhibitions; Museums (*in part*)

MISTRY, RAMILA. Free-lance Industrial Writer, London.
Industrial Review: *Glass*

MITCHELL, K. K. Lecturer, Department of Physical Education, University of Leeds, England. Director, English Basket Ball Association.
Basketball (*in part*)

MODIANO, MARIO. Athens Correspondent, *The Times*, London.
Biographies (*in part*); **Greece**

MONACO, ALBERT M., JR. Executive Director, United States Volleyball Association, Colorado Springs, Colo.
Court Games: *Volleyball*

MOORE, GERALD. Dean of Arts, University of Jos, Nigeria. Author of *Twelve African Writers; Wole Soyinka; Modern Poetry from Africa.*
Literature: *Special Report*

MOORE, JOHN E. Hydrologist, Reston, Va.
Earth Sciences: *Hydrology*

MORRISON, DONALD. Senior Editor, *Time* magazine.
Publishing: *Newspapers* (*in part*)

MORTIMER, MOLLY. Commonwealth Correspondent, *The Spectator*, London. Author of *Trusteeship in Practice; Kenya.*
Commonwealth of Nations; Dependent States (*in part*); **Nigeria.**

MOSEY, CHRIS. Associate Editor, *Sweden Now*, Stockholm; Swedish Correspondent, *The Observer, Daily Mail*, and *The Times Educational Supplement.* Contributor to *The Boat People.*
Sweden

MOSHANSKY, MOZELLE A. Music Journalist and Writer, *International Music Guide.*
Biographies (*in part*); **Music:** *Classical*

MUCK, TERRY CHARLES. Editor, *Leadership* magazine, Carol Stream, Ill.
Court Games: *Handball*

MUGABE, ROBERT G. Prime Minister of Zimbabwe.
Feature Article: *Struggling for Nationhood: The Birth of Zimbabwe*

NAYLOR, ERNEST. Professor of Marine Biology, University of Liverpool; Director, Marine Biological Laboratory, Port Erin, Isle of Man. Author of *British Marine Isopods.* Co-editor, *Estuarine, Coastal and Shelf Science.*
Life Sciences: *Marine Biology*

NEILL, JOHN. Product Development Manager, Walker Engineering Ltd.; Consultant, Submerged Combustion Ltd. Author of *Climbers' Club Guides; Cwm Silyn and Tremadoc, Snowdon South; Alpine Club Guide: Selected Climbs in the Pennine Alps.*
Mountaineering

NELSON, BERT. Editor, *Track and Field News.* Author of *Little Red Book; The Decathlon Book; Olympic Track and Field; Of People and Things.*
Track and Field Sports

NETSCHERT, BRUCE C. Vice-President, National Economic Research Associates, Inc., Washington, D.C. Author of *The Future Supply of Oil and Gas.* Co-author of *Energy in the American Economy: 1850–1975.*
Energy: *World Summary*

NEUSNER, JACOB. University Professor, Brown University, Providence, R.I. Author of *Invitation to the Talmud; A History of the Mishnaic Law of Purities.*
Religion: *Judaism*

NOEL, H. S. Free-lance Journalist; formerly Managing Editor, *World Fishing*, London.
Fisheries

NORMAN, GERALDINE. Saleroom Correspondent, *The Times*, London. Author of *The Sale of Works of Art; Nineteenth Century Painters and Painting: A Dictionary;* Co-author of *The Fake's Progress.*
Art Sales

NYREN, KARL. Senior Editor, *Library Journal;* Editor, *LJ/SLJ Hotline*, New York City.
Libraries (*in part*)

OLNEY, P. J. Curator of Birds, Zoological Society of London. Editor, *International Zoo Yearbook.* Co-editor of *Birds of the Western Palearctic.*
Zoos and Botanical Gardens: *Zoos*

OSBORNE, KEITH. Editor, *Rowing, 1961–63;* Honorary Editor, *British Rowing Almanack, 1961– .* Author of *Boat Racing in Britain, 1715–1975.*
Rowing

OSTERBIND, CARTER C. Director, Gerontology Center, and Professor of Economics, University of Florida. Editor of *Income in Retirement; Migration, Mobility, and Aging;* and others.
Industrial Review: *Building and Construction*

PAGE, SHEILA A. B. Research Officer, National Institute of Economic and Social Research, London.
Economy, World (*in part*)

PALMER, JOHN. European Editor, *The Guardian*, London.
European Unity

PALMER, S. B. Senior Lecturer, Department of Applied Physics, University of Hull, England.
Physics

PARKER, SANDY. Publisher of weekly international newsletter on fur industry.
Industrial Review: *Furs*

PAUL, CHARLES ROBERT, JR. Director of Communications, U.S. Olympic Committee, Colorado Springs, Colo. Author of *The Olympic Games.*
Gymnastics and Weight Lifting

PENFOLD, ROBIN C. Free-lance Writer specializing in industrial topics. Editor, *Shell Polymers.* Author of *A Journalist's Guide to Plastics.*
Industrial Review: *Plastics*

PERTILE, LINO. Lecturer in Italian, University of Sussex, England.
Literature: *Italian*

PETHERICK, KARIN. Reader in Swedish, University of London.
Literature: *Swedish*

PFEFFER, IRVING. Attorney. Chairman, Pacific American Group, Inc. Author of *The Financing of Small Business; Perspectives on Insurance.*
Stock Exchanges (*in part*)

PHINNEY, ALLISON W. Manager, Committees on Publication, The First Church of Christ, Scientist, Boston.
Religion: *Church of Christ, Scientist*

PINFOLD, GEOFFREY M. Associate, NCL Consulting Engineers, London. Author of *Reinforced Concrete Chimneys and Towers.*
Engineering Projects: *Buildings*

PLOTKIN, MANUEL D. Division Vice-President and Group Practice Director, Management Consulting Division, Austin Company; formerly Director of the U.S. Census Bureau.
Feature Article: *The Changing Face of America*

POPPELIERS, JOHN. Chief, Section for Operations and Training, Cultural Heritage Division, UNESCO, Paris.
Historic Preservation

POST, AVERY D. President, United Church of Christ, New York City.
Religion: *United Church of Christ*

PRASAD, H. Y. SHARADA. Information Adviser to the Prime Minister, New Delhi, India.
Biographies (*in part*); **India**

RANGER, ROBIN. Visiting Associate Professor, Defense and Strategic Studies Program, University of Southern California, Associate Professor, Department of Political Science, St. Francis Xavier University, Antigonish, Nova Scotia; Department of National Defence Fellow in Strategic Studies (1978–79); NATO Fellow, 1980–81. Author of *Arms and Politics, 1958–1978; Arms Control in a Changing Political Context.*
Defense; Defense: *Special Report*

RASKIN, A. H. Associate Director, National News Council, New York City. Co-author of *David Dubinsky: A Life with Labor.*
Industrial Relations: *Special Report*

RAY, G. F. Senior Research Fellow, National Institute of Economic and Social Research, London; Visiting Professor, University of Surrey, Guildford, England.
Industrial Review: *Introduction*

READ, ANTHONY A. Director, Book Development Council, London.
Publishing: *Books* (*in part*)

REBELO, L. S. Lecturer, Department of Portuguese Studies, King's College, University of London.
Literature: *Portuguese* (*in part*)

REICHELDERFER, F. W. Consultant on Atmospheric Sciences; formerly Director, Weather Bureau, U.S. Department of Commerce, Washington, D.C.
Earth Sciences: *Meteorology*

REID, J. H. Senior Lecturer in German, University of Nottingham, England. Co-editor of *Renaissance and Modern Studies.* Author of *Heinrich Böll: Withdrawal and Re-emergence;* Co-author of *Critical Strategies: German Fiction in the Twentieth Century.*
Literature: *German*

RIPLEY, MICHAEL D. Public Relations Officer, Brewers' Society, U.K.; formerly Editor, *Brewing Review.*
Industrial Review: *Alcoholic Beverages* (*in part*)

ROBINSON, DAVID. Film Critic, *The Times*, London. Author of *Buster Keaton; The Great Funnies—A History of Screen Comedy; A History of World Cinema.*
Motion Pictures (*in part*)

SAEKI, SHOICHI. Professor of Literature, University of Tokyo. Author of *In Search of Japanese Ego*.
Literature: *Japanese*

SAINT-AMOUR, ROBERT. Professor, Department of Literary Studies, University of Quebec at Montreal.
Literature: *French (in part)*

SARAHETE, YRJÖ. General Secretary, Fédération Internationale des Quilleurs, Helsinki.
Bowling: *Tenpin Bowling (in part)*

SARMIENTO, SERGIO. Editor in Chief, *Enciclopedia Barsa*, Encyclopædia Britannica Publishers, Inc.
Baseball *(in part)*

SCHOENFIELD, ALBERT. Formerly Publisher, *Swimming World*; Vice-Chairman, U.S. Olympic Swimming Committee. U.S. Representative to FINA Technical Committee. Contributor to *The Technique of Water Polo*; *The History of Swimming*; *Competitive Swimming as I See It*; *International Swimming and Water Polo* magazine.
Swimming

SCHÖPFLIN, GEORGE. Lecturer in East European Political Institutions, London School of Economics and School of Slavonic and East European Studies, University of London.
Czechoslovakia

SCHULMAN, ELIAS. Professor, Queens College, City University of New York. Author of *Israel Tsinberg, His Life and Works*; *A History of Yiddish Literature in America*; *Soviet-Yiddish Literature*; *Portraits and Studies*.
Literature: *Yiddish (in part)*

SEARS, ROBERT N. Editor, National Rifle Association, Washington, D.C.
Target Sports: *Shooting*

SHACKLEFORD, PETER. Director, International Tourism Consultants.
Industrial Review: *Tourism*

SHARPE, MITCHELL R. Science Writer; Historian, Alabama Space and Rocket Center, Huntsville. Author of *The Rocket Team*; *Living in Space: The Environment of the Astronaut*; *"It Is I, Seagull": Valentina Tereshkova, First Woman in Space*; *Satellites and Probes, the Development of Unmanned Spaceflight*.
Space Exploration

SHAW, T. R. Associate Editor, *International Journal of Speleology*. Author of *History of Cave Science*.
Speleology

SHENK, CLAYTON B. Honorary President, U.S. National Archery Association.
Target Sports: *Archery*

SHEPHERD, MELINDA. Copy Editor, *Encyclopædia Britannica*.
Biographies *(in part)*

SIMPSON, NOEL. Managing Director, Sydney Bloodstock Proprietary Ltd., Sydney, Australia.
Equestrian Sports: *Harness Racing*

SMEDLEY, GLENN B. Public Relations Director, American Numismatic Association.
Philately and Numismatics: *Coins*

SMITH, REUBEN W. Dean, Graduate School, and Professor of History, University of the Pacific, Stockton, Calif. Editor of *Venture of Islam* by M. G. S. Hodgson.
Religion: *Islam*

SMOGORZEWSKI, K. M. Writer on contemporary history. Founder and Editor, *Free Europe*, London. Author of *The United States and Great Britain*; *Poland's Access to the Sea*.
Albania; Andorra; Biographies *(in part)*; **Bulgaria; Feature Article:** *"Not a single Polish problem can be solved by violence"*; **Hungary; Liechtenstein; Luxembourg; Monaco; Mongolia; Poland; Political Parties; Romania; San Marino**

SPELMAN, ROBERT A. President, Home Furnishings Services, Washington, D.C.
Industrial Review: *Furniture*

STAERK, MELANIE. Member, Swiss Press Association. Former Member, Swiss National Commission for UNESCO.
Switzerland

STEEN, LYNN ARTHUR. Professor of Mathematics, St. Olaf College, Northfield, Minn. Author of *Mathematics Today*; *Counterexamples in Topology*; *Annotated Bibliography of Expository Writing in the Mathematical Sciences*.
Mathematics

STERN, IRWIN. Assistant Professor of Portuguese, Columbia University, New York City. Author of *Júlio Dinis e o romance português (1860–1870)*; Co-editor of *Modern Iberian Literature: A Library of Literary Criticism*.
Literature: *Portuguese (in part)*

STEVENSON, TOM. Garden Columnist, *Washington Post*; Washington Post-Los Angeles Times News Service. Author of *Pruning Guide for Trees, Shrubs, and Vines*; *Lawn Guide*.
Gardening *(in part)*

STONE, GEOFFREY R. Professor of Law, University of Chicago Law School. Author of numerous articles on constitutional law; currently at work on *Constitutional Law: Cases and Other Problems*.
Law: *Special Report*

STØVERUD, TORBJØRN. W. P. Ker Senior Lecturer in Norwegian, University College, London.
Literature: *Norwegian*

STRAUSS, MICHAEL. Ski and Sports Writer, *New York Times*. Author of *Ski Areas, U.S.A.*
Combat Sports: *Fencing*

SULLIVAN, H. PATRICK. Dean of the College and Professor of Religion, Vassar College, Poughkeepsie, N.Y.
Religion: *Hinduism*

SWEETINBURGH, THELMA. Paris Fashion Correspondent for the British Wool Textile Industry.
Fashion and Dress *(in part)*

SWIFT, RICHARD N. Professor of Politics, New York University, New York City. Author of *International Law: Current and Classic*; *World Affairs and the College Curriculum*.
United Nations

SYNAN, VINSON. Assistant General Superintendent, Pentecostal Holiness Church. Author of *The Holiness-Pentecostal Movement*; *The Old Time Power*.
Religion: *Pentecostal Churches*

TAISHOFF, SOL J. Editor, *Broadcasting*, Washington, D.C.
Television and Radio *(in part)*

TALLAN, NORMAN M. Chief Scientist, Materials Laboratory, Wright-Patterson Air Force Base, Dayton, Ohio. Editor of *Electrical Conductivity in Ceramics and Glass*.
Materials Sciences: *Ceramics*

TATTERSALL, ARTHUR. Textile Trade Statistician, Manchester, England.
Industrial Review: *Textiles (in part)*

TERRY, WALTER, JR. Dance Critic, *Saturday Review* magazine, New York City. Author of *The Dance in America*; *Great Male Dancers of the Ballet*.
Dance *(in part)*

THEINER, GEORGE. Assistant Editor, *Index on Censorship*, London. Co-author of *The Kill Dog*; editor of *New Writing in Czechoslovakia*; translator of *Poetry of Miroslav Holub*.
Literature: *Eastern European; Russian (in part)*

THOMAS, HARFORD. Retired City and Financial Editor, *The Guardian*, London.
Biographies *(in part)*

THOMAS, THEODORE V. Free-lance Journalist and Press Consultant. Editor (1961–79), *British Toys and Hobbies*.
Games and Toys

THOREN, BARBARA. Art Critic, *Japan Times*, Tokyo.
Biographies *(in part)*

TINGAY, LANCE. Formerly Lawn Tennis Correspondent, the *Daily Telegraph*, London. Author of *100 Years of Wimbledon*; *Tennis, A Pictorial History*.
Tennis

TINKER, JON. Director, Earthscan, a service of the International Institute for Environment and Development.
Environment: *Special Report*

TOWNSEND, EDWARD T. National Labor Correspondent, *Christian Science Monitor*; Editor and Consultant, Manpower Education Institute, New York City. Retired Associate Editor, *Business Week* magazine.
Industrial Relations *(sidebar)*

TRIGG, ROBERT H. Assistant Vice-President, Economic Research, New York Stock Exchange.
Stock Exchanges *(in part)*

TRILLING, OSSIA. Vice-President, International Association of Theatre Critics (1956–77). Co-editor and Contributor, *International Theatre*. Contributor, BBC, the *Financial Times*, London.
Biographies *(in part)*; **Theatre** *(in part)*

ULLMANN, LIV. International Film and Stage Star; films include *Persona*; *Cries and Whispers*; *Scenes from a Marriage*. Author of *Changing*.
African Affairs: *Special Report (in part)*

UNHCR. The Office of the United Nations High Commissioner for Refugees.
Refugees

UNNY, GOVINDAN. Agence France-Presse Special Correspondent for India, Nepal, and Sri Lanka.
Afghanistan; Bangladesh; Bhutan; Biographies (*in part*)**; Burma; Nepal; Pakistan; Sri Lanka**

VALE, NORMAN K. Retired Director of News Services, The United Church of Canada.
Religion: *United Church of Canada*

van den HOVEN, ISOLA. Writer on Consumer Affairs, The Hague, Neth.
Consumerism (*in part*)

VERDI, ROBERT WILLIAM. Sportswriter, *Chicago Tribune.*
Baseball (*in part*)

VINT, ARTHUR KINGSLEY. Counselor, International Table Tennis Federation, Hastings, East Sussex, England.
Table Tennis

WARD, PETER. Owner and Operator, Ward News Service, Ottawa; Parliamentary Reporter and Commentator.
Canada: *Special Report*

WARD-THOMAS, P. A. Golf Correspondent, *Country Life,* London.
Golf

WARNER, ANTONY C. Editor, *Drinks Marketing,* London.
Industrial Review: *Alcoholic Beverages* (*in part*)

WATSON, LOUISE. Assistant Editor, Encyclopædia Britannica, London.
Biographies (*in part*)

WAY, DIANE LOIS. Historical Researcher, Ontario Historical Studies Series.
Biographies (*in part*)

WHELAN, JOHN. Deputy Editor and Chief News Editor, *Middle East Economic Digest,* London.
Bahrain; Biographies (*in part*)**; Egypt; Iraq; Jordan; Kuwait; Lebanon; Middle Eastern Affairs; Oman; Qatar; Saudi Arabia; Syria; United Arab Emirates; Yemen, People's Democratic Republic of; Yemen Arab Republic**

WHITTINGHAM, RICHARD. Free-lance Writer and Editor. Author of *Martial Justice* and many other books on contemporary affairs.
Feature Article: *Our Changing Cities*

WIJNGAARD, BARBARA. Economist, Group Economics Department, Lloyds Bank Ltd., London.
Argentina

WILKINSON, GORDON. Information Consultant and Free-lance Science Writer; formerly Chemistry Consultant, *New Scientist,* London. Author of *Industrial Timber Preservation.*
Chemistry

WILKINSON, JOHN R. Sports Writer, East Midland Provincial Newspapers Ltd., U.K.
Cycling

WILLEY, DAVID DOUGLAS. Rome Correspondent, BBC.
Biographies (*in part*)**; Italy**

WILLIAMS, MICHAEL H. Director of Information Services, International Headquarters, Salvation Army.
Religion: *Salvation Army*

WILLIAMS, RAYMOND L. Assistant Professor of Spanish, Washington University, St. Louis, Mo. Author of *La novela colombiana contemporanea; Aproximaciones a Gustavo Álvarez Gardeazabal.*
Literature: *Spanish* (*in part*)

WILLIAMSON, TREVOR. Chief Sports Subeditor, *Daily Telegraph,* London.
Biographies (*in part*)**; Football:** *Association Football*

WILSON, MICHAEL. Consultant Editor, Jane's Publishing Co. Ltd.
Industrial Review: *Aerospace*

WITTE, RANDALL E. Associate Editor, *The Western Horseman* magazine, Colorado Springs, Colo.
Rodeo

WOOD, CHRISTINA. Free-lance Sportswriter.
Racket Games: *Rackets; Real Tennis*

WOOD, KENNETH H. Editor, *Adventist Review.* Author of *Meditations for Moderns; Relevant Religion;* co-author of *His Initials Were F.D.N.*
Religion: *Seventh-day Adventist Church*

WOODS, ELIZABETH. Writer. Author of *The Yellow Volkswagen; Gone; Men; The Amateur.*
Literature: *English* (*in part*)

WOOLLER, MICHAEL. Economist, Group Economics Department, Lloyds Bank Ltd., London.
Biographies (*in part*)**; Bolivia; Portugal; Spain; Uruguay**

WOOLLEY, DAVID. Editor, *Airports International,* London.
Transportation (*in part*)

WORSNOP, RICHARD L. Associate Editor, Editorial Research Reports, Washington, D.C.
United States

WRIGHT, ALMON R. Retired Senior Historian, U.S. Department of State.
Panama

WYLLIE, PETER JOHN. Homer J. Livingston Professor and Chairman, Department of Geophysical Sciences, University of Chicago. Author of *The Dynamic Earth; The Way the Earth Works.*
Earth Sciences: *Geology and Geochemistry*

YANG, WINSTON L. Y. Professor of Chinese Studies, Department of Asian Studies, Seton Hall University, South Orange, N.J. Author of *Modern Chinese Fiction; Teng Hsiao-p'ing: A Political Biography* (forthcoming).
Literature: *Chinese* (*in part*)

YOUNG, M. NORVEL. Chancellor, Pepperdine University, Malibu, California; Chairman of the Board, 20th Century Christian Publishing Company. Author of *Preachers of Today; History of Colleges Connected with Churches of Christ; The Church Is Building.*
Religion: *Churches of Christ*

YOUNG, SUSAN. News Editor, *Church Times,* London.
Religion: *Anglican Communion*

Index

The black type entries are article headings in the *Book of the Year*. These black type article entries do not show page notations because they are to be found in their alphabetical position in the body of the book. They show the dates of the issues of the *Book of the Year* in which the articles appear. For example "Archaeology 82, 81, 80" indicates that the article "Archaeology" is to be found in the 1982, 1981, and 1980 *Book of the Year*.

The light type headings that are indented under black type article headings refer to material elsewhere in the text related to the subject under which they are listed. The light type headings that are not indented refer to information in the text not given a special article. Biographies and obituaries are listed as cross references to the sections "Biographies" and "Obituaries" within the article "*People of the Year*." References to illustrations are preceded by the abbreviation "il."

All headings, whether consisting of a single word or more, are treated for the purpose of alphabetization as single complete headings. Names beginning with "Mc" and "Mac" are alphabetized as "Mac"; "St." is treated as "Saint."

V

W

X

Y

Z

Now there's a way to identify all your fine books, and carry papers, personal belongings and books around with you with flair and style. As part of our continuing service to you, Encyclopaedia Britannica is proud to be able to offer you the fine quality items shown on the next page.

Booklovers will love the heavy-duty personalized **Ex Libris** embosser. Now you can personalize all your fine books with the mark of distinction, just the way all the fine libraries of the world do.

The fashionably designed tote bag, decorated with the Britannica thistle, has been specially made for our patrons. Constructed from heavy-duty canvas, it gives you an easy, convenient way to carry books, papers, personal belongings, even shoes or any other daily necessities.

To order either of these items, please type or print your name, address and zip code on a plain sheet of paper along with the description and quantity of the items you are ordering (note special instructions for ordering the embosser). Please send a check or money order only (your money will be refunded in full if you are not delighted) for the full amount of purchase, including postage and handling, to:

17 68

Britannica Home Library Service
Attn: Yearbook Department
Post Office Box 6137
Chicago, Illinois 60680

(Please make remittance payable to: Britannica Home Library Service)

IN THE
BRITANNICA TRADITION
OF QUALITY...

EX LIBRIS
PERSONAL EMBOSSER

A mark of distinction for your fine books. A book embosser just like the ones used in libraries. The 1½″ seal imprints "Library of _____" (with the name of your choice) and up to three centered initials. Please type or print clearly BOTH full name (up to 26 letters including spaces between names) and up to three initials. Please allow six weeks for delivery.

Just **$20.00**

plus $2.00 shipping and handling

ENCYCLOPAEDIA BRITANNICA
TOTE BAG

This stylishly designed tote bag is useful for carrying your books, records, papers —even a spare pair of shoes. Warm earth-brown, sturdy cotton canvas, to withstand hard school use or as a shopping carry-all. Britannica thistle emblem in light golden color adds attractive style accent. Two extra pockets for small items and sundries. Please allow two to three weeks for delivery.

Only **$12.95**

plus $2.95 shipping and handling

This offer available only in the United States.
Illinois residents please add sales tax.